CURRICULUM

THE EMC MASTERPIECE SERIES

Literature

and the Language Arts

GRADES 6–12

Discovering Literature
Grade 6

Exploring Literature
Grade 7

Responding to Literature
Grade 8

Experiencing Literature
Grade 9

Understanding Literature
Grade 10

The American Tradition
Grade 11

The British Tradition
Grade 12

World Literature

We Speak Your Language

CORE COMPONENTS

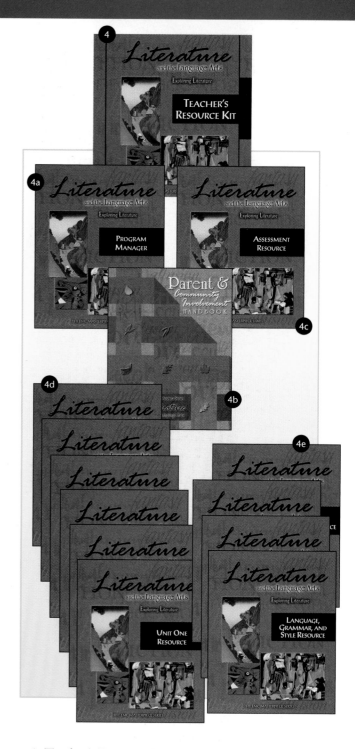

THE EMC MASTERPIECE SERIES

Literature and the Language Arts

1. Pupil's Edition with Guided Writing CD-ROM
2. Annotated Teacher's Edition
   Annotated Teacher's Edition CD-ROM
3. Literacy Resource
   3a. Lesson Plans
   3b. Reading Strategies

4. Teacher's Resource Kit
   4a. Program Manager
   4b. Parent & Community Involvement Handbook
   4c. Assessment Resource
   4d. Twelve Unit Resource Books
   4e. Eight Language Arts Skills Resource Books

CORE COMPONENTS

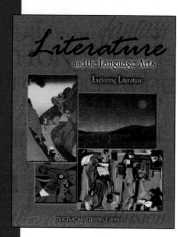

❶ PUPIL'S EDITION

- Mix of easy, moderate, and challenging selections
- Process approach to reading grants each student access to every selection
- Prereading pages tap prior experiences, build background knowledge, and engage interest
- Embedded, fact-based Guided Reading questions check comprehension and call out key points
- Graduated post-reading questions develop higher-level thinking ability
- Skill Builders for grades 6-8 and Integrating the Language Arts in grades 9-12 provide full integration of language arts skills following the literature selections
- Writer's Journal following each selection provides easy, moderate, and challenging critical and creative writing prompts
- Guided Writing lesson after each of the twelve literature units provides:
    - direct, step-by-step guidance for each stage of the writing process
    - professional and student models to help students explore a variety of modes and forms
    - language, grammar, and style lesson integrated within the writing lesson
    - Guided Writing software support (see ⓫ below)

❷ ANNOTATED TEACHER'S EDITION

- Teacher pages cover best practice for using *Literature and the Language Arts* to meet goals in reading, literature study, writing, other language arts skills, and collaborative learning
- Cross-Curricular Connections and Teaching the Multiple Intelligences provide varied, engaging activities
- Individual Learning Strategies offer individualized instruction for:
    - Motivation
    - Reading proficiency
    - English language learning
    - Special needs
    - Enrichment
- Answer key and list of ancillary materials for each selection
- Historical, literary, biographical, and other background information throughout the margins

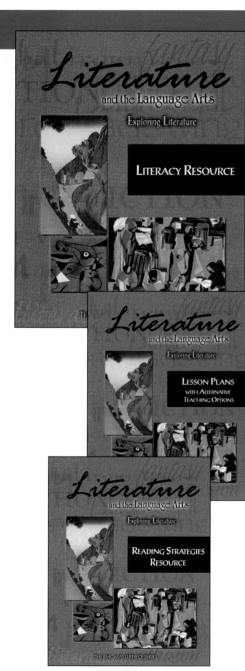

③ LITERACY RESOURCE BINDER

The Literacy Resource binder provides comprehensive support for making the quality literature in *Literature and the Language Arts* accessible to all students.

③a Lesson Plans and Alternative Teaching Options with Readability Guides

Lesson Plans for each selection include:
- Readability Guides that rate each selection as easy, moderate, or challenging, based on readability scales, author's style, subject matter, vocabulary, syntax, and selection length
- Lesson Plans that serve as road map to the entire program, providing overview of all components needed to teach each literature selection
- Ideas for whole-group and flexible-group instruction
- Strategies to address readability considerations
- Meaningful before-reading, during-reading, and after-reading activities
- Alternative teaching options and strategies for teaching developing readers, advanced readers, and English language learners
- Homework suggestions

③b Reading Strategies Resource

This resource provides step-by-step instructions on how to teach reading strategies in general and for each selection in the program. Each integrated Reading Strategies Mini-Lesson includes:
- A Student Guidesheet with reading strategy identification (based on readability level), instruction, and practice
- Standardized Test Practice specific to the reading strategy in the Mini-Lesson
- Teaching Notes with comprehensive guidance on teaching reading strategies and developing test practice skills with students of varying abilities

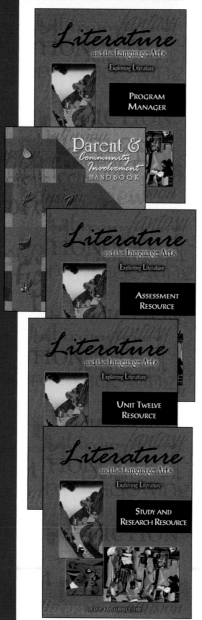

❹ TEACHER'S RESOURCE KIT

The Teacher's Resource Kit for each level includes the following components:

❹ₐ Program Manager
- Provides thorough scope and sequence charts across each grade level
- Offers a clear, ready-to-use lesson planning guide with timed activities suited for a variety of approaches and scheduling options (including block scheduling)

❹ᵦ Parent and Community Involvement Handbook
- Helps parents assist their children with their studies
- Includes study logs, parent guides, activity lists, suggested reading lists, and additional references
- Features introductory letter to parents in English and Spanish
- *Manual para Padres y Comunidades* (Spanish version) available upon request; see ❼ᵦ below

❹ᵪ Assessment Resource
The Assessment Resource provides blackline masters for:
- Portfolio assessment forms
- Writing rubrics
- Language Arts Survey worksheets, peer and self-evaluation forms, and assessment forms
- Comprehensive Tests: Literature
- Comprehensive Tests: Language Arts Skills
- Index of Selection and Unit Tests
- Test-taking skills worksheets and resources
- Test preparation resources

❹_d Unit Resource Books
Each of the twelve Unit Resource Books pulls together support materials for each selection in the unit, including:
- Selection Worksheets
- Selection Check Tests
- Selection Tests
- Unit Review/Study Guides
- Unit Tests
- Answer Keys
- Additional reading and research support

❹ₑ Skills Resource Books
The Language Arts Skills Resource books contain blackline masters of exercises keyed to the Language Arts Survey section of the student text-books. They provide additional skill exercises in these subject areas:
- Reading
- Writing
- Language, Grammar, and Style
- Speaking and Listening
- Study and Research
- Applied English
- Vocabulary (lessons integrated with the literature selections)
- Word Study (30 weekly stand-alone vocabulary lessons and fun activities with a comprehensive guide to teaching and modeling word study)

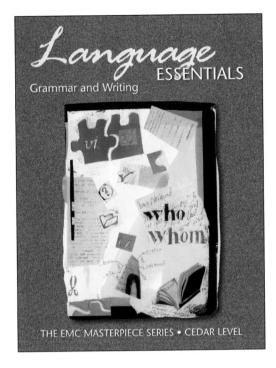

⑤ LANGUAGE ESSENTIALS

Language Essentials provides in-depth instruction and practice for grammar, usage and mechanics, and the writing process; instruction extends lessons in *Literature and the Language Arts* for teachers who want more intensive language, grammar, and style practice.

- Literature models and practice sentences are contextually related to the selections in the corresponding literature textbook
- A unique three-step approach to the Try It Yourself practice exercises gives students the opportunity to:
  - *Identify* grammar concepts in literature models or sample sentences
  - *Understand* the usage of grammar concepts and correct errors in usage
  - *Use* grammar concepts correctly in their own writing
- A special unit covers etiquette and style for electronic communications, including netiquette for communicating on the Internet, Internet searches, and Internet source citations
- Each level includes a *Language Essentials Resource* book with blackline masters to accompany the Try It Yourself exercises, writing assignments, and unit reviews, and an answer key for the exercises in the textbook and resource book

⑥ VISUAL LITERACY RESOURCE

⑥ₐ Visual Literacy Resource I: Reading & Writing Skills Transparencies

Address the needs of visual learners with transparencies of
- Daily oral language (grades 6-9)
- Graphic organizers
- Student model drafts
- Whole class activities to engage all students

⑥ᵦ Visual Literacy Resource II: Fine Art Transparencies
- Rich collection of full-color fine art transparencies
- Activities integrating fine art with the literature selections throughout the program
- Questions to help students develop their critical viewing skills

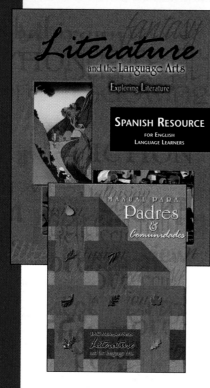

⑦ RESOURCES FOR ENGLISH LANGUAGE LEARNERS

⑦ₐ Spanish Resource for English Language Learners (Grades 6–10)
- Designed to enhance the ability of Spanish-speaking students to understand the selections, participate in class discussions, and make the transition to English-language learning
- Blackline masters, in Spanish, of the study materials for before, during, and after reading, including Guided Reading questions

⑦ᵦ *Manual para Padres y Comunidades*
Spanish version of the Parent and Community Involvement Handbook:
- Helps Spanish-speaking parents assist their children with their studies
- Includes study log blackline masters, parent guides, activity lists, suggested reading lists, and additional references
- Available free with the program upon request

⑧ ACCESS EDITION LIBRARY

⑧ₐ Access Editions
Each Access Edition contains:
- The complete literary work
- A historical introduction, including an explanation of literary or philosophical movements relevant to the work
- A biographical introduction with a time line of the author's life
- Art, including explanatory illustrations, maps, genealogies and plot diagrams, as appropriate to the text
- Study apparatus for each chapter or section, including
  - Guided Reading questions
  - Words for Everyday Use entries for point-of-use vocabulary development
  - Footnotes
  - Responding to the Selection questions
  - Investigate, Inquire, and Imagine questions (with recall, interpretation, and higher-level questions to assure your students a close and accessible reading of the text)
  - Understanding Literature questions covering literary terms
  - Prompts for creative writing, critical writing, and research projects
  - Many titles also include:
    - Related readings
    - Critical viewing questions

⑧ᵦ Access Edition Assessment Manuals
Each Access Edition title is supplemented with an Assessment Manual that includes:
- An Answer Key
- Graphic Organizers
- Vocabulary and Literary Terms Review
- Exam Masters
- Evaluation Forms

TECHNOLOGY TOOLS

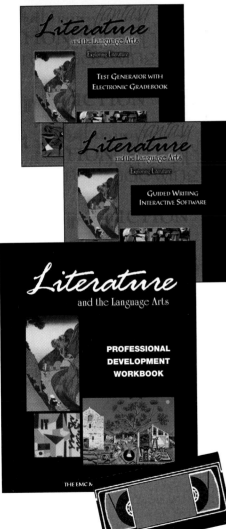

❾ ATE ON CD-ROM

- View on-screen or print selections instead of carrying the textbook home to plan classes
- Preview and print blackline masters from Resource books
- Sample Audio Library selections using Quick Time
- Connect to Internet sites in textbook via hyperlinks
- Available in Windows and Macintosh formats

❿ TEST GENERATOR AND CLASSROOM ADMINISTRATOR ELECTRONIC GRADEBOOK

- Test Generator allows you to generate customized true/false, multiple choice, short answer, and essay tests based on all selection check tests, selection tests, and unit tests in each textbook
- Classroom Administrator Electronic Gradebook helps manage grades electronically with option of posting scores to a network or website for students and parents
- Windows and Macintosh formats

⓫ GUIDED WRITING ON CD-ROM

The Guided Writing Interactive Software builds on the Guided Writing and integrated Language, Grammar, and Style lessons in the textbook. The "writer-friendly" word processor includes:
- Capacity for self-, peer, and teacher evaluation notes
- Spelling and grammar utilities
- Hypertext links providing help specific to the writing task
- Printable graphic organizers, checklists, and student handouts
- Portfolio management system for teachers
- Windows and Macintosh compatability

⓬ PROFESSIONAL DEVELOPMENT LIBRARY

⓬ₐ Professional Development Videos
- Modeling of practical techniques and strategies for classroom management as well as teaching reading, vocabulary, and word study
- Integration of all techniques with the *Literature and the Language Arts* program

⓬ᵦ Professional Development Workbook
- Video transcripts with additional information on each teaching technique
- Questions to help teachers adapt techniques to their classrooms
- Research summaries
- References for additional information

⓭ AUDIO LIBRARY

- Authentic, dramatic recordings of most literature selections in the textbooks
- Recordings by authors, professional actors, and literary scholars
- Available on audiocassette and audio CD

⓮ VIDEO LIBRARY

- Author biographies, documentaries, feature-length films
- Titles available in VHS and DVD format
- Videos selected to tie in to specific textbook selections, themes, and course of study

⓯ ELECTRONIC LIBRARY ON CD-ROM

- More than 20,000 pages of literary classics
- 120 long selections, including epic poems, novels, plays, non-fiction, and poetry, as well as 194 short selections, which include poetry and excerpts
- Ability to view on screen or print out individual selections instead of carrying multiple texts to plan classes
- Electronic Library Guide with teaching suggestions, enrich-ment activities, and reading strategies guidesheets

⓰ LITERATURE INTERNET RESOURCE CENTER

- Internet links and activities for most literature selections in *Literature and the Language Arts*
- Literary links
- Professional development, scholarship, and grant opportunities
- Workshops
- Standardized test preparation resources
- State-specific information
- Teaching tools
- Online reference materials

EMCParadigm
WE SPEAK YOUR LANGUAGE

Dear Language Arts Educator:

On behalf of EMC/Paradigm Publishing's language arts editorial team, I am excited to share with you *The EMC Masterpiece Series, Literature and the Language Arts* textbook program—the result of ongoing, intensive collaboration between our editorial team and educators across the country. What you discover in this program will, I hope, reflect the passion for great literature and the inspired teaching that shaped it.

Most language arts educators are deeply invested in literature. We enter into a teaching career because something we experienced through reading first transformed our own lives. But even the most inspired teachers among us find it increasingly difficult to share our love of literature with our students in a way that really takes hold. As reading scores attest, students today struggle with comprehension. They tell us the vocabulary is too difficult. They say they can't relate to the very literature that we know will help them find their place in the world.

The EMC Masterpiece Series, Literature and the Language Arts responds to these challenges by following through on the belief that all students, even those who are struggling, can read great literature—and even be transformed by it. Look over our program and you'll see comprehensive instruction in reading strategies paired with literary works that have the power to change lives. EMC/Paradigm carefully structures the *Literature and the Language Arts* program, helping students to lay a foundation with literal, fact-based questions during reading and to build higher-level thinking skills after reading. We provide lesson plans and readability guides that consider difficulty and ease factors; we then provide students with direct instruction in reading strategies designed to help them achieve reading success. Our writing program and other language arts skills instruction are integrated within the literature units and, like the literature selections, include individual learning strategies that meet students where they are and lead them toward academic success.

Emerson said, " 'Tis the good reader that makes the good book." At EMC/Paradigm, we believe this—and we also believe that a good textbook program can help make a good reader. We hope that you discover, as so many other language arts teachers have, that *Literature and the Language Arts* is *that* textbook program.

Sincerely,

Laurie Skiba

Laurie Skiba
Managing Editor
Literature and the Language Arts

Meeting Your Teaching Goals with the *EMC Masterpiece Series, Literature and the Language Arts*

Contents

Overview

The grades 9 and 10 textbooks in *The EMC Masterpiece Series, Literature and the Language Arts*, are each divided into three parts. Part One takes a genre-based approach to literature, and Part Two takes a theme-based approach. Part Three is the Language Arts Survey, a handbook of essential language arts skills.

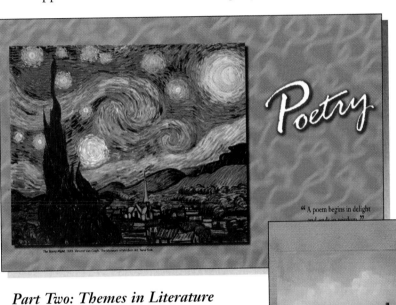

Part One: Genres in Literature *contains six units building understanding in the five major literary genres—the oral tradition, fiction, poetry, drama, and nonfiction, as well as in informational and visual media.*

Part Two: Themes in Literature *presents literature using a thematic approach. It consists of six units organized by themes designed to appeal to high school readers.*

Part Three: Language Arts Survey *is a comprehensive handbook of essential language arts skills, including reading; writing; language, grammar, and style; speaking and listening; study and research; and applied English.*

Teachers who wish to take a theme-based approach to the entire book should consult the **Thematic Organization Chart** starting on page T34. Teachers who wish to emphasize genre throughout the year should consult the **Selections by Genre** pages starting on page T37.

Following the presentation of high-quality literature selections, each literature unit concludes with a **Unit Review**, including vocabulary and literary terms review and **Reflecting on Your Reading** questions for discussion or writing. Each literature unit also includes a **For Your Reading List** feature that encourages independent reading and a **Guided Writing lesson** that integrates a lesson in language, grammar, and style.

Part Three, the **Language Arts Survey**, provides a comprehensive overview of the complete range of language arts skills. The survey is divided into six sections, as follows:

- Reading Resource
- Writing Resource
- Language, Grammar, and Style Resource
- Speaking and Listening Resource
- Study and Research Resource
- Applied English Resource

Students are asked to refer to these sections when doing writing or language arts skills activities following each literature selection and at the end of each literature unit. Teachers wishing to give their students additional practice in any of these skills areas will

find, for each lesson in the Language Arts Survey, a corresponding worksheet in one of the **Skills Resource books** found in the Teacher's Resource Kit. Teachers wishing to present whole units related to specific language arts skills can have students work through parts of the Language Arts Survey, doing the activities found in the Skills Resource books.

The **Handbook of Literary Terms** defines and provides examples of terms for literary concepts, techniques, and genres. The **Glossary** collects all the Words for Everyday Use from the literature selections and provides both pronunciations and definitions. The text ends with **indexes** of titles and authors, skills, Internet sites, and fine art.

*An **Elements of Genre** feature begins each genre-based unit with information about key literary concepts.*

*An **Echoes** feature starts each theme-based unit with several quotations geared to get students thinking about the theme.*

APPROACHES TO *LITERATURE AND THE LANGUAGE ARTS*

Literature and the Language Arts contains a number of features that allow you the flexibility to organize your instruction to best suit your preferences and your district's requirements. The following chart offers some tips for using your chosen approach to the text.

FEATURES OF THE PROGRAM, BY APPROACH

Genre Approach
- Units 1–5 provide an overview of the five traditional literary genres (the oral tradition, poetry, fiction, drama, and nonfiction). Unit 6 helps students to extend their literacy skills to interpreting informational and visual media.
- The Selections by Genre pages beginning on page T37 list all the selections in the book by genres. Use the chart to find examples of the types of literature you wish to teach. The selections are arranged in chronological order to help your class trace the historical development of the several genres.
- The Language Arts Survey, Writing Resource, provides instruction in techniques that are characteristic of the various genres of writing.
- Questions for Understanding Literature following selections help students understand the use of literary techniques.
- Reflecting on Your Reading questions in the Unit Review relate matters of genre and literary technique to thematic issues.

Thematic Approach
- Units 7–12 provide selections organized by theme.
- The **Echoes** page that opens each theme-based unit offers intriguing quotations chosen to get students thinking about the theme.
- The Thematic Organization chart on pages T34–T36 lists all the selections in the book under forty-seven major themes.
- Writer's Journal prompts following selections ask students to explore and develop their thoughts about thematic topics.
- Reflecting on Your Reading questions in the Unit Review help students explore thematic relations among selections.

Writing Approach
- Writer's Journal activities following each selection use the literature as a springboard for engaging writing assignments that require both creative and critical thinking skills.
- Guided Writing lessons at the end of each unit provide direct instruction that integrates the writing process with the study of literature and the development of other language arts skills.

- The Guided Writing Interactive Software on CD-ROM provides an electronic version of all end-of-unit Guided Writing lessons in the textbook, along with additional electronic support.
- The Selections by Genre pages beginning on page T37 list all the selections in the book under five genres of writing. Use the chart to find examples of the types of writing you wish to teach.
- The Writing Resource in the Language Arts Survey provides instruction in all phases of writing, editing, and proofreading, student and peer evaluation, publishing and presenting, and reflecting on the writing process.
- The Writing Resource book provides guided exercises in all writing phases. These worksheets are keyed to the instructional text in the Language Arts Survey.

Skills Approach
- The Language Arts Survey, following Unit 12, provides instruction in the range of language arts skills and concepts, including reading; writing; language, grammar and style; speaking and listening; study and research; and applied English.
- Use the Scope and Sequence Charts in the Program Manager to locate additional exercises in specific language arts skills.
- The Resource Books in the Teacher's Resource Kit provide guided exercises in the range of language arts skills: reading; writing; language, grammar and style; speaking and listening; study and research; applied English; critical thinking; and testing. These worksheets are coordinated with the instructional text in the Language Arts Survey.
- The Assessment Resource contains skills tests for reading; writing; language, grammar, and style; speaking and listening; study and research; applied English; critical thinking; and testing. These materials are coordinated with the instructional text in the Language Arts Survey and with the worksheets in the Resource books.

T5

Teaching Reading with *Literature and the Language Arts*

Reading is a complex cognitive process. Good readers interact with a text in multiple ways: connecting with the topic, making predictions, asking questions, visualizing the action, drawing tentative conclusions and testing them as they read further. Proficient readers monitor their own comprehension and make adjustments as necessary. Because these behaviors are usually invisible, they are not always apparent to students. *Literature and the Language Arts* makes these implicit reading behaviors explicit.

The student textbook is the primary tool for teaching reading skills and strategies. A good place to start is the **Reading Resource**, which is located in the Language Arts Survey, part three of the textbook. This resource provides an overview of the purposes and processes of reading, covering such topics as identifying a writer's purpose and point of view, distinguishing fact from opinion, reading actively, and interpreting graphic aids. Practice in each of these skills can be found in the Reading Resource book in the Teacher's Resource Kit. The Reading Resource in the textbook also introduces strategies for developing vocabulary, including using context clues, identifying word parts, understanding word origins, and distinguishing between denotations and connotations. Vocabulary strategies are reinforced and practiced not only in the Reading Resource book but also in two other ancillaries in the Teacher's Resource Kit: the Vocabulary Resource and the Word Study Resource.

Another part of the Language Arts Survey, the **Study and Research Resource**, provides further instruction in distinguishing fact from opinion; identifying and evaluating persuasive techniques, false arguments, and propaganda; thinking critically; and summarizing information. In the Teacher's Resource Kit, you will find a Study and Research Resource book with blackline masters practicing each of these skills.

At the heart of the textbook and reading instruction is the literature selection itself. Coverage of each literature selection is structured according to what proficient readers do before reading, during reading, and after reading. Each selection consists of a prereading page, the selection itself, and a set of postreading pages.

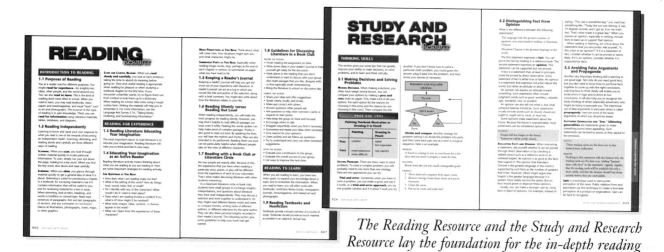

The Reading Resource and the Study and Research Resource lay the foundation for the in-depth reading instruction that accompanies each literature selection.

Sample Prereading Page

Literary Tools *introduces literary techniques or concepts that will help the reader understand the selection.*

A **Graphic Organizer** *is provided in prereading or post-reading for visual learners.*

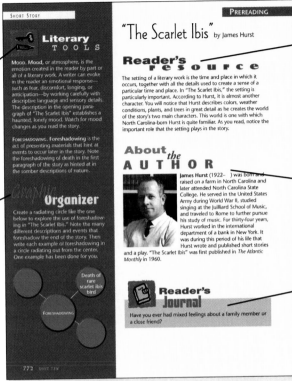

SHORT STORY

PREREADING

"The Scarlet Ibis" by James Hurst

Literary TOOLS

MOOD. **Mood**, or atmosphere, is the emotion created in the reader by part or all of a literary work. A writer can evoke in the reader an emotional response—such as fear, discomfort, longing, or anticipation—by working carefully with descriptive language and sensory details. The description in the opening paragraph of "The Scarlet Ibis" establishes a haunted, lonely mood. Watch for mood changes as you read the story.

FORESHADOWING. **Foreshadowing** is the act of presenting materials that hint at events to occur later in the story. Note the foreshadowing of death in the first paragraph of the story as hinted at in the somber descriptions of nature.

Graphic Organizer

Create a radiating circle like the one below to explore the use of foreshadowing in "The Scarlet Ibis." Note the many different descriptions and events that foreshadow the end of the story. Then write each example of foreshadowing in a circle radiating out from the center. One example has been done for you.

Death of rare scarlet ibis bird

FORESHADOWING

772 UNIT TEN

Reader's resource

The setting of a literary work is the time and place in which it occurs, together with all the details used to create a sense of a particular time and place. In "The Scarlet Ibis," the setting is particularly important. According to Hurst, it is almost another character. You will notice that Hurst describes colors, weather conditions, plants, and trees in great detail as he creates the world of the story's two main characters. This world is one with which North Carolina-born Hurst is quite familiar. As you read, notice the important role that the setting plays in the story.

About the AUTHOR

James Hurst (1922–) was born and raised on a farm in North Carolina and later attended North Carolina State College. He served in the United States Army during World War II, studied singing at the Juilliard School of Music, and traveled to Rome to further pursue his study of music. For thirty-four years, Hurst worked in the international department of a bank in New York. It was during this period of his life that Hurst wrote and published short stories and a play. "The Scarlet Ibis" was first published in *The Atlantic Monthly* in 1960.

Reader's Journal

Have you ever had mixed feelings about a family member or a close friend?

Reader's Resource *provides keys to comprehension of the selection; it includes cross-curricular and contextual information designed to help students prepare for the literature selection.*

About the Author *provides contextual information about the author's life and the period in which he or she lived.*

Reader's Journal *activities help create the anticipatory set by relating the literature to students' own lives.*

Before Reading

The dual purpose of the **prereading page** is to help students connect with the context of the literature they are about to read while giving them an active reading strategy to carry out while reading.

The **Reader's Journal** activity taps each student's prior knowledge and experiences by raising a central theme from the selection and asking the student to relate that theme to his or her own life. After writing about or discussing this topic, students will be thinking about the theme of the selection in terms of their own lives and will be more likely to relate personally to the selection. Responses to the Reader's Journal can be recorded on the **Selection Worksheets** found in the **Unit Resource** books or on

students' own paper. These prompts can also be used as whole-class or small-group discussion topics.

The **Reader's Resource** and **About the Author** features on the prereading page build the background knowledge students need to understand the selection. Often, this background information consists of cross-curricular connections, explaining, for example, historical allusions, geographical information, or scientific discoveries that play a role in the selection.

Each prereading page also contains a **Literary Tools** feature, which introduces literary techniques or concepts that will help the reader understand the selection. Literary Tools also gives students an active reading strategy

for approaching the selection. Additional support for using reading strategies can be found in the **Reading Strategy Mini-Lessons** in the **Reading Strategies Resource**, which is located in the Literacy Resource binder.

The active reading strategy often includes a **Graphic Organizer** providing a structured, visual way for students to represent organizational patterns and practice note-taking. Students can either copy the Graphic Organizer from the prereading page onto their own paper or use the printed version on the Selection Worksheet in the Unit Resource books. The concepts introduced in Literary Tools and tracked in the Graphic Organizer are reinforced in the Understanding Literature section of the post-reading pages.

During Reading

In the **during-reading** phase, students activate the reading strategy introduced in the pre-reading phase. The **Reading Strategies Resource** contains mini-lessons with both a **Student Guidesheet** and **Teaching Notes** that will help you model and practice use of this strategy during in-class reading.

Throughout the selection, students can also take advantage of **Guided Reading questions** embedded in the text. These fact-based, literal comprehension questions check students' understanding as they read and call out key points from the selection. The Guided Reading questions also model for students how to ask questions as they read.

Students can record their answers to the questions on the Selection Worksheet or on their own paper. (Answers are provided in the margins of the Annotated Teacher's Edition.) Some students might use the Guided Reading questions more than others, and some might use them only when they find they are having trouble staying focused on the reading.

After Reading

Having used these supports to comprehend the text, students are prepared to reflect on the reading experience during the **after-reading phase**. At this stage, students move from basic comprehension into higher-level thinking, confirming main ideas and supporting details, forming inferences about words and text, making judgments about what they have read, and comparing and contrasting selections. The after-reading activities in *Literature and the Language Arts* provide the support students need to take this step successfully.

The first post-reading activity is the **Respond to the Selection** prompt, which asks students to react personally to what they have read. The Respond to the Selection activity is followed by **Investigate, Inquire, and Imagine** questions that take students through the selection step by step, building upon their responses and refining them through questions of increasing complexity. These questions are paired and connected by arrows to remind students that their

Sample Selection Page

Guided Reading questions guide *students through the selection and help them to recognize and understand important ideas and key points. The questions help all students reach a basic understanding of the selection.*

Footnotes explain obscure references, *unusual usages, and terms meant to enter students' passive vocabularies and are defined separately from active vocabulary.*

The **Words for Everyday Use** *feature, included in selections at point of use, defines and gives pronunciations for difficult terms meant to enter students' active vocabularies. A contextual sentence for each term increases vocabulary development.*

answers to more complex questions should build on answers to more concrete questions. The most basic pairing, **Recall/Interpret**, is followed by **Analyze/Synthesize**, and finally by either **Evaluate/Extend** or **Perspective/Empathy**. This feature is illustrated on page T11.

Investigate, Inquire, and Imagine question sets are structured to develop different levels of cognitive skill based on *Bloom's Taxonomy of Educational Objectives*. Since its publication in 1956, Bloom's taxonomy has been the most widely employed system for labeling levels of cognitive processing and constructing tests. The primary levels of cognition in Bloom's taxonomy include the following:

1. Knowledge: involves the recall of specifics, methods, and processes
2. Comprehension: represents the lowest level of understanding
3. Application: uses abstractions in particular and concrete situations
4. Analysis: breaks down communication into its elements or parts
5. Synthesis: brings together elements and parts to form a whole
6. Evaluation: makes judgments about the value of material and methods

The questions in Investigate, Inquire, and Imagine take the students through these six levels of the cognitive domain, as well as taking them a step further by developing their appreciation of other perspectives and empathy for other people.

- Recall questions ensure that students remember the basic key facts from the selections (knowledge).
- Interpret questions use facts from Recall questions as a basis for valid interpretation (comprehension).
- Analyze questions ask readers to classify, compare and contrast, and identify relationships between ideas (analysis).
- Synthesize questions are linked to Analyze questions and ask readers to integrate, restructure, predict, elaborate, and summarize (synthesis).
- Evaluate questions ask students to appraise, assess, critique, and make judgments about certain aspects of a selection (evaluation).
- Extend questions are paired with Evaluate questions and allow readers to try out their understanding in a different context: a student's own experience, a contemporary real world situation, or another literary or artistic work (application).
- Perspective questions develop insight and self-knowledge by encouraging students to look for and value alternative perspectives.

- Empathy questions complement Perspective questions and facilitate knowledge of others by asking students to demonstrate understanding of another person's worldview.

Because students are frequently unfamiliar with literary terminology and its applications, such terminology does not appear in the questions for Investigate, Inquire, and Imagine. Instead, literary terminology and techniques are covered in the next part of the post-reading apparatus, which is called **Understanding Literature**. This feature is covered in more detail in the next section.

All of these features provide support for students as they develop their ability to read and make sense of texts. Of course, our hope is that students will internalize these skills and become lifelong readers. The **For Your Reading List** activity at the end of each unit directs students to additional reading they might enjoy and helps them develop and articulate personal reading preferences.

Investigate, Inquire, Imagine	Bloom's Taxonomy
Recall	Knowledge
Interpret	Comprehension
Analyze	Analysis
Synthesize	Synthesis
Evaluate	Evaluation
Extend	Application
Alternate Question Set	
Perspective	Insight and self-knowledge
Empathy	Knowledge of others

Gains in Critical Thinking

Teaching Literature with *Literature and the Language Arts*

Experiencing Literature and *Understanding Literature* are designed to introduce students to the stylistic, thematic, and technical qualities of a variety of high-quality, engaging literary works from many different cultures and perspectives. The study of relationships among literary elements, techniques, and genres is an essential part of this goal.

Textbook units are based on either genre or theme, and each unit's apparatus is designed to provoke reflection on the genre or theme in question. Genre units begin with an **Elements of Genre** feature that introduces definitions and examples of key literary concepts for students to use as they work their way through the unit. For example, the Elements of Poetry page at the beginning of Unit Two covers the types of poetry and introduces techniques related to imagery, shape, sound, and meaning. Thematic units begin with a page of **Echoes**, quotations that get students thinking about the theme and comparing and contrasting perspectives

Sample Reflecting On Your Reading Section

Theme and Genre questions ask students to synthesize ideas from multiple selections and compare and contrast literary themes and techniques.

on it from the start. At the end of each unit, the **Reflecting on Your Reading** section asks students to compare and contrast themes, synthesize information from multiple texts, and draw conclusions about genre; this reflection often takes the form of both small group and individual activities.

Most literature instruction takes place in the context of individual selections. Appropriate literary elements such as setting, plot, character, and conflict, and techniques such as symbolism, figurative language, and foreshadowing are introduced and explained in the **Literary Tools** feature on the prereading page for each selection. Then, students are asked to note, as they read, how the author has used the elements and techniques. These same devices are then reinforced and discussed in the **Understanding Literature** section of the post-reading pages.

Beyond a technical understanding of literary genres, elements, and techniques, students gain practice recognizing and articulating personal responses to characters, events, motives, and conflicts. The **Reader's Journal** activity on the prereading page asks students to connect the theme of the selection they are about to read to their own lives. The **Respond to the Selection** prompt, which comes immediately after the selection, asks students to respond personally to what they have just read.

Discussions based on these prompts can help students understand how readers respond differently to texts based on their background knowledge, purpose, and point of view. Selections have been chosen to reflect a broad range of viewpoints, and students are encouraged to consider how literature reflects diverse voices. Specifically,

Sample Post-Reading Page

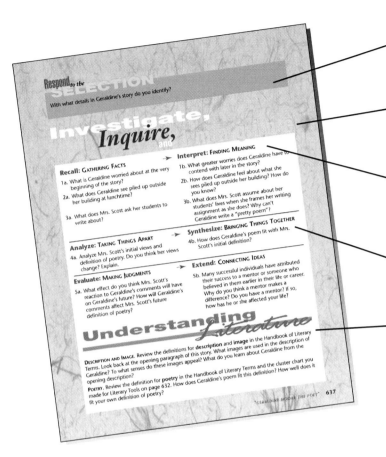

Respond to the Selection is a *reader response* activity designed to elicit an affective response to the selection.

Investigate, Inquire, and Imagine takes students through the work step by step, building from their individual responses a complete interpretation of the selection.

Recall questions address comprehension of key facts from the selection. *Interpret* questions, keyed to the Recall questions by arrows, evoke interpretations based on evidence from the selection.

Paired questions such as *Analyze / Synthesize*, *Evaluate / Extend*, and *Perspective / Empathy* lead students to higher-level thinking.

Understanding Literature questions reinforce the Literary Tools introduced in prereading and provide selection-related study of literary movements, genres, and techniques.

Perspective and **Empathy** questions in the **Investigate, Inquire, and Imagine** section of the post-reading material help students look for and value diverse perspectives and empathize with others. **Extend** questions ask students to compare and contrast one selection with another selection, with a real-world situation, or with their own experiences. Also, **Related Readings** included with many main selections offer different perspectives on a common theme. For example, in the grade nine text, the short story "The Leap" by Native American writer Louise Erdrich is paired with African-American writer Nikki Giovanni's poem "Her Flying Trapeze."

From selection to selection, the **Investigate, Inquire, and Imagine** questions ask students to look at literature through a variety of critical lenses.

At the end of each unit, the **Reflecting on Your Reading** section asks students to synthesize ideas from the selections they have read. Genre-based questions explore relationships among style, genre, and impact, and theme-based questions deal with the expression of universal themes and ideas as manifested in unique, culturally informed texts.

Using *Literature and the Language Arts*, students gain a broad understanding of literary themes, genres, and techniques as they learn to appreciate literary works.

Teaching Writing with *Literature and the Language Arts*

Literature and the Language Arts takes a process and portfolio approach to writing instruction and incorporates frequent opportunities for writing practice.

The process approach breaks the act of writing into manageable steps, with guidance and feedback at each step. Students are trained in techniques for prewriting, drafting, evaluating their drafts by themselves and with peers, revising, and publishing. They are also given opportunities to reflect on the process and consider what they would change next time.

Writing portfolios and evaluation forms are used to track development of pieces of writing over time.

Explicit Instruction on the Writing Process

The **Writing Resource**, which comprises part two of the Language Arts Survey at the back of the textbook, surveys the entire writing process from prewriting through drafting, self- and peer evaluation, revising, proofreading, publishing and presenting, and reflecting on the process. This section of the Language Arts Survey is divided into fifty lessons. Additional practice activities for each lesson can be found in the Writing Resource book in the Teacher's Resource Kit.

In the Assessment Resource book, also located in the Teacher's Resource Kit, you will find Writing Skills Comprehensive Test 3.1. Designed to assess students' familiarity with basic writing concepts and skills, this test may be used as a pre-test or a post-test as you assess students' preparedness for real-world writing as well as standardized tests.

Frequent Writing Practice

The basic skills instruction in the Writing Resource prepares students to benefit from the frequent writing practice opportunities throughout *Literature and the Language Arts*. These opportunities take three principle forms: Writer's Journal prompts accompanying each literature selection, guided essay prompts on each selection and unit test, and Guided Writing lessons at the end of each unit.

The **Writer's Journal** activities following each selection use the literature selection as a springboard for engaging quick-writing assignments that require both creative and critical thinking skills. Every literary selection includes three writing prompts. Although they are not labeled as such for the students, you should know that they are graded 1) simple, 2) moderate, and 3) challenging.

Essay questions on **Selection Tests** and **Unit Tests** involve prewriting as well as writing prompts, reminding students to take time to organize their thoughts before they draft their responses. The prewriting sections often include a graphic organizer, helping students learn to use systems to structure their ideas. Through these repeated reminders to use the writing process, students internalize the steps and begin to use them on their own.

More extended writing projects can be found in the Guided Writing lessons at the end of each unit. These step-by-step lessons are described in detail below.

Hands-On, Guided Writing Instruction

Literature and the Language Arts offers complete, direct writing instruction that integrates the writing process with the study of literature and the development of other key language arts skills. At the end of each of twelve literature units, a **Guided Writing lesson** provides direct, step-by-step instruction in the writing process, working with a particular mode. This lesson is integrated with the following:
(1) the literature in the unit
(2) a Language, Grammar, and Style lesson that teaches key concepts in the context of writing

(3) the Language Arts Survey in the textbook
(4) the Resource books in the Teacher's Resource Kit
(5) the Guided Writing software

The writing assignment ties directly to the literature unit studied, frequently using literature in that unit as a Professional Model that students are invited to examine as they prepare to write. In some cases, a Student Model introduces the writing assignment. At other times, a Student Model appears later in the lesson to show the stages of drafting and revision.

As students enter the Prewriting stage, they are asked to consider voice, audience, and strategy in the Finding Your Voice, Identifying Your Audience, and Writing with a Plan sections before entering the Drafting stage. This section coaches them through the process of organizing their words and getting them down on paper. Then students are shown a Student Model in draft form that contains self- and peer evaluation comments. A student-friendly evaluation checklist

provides a rubric for students to use in the Self- and Peer Evaluation stage. Students are then led through the Revising, Proofreading, Publishing and Presenting, and Reflecting stages.

Students are also introduced to a key Language, Grammar, and Style concept within the Guided Writing lesson. Designed with the idea that grammar is best taught in the context of writing rather than in isolation, the Language, Grammar, and Style lesson offers solid instruction by helping students to 1) identify correct grammatical usage in the Professional Model, 2) revise incorrect grammatical usage in the Student Model and examples, and 3) demonstrate correct grammatical usage in their own work. Throughout this lesson, students can refer to the Language, Grammar, and Style Resource of the Language Arts Survey for additional support.

Finally, the **Guided Writing Interactive Software**, included on CD-ROM at the back of each student and annotated teacher's edition of the textbook, provides extended lessons and a writer-friendly word-processor that allows self-, peer, and teacher evaluation comments to be delivered electronically. Using this software, students write to communicate, using electronic sticky notes to convey their comments. While the print lessons do not depend on software for students to complete the assignments, the electronic version of the Guided Writing program provides printable worksheets, graphic organizers, checklists, and student models; spelling and grammar utilities; hypertext links providing help specific to the writing task; and a portfolio management system for teachers.

Students examine a Professional Model as they prepare to write.

Note: Teachers who wish to do so can teach the Guided Writing program as a separate composition course by using the Guided Writing lessons at the end of each of the twelve literature units, the Writing Resource in the Language Arts Survey in its entirety, the Writing Resource book in the Teacher's Resource Kit, and the Guided Writing Interactive Software at the back of the book.

Process for Writing Assignments

See the chart on page T15 for a recommended sequence of activities you can follow with the writing assignments at the end of each unit. Steps 1–11 may be repeated for each writing assignment. Then, periodically, step 12 should also be completed.

Assessing Student Writing

See the introduction to the **Assessment Resource** in the Teacher's Resource Kit for a thorough discussion of both analytic and holistic assessment of writing. The Assessment Resource also contains Comprehensive Portfolio Evaluation Forms. Rubrics for evaluating each Guided Writing lesson have been modeled after those used to evaluate writing on standardized tests; they can be found in the **Writing Resource**.

Reports and Research Papers

Literature and the Language Arts contains complete materials for instruction in research and report-writing. The Research Skills section of the Study and Research Resource in the Language Arts Survey, covers research procedures, from using the library to documenting print and Internet sources. The Reflecting on Your

Students are given clear instruction in the Revising and Proofreading stages.

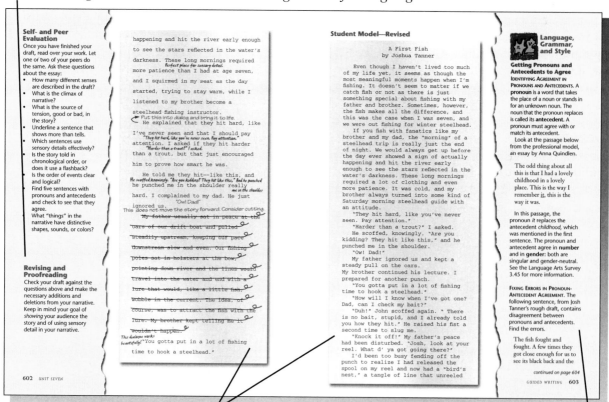

The Student Model is shown in draft and revised versions whenever possible.

An integrated Language, Grammar, and Style lesson teaches concepts in the context of student writing

T14

Reading questions that appear at the end of each Unit Review make excellent topics for extended reports or research papers.

Remedial Exercises in Specific Writing Skills

As you evaluate your students' writing, you will discover consistent areas of weakness. One student may have trouble making transitions, while another may consistently use serial commas incorrectly. The Language Arts Survey in the student edition and the accompanying Resource book provide ample activities for remediation of recurring problems. Most of the instruction and activities in the Writing and Language, Grammar, and Style sections of the Language Arts Survey are useful for this purpose. Thus, if a student has a tendency to write sentence fragments, you can have him or her read the Language Arts Survey 3.33, "Correcting Sentence Fragments." That student can then do corresponding worksheet 3.33 in the Language, Grammar, and Style Resource book. If a student has problems organizing his or her ideas, you can have him or her read Language Arts Survey 2.24–2.27, "Organizing Ideas" and complete the corresponding worksheets in the Writing Resource book. Thus, you can use the Language Arts Survey and the Resource books to individualize your writing instruction and to target it to remediate particular writing problems your students encounter.

PROCESS FOR WRITING ASSIGNMENTS

1. WHOLE CLASS: Study of the literature selection in the student edition textbook, along with its corresponding instructional apparatus

2. TEACHER: Introduction of the writing prompt from the student text

3. STUDENT: Prewriting (with reference to any applicable prewriting lessons in the Writing Resource section of the Language Arts Survey)

4. STUDENT: Drafting (with reference to the drafting lesson in the Writing Resource section of the Language Arts Survey)

5. STUDENT: Sharing of draft with one or more peers

6. STUDENT and PEER(S): Evaluation of the draft and conferencing with one another and with the teacher if necessary (with reference to the Analytic Scale for Evaluation from the Annotated Teacher's Edition and/or the general evaluation forms and revision checklists in the Assessment Resource)

7. STUDENT: Revising (with reference to the Revision and Proofreading Checklists in the Assessment Resource, and to the revision section of the Writing Resource section of the Language Arts Survey)

8. STUDENT: Proofreading and preparation of the final manuscript (with reference to the Revising and Proofreading Checklists in the Assessment Resource, and to the proofreading and manuscript preparation lessons in the Writing Resource section of the Language Arts Survey) and completion of the Writing Summary Form in the Assessment Resource

9. STUDENT and PEER(S): Publishing and/or presenting of the completed draft (with reference to the lesson on publishing and presenting in the Writing Resource section of the Language Arts Survey)

10. STUDENT and TEACHER: Assessment and/or conferencing with regard to the completed work

11. STUDENT: Decision as to whether to place the completed work in the student's Writing Portfolio

12. STUDENT and TEACHER: Evaluating the student's Writing Portfolio (using the Comprehensive Portfolio Evaluation Form: Teacher and the Comprehensive Portfolio Evaluation Form: Student in the Assessment Resource) and holding a teacher-student conference to discuss the evaluation and to set goals for future writing improvement

Teaching Language, Grammar, and Style with *Literature and the Language Arts*

The EMC Masterpiece Series encourages students to think about language as a powerful and complex tool for conveying meaning. This means, for one thing, that the study of language is introduced with a consideration of such broad concepts as formal and informal English; register, tone, and voice; irony, sarcasm, and rudeness; and dialect. It also means that language rules and skills—including grammar, usage, mechanics, spelling, and vocabulary—are taught, not in isolation, but in meaning-making contexts.

Language, Grammar, and Style activities are featured throughout the twelve literature units in post-reading activities called Integrating the Language Arts. These activities first direct students to read a particular lesson from the **Language, Grammar, and Style Resource** in the Language Arts Survey. Students are then asked to complete an exercise using the concept from the lesson to work with passages

from the literature they have just read. Teachers who find that their students need more practice with the concept can assign the corresponding worksheet from the **Language, Grammar, and Style Resource book** found in the Teacher's Resource Kit.

Sample Language, Grammar, and Style Activity

Language, Grammar, and Style activities practice language skills using passages from the selection students have just read.

Language Essentials is a comprehensive grammar and writing textbook integrated with the literature in *Literature and the Language Arts*.

Students are also introduced to a key language, grammar, and style concept within the Guided Writing lesson at the end of each literature unit. These **Language, Grammar, and Style lessons**, like the Language, Grammar, and Style activities through the unit, teach concepts within a context of meaning-making. Each lesson asks students to identify correct usage in a professional model, revise incorrect usage in a student model, and demonstrate correct usage in their own writing. Throughout this lesson, students are once again directed to the Language, Grammar, and Style Resource for additional support.

Language Essentials, a comprehensive grammar and writing textbook integrated with *Literature and the Language Arts*, provides even more practice in language, grammar, and style using passages from the literature book. Each level includes a *Language Essentials Resource book* with blackline masters to accompany exercises, writing assignments, and unit reviews.

The development of language, the impact on it of culture and time period, and the use of literary devices and powerful language to shape reactions, perceptions, and beliefs is further emphasized in two ancillary

resources: the Vocabulary Resource and the Word Study Resource. The **Vocabulary Resource**, correlated to the selections in the textbook, builds a rich, conceptual context for learning the Words for Everyday Use while covering such topics as morphemes, word origins, connotation and denotation, proverbs and other expressions, and semantic families. The **Word Study Resource** combines instruction, exercises, fun activities, and metacognitive reviews to teach word attack strategies and explore the characteristics of language.

Teaching the Other Language Arts Skills with *Literature and the Language Arts*

As an integrated literature and language arts program, *The EMC Masterpiece Series* combines the study of literature with instruction in study and research; speaking and listening; visual and media literacy; and applied English, giving students a meaningful context for learning new skills.

Language arts activities are featured throughout the twelve literature units in post-reading activities called **Integrating the Language Arts**. For example, a Speaking and Listening activity following the "I Have a Dream" speech by Martin Luther King, Jr. asks students to prepare a speech to convince their classmates of their visions for a better world. The instructions for this activity refer students to a section of the Speaking and Listening Resource in the Language Arts Survey for a lesson on preparing a speech. Another activity asks students to prepare a book jacket that represents visually Roger Williams's views of Native Americans. Other activities guide students in conducting research on a topic related to the selection, representing information visually, writing grant proposals, and more. Similarly, **Internet activities** for each selection address even more language arts skills.

In Integrating the Language Arts activities, students are referred to sections of the Language Arts Survey. The **Speaking and Listening Resource**, comprising part four of the Survey, provides compact lessons on such topics as communicating in small and large groups; understanding communication styles and cultural barriers; public speaking; and creating multimedia presentations. In addition, the **Study and Research Resource**—part five of the Language Arts Survey—contains strategies for critical thinking, test-taking, and using and evaluating information sources, including the media. Part six of the Survey, the **Applied English Resource**, focuses on practical applications of language arts skills in the world beyond school.

Sample Post-Reading Page

Integrating the Language Arts activities provide integrated activities in language arts areas, including language, grammar, and style; speaking and listening; study and research; applied English; collaborative learning; media literacy; vocabulary development; and critical thinking.

*Language arts **Skills Resource books** offer practice for each lesson in the corresponding sections of the Language Arts Survey.*

Language arts **Skills Resource books** in the Teacher's Resource Kit correspond to each of these sections of the Language Arts Survey and provide blackline masters with exercises keyed to each lesson in the Survey. These exercises offer a way for teachers to make sure students are mastering basic concepts.

Practice in understanding and creating visual material and thinking critically about images is emphasized throughout the program. Media Literacy activities in Integrating the Language Arts ask students to identify pro-

paganda in advertisements, create collages, represent events visually, reflect on talk show communication, and more.

Visual art throughout the book is accompanied by Art Notes which offer succinct background on the work, often followed by a Critical Viewing question. The supplemental Visual Literacy Resources I and II are based on the notion that visual literacy, or the ability to understand and produce visual messages, is becoming increasingly important as more information and entertainment is acquired through

non-print media such as television and the Internet. **Visual Literacy Resource I** contains resources for using visual learning techniques to teach literacy: these resources include reading strategies transparencies, writing transparencies, and selection transparencies with Daily Oral Language exercises and graphic organizers. **Visual Literacy Resource II** contains fine art transparencies and accompanying blackline masters; these worksheets feature additional information on the artist and artwork as well as Critical Viewing questions.

Preparing for State and National Standardized Tests
with *Literature and the Language Arts*

As you have seen, *Literature and the Language Arts* has been designed to address the competencies that make up state standards and determine success on national standardized tests. By using this program, you help students learn the strategies and develop the higher-level thinking skills they need to succeed on state proficiency tests, college entrance exams, and other standardized tests. In addition to this thorough, general preparation, explicit test practice is integrated into the program in several places.

The **Reading Strategies Resource**, also located in the Literacy Resource binder, is specifically designed to help students internalize the reading strategies they need to answer reading comprehension questions successfully. Each **Reading Strategy Mini-Lesson** culminates in a **Test Practice** page that asks students to demonstrate their successful use of the reading strategy by answering sample multiple-choice or extended-response test questions. The **Teaching Notes** for each Reading Strategy Mini-Lesson include sample think alouds that model effective ways to approach these standardized test questions.

Test-taking strategies are covered in the **Study and Research Resource**, part five of the

Language Arts Survey. This resource covers analogy, synonym and antonym, sentence completion, reading comprehension, and essay questions. The corresponding worksheets in the **Study and Research Resource book** offer exercises that practice these skills.

Also in the Teacher's Resource Kit are the **Vocabulary Resource** and the **Word Study Resource**. These two ancillaries contain instruction on and practice in word attack strategies students can use to answer standardized test questions.

Finally, the selection and unit tests in the **Unit Resource books** guide students in answering essay questions similar to those they will encounter on standardized tests. For each essay question, a prewriting prompt reminds students to plan their responses before they begin to write. After working through these prompts for an entire year, students will have internalized this process and will be able to use it on high-stakes tests.

Each Reading Strategy Mini-Lesson in the Reading Strategies Resource includes Test Practice. Students are asked to use the reading strategy to answer multiple-choice or extended-response questions.

Alternative Teaching Options

Using Flexible Groups

Flexible grouping involves using different group configurations—whole class, small group, and paired—for varying lengths of time, depending on the learning task. For a detailed description of how to use flexible grouping and design effective group activities, see the **Professional Development Library**, which contains three videos modeling effective teaching techniques and a workbook with more information on each technique.

Many of the **Integrating the Language Arts** activities that follow each literature selection are designated as **Collaborative Learning** activities. You can find other flexible grouping ideas for each selection in the **Lesson Plans with Alternative Teaching Options** in a section called "Flexible Grouping Suggestions."

TEACHING STUDENTS TO WORK COOPERATIVELY

PREPARING STUDENTS FOR SMALL GROUP WORK

PARTICIPATION
- Review/preteach vocabulary and cultural concepts for nonnative speakers.
- Begin with a nongraded, fun, get-to-know-one-another activity.
- Take steps to ensure that group members know each other's names.
- Assign tasks that call on multiple intelligences.
- Ask questions that call for personal response and interpretation.
- Value interpretations that differ from your own.
- Have students determine the wording of their topics or questions.
- Don't talk too much.
- Model tentativeness and openness.
- Model courtesy and respect for all.
- Respond only holistically and orally to early drafts and initial products.
- Avoid judging early drafts; discuss ideas rather than expression.
- Discuss anonymous samples.
- Praise students for taking risks.
- Require (only) positive feedback from peers.
- Use joint grading for group work: (1) everyone in the group receives the average among the group; (2) everyone receives the lowest grade among the group; (3) a final product is graded and everyone receives that grade.

LEADERSHIP
- Ask students to conduct lessons.
- Rotate leadership assignments in groups.
- Appoint two group leaders—one to learn from the other.
- Model and give direct instruction and practice in asking questions.
- Model and give direct instruction and practice in reporting a summary.
- Model and give direct instruction and practice in involving nonparticipants.
- Model and give direct instruction and practice in restraining dominators.
- Model and give direct instruction and practice in providing positive feedback.
- Model and give direct instruction and practice in providing constructive feedback.

LISTENING/DISCUSSING
- Model, explain, and encourage attentive listening, eye contact, and not interrupting.
- Give practice in paraphrasing students' words and your own.
- Ask students to identify good speaking and listening habits and skills.
- Ask students to evaluate group processes and their roles in their groups (use Assessment Resource form 1.4.3 and Language Arts Survey 6.12, "Working on a Team").

FORMING GROUPS
- Groups should contain a maximum of six students for a complex task, a maximum of four otherwise.
- For peer writing groups, two may be the ideal size. Require periodically that students change partners.
- In the prewriting stage, it can be helpful to match those who share a primary language other than English.
- Working groups should contain students of varied abilities.
- Allow groups to vary their seating arrangements (suggest possibilities).

GUIDING AND MONITORING
- Give specific tasks.
- Explain criteria for success.
- Assign roles in groups, or assign groups to distribute roles.
- When assigning roles in groups, divide responsibilities to assure interdependence and cooperation. One workable division of responsibilities includes (1) a discussion leader/facilitator; (2) a recorder; (3) a reporter; (4) a materials manager.
- Specify desired behaviors (see "Preparing Students for Small Group Work," above).
- Monitor group interactions and advise when appropriate.
- Intervene to diffuse conflict and to foster collaborative skills.
- When intervening in group work, ask a question rather than giving advice directly.
- If multiple groups have the same problem, interrupt the process and clarify or reteach.

CLOSURE AND ASSESSMENT
- Ask for sharing of a product.
- Both students and teacher should assess the quality of the product. Assessment can be among the entire class or only within groups.
- Both students and teacher should assess the quality of the group processes and communication.

Differentiating Instruction

Students come to your classroom with varying degrees of preparedness, differing learning styles and cultural backgrounds, and various interests and motivations. Addressing such diverse students in one class period is one of the biggest challenges facing teachers today.

You can meet these diverse needs through differentiated instruction, which simply means allowing different students to learn in different ways or about different aspects of a general topic. Practical strategies for differentiating instruction are modeled in the **Professional Development Library** videos and described in more detail in the accompanying **Professional Development Workbook**.

The **Lesson Plans with Alternative Teaching Options** identify activities that will allow you to differentiate instruction. For example, the **Individual Learning Strategies** refer you to activities in the Annotated Teacher's Edition designed for students who could benefit from help with motivation, reading proficiency, English language learning, special needs, and enrichment. In addition, the **Strategies for Developing Readers** are good activities for short-term, homogenous groups dedicated to skill development.

TEACHING MULTIPLE INTELLIGENCES

- Use multiple modes of expression: e.g., read selections aloud; read questions aloud; use visual aids—charts, graphs, tables, or other graphics, art, and films; play songs; and perform demonstrations.
- Encourage students to use multiple modes of expression, including nonverbal expressions and performances such as drawing, painting, collage, sculpture, dance and choreography, acting and oral interpretation, photography, filmmaking, video production, and musicianship and singing.
- Ask students to read aloud.
- Precede written work with a related oral activity.
- Teach students to use graphic aids for understanding and for studying.
- Facilitate group work.
- Use cooperative learning.
- Allow students ample thinking time.

TEACHING ENGLISH LANGUAGE LEARNERS

- Ask students to read aloud.
- Precede written work with a related oral activity.
- Use cooperative learning.
- Allow ample thinking time.
- When using small groups, pair with English-proficient students.
- Provide ample opportunity for nongraded, even nonevaluated, writing in English.
- Use multiple modes of expression: e.g., read selections aloud; read questions aloud; use visual aids—charts, graphs, tables, or other graphics, art, and films; play songs; and perform demonstrations.
- Encourage students to use multiple modes of expression, including nonverbal expressions and performances such as drawing, painting, collage, sculpture, dance and choreography, acting and oral interpretation, photography, filmmaking, video production, and musicianship and singing.

Teaching to Develop Students' Multiple Intelligences and to Accommodate Diverse Learning Styles

Activities using multiple intelligences are identified by green icons. See the legend on page T25. Use the techniques in the chart at left to teach and encourage students with diverse intellectual strengths and learning styles and to help all students use and develop the full range of their abilities.

Teaching English Language Learners

Use the techniques in the chart at left to facilitate learning and participation for students whose native language is not English.

Teaching Students with Diverse Cultural Backgrounds

Use the techniques in the chart at right to facilitate learning and participation for students with diverse cultural backgrounds.

Teaching Students with Special Needs

Students with special needs may include students with learning disabilities or students who are mentally challenged. Use the techniques in the chart at right and the suggestions for students with special needs in the Individual Learning Strategies boxes in the Teacher's Edition to help students with special needs succeed in your classroom.

Teaching Students with Special Academic Gifts and Talents

Just as students who work below grade level may lose interest because tasks are too difficult, students with special academic gifts and talents may lose interest because they complete work quickly or because they are not sufficiently challenged.

Activities involving other curricular areas are identified by brown icons and those honoring multiple intelligences are keyed by green icons in the margins of the Teacher's Edition. See the legend on page T25.

TEACHING STUDENTS WITH DIVERSE CULTURAL BACKGROUNDS

- Encourage discussion of cultural differences; invite students to share contrasting experiences; invite them to discuss events and characters from the selections that strike them as odd. Rely on students for your cultural information; be aware that you are liable to overlook differences unless you can take a different point of view.
- Use multiple modes of expression: e.g., read selections aloud; read questions aloud; use visual aids—charts, graphs, tables, or other graphics, art, and films; play songs; and perform demonstrations.
- Encourage students to use multiple modes of expression, including nonverbal expressions and performances such as drawing, painting, collage, sculpture, dance and choreography, acting and oral interpretation, photography, filmmaking, video production, and musicianship and singing.
- Precede written work with a related oral activity.
- Use cooperative learning.
- Allow ample thinking time.
- When using small groups, pair with English-proficient students.
- Preview/explain culturally loaded terms and names.
- Discuss idioms and word origins.
- Discuss topics with universal appeal and relevance—for instance, independence versus family ties, independence versus friendship, or identity.
- Discuss literature from both an "insider" and an "outsider" perspective.

TEACHING STUDENTS WITH SPECIAL NEEDS

- Discover the particular effects of each individual's disability and try to fill gaps.
- Allow ample thinking time.
- Seat students in front.
- Repeat important ideas frequently.
- Summarize and check students' bearings frequently.
- Monitor progress frequently.
- On larger projects, provide step-by-step guidance.
- Precede written work with a related oral activity.
- Use cooperative learning.
- Use multiple modes of expression: e.g., read selections aloud; read questions aloud; use visual aids—charts, graphs, tables, or other graphics, art, and films; play songs; and perform demonstrations.
- Encourage students to use multiple modes of expression, including nonverbal expressions and performances such as drawing, painting, collage, sculpture, dance and choreography, acting and oral interpretation, photography, filmmaking, video production, and musicianship and singing.

TEACHING STUDENTS WITH SPECIAL ACADEMIC GIFTS AND TALENTS

- Encourage students to use multiple modes of expression, including nonverbal expressions and performances such as drawing, painting, collage, sculpture, dance and choreography, acting and oral interpretation, photography, filmmaking, video production, and musicianship and singing.
- Use cooperative learning.
- Allow ample thinking time.
- Involve students in the planning, preparation, and presentation or conduct of lessons.
- Provide or encourage extension activities once mastery is demonstrated.
- Provide or encourage self-guided activities and independent research.

Additional Resources for Language Arts Teachers

Literature and the Language Arts is a research-based program. For a complete list of the primary studies on which the series is based, please contact EMC/Paradigm Publishing. The following is a list of resources helpful for classroom teachers.

TEACHING READING/LITERATURE

Allen, J. (2000). *Yellow brick roads: Shared and guided paths to independent reading 4–12.* Portland, Maine: Stenhouse Publishers.

Allington, R. (2002). *What really matters for struggling readers.* New York: Longman.

Alvermann, D. E. (2001). *Effective literacy instruction for adolescents.* Chicago, IL: National Reading Conference.

Burke, Jim. (2000). *Reading reminders: Tools, tips, and techniques.* Portsmouth, NH: Boynton/Cook.

Curtis, M. E. (2002). *Adolescent reading research since 1990.* Cambridge, MA: Center for Special Education, Lesley University.

Duke, Nell K. and Pearson, P. D. (2002). Effective practices for developing reading comprehension. In A. E. Farstrup and S. Jay Samuels, eds. *What research has to say about reading instruction.* Newark, DE: International Reading Association.

Ericson, B. O., ed. (2001). *Teaching reading in high school English classes.* Urbana, IL: National Council of Teachers of English.

Graves, M. F. and Graves, B. B. (1994). *Scaffolding reading experiences: Designs for student success.* Norwood, MA: Christopher-Gordon.

Graves, M. F., Palmer, R. J., and Furniss, D. W. (1976). *Structuring reading assignments for English classes.* Urbana, IL: National Council of Teachers of English.

Harvey, S. and Goudvis, A. (2001). *Strategies that work: Teaching comprehension to enhance understanding.* York, ME: Stenhouse Publishers.

Keene, E. O. and Zimmerman, S. (1997). *Mosaic of thought: Teaching comprehension in a reader's workshop.* Portsmouth, NH: Heinemann.

Langer, J. A., ed. (1992). *Literature instruction: A focus on student response.* Urbana, IL: National Council of Teachers of English.

Levin, J. R. and Pressley, M. (1981). Improving children's prose comprehension: Selected strategies that seem to succeed. In C. M. Santa and B. L. Hayes, eds.

Children's prose comprehension: Research and practice. Newark, DE: International Reading Association.

Marzano, R. J., Pickering, D. J., and Pollock, J. E. (2001). *Classroom instruction that works: Research-based strategies for increasing student achievement.* Alexandria, VA: Association for Supervision and Curriculum Development.

Newell, G. E. and Durst, R. K. (1993). *Exploring texts: The roles of discussion and writing in the teaching and learning of literature.* Norwood, MA: Christopher-Gordon.

Nims, J. F. and Mason, D. (2000). *Western wind: An introduction to poetry,* 4th ed. Boston: McGraw-Hill.

Probst, R. *Response and analysis: Teaching literature in junior and senior high school.* Portsmouth, NH: Heinemann.

Rosenblatt, L. (1938, 1996). *Literature as exploration,* 5th ed. New York: MLA.

Smith, M. W. and Wilhelm. J. D. (2002). *"Reading don't fix no Chevys": Literacy in the lives of young men.* Portsmouth, NH: Heinemann.

Tovani, C. (2000). *I read it, but I don't get it: Comprehension strategies for adolescent readers.* Portland, Maine: Stenhouse Publishers.

Wilhelm, J. D. (2001). *Improving comprehension with think aloud strategies.* New York: Scholastic.

Wilhelm, J. D. and Smith, M. W. (1996). *"You gotta BE the book": Teaching engaged and reflective reading with adolescents.* New York: Teachers College Press.

TEACHING CRITICAL THINKING

Bloom, B. S., ed. (1956, 1984). *Taxonomy of educational objectives: The classification of educational goals, Handbook I, cognitive domain.* New York: Longmans, Green.

Costa, A. L. (1991). *Developing minds: A resource book for teaching thinking.* Rev. ed. 2 Vols. Alexandria, VA: ASCD.

Gardner, H. (1999). *The unschooled mind: How children learn and how schools should teach.* New York: Basic.

Nickerson, R. S., D. N. Perkins, and E. E. Smith. *The teaching of thinking.* Hillsdale, NJ: Erlbaum, 1985.

Pressley, M. et al. (1990). *Cognitive strategy instruction that really improves children's academic performance.* Campbridge, MA: Brookline.

Resnick, L. B. (1987). *Education and learning to think.* Washington, DC: Natl. Academy P.

Rogoff, B. (1989). *Apprenticeship in thinking.* New York: Cambridge UP.

TEACHING WRITING/USAGE/GRAMMAR

Behrens, L. and Rosen, L. J. (2002). *Writing and reading across the curriculum,* 8th ed. New York: Addison Wesley Longman, Inc.

Dellinger, D. G. *Out of the heart: How to design writing assignments for high school courses.* Berkeley: Bay Area Writing Project.

Elbow, P. (1981). *Writing with power: Techniques for mastering the writing process.* New York: Oxford UP.

Flower, L. S. (1985). *Problem-solving strategies in sriting.* 2nd ed. Orlando: Harcourt.

Follett, W. and Wensburg, E. (1998). *Modern English usage: A guide.* New York: Hill and Wang, Inc.

Flood, J., Lapp, D., Squire, J., and Jensen, J. M. (2003). *Handbook of research on teaching the English language arts.* Mahwah, NJ: Lawrence Erlbaum Associates, Publishers.

Fowler, H. W. (1983). *Modern English usage,* 2nd ed. New York: Oxford University Press.

Garner, B. A. (1998). *A dictionary of modern American usage.* New York: Oxford University Press.

Hillocks, G., Jr. (1986). *Research on written composition: New directions for teaching.* Urbana, IL: Educational Resource Information Center and National Conference on Research in English.

Hillocks, G., Jr., and Smith, M. W. (2003). *Grammars and literacy learning.* Mahwah, NJ: Lawrence Erlbaum Associates, Publishers.

Purves, A., Papa, L., and Jordon, S. (1994). *Encyclopedia of English studies and language arts,* vol.1. New York: Scholastic. A

Romano, T. (1987). *Clearing the way: Working with teenage writers.* Portsmouth, NH: Heinemann.

Sebranek, P., Meyer, V., and Kemper, D. (1995). *Write source 2000: A guide to writing, thinking, and learning.* Burlington, WI: Write Source Educational Publishing House.

Sebranek, P., Meyer, V., and Kemper, D. (1992). *Writers inc.* Burlington, WI: Write Source Educational Publishing House.

Shaughnessy, M. (1977). *Errors and expectations.* New York: Oxford UP.

University of Chicago Press, The. (1993). *The Chicago manual of style,* 14th ed. Chicago, IL: The University of Chicago Press.

Weaver, C. (1996). *Teaching grammar in context.* Portsmouth, NH: Boynton/Cook.

ASSESSMENT

California Assessment Program. (1990). *The California Assessment Program: A Position Paper on Testing and Instruction.* Sacramento, CA: CAP.

Cambourne, B., and J. Turbil. (1991). "Assessment in Whole-Language Classrooms: Theory into Practice." *Elementary School Journal* 90: 337–349.

García, G. E., and P. D. Pearson. (1994). "Assessment and Diversity." *Review of Research in Education* 20: 337–391.

Gronlund, N. E., and R. L. Linn. (1990). *Measurement and Evaluation in Teaching.* 6th ed. New York: Macmillan.

Herman, J. L., P. R. Aschbacher, and L. Winters. (1992). *A Practical Guide to Alternative Assessment.* Alexandria, VA: ASCD.

Johnston, P. H. (1992). *Constructive Evaluation of Literate Activity.* White Plains, NY: Longman.

Smith, M. A., and M. Ylvisaker, eds. (1994). *Teacher's Voices: Portfolios in the Classroom.* Berkeley, CA: Natl. Writing Project.

Wolf, D., et al. (1991). "To Use Their Minds Well: Investigating New Forms of Student Assessment." *Review of Research in Education* 17: 31–74.

Yancey, K. B., ed. (1992) *Portfolios in the Writing Classroom.* Urbana, IL: NCTE.

TEACHING SPECIAL POPULATIONS

Banks, J., and C. M. Banks, eds. (1993). *Multicultural Education: Issues and Perspectives.* 2nd ed. Boston: Allyn.

Brooks, C., ed. (1985). *Tapping Potential: English and the Language Arts for the Black Learner.* Urbana, IL: NCTE.

Cummins, J. (1989). *Empowering Minority Students.* Sacramento, CA: CA Assoc. for Bilingual Education.

Farr, M., and H. Daniels. (1986). *Language Diversity and Writing Instruction.* New York: ERIC Clearinghouse on Urban Education/Columbia UP.

Garcia, E. E. (1993). "Language, Culture, and Education." *Review of Research in Education* 19: 51–98.

Haberman, M. (1991). "The Pedagogy of Poverty versus Good Teaching." *Phi Delta Kappan*: 290–294.

Hernandez, H. (1989). *Multicultural Education: A Teacher's Guide to Content and Process.* Columbus, OH: Merrill.

Kronick, D. (1988). *New Approaches to Learning Disabilities.* Philadelphia, PA: Grune & Stratton.

Marik, R (1982). *Special Education Students Write: Classroom Activities and Assignments.* Berkeley, CA: Bay Area Writing Project.

Shade, B. J. (1989). *Culture, Style, and the Educative Process.* Springfield, IL: Charles Thomas.

Slavin, R., N. Karweit, and N. Madden, eds. (1989). *Effective Programs for Students at Risk.* Boston: Allyn.

West, W. W. (1980). *Teaching the Gifted and Talented in the English Classroom.* Washington, DC: NEA.

GENDER ISSUES

Brown, L. M., and C. Gilligan. (1992). *Meeting at the Crossroads: Women's Psychology and Girls' Development.* Cambridge: Harvard UP.

Gilbert, P. (1989). *Gender, Literacy, and the Classroom.* Carlton South, Victoria: Austral. Reading Assn.

Sadker, M., and D. Sadker. (1994). *Failing at Fairness: How Schools Cheat Girls.* New York: Scribner's.

Sadker, M., D. Sadker, and S. Klein. (1991). "The Issue of Gender in Elementary and Secondary Education." *Review of Research in Education* 17: 269–334.

Wellesley College Center for Research on Women. (1992). *How Schools Shortchange Girls: The AAUW Report.* Washington, DC: American Assn. of Univ. Women.

TEACHING HIGH SCHOOL STUDENTS

Applebee, A. N. (1978). *The Child's Concept of Story: Ages Two to Seventeen.* Chicago: U of Chicago P.

Flavell, J. (1985). *Cognitive Development.* 2nd ed. Englewood Cliffs, NJ: Prentice.

Kohlberg, L. (1970). "Education for Justice: A Modern Statement of the Platonic View." *Five Lectures on Moral Education.* Ed. N. F. Sizer and T. R. Sizer. Cambridge: Harvard UP.

KEY TO ICONS

Cross-Curriculum Icons

 Arts and Humanities

 Mathematics and Sciences

 Social Studies

 Applied Arts

Multiple Intelligence Icons

 Musical Intelligence
Ability to produce and to appreciate forms of musical expression

 Logical-Mathematical Intelligence
Ability to reason and to discern logical or numerical patterns

 Spatial Intelligence
Ability to configure space to pose and solve problems

 Kinesthetic Intelligence
Ability to use the body effectively to solve problems

 Interpersonal/Intrapersonal Intelligence
Ability to respond to the needs of others, self

Naturalist Intelligence
Ability to respond to surrounding environment

SCANS Icons

 Managing Resources
Identifies, organizes, plans, allocates time, money, materials, space, human resources

 Interpersonal Skills
Works with others as member of team

 Information Skills
Acquires, evaluates, organizes, maintains, interprets, communicates, and processes information

 Systems Skills
Understands complex inter-relationships

 Technology Skills
Selects, applies, and maintains appropriate technology to perform tasks and solve problems

 Basic Skills
Reads, writes, performs arithmetic and mathematical operations, and listens and speaks well

 Thinking Skills
Thinks creatively, makes decisions, solves problems, visualizes, knows how to learn, and reasons

 Personal Qualities
Displays responsibility, self-esteem, sociability, self-management, and integrity and honesty

Using the Annotated Teacher's Edition

The *Annotated Teacher's Edition* is designed to be as "teacher-friendly" as possible. Answers for exercises are usually provided on the same pages as the exercises themselves. All items are color-coded:

- white backgrounds: answers to student edition questions, exercises, and selection check tests
- green backgrounds: supplementary notes and background information

- pink backgrounds: quotes and cross-curricular connections and activities
- blue backgrounds: additional resources, questions and activities

Sample Unit Opening Pages

*The **Unit Skills Outline** lists the skills taught in the student edition and in additional activities in this Annotated Teacher's Edition.*

***Cross-Curricular Connections** lists the cross-curricular activities from the unit.*

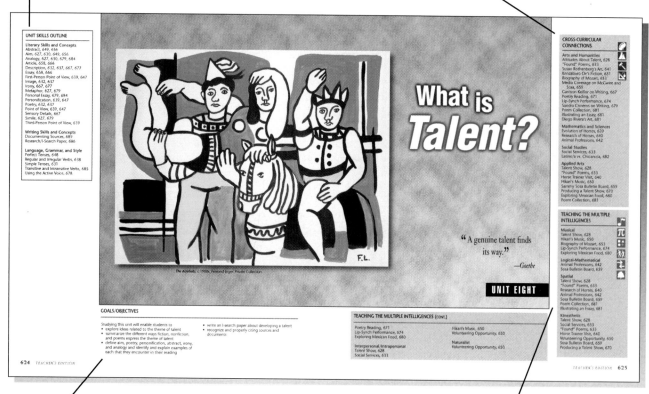

*A list of **Goals/Objectives** helps you plan overall intended learning outcomes for the unit. Affective goals are consistent with the philosophy of the program and its emphasis on reader involvement. Cognitive goals encompass content, literary technique, interpretation in historical context, and concepts taught in the Guided Writing lesson at the end of the unit.*

***Teaching the Multiple Intelligences** lists activities from the unit that call for the exercise of students' multiple intelligences.*

Sample Unit Review Pages

Additional Resources notes identify assessment materials for the unit and study guides and worksheets for student review and practice.

Vocabulary Development notes provide an activity for reinforcing vocabulary acquisition as students prepare for the unit test. Additional vocabulary development work is available in the Vocabulary Resource and Word Study Resource, which are part of the Teacher's Resource Kit.

Reflecting on Your Reading questions extend the ideas presented throughout the unit. These questions, which are appropriate prompts for writing, research, or discussion, cover genres and themes in a way that allows students to synthesize the material from the unit.

For Your Reading List highlights books suitable for independent reading, along with an **Independent Reading Activity** to help students extend their reading experience beyond the classroom and develop a passion for lifelong learning.

Sample Prereading Page

Additional Resources *notes identify materials from the Teacher's Resource Kit to use in teaching the selection: worksheets from the Unit Resource book and from the language arts Skills Resource books, and selection check tests and tests from the Unit Resource book.*

*Color-coded **icons** identify at a glance **cross-curricular** activities (brown), **multiple intelligences** activities (green), and **SCANS** (Secretary's Commission on Achieving Necessary Skills) activities (blue). A key to these icons is provided on page T25 of this Annotated Teacher's Edition.*

Vocabulary from the Selection *notes provide a comprehensive list of the Words for Everyday Use from the selection.*

Reader's Journal Notes *give suggestions for helping students relate the topic to their experience, anticipate questions or difficulties students may have, or provide additional prompts for students who have trouble starting. Special attention is given to problems that may arise from student diversity.*

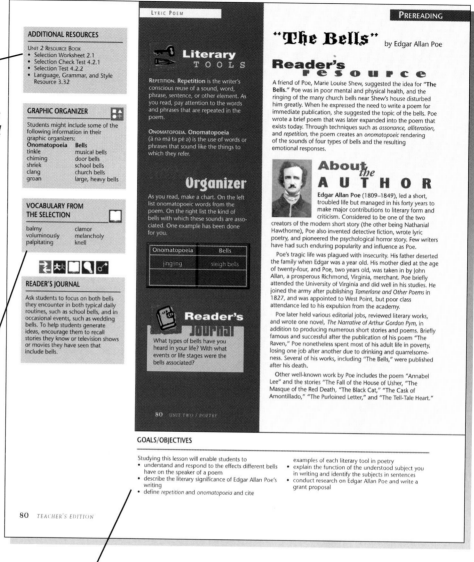

*A list of **Goals/Objectives** helps you plan intended learning outcomes for the selection. Affective goals are consistent with the philosophy of the program and its emphasis on reader involvement. Cognitive goals encompass content, literary technique, interpretation of the selection in historical context, and language arts skills taught in the student text.*

Sample Selection Page

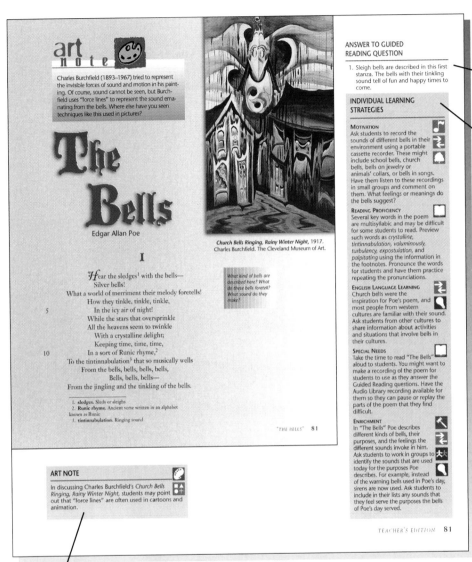

art note

Charles Burchfield (1893–1967) tried to represent the invisible forces of sound and motion in his painting. Of course, sound cannot be seen, but Burchfield uses "force lines" to represent the sound emanating from the bells. Where else have you seen techniques like this used in pictures?

The Bells

Edgar Allan Poe

I

Hear the sledges¹ with the bells—
    Silver bells!
What a world of merriment their melody foretells!
        How they tinkle, tinkle, tinkle,
            In the icy air of night!
        While the stars that oversprinkle
        All the heavens seem to twinkle
            With a crystalline delight;
            Keeping time, time, time,
            In a sort of Runic rhyme,²
To the tintinnabulation³ that so musically wells
        From the bells, bells, bells, bells,
                Bells, bells, bells—
From the jingling and the tinkling of the bells.

1. **sledges.** Sleds or sleighs
2. **Runic rhyme.** Ancient verse written in an alphabet known as Runic
3. **tintinnabulation.** Ringing sound

"THE BELLS" **81**

Church Bells Ringing, Rainy Winter Night, 1917.
Charles Burchfield. The Cleveland Museum of Art.

What kind of bells are described here? What do these bells foretell? What sound do they make?

ART NOTE

In discussing Charles Burchfield's *Church Bells Ringing, Rainy Winter Night,* students may point out that "force lines" are often used in cartoons and animation.

ANSWER TO GUIDED READING QUESTION

1. Sleigh bells are described in this first stanza. The bells with their tinkling sound tell of fun and happy times to come.

INDIVIDUAL LEARNING STRATEGIES

MOTIVATION
Ask students to record the sounds of different bells in their environment using a portable cassette recorder. These might include school bells, church bells, bells on jewelry or animals' collars, or bells in songs. Have them listen to these recordings in small groups and comment on them. What feelings or meanings do the bells suggest?

READING PROFICIENCY
Several key words in the poem are multisyllabic and may be difficult for some students to read. Preview such words as *crystalline, tintinnabulation, voluminously, turbulency, expostulation,* and *palpitating* using the information in the footnotes. Pronounce the words for students and have them practice repeating the pronunciations.

ENGLISH LANGUAGE LEARNING
Church bells were the inspiration for Poe's poem, and most people from western cultures are familiar with their sound. Ask students from other cultures to share information about activities and situations that involve bells in their cultures.

SPECIAL NEEDS
Take the time to read "The Bells" aloud to students. You might want to make a recording of the poem for students to use as they answer the Guided Reading questions. Have the Audio Library recording available for them so they can pause or replay the parts of the poem that they find difficult.

ENRICHMENT
In "The Bells" Poe describes different kinds of bells, their purposes, and the feelings the different sounds invoke in him. Ask students to work in groups to identify the sounds that are used today for the purposes Poe describes. For example, instead of the warning bells used in Poe's day, sirens are now used. Ask students to include in their lists any sounds that they feel serve the purposes the bells of Poe's day served.

TEACHER'S EDITION **81**

Answers to Guided Reading questions *are keyed to questions in the student edition.*

Individual Learning Strategies *notes provide additional lesson plans for individual instruction in the following areas:*

- ***Motivation*** *strategies encourage students to take an interest in the selection and relate it to their own lives.*
- ***Reading Proficiency*** *activities focus on developing reading skills and present reading strategies to help students with reading difficulties.*
- ***English Language Learning*** *activities provide support for students whose native language is not English, including* ***Additional Vocabulary*** *to help you offer instruction before students encounter difficulty in reading.*
- ***Special Needs*** *activities offer assistance in planning instruction for students with learning disabilities and mentally challenged students to help them succeed in your classroom.*
- ***Enrichment*** *activities challenge academically gifted students and provide opportunities for independent study and self-guided research.*

The ***Art Note*** *feature provides a visual literacy component that connects fine art to the literature studied.*

Internet Resources *notes (not shown) connect you with a wealth of online resources that provide additional information on authors and literary selections, links to related readings, and Internet activities.*

Historical, Literary, Bibliography, *and* ***Art Notes*** *provide additional information to enhance the reading of the selections.*

Cross-Curricular Connections and Activities *(not shown) are supplementary activities that involve knowledge, skills, research, and resources from disciplines other than language arts.*

Cross-references *(not shown) to additional instruction, worksheets, and assessment materials are provided throughout the annotations.*

Sample Selection Post-Reading Page

Notes on the **Respond to the Selection** questions help you help students relate the topic to their experience, anticipate questions or difficulties students might have, or suggest alternative formats (such as large or small group discussion or role playing). These notes give special attention to concerns of diversity.

Answers to Investigate, Inquire, Imagine give sample responses to Recall/Interpret, Analyze/Synthesize, Evaluate/Extend, and Perspective/Empathy question sets.

RESPOND TO THE SELECTION

Responses will vary. Both poems generate an emotion of gratefulness. Kenyon opposes everyday descriptions against an "otherwise" that makes her grateful for what she has now. Hall is grateful for his writing, which represents his "one task and desire."

ANSWERS TO INVESTIGATE, INQUIRE, AND IMAGINE

RECALL
1a. She says she got out of bed "on two strong legs."
2a. She says that one day "it will be otherwise."
3a. He sees a "bluish / mounded softness where / the Honda was."
4a. He sits at his desk "for this day's lifelong / engagement with the one task and desire."

INTERPRET
1b. She is saying that she is healthy and strong.
2b. She is referring to a time when she will not be healthy, might not have enough to eat, and might not have a partner with whom to share her life.
3b. The speaker is describing his snow-covered car in the early morning light.
4b. A day's work can be "lifelong" because it is part of a continuum connecting the work of the day before and tomorrow. The "one task and desire" is the speaker's desire to write.

ANALYZE
5a. The speakers of "Otherwise" and "The Old Life" both write in the morning and share a passion for writing poetry. Both speakers eat breakfast before beginning to write, even though they enjoy eating different foods. What differs between them is the other activities that precede the beginning of their work day. The speaker of "Otherwise" takes the dog for a walk (doing something physical), while the speaker of "The Old Life" reads the newspaper (doing something intellectual).

SYNTHESIZE
5b. The speaker of "Otherwise" lies down with her mate at noon. She eats dinner with him "at a table with silver / candlesticks." The speaker of "The Old Life" gets

---

Respond*to the*
SELECTIONS

How do the speakers of both poems feel about the day they have described? What emotion do the poems generate?

Investigate, Inquire, and Imagine

Recall: GATHERING FACTS
1a. In "Otherwise," what does the speaker say about getting out of bed?
2a. In "Otherwise," what does the speaker say will happen "one day"?
3a. In "The Old Life," what does the speaker see when he awakes?
4a. In "The Old Life," why does the speaker sit at his desk?

Interpret: FINDING MEANING
1b. What comment is the speaker making about her health?
2b. What alternate realities do you think the speaker is referring to?
3b. What is the speaker describing?
4b. How can a day's work be "lifelong"? What is the "one task and desire"?

Analyze: TAKING THINGS APART →
5a. Compare and contrast the speakers' mornings in "Otherwise" and " The Old Life."

Synthesize: BRINGING THINGS TOGETHER
5b. How do the speakers of both poems interact? Sometimes the speaker of a poem is the poet himself or herself, but sometimes the speaker is a voice assumed by the poet. Which is the case for "Otherwise" and "The Old Life"? How can you tell?

Evaluate: MAKING JUDGMENTS
6a. According to Hall, American poetry after 1950 is "a poetry of experiences more than of ideas. The experience is presented often without comment, and the words of the description must supply the emotion which the experience generates. . . ." Do "Otherwise" and "The Old Life" support this assessment of contemporary poetry?

Extend: CONNECTING IDEAS
6b. What do you think Jane Kenyon and Donald Hall value most in life? What leads you to this conclusion?

Understanding *Literature*

REPETITION. Review the definition for **repetition** in the Handbook of Literary Terms. What is repeated in "Otherwise" and "The Old Life"? What is the effect of this repetition?

DESCRIPTION. Review the definition for **description** in the Handbook of Literary Terms and the chart you made for Literary Tools on page 832. How would the poems be different without the use of sensory details? Which sensory detail in each poem do you find the most striking? Why?

836 UNIT ELEVEN / JOURNEYS

ANSWERS TO INVESTIGATE, INQUIRE, AND IMAGINE (CONT.)

coffee for his mate in the morning while she's still "half-asleep." Knowing from the Reader's Resource and About the Authors that Jane Kenyon and Donald Hall were married, and noticing that the speaker of "The Old Life" calls his mate Jane, students should be able to tell that in each poem, the speaker is the poet. The poets are talking about their own lives and are not assuming a different voice.

EVALUATE
6a. Yes. Each poet describes a typical, routine day. Kenyon and Hall do not comment on their experiences. There is no philosophical aside to the reader telling him or her how to interpret their experiences. Their descriptions "supply the emotion which the experience generates" through the use of sensory details that evoke a realistic life.

Continued on page 837

836 *TEACHER'S EDITION*

Writer's Journal

1. Write a **paragraph** describing the "otherwise" situations that Kenyon hints at in "Otherwise." Tell how her life might be different in the future.
2. Imagine that you are Donald Hall. Write a **journal entry** describing your frustration or joy with your work in the afternoon.
3. Write a **poem** describing a part of your day or a daily routine. Choose sensory details designed to evoke a particular emotion in your reader.

Integrating the Language Arts

Language, Grammar, and Style

USING VIVID VERBS. Read the Language Arts Survey 3.39, "Adding Colorful Language to Sentences." Then rewrite the following sentences using vivid verbs.

1. Donald made strong coffee.
2. He relaxed in the blue chair.
3. He took the snow off the Honda.
4. Jane said, "Thank you for the coffee."
5. She ate cereal and a peach.

Speaking and Listening

POETRY READING. Imagine that you are Jane Kenyon and you have agreed to give a poetry reading at a bookstore in your area. Select three or four poems that you consider representative of your work and interesting to an audience. Prepare an introduction for each poem. This might be a story about how you came to write the poem, a summary of the poem, or an anecdote intended to pique your audience's interest. Then decide what tone, facial expression, gestures, and body language to use for each poem. Finally, present your poetry reading to the class. Before your presentation, you might want to review the Language Arts Survey 4.19, "Oral Interpretation of Poetry."

Applied English

FLYER. Imagine that you own a bookstore in New Hampshire and have convinced Donald Hall to read from his poetry for your customers. Having read " The Old Life," you know something of what he values, but you may want to find others of his later works and read them as well. Create a flyer to be sent to your best customers advertising the reading and inviting them to come. You will want to describe it in such a way that your customers will not want to miss it, even if they have never read Hall.

"OTHERWISE" AND "THE OLD LIFE" **837**

ANSWERS TO INVESTIGATE, INQUIRE, AND IMAGINE (CONT. FROM PAGE 836)

EXTEND
6b. *Responses will vary.* Each mentions a profound love for his or her work. Each poet places the other in a central place in the poem. And each mentions several simple things in his or her daily routine. We can conclude from this that they love their work, they love each other, and they appreciate the fact that they are alive and able to enjoy simple things.

TEACHER'S EDITION **837**

ANSWERS TO INTEGRATING THE LANGUAGE ARTS

Language, Grammar, and Style
Responses will vary. Possible responses are given.
1. Donald brewed strong coffee.
2. He stretched out in the blue chair.
3. He broomed the snow off the Honda.
4. Jane murmured thank you for the coffee.
5. She breakfasted on cereal and a peach.

Speaking and Listening
Encourage students to work with a partner to practice their poetry readings and get constructive feedback before they present their reading.

Applied English
Ask students to read through 6.9, "Delivering a Press Release," in the Language Arts Survey before they begin this activity.

ANSWERS TO UNDERSTANDING LITERATURE

REPETITION. The sentence "It might have been otherwise" is repeated in "Otherwise." The effect of this repetition is to make the reader focus on all the speaker has to be grateful for, which might someday be taken away from her. In "The Old Life" the color blue is repeated. First there is the "bluish mounded softness" describing the car covered with snow. Then there is the blue of the chair and the blue-berry of the bagels. The effect of this repetition is to call to mind the bluish half-light of early morning and the poet's awakening state of mind as he prepares for another day's work.

DESCRIPTION. *Responses will vary.* Without sensory details, the poems would be bare, and the specific events in the lives of these poets would seem more ordinary.

Sample Selection Post-Reading Page

Answers to Integrating the Language Arts provide model answers for Language Grammar, and Style; Speaking and Listening; Critical Thinking; Study and Research; Media Literacy; Collaborative Learning; Vocabulary; and Applied English activities.

Answers to Understanding Literature provide possible answers for these questions about literary techniques.

Selection Check Test with Answers (not shown) includes the questions with answers and appears on or near the last page of each selection. You can photocopy the test from the Unit Resource book and distribute it, or you can present the questions orally.

Literature and the Language Arts: Understanding Literature

ART NOTES

Totem Pole, Inuit Artist

Granary Door, Dogon Artist

On the Seekonk, Edward Mitchell Bannister

Landscape of the Four Seasons, Shen Shih-ch'ing

Mt. Cortezo; in Hereto Provience near Mexico City Mexico, Joseph Yoakum

The Human Condition, Rene Magritte

Scorched Earth, Clear-cut Logging on Native Sovereign Land, Shaman Coming to Fix, Lawrence Paul Yuxweluptun

Melancholia: On the Beach, Edvard Munch

Angel of Destiny, Odilon Redon

Cornfield with Crows, Vincent van Gogh

Mona Lisa, Leonardo da Vinci

Dislocation, Kuange Jian

Autobiography: Water / Ancestors / Middle Passage / Family Ghosts, Howardena Pindell

An American Diary, Roger Shimomura

Antigone, Marie Spartali Stillman

Interrupted Journey, Samuel Bak

Words For Everyday Use
Literary Tools
Reflecting on Your Reading

Thematic Organization Chart

The chart on these pages lists forty-seven common literary themes and identifies the selections in this book that deal with these themes. Choose the themes you wish to teach in your course, and use the chart to identify selections that deal with those themes.

Selection	AGE	ALIENATION	ART AND ARTISTRY	BEAUTY	BIRTH	CONFUSION	COURAGE AND FEAR	DEATH	DISCOVERING AND LEARNING	DIVERSITY AND PLURALISM	DRAMA AND ACTING	EXILE	FAITH	FAMILY	FREEDOM	FRIENDSHIP	THE FUTURE	GIVING	GOD	GREED AND AMBITION	GROWTH/GROWING UP	HERO/HEROISM	HOME AND COUNTRY	HONESTY	HOPE	IDENTITY	IMAGINATION	INDEPENDENCE	JUSTICE	KNOWLEDGE/WISDOM	LAW AND CUSTOM	LEADERSHIP AND AUTHORITY	LOSS AND REMEMBRANCE	LOVE	NATURE	ORDER/DISORDER	PARENTS AND CHILDREN	PEACE	PRIDE AND VANITY	RELIGION	SCIENCE	STRUGGLE	TECHNOLOGY	TRUTH/REALITY	WAR	WORK	WRITING AND BOOKS
UNIT 1																																															
"Magic Words," 6			●																						●	●									●												
from *The Greek Myths* "The Five Ages of Man," 10																			●		●				●										●						●			●			
"Orpheus," 12			●				●	●																																							
from the *Popol Vuh*, 16					●														●																●	●				●							
"Popocatépetl and Ixtacihuatl," 23													●						●											●		●	●	●			●										
from *King Arthur and His Knights of the Round Table*, 32																						●								●		●							●								
from *Le Morte d'Arthur*, 45								●											●				●							●		●							●	●		●			●		
"Sundiata Keita, the Legend and the King," 54					●		●	●				●							●			●	●									●										●			●		
UNIT 2																																															
"36. In the late-afternoon light the tops of the breadfruit leaves," 78																																			●												
"The Bean Eaters," 83	●																								●	●				●																	
"Dream Variations," 88		●													●				●						●	●									●												
"The Dance," 92																																															
"Ars Poetica," 96		●																																	●												●
"Poetry," 101																																															●
"The Gazelle," 106				●																															●												
"Afternoon," 108	●							●																									●		●												
"Success is counted sweetest. . .," 111								●																		●							●									●			●		
"The Mystery of Emily Dickinson," 113																																						●									●
"I heard my love. . .," 116																																	●	●													
"A Tree Telling of Orpheus," 120			●	●			●	●																						●			●		●												
from "Holidays," 128																									●	●																					
"The Drowned Maid" from the *Kalevala*, 134														●											●		●						●			●											
"In the Blue Woodland," 142														●											●								●			●											
"Musical Adaption of the *Kalevala* Presented at Guthrie Theater Lab," 143		●									●			●																			●			●											
"Participating in a Poetry Slam," 146																																															●
UNIT 3																																															
"Lather and Nothing Else," 164						●	●	●	●																●					●									●			●					
"The Black Cat," 171						●	●	●																			●				●					●						●					
"The Open Window," 183			●				●	●	●																	●																		●			
"The Moment Before the Gun Went Off," 190								●																	●											●	●				●	●					
"The Necklace," 198				●				●											●																				●								
"I Stand Here Ironing," 208									●																●	●											●					●					

T34

Selection	Themes marked
"Like the Sun," 218	Alienation; Honesty; Truth/Reality
"The Enchanted Garden," 224	Alienation; Beauty; Confusion; Courage and Fear; Love
UNIT 4	
The Tragedy of Julius Cæsar, 242	Confusion; Death; Diversity and Pluralism; Freedom; Greed and Ambition; Home and Country; Justice; Leadership and Authority; Order/Disorder; Religion; War
from *The Prince,* 339	Greed and Ambition; Home and Country; Leadership and Authority
"One-Act Play Competition," 345	Drama and Acting
UNIT 5	
from *The Diary of a Young Girl,* 364	Confusion; Courage and Fear; Faith; Family; Freedom; Friendship; Growth/Growing Up; Hope; Identity; Love; Parents and Children; Peace; Religion; War; Writing and Books
from *The Drowned and the Saved,* 382	Courage and Fear; Faith; Freedom; Struggle; War
"Harriet Tubman: The Moses of Her People," 386	Courage and Fear; Exile; Freedom; Hero/Heroism; Hope; Leadership and Authority; Struggle
"Montgomery Boycott," 395	Courage and Fear; Exile; Freedom; Family; Hero/Heroism; Independence; Leadership and Authority; Struggle
"The Man Who Mistook His Wife for a Hat," 405	Confusion; Pride and Vanity
"Ice and Light," 417	Beauty; Nature
"The Last Bison," 425	Death; Discovering and Learning; Hope; Nature; Order/Disorder; Struggle
"Yonder sky that has wept tears of compassion. . .," 433	Alienation; Discovering and Learning; Faith; Family; God; Home and Country; Loss and Remembrance; Love; Peace; War
from *The Diving Bell and the Butterfly*	
"The Alphabet," 440	Courage and Fear; Loss and Remembrance; Struggle
"Paris," 442	Loss and Remembrance; Struggle
"The United Nations Essay Writing Contest," 446	Writing and Books
UNIT 6	
"Under the Crack of Reality," 466	Art and Artistry; Beauty
"One Evening," 471	Age; Art and Artistry; Death; Knowledge/Wisdom; Parents and Children; Peace
"Beware the Unruly Sun," 475	Science
"How to Write a Letter," 482	Art and Artistry; Friendship; Giving
"Into the Electronic Millennium," 488	Technology
from "The New Pandora's Box: An Interview with Sven Birkerts," 495	Technology
from *The Victorian Internet,* 499	Technology
"Internet and E-mail," 505	Technology
"The 21st Century," 508	The Future; Imagination
UNIT 7	
"The Waking," 523	Alienation; Hope; Science
"The Happy Man," 528	Confusion; Family; Law and Custom; War
"Land Enough for a Man," 538	Death; Discovering and Learning; Greed and Ambition; Peace; Work
"The Thief," 551	Death; Friendship; Greed and Ambition; Honesty; Hope; Science; Truth/Reality
"The Liar," 563	Hero/Heroism; Honesty
"Third Bank of the River," 581	Alienation; Confusion; Family; Knowledge/Wisdom; Parents and Children; Truth/Reality
"Heraclitus," 585	Truth/Reality
from *How Reading Changed My Life,* 588	Death; Greed and Ambition
UNIT 8	
"A Smart Cookie," 611	Growth/Growing Up; Hero/Heroism; Knowledge/Wisdom; Parents and Children
"Curiositá," 615	Discovering and Learning; Home and Country; Work
"The Major Accomplishments of Leonardo da Vinci," 620	Discovering and Learning; Home and Country; Knowledge/Wisdom; Work

Selections cross-referenced by theme. A bullet (●) indicates that the selection addresses the theme named in that column.

Selection	AGE	ALIENATION	ART AND ARTISTRY	BEAUTY	BIRTH	CONFUSION	COURAGE AND FEAR	DEATH	DISCOVERING AND LEARNING	DIVERSITY AND PLURALISM	DRAMA AND ACTING	EXILE	FAITH	FAMILY	FREEDOM	FRIENDSHIP	THE FUTURE	GIVING	GOD	GREED AND AMBITION	GROWTH/GROWING UP	HERO/HEROISM	HOME AND COUNTRY	HONESTY	HOPE	IDENTITY	IMAGINATION	INDEPENDENCE	JUSTICE	KNOWLEDGE/WISDOM	LAW AND CUSTOM	LEADERSHIP AND AUTHORITY	LOSS AND REMEMBRANCE	LOVE	NATURE	ORDER/DISORDER	PARENTS AND CHILDREN	PEACE	PRIDE AND VANITY	RELIGION	SCIENCE	STRUGGLE	TECHNOLOGY	TRUTH/REALITY	WAR	WORK	WRITING AND BOOKS
"Rules of the Game," 625														●						●						●											●				●						
"The Rules of Chess," 637									●																																						
from *My Left Foot*, 642		●				●	●	●	●					●										●													●				●					
from *Albert Einstein: A Biography*, 650									●																					●											●		●			
"Einstein's Theory of Relativity," 657									●																					●											●		●			
"The Roots of Genius?," 658									●																					●											●		●			
"My Credo," 659									●					●									●		●								●							●						
"Engineer-Private Paul Klee Misplaces an Aircraft Between Milbertshofen and Cambrai," 662																																															
"Flowers for Algernon," 669		●					●	●	●			●				●	●		●						●	●				●			●		●				●	●	●	●			●	●	
"Short Assignments," 693									●																												●										●
UNIT 9																																															
"Simple Song," 711		●							●																								●														
"Prayer to the Pacific," 715													●									●			●										●												
"The Cabuliwallah," 720	●	●							●				●			●											●	●	●					●													
"New Dog," 729								●																									●	●								●				
"1910," 734									●																●			●														●				
"Not Knowing in Aztlán," 737									●																●			●														●				
"The Legend," 740		●						●	●																																					
"A White Woman of Color," 745									●																																					
"Something Could Happen to You," 755								●	●											●					●												●										
"On Loan to the Lonely," 761																									●																						●
"After You, My Dear Alphonse," 764									●						●																																
"I Remember, I Believe," 770									●			●														●		●																			
UNIT 10																																															
"Dead Men's Path," 785		●											●										●													●										
"One of Grandma Selma's Stories," 791						●	●		●				●																													●				
"The Gift of Cochise," 795							●						●												●			●																		
"Chee's Daughter," 809							●							●					●						●							●	●		●											
"Freeway 280," 821														●																			●													
"The Road from Ballygunge," 824														●											●	●			●																	
from *Desert Exile: The Uprooting of a Japanese American Family*, 833		●					●		●																●								●									●		●			
from *When Heaven and Earth Changed Places*, 843		●					●		●																●																	●			●		
UNIT 11																																															
Antigone, 863							●						●						●										●		●	●				●											
UNIT 12																																															
"House Taken Over," 917		●																																		●								●			
"Casa" / "House," 923																							●		●																						
"A Very Old Man with Enormous Wings," 926										●										●																				●							
"East Song," 933																										●						●															
"The Adventure of the Speckled Band," 936						●	●	●												●						●			●		●																
"The Pedestrian," 958		●															●														●				●							●	●				
"By the Waters of Babylon," 965						●	●	●									●													●											●	●	●	●			
The Hitchhiker, 978							●	●																																		●					
from *The Vanishing Hitchhiker*, 989																																										●					

Selections by Genre

These pages list all the selections in this book, organized by genre. Choose the genres you wish to teach in your course, and use the list to identify selections that represent those genres.

Literature
and the Language Arts
Understanding Literature

THE EMC MASTERPIECE SERIES

SECOND EDITION

EMCParadigm Publishing Saint Paul, Minnesota

Staff Credits

Editorial

Laurie Skiba
Editor

Brenda Owens
Associate Editor

Lori Ann Coleman
Associate Editor

Diana Moen
Associate Editor

Jennifer Joline Anderson
Assistant Editor

Gia Marie Garbinsky
Assistant Editor

Janice Johnson
Curriculum Specialist

Paul Spencer
Art and Photo Researcher

Chris Bohen
Editorial Assistant

Katherine S. Link
Editorial Assistant

Design

Shelley Clubb
Production Manager

Jennifer Wreisner
Senior Designer

C. Vern Johnson
Senior Designer

Michelle Lewis
Senior Design Specialist

Julie L. Hansen
Design Specialist

Cover Credits

Cover Designer: C. Vern Johnson

The Human Condition, 1934. René Magritte.
Tahitian Pastoral Scene, 1893. Paul Gauguin.
The Farm, 1921–1922. Joan Miró.
The Persistence of Memory, 1931. Salvador Dalí.

ISBN 0-8219-2135-5 (Student Edition)   ISBN 0-8219-2136-3 (Annotated Teacher's Edition)
© 2005, 2003, 2001 by EMC Corporation

Published by EMC/Paradigm Publishing
875 Montreal Way
St. Paul, Minnesota 55102
800-328-1452
www.emcp.com
E-mail: educate@emcp.com

Printed in the United States of America.
11 10 9 8 7 6 5 4   XXX   06 05

Literature
and the Language Arts

SECOND EDITION

REDWOOD LEVEL
DISCOVERING LITERATURE

WILLOW LEVEL
UNDERSTANDING LITERATURE

CEDAR LEVEL
EXPLORING LITERATURE

PINE LEVEL
THE AMERICAN TRADITION

OAK LEVEL
RESPONDING TO LITERATURE

MAPLE LEVEL
THE BRITISH TRADITION

BIRCH LEVEL
EXPERIENCING LITERATURE

CYPRESS LEVEL
WORLD LITERATURE

Consultants and Writers

Senior Consultant
Dr. Edmund J. Farrell
Emeritus Professor of English Education
University of Texas at Austin
Austin, Texas

Gwendolyn Alexander
Educational Consultant
Washington, DC

Amy Bergstrom
Instructor
English Education Department
University of Minnesota
Duluth, Minnesota

Diana Blythe
Senior Content Manager
Humanities Software,
    a division of Advantage
    Learning Systems, Inc.
Hood River, Oregon

Cherie Boen
National Board Certified
    Teacher
Educational Consultant
Minneapolis, Minnesota

Gloria Canson
English Instructor
Roosevelt High School
Portland, Oregon

Linda Christopherson
Educational Writer
Charlotte, North Carolina

Mary Curfman
Language Arts Supervisor
Department of Curriculum
    and Professional Development
Clark County Schools
Las Vegas, Nevada

Deanna and Roger Hebbert
Educational Writers
Longmont, Colorado

Tim Fisher
Educational Writer
Minneapolis, Minnesota

Sheila Griffin
Educational Writer
Waukesha, Wisconsin

Sara Hyry
Freelance Education Writer
Easthampton, Massachusetts

Christina Kolb
Educational Writer
Newton, Massachusetts

Sharon Kremer
English Department Chair
A. O. Calhoun Middle School
Denton, Texas

Jon Madian
Senior Instructional Designer
Humanities Software,
    a division of Advantage
    Learning Systems, Inc.
Hood River, Oregon

Beverly Martin
Managing Editor
Humanities Software,
    a division of Advantage
    Learning Systems, Inc.
Hood River, Oregon

Chris Nelson
Educational Writer
Northfield, Minnesota

Laura Mezner Nelson
Educational Writer
Minnetonka, Minnesota

Margaret Palmer
English Department Chair
Samuel Clemens High School
Shertz, Texas

David Rathbun
English Instructor
South High School
Minneapolis, Minnesota

Cassandra Sagan
Educational Writer
Portland, Oregon

Eric Schneider
English Instructor
Patrick Henry High School
Minneapolis, Minnesota

Elnora Shields
Educational Consultant
Durham, North Carolina

Dr. Jane S. Shoaf
Educational Consultant
Edenton, North Carolina

Kendra Sisserson
Research Associate
University of Chicago
Chicago, Illinois

Brady Smith
Language Arts Teacher
Portland, Oregon

James W. Swanson
Educational Consultant
Minneapolis, Minnesota

Anita Usmiani
Language Arts Supervisor
Hamilton Township School
    District
Hamilton, New Jersey

Hope Vasholz
Teacher of English
Hammond High School
Columbia, Maryland

Dr. Gary Wiener
Language Arts Chair
Brighton High School
Rochester, New York

PART ONE • Genres in Literature

The Oyster Gatherers of Cancale, c.1878. John Singer Sargent.

◀ Dramatic recording included in Audio Library

✎ Additional reading support provided in *The EMC Write-In Reader*

☉ Guided Writing Interactive Software on CD-ROM

Diner, c.1971. Richard Estes.

◄ Dramatic recording included in Audio Library

✎ Additional reading support provided in *The EMC Write-In Reader*

◉ Guided Writing Interactive Software on CD-ROM

◀ Dramatic recording included in Audio Library   ✎ Additional reading support provided in The EMC Write-In Reader   ◉ Guided Writing Interactive Software on CD-ROM

◀ Dramatic recording included in Audio Library   ✐ Additional reading support provided in *The EMC Write-In Reader*   ☮ Guided Writing Interactive Software on CD-ROM

Artist's Garden at Vétheuil, 1880.
Claude Monet.

PART TWO • Themes in Literature

Melancholia: On the Beach, 1896. Edvard Munch.

UNIT 8   The Genius Within

GUIDED WRITING ⊚   699

The Research Paper: Writing a Biography/Exploring Genius
LANGUAGE, GRAMMAR, AND STYLE: **Effective Documentation**

UNIT 9   Diversity and Community

GUIDED WRITING ⊚   774

Informative Writing: Writing a Cause and Effect Essay
LANGUAGE, GRAMMAR, AND STYLE: **Standard, Formal English**

◀ Dramatic recording included in Audio Library

✎ Additional reading support provided in *The EMC Write-In Reader*

⊚ Guided Writing Interactive Software on CD-ROM

UNIT 10   Cultures in Conflict

The Rule of Light, 1944. René Magritte.

UNIT 11   What We Live By

◀ Dramatic recording included in Audio Library   🖉 Additional reading support provided in *The EMC Write-In Reader*   ◉ Guided Writing Interactive Software on CD-ROM

UNIT 12   Other Worlds

◀ Dramatic recording included in Audio Library   ✐ Additional reading support provided in *The EMC Write-In Reader*   💿 Guided Writing Interactive Software on CD-ROM

PART THREE • Language Arts Survey
A Handbook of Essential Skills

To the Student

Features of Your Textbook

A Guide for Reading

When you open your *EMC Masterpiece Series* textbook, you will find great literature, both classic and contemporary, by a wide variety of authors. You will also find useful step-by-step study strategies for each selection, helpful background information, and activities that allow you to relate the literature to your own experiences and share your point of view.

The **Guided Reading** program in this *EMC Masterpiece Series* book gives you tips before, during, and after you read each selection. Read on for a description of the features you will find in your textbook.

- **Reader's Resource** gives you background and other information you'll need for the reading.
- **Literary Tools** features point out and explain literary techniques that are used in the selection.
- A **Graphic Organizer** is provided to help you sort out the important points on paper.
- **Guided Reading Questions** within the selection help you check your understanding of the reading.
- **Words for Everyday Use** includes the definition and pronunciation for new vocabulary. A sample sentence demonstrates the use of the word in context.
- **Footnotes** explain unfamiliar terms or unusual words.
- **Art Note** features provide information about the history, culture, or artistic technique of the fine art throughout the textbook and foster critical viewing of the art.
- **Respond to the Selection** allows you to relate the literature to your own experiences.

- **Investigate, Inquire, and Imagine** contains questions you need to perfect your understanding of the reading, from basic recalling and interpreting to questions that ask you to analyze, synthesize, evaluate, and extend your ideas. Some questions also ask you to look at a specific point of view, or examine a different perspective.
- **Understanding Literature** follows up on the literary techniques introduced in Reader's Toolbox and asks you questions to further your understanding.
- **Writer's Journal** gives you three quick-writing options to help you build writing skills.
- **Integrating the Language Arts** contains creative activities that tie literature to other language arts areas such as grammar, vocabulary development, public speaking, study and research, collaborative learning, media literacy, and applied English.

A Guide for Writing

At the end of each unit of your textbook you will find a **Guided Writing** activity that takes you through the steps of the writing process. The lesson includes models from professional writers and students. Also included are graphic organizers, questions to get you thinking, and an integrated **Language, Grammar, and Style** lesson to help you brush up on grammar points.

A Guide for Language Arts Skills

The **Language Arts Survey** in the back of your textbook is your resource for information about how to use the English language effectively. It includes tips on what you need to know to write, speak, and read effectively. There are six sections in the Language Arts Survey: the **Reading Resource**, the **Writing Resource**, the **Language, Grammar, and Style Resource**, the **Speaking and Listening Resource**, the **Study and Research Resource**, and the **Applied English Resource**. Do you need to correct a passive sentence? include an Internet site in a research paper? interview someone in the community? write a letter? It's all here for you.

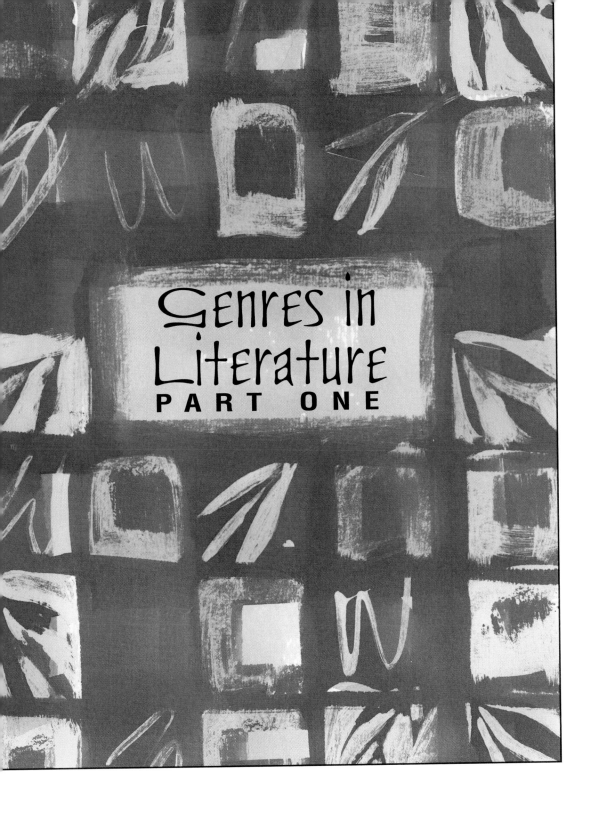

Genres in Literature
PART ONE

Geese in Flight, c.1850. Lelia T. Bauman. National Gallery of Art, Washington, DC.

GOALS/OBJECTIVES

Studying this unit will enable students to
- explore different kinds of literature from the oral tradition
- understand the influence the oral tradition has had on literature of the past and of the present
- define *oral tradition, transcription, translation, myth, muse, chronological order, legend, folk tale, foreshadowing, motif, dramatic irony, tragedy, tragic flaw,* and *dialogue* and identify examples of each that they encounter in their reading
- create a time capsule
- demonstrate the ability to write paragraphs with topic sentences

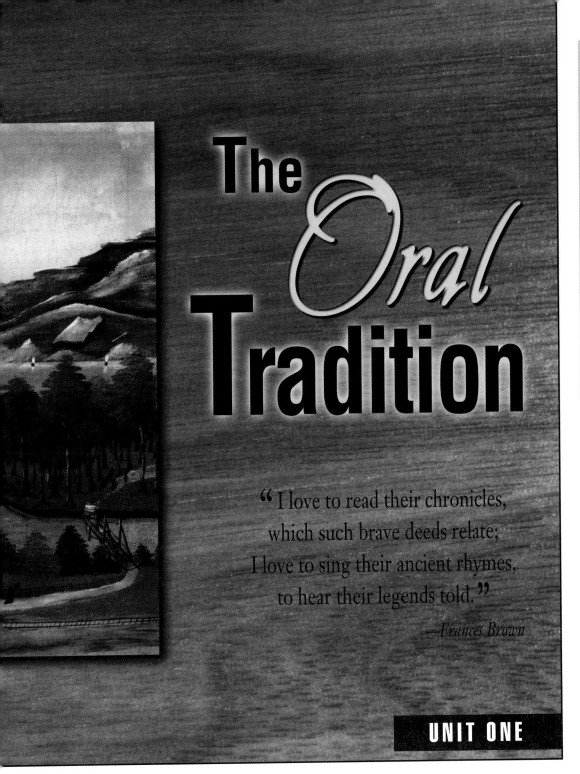

The *Oral* Tradition

> " I love to read their chronicles,
> which such brave deeds relate;
> I love to sing their ancient rhymes,
> to hear their legends told. "
>
> —*Frances Brown*

UNIT ONE

CROSS-CURRICULAR CONNECTIONS

Arts and Humanities
African Legends, 57
Arthurian Art, 37
A Connecticut Yankee in King Arthur's Court, 35
Mayan god, Huracan, 19
Merlin the Magician, 34
Mythological Art, 12
Quetzalcoatl Myth, 26
Script Writing and Performance, 24

Mathematics and Sciences
Geography of Mexico City, 25
Stages of Human Development, 56

Social Studies
Aztec Culture, 27
Battle of Camlan, 48Geography of Mexico City, 25
Inuit People, 6
Jousting and Fencing, 40
Role of Religion during the Fifth and Sixth Centuries, 38
Sacred Mayan Sites, 18

TEACHING THE MULTIPLE INTELLIGENCES

Logical-Mathematical
Quetzalcoatl Myth, 26

Spatial
Arthurian Art, 37
Mythological Art, 12
Stages of Human Development, 56

Kinesthetic
Jousting and Fencing, 40
Script Writing and Performance, 24

Interpersonal/Intrapersonal
Aztec Culture, 27
Battle of Camlan, 48
Script Writing and Performance, 24

ADDITIONAL QUESTIONS AND ACTIVITIES

Have each student choose a favorite story from the oral tradition to share in a small group. After each student has shared his or her story, have groups discuss the common features of the stories. Did the characters possess supernatural powers? Did the stories have happy endings? Was there an evil force to overcome? When they have identified the common features, have students discuss what these features add to the stories.

LITERARY TECHNIQUE

ORAL TRADITION. An **oral tradition** is a work, an idea, or a custom that is passed by word of mouth from generation to generation. Point out to students that works from the oral tradition often vary in retelling.

ELEMENTS *of* THE ORAL TRADITION

Are there favorite stories that people in your family like to tell? When you were a child, did people tell you bedtime stories? Did you learn rhymes and jingles and songs from your friends? Have you ever sat around a campfire and told ghost stories? Have you ever heard a minister, priest, rabbi, or teacher tell a story to make a point? If so, then you have experienced the oral tradition.

One good definition of human beings is that we are storytelling creatures. Long before people invented writing, they were telling stories about their gods and heroes and experiences. The best of these stories were passed by word of mouth from generation to generation to form the basis of the literature that we know today. Some early stories were told in the form of poems. Some were in the form of songs. Others were in the form of what we would now call prose tales.

The passing of stories, poems, and songs by word of mouth from person to person is called oral transmission. The body of work created in this way in a particular culture is called that culture's **oral tradition.**

Types of Oral Literature

MYTHS. Myths are stories that explain objects or events in the natural world as resulting from the action of some supernatural force or entity, most often a god. Every early culture around the globe has produced its own myths. This unit includes two Greek myths, "The Five Ages of Man" and "Orpheus," told by Robert Graves, and a selection from the *Popol Vuh,* a sacred epic of Quiché Mayan mythology.

LEGENDS. Legends are stories coming down from the past, often based on real events or characters from older times. Unlike myths, legends are popularly regarded as historical; however, they may contain elements that are fantastic or unverifiable. An example of a legend is the story of George Washington chopping down the cherry tree. An example in this unit is "Sundiata Keita, the Legend and the King," which tells of Sundiata Keita, a legendary king of Mali. Other legends in this unit include the tales of King Arthur, a legendary king of Great Britain.

FOLK TALES. Folk tales are brief stories passed by word-of-mouth from generation to generation. "Popocatépetl and Ixtacihuatl," an Aztec story in this unit, can be considered a folk tale. However, it can also be considered a myth or a legend. The works of the oral tradition all share characteristics, the most important of which is that they have all been passed by word of mouth from generation to generation. Thus many folk tales can also be called legends, myths, tall tales, and so forth.

TALL TALES. Tall tales are also folk tales. Tall tales are often light-hearted or humorous, and contain highly exaggerated, unrealistic elements. The stories of Paul Bunyan and Pecos Bill are tall tales.

FAIRY TALES. Fairy tales are stories that deal with mischievous spirits and other supernatural occurrences, often in medieval settings. The name is generally applied to stories of the kinds collected by Charles Perrault in France and the Brothers Grimm in Germany or told by Hans Christian Andersen of Denmark. "Cinderella" and "The Little Mermaid" are famous examples.

PARABLES. Parables are very brief stories told to teach a moral lesson. The most famous parables are those told by Jesus in the Bible.

FABLES. Fables are brief stories, often with animal characters, told to express a moral. Famous fables include those of Æsop and Jean de La Fontaine.

FOLK SONGS. Folk songs are traditional or composed songs typically made up of stanzas, a refrain, and a simple melody. A form of folk literature, folk songs are expressions of commonly shared ideas or feelings and may be

Screen. Thai Artist. Prince Rangsit Collection, Bangkok, Thailand.

narrative or lyric in style. Traditional folk songs are anonymous songs that have been transmitted orally.

SPIRITUALS. Spirituals are religious songs from the African-American folk tradition.

EPICS. Epics are long stories, often told in verse, involving heroes and gods. Epics have long been passed on orally and may have anony-

mous authors. Grand in length and scope, an epic provides a portrait of an entire culture, of the legends, beliefs, values, laws, arts, and ways of life of a people.

PROVERBS. Proverbs, or *adages,* are traditional sayings, such as "You can lead a horse to water, but you can't make it drink" or the title of Shakespeare's play *All's Well That Ends Well.*

ELEMENTS OF THE ORAL TRADITION   5

BIBLIOGRAPHIC NOTE

Students may be interested in investigating the following anthologies of folk tales:

Ragan, Kathleen and Yolen, Jane. *Fearless Girls, Wise Women, and Beloved Sisters: Heroines in Folktales from Around the World.* W. W. Norton and Company, 1998.

Abrahams, Roger D. and Frank, Dan. *African Folktales: Traditional Stories of the Black World.* Pantheon Books, 1983.

GENRE CHECK TEST 4.1.1 WITH ANSWERS

Literary Tools
MATCHING
Match each literary term with the best description. You may not use every term, and you may use some terms more than once.

 a. myth   b. tall tale
 c. legend   d. oral tradition
       e. spiritual

1. story that may contain elements of fantasy but is generally based on real events or people; **c**
2. produced by a culture as a way of explaining objects or events in nature; **a**
3. passing of stories, poems, and songs by word of mouth; **d**
4. religious songs from the African-American folk tradition; **e**
5. one example is the story of George Washington chopping down the cherry tree; **c**

TRUE OR FALSE
1. "Haste makes waste" is an example of a proverb. **True**
2. A theme is a central idea in a literary work. **True**
3. Refrain is found only in song, and repetition is found only in poetry. **False**
4. The oral tradition of the United States has origins in Native American culture, Europe, Asia, and Africa. **True**
5. Stories about Pecos Bill and Paul Bunyan are examples of legends. **False**

ADDITIONAL RESOURCES

UNIT 1 RESOURCE BOOK
- Selection Worksheet 1.1
- Selection Check Test 4.1.3
- Selection Test 4.1.4
- Language, Grammar, and Style Resource 3.17
- Speaking and Listening Resource 4.14

CROSS-CURRICULAR CONNECTIONS

SOCIAL STUDIES. The term "Inuit" is now often preferred to the term "Eskimo" as a name for the indigenous arctic and sub-arctic cultures. "Eskimo" is a Cree word meaning "eater of raw meat." The name actually honors the survival skills of the Eskimo people. Eating raw meat enabled the Eskimo to take in Vitamin C and thus avoid scurvy.

READER'S JOURNAL

Say to your students: "Don't think of a blue cow." Then point out that it is difficult to avoid thinking about a blue cow, simply because they heard the words. Explain that words seem to have a direct connection to our imaginations, making us feel certain ways and think about different things. In that sense, words are powerful and magical.

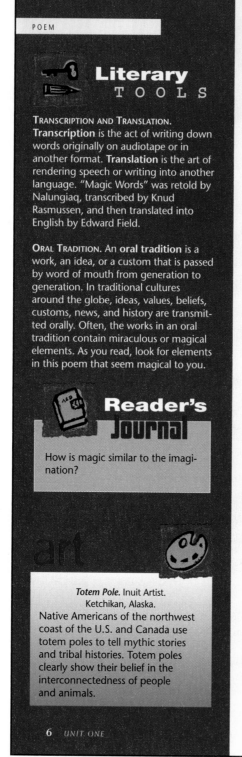

Literary TOOLS

TRANSCRIPTION AND TRANSLATION. Transcription is the act of writing down words originally on audiotape or in another format. **Translation** is the art of rendering speech or writing into another language. "Magic Words" was retold by Nalungiaq, transcribed by Knud Rasmussen, and then translated into English by Edward Field.

ORAL TRADITION. An **oral tradition** is a work, an idea, or a custom that is passed by word of mouth from generation to generation. In traditional cultures around the globe, ideas, values, beliefs, customs, news, and history are transmitted orally. Often, the works in an oral tradition contain miraculous or magical elements. As you read, look for elements in this poem that seem magical to you.

Reader's Journal

How is magic similar to the imagination?

art

Totem Pole. Inuit Artist. Ketchikan, Alaska.
Native Americans of the northwest coast of the U.S. and Canada use totem poles to tell mythic stories and tribal histories. Totem poles clearly show their belief in the interconnectedness of people and animals.

6 *UNIT ONE*

"MAGIC WORDS"
by Nalungiaq, translated by Edward Field

Reader's resource

HISTORY AND CULTURE CONNECTION. The Netsilik Inuit, who call themselves the "people of the seal," live in a remote area of Canada above the Arctic Circle, in one of the bleakest regions of the world. Winter there lasts ten months, the temperature drops to fifty degrees below zero, and the ocean freezes solid. Like other Inuit peoples living in the Arctic and subarctic areas of Canada, Greenland, Alaska, and Siberia, the Netsilik are well adapted to this harsh environment and live in close harmony with nature. As is true of many peoples around the globe, the Inuit have felt the encroachment of modern civilization on their traditional way of life. This poem expresses a Netsilik priest's or shaman's belief that at one time words had magical powers that they no longer have today.

CULTURE CONNECTION. "Magic Words" is taken from the oral tradition of the Inuit people. It teaches that words have enormous power to bring things into existence. Although modern-day residents of Europe, Canada, and the United States might scoff at the idea that words literally have magical power, the poem reminds readers that words can create objects, people, animals, and places in the imagination. The poem can be read as a celebration of the power of literature to bring worlds of the imagination into existence.

About the AUTHOR

Nalungiaq, an Inuit (Eskimo) woman, reported that she learned the song **"Magic Words"** from an elderly uncle named Unaraluk. Unaraluk was a shaman, a kind of sorcerer or priest. The song was first written down by Danish explorer Knud Rasmussen. Rasmussen, who was part Inuit and spoke the Inuit language, lived for some time with the Netsilik people during his expedition across arctic America, known as the Fifth Thule Expedition (1921–1924). He collected many Netsilik legends and tales in the desire to learn about the unique view such an isolated people had developed of their world and the universe. Poet Edward Field translated many of these stories. "Magic Words" is also included in Jerome Rothenberg's collection of traditional Native American poetry, *Shaking the Pumpkin*.

GOALS/OBJECTIVES

Studying this lesson will enable students to
- interpret and appreciate a poem about magic passed down through the Inuit oral tradition
- describe aspects of the Inuit culture and discuss Inuit beliefs as described in a poem
- define *transcription* and *translation* and discuss how these processes might affect the interpretation of literature
- define *oral tradition* and explain how the term relates to the selection
- work collaboratively to retell well-known children's stories orally
- conduct and transcribe an interview

MAGIC WORDS

Nalungiaq, translated by
Edward Field

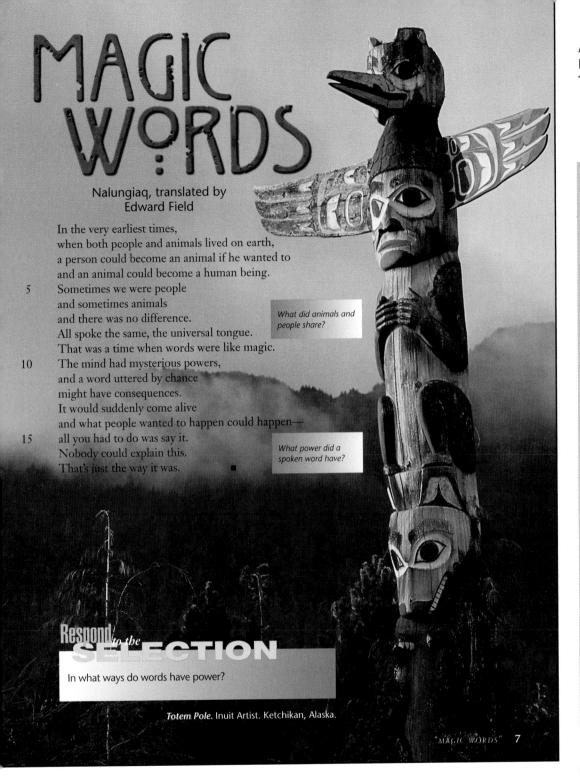

In the very earliest times,
when both people and animals lived on earth,
a person could become an animal if he wanted to
and an animal could become a human being.
5   Sometimes we were people
and sometimes animals
and there was no difference.
All spoke the same, the universal tongue.
That was a time when words were like magic.
10   The mind had mysterious powers,
and a word uttered by chance
might have consequences.
It would suddenly come alive
and what people wanted to happen could happen—
15   all you had to do was say it.
Nobody could explain this.
That's just the way it was.

> *What did animals and people share?*

> *What power did a spoken word have?*

Respond *to the* SELECTION

In what ways do words have power?

Totem Pole. Inuit Artist. Ketchikan, Alaska.

"MAGIC WORDS"   7

1. Animals and people shared the same language—"the universal tongue."
2. A spoken word could come alive and make things happen for people.

INDIVIDUAL LEARNING STRATEGIES

MOTIVATION
Ask students to work in small groups to create an encyclopedia entry for the word *magic*. Ask them to first brainstorm ideas about magic, and then write a definition for the word. Have them embellish their entries with different examples, stories, and representations of magic.

READING PROFICIENCY
Read the poem aloud to students, or have them work with a partner to read it aloud. Remind students to pay attention to the punctuation in the poem, pausing at commas and stopping at periods.

ENGLISH LANGUAGE LEARNING
Review with students the information provided in the Reader's Resource on page 6 to help them understand the background of the selection.

SPECIAL NEEDS
Encourage students to focus on the Guided Reading and Recall questions to ensure they grasp the main ideas of the poem.

ENRICHMENT
Ask students to research the Inuit culture and choose one aspect of daily life or history that particularly interests them. For example, students might research the language, hunting and fishing techniques, populations and locations, or beliefs and traditions. Have students present their findings in a brief report.

SELECTION CHECK TEST 4.1.3 WITH ANSWERS

Checking Your Reading
1. What could a person do in early times? **A person could become an animal.**
2. What could an animal do in early times? **An animal could become a person.**
3. What kind of magic did words have in early times? **What people wanted to happen could happen just by saying it.**

Literary Tools
Fill in the blanks using the following terms.

transcription   translation   oral tradition

1. The act of writing or rendering speech into another language is called **translation**.

(Continued on page 8)

RESPOND TO THE SELECTION

As an alternative question, ask students to define *good life* and what creates or denies such a life. Students might consider human connectedness with nature and the effects changing technological discoveries have had on various aspects of life.

2. <u>Transcription</u> is when a person writes down words that were originally on audiotape or in another format.
3. Any work that is passed down by word or mouth from generation to generation is considered <u>**oral tradition**</u>.

ANSWERS TO INVESTIGATE, INQUIRE, AND IMAGINE

RECALL
1a. The speaker is referring to the "very earliest times."
2a. A person could become an animal and an animal could become a human. At that time everybody spoke the same language.
3a. A word "uttered by chance" might come alive. What people wanted to happen could happen.

INTERPRET
1b. The speaker thinks that life is different now as indicated by the use of the past tense and the explanation that the events took place in the earliest times.
2b. Students might suggest that in the earliest times, people had to struggle to survive, just as the animals did. They may not have had a language of their own and communicated through simple sounds and body movements. They did not have many of the tools, skills, and technology that they have today that make human life so different from that of the animals.
3b. Words had strange consequences. They could make anything happen.

ANALYZE
4a. The speaker says that people and animals once spoke the same language and were inter-changeable. People could make things come alive and make things happen just by saying words.

SYNTHESIZE
4b. The speaker suggests that life was easier long ago. Words and the mind were powerful and magical, and people could get what they wanted just by saying it.

EVALUATE
5a. People today, at least in our culture, are not as deeply connected to animals and the natural world as they were in the time referred to by the speaker. Cities and technology have caused a decline in the

Investigate, Inquire, and Imagine

Recall: GATHERING FACTS

1a. What time is the speaker of the poem talking about, according to line 1?

2a. According to lines 3 and 4, what could people and animals do in that time? What observation does the speaker make in line 8 about language in that time?

3a. According to the speaker, what strange consequences used to result from a word "uttered by chance"?

Interpret: FINDING MEANING

1b. Does the speaker think that life today is different? How do you know?

2b. What might this suggest about the way of life of the earliest Inuit peoples?

3b. What was magical about words in the earlier time?

Analyze: TAKING THINGS APART

4a. What evidence does the speaker offer that people in earlier times lived in close harmony with nature and had powers they do not have today?

Synthesize: BRINGING THINGS TOGETHER

4b. Does the speaker believe that life is harder or easier for people today? Explain.

Evaluate: MAKING JUDGMENTS

5a. Do you believe that people today view themselves as deeply connected to animals and the natural world? What aspects of modern life make such connections less direct than they once were?

Extend: CONNECTING IDEAS

5b. In what sense do words still perform magically every time a person reads a poem, story, or play?

Understanding Literature

TRANSCRIPTION AND TRANSLATION. Review the definitions for **transcription** and **translation** in the Handbook of Literary Terms. How might "Magic Words" have been affected by having been retold so many times, then transcribed and translated into an entirely different language? People who transcribe text try to write down word for word everything that is said, without leaving anything out or rewording. Translators try to preserve the original meaning of the text while using different words to express ideas. Why do you think it is important for them to avoid rewording or changing the original meaning of the text?

ORAL TRADITION. Review the definition for **oral tradition** in Literary Tools on page six. How, according to the shaman, did the world as it once was differ from the world today? Create a Venn diagram like the one below to show the similarities and differences between the past and present. Refer to the Language Arts Survey 2.16, "Completing Venn Diagrams."

World in Earliest Times   World Today

8   *UNIT ONE / THE ORAL TRADITION*

ANSWERS TO INVESTIGATE, INQUIRE, AND IMAGINE (CONT.)

contact humans have with nature, and have made humans' lives very different from those of animals in the wild.

EXTEND
5b. Words are still magical in that literature allows us to experience other worlds, characters, and situations that live in the imagination.

ANSWERS TO UNDERSTANDING LITERATURE

TRANSCRIPTION AND TRANSLATION. Some of the details of the story may have been lost as the story was told and retold over many generations. When the story was translated, it may have lost some of its original meaning because the particular words used in the Inuit language may not have had direct equivalents in English. Also, Edward Field may have had to change the syntax, or word order, of the song so that it would sound
(Continued on page 9)

Writer's Journal

1. Imagine that you have the power to make things happen just by saying them. Write three **wishes** you would like to come true.
2. Strange things, such as people turning into animals, can often happen in dreams. Recall a dream you had once, and write a **dream report** describing it. Dreams disappear quickly. If you cannot recall one, you may wish to keep a notebook beside your bed so that when you wake up, you can immediately write down what happened in your dream.
3. "Magic Words" teaches us that words can be used to create people, places, and things that did not exist before. Writers use words to perform magic all the time. Try doing some of this magic yourself. Close your eyes and create a place in your imagination. Then write a **description** of your place.

Integrating the Language Arts

Language, Grammar, and Style

FUNCTIONS OF SENTENCES. Sentences are the basic unit of expression in the English language. Four different kinds of sentences express four different kinds of thoughts and feelings, and each has characteristic end punctuation: **declarative, interrogative, imperative,** and **exclamatory.** For more information refer to the Language Arts Survey 3.17, "Functions of Sentences."

Identify the function of each sentence below by writing <u>dec</u> (declarative), <u>int</u> (interrogative), <u>imp</u> (imperative) or <u>exc</u> (exclamatory). Add appropriate end punctuation.

1. Have you read the poem "Magic Words"
2. Tell me about how words used to be magical
3. Wow, I can't believe that people could once talk to animals
4. The Inuit had many legends and tales from long ago
5. What do you know about the Inuit people

Speaking and Listening & Collaborative Learning

STORYTELLING. Many children's stories, such as "Cinderella," "The Frog Prince," and "Beauty and the Beast," contain elements of magic. Work with other students to brainstorm a list of such stories. You may want to consult the children's section in your school or community library. Take turns telling these stories to one another orally. Then discuss how stories change when they are told orally and not written down.

Applied English & Speaking and Listening

INTERVIEW AND TRANSCRIPTION. Interview an older person—a grandparent, a neighbor, or a resident of a local nursing home—about what life was like long before you were born. Read the Language Arts Survey 4.14, "Conducting an Interview." Then, prepare a list of questions. Ask the person's permission to tape record the interview. When your interview is complete, play back the tape and transcribe, or write down, everything that was said.

ANSWERS TO INTEGRATING THE LANGUAGE ARTS (CONT.)

Language, Grammar, and Style
1. Have you read the poem "Magic Words"? (<u>int</u>)
2. Tell me about how words used to be magical. (<u>imp</u>—an exclamation point could also be used)
3. Wow, I can't believe that people could once talk to animals! (<u>exc</u>)
4. The Inuit had many legends and tales from long ago. (<u>dec</u>)
5. What do you know about the Inuit people? (<u>int</u>)

ANSWERS TO UNDERSTANDING LITERATURE (CONT.)

natural in English. Transcribers should write the words exactly as they were said to avoid misinterpretation. Also, it is important for the translator to stay close to the original meaning of the text because otherwise, the cultural information we learn from reading such songs will be inaccurate.

ORAL TRADITION. In the time described in the poem, humans were more closely interrelated with the natural world, especially animals. Communication was easier because there were no language barriers. Words had the power to make things happen.

GRAPHIC ORGANIZER

Students may include the following in their Venn diagrams: **Earliest Times:** Humans could become animals and animals could become human; there was no difference between humans and animals; all spoke the same language; words were magic and could come alive; the mind had mysterious powers and people could make things happen just by saying words. **Today:** Humans and animals are different and live in different worlds; humans and animals do not speak the same language; words are no longer magic; people cannot make things happen just by saying words. In the overlapping space, students might write: People and animals live on Earth together; people and animals are companions; words can be used to create people, places, and things that did not exist before.

ANSWERS TO INTEGRATING THE LANGUAGE ARTS

Speaking and Listening & Collaborative Learning
Refer students to the Language Arts Survey 4.19, "Oral Interpretation," for tips on reading their stories aloud. Students can discuss what magic accomplished in each story: what change it made, what made it possible, and why magic is popular in children's literature. Ask students if they think magic is as common in literature written for adults. Why might this be so?

ADDITIONAL RESOURCES

UNIT 1 RESOURCE BOOK
- Selection Worksheet 1.2
- Selection Check Test 4.1.5
- Selection Test 4.1.6
- Language, Grammar, and Style Resource 3.19

VOCABULARY FROM THE SELECTION

degenerate   reverently
insolent   spontaneously
plaintive

GRAPHIC ORGANIZER

Students might include the following:
Zeus—quarreled with Hera; destroyed the silver race
Apollo—gave Orpheus a lyre
Hades—took Orpheus's wife Eurydice back to the underworld
Dionysus—set the Maenads upon Orpheus

READER'S JOURNAL

Ask students to jot down ideas about why a certain figure might have been used in the pictures. What qualities does that figure represent? Ask them to consider how the figures of Greek mythology remain with us today.

Literary TOOLS

MUSE. The **Muses**, the nine daughters of Zeus and Mnemosyne (ni mä' sən ē), the goddess of memory, were believed to inspire aspects of the arts and sciences. Calliope (kə lī' ə pē), said to be Orpheus's mother, was the Muse of epic poetry. The other Muses were linked individually with history, lyrical poetry, music, tragedy, sacred choral poetry, choral dance and song, comedy, and astronomy. Look for the appearance of the Muses as you read "Orpheus."

MYTH. A **myth** is a story that explains objects or events in the natural world as resulting from the action of some supernatural force or entity, most often a god. Every early culture around the globe has produced its own myths. As you read this selection, look for gods that are mentioned. Record their names and their actions in the graphic organizer below.

Graphic Organizer

GODS

Prometheus

some say he created humans

Reader's Journal

List places where you have read about or seen the influence of Greek mythology. These might be pictures used in advertisements, names of sports teams, or even descriptions of characters in a book, movie, or television show.

from *The Greek Myths*
"The Five Ages of Man" and "Orpheus"
by Robert Graves

Reader's resource

"The Five Ages of Man" and "Orpheus" appear in Robert Graves's book *The Greek Myths,* a dictionary-style work that contains explanations of many classic Greek myths. These myths probably grew out of Greece's early feudal culture of the Mycenaean Age (1580–1100 BC). "The Five Ages of Man" traces the history of humankind. "Orpheus" tells several tales about the mythical poet and musician Orpheus (ôr' fē əs).

Dionysus (dī' ō nī' səs), the god of wine and fertility, plays an important role in "Orpheus." His followers were the **Maenads** (mē nadz), a wild group of women, and he demanded sacrifice be paid to him. In this selection, he becomes angry with Orpheus, whose values contradict his. Other Greek gods mentioned in this selection include **Zeus** (züs), king of all the gods; **Hera** (hā rə), Zeus's wife; **Athene** (ə thē' nə), goddess of wisdom; **Hades** (hā' dēz), the god of the underworld; and **Helius** (hē' lē əs), or Apollo, the sun god. Also mentioned are two Titans, or earlier gods who were thrown out of power by the gods led by Zeus. One is **Prometheus** (prō mē' thē əs), who according to some myths created the first humans and then was punished by Zeus for giving humans the gift of fire; the other is **Cronus** (crō' nəs), Zeus's father.

About the AUTHOR

Robert Graves (1895–1985), like so many of his generation, was profoundly influenced by his experiences as a soldier in World War I, and this influence is apparent in much of his writing. His classic autobiography, *Goodbye to All That,* focuses ruthlessly on his own wartime nightmare. Although he was born in England and served England in battle, Graves spent most of his adult life on the island of Majorca, Spain. There he wrote lyric poetry, fiction, and nonfiction works related to history, often that of the Classical Era (the height of the cultures of ancient Greek and Rome). He was also known for his learned studies in mythology.

GOALS/OBJECTIVES

Studying this lesson will enable students to
- enjoy and appreciate two retellings of popular Greek myths
- recognize and discuss the influences of Greek mythology throughout the ages
- define *myth* and *muse* and note the function of the Muses in mythology
- demonstrate an ability to identify complete subjects and predicates in sentences
- work collaboratively to create a comic strip based on a mythological character

FROM The GREEK Myths

Robert Graves

THE FIVE AGES OF MAN

Some deny that Prometheus created men, or that any man sprang from a serpent's teeth.[1] They say that Earth bore them spontaneously, as the best of her fruits, especially in the soil of Attica, and that Alalcomeneus was the first man to appear, by Lake Copais in Boeotia,[2] before even the Moon was. He acted as Zeus's counsellor on the occasion of his quarrel with Hera, and as tutor to Athene while she was still a girl.

These men were the so-called golden race, subjects of Cronus, who lived without cares or labour, eating only acorns, wild fruit, and honey that dripped from the trees, drinking the milk of sheep and goats, never growing old, dancing, and laughing much; death, to them, was no more terrible than sleep. They are all gone now, but their spirits survive as genii[3] of happy music retreats, givers of good fortune, and upholders of justice.

> *What are the lives of humans like in the Golden Age?*

Next came a silver race, eaters of bread, likewise divinely created. The men were utterly subject to their mothers and dared not disobey them, although they might live to be a hundred years old. They were quarrelsome and ignorant, and never sacrificed to the gods but, at least, did not make war on one another. Zeus destroyed them all.

Next came a brazen[4] race, who fell like fruits from the ash-trees, and were armed with brazen weapons. They ate flesh as well as bread, and delighted in war, being insolent and pitiless men. Black Death has seized them all.

The fourth race of man was brazen too, but nobler and more generous, being begotten by the gods on mortal mothers. They fought gloriously in the siege of Thebes, the expedition of the Argonauts, and the Trojan War. These became heroes, and dwell in the Elysian Fields.[5]

The fifth race is the present race of iron, unworthy descendants of the fourth. They are degenerate, cruel, unjust, malicious, libidinous, unfilial, treacherous.

> *What is the present age? What are the people in it like?*

THE FIVE AGES OF MAN
1. **Prometheus . . . serpent's teeth.** Reference to other Greek creation myths
2. **Boeotia.** District in east-central Greece
3. **genii.** Guardian spirits
4. **brazen.** Brass
5. **Elysian Fields.** Paradise for virtuous people after death

words for everyday use

spon • ta • ne • ous • ly (spän tā′ nē əs lē) adv., in a natural way, without outside influence. *Jacob's love for painting developed spontaneously; his parents did not push him to develop his artistic talents.*

in • so • lent (in′ sə lənt) adj., boldly disrespectful. *The insolent student talked back to his teacher.*

de • gen • er • ate (dē jen′ ər it) adj., having sunk below a former condition. *He had sunk to such lows that he would steal from his own mother.*

---

1. The golden race lived carefree, happy lives, eating the fruits of the Earth and celebrating often.
2. The present age is the race of iron. These people are unkind, disrespectful, and unjust.

INDIVIDUAL LEARNING STRATEGIES

MOTIVATION
Have students work in small groups and discuss what life might have been like for people who lived three- to four thousand years ago. Point out that these people did not have the benefit of scientific and technological discoveries that we have today. Then ask them to discuss how these early people might have explained natural phenomena, such as thunder, lightning, stars, and so on. Lead students to understand that early cultures created myths to explain these things.

READING PROFICIENCY
Work with students to preview these selections and identify any words that they have difficulty understanding or pronouncing, such as: Alalcomeneus (a läl cō mā′ nəs), Thebes (thēbs), Oeagrus (ō a′grəs), Eurydice (yoo ri′ də sē), and Agriope (a grī ′ō pē). Help students become more comfortable with these words before they read the selections.

ENGLISH LANGUAGE LEARNING
The strategies for Reading Proficiency above will also benefit English language learners. In addition, you might encourage students to share popular myths or stories from their original cultures.

SPECIAL NEEDS
Encourage students to listen to an audio recording of the selection as they read along in their books. Frequently monitor their comprehension as they read these myths to ensure that they do not become frustrated with the numerous unfamiliar words they encounter.

INDIVIDUAL LEARNING STRATEGIES (CONT.)

ENRICHMENT
Students might enjoy holding a mythology storytelling festival. Have each student choose a different myth to learn. You might allow students to choose myths from any culture, or you

might ask them to focus on Greek mythology. Once students have read their myths, have the groups share them by enacting them. Encourage costumes, props, and scenery.

MYTHOLOGICAL ART. Explain to students that artists throughout the centuries have been inspired by mythological stories and characters. Ask pairs of students to perform research to find an artwork inspired by a Greek mythology. Have them photocopy or print out an illustration of the artwork, and learn about the character or myth depicted. Finally, ask each pair to share their research with the class by showing a picture of the artwork and briefly explaining the mythological story that inspired it.

INTERNET RESOURCES

If students are interested in learning more about mythology, direct them to **The Encyclopedia Mythica** at http://www.pantheon.org/mythica. This site includes over 5,700 articles, 300 illustrations, maps, and genealogy tables that cover more than 25 areas of mythology.

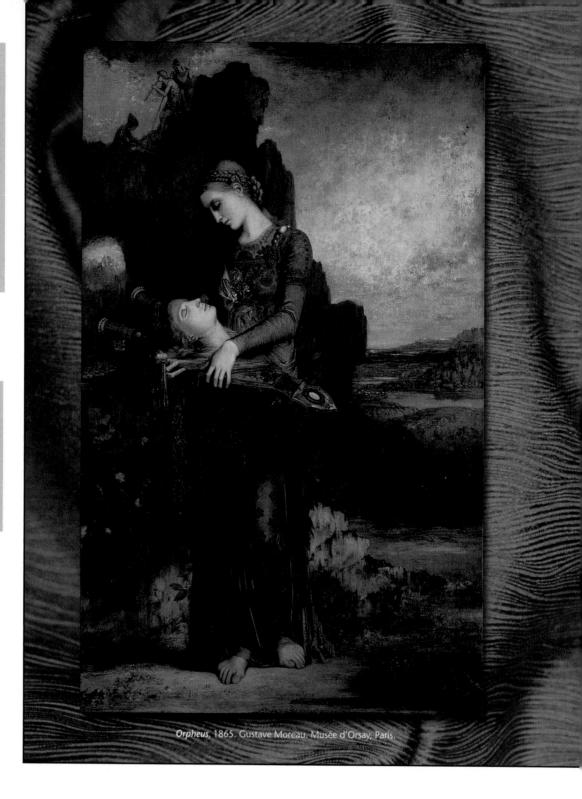

Orpheus, 1865. Gustave Moreau. Musée d'Orsay, Paris.

ORPHEUS

Orpheus, son of the Thracian King Oeagrus and the Muse Calliope,[1] was the most famous poet and musician who ever lived. Apollo presented him with a lyre, and the Muses taught him its use, so that he not only enchanted wild beasts, but made the trees and rocks move from their places to follow the sound of his music. At Zone in Thrace[2] a number of ancient mountain oaks are still standing in the pattern of one of his dances, just as he left them.

After a visit to Egypt, Orpheus joined the Argonauts,[3] with whom he sailed to Colchis, his music helping them to overcome many difficulties—and, on his return, married Eurydice, whom some called Agriope, and settled among the savage Cicones of Thrace.

One day, near Tempe, in the valley of the river Peneius, Eurydice met Aristaeus, who tried to force her. She trod on a serpent as she fled, and died of its bite; but Orpheus boldly descended into Tartarus,[4] hoping to fetch her back. He used the passage which opens at Aornum in Thesprotis and, on his arrival, not only charmed the ferryman Charon, the Dog Cerberus,[5] and the three Judges of the Dead with his plaintive music, but temporarily suspended the tortures of the damned; and so far soothed the savage heart of Hades that he won leave to restore Eurydice to the upper world. Hades made a single condition: that Orpheus might not look behind him until she was safely back under the light of the sun. Eurydice followed Orpheus up through the dark passage, guided by the sounds of his lyre, and it was only when he reached the sunlight again that he turned to see whether she were still behind him, and so lost her for ever.

> What is Orpheus's special skill? How powerful is this skill?

> What is Orpheus's great accomplishment? How does he achieve it?

When Dionysus invaded Thrace, Orpheus neglected to honour him, but taught other sacred mysteries and preached the evil of sacrificial murder to the men of Thrace, who listened reverently. Every morning he would rise to greet the dawn on the summit of Mount Pangaeum, preaching that Helius, whom he named Apollo, was the greatest of all gods. In vexation, Dionysus set the Maenads[6] upon him at Deium in Macedonia. First waiting until their husbands had entered Apollo's temple, where Orpheus served as priest, they seized the weapons stacked outside, burst in, murdered their husbands, and tore Orpheus limb from limb. His head they threw into the river Hebrus, but it floated, still singing, down to the sea, and was carried to the island of Lesbos.

Tearfully, the Muses collected his limbs and buried them at Leibethra, at the foot of Mount Olympus,[7] where the nightingales now sing sweeter than anywhere else in the world. The Maenads had attempted to cleanse themselves of Orpheus's blood in the river Helicorn; but the River-god dived under the ground and disappeared for the space of nearly four miles, emerging with a different name, the Baphyra. Thus he avoided becoming an accessory to the murder. ∎

ORPHEUS

1. **Calliope** (kə lī′ ə pē′). Muse of eloquence and epic poetry
2. **Thrace.** Ancient region in the Balkan Peninsula of Greece, north of the Aegean Sea
3. **Argonauts.** Men who sail with the hero Jason to search for the Golden Fleece in Greek myth
4. **Tartarus.** Infernal abyss below Hades, which is the home of the dead, and ruled by Hades, the god of the underworld
5. **Charon, the Dog Cerberus.** Charon was the boatman who led the dead across the river Styx into Hades; Cerberus was a three-headed dog who guarded the gate of Hades.
6. **Maenads** (mē′ nadz). Wild group of women who worshipped Dionysus, the god of revelry
7. **Mount Olympus.** Mountain where the gods live

---

words for everyday use

plain • tive (plān′ tiv) adj., mournful; sad. At the funeral, the pastor read the eulogy in a plaintive voice.

rev • er • ent • ly (rev′ ər ənt lē) adv., in a manner suggesting deep respect, love, or awe. At the church service, the altar boy lit the candles reverently.

ANSWERS TO GUIDED READING QUESTIONS

1. Orpheus's special skill was playing the lyre. His skill was so powerful that he could calm wild beasts and cause trees and rocks to move and follow the sound of his music.
2. Orpheus convinced Hades, the god of the underworld, to allow Eurydice to return back to Earth. He achieves this feat by soothing Hades's savage heart with his music.

SELECTION CHECK TEST 4.1.5 WITH ANSWERS

Checking Your Reading
1. What do some people deny in "The Five Ages of Man"? **Some people deny that Prometheus created man.**
2. How was the golden race of man created in "The Five Ages of Man"? **It is said that Earth bore humans spontaneously.**
3. What are the five ages of man? **The five ages of man consists of the golden race, the silver race, the brazen race, a second type of brazen race, and the iron race.**
4. Who is Orpheus? **He is the most famous poet and musician who ever lived.**
5. How was Orpheus killed? **He was cut from limb to limb by the Maenads.**

Vocabulary in Context
Fill in each blank below with the most appropriate word from the following Words for Everyday Use.

> spontaneously   insolent
> reverently   degenerate

1. Our plans for the weekend came up **spontaneously**; we didn't plan to go on a picnic.
2. The newlyweds looked at each other **reverently**.
3. My grandpa sunk deeper into a **degenerate** condition due to his declining health.

Literary Tools
Fill in the blanks using the following terms.

> Muse   myth   Prometheus
> Zeus

1. A **myth** is a story that explains objects or events in the natural as resulting from supernatural forces.
2. Some people believe that **Prometheus** first created humans and gave them the gift of fire.
3. Shakespeare counted on a **Muse** to inspire him to write love sonnets and plays.

ANSWERS TO INVESTIGATE, INQUIRE, AND IMAGINE

RECALL

1a. The first race of humans is called the golden race.

2a. The gods create and Zeus destroys the second race. The third race is seized by Black Death. Members of the fourth race become heroes and dwell in the Elysian Fields. The fifth race remains.

3a. Orpheus is the son of King Oeagrus and the Muse Calliope. He is best known for his music. Orpheus is slaughtered by the Maenads.

INTERPRET

1b. The first race of humans is gone; it is not explained why they are gone. These people's spirits watch over music retreats, give good fortune, and uphold justice.

2b. Students will probably say that the first race, the golden race, was the most admirable and that the fifth race is the least admirable.

3b. Orpheus persuades natural elements to follow him, charms his way into the underworld to rescue his wife, leads her out in darkness with his music, and convinces men to abandon sacrificial murder. Dionysus becomes angry because Orpheus refuses to honor him, and instead calls Apollo the greatest of all gods.

ANALYZE

4a. The people change from silver to bronze to iron. They evolve from obedient yet quarrelsome and ignorant (second race) to insolent and warlike (third race), to generous and heroic (fourth race), to cruel and unjust (fifth and current race).

SYNTHESIZE

4b. Based on the myth, students might infer that Greeks had a negative attitude toward human nature in their time. They seem to have felt that human nature had become immoral and treacherous and gradually deteriorated from a pure and joyful state (golden age) to an unjust, cruel, and malicious state.

Respond *to the* SELECTION

Which excerpt did you find more interesting, "The Five Ages of Man" or "Orpheus"? Why?

Investigate, *Inquire,* and Imagine

Recall: GATHERING FACTS

1a. What is the first race of humans called?

2a. Who creates the second race? What becomes of this race? What are the fates of the races that follow?

3a. Who is Orpheus? For what is he best known? What happens to Orpheus at the hands of Dionysus?

→ **Interpret:** FINDING MEANING

1b. What becomes of the first race of humans? How is their influence felt today?

2b. Which of the five races seems to have been the most admirable? the least admirable?

3b. How do Orpheus's talents help him during his life? Why is Dionysus angry with Orpheus?

Analyze: TAKING THINGS APART

4a. Analyze how the materials and qualities associated with each successive race in "The Five Ages of Man" evolve, or change.

→ **Synthesize:** BRINGING THINGS TOGETHER

4b. Based on your analysis, what can you infer about classical Greek attitudes toward the state of human nature in their own time? What did they probably think had happened to human nature over time?

Evaluate: MAKING JUDGMENTS

5a. Based on the different stories about Orpheus, what is your opinion of Orpheus's character? What is your opinion of Zeus? of Dionysus?

→ **Extend:** CONNECTING IDEAS

5b. Based on these selections from *The Greek Myths,* what can you conclude about the Greeks' view of their gods? about the world in general?

Understanding *Literature*

MUSE. Review the definition for **Muse** in the Handbook of Literary Terms. Why might the Muses be associated with Orpheus? How did their burial of him at the foot of Mount Olympus inspire new art to replace that which was lost with his death? Have you ever heard the term "muse" used to mean artistic inspiration? If so, explain.

MYTH. Review the definition for **myth** in the Handbook of Literary Terms. What characteristics of a myth can you find in this selection from *The Greek Myths?* If you have read the selection from the *Popol Vuh,* explain how the myth "The Five Ages of Man" is similar to it.

ANSWERS TO INVESTIGATE, INQUIRE, AND IMAGINE (CONT.)

EVALUATE

5a. Orpheus seems brave, loyal, and talented, but sometimes overconfident and unable to accept limitations. They may admire his opposition to "murderous sacrifice." Students may find Zeus violent and unjust, based on his destruction of the silver race, and Dionysus proud and vengeful.

EXTEND

5b. Greeks viewed their gods as having the same range of virtues and faults as humans. They viewed their gods as impulsive, irrational, vengeful, and violent. They may have viewed their world in general as insecure, full of violence and injustice. The fact that four races of man had been wiped out prior to the current one suggests that the Greeks felt that they too might be destroyed by the gods.

Writer's Journal

1. Write a **wish list** of characteristics you would like to see in the Sixth Age of humans, if the gods decided to create a new group of humans.
2. Write a paragraph-long **character sketch** of Orpheus, based on what you learned about him in this selection.
3. Imagine that you are a friend of Orpheus and Eurydice and are outraged at what happened to Eurydice. Write an **appeal** to the gods explaining why you think Hades should not have been so strict in enforcing his "single condition."

Integrating the Language Arts

Language, Grammar, and Style

COMPLETE SUBJECTS AND PREDICATES. Read the Language Arts Survey 3.19, "Finding the Complete Subject and Complete Predicate in a Sentence." Then, in each of the sentences below, underline the complete subject once and the complete predicate twice.

EXAMPLE   The Greek myths originated in ancient times.

1. Greek myths involved gods who had human characteristics but superhuman abilities.
2. Many of the gods resided at the top of Mount Olympus.
3. People went to Hades, the underworld, after they died.
4. Heroes went to the Elysian Fields, which was a sort of heaven or paradise.
5. Bards such as Homer were inspired to write beautiful epic poems about Greek myths.

Media Literacy

CREATING A COMIC STRIP. According to Robert Graves, Greek mythology was "no more mysterious … [than a] modern election cartoon." Certainly, the figures in mythology were often simplified as cartoon characters must be. Choose one of the stories from the selection and create a comic strip or cartoon capturing its central plot and theme. You may want to look at current political and literary cartoons, as well as ordinary comic strips, to gain a sense of their style and approach. Then, reread the selection with the goal of choosing a portion to depict in your cartoon. A character chart, in which you note the characteristics of various figures, may help you envision your drawing.

Collaborative Learning

ILLUSTRATING THE AGES. With a partner, choose one of the "Five Ages of Man" that you think would be particularly visually striking. Remembering that myths often deviate from reality, illustrate your chosen age using your imagination to depict how humans might have looked at that time. The class can then display their pictures and have other students try to guess the age that served as inspiration for the drawing.

ANSWERS TO UNDERSTANDING LITERATURE

MYTH. This selection from *The Greek Myths* offers an explanation of the creation of humans. It explains the position of some oak trees as being the result of the music of Orpheus, and the existence of the sweetest-singing nightingales as existing because of the death of Orpheus. It also explains the unusual route of a river that runs underground for four miles as having been caused by the actions of the River-god.

MUSE. The Muses probably are associated with Orpheus because they, like Orpheus, share a love of the arts. The burial of the great musician prompted a more beautiful song of the nightingale in the spot where he was buried.

ADDITIONAL RESOURCES

UNIT 1 RESOURCE BOOK
- Selection Worksheet 1.3
- Selection Check Test 4.1.7
- Selection Test 4.1.8
- Language, Grammar, and Style Resource 3.33

GRAPHIC ORGANIZER

Students may include the following events in their sequence charts: gods create birds and animals and assign homes to them; gods tell the animals to speak the gods' names but the animals cannot; gods condemn the animals to be eaten; gods create a human being of earth and mud; being melts away; gods call upon the soothsayers and cast lots of corn and *tzité;* gods create humans from wood; wooden beings multiply and roam the earth but have no souls nor minds.

READER'S JOURNAL

Why do you think there is so much controversy surrounding the creation of the world—especially between creationists and evolutionists?

VOCABULARY FROM THE SELECTION

condemn	ravine
diviner	soothsayer
invoke	venerate

 Literary
T O O L S

MYTH. A myth is a story that explains objects or events in the natural world as resulting from the action of some supernatural force or entity, most often a god. As you read this selection, look for references to gods. What are some of the names given to these gods?

CHRONOLOGICAL ORDER. Chronological order is the arrangement of details in the order of their occurrence. Create a sequence chart like the one below to organize the events in the order they occur.

Graphic
Organizer

Fill in the boxes of your sequence chart with the most important events in the selection from the *Popol Vuh*. Be as brief as possible.

They made the small wild animals	→	
	→	

 Reader's
Journal

Throughout history, people have tried to explain the creation of the world. How do you believe the world was created? Answer this question in detail in your journal.

---

from the POPOL VUH

Anonymous, English version by Delia Goetz and Sylvanus G. Morley, from the Spanish translation by Adrián Recinos

Reader's resource

The *Popol Vuh* contains a story of creation that recounts the reasons for—and difficulties of—bringing human beings and other creatures into the world. It teaches how the gods created humans. The Maya had many names for their creator gods. They believed that such gods had a dual nature, combining both female and male, mother and father. Other gods were made up of multiple beings as well.

HISTORY CONNECTION. The highly developed culture of the Maya flourished from about AD 250–900. The Maya reached great intellectual and artistic heights, developing a form of hieroglyphic writing, working with gold and other precious metals, and building great stone palaces and stepped pyramids. Mayan astronomy and mathematics were highly advanced. The time of Mayan glory came to an abrupt and inexplicable end. Large lowland cities were left vacant, and although cities on the highland of the Yucatán peninsula continued to thrive for a while, by the sixteenth century, the time the Spanish arrived in the Americas, the Maya were living and farming in small villages, all their great cities abandoned to the encroaching jungle.

About the AUTHOR

The *Popol Vuh* or "The Book of the Community" is a sacred epic of the Quiché Maya, a people who inhabited present-day Guatemala from the beginning of the eleventh century. It was written sometime between 1554 and 1558, after the Quiché Maya had been conquered by Pedro de Alvarado in 1524. The original *Popol Vuh* was destroyed by the Spanish, who burned many such documents in the belief that native texts were pagan and therefore evil. The author of the present version was probably a Quiché Mayan who had been taught to write with the Latin alphabet. Because of the elegance and sophistication of the work, many scholars believe that the author must have been a highly educated member of the Quiché royal family. He or she wrote the book in the hope of preserving some of the stories from the Quiché oral tradition.

The original manuscript of the *Popol Vuh* was hidden for more than 150 years until it was found, in the seventeenth century, by Father Francisco Ximénez, a parish priest who lived in the mountains of Guatemala. Ximénez translated the work into Spanish. Thereafter the original book was lost, but thanks to Father Ximénez's translation, the beliefs, legends, and customs of this fascinating people of the early Americas have been preserved.

GOALS/OBJECTIVES

Studying this lesson will enable students to
- interpret and appreciate a retelling of a Mayan creation myth
- discuss different beliefs about creation across cultures
- define *myth* and explain how the term relates to the selection

- define *chronological order* and note words in literature that signal the time order of events
- write a job interview and work with a partner to conduct an interview
- work collaboratively to research the Mayan culture

FROM THE POPOL VUH

Anonymous, English version by Delia Goetz and Sylvanus G. Morley, from the Spanish translation by Adrián Recinos

Then they made the small wild animals, the guardians of the woods, the spirits of the mountains,[1] the deer, the birds, pumas, jaguars, serpents, snakes, vipers, guardians of the thickets.

And the Forefathers asked: "Shall there be only silence and calm under the trees, under the vines? It is well that hereafter there be someone to guard them."

So they said when they meditated and talked. Promptly the deer and the birds were created. Immediately they gave homes to the deer and the birds. "You, deer, shall sleep in the fields by the river bank and in the <u>ravines</u>. Here you shall be amongst the thicket, amongst the pasture; in the woods you shall multiply, you shall walk on four feet and they will support you. Thus be it done!" So it was they spoke.

Then they also assigned homes to the birds big and small. "You shall live in the trees and in the vines. There you shall make your nests; there you shall multiply; there you shall increase in the branches of the trees and in the vines." Thus the deer and the birds were told; they did their duty at once, and all sought their homes and their nests.

---

1. **spirits of the mountains.** In ancient times the Maya believed that forests were filled with spirits that acted as guardians.

words for everyday use

ra • vine (rə vēn′) *n.*, long, deep hollow in the earth's surface. *Loliwag River dried up after the Conifer Dam was built, but a deep <u>ravine</u> marks where the water used to flow.*

Ask students the following questions:
1. According to the *Popol Vuh*, who is responsible for creating the small wild animals?
2. What two kinds of animals are the first to be created?

Answers
1. The Forefathers (of the Mayan culture) create the small wild animals.
2. The first animals created are deer and birds.

INDIVIDUAL LEARNING STRATEGIES

MOTIVATION
Ask students to work in small groups to discuss creation myths about which they have heard or read. Prompt them with the names of different cultures, such as Native American, Asian, African, and so on. Encourage them to include biblical stories and scientific theories. Have each group share the stories they discussed with the class.

READING PROFICIENCY
Before students begin reading this selection, preview the footnotes, which include the pronunciations and descriptions of many of the unfamiliar names mentioned in the myth. Also, encourage students to fill in a graphic organizer that keeps track of the sequence of events in the story.

ENGLISH LANGUAGE LEARNING
As mentioned in strategies for Reading Proficiency above, preview the footnotes of the selection with students. You might ask Spanish-speaking students if they are able to help the class master the pronunciations of the words in the footnotes. You might also encourage students from other cultures to share creation stories from their cultures.

SPECIAL NEEDS
Help students understand the uncommon dialogue in this selection by reading the selection aloud. You might read the narrative part of the story and have volunteers read the passages in quotation marks. As you work through the selection with students, discuss the Guided Reading questions aloud.

INDIVIDUAL LEARNING STRATEGIES (CONT.)

ENRICHMENT
Ask students to work with a partner to research and compare two creation stories from different cultures. Ask each student to research the story of creation from a culture of their choice. Each student in a pair should choose a culture different from the one chosen by his or her partner. Have students share their stories with partners and compare the similarities and differences between each culture's story.

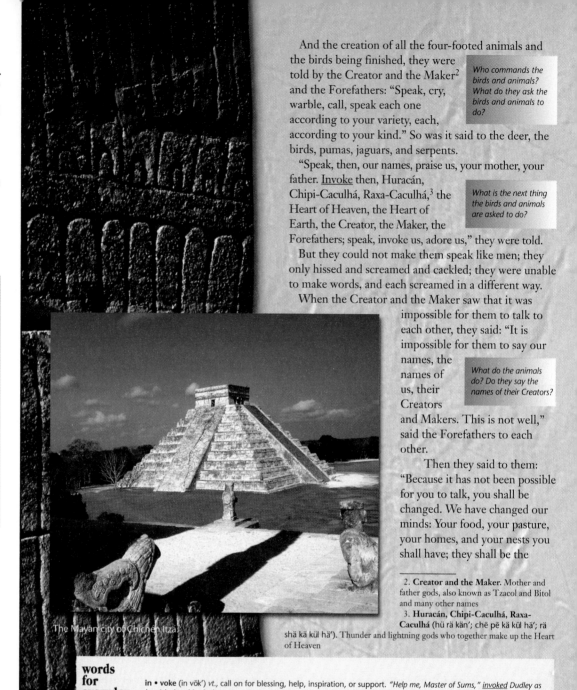

The Mayan city of Chichen Itza.

And the creation of all the four-footed animals and the birds being finished, they were told by the Creator and the Maker[2] and the Forefathers: "Speak, cry, warble, call, speak each one according to your variety, each, according to your kind." So was it said to the deer, the birds, pumas, jaguars, and serpents.

Who commands the birds and animals? What do they ask the birds and animals to do?

"Speak, then, our names, praise us, your mother, your father. Invoke then, Huracán, Chipi-Caculhá, Raxa-Caculhá,[3] the Heart of Heaven, the Heart of Earth, the Creator, the Maker, the Forefathers; speak, invoke us, adore us," they were told.

What is the next thing the birds and animals are asked to do?

But they could not make them speak like men; they only hissed and screamed and cackled; they were unable to make words, and each screamed in a different way. When the Creator and the Maker saw that it was impossible for them to talk to each other, they said: "It is impossible for them to say our names, the names of us, their Creators and Makers. This is not well," said the Forefathers to each other.

What do the animals do? Do they say the names of their Creators?

Then they said to them: "Because it has not been possible for you to talk, you shall be changed. We have changed our minds: Your food, your pasture, your homes, and your nests you shall have; they shall be the

---

2. **Creator and the Maker.** Mother and father gods, also known as Tzacol and Bitol and many other names
3. **Huracán, Chipi-Caculhá, Raxa-Caculhá** (hü rä kän'; chē pē kä kül hä'; rä shä kä kül hä'). Thunder and lightning gods who together make up the Heart of Heaven

words for everyday use

in • voke (in vōk') *vt.*, call on for blessing, help, inspiration, or support. *"Help me, Master of Sums," invoked Dudley as he picked up his algebra test.*

ravines and the woods, because it has not been possible for you to adore us or invoke us. There shall be those who adore us, we shall make other [beings] who shall be obedient. Accept your destiny: your flesh shall be torn to pieces. So shall it be. This shall be your lot." So they said, when they made known their will to the large and small animals which are on the face of the earth.

They wished to give them another trial; they wished to make another attempt; they wished to make [all living things] adore them.

But they could not understand each other's speech; they could succeed in nothing, and could do nothing.

What happens to the animals and birds because of their failure?

For this reason they were sacrificed, and the animals which were on earth were condemned to be killed and eaten.

For this reason another attempt had to be made to create and make men by the Creator, the Maker, and the Forefathers.

Why do the Creator, the Maker, and the Forefathers decide to create humankind?

"Let us try again! Already dawn draws near: Let us make him who shall nourish and sustain us! What shall we do to be invoked, in order to be remembered on earth? We have already tried with our first creations, our first creatures; but we could not make them praise and venerate us. So, then, let us try to make obedient, respectful beings who will nourish and sustain us." Thus they spoke.

Then was the creation and the formation. Of earth, of mud, they made [man's] flesh. But they saw that it was not good. It melted away, it was soft, did not move, had no strength, it fell down, it was limp, it could not move its head, its face fell to one side, its sight was blurred, it could not look behind. At first it spoke, but had no mind. Quickly it soaked in the water and could not stand.

And the Creator and the Maker said: "Let us try again because our creatures will not be able to walk nor multiply. Let us consider this," they said.

Then they broke up and destroyed their work and their creation. And they said: "What shall we do to perfect it, in order that our worshipers, our invokers, will be successful?"

Thus they spoke when they conferred again: "Let us say again to Xpiyacoc, Xmucané,[4] Hunahpú-Vuch, Hunahpú-Utiú:[5] 'Cast your lot again. Try to create again.'" In this manner the Creator and the Maker spoke to Xpiyacoc and Xmucané.

Then they spoke to those soothsayers, the Grandmother of the Day, the Grandmother of the Dawn, as they were called by the Creator and the Maker, and whose names were Xpiyacoc and Xmucané.

And said Huracán, Tepeu, and Gucumatz[6] when they spoke to the soothsayer, to the Maker, who are the diviners: "You must work together and find the means so that man, whom we shall make, man, whom we are going to make, will nourish and sustain us, invoke and remember us."

"Enter, then, into council, grandmother, grandfather, our grandmother, our grandfather, Xpiyacoc, Xmucané, make light, make dawn, have us invoked, have us adored, have us

---

4. **Xpiyacoc, Xmucané** (shēp yä kōk'; shmü kä nä'). Old man and woman, Grandfather and Grandmother; a Creator-couple responsible for making the material things of the world

5. **Hunahpú-Vuch, Hunahpú-Utiú** (hü nä pǘ üch; hü nä pǘ ü tyü'). Other names for the Grandfather and Grandmother. Hunahpú-Vuch was goddess of the dawn; Hunahpú-Utiú was god of the night.

6. **Tepeu, and Gucumatz** (tä pä ǘ; gü kü mätz'). Other names for the Creator and the Maker. Tepeu meant king; Gucumatz was a serpent covered with green feathers, the equivalent of the Mexican Kukulcán and the Aztec Quetzalcoatl

---

words for everyday use

con • demn (kən dem') vt., pronounce judgement against; sentence. *The armed robber was condemned to twenty years in prison.*

ven • er • ate (ven' ər āt) vt., worship. *Chloe venerated Gordie until she found out what a scoundrel he was.*

sooth • say • er (sooth' sā ər) n., person who professes to foretell the future. *Marcel asked the soothsayer what the future held for him.*

di • vin • er (də vīn' ər) n., one who tries to foretell the future. *Unhappy with the soothsayer's prediction, he tried another diviner whose answer pleased him.*

1. The animals on Earth were condemned to be killed and eaten because of their failure.
2. The Creator, the Maker, and the Forefathers create humankind in order to have a race of creatures that will praise and venerate them.

CROSS-CURRICULAR CONNECTIONS

MYTHOLOGY. Huracan, the Mayan god of wind and storm, was responsible for punishing the first humans with the flood that destroyed them. It is believed that our modern word *hurricane* comes from his name.

1. The creators want to make humans from grains of corn and *tzite,* a type of tree. They will know if this is the right substance by the outcome of the divination.
2. The wooden figures live and reproduce, but they do not have souls or minds. They do not satisfy their creators because they did not remember—and could not praise—them.

SELECTION CHECK TEST 4.1.7 WITH ANSWERS

Checking Your Reading

1. What is the aim or purpose of *Popol Vuh*? **The aim of this story is to tell the story of how the gods created humans.**
2. Why were deer and birds created? **They were created to guard the trees and the vines.**
3. Why were the animals condemned to be killed and eaten? **The animals were condemned in this way because they could not praise or worship their Creator and Makers.**
4. How was man's flesh formed the first time? **Man's flesh was formed out of mud.**
5. What was the next substance used to form man? **Wood was used to form man.**

Vocabulary in Context

Fill in each blank below with the most appropriate word from the following Words for Everyday Use. You may have to change the tense of the word.

ravine   venerate   diviner
condemn   invoke

1. The murderer was **condemned** to life imprisonment.
2. I went to a **diviner** to find out what the future held for me.
3. During our hike, my sunglasses fell down the deep **ravine**.
4. Donell **invoked** me to help him with his homework.
5. My grandfather **venerated** my grandmother during their long marriage.

Literary Tools

Fill in the blanks using the following terms.

myth   chronological order

1. It is best to use **chronological order** when giving directions.
2. Popol Vuh is an example of a Mayan **myth**.

---

remembered by created man, by made man, by mortal man. Thus be it done.

"Let your nature be known, Hunahpú-Vuch, Hunahpú-Utiú, twice mother, twice father, Nim-Ac, Nima-Tziís,[7] the master of emeralds, the worker in jewels, the sculptor, the carver, the maker of beautiful plates, the maker of green gourds, the master of resin, the master Toltecat,[8] grandmother of the sun, grandmother of dawn, as you will be called by our works and our creatures.

"Cast the lot with your grains of corn and the *tzité.*[9] Do it thus, and we shall know if we are to make, or carve his mouth and eyes out of wood." Thus the diviners were told.

> *Of what do the creators want to make humans? How will they determine if this is the right substance?*

They went down at once to make their divination, and cast their lots with the corn and the *tzité.* "Fate! Creature!" said an old woman and an old man. And this old man was the one who cast the lots with *tzité,* the one called Xpiyacoc. And the old woman was the diviner, the maker, called Chiracán Xmucané.

Beginning the divination, they said: "Get together, grasp each other! Speak, that we may hear." They said, "Say if it is well that the wood be got together and that it be carved by the Creator and the Maker, and if this [man of wood] is he who must nourish and sustain us when there is light when it is day!

"Thou, corn; thou, *tzité;* thou, fate; thou, creature; get together, take each other," they said to the corn, to the *tzité,* to fate, to the creature. "Come to sacrifice here, Heart of Heaven; do not punish Tepeu and Gucumatz!"[10]

Then they talked and spoke the truth: "Your figures of wood shall come out well; they shall speak and talk on earth."

"So may it be," they answered when they spoke.

And instantly the figures were made of wood. They looked like men, talked like men, and populated the surface of the earth.

They existed and multiplied; they had daughters, they had sons, these wooden figures; but they did not have souls, nor minds, they did not remember their Creator, their Maker; they walked on all fours, aimlessly.

They no longer remembered the Heart of Heaven and therefore they fell out of favor. It was merely a trial, an attempt at man. At first they spoke, but their face was without expression; their feet and hands had no strength; they

> *What do the wooden figures do? What is wrong with the first humans? Do they satisfy their creators?*

had no blood, nor substance, nor moisture, nor flesh; their cheeks were dry, their feet and hands were dry, and their flesh was yellow.

Therefore, they no longer thought of their Creator nor their Maker, nor of those who made them and cared for them.

These were the first men who existed in great numbers on the face of the earth. ■

---

7. **Nim-Ac, Nima-Tziís** (nēm ăk'; nē mä' tzē ēs'). Other names for the Creator and the Maker. Nim-Ac was the Father and Nima-Tziís was the Mother.
8. **Toltecat** (tôl' te kät). Silversmith, worker of silver—a valued occupation
9. *tzité* (tzē tä'). Tree whose wood is used for making fences. The red grains of its fruit are used for fortunetelling, along with the grains of corn.
10. **"Come...Gucumatz!"** The speakers are inviting the Heart of Heaven to join in the casting of lots and ensure the success of the diviners.

Respond *to the* SELECTION

What ideas or beliefs expressed in this myth seemed strange or unfamiliar to you? Which of your beliefs might seem strange to a person from the ancient Mayan culture?

RESPOND TO THE SELECTION

If students could discuss this creation story with someone of the ancient Mayan culture, what might they say? What comments or questions might they have about the story?

Investigate, Inquire, and Imagine

Recall: GATHERING FACTS

1a. For what purpose did the creator gods create the deer and the birds?

2a. What instructions do the creators give all the creatures once the deer and the birds have been assigned their homes?

3a. From what material do the creators attempt to make the first humans? What attributes are lacking in the second group of humans?

Interpret: FINDING MEANING

1b. In what way do the creators change their minds about the creatures' destiny?

2b. What prevents the creators from regarding their first creations as successes?

3b. How is the creation of the first human seen as a second failing?

Analyze: TAKING THINGS APART

4a. Compare the second group of humans to the previous creations of the creators. In comparison to these, what suggests that the creators regard the second group of humans as at least a partial success?

Synthesize: BRINGING THINGS TOGETHER

4b. What in the creation of humans suggests that they could be a higher order of beings than the other creatures?

Evaluate: MAKING JUDGMENTS

5a. What kind of relationship between the earthly and spiritual worlds is established in this creation story? Based on their desires and their actions, what is your opinion of the creator gods? Explain.

Extend: CONNECTING IDEAS

5b. Design a third group of humans that would satisfy the desires of the creator gods. What abilities and attributes would this third group possess? Of what materials would you make these new humans?

Understanding Literature

MYTH. Review the definition for **myth** in the Handbook of Literary Terms. What characteristics of a myth can you find in this selection from the *Popol Vuh?* Cultures from around the world have created their own unique myths, and many focus on similar issues. Thus, there may be several myths from different parts of the world explaining the same events. What other myths do you know that offer alternative explanations for the events explained in the *Popol Vuh?*

CHRONOLOGICAL ORDER. Review the definition for **chronological order** in the Handbook of Literary Terms. Recall that writers, or storytellers, may use signal words such as *then, next,* and *before* to guide readers through the sequence of events. Why would chronological order be an appropriate organization for a creation story? What signal words can you identify in the selection from the *Popol Vuh?*

RECALL

1a. The deer and birds are created to guard the trees.

2a. The creators instruct the deer and the birds to speak in order to praise, invoke, and adore them.

3a. The first humans are made of earth and mud. The second group lack souls, minds, and memories.

INTERPRET

1b. The creators decide that the creatures will be used for food because they are not able to honor their creators. It will be their destiny to be killed and eaten.

2b. The creatures cannot speak to one another or to the creators. This inability prevents them from fulfilling their purpose of praising their makers.

3b. The first human being is a failure because it is so fluid that it cannot walk, talk, or multiply.

ANALYZE

4a. The first group of creatures cannot speak. The first human, made of mud, dissolves; it cannot speak or move. The second group of humans speak and move like real human beings. They can reproduce and populate the earth, but like the other two groups, they cannot praise their creators. The creators allow the second group of humans to live, rather than destroying them as they did the first group.

SYNTHESIZE

4b. They are specifically created to praise and venerate the creators. Extra effort is taken by the creators, for example, in including the soothsayers in the process to ensure the success of these humans.

EVALUATE

5a. The relationship established is ever changing; the spiritual world creates and then recreates the earthly world, always working toward greater success. The spiritual world is in complete control of the earthly one; the earth's creatures are at the mercy of the gods. Students may say that the creator gods are demanding and cruel. Some may say that they are egotistical in that they desire so much praise. Others may say that the gods are simply trying to create feeling beings who can appreciate the gift of life.

EXTEND

5b. *Responses will vary.* Students might say that the third group must have the ability to praise and fear the gods. They should have a full range of emotions; strength in their feet and hands; and blood, substance, and moisture, just as real human beings have.

ANSWERS TO UNDERSTANDING LITERATURE

MYTH. This selection from *The Popol Vuh* is a myth because it offers an explanation of the creation of animals and humans as being performed by gods. There are many creation stories. Students might suggest the creation story in Genesis, the Greek myth of Prometheus, or the Norse creation myth told in the *Eddas* in which men are made from an ash tree and women from an elm.

(Continued on page 22)

CHRONOLOGICAL ORDER. A creation story is a story that explains the process of creating the world. It makes sense to explain what happened in the order that it happened in this type of story. Signal words include "**Then** they made," "**Then** they assigned," "**Then** they said to them," "**Then** was the creation," and "**At first . . . but.**"

ANSWERS TO INTEGRATING THE LANGUAGE ARTS

Language, Grammar, and Style
Students may correct the fragments in a variety of ways.
1. The creator gods <u>were disappointed with the animals.</u>
2. Fragment; The animals <u>were not able to praise them.</u>
3. Because of this, they <u>created a creature from mud.</u>
4. Fragment; They <u>saw this creature dissolve;</u> they <u>were unable to speak clearly.</u>
5. The next being they created <u>was made out of wood.</u>

Applied English & Collaborative Learning
Encourage students to refer to the Language Arts Survey 4.10, "Asking and Answering Questions," and 4.14, "Conducting an Interview." To help them create job-related questions, you might ask them to review the Language Arts Survey 6.8, "Writing a Résumé."

Study and Research & Media Literacy
For this activity, ask students to review the Language Arts Survey 5.20, "Using Reference Works," and 5.26, "Using the Internet." Once students have completed their research, ask them to read 6.11, "Displaying Effective Visual Information."

Writer's Journal

1. Imagine that you are one of the creation gods and write a **want ad** to be published in your heavenly newspaper describing the type of human being you are looking for to populate the earth. Keep your ad brief, and use abbreviations as long as they are easily understood by the average reader.
2. Write a **birth announcement** heralding the "birth" of the first humans, the ones made of wood. Be sure to include on your announcement the "parents" of these humans—the Mother and Father gods (include all their various names), and a brief description of the newborn.
3. Imagine you are a scientist and create a **design scheme** for a human being to be presented to the Mayan creation gods. Use your knowledge of human anatomy, but don't worry about being correct in every detail.

Integrating the Language Arts

Language, Grammar, and Style

IDENTIFYING AND CORRECTING SENTENCE FRAGMENTS. Read the Language Arts Survey 3.33, "Correcting Sentence Fragments." Then complete the following exercise.
If the group of words is a complete sentence, underline the complete subject once and the complete predicate twice. If it is a fragment, add material to make the group of words into a complete sentence.
1. The creator gods were disappointed with the animals.
2. Who were not able to praise them.
3. Because of this, they created a new creature from mud.
4. Saw this creature dissolve, unable to speak clearly.
5. The next being they created was made out of wood.

Applied English & Collaborative Learning

JOB INTERVIEW. The creations in the *Popol Vuh* did not all live up to the creators' expectations. Write the text of an interview between yourself, as a creator, and a creation to determine whether or not you wish to keep the creation. Be sure to indicate in your questions your requirements for the "job" of the creation. When you have finished writing both the questions and answers of the imaginary interviewee, you might want to find a partner and act out the interviews together in a role-play.

Study and Research & Media Literacy

RESEARCHING THE QUICHÉ MAYA. As a class, learn more about the Quiché people and the place in which they lived. Divide your research into geography and climate, animals and vegetation, housing and diet, and cultural traditions. You may also choose to investigate what exactly happened to all the Maya codices, or documents written on bark paper, when the Spanish arrived. Form groups of three or four people to research these various subjects using library or Internet resources. Then, within each group, plan a presentation of your findings that utilizes visual materials.

"Popocatépetl and Ixtacihuatl"

Retold by Julie Piggott

Reader's resource

"Popocatépetl and Ixtacihuatl" is an Aztec tale which explains the presence of a snow-capped volcano called Popocatépetl (pō′ pō ka tā′ pet′l), or "smoking mountain" in the Aztec language, and its twin mountain, Ixtacihuatl (ēs′ tä sē′ wä təl), or "white woman."

HISTORY CONNECTION. "Popocatépetl and Ixtacihuatl" takes place in the Aztec capital of Tenochtitlan (tā nōch′ tēt län′), a city built in about 1325 roughly on the site where Mexico City now stands. The settlement began on two islands in Lake Texcoco (tes kō′ kō′) and expanded rapidly to become a city with hundreds of buildings, an extensive canal system, and an estimated population of three hundred thousand. The Aztecs began as a nomadic tribe, but by the fifteenth century had taken shape as a sophisticated and intellectual society which has been a fascinating subject for scholars today. Both art and architecture, as well as mathematical studies, agriculture, and trade, contributed to a well-rounded empire, which covered about seventy-five thousand square miles and had a population of about five million people. In 1521, however, the Aztec civilization came to an end. Spanish conquistadors, led by Hernán Cortés, wanted gold, which the Aztecs had in plenty. Cortés and the Spaniards enlisted the help of a rival group of indigenous people and arrived at Tenochtitlan, where the Aztec emperor Moctezuma welcomed the Spaniards as guests. Cortés imprisoned his host and waged war against the Aztecs for several months. The conquistadors founded Mexico City on the rubble of the shattered Aztec capital.

Graphic Organizer

Examples of Foreshadowing	Prediction
Some doubt Emperor's Wisdom	The Emperor may do something foolish.

Literary TOOLS

MYTH, LEGEND, AND FOLK TALE. A myth is a story that explains objects or events in the natural world as resulting from the action of some supernatural force or entity, most often a god. Features of myth are shared by other works from the oral tradition. A **legend** is a story coming down from the past, often based on real events or characters from older times. Unlike myths, legends are popularly regarded as historical; however, they may contain elements that are fantastic or unverifiable. A **folk tale** is a brief story that, like myths and legends, was passed by word-of-mouth from generation to generation. It is characteristically anonymous, timeless, and placeless. The selection "Popocatépetl and Ixtacihuatl" could be considered as any one of these three. As you read, decide which definition best fits the story.

FORESHADOWING. Foreshadowing is the act of presenting materials that hint at events to occur later in the story. Foreshadowing may take the form of actual plot elements or be embodied in the mood a writer creates. As you read, look for events or details that seem ominous or seem to foreshadow what will happen later in the story. Record these in a Graphic Organizer like the one on this page. In the right column, write a prediction of what you think will happen based on each event or detail.

Reader's Journal

What stories do you know that deal with young lovers who meet with difficulty or opposition?

ADDITIONAL RESOURCES

UNIT 1 RESOURCE BOOK
- Selection Worksheet 1.4
- Selection Check Test 4.1.9
- Selection Test 4.1.10
- Language, Grammar, and Style Resource 3.21

GRAPHIC ORGANIZER

- **Foreshadowing:** strength and constancy of the love between Ixta and Popo
  Prediction: Ixta and Popo will marry
- **Foreshadowing:** the Emperor's refusal of Ixta and Popo marrying
  Prediction: Ixta and/or Popo will experience or die of a broken heart.
- **Foreshadowing:** some of the warriors are jealous of Popo
  Prediction: they will do something to ruin Popo's happiness with Ixta

READER'S JOURNAL

What difficulties do young lovers face today? What makes a relationship between two young people stressful or hard?

GOALS/OBJECTIVES

Studying this lesson will enable students to
- interpret and appreciate an Aztec myth that explains the origin of a volcano and a mountain
- learn about the Aztec culture and discuss the role myths played in early civilizations
- define *myth, legend,* and *folk tale* and explain how these terms relate to the selection
- define *foreshadowing* and identify examples of this literary technique in literature
- demonstrate an ability to find the simple subject in sentences
- work collaboratively to research and compare folk tales, myths, and legends from various cultures

MOTIVATION
Ask students to work in small groups to discuss stories they know about star-crossed lovers, such as Shakespeare's *Romeo and Juliet*. Encourage students to bring into the conversations examples from popular culture. Ask them to identify common themes that permeate each story.

READING PROFICIENCY
Read through the Reader's Resource on page 23 with students, carefully pronouncing each name and asking students to practice their pronunciation with you. You might also ask students to focus on the Guided Reading and Recall questions to help them grasp the main events and ideas of the myth.

ENGLISH LANGUAGE LEARNING
The strategies for Reading Proficiency above will also benefit English language learners. Encourage students from other cultures to share any stories from their original cultures that explain the presence of natural elements.

SPECIAL NEEDS
Students will benefit from listening to an audio recording of the myth as they read along in their texts. Remind students to pause the tape and write questions or seek help when they encounter a passage that confuses them.

ENRICHMENT
Ask students to work with a partner to research and perform other myths, legends, folk tales, or tall tales that explain the presence of natural elements. Give the paired students time to read and discuss their selection, write a script, and rehearse their performance. Then have them perform their piece as the rest of the class rates the creativity used for the explanation in each story. You might have students vote to choose a class favorite.

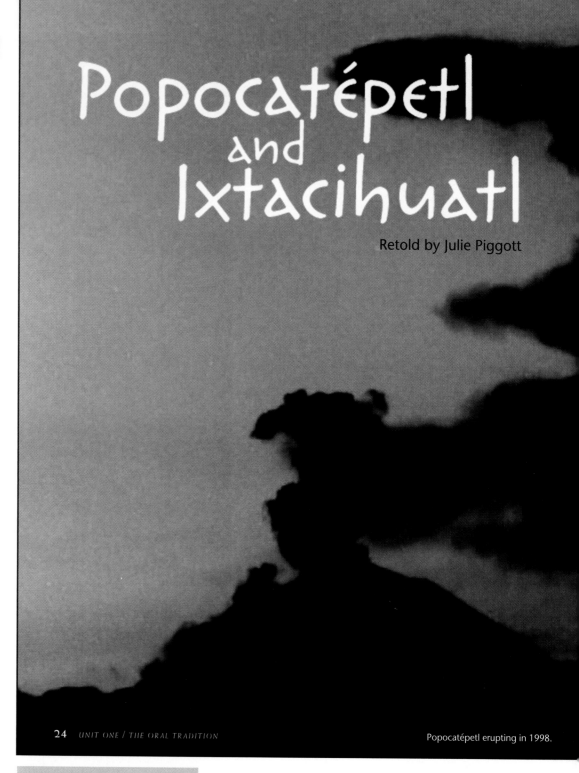

Popocatépetl and Ixtacihuatl

Retold by Julie Piggott

Popocatépetl erupting in 1998.

VOCABULARY FROM THE SELECTION

adamant	edifice
apprehensive	emit
behest	refute
besiege	resinous
brandish	trebly
brine	unanimous
decree	vanquish

There was once an Aztec emperor in Tenochtitlan. He was very powerful. Some thought he was wise as well, while others doubted his wisdom.

What opinion of the Emperor do the people hold?

He was born a ruler and a warrior; and he kept at bay those tribes living in and beyond the mountains surrounding the Valley of Mexico, with its huge lake called Texcoco in which Tenochtitlan was built. His power was absolute, and the splendor in which he lived was very great.

It is not known for how many years the Emperor ruled Tenochtitlan, but it is known that he lived to a great age. However, it was not until he was in his middle years that his wife gave him an heir, a girl. The Emperor and Empress loved the princess very much, and she was their only child. She was a dutiful daughter and learned all she could from her father about the art of ruling, for she knew that when he died, she would reign in his stead in Tenochtitlan.

Her name was Ixtacihuatl. Her parents and her friends called her Ixta. She had a pleasant disposition and, as a result, she had many friends. The great palace where she lived with the Emperor and Empress rang with their laughter when they came to the parties her parents gave for her. As well as being a delightful companion, Ixta was also very pretty, even beautiful.

Her childhood was happy, and she was content enough when she became a young woman. But by then she was fully aware of the great responsibilities which would be hers when her father died, and she became serious and studious and did not enjoy parties as much as she had done when younger.

Another reason for her being so serious was that she was in love. This in itself was a joyous thing, but the Emperor forbade her to marry. He wanted her to reign and rule alone when he died, for he trusted no one, not even his wife, to rule as he did except his much loved only child, Ixta. This was why there were some who doubted the wisdom of the Emperor; for, by not allowing his heiress to marry, he showed a selfishness and shortsightedness toward his daughter and his empire

What does the Emperor forbid Ixta to do? Why? What do the people think of the Emperor because of his decision?

which many considered was not truly wise. An emperor, they felt, who was not truly wise could not also be truly great or even truly powerful.

CROSS-CURRICULAR ACTIVITIES

GEOGRAPHY OF MEXICO CITY. Have students research the volcano Popocatépetl. Is the volcano still active? If not, when was it last active? How tall is it? How are volcanoes formed? Students could also research the draining of Lake Texcoco and other lakes which allowed Mexico City to expand over the entire valley. What problems are occurring in Mexico City as a result of its having been built on such marshy land? What problems have arisen because of the high mountains that surround the city?

1. The Emperor realized that he was
   no longer powerful and that his
   domain was in danger.
2. The Emperor bribes his warriors by
   offering the hand of his daughter,
   Ixta, and equal rule of his kingdom
   to the warrior that defeated the
   enemies.
3. Ixta was fearful of her father's bribe
   because she wanted to marry only
   Popo.

CROSS-CURRICULAR CONNECTIONS

MYTHOLOGY. Quetzalcoatl was
one of the major gods worshipped
by the Aztecs. He was believed to be
responsible for creation and was a
god of wind, water, and fertility. He
is also often credited with introducing the Aztec calendar.

One myth claims that
Quetzalcoatl was driven into exile
but would return or "come again."
According to legend, the Aztec king
Montezuma II believed that Hernán
Cortés, arriving at Tenochtitlan, was
the returning Quetzalcoatl. Some
believe this is why Montezuma
welcomed Cortés as an honored
guest.

INTERNET RESOURCES

If students are interested in
learning more about the Aztec
calendar, direct them to the Internet
site http://azteccalendar.com. This
site translates the current date into
the corresponding Aztec calendar
day and provides an explanation of
the basics of the Aztec calendar.

The man with whom Ixta was in love was also
in love with her. Had they been allowed to
marry, their state could have been doubly joyous. His name was Popocatépetl, and Ixta and
his friends all called him Popo. He was a warrior in the service of the Emperor, tall and
strong, with a capacity for gentleness, and very
brave. He and Ixta loved each other very much,
and while they were content and even happy
when they were together, true joy was not theirs
because the Emperor continued to insist that
Ixta should not be married when the time came
for her to take on her father's responsibilities.

This unfortunate but moderately happy relationship between Ixta and Popo continued for
several years, the couple pleading with the
Emperor at regular intervals and the Emperor
remaining constantly <u>adamant</u>. Popo loved Ixta
no less for her father's stubbornness; and she
loved him no less while she studied, as her
father demanded she should do, the art of ruling
in preparation for her reign.

When the Emperor became very old, he also
became ill. In his feebleness, he channeled all
his failing energies toward instructing Ixta in
statecraft,[1] for he was no longer able to exercise
that craft himself. So it was that his enemies, the
tribes who lived in the mountains and beyond,
realized that the great Emperor in Tenochtitlan
was great no longer, for he was only teaching his
daughter to rule and not ruling himself.

The tribesmen came nearer and nearer to
Tenochtitlan until the city was <u>besieged</u>. At last
the Emperor realized him-
self that he was great no
longer, that his power was
nearly gone, and that his
domain was in dire peril.[2]

What does the Emperor realize about himself? What danger does he see?

Warrior though he long had been, he was now
too old and too ill to lead his fighting men into
battle. At last he understood that, unless his
enemies were frustrated in their efforts to enter
and lay waste to Tenochtitlan, not only would
he no longer be Emperor but his daughter
would never be Empress.

Instead of appointing one of his warriors to
lead the rest into battle on his behalf, he offered
a bribe to all of them. Perhaps it was that his
wisdom, if wisdom he had,
had forsaken him; or per-
haps he acted from fear. Or

What bribe does the Emperor offer? Why?

perhaps he simply changed his mind. But the
bribe he offered to whichever warrior succeeded
in lifting the siege of Tenochtitlan and defeating
the enemies in and around the Valley of Mexico
was both the hand of his daughter and the equal
right to reign and rule, with her, in
Tenochtitlan. Furthermore, he decreed that
directly he learned that his enemies had been
defeated, he would instantly cease to be
Emperor himself. Ixta would not have to wait
until her father died to become Empress; and, if
her father should die of his illness or old age
before his enemies were <u>vanquished</u>, he further
<u>decreed</u> that he who overcame the surrounding
enemies should marry the princess whether he,
the Emperor, lived or not.

Ixta was fearful when she heard of her father's
bribe to his warriors, for the only one whom she
had any wish to marry was
Popo; and she wanted to
marry him, and only him,
very much indeed.

How does Ixta feel when she hears of her father's bribe?

The warriors, however, were glad when they
heard of the decree. There was not one of them
who would not have been glad to have the
princess as his wife, and they all relished the

---

1. **statecraft.** Ability, wisdom, and methods of someone who
manages public affairs
2. **dire peril.** Great danger

---

words for everyday use

ad • a • mant (ad′ ə mənt) *adj.*, unshakeable; not giving in. *Luan begged me to reconsider, but I remained <u>adamant</u> in my decision.*

be • siege (bē sēj′) *vt.*, close in on and attack. *As the defendant left the courtroom he was <u>besieged</u> with angry shouts from the crowd and questions from reporters.*

van • quish (van′ kwish) *vt.*, conquer. *After their enemies were <u>vanquished</u>, the warriors celebrated with a joyous banquet.*

de • cree (dē krē′) *vt.*, order officially. *Ms. Kwillian <u>decreed</u> that anyone talking during the test would fail.*

chance of becoming Emperor.

And so the warriors went to war at their ruler's <u>behest</u>, and each fought <u>trebly</u> hard; for each was fighting not only for the safety of Tenochtitlan and the surrounding valley, but for the delightful bride and for the right to be the Emperor himself.

Even though the warriors fought with great skill, and even though each one exhibited a courage he did not know he possessed, the war was a long one. The Emperor's enemies were firmly entrenched around Lake Texcoco and Tenochtitlan by the time the warriors were sent to war; and as battle followed battle, the final outcome was uncertain.

The warriors took a variety of weapons with them; wooden clubs edged with sharp blades of obsidian,[3] obsidian machetes,[4] javelins[5] which they hurled at their enemies from troughed throwing boards,[6] bows and arrows, slings and spears set with obsidian fragments, and lances, too. Many of them carried shields woven from wicker and covered in tough hide and most wore armor made of thick quilted cotton soaked in <u>brine</u>.

The war was long and fierce. Most of the warriors fought together and in unison, but some fought alone. As time went on, natural leaders emerged and, of these, undoubtedly Popo was the best. Finally, it was he, <u>brandishing</u> his club

How do the warriors feel when they hear the Emperor's decree?

and shield, who led the great charge of running warriors across the valley, with their enemies fleeing before them to the safety of the coastal plains and jungles beyond the mountains.

The warriors acclaimed Popo as the man most responsible for the victory; and, weary though they all were, they set off for Tenochtitlan to report to the Emperor and for Popo to claim Ixta as his wife at last.

But a few of those warriors were jealous of Popo. Since they knew none of them could rightly claim the victory for himself (the decision among the Emperor's fighting men that Popo was responsible for the victory had been <u>unanimous</u>), they wanted to spoil for him and for Ixta the delights which the Emperor had promised.

These few men slipped away from the rest at night and made their way to Tenochtitlan ahead of all the others. They reached the capital two days later, having traveled without sleep all the way, and quickly let it be known that, although the Emperor's warriors had been successful against his enemies, the warrior Popo had been killed in battle.

Who is most responsible for victory according to the warriors? In what way is this warrior to be rewarded? Why do some of the warriors want to ruin Popo's happiness?

---

3. **obsidian.** Hard, black volcanic rock
4. **machetes.** Heavy-bladed knives
5. **javelins.** Throwing spears
6. **throwing boards.** Hollowed, narrow wooden paddle with which to throw

words for everyday use

be • hest (bē hest') *n.*, command. *Sarah took out the garbage at her father's <u>behest</u>.*
tre • bly (treb' lē) *adv.*, extremely; three times as. *After hearing of Amy's accomplishments on the flute, piano, and guitar, I was <u>trebly</u> impressed.*
brine (brīn) *n.*, salt water. *After swimming in the ocean, Loren washed the <u>brine</u> from her clothes.*
bran • dish (bran' dish) *vt.*, wave; exhibit. *Minerva proudly <u>brandished</u> the first copy of the newspaper with her picture on the front page.*
u • nan • i • mous (yoo nan' ə məs) *adj.*, in complete agreement. *I expected Lionel to oppose the proposition, but the decision was <u>unanimous</u>.*

"POPOCATÉPETL AND IXTACIHUATL" **27**

And so the warriors went to war at their ruler's behest, and each fought trebly hard . . .

ANSWERS TO GUIDED READING QUESTIONS

1. The warriors, each one eager to marry Ixta and rule the kingdom, were very pleased with the Emperor's decree.
2. Popo is most responsible for the victory. Popo, according to the Emperor's decree, should be rewarded by marrying Ixta and sharing rule of the kingdom. Some of the warriors wanted to ruin Popo's happiness because they were jealous of him and the reward he would receive.

CROSS-CURRICULAR ACTIVITIES

HISTORY. Ask students to research the history surrounding the Aztec culture. Students might choose to focus on Montezuma II, Hernán Cortés, or the development of Mexico City. Others might choose to focus on information about the daily lives of people during the Aztec civilization. Ask students to present their research in the form of a one-page report. You might consider having students share their findings in small groups or in the form of a brief oral presentation.

ANSWER TO GUIDED READING QUESTION

1. The warriors tell the Emperor that Popo was killed in battle.

ADDITIONAL QUESTIONS AND ACTIVITIES

Ask students the following questions:

1. What do the warriors tell the Emperor when he demands to know which warrior was responsible for the victory?
2. What happens to Ixta after she hears of Popo's death?
3. How does Popo punish the jealous warriors who falsely reported his death?

Answers

1. None of the warriors would claim the honor and refused to answer the Emperor's questions.
2. Ixta retires to her room, becomes very ill, and dies.
3. Popo kills each of them in single combat with his obsidian studded club.

It was a foolish and cruel lie which those warriors told their Emperor, and they told it for no reason other than that they were jealous of Popo.

What do the warriors tell the Emperor? Why?

When the Emperor heard this, he demanded that Popo's body be brought to him so that he might arrange a fitting burial. He knew the man his daughter had loved would have died courageously. The jealous warriors looked at one another and said nothing. Then one of them told the Emperor that Popo had been killed on the edge of Lake Texcoco and that his body had fallen into the water and no man had been able to retrieve it. The Emperor was saddened to hear this.

After a little while, he demanded to be told which of his warriors had been responsible for the victory; but none of the fighting men before him dared claim the successful outcome of the war for himself, for each knew the others would refute him. So they were silent. This puzzled the Emperor, and he decided to wait for the main body of his warriors to return and not to press the few who had brought the news of the victory and of Popo's death.

Then the Emperor sent for his wife and his daughter and told them their enemies had been overcome. The Empress was thoroughly excited and relieved at the news. Ixta was only apprehensive. The Emperor, seeing her anxious face, told her quickly that Popo was dead. He went on to say that the warrior's body had been lost in the waters of Lake Texcoco; and again it was as though his wisdom had left him, for he spoke at some length of his not yet being able to tell Ixta who her husband would be and who would become Emperor when the main body of warriors returned to Tenochtitlan.

But Ixta heard nothing of what he told her, only that her beloved Popo was dead. She went to her room and lay down. Her mother followed her and saw at once she was very ill. Witch doctors were sent for, but they could not help the princess, and neither could her parents. Her illness had no name, unless it was the illness of a broken heart. Princess Ixtacihuatl did not wish to live if Popocatépetl was dead, and so she died herself.

The day after her death, Popo returned to Tenochtitlan with all the other surviving warriors. They went straight to the palace and, with much cheering, told the Emperor that his enemies had been routed and that Popo was the undoubted victor of the conflict.

The Emperor praised his warriors and pronounced Popo to be the new Emperor in his place. When the young man asked first to see Ixta, begging that they should be married at once before being jointly proclaimed Emperor and Empress, the Emperor had to tell Popo of Ixta's death and how it had happened.

Popo spoke not a word.

He gestured the assembled warriors to follow him, and together they sought out the few jealous men who had given the false news of his death to the Emperor. With the army of warriors watching, Popo killed each one in single combat with his obsidian studded club. No one tried to stop him.

That task accomplished, Popo returned to the palace and, still without speaking and still wearing his stiff cotton armor, went to Ixta's room. He gently lifted her body and carried it out of the palace and out of the city, and no one tried to stop him doing that either. All the warriors followed him in silence.

When he had walked some miles, he gestured to them again, and they built a huge pile of stones in the shape of a pyramid. They all worked together and they worked fast, while

---

words for everyday use

re • fute (ri fyōōt′) *vt.*, prove to be wrong. *Angela refuted Tony's accusation that she was lazy by showing him the work she had done on their project while he was sleeping.*

ap • pre • hen • sive (ap′ rē hen′ siv) *adj.*, fearful; nervous. *Despite hours spent studying, Paul was apprehensive that he might not pass the test.*

Popo stood and watched, holding the body of the princess in his arms. By sunset the mighty <u>edifice</u> was finished. Popo climbed it alone, carrying Ixta's corpse with him. There, at the very top, under the heap of stones, he buried the young woman he had loved so well and for so long and who had died for the love of him.

That night Popo slept alone at the top of the pyramid by Ixta's grave. In the morning he came down and spoke for the first time since the Emperor had told him the princess was dead. He told the warriors to build another pyramid, a little to the southeast of the one which held Ixta's body, and to build it higher than the other.

He told them, too, to tell the Emperor on his behalf that he, Popocatépetl, would never reign and rule in Tenochtitlan. He would keep watch over the grave of the Princess Ixtacihuatl for the rest of his life.

What does Popo have the warriors build? What does he do with Ixta's body?

The messages to the Emperor were the last words Popo ever spoke. Well before the evening, the second mighty pile of stones was built. Popo climbed it and stood at the top, taking a torch of <u>resinous</u> pine wood with him.

And when he reached the top, he lit the torch, and the warriors below saw the white smoke rise against the blue sky; and they watched as the sun began to set, and the smoke turned pink and then a deep red, the color of blood.

So Popocatépetl stood there, holding the torch of memory of Ixtacihuatl, for the rest of his days.

The snows came, and, as the years went by, the pyramids of stone became high, white-capped mountains. Even now the one called Popocatépetl <u>emits</u> smoke in memory of the princess whose body lies in the mountain which bears her name.

What does Popo do to honor the memory of Ixta? What happens to the pyramids?

■

words for everyday use

ed • i • fice (ed' i fis) *n.*, structure. *The old abandoned building was torn down to make room for a new <u>edifice</u>.*
res • in • ous (rez' ən əs) *adj.*, having resin—a clear, yellowish-brown substance that comes from trees or plants. *Joan built a fire using <u>resinous</u> wood and it smoked quite a bit.*
e • mit (ē mit') *vt.*, give off. *The honeysuckle by the railroad tracks <u>emits</u> a sweet, heavy scent.*

Respond *to the* SELECTION

How do you feel when you have played by the rules, only to lose to someone who cheats or plays unfairly?

ANSWERS TO GUIDED READING QUESTIONS

1. Popo has the warriors build a huge pyramid with stones. He buries Ixta's body at the top of the pyramid.
2. Popo sends a message to the Emperor saying that he will not rule, but that he will keep watch over Ixta's body for the rest of his life. Then he climbs a second pyramid, lights a torch, and holds it in Ixta's memory until he himself dies. The pyramids become high, snow-capped mountains. The one called Popocatépetl is a volcano.

RESPOND TO THE SELECTION

Imagine you are Ixta. How would you have responded to the news of Popo's death? Who do you think is to blame for her death?

SELECTION CHECK TEST 4.1.9 WITH ANSWERS

Checking Your Reading
1. Describe Ixtacihuatl. **She is the heir to her father's empire, she has a sweet disposition, and is very beautiful.**
2. Why did the Emperor forbid his daughter to marry? **He wanted her to reign alone because he trusted no one but his daughter.**
3. Describe Popocatépetl. **He is a tall, strong, brave, gentle warrior.**
4. What did the bribe consist of that the Emperor offered to his warriors? **The bribe was that whoever could defeat the enemy attacks on his empire would win his daughter's hand in marriage and have equal right to rule.**
5. What did the warriors tell the Emperor? **They told the Emperor that Popocatépetl died in the war.**

Vocabulary in Context
Fill in each blank below with the most appropriate word from the following Words for Everyday Use. You may have to change the tense of the words.

adamant   vanquish
decree   brine   refute
emit

1. The **brine** dried out my skin and made my hair stiff.

SELECTION CHECK TEST 4.1.9 WITH ANSWERS (CONT.)

2. The king sent out a **decree** that all maidens must attend the ball.
3. I could tell from the odor that was **emitted** from the milk carton that it was old.
4. Jesse was **adamant** about paying the dinner bill.
5. After the lioness **vanquished** the deer, she feasted on it.

Literary Tools
Fill in the blanks using the following terms.

legend   folk tale   myth
foreshadowing

1. A **legend** is a story that is passed down from generation to generation, but it is often based on real events or characters.
2. **Foreshadowing** is used to give reader a hint of what will occur later in the story.
3. A **folk tale** is a story that is often placeless, timeless, and anonymous.

RECALL

1a. The Emperor wants his daughter to rule Tenochtitlan after his death. He forbids her to marry.

2a. As the Emperor grows old and sick, enemy tribes, recognizing the Emperor's focus on his daughter's education, begin to invade the empire. The Emperor offers a bribe to his warriors, giving the finest the right to marry Ixta and rule the empire without waiting for the Emperor's death.

3a. Most of the warriors celebrate Popo's right to finally marry Ixta. A few falsely report that Popo has been killed. Ixta dies of a broken heart. She believes Popo is dead.

INTERPRET

1b. The Emperor restricts Ixta because he doesn't trust anyone else to rule in his stead. He worries that a husband might influence Ixta. She willingly studies to become an effective ruler though she tries to persuade her father to let her marry.

2b. He is old and frightened. He might have lost his wisdom or have changed his mind about letting Ixta marry.

3b. Jealousy drives some of the warriors to betray Popo. Popo hasn't the heart to rule without Ixta. He commands the building of two pyramids, one for Ixta's grave and one for himself. He then stands guard on his pyramid for the rest of his life, a torch in his hand.

ANALYZE

4a. Both are heartbroken; both give up the privileges and responsibilities of their lives. Ixta dies, while Popo withdraws from life.

SYNTHESIZE

4b. The pyramids become mountains in Mexico, one an active volcano. The story was probably created to explain the smoke and eruptions of Popocatépetl.

EVALUATE

5a. Students may say that the Emperor, as well as the soldiers who falsely reported Popo's death, are to blame for the tragedy. They may hold the soldiers more at fault because their act was deliberately malicious while the Emperor's actions were a result of poor judgment. Students may suggest that the Emperor could have prevented the tragedy by allowing Popo and Ixta to marry. He also should never have promised his

---

Investigate, Inquire, and Imagine

Recall: GATHERING FACTS

1a. What does the Emperor expect of his daughter? What does he forbid her to do?

2a. What combined factors undermine the Emperor's power? What actions does the Emperor take in response to the threats to his domain?

3a. After Popo's victory, how do some of his fellow warriors behave? How does Ixta respond to the news about Popo's performance in battle? What does she do? Why?

Interpret: FINDING MEANING

1b. What reason does the Emperor have for the one restriction he places on Ixta? How does Ixta respond to her father's wishes?

2b. According to the story, why does the Emperor respond as he does to the threats against the empire?

3b. What emotion drives some of the warriors to betray Popo? Why does Popo refuse to rule Tenochtitlan? What does he do instead?

Analyze: TAKING THINGS APART

4a. How are the reactions of Popo and Ixta to their separation similar? How are their reactions different?

Synthesize: BRINGING THINGS TOGETHER

4b. What do the two pyramids become? Why do you think the people of Tenochtitlan developed this story?

Evaluate: MAKING JUDGMENTS

5a. Which people are to blame for the tragic end of the two lovers? Who is most at fault, in your opinion, and why? What could have been done to prevent the tragedy?

Extend: CONNECTING IDEAS

5b. What morals, or messages, can be taken from this story? What does the story tell you about the values of the Aztec people?

Understanding Literature

MYTH, LEGEND, AND FOLK TALE. Review the definitions for **myth**, **legend**, and **folk tale** in the Handbook of Literary Terms. Myths, legends, and folk tales are all works from the oral tradition, and all share certain characteristics. "Popocatépetl and Ixtacihuatl" has characteristics of all three types. What characteristics of a myth are found in the story? What characteristics of a legend and a folk tale are found in the story?

FORESHADOWING. Review the definition for **foreshadowing** in the Handbook of Literary Terms and the chart you completed for Literary Tools on page 23. Find three examples of foreshadowing in "Popocatépetl and Ixtacihuatl." What events are foreshadowed?

ANSWERS TO INVESTIGATE, INQUIRE, AND IMAGINE (CONT.)

daughter to the most valiant warrior.

EXTEND

5b. *Responses will vary.* One moral that could be taken from the story is that no one should stand in the way of true love, as the Emperor did. Another message could be that a leader should not encourage his troops to compete against one another for a goal, but rather promote unity

among them. Yet another might be a warning against treating one's daughter like property to be awarded as a prize. Based on this story, students might say that the Aztecs valued love, commitment, honesty, and heroism in battle.

Answers to Understanding Literature can be found on page 31.

Writer's Journal

1. The story of Popo and Ixta does not contain dialogue. Select one of the scenes in the story and write **dialogue** for it. For example, you might choose to write the dialogue between Ixta and her father as she pleads to be allowed to marry Popo.
2. Imagine that you are an advice columnist and that the Emperor, before making any decisions about war or about his daughter's fate, writes for advice on how to handle his various troubles. Write an **advice column** including the Emperor's letter and your advice to him.
3. Write a **lament**, a sorrowful piece of writing, that expresses the sadness of Popo at the end of the story. Your lament can be a poem, a song, or an essay.

Integrating the Language Arts

Language, Grammar, and Style

FINDING THE SIMPLE SUBJECT. Read the Language Arts Survey 3.21, "How to Find the Simple Subject and Verb." In the following sentences, underline the simple subject once and the verb twice. Be sure to find the verb before you identify the simple subject.

EXAMPLE   The great Aztec <u>civilization</u> <u>fell</u> from glory when the Spanish arrived.

1. The fascinating Aztec legends, however, have survived the centuries.
2. One of these legends is the story of Popocatépetl and Ixtacihuatl.
3. The young Ixta was in love with the warrior Popo.
4. Unfortunately, the strict Emperor forbade their marriage.
5. The sad events that followed explain the existence of two volcanoes in Mexico.

Applied English

CREATING A PLAQUE. Write the text for a plaque explaining the origin of an important natural or human-made element in your community. This could be a canal, a dam, a rock formation, a river, or some other geographical element. Why does this element have its name? How did it come into being? Use the folk tale genre to create your explanation. Let your mind wander, and use your imagination to think of a creative reason for how the element came to exist. Explore fantastic events, such as the work of a giant, for example, as well as realistic events, such as the movement of glaciers. Then ask yourself: What questions do I need to answer to complete my explanation? As you write the text for your plaque, try to respond to the questions you have identified.

Media Literacy & Collaborative Learning

STORYTELLING. The indigenous peoples of Mexico and Central and South America have a rich oral tradition. Using library or Internet resources, gather some other folk tales, myths, or legends from these regions. On the Internet, use keywords such as "legend," "myth," "folk tale," or be more specific and write "Latin American legends," or "Aztec myths," for example. Choose one story and read it aloud to your classmates. Then, as a class, discuss the similarities and differences among the stories. Include "Popocatépetl and Ixtacihuatl" in your discussion.

ANSWERS TO UNDERSTANDING LITERATURE

MYTH, LEGEND, AND FOLK TALE. *Responses will vary.* Students may say that the story is like a myth because it explains objects and events in the natural world: the two mountains and the eruptions and smoke coming from one of the mountains. Although gods do not enter the story, there is an element of the supernatural in that Popo lives on through the smoke coming from the mountain that bears his name. The story is like a legend in that it may have been popularly regarded as true, and the characters may be partly based on actual figures from Aztec royalty, although this is not verifiable. The story is like a folk tale in that it could have taken place at any time, and begins simply with the phrase, "There was once an Aztec emperor in Tenochtitlan."

FORESHADOWING. The early doubts about the Emperor's wisdom and the feeling that he is selfish and shortsighted foreshadow his poor decision regarding the bribe. The strength and constancy of the love between Ixta and Popo combined with their early troubles foreshadow Ixta's death of a broken heart. The desire of some of the warriors to ruin Popo's happiness foreshadows the tragedy at the end of the story.

ANSWERS TO INTEGRATING THE LANGUAGE ARTS

Language, Grammar, and Style
1. The fascinating Aztec <u>legends</u>, however, <u>have survived</u> the centuries.
2. One of these <u>legends</u> <u>is</u> the story of Popocatépetl and Ixtacihuatl.
3. The young <u>Ixta</u> <u>was</u> in love with the warrior Popo.
4. Unfortunately, the strict <u>Emperor</u> <u>forbade</u> their marriage.
5. The sad <u>events</u> that followed <u>explain</u> the existence of two volcanoes in Mexico.

Applied English
Consider allowing students to work with partners or in small groups to brainstorm possible creative reasons for their elements' existence. You might direct students to research other popular folk tales or tall tales that explain the origin of natural elements, such as the Pecos Bill tall tales.

Media Literacy & Collaborative Learning
Refer students to the Language Arts Survey 4.19, "Oral Interpretation." Students can use the tips provided to prepare to share their stories with the class.

ADDITIONAL RESOURCES

UNIT 1 RESOURCE BOOK
- Selection Worksheet 1.5
- Selection Check Test 4.1.11
- Selection Test 4.1.12
- Language, Grammar, and Style Resource 3.7

VOCABULARY FROM THE SELECTION

churl   ravage
homage   vengeance

GRAPHIC ORGANIZER

- **Motif:** the trial or quest
  Appearance in Story: the trial is pulling the sword out of the stone and anvil
- **Motif:** a humble person transformed into a position of high status
  Appearance in Story: Arthur's transformation from a common youth to a king
- **Motif:** three wishes
  Appearance in Story: the three magical gifts given to Arthur by the fairies and elves when he was born

READER'S JOURNAL

Encourage students to include in their journal entries examples of people whom they believe are good leaders. Ask them to explain why they believe these people are good leaders.

Literary TOOLS

LEGEND. A **legend** is a story coming down from the past, often based on real events or characters from older times. Unlike myths, legends are popularly regarded as historical; however, they may contain elements that are fantastic or unverifiable. As you read this story of King Arthur, look for elements of a legend.

MOTIF. A **motif** is any element that recurs in one or more works of literature or art. Some common motifs in folk tales include a trial or quest, three wishes, and transformation from humble being to one of exceptional status. As you read, look for familiar motifs in this selection from *King Arthur and His Knights of the Round Table*. List these in a graphic organizer like the one below.

Graphic Organizer

Common Folk Tale Motif	How it appears in King Arthur's story

Reader's Journal

What qualities are important for leadership, in your opinion?

from King Arthur and His Knights of the Round Table

Retold by Roger Lancelyn Green

Reader's resource

HISTORY CONNECTION. *King Arthur and His Knights of the Round Table,* like other Arthurian legends, is set in England in approximately the fifth or sixth century AD. Some of the earliest inhabitants of Britain included the Picts and the Celts, who migrated from central Europe. From the first to the fifth century AD the Romans ruled most of what we know as Britain, until attacks by Saxons from Germany and Denmark weakened the colony. This is the historical backdrop for the following story, which is based upon the tale of a real sixth-century Celtic chieftain named Arthur. Upon the death of legendary King Uther, further division and lack of leadership left Britain nearly in ruins. Into this confusion young King Arthur strode to take command.

This excerpt, from Roger Lancelyn Green's first volume of four about King Arthur, retells the story of Arthur's birth and rise to leadership. Like many other chronicles of King Arthur, Roger Lancelyn Green's story is based primarily on Thomas Malory's *Le Morte d'Arthur* (see page 45). However, Green also added material from several other texts—British, French, and even Latin poetry, prose, and analysis—in an effort to pull together a coherent overview of the Arthur story. As you read, you will notice British spellings such as *centre* for *center* and *armour* for *armor*.

About the AUTHOR

Roger Lancelyn Green (1918–1987) was born in Norwich, England. An important goal of his writing was to share with young readers great stories and legends of the ancient world, including national legends of Great Britain. Though Green followed many professional paths including actor, librarian, antiquarian bookseller, and editor, it is for his work in retelling historic stories and legends that he is best known. Green based his versions on careful research and thoughtful analysis of the many sources available to him. He then channeled all his findings through his passion for legend, believing that something new can always be found in the retelling of a legend. Not surprisingly, given Green's love of historical culture and literature, his most successful original works are also historic stories.

GOALS/OBJECTIVES

Studying this lesson will enable students to
- enjoy an excerpt that depicts the history and exciting adventures of the legendary King Arthur
- discuss different perspectives of leadership and heroism
- define *legend* and *motif* and explain how these terms relate to the selection

- demonstrate an ability to identify the parts of speech and their functions in a paragraph
- compare film representations of the Arthurian legend to literary representations

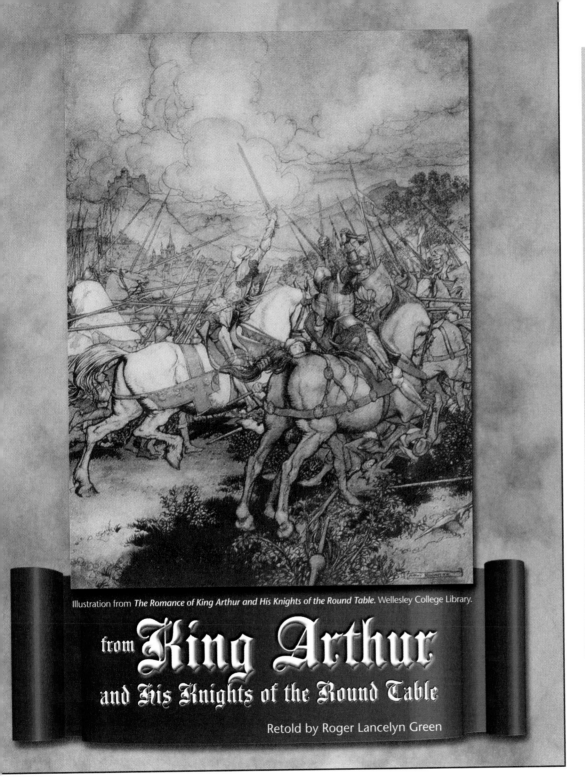

Illustration from *The Romance of King Arthur and His Knights of the Round Table.* Wellesley College Library.

from King Arthur
and His Knights of the Round Table

Retold by Roger Lancelyn Green

1. Merlin carries the baby down a secret path in the middle of the night, and no one knows what happened to it but him.
2. The Saxons made war against King Uther, ending his happiness. They sent a traitor to serve the king, and this traitor poisoned the king and others.
3. Because King Uther's knights were fighting over who should rule, the Saxons conquered more and more of Britain.

LITERARY NOTE

To many modern readers, the name Merlin is synonymous with "magician." In fact, the name comes from the Welsh name "Myrrdin." Legend says that a Welsh man named Myrrdin actually existed in the late sixth century. He was a bard, or an official poet, who traveled throughout the country performing national celebrations. Some say that Myrrdin was a prophet who foresaw a major Celtic conflict. The Merlin of Arthurian legend demonstrated a similar knowledge of events to come.

Merlin is closely associated with Arthur throughout Arthur's life and reign. In fact, some versions of Arthurian legend credit Merlin with creating the test to prove Arthur's right to rule: the sword in the stone.

CHAPTER I
THE TWO SWORDS

After wicked King Vortigern had first invited the Saxons to settle in Britain and help him to fight the Picts and Scots, the land was never long at peace. Although so much of it was covered with thick forests, much also was beautiful open country, with little villages and towns, country houses and cottages, as the Romans had left it not many years before. Having once seen it, the Saxons could never again be contented with their savage, unfruitful homes in Germany and Denmark; and year by year more and more of them came stealing across the North Sea in their long ships, to kill or drive out the Britons and settle in their homes.

Vortigern was dead, and Aurelius Ambrosius, last of the Romans, was dead too, when Uther Pendragon, whom some call the brother of Ambrosius, led the Britons. He defeated the Saxons in many battles, and brought peace to the southern lands where he was king—to London, and to Winchester, which was then called Camelot, and to Cornwall where Gorlois his loyal follower was duke. But Uther fell in love with Gorlois's wife, the lovely Igrayne, and there was battle between them, until Gorlois fell, and Uther married his widow.

He visited her first in the haunted castle of Tintagel, the dark castle by the Cornish sea, and Merlin the enchanter watched over their love. One child was born to Uther and Igrayne—but what became of that baby boy only the wise Merlin could have told, for he carried it away by a secret path down the cliff side in the dead of night, and no word was spoken of its fate.

What happens to the son of Uther and Igrayne?

Uther had no other children, though Igrayne and Gorlois had three daughters; two of these were grown-up when Igrayne became queen, and were married—Morgawse to Lot, King of Orkney,[1] and Elaine to Nantres, King of Garlot: they had sons who in after days were among the bravest Knights of the Round Table. But the third daughter, Morgana le Fay, was still only a child, and she was sent to school in a nunnery; yet, by some means, she learnt much magic, which she used wickedly.

King Uther Pendragon had only a little while of happiness with the fair Igrayne, for soon the Saxons made war against him once more, and sent a traitor to serve him, who poisoned the King and many of his followers.

What ends King Uther's happiness?

Then the land fell upon days more evil and wretched than any which had gone before. King Uther's knights fought amongst themselves, quarrelling as to who should rule; and the Saxons, seeing that there was no strong man to lead the Britons against them, conquered more and more of Britain.

What happens to Britain after Uther's death?

Years of strife and misery went by, until the appointed time was at hand. Then Merlin, the good enchanter, came out from the deep, mysterious valleys of North Wales, which in those days was called Gwynedd, through Powys or South Wales, and passed on his way to London. And so great was his fame that neither Saxon nor Briton dared molest him.

Merlin came to London and spoke with the Archbishop; and a great gathering of knights was called for Christmas Day—so great that all of them could not find a place in the abbey church, so that some were forced to gather in the churchyard.

In the middle of the service, there arose suddenly a murmur of wonder outside the abbey: for there was seen, though no man saw it come, a great square slab of marble-stone in the churchyard, and on the stone an anvil[2] of iron, and set point downwards a great, shining sword of steel thrust deeply into the anvil.

"Stir not till the service be done," commanded the Archbishop when this marvel was made known to him. "But pray the more unto God

---

1. **Orkney.** Region of Scotland
2. **anvil.** Heavy iron block on which metal is hammered into shape

Whoso pulleth out this sword from this stone and anvil is the true-born king of all Britain.

that we may find a remedy for the sore wounds of our land."

When the service was ended the Archbishop and the lords and knights who had been within the abbey came out to see the wonder of the sword. Round about the anvil they found letters of gold set in the great stone, and the letters read thus:

WHOSO PULLETH OUT THIS SWORD FROM THIS STONE AND ANVIL IS THE TRUE-BORN KING OF ALL BRITAIN.

When they saw this, many and many a man tried to pull out the sword—but not one of them could stir it a hair's breadth.

"He is not here," said the Archbishop. "But doubt not that God will send us our King. Let messengers be sent through all the land to tell what is written on the stone: and upon New Year's Day we will hold a great tournament, and see whether our King is amongst those who come to joust. Until then, I counsel that we appoint ten knights to guard the stone, and set a rich pavilion over it."

All this was done, and upon New Year's Day a great host of knights met together. But none as yet could draw forth the sword out of the stone. Then they went all a little way off, and pitched tents, and held a tournament or sham fight, trying their strength and skill at jousting with long lances of wood, or fighting with broad-swords.

It happened that among those who came was the good knight Sir Ector, and his son Kay, who had been made a knight not many months before; and with them came Arthur, Sir Kay's young brother, a youth of scarcely sixteen years of age.

Riding to the jousts, Sir Kay found suddenly that he had left his sword in his lodgings, and he asked Arthur to ride back and fetch it for him.

"Certainly I will," said Arthur, who was always ready to do anything for other people, and back he rode to the town. But Sir Kay's mother had locked the door, and gone out to see the tournament, so that Arthur could not get into the lodgings at all.

This troubled Arthur very much. "My brother Kay must have a sword," he thought, as he rode slowly back. "It will be a shame and a matter for unkind jests if so young a knight comes to the jousts without a sword. But where can I find him one? . . . I know! I saw one sticking in an anvil in the churchyard, I'll fetch that: it's doing no good there!"

So Arthur set spurs to his horse and came to the churchyard. Tying his horse to the stile, he ran to the tent which had been set over the stone—and found that all ten of the guardian knights had also gone to the tournament. Without stopping to read what was written on the stone, Arthur pulled out the sword at a touch, ran back to his horse, and in a few minutes had caught up with Sir Kay and handed it over to him.

Why does Arthur take the sword from the anvil?

Arthur knew nothing of what sword it was, but Kay had already tried to pull it from the anvil, and saw at a glance that it was the same one. Instantly he rode to his father Sir Ector, and said:

"Sir! Look, here is the sword out of the stone! So you see I must be the true-born King of all Britain!"

What does Kay know about the sword that Arthur does not know? What does Kay try to claim?

But Sir Ector knew better than to believe Sir Kay too readily. Instead, he rode back with him to the church, and there made him swear a solemn oath with his hands on the Bible to say truly how he came by the sword.

ANSWERS TO GUIDED READING QUESTIONS

1. Arthur takes the sword for his brother Kay to use in the New Year's Day jousts.
2. Kay knows that the sword was the one in the anvil and that whoever pulled that sword from the anvil was "the true-born king of all Britain." Kay tries to claim that he, not Arthur, pulled the sword from the anvil.

BIBLIOGRAPHIC NOTE

If students are interested in reading a twist on Arthurian legend, suggest:

Twain, Mark. *A Connecticut Yankee in King Arthur's Court.*

1. Sir Ector kneels before Arthur and proclaims him "the true-born king" of Britain. Arthur is confused and upset to hear the news and see his father kneeling before him.
2. Arthur pledges himself "to the service of God and my people, to the righting of wrongs, to the driving-out of evil, to the bringing of peace and plenty to my land."

ADDITIONAL QUESTIONS
AND ACTIVITIES

Ask students the following questions:
1. Once Arthur tells the story of how he obtained the sword, what does Sir Ector command him to do?
2. What happens after Arthur sets the sword back into the anvil?
3. Why do the people finally, at Pentecost, accept Arthur as king?

Answers
1. Sir Ector commands Arthur to replace the sword and draw it out again while he watches.
2. Both Sir Kay and Sir Ector try to remove the sword to no avail; then Arthur easily draws the sword out.
3. By Pentecost, kings, knights, and barons from near and far had tried to remove the sword, but only Arthur could do it.

"My brother Arthur brought it to me," said Kay, with a sigh.

"And how did *you* get the sword?" asked Sir Ector.

"Sir, I will tell you," said Arthur, fearing that he had done wrong. "Kay sent me to fetch his sword, but I could not come to it. Then I remembered having seen this sword sticking uselessly into an anvil in the churchyard. I thought it could be put to a better use in my brother's hand—so I fetched it."

"Did you find no knights guarding the sword?" asked Sir Ector.

"Never a one," said Arthur.

"Well, put the sword back into the anvil, and let us see you draw it out," commanded Sir Ector.

"That's easily done," said Arthur, puzzled by all this trouble over a sword, and he set it back easily into the anvil.

Then Sir Kay seized it by the hilt and pulled his hardest: but struggle and strain as he might, he could not move it by a hair's breadth. Sir Ector tried also, but with no better success.

"Pull it out," he said to Arthur.

And Arthur, more and more bewildered, put his hand to the hilt and drew forth the sword as if out of a well-greased scabbard.[3]

"Now," said Sir Ector, kneeling before Arthur and bowing his head in reverence, "I understand that you and none other are the true-born King of this land."

"Why? Oh, why is it I? Why do you kneel to me, my father?" cried Arthur.

What does Sir Ector do when Arthur has proven he can pull the sword from the anvil? What is Arthur's reaction?

"It is God's will that whoso might draw forth the sword out of the stone and out of the anvil is the true-born King of Britain," said Sir Ector. "Moreover, though I love you well, you are no son of mine. For Merlin brought you to me when you were a small child, and bade me bring you up as my own son!"

"Then if I am indeed King," said Arthur, bowing his head over the cross-hilt of the sword, "I hereby pledge myself to the service of God and of my people, to the righting of wrongs, to the driving-out of evil, to the bringing of peace and plenty to my land . . . Good sir, you have been as a father to me since ever I can remember, be still near me with a father's love and a father's counsel and advice . . . Kay, my foster-brother, be you seneschal[4] over all my lands and a true knight of my court."

What pledge does Arthur make?

After this they went to the Archbishop and told him all. But the knights and barons were filled with rage and jealousy, and refused to believe that Arthur was the true-born King. So the choice was put off until Easter; and at Easter once more until Whitsun, or Pentecost[5] as it then was called: but still, though many kings and knights came to try their strength, Arthur alone could pull out the sword.

Then all the people cried: "Arthur! We will have Arthur! By God's will he is our King! God save King Arthur!" And they knelt down before him, the noble and the humble together, the rich and the poor, and cried him mercy for delaying him so long. And Arthur forgave them readily, and kneeling down himself he gave the wondrous sword to the Archbishop and received of him the high and holy order of Knighthood. And then came all the earls and barons, the knights and squires, and did <u>homage</u> to Arthur, swearing to serve and obey him as was their duty.

King Arthur now gathered together all the hosts of Britain, and with the pick of the older knights who had served his father and the

---

3. **scabbard.** Case or sheath for a sword
4. **seneschal.** Person in charge of lands or resources
5. **Whitsun, or Pentecost.** Christian festival seven Sundays after Easter

**words
for
everyday
use**

hom • age (häm′ ij) *n.,* acts done to show honor and respect. *Jergen knelt in <u>homage</u> before the king.*

younger knights whose chief desire was to show their courage and loyalty, he set out to do battle with the Saxons and to punish all those thieves and robbers who had <u>ravaged</u> the land for many years, doing cruel and shameful deeds.

Before long he had brought peace and safety to the southern parts of Britain, making his capital at Camelot. But the other kings who ruled then in and about Britain—the Kings of Orkney and Lothian, of Gwynedd and Powys, of Gorre and Garlot—grew jealous of this unknown boy who was calling himself King of all Britain, and sent word that they were coming to visit him with gifts—but that their gifts would be given with sharp swords between the head and shoulders.

Then Merlin came suddenly to Arthur and led him to the city of Caerleon in South Wales, into a strong tower well provisioned for a siege. The hostile kings came also to Caerleon and surrounded the tower: but they could not break in, to kill Arthur and his faithful followers.

Merlin came out of the tower after fifteen days, stood upon the steps in the gateway and asked all the angry kings and knights why they came in arms against King Arthur.

What does Merlin do to protect Arthur?

"Why have you made that boy, that Arthur, our King?" they shouted.

"Be silent and listen, all of you!" commanded Merlin, and a great quiet fell upon all who were gathered together, an awe and a wonder as the good enchanter spoke to them.

"I will tell you of wondrous things," he said. "Arthur is indeed your King, the rightful King of all this land—yes, and of Wales too, of Ireland and Scotland and Orkney also, and of Armorica[6] beyond the sea; and he shall rule other lands also.

He is the true and only son of the good King Uther Pendragon! Of his birth and of the things which should befall when he was King, I knew by my holy arts. Uther came to Tintagel in the form of Gorlois three hours after Gorlois was dead: then and thus he comforted the Lady Igrayne and won her to be his wife. But, so my knowledge told me, their son, this Arthur, was born to great and wondrous things. A little while after his birth at dark Tintagel, Uther, who hearkened to

What does Merlin explain about Arthur? Why is this related to the people's acceptance of Arthur as king?

---

6. **Armorica.** Brittany, in France

words for everyday use

rav • age (rav' ij) *vt.*, destroy; ruin. *The storm <u>ravaged</u> the towns up and down the shore, leaving behind a wake of destruction and despair.*

1. Merlin leads Arthur into a strong tower well that protects him from the siege of angry kings.
2. Merlin explains that Arthur is the son of King Uther. The people accept Arthur because he was the son of their last good king.

CROSS-CURRICULAR ACTIVITIES

ARTHURIAN ART. Ask students to perform library or Internet research to find artworks inspired by Arthurian legend, such as *The Lady of Shalott* by J. W. Waterhouse. (If students have trouble with their research, direct them to the Internet site **Arthurian Artists** at http://www.celtic-twilight.com/artists.) Ask them to choose a favorite piece and make a photocopy or printout of it. Then have them learn the story of the scene or character depicted. Have them write two paragraphs about the piece: one that gives some background information about the artwork and the artist, and one that gives background information about the scene or character from Arthurian legend that is depicted.

1. The people feel that "they were at the beginning of a time of wonders." They accept their enchanted king and vow to be faithful subjects.
2. Arthur makes plans to protect the country from enemies, to build and rebuild churches, and to bring peace to all of his subjects.

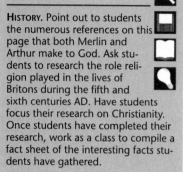

CROSS-CURRICULAR ACTIVITIES

HISTORY. Point out to students the numerous references on this page that both Merlin and Arthur make to God. Ask students to research the role religion played in the lives of Britons during the fifth and sixth centuries AD. Have students focus their research on Christianity. Once students have completed their research, work as a class to compile a fact sheet of the interesting facts students have gathered.

---

my words, gave the child into my care, and I bore him to Avalon, the Land of Mystery. And the Dwellers in Avalon—you know them not, but you would call them Fairies and Elves—cast a pure and great enchantment upon the child, a magic most strong. Three gifts they gave to Arthur: that he should be the best of all knights; that he should be the greatest king this land shall ever know; and that he should live long—longer than any man shall ever know. These, the virtues of a good and generous prince, the Dwellers in Avalon gave to Arthur. And in Avalon the elves are forging Excalibur to be the sword of his right—the clean flashing blade that shall be raised only in the cause of right, shining on the earth until the time comes when they shall call it back again. . . . Arthur is your King! Year by year as he reigns, his kingdom shall grow—not Britain, nor the islands of the seas, no, nor Armorica and Gaul[7]—but Logres,[8] the land of blessing, God's Kingdom upon earth, which Arthur shall show you for a little space before the darkness falls again."

There was silence for a while when Merlin had finished speaking, for all those who heard him felt that they were at the beginning of a time of wonders, and that Arthur was more than just a King who ruled because his father had been King, or because he was the strongest man amongst them.

How do the people feel after Merlin speaks? What do they think of their new king?

Suddenly they all knelt before him where he stood above Merlin on the steps of the tower, and with one voice promised to be his true and faithful subjects all the days of their lives.

Then the Archbishop set the crown upon Arthur's head, and the people cheered him once more: and this was the real beginning of his reign.

"Tomorrow we will begin to collect our forces," said King Arthur. "And when all are gathered together, we march to the north and to the east to do battle with the Saxons and drive them out of Britain. Then we will build castles and set guards along the coast so that never again may they invade us: we will rebuild the churches which they have destroyed, and build new ones to the glory of God; and our knights shall ride about the country punishing all those who break the peace and do ill to any. And if any man or woman, be he or she the greatest or the least of my subjects, be in any trouble, or have complaint against any man, let them come to me, and never shall their sorrow go uncomforted and their wrong unrighted."

What plans does Arthur set forth as king?

King Arthur feasted that day in the great castle of Caerleon: but before ever the feast was ended there befell the first of the marvelous adventures that were to happen in the wonderland of Logres during his reign.

Suddenly into the courtyard there rode a young squire, leading another horse, across the saddle of which lay the body of a knight but newly slain.

"<u>Vengeance</u>, lord King!" cried the squire, when Arthur came from the hall to learn what this might mean. "Give me vengeance! Here lies Sir Miles, dead upon his steed, as goodly a knight and as brave as any in the land. In the forest not many leagues[9] from here King Pellinore has set up his pavilion beside the high road, by a well of fresh water, and he goes about to slay all knights that pass this way. Wherefore I pray you that my master be honourably buried, and that some knight ride out to avenge his death."

There was a certain squire in Arthur's court, whose name was Gryflet, no older than Arthur

---

7. **Gaul.** France
8. **Logres.** Kingdom of Britain ruled by Arthur
9. **leagues.** Units of measurement equal to about three miles

---

words for everyday use

ven• geance (ven′ jəns) *n.,* return of an injury for an injury; revenge. *I tried to make Arden forgive and forget, but she was out for <u>vengeance</u>.*

himself, and now he fell on his knees before the King and begged him for all his service to make him a knight so that he might go out and fight with Pellinore.

"You are not old enough yet for such a battle," said King Arthur, "nor have you grown great enough in strength."

"Yet, make me a knight!" begged Gryflet.

"My lord," said Merlin quietly to Arthur, "it were a great pity to lose Gryflet, for he would be a passing good man when he comes of age, and would be your faithful knight all his life . . . Pellinore is the strongest man in the world now bearing arms, and surely Gryflet will be slain if they come to sword strokes."

King Arthur nodded, and turned again to his young squire: "Gryflet," he said, "kneel, and I will make you a knight according to your wish." And when this was done, he went on: "And now, Sir Gryflet, since I have made you knight, surely you owe me a gift."

"My lord, whatever you shall ask is yours," said Gryflet.

"Promise me then," commanded Arthur, "by your honour as a knight, that when you come upon King Pellinore by the well in the forest, you joust but with your spears and, on horseback or on foot, fight with him in no other wise."[10]

Why does Arthur make Gryflet a knight? What does he ask in return?

"That will I promise you," said Gryflet; and then he took his horse in great haste, snatched up his spear, slung his shield on his left arm, and went off in a cloud of dust until he came to the well-side in the forest. And there he saw a rich pavilion, and before it a horse ready saddled and bridled, and at the side a tree on which hung a shield painted in bright colours, and by it a great spear.

Sir Gryflet hit the shield with the butt of his own spear so hard that it came clattering to the ground, and King Pellinore came out of the pavilion—a tall, strong man as fierce as a lion.

"Sir knight!" he cried, "why smote you down my shield?"

"Sir, for that I would joust with you!" answered Gryflet.

"It were better that you did not," said King Pellinore. "You are but a new, young knight, and not so strong as I!"

"In spite of that, I will joust with you," repeated Gryflet.

"Well, this is by no desire of mine," said King Pellinore as he buckled on his armour, "but let things fall as they must. Whose knight are you?"

"Sir, I am one of King Arthur's court!" cried Gryflet. And with that they rode away in either direction along the road, then turned their horses, set their spears in rest, and galloped at one another as hard as they could. Sir Gryflet's spear struck the shield of King Pellinore and broke all to pieces: but King Pellinore's spear went straight through Gryflet's shield, deep into his side, and there broke off short. And Sir Gryflet and his horse fell upon the ground.

King Pellinore came and bent over Sir Gryflet, who lay still where he had fallen, and unloosed his helmet. "Well, this was a brave youth," said Pellinore, "and if he lives, will be a mighty knight." Then he placed Gryflet across the saddle, and the horse galloped back to Caerleon with none to guide it.

Arthur was very wroth when he saw how badly

What is Pellinore's opinion of Sir Gryflet?

---

10. **in no other wise.** In no other way

'**You are not old enough yet for such a battle,' said King Arthur, 'nor have you grown great enough in strength.'**

ANSWERS TO GUIDED READING QUESTIONS

1. Merlin advises Arthur that Gryflet will be a great and faithful knight as he grows and gets stronger. Arthur asks that Gryflet only joust with Pellinore using spears.
2. Pellinore believes that Gryflet will make a brave and mighty knight if he lives.

ADDITIONAL QUESTIONS AND ACTIVITIES

Ask students the following questions:

1. Why does Arthur initially refuse to make Gryflet a knight?
2. How does King Pellinore first respond to Gryflet's challenge? What is his explanation?
3. What happens to Gryflet during his joust with Pellinore?

Answers

1. Arthur refuses because he says Gryflet is not old enough or strong enough for battle.
2. Pellinore first refuses the challenge, saying that the knight is not old enough or strong enough to be a worthy opponent.
3. Gryflet was hurt badly by Pellinore's spear.

1. Arthur thinks that he has saved Merlin's life. Merlin had tried to prevent Arthur from seeking a battle with Pellinore.
2. Arthur thinks that death is more honorable than surrender. Students might suggest that Arthur is very stubborn, refusing to abandon his beliefs even when faced with death.

CROSS-CURRICULAR
ACTIVITIES

PHYSICAL EDUCATION. Have students work with a partner to research either jousting or fencing. Ask students to focus on one aspect of the sport they choose, such as history, purposes, techniques, or modern practice. Try to guide the activity so that each pair reports on a different aspect of each sport. Encourage students with strong kinesthetic skills to research the sport's techniques and demonstrate some examples for the class. Have other pairs present their research in short oral reports.

hurt was Sir Gryflet, and at once he put on his own armour, closed the vizor of his helmet so that no one could see his face, and with spear in hand rode hard into the forest to be revenged upon King Pellinore.

But on his way he found three robbers attacking Merlin, and they seemed like to beat him to death with great clubs.

"Fly, <u>churls</u>!" cried Arthur, riding at them furiously, and the three cowards turned and fled when they saw the knight charging at them.

"Ah, Merlin," said Arthur, "for all your wisdom and your magic, you would have been murdered in a few minutes if I had not come to your rescue!"

"Not so," answered Merlin, smiling his mysterious smile. "Easily could I have saved myself, had I willed it. It is you who draw near to your death—for you go towards it in your pride, if God does not aid you."

> What does Arthur think he has done when he sends the churls away? What had Merlin actually done?

But Arthur would not take heed of Merlin's wisdom, and rode fiercely on until he came to the rich pavilion by the well. And there sat King Pellinore upon his great war-horse, waiting for him.

"Sir knight!" cried Arthur, "why stand you here, fighting and striking down all the knights who ride this way?"

"It is my custom to do so," answered Pellinore sternly. "And if any man would make me change my custom, let him try at his peril!"

"I will make you change it!" cried Arthur.

"And I will defend my custom," replied Pellinore quietly.

Then they drew apart, and came riding together at full tilt, so hard that both spears shivered into little pieces as each hit the centre of the other's shield. Arthur would have drawn his sword then, but Pellinore said:

"Not so, let us run together with spears yet again."

"So I would," said Arthur, "if I had another spear!"

"I have plenty," answered Pellinore, and he shouted to his squire to bring two out of the pavilion.

Once more the two kings jousted together; and once more their spears broke into fragments without either of them being struck from his horse. A third time they jousted, and Arthur's spear broke, but King Pellinore's struck him so hard in the middle of the shield that horse and man fell to the earth.

But Arthur sprang to his feet in a great fury, drawing his sword and shouting defiance at Pellinore, who thereupon came down from his horse and drew his own sword. Then began a fierce battle, with many great strokes; they hacked and hewed at one another, cutting pieces off their shields and armour, and suffering each of them so many wounds that the trampled grass in front of the pavilion was stained with red. They rested once, and then charged each other again: but their swords met together with so mighty a crash that Arthur's broke in two, leaving him with the useless hilt in his hand.

"Ah-ha!" cried King Pellinore. "Now you are in my power, to slay or spare as I will! And I will kill you forthwith, unless you kneel and yield to me, confessing yourself to be a knight of little worth."

"There are two ways with that," cried Arthur, mad with shame and fury. "Death is welcome when it comes; but to yield—never!" And with that he leapt in under Pellinore's sword, seized him round the waist and hurled him to the ground. They struggled there for a while, but Pellinore was still the strongest, and presently he tore off Arthur's helmet and took up his sword to cut his head off also.

> What does Arthur think of surrender? What does this tell you about his values?

words
for
everyday
use

churl (chǔrl) n., surly, mean person. "What a <u>churl</u>!" Helen sputtered after the cashier slammed down her change with a surly glare.

But Merlin came suddenly and laid his hand on Pellinore's shoulder: "Knight," he said, "hold your hand and do not strike this stroke. For if you do the hope of Logres dies, and you put this land of Britain into the greatest ruin and desolation that ever a country suffered."

What does Merlin do to save Arthur's life again?

"Who is it?" asked Pellinore.

"This is King Arthur!" said Merlin.

For a moment Pellinore was tempted to strike the blow: for he feared that if Arthur lived, he would never forgive him for what he had done. But Merlin smiled quietly, and placed his hand on Pellinore's head. And at once all the anger and fear went from his mind, and he sank back quietly against the tree beside the well of clear water, and passed into a deep sleep.

Merlin helped King Arthur, who was sorely wounded, to mount his horse, and led him away into the forest.

"Alas, Merlin, what have you done?" asked Arthur; for now he had put from him all the pride and wilfulness which had so nearly caused his death. "You have killed this good knight by your magic—and I would rather have lost my kingdom than that one so brave and mighty should die thus."

"Cease to trouble," said Merlin. "For all things work by the will of God and to the glory of Logres. He is more like to live than you are, for you are sorely wounded, and he does but sleep . . . I told you how mighty a fighter he was. This is King Pellinore who in time to come shall do you good service. And his sons, Sir Tor and Sir Lamorak, shall be among the bravest of your knights."

Then Merlin brought Arthur to a hermitage where lived a good old man who was a clever leech, or healer of wounds. And in three days he was nearly cured, and could ride once more and fight as strongly as ever.

"Alas," said Arthur as they rode through the forest. "Now I have no sword."

"Let not that trouble you," said Merlin. "There was no virtue in the sword which is lost: it has served its purpose. But near here your own sword awaits you: it was made in Avalon by fairy craft, made for you alone until you must return it ere you journey to Avalon yourself. It is called Excalibur, and none may stand against its stroke: and with it you shall bring freedom and peace to Logres. This is the hour appointed when Excalibur shall be placed in your hand—for now you will grasp its hilt in all humility, and draw it only to defend the right."

Why is this time chosen for Arthur to receive Excalibur? What has Arthur learned?

Deeper and deeper into the forest they went, and before long the hills rose on either side until they were riding through a narrow valley that wound through dark mountains. And at last they came to a narrow pass in the rocks, and beyond it, in a cup of the mountains, Arthur saw a strange lake. All around it the hills rose darkly and desolately, but the lake water was of the clearest, sunniest blue, and the shore was covered thickly in fresh green grass and flowers. Over the brow of a little rise beyond the lake, the mountains opened out into a great plain, and beyond it was water, half hidden in mist, and broken with many islands.

"This is the Lake of the Fairy Palace," said Merlin, "and beyond the lake, over the brow of the hill yonder, lies the plain of Camlann where the last battle shall be fought, and you shall fall beneath the stroke of the Evil Knight. And beyond the plain lies Avalon, hidden in the mist and the mysterious waters . . . Go down now and speak with the Lady of the Lake, while I wait for you here."

What event is foretold here? What effect does this information have on Arthur?

Leaving his horse with Merlin, Arthur went down the steep path to the side of the magic lake. Standing on the shore, he looked out across the quiet blue water—and there in the very centre of the Lake he saw an arm clothed in white samite[11] with a hand holding above the surface a wondrous sword with a golden hilt set with jewels, and a jewelled scabbard and belt.

---

11. **samite.** Heavy silk cloth, often interwoven with gold or silver, commonly worn in the Middle Ages

ANSWERS TO GUIDED READING QUESTIONS

1. The Lady of the Lake asks Arthur to give her a gift when she asks for one.
2. Merlin advises Arthur to refrain from fighting with Pellinore once more. Arthur heeds Merlin's advice. Students might say that Arthur is learning from his past mistakes. They might suggest that he has learned to be more humble.
3. Merlin explains that Arthur cannot be mortally wounded while he wears the scabbard. He also explains that a woman close to Arthur will try to steal the sword and scabbard from him. Students might suggest that Arthur's death will be the result of his scabbard and sword being stolen.

SELECTION CHECK TEST 4.1.11 WITH ANSWERS

Checking Your Reading

1. What text was written in gold on the great stone? **"Whoso pulleth out this sword from this stone and anvil is the true-born king of all Britain" was written on the stone.**
2. How many knights were sent to guard the stone? **Ten knights were commanded to guard the stone.**
3. Who pulled the sword out of the stone? **Arthur pulled out the sword.**
4. What does Arthur pledge to do during his reign as king? **He pledges to serve God and his people by righting wrongs, driving out evil, and by bringing peace and plenty to his land.**
5. What does Merlin tell Arthur about his pride? **He tells him that his pride draws him near to death.**

Vocabulary in Context
Fill in each blank below with the most appropriate word from the following Words for Everyday Use. You may have to change the tense of the word.

homage   ravage   vengeance
              churl

1. Our old neighbor down the street is known to be a <u>churl</u> because he is so unfriendly.
2. I went to pay <u>homage</u> to my grandfather by visiting his tomb on Memorial Day.
3. The tornado <u>ravaged</u> the city, destroying everything in its path.

And then Arthur saw a beautiful damsel dressed in pale blue silk with a golden girdle, who walked across the water until she stood before him on the shore.

"I am the Lady of the Lake," she said, "and I am come to tell you that your sword Excalibur awaits you yonder. Do you wish to take the sword and wear it at your side?"

"Damsel," said Arthur, "that is indeed my wish."

"For long I have guarded the sword," said the Lady of the Lake. "Give me but a gift when I shall come to ask you for one, and the sword shall be yours."

> What does the Lady of the Lake ask of Arthur?

"By my faith," answered Arthur, "I swear to give you whatsoever gift you shall ask for."

"Enter into this boat, then," said the Lady of the Lake. And Arthur saw a barge floating on the water before him, into which he stepped. The Lady of the Lake stood on the shore behind him, but the barge moved across the water as if unseen hands drew it by the keel, until Arthur came beside the arm clothed in white samite. Leaning out, he took the sword and the scabbard: and at once the arm and the hand which had held it sank quietly out of sight beneath the blue waters.

Then the barge brought Arthur to the shore where the Lady of the Lake had stood: but now she was gone also. He tied the barge to a tree-root which curved over the waterside, and strode joyfully up the steep path to the pass, buckling the sword Excalibur to his side as he went.

Merlin awaited him with the horses, and together they rode away into the forest, and back by many winding paths until they drew near the river which lay between them and Caerleon, and came to the straight, paved road leading to the city.

"In a little while," said Merlin, "King Pellinore will come riding towards us. For he has ceased to do battle with all who pass through the forest, having seen a Questing Beast which he must follow now for many years."

"Then I will fight with him once more," cried Arthur. "Now that I have so good a sword as Excalibur maybe I shall overcome and slay him!"

Merlin shook his head: "Let him pass," he said, "for so I counsel you. He is a brave knight and a mighty, and in days to come he will do you good service, and he and his sons shall be among the bravest in your court."

> What advice does Merlin give Arthur? Does Arthur heed the advice? What change in Arthur does his reaction to Merlin's advice demonstrate?

"I will do as you advise me," said Arthur. But he looked upon the sword Excalibur, and sighed.

"Which like you better, the sword or the scabbard?" asked Merlin.

"I like the sword!" cried Arthur.

"Then are you the more unwise," said Merlin gravely. "The scabbard is worth ten such swords: for while you wear that magic scabbard you shall lose but little blood, however sorely you are wounded. Keep well that scabbard, and have good care of it after I am gone from you, for a certain wicked lady who is nearly related to you shall seek to steal both sword and scabbard."

> What magic does Merlin explain? What warning does he give Arthur? What do you think might happen based on this warning?

They rode on, and in a little while met King Pellinore—who rode past as if he had not seen them.

"I marvel," said Arthur, "that he did not even speak to us!"

"He saw you not," answered Merlin, "for my magic was upon him. But had you striven to stay him in your pride, then he would have seen you well enough."

Before long they came to Caerleon, and his knights welcomed Arthur joyfully. And when they heard of his adventures, they were surprised that he should thus have gone into danger alone. But all the bravest and noblest of them rejoiced exceedingly that they had such a king, one who would risk his life in an adventure as other ordinary knights did. ∎

SELECTION CHECK TEST 4.1.11 WITH ANSWERS (CONT.)

Literary Tools
Fill in the blanks using the following terms.

legend   motif   Celtic

1. Arthur is a <u>Celtic</u> chieftain from the sixth century.
2. The quest <u>motif</u> is found throughout medieval literature.
3. Unlike myths, a <u>legend</u> is regarded as historically based.

Respond *to the* SELECTION

If you had lived in King Arthur's time, would you have endorsed him as king? Would you have become a follower? Why, or why not?

Investigate, Inquire, and Imagine

Recall: GATHERING FACTS

1a. What is the story of Arthur's birth? Who were his parents and how does he interact with them in his early years?

2a. When and where were the terms set out to select Britain's new king? What were those terms? How were they met and by whom?

3a. What happens during Arthur's battle with King Pellinore?

Interpret: FINDING MEANING

1b. What were the causes of the troubles facing Britain at the time of Arthur's birth?

2b. How does Arthur envision his new role? How does he hope to change Britain's situation? What promises does he make to the people?

3b. What does Arthur's behavior with King Pellinore reveal about his character?

Analyze: TAKING THINGS APART

4a. Analyze the role Merlin plays in Arthur's early years and in his transformation to king. What special gifts does Arthur have as a result of Merlin's guidance? What signs of magic are there in Merlin's interaction with Arthur?

Synthesize: BRINGING THINGS TOGETHER

4b. How does Arthur's relationship with Merlin change by the end of the excerpt?

Evaluate: MAKING JUDGMENTS

5a. Why do you think the people of Britain believed Arthur's claim to the throne? Why was his leadership so compellingly attractive?

Extend: CONNECTING IDEAS

5b. What does this story suggest about the rest of Arthur's life and reign as king?

Understanding *Literature*

LEGEND. Review the definition for **legend** in the Handbook of Literary Terms. What makes the story of King Arthur a legend?

MOTIF. Review the definition for **motif** in the Handbook of Literary Terms and the chart you made for Literary Tools on page 32. What motifs can you identify in *King Arthur and His Knights of the Round Table?* What can you infer about Arthur from these occurrences?

FROM KING ARTHUR AND HIS KNIGHTS OF THE ROUND TABLE **43**

ANSWERS TO INVESTIGATE, INQUIRE, AND IMAGINE (CONT.)

by setting the challenge of the sword in the stone and by telling the knights and citizens about Arthur's birth. As a result of Merlin's guidance, Arthur will be the best of all knights, the greatest king the land will know, and will live longer than any man shall know. Signs of magic include Merlin's knowledge of Arthur's future and the future of others, his relationship with the fairies of

Avalon, his ability to put Pellinore to sleep and keep him from seeing Arthur, and his link to the Lady of the Lake.

SYNTHESIZE

4b. Arthur begins to take Merlin's advice, recognizing its value and learning to control his own pride.

(Continued on page 44)

RESPOND TO THE SELECTION

Students might begin by referring to their response to the Reader's Journal activity, in which they described the qualities a leader should have.

ANSWERS TO INVESTIGATE, INQUIRE, AND IMAGINE

RECALL

1a. Arthur was born of King Uther and Igrayne, the widow of Gorlois, who was slain by Uther in battle. Arthur doesn't see his real parents after his birth because Merlin the enchanter—knowing Arthur's future importance—takes him away for safety. Arthur is raised by Sir Ector, whom he believes to be his father.

2a. Many years after Arthur's birth, in London at a meeting of the knights called by Merlin and the Archbishop, the terms to determine the new king are set. It is decided that the knight who can pull the sword from the stone and anvil is Britain's trueborn king. Arthur, without realizing that he is taking the test, pulls out the sword to replace the one his brother forgot at home and meets these terms.

3a. When Arthur fights Pellinore, he risks being killed when Merlin steps in and tells Pellinore that Arthur is king. With a spell Merlin begins to transform Pellinore into a loyal and brave knight.

INTERPRET

1b. Saxon aggression had left the country weak. Uther's death resulted in factional fighting among knights. Without clear leadership, Britain lost more territory to the Saxons.

2b. Arthur hopes to be a just king. He wants to repel the Saxons from Britain, regain control of British lands, and build a defense so that no such invasion will ever recur. He promises peace, safety, and fair redress of grievances to all the people, both humble and great.

3b. Arthur is extremely proud, stubborn, and has a terrible temper.

ANALYZE

4a. Merlin watches over Arthur from the time of his conception, first guarding the meeting between Uther and Igrayne, then taking the baby away in secret. He later ensures Arthur's rise to the throne

ANSWERS TO INVESTIGATE, INQUIRE, AND IMAGINE (CONT.)

EVALUATE

5a. The fact that only Arthur could pull the sword from the stone convinced the people that God willed that Arthur should be king. The people of Britain were hungry for a true leader, one who would unite him against their enemies. Arthur's inherent goodness and the presence of Merlin's magic made Arthur seem special.

EXTEND

5b. The story suggests that Arthur will be a much-loved and just king, will lead the knights in many battles to improve Britain's situation, and will die in battle but may return to life later through magical means.

ANSWERS TO UNDERSTANDING LITERATURE

LEGEND. The story of King Arthur is a legend because it was passed down through generations before being recorded in writing. Also, it is based on real events from the history of Great Britain—there was confusion as to who should rule—and characters from the distant past—Arthur is probably based on a real king. Many elements of the story are fantastic and unverifiable, such as the element of magic and the fact that Arthur was able to pull the sword from the stone.

MOTIF. Motifs in the selection include: the trial or quest, three wishes, and a humble being transformed into one of exceptional status. The trial (test) is pulling the sword out of the stone and anvil. This brought about Arthur's transformation from a person of humble status to one of exceptional status. The three wishes are rather the three magical gifts (to be the best of all knights, to be the greatest king ever known, and to live a very long life) given to Arthur by the fairies and elves when he was born. The reader can infer that Arthur is a deserving folk tale hero, one on whom fortune smiles.

ANSWERS TO INTEGRATING THE LANGUAGE ARTS

Language, Grammar, and Style
1. linker; conj.
2. interrupter; int.
3. expresser; v.
4. namer; n.
5. modifier; adv.

Writer's Journal

1. Now that you know the story of Arthur's birth and early years, how do you think his reign as king will unfold? Write four **fortune cookie inserts** that offer predictions of various stages of Arthur's future.
2. Write a **comic strip** depicting a brief scene from Arthur's story.
3. In this selection, King Arthur declares some of the goals he wishes to achieve as king. In your own words, write a **speech** he might have delivered to the people of Britain about what they can expect from him.

Integrating the Language Arts

Language, Grammar, and Style

IDENTIFYING THE PARTS OF SPEECH AND THEIR FUNCTIONS. Read the Language Arts Survey 3.7, "Grammar Reference Chart—Parts of Speech Overview." Then identify the function of each italicized word in the following paragraph, and tell what part of speech it is. Use *n.* for noun, *pro.* for pronoun, *v.* for verb, *adj.* for adjective, *adv.* for adverb, *prep.* for preposition, *conj.* for conjunction, and *int.* for interjection.

The Arthurian legends have captured the imaginations of writers [1] *and* storytellers for hundreds of years. [2] *True,* the legends have a historical basis, but most details about the Celtic warrior are embellishments rather than facts. Historians [3] *have determined* that the first references to Arthur appear in Welsh literature from the sixth century. [4] *References* to Arthur appear [5] *again* in the twelfth century in <u>The History of the Kings of Britain</u>. At this time, Merlin, Guinevere, Gawain, and other [6] *legendary* figures commonly associated [7] *with* the Arthurian legends are mentioned. Arthur became the subject of medieval poems in France. [8] *His* story eventually [9] *returned* across the English Channel to inspire the unknown author of <u>Sir Gawain and the Green Knight</u> and Sir Thomas Malory, the author of <u>Le Morte d'Arthur</u>, one of the [10] *greatest* retellings of the Arthurian legends.

Study and Research & Applied English

DESIGNING ARTHURIAN COSTUMES. The Arthurian legend has been depicted many times in art as well as in literature. Research art depicting Arthurian legends to learn more about the manner of dress during Arthurian times. Some illustrations are in this book. Design your own costumes for this story of Arthur or another Arthurian legend of your choice. Explain the purpose or significance of various parts of your costume, and indicate what type of material would be used to create the costume.

Media Literacy

REVIEWING MOVIES ON ARTHURIAN THEMES. Several movies have been made that relate to the story of King Arthur, including *Excalibur* (1981), *First Knight* (1995), *Knights of the Round Table* (1953), and *Camelot* (1967). Choose one of these movies to watch and write a movie review about. Compare the plot of the movie to the selection you have just read as well as to the selection from *Le Morte d'Arthur* on page 45. Does the movie share any of the same plot elements or characters? If so, how do the portrayals and the language compare with those in the literature?

ANSWERS TO INTEGRATING THE LANGUAGE ARTS (CONT.)

6. modifier; adj.
7. linker; prep.
8. namer; pro.
9. expresser; v.
10. modifier; adj.

Study and Research & Applied English
You might have students work in groups to complete this activity. Suggest that they consult theater costuming books to find ideas. If students find it difficult to represent their ideas visually, encourage them to seek the advice of an art teacher.

Media Literacy
Ask students to read the Language Arts Survey 5.30, "Evaluating Information and Media Sources," before they begin this activity. Help students create a list of criteria on which they can base their comparisons, including such elements as themes, motifs, style, characters, and point of view.

from Le Morte d'Arthur

by Sir Thomas Malory

Reader's resource

Le Morte d'Arthur pulled together many different legends about the historical figure of Arthur, a brave sixth-century British chieftain. In developing his King Arthur, Malory apparently drew on Geoffrey of Monmouth's twelfth-century *Historia Regum Brittaniæ*, which in turn can be traced to a variety of sources. In blending these many legends, Malory paints a picture of King Arthur as a great hero, a leader of the daring and chivalrous knights of the Round Table, the husband of Guinevere, and a just and benevolent king.

The following excerpt appears in the last of the twenty-one books in Malory's story. As the excerpt begins, Arthur prepares to fight Sir Mordred, his illegitimate son, to avenge Mordred's attempt to assume the throne and marry his stepmother, Queen Guenever, or Guinevere.

About the AUTHOR

Sir Thomas Malory (*circa* 1374–1471) was an English knight. While little is known about his early life, he is believed to have lived on his family's estates at Warwickshire and Northamptonshire, England. Malory fought in the Hundred Years' War between England and France, after which he took over his father's estates, for a time representing Warwickshire in the English Parliament. Later in life, however, Malory's fortunes evidently changed. Some say he committed a series of crimes, including poaching, extortion, robbery, and murder; others say he was the victim of political entanglements. In any case, Malory was arrested on several occasions and spent much of his later life in prison, dying there in 1471. Scholars believe that Malory did most of his writing as a prisoner. His work about King Arthur was originally titled *The Book of King Arthur and His Knights of the Round Table* and was made up of eight separate romances. When the book was printed in 1485, it was given the title *Le Morte d'Arthur* (*The Death of Arthur*), which was a somewhat misleading title, since the work actually deals with Arthur's life.

Literary TOOLS

DRAMATIC IRONY. Dramatic irony is a situation in which something is known by the reader or audience but unknown to the characters. As you read this selection, look for an example of dramatic irony.

TRAGEDY AND TRAGIC FLAW. A tragedy is a work of literature that tells the story of the fall of a person of high status. A **tragic flaw** is a personal weakness that brings about the fall of a character in a tragedy. As you read this selection, decide whether it can be considered a tragedy.

Reader's Journal

What do you know about King Arthur and the Arthurian legends? What would you like to know?

ADDITIONAL RESOURCES

UNIT 1 RESOURCE BOOK
- Selection Worksheet 1.6
- Selection Check Test 4.1.13
- Selection Test 4.1.14

VOCABULARY FROM THE SELECTION

avenge
proffer

READER'S JOURNAL

Students might discuss the Arthurian legends as a class. Ask them to consider why there are often discrepancies in stories such as myths and legends.

GOALS/OBJECTIVES

Studying this lesson will enable students to
- appreciate a story about the death of King Arthur
- briefly describe how Sir Thomas Malory composed the book from which this excerpt is taken

- define *dramatic irony, tragedy,* and *tragic flaw* and recognize these literary elements in the selection
- write a television news report

ANSWER TO GUIDED READING QUESTION

1. He dreams that he is sitting on a platform and below him are hideous creatures. He falls among the creatures and is killed by them. The dream may mean that King Arthur's death is near.

INDIVIDUAL LEARNING STRATEGIES

MOTIVATION
Write the word *legend* on the board. Ask students to list characteristics of legends. Discuss how characters in legends often have mythical qualities and strengths.

READING PROFICIENCY
Read the selection aloud to the class or play the selection from the Audio Library. Pause after each chapter, and give the class an opportunity to discuss and summarize the events that occurred. Clarify any confusing passages.

ENGLISH LANGUAGE LEARNERS
Help students who have difficulty with the language of the selection by explaining that many words have contemporary equivalents—for example, *betwixt* and *between* and *tomorn* and *tomorrow*. Also point out that the suffix *–eth* is sometimes added to contemporary verbs, such as *lieth*.

SPECIAL NEEDS
Have students read the short descriptions after each chapter title. For each description, students should write a prediction for the chapter. What do they think will happen as a result of the event described? How do they think these things will come to pass? After students write their predictions, have them read the chapters and compare their predictions with the actual occurrences.

ENRICHMENT
Challenge students to read the entirety of Malory's *Le Morte d'Arthur* and write a review of the book. In their reviews, they should summarize the plot, as well as evaluate the work and put forth their recommendations.

Illustration from *The Romance of King Arthur and His Knights of the Round Table.* Wellesley College Library.

from

Le Morte d'Arthur

Sir Thomas Malory

FROM BOOK XXI CHAPTER 3

HOW AFTER, SIR GAWAIN'S GHOST APPEARED TO KING ARTHUR, AND WARNED HIM THAT HE SHOULD NOT FIGHT THAT DAY

And then King Arthur drew him with his host down by the seaside westward toward Salisbury; and there was a day assigned betwixt King Arthur and Sir Mordred, that they should meet upon a down beside Salisbury, and not far from the seaside; and this day was assigned on a Monday after Trinity Sunday, whereof King Arthur was passing glad, that he might be avenged upon Sir Mordred.

Then Sir Mordred araised much people about London, for they of Kent, Sussex and Surrey, Essex, and of Suffolk, and of Norfolk, held the most part with Sir Mordred; and many a full noble knight drew unto Sir Mordred and to the king; but they loved Sir Launcelot drew unto Sir Mordred.

So upon Trinity Sunday at night, King Arthur dreamed a wonderful dream, and that was this: that him seemed he sat upon a chaflet[1] in a chair, and the chair was fast to a wheel, and thereupon sat King Arthur in the richest cloth of gold that might be made; and the king thought there was under him, far from him, an hideous deep black water, and therein were all

---

1. **chaflet.** Platform

manner of serpents, and worms, and wild beasts, foul and horrible; and suddenly the king thought the wheel turned up-so-down, and he fell among the serpents, and every beast took him by a limb; and then the king cried as he lay in his bed and slept, "Help."

> What dream does Arthur have? What might this dream mean?

And then knights, squires, and yeomen, awaked the king; and then he was so amazed that he wist[2] not where he was; and then he fell on slumbering again, not sleeping nor thoroughly waking.

So the king seemed verily that there came Sir Gawain unto him with a number of fair ladies with him. And when King Arthur saw him, then he said, "Welcome my sister's son; I weened[3] thou hadst been dead, and now I see thee alive, much am I beholding unto Almighty Jesu. O fair nephew and my sister's son, what be these ladies that hither be come with you?"

"Sir," said Sir Gawain, "all these be ladies for whom I have foughten when I was man living, and all these are those that I did battle for in righteous quarrel; and God hath given them that grace at their great prayer, because I did battle for them, that they should bring me hither unto you: thus much hath God given me leave, for to warn you of your death; for and ye fight as tomorn with Sir Mordred, as ye both have assigned, doubt ye not ye must be slain, and the most part of your people on both parties. And for the great grace and goodness that Almighty Jesu hath unto you, and for pity of you, and many more other good men there shall be slain, God hath sent me to you of his special grace, to give you warning that in no wise ye do battle as tomorn, but that ye take a treaty for a month day; and <u>proffer</u> you largely, so as tomorn to be put in a delay. For within a month shall come Sir Launcelot with all his noble knights, and rescue you worshipfully, and slay Sir Mordred, and all that ever will hold with him."

> What warning does Sir Gawain give? What reason does he give for postponing the battle?

Then Sir Gawain and all the ladies vanished. And anon[4] the king called upon his knights, squires, and yeomen, and charged them wightly[5] to fetch his noble lords and wise bishops unto him. And when they were come, the king told them his avision, what Sir Gawain had told him, and warned him that if he fought on the morn he should be slain.

Then the king commanded Sir Lucan the Butler, and his brother Sir Bedevere, with two bishops with them, and charged them in any wise, and they might: "Take a treaty for a month day with Sir Mordred, and spare not, proffer him lands and goods as much as ye think best."

So then they departed, and came to Sir Mordred, where he had a grim host of an hundred thousand men. And there they entreated Sir Mordred long time; and at the last Sir Mordred was agreed for to have Cornwall and Kent, by Arthur's days; after, all England, after the days of King Arthur.

BOOK XXI CHAPTER 4
HOW BY MISADVENTURE OF AN ADDER[6] THE BATTLE BEGAN, WHERE MORDRED WAS SLAIN, AND ARTHUR HURT TO THE DEATH

---

2. **wist.** Knew
3. **weened.** Thought
4. **anon.** Immediately
5. **wightly.** Valiantly
6. **ADDER.** Poisonous snake

---

words for everyday use

prof • fer (präf′ ər) vi., offer. *Felipe grudgingly took the hand that Martina <u>proffered</u> to help him get up.*

ANSWERS TO GUIDED READING QUESTIONS

1. Arthur warns that if a sword is drawn, his companions must battle and slay the enemy.
2. Mordred gives the same warning to his companions.
3. A snake bites a knight, and that knight draws his sword to kill the snake.

CROSS-CURRICULAR ACTIVITIES

HISTORY. Have students research the Battle of Camlan, the final battle of King Arthur's reign depicted in the text. Students should report the approximate year in which it occurred, as well as the theories on the location of the battle. Challenge students to investigate the kinds of weapons and means of fighting used in this battle. Invite volunteers to share their findings with the rest of the class.

Then were they condescended that King Arthur and Sir Mordred should meet betwixt both their hosts, and every each of them should bring fourteen persons; and they came with this word unto Arthur.

Then said he, "I am glad that this is done": and so he went into the field.

And when Arthur should depart, he warned all his host that and they see any sword drawn, "look ye come on fiercely, and slay that traitor, Sir Mordred, for I in no wise trust him."

> What warning does Arthur give?

In likewise Sir Mordred warned his host that: "And ye see any sword drawn, look that ye come on fiercely, and so slay all that ever before you standeth; for in no wise I will not trust for this treaty, for I know well my father will be <u>avenged</u> on me."

> What warning does Mordred give?

And so they met as their pointment was, and so they were agreed and accorded thoroughly; and wine was fetched, and they drank.

Right soon came an adder out of a little heath bush, and it stung a knight on the foot. And when the knight felt him stungen, he looked down and saw the adder, and then he drew his sword to slay the adder, and thought of none other harm. And when the host on both parties saw that sword drawn, then they blew beams,[7] trumpets, and horns, and shouted grimly. And so both hosts dressed them together.

> What innocent action starts the battle?

And King Arthur took his horse, and said, "Alas this unhappy day!" and so rode to his party. And Sir Mordred in likewise. And never was there seen a more dolefuller battle in no Christian land; for there was but rushing and riding, foining[8] and striking, and many a grim word was there spoken either to other, and many a deadly stroke. But ever King Arthur rode throughout the battle of Sir Mordred many times, and did full nobly as a noble king should, and at all times he fainted never; and Sir Mordred that day put him in devoir,[9] and in great peril. And thus they fought all the long day, and never stinted[10] till the noble knights were laid to the cold earth; and ever they fought still till it was near night, and by that time was there an hundred thousand laid dead upon the down. Then was Arthur wood wroth[11] out of measure, when he saw his people so slain from him.

Then the king looked about him, and then was he ware, of all his host and of all his good knights, were left no more alive but two knights; that one was Sir Lucan the Butler, and his brother Sir Bedevere, and they were full sore wounded.

"Jesu mercy," said the king, "where are all my noble knights becomen? Alas that ever I should see this doleful day, for now," said Arthur, "I am come to mine end. But would to God that I wist where were that traitor Sir Mordred, that hath caused all this mischief."

Then was King Arthur ware[12] where Sir Mordred leaned upon his sword among a great heap of dead men.

"Now give me my spear," said Arthur unto Sir Lucan, "for yonder I have espied the traitor that all this woe hath wrought."

"Sir, let him be," said Sir Lucan, "for he is unhappy; and if ye pass this unhappy day ye shall be right well revenged upon him. Good lord, remember ye of your night's dream, and what the

---

7. **beams.** Bugles
8. **foining.** Thrusting a spear
9. **devoir.** Knightly duty
10. **stinted.** Stopped
11. **wood wroth.** Out of his mind with rage
12. **ware.** Aware

words for everyday use

a • venge (ə venj′) vi., get revenge for an injury or wrong. *The caped crusader vowed to <u>avenge</u> the wrongs visited on the people of the ravaged village.*

48 UNIT ONE / THE ORAL TRADITION

spirit of Sir Gawain told you this night, yet God of his great goodness hath preserved you hitherto. Therefore, for God's sake, my lord, leave off by this, for blessed be God ye have won the field, for here we be three alive, and with Sir Mordred is none alive; and if ye leave off now this wicked day of destiny is past."

"Tide[13] me death, betide me life," saith the king, "now I see him yonder alone he shall never escape mine hands, for at a better avail shall I never have him."

How is Arthur again warned of his fate and about Mordred? Why does Arthur pursue his vengeance on Mordred despite all the warnings he has been given?

"God speed you well," said Sir Bedevere.

Then the king gat his spear in both his hands, and ran toward Sir Mordred, crying, "Traitor, now is thy death day come."

And when Sir Mordred heard Sir Arthur, he ran until him with his sword drawn in his hand. And there King Arthur smote[14] Sir Mordred under the shield, with a foin of his spear, throughout the body, more than a fathom. And when Sir Mordred felt that he had his death's wound he thrust himself with the might that he had up to the bur[15] of King Arthur's spear. And right so he smote his father Arthur, with his sword holden in both his hands, on the side of the head, that the sword pierced the helmet and the brain pan, and therewithal Sir Mordred fell stark dead to the earth; and the noble Arthur fell in a swoon to the earth and there he swooned ofttimes.

And Sir Lucan the Butler and Sir Bedevere ofttimes heave him up. And so weakly they led him betwixt them both, to a little chapel not far from the seaside. And when the king was there he thought him well eased. Then heard they people cry in the field.

"Now go thou, Sir Lucan," said the king, "and do me to wit what betokens that noise in the field."

So Sir Lucan departed, for he was grievously wounded in many places. And so as he yede,[16] he saw and hearkened by the moonlight, how that pillers[17] and robbers were comen into the field, to pill and to rob many a full noble knight of brooches, and beads, of many a good ring, and of many a rich jewel; and who that were not dead all out, there they slew them for their harness and their riches. When Sir Lucan understood this work, he came to the king as soon as he might, and told him all what he had heard and seen.

"Therefore by my rede,"[18] said Sir Lucan, "it is best that we bring you to some town."

"I would it were so," said the king.

BOOK XXI CHAPTER 5
HOW KING ARTHUR COMMANDED TO CAST HIS SWORD EXCALIBUR INTO THE WATER, AND HOW HE WAS DELIVERED TO LADIES IN A BARGE

"But I may not stand, mine head works so. Ah Sir Launcelot," said King Arthur, "this day have I sore missed thee: alas, that ever I was against thee, for now have I my death, whereof Sir Gawain me warned in my dream."

Then Sir Lucan took up the king the one part, and Sir Bedevere the other part, and in the lifting the king swooned; and Sir Lucan fell in a swoon with the lift, that the part of his guts fell out of his body, and therewith the noble knight's heart brast. And when the king awoke, he beheld Sir Lucan, how he lay foaming at the mouth, and part of his guts lay at his feet.

"Alas," said the king, "this is to me a full heavy sight, to see this noble duke so die for my sake, for he would have holpen me, that had more need of help than I. Alas, he would not complain him, his heart was so set to help me: now Jesu have mercy upon his soul!"

Then Sir Bedevere wept for the death of his brother.

"Leave this mourning and weeping," said the king, "for all this will not avail me, for wit thou

13. **Tide.** Happen to; befall
14. **smote.** Hit
15. **bur.** Hand guard on a spear
16. **yede.** Went
17. **pillers.** Pillagers, plunderers
18. **rede.** Advice

1. He finally throws the sword into the lake. He witnesses an arm come out of the water and catch the sword, brandish it three times, and then vanish into the water.

ADDITIONAL QUESTIONS AND ACTIVITIES

Have students research Avilion, or Avalon, the place to which Arthur is taken on the barge. Students should focus on the mythical aspects of the location. Explain to students that Avalon played a large part in the Arthurian legends. Have students give oral presentations on their discoveries about Avalon.

INTERNET RESOURCES

The **Arthurian A 2 Z Listing** at http://www.mystical-www.co.uk provides descriptions of characters and places, as well as an overview of the relationships between characters. Challenge students to use this site to gather information about one of the characters in this excerpt.

---

well and I might live myself, the death of Sir Lucan would grieve me evermore; but my time hieth fast," said the king. "Therefore," said Arthur unto Sir Bedevere, "take thou Excalibur, my good sword, and go with it to yonder water side, and when thou comest there I charge thee throw my sword in that water, and come again and tell me what thou there seest."

"My lord," said Bedevere, "your commandment shall be done, and lightly bring you word again."

So Sir Bedevere departed, and by the way he beheld that noble sword, that the pommel and the haft[19] was all of precious stones; and then he said to himself, "If I throw this rich sword in the water, thereof shall never come good, but harm and loss." And then Sir Bedevere hid Excalibur under a tree.

And so, as soon as he might, he came again unto the king, and said he had been at the water, and had thrown the sword into the water.

"What saw thou there?" said the king.

"Sir," he said, "I saw nothing but waves and winds."

"That is untruly said of thee," said the king, "therefore go thou lightly again, and do my commandment; as thou art to me leve[20] and dear, spare not, but throw it in."

Then Sir Bedevere returned again, and took the sword in his hand; and then him thought sin and shame to throw away that noble sword, and so eft[21] he hid the sword, and returned again, and told to the king that he had been at the water and done his commandment.

"What saw thou there?" said the king.

"Sir," he said, "I saw nothing but the waters wap and waves wan."

"Ah, traitor untrue," said King Arthur, "now hast thou betrayed me twice. Who would have weened that thou that hast been to me so leve and dear, and thou art named a noble knight, and would betray me for the riches of the sword? But now go again lightly, for thy long tarrying putteth me in great jeopardy of my life, for I have taken cold. And but if thou do now as I bid thee, if ever I may see thee, I shall slay thee with mine

own hands; for thou wouldst for my rich sword see me dead."

Then Sir Bedevere departed, and went to the sword, and lightly took it up, and went to the water side; and there he bound the girdle about the hilts, and then he threw the sword as far into the water as he might; and there came an arm and an hand above the water and met it, and caught it, and so shook it thrice and brandished, and then vanished away the hand with the sword in the water. So Sir Bedevere came again to the king, and told him what he saw.

After lying to Arthur twice, how does Bedevere finally fulfill Arthur's wish? What does he see?

"Alas," said the king, "help me hence, for I dread me I have tarried over long."

Then Sir Bedevere took the king upon his back, and so went with him to that water side. And when they were at the water side, even fast by the bank hoved a little barge with many fair ladies in it, and among them all was a queen, and all they had black hoods, and all they wept and shrieked when they saw King Arthur.

"Now put me into the barge," said the king.

And so he did softly; and there received him three queens with great mourning; and so they set them down, and in one of their laps King Arthur laid his head.

And then that queen said, "Ah, dear brother, why have ye tarried so long from me? Alas, this wound on your head hath caught over-much cold."

And so then they rowed from the land, and Sir Bedevere beheld all those ladies go from him.

Then Sir Bedevere cried, "Ah my lord Arthur, what shall become of me, now ye go from me and leave me here alone among mine enemies?"

"Comfort thyself," said the king, "and do as well as thou mayest, for in me is no trust for to trust in; for I will into the vale of Avilion to heal

---

19. **pommel and the haft.** Hilt of a sword and the knob on the end of it
20. **leve.** Dear, pleasing
21. **eft.** Again

me of my grievous wound: and if thou hear never more of me, pray for my soul."

But ever the queens and ladies wept and shrieked, that it was pity to hear. And as soon as Sir Bedevere had lost the sight of the barge, he wept and wailed, and so took the forest; and so he went all that night, and in the morning he was ware betwixt two holts hoar,[22] of a chapel and an hermitage.

BOOK XXI CHAPTER 6

HOW SIR BEDEVERE FOUND HIM ON THE MORN DEAD IN AN HERMITAGE, AND HOW HE ABODE THERE WITH THE HERMIT

Then was Sir Bedevere glad, and thither he went; and when he came into the chapel, he saw where lay an hermit grovelling on all four, there fast by a tomb was new graven. When the hermit saw Sir Bedevere he knew him well, for he was but little tofore Bishop of Canterbury, that Sir Mordred flemed.[23] "Sir," said Sir Bedevere, "what man is there interred that ye pray so fast for?"

"Fair son," said the hermit, "I wot not verily, but by deeming. But this night, at midnight, here came a number of ladies, and brought hither a dead corpse, and prayed me to bury him; and here they offered an hundred tapers, and they gave me an hundred bezants.[24]

"Alas," said Sir Bedevere, "that was my lord King Arthur, that here lieth buried in this chapel."

Then Sir Bedevere swooned; and when he awoke he prayed the hermit he might abide with him still there, to live with fasting and prayers. "For from hence will I never go," said Sir Bedevere, "by my will, but all the days of my life here to pray for my lord Arthur."

"Ye are welcome to me," said the hermit, "for I know you better than ye ween that I do. Ye are the bold Bedevere, and the full noble duke, Sir Lucan the Butler, was your brother."

Then Sir Bedevere told the hermit all as ye have heard tofore. So there bode Sir Bedevere with the hermit that was tofore Bishop of Canterbury, and there Sir Bedevere put upon him poor clothes, and served the hermit full lowly in fasting and in prayers.

Thus of Arthur I find never more written in books that be authorised, nor more of the very certainty of his death heard I never read, but thus was he led away in a ship wherein were three queens; that one was King Arthur's sister, Queen Morgan le Fay; the other was the Queen of Northgales; the third was the Queen of the Waste Lands. Also there was Nimue, the chief lady of the lake, that had wedded Pelleas the good knight; and this lady had done much for King Arthur, for she would never suffer Sir Pelleas to be in no place where he should be in danger of his life; and so he lived to the uttermost of his days with her in great rest. More of the death of King Arthur could I never find, but that ladies brought him to his burials; and such one was buried there, that the hermit bare witness that sometime was Bishop of Canterbury, but yet the hermit knew not in certain that he was verily the body of King Arthur; for this tale Sir Bedevere, knight of the Table Round, made it to be written.

Did the hermit bury Arthur's body?

FROM BOOK XXI CHAPTER 7

OF THE OPINION OF SOME MEN OF THE DEATH OF KING ARTHUR; AND HOW QUEEN GUENEVER MADE HER A NUN IN ALMESBURY

Yet some men say in many parts of England that King Arthur is not dead, but had by the will of Our Lord Jesu into another place; and men say that he shall come again, and he shall win the holy cross. I will not say that it shall be so, but rather I will say, here in this world he changed his life. But many men say that there is written upon his tomb this verse: HIC IACET ARTHURUS, REX QUONDAM REXQUE FUTURUS.[25] ∎

---

22. **holts hoar.** Frosted woods
23. **tofore . . . flemed.** The hermit was, not long ago, the Bishop of Canterbury, whom Sir Mordred flemed, or made to flee.
24. **bezants.** Gold coins
25. **HIC . . . FUTURUS.** Here lies Arthur, who was king and will be king again.

1. The hermit buried a body, but he was not certain that it was King Arthur.

SELECTION CHECK TEST 4.1.13 WITH ANSWERS

Checking Your Reading

1. Why did King Arthur yell for help in his sleep? **He dreamed that he fell among serpents and beasts who took hold of his limbs.**
2. What two knights of King Arthur's survived the battle between Sir Mordred and himself? **Sir Lucan the butler and Sir Bedevere, his brother, survived the battle.**
3. Who killed Sir Mordred? **King Arthur killed Sir Mordred.**
4. What is an Excalibur? **The Excalibur is the name of King Arthur's sword.**
5. What do men say about King Arthur and his death? **Men say that he is not really dead, but in another place. They also say that he will come back again and win the holy cross.**

Vocabulary in Context
Fill in each blank below with the most appropriate word from the following Words for Everyday Use. You may have to change the tense of the word.

proffer   avenge

1. I planned to **avenge** the wrong done to my sister by punishing the boy who called her names.
2. Julia **proffered** dessert after the dinner dishes were cleared away.

Literary Tools
Fill in the blanks using the following terms.

tragedy   dramatic irony
tragic flaw

1. **Dramatic irony** occurs when the audience knows something that is unknown to the characters in the story.
2. Some critics say that Macbeth's **tragic flaw** is his greed for power.
3. *Le Morte d' Arthur* is a **tragedy** because it tells the story of King Arthur's fall and death.

RESPOND TO THE SELECTION

What makes Arthur's leadership and status as a mythical hero legendary? Do you think he deserves such legendary status? Why, or why not?

ANSWERS TO INVESTIGATE, INQUIRE, AND IMAGINE

RECALL

1a. Sir Gawain appears to Arthur with several ladies. These visitors appear to Arthur in a dream.

2a. Mordred will receive Cornwall and Kent during Arthur's lifetime and the rest of England after Arthur's death. The treaty is not honored because both parties mistrust the other and come to the treaty ceremony with full armies of suspicious knights. When a soldier draws his sword to kill a snake, all the knights burst into battle.

3a. Most of Arthur's soldiers are killed or seriously wounded during the battle. Lucan advises Arthur to let Mordred be and give up the battle, lest Arthur be killed as his dream had earlier predicted.

INTERPRET

1b. Arthur does not want to fight Mordred because he believes he will die in the battle. His dream convinces him of this, first with awful serpent-filled waters that symbolize death, and then his fears are confirmed by the words of Sir Gawain who predicts Arthur's death in battle.

2b. Both say they do not trust the other; both warn their companions to be ready for battle.

3b. Arthur is angry at the slaying of his loyal soldiers. He believes Mordred has betrayed the treaty.

ANALYZE

4a. *Responses will vary.* Betrayal of loyalty, as when Mordred appears to breach the treaty, is a grievous crime. Arthur is very upset when Bedevere fails to follow instructions about throwing the sword in the lake because such disobedience shows a lack of loyalty.

SYNTHESIZE

4b. *Responses will vary.* Students may say that kings rely on the loyalty of their subjects to maintain order in their kingdoms. In the code of chivalry, loyalty is among the most highly valued virtues, worth dying for.

Respond to the SELECTION

What surprised you about the circumstances surrounding Arthur's death? Why?

Investigate, Inquire, and Imagine

Recall: GATHERING FACTS

1a. Who speaks to Arthur the night before his battle with Mordred? In what context do his visitors appear?

2a. What treaty does Arthur propose to Mordred? Is the treaty honored? Why, or why not?

3a. What happens to Arthur's soldiers during the battle? What advice does Sir Lucan give Arthur about the battle?

Interpret: FINDING MEANING

1b. Why does Arthur not want to fight Mordred? How does Arthur's dream contribute to his feelings?

2b. How do Arthur's and Mordred's words about each other create a feeling of impending doom?

3b. Why is Arthur determined to continue with the fight?

Analyze: TAKING THINGS APART

4a. In what way is loyalty, or lack of same, demonstrated in the story of Arthur?

Synthesize: BRINGING THINGS TOGETHER

4b. Why might loyalty have been so highly valued for the people who first told this story?

Evaluate: MAKING JUDGMENTS

5a. What is the cause of Arthur's death? What condition is he in when he is last seen? What indications are there that Arthur may not, in fact, have died after the battle?

Extend: CONNECTING IDEAS

5b. Why do you think the legend is written to suggest that Arthur will return as king one day? Why might this idea be appealing to readers?

Understanding Literature

DRAMATIC IRONY. Review the definition for **dramatic irony** in the Handbook of Literary Terms. Although Arthur and Mordred agree to a truce, the battle begins when a knight raises his sword to kill a snake. Why is this situation an example of dramatic irony? How does this irony affect the tone of the story?

TRAGEDY AND TRAGIC FLAW. Review the definitions for **tragedy** and **tragic flaw** in the Handbook of Literary Terms. How does this story fit the definition of a tragedy? What tragic flaw brings about Arthur's fall?

ANSWERS TO INVESTIGATE, INQUIRE, AND IMAGINE (CONT.)

EVALUATE

5a. Arthur insists on battling singly with Mordred until both are gravely wounded. Arthur is last seen lying weakly in a barge bound for Avilion. Lack of detail about his burial, rumor from around the land that Arthur still lives, and the presence of magic during his lifetime suggest the possibility that Arthur may not have died after the battle.

EXTEND

5b. Arthur is such a heroic figure that storytellers and readers alike want to believe he will return some day. People want to have faith that justice and heroism will be rewarded over betrayal and evil. Arthur's return would confirm such faith.

Writer's Journal

1. A **eulogy** is a formal piece of writing or a speech that praises a person who has died. Write a short eulogy for Arthur. Try to paint a vivid picture of this legendary hero and the reasons to honor his memory. You might write it from the point of view of one of Arthur's loyal knights.

2. Write an alternative **ending** for this story that shows King Arthur alive. How do you explain the body that was buried by the hermit? How did Arthur escape death, and what did he do next?

3. This selection contains many archaic, or old, words and expressions. Imagine you wanted to tell this story to a child. Write a brief **retelling** of the story using everyday language.

Integrating the Language Arts

Language, Grammar, and Style

USING THE PARTS OF SPEECH IN WRITING. Many words in English can be used as more than one part of speech. Identify the part of speech of each italicized word in the sentences below. Then, write a new sentence using each word as the part of speech given in parentheses.

EXAMPLE   Medieval knights wore heavy suits of *mail* into battle. (Use as a verb.)

    mail = noun   <u>Mail</u> the letters before the end of the day.

1. "*Say*," asked Irena, "do you remember the name of King Arthur's wife?" (Use as a verb.)
2. Arthur's knights beat *back* the advancing enemy. (Use as a noun.)
3. Bedevere stayed *close* to his brother throughout the battle. (Use as an adjective.)
4. Arthur called *out* to Mordred as he charged toward him with a spear. (Use as a preposition.)
5. In some retellings of the Arthurian legend, the mortally *wounded* Arthur is taken to Avalon. (Use as a verb.)

Media Literacy & Collaborative Learning

WRITING A TELEVISION NEWS REPORT. Today's reporters often experience war firsthand. Television viewers have a closer sense of the action as they view battle footage, hear reports from war-torn cities, and see stricken refugees and military victims on their screen. Work with a small group of classmates to report the battle between Arthur and Mordred. Let each person focus on an aspect of the conflict, for example, troop movements, truce negotiations, the history of the conflict, or battlefront updates. Another group member can be the news anchor who coordinates stories among the reporters and organizes the sequence in which information and images will be presented. If possible, videotape your television news report.

DRAMATIC IRONY. When the knight raises his sword, the reader knows that he is doing so to kill a snake that has bitten him. The other participants in the story are unaware of his reasons. The senseless reason for the beginning of the battle makes the carnage of the fight all the more horrifying. It also seems that the fighting and Arthur's death were inevitable, for despite all the warnings given, the battle takes place.

TRAGEDY AND TRAGIC FLAW. The story of King Arthur is a tragedy because it depicts the fall of a person of high status. It celebrates King Arthur's courage and dignity in the face of his inevitable death. Arthur's tragic flaw is his pride, which makes him desire revenge against Mordred for having killed so many of his men. He is unable to give up a chance at vengeance despite the many warnings he has been given, and this leads to his fall.

ANSWERS TO INTEGRATING THE LANGUAGE ARTS

Language, Grammar, and Style
Students' sentences will vary, but they should use the correct part of speech.
1. int.
2. adv.
3. adv.
4. adv.
5. adj.

Media Literacy & Collaborative Learning
Allow students ample time to practice their news reports before presenting them to the class.

ADDITIONAL RESOURCES

UNIT 1 RESOURCE BOOK
- Selection Worksheet 1.7
- Selection Check Test 4.1.15
- Selection Test 4.1.16

VOCABULARY FROM THE SELECTION

benevolent	envoy
boisterous	refuge
coerce	rigorous
disperse	vanquished

READER'S JOURNAL

Ask students to explain how their end goal helped to motivate them, what support they received from other people, and how this support helped them. Students may begin by brainstorming a list of things that they have achieved during their lives and a list of things they still want to achieve. How did they go about achieving what they did? Was the feeling they had after their achievements different from what they expected they would feel? If so, how? What kinds of help do they think they will need in order to complete future achievements?

Literary TOOLS

ORAL TRADITION AND LEGEND. An oral tradition is a work, an idea, or a custom that is passed by word of mouth from generation to generation. A **legend** is a story coming down from the past, often based on real events or characters from older times. They are popularly regarded as historical, but may contain elements that are fantastic or unverifiable. As you read "Sundiata Keita, the Legend and the King," decide which elements are fact and which might be fiction. How do the writers of this selection say that Sundiata should be viewed?

DIALOGUE. Dialogue is conversation involving two or more people or characters. This selection includes dialogue between Sundiata and Sumanguru, the ruler of Mali. What does this dialogue reveal about the two characters?

Reader's Journal

Have you ever had to overcome a great difficulty to achieve something? Explain.

"Sundiata Keita, the Legend and the King"

from *The Royal Kingdoms of Ghana, Mali, and Songhay: Life In Medieval Africa*

by Patricia and Fredrick McKissack

Reader's resource

GEOGRAPHY AND HISTORY CONNECTION. A landlocked country in western Africa, the Republic of Mali is crossed by most of the major trade routes of Africa. Between AD 500 and AD 1700, the kingdom of Mali flourished along with the kingdoms of Ghana and Songhay. The prosperity of these countries was based on gold, salt, and the slave trade. After the fall of Ghana in 1200, Mali became the dominant power in the region for three hundred years. Around the year 1235, the Keita kings of Mali came to the height of their power during the reign of Sundiata. Sundiata overcame an inability to walk and became a powerful king and hero.

About the AUTHORS

Patricia and Fredrick McKissack have written many books for young people. Their writings have received such honors as the Coretta Scott King Award, the Jane Addams Book Award, and a Newbery Honor. In *The Royal Kingdoms of Ghana, Mali, and Songhay*, from which this selection is taken, they tried to capture the excitement that they experienced during an exploration of these kingdoms of western Africa.

art note

Granary Door. Dogon Artist. Sangha, Mali.

Dogon artists work individually and collectively in workshops. For large projects, experienced apprentices cut the preliminary shapes, the master carver does the final cutting and the youngest apprentices, who start at age 10, smooth the surface. Traditional African art is often thought to be unchanged through the centuries, but the master artist brings his individual style to the sculpture. This door is carved with ancestor figures who protect the grain stored inside.

GOALS/OBJECTIVES

Studying this lesson will enable students to
- empathize with and understand the challenges of a boy who struggled to become a leader of his people
- discuss the development and importance of the oral tradition in early civilizations
- define *oral tradition* and *legend* and explain how the terms relate to the selection
- define *dialogue* and analyze the dialogue in a literary work
- work collaboratively to stage and perform a dramatic interpretation of "Sundiata Keita"
- conduct research on African history

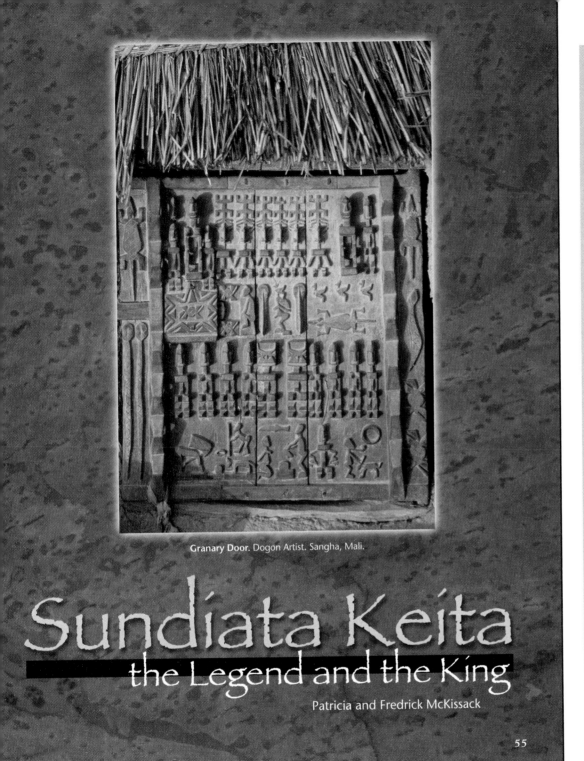

Granary Door. Dogon Artist. Sangha, Mali.

Sundiata Keita
the Legend and the King

Patricia and Fredrick McKissack

55

INDIVIDUAL LEARNING STRATEGIES

MOTIVATION
Ask students to recall some names of people who overcame physical challenges against the odds. Prompt students' thinking by mentioning such people as Helen Keller, actor Christopher Reeve, and cyclist Lance Armstrong. Initiate a discussion about what personal qualities or circumstances might motivate a person to surpass their "limitations."

READING PROFICIENCY
Work with students to help them understand the Vocabulary from the Selection and the footnotes before they begin reading. You might skim the selection with students, identifying unfamiliar names and places and practicing pronunciation with them.

ENGLISH LANGUAGE LEARNING
The strategies for Reading Proficiency above will also benefit students learning English. You might also define these words and phrases from the selection:
humiliate—embarrass; destroy one's self-respect
ill omen—indication of bad things to come
cinder—ashes
torrent—rush of liquid

SPECIAL NEEDS
Celebrate the aspects of the oral tradition in this selection by reading it aloud to students. Give students clear direction by having them write the Guided Reading questions in their notebooks, and note any answers they hear as you read. Once you have finished reading, encourage students to return to the text to double-check their answers.

ENRICHMENT
Encourage students to research symbolism in African culture, particularly the symbolism associated with an individual's clan, as mentioned at the end of this excerpt. You might have students focus on the Mali people in order to narrow their research. Encourage students to gather in small groups to share their findings, which should include illustrations of symbols along with factual material.

1. Sundiata is compared to King
   Arthur and George Washington.
   Like Arthur, he was a "warrior
   king," and he "united a weak and
   scattered people." Like
   Washington, he is honored as the
   founder of his nation. There is no
   evidence that King Arthur actually
   lived, but there is evidence that
   both Washington and Sundiata
   lived.
2. Sassouma was jealous of Sogolon
   and hated Sundiata. She planned to
   destroy Sundiata and his mother so
   her son would rule Mali, not
   Sundiata.

CROSS-CURRICULAR ACTIVITIES

PHYSIOLOGY. This excerpt
explains that Sundiata had a
physical handicap because he
could not walk by the age of
seven. Ask students to research
the basic stages of human
development, focusing on the
stages of birth to age seven. Have
students create a poster that explains
at least one stage of development.
Encourage them to include pictures
and illustrations on their posters.

At a time when the Mande[1] people needed a leader one came, and his name was Sogolon-Djata, a member of the Keita clan, who had ruled in Mali for three centuries. Maghan Kon Fatta, the king, was his father, and his mother was Sogolon Kedjou, a hunchback. In the rapidly spoken language of the Mandinka,[2] his name, Sogolon-Djata, became Sundiata, "The Hungering Lion."

Sundiata Keita is the King Arthur and George Washington of Mali.[3] He was a warrior-king who united a weak and scattered people, and, under his <u>benevolent</u> leadership, ushered in a glorious period of peace and prosperity. However, Arthur is a mythical king; there is no evidence that he ever lived. There are many legends about Washington, but he was definitely a real person. Sundiata's story is full of legend, but he, too, really lived. Like Washington, he is honored as a great man, the founder of his nation. As we learn more about him, we will be able to see him as a person with good and bad sides. Sundiata should be seen as a three-dimensional man of his time and not just a mythic figure.

To whom is Sundiata Keita compared? How was he like these people? How did he differ from them?

The Keita griots[4] of Mali, who preserved the history and wisdom of their great kings, have told the story of Sundiata for centuries. Mamadou Kouyate, from the village of Djeliba Koro, begins the tale:

> Listen then, sons of Mali, children of the black people, listen to my word, for I am going to tell you of Sundiata, the father of the Bright Country, of the savanna[5] land, the ancestor of those who draw the bow, the master of a hundred <u>vanquished</u> kings.

Two hunters told Maghan Kon Fatta that if he married Sogolon, their son would be a leader without equal, and so the king did. The day Sundiata was born a storm foretold of his greatness. "The lion child, the buffalo child is born," said the midwife.[6] "The Almighty has made the thunder peal, the white sky has lit up and the earth has trembled."

Maghan Kon Fatta favored Sundiata and his mother, which angered his first wife, Sassouma Berete. Sassouma's jealousy of Sogolon was matched only by her hatred of Sundiata. She plotted to destroy them both to make sure her son, Prince Dankaran Touman, would become king after King Fatta died.

How did Sassouma Berete feel about Sundiata and his mother? What did she plan to do?

As Sundiata grew, the situation took an odd twist. Sundiata was seven years old, yet he couldn't walk! People were shocked and surprised to see a boy his age crawling around like a baby. Sassouma used every opportunity to embarrass Sogolon and hurl insults at her son. She pushed her beautiful child up front during all ceremonies, so he could be seen and adored.

As long as the king lived, Sundiata was protected and Sassouma's scheming was kept in check, but Maghan Kon Fatta died when Sundiata was very young. Against Fatta's wishes, the royal council was <u>coerced</u> into making Touman the mansa,[7] and Sassouma became the power behind the throne.

Free to carry out her threats, she did her best to humiliate Sogolon and her children. Sogolon was forced to live in a storage hut out behind

---

1. **Mande.** Any member of a group of people native to western Africa
2. **Mandinka.** Subgroup of the Mande
3. **Mali.** Inland nation in western Africa
4. **griots.** Storytellers, bards from West Africa
5. **savanna.** Flat grassland
6. **midwife.** Person who assists women in childbirth
7. **mansa.** Heir to the throne

---

words for everyday use

be • nev • o • lent (bə nev′ ə lənt) *adj.,* kindly or charitable. *The <u>benevolent</u> queen allowed her subjects to pay her in taxes only what they could afford, and her kindness was rewarded with loyal support.*

van • quished (vaŋ′ kwishd) *adj.,* beaten or conquered in battle. *The <u>vanquished</u> ruler was sent by his conquerer to live in another kingdom.*

co • erce (kō urs′) *vt.,* force by intimidation to do something. *The police detective was able to <u>coerce</u> a confession out of the suspect by threatening to arrest her family.*

the palace and Sassouma encouraged children to tease and poke fun at them. In spite of her efforts, Sundiata made two friends, Manding Bory, his half-brother, and Balla Fasseke, his teacher.

Just at this time, Sumanguru's army captured Mali. He spared the lives of Touman, who could be controlled through his mother, and Sundiata, who seemed harmless. Before leaving the city Sumanguru mocked the Mandinka, saying they were a weak and spineless people, like their king's son.

Balla Fasseke was sent as an <u>envoy</u> to Sumanguru, but after hearing Balla Fasseke speak, the king decided to keep him there to be his personal griot. After that Sundiata was determined to overcome his physical handicap.

Oh, day, what a beautiful day,
Oh, day, day of joy;
Allah Almighty, you never created a finer day.
So my son is going to walk!

With the help of a blacksmith—remember the power of the blacksmiths—who made braces for his legs, and the loving support of his family, Sundiata learned to walk upright. On that day his mother sang:

> How did Sundiata learn to walk?

Oh, day, what a beautiful day,
Oh, day, day of joy;
Allah Almighty, you never created a finer day.
So my son is going to walk!

Through <u>rigorous</u> exercise and hard work the young prince grew tall and strong and became a very good archer. A prince needed to be fit, but Sogolon taught her son that a good ruler also needed to be wise. She taught Sundiata to respect Mandinka customs and traditions, their history and law.

When Sassouma heard that Sundiata could walk, she went to the Nine Witches of Mali and asked them to kill him. They tried, but Sundiata's kind heart weakened the witches' powers. Knowing that Sassouma would not stop until she had killed Sundiata, Sogolon fled with her children. Sundiata hated to leave his friends, but he had to go.

No one would take them in, because they were afraid of Sassouma's revenge. At last they found refuge with the distant king of Mema. Mema was probably what was left of the old kingdom of Ghana.[8] There Sundiata lived in exile, where he distinguished himself as a warrior-hunter.

Over the years, Sumanguru's taxes increased so much that Mali couldn't pay them. Sumanguru's army advanced against the Mandinka people at Kangaba. Touman and Sassouma fled, but loyal subjects sent a message to Sundiata, asking him to come home. The Mandinka warriors weren't afraid to fight, but they needed a general.

> Why did Sundiata return to his people?

The king of Mema loved Sundiata as a son, so he raised an army with troops and cavalry to help fight the wicked ruler. Even the king's sons joined Sundiata. With Sogolon's blessings, the young prince of Mali was at last ready to fulfill his destiny.

---

8. **Ghana.** Nation in Africa

---

words for everyday use

en • voy (än′ voi) *n.*, agent who transacts diplomatic business. *The president sent a diplomatic <u>envoy</u> on a mission to England in order to complete the business transaction.*

rig • or • ous (rig′ ər əs) *adj.*, extremely harsh or severe. *Her <u>rigorous</u> training schedule called for waking up at five o'clock in the morning and running six miles before breakfast.*

1. Sundiata learned to walk by using leg braces forged by a blacksmith. The support of his family also helped him.
2. Sundiata returned to his people to lead the Mandinka warriors in battle against Sumanguru.

BIBLIOGRAPHIC NOTE

If students are interested in learning more about African legends, folk tales, and myths, suggest the following:

Ford, Clyde W. *The Hero With an African Face: Mythic Wisdom of Traditional Africa.* Bantam, 1999.

Radin, Paul. Ed. *African Folktales.* Schocken Books, 1983.

1. Sumanguru claims to be "the mighty silk-cotton tree"—a tree higher than all the others. Sundiata claims to be one that climbs to the tops of the highest trees.
2. Sumanguru fled when he saw a rooster nail that had been dipped in blood on an arrow Sundiata shot at him.

ADDITIONAL QUESTIONS AND ACTIVITIES

Have students work in pairs to research the role of griots in African society. Then have them compare that role to people who held similar positions in other cultures, such as the epic poets of ancient Greece and Rome or the bards in Celtic and Welsh history. Ask students to present their research in a report and to conclude the report with their opinions on how important and respected these "official poets and musicians" were in their day.

SELECTION CHECK TEST 4.1.15 WITH ANSWERS

Checking Your Reading

1. For how long did Sogolon-Djata rule? **He ruled in Mali for three centuries.**
2. To whom is Sundiata Keita compared? **He is compared to George Washington and King Arthur.**
3. What was Sundiata unable to do at the age of seven? **He was unable to walk.**
4. What helped Sundiata to overcome his physical handicap? **The leg braces made by a blacksmith and the support from his family helped Sundiata to walk.**
5. What did Sassouma ask the Nine Witches of Mali? **She asked them to kill Sundiata.**

(Continued on page 59)

All along the way, the Mandinka army scored victory after victory against Sumanguru's forces. As the people were freed, they joined Sundiata in his march against the oppressive Susu[9] regime.

After five years, the two armies met in the plain of Kirina (Krina).[10] Sundiata pitched his camp at Dayala in the valley of the Niger.[11] Sumanguru's army stood at Kirina. The night before the battle, Sumanguru visited Sundiata in the form of an owl, a bird of ill omen among the Mande.

SUMANGURU: I am the king of Mali by force of arms. My rights have been established by conquest.

SUNDIATA: Then I will take Mali from you by force of arms and chase you from my kingdom.

SUMANGURU: Know that I am the wild yam of the rocks; nothing will make me leave Mali.

SUNDIATA: Know that I have in my camp seven master smiths who will shatter the rocks. Then, yam, I will eat you.

SUMANGURU: I am the poisonous mushroom that made the fearless vomit.

SUNDIATA: As for me I am the ravenous cock, the poison does not matter to me.

SUMANGURU: Behave yourself, little boy, or you will burn your foot, for I am the red-hot cinder.

SUNDIATA: But me, I am the rain that extinguishes the cinder; I am the boisterous torrent that will carry you off.

SUMANGURU: I am the mighty silk-cotton tree that looks from on high on the tops of other trees.

What is the last thing Sumanguru claimed to be? What response did Sundiata have?

SUNDIATA: And I, I am the creeper that climbs to the top of the forest giant.

SUMANGURU: Enough of this argument. You shall not have Mali.

SUNDIATA: Know that there is not room for two kings on the same skin, Sumanguru; you will let me have your place.

Sumanguru was shaken by Sundiata's self-confidence, although he was sure his magic would protect him. But Sundiata's blacksmith was also a well-known wizard. He made a poison from the blood of a white rooster stolen from Sumanguru's camp. Then he dipped the rooster's nail into the blood and fastened it to an arrow.

In the story the griots tell, the battle at Kirina is a classic tale of good versus evil. The Mandinka warriors fought nobly. When the battle looked like it was going against the Susu, Sumanguru hid behind his men. At just the right moment, Sundiata shot the arrow. It barely grazed Sumanguru's shoulder, but it was enough. Seeing the rooster nail caused him to tremble and scream. Then, turning his horse toward the mountains, he fled. Sundiata followed, but Sumanguru was never heard from again. Some say he was swallowed by the mountains. Without their leader the Susu army was defeated and dispersed.

What caused Sumanguru to flee?

Sundiata was reunited with Balla Fasseke, who became his griot, and his good friend and half-brother, Manding Bory. The griot hailed him, saying, "Sundiata, Maghan Sundiata, hail, king of Mali, in the name of the twelve kings of the Bright Country, I salute you as Mansa." To

---

9. **Susu.** Agricultural people living mainly in the African nations of Guinea and Sierra Leone
10. **plain of Kirina (Krina).** Wide, open flatlands in Mali
11. **Niger.** River that flows from the northeast border of Guinea through Mali, Niger, and Nigeria, where it empties into the Atlantic Ocean

words for everyday use

bois • ter • ous (bois' tər əs) *adj.*, stormy or turbulent. *The boisterous baseball fans became even rowdier after their team won the World Series.*

dis • perse (dis pʉrs') *vi.*, break up and scatter about. *The crowd dispersed peacefully after the fireworks display, going their separate ways with little trouble.*

celebrate their liberation, Balla Fasseke wrote a song that griots still sing:

Niama,[12] Niama, Niama,
You, you serve as a shelter for all,
All come to seek refuge under you.
And as for you, Niama,
Nothing serves you for shelter,
God alone protects you.

Sundiata crushed the Susu's stronghold, forever destroying the Susu and their dynasty.

Because of his courage and leadership, Sundiata was chosen to be mansa of Mali, which he ruled from 1230 to 1255. Mali means "the hippopotamus," which is often used in association with Sundiata, as are the lion, the symbol of the Keita clan, and the buffalo of his mother's clan.

> What symbols were often used in association with Sundiata?

According to the griots' story, Sundiata began his rule by first moving his seat of government from Kangaba to Niani, the place of his birth. Then he established a solid hold over the gold and salt trade that had been the source of Ghana's wealth. ∎

12. **Niama.** Mande word that could mean "leader"

---

words for everyday use

ref • uge (ref´ yŏŏj) *n.,* place of shelter and safety. *The store's awning was our refuge from the sudden downpour.*

Respond to the SELECTION

Do you think Sundiata would be a good leader? Why, or why not? Would you want Sundiata to be your ruler?

ANSWER TO GUIDED READING QUESTION

1. The symbols used in association with Sundiata include the hippopotamus, the lion, the symbol of the Keita clan, and the buffalo of his mother's clan.

SELECTION CHECK TEST 4.1.15 WITH ANSWERS (CONT.)

Vocabulary in Context
Fill in each blank below with the most appropriate word from the following Words for Everyday Use. You may have to change the tense of the word.

benevolent	coerce	envoy
rigorous	boisterous	
disperse	refuge	

1. Compared to high school, college requires a more **rigorous** study schedule.
2. The woman is known for her **benevolence** because she is always volunteering at shelters.
3. My girlfriends **coerced** me to buy the dress even though I didn't really need it.
4. The speaker's **boisterous** laugh filled the auditorium.
5. The coach told the team to **disperse** so they could start their running exercises.

Literary Tools
Fill in the blanks using the following terms.

legend	oral tradition	dialogue

1. Even though elements of a(n) **legend** are fantastic and unverifiable, it is still regarded as historical.
2. A conversation that involves at least two people is called a(n) **dialogue**.
3. A work, an idea, or a custom that is passed down by word of mouth is called **oral tradition**.

RESPOND TO THE SELECTION

Ask students to make a list of the qualities they think a good ruler needs to have, or, if they made such a list in Prereading for the King Arthur legend on page 32, look back at that list. What qualities on the list does Sundiata have? What qualities does he lack? How do King Arthur and George Washington compare to Sundiata according to students' lists?

RECALL

1a. The name Sundiata means "the Hungering Lion." Sundiata is compared to King Arthur and George Washington.

2a. On the day Sundiata was born, a storm foretold of his greatness as a leader. The storm was said to be caused by the "Almighty," who made the thunder peal and the sky light up. Sassouma Berete, the first wife of Maghan Kon Fatta, was jealous of Sundiata and his mother.

3a. People were surprised that when Sundiata was seven years old, he still could not walk. A blacksmith helped him overcome this problem by making braces for his legs. Sundiata found refuge with the king of Mema after he was forced to leave. He came back to lead an army that was raised to fight Sumanguru, Mali's wicked ruler.

INTERPRET

1b. Sundiata was like King Arthur in that he was a warrior-king who united people and "ushered in a glorious period of peace and prosperity." He, like Washington, was honored as a great man who founded his country. He was different from Arthur in that, according to the authors, Arthur was a mythical king, and Sundiata Keita really lived. He differed from Washington in that more of what was known about Sundiata came from legend, because Sundiata Keita lived in the more distant past.

2b. Sundiata Keita met the expectations of his birth by becoming a leader without equal. Sundiata stood in the way of Sassouma Berete by making friends with his half-brother and his teacher, and by overcoming his physical handicap.

3b. People viewed Sundiata as harmless and weak because of his inability to walk. Sundiata and his family left because his life was threatened by Sassouma. The battle between the Mandinka and Sumanguru and his army was the classic battle of good versus evil, with the Mandinka fighting nobly and Sumanguru hiding behind his men.

ANALYZE

4a. Sundiata is the noble hero of the story, while Sumanguru is a wicked coward. Sumanguru's evil character is revealed in the way he first mocks the Mandinka, then increases taxes to an intolerable level, and prepares to attack the Mandinka, who cannot afford to pay. He visits Sundiata as an owl, a bird of ill

Investigate,
Inquire,
and **Imagine**

Recall: GATHERING FACTS

1a. What does the name Sundiata mean? To what two legendary figures is Sundiata Keita compared?

2a. What happened on the day Sundiata was born? What significance was given to this event? Who was jealous of Sundiata?

3a. What surprised people about the seven-year-old Sundiata? Who helped him overcome this problem? Where did Sundiata go when he was forced to leave? Why did he come back?

Analyze: TAKING THINGS APART

4a. Compare the character of Sundiata in this story to that of Sumanguru. What do their actions and behavior tell you about each man?

Evaluate: MAKING JUDGMENTS

5a. Do you think that the authors are successful in portraying Sundiata as a "man of his time" or do they only show him as a "mythic figure"?

Interpret: FINDING MEANING

1b. According to the selection, in what ways was Sundiata Keita like both of the people to whom he is compared?

2b. Did Sundiata live up to the expectations of his birth? How did Sundiata stand in the way of Sassouma Berete and her plans?

3b. How did Sundiata's problem affect the way that other people viewed him? Why did Sundiata leave his friends and home? What was the battle like between the Mandinka and Sumanguru and his army?

Synthesize: BRINGING THINGS TOGETHER

4b. What qualities made Sundiata a good leader? What about his early life makes his accomplishments especially admirable?

Extend: CONNECTING IDEAS

5b. Compare Sundiata to King Arthur as portrayed in the legends on pages 32 and 45. What similarities and differences can you find? For example, how was each man's future greatness predicted from the time of his birth? How did God's will fit into the destiny of each man? In what ways did each man embody the motif of a transformation from humble being to one of exceptional status?

Understanding *Literature*

ORAL TRADITION AND LEGEND. Review the definition for **oral tradition** in the Handbook of Literary Terms. Materials transmitted orally may be simplified in the retelling. The story of Sundiata Keita was passed down in spoken form by the storytellers, or *griots,* of West Africa. The storytellers may have invented specific details over the years, so that the story is probably not word for word the exact truth of what happened. What elements in this version of the story of Sundiata are true, and which are probably invented or recreated by the teller? Often, works in an oral tradition contain miraculous or magical elements. What magical elements appear in this story?

ANSWERS TO INVESTIGATE, INQUIRE, AND IMAGINE (CONT.)

omen which represents his wicked character. Sumanguru shows cowardice: he hides behind his men and runs screaming when scratched by an arrow. Sundiata's character is revealed in the way he defeats his disability and distinguishes himself as a warrior-hunter. He reveals his bravery by standing up to the powerful Sumanguru.

SYNTHESIZE

4b. Sundiata's leadership traits are his self-confidence, courage, and leadership. He is also a good leader because he has heeded his mother's advice and learned to respect the culture, history, and law of his people. He is also determined and willing to do hard work.

(Continued on page 61)

DIALOGUE. Review the definition for **dialogue** in the Handbook of Literary Terms. What does the dialogue between Sundiata and Sumanguru add to this story? How does it differ from the rest of the story? What kinds of imagery are used? Who emerges as the winner of the exchange? How does it affect the outcome of the story? Griots, or storytellers from West Africa, often acted out the stories they told. What about the dialogue is entertaining?

Writer's Journal

1. In the dialogue between Sundiata and Sumanguru, the two men hurl insults and boasts at one another. Write three more **boasts** that Sumanguru may have made and the **insults** that Sundiata could hurl back in response.

2. In this story, songs are used to herald joyous events. Write the **lyrics** for another short song that could have been added to the story. Make sure the lyrics are related to an event in the story, whether good or bad.

3. Based on the information given in this story, write a brief **encyclopedia entry** for Sundiata Keita. Include the important facts about Sundiata's life as well as some of what "some say" about him.

Integrating the Language Arts

Collaborative Learning

STAGING A PLAY. The griots of West Africa who told the story of Sundiata Keita often acted out scenes and used music and body movement to make the story come alive for the listener. As a class, adapt the story of Sundiata Keita into the form of a play. Divide the play into scenes, and form groups of four or five students to create the dialogue for each scene. The scene between Sundiata and Sumanguru already contains dialogue, but you may add some at the beginning and end of the scene if you choose. Some students who are musically inclined may write music or establish a melody for the songs included in the story. Create a list of the characters you will need, including the soldiers in the battle scene. You may wish to find or make simple props to be used in the play, or the actors may simply mime, pretending these objects are there. When you have finished writing the play, perform it for another class or to a larger group in your school to inform fellow students of an important figure in African history.

Study and Research

RESEARCHING AFRICAN HISTORY. Many Americans are unaware of the complex history of Africa. Conduct research on the history of an African nation of your choice. Be sure to consult a current source, since the names of some countries have changed in recent years. Find out information about past leaders of these nations, from the times of tribal rule to colonial government (if the country was colonized by a foreign land) and the form of government in place today. What groups of people live in the country today? What languages are spoken? Are there any legendary heroes from the country you chose? Compile the information you found into a report to be handed in to your teacher.

ANSWERS TO INTEGRATING THE LANGUAGE ARTS

Collaborative Learning
Encourage students to perform some research on the basic techniques of dramatic presentations for guidance with this activity. You might ask them to consult the Internet or theater books to find information on props, costumes, or pantomime movements.

Study and Research
Before they begin their research, suggest that students refer to Language Arts Survey 5.19, "How to Locate Library Materials," 5.20, "Using Reference Works," 5.26, "Using the Internet," and 5.36, "Documenting Sources."

ANSWERS TO UNDERSTANDING LITERATURE (CONT.)

emerges as the winner of the exchange. Sumanguru is shaken by Sundiata's self-confidence and foreshadows Sundiata's triumph over Sumanguru. The exchange is dramatic and confrontational. Students may say that they find the insults original and humorous.

ANSWERS TO INVESTIGATE, INQUIRE, AND IMAGINE (CONT.)

EVALUATE
5a. Some students will say that Sundiata seems a mythic figure and cite evidence such as his use of a poisoned rooster nail to defeat Sumanguru. They may find Sundiata somewhat idealized in the selection. Others will say that Sundiata seems a "man of his time" and cite evidence such as his moving the seat of government and establishing a hold over trade.

EXTEND
5b. *Responses will vary.* If students did not read the selections on King Arthur, they may choose another legendary hero. Merlin predicted King Arthur's greatness from the time of his birth by Merlin, while Sundiata's was foretold by a storm that alerted the midwife that here was a "lion child." God's will created that storm and enabled Arthur to pull the sword from the stone. Arthur was taken from his royal parents at birth and raised by another family, thus no one guessed he was really the heir to the throne of Britain. Sundiata was banished from his home first when his father died, when he and his family were forced to live in a shack out back of the palace, and later when his life was threatened. His disability also made him appear humble. However, both men emerged from their obscure status to claim their royal birthrights and become powerful kings.

ANSWERS TO UNDERSTANDING LITERATURE

ORAL TRADITION AND LEGEND. The specific words of the citizens of Mali, the songs, and the magical occurrences were probably added by the storytellers to make the history come alive. The names of the principal characters, their parentage, and the places mentions are probably true. Magical elements in the story include the storm predicting Sundiata's greatness and the encounter in which Sumanguru visits Sundiata in the form of an owl.

DIALOGUE. *Responses will vary.* Students may say that the dialogue adds drama and humor to the story. In present tense, it gives a more immediate feel than the rest of the story. It is the first time two characters are speaking to each other; until this point, the narrator has informed the reader of events. Images of nature ("wild yam of the rocks," "rain that extinguishes the cinder," "mighty silk cotton tree") are related to conflict and battle. Sundiata

GUIDED WRITING
Software

See the Guided Writing Software for an extended version of this lesson that includes printable graphic organizers, extensive student models and student-friendly checklists, and self-, peer, and teacher evaluation features.

PERSONAL/EXPRESSIVE WRITING

"What moves men of genius, or rather what inspires their work, is not new ideas, but their obsession with the idea that what has already been said is still not enough."

—*Eugene Delacroix*

We live in a complex, densely populated world, thus your time capsule is limited in size. Think small. You cannot include a television set, a CD player, or the car of your dreams. You could include tapes or recordings and make arrangements for common space for the antique implements to play them. Or you could choose photographs and scripts that wouldn't require equipment. How will you determine what to place in your limited space allocation?

Guided Writing

CREATING A TIME CAPSULE

The value of history is to remind us of where we've been so that we can learn from the past and improve our future, perhaps even avoid the errors of our ancestors. Each generation seeks to codify its experiences, enumerate its insights, and pass them on. You've read myths, legends, and poems that demonstrate the attainment of values, the lessons learned, the paths to follow. In which ways could you capture the essence of the twenty-first century and pass it on?

WRITING ASSIGNMENT. Create a small time capsule (no bigger than a shoe box) that represents your generation and the society you live in. You will be writing an explanation of your time capsule, to be opened in the year 2088 by your great-grandchildren's generation. Imagine that the capsules will be stored in a sealed chamber in your city hall (and relocated if a highway comes through!). Your insights will be crucial to future generations' comprehension of turn-of-the-century perspectives, just as a letter written by your own great-grandparents is meaningful to your understanding of the way life felt in 1900.

Student Model

from "Optimism" by Trasy Van Slooten

Hello, my grandchildren. I hope you find this time capsule interesting, and that you are in good health. I participated in this project to show you what it was like when I was a teenager, and to share my opinions about what the year 2000 was all about. Even though I'm only sixteen right now, you know me as Great Grandma. The year you are reading this should be 2088. Maybe by this time they will have found a miracle drug to keep me living to age 100, and I can open this with you. It is a time of medical miracles. Or, perhaps I've passed peacefully into Summerland. My hands have placed in this capsule three items:

A color, wide-angle picture of a rainforest

Something called a "tongue ring"

A guitar string

This time capsule represents what I foresee as important crossroads for the world around me, crossroads at which I hope my generation made the right decisions. I know you may be using jetpacks for transportation instead of cars, and you may take your vacations on Mars, so these items and their significance may seem petty and foolish. Try to keep an open mind; I think I can explain it all.

A rainforest is something you've likely never seen before. You have probably heard of them in recent folklore, but never realized their importance. Rainforests were great masses of land with trees taller than you could see and just as wide. There were millions of creatures living in them, from insects to monkeys to birds, millions of species. They were sacred to many people for their beauty and magical spirits. Industrialization and "progress" came along and needed a place to build, and builders needed wood. After years of stripping both resources and beauty, bit by bit, from the rainforests, they were all destroyed. Many species died along with the magic of nature. Your generation surely is helping to reconstruct the rainforests, or the world you live in may be dying. Were we able to preserve DNA and reconstruct what we lost?

EXAMINING THE MODEL. "Optimism" demonstrates the thoughtful selection of a perspective, in Trasy's case one of concern, and her subsequent identification of items that would fit in the capsule and symbolize the concern. She has written in the first person, "I" and "you," because it is her statement to a future generation. She has thus personalized her approach.

Notice how she ties it together with questions addressed to the audience that opens the capsule, finalizing each paragraph of explanation with a question.

She begins her essay by noting the passage of time, almost like a letter from the past, and her reference to crossroads. Her voice is thoughtful and respectful of her descendents' lives.

Prewriting

FINDING YOUR VOICE. Voice is the quality of a work that tells you that one person in particular wrote it. Your voice in this essay will be necessarily connected to your feelings. You may choose a respectful and formal approach, as Trasy has done, or you could write in the casual jargon of a teenager. Doing so would make your description reflect your generation's speech patterns—the

"Things do not change; we change."
—Henry David Thoreau

Understanding Register

A **register** is a subset of language usage specific to a particular relationship between people. In talking to a friend or writing him or her a letter, you would usually use a register that is casual, warm, and open. In talking or writing to a young child, you would typically speak in a register that is nonthreatening and easy to understand. In speaking to or corresponding with an official such as a police officer or a government clerk, you would use a register that is polite but direct—the same register that you would expect that person to use with you. The words you choose, the grammar you employ to say those words, and your tone of voice will change depending on the register in which you are speaking or writing.

How would you characterize the register Trasy uses in addressing her future grandchildren? How might her register change if she were addressing her peers? her high school principal?

INDIVIDUAL LEARNING STRATEGIES

MOTIVATION
Have students, as a class, brainstorm events, ideas, people, etc., that they think most represent their generation. Then have them find objects that symbolize those generational themes.

READING PROFICIENCY
As students read the Guided Writing lesson, you may want to refer them to the Language Arts Survey 1.12, "Seeking Knowledge as an Active Reader," to help them understand the instructions given in the lesson.

ENGLISH LANGUAGE LEARNING
As students read the Guided Writing lesson, have them keep notes of phrases or directions they find difficult to understand. You may want to have a brief conference with students to make sure they understand what the purpose of the lesson is.

SPECIAL NEEDS
You may want to simplify this lesson by asking students to create a time capsule of the history of their own lives. Even simpler, students may choose to create a time line of their lives.

ENRICHMENT
Students may want to challenge themselves by recording the step-by-step procedures the class takes in creating their time capsule. Students may choose to edit their video recording to show to the rest of class and to ultimately include it in the time capsule.

Prewriting

FINDING YOUR VOICE. For more information on voice, refer students to the Language Arts Survey 2.5, "Finding Your Voice," and 3.3, "Register, Tone, and Voice."

continued on page 64

IDENTIFYING YOUR AUDIENCE. This section gives students the option of addressing their great-grandchildren or a different audience. As students decide on an audience, have them discuss the different approaches that could be used for each audience.

WRITING WITH A PLAN. This section provides several options designed to generate ideas for their time capsule. For additional ways in helping students generate ideas for their time capsule and essay, refer students to Language Arts Survey 2.9–2.23, "Gathering Ideas."

> "I have made my world and it is a much better world than I ever see outside."
> —Louise Nevelson

IDENTIFYING YOUR AUDIENCE. Trasy has addressed her remarks to her great-grandchildren. You could select the same audience, or you could envision a different audience in 2088. Perhaps you'd want to address your remarks to those who survive from your own generation.

reader would be able to hear you speak in a conversational tone, relaying your ideas as a teen from one time period to a teen in a different time and space. Be careful, however, if you write conversationally, to explain your terminology as you proceed. The year 2088 will have its own set of slang terms and be unfamiliar with yours.

WRITING WITH A PLAN. Your class needs a framework for deciding the criteria about what to include in the time capsules. In general, start with a commitment to ideas worth passing on to future generations. While each capsule will be a personal one, it should also demonstrate cultural significance for America in the world of the early twenty-first century. It is possible to target items that are simply popular in our present time, but look beneath that popularity to its cultural implications. Trasy models this in her selection of a tongue ring.

Searching for what is important right now can be facilitated by surveying:

- television programs
- computer games
- magazines
- newspapers, especially your school newspaper

A class session devoted to this kind of personal searching would unveil many realities that are joyful as well as disturbing.

If you'd like to include video clips, music, or software, come to consensus about including equipment to make them accessible to the year 2088. Perhaps your storage facility will have a space devoted to equipment.

You are allowed to dictate space requirements—this is your show! Keep individual capsules small, however. It will force you to choose your items thoughtfully. And don't take an easy approach by choosing a film that attempts to capture where we are today—you can assume films from this turn-of-the-century moment will be archived and accessible to all. What you have to offer goes beyond films by providing a personal perspective.

The outline for your essay has three fundamental sections:

Introduction:
- identifies and grabs the attention of your audience
- explains why you are putting a time capsule together
- plants the seed you will return to in the conclusion, the theme of your message to the future

Body:
- lists the items you have included
- explains the criteria used to determine items to include
- contains paragraphs describing each item and its significance

Conclusion:
- returns to the pivotal idea behind your capsule
- reflects about importance and impact

There are as many items to consider including in a time capsule as there are people in our world. Pinpointing the areas you think worthy of future reflection is easier if you chart out your own concerns, or, taking a different tack, your own joys in life as it is. Brainstorm possible categories of both concern and joy with your classmates. Examine Trasy's initial charting for the categories she explored: the environment, individuality, and violence.

Student Model—Graphic Organizer

Current issue	Cause for concern	Cause for celebration	What would symbolize 2000?
The environment	destruction	electric cars	rainforests, cars a battery
Individuality	cliques in conflict	mixed clique activities	body piercings photograph of teens together
One world	ethnic wars	music pulls world's teens together	video of Bosnia guitar string

To help you analyze the perspective you want to share, complete a graphic organizer like the one above. Trasy's initial chart let her explore her thoughts on the environment, individuality, and violence. Other possible categories could include health, technology, spirituality, family life, consumerism, education, freedom, population, war, and peace.

Trasy decided to focus on the concerns she has. She could have just as easily focused on the "good news" about her generation. But because she wanted to emphasize putting her faith in the generations to come, she chose to present the problems she hoped would be solved.

Drafting

Writing the first draft of your essay could involve your explanations for the three items you are choosing. Your overriding theme may come to you as you write. Is there a commonality to your selections—to your concerns and sources of celebration?

You could also begin to write by stating a message you would want to put on a poster for the eyes of the future. Trasy's initial thoughts for her theme were:

Choosing Objects for Your Time Capsule

In choosing the items for your time capsule, you can explore many options for gathering ideas. One of these is **brainstorming**. When you brainstorm, you think of as many ideas as you can, as quickly as you can, without stopping to evaluate or criticize your ideas. You might also look for ideas from professional models. **Professional models** are works by published authors and can serve as a springboard to help you know what you really think about things. A **personal journal** can also be an excellent source of ideas. Reflecting on journal entries can reveal things that are important to you. If you found, for example, that you had written several entries on health and diet concerns, you might want to include an object in your time capsule that symbolized this issue.

See the Language Arts Survey 2.9–2.23, "Gathering Ideas," for more ways to choose objects for your time capsule.

"People move forward into the future out of the way they comprehend the past. When we don't understand something in our past, we are therefore crippled."
—Norman Mailer

STUDENT MODEL—
GRAPHIC ORGANIZER

See the Writing Resource book for a blackline master of the graphic organizer for this lesson.

Drafting

Encourage students to work through the graphic organizer on page 65 to help them generate the theme and the supporting paragraphs of their essay.

Self- and Peer Evaluation

Use the checklist on page 66 for self- and peer evaluation. The checklist is intended to act as a student-friendly rubric to help students identify specific evidence of writing strengths and areas needing improvement. Make sure they provide concrete suggestions for improvement or specific evidence of why the writing works.

Revising and Proofreading

A handout of the proofreading checklist is available in the Teacher's Resource Kit, Writing Resource book 2.45.

Delivering and Receiving Helpful Criticism

To deliver helpful criticism in peer evaluations, follow these guidelines.

- **Be focused.** Concentrate on content, organization, and style. Fix spelling and punctuation errors at the proofreading stage.
- **Be positive.** Let the writer know what he or she has done right.
- **Be specific.** Give the writer concrete ideas for improving his or her work.
- **Be tactful.** Consider the other person's feelings. Do not criticize the writer. Instead, focus on the writing.

To benefit from criticism,

- **Tell your evaluator specific concerns.** If you are wondering if your writing is clear, ask the evaluator if he or she understands it.
- **Ask questions to clarify comments** that your evaluator makes.
- **Accept your evaluator's comments graciously.** Remember that criticism can help you to identify weaknesses and produce better work through revision. If, on the other hand, you think that a given suggestion will not truly improve your writing, you do not have to follow it. There are many ways to strengthen writing. By reflecting on reviewer comments and your own self-evaluation, you will be ready to go on to the next step: revision.

We need to take action to save our world and the beauty of the human body.
The objects she chose reinforced that idea.

Remember that the first draft of any piece of writing is just that—the first. In your next step, you will examine what you seem to be saying and evaluate your structure.

Self- and Peer Evaluation

Ask yourself if you truly believe that each item you have chosen is significant. If you included an item merely to complete the assignment, your completed essay may not ring true to either you or your peers. Use the following questions below to guide you in making revisions of your first draft. If time allows, have another student evaluate your paper.

- Where is the statement of theme for the essay?
- Where do you find support for the theme?
- What is the perspective of the essay—that is, what is the writer's general attitude about the future?
- Does the essay contain an introduction, a body, and a conclusion?
- Has each object in the time capsule been discussed?
- How does the introduction grab the attention of the audience?
- Where does the writer reflect on the importance of his or her theme?
- Has the writer explained his or her criteria for selecting items to include in the time capsule?
- Are the objects in the time capsule good choices? Why, or why not?
- Has the writer reached out with a vision for a future audience?
- What is the topic sentence of each paragraph?

Revising and Proofreading

Review your self- and peer evaluations. Revise your writing after considering your comments. Finally, revise your rough draft for surface errors. Refer to the Language Arts Survey 2.41–2.45 for more information on revising and proofreading.

Student Model—Revised

"Optimism" by Trasy Van Slooten

Hello, my grandchildren. I hope you find this time capsule interesting, and that you are in good health. I participated in this project to show you what it was like when I was a teenager, and to share my opinions about what the year 2000 was all about.

you are reading this should be 2088. Maybe by this time they will have found a miracle drug to keep me living to age 100, and I can open this with you. It is a time of medical miracles. Or, perhaps I've passed peacefully into Summerland. My hands have placed in this capsule three items:

A color, wide-angle picture of a rainforest

Something called a "tongue ring"

A guitar string

This time capsule represents what I foresee as important crossroads for the world around me, crossroads at which I hope my generation made the right decisions. I know you may be using jetpacks for transportation instead of cars, and you may take your vacations on Mars, so these items and their significance may seem petty and foolish. Try to keep an open mind; I think I can explain it all.

A rainforest is something you've likely never seen before. You have probably heard of them in recent folklore, but never realized their importance. Rainforests were great masses of land with trees taller than you could see and just as wide. There were millions of creatures living in them, from insects to monkeys to birds, millions of species. They were sacred to many people for their beauty and magical spirits. Industrialization and "progress" came along and needed a place to build, and builders needed wood. After years of stripping both resources and beauty, bit by bit, from the rainforests, they were all destroyed. Many species died along with the magic of nature. Your generation surely is helping to reconstruct the rainforests, or the world you live in may be dying. Were we able to preserve DNA and reconstruct what we lost?

I have placed a tongue ring in this capsule because it currently has become the latest and greatest craze. Everyone has to have one, and even children in

Language, Grammar, and Style

Paragraphs with Topic Sentences

IDENTIFYING PARAGRAPHS WITH TOPIC SENTENCES. A paragraph often includes a topic sentence that presents its main idea. The topic sentence can be placed at the beginning, middle, or end of the paragraph. Most paragraphs also contain two or more sentences related to the topic sentence. These sentences may illustrate, back up, or elaborate on the topic sentence.

The **main idea** is the foundation of the paragraph. To write clearly and convincingly, you must write topic sentences that are lucid enough to be imbedded in the reader's memory.

In her paragraph about the tongue ring, Trasy's topic sentence is very late in the paragraph and has a strong message.

It makes me wonder how far society will go with self-mutilation.

Topic sentences do not always have to be at the beginning of a paragraph. However, Trasy could have placed hers at the beginning if she had wanted to start out the paragraph with a jolt.

FIXING PARAGRAPHS WITH TOPIC SENTENCES. If peer reviewers are unsure about your topic sentences or mark sentences you don't consider to be the main idea of the paragraph, you probably need to revise your writing.

continued on page 68

Language, Grammar, and Style

Paragraphs with Topic Sentences
LESSON OVERVIEW
In this lesson, students will be asked to do the following:
- Identify Paragraphs with Topic Sentences, 67
- Fix Paragraphs with Topic Sentences, 67
- Use Topic Sentences Effectively, 68

INTRODUCING THE SKILL. Explain to students that the topic sentence in each paragraph is the foundation of the paragraph. Therefore, the topic sentence must be written in a clear, coherent, and convincing way in order to develop a strong paragraph.

PREVIEWING THE SKILL. Refer student to the Language Arts Survey 2.26, "Writing Main Ideas and Supporting Details," for more information on topic sentences.

continued on page 68

Watch out for paragraphs that don't seem to have a topic sentence. Sometimes a missing topic sentence signals a lack of focus.

Trasy's paragraph about the rainforests has no topic sentence. Write a topic sentence that will tie the paragraph together.

A rainforest is something you've likely never seen before. You have probably heard of them in recent folklore, but never realized their importance. Rainforests were great masses of land with trees taller than you could see and just as wide. There were millions of creatures living in them, from insects to monkeys to birds, millions of species. They were sacred to many people for their beauty and magical spirits. Industrialization and companies came along and needed a place to build, and builders needed wood. After years of stripping both resources and beauty, bit by bit, from the rainforests, they were all destroyed. Many species died along with the magic of nature. Were we able to preserve DNA and reconstruct what we lost?

USING TOPIC SENTENCES EFFECTIVELY. Now, write an outline of your essay. Record the topic sentence of each paragraph (label these with Roman numerals I, II, III, IV, and so on) and list the supporting ideas under it (label these with

continued on page 69

Language, Grammar, and Style (CONT.)

PRACTICING THE SKILL. For additional practice, have students exchange their drafts with a partner. Each student should then underline the topic sentence for each paragraph. If students have difficulty finding a topic sentence, have them suggest to their partner ways in which to write a topic sentence based on the suggestions given in this lesson.

elementary grades are beginning to participate in this fad. Some tribes in Africa have traditions of stretching certain parts of their bodies. For example, some stretch, or "gage," their bottom lip, their ears, even their necks. "Gage" means that they create actual holes in the tissue and then stretch the skin to a certain size. These traditions are starting to show up in the United States. It is slowly becoming socially acceptable to have different types of piercing and various gages. How far will it go? It makes me wonder how far society will go with self-mutilation. I hope this tongue ring is quite foreign to you; otherwise, you probably have one. Or has the beauty of the healthy human body returned to a level of respect and honor? Has the beauty of the individual achieved higher status than the group identity of fads and crazes?

The year 2000 is a year of musical trends that cover the spectrum—but it's clear that most young people enjoy a more mellow type of music than in the past two decades. We've moved away from the hard rock, squealing screeching guitars with not-so-nice connotations. Not that this kind of music is gone from the horizon, but it's looked at nostalgically now rather than taking center stage. There is so much to choose from, and much of it comes to us from the rest of the world. We have multi-ethnic sounds in our music that steer us toward multi-ethnic appreciation of one another. Music binds. Has it continued to bring us even closer? Is your world singing the languages of other countries, widening horizons and appreciation for all people?

These items will enlighten you about our times of confusion and concern about our social and our physical environment. Each one represents a crossroads in our blue-green world floating in infinite space, our definition of purity in our bodies and our unique individuality, and

our desire for peace among diversity.
You will know if we chose correctly when
the fork in the road appeared. I trust
you will think back to my time of
change, and you will know you exist
because I believed you, and your
ancestors, would have the power to make
life harmonious again.

Publishing and Presenting

Each capsule embodies the philosophy of each individual in your class, and taken together, a philosophy for your generation.

Presenting the items you have selected and giving the rationale for each would be an illuminating final public sharing. Your speech to the class should not be a simple reading of your essay. Distill your thoughts and present your capsule's contents, using the actual items as visual aids.

Your audience for this speech is, of course, the very people who can help you celebrate advances and progress or help correct the problems and confront the concerns that you have targeted. Your approach may be to convince your audience to continue making progress or take action in a new direction to address concerns. If you believe these are the best of times, emphasize what you think is being done right. This adds action to your theme, exhorts your peers to take your philosophy to heart and reinforce a trend, or to be part of a new direction. This kind of speech would be persuasive in purpose. Or you may take the approach of thoughtfully examining your selections and sharing your insights with the audience. In this case your purpose would be to inform.

Reflecting

Trasy initially thought she would include an article about the "mosh pit" at a rock concert. On second thought, she decided to leave it out because she felt that teen behavior at concerts was only truly controversial in the eyes of parents, and did not seem to be an important enough issue to discuss.

Upon reflection, Trasy decided to focus on issues she found to be more important: the value of our ecosystem, the value of the individual, and the value of music that brings cultures together.

What do your choices for your time capsule reflect about you and what you value? What does your perspective about them reveal about yourself? about your generation and the time in which you live?

letters A, B, C, and so on). An outline covers the major points you make, idea by idea. The perfect test of an essay is whether you can outline it this way. Remember that your topic sentences must link back to your theme. If you have trouble finding the topic sentence in each paragraph, go back and add a more clear topic sentence. For review, refer to the Language Arts Survey 2.24, "Writing Paragraphs."

Maintaining a Writing Portfolio

A **writing portfolio** is a collection of your writing. Your teacher may instruct you to keep either a complete portfolio or a selected portfolio. A **complete portfolio** includes all the pieces that you write; it may also include the first draft through finished product. A **selected portfolio** contains only your very best pieces of writing.

Displaying your work in a portfolio may involve clean, printed copies of final papers. It can also include photographs of multimedia displays carefully documenting each section or aspect of the display, along with the accompanying printed script. If your work is published on an Internet site, your teacher may want you to represent this work in a portfolio by printing each page and link to preserve your product long after the Internet site is no longer available.

Publishing and Presenting

Students may be interested in burying their time capsules together as a class after they have presented their time capsules. Students will need permission from the principal to dig an area on school property before they begin this activity.

Reflecting

Allow students to answer these questions in their journals. Then ask them to work their responses into a comparison-contrast essay on values they hold versus the values their generation holds.

VOCABULARY DEVELOPMENT

Give students the following exercise: Choose twenty words from the Words for Everyday Use list on page 70. Use each word in a sentence, along with context clues to help a reader clearly identify the word. (See the Language Arts Survey 1.16, "Using Context Clues to Estimate Word Meaning.") Next, rewrite your sentences as a fill-in-the-blank quiz, omitting the vocabulary word from each. Exchange papers with a partner and try to complete his or her quiz, choosing from the list of vocabulary words on page 70.

REFLECTING ON YOUR READING

The prompts in Reflecting on Your Reading are suitable as topics for research papers. Refer to the Language Arts Survey 5.18–5.45, "Research Skills." (To evaluate papers, see the evaluation forms for writing, revising, and proofreading in the Assessment Resource book.)

The prompts in Reflecting on Your Reading can also be adapted for use as topics for oral reports or debates. Refer students to the Speaking and Listening Resource in the Language Arts Survey. (To evaluate these projects, see the evaluation forms in the Assessment Resource book.)

UNIT 1 review
The Oral Tradition

Words for Everyday Use

Check your knowledge of the following vocabulary words from the selections in this unit. Write short sentences using the words in context to make the meaning clear. To review the definition or usage of a word, refer to the page number listed or the Glossary of Words for Everyday Use.

adamant, 26	coerce, 56	insolent, 11	rigorous, 57
apprehensive, 28	condemn, 19	invoke, 18	soothsayer, 19
avenge, 48	decree, 26	plaintive, 13	spontaneously, 11
behest, 27	degenerate, 11	proffer, 47	trebly, 27
benevolent, 56	disperse, 58	ravage, 37	unanimous, 27
besiege, 26	diviner, 19	ravine, 17	vanquish, 26
boisterous, 58	edifice, 29	refuge, 59	vanquished, 56
brandish, 27	emit, 29	refute, 28	venerate, 19
brine, 27	envoy, 57	resinous, 29	vengeance, 38
churl, 40	homage, 36	reverently, 13	

Literary Tools

Define the following terms, giving concrete examples of how they are used in the selections in this unit. To review a term, refer to the page number indicated or to the Handbook of Literary Terms.

chronological order, 16	legend, 23, 32, 54	tragedy, 45
dialogue, 54	motif, 32	tragic flaw, 45
dramatic irony, 45	Muse, 10	transcription, 6
folk tale, 23	myth, 10, 16, 23	translation, 6
foreshadowing, 23	oral tradition, 6, 54	

Reflecting on your reading

Genre Studies

1. **MYTHS AND LEGENDS.** What do myths and legends have in common? What are the differences between myths and legends? Explain, using examples from the unit.

2. **ORAL TRADITION.** How do selections from the oral tradition present historical facts, descriptions, and magical events differently from other literary forms? Explain, using examples from the unit.

Thematic Studies

3. **CREATION STORIES.** Compare and contrast the creation story in "The Five Ages of Man" with the story in the selection from the *Popol Vuh*. How were people's ideas about their own creation and about their gods similar in ancient Greece and in ancient Central America?

4. **TRANSFORMATION.** Transformation, or changing form, is a common motif in folklore. Why might this idea be common? Find examples of transformation in the unit.

5. **LEADERSHIP.** The idea of leadership is important in "Popocatépetl and Ixtacihuatl," the selections from the King Arthur legends, and the story of Sundiata Keita. What does each of these selections reveal about the qualities a leader should have? How are Sundiata and Arthur similar and different, and how do both men compare to the Emperor of Tenochtitlan and to Popo? Would Popo have made a good leader?

for your READING LIST

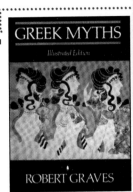

The Greek Myths by Robert Graves. Graves retells the stories of the most important Greek gods and heroes, relating the adventures of Theseus, Oedipus, Heracles, the Argonauts, and the Trojan War in simple, modern language. He summarizes stories, such as the *Iliad* and the *Odyssey*, from ancient storytellers like Hesiod, Homer, and Virgil. Graves also provides commentary and context for the myths, discussing the political and social life of ancient Greece. The index, maps, illustrations, and the organization of the book as a whole make this an excellent resource for students of Greek and Roman mythology.

Independent Reading Activity

STORYTELLING. Choose a story from this unit and read it out loud, either to a friend or just to yourself. Then set the book aside and retell the story as you remember it. Did it change at all? Tell this story or a story from your own life to a friend, group of friends, or classmates. You might want to embellish on it, or to highlight certain sections that you like best. How is telling a story different from reading it? What makes a story fun to tell? If you are in a group, take turns telling stories. How is listening to a story different from reading it on the page? What makes a good story fun to listen to?

Selections for Additional Reading

Black Elk Speaks: Being the Life Story of a Holy Man of the Oglala Sioux as told to John G. Neihardt. In 1930, when Black Elk was an old man, he told his life story to Neihardt, who transcribed his words as Black Elk's son, Ben, translated. Black Elk was a cousin to Crazy Horse. He fought in the battle against General Custer and saw his people's land taken by white soldiers. Black Elk tells his story the way he saw it.

The Once and Future King by T. H. White. This captivating epic novel retells the story of young Arthur, from when he is first apprenticed to Merlin the Magician through his adventures as king. If you like the legend of King Arthur, you will not be able to put this book down.

The Wishing Bone Cycle, Narrative Poems from the Swampy Cree Indians, gathered and translated by Howard A. Norman. Norman retells these poems from traditional Cree storytellers Jacob Nibenegenesabe and Samuel Makidemewabe. The poems include Trickster narratives, sacred stories, and naming stories.

Robert Graves falls into the category of being a classicist and a mythologist with the writing of his book *The Greek Myths*. Graves chronicles the most famous Greek legends and myths while offering his own interpretation of them, taking into account the historical, political, social, and cultural world of Greece at that time. Because of this, *The Greek Myths* has become a reference book for both scholars and for the casual reader.

Independent Reading Activity
Before students begin the storytelling activity under the Independent Reading Activity, encourage them to tell an impromptu story about a family trip or an outing with friends. This pre-storytelling activity should help ease the nerves of students who may be uncomfortable telling stories. Also refer students to the Language Arts Survey 4.20, "Telling a Story." This section provides helpful tips on telling a story that is both effective and engaging.

UNIT SKILLS OUTLINE

The Oyster Gatherers of Cancale, 1878. John Singer Sargent. Corcoran Gallery of Art, Washington, DC.

GOALS/OBJECTIVES

Studying this unit will enable students to
- respond to several different types of poems
- discuss different definitions of poetry and approaches to poetry
- define *personification, image, imagery, tone, repetition, mood, run-on line, simile, paradox, stanza, abstract and concrete words and phrases, rhyme, scheme, rhythm, narrative poem, inversion, meter, allusion, point of view,* and *parallelism* and identify and explain examples of each that they encounter in their reading
- write a personal interpretation of a poem
- Identify and use context clues to define words

Poetry

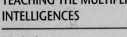

" A poem should not mean
But be. "

—*Archibald Macleish*

UNIT TWO

ELEMENTS of POETRY

The word "poem" comes from the Greek root *poíema,* which means "work," and is derived from *poieín,* "to make." Finding a good definition for poetry is difficult, especially because poems can take so many forms. Poetry does not have to be written down; it can be chanted or sung, spontaneous or memorized. Some poems rhyme and have regular, rhythmical patterns, but others do not. Many poems depend on special devices of sound such as onomatopoeia and alliteration, and many use special techniques of meaning such as metaphor and symbolism. Some are simply designs or word pictures, like this concrete poem:

```
                     O    O
        B A L L          N
```

Poetry differs from prose in that it compresses more meaning into fewer words, and often uses meter, rhyme, rhythm, and techniques such as metaphor and simile. Poetry is often arranged in lines and stanzas as opposed to sentences and paragraphs, and it can be more free in the ordering of words and the use of punctuation. One thing that all poems have in common is that they use imaginative language carefully chosen and arranged to communicate experiences, thoughts, or emotions. Here are some interesting definitions of poetry put forward by important literary figures from the past:

Poetry is . . .

"the spontaneous overflow of powerful feelings."
—William Wordsworth

"the best words in the best order."
—Samuel Taylor Coleridge

"the record of the best and happiest moments of the happiest and best minds."
—Percy Bysshe Shelley

"[language that] strike[s] the reader as a wording of his own highest thoughts, and appear[s] almost a remembrance."
—John Keats

"musical thought."
—Thomas Carlyle

"conceived and composed in the soul."
—Matthew Arnold

"a mixture of common sense, which not all have, with an uncommon sense, which very few have."
—John Masefield

"the supreme fiction."
—Wallace Stevens

"what gets lost in translation."
—Robert Frost

"not an assertion of truth, but the making of that truth more fully real to us."
—T. S. Eliot

TYPES OF POETRY

NARRATIVE POETRY. A **narrative poem** is a verse that tells a story. "A Tree Telling of Orpheus" in this unit is an example of a narrative poem.

DRAMATIC POETRY. A **dramatic poem** is a verse that relies heavily on dramatic elements such as **monologue** (speech by a single character) or **dialogue** (conversation involving two or more characters). Often dramatic poems are narratives as well. In other words, they often tell stories. A **dramatic monologue** is a poem that presents the speech of a single character in a dramatic situation. Mark Doty's "New Dog" (Unit 9) could be considered a dramatic poem.

LYRIC POETRY. A **lyric poem** is a highly musical verse that expresses the emotions of a speaker. There are many types of lyric poems. Among the most common types are the following:

SONNET. A **sonnet** is a fourteen-line poem that follows one of a number of different rhyme schemes. Many sonnets deal with the subject of love.

ODE. An **ode** is a lofty lyric poem on a serious theme. It may employ alternating stanza patterns, developed from the choral ode of Greek

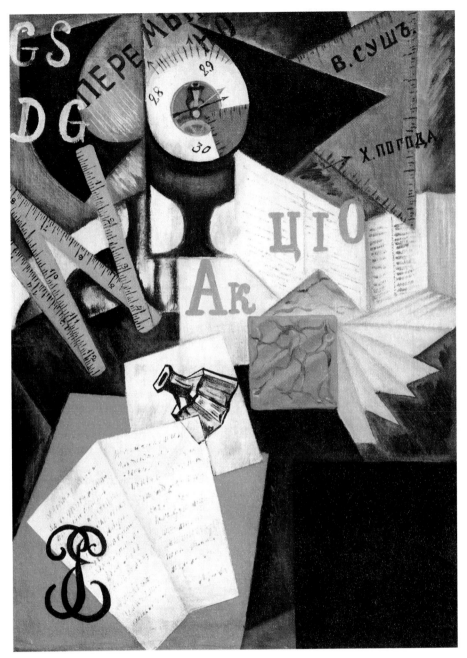

Desk, c.1918. Olga Vladimirovna Rozanova.

Quotables

"It is difficult / to get the news from poems / yet men die miserably every day / for lack / of what is found there."

—William Carlos Williams

INTERNET RESOURCES

If students need proof that poetry matters to all kinds of people, have them visit the website for the **Favorite Poem Project** at http://www.favoritepoem.org. Organized by poet Robert Pinsky, this project records Americans reciting their favorite poems and briefly explaining the poem's importance to them. Tapes from the project (1997–2000) will become part of the Library of Congress archives. An anthology of the poems, *Americans' Favorite Poems,* has been published by W. W. Norton.

ART NOTE

Desk, c.1918. Olga Vladimirovna Rozanova. **Olga Rozanova** (1886–1918) was a Russian artist associated with Suprematism, an abstract style that sought "supremacy of pure feeling or perception in the pictorial arts" over narrative or realistic depictions. Shapes and colors would express feeling rather than objective meaning.

Point out that meter is closely related to the idea of rhythm. *Rhythm* is the pattern of beats or stresses in a line of poetry (or prose). Ask students to give examples of rhythms from everyday life, such as the throb of a heart beating, the beat of drums playing in a marching band, or the clip-clop of horses' hooves on pavement. Explain that when the rhythm of the lines is regular and occurs throughout the poem, the poem is said to have a *meter*.

Have students say aloud the examples of metrical feet in the chart and then give examples of other words that have the same combination of strongly and weakly stressed syllables. In the table of metrical lines, have them read aloud the examples of *trimeter* and *pentameter*.

BIBLIOGRAPHIC NOTE

The following is a lively and insightful guide for reluctant readers of poetry and those who teach them:

John Timpane. *It Could Be Verse: Anybody's Guide to Poetry*. Ten Speed Press, 1995.

---

dramatic poetry. These stanza patterns are called the *strophe*, the *antistrophe*, and the *epode*. However, not all odes follow this pattern.

FREE VERSE. Free verse is poetry that avoids use of regular rhyme, rhythm, meter, or division into stanzas. Examples of free verse poems include "Afternoon" and "The Mystery of Emily Dickinson" in this unit.

ELEGIAC LYRIC. An elegaic lyric expresses a speaker's feelings of loss, often because of the death of a loved one or friend.

IMAGIST POEM. An imagist poem is a lyric that presents a single vivid picture in words.

TECHNIQUES OF POETRY: METER AND STANZA FORM

METRICAL VERSE follows a set rhythmical pattern. **FREE VERSE**, or *vers libre*, does not. Instead, it follows the rhythms of ordinary speech.

METER. The **meter** of a poem is its rhythmical pattern. English verse usually is described as being made up of rhythmical units called **feet**. A **foot** consists of some combination of **weakly stressed** (˘) and **strongly stressed** (/) syllables, as follows:

TYPE OF FOOT	PATTERN	EXAMPLE
iamb, or **iambic foot**	˘ /	afraid
trochee, or **trochaic foot**	/ ˘	freedom
anapest, or **anapestic foot**	˘ ˘ /	in a flash
dactyl, or **dactylic foot**	/ ˘ ˘	feverish
spondee, or **spondaic foot**	/ /	baseball

Some writers on meter also use the term **pyrrhee**, or **pyrrhic foot**, to describe a foot with two weak stresses, as follows:

anapest			pyrrhee	
˘	˘	/	˘	˘
un	re	li	a	ble

The following terms are used to describe the number of feet in a line of poetry:

TERM	# OF FEET	EXAMPLE
monometer	one foot	˘ / Today
		˘ / We play
dimeter	two feet	/ ˘ ˘ / ˘ Following | closely
		/ ˘ ˘ / ˘ Through the | forest
trimeter	three feet	˘ / ˘ / ˘ / God shed | His light | on thee
tetrameter	four feet	/ ˘ ˘ / ˘ / ˘ / In the | greenest | of our | valleys
pentameter	five feet	˘ / ˘ / ˘ / A vast | re pub | lic famed|
		˘ / ˘ / through ev | ry clime
hexameter or Alexandrine	six feet	˘ / ˘ / ˘ / In o | ther's eyes | we see |
		˘ / ˘ / ˘ / ourselves | the truth |

A complete description of the meter of a line includes both the term for the type of foot that predominates in the line and the term for the number of feet in the line. The most common meters in English are **iambic tetrameter** and **iambic pentameter**.

STANZA FORM. A **stanza** is a group of lines in a poem. The following are some common types of stanza:

COUPLET (*two lines*)

We dance round in a ring and suppose,
But the Secret sits in the middle and knows.
—Robert Frost, "The Secret Sits"

TRIPLET OR TERCET (*three lines*)

Children picking up our bones
Will never know that these were once
As quick as foxes on the hill;
—Wallace Stevens, "A Postcard from the Volcano"

SELECTION CHECK TEST 4.2.1 WITH ANSWERS (CONT.)

True or False
1. Rhythm is the repetition of sounds at the ends of words. **False**
2. The line "Once upon a midnight dreary, while I pondered, weak and weary" illustrates internal rhyme. **True**
3. Consonance is used in the phrase "While I nodded, nearly napping." **True**
4. Alliteration is the repetition of initial consonant sounds. **True**
5. Words like *click, snap,* and *pow* illustrate assonance. **False**

QUATRAIN (*four lines*)

By the rude bridge that arched the flood,
   Their flag to April's breeze unfurl'd,
Here once the embattled farmers stood,
   And fired the shot heard round the world.

      —Ralph Waldo Emerson, "Hymn Sung
        at the Completion of the Concord
        Monument, April 19, 1836"

QUINTAIN (*five lines*)

Gaunt the shadow on your green,
   Shenandoah!
The cut is on the crown
   (Lo, John Brown),
And the stabs shall heal no more.

      —Herman Melville, "The Portent"

SESTET (*six lines*)

Over these writings I bent my head.
Now you are considering them. If you
turn away I will look up: a bridge
that was there will be gone.
For the rest of your life I will stand here,
reaching across.

      —William Stafford, "Sending These Messages"

HEPTASTICH (*seven lines*)

In Heaven a spirit doth dwell
   "Whose heart-strings are a lute;"
None sing so wildly well
As the angel Israfel,
And the giddy stars (so legends tell)
Ceasing their hymns, attend the spell
   Of his voice, all mute.

      —Edgar Allan Poe, "Israfel"

OCTAVE (*eight lines*)

The God who made New Hampshire
Taunted the lofty land
With little men;—
Small bat and wren
House in the oak:—
If earth-fire cleave
The upheaved land, and bury the folk,
The southern crocodile would grieve.

      —Ralph Waldo Emerson,
        "Ode, Inscribed to
        W. H. Channing"

TECHNIQUES OF POETRY: SOUND*

RHYTHM. The **rhythm** is the pattern of beats or stresses in a line of verse or prose. A regular rhythmic pattern is called a **meter**.

RHYME. Rhyme is the repetition of sounds at the ends of words. The following are some types of rhyme:

END RHYME. End rhyme is rhyme that occurs at the ends of lines.

INTERNAL RHYME. Internal rhyme is the use of rhyming words within lines.

SLANT RHYME. A **slant rhyme**, half rhyme, near rhyme, or off rhyme is the substitution of assonance or consonance for true rhyme. The pairs *world/boiled* and *bear/bore* are examples.

ALLITERATION. Alliteration is the repetition of initial consonant sounds. Some writers also use the term to describe repeated initial vowel sounds. Derek Walcott's "36. In late-afternoon light the tops of the breadfruit leaves" contains the following example of alliteration: "In late-afternoon light the tops of the breadfruit leaves / are lemon and the lower leaves. . ."

ASSONANCE. Assonance is the repetition of vowel sounds in stressed syllables that end with different consonant sounds, as in "dolls and cloths" in "The Bean Eaters" in this unit.

CONSONANCE. Consonance is a kind of slant rhyme in which the ending consonant sounds of two words match, but the preceding vowel sound does not, as in the words *wind* and *sound*.

ONOMATOPOEIA. Onomatopoeia is the use of words or phrases that sound like the things to which they refer. Examples of onomatopoeia include words such as *pow, caw, clink,* and *murmur.*

*Note: These techniques are used commonly, but not exclusively, in poetry.

ELEMENTS OF POETRY   77

ADDITIONAL QUESTIONS AND ACTIVITIES

Ask students to look for examples of sound techniques in the stanzas on pages 76–77. Have them read the example out loud and then explain which words or parts demonstrate the technique.

GENRE CHECK TEST 4.2.1 WITH ANSWERS

Short Answer
1. Why is it difficult to find a good definition for poetry? **It is difficult to find one good definition because poetry can take so many forms.**
2. Name one way in which poetry differs from prose. *Responses will vary.* **Students may name one of the following differences: poetry compresses more meaning into fewer words; it uses meter, rhyme, and rhythm; it relies heavily on literary techniques such as metaphor and simile; it is often arranged in lines and stanzas as opposed to sentences and paragraphs; and it can be more free in the ordering of words and the use of punctuation.**
3. What do all poems have in common? **All poems use imaginative language carefully chosen and arranged to communicate experiences, thoughts, or emotions.**

Matching
Match each type of stanza with its description. You may not use every letter, and you may use some letters more than once.

a. narrative poetry
b. sonnet
c. ode
d. lyric poetry
e. dramatic poetry
f. free verse
g. imagist poem

1. highly musical verse that expresses the emotions of the speaker; **d**
2. relies heavily on dramatic elements such as monologue or dialogue; **e**
3. has fourteen lines and follows one of a number of different rhyme schemes; **b**
4. lofty lyric poem on a serious theme; **c**
5. avoids use of regular rhyme, rhythm, meter, or division into stanzas; **f**

SELECTION CHECK TEST 4.2.1 WITH ANSWERS (CONT.)

Techniques of Poetry
Mark the stressed and unstressed syllable in the following line:

˘   /   ˘   ˘   /   ˘   ˘   /
We dance round in a ring and suppose

˘   ˘   /   ˘   ˘   /   ˘   ˘   /   ˘   /
But the Secret sits in the middle and knows

Matching
Match each type of stanza with its description. You may not use every letter.
  a. sestet   b. triplet   c. hepastich   d. quintain
      e. couplet   f. octave   g. quatrain

1. eight-line stanza; **f**
2. three-line stanza; **b**
3. four-line stanza; **g**
4. seven-line stanza; **c**
5. two-line stanza; **e**

ADDITIONAL RESOURCES

UNIT 2 RESOURCE BOOK
- Selection Worksheet 2.1
- Selection Check Test 4.2.3
- Selection Test 4.2.4
- Language, Grammar, and Style Resource 3.17
- Speaking and Listening Resource 4.19

GRAPHIC ORGANIZER

Responses will vary. Images might include the following: grass, sides of house, rooster blazing in the light; lit bulbs of lighthouse; silhouettes of fishermen in postcard sunset; smell of baked bread; hum of mosquitoes; darkening road-ruts and faces; indigo sea; plane with green and red wing-lights; stars coming out; droning of planes.

READER'S JOURNAL

Students might enjoy discussing their preferences and observations in small groups.

Literary TOOLS

PERSONIFICATION. Personification is a figure of speech in which an idea, animal, or thing is described as if it were a person. As you read, try to find three examples of personification in the poem.

IMAGE AND IMAGERY. An **image** is language that creates a concrete representation of an object or an experience. The images in a literary work are referred to, collectively, as the work's **imagery**.

Graphic Organizer

As you read, make a cluster chart to list images from the poem. One example has been done for you.

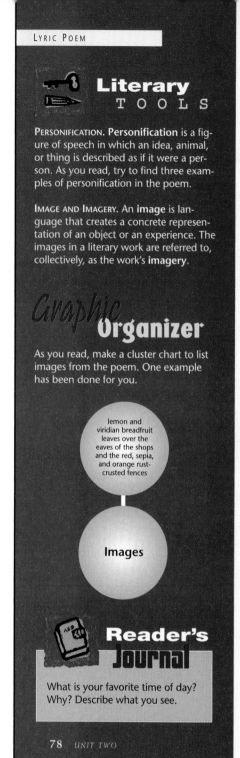

> lemon and viridian breadfruit leaves over the eaves of the shops and the red, sepia, and orange rust-crusted fences

> Images

Reader's Journal

What is your favorite time of day? Why? Describe what you see.

"36. In late-afternoon light the tops of the breadfruit leaves"
by Derek Walcott

Reader's resource

"36. In late-afternoon light the tops of the breadfruit leaves" describes a tropical setting in changing light. It is a prose poem, which is a work of prose, usually a short work, that makes such extensive use of poetic language, like figures of speech and words that echo their sense, that the line between prose and poetry becomes blurred.

About the AUTHOR

Derek Walcott (1930–) is a poet and playwright whose works explore the Caribbean cultural experience. He began his writing career when he was a teenager, and by the age of nineteen he had published twenty-five poems. Born on the Caribbean island of St. Lucia, Walcott attended the University of the West Indies in Jamaica. After graduating, he taught at schools in St. Lucia, Grenada, and Jamaica. He then moved to Trinidad, where he wrote articles and essays for newspapers and journals. Since the 1950s he has lived in the United States, but he continues to spend part of each year in the West Indies.

Walcott's poetry collections include *In a Green Night: Poems 1948–1960* (1962), which celebrates the Caribbean landscape's natural beauty; *Selected Poems* (1964), *The Castaway* (1965), and *The Gulf* (1969), which explore his feelings of personal isolation as a man caught between his European cultural orientation and the black folk cultures of his native Caribbean; *Another Life* (1973), which tells the story of his life; *Midsummer* (1984), which discusses his situation as a black writer in America who has become increasingly estranged from his Caribbean homeland; *Omeros* (1990), which recalls the dramas of Homer in a Caribbean setting; and *Tiepolo's Hound* (2000), which explores the relationship between the poet and the painter Pissarro. Walcott has also written numerous plays. In 1992 he was awarded the Nobel Prize for literature.

GOALS/OBJECTIVES

Studying this lesson will enable students to
- appreciate a poem about a tropical setting
- briefly explain who Derek Walcott is and describe his literary accomplishments
- define *image, imagery,* and *personification* and identify examples of each that they encounter in their reading
- identify functions of sentences
- conduct research to gather information about a Caribbean island

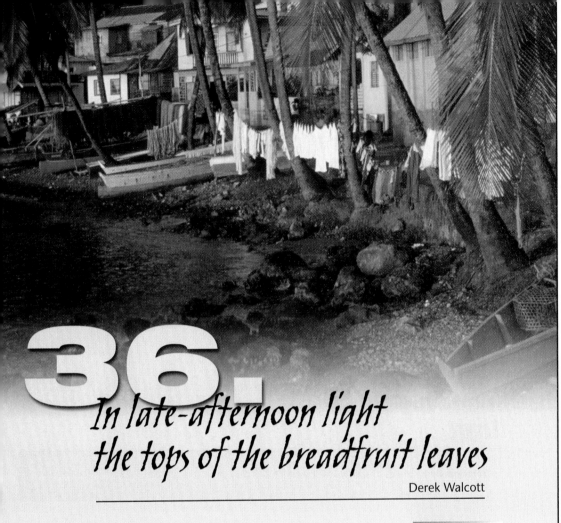

36.

In late-afternoon light the tops of the breadfruit leaves

Derek Walcott

In late-afternoon light the tops of the breadfruit leaves

are lemon and the lower leaves a waxen <u>viridian</u>

with the shaped shadows greenish black over the <u>eaves</u>

of the shops and the rust-crusted fences that are Indian

red, <u>sepia</u>, and often orange; but by then the light has

ripened and grass and the sides of the houses and even a

> What color are the breadfruit leaves in "late-afternoon light"?

words for everyday use	**vi • rid • i • an** (və riʹ dē ən) *adj.*, chrome green. *June watered the <u>viridian</u> plant.*
	eaves (ēvz) *n.*, the lower border of a roof that overhangs the wall. *Pigeons sat on the <u>eaves</u> of Walter's house.*
	se • pia (sēʹ pē ə) *adj.*, brownish gray to dark olive brown color. *The <u>sepia</u> photograph showed a lady in an Edwardian dress.*

ANSWER TO GUIDED READING QUESTION

1. The top leaves are lemon, and the lower leaves are a "waxen viridian."

INDIVIDUAL LEARNING STRATEGIES

MOTIVATION
In small groups, have students create a word web for "Tropical Island." To put the activity in context and help them brainstorm, have them first study a globe or maps to find islands that are in the tropics. Suggest that they draw three main branches for "Sights," "Sounds," and "Smells" in their webs. Then ask them to brainstorm details in each category for ten minutes to complete their web.

READING PROFICIENCY
Read the poem aloud to students to help them become aware of its prose form and the many poetic images the author uses.

ENGLISH LANGUAGE LEARNING
Point out the following vocabulary words:
breadfruit—tropical tree with round fruits that look like bread when baked
silhouette—dark outline against a light background
tangible—possible to touch
dusk—darkness as night falls
infinity—unbounded time and space

SPECIAL NEEDS
Encourage students to work with a partner to write answers for the Guided Reading questions and the Recall questions in the Investigate, Inquire, and Imagine section. Then check their comprehension with the Selection Check Test.

ENRICHMENT
Interested students might enjoy locating other works by Derek Walcott, as well as researching his life. Have students write a one-page analysis of one of Walcott's poems, focusing on his imagery, or a one-page biography.

VOCABULARY FROM THE SELECTION

eaves	satrap
novena	sepia
protract	viridian

1. The time of day is sunset.
2. The speaker sees green and red airplane lights and stars in the night sky.

CROSS-CURRICULAR ACTIVITIES

GEOGRAPHY. Ask students to use a globe or world map to locate the places in the West Indies where Derek Walcott has lived. Have them create an outline map of the Caribbean region and mark the places on the map. Then have them find out why the region is sometimes called the West Indies.

RESPOND TO THE SELECTION

As an alternate activity, have students paint pictures or color samples that fit the lines in the poem that show awareness of color.

SELECTION CHECK TEST 4.2.3 WITH ANSWERS

Checking Your Reading
1. What color are the breadfruit leaves? **The tops of the leaves are yellow and the lower leaves are green.**
2. What are people doing in the cathedral? **They are saying the novena, or a Roman Catholic prayer.**
3. What smells and sounds are described in the poem? **The smell of baked bread and the hum of mosquitoes are described.**
4. How is the sand personified? **The sand is described to be exhaling—as if sand can breathe.**
5. In which direction are the planes headed? **They are headed north.**

Vocabulary in Context
Fill each blank with the most appropriate word from the following Words for Everyday Use. You may have to change the tense of the words.

viridian   eaves
sepia   protract

1. The woman's **sepia** colored skin made her look exotic among the white-faced crowd.
2. The **eaves** along the house needed

---

rooster crossing a yard blazes like a satrap;[1] the lighthouse

is already on, and bulbs, and they are saying the novena[2]

in the cathedral and the fishermen consciously become

silhouettes in the postcard sunset: this is when a

powerful smell of baked bread drifts and when the hum

of mosquitoes becomes tangible, when the road-ruts

deepen and faces that I love harder every year turn

towards the dusk and deepen also under the coconuts.

It is indigo now and the sea will continue to burn

until the last plane crosses with its green and red

wing-lights headed north and it is now definitely

night and the stars come where they were ordered

to protract the idea of patterns to infinity

and the sand exhales and there on the edge of the sea

green and red lights droning where stars and fireflies breed. ▪

What time of day is it when the fishermen look like silhouettes?

What does the speaker see in the night sky?

1. **satrap.** Ruler in ancient Persia
2. **novena.** Roman Catholic period of prayer lasting nine consecutive days

Respond *to the* SELECTION

What lines in the poem show that the speaker is aware of shades of color?

words for everyday use

tan • gi • ble (tan' jə bəl) *adj.*, capable of being perceived by the senses, especially by the sense of touch. *There was a tangible change in the climage as we drove south; I felt beads of sweat on my forehead and struggled to breathe the humid air.*

pro • tract (prō trakt') *vt.*, prolong. *The widow protracted her period of mourning.*

SELECTION CHECK TEST 4.2.3 WITH ANSWERS (CONT.)

to be replaced because they began to rust.
3. Dorian looked like a chameleon in his **viridian** suit.
4. The blistering sun **protracted** our discomfort.
5. The rosebush has a **tangible** characteristic—its lovely fragrance.

Literary Tools
Fill in the blanks using the following terms.

personification   image   imagery

1. "The storm roared through town, expressing its anger" is an example of **personification**.
2. A(n) **image** is a concrete representation of an object or an experience.
3. Poets use **imagery** to paint vivid pictures in the reader's mind.

Investigate, *Inquire,* and Imagine

Recall: GATHERING FACTS

1a. What time of day is it when the poem begins? What time of day is it when the poem ends?

2a. What kind of a setting does the speaker describe?

→ Interpret: FINDING MEANING

1b. How does the speaker feel about nighttime? How can you tell?

2b. Is the speaker a tourist or a resident? How do you know?

Analyze: TAKING THINGS APART

3a. Identify the categories of things that the speaker describes. Also identify vivid verbs used in the poem. Why do you think the poet chose each one? For example, what does it mean for the light to "ripen"? What image does this vivid verb evoke?

→ Synthesize: BRINGING THINGS TOGETHER

3b. What element pushes the poem forward?

Evaluate: MAKING JUDGMENTS

4a. How well does this poem describe the changing light? Would the poem be more or less effective if it described just one object or person in that changing light?

→ Extend: CONNECTING IDEAS

4b. Describe the light as it is right now where you are.

Understanding *Literature*

PERSONIFICATION. Review the definition for **personification** in the Handbook of Literary Terms. What examples of personification did you find in the poem? What is the effect of this personification?

IMAGE AND IMAGERY. Review the definitions for **image** and **imagery** in the Handbook of Literary Terms and the cluster chart you made for Literary Tools on page 78. To which senses does the imagery in the poem appeal? What is your favorite image in the poem? Why?

"36 IN LATE-AFTERNOON LIGHT THE TOPS OF THE BREADFRUIT LEAVES" **81**

RECALL

1a. It is late afternoon at the beginning of the poem. By the end of the poem, night has arrived.

2a. The speaker describes a tropical island setting, as indicated by the coconut and breadfruit trees as well as the sea and sand.

INTERPRET

1b. The speaker thinks nighttime is an almost magical time. The sand exhales and red lights drone as if they were alive.

2b. The speaker is a resident. He speaks of faces that he loves "harder every year."

ANALYZE

3a. The speaker describes plants, animals, people, and objects. Vivid verbs include "ripen," "blazes," "drifts," "crosses," and "exhales." The light ripening evokes an image of fruit; for light to ripen, it becomes its most intense or saturated before fading into night.

SYNTHESIZE

3b. The changing light as day turns into night pushes the poem forward.

EVALUATE

4a. *Responses will vary.* Describing just one object or person would be less effective since it would not capture the whole scene or transport the reader to that scene.

EXTEND

4b. *Responses will vary.*

ANSWERS TO UNDERSTANDING LITERATURE

PERSONIFICATION. The stars come "where they were ordered," the "sand exhales," and the stars "breed." These examples of personification make the night seem to come alive.

IMAGE AND IMAGERY. The images suggest that the man is walking from his house through the village to the sea. The poem's imagery appeals to the senses of sight, smell, and sound. *Responses will vary.*

ANSWERS TO INTEGRATING THE LANGUAGE ARTS

Language, Grammar, and Style
1. declarative
2. exclamatory
3. interrogative
4. declarative
5. imperative

Study and Research
Ask those who listen to the presentations to take notes. Then ask each listener to state two new facts they learned about St. Lucia.

Collaborative Learning
In their introductions, students may wish to mention the types of poems chosen (lyric, narrative, dramatic), the subject matter, and any features the poems have in common, such as tone, mood, or use of figurative language. Have them use the Handbook of Literary Terms if they need to review these terms. Oral readings should show evidence of study and rehearsal, such as clear pronunciation of words, effective use of voice and gesture, and phrasing that shows an understanding of the poet's meaning.

Writer's Journal

1. Write a **postcard** to a friend in the United States describing the island setting of the poem.
2. Imagine you are the speaker. Write a **journal entry** about how things on your island look different to you during the day.
3. Write a **lyric** or **prose poem** describing the light of dusk and nightfall where you live. Fill it with imagery and figurative language.

Integrating the Language Arts

Language, Grammar, and Style

FUNCTIONS OF SENTENCES. Read the Language Arts Survey 3.17, "Functions of Sentences." Then identify each of the following sentences as declarative, interrogative, imperative, or exclamatory.

1. In late-afternoon light the tops of the breadfruit leaves are lemon.
2. How the rooster blazes!
3. Where are the fishermen in the postcard sunset?
4. The faces I love harder every year turn towards the dusk.
5. Watch the stars and fireflies breed!

Study and Research

RESEARCHING ST. LUCIA. Research an aspect of St. Lucia, the Caribbean island where Derek Walcott was born. Topics to consider include demography, geography, government, economy, tourism, and colonial rule. Prepare a graphic to accompany your information and make a presentation to a small group of your classmates. If you are interested in doing some of your research online, access the St. Lucia Internet site at http://landow.stg.brown.edu/post/caribbean/stlucia/stluciaov.html.

Collaborative Learning

EXAMINING BINARY OPPOSITES. As a poet, Derek Walcott has consistently taken on the binary opposites that define his life: white and black, colonizer and colonized, British and West Indian. With a classmate explore one of these binary pairs. Find poems that reflect the binary opposites you chose. Prepare an introduction for the poems. Decide what tone, facial expressions, volume, and body posture to use for your presentation. Then make your presentation to the class. To help you prepare, you might find it useful to refer to the Language Arts Survey 4.19, "Oral Interpretation."

"The Bean Eaters"
by Gwendolyn Brooks

Reader's resource

"**The Bean Eaters**" was inspired by Vincent van Gogh's painting *The Potato Eaters,* shown on the next page. Both the poem and the painting provide a glimpse into the everyday lives of poor people, people who must struggle to get by. "The Bean Eaters," like much of Gwendolyn Brooks's writing, depicts life in an urban black neighborhood. It shows the hardships faced by black people in America, but it also shows the beauty in their lives. Although the elderly couple in the poem "eat beans mostly" and "dinner is a casual affair," they enjoy rich memories of the past.

About the AUTHOR

Gwendolyn Brooks (1917–2000) was born in Topeka, Kansas, and raised in Chicago. Brooks published her first poem, "Eventide," when she was only thirteen. A few years later, she met famous black poets James Weldon Johnson and Langston Hughes, who encouraged her writing. Brooks graduated from Wilson Junior College in 1936, got married in 1938, and had her first child, Henry, in 1940. Meanwhile, she continued to write. In 1945 she published her first book of poetry, *A Street in Bronzeville.* This book of poems about life in an inner-city black neighborhood brought her instant success and critical acclaim. Her second book of poems, *Annie Allen* (1949), won the 1950 Pulitzer Prize in poetry, making Gwendolyn Brooks the first African American ever to win this prestigious award.

Brooks went on to write over twenty books of poetry, including *The Bean Eaters* (1960), from which the poem "The Bean Eaters" was taken. She also wrote a novel, *Maud Martha* (1953); a children's poetry book; and an two-part autobiography. She won numerous awards and fellowships, and earned more than fifty honorary degrees from colleges and universities. In 1968 she was named Poet Laureate of Illinois, and from 1985–1986 she was Consultant in Poetry to the Library of Congress. In her writing, Brooks depicted the struggles of black people and explored how ethnic identity affects people's lives. After 1968, she joined the Black Arts movement founded by poet Leroi Jones (Imamu Amiri Baraka) and, with other African-American writers and activists, she worked to fight racism and to encourage African-American writing.

Literary TOOLS

TONE. Tone is the emotional attitude toward the reader or toward the subject implied by a literary work. As you read, determine the tone of this poem.

IMAGE. An image is language that creates a concrete representation of an object or an experience. As you read, pay attention to the images in the poem.

Organizer

As you read, make a chart to list strong images in the poem and the sense(s) that they appeal to. One example has been done for you.

IMAGE	SENSE(S)
beans	taste sight smell

Reader's Journal

What objects do you have around you in your room? What do they say about who you are?

ADDITIONAL RESOURCES

UNIT 2 RESOURCE BOOK
- Selection Worksheet 2.2
- Selection Check Test 4.2.5
- Selection Test 4.2.6
- Language, Grammar, and Style Resource 3.21
- Speaking and Listening Resource 4.19
- Study and Research Resource 5.40

GRAPHIC ORGANIZER

Responses will vary. Students may suggest the following: yellow pair (sight); chipped china (sight, touch); creaky wooden table (hearing); tin flatware (sight and touch); putting on clothes and putting things away (touch); beads and receipts and dolls and cloths, tobacco crumbs, vases and fringes (sight, touch)

READER'S JOURNAL

As an alternate activity, you might have students bring an object from their room to class and discuss in small groups why that object is important to them and what it reveals about who they are.

GOALS/OBJECTIVES

Studying this lesson will enable students to
- appreciate a poem about ordinary people
- explain how Brooks was inspired by a visual work of art in composing her poem
- define *tone* and explain how the words and phrases in a poem contribute to its tone
- define *image* and highlight examples of different sense images in "The Bean Eaters"
- identify verbs in sentences
- create a bibliography of Brooks's writings
- celebrate poetry by participating in a poetry recital

The Potato Eaters, 1885. Vincent van Gogh.

The Potato Eaters is considered by many scholars to be **Vincent van Gogh's** (1853–1890) first great achievement in painting. A few years earlier, he had been frustrated in his attempts to minister to impoverished miners, but this painting reflects his continuing concern for the poor. Have students compare this painting to van Gogh's later *Wheatfield with Crows* (page 608) for differences in subject matter, as well as stylistic changes in brushstroke and color.

Invite students to respond to van Gogh's painting by writing a poem titled "The Potato Eaters." Before they begin, ask them to study the painting and make notes as they imagine what the daily lives of the people in the peasant family might be like. What are their daily routines? What work do they do? What do they think and talk about? What things do they keep in the rooms of their cottage? Students might wish to pattern their poems after Brooks's poem or choose a form of their own.

INDIVIDUAL LEARNING STRATEGIES

MOTIVATION

Students might enjoy finding a poem by Gwendolyn Brooks that they especially like and copying it onto a sheet of paper. Or they might prefer to "translate" the poem into a visual image that conveys the subject of the poem and author's attitude toward the subject.

READING PROFICIENCY

Read the poem aloud to students before they read it on their own.

ENGLISH LANGUAGE LEARNING

Point out the following vocabulary word:
twinge—sharp, sudden pain

SPECIAL NEEDS

Point out the footnotes before students begin reading. Have students answer the Guided Reading questions and the Recall questions in the Investigate, Inquire, and Imagine section with a partner.

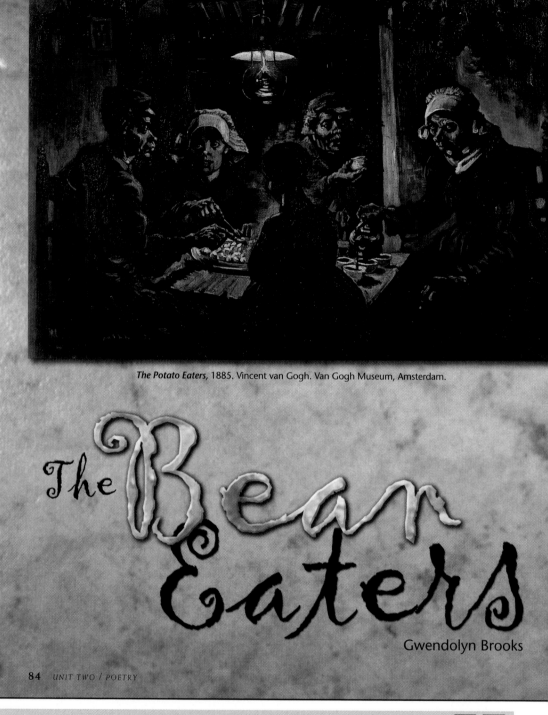

The Potato Eaters, 1885. Vincent van Gogh. Van Gogh Museum, Amsterdam.

The Bean Eaters

Gwendolyn Brooks

INDIVIDUAL LEARNING STRATEGIES (CONT.)

ENRICHMENT

Invite interested students to compare and contrast the images and tone Brooks uses in "The Bean Eaters" with those Derek Walcott uses in the poem on page 79. Have them analyze these features of the two poems in one or more paragraphs. Students may wish to conclude by stating which poem they enjoyed more, and why.

They eat beans mostly, this old yellow pair.

Dinner is a casual affair.

Plain chipware[1] on a plain and creaking wood,

Tin flatware.[2]

What have the two already done? What do they continue to do?

5   Two who are Mostly Good.

Two who have lived their day,

But keep on putting on their clothes

And putting things away.

And remembering . . .

10   Remembering, with twinklings and twinges,

As they lean over the beans in their rented back room

        that is full of beads and receipts[3] and dolls and cloths,

        tobacco crumbs, vases and fringes.   ■

What items are in this couple's apartment?

---

1. **chipware.** China dishes that have been chipped
2. **flatware.** Forks, knives, and spoons
3. **receipts.** Formal written notices that payment for goods or services has been received

Respond to the SELECTION

How do you feel about the people in this poem? How do you think the speaker feels about them?

ANSWER TO GUIDED READING QUESTIONS

1. Day after day, the two have eaten a dinner of beans on creaky wooden table using broken plates and tin flatware, have put on their clothes, and have put things away.
2. Beads, receipts, dolls, clothes, tobacco crumbs, vases, and fringes are all items in their apartment.

SELECTION CHECK TEST 4.2.5 WITH ANSWERS

Checking Your Reading
1. What does the couple usually eat? **They eat beans mostly.**
2. In what way is dinner a "casual affair"? **They use plain china and tin flatware.**
3. Describe the couple. **The couple is described to be "mostly good." They are also simple people with simple lives.**
4. What items are in their apartment? **Beads, receipts, dolls, and cloths are just some of the things that are in their apartment.**
5. What do you think the couple is remembering? *Responses will vary.*

Literary Tools
Fill in the blanks using the following terms.

    tone   image

1. One **image** that is developed in the poem is that of a couple eating beans.
2. The emotional attitude toward the reader or subject in a work is called **tone**.

RESPOND TO THE SELECTION

As an alternate activity, have students respond to one of these questions: Do they admire the couple in the poem? Have they known anyone who was like the couple in some way? Do they think the two are happy with the way they have lived and are living?

LITERARY TECHNIQUE

REPETITION. Repetition is the reuse of a sound, word, phrase, or other element. Have students identify examples of repetition in the poem. Also ask how the author's use of repetition enhances the poem.
Answers
Words and phrases repeated in this poem are "beans," "Two who," "putting," and "remembering."

The author's use of repetition impresses certain images and traits of the couple on the reader's mind. Repetition also helps to unify the poem, establish a rhythm, and create a feeling of simplicity, which reflects the simplicity of the couple's life.

ANSWERS TO INVESTIGATE, INQUIRE, AND IMAGINE

RECALL

1a. Details about what and how the people eat and what they do each day are given in the poem.

2a. They remember both pleasant and unpleasant memories.

INTERPRET

1b. The details, such as the chipped china, having mostly beans for dinner, and living in a rented back room, suggest that they lead a simple life and do not have much money.

2b. These people were probably honest, hardworking people who held ordinary jobs and made a modest income. They are left with their memories and a few possessions, some of which may once have played an important role in their lives.

ANALYZE

3a. The couple has some good memories ("twinklings") that they look back on with joy. They also have some painful memories ("twinges") that bother them.

SYNTHESIZE

3b. The poem implies that most people are average, hardworking, honest people who live modestly and cherish their memories, whether good or bad.

PERSPECTIVE

4a. *Responses will vary.* The poem is realistic in that many families that are poor rely on the same inexpensive foods day after day.

EMPATHY

4b. The poem indicates that the couple is set in their ways and do not need wealth or luxuries to feel content. So even if they won the lottery, they might not change their lives radically.

Investigate, Inquire, and Imagine

Recall: GATHERING FACTS

1a. What details are given about the physical surroundings and the activities of the couple in the poem?

2a. What does the couple in the poem do as they "lean over the beans in their rented back room"?

Interpret: FINDING MEANING

1b. What might the details about physical surroundings and activities say about the lives these people lead?

2b. What sort of lives might these people have had? With what are they left?

Analyze: TAKING THINGS APART

3a. Analyze the nature of the couple's memories.

Synthesize: BRINGING THINGS TOGETHER

3b. What might this poem be saying about most people's lives?

Perspective: LOOKING AT OTHER VIEWS

4a. Do you think it is realistic that the couple eats beans so frequently? Explain your answer.

Empathy: SEEING FROM INSIDE

4b. If you were one of these people, how would your life change if you won the lottery?

Understanding Literature

TONE. Review the definition for **tone** in the Handbook of Literary Terms. What is the tone of this poem? What specific phrases create this tone?

IMAGE. Review the definition for **image** in the Handbook of Literary Terms and the chart you made for Literary Tools on page 83. What are some of the strongest images in this poem? To what senses do they appeal? What images help to characterize the couple in the poem?

Writer's Journal

1. Write an **inventory** of the couple's possessions.

2. Imagine you are one of the people in this poem. Write a **journal entry** about a memory that gives you "twinges."

3. Write a **dialogue** between the two people in this poem as they "lean over the beans in their rented back room." Express their past regrets and future hopes.

ANSWERS TO UNDERSTANDING LITERATURE

TONE. The tone in this poem is one of respect or quiet admiration. Phrases that create this tone include "Mostly Good," "lived their day," "keep on," and "Remembering, with twinklings and twinges."

IMAGE. Strong images in the poem include the beans the couple eat, the chipped china, the creaky wooden table, the tin flatware, putting on clothes, putting things away, and the items that fill their room. These images appeal to the senses of taste, sight, touch, and hearing. Images that help characterize the couple are "old yellow pair" and the image of the two leaning over their simple meal in the cluttered, rented back room.

Integrating the Language Arts

Language, Grammar, and Style

FINDING THE VERB. Read the Language Arts Survey 3.21, "How to Find the Simple Subject and Verb." Then list the verb for each of the following sentences.

1. The old man and woman were eating beans again.
2. They have been using plain chipware and tin flatware.
3. They continually put things away.
4. They live in a rented back room.
5. They had accumulated beads, receipts, dolls and cloths.

Speaking and Listening & Collaborative Learning

DISCUSSION. With several classmates, discuss Vincent van Gogh's *The Potato Eaters*, shown on page 84. Compare and contrast the painting with the poem "The Bean Eaters." To what social class do the people in the painting and in the poem belong? What are the people wearing? What are they eating? What can the people expect for their lives in the future? What is the relationship between the people in the painting and in the poem? What feeling did van Gogh and Brooks want to convey in the painting and in the poem?

Media Literacy

BIBLIOGRAPHY. Create a complete bibliography for Gwendolyn Brooks's writings. You will find it useful to consult The Academy of American Poets Internet site at http://www.poets.org/lit/POET/gbrooks.htm. For help in writing bibliographic entries, read the Language Arts Survey 5.40, "Making Bibliographies and Bibliography Cards."

Collaborative Learning

POETRY RECITAL. Some of the themes apparent in Gwendolyn Brooks's writings include African-American pride, African-American identity and solidarity, African-American humanism, African-American leadership, and *caritas*, a maternal vision. Working with several classmates, find poems by Brooks that exemplify these themes. Then write an introduction for each poem exploring its theme. Practice which facial expressions, body language, gestures, and tone to use when reciting these poems. Finally, present your selection of poems to the class. In preparation for your poetry recital, you might want to read the Language Arts Survey 4.19, "Oral Interpretation."

Language, Grammar, and Style
1. were eating
2. have been using
3. put
4. live
5. had accumulated

Speaking and Listening & Collaborative Learning
Encourage students to locate and discuss other paintings and drawings of peasants by van Gogh in small groups. Ask them if all the works express the same tone.

Media Literacy
Make sure students' entries are in correct bibliographic form and include a range of works both by and about Brooks.

Collaborative Learning
You may want to assess presentations on the following points:
- **INTRODUCTION.** Is the introduction well organized and does it highlight important aspects of the poems, such as theme, content, and style?
- **CLARITY OF DELIVERY.** Are all words pronounced correctly and is the flow of the poem easy for the listener to follow?
- **EXPRESSIVENESS OF DELIVERY.** Are facial expression, body language, gestures, and tone of voice used appropriately and effectively?

ADDITIONAL RESOURCES

UNIT 2 RESOURCE BOOK
- Selection Worksheet 2.3
- Selection Check Test 4.2.7
- Selection Test 4.2.8
- Language, Grammar, and Style Resource 3.21

GRAPHIC ORGANIZER

Other examples of repetition that students should list in students' cluster charts are "the sun," "whirl," "dance," "day is done," "tree," "night," and "like me."

READER'S JOURNAL

As an alternate activity, have students write about activities or thoughts that give them a sense of freedom and joy. Do they ever think about having greater freedom in their life than they do now?

INDIVIDUAL LEARNING STRATEGIES

MOTIVATION
Students might enjoy creating their own poem on the subject of "dreams." Encourage them to use repetition—of sounds, words, phrases, or images—in their poem.

READING PROFICIENCY
Students might benefit from hearing the poem read aloud or on audiocassette. Ask students to notice words or phrases that are repeated in the poem and to jot them down while listening.

ENGLISH LANGUAGE LEARNING
Review or explain the meaning of the punctuation marks used in the poem, including the comma, period, dash, and ellipsis.

SPECIAL NEEDS
On a printed copy of the poem, ask students to circle "fling my arms wide," "place of the sun," "whirl," and "dance" in the first stanza and identify the mood these

(Continued on page 89)

Literary TOOLS

MOOD. Mood, or atmosphere, is the emotion created in the reader by all or part of a literary work. As you read, consider the mood of the poem.

REPETITION. Repetition is a writer's conscious reuse of a sound, word, phrase, sentence, or other element. Look for examples of repetition in the poem.

Graphic Organizer

As you read, make a cluster chart listing the examples of repetition in the poem. One example has been done for you.

"To fling my arms wide."

Repetition

Reader's Journal

When do you feel a sense of celebration in life?

"Dream Variations"
by Langston Hughes

Reader's resource

Langston Hughes's work is concerned with the lives of African Americans, particularly those who live in cities. Hughes was a leading figure of the Harlem Renaissance, a period in which art, literature, and music by African-American artists flourished in Harlem, an area of New York City. Hughes's poetry reflects the spontaneity and lyricism of Harlem jazz at that time. **"Dream Variations"** deals with a common theme in Hughes's writing— African-American pride.

About the AUTHOR

Langston Hughes (1902–1967) was born in Joplin, Missouri, and grew up in Lawrence, Kentucky, and Cleveland, Ohio. He came from a family of abolitionists, who fought for the end of slavery in the United States. Hughes started writing at an early age and published poetry and fiction in his high school magazine. After attending Columbia University for one year and working at a series of odd jobs while developing his skills as a writer. He enrolled at Lincoln University in Pennsylvania, graduating in 1929. By that time, he had published two books of poetry and had become known as a versatile and gifted poet. Hughes became concerned with political issues in the United States and other countries. For twenty years he worked as a columnist for an African-American weekly publication, *The Chicago Defender*. He also wrote the lyrics for a Broadway musical, *Street Scene*. Hughes eventually settled in Harlem, New York, and produced several volumes of poetry as well as a novel and an autobiography.

art note

On the Seekonk, 1892. Edward Mitchell Bannister.

Edward M. Bannister (1827–1901) was hailed as one of the greatest artists of his generation and was the first African American to win a national award in art. This watercolor sketch has a lighter feel than his more familiar oil paintings, which are dense and detailed. Do you think the painting reflects the mood of Hughes's poem?

GOALS/OBJECTIVES

Studying this lesson will enable students to
- empathize with the feelings of the speaker about his dream
- summarize the background and writing career of Langston Hughes

- define *mood* and *repetition* and point out examples of each in the poem
- identify nouns of direct address in sentences
- work collaboratively to research the Harlem Renaissance

Dream VARIATIONS
Langston Hughes

To fling my arms wide
In some place of the sun,
To whirl and to dance
Till the white day is done.
5   Then rest at cool evening
Beneath a tall tree
While night comes on gently,
        Dark like me—
That is my dream!

10   To fling my arms wide
In the face of the sun,
Dance! Whirl! Whirl!
Till the quick day is done.
Rest at pale evening . . .
15   A tall, slim tree . . .
Night coming tenderly
        Black like me.

On the Seekonk, 1892. Edward Mitchell Bannister. National Museum of American Art, Washington, DC.

What does the speaker want to do during the day?

What does the speaker want to do during the evening?

"DREAM VARIATIONS"   89

1. The speaker wants to whirl around and dance during the day.
2. The speaker wants to rest beneath a tree during the evening.

INDIVIDUAL LEARNING STRATEGIES (CONT.)

words suggest. Then help them see that the words "To" and "dream" show that this joy is not yet a reality for the speaker, so the poem's mood includes longing as well as joy.

ENRICHMENT
Invite interested students to create dance movements to accompany an oral reading of the poem.

SELECTION CHECK TEST 4.2.7 WITH ANSWERS

Checking Your Reading
1. What does the speaker want to do in the sun? **He wants to whirl around and dance.**
2. What does the speaker want to do at night? **He wants to rest beneath a tree.**
3. To what does he compare the night? **He compares the night to himself; it is "dark like me."**

Literary Tools
Fill in the blanks using the following terms.

        mood   repetition

1. The emotion created in the reader by a particular literary work is called **mood**.
2. The line "To fling my arms wide" is an example of **repetition** because it is used more than once.

RESPOND TO THE SELECTION

Ask students if they associate the same feelings with day and night that the speaker in the poem does.

ANSWERS TO INVESTIGATE, INQUIRE, AND IMAGINE

RECALL

1a. The speaker uses the adjective *white* to describe day in line 4 and *quick* to describe day in line 13.

2a. The speaker will rest at evening. The words *cool* and *pale* are used to describe evening in lines 5 and 14. The speaker will rest beneath a tree. He uses the adverbs *gently* and *tenderly* to describe the approach of night.

INTERPRET

1b. The speaker dreams of embracing the sunlight and of whirling and dancing all day. He wants to be joyous and free of restraint during daily life.

2b. The speaker thinks of night as gentle, tender, and black like he is. The speaker associates peacefulness, rest, and contentment with night and with being African American.

ANALYZE

3a. Line 9, "That is my dream!," makes it clear that the joy and freedom the poet describes in lines 1–8 are not yet a reality for him.

SYNTHESIZE

3b. The speaker's dream is to be free and active all day long and to rest peacefully at the end of the day.

EVALUATE

4a. The tone is celebratory. This tone is in synch with the speaker's goals because he wants to embrace life and live it to the fullest.

EXTEND

4b. *Responses will vary.* The couple in "The Bean Eaters" seem to move slowly through their life, which follows a predictable pattern. In contrast, the speaker in "Dream Variations" whirls and dances, finding joy and excitement in living spontaneously.

Respond to the SELECTION

What feelings in this poem are associated with day? with night?

Investigate, Inquire, and Imagine

Recall: GATHERING FACTS

1a. What adjectives does the speaker use to describe day in lines 4 and 13 of the poem?

2a. When and where will the speaker rest? What adjectives does the speaker use to describe evening in lines 5 and 14? What adverbs are used to describe the approach of night in lines 7 and 16?

Interpret: FINDING MEANING

1b. What does the speaker dream of being able to do during the day? What attitude does he want to have toward daily life?

2b. How does the speaker feel about night? What emotions does the speaker associate with night and with being African American?

Analyze: TAKING THINGS APART

3a. Identify lines in the poem that suggest the speaker might feel uncomfortable or out of place in his life as it is now.

Synthesize: BRINGING THINGS TOGETHER

3b. What is the speaker's dream?

Evaluate: MAKING JUDGMENTS

4a. Evaluate whether the tone of the poem is in harmony with the speaker's goals for his life.

Extend: CONNECTING IDEAS

4b. How are the lives of the couple in "The Bean Eaters" different from the speaker's dream for his life in "Dream Variations"?

Understanding Literature

MOOD. Review the definition for **mood** in the Handbook of Literary Tools. What is the mood of this poem? Does the mood change? What specific words and phrases create this mood?

REPETITION. Review the definition for **repetition** in the Handbook of Literary Terms and the cluster chart you made for Literary Tools on page 88. What is repeated in this poem? How is the reader affected by this unified repetition?

ANSWERS TO UNDERSTANDING LITERATURE

MOOD. The mood of the poem is one of longing for freedom and happiness. The mood is consistent throughout the poem, although day is associated with jubilation and night with peacefulness and tenderness. Words and phrases that create the mood are "fling my arms wide," "whirl," "dance," "gently," "tenderly," and "That is my dream!"

REPETITION. The actions of flinging arms wide in the sun, whirling, dancing, and resting as night approaches are repeated. The reader is caught up in the excitement and joy of the speaker's dream.

Writer's Journal

1. Write a **birthday card verse** for the speaker, encouraging him to celebrate his birthday in a way consistent with his personality.
2. Imagine you are the speaker. Write a **daily planner entry** for the weekend. List the activities you plan to engage in to live out part of your dream for your life.
3. Imagine you are the speaker. Write a **note** to a friend who is depressed, explaining your philosophy of life and giving him or her encouragement.

Integrating the Language Arts

Language, Grammar, and Style

COMPOUND SIMPLE SUBJECTS AND COMPOUND VERBS. Read the Language Arts Survey 3.21, "How to Find the Simple Subject and Verb." Then identify the simple subject and verb for each of the following sentences.

1. The Harlem Renaissance and the New Negro Movement refer to the same period.
2. Outstanding literary vigor and creativity by African Americans occurred during the 1920s.
3. The movement was centered in Harlem and altered the character of African-American literature.
4. Sophisticated explorations of black life and culture revealed and stimulated a new confidence and racial pride.
5. During this time period, Langston Hughes and Zora Neale Hurston collaborated on a play called *Mule Bone*.

Study and Research & Collaborative Learning

HARLEM RENAISSANCE. Langston Hughes was a leading figure of the Harlem Renaissance. Research the Harlem Renaissance with several classmates. Then have each group member select a work by a writer, artist, or musician who participated in that movement. Write an introduction for the piece you chose. Then present your introduction and share the piece of writing, art, or music with the class. If you want to research a poetry or prose selection online, you might find Northern Kentucky University's Poetry and Prose of the Harlem Renaissance site helpful at http://www.nku.edu/~diesmanij/poetryindex.html. If you want to research a piece of art, contact the University of Texas at Arlington's Harlem Renaissance Art site at http://www.uta.edu/english/V/students/collab13/lbc.html. For those of you interested in music, the University of Kansas's Horn-Blowing and More site at http://falcon.cc.ukans.edu/~adday/ will get you started.

Media Literacy

ONLINE WORKSHEET. Visit the Think Quest Library Internet site for Langston Hughes at http://tqd.advanced.org/3453/less_act/e_lh1.html. After reading a biography of Langston Hughes, you will be asked to answer some questions about his life and to describe the movement in which he participated. Then you will be asked to read another of his poems and analyze it.

ANSWERS TO INTEGRATING THE LANGUAGE ARTS

Language, Grammar, and Style
1. SS: Harlem Renaissance and New Negro Movement; V: refer
2. SS: vigor and creativity; V: occurred
3. SS: movement; V: was centered
4. SS: black life and culture; V: revealed and stimulated
5. SS: Langston Hughes and Zora Neale Hurston; V: collaborated

Study and Research & Collaborative Learning
You may wish to group student presentations by art form or alternate writers, artists, and musicians. In either case, ask students to look for and comment on connections across art forms and similarities and differences among artists within each form.

Media Literacy
Have students work on this activity individually. Ask students to share their poem analyses in small groups after reading the poem they selected out loud.

ADDITIONAL RESOURCES

UNIT 2 RESOURCE BOOK
- Selection Worksheet 2.4
- Selection Check Test 4.2.9
- Selection Test 4.2.10
- Language, Grammar, and Style Resource 3.32

GRAPHIC ORGANIZER

Other repeated elements in the poem include the following: The phrase "In Brueghel's great picture, The Kermess"; words for body parts: *bellies, hips, butts, shanks*; words ending in *–ing*.

READER'S JOURNAL

Ask students to write a short description of what dance means to them. Do they enjoy watching dance performances? Do they enjoy dancing themselves? Why, or why not?

INDIVIDUAL LEARNING STRATEGIES

MOTIVATION
Students might enjoy researching medieval folk music of the 1500s that uses bagpipes, fiddles, and other instruments. Ask students to bring in a recording to play for the class. Students should be prepared to share some information about the music with the class.

READING PROFICIENCY
Have students listen to a recording of the poem before they begin. As they listen, ask them to lightly clap their hands to match the stressed and unstressed beats they hear. You may wish to demonstrate this for the first few lines or clap along with the students throughout the poem.

ENGLISH LANGUAGE LEARNING
Point out the following vocabulary words:
blare—loud, harsh sound
rollicking—carefree and joyous
(Continued on page 93)

Literary TOOLS

RUN-ON LINE AND RHYTHM. A **run-on line** is a line of verse in which the sense or the grammatical structure does not end with the end of the line, but rather is continued on one or more subsequent lines. **Rhythm** is the pattern of beats or stresses in a line of verse or prose. As you read, determine the effect of the run-on lines upon the rhythm of the poem.

REPETITION. Repetition is a writer's conscious reuse of a sound, word, phrase, sentence, or other element.

Graphic Organizer

As you read, make a cluster chart to list the examples of repetition in the poem.

round

Repetition

Reader's Journal

Describe a painting or photograph that captured your imagination or drew you into its story.

"The Dance"
by William Carlos Williams

Reader's resource

"**The Dance**" was published in William Carlos Williams's collection of poetry *The Wedge* in 1944.

ART CONNECTION. "The Dance" describes the dance in Brueghel's painting *Wedding Dance in the Open Air,* which Williams refers to as *The Kermess.* Pieter Brueghel the Elder was a Flemish painter who lived from *circa* 1525 to 1569. Nicknamed "the Peasant Brueghel," he used his powers of minute observation in depicting the living world of field and forest and of sturdy peasants at work and play. He is perhaps best known for his scenes of daily life. His people are stubby in proportion, but lively and solid. His color is remarkably sensitive, as is his feeling for landscape.

About the AUTHOR

William Carlos Williams (1883–1963) was born in Rutherford, New Jersey. After graduating from high school, he began studying to become a dentist, but he soon switched to medicine. In college he met and became friends with Ezra Pound, who would become one of the most influential American literary figures, and Hilda Doolittle, who later achieved fame as the poet and novelist H. D. These relationships fed his interest in literature and poetry and changed his career plans even as he was completing his medical internship in New York City and doing postgraduate study in Leipzig, Germany. In 1912, Williams married and settled in Rutherford, where he began his medical practice. Specializing in pediatrics, Williams delivered thousands of babies, made house calls, and gained a reputation as a dedicated, old-fashioned doctor. He lived and practiced medicine in Rutherford for the rest of his life. It was an occupation that supported his poetry and his other writing. Active in local politics and co-founder of several small magazines, in the 1930s and 1940s he occasionally supported leftist causes, which later resulted in his not being named consultant in poetry at the Library of Congress. A heart attack in 1948 and a series of strokes later caused him to cede his medical practice to one of his two sons, and by 1961 he had stopped writing because of his health. Williams was awarded the Pulitzer Prize in 1962, the Bollingen Prize in 1953, and the National Book Award in 1950, among other honors. His works include *Spring and All* (1923), *The Edge of the Knife* (1932), *The Wedge* (1944), an epic poem with a city as its hero, *Paterson* (1946–1958), and *Pictures from Brueghel* (1962).

GOALS/OBJECTIVES

Studying this lesson will enable students to
- enjoy a lively poem about a work of art
- understand connections between visual and verbal forms of art
- define *run-on line* and *rhythm* and identify and explain examples of each that they encounter in their reading
- define *repetition* and recognize a variety of repeated elements in the selection

Wedding Dance in the Open Air, 1566. Pieter Brueghel the Elder. Detroit Institute of Arts.

The Dance

William Carlos Williams

In Brueghel's great picture, The Kermess,[1]
the dancers go round, they go round and
around, the squeal and the blare and the
tweedle of bagpipes, a bugle and fiddles
5   tipping their bellies (round as the thick-
sided glasses whose wash they impound)[2]
their hips and their bellies off balance
to turn them. Kicking and rolling about
the Fair Grounds, swinging their butts, those
10   shanks[3] must be sound to bear up under such
rollicking measures, prance as they dance
in Brueghel's great picture, The Kermess.

---

1. **Brueghel's . . . The Kermess.** Refers to *Wedding Dance in the Open Air* by Flemish painter Pieter Brueghel the Elder (*circa* 1525–1569)
2. **wash they impound.** Beverage they drink
3. **shanks.** Upper legs

INTERNET RESOURCES

For a sampling of Williams's poems, students can visit the website of the **Academy of American Poets** at http://www.poets.org.

INDIVIDUAL LEARNING STRATEGIES (CONT.)

SPECIAL NEEDS
Ask students to study Bruegel's picture of the wedding dance and then listen carefully to an oral reading of the poem. Based on what they see and what they hear, have a group of students try dancing as Bruegel's peasants might have danced.

ENRICHMENT
Have students do a detailed analysis of the rhythm of the "The Dance." Suggest they begin by typing a double-spaced copy of the poem and then mark the stressed and unstressed syllables in every line. Have students write a brief essay on their analysis.

SELECTION CHECK TEST 4.2.9 WITH ANSWERS

Checking Your Reading
1. What painting is referred to in "The Dance"? *The Kermess* **by Brueghel is referred to in the poem.**
2. What instruments are people playing in the painting? **They are playing bagpipes, bugles, and fiddles.**
3. Describe the way the people are dancing. **They are kicking and rolling about and swinging their hips and butts.**

Literary Tools
Fill in the blanks using the following terms.

rhythm   run-on line   repetition

1. "The Dance" is an example of a **run-on line** because the line of verse doesn't stop at the end of the line.
2. The **rhythm** or the pattern of beats in the poem is very distinct.
3. The writer's conscious reuse of a sound, word, or phrase is called **repetition**.

RESPOND TO THE SELECTION

As an alternative activity, ask students where they would take a breath, or breaths, if they were giving an oral interpretation of "The Dance."

ANSWERS TO INVESTIGATE, INQUIRE, AND IMAGINE

RECALL
1a. The dancers dance and "go round . . . and around." They tip their bellies, turn, and kick and roll about the Fair Grounds.
2a. Bagpipes, a bugle, and fiddles are making the music.

INTERPRET
1b. The dancers are kicking, rolling about, "swinging their butts," and prancing.
2b. The musical instruments are described as squealing, blaring, and tweedling.

ANALYZE
3a. The poem ends with the same words with which it began: "In Brueghel's great picture, The Kermess."

SYNTHESIZE
3b. The sentences run into one another, creating a sense of commotion, constant movement, and energy for the reader.

PERSPECTIVE
4a. The dancers, whose movements are detailed in the poem, had the most impact on the poet.

EMPATHY
4b. *Responses will vary.* The atmosphere of the dance is festive and lively.

Respond to the SELECTION

What emotions would you have experienced if you were one of the dancers in the poem?

Investigate, Inquire, and Imagine

Recall: GATHERING FACTS

1a. What do the dancers do "In Brueghel's great picture"?
2a. What instruments are making the music?

Interpret: FINDING MEANING

1b. What actions on the part of the dancers suggest celebration and enjoyment?
2b. What sounds of the instruments support "the rollicking measures" they create?

Analyze: TAKING THINGS APART

3a. How does the poem come full circle?

Synthesize: BRINGING THINGS TOGETHER

3b. As the dancers "go round" in the painting, how does the poem "go round" on the page?

Perspective: LOOKING AT OTHER VIEWS

4a. Which part of the painting had the most impact on William Carlos Williams?

Empathy: SEEING FROM INSIDE

4b. If you were one of the dancers described in the poem, how would you describe the atmosphere of the dance?

Understanding Literature

RUN-ON LINE AND RHYTHM. Review the definitions for **run-on line** and **rhythm**. Then read the poem aloud to a partner. What effect do the run-on lines have upon the rhythm of "The Dance"? How would you describe the rhythm? You may wish to mark the stressed syllables in each line in order to "see" the rhythm more clearly.

REPETITION. Review the definition for **repetition** in the Handbook of Literary Terms and the cluster chart you made for Literary Tools on page 92. What words and phrases are repeated in the poem? What is the effect of these repetitions?

ANSWERS TO UNDERSTANDING LITERATURE

RUN-ON LINE AND RHYTHM. The run-on lines suggest the nonstop movement of the dancers and help to create a fast-paced rollicking rhythm. The rhythm of the poem, with many stressed beats close together, reflects the rhythm of the music and the event.

REPETITION. The phrase "In Brueghel's great picture" is repeated, and the word *round* is repeated. In addition, references to bellies, hips, butts, and shanks are scattered throughout the poem, and one-syllable words occur frequently. These repeated elements make the dance more vivid in the reader's mind and suggest the lively and endless movement of the dancers.

Writer's Journal

1. Imagine you are one of the musicians at the dance. Write a **journal entry** describing what you saw in front of you as you performed.

2. Write a **descriptive paragraph** about a work of art that you find interesting. In the paragraph, tell what you see when you look at the work of art, describing as clearly as possible what is happening in that work.

3. Write a **critical interpretation** that analyzes how the content of "The Dance" is reflected in the meter, or rhythm, of the poem. Use lines from the poem, with the stressed and unstressed syllables marked, to support your interpretation.

Integrating the Language Arts

Language, Grammar, and Style

UNDERSTOOD SUBJECT: *You.* Read the Language Arts Survey 3.32, "Avoiding Problems Caused by Understood Subjects and Nouns of Direct Address." Then identify the subject and verb for each of the following sentences.

1. Go round and round!
2. Hear the squeal and the blare of bagpipes!
3. The dancers tip their bellies.
4. They dance about the Fair Grounds.
5. Anneke, you look just like a dancer in Brueghel's great picture, *The Kermess*.

Study and Research & Collaborative Learning

ART HISTORY. Form small groups of three or four students to research the life and art of the sixteenth-century Flemish painter Pieter Brueghel the Elder. Assign to each group one of the following topics: biography, paintings, style, social and historical context, and works of other sixteenth-century Flemish painters. After completing the research, have each group present its findings to the rest of the class.

Critical Thinking

COMPARISON AND CONTRAST ESSAY. Another poet who was inspired by a Brueghel painting to write a poem was W. H. Auden, who wrote "Musée des Beaux Arts." Compare and contrast the aim, subject, and theme of Auden's poem with Williams's "The Dance."

Collaborative Learning & Speaking and Listening

ART IDENTIFICATION. Post reproductions of famous paintings around the classroom and make a list of each painting's title and artist. Then cover the paintings. Working with several classmates, take turns describing each painting. Begin with the most subtle details and conclude with the most obvious. The group member who first identifies the painting and its artist earns a point. When all the paintings have been described, the classmate in your group with the highest number of points is the winner.

ANSWERS TO INTEGRATING THE LANGUAGE ARTS

Language, Grammar, and Style
1. S: You; V: Go
2. S: You; V: hear
3. S: dancers; V: tip
4. S: They; V: dance
5. S: Anneke; V: look

Study and Research & Collaborative Learning
Ask students to document their research by listing their sources in alphabetical order and in correct bibliographic form. Encourage them to use print, multimedia, and Internet resources.

Critical Thinking
Students may note that Auden uses Bruegel's painting *Icarus* to illustrate his thesis about suffering, whereas Williams is concerned with concrete particulars rather than abstract ideas. Williams's poem has more immediacy, while Auden's is more reflective.

Collaborative Learning & Speaking and Listening
Suggest that one person in the group act as coordinator to identify correct and incorrect answers.

VOCABULARY FROM THE SELECTION

palpable

GRAPHIC ORGANIZER

Students should consider the following similes:
- "Dumb / As old medallions to the thumb." *Tenor:* poem. *Vehicle:* old medallions.
- "Silent as the sleeve-worn stone / Of casement ledges . . . " *Tenor:* poem. *Vehicle:* sleeve-worn stone.
- "A poem should be wordless / As the flight of birds." *Tenor:* poem. *Vehicle:* flight of birds.
- "A poem should be motionless in time / As the moon climbs." *Tenor:* poem. *Vehicle:* climbing moon.

READER'S JOURNAL

Invite students to write and complete the sentence "A poem should be . . ." at least three times. In each sentence they should state an important quality of a good or engaging poem.

Literary
T O O L S

PARADOX. A **paradox** is a seemingly contradictory statement, idea, or event. As you read, determine what paradox exists in these lines: "A poem should be wordless / As the flight of birds."

SIMILE. A **simile** is a comparison using *like* or *as*. This figure of speech invites the reader to make a comparison between two things. The two "things" involved are the writer's actual subject, the *tenor* of the simile, and another thing to which the subject is likened, the *vehicle* of the metaphor. Look for similes in "Ars Poetica."

Graphic Organizer

As you read, make a chart listing the tenor and vehicle for each simile in the poem. One example has been done for you.

TENOR	VEHICLE
poem	globed fruit

Reader's Journal

What characteristics do good poems and song lyrics have in common that bad ones lack?

"Ars Poetica"
by Archibald MacLeish

Reader's
r e s o u r c e

In a sense, a blade of grass or a cloud in the sky doesn't mean anything. It simply is. It exists. In **"Ars Poetica,"** the title of which means "The Art of Poetry" in Latin, MacLeish argues that a poem is like a blade of grass or a cloud in that respect. In his words, "A poem should not mean / But be." This idea was a central one to the New Criticism, which was a method of literary criticism that became popular after World War I. The New Critics disregarded the emotional effect of the work upon the reader. MacLeish's idea was also central to the Imagist movement of the early 1900s. Imagism championed short verse free of anything except images. "Ars Poetica" was published in MacLeish's collection of poetry *Streets in the Moon* (1926).

About *the*
A U T H O R

Archibald MacLeish (1892–1982), born in Glencoe, Illinois, graduated from Yale in 1915 and earned a law degree from Harvard in 1919. He practiced law in Boston from 1920 to 1923 and lived in France from 1923 to 1928. MacLeish's military experience in World War I and his experiences during the Great Depression in the United States shaped and forged his intellectual interests and work. As his social awareness grew, it was reflected in his writing. MacLeish was Librarian of Congress (1939–1944), Assistant Secretary of State (1944–1945), Boylston Professor at Harvard (1949–1962), and a lecturer at Amherst College (1963–1967). A prolific writer, he was awarded three Pulitzers, two for poetry (*Conquistador* in 1933 and *Collected Poems, 1917–1952* in 1953) and one for drama (*J. B.* in 1958). The play *J. B.* treated the biblical story of Job in a modern setting and idiom. MacLeish's other works include *New Found Land* (1930), *Public Speech* (1936), *The Fall of the City* (1937), *Songs for Eve* (1954), *The Wild Old Wicked Man* (1968), and *Herakles* (1967).

GOALS/OBJECTIVES

Studying this lesson will enable students to
- enjoy a poem about the nature of poetry
- describe the accomplishments of Archibald MacLeish and explain his philosophy as a poet

- define *paradox* and *simile* and identify and explain how these terms apply to "Ars Poetica"
- identify subject, verb, and direct object in sentences
- research the work of other Imagist poets

Leaves in Pond, 1956. Brett Weston.

ArsPoetica

Archibald MacLeish

A poem should be <u>palpable</u> and mute
As a globed fruit,

Dumb
As old medallions[1] to the thumb,

---

1. **medallions.** Medals

INDIVIDUAL LEARNING STRATEGIES

MOTIVATION
Have students study the photograph on page 97. Do they think this image is a fitting one for a poem about the art of poetry? For example, is poetry a reflection of the real world? Can things in nature serve as representations of things in human experience? Have students give a written or oral response to these questions, citing specific examples.

READING PROFICIENCY
Ask students to close their eyes and take three slow, quiet breaths. With eyes still closed, have them listen to the poem read aloud. Afterward, ask them which images lingered in their mind.

ENGLISH LANGUAGE LEARNING
Point out the following vocabulary words:
mute—unable to speak
dumb—lacking the power to speak
casement—window that opens from the sides

SPECIAL NEEDS
Students may have trouble with the idea of paradox. Give some everyday examples: a dead person who lives on, the wisdom of children, a silence that says more than words. Explain that a paradox is something that seems to go against common sense yet may be true. With this definition in mind, help students explore each paradox in the poem one at a time.

ENRICHMENT
After resolving the paradox in lines 7–8, interested students might like to examine other paradoxes in the poem, such as those in lines 1–6 and 15–16. Or they might wish to explore whether the poem lives up to the author's credo "A poem should not mean / But be." Have them write a short essay on one of these subjects.

SCIENCE. Ask students to do research to find out the actual speed at which the moon travels in its orbit around the earth. Also have them find out how many hours elapse between the rising and setting of the moon at different times of the year. Some students might enjoy drawing a diagram or creating a model to explain why the moon's travel time from horizon to horizon is shorter in winter and longer in summer.

SELECTION CHECK TEST 4.2.11 WITH ANSWERS

Checking Your Reading

1. In your opinion, why should a poem be "palpable"? *Responses will vary.* **A poem should be clear and easily perceived so people can understand its message.**
2. What should be "motionless in time"? **A poem should be motionless in time.**
3. How silent should a poem be? **It should be as silent as stone.**
4. What abstract concept is described by "an empty doorway"? **Grief is represented by the empty doorway.**
5. In summary, what should a poem be according to the speaker of "Ars Poetica"? **"A poem should not mean / But be."**

Vocabulary in Context
Write a contextual sentence using the word *palpable*.
Responses will vary.

Literary Tools
Fill in the blanks using the following terms.

paradox   simile   tenor   vehicle

1. A **simile** is a comparison using *like* or *as*.
2. An idea, statement, or event that seems to be contradictory is called a **paradox**.
3. The actual subject of the simile is called a **tenor**.

5   Silent as the sleeve-worn stone
Of casement ledges where the moss has grown—

A poem should be wordless
As the flight of birds.

A poem should be motionless in time
10   As the moon climbs,

Leaving, as the moon releases
Twig by twig the night-entangled trees,

Leaving, as the moon behind the winter leaves,
Memory by memory the mind—

15   A poem should be motionless in time
As the moon climbs.

A poem should be equal to:
Not true.

For all the history of grief
20   An empty doorway and a maple leaf.

For love
The leaning grasses and two lights above the sea—

A poem should not mean
But be.

■

words for everyday use
pal • pa • ble (pal′ pə bəl) *adj.*, capable of being handled, touched, or felt. *There was a palpable lump on the baby's forehead after she fell from the chair.*

Respond *to the* SELECTION

Imagine that you are a photographer who has been asked to provide a concrete image as a striking metaphor for the art of poetry. In your journal, brainstorm a list of possible images, noting your thoughts beside each one.

98   *UNIT TWO / POETRY*

RESPOND TO THE SELECTION

As an alternate activity, have students browse through magazines, cutting out pictures and images that reflect the art of poetry. Then, using the pictures, make a collage.

Investigate, *Inquire,* and imagine

Recall: GATHERING FACTS

1a. What does it mean to be palpable? What, according to the speaker, should be "palpable and mute"?

2a. According to the speaker, what should be "motionless in time"?

3a. How might a poem express a "history of grief"? How might it express love?

Interpret: FINDING MEANING

1b. In what sense should a poem be "palpable"?

2b. What gives the moon the appearance of stillness despite its movement? How might a really good poem lead a reader or listener from part to part without that person being aware of its progression?

3b. Near the end of the poem, the speaker gives examples of how concrete images might be used in place of abstract concepts such as grief and love. What do these images have in common with grief and love?

Analyze: TAKING THINGS APART

4a. Consider the following phrases from the poem:
"all the history of grief"
"An empty doorway and a maple leaf"
The speaker says "A poem should not mean / But be." Which of these lines "means" in the speaker's sense? Which line, in the speaker's sense, simply "is"?

Synthesize: BRINGING THINGS TOGETHER

4b. What kind of poetry do you think the speaker of this poem prefers? Why?

Perspective: LOOKING AT OTHER VIEWS

5a. Would the speaker approve of Gwendolyn Brooks's poem "The Bean Eaters"? Why, or why not?

Empathy: SEEING FROM INSIDE

5b. If you were the speaker, what image would you use to express celebration in your poem?

Understanding *Literature*

PARADOX. Review the definition for **paradox** in the Handbook of Literary Terms. What paradox exists in these lines: "A poem should be wordless / As the flight of birds"? How can the paradox be resolved into a coherent, noncontradictory idea? In other words, how can a poem appear to be wordless and yet be composed of words?

SIMILE. Review the definition for **simile** in the Handbook of Literary Terms and the chart you made for Literary Tools on page 96. What tenor do all the similes share? What qualities do the tenor and vehicle share in the simile "A poem should be palpable and mute / As a globed fruit"?

"ARS POETICA" 99

ANSWERS TO UNDERSTANDING LITERATURE

PARADOX. The paradox is that because a poem is made of words, it seems strange to say that a poem should be "wordless." One might resolve the paradox by saying that a poem should use words in a way that makes the reader unaware of the words but only the images and meanings they suggest.

SIMILE. The tenor for all the similes is a poem. In the simile, the qualities shared by a poem and globed fruit are silence and being concrete.

ANSWERS TO INVESTIGATE, INQUIRE, AND IMAGINE

RECALL

1a. To be palpable is to be clear and easily understood. A poem should be "palpable and mute."

2a. According to the speaker, a poem should be "motionless in time."

3a. A poem might express a "history of grief" with "An empty doorway and a maple leaf." It might express love with "The leaning grasses and two lights above the sea."

INTERPRET

1b. Students might say that a poem should be palpable in the sense that it should use clear and concise imagery and create pictures in the reader's mind.

2b. Because the moon is so far away and thus appears to move very slowly, one does not notice its movement. A good poem might lead a reader or listener from part to part without the reader's sensing the progression by using language in careful and subtle ways.

3b. An empty doorway could signify a person's leaving, which could cause grief to another. A maple leaf in fall could represent an ending; a single leaf could suggest loneliness. Leaning grasses and lights about the sea describe a romantic setting. Leaning grasses might also suggest gentleness and the two lights, perhaps stars, might suggest hopefulness or two people in love.

ANALYZE

4a. The line "all the history of grief" "means" in the speaker's sense. The line "An empty doorway and a maple leaf" simply "is."

SYNTHESIZE

4b. The speaker of the poem most likely prefers poetry that is rich with imagery and creates vivid pictures in the reader's mind. He uses such images in his own poem and expresses this philosophy of poetry in the line "A poem should not mean / But be."

PERSPECTIVE

5a. *Responses will vary.* The speaker would probably approve of "The Bean Eaters" because it uses vivid images to depict the old age of a poor couple. The images speak for themselves without the poet supplying a "history" of the couple or the meaning of the images.

EMPATHY

5b. *Responses will vary.*

ANSWERS TO INTEGRATING THE LANGUAGE ARTS

Language, Grammar, and Style
1. S: MacLeish; V: studied; DO: law
2. S: He; V: perfected; DO: poetic craft
3. S: Ezra Pound and T. S. Eliot; V: influenced; DO: MacLeish
4. S: MacLeish; V: wrote; DO: poems
5. S: students; V: read; DO: "Ars Poetica"

Study and Research & Media Literacy
Have students write a one-page report on their findings.

Study and Research
If students print out their findings, have them number each catalog record to match the list and note the search term they used at the top of the page. Alternatively, you might have students write a bibliographic entry for each item.

Media Literacy
Encourage students to illustrate the cover or inside pages of their booklets with simple, striking images. Some students might also like to explore unusual formats for their booklets, such as accordion pages or mini-sized pages for very short poems. The poems and introduction could be handwritten or typed. In either case, students should proofread all text for correct spelling, punctuation, and legibility.

Writer's Journal

1. Write an **image** for the poem that suggests death.
2. Imagine you are the speaker of the poem. Write your **credo** as a poet. A credo is a creed, or statement of belief.
3. Choose a subject that is especially vivid in your imagination and write an **Imagist poem** about it. Make a list of words that describes how the subject looks, sounds, tastes, feels, or smells. Then write a few lines that create a vivid picture of the subject. Keep all abstract statements of emotion out of your poem.

Integrating the Language Arts

Language, Grammar, and Style

SENTENCE COMPLETERS FOR ACTION VERBS #1. Read the Language Arts Survey 3.22, "Sentence Completers for Action Verbs." Then identify the subject, verb, and direct object for each of the following sentences.

1. MacLeish studied law at Harvard.
2. He perfected his poetic craft in France.
3. Ezra Pound and T. S. Eliot influenced MacLeish.
4. MacLeish wrote some public poems to protest the growing fascism in Europe.
5. Many students read "Ars Poetica" in anthologies.

Study and Research & Media Literacy

LIBRARY OF CONGRESS. Archibald MacLeish became Librarian of Congress in 1939. Research the role of the U.S. Library of Congress in Washington, DC. Who were some of the other Librarians of Congress? Why was MacLeish chosen for the position? What changes was he responsible for? As you begin your research, you may wish to visit the following Internet page on the Library of Congress website: http://lcweb.loc.gov/loc/legacy/librs.html.

Study and Research

USING SEARCHING TOOLS. Read the Language Arts Survey 5.19, "How to Locate Library Materials." Then, use your library's computerized catalog to search for and provide a source of information about each of the following items.

1. MacLeish, Archibald
2. "Ars Poetica"
3. *Conquistador*
4. Imagism
5. William Carlos Williams
6. The New Criticism
7. *J. B.*
8. Gwendolyn Brooks

Media Literacy

IMAGIST POETRY BOOKLET. Use the Internet to locate poems by Imagist poets such as Hilda Doolittle, Ezra Pound, Richard Aldington, F. S. Flint, John Gould Fletcher, Amy Lowell, William Carlos Williams, and Harriet Monroe. Then make a poetry booklet of your favorite Imagist poems. Write a short introduction for your poetry booklet about the aims of the Imagist movement. You can find information about Imagist poetry at the following site, maintained by the English department of the University of Pennsylvania: http://www.english.upenn.edu/~afilreis/88v/imagism-def.html/.

"POETRY"

by Marianne Moore

Reader's resource

Marianne Moore is often called a "poet's poet" because of her complex and subtle use of poetic technique. In using the entire stanza, rather than the word, line, image, or clause, as the unit of the poem, "Poetry" is characteristic of Moore's verse. The poem is also characteristic in its use of a catalog of particulars to define a general term, such as *poetry*. "Poetry" first appeared in Moore's poetry collection *Observations,* which was published in 1924.

About the AUTHOR

Marianne Moore (1887–1972) was born in Kirkwood, Missouri. After graduating from Bryn Mawr College in 1909, she got a job as schoolteacher at the U.S. Indian School in Carlisle, Pennsylvania. In 1918, Moore and her mother moved to New York City, where Moore became an assistant at the New York Public Library. Meanwhile, Marianne Moore wrote poetry. Beginning in 1915, she had her poems published in an English literary magazine called *Egoist.* Two of her friends, recognizing Moore's genius, conspired to get a book of Moore's poetry published without telling her. That first book, entitled simply *Poems,* came out in 1921.

While in New York City, Moore met other poets, such as William Carlos Williams and Wallace Stevens, and began to contribute to the *Dial,* a prestigious literary magazine. Her second poetry collection, *Observations* (1924), won a Dial writing award. After that, Moore worked as the editor of the *Dial,* and continued to do so until the magazine folded in 1929. Moore often made animals the subject of her musings and was a frequent visitor to the Bronx Zoo. She was also a lifelong fan of the Brooklyn Dodgers baseball team, and was once invited to throw out the first ball of the season. Moore and her mother had a close relationship, and they lived together until her mother died.

Throughout her life, Marianne Moore was widely recognized for her writing. Among her many honors were the Bollingen prize, the National Book Award, and the Pulitzer Prize. A collection of her poetry, entitled *The Complete Poems of Marianne Moore,* appeared in 1967.

Literary TOOLS

STANZA. A **stanza** is a group of lines in a poem. Some types of stanzas include the couplet, triplet, quatrain, and quintain. Refer to the Handbook of Literary Terms under "stanza" for the names of additional types of stanzas. As you read, identify the two types of stanzas that are used in the selection.

ABSTRACT AND CONCRETE. An **abstract** word or phrase is one that refers to something that cannot be directly perceived by the senses. *Truth, love, force, theory,* and *sadness* are examples of abstract terms. A **concrete** word or phrase is one that names or describes something that can be directly perceived by one or more of the five senses. *Book, pool, light, garden,* and *car* are examples of concrete terms.

Graphic Organizer

As you read, make a chart. On the left write abstract terms that are mentioned in the poem. On the right write the concrete words or phrases that describe the abstract terms. One example has been done for you.

ABSTRACT TERMS	CONCRETE TERMS
the genuine	hands eyes hair

Reader's Journal

What does poetry mean to you? What types of poems do you enjoy?

ADDITIONAL RESOURCES

UNIT 2 RESOURCE BOOK
- Selection Worksheet 2.6
- Selection Check Test 4.2.13
- Selection Test 4.2.14
- Language, Grammar, and Style Resource 3.22, 3.52

VOCABULARY FROM THE SELECTION

dilate	triviality
insolence	valid
prominence	

GRAPHIC ORGANIZER

Students should include the following abstract and concrete terms:
- what we cannot understand (lines 14–15): bat holding upside down, elephants pushing, . . . the statistician
- poetry (lines 26, 30): imaginary gardens, real toads

READER'S JOURNAL

You may want to define poetry as a class by listing its characteristics on the board. Some students may have fairly narrow notions about what poetry is (e.g., that it rhymes, that it is often about love) that you may want to expand on.

GOALS/OBJECTIVES

Studying this lesson will enable students to
- appreciate a complex poem about poetry itself
- discuss different perspectives on what poetry is and explain the idea of poetry as developed in Moore's poem
- define *stanza* and explain how it applies to "Poetry"

- define and recognize examples of *abstract* and *concrete* words and phrases in the selection
- identify subjects, verbs, and direct and indirect objects in sentences
- define abstract nouns using concrete nouns

1. The speaker dislikes poetry.

INDIVIDUAL LEARNING STRATEGIES

MOTIVATION
To sample Moore's work, students might enjoy reading aloud to each other from one of her poetry collections. Suggest that students browse and skim for poems that seem interesting to them. Then have them take turns reading, commenting if they wish.

READING PROFICIENCY
Moore uses complex sentence structure in her poem. Play an audio-cassette of the poem twice to help students follow Moore's statements. Students may also have trouble with some of the words in the poem. Before they read, go over the footnotes and vocabulary words as a class or in small groups to ensure that students understand all the words.

ENGLISH LANGUAGE LEARNING
Point out the following vocabulary words and expressions:
contempt—hatred
unintelligible—unable to be understood
literalist—person who stresses facts
phenomena—events and objects known through the senses

SPECIAL NEEDS
Encourage students to work with a partner or in a small group to write answers for the Guided Reading questions and the Recall questions in the Investigate, Inquire, and Imagine section.

ENRICHMENT
Invite pairs or small groups of students to present an oral interpretation of Moore's poem. They may wish to review Language Arts Survey 4.19, "Oral Interpretation," before beginning.

At the Table, 1930s. Karl Hofer. Private Collection.

I, too, dislike it: there are things that are important beyond all
    this fiddle.[1]
    Reading it, however, with a perfect contempt for it, one
      discovers in
5   it after all, a place for the genuine
        Hands that can grasp, eyes

What does the speaker dislike?

---

1. **fiddle.** Nonsense

Marianne Moore

that can <u>dilate</u>, hair that can rise
    if it must, these things are important not because a

What real things can poetry describe?

high-sounding interpretation can be put upon them but because
10   they are
useful. When they become so derivative[2] as to become
    unintelligible,
the same thing may be said for all of us, that we
    do not admire what
15   we cannot understand: the bat
        holding on upside down or in quest of something to

eat, elephants pushing, a wild horse taking a roll, a tireless wolf
    under
a tree, the immovable[3] critic twitching his skin like a horse
20   that feels a flea, the base-
ball fan, the statistician[4]—
    nor is it <u>valid</u>
        to discriminate against "business documents and

school-books"; all these phenomena are important. One must
    make a distinction
25   however: when dragged into <u>prominence</u> by half poets the
        result is not poetry,
nor till the poets among us can be
    "literalists of
    the imagination"[5]—above
<u>insolence</u> and <u>triviality</u> and can present

What does poetry combine with imagination?

30   for inspection, "imaginary gardens with real toads in them," shall
    we have
it. In the meantime, if you demand on the one hand,
    the raw material[6] of poetry in
    all its rawness and
35   that which is on the other hand
        genuine, then you are interested in poetry. ∎

2. **derivative.** Imitative
3. **immovable.** Stubborn
4. **statistician.** Expert in statistics
5. **"literalists of the imagination."** Term from W. B. Yeats's *Ideas of Good and Evil*
6. **raw material.** Basic ingredients

words for everyday use

di • late (dī´lāt) *vi.*, become larger or wider. *I had to wear dark glasses outside after the optometrist <u>dilated</u> my eyes.*
val • id (val´id) *adj.*, sound; just. *Mark's criticism of the play was <u>valid</u>; the acting was melodramatic.*
prom • i • nence (prom´ə nəns) *n.*, conspicuousness. *Martin Luther King, Jr., rose to national <u>prominence</u> when he led the successful boycott of buses in Montgomery, Alabama.*
in • so • lence (in´sə ləns) *n.*, disrespectfulness. *When Jared talked back to his father, his father said, "I won't tolerate <u>insolence</u>."*
triv • i • al • i • ty (triv´ē al´i tē) *n.*, something insignificant. *Chandra criticized the <u>triviality</u> of her local news broadcast.*

ANSWERS TO GUIDED READING QUESTIONS

1. Poetry can describe hands that can grasp, eyes that can dilate, and hair that can rise.
2. Poetry combines literal observations, or facts, with imagination.

SELECTION CHECK TEST 4.2.13 WITH ANSWERS

Checking Your Reading
1. How does the speaker feel about reading poetry? **The speaker feels contempt for it.**
2. What makes poetry important? **The usefulness of poetry makes it important.**
3. How does the speaker feel about "high-sounding interpretation"? **The speaker thinks it is unimportant and can be unintelligible.**
4. How does one know if he or she is interested in poetry according to the speaker? **One knows if he or she demands the basic ingredients of poetry and demands it to be genuine.**
5. What were some of your favorite images in the poem? *Responses will vary.*

Vocabulary in Context
Fill in each blank with the most appropriate word from the following Words for Everyday Use. You may have to change the tense of the word.

dilate	valid	prominence
	insolence	triviality

1. John made a <u>valid</u> point about not walking around the streets past 10 P.M.
2. Because of the mayor's <u>prominence</u>, he was able to influence the people to end their strike.
3. The <u>triviality</u> of our conversation emphasized the superficiality of the relationship.

Literary Tools
Fill in the blanks using the following terms.

stanza	abstract	concrete

1. "Porch light" and "red dress" are examples of <u>concrete</u> terms.
2. Something that cannot be directly perceived by the senses is considered to be <u>abstract</u>.
3. A <u>stanza</u> is a group of lines in a poem.

Have students write about whether the selection gave them a new perspective on what poetry is.

ANSWERS TO INVESTIGATE, INQUIRE, AND IMAGINE

RECALL

1a. The phrase "all this fiddle" refers to poetry, most likely to those aspects that are unnatural, unrealistic, or abstract.

2a. We do not admire what we do not understand.

3a. We must make a distinction between what "half poets" create, which is "not poetry," and poetry created by "literalists of the imagination."

INTERPRET

1b. They are useful; that is, they enable the organism to interact with and react to the environment.

2b. "Elephants pushing" is an example of what we do not admire because we cannot understand it.

3b. She has contempt for the work of half poets.

ANALYZE

4a. The half poet simply drags whatever he or she considers important into prominence. The true poet, on the other hand, rises above insolence and triviality as a "literalist of the imagination," who presents for inspection "imaginary gardens with real toads in them."

SYNTHESIZE

4b. The reader or listener should demand "the raw material of poetry in / all its rawness" and "that which is on the other hand genuine." In other words, he or she should demand something concrete and something imaginative or abstract.

EVALUATE

5a. *Responses will vary.*

EXTEND

5b. *Responses will vary.*

Respond *to the* SELECTION

Why does the speaker assume that you, too, dislike poetry?

Investigate, *Inquire,* and imagine

Recall: GATHERING FACTS

1a. To what does "all this fiddle" refer?

2a. What do we not admire?

3a. About what must we "make a distinction"?

Interpret: FINDING MEANING

1b. What quality do "Hands that can grasp" and "eyes / that can dilate" have in common?

2b. Of what is the phrase "elephants pushing" an example?

3b. What is the speaker's attitude toward what the half poets create?

Analyze: TAKING THINGS APART

4a. Compare and contrast the half poet and the true poet.

Synthesize: BRINGING THINGS TOGETHER

4b. Summarize what demands the reader or listener should make on poetry.

Evaluate: MAKING JUDGMENTS

5a. Evaluate whether Moore's own poem "Poetry," according to her definition, is written by a half poet or a real poet.

Extend: CONNECTING IDEAS

5b. Assess a poem in this unit in terms of Moore's definition of poetry.

Understanding *Literature*

STANZA. Review the definition for **stanza** in the Handbook of Literary Terms. What two types of stanzas are used in the selection?

ABSTRACT AND CONCRETE. Review the definition for **abstract** and **concrete** in the Handbook of Literary Terms. Then look at the chart you made in Literary Tools on page 101. How does Moore use abstract and concrete terms to define good poetry?

ANSWERS TO UNDERSTANDING LITERATURE

STANZA. This poem makes use of seven- and eight-line stanzas. A seven-line stanza is a heptastich. An eight-line stanza is an octave.

ABSTRACT AND CONCRETE. The abstract word "poetry" is described by "imaginary gardens" with "real toads," two concrete terms.

Writer's Journal

1. The speaker says of poetry, "I, too, dislike it." Write a **letter** to the speaker, explaining why you do or do not dislike poetry.

2. In the second and third stanzas the speaker gives examples of what is not understandable. Write a **list** to share with a classmate of additional things we cannot admire because we do not understand them.

3. Write a **lyric poem** outlining your own definition of poetry.

Integrating the Language Arts

Language, Grammar, and Style

SENTENCE COMPLETERS FOR ACTION VERBS #2. Read the Language Arts Survey 3.22, "Sentence Completers for Action Verbs: Direct and Indirect Objects." Then identify the subject, verb, direct object, and indirect object if one is present.

1. After college, Moore contributed poetry and criticism to many journals.
2. In 1925 the poet took the job of editing *The Dial,* an influential American journal of literature and arts.
3. LaFontaine's fables gave her the idea to translate.
4. Moore won the admiration of fellow poets throughout her long career.
5. Her work shows us moral and intellectual insights from her close and accurate observation of objective detail.

Language, Grammar, and Style

CONCRETE AND ABSTRACT NOUNS. Read the Language Arts Survey 3.52, "Concrete Nouns and Abstract Nouns." Then, for each of the abstract nouns listed below, write a definition using a concrete noun and underline the concrete noun.

1. citizenship
2. graduation
3. espionage
4. agriculture
5. automation

Collaborative Learning

DEFINING POETRY. With two or three classmates, write a definition of poetry that makes sense to you. Use abstract and concrete language.

Study and Research

RESEARCHING ON THE INTERNET. With a partner, use the Internet to research Marianne Moore's poetry. Visit at least five different websites, and be sure to record the Internet address for each. You might start with the website of the Academy of American Poets, at http://www.poets.org/. See if you can find any of Moore's poems online. If possible, print these out. Then look for comments other people have made about Moore's work. Can you find any quotes from other poets? What other poets was Moore associated with? How does she fit in with the Imagist movement? the Modernist movement? When you have finished your research, turn in a research log that shows each site you visited and what you learned at each site.

Language, Grammar, and Style
SENTENCE COMPLETERS FOR ACTION VERBS #2

1. S: Moore; V: contributed; DO: poetry and criticism; IO: journals
2. S: poet; V: took; DO: job
3. S: LaFontaine's fables; V: gave; DO: idea; IO: her
4. S: Moore; V: won; DO: admiration
5. S: Work; V: shows; DO: insights; IO: us

Language, Grammar, and Style
CONCRETE AND ABSTRACT NOUNS

1. Citizenship, for adults, means having the right to vote.
2. Graduation is marked by receiving a diploma.
3. Espionage occurs when a spy steals secrets.
4. Agriculture is the practice of growing crops.
5. Automation is the use of machines, such as computer-programmed robots, to do work.

VOCABULARY FROM THE SELECTION

enchanted   isolated
feature

GRAPHIC ORGANIZER

Stanza 2: through, rose-, who, eyes: *abac*
Stanza 3: gun, neck, when: *abc*
Stanza 4: place, look, face: *aba*

READER'S JOURNAL

Students might find it helpful to complete a cluster chart listing qualities and traits they attribute to the animal of their choice. Have students read the Language Arts Survey 2.13, "Clustering," first.

LYRIC POEM

Literary
T O O L S

INVERSION. An **inversion** is a poetic technique in which the normal order of words in an utterance is altered. As you read the poem, find an example of inversion in the final stanza.

RHYME SCHEME. A **rhyme scheme** is a pattern of end rhymes, or rhymes at the ends of lines of verse. The rhyme scheme of a poem is designated by letters, with matching letters signifying matching sounds. For example, a rhyme scheme in which the first two lines rhyme together and the third and fourth lines rhyme together would be expressed as an *aabb* rhyme scheme.

Graphic
Organizer

As you read, make a chart listing the last word of each line and the rhyme scheme for each stanza. The first stanza has been done for you.

LAST WORDS	RHYME SCHEME
words rhyme stirs climb	*abcb*

Reader's
Journal

Select an animal that you find beautiful or intriguing. What qualities and traits do you attribute to the animal?

106 *UNIT TWO*

"The Gazelle"
by Rainer Maria Rilke

Reader's
resource

"**The Gazelle**" was published in Rainer Maria Rilke's collection of poetry *New Poems*, which appeared in 1907–1908. In this poem Rilke makes comparisons about aspects of the gazelle in whose beauty the poet sees "the harmony of pure rhyme."

About *the*
AUTHOR

Rainer Maria Rilke (1875–1926) was a German poet considered by many to be one of the most important lyric poets of the twentieth century. His poetry has been translated into many languages. Rilke's early collections are not considered to be his best; however, after writing them, he paid two visits to Russia which are said to have deepened his religious beliefs and to have given his work greater depth. Rilke worked for a time as secretary to the French sculptor Rodin, and the relationship influenced some of his poetry. Among Rilke's most popular poetry collections are *Neue Gedichte* (*New Poems*) and *Die Sonette an Orpheus* (*Sonnets to Orpheus*). His personal letters and correspondence also have literary value. In *Letter to a Young Poet*, Rilke gives advice to a young poet.

GOALS/OBJECTIVES

Studying this lesson will enable students to
- enjoy a lyric poem about an animal
- identify Rainer Maria Rilke as a lyric poet and describe his literary contributions
- define *inversion* and give an example of this element in "The Gazelle"

- define *rhyme scheme* and identify the rhyme scheme in a specific poem
- work with contractions in sentences
- visit a photo gallery on the Internet of Rilke's life

The Gazelle[1]

Rainer Maria Rilke

Gazella Dorcas[2]

<u>Enchanted</u> thing: how can two chosen words
ever attain the harmony of pure rhyme
that pulses through you as your body stirs?
Out of your forehead branch and lyre climb,

5   and all your <u>features</u> pass in simile,[3] through
the songs of love whose words, as light as rose-
petals, rest on the face of someone who
has put his book away and shut his eyes:

to see you: tensed, as if each leg were a gun
10   loaded with leaps, but not fired while your neck
holds your head still, listening: as when,

while swimming in some <u>isolated</u> place,
a girl hears leaves rustle, and turns to look:
the forest pool reflected in her face. ∎

What enchanted, harmonious thing is being described in the opening lines?

Of what songs, or poems, does the gazelle remind the speaker?

1. **Gazelle.** Swift, timid, deer-like animal native to Africa
2. ***Gazella Dorcas.*** Scientific name of small, northern African gazelle with horns shaped like a lyre (a type of harp)
3. **all . . . simile.** All your features can be compared to other things

words for everyday use

en • chant • ed (en chant' əd) *adj.*, invested with magical powers. *The trees danced in the <u>enchanted</u> forest.*
fea • ture (fē' chər) *n.*, distinct part or quality. *One <u>feature</u> that Carol liked about her house was the gabled roof.*
i • so • lat • ed (ī' sə lāt' əd) *adj.*, separate; remote. *I love to picnic in <u>isolated</u> places that are far away from the city.*

CROSS-CURRICULAR ACTIVITIES

MUSIC. Ask students to design a soundtrack to be used as musical background for an oral reading of the poems, "The Gazelle" or "Afternoon." Give them the choice of annotating a copy of the poem with the type of music, musical instruments, or musical effects they would use at different points or locating actual musical excerpts that fit the content and mood of the poem. If students select musical excerpts, have them play them for the class and explain their choices.

SELECTION CHECK TEST 4.2.15 WITH ANSWERS

Checking Your Reading
1. What are words compared to in lines 6 and 7? **Words are compared to rose petals.**
2. Where do the words rest? **The words rest "on the face of someone who has put his book away and shut his eyes."**
3. How are the gazelle's legs described? **They are described as "a gun loaded with leaps."**

Vocabulary in Context
Fill in each blank below with the most appropriate word from the following Words for Everyday Use. You may have to change the tense of the word.

    enchanted   feature   isolated

1. The **enchanted** woman bewitched us with her beautiful song.
2. We put the dogs in **isolation** because our guests were allergic to them.
3. My friend's best **feature** is his ability to make people laugh.

Literary Tools
1. What is inversion? **An inversion is a technique used in poems where the normal order of words is altered.**
2. What is the rhyme scheme of the third and forth stanza? **The rhyme scheme is** *abacdc.*

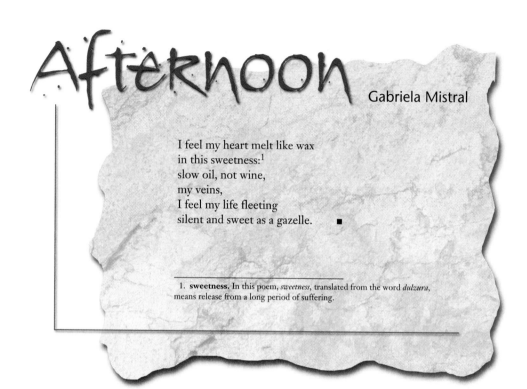

Afternoon

Gabriela Mistral

I feel my heart melt like wax
in this sweetness:[1]
slow oil, not wine,
my veins,
I feel my life fleeting
silent and sweet as a gazelle. ■

---

1. **sweetness.** In this poem, *sweetness,* translated from the word *dulzura,* means release from a long period of suffering.

About the Related Reading
Gabriela Mistral (1889–1957) was one of the most popular poets in the Spanish-speaking countries of Latin America. In 1945 she became the first Latin American woman to receive the Nobel Prize for literature. Mistral's work often explores large issues within the human experience, such as death and birth. **"Afternoon"** focuses on the human emotions surrounding aging and approaching death. Mistral's unique, vivid imagery evokes in only a few lines a strong emotional response. "Afternoon" was published in Mistral's collection of poetry *Lagar* in 1954.

Respond *to the* SELECTION

Have you ever experienced something so beautiful that it was almost impossible to describe to someone? Choose such an experience and try to put it into words.

Investigate, *Inquire,* and Imagine

Recall: GATHERING FACTS

1a. What are the two "chosen words" referred to in the first line of "The Gazelle"? What pulses through the body of the subject of the poem?

2a. To what is each leg of the animal compared in stanza 3 of "The Gazelle"?

Interpret: FINDING MEANING

1b. What does the speaker feel toward the subject of the poem? Which details in stanza 1 convey this feeling?

2b. What similarities exist between a loaded gun and the legs of a gazelle?

Analyze: TAKING THINGS APART

3a. In "The Gazelle," how would you describe the girl referred to in stanza 4 and the gazelle?

Synthesize: BRINGING THINGS TOGETHER

3b. Why does Rilke compare a girl "swimming in some isolated place" to a gazelle? What aspect of the gazelle is he trying to convey with this image?

Evaluate: MAKING JUDGMENTS

4a. In the poem "Afternoon" what would be the difference between slow oil and wine flowing in a person's veins? Why might Mistral have chosen those two liquids for the poem?

Extend: CONNECTING IDEAS

4b. Compare and contrast the characteristics of the gazelle in the Rilke and Mistral poems.

Understanding *Literature*

INVERSION. Review the definition for **inversion** in the Handbook of Literary Terms. Consider the last line of the poem, "the forest pool reflected in her face." What would the line say if you switched the words *forest pool* and *face?* Which is the more common phrase? Why do you think the author chose to invert this idea? What inversions can you think of?

RHYME SCHEME. Review the definition for **rhyme scheme** in the Handbook of Literary Terms and the chart you made for Literary Tools on page 106. What is the rhyme scheme of the poem?

"THE GAZELLE" 109

ANSWERS TO UNDERSTANDING LITERATURE

INVERSION. The last line would say "her face reflected in the forest pool," which is the more common phrase. The author may have chosen to invert this idea to show how the natural world affects individuals. Students might come up with inversions like these: a hand brushing hair/hair brushing a hand; the sun rising above the mountains/mountains rising above the sun.

RHYME SCHEME. The rhyme scheme of the poem is *abcb abac abc aba.*

Language, Grammar, and Style
1. cannot
2. will not
3. do not
4. should not
5. have not

Media Literacy & Study and Research
Encourage students to print the photographs they find if possible. Ask volunteers to read their descriptions while displaying or projecting the photographs on an overhead projector for the class.

Applied English
Have students get together in small groups to read their letters aloud.

Writer's Journal

1. Imagine you are the speaker. Write a **nature log** about the gazelle that you have just observed. Describe his appearance and actions.
2. Speaking to the gazelle, Rilke says, "all your features pass in simile." Write a **simile** comparing an aspect of an animal to something else. (A simile is a comparison using *like* or *as*.)
3. Write a three- or four-line **stanza** about an animal, using Rilke's rhyme scheme for one of the stanzas of this poem. Address the animal using *you* and *your*.

Integrating the Language Arts

Language, Grammar, and Style

CONTRACTIONS. Read the Language Arts Survey 3.29, "Working with Negatives and Contractions." Then write out all contractions in the following sentences.

1. According to Rilke, two chosen words can't attain the harmony of pure rhyme evident in the gazelle.
2. The forehead branch and lyre won't stop climbing.
3. Why don't you like words as light as rose petals?
4. The observer shouldn't move a muscle when a gazelle passes by.
5. Why haven't you swum in an isolated place?

Media Literacy & Study and Research

PHOTO GALLERY. Visit Middle Tennessee State University's Rainer Maria Rilke website at http://www.mtsu.edu/~dlavery/rmrpics.htm where you will find a photo gallery about Rilke's life. Read biographical information about Rilke's life in the library or on the Internet. Then write a paragraph describing six of the photos in the photo gallery, explaining the influence these people or places had on Rilke. For portraits of Rilke, explain what was going on in his life during that time period or describe his personality and appearance.

Applied English

PERSONAL LETTER. Imagine you are the young poet with whom Rilke corresponded with in his *Letter to a Young Poet*. Read part of this book of correspondence. Then write a letter to Rilke telling him what advice you find helpful and plan to follow.

"Success is counted sweetest . . ."
by Emily Dickinson

Reader's resource

Most of Emily Dickinson's work focused closely on one aspect of life or human nature, such as love, death, or spirituality. Because of the quiet, secluded life Dickinson led, people are often amazed at the power, diversity, and timelessness of her poetry. Her work has been translated into other languages and read by millions of people around the world. **"Success is counted sweetest . . ."** discusses the true nature of success and who can really appreciate it.

Amherst College Archives and Special Collections

About *the* AUTHOR

Emily Dickinson (1830–1886) was born in Amherst, Massachusetts. Dickinson's life was outwardly rather uneventful, and she wrote most of her poems in the same house. Only once did she venture outside of Massachusetts, and only a few times did she leave her small village. Dickinson consciously chose to live in a quiet, secluded manner, associating with a small circle of friends and family. Her surprisingly passionate, witty, and insightful verse reveals an eventful inner life, nourished by seclusion and privacy. Seven of her poems were published in her own lifetime without her knowledge. A complete collection of her work (edited by Thomas Johnson and Theodora Ward) was available for the first time in 1955.

At her death, which occurred in her house in Amherst, Massachusetts, where she was born, Dickinson had produced over one thousand poems. These explored a tremendous range of subjects in language remarkable for its wit, inventiveness, and economy of expression. Taken as a whole, her verses, most of them quite brief, present a complex self-portrait, a sort of spiritual autobiography. Her voice is alternately humble and proud, intimate and aloof, ecstatic and sorrowful, but always questioning, reflective, and intensely alive. She was a keen observer of particulars, but capable of sudden, breathtaking generalizations that synthesized these particulars into truths.

Literary TOOLS

RHYME. Rhyme is the repetition of sounds at the ends of words. Types of rhyme include **end rhyme**, the use of rhyming words at the ends of lines; **exact rhyme**, in which the rhyming words end with the same sound or sounds; and **slant rhyme**, in which the rhyming sounds are similar but not identical. An example of exact rhyme is the word pair *stale/fail*. An example of slant rhyme is the word pair *rot/rock*. As you read, determine the types of rhymes used in the poem.

METER. The **meter** of a poem is its rhythmical pattern. English verse usually is described as being made up of rhythmical units called **feet**. This poem is written primarily in **iambs**, a type of poetic foot in which an unstressed syllable is followed by a stressed syllable, as in the words *afraid* and *release*. However, Dickinson varies the meter in her poem.

Graphic Organizer

As you read, mark the stress pattern of this poem. The first line has been done for you.

Success is counted sweetest

Reader's Journal

When have you experienced success? How have you felt when you wanted to succeed but did not?

ADDITIONAL RESOURCES

UNIT 2 RESOURCE BOOK
- Selection Worksheet 2.8
- Selection Check Test 4.2.17
- Selection Test 4.2.18
- Reading Resource 1.17
- Language, Grammar, and Style Resource 3.66, 3.67
- Speaking and Listening Resource 4.19

GRAPHIC ORGANIZER

Students should mark the stress pattern as follows:

Success is counted sweetest
By those who ne'er succeed.
To comprehend a nectar
Requires sorest need.

Not one of all the purple Host
Who took the Flag today
Can tell the definition
So clear of Victory

As he defeated—dying—
On whose forbidden ear
The distant strains of triumph
Burst agonized and clear!

READER'S JOURNAL

As an alternative activity, have students brainstorm a time when they succeeded at something they wanted to achieve and a time when they failed to succeed. What feelings do they associate with success and failure?

GOALS/OBJECTIVES

Studying this lesson will enable students to
- appreciate a poem about success
- describe Emily Dickinson's life and how it contrasted with her poetry
- define *rhyme* and locate and explain examples of rhyme in the selection
- define *meter* and discuss the varied meter in Dickinson's poem
- identify personal and indefinite pronouns in sentences
- find the etymology of various words
- discuss Dickinson's work and the type of life she led

1. The person who can provide the clearest definition of victory is he who is defeated or dying.

INDIVIDUAL LEARNING STRATEGIES

MOTIVATION
Have students make a time line on which they list American women poets whose work is widely respected. Have them use reference works to find the dates for each poet's birth date and mark and label it on the time line.

READING PROFICIENCY
Point out that Dickinson's use of dashes in line 9, and in her poetry as a whole, is unconventional. Here, instead of signaling a sudden change of thought, the dashes serve more to make the reader pause and pay special attention to the word they surround.

ENGLISH LANGUAGE LEARNING
Give students the following vocabulary words:
counted—valued
sorest—most desperate
host—army
strain—portion of a piece of music or a speech

SPECIAL NEEDS
To get a clearer idea of the meter, and where it changes, students may benefit from hearing the poem read aloud.

ENRICHMENT
Challenge students to unravel the meaning of the phrase "forbidden ear" in line 10 of the poem.

RESPOND TO THE SELECTION

Encourage students to think back to a time when they have fallen short of success. Did success seem at that moment to be a far-off, much-desired condition?

Success is counted sweetest . . .

Emily Dickinson

Success is counted sweetest
By those who ne'er succeed.
To comprehend a nectar[1]
Requires sorest need.

5   Not one of all the purple Host
Who took the Flag today[2]
Can tell the definition
So clear of Victory

As he defeated—dying—
10   On whose forbidden ear
The distant strains of triumph
Burst agonized and clear! ■

> *According to the speaker, who can provide the clearest definition of victory?*

---

1. **nectar.** Sweet liquid; here the speaker means "reward."
2. **purple Host/Who took the Flag today.** The speaker means "honored soldiers."

Respond *to the* SELECTION

Do you agree with the idea expressed by the speaker of this poem about who appreciates success the most? Personally, do you appreciate success most when you have attained it or when you have fallen short of it?

The Mystery of Emily Dickinson

Marvin Bell

Sometimes the weather goes on for days
but you were different. You were divine.
While the others wrote more and longer,
you wrote much more and much shorter.
I held your white dress once: 12 buttons.
In the cupola, the wasps struck glass
as hard to escape as you hit your sound
again and again asking Welcome. No one.

Except for you, it were a trifle:
This morning, not much after dawn,
in level country, not New England's,
through leftovers of summer rain I
went out rag-tag to the curb, only
a sleepy householder at his routine
bending to trash, when a young girl
in a white dress your size passed,

so softly!, carrying her shoes. It must be
she surprised me—her barefoot quick-step
and the earliness of the hour; your dress—
or surely I'd have spoken of it sooner.
I should have called to her, but a neighbor
wore that look you see against happiness.
I won't say anything would have happened
unless there was time, and eternity's plenty. ∎

About the Related Reading

Poet and writer **Marvin Bell** encourages young people to find poetry in their everyday lives. "The words of songs are a kind of poetry," he says. Contemplating Emily Dickinson in his poem **"The Mystery of Emily Dickinson,"** Bell tells of his experience of holding one of her dresses, which opens up a possibility in his own life, one that is all the sweeter for not being actualized.

Quotables

"The Soul selects her own
Society—
Then—shuts the Door—
To her divine Majority—"

—Emily Dickinson

SELECTION CHECK TEST 4.2.17 WITH ANSWERS

Checking Your Reading

1. By whom is success counted sweetest? **Success is counted sweetest by those who never succeed.**
2. Who is the "purple Host who took the Flag today"? **The "purple Host" is a group of soldiers being honored in a ceremony.**
3. Who can best tell the definition of victory? **The person who is defeated or dying can best tell the definition of victory.**

Literary Tools

1. Give an example of an exact rhyme from the "Success is counted sweetest..." **An exact rhyme occurs in lines 2 and 4— succeed/need.**
2. What is a slant rhyme? **A slant rhyme is a rhyme between words that sound similar but is not identical.**
3. What is meter? **Meter is the rhythmical pattern in a poem.**

ANSWERS TO INVESTIGATE,
INQUIRE, AND IMAGINE

RECALL

1a. Success is counted sweetest by those who never succeed.

2a. The sounds of triumph are particularly painful and clear on the ears of the defeated and dying.

INTERPRET

1b. The speaker feels that victory or success is never fully appreciated unless a person feels a great need for it.

2b. The sounds of victory might be clearer to those who have failed or who have not yet attained success because they want it so much and feel it is far off or impossible to achieve.

ANALYZE

3a. The value of success seems to increase in direct proportion with one's need for and distance from it.

SYNTHESIZE

3b. Those who always win may not appreciate their easily won victories, while those who never win may magnify the importance of the victories they feel will never come to them.

PERSPECTIVE

4a. *Responses will vary.* Some students may say that Dickinson did not seem to have been driven to achieve worldly success in her lifetime, and thus chose to write about success as an observer. Others might note that she wanted to make a universal rather than personal statement in the poem.

EMPATHY

4b. *Responses will vary.* Some students may speculate that Dickinson probably felt successful in maintaining close personal relationships with important people in her life.

Investigate, Inquire, and Imagine

Recall: GATHERING FACTS

1a. For whom is success "counted sweetest"?

2a. On whose ear are the sounds of triumph particularly painful and clear?

Interpret: FINDING MEANING

1b. What role does "need" play in the appreciation of victory or success?

2b. Why might the sounds of victory be clearer to certain people?

Analyze: TAKING THINGS APART

3a. Analyze how distance and need apply to the idea of success as expressed in the poem.

Synthesize: BRINGING THINGS TOGETHER

3b. How does the speaker feel about those who always win, those who never win, and their different concepts of victory?

Perspective: LOOKING AT OTHER VIEWS

4a. Much of Emily Dickinson's poetry is personal and subjective. Why do you think she chose to discuss success objectively rather than through her own experience with it?

Empathy: SEEING FROM INSIDE

4b. If you were Emily Dickinson, what would you count as successes in your life?

Understanding Literature

RHYME. Review the definition for **rhyme** in the Handbook of Literary Terms. What types of rhymes are used in this poem? What are the effects of these types of rhymes? Does the rhyming in the poem enhance or undercut the poem's theme?

METER. Review the definition for **meter** in the Handbook of Literary Terms and the stress pattern you completed for Literary Tools on page 111. Where in the poem does the meter vary? What is the effect of changing the meter? Point out the word that is emphasized because of this change. Why do you think Dickinson chose to emphasize this word?

Writer's Journal

1. Write a **review** of a book, movie, or TV show in which a character experienced victory and appreciated it because of his or her struggle.

2. Successes do not have to be large triumphs such as trophies won or bonuses earned. Write a **letter** congratulating a friend for the small triumphs of daily life he or she has won.

3. Dickinson expresses a different idea about success in each stanza. Try to think of a fourth variation on Dickinson's theme, and write a fourth **stanza** for the poem.

ANSWERS TO UNDERSTANDING LITERATURE

RHYME. Two types of end rhyme are used in this poem: exact rhyme (lines 2 and 4, 10 and 12) and slant rhyme (lines 6 and 8). The effect of this rhyme is to emphasize the ideas behind the rhyming words. The rhyme enhances the theme of the poem by focusing the reader's attention on related ideas such as "succeed" and "need."

METER. The meter varies in line 9 of the poem. The effect of changing the meter is to make the reader pause and take notice of the word that ends the line— *dying.* Dickinson may have emphasized this word because it is the dying, who can never succeed, who appreciate success most.

Integrating the Language Arts

Language, Grammar, and Style

PERSONAL AND INDEFINITE PRONOUNS. Read the Language Arts Survey 3.54, "Types of Pronouns." Then identify the personal pronouns and the indefinite pronouns in the following sentences.

1. Emily Dickinson? Anyone can appreciate her poetry.
2. Few people during her life knew she was writing volumes of verse.
3. A recluse, she socialized with almost no one.
4. The editors of the *Springfield Republican?* They took an interest in some literary matters.
5. You can read something about their correspondence with Dickinson in her biography.

Vocabulary

ETYMOLOGIES. Read the information about etymologies in the Language Arts Survey 1.17, "Using a Dictionary." Using a dictionary that gives etymologies, list the Latin word that gives *victory* and *triumph* come from. Then make a list of other English words related to *victory* and *triumph*.

Collaborative Learning & Speaking and Listening

INTERVIEW. Read the Related Reading, "The Mystery of Emily Dickinson" by Marvin Bell. Like "Success is counted sweetest . . .," Bell's poem is about possibilities. With your classmate, conduct two interviews. For the first, one classmate interviews Emily Dickinson about the possibilities expressed in her poem, while the other classmate plays the role of Emily Dickinson. For the second, one classmate interviews Marvin Bell about the possibilities expressed in his poem, while the other classmate plays the role of Marvin Bell. When you have completed the interviews, hold a class discussion about what you learned about possibilities from the two poems.

Speaking and Listening & Study and Research

DISCUSSION. Read or see *The Belle of Amherst*, a 1976 play by William Luce based on the life of Emily Dickinson. Next, research what life was like for women in the 1800s. Finally, hold a class discussion about Dickinson's life and work. Was her quiet life common for a woman in her position? What do you think was expected of her by her family and friends? Why do you think she was able to create verse that so many people today find important and inspiring? Do you believe it is necessary for poets and other artists to travel the world and live exciting lives in order to have ideas and insight?

Language, Grammar, and Style
1. PP: her; IP: anyone
2. PP: her, she; IP: few
3. PP: she; IP: no one
4. PP: They; IP: some
5. PP: their, her; IP: something

Vocabulary
You might want to have students create word webs instead of lists and ask them to cluster related words. For example, they might group words by part of speech.

Collaborative Learning & Speaking and Listening
To help students explore the possibilities in Bell's poem before they conduct their interviews, have them answer the questions on page 114 as well as the following:
1. What quality in Dickinson's poetry does the speaker seem to highlight in the first stanza?
2. What is there plenty of time for, according to the speaker?
Answers
1. The speaker seems to highlight the intensity of Dickinson's poetry.
2. There is plenty of time to explore the mystery of Emily Dickinson's poetry—to get to know the young girl.

Speaking and Listening & Study and Research
If time is limited, you might play an excerpt from an audiotape of the play or show students a portion of the film. In their research, encourage students to investigate firsthand accounts or look for quotations by women who lived during that time. You might save the last discussion question for a writing or journal activity.

ADDITIONAL RESOURCES

UNIT 2 RESOURCE BOOK
- Selection Worksheet 2.9
- Selection Check Test 4.2.19
- Selection Test 4.2.20
- Language, Grammar, and Style Resource 3.66, 3.67
- Speaking and Listening Resource 4.19

READER'S JOURNAL

Ask students if they associate a certain image or atmosphere with their experience. How would they describe that image or atmosphere?

INDIVIDUAL LEARNING STRATEGIES

MOTIVATION
Ask groups of students to write a short screenplay for a scene in a film in which two people in love must say farewell. Have them decide the reason for the parting, the scene where it will take place, and other important background details. They should then write both dialogue and stage directions for the scene. For a film, these could include what the camera will focus on as well as the items listed under "stage directions" in the Handbook of Literary Terms.

READING PROFICIENCY
Have student read the poem aloud to a partner. Before they read, ask them to read silently and think about how they can use the tone of their voice to reflect the tone of the poem.

ENGLISH LANGUAGE LEARNING
Point out that the names of the Chinese cities are pronounced as written.

SPECIAL NEEDS
Students might be puzzled by the speaker's shift of address in lines 3–4. Help students identify the third-person and first-person pronouns that signal this shift.

(Continued on page 117)

Literary TOOLS

IMAGE. An **image** is language that creates a concrete representation of an object or an experience. What image do you find in "I heard my love . . ."?

TONE. Tone is the emotional attitude toward the reader or toward the subject implied by a literary work. As you read, determine the tone of the poem.

Reader's Journal

Have you ever experienced so strong an emotion that time seemed to stand still for a moment? Write about your experience and the powerful emotions it evoked in you.

116 *UNIT TWO*

"I heard my love . . ."
by Tzu Yeh

Reader's resource

Like many short poems, "I heard my love . . ." depends on the power of a single image to express a strong emotion or to carry the reader to another place and time. Poets and lyricists from all cultures and times have used images from nature to reflect human experiences. As you read this poem, close your eyes and try to picture the image the author creates.

About the AUTHOR

Tzu Yeh (sixth century) was a woman said to have written a collection of one hundred and twenty-four short, popular songs, often about love. However, people now believe that these songs were actually written over a period of about three hundred years by many different authors living in Soochow and Nanking, areas of southern China.

art note

Landscape of the Four Seasons, 1600s. Shen Shih-ch'ing.

Chinese landscape painters of the Ming dynasty saw their works as visual poetry which expressed the harmony and simplicity of nature. What similarities do you see in the method of the poet and the painter?

GOALS/OBJECTIVES

Studying this lesson will enable students to
- respond to a brief lyric love poem
- identify Tzu Yeh as a lyric poet and describe her literary contributions
- define *image* and recognize the central image in a poem

- define *tone* and determine the tone of a poem
- identify adjectives and adverbs in sentences
- create a map of China

Landscape of the Four Seasons, 1600s. Shen Shih-ch'ing.

"I heard my love . . ."

Tzu Yeh

I heard my love was going to Yang-chou[1]

And went with him as far as Ch'u-shan.[2]

For a moment when you held me fast in your outstretched arms

I thought the river stood still and did not flow.　　　■

---

1. **Yang-chou.** City in south-central China, north of the Yangtze River
2. **Ch'u-shan.** City in eastern China

CROSS-CURRICULAR ACTIVITIES

SOCIAL STUDIES. Have students use a CD–ROM or print encyclopedia to locate three important facts about the city of Yang-chou in modern or ancient times. Have them share their findings with the class.

SELECTION CHECK TEST 4.2.19 WITH ANSWERS

Checking Your Reading
1. What did the speaker hear about her love? **The speaker heard that her love was going to a city called Yang-chou.**
2. In what city did the speaker end up? **The speaker ended up in Ch'u-shan.**
3. What did the river seem to do while the speaker's love held her in his arms? **The river seemed to stand still.**

Literary Tools
1. What image can be found in the last line of the poem? **The image of the river standing still and not flowing is in the poem.**
2. How do you think the speaker feels? What is the overall tone of the poem? *Responses will vary.* **Students may say that the tone is one of longing. At the same time, it conveys the joy of being in love.**

INDIVIDUAL LEARNING STRATEGIES (CONT.)

ENRICHMENT
Students might read several haiku, which also use powerful natural imagery. Then have students write their own haiku in which human emotions change the speaker's perception of nature. The poems should be written in the proper form for haiku (one five-syllable line, one seven-syllable line, and a final five-syllable line).

ART NOTE

Landscape of the Four Seasons, 1600s. Shen Shih-ch'ing. Like the poem, the painting is very simplified. The painter has left plenty of open space in the composition, which is similar to the way the poet has left out specific details.

RESPOND TO THE SELECTION

Students might compare the literal and symbolic meanings of the last two lines of the poem. Do students think the river really stopped flowing? If not, what could the speaker of the poem mean? Encourage students to think of other ways the poet could have expressed the same idea.

ANSWERS TO INVESTIGATE, INQUIRE, AND IMAGINE

RECALL
1a. The speaker's love was going to a distant city in China and the speaker went with him as far as Ch'u-shan.
2a. The people in the poem love each other.

INTERPRET
1b. She does not want to part from her love.
2b. The river seems to stop flowing. The speaker was so romantically moved by the farewell embrace of her love that time and motion seemed frozen.

ANALYZE
3a. In the first two lines, the speaker might be talking to a friend or relative. In the last two lines, the speaker is talking to her love.

SYNTHESIZE
3b. The speaker speaks these four lines in her love's absence. The purpose of the first two lines is for the speaker to explain why she went away. The purpose of the last two lines is to remind the speaker of her love's love and to comfort herself in his absence.

Respond *to the*
SELECTION

What sort of feeling does this poem express? Is it similar in theme to any popular songs of today? Explain.

Investigate, Inquire, *and* Imagine

Recall: GATHERING FACTS

1a. What situation is described in the first two lines of the poem?

2a. How do the two people in this poem feel about each other?

Interpret: FINDING MEANING

1b. Why does the speaker travel with her love?

2b. What does the river seem to do? Why?

Analyze: TAKING THINGS APART

3a. Identify whom the speaker is addressing in the first two lines and in the last two lines.

Synthesize: BRINGING THINGS TOGETHER

3b. When does the speaker speak these four lines? What is the purpose of the first two lines? What is the purpose of the last two lines?

Understanding *Literature*

IMAGE. Review the definition for **image** in Literary Tools in Prereading. An image is also the vivid mental picture created in the reader's mind by the language. What mental picture is created in your mind when you read "I heard my love . . ."? What sense does this image appeal to?

TONE. Review the definition for **tone** in the Handbook of Literary Terms. Examples of the different tones that a work may have include familiar, ironic, playful, sarcastic, serious, and sincere. What is the tone of the poem? How does the speaker feel? How do you know?

ANSWERS TO UNDERSTANDING LITERATURE

IMAGE. The image is of the speaker being held in her love's outstretched arms. This image appeals to the sense of touch.

TONE. The tone of the poem is longing. The speaker feels the joyful emotion of love as well as sadness at being separated from her love. In his absence, she longs for him. The speaker's feelings are evident in her remembrance of their farewell embrace, which was so intense that the "river seemed to stop flowing," or time seemed to stand still.

Writer's Journal

1. Imagine you are the speaker. Write a **letter** to your love telling him what happened to you when you parted and how you feel about him.

2. Write **song lyrics** that express longing for something or someone.

3. On one sheet of paper, freewrite some images of nature, scenes in school or home, or familiar objects. Your images can be beautiful, strange, or unpleasant. On another sheet of paper, freewrite about some of the most important feelings and experiences you have had. Include feelings of sadness, happiness, anger, and excitement. Then try to connect one feeling to one of your images. Finally, write your own short **verse** in which you focus on a single feeling and a single image. You might start your poem by describing a situation, and then end your poem with one or two lines that express a particular feeling about the situation.

Integrating the Language Arts

Language, Grammar, and Style

MODIFIERS: ADJECTIVES AND ADVERBS. Read the Language Arts Survey 3.66, "Adjectives" and 3.67, "Adverbs." Then identify each underlined word as an adjective or an adverb.

1. The speaker was really in love with her <u>ardent</u> lover.
2. He told her <u>sadly</u> that he had to go away on a long trip.
3. She went with him <u>gladly</u> to busy Ch'u-shan.
4. When they said their last goodbye, her lover held her in his <u>outstretched</u> arms.
5. It seemed to the <u>dejected</u> speaker that the river was not flowing perceptibly.

Speaking and Listening & Collaborative Learning

ORAL INTERPRETATION. Form small groups of three or four students. As a group, select several love poems. Then find a piece of visual art that expresses the theme of each poem. Interpret your poems for the class, deciding what tone, facial expressions, gestures, and body language to use. Then explain why the piece of visual art goes with the poem. Before you present your poems, read the Language Arts Survey 4.19, "Oral Interpretation."

Collaborative Learning

MAP OF CHINA. With a classmate, make a map of China. On the map label the cities of Yang-chou and Ch'u-shan.

ANSWERS TO INTEGRATING THE LANGUAGE ARTS

Language, Grammar, and Style
1. adjective
2. adverb
3. adverb
4. adjective
5. adjective; adverb

Speaking and Listening & Collaborative Learning
Set up a time for the groups to present their poems to the class. To evaluate student performance, see the evaluation from in the Assessment Resource book.

Collaborative Learning
Encourage students to consult a detailed atlas of China to find the two cities. Ask them to also label the major modern cities of China, such as Beijing, Shanghai, and Hong Kong, on the map, in a different color, and major rivers or canals near the two cities mentioned in the poem.

ADDITIONAL RESOURCES

UNIT 2 RESOURCE BOOK
- Selection Worksheet 2.10
- Selection Check Test 4.2.21
- Selection Test 4.2.22
- Language, Grammar, and Style Resource 3.29
- Study and Research Resource 5.18

VOCABULARY FROM THE SELECTION

anguish   knoll
asunder   rivery
fell

GRAPHIC ORGANIZER

In lines 145–146, Orpheus makes his earth-journey and lost what he sought. In lines 147–148, Orpheus is killed violently. In lines 149–150, Orpheus's head sings in death as he is swept out to sea.

READER'S JOURNAL

Ask students to spend time freewriting about books, movies, music, paintings, and photographs they enjoy. Encourage them to list everything that comes to mind, even things that they have never thought of as "art." Then ask them to think about why these different things appeal to them.

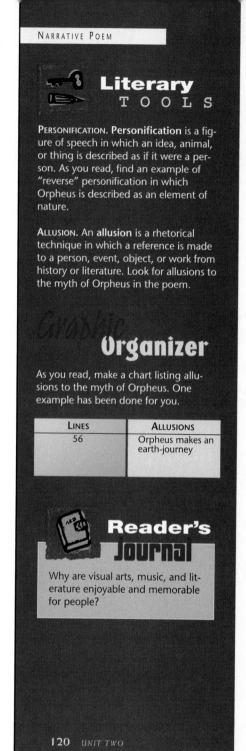

Literary TOOLS

PERSONIFICATION. Personification is a figure of speech in which an idea, animal, or thing is described as if it were a person. As you read, find an example of "reverse" personification in which Orpheus is described as an element of nature.

ALLUSION. An **allusion** is a rhetorical technique in which a reference is made to a person, event, object, or work from history or literature. Look for allusions to the myth of Orpheus in the poem.

Graphic Organizer

As you read, make a chart listing allusions to the myth of Orpheus. One example has been done for you.

LINES	ALLUSIONS
56	Orpheus makes an earth-journey

Reader's Journal

Why are visual arts, music, and literature enjoyable and memorable for people?

"A Tree Telling of Orpheus"
by Denise Levertov

Reader's resource

Denise Levertov's poem **"A Tree Telling of Orpheus,"** which first appeared in *Stony Brook* (1968), makes allusions to the myth of Orpheus. According to Greek mythology, Orpheus, the son of a Muse, was a gifted poet-musician. His music was said to be so beautiful and magical that it made animals and trees dance and rocks grow ears. Orpheus was very much in love with his wife, Eurydice, and when she died from a snake bite he was devastated. He went to the land of the dead and begged Hades, king of the underworld, to allow Eurydice to come back home to him. His beautiful music and his sadness moved Hades. Hades agreed to let Orpheus take Eurydice back, but he set one condition. Orpheus was forbidden to look back as they left the land of the dead. The couple went happily on their way. Just before they made it into the upper world, Orpheus looked back to share his joy with Eurydice—and she disappeared forever.

Orpheus was later killed in a violent manner by the women of Thrace. His head and his lyre, still making music, were floated down the river Hebrus into the city of Lesbos. There the head of Orpheus became an oracle, or a source of knowledge and wisdom.

About the AUTHOR

Denise Levertov (1923–1997) ws an American poet who was born in Essex, England, where she grew up and was educated at home by her mother. Her father, a Russian Jew, became an Anglican minister. During World War II, Levertov worked as a civilian nurse in London. Her first book of poetry, *The Double Image*, was published in 1946. In 1948 she immigrated to the United States, and in 1955 she became an American citizen. Levertov published over a dozen books of poetry and two books of essays. She also taught at universities, worked as a poetry editor for the journal *The Nation*, and was open about her concern for important social issues.

GOALS/OBJECTIVES

Studying this lesson will enable students to
- interpret and appreciate a poem about how art affects the individual
- describe the myth of Orpheus and explain how it is central to Levertov's poem
- identify, define, and illustrate with examples the terms *personification* and *allusion*
- identify and correct double negatives in sentences
- demonstrate the ability to retell Greek myths

Orpheus Singing His Lament for Eurydice, c.1865–70. Jean-Baptiste-Camille Corot. Kimbell Art Museum, Fort Worth, Texas.

A Tree Telling of Orpheus

Denise Levertov

White dawn. Stillness.   When the rippling began
    I took it for sea-wind, coming to our valley with rumors
    of salt, of treeless horizons. But the white fog
didn't stir; the leaves of my brothers remained outstretched,
5   unmoving.
        Yet the rippling drew nearer—and then
my own outermost branches began to tingle, almost as if
fire had been lit below them, too close, and their twig-tips
were drying and curling.

ANSWERS TO GUIDED READING QUESTIONS

1. The tree sees a man. He carries a lyre, a musical instrument with a curved frame that has strings running across it.
2. The tree hears the music of the lyre and the words of the man singing. The tree listens and takes the singer's language into its roots and bark and knows the meaning of all the man's words.

Quotables

"When I was twelve I had the temerity to send some poems to T. S. Eliot, even though I had not shown them even to my sister, and certainly to no one else. Months later, when I had forgotten all about this impulsive act, a two- or even three-page typewritten letter from him arrived, full of excellent advice."

—Denise Levertov

ADDITIONAL QUESTIONS AND ACTIVITIES

Ask students whether poetry, song, or instrumental music has the strongest emotional effect on them. Have them describe the effects, both during and after the experience.

---

10   Yet I was not afraid, only
           deeply alert.

     I was the first to see him,[1] for I grew
       out on the pasture slope, beyond the forest.
    He was a man, it seemed: the two
15   moving stems, the short trunk, the two
    arm-branches, flexible, each with five leafless
              twigs at their ends,
    and the head that's crowned by brown or gold grass,
    bearing a face not like the beaked face of a bird,
20   more like a flower's.
           He carried a burden made of
    some cut branch bent while it was green,
    strands of a vine tight-stretched across it. From this,
    when he touched it, and from his voice
25   which unlike the wind's voice had no need of our
    leaves and branches to complete its sound,
           came the ripple.
    But it was now no longer a ripple (he had come near and
    stopped in my first shadow) it was a wave that bathed me
30   as if rain
         rose from below and around me
       instead of falling.
    And what I felt was no longer a dry tingling:
      I seemed to be singing as he sang, I seemed to know
35   what the lark knows; all my sap
       was mounting towards the sun that by now
        had risen, the mist was rising, the grass
  was drying, yet my roots felt music moisten them
  deep under earth.

40   He came still closer, leaned on my trunk:
       the bark thrilled like a leaf still-folded.
    Music! There was no twig of me not
         trembling with joy and fear.

    Then as he sang
45   it was no longer sounds only that made the music:
    he spoke, and as no tree listens I listened, and language
       came into my roots
          out of the earth,
      into my bark

Whom does the tree see? What does this person carry?

What does the tree hear? How does the tree react?

---

1. **him.** Orpheus, the poet-musician of Greek mythology

50 out of the air,
        into the pores of my greenest shoots
                gently as dew
and there was no word he sang but I knew its meaning.
He told of journeys,

Of what journeys does the tree hear?

55   of where sun and moon go while we stand in dark,
        of an earth-journey he dreamed he would take some day
deeper than roots . . .
He told of the dreams of man, wars, passions, griefs,
                and I, a tree, understood words—ah, it seemed
60 my thick bark would split like a sapling's that
                        grew too fast in the spring
        when a late frost wounds it.

                                Fire he sang,
        that trees fear, and I, a tree, rejoiced in its flames.
65 New buds broke forth from me though it was full summer.
        As though his lyre[2] (now I knew its name)
                were both frost and fire, its chords flamed
up to the crown of me.
                I was seed again.
70   I was fern in the swamp.
                        I was coal.

What breaks forth from the tree? How is the tree transformed?

And at the heart of my wood
(so close I was to becoming man or a god)
        there was a kind of silence, a kind of sickness,
75   something akin to what men call boredom,
                                something
(the poem descended a scale, a stream over stones)
        that gives to a candle a coldness
                in the midst of its burning, he said.

80 It was then,
        when in the blaze of his power that
                        reached me and changed me
        I thought I should fall my length,
that the singer began
85   to leave me.   Slowly
        moved from my noon shadow
                        to open light,
words leaping and dancing over his shoulders
back to me

---

2. **lyre.** A small stringed instrument of the harp family, used by the ancient Greeks to accompany singers

ANSWERS TO GUIDED READING QUESTIONS

1. The tree hears of the journey the musician will take some day on earth.
2. New buds break forth from the tree. The tree is transformed into seed, fern in a swamp, and coal. It comes close to becoming a man or god.

ADDITIONAL QUESTIONS AND ACTIVITIES

Ask students to compare Levertov's description of the effect of music on the listener with MacLeish's description of the effect of poetry in "Ars Poetica." In comparing the poems, ask them to pay special attention to lines 80–92, lines 153–162 in Levertov's poem, and lines 9–16 in MacLeish's poem. How is the effect of a work of art similar in each selection?
Answer
In both poems, the poem or song affects the listener memories, giving the listener a heightened sense of their experiences and emotions.

BIBLIOGRAPHIC NOTE

Students might enjoy reading to each other from the one of the following collections by Levertov:
Collected Earlier Poems: 1940–1960. New York: New Directions, 1979.
Relearning the Alphabet. New York: New Directions, 1970.
They might also enjoy exploring Levertov's views on poetry in the following nonfiction books:
The Poet in the World. New York: New Directions, 1973
Light Up the Cave. New York: New Directions, 1981.

90   rivery sweep of lyre-tones becoming
  slowly again

       ripple.

   And I
      in terror
95   but not in doubt of
            what I must do
in anguish, in haste,
       wrenched from the earth root after root,
the soil heaving and cracking, the moss tearing asunder—
100 and behind me the others: my brothers
forgotten since dawn. In the forest
they too had heard,
and were pulling their roots in pain
out of a thousand years' layers of dead leaves,
105   rolling the rocks away,

         breaking themselves
              out of
           their depths.
You would have thought we would lose the sound of the lyre,
110   of the singing
so dreadful the storm-sounds were, where there was no storm,
        no wind but the rush of our
     branches moving, our trunks breasting the air.
      But the music!
115   The music reached us.

Clumsily,
    stumbling over our own roots,
        rustling our leaves
          in answer,
120 we moved, we followed.

All day we followed, up hill and down.
         We learned to dance,
for he would stop, where the ground was flat,
        and words he said
125 taught us to leap and to wind in and out
around one another in figures the lyre's measure designed.

> **What does the tree wrench from the earth?**

> **What do the trees clumsily do?**

words for everyday use

riv • er • y (riv′ ər ē) *adj.,* riverlike. *The rivery stream of light washed the fruit on my table.*
an • guish (aŋ′ gwish) *n.,* great suffering from worry or pain. *We saw the hurt and anguish on the faces of the victims whose houses were destroyed by the hurricane.*
a • sun • der (ə sun′ dər) *adv.,* into pieces or parts. *Our original plans fell asunder, so we had to plan a different trip.*

The singer
              laughed till he wept to see us, he was so glad.
                                              At sunset
130   we came to this place I stand in, this <u>knoll</u>
      with its ancient grove that was bare grass then.
              In the last light of that day his song became
      farewell.
              He stilled our longing.
135   He sang our sun-dried roots back into earth,
      watered them: all-night rain of music so quiet
                                      we could almost
              not hear it in the
                              moonless dark.
140   By dawn he was gone.
                      We have stood here since,
      in our new life.
              We have waited.
                      He does not return.
145   It is said he made his earth-journey, and lost
      what he sought.
              It is said they <u>felled</u> him
      and cut up his limbs for firewood.
                      And it is said
150   his head still sang and was swept out to sea singing.
      Perhaps he will not return.
                      But what we have lived
      comes back to us.
              We see more.
                              We feel, as our rings increase,
155   something that lifts our branches, that stretches our furthest
                                              leaf-tips
      further.
              The wind, the birds,
                              do not sound poorer but clearer,
160   recalling our agony, and the way we danced.
      The music!   ■

What does the musician
do for the trees?

Why will the musician
probably not return?

In what way is the tree
permanently changed?

**words
for
everyday
use**

knoll (nōl) *n.*, mound. *I stopped to sit on the <u>knoll</u> in the woods and eat my sandwich.*
fell (fel) *vt.*, knock or cut down. *The hero <u>felled</u> the evil villian and stood triumphantly over his foe.*

"A TREE TELLING OF ORPHEUS"   125

ANSWERS TO GUIDED
READING QUESTIONS

1. The musician stills the longing of
   the trees and sings their dried-out
   roots back into the earth and
   waters them.
2. He will probably not return because
   it is said that he was killed and cut
   up, and his head was swept out to
   sea.
3. The tree now sees more, and it feels
   something that lifts it up and
   stretches it. It is more sensitive now
   to other sounds, and its own
   memories of pain and joy are more
   vivid.

SELECTION CHECK TEST 4.2.21 WITH ANSWERS

Checking Your Reading
1. Who is the speaker of this poem?
   The speaker is a tree.
2. What is the speaker's reaction to
   the rippling that is drawing nearer?
   **The speaker reacts by becoming
   more alert.**
3. Whom does the tree see? **He sees a
   man who is named Orpheus, the
   Greek mythical poet and
   musician.**
4. What is the rippling? **It is the
   sound of music.**
5. What did the trees learn to do?
   **They learned to dance to the
   music.**

Vocabulary in Context
Fill in each blank below with the most
appropriate word from the following
Words for Everyday Use. You may have
to change the tense of the word.

    rivery   anguish   asunder
           knoll   fell

1. The old man was last seen sitting
   on a(n) **knoll**, resting with his
   hands laid on his lap.
2. The **anguish** of my mother's death
   led me into a deep depression.
3. His **rivery** words seemed to wash
   away my sadness.

Literary Tools
1. Describe your favorite image from
   the poem. *Responses will vary.*
2. What is personified in the poem? **A
   tree is personified.**
3. To what or to whom does the
   poem make allusions? **The poem
   alludes to Orpheus, a Greek
   mythical poet and musician.**

RESPOND TO THE SELECTION

Students should consider especially lines 152–162.

ANSWERS TO INVESTIGATE, INQUIRE, AND IMAGINE

RECALL

1a. The tree, when it first sees Orpheus, is growing in a pasture slope beyond the forest. The tree does not stay in one place. It, along with the other trees, rips its roots from the earth to follow Orpheus's beautiful music. Orpheus stops where the ground is flat so the trees can dance to his music.

2a. The subjects of Orpheus's songs are the earth-journey he would some day take below the earth's surface as well as the dreams of man, wars, passions, and griefs.

INTERPRET

1b. The tree describes Orpheus as having stems, branches, and a trunk instead of fingers, arms, and a body. This is how a tree might see a man. The ripple the tree hears is music from Orpheus's lyre.

2b. The tree now feels more alive and aware. The music is a sound the tree has never heard before, and the songs tell tales the tree has never heard before. Lines 69–71 show that the tree, through the music, is able to experience other forms of being or different stages of its existence, demonstrating heightened self-awareness.

ANALYZE

3a. The tree is transformed and will never be the same again. It says, "We see more," meaning its ability to appreciate the joys and agonies of life have been expanded. Besides seeing more, the tree feels more, and hears more clearly after its experience of hearing Orpheus's music.

SYNTHESIZE

3b. Art has the power to transform people by opening their eyes to new ideas and experiences. It is uplifting and stretches their understanding.

PERSPECTIVE

4a. *Responses will vary.* The tree might be more sensitive to the touch of birds that come to sit on its branches.

EMPATHY

4b. *Responses will vary.*

Respond *to the* SELECTION

How does the speaker in this poem feel about the experience being described?

Investigate, Inquire, and Imagine

Recall: GATHERING FACTS

1a. Where is the tree when it first sees Orpheus? Does the tree stay in one place? What does it do? How does Orpheus treat the tree when he witnesses the tree's behavior?

2a. Name the subjects of the songs of Orpheus.

Interpret: FINDING MEANING

1b. How does the tree describe Orpheus? Why might the tree describe him in this way? What is the ripple that the tree hears in line 27?

2b. How does music change the tree? Why does it have this effect? How do lines 69–71 show how much the tree has learned about life?

Analyze: TAKING THINGS APART

3a. Identify what happens to the tree after Orpheus's departure.

Synthesize: BRINGING THINGS TOGETHER

3b. What might this poem be saying about art in general?

Perspective: LOOKING AT OTHER VIEWS

4a. The tree says that, after Orpheus's departure, "The wind, the birds, / do not sound poorer but clearer." What other senses besides hearing could be affected by Orpheus's music? How?

Empathy: SEEING FROM INSIDE

4b. If you were the speaker, how would you feel if a new music maker came into your life? Would you compare his or her music to Orpheus's and find it wanting, or would you rejoice in the gift of music again?

Understanding Literature

PERSONIFICATION. Review the definition for **personification** in the Handbook of Literary Terms. What example of "reverse" personification did you find in the tree's description of Orpheus? How is the poem in its entirety an example of personification?

ALLUSION. Review the definition for **allusion** in the Handbook of Literary Terms and the chart you made for Literary Tools on page 120. Where in the poem did you find specific references to the myth of Orpheus? What parts of the Orpheus myth do they relate?

126   *UNIT TWO / POETRY*

ANSWERS TO UNDERSTANDING LITERATURE

PERSONIFICATION. The tree describes Orpheus as having a trunk, a stem, twigs, and grass for hair, as if Orpheus were a tree or a plant. The poem in its entirety is an example of personification because the tree has thoughts, ideas, and feelings as if it were a person.

ALLUSION. Lines 56 and 145 allude to Orpheus's journey to the underworld in search of Eurydice. Lines 147–148 allude to Orpheus's violent death. Lines 149–150 allude to what happens after Orpheus's death when his head floats down the river Hebrus into the city of Lesbos.

Writer's Journal

1. Imagine you are the tree. Write an **appeal** to Orpheus to come back. Explain to him what his music meant to you and why you need him to return.

2. Imagine that a lyre is left in the forest for someone to play to the trees after Orpheus's departure. As Orpheus, write **directions** for the new musician, telling him how to play and sing.

3. Freewrite about the details of a favorite book, song, movie, painting, or photograph that has touched you. Why was it special? Did it change your life, or was the experience more subtle than that? How did it relate to your life? Then, using your notes, write a **paragraph** describing the work of art and how it affected you. Try to express to your reader what was special about this work.

Integrating the Language Arts

Language, Grammar, and Style

AVOIDING DOUBLE NEGATIVES. Read the Language Arts Survey 3.29, "Working with Negatives and Contractions." Then change the double negatives in the following sentences. Write *Correct* if the sentence is without errors.

1. The white fog didn't never stir.
2. The instrument the man carried doesn't make no sound the tree has ever heard before.
3. The trees don't never stay in one place when he plays.
4. They don't have any bare branches in summer.
5. Orpheus can't sing no more songs.

Media Literacy

GREEK ALLUSIONS IN TITLES. Using the Internet, make a list of titles of books that have references to Greek mythology. A good place to look on the Internet is Amazon Books at http://www.amazon.com. For example, if you key in "Orpheus," you would find *The Lyre of Orpheus* by Robertson Davies. Then classify the book as poetry, fiction, or nonfiction. Davies' book is fiction. Finally, give the call numbers you would need to locate the book in the library for books that are not fiction. Works of fiction, like Davies' book, are shelved alphabetically in the fiction section. To refer to the Dewey decimal system, read the Language Arts Survey 5.18, "How Library Materials are Organized."

Speaking and Listening & Collaborative Learning

STORYTELLING. With the help of your teacher, make up a short list of Greek myths to read. Make note cards for each myth, listing descriptions of the important characters and putting the main events in chronological order. Then put the names of each story on slips of paper and put them in a bag. With several classmates, take turns drawing a story from the bag and telling the story to your group. Be sure to include appropriate tone, gestures, facial expressions, and body language in telling your story.

ANSWERS TO INTEGRATING THE LANGUAGE ARTS

Language, Grammar, and Style
1. The white fog didn't ever stir.
2. The instrument the man carried doesn't make any sound the tree has ever heard before.
3. The trees don't ever stay in one place when he plays.
4. *Correct*
5. Orpheus can't sing any more songs.

Media Literacy
Ask students to list six to ten books that include poetry, fiction, and nonfiction titles. If students find a nonfiction title that interests them, have them get the book from the shelf and then write a "book blurb," or short summary. To write the blurb, ask them to skim the table of contents and read the part or all of the book's preface or introduction.

Speaking and Listening & Collaborative Learning
A sample note card might look like this:
"Myth of Orpheus"
Characters: Orpheus, a gifted poet-musician; Eurydice, his wife; Hades, king of the underworld
Main Events:
1. Orpheus and Eurydice are deeply in love.
2. Eurydice dies from a snake bite and Orpheus is devastated.
3. Orpheus goes to the land of the dead to beg Hades to let Eurydice return.
4. Hades, moved by Orpheus's sadness and music, agrees.
5. Hades sets one condition: Orpheus must not look back at Eurydice as they leave.
6. Just before entering the upper world, Orpheus looks back to share his joy with his wife.
7. Eurydice disappears forever.

GRAPHIC ORGANIZER

The selection repeats many present-tense phrases beginning with *I,* such as "I walk," "I feel," "I put," and "I can see." "Should I" and "perhaps" are also repeated.

READER'S JOURNAL

You might have students complete this journal entry as a homework assignment. Ask them to take their journals home and sit by themselves in a quiet and out-of-the-way spot. Tell students to let their thoughts move in and out of their heads freely. After several minutes, they should take notes on the thoughts they had.

PROSE POEM

Literary
T O O L S

POINT OF VIEW. Point of view is the vantage point from which a story is told. Stories and poems are typically written from a *first-person point of view,* in which the narrator uses words such as *I* and *we,* or from a *third-person point of view,* in which the narrator uses words such as *he, she, it,* and *they.* Identify which point of view is used in this prose poem.

REPETITION. Repetition is a writer's conscious reuse of a sound, word, phrase, sentence, or other element. Look for examples of repetition in the poem.

Graphic Organizer

As you read, make a cluster chart listing the examples of repetition you find in the poem. One example has been done for you.

> I sit on the porch facing the mountains.

> repetition

Reader's Journal

How would you pass the time in the solitude of a secluded setting?

128   *UNIT TWO*

---

from "Holidays"
by Jamaica Kincaid

Reader's resource

"Holidays," published in Jamaica Kincaid's collection called *At the Bottom of the River* (1983), is a prose poem. A prose poem is a work of prose, usually a short work, that makes extensive use of poetic language, such as figures of speech and words that echo their sense, so that the line between prose and poetry becomes blurred. This selection from "Holidays" is prose in that it is written with complete sentences in the form of paragraphs. However, it is such a compact collection of vivid details that it is poetic to the ear.

About *the* AUTHOR

Jamaica Kincaid (1949–) was born on the island of St. John's, Antigua, as Elaine Potter Richardson. There she completed her secondary education under the British system because of Antigua's status as a British colony until 1967. In 1965 she went to Westchester, New York to work as an *au pair* (live-in maid and nanny). After leaving the family for which she worked, Kincaid went on to study photography at the New York School for Social Research, and also attended Franconia College in New Hampshire for a year. Her first published writing was a series of articles for *Ingenue* magazine. In 1973, she changed her name to Jamaica Kincaid because her family disapproved of her writing. When asked why she did not change her name to an African name, Kincaid replied, "the connection I have to Africa is the color of my skin and that doesn't seem enough to have changed it to an African name."

As a freelance writer, Kincaid has published articles and short stories in *The New Yorker, Rolling Stone, Ms.,* and the *Paris Review.* She has also worked as a staff writer for *The New Yorker.* Her collection *At the Bottom of the River* (1983) won the Morton Dauwen Zabel Award from the American Academy and Institute of Arts and Letters. Kincaid's most recent work is the novel *The Autobiography of My Mother,* which was published in 1996.

GOALS/OBJECTIVES

Studying this lesson will enable students to
- enjoy a prose poem
- identify Jamaica Kincaid and briefly describe her literary accomplishments
- define *point of view* and recognize the point of view in the selection

- define *repetition* and identify elements of repetition in the poem
- identify pronouns as subjects or direct objects in sentences
- plan a dream vacation

from **Holidays**

Jamaica Kincaid

I sit on the porch facing the mountains. I sit on a wicker couch looking out the window at a field of day lilies. I walk into a room where someone—an artist, maybe—has stored some empty canvases. I drink a glass of water. I put the empty glass, from which I have just drunk the water, on a table. I notice two flies, one sitting on top of the other, flying around the room. I scratch my scalp, I scratch my thighs. I lift my arms up and stretch them above my head. I sigh. I spin on my heels once. I walk around the dining-room table three times. I see a book lying on the dining-room table and I pick it up. The book is called *An Illustrated Encyclopedia of Butterflies and Moths*. I leaf through the book, looking only at the pictures, which are bright and beautiful. From my looking through the book, the word "thorax"[1] sticks in my mind. "Thorax," I say, "thorax, thorax," I don't know how many times. I bend over and touch my toes. I stay in that position until I count to one hundred. As I count, I pretend to be counting off balls on a ball frame. As I count the balls, I pretend that they are the colors red, green, blue, and yellow. I walk over to the fireplace. Standing in front of the fireplace, I try to write my name in the dead ashes with my big toe. I cannot write my name in the dead ashes with my big toe. My big toe, now dirty, I try to clean by rubbing it vigorously on a clean royal-blue rug. The royal-blue rug now has a dark spot, and my big toe has a strong burning sensation. Oh, sensation. I am filled with sensation. I feel—oh, how I feel. I feel, I feel, I feel. I have no words right now for how I feel.

I take a walk down the road in my bare feet. I feel the stones on the road, hard and sharp against my soft, almost pink soles. Also, I feel the hot sun beating down on my bare neck. It is midday. Did I say that? Must I say that? Oh, me, oh my. The road on which I walk barefoot leads to the store—the village store. Should I go to the village store or should I not go to

> *What is the speaker facing at the beginning of the poem?*

> *What sensations does the speaker experience?*

---

1. **thorax.** Part of a mammal's or insect's body between the head and the abdomen

ANSWERS TO GUIDED READING QUESTIONS

1. The speaker is facing the mountains as she sits on the porch.
2. The speaker experiences the sensations of sharp stones against her bare feet as she walks down the road and the hot sun beating down on her bare neck.

INDIVIDUAL LEARNING STRATEGIES

MOTIVATION
Have students create a word web for "Tropical Island." In their webs, ask them to list and group the sights, sounds, and activities that come to mind when they think of a tropical island.

READING PROFICIENCY
Use several subject-verb combinations from students' completed graphic organizer to point out that the selection is written in the first-person point of view. You might want to work with students to convert several examples to first-person plural and third-person singular, so they can see when the verb form changes and when it does not.

ENGLISH LANGUAGE LEARNING
The simple sentence structure, use of repetition, and manageable vocabulary make this selection a good one for English language learners to read aloud in a small group. Suggest that the group divide the selection into five or six roughly equal sections, stopping and starting at a sentence break.

SPECIAL NEEDS
Ask students what words and ideas they associate with vacations. In general do they think of vacations as exciting or relaxing?

ENRICHMENT
Students might be interested in researching the literary technique called *stream of consciousness*, in which the writer presents the flow of feelings, thoughts, and impressions as they occur in the mind. Have students locate books by writers who use this style and read excerpts from the works aloud.

ANSWER TO GUIDED READING QUESTION

1. The speaker notices the parts of her body that she can see and feel. The speaker notices a bumblebee flying around, the book in her lap, and ten ants wrestling with a bit of food. The decisions she thinks about are whether to make herself a drink, to write a letter, or to take a nap. Her state of mind is restless.

CROSS-CURRICULAR ACTIVITIES

GEOGRAPHY. Have students make guesses about the poem's general and specific setting using details from the poem and the author's background. Ask them to focus on details related to climate, landscape, and insect life that are given in the poem. Then have them use a physical map of the Caribbean area to locate countries with areas that fit the details they have gathered.
Answer
The setting is most likely a rural area of a Caribbean country that contains mountains.

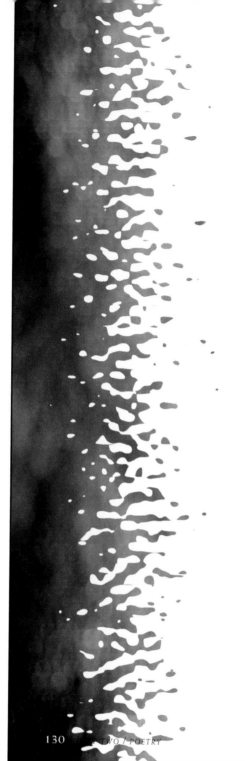

the village store? I can if I want. If I go to the village store, I can buy a peach. The peach will be warm from sitting in a box in the sun. The peach will not taste sweet and the peach will not taste sour. I will know that I am eating a peach only by looking at it. I will not go to the store. I will sit on the porch facing the mountains.

I sit on the porch facing the mountains. The porch is airy and spacious. I am the only person sitting on the porch. I look at myself. I can see myself. That is, I can see my chest, my abdomen, my legs, and my arms. I cannot see my hair, my ears, my face, or my collarbone. I can feel them, though. My nose is moist with sweat. Locking my fingers, I put my hands on my head. I see a bee, a large bumblebee, flying around aimlessly. I remove my hands from resting on my head, because my arms are tired. But also I have just remembered a superstition: if you sit with your hands on your head, you will kill your mother. I have many superstitions. I believe all of them. Should I read a book? Should I make myself something to drink? But what? And hot or cold? Should I write a letter? I should write a letter. I will write a letter. "Dear So-and-So, I am . . . and then I got the brilliant idea . . . I was very amusing . . . I had enough, I said . . . I saw what I came to see, I thought
. . . I am laughing all the way to the poorhouse. I grinned . . . I just don't know anymore. I remain, etc." I like my letter. Perhaps I shall keep my letter to myself. I fold up the letter I have just written and put it between the pages of the book I am trying to read. The book is lying in my lap. I look around me, trying to find something on which to focus my eyes. I see ten ants. I count them as they wrestle with a speck of food. I am not fascinated by that. I see my toes moving up and down as if they were tapping out a beat. Why are my toes tapping? I am fascinated by that. A song is going through my mind. It goes, "There was a man from British Guiana, Who used to play a piana. His foot slipped, His trousers ripped . . ." I see, I see. Yes. Now. Suddenly I am tired. I am yawning. Perhaps I will take a nap. Perhaps I will take a long nap. Perhaps I will take a nice long nap. Perhaps, while taking my nap, I will have a dream, a dream in which I am not sitting on the porch facing the mountains. ∎

What does the speaker notice about herself and her surroundings? What decisions does the speaker think about making? What is the speaker's state of mind?

Mt. Cortezo; in Hureto Provience near Mexico City, Mexico, c.1960–1970. Joseph Yoakum.
National Museum of American Art, Washington, DC.

art note

Mt. Cortezo; in Hureto Provience near Mexico City, Mexico, c.1960–1970. Joseph Yoakum.

The art of **Joseph Yoakum** (*circa* 1886–1972) is called "Outsider Art," because Yoakum worked outside the established art system. Although he had no training in art and only began drawing in his seventies, he had an enormous influence on young artists who discovered him in Chicago. They were inspired by his fanciful drawings of places, some of which he may have visited but many of which came from his imagination.

Respond *to the* SELECTION

Do you think the speaker in the selection is enjoying her solitude?

Ask students if they have ever had some of the same thoughts or made the same kinds of observations that the speaker does when sitting quietly "doing nothing."

SELECTION CHECK TEST 4.2.23 WITH ANSWERS

Checking Your Reading

1. What is the speaker looking out to in the beginning of the poem? **The speaker is looking out to a field of day lilies.**
2. What does the speaker notice in the room? **She notices two flies flying about in the room.**
3. What word does the speaker repeat over and over? **She repeats the word, "thorax."**
4. What does the speaker try to do with her big toe? **She tries to write her name in the dead ashes with it.**
5. What is the superstition the speaker remembers while sitting out on the porch? **She remembers, "If you sit with your hands on your head, you will kill your mother."**

Literary Tools

1. From what point of view is this poem told? **It is told from the first-person point of view.**
2. Give an example of repetition that is used in the poem. **The sentence, "I sit on the porch facing the mountains" is repeated throughout the poem.**
3. What is a prose poem? **A prose poem is a work of prose that is filled with poetic language; therefore, it is hard to distinguish the prose from poetry.**

RESPOND TO THE SELECTION

Do you enjoy being by yourself? How do you feel about solitude?

RECALL

1a. At the beginning and at the end of the poem, the speaker sits on the porch facing the mountains.

2a. The speaker tries to write her name in the ashes with her big toe. She then tries to clean her big toe by rubbing it on the carpet. This causes the carpet to become dirty.

3a. As the speaker walks down the road, she tries to decide if she should go to the village store or not. Later, she must decide if she should read a book, make herself something to drink, or write a letter. These would normally be considered easy and unimportant decisions.

INTERPRET

1b. She is on holiday. One can assume that the speaker is not at the place in which she lives because in the opening paragraph she seems unfamiliar with several items in the room, such as the artist's canvases.

2b. The speaker feels a burning sensation in her toe after the ash incident. She then goes for a walk in her bare feet and experiences other sensations: sharp rocks under her feet and the sun on her neck.

3b. The speaker says that the peach will be warm from the sun and rather tasteless. The speaker herself might feel this way.

ANALYZE

4a. *Responses will vary.* The speaker could be described as reflective, indecisive, restless, intelligent, or lazy.

SYNTHESIZE

4b. The speaker's actions suggest that she is bored or restless. Although she is not doing much on her holiday, she does seem to have a creative and active mind.

PERSPECTIVE

5a. The speaker would probably remember drawing her name in ashes, walking to the store, watching a bee and some ants, and thinking about her freedom and the options she has for her day.

EMPATHY

5b. *Responses will vary.* Students who enjoy inactivity will probably say that they would regret going home and would miss their lazy holiday. Students who enjoy activity will probably say that they would be happy to go home and resume a more active life.

Investigate, *Inquire*, and Imagine

Recall: GATHERING FACTS

1a. Where is the speaker at the beginning and at the end of this poem?

2a. What does the speaker try to do with the ashes from the fireplace? What does she do after this attempt? What are the results of her cleansing efforts?

3a. What decision does the speaker have to make as she walks down the road? What other decisions does she have to make? Are these difficult or important decisions?

Interpret: FINDING MEANING

1b. Why is the speaker at this particular place? Is this where she normally lives? How can you tell?

2b. What does the speaker feel after the ash incident? What does she do next? What connection is there between the ash incident and the activity that follows?

3b. In what way is the speaker's description of the peach she could buy similar to her feelings?

Analyze: TAKING THINGS APART

4a. Identify adjectives that describe the speaker.

Synthesize: BRINGING THINGS TOGETHER

4b. What is the speaker's attitude about where she is and what she is doing?

Perspective: LOOKING AT OTHER VIEWS

5a. What would the speaker remember about her day?

Empathy: SEEING FROM INSIDE

5b. If you were the speaker, how would you feel about going home after your inactive holiday?

Understanding *Literature*

POINT OF VIEW. Review the definition for **point of view** in the Handbook of Literary Terms. What point of view is used in the selection? Why did Kincaid choose this point of view?

REPETITION. Review the definition of **repetition** in Literary Tools on page 128. What sentences and phrases does the speaker repeat? What patterns do you find in these repetitions?

Writer's Journal

1. Write a **billboard sign** for the vacation spot where the speaker finds herself. Think of words that make the place seem appealing to would-be tourists.

2. Imagine you are the speaker. Complete the **letter** that you are considering writing in paragraph 2.

3. Freewrite about being in a specific place. What are you aware of while you are there? What do you think about? What actions do you take? Then, based on your freewrite, write a **prose poem** that focuses on being in that place.

ANSWERS TO UNDERSTANDING LITERATURE

POINT OF VIEW. This selection uses a first-person point of view. Kincaid probably chose this point of view because "Holidays" is mostly composed of thoughts the speaker is having and only the speaker can tell us exactly what is in her own head.

REPETITION. The speaker repeats the sentence "I sit on the porch facing the mountains," which she uses as a transition into a new series of thoughts. She repeats present-tense phrases such as "I walk," "I feel," "I put," and "I can see," which lend a directness to her account. The repetition of "should I" and "perhaps" indicate her continued indecisiveness at what actions she should take next.

Integrating the Language Arts

Language, Grammar, and Style

PRONOUNS AS SUBJECTS AND OBJECTS. Read the Language Arts Survey 3.54–3.56. Then identify the following underlined personal and indefinite pronouns as subjects or direct objects.

1. <u>Someone</u> has stored empty canvases in the room.
2. The flies? I notice <u>them</u> flying around the room.
3. The book? <u>It</u> is called *An Illustrated Encyclopedia of Butterflies and Moths.*
4. No <u>one</u> comes to visit me.
5. The letter? I write <u>it</u> to stave off my boredom.

Media Literacy

DREAM VACATION. Plan a week-long trip to a location you have always wanted to visit. First, find out how much the airfare costs by locating an airline on-line. Then locate an Internet site about your desired location by entering a key word, such as "Hawaii." Find a hotel and write out an itinerary, listing where you will go and what you will do each day.

Study and Research

BIOGRAPHY. Jamaica Kincaid was born in Antigua, an island in the Caribbean. Research the life of another prominent person of Caribbean heritage and describe his or her contributions. If you want to do your research on the Internet, one site you will find useful is Southern Illinois University's Prominent People of Caribbean Heritage at http://www.siu.edu/~carib/people.html.

Media Literacy & Study and Research

BIOGRAPHICAL CRITICISM. Locate a site on the Internet listing Jamaica Kincaid's literary works. To find such a site, enter "Jamaica Kincaid." Choose one of her books and read a review about it. One place to locate book reviews is http://www.amazon.com. Then read a biography about her; you might even be able to use the same Internet site you used to find the bibliography. Finally, write a paragraph analyzing the connection between Kincaid's real life and her writing. What events in her life has she written about? How did they affect her? What attitude does she take toward these events? Answer these and other pertinent questions that arise during your research.

ANSWERS TO INTEGRATING THE LANGUAGE ARTS

Language, Grammar, and Style
1. subject
2. direct object
3. subject
4. subject
5. direct object

Media Literacy
Remind students that they can use a Boolean search that combines the term "Hawaii" with "vacations," "travel," or "tourism." They may also obtain travel information directly from the home page of the Internet service provider.

Study and Research
Ask students to read about several persons in different categories before making their selection. Assign a score from 1 to 25 for each grading criterion below. (See the evaluation forms for writing, revising, and proofreading in the Assessment Resource book.)

BIOGRAPHY
- **CONTENT/UNITY.** The biography describes the life and achievements of a prominent person of Caribbean heritage.
- **ORGANIZATION/COHERENCE.** Events of the person's life are described in chronological order.
- **LANGUAGE/STYLE.** The biography uses vivid and precise nouns, verbs, and modifiers.
- **CONVENTIONS.** The biography avoids errors in spelling, grammar, usage, mechanics, and manuscript form.

Media Literacy & Study and Research
An excellent site for Jamaica Kincaid is maintained by George P. Landow at http://landow.stg.brown.edu/post/caribbean/kincaid/kincaidov.html. Assign a score from 1 to 25 for each grading criterion below. (See the evaluation forms for writing, revising, and proofreading in the Assessment Resource book.)

PARAGRAPH
- **CONTENT/UNITY.** The paragraph makes a connection between Jamaica Kincaid's life and her writing.
- **ORGANIZATION/COHERENCE.** Thoughts and ideas are arranged in an appropriate way and are communicated coherently to the reader.
- **LANGUAGE/STYLE.** The paragraph uses formal language.
- **CONVENTIONS.** The paragraph avoids errors in spelling, grammar, usage, mechanics, and manuscript form.

ADDITIONAL RESOURCES

UNIT 2 RESOURCE BOOK
- Selection Worksheet 2.12
- Selection Check Test 4.2.25
- Selection Test 4.2.26
- Language, Grammar, and Style Resource 3.45
- Speaking and Listening Resource 4.19

VOCABULARY FROM THE SELECTION

detain
lament
wrench

GRAPHIC ORGANIZER

Students should include most of the following examples of repetition, and may include others, in their cluster charts: "I have cause to weep / woes to complain of!"; "For this I weep . . . / for this I weep and complain"; "to be sister to whitefish" / and brother to the fishes!"; "and there I, a hen, was lost / I, a bird, untimely died"; "Who now will carry the news / will tell it by word of mouth / to the maid's famous / home, to the fair farm?"; "One tear rolled, another rolled / her plentiful waters rolled."

READER'S JOURNAL

What advice would you give to a friend if he or she was in a situation similar to the one described in the Reader's Journal?

Literary
T O O L S

PARALLELISM. Parallelism is a rhetorical technique in which a writer emphasizes the equal value or weight of two or more ideas by expressing them in the same grammatical form. As you read, look for an example of parallelism.

REPETITION. Repetition is a writer's conscious reuse of a sound, word, phrase, sentence, or other element. As you read, look for examples of repetition.

Graphic
Organizer

Make a cluster chart like the one below and fill it in with several examples of repetition from the selection.

> I live in tight clothes/I grow on breadcrusts/ by my good father/with my dear mother.

> **repetition**

Reader's
Journal

How would it feel to have someone interested in you romantically that you did not like? What would be the best way to deal with the situation?

134 *UNIT TWO*

"The Drowned Maid" from the *Kalevala*

by Elias Lönnrot, translated by Elias Bosley

Reader's
r e s o u r c e

The *Kalevala* is a Finnish epic. An *epic* is a long story, often told in verse, involving heroes and gods. Väinämönen is a powerful seer with supernatural origins who courts a young maiden, Aino, in Kalevala, the "land of heroes" which is the dwelling place of the poem's chief characters.

The first edition of Lönnrot's *Kalevala* appeared in 1835. Lönnrot and his colleagues continued to collect folk poetry, and using this new material, Lönnrot published a second, expanded version of the *Kalevala* in 1849. The second edition of the *Kalevala* is the version that has been read in Finland ever since and upon which most translations are based. This poetic song tradition has been part of the oral tradition among speakers of Balto-Finnic languages for two thousand years.

CULTURE CONNECTION. When the *Kalevala* first appeared in print in 1835, Finland had been an Autonomous Grand Duchy for a quarter of a century. Prior to this, until 1809, Finland had been a part of the Swedish empire. The *Kalevala* marked an important turning point for Finnish-language culture, and bolstered the Finns' self-confidence and faith in their language and culture. It also caused a stir abroad by bringing a small unknown people to the attention of other Europeans.

About *the*
A U T H O R

Elias Lönnrot (1802–1884) created the Finnish national epic, the *Kalevala*, from short ballads and lyric poems collected from oral tradition. He also published "Old Songs and Ballads of the Finnish People" and other collections. From 1853 to 1862 he taught Finnish language and literature at the University of Helsinki. Lönnrot promoted Finnish as a national language (Swedish had previously been predominant) and paved the way for the birth of modern Finnish literature.

GOALS/OBJECTIVES

Studying this lesson will enable students to
- appreciate a folk epic from another country
- explain how the *Kalevala* came into being as a work of literature
- define *parallelism* and recognize this technique in the selection

- define *repetition* and describe its use and function in the selection
- demonstrate the ability to get pronouns and antecedents to agree
- conduct research on oral epics

The DROWNED *Maid*

FROM THE *KALEVALA*

Elias Lönnrot

Now, that Aino, the young maid
young Joukahainen's sister
went for a broom from the grove
and for bath-whisks[1] from the scrub;
broke off one for
    her father
another for her
    mother
    gathered a third too
for her full-blooded brother.
She was just stepping homeward
    tripping through alders
when old Väinämöinen came.
He saw the maid in the grove
the fine-hemmed in the grasses
and uttered a word, spoke thus:
"Don't for anyone, young maid
    except me, young maid
wear the beads
    around your
    neck
set the cross upon
    your breast
put your head into a braid
    bind your hair with silk!'

The maid put this into words:
'Not for you nor anyone
do I wear crosses upon
my breast, tie my hair with silk.
I don't care for cogware,[2] for

Where is Aino? What is she looking for?

Who comes to Aino? What does he say?

---

1. **bath-whisks.** Tree branches used for cleaning the skin in the sauna
2. **cogware.** A kind of coarse cloth worn by the poorer classes

"THE DROWNED MAID" **135**

Aino Myth [Detail], 1891. Akseli Gallen-Kallela.
The Museum of Finnish Art, Ateneum, Helsinki.

1. She takes off the cross, her rings
and beads, and the silk threads in
her hair and leaves them on the
ground. Weeping, she goes home
to the farm.

**ADDITIONAL QUESTIONS
AND ACTIVITIES** π

What effect is created by the
frequent repetition of Aino's
words "For this I weep"? What practical value would the use of repetition have in a long oral work of literature?
Answers
Aino is replying to the repeated
question, "Why are you weeping?"
from her father, brother, and sister.
The repetitions in her answer underscore the depth of her sadness. In a
long oral work, repetition would
help the listener keep track of the
action and clearly understand the
feelings of the characters.

---

wheat slices I don't complain:
    I live in tight clothes
    I grow on breadcrusts
    by my good father
    with my dear mother."

She <u>wrenched</u> the cross from her breast
and the rings from her finger
the beads she shook from her neck
and the red threads off her head
left them on the ground for the ground's sake
in the grove for the grove's sake
    and went weeping
    home
    wailing to the farm.

Her father at the window
sat adorning an axe haft:[3]
"Why are you weeping, poor girl
    poor girl, young maiden?"

    "I have cause to weep
    woes to complain of!
For this I weep, my papa
for this I weep and complain:
the cross came loose from my breast
the bauble[4] shook from my belt
from my breast the silver cross
the copper threads off my belt."

Her brother at the gateway
is carving collar-bow wood:
"Why do you weep, poor sister
    poor sister, young maid?"

    "I have cause to weep
    woes to complain of!
For this I weep, poor brother
for this I weep and complain:
the ring slipped off my finger

and the beads fell from my neck
the gold ring from my finger
from my neck the silver beads."

Her sister at the floor seam
is weaving a belt of gold:
"Why do you weep, poor sister
    poor sister, young maid?"

    "The weeper has cause
    she who whines has woes!
For this I weep, poor sister
for this I weep and complain:
the gold came loose from my brows
and the silver from my hair
and the blue silks from my eyes
the red ribbons off my head."

Her mother on the shed step
is skimming cream off the milk:
"Why are you weeping, poor girl
    poor girl, young maiden?"

"O mamma who carried me
O mother who suckled me!
    There are dark causes
    very low spirits!
For this I weep, poor mother
for this, mamma, complain: I
went for a broom from the grove
for bath-whisk tips from the scrub
broke off one for my father
another for my mother
    gathered a third too
for my full-blooded brother.
I began to step homeward
was just stepping through the glade
when from the dell, from the land

---

3. **haft.** Handle
4. **bauble.** Inexpensive ornamentation

> *What is Aino's reaction
> to old Väinämöinen's
> proposal?*

**words
for
everyday
use**   wrench (rench) *vt.,* pull or strain at something with violent twisting or straining. *Joe <u>wrenched</u> the hubcap from the car.*

burnt over, the Great One said:
'Don't for anyone, poor maid
    except me, poor maid
wear the beads around your neck
set the cross upon your breast
put your head into a braid
    bind your hair with silk!'
I wrenched the cross from my breast
beads I shook from my neck
and the blue threads from my eyes
and the red threads off my head
cast them on the ground for the ground's sake
in the grove for the grove's sake
and I put this into words:
'Not for you nor anyone
do I wear the cross upòn
my breast, tie my head with silk.
I don't care for cogware, for
wheat slices I don't complain:
    I live in tight clothes
    I grow on breadcrusts
    by my good father
    with my dear mother.'"

The mother put this in words
the eldest spoke to her child:
    "Don't weep, my daughter
fruit of my youth, don't <u>lament</u>!
One year eat melted butter:
you'll grow plumper than others;
    the next year eat pork:
you'll grow sleeker than others;
a third year eat cream pancakes:
you'll grow fairer than others.
Step to the shed on the hill
    open the best shed:
there is chest on top of chest
    and box beside box.
    Open the best chest
    slam the bright lid back:

inside are six golden belts
    and seven blue skirts
all woven by Moon-
    daughter
finished off by Sun-daughter.

What does Aino's mother say she can find in the chest in the shed?

"Long since, when I was a maid
and lived as a lass, I went
for berries in the forest
raspberries under the slope.
I heard Moon-daughter weaving
    Sun-daughter spinning
    beside blue backwoods
at the edge of a sweet grove.
    I went up to them
    I came close, approached;
I began to beg of them
    I uttered and said:
'Give, Moon-daughter, of your gold
Sun-daughter, of your silver
to this girl who has nothing
    to this child who begs!'
Moon-daughter gave of her
    gold
Sun-daughter of her silver:
I put the gold on my brows
on my head the good silver
    and came home a flower
to my father's yards a joy.
I wore them for one day, two
    till on the third day
I stripped the gold from my brows
from my head the good silver
took them to the hilltop shed
put them under the chest lid:
there they have been ever since
all this time unlooked upon.

What did Moon-daughter and Sun-daughter give to Aino's mother when she was a maid?

"Bind now the silks to your eyes
and to your brows lift the gold

ANSWERS TO GUIDED READING QUESTIONS

1. Aino's mother says her daughter can find six golden belts and seven blue skirts made by Moon-daughter and Sun-daughter in the chest.
2. Moon-daughter gave her gold and Sun-daughter gave her silver.

INTERNET RESOURCES

The Finnish Literature Society at http://virtual.finland.fi/finfo/english/kaleva.thml provides excellent information on the origin, content, and influence of the *Kalevala*. Topics include the songs behind the *Kalevala*, Finnish culture in the early 1800s, and summaries of the different poems that make up the epic, among others. Invite students to explore the site. Have them report on the part of the topic that they found most interesting.

words for everyday use

la • ment (lə ment´) *vi.,* express sorrow or grieve; regret strongly. *June <u>lamented</u> the loss of her overtime hours.*

1. Lucky people's feelings are compared to "water stirring / or a ripple on a trough." Luckless people's feelings are compared to "hard snow under a ridge" and "water in a deep well."
2. Aino is grieving because her parents have promised her in marriage to Väinämöinen, whom she sees as an "old man" and a "dodderer."

LITERARY NOTE

Henry Wadsworth Longfellow was influenced by both the style and meter of the *Kalevala* in writing his own epic poem *The Song of Hiawatha*. The original *Kalevala* is written in a meter based on the trochee, a metric unit with one strong and one weak stress. This singsong meter is can be heard in this passage from the opening of Longfellow's poem:
"In the vale of Tawasentha,
In the green and silent valley,
By the pleasant water-courses,
Dwelt the singer Nawadaha."

around your neck the bright beads
the gold crosses on your breasts!
Put on a shirt of linen
one of hempen lawn[5] on top;
pull on a skirt of broadcloth
on top of it a silk belt
    fine stockings of silk
    handsome leather shoes!
Twine your hair into a braid
tie it with ribbons of silk
on your fingers put gold rings
and on your hands gold bracelets!
Like that you will come back home
you will step in from the shed
to be your kinsfolk's sweetness
the softness of all your clan:
you will walk the lanes a flower
you will roam a raspberry
more graceful than you once were
better than you were before."

The mother put that in words
that's what she said to her child
but the daughter did not heed
did not hear the mother's words:
she went weeping to the yard
pining into the farmyard.
    She says with this word
    she spoke with this speech:
"How do the lucky ones feel
and how do the blessed think?
This is how the lucky feel
    how the blessed think—
    like water stirring
or a ripple on a trough.
But how do the luckless feel
and how do the callous think?
This is how the luckless feel
    how the callous think—
like hard snow under a ridge
like water in a deep well.
    Often in my gloom
now, often, a gloomy child
my mood is to tread dead grass
and through undergrowth to crawl

What are the lucky people's feelings compared to? What are luckless people's feelings compared to?

on turf to loiter
in a bush to roll about—
my mood no better than tar
my heart no whiter than coal.
Better it would be for me
and better it would have been
had I not been born, not grown
    not sprung to full size
    in these evil days
    in this joyless world.
Had I died a six-night-old
and been lost an eight-night-old
I would not have needed much—
    a span of linen
    a tiny field edge
a few tears from my mother
still fewer from my father
not even a few from my brother."

She wept one day, she wept two.
Her mother began to ask:
"Why are you weeping, poor lass
why, woebegone, complaining?"

"This is why I, poor lass, weep
    all my time complain:
you have given luckless me
and your own child you have pledged
made me care for an old man
gladden an aged man, be
refuge for a dodderer[6]
shelter for a nook-haunter.[7]
Sooner had you bidden me
go below the deep billows
to be sister to whitefish
and brother to the fishes!
Better to be in the sea
to dwell below the billows
to be sister to whitefish
and brother to the fishes

What is the cause of Aino's grief?

---

5. **hempen lawn.** Cloth made of hemp, a fiber used to make rope
6. **dodderer.** One who trembles from weakness or old age
7. **nook-haunter.** One who haunts, or frequents, secluded or sheltered places

than to care for an old man
be a dodderer's refuge
one who trips on his stockings
who falls over a dry twig."

Then she stepped to the shed-hill
    stepped inside the shed
    opened the best chest
    slammed the bright lid back
and she found six golden belts
    and seven blue skirts
    and she put them on
    she decks her body.
She set the gold on her brows
the silver upon her hair
the blue silks upon her eyes
the red threads upon her head.
    The she stepped away
across one glade, along two;
    she roamed swamps, roamed lands
    roamed gloomy backwoods.
    She sang as she went
    uttered as she roamed:
"In my heart there is a hurt
in my head there is an ache
but the hurt would not hurt more
and the ache would not more ache
if I, hapless, were to die
    were cut off, mean one
    from these great sorrows
    from these low spirits.
Now would be the time for me
    to part from this world—
the time to go to Death, the
age to come to Tuonela:
father would not weep for me
mother would not take it ill
sister's face would not be wet
brother's eyes would not shed tears
though I rolled in the water

What does Aino put on in the shed?

Where does Aino roam?

fell into the fishy sea
down below the deep billows
    upon the black mud."

She stepped one day, she stepped two
    till on the third day
    she came upon sea
    faced a reedy shore:
there the night overtakes her
    the dark <u>detains</u> her.
There the lass wept all evening
    whimpered all night long
on a wet rock on the shore
    at the broad bay-end.

Early in the morning she
looked out at a headland's tip:
three maids at the headland's tip
there were, bathing in the sea!
The maid Aino would be fourth
and the slip of a girl fifth!
She cast her shirt on willow
her skirt upon an aspen
her stockings on the bare ground
her shoes upon the wet rock
her beads on the sandy shore
her rings upon the shingle.
A rock was bright on the main
a boulder glittering gold:
she strove to swim to the rock
she would flee to the boulder.
    Then, when she got there
    she sits herself down
    upon the bright rock
on the glittering boulder:
the rock plopped in the water
    the boulder sank down
    the maid with the rock
Aino beside the boulder.

ANSWERS TO GUIDED READING QUESTIONS

1. She puts on the gold, silver, and blue silks, and the red threads she finds in the chest in the shed.
2. Aino roams swamps and "gloomy backwoods."

LITERARY NOTE

In the *Kalevala,* Tuonela is the Kingdom of Death, similar to Hades, the underground abode of the dead in Greek mythology.

1. Aino drowns in the sea.
2. The hare carries the news of Aino's death back to the farm.

LITERARY TECHNIQUE

Foreshadowing. Foreshadowing is the presenting of information that hints at events to occur later in a story. What earlier comments by Aino foreshadow her death in the sea? What do these comments show about her state of mind?
Answers
As she wanders and weeps, she says "Now would be the time for me / to part from this world—the time to go to Death" and, to her mother, she says, "Better to be in the sea / to dwell below the billows . . . than to care for an old man." Her state of mind is one of sad desperation.

That is where the hen was lost
    there the poor lass died.
She said while she was
    dying
spoke as she was still rolling:
"I went to bathe in the sea
arrived to swim in the main
and there I, a hen, was lost
I, a bird, untimely died:
    let not my father
    ever in this world
    draw any fishes
    from this mighty main!
I went to wash at the shore
I went to bathe in the sea
and there I, a hen, was lost
I, a bird, untimely died:
    let not my mother
    ever in this world
    put water in dough
    from the broad home-bay!
I went to wash at the shore
I went to bathe in the sea
and there I, a hen, was lost
I, a bird, untimely died:
    let not my brother
    ever in this world
    water his war-horse
    upon the seashore!
I went to wash at the shore
I went to bathe in the sea
and there I, a hen, was lost
I, a bird, untimely died:
    let not my sister
    ever in this world
    wash her eyes here, at
    the home-bay landing!
    Waters of the sea
    so much blood of mine;
    fishes of the sea
    so much flesh of mine;
    brushwood on the shore
    is a poor one's ribs;
    grasses of the shore
    are her tousled hair."

What happens to Aino?

Such the death of the young maid
end of the fair little hen.

Who now will carry the news
will tell it by word of mouth
    to the maid's famous
    home, to the fair farm?
A bear will carry the news
will tell it by word of mouth!
But the bear does not: it was
lost among a herd of cows.
Who now will carry the news
will tell it by word of mouth
    to the maid's famous
    home, to the fair farm?
A wolf will carry the news
will tell it by word of mouth!
But the wolf does not: it was
lost among a flock of sheep.
Who now will carry the news
will tell it by word of mouth
    to the maid's famous
    home, to the fair farm?
A fox will carry the news
will tell it by word of mouth!
But the fox does not: it was
lost among a flock of geese.
Who now will carry the news
Will tell it by word of mouth
    to the maid's famous
    home, to the fair farm?
A hare will carry the news
will tell it by word of mouth!
The hare said for sure: "The news
will not be lost on this
    man!"
    And the hare ran off
    the long-ear lolloped
    the wry-leg rushed off
    the cross-mouth careered
    to the maid's famous
    home, to the fair farm.

To the sauna threshold it
ran, on the the threshold it squats.

Who carries the news of Aino's death back to the farm?

The sauna is full of maids;
whisks in hand they greet: "Sly one
have you come here to be cooked
pop-eye, to be roasted for
        the master's supper
        the mistress's meal
        for the daughter's snacks
        or for the son's lunch?"

The hare manages to say
and the round-eye to speak out:
"Perhaps the Devil has come
        to stew in the pans!
I have come carrying news
to tell it by word of mouth:
        the fair has fallen
the tin-breast has pined away
sunken the silver-buckle
the copper-belt slipped away—
gone into the wanton sea
        down to the vast deeps
to be sister to whitefish
and brother to the fishes."

The mother started weeping
and a stream of tears rolling
and then she began to say
the woebegone to complain:
        "Don't, luckless mothers
        ever in this world
        don't lull your daughters
        or rock your children,
to marry against their will
as I, a luckless mother
        have lulled my daughters
        reared my little hens."

What does Aino's mother regret?

The mother wept, a tear rolled:
her plentiful waters rolled
        out of her blue eyes
        to her luckless cheeks.
One tear rolled, another rolled
her plentiful waters rolled
        from her luckless cheeks
        to her ample breasts.

One tear rolled, another rolled
her plentiful waters rolled
        from her ample breasts
        upon her fine hems.
One tear rolled, another rolled
her plentiful waters rolled
        down from her fine hems
upon her red-topped stockings.
One tear rolled, another rolled
her plentiful waters rolled
down from her red-topped stockings
to her gilded[8] shoe-uppers.
One tear rolled, another rolled
her plentiful waters rolled
from her gilded shoe-uppers
to the ground beneath her feet;
they rolled to the ground for the ground's sake
to the water for the water's sake.
The waters reaching the ground
began to form a river
        and three rivers grew
        from the tears she wept
        that came from her
        head
that went from beneath her brow.
        In each river grew
        three fiery rapids;
        on each rapid's foam
        three crags[9] sprouted up
        and on each crag's edge
        a golden knoll[10] rose
        and on each knoll's peak
        there grew three birches;
        in each birch's top
there were three golden cuckoos.

The cuckoos started calling:
        the first called *love, love!*
the second *bridegroom, bridegroom!*
        and the third *joy, joy!*
        That which called *love, love!*
        called out for three months

What forms from the tears of Aino's mother?

---

8. **gilded.** Stitched or decorated with gold
9. **crags.** Steep, rugged rocks or cliffs
10. **knoll.** Small round hill

"THE DROWNED MAID" **141**

ANSWERS TO GUIDED
READING QUESTIONS

1. Aino's mother regrets requiring her daughter to marry against her will.
2. Three rivers form from the tears of Aino's mother.

CROSS-CURRICULAR
CONNECTIONS

MUSIC. The *Kalevala* inspired several major musical works by the Finnish composer Jean Sibelius (1865–1957). Among these was a four-part symphonic work about one of the heroes of the poem, an adventurer and warrior named Lemminkäinen.

In the work's third part, *The Swan of Tuonela,* Lemminkäinen begins a journey to the Kingdom of Death. To win the hand of a beautiful maid, he must complete certain tasks, including shooting the swan on the river of black water that surrounds the kingdom. The mournful mood of the tone poem (a lyric symphonic work that creates musical pictures in the listener's mind) is emphasized by the low string parts and a muted horn representing the song of the swan.

ADDITIONAL QUESTIONS
AND ACTIVITIES

Ask students the following questions:
1. Who is Ruth MacKenzie?
2. What did MacKenzie want to do with the vocal sounds of Finland and Sweden?
3. Why did MacKenzie sing songs in both Finnish and English in the musical production of the *Kalevala*?
Answers
1. Ruth MacKenzie is a singer, writer, and an actor in Minneapolis, Minnesota.
2. She wanted to "house these sounds within [her] body."
3. In order to communicate the story of Aino, she felt she needed to sing her songs in both Finnish and English.

ANSWER TO GUIDED
READING QUESTION

1. The cuckoo's song is a song of
   mourning for Aino's mother.

to the loveless girl
   lying in the sea;
that which called *bridegroom, bridegroom!*
   called out for six months
to the comfortless bridegroom
   sitting and longing;
   that which called *joy, joy!*
called out for all her lifetime
to the mother without joy
   weeping all her days.

The mother put this in words
listening to the cuckoo:

'Let a luckless mother not
listen long to the cuckoo!
When the cuckoo is calling
   my heart is throbbing
tears come to my eyes
   waters down my cheeks
flow thicker than peas
   and fatter than beans:
by an ell[11] my life passes
by a span my frame grows old
my whole body is blighted
when I hear the spring cuckoo." ∎

11. **ell.** Archaic unit of measurement

*Is the cuckoo's song a
song of joy or mourning
for Aino's mother?*

RELATED READING

In the Blue Woodland

from *Kalevala: Dream of the Salmon Maiden*
by Ruth MacKenzie
Song lyrics adapted from Eino Friberg's translation of the *Kalevala*.

Long, long ago, in my girlhood
I went berrying, berry picking on a hillside.
Out in the cloudberries, raspberries
There I heard the Moonmaid sigh.

Daughter of the Moon, she sat to weaving
And her sister sun, bright, Sunsister spinning
In the far blue, the blue woodland
There I saw blue dresses of the eternities.

Anna Kuutar, kultiasi
Päivätär hopeitasi[1]
O how softly, how softly,
I stepped into the blue, stepped into the blue
   woodland
Whispering these words I've kept in secret
Kept in secret but I now repeat to you.

Anna Kuutar, kultiasi
Päivätär hopeitasi
(Give me good Moonmaid of your gold
Give sweet Sunlight your silver stole)
Wrap me around in your bright arms
Give good Moon what this child desires.

Gold on my brow and sleeves of silver
I came to my homegates, I came home then like
   a flower
Wearing the moonlight, the sunlight,
The very sky above, gifts of light and love and
   power.

   Wore them one day, then another
Seven blue dresses, six golden girdles wait you
   As a joy to father's farmyard
This I have kept for you, all from that distant
   girlhood
   But already on the third day
Clang the richest locker up, you behold the
   moon.
   Took the gold from off my forehead
And I saved it all for you my daughter. ∎

1. English translation of the Finnish: Give me good Moonmaid of
your gold; Give sweet Sunlight your silver stole.

INSIGHTS

Musical Adaptation of the *Kalevala* Presented at Guthrie Theater Lab

In June of 1998 the Frank Theatre, the Guthrie Theater, and the Walker Art Center presented *Kalevala: Dream of the Salmon Maiden*, a musical adaptation of the *Kalevala* on the Guthrie Lab stage in Minneapolis, Minnesota. The production was written, composed, and adapted by Ruth

Ruth MacKenzie and cast in *Kalevala: Dream of the Salmon Maiden*. Photo by Ann Marsden.

MacKenzie, a singer, writer, and actor who has explored many creative and performing arenas.

"The first time I heard the vocal sounds of Finland and Sweden, I was hooked. I wanted to house these sounds within my own body," MacKenzie said. In 1994, she studied in Finland and Sweden, as well as working at home experimenting with vocal sounds and "driving my dog nuts. As I learned more about these singing traditions, I wanted to put the songs within the context of a story because in the Finno-Ugrian tradition the singer is the storyteller. The singer is the magician."

In the musical production, three vocalists sing the story of Aino from the *Kalevala*, as it is dramatized by interpretive dancers. MacKenzie interprets the story as "honoring the untamable within each of us." In this section of the *Kalevala* the young maiden Aino eludes the advances of Väinämöinen, a 900-year-old magician, by transforming herself into a salmon in search of her own truth. MacKenzie decided on this story because she felt it resonated with her own path. "Just as Aino, I was going about my business when fate intervened (a concert in Kaustinen, Finland), setting me on a path that has been unpredictable and transformative."

The production was directed by Wendy Knox and choreographed by Wynn Fricke. The presentation included *kulning* (a high-pitched Swedish song for calling animals), Ingrian Choral work, Itku Virsi (crying hymns), and *trallning* (Swedish cat singing). In order to communicate the story of Aino, MacKenzie decided to sing in both Finnish and English. She used traditional Finnish and Swedish melodies and created new melodies inspired by the tradition. MacKenzie integrated Finnish text with English text so that audiences could hear the original language as well as the poetry that is part of this tradition. "I've taken the original *Kalevala* text and interwoven poems from other Finno-Ugrian song lyric sources to broaden the emotional and metaphysical landscape from which the story is told. But truly at the heart of this work is the voice, the untamed voice."

MacKenzie received a 1995 Fellowship grant from the Minnesota State Arts Board for her performance work of Scandinavian and Finno-Ugrian singing styles, a 1996 Diverse Visions Grant from Intermedia Arts, and a 1994 Jerome Foundation Travel/Study grant. She was awarded Artist of the Year in 1997 by both the Minneapolis *Star Tribune* and *City Pages* newspapers for her production of *Kalevala, Dream of the Salmon Maiden*. A compact disk recording of the performance is also available from Omnium. For more information and to listen to the audio recording visit the website at http://www.omnium.com/kalevala/. ∎

"THE DROWNED MAID" 143

SELECTION CHECK TEST 4.2.25 WITH ANSWERS

Checking Your Reading
1. What is the young maiden's name? **Her name is Aino.**
2. What instructions did Vainamoinen give to Aino? **He told her to wear beads around her neck, set the cross on her breast, put a braid into her hair, and to bind her hair with silk; however, these things must only be done for him.**
3. How does Aino react to Vainamoinen's instructions? **She throws everything he gave her onto the ground and runs away from him.**
4. What does Aino's mother tell her to eat? **She tells her to eat melted butter, pork, and cream pancakes.**
5. How does Aino die? **She is pulled down by a rock that sinks into the sea.**

Vocabulary in Context
Fill in each blank below with the most appropriate word from the following Words for Everyday Use. You may have to change the tense of the word.

    wrench   lament   detain

1. We were **detained** at the airport due to a storm.
2. Jonah **wrenched** off his tie after a long day of work.
3. Clarence **lamented** the loss of his car keys.

Literary Tools
Fill in the blanks using the following terms.

    repetition   parallelism   epic
                Balto-Finnic

1. A(n) **epic** is a long story, told in verse, that involves heroes and gods.
2. **Repetition** is a writer's conscious reuse of a word, phrase, or sound.
3. The rhetorical technique in which a writer emphasizes the equality of two or more ideas by using the same grammatical format is called **parallelism**.

TEACHER'S EDITION **143**

RESPOND TO THE SELECTION

Have students make a list of alternative actions that Aino could have taken instead of drowning herself. You might have students vote on the best idea for getting Aino out of her betrothal.

ANSWERS TO INVESTIGATE, INQUIRE, AND IMAGINE

RECALL

1a. Aino throws off those adornments and leaves them all on the ground and returns home weeping.

2a. She roams swamps and "gloomy backwoods" and finally arrives at the sea.

3a. She drowns, becoming "sister to whitefish / and brother to the fishes."

INTERPRET

1b. Aino does not love Väinämöinen and is not interested in his advances.

2b. Aino leaves home because her parents have betrothed her to old Väinämöinen, whom she does not want to marry.

3b. *Responses will vary.* The part of the poem describing her death says only that she "went to bathe in the sea . . . and untimely, died." But her earlier words—"the hurt would not hurt more . . . if I, hapless, were to die"—suggest that suicide was her planned method of escape from an unbearable situation.

ANALYZE

4a. Aino says, "Waters of the sea / so much blood of mine; / fishes of the sea / so much flesh of mine." As she dies, Aino identifies herself with the sea—the waters are her blood and the fish her flesh.

SYNTHESIZE

4b. Water is tied to sadness. First, in her sadness, Aino drowns herself in the sea. Then, after Aino's death, her mother cries in grief to such an extent that her tears form three rivers.

(Continued on page 145)

Respond to the SELECTION

How well do you think Aino handled the situation of being betrothed to someone she did not love?

Investigate, Inquire, and Imagine

Recall: GATHERING FACTS

1a. When Väinämöinen asks Aino to wear her adornments for him alone, what does Aino do?

2a. When Aino leaves the farm, her home, where does she go?

3a. What happens to Aino when she bathes in the sea?

Interpret: FINDING MEANING

1b. What does Aino's response reveal about her feelings for Väinämöinen?

2b. Why does Aino leave home?

3b. Is Aino's death intentional?

Analyze: TAKING THINGS APART

4a. Analyze Aino's affinity with the sea.

Synthesize: BRINGING THINGS TOGETHER

4b. To what emotion is water tied in this selection?

Perspective: LOOKING AT OTHER VIEWS

5a. How do you predict the mother will arrange a wedding for her other daughter, now that Aino is dead?

Empathy: SEEING FFROM INSIDE

5b. If you were Aino's mother, how would you view the hare after Aino's death?

Understanding Literature

PARALLELISM. Review the definition of **parallelism** in the Handbook of Literary Terms. After the death of Aino is announced on page 141, what example of parallelism do you find as the narrator announces who might deliver the news to Aino's family? What effect does this example of parallelism have on the story?

REPETITION. Review the definition of **repetition** in the Handbook of Literary Terms and the cluster chart you made on page 134. Which example of repetition demonstrates how upset Aino was by Väinämöinen's advances? Which example of repetition serves to foreshadow Aino's death? Which example of repetition reinforces the mother's grief?

144 UNIT TWO / POETRY

ANSWERS TO UNDERSTANDING LITERATURE

PARALLELISM. Parallelism is found in the use of the future tense: "A bear (wolf, fox, hare) will carry the news / will tell it by word of mouth!" This example of parallelism has the effect of creating suspense, as the reader wonders how the parents will learn of Aino's death.

REPETITION. "I have cause to weep / woes to complain of!" is the example of repetition that demonstrates how upset Aino was by Väinämöinen's advances. "To be sister to whitefish / and brother to the fishes" serves to foreshadow Aino's death. "One tear rolled, another rolled / her plentiful waters rolled" reinforces the mother's grief.

Writer's Journal

1. Imagine you are Väinämöinen. Write a **love note** to Aino expressing how you feel and your response to her behavior in the grove.
2. Imagine Aino writes to the newspaper for advice on how to get out of her engagement. Write an **advice column** offering a solution to her problem.
3. Write a **ballad** summarizing the main events of "The Drowned Maid." A ballad is a simple narrative poem in four-line stanzas, usually meant to be sung and usually rhyming *abcb*.

Integrating the Language Arts

Language, Grammar, and Style

AGREEMENT OF PRONOUNS AND ANTECEDENTS. Read the Language Arts Survey 3.45, "Getting Pronouns and Antecedents to Agree." Then rewrite the following sentences so that the pronouns and antecedents agree. If a sentence has no errors, write *Correct*.

1. Old Väinämöinen wanted to ask the maid for his hand in marriage.
2. The maid wrenched the cross from her breast and threw it on the ground in protest.
3. The maid's father asked their question: Why are you crying, daughter?
4. Aino cast aside his clothes and swam in the sea.
5. The mother decided parents shouldn't make children marry against his will.

Speaking and Listening

ORAL INTERPRETATION. In groups of three, practice reciting the meeting of Väinämöinen and Aino in the grove. Have the first student play the role of the narrator, the second student play the role of Väinämöinen, and the third student play the role of Aino. Decide what gestures, tone, facial expressions, and body posture you should use. Then present an oral interpretation to the class. Refer to the Language Arts Survey 4.19, "Oral Interpretation" for tips on how to analyze the narrator and characters of a narrative poem.

Study and Research

WORLD EPICS. Research another epic besides the *Kalevala*, such as Homer's *Iliad* or *Odyssey*, Virgil's *Aeneid*, Dante's *The Divine Comedy*, the Old English *Beowulf*, or Milton's *Paradise Lost*. Then, in small groups, relate what your epic is about, and give a plot outline. Explain what makes your epic an epic. What heroes and gods are portrayed? What does the epic reveal about the legends, beliefs, values, laws, arts, and ways of life of those people?

PERSPECTIVE

5a. Toward the end of the selection, the mother advises other mothers: "Don't, luckless mothers / ever in this world / don't lull your daughters / or rock your children / to marry against their will." From Aino's death the mother has learned not to force a daughter to marry someone against her will. She will probably make sure that her other daughter approves of her betrothed before arranging the wedding.

EMPATHY

5b. *Responses will vary.*

ANSWERS TO INTEGRATING THE LANGUAGE ARTS

Language, Grammar, and Style

1. Old Väinämöinen wanted to ask the maid for her hand in marriage.
2. *Correct*
3. The maid's father asked her the question: Why are you crying, daughter?
4. Aino cast aside her clothes and swam in the sea.
5. The mother decided parents shouldn't make children marry against their will.

Speaking and Listening

Students might also benefit from reviewing the elements of verbal and nonverbal communication in the Language Arts Survey 4.1 as they plan how to interpret the poem.

Study and Research

Encourage students to consult specialized encyclopedias with articles about literary or traditional epics.

ADDITIONAL QUESTIONS AND ACTIVITIES

Ask students the following questions:
1. What is a poetry slam?
2. With what does Bao Phi like to combine poetry?
3. What overriding theme(s) is found in Bao Phi's poetry?

Answers
1. A poetry slam is a competition of words that is part poetry reading and part sports meet.
2. Bao Phi likes to combine poetry with music.
3. The theme of struggle—the struggle of being Asian American in the United States and the struggle of facing racism—is found in his poetry.

Language Arts *in Action*

PARTICIPATING IN A POETRY SLAM

What is a poetry slam? It's a competition of the spoken word—part poetry reading and part sports meet. "Slam" is a word borrowed from the world of sports. The term *slam* or *grand slam* can be found in baseball, golf, and tennis. Slams were invented in the mid–1980s to help bring poetry to a wider audience and make it more of a recreational event. The first slam-type events were held in boxing rings with poets decked out in boxing gloves and shorts, and crowds got rowdy. Now, slams have caught on across the country—over 40 states now hold regular poetry slams at local cafés, clubs, bookstores, pizza parlors, libraries, or other public places.

At most poetry slams, anyone can enter the competition. Judges are chosen randomly from the audience, and score poets on a scale from 0.0 to 10.0. The audience is encouraged to cheer or boo a judge's score. At the end of the evening, the poet with the highest score wins the slam. At the end of a slam season, many cities and regions choose a team of four poets to send to the National Poetry Slam held each year in a different state.

Thien-bao Thuc Phi, a 25-year-old poet from Minneapolis, has been chosen three years in a row to participate in the National Poetry Slam with the Minnesota Slam Team. He writes poems about love and about life in America from his perspective as an Asian American. Bao was born in Vietnam; he and his family were refugees from the war, and fled to the United States in the 1970s. Bao Phi is interested in combining his poetry with music. On his new CD, *Flares,* he accompanies his words with instrumentals including the taiko drum, flute, and beatbox.

On the facing page is one of the poems Bao has slammed with. Like many of his poems, it deals with the struggle for Asian Americans to find a place in American culture while fighting racism and racial stereotyping. In the poem, Bao refers to Lawson Fusao Inada, a Japanese-American poet and musician; Nellie Wong, a Chinese-American poet and union activist; and Thien Minh Ly, a 24-year-old Vietnamese man and graduate of UCLA who fell victim to a racially motivated hate crime in 1996.

1999 Minnesota Poetry Slam Team.
L–R: Matthew John Conley,
Meghan McInerney,
Thien-bao Thuc Phi,
Diego Vázquez, Jr., Slam Master

146 UNIT TWO

Where Is Our Blues?

Asian america, where is our blues?

I went looking for it
in my corner of the world called tundra
whispering bilingual riddles that turned
into the ghosts of breath in the air
yes I went looking for our blues
while overhead the stars lit up like flares
Asian america, I went looking for you.

I thought I found you
on Nicollet Avenue,
knew you were cold and just for a moment
I felt warm
so I wanted to wrap you in my arms
ask you to sing your favorite song
while the shadows from the hanging ducks
slashed sharp across the sidewalk:
they lengthen, we use them to tell time
we let our minds rhyme
but I was chasing that radiant silhouette
called love,
and I lost you.

So I drew a map by connecting
the internment camps
hopped in a Nissan, listened to the
ching chong lights-on warning tone,
turned on the Sanyo radio,
asked Lawson Fusao Inada for
direction,
inflection,
a blues infection.
He told me to look up and
follow the concentration constellation:
sometimes
our blues rhymes.

I thought I saw Nellie Wong
but it was just steam in the shape of a poetess
by the docks in Seattle,
in a black night the yellow lights through smoke
can paint a yellow ghost of a girl
who billows in the wind to become
steam woman, substantial,
warm, haunting.

I wandered down to Little Sai Gon
looked for our blues in a tricolor dessert.
This is when I wanted to go to UCLA
ask Thien Minh Ly the way.
But he couldn't answer, his mouth
full of blood, his body full of holes,
so I followed his directions
to the blues and just cried, y'all,
I just cried and cried.

Asian america,
I'm just one of your sons.
who was transmitted in black and white
but grew up in color,
who carries blue like a berry
in my heart
blue like a river in my body
blue like an echoing whisper
in my mind
blue like incense smoke
in my spirit
blue like the missing song of my love
in my soul

blue
paints the testimony
of my hands
blue fills my home
and spills out the door
into the street
Asian america,
all the streets towards you are blue.

Asian america
where is our blues?
it's here.
oh, it's here

here it is

Thien-bao Thuc Phi

ADDITIONAL QUESTIONS AND ACTIVITIES

Encourage students to form their own poetry slam. They may want to compete, using a poem they have written themselves or a poem written by their favorite poet. Students should decide who is going to compete and who will act as judges. There should be at least five judges present. You may want to set the rules for the contest—what each contestant will be judged on, how much time each contestant gets to read their poem, and how each performance will be scored.

Interview with Thien-Bao Thuc Phi

We talked to Bao Phi about his experiences with poetry and slamming.

How did you first become interested in poetry? Did you always know you wanted to be a poet or was it something that happened by accident?

I actually started to sketch/draw when I was 5—and to some extent, I'm very visually oriented. I began writing fiction when I was in fourth grade, as an escape from the reality of my surroundings (refugee, poverty, violence, etc). I fell in love with books at a young age, because my family was poor and we couldn't afford toys: I would walk by myself to the neighborhood library and read all day, or check out some books. Poetry came later—inspired by hip hop and poets such as Lawson Fusao Inada, Quincy Troupe and Ntozake Shange, I began to seriously write poetry when I was 15 (ten years ago). I wrote because I felt the need to—when I was younger, I didn't necessarily think I was going to be a poet.

Did you go to college and major in literature? What classes have you taken that have helped your writing?

Yes, I majored in Creative Writing. All the classes helped me, to some extent.

When do you sit down to write? Do you have a sort of ritual, such as a time of day you usually write, or where you like to sit? Do you write something every day, or just whenever you feel like it?

I try to write every day. I don't have any particular rituals or set a time for it—in a way, that would be too constraining. Although writing is about dedication and work, it's also about the need to express. Sometimes you can't get there if you try overly hard.

How did you get started slamming? Were you nervous at first about sharing your poems in a competition? Do you think it is really possible to "judge" poetry just as you would judge a dive or other athletic performance or is it more subjective?

Slamming is something I stumbled onto—I wasn't even sure what it was when I competed for the first time. I wasn't too shy about the competition aspect, because in college I competed on the speech team. In a way, I think it's possible to judge poetry to a degree: some poems and performances are more polished than others. But when you get poets who are about the same level, that's when it gets really subjective.

What does your family think of your poetry?

In Viet Nam, poetry is regarded as one of the highest forms of art. My family is proud, but at the same time they are worried about whether or not I can make a living doing this. They know that poetry isn't as highly regarded here as it is back in the homeland.

Which poets do you enjoy reading?

Sherman Alexie, Quincy Troupe, Lawson Inada, Ntozake Shange, Nellie Wong, Jessica Hagedorn, Marilyn Chin, Philip Levine, David Mura, Joanna Kadi, Vijit Ramchandani, Dwight Okita, Cornelius Eady, Mai Neng Moua, Venessa Fuentes, Willie Perdomo, Sonia Sanchez, Zoli Hall, Sarah Jones, Saul Williams, Emily Chang, Anida Esguerra, Marlon Esguerra, Dennis Kim, Beau Sia, Pablo Neruda...

If you would like to get involved in poetry slamming, visit the National Poetry Slam homepage at http://www.poetryslam.com, or do a general search of the Internet for poetry slam-related sites. If there are no slam events being held in your area, start your own! You can hold a competition at your school or at a local hangout. Whether competing on teams as individuals, all slammers must follow these rules:

- All work must be original to the poet
- No props, costumes, or background music may be used
- Performances are limited to three minutes

Generally, points are taken off if a poet goes over the time limit. Competitors should rehearse before the performance to be sure they won't go over time. Judges can make their decisions based on a set of criteria you determine beforehand, such as value of content, emotional effect, originality, and delivery. The audience should respect both the competitors and the judges. ∎

148 *UNIT TWO*

LESSON OVERVIEW

Interpreting a Poem
Student Model, 149
Examining the Model, 149
Prewriting, 150
Finding Your Voice, 150
Identifying Your Audience, 150
Writing with a Plan, 151
Student Model—Graphic Organizer, 151
Drafting, 152
Self- and Peer Evaluation, 152
Revising and Proofreading, 153
Student Model (continued), 153
Publishing and Presenting, 155
Reflecting, 155

Language, Grammar, and Style
WRITING WITH CONTEXT CLUES
Identifying Context Clues to Define Words, 153
Fixing Unclear Writing by Adding Context Clues, 155
Using Context Clues Effectively, 155

> "Genuine poetry can communicate before it is understood."
> —T. S. Eliot

INTERPRETING A POEM

When we encounter art in any form, including poetry, we usually receive it and then rate it—is it good? Is it beautiful? Do I like it? Only sometimes do we think, "Why do I like it?" or "How do I know it's beautiful?" It is important to ask those questions, however, because those are the questions that best allow art to do one of its jobs: to tell us about ourselves.

Too often people think a poem can mean anything—after all, it's all personal interpretation, isn't it? That's only partially true. Intelligent people seriously regard only interpretations that are supported by reasonable examples.

WRITING ASSIGNMENT. In this lesson, you'll get the chance to ask those questions about one of the poems you've just read. Your assignment is to write a *poem explication*, a thorough analysis of a poem that explores its meaning and the literary techniques the poet used to create that meaning. As such, an explication should not concern itself too much with the idea of *if* it is good or beautiful as much as *how* it is good or beautiful.

For this assignment, you will offer your personal interpretation of a poem, but then back it up objectively. As you finalize your paper, you can look forward to a better understanding of a poet, a poem and, most important, your own relationship to great writing.

Student Model

from "Dreaming a Reward for the Dream"
by Silvano Ortiz

Langston Hughes was the first African-American poet to make a living from just his writing. He was a main figure of the Harlem Renaissance, a rebirth of African-American culture in the 1930s. His legacy was that he mixed jazz techniques with traditional poetry to create powerful works that spoke to his generation. However, Hughes was still a black man living in America at a time when segregation was allowed by law. So he felt oppressed in spite of his success. In "Dream Variations," all of these factors burst from two stanzas that look simple, but are

EXAMINING THE MODEL. The writer of the model clearly had a close, personal experience with Hughes's poem. Still, Silvano's essay concerns itself with the devices and techniques Hughes used to create meaning. His introduction demonstrates a bias toward the poem, in phrases like, "...to create powerful works" and "that spoke to his

continued on page 150

GUIDED WRITING
Software

See the Guided Writing Software for an extended version of this lesson that includes printable graphic organizers, extensive student models and student-friendly checklists, and self-, peer, and teacher evaluation features.

MOTIVATION
Have students discuss the poem they like best from Unit 2. Then have them explain why they liked it the best. Explain to students that liking a poem is a good first step toward explicating a poem.

READING PROFICIENCY
Have students read the Student Model on pages 149–154. This will help them to get a better sense of the writing they should strive to produce for this lesson.

ENGLISH LANGUAGE LEARNING
Pair students with a native English speaker as they work on completing their graphic organizer. The native English speaker can review the completed graphic organizer with them and make sure it demonstrates understanding of the lesson.

SPECIAL NEEDS
This activity may be difficult for students with special needs. You may want to simplify this assignment by having students offering their personal feelings about a poem—such as whether they like it or not—and explaining why they feel that way.

ENRICHMENT
Students may be interested in submitting their poem explication to the school newspaper or a literary website on the Internet. Before students do this, however, you may suggest that they go through an editing stage with you to make sure their paper is polished and free of grammatical errors.

Prewriting

FINDING YOUR VOICE. For this assignment, students may want to blend both formal and informal language in their paper. Refer students to the Language Arts Survey 3.2, "Formal and Informal English."

IDENTIFYING YOUR AUDIENCE. Help students identify their audience for this assignment. They may need to prepare their papers for you, the instructor, but may also need to prepare them for their classmates, as well. Refer to Language Arts Survey 2.4, "Identifying Your Audience."

continued on page 151

generation," but he doesn't use "I" or "you," which would be too informal. Note that Silvano doesn't need to use "I"—it's his essay: the reader assumes the thoughts are his.

Once he states his idea about what the poem is about and lets the reader know he likes the poem, Silvano uses the next part of his paper for an objective description of Hughes's techniques.

The overall effect of the piece demonstrates the basic effective technique for writing essays: state a position and then prove it.

really complex. This poem is an expression of the frustration the speaker feels as a creative African-American working within a dominant white culture. It uses images of nature and dance, rhyme and jazz techniques to make this point.

The main images in the poem are the dance, the sun and a tree in cool evening. These represent creative expression, oppression and reward, respectively. Hughes uses exciting words like "whirl" and "fling" to give the reader a picture of a free-form dance, the way people dance to jazz, instead of a more formal dance like ballet. It is a releasing action. The dancer is dancing in the sunlight, but the sunlight doesn't seem to be the good thing it usually is—in the first stanza it's just there: "some place of the sun." In the second stanza, the sun is something to be defied. Further, the sun makes a "white day" in which the dancer dances. This must be interpreted as a reference to white dominance in general. The third image, the tree in the evening, represents the reward. It's like a release from the struggle against the oppression. When all these images are taken together, they present a kind of plot: the speaker creatively dances against the sun that is whiteness, an exuberant dance of freedom, and earns a rest beneath a tall tree as his natural state—Blackness—returns to him.

Prewriting

FINDING YOUR VOICE. The poetry you have read in this unit sometimes uses elevated language to make its point. Devices like repetition and classical allusions create "poetic" voices that almost seem to come from somewhere above us. You don't need to use this same kind of voice in your essay just because you're writing about it. On the other hand, the feelings expressed by these poems demand a little respect, so you also won't want to use the same voice you use when talking to your friends in the hall. Use a true, thoughtful voice to speak confidently and honestly of important issues in an academic setting.

IDENTIFYING YOUR AUDIENCE. As part of deciding on an appropriate voice for your essay, consider who will be reading it. Your audience for this paper will include other students like you who have read the poem but don't know as much about it as you do. It's your job to fill them in on what it's about.

When identifying an audience, you should also consider how you will be publishing this essay. For instance, if you plan to post this essay to an Internet site featuring student work, you should include more detail. The wider you make the audience, the more you must assume that they won't know much about the poem or the poet.

WRITING WITH A PLAN. Good poetry spirals and surprises you—that's what makes it so fun to read! However, sometimes that's what makes it frustrating, too. In order to prepare yourself for the experience of encountering great poetry, make a reading plan. Follow the plan through to the end, and you'll probably emerge with a clear understanding of the poem.

Read the poem you are explicating several times. Then read and discuss it in a small group with others who have chosen different poems. Listen to the way your classmates have interpreted their poems, but also pay close attention to what you say about the poem you have selected—you might be surprised by how much thinking you've already done about it.

Right after your small group work, take a moment to write down what you have discovered about your poem. What is this poem about? How does it make you feel? What literary techniques are used in the poem? Then share your notes as a group.

Now that you've generated some thoughts about your poem, you need to write and organize them. As you organize, work in the general order in which your paper might take shape. That is, begin with a general statement, and then decide why you know this is true. At the end, sum up the thoughts you've generated and you'll have a thesis statement. Silvano organized his thoughts this way:

Student Model—Graphic Organizer

Name of Poem	"Dream Variations"
Poet	Langston Hughes
Biography Note #1	first African American to support himself exclusively from his writing.
Biography Note #2	Harlem Renaissance
What this poem is about	Dancing, being creative and excited, even if you're held back by something – relates to black/white relations, but not only – and if you do it, you'll be rewarded. But it is a dream…

How to Read A Poem
Read with the eye
Observe the way the poet has laid out the poem on the page—the lengths of the lines, the gaps between sections, the spaces around the words and everything that gives the poem shape. Try to look at a poem as you might a painting or a sculpture. How does the shape affect your experience with the poem?

Read with the ear
Read the poem out loud to yourself or to someone else, or both. Poetry's earliest roots are in song. Good poems come alive and create music when read aloud. Try to hear that music as you read through the poem. How does the music help communicate the meaning of the poem?

Respond to what is unique
After you've read the poem with your eyes and ears, try to find its heart. What makes this poem unique? Why did this poem need to be written? Jot a few notes to yourself about the unique character of the poem.

Think about what is general
Although each poem is unique, all poems share some features. They are:
- composed of words
- narrowly focused
- crafted to unite thought and emotion
- shaped in a particular and intentional form

Keep these four features in mind as you talk and write about your poem.

Prewriting (CONT.)

WRITING WITH A PLAN. Schedule brief, individual conferences to make sure students have a clear focus and topic for their poem explication. You may suggest that students bring along three possible thesis statements to their conference.

Student Model— Graphic Organizer

See the Writing Resource book for a blackline master of the graphic organizer for this lesson.

Self- and Peer Evaluation

Read through your draft with your thesis statement in mind.

- What is your thesis? How well does your paper prove it?
- Does everything in the essay relate to the thesis? What should you add or delete to strengthen your thesis?

When you have a solid draft, have someone from your identified audience read it. Ask your peer reviewer to do three things:

- read your paper out loud to you
- tell you what your paper is about
- point to the exact place where they knew what your paper was about

Don't argue with or correct your reader. Simply thank that person and go on to the next steps.

- What did you notice about your essay when you heard it read aloud? What weak arguments did you notice?
- What about the reader's comments surprised you? What should you change based on this response?
- Did your reader see the essay you thought you wrote? Why, or why not?

Sit down immediately and write notes to yourself about what you heard, as well as possible solutions.

If there is time, you may want someone else to evaluate your paper.

continued on page 153

How I know this? #1	The images tell a story that says that—	dance, tree, sun
How I know this? #2	the sounds — they emphasize the dance vs. the rest	rhyme scheme/ no rhyme scheme "eeeee" sounds
How I know this? #3	the way the poem sounds like jazz — changes from one stanza to the next make emphasis for clarification	variations on a theme, "some place" vs. in your face
MY THESIS STATEMENT	Langston Hughes's poem "Dream Variations" is an expression of the frustration the speaker feels as a creative African American oppressed by a dominant white culture. The poem uses images like the tree, the sun and the dance, as well as consonance and jazz techniques, to make its point.	

Notice how this chart converted nicely into the five paragraphs of Silvano's essay. He started with biographical information and what the poem is about, and then went straight through "How I know this" numbers one, two, and three, following the chart. In the organizational chart his thesis statement comes last, but notice how it sounds a lot like his conclusion. A strong conclusion restates your thesis and supporting statements.

Drafting

Your reading and organization have generated some great ideas about a complex subject; don't be surprised if it comes out a bit jumbled at first. Keep two things in mind as you write:

- your thesis statement—*why* are you writing this?
- your audience—to *whom* are you talking?

Also, remember to write in an honest, confident voice appropriate to the assignment.

On the first draft, just write without correcting yourself. If you are composing on a word processor, try not to delete whole blocks of text at once. If you need to make a big change, just move that section to the bottom of your essay so it will be there if you change your mind. For tips on writing and supporting your thesis, see the Language Arts Survey 2.25, "Writing a Thesis Statement" and 2.26, "Writing Main Ideas and Supporting Details."

Revising and Proofreading

As you begin to revise, keep your peer evaluation comments in mind, as well as those in your self-evaluation. Imagine each paragraph in the body of your essay as an arrow that points to a concept. Does every paragraph point toward a concept in your thesis statement? If not, you might need to sharpen the paragraph or broaden your thesis statement.

Also watch out for the over-writing sometimes found in poetry explications. Poetry reading can be an emotional experience, but writing about it requires a more objective view.

The following is the remainder of Silvano's explication of Langston Hughes's poem "Dream Variations."

Student Model (continued)

This "plot" is reinforced by Hughes's use of rhyme and assonance. The first stanza splits in half and the fifth line is a transition between the two halves. In the first half, the rhyme scheme is irregular like a modern dance (abcb) with the word "to" keeping beat. At the end of the fifth line, the word "evening" has a long "e" sound that creates assonance with the long "e" sounds at the ends of the next three lines. The long "e" is a soothing, cool sound at the end of each line. It also slows down the reader. In this way, the jumbled freedom dance of the first half is mellowed out and a relaxing rest under a tall tree follows it as evening covers the hero. This same general pattern happens in the second stanza. This time the differences between the halves are even more obvious. Hughes puts in even more excitement into the first half with "Dance! Whirl! Whirl!" and relaxes the second half by use of the ellipses at the end of two lines that force the poem to slow down.

When Hughes repeats a thought the second time through like that he is working in the jazz methods that influenced the whole Harlem Renaissance. In jazz, a theme is introduced and then each instrument takes a turn trying out

Revise your paper once more. Then have a peer answer these questions:

- Does the writer prove the thesis?
- Does everything in the essay relate to the thesis?
- Is there anything that should be eliminated or added to the thesis?
- Has the writer used examples from the poem to support his or her ideas?
- What poetic techniques does the paper discuss?
- Where has the writer included contextual clues to help the reader understand his or her meaning?

 Language, Grammar, and Style

Writing with Context Clues

IDENTIFYING CONTEXT CLUES TO DEFINE WORDS. When you come across an unfamiliar word while reading, but don't have access to a dictionary, what do you do? Often, you can figure out what a word means by using context clues. To do this, you use the familiar words around it to deduce the meaning of the unfamiliar.

continued on page 154

Revising and Proofreading

A handout of the proofreading checklist is available in the Teacher's Resource Kit, Writing Resource book 2.45.

Language, Grammar, and Style

Writing with Context Clues
LESSON OVERVIEW
In this lesson, students will be asked to do the following:
- Identify Context Clues to Define Words, 153
- Fix Unclear Writing by Adding Context Clues, 155
- Use Context Clues Effectively, 155

INTRODUCING THE SKILL. Explain to students that being able to derive meaning of words that are unfamiliar to them through the use of context clues is a sign of becoming a proficient reader. Also, this skill will make their reading go faster because they don't have to stop and look up the unfamiliar word in the dictionary.

continued on page 154

PREVIEWING THE SKILL. Refer students to the Words for Everyday Use in previous selections they have read. Have them read the contextual sentence that is written after the definition. Point out to students how the contextual sentence hints at the definition of the vocabulary word.

PRACTICING THE SKILL. For additional practice, have students select ten words from the Words for Everyday Use listed on page 156 and write contextual sentences for each word.

One type of context clue is *restatement*. Sometimes the writer tells you the meaning of the word by stating the thought again nearby, in familiar words.

RESTATEMENT

George razed the city. He absolutely destroyed it.

Here, restatement provides a contextual clue that "razed" must mean something like "absolutely destroyed." If the author doesn't give clues in the next sentence, he or she might define an obscure word right in the sentence itself. This is called *apposition*.

APPOSITION

Hughes made great use of consonance, the use of similar sounds to create unity and rhythm.

Here, the author has helped out the reader with what might be a difficult term because the success of the essay depends, in part, on the reader understanding the concept of consonance.

Sometimes, *examples* given in a sentence will offer context clues.

EXAMPLES

The words *dad, radar,* and *tenet* are all palindromes.

By looking at the examples, you see that "palindrome" means a word that can be read forward or backward.

The key factor in figuring out context clues is common sense. Use it to make your reading experiences more smooth and enjoyable.

continued on page 155

154 *UNIT TWO*

variations on that theme. In "Dream Variations" the theme is introduced in the first stanza with hints about where it will go. In the second part, the theme is restated, only more powerfully, with only a few changes. For example, the first stanza says the sun is a general "some place," but in the second stanza the dancer is right "in the face" of the sun. "In your face" maybe did not mean quite the same thing in the 1930s that it does now, but this is still stronger wording and emotion. As another example, the "day" changes from "white" to "quick." This is a different note meant to complement the first. Together, they relate the idea that the whiteness, though dominant, will not last forever. It will be replaced by the "rest at pale evening" earned by the dance which becomes more frantic and energetic in the second stanza. But, just as the dance is more dramatic, the response to it is that much more relaxed also, since the ellipses nearly stop the poem.

Still, the reader does make it through the poem, and is probably better for it. Since we know that Hughes was a certain kind of person living in a certain time, we think the poem is about black and white relationships. It probably is, especially since Hughes once said that he thought his job was to "explain and illuminate the Negro condition in America." However, this poem goes beyond the subject of race relations. Using striking images, sound and jazz techniques, it talks about the struggle of any human to dance in the harsh glare of the world, and of the dreamed-of reward for dreaming at all.

Publishing and Presenting

Poetry explications are a great way to get other people to read a poem that touched you by offering objective reasons for its qualities. Where might you publish or present your essay to reach the people you think should read the poem? Maybe you could combine your essay with your classmates' and make a resource book for your library or a bulletin board display to help other students evaluate which poets they might want to read. The point of writing is, after all, communication, so be sure to get your thoughts out there where the world can admire them!

Reflecting

So often we go through our day consuming art of various sorts —wall murals, songs on the radio, a friend's doodle—without examining our relationship to it or how it works. What did the artist do to make something happen in our heads or hearts? Poetry explications are a great way to explore that question. What else around you could be "explicated"? What does your favorite song have or do that your least favorite doesn't? Can you explicate things that aren't strictly "art"? Can you explicate the sun?

FIXING UNCLEAR WRITING BY ADDING CONTEXT CLUES. Do you know the meanings of the words *smorked* and *pracup*? Read the following sentence.

I smorked the pracup, a tall, leafy one, and it shattered into many pieces.

What part of speech is *smorked*? How about *pracup*? What sort of object is a *pracup*? Does the word *smorked* refer to a gentle action, or a more violent one? How do you know all of this?

It doesn't really matter that *smorked* and *pracup* are not real words. Just by looking at their places in the sentence and the words around them— their context—you were able to determine many things about them.

Read through the student model on pages 153 and 154. What context clues could you add to help the reader understand *consonance*, *ellipses*, and *Harlem Renaissance*?

USING CONTEXT CLUES EFFECTIVELY. Read through your essay and look for terms and expressions that are important to your point, but which might be unfamiliar to your audience. Some examples might be literary terms, technical terms, or words particular to your poet's age or society. What context clues could you add to help the reader understand?

Publishing and Presenting

Students may also be interested in turning their poetry explications into a persuasive essay or speech, persuading their audience to see a poem from their perspective or to simply get others to read it.

Reflecting

Encourage students to write a journal entry reflecting on one or more of the questions provided.

UNIT 2 review
Poetry

Words for Everyday Use

Check your knowledge of the following vocabulary words from the selections in this unit. Write a short sentence using these words in context to make the meaning clear. To review the definition or usage of a word, refer back to the page number listed or the Glossary of Words for Everyday Use.

anguish, 124	feature, 107	palpable, 98	valid, 103
asunder, 124	fell, 125	prominence, 103	viridian, 79
detain, 139	insolence, 103	protract, 80	wrench, 136
dilate, 103	isolated, 107	rivery, 124	
eaves, 79	knoll, 125	sepia, 79	
enchanted, 107	lament, 137	triviality, 103	

Literary Tools

Define the following terms, giving concrete examples of how they are used in the selections in this unit. To review a term, refer to the page number indicated or the Handbook of Literary Terms.

abstract, 101	mood, 88	rhyme scheme, 106
allusion, 120	paradox, 96	rhythm, 92
concrete, 101	parallelism, 134	run-on line, 92
image, 78, 83, 116	personification, 78, 120	simile, 96
imagery, 78	point of view, 128	stanza, 101
inversion, 106	repetition, 88, 92, 128, 134	tone, 83, 116
meter, 111	rhyme, 111	

Reflecting on your reading

Genre Studies

1. **LYRIC AND NARRATIVE POETRY.** Select a lyric poem and a narrative poem from the unit and explain how they differ. Use specific examples from the poems to define what a lyric poem and a narrative poem are.

2. **TECHNIQUES OF SOUND.** What examples can you find in the unit of the sound techniques of repetition, rhyme, and rhythm? Explain their effects, using examples from several poems.

3. **FIGURATIVE LANGUAGE.** Find examples of figurative language in the selections from this unit, specifically, personification and simile. What idea is expressed by each example?

4. **EPIC.** What characteristics make the *Kalevala* an epic?

Thematic Studies

5. **POETRY.** Discuss the definitions of poetry presented by Archibald MacLeish in "Ars Poetica" and Marianne Moore in "Poetry." How do their views differ? How are they similar? Which, do you think, comes closest to defining what poetry should be?

6. **CELEBRATION.** What is being celebrated in Langston Hughes's "Dream Variations" and in William Carlos Williams's "The Dance"? What meaning do the poets attribute to the moments in time that they describe? Are these moments happening now or in the future?

7. **TRANSFORMATION.** What transforms the tree in "A Tree Telling of Orpheus"? What transforms the speaker in "I heard my love. . ."? How are these transforming experiences the same? How are they different?

8. **GRIEF.** How do the mother in the *Kalevala* and the tree in "A Tree Telling of Orpheus" grieve when they lose their loved ones? Besides death and absence, what other topics could a poet write about to express grief?

for your READING LIST

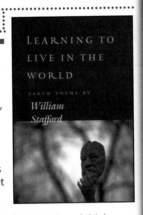

LEARNING TO LIVE IN THE WORLD

EARTH POEMS BY

William Stafford

Learning to Live in the World: Earth Poems by William Stafford. The fifty poems in this small but beautiful collection are about nature and about being human on earth. His poems explore the solitude of the wilderness, but also the complex world of relationships. All of the poems are connected by the theme of loving and keeping the earth.

Independent Reading Activity

READING POETRY IN NATURE. If the weather permits, carry a book of poems with you while you walk around outside. You may want to choose a poet who loves nature, like Emily Dickinson, Walt Whitman, or William Stafford. It could be an anthology of Native American poets. Every once in a while, open the book and read a poem. Then close it and continue walking, or sit and think, or watch the sky, or just sit in the sun and read. How does being in nature affect your experience of reading? How does reading poetry affect your experience of being outside in nature? You might find yourself thinking and seeing in ways you never have before.

Selections for Additional Reading

I Feel a Little Jumpy Around You: A Book of Her Poems and His Poems Collected in Pairs by Naomi Shihab Nye (editor), and Paul B. Janeczko (editor). The poems in this anthology are meant to be read in pairs—one by a woman and one by a man for each similar theme. There is much humor and wisdom in what turns out to be a universally human, rather than gender specific, view of life.

Letters to a Young Poet by Rainer Maria Rilke. Imagine writing to a poet you admire, and having that poet write back. This book contains ten letters written by the famous German poet Rilke in response to a young man seeking his help. Rilke offers much more than advice in writing: he speaks of matters of the heart and soul.

New and Selected Poems by Gary Soto. This collection spans Soto's thirty-year career as a poet from beginning to present. He pulls his favorite poems from seven of his books, including *The Elements of San Joaquin, The Tale of Sunlight,* and *Where Sparrows Work Hard.*

FOR YOUR READING LIST

Students will love William Stafford's *Learning to Live in the World,* a brief book of poems written in simple language and reflecting a relaxed tone. The fifty nature poems speak on solitude and loneliness. They also speak about how humans can bond with nature. This book of poems is not solely for wilderness lovers. The references to relationships between humankind and the images of hope and beauty will also draw readers to this powerful and inspiring book.

Independent Reading Activity
You may want to prepare your students for this nature outing by asking them to bring their own poems they have written about nature or to bring a nature poem written by their favorite poet. They will have the opportunity to read these poems during a group discussion session. Also during one of the group discussions, have students reflect on their connection with nature and how it inspires or motivates them. Ask students to share these reflections throughout the course of the day.

Diner, 1971. Richard Estes. Hirshhorn Museum, Washington, DC.

GOALS/OBJECTIVES

Studying this unit will enable students to
- enjoy and appreciate several short stories
- understand different elements of fiction
- explain *character, conflict, flashback, irony, motivation, plot, stereotype, theme, narrator, point of view, setting, mood,* and *foreshadowing* and recognize the use of these techniques in the selection they read
- write an analysis of a plot
- demonstrate an understanding of subject-verb agreement in sentence writing

Fiction

UNIT THREE

ADDITIONAL RESOURCES

UNIT 3 RESOURCE BOOK
- Genre Check Test 4.3.1
- Genre Test 4.3.2

BIOGRAPHICAL NOTE

Miguel de Cervantes Saavedra (1547–1616) was a Spanish writer of the Golden Age. His satiric novel *Don Quixote* is one of the masterpieces of world literature. When he was just a student, his first poems were published to commemorate the death of the Spanish queen. Later Cervantes joined a Spanish regiment in Naples. He lost the use of this left hand in a battle and then, when returning to Spain, he was captured by pirates. He was taken to Algeria as a slave, and after unsuccessful attempts to escape, he was ransomed in 1580 by family and friends. When he returned he resumed his writing and supplemented his income working as a tax collector, a role which landed him in prison several times. Cervantes's most important work is called in full *The Ingenious Hidalgo of Don Quixote de la Mancha*. It has been translated into all modern languages and has appeared in some 700 editions. It has been the subject of a variety of other works including operas, films, paintings, and the American musical *Man of La Mancha* (1965) by Mitch Leigh.

The term *fiction* comes from the Latin *fictio*, meaning "something invented." Thus fiction is any prose writing that tells an invented or imaginary story. Some fiction, the historical novel, for example, is based on fact, while other forms, such as the fantasy tale, are highly unrealistic. Fictional works also vary in structure and length, from the newly recognized **short short** (a very brief short story) to the book-length **novel**. Other forms include the traditional **short story** and the **novella**, a fictional work of intermediate length.

The Development of Fiction

The oldest fictions are the prose stories told in the oral tradition, which include myths, legends, and fables. Early written prose fictions include Petronius's *Satyricon* and Apuleius's *The Golden Ass*, written by Romans in the first and second centuries. The first novel, *The Tale of Genji*, was written by a Japanese woman, Lady Murasaki Shikibu, in the eleventh century. Early fictions from Europe include Boccaccio's *Decameron*, a collection of short prose tales written in the mid-fourteenth century, and Cervantes's *Don Quixote*, a satire of medieval romance tales written in the early seventeenth century.

The Novel

The novel developed from various kinds of nonfictional writing, including autobiographies, biographies, travel sketches, journals, and letters. Aruguably the first full-fledged novel in English was Aphra Behn's *Oroonoko*, published in 1688. Other early novels in English include Daniel Defoe's *Robinson Crusoe* (1719) and *Moll Flanders* (1722), and Samuel Richardson's *Pamela* (1740) and *Clarissa* (1747–1748). By the mid-1800s, the novel had become a popular form in the United States. Important American novelists include Nathaniel Hawthorne (1804–1864), Herman Melville (1819–1891), Mark Twain (1835–1910), Henry James (1843–1916), Kate Chopin (1850–1904), Edith Wharton (1862–1937), Stephen Crane (1871–1945), Willa Cather (1873–1947), Zora Neale Hurston (1891–1960), F. Scott Fitzgerald (1896–1940), William Faulkner (1897–1962), Ernest Hemingway (1899–1961), Richard Wright (1908–1960), John Steinbeck (1902–1968), Eudora Welty (1909–), Saul Bellow (1915–), James Baldwin (1924–1987), Toni Morrison (1931–), John Updike (1932–), and Alice Walker (1944–).

Important novelists from around the world include Honoré de Balzac (1799–1850), Victor Hugo (1802–1885), and Marcel Proust (1871–1922) from France; Jane Austen (1775–1817), Emily Brontë (1818–1848), and James Joyce (1882–1941) from Great Britain; Fyodor Dostoyevsky (1821–1881) and Leo Tolstoy (1828–1910) from Russia; Yasunari Kawabata (1899–1972) from Japan; Kamala Markandaya (1923–) from India; Gabriel García Márquez (1928–) from Colombia; Chinua Achebe (1930–) from Nigeria; Mexican authors Carlos Fuentes (1928–) and Laura Esquivel (1950–); Isabel Allende (1942–) from Chile; Julia Álvarez (1950–) from the Dominican Republic; and Mark Mathabane (1960–) from South Africa.

The Short Story

The short story genre, or type, originated in the United States. Important American figures in the development of the short story include Washington Irving (1783–1859), Nathaniel Hawthorne (1804–1864), and Edgar Allan Poe (1809–1849). Poe was instrumental in defining the genre, which he described as a short work that creates a single dominant impression on the reader. According to Poe, every detail in a short story should contribute to creating that overall impression or effect.

The Human Condition, 1934. René Magritte. National Gallery of Art, Washington, DC.

 art **note**

The Human Condition, 1934. René Magritte.

While many Surrealists, such as Salvador Dalí and Joan Miró, painted wholly imaginary worlds, **René Magritte** (1898–1967) painted clearly defined situations that are only slightly skewed from reality. His work often raises questions about the artificiality of the arts. At first, we may perceive that the landscape through the window is real and the painting that obscures it is a representation, but, in fact, the entire scene is fictitious. Why did Magritte title his painting The Human Condition?

ELEMENTS OF FICTION   161

ART NOTE

By titling his painting The Human Condition, Magritte may be saying that the human condition is our difficulty in discerning reality from illusion.

GENRE CHECK TEST 4.3.1 WITH ANSWERS

Checking Your Reading
Match the following literary terms about characters with the sentences below.

major character   minor character
static character   dynamic character
stock character   protagonist
antagonist

1. A **stock character** appears over and over in several different literary works.
2. The **antagonist** creates difficulties for the main character of a literary work.
3. A **dynamic character** undergoes growth and/or changes during the course of a work.
4. Because short stories are not long and usually only develop a single plot line, most have only one or two **major characters**.
5. The main character of a work is also known as the **protagonist**.

Short Answer
1. What is the difference between a one-dimensional and a three-dimensional character? **A one-dimensional character exhibits only one trait; a three-dimensional character is more complex, like a real human being.**
2. What is meant by *motivation* in a literary work? **Motivation is a force that provokes a character to think, feel, or behave in a certain way.**
3. How does a writer create mood? **A writer uses concrete details to create mood.**
4. In a broad sense, what does understanding of a story's setting help the reader grasp?

There are many short stories in this textbook. In this unit, you will find among others "The Black Cat" by Edgar Allan Poe, "The Open Window" by Saki, "The Moment Before the Gun Went Off" by Nadine Gordimer, and "I Stand Here Ironing" by Tillie Olsen. Elsewhere in the book you will find "The Thief" by Junichiro Tanizaki (Unit 7), "The Cabuliwallah" by Rabindranath Tagore (Unit 9), "Dead Men's Path" by Chinua Achebe (Unit 10), and "A Very Old Man with Enormous Wings" by Gabriel García Márquez (Unit 12).

ELEMENTS OF FICTION

CHARACTER. A character is a person (or sometimes an animal) who figures in the action of a story. The following are some useful terms for describing characters:

A **protagonist,** or **main character**, is the central figure in a story.

An **antagonist** is a character who is pitted against a protagonist.

A **major character** is one with a significant role in the action of a story. A **minor character** is one who plays a lesser role. Because of limitations of length and focus, most short stories have, at most, one or two major characters.

A **one-dimensional character, flat character,** or **caricature** is one who exhibits a single dominant quality, or **character trait.**

A **three-dimensional, full,** or **rounded character** is one who exhibits the complexity of traits associated with actual human beings.

A **static character** is one who does not change during the course of the story.

A **dynamic character** is one who does change during the course of the story.

A **stock character** is one found again and again in different literary works. Examples of stock characters include the mad scientist and the absent-minded professor.

Motivation is a force that moves a character to think, feel, or behave in a certain way. For example, a character may be **motivated** by

greed, love, or friendship. The particular reasons or causes behind a character's actions are his or her **motives.**

CHARACTERIZATION. Characterization is the use of literary techniques to create a character. Writers use three major techniques to create characters: direct description, portrayal of characters' behavior, and representations of characters' internal states. When using direct description, the writer, through a speaker, a narrator, or another character, simply comments on the character, telling the reader about such matters as the character's appearance, habits, dress, background, personality, motivations, and so on. Skillful writers are able to create characterizations through a few well-chosen, significant details. In portrayal of a character's behavior, the writer presents the actions and speech of the character, allowing the reader to draw his or her own conclusions from what the character says or does. When using representations of internal states, the writer reveals directly the character's private thoughts and emotions, often by means of what is known as the *internal monologue.*

SETTING AND MOOD. The **setting** is the time and place in which a story occurs, together with all the details used to create a sense of a particular time and place. The **mood** is the emotion created in the reader by part or all of a literary work. A writer creates mood through judicious use of concrete details. These details might include descriptions of the setting, of characters, and of events. In fiction, setting is most often revealed by means of description of such elements as landscape, scenery, buildings, furniture, clothing, weather, and the season. It also can be revealed by how characters talk and behave. In its widest sense, setting includes the general social, political, moral, and psychological conditions in which characters find themselves. Many American novels and short stories deal with particular regions of the country (New York City, the western frontier, small towns in the South or Midwest, and so on). Writing in which particular settings play an important role is called **regional fiction.** The

GENRE CHECK TEST 4.3.1 WITH ANSWERS (CONT.)

Understanding a story's setting can suggest such concepts as the weather, the constraints, and the political and social climate in which the characters operate.

5. Identify and define the two types of conflict characters face in literary works. **External conflict is a struggle that takes place between a character and some outside force. An internal conflict takes place within a character.**

(Continued on page 163)

details used to create a particular regional setting are called **local color.**

CONFLICT. A **conflict** is a struggle between two forces in a literary work. A plot involves the introduction, development, and eventual resolution of a conflict. One side of the central conflict in a work of fiction usually is taken by the main character. That character may struggle against another character, against the forces of nature, against society or social norms, against fate, or against some element within himself or herself. A struggle that takes place between a character and some outside force is called an **external conflict.** A struggle that takes place within a character is called an **internal conflict.**

PLOT. A **plot** is a series of events related to a central **conflict,** or struggle. Often the events of a plot are causally connected. The English novelist E. M. Forster explained, famously, that if the king dies and then the queen dies, that is a story, but if the king dies and then the queen dies of grief, that is a plot. A typical plot involves the following elements:

The **exposition,** or **introduction,** sets the tone and mood, introduces the characters and the setting, and provides necessary background information.

The **inciting incident** is the event that introduces the central conflict.

The **rising action,** or **complication,** develops the conflict to a high point of intensity.

The **climax** is the high point of interest or suspense.

The **crisis,** or **turning point,** often the same event as the climax, is the point in the plot where something decisive happens to determine the future course of events and the eventual working out of the conflict.

The **falling action** is all the events that follow the climax.

The **resolution** is the point at which the central conflict is ended, or resolved.

The **dénouement** is any material that follows the resolution and that ties up loose ends.

Plots are often illustrated using the diagram shown below, known as a plot pyramid. However, many plots do not include all of these elements, and in short stories, the climax often occurs very late in the plot.

THEME. A **theme** is a central idea in a literary work. A long work such as a novel may deal with several interrelated themes.

PLOT PYRAMID

Climax

Rising Action

Falling Action

Exposition

Dénouement

Inciting Incident

Resolution

ADDITIONAL QUESTIONS AND ACTIVITIES

Encourage students to create a plot pyramid for stories or novels they read on their own. This will help students realize the thought process an author undergoes to make everything in the story work together with the ultimate goal of solving one or more conflicts.

GENRE CHECK TEST 4.3.1 WITH ANSWERS (CONT.)

Plot Pyramid
Identify each element on the chart below, and tell what occurs in a work of fiction at that point. The first and last elements are done as examples.

Element/What the element contributes to the plot
Introduction/Exposition
Sets the tone and mood, introduces the characters and the setting and provides background information.

1. **Inciting Incident**
   Introduces the central conflict
2. **Rising Action/Complication**
   Develops the conflict to a high point of intensity
3. **Climax/Crisis/Turning Point**
   High point of interest or suspense; the point in the plot where something decisive happens to determine the course of events through the rest of the work, including the eventual working out of the central conflict
4. **Falling Action**
   All events that follow the climax, leading toward a resolution of the central conflict
5. **Resolution**
   The point at which the central conflict is ended, or resolved
Denouement
Any material that follows the resolution and ties up loose ends.

Plot Pyramid

3

2

4

Introduction/ Exposition

Dénouement

1

5

ADDITIONAL RESOURCES

UNIT 3 RESOURCE BOOK
- Selection Worksheet 3.1
- Selection Check Test 4.3.3
- Selection Test 4.3.4
- Language, Grammar, and Style Resource 3.38

GRAPHIC ORGANIZER

Students might include the following in their charts:

Pros
- "...it would be so easy to kill him. He deserves it."
- "He would feel no pain. He would not suffer at all."
- The revolutionaries would call him a hero: "The avenger of our people. A name to remember."

Cons
- "A good barber stakes his reputation on not permitting that [bleeding] to happen to any of his customers."
- "No one deserves the sacrifice others make in becoming assassins . . . everything becomes a sea of blood."
- ". . . what would I do with the body? I would have to flee. . . . But they [Captain Torres's men] would follow until they caught up with me."
- His enemies would call him a "murderer" who had done a "cowardly thing."
- "I do my work honorably. I don't want to stain my hands with blood."

READER'S JOURNAL

As an alternate activity, have students write about the emotions that face-to-face confrontations can trigger. What are the consequences of controlling or not controlling emotions during a confrontation? What are some ways to avoid negative confrontations?

Literary TOOLS

NARRATOR AND POINT OF VIEW. A **narrator** is one who tells a story. **Point of view** is the vantage point from which a story is told. Stories are often written from a *first-person point of view,* in which the narrator uses words such as *I* and *we.* In this selection, the narrator is the town barber, and the story is told from his point of view. As you read, note how the story reveals the private, internal thoughts of the narrator as he struggles with his dual roles of good barber and loyal revolutionary.

SETTING AND MOOD. The **setting** of a literary work is the time and place in which it occurs, together with all the details used to create a sense of a particular time and place. **Mood,** or **atmosphere,** is the emotion created in the reader by part or all of a literary work. As you read, consider how mood is created when Captain Torres walks into the barbershop.

Graphic Organizer

Much of the tension in the story stems from the narrator's internal conflict over whether or not he should kill Captain Torres. Make a pro and con chart like the one below. As you read the story, indicate the reasons the barber considers killing the Captain (the *pros*) and the drawbacks he visualizes for choosing murder (the *cons*).

KILLING THE CAPTAIN	
Pros	"...it would be so easy to kill him."
Cons	The barber was "secretly a revolutionary, but at the same time...a conscientious barber."

164   *UNIT THREE*

"Lather and Nothing Else"

by Hernando Téllez

Reader's resource

An **internal monologue** presents the private sensations, thoughts, and emotions of a character. The reader is allowed to step inside the character's mind and overhear what is going on in there. **"Lather and Nothing Else"** uses an internal monologue to reveal the private thoughts and emotions of the narrator, the barber. The inner thoughts of the barber are interspersed with vivid descriptions of his actions. This combination of private thought and action engages the reader of this suspenseful story.

About *the* AUTHOR

Hernando Téllez (1908–1966) was born in Bogotá, Colombia. Téllez served in the Colombian Parliament. Later, in Paris, he served as Colombia's ambassador to the United Nations Educational, Scientific, and Cultural Organization (UNESCO). A career politician with a great interest in writing, Téllez published many articles about political topics in newspapers and magazines. His short story collection *Ashes for the Wind and Other Stories* includes "Lather and Nothing Else."

Reader's Journal

If you worked in a service profession, such as a barber, a salesperson, or a waiter or waitress, and discovered you were serving an enemy, how might you behave? What choices would you make?

GOALS/OBJECTIVES

Studying this lesson will enable students to
- empathize with a narrator's feelings and understand his perspective
- explain the link between the writings and political career of Hernando Téllez
- define *internal monologue* and explain why an author might use this literary technique

- define and distinguish *narrator* and *point of view* and recognize these features in a short story
- compare and contrast *setting* and *mood* and describe these features in a short story
- research a current example of political instability in the world

Lather and Nothing Else

Hernando Téllez

At The Barber's, 1912. Marc Chagall. Musée National d'Art Moderne, Paris.

H e came in without a word. I was stropping[1] my best razor. And when I recognized him, I started to shake. But he did not notice.

How does the barber react to the customer?

To cover my nervousness, I went on honing[2] the razor. I tried the edge with the tip of my thumb and took another look at it against the light.

---

1. **stropping.** Sharpening by rubbing back and forth on a thick piece of leather, the strop
2. **honing.** Sharpening

"LATHER AND NOTHING ELSE"   165

INDIVIDUAL LEARNING STRATEGIES

MOTIVATION
Ask students to list jobs that involve being responsible for the lives or safety of others. Ask students whether any of these jobs appeal to them. How might being responsible for others' safety be a source of stress? How might it be a source of pride?

READING PROFICIENCY
Ask students to select portions of the story to read aloud and record. Encourage them to read the chosen portions with the emotional tone that the words suggest.

ENGLISH LANGUAGE LEARNING
Use passages from the story to give students practice in using quotation marks with dialogue. First, review with students the Language Arts Survey 3.92, "Quotation Marks." Then provide a typed copy of several consecutive paragraphs but omit the quotation marks. Ask them to insert the quotation marks at the correct points. Tell them reading the sentences aloud may help them.

SPECIAL NEEDS
Help students focus on the Guided Reading questions in the selection.

ENRICHMENT
Have students do research on the history of government in Colombia during the last hundred years. Students might wish to create a time line of political developments, or they might compare the political climate during Téllez's adult lifetime with that in Colombia today.

ART NOTE

Marc Chagall (1887–1985) painted *At the Barber's* in Paris, shortly before returning to his native Russia. Have students contrast the mood of the story with the mood of *At the Barber's*. Have them focus on the colors, painting style, and the expressions and postures of the figures. Then ask them to create their own painting or drawing for the story. Before they begin, have them review the story to list details to convey in their painting.

VOCABULARY FROM THE SELECTION

conscientious	regime
emit	rejuvenate
foray	revolutionary
indelible	tranquil
indifference	venture
minutely	

Meanwhile he was taking off his cartridge-studded[3] belt with the pistol holster suspended from it. He put it on a hook in the wardrobe and hung his cap above it. Then he turned full around toward me and, loosening his tie, remarked, "It's hot as the devil, I want a shave." With that he took his seat.

I estimated he had a four-days' growth of beard, the four days he had been gone on the last foray after our men. His face looked burnt, tanned by the sun.

I started to lay on the first coat of lather. He kept his eyes closed.

I started to work carefully on the shaving soap. I scraped some slices from the cake, dropped them into the mug, then added a little lukewarm water, and stirred with the brush. The lather soon began to rise.

"The fellows in the troop must have just about as much beard as I." I went on stirring up lather. "But we did very well, you know. We caught the leaders. Some of them we brought back dead; others are still alive. But they'll all be dead soon."

"How many did you take?" I asked.

"Fourteen. We had to go pretty far in to find them. But now they're paying for it. And not one will escape; not a single one."

He leaned back in the chair when he saw the brush in my hand, full of lather. I had not yet put the sheet on him. I was certainly flustered. Taking a sheet from the drawer, I tied it around my customer's neck.

He went on talking. He evidently took it for granted that I was on the side of the existing regime.

"The people must have gotten a scare with what happened the other day," he said.

"Yes," I replied, as I finished tying the knot against his nape, which smelt of sweat.

"Good show, wasn't it?"

"Very good," I answered, turning my attention now to the brush. The man closed his eyes wearily and awaited the cool caress of the lather.

I had never had him so close before. The day he ordered the people to file through the schoolyard to look upon the four rebels hanging there, my path had crossed his briefly. But the sight of those mutilated bodies kept me from paying attention to the face of the man who had been directing it all and whom I now had in my hands.

It was not a disagreeable face, certainly. And the beard, which aged him a bit, was not unbecoming. His name was Torres. Captain Torres.

I started to lay on the first coat of lather. He kept his eyes closed.

"I would love to catch a nap," he said, "but there's a lot to be done this evening."

I lifted the brush and asked, with pretended indifference: "A firing party?"

"Something of the sort," he replied, "but slower."

"All of them?"

"No, just a few."

I went on lathering his face. My hands began to tremble again. The man could not be aware of this, which was lucky for me. But I wished he had not come in. Probably many of our men had seen him enter the shop. And with the enemy in my house I felt a certain responsibility.

---

3. **cartridge-studded.** Adorned with bullets

words for everyday use	for • ay (fôr′ā) *n.*, raid; attack. *When the kids at the party were hungry, they made a foray on the refrigerator that was as noisy as a raid on a military supply storage area.*
	re • gime (rə zhēm′) *n.*, government; administration in power. *If you like the existing political system, you call those in power "the government"; if you dislike the system, you call those in power "the regime."*
	in • dif • fer • ence (in dif′ər əns) *n.*, lack of concern. *I view a snowstorm in April with complete indifference because I know the snow will soon melt.*

I would have to shave his beard just like any other, carefully, neatly, just as though he were a good customer, taking heed that not a single pore should emit a drop of blood. Seeing to it that the blade did not slip in the small whorls.[4] Taking care that the skin was left clean, soft, shining, so that when I passed the back of my hand over it not a single hair should be felt. Yes. I was secretly a revolutionary, but at the same time I was a conscientious barber, proud of the way I did my job. And that four-day beard presented a challenge.

I took up the razor, opened the handle wide, releasing the blade, and started to work, downward from one sideburn. The blade responded to perfection. The hair was tough and hard; not very long, but thick. Little by little the skin began to show through. The razor gave its usual sound as it gathered up layers of soap mixed with bits of hair. I paused to wipe it clean, and taking up the strop once more went about improving its edge, for I am a painstaking barber.

The man, who had kept his eyes closed, now opened them, put a hand out from under the sheet, felt of the part of his face that was emerging from the lather, and said to me, "Come at six o'clock this evening to the school."

What is going to happen at six o'clock at the school?

"Will it be like the other day?" I asked, stiff with horror.

"It may be even better," he replied.

"What are you planning to do?"

"I'm not sure yet. But we'll have a good time."

Once more he leaned back and shut his eyes. I came closer, the razor on high.

"Are you going to punish all of them?" I timidly ventured.

"Yes, all of them."

The lather was drying on his face. I must hurry. Through the mirror, I took a look at the street. It appeared about as usual; there was the grocery shop with two or three customers. Then I glanced at the clock, two-thirty.

The razor kept descending. Now from the other sideburn downward. It was a blue beard, a thick one. He should let it grow like some poets, or some priests. It would suit him well. Many people would not recognize him. And that would be a good thing for him, I thought, as I went gently over all the throat line.[5] At this point you really had to handle your blade skillfully, because the hair, while scantier, tended to fall into small whorls. It was a curly beard. The pores might open, minutely, in this area and let out a tiny drop of blood. A good barber like myself stakes his reputation on not permitting that to happen to any of his customers.

On what does a good barber stake his reputation?

And this was indeed a special customer. How many of ours had he sent to their death? How many had he mutilated? It was best not to think about it. Torres did not know I was his enemy. Neither he nor the others knew it. It was a secret shared by very few, just because that made it possible for me to inform the revolutionaries about Torres's activities in the town and what he planned to do every time he went on one of his raids to hunt down rebels. So it was going to be very difficult to explain how it was that I had him in my hands and then let him go in peace, alive, clean-shaven.

What is going to be difficult for the barber to explain?

His beard had now almost entirely disappeared. He looked younger, several years younger than

---

4. **whorls.** Clusters or curls of hair
5. **throat line.** Area under the chin across the front of the neck

---

words for everyday use

e • mit (ē mit´) vt., discharge; send out. *The astronauts landed near the spot where the mysterious radio beacon was emitting a faint signal.*
rev • o • lu • tion • ar • y (rev´ə loo¯´shən er ē) n., one who seeks to overthrow a government. *The United States was founded by both sober statesmen and wild-eyed revolutionaries.*
con • sci • en • tious (kän´she en´shəs) adj., scrupulous; governed by what one knows is right. *In contrast to her twin brother, Allen, who was utterly irresponsible, Ellen was highly conscientious.*
ven • ture (ven´chər) vi., do at some risk. *Although Dean was frightened of heights, he ventured up the ladder to rescue the little girl's mewing kitten.*
mi • nute • ly (mī noo¯t´ lē) adv., to a very small degree. *I would not have thought that such a huge mess as I found in the refrigerator could be traced to a minutely leaking carton of milk.*

---

1. The barber imagines cutting Captain Torres's throat. He imagines the blood would flow over the sheet, onto the floor, and into the street. He imagines that some people would say he was a coward, while others would praise him as an avenger of the people.

SELECTION CHECK TEST 4.3.3 WITH ANSWERS

Checking Your Reading

1. Who is the barber's customer? **The customer is Torres, a captain in the current oppressive regime.**
2. What does the barber believe his customer does not know about him? **He thinks his customer doesn't realize that he is a revolutionary.**
3. What is displayed in the schoolyard? **The bodies of rebels hang in the schoolyard.**
4. What choice must the barber make as he shaves his customer? **He must choose whether or not to murder Torres.**
5. What does the barber's customer say was his real reason for coming into the shop? **He says he knew the barber was a revolutionary and he came in to see if the barber would murder him or not.**

Vocabulary in Context

Fill in each blank with the most appropriate word from the following Words for Everyday Use. You may have to change the tense of the word.

indelible   foray   rejuvenate   emit
minutely   indifference   tranquil

1. The girls squealed as the boys launched a **foray** on their fort.
2. Veronica tried to show **indifference** when her plane hit turbulence, but she was actually very frightened.
3. Once we passed the rapids, we relaxed as the river water became more **tranquil**.
4. We were exhausted, but our short vacation **rejuvenated** us.
5. Larry's weekend at U. S. Space Camp left such **indelible** memories that he told his stories over and over.

Literary Tools

Fill in the blanks below with the following terms.

narrator   first-person point of view
third-person point of view   setting
mood

---

when he had come in. I suppose that always happens to men who enter and leave barbershops. Under the strokes of my razor Torres was <u>rejuvenated</u>; yes, because I am a good barber, the best in this town, and I say this in all modesty.

A little more lather here under the chin, on the Adam's apple, right near the great vein.[6] How hot it is! Torres must be sweating just as I am. But he is not afraid. He is a <u>tranquil</u> man, who is not even giving thought to what he will do to his prisoners this evening. I, on the other hand, polishing his skin with this razor but avoiding the drawing of blood, careful with every stroke—I cannot keep my thoughts in order.

Confound the hour he entered my shop! I am a revolutionary but not a murderer. And it would be so easy to kill him. He deserves it. Or does he? No! No one deserves the sacrifice others make in becoming assassins. What is to be gained by it? Nothing. Others and still others keep coming, and the first kill the second, and then these kill the next, and so on until everything becomes a sea of blood. I could cut his throat, so, swish, swish! He would not even have time to moan, and with his eyes shut he would not even see the shine of the razor or the gleam in my eye.

But I'm shaking like a regular murderer. From his throat a stream of blood would flow on the sheet, over the chair, down on my hands, onto the floor. I would have to close the door. But the blood would go flowing along the floor, warm, <u>indelible</u>, not to be staunched,[7] until it reached the street like a small scarlet river.

I'm sure that with a good strong blow, a deep cut, he would feel no pain. He would not suffer at all. And what would I do then with the body? Where would I hide it? I would have to flee, leave all this behind, take shelter far away, very far away. But they would follow until they caught up with me. "The murderer of Captain Torres. He slit his throat while he was shaving him. What a cowardly thing to do!"

And others would say, "The avenger of our people. A name to remember"—my name here. "He was the town barber. No one knew he was fighting for our cause."

And so, which will it be? Murderer or hero? My fate hangs on the edge of this razor blade.

I can turn my wrist slightly, put a bit more pressure on the blade, let it sink in. The skin will yield like silk, like rubber, like the strop. There is nothing more tender than a man's skin, and the blood is always there, ready to burst forth. A razor like this cannot fail. It is the best one I have.

But I don't want to be a murderer. No, sir. You came in to be shaved. And I do my work honorably. I don't want to stain my hands with blood. Just with lather, and nothing else. You are an executioner; I am only a barber. Each one to his job. That's it. Each one to his job.

The chin was now clean, polished, soft. The man got up and looked at himself in the glass. He ran his hand over the skin and felt its freshness, its newness.

"Thanks," he said. He walked to the wardrobe for his belt, his pistol, and his cap. I must have been very pale, and I felt my shirt soaked with sweat. Torres finished adjusting his belt buckle, straightened his gun in its holster, and smoothing his hair mechanically, put on his cap. From his trousers pocket he took some coins to pay for the shave. And he started toward the door. On the threshold he stopped for a moment, and turning toward me, he said, "They told me you would kill me. I came to find out if it was true. But it's not easy to kill. I know what I'm talking about." ∎

What does the barber imagine doing? What would happen? What does he imagine people would say?

---

6. **great vein.** Carotid artery—large blood vessel in the neck
7. **staunched.** Stopped

---

words for everyday use	**re • ju • ve • nate** (ri jōō´və nāt) *vt.*, make feel young again. *In the hope of being <u>rejuvenated</u>, the explorer searched for the Fountain of Youth until he died.*
	tran • quil (tran´kwil) *adj.*, calm; serene. *During Christine's early years she suffered greatly from turmoil and confusion, but as she grew, she became more <u>tranquil</u> and sure of herself.*
	in • del • i • ble (in del´ə bəl) *adj.*, permanent; incapable of being erased or removed. *The practical joke went sour when the ink Rodney splashed on Danforth, which was supposed to wash out with water, proved to be <u>indelible</u>.*

SELECTION CHECK TEST 4.3.3 WITH ANSWERS (CONT.)

1. To create setting, a writer uses details to suggest a sense of time and place.
2. If a narrator tells a story using pronouns such as *I* or *we*, then the story is in **first-person point of view**.
3. A **narrator** may or may not be part of the action of a story.
4. The **narrator** in "Lather and Nothing Else" is a barber.
5. A story told by a narrator who is not part of the action is told in **third-person point of view**.

Respond *to the* SELECTION

Which of the barber's reasons for not killing Captain Torres did you find most persuasive?

Investigate, *Inquire,* and Imagine

Recall: GATHERING FACTS → **Interpret:** FINDING MEANING

1a. Describe Torres's entrance into the barber shop. Describe the barber's reaction to Torres's entrance.

2a. When did the narrator last cross paths with Torres? What kept him from looking at Torres's face then?

3a. What does the narrator say about his fate?

1b. What might these details reveal about each character?

2b. How is the narrator's confrontation in the barber shop with Torres different from the last time they crossed paths?

3b. What do you think he means by this?

Analyze: TAKING THINGS APART → **Synthesize:** BRINGING THINGS TOGETHER

4a. Identify the relationship that exists between the narrator and Captain Torres. How are their occupations compared and contrasted in the selection?

4b. What is Captain Torres's real purpose in coming to the narrator for a shave? What does this reveal about his character? What does Torres admit at the end of the story? What does this reveal about his character?

Evaluate: MAKING JUDGMENTS → **Extend:** CONNECTING IDEAS

5a. To what extent is each of the characters at the mercy of the other?

5b. Do you think the use of violence to bring about political change can be justified? If so, at what point does political violence cease to be justified? If not, how can political change to be brought about if the party in power will not allow compromises?

Understanding *Literature*

NARRATOR AND POINT OF VIEW. Review the definitions for **narrator** and **point of view** in the Handbook of Literary Terms. Which passages in the selection reveal the narrator's love of his work as a barber? Which passages reveal his dedication to the revolution? How would the story be different if told from a third-person point of view? If Torres were the narrator?

SETTING AND MOOD. Review the definitions for **setting** and **mood** in the Handbook of Literary Terms. What kind of mood does the scene in the barber shop create for the reader? Identify specific details that contribute to creating this mood.

"LATHER AND NOTHING ELSE" **169**

ANSWERS TO INVESTIGATE, INQUIRE, AND IMAGINE (CONT.)

SYNTHESIZE

4b. *Responses will vary.* Captain Torres came to find out if the barber would kill him. This statement shows that Captain Torres suspected the barber is a revolutionary. The fact that the Captain placed his life in the barber's hands shows his determination to serve a political cause as well as personal daring. At the end, Torres admits that it's not easy to kill. This statement may show a more human side of

Torres; he seems to empathize with the barber and be perceptive about human nature.

EXTEND

5b. Some students may say that violence is never justified. Others may say that if peaceful means have been exhausted violent means may be necessary; they may cite the American Revolution as an example.

(Continued on page 170)

RESPOND TO THE SELECTION

As an alternate activity, have students respond to the barber's statement, "No one deserves the sacrifice others make in becoming assassins." What would a person who becomes an assassin have to lose?

ANSWERS TO INVESTIGATE, INQUIRE, AND IMAGINE

RECALL

1a. Torres comes in without a word, takes off his gun belt, and hangs up his cap. He then says, "It's hot as the devil, I want a shave." The barber begins to shake from nervousness. He continues to sharpen his razor to hide his fear.

2a. The narrator last crossed paths with Torres on the day Torres ordered people to look at four rebels who had been hanged in the schoolyard. The sight of the mutilated bodies kept the barber from looking at Torres.

3a. The narrator says, "My fate hangs on the edge of this razor blade."

INTERPRET

1b. Torres appears to be a confident man who takes control and makes himself at home wherever he is. The barber appears less self-assured, reflective, and cautious.

2b. The meeting in the barber shop is more intimate; in the schoolyard the barber didn't look at Torres; in the shop he touches and studies Torres's face. The barber was ordered to the schoolyard, while Torres comes to the shop by choice. In the first encounter, Torres, in control, flaunts his brutality. In the barbershop, the barber has control because he holds a knife to his customer's neck.

3b. The narrator is contemplating cutting Captain Torres's throat with his razor and considering the consequences of this action.

ANALYZE

4a. On the surface, the relationship is one of barber and customer. In reality, the two are enemies; Torres is a military officer who represents an oppressive government, while the barber is a revolutionary who opposes this violent authority. The two men's jobs are compared and contrasted in this narrator's quote: "I don't want to stain my hands with blood. Just with lather, and nothing else. You are an executioner; I am only a barber. Each one to his job."

TEACHER'S EDITION **169**

EVALUATE

5a. *Responses will vary.* Though Captain Torres was in one sense at the barber's mercy as he received a shave from him, the barber is essentially at the mercy of the brutal political regime represented by Captain Torres.

ANSWERS TO UNDERSTANDING LITERATURE

NARRATOR AND POINT OF VIEW. Passages that reveal the narrator's love of his work describe his care in stropping his razor, scraping slices from the cake of soap, and shaving difficult spots without cutting the skin, and his pride in making his customers look younger. Passages that reveal his dedication to the revolution include his statement that "with the enemy in my house I felt a certain responsibility" and his desire to be seen as an "avenger of our the people."

SETTING AND MOOD. The mood in the barber shop is one of tension. Concrete details such as the nervous shaking and sweating of the narrator, the narrator's recounting of the hanging and mutilation of the rebels in the schoolyard, the captain's talk of more punishment for the rebels, and the narrator's thoughts of murder as he holds a razor to the captain's throat all contribute to the tense atmosphere.

ANSWERS TO INTEGRATING THE LANGUAGE ARTS

Language, Grammar, and Style
1. Torres <u>was silent</u>; the barber <u>was nervous</u>; the atmosphere <u>was tense</u>.
2. Torres is intelligent, he is ruthless, and he has a good deal of confidence.
3. He took up the razor, he opened the handle, and he started to work.
4. Patiently, the barber lathered his face; dutifully, he took up the razor; nervously, he shaved his beard.
5. <u>While shaving Torres</u>, the barber thought about killing him; <u>after debating the consequences</u>, he decided against murder.

Study and Research & Media Literacy
Remind students to provide enough background so outsiders can understand the basis for the conflict. Students might want to watch several television news reports on unstable political situa-

---

Writer's Journal

1. Hyperbole is exaggeration for literary effect. Téllez uses an example of hyperbole in his description of the stream of blood flowing out the door and into the street. Write your own example of **hyperbole.**

2. Write a **descriptive paragraph** that describes an approaching storm. To create a mood of anticipation or foreboding, provide concrete details that describe the sights, sounds, and smells that signal the storm.

3. "Lather and Nothing Else" provides the reader with a detailed description of each step the barber takes in shaving Torres's beard. Write **step-by-step instructions** for a task you perform frequently or well so that someone who has never performed that task will know how to proceed.

Integrating the Language Arts

Language, Grammar, and Style

ACHIEVING PARALLELISM. Read the Language Arts Survey 3.38, "Achieving Parallelism." Parallel structure calls attention to coordinating ideas, creating symmetry that emphasizes important points. Parallelism is achieved by pairing the same grammatical form of individual words, phrases, clauses, or sentences. Evaluate the following sentences. If a sentence demonstrates parallelism, underline the words that create that parallelism. If a sentence does not achieve parallelism, rewrite it to achieve parallelism.
1. Torres was silent; the barber was nervous; the atmosphere was tense.
2. Torres is intelligent, ruthless, and has a good deal of confidence.
3. He took up the razor, opened the handle, and started to work.
4. Patiently, the barber lathered his face; dutifully, he took up the razor, and with great nervousness, he shaved his beard.
5. While shaving Torres, the barber thought about killing him; after debating the consequences, he decided against murder.

Study and Research & Media Literacy

TELEVISION REPORT. Use the Internet, newspaper, and/or periodicals to conduct research on a current example of political instability in the world. Is violence being used by the party in power to control the people? Are other methods of control, such as a hostile police presence or forced taxes being used? Are there factions of people using violence to bring about political change? Are any groups using nonviolent methods like civil disobedience? What are the basic issues around which the conflict revolves? Report on the situation as if you were a television reporter.

Collaborative Learning & Speaking and Listening

WRITING A DRAMATIC SKIT. Collaborate with a partner to write a dramatic skit that continues the plot of the story. Begin your skit by having the barber respond to Captain Torres's remark, "They told me you would kill me. I came to find out if it was true. But it's not easy to kill. I know what I'm talking about." Write two parts, one for the barber and one for Captain Torres. Rehearse your skit and present it to the rest of the class.

170 UNIT THREE / FICTION

ANSWERS TO INTEGRATING THE LANGUAGE ARTS (CONT.)

tions to note the typical content and format of such reports. Possible sources include the "NewsHour with Jim Lehrer" on PBS and news programs on CNN. Have students limit their reports to 10 minutes.

Collaborative Learning & Speaking and Listening
Tell students their skits should be short (1-2 minutes).

Ask students to consider questions such as these as they plan their skits: Does Torres know for certain that the barber is a revolutionary? Will the barber continue to pretend he is not a revolutionary? Can the barber now do anything to help the people? Does the barber now have a different view of the captain?

"The Black Cat"
by Edgar Allan Poe

Reader's resource

Published in the August 19, 1843, issue of the *U.S. Saturday Post* and republished in Poe's 1845 collection *Tales*, **"The Black Cat"** is considered one of Poe's greatest horror tales. Two other horror tales, "The Tell-Tale Heart" and "The Murders in the Rue Morgue" also appeared in 1843, a year in which Poe was trying to establish his own literary journal.

Language that might have more than one meaning is ambiguous. The entirety of "The Black Cat" is ambiguous because it can be read in one of two ways—as a tale about supernatural events told by a sane narrator, or as a tale in which an insane narrator relates his hallucinations. Poe was one of the first writers to use this technique, which is now common among horror writers.

About the AUTHOR

Edgar Allan Poe (1809–1849) was born in Boston, Massachusetts. The son of traveling actors, he was orphaned before he was three years old. Raised by John Allan of Richmond, Virginia, Poe was educated primarily at classical academies in England, where he excelled in languages. In 1827, Poe enlisted in the United States Army and published his first work, *Tamerlane and Other Poems*. Three years later, Poe entered West Point, but after an argument with John Allan, he deliberately provoked his own discharge. Cut off from receiving any further financial support from Allan, Poe supported himself by literary journalism, barely staying one step ahead of poverty throughout his life. Beginning in 1843, Poe gave lectures on American poetry for the "Poets and Poetry of America" circuit, traveling to Philadelphia and New York. While lecturing, he continued to publish in a variety of journals and magazines. The publication of "The Raven" brought him brief fame in the United States, where, until the twentieth century, most of his work remained relatively unpopular. In England and France, however, Poe's literary influence was strongly felt in his own century. Because of Poe's fondness for telling romantic tales about his own life, accurate biographies of the writer have been difficult to construct.

Literary TOOLS

FLASHBACK. A **flashback** is a section of a literary work that presents an event or series of events that occurred earlier than the current time in the work. As you read, note how Poe uses this technique in "The Black Cat."

PLOT AND CONFLICT. A **plot** is a series of events related to a central conflict or struggle. A typical plot involves the introduction of a conflict, its development, and eventual resolution. A **conflict** is a struggle between two forces in a literary work. A struggle that takes place between a character and some outside force is called an **external conflict**. A struggle that takes place within a character is called an **internal conflict**. As you read, pay attention to plot twists and various conflicts.

Reader's Journal

Recall the scariest horror story you've read or the scariest horror film you've seen. What aspects of the story or film did you find most frightening? Why?

ADDITIONAL RESOURCES

UNIT 3 RESOURCE BOOK
- Selection Worksheet 3.2
- Selection Check Test 4.3.5
- Selection Test 4.3.6
- Reading Resource 1.19
- Language, Grammar, and Style Resource 3.23

VOCABULARY FROM THE SELECTION

allusion	incumbent
anomalous	inscrutability
apparition	intemperate
atrocity	jeopardize
aversion	latter
bravado	lime
cherish	odious
conflagration	perverseness
conjointly	premises
consign	procure
constitute	remorse
debauch	render
deliberate	repose
docility	reverberation
equivocal	solicit
expedient	succumb
expound	succinctly
goaded	uncongenial
imperceptible	ungovernable
inclination	

GOALS/OBJECTIVES

Studying this lesson will enable students to
- enjoy an ambiguous, suspenseful story
- describe Edgar Allan Poe's literary accomplishments
- define *flashback* and explain how Poe uses this technique in the story
- define *plot* and *conflict* and recognize the two forms of conflict in Poe's story
- identify the meanings of prefixes and suffixes as a way of expanding vocabulary
- use the format of a mock trial to evaluate a character's guilt or innocence

Sita and Sarita, c.1921. Cecilia Beaux. Corcoran Gallery of Art, Washington, DC.

The Black Cat

Edgar Allan Poe

For the most wild yet most homely[1] narrative which I am about to pen, I neither expect nor <u>solicit</u> belief. Mad indeed would I be to expect it, in a case where my very senses reject their own evidence. Yet, mad am I not—and very surely do I not dream. But tomorrow I die, and today I would unburden my soul. My immediate purpose is to place before the world, plainly, <u>succinctly</u>, and without comment, a series of mere household events. In their consequences, these events have terrified—have tortured—have destroyed me. Yet I will not attempt to <u>expound</u> them. To me, they have presented little but horror—to many they will seem less terrible than *baroques.*[2] Hereafter, perhaps, some intellect may be found which will reduce my phantasm[3] to the commonplace—some intellect more calm, more log-

---

1. **homely.** Simple, plain
2. **baroques.** Grotesque or whimsical designs, in the style of the Baroque period (*circa* 1600–1750)
3. **phantasm.** Specter or ghost

---

words for everyday use

so • lic • it (sə lis´it) *vt.,* ask earnestly or pleadingly. *I wish to <u>solicit</u> your advice about an important matter.*

suc • cinct • ly (suk siŋkt´lē) *adv.,* in a concise manner. *After <u>succinctly</u> explaining the procedure, the physician asked if anyone had any questions.*

ex • pound (eks pound´) *vt.,* explain in detail point by point. *The audience wilted from boredom as the speaker continued to <u>expound</u> the details of his scientific theory.*

ical, and far less excitable than my own, which will perceive, in the circumstances I detail with awe, nothing more than an ordinary succession of very natural causes and effects.

From my infancy I was noted for the docility and humanity of my disposition. My tenderness of heart was even so conspicuous as to make me the jest of my companions. I was especially fond of animals, and was indulged by my parents with a great variety of pets. With these I spent most of my time, and never was so happy as when feeding and caressing them. This peculiarity of character grew with my growth, and, in my manhood, I derived from it one of my principal sources of pleasure. To those who have cherished an affection for a faithful and sagacious[4] dog, I need hardly be at the trouble of explaining the nature or the intensity of the gratification thus derivable.[5] There is something in the unselfish and self-sacrificing love of a brute, which goes directly to the heart of him who has had frequent occasion to test the paltry friendship and gossamer fidelity[6] of mere *Man*.

I married early, and was happy to find in my wife a disposition not uncongenial with my own. Observing my partiality for domestic pets, she lost no opportunity of procuring those of the most agreeable kind. We had birds, goldfish, a fine dog, rabbits, a small monkey, and a *cat*.

This latter was a remarkably large and beautiful animal, entirely black, and sagacious to an astonishing degree. In speaking of his intelligence, my wife, who at heart was not a little tinctured[7] with superstition, made frequent allusion to the ancient popular notion, which regarded all black cats as witches in disguise. Not that she was ever *serious* upon this point—and I mention the matter at all for no better reason than that it happens, just now, to be remembered.

Pluto[8]—this was the cat's name—was my favorite pet and playmate. I alone fed him, and he attended me wherever I went about the house. It was even with difficulty that I could prevent him from following me through the streets.

Our friendship lasted, in this manner, for several years, during which my general temperament and character—through the instrumentality of the Fiend Intemperance[9]—had (I blush to confess it) experienced a radical alteration for the worse. I grew, day by day, more moody, more irritable, more regardless of the feelings of others. I suffered[10] myself to use intemperate language to my wife. At length, I even offered her personal violence. My pets, of course, were made to feel the change in my disposition. I not only neglected, but ill-used them. For Pluto, however, I still retained sufficient regard to restrain me from maltreating him, as I made no scruple of maltreating the rabbits, the monkey, or even the

4. **sagacious.** Wise
5. **derivable.** Received
6. **paltry . . . fidelity.** *Paltry*—almost worthless; *gossamer fidelity*—light, flimsy loyalty
7. **tinctured.** Stained
8. **Pluto.** The cat was named for the Greek god of the underworld, whom the Romans called Pluto.
9. **Fiend Intemperance.** Substance abuse, particularly of alcohol
10. **suffered.** Allowed

> **What makes the speaker "the jest of his companions"? How is the speaker indulged by his parents? How does he spend most of his time?**

> **Who becomes the speaker's favorite pet?**

> **What happens to the speaker's temperament? Why? How does this change affect the pets?**

words for everyday use	
	do • cil • i • ty (dō sil′ə tē) *n.*, state of being easily managed. *Maria picked the smallest puppy from the litter because of his docility and sweet face.*
	cher • ish (cher′ish) *vt.*, hold dear. *They cherish their quiet evenings spent sitting on the front porch.*
	un • con • ge • ni • al (un kən jēn′yəl) *adj.*, incompatible. *Tomatoes and potatoes are uncongenial companion plants in the garden.*
	lat • ter (lat′ər) *adj.*, last mentioned. *Of all their children, Mary, Joseph, and Jasmine, the latter looks most like her mother.*
	al • lu • sion (ə lü′zhən) *n.*, indirect reference. *The poet frequently made allusion to youth, a topic with which he was obsessed.*
	in • tem • per • ate (in tem′pər it) *adj.*, lacking restraint. *Because of her intemperate spending practices, Allison decided against opening another charge account.*

ANSWERS TO GUIDED READING QUESTIONS

1. The speaker's tenderness of heart made him "the jest of his companions." His parents indulged him by giving him a variety of pets, with whom he spent most of his time.
2. Pluto, a large black cat, becomes the speaker's favorite pet.
3. The speaker's temperament becomes moody and irritable due to the effect of alcohol. This radical change leads the speaker to neglect and mistreat his pets.

ANSWERS TO GUIDED READING QUESTIONS

1. The speaker feels remorse and horror at having hurt the cat, but this feeling is not very strong and his soul remains "untouched" by the terrible deed.
2. The speaker hangs the cat, perversely, because it had loved him and given him no reason for offense and because he knew he was committing a sin.

CROSS-CURRICULAR ACTIVITIES

HEALTH. In this passage the narrator confesses that he is an alcoholic. Ask students to visit the website of a recognized organization that helps people deal with this problem, such as Alcoholics Anonymous. Have them list the symptoms of this disease. Encourage students to do additional research at the site they select. Some students might like to write a short report on the organization's philosophy and treatment program. Others might like to write about why alcoholism can be considered a disease.

---

dog, when, by accident, or through affection, they came in my way. But my disease grew upon me—for what disease is like Alcohol!—and at length even Pluto, who was now becoming old, and consequently somewhat peevish[11]—even Pluto began to experience the effects of my ill temper.

One night, returning home, much intoxicated, from one of my haunts about town, I fancied that the cat avoided my presence. I seized him; when, in his fright at my violence, he inflicted a slight wound upon my hand with his teeth. The fury of a demon instantly possessed me.[12] I knew myself no longer. My original soul seemed, at once, to take its flight from my body; and a more than fiendish malevolence, gin-nurtured,[13] thrilled every fiber of my frame. I took from my waistcoat-pocket a penknife, opened it, grasped the poor beast by the throat, and deliberately cut one of its eyes from the socket! I blush, I burn, I shudder, while I pen the damnable <u>atrocity</u>.

When reason returned with the morning—when I had slept off the fumes of the night's <u>debauch</u>—I experienced a sentiment half of horror, half of remorse, for the crime of which I had been guilty; but it was, at best, a feeble and <u>equivocal</u> feeling, and the soul remained untouched. I again plunged into excess, and soon drowned in wine all memory of the deed.

In the meantime the cat slowly recovered. The socket of the lost eye presented, it is true, a frightful appearance, but he no longer appeared to suffer any pain. He went about the house as usual, but, as might be expected, fled in extreme terror at my approach. I had so much of my old heart left, as to be at first

> *How does the speaker feel about having hurt the cat the first time?*

grieved by this evident dislike on the part of a creature which had once so loved me. But this feeling soon gave place to irritation. And then came, as if to my final and irrevocable overthrow,[14] the spirit of <u>PERVERSENESS</u>. Of this spirit philosophy takes no account. Yet I am not more sure that my soul lives, than I am that perverseness is one of the primitive impulses of the human heart—one of the indivisible primary faculties, or sentiments, which give direction to the character of Man. Who has not, a hundred times, found himself committing a vile or a stupid action, for no other reason than because he knows he should *not?* Have we not a perpetual <u>inclination</u>, in the teeth of our best judgment, to violate that which is *Law,* merely because we understand it to be such? This spirit of perverseness, I say, came to my final overthrow. It was this unfathomable[15] longing of the soul *to vex itself*—to offer violence to its own nature—to do wrong for the wrong's sake only—that urged me to continue and finally to consummate[16] the injury I had inflicted upon the unoffending brute. One morning, in cold blood, I slipped a noose about its neck and hung it to the limb of a tree;—hung it with the tears streaming from my eyes, and with the bitterest remorse at my heart;—hung it *because* I knew that it had loved me, and *because* I felt it had given me no reason of offense;—hung it *because* I knew that in so doing I was committing a sin—a deadly sin that

> *Why does the speaker hang the cat?*

---

11. **peevish.** Cranky; bad-tempered
12. **possessed me.** Held me
13. **gin-nurtured.** Caused by drinking gin, a hard liquor
14. **irrevocable overthrow.** Unavoidable downfall
15. **unfathomable.** Not thoroughly understood
16. **consummate.** Bring to completion

---

words for everyday use

a • troc • i • ty (ə träs´ə tē) *n.,* cruel or evil act. *The prisoner of war remembered the <u>atrocity</u> committed against him for the rest of his life.*

de • bauch (dē bôch´) *n.,* extreme indulgence of one's appetites. *After eating an entire gallon of chocolate almond fudge ice cream, the twins paid for their <u>debauch</u> with severe stomach aches.*

e • quiv • o • cal (ē kwiv´ə kəl) *adj.,* uncertain; undecided. *Because of my experiences with both his fury and his kindness, I maintained an <u>equivocal</u> opinion.*

per • verse • ness (pər vʉrs´nəs) *n.,* deviation from what is considered right or good. *Children who commit acts of <u>perverseness</u> often become seriously troubled adults.*

in • cli • na • tion (in´ klə nā´ shən) *n.,* tendency. *On such a dreary morning, her <u>inclination</u> to stay in bed was understandable.*

would so <u>jeopardize</u> my immortal soul as to place it—if such a thing were possible—even beyond the reach of the infinite mercy of the Most Merciful and Most Terrible God.

On the night of the day on which this most cruel deed was done, I was aroused from sleep by the cry of fire. The curtains of my bed were in flames. The whole house was blazing. It was with great difficulty that my wife, a servant, and myself, made our escape from the <u>conflagration</u>. The destruction was complete. My entire worldly wealth was swallowed up, and I resigned myself thenceforward[17] to despair.

What happens to the speaker the night after the abuse of the cat? What is the speaker's mindset after this event?

I am above the weakness of seeking to establish a sequence of cause and effect, between the disaster and the atrocity. But I am detailing a chain of facts—and wish not to leave even a possible link imperfect. On the day succeeding the fire, I visited the ruins. The walls, with one exception, had fallen in. This exception was found in a compartment wall, not very thick, which stood about the middle of the house, and against which had rested the head of my bed. The plastering had here, in great measure, resisted the action of the fire—a fact which I attributed to its having been recently spread. About this wall a dense crowd were collected, and many persons seemed to be examining a particular portion of it with very minute and

He went about the house as usual, but, as might be expected, fled in extreme terror at my approach.

eager attention. The words "strange!" "singular!" and other similar expressions, excited my curiosity. I approached and saw, as if graven in *bas-relief*[18] upon the white surface, the figure of a gigantic *cat*. The impression was given with an accuracy truly marvellous. There was a rope about the animal's neck.

What figure does the speaker see? What is on this figure?

When I first beheld this <u>apparition</u>—for I could scarcely regard it as less—my wonder and my terror were extreme. But at length reflection came to my aid. The cat, I remembered, had been hung in a garden adjacent to the house. Upon the alarm of fire, this garden had been immediately filled by the crowd—by some one of whom the animal must have been cut from the tree and thrown, through an open window, into my chamber.[19] This had probably been done with the view of arousing me from sleep. The falling of other walls had compressed the victim of my cruelty into the substance of the freshly-spread plaster; the <u>lime</u> of which, with the flames, and the *ammonia* from the carcass,[20] had then accomplished the portraiture as I saw it.

---

17. **thenceforward.** From then on
18. **graven in *bas-relief*.** Carved so that it stands out against a wall or flat surface
19. **chamber.** Room
20. ***ammonia* from the carcass.** Colorless strong-smelling gas made of nitrogen and hydrogen; it is a compound produced by a decaying human or animal body.

---

words for everyday use

jeop • ard • ize (jep´ər dīz´) *vt.,* risk; endanger. *The thunder and darkening sky could <u>jeopardize</u> our plans for an outdoor picnic.*
con • fla • gra • tion (kän′ flə grā´ shən) *n.,* large, destructive fire. *To the horror of the villagers, the <u>conflagration</u> jumped the water barriers and burned a destructive path toward the village.*
ap • pa • ri • tion (ap´ə rish´ən) *n.,* anything that appears suddenly, or in an extraordinary way. *She blinked her eyes, but she couldn't shake from view the <u>apparition</u> of the young, smiling woman.*
lime (līm) *n.,* calcium oxide, a white substance used in making mortar and cement. *Some soils naturally contain a high percentage of <u>lime</u>.*

ANSWERS TO GUIDED READING QUESTIONS

1. The speaker's house catches fire and is completely destroyed. After this event, the speaker's mindset is one of despair.
2. The speaker sees the impression of a gigantic cat in the plaster wall above his bed. A rope is wrapped around the neck of the cat.

ADDITIONAL QUESTIONS AND ACTIVITIES

Ask students how the narrator explains the apparition of the gigantic cat? How might the narrator's state of mind have influenced what he saw?
Answer
He hypothesizes that someone threw the hanged cat into his room to wake him up during the fire. The cat's body, he speculates, was compressed into the recently spread, and therefore soft, plaster on the wall and then coated over as the fire's heat and fumes from the decaying animal further softened it. The narrator's despair at seeing his house destroyed, and possibly feelings of guilt, may have influenced what he saw—the image of a cat with a rope around its neck.

1. The speaker lets the cat follow him home.
2. The speaker begins to dislike the cat. This feeling is intensified by the fact that the cat, like Pluto, "had been deprived of one of its eyes."

ADDITIONAL QUESTIONS
AND ACTIVITIES

Where does the narrator typically hang out? How does the speaker describe his condition while in these "vile haunts"?
Answer
He hangs out in taverns that have a bad reputation. The narrator describes his condition as "half stupefied."

Although I thus readily accounted to my reason,[21] if not altogether to my conscience, for the startling fact just detailed, it did not the less fail to make a deep impression upon my fancy.[22] For months I could not rid myself of the phantasm of the cat; and, during this period, there came back into my spirit a half-sentiment that seemed, but was not, <u>remorse</u>. I went so far as to regret the loss of the animal, and to look about me, among the vile haunts which I now habitually frequented, for another pet of the same species, and of somewhat similar appearance, with which to supply its place.

One night as I sat, half stupefied, in a den of more than infamy,[23] my attention was suddenly drawn to some black object, <u>reposing</u> upon the head of one of the immense hogsheads[24] of gin, or of rum, which <u>constituted</u> the chief furniture of the apartment. I had been looking steadily at the top of this hogshead for some minutes, and what now caused me surprise was the fact that I had not sooner perceived the object thereupon. I approached it, and touched it with my hand. It was a black cat—a very large one—fully as large as Pluto, and closely resembling him in every respect but one. Pluto had not a white hair upon any portion of his body; but this cat had a large, although indefinite splotch of white, covering nearly the whole region of the breast.

Upon my touching him, he immediately arose, purred loudly, rubbed against my hand, and appeared delighted with my notice. This, then, was the very creature of which I was in search. I at once offered to purchase it of the landlord; but this person made no claim to it—knew nothing of it—had never seen it before.

I continued my caresses, and when I prepared to go home, the animal evinced a disposition[25] to accompany

What does the speaker do with the cat that he sees?

me. I permitted it to do so; occasionally stooping and patting it as I proceeded. When it reached the house it domesticated itself at once, and became immediately a great favorite with my wife.

For my own part, I soon found a dislike to it arising within me. This was just the reverse of what I had anticipated; but—I know not how or why it was—its evident fondness for myself rather disgusted and annoyed me. By slow degrees these feelings of disgust and annoyance rose into the bitterness of hatred. I avoided the creature; a certain sense of shame, and the remembrance of my former deed of cruelty, preventing me from physically abusing it. I did not, for some weeks, strike, or otherwise violently ill use it; but gradually—very gradually—I came to look upon it with unutterable loathing, and to flee silently from its <u>odious</u> presence, as from the breath of a pestilence.[26]

What added, no doubt, to my hatred of the beast, was the discovery, on the morning after I brought it home, that, like Pluto, it also had been deprived of one of its eyes. This circumstance, however, only endeared it to my wife, who, as I have already said, possessed, in a high degree, that humanity of feeling which had once been my distinguishing trait,[27] and the source of many of my simplest and purest pleasures.

How does the speaker begin to feel about the cat? What strange characteristic of the cat intensifies these feelings?

---

21. **accounted to my reason.** Explained to myself
22. **fancy.** Imagination
23. **den of more than infamy.** Tavern with a particularly bad reputation
24. **hogsheads.** Large barrels holding from sixty-three to one hundred and forty gallons
25. **evinced a disposition.** Appeared to want
26. **pestilence.** Communicable disease
27. **distinguishing trait.** Identifying characteristic

---

words for everyday use

re • morse (ri môrs´) *n.*, deep sense of guilt. *The convict showed no apparent <u>remorse</u> for her crime.*
re • pose (ri pōz´) *vt.*, lie, rest, or be supported on. *While <u>reposing</u> in her hammock, the ever-hopeful gardener dreamed of giant tomatoes and succulent sweet corn.*
con • sti • tute (kän´ stə tōōt´) *vt.*, form the components or elements of. *Wheat flour, bananas, and oatmeal <u>constituted</u> the primary ingredients of the banana bread.*
o • di • ous (ō´ dē əs) *adj.*, disgusting; offensive. *Opinion polls indicated that the public believed the candidate was an <u>odious</u>*

With my aversion to this cat, however, its partiality for myself seemed to increase. It followed my footsteps with a pertinacity[28] which it would be difficult to make the reader comprehend. Whenever I sat, it would crouch beneath my chair, or spring upon my knees, covering me with its loathsome caresses. If I arose to walk it would get between my feet and thus nearly throw me down, or, fastening its long and sharp claws in my dress, clamber, in this manner, to my breast. At such times, although I longed to destroy it with a blow, I was yet withheld from so doing, partly by a memory of my former crime, but chiefly—let me confess it at once—by absolute *dread* of the beast.

This dread was not exactly a dread of physical evil—and yet I should be at a loss how otherwise to define it. I am almost ashamed to own—yes, even in this felon's cell, I am almost ashamed to own—that the terror and horror with which the animal inspired me, had been heightened by one of the merest chimeras[29] it would be possible to conceive. My wife had called my attention, more than once, to the character of the mark of white hair, of which I have spoken, and which constituted the sole visible difference between the strange beast and the one I had destroyed. The reader will remember that this mark, although large, had been originally very indefinite; but, by slow degrees— degrees nearly imperceptible, and which for a long time my reason struggled to reject as fanciful—it had, at length, assumed a rigorous distinctness of outline. It was now the representation of an object that I shudder to name—and for this, above all, I loathed, and dreaded, and would have rid myself of the monster *had I dared*—it was now, I say, the image of a hideous—of a ghastly thing—of the GALLOWS![30]—oh, mournful and terrible engine of Horror and of Crime—of Agony and of Death!

And now was I indeed wretched beyond the wretchedness of mere Humanity. And *a brute beast*—whose fellow I had contemptuously destroyed—*a brute beast* to work out for *me*—for me, a man fashioned in the image of the High God—so much of insufferable woe! Alas! neither by day nor by night knew I the blessing of rest any more! During the former the creature left me no moment alone, and in the latter I started hourly from dreams of unutterable fear to find the hot breath of *the thing* upon my face, and its vast weight—an incarnate nightmare that I had no power to shake off—incumbent eternally upon my *heart!*

Beneath the pressure of torments such as these the feeble remnant of the good within me succumbed. Evil thoughts became my sole intimates[31]—the darkest and most evil of thoughts. The moodiness of my usual temper increased to hatred of all things and of all mankind; while from the sudden, frequent, and ungovernable outbursts of a fury to which I now blindly abandoned myself, my uncomplaining wife, alas, was the most usual and the most patient of sufferers.

One day she accompanied me, upon some household errand, into the cellar of the old building which our poverty compelled us to

> *What distinguishes the new cat from Pluto? How does this distinguishing feature change shape? What does this feature finally look like?*

> *Why does the speaker develop a hatred for all things?*

---

28. **pertinacity.** Persistence
29. **chimeras.** Illusions or fabrications of the mind
30. **GALLOWS.** Upright frames used for hanging people
31. **intimates.** Close friends

---

words for everyday use

a • ver • sion (ə vur′zhən) *n.*, loathing or revulsion. *Heidi's aversion toward television was not shared by many of her friends.*
im • per • cep • ti • ble (im′pər sep′tə bəl) *adj.*, subtle; so as not to be easily perceived. *A slight breeze brought some relief, although it was nearly imperceptible, to the laborers working in the sun.*
in • cum • bent (in kum′bənt) *n.*, lying or pressing with its weight on something else. *Incumbent on the young boy's heart was the death of his beloved dog.*
suc • cumb (sə kum′) *vi.*, give way to; yield. *Several of the hikers succumbed to the heat.*
un • gov • ern • a • ble (un guv′ərn ə bəl) *adj.*, unable to be controlled. *The child's ungovernable behavior distressed his parents greatly.*

ANSWERS TO GUIDED READING QUESTIONS

1. The new cat has a mark of white hair on its chest. This feature slowly changes shape until it forms the distinct outline of a gallows.
2. The speaker develops a hatred of all things because of "the pressure of torments." The cat with the gallows marking will not leave him alone and causes him to have "dreams of unutterable fear."

LITERARY TECHNIQUE

MOOD. Mood, or *atmosphere*, is the emotion created in the reader by part or all of a literary work. A writer creates a mood through descriptive language and sensory details. What mood, or emotion, dominates this part of the story? What language and concrete details on page 177 contribute to this mood?
Answers
The mood is one of dread and horror. Language contributing to this mood includes words of the narrator that reveal his torment and paranoia, such as "And now was I indeed wretched beyond the wretchedness of mere humanity." Concrete details include the white mark on the black cat, which looks like a gallows to the narrator, the fact that the narrator wakes hourly from "dreams of unutterable fear," and the phrase "in this felon's cell," which tells the reader the narrator is in prison for a serious crime that has not yet been revealed.

inhabit. The cat followed me down the steep stairs, and, nearly throwing me headlong, exasperated me to madness. Uplifting an axe, and forgetting in my wrath the childish dread which had hitherto stayed my hand, I aimed a blow at the animal, which, of course, would have proved instantly fatal had it descended as I wished. But this blow was arrested by the hand of my wife. Goaded by the interference into a rage more than demoniacal, I withdrew my arm from her grasp and buried the axe in her brain. She fell dead upon the spot without a groan.

What happens when the speaker tries to hit the cat with an ax?

This hideous murder accomplished, I set myself forthwith, and with entire deliberation, to the task of concealing the body. I knew that I could not remove it from the house, either by day or by night, without the risk of being observed by the neighbors. Many projects entered my mind. At one period I thought of cutting the corpse into minute fragments, and destroying them by fire. At another, I resolved to dig a grave for it in the floor of the cellar. Again, I deliberated about casting it in the well in the yard—about packing it in a box, as if merchandise, with the usual arrangements, and so getting a porter to take it from the house. Finally I hit upon what I considered a far better expedient than either of these. I determined to wall it up in the cellar, as the monks of the Middle Ages are recorded to have walled up their victims.

For a purpose such as this the cellar was well adapted. Its walls were loosely constructed, and had lately been plastered throughout with a rough plaster, which the dampness of the atmosphere had prevented from hardening.

Moreover, in one of the walls was a projection, caused by a false chimney, or fireplace, that had been filled up and made to resemble the rest of the cellar. I made no doubt that I could readily displace the bricks at this point, insert the corpse, and wall the whole up as before, so that no eye could detect any thing suspicious.

Where does the speaker decide to hide the body?

And in this calculation I was not deceived. By means of a crowbar I easily dislodged the bricks, and, having carefully deposited the body against the inner wall, I propped it in that position, while with little trouble I relaid the whole structure as it originally stood. Having procured mortar, sand, and hair, with every possible precaution, I prepared a plaster which could not be distinguished from the old, and with this I very carefully went over the new brick-work. When I had finished, I felt satisfied that all was right. The wall did not present the slightest appearance of having been disturbed. The rubbish on the floor was picked up with the minutest care. I looked around triumphantly, and said to myself: "Here at least, then, my labor has not been in vain."

My next step was to look for the beast which had been the cause of so much wretchedness; for I had, at length, firmly resolved to put it to death. Had I been able to meet with it at the moment, there could have been no doubt of its fate; but it appeared that the crafty animal had been alarmed at the violence of my previous anger, and forbore[32] to present itself in my present mood. It is impossible to describe or to imagine the deep, the blissful sense of relief which the absence of the detested creature

---

32. **forbore.** Decided not

words for everyday use	
goad • ed (gōd´əd) *part.*, prodded into action. *Threats from the Department of Health goaded the negligent landlord into making improvements.*
de • lib • er • ate (di lib´ər āt´) *vt.*, think about or consider carefully. *With only thirty seconds left in the final quarter, the coach deliberated about the team's last play.*
ex • pe • di • ent (ek spē´ dē ənt) *n.*, resource suited to the occasion. *The young designer's idea proved to be a more efficient expedient than the previous solution.*
pro • cure (prō kyo͞or´) *vt.*, get or obtain. *After he procured his meager rations of bacon, beans, and tinned milk, the elderly pensioner walked home.*

occasioned[33] in my bosom. It did not make its appearance during the night; and thus for one night, at least, since its introduction into the house, I soundly and tranquilly slept; aye, *slept* even with the burden of murder upon my soul.

> *How does the speaker feel about the absence of the cat?*

The second and the third day passed, and still my tormentor came not. Once again I breathed as a freeman. The monster, in terror, had fled the <u>premises</u> for ever! I should behold it no more! My happiness was supreme! The guilt of my dark deed disturbed me but little. Some few inquiries had been made, but these had been readily answered. Even a search had been instituted—but of course nothing was to be discovered. I looked upon my future felicity[34] as secured.

> **The guilt of my dark deed disturbed me but little.**

Upon the fourth day of the assassination, a party of the police came, very unexpectedly, into the house, and proceeded again to make rigorous investigation of the premises. Secure, however, in the <u>inscrutability</u> of my place of concealment, I felt no embarrassment whatever. The officers bade[35] me accompany them in their search. They left no nook or corner unexplored. At length, for the third or fourth time, they descended into the cellar. I quivered not in a

> *Who comes to the speaker's house? What do they do? What is the speaker's reaction?*

muscle. My heart beat calmly as that of one who slumbers in innocence. I walked the cellar from end to end. I folded my arms upon my bosom, and roamed easily to and fro. The police were thoroughly satisfied and prepared to depart. The glee at my heart was too strong to be restrained. I burned to say if but one word, by way of triumph, and to <u>render</u> doubly sure their assurance of my guiltlessness.

"Gentlemen," I said at last, as the party ascended the steps, "I delight to have allayed your suspicions. I wish you all health and a little more courtesy. By the bye, gentlemen, this—this is a very well-constructed house," (in the rabid desire to say something easily, I scarcely knew what I uttered at all),—"I may say an *excellently* well-constructed house. These walls—are you going, gentlemen?—these walls are solidly put together"; and here, through the mere frenzy of <u>bravado</u>, I rapped heavily with a cane which I held in my hand, upon that very portion of the brickwork behind which stood the corpse of the wife of my bosom.

But may God shield and deliver me from the fangs of the Arch-Fiend! No sooner had the <u>reverberation</u> of my blows sunk into silence, than I was answered by a voice from within the

---

33. **occasioned.** Caused
34. **felicity.** Happiness
35. **bade.** Asked

words for everyday use

prem • is • es (prem´ is əs) *n.*, house and its land. *The realtor couldn't recall how long the <u>premises</u> had been vacated.*
in • scru • ta • bil • i • ty (in skrōōt´ə bil´ə tē) *n.*, complete obscurity. *The famous actor's <u>inscrutability</u> was achieved with the aid of a masterful disguise.*
ren • der (ren´ dər) *vt.*, cause to be or become. *To <u>render</u> the squawking parrot silent, she threw a pillowcase over its cage.*
bra • va • do (brə vä´ dō) *n.*, false courage. *In a show of <u>bravado</u>, the circus clown stood tall and puffed out his chest.*
re • ver • ber • a • tion (ri vʉr´ bər ā´ shən) *n.*, echoed sound. *The <u>reverberation</u> from the bass guitar could be felt throughout the amphitheater.*

1. The speaker feels great relief when the cat is absent.
2. A group of police officers comes to the speaker's house and searches it. The speaker reacts with "no embarrassment whatever" and without fear.

INTERNET RESOURCES

To learn more about Poe's life and writing career, encourage students to take a tour of the **Edgar Allan Poe Museum in Richmond, Virginia**, at the museum's website: <u>http://www.poemuseum.org</u>.

LITERARY TECHNIQUE

FORESHADOWING. Foreshadowing is the use of materials to hint at events that will occur later in the story. Ask students what examples of foreshadowing they can find in the story.
Answer
The image of the first black cat in the plaster wall foreshadows the entombment of the second black cat behind the wall. The image of the gallows on the second black cat foreshadows the narrator's death by hanging for his crime.

1. When the visitors are about to
leave, the speaker raps on the cellar
wall to show how strong the walls
are. A sobbing cry comes from
inside the wall.
2. The cat has been sealed into the
wall along with the speaker's
dead wife.

SELECTION CHECK TEST 4.3.5
WITH ANSWERS

Checking Your Reading
1. Why does the narrator write this
story? **He is about to be executed.**
2. What does the narrator claim
caused his personality to change
over the years? **He became an
alcoholic.**
3. What reason does the narrator give
for killing Pluto? *Responses may
vary;* **he attributes it to perversity,
to the desire to do that which is
forbidden.**
4. Why is a crowd gathered around
the ruins of the narrator's burned
house? **It is gathered around a
silhouette of a black cat with a
rope around its neck.**
5. How does the black cat help the
police find the body of the
narrator's wife? **The cat, entombed
with the wife, shrieks.**

Vocabulary in Context
Fill in each blank below with the most
appropriate word from the following
Words for Everyday Use. You may have
to change the tense of the word.

docility   allusion   uncongenial
debauch   expound   jeopardize
cherish

1. As a puppy, Fenway was a handful,
but as an adult dog he is a model
of **docility**.
2. Guy pursued success as a dancer,
but he **cherished** his privacy so
much that he wasn't sure he
wanted to be famous.
3. My father and stepfather get along,
but my mother and stepmother are
uncongenial.
4. I enjoy *The New York Times* because
it **expounds** upon important issues.
5. Dan knew he was **jeopardizing** his
career when he refused to move to
a bigger city.

Literary Tools

flashback   ambiguous   plot
external conflict   internal conflict
development   resolution

1. Like many of Poe's stories, "The
Black Cat" is **ambiguous** and
doesn't offer an easy interpretation.

---

tomb!—by a cry, at first muffled and broken, like
the sobbing of a child, and then quickly swelling
into one long, loud, and continuous scream,
utterly <u>anomalous</u> and inhuman—a howl—a
wailing shriek, half of hor-
ror and half of triumph,
such as might have arisen
only out of hell, <u>conjointly</u>
from the throats of the damned in their agony
and of the demons that exult in the damnation.

*What happens when
the visitors are about to
leave?*

Of my own thoughts it is folly to speak.
Swooning, I staggered to the opposite wall. For
one instant the party on the stairs remained
motionless, through extremity of terror and awe.
In the next a dozen stout arms were toiling at the
wall. It fell bodily. The corpse, already greatly
decayed and clotted with gore, stood erect before
the eyes of the spectators. Upon its head, with
red extended mouth and solitary eye of fire, sat
the hideous beast whose
craft had seduced me into
murder, and whose inform-
ing voice had <u>consigned</u> me to the hangman. I
had walled the monster up within the tomb. ∎

*Where had the cat
been?*

words for everyday use	a • nom • a • lous (ə näm´ə ləs) *adj.*, inconsistent or contradicting. *The appearance of the entire family, seated together at the kitchen table for breakfast, was an <u>anomalous</u> sight.* con • joint • ly (kən joint´ lē) *adv.*, in a united or combined manner. *The baritone and tenor sections <u>conjointly</u> sang the final verses of the song.* con • sign (kən sīn´) *vt.*, hand over or deliver. *After she had <u>consigned</u> the telegram to its recipient, the messenger rode away on her bicycle.*

Respond to the SELECTION

What aspect of this story did you find the most horrifying? Why?

SELECTION CHECK TEST 4.3.5 WITH ANSWERS (CONT.)

2. The **plot** of a story is the sequence of events that
revolve around the central conflict.
3. When a character deals with a struggle within him-
or herself, he or she faces a(n) **internal conflict**.
4. **Flashbacks** present events that occurred earlier
than the current time of the work.
5. Near a story's conclusion, the **resolution** of the
plot is revealed.

RESPOND TO THE SELECTION

Ask students if they have ever witnessed someone treating an animal
cruelly. Do they think the person
was motivated by perverseness, as
the narrator in "The Black Cat" was?
Explain.

Investigate, *Inquire,* and Imagine

Recall: GATHERING FACTS

1a. What is the narrator's "immediate purpose" in writing his "most wild yet most homely narrative"?

2a. What features do Pluto and the black cat have in common?

3a. What causes the narrator to murder his wife?

Interpret: FINDING MEANING

1b. What is the probable reason that the narrator would be "mad" to expect readers to believe his tale?

2b. What later event is foreshadowed by the black cat's white mark?

3b. What false securities allow the narrator to remain calm after the murder?

Analyze: TAKING THINGS APART

4a. Identify specific details that are particularly effective in creating an atmosphere of horror in the story.

Synthesize: BRINGING THINGS TOGETHER

4b. What is the narrator's definition of perverseness? What acts of perversity does the narrator commit? In what way is the telling of the story an act of perversity on the part of the narrator?

Evaluate: MAKING JUDGMENTS

5a. In your opinion, is the narrator reliable? Why, or why not?

Extend: CONNECTING IDEAS

5b. Do you think Poe wrote this story simply to engage readers by appealing to their fascination for the morbid? Or do you think Poe had a deeper message? If so, what might this message be?

Understanding *Literature*

FLASHBACK. Review the definition for **flashback** in the Handbook of Literary Terms. With what final event does the story open? Where is the narrator as he "pens" his tale?

PLOT AND CONFLICT. Review the definitions for **plot** and **conflict** in the Handbook of Literary Terms. Use the plot pyramid below as a guide for tracking points of plot in the story you've just read. Identify each element of plot by summarizing events from the story next to the appropriate part of the plot pyramid. You may want to refer to the Elements of Fiction on page 163 for a review of all the elements of plot.

Rising action
cat has patch of fur that takes shape of gallows
finds replacement for Pluto
narrator feels fear and hatred for cat

What conflicts does the narrator face during the course of the story? Would you characterize each conflict as an internal or external conflict? How is each conflict resolved? Explain how conflict drives the plot forward in this story.

RECALL

1a. His immediate purpose is "to place before the world" a plain and objective account of a series of "mere household events."

2a. Both cats are fond of the narrator, are large and black, and have only one eye.

3a. He becomes demoniacally angry when his wife prevents him from killing the cat with an ax by grabbing his arm. In his rage, he kills her instead.

INTERPRET

1b. He would be "mad" to expect readers to believe his tale because the events seem too fantastic to be true and the narrator's immoral behavior in the tale may seem too horrifying to be believable.

2b. The narrator's expected sentence of death by hanging for murdering his wife is foreshadowed by the white gallows outlined on the cat's chest.

3b. He remains calm because he believes that the cat has run away and he is certain that he left no trace of his actions when he entombed his wife in the cellar wall.

ANALYZE

4a. Details contributing to the atmosphere of horror include the descriptions of gouging out the cat's eye and hanging the cat dead, the image of the narrator driving an ax through his wife's brain, and the narrator's many comments that reveal his cold-blooded attitude.

SYNTHESIZE

4b. The narrator defines perverseness as the "inclination . . . to violate that which is Law, merely because we understand it to be such" or the "longing . . . to do wrong for the wrong's sake only." His acts of perversity include maiming his pet cat when it bites him out fear, hanging the cat after it comes to dislike him, and killing his wife because she tried to keep him from harming the second cat. The telling of the story may be perverse because people who commit evil deeds often do not confess them.

EVALUATE

5a. Students who feel the narrator is unreliable may cite his alcoholism, which would impair his perception. He relates certain implausible events without question, such as the impression of a gigantic cat in the plaster above the bed and the change in the black cat's white markings. These may only be the narrator's imaginings, which he

---

cannot distinguish from reality. Students who feel the narrator is reliable may note his claim at the beginning that he is not mad and wants to unburden his soul by confessing, his seeming perceptiveness about his changing states of mind, his admission that the events are startling, and the general coherence of the story. He may be the reliable narrator of an incredible tale.

EXTEND

5b. *Responses will vary.* A deeper message may be that alcohol abuse can destroy one's character and ruin one's life.

ANSWERS TO UNDERSTANDING LITERATURE

FLASHBACK. The story opens with the narrator's final day of life in prison, where he pens his tale. He says "tomorrow I die," and the explanation for his impending death is revealed in his tale.

(Continued on page 182)

ANSWERS TO UNDERSTANDING LITERATURE (CONT.)

Plot and Conflict. The plot pyramid should include information similar to the following.

Exposition. Narrator has always loved animals; has a favorite cat named Pluto.

Inciting Incident. He becomes an alcoholic, grows moody and irritable. One night he cuts one of Pluto's eyes out when Pluto irritates him. He hangs Pluto from a tree.

Rising Action. Narrator's house burns down. Impression of a cat appears on a still-standing wall. Narrator finds a replacement cat who closely resembles Pluto and follows him everywhere. A patch of white on its breast slowly begins to resemble a gallows. Sight of the cat torments him.

Climax. Cat follows him into the cellar and nearly causes him to fall. In a rage, the narrator tries to kill it with an ax. When his wife intervenes, he kills her.

Falling Action. Narrator hides wife's body inside wall of cellar without a trace, and the cat disappears. Narrator feels secure. Police come to search house. Narrator remains calm.

Resolution. As police tour the cellar, they hear a shriek from inside wall. Police dig through to find the corpse of the narrator's wife and the black cat that had cried out. The narrator is sentenced to be hanged.

Conflict. The speaker faces several conflicts. He struggles against alcoholism, self-hatred, and growing madness—all internal conflicts. These internal conflicts are not resolved. They drive the plot forward by causing specific actions. For example, his alcohol-induced irritability causes him to overreact when Pluto bites him out of fear and when the second cat nearly trips him.

ANSWERS TO INTEGRATING THE LANGUAGE ARTS

Language, Grammar, and Style
1. Edgar Allan Poe (subject); is (predicate); author (predicate noun)
2. narrator (subject); becomes (predicate); evil (predicate adjective)
3. narrator's pets and his wife (subject); are (predicate); ones (predicate pronoun).
4. narrator (subject); appears (predicate); calm (predicate adjective)

Writer's Journal

1. Write the **obituary** that might appear in the local newspaper after the narrator's death.

2. Write a **letter** to a friend describing an incident that happened to you or an event you took part in recently. Begin your letter in the present and use the technique of flashback to tell about the incident or event.

3. Imagine that once the narrator's crimes have been exposed, a local reporter interviews one of the narrator's neighbors about anything unusual heard or witnessed at the narrator's residence during the time that the narrator lived there. In narrative form or question-and-answer format, write a short **newspaper article** that reveals the neighbor's responses.

Integrating the Language Arts

Language, Grammar, and Style

COMPLETERS FOR LINKING VERBS: PREDICATE NOUNS, PRONOUNS, AND ADJECTIVES. Refer to the Language Arts Survey, 3.23, "Sentence Completers for Linking Verbs: Predicate Nouns, Pronouns, and Adjectives." In each sentence below, identify the subject, the linking verb, and its complement, and label each complement as a predicate noun, pronoun, or adjective.

1. Edgar Allan Poe is the author of many tales of horror.
2. The narrator of "The Black Cat" becomes increasingly evil.
3. The narrator's pets and his wife are the ones who suffer.
4. When the police arrive, the narrator appears calm.
5. Pluto is the narrator's antagonist.

Vocabulary Development & Collaborative Learning

PREFIXES AND SUFFIXES. Read the Language Arts Survey 1.19, "Learning Base Words, Prefixes, and Suffixes." This story has a lengthy vocabulary list, and the words include numerous prefixes and suffixes. Form small groups and work together to gather as many prefixes and suffixes as you can find from the Words for Everyday Use list for the selection. Use a dictionary to identify the meaning of each prefix and suffix. Share your lists with other groups in your class.

Speaking and Listening & Collaborative Learning

MOCK TRIAL. Hold a mock trial in which you determine whether the defendant—the narrator—is guilty of premeditated murder or not guilty by reason of insanity. Work in groups large enough to assign the roles of judge, narrator, defense attorney, prosecuting attorney, and jury. Work together to develop arguments for and against the narrator, using details and events from the text as evidence.

ANSWERS TO INTEGRATING THE LANGUAGE ARTS (CONT.)

5. Pluto (subject); is (predicate); antagonist (predicate noun)

Vocabulary Development & Collaborative Learning
Have students relate the meaning of the prefix or suffix to the meaning of the entire word. You may wish to have them makes webs to group words with the same

prefix or suffix or words that are the same part of speech.

Speaking and Listening & Collaborative Learning
Remind each side to consider the arguments that will be used against them so they can prepare counterarguments.

"The Open Window"
by Saki

Reader's resource

Letters of introduction, formal visits, and polite conversation with total strangers are revealed as empty and trite in **"The Open Window,"** a thematic farce on the conventions of social etiquette.

CHARACTERIZATION. Characterization is the use of literary techniques to create a character. In "The Open Window," the character of Framton Nuttel is created through direct description and portrayal of behavior, two techniques of characterization. Placed opposite the ineffective and earnest character of Nuttel is Vera. Note how Vera has a rather unconventional approach to formal visits and polite conversation with strangers.

About the AUTHOR

Hector Hugh Munro (1870–1916) was born in Scotland. He later took the pseudonym **Saki** from a character in Edward Fitzgerald's translation of the *Rubáiyát of Omar Khayyám.* Mostly known for his witty short stories, of which this selection is an example, Saki wrote a series in which two young men, Reginald and Clovis, happily satirize the conventional adult world. Some of Saki's stories, however, such as "Sredni Vashtar" and "The Muse on the Hill," are rather somber. At the age of forty-four, Saki volunteered for active service in World War I; he was killed in action. Among Saki's short story collections are *Reginald, The Chronicles of Clovis, Beasts and Super Beasts,* and *The Square Egg.* His other works include two novels, three plays, and one history book. Except for his earliest writings, Saki's work is collected in *The Complete Works of Saki,* published in 1976.

Literary TOOLS

PLOT AND CONFLICT. A **plot** is a series of events related to a central conflict, or struggle. A typical plot involves the introduction of a conflict, its development, and its eventual resolution. A **conflict** is a struggle between two forces in a literary work. A struggle that takes place between a character and some outside force is called an *external conflict.* A struggle that takes place within a character is called an *internal conflict.* As you read, jot down a summary of the events that occur in the story.

IRONY. Irony is a difference between appearance and reality. Types of irony include the following: *dramatic irony,* in which something is known by the reader or audience but is unknown to the characters; *verbal irony,* in which a statement is made that implies its opposite; and *irony of situation,* in which an event occurs that violates the expectations of the characters, the reader, or the audience. As you read, contemplate which form of irony occurs in "The Open Window."

Reader's Journal

Think about a social situation in which you were expected to behave in a certain way. Did you, or did you not, behave in the manner expected of you? Why?

ADDITIONAL RESOURCES

UNIT 3 RESOURCE BOOK
- Selection Worksheet 3.3
- Selection Check Test 4.3.7
- Selection Test 4.3.8
- Language, Grammar, and Style Resource 3.94, 3.95–3.99

VOCABULARY FROM THE SELECTION

convey	ghastly
delusion	imminent
duly	migrate
engulf	self-possessed
falteringly	

READER'S JOURNAL

As an alternate activity, ask students to think about social conventions that are part of their everyday lives. What is the polite or expected thing to do in various social situations? Have students make a list of these conventions. You may also want to have them note which conventions they feel are useful and which they feel are outdated.

GOALS/OBJECTIVES

Studying this lesson will enable students to
- enjoy a short story
- identify Saki and describe his literary accomplishments
- define *plot, conflict,* and *characterization* and identify examples of each in the story
- explain what *irony* is and identify the type of irony Saki uses in "The Open Window"
- demonstrate an ability to use correct capitalization
- create a sitcom that demonstrates one or more types of irony

MOTIVATION

Have students create a two-column characterization chart for the two main characters in the story. Have them list Mr. Nuttel and Vera across the top and the headings "Direct Description" and "Behavior" along the left side. Have them fill in the chart with details for each character as they read.

READING PROFICIENCY

Have students practice reading the story aloud with a partner.

ENGLISH LANGUAGE LEARNING

Share with students the following additional vocabulary:

rectory—residence of a local minister
moor—broad area of open, rolling land with few trees
scarcity—inadequate supply
bolt—move suddenly
romance—imaginary or exaggerated story

SPECIAL NEEDS

To help put the story in context, explain that in the late nineteenth and early twentieth century newcomers to an area often carried a letter of introduction. This letter was written by someone who had personal connections in the area. It usually stated the newcomer's family connections, qualifications, reputation, and interests. Such letters helped the newcomers settle in to their new surroundings and gain social acceptance.

ENRICHMENT

Have students imagine that a friend is going to be an exchange student in another country where they know someone. Have them write a letter to the person they know introducing their friend. The letter should present the friend in a way that makes a positive impression. It might also suggest something the letter receiver could do to make your friend feel more at home in a new place.

The Girl by the Window, Harry Morley.

The OPEN Window

Saki

"My aunt will be down presently,[1] Mr. Nuttel," said a very self-possessed young lady of fifteen; "in the meantime you must try and put up with me."

Framton Nuttel endeavored[2] to say the correct something which should duly flatter the niece of the moment without unduly discounting[3] the aunt that was to come. Privately he doubted more than ever whether these formal visits on a succession of total strangers would do much towards helping the nerve cure which he was supposed to be undergoing.

What are Framton Nuttel's feelings on formal social situations?

"I know how it will be," his sister had said when he was preparing to migrate to this rural retreat; "you will bury yourself down there and not speak to a living soul, and your nerves will be worse than ever from moping. I shall just give you letters of introduction to all the people I know there. Some of them, as far as I can remember, were quite nice."

Framton wondered whether Mrs. Sappleton, the lady to whom he was presenting one of the letters of introduction, came into the nice division.

"Do you know many of the people round here?" asked the niece when she judged that they had had sufficient silent communion.[4]

"Hardly a soul," said Framton. "My sister was staying here, at the rectory,[5] you know, some four years ago, and she gave me letters of introduction to some of the people here."

He made the last statement in a tone of distinct regret.

"Then you know practically nothing about my aunt?" pursued the self-possessed young lady.

"Only her name and address," admitted the caller. He was wondering whether Mrs. Sappleton was in the married or widowed state. An undefinable something about the room seemed to suggest masculine habitation.

"Her great tragedy happened just three years ago," said the child; "that would be since your sister's time."

---

1. **presently.** Soon; in a little while
2. **endeavored.** Tried; attempted
3. **unduly discounting.** Improperly disregarding
4. **communion.** Sharing of thoughts
5. **rectory.** A residence of a parish priest

---

words for everyday use

self- • pos • sessed (self´ pə zesd´) *adj.,* confident, composed. *A self-possessed speaker in any situation, she was undaunted by the hecklers in the audience.*
du • ly (dōō´ lē) *adv.,* as required, sufficiently. *The bold applicant asked the company president if she was duly impressed with his qualifications.*
mi • grate (mī´grāt´) *vi.,* move from one place to another. *In early winter, flocks of birds migrate south to warmer climates.*

ANSWER TO GUIDED READING QUESTION

1. Framton Nuttel doubts that social visits will help cure his nervousness.

CROSS-CURRICULAR ACTIVITIES

SCIENCE. Tell students that the word *moor* is a clue to the setting of the story, which may take place in rural Scotland or another part of Great Britain. Have students locate photographs of moors in travel books about Great Britain and gather information about the animals and plants that live in this environment.

1. The niece explains that her aunt's husband and two brothers went off shooting one day through the window and never came back. She says the window is kept open by her aunt because she thinks the hunting party will "walk in at that window just as they used to do."

"Her tragedy?" asked Framton; somehow in this restful country spot tragedies seemed out of place.

"You may wonder why we keep that window wide open on an October afternoon," said the niece, indicating a large French window that opened on to a lawn.

"It is quite warm for the time of the year," said Framton; "but has that window got anything to do with the tragedy?"

"Out through that window, three years ago to a day, her husband and her two young brothers went off for their day's shooting. They never came back. In crossing the moor to their favorite snipe-shooting[6] ground they were all three <u>engulfed</u> in a treacherous piece of bog.[7] It had been that dreadful wet summer, you know, and places that were safe in other years gave way suddenly without warning. Their bodies were never recovered. That was the dreadful part of it." Here the child's voice lost its self-possessed note and became <u>falteringly</u> human. "Poor aunt always thinks that they will come back some day, they and the little brown spaniel that was lost with them, and walk in at that window just as they used to do. That is why the window is kept open every evening till it is quite dusk. Poor dear aunt, she has often told me how they went out, her husband with his white waterproof coat over his arm, and Ronnie, her youngest brother, singing, 'Bertie, why do

What explanation does the girl give for the open window?

I hope you don't mind
the open window . . .

you bound?'[8] as he always did to tease her, because she said it got on her nerves. Do you know, sometimes on still, quiet evenings like this, I almost get a creepy feeling that they will all walk in through that window—"

She broke off with a little shudder. It was a relief to Framton when the aunt bustled into the room with a whirl of apologies for being late in making her appearance.

"I hope Vera has been amusing you?" she said.

"She has been very interesting," said Framton.

"I hope you don't mind the open window," said Mrs. Sappleton briskly; "my husband and brothers will be home directly from shooting, and they always come in this way. They've been out for snipe in the marshes today, so they'll make a fine mess over my poor carpets. So like you men-folk, isn't it?"

She rattled on cheerfully about the shooting and the scarcity of birds, and the prospects for duck in the winter. To Framton, it was all purely horrible. He made a desperate but only partially successful effort to turn the talk on to a less <u>ghastly</u> topic; he was conscious that his hostess was giving him only a fragment of her attention, and her eyes were constantly straying past him to the open window

---

6. **snipe-shooting.** Bird-hunting
7. **bog.** Wet, spongy ground
8. **'Bertie . . . bound?'** Line from a popular song

words for everyday use

en • gulf (en gulf´) *vt.,* swallow up. *The foamy waves <u>engulfed</u> the children's sand castle.*
fal • ter • ing • ly (fôl´ tər iŋ lē) *adv.,* uncertainly, unsteadily. *Not expecting a gesture of kindness, he <u>falteringly</u> took her hand.*
ghast • ly (gast´ lē) *adj.,* horrible; frightful. *The <u>ghastly</u> wound on his leg required over fifty stitches.*

and the lawn beyond. It was certainly an unfortunate coincidence that he should have paid his visit on this tragic anniversary.

"The doctors agree in ordering me complete rest, an absence of mental excitement, and avoidance of anything in the nature of violent physical exercise," announced Framton, who labored under the tolerably widespread <u>delusion</u> that total strangers and chance acquaintances are hungry for the least detail of one's ailments and infirmities,[9] their cause and cure. "On the matter of diet they are not so much in agreement," he continued.

> *What does Framton think is a good topic of conversation?*

"No?" said Mrs. Sappleton, in a voice which only replaced a yawn at the last moment. Then she suddenly brightened into alert attention—but not to what Framton was saying.

"Here they are at last!" she cried. "Just in time for tea, and don't they look as if they were muddy up to the eyes!"

Framton shivered slightly and turned towards the niece with a look intended to <u>convey</u> sympathetic comprehension. The child was staring out through the open window with dazed horror in her eyes. In a chill shock of nameless fear Framton swung around in his seat and looked in the same direction.

In the deepening twilight three figures were walking across the lawn towards the window; they all carried guns under their arms, and one of them was additionally burdened with a white coat hung over his shoulders. A tired brown spaniel kept close at their heels. Noiselessly they neared the house, and then a hoarse young voice chanted out of the dusk: "I said, Bertie, why do you bound?"

Framton grabbed wildly at his stick and hat; the hall-door, the gravel-drive, and the front gate were dimly noted stages in his headlong retreat. A cyclist coming along the road had to run into the hedge to avoid <u>imminent</u> collision.

"Here we are, my dear," said the bearer of the white mackintosh,[10] coming in through the window; "fairly muddy, but most of it's dry. Who was that who bolted out as we came up?"

"A most extraordinary man, a Mr. Nuttel," said Mrs. Sappleton; "could only talk about his illnesses, and dashed off without a word of good-bye or apology when you arrived. One would think he had seen a ghost."

"I expect it was the spaniel," said the niece calmly; "he told me he had a horror of dogs. He was once hunted into a cemetery somewhere on the banks of the Ganges by a pack of pariah dogs,[11] and had to spend the night in a newly dug grave with the creatures snarling and grinning and foaming just above him. Enough to make any one lose their nerve."

Romance at short notice was her speciality. ∎

> *What does the last line explain about the girl?*

---

9. **infirmities.** Physical weaknesses or defects
10. **mackintosh.** Waterproof outer coat
11. **Ganges . . dogs.** *Ganges*—river in India; *pariah dogs*—outcast dogs, rejected by others

---

words for everyday use

de • lu • sion (di loō´ zhən) *n.*, false belief or opinion. *Suffering from paranoia, the patient lived with the <u>delusion</u> that others wished him harm.*

con • vey (kən vā´) *vt.*, make known. *To <u>convey</u> her disbelief at the jury's decision, the defense attorney shook her head and arched her eyebrows.*

im • mi • nent (im´ ə nənt) *adj.*, impending; threatening. *The dark clouds and high humidity suggested an <u>imminent</u> thunderstorm.*

Respond *to the* SELECTION

Why do you think Vera does what she does?

---

1. Framton thinks that the causes and cures of ailments and infirmities are good topics of conversation.
2. The last line reveals that Vera had made up the story about her relatives dying. Because Framton believed the hunters were dead, he was frightened into leaving when they showed up.

RESPOND TO THE SELECTION

As an alternate activity, ask students if they have ever known someone like Vera. How did the person behave? What might explain the person's behavior?

SELECTION CHECK TEST 4.3.7 WITH ANSWERS

Checking Your Reading

1. Why has Nuttel come to town? **His doctors have ordered him to rest.**
2. Why is the window left open, according to Vera? **She says her aunt's husband and brothers died in a hunting accident three years ago. The window is left open because the aunt is sure they will return.**
3. What does Mrs. Sappleton talk about when she joins Nuttel and Vera? **She talks about her husband and his brothers returning from hunting.**
4. How does Vera explain Nuttel's sudden departure? **She says he is afraid of dogs.**
5. What is Vera's "specialty"? **Romance, or making up stories, is her specialty.**

Vocabulary in Context

Fill in each blank with the most appropriate word from the following Words for Everyday Use. You may have to change the tense of the word.

imminent   engulf   migrate
duly   ghastly   convey

1. After the IRS audited the Marshalls, they **duly** collected receipts and kept records.
2. The circus **migrated** from one town to the next all summer.
3. The forest fire completely **engulfed** the trees in its path.
4. The police refused to release the **ghastly** details about the crime.

SELECTION CHECK TEST 4.3.7 WITH ANSWERS (CONT.)

5. Mrs. Kellar **conveyed** her displeasure with raised eyebrows.

Literary Tools

dramatic irony   verbal irony   irony of situation
characterization   internal conflict
external conflict   plot

1. When an event counters what the characters expect, the writer is using **irony of situation**.
2. If the reader is aware of something that a character is not aware of, then the writer is using **dramatic irony**.
3. A struggle between a character and an outside force is a(n) **external conflict**.
4. Saki describes Framton Nuttel through direct description and portrayal of behavior, two techniques of **characterization**.
5. A typical **plot** involves the introduction, development, and resolution of a conflict.

RECALL

1a. Framton makes these formal visits at the recommendation of his sister to try to help cure his nervous disorder. She gives him letters of introduction to help him get out and meet other people.

2a. Vera asks Framton, "Do you know many of the people round here?" and "Then you know practically nothing about my aunt?"

3a. Vera directs Framton's attention to the window by mentioning her aunt's "great tragedy" and saying, "You may wonder why we keep that window open on an October afternoon." Framton responds by asking what the window has to do with the tragedy.

INTERPRET

1b. Framton keeps to himself and does not have many social encounters.

2b. She wants to confirm that Framton has no knowledge about her aunt so she can try out a fictional tale about her.

3b. Vera's actions suggest that she is inventive, crafty, and likes to deceive others.

ANALYZE

4a. Vera begins by questioning Framton about who he knows and what he knows about her aunt. She mentions the tragedy first to arouse Framton's curiosity and sympathy, and then the open window. She tells her story dramatically, with appropriate emotion, and when the hunters return, stares out the window with "dazed horror" as if shocked. This convinces Framton that her story is true and the men must be ghosts.

SYNTHESIZE

4b. The second story reveals that Vera is capable of lying, since Mr. Nuttel never told her a story about his horror of dogs. The story also reveals that she has the ability to make up wild stories on the spot.

PERSPECTIVE

5a. Saki may be saying that making social connections through formal means such as letters of introduction is forced and pointless. Mr. Nuttel and Mrs. Sappleton seem to have nothing in common and are unlikely to develop a sincere connection. Saki also shows that politeness and sympathy do not always govern social inter-actions, as Vera creates her own excitement at Mr. Nuttel's expense.

EMPATHY

5b. *Responses will vary.*

Investigate Inquire, and Imagine

Recall: GATHERING FACTS

1a. Why does Framton make "formal visits on a succession of total strangers"? Why does Framton's sister give him letters of introduction to people she knows?

2a. What does Vera ask Framton about the "people round here"? about her aunt?

3a. How does Vera direct Framton's attention to the open window? How does Framton respond?

Interpret: FINDING MEANING

1b. What might this suggest about the character of Framton?

2b. Why do you think she asks these questions?

3b. What might this suggest about the character of Vera?

Analyze: TAKING THINGS APART

4a. Review the story, and note the various tactics Vera employs to successfully create "romance at short notice."

Synthesize: BRINGING THINGS TOGETHER

4b. What is the purpose of Vera's story about Framton Nuttel's "horror of dogs"?

Perspective: LOOKING AT OTHER VIEWS

5a. What is Saki saying about the social conventions of the time period?

Empathy: SEEING FROM INSIDE

5b. Imagine yourself in Framton's place—new to an unfamiliar community with a doctor's orders to avoid mental excitement and physical exertion. You discover Vera's lie. Do you confront her? If so, what will you say? Will you continue to try meeting other members of the community using letters of introduction? Will you tell them about Vera's story? Why, or why not?

Understanding Literature

PLOT AND CONFLICT. Review the definitions for plot and conflict in Literary Tools on page 183. Look back at your summary of events in the story. Categorize the events in terms of plot by placing each event next the appropriate term on a plot pyramid like the one below. Next identify conflict(s) in the story. Classify the conflict(s) you identify as internal or external, and explain your answer(s).

Exposition · Inciting Incident · Rising Action · Climax · Falling Action · Resolution · Dénouement

IRONY. Review the definition for **irony** in the Handbook of Literary Terms. Which type of irony occurs in "The Open Window"? Explain your answer. Cite specific examples of irony that occur in the story. How important to the success of this story is the author's use of irony? Explain your answer.

ANSWERS TO UNDERSTANDING LITERATURE

PLOT AND CONFLICT. Students' plot pyramids should include information similar to the following.

Exposition. The nervous Framton and self-possessed Vera meet.

Inciting incident. Vera mentions her aunt's "great tragedy" and the open window.

Rising action. Vera dramatically relates a story about how her aunt's husband and two brothers left through the window to go hunting and never returned.

Climax. As Framton chats with Mrs. Sappleton, the three hunters and their dog stroll toward the open window.

Falling action. Framton runs from the house. Vera concocts a story about Framton's horror of dogs. Conflicts include the external struggle between Framton and Vera and the internal struggle within Framton between

(Continued on page 189)

Writer's Journal

1. Write Vera's **diary entry** for the evening she scared off Framton.

2. In the time period of the story, a newcomer to town usually carried a letter of introduction. A social résumé, the letter usually stated the newcomer's family connections, qualifications, reputation, and interests. Based on what you know about Framton and his sister from the story, and filling the rest in with your own imagination, write the **letter of introduction** Framton presents to Mrs. Sappleton.

3. Consider the conventions involved with social activities as simple as dining in a restaurant; watching movies, plays, or concerts; and attending birthday parties or weddings. Select such an experience, and write a set of **guidelines** for a visitor who is unfamiliar with the social conventions associated with this activity.

Integrating the Language Arts

Language, Grammar, and Style

PROOFREADING FOR ERRORS IN CAPITALIZATION. Review the Language Arts Survey 3.94, "Editing for Capitalization Errors" and sections 3.95–3.99. Then examine the sentences below and correct any capitalization errors.

1. A tired brown Spaniel kept close at their heels.
2. Then you know practically nothing about my Aunt?
3. You may wonder why we keep that large french window open on an october afternoon.
4. It had been that dreadful wet Summer, you know.
5. The Doctors agree in ordering me complete rest.

Study and Research

COMPARISON AND CONTRAST REPORT. Research the social conventions of another time period in American or world history. Provide as much information as you can explaining the reasons behind the conventions. Write a report comparing and contrasting these conventions (or rules of etiquette) to modern day conventions for similar situations and providing some of the reasons behind modern day conventions.

Speaking and Listening & Collaborative Learning

SITCOM. Work together in a small group to write a situation comedy that features two or more characters in a conventional social situation and that yields ironic results. Employ one or more types of irony in creating your sitcom. You may want to review the definition of each type of irony in the Handbook of Literary Terms. Act out the sitcom for your classmates.

ANSWERS TO UNDERSTANDING LITERATURE (CONT.)

his nervous and reclusive tendencies and his decision to try to calm his nerves by meeting total strangers.

IRONY. The dramatic irony in the story is that the reader knows (at least sooner than Nuttel) that Vera's story is a lie, while Nuttel does not. Situational irony occurs (1) when the hunters return, violating Nuttel's expectation that they are dead, (2) when Nuttel expects to be welcomed by "nice" people but ends up being driven away, and (3) Nuttel expects to calm himself through social interaction but ends up highly agitated.

ANSWERS TO INTEGRATING THE LANGUAGE ARTS

Language, Grammar, and Style
1. A tired brown **spaniel** kept close at their heels.
2. Then you know practically nothing about my **aunt**?
3. You may wonder why we keep that large **French** window open on an **October** afternoon.
4. It had been that dreadful wet **summer**, you know.
5. The **doctors** agree in ordering me complete rest.
6. He was once hunted into a **cemetery** somewhere on the **banks** of the Ganges by a pack of pariah dogs.
7. Vera should have received an Academy **Award** for her performance.

Study and Research
Some students might like to focus on social conventions related to dating and marriage.

Speaking and Listening & Collaborative Learning
After each group has presented its sitcom, have students identify the types of irony used.

ADDITIONAL RESOURCES

UNIT 3 RESOURCE BOOK
• Selection Worksheet 3.4
• Selection Check Test 4.3.9
• Selection Test 4.3.10
• Language, Grammar, and Style Resource 3.22

GRAPHIC ORGANIZER

Groups of People
Afrikaner farmers; Americans and English (overseas people); white people in the South African cities; anti-apartheid agitators; black parents; young black wives

Stereotypes Revealed
treat blacks brutally; have no respect for black lives; see all whites in the same light; don't believe that whites can have blacks as friends; think all blacks are like the bigmouth agitators in town; are never satisfied with anything the government does; expose their children to everything; are often pregnant

READER'S JOURNAL

Literary TOOLS

POINT OF VIEW. Point of view is the vantage point from which a story is told. In stories written from a *first-person point of view,* the narrator may be a participant or witness of the action. In stories told from a *third-person point of view,* the narrator generally stands outside the action. Writers achieve a wide variety of ends by varying the characteristics of the narrator chosen for a particular work. Of primary importance is the choice of the narrator's point of view. Will the narrator be omniscient, knowing all things including the internal workings of the minds of the characters of the story, or will the narrator be limited in his or her knowledge? Will the narrator be reliable or unreliable—that is, will the reader be able to trust the narrator's statements? As you read "The Moment Before the Gun Went Off," identify the point of view from which the story is told.

STEREOTYPE. A stereotype is an uncritically accepted, fixed or conventional idea, particularly such an idea held about whole groups of people. As you read, keep track of those groups of people about whom the narrator makes stereotypical comments. Use the model below as a guide, filling in the left column only as you read the story for the first time.

Organizer

GROUPS OF PEOPLE	STEREOTYPES REVEALED
Americans and English	

190 UNIT THREE

"The Moment Before the Gun Went Off"
by Nadine Gordimer

Reader's resource

Under apartheid, a policy of racial segregation and political and economic discrimination, a person's race determines what rights he or she has. In 1948, an all-white South African government ensured white political and economic dominance under law through the system of apartheid, a system that allowed the government to force millions of blacks to live in independent homelands or in separated urban townships. Officials required blacks to carry identification papers and revoked their South African citizenship. During the 1950s, as more and more apartheid laws came into being, resistance grew among black communities. Apartheid in South Africa finally came to an end in 1991.

"The Moment Before the Gun Went Off" takes place in South Africa during the time when the policy of apartheid was being dismantled. This story appeared in the 1991 collection *Jump and Other Stories* by South African writer Nadine Gordimer.

About the AUTHOR

Nadine Gordimer was born in a small mining town outside Johannesburg, South Africa, on November 20, 1923. She began writing at a young age, publishing her first short story in a South African magazine while she was still in her teens. In 1949, she published *Face to Face,* her first collection of short stories. An English-speaking Jew living in South Africa during apartheid, Gordimer, who has been called "the conscience of South Africa," has been politically active for most of her life and has written much about race relationships in her native land. At times, some of her books have been banned in South Africa. Today, Gordimer is the author of numerous novels and short story collections, a few volumes of literary criticism, and many articles, speeches, and lectures. In 1991, she won the Nobel Prize for literature.

Reader's Journal

Have you ever been involved in a social situation that influenced how you treated certain people or made you feel as though you couldn't tell the truth about some aspect of your life? If so, write about this in your journal. If not, consider how you might react to such a situation.

GOALS/OBJECTIVES

Studying this lesson will enable students to
• interpret a story that explores the impact of racial stereotyping
• explain why writer Nadine Gordimer has been called "the conscience of South Africa"
• define *point of view* and explain which type of point of view applies to the story
• define *stereotype* and give examples from the story
• identify direct and indirect objects in sentences
• conduct research on the history of apartheid in South Africa

The MOMENT Before the Gun Went Off

Nadine Gordimer

Marais Van der Vyver shot one of his farm laborers, dead. An accident, there are accidents with guns every day of the week—children playing a fatal game with a father's revolver in the cities where guns are <u>domestic</u> objects, nowadays, hunting mishaps like this one, in the country—but these won't be reported all over the world. Van der Vyver knows his will be. He knows that the story of the Afrikaner[1] farmer—regional leader of the National Party[2] and commandant[3] of the local security commando[4]— shooting a black man who worked for him will fit exactly *their* version of South Africa, it's made for them. They'll be able to use it in their boycott and <u>divestment</u> campaigns, it'll be another piece of evidence in their truth about the country. The papers at home will quote the story as it has appeared in the <u>overseas</u> press, and in the back and forth he and the black man will become those crudely drawn figures on anti-apartheid banners, units in statistics of white brutality against blacks quoted at the United Nations—he, whom they will gleefully be able to call "a leading member" of the ruling Party.

People in the farming community understand how he must feel. Bad enough to have killed a man, without helping the Party's, the government's, the country's enemies as well. They see the truth of that. They know, reading the Sunday papers, that when Van der Vyver is quoted saying he is "terribly shocked," he will "look after the wife and children," none of those Americans and

> *What did Marais Van der Vyver do?*

> *Who understands the way Van der Vyver must feel? Who won't believe that Van der Vyver is "terribly shocked" and will "look after the wife and children"?*

---

1. **Afrikaner.** A South African of European descent whose native language is Afrikaans
2. **National Party.** Ruling political party in South Africa from 1948–1994; initiated policy of apartheid
3. **commandant.** Commanding officer
4. **commando.** An organized force of Boer—South Africans of Dutch or Huguenot descent—troops in South Africa.

words for everyday use

do • mes • tic (də məs′ tik) *adj.,* of or relating to the household or the family. *I much prefer <u>domestic</u> activities like cooking and sewing to running errands.*
di • vest • ment (dī vest′ mənt) *n.,* deprivation of property, authority, or title. *The family had no choice but to come to terms with the <u>divestment</u> they suffered as a result of the failing of their business.*
over • seas (ō var sēz′) *adj.,* situated, originating in, or relating to lands beyond the sea. *Janice is very much looking forward to her <u>overseas</u> travel from New York to Paris.*

"THE MOMENT BEFORE THE GUN WENT OFF" 191

1. Most farmers have a "particular black boy" they like to take out on their lands with them—"a kind of a friend." They also have white friends whom they invite to their houses, pray with in church, and work with on the Party committee.
2. Van der Vyver was sure the gun wasn't loaded. The gun had belonged to his father, who never kept loaded guns in the house.

CROSS-CURRICULAR ACTIVITIES

GEOGRAPHY. Have students locate South Africa on a map and then work in small groups to list at least ten facts about the political, physical, and human geography of the country. Suggest that students list questions they have first. For example: What and where are the largest cities? What does the landscape look like? What wild animals are common in South Africa? What crops are raised by farmers? What different ethnic groups live in South Africa? Ask them to share their facts in each category with the class.

VOCABULARY FROM THE SELECTION

callously
cull
overseas

domestic
divestment

English, and none of those people at home who want to destroy the white man's power will believe him. And how they will sneer when he even says of the farm boy (according to one paper, if you can trust any of those reporters), "He was my friend, I always took him hunting with me." Those city and overseas people don't know it's true: farmers usually have one particular black boy they like to take along with them in the lands; you could call it a kind of friend, yes, friends are not only your own white people, like yourself, whom you take into your house, pray with in church, and work with on the Party committee. But how can those others know that? They don't want to know it. They think all blacks are like the bigmouth agitators in town. And Van der Vyver's face in the photographs, strangely opened by distress—everyone in the district remembers Marais Van der Vyver as a little boy who would go away and hide himself if he caught him smiling at him, and everyone knows him now as a man who hides any change of expression round his mouth behind a thick, soft mustache, and in his eyes by always looking at some object in hand, a leaf or a crop fingered, pen or stone picked up, while concentrating on what he is saying, or while listening to you. It just goes to show what shock can do; when you look at the newspaper photographs you feel like apologizing, as if you had stared in on some room where you should not be.

What different types of "friends" do most farmers have?

There will be an inquiry; there had better be, to stop the assumption of yet another case of brutality against farm workers, although there's nothing in doubt—an accident, and all the facts fully admitted by Van der Vyver. He made a statement when he arrived at the police station

with the dead man in his *bakkie*.[5] Captain Beetge knows him well, of course; he gave him brandy. He was shaking, this big, calm, clever son of Willem Van der Vyver, who inherited the old man's best farm. The black was stone dead, nothing to be done for him. Beetge will not tell anyone that after the brandy Van der Vyver wept. He sobbed, snot running onto his hands, like a dirty kid. The captain was ashamed for him, and walked out to give him a chance to recover himself.

Marais Van der Vyver left his house at three in the afternoon to <u>cull</u> a buck from the family of kudu[6] he protects in the bush areas of his farm. He is interested in wildlife and sees it as the farmers' sacred duty to raise game as well as cattle. As usual, he called at his shed to pick up Lucas, a twenty-year-old farmhand who had shown mechanical aptitude and whom Van der Vyver himself had taught to maintain tractors and other farm machinery. He hooted, and Lucas followed the familiar routine, jumping onto the back of the truck. He liked to travel standing up there, spotting game before his employer did. He would lean forward, bracing against the cab below him.

Van der Vyver had a rifle and .30 caliber ammunition beside him in the cab. The rifle was one of his father's, because his own was at the gunsmith's in town. Since his father died (Beetge's sergeant wrote "passed on") no one had used the rifle, and so when he took it from a cupboard he was sure it was not loaded. His father had never allowed a loaded gun in the house, he himself had been taught since childhood never

What was Van der Vyver sure about? Why?

---

5. *bakkie.* Pickup truck
6. **kudu.** African antelope

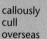

words for everyday use

cull (kul) *vt.,* to select from a group. *The photographer planned to <u>cull</u> his best shots and send them to the gallery owner.*

Homage to Chris Hani, 1993. Willie Bester. Private Collection.

1. The jolt from the pothole caused the rifle to fire. The bullet went through the roof of the truck cab, killing Lucas, who was standing up on the back of the truck to spot game.
2. The narrator says nothing can satisfy blacks or whites who oppose apartheid.

ART NOTE

Willie Bester (1956–) is a South African who studied art part time while working as a dental assistant, until deciding to become a full-time artist at age 35. He works mainly in mixed media on wood, using newspaper, graffiti, tin cups, wire, ammunition cases, photographs, and found objects gathered from the very places he portrays in his art. This mass of material gives a sense of the confusion of life under apartheid.

---

to ride with a loaded weapon in a vehicle. But this gun was loaded. On a dirt track, Lucas thumped his fist on the cab roof three times to signal: look left. Having seen the white-ripple-marked flank of a kudu, and its fine horns raking through disguising bush, Van der Vyver drove rather fast over a pothole. The jolt fired the rifle. Upright, it was pointing straight through the cab roof at the head of Lucas. The bullet pierced the roof and entered Lucas's brain by way of his throat.

What happened when Van der Vyver drove fast over a pothole?

That is the statement of what happened. Although a man of such standing in the district, Van der Vyver had to go through the ritual of swearing that it was the truth. It has gone on record, and will be there in the archive of the local police station as long as Van der Vyver lives, and beyond that, through the lives of his children, Magnus, Helena, and Karel—unless things in the country get worse, the example of black mobs in the town spreads to the rural areas and the place is burned down as many urban police stations have been. Because nothing the government can do will appease the agitators and the whites who encourage them. Nothing satisfies them, in the cities: blacks can sit and drink in white hotels now, the Immorality Act has gone, blacks can sleep with whites . . . It's not even a crime anymore.

Whom does the narrator say cannot be satisfied?

Van der Vyver has a high, barbed security fence round his farmhouse and garden which

1. He has a high, barbed-wire security fence around his farmhouse. Like other farmers, he has an aerial in his backyard and on all his vehicles. The aerials allow farmers in the district to stay in touch by radio 24 hours a day and get help if they are hurt by anti-apartheid attackers.
2. It is obvious that Van der Vyver provided money for the funeral.
3. Van der Vyver doesn't notice that his wife is always supportive.

INTERNET RESOURCES

Students might be interested to learn about the long-term relationship between Thomas Jefferson and Sally Hemings, who was a slave in his household at Monticello. Scientists now believe, based on a rigorous DNA study, that Thomas Jefferson was the likely father of all six of Sally Hemings's children. Students can learn more about this research study at the website for the **Thomas Jefferson Memorial Foundation** at http://www.monticello.org/plantation/heggins_report.html. To introduce or conclude this activity, ask students if they think interracial dating and marriage has a generally positive or negative effect on racial stereotyping and racial discrimination.

LITERARY TECHNIQUE

IRONY. Irony is a difference between appearance and reality. *Situational irony* refers to the occurrence of an event that violates the expectations of the characters or the reader. Ask students why the situation revealed at the end of the story is ironic.
Answer
The revelation that Lucas is Van der Vyver's son violates the reader's expectation because earlier Van der Vyver called him his friend and he never treated Lucas with the kind of affection and attention that a father typically shows a son.

---

his wife, Alida, thinks spoils completely the effect of her artificial stream with its tree ferns beneath the jacarandas.[6] There is an aerial soaring like a flagpole in the backyard. All his vehicles, including the truck in which the black man died, have aerials that swing their whips when the driver hits a pothole: they are part of the security system the farmers in the district maintain, each farm in touch with every other by radio, twenty-four hours out of twenty-four. It has already happened that infiltrators from over the border have mined remote farm roads, killing white farmers and their families out on their own property for a Sunday picnic. The pothole could have set off a land mine, and Van der Vyver might have died with his farm boy. When neighbors use the communications system to call up and say they are sorry about "that business" with one of Van der Vyver's boys, there goes unsaid: it could have been worse.

In what ways does Van der Vyver maintain security on his farm?

It is obvious from the quality and fittings of the coffin that the farmer has provided money for the funeral. And an elaborate funeral means a great deal to blacks; look how they will deprive themselves of the little they have, in their lifetime, keeping up payments to a burial society so they won't go in boxwood[7] to an unmarked grave. The young wife is pregnant (of course) and another little one, a boy wearing red shoes several sizes too large, leans under her jutting belly. He is too young to understand what has happened, what he is witnessing that

What is obvious from the quality and fittings of the coffin?

day, but neither whines nor plays about; he is solemn without knowing why. Blacks expose small children to everything, they don't protect them from the sight of fear and pain the way whites do theirs. It is the young wife who rolls her head and cries like a child, sobbing on the breast of this relative and that. All present work for Van der Vyver or are the families of those who work; in the weeding and harvest seasons, the women and children work for him too, carried at sunrise to the fields, wrapped in their blankets, on a truck, singing. The dead man's mother is a woman who can't be more than in her late thirties (they start bearing children at puberty), but she is heavily mature in a black dress, standing between her own parents, who were already working for old Van der Vyver when Marais, like their daughter, was a child. The parents hold her as if she were a prisoner or a crazy woman to be restrained. But she says nothing, does nothing. She does not look up; she does not look at Van der Vyver, whose gun went off in the truck, she stares at the grave. Nothing will make her look up; there need be no fear that she will look up, at him. His wife, Alida, is beside him. To show the proper respect, as for any white funeral, she is wearing the navy blue and cream hat she wears to church this summer. She is always supportive, although he doesn't seem to notice it; this coldness and reserve—his mother

> Nothing will make her look up; there need be no fear that she will look up, at him.

What doesn't Van der Vyver notice about his wife?

---

6. **jacarandas.** A type of creeping, flowering, tropical tree
7. **boxwood.** Close-grained, heavy, hard wood

says he didn't mix well as a child—she accepts for herself but regrets that it has prevented him from being nominated, as he should be, to stand as the Party's parliamentary candidate for the district. He does not let her clothing, or that of anyone else gathered closely, make contact with him. He, too, stares at the grave. The dead man's mother and he stare at the grave in communication like that between the black man outside and the white man inside the cab the moment before the gun went off.

The moment before the gun went off was a moment of high excitement shared through the roof of the cab, as the bullet was to pass, between the young black man outside and the white farmer inside the vehicle. There were such moments, without explanation, between them, although often around the farm the farmer would pass the young man without returning a greeting, as if he did not recognize him. When the bullet went off what Van der Vyver saw was the kudu stumble in fright at the report and gallop away. Then he heard the thud behind

> What type of moments did the farmer and Lucas sometimes share? At other times, how would the farmer act to Lucas?

him, and past the window saw the young man fall out of the vehicle. He was sure he had leapt up and toppled—in fright, like the buck. The farmer was almost laughing with relief, ready to tease, as he opened his door, it did not seem possible that a bullet passing through the roof could have done harm.

The young man did not laugh with him at his own fright. The farmer carried him in his arms, to the truck. He was sure, sure he could not be dead. But the young black man's blood was all over the farmer's clothes, soaking against his flesh as he drove.

How will they ever know, when they file newspaper clippings, evidence, proof, when they look at the photographs and see his face—guilty! guilty! they are right!—how will they know, when the police stations burn with all the evidence of what has happened now, and what the law made a crime in the past? How could they know that *they do not know*. Anything. The young black <u>callously</u> shot through the negligence of the white man was not the farmer's boy; he was his son. ∎

> Who was Lucas?

words for everyday use

cal • lous • ly (ka′ ləs lē) *adv.*, insensitively, uncaringly. *Anton acted <u>callously</u> when he insulted Kurt in front of a group of others.*

Respond to the SELECTION

Do you think Van der Vyver's life will change at all following Lucas's funeral? If so, how? If not, why not?

"THE MOMENT BEFORE THE GUN WENT OFF" 195

SELECTION CHECK TEST 4.3.9 WITH ANSWERS (CONT.)

1. "The Moment Before the Gun Went Off" is told in **third-person point of view**.
2. If a narrator knows the internal workings of the minds of all the characters, then he or she is **omniscient**.
3. A reader must decide if he or she trusts the narrator, deeming him or her **reliable**.

RESPOND TO THE SELECTION

As an alternate activity, ask students what opinion they hold of Van der Vyver at the end of the story, and why.

ANSWERS TO GUIDED READING QUESTIONS

1. Van der Vyver and Lucas sometimes shared moments of excitement, like "the moment before the gun went off." At other times, Van der Vyver would ignore Lucas.
2. Lucas was Van der Vyver's son.

SELECTION CHECK TEST 4.3.9 WITH ANSWERS

Checking Your Reading
1. Why does Van der Vyver expect news of the shooting to spread around the world? **He expects news to spread because the world will think it a typical shooting of a black man by a white South African.**
2. What will Captain Beetge not tell about Van der Vyver? **He will not tell how Van der Vyver sobbed when he told the story.**
3. How was Lucas killed? **Van der Vyver's gun, which he thought was not loaded, went off when the truck hit a pothole and shot Lucas through the truck's roof.**
4. Over the years, how have the rules changed between races in South Africa? **The rules have relaxed, allowing blacks more freedoms and the two races more opportunities to intermingle.**
5. At the end of the story, what do we learn about Lucas? **We learn he was Van der Vyver's son.**

Vocabulary in Context
Fill in each blank below with the most appropriate word from the following Words for Everyday Use. You may have to change the tense of the word.

> callously   cull   domestic
> divestment   overseas

1. Since she works long hours, Saundra reserves her **domestic** chores for weekends.
2. Catherine remarked that she hadn't seen Whitney since her friend moved **overseas**.
3. The king fled the country after parliament supported the **divestment** of his title.
4. The machine **culled** weeds from the crop, but we checked each batch to be sure.
5. Scrooge **callously** forced his employee to work on Christmas Day.

Literary Tools

> omniscient   limited   reliable
> unreliable   first-person point of view
> third-person point of view

RECALL

1a. The accident is different because it involves a white man killing a black man and happens in South Africa during a time of tense racial tension. The narrator says the story will be reported all over the world, that countries opposing apartheid will use the story to justify boycotts and divestments against South Africa, that overseas stories picked up in local papers will fan anti-apartheid demonstrations, and that Van der Vyver and Lucas will become stereotypes in the conflict.

2a. The narrator describes it as "a moment of high excitement" like others between the young black man and white farmer that were shared "without explanation." The narrator compares the moment to the communication between Van der Vyver and Lucas's mother as they stare at Lucas's gravesite.

3a. Van der Vyver was sure the gun was not loaded because it had been his father's, and his father never allowed loaded guns in the house.

INTERPRET

1b. At the beginning of the story, the narrator seems to sympathize with Van der Vyver, concerned how the shooting will be portrayed in the media and about the scrutiny Van der Vyver will face.

2b. *Responses will vary.* The description shows that the two men could only share each other's company in certain situations, such as hunting. They are together yet separated, not only by the cab of the truck, but by restrictive rules about race. Yet by sharing this exciting part of their lives, they develop a deep but unspoken bond. The comparison of the moment before the gun went off and the moment Van der Vyver and Lucas's mother share at the gravesite shows that blacks and white in South Africa, despite racial discrimination and unrest, were often emotionally connected.

3b. *Responses will vary.* The loaded gun might symbolize the racial tension in apartheid South Africa that can easily erupt into violence.

ANALYZE

4a. Details include Van der Vyver's shyness as a little boy; his sobbing like a child when he makes his statement to the police; his mustache and always averted gaze, which hide his expression; the fact that he sometimes avoided greeting Lucas; the fact that he promptly reported what happened;

Investigate, Inquire, and Imagine

Recall: GATHERING FACTS

1a. How is Van der Vyver's accident different from other gun accidents? What does the narrator say will happen to the story?

2a. How does the narrator describe "the moment before the gun went off"? To what does the narrator compare that moment?

3a. Why was Van der Vyver sure the gun wasn't loaded?

Interpret: FINDING MEANING

1b. At this point, with whom—Van der Vyver or Lucas—do the narrator's sympathies seem to lie?

2b. In what ways does the description of "the moment before the gun went off" offer insight into the relationship between Van der Vyver and Lucas? How does the comparison the author makes offer insight into the larger picture of race relations in South Africa at the time the story took place?

3b. What might the loaded gun symbolize?

Analyze: TAKING THINGS APART

4a. Gather details from the story that provide insight to the character of Van der Vyver.

Synthesize: BRINGING THINGS TOGETHER

4b. What kind of man do you believe Van der Vyver to be? How do you think he felt about Lucas?

Perspective: LOOKING AT OTHER VIEWS

5a. At the end of the story, the narrator reveals to the reader information about Van der Vyver and Lucas. How does the revelation bring to light the narrator's true perspective on the events that take place in the story?

Empathy: SEEING FROM INSIDE

5b. Consider the secret surrounding Van der Vyver's relationship to Lucas and the social and political climate in South Africa at the time the story takes place. Imagine you are Lucas's mother at the funeral. What are you thinking? feeling? Why do you act as you do at the funeral?

Understanding Literature

POINT OF VIEW. Review the definition for **point of view** in Literary Tools in Prereading. From what point of view is "The Moment Before the Gun Went Off" told? Is the narrator's perspective limited or omniscient? Do you believe the narrator's account of the events in the story is accurate? Do you believe the narrator's account of the story expresses the narrator's perspective of the events? Why do you think the author reveals the relationship between Van der Vyver and Lucas at the end of the story?

STEREOTYPE. Review the definition for **stereotype** in Literary Tools in Prereading. Look back to the chart you kept to record groups of people about whom the narrator makes stereotypical judgments. Complete the chart, noting specific examples of generalizations the narrator makes throughout the story. Do the narrator's stereotypical remarks influence the telling of the story? Do the narrator's apparent prejudices influence the reader's reaction to the story? Why do you think the author chose to have the narrator employ so many stereotypes throughout the story?

ANSWERS TO INVESTIGATE, INQUIRE, AND IMAGINE (CONT.)

and the fact that he doesn't let anyone else's clothing touch him at Lucas's funeral. These details show that Van der Vyver did not express emotion openly, loved his son but did not treat him as a son, and was honest and responsible.

SYNTHESIZE

4b. *Responses will vary.* Students should see that Van der Vyver is a complex character with both strong and weak points who was shaped by the social world in which he lived.

PERSPECTIVE

5a. *Responses will vary.* Throughout the story the narrator appears sympathetic to Van der Vyver's plight. The revelation in the last paragraph suggests that the narrator condemns Van der Vyver.

EMPATHY

5b. *Responses will vary.*

Writer's Journal

1. Write a **newspaper headline** about the shooting incident that might appear in Van der Vyver's local newspaper and one that might appear in a paper in the United States or the United Kingdom.
2. Write Alida Van der Vyver's **diary entry** the day of the funeral, chronicling her feelings about her husband's behavior at the cemetery.
3. Use the phrase, "The moment before the . . ." as a writing prompt. Begin with those words and **freewrite** in your journal for five to ten minutes.

Integrating the Language Arts

Language, Grammar, and Style

COMPLETERS FOR ACTION VERBS: DIRECT AND INDIRECT OBJECTS. Direct and indirect objects are completers for action verbs. **Direct objects** receive the action of the verb and answer the questions *what?* or *whom?* after the verb. **Indirect objects** tell *to* or *for whom* or *what* the action of the verb is executed. Review the Language Arts Survey 3.22, "Sentence Completers for Action Verbs: Direct and Indirect Objects," and identify direct and indirect objects in the sentences below.

1. Van der Vyver shot Lucas.
2. A bullet pierced the roof of the cab and killed Lucas.
3. He gave Captain Beetge a statement.
4. At the funeral, Lucas's grandparents hold their daughter, but she says nothing, does nothing.
5. "The Moment Before the Gun Went Off" tells the reader the story of this tragedy.

Study and Research

RESEARCHING SOUTH AFRICAN HISTORY. Use library resources and/or the Internet to conduct research on the history of apartheid in South Africa. In your own words, define apartheid and the restrictions it imposed on non-white members of the South African population. Identify some of the events that directly preceded apartheid in South Africa. Tell when the policy began and how it was brought to an end. Describe what life is like in South Africa today.

ANSWERS TO UNDERSTANDING LITERATURE

POINT OF VIEW. The point of view is third-person omniscient. The narrator stands outside the action and "knows all things." The narrator is reliable in giving an accurate account of the shooting incident, the political climate in South Africa, and the characters' actions. The story seems to express the narrator's perspective on the events, though it is not fully revealed until the last paragraph. Students may say that the revelation at the end has caused them to rethink their response to Van der Vyver. If they thought that before he had been unjustly painted as a typical white racist, now they see him as guilty of letting racism (his own or society's) define his relationship to his son.

STEREOTYPE. The narrator's stereotypical remarks expose the reader to the typical thoughts of those who are anti- and pro-apartheid. The remarks influence the telling of the story in that they imply primarily that South African whites have been unfairly stereotyped. The narrator's apparent sympathy for Van der Vyver tends to make the reader feel sympathetic toward him too. The author may have had the narrator express racial stereotypes to help readers understand the depth and complexity of racial prejudice.

ANSWERS TO INTEGRATING THE LANGUAGE ARTS

Language, Grammar, and Style
1. Lucas (direct object)
2. roof, Lucas (direct objects)
3. Captain Beetge (indirect object); statement (direct object)
4. daughter, nothing, nothing (direct objects)
5. reader (indirect object); story (direct object)

Study and Research
Have students prepare a written or oral report of their findings. To evaluate reports, assign 25 points for each grading criterion below, for a total of 100 points.

WRITTEN OR ORAL REPORT
- **Content/Unity.** The report defines apartheid, describes key events that led to its establishment, and summarizes life in South Africa during and after apartheid.
- **Organization/Coherence.** Paragraphs have a clear topic sentence, include supporting sentences, and use transitions to connect ideas.
- **Language/Style.** The report is written in formal language.
- **CONVENTIONS.** The report avoids errors in spelling, grammar, usage, mechanics, and manuscript form.

ADDITIONAL RESOURCES

UNIT 3 RESOURCE BOOK
• Selection Worksheet 3.5
• Selection Check Test 4.3.11
• Selection Test 4.3.12

GRAPHIC ORGANIZER

Students might include the following motivations in their charts:

Before the ball:
• Feels ashamed of her poverty
• Feels she was born to have a life of luxury
• Longs to own beautiful things
• Wants to be admired at the ball
These things motivate her to daydream about a life of luxury, to insist on an expensive dress for the ball, and to borrow her friend's diamond necklace.

At the ball:
• Feels pride in being the prettiest woman at the ball
• Feels embarrassed by her ordinary coat
These things motivate her to dance with enthusiasm and be sociable; to hurry away from the ball.

After losing the necklace:
• Needs to pay off huge debt
• Feels pride in paying off the debt
Her poverty motivates her to take on all the household chores and to spend wisely. Her pride in paying the debt motivates her to tell her friend the truth about losing the necklace.

READER'S JOURNAL

Students might also consider the effect that advertising has on fostering a desire for wealth or material possessions.

Literary TOOLS

FORESHADOWING. Foreshadowing is the act of presenting materials that hint at events to occur later in the story. As you read, pay close attention to clues that foreshadow events to come, and based on those clues, anticipate how the story will end.

CHARACTER AND MOTIVATION. A **character** is a person who figures in the action of the work. A *protagonist,* or *main character,* is the central literary figure in a literary work. A **motivation** is a force that moves a character to think, feel, or behave in a certain way.

Organizer

As you read the story, make a cluster chart of the forces that motivate Mme. Loisel to behave as she does.

Ashamed of her poverty

Mme. Loisel's motivations

Reader's JOURNAL

Have you ever envied the apparent wealth or material possessions of someone else? Would having those things make your life better? Why, or why not?

198 UNIT THREE

"The Necklace"
by Guy de Maupassant

Reader's resource

Naturalism was a literary movement of the late nineteenth and early twentieth centuries that saw actions and events as resulting inevitably from biological or environmental forces. Unemotional narration, meticulous detail, and accurate historical background are three of the techniques that marked the work of Maupassant and other Naturalist writers. In revolt against the Romantic school and its emphasis on subjectivity and imagination, the Naturalist writers sought to portray human beings and the society in which they live as accurately and truthfully as possible.

CULTURE CONNECTION. Maupassant selected the subjects of his short stories from peasant life in Normandy, the Franco-Prussian War, the behavior of the middle class, and the fashionable life of Paris. Telling his stories with a tone of detachment, Maupassant also infused them with a fine sense of irony that can be seen in "The Necklace."

About the AUTHOR

Guy de Maupassant (1850–1893) was born in Normandy, France, near the town of Dieppe. After joining the French Army and fighting in the Franco-Prussian War, Maupassant moved to Paris where he met many famous writers including Gustave Flaubert. Studying under Flaubert, Maupassant was greatly influenced by the style and techniques of the Naturalist school. Maupassant's short story "Boule de suif," published in 1880, established his reputation as a writer. From 1880 to 1890, Maupassant wrote six novels and more than three hundred short stories. He is widely considered to be the greatest French short-story writer.

GOALS/OBJECTIVES

Studying this lesson will enable students to
• enjoy a short story with an ironic ending
• explain how "The Necklace" reflects the style and techniques of Naturalism
• define and identify examples of *foreshadowing* in the story

• define *character* and *motivation* and identify the *motivations* of the main character in "The Necklace"
• translate late-nineteenth-century terms into modern vocabulary
• write detailed descriptive passages from observations

The Necklace

Guy de Maupassant

The New Necklace, 1910. William McGregor Paxton.
Museum of Fine Arts, Boston.

She was one of those pretty, charming young ladies; born, as if through an error of destiny, into a family of clerks. She had no dowry,[1] no hopes, no means of becoming known, appreciated, loved, and married by a man either rich or distinguished; and she allowed herself to marry a petty clerk in the office of the Board of Education.

She was simple, not being able to adorn herself, but she was unhappy, as one out of her class; for women belong to no caste, no race, their grace, their beauty and

In what way is the young woman described?

---
1. **dowry.** Wealth to be given by a bride to her husband when she marries

"THE NECKLACE" 199

ART NOTE

The New Necklace, 1910. William McGregor Paxton
William McGregor Paxton (1869–1941) was a prominent member of what is known as the Boston School, a group of painters who represented the extension of the French academic tradition in America. (Jacques-Louis David is considered the epitome of the academic style; see *The Death of Socrates* page 860.) Ask students if the decorations and clothing fit the scene at Mme. Forestier's house.

1. The husband is content with simple food and a simple life and does not appear to crave luxuries as his wife does.
2. The young woman's desires might be characterized as materialistic, wishful, or unrealistic.

**CROSS-CURRICULAR
ACTIVITIES**

ART. Invite students to research the clothing and hairstyles worn by women and men of the middle and upper classes in the late nineteenth century, in both Europe and the United States. Have them create a poster, full-size cutout, or multiple drawings to present their findings and label or discuss specific details shown on their visuals.

---

their charm serving them in the place of birth and family. Their inborn <u>finesse</u>, their instinctive elegance, their <u>suppleness</u> of wit, are their only aristocracy, making some daughters of the people the equal of great ladies.

She suffered <u>incessantly</u>, feeling herself born for all delicacies and luxuries. She suffered from the poverty of her apartment, the shabby walls, the worn chairs and the faded stuffs. All these things, which another woman of her station would not have noticed, tortured and angered her. The sight of the little Breton,[2] who made this humble home, awoke in her sad regrets and desperate dreams. She thought of quiet antechambers with their oriental hangings lighted by high bronze torches and of the two great footmen in short trousers who sleep in the large armchairs, made sleepy by the heavy air from the heating apparatus. She thought of large drawing rooms hung in old silks, of graceful pieces of furniture carrying bric-a-brac[3] of <u>inestimable</u> value and of the little perfumed coquettish apartments made for five o'clock chats with most intimate friends, men known and sought after, whose attention all women envied and desired.

When she seated herself for dinner before the round table, where the tablecloth had been used three days, opposite her husband who uncovered the tureen with a delighted air, saying: "Oh! the good potpie! I know nothing better than that," she would think of the elegant dinners, of the shining silver, of the tapestries[4] peopling the walls with ancient personages and rare birds in the midst of fairy forests; she

In what ways does the husband differ from his wife?

thought of the exquisite food served on marvelous dishes, of the whispered gallantries, listened to with the smile of the Sphinx[5] while eating the rose-colored flesh of the trout or a chicken's wing.

She had neither frocks nor jewels, nothing. And she loved only those things. She felt that she was made for them. She had such a desire to please, to be sought after, to be clever and courted.

She had a rich friend, a schoolmate at the convent,[6] whom she did not like to visit. She suffered so much when she returned. And she wept for whole days from <u>chagrin</u>, from regret, from despair and disappointment.

In what way would you characterize the desires of the young woman?

◆　◆　◆

One evening her husband returned, <u>elated</u>, bearing in his hand a large envelope.

"Here, he said, "here is something for you."

She quickly tore open the wrapper and drew out a printed card on which were inscribed these words:

The Minister of Public Instruction and Madame George Ramponneau ask the honor of M. and Mme. Loisel's company Monday evening, January 18, at the Minister's residence.

---

2. **Breton.** Someone from Brittany, a rural province of France
3. **bric-a-brac.** Decorations
4. **tapestries.** Woven wall hangings
5. **Sphinx.** In Greek myth, a creature with the body of a lion and the head of a woman that demanded that passersby in Thebes answer its riddles
6. **convent.** Residence for Catholic nuns; sometimes also a school for girls

---

words for everyday use

fi • nesse (fə nes´) *n.,* ability to handle difficult situations diplomatically. *When nations are in conflict they do better to rely on the <u>finesse</u> of diplomats and negotiators than on violence and threats to settle their differences.*

sup • ple • ness (sup´əl nes) *n.,* flexibility. *I considered myself very flexible, but the <u>suppleness</u> of my new yoga instructor was far greater than mine.*

in • ces • sant • ly (in ses´ ənt lē) *adv.,* constantly, endlessly. *City dwellers who vacation in the country sometimes find they miss the traffic that roars <u>incessantly</u>, night and day, along the city streets.*

in • es • ti • ma • ble (in es´ tə mə bəl) *adj.,* too valuable to be measured; invaluable. *The value of a gift can be estimated in dollars and cents, but the value of the generosity behind the gift is <u>inestimable</u>.*

cha • grin (shə grin´) *n.,* feeling of severe embarrassment and annoyance. *The artist felt <u>chagrin</u> when her painting was described in the local papers as "second-rate."*

e • lat • ed (ē lāt ´ed) *part.,* filled with joy. *Suzie's parents were <u>elated</u> when she decided to finish school rather than drop out.*

200　*UNIT THREE / FICTION*

Instead of being delighted, as her husband had hoped, she threw the invitation spitefully upon the table, murmuring:

"What do you suppose I want with that?"

"But, my dearie, I thought it would make you happy. You never go out, and this is an occasion, and a fine one! I had a great deal of trouble to get it. Everybody wishes one, and it is very select; not many are given to employees. You will see the whole official world there."

She looked at him with an irritated eye and declared impatiently: "What do you suppose I have to wear to such a thing as that?"

He had not thought of that; he stammered:

"Why, the dress you wear when we go to the theater. It seems very pretty to me."

He was silent, <u>stupefied</u>, in dismay, at the sight of his wife weeping. Two great tears fell slowly from the corners of her eyes toward the corners of her mouth; he stammered:

"What is the matter? What is the matter?"

By a violent effort she had controlled her vexation and responded in a calm voice, wiping her moist cheeks:

"Nothing. Only I have no *What first disturbs Mme. Loisel?* dress and consequently I cannot go to this affair. Give your card to some colleague whose wife is better filled out than I."

He was grieved but answered:

"Let us see, Matilda. How much would a suitable costume cost, something that would serve for other occasions, something very simple?"

She reflected for some seconds, making estimates and thinking of a sum that she could ask for without bringing with it an immediate refusal and a frightened exclamation from the economical clerk.

Finally she said in a hesitating voice: "I cannot tell exactly, but it seems to me that four hundred francs[7] ought to cover it."

He turned a little pale, for he had saved just this sum to buy a gun that he might be able to join some hunting parties the next summer, on the plains at Nanterre,[8] with some friends who went to shoot larks up there on Sunday. Nevertheless, he answered:

"Very well. I will give you four hundred francs. But try to have a pretty dress."

♦   ♦   ♦

The day of the ball approached, and Mme. Loisel seemed sad, disturbed, anxious. Nevertheless, her dress was nearly ready. Her husband said to her one evening: "What is the matter with you? You have acted strangely for two or three days."

And she responded: "I am *What next disturbs Mme. Loisel?* vexed not to have a jewel, not one stone, nothing to adorn myself with. I shall have such a poverty-laden look. I would prefer not to go to this party."

He replied: "You can wear some natural flowers. At this season they look very chic. For ten francs you can have two or three magnificent roses."

She was not convinced. "No," she replied, "there is nothing more humiliating than to have a shabby air in the midst of rich women."

Then her husband cried out: "How stupid we are! Go and find your friend Madame Forestier and ask her to lend you her jewels. You are well enough *What does Mme. Loisel resolve to do?* acquainted with her to do this."

She uttered a cry of joy. "It is true!" she said. "I had not thought of that."

7. **francs.** French currency
8. **Nanterre.** Suburb of Paris, France

words for everyday use

stu • pe • fied (stōō´ pə fīd) *adj.,* stunned; bewildered. *He stood <u>stupefied</u> with horror as all his hard-earned cash blew away in the wind.*

1. Mme. Loisel is disturbed because she has no dress to wear to such a gala event.
2. She is disturbed because she does not have a single jewel and fears she will look "poverty-laden."
3. She resolves to ask Mme. Forestier to lend her some jewelry for the party.

LITERARY NOTE

NATURALISM. **Naturalism** is closely related to Realism. While romantic writers emphasized characters and situations that were more adventurous, exotic, and heroic than ordinary life, Naturalists wrote about the everyday world. Characters in naturalistic works are usually from the middle or working class. Their lives are not only ordinary, but often dull and unhappy.

Naturalists also shared a particular philosophy about life. They believed that human behavior is governed by two kinds of natural forces: instinct and environment. Instinct includes forces such as hunger or greed. Environment refers primarily to a person's social environment, including their family and class.

The next day she took herself to her friend's house and related her story of distress. Mme. Forestier went to her closet with the glass doors, took out a large jewel case, brought it, opened it and said: "Choose, my dear."

She saw at first some bracelets, then a collar of pearls, then a Venetian cross of gold and jewels and of admirable workmanship. She tried the jewels before the glass, hesitated, but could neither decide to take them nor leave them. Then she asked:

"Have you nothing more?"

"Why, yes. Look for yourself. I do not know what will please you."

Suddenly she discovered in a black satin box a superb necklace of diamonds, and her heart beat fast with an <u>immoderate</u> desire. Her hands trembled as she took them up. She placed them about her throat, against her dress, and remained in ectasy before them. Then she asked in a hesitating voice full of anxiety:

> *What does Mme. Loisel borrow? How does she feel about this object?*

"Could you lend me this? Only this?"

"Why, yes, certainly."

She fell upon the neck of her friend, embraced her with passion, then went away with her treasure.

❖ ❖ ❖

The day of the ball arrived. Mme. Loisel was a great success. She was the prettiest of all, elegant, gracious, smiling and full of joy. All the men noticed her, asked her name and wanted to be presented.

> *Was Mme. Loisel's night a success? Why was it so enjoyable?*

All the members of the Cabinet wished to waltz with her. The minister of education paid her some attention.

She danced with enthusiasm, with passion, intoxicated with pleasure, thinking of nothing, in the triumph of her beauty, in the glory of her success, in a kind of cloud of happiness that came of all this <u>homage</u> and all this admiration, of all these awakened desires and this victory so complete and sweet to the heart of woman.

She went home toward four o'clock in the morning. Her husband had been half asleep in one of the little salons[9] since midnight, with three other gentlemen whose wives were enjoying themselves very much.

He threw around her shoulders the wraps they had carried for the coming home, modest garments of everyday wear, whose poverty clashed with the elegance of the ball costume. She felt this and wished to hurry away in order not to be noticed by the other women who were wrapping themselves in rich furs.

Loisel detained her. "Wait," said he. "You will catch cold out there. I am going to call a cab."

But she would not listen and descended the steps rapidly. When they were in the street they found no carriage, and they began to seek for one, hailing the coachmen whom they saw at a distance.

They walked along toward the Seine,[10] hopeless and shivering. Finally they found on the dock one of those old <u>nocturnal</u> coupés[11] that one sees in Paris after nightfall, as if they were ashamed of their misery by day.

It took them as far as their door in Martyr Street,[12] and they went wearily up to their apartment. It was all over for her. And on his part he remembered that he would have to be at the office by ten o'clock.

---

9. **little salons.** Little rooms or booths alongside a ballroom floor
10. **Seine.** River that runs through Paris
11. **coupés.** Carriages
12. **Martyr Street.** A martyr is someone who dies for a good cause

words for everyday use	
im • mod • er • ate (im mäd′ ər it) *adj.,* excessive, unrestrained. *<u>Immoderate</u> praise can be embarrassing.*
hom • age (häm′ ij) *n.,* action to show honor or respect. *The film industry paid <u>homage</u> to the aging actor by giving him a special award in recognition of his many excellent film roles.*
noc • tur • nal (näk tʉr′ nəl) *adj.,* active at night. *The exterminator told Ellen that the noise she heard in her walls at night must be a mouse and not a squirrel, because mice are <u>nocturnal</u>, but squirrels are active only during the day.*

She removed the wraps from her shoulders before the glass for a final view of herself in her glory. Suddenly she uttered a cry. Her necklace was not around her neck.

Her husband, already half undressed, asked: "What is the matter?"

She turned toward him excitedly:

"I have—I have—I no longer have Madame Forestier's necklace."

He arose in dismay: "What! How is that? It is not possible."

And they looked in the folds of the dress, in the folds of the mantle, in the pockets, everywhere. They could not find it.

He asked: "You are sure you still had it when we left the house?"

"Yes, I felt it in the vestibule as we came out."

"But if you had lost it in the street we should have heard it fall. It must be in the cab."

"Yes. It is probable. Did you take the number?"

"No. And you, did you notice what it was?"

"No."

They looked at each other, utterly cast down. Finally Loisel dressed himself again.

"I am going," said he, "over the track where we went on foot, to see if I can find it."

And he went. She remained in her evening gown, not having the force to go to bed, stretched upon a chair, without ambition or thoughts.

Toward seven o'clock her husband returned. He had found nothing.

He went to the police and to the cab offices and put an advertisement in the newspapers, offering a reward; he did everything that afforded them a suspicion of hope.

She waited all day in a state of bewilderment before this frightful disaster. Loisel returned at evening, with his face harrowed[13] and pale, and had discovered nothing.

"It will be necessary," said he, "to write to your friend that you have broken the clasp of the necklace and that you will have it repaired. That will give us time to turn around."

She wrote as he dictated.

"I have—I have—I no longer have Madame Forestier's necklace."

◆ ◆ ◆

At the end of a week they had lost all hope. And Loisel, older by five years, declared:

"We must take measures to replace this jewel."

The next day they took the box which had inclosed it to the jeweler whose name was on the inside. He consulted his books.

"It is not I, madame," said he, "who sold this necklace; I only furnished the casket."[14]

Then they went from jeweler to jeweler, seeking a necklace like the other one, consulting their memories, and ill, both of them, with chagrin and anxiety.

In a shop of the Palais-Royal they found a chaplet of diamonds which seemed to them exactly like the one they had lost. It was valued at forty thousand francs. They could get it for thirty-six thousand.

They begged the jeweler not to sell it for three days. And they made an arrangement by which they might return it for thirty-four thou-

---

13. **harrowed.** Lined
14. **casket.** Case

What emotions does Mme. Loisel feel about the lost necklace? What does the couple decide to do about it?

ANSWER TO GUIDED READING QUESTION

1. Mme. Loisel was bewildered and fearful about the lost necklace. When the couple are unable to find it, they decide to write a note to Mme. Forestier telling her that the clasp of the necklace broke and needs to be repaired. They use this ploy to buy time to find a solution to the problem.

INTERNET RESOURCES

The "voluntary simplicity" movement has spread in recent years among people who question the idea that people are fulfilled by having a substantial amount of money and material possessions. Students might be interested in exploring the **"Simplicity Resource Guide"** at http://www.gallagherpress.com/pierce/whatisvs.htm to find out more about this philosophy and lifestyle. After doing some reading at the site, ask them to create a poster listing **"Ten Ways to Simplify Your Life."** Have them discuss whether the philosophy of simplicity described at the site is one they could embrace.

1. After losing the necklace, Mme. Loisel is forced to live a "life of necessity." She and her husband must repay the huge debt they have after purchasing a replacement necklace. To do this, they give up their maid and move to cheap lodgings. Mme. Loisel must do all the household chores, including washing the dishes and clothes and taking out the garbage. She now dresses very plainly and must haggle at the grocer's to reduce expenses.
2. Mme. Loisel still dreams of the evening party and all the flattery she received for her beauty. She has learned that a small thing can ruin a person or save a person but does not seem to feel responsible for her situation.

ADDITIONAL QUESTIONS AND ACTIVITIES

Have students create a word web in which they list words that could describe Mme. Loisel at different stages in the story.
Answers
Before losing the necklace: self-centered, dissatisfied, dreamy, pretty, charming, materialistic, vain, envious, middle-class.
After losing the necklace: lower-middle-class, hard-working, realistic, strong, ordinary, responsible, dreamy.

SELECTION CHECK TEST 4.3.11 WITH ANSWERS

Checking Your Reading
1. Why is Mme. Loisel unhappy with her lot in life? **She wishes she were wealthier.**
2. How does Mme. Loisel respond to the invitation to the ball? **She is distressed that she has nothing appropriate to wear. She is excited once she gets a new dress and borrows the necklace.**
3. Why is Mme. Forestier annoyed when Mme. Loisel returns the necklace? **Mme. Loisel did not return it promptly.**
4. What happens to Mme. Loisel over the years? **Her hard circumstances age her.**
5. What does Mme. Forestier tell Mme. Loisel about the necklace? **It was fake.**

---

sand francs if they found the other one before the end of February.

Loisel possessed eighteen thousand francs which his father had left him. He borrowed the rest.

He borrowed it, asking for a thousand francs of one, five hundred of another, five louis of this one and three louis of that one. He gave notes, made ruinous promises, took money of <u>usurers</u> and the whole race of lenders. He compromised his whole existence, in fact, risked his signature without even knowing whether he could make it good or not, and, harassed by anxiety for the future, by the black misery which surrounded him and by the prospect of all physical privations and moral torture, he went to get the new necklace, depositing on the merchant's counter thirty-six thousand francs.

When Mme. Loisel took back the jewels to Mme. Forestier the latter said to her in a frigid tone:

"You should have returned them to me sooner, for I might have needed them."

She did open the jewel box as her friend feared she would. If she should perceive the substitution what would she think? What should she say? Would she take her for a robber?

◆ ◆ ◆

Mme. Loisel now knew the horrible life of necessity. She did her part, however, completely, heroically. It was necessary to pay this frightful debt. She would pay it. They sent away the maid; they changed their lodgings; they rented some rooms under a mansard roof.[15]

She learned the heavy cares of a household, the <u>odious</u> work of a kitchen. She washed the dishes,

In what way has losing the necklace changed Mme. Loisel's life?

using her rosy nails upon the greasy pots and the bottoms of the stewpans. She washed the soiled linen, the chemises and dishcloths, which she hung on the line to dry; she took down the refuse to the street each morning and brought up the water, stopping at each landing to breathe. And, clothed like a woman of the people, she went to the grocer's, the butcher's and the fruiterer's with her basket on her arm, shopping, haggling to the last sou her miserable money.

Every month it was necessary to renew some notes, thus obtaining time, and to pay others.

The husband worked evenings, putting the books of some merchants in order, and nights he often did copying at five sous a page.

And this life lasted for ten years.

At the end of ten years they had restored all, all, with interest of the usurer, and accumulated interest, besides.

Mme. Loisel seemed old now. She had become a strong, hard woman, the crude woman of the poor household. Her hair badly dressed, her skirts awry, her hands red, she spoke in a loud tone and washed the floors in large pails of water. But sometimes, when her husband was at the office, she would seat herself before the window and think of that evening party of former times, of that ball where she was so beautiful and so flattered.

In what ways has Mme. Loisel remained the same? What knowledge has she gained?

How would it have been if she had not lost that necklace? Who knows? Who knows? How singular is life and how full of changes! How small a thing will ruin or save one!

---

15. **mansard roof.** Roof with two slopes on each of the four sides, named for French architect François Mansard (1598–1666)

words for everyday use

u • sur • er (yōō´ zhər ər) *n.*, person who lends at an extremely high interest rate. *The Italian poet Dante, like most medieval Christians, considered lending money at interest immoral and believed the <u>usurers</u> who did this would suffer torment in hell after death.*

o • di • ous (ō´ dē əs) *adj.*, hateful and offensive. *When he was young, he did not mind heavy tasks like carrying water or digging holes, but he thought raking leaves was <u>odious</u> and unbearable.*

SELECTION CHECK TEST 4.3.11 WITH ANSWERS (CONT.)

Vocabulary in Context
Fill in each blank below with the most appropriate word from the following Words for Everyday Use. You may have to change the tense of the word.

homage   immoderate   incessantly
odious   nocturnal   chagrin

1. Maria found the painting **odious**, but Manuel found them provoking and interesting.
2. Sasha was **nocturnal** and preferred to work what others called the Graveyard Shift.
3. Many pay **homage** to American industry, buying products marked "Made in USA."
4. After LaTonya left for college, her mother worried about her **incessantly**.
5. Much to Antonio's **chagrin**, his partners rejected his new plan.

(Continued on page 205)

♦ ♦ ♦

One Sunday, as she was taking a walk in the Champs Elysées to rid herself of the cares of the week, she suddenly perceived a woman walking with a child. It was Mme. Forestier, still young, still pretty, still attractive. Mme. Loisel was affected. Should she speak to her? Yes, certainly. And now that she had paid, she would tell her all. Why not?

She approached her. "Good morning, Jeanne."

Her friend did not recognise her and was astonished to be so familiarly addressed by this common personage. She stammered:

"But, madame—I do not know—You must be mistaken."

"No, I am Matilda Loisel."

Her friend uttered a cry of astonishment: "Oh! my poor Matilda! How you have changed."

"Yes, I have had some hard days since I saw you, and some miserable ones—and all because of you."

"Because of me? How is that?"

"You recall the diamond necklace that you loaned me to wear to the minister's ball?"

Whom does Mme. Loisel blame for her misery? Is her blame well placed?

"Yes, very well."

"Well, I lost it."

"How is that, since you returned it to me?"

"I returned another to you exactly like it. And it has taken us ten years to pay for it. You can understand that it was not easy for us who have nothing. But it is finished, and I am decently content."

Mme. Forestier stopped short. She said: "You say that you bought a diamond necklace to replace mine?"

"Yes. You did not perceive it then? They were just alike."

And she smiled with a proud and simple joy. Mme. Forestier was touched and took both her hands as she replied:

"Oh, my poor Matilda! Mine were false. They were not worth over five hundred francs!" ■

Respond *to the* SELECTION

Imagine that you are Mme. Loisel. How would you feel after finding out the original diamond necklace was false?

ANSWER TO GUIDED READING QUESTION

1. Mme. Loisel blames her friend, Mme. Forestier, for her misery. Her blame is poorly placed. Her friend did Mme. Loisel a favor by lending her the necklace. Mme. Loisel sought the necklace because she was not satisfied with the idea of wearing flowers instead of jewels to the ball. Therefore she is more to blame than Mme. Forestier.

RESPOND TO THE SELECTION

As an alternate activity, ask students what might have happened if Mme. Loisel had confessed the loss of the necklace immediately to her friend? Can they understand her desire to conceal what happened? Explain.

SELECTION CHECK TEST 4.3.11 WITH ANSWERS (CONT.)

Literary Tools

Naturalism   Romanticism
foreshadowing   character
motivation   tone   protagonist
antagonist   irony

1. Like most of de Maupassant's stories, "The Necklace" has a **tone** of detachment.
2. Madame Forestier's concluding comment gives the story's ending **irony**.
3. The **protagonist** of "The Necklace" is Madame Loisel.
4. Believers in **Naturalism** claim that events are shaped from forces not in our control.
5. Unemotional narration, careful detail, and accurate history are traits of **Naturalism**.

RECALL

1a. She was born into a family of clerks.
2a. He gives her an invitation to a formal ball.
3a. She feels she must have some jewels, which she borrows from a rich friend.

INTERPRET

1b. Thoughts that show she feels she should have been born to an aristocratic life include feeling tortured as she looks at her small apartment and shabby furnishing and daydreaming about luxurious, well-heated drawing rooms, footmen in short trousers, and graceful pieces of furniture and expensive decorations.
2b. Her husband takes a great deal of trouble to obtain an invitation to the ball, gives his wife the money he has been saving for a gun so she can buy a dress, and endures the ball for her sake.
3b. Actions demonstrating her feeling of triumph include dancing with enthusiasm and passion, "intoxicated with pleasure, thinking of nothing" and feeling she is in a cloud of happiness.

ANALYZE

4a. The irony of situation is that Mme. Loisel longs for a life of ease and luxury but ends up with a life of drudgery and poverty.

SYNTHESIZE

4b. *Responses will vary.* The necklace symbolizes Mme. Loisel's desire to surround herself with and display beauty and luxury. Just as the necklace quickly disappears, so does "the cloud of happiness" she experienced in her elegant finery at the ball. Also, the necklace seems to be expensive but is fake; in the same, the narrator may be suggesting that Mme. Loisel's dream of owning elegant things is an empty one.

EVALUATE

5a. *Responses will vary.* Mme. Loisel may have chosen to tell her friend the truth because she felt she had now "paid her dues" or that she had nothing to lose by telling the truth now because of her lower social status. Some students may say Mme. Loisel was justified in blaming her friend because Mme. Forestier failed to tell her the necklace was fake at the time she borrowed it. Others may say that Mme. Loisel could have avoided her fate if she had confessed the loss of the necklace right after it happened.

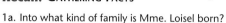

Investigate, Inquire, and Imagine

Recall: GATHERING FACTS

1a. Into what kind of family is Mme. Loisel born?

2a. What does Mme. Loisel's husband give to her, hoping that she will be delighted?

3a. What does Mme. Loisel feel she must have in order to make her ball ensemble complete?

Interpret: FINDING MEANING

1b. What thoughts on the part of Mme. Loisel show that she feels she should have been born to an aristocratic life?

2b. What actions on the part of the husband show that he places his wife's happiness above his own?

3b. What actions on the part of Mme. Loisel emphasize her feeling of triumph at the dance?

Analyze: TAKING THINGS APART

4a. *Irony of situation* exists in a literary work when an event occurs that violates the expectations of the characters, the reader, or the audience. Identify the irony of situation in "The Necklace."

Synthesize: BRINGING THINGS TOGETHER

4b. How is Mme. Loisel's life symbolized by the necklace?

Evaluate: MAKING JUDGMENTS

5a. Why do you think that Mme. Loisel chose to tell Mme. Forestier the truth when she saw her walking? Do you think Mme. Loisel was justified in blaming Mme. Forestier for the hardships she had suffered? Why, or why not?

Extend: CONNECTING IDEAS

5b. What sort of relationship between human beings and their social environment is described in this short story?

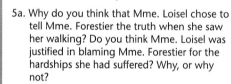

Understanding Literature

FORESHADOWING. Review the definition for **foreshadowing** in the Handbook of Literary Terms. Is the ending of the story a complete surprise, or is the true value of the diamond necklace partly foreshadowed? If it was foreshadowed, what clues foreshadow it?

CHARACTER AND MOTIVATION. Review the definitions for **character** and **motivation** and the cluster chart you made for Literary Tools in Prereading. What motivates Mme. Loisel to borrow the necklace from her friend? Why doesn't she tell Mme. Forestier the truth about losing the necklace right after it happens? In your own words, explain the price Mme. Loisel pays for allowing pride and envy dictate how she behaves.

EXTEND

5b. *Responses will vary.* Human beings seem to be strongly influenced in their attitudes and desires by their social class. The differences between the classes fosters envy in the main character, who sees herself as a have-not.

ANSWERS TO UNDERSTANDING LITERATURE

FORESHADOWING. The falseness of the necklace was partly foreshadowed. One clue is that Mme. Forestier kept the necklace apart from her other jewels and did not seem at all concerned about lending the necklace to Mme. Loisel. Another is that the jeweler whose name was on the case did not make the necklace itself.
(Continued on page 207)

Writer's Journal

1. Imagine that Mme. Loisel decided to write Mme. Forestier first to ask if she could borrow some jewels. Write this **letter** in which Mme. Loisel sets out her reasons for needing the jewels and pleads with her friend to let her borrow them. Remember to write in the character of Mme. Loisel and give reasons she might give for wishing to wear jewels on the night of the ball.

2. Write the **dialogue** for the conversation Mme. Loisel and her husband might have after she finds out the necklace was fake.

3. Write a short **short story** about a character who is faced with a conflict in a particular social environment. Relate the details of the character's life with accuracy; use third-person point of view.

Integrating the Language Arts

Vocabulary Development

ARCHAIC LANGUAGE. Some of the words used in this story reflect aspects of late nineteenth-century life and may not be familiar to you. Review the list of such terms below as noted in phrases from the story. Write a possible modern parallel for each term. Consult a dictionary if necessary. One example has been done for you.

1. "she allowed herself to marry a petty <u>clerk</u>" Modern parallel: a low-level office worker

2. "for women belong to no <u>caste</u>"

3. "She thought of quiet <u>antechambers</u>"

4. "two great <u>footmen</u> in short trousers"

5. "large <u>drawing rooms</u>"

6. "She had neither <u>frocks</u> nor jewels"

7. "She removed the wraps from her shoulders before the <u>glass</u> for a final view of herself in her glory."

8. "She washed the soiled linen, the <u>chemises</u> and dishcloths."

9. "she went to the grocer's, the butcher's and the <u>fruiterer's</u>"

10. "he threw around her shoulders the <u>wraps</u> they had carried"

Collaborative Learning

OBSERVATION AND DESCRIPTION GAME. As a class, bring in a variety of interesting and detailed photographs from magazines or books, particularly photographs of people and places. Arrange the photographs on a display table, and let everyone in the class look closely at them. Each student should select a favorite photograph without letting anyone else know which one he or she has chosen. Each student should then write a paragraph that describes the photographic image he or she has chosen, using only the most specific details. Take turns reading aloud each descriptive paragraph. Everyone else in the class should try to guess from the description the chosen photograph.

Media Literacy & Speaking and Listening

TALK SHOW. Use the Loisel's story as the topic for a talk show. Divide into groups of four, and choose roles: Mme. Loisel, M. Loisel, Mme. Forestier, and the show host. The host should be prepared to ask questions about how the incident with the necklace changed lives and relationships, and the characters should be prepared to answer the questions. After rehearsing, perform your show for your class.

"THE NECKLACE" **207**

VOCABULARY FROM THE SELECTION

anonymity	glib
articulate	implore
coherent	laceration
communicative	preen
corrode	prestige
decree	ravaged
delirious	replica
denunciation	rigidity
dredge	shoddy
eddy	tenancy
engulf	

GRAPHIC ORGANIZER

Students might include the following attributes in their charts: beautiful as a baby, anxious, quiet, uncomplaining, somber, comical, skeleton thin, dark and foreign-looking, slow to learn, slow to develop physically, vulnerable, responsible, confident in front of an audience, sometimes communicative, pessimistic

READER'S JOURNAL

Students might consider things they have learned from their parents or other adult caregivers and different parenting styles they have observed.

CHARACTER

Literary TOOLS

THEME. A **theme** is a central idea in a literary work. As you read, consider what themes Tillie Olsen intends to convey to readers in "I Stand Here Ironing."

CHARACTERIZATION. Characterization is the use of literary techniques to create a character. Writers use three major techniques to create characters: direct description, portrayal of characters' behavior, and representations of characters' internal states. When using representations of internal states, the writer reveals directly the character's private thoughts and emotions, often by means of what is known as the *internal monologue.* In this story the personalities of both the mother and the daughter are revealed through the mother's internal monologue.

Graphic Organizer

As you read the story, create a cluster chart of character attributes of Emily that are revealed through her mother's internal monologue.

Reader's Journal

How can parents help their children to grow up happy, confident, and secure?

208   *UNIT THREE*

"I Stand Here Ironing"

by Tillie Olsen

Reader's resource

"**I Stand Here Ironing**" shows characteristics common to much of the great short fiction produced in the United States in the past few decades. This fiction is often written in the first person, employing a narrator who tells his or her own story, and often deals with significant issues involving relationships with others. The first-person narrators so common to contemporary fiction tend to relate intense, private experiences, but they do so in what has come to be known as a *Minimalist* style marked by concreteness, compression of language, the inclusion of no more details than are absolutely necessary to advance the story, and avoidance of direct statements of the narrator's feelings. As you read this story, notice that the details speak for themselves, revealing clearly the narrator's pain, pride, defensiveness, and other emotions by letting the narrator's tone and the details of the story speak for themselves. Also note that the basic situation to which the narrator responds is given only the barest of outlines, providing just enough background information to let the reader know what is going on.

About the AUTHOR

Tillie Olsen (1913–) was born in Nebraska to parents who escaped from Russia during the political repression of 1905. Olsen dropped out of high school and worked at various jobs while raising her children. "My great colleges were the worlds of work, motherhood, struggle, and literature," she says of herself. When still in her teens, she began writing a novel, *Yonnondio,* a chapter of which was published in the prestigious *Partisan Review* in 1934. Work, union activities, and, above all, duties as a mother consumed her time for many years; however, when her youngest child enrolled in school, she began writing again in earnest, assisted by a writing fellowship received in 1956 and a Ford grant received in 1959. The title story of her collection *Tell Me a Riddle* won the O. Henry Award in 1961, one of many awards she has received for her works. *Yonnondio: From the Thirties,* the story of a family struggling through the Great Depression, was finally completed for publication in 1974. Her collection of essays and lectures, *Silences* (1978), champions writers whose voices have been silenced because of their class or gender.

GOALS/OBJECTIVES

Studying this lesson will enable students to
- appreciate a contemporary short story in the Minimalist style
- describe Tillie Olsen's literary accomplishments
- define *theme* and identify possible themes of "I Stand Here Ironing"

- define *characterization* and recognize the use of this technique in the selection
- create a comparison and contrast chart
- write a business letter

I Stand Here IRONING

Tillie Olsen

I stand here ironing, and what you asked me moves tormented back and forth with the iron.

"I wish you could manage the time to come in and talk with me about your daughter. I'm sure you can help me understand her. She's a youngster who needs help and whom I'm deeply interested in helping."

"Who needs help." Even if I came, what good would it do? You think because I am her mother I have a key, or that in some way you could use me as a key? She has lived for nineteen years.

Nancy Selvage, 1967. Alice Neel. Rhode Island School of Design Museum of Art, Providence.

INDIVIDUAL LEARNING STRATEGIES

MOTIVATION
Have students choose a family member or friend they know well and characterize that person in three different ways: by describing them directly, by portraying their behavior, and by representing their internal state of mind. They should write three separate paragraphs and limit themselves to just one approach in each paragraph.

READING PROFICIENCY
Work with students to make a plot map of the events that occur as Emily grows up. Make sure students understand the cause and effect relationships between events.

ENGLISH LANGUAGE LEARNING
Students may have trouble with some sentences that are written in a more stream-of-consciousness style or have a more complex syntax. Read these sentences aloud to students, and paraphrase them in simpler, more conventional form.

SPECIAL NEEDS
Allow time for students to discuss the mixed feelings the speaker has about how she has raised her daughter and both the positive and negative aspects of her daughter's life.

ENRICHMENT
Have students write an internal monologue in which they reflect on whether or not they did the right thing concerning another person. The monologue should reveal their various thoughts and emotions concerning what happened. Alternatively, they might write an internal monologue from Emily's point of view in which she reflects on her years growing up and her relationship with her mother. Students may wish to perform their monologues for the class.

ART NOTE

Nancy Selvage, 1967. Alice Neel.
Alice Neel (1900–1984) said that her paintings revealed about the people in them "all their character and social standing—what the world has done to them, and their retaliation." She achieved this with slight distortions that exaggerate and call attention to expressions and postures. Her subjects were usually family or friends and one gets a sense of the relationship between artist and sitter. With *Nancy Selvage,* Neel portrays her daughter-in-law. Ask students to describe the character and demeanor of the woman in the painting and compare her to Emily in "I Stand Here Ironing."

1. The speaker believes she will be
interrupted or that she will be
overwhelmed with guilt.
2. Emily seems nervous and has lost
her baby loveliness.

There is all that life that has happened outside of me, beyond me.

And when is there time to remember, to sift, to weigh, to estimate, to total? I will start and there will be an interruption and I will have to gather it all together again. Or I will become engulfed with all I did or did not do, with what should have been and what cannot be helped.

She was a beautiful baby. The first and only one of our five that was beautiful at birth. You do not guess how new and uneasy her tenancy in her now-loveliness. You did not know her all those years she was thought homely, or see her poring over her baby pictures, making me tell her over and over how beautiful she had been—and would be, I would tell her—and was now, to the seeing eye. But the seeing eyes were few or nonexistent. Including mine.

I nursed her. They feel that's important nowadays. I nursed all the children, but with her, with all the fierce rigidity of first motherhood, I did like the books then said. Though her cries battered me to trembling and my breasts ached with swollenness, I waited till the clock decreed.

Why do I put that first? I do not even know if it matters, or if it explains anything.

She was a beautiful baby. She blew shining bubbles of sound. She loved motion, loved light, loved color and music and textures. She would lie on the floor in her blue overalls, patting the surface so hard in ecstasy her hands and feet would blur. She was a miracle to me, but when she was eight months old, I had to leave her daytimes with the woman downstairs, to whom she was no miracle at all, for I worked or looked for work and for Emily's father, who "could no

What does the speaker believe will happen if she tries to remember her daughter's life?

longer endure" (he wrote in his goodbye note) "sharing want with us."

I was nineteen. It was the pre-relief, pre-WPA world of the depression.[1] I would start running as soon as I got off the streetcar, running up the stairs, the place smelling sour, and awake or asleep to startle awake, when she saw me, would break into a clogged weeping that could not be comforted, a weeping I can yet hear.

After a while I found a job hashing[2] at night so I could be with her days, and it was better. But it came to where I had to bring her to his family and leave her.

It took a long time to raise the money for her fare back. Then she got chicken pox, and I had to wait longer. When she finally came, I hardly knew her, walking quick and nervous like her father, looking like her father, thin, and dressed in a shoddy red that yellowed her skin and glared at the pockmarks. All the baby loveliness gone.

What changes have occurred in Emily when she returns?

She was two. Old enough for nursery school they said, and I did not know then what I know now—the fatigue of the long day, and the lacerations of group life in the nurseries that are only parking places for children.

Except that it would have made no difference if I had known. It was the only place there was. It was the only way we could be together, the only way I could hold a job.

And even without knowing, I knew. I knew the teacher was evil because all these years it has

---

1. **pre-relief . . . depression.** The WPA (Works Progress Administration) was one of several relief programs instituted by the government during the Great Depression to help the poor and unemployed.
2. **hashing.** Serving hash (chopped mixture of meat and vegetables) in a diner

---

words for everyday use

en • gulf (en gulf´) vt., overwhelm. *The next wave will engulf our sand castle.*

ten • an • cy (ten´ ən sē) n., occupation of something by right. *Our tenancy in this home will end on Saturday when the new family moves in.*

ri • gid • i • ty (ri jid´ ə tē) n., state of being inflexible. *The retired colonel's unwavering ideas about household management showed his stubborn rigidity.*

de • cree (dē krē´) vt., order. *The queen decreed that her birthday would be celebrated with festivities throughout the land.*

shod • dy (shäd´ ē) adj., poorly made; cheap, inferior. *The porch construction was shoddy, and it did not weather the storm.*

lac • er • a • tion (las´ər ā´ shən) n., wound; distress. *The nurse bandaged the laceration on the child's heel.*

curdled into my memory, the little boy hunched in the corner, her rasp, "Why aren't you outside, because Alvin hits you? That's no reason, go out, scaredy." I knew Emily hated it even if she did not clutch and <u>implore</u> "Don't go, Mommy" like the other children, mornings.

She always had a reason why we should stay home. Momma, you look sick. Momma, I feel sick. Momma, the teachers aren't there today, they're sick. Momma, there was a fire there last night. Momma, it's a holiday today, no school, they told me.

But never a direct protest, never rebellion. I think of our others in their three-, four-year-oldness—the explosions, the tempers, the <u>denunciations</u>, the demands—and I feel suddenly ill. I put the iron down. What in me demanded that goodness in her? And what was the cost, the cost to her of such goodness?

The old man living in the back once said in his gentle way: "You should smile at Emily more when you look at her." What *was* in my face when I looked at her? I loved her. There were all the acts of love.

It was only with the others I remembered what he said, and it was the face of joy, and not of care or tightness or worry I turned to them— too late for Emily. She does not smile easily, let alone almost always as her brothers and sisters do. Her face

is closed and somber, but when she wants, how fluid. You must have seen it in her pantomimes;[3] you spoke of her rare gift for comedy on the stage that rouses a laughter out of the audience so dear they applaud and applaud and do not want to let her go.

Where does it come from, that comedy? There was none of it in her when she came back to me that second time, after I had had to send her away again. She had a new daddy now to learn to love, and I think perhaps it was a better time.

Except when we left her alone nights, telling ourselves she was old enough. "Can't you go some other time, Mommy, like tomorrow?" she would ask. "Will it be just a little while you'll be gone? Do you promise?"

The time we came back, the front door open, the clock on the floor in the hall. She rigid awake. "It wasn't just a little while. I didn't cry. Three times I called you, just three times, and then I ran downstairs to open the door so you could come faster. The clock talked loud. I threw it away; it scared me when it talked."

She said the clock talked loud again that night when I went to the hospital to have Susan. She was <u>delirious</u> with the fever that comes before red measles, but she was fully conscious all the

I LOVED HER.
There were all the acts of love.

What does Emily not do easily?

---

3. **pantomimes.** Acting without words, using only actions and gestures

words for everyday use

im • plore (im plôr´) vt., beg. *I implore you not to miss an opportunity to exercise your right to vote.*
de • nun • ci • a • tion (dē nun´ sē ā´ shən) n., criticism; speaking against. *No denunciation will change the behavior of an adult committed to serving himself above others.*
de • lir • i • ous (di lir´ ē əs) adj., hallucinating; restless and confused. *The night before the performance, we were delirious with excitement and nervousness.*

1. Emily does not smile easily.

CROSS-CURRICULAR ACTIVITIES

PSYCHOLOGY. Emily weeps inconsolably when she is left with other caretakers as an infant. Later, after her mother remarries, she acts up when her parents leave her alone to go out at night. Ask students to do research about "separation anxiety" in children using print or electronic resources. Have students share their findings as they discuss whether Emily's anxiety about being alone or away from her mother is typical or atypical for a young child. What might explain the intensity of Emily's responses?

1. The home looks beautiful and well kept on the outside, but the children are treated insensitively and cannot have any physical contact with their visiting families.

Quotables

"I know that I haven't powers enough to divide myself into one who earns and one who creates."

—Tillie Olsen

week I was gone and the week after we were home, when she could not come near the new baby or me.

She did not get well. She stayed skeleton thin, not wanting to eat, and night after night she had nightmares. She would call for me, and I would rouse from exhaustion to sleepily call back, "You're all right, darling—go to sleep—it's just a dream," and if she still called, in a sterner voice, "now go to sleep Emily, there's nothing to hurt you." Twice, only twice, when I had to get up for Susan anyhow, I went in to sit with her.

Now, when it is too late (as if she would let me hold and comfort her like I do the others), I get up and go to her at once at her moan or restless stirring. "Are you awake, Emily? Can I get you something?" And the answer is always the same: "No, I'm all right, go back to sleep, Mother."

They persuaded me at the clinic to send her away to a convalescent home[4] in the country where "she can have the kind of food and care you can't manage for her, and you'll be free to concentrate on the new baby." They still send children to that place. I see pictures on the society page of sleek young women planning affairs to raise money for it, or dancing at the affairs, or decorating Easter eggs or filling Christmas stockings for the children.

They never have a picture of the children, so I do not know if the girls still wear those gigantic red bows and the <u>ravaged</u> looks on the every other Sunday when parents can come to visit "unless otherwise notified"—as we were notified the first six weeks.

Oh, it is a handsome place, green lawns and tall trees and fluted flower beds. High up on the balconies of each cottage the children stand, the girls in their red bows and white dresses, the boys in white suits and giant red ties. The par-

ents stand below shrieking up to be heard and the children shriek down to be heard, and between them the invisible wall "Not to Be Contaminated by Parental Germs or Physical Affection."

There was a tiny girl who always stood hand in hand with Emily. Her parents never came. One visit she was gone. "They moved her to Rose Cottage," Emily shouted in explanation. "They don't like you to love anybody here."

She wrote once a week, the labored writing of a seven-year-old. "I am fine. How is the baby. If I write my leter nicly I will have a star. Love." There never was a star. We wrote every other day, letters she could never hold or keep but only hear read—once. "We simply do not have room for children to keep any personal possessions," they patiently explained when we pieced one Sunday's shrieking together to plead how much it would mean to Emily, who loved so to keep things, to be allowed to keep her letters and cards.

How does the description of the surroundings of the convalescent home differ from the description of the children's lives there?

Each visit she looked frailer. "She isn't eating," they told us. (They had runny eggs for breakfast or mush with lumps, Emily said later; I'd hold it in my mouth and not swallow. Nothing ever tasted good, just when they had chicken.)

It took us eight months to get her released home, and only the fact that she gained back so little of her seven lost pounds convinced the social worker.

I used to try to hold and love her after she came back, but her body would stay stiff, and after a while she'd push away. She ate little.

---

4. **convalescent home.** Place where one can recover from illness and regain strength and health

words for everyday use   rav • aged (rav´ijd) *adj.,* ruined; devastated. *After making her way through the crowd of excited fans, the rock star had a* <u>ravaged</u> *appearance.*

Food sickened her, and I think much of life too. Oh, she had physical lightness and brightness, twinkling by on skates, bouncing like a ball up and down, up and down, over the jump rope, skimming over the hill; but these were momentary.

> *What sickened Emily? What words are used to describe her actions?*

She fretted about her appearance, thin and dark and foreign-looking at a time when every little girl was supposed to look or thought she should look a chubby blonde <u>replica</u> of Shirley Temple.[5] The doorbell sometimes rang for her, but no one seemed to come and play in the house or be a best friend. Maybe because we moved so much.

There was a boy she loved painfully through two school semesters. Months later she told me how she had taken pennies from my purse to buy him candy. "Licorice was his favorite and I brought him some every day, but he still liked Jennifer better'n me. Why, Mommy?" The kind of question for which there is no answer.

School was a worry to her. She was not <u>glib</u> or quick in a world where glibness and quickness were easily confused with ability to learn. To her overworked and exasperated teachers she was an overconscientious "slow learner" who kept trying to catch up and was absent entirely too often.

I let her be absent, though sometimes the illness was imaginary. How different from my now-strictness about attendance with the others. I wasn't working. We had a new baby, I was home anyhow. Sometimes, after Susan grew old enough, I would keep her home from school, too, to have them all together.

Mostly Emily had asthma, and her breathing, harsh and labored, would fill the house with a curiously tranquil sound. I would bring the two old dresser mirrors and her boxes of collections to her bed. She would select beads and single earrings, bottle tops and shells, dried flowers and pebbles, old postcards and scraps, all sorts of oddments; then she and Susan would play Kingdom, setting up landscapes and furniture, peopling them with action.

Those were the only times of peaceful companionship between her and Susan. I have edged away from it, that poisonous feeling between them, that terrible balancing of hurts and needs I had to do between the two, and did so badly, those earlier years.

Oh, there are conflicts between the others too, each one human, needing, demanding, hurting, taking—but only between Emily and Susan, no, Emily toward Susan, that <u>corroding</u> resentment. It seems so obvious on the surface, yet it is not obvious. Susan, the second child, Susan, golden- and curly-haired and chubby, quick and <u>articulate</u> and assured, everything in appearance and manner Emily was not. Susan, not able to resist Emily's precious things, losing or sometimes clumsily breaking them; Susan telling jokes and riddles to company for applause, while Emily sat silent (to say to me later: that was *my* riddle, Mother, I told it to Susan); Susan, who for all the five years' difference of age was just a year behind Emily in developing physically.

> *How did Emily feel toward Susan? In what ways were they different?*

I am glad for that slow physical development that widened the differ-

> *Why is the speaker glad for Emily's slow physical development?*

---

5. **Shirley Temple.** (1928–), famous child actress of the 1930s

---

words for everyday use

rep • li • ca (rep´li kə) *n.,* copy. *Even an expert can be fooled by a good <u>replica</u> of a piece of fine art.*

glib (glib) *adj.,* able to speak in a smooth, easy manner. *The governor's <u>glib</u> remarks about every cloud having a silver lining were not at all comforting to the flood victims.*

cor • rode (kə rōd´) *vt.,* eat away, weaken or destroy gradually. *Rust <u>corroded</u> the car's fender, until finally the fender fell off.*

ar • tic • u • late (är tik´yo͞o lit) *adj.,* able to express oneself easily and clearly. *Leon has the qualities of a good speaker; he is <u>articulate</u> and comfortable in front of large audiences.*

1. Food sickened Emily. Her actions are described as having "lightness and brightness." She twinkles by on skates, bounces up and down like a ball, jumps rope, and skims over the hill, but her lively activity is momentary.
2. Emily felt resentful toward Susan. Susan is golden- and curly-haired, chubby, quick, articulate, and assured. Emily, in contrast, is "thin and dark and foreign-looking," friendless, a "slow learner," and unsure of herself.
3. The speaker is glad for Emily's slow physical development because it keeps her from being caught up in teenage competition about looks.

LITERARY TECHNIQUE

AIM. A writer's **aim** is his or her purpose or goal. People may write to inform, entertain, make a point, reflect, or persuade. Ask students to look for statements by the author/narrator that suggest her aim in writing "I Stand Here Ironing."

Answers

Olsen's main aim is to reflect. She reflects on her relationship with her daughter and tries to explain why her daughter became the person she did. Another aim is to make a point, or at least raise a question, about how much influence parents have over their children and how much control any person has over the circumstances of his or her own life. Statements that relate to the writer's aim include "And when is there time to remember, to sift, to weigh, to estimate, to total?" (210), "What did I start to gather together, to try and make coherent?" (214), and "I will never total it all" (215).

ANSWERS TO GUIDED READING QUESTIONS

1. Emily invented the word *shoogily,* which means "comfort."
2. The speaker suggests that Emily try doing her funny imitations and skits in a school talent show. Emily competes and wins first prize.

ADDITIONAL QUESTIONS AND ACTIVITIES

Ask students what the speaker means when she says of Emily, "In this and other ways she leaves her seal." The fact that the speaker says this aloud suggests its importance. Why is this an important realization for the speaker?
Answer
Emily has left an impression on other family members and helped shape her family's character. The narrator may feel grateful to Emily for looking after her siblings like a second mom or feel appreciation for her inventiveness and creativity.

SELECTION CHECK TEST 4.3.13 WITH ANSWERS

Checking Your Reading

1. What has the mother been asked to do? **She's been asked to come to school to talk about Emily.**
2. Why had the mother left Emily with her husband's family? **She was too busy working to take care of Emily, and Emily's father had left the family.**
3. How did the mother communicate with Emily when she visited her at the convalescent home? **She shouted up to Emily as she stood on a balcony.**
4. At what has Emily succeeded? **Emily has succeeded in stage shows.**
5. Why does Emily claim that midterms are not important? **Emily believes everyone will soon be killed by an atom bomb.**

Vocabulary in Context
Fill in each blank with the most appropriate word from the following Words for Everyday Use. You may have to change the tense of the word.

implore   corrode   laceration
ravaged   tenancy   rigidity   preen

1. Ralph learned the **rigidity** of the rules when he was fired for being late the first time.

(Continued on page 215)

---

ence between her and her contemporaries, though she suffered over it. She was too vulnerable for that terrible world of youthful competition, of preening and parading, of constant measuring of yourself against every other, of envy, "If I had that copper hair," "If I had that skin . . . ." She tormented herself enough about not looking like the others, there was enough of the unsureness, the having to be conscious of words before you speak, the constant caring—what are they thinking of me?—without having it all magnified by the merciless physical drives.

Ronnie is calling. He is wet and I change him. It is rare there is such a cry now. That time of motherhood is almost behind me when the ear is not one's own but must always be racked and listening for the child cry, the child call. We sit for a while and I hold him, looking out over the city spread in charcoal with its soft aisles of light. "*Shoogily,*" he breathes and curls closer. I carry him back to bed, asleep. *Shoogily.* A funny word, a family word, inherited from Emily, invented by her to say: *comfort.*

What special family word did Emily invent? What does it mean?

In this and other ways she leaves her seal, I say aloud. And startle at my saying it. What do I mean? What did I start to gather together, to try and make coherent? I was at the terrible, growing years. War years. I do not remember them well. I was working, there were four smaller ones now, there was not time for her. She had to help be a mother, and housekeeper, and shopper. She had to set her seal. Mornings of crisis and near hysteria trying to get lunches packed, hair combed, coats and shoes found, everyone to school or child care on time, the baby ready for transportation. And always the paper scribbled on by a smaller one, the book looked at by Susan then mislaid, the homework not done. Running out to

that huge school where she was one, she was lost, she was a drop; suffering over her unpreparedness, stammering and unsure in her classes.

There was so little time left at night after the kids were bedded down. She would struggle over books, always eating (it was in those years she developed her enormous appetite that is legendary in our family), and I would be ironing, or preparing food for the next day, or writing V-mail[6] to Bill, or tending the baby. Sometimes, to make me laugh, or out of her despair, she would imitate happenings or types at school.

I think I said once: "Why don't you do something like this in the school amateur shows?" One morning she phoned me at work, hardly understandable through the weeping: "Mother, I did it. I won, I won; they gave me first prize; they clapped and clapped and wouldn't let me go."

What does the speaker suggest Emily do? What does Emily do?

Now suddenly she was Somebody, and as imprisoned in her difference as she had been in her anonymity.

She began to be asked to perform at other high schools, even in colleges, then at city and statewide affairs. The first one we went to, I only recognized her that first moment when thin, shy, she almost drowned herself into the curtains. Then: Was this Emily? the control, the command, the convulsing and deadly clowning, the spell, then the roaring, stamping audience, unwilling to let this rare and precious laughter out of their lives.

Afterward: You ought to do something about her with a gift like that—but without money or knowing how, what does one do? We have left it

---

6. **V-mail.** Mail to or from the armed forces in World War II, reduced to microfilm to save shipping space

words for everyday use

preen (prēn´) vi., dress or groom oneself in a fussy, vain way. *The canary would preen itself in the mirror every morning.*
co • her • ent (kō hir´ənt) adj., logically connected; making sense. *The boy's alibi was coherent, and the judge believed him.*
an • o • nym • i • ty (an´ə nim´ə tē) n., condition of having no special or distinguishing qualities. *Many people prefer anonymity to fame.*

all to her, and the gift has as often <u>eddied</u> inside, clogged and clotted, as been used and growing.

She is coming. She runs up the stairs two at a time with her light, graceful step, and I know she is happy tonight. Whatever it was that occasioned your call did not happen today.

How does the speaker know Emily is happy?

"Aren't you ever going to finish the ironing, Mother? Whistler[7] painted his mother in a rocker. I'd have to paint mine standing over an ironing board." This is one of her <u>communicative</u> nights, and she tells me everything and nothing as she fixes herself a plate of food out of the icebox.

She is so lovely. Why did you want me to come in at all? Why were you concerned? She will find her way.

She starts up the stairs to bed. "Don't get *me* up with the rest in the morning." "But I thought you were having midterms." "Oh, those," she comes back in, kisses me, and says quite lightly, "in a couple of years when we'll be atom-dead, they won't matter a bit."

What does Emily believe about the future?

She has said it before. She *believes* it. But because I have been <u>dredging</u> the past, and all that compounds a human being is so heavy and meaningful in me, I cannot endure it tonight.

I will never total it all. I will never come in to say: She was a child seldom smiled at. Her father left me before she was a year old. I had to work away from her her first six years when there was work, or I sent her home and to his relatives. There were years she had care she hated. She was dark and thin and foreign-looking in a world where the <u>prestige</u> went to blondness and curly hair and dimples; she was slow where glibness was prized. She was a child of anxious, not proud, love. We were poor and could not afford for her the soil of easy growth. I was a young mother, I was a distracted mother. There were the other children pushing up, demanding. Her younger sister seemed all that she was not. There were years she did not let me touch her. She kept too much in herself; her life has been such she had to keep too much in herself. My wisdom came too late. She has much to her and probably little will come of it. She is a child of her age, of depression, of war, of fear.

Let her be. So all that is in her will not bloom—but in how many does it? There is still enough left to live by. Only help her to know—help make it so there is cause for her to know—that she is more than this dress on the ironing board, helpless before the iron. ■

What does the speaker seem to be saying about people fulfilling their potential?

---

7. **Whistler.** James Abbott McNeil Whistler (1834–1903), American painter in England, best known for the portrait of his mother in a rocking chair

---

words for everyday use

ed • dy (ed´ē) *v.,* move with a circular motion against the main current. *The leaf fell into the water,* <u>eddied</u> *a moment behind a rock, then slipped free and rapidly disappeared downstream.*

com • mu • ni • ca • tive (kə my\=oo´ni kāt´iv) *adj.,* talkative; giving information readily. *A good attorney knows when to be* <u>communicative</u> *and when to be silent.*

dredge (drej) *vt.,* dig up (in search of something). *We shall have to* <u>dredge</u> *the pond to find the missing boat.*

pres • tige (pres tēzh´) *n.,* reputation; power to impress. *The mayor's* <u>prestige</u> *had been hard-earned, but after six years in office, she was almost universally respected.*

Respond *to the* SELECTION

If you were Emily, would you be understanding of your mother's difficult life and her inability to provide you with much support, or would you be hurt, disappointed, or angered by her actions? Explain your answer.

1. The speaker knows Emily is happy because of her light, graceful step as she runs up the stairs two at a time.
2. Emily believes that in a couple of years everyone will be killed by an atom bomb.
3. The speaker seems to be saying that few people reach their full potential.

SELECTION CHECK TEST 4.3.13 WITH ANSWERS (CONT.)

2. The doctor said Trent was lucky to have only <u>lacerations</u> from his motorcycle crash.
3. The Red Cross volunteers raced to the village that had been <u>ravaged</u> by the storm.
4. The constant salt water and strong winds <u>corroded</u> the seawall.
5. "You'd be on time if you didn't spend so much time <u>preening</u>," Malcolm snapped.

Literary Tools
1. What are the three common techniques writers use to create characters? **The three main techniques of characterization are direct description, description of a character's behavior, and description of a character's inner state of mind.**
2. Identify two traits of the Minimalist style. **Responses may include concreteness, compression of language, no unnecessary details, or avoidance of direct statements about the character's feelings.**
3. What is a possible theme for this selection? *Responses will vary.* **A possible theme may be that although our lives are not perfect, and few people seldom reach their full potential, we make do with what we have, and find our way.**
4. What is an internal monologue? **Internal monologue is a character's thoughts organized as a monologue.**
5. Who is the main character in this story? **The mother is the main character.**

RESPOND TO THE SELECTION

As an alternate activity, ask students to find evidence in the story that the mother is proud of her daughter and wants her to succeed.

RECALL

1a. She is ironing and thinking about her daughter's life. A request from someone at the school for a meeting sets her to thinking about her daughter.

2a. The mother was abandoned by Emily's father and had to earn a living while caring for Emily during the depression. Emily was isolated by her homely appearance, her slow physical development, her childhood illnesses, her stay at a strict convalescent home, her teenage role as a second mother in the family, and her own serious nature.

3a. She has a talent for mimicry and comedy.

INTERPRET

1b. A teacher or counselor or Emily's drama coach might have made the request. Emily might have few friends, be doing poorly in school, or be frequently absent.

2b. Emily helps shape the character of her family, grows up to become a perceptive person, and finds an outlet for her special talent.

3b. Emily might have developed this talent because in her quietness she could closely study the behavior of other people. Comedy might also have been a way of gaining attention or distinguishing herself within her family. Isolation, or detachment from others, might give a comedic actor a more objective, critical, or cynical perspective; the actor could exploit this by highlighting or exposing human weaknesses to comic effect.

ANALYZE

4a. Emily seems aloof and disconnected from her mother. Her mother has no high hopes or dreams for her; while she recognizes her specialness, she says "probably little will come of it." She hopes only that Emily will discover that she is not helpless in life.

SYNTHESIZE

4b. Emily's mother may be referring to wisdom in parenting. She has learned the importance of providing comfort, consistent attention, and positive reinforcement to a young child—something she did not know until she began raising her later children. She feels she has failed her daughter. She has not learned that human beings have the power to overcome early deprivations and succeed in spite of them, or even because of them.

Investigate, Inquire, and Imagine

Recall: GATHERING FACTS

1a. What is Emily's mother doing throughout the story? What request sets her to thinking about her daughter?

2a. What circumstances in Emily's mother's life made Emily's young life difficult? What circumstances isolated Emily from others?

3a. What talent does Emily discover that she has?

Interpret: FINDING MEANING

1b. Who do you think might have made the request to Emily's mother? What kind of problem do you think Emily might have?

2b. In what way has Emily managed to become successful despite the pain of her childhood?

3b. Why might Emily have developed this particular talent? What perspective does isolation give that a comedic actor might exploit?

Analyze: TAKING THINGS APART

4a. What attitude does Emily seem to have toward her mother? What hopes and dreams does the narrator have for Emily?

Synthesize: BRINGING THINGS TOGETHER

4b. When Emily's mother says, "My wisdom came too late. She has much to her and probably little will come of it," to what wisdom is she referring? What has she learned? Given the second half of her statement, what has she not learned?

Evaluate: MAKING JUDGMENTS

5a. Why does Emily's mother feel incapable of helping her daughter? How do you feel about this aspect of her mother's character? Explain.

Extend: CONNECTING IDEAS

5b. Emily's mother says of Emily, "So all that is in her will not bloom—but in how many does it? There is still enough left to live by." To what has the mother resigned herself? What do you think of this philosophy of life?

Understanding Literature

THEME. Review the definition for **theme** in the Handbook of Literary Terms. What attitude does the mother in this story have about helping her daughter? What circumstances in the mother's life have led her to develop this attitude?

CHARACTERIZATION. Review the definition for **characterization** and the cluster chart you made for Literary Tools in Prereading. While the narrator in this story talks about her daughter, the story is not really about the daughter; it is about the narrator herself. The mother asks the unnamed person who has contacted her to "help [Emily] to know…that she is more than this dress on the ironing board, helpless before the iron." In what sense is the mother like the dress on the ironing board? In what ways does she feel helpless? What circumstances have contributed to making her feel that way?

EVALUATE

5a. Emily's mother may feel incapable of helping her daughter because she could not help herself much when she was a young adult.

EXTEND

5b. The mother has resigned herself to the fact that most people do not fulfill their potential. Students may say that living up to one's talents and dreams requires hard work, persistence, and some luck.

THEME. The mother's attitude is that she, and others, cannot help her daughter at this point: "Let her be." The need to work for a living, the hard times of the depression, and the fact that she had to look after an infant daughter alone may have led her to develop this attitude. Because of these circumstances, the mother (and the author) may feel that life is not perfect, and that few people can ever reach their full potential, but rather must make do with what they have and find their own imperfect happiness.

(Continued on page 216)

Writer's Journal

1. Write your own **guidelines** for parents of teenagers on ways to develop and enhance teens' self-esteem.

2. Imagine that you are an advice columnist. Emily has written to you for help in overcoming her lack of self-confidence. Write an **advice column** giving her encouragement.

3. Pretend that you write for the school newspaper. Write a short **promotional article** for the paper encouraging students to attend Emily's comedic performance. The article should include the type of function; the location, date, and time; a short biography on Emily; and information about her performance.

Integrating the Language Arts

Language, Grammar, and Style

WRITING GRAMMATICAL SENTENCES. "I Stand Here Ironing" is told from a first-person point of view. It presents an internal monologue—the thoughts, associations, and impressions that float through the mind of the central character. To render the narrator's stream-of-consciousness realistically, Tillie Olsen has occasionally scrambled the grammar of her sentences. Rewrite each of the following sentences from the story using more conventional grammar.

1. You do not guess how new and uneasy her tenancy in her now-loveliness.

2. I would start running as soon as I got off the streetcar, running up the stairs, the place smelling sour, and awake or asleep to startle awake, when she saw me, she would break into a clogged weeping that could not be comforted, a weeping I can yet hear.

3. But it came to where I had to bring her to his family and leave her.

4. "Why aren't you outside, because Alvin hits you? That's no reason, go out, scaredy."

5. Oh, there are conflicts between the others, too, each one human, needing, demanding, hurting, taking—but only between Emily and Susan, no, Emily toward Susan, that corroding resentment.

Applied English

PROFESSIONAL LETTER. Imagine that you are a school counselor and that you have received a letter from Emily's mother that reads as follows:

Let her be. So all that is in her will not bloom—but in how many does it? There is still enough left to live by. Only help her to know—help make it so there is cause for her to know—that she is more than this dress on the ironing board, helpless before the iron.

Write a letter addressed to Emily's mother that states your response. Follow proper business letter form as described in the Language Arts Survey 6.5, "Writing a Business Letter."

Critical Thinking

COMPARING AND CONTRASTING. Read the Language Arts Survey 5.10, "Comparing and Contrasting." Then, as you read the selection, compare and contrast the mother's actions toward Emily with her actions toward her other children.

ANSWERS TO INTEGRATING THE LANGUAGE ARTS (CONT.)

Differences
- Often left Emily in the care of a neighbor or her husband's family, during work, when she was 8 months to 2 years old
- Placed Emily in a nursery school when she was very young
- Seldom smiled at Emily
- Sent Emily to a convalescent home for several months after an illness
- Allowed her to help be a mother to the younger children

ANSWERS TO UNDERSTANDING LITERATURE (CONT.)

CHARACTERIZATION. The mother may feel that the circumstances of her own life have pressed against her and "flattened" her goals and dreams. She has felt helpless before the circumstances of her life, including balancing the need to work with her duties as a mother.

ANSWERS TO INTEGRATING THE LANGUAGE ARTS

Language, Grammar, and Style
Responses will vary.
1. You don't know how uneasy Emily is about the loveliness she has now.
2. When I ran up the stairs in the sour-smelling place, I would find her awake or asleep, and when she saw me she would weep so hard that I can still hear it.
3. Eventually I had no choice but to leave her with his family.
4. You shouldn't be afraid to go outside because Alvin hits you. Go out, scaredy-cat.
5. The others had disagreements too, because of their needs and demands or because they hurt or took something from each other, but Emily developed a destructive resentment toward Susan.

Applied English
Assign a score from 10 to 25 for each grading criterion below. (For more detailed evaluation, see the evaluation forms for writing, revising, and proofreading in the Assessment Resource.)

PROFESSIONAL LETTER
- **Content/Unity.** The letter presents a logical response to the mother's views.
- **Organization/Coherence.** The ideas in the letter are organized in a logical framework and connected with logical transitions.
- **Language/Style.** The writer uses vivid and precise nouns, verbs, and modifiers.
- **Conventions.** The letter uses business letter form and avoids errors in spelling, grammar, usage, and mechanics.

Critical Thinking
Students might use a chart to list the similarities and differences such as the following:
Similarities
- Nursed all her children
- Loved and looked after them
- Holds them

GRAPHIC ORGANIZER

Students might include the following in their charts:
Challenge 1
Pros: Wife probably won't serve the same food again.
Cons: Wife's feelings will be hurt.
Challenge 2
Pros: Sekhar can finally say what he thinks of the man.
Cons: Other will think Sekhar insensitive for speaking unkindly about a person who is dead.
Challenge 3
Pros: Others will be saved from having to listen to the terrible singing. Headmaster will save himself further embarrassment singing for others. Headmaster will save money by not spending it on ineffective music lessons.
Cons: Headmaster may hold a grudge against Sekhar, leading him to make Sekhar's work more difficult or not promote him.

READER'S JOURNAL

Students might wish to share their truth-telling experiences with a partner or small group.

THEME

Literary TOOLS

IRONY. **Irony** is a difference between appearance and reality. In *irony of situation* an event occurs that violates the expectations of the characters, the reader, or the audience. Look for examples of situation irony as you read the story.

THEME. A **theme** is a central idea in a literary work. With gentle humor, in "Like the Sun" Narayan explores themes about truth and its possible consequences.

Graphic Organizer

Create a pro and con chart to keep track throughout the story of Sekhar's reasoning and the author's treatment of themes about truth and its possible consequences. Refer to the Language Arts Survey, 5.1 "Making Decisions and Solving Problems" for guidance. Note the pros and cons of each decision to tell the truth.

Main Proposition: To take one day in the year to give and take absolute Truth whatever may happen.
Challenge #1: Tell wife truth about her cooking.
Pros:
Cons:
Challenge #2: Tell truth about someone who has died.
Pros:
Cons:
Challenge #3: Tell headmaster truth about his singing.
Pros:
Cons:

"Like the Sun"

by R. K. Narayan

Reader's resource

The *setting* of a literary work is the time and place in which it occurs, together with all the details used to create a sense of a particular time and place. Written in a style noted for its elegance and simplicity, Narayan's stories, including "**Like the Sun**," are set in the imaginary town of Malgudi, located in southern India. Through the ordinary experiences of the characters in this town, Narayan perceptively portrays the quirkiness of human relationships and the ironies of daily life.

About the AUTHOR

R. K. Narayan (1906–2001) was born in Madras, India. After completing his education, he taught in a small village school. Narayan left teaching to devote himself full time to writing, and in 1935 he published his first novel, *Swami and Friends.* Two other early works, *The Bachelor of Arts* and *Mr. Sampath,* helped establish his reputation internationally. *The Financial Expert* (1952), his first novel to be published in the United States, was followed by a number of other novels, *The English Teacher* (1953), *The Man-Eater of Malgudi* (1961), *The Painter of Signs* (1976), and *A Tiger for Malgudi* (1983). Among his short-story collections are *Malgudi Days* (1982), and *The Grandmother's Tale and Selected Stories* (1994). In 1974, Narayan published *My Days,* a volume of memoirs, and in 1989, an additional volume of nonfiction, *A Story Teller's World.*

Reader's Journal

Have you ever told someone the absolute truth in response to a difficult question? What was the person's response? What does it feel like to have someone tell you the absolute truth?

GOALS/OBJECTIVES

Studying this lesson will enable students to
- appreciate what it might be like to tell someone the cold truth about something
- describe R. K. Narayan's origins and literary accomplishments

- define *irony* and *theme* and recognize these literary features in the selection
- do research on Indian music
- conduct a poll about telling the truth

Like the SUN

R. K. Narayan

ANSWERS TO GUIDED READING QUESTIONS

1. Truth is like the sun because "no human being can ever look it straight in the face without blinking or being dazed."
2. Sekhar sets apart a day to tell and accept "absolute Truth." Sekhar does this as "a secret plan between him and eternity."

INDIVIDUAL LEARNING STRATEGIES

MOTIVATION
Ask students if they appreciate it when a friend or family member gives them frank criticism. How do they usually feel after they have received negative criticism? Then have students discuss the following questions: Do they think that telling the truth bluntly is best, or should a person be more tactful or indirect when telling someone the truth? What is the meaning of terms and phrases such as "naked truth," "cold, hard truth," "half-truth," and "sugar-coating the truth"? What do these phrases suggest about the effect that telling the truth has on people?

READING PROFICIENCY
Direct students' attention to the Words for Everyday Use and the footnotes for the selection.

ENGLISH LANGUAGE LEARNING
Students might describe truth-telling practices or courtesies in their country of origin. In general, do people try to tell the truth in a way that is not shocking?

SPECIAL NEEDS
Tell students that the main character in the story is a teacher who has decided to perform an experiment among his family and fellow workers. For one day he will treat them all differently in one important way.

ENRICHMENT
Students might enjoy compiling a booklet of sayings about telling the truth. Have them include statements from Narayan's story such as "Truth is like the sun" and "Truth requires as much strength to give as to receive." Other sayings can be ones students compose themselves or statements gathered from books of quotations, works of fiction, and even magazines and newspapers. The booklet should help readers understand "the truth about truth."

Truth, Sekhar reflected, is like the sun. I suppose no human being can ever look it straight in the face without blinking or being dazed. He realized that, morning till night, the essence of human relationships consisted in tempering truth so that it might not shock. This day he set apart as a unique day—at least one day in the year we must give and take absolute Truth whatever may happen. Otherwise life is not worth living. The day ahead seemed to him full of possibilities. He told no one of his experiment. It was a quiet resolve, a secret pact between him and eternity.

How is truth like the sun?

For what purpose does Sekhar set apart a day? Why does he do this?

The very first test came while his wife served him his morning meal. He showed hesitation over a tidbit, which she had thought was her culinary masterpiece. She asked, "Why, isn't it good?" At other times he would have said, considering her feelings in the matter, "I feel full up; that's all." But today he said, "It isn't good. I'm unable to swallow it." He saw her wince and said to himself, Can't be helped. Truth is like the sun.

His next trial was in the common room when one of his colleagues came up and said, "Did you hear of the death of so and so? Don't you

words for everyday use

tem • per (tem´pər) *vt.*, reduce in intensity; moderate. *After tempering his anger, he resumed his discussion with his boss.*

re • solve (ri zälv´) *n.*, intention. *Their resolve to start jogging diminished by the next morning.*

"LIKE THE SUN" 219

VOCABULARY FROM THE SELECTION

ingratiating temper
resolve tentatively
scrutinize

ANSWERS TO GUIDED READING QUESTIONS

1. Sekhar probably will experience another conflict caused by telling the truth.
2. The headmaster is obsessed with his music. His ambition in life is to forget himself in music.

ADDITIONAL QUESTIONS AND ACTIVITIES

Remind students that studying a person's facial expression, eye contact, tone of voice, gestures, and posture can help them understand a speaker's true feelings about something. Sometimes people say one thing, but their body language reveals a different opinion, attitude, or feeling. For example, a person might say "I'm happy to meet you" but use a bored tone of voice and avoid eye contact.

Have students explore the relationship between body language and telling the truth by videotaping short skits involving two students. One student should ask for or express an opinion about something, and the other should respond both verbally and nonverbally. Students in the audience should evaluate whether the responder's body language matches the verbal message or whether it sends a different message.

think it a pity?" "No," Sekhar answered. "He was such a fine man—" the other began. But Sekhar cut him short with: "Far from it. He always struck me as a mean and selfish brute."

During the last period, when he was teaching geography for Third Form A, Sekhar received a note from the headmaster: "Please see me before you go home." Sekhar said to himself: It must be about these horrible test papers. A hundred papers in the boys' scrawls; he had shirked this work for weeks, feeling all the time as if a sword were hanging over his head.

The bell rang and the boys burst out of the class.

Sekhar paused for a moment outside the headmaster's room to button up his coat; that was another subject the headmaster always sermonized[1] about.

He stepped in with a very polite "Good evening, sir."

The headmaster looked up at him in a very friendly manner and asked, "Are you free this evening?"

Sekhar replied, "Just some outing which I have promised the children at home—"

"Well, you can take them out another day. Come home with me now."

"Oh . . . yes, sir, certainly . . . " And then he added timidly, "Anything special, sir?"

"Yes," replied the headmaster, smiling to himself . . . "You didn't know my weakness for music?"

"Oh, yes, sir . . ."

"I've been learning and practicing secretly, and now I want you to hear me this evening. I've engaged a drummer and a violinist to accompany me—this is the first time I'm doing it full dress[2] and I want your opinion. I know it will be valuable."

What might you expect to happen based on Sekhar's experience so far with his day of truth?

Sekhar's taste in music was well known. He was one of the most dreaded music critics in the town. But he never anticipated his musical inclinations would lead him to this trial. . . ."Rather a surprise for you, isn't it?" asked the headmaster. "I've spent a fortune on it behind closed doors. . . ." They started for the headmaster's house. "God hasn't given me a child, but at least let him not deny me the consolation of music," the headmaster said, pathetically, as they walked. He incessantly chattered about music: how he began one day out of sheer boredom; how his teacher at first laughed at him and then gave him hope; how his ambition in life was to forget himself in music.

How does the headmaster feel about music?

At home the headmaster proved very ingratiating. He sat Sekhar on a red silk carpet, set before him several dishes of delicacies, and fussed over him as if he were a son-in-law of the house. He even said, "Well, you must listen with a free mind. Don't worry about these test papers." He added half humorously, "I will give you a week's time."

"Make it ten days, sir," Sekhar pleaded.

"All right, granted," the headmaster said generously. Sekhar felt really relieved now—he would attack them at the rate of ten a day and get rid of the nuisance.

The headmaster lighted incense sticks. "Just to create the right atmosphere," he explained. A drummer and a violinist, already seated on a Rangoon mat,[3] were waiting for him. The headmaster sat down between them like a professional at a concert, cleared his throat, and

---

1. **sermonized.** Gave lectures
2. **full dress.** Dress rehearsal; final practice before a performance
3. **Rangoon mat.** Woven mat from the seaport capital of Burma

words for everyday use

in • gra • ti • at • ing (in grā´ shē āt iŋ) *adj.,* seeking another's favor by conscious effort. *Her ingratiating behavior soon got on my nerves.*

began an alapana,[4] and paused to ask, "Isn't it good Kalyani?"[5] Sekhar pretended not to have heard the question. The headmaster went on to sing a full song composed by Thyagaraja[6] and followed it with two more. All the time the headmaster was singing, Sekhar went on commenting within himself. He croaks like a dozen frogs. He is bellowing like a buffalo. Now he sounds like loose window shutters in a storm.

The incense sticks burnt low. Sekhar's head throbbed with the medley of sounds that had assailed his eardrums for a couple of hours now. He felt half stupefied. The headmaster had gone nearly hoarse, when he paused to ask, "Shall I go on?" Sekhar replied, "Please don't, sir, I think this will do. . . ." The headmaster looked stunned. His face was beaded with perspiration. Sekhar felt the greatest pity for him. But he felt he could not help it. No judge delivering a sentence felt more pained and helpless. Sekhar noticed that the headmaster's wife peeped in from the kitchen, with eager curiosity. The drummer and the violinist put away their burdens with an air of relief. The headmaster removed his spectacles, mopped his brow, and asked, "Now, come out with your opinion."

"Can't I give it tomorrow, sir?" Sekhar asked tentatively.

> Why does Sekhar want to wait until tomorrow?

"No. I want it immediately—your frank opinion. Was it good?"

"No, sir . . . ," Sekhar replied.

"Oh! . . . Is there any use continuing my lessons?"

"Absolutely none, sir . . . ," Sekhar said with his voice trembling. He felt very unhappy that he could not speak more soothingly. Truth, he reflected, required as much strength to give as to receive.

All the way home he felt worried. He felt that his official life was not going to be smooth sail-

ing hereafter. There were questions of increment and confirmation[7] and so on, all depending upon the headmaster's goodwill. All kinds of worries seemed to be in store for him. . . . Did not Harischandra[8] lose his throne, wife, child, because he would speak nothing less than the absolute Truth, whatever happened?

> What happened to Harischandra when he spoke only the truth?

At home his wife served him with a sullen face. He knew she was still angry with him for his remark of the morning. Two casualties for today, Sekhar said to himself. If I practice it for a week, I don't think I shall have a single friend left.

He received a call from the headmaster in his classroom next day. He went up apprehensively.

"Your suggestion was useful. I have paid off the music master. No one would tell me the truth about my music all these days. Why such antics at my age! Thank you. By the way, what about those test papers?"

"You gave me ten days, sir, for correcting them."

> What does the headmaster have to say about Sekhar's opinion of his music? How do you think he really feels?

"Oh, I've reconsidered it. I must positively have them here tomorrow. . . ." A hundred papers in a day! That meant all night's sitting up! "Give me a couple of days, sir . . . ."

"No. I must have them tomorrow morning. And remember, every paper must be scrutinized."

"Yes, sir," Sekhar said, feeling that sitting up all night with a hundred test papers was a small price to pay for the luxury of practicing Truth. ■

---

4. **alapana.** Classical Indian music that is improvised
5. **Kalyani.** Folk song from Mysore, a state in what is now India
6. **Thyagaraja.** Indian composer (1756–1847)
7. **increment and confirmation.** Raise and recognition (as for an employee)
8. **Harischandra.** Ancient ruler of Mysore

---

words for everyday use

ten • ta • tive • ly (ten′tə tiv lē) adv., hesitantly, timidly; uncertainly. _Tentatively, the child tried to touch the dog's wagging tail._
scru • ti • nize (skrōōt′'n īz′) vt., look at carefully. _The witness scrutinized every person in the police lineup._

RESPOND TO THE SELECTION

As an alternate activity, ask students under what conditions it might be important or necessary to speak the truth bluntly to someone.

ANSWERS TO INVESTIGATE, INQUIRE, AND IMAGINE

RECALL

1a. Sekhar resolves to undertake the "experiment" of telling the truth—the absolute truth—for one day, "whatever may happen."

2a. The "first test" in Sekhar's experiment occurs at his breakfast meal, when his wife serves him her "culinary masterpiece" and he tells her, "It isn't good."

3a. The headmaster wants Sekhar's opinion about his singing abilities.

INTERPRET

1b. He decides that unless he is willing to speak the absolute truth for one day out of each year, "life is not worth living."

2b. She winces in response to Sekhar's remark.

3b. The headmaster's seriousness about his singing is shown by the fact that he has spent much money on lessons, engaged a drummer and violinist to accompany him, and asked Sekhar, a music critic, to hear his performance. He has also made detailed preparations for his performance including lighting incense sticks "to create the right atmosphere."

ANALYZE

4a. Others who seem to agree with Sekhar about his headmaster's music are the drummer and the violinist, who put away their instruments "with an air of relief."

SYNTHESIZE

4b. *Responses will vary.* The headmaster might have performed for a huge crowd only to be embarrassed by their lack of enthusiasm for his ability or by a review in the newspaper ridiculing his singing. Had this happened, he might have been upset with Sekhar for not leveling with him earlier about his abilities.

EVALUATE

5a. *Responses will vary.* Softening, or tempering, the truth is necessary if human relationships are to remain strong. When Sekhar sees that truth-telling has a price, that it can hurt others as well as his own well-being, he understands that truth is

---

Respond *to the* SELECTION

Why might it be difficult to practice absolute truth in daily life? Is there a point when telling the truth can be brutal or cruel? How can you be both honest and considerate of other people's feelings?

Investigate, *Inquire,* and Imagine

Recall: GATHERING FACTS

1a. What "experiment" does Sekhar resolve to undertake for one day?

2a. What is the "first test" in Sekhar's experiment?

3a. About what does the headmaster want Sekhar's opinion?

Interpret: FINDING MEANING

1b. Why does Sekhar decide to set aside the day for his experiment?

2b. What actions on the part of Sekhar's wife show the stinging effect truth can have?

3b. What actions on the part of the headmaster show that he takes his singing ability seriously?

Analyze: TAKING THINGS APART

4a. Identify indications in the story showing that others concur with Sekhar's opinion of the headmaster's musical ability.

Synthesize: BRINGING THINGS TOGETHER

4b. Predict what the long-term consequences might have been had Sekhar not told the headmaster the truth about his singing ability.

Evaluate: MAKING JUDGMENTS

5a. What relationship between human interaction and truth is described in this story? How does Sekhar come to understand that practicing truth is a luxury?

Extend: CONNECTING IDEAS

5b. What significance does the legend of Harischandra have to Sekhar's situation? Think of other situations in which it might be difficult to tell the truth.

Understanding *Literature*

IRONY. Review the definition for **irony** in the Handbook of Literary Terms. In what way is Sekhar's "first test" at his morning meal an example of irony of situation? How are the expectations of Sekhar's wife violated? What major example of irony of situation occurs that violates Sekhar's expectations for his experiment?

THEME. Review the definition for **theme** and the pro and con chart you completed for Literary Tools in Prereading. What does Sekhar learn about the consequences of telling the truth? Develop two or three thematic statements about truth based on what he learns.

ANSWERS TO INVESTIGATE, INQUIRE, AND IMAGINE (CONT.)

a luxury; it can only be practiced by someone who does not depend on the good will of others.

EXTEND

5b. The legend is significant because it reveals Sekhar's state of mind. He feels that, like Harischandra, he will not have a single friend left if he continues to speak the absolute truth.

ANSWERS TO UNDERSTANDING LITERATURE

IRONY. At the morning meal, Sekhar's wife expects that her husband will compliment her "culinary masterpiece," whether he likes it or not. He violates this expectation when he tells her it is not good and he cannot swallow it. Sekhar expects that his experiment will make him feel better about himself. But after his third test, with the headmaster, he finds himself worry-

(Continued on page 223)

Writer's Journal

1. Write three **similes** comparing the sounds of certain types of music or particular instruments to other sounds.

2. Suppose that the headmaster had made his singing debut in a small concert hall rather than in the private audience of Sekhar. Imagine that you are a music reviewer for the local newspaper who has attended the performance. Write your **music review** including such information as a brief biography of the performer, the type of music performed, the quality of the performer and the accompanists, the length of the performance, the comfort and ambiance of the concert hall, etc. Use details from the story when possible, but fill in with your own imagination as necessary.

3. A parable is a very brief story told to teach a moral lesson. Write a **parable** that teaches a humorous lesson about telling the truth.

Integrating the Language Arts

Language, Grammar, and Style

PREPOSITION REVIEW. Read the Language Arts Survey 3.30, "Identifying Prepositional Phrases." A **preposition** is a word that shows a relationship between a noun or a pronoun, its object, and some other word in a sentence. A preposition introduces a **prepositional phrase.** Common prepositions include the following: *about, after, among, at, before, behind, beside, by, down, for, from, in, of, off, through, until, upon, with.* Read through the story to find ten sentences with prepositional phrases. Copy the sentences, underline the prepositional phrases, and circle the prepositions.

EXAMPLE: He told no one (of) his experiment.

Study and Research

INDIAN MUSIC. Research the music of India, and write a written report. You may want to give a broad overview of the country's music or concentrate on a particular composer, singer, instrumentalist, instrument, time period, etc. Check your library for recordings of the type of music you selected or for works by the musician/composer you chose, and bring these in to share with the class. You may find it helpful to visit Ohio State University's Indian Classical Arts Home Page at http://www.cis.ohio-state.edu/~sundar/ for more information on different types of classical music from India.

Speaking and Listening & Collaborative Learning

TRUTH POLL. As a class, brainstorm a list of questions to include in a poll about telling the truth. For example, you might ask questions such as these: In what kind of situation do you always tell the truth? Have you ever softened the truth to spare someone's feelings? Narrow the list down to five or six questions. Then form small groups of three or four students. As a group, decide on a place to poll individuals, such as the library, grocery store, or youth center. (Be certain to ask a supervisor or manager in advance for permission to poll individuals.) After each group has completed its poll, list each group's results on the chalkboard. Then combine the results for the entire class.

ANSWERS TO UNDERSTANDING LITERATURE (CONT.)

ing about his future. He knows he has jeopardized his headmaster's goodwill, which he needs in order to enjoy his work and advance in his career.

THEME. It requires as much strength to give the truth as to receive it. The price of telling the absolute truth is too high. Softening the truth is often necessary to maintain goodwill.

ANSWERS TO INTEGRATING THE LANGUAGE ARTS

Study and Research
When students share their examples of Indian music, ask them to play excerpts from three contrasting selections. For each selection, have them identify the instruments used, the composer or performer, and other details about the selection or type of music that will help listeners appreciate it.

Speaking and Listening & Collaborative Learning
Ask students to use multiple-choice questions in their poll. You may wish to evaluate the survey form separately by assigning up to 25 points for each grading criterion below, for a total of 100 points.

TRUTH POLL
- **Content/Unity.** The survey form has an appropriate heading and questions cover important points about telling the truth.
- **Organization/Coherence.** Questions are numbered and answer choices are arranged in a consistent manner. Each question covers a different point.
- **Language/Style.** Instructions, questions, and answer choices are worded clearly and concisely.
- **Conventions.** The survey form avoids errors in spelling, grammar, usage, and mechanics.

ADDITIONAL RESOURCES

UNIT 3 RESOURCE BOOK
- Selection Worksheet 3.8
- Selection Check Test 4.3.17
- Selection Test 4.3.18
- Language, Grammar, and Style Resource 3.33

GRAPHIC ORGANIZER

Students might include the following in their charts:

Sight
"sharp bends in the path and high, curling eucalyptus leaves and patches of sky"
"flower beds filled with neat rows of petunias and convolvulus, and paths and balustrades and rows of box trees"
"a large villa with flashing window panes and yellow-and-orange curtains"
"seeing only the blue from the tiles and his pink hands like goldfish"

Hearing
"Everything was quiet; not a leaf was stirring."
"taking care not to crunch the gravel"
"[the wheelbarrow] creaked like a whistle at every turn"
"a long somber boom" [from the gong]
"the pounding of their hearts"

Touch
"burning hot" railroad tracks
"their hair full of dry leaves and moss"

Taste
"They could not really enjoy the tea and cake, for nothing seemed to have any taste."

Smell
No direct references

READER'S JOURNAL

Students may wish to write about a place that is familiar to them, a place they have always wanted to go, or an imaginary place. Encourage them to write about what they can see, hear, smell, and touch in this special place.

Literary TOOLS

THEME. A **theme** is a central idea in a literary work. As you read "The Enchanted Garden" try to determine the central theme of the story.

SETTING. The **setting** of a literary work is the time and place in which it occurs, together with all the details used to create a sense of a particular time and place. In this selection, setting is revealed by describing such elements as landscape, scenery, buildings, objects, and so on.

Graphic Organizer

From the author's descriptions of the garden and the children's play during their outing, the reader can readily envision the settings. Create a sensory detail chart like the one below to examine how Calvino uses the senses to provide illustrative descriptions.

Sensory Details Chart	
Sight:	the children saw the train suddenly appear
Hearing:	
Touch:	
Taste:	
Smell:	

"The Enchanted Garden"
by Italo Calvino

Reader's resource

"The Enchanted Garden" is a realistic short story with elements of fantasy. Taken from Calvino's collection *Difficult Loves*, the selection is written in lyrical and sharply realistic prose, particularly the descriptive passages of the garden grounds that Giovannino and Serenella find by chance. Chance is an invisible character in "The Enchanted Garden," governing the children's discovery of the garden, which is itself a metaphor for beauty and enchantment.

About the AUTHOR

Italo Calvino (1923–1985) was born in Santiago de las Vegas, Cuba. In his youth, Calvino left Cuba for Italy, where he joined the Italian Resistance during World War II. After the war, Calvino moved to Turin, Italy. He wrote his first novel, *The Path to the Nest of Spiders,* when he was only twenty-four years old. In the 1950s, Calvino turned his attention to writing fantasy and allegory. *The Cloven Viscount, The Baron in the Tree,* and *The Nonexistent Knight,* three novels from this period, brought Calvino international recognition. In 1960, the three novels were reissued as a trilogy, titled *Our Ancestors.* Calvino's other works include *Italian Fables, Difficult Loves,* and *Mr. Palomar.*

Reader's Journal

If you could have a special place to explore, what would it look like?

GOALS/OBJECTIVES

Studying this lesson will enable students to
- appreciate a short story that contains elements of fantasy
- summarize the life and writing career of Italo Calvino
- define *theme* and identify a possible theme of the story
- define *setting* and explain its importance in the story
- give an oral book report

The Enchanted Garden

Italo Calvino

Giovannino and Serenella were strolling along the railroad tracks. Below was a scaly sea of somber, clear blue; above, a sky lightly streaked with white clouds. The railroad tracks were shimmering and burning hot. It was fun going along the tracks, there were so many games to play—he balancing on one rail and holding her hand while she walked along on the other, or else both jumping from one sleeper[1] to the next without ever letting their feet touch the stones in between. Giovannino and Serenella had been out looking for crabs, and now they had decided to explore the railroad tracks as far as the tunnel. He liked playing with Serenella, for she did not behave as all the other little girls did, forever getting frightened or bursting into tears at every joke. Whenever Giovannino said, "Let's go there," or "Let's do this," Serenella followed without a word.

Ping! They both gave a start and looked up. A telephone wire had snapped off the top of the pole. It sounded like an iron stork shutting its beak in a hurry. They stood with their noses in the air and watched. What a pity not to have seen it! Now it would never happen again.

> Why does Giovannino like playing with Serenella?

---

1. **sleeper.** British word for a tie supporting a railroad track

"THE ENCHANTED GARDEN" 225

ANSWER TO GUIDED READING QUESTION

1. He likes playing with Serenella because she does not get frightened or burst into tears at every joke and she is eager to follow him on his adventures.

INDIVIDUAL LEARNING STRATEGIES

MOTIVATION
To help students prepare to consider the fantasy elements in the story, have them brainstorm ideas about what an "enchanted garden" would be like. What things might grow there? What would it look like? What might happen there?

READING PROFICIENCY
Tell students that while some stories could be set in any number of places, the setting in "The Enchanted Garden" is critical to both the action and the theme of the story.

ENGLISH LANGUAGE LEARNING
Share with students these additional vocabulary words:
parry—deflect
chaise longue—couchlike chair
furtively—sneakily

SPECIAL NEEDS
Ask students to keep a list of elements that are surprising, unrealistic, or out of place as they read the story. Make sure students notice how the children arrive in the garden.

ENRICHMENT
Invite students to write about the role chance plays in life. Have they or someone close to them experienced a chance discovery or chance encounter that affected their life? How does the element of chance add to one's enjoyment in life?

VOCABULARY FROM THE SELECTION

impenetrable	somber
residue	subside

"There's a train coming," said Giovannino. Serenella did not move from the rail. "Where from?" she asked.

Giovannino looked around in a knowledgeable way. He pointed at the black hole of the tunnel, which showed clear one moment, then misty the next, through the invisible heat haze rising from the stony track.

"From there," he said. It was as though they already heard a snort from the darkness of the tunnel, and saw the train suddenly appear, belching out fire and smoke, the wheels mercilessly eating up the rails as it hurtled toward them.

"Where shall we go, Giovannino?"

There were big gray aloes[2] down by the sea, surrounded by dense, <u>impenetrable</u> nettles, while up the hillside ran a rambling hedge with thick leaves but no flowers. There was still no sign of the train; perhaps it was coasting, with the engine cut off, and would jump out at them all of a sudden. But Giovannino had now found an opening in the hedge. "This way," he called.

> Why do Giovannino and Serenella crawl through the hedge?

The fence under the rambling hedge was an old bent rail. At one point it twisted about on the ground like the corner of a sheet of paper. Giovannino had slipped into the hole and already half vanished.

"Give me a hand, Giovannino."

They found themselves in the corner of a garden, on all fours in a flower bed, with their hair full of dry leaves and moss. Everything was quiet; not a leaf was stirring.

> Where do they find themselves?

"Come on," said Giovannino, and Serenella nodded in reply.

There were big old flesh-colored eucalyptus trees[3] and winding gravel paths. Giovannino

and Serenella tiptoed along the paths, taking care not to crunch the gravel. Suppose the owners appeared now?

Everything was so beautiful: sharp bends in the path and high, curling eucalyptus leaves and patches of sky. But there was always the worrying thought that it was not their garden, and that they might be chased away any moment. Yet not a sound could be heard. A flight of chattering sparrows rose from a clump of arbutus[4] at a turn in the path. Then all was silent again. Perhaps it was an abandoned garden?

> How do they feel about being in the garden?

But the shade of the big trees came to an end, and they found themselves under the open sky facing flower beds filled with neat rows of petunias and convolvulus,[5] and paths and balustrades[6] and rows of box trees. And up at the end of the garden was a large villa with flashing window panes and yellow-and-orange curtains.

And it was all quite deserted. The two children crept forward, treading carefully over the gravel: perhaps the windows would suddenly be flung open, and angry ladies and gentlemen appear on the terraces to unleash great dogs down the paths. Now they found a wheelbarrow standing near a ditch. Giovannino picked it up by the handles and began pushing it along: it creaked like a whistle at every turn. Serenella seated herself in it and they moved slowly for-

---

2. **aloes.** Plants of the lily family with large fleshy leaves, native to Africa

3. **eucalyptus trees.** Tall, minty-smelling evergreens of the myrtle family, native to Australia

4. **arbutus.** Trees or shrubs of the heath family, featuring clusters of flowers and strawberry-like fruit

5. **convolvulus.** Trailing plants of the morning glory family with funnel-shaped blooms

6. **balustrades.** Staircase railings held up by posts

words for everyday use	im • pen • e • tra • ble (im pen´i trə bəl) *adj.*, incapable of being passed through. *The dense thicket was <u>impenetrable</u>, so we had to walk all the way around it.*

ward, Giovannino pushing the barrow with her on top, along the flower beds and fountains.

Every now and then Serenella would point to a flower and say in a low voice, "That one," and Giovannino would put the barrow down, pluck it, and give it to her. Soon she had a lovely bouquet.

Eventually the gravel ended and they reached an open space paved in bricks and mortar. In the middle of this space was a big empty rectangle: a swimming pool. They crept up to the edge; it was lined with blue tiles and filled to the brim with clear water. How lovely it would be to swim in!

"Shall we go for a dip?" Giovannino asked Serenella. The idea must have been quite dangerous if he asked her instead of just saying, "In we go!" But the water was so clear and blue, and Serenella was never afraid. She jumped off the barrow and put her bunch of flowers in it. They were already in bathing suits, since they'd been out for crabs before. Giovannino plunged in—not from the diving board, because the splash would have made too much noise, but from the

What indicates that swimming in the pool is different from other activities?

edge of the pool. Down and down he went with his eyes wide open, seeing only the blue from the tiles and his pink hands like goldfish; it was not the same as under the sea, full of shapeless green-black shadows. A pink form appeared above him: Serenella! He took her hand and they swam up to the surface, a bit anxiously. No, there was no one watching them at all. But it was not so nice as they'd thought it would be; they always had that uncomfortable feeling that they had no right to any of this, and might be chased out at any moment.

They scrambled out of the water, and there beside the swimming pool they found a Ping-Pong table. Instantly Giovannino picked up the paddle and hit the ball, and Serenella, on the other side, was quick to return his shot. And so they went on playing, though giving only light taps at the ball, in case someone in the villa heard them. Then Giovannino, in trying to parry a shot that had bounced high, sent the ball sailing away through the air and smack against a gong hanging in a pergola.[7] There was a long,

Artist's Garden at Vétheuil, 1880. Claude Monet. National Gallery of Art, Washington, DC.

---

7. **pergola.** An arbor

1. Swimming in the pool is different because it seems dangerous, causing Giovannino to ask Serenella if they should take a dip, instead of plunging in as he normally would do.

ADDITIONAL QUESTIONS AND ACTIVITIES

- Have students locate paintings of gardens by artists from different periods and countries in books from the library. Have them identify the one garden that seems most "enchanting" to them and share their pictures in small groups.

- Ask students what the expression "too much of a good thing" means. Then ask them how they would feel if they were suddenly granted all the "lovely, comfortable things" that they could want.

ART NOTE

Claude Monet (1840–1926) was an originator of the Impressionist style, which was concerned with representing the effects of light and color in nature. Monet moved to Vétheuil because of the quality of light found there and even constructed gardens especially to serve as subjects in his paintings. Ask students to examine *Artist's Garden at Vétheuil* and discuss in what ways the Impressionist style is suited to representing a flower garden.

1. When the ball sounds the gong, two menservants appear carrying trays for tea.
2. The children can't enjoy the wonders of the garden because they keep feeling that they are only there by luck and will have to explain to someone why they are there.
3. The boy in the house acts very worried, as though it is a mistake that he was granted all the wonderful things in the villa and in the garden.

SELECTION CHECK TEST 4.3.17 WITH ANSWERS

Checking Your Reading

1. How do Giovannino and Serenella get to the garden? **They crawl through an opening in a hedge by the train track.**
2. How do the children entertain themselves in the garden? *Responses will vary.* **They swim, pick flowers, ride in a wheelbarrow, and play Ping-Pong.**
3. What feeling keeps the children from completely enjoying the garden? **The feeling that they will be chased out at any moment keeps them from completely enjoying it.**
4. What do the children see when they look in the villa's window? **They see a boy.**
5. What does Giovannino admire about Serenella, compared to other girls? **He admires that she is never afraid.**

Literary Tools

1. What elements of this story are realistic? *Responses will vary.* **They could include the children playing and the descriptions of the garden.**
2. What elements are unrealistic? *Responses will vary.* **They could include the appearance of all the things the children love, the boy in the house, and the garden.**
3. Why is setting particularly important to this story? **This story is about the discovery of an enchanted garden; the garden is essentially a character in the story.**
4. What is unclear about the setting of this story? *Responses will vary.* **Settings consist of time and place; the time this story takes place is unclear. The origins of the garden are also vague.**

somber boom. The two children crouched down behind a clump of ranunculus.[8] At once two menservants in white coats appeared, carrying big trays; when they had put the trays down on a round table under an orange-and-yellow-striped umbrella, off they went.

What happens when the ball sounds the gong?

Giovannino and Serenella crept up to the table. There was tea, milk, and sponge cake. They had only to sit down and help themselves. They poured out two cups of tea and cut two slices of cake. But somehow they did not feel at all at ease, and sat perched on the edge of their chairs, their knees shaking. And they could not really enjoy the tea and cake, for nothing seemed to have any taste. Everything in the garden was like that: lovely but impossible to enjoy properly, with that worrying feeling inside that they were only there through an odd stroke of luck, and the fear that they'd soon have to give an account of themselves.

Why can't the children enjoy any of the wonders of the garden?

Very quietly they tiptoed up to the villa. Between the slits of a Venetian blind they saw a beautiful shady room, with collections of butterflies hanging on the walls. And in the room was a pale little boy. Lucky boy, he must be the owner of this villa and garden. He was stretched out on a chaise longue, turning the pages of a large book filled with figures. He had big white hands and wore pajamas buttoned up to the neck, though it was summer.

As the two children went on peeping through the slits, the pounding of their hearts gradually subsided. Why, the little rich boy seemed to be sitting there and turning the pages and glancing around with more anxiety and worry than their own. Then he got up and tiptoed around, as if he were afraid that at any moment someone would come and turn him out, as if he felt that that book, that chaise longue, and those butterflies framed on the wall, the garden and games and tea trays, the swimming pool and paths, were only granted to him by some enormous mistake, as if he were incapable of enjoying them and felt the bitterness of the mistake as his own fault.

How does the boy in the house behave?

The pale boy was wandering about his shady room furtively, touching with his white fingers the edges of the cases studded with butterflies; then he stopped to listen. The pounding of Giovannino and Serenella's hearts, which had died down, now got harder than ever. Perhaps it was the fear of a spell that hung over this villa and garden and over all these lovely, comfortable things, the residue of some injustice committed long ago.

Clouds darkened the sun. Very quietly Giovannino and Serenella crept away. They went back along the same paths they had come, stepping fast but never at a run. And they went through the hedge again on all fours. Between the aloes they found a path leading down to the small, stony beach, with banks of seaweed along the shore. Then they invented a wonderful new game: a seaweed fight. They threw great handfuls of it in each other's faces till late in the afternoon. And Serenella never once cried. ∎

---

8. **ranunculus.** Medicinal plant

words for everyday use	som • ber (säm´bər) *adj.*, dark and gloomy. *The bassoon sounded a long and low, somber sound.*
	sub • side (səb sīd´) *vi.*, become less intense. *After rising for a month, the Mississippi River finally peaked, then subsided, leaving behind a disaster of mud and ruin.*
	res • i • due (rez´ə dōō´) *n.*, leftover or remainder. *The powder left a sparkling residue on her fingertips.*

228 *UNIT THREE / FICTION*

SELECTION CHECK TEST 4.3.17 WITH ANSWERS (CONT.)

5. What is a possible theme for this story? *Responses will vary.* **The story could be about longing, imagination, or the friendship between the children. The theme might also be that it is better to lead a simple life than to live in luxury and opulence and always feel guilty about it.**

Respond *to the* SELECTION

Why might a garden such as the one described in the story seem unreal? Have you ever experienced a place so beautiful it seemed imaginary?

Investigate, Inquire, *and* Imagine

Recall: GATHERING FACTS

1a. What occurrence makes Serenella and Giovannino leave the railroad tracks?

2a. Where do the children find themselves after slipping through the hole in the hedge?

3a. What happens as a result of the Ping-Pong ball hitting the gong?

Interpret: FINDING MEANING

1b. What actions on the part of Serenella make her a good friend for Giovannino?

2b. What details about the garden emphasize its beauty?

3b. What is the reason that the children do not enjoy the tea and cake?

Analyze: TAKING THINGS APART

4a. Compare and contrast the little pale boy with Giovannino and Serenella.

Synthesize: BRINGING THINGS TOGETHER

4b. Why do you think none of the children were able to enjoy the garden?

Evaluate: MAKING JUDGMENTS

5a. What elements in the garden emphasize the feeling of otherworldiness?

Extend: CONNECTING IDEAS

5b. An *allusion* is a rhetorical technique in which reference is made to a person, event, object, or work from history or literature. At the end of the story, the narrator alludes to or refers to "the residue of some injustice committed long ago." To what biblical story might the author be alluding?

Understanding *Literature*

THEME. Review the definition for **theme** in Literary Tools in Prereading. Throughout the story, Giovannino and Serenella are anxious about their presence in the garden, feeling that they have no right to be in such a beautiful place. They notice that the pale boy seems as anxious as they are about his environment. What do you think is the central theme of this story?

SETTING. Review the definition for **setting** in the Handbook of Literary Terms. Identify specific details that are particularly effective in creating the setting of the enchanted garden. How do these details create a sense of enchantment?

"THE ENCHANTED GARDEN" **229**

ANSWERS TO INVESTIGATE, INQUIRE, AND IMAGINE (CONT.)

EXTEND

5b. The event might allude to a well-known event from the Bible that also took place in a beautiful and bountiful garden: Adam and Eve's eating of the forbidden fruit in the Garden of Eden, for which God expelled them and punished them.

ANSWERS TO UNDERSTANDING LITERATURE

THEME. Students should take into account both the overwhelming beauty and pleasure offered by the garden as well as the children's uneasiness about being there. Possible themes: People find it difficult to enjoy something they feel they don't deserve or that they know others can never enjoy. Simple pleasures in life are sweeter, because the very rich have the burden of guilt, knowing that they do not truly deserve to have so much more than everyone else.

(Continued on page 230)

RESPOND TO THE SELECTION

As an alternate activity, have students compare how the children act and feel in the scenes that take place before and after their time in the garden, as they walk along the railroad track and as they have a seaweed fight on the beach.

ANSWERS TO INVESTIGATE, INQUIRE, AND IMAGINE

RECALL

1a. The approach of an oncoming train makes the children leave the tracks.

2a. They find themselves in the corner of a garden, on all fours in a flower bed.

3a. When the Ping-Pong ball hits the gong, two servants come out of the house and set trays of tea and cake on a table.

INTERPRET

1b. Serenella is a good friend for Giovannino because she is willing to go anywhere and explore anything with him.

2b. Details that emphasize the garden's beauty include the old eucalyptus trees, the winding gravel paths, the flower beds, the large villa, and the blue-tiled swimming pool.

3b. The tea and cakes seem flavorless to the children because they fear that someone will show up and make them account for themselves.

ANALYZE

4a. Unlike Giovannino and Serenella, the pale little boy is rich and is apparently the owner of the garden and villa, whereas they are in the garden by luck. Like them, he is anxious and feels that someone might show up at any moment and turn him out of the garden; in fact, he is even more uneasy than they are.

SYNTHESIZE

4b. They feel they have no right to be in such a beautiful place.

EVALUATE

5a. The otherworldliness of the garden is emphasized by unusual or unlike occurrences such as the sudden appearance of the menservants who take no notice of the children; the unlikely placement of a Ping-Pong table beside the swimming pool; and by the overwhelming beauty of the garden.

ANSWERS TO UNDERSTANDING LITERATURE (CONT.)

SETTING. The garden seems enchanting because of the mysterious way in which the children enter it, by slipping into a hole. Also contributing to the sense of enchantment are the many winding paths and abundant flowers and plants, the fact the children have the garden all to themselves, the accidental way in which the servants are summoned when Giovannino sounds the Gong with a Ping-Pong ball, and the presence of so many things for children to enjoy such as a swimming pool, a Ping-Pong table, and treats under a bright umbrella.

ANSWERS TO INTEGRATING THE LANGUAGE ARTS

Language, Grammar, and Style
1. Fragment. Students' complete sentences will vary.
2. Complete sentence. Complete subject: Giovannino and Serenella Complete predicate: discover a secret garden.
3. Fragment. Students' complete sentences will vary.
4. Complete sentence. Complete subject: They Complete predicate: see a young boy filled with anxiety in the house.
5. Fragment. Students' complete sentences will vary.

Speaking and Listening
Suggest that students read one or more excerpts from the book to give the audience a sense of the setting and characters as well as the author's writing style.

Study and Research
Students may wish to work in pairs or small groups on this project.

Writer's Journal

1. Imagine that you could design your own enchanted garden. Write a **wish list** of all the special things you would include in it.

2. Pretend that you are Giovannino or Serenella and you are writing a **letter** to your grandmother to tell her of the garden you explored. Write about what you found most enchanting in the garden. Use your own words, but base your descriptions on the details from the story.

3. Write a **descriptive paragraph** about a place that appears realistic but contains highly unrealistic, or fantastic, elements. Through the use of precise details, convey a definite atmosphere, such as beauty, peacefulness, chaos, or starkness.

Integrating the Language Arts

Language, Grammar, and Style

IDENTIFYING AND CORRECTING SENTENCE FRAGMENTS. A sentence fragment is a piece of a sentence. It might be a subject or part of a predicate. Fragments are not complete sentences because they don't express complete thoughts. Refer to the Language Arts Survey 3.33, "Correcting Sentence Fragments" for examples. Classify each example below as a complete sentence or a sentence fragment. For each sentence, underline the complete subject and complete predicate. Revise each fragment to make it a complete sentence.

1. To get out of the way of the oncoming train.
2. Giovannino and Serenella discover a secret garden.
3. At all times a feeling as though they don't belong there.
4. They see a young boy filled with anxiety in the house.
5. Quietly crept away to the beach.

Speaking and Listening

ORAL BOOK REPORT. To become acquainted with other examples of fantasy literature, select a book such as *Alice in Wonderland, The Hobbit,* one of the *Chronicles of Narnia,* a Harry Potter book, or another suggested by a librarian or teacher. If you have access to the Internet, you may want to refer to the Open Directory Project's links to fantasy literature at http://dmoz.org/Arts/Literature/Genres/Fantasy/. After selecting and reading your book, prepare an oral report on the book detailing the characters, the setting, the theme, and a discussion of what role fantasy plays in the story.

Study and Research

DESIGN YOUR OWN GARDEN. If you could design a garden what would it look like? Would it be a flower garden, a vegetable garden, a windowsill garden, or a Japanese rock garden? Would you have a cactus garden in the desert or a water lily garden by a pond? Decide where you would plant your garden (i.e. in Paris, in Honolulu, in Phoenix?) and research the types of plants that grow in that environment. Select several varieties for your garden and write why you chose them. You may also want to draw up a blueprint of how you would arrange your garden.

Guided Writing

ANALYZING A PLOT

What makes a good story? Why do some stories "work" while others don't? Are there certain elements that all stories have in common? As you approach the end of this unit, you should be able to respond to these questions. Take "Little Red Riding Hood" for example. The story begins "once there was a little girl who lived in the wood," and she "had to deliver some food to her granny." These statements set up the whole story. Later, she meets the wolf on the way to grandma's house, gets eaten, and eventually, is miraculously saved by a woodsman. The woodsman kills the wolf and everybody lives happily ever after. Almost every story has the same elements as "Little Red Riding Hood." These elements combine to make the plot.

WRITING ASSIGNMENT. Your assignment is to analyze a short story using the elements of plot that you will learn about in this unit. It should help you understand what makes a good story.

Student Model

from "Here, Kitty, Kitty: Analyzing Poe's 'The Black Cat'"
by Goyh Saephan

"The Black Cat" by Edgar Allan Poe is a gruesome story about a man's fall into cruelty and madness. This is a good piece of writing, though—this story "works." Poe has combined all the elements of plot to build a good story.

The exposition successfully sets the mood. The purpose of exposition—to set the tone and mood, introduce the characters and setting, and provide necessary background information—is achieved. In the exposition the narrator of the story, the main character, tells the reader that he is a kind, animal-loving person. He has a wife and many household pets, particularly a black cat named Pluto. He seems to be an almost normal man except for a few hints to the contrary that Poe plants. First he admits that he did have one "peculiarity of character" that involved preferring the company of animals to people, spending most of this time "feeding and caressing" his pets as a youngster. This peculiarity, he says, grew with him and in

---

"There are only two or three human stories, and they go on repeating themselves as fiercely as if they had never happened before."

—Willa Cather

Read Edgar Allan Poe's "The Black Cat" on page 172.

EXAMINING THE MODEL. Goyh Saephan, a sophomore, analyzes each element in the plot of "The Black Cat" to show the structure of the story. The first paragraph clearly outlines what his paper will do. Each of the following paragraphs deals with plot elements. Goyh first defines each element of the plot, and then he takes examples from the story to explain how those elements work. He gives quotes to back up his assertions. He will close his paper with a summary of what he has done.

GUIDED WRITING
Software

See the Guided Writing Software for an extended version of this lesson that includes printable graphic organizers, extensive student models and student-friendly checklists, and self-, peer, and teacher evaluation features.

INDIVIDUAL LEARNING STRATEGIES

MOTIVATION
Ask students to list five qualities that they think make a good story, based on the short stories they read from Unit 3.

READING PROFICIENCY
Encourage students to read the Guided Writing lesson one section at a time, summarizing each section as they work through the lesson.

ENGLISH LANGUAGE LEARNING
As students read the Guided Writing lesson, have them keep notes in their reading or phrases they find difficult to understand. Then encourage them to use context clues or help from the text to uncover meaning.

SPECIAL NEEDS
Encourage students to concentrate on completing the graphic organizer. You may also want to pair them up with an advanced student who can help them work their final draft into complete sentences.

ENRICHMENT
For this lesson, allow students to act as peer instructors for students struggling with reading proficiency, English language learners, or students with special needs.

Prewriting

FINDING YOUR VOICE. To help students find their natural voice, allow them time to freewrite about various topics such as school, future, family, etc. Then have them reread what they have written and describe the voice that they use.

IDENTIFYING YOUR AUDIENCE. Remind students that a plot analysis is not a paper that retells the plot of the story. Instead, it identifies plot elements and critiques the effectiveness of the plot while supporting their judgments with examples from the story.

WRITING WITH A PLAN. As students reread the selection they choose to analyze, encourage them to fill out the graphic organizer as they read. Students may also want to keep a notebook handy to make extra notes about critiques or ideas that come up in their rereading of the selection.

Understanding Plot
A **plot** is a series of events related to a central **conflict**, or struggle. Each element has a different purpose.

- The **exposition**, or **introduction**, sets the tone and mood, introduces the characters and the setting, and provides necessary background information.
- The **inciting incident** is the event that introduces the central conflict.
- The **rising action**, or **complication**, develops the conflict to a high point of intensity.
- The **climax** is the high point of interest or suspense in the plot.
- The **falling action** is all the events that follow the climax.
- The **resolution** is the point at which the central conflict is ended, or resolved.
- The **dénouement** is any material that follows the resolution and ties up loose ends.

his manhood he "derived from it one of my principal sources of pleasure." So the reader isn't quite sure what to make of him, other than he may be a bit odd.

The second element is the inciting incident, or the event that introduces the central conflict. The central conflict of the story is that the man becomes an alcoholic and cruel. The narrator describes the effect of his disease: "I grew, day by day, more moody, more irritable, more regardless of the feelings of others" (page 173). He also begins to mistreat his wife and pets. One night he comes home drunk and cuts out one of Pluto's eyes! Now the reader wonders whether alcoholism is the man's only disease. Increasingly, the reader wonders if the narrator isn't crazy. After this incident, he says he starts *really* to be bothered by the cat, as if he weren't before!

Prewriting

FINDING YOUR VOICE. Use your natural voice, one that expresses a commitment to what you have learned about the story you have analyzed. Your voice should demonstrate your understanding of the language you have learned regarding the elements of plot. Most analysis is somewhat formal, so you should avoid casual language like slang. However, do include fresh descriptions, humor, or other language that shows honesty and conviction. Goyh chose a title that illustrates the chilling perverseness of the tale he describes. His voice is evident there.

IDENTIFYING YOUR AUDIENCE. Your audience for this will be your classmates and teacher. Keep in mind that this audience may have read the story you choose to analyze, but if you care to publish for a larger audience, not everyone may have done so. Therefore, in your paper you should give enough examples to make your analysis understandable to anyone.

WRITING WITH A PLAN. Obviously, it is necessary to read the story that you plan to analyze first. You should plan to reread it, or parts of it, while you do your analysis. After you have read it the first time, go back over it and skim it to search for the different plot elements and to look for quotes that you might use in your writing. Next, complete a plot chart that is specific to your story. Your analysis should refer to each of the seven plot elements, so your plot chart will help ensure that you discuss them all.

The following is Goyh's completed chart.

Student Model—Graphic Organizer

Introduction paragraph: title and author ("The Black Cat," Edgar Allan Poe); hook the reader's interest (with the word "gruesome"); explain how the plot elements work (Poe builds interest to a peak)

1. **Exposition:** The characters: young man, the narrator (and he says he's an animal lover), wife and pet cat Pluto. Mood: unsettled because the man seems a little strange.

2. **Inciting incident:** The young man becomes an alcoholic. He grows more moody; cuts the cat's eye out.

3. **Rising action:** The man hangs his cat; his house burns down; finds another cat.

4. **Climax:** kills his wife for trying to stop him from killing the new cat

5. **Falling action:** walls up his dead wife in the cellar (cat too)

6. **Resolution:** The narrator sleeps well, thinks the conflict is over.

7. **Dénouement:** The police find his wife's body when the cat meows.

Conclusion: wrap up what I've done: say that the plot elements worked together to pull the story along. (Refers back to the introduction).

Drafting

With your story and your completed plot chart in front of you, it is time to use your insights to analyze your story.

Concentrate on getting your ideas down on paper. Don't worry about mechanics at this point. Your analysis will consist of your thoughts about how the different elements worked together in this story. In other words, how did the exposition successfully set the mood? Where did the rising action increase the level of intensity to make the climax the true high point of the story? Was the conflict resolved in a believable and creative way in the resolution? Your draft should expand on the list you completed in your graphic organizer. Try to combine elements, quotes, and analysis into a fluid piece of writing.

Another important part of a plot analysis is using quotes from the story. When you use quotes, you use the story itself to support your analysis. Write down two or three quotes from your story that you may use in your analysis. Don't forget to use quotation marks, and copy the quoted passage word for word exactly as it appears in the story. Notice how Goyh uses quotes in his essay.

Self- and Peer Evaluation

Use the following questions to complete a self- and peer evaluation:

- Where in the introduction are the title of the story and the author mentioned?
- How does the writer capture interest in the introduction?
- Does the paper discuss all seven of the plot elements?
- Where does the writing seem to flow from one paragraph to another?
- Is there a place where the writing could be revised to be more fluent?
- Where are the insights of the writer clear?
- Where are there quotes to support the writer's points? Do they fit into the piece without being awkward?
- Is the analysis written in such a way that someone who has not read the story could still understand it?
- How does the conclusion wrap up the paper?
- Where, if anywhere, are there problems with subject-verb agreement?
- Where, if anywhere, do errors in spelling and punctuation occur?

Language, Grammar, and Style

Subject-Verb Agreement
IDENTIFYING SUBJECT-VERB AGREEMENT. The subject of a sentence can be singular or plural. A subject that is singular must be used with the singular form of the verb in the sentence, a plural subject with the plural form of the verb. This is called **subject-verb agreement**. In the student model, Goyh writes:

> The exposition, the first element of plot, successfully sets the mood.

Exposition is the subject of the sentence, and it is singular, so the correct form of the verb is *sets*.

Identify the subject in the following sentence and determine whether it and the verb should be singular or plural.

> This part among all the sections ties up loose ends.

Part is the subject, so *ties* is the correct verb.

In the next sentence, the subject is *ends*, so the plural verb *are* is correct.

> All ends are tied up when the police discover his wife's body.

Another confusing aspect is when the subject is a collective noun, like "team" or "orchestra." Even though these are groups of people, they are

continued on page 235

Revising and Proofreading

Based on the responses of your self- and peer evaluations, make changes in your essay that will help your audience better understand your analysis. Don't hesitate to tweak your thesis so it says what you want it to say. When you are finished revising, proofread your paper for errors in conventions such as spelling and punctuation.

Here is the remainder of Goyh's complete plot analysis.

Student Model (continued)

> The conflict comes to a higher point of intensity in the next element, rising action. He becomes so irritated by the cat that he ends up hanging it from a limb of a tree. His drive to kill is what he calls "...the spirit of perverseness." That's further proof that he is mad. But Poe introduces yet another element: The night he kills the cat his house burns down. Also mysteriously, an image of the cat, with a noose around its neck, appears on the wall of the burned house. Poe definitely adds suspense to the story by giving it this supernatural touch.
>
> The fourth element is the climax, the true high point of the story. The climax is shocking. The narrator ends up murdering his wife when she interferes with his trying to axe another cat. Throughout the whole story, the narrator talks about how much he loves his wife and how good she is to him through everything. He also talks about how much he loves his new cat, and how, the more the cat loves him, the more he begins to hate it. In fact, it is the cat's always wanting to be near him that causes him to want to kill it. He feels it is trying to trip him, so he swings at it with an axe. His wife stops the axe, so he, in his anger, turns the axe on his wife and kills her. After murdering his wife he walls her up in the cellar wall, and that is the fifth element, the falling action. The falling action is all the events that follow the climax. He feels no remorse at this point. He is outwardly and profoundly crazy. Surely

even the most forgiving reader has lost all sympathy for him by now.

Following the falling action is the resolution. This is the point at which the central conflict is resolved. The narrator believes all of his problems are solved when the cat doesn't return, "...and thus for one night at least, since its introduction into the house, I soundly and tranquilly slept, aye, slept even with the burden of murder upon my soul." All offending creatures are now out of his life, so the conflict seems to be resolved.

The final element of plot is the denouement. This part ties up loose ends. All bits are tied up when the police discover his wife's body. The one thing that he loathes, the black cat, which he had accidentally walled up with his dead wife, gives him away. It's ironic and fitting that the cat should be the one to cause the man to get caught. It's a delicious denouement.

Edgar Allan Poe creatively combined all the plot elements in the story to make it work. From exposition through denouement, the reader is pulled along the trail of madness. He builds the story so that an idea he starts with, the narrator's oddness, becomes full-blown madness by the end. The reader tries at first to be sympathetic to the narrator, who says that he is kind, but by the end Poe makes sure readers loathe him for his unspeakable cruelty.

Publishing and Presenting

You will be expected to share these with other students in a read-aloud in class. Your analysis contains a fair amount of your insights, so each person's essay should be different. Discuss each story again, after hearing one another's insights.

Reflecting

What things did you discover about the story when you looked at it a second and third time that you missed the first time through? What did you learn when you heard others' reactions to the same story? Have your insights deepened even further? How might being an insightful reader help you to become a better writer?

singular when they refer to the group as a unit:

> The team runs laps every day.

But they are plural when referring to the members of the group as individuals:

> The orchestra play their instruments well.

The key is to identify the subject first, and to make sure your verb agrees. It often helps to read your writing aloud to discover any errors in agreement.

FIXING ERRORS IN SUBJECT-VERB AGREEMENT.
The following sentences from an early draft of the student model have errors in subject-verb agreement. Fix them.

> Both the wife and the cat is walled up in the cellar.

> Those elements of the plot clearly shows Poe's mastery as a writer.

> Each of the policemen know he is hiding the truth when the cat meows.

USING SUBJECT-VERB AGREEMENT.
When you check your writing, determine whether each subject is singular or plural and make sure the verb agrees with it. Read your sentences aloud and check to see that singular subjects have singular verbs and plural subjects have plural verbs. Make necessary changes to improve the readability of your paper.

For more information, see the Language Arts Survey 3.40, "Getting Subject and Verb to Agree."

PREVIEWING THE SKILL. Refer students to the Language Arts Survey 3.40, "Getting Subject and Verb to Agree." For a summary of related parts of speech before conducting the lesson, see the Language Arts Survey 3.53, "Collective Nouns," and 3.56, "Indefinite Pronouns."

PRACTICING THE SKILL. For additional practice, have students work through the exercises in the Language, Grammar, and Style Resource Book 3.40, "Getting Subject and Verb to Agree," in the Teacher's Resource Kit.

Publishing and Presenting

Students' plot analyses could make excellent persuasive speeches. You may want to give extra credit to those students who present their plot analyses as a persuasive speech.

Reflecting

Allow students to answer these questions in their journals. Then have them get into small groups and discuss their responses to this lesson and the experience of analyzing a story's plot.

UNIT 3 review
Fiction

Words for Everyday Use

Check your knowledge of the following vocabulary words from the selections in this unit. Write a short sentence using each of these words in context to make the meaning clear. To review the definition or usage of a word, refer to the page number listed or to the Glossary of Words for Everyday Use.

allusion, 173
anomalous, 180
anonymity, 214
apparition, 175
articulate, 213
atrocity, 174
aversion, 177
bravado, 179
callously, 195
chagrin, 200
cherish, 173
coherent, 214
communicative, 215
conflagration, 175
conjointly, 180
conscientious, 167
consign, 180
constitute, 176
convey, 187
corroding, 213
cull, 192
debauch, 174
decree, 210
deliberate, 178
delirious, 211
delusion, 187

denunciation, 211
divestment, 191
docility, 173
domestic, 191
dredge, 215
duly, 185
eddy, 215
elated, 200
emit, 167
engulf, 186, 210
equivocal, 174
expedient, 178
expound, 172
falteringly, 186
finesse, 200
foray, 166
ghastly, 186
glib, 213
goaded, 178
homage, 202
imminent, 187
immoderate, 202
impenetrable, 226
imperceptible, 177
implore, 211
incessantly, 200

inclination, 174
incumbent, 177
indelible, 168
indifference, 166
inestimable, 200
ingratiating, 220
inscrutability, 179
intemperate, 173
jeopardize, 175
laceration, 210
latter, 173
lime, 175
migrate, 185
minutely, 167
nocturnal, 202
odious, 176, 204
overseas, 191
perverseness, 174
preen, 214
premises, 179
prestige, 215
procure, 178
ravaged, 212
regime, 166
rejuvenate, 168
remorse, 176

render, 179
replica, 213
repose, 176
residue, 228
resolve, 219
reverberation, 179
revolutionary, 167
rigidity, 210
scrutinize, 221
self-possessed, 185
shoddy, 210
solicit, 172
somber, 228
stupefied, 201
subside, 228
succinctly, 172
succumb, 177
suppleness, 200
temper, 219
tenancy, 210
tentatively, 221
tranquil, 168
uncongenial, 173
ungovernable, 177
usurer, 204
venture, 167

Literary Tools

Define each of the following terms, giving concrete examples of how they are used in the selections in this unit. To review a term, refer to the page number indicated or to the Handbook of Literary Terms.

character, 198
characterization, 208
conflict, 171, 183
flashback, 171
foreshadowing, 198

irony, 183, 218
mood, 164
motivation, 198
narrator, 164
plot, 171, 183

point of view, 164, 190
setting, 164, 224
stereotype, 190
theme, 208, 218, 224

Reflecting on your reading

Genre Studies

1. In some works of literature, *where* is just as important as *who* and *what*. The setting of a short story can exert a powerful influence over characters and their actions. Identify the settings of

"Lather and Nothing Else," "The Open Window," and "The Enchanted Garden." What mood does setting create in each story? In what ways does setting influence the development of the story or the characters' actions in each selection?

2. English author E. M. Forster said, "'The king died and then the queen died' is a story. 'The king died, and then the queen died of grief' is a plot." Consider this statement and, in your own words, explain what you think Forster meant. Next, apply your understanding of Forster's definition to one of the stories from this unit. Cite specific examples of how plot functions in the story and comment on how it illustrates or deviates from Forster's definition.

Thematic Studies

3. Review the definition for *theme* in the Handbook of Literary Terms. Examine a selection from the unit in terms of the way it handles theme. Does the story strongly convey one or more themes, or do other literary elements play a more prominent role? If the story does clearly express a theme (or themes), what is the theme (or themes), and what events in the story contribute to the development of the theme (or themes)?

4. Much of prose literature is filled with dynamic characters, characters who change in some way over the course of the story's action. Examine the dynamic characters in "The Black Cat," "The Necklace," and "Like the Sun." In what ways do the characters develop and change?

for your READING LIST

Ethan Frome by Edith Wharton. A terrible accident has left Ethan Frome a disfigured, broken man. What tragic story lies behind Ethan's tortured face? The narrator leads you through one compelling vision of Ethan's story in this vivid tale of life in the stark New England countryside. A film version of the novel was released in 1993 starring Liam Neeson. Wharton, author of many acclaimed works, including the Pulitzer Prize-winning *Age of Innocence*, is considered to be one of America's best writers.

ETHAN FROME

Edith Wharton

EMC MASTERPIECE SERIES
ACCESS EDITION

Independent Reading Activity

RESPONDING TO FICTION. What makes a short story or a novel good? What elements make good fiction? Often you can tell just by paying attention to your own responses as you read. Choose a short story, either from this unit or by another author that you are familiar with, and ask yourself these questions as you read. How does the plot work? At what point, if any, are you gripped with interest or suspense or confusion, or feel sad or happy by what is happening? What is the conflict? How is it resolved? How do you feel about the characters? Take some notes as you read the story, and afterwards write up a brief response to it.

Selections for Additional Reading

Ultimate Sports: Short Stories by Outstanding Writers for Young Adults, edited by Donald R. Gallo. This compilation of short stories by popular young adult authors contains sixteen short stories with sports settings or themes.

Local Girls by Alice Hoffman. Alice Hoffman stories have a quality of the magical and the lyrical, perhaps because she claims her greatest influence has been fairy tales. These connected short stories follow the life of Gretel through her teenage years, from when she is a young girl until she is old enough to leave home.

Literary Skills and Concepts

Writing Skills and Concepts

Language, Grammar, and Style

TEACHING THE MULTIPLE INTELLIGENCES

Musical

Logical-Mathematical

Spatial
(Continued on page 239)

Ronin Fighting Scene from Chushingura Play, c.1830. Utagawa Kunisada. Bass Museum of Art, Miami Beach, Florida.

GOALS/OBJECTIVES

Studying this unit will enable students to
- describe and appreciate William Shakespeare's literary accomplishments and explain the historical significance of his writings
- recognize and give examples of blank verse
- define and illustrate with examples the literary techniques of *carastrophe, central conflict, character, climax, falling action, foreshadowing, irony, motif, repetition,* and *simile*
- read a selection from Machiavelli's *The Prince* and relate its ideas about leadership to ideas in *Julius Cæsar*
- write an extended definition
- identify, edit for, and use sentence variety in their writing

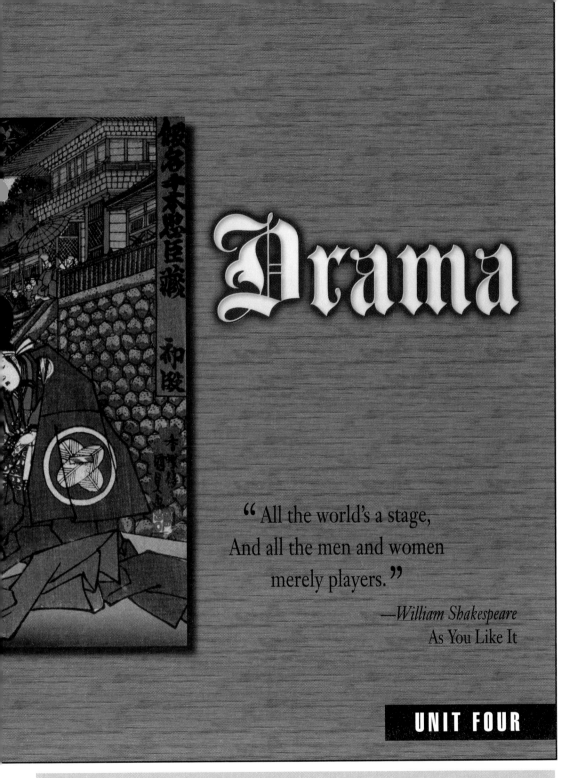

Drama

" All the world's a stage,
And all the men and women
merely players. "

—*William Shakespeare*
As You Like It

UNIT FOUR

ART NOTE

Ronin Fighting Scene from Chushingura Play, c.1830. Utagawa Kunisada.
Utagawa Kunisada (1786–1864) was a master of Japanese woodblock printmaking, a style of art known as *ukiyo-e,* or "pictures of the floating world." Kunisada was famous for making pictures of popular actors, but also for his beautiful landscapes, which he often incorporated into the background of his works. The print on pages 238–239, *Ronin Fighting Scene from Chushingura Play,* depicts a scene from *Kanadehon Chushingura (The Treasury of Loyal Retainers),* the most popular kabuki play ever produced. Kabuki, a traditional form of Japanese theater which originated in the 17th century, is highly stylized. The actors, all male (even those playing the female parts, just as in Shakespearean times), wear elaborate costumes and white face makeup. Dancing and musical accompaniment are a part of kabuki.

Chushingura tells the story of forty-seven masterless samurai, or *ronin,* who on the night of January 30, 1703, avenged the wrongful death of their former master and then committed ritual suicide. These ronin are regarded as heroes in Japan for their loyalty and resolute action. The story has been adapted into several movies, including *The Loyal Forty-Seven Ronin* (1941–1942, directed by Kenji Mizoguchi), and *Chushingura* (1962, directed by Hiroshi Inagaki). These movies are available with English subtitles.

As noted above, kabuki theater is highly stylized. Explain to students that stylized means "representing a conventional style, not naturalistic." For example, the actors in kabuki do not look "natural"—they wear highly exaggerated makeup—and they do not speak in a realistic manner, but rather sing their lines. The actors portraying females are in fact males speaking in a high falsetto. Ask students to examine the print *Ronin Fighting Scene.* Would they describe it as stylized or realistic? Does it portray nature as it really is, or is it following a conventional style?

ELEMENTS of DRAMA

Drama is literature enacted in front of an audience by people who play the parts of the characters. No one knows for certain how drama originated, but we do know that ritual performances have been held by people around the globe since long before the beginning of recorded history.

The first literary dramas were created long ago in ancient Greece and may have developed from reenactments of ritual sacrifices to the gods. According to one theory, people in ancient Greece would come together to sacrifice an animal—often a goat—to win a god's favor. Eventually, that sacrifice developed into an elaborate show involving an actor, a priest, and a chorus with whom the priest interacted. In fact, the ancient Greek word *tragōidia,* from which our word *tragedy* derives, meant "song of the goats." In the fifth century BC, the Greek playwright Aeschylus added a second actor, and drama as we know it was born.

Types of Stages

In classical times, dramas were performed in open-air amphitheaters, or **arena stages**. In the Middle Ages, plays were often produced on the backs of wagons in the courtyards of inns. From these developed the **thrust stage** used in Elizabethan England, a platform that jutted into an area open to the sky. In the nineteenth and twentieth centuries, the **proscenium stage**, or **picture stage**, became common. Such a stage is a box-like area with three walls (or curtains) and a removed "fourth wall" through which the audience views the action.

Types of Drama

Most dramas can be classified as either comedies or tragedies. A **comedy**, in its original sense, was any work with a happy ending. The term is widely used today to refer to any humorous work, especially one prepared for the stage or the screen. A **tragedy** initially was a drama that told the story of the fall of a person of high status, though in recent years the word has been used to describe any play about the downfall of a central character, or protagonist, who wins the audience's sympathies in some way.

ELEMENTS OF DRAMA

PLAYWRIGHT. The author of a play is the **playwright**. The relationship between a playwright and the play is more tenuous than that of an ordinary author to his or her text. A novelist or poet has enormous control over the form in which his or her work will be presented to its audience, the reader. A playwright, in contrast, must depend upon the interpretations given his or her work by producers, directors, set designers, actors, and other persons involved in producing the work for the stage. The playwright's art involves the collaboration of many people.

SCRIPT. A **script** is the written form of the play. It contains stage directions and dialogue and may be divided into acts and scenes. Scripts for television screenplays include instructions for how the play should be filmed.

DIALOGUE. Dialogue is the term used to describe the speech of actors in a play. The dialogue usually consists of the characters' names and the words or other utterances to be spoken by the actors. The dialogue of a play may contain many **monologues**, or long speeches given by actors. A speech given by a lone character on stage is called a **soliloquy**. A statement intended to be heard by the audience or by a single other character but not by other characters on the stage is called an **aside**.

ACTS AND SCENES. An **act** is a major division of a drama. The plays of ancient Rome and of Elizabethan England were typically divided into **five acts**. Shakespeare's *Julius Cæsar,* in this unit, consists of five acts. In the Modern Era, **three-act** and **one-act** plays are quite

CROSS-CURRICULAR ACTIVITIES

ARTS AND MUSIC. Ask interested students to research kabuki theater and prepare an oral report to be shared with the class. They may do this activity alone or in a small group. They should find out details about the kind of music used in kabuki, such as the musical instruments used and the type of songs sung by the actors; the type of dance or body expression; and details about the costumes. Students should look for photographs of kabuki productions in magazines or in books, or if possible a videotape of a kabuki production to share with the class.

common. The acts may be divided into scenes. Typically, a **scene** begins with the entrance of one or more characters. The time and place of acts or scenes may change from one to the next.

STAGE DIRECTIONS. Stage directions are notes provided by the playwright to describe how something should be presented or performed on the stage. Stage directions often describe elements of the **spectacle**, such as lighting, music, sound effects, costumes, properties (props), or set design. They also may describe entrances and exits, the movements of characters, facial expressions, gestures, body language, tone of voice, or other elements related to the acting of the play. Sometimes, stage directions provide historical or background information. Stage directions usually are printed in italics and enclosed in brackets or parentheses. In stage directions, the parts of the stage are often described using the terms *up, down, right, left,* and *center,* which describe stage areas from the point of view of the actors.

STAGE AREAS.

THE PARTS OF A STAGE

Up Right	Up Center	Up Left
Right Center	Center	Left Center
Down Right	Down Center	Down Left

Audience

THE SPECTACLE

SPECTACLE. The **spectacle** is all the elements of the drama presented to the senses of the audience—the lights, sets, curtains, costumes, makeup, music, sound effects, properties, and movements of the actors, including any special movement such as pantomime or dance. Spectacle is one major feature that differentiates dramatic from nondramatic works. The following chart describes common parts of the spectacle.

ELEMENT OF SPECTACLE	DESCRIPTION
Stage	This is the area in which the action is performed. An **arena stage,** or **theater in the round,** is one in which the audience stands or sits around a circular or semicircular open space. A **thrust stage** is one that extends into the audience, which is situated on three sides of the playing area. A **proscenium,** or **picture stage,** is one that has an arch around an opening that acts as a removed "fourth wall."
Set	The set is everything placed upon the stage to give the impression of a particular setting, or time and place. Sets often include walls, furnishings, and painted backdrops.
Properties	Properties are items that can be carried on and off the stage by actors or manipulated by actors during scenes. Examples of properties include books, fans, gavels, and walking sticks.
Sound effects	These are sounds introduced to create mood or to indicate the presence of something. Common sound effects include thunder, ringing telephones, and police sirens.
Blocking	This is the act of determining how actors will move on a stage. Blocking is almost always done by the director of the play.

ELEMENTS OF DRAMA 241

GRAPHIC ORGANIZER

MOTIF. Students may include in their cluster charts the following examples of disorder in nature: man's hand on fire, but not burned; lion near the Capitol; men in flames walking the streets; owl hooting in market in middle of day.

LITERARY/HISTORICAL NOTE

You might inform students that in his age, Shakespeare was popular not only with the intellectual elite but with the common people as well. His plays drew crowds composed of members of the nobility and throngs of commoners; attending a Shakespearean play, in a sense, was one of the few democratic experiences in an age in which the class system was distinctly stratified. Encourage students to look for scenes in *Julius Cæsar* that seem aimed to please the common people who composed the body of Shakespeare's audience.

ADDITIONAL QUESTIONS AND ACTIVITIES

Have students work in pairs to analyze the meter of a few lines from the play. Students can write out the lines, then divide them into feet and mark strong and weak stresses. If students have difficulty hearing stresses, suggest that one student read the lines aloud while the other listens for stress.

PLAY

Literary TOOLS

CHARACTER. A **character** is a person who figures in the action of a literary work. Some critics have said that Shakespeare's play ought to be called *Brutus* instead of *Julius Cæsar* because Brutus is the play's main character. As you read act 1, consider what sort of person Brutus is. What motivates him? What conflicting feelings does he have?

PLOT, CENTRAL CONFLICT, AND INCITING INCIDENT. A **plot** is a series of events related to a central *conflict,* or struggle. The event that introduces the central conflict is called the **inciting incident**. As you read act 1, determine what the central conflict or struggle is for Brutus.

MOTIF. A **motif** is any element that recurs in one or more works of literature or art. The motif of disorder in nature runs throughout much of Shakespeare's work and usually signifies the disorder of the political state. As you read *Julius Cæsar*, note the motif of disorder in nature as it occurs and jot the details down on a cluster chart as illustrated below.

Graphic Organizer

Create a cluster chart like the one below to record examples of disorder in nature in act 1. One example has been filled in for you. You will want to continue to fill in this chart as you read the entire play and ask yourself what, specifically, is out of order in the political state?

- Disorder in Nature
- storm "dropping fire"

242 UNIT FOUR

The Tragedy of Julius Cæsar
by William Shakespeare

Reader's resource

Background: Theater in Shakespeare's Day. The Globe Theater, in which *The Tragedy of Julius Cæsar* was first performed, is described in one of Shakespeare's plays as a "wooden O." The theater, which had eight sides and was open in the middle, was nearly circular. The stage jutted into the center of this open area. Some members of the audience stood or sat in the three tiers of seats inside the walls of the theater. Most, however, paid a penny for admittance and stood around the stage on three sides. These audience members were the "groundlings." Part of the stage was covered by a canopy supported by two pillars. Doors on the sides of the stage allowed for entrances and exits. Trap doors in the floor of the stage made it possible for actors to appear or disappear. Backstage center was an area known as the "tiring house," in which actors could change. This area could be opened for interior scenes. Above the tiring house was a second-story balcony, which could be used to represent a hilltop, a lookout, an upper room, or, of course, a balcony. A third level above the balcony provided a space for musicians and sound-effects technicians.

The theater in Shakespeare's day used little in the way of scenery. The audience had to imagine the setting based on characters' descriptions and properties (small objects, such as swords or crowns, that could be carried on and off stage). In a modern performance of a historical play like *Julius Cæsar*, the actors would most likely be dressed in period costumes such as togas. However, in Shakespeare's day, actors wore standard contemporary Elizabethan dress. As you read *Julius Cæsar*, you may notice that there are other elements of the play that are historically inaccurate. For example, in the play Shakespeare refers to clocks striking, despite the fact that such clocks did not exist in Roman times. Another unrealistic element that you would notice if you were to go back to the Globe to view this play is that the actors were all men or boys. In Shakespeare's time it was considered improper for women to act in plays.

Technique. Most of *Julius Cæsar* is written in **blank verse.** Blank verse is unrhymed iambic pentameter. Each line consists of five feet, each made up of a weakly stressed syllable followed by a strongly stressed one. The following are some typical lines:

˘ / ˘ / ˘ / ˘ / ˘ /
Are all | thy con | quests, glo | ries, tri | umphs, spoils,

/ ˘ / ˘ / ˘ / ˘ /
Shrunk to | this lit | tle mea | sure? Fare | thee well.

Blank verse has a noble, heroic quality appropriate to this play about the fall of a great leader.

The Globe

The Kingdom and Republic of Rome. Roman legend held that the city was founded on the banks of the river Tiber by two brothers, Romulus and Remus, sons of the war god Mars. According to the legend, when the boys were still babies, they were thrown into the river by their mother's brother. A she-wolf discovered the nearly drowned babies on the riverbank and nursed them back to health. Later adopted by a shepherd who raised them, the boys grew up to found a city, named for Romulus, that would come to rule the Western world.

Traditionally, the belief is that Rome was founded in 753 BC and was ruled in the ensuing centuries by a succession of seven kings. In about 509 BC, the last of these kings

The Globe Theater

was overthrown and a republic was established, ruled by a senate and by elected officials, the consuls and tribunes. During the four centuries of the existence of the republic, Rome grew to become a great power, first by subduing its immediate neighbors, then by defeating the mighty empire of Carthage, located across the Mediterranean Sea on the coast of northern Africa. At the time of the death of Julius Cæsar in 44 BC, Rome controlled much of Europe, northern Africa, and Asia Minor.

Julius Cæsar. Gaius Julius Cæsar was born on the twelfth or thirteenth of July, sometime around the year 100 BC, into a noble Roman family. One of the ablest leaders the world has known, Cæsar bore a name that became forever synonymous with power and leadership. The Russian word *czar*, the German *kaiser*, and the Arabic *qaysar*, meaning "king" or "ruler," are all variations on his name. The month of July is also named after him.

As a young man, Cæsar left Rome to travel to the Greek city of Rhodes, where he intended to study oratory, or public speaking. On the way, he was captured by pirates, who released him after he raised a large ransom. Cæsar retaliated by gathering a private naval force, capturing the pirates, and crucifying them. Over succeeding years, Cæsar moved steadily up the political ladder in Rome, holding a number of important posts, culminating in his election to the post of consul in 59 BC, a position which made him one of two chief rulers of the Roman Empire.

THE TRAGEDY OF JULIUS CÆSAR 243

HISTORICAL NOTE

- Roman generals received their training on the field, as it was assumed that members of the nobility instinctively knew military tactics. Cæsar was, in fact, a better politician than general. He wrote extensively about his military campaigns in Gaul, portraying them in their best possible light in order to gain popularity.

- You may also wish to inform students that when Cæsar crossed the Rubicon and entered Rome at the head of his army, he was flouting a time-honored tradition of the Roman Republic. It was forbidden for generals to enter the city at the head of an army; this tradition was maintained to prevent precisely what followed Cæsar's crossing of the Rubicon—civil war. Cæsar's blatant disregard for the traditions of the Roman Republic do lend credence to the conspirators' fears that the politically ambitious Cæsar intended to dismantle the Republic entirely.

INDIVIDUAL LEARNING STRATEGIES

MOTIVATION
Ask students to discuss which they consider the better form of government: a monarchy, in which a king or queen rules absolutely, or a republic, in which representatives of the people make the laws. Ask them to answer the following questions: What are the pros and cons of each form of government? Why might people who live in a republic not want to change to living under the rule of a monarch?

READING PROFICIENCY
Many students may find the language of Shakespeare's time difficult. Go over with them the Words for Everyday Use and the footnotes, then encourage them to read through each scene with a partner, answering the Guided Reading Questions as they go and summing up the main point of each scene.

ENGLISH LANGUAGE LEARNING
In addition to going over the Words for Everyday Use and footnotes, you may wish to review with students the archaic language and the additional vocabulary below.
sate—sat
strew—throw
offal—refuse, garbage
livelong—whole; entire
intermit—stop
exalted—praised; glorified
gusty—windy

Between 58 BC and 50 BC, Cæsar conducted a series of brilliant military campaigns that won for Rome all of Gaul (modern-day France) and that extended Roman power as far north as Britain. Members of the nobility, or patricians, in Rome came to fear Cæsar because he commanded a large army made up of fiercely loyal troops and because he was much loved by the common people, or plebeians, of the city. Fearing that Cæsar would make himself king and overthrow the republic, the patricians of the senate voted on January 1, 49 BC, to have Cæsar lay down his command. Cæsar refused and instead led his troops across the Rubicon, a small river between Gaul and Italy, initiating a civil war that lasted from 49 BC to 45 BC. In the civil war, Cæsar defeated the forces of his former ally, the Roman general Pompey. After returning to Rome and assuming the title of dictator, he left in 45 BC for the province of Farther Spain to put down a revolt led by Pompey's sons. Shakespeare's play begins with Cæsar's return to Rome after his campaign in Spain. Basing his play on material taken from Sir Thomas North's translation of *Lives of the Noble Greeks and Romans,* by the ancient Greek writer Plutarch, Shakespeare heightens the drama of the events that followed Cæsar's return by compressing three years of action into five acts.

Close-up of Roman Colosseum

On Reading Shakespeare. *The Tragedy of Julius Cæsar* was written about four hundred years ago. Since that time, the English language has changed considerably, and you will therefore find that reading Shakespeare presents some special challenges. The editors of this text have provided footnotes to help you understand words and phrases that have changed in meaning since Shakespeare's day. However, try not to get bogged down in these footnotes. Remember that a play is a dramatic action and should move quickly. First read through each scene without looking at the footnotes, so that you can get a general sense of what is happening. Then reread the scene, referring to the footnotes to discern details. In addition to reading the play, you may want to listen to a recording of it or watch a production on film, videotape, or CD. All drama comes alive when performed by actors and is best experienced in that way.

INDIVIDUAL LEARNING STRATEGIES (CONT.)

mark—notice
mettle—quality of character
wrought—shaped

SPECIAL NEEDS
Students will find it helpful to hear the selection read out loud. Either read out loud to students or have them alternate reading aloud. Make sure students focus on the Guided Reading Questions and the

Recall questions in the Investigate, Inquire, and Imagine section.

ENRICHMENT
In act 1, the reader learns that Julius Cæsar has just returned from defeating the sons of Pompey. Have students research Cæsar's relationship with Pompey. Students should learn about the First

Triumvirate, when it was formed, what Cæsar's role was in the Gallic Wars, and what happened to start Cæsar's quarrel with Pompey. Under Cæsar, Rome became a great and powerful empire. Ask students to find out what territories were held by Rome at the time of Cæsar's death. They can write a short report to be shared with the class.

About *the* AUTHOR

William Shakespeare (1564–1616), born in the English town of Stratford-upon-Avon to Mary Arden and John Shakespeare, is widely considered to be the greatest play-wright who ever lived. Very little is known of Shakespeare's early life. His mother was from a well-to-do local family. His father was a politician and glove maker who eventually became bailiff of Stratford-upon-Avon, a post equivalent to mayor. Shakespeare attended the local grammar school and may have worked for some time thereafter as a school teacher. In 1582, at the age of eighteen, Shakespeare married a woman named Anne Hathaway, who was twenty-six. The couple had three children, Susanna, Hamnet, and Judith.

By 1592, Shakespeare was living in London and working in the theater. Shakespeare's theater company, the Lord Chamberlain's Men, became the most popular group of actors in the city, performing at the Globe Theater and in a small-er indoor theater called Blackfriars. The company enjoyed royal support and in 1594 per-formed two plays before Queen Elizabeth I. In 1603, after the death of Queen Elizabeth, the company became servants of the new king, James I, and changed their name to the King's Men.

In 1597 Shakespeare bought a large house in Stratford-upon-Avon called New Place. Thereafter he divided his time between Stratford-upon-Avon and London. Despite a busy career as actor and theater owner, Shakespeare managed to write at least thirty-six plays and some of the finest poetry in the English language, including a series of famous son-nets. His plays include comedies such as *The Taming of the Shrew* and *The Merchant of Venice;* histories such as *Richard the Third* and *Henry the Fifth;* tragedies such as *Hamlet, Othello, King Lear,* and *Macbeth;* and romances such as *The Winter's Tale* and *The Tempest. The Tragedy of Julius Cæsar,* which is both a history and a tragedy, was first performed on September 21, 1599, at the Globe Theater. In or around 1611, Shakespeare retired to Stratford-upon-Avon a wealthy and successful man. There, on April 25, 1616, he was buried in Holy Trinity Church. Carved in stone above his grave are the following lines, believed to have been written by Shakespeare himself:

> Good friend, for Jesus sake forbeare,
> To digg the dust enclosèd heare!
> Blest be the man that spares thes stones,
> And curst be he that moves my bones.

Reader's Journal

How would you feel if a very popular and effective military leader attempted to declare himself king over our own representative form of government?

ART NOTE

Temple of Vesta in the Roman Forum. The Temple of Vesta depicted in the photograph on page 246 is located in Rome, Italy, in the ruins of the Roman Forum. Vesta was the Roman goddess of the hearth. As ancient peoples lacked ready sources of fire, Vesta, goddess of the ever-burning hearth fire, was important to both individual households and the state. Worship of Vesta was popular, involving many rites and a week of festival. Vesta's shrine was traditionally circular, to symbolize both the hearth and the shape of early dwellings.

The Roman Forum was a market and meeting place in ancient Rome. Students will have an opportunity to research the Forum in a Study and Research activity on page 308.

CROSS-CURRICULAR ACTIVITIES

HISTORY. Students might research the sweeping changes in the religious history of Rome. Some students might research the gods and goddesses central to the religion of pre-Christian Rome, focusing on what the gods and goddesses reveal about the values of the Roman people. Other students may be interested in studying the rise of Christianity in Rome.

CROSS-CURRICULAR ACTIVITIES

APPLIED ARTS. Explain that a prop master is the person responsible for finding and keeping track of all properties, or props, used by actors in a play. Suggest that students assume the role of prop master as they read. Encourage students not only to make a list of props specifically mentioned in the script (such as swords and letters) but also to think of props that might help create the scene on stage.

The Tragedy of Julius Cæsar

William Shakespeare

Temple of Vesta in the Roman Forum.

CHARACTERS IN THE PLAY

JULIUS CÆSAR
OCTAVIUS CÆSAR
MARK ANTONY
M. AEMILIUS LEPIDUS } *triumvirs[1] after the death of Julius Cæsar*

CICERO
PUBLIUS
POPILIUS LENA } *senators*

MARCUS BRUTUS
CASSIUS
CASCA
TREBONIUS
CAIUS LIGARIUS
DECIUS BRUTUS
METELLUS CIMBER
CINNA } *conspirators against Julius Cæsar*

FLAVIUS *and* MURELLUS, *tribunes[2]*
ARTEMIDORUS OF CNIDOS, *a teacher of rhetoric[3]*
SOOTHSAYER[4]

CINNA, *a poet*
Another POET
LUCILIUS
TITINIUS
MESSALA
Young CATO
VOLUMNIUS
FLAVIUS } *friends to Brutus and Cassius*

VARRUS
CLITUS
CLAUDIO
STRATO
LUCIUS
DARDANIUS } *servants to Brutus*

PINDARUS, *servant to Cassius*
CALPHURNIA, *wife to Cæsar*
PORTIA, *wife to Brutus*
SENATORS, CITIZENS, GUARDS, ATTENDANTS, *etc.*

SCENES: *Rome; near Sardis; near Philippi*

1. *triumvirs.* In ancient Rome, three administrators who shared power equally among themselves
2. *tribunes.* In ancient Rome, administrators elected to protect the rights of the plebeians, or common people
3. *rhetoric.* Art of public speaking and persuasion
4. SOOTHSAYER. Fortune-teller; literally, a "truth teller"

246   UNIT FOUR / DRAMA

VOCABULARY FROM THE SELECTION

apparel	construe	fawn	prodigy	surly	wretched
cogitation	countenance	impart	replication	tempest	yoke
concave	cull	infuse	servile	throng	
conjointly	endure	portentous	sinew	underling	

ACT 1
SCENE 1: street in Rome

Enter FLAVIUS, MURELLUS, *and certain* COMMONERS *over the stage.*

FLAVIUS. Hence! home, you idle creatures, get you home!
Is this a holiday? What, know you not,
Being mechanical,[1] you ought not walk
Upon a laboring day without the sign

5 Of your profession?[2] Speak, what trade art thou?

CARPENTER. Why, sir, a carpenter.

MURELLUS. Where is thy leather apron and thy rule?
What dost thou with thy best <u>apparel</u> on?
You, sir, what trade are you?

10 **COBBLER.** Truly, sir, in respect of a fine workman,[3] I am but, as you would say, a
cobbler.[4]

MURELLUS. But what trade art thou? Answer me directly.[5]

COBBLER. A trade, sir, that I hope I may use with a safe conscience, which is indeed,
sir, a mender of bad soles.[6]

15 **FLAVIUS.** What trade, thou knave? thou naughty knave, what trade?

COBBLER. Nay, I beseech you, sir, be not out with me; yet if you be out,[7] sir, I can
mend you.

MURELLUS. What mean'st thou by that? Mend me, thou saucy[8] fellow?

COBBLER. Why, sir, cobble you.

20 **FLAVIUS.** Thou art a cobbler, art thou?

COBBLER. Truly, sir, all that I live by is with the awl: I meddle with no tradesman's
matters, nor women's matters; but withal[9] I am indeed, sir, a surgeon to old shoes; when
they are in great danger, I recover[10] them. As proper men as ever trod upon neat's-leather[11]
have gone upon my handiwork.

25 **FLAVIUS.** But wherefore art not in thy shop today?
Why dost thou lead these men about the streets?

ACT 1, SCENE 1
1. **Being mechanical.** Being workmen
2. **sign/Of your profession.** Tools and uniforms
3. **in respect . . . workman.** Compared to a master craftsman
4. **a cobbler.** Pun meaning both "a bungler" and "a shoemaker"
5. **directly.** Plainly, without puns or double talk
6. **soles.** Pun on the word *souls*

7. **if you be out.** Punning phrase meaning both "if your shoes
are worn out" and "if you are put out, or angry"
8. **saucy.** Rude or impertinent
9. **withal.** Pun meaning both "yet" and "with an awl"
10. **recover.** Pun meaning both "to make better" and "to resole"
11. **neat's-leather.** Cowhide

**words
for
everyday
use**   ap • par • el (ə per′əl) *n.,* clothing. *The young girl grew so quickly that all her old <u>apparel</u> no longer fit.*

LITERARY TECHNIQUE

Scenes such as act 1, scene 1 are often referred to as *window scenes* in the study of Shakespeare because, like a window, such scenes allow some light to be shed upon the action of the play. Window scenes often involve minor characters or commoners who do not figure in the action of the rest of the play, and these characters typically comment on the social or political climate in which the play is situated. Shakespeare frequently uses window scenes in his histories, although similar scenes appear in his other works and serve as commentary on characters' actions and the play's events.

ADDITIONAL QUESTIONS AND ACTIVITIES

Ask students to discuss the language of the cobbler in this scene. What two levels of meaning are present in the cobbler's speech? What is significant about the cobbler's claiming to be "a mender of bad soles"? What does the play on words indicate might be the subject of this play?
Answers
The cobbler's speech is a pun that implies he is both a mender of the bottoms of worn shoes and a mender of bad souls. The cobbler implies by his speech that there are as many bad souls in Rome as there are worn shoes. The play on "bad souls" indicates that this play will have a serious theme and possibly be about the negative traits that exist in humans.

INTERNET RESOURCES

In scene 1, Murellus notes that the commoners are wearing their best apparel. Students may be interested in researching the apparel of ancient Rome. What did common people wear? What was a *tunica*, a *toga*, a *stola*, or a *palla*? A wealth of information is available on the Internet. One good site is the **Tulane University Theater Pages**, which contain information about costume, hairstyles, and jewelry from different time periods—illustrated with art and sculpture of the day. Take a look at the following address for the

INTERNET RESOURCES (CONT.)

costumes of ancient Rome:
http://ps.theatre.tulane.
edu/Period.Styles/
Costumes/text/Rome/
Roman.Intro.html.
Another site is the **Timeline of Costume History** at http://www.

costumes.org/pages/timelinepages/
ancientrome1.htm.
Other links can be found at
http://www.costumes.org/pages/ro
manlnx.htm. Students might visit
these sites and then imagine they
are costume designers for a

production of *Julius Cæsar.* They
could then describe, or draw and
label, costume and hairstyle designs
for each of the characters in act 1. If
students do not have access to the
Internet, they may find many
resources at the local library.

COBBLER.   Truly, sir, to wear out their shoes, to get myself into more work. But indeed, sir, we make holiday to see Cæsar, and to rejoice in his triumph.[12]

MURELLUS.   Wherefore rejoice? What conquest brings he home?
30 What tributaries[13] follow him to Rome,
To grace in captive bonds his chariot-wheels?
You blocks, you stones, you worse than senseless things!
O you hard hearts, you cruel men of Rome,
Knew you not Pompey?[14] Many a time and oft
35 Have you climb'd up to walls and battlements,
To tow'rs and windows, yea, to chimney-tops,
Your infants in your arms, and there have sate
The livelong day, with patient expectation,
To see great Pompey pass the streets of Rome;
40 And when you saw his chariot but appear,
Have you not made an universal shout,
That Tiber[15] trembled underneath her banks
To hear the replication of your sounds
Made in her concave shores?
45 And do you now put on your best attire?
And do you now cull out a holiday?
And do you now strew flowers in his way,
That comes in triumph over Pompey's blood?[16]
Be gone!
50 Run to your houses, fall upon your knees,
Pray to the gods to intermit the plague
That needs must light on this ingratitude.[17]

FLAVIUS.   Go, go, good countrymen, and for this fault
Assemble all the poor men of your sort;
55 Draw them to Tiber banks, and weep your tears
Into the channel, till the lowest stream
Do kiss the most exalted shores of all.

Exeunt[18] *all the* COMMONERS.

See whe'er their basest metal be not mov'd;[19]
They vanish tongue-tied in their guiltiness.

Why are the commoners in the streets?

Whom has Cæsar defeated?

---

12. **triumph.** Procession in the streets made by a returning or conquering hero
13. **tributaries.** Subdued or conquered persons who will pay tribute, or protection money, to Rome
14. **Pompey.** Roman general and statesman, former triumvir who ruled with Cæsar and Crassus, defeated by Cæsar in the Roman Civil War and murdered in Egypt
15. **Tiber.** River on the banks of which Rome was built
16. **Pompey's blood.** Cæsar has just returned from defeating the sons of Pompey in the province of Farther Spain.
17. **Pray . . . ingratitude.** Murellus warns that the disrespect shown for Pompey may anger the gods.
18. *Exeunt.* Exit by two or more persons
19. **See . . . mov'd.** Notice that their most basic selves are affected.

words for everyday use

rep • li • ca • tion (rep′lə kā′shən) *n.*, repetition, echo. *The parrot's exact replication of human words and sounds was startling.*

con • cave (kän kāv′) *adj.*, curved inward. *The light was focused on a single point by a concave lens.*

cull (kul) *vt.*, pick; select. *Jason's team had the advantage over Lou's because Jason had culled the better players from the group of boys.*

60   Go you down that way towards the Capitol,[20]
    This way will I. Disrobe the images,
    If you do find them deck'd with ceremonies.[21]

MURELLUS.   May we do so?
    You know it is the feast of Lupercal.[22]

65 **FLAVIUS.**   It is no matter, let no images
    Be hung with Cæsar's trophies.[23] I'll about,
    And drive away the vulgar[24] from the streets;
    So do you too, where you perceive them thick.
    These growing feathers pluck'd from Cæsar's wing
70   Will make him fly an ordinary pitch,[25]
    Who else would soar above the view of men,
    And keep us all in <u>servile</u> fearfulness.

                                                  Exeunt.

SCENE 2: PUBLIC PLACE IN ROME

Enter CÆSAR, ANTONY *for the course,*[1] CALPHURNIA, PORTIA, DECIUS, CICERO, BRUTUS, CASSIUS, CASCA, CITIZENS, *and a* SOOTHSAYER; *after them* MURELLUS *and* FLAVIUS.

CÆSAR.   Calphurnia!

CASCA.   Peace ho, Cæsar speaks.

CÆSAR.   Calphurnia!

CALPHURNIA.   Here, my lord.

CÆSAR.   Stand you directly in Antonio's[2] way
    When he doth run his course. Antonio!

5 **ANTONY.**   Cæsar, my lord?

CÆSAR.   Forget not in your speed, Antonio,
    To touch Calphurnia; for our elders say,
    The barren, touched in this holy chase,
    Shake off their sterile curse.[3]

ANTONY.   I shall remember:

---

20. **Capitol.** Temple of Jupiter on the Capitoline Hill in Rome
21. **Disrobe . . . ceremonies.** If you find that the statues of Cæsar have ceremonies, or ornaments, on them, take them off. Murellus is worried that Cæsar's supporters may have placed kingly garments or crowns on Cæsar's statues.
22. **the feast of Lupercal.** Fertility festival held on the fifteenth of February
23. **trophies.** Ornaments
24. **vulgar.** Common people

25. **pitch.** Height

ACT 1, SCENE 2
1. *for the course.* Dressed for a ceremonial race through the city held on the feast day known as the Lupercalia
2. **Antonio's.** Mark Antony's
3. **The barren . . . curse.** Cæsar's wife, Calphurnia, had borne no children, and so Cæsar was without an heir.

| words for everyday use | **ser • vile** (sʉr´vəl *or* sʉr´vīl) *adj.,* slavelike, submissive. *Because we were afraid of the tyrant, we developed a <u>servile</u> manner and would do whatever she asked when in her presence.* |

ADDITIONAL QUESTIONS AND ACTIVITIES

Ask students the following comprehension questions relating to what they just read in act 1, scene 1: Why does Murellus remind the people of Pompey? How do Murellus and Flavius feel about Cæsar's coming in triumph into the city? According to Flavius, why is Cæsar to be feared?

Answers

Murellus reminds the people of Pompey in order to show them how fickle they are behaving. He points out that while they now cheered for Cæsar, they once cheered for Pompey, whom Cæsar defeated. Murellus and Flavius feel that Cæsar is an upstart who is ruling unlawfully. Flavius says that Cæsar is to be feared because he is gaining popularity and may assume the role of king.

INTERNET RESOURCES

Students may be interested in researching an aspect of life in ancient Rome. A nearly overwhelming amount of information is available on the Internet. Students may enjoy a simple overview of Roman life such as that found at the **EduWeb site of Nettlesworth Primary School**, at http://atschool.eduweb.co.uk/ nettsch/time/romans.html. Although the site was developed for younger children, it does provide a peek into several aspects of Roman life and includes visuals that students may appreciate. Another entertaining site is **Daily Life in Ancient Rome** at http://members.aol.com/Donnclass/ Romelife.html. Because sites change and disappear so frequently, you might wish to conduct your own search on "life in ancient Rome." Also, you may want to explore some of the sites yourself and direct students to a select few, rather than have students delve into a potentially endless web search.

1. The soothsayer says, "Beware the ides of March."
2. Cassius notices that Brutus has not seemed as friendly toward him as he once did.

HISTORICAL NOTE

The ides was a specific date that occurred in the middle of each month of the Roman calendar. In March, May, July, and October, the ides fell on the fifteenth day of the month. In all other months, it occurred on the thirteenth day.

LITERARY TECHNIQUE

REPETITION. **Repetition** is the writer's conscious reuse of a sound, word, phrase, sentence, or other element. Shakespeare makes use of repetition in order to emphasize the words of the Soothsayer. "The ides of March" becomes a phrase that recurs throughout the first acts of the play. Shakespeare further emphasizes the Soothsayer's warning in act 1, scene 2, by having Cæsar single out the Soothsayer for a moment on stage and command him, "Speak once again." The repeated warning casts a pall over the action of the play and alerts the audience to the play's tragic nature.

CROSS-CURRICULAR ACTIVITIES

MATH. Students might be interested in reviewing Roman numerals. Remind them that the Romans used the letters I, V, X, L, C, D, and M to represent numbers, as shown below.
 I = 1   V = 5   X = 10   L = 50
 C = 100   D = 500   M = 1000
Letters are placed before or after each other to lower or increase their value.
 XV = 15   MXI = 1011
MCMLVII = 1957 MM = 2000
Ask students to write in Roman numerals the years the following events occurred. (They should refer to Reader's Resource on pages 242–245 for this information). They may then draw a rough time line including all the events.
Rome founded (traditionally held date)

---

10 When Cæsar says, "Do this," it is perform'd.

CÆSAR. Set on, and leave no ceremony out.

Flourish.[4]

SOOTHSAYER. Cæsar!

CÆSAR. Ha? who calls?

CASCA. Bid every noise be still; peace yet again!

15 **CÆSAR.** Who is it in the press[5] that calls on me?
I hear a tongue shriller than all the music
Cry "Cæsar!" Speak, Cæsar is turn'd to hear.

SOOTHSAYER. Beware the ides of March.[6]

CÆSAR.   What man is that?

BRUTUS. A soothsayer bids you beware the ides of March.

20 **CÆSAR.** Set him before me, let me see his face.

CASSIUS. Fellow, come from the <u>throng</u>, look upon Cæsar.

CÆSAR. What say'st thou to me now? Speak once again.

SOOTHSAYER. Beware the ides of March.

CÆSAR. He is a dreamer, let us leave him. Pass.

Sennet.[7] *Exeunt. Manent*[8] BRUTUS *and* CASSIUS.

25 **CASSIUS.** Will you go see the order of the course?[9]

BRUTUS. Not I.

CASSIUS. I pray you do.

BRUTUS. I am not gamesome;[10] I do lack some part
Of that quick spirit that is in Antony.

30 Let me not hinder, Cassius, your desires;
I'll leave you.

CASSIUS. Brutus, I do observe you now of late;
I have not from your eyes that gentleness
And show of love as I was wont to[11] have.

35 You bear too stubborn and too strange a hand
Over your friend that loves you.

> *What does the soothsayer say to Cæsar?*

> *What does Cassius notice about Brutus?*

---

4. *Flourish.* Sounding of trumpets
5. **press.** Press of bodies; crowd
6. **the ides of March.** The fifteenth of March
7. *Sennet.* Sounding of trumpets to mark, ceremoniously, an entrance or an exit
8. *Manent.* They remain
9. **see the order of the course.** Watch the progress of the race
10. **gamesome.** In the mood for games; merry
11. **was wont to.** Used to

> **words for everyday use**
> **throng** (thrôn) *n.*, crowd, gang; group. *We pushed our way through the <u>throng</u> to get to the front of the stage.*

CROSS-CURRICULAR ACTIVITIES (CONT.)

Roman Republic founded; Cæsar born, elected consul, conducted military campaigns, patricians voted to have him | lay down command; Cæsar crossed Rubicon (beginning a civil war), civil war ends, goes to Farther Spain to put down | Pompey's sons, is killed (44 BC); birth and death of Shakespeare; your birth.

BRUTUS.   Cassius,
Be not deceiv'd. If I have veil'd my look,
I turn the trouble of my <u>countenance</u>
Merely upon myself.[12] Vexed I am

40 Of late with passions of some difference,[13]
Conceptions only proper to myself,
Which give some soil, perhaps, to my behaviors;[14]
But let not therefore my good friends be griev'd
(Among which number, Cassius, be you one),

45 Nor <u>construe</u> any further my neglect,
Than that poor Brutus, with himself at war,
Forgets the shows of love to other men.

CASSIUS.   Then, Brutus, I have much mistook your passion,
By means whereof[15] this breast of mine hath buried

50 Thoughts of great value, worthy <u>cogitations</u>.
Tell me, good Brutus, can you see your face?

BRUTUS.   No, Cassius; for the eye sees not itself
But by reflection, by some other things.

CASSIUS.   'Tis just,[16]

55 And it is very much lamented, Brutus,
That you have no such mirrors as will turn
Your hidden worthiness into your eye,[17]
That you might see your shadow.[18] I have heard
Where many of the best respect in Rome

60 (Except immortal[19] Cæsar), speaking of Brutus
And groaning underneath this age's <u>yoke</u>,
Have wish'd that noble Brutus had his eyes.

BRUTUS.   Into what dangers would you lead me, Cassius,
That you would have me seek into myself

65 For that which is not in me?

CASSIUS.   Therefore,[20] good Brutus, be prepar'd to hear;
And since you know you cannot see yourself
So well as by reflection, I, your glass,
Will modestly discover to yourself

How does Brutus explain his changed behavior?

---

12. **If I . . . myself.** If I have seemed distant, it is because something in myself is troubling me.
13. **passions of some difference.** Conflicting feelings
14. **give some soil . . . behaviors.** Provide a growing place for my actions
15. **By means whereof.** As a consequence of which

16. **'Tis just.** That is so
17. **will turn . . . your eye.** Show you how worthy you are
18. **shadow.** Reflection
19. **immortal.** Cassius may be using this word as a contemptuous exaggeration.
20. **Therefore.** In answer to that

---

words for everyday use

coun • te • nance (koun'tə nəns) *n.*, face; looks. *Kim said she did not mind staying late, but her <u>countenance</u> revealed a different story.*

con • strue (kən strōō') *vt.*, analyze; interpret. *His wild and antic behavior caused onlookers to <u>construe</u> that he was searching for attention.*

cog • i • ta • tion (käj'ə tā'shən) *n.*, thought. *The hermit had his best <u>cogitations</u> about the meaning of life while sitting quietly by the brook, watching trout glide past.*

yoke (yōk) *n.*, anything that harnesses or reduces to servitude, like the wooden yoke used around the necks of cattle. *The oxen strained against their <u>yokes</u> to pull the heavy load.*

ACT 1, SCENE 2 / THE TRAGEDY OF JULIUS CÆSAR   **251**

ANSWER TO GUIDED READING QUESTION

1. Brutus says he is troubled by some conflicting feelings, and has not changed his feelings for Cassius.

ADDITIONAL QUESTIONS AND ACTIVITIES

Are Brutus and Cassius friends? How do you know?
Answers
Brutus and Cassius are good friends. Cassius is concerned about the change in Brutus's mood; he notices that "I have not from your eyes that gentleness / And show of love as I was wont to have." In turn, Brutus counts Cassius among his "good friends" and acknowledges Cassius's concern for him.

CROSS-CURRICULAR ACTIVITIES

APPLIED ARTS. In lines 55–70, Cassius attempts to appeal to Brutus's sense of vanity, and says he laments that Brutus has "no such mirrors" that will reveal his own greatness to him. Ask students whether they think mirrors existed in Roman times, or whether Shakespeare is employing an anachronism. When were mirrors invented? If the Romans had mirrors, how were they made? How were they different from the mirrors produced in Shakespeare's time and those produced today? Students should also be able to explain how mirrors work to reflect our own image back to us.

ADDITIONAL QUESTIONS AND ACTIVITIES

You might ask students to pay close attention to the contradictory feelings Brutus expresses about Cæsar in lines 79–89. Ask them why Brutus might be so concerned with the welfare of the Republic. Why might he, at the same time, feel loyalty and love for Cæsar? Are loyalty to Cæsar and loyalty to the Republic two irreconcilable values? Ask students to predict which sentiment will prove to have the stronger hold over Brutus.

70   That of yourself which you yet know not of.
     And be not jealous on me,[21] gentle Brutus:
     Were I a common laughter,[22] or did use
     To stale with ordinary oaths my love
     To every new protester;[23] if you know
75   That I do <u>fawn</u> on men and hug them hard,
     And after scandal[24] them; or if you know
     That I profess myself in banqueting
     To all the rout,[25] then hold me dangerous.

Flourish and shout.

BRUTUS.   What means this shouting? I do fear the people
     Choose Cæsar for their king.

What does Brutus suspect is the reason for the shouting?

80   **CASSIUS.**   Aye, do you fear it?
     Then must I think you would not have it so.

BRUTUS.   I would not, Cassius, yet I love him well.
     But wherefore do you hold me here so long?
     What is it that you would <u>impart</u> to me?
85   If it be aught toward the general good,[26]
     Set honor in one eye and death i' th' other,
     And I will look on both indifferently;[27]
     For let the gods so speed me[28] as I love
     The name of honor more than I fear death.

What does Brutus love more than he fears death?

90   **CASSIUS.**   I know that virtue to be in you, Brutus,
     As well as I do know your outward favor.[29]
     Well, honor is the subject of my story:
     I cannot tell what you and other men
     Think of this life; but, for my single self,
95   I had as lief[30] not be as live to be
     In awe of such a thing as I myself.[31]
     I was born free as Cæsar, so were you;
     We both have fed as well, and we can both
     Endure the winter's cold as well as he;

21. **jealous on me.** Suspicious of me
22. **a common laughter.** Someone whom people easily dismiss as laughable
23. **stale . . . protester.** Make my love seem less valuable and more ordinary by expressing it all the time
24. **scandal.** Slander
25. **profess . . . rout.** Declare my friendship by holding banquets for the rabble
26. **aught toward the general good.** Anything for the common welfare

27. **Set honor . . . indifferently.** Brutus is expressing his belief that he would willingly face death in order to preserve his honor and that he considers whatever serves the public welfare to be honorable.
28. **speed me.** Bring me good fortune
29. **outward favor.** Appearance
30. **as lief.** As soon
31. **of such a thing as I myself.** Of someone no greater than but rather just like me

words for everyday use	
fawn (fôn) *vi.,* show excessive friendliness; flatter. *While some parents love their children to excess, this couple* <u>fawned</u> *over their child, satisfying her every whim.*
im • part (im pärt´) *vt.,* get across; give. *The point the speaker* <u>imparted</u> *was that reform was needed in order to survive as a nation.*

100 For once, upon a raw and gusty day,
The troubled Tiber chafing[32] with her shores,
Cæsar said to me, "Dar'st thou, Cassius, now
Leap in with me into this angry flood,
And swim to yonder point?" Upon the word,
105 Accoutred[33] as I was, I plunged in,
And bade him follow; so indeed he did.
The torrent roar'd, and we did buffet it
With lusty sinews, throwing it aside
And stemming it with hearts of controversy;[34]
110 But ere we could arrive the point propos'd,
Cæsar cried, "Help me, Cassius, or I sink!"
I, as Aeneas,[35] our great ancestor,
Did from the flames of Troy upon his shoulder
The old Anchises[36] bear, so from the waves of Tiber
115 Did I the tired Cæsar. And this man
Is now become a god, and Cassius is
A wretched creature, and must bend his body
If Cæsar carelessly but nod on him.
He had a fever when he was in Spain,
120 And when the fit was on him, I did mark
How he did shake—'tis true, this god did shake;
His coward lips did from their color fly,[37]
And that same eye whose bend[38] doth awe the world
Did lose his[39] lustre; I did hear him groan;
125 Aye, and that tongue of his that bade the Romans
Mark him, and write his speeches in their books,
Alas, it cried, "Give me some drink, Titinius,"
As a sick girl. Ye gods, it doth amaze me
A man of such a feeble temper[40] should
130 So get the start of[41] the majestic world
And bear the palm[42] alone.

Shout. Flourish.

BRUTUS. Another general shout!

---

32. **chafing.** Contending, fighting
33. **Accoutred.** Dressed (in battle gear)
34. **stemming . . . controversy.** Moving through the water in aggressive competition
35. **Aeneas.** In later myth, the founder of Rome
36. **Troy . . . Anchises.** In classical myth, the city of Troy was destroyed by the Greeks, and Aeneas carried his father from the ruins of the city.

37. **coward lips . . . fly.** The color drained from his lips as a coward runs from the colors of a battle flag or banner.
38. **bend.** Glance
39. **his.** Its
40. **feeble temper.** Weak or sickly constitution
41. **get the start of.** Get ahead of, outdistance
42. **bear the palm.** Carry the prize of victory

words for everyday use

sin • ew (sin´yoo) *n.,* muscle. *I felt the effects of the heavy lifting in every joint and* sinew *of my body.*

wretch • ed (rech´id) *adj.,* miserable; deeply unhappy. *The baby birds that had fallen from their nest looked so* wretched *that we just had to try to help them.*

DESCRIPTION. Description is a type of writing that portrays a character, an object, or a scene. Descriptions make use of *sensory details*—words and phrases that describe how things look, sound, smell, taste, or feel. Effective descriptions contain precise nouns, verbs, adverbs, and adjectives. Have students pay close attention to Cassius's description of Cæsar in lines 110–128. Ask them to note what sensory details Cassius uses to portray Cæsar as weak and ineffectual. Ask them to whom Cassius compares himself in lines 112–115. In what way does this comparison affect the description of Cæsar? Ask students whether or not they find this description of Cæsar convincing.

Answers
Cassius describes Cæsar as "old Anchises," as "tired," as having a fever and shaking, as having "coward lips" and eyes that have lost their "lustre," and as a "sick girl." Cassius compares himself to Aeneas bearing the aged body of Anchises (Cæsar). This comparison of Cassius to a hero is so exaggerated that it throws doubt upon his description of Cæsar. Students may say that they find the description of Cæsar to be exaggerated.

1. Cassius says that Brutus's name is equal to Cæsar's.

• Ask students to state what view of fate Cassius expresses in lines 139–141. Does he believe that humans are the masters of their own fates, or does he believe that the destiny of humans is written in the stars?
• In a small group, discuss Cassius's attitude toward Cæsar and toward power. You might also consult a dictionary for definitions of the words envy and jealousy. Which word better describes Cassius's attitude toward Cæsar? Why?

Answers
Cassius believes that humans are "at some time" masters of their fates. Students might suggest that Cassius is envious of the power that Cæsar wields.

CROSS-CURRICULAR ACTIVITIES

• Ask students to research the ancient world's conception of fate. Students may wish to read the works of Greek playwrights such as Sophocles and Æschylus, both of whom were concerned with the balance between humans' destiny and their free will. Students can research depictions of fate and agents of fate, such as the Furies, in Greek and Roman mythology.
• Students can hold a debate on the issue of how much free will humans exert over their destinies. Students can role play as supporters and opponents of Cassius's view.

I do believe that these applauses are
For some new honors that are heap'd on Cæsar.

135 **CASSIUS.**   Why, man, he doth bestride the narrow world
Like a Colossus,[43] and we petty men
Walk under his huge legs, and peep about
To find ourselves dishonorable graves.
Men at some time are masters of their fates;
140 The fault, dear Brutus, is not in our stars,[44]
But in ourselves, that we are underlings.
Brutus and Cæsar: what should be in that "Cæsar"?
Why should that name be sounded more than yours?
Write them together, yours is as fair a name;
145 Sound them, it doth become[45] the mouth as well;
Weigh them, it is as heavy; conjure[46] with 'em,
"Brutus" will start a spirit[47] as soon as "Cæsar."
Now in the names of all the gods at once,
Upon what meat doth this our Cæsar feed
150 That he is grown so great? Age, thou art sham'd!
Rome, thou hast lost the breed of noble bloods!
When went there by an age since the great flood
But it was fam'd with more than with one man?[48]
When could they say, till now, that talk'd of Rome,
155 That her wide walks encompass'd but one man?
Now is it Rome indeed and room enough,
When there is in it but one only man.[49]
O! you and I have heard our fathers say
There was a Brutus[50] once that would have brook'd
160 Th' eternal devil to keep his state in Rome
As easily as a king.[51]

BRUTUS.   That you do love me, I am nothing jealous;[52]
What you would work me to, I have some aim.[53]
How I have thought of this, and of these times,

Whose name is equal to Cæsar's, according to Cassius?

---

43. **Colossus.** Gigantic statue, like that of the Colossus of Rhodes, under whose legs ships sailed
44. **stars.** Reference to the belief that human destiny is governed by the stars
45. **become.** Suit
46. **conjure.** Do magic, call up spirits
47. **start a spirit.** Call up a ghost, inspire people
48. **But it was . . . man.** Cassius is saying that every age has had more than one famous person.
49. **Now is it Rome . . . man.** Cassius puns on the words *Rome*

and *room*, calling attention to the fact that in Rome there is room enough for only one great man, Cæsar.
50. **Brutus.** Lucius Junius Brutus, who led the defeat of the Etruscan kings in ancient Rome and then helped to establish the republic
51. **that would have brook'd . . . king.** Who would have tolerated the devil himself to live in Rome rather than a king
52. **am nothing jealous.** Do not doubt
53. **aim.** Understanding

words for everyday use   **un • der • ling** (un′dər liŋ) *n.*, person of low status; servant. *The leader of the group of bandits never did any of the dirty work himself, but he would have one of his* underlings *perform the deed.*

INTERNET RESOURCES

In line 136, Cassius compares Cæsar to a "Colossus," an enormous statue like the Colossus of Rhodes. Inform students that the Colossus of Rhodes was one of the seven wonders of the ancient world, and ask them to research the great statue. Who built it, in whose honor was it built, what materials were used, how tall was it, where was it located, and is it still standing today? They should also find out what the other six wonders were, and what technology and materials were needed to build each of these wonders. Encourage them to find this information at the Seven Wonders of the World, an award-winning website located at http://ce.eng.usf.edu/pharos/wonders/. As a follow-up, ask students to comment on what they think motivates people to create "wonders."

165 I shall recount hereafter. For this present,
     I would not (so with love I might entreat you)
     Be any further mov'd. What you have said
     I will consider; what you have to say
     I will with patience hear, and find a time
170 Both meet to hear and answer such high things.
     Till then, my noble friend, chew upon this:
     Brutus had rather be a villager
     Than to repute himself a son of Rome
     Under these hard conditions as this time
175 Is like to lay upon us.

     CASSIUS. I am glad that my weak words
     Have struck but thus much show of fire from Brutus.

     Enter CÆSAR and his TRAIN.[54]

     BRUTUS. The games are done, and Cæsar is returning.

     CASSIUS. As they pass by, pluck Casca by the sleeve,
180 And he will (after his sour fashion) tell you
     What hath proceeded worthy note today.

     BRUTUS. I will do so. But look you, Cassius,
     The angry spot doth glow on Cæsar's brow,
     And all the rest look like a chidden train:
185 Calphurnia's cheek is pale, and Cicero
     Looks with such ferret[55] and such fiery eyes
     As we have seen him in the Capitol,
     Being cross'd in conference[56] by some senators.

     CASSIUS. Casca will tell us what the matter is.

190 CÆSAR. Antonio!

     ANTONY. Cæsar?

     CÆSAR. Let me have men about me that are fat,
     Sleek-headed men and such as sleep a-nights.
     Yond Cassius has a lean and hungry look,
195 He thinks too much; such men are dangerous.

     ANTONY. Fear him not, Cæsar, he's not dangerous,
     He is a noble Roman, and well given.[57]

     CÆSAR. Would he were fatter! but I fear him not.
     Yet if my name[58] were liable to fear,
200 I do not know the man I should avoid
     So soon as that spare Cassius. He reads much,
     He is a great observer, and he looks

---

54. **TRAIN.** Companions, attendants
55. **ferret.** Like a ferret or weasel, known for quickness and evasiveness

56. **cross'd in conference.** Engaged in debate
57. **well given.** Well disposed (toward Cæsar)
58. **my name.** A person with my fame and power

> *What does Brutus agree to do in response to Cassius's remarks?*

> *How does Cassius look to Caesar?*

ANSWERS TO GUIDED READING QUESTIONS

1. Brutus promises to think about what Cassius has said and to answer him when the time is appropriate.
2. Cæsar says "Cassius has a lean and hungry look."

ADDITIONAL QUESTIONS AND ACTIVITIES

Cæsar is wary of Cassius's "lean and hungry look" and says, "He thinks too much; such men are dangerous." Ask students whether Cæsar is correct to fear Cassius.

You might also wish to encourage a discussion on the traits Cæsar finds objectionable in Cassius, namely that he thinks, reads, observes, has a self-mocking smile, and does not divert himself with plays or music. Ask students whether these are objectionable traits. Why might Cæsar find someone with these traits to be dangerous? Do Cæsar's fears imply that Cæsar may be doing something a well-read, serious-minded man might find inappropriate?

1. The crown was offered to Cæsar three times, and each time he rejected it. Casca believes that he rejected it less strongly each time.
2. Casca believes that Cæsar actually wanted to accept the crown.

HISTORICAL NOTE

Since ancient times, the number three has had special meaning. An Elizabethan audience probably would have recognized the symbolism of the crown being offered to Cæsar three times. Greek philosopher Pythagoras declared three the perfect number because it symbolizes the "beginning, middle, and end." Likewise, both Greek and Roman mythology are filled with instances of the number three: the three Fates, the three gods (Zeus, Poseidon, and Hades) who rule the world, and so on.

The numbers seven and thirteen have also had significance in Western culture: seven first as a "magical" number and then attributed as God's number in the Judeo-Christian Bible. The number thirteen has been considered symbolic of bad luck.

Ask students what the numbers three, seven, and thirteen have in common, in mathematical terms.
Answer
All three are prime numbers, meaning they are only divisible by themselves and one.

Quite through the deeds of men.[59] He loves no plays,
As thou dost, Antony; he hears no music;
205 Seldom he smiles, and smiles in such a sort
As if he mock'd himself, and scorn'd his spirit
That could be mov'd to smile at anything.
Such men as he be never at heart's ease
Whiles they behold a greater than themselves,
210 And therefore are they very dangerous.
I rather tell thee what is to be fear'd
Than what I fear; for always I am Cæsar.
Come on my right hand, for this ear is deaf,
And tell me truly what thou think'st of him.

Sennet. Exeunt CÆSAR *and his* TRAIN. CASCA *stays.*

215 **CASCA.**   You pull'd me by the cloak, would you speak with me?

BRUTUS.   Aye, Casca, tell us what hath chanc'd today
That Cæsar looks so sad.[60]

CASCA.   Why, you were with him, were you not?

BRUTUS.   I should not then ask Casca what had chanc'd.

220 **CASCA.**   Why, there was a crown offer'd him; and being offer'd him, he put it by with the back of his hand thus, and then the people fell a-shouting.

BRUTUS.   What was the second noise for?

CASCA.   Why, for that too.

CASSIUS.   They shouted thrice;[61] what was the last cry for?

225 **CASCA.**   Why, for that too.

BRUTUS.   Was the crown offer'd him thrice?

CASCA.   Aye, marry,[62] was't,[63] and he put it by thrice, every time gentler than other; and at every putting-by mine honest neighbors shouted.

What was offered to Cæsar three times? How did he react?

CASSIUS.   Who offer'd him the crown?

230 **CASCA.**   Why, Antony.

BRUTUS.   Tell us the manner of it, gentle Casca.

CASCA.   I can as well be hang'd as tell the manner of it: it was mere foolery, I did not mark it. I saw Mark Antony offer him a crown—yet 'twas not a crown neither, 'twas one of these coronets[64]—and as I told you, he put it by once; but for
235 all that, to my thinking, he would fain[65] have had it. Then he offer'd it to him again; then he put it by again; but, to my thinking, he was very loath[66] to lay his fingers off it. And then he offered it the third time; he put it the third

What did Casca think Cæsar wanted to do?

59. **looks/Quite through . . . men.** Sees the motivations behind men's actions
60. **sad.** Serious, troubled
61. **thrice.** Three times
62. **marry.** Oath meaning "truly" or "indeed"
63. **was't.** It was
64. **coronets.** Little crowns
65. **fain.** Willingly, gladly
66. **loath.** Unwilling

time by; and still[67] as he refus'd it, the rabblement howted,[68] and clapp'd their
chopp'd[69] hands, and threw up their sweaty nightcaps, and utter'd such a deal of
stinking breath because Cæsar refus'd the crown, that it
240 had, almost, chok'd Cæsar, for he swounded,[70] and fell down at it; and for mine own
part, I durst[71] not laugh, for fear of opening my lips and receiving the bad air.[72]

    CASSIUS.   But soft[73] I pray you; what, did Cæsar swound?

    CASCA.   He fell down in the market-place, and foam'd at mouth, and was
speechless.

What did Cæsar do in the marketplace?

245   BRUTUS.   'Tis very like, he hath the falling sickness.[74]

    CASSIUS.   No, Cæsar hath it not; but you, and I,
And honest Casca, we have the falling sickness.[75]

    CASCA.   I know not what you mean by that, but I am sure Cæsar fell down. If the
tag-rag people did not clap him and hiss him, according as he pleas'd and displeas'd
250 them, as they use to do the players in the theater,[76] I am no true man.

    BRUTUS.   What said he when he came unto himself?

    CASCA.   Marry, before he fell down, when he perceiv'd the common herd was glad he
refus'd the crown, he pluck'd me ope his doublet,[77] and offered them his throat to cut.
And[78] I had been a man of any occupation,[79] if I would not have taken him at a word,[80] I
255 would I might go to hell among the rogues. And so he fell. When he came to himself
again, he said, if he had done or said anything amiss, he desir'd their worships to think it
was his infirmity. Three or four wenches, where I stood, cried, "Alas, good soul!" and
forgave him with all their hearts. But there's no heed to be taken of them; if Cæsar had
stabb'd their mothers, they would have done no less.

260   BRUTUS.   And after that, he came thus sad away?

    CASCA.   Aye.

    CASSIUS.   Did Cicero say anything?

    CASCA.   Aye, he spoke Greek.

    CASSIUS.   To what effect?

265   CASCA.   Nay, and I tell you that, I'll ne'er look you i' th' face again. But those that
understood him smil'd at one another, and shook their heads; but, for mine own part, it
was Greek to me.[81] I could tell you more news too. Murellus and Flavius, for pulling
scarfs off Cæsar's images, are put to silence.[82] Fare you well. There was more foolery yet,
if I could remember it.

---

67. **still.** Each time
68. **howted.** Howled
69. **chopp'd.** Chapped or rough from working
70. **swounded.** Swooned, fainted
71. **durst.** Dared
72. **receiving the bad air.** Breathing or smelling the bad odor
73. **soft.** Pause, hold on
74. **falling sickness.** Epilepsy
75. **No . . . sickness.** Cassius is implying that while Cæsar's power increases, that of others, such as Brutus, Casca, and he, declines.

76. **If the tag-rag . . . theater.** Casca implies that a noble Roman, unlike Cæsar, should be above the approval or disapproval of commoners.
77. **pluck'd me ope his doublet.** Opened his jacket
78. **And.** If
79. **a man of any occupation.** Member of the working classes or a man of action
80. **if I . . . word.** Had I not taken him literally (and cut his throat)
81. **Greek to me.** Unintelligible to me
82. **put to silence.** Deprived of their political posts or executed

1. Cæsar had a seizure—he "fell down in the market-place and foam'd at the mouth, and was speechless."

ADDITIONAL QUESTIONS AND ACTIVITIES

Point out to students that the line "it was Greek to me" (spoken by Casca, lines 266–267) is a common expression even today. Have they ever heard the expression "It's Greek to me" to mean, "it makes no sense to me"? Inform students that while most Romans learned Greek in school, their first language was Latin. Latin, in turn, borrowed a lot from ancient Greek. Ask students to research the Latin language. If possible, they should locate a table showing the way the alphabet was written. What did the Latin alphabet look like? Where was that alphabet derived from?

Inform students that Latin is no longer in widespread use, and for that reason is considered a "dead language." However, it is still the official language of Vatican City, the home of the Pope, and of the Roman Catholic Church. Although Latin is rarely taught in American schools these days, it is helpful to become familiar with Latin roots because English vocabulary is in large part based on ancient Greek and Latin. Share with students the table of Greek and Latin roots at the bottom of this page of the teacher's edition. Then, ask them to name other English words with the Latin prefixes *mal–*, *sup–*, *circum–*, *com–*, *trans–*, *uni–*, and *multi–*.

FROM GREEK	FROM LATIN	MEANING OF GREEK AND LATIN ROOTS
dys • trophy	mal • nutrition	"bad-nourishment"
hypo • thesis	sup • position	"under-put"
peri • phrasis	circum • locution	"around-say"
sym • pathy	com • passion	"with-feel"
dia • phanous	trans • parent	"through-show"
mono • morphic	uni • form	"one-form"
poly • glottal	multi • lingual	"many-tongued"

1. Cæsar loves Brutus but dislikes
Cassius.

LITERARY TECHNIQUE

Soliloquy. A **soliloquy** is a
speech delivered by a lone
character that reveals the speaker's
thoughts and feelings. Inform
students that soliloquies are an
essential part of Shakespeare's plays
and, when coming across a
soliloquy, they should be observant
of the way in which the character
speaking is further developed.

In lines 289–303, Cassius delivers
a soliloquy that reveals his thoughts
and feelings about Brutus. Ask
students what Cassius says he would
do if he were in Brutus's position.
What is revealed about Cassius's
motivation for plotting against
Cæsar?

Answers
Cassius says that if he were in
Brutus's position, he would not be
persuaded to turn against Cæsar.
Cassius reveals that he is
motivated by jealousy of Cæsar and a desire to
seek revenge for Cæsar's dislike of
him ("Cæsar doth bear me hard").

ADDITIONAL QUESTIONS
AND ACTIVITIES

Ask students the following comprehension
questions relating to what they
just read in act 1, scene 2:
What does Cassius attempt to
persuade Brutus to do? How does
Brutus respond? What fear do Brutus,
Cassius, and Casca share? Why are
they worried about Cæsar's reaction to
Mark Antony's offering him a crown in
front of the crowd of common people?
What attitude does Casca have toward
the common people of Rome?
Answers
Cassius attempts to persuade Brutus
to turn against Cæsar. Brutus
responds by saying he will think
about the matter. Brutus, Cassius,
and Casca fear that Cæsar will
accept the crown and become king
of Rome. They are worried about
Cæsar's reaction because it seemed
that Cæsar really desired to accept
the crown and was only refusing it to
encourage the people to believe him
modest and unambitious and thus to
support his becoming a monarch.

---

270   **Cassius.**   Will you sup with me tonight, Casca?

     Casca.   No, I am promis'd forth.[83]

     Cassius.   Will you dine with me tomorrow?

     Casca.   Aye, if I be alive, and your mind hold, and your dinner worth the eating.

     Cassius.   Good, I will expect you.

275   **Casca.**   Do so. Farewell both.   *Exit.*

     Brutus.   What a blunt fellow is this grown to be!
He was quick mettle[84] when he went to school.

     Cassius.   So is he now in execution
Of any bold or noble enterprise,
280   However he puts on this tardy form.[85]
This rudeness is a sauce to his good wit,
Which gives men stomach to digest his words
With better appetite.[86]

     Brutus.   And so it is. For this time I will leave you;
285   Tomorrow, if you please to speak with me,
I will come home to you; or, if you will,
Come home to me, and I will wait for you.

     Cassius.   I will do so; till then, think of the world.[87]

                             Exit Brutus.

     Well, Brutus, thou art noble; yet I see
290   Thy honorable mettle may be wrought
From that it is dispos'd;[88] therefore it is meet
That noble minds keep ever with their likes;
For who so firm that cannot be seduc'd?
Cæsar doth bear me hard,[89] but he loves Brutus.
295   If I were Brutus now and he were Cassius,
He should not humor me.[90] I will this night,
In several hands,[91] in at his windows throw,
As if they came from several citizens,
Writings, all tending to[92] the great opinion
300   That Rome holds of his name; wherein obscurely
Cæsar's ambition shall be glanced at.

*How does Cæsar feel
about Brutus? How
does he feel about
Cassius?*

---

83. **I am promis'd forth.** I have a previous engagement.
84. **quick mettle.** A lively spirit
85. **tardy form.** Show of caution and deliberation
86. **rudeness . . . appetite.** As a sauce makes a meal easier to
digest, so does Casca's bluntness make it easier for people to
accept the intelligence, or wit, of his words.

87. **think of the world.** Think about the state of the world today.
88. **be wrought . . . dispos'd.** Be turned from its predispositions
89. **bear me hard.** Dislike me
90. **humor me.** Persuade me
91. **in several hands.** In different handwritings
92. **tending to.** Dealing with

ADDITIONAL QUESTIONS AND ACTIVITIES (CONT.)

Casca seems to view the common people of Rome as
blind followers, who are easily taken in by Cæsar's
charisma and would adore him even if he stabbed
their mothers.

And after this let Cæsar seat him sure,[93]
For we will shake him, or worse days endure.

Exit.

SCENE 3: STREET IN ROME

Thunder and lightning. Enter from opposite sides CASCA *with his sword drawn and* CICERO.

CICERO.   Good even,[1] Casca; brought you Cæsar home?
Why are you breathless, and why stare you so?

CASCA.   Are not you mov'd, when all the sway of earth[2]
Shakes like a thing unfirm? O Cicero,
5   I have seen tempests when the scolding winds
Have riv'd[3] the knotty oaks, and I have seen
Th' ambitious ocean swell, and rage, and foam,
To be exalted with[4] the threat'ning clouds;
But never till tonight, never till now,
10   Did I go through a tempest dropping fire.
Either there is a civil strife in heaven,
Or else the world, too saucy[5] with the gods,
Incenses them to send destruction.

CICERO.   Why, saw you anything more wonderful?

15   **CASCA.**   A common slave—you know him well by sight—
Held up his left hand which did flame and burn
Like twenty torches join'd; and yet his hand,
Not sensible of fire, remain'd unscorch'd.
Besides—I ha' not since put up my sword—
20   Against[6] the Capitol I met a lion,
Who glaz'd[7] upon me, and went surly by,
Without annoying me. And there were drawn
Upon a heap[8] a hundred ghastly women,[9]
Transformed with their fear, who swore they saw
25   Men, all in fire, walk up and down the streets.
And yesterday the bird of night[10] did sit

> What sort of weather has Casca encountered?

---

93. **seat him sure.** Make himself secure

ACT 1, SCENE 3
1. **even.** Evening
2. **all the sway of earth.** Whole pattern or rule of things
3. **riv'd.** Split open
4. **exalted with.** Raised up to

5. **saucy.** Rude or impertinent
6. **Against.** Near
7. **glaz'd.** Gazed
8. **drawn / Upon a heap.** Gathered together in a huddle
9. **ghastly women.** Women white like ghosts
10. **bird of night.** Owl

words for everyday use	en • dure (en door´) *vt.,* live through. *Despite undergoing many hardships such as natural disaster, failed crops, and famine, the pioneers of the American West endured.* tem • pest (tem´pist) *n.,* storm. *King Lear was sent out by his ungrateful children into a tempest, and he raged outside in the lightning, wind, and rain.* sur • ly (sur´lē) *adj.,* bad-tempered; rude; hostile. *No one found it pleasant to be around Steve in the morning because his behavior was so surly.*

LITERARY TECHNIQUE

MOTIF. A motif is any element that recurs in one or more works of literature or art. The motif of natural disorder runs throughout much of Shakespeare's work and usually signifies the disorder of the political state. Students should be informed that when reading Shakespeare, they should pay close attention to storms or any other disruption in the natural order as an indication of something being drastically wrong with the world of men.

Quotables

"And through this distemperature, we see / The seasons alter: hoary-headed frosts / Fall in the fresh lap of the crimson rose, / And on old Hiems' thin and icy crown / An odorous chaplet of sweet summer buds / Is, as in mockery, set."

—William Shakespeare,
A Midsummer Night's Dream

"Blow, winds, and crack your cheeks! rage, blow! / You cataracts and hurricanoes, spout / Till you have drench'd our steeples, drown'd the cocks! / You sulph'rous and thought-executing fires, / Vaunt-couriers of oak-cleaving thunderbolts, / Singe my white head! And thou, all-shaking thunder, / Strike flat the thick rotundity o' th' world! / Crack nature's moulds, all germains spill at once / That makes ingrateful man!"

—William Shakespeare,
The Tragedy of King Lear

Even at noon-day upon the market-place,
Howting[11] and shrieking. When these <u>prodigies</u>
Do so <u>conjointly</u> meet, let not men say,

30   "These are their reasons, they are natural";
For I believe they are <u>portentous</u> things
Unto the climate that they point upon.[12]

CICERO.   Indeed, it is a strange-disposed[13] time;
But men may construe things after their fashion

35   Clean from the purpose of the things themselves.[14]
Comes Cæsar to the Capitol tomorrow?

CASCA.   He doth; for he did bid Antonio
Send word to you he would be there tomorrow.

CICERO.   Good night then, Casca; this disturbed sky
Is not to walk in.[15]

40   **CASCA.**   Farewell, Cicero.

                    Exit CICERO.

Enter CASSIUS.

CASSIUS.   Who's there?

CASCA.   A Roman.

CASSIUS.   Casca, by your voice.

CASCA.   Your ear is good. Cassius, what night is this!

CASSIUS.   A very pleasing night to honest men.

CASCA.   Who ever knew the heavens menace so?

45   **CASSIUS.**   Those that have known the earth so full of faults.
For my part, I have walk'd about the streets,
Submitting me unto the perilous night;
And thus unbraced,[16] Casca, as you see,
Have bar'd my bosom to the thunder-stone;[17]

50   And when the cross[18] blue lightning seem'd to open
The breast of heaven, I did present myself
Even in the aim and very flash of it.

CASCA.   But wherefore[19] did you so much tempt the heavens?

---

11. **Howting.** Hooting
12. **they are . . . upon.** They are ominous signs of things to come in the climate, or region, in which they occur.
13. **strange-disposed.** Unusual, abnormal
14. **men may . . . themselves.** Men are capable of misunderstanding the actual meaning of things.

15. **in.** Under
16. **unbraced.** With jacket open
17. **thunder-stone.** Lightning, thunderbolt
18. **cross.** Jagged or zigzagged
19. **wherefore.** Why

---

words for everyday use

pro • di • gy (präd′ə jē) *n.,* exceptional person or thing. *Mozart was considered by many to be a child <u>prodigy</u> as his musical ability was displayed at such an early age.*

con • joint • ly (kən joint ′lē) *adv.,* in a joined-together manner. *He could handle many different projects <u>conjointly</u>.*

por • ten • tous (pôr ten′təs) *adj.,* ominous; foreboding; predictive. *The words of the wise man proved <u>portentous</u> because everything happened just as he had foreseen.*

It is the part[20] of men to fear and tremble

55　When the most mighty gods by tokens send
　　Such dreadful heralds to astonish us.

What does Casca believe is the cause of the storm?

　　Cassius.　You are dull, Casca; and those sparks of life
　　That should be in a Roman you do want,[21]
　　Or else you use not. You look pale, and gaze,
60　And put on fear, and cast yourself in wonder,
　　To see the strange impatience of the heavens;
　　But if you would consider the true cause
　　Why all these fires, why all these gliding ghosts,
　　Why birds and beasts from quality and kind,[22]
65　Why old men, fools, and children calculate,[23]
　　Why all these things change from their ordinance,[24]
　　Their natures, and preformed faculties,[25]
　　To monstrous quality—why, you shall find
　　That heaven hath <u>infus'd</u> them with these spirits,
70　To make them instruments of fear and warning
　　Unto some monstrous state.[26]
　　Now could I, Casca, name to thee a man
　　Most like this dreadful night,
　　That thunders, lightens, opens graves, and roars
75　As doth the lion in the Capitol—
　　A man no mightier than thyself, or me,
　　In personal action, yet prodigious[27] grown,
　　And fearful, as these strange eruptions are.

　　Casca.　'Tis Cæsar that you mean; is it not, Cassius?

80　**Cassius.**　Let it be who it is; for Romans now
　　Have thews[28] and limbs like to their ancestors;
　　But woe the while,[29] our fathers' minds are dead,
　　And we are govern'd with our mothers' spirits;
　　Our yoke and sufferance[30] show us womanish.

85　**Casca.**　Indeed, they say, the senators tomorrow
　　Mean to establish Cæsar as a king;

---

20. **part.** Role
21. **want.** Lack
22. **from quality and kind.** Not displaying their normal characteristics and natures
23. **calculate.** Prophesy
24. **ordinance.** Usual ways of being
25. **preformed faculties.** Innate or inborn qualities

26. **Unto some monstrous state.** About the coming of some terrible state of affairs
27. **prodigious.** Ominous and enormous
28. **thews.** Sinews or muscles
29. **woe the while.** Pity the times
30. **yoke and sufferance.** Servitude and the acceptance of it

words for everyday use　in • fuse (in fyōōz´) *vt.*, inspire; fill. *Just when she thought she could work no longer, she was <u>infused</u> with a new burst of energy.*

ANSWER TO GUIDED READING QUESTION

1. Casca believes the gods have sent the storm to frighten the people of Rome.

ADDITIONAL QUESTIONS AND ACTIVITIES

Ask students how Cassius interprets the disorder of the natural world. Do students feel that Cassius's interpretation of the chaos in Rome is correct?
Answers
Responses will vary. Cassius believes the disorder in nature is a result of Cæsar's attempt to gain absolute political power. Students may either agree or disagree with Cassius's interpretation but should support their positions with evidence from the text.

HISTORICAL NOTE

Remind students that the people who lived in Shakespeare's day are called Elizabethans, after their great monarch Queen Elizabeth I. The Elizabethans were extremely superstitious. They believed in astrology, magic, witchcraft, good and bad omens, ghosts, fortune-telling, and alchemy. Belief in the supernatural was common, and Queen Elizabeth's successor, James I, wrote a popular work on witchcraft, the *Daemonologie,* in 1599. Ask students the following questions: Do you share any of the beliefs of the Elizabethans? How would you feel if, like Cicero, Cassius, Casca, and others in this act, you had seen strange apparitions and heard fearful prophecies? How did Shakespeare's descriptions of the abnormal events of the times affect you? How do you think these descriptions might have affected an Elizabethan audience?

1. Cassius says that Cæsar could take power only because Romans have been passive and allowed it to happen.
2. Casca vows that if Cassius leads a group to redress, or make amends for, the excessive power Cæsar has gained, he will join and go to whatever lengths the group chooses.

LITERARY TECHNIQUE

METAPHOR. A **metaphor** is a figure of speech in which one thing is spoken or written about as if it were another. This figure of speech invites the reader to make a comparison betweeen the two things. The two "things" involved are the writer's actual subject, the *tenor* of the metaphor, and another thing to which the subject is likened, the *vehicle* of the metaphor. In lines 104–106, Cassius declares, "Poor man, I know that [Cæsar] would not be a wolf / But that he sees the Romans are but sheep; / He were no lion, were not Romans hinds." To what two things does Cassius compare Cæsar? How are these things alike? To what two things does he compare Romans? How are these things alike? What is the effect of these comparisons?
Answers
Cassius compares Cæsar to a wolf and a lion; he compares Romans to sheep and hinds, or deer. Like a wolf and a lion, Cæsar is powerful and to be feared. Like the Romans, sheep and deer are timid creatures; they are preyed upon by the wolf and the lion. The effect of the comparisons is to point out Cassius's belief that Cæsar is only assuming the powerful role of king because he senses that the Romans will not defy him.

ADDITIONAL QUESTIONS AND ACTIVITIES

Point out to students that the words "tyrant" and "tyranny," in lines 92 and 100 respectively, come from the Latin *tyrannus*, which came from the Greek *tyrannos*, for absolute ruler. Ask them to look up the following additional words from this page in a dictionary and name the Latin root for each: deliver, retentive, dismiss, cancel, captivity, illuminate.

And he shall wear his crown by sea and land,
In every place, save here in Italy.

CASSIUS. I know where I will wear this dagger then;
90   Cassius from bondage will deliver Cassius.[31]
Therein, ye gods, you make the weak most strong;
Therein, ye gods, you tyrants do defeat;
Nor stony tower, nor walls of beaten brass,
Nor airless dungeon, nor strong links of iron,
95   Can be retentive to the strength of spirit;[32]
But life, being weary of these worldly bars,
Never lacks power to dismiss itself.
If I know this, know all the world besides,
That part of tyranny that I do bear
I can shake off at pleasure.   *Thunder still.*

100 **CASCA.**   So can I;
So every bondman[33] in his own hand bears
The power to cancel his captivity.

CASSIUS. And why should Cæsar be a tyrant then?
Poor man, I know he would not be a wolf
105   But that he sees the Romans are but sheep;
He were no lion, were not Romans hinds.[34]
Those that with haste will make a mighty fire
Begin it with weak straws. What trash is Rome?
What rubbish and what offal? when it serves
110   For the base matter to illuminate
So vile a thing as Cæsar! But, O grief,
Where hast thou led me? I, perhaps, speak this
Before a willing bondman; then I know
My answer must be made. But I am arm'd,
115   And dangers are to me indifferent.[35]

CASCA. You speak to Casca, and to such a man
That is no fleering[36] tell-tale. Hold, my hand.
Be factious[37] for redress of all these griefs,
And I will set this foot of mine as far
As who goes farthest.

120 **CASSIUS.**   There's a bargain made.
Now know you, Casca, I have mov'd already
Some certain of the noblest-minded Romans
To undergo with me an enterprise

Why has Cæsar been able to take power, according to Cassius?

What does Casca vow to Cassius?

---

31. **will deliver Cassius.** That is, by killing himself
32. **Nor stony . . . spirit.** This idea was later expressed by poet Richard Lovelace: "Stone walls do not a prison make/Nor iron bars a cage," because the spirit cannot be contained.
33. **bondman.** Serf or slave
34. **hinds.** Deer
35. **indifferent.** Of little consequence
36. **fleering.** Flattering
37. **factious.** Willing to start a faction, or political organization

---

ADDITIONAL QUESTIONS AND ACTIVITIES (CONT.)

Answers
deliver: fr. L *de–* + *liberare* to liberate; **retentive:** fr. L *retentus*, pp. of *retinere*; **dismiss:** modif. of L *dimissus*, pp. of *dis–* apart + *mittere* to send; **cancel:** fr. L, to make like a lattice, fr. *cancelli* (pl.) dim. of *cancer* lattice); **captivity:** fr. L *captivus*; **illuminate:** fr. L *illuminatus*, pp. of *illuminare*, fr. *in–* + *luminare* to light up.

"Death is better, a milder fate than tyranny."

—Aeschylus (525–456 BC)
Greek philosopher

Of honorable-dangerous consequence;
125 And I do know, by this they stay[38] for me
     In Pompey's Porch;[39] for now, this fearful night,
     There is no stir or walking in the streets;
     And the complexion of the element[40]
     In favor's[41] like the work we have in hand,
130 Most bloody, fiery, and most terrible.

     Enter CINNA.

     CASCA. Stand close[42] a while, for here comes one in haste.

     CASSIUS. 'Tis Cinna, I do know him by his gait,
     He is a friend. Cinna, where haste you so?

     CINNA. To find out you. Who's that? Metellus Cimber?

135 **CASSIUS.** No, it is Casca, one incorporate[43]
     To our attempts. Am I not stay'd for, Cinna?

     CINNA. I am glad on't.[44] What a fearful night is this!
     There's two or three of us have seen strange sights.

     CASSIUS. Am I not stay'd for? Tell me.

     CINNA.   Yes, you are.
140 O Cassius, if you could
     But win the noble Brutus to our party—

     CASSIUS. Be you content. Good Cinna, take this paper,
     And look you lay it in the praetor's[45] chair,
     Where Brutus may but find it; and throw this
145 In at his window; set this up with wax
     Upon old Brutus'[46] statue. All this done,
     Repair[47] to Pompey's Porch, where you shall find us.
     Is[48] Decius Brutus and Trebonius there?

     CINNA. All but Metellus Cimber, and he's gone
150 To seek you at your house. Well, I will hie,[49]
     And so bestow these papers as you bade me.

     CASSIUS. That done, repair to Pompey's theater.

                                        Exit CINNA.

     Come, Casca, you and I will yet, ere day,
     See Brutus at his house. Three parts of him
155 Is[50] ours already, and the man entire
     Upon the next encounter yields him ours.

---

38. **by this they stay.** By this time they wait
39. **Pompey's Porch.** By the covered walk, or portico, in front of Pompey's theater
40. **complexion of the element.** Appearance of the heavens
41. **favor's.** Appearance is
42. **close.** Nearby
43. **incorporate.** Bound
44. **on't.** Of it

45. **praetor's.** Brutus is praetor, or chief magistrate, of Rome.
46. **old Brutus'.** Lucius Junius Brutus, founder of the republic and symbol of republican ideals
47. **Repair.** Go
48. **Is.** Are
49. **hie.** Make haste
50. **Is.** Are

Checking Your Reading
1. What warning does the Soothsayer give Cæsar? **He warns Cæsar, "Beware the ides of March."**
2. Who recalls saving Cæsar from drowning when they were young? **Cassius recalls saving Cæsar from drowning when he was young.**
3. What complaint does Cassius have about Cæsar? **He complains that Cæsar is actually a weak person who has no right to the power he now commands over others.**
4. What does Cæsar refuse three times? **He refuses the crown.**
5. Whom does Cassius want to join the conspiracy? **He wants Brutus to join.**

Vocabulary in Context
Fill in each blank with the most appropriate word from the *Words for Everyday Use* from *The Tragedy of Julius Cæsar.* You may have to change the tense of the word.

wretched	cull	endure	underling
	tempest	construe	apparel

1. Mrs. Tinsmore reminded the children to **cull** the best vegetables for her stew.
2. Sylvia enjoys modern art even though she finds its meaning difficult to **construe**.
3. Justin felt **wretched** his first semester at college, but by spring his mood improved.
4. The CEO announced that everyone, even **underlings**, would receive a bonus.
5. Only by the courageous act of the captain did the ship survive the **tempest**.

Literary Tools
The dramatic plot of a play revolves around a central conflict and follows the same pattern as in fiction. Identify each plot element.

In each blank above, place the letter of the plot element that fits that position.
a. resolution
b. falling action
c. rising action
d. inciting incident
e. dénouement
f. exposition
g. climax
h. crisis

1. The group of conspirators needs Brutus because his high standing in the minds of Romans will lend virtue and worthiness to their cause.

LITERARY TECHNIQUE

SIMILE. A **simile** is a comparison using *like* or *as*. Casca describes Brutus with the following simile: "And that which would appear offense in us, / His countenance, like richest alchemy, / Will change to virtue and worthiness." Ask students to what Casca is comparing Brutus's reputation. Why is Brutus so instrumental to the conspirators' plot?
Answers
Casca is comparing Brutus's reputation to the "science" of alchemy, which sought to transform base metals to gold. Brutus is instrumental to the plot because he is well respected.

CROSS-CURRICULAR ACTIVITIES

SCIENCE. Point out to students that the actor pictured on page 264 is wearing a crown of laurel leaves. Ask them to research the laurel plant. What is its scientific name and family name? What does it look like, and to what region is it native? When was it originally used to make crowns, and what did these crowns signify? To extend the activity, you may wish to have students research the climate of Rome today. They should identify some of the crops and vegetation native to the region.

CASCA. O, he sits high in all the people's hearts;
And that which would appear offense in us,
His countenance, like richest alchemy,
160 Will change to virtue and to worthiness.[51]

CASSIUS.   Him and his worth, and our great need of him,
You have right well conceited.[52] Let us go,
For it is after midnight, and ere day
We will awake him and be sure of him.

Exeunt.

Why does the group need Brutus?

---

51. **that which . . . worthiness.** What would offend the populace if we did it will be considered virtuous and worthy if Brutus does it (alchemy: ancient pseudoscience in which people attempted to turn base metals into gold).
52. **conceited.** Described in an elaborate metaphor, or conceit

Martin Benrath as Julius Cæsar and Rosel Zech as Calphurnia in a production of *Julius Cæsar* at the Edinburgh International Arts Festival, 1993.

Respond *to the* SELECTION

At what point do you think it is dangerous for one person to become too powerful or popular? Explain.

Investigate, Inquire, *and* Imagine

Recall: GATHERING FACTS

1a. What traits does Cæsar object to in Cassius?

2a. What is Brutus's response when Cassius suggests that Brutus would not like to see Cæsar crowned king?

3a. To what work of art does Cassius compare Cæsar?

Interpret: FINDING MEANING

1b. Why might Cæsar object to these traits? What about them seems dangerous to him?

2b. What conflicting feelings does Brutus have about Cæsar?

3b. How does Cæsar make Cassius feel?

Analyze: TAKING THINGS APART

4a. Identify the arguments Cassius uses to persuade Brutus to join the conspiracy against Cæsar.

Synthesize: BRINGING THINGS TOGETHER

4b. How effective do you predict these arguments will be with Brutus? Will he be persuaded to join the conspirators? Why do you think Cassius chooses these arguments?

Evaluate: MAKING JUDGMENTS

5a. In your opinion, which of these characters is more honorable: Cassius, Cæsar, or Brutus? Explain.

Extend: CONNECTING IDEAS

5b. The term "honor" is one that is used frequently but not always defined by the user. In your opinion, what does it mean to be "honorable"? Do you believe it means the same thing to most Americans? Why, or why not?

Understanding *Literature*

CHARACTER. Review the definition for **character** in the Handbook of Literary Terms. Some critics have said that Shakespeare's play ought to be called *Brutus* instead of *Julius Cæsar* because Brutus is the play's main character. What is Brutus like? What motivates him? What conflicting feelings does he have?

MOTIF. Review the definition for **motif** in the Handbook of Literary Terms. The motif of disorder in nature runs throughout much of Shakespeare's work and usually signifies the disorder of the political state. Review the cluster chart you completed for Literary Tools in Prereading on page 242. What do you believe is out of order in the political state, giving rise to these signs of disorder in the natural world?

ACT 1 / THE TRAGEDY OF JULIUS CÆSAR **265**

ANSWERS TO INVESTIGATE, INQUIRE, AND IMAGINE (CONT.)

SYNTHESIZE

4b. *Responses will vary.* Brutus has said that he loves honor more than he fears death and that he considers anything that serves the common good to be honorable. He tells Cassius that he loves Cæsar but does not believe he should be crowned king. He promises to think further about Cassius's words and says he would "rather be a villager than to repute himself a son of Rome under these hard conditions." Students may interpret these comments as evidence that Brutus may be swayed. They are evidence that Brutus is concerned with preserving the republic and may, therefore, be moved to prevent Cæsar from rising above it. Cassius chooses these arguments because he has a good understanding of what motivates Brutus.

(Continued on page 266)

RESPOND TO THE SELECTION

Students might think of examples from their own experience, history, or current events in which popular or powerful people have abused their power. Why might people in a position of power be tempted to disregard certain boundaries?

ANSWERS TO INVESTIGATE, INQUIRE, AND IMAGINE

RECALL

1a. Cæsar objects to the fact that Cassius "thinks too much," reads a great deal, is restless and hungry rather than content and happy, and is a keen observer who is capable of guessing people's motivations. He senses that Cassius is a dangerous man who will never be comfortable while another person is more powerful than himself.

2a. Brutus says, "I would not, Cassius, yet I love him well."

3a. Cassius compares Cæsar to a colossus, or a giant statue.

INTERPRET

1b. Cæsar might object to these traits in Cassius because they might make Cassius very independent—less likely to follow the leadership of another or become swayed by popular opinion—and more likely to question and challenge Cæsar.

2b. Brutus likes and respects Cæsar but he does not believe that he should be crowned king.

3b. Cassius feels angry and resentful because Cæsar has overstepped his bounds and unjustly assumed a godlike position. Cassius also seems to resent the fact that Cæsar dislikes him.

ANALYZE

4a. Cassius tells Brutus that men are masters of their own fates at times and that the only reason Cæsar is set above other men is that they have been passive and allowed it to happen. He tells the story of having to rescue Cæsar from the river Tiber to point out that Cæsar is no god but a mere mortal. He speaks of the injustice of this and says that Brutus's ancestor, Lucius Junius Brutus who helped to found Rome, would not have allowed one man to be set above others as king. He appeals to Brutus's pride and says that Cæsar is no more noble than Brutus. He tells Brutus that he should consider how others see him and know that his virtue and worthiness is equal, in the eyes of others, to that of Cæsar.

EVALUATE

5a. *Responses will vary.* Students may say that Cassius is less than honorable since he is willing to deliberately mislead and manipulate Brutus into joining the conspiracy by placing forged letters in his window. Others may point out that Cæsar is afraid of Cassius because he thinks too much and reads widely. If he fears the observant eye of an educated and thoughtful man, perhaps Cæsar's intentions are less than honorable as well. Brutus appears to be the most honorable of the three so far in the play.

EXTEND

5b. *Responses will vary.* Students may wish to use a graphic organizer to explore the concept of honor. Refer them to the Language Arts Survey 2.13, "Clustering." Have students create a cluster chart around the word *honor.*

ANSWERS TO UNDERSTANDING LITERATURE

CHARACTER. Brutus is trusting and well-intentioned, but troubled. He is motivated by his love for the Roman Republic. Brutus is conflicted over whether to support Cæsar or join a plot against him: he loves Cæsar, but fears that Cæsar may attempt to become king and destroy the republic.

MOTIF. *Responses will vary.* At the beginning of the play, it appears that the overreaching ambition of Cæsar, which threatens the republic, is what is out of order in the political state. Later in act 1, however, it appears that the plot against Cæsar may also be considered unnatural and wrong.

PLOT, CENTRAL CONFLICT, AND INCITING INCIDENT. The central conflict is between Brutus's love for Cæsar and his love for the Republic. Cassius speaks to Brutus to find out if he is also against Cæsar being crowned and to attempt to sway him to join the conspiracy against Cæsar.

PLOT, CENTRAL CONFLICT, AND INCITING INCIDENT. Review the definition for **plot** in the Handbook of Literary Terms, and note the information given for **central conflict** and **inciting incident**. What struggle on the part of Brutus is introduced in lines 78–89 of act 1, scene 2? Why does Cassius speak with Brutus in scene 2? As you read *Julius Cæsar*, create a plot pyramid like the one below, diagramming the elements of plot as they develop. Now, note on the pyramid the central conflict.

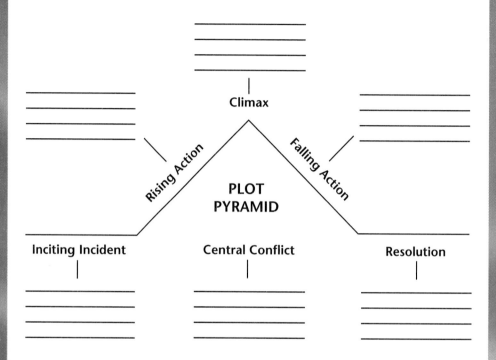

Writer's Journal

1. Write an **announcement** that might be hung in the square proclaiming Cæsar's victorious return from battle and announcing the Feast of Lupercalia. Invite all Romans to come out to welcome him and take part in the festivities.

2. Although there were no newspapers or advice columns in ancient Rome, imagine that you are an advice columnist at the time of Julius Cæsar and that you have received a letter from "A Troubled Senator," who asks for guidance with a moral dilemma he faces. He says, "I fear that Cæsar will proclaim himself king and end this glorious republican form of government we have established. Yet to stop him, it is said that we must kill him. I respect and admire him, despite his overreaching ambition. What should I do?" Respond to "Troubled Senator" in your **advice column**.

3. Review Cassius's soliloquy in act 1, scene 2, lines 289–303. Shakespearean English is often challenging for modern readers and listeners. **Paraphrase** Cassius's words, attempting to keep the original meaning, but using your own words.

Integrating the Language Arts

Study and Research

RESEARCHING EPILEPSY. The "falling sickness" that Casca and Brutus ascribe to Cæsar is commonly thought to have been epilepsy. Though this condition even now is not fully understood, it has been subject to many misunderstandings. Using Internet, library, and community resources, research the nature and treatment of this condition, including the different types of epilepsy. What have the misconceptions about it been? What is the truth? Throughout history, many famous and talented figures have suffered from epilepsy. Who were/are they? You may wish to share your findings with your class in an oral presentation.

Collaborative Learning

RESEARCHING THE REPUBLIC. Brutus is much concerned with preserving the republican form of government in Rome. With a group of three or four other students, research the meaning of "republic" as a form of government. Compare the government of Rome to our own form of government. How is our government similar to that of Rome? How is it different? Share your findings with your class.

Media Literacy

MOVIE VERSIONS OF *JULIUS CÆSAR*. Go to a video store or library and locate movie versions of *Julius Cæsar*. Joseph L. Mankiewicz's 1953 version, starring Marlon Brando and James Mason, and Stuart Burge's 1970 version, starring Charlton Heston and Jason Robards, are two that you might find. Play act 1 of both versions. Then compare and contrast them. Which actors did you find more effective? Which movie had better background scenery? What was similar and different about each interpretation? Finally, imagine you were directing a brand-new movie version of *Julius Cæsar*. Decide which Hollywood actor you would choose for the roles of Julius Cæsar, Brutus, Cassius, and Casca, and explain your choices.

ANSWERS TO INTEGRATING THE LANGUAGE ARTS

Study and Research
Some famous characters in history thought to have had epilepsy include Socrates, Peter the Great, Napoleon, Vincent van Gogh, and Alfred Nobel.

Collaborative Learning
Direct students to the Language Arts Survey 5.10, "Comparing and Contrasting," for help in completing this activity.

Media Literacy
Students should refer to the Language Arts Survey 5.10, "Comparing and Contrasting," and 5.32, "How to Evaluate a Film," before working on this activity.

HISTORICAL NOTE

One of the most famous accounts of the legend of the founding of Rome was given by Roman historian **Titus Livius** (59 BC–AD 17), better known as Livy. His version of the legend is found in the first book of his complete history of Rome, *Ab Urbe Condita,* or *From the Founding of the City.* The history was originally made up of 142 books. However, only books 1 through 10 and 21 through 35 remain today. Text of Livy's history can be found online at **The Perseus Project** website, an evolving digital library with information about ancient Greece and Rome, at http://www.perseus.tufts.edu/.

Histories were popular in Rome; Romans were interested in and proud of their past. Among Rome's many historians were Sallust, Tacitus, the elder Cato, and Julius Cæsar himself. A complete history of Rome was not unique in itself. Livy's innovation lay in trying to understand history by examining the character of historical figures. In fact, he is known to sacrifice accuracy to focus on character. Point out to students that a historical play such as *Julius Cæsar* does this to an even greater degree. It interprets history, rather than reporting it as it actually occurred.

GRAPHIC ORGANIZER

lines 32–34: Tenor: Cæsar; Vehicle: a serpent's egg
lines 63–69: Tenor: a man's mind; Vehicle: a little kingdom suffering an insurrection or civil war
lines 171–174: Tenor: method of killing Cæsar; Vehicle: carving meat: "carve him as a dish fit for the gods"

READER'S JOURNAL

Ask students to write about what they did to solve the dilemma, and why.

ART NOTE

View of Rome. Antonio Canaletto (Giovanni Antonio Canale). **Giovanni Antonio Canaletto** (1697–1768) was an Italian topographical painter who was best known for his paintings of Venice and the Italian landscape.

VOCABULARY FROM THE SELECTION

amiss	insurrection
augment	interim
carcass	interpose
commend	lament
constancy	particle
entrails	portent
entreat	redress
expound	resolution
horrid	suffice
imminent	visage
instigation	

Literary TOOLS

PLOT AND COMPLICATION. A **plot** is a series of events related to a central conflict or struggle. The **complication** develops the conflict to a high point of intensity. As you read act 2, note the events that develop the central conflict in which Brutus is involved.

SIMILE. A **simile** is a comparison using *like* or *as*. Like metaphors, similes can be analyzed into two parts, the *tenor* (or subject being described) and the *vehicle* (or object being used in the description). Brutus uses several similes in act 2 that help reveal his state of mind and the internal struggle in which he finds himself.

Graphic Organizer

As you read note the similes in the following passages: scene 1, lines 32–34, lines 63–69 and lines 171–174. On the following chart write the tenor and vehicle of each simile.

Tenor	Vehicle

Reader's Journal

When have you faced a moral dilemma and had to choose between two courses of action, neither of which was completely right or wrong?

View of Rome, [Detail]. *Antonio Canaletto (Giovanni Antonio Canale).*

ACT 2

SCENE 1: Brutus's garden in Rome

Enter BRUTUS *in his orchard.*[1]

BRUTUS.   What, Lucius, ho!
I cannot by the progress of the stars
Give guess how near to day. Lucius, I say!
I would it were my fault to sleep so soundly.
5   When, Lucius, when? Awake, I say! What, Lucius!

Enter LUCIUS.

LUCIUS.   Call'd you, my lord?

BRUTUS.   Get me a taper[2] in my study, Lucius.
When it is lighted, come and call me here.

LUCIUS.   I will, my lord.   *Exit* LUCIUS.

ACT 2, SCENE 1
1. *orchard.* Garden
2. **taper.** Candle

10   **BRUTUS.**   It must be by his death; and for my part,
I know no personal cause to spurn³ at him,
But for the general.⁴ He would be crown'd:
How that might change his nature, there's the question.
It is the bright day that brings forth the adder,⁵
15   And that craves⁶ wary walking. Crown him that,
And then I grant we put a sting in him
That at his will he may do danger with.⁷
Th' abuse of greatness is when it disjoins
Remorse from power;⁸ and to speak truth of Cæsar,
20   I have not known when his affections sway'd⁹
More than his reason. But 'tis a common proof¹⁰
That lowliness¹¹ is young ambition's ladder,
Whereto the climber-upward turns his face;
But when he once attains the upmost round,¹²
25   He then unto the ladder turns his back,
Looks in the clouds, scorning the base degrees
By which he did ascend. So Cæsar may;
Then lest he may, prevent.¹³ And since the quarrel
Will bear no color for the thing he is,¹⁴
30   Fashion it thus: that what he is, <u>augmented</u>,
Would run to these and these extremities;
And therefore think him as a serpent's egg,
Which, hatch'd, would as his kind grow mischievous,
And kill him in the shell.

Enter LUCIUS.

35   **LUCIUS.**   The taper burneth in your closet,¹⁵ sir.
Searching the window for a flint,¹⁶ I found
This paper, thus seal'd up, and I am sure
It did not lie there when I went to bed.

Gives him the letter.

BRUTUS.   Get you to bed again, it is not day.

> *What does Brutus think is the only way to preserve the common good?*

> Brutus worries that Cæsar's nature will change when what happens?

> To what does Brutus compare Cæsar?

> What has Lucius found and given to Brutus?

---

3. **spurn.** Goad or kick
4. **the general.** The general welfare or common good
5. **adder.** Type of poisonous snake
6. **craves.** Requires or demands
7. **we put . . . with.** Brutus is making the point that power corrupts.
8. **disjoins/Remorse from power.** Makes the powerful no longer merciful
9. **affections sway'd.** Feelings moved him
10. **'tis a common proof.** It is commonly proved or shown

11. **lowliness.** Pretended humility
12. **round.** Rung
13. **prevent.** The word is said by Brutus as a command or exhortation to himself.
14. **Will bear no . . . he is.** Will not be excused by something terrible in Cæsar himself
15. **closet.** Room
16. **flint.** Piece of stone that creates a spark with which to light the candle

---

words for everyday use

aug • ment (ôg ment´) *vt.*, increase; add to. *Sharon decided to* <u>augment</u> *her income by taking a second job.*

ANSWERS TO GUIDED READING QUESTIONS

1. Brutus thinks "his [Cæsar's] death" is the only recourse to preserve the common good.
2. Brutus worries that Cæsar's nature will change when he is crowned.
3. Brutus compares Cæsar to a serpent's egg "Which, hatch'd, would as his kind grow mischievous."
4. Lucius has found one of the forged letters planted at Cassius's direction.

INDIVIDUAL LEARNING STRATEGIES

MOTIVATION
As they read act 2, ask students to consider the moral dilemma faced by Brutus. He doesn't want Cæsar to become king, for that would mean an end to the republic that he loves. However, he has no personal grudge against Cæsar that would lead him to take action against him. What do students think Brutus should do?

READING PROFICIENCY
Many students may find the language of Shakespeare's time difficult. Go over with them the Words for Everyday Use and the footnotes, then encourage them to read through each scene with a partner, answering the Guided Reading Questions as they go and summing up the main point of each scene.

ENGLISH LANGUAGE LEARNING
In addition to going over the Words for Everyday Use and footnotes, you may wish to review with students the archaic language and the additional vocabulary below.
affability—friendly manner
contagion—bacteria or other substance that causes a communicable disease
suitors—people who request something

SPECIAL NEEDS
Students will find it helpful to hear the selection read out loud. Make sure students focus on the Guided Reading Questions and the Recall questions in the Investigate, Inquire, and Imagine section.

ENRICHMENT
Ask students to research the Roman calendar and Julius Cæsar's contribution to it. Their research should answer the following questions: Whose calendar did the Romans borrow and adapt? When was the first Roman calendar established? How

---

LITERARY TECHNIQUE

ALLUSION. An **allusion** is a figure of speech in which a reference is made to a person, event, object, or work from history or literature. Ask students if they can identify the allusion in lines 32–34. The simile used in those lines is an allusion to the serpent who tempts Eve in the book of Genesis in the Bible.

INDIVIDUAL LEARNING STRATEGIES (CONT.)

many months and days in a year did the calendar originally have? Who changed it to 12 months and 365 days? Why did Cæsar need to change the calendar, and how did he change it? Why was the year 46 called "the year of confusion"? Which month is named after Cæsar?

40   Is not tomorrow, boy, the ides of March?

LUCIUS.   I know not, sir.

BRUTUS.   Look in the calendar, and bring me word.

LUCIUS.   I will, sir.   *Exit* LUCIUS.

BRUTUS.   The exhalations[17] whizzing in the air

45   Give so much light that I may read by them.

                             Opens the letter and reads.

> "Brutus, thou sleep'st; awake, and see thyself!
> Shall Rome, etc. Speak, strike, <u>redress</u>!"
> "Brutus, thou sleep'st, awake!"
> Such <u>instigations</u> have been often dropp'd

50   Where I have took[18] them up.
"Shall Rome, etc." Thus must I piece it out:[19]
Shall Rome stand under one man's awe? What, Rome?
My ancestors did from the streets of Rome
The Tarquin[20] drive when he was call'd a king.

55   "Speak, strike, redress!" Am I <u>entreated</u>
To speak and strike? O Rome, I make thee promise,
If the redress will follow, thou receivest
Thy full petition[21] at the hand of Brutus!

Enter LUCIUS.

LUCIUS.   Sir, March is wasted fifteen days.

                            Knock within.

60   **BRUTUS.**   'Tis good. Go to the gate. Somebody knocks.   *Exit* LUCIUS.
Since Cassius first did whet[22] me against Cæsar,
I have not slept.
Between the acting of a dreadful thing
And the first motion, all the <u>interim</u> is

65   Like a phantasma[23] or a hideous dream.
The genius and the mortal instruments[24]
Are then in council; and the state of a man,
Like to a little kingdom, suffers then
The nature[25] of an <u>insurrection</u>.

> *What does the letter urge Brutus to do?*

> *What is the date?*

---

17. **exhalations.** Meteors (omens of important events)
18. **took.** Taken
19. **piece it out.** Explain this matter
20. **Tarquin.** Last king of Rome
21. **thy full petition.** All that you ask for
22. **whet.** Sharpen, incite
23. **phantasma.** Fantastic imagining
24. **genius and the mortal instruments.** Reasoning spirit and the physical body that will carry out its intentions
25. **The nature.** A kind

---

words for everyday use

re • dress (ri dres´) *vt.*, right a wrong; rectify. *The former villain had a change of heart and decided to <u>redress</u> the wrongs he had done to others.*

in • sti • ga • tion (in stə gā´ shən) *n.*, incitement; something that urges one to act. *Because of Bill's <u>instigation</u>, I decided I could attempt to climb the mountain after all.*

en • treat (en trēt´) *vt.*, implore; strongly request. *I <u>entreated</u> my parents to let me stay out one hour later than my usual curfew, but I couldn't change their minds.*

in • ter • im (in´ tər im) *n.*, in-between time. *Some people find the halftime of a game too long, but others enjoy the <u>interim</u>.*

in • sur • rec • tion (in´ sə rek´ shən) *n.*, rebellion. *The ruler had such power that she was able to squash the <u>insurrection</u> without any loss to her forces, but with heavy losses to the rebel army.*

Enter LUCIUS.

70 **LUCIUS.** Sir, 'tis your brother Cassius at the door,
Who doth desire to see you.

BRUTUS.   Is he alone?

LUCIUS. No, sir, there are more with him.

BRUTUS.   Do you know them?

LUCIUS. No, sir, their hats are pluck'd about[26] their ears
And half their faces buried in their cloaks,
75 That by no means I may discover[27] them
By any mark of favor.

BRUTUS.   Let 'em enter.   *Exit* LUCIUS.
They are the faction. O Conspiracy,
Sham'st thou to show thy dang'rous brow by night,
When evils are most free? O then, by day
80 Where wilt thou find a cavern dark enough
To mask thy monstrous <u>visage</u>? Seek none, Conspiracy!
Hide it in smiles and affability,
For if thou path,[28] thy native semblance[29] on,
Not Erebus[30] itself were dim enough
85 To hide thee from prevention.

Enter the conspirators, CASSIUS, CASCA, DECIUS, CINNA, METELLUS, *and* TREBONIUS.

CASSIUS. I think we are too bold upon your rest.
Good morrow, Brutus, do we trouble you?

BRUTUS. I have been up this hour, awake all night.
Know I these men that come along with you?

90 **CASSIUS.** Yes, every man of them; and no man here
But honors you, and every one doth wish
You had but that opinion of yourself
Which every noble Roman bears of you.
This is Trebonius.

BRUTUS.   He is welcome hither.[31]

CASSIUS. This, Decius Brutus.

---

26. **pluck'd about.** Drawn down to
27. **discover.** Recognize
28. **path.** Step
29. **native semblance.** Normal look

30. **Erebus.** In Greek and Roman myth, a dark place in the underworld
31. **hither.** Here

words for everyday use

vis • age (viz´ ij) *n.,* face; appearance. *We were tempted to ask Hank how he did on the test, but when we saw the frown upon his <u>visage</u> we knew the answer.*

ANSWER TO GUIDED READING QUESTION

1. Cassius says that each of the conspirators wishes that Brutus had the same high opinion of himself that "every noble Roman" has of him.

Quotables

"Ay, now the plot thickens very much upon us."

—George Villiers, Second Duke of Buckingham

What does each of the conspirators wish, according to Cassius?

1. Cassius proposes the conspirators all swear an oath on their plan. Brutus objects and says that noble Romans need not swear oaths. He feels that the cause is right and noble enough to bind them and if it is not, they should not undertake it.

95 **BRUTUS.** He is welcome too.

CASSIUS. This, Casca; this, Cinna; and this, Metellus Cimber.

BRUTUS. They are all welcome.
What watchful cares[32] do <u>interpose</u> themselves
Betwixt[33] your eyes and night?

100 **CASSIUS.** Shall I entreat a word?

They whisper.

DECIUS. Here lies the east; doth not the day break here?

CASCA. No.

CINNA. O, pardon, sir, it doth; and yon grey lines
That fret[34] the clouds are messengers of day.

105 **CASCA.** You shall confess that you are both deceiv'd.
Here, as I point my sword, the sun arises,
Which is a great way growing on the south,[35]
Weighing[36] the youthful season of the year.
Some two months hence, up higher toward the north
110 He first presents his fire, and the high[37] east
Stands, as the Capitol, directly here.

BRUTUS. Give me your hands all over,[38] one by one.

CASSIUS. And let us swear our <u>resolution</u>.

BRUTUS. No, not an oath! If not the face of men,
115 The sufferance of[39] our souls, the time's abuse[40]—
If these be motives weak, break off betimes,[41]
And every man hence to his idle bed;
So let highsighted tyranny range on,
Till each man drop by lottery.[42] But if these
120 (As I am sure they do) bear fire enough
To kindle cowards, and to steel with valor
The melting spirits of women, then, countrymen,
What need we any spur but our own cause
To prick us to redress? what other bond
125 Than secret Romans, that have spoke the word

What does Cassius propose? How does Brutus react?

---

32. **watchful cares.** Cares that keep you awake
33. **Betwixt.** Between
34. **fret.** Streak across, like the frets, or bands of metal, on a lute
35. **a great way . . . south.** Further to the south
36. **Weighing.** Judging
37. **high.** Due

38. **all over.** All turned over, palm down, one on top of the other
39. **sufferance of.** Things suffered by
40. **time's abuse.** Abuses, or misdeeds, of our day
41. **betimes.** At once
42. **by lottery.** By chance

words for everyday use

in • ter • pose (in′ tər pōz′) *vt.,* place or come between. *The referee interposed himself between the argumentative wrestlers.*

res • o • lu • tion (rez′ ə lōō′shən) *n.,* determination. *Her New Year's <u>resolution</u> was to be kinder to her younger brother no matter how he irked her.*

And will not palter?[43] and what other oath
Than honesty to honesty engag'd
That this shall be, or we will fall for it?
Swear priests and cowards, and men cautelous,[44]
130 Old feeble carrions,[45] and such suffering souls
That welcome wrongs; unto bad causes swear
Such creatures as men doubt; but do not stain
The even virtue of our enterprise,
Nor th' insuppressive mettle[46] of our spirits,
135 To think that or our cause or our performance[47]
Did need an oath; when every drop of blood
That every Roman bears, and nobly bears,
Is guilty of a several bastardy,[48]
If he do break the smallest particle
140 Of any promise that hath pass'd from him.

    CASSIUS.   But what of Cicero? Shall we sound him?
I think he will stand very strong with us.

    CASCA. Let us not leave him out.

    CINNA.   No, by no means.

    METELLUS.   O, let us have him, for his silver hairs
145 Will purchase us a good opinion,
And buy men's voices to commend our deeds.
It shall be said his judgment rul'd our hands;
Our youths and wildness shall no whit appear,
But all be buried in his gravity.[49]

150 **BRUTUS.**   O, name him not; let us not break with[50] him,
For he will never follow anything
That other men begin.

    CASSIUS.   Then leave him out.

    CASCA.   Indeed he is not fit.

    DECIUS.   Shall no man else be touch'd but only Cæsar?

155 **CASSIUS.**   Decius, well urg'd. I think it is not meet,[51]

---

43. **palter.** Speak in double talk
44. **cautelous.** Full of deception
45. **carrions.** Literally, pieces of dead flesh; figuratively, people who are almost dead
46. **insuppressive mettle.** Unyielding nature

47. **or our cause . . . performance.** Either our cause or our performance
48. **Is guilty . . . bastardy.** Shows ourselves not truly Romans
49. **gravity.** Seriousness
50. **break with.** Share the secret
51. **meet.** OK, acceptable

**words
for
everyday
use**

par • ti • cle (pärt´ i kəl) *n.*, tiny bit. *The miserly gold miner was determined not to lose one particle of gold dust, and he ventured into the abandoned mine to collect the last few bits.*

com • mend (kə mend´) *vt.*, praise. *Since Jose was the teacher's favorite student, she commended him highly to potential employers.*

**ADDITIONAL QUESTIONS
AND ACTIVITIES**

Ask students the following questions about Brutus's speech in lines 114–140:
- Why doesn't Brutus want the conspirators to swear an oath upon the course they have determined to take?
- What is Brutus's conception of Romans? of honor? Why is it that Romans do not need to swear an oath?
- Is Brutus overly generous in evaluating the honesty of his fellow Romans? Why might he make this mistake?

Answers
Brutus doesn't want the conspirators to swear an oath because he feels only cowards and evildoers must take such oaths. Brutus thinks that Romans are by nature very honorable; he thinks that honor is one of the most important values. Romans are so honorable that they need not swear oaths. Students may say that Brutus is overly generous; he believes others honorable because he himself is honorable.

LITERARY/HISTORICAL NOTE

In line 165 and following, Brutus metaphorically describes Antony as a limb of Cæsar. You might wish to tell students that this comparison is a reference to the Elizabethan conception of the king's two bodies. According to Elizabethan notions of kingship, a king had two bodies: a physical and mortal body, and a political and immortal body. Shakespeare is describing Cæsar as a typical Elizabethan monarch would be described—as possessing a physical body that will die when the conspirators "cut the head off," as well as possessing the authority of kingship, or a "kingly" body, that will continue to exist even after physical death. Antony, here, is described as the limb of kingship, indicating that he will take on Cæsar's political power once Cæsar's physical body is destroyed. While this concept had not yet evolved in Cæsar's time, it would have had contemporary significance to Shakespeare's audience.

Mark Antony, so well belov'd of Cæsar,
Should outlive Cæsar. We shall find of him
A shrewd contriver; and you know, his means,
If he improve them, may well stretch so far
160 As to annoy[52] us all; which to prevent,
Let Antony and Cæsar fall together.

BRUTUS. Our course will seem too bloody, Caius Cassius
To cut the head off and then hack the limbs[53]—
Like wrath in death and envy afterwards;[54]
165 For Antony is but a limb of Cæsar.
Let's be sacrificers, but not butchers, Caius.
We all stand up against the spirit of Cæsar,
And in the spirit of men there is no blood;
O that we then could come by[55] Cæsar's spirit,
170 And not dismember Cæsar! But, alas,
Cæsar must bleed for it! And, gentle friends,
Let's kill him boldly, but not wrathfully;
Let's carve him as a dish fit for the gods,
Not hew him as a carcass fit for hounds;
175 And let our hearts, as subtle masters do,
Stir up their servants to an act of rage,
And after seem to chide 'em. This shall make
Our purpose necessary, and not envious;
Which so appearing to the common eyes,
180 We shall be called purgers,[56] not murderers.
And for Mark Antony, think not of him;
For he can do no more than Cæsar's arm
When Cæsar's head is off.

CASSIUS.   Yet I fear him,
For in the ingrafted[57] love he bears to Cæsar—

185 **BRUTUS.** Alas, good Cassius, do not think of him.
If he love Cæsar, all that he can do
Is to himself—take thought[58] and die for Cæsar;
And that were much he should, for he is given
To sports, to wildness, and much company.

Who else does Cassius propose they kill?

How does Brutus respond?

How will the plot look to the common eye, according to Brutus?

---

52. **annoy.** Hurt
53. **cut the head . . . the limbs.** Kill Cæsar and then also kill his supporters
54. **Like wrath . . . afterwards.** Brutus is saying that killing Cæsar should not be made to seem a matter of anger or malice.
55. **come by.** Possess
56. **purgers.** Ones who get rid of, or cleanse, something
57. **ingrafted.** Joined, as the limb of one tree might be grafted onto the trunk of another
58. **take thought.** Brood or mourn

---

words for everyday use
car • cass (kär´ kəs) *n.*, body of a slain animal. *The carcass of the slain deer was a pitiful sight.*

190 **TREBONIUS.**   There is no fear in him; let him not die,
For he will live, and laugh at this hereafter.

Clock strikes.

BRUTUS.   Peace, count the clock.

CASSIUS.   The clock hath stricken three.

TREBONIUS.   'Tis time to part.

CASSIUS.   But it is doubtful yet
Whether Cæsar will come forth today or no;
195 For he is superstitious grown of late,
Quite from the main opinion[59] he held once
Of fantasy, of dreams, and ceremonies.[60]
It may be these apparent prodigies,[61]
The unaccustom'd terror of this night,
200 And the persuasion of his augurers[62]
May hold him from the Capitol today.

DECIUS.   Never fear that. If he be so resolv'd,
I can o'ersway him;[63] for he loves to hear
That unicorns may be betray'd with trees,[64]
205 And bears with glasses,[65] elephants with holes,[66]
Lions with toils,[67] and men with flatterers;
But when I tell him he hates flatterers
He says he does, being then most flattered.
Let me work;
210 For I can give his humor[68] the true bent,[69]
And I will bring him to the Capitol.

CASSIUS.   Nay, we will all of us be there to fetch him.

BRUTUS.   By the eighth hour; is that the uttermost?

CINNA.   Be that the uttermost, and fail not then.

215 **METELLUS.**   Caius Ligarius doth bear Cæsar hard,[70]
Who rated[71] him for speaking well of Pompey;
I wonder none of you have thought of him.

BRUTUS.   Now, good Metellus, go along by[72] him.
He loves me well, and I have given him reasons;
220 Send him but hither, and I'll fashion[73] him.

CASSIUS.   The morning comes upon 's.[74] We'll leave you, Brutus,

> What will Decius do if Cæsar refuses to come out?

---

59. **Quite from the main opinion.** Very different from the strong opinion
60. **ceremonies.** Rituals held to predict the future
61. **apparent prodigies.** Observable omens
62. **augurers.** People who read omens to foretell the future
63. **o'ersway him.** Convince him otherwise
64. **betray'd with trees.** Tricked into burying its horn into a tree and so captured
65. **glasses.** Looking glasses, or mirrors

66. **holes.** Pits dug into the ground
67. **toils.** Nets
68. **humor.** State of mind
69. **true bent.** Right direction
70. **bear Cæsar hard.** Dislike Cæsar
71. **rated.** Chastised
72. **along by.** To
73. **fashion.** Mold, shape, convince
74. **The morning comes upon 's.** The sun is up.

ACT 2, SCENE 1 / THE TRAGEDY OF JULIUS CÆSAR   **275**

ANSWER TO GUIDED READING QUESTION

1. Decius will flatter Cæsar and persuade him to come to the Senate.

LITERARY TECHNIQUE

ANACHRONISM. An **anachronism** is a reference to something that did not exist at the time being described. Thus, a reference to a computer in a story taking place during the Civil War would be an anachronism because computers had not been invented during the nineteenth century. Point out to students Shakespeare's anachronism in scene 1—the striking of a clock. Since clocks were not invented until the late 1000s, by the Chinese, there could not really have been a clock in Brutus's home. Brutus would likely have used a sundial or an hourglass to tell time. Ask students if they think Shakespeare had a reason for including a clock even though he probably knew it was an anachronism. What does the chiming of the clock add to the scene?

And, friends, disperse yourselves; but all remember
What you have said, and show yourselves true Romans.

BRUTUS.   Good gentlemen, look fresh and merrily;
225 Let not our looks put on our purposes,
But bear it[75] as our Roman actors do,
With untir'd spirits and formal constancy.[76]
And so good morrow to you every one.

Exeunt. Manet BRUTUS.

Boy! Lucius! Fast asleep? It is no matter,
230 Enjoy the honey-heavy dew of slumber.
Thou hast no figures[77] nor no fantasies,
Which busy care draws in the brains of men;
Therefore thou sleep'st so sound.

Enter PORTIA.

PORTIA.   Brutus, my lord!

BRUTUS.   Portia! What mean you? Wherefore[78] rise you now?
235 It is not for[79] your health thus to commit
Your weak condition to the raw cold morning.

PORTIA.   Nor for yours neither. Y' have ungently, Brutus,
Stole from my bed; and yesternight[80] at supper
You suddenly arose and walk'd about,
240 Musing and sighing, with your arms across;
And when I ask'd you what the matter was,
You star'd upon me with ungentle looks.
I urg'd you further; then you scratch'd your head
And too impatiently stamp'd with your foot.
245 Yet I insisted, yet you answer'd not,
But with an angry wafter[81] of your hand
Gave sign for me to leave you. So I did,
Fearing to strengthen that impatience
Which seem'd too much enkindled; and withal[82]
250 Hoping it was but an effect of humor,[83]
Which sometime hath his hour with every man.
It will not let you eat, nor talk, nor sleep;
And could it work so much upon your shape
As it hath much prevail'd on your condition,
255 I should not know you Brutus. Dear my lord,
Make me acquainted with your cause of grief.

BRUTUS.   I am not well in health, and that is all.

---

75. **bear it.** Perform the role
76. **formal constancy.** Unfaltering dignity
77. **figures.** Wild imaginings
78. **Wherefore.** Why
79. **for.** Good for

80. **yesternight.** Last night
81. **wafter.** Waving
82. **withal.** Also
83. **humor.** Ill spirits

PORTIA. Brutus is wise, and were he not in health,
He would embrace the means to come by it.

260 **BRUTUS.** Why, so I do. Good Portia, go to bed.

PORTIA. Is Brutus sick? and is it physical[84]
To walk unbraced[85] and suck up the humors[86]
Of the dank morning? What, is Brutus sick?
And will he steal out of his wholesome bed
265 To dare the vile contagion of the night,
And tempt the rheumy and unpurged[87] air
To add unto his sickness? No, my Brutus,
You have some sick offense within your mind,
Which, by the right and virtue of my place,[88]
270 I ought to know of; and upon my knees
I charm you, by my once commended beauty,
By all your vows of love, and that great vow
Which did incorporate[89] and make us one,
That you unfold to me, yourself, your half,
275 Why you are heavy, and what men tonight
Have had resort to you; for here have been
Some six or seven, who did hide their faces
Even from darkness.

BRUTUS.   Kneel not, gentle Portia.

PORTIA. I should not need, if you were gentle Brutus.
280 Within the bond of marriage, tell me, Brutus,
Is it excepted[90] I should know no secrets
That appertain[91] to you? Am I yourself
But, as it were, in sort or limitation.[92]
To keep with you at meals, comfort your bed,
285 And talk to you sometimes? Dwell I but in the suburbs[93]
Of your good pleasure? If it be no more,
Portia is Brutus' harlot, not his wife.

BRUTUS. You are my true and honorable wife,
As dear to me as are the ruddy[94] drops
290 That visit my sad heart.

PORTIA. If this were true, then should I[95] know this secret.
I grant I am a woman; but withal
A woman that Lord Brutus took to wife.
I grant I am a woman; but withal

84. **physical.** Good for the body
85. **unbraced.** Not buttoned up
86. **humors.** Dampness and cold
87. **rheumy and unpurged.** Damp and impure
88. **my place.** Portia's position as his wife
89. **incorporate.** Join together
90. **excepted.** Specified, required

91. **appertain.** Relate
92. **in sort or limitation.** Of such a kind or so limited
93. **suburbs.** Outskirts of a city, where theaters, taverns, and houses of ill repute were to be found
94. **ruddy.** Red
95. **should I.** I should

What concerns Portia?

ANSWER TO GUIDED READING QUESTION

1. Portia worries that Brutus is troubled by something.

ADDITIONAL QUESTIONS AND ACTIVITIES

Brutus instructs the conspirators to "look fresh and merrily; / Let not our looks put on our purposes, / But bear it as our Roman actors do, / With untir'd spirits and formal constancy." Does Brutus follow his own advice? Who sees through his act?
Answers
No, Brutus does not follow his own advice. Brutus cannot deceive Portia, his wife, who knows that something grave is troubling her husband.

HISTORICAL NOTE

Plutarch's account of this encounter explains that Portia, distressed over the change in Brutus's behavior, tested her resolve by inflicting a wound on her thigh. She became feverish and weak as a result of her wound. In revealing her self-inflicted wound to Brutus, she hopes to prove to her husband that she can bear any pain or burden.

ADDITIONAL QUESTIONS AND ACTIVITIES

In Rome during the first century BC, married noblewomen possessed a certain degree of influence. Although they could not hold governmental positions, they could own property and sometimes had a role in making decisions with their powerful husbands. What influence, if any, does Portia seem to have with Brutus? How does she define herself?
Answers
Portia seems to have Brutus's respect; he listens to her concerns and calls her his "true and honorable wife." However, Portia must define herself and her worth by the men in her life: "I grant I am a woman; but withal / A woman that Lord Brutus took to wife. / I grant I am a woman; but withal / A woman well reputed, Cato's daughter. / Think you I am no stronger than my sex, / Being so father'd and so husbanded?"

---

295   A woman well reputed, Cato's[96] daughter.
      Think you I am no stronger than my sex,
      Being so father'd and so husbanded?
      Tell me your counsels,[97] I will not disclose 'em.
      I have made strong proof of my <u>constancy</u>,
300   Giving myself a voluntary wound
      Here, in the thigh; can I bear that with patience,
      And not my husband's secrets?

BRUTUS.   O ye gods !
      Render me worthy of this noble wife!

                                Knock.

      Hark, hark, one knocks! Portia, go in a while,
305   And by and by thy bosom shall partake
      The secrets of my heart.
      All my engagements I will construe to thee,
      All the charactery of[98] my sad brows.
      Leave me with haste.   *Exit* PORTIA.
             Lucius, who's that knocks?

Enter LUCIUS *and* CAIUS LIGARIUS.

310 **LUCIUS.**   Here is a sick man that would speak with you.

BRUTUS.   Caius Ligarius, that Metellus spake of.
      Boy, stand aside. Caius Ligarius, how?[99]   *Exit* LUCIUS.

LIGARIUS.   Vouchsafe[100] good morrow from a feeble tongue.

BRUTUS.   O, what a time have you chose out, brave Caius,
315   To wear a kerchief![101] Would you were not sick!

LIGARIUS.   I am not sick, if Brutus have in hand
      Any exploit worthy the name of honor.

BRUTUS.   Such an exploit have I in hand, Ligarius,
      Had you a healthful ear to hear of it.

320 **LIGARIUS.**   By all the gods that Romans bow before,
      I here discard my sickness! Soul of Rome!
      Brave son, deriv'd from honorable loins![102]
      Thou, like an exorcist, hast conjur'd up

> What does Portia demand?

---

96. **Cato's.** Marcus Porcius Cato, an ally of Pompey's against Cæsar, who was known for his nobility and integrity
97. **counsels.** Secrets
98. **charactery of.** Writing found on (that is, the troubled look)
99. **how.** How are you?

100. **Vouchsafe.** Agree to accept
101. **wear a kerchief.** To be sick
102. **loins.** Thighs. The reference is to Brutus's heritage. He is descended from Lucius Junius Brutus, who helped to establish the Roman Republic by overthrowing a king.

---

words for everyday use
   con • stan • cy (kän´stən sē) *n.*, faithfulness; resolve; unchangeableness. *Advertisers rely on consumers' <u>constancy</u> to particular product brands.*

---

278   *UNIT FOUR / DRAMA*

My mortified[103] spirit. Now bid me run,
325 And I will strive with things impossible,
Yea, get the better of them. What's to do?

BRUTUS.   A piece of work that will make sick men whole.

LIGARIUS.   But are not some whole that we must make sick?

BRUTUS.   That must we also. What it is, my Caius,
330 I shall unfold to thee, as we are going,
To whom it must be done.

LIGARIUS.   Set on your foot
And with a heart new-fir'd I follow you,
To do I know not what; but it <u>sufficeth</u>
That Brutus leads me on.   *Thunder.*

BRUTUS.   Follow me then.

                                                              Exeunt.

SCENE 2: THE HOME OF JULIUS CÆSAR

Thunder and lightning. Enter JULIUS CÆSAR *in his nightgown.*

CÆSAR.   Nor[1] heaven nor earth have been at peace tonight.
Thrice hath Calphurnia in her sleep cried out,
"Help, ho! they murther[2] Cæsar!" Who's within?

Enter a SERVANT.

SERVANT.   My lord?

5 **CÆSAR.**   Go bid the priests do present sacrifice,[3]
And bring me their opinions of success.[4]

SERVANT.   I will, my lord.   *Exit.*

Enter CALPHURNIA.

CALPHURNIA.   What mean you, Cæsar? Think you to walk forth?
You shall not stir out of your house today.

10 **CÆSAR.**   Cæsar shall forth; the things that threaten'd me
Ne'er look'd but on my back; when they shall see
The face of Cæsar, they are vanished.

> What has Calphurnia
> cried out in her sleep?

---

103. **mortified.** Deadened

ACT 2, SCENE 2
  1. **Nor.** Neither
  2. **murther.** Murder

3. **do present sacrifice.** Immediately perform a
sacrifice (and read the omens)
4. **opinions of success.** Predictions about whether
I shall be successful

**words
for
everyday
use**
  suf • fice (sə fīs´) *vi.,* be enough; be sufficient. *"Well,"* said my mom as she put the enormous bowl of steaming pasta on
the table, *"do you think that this will <u>suffice</u>?"*

1. Calphurnia has cried out "Help, ho!
They murther Cæsar!" in her sleep.

**ADDITIONAL QUESTIONS
AND ACTIVITIES**

Ask students the following
comprehension questions relating to
what they just read in act 2, scene 1.

• What does Portia ask Brutus to
do? What sort of person does
Portia reveal herself to be? Why
does Brutus say, "Render me
worthy of this noble wife"? Do
you believe that Portia has a right
to know what Brutus is planning
to do? Why, or why not?

• Why might Shakespeare have
ended this scene with a man who
is willing to do anything
suggested by Brutus? What does
this tell us about Brutus's
reputation? What does this tell us
about the importance of Brutus to
the conspiracy?

Answers

• Portia asks Brutus to take her into
his confidence. She reveals herself
to be a strong and loyal woman,
willing to bear physical pain rather
than betray the confidence of her
husband. Brutus says this because
he realizes that Portia is "noble,"
loyal, and strong—in short, an
excellent wife. Students will
probably say that Portia deserves
to know what her husband is
planning. As his wife, she should
be involved in any major decisions
he makes.

• By ending scene 1 with Ligarius's
declaration that he will follow
Brutus no matter what the plan is,
Shakespeare may have intended
to show that Brutus's reputation
and opinion were valued by the
Roman community and also to
illustrate how easily people are
swayed to take part in violence.
Brutus's reputation is as one of the
foremost men of Rome. Brutus is
instrumental to the success of the
conspirators.

1. Calphurnia reports sightings of a lioness giving birth in the street, fiery warriors in the clouds, blood drizzling on the Capitol, and shrieking ghosts.

CALPHURNIA. Cæsar, I never stood on ceremonies,[5]
Yet now they fright[6] me. There is one within,
15 Besides the things that we have heard and seen,
Recounts most <u>horrid</u> sights seen by the watch.[7]
A lioness hath whelped[8] in the streets,
And graves have yawn'd and yielded up their dead;
Fierce fiery warriors fight upon the clouds
20 In ranks and squadrons and right form[9] of war,
Which drizzled blood upon the Capitol;
The noise of battle hurtled in the air;
Horses did neigh, and dying men did groan,
And ghosts did shriek and squeal about the streets.
25 O Cæsar, these things are beyond all use,[10]
And I do fear them.

CÆSAR.   What can be avoided
Whose end is purpos'd by the mighty gods?
Yet Cæsar shall go forth; for these predictions
Are to the world in general as to Cæsar.[11]

30 **CALPHURNIA.** When beggars die there are no comets seen;
The heavens themselves blaze forth the death of princes.

CÆSAR. Cowards die many times before their deaths,
The valiant never taste of death but once.
Of all the wonders that I yet have heard,
35 It seems to me most strange that men should fear,
Seeing that death, a necessary end,
Will come when it will come.

Enter a SERVANT.

                    What say the augurers?[12]

SERVANT. They would not have you to stir forth today.
Plucking the <u>entrails</u> of an offering forth,
40 They could not find a heart within the beast.

CÆSAR. The gods do this in shame of cowardice;
Cæsar should be a beast without a heart
If he should stay at home today for fear.

What omens does Calphurnia report?

---

5. **stood on ceremonies.** Believed in omens
6. **fright.** Frighten
7. **watch.** Watchman
8. **whelped.** Given birth
9. **right form.** Proper formations

10. **beyond all use.** Outside of all normal experience
11. **Are to . . . Cæsar.** Apply as much to the rest of the world as they do to me
12. **augurers.** Religious officials of ancient Rome who foretold the future by reading signs and omens

words for everyday use

hor • rid (hōr´ id) *adj.,* terrible; horrible. *The smell of the garbage after two days in the sun was absolutely <u>horrid</u>.*

en • trails (en´ trālz) *n. pl.,* inner organs, viscera. *The movie was so frightening Eric could feel it in his <u>entrails</u>; he felt so nauseous that he could not watch it anymore.*

No, Cæsar shall not; Danger knows full well
45 That Cæsar is more dangerous than he.
  We are two lions litter'd[13] in one day,
  And I the elder and more terrible;
  And Cæsar shall go forth.

  CALPHURNIA.   Alas, my lord,
  Your wisdom is consum'd in confidence.
50 Do not go forth today; call it my fear
  That keeps you in the house, and not your own.
  We'll send Mark Antony to the Senate house
  And he shall say you are not well today.
  Let me, upon my knee, prevail in this.

55 **CÆSAR.** Mark Antony shall say I am not well,
  And for thy humor[14] I will stay at home.

  Enter DECIUS.

  Here's Decius Brutus; he shall tell them so.

  DECIUS. Cæsar, all hail! Good morrow, worthy Cæsar,
  I come to fetch you to the Senate house.

60 **CÆSAR.** And you are come in very happy time
  To bear my greeting to the senators,
  And tell them that I will not come today.
  Cannot, is false; and that I dare not, falser:
  I will not come today. Tell them so, Decius.

  CALPHURNIA. Say he is sick.

65 **CÆSAR.**   Shall Cæsar send a lie?
  Have I in conquest stretch'd mine arm so far,
  To be afeard to tell greybeards the truth?
  Decius, go tell them Cæsar will not come.

  DECIUS. Most mighty Cæsar, let me know some cause,
70 Lest I be laugh'd at when I tell them so.

  CÆSAR. The cause is in my will, I will not come:
  That is enough to satisfy the Senate.
  But for your private satisfaction,
  Because I love you, I will let you know.
75 Calphurnia here, my wife, stays[15] me at home:
  She dreamt tonight she saw my statue,
  Which, like a fountain with an hundred spouts,
  Did run pure blood; and many lusty Romans
  Came smiling and did bathe their hands in it.

What does Calphurnia beg of Cæsar? How does Cæsar respond?

What has Calphurnia dreamed?

---

13. **litter'd.** Born
14. **for thy humor.** At your insistence, to please you
15. **stays.** Keeps

ANSWERS TO GUIDED READING QUESTIONS

1. Calphurnia begs Cæsar not to go out of the house that day. Cæsar agrees to stay home.
2. Calphurnia dreamed that a statue of Cæsar poured blood from a hundred spouts and Romans bathed their hands in it.

ADDITIONAL QUESTIONS AND ACTIVITIES

What are Cæsar's reactions to Calphurnia's warnings? Why doesn't he listen to her? Does he seem to respect her opinions or wishes?
Answers
Calphurnia dreams that Cæsar is murdered. (Cæsar later says she dreamt that a statue of Cæsar spurted blood and Romans washed their hands in the blood.) She is afraid that something awful might befall Cæsar. Cæsar dismisses Calphurnia's warnings. He ignores her warnings so as to impress Decius. Cæsar seems to have little respect for his wife's opinions and wishes.

LITERARY TECHNIQUE

FORESHADOWING. Foreshadowing is the act of presenting materials that hint at events to occur later in a story. Have students note examples of foreshadowing as they occur in this scene. Then ask students why Cæsar's fate seems obvious to everyone but Cæsar. Is his belief in his own infallibility and immortality an essential part of his character?

1. Decius says the dream means that
Cæsar's blood will revive Rome and
that great men will show their
allegiance to him.
2. Cæsar decides to go to the Senate.

CROSS-CURRICULAR ACTIVITIES

SCIENCE. Students might be
interested in researching dreams and
their interpretations. Students should
look at different psychological
interpretations as well as examine
the work of neurologists. They
should also try to answer the
following questions: Why might
people be fascinated with dreams?
Why are dreams open to many
different interpretations?

ADDITIONAL QUESTIONS AND ACTIVITIES

As act 2, scene 2 is filled with
references to dreams, you
might ask students to what extent
the plot that is unfolding around
Cæsar is like a dream or nightmare.
When events in our lives are out of
our control, why might we feel we
are in a dreamlike state?

Quotables

"What is life? A frenzy. What is life?
An illusion, a shadow, a fiction. And
the greatest good is of slight
worth, as all life is a dream, and
dreams are dreams."
—Pedro Calderón de la Barca

ADDITIONAL QUESTIONS AND ACTIVITIES

Have students write their own letters
of warning to Cæsar.

80　And these does she apply for[16] warnings and <u>portents</u>
And evils <u>imminent</u>, and on her knee
Hath begg'd that I will stay at home today.

DECIUS.　This dream is all <u>amiss</u> interpreted,
It was a vision fair and fortunate.
85　Your statue spouting blood in many pipes,
In which so many smiling Romans bath'd,
Signifies that from you great Rome shall suck
Reviving blood, and that great men shall press
For tinctures, stains, relics, and cognizance.[17]
90　This by Calphurnia's dream is signified.

CÆSAR.　And this way have you well <u>expounded</u> it.

DECIUS.　I have, when you have heard what I can say;
And know it now: the Senate have concluded
To give this day a crown to mighty Cæsar.
95　If you shall send them word you will not come,
Their minds may change. Besides, it were a mock
Apt to be render'd,[18] for someone to say
"Break up the Senate till another time,
When Cæsar's wife shall meet with[19] better dreams."
100　If Cæsar hide himself, shall they not whisper,
"Lo Cæsar is afraid"?
Pardon me, Cæsar, for my dear, dear love
To your proceeding[20] bids me tell you this;
And reason to my love is liable.[21]

105　CÆSAR.　How foolish do your fears seem now, Calphurnia!
I am ashamed I did yield to them.
Give me my robe, for I will go.

Enter BRUTUS, LIGARIUS, METELLUS, CASCA, TREBONIUS, CINNA, *and* PUBLIUS.

And look where Publius is come to fetch me.

PUBLIUS.　Good morrow, Cæsar.

CÆSAR.　　　　　　　　　　Welcome, Publius.
110　What, Brutus, are you stirr'd so early too?
Good morrow, Casca. Caius Ligarius,

How does Decius interpret this dream?

What does Cæsar ultimately decide to do?

---

16. **apply for.** Explain as
17. **tinctures . . . cognizance.** Signs showing their allegiance
to Cæsar
18. **mock . . . render'd.** Something likely to be said in mockery
19. **meet with.** Have
20. **proceeding.** Advancing, moving forward
21. **reason . . . liable.** My thinking is based upon my love for you

---

words for everyday use	**por • tent** (pôr´ tent´) *n.*, sign; omen. *We interpreted the thunder as a <u>portent</u> of doom.* **im • mi • nent** (im´ ə nənt) *adj.*, about to occur. *When we heard the thunder we knew that lightning was <u>imminent</u>.* **a • miss** (ə mis´) *adv.*, wrongly; improperly. *When we smelled smoke after lightning struck the house, we knew that something was <u>amiss</u>.* **ex • pound** (eks pound´) *vt.*, explain; give more information about. *We tried to <u>expound</u> the danger we were in to the fire department as clearly and quickly as possible.*

Cæsar was ne'er so much your enemy
As that same ague[22] which hath made you lean.
What is't a' clock?[23]

BRUTUS.   Cæsar, 'tis strucken[24] eight.

115   **CÆSAR.**   I thank you for your pains and courtesy.

Enter ANTONY.

See, Antony, that revels long a-nights,
Is notwithstanding up. Good morrow, Antony.

ANTONY.   So to most noble Cæsar.

CÆSAR.   Bid them prepare within;
I am to blame to be thus waited for.
120   Now, Cinna; now, Metellus; what, Trebonius:
I have an hour's talk in store for you;
Remember that you call on me today;
Be near me, that I may remember you.

TREBONIUS.   Cæsar, I will; [*aside*] and so near will I be,
125   That your best friends shall wish I had been further.

CÆSAR.   Good friends, go in, and taste some wine with me,
And we, like friends, will straightway go together.

BRUTUS.   [*Aside.*] That every like is not the same,[25] O Cæsar,
The heart of Brutus earns[26] to think upon!

Exeunt.

SCENE 3: A STREET IN ROME NEAR THE CAPITOL

Enter ARTEMIDORUS *reading a paper.*

ARTEMIDORUS.   "Cæsar, beware of Brutus; take heed of Cassius; come not near Casca;
have an eye to Cinna; trust not Trebonius; mark well Metellus Cimber; Decius Brutus
loves thee not; thou hast wrong'd Caius Ligarius. There is but one mind in all these
men, and it is bent against Cæsar. If thou beest[1] not immortal, look about you; security
5   gives way to conspiracy. The mighty gods defend thee!
        Thy lover,[2]
                    Artemidorus."
Here will I stand till Cæsar pass along,
And as a suitor[3] will I give him this.

---

22. **ague.** Fever
23. **What is't a' clock.** What time is it?
24. **'tis strucken.** It has struck
25. **every like . . . same.** Being like something is not being
identical with it. Brutus is saying that some of those present are
only like friends, not actually friends.

26. **earns.** Grieves

ACT 2, SCENE 3
1. **thou beest.** You are
2. **lover.** Friend
3. **as a suitor.** Like someone asking a favor

LITERARY TECHNIQUE

ASIDE. An **aside** is a statement made by
a character in a play, intended to be
heard by the audience but not by
other characters on the stage. Who
makes an aside in this scene? Who is
not meant to hear the statement?
Why?
Answers
Trebonius and Brutus make asides in
this scene. Cæsar is not meant to hear
these statements because they reveal
Trebonius's treacherous intentions and
Brutus's betrayal.

ADDITIONAL QUESTIONS
AND ACTIVITIES

Ask students the following comprehension questions relating to what they
just read in act 2, scene 2.
    In what way does Decius fulfill in this
scene his earlier promise to flatter
Cæsar and thus bring him to the
Capitol? What emotions does Decius
play upon to induce Cæsar to come
with him? How does Decius know what
emotions would influence Cæsar?

SELECTION CHECK TEST 4.4.7
WITH ANSWERS

Checking Your Reading
1. What does Lucius find and give to
   Brutus? **He gives a letter to Brutus.**
2. What does Brutus decide to do
   regarding Cæsar? **He joins the plot
   against him.**
3. What does Brutus convince Cassius
   to do regarding Antony? **He
   convinces him not to kill Antony.**
4. What does Portia ask Brutus to do?
   Portia asks Brutus to confide in her.
5. What request of Calphurnia's does
   Cæsar refuse? **Calphurnia asks
   Cæsar to remain at home that
   day, but he refuses.**

Vocabulary in Context
Fill in each blank with the most
appropriate word from the following
Words for Everyday Use from *The Tragedy
of Julius Cæsar.* You may have to change
the tense of the word.

    imminent   augment   interpose
portent   suffice   commend   particle

1. The baker skillfully **interposed** a
   layer of marzipan between layers of
   sponge cake.
2. The doctor found a **particle** of glass
   in Mark's eye.

3. The coach **commended** Mark for his efforts in the game.
4. The sailors rationed their water so it would **suffice** for the whole trip.
5. The fans prepared for the **imminent** arrival of the movie stars.

Literary Tools
Fill in the blanks using the following terms. You may
not use every term, and you may use some terms more
than once.

tenor   vehicle   conflict   inciting incident
character   complication   motif

1. In a simile, the **tenor** is the subject being described.
2. In a plot, the **complication** develops the conflict to
   a high point of intensity.
3. Any element that recurs in one or more works of
   literature or art is a(n) **motif**.
4. The plot of a literary work revolves around a
   central **conflict**.
5. There is debate over whether Cæsar or Brutus is
   the central **character** of this play.

1. Artemidorus laments that "virtue cannot live / Out of the teeth of emulation." In other words, he laments that no virtuous person can exist without having jealous and destructive rivals.

LITERARY TECHNIQUE

SUSPENSE. **Suspense** is a feeling of expectation, anxiousness, or curiosity created by questions raised in the mind of a reader or viewer. Ask students the following questions: How does scene 4, at the end of act 2, help to build suspense about what will happen in the next act? What do you think will happen when Cæsar arrives at the Capitol?

ADDITIONAL QUESTIONS AND ACTIVITIES

Ask students to reread lines 6–9, spoken by Portia, and then ask them the following questions: Does Portia know what Brutus is going to do at the Capitol? How can you tell? What stereotypes does Portia express about women? Explain. Ask students how they feel about these stereotypes.
Answers
Portia does know what Brutus is going to do, as evidenced by her struggle to "keep counsel," or to keep a Brutus's secret. Portia expresses three stereotypes about women: that women have weak minds, that they have weak bodies, and that they have trouble keeping secrets. She distinguishes herself from most women by saying that she has "a man's mind," meaning she believes she is uncharacteristically intelligent for a woman; however, she says that she has "a woman's might," meaning that she is as weak as any other woman (in her opinion). Students will probably feel that these stereotypes are sexist and insulting toward women. You may add that these stereotypes were familiar ones in Shakespeare's day, and that Shakespeare's audience would probably have accepted them as fact.

---

10   My heart <u>laments</u> that virtue cannot live
Out of the teeth of emulation.[4]
If thou read this, O Cæsar, thou mayest live;
If not, the Fates with traitors do contrive.

Exit.

> What does
> Artemidorus lament?

SCENE 4: IN FRONT OF BRUTUS' HOUSE

Enter PORTIA *and* LUCIUS.

PORTIA.   I prithee,[1] boy, run to the Senate house;
Stay not to answer me, but get thee gone.
Why dost thou stay?

LUCIUS.   To know my errand, madam.

PORTIA.   I would have had thee there and here again
5   Ere I can tell thee what thou shouldst do there.—
O constancy,[2] be strong upon my side,
Set a huge mountain 'tween my heart and tongue!
I have a man's mind, but a woman's might.
How hard it is for women to keep counsel![3]—
Art thou here yet?

10   LUCIUS.   Madam, what should I do?
Run to the Capitol, and nothing else?
And so return to you, and nothing else?

PORTIA.   Yes, bring me word, boy, if thy lord look well,
For he went sickly forth; and take good note
15   What Cæsar doth, what suitors press to him.
Hark, boy, what noise is that?

LUCIUS.   I hear none, madam.

PORTIA.   Prithee listen well;
I heard a bustling rumor,[4] like a fray,[5]
And the wind brings it from the Capitol.

20   LUCIUS.   Sooth,[6] madam, I hear nothing.

Enter the SOOTHSAYER.

---

4. **Out of . . . emulation.** Outside the destructive reach (the bite) of rivalry

ACT 2, SCENE 4
1. **prithee.** Pray thee, request

2. **constancy.** Will
3. **counsel.** Secrets
4. **rumor.** Noise
5. **fray.** Battle
6. **Sooth.** Truthfully

words for everyday use   la • ment (lə ment´) *vt.*, regret deeply; grieve. *The mourners <u>lamented</u> the passing of their beloved friend.*

PORTIA. Come hither, fellow; which way hast thou been?

SOOTHSAYER. At mine own house, good lady.

PORTIA. What is't a' clock?

SOOTHSAYER. About the ninth hour, lady.

PORTIA. Is Cæsar yet gone to the Capitol?

25 **SOOTHSAYER.** Madam, not yet; I go to take my stand,
To see him pass on to the Capitol.

PORTIA. Thou hast some suit to Cæsar, hast thou not?

SOOTHSAYER. That I have, lady, if it will please Cæsar
To be so good to Cæsar as to hear me:
30 I shall beseech[7] him to befriend himself.

PORTIA. Why, know'st thou any harm's intended towards him?

SOOTHSAYER. None that I know will be, much that I fear may chance.[8]
Good morrow to you. Here the street is narrow;
The throng that follows Cæsar at the heels,
35 Of senators, of praetors,[9] common suitors,
Will crowd a feeble man almost to death.
I'll get me to a place more void,[10] and there
Speak to great Cæsar as he comes along.

Exit.

PORTIA. I must go in. Aye me! How weak a thing
40 The heart of woman is! O Brutus,
The heavens speed thee in thine enterprise!
Sure the boy heard me.—Brutus hath a suit
That Cæsar will not grant.—O, I grow faint.—
Run, Lucius, and commend me[11] to my lord,
45 Say I am merry. Come to me again,
And bring me word what he doth say to thee.

Exeunt severally.

---

7. **beseech.** Beg, ask
8. **chance.** Occur, happen
9. **praetors.** Magistrates
10. **void.** Empty
11. **commend me.** Give my best wishes

Respond *to the* **SELECTION**

Do you agree with Cæsar's decision to go to the Capitol? Why, or why not?

RESPOND TO THE SELECTION

Ask students what their opinion of Cæsar is after having read this act. Do they see him as foolish or brave, or how else do they see him?

ADDITIONAL QUESTIONS AND ACTIVITIES

Ask students the following comprehension questions relating to what they just read in act 2, scenes 3 and 4.
- What message does Artemidorus intend to give to Cæsar?
- Why is Portia so upset? About what is she worried? What does the Soothsayer tell Portia?
- At the end of this scene, what message does Portia ask Lucius to give to Brutus? How is she like her husband in this regard?

Answers
Artemidorus plans to give Cæsar a letter warning him to beware of Brutus, Cassius, Casca, Cinna, Trebonius, Metellus Cimber, and Caius Ligarius, all of whom are conspiring to kill Cæsar. Portia is upset because she senses that something terrible is about to happen. The Soothsayer tells her that he fears something might happen to Cæsar. Portia sends a message to her husband telling him that she is well. Like Brutus, she feels she must maintain an outward appearance of calm even though she is deeply troubled.

RECALL

1a. Brutus has decided to join the conspiracy to kill Cæsar.

2a. Cassius initiates the plot and recruits members of the conspiracy, but Brutus makes the decisions to not swear oaths and to not kill Mark Antony.

3a. Brutus compares killing Cæsar to carving meat and says they should "carve him as a dish fit for the gods, / Not hew him as a carcass fit for hounds."

INTERPRET

1b. Brutus is motivated by his desire to preserve the republic, which he believes is in the best interest of the common good.

2b. *Responses will vary.* Some students may feel that Brutus is the actual leader, once he agrees to join, as he overrules Cassius on several critical decisions.

3b. *Responses will vary.* Brutus is not describing the way Cæsar is to be stabbed. He is still uncomfortable with the idea of killing Cæsar and he is attempting to convince himself that this is a noble thing to do, rather than a vicious attack on his friend.

ANALYZE

4a. Brutus listens to his wife's concerns. She argues that if he will only share his bed and table with her, but not share with her the deepest concerns that trouble him, then she is no more than his "harlot." When she inflicts a wound in her thigh to prove to him that she will honor his confidence and not reveal his troubles to others, he says "O ye gods! / Render me worthy of this noble wife!" He agrees to tell her all. Cæsar agrees to stay home, in deference to Calphurnia's fears for him, until Decius arrives and hints that he will be thought weak if he surrenders to his wife's wishes. At this, Cæsar changes his mind, calls Calphurnia's fears "foolish," and says he is ashamed that he listened to her.

SYNTHESIZE

4b. *Responses will vary.* Some students will point out that Cæsar allows his pride to overrule his concern for his wife. You may wish to point out to students that an Elizabethan audience would have been very superstitious and would have taken the dreams and omens very seriously. Therefore Shakespeare may have intended for us to interpret Cæsar's actions as foolhardy. Students may say that Brutus's actions are honorable and loyal.

Investigate, Inquire, and Imagine

Recall: GATHERING FACTS ➤

1a. What has Brutus decided to do at the beginning of act 2?

2a. Who initiates the plot against Cæsar? Who makes the ultimate decisions about how it will be carried out, such as whether or not to swear oaths and whether or not to kill Mark Antony as well?

3a. In scene 1, lines 171–174, Brutus uses a simile that compares the actual killing of Cæsar to something else. To what does he compare it?

Interpret: FINDING MEANING

1b. What do you think is Brutus's motive for joining the conspiracy?

2b. Who do you think is the leader of the conspiracy?

3b. Why do you think he uses this comparison? Is he attempting to describe the way Cæsar will be stabbed, or is he commenting on the right or wrong nature of the act itself?

Analyze: TAKING THINGS APART ➤

4a. Compare Brutus's reaction to Portia's fears with Cæsar's reaction to Calphurnia's fears. To what degree does each man listen to his wife's concerns or agree to respond to them?

Synthesize: BRINGING THINGS TOGETHER

4b. What conclusions can you draw about the character of each man based on this?

Evaluate: MAKING JUDGMENTS ➤

5a. In act 2, scene 1, Brutus delivers a soliloquy in which he wrestles with whether or not killing Cæsar is justified. Examine this soliloquy, lines 10–34, in which Brutus constructs a rationale for the murder and paraphrase it in your own words. Then, evaluate his reasoning. Is his thinking sound, or is he stretching to come up with reasons for killing Cæsar?

Extend: CONNECTING IDEAS

5b. Lord Acton, a British nobleman, said in 1887, "Power tends to corrupt and absolute power corrupts absolutely." What do you think he meant? What examples can you cite from your own experience, history, or current events of people who have abused their power? Why might someone in a position of power be tempted to disregard the established boundaries of his or her power?

Understanding Literature

PLOT AND COMPLICATION. Review the definition for **plot** in the Handbook of Literary Terms. What events occur in act 2 that develop the central conflict in which Brutus is involved? What important decision does Brutus make and why? On the plot pyramid you began in act 1, enter the events from act 2 that complicate the plot of *Julius Cæsar*.

SIMILE. Review the definition for **simile** in the Handbook of Literary Terms and the simile chart you completed in Literary Tools on page 268. How would you describe Brutus's state of mind in act 2? What is the basis of his internal struggle?

EVALUATE

5a. *Responses will vary.* Brutus says he knows no reason to oppose Cæsar other than for the common good, but then speculates that Cæsar might change his nature once crowned. He says that many have risen from lowliness and, once at the top, have failed to acknowledge the lowly they left behind. He says that, since this is possible, Cæsar should be prevented. As the plot cannot be excused by anything terrible in Cæsar himself, it must be justified by the warning that if Cæsar is crowned and given more power, he may become like a snake's egg—harmless but full of dangerous potential. It seems that Brutus is basing his justification on the *possibility* that Cæsar will abuse his power and not on any solid confirmation of any danger.

EXTEND

5b. *Responses will vary.* The saying means that unlimited power will lead to total corruption. Many feel that it is human nature to desire power and to use it for personal gain in the absence of any limits or checks on that power.

Writer's Journal

1. Write a **journal entry** that Portia might have written at the end of act 2, scene 1, after having begged Brutus to tell her what troubled him and getting no answer.

2. Imagine that you are a Roman citizen who has seen the omens and overheard some of the conspirators talking. Write your own **letter** to Cæsar warning him of the danger he may encounter.

3. Imagine that you are Brutus and have decided to first try to sway Cæsar by appealing to him personally, as a friend. Write a **personal letter** to Cæsar, outlining your concerns as well as your respect for him and ask for assurance that he will preserve the republic and not attempt to become king.

Integrating the Language Arts

Language, Grammar, and Style

USING COMMAS AND SEMICOLONS. Review the the Language Arts Survey, 3.87, "Commas," 3.88, "Semicolons," and 3.89, "Colons." Then rewrite the following sentences using commas, semicolons, and colons where appropriate.

1. Brutus joined Cassius Casca Cinna and Metellus in a conspiracy to kill Cæsar.

2. Brutus found himself struggling with two opposing ideals loyalty to his leader Cæsar and loyalty to the republic of Rome.

3. Cassius who feared Cæsar would declare himself king was determined to stop him.

4. Antony was Cæsar's friend and right-hand man Octavius was Cæsar's nephew.

5. The minor characters of this play include Portia Brutus's wife Calphurnia Cæsar's wife a soothsayer and several senators and citizens of Rome.

Study and Research & Collaborative Learning

RESEARCHING THE WOMEN OF ROMAN TIMES. Working with a partner, research what life was like for women of the nobility in Rome around the time of Julius Cæsar. You may use Internet or library resources. What roles did women play in society and in the home? Were they likely to be educated as well as their male peers? Compare your findings to the depiction of the relationship between Brutus and his wife, Portia. Was their relationship typical or atypical?

Critical Thinking

PRO AND CON CHART. Review the Language Arts Survey 5.1, "Making Decisions and Solving Problems." Then imagine that you are Brutus and must make a decision about what to do with regard to Cæsar. Complete a pro and con chart about your decision.

ANSWERS TO INTEGRATING THE LANGUAGE ARTS

Language, Grammar, and Style

1. Brutus joined Cassius, Casca, Cinna and Metellus in a conspiracy to kill Cæsar.

2. Brutus found himself struggling with two opposing ideals: loyalty to his leader, Cæsar, and loyalty to the republic of Rome.

3. Cassius, who feared Cæsar would declare himself king, was determined to stop him.

4. Antony was Cæsar's friend and right-hand man; Octavius was Cæsar's nephew.

5. The minor characters of this play include Portia, Brutus's wife; Calphurnia, Cæsar's wife; a soothsayer; and several senators and citizens of Rome.

Study and Research & Collaborative Learning

Many books are available on the subject of women in classical times. You may direct students' attention to any of the following:

Cantarella, Eva. *Pandora's Daughters.* Baltimore: The Johns Hopkins University Press, 1987.

Clark, Gillian. *Women in the Ancient World.* Oxford: Oxford University Press, 1989.

Demand, Nancy. *Birth, Death, and Motherhood in Classical Greece.* Baltimore: The Johns Hopkins University Press, 1994.

Foshel, Sandra R. & Murnaghan, Sheila, eds. *Women and Slaves in Greco-Roman Culture.* London: Routledge, 1988.

Lefkowitz, Mary R. & Fant, Maureen B. *Women In Greece and Rome.* Toronto: Samuel-Stevens, 1977.

Lefkowitz, Mary R. & Fant, Maureen B. *Women's Life in Greece and Rome.* Baltimore: The Johns Hopkins University Press, 1982.

Massey, Michael. *Women in Ancient Greece and Rome.* New York: Cambridge University Press, 1988.

McAuslan, Ian & Walcot, Peter, eds. *Women in Antiquity.* Oxford: Oxford University Press, 1996.

Patterson, Cynthia B. *The Family in Greek History.* Cambridge: Harvard University Press, 1998.

Pomeroy, Sarah B. *Goddesses, Whores, Wives and Slaves: Women in Classical Antiquity.* New York: Shocken Books, 1975.

ANSWERS TO UNDERSTANDING LITERATURE

PLOT AND COMPLICATION. The complication is Brutus's decision to join the conspirators and his sucessful effort to convince them not to kill Mark Antony. Brutus decides to join the conspiracy and kill Cæsar to protect the republic.

SIMILE. Brutus is troubled; he is unable to sleep. His internal struggle is based on whether or not killing Cæsar is the morally correct thing to do. He is struggling with two opposing ideals: loyalty to his leader, Cæsar, and loyalty to the republic of Rome.

ADDITIONAL RESOURCES

UNIT 4 RESOURCE BOOK
• Selection Worksheet 4.3
• Selection Check Test 4.4.9
• Selection Test 4.4.10

READER'S JOURNAL

Ask students whether they think that Portia could have stopped Brutus from carrying out his plan. Why, or why not?

ART NOTE

The Roman Forum, pictured in the photograph on page 288, was the heart of Rome; it was where the Senate was located, where people gathered in times of crisis to hear people speak from the *rostrum,* and where Antony exhibited the body of Cæsar. The Forum was not only a government site for meetings and courts of law, but also a social center, featuring gladiatorial combat and open-air markets. After the Republican period, it became a religious site as well, and many important temples were built there. Students will have the opportunity to research the Roman Forum in an activity on page 308.

ANSWER TO GUIDED READING QUESTION

1. The date is March 15—the ides of March.

VOCABULARY FROM THE SELECTION

bequeath	malice
commonwealth	puissant
cur	reverence
decree	utterance
discourse	valiant
grievous	valor
inter	

Literary TOOLS

REPETITION AND IRONY. Repetition is the writer's conscious reuse of a word, phrase, sentence or clause. **Irony** is a difference between appearance and reality. *Verbal irony* occurs when a statement is made that implies its opposite. As you read act 3, notice the use of repetition and irony in Mark Antony's speech in scene 2. What effect does he achieve with these techniques?

PLOT, CLIMAX, AND CRISIS. In a **plot,** the **climax** is the high point of interest or suspense. The **crisis** is the point in the plot where something decisive happens to determine the future course of events and the eventual working out of the conflict. As you read act 3, consider what the climax and the crisis are.

Reader's Journal

What would you do if you were Portia and discovered the plot in which Brutus is involved?

Temple of Vesta in the Roman Forum.

ACT 3

SCENE 1: ROME IN FRONT OF THE CAPITOL

Flourish. Enter CÆSAR, BRUTUS, CASSIUS, CASCA, DECIUS, METELLUS, TREBONIUS, CINNA, ANTONY, LEPIDUS, ARTEMIDORUS, PUBLIUS, POPILIUS, *and the* SOOTHSAYER.

CÆSAR. The ides of March[1] are come. ⟶ *What is the date?*

SOOTHSAYER. Ay, Cæsar, but not gone.

ARTEMIDORUS. Hail, Cæsar! Read this schedule.

DECIUS. Trebonius doth desire you to o'er-read

5 (At your best leisure) this his humble suit.

ACT 3, SCENE 1
1. **ides of March.** Fifteenth of March

HISTORICAL NOTE

• According to Plutarch's *Lives,* Cæsar wanted to read Artemidorus's "suit," but could not get to it. You might ask students why Shakespeare may have chosen to change this detail of the source from which he adapted this tragic history. In what way is Cæsar's line, "What touches us ourself shall be last serv'd" more in keeping with the character Shakespeare has given him?
• You might also point out to students Cæsar's use of the royal *we.*

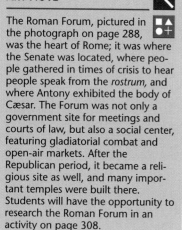

ARTEMIDORUS.   O Cæsar, read mine first; for mine's a suit
That touches Cæsar nearer. Read it, great Cæsar.

    CÆSAR.   What touches us ourself shall be last serv'd.

    ARTEMIDORUS.   Delay not, Cæsar, read it instantly.

    CÆSAR.   What, is the fellow mad?

10   **PUBLIUS.**   Sirrah,[2] give place.

    CASSIUS.   What, urge you your petitions in the street?
Come to the Capitol.

    CÆSAR enters the Capitol, the rest following.

    POPILIUS.   I wish your enterprise today may thrive.

    CASSIUS.   What enterprise, Popilius?

    POPILIUS.   Fare you well.

    Leaves him and joins CÆSAR.

15   **BRUTUS.**   What said Popilius Lena?

    CASSIUS.   He wish'd today our enterprise might thrive.
I fear our purpose is discovered.

    BRUTUS.   Look how he makes to[3] Cæsar; mark him.

    CASSIUS.   Casca, be sudden, for we fear prevention.

20   Brutus, what shall be done? If this be known,
Cassius or Cæsar never shall turn back,
For I will slay myself.

    BRUTUS.   Cassius, be constant;[4]
Popilius Lena speaks not of our purposes,
For look he smiles, and Cæsar doth not change.

25   **CASSIUS.**   Trebonius knows his time; for look you, Brutus,
He draws Mark Antony out of the way.

    Exeunt ANTONY and TREBONIUS.

    DECIUS.   Where is Metellus Cimber? Let him go
And presently prefer[5] his suit to Cæsar.

    BRUTUS.   He is address'd;[6] press near and second him.

30   **CINNA.**   Casca, you are the first that rears your hand.

    CÆSAR.   Are we all ready? What is now amiss
That Cæsar and his Senate must redress?

---

2. **Sirrah.** Contemptuous term or address used toward an
inferior individual
3. **makes to.** Heads toward

4. **constant.** Steady
5. **presently prefer.** Immediately present
6. **address'd.** Ready

> *How does Cæsar respond to the letter Artemidorus offers?*

> *What does Trebonius do?*

1. Cæsar refuses to read it, saying that what pertains to him personally shall be read last.
2. Trebonius draws Antony away from Cæsar.

INDIVIDUAL LEARNING STRATEGIES

MOTIVATION
Assign each student a role for act 3, scene 1, and have them prepare to enact their parts in an informal performance. If your class is large, you may divide the class into two groups. Emphasize that the energy level and tension is high in this climactic scene, and encourage students to read expressively.

READING PROFICIENCY
After they have read act 3, scene 1, have students listen to act 3, scene 2, on the EMC Masterpiece Series Audio Library. In addition, have them answer the Guided Reading and Recall questions in groups of two. As a class, go over the rest of the questions in Investigate, Inquire, and Imagine. Share with them the additional vocabulary below.

ENGLISH LANGUAGE LEARNING
You may wish to review with students the following additional vocabulary before they read the selection.
suit—request or petition (archaic)
parchment—paper or document (archaic)
unassailable—not able to be attacked or moved
prostrate—lying face down in submission
pulpit—raised platform for giving a speech or sermon
carrion—dead and decaying
rendered—given
legacy—anything handed down, as from an ancestor
arbors—gardens or lawns

SPECIAL NEEDS
If students have not already completed a pro and con chart as suggested in the Study and Research activity on page 287, have them do this now. They may debate the issue of whether Brutus should go along with the conspirators' plot or stop them before it is too late.

ENRICHMENT
Encourage interested students to examine Shakespeare's *The*

INDIVIDUAL LEARNING STRATEGIES (CONT.)

Tragedy of Antony and Cleopatra, a play of great lyrical and tragic intensity in which Mark Antony is ascribed a very different character than that which he is given in *Julius Cæsar.* An excellent, if ambitious, project for a student would be a comparative analysis of the character of Mark Antony as presented in these two plays.

1. Metellus appeals to Cæsar to allow the return of his brother, whom Cæsar has banished.
2. Brutus and Cassius also ask Cæsar to repeal the banishment of Publius Cimber. Cæsar refuses to change his position on the matter, saying "I am constant as the northern star, / Of whose true-fix'd and resting quality / There is no fellow in the firmament."

LITERARY TECHNIQUE

IMAGE AND OBJECTIVE CORRELATIVE. An **image** is a word or phrase that names something that can be seen, heard, touched, tasted, or smelled. An **objective correlative** is a group of images that together create a particular emotion in the reader. What group of images does Cæsar use to describe himself? What is the effect of this group of images? What is the effect of Cæsar describing himself in this manner at this particular time? Do students think his words strengthen the conspirators' resolve? If so, why?

CROSS-CURRICULAR ACTIVITIES

ASTRONOMY. In lines 60–63, Cæsar compares himself to the northern star, saying that the northern star is the only star that is "fix'd," or unmoving. Ask students to research the northern star. By what other name is it known? Why does it not appear to move as the other stars do? As an alternative, you may have students research Romans' knowledge of astronomy. What did the Romans know and believe about the stars and the planets? Which of the planets are named for Roman gods?

METELLUS.   Most high, most mighty, and most <u>puissant</u> Cæsar,
Metellus Cimber throws before thy seat
An humble heart.   *Kneeling.*

35   **CÆSAR.**   I must prevent thee, Cimber.
These couchings and these lowly courtesies[7]
Might fire the blood of ordinary men,
And turn preordinance and first decree[8]
Into the law of children.[9] Be not fond

40   To[10] think that Cæsar bears such rebel[11] blood
That will be thaw'd from the true quality
With that which melteth fools—I mean sweet words,
Low-crooked curtsies, and base spaniel fawning.
Thy brother by <u>decree</u> is banished;

45   If thou dost bend, and pray, and fawn for him,
I spurn[12] thee like a <u>cur</u> out of my way.
Know, Cæsar doth not wrong, nor without cause
Will he be satisfied.[13]

METELLUS.   Is there no voice more worthy than my own,

50   To sound more sweetly in great Cæsar's ear
For the repealing of my banish'd brother?

BRUTUS.   I kiss thy hand, but not in flattery, Cæsar;
Desiring thee that Publius Cimber may
Have an immediate freedom of repeal.[14]

CÆSAR.   What, Brutus?

55   **CASSIUS.**   Pardon, Cæsar! Cæsar, pardon!
As low as to thy foot doth Cassius fall,
To beg enfranchisement[15] for Publius Cimber.

CÆSAR.   I could be well mov'd, if I were as you;
If I could pray to move, prayers would move me;

60   But I am constant as the northern star,
Of whose true-fix'd and resting quality
There is no fellow[16] in the firmament.[17]
The skies are painted with unnumb'red sparks,
They are all fire, and every one doth shine;

(margin) What does Metellus want from Cæsar?

(margin) What do Brutus and Cassius ask of Cæsar? How does Cæsar respond? To what does he compare himself?

---

7. **courtesies.** Bows
8. **preordinance and first decree.** Earlier made laws
9. **the law of children.** Children's games to be changed at whim
10. **fond / To.** So absurd as to
11. **rebel.** Rebellious
12. **spurn.** Kick
13. **Will he be satisfied.** Moved to change his mind
14. **freedom of repeal.** Permission to be recalled from exile
15. **enfranchisement.** Here, Cassius means reinstatement as a full citizen
16. **fellow.** Equal
17. **firmament.** Sky

words for everyday use

pu • is • sant (pyoo͞´ĭ sənt) *adj.*, strong; powerful. *Absolute monarchs are known for their <u>puissant</u> control over their country and subjects.*

de • cree (dĭ krē´) *n.*, order. *The banished woman's family begged the king to reverse his <u>decree</u>.*

cur (kʉr) *n.*, dog; mongrel. *A flea-bitten <u>cur</u> harassed the postal worker as he attempted to deliver mail along his route.*

65   But there's but one in all doth hold his place.
      So in the world: 'tis furnish'd well with men,
      And men are flesh and blood, and apprehensive;[18]
      Yet in the number I do know but one
      That unassailable holds on his rank,[19]
70   Unshak'd of motion; and that I am he,
      Let me a little show it, even in this—
      That I was constant Cimber should be banish'd
      And constant do remain to keep him so.

CINNA. O Cæsar—

CÆSAR.   Hence! Wilt thou lift up Olympus?[20]

DECIUS. Great Cæsar—

75   **CÆSAR.**   Doth not Brutus bootless[21] kneel?

CASCA. Speak hands for me!

          They stab CÆSAR.

CÆSAR. *Et tu,*[22] *Brute?*—Then fall Cæsar!

          Dies.

CINNA. Liberty! Freedom! Tyranny is dead!
      Run hence, proclaim, cry it about the streets.

80   **CASSIUS.** Some to the common pulpits,[23] and cry out,
      "Liberty, freedom, and enfranchisement!"[24]

BRUTUS. People and senators, be not affrighted;[25]
      Fly not, stand still; ambition's debt is paid.

CASCA. Go to the pulpit, Brutus.

DECIUS.   And Cassius too.

85   **BRUTUS.** Where's Publius?

CINNA. Here, quite confounded with[26] this mutiny.

METELLUS. Stand fast together, lest some friend of Cæsar's
      Should chance[27]—

BRUTUS. Talk not of standing. Publius, good cheer,
90   There is no harm intended to your person,
      Nor to no Roman else.[28] So tell them, Publius.

CASSIUS. And leave us, Publius, lest that the people,
      Rushing on us, should do your age some mischief.

BRUTUS. Do so, and let no man abide[29] this deed,

What are Cæsar's last words, and to whom are they directed? What do the killers shout after Cæsar is dead?

---

18. **apprehensive.** Capable of reason
19. **holds on his rank.** Holds his position
20. **Olympus.** In Greek myth, the mountain that is home to the gods
21. **bootless.** In vain
22. **Et tu.** Latin for *and you*
23. **pulpits.** Platforms for public speakers

24. **enfranchisement.** Full citizenship rights
25. **affrighted.** Frightened
26. **confounded with.** Overwhelmed by
27. **chance.** Happen
28. **no Roman else.** Any other Roman
29. **abide.** Suffer the consequences of

1. Cæsar's dying words are to Brutus. He says, *"Et tu, Brute?*—Then fall Cæsar." The killers shout "Liberty! Freedom! Tyranny is dead!" and "Liberty, freedom, and enfranchisement!"

ADDITIONAL QUESTIONS AND ACTIVITIES

Ask students the following questions: What is the effect of Cæsar's last words? Why do they make him a more sympathetic character?
Answer
Responses will vary. Cæsar's last words reveal that he trusted and loved Brutus and is surprised by Brutus's betrayal most of all. These words make Cæsar more sympathetic because they reveal his trusting nature.

ANSWERS TO GUIDED READING QUESTIONS

1. According to Brutus, no one but the doers should suffer the consequences.
2. Brutus suggests they each bathe their hands in Cæsar's blood and go into the marketplace shouting, "Peace, freedom and liberty!"

LITERARY NOTE

IRONY. Irony is a difference between appearance and reality. What is peculiar about the desire Brutus expresses in lines 105–110? Why might bathing hands in blood and waving bloody weapons be inappropriate? What is ironic about their doing so while shouting, "Peace, freedom, and liberty"? What is Shakespeare revealing about the conspirators' reasoning and that of Brutus in particular?
Answers
Students may say that celebrating someone's murder is highly inappropriate behavior. A cry of "Peace, freedom, and liberty" is ironic because murderers are abroad waving bloody hands and daggers, and bloodthirsty murderers are not conducive to peace, freedom, or liberty. Shakespeare is revealing that Brutus and the conspirators have muddled reasoning.

LITERARY NOTE

You might draw students' attention to Brutus's statement in line 114, "How many times shall Cæsar bleed in sport," and Cassius's response in lines 116–118, "So oft as that shall be, / So often shall the knot of us be call'd / The men that gave their country liberty." Indicate that at this point Shakespeare for a moment lets the conventions of the play slip and reminds his audience that this, after all, is just a play about Cæsar. You should also explain the irony, or difference between appearance and reality, that occurs when the murderers, who are steeped in blood, imagine the audience as viewing them as heroes of liberty.

---

95 But we the doers.

Exeunt all but the Conspirators.

Enter TREBONIUS.

CASSIUS.   Where is Antony?

TREBONIUS.   Fled to his house amaz'd.
Men, wives, and children stare, cry out, and run,
As[30] it were doomsday.

BRUTUS.   Fates, we will know your pleasures.
That we shall die, we know, 'tis but the time,
100 And drawing days out, that men stand upon.[31]

CASCA.   Why, he that cuts off twenty years of life
Cuts off so many[32] years of fearing death.

BRUTUS.   Grant that, and then is death a benefit;
So are we Cæsar's friends, that have abridg'd
105 His time of fearing death. Stoop, Romans, stoop,
And let us bathe our hands in Cæsar's blood
Up to the elbows, and besmear our swords;
Then walk we forth, even to the marketplace,[33]
And waving our red weapons o'er our heads,
110 Let's all cry, "Peace, freedom, and liberty!"

CASSIUS.   Stoop then, and wash. How many ages hence
Shall this our lofty scene be acted over
In states unborn and accents[34] yet unknown!

BRUTUS.   How many times shall Cæsar bleed in sport,[35]
115 That now on Pompey's basis[36] lies along
No worthier than the dust!

CASSIUS.   So oft as that shall be,
So often shall the knot[37] of us be call'd
The men that gave their country liberty.

DECIUS.   What, shall we forth?

CASSIUS.   Ay, every man away.
120 Brutus shall lead, and we will grace his heels
With the most boldest and best hearts of Rome.

Enter a SERVANT.

BRUTUS.   Soft, who comes here? A friend of Antony's.

SERVANT.   Thus, Brutus, did my master bid me kneel;
Thus did Mark Antony bid me fall down;

Who should suffer the consequences of what the conspirators have done?

What does Brutus suggest the conspirators do?

---

30. **As.** As if
31. **stand upon.** Worry about
32. **so many.** As many
33. **marketplace.** The Forum
34. **accents.** Languages
35. **in sport.** In entertainments, such as plays
36. **Pompey's basis.** Pedestal of Pompey's statue
37. **knot.** Group

125   And being prostrate, thus he bade me say:
     Brutus is noble, wise, <u>valiant</u>, and honest;
     Cæsar was mighty, bold, royal, and loving.
     Say, I love Brutus, and I honor him;
     Say, I fear'd Cæsar, honor'd him, and lov'd him.
130   If Brutus will vouchsafe that Antony
     May safely come to him, and be resolv'd
     How Cæsar hath deserv'd to lie in death,
     Mark Antony shall not love Cæsar dead
     So well as Brutus living; but will follow

What does Antony request of Brutus? What does he promise Brutus in return?

135   The fortunes and affairs of noble Brutus
     Thorough the hazards of this untrod[38] state
     With all true faith. So says my master Antony.

    BRUTUS.   Thy master is a wise and valiant Roman,
     I never thought him worse.
140   Tell him, so please him come unto this place,
     He shall be satisfied; and, by my honor,
     Depart untouch'd.

    SERVANT.   I'll fetch him presently.[39]   *Exit* SERVANT.

    BRUTUS.   I know that we shall have him well to friend.[40]

    CASSIUS.   I wish we may; but yet have I a mind
145   That fears him much; and my misgiving still
     Falls shrewdly to the purpose.[41]

    Enter ANTONY.

    BRUTUS.   But here comes Antony. Welcome, Mark Antony!

    ANTONY.   O mighty Cæsar! dost thou lie so low?
     Are all thy conquests, glories, triumphs,[42] spoils,
150   Shrunk to this little measure? Fare thee well!
     I know not, gentlemen, what you intend,
     Who else must be let blood,[43] who else is rank;[44]
     If I myself, there is no hour so fit
     As Cæsar's death's hour, nor no instrument
155   Of half that worth as those your swords, made rich
     With the most noble blood of all this world.

How does Antony react upon seeing Cæsar's body? What does he beg of the conspirators?

---

38. **untrod.** Not previously explored, new
39. **presently.** At once
40. **well to friend.** As a good friend
41. **misgiving . . . purpose.** Doubts usually prove to be well-founded.
42. **triumphs.** Processions
43. **let blood.** Bled, as was done in the past to cure disease
44. **rank.** Sick

words for everyday use
    val • iant (val´yənt) *adj.,* full of courage; brave. *The <u>valiant</u> knight fought off eight opponents after he had been wounded.*

ANSWERS TO GUIDED READING QUESTIONS

1. Antony requests that he be allowed to return safely to the Capitol and hear an explanation for Cæsar's death. In return, Antony promises that he will be loyal to Brutus and follow him.
2. Antony wonders sadly how all of Cæsar's mighty conquests have come down to this end. He beseeches the conspirators to kill him, too, if they must, with the same weapons used to kill Cæsar.

ADDITIONAL QUESTIONS AND ACTIVITIES

Ask students the following questions: The rules governing English have changed since Shakespeare's time. What about Cassius's statement in lines 120–121 would be considered incorrect usage today? How would the lines be stated in modern English? If you need help, refer to the Language Arts Survey 3.65, "Modifiers—Adjectives and Adverbs."
Answer
Cassius refers to their hearts as "the most boldest and best hearts of Rome." In modern English, the phrase would be "the boldest and best hearts." "Most" is not needed.

ADDITIONAL QUESTIONS AND ACTIVITIES

Ask students the following questions: What does Antony's servant reveal about his master's feelings for Brutus? for Cæsar? How do those feelings compare? What might Antony's feelings reveal about his motives?
Answers
Antony loves and honors Brutus, and he loved, honored, and feared Cæsar. One might infer that Antony is saying he does not fear Brutus; therefore, he might attempt revenge for Cæsar's murder.

ANSWERS TO GUIDED READING QUESTIONS

1. Brutus and Cassius tell Antony they love and revere him and mean him no harm. They promise him a prominent place in the new government.
2. Antony shakes the bloody hand of each of the conspirators.

LITERARY NOTE

You might point out to students that the scene described on page 294 would be particularly striking on stage. Encourage students to visualize the action: Mark Antony singles out each conspirator and grasps each blood-covered hand; as a result, Mark Antony too would become covered in blood. Suggest to students that this dramatic scene is meant to emphasize that Antony is not aligning himself with the conspirators but disgusted by them; he shakes the conspirators' hands not as a sign of allegiance but almost as a resolution to take revenge upon each and every man involved.

I do beseech ye, if you bear me hard,[45]
Now, whilst your purpled hands do reek and smoke,[46]
Fulfill your pleasure. Live a thousand years,
160 I shall not find myself so apt to die;
No place will please me so, no mean[47] of death,
As here by Cæsar, and by you cut off,
The choice and master spirits of this age.

    BRUTUS.   O Antony! beg not your death of us.
165 Though now we must appear bloody and cruel,
As by our hands and this our present act
You see we do, yet see you but our hands,
And this the bleeding business they have done.
Our hearts you see not, they are pitiful;[48]
170 And pity to the general wrong of Rome—
As fire drives out fire, so pity pity—
Hath done this deed on Cæsar.[49] For your part,
To you our swords have leaden points, Mark Antony;
Our arms in strength of <u>malice</u>, and our hearts
175 Of brothers' temper, do receive you in
With all kind love, good thoughts, and <u>reverence</u>.

    CASSIUS.   Your voice shall be as strong as any man's
In the disposing of new dignities.[50]

    BRUTUS.   Only be patient till we have appeas'd
180 The multitude, beside themselves with fear,
And then we will deliver[51] you the cause
Why I, that did love Cæsar when I strook him,
Have thus proceeded.

    ANTONY.   I doubt not of your wisdom.
Let each man render me his bloody hand.
185 First, Marcus Brutus, will I shake with you;
Next, Caius Cassius, do I take your hand;
Now, Decius Brutus, yours; now yours, Metellus;
Yours, Cinna; and, my valiant Casca, yours;
Though last, not least in love, yours, good Trebonius.
190 Gentlemen all—alas, what shall I say?

> *What feelings do Brutus and Cassius express toward Antony?*

> *What does Antony do?*

---

45. **bear me hard.** Dislike me
46. **smoke.** Steam with warm blood
47. **mean.** Means
48. **pitiful.** Full of pity

49. **pity to . . . Cæsar.** Our pity for Rome caused us to act as we have.
50. **dignities.** Titles, public offices
51. **deliver.** Explain to

words for everyday use

mal • ice (mal´is) *n.,* desire to do harm. *The reporter told the politician privately that she had no feelings of <u>malice</u>, she was just doing her job.*

rev • er • ence (rev´ər əns) *n.,* feelings of respect, care, or love. *The children looked at their grandmother with <u>reverence</u> and love.*

My credit[52] now stands on such slippery ground
That one of two bad ways you must conceit[53] me,
Either a coward or a flatterer.
That I did love thee, Cæsar, O, 'tis true;
195 If then thy spirit look upon us now,
Shall it not grieve thee dearer than thy death,
To see thy Antony making his peace,
Shaking the bloody fingers of thy foes,
Most noble! in the presence of thy corse?[54]
200 Had I as many eyes as thou hast wounds,
Weeping as fast as they stream forth thy blood,
It would become me better than to close
In terms of friendship with thine enemies.
Pardon me, Julius! Here wast thou bay'd,[55] brave hart,[56]
205 Here didst thou fall, and here thy hunters stand,
Sign'd in thy spoil, and crimson'd in thy lethe.[57]
O world! thou wast the forest to this hart,
And this indeed, O world, the heart of thee.
How like a deer, strooken[58] by many princes,
210 Dost thou here lie!

CASSIUS.   Mark Antony—

ANTONY.   Pardon me, Caius Cassius!
The enemies of Cæsar shall say this:
Then, in a friend, it is cold modesty.

CASSIUS.   I blame you not for praising Cæsar so,
215 But what compact mean you to have with us?
Will you be prick'd in number[59] of our friends,
Or shall we on, and not depend on you?

ANTONY.   Therefore I took your hands, but was indeed
Sway'd from the point, by looking down on Cæsar.
220 Friends am I with you all, and love you all,
Upon this hope, that you shall give me reasons
Why, and wherein, Cæsar was dangerous.

BRUTUS.   Or else were this a savage spectacle.
Our reasons are so full of good regard
225 That were you, Antony, the son of Cæsar,
You should be satisfied.

ANTONY.   That's all I seek,

---

52. **credit.** Reputation
53. **conceit.** Perceive
54. **corse.** Body
55. **bay'd.** Chased down, brought to bay
56. **hart.** Deer, with a pun to *heart*

57. **lethe.** Blood. In Greek myth, Lethe was a river from which the dead in Hades drank, causing them to forget and to give up their former lives.
58. **strooken.** Struck
59. **prick'd in number.** Counted as one

ANSWER TO GUIDED READING QUESTION

1. Antony fears he will be perceived as either a flatterer or a coward because he loved Cæsar but has quickly forgiven and promised loyalty to the conspirators.

LITERARY TECHNIQUE

METAPHOR. A **metaphor** is a figure of speech in which one thing is spoken or written about as if it were another. Ask students what metaphor Antony uses to describe the death of Cæsar in lines 204–206. To what is Cæsar compared? To what are the conspirators compared? What feelings about Cæsar and his murderers are revealed by Antony's choice of this metaphor?
Answers
Antony says that Cæsar was a hart, or deer, chased down and slain by hunters. Cæsar is compared to a hart; the conspirators are compared to hunters. Antony's sympathy with Cæsar and disgust for his murderers is revealed by this metaphor.

HISTORICAL NOTE

Some historians have speculated that Brutus may have been Cæsar's illegitimate son. This cannot be proved or disproved. However, if it is true, lines 225–226, spoken by Brutus, have a deeper meaning.

1. Cassius fears that the speech will move the people and rouse their sympathy for Cæsar.

ADDITIONAL QUESTIONS AND ACTIVITIES

- On what condition does Antony say he will join Brutus and Cassius?
- What restrictions does Brutus place on Antony's speech at Cæsar's funeral?

Answers

Antony says he will join the conspirators when he hears their explanation of why Cæsar was dangerous. Brutus restricts Antony from blaming the conspirators and requires him to acknowledge that he speaks with Brutus's permission.

CROSS-CURRICULAR ACTIVITIES

SOCIAL STUDIES. In lines 240–241, Brutus states that Cæsar shall receive "all true rites and lawful ceremonies." Students may be interested in researching funeral customs in ancient Rome. What were funerals like in pre-Christian Rome? Where did people expect to go after death? You may refer them to the book *Death and Burial in the Roman World* by J. M. C. Toynbee (1971; pbk 1996), (Baltimore & London: Johns Hopkins Univ. Press). You may note to students that Cæsar's grave is located in the remains of The Cæsars' Church *(Templum Divii Iulii)* in the northern part of the Roman Forum and receives thousands of visitors a year. Some tour guides have been known to add drama to the tour by performing Mark Antony's speech at Cæsar's grave.

And am, moreover, suitor[60] that I may
Produce his body to the marketplace,
And in the pulpit, as becomes a friend,
230 Speak in the order of[61] his funeral.

BRUTUS.   You shall, Mark Antony.

CASSIUS.   Brutus, a word with you.
Aside to Brutus. You know not what you do. Do not consent
That Antony speak in his funeral.
Know you how much the people may be mov'd
By that which he will utter?

235 **BRUTUS.**   By your pardon—
I will myself into the pulpit first,
And show the reason of our Cæsar's death.
What Antony shall speak, I will protest
He speaks by leave and by permission;
240 And that we are contented Cæsar shall
Have all true rites and lawful ceremonies.
It shall advantage[62] more than do us wrong.

CASSIUS.   I know not what may fall,[63] I like it not.

BRUTUS.   Mark Antony, here take you Cæsar's body.
245 You shall not in your funeral speech blame us,
But speak all good you can devise of Cæsar,
And say you do 't by our permission;
Else shall you not have any hand at all
About his funeral. And you shall speak
250 In the same pulpit whereto I am going,
After my speech is ended.

ANTONY.   Be it so;
I do desire no more.

BRUTUS.   Prepare the body then, and follow us.

Exeunt. Manet ANTONY.

ANTONY.   O, pardon me, thou bleeding piece of earth,[64]
255 That I am meek and gentle with these butchers!
Thou art the ruins of the noblest man
That ever lived in the tide of times.
Woe to the hand that shed this costly blood!
Over thy wounds now do I prophesy
260 (Which like dumb mouths do ope[65] their ruby lips

Why does Cassius warn Brutus against allowing Antony to speak at the funeral?

---

60. **suitor.** Petitioner
61. **in the order of.** In the ceremonies conducted for
62. **advantage.** Help, aid
63. **may fall.** May occur
64. **thou . . . earth.** Cæsar
65. **ope.** Open

HISTORICAL NOTE

Elizabethans believed that the wounds of the dead would open, almost as if to speak in accusation, when the murderer or murderers were in the presence of the deceased. This belief is reflected in lines 260–261, in which Antony describes Cæsar's wounds as opening like speechless mouths to beg him to speak for them. Similar scenes occur in other works of Shakespeare, most notably in *The Tragedy of Richard III,* in which Richard woos Anne over the body of her father-in-law.

To beg the voice and <u>utterance</u> of my tongue)
A curse shall light upon the limbs of men;
Domestic fury and fierce civil strife
Shall cumber[66] all the parts of Italy;

What does Antony say will happen as a result of Cæsar's death?

265 Blood and destruction shall be so in use,
And dreadful objects so familiar,
That mothers shall but smile when they behold
Their infants quartered with the hands of war;
All pity chok'd with custom of[67] fell[68] deeds;

270 And Cæsar's spirit, ranging[69] for revenge,
With Ate[70] by his side come hot from hell,
Shall in these confines with a monarch's voice
Cry "Havoc!" and let slip[71] the dogs of war,
That this foul deed shall smell above the earth

275 With carrion men, groaning for burial.

Enter Octavio's[72] SERVANT.

You serve Octavius Cæsar, do you not?

SERVANT.   I do, Mark Antony.

ANTONY.   Cæsar did write for him to come to Rome.

SERVANT.   He did receive his letters and is coming,
280 And bid me say to you by word of mouth—
O Cæsar!— [*Seeing the body.*]

ANTONY.   Thy heart is big; get thee apart and weep.
Passion, I see, is catching, for mine eyes,
Seeing those beads of sorrow stand in thine,
285 Began to water. Is thy master coming?

SERVANT.   He lies tonight within seven leagues of Rome.

ANTONY.   Post[73] back with speed, and tell him what hath chanc'd.[74]
Here is a mourning Rome, a dangerous Rome,
No Rome of safety for Octavius yet;
290 Hie hence,[75] and tell him so. Yet stay awhile,
Thou shalt not back till I have borne this corse
Into the marketplace. There shall I try,
In my oration, how the people take

Who is coming to Rome? What message does Antony send this person?

---

66. **cumber.** Help, aid
67. **with custom of.** By familiarity with
68. **fell.** Terrible; cruel
69. **ranging.** Roving
70. **Ate.** Greek goddess of discord
71. **let slip.** Unhook from their leashes

72. *Octavio's.* Gaius Octavius, grand nephew and heir to Julius Cæsar; later Augustus Cæsar, the first of the Roman emperors
73. **Post.** Ride
74. **chanc'd.** Happened
75. **Hie hence.** Hurry from here

words for everyday use

ut • ter • ance (ut´ər əns) *n., speech. The <u>utterances</u> of the poet were so beautiful that all her listeners left feeling radiant.*

---

1. The plebeians demand to hear why
Cæsar has been killed. Cassius and
Brutus will each speak to the people
and give them the reasons for their
leader's death.

ADDITIONAL QUESTIONS AND ACTIVITIES

Ask students the following
comprehension questions relating to
what they just read in act 3, scene 1:
- Whom has Cæsar banished? Does
he change his mind? Why, or why
not? What does his unwillingness
to pardon this person reveal about
his character? What type of leader
do you think Cæsar was?
- What does Mark Antony reveal in
his passionate words over Cæsar's
dead body (lines 255–257)? In
what way does Antony seem
different than Cæsar as a
politician?
- What explanation of his actions
does Brutus offer Mark Antony?
Do you think Brutus is sincere? Do
you consider Brutus a good man?
a confused man? Explain.
- Why do you think Antony sends
word to Octavius at the end of
this scene? What is Antony
planning?

Answers
Cæsar has banished Metellus
Cimber's brother, Publius Cimber.
Cæsar does not change his mind
because, as he says, he is as
determined and as fixed as "the
northern star." *Responses will vary.*
This suggests that Cæsar was a firm
ruler who meted out justice firmly,
but would not act in a contradictory
manner. Mark Antony reveals that he
has been feigning regard for Cæsar's
killers and plans to wage war against
the conspirators. He seems craftier
than Cæsar; he is willing to present a
false face to achieve his personal
goals, unlike Cæsar who strove to be
as fixed and as constant as "the
northern star." Brutus says that
although the conspirators have
bleeding hands, they have pitiful and
compassionate hearts and merely
acted for the good of the country.
Responses will vary. Brutus is sincere,
but confused. He has just committed
a callous act and is saying he has a
compassionate heart. Mark Antony
wishes to join forces with Octavius
against Brutus and the conspirators.
Antony is probably planning to seize
control of the government.

The cruel issue[76] of these bloody men,
295 According to the which[77] thou shalt <u>discourse</u>
To young Octavius of the state of things.
Lend me your hand. *Exeunt with* CÆSAR'S *body.*

SCENE 2: THE ROMAN FORUM

Enter BRUTUS *and* CASSIUS *with the* PLEBEIANS.[1]

PLEBEIANS. We will be satisfied! Let us be satisfied!

BRUTUS. Then follow me, and give me audience, friends.
Cassius, go you into the other street,
And part the numbers.[2]
5 Those that will hear me speak, let 'em stay here;
Those that will follow Cassius, go with him;
And public reasons shall be rendered
Of Cæsar's death.

1. PLEBEIAN. I will hear Brutus speak.

2. PLEBEIAN. I will hear Cassius, and compare their reasons,
10 When severally[3] we hear them rendered.

Exit Cassius with some of the Plebeians.
Brutus goes into the pulpit.

3. PLEBEIAN. The noble Brutus is[4] ascended; silence!

BRUTUS. Be patient till the last.[5]
Romans, countrymen, and lovers,[6] hear me for my cause, and be silent, that you may hear.
Believe me for mine honor, and have respect to[7] mine honor, that you may believe.
15 Censure[8] me in your wisdom, and awake your senses, that you may the better judge. If
there be any in this assembly, any dear friend of Cæsar's, to him I say, that Brutus' love to
Cæsar was no less than his. If then that friend demand why Brutus rose against Cæsar, this
is my answer: Not that I lov'd Cæsar less, but that I lov'd Rome more. Had you rather
Cæsar were living, and die all slaves, than that Cæsar were dead, to live all freemen? As
20 Cæsar lov'd me, I weep for him; as he was fortunate, I rejoice at it; as he was valiant, I
honor him; but, as he was ambitious, I slew him. There is tears for his love; joy for his

> What do the plebeians
> demand? How will
> Brutus and Cassius
> fulfill the demand?

---

76. **issue.** Consequences
77. **the which.** The outcome of which (Antony plans to use his
speech as an occasion to test the attitudes of the people about the
killing of Cæsar.)

ACT 3, SCENE 2
1. **PLEBEIANS.** Common people

2. **part the numbers.** Divide up the crowd
3. **severally.** Separately
4. **is.** Has
5. **last.** End
6. **lovers.** Friends
7. **to.** For
8. **Censure.** Judge

**words
for
everyday
use** dis • course (dis´kôrs´) *vi.,* speak. *Listening to the professor* <u>discourse</u> *upon almost any topic was an illuminating experience.*

fortune; honor for his <u>valor</u>; and death for his ambition. Who is here so base[9] that would be a bondman?[10] If any, speak, for him have I offended. Who is here so rude[11] that would not be a Roman? If any, speak, for him
25   have I offended. Who is here so vile that will not love his country? If any, speak, for him have I offended. I pause for a reply.

What does Brutus say would have happened had Cæsar not been killed? What was Cæsar's crime?

ALL.   None, Brutus, none.

BRUTUS.   Then none have I offended. I have done no more to Cæsar than you shall do to Brutus. The question of his death is enroll'd[12] in the Capitol: his glory not extenuated,[13]
30   wherein he was worthy; nor his offences enforc'd,[14] for which he suffer'd death.

Enter MARK ANTONY *and others with Cæsar's body.*

Here comes his body, mourn'd by Mark Antony, who, though he had no hand in his death, shall receive the benefit of his dying, a place in the <u>commonwealth</u>, as which of you shall not? With this I depart, that, as I slew my best lover[15] for the good of Rome, I have the same dagger for myself, when it shall please
35   my country to need my death.

What does Brutus offer the people? How do they respond?

ALL.   Live, Brutus, live, live!

1. PLEBEIAN.   Bring him with triumph home unto his house.

2. PLEBEIAN.   Give him a statue with his ancestors.

3. PLEBEIAN.   Let him be Cæsar.

4. PLEBEIAN.   Cæsar's better parts
Shall be crown'd in Brutus.

40   **1. PLEBEIAN.**   We'll bring him to his house
With shouts and clamors.

BRUTUS.   My countrymen—

2. PLEBEIAN.   Peace, silence! Brutus speaks.

1. PLEBEIAN.   Peace ho!

BRUTUS.   Good countrymen, let me depart alone,
And, for my sake, stay here with Antony.
45   Do grace to Cæsar's corpse, and grace his speech
Tending to Cæsar's glories, which Mark Antony
(By our permission) is allow'd to make.
I do entreat you, not a man depart,

---

9. **base.** Low
10. **bondman.** Servant, slave
11. **so rude.** Barbarous
12. **question . . . is enroll'd.** Reasons for his death have

been recorded
13. **extenuated.** Lessened
14. **enforc'd.** Forced, exaggerated
15. **lover.** Friend

words for everyday use

val • or (val´ər) *n.,* courage or bravery. *In some medieval works, women are portrayed as knights of great <u>valor</u>.*

com • mon • wealth (käm´ən welth´) *n.,* republic. *Members of the <u>commonwealth</u> elect officials to represent them.*

ANSWERS TO GUIDED READING QUESTIONS

1. Brutus says that if Cæsar had not been killed, the people would have become slaves. Cæsar's crime, according to Brutus, was ambition.
2. Brutus offers the people his life, saying that he will slay himself just as he slayed Cæsar. The people shout, "Live, Brutus, live!" They say they will crown him and bring him to his house "with shouts and clamors."

ADDITIONAL QUESTIONS AND ACTIVITIES

Have students keep track of the mob's reaction to the speakers throughout this scene. Ask them the following about the mob's reaction to Brutus's speech: What indication is there that the plebeians do not truly understand Brutus's reasons for Cæsar's being slain?
Answer
The plebeians are willing to make Brutus king. They do not understand that the reason Brutus helped kill Cæsar was because he is opposed to a monarchy in Rome.

1. The crowd says that Cæsar was a tyrant and that Rome is better off without him.
2. Antony says that the purpose of his speech is to bury Cæsar, not to praise him. He says that the "evil" that Cæsar has done will live on, whereas the good will be buried with him.

LITERARY NOTE

You may wish to help students compare Brutus's prose speech to that of Antony which is written in blank verse. You should ask students in what way Shakespeare was characterizing these two men by choosing to have one speak in prose and the other speak in verse. You might then suggest that prose is in keeping with Brutus's character because it is straightforward, everyday language, and Brutus is speaking to honorably explain his actions. Antony may speak in the more elevated language of verse because he has an agenda—to eloquently move his audience to turn against Brutus. Since Antony has a more complex purpose in speaking, he makes use of many rhetorical devices such as repetition and verbal irony. By comparing the two speeches, students should be able to see readily why Antony's speech might have moved the crowd to greater fervor.

CROSS-CURRICULAR ACTIVITIES

MUSIC. Students may wish to compose a rap based on Mark Antony's speech. They may simply recite his speech as a rapper would, or they might set the speech to music or rephrase it in their own words and then perform it in front of the class.

Save I alone, till Antony have spoke.[16]   *Exit.*

50 **1. PLEBEIAN.**   Stay ho, and let us hear Mark Antony.

3. PLEBEIAN.   Let him go up into the public chair,
We'll hear him. Noble Antony, go up.

ANTONY.   For Brutus' sake, I am beholding to you. *Goes into the pulpit.*

4. PLEBEIAN.   What does he say of Brutus?

3. PLEBEIAN.   He says, for Brutus' sake
He finds himself beholding to us all.

55 **4. PLEBEIAN.**   'Twere best he speak no harm of Brutus here!

1. PLEBEIAN.   This Cæsar was a tyrant.

3. PLEBEIAN.   Nay, that's certain:
We are blest that Rome is rid of him.

2. PLEBEIAN.   Peace, let us hear what Antony can say.

ANTONY.   You gentle Romans—

60 **ALL.**   Peace ho, let us hear him.

ANTONY.   Friends, Romans, countrymen, lend me your ears!
I come to bury Cæsar, not to praise him.
The evil that men do lives after them,
The good is oft <u>interred</u> with their bones;
65 So let it be with Cæsar. The noble Brutus
Hath told you Cæsar was ambitious;
If it were so, it was a <u>grievous</u> fault,
And grievously hath Cæsar answer'd it.
Here, under leave of Brutus and the rest
70 (For Brutus is an honorable man,
So are they all, all honorable men),
Come I to speak in Cæsar's funeral.
He was my friend, faithful and just to me;
But Brutus says he was ambitious,
75 And Brutus is an honorable man.
He hath brought many captives home to Rome,
Whose ransoms did the general coffers[17] fill;
Did this in Cæsar seem ambitious?
When that the poor have cried, Cæsar hath wept;
80 Ambition should be made of sterner stuff:

What is the crowd's opinion of Cæsar after Brutus's speech?

What does Antony say is the purpose of his speech? What does he say will live on after Cæsar dies, and what will be buried with Cæsar?

16. **have spoke.** Has spoken
17. **general coffers.** The treasury of the Republic

words for everyday use

in • ter (in tur´) vt., bury. *Since the sailors were not able to <u>inter</u> their comrade's remains, they gave him an honorable burial at sea.*
griev • ous (grēv´əs) adj., very serious; grave. *That is not just a slight mistake—that's a <u>grievous</u> error!*

Yet Brutus says he was ambitious,
And Brutus is an honorable man.
You all did see that on the Lupercal
I thrice presented him a kingly crown,
85 Which he did thrice refuse. Was this ambition?
Yet Brutus says he was ambitious,
And sure[18] he is an honorable man.
I speak not to disprove what Brutus spoke,
But here I am to speak what I do know.
90 You all did love him once, not without cause;
What cause withholds you then to mourn for him?
O judgment! thou art fled to brutish beasts,
And men have lost their reason. Bear with me,
My heart is in the coffin there with Cæsar,
95 And I must pause till it come back to me.

    1. PLEBEIAN.   Methinks there is much reason in his sayings.

    2. PLEBEIAN.   If thou consider rightly of the matter,
Cæsar has had great wrong.

    3. PLEBEIAN.   Has he, masters?
I fear there will a worse come in his place.

100   **4. PLEBEIAN.**   Mark'd ye his words? He would not take the crown,
Therefore 'tis certain he was not ambitious.

    1. PLEBEIAN.   If it be found so, some will dear abide it.[19]

    2. PLEBEIAN.   Poor soul, his eyes are red as fire with weeping.

    3. PLEBEIAN.   There's not a nobler man in Rome than Antony.

105   **4. PLEBEIAN.**   Now mark him, he begins again to speak.

    ANTONY.   But yesterday the word of Cæsar might
Have stood against the world; now lies he there,
And none so poor to[20] do him reverence.
O masters! if I were dispos'd to stir
110 Your hearts and minds to mutiny and rage,
I should do Brutus wrong, and Cassius wrong,
Who (you all know) are honorable men.
I will not do them wrong; I rather choose
To wrong the dead, to wrong myself and you,
115 Than I will wrong such honorable men.
But here's a parchment with the seal of Cæsar,
I found it in his closet, 'tis his will.
Let but the commons hear this testament—
Which, pardon me, I do not mean to read—
120 And they would go and kiss dead Cæsar's wounds,

---

18. **sure.** Certainly
19. **some . . . it.** Some (the conspirators) will pay dearly for it.
20. **poor to.** Low ranking as to

**ANSWER TO GUIDED
READING QUESTION**

What three reasons does Antony give to "disprove" the charge that Cæsar was "ambitious"? What phrase does he repeat?

1. Antony repeats the phrase "Yet Brutus says he was ambitious, / And Brutus is an honorable man." At the same time, he denies that Cæsar was ambitious, pointing out that Cæsar gave all the money from the ransom of prisoners of war to the people, that Cæsar had sympathy for the poor; and that he refused the crown three times when offered it.

Quotables

"There come now no Kings
   nor Cæsars

Nor gold-giving lords like those
   gone.

Howe'er in mirth most magnified,

Whoe'er lived in life most lordliest,

Drear all this excellence, delights
   undurable!

Waneth the watch, but the world
   holdeth.

Tomb hideth trouble. The blade is
   layed low.

Earthly glory ageth and seareth."

             —Ezra Pound,
             The Seafarer

LITERARY NOTE

The above quotation is taken from Ezra Pound's reworking of the Old English elegy *The Seafarer.* You might wish to share other works from both the Latin and English elegiac traditions in order to give students a firmer basis for understanding Antony's funeral oration as part of a tradition of literature about loss.

ADDITIONAL QUESTIONS AND ACTIVITIES

Hold a debate in which students discuss the justice of Cæsar's murder. Appoint one person as a moderator; this person should suggest topics of discussion and mediate any intense arguments during the discussion. The other group members should divide evenly into two groups: those who believe Cæsar's murder was just and those who believe his murder was unjust. You might want to refer students to the background on Julius Cæsar on pages 243–244.

1. Antony says he must not read it, lest
he "inflame" their wills and make
them do crazy things when they
learn that he has left his possessions
to them.
2. The crowd now calls the
conspirators traitors, villains, and
murderers.

And dip their napkins in his sacred blood;
Yea, beg a hair of him for memory,
And dying, mention it within their wills,
<u>Bequeathing</u> it as a rich legacy
Unto their issue.[21]

125 **4. PLEBEIAN.** We'll hear the will. Read it, Mark Antony.

ALL. The will, the will! we will hear Cæsar's will.

ANTONY. Have patience, gentle friends, I must not read it.
It is not meet[22] you know how Cæsar lov'd you:
You are not wood, you are not stones, but men;

130 And, being men, hearing the will of Cæsar,
It will inflame you, it will make you mad.
'Tis good you know not that you are his heirs,
For if you should, O, what would come of it?

4. PLEBEIAN. Read the will, we'll hear it, Antony.

135 You shall read us the will, Cæsar's will.

ANTONY. Will you be patient? Will you stay[23] awhile?
I have o'ershot myself[24] to tell you of it.
I fear I wrong the honorable men
Whose daggers have stabb'd Cæsar; I do fear it.

140 **4. PLEBEIAN.** They were traitors; honorable men!

ALL. The will! the testament!

2. PLEBEIAN. They were villains, murderers. The will, read the will!

ANTONY. You will compel me then to read the will?
Then make a ring about the corpse of Cæsar,

145 And let me show you him that made the will.
Shall I descend? and will you give me leave?[25]

ALL. Come down.

2. PLEBEIAN. Descend.

3. PLEBEIAN. You shall have leave.

ANTONY comes down from the pulpit.

150 **4. PLEBEIAN.** A ring, stand round.

1. PLEBEIAN. Stand from the hearse, stand from the body.

> *What does Antony say
> when the plebeians
> insist on hearing
> Cæsar's will?*

> *What is the crowd's
> opinion of the
> conspirators now?*

---

21. **issue.** Descendants, heirs
22. **meet.** Proper, suitable
23. **stay.** Wait

24. **o'ershot myself.** Gone too far
25. **give me leave.** Allow me to

**words
for
everyday
use**
be • queath (bē kwēth´) *vt.*, hand down; pass on. *My grandfather <u>bequeathed</u> his gold pocket watch to my father.*

2. PLEBEIAN. Room for Antony, most noble Antony.

ANTONY. Nay, press not so upon me, stand far off.

ALL. Stand back; room, bear back!

155 **ANTONY.** If you have tears, prepare to shed them now.
You all do know this mantle. I remember
The first time ever Cæsar put it on;
'Twas on a summer's evening, in his tent,
That day he overcame the Nervii.

160 Look, in this place ran Cassius' dagger through;
See what a rent the envious Casca made;
Through this the well-beloved Brutus stabb'd,
And as he pluck'd his cursed steel away,
Mark how the blood of Cæsar followed it,

165 As rushing out of doors to be resolv'd
If Brutus so unkindly[26] knock'd or no;
For Brutus, as you know, was Cæsar's angel.
Judge, O you gods, how dearly Cæsar lov'd him!
This was the most unkindest cut of all;

170 For when the noble Cæsar saw him stab,
Ingratitude, more strong than traitors' arms,
Quite vanquish'd him. Then burst his mighty heart,
And in his mantle muffling up his face,
Even at the base of Pompey's statue

175 (Which all the while ran blood) great Cæsar fell.
O, what a fall was there, my countrymen!
Then I, and you, and all of us fell down,
Whilst bloody treason flourish'd over us.
O now you weep, and I perceive you feel

180 The dint[27] of pity. These are gracious drops.
Kind souls, what weep you when you but behold
Our Cæsar's vesture[28] wounded? Look you here,
Lifting CÆSAR's mantle.
Here is himself, marr'd as you see with traitors.

1. PLEBEIAN. O piteous spectacle!

185 **2. PLEBEIAN.** O noble Cæsar!

3. PLEBEIAN. O woeful day!

4. PLEBEIAN. O traitors, villains!

1. PLEBEIAN. O most bloody sight!

2. PLEBEIAN. We will be reveng'd!

190 **ALL.** Revenge! About! Seek! Burn! Fire! Kill!
Slay! Let not a traitor live!

---

26. **unkindly.** Unnaturally
27. **dint.** Stroke

28. **vesture.** Clothing

ACT 3, SCENE 2 / THE TRAGEDY OF JULIUS CÆSAR **303**

What does Antony show the crowd?

What does Antony now call the conspirators?

1. Antony claims he did not mean to stir the people "To such a sudden flood of mutiny." He claims that while Brutus is a skillful orator, he himself is but a "plain blunt man" with "neither wit, nor words...nor the power of speech / To stir men's blood.")
2. Cæsar has left each person 75 drachmas and has left his private gardens to the public.

CROSS-CURRICULAR ACTIVITIES

SOCIAL STUDIES. Antony rouses the plebeians and helps to create a vigilante mob. In a group, discuss the factors that can create a mob. What roles do emotion, economics, and politics play? What other elements might incite people to mob action? Groups can share their ideas with the rest of the class.

ANTONY. Stay, countrymen.

1. PLEBEIAN. Peace there, hear the noble Antony.

2. PLEBEIAN. We'll hear him, we'll follow him, we'll die with him.

195 **ANTONY.** Good friends, sweet friends, let me not stir you up
To such a sudden flood of mutiny.
They that have done this deed are honorable.
What private griefs they have, alas, I know not,
That made them do it. They are wise and honorable,
200 And will no doubt with reasons answer you.
I come not, friends, to steal away your hearts.
I am no orator, as Brutus is;
But (as you know me all) a plain blunt man
That love^{29} my friend, and that they know full well
205 That gave me public leave to speak of him.
For I have neither wit, nor words,^{30} nor worth,
Action, nor utterance, nor the power of speech
To stir men's blood; I only speak right on.^{31}
I tell you that which you yourselves do know,
210 Show you sweet Cæsar's wounds, poor, poor, dumb mouths,
And bid them speak for me. But were I Brutus,
And Brutus Antony, there were an Antony
Would ruffle up your spirits, and put a tongue
In every wound of Cæsar, that should move
215 The stones of Rome to rise and mutiny.

ALL. We'll mutiny.

1. PLEBEIAN. We'll burn the house of Brutus.

3. PLEBEIAN. Away then, come, seek the conspirators.

ANTONY. Yet hear me, countrymen, yet hear me speak.

ALL. Peace ho, hear Antony, most noble Antony!

220 **ANTONY.** Why, friends, you go to do you know not what.
Wherein hath Cæsar thus deserv'd your loves?
Alas you know not! I must tell you then:
You have forgot the will I told you of.

ALL. Most true. The will! Let's stay and hear the will.

225 **ANTONY.** Here is the will, and under Cæsar's seal:
To every Roman citizen he gives,
To every several man, seventy-five drachmas.

2. PLEBEIAN. Most noble Cæsar! we'll revenge his death.

3. PLEBEIAN. O royal Cæsar!

What does Antony say he did not mean to do? According to Antony, how does he differ from Brutus?

What has Cæsar left to the people in his will?

---

29. **That love.** Loved
30. **words.** Fluency; ease with words
31. **right on.** Directly, from the heart, not as a trained speaker

304   *UNIT FOUR / DRAMA*

230 **ANTONY.**   Hear me with patience.

ALL.   Peace ho!

ANTONY.   Moreover, he hath left you all his walks,
His private arbors and new-planted orchards,
On this side Tiber;³² he hath left them you,
235 And to your heirs for ever—common pleasures,³³
To walk abroad and recreate³⁴ yourselves.
Here was a Cæsar! when comes such another?

1. PLEBEIAN.   Never, never! Come, away, away!
We'll burn his body in the holy place,
240 And with the brands fire the traitors' houses.
Take up the body.

2. PLEBEIAN.   Go fetch fire.

3. PLEBEIAN.   Pluck down benches.

4. PLEBEIAN.   Pluck down forms,³⁵ windows,³⁶ anything.

Exeunt PLEBEIANS *with the body.*

245 **ANTONY.**   Now let it work. Mischief, thou art afoot,
Take thou what course thou wilt!

Enter SERVANT.

How now, fellow?

SERVANT.   Sir, Octavius is³⁷ already come to Rome.

ANTONY.   Where is he?

SERVANT.   He and Lepidus are at Cæsar's house.

250 **ANTONY.**   And thither will I straight to visit him;
He comes upon a wish.³⁸ Fortune is merry,
And in this mood will give us any thing.

SERVANT.   I heard him say, Brutus and Cassius
Are rid³⁹ like madmen through the gates of Rome.

255 **ANTONY.**   Belike⁴⁰ they had some notice⁴¹ of the people,
How I had mov'd them. Bring me to Octavius.

Exeunt.

SCENE 3: A STREET IN ROME

Enter CINNA *the poet, and after him the* PLEBEIANS.

CINNA.   I dreamt tonight¹ that I did feast with Cæsar,

---

32. **this side Tiber.** On this side of the Tiber river
33. **pleasures.** Public places of rest and relaxation
34. **recreate.** Enjoy
35. **forms.** Benches
36. **windows.** Shutters
37. **is.** Has
38. **upon a wish.** As I wished

39. **Are rid.** Have ridden
40. **Belike.** Most likely
41. **notice.** News

ACT 3, SCENE 3
  1. **tonight.** Last night

ACT 3, SCENE 3 / THE TRAGEDY OF JULIUS CÆSAR   **305**

Margin notes:

What does the mob leave to do?

Who has arrived in Rome? Where are Brutus and Cassius?

What dream did Cinna have?

ANSWERS TO GUIDED READING QUESTIONS

1. The mob leaves the Forum to cremate Cæsar's body and to burn the houses of the conspirators.
2. Octavius has arrived with Lepidus, and Brutus and Cassius have fled Rome.
3. He dreamt that he dined with Cæsar.

LITERARY TECHNIQUE

Antony's words in lines 245–246, "Now let it work. Mischief, thou art afoot, / Take thou what course thou wilt!" are similar to those of one of Shakespeare's most memorable villains. In *The Tragedy of Othello, Moor of Venice*, Iago says of his schemes, "Work on, / My medicine, work! Thus credulous fools are caught" (act 4, scene 1, line 45). Why might Shakespeare characterize Antony as a villain? Does the portrayal of Antony as a villain make the character of Brutus seem more sympathetic and appealing?

ANSWER TO GUIDED READING QUESTION

1. Cinna is killed by the mob, who mistake him for one of the conspirators.

SELECTION CHECK TEST 4.4.9 WITH ANSWERS

Checking Your Reading
1. What request from Metellus Cimber does Cæsar deny? **Cæsar refuses to recall the banishment of Cimber's brother.**
2. Whom does Cæsar address in his dying words? **Cæsar addresses Brutus.**
3. Who shakes each man's bloody hand? **Antony shakes each man's bloody hand.**
4. What effect does Brutus's speech have on the people? **The people are convinced that Cæsar deserved to die and are ready to crown Brutus.**
5. What effect does Antony's speech have on the people? **They turn against Brutus and support Antony.**

Vocabulary in Context
Fill in each blank with the most appropriate word from the following *Words for Everyday Use* from *The Tragedy of Julius Cæsar,* act 3. You may have to change the tense of the word.

grievous malice valiant inter
discourse reverence cur

1. Mrs. Wilkes warned the children to stay away from the stray **cur**.
2. The soldier was given a medal to honor his **valiant** acts in the battle.
3. On Halloween, Linus waited with **reverence** for the Great Pumpkin to appear.
4. The Coast Guard operator told the fishermen that to head toward the storm would be a **grievous** mistake.
5. The crowd gasped at the glint of **malice** in the villain's eye as he stalked the hero.

Literary Tools
Fill in the blanks using the following terms. You may not use every term, and you may use some terms more than once.

repetition verbal irony plot
climax crisis

1. In a plot, the **crisis** is the point where something decisive happens to determine the future course of events and the eventual working out of the conflict.

And things unluckily charge my fantasy.
I have no will to wander forth of² doors,
Yet something leads me forth.

5 **1. PLEBEIAN.** What is your name?

2. PLEBEIAN. Whither are you going?

3. PLEBEIAN. Where do you dwell?

4. PLEBEIAN. Are you a married man or a bachelor?

2. PLEBEIAN. Answer every man directly.

10 **1. PLEBEIAN.** Aye, and briefly.

4. PLEBEIAN. Aye, and wisely.

3. PLEBEIAN. Aye, and truly, you were best.³

CINNA. What is my name? Whither am I going? Where do I dwell? Am I a married man or a bachelor? Then to answer every man directly and briefly, wisely and truly:

15 wisely, I say, I am a bachelor.

2. PLEBEIAN. That's as much as to say, they are fools that marry. You'll bear me a bang⁴ for that, I fear. Proceed directly.

CINNA. Directly, I am going to Cæsar's funeral.

1. PLEBEIAN. As a friend or an enemy?

20 **CINNA.** As a friend.

2. PLEBEIAN. That matter is answer'd directly.

4. PLEBEIAN. For your dwelling—briefly.

CINNA. Briefly, I dwell by the Capitol.

3. PLEBEIAN. Your name, sir, truly.

25 **CINNA.** Truly, my name is Cinna.

1. PLEBEIAN. Tear him to pieces, he's a conspirator.

CINNA. I am Cinna the poet, I am Cinna the poet.

4. PLEBEIAN. Tear him for his bad verses, tear him for his bad verses.

CINNA. I am not Cinna the conspirator.

30 **4. PLEBEIAN.** It is no matter, his name's Cinna. Pluck but his name out of his heart, and turn him going.⁵

3. PLEBEIAN. Tear him, tear him! Come, brands ho, firebrands! To Brutus', to Cassius'; burn all! Some to Decius' house, and some to Casca's; some to Ligarius'. Away, go!

Exeunt all the Plebeians dragging off Cinna.

What happens to Cinna?

---
2. **forth of.** Out of
3. **were best.** Had better
4. **bear me a bang.** Be beaten by me
5. **turn him going.** Send him away, kill him

UNIT FOUR / DRAMA

SELECTION CHECK TEST 4.4.9 WITH ANSWERS (CONT.)

2. **Verbal irony** occurs when a statement is made that implies its opposite.
3. A writer uses **repetition** when he or she repeats a word, phrase, or sentence to emphasize its importance.

Short Answer
1. What is the true purpose of Brutus's speech at Cæsar's funeral? **Brutus seeks to explain why he and the conspirators slew Cæsar.**
2. What is the true purpose of Antony's speech at Cæsar's funeral? **Antony wishes to win the favor of the crowd and turn them against Brutus and the conspirators.**

TEACHER'S EDITION

What do you predict will happen next? What will Antony's next move be?

Investigate, Inquire, *and* Imagine

Recall: GATHERING FACTS

1a. What were Cæsar's last words?

2a. Who does not trust Mark Antony? Who does trust him? Which actions on his part make him seen trustworthy? Which make him seem untrustworthy?

3a. What does Brutus tell the crowd regarding Antony at the end of his speech?

Interpret: FINDING MEANING

1b. What do Cæsar's last words reveal about him? What feelings did he have for Brutus?

2b. What do the characters' differing reactions to Mark Antony reveal about them? Whose trusting nature is similar to Cæsar's? What is ironic about this?

3b. Why do you think Brutus allows Antony to give a funeral oration for Cæsar? What does his action reveal about him? Is this action a mistake? Why, or why not?

Analyze: TAKING THINGS APART

4a. Compare the speeches delivered on the steps of the Forum by Brutus and by Mark Antony. Analyze the content and purpose of each speech as well as its tone and style. How are they different, and how are they similar?

Synthesize: BRINGING THINGS TOGETHER

4b. What conclusions do you draw about the character of each man based on your analysis of their speeches?

Evaluate: MAKING JUDGMENTS

5a. Evaluate the impact of Mark Antony's speech on the crowd. What do you think he hoped to accomplish with this speech? Why? Using evidence from the text of the speech, explain whether or not it was effective in achieving his goal.

Extend: CONNECTING IDEAS

5b. Why do you think mob mentality is often considered dangerous? When have you been part of a crowd that acted in ways you would not if alone? What examples of mob mentality can you recall from history or recent world and national events? Are they all negative examples?

Understanding *Literature*

REPETITION AND IRONY. Review the definitions for **repetition** and **irony** in the Handbook of Literary Terms. What word does Antony repeat many times to describe the conspirators? What does he really want the crowd to think of them? What makes Antony's description ironic?

ACT 3 / THE TRAGEDY OF JULIUS CÆSAR   **307**

RESPOND TO THE SELECTION

When answering this question, students should also consider what they judged to be Antony's motivation for acting as he does.

ANSWERS TO INVESTIGATE, INQUIRE, AND IMAGINE

RECALL

1a. Cæsar's last words were, "*Et tu, Brute?*—Then fall Cæsar!"

2a. Cassius does not trust Mark Antony, while Brutus does trust him. Antony's appeal to the conspirators to do with him what they will makes him seem trustworthy. His preoccupation with the horrible nature of the crime, his shaking of the bloody hands of the conspirators and his great desire to make a funeral oration for Cæsar make him seem untrustworthy.

3a. Brutus tells the crowd that Antony was not involved in the murder of Cæsar and is present to mourn him.

INTERPRET

1b. Cæsar's last words reveal that he was a trusting person who is surprised to find himself betrayed by Brutus. He apparently liked, respected, and trusted Brutus.

2b. Cassius is revealed to be a suspicious person, while Brutus is revealed to be trusting. Brutus's nature is similar to Cæsar's. This is ironic not only because Brutus has just betrayed and murdered Cæsar, but because Brutus does not realize that he is running the same risk that Cæsar did because of his trusting nature.

3b. Brutus allows Antony to speak because Brutus feels guilty about killing Cæsar. His action reveals him to be a trusting person who expects others to act according to their word. This is a mistake because encouraging the crowd to mourn Cæsar can only risk inflaming them against Cæsar's killers. As it turns out, allowing Antony to speak leads directly to the mob violence in scene 3.

ANSWERS TO INVESTIGATE, INQUIRE, AND IMAGINE (CONT.)

ANALYZE

4a. Brutus speaks to explain the conspiracy and murder to the crowd and, at the end, tests the crowd's reaction to see if they agree the act was justified. Antony wishes to test the crowd's reaction as well, but he also hopes to rouse the crowd's emotions against the conspirators. Brutus speaks briefly and directly, saying simply that he honors Cæsar's valiant accomplishments, but killed Cæsar because his ambition posed a danger to the Roman Republic. Antony speaks at length about Cæsar's virtues and uses Cæsar's will to inflame the crowd. Brutus speaks in prose while Antony speaks in blank verse, using repetition and a generally more elevated language.

SYNTHESIZE

4b. It seems that Shakespeare intended for the reader to see Brutus as plain-spoken, direct and honest, and Antony as more cunning and calculating—

(Continued on page 308)

ANSWERS TO INVESTIGATE, INQUIRE, AND IMAGINE (CONT.)

perhaps also dishonest. Brutus may also seem a bit naïve and trusting, in not anticipating what Antony might say. Antony seems the more skillful politician as he is more effective at manipulating the emotions of the crowd.

EVALUATE

5a. Antony is grieved by Cæsar's death and hopes to gauge the Roman people's reaction to the assassination. He has hidden his true feelings from the conspirators but hopes that, if the people are as horrified as he is at the death of Cæsar, he might rouse them to action. At the end of Brutus's speech, the crowd is sympathetic to the conspirators. By the end, however, their mood has changed. Antony uses irony in his speech, repeatedly saying that Brutus is an honorable man, as he points out what seems to be the results of a very dishonorable act—the murder of Cæsar. The crowd reacts to this ironic contradiction and is moved by Antony's grief. He gives evidence that Cæsar was not ambitious, shows his wounds and reads Cæsar's will granting money and land to the people. Antony's speech is quite effective in turning the crowd's feelings against the conspirators and rousing them to violent action against them.

EXTEND

5b. *Responses will vary.* Students should note that the mob in act 3 changed its mind dramatically and rather quickly. Mob mentality seems to be characterized by little individual thought, and therefore mobs are relatively easily swayed by emotions to do things the individuals involved would never do. Individuals seem to suspend their own judgment to "go along with the crowd," perhaps doubting their own thoughts when so many others feel differently. Individuals also draw courage from the crowd to do things they would fear to do alone. Some examples from history include lynchings, destructive protest, and looting during riots. Some mob actions that may be considered positive include the student uprising in Tiananmen Square in Beijing and the storming of the Bastille during the French Revolution.

PLOT, CLIMAX, AND CRISIS. Review the definition for **plot** in the Handbook of Literary Terms, noting the entries for **climax** and **crisis**. What is the climax of *Julius Cæsar*? At what point is the crisis—the point at which the fortunes of Brutus take a turn for the worse? Note these points on the plot pyramid you began in act 1.

Writer's Journal

1. Newspapers did not exist in ancient Rome, but if they had, the events of act 3 would have made banner headlines. Imagine that you are the editor of a newspaper in Rome. Write the **headlines** you would have written for the next day's edition.
2. Imagine that you are a law enforcement officer for the state of Rome. Write a **wanted poster** for Brutus and Cassius, describing the "criminals" and their "crime," and asking for information or help in their apprehension.
3. The rhetorical techniques used by Mark Antony in his funeral oration are excellent material for parody. A parody is a literary work that imitates another work for humorous, often satirical purposes. Write a **parody** of Antony's speech on a topic of your choice. Be sure to use the rhetorical techniques Antony uses, such as repetition and irony.

Integrating the Language Arts

Study and Research

RESEARCHING THE ROMAN FORUM. Using Internet and library resources, research the Roman Forum. What did it look like in Julius Cæsar's day? What took place there? How did its purpose in Roman society change over the years? How does it look today? You may wish to make a presentation to the class on your findings, using pictures and illustrations.

Media Literacy & Collaborative Learning

NEWSCAST OF CÆSAR'S MURDER. Working in small groups, imagine that you are a modern-day television news team who has just received, on the ides of March, the breaking news of the murder of Julius Cæsar in the Senate. Develop a newscast covering the story, perhaps using on-scene interviews with the conspirators, witnesses, local authorities, and anyone else you think can help shed light on the day's tragic events. Present your live newscast to the class.

Speaking and Listening

DELIVERING A SPEECH. Mark Antony's funeral oration is one of the most famous speeches in all of literature. Memorize act 3, scene 2, lines 61–95. It may help you to divide the section into parts and then repeat each part separately until you have memorized them all. Then repeat two of the parts together. Once you have memorized that chunk, continue to add on parts one at a time until you can repeat all the lines together. Then practice delivering this portion of Antony's speech orally. You may experiment with different emotional tones as you recite the lines. Try anger, fear, and sadness. How does each change the impact of the speech? Deliver the speech to your class.

ANSWERS TO UNDERSTANDING LITERATURE

REPETITION AND IRONY. Antony repeats the word "honorable." The speech is ironic because Antony describes the dishonorable actions of the conspirators all the while calling them "honorable."

PLOT, CLIMAX, AND CRISIS. The stabbing of Cæsar is the most dramatic event of the play and constitutes the climax. The bloody and violent nature of the scene, particularly as each of the conspirators bathes his hands in Cæsar's blood, might horrify an audience. The fortunes of the central character, Brutus, are reversed when Antony sways the crowd against the conspirators and Brutus.

Literary TOOLS

PLOT AND FALLING ACTION. The **plot** is a series of events related to a central conflict, or struggle. The **falling action** is all the events that follow the climax. During the falling action of a tragedy, the fortunes of the main character decline. As you read act 4, determine whether or not the fortunes of Brutus have begun to decline and if so, how.

FORESHADOWING. Foreshadowing is the act of presenting materials that hint at events to occur later in a plot. In acts 1, 2 and 3, the mysterious occurrences of disorder in the natural world foreshadowed the disorder in the political state. In act 4, you will note other instances of foreshadowing.

Reader's Journal

Write about a time when you lost admiration for someone in a leadership position who disappointed you greatly.

ADDITIONAL RESOURCES

UNIT 4 RESOURCE BOOK
- Selection Worksheet 4.4
- Selection Check Test 4.4.11
- Selection Test 4.4.12
- Speaking and Listening Resource 4.1

ART NOTE

Athena was one of the most important goddesses in the ancient Greek religion. She was the protector of the city of Athens, which carries her name, and a goddess of war, wisdom, justice, and handicraft. In the Roman period, she was associated with the goddess Minerva. Minerva was a goddess of handicrafts, the arts, and war. After a series of successful battles and explorations, Pompey built a temple to Minerva, indicating that she was also associated with victory.

READER'S JOURNAL

Students might write about corruption in politics, or they might write about a role model, such as a sports figure, who committed a crime or an unwise act.

ANSWER TO GUIDED READING QUESTION

1. Antony, Octavius, and Lepidus are deciding who should be killed and who should be allowed to live.

VOCABULARY FROM THE SELECTION

apparition   corporal
chastisement   infirmity

Temple of Athena in Paestum.

ACT 4

SCENE 1: ANTONY'S HOUSE IN ROME

Enter ANTONY, OCTAVIUS, *and* LEPIDUS.

ANTONY. These many then shall die, their names are prick'd.[1]

> *What decisions are Antony, Octavius, and Lepidus making?*

OCTAVIUS. Your brother too must die; consent you, Lepidus?

LEPIDUS. I do consent—

OCTAVIUS.   Prick him down, Antony.

LEPIDUS. Upon condition Publius shall not live,
5   Who is your sister's son, Mark Antony.

ACT 4, SCENE 1
1. **prick'd.** Marked off

1. Antony has little respect for Lepidus: he considers him to be like an ass whose job it is to bear heavy loads. He plans to use Lepidus to bear the burden of the accusations that they must face. When they have gotten through the hard times, Antony hints, they will get rid of Lepidus—or let him "graze in commons" like an unoccupied ass. Antony further says that Lepidus should be spoken of as property, just as a horse would be.

INDIVIDUAL LEARNING STRATEGIES

MOTIVATION
Ask students to imagine that they are one of the people closest to the leaders of the Roman Empire. They should then read the Language Arts Survey 5.1, "Making Decisions and Solving Problems," and create a pro and con chart listing the positive and negative aspects of each leader: Cæsar, Brutus, Antony, and Cassius. They should also think of the similarities and differences among the leaders. Do any of them share similar traits? Do any of them have opposing traits?

READING PROFICIENCY
Go over with students the Words for Everyday Use and the footnotes, then encourage them to read through each scene with a partner, answering the Guided Reading Questions as they go and summing up the main point of each scene.

ENGLISH LANGUAGE LEARNING
You may wish to review with students the additional vocabulary below.
proscription—publication of the names of those to be put to death or banished (archaic)
levying—collecting; gathering
covert—hidden; concealed
wrangle—argue; quarrel
vaunting—boasting; bragging

SPECIAL NEEDS
Students will find it helpful to hear the selection read out loud. Either read out loud to students or have them alternate reading aloud. Make sure students focus on the Guided Reading Questions and the Recall questions in the Investigate, Inquire, and Imagine section.

ANTONY. He shall not live; look, with a spot[2] I damn him.
But, Lepidus, go you to Cæsar's house;
Fetch the will hither, and we shall determine
How to cut off some charge in legacies.[3]

10 **LEPIDUS.** What? shall I find you here?

OCTAVIUS. Or here or at the Capitol.

Exit LEPIDUS.

ANTONY. This is a slight unmeritable[4] man,
Meet[5] to be sent on errands; is it fit,
The threefold world[6] divided, he should stand
One of the three to share it?

15 **OCTAVIUS.** So you thought him,
And took his voice[7] who should be prick'd to die
In our black sentence[8] and proscription.[9]

ANTONY. Octavius, I have seen more days than you,
And though we lay these honors on this man
20 To ease ourselves of divers[10] sland'rous loads,[11]
He shall but bear them as the ass bears gold,
To groan and sweat under the business,
Either led or driven, as we point the way;
And having brought our treasure where we will,
25 Then take we down his load, and turn him off
(Like to the empty ass) to shake his ears
And graze in commons.[12]

OCTAVIUS. You may do your will;
But he's a tried and valiant soldier.

ANTONY. So is my horse, Octavius, and for that
30 I do appoint him store[13] of provender.[14]
It is a creature that I teach to fight,
To wind, to stop, to run directly on,
His corporal motion govern'd by my spirit;

What is Antony's assessment of Lepidus? How does he plan to use him?

---

2. **a spot.** Mark
3. **off . . . legacies.** Reduce the cost of the bequests left in the will
4. **unmeritable.** Undeserving; lacking in worth
5. **Meet.** Appropriate
6. **threefold world.** The Roman Empire spanned Europe, Asia, and Africa.
7. **voice.** Vote
8. **black sentence.** Death sentence

9. **proscription.** Publishing of the name of a person condemned to death or exile
10. **divers.** Various
11. **sland'rous loads.** Accusations
12. **commons.** Pun referring both to a public pastureland and to the lower order of society, the common people
13. **appoint him store.** Provide to him
14. **provender.** Fodder

words for everyday use
cor • por • al (kôr′ pə rəl) *adj.,* having to do with the body. *Luke said that the mysterious figure we had been so frightened by could not have been a spirit but must have been a corporal creature.*

INDIVIDUAL LEARNING STRATEGIES (CONT.)

ENRICHMENT
Tell students that the assassination of Cæsar is one of the most well-known in world history. Ask them to research another political assassination, such as that of Archduke Ferdinand of Austria in 1914, or that of one of the American presidents Lincoln, Garfield, McKinley, and Kennedy.

And in some taste is Lepidus but so:[15]
35   He must be taught, and train'd, and bid go forth;
      A barren-spirited fellow; one that feeds
      On objects, arts, and imitations,
      Which, out of use and stal'd by other men,
      Begin his fashion.[16] Do not talk of him
40   But as a property. And now, Octavius,
      Listen great things. Brutus and Cassius
      Are levying powers; we must straight make head;[17]
      Therefore let our alliance be combin'd,[18]
      Our best friends made, our means stretch'd,
45   And let us presently[19] go sit in council,
      How covert matters may be best disclos'd[20]
      And open perils surest answered.

      OCTAVIUS.   Let us do so; for we are at the stake,
      And bay'd about with many enemies,
50   And some that smile have in their hearts, I fear,
      Millions of mischiefs.

                                                    Exeunt.

What are Brutus and Cassius doing? What must Antony and Octavius do?

SCENE 2: CAMP NEAR SARDIS, IN FRONT OF BRUTUS'S TENT

Drum. Enter BRUTUS, LUCILIUS, LUCIUS, *and the army.* TITINIUS *and* PINDARUS *meet them.*

BRUTUS.   Stand ho!

LUCILIUS.   Give the word ho! and stand.

BRUTUS.   What now, Lucilius, is Cassius near?

LUCILIUS.   He is at hand, and Pindarus is come
5   To do you salutation[1] from his master.

BRUTUS.   He greets me well. Your master, Pindarus,
      In his own change, or by ill officers,
      Hath given me some worthy cause to wish
      Things done undone; but if he be at hand[2]
      I shall be satisfied.

10   **PINDARUS.**   I do not doubt
      But that my noble master will appear
      Such as he is, full of regard[3] and honor.

      BRUTUS.   He is not doubted. A word, Lucilius,

---

15. **in some . . . but so.** Lepidus is no different.
16. **Begin his fashion.** Antony is saying that Lepidus is a follower, one who pursues interests after others have taken them up.
17. **make head.** Raise an army
18. **combin'd.** Added to
19. **presently.** At once
20. **covert . . . disclos'd.** Hidden or secret plans (on the part of Brutus and Cassius) may best be uncovered.

ACT 4, SCENE 2
1. **To do you salutation.** To bring you greetings
2. **be at hand.** Will join us again
3. **full of regard.** Worthy of being held in high regard

1. Brutus and Cassius are gathering their forces, and so Antony and Octavius must gather an army and plot a way to undermine their enemies' plans.

LITERARY TECHNIQUE

CHARACTERIZATION.
Characterization is the use of literary techniques to create a character. Writers use three major techniques to create characters: direct description, portrayal of characters' behavior, and representations of characters' internal states. Ask students what is revealed about Antony through his behavior in this scene. Do they like him? Why, or why not? Ask students why Shakespeare might have chosen to reveal a distasteful element of Antony's character immediately after his effective and rousing speech in the Forum. What do students think Shakespeare's attitude toward Antony might have been?

ADDITIONAL QUESTIONS AND ACTIVITIES

Ask students the following comprehension questions relating to what they just read in act 4, scene 1: What are Antony and Lepidus willing to do in order to further their own political plans? What does Antony intend to do with the legacies set forth in Cæsar's will?
Answers
Antony and Lepidus are willing to sacrifice relatives in order to further their own plans. Antony intends to reduce the amount of the legacy that is supposed to be given to the Roman populace.

ANSWERS TO GUIDED READING QUESTIONS

1. Brutus tells Cassius's servant that Cassius has given him reason "to wish / Things done undone." In other words, Brutus is beginning to doubt whether they did the right thing in killing Cæsar. Cassius's attitude has changed, whether through his own will or the influence of others.
2. Brutus urges Cassius to speak softly and to take their disagreement into the tent so that their men will not overhear.

Quotables

"Friendships begin with liking or gratitude—roots that can be pulled up."

—George Eliot

How he receiv'd you; let me be resolv'd.[4]

15 **LUCILIUS.** With courtesy and with respect enough,
But not with such familiar instances,[5]
Nor with such free and friendly conference,[6]
As he hath us'd of old.[7]

BRUTUS. Thou hast describ'd
A hot friend cooling. Ever note, Lucilius,
20 When love begins to sicken and decay
It useth an enforced ceremony.[8]
There are no tricks in plain and simple faith;
But hollow[9] men, like horses hot at hand,[10]
Make gallant show and promise of their mettle;[11]   *Low march within.*
25 But when they should endure the bloody spur,
They fall[12] their crests, and like deceitful jades[13]
Sink in the trial.[14] Comes his army on?

LUCILIUS. They mean this night in Sardis to be quarter'd.
The greater part, the horse in general,[15]
Are come with Cassius.

Enter CASSIUS *and his powers.*

30 **BRUTUS.** Hark, he is arriv'd.
March gently on to meet him.

CASSIUS. Stand ho!

BRUTUS. Stand ho! Speak the word along.

1. SOLDIER. Stand!

35 **2. SOLDIER.** Stand!

3. SOLDIER. Stand!

CASSIUS. Most noble brother, you have done me wrong.

BRUTUS. Judge me, you gods! wrong I mine enemies?
And if not so, how should I wrong a brother?

40 **CASSIUS.** Brutus, this sober[16] form of yours hides wrongs,
And when you do them—

BRUTUS. Cassius, be content,
Speak your griefs softly; I do know you well.
Before the eyes of both our armies here
(Which should perceive nothing but love from us)
45 Let us not wrangle. Bid them move away;

What does Brutus say Cassius has done? How has Cassius changed?

What does Brutus urge Cassius to do?

---

4. **resolv'd.** Told in full
5. **familiar instances.** Friendly actions
6. **conference.** Discussion, talk
7. **of old.** In the past
8. **enforced ceremony.** Forced civility or formality
9. **hollow.** Phony, insincere
10. **hot at hand.** Too spirited at the beginning (as of a race)
11. **mettle.** Ability
12. **fall.** Drop
13. **deceitful jades.** Poor horses, nags
14. **Sink in the trial.** Fail to meet the challenge
15. **horse in general.** Cavalry as a whole
16. **sober.** Somber

Then in my tent, Cassius, enlarge[17] your griefs,
And I will give you audience.

CASSIUS. Pindarus,
Bid our commanders lead their charges[18] off
A little from this ground.

50 **BRUTUS.** Lucius, do you the like, and let no man
Come to our tent till we have done our conference.
Let Lucilius and Titinius guard our door.

Exeunt. Manent BRUTUS *and* CASSIUS, *who withdraw into* BRUTUS's *tent, while* LUCILIUS *and* TITINIUS *mount guard without.*

SCENE 3: INTERIOR OF BRUTUS'S TENT

CASSIUS. That you have wrong'd me doth appear in this:
You have condemn'd and noted[1] Lucius Pella
For taking bribes here of the Sardians;
Wherein my letters, praying on his side,
5 Because I knew the man, was[2] slighted off.[3]

BRUTUS. You wrong'd yourself to write in such a case.

CASSIUS. In such a time as this it is not meet[4]
That every nice[5] offense should bear his comment.[6]

BRUTUS. Let me tell you, Cassius, you yourself
10 Are much condemn'd to have an itching palm,
To sell and mart[7] your offices for gold
To undeservers.

CASSIUS. I, an itching palm?
You know that you are Brutus that speaks this,
Or, by the gods, this speech were else your last.

15 **BRUTUS.** The name of Cassius honors this corruption,
And <u>chastisement</u> doth therefore hide his head.

CASSIUS. Chastisement?

BRUTUS. Remember March, the ides of March remember:
Did not great Julius bleed for justice' sake?

> In what way has Brutus "wrong'd" Cassius? Of what does Brutus accuse Cassius?

---

17. **enlarge.** Expand upon
18. **charges.** Soldiers

ACT 4, SCENE 3
1. **noted.** Marked for disgrace
2. **was.** Were

3. **slighted off.** Ignored
4. **meet.** Fit, appropriate
5. **nice.** Small
6. **bear his comment.** Require criticism; *his*—its
7. **mart.** Market

words for everyday use
chas • tise • ment (chas´tīz´mənt) *n.,* scolding; condemnation. *The public <u>chastisement</u> caused Zara much embarrassment.*

1. According to Cassius, Brutus has wronged him by condemning Lucius Pella, a man accused of accepting bribes. Cassius had defended Pella, and is angry that Brutus opposed him. Brutus accuses Cassius of having "an itching palm," implying that he accepts bribes as well.

1. Brutus felt that when they killed
    Julius Cæsar, they did so in the
    name of justice. They wanted to set
    things right in the Roman Republic.
    If they themselves are corrupt and
    injust, then Cæsar died for nothing.
2. Brutus and Cassius are arguing over
    which of them is the better soldier.

20   What villain touch'd his body, that did stab
      And not for justice? What? shall one of us,
      That struck the foremost man of all this world
      But for supporting robbers, shall we now
      Contaminate our fingers with base bribes?
25   And sell the mighty space of our large honors
      For so much trash as may be grasped thus?
      I had rather be a dog, and bay the moon,
      Than such a Roman.

CASSIUS.   Brutus, bait not me,
      I'll not endure it. You forget yourself
30   To hedge me in.[8] I am a soldier, I,
      Older in practice, abler than yourself
      To make conditions.

BRUTUS.   Go to; you are not, Cassius.

CASSIUS.   I am.

BRUTUS.   I say you are not.

35   **CASSIUS.**   Urge me no more, I shall forget myself;
      Have mind upon your health; tempt me no farther.

BRUTUS.   Away, slight man!

CASSIUS.   Is't possible?

BRUTUS.   Hear me, for I will speak.
      Must I give way and room to your rash choler?[9]
40   Shall I be frighted[10] when a madman stares?

CASSIUS.   O ye gods, ye gods, must I endure all this?

BRUTUS.   All this? ay, more. Fret till your proud heart break;
      Go show your slaves how choleric[11] you are,
      And make your bondmen[12] tremble. Must I bouge?[13]
45   Must I observe you? Must I stand and crouch
      Under your testy humor?[14] By the gods,
      You shall digest the venom of your spleen[15]
      Though it do split you; for, from this day forth,
      I'll use you for my mirth, yea, for my laughter,
      When you are waspish.

50   **CASSIUS.**   Is it come to this?

BRUTUS.   You say you are a better soldier:
      Let it appear so; make your vaunting true,

Why is Brutus especially outraged that Cassius would accept bribes or defend others who do so?

What do Brutus and Cassius argue about now?

---

8. **hedge me in.** Close me in, limit my freedom
9. **choler.** Anger
10. **frighted.** Frightened
11. **choleric.** Angry
12. **bondmen.** Slaves

13. **bouge.** Budge, move
14. **humor.** Disposition
15. **spleen.** Organ considered by Elizabethans
to be the seat of strong emotions

And it shall please me well. For mine own part,
I shall be glad to learn of noble men.

55   **CASSIUS.**   You wrong me every way; you wrong me, Brutus:
I said an elder soldier, not a better.
Did I say "better"?

    BRUTUS.   If you did, I care not.

    CASSIUS.   When Cæsar liv'd, he durst[16] not thus have mov'd me.

    BRUTUS.   Peace, peace, you durst not so have tempted him.

60   **CASSIUS.**   I durst not?

    BRUTUS.   No.

    CASSIUS.   What? durst not tempt him?

    BRUTUS.   For your life you durst not.

    CASSIUS.   Do not presume too much upon my love,
I may do that I shall be sorry for.

65   **BRUTUS.**   You have done that you should be sorry for.
There is no terror, Cassius, in your threats;
For I am arm'd so strong in honesty
That they pass by me as the idle wind,
Which I respect[17] not. I did send to you
70 For certain sums of gold, which you denied me;
For I can raise no money by vile means.
By heaven, I had rather coin my heart
And drop my blood for drachmas[18] than to wring
From the hard hands of peasants their vile trash
75 By any indirection.[19] I did send
To you for gold to pay my legions,[20]
Which you denied me. Was that done like Cassius?
Should I have answer'd Caius Cassius so?
When Marcus Brutus grows so covetous
80 To lock such rascal counters[21] from his friends,
Be ready, gods, with all your thunderbolts,
Dash him to pieces!

    CASSIUS.   I denied you not.

    BRUTUS.   You did.

    CASSIUS.   I did not. He was but a fool that brought
85 My answer back. Brutus hath riv'd[22] my heart.

> *What new complaint does Brutus have about Cassius? How does Cassius respond?*

---

16. **durst.** Dared
17. **respect.** Fear
18. **drachmas.** Ancient silver coins
19. **indirection.** Cunning or false means

20. **legions.** Military divisions with three to six thousand soldiers
21. **rascal counters.** Coins of little worth
22. **riv'd.** Broken

ANSWER TO GUIDED
READING QUESTION

1. Brutus now complains that Cassius would not send him money he asked for to pay his soldiers. Cassius responds that his messenger must have made a mistake.

Quotables

"THIS IS A rotten argument, but it should be good enough for their lordships on a hot summer afternoon."

—Anonymous

1. Cassius urges Brutus to go ahead
   and kill him if he truly believes he is
   guilty of withholding money from
   him. Cassius points out that after all,
   Brutus loved Cæsar better than he
   ever loved Cassius, and yet he still
   killed Cæsar.

A friend should bear his friend's <u>infirmities</u>;
But Brutus makes mine greater than they are.

BRUTUS.   I do not, till you practice them on me.

CASSIUS.   You love me not.

BRUTUS.   I do not like your faults.

90   **CASSIUS.**   A friendly eye could never see such faults.

BRUTUS.   A flatterer's would not, though they do appear
As huge as high Olympus.

CASSIUS.   Come, Antony, and young Octavius, come,
Revenge yourselves alone on Cassius,
95   For Cassius is a-weary of the world;
Hated by one he loves, brav'd[23] by his brother,
Check'd like a bondman, all his faults observ'd,
Set in a note-book, learn'd, and conn'd by rote,[24]
To cast into my teeth. O, I could weep
100   My spirit from mine eyes! There is my dagger,
And here my naked breast; within, a heart
Dearer than Pluto's mine,[25] richer than gold:
If that thou be'st a Roman, take it forth.
I, that denied thee gold, will give my heart:
105   Strike as thou didst at Cæsar; for I know,
When thou didst hate him worst, thou lovedst him better
Than ever thou lovedst Cassius.

BRUTUS.   Sheathe your dagger.
Be angry when you will, it shall have scope;[26]
Do what you will, dishonor shall be humor.[27]
110   O Cassius, you are yoked with a lamb[28]
That carries anger as the flint bears fire,
Who, much enforced, shows a hasty spark,
And straight is cold again.

CASSIUS.   Hath Cassius liv'd
To be but mirth and laughter to his Brutus,
115   When grief and blood ill-temper'd vexeth him?

BRUTUS.   When I spoke that, I was ill-temper'd too.

*What does Cassius
urge Brutus to do?
Why?*

---

23. **brav'd.** Defied
24. **conn'd by rote.** Memorized
25. **Pluto's mine.** Treasures found in the earth; Pluto,
Roman god of the underworld, is here mixed up with
Plutus, the god of riches.

26. **scope.** Free play; range
27. **dishonor shall be humor.** I shall interpret your
insults (dishonor) as due to your disposition, or temper.
28. **yoked with a lamb.** Alternate between anger and
gentleness like that of a lamb

**words
for
everyday
use**   in • fir • mi • ty (in fur´mə tē) *n.*, sickness; weakness. *I was feeling too sick and weak to compete in the marathon
because I had an <u>infirmity</u> that left me bedridden.*

CASSIUS. Do you confess so much? Give me your hand.

BRUTUS. And my heart too.

CASSIUS. O Brutus!

BRUTUS. What's the matter?

CASSIUS. Have not you love enough to bear with me,
120 When that rash humor which my mother gave me
Makes me forgetful?

BRUTUS. Yes, Cassius, and from henceforth,
When you are over-earnest[29] with your Brutus,
He'll think your mother chides,[30] and leave you so.

Enter a POET, *to* LUCILIUS *and* TITINIUS, *as they stand on guard.*

POET. Let me go in to see the generals.
125 There is some grudge between 'em; 'tis not meet
They be alone.

LUCILIUS. You shall not come to them.

POET. Nothing but death shall stay me.

BRUTUS and CASSIUS step out of the tent.

CASSIUS. How now? what's the matter?

130 **POET.** For shame, you generals! what do you mean?
Love, and be friends, as two such men should be,
For I have seen more years, I'm sure, than ye.

CASSIUS. Ha, ha! how vildly[31] doth this cynic[32] rhyme!

BRUTUS. Get you hence, sirrah; saucy[33] fellow, hence!

135 **CASSIUS.** Bear with him, Brutus, 'tis his fashion.

BRUTUS. I'll know his humor, when he knows his time.[34]
What should the wars do with these jigging[35] fools?
Companion,[36] hence!

CASSIUS. Away, away, be gone!

Exit POET.

BRUTUS. Lucilius and Titinius, bid the commanders
140 Prepare to lodge their companies tonight.

CASSIUS. And come yourselves, and bring Messala with you
Immediately to us.

Exeunt LUCILIUS *and* TITINIUS.

BRUTUS. [*To* LUCIUS *within.*] Lucius, a bowl of wine!

---

29. **over-earnest.** Overly upset
30. **He'll . . . chides.** He will attribute your actions
to inherited bad temper.
31. **vildly.** Vilely
32. **cynic.** Worldly philosopher

33. **saucy.** Impertinent
34. **I'll know . . . his time.** I'll accept his temperament
when he chooses an appropriate time to display it.
35. **jigging.** Rhyming
36. **Companion.** Low person

How do Brutus and Cassius resolve their fight?

ANSWER TO GUIDED
READING QUESTION

1. The two men apologize.

CROSS-CURRICULAR ACTIVITIES

Although the bickering between Brutus and Cassius indicates serious problems, scene 3 is also somewhat comical. The two generals engage in a childish exchange of name-calling, and their dialogue is reduced to the level of "'I am,' 'I say you are not.'" Suggest that students enact part of this scene between Brutus and Cassius with a partner. As students discuss and practice their scenes, encourage them to determine their characters' motivations. Also, students should decide the tone of the scene. Is it comic? heated and intense? a combination of emotions? When students are ready, have them perform their scenes for the class. Students might think about wearing costumes or using props to emphasize the scene's dramatic potential.

ANSWERS TO GUIDED READING QUESTIONS

1. Portia has killed herself out of grief at Brutus's absence and fear of Antony's and Octavius's growing power.
2. Brutus has learned that Octavius and Antony are preparing to attack them, and are headed for Philippi. Messala further tells him that the two men have put to death a hundred senators.

ADDITIONAL QUESTIONS AND ACTIVITIES

What tragic news does Brutus relate to Cassius? Why is Cassius especially shocked to hear this news?
Answers
Brutus relates that his wife, Portia, is dead. Cassius is shocked to hear this news because he cannot believe Brutus's composure; he exclaims, "How scap'd I killing when I cross'd you so?"

BRUTUS and CASSIUS return into the tent.

CASSIUS.   I did not think you could have been so angry.

BRUTUS.   O Cassius, I am sick of[37] many griefs.

145 **CASSIUS.**   Of your philosophy you make no use,
If you give place to accidental evils.[38]

BRUTUS.   No man bears sorrow better. Portia is dead.

CASSIUS.   Ha? Portia?

BRUTUS.   She is dead.

150 **CASSIUS.**   How scap'd I killing when I cross'd you so?
O insupportable and touching loss!
Upon what sickness?

BRUTUS.   Impatient of[39] my absence,
And grief that young Octavius with Mark Antony
Have made themselves so strong—for with her death

155 That tidings came. With this she fell distract,[40]
And (her attendants absent) swallow'd fire.[41]

CASSIUS.   And died so?

BRUTUS.   Even so.

CASSIUS.   O ye immortal gods!

Enter the Boy LUCIUS with wine and tapers.

BRUTUS.   Speak no more of her. Give me a bowl of wine.
In this I bury all unkindness, Cassius.   *Drinks.*

160 **CASSIUS.**   My heart is thirsty for that noble pledge.
Fill, Lucius, till the wine o'erswell the cup;
I cannot drink too much of Brutus' love.

Drinks. Exit LUCIUS.

Enter TITINIUS and MESSALA.

BRUTUS.   Come in, Titinius. Welcome, good Messala.
Now sit we close about this taper here,

165 And call in question our necessities.[42]

CASSIUS.   Portia, art thou gone?

BRUTUS.   No more, I pray you.
Messala, I have here received letters
That young Octavius and Mark Antony
Come down upon us with a mighty power,

> What has happened to make Brutus so quick to anger and so given to emotion?

> What news does Brutus receive about Octavius and Antony?

---

37. **of.** From
38. **accidental evils.** The stoic philosophers taught that one should avoid displays of emotion and cultivate indifference to the tides of fortune.
39. **Impatient of.** Not able to endure
40. **fell distract.** Became crazed
41. **swallow'd fire.** According to Plutarch's *Lives*, she swallowed live coals.
42. **call . . . necessities.** Consider what we must do

170 Bending their expedition toward Philippi.

MESSALA.   Myself have letters of the self-same tenure.[43]

BRUTUS.   With what addition?

MESSALA.   That by proscription and bills of outlawry
Octavius, Antony, and Lepidus
175 Have put to death an hundred senators.

BRUTUS.   Therein our letters do not well agree;
Mine speak of seventy senators that died
By their proscriptions, Cicero being one.

CASSIUS.   Cicero one?

MESSALA.   Cicero is dead,
180 And by that order of proscription.
Had you your letters from your wife, my lord?

BRUTUS.   No, Messala.

MESSALA.   Nor nothing in your letters writ of her?

BRUTUS.   Nothing, Messala.

MESSALA.   That, methinks, is strange.

185 **BRUTUS.**   Why ask you? Hear you aught of her in yours?

MESSALA.   No, my lord.

BRUTUS.   Now as you are a Roman tell me true.

MESSALA.   Then like a Roman bear the truth I tell:
For certain she is dead, and by strange manner.

190 **BRUTUS.**   Why, farewell, Portia. We must die, Messala.
With meditating that she must die once,[44]
I have the patience to endure it now.

MESSALA.   Even so great men great losses should endure.

CASSIUS.   I have as much of this in art[45] as you,
195 But yet my nature could not bear it so.

BRUTUS.   Well, to our work alive.[46] What do you think
Of marching to Philippi presently?

CASSIUS.   I do not think it good.

BRUTUS.   Your reason?

CASSIUS.   This it is:
'Tis better that the enemy seek us;
200 So shall he waste his means, weary his soldiers,
Doing himself offense, whilst we, lying still,

> *What is Cassius's opinion about marching to Philippi to meet Antony and Octavius?*

---

43. **tenure.** Import
44. **With . . . once.** By thinking on the fact that death is inevitable

45. **have . . . art.** Know as much of this stoic philosophy
46. **to our work alive.** Let's act like the living.

ANSWER TO GUIDED READING QUESTION

1. Cassius feels it is best to wait for them at Sardis and save their army's strength.

ADDITIONAL QUESTIONS AND ACTIVITIES

- What tactics do Brutus and Cassius discuss regarding Philippi?
- What does Messala reveal that Octavius, Antony, and Lepidus have been doing in Rome? What could Cassius's nature not bear?

Answer
Cassius proposes letting the enemy come to them; in doing so, the enemy army will use some of its resources and not be as well rested. Brutus counters that plan by pointing out that the enemy armies will probably recruit more members along the way and thus gain a greater advantage. Messala reveals that Octavius, Antony, and Lepidus have put to death a hundred Roman senators. Cassius's nature could not bear the death of a loved one as stoically as Brutus's nature.

Are full of rest, defense, and nimbleness.

BRUTUS.   Good reasons must of force give place to better:
The people 'twixt Philippi and this ground
205 Do stand but in a forc'd affection,
For they have grudg'd us contribution.
The enemy, marching along by them,
By them shall make a fuller number up,
Come on refresh'd, new-added, and encourag'd;
210 From which advantage shall we cut him off
If at Philippi we do face him there,
These people at our back.

CASSIUS.   Hear me, good brother.

BRUTUS.   Under your pardon. You must note beside
That we have tried the utmost of [47] our friends,
215 Our legions are brimful, our cause is ripe:
The enemy increaseth every day;
We, at the height, are ready to decline.
There is a tide in the affairs of men,
Which taken at the flood, leads on to fortune;
220 Omitted, all the voyage of their life
Is bound in shallows [48] and in miseries.
On such a full sea are we now afloat,
And we must take the current when it serves,
Or lose our ventures.

To what does Brutus compare the success in life of some people and the failure?

CASSIUS.   Then with your will go on;
225 We'll along ourselves, and meet them at Philippi.

BRUTUS.   The deep of night is [49] crept upon our talk,
And nature must obey necessity,
Which we will niggard with a little rest. [50]
There is no more to say?

CASSIUS.   No more. Good night.
230 Early tomorrow will we rise, and hence.

BRUTUS. Lucius!

Enter LUCIUS.

My gown.

Exit LUCIUS.

Farewell, good Messala.
Good night, Titinius. Noble, noble Cassius,

What do the two men decide to do?

---

47. **tried the utmost of.** Got all the support that we shall be able to get
48. **bound in shallows.** Limited to shallow waters (confined to a harbor)

49. **is.** Has
50. **niggard with a little rest.** Shortchange by allowing ourselves but a little sleep

Good night, and good repose.

Cassius. O my dear brother!
This was an ill beginning of the night.
235 Never come such division 'tween our souls!
Let it not, Brutus.

Enter Lucius *with the gown.*

Brutus. Everything is well.

Cassius. Good night, my lord.

Brutus. Good night, good brother.

Titinius, Messala. Good night, Lord Brutus.

Brutus. Farewell every one.
Exeunt all but Brutus *and* Lucius.
Give me the gown. Where is thy instrument?[51]

Lucius. Here in the tent.

240 **Brutus.** What, thou speak'st drowsily?
Poor knave, I blame thee not, thou art o'erwatch'd.[52]
Call Claudio and some other of my men,
I'll have them sleep on cushions in my tent.

Lucius. Varrus and Claudio!

Enter Varrus *and* Claudio.

245 **Varrus.** Calls my lord?

Brutus. I pray you, sirs, lie in my tent and sleep;
It may be I shall raise you by and by
On business to my brother Cassius.

Varrus. So please you, we will stand and watch your pleasure.

250 **Brutus.** I will not have it so. Lie down, good sirs,
It may be I shall otherwise bethink me.[53]

Varrus *and* Claudio *lie down.*

Look, Lucius, here's the book I sought for so;
I put it in the pocket of my gown.

Lucius. I was sure your lordship did not give it me.

255 **Brutus.** Bear with me, good boy, I am much forgetful.
Canst thou hold up thy heavy eyes awhile,
And touch thy instrument a strain or two?

---

51. **instrument.** Lute, perhaps, to play a song for Brutus
52. **o'erwatch'd.** Overly tired
53. **otherwise bethink me.** Change my mind

CROSS-CURRICULAR ACTIVITIES

Music. In this scene, Brutus asks his servant Lucius to play him a song on his lute. Ask students to decide what kind of music Lucius should play. If they were staging a performance of *Julius Cæsar*, would they select a slow, sad song that echoes the melancholy mood of the scene, or an upbeat one, one designed to lift up Brutus's spirits and also to provide contrast? Ask students who play a string instrument such as a cello, violin, or guitar to select a song they think would be fitting for this scene and play it for the class. They should then explain why they think the song fits the scene.

1. The ghost of Cæsar appears and tells Brutus that they will see each other at Philippi.

ADDITIONAL QUESTIONS AND ACTIVITIES

How does Brutus react upon seeing Cæsar's ghost? How does this reaction compare to his behavior earlier in this act?
Answers
Brutus reacts rather calmly upon seeing the ghost. Although he says that the ghost "mak'st my blood cold, and my hair to stare," he still maintains his composure. As with his calm demeanor when telling Cassius of Portia's death, Brutus seems to be trying to maintain a stoic attitude.

LITERARY NOTE

Ghosts frequently appear in Shakespeare's plays and usually indicate a guilty conscience or a troubled psyche. In Shakespeare's histories and historical tragedies, the appearance of a ghost also typically foreshadows a character's defeat or downfall. One scene similar to this ghost scene is in *The Tragedy of Richard III,* act 5, scene 3, in which Richard is confronted by the ghosts of the many people he has murdered; the ghosts all urge Richard to "Despair and die!" and Richard is slain in the next day's battle. Another famous scene occurs in *The Tragedy of Macbeth,* act 3, scene 4, in which Macbeth is confronted by the gory ghost of his victim and former friend, Banquo.

LUCIUS.   Ay, my lord, an't[54] please you.

BRUTUS.   It does, my boy.
I trouble thee too much, but thou art willing.

260 **LUCIUS.**   It is my duty, sir.

BRUTUS.   I should not urge thy duty past thy might;
I know young bloods look for a time of rest.

LUCIUS.   I have slept, my lord, already.

BRUTUS.   It was well done, and thou shalt sleep again;
265 I will not hold thee long. If I do live,
I will be good to thee.   *Music, and a song.*
This is a sleepy tune. O murd'rous slumber!
Layest thou thy leaden mace[55] upon my boy,
That plays thee music? Gentle knave, good night;
270 I will not do thee so much wrong to wake thee.
If thou dost nod, thou break'st thy instrument,
I'll take it from thee; and, good boy, good night.
Let me see, let me see; is not the leaf turn'd down
Where I left reading? Here it is, I think.

Enter the GHOST OF CÆSAR.

275 How ill this taper burns! Ha! who comes here?
I think it is the weakness of mine eyes
That shapes this monstrous <u>apparition</u>.
It comes upon me. Art thou any thing?
Art thou some god, some angel, or some devil
280 That mak'st my blood cold, and my hair to stare?[56]
Speak to me what thou art.

GHOST.   Thy evil spirit, Brutus.

BRUTUS.   Why com'st thou?

GHOST.   To tell thee thou shalt see me at Philippi.

BRUTUS.   Well; then I shall see thee again?

285 **GHOST.**   Aye, at Philippi.

BRUTUS.   Why, I will see thee at Philippi then.

                                    Exit GHOST.

What apparition appears before Brutus? What does it tell him?

---

54. **an't.** If it
55. **mace.** Club
56. **stare.** Stand up

---

words for everyday use   ap • pa • ri • tion (ap´ə rish´ən) *n.,* ghost. *The resident of the Scottish castle claimed that an <u>apparition</u> walked the cold stone halls at night.*

---

322   *UNIT FOUR / DRAMA*

Now I have taken heart thou vanishest.
Ill spirit, I would hold more talk with thee.
Boy, Lucius! Varrus! Claudio! Sirs, awake!
290 Claudio!

LUCIUS. The strings, my lord, are false.[57]

BRUTUS. He thinks he still is at his instrument.
Lucius, awake!

LUCIUS. My lord?

295 **BRUTUS.** Didst thou dream, Lucius, that thou so criedst out?

LUCIUS. My lord, I do not know that I did cry.

BRUTUS. Yes, that thou didst. Didst thou see any thing?

LUCIUS. Nothing, my lord.

BRUTUS. Sleep again, Lucius. Sirrah Claudio!
300 [*To* VARRUS.] Fellow thou, awake!

VARRUS. My lord?

CLAUDIO. My lord?

BRUTUS. Why did you so cry out, sirs, in your sleep?

VARRUS, CLAUDIO. Did we, my lord?

BRUTUS.   Aye. Saw you any thing?

VARRUS. No, my lord, I saw nothing.

305 **CLAUDIO.** Nor I, my lord.

BRUTUS. Go and commend me[58] to my brother Cassius;
Bid him set on his pow'rs betimes before,[59]
And we will follow.

VARRUS, CLAUDIO. It shall be done, my lord.

Exeunt.

---

57. **false.** Out of tune
58. **commend me.** Give my regards
59. **set on . . . before.** Advance his troops ahead of mine

Respond *to the*
SELECTION

How do you react to sorrow or grief? Do you try to push your grief aside to concentrate on something else or do you dwell on your sadness for a time?

RESPOND TO THE SELECTION

If students have experienced a painful loss, have they tried to push their grief aside and to concentrate on something else (as Brutus does), or have they dwelt on their sadness (as Cassius seems to want Brutus to do)? Students can discuss grief and people's reactions to it. You might mention that people grieve in different ways and that a stoical reaction like that of Brutus does not necessarily signify indifference.

Checking Your Reading
1. What list are Antony and his men preparing? **They are preparing a list of the Romans who must die.**
2. How does Portia die? **Portia commits suicide by swallowing coals.**
3. With whom does Brutus fight bitterly? **Brutus fights with Cassius.**
4. How does this fight conclude? **The two men make up.**
5. What does the ghost say to Brutus? **The ghost says he will see him at Philippi.**

Vocabulary in Context
Fill in each blank with the most appropriate word from the following *Words for Everyday Use* from *The Tragedy of Julius Caesar.* You may have to change the tense of the word.

corporal   infirmity   apparition
chastisement

1. When Paul saw the broken glass, he knew he was in for **chastisement**.
2. Many colonists suffered **infirmity** during the long voyage to the New World.
3. The set designers used fishing line to make the **apparition** appear to fly.

Literary Tools
Fill in the blanks using the following terms. You may not use every term, and you may use some terms more than once.

plot   falling action   crisis
foreshadowing   motif

1. Presenting materials that hint at events to occur later in the plot is **foreshadowing**.
2. The **falling action** is all the events that follow the climax.
3. The **plot** is a series of events relating to a central conflict.

ANSWERS TO INVESTIGATE, INQUIRE, AND IMAGINE

RECALL

1a. Lepidus, Antony and Octavius are deciding which Romans shall live and which shall die. Antony wants to reduce the cost of the legacies in Cæsar's will—in other words, he does not want to fully honor the will.

2a. Brutus and Cassius argue about a number of relatively unimportant things, including who is the better soldier. They disagree over how to deal with a man accused of taking bribes and Brutus accuses Cassius of taking bribes. They also argue over whether or not Cassius has sent the money he promised to cover the expenses of the soldiers.

3a. Brutus tells Cassius that Portia has killed herself by swallowing fire.

INTERPRET

1b. Antony, Octavius and Lepidus are ruthless, opportunistic and ambitious. Antony, in particular, seems mercenary and hypocritical, willing to use the words of Cæsar, whom he supposedly loved and respected, to his own political advantage and ignore them when they no longer serve his purpose.

2b. Brutus and Cassius are arguing over minor matters, probably because of the stress they are under. They are concerned about the future and the threat from Antony and Octavius and Brutus has begun to have second thoughts about whether the killing of Cæsar was the right thing to do.

3b. Brutus is sad but attempts to put his grief aside in the manner of a stoic. Cassius is also saddened when he hears, and is surprised at Brutus's ability to contain his emotions. Brutus and Cassius have been quarreling and after he tells Cassius of Portia's death, Brutus says he wishes to "bury all unkindness." Cassius responds, "My heart is thirsty for that noble pledge." The two men stop their quarreling.

ANALYZE

4a. Cassius argues for waiting at Sardis, believing that the opposing army will use up its resources and will be tired when it arrives while their own army will be well rested. Brutus disagrees, believing that the people who live between Philippi and Sardis are only grudgingly sympathetic to their cause. He fears that Antony and Octavius will be able to recruit many new soldiers along the way and arrive, larger and more powerful than ever, to confront them. Brutus argues for marching to Philippi and confronting Antony and Octavius

Investigate, *Inquire*, and Imagine

Recall: GATHERING FACTS

1a. About what are Lepidus, Antony, and Octavius deciding at the beginning of act 4? What does Antony want to do about the promises in Cæsar's will?

2a. What do Brutus and Cassius argue about in scene 3?

3a. What tragic news does Brutus share with Cassius in scene 3?

Interpret: FINDING MEANING

1b. What does it tell you about Antony and Lepidus that they are willing to sacrifice relatives who oppose their political plans? What does Antony's plan for Cæsar's legacy tell you about his character?

2b. Are Cassius and Brutus arguing over important matters? Why do you think they are arguing in this manner?

3b. How has this news affected Brutus? How does it affect Cassius and his relationship with Brutus?

Analyze: TAKING THINGS APART

4a. In scene 3, Brutus and Cassius disagree over whether to confront the army of Antony and Octavius at Philippi or to wait for the enemy to come to them, near Sardis. Outline the arguments on either side of this question.

Synthesize: BRINGING THINGS TOGETHER

4b. Which argument seems more persuasive to you? How do the appearance of Cæsar's ghost and his words to Brutus affect your answer?

Evaluate: MAKING JUDGMENTS

5a. Evaluate the nature of the relationship between Brutus and Cassius. Would you call it friendship or more of a working partnership? Support your conclusion with evidence from the text. The relationship between the two men suffers some severe strain in act 4. What do you predict for their relationship in act 5?

Extend: CONNECTING IDEAS

5b. Upon hearing that Cassius seems less friendly, Brutus observes, "When love begins to sicken and decay / It useth an enforced ceremony." Do you agree? Have you ever noticed people behaving in a forced and coldly civil manner as their friendship fades? Has this behavior ever occurred with one of your friendships?

Understanding *Literature*

PLOT AND FALLING ACTION. Review the definition for **plot** in the Handbook of Literary Terms, noting the entry for **falling action**. During the falling action of a tragedy, the fortunes of the main character decline. What misfortunes does Brutus suffer in this act? What has happened to his relationship with Cassius? What has happened to his wife? What immediate threat does he face?

FORESHADOWING. Review the definition for **foreshadowing** in the Handbook of Literary Terms. What do you think the appearance of the ghost foreshadows? If the ghost is not real, what does its appearance to Brutus tell you about Brutus's state of mind? Why might he be feeling this way?

ANSWERS TO INVESTIGATE, INQUIRE, AND IMAGINE (CONT.)

there. He compares their situation to the tides and says they are at high tide—their army is large and strong and the time to strike is now. If they wait, he fears, they will lose the advantage they have.

SYNTHESIZE

4b. *Responses will vary.* Some students will feel that the appearance of Cæsar's ghost and its promise to see Brutus again in Philippi is an omen that the battle will bring defeat to Brutus. Ghosts frequently appear in Shakespeare's plays to indicate a guilty conscience or as an omen of impending doom or defeat.

EVALUATE

5a. *Responses will vary.* Some students will feel that Cassius's willingness to deceive Brutus with forged letters evidences more of a working relationship than a true friendship in which the two people genuinely care for one another. And yet, Cassius seems to truly grieve for Brutus when Portia dies. Perhaps the relationship began as a working relationship that grew into friendship.

EXTEND

5b. *Responses will vary.*

Writer's Journal

1. Write an **epitaph** for Portia, who has killed herself in act 4. Give thought to what you know of her character, and write a brief epitaph that conveys something important about her life.

2. Brutus's words in scene 3, lines 218–223 are often quoted. Study these lines and **paraphrase** them. Be sure to capture the meaning while using your own, modern English.

3. If you were Brutus, sitting alone in your tent the night before the battle with Octavius and Antony, your mind would likely be filled with thoughts of what has happened thus far and speculation about the outcome of the next day's battle. What would you say to Cæsar if you had opportunity to speak with him? Write an imaginary **dialogue** with Cæsar, telling him what is on your mind.

Integrating the Language Arts

Speaking and Listening & Collaborative Learning

ANALYZING CHARACTER MOTIVATION. Although the bickering between Brutus and Cassius in scene 3 indicates serious problems between the two, it is somewhat comical that two generals would engage in a childish exchange of name-calling. In pairs, study this scene and discuss the motivation of the characters. What causes them to behave this way? What do you think the tone of the scene should be—comic? heated and intense? some combination of emotions? Practice enacting this scene in different tones, then choose one and read it for your class. Refer to the Language Arts Survey 4.1, "Verbal and Nonverbal Communication," for notes about tone.

Study and Research

RESEARCHING STOICISM. Using Internet and library resources, research the philosophy of Stoicism advocated by Brutus. When was it first introduced? Which philosophers are linked to Stoicism? What elements of this philosophy do you like? Which do you dislike? Write a report of your findings.

Study and Research

RESEARCHING ANCIENT ROME. Using library and Internet resources, research the geography of ancient Rome and the surrounding lands. Note the locations of Philippi and Sardis, including the topography of the area. What conclusions can you draw about the decision made by Brutus and Cassius to march to Phillippi and do battle with Antony and Octavius there, as opposed to waiting at Sardis? Share your findings with your class.

ANSWERS TO UNDERSTANDING LITERATURE

PLOT AND FALLING ACTION. Brutus's many misfortunes include the following: his wife has died, he is unable to raise money to support his army, Octavius and Antony have raised a large army against Brutus, he cannot sleep, and he is haunted by the ghost of Cæsar. He no longer respects Cassius, and their relationship is weakening. He is threatened not only with losing control of Rome but with death as well.

FORESHADOWING. The appearance of the ghost foreshadows Brutus's defeat. If the ghost is not real, it signifies Brutus's disturbed state of mind. His conscience is guilty because of Cæsar's murder, he may be feeling almost mad because he has lost his wife and his reputation as a Roman citizen, and he may lose his life.

ADDITIONAL RESOURCES

UNIT 4 RESOURCE BOOK
- Selection Worksheet 4.5
- Selection Check Test 4.4.13
- Selection Test 4.4.14
- Language, Grammar, and Style Resource 3.47
- Speaking and Listening Resource 4.21
- Study and Research Resource 5.1

READER'S JOURNAL

If students have trouble relating to this question, you might ask them whether they know a veteran of war. If so, what do they know of the veteran's experiences? What do students imagine might happen to them if they were to go into battle? What would their fears be? What would their hopes be?

ART NOTE

A basilica was a Roman building, rectangular in shape and flanked by columns. These structures were typically used as marketplaces, public halls, and courtrooms.

ANSWER TO GUIDED READING QUESTION

1. Octavius says "our hopes are answered." In other words, he is pleased they have come down from their hilltop position to do battle at Philippi.

CROSS-CURRICULAR ACTIVITIES

APPLIED ARTS. The photograph on page 326 shows the remains of a basilica with Roman columns. Inform students that there were five types of columns in classical architecture, and these represented the five classical "orders," or styles, of architecture. These were the Doric, Ionic, Corinthian, Tuscan, and Composite. Ask students to consult an encyclopedia for more information about each of these styles and for diagrams of each type of column. They should copy the diagrams in their notebooks and

CROSS-CURRICULAR ACTIVITIES (CONT.)

label each part—the cornice, frieze, architrave, capital, column, and pedestal—as they appear. Then they should note the main characteristics of each style of column and, looking at the photograph, should tell which order best describes the columns of the basilica.

Literary
TOOLS

PLOT AND CATASTROPHE. The **plot** is a series of events related to a central conflict, or struggle. The **catastrophe** in a tragedy is the event that marks the ultimate fall of the central character. In act 5, what is the catastrophe?

TRAGIC FLAW. A **tragic flaw** is a personal weakness that brings about the fall of a character in a tragedy. After you have read act 5, decide what is Brutus's tragic flaw.

Reader's
Journal

How would it feel to face going into battle?

Roman columns and basilica.

ACT 5

SCENE 1: THE BATTLEGROUND AT PHILIPPI

Enter OCTAVIUS, ANTONY, *and their army.*

OCTAVIUS. Now, Antony, our hopes are answered.
You said the enemy would not come down,
But keep the hills and upper regions.
It proves not so: their battles[1] are at hand;
5   They mean to warn[2] us at Philippi here,
Answering before we do demand of them.

ANTONY. Tut, I am in their bosoms,[3] and I know
Wherefore they do it. They could be content

How does Octavius feel about Brutus and Cassius coming to Philippi to challenge Antony and him?

ACT 5, SCENE 1
1. **battles.** Battalions; armies
2. **warn.** Challenge
3. **I am . . . bosoms.** I know their hearts (plans).

VOCABULARY FROM THE SELECTION

disconsolate   garland
engender   misconstrue
ensign   presage

To visit other places, and come down
10   With fearful bravery, thinking by this face[4]
To fasten in our thoughts that they have courage;
But 'tis not so.

Enter a MESSENGER.

MESSENGER.   Prepare you, generals.
The enemy comes on in gallant show;
15   Their bloody sign of battle is hung out,
And something to be done immediately.

ANTONY.   Octavius, lead your battle softly on
Upon the left hand of the even field.

OCTAVIUS.   Upon the right hand I, keep thou the left.

20   ANTONY.   Why do you cross me in this exigent?[5]

OCTAVIUS.   I do not cross you; but I will do so.

Drum. Enter BRUTUS, CASSIUS, *and their army;*
LUCILIUS, TITINIUS, MESSALA, *and others.*

BRUTUS.   They stand, and would have parley.[6]

CASSIUS.   Stand fast, Titinius; we must out and talk.

OCTAVIUS.   Mark Antony, shall we give sign of battle?

25   ANTONY.   No, Cæsar, we will answer on their charge.[7]
Make forth, the generals would have some words.

OCTAVIUS.   Stir not until the signal.

BRUTUS.   Words before blows; is it so, countrymen?

OCTAVIUS.   Not that we love words better, as you do.

30   BRUTUS.   Good words are better than bad strokes, Octavius.

ANTONY.   In your bad strokes, Brutus, you give good words;
Witness the hole you made in Cæsar's heart,
Crying, "Long live! Hail, Cæsar!"

CASSIUS.   Antony,
The posture[8] of your blows are yet unknown;
35   But for your words, they rob the Hybla[9] bees,
And leave them honeyless.

ANTONY.   Not stingless too?

BRUTUS.   O yes, and soundless too;
For you have stol'n their buzzing, Antony,
And very wisely threat before you sting.

40   ANTONY.   Villains! you did not so, when your vile daggers

March.

> What do Antony and
> Octavius argue about?

---

4. **face.** Look; appearance
5. **cross . . . exigent.** Contradict me in this emergency
6. **have parley.** Speak; confer
7. **answer on their charge.** React when they attack
8. **posture.** Strength or nature
9. **Hybla.** Town in Sicily known for beehives and honey

1. Antony and Octavius argue about which army will take the left side of the field and which will take the right.

INDIVIDUAL LEARNING STRATEGIES

MOTIVATION
Read to students Wilfred Owen's "Dulce et Decorum Est," a twentieth-century poem about the horrors of war. Also have them read the quote on this page by Oscar Wilde. What are their attitudes toward war? Is it ever justifiable, and in what circumstances?

READING PROFICIENCY
Go over with students the Words for Everyday Use and the footnotes, then encourage them to read through each scene with a partner, answering the Guided Reading Questions as they go and summing up the main point of each scene.

ENGLISH LANGUAGE LEARNING
You may wish to review with students the additional vocabulary below.
kites—birds of prey
tarry—wait; linger

SPECIAL NEEDS
Students will find it helpful to hear the selection read out loud. Either read out loud to students or have them alternate reading aloud. Make sure students focus on the Guided Reading Questions and the Recall questions in the Investigate, Inquire, and Imagine section.

ENRICHMENT
Have students research the history of the Roman Republic. How did it start? How long did it last? What form of government came after Cæsar was assassinated, and who was in power? Also, ask students to define the *Pax Romana*.

CROSS-CURRICULAR ACTIVITIES

GEOGRAPHY. As students read the description of the battle, they may wish to have a visual in mind. Brutus and Cassius have left their camp at Sardis for Philippi. Sardis, a city dating back to the 1300s BC, was the capital of the ancient kingdom of Lydia. It is located on a site a little east of present-day Izmir, Turkey. Philippi was an ancient town in northeastern Greece, in north-central Macedonia. Ask students to locate a map that shows Sardis, and one that shows Philippi, and then to find the approximate location of these sites on a modern-day map. How close are these sites to Rome? What is the topography like? Were there bodies of water or mountains nearby? Maps of the ancient world, often showing the boundaries of the Roman Empire, can be found in many world atlases.

Quotables

"As long as war is regarded as wicked, it will always have its fascination. When it is looked upon as vulgar, it will cease to be popular."

—Oscar Wilde

1. Cassius tells Brutus he has himself to thank for Antony's curses. Had Brutus listened to Cassius, Antony would have been killed along with Cæsar.

What change has occurred on the side of Antony and Octavius? What does this change indicate about the future of Rome?
Answers
Octavius has clearly asserted himself as leader. When Antony attempted to direct the course of battle, Octavius simply told him that he would make his own decisions. After this point, Antony refers to him as Cæsar and Octavius also calls himself by that name (line 55). This change indicates that Octavius, not Antony, will rule Rome if they win the battle.

Hack'd one another[10] in the sides of Cæsar.
You show'd your teeth like apes, and fawn'd like hounds,
And bow'd like bondmen, kissing Cæsar's feet;
Whilst damned Casca, like a cur, behind
45   Strook[11] Cæsar on the neck. O you flatterers!

CASSIUS.   Flatterers? Now, Brutus, thank yourself;
This tongue had not offended so today,
If Cassius might have rul'd.[12]

OCTAVIUS.   Come, come, the cause. If arguing make us sweat,
50   The proof of it will turn to redder drops.
Look,
I draw a sword against conspirators;
When think you that the sword goes up again?[13]
Never, till Cæsar's three and thirty wounds
55   Be well aveng'd; or till another Cæsar
Have added slaughter to the sword of traitors.[14]

BRUTUS.   Cæsar, thou canst not die by traitors' hands,
Unless thou bring'st them with thee.

CASSIUS.   So I hope;
I was not born to die on Brutus' sword.

60   **BRUTUS.**   O, if thou wert the noblest of thy strain,[15]
Young man, thou couldst not die more honorable.

CASSIUS.   A peevish schoolboy,[16] worthless of such honor,
Join'd with a masker[17] and a reveller!

ANTONY.   Old Cassius still!

OCTAVIUS.   Come, Antony; away!
65   Defiance, traitors, hurl we in your teeth.
If you dare fight today, come to the field;
If not, when you have stomachs.

                              Exeunt OCTAVIUS, ANTONY, *and army.*

CASSIUS.   Why now blow wind, swell billow, and swim bark![18]
The storm is up, and all is on the hazard.[19]

BRUTUS.   Ho, Lucilius, hark, a word with you.

                              LUCILIUS *and then* MESSALA *stand forth.*

70   **LUCILIUS.**   My lord.

For what does Cassius tell Brutus he has himself to thank?

---

10. **one another.** One after the other
11. **Strook.** Struck
12. **Cassius might have rul'd.** Cassius had urged that Antony be killed along with Cæsar.
13. **goes up again.** Will be resheathed
14. **till another . . . sword of traitors.** Until these traitors have killed another Cæsar, Octavius himself

15. **thy strain.** Your family
16. **peevish schoolboy.** Octavius was twenty-one years old at the time of the battle.
17. **masker.** One who attends masked balls
18. **swim bark.** Sail ship
19. **on the hazard.** Risked

BRUTUS and LUCILIUS converse apart.

CASSIUS. Messala!

MESSALA. What says my general?

CASSIUS. Messala,
This is my birthday; as this very day
Was Cassius born. Give me thy hand, Messala.
Be thou my witness that against my will
75 (As Pompey was) am I compell'd to set
Upon[20] one battle all our liberties.
You know that I held Epicurus[21] strong,
And his opinion; now I change my mind,
And partly credit things that do presage.
80 Coming from Sardis, on our former[22] ensign
Two mighty eagles fell, and there they perch'd,
Gorging and feeding from our soldiers' hands,
Who to Philippi here consorted[23] us.
This morning are they fled away and gone,
85 And in their steads[24] do ravens, crows, and kites
Fly o'er our heads, and downward look on us
As we were sickly prey. Their shadows seem
A canopy most fatal, under which
Our army lies, ready to give up the ghost.

MESSALA. Believe not so.

90 **CASSIUS.** I but believe it partly,
For I am fresh of spirit, and resolv'd
To meet all perils very constantly.[25]

BRUTUS. Even so, Lucilius.

CASSIUS. Now, most noble Brutus,
The gods today stand friendly, that we may,
95 Lovers[26] in peace, lead on our days to age!
But since the affairs of men rest still incertain,[27]
Let's reason with the worst that may befall.[28]
If we do lose this battle, then is this
The very last time we shall speak together:

What evil omen did Cassius witness? What does this omen seem to foretell?

---

20. **set / Upon.** Risk in
21. **Epicurus.** Greek philosopher who did not believe in omens
22. **former.** Foremost
23. **consorted.** Accompanied

24. **steads.** Places
25. **constantly.** Firmly; resolutely
26. **Lovers.** Friends
27. **incertain.** Uncertain
28. **reason . . . befall.** Expect the worst

words for everyday use

pre • sage (prē sāj´) vi., foretell; warn. *Some superstitious people believe that a black cat presages bad luck.*

en • sign (en´sīn´) n., flag; banner. *The soldier who bore the ensign was proud because his flag emerged intact from the battle.*

1. Cassius saw two eagles perch on their army's foremost flag and feed hungrily from the soldiers' hands. Then the eagles, who had been flown with the troops all the way to Philippi, fled. In their place, scavenger birds flew in, circling, as if looking for "sickly prey." This omen seems to Cassius to foretell death for the troops.

1. Brutus will have patience and wait for whatever destiny, or providence, has in store. He will not take his own life, because a stoic would view suicide as cowardly.

ADDITIONAL QUESTIONS AND ACTIVITIES

Brutus and Cassius say farewell to each other before the battle. Do you think they will see each other again? What do you think might happen to Brutus? to Cassius? Students may either discuss these questions or answer them in their journals.

HISTORICAL NOTE

When Brutus says he will never "go bound to Rome," he is referring to an element of the triumph. The triumph was a ritual procession that was the highest honor that could be given to a victorious general. The procession was led by the Senate and followed by sacrificial animals and the defeated prisoners in chains. Behind the prisoners, the victorious general rode in a chariot. The triumph was a spectacle that emphasized the glory of the victor and the humiliation of the defeated.

ADDITIONAL QUESTIONS AND ACTIVITIES

Ask students the following comprehension questions relating to what they just read in act 5, scene 1:
What do Brutus, Cassius, Antony, and Octavius do before the battle begins? Does each side in this battle believe that its cause is just? Explain. What do Brutus and Cassius say to one another at the end of the scene? Why do you think they say these things? How confident are they about the outcome of the battle? Explain.
Answers
Brutus, Cassius, Antony, and Octavius meet and talk before the battle begins. *Responses will vary.* Each side does believe its cause is just. Brutus and Cassius feel they are defending the Republic, and Antony

---

100 What are you then determined to do?

BRUTUS. Even by the rule of that philosophy[29]
By which I did blame Cato[30] for the death
Which he did give himself—I know not how,
But I do find it cowardly and vile,
105 For fear of what might fall, so to prevent[31]
The time[32] of life—arming myself with patience
To stay the providence[33] of some high powers
That govern us below.

CASSIUS.   Then, if we lose this battle,
You are contented to be led in triumph
110 Thorough[34] the streets of Rome?

BRUTUS. No, Cassius, no. Think not, thou noble Roman,
That ever Brutus will go bound to Rome;
He bears too great a mind. But this same day
Must end that work the ides of March begun.
115 And whether we shall meet again I know not;
Therefore our everlasting farewell take:
For ever, and for ever, farewell, Cassius!
If we do meet again, why, we shall smile;
If not, why then this parting was well made.

120 **CASSIUS.** For ever, and for ever, farewell, Brutus!
If we do meet again, we'll smile indeed;
If not, 'tis true this parting was well made.

BRUTUS. Why then lead on. O, that a man might know
The end of this day's business ere it come!
125 But it sufficeth that the day will end,
And then the end is known. Come ho, away!   *Exeunt.*

SCENE 2: THE BATTLEGROUND AT PHILIPPI

Alarum.[1] *Enter* BRUTUS *and* MESSALA.

BRUTUS. Ride, ride, Messala, ride, and give these bills[2]
Unto the legions on the other side.

                                    Loud alarum.

Let them set on[3] at once; for I perceive
But cold demeanor[4] in Octavio's wing,

> *What does Brutus vow not to do if they lose the battle?*

---

29. **that philosophy.** Stoicism
30. **Cato.** Marcus Porcius Cato, Brutus's father-in-law, who fought with Pompey against Cæsar and committed suicide rather than surrender
31. **prevent.** Decide
32. **time.** Length
33. **stay the providence.** Await the pleasure
34. **Thorough.** Through

ACT 5, SCENE 2
1. *Alarum.* Call to battle
2. **bills.** Written orders
3. **set on.** Go forward; charge
4. **cold demeanor.** Lack of spirit; weakness

330 *UNIT FOUR / DRAMA*

ADDITIONAL QUESTIONS AND ACTIVITIES (CONT.)

and Octavius feel they are revenging Cæsar and punishing vile murderers. Brutus and Cassius bid farewell to one another. *Responses will vary.* They sense the downward course of their fates and would rather die than be taken captive in battle and led in chains through Rome. Brutus and Cassius are not very confident as evidenced by the fact that they discuss very seriously the prospect of losing. Brutus and Cassius are outnumbered by Antony and Octavius's forces.

5 And sudden push gives them the overthrow.
 Ride, ride, Messala, let them all come down.

Exeunt.

SCENE 3: THE BATTLEGROUND AT PHILIPPI

Alarums. Enter CASSIUS *and* TITINIUS.

CASSIUS. O, look, Titinius, look, the villains[1] fly!
Myself have to mine own[2] turn'd enemy.
This ensign here of mine was turning back;
I slew the coward, and did take it from him.

5 **TITINIUS.** O Cassius, Brutus gave the word too early,
Who, having some advantage on Octavius,
Took it too eagerly. His soldiers fell to spoil,
Whilst we by Antony are all enclos'd.

Enter PINDARUS.

PINDARUS. Fly further off, my lord, fly further off;
10 Mark Antony is in your tents, my lord;
Fly therefore, noble Cassius, fly far off.

CASSIUS. This hill is far enough. Look, look, Titinius,
Are those my tents where I perceive the fire?

TITINIUS. They are, my lord.

CASSIUS.   Titinius, if thou lovest me,
15 Mount thou my horse, and hide thy spurs in him
Till he have brought thee up to yonder troops
And here again, that I may rest assur'd
Whether yond troops are friend or enemy.

TITINIUS. I will be here again, even with a thought.[3]   *Exit.*

20 **CASSIUS.** Go, Pindarus, get higher on that hill;
My sight was ever thick; regard Titinius,
And tell me what thou not'st about the field.

PINDARUS goes up.

This day I breathed first: time is come round,
And where I did begin, there shall I end;
25 My life is run his compass.[4] Sirrah, what news?

PINDARUS. [*Above.*] O my lord!

CASSIUS. What news?

PINDARUS. Titinius is enclosed round about

ACT 5, SCENE 3
 1. **villains.** Cowards
 2. **mine own.** My own soldiers (because of their cowardice)

3. **even with a thought.** As quickly as a thought
4. **is run his compass.** Has run its course; is finished

Sidebar prompts:
- What is happening to Cassius's army?
- What news do Titinius and Pindarus give Cassius?

ANSWERS TO GUIDED READING QUESTIONS

1. Pindarus reports that Titinius has been surrounded and captured by enemy troops.
2. Cassius orders Pindarus to kill him with a sword.
3. Octavius was defeated by Brutus, while Cassius was defeated by Antony. This news, according to Titinius, would "comfort" Cassius.

ADDITIONAL QUESTIONS AND ACTIVITIES

Why does Cassius despair? Has he done so too soon? What does Messala say about Cassius's death? In what way is Cassius's death typical of his character?
Answers
Cassius despairs because he believes that Octavius and Antony's forces have overcome his forces, overrun his camp, and taken his best friend prisoner. He has despaired and chosen to end his life too soon, for Messala and Titinius return with news of Brutus's success. Messala says, "Mistrust of good success hath done this deed. O hateful error, melancholy's child." Cassius's death is typical of his character because he is a highly emotional, hot-tempered individual; just as he acted on his emotions in life, he has acted on emotions that needlessly led to his death.

---

30   With horsemen, that make to him on the spur,
  Yet he spurs on. Now they are almost on him.
  Now, Titinius! Now some light.[5] O, he lights too.
  He's ta'en. [*Shout.*] And hark, they shout for joy.

  CASSIUS. Come down, behold no more.
  O, coward that I am, to live so long,
35   To see my best friend ta'en before my face!

                        PINDARUS *descends.*

  Come hither, sirrah.
  In Parthia did I take thee prisoner,
  And then I swore thee, saving of thy life,
  That whatsoever I did bid thee do,
40   Thou shouldst attempt it. Come now, keep thine oath;
  Now be a freeman, and with this good sword,
  That ran through Cæsar's bowels, search this bosom.
  Stand not to answer; here, take thou the hilts,
  And when my face is cover'd, as 'tis now,
45   Guide thou the sword. [PINDARUS *stabs him.*] Cæsar, thou art reveng'd,
  Even with the sword that kill'd thee.   *Dies.*

  PINDARUS. So, I am free; yet would not so have been,
  Durst I have done my will. O Cassius,
  Far from this country Pindarus shall run,
50   Where never Roman shall take note of him.

                          Exit.

  Enter TITINIUS *and* MESSALA.

  MESSALA. It is but change, Titinius; for Octavius
  Is overthrown by noble Brutus' power,
  As Cassius' legions are by Antony.

  TITINIUS. These tidings will well comfort Cassius.

  MESSALA. Where did you leave him?

55   **TITINIUS.**   All <u>disconsolate</u>,
  With Pindarus his bondman, on this hill.

  MESSALA. Is not that he that lies upon the ground?

  TITINIUS. He lies not like the living. O my heart!

  MESSALA. Is not that he?

---

5. **light.** Dismount

What does Pindarus say has happened to Titinius?

What does Cassius order Pindarus to do?

What is the result of the day's battle? How would Cassius feel about this result?

---

words for everyday use

dis • con • so • late (dis kän´sə lit) *adj.,* unhappy; not to be comforted. *The little boy who lost his stuffed zebra was* <u>disconsolate</u>; *neither cookies and milk nor his mother's hugs could make him stop crying.*

TITINIUS.   No, this was he, Messala,

60 But Cassius is no more. O setting sun,
As in thy red rays thou dost sink tonight,
So in his red blood Cassius' day is set!
The sun of Rome is set. Our day is gone,
Clouds, dews, and dangers come; our deeds are done!

65 Mistrust of[6] my success hath done this deed.

MESSALA.   Mistrust of good success hath done this deed.
O hateful error, melancholy's child,
Why dost thou show to the apt thoughts of men
The things that are not? O error, soon conceiv'd,

70 Thou never com'st unto a happy birth,
But kill'st the mother that <u>engend'red</u> thee!

TITINIUS.   What, Pindarus? Where art thou, Pindarus?

MESSALA.   Seek him, Titinius, whilst I go to meet
The noble Brutus, thrusting this report

75 Into his ears; I may say "thrusting" it;
For piercing steel, and darts envenomed,
Shall be as welcome to the ears of Brutus
As tidings of this sight.

TITINIUS.   Hie you, Messala,
And I will seek for Pindarus the while.

Exit MESSALA.

80 Why didst thou send me forth, brave Cassius?
Did I not meet thy friends? and did not they
Put on my brows this wreath of victory,[7]
And bid me give it thee? Didst thou not hear their shouts?
Alas, thou hast <u>misconstrued</u> every thing.

> Who were the men Pindarus had seen surrounding Titinius and shouting?

85 But hold thee, take this <u>garland</u> on thy brow;
Thy Brutus bid me give it thee, and I
Will do his bidding. Brutus, come apace,[8]
And see how I regarded Caius Cassius.
By your leave, gods!—this is a Roman's part.

> What does Titinius do?

90 Come, Cassius' sword, and find Titinius' heart.   *Dies.*

Alarum. Enter BRUTUS, MESSALA, *young* CATO, STRATO, VOLUMNIUS, *and* LUCILIUS.

---

6. **Mistrust of.** Lack of belief in
7. **Put . . . wreath of victory.** In Rome and in Greece,
victory in battle or in an athletic competition was often signified
by awarding the victor a crown or wreath of laurel.
8. **apace.** Quickly

words for everyday use	**en • gen • der** (en jen′dər) *vt.,* give birth to; produce. *The writer described her work as if it were her child, <u>engendered</u> by her imagination.* **mis • con • strue** (mis′kən strōō′) *vt.,* misinterpret; misunderstand. *"I don't want you to <u>misconstrue</u> my meaning, so listen carefully," Lorenzo told his employee.* **gar • land** (gär′lənd) *n.,* wreath or chain of flowers or leaves. *The children sat in a butterfly-covered field, making <u>garlands</u> of daisies to wear around their necks.*

1. The men who surrounded Titinius were Brutus's troops, who shouted with joy at their victory.
2. Titinius kills himself with Cassius's sword.

LITERARY TECHNIQUE

IRONY. Irony is a difference between appearance and reality. In *irony of situation,* something happens that violates the expectations of the characters, the reader, or the audience. What irony of situation does Titinius reveal?
Answer
He reveals that he was not surrounded by the enemy who shouted his defeat but by friends who shouted his victory. Pindarus misconstrued the scene that lead Cassius to rashly end his life.

1. Lucilius pretends to be Brutus and is taken captive by Antony's men.

Ask students the following questions relating to what they just read in act 5, scene 3:

• Whose troops have fought whom? Who has been victorious? What does Cassius misunderstand, and what does he do as a result? What do Messala's words tell us about the error of taking one's life (see lines 66–71)?

Answers
At the beginning of the scene, Brutus's troops fought Octavius's, and Antony's troops fought Cassius's. Brutus triumphed over Octavius, but Antony was victorious over Cassius. Cassius mistakenly believes that Titinius has been overcome, and he kills himself in despair. *Responses will vary.* Messala's words indicate that mistrust and lack of faith lead some to rashly take their own lives when they are overcome by melancholy.

CHARACTERIZATION. Characterization is the use of literary techniques to create a character. Writers use three major techniques to create characters: direct description, portrayal of characters' behavior, and representations of characters' internal states. In lines 101–103, Brutus says, "I owe moe tears / To this dead man than you shall see me pay. / I shall find time, Cassius; I shall find time." Is this reaction typical of Brutus? How does it compare to his reaction to Portia's death?

Answers
This reaction is typical of Brutus. He suffers the loss of his dearest friend but can't allow himself to mourn. One wonders when he "shall find time."

BRUTUS. Where, where, Messala, doth his body lie?

MESSALA. Lo yonder, and Titinius mourning it.

BRUTUS. Titinius' face is upward.

CATO. He is slain.

BRUTUS. O Julius Cæsar, thou art mighty yet!
95 Thy spirit walks abroad, and turns our swords
In our own proper[9] entrails.   *Low alarums.*

CATO. Brave Titinius!
Look whe'er he have not crown'd dead Cassius![10]

BRUTUS. Are yet two Romans living such as these?
The last of all the Romans, fare thee well!
100 It is impossible that ever Rome
Should breed thy fellow.[11] Friends, I owe moe tears
To this dead man than you shall see me pay.
I shall find time, Cassius; I shall find time.
Come therefore, and to Thasos[12] send his body;
105 His funerals shall not be in our camp,
Lest it discomfort us. Lucilius, come,
And come, young Cato, let us to the field,
Labio and Flavio set our battles on.
'Tis three a' clock, and, Romans, yet ere night
110 We shall try fortune[13] in a second fight.

       Exeunt.

SCENE 4: THE BATTLEGROUND AT PHILIPPI

Alarum. Enter BRUTUS, MESSALA, *young* CATO, LUCILIUS, *and* FLAVIUS.

BRUTUS. Yet, countrymen! O yet, hold up your heads! *Exit.*

CATO. What bastard doth not? Who will go with me?
I will proclaim my name about the field.
I am the son of Marcus Cato, ho!
5 A foe to tyrants, and my country's friend.
I am the son of Marcus Cato, ho!

Enter SOLDIERS *and fight.*

LUCILIUS. And I am Brutus, Marcus Brutus, I,
Brutus, my country's friend; know me for Brutus!

     Young CATO *is slain.*

O young and noble Cato, art thou down?

Whom does Lucilius pretend to be? What happens to him?

---

9. **own proper.** Very own
10. **Look . . . Cassius!** Notice that he has crowned the dead Cassius!
11. **fellow.** Equal
12. **Thasos.** Nearby island
13. **try fortune.** Take our chances

10   Why, now thou diest as bravely as Titinius,
And mayst be honor'd, being Cato's son.

1. SOLDIER.   Yield, or thou diest.

LUCILIUS.   Only I yield to die;[1]
There is so much that thou wilt[2] kill me straight:
Kill Brutus, and be honor'd in his death.

15   **1. SOLDIER.**   We must not. A noble prisoner!

Enter ANTONY.

2. SOLDIER.   Room ho! Tell Antony, Brutus is ta'en.

1. SOLDIER.   I'll tell the news. Here comes the general.
Brutus is ta'en, Brutus is ta'en, my lord!

ANTONY.   Where is he?

20   **LUCILIUS.**   Safe, Antony, Brutus is safe enough.
I dare assure thee that no enemy
Shall ever take alive the noble Brutus;
The gods defend him from so great a shame!
When you do find him, or alive or dead,
25   He will be found like Brutus, like himself.

ANTONY.   This is not Brutus, friend, but, I assure you,
A prize no less in worth. Keep this man safe,
Give him all kindness; I had rather have
Such men my friends than enemies. Go on,
30   And see whe'er Brutus be alive or dead,
And bring us word unto Octavius' tent
How every thing is chanc'd.[3]

Exeunt.

SCENE 5: THE BATTLEGROUND AT PHILIPPI

Enter BRUTUS, DARDANIUS, CLITUS, STRATO, *and* VOLUMNIUS.

BRUTUS.   Come, poor remains of[1] friends, rest on this rock.

CLITUS.   Statilius show'd the torchlight, but, my lord,
He came not back. He is or ta'en or slain.

BRUTUS.   Sit thee down, Clitus; slaying is the word,
5   It is a deed in fashion. Hark thee, Clitus.

Whispering.

CLITUS.   What, I, my lord? No, not for all the world.

ACT 5, SCENE 4
1. **Only . . . die.** I yield only to die.
2. **so much . . . thou wilt.** Good reason for you to
3. **is chanc'd.** Has happened

ACT 5, SCENE 5
1. **remains of.** Remaining

HISTORICAL NOTE

In ancient times, most battles involved hand-to-hand combat. Opposing soldiers would face each other with swords or similar handheld weaponry in a battle to the death. Soldiers also used javelins and spears, which could be thrown from a distance. It was not until the invention of gunpowder in the fifteenth century that warfare became more mechanized.

1. Brutus has seen Cæsar's ghost twice and believes his "hour has come."
2. Brutus asks Volumnius to kill him, saying that it is nobler to kill oneself than to wait for the victorious enemy to do it.

SELECTION CHECK TEST 4.4.13 WITH ANSWERS

Checking Your Reading
1. What do Brutus and Cassius say to each other as they leave for battle? **They bid each other farewell.**
2. What does Cassius order Pindarus to do? **He orders him to stab him.**
3. Which of the conspirators is successful in battle? **Brutus is successful in battle.**
4. How does Brutus die? **He has Strato hold his sword and then runs onto it.**
5. Whom does Antony call "the noblest Roman of all"? **He says this of Brutus.**

Vocabulary in Context
Fill in each blank with the most appropriate word from the following *Words for Everyday Use* from *The Tragedy of Julius Cæsar.* You may have to change the tense of the word.

disconsolate   misconstrue   engender
    ensign   garland   presage

1. The new recruit's job was to unfurl the ship's **ensign** each morning.
2. Brittany was **disconsolate** when the all the passengers had deplaned and Ray was not among them.
3. Sarah chose to wear a **garland** instead of a veil with her wedding gown.
4. With months of hard work, the troupe **engendered** a successful play.
5. **Misconstruing** the catcher's signal, the pitcher threw a fastball straight to the opposite team's best hitter.

Literary Tools
A plot pyramid shows the major points or stages of a plot. Label the plot pyramid by filling in each space with one of the following stages: climax, resolution, inciting incident, falling action, rising action, dénouement.

Brutus.   Peace then, no words.

Clitus.   I'll rather kill myself.

Brutus.   Hark thee, Dardanius.

Whispering.

Dardanius.   Shall I do such a deed?

Clitus.   O Dardanius!

10 **Dardanius.**   O Clitus!

Clitus.   What ill request did Brutus make to thee?

Dardanius.   To kill him, Clitus. Look, he meditates.

Clitus.   Now is that noble vessel full of grief,
That it runs over even at his eyes.

15 **Brutus.**   Come hither, good Volumnius; list[2] a word.

Volumnius.   What says my lord?

Brutus.   Why, this, Volumnius:
The ghost of Cæsar hath appear'd to me
Two several times by night; at Sardis once,
And this last night, here in Philippi fields.
I know my hour is come.

> *What has Brutus seen twice? What does this vision mean to him?*

20 **Volumnius.**   Not so, my lord.

Brutus.   Nay, I am sure it is, Volumnius.
Thou seest the world,[3] Volumnius, how it goes;
Our enemies have beat us to the pit.   *Low alarums.*
It is more worthy to leap in ourselves
25 Than tarry till they push us. Good Volumnius,
Thou know'st that we two went to school together;
Even for that our love of old, I prithee
Hold thou my sword-hilts, whilest I run on it.

> *What does Brutus ask of Volumnius? Why?*

Volumnius.   That's not an office for a friend, my lord.

Alarum still.

30 **Clitus.**   Fly, fly, my lord, there is no tarrying here.

Brutus.   Farewell to you, and you, and you, Volumnius.
Strato, thou hast been all this while asleep;
Farewell to thee too, Strato. Countrymen,
My heart doth joy that yet in all my life
35 I found no man but he was true to me.
I shall have glory by this losing day

---

2. **list.** Listen to
3. **Thou seest the world.** You know how things are.

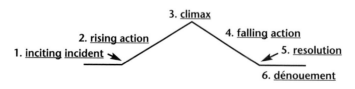

3. climax
2. rising action
4. falling action
1. inciting incident
5. resolution
6. dénouement

(Continued on page 337)

More than Octavius and Mark Antony
By this vile conquest shall attain unto.
So fare you well at once, for Brutus' tongue
40 Hath almost ended his live's history.
Night hangs upon mine eyes, my bones would rest,
That have but labor'd to attain this hour.

Alarum. Cry within, "Fly, fly, fly!"

CLITUS.   Fly, my lord, fly.

BRUTUS.   Hence! I will follow.

Exeunt CLITUS, DARDANIUS, *and* VOLUMNIUS.

I prithee, Strato, stay thou by thy lord.
45 Thou art a fellow of a good respect;[4]
Thy life hath had some smatch[5] of honor in it.
Hold then my sword, and turn away thy face,
While I do run upon it. Wilt thou, Strato?

STRATO.   Give me your hand first. Fare you well, my lord.

50 **BRUTUS.**   Farewell, good Strato.

Runs on his sword.
                          Cæsar, now be still,
I kill'd not thee with half so good a will.   *Dies.*

Alarum. Retreat. Enter ANTONY, OCTAVIUS, MESSALA, LUCILIUS, *and the army.*

OCTAVIUS.   What man is that?

MESSALA.   My master's man. Strato, where is thy master?

STRATO.   Free from the bondage you are in, Messala;
55 The conquerors can but make a fire of him;
For Brutus only overcame himself
And no man else hath honor by his death.

LUCILIUS.   So Brutus should be found. I thank thee, Brutus,
That thou hast prov'd Lucilius' saying true.

60 **OCTAVIUS.**   All that serv'd Brutus, I will entertain them.[6]
Fellow, wilt thou bestow[7] thy time with me?

STRATO.   Ay, if Messala will prefer[8] me to you.

OCTAVIUS.   Do so, good Messala.

MESSALA.   How died my master, Strato?

65 **STRATA.**   I held the sword, and he did run on it.

MESSALA.   Octavius, then take him to follow thee,

> How does Brutus die? What are his dying words, and to whom does he address them?

---

4. **respect.** Reputation
5. **smatch.** Taste
6. **entertain them.** Take them into my service
7. **bestow.** Spend
8. **prefer.** Recommend

1. Brutus kills himself by falling on a sword held by Strato. In his last words, he tells Cæsar to rest and says that he killed himself more willingly than he killed Cæsar.

BIOGRAPHICAL NOTE

Shakespeare is just one of the many writers who have been intrigued by the dramatic history of Julius Cæsar. In *The Inferno,* Italian poet Dante depicts the nine circles of hell; the ninth circle, which is the last and most terrible, is reserved for traitors—those who betrayed their family and country. Special torment is given to Judas Iscariot, who betrayed Jesus, and to Brutus and Cassius, Julius Cæsar's betrayers.

**SELECTION CHECK TEST 4.4.13
WITH ANSWERS** (CONT.)

Short Answer
1. What *background information* was given in the introduction? **The introduction gives the recent history of and state of things in Rome; the people's feelings toward Cæsar; the Soothsayer's warning; the perspectives and personalities of Cassius, Brutus, and Cæsar.**
2. What events comprised the *rising action,* or *complication?* **The primary focus of the rising action is the persuasion of Brutus to participate in the conspiracy against Cæsar.**
3. What event was the *climax?* the *crisis?* **The climax was the murder of Cæsar; the crisis occurs when Antony convinces the crowd to support him instead of Brutus.**
4. What events comprise the *falling action?* **Brutus's fortunes decline; the conspirators' bond grows fractious; and Antony gains power.**
5. What events provided the *dénouement?* **The events after Brutus's death are the dénouement: Antony discovers Brutus's body, calls him "the noblest Roman of them all," acknowledges that Brutus thought he was acting in the best interest of Rome; Octavius announces that Brutus will receive a hero's funeral.**

1. Antony says that Brutus killed Cæsar through a desire for the common good, while the other conspirators were motivated by envy.

LITERARY TECHNIQUE

IRONY. **Irony** is a difference between appearance and reality. You might wish to explain to students the irony present in Octavius's final couplet, "So call the field to rest, and let's away, / To part the glories of this happy day." Point out that two characters have just died violently on stage, making the word *happy* seem inappropriate. Also explain that there is a sense that the tragedy will continue; Octavius and Antony seem to have learned nothing from the play's actions; they are eager to divide up the spoils of war. In fact, Antony and Octavius fought their own war soon after the death of Brutus.

CROSS-CURRICULAR ACTIVITIES

HISTORY. Ask students to research the history of Rome in the years immediately following the death of Cæsar. They may use library or Internet resources. Have them answer the following questions: How closely does the play mirror reality? Did the conspiracy achieve its ultimate goal of preserving the Republic from the rule of dictators and emperors? Share your findings with your class.

ADDITIONAL QUESTIONS AND ACTIVITIES

Ask students to write about the following questions in their journals: Did the plot to kill Cæsar work to achieve Brutus's goal, to preserve the republic? If Brutus were allowed to go back in time, do you think he would make the same decision? Why, or why not?

That did the latest[9] service to my master.

ANTONY. This was the noblest Roman of them all:
All the conspirators, save only he,
70 Did that they did in envy of great Cæsar;
He, only in a general honest thought
And common good to all,[10] made one of them.[11]
His life was gentle,[12] and the elements[13]
So mix'd in him that Nature might stand up
75 And say to all the world, "This was a man!"

OCTAVIUS. According to his virtue[14] let us use[15] him,
With all respect and rites of burial.
Within my tent his bones tonight shall lie,
Most like a soldier, ordered honorably.[16]
80 So call the field[17] to rest, and let's away,
To part the glories[18] of this happy day.

Exeunt omnes.[19] ∎

According to Antony, what set Brutus apart from the other conspirators?

---

9. **latest.** Last
10. **general . . . all.** With thought for the good of all
11. **made one of them.** Joined them
12. **gentle.** Noble
13. **elements.** Four elements: earth, air, fire, and water
14. **virtue.** Worth

15. **use.** Act toward
16. **ordered honorably.** Treated with honor
17. **field.** Military forces
18. **To part the glories.** Divide the spoils
19. *omnes.* All

Respond *to the* SELECTION

Do you agree with Antony's final judgment of Brutus? Why, or why not?

RESPOND TO THE SELECTION

Students might wish to discuss why Antony, who has spoken so harshly of Brutus and the conspirators, gives this moving tribute to Brutus. Why might we respect our opponents?

from The Prince

Niccolò Machiavelli

Chapter 15:
Of the Things for Which Men, and Especially Princes, Are Praised or Blamed

It now remains to be seen what are the methods and rules for a prince as regards his subjects and friends. And as I know that many have written of this, I fear that my writing about it may be deemed presumptuous, differing as I do, especially in this matter, from the opinions of others. But my intention being to write something of use to those who understand, it appears to me more proper to go to the real truth of the matter than to its imagination; and many have imagined republics and principalities which have never been seen or known to exist in reality; for how we live is so far removed from how we ought to live, that he who abandons what is done for what ought to be done, will rather learn to bring about his own ruin than his preservation. A man who wishes to make a profession of goodness in everything must necessarily come to grief among so many who are not good. Therefore it is necessary for a prince, who wishes to maintain himself, to learn how not to be good, and use this knowledge and not use it, according to the necessity of the case.

Leaving on one side, then, those things which concern only an imaginary prince, and speaking of those that are real, I state that all men, and especially princes, who are placed at a greater height, are reputed for certain qualities which bring them either praise or blame. Thus one is considered liberal, another *misero* or miserly (using a Tuscan term, seeing that *avaro* still means one who is rapaciously acquisitive[1] and *misero* one who makes grudging[2] use of his own); one a free giver, another rapacious; one cruel, another merciful; one a breaker of his word, another trustworthy; one effeminate and pusillanimous,[3] another fierce and high-spirited; one humane,[4] another haughty; one lascivious,[5] another chaste; one frank, another astute[6]; one hard, another easy; one serious, another frivolous; one religious, another an unbeliever, and so on. I know that everyone will admit that it would be highly praiseworthy in a prince to possess all the above-named qualities that are reputed good, but as they cannot all be possessed or observed, human conditions not permitting of it, it is necessary that he should be prudent enough to avoid the scandal of those vices which would lose him the state, and guard himself if possible against those which will not lose it him, but if not able to, he can indulge them with less scruple. And yet he must not mind incurring the scandal of those vices, without which it would be difficult to save the state, for if one considers well, it will be found that some things which

---

1. **rapaciously acquisitive.** Greedily seeking to gain wealth
2. **grudging.** Reluctant
3. **pusillanimous.** Cowardly
4. **humane.** Merciful; considerate of human life
5. **lascivious.** Lustful
6. **astute.** Clever

ADDITIONAL QUESTIONS AND ACTIVITIES

This selection may be difficult for students because it contains sentences with many clauses, some non-standard comma usage, and some unfamiliar vocabulary. You may wish to read the selection aloud for students and then to ask volunteers to paraphrase as you go along. Ask students the following questions about what they read in chapter 15:

- According to Machiavelli, what will happen to people who do "what ought to be done" instead of what everyone else does? Why is it foolish to strive for goodness in everything? What must a prince learn in order to maintain power?
- According to Machiavelli, is it possible for a prince to possess all of the good qualities he names? Why, or why not? Which vices, or faults, should a prince particularly avoid? Which vices can he, if necessary, indulge in with less scruple, or guilt? Which scandal must he not mind bringing upon himself, and why?
- What can some things that seem virtues lead to, if followed? What can some things that seem vices lead to?

Answers

- People who do "what ought to be done" will bring about their own ruin. It is foolish to strive for goodness because there are too many bad people in the world, and they are all willing to win by unfair tactics. A prince must learn "how not to be good," or in other words, how to use sneaky and unfair tactics, in order to maintain power.
- According to Machiavelli, a prince can never possess all of these qualities because human conditions will not permit it. A prince must particularly avoid faults that will cause him to lose power, but may indulge in others that won't harm his power. He must not mind, or care about, causing scandal about things he must do in order to stay in power.
- Some things that seem like virtues lead to ruin, and others that seem like faults lead to security and well-being. You may point out to students that this is a paradox.

ADDITIONAL QUESTIONS AND ACTIVITIES

Ask students to work in groups to describe the kind of leader Machiavelli would praise, based on what they learned in chapter 15. Would a Machiavellian leader be likely to lie to his or her subjects in order to avoid scandal or opposition? Would he or she ever commit human rights violations by, for example, secretly killing those people who protested his or her form of government? How would a Machiavellian leader react if he or she learned that the sacrifice of thousands of soldiers might be necessary to put down an attack on the country's borders?

Ask students the following questions about what they read in chapter 16:

- For a prince, what is the danger of being liberal, or generous, in a virtuous and proper way? What is the danger in being overly generous and putting on sumptuous displays?
- Why shouldn't a ruler be afraid of being called "miserly"? What will people come to realize about him? What famous examples does Machiavelli give of great rulers who were called miserly, or niggardly?
- Through what quality is Cæsar said to have attained the Roman Empire? What might have happened to his empire if he had not changed his ways?
- Whose wealth can a leader afford to spend liberally? Why is liberality of this sort necessary for a prince who marches with his armies? What are the most important things a prince must guard against? What will lead to these things?

Answers

- The danger of being generous in a virtuous and proper way is that nobody will notice, and they will accuse the prince of not being generous enough. On the other hand, if a prince is too generous, he will lose all of his resources and will end up overtaxing people and seizing people's money unfairly, and people will begin to hate him.
- A ruler shouldn't be afraid of being called "miserly" because in the long run, people will realize that his so-called miserly ways allow him to defend the country and undertake enterprises. Machiavelli mentions Pope Julius II, Louis XII of France, and Ferdinand II of Spain.
- Cæsar is said to have gained the empire through being generous, but according to Machiavelli, if Cæsar had lived and not begun to cut costs, he would have destroyed it.
- A leader can afford to spend other people's wealth. For example, while marching with armies, a leader needs to allow his troops to take the wealth of conquered cities, or else the troops will not follow him. The most important things to guard against are being despicable or hated. Liberality will lead to these things.

seem virtues would, if followed, lead to one's ruin, and some others which appear vices result in one's greater security and wellbeing.

Chapter 16:
Of Liberality and Niggardliness[7]

Beginning now with the first qualities above named, I say that it would be well to be considered liberal; nevertheless liberality such as the world understands it will injure you, because if used virtuously and in the proper way, it will not be known, and you will incur the disgrace of the contrary vice. But one who wishes to obtain the reputation of liberality among men, must not omit every kind of sumptuous[8] display, and to such an extent that a prince of this character will consume by such means all his resources, and will be at last compelled, if he wishes to maintain his name for liberality, to impose heavy taxes on his people, become extortionate,[9] and do everything possible to obtain money. This will make his subjects begin to hate him, and he will be little esteemed being poor, so that having by this liberality injured many and benefited but few, he will feel the first little disturbance and be endangered by every peril. If he recognizes this and wishes to change his system, he incurs at once the charge of niggardliness.

A prince, therefore, not being able to exercise this virtue of liberality without risk if it be known, must not, if he be prudent,[10] object to being called miserly. In course of time he will be thought more liberal, when it is seen that by his parsimony his revenue is sufficient, that he can defend himself against those who make war on him, and undertake enterprises without burdening his people, so that he is really liberal to all those from whom he does not take, who are infinite in number, and niggardly to all to whom he does not give, who are few. In our times we have seen nothing great done except by those who have been esteemed niggardly; the others have all been ruined. Pope Julius II,[11] although he

had made use of a reputation for liberality in order to attain the papacy, did not seek to retain it afterwards, so that he might be able to wage war. The present King of France[12] has carried on so many wars without imposing an extraordinary tax, because his extra expenses were covered by the parsimony he had so long practiced. The present King of Spain,[13] if he had been thought liberal, would not have engaged in and been successful in so many enterprises.

For these reasons a prince must care little for the reputation of being a miser, if he wishes to avoid robbing his subjects, if he wishes to be able to defend himself, to avoid becoming poor and contemptible, and not to be forced to become rapacious; this niggardliness is one of those vices which enable him to reign. If it is said that Cæsar[14] attained the empire through liberality, and that many others have reached the highest positions through being liberal or being thought so, I would reply that you are either a prince already or else on the way to become one. In the first case, this liberality is harmful; in the second, it is certainly necessary to be considered liberal. Cæsar was one of those who wished to attain the mastery over Rome, but if after attaining it he had lived and had not moderated his expenses, he would have destroyed that empire. And should any one reply that there have been many princes, who have done great things with their armies, who have been thought extremely liberal, I would answer by saying that the prince may either spend his own wealth and that of his subjects or the wealth of others. In

---

7. **Liberality and Niggardliness.** Generosity and stinginess
8. **sumptuous.** Lavish, opulent, fancy
9. **extortionate.** Extorting, or unfairly seizing, the property and goods of others
10. **prudent.** Wise
11. **Pope Julius II.** Pope who served from 1503–1513 and restored the Papal lands to the Church. He also sponsored Renaissance artists such as Michelangelo and Raphael.
12. **present King of France.** Refers to Louis XII (1462–1515)
13. **present King of Spain.** Refers to Ferdinand II (1452–1516), a king who drove the Moors from Spain and unified the country
14. **Cæsar.** Julius Cæsar (c.102–44 BC)

LITERARY TECHNIQUE

PARADOX. A **paradox** is a seemingly contradictory statement, idea, or event. All forms of irony involve paradox. Point out to students the paradox at the end of chapter 15: "some things which seem virtues would, if followed, lead to one's ruin, and some others which appear vices result in one's greater security and well-being." Ask students to restate the paradox in fewer words, and then to explain why it is a paradox. Finally, ask them to identify a paradox in the first paragraph of chapter 16.

the first case he must be sparing, but for the rest he must not neglect to be very liberal. The liberality is very necessary to a prince who marches with his armies, and lives by plunder, sack and ransom, and is dealing with the wealth of others, for without it he would not be followed by his soldiers. And you may be very generous indeed with what is not the property of yourself or your subjects, as were Cyrus, Cæsar, and Alexander;[15] for spending the wealth of others will not diminish your reputation, but increase it, only spending your own resources will injure you. There is nothing which destroys itself so much as liberality, for by using it you lose the power of using it, and become either poor and despicable, or, to escape poverty, rapacious and hated. And of all things that a prince must guard against, the most important are being despicable or hated, and liberality will lead you to one or the other of these conditions. It is, therefore, wiser to have the name of a miser, which produces disgrace without hatred, than to incur of necessity the name of being rapacious, which produces both disgrace and hatred.

Chapter 18:
In What Way Princes Must Keep Faith

How laudable[16] it is for a prince to keep good faith and live with integrity, and not with astuteness, everyone knows. Still the experience of our times shows those princes to have done great things who have had little regard for good faith, and have been able by astuteness to confuse men's brains, and who have ultimately overcome those who have made loyalty their foundation.

You must know, then, that there are two methods of fighting, the one by law, the other by force: the first method is that of men, the second of beasts; but as the first method is often insufficient, one must have recourse to the second. It is therefore necessary for a prince to know well how to use both the beast and the man. This was covertly taught to rulers by ancient writers, who relate how Achilles[17] and many others of those ancient princes were given to Chiron the centaur[18] to be brought up and educated under his discipline. The parable of this semi-animal, semi-human teacher is meant to indicate that a prince must know how to use both natures, and that the one without the other is not durable.

A prince being thus obliged to know well how to act as a beast must imitate the fox and the lion, for the lion cannot protect himself from traps, and the fox cannot defend himself from wolves. One must therefore be a fox to recognize traps, and a lion to frighten wolves. Those that wish to be only lions do not understand this. Therefore, a prudent ruler ought not to keep faith when by so doing it would be against his interest, and when the reasons which made him bind himself no longer exist. If men were all good, this precept[19] would not be a good one; but as they are bad, and would not observe their faith with you, so you are not bound to keep faith with them. Nor have legitimate grounds ever failed a prince who wished to show colorable excuse for the non-fulfillment of his promise. Of this one could furnish an infinite number of modern examples, and show how many times peace has been broken, and how many promises rendered worthless, by the faithlessness of princes, and those that have been best able to imitate the fox have succeeded best. But it is necessary to be able to disguise this character well, and to be a great feigner and dissembler;[20] and men are so simple and so ready to obey present necessities, that one who deceives will always find those who allow themselves to be deceived.

15. **Cyrus...Alexander.** Cyrus the Great (died 529 BC) founded the Persian Empire; Alexander the Great (356–323 BC) was king of Macedonia and one of the greatest leaders of all time. He conquered Greece and much of Asia.
16. **laudable.** Praiseworthy
17. **Achilles.** Mythological Greek hero of the Trojan War
18. **Chiron the centaur.** A figure of Greek mythology who had the torso and head of a man but the body of a horse
19. **precept.** Law or guideline
20. **feigner and dissembler.** Pretender; liar; sneak

FROM THE PRINCE

ADDITIONAL QUESTIONS AND ACTIVITIES

Ask students to form groups to discuss the saying "the end justifies the means." Can they think of any times in history or in current events when leaders have achieved their goals, but caused human rights violations and/or another kind of damage in order to do so? Students may research dictators around the world who have used Machiavellian tactics to stay in power. Can they think of a more everyday example of an individual doing "whatever it takes" to achieve a goal?

Answers
Responses will vary. Some examples you might cite are military takeovers in Argentina and Chile. Students may be able to think of many everyday examples of an individual doing "whatever it takes."

Ask students the following questions:
- According to Machiavelli, what is more important than possessing the virtues of mercy, faith, integrity, humanity, and religion? What is a prince often obliged to do in order to maintain the state? What must he be able to do if constrained, or in a tight spot?
- According to Machiavelli, how do people in general judge their rulers? What does he say about the "vulgar" people? What does Machiavelli mean by the statement "the end justifies the means"?

Answers
- It is more important to seem to have these virtues than to actually possess them. A prince is often obliged to act against these virtues in order to maintain the state. If in a tight spot, he may have to do evil.
- According to Machiavelli, people in general judge by what they see; they judge by appearances. The "vulgar" are always taken in by appearances. The statement "the end justifies the means" means that if the result you bring is popular with the people, the people will forgive whatever actions you took in order to achieve that result.

ADDITIONAL QUESTIONS AND ACTIVITIES

Ask students if they have heard the phrase, "Might makes right," meaning whoever is strongest has the right to rule. Students should discuss what they think of this expression. They may also give examples of occurrences throughout history that have involved the strong taking over the weak.

Answers
Responses will vary. There are innumerable examples of the strong taking over the weak. You should point out that empires such as Rome were built on this precept. On the other hand, you may point out examples of how the "weak" can reclaim power through organized protest and rebellion. Some examples include labor union organizers in the United States, women who fought for suffrage and for equal rights, and rebels who started revolutions against oppressive powers all over the world.

I will only mention one modern instance. Alexander VI[21] did nothing else but deceive men, he thought of nothing else, and found the occasion for it; no man was ever more able to give assurances, or affirmed things with stronger oaths, and no man observed them less; however, he always succeeded in his deceptions, as he well knew this aspect of things.

It is not, therefore, necessary for a prince to have all the above-named qualities, but it is very necessary to seem to have them. I would even be bold to say that to possess them and always to observe them is dangerous, but to appear to possess them is useful. Thus it is well to seem merciful, faithful, humane, sincere, religious, and also to be so; but you must have the mind so disposed that when it is needful to be otherwise you may be able to change to the opposite qualities. And it must be understood that a prince, and especially a new prince, cannot observe all those things which are considered good in men, being often obliged, in order to maintain the state, to act against faith, against charity, against humanity, and against religion. And, therefore, he must have a mind disposed to adapt itself according to the wind, and as the variations of fortune dictate, and, as I said before, not deviate from what is good, if possible, but be able to do evil if constrained.

A prince must take great care that nothing goes out of his mouth which is not full of the above-named five qualities, and, to see and hear him, he should seem to be all mercy, faith, integrity, humanity, and religion. And nothing is more necessary than to seem to have this last quality, for men in general judge more by the eyes than by the hands, for everyone can see, but very few have to feel. Everybody sees what you appear to be, few feel what you are, and those few will not dare to oppose themselves to the many, who have the majesty of the state to defend them; and in the actions of men, and especially of princes, from which there is no appeal, the end justifies the means. Let a prince therefore aim at conquering and maintaining the state, and the means will always be judged honorable and praised by everyone, for the vulgar[22] is always taken by appearances and the issue of the event; and the world consists only of the vulgar, and the few who are not vulgar are isolated when the many have a rallying point in the prince. A certain prince of the present time, whom it is well not to name, never does anything but preach peace and good faith, but he is really a great enemy to both, and either of them, had he observed them, would have lost him state or reputation on many occasions. ∎

---

21. **Alexander VI.** Pope who served from 1492–1503. He was ambitious, a great political strategist who used his position to help build up the power of his son and daughter. However, his religious values were lacking and many considered him unscrupulous.
22. **vulgar.** Common people; the general public—this word is used insultingly

ABOUT THE RELATED READING

Niccolò Machiavelli (1469–1527) was a citizen of Florence, Italy, and served as a government official with diplomatic duties. When Spanish forces overthrew the Florentine Republic, he was forced out of office. Poor and desperate to find favor with the Medici princes who now ruled the city, Machiavelli devoted himself to studying and writing about the art of rule. This selection is from his most famous work, *The Prince,* which was dedicated to a member of the Medici family. The work attempts to discuss the ways in which a prince (meaning a ruler in general, not just a young one) should conduct himself in order to gain and maintain power. Machiavelli did not concern himself with how a ruler should *ideally* act, but rather, with how a ruler *had* to act in order to be successful. Accordingly, he stressed that rulers should appear to have all of the kingly virtues, but in reality, that they should be tyrants and act as immoral and calculating as need be, since, as he perceived it, the world was cruel and nobody played fair. Mostly because of this cynical philosophy Machiavelli wrote about in *The Prince,* the term *Machiavellian* came to mean an amoral cunning and a willingness to justify any action through the goal of supreme power.

342 UNIT FOUR / DRAMA

ANSWERS TO INTEGRATING THE LANGUAGE ARTS (FROM PAGE 344)

Language, Grammar, and Style
1. In writing *Julius Cæsar,* Shakespeare was most influenced by Plutarch's *Lives.*
2. Of Mark Antony and Brutus, who do you think loved Cæsar more?
3. Some critics believe *Julius Cæsar* is the weakest of Shakespeare's various history plays.
4. Mark Antony spoke eloquently at Cæsar's funeral.
5. What became of those conspirators after Cæsar's death?

1. good
2. well
3. bad
4. most
5. those

Investigate, Inquire and Imagine

Recall: GATHERING FACTS

1a. What do Brutus and Cassius say to one another at the end of scene 1?

2a. Whose troops have fought whom? Who has been victorious? Who has not?

3a. What does Antony call Brutus at the end of the play?

Interpret: FINDING MEANING

1b. Do Brutus and Cassius seem confident of victory? Why, or why not?

2b. What fatal error does Cassius make?

3b. Why does Antony think more highly of Brutus than of the other conspirators?

Analyze: TAKING THINGS APART

4a. Some critics have suggested that Brutus overruled Cassius on three pivotal decisions in this play: the decision to not kill Antony, the decision to allow Antony to make a funeral oration for Cæsar, and the decision to march to Philippi rather than wait on the strategically preferable high ground at Sardis for Antony's and Octavius's armies. In what way did these decisions help determine the outcome of the play? Do you agree that they were crucial? Were these mistakes?

Synthesize: BRINGING THINGS TOGETHER

4b. What do you conclude about Brutus's character from his decisions to overrule Cassius on these points? Why do you think Cassius acceded on each occasion? Which of the two men do you find to be the better military strategist? Which do you find to be the more honorable person? Why?

Evaluate: MAKING JUDGMENTS

5a. Do you feel that the murder of Cæsar was justified? Why, or why not? Can you think of other options the conspirators might have pursued to achieve their goal?

Extend: CONNECTING IDEAS

5b. In the first half of the play, omens and signs of disorder in the natural world seem to point to disorder in the affairs of man. Some characters believed the signs indicated that Cæsar's growing power was unnatural and angered the gods. Another interpretation is that the omens pointed to the plot to kill Cæsar as being unnatural. Which do you think is the interpretation intended by Shakespeare? Has Shakespeare made it clear who is right and who is wrong? What is your opinion as why he did or did not do so?

Understanding *Literature*

PLOT AND CATASTROPHE. Review the definitions for **plot** and **catastrophe** in the Handbook of Literary Terms. What is the catastrophe that occurs in act 5? Complete the plot pyramid you began in act 1.

TRAGIC FLAW. Review the definition for **tragic flaw** in the Handbook of Literary Terms. What is Brutus's tragic flaw? Give evidence to support your answer.

ANSWERS TO INVESTIGATE, INQUIRE, AND IMAGINE

RECALL

1a. Brutus and Cassius say goodbye to one another at the end of scene 1.

2a. Brutus's troops fought those of Octavius and Cassius's troops fought those of Mark Antony. Brutus was victorious over Octavius but Antony soundly defeated Cassius.

3a. Antony calls Brutus "the noblest Roman of them all."

INTERPRET

1b. Brutus and Cassius do not seem confident of victory. They say goodbye to each other because they believe they may not see each other again. They seriously discuss the possibility of losing and whether or not they will commit suicide to avoid being led through the streets of Rome, bound, in front of the victorious Antony and Octavius.

2b. Cassius makes the fatal error of thinking that Titinius has been taken by Antony's troops, when, in fact, he has been greeted loudly by Brutus's victorious troops. Cassius incorrectly assumes that he and Brutus have been defeated and orders Pindarus to kill him.

3b. Antony thinks more highly of Brutus than of the other conspirators because he believes Brutus acted not out of envy but out of a desire to do what was best for Rome.

ANALYZE

4a. The decision to allow Antony to live sets up the possibility that Antony will attempt to avenge the death of Cæsar, which he, of course, does in the final act. Allowing him to make a funeral oration allows Antony to stir up the crowd against the conspirators and gives Antony the confidence that he can raise an army to defeat Brutus and Cassius. In deciding to march to Philippi, Brutus gives up the strategic advantage of the hills of Sardis. When he learns of this, Octavius says to Antony, "Our hopes are answered." Certainly, from the standpoint of their own survival, these decisions were mistakes. Some students will feel that killing under any circumstances is wrong and that Brutus and Cassius meet their own deaths because of their involvement in Cæsar's death, regardless of what they decided about Antony and the battle.

ANSWERS TO INVESTIGATE, INQUIRE, AND IMAGINE (CONT.)

SYNTHESIZE

4b. *Responses will vary.* It may be said that Brutus is too trusting of Antony. It may also be said that Brutus fails to listen to the counsel of others and trusts his own instincts too readily. Had he followed Cassius's advice on these three decisions, he would likely have lived. Cassius will seem to be the better military strategist. Others will feel that Brutus is a more honorable man and could not bring himself to kill yet another person.

EVALUATE

5a. *Responses will vary.* Some students will agree with Brutus that Cæsar's death was required to save the republic. Others will feel that the conspirators should have brought their concerns to Cæsar directly or to the Senate for resolution. On the evidence in the text, it appears that the murder was the only option the conspirators considered. Some students will feel that murder is never justified and that Cæsar's death only brought more trouble to Rome.

ANSWERS TO INVESTIGATE, INQUIRE, AND IMAGINE (CONT.)

EXTEND

5b. The omens and signs of disorder in the natural world may be interpreted as signs that Cæsar has violated natural law and that his rise to power is wrong. They may also be interpreted as meaning that the plot against Cæsar is unnatural and wrong. Many critics feel that Shakespeare intended this moral ambiguity to point out that, no matter how wrong Cæsar's actions, violent "solutions" only breed more violence and chaos. In fact, after the defeat of Brutus and Cassius, the next several years saw more chaos and war in Rome with Octavius and Antony battling each other for power.

ANSWERS TO UNDERSTANDING LITERATURE

PLOT AND CATASTROPHE. The catastrophe is Brutus's suicide. Students should have completed the plot pyramids they began after reading act 1. *Responses will vary. Possible responses are given.* **Inciting Incident:** Cæsar is offered the crown, triggering fears among the senators that his power is growing too great; Cassius approaches Brutus to encourage him to join a conspiracy against Cæsar. **Central Conflict:** One central conflict is between Cæsar and those who plot to kill him. The other, and more psychological conflict, is Brutus's struggle between his love for Cæsar and his love for the Republic. **Complication:** Brutus decides to join the conspirators and successfully convinces them not to kill Antony. **Climax:** Cæsar is stabbed. **Crisis:** The fortunes of the central character, Brutus, are reversed when Antony sways the crowd against the conspirators and Brutus. **Falling Action:** Cassius and Brutus to raise troops for a battle against Antony and Octavian. They feel less than confident they will win. The ghost of Cæsar appears to Brutus. Brutus's troops defeat those of Octavian, but Cassius's troops are beaten by Antony's. Cassius kills himself because of a tragic mistake. **Catastrophe:** Brutus kills himself rather than be captured by the enemy. He calls out to Cæsar that Cæsar can now rest.

TRAGIC FLAW. *Responses will vary.* Brutus's main tragic flaw is his trust in human nature. He did not recognize, or chose to ignore, the selfish motives of the other conspirators. He believed that the Romans would follow his reasoning for

---

Writer's Journal

1. Imagine the scene on the battleground at Philippi after Brutus's death. Write a **descriptive paragraph** about this scene, using sensory details to bring the scene to life for your reader.

2. Write an **obituary** for Brutus. You may want to review several obituaries in your local newspaper to note the kind of things that are customarily included about the deceased and his or her life. What are the most important things to say about Brutus and his life?

3. Write an **epilogue** for *Julius Cæsar*. An epilogue may be a brief summary of the meaning or moral of the preceding work. What do you think the moral of this play should be?

Integrating the Language Arts

Language, Grammar, and Style

CORRECTING AND AVOIDING ERRORS IN MODIFIER USAGE. A **modifier** is a word that modifies—that is, changes or explains—the meaning of another word. When editing your writing, you should watch for common errors in modifier usage. Read the Language Arts Survey 3.47, "Recognizing Other Problems with Modifiers." Then correct the errors in the sentences below.

1. In writing *Julius Cæsar,* Shakespeare was influencedest by Plutarch's *Lives.*
2. Of Mark Antony and Brutus, who do you think loved Cæsar most?
3. Some critics believe *Julius Cæsar* is the weaker of Shakespeare's various history plays.
4. Mark Antony spoke eloquent at Cæsar's funeral.
5. What became of them conspirators after Cæsar's death?

In the following sentences, choose the correct word from within the parentheses.

1. I feel very (good, well) about today's performance!
2. Emma read the part of Calphurnia (good, well).
3. Tim felt (bad, badly) when he forgot his lines during the play!
4. Of all the conspirators, I think Brutus was the (more, most) despicable.
5. Mark Antony was plotting against (them, those) who had killed Cæsar.

Speaking and Listening & Collaborative Learning

HOLDING A DEBATE. Conduct a debate on the issue of whether or not Cæsar's murder was justified. Working in small groups, each of which has taken one side or the other of this question, develop arguments and evidence to support your side of the debate. Then, with one student appointed as moderator, conduct your debate for the class. As part of your preparation, review the Language Arts Survey 4.21, "Participating in a Debate" and 5.1, "Making Decisions and Solving Problems." You may want to complete a pro and con chart on this question to help formulate your arguments.

344 *UNIT FOUR / DRAMA*

ANSWERS TO UNDERSTANDING LITERATURE (CONT.)

killing Cæsar. He ignored Cassius's warnings and misplaced his trust in Antony. Students might also point out that Brutus trusts his own instincts too much when he overrules Cassius on three critical decisions that set up the defeat of the conspirators on the battlefield. Some would call this flaw pride. Brutus's total faith in himself and his own opinions leads him to ignore the advice of others. He takes the counsel of no one—he puts Portia off, he overrules Cassius numerous times and asks advice of no one. Ironically, this sort of pride is the same flaw that leads Cæsar to overreach and leads to his fall as well.

Answers to INTEGRATING THE LANGUAGE ARTS can be found on page 342.

Language Arts in Action

One-Act PLAY COMPETITION

Many high schools have two major theater shows a year, one in the spring and one in the fall, with no shows from November to March. During this "down time," some student actors keep their acting skills honed by entering in their state's One-Act Play Competition. These tournaments are a chance for students from different schools to meet and pit their acting skills against one another for fun and recognition.

For the Minnesota State High School League (MSHSL) the One-Act Play Competition season begins sometime between late November and early December. Adult directors will have already chosen a play and, if needed, have edited and cut it down to the required thirty-five-minute length. The variety of plays chosen runs from true one-acts to cut-down full-length plays, from Greek and Shakespearean to modern and from comedy to tragedy. Rather than leaning toward one genre or another, competitions are often very diverse. Directors may even write their own plays.

Auditions are held to select the actors. As directors are limited by rule to a combined total cast and stage crew of not more than twenty, students will often find themselves with more than one character to play, which is a challenge. Switching roles during a thirty-five–minute performance can mean some very fast costume changes!

With so few people allowed in the production everyone is expected to assist the stage crew in some fashion, whether in helping build the set, painting backgrounds, moving set pieces during the performance, or helping with one of many other tasks needed for a successful show. The core of the stage crew is made up of volunteers, often people who didn't land a part in the play itself. Actors learn quickly that the best way to get into theater is to join the crew and get experience from watching those who did make it.

Rehearsal lasts only four to five weeks. Thus, many long days of intensive work are needed to sharpen up the production. The first thing a direc-

Photo Credit Steve Estenson

The cast of Park High School's 1998 One-Act Play.

ADDITIONAL QUESTIONS AND ACTIVITIES

Why is it important for directors to consider carefully any cuts they make to a play? What are stage directions, and why are they important? What does the stage crew do while the actors practice the play? What challenges are involved in their work? Why are costumes important? Are they judged?

Answers

It is important for directors to consider carefully the cuts they make since every cut slightly changes the information the audience receives. If the wrong cuts are made, the significance of the play or parts of its plot may be lost, and the performance could be ranked poorly in competition. Stage directions tell actors where they will be and how they need to move during a scene. These are important because they may affect plot development or the meaning of a line, they help indicate where the audience's center of attention should be, and they can be used to develop a "stage picture," or artistic arrangement of the cast in a scene. Movement can also help pull off a joke or a gag on stage. While the actors practice, the stage crew is at work building a set. Their job is challenging because they have to make sure the set pieces are easy to move around, are easily transportable, and yet sturdy. Costumes are important because they help place the show in a cultural or historical context if needed and provide style and personality to the characters. However, they are not judged.

tor does with a new cast is to have them read straight through the play from beginning to end. This allows him or her to judge approximately how long the play will run, and gives the actors a chance to start developing their characters. If a play looks as if it is going to run past the maximum thirty-five minutes, scenes or dialogues of lesser importance are cut to conserve time. Directors consider carefully any cuts they make since every cut slightly changes the information the audience receives. If the significance of the play or parts of the plot are lost, the performance could be ranked poorly in competition.

Left to right: Erin Gebhart, Luis Pereira, Emily Lee, and Arthur Anfan onstage during 1998's "Curate Shakespeare: *As You Like It.*"

Photo Credit Steve Estenson

After the initial readings, the directors begin giving "stage directions," which tell actors where they will be and how they need to move during a scene. Good placement and movement instructions are crucial. They may affect plot development or the meaning of a line, they help indicate where the audience's center of attention should be, and they can be used to develop a "stage picture," or artistic arrangement of the cast in a scene. Of course, movement can also be very important in pulling off a good joke or sight gag. Over the next few weeks the actors will hone these movements, as well as their clarity of voice, inflection, timing—everything that is important to making a good show.

While the actors practice, the crew is hard at work constructing the set. One-Act Play Competition sets provide unique challenges to those who design them. Every piece must be easy to move around, and there can be no static (fixed in place) set pieces, as a show must by rule be able to set up in ten minutes and clear the stage afterward in five. Set pieces must be easily transportable by car or van, as shows move from school to school as they advance through each round of competition. They must also be sturdy, especially if cast members will have to put their weight on them. Although plays are not judged on the quality of their sets (based mainly on show budget), a bad set can influence enjoyment of the performance and thus how it gets ranked. Costumes, as well, are not judged, but contribute greatly to placing the show in a cultural or historical context if needed and provide style and personality to characters.

Once the actors have begun to solidify their performances the director will first bring in the set elements, then costumes, and finally start to run full dress rehearsals. Around this time there will also be a tech rehearsal if the director has chosen to use special lighting schemes or music. As musicals are not allowed, music must be either ambient (background) music or other music that does not, by itself, advance the plot. During a tech rehearsal the focus is not on the actors' performance, but instead on the timing of the sound and light cues. Often the technical crew will only have one day dedicated to their work. As a result, tech rehearsals can be quite long. An eight-hour tech day is not unusual, and ten hours, with breaks, is not unheard of.

By competition time directors hope to have the play polished and ready, with a week of full dress rehearsals if they are lucky. Final script cuts would have been made a week or two before, to allow the cast to adjust to any changes in their lines. If cuts are made in the last week of rehearsals it is easy for the actors to forget which lines have been cut and which are still in. If the play is running overtime, however, the director has no choice. Running over thirty-five minutes in competition means disqualification.

All of the days of preparation culminate in the sub-section competition. Each of the eight sections in the MSHSL splits up its schools by size, with schools of fewer than 800 students participating in Class A competition and those with greater than 800 in Class AA. The classes are then split into separate sub-sections, usually with four schools in each. These four compete in one night of performances at the same theater, with the top two schools going on to section finals. Receiving a winning rank depends on actors delivering their lines clearly and with the proper emotion. They must have developed their characters well. The cuts in the script must not have interfered with the plot or understanding of the play. Movement, facial expression, and body language must be clean and expressive. Overall, the play must be successful in delivering its message.

All of the schools that advance to section finals then compete with each other for the section title. Competition at this level becomes even fiercer, as poorer performances have been weeded out at the sub-section. Only the number one cast from the section tournament gets the honor of participating in the Minnesota One-Act Play Festival. This festival is held in the 1000-seat O'Shaughnessy Auditorium of the College of St. Catherine in St. Paul. There are two days of performances, one for Class A schools and one for Class AA. Performances do not compete against each other for rank, but they are graded. Each judge analyzes the play and may give it a "star" if they deem it a superior performance. Two of the three judges must "star" a play for it to receive "starred" status, the highest ranking in the whole tournament. There is no limit to the number of plays that can star at state. One, none, or all could, depending on the year. The starred plays from every year are listed in the program at each state festival. After this exhausting, but rewarding, experience, directors, cast, and crew return the set to their home school, celebrate the good and discuss the bad points of the experience, and prepare for their spring theater season.

- What is the purpose of a tech rehearsal?
- Why is it not a good idea to make script cuts in the last week of rehearsals? Why is it necessary to do so in some cases?
- Who competes in the sub-section competition? Which schools compete in the Class A competition, and which compete in the Class AA? What are the criteria used for judging performances in the sub-section competition? Who goes on to compete for the section title?
- Who can participate in the Minnesota One-Act Play Festival? Do these performances compete against each other? Explain. What honor do the best plays receive?

Answers
A tech rehearsal is held in order to establish the timing for the sound and light cues. It's not a good idea to make script cuts in the last week of rehearsals because the actors may become confused. However, it is necessary if the play runs over the 35-minute time limit. Everyone in all eight sections of the MSHSL competes in the sub-section competition. Schools with fewer than 800 students compete in the Class A competition, and larger school compete in the Class AA. Performances are judged by the clarity and expressiveness of the actors' delivery, by the development of the characters, by whether any cuts made to the play have interfered with the storyline or understanding of the play, and by the effectiveness of the movement, facial expression, and body language used by the actors. Overall, the play must be successful in delivering its message. The top two schools in each sub-section go on to section finals, where they compete for the section title. The number one school from each of the eight sections gets to participate in the One-Act Play Festival. These performances do not compete against each other, but the plays judged to be superior are awarded a star. The starred plays from every year are listed in the program at each state festival.

CROSS-CURRICULAR ACTIVITIES

ARTS AND HUMANITIES. You might invite the school drama teacher to visit the class and talk about any one-act play competitions in your home state. Or, if there are none, he or she could discuss local playwriting workshops, community theater opportunities, or upcoming school productions. Students may wish to collaborate with the acting teacher on a production of *Julius Cæsar*. The scale of the production would depend on the time you are able to devote to such a project. Students could stage individual scenes from the play, with makeshift costumes and a few props, or they could collaborate with the acting class on a full-fledged school production.

GUIDED WRITING
Software

See the Guided Writing Software for an extended version of this lesson that includes printable graphic organizers, extensive student models and student-friendly checklists, and self-, peer, and teacher evaluation features.

"It's true that heroes are inspiring, but mustn't they also do some rescuing if they are to be worthy of their name? Would Wonder Woman matter if she only sent commiserating telegrams to the distressed?"

—Jeannette Winterson

EXAMINING THE MODEL. Notice how Nazarali-Stranieri begins to define the qualities of a good leader by describing the "traditional confusion of leadership with power." What words or phrases let you know that she is not in agreement with this definition? Is her argument convincing? Do you

continued on page 349

348 *UNIT FOUR*

Guided Writing

WRITING AN EXTENDED DEFINITION / DEFINING A GOOD LEADER

Julius Caesar is one of the most celebrated leaders of world history. He created the First Triumvirate, in which opposing political forces shared power equally, and was responsible for many social reforms, including fair wages for workers and extending the rights of Roman citizenship to those who lived in the lands that his powerful army had suppressed and conquered. His very name is embedded in the language of the world: the month of July; the titles of power, *Kaiser* and *Czar;* his birth story is told by the surgical procedure known as "Caesarian section."

Through relentless military might, political manipulation, bribery, and self-interest, Caesar eventually acquired power over all aspects of Roman life—religious, political, and economic—and was named Dictator for Life. The ruling class, fearing his power, brutally murdered him. Although Caesar was a powerful leader, he was not what people today consider a good leader. These days people are looking for a very different kind of leader. Who are the leaders you admire in your school, church, community, or in the world? Who are the leaders you are willing to follow?

WRITING ASSIGNMENT. In this assignment you will write a persuasive essay defining what you consider to be the qualities of a good leader by describing someone who manifests these qualities.

Professional Model

excerpted from the prize-winning essay "The Most Influential Leader of the Twentieth Century" by Farah Nazarali-Stranieri

In 1978, James McGregor Burns wrote about the dearth of leadership—"one of the most universal cravings of our time is a hunger for compelling and creative leadership." McGregor Burns's search for "moral leadership" reveals the tragedy of leadership studies—the confusion of leadership with power. Traditionally, leaders have been defined as those who hold power; allowing presidents/prime ministers and military generals, regardless of their accomplishments, to be considered leaders. Leadership studies have been further detracted from "moral leadership" because of the confusion of leadership with management. Norman Rockefeller, Henry Ford, and Bill Gates are considered leaders for the economic power they amassed. The confusion of leadership with power and leadership with management has led to a model of leadership that is Machiavellian (manipulative), hierarchical, authoritative, impersonal, elitist, and self-interested.

The person I believe to be the greatest leader of the twentieth century exhibited none of the qualities named above. This person held no official political title; he commanded no army and he amassed no great wealth. He did, however, have tremendous influence. This truly exemplary leader derived his power from the conscious citizenry. The leader I am referring to is Mahatma Gandhi.

Instrumental in the Indian Independence movement, Gandhi's influence extended beyond the borders of India to the rest of the world. Gandhi's philosophy of non-violence inspired millions, including the great American civil rights leader—Martin Luther King, Jr. A simple, pious man, Gandhi identified with and won the hearts of India's most politically and economically marginalized people. He spent his life fighting to overcome modern forms of enslavement and oppression—caste oppression, religious hatred, gender oppression, and, what he saw as the worst form of violence, poverty. The purpose of this essay is to outline Gandhi's philosophy of non-violence and its influence worldwide as well as the strategies and characteristics that made Gandhi successful.

Prewriting

FINDING YOUR VOICE. Since the object of this assignment is to persuade your audience that your definition of a good leader is an effective definition, you will have to feel strongly about your subject matter. You will then be able to allow the power of your personal conviction and attitude to show through the tone of your writing, your choice of words, and the structure of your sentences.

Notice the strong word choices Nazarali-Stranieri makes in her essay. She describes Gandhi as a "leader [who] derived his power from the conscious citizenry." From where does your leader derive her or his power? How does (did) this person wield or emanate the power necessary to lead?

agree or disagree with her definition of what makes a good leader? Why? As you develop your own definition of what a good leader is, it will help you to select a person who exemplifies these traits.

Clearly, the writer is passionate about her chosen subject; it is easy to imagine that the life and work of Mahatma Gandhi have had a great impact on her own course in life. Notice that Nazarali-Stranieri puts the subject of leadership in perspective; she clearly states who she thinks is the greatest leader of the twentieth century, and why; she gives a list of the leadership qualities which Gandhi exemplified. As suggested by the last sentence of the excerpt, her essay goes on to describe his philosophy of non-violence, and the strategies and characteristics that made Gandhi one of the most influential leaders of the twentieth century, and beyond.

"People seldom see the halting and painful steps by which the most significant success is achieved."
—Anne Sullivan

INDIVIDUAL LEARNING STRATEGIES

MOTIVATION
Have students brainstorm in groups of four the qualities that make a good leader. Then have them list names of people (famous or civilians) who they think exemplify these qualities. Finally, have students choose a person from the list to represent their definition of a good leader.

READING PROFICIENCY
Encourage students to read the Professional Model and the Student Model—Revised to get a sense of how the tone and language sounds as they work through the lesson. You may want to refer students to the Language Arts Survey 1.6, "Reading Silently versus Reading Out Loud."

ENGLISH LANGUAGE LEARNING
See strategies for Reading Proficiency above that will help students who are English language learners. You may also encourage students to write about a leader from their country and to define good leadership from their culture's standards.

SPECIAL NEEDS
Students with special needs may have difficulty completing the Graphic Organizer. Have them pair with another student who can help them complete the Graphic Organizer and use it to help them draft their paper.

ENRICHMENT
Students may want to take this activity a step further by displaying visual aids with their paper. They may want to include photos of the person they wrote about. And depending on the work the person has done, students may want to show photographs of the person working in society and visually show the positive impacts he or she has made through graphs or charts.

Prewriting

FINDING YOUR VOICE. Have students read the Professional Model. Have them describe the tone and voice of the speaker in the model. Then encourage students to work toward this convicting and powerful tone as they develop their own voice.

(Continued on page 350)

IDENTIFYING YOUR AUDIENCE. Refer students to the Language Arts Survey 2.4, "Identifying Your Audience" for a helpful chart on "Thinking about Your Audience."

WRITING WITH A PLAN. Refer students to the Language Arts Survey 2.24, "Writing Paragraphs," 2.25, "Writing a Thesis Statement," and 2.26, "Writing Main Ideas and Supporting Details," as they begin to write their paper.

Defining Leadership

Webster's Dictionary defines a leader as one who: "1) goes before or with to show the way; 2) conducts by holding and guiding; 3) influences or induces."

Extending the Definition:

We generally think of the dictionary as the source of definitions, but dictionary definitions are general and limited in scope. For example, Webster's Dictionary defines a peanut as "the pod or the enclosed edible seed of a plant of the legume family." If you wanted to define what a peanut is to someone who had never seen or tasted one, you would need to go beyond the dictionary definition and examine a peanut more closely, describing it using images and details, comparing the peanut (the unknown) to things that are familiar (the known). You would want to draw a picture or, better yet, give the person an actual peanut to see, touch, and taste.

"Playing small doesn't serve the world."
—*Nelson Mandela*

IDENTIFYING YOUR AUDIENCE. As Farah Nazarali-Stranieri quotes in the essay model, "one of the most universal cravings of our time is a hunger for compelling and creative leadership." The development and success of student leadership training programs nationwide suggests that many adults are looking to youth and to the future to provide creative solutions for some of our vital leadership needs. People want to hear what you have to say. If you write with an eye toward publishing on the Internet, in the "Op Ed" section of your local newspaper, or in the nationally syndicated Sunday news magazines, you will have the opportunity to affect many people with your ideas and convictions. Does your neighborhood, church, or community have a newsletter?

WRITING WITH A PLAN. Working with a group, brainstorm names of leaders who have inspired you to action or personal growth. Remember, in a brainstorm, all ideas are acceptable. Someone might name a scout leader who helped her overcome a fear of kayaking through rapids; someone else might name a band leader who miraculously brought the high school band into perfect harmony. You could name world famous leaders, like Nelson Mandela or Joan of Arc; people such as Helen Keller or Franklin Roosevelt, who overcame great personal obstacles and went on to lead others; or someone in your own community who effectively organized a stream clean-up or meals for the homeless. Whom do you admire or emulate?

The more research you do, and the more information, ideas and material you gather before you actually begin drafting your essay, the easier your writing will be. The object of the essay is to **extend the definition** of what a good leader is by describing someone whom you consider to be a good leader. If you choose a famous leader, research that person in the library or on the Internet.

If you select a local leader, interview that person or talk to people who have worked with him or her. Plan your questions in advance. Be specific. Rather than asking, "How would you define a good leader?" or "What do you think makes you such a good leader?", you might ask what strategies and practices this person employed to complete a certain project successfully. What mistakes or setbacks did this person experience, and what did he or she learn from them? What advice does this person have for others who take on or find themselves in positions of leadership? What leaders does he or she admire, and why? By listening to the answers this person gives, you can learn the specifics of what is involved in being a successful leader.

The following cubing exercise can be helpful in articulating and expanding your definition of a good leader. It asks you to break down your subject using six steps, one for each side of a cube: Classify, Describe, Locate, Analyze, Differentiate, and Apply. Analyzing your subject in this way offers you a different set of questions through which to derive information, images, and ideas. The three-dimensional cube is a way to offer you a new perspective.

Use all six sides of the cube. Even if a question doesn't obviously apply to your subject, it might offer a creative vantage point from which to observe your ideas and material.

Jot down words and phrases that come to mind. Write quickly. Even if an idea seems silly, write it down. You don't have to use all your notes in your essay.

Here is how Yolanda filled in her cube.

Student Model—Graphic Organizer

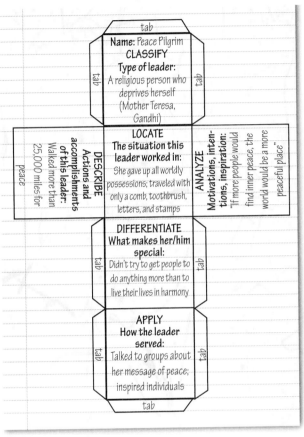

"Very few writers really know what they are doing until they've done it. They do not type a few stiff warm-up sentences and then find themselves bounding along like huskies across the snow. We all often feel like we are pulling teeth, even those writers whose prose ends up being the most natural and fluid. The right words and sentences just do not come pouring out like ticker tape most of the time."

—Anne Lamott

Drafting

Once you have finished your research and have your notes and completed cube handy, you are ready to begin writing your first draft. For this draft you don't need to be concerned with spelling or rules of grammar, or even writing in complete sentences; those concerns will be addressed in the revising and proofreading stage. For now, just allow your voice and ideas to flow freely. Create an inspiring, evocative portrait and presentation of your chosen leader.

Self- and Peer Evaluation

After completing your first draft, it is time to evaluate, edit, and revise your work. You can either do a self-evaluation, or if time permits, get one or two peer evaluations to help you see if you are making your points coherently. Use these questions to help evaluate your paper or that of a classmate.

- Where does the paper clearly state the definition of a good leader? Is the definition convincing?
- What leadership qualities does the essay describe?
- How do you respond as you read about this leader? What inspires or motivates you to want to know more about this person?

continued on page 352

Student Model— Graphic Organizer

See the Writing Resource for a black-line master of the graphic organizer for this lesson.

Self- and Peer Evaluation

Use the checklist on pages 351–352 for self- and peer evaluation. The checklist is intended to act as a student-friendly rubric to help students identify specific evidence of writing strengths and areas needing improvement. Make sure they provide concrete suggestions for improvement or specific evidence of why the writing works.

Drafting

Encourage students to use their completed graphic organizer on page 351 to help them make sure they have gathered the essential information for their essays. For additional help, refer students to the Language Arts Survey 2.31–2.36, "Drafting."

- What most impresses you about this leader? What else do you want to learn about him or her?
- Which, if any, of this leader's principles do you want to apply to your own life?
- Is the voice in the essay believable? Is it compelling and engaging? Do you feel as if the writer is speaking to you?
- Is the voice appropriate for publication in the newspaper editorial section, or is it too casual and conversational?
- Where, if anywhere, could stronger, more interesting or evocative words could be used?
- Where, if anywhere, does the writer repeat words and phrases excessively?
- Where does the writer employ a variety of sentence structures to keep the tone of the essay lively? Which paragraphs would benefit from more sentence variety?

Your completed essay must have an introduction, a body, and a conclusion, so write your first draft with this in mind. The model excerpted here is an excellent structural example. The writer clearly states her perspective, introduces her subject, and outlines what she will write about in the rest of the essay.

Student Model—Draft

This is the way of peace.
Overcome evil with good,
Falsehood with truth,
And hatred with love. (Nichols)

from "~~PEACE PILGRIM~~: Leading by Example" by Yolanda Mays

can you start with a quote

To me, a good leader is one who

be specific: How does p live her life?

leads by her example and by how she

lives her life. ~~She is not reaching out~~

~~and trying to get people to follow~~

~~them,~~ she just does. As my dad always

says, "Run it up the flagpole and see

who salutes." To me, a simple woman who

called herself Peace Pilgrim exemplifies

and defines what it means to be a ~~really~~

good leader; she was "an American

saint." (~~Dan~~ Millman) Not only did her

life and teachings inspire many people

while she was alive, but she continues

to inspire people even after death.

Her message was at once simple and

profound: if more people would find

inner peace, the world would be a more

peaceful place. From 1953 until her

death in 1981 she walked on foot across

the United States seven times, and

Long sentence here. Break it up.

several times across Mexico and Canada,

carrying no money, but only a comb, a

toothbrush, letters and stamps. ~ *Finish to make a sentence*

she traveled on foot, committed to her vows.

Originally she vowed to walk 10,000

miles; then she ~upped~ it to 25,000, and

slang *increased*

after that she just stopped counting.

~She had made this vow:~ "I shall remain a

wanderer ∧ until mankind has learned the

", she vowed

way of peace, walking until I am given

shelter and fasting until I am given

food." ~She~ spoke at universities,

Peace Pilgrim

churches, and libraries ~everywhere~, to

repeats

newspaper reporters and radio

interviewers, on campuses, and on the

streets, everywhere giving her message

of peace. She did not try to encourage

people to follow in her exact

footsteps, giving up everything—name,

home, money, security—and walk back and

forth across the country, she just

emanated peace and wisdom and

encouraged others to discover how to

live their own lives in harmony.

Revising and Proofreading

Good writing takes time. It is best to consider the evaluation comments for at least a day before writing your final draft. Experiment with sentence structure. Try replacing lifeless verbs with more expressive ones. Trust your instincts: if a phrase or sentence feels confusing, drab, or clunky, revise or delete it.

Remember also to proofread your essay. See the Language Arts Survey 2.45 for a proofreading checklist.

Language, Grammar, and Style

Sentence Variety

IDENTIFYING SENTENCE VARIETY. Unless you are writing lullabies, your goal as a writer is to keep your audience awake, informed, and interested. Varying the structure and length of your sentences is one way to achieve this.

Take a **simple sentence,** one independent clause made up of a complete subject and predicate, and see how many ways you can rewrite it without distorting the original meaning.

The cat sat in the window.

Replace the nouns and verbs with more descriptive ones, and add a few adjectives:

The blue-eyed Siamese curled in the sunlit window.

Add one or more details:

The blue-eyed Siamese curled in the window, asleep.

Add the detail in different places:

Asleep, the blue-eyed Siamese curled in the window.

The sleeping Siamese curled in a patch of sunlight.

The blue-eyed cat, curled in the sunlight, slept all morning.

continued on page 354

Language, Grammar, and Style

Sentence Variety

LESSON OVERVIEW
In this lesson, students will be asked to do the following:
Identifying Sentence Variety, 353
Fixing Sentence Variety, 355
Using Sentence Variety, 356

INTRODUCING THE SKILL. Explain to students that learning to use sentence variety will help them improve their writing. Achieving sentence variety will keep readers interested in what they are reading.

continued on page 354

Revising and Proofreading

A handout of the proofreading checklist is available in the Teacher's Resource Kit, Writing Resource book 2.45.

Language, Grammar, and Style (CONT.)

PREVIEWING THE SKILL. Refer students to the Language Arts Survey 3.36, "Combining and Expanding Sentences." This is the basis of the Language, Grammar, and Style lesson.

continued on page 355

You can add an imaginative detail or description:

> Like a furry gray comma, my cat slept in the window.

You can start with a prepositional phrase:

> In the window, the blue-eyed cat slept.

> Across the room, the cat sat in the window.

You can add a phrase that shows when the action takes place:

> After leaving the dead bird on the kitchen table like a gift, the cat went to sleep on the window sill.

> When the snow falls, my cat sits in the window and waits.

You can add a phrase that acts like an adjective:

> Sitting in the window, Furly curls in sleep.

> The Siamese, curled like a question mark, slept in the sunlight.

You can expand the original into two sentences:

> The sunlight streamed in the window. My cat, like a furry gray comma, slept on the sill.

You can add action or details by using a colon or semi-colon to divide the parts of the sentence:

> In the window I saw a beautiful sight: my cat was curled in the sunlight, peacefully asleep.

continued on page 355

Student Model—Revised

Peace Pilgrim: Leading by Example
by Yolanda Mays

"This is the way of peace.
Overcome evil with good,
Falsehood with truth,
And hatred with love." (Nichols)

A good leader is one who leads by example. Because she lives her life with strength and integrity, people will follow her. As my dad always says, "Run it up the flagpole and see who salutes." To me, a simple woman who called herself Peace Pilgrim exemplifies and defines what it means to be an outstanding leader; she was "an American saint." (Millman) Even after her death, many people continue to be inspired by her life and teachings.

Her message was at once simple and profound: if more people would find inner peace, the world would become a more peaceful place. From 1953 until her death in 1981, she walked on foot across the United States seven times, and several times across Mexico and Canada. Carrying no money or sleeping bag, but only a comb, a toothbrush, letters and stamps, she traveled on foot, committed to her vows.

Originally, she vowed to walk 10,000 miles; then she increased it to 25,000; and after walking 25,000 miles she just stopped counting. "I shall remain a wanderer," she vowed, "until mankind has learned the way of peace, walking until I am given shelter and fasting until I am given food." Peace Pilgrim spoke at universities, churches, and libraries, to newspaper reporters and radio interviewers, on campuses, and on the streets, everywhere delivering her message of peace. She did not try to encourage people to follow in her exact footsteps, giving up everything as she had. She just emanated peace and wisdom and encouraged others to discover how to live their own lives peacefully.

Peace Pilgrim did not simply wake up one morning, walk out the door, and never come back. One night, while walking in the woods, she realized that her mission in life was to work for peace. Then she began fifteen years of what she called preparation, doing volunteer work for peace organizations and helping people who had physical, emotional, and mental problems (Pilgrim).

After her death in 1981 in a head-on collision while being driven to a speaking engagement, her friends published a book about her life, written in Peace Pilgrim's own words which had been collected from letters, a newsletter she published, and taped speeches. Dozens of Internet sites offer her story as well as a place to discuss her teachings with others. Inspired by Peace Pilgrim, many people have set out on similar pilgrimages. The day before her death, responding to an interviewer who said that she seemed to be a most happy person, "I certainly am a happy person. Who could know God and not be joyous?" Peace Pilgrim not only led, she led joyously and rightly by example.

Works Cited

Nichols, Bruce. The Peace Pilgrim Home Page, Sept. 1999. 25 April 2000 <http:/www.peacepilgrim.com/>

Pilgrim, Peace. Peace Pilgrim: Her Life and Work in Her Own Words. Ed. by Friends of Peace Pilgrim, Ocean Tree Books, 1982

Millman, Dan. Quotation from the back cover of Peace Pilgrim: Her Life and Work in Her Own Words

The cat sat in the window; all was well with the world.

You can use a conjunction to combine two phrases:

The cat curled in the sunlight <u>and</u> fell asleep.

Sun poured through the window, <u>but</u> the cat slept as if it were midnight.

You can start with the word *if*:

If there's one patch of sunlight anywhere in the house, you will find my Siamese cat asleep there.

What other ways can you alter the structure of the original sentence? For more information, see the Language Arts Survey 3.36, "Combining and Expanding Sentences."

Notice how the author of the professional model on page 348 varies the length and structure of her sentences in ways that keep her writing persuasive and interesting.

Examine these three sentences from Farah Nazarali-Stranieri's essay, and explain how she varies the structure.

Instrumental in the Indian Independence movement, Gandhi's influence extended beyond the borders of India to the rest of the world.

Gandhi's philosophy of non-violence inspired millions, including the great American civil rights leader—Martin Luther King, Jr.

A simple, pious man, Gandhi identified with and won the hearts of India's most politically and economically marginalized people.

continued on page 356

Language, Grammar, and Style (CONT.)

PRACTICING THE SKILL. For additional practice, have students work through the exercises in the Language, Grammar, and Style Resource book, 3.36, "Combining and Expanding Sentences," located in the Teacher's Resource Kit.

For more ideas on publishing and presenting, direct students to the Language Arts Survey 2.47, "Publishing and Presenting Your Work," and 2.49, "Sharing Your Work with Others." These sections provide numerous ways in which students can display their work.

Reflecting

The questions in this section are appropriate prompts for interested students who may want to write a paper on bad leaders and the effects of bad leadership on a people, a country, and/or a nation.

REVISING FOR SENTENCE VARIETY. Examine these two sentences from the student model. They are of nearly equal length, and both begin with the subject. Rewrite them by varying the sentence structures while retaining their original meanings.

> There are dozens of websites offering her teachings and a place to discuss how she has affected your life. Many people have been inspired to set off on foot on their own pilgrimages.

USING A VARIETY OF SENTENCES. Examine your essay for sentence variety. Experiment with rewriting some of your key sentences in different ways. Have fun scrambling and reconstructing your sentences; you might discover some new meaning you hadn't originally intended.

Publishing and Presenting

Now it's time to print your essay and share it with classmates. You might want to send copies to leaders in your school or community. Try to publish in your local newspaper or on the Internet. Remember that the only way to become a published writer is to keep sending out your work. You will end up with a stack of rejection letters; many professional writers collect these to inspire and motivate themselves to try try again.

Reflecting

How has researching and writing this essay, and listening to your classmates' essays, changed or strengthened your ideas about good leadership? Consider the various leaders whom you have followed in your life, and what sort of effect those experiences have had on you.

As you bring to a close your reading of Shakespeare's *Julius Caesar*, you might discuss with your classmates the devastating effects of bad leadership in your life and in the world. What are the attributes of a bad leader? Have you ever been led astray, or seen others close to you led astray? How can you recognize a bad leader, and how can you protect yourself against one? How would the leaders in your essays respond to Machiavelli's ideas of how to lead? How would you respond?

UNIT 4 review
Drama

ADDITIONAL RESOURCES

UNIT 4 RESOURCE BOOK
- Vocabulary Worksheet: Unit 4
- Study Guide: Unit 4 Test
- Unit 4 Test

Words for Everyday Use

Check your knowledge of the following vocabulary words from this unit. Write a short sentence using these words in context to make the meaning clear. To review the definition or usage of a word, refer to the page number listed or to the Glossary of Words for Everyday Use.

amiss, 282
apparel, 247
apparition, 322
augment, 269
bequeath, 302
carcass, 274
chastisement, 313
cogitation, 251
commend, 273
commonwealth, 299
concave, 248
conjointly, 260
constancy, 278
construe, 251
corporal, 310
countenance, 251
cull, 248
cur, 290
decree, 290
disconsolate, 332
discourse, 298
endure, 259

engender, 333
ensign, 329
entrails, 280
entreat, 270
expound, 282
fawn, 252
garland, 333
grievous, 300
horrid, 280
imminent, 282
impart, 252
infirmity, 316
infuse, 261
instigation, 270
insurrection, 270
inter, 300
interim, 270
interpose, 272
lament, 284
malice, 294
misconstrue, 333
particle, 273

portent, 282
portentous, 260
presage, 329
prodigy, 260
puissant, 290
redress, 270
replication, 248
resolution, 272
reverence, 294
servile, 249
sinew, 253
suffice, 279
surly, 259
tempest, 259
throng, 250
underling, 254
utterance, 297
valiant, 293
valor, 299
visage, 271
wretched, 253
yoke, 251

Literary Tools

Define the following terms, giving concrete examples of how they are used in this unit. To review a term, refer to the page number indicated or to the Handbook of Literary Terms.

catastrophe, 326
central conflict, 242
character, 242
climax, 288
complication, 268
crisis, 288

falling action, 309
foreshadowing, 309
inciting incident, 242
irony, 288
motif, 242

plot, 242, 268, 288,
  309, 326
repetition, 288
simile, 268
tragic flaw, 326

VOCABULARY DEVELOPMENT

Give students the following exercise: Each student should select ten words from the list on page 357 and write "riddles" describing the words. The students can then exchange papers with classmates who must determine the answers to the riddles.

EXAMPLE
Not only is this a storm marked by strong winds, but it is also used as the title of one of Shakespeare's plays.
(Answer: tempest)

Reflecting on your reading

Genre Studies

1. **SPEECHES.** Both Brutus and Mark Antony deliver speeches in act 3, scene 2 of *Julius Cæsar.* Compare these two speeches, analyzing them for content, purpose, tone, and style. How are they different and similar? To what emotions does each speech appeal? Which speech is the more persuasive? Which man would you judge as the better orator, and why?

2. **TRAGEDY.** What is a tragedy? What makes this play tragic? Who is the tragic hero and what is this hero's tragic flaw?

3. **CONFLICT IN A DRAMA.** In act 1, scene 2 of the play, Brutus describes himself in these words, "Poor Brutus, with himself at war, / Forgets the shows of love to other men." To what extent is Brutus at war with himself? Has he misjudged the course of action he should take? In what sense is Brutus's internal conflict also the central conflict of the drama? Support your answer with examples from the text.

Thematic Studies

4. **MORAL AND POLITICAL RELATIVITY.** With whom did your sympathies lie in *Julius Cæsar?* Did you find your sympathies wavering between Cæsar, Brutus, and Antony? Why might Shakespeare have made firm moral and political ground elusive in this play? Do you think that Shakespeare deliberately invites you to share in the same fickle mentality as the crowd in the play? Explain your answer.

5. **VIEWS OF THE PLEBEIANS.** The general populace, or common people, of Rome were referred to as plebeians, while the upper class of rulers and scholars were called the patricians. Which of Machiavelli's ideas about plebeians are supported in *Julius Cæsar?* For example, are the public portrayed as selfish, changeable, ignorant, or lacking in gratitude? You may wish to especially focus on how the plebeians are portrayed in act 1, scene 1 and in act 3. Cite passages from the play to support your answer.

6. **THE END JUSTIFIES THE MEANS.** Consider the phrase "the end justifies the means" as used by Machiavelli in Chapter 18 of *The Prince.* In your opinion, did Brutus's goal of preserving the republic justify his support of the conspirators, or was there no excuse for his betrayal of a friend?

7. **THE MACHIAVELLIAN RULER.** In what ways does Julius Cæsar fit the Machiavellian view of what a prince should be like? Is he generous or miserly with the people? Is he a lion or a fox, or both? In what ways do the conspirators, in particular Cassius, fit the Machiavellian model? Is there sufficient evidence in the play to suggest that Cæsar was indeed seeking to gain absolute power over Rome, or do you think that he was truly a noble person who would have refused the crown?

for your READING LIST

A Midsummer Night's Dream by William Shakespeare. Now that you have read at least one play by the great bard, you may want to try another. In one of his finest and most imaginative comedies, Shakespeare explores the madness of love. The story is set in a wood outside Athens, where two young couples in romantic confusion encounter a band of mischievous fairies who can alter human affections (and shapes!) with potions and magic. The chaos, misunderstandings, and arguments that stem from this chance encounter reveal love's comic side.

Independent Reading Activity

DRAMATIC READING. Plays are meant to be read aloud, to be performed. Reading the words out loud brings them to life. Often the action and themes in plays are very immediate and urgent. Choose one of the suggested plays in this unit, or find another play that you like, and with a few friends or classmates, read the play aloud. Sit in a circle, share copies of the play, or see that each person has their own copy, divide up the roles, and simply read the play out loud. You will find the play come to life as the humor emerges, as well as the tragedy. As you get into the reading, you might want to add small dramatic touches: stand as you read, move your arms, walk around the room, or sit or stand close to or far from the other characters. Add your own interpretation. Reading a play out loud requires very few props to bring out the drama.

Selections for Additional Reading

Our Town by Thornton Wilder. Wilder's Pulitzer-Prize-winning drama in three acts, produced and published in 1938, is a classic portrayal of small-town American life. Considered innovative for its lack of props and scenery and revered for its sentimental but realistic depictions of middle-class America, *Our Town* soon became a staple of American theater.

Waiting for Godot by Samuel Beckett. Two tramps meet on a country road at dusk to wait for the promised arrival of a mysterious man called Godot. The longer they wait, the more desperate they become—and their behavior becomes more and more absurd as they try to find ways to relieve their boredom. So long as Godot does not come to resolve their waiting, their lives always remain futile and pointless. This comical yet tragic play explores the ideas of Existentialism, a twentieth-century school of thought that holds that life is essentially absurd and meaningless. When *Waiting for Godot* premiered in Paris in 1953, many people thought it was bizarre. However, the play slowly gained popularity, and today it is considered a classic.

Screenplay, the Foundations of Screenwriting: A Step-by-Step Guide from Concept to Finished Script by Syd Field. Have you ever thought about writing your own play, movie script, or television show? Field's book takes you through each step of the process, from forming an idea, to developing characters, to creating scenes. It is an absorbing and accessible book, as well as a valuable resource for aspiring screenwriters.

FOR YOUR READING LIST

A comedy full of twists and turns in the plot, love triangles, and a forest full of fairies, *A Midsummer Night's Dream* contains the recipe for a humorous and delightful ride into the realm of the imagination. Students will revel in the chaos and confusion that takes place in the forest. They will be entertained by the hilarious and somewhat naïve Bottom and his "relationship" with the Queen of the Fairies. *A Midsummer Night's Dream* is a refreshing and perfect follow-up to the serious and tragic *Julius Cæsar*.

Independent Reading Activity
Refer students to the Language Arts Survey 4.19, "Oral Interpretation," for helpful guidelines in reading a dramatic piece of work. Encourage students to prepare their dramatic reading by reading the play aloud several times to get a feel for the inflection, pitch, tone, and timing of the characters. You may want to motivate students to practice by putting on a contest: whichever group does the most creative and expressive reading wins the opportunity to tape-record their reading and make it available to the audio library in their classroom or school library.

Foreign Correspondent, 1987. Graham Dean. Williamson Art Gallery and Museum, Birkenhead, England.

GOALS/OBJECTIVES

Studying this unit will enable students to
- enjoy reading nonfiction
- describe and give an example of an autobiography, a memoir, a diary, a biography, a speech, and an essay
- define literary terms such as *description, style, allusion, dialogue, mood,* and *imagery* and identify and explain examples of each that they encounter in their reading
- understand *aim* and *point of view* and identify both in their reading of nonfiction
- compose and deliver a persuasive speech
- identify and demonstrate effective use of formal and informal English

Nonfiction

“ 'Tis strange but true; for truth is always strange; Stranger than fiction. ”

—*George Gordon, Lord Byron*

UNIT FIVE

(Continued on page 458)

GENRE CHECK TEST 4.5.1 WITH ANSWERS

Literary Tools

1. What is nonfiction? **Nonfiction is prose writing that deals with real, not imagined, people and experiences. It also explores thoughts and ideas.**
2. What are two examples of public records? **Public records include sermons, speeches, political tracts, deeds, contracts, constitutions, and laws.**
3. What is the difference between a biography and an autobiography? **Both are stories of a person's life; a biography is written by another person and an autobiography is written by the person himself or herself.**
4. What is a history? **A history is an account of a past event.**
5. What characterizes a good essay? **A good essay develops a single idea and is characterized by unity and coherence.**

Structure in Nonfiction

MATCHING

Match each type of writing with the best description. You may use some choices more than once, and you may not use every choice.

a. description
b. analysis
c. narration
d. comparison-contrast
e. dialogue

1. uses chronological order as a method of organization; **c**
2. presents words as they are actually spoken by people; **e**
3. portrays in words how things look, sound, smell, taste, or feel; **a**
4. presents similarities and differences; **d**
5. breaks something into its parts and shows how the parts are related; **b**

Purposes in Nonfiction

SHORT ANSWER

1. What is a writer's purpose, or aim? **A writer's purpose, or aim, is the goal he or she wants to accomplish with a piece of writing.**
2. What is the writer's purpose when he or she uses the imaginative mode? **The purpose of using imaginative mode is to entertain, enrich, enlighten, and/or share a unique perspective.**

ELEMENTS of NONFICTION

Nonfiction is prose writing that deals with real, not imagined, people and experiences. It also explores thoughts and ideas.

Forms of Nonfiction

Histories provide accounts of past events. The textbook you use in history class is a perfect example. Of importance to historians in preparing histories are many types of **public records,** also nonfiction. These include **speeches, sermons, contracts, deeds, constitutions, laws,** and **political tracts.** One example in this textbook is Chief Seattle's speech "Yonder sky that has wept tears of compassion . . ." (Unit 5).

Other types of nonfiction, closely related to histories, are **biographies** and **autobiographies,** which can be thought of as histories of individual people. A biography is the story of a person's life. An autobiography is the story of a person's life, written by that person. Langston Hughes's "Harriet Tubman: The Moses of Her People" (Unit 5), Coretta Scott King's "Montgomery Boycott" (Unit 5), and the excerpt from *Albert Einstein: A Biography* by Albrecht Fölsing (Unit 8), are examples of biography. Examples of autobiography include the excerpts from Anne Frank's *The Diary of a Young Girl* (Unit 5), Christy Brown's *My Left Foot* (Unit 8), Yoshiko Uchida's *Desert Exile: The Uprooting of a Japanese-American Family* (Unit 10), and Le Ly Hayslip's *When Heaven and Earth Changed Places* (Unit 10).

Letters, diaries, and **journals,** which are often used by biographers as source material, are also considered nonfiction. The excerpt from *The Diary of a Young Girl* by Anne Frank (Unit 5) is an example of a diary.

An **essay** is a brief work of prose nonfiction. The original meaning of essay was "a trial or attempt," and the word retains some of this original force. An essay need not be a complete or exhaustive treatment of a subject but rather a tentative exploration of it. A good essay develops a single idea and is characterized by unity and coherence. Oliver Sacks's "The Man Who Mistook His Wife for a Hat" (Unit 5) and David Quammen's "The Last Bison" (Unit 5) are examples of essays (Unit 5). A **personal essay** is a short work of nonfictional prose on a single topic related to the life or interests of the writer. Personal essays are characterized by an intimate and informal style and tone. They are often, but not always, written in the first person. Examples of personal essays in this textbook include the excerpts from Anna Quindlen's *How Reading Changed My Life* (Unit 7), Anne Lamott's *Bird by Bird* (Unit 8), and Bharati Mukherjee's "The Road from Ballygunge" (Unit 10). **Creative nonfiction** is nonfiction that incorporates some elements of fiction writing, such as imaginative description. One example is "Ice and Light" from Barry Lopez's *Arctic Dreams* (Unit 5).

An **article** is a brief work of nonfiction on a specific topic. The term *article* is typically used of encyclopedia entries and short nonfiction works that appear in newspapers and popular magazines. The term is sometimes used as a synonym of *essay,* though the latter term often connotes a more serious, important, or lasting work. Examples of articles include "Beware the Unruly Sun" by Claudia Kalb (Unit 6) and "The Roots of Genius?" by Steven Levy (Unit 8).

How-to writing, or writing that explains a procedure or strategy, is also nonfiction. One example of how-to writing is Garrison Keillor's "How to Write a Letter" (Unit 6).

Purposes in Nonfiction

PURPOSE. A writer's **purpose,** or **aim,** is what he or she wants to accomplish. All writing, including nonfiction, is generally produced with some overall purpose in mind. The following chart classifies modes, or categories, of prose writing by purpose.

GENRE CHECK TEST 4.5.1 WITH ANSWERS (CONT.)

3. Give three examples of persuasive/argumentative writing. **Responses will vary, but could include editorial, petition, advertisement, campaign speech, debate, graffiti, grant application, invitation, letter of complaint, movie review, nomination speech, press release, sermon, slogan, etc.**

4. What is the main purpose of expository/informative writing? **The main purpose is to inform.**
5. If a writer's purpose is to reflect on a significant event in his or her life, what mode of writing would he or she use? **The personal/expressive mode is used for reflection.**

MODE OF WRITING	PURPOSE	EXAMPLE
expository / informative	to inform	news article, research report
imaginative	to entertain, enrich, enlighten, and/or use an artistic medium such as fiction, poetry, or creative nonfiction, to share a perspective	poem, short story, humorous essay
narrative	to share a story about an event, often to make a point	biography, family history
personal / expressive	to reflect	diary entry, personal letter
persuasive / argumentative	to persuade readers or listeners to respond in some way, such as to agree with a position, change a view on an issue, reach an agreement, or perform an action	editorial, petition

Note that a written work can have more than one purpose. For example, a nonfiction work may start with a brief story, or narrative, to introduce the topic or to make a point. It may then incorporate imaginative writing, provide information, express a personal reaction to that information, and strive to persuade the reader to adopt the writer's view. The emerging form known as "creative nonfiction" in fact combines purposes and aims in new ways.

For more information, consult the Language Arts Survey 2.3, "Identifying Your Purpose."

Structure in Nonfiction

A writer may structure, or organize, a piece of writing in different ways in order to communicate more clearly. The following chart describes types of writing that are commonly used in nonfiction, and how these types are typically structured.

TYPE OF WRITING	STRUCTURE OR ORGANIZATIONAL METHOD
Narration	As with the narrative mode, writing with this method tells a story or describes events using time, or chronological order, as a way of organization.
Dialogue	Writing using this method presents words as they are actually spoken by people. Quotation marks are usually used to set off direct speech.
Description	Writing with this method portrays in words how things look, sound, smell, taste, or feel. Descriptive writing frequently uses spatial order as a way of organization.
Exposition	Writing using this method presents facts or opinions in an organized manner. There are many ways to organize exposition. The following are some of the most common. **Analysis** breaks something into its parts and shows how the parts are related. **Classification** places subjects into categories, or classes, according to their properties or characteristics. **Comparison-contrast** presents similarities as it compares two things and presents differences as it contrasts them. **Process / How-to** writing presents the steps in a process or gives the reader directions on how to do something.

ADDITIONAL RESOURCES

UNIT 5 RESOURCE BOOK
- Selection Worksheet 5.1
- Selection Check Test 4.5.3
- Selection Test 4.5.4
- Study and Research Resource 5.26, 5.30

GRAPHIC ORGANIZER

A	B	C, D	E	F, G
1921	1929	1933	1934	1940

H	I, J, K	L, M, N, O, P
1941	1942 1943	1944

Q, R, S
1945

A Hitler becomes leader of Nazi party
B Anne born on June 12, 1929
C Hitler becomes chancellor of Germany
D Frank family emigrates to Amsterdam, Holland
E Anne starts school at Montessori Kindergarten
F Germans invade Holland
G Anti-Jewish decrees start in Holland
H Anne required to transfer to Jewish Secondary School
I Anne starts diary on June 14
J Margot receives deportation notice on July 5
K Frank family goes into hiding on July 6
L Anne experiences first kiss from Peter on April 15
M D-Day—Allied forces invade Europe on June 6
N Anne's last diary entry on August 1
O Hideout invaded by Gestapo on August 4; families sent to Auschwitz
P Anne moved to Belsen concentration camp in October
Q Anne died at Belsen in March; not yet 16
R Victory in Europe Day on May 8
S Victory in Japan Day on September 2

READER'S JOURNAL

What makes a person's diary unique? How is a diary different from a poem or story?

Literary TOOLS

DIARY. A **diary** is a day-to-day record of a person's activities, experiences, thoughts, and feelings. As you read the diary excerpts, contemplate what you learn about Anne through her words.

DESCRIPTION. Description is a type of writing that portrays a character, an object, or a scene. Descriptions make use of sensory details—words and phrases that describe how things look, sound, smell, taste, or feel. Look for some detailed descriptions of people and places in Anne's diary.

Graphic Organizer

Using background information from the Reader's Resource as well as details from Anne's diary, create a time line noting both details of Anne's life and the political changes in Germany. This will help you see how Anne's life changes as the political turmoil and resulting war progress. Follow the style shown below.

Time Line: Life of Anne Frank/Political Turmoil in Germany during WWII

A Hitler became leader of Nazi party
B Anne born on June 12, 1929

Reader's Journal

What kinds of things have you written about in a diary or would write about if you were to keep one?

from *The Diary of a Young Girl*

by Anne Frank

Reader's resource

WORLD HISTORY CONNECTION. Following World War I, the new government of Germany faced a number of problems. The government was unpopular because of its connection with the Treaty of Versailles, which had decreed Germany solely responsible for the war, stripped it of its territories, and destroyed its once powerful military. The government was ineffective because no one political party was able to gain a majority in the Reichstag, the legislative assembly. Opposition to the government gave rise to several new political parties, including the National Socialist German Worker's Party, or the Nazi Party. Promises to restore Germany to its former power and to provide jobs and prosperity for all appealed to many people. In 1921, Adolf Hitler became the *führer*, or leader, of the Nazi Party. Hitler was willing to use any means to achieve his goals, including lies and violence. He blamed the decline of Germany on the Jews and claimed that the Germans were the "master race" who should rule over all others.

A worldwide depression in the late 1920s created a new audience for the Nazi party and for Hitler, who appealed to national pride, simplified complex issues, and offered to assume full responsibility if given full power. On January 30, 1933, Hitler became chancellor of Germany. He demanded and was granted emergency powers by the Reichstag, which was immediately dissolved. After gaining absolute power over Germany, Hitler quickly put his anti-Jewish programs into effect. The new laws barred Jews from civil service, teaching, and work in the media. Further restrictions on employment followed, and many Jews lost their means of livelihood. These repressive laws and raids by the Gestapo, or secret police, made life increasingly difficult and dangerous for Jews in Germany.

Otto Frank recognized the growing danger and moved his family to Holland, which had a long reputation for accepting persecuted people. Many Jews sought refuge in that country, but the German invasion in 1940 brought similar repressive measures to Holland. Since Jews were being regularly deported to concentration camps, the Franks prepared to go into hiding with another family, the Van Daans, a name Anne gave in her diary for the Van Pels family. However, they were forced into their "Secret Annexe" ahead of schedule.

GOALS/OBJECTIVES

Studying this lesson will enable students to
- experience Anne Frank's feelings of fear, joy, despair, and hope during the years she and her family hid from the Nazis
- interpret and explain the tragic connections between the Nazi Holocaust and Anne Frank's writing
- define *diary* and explain how Anne Frank used hers and define *description* and note what Anne typically described in her accounts
- write a description of your living arrangements, a packing list of the items you would take if in Anne's situation, and a memorial speech describing Anne Frank's positive qualities
- put on a play about Anne Frank's life, research other aspects of the Holocaust, and read and summarize media interviews with Holocaust survivors

Anne kept a diary which began on June 14, 1942, less than a month before her family went into hiding. She continued to write in her diary throughout the families' stay in the "Secret Annexe." The last entry Anne wrote was dated August 1, 1944. Three days later, the hiding place was invaded by the Gestapo, who had been told of their whereabouts by a Dutch informer. The Franks and Van Daans were put on a freight train to Auschwitz, a concentration camp in Poland. At Auschwitz, healthy prisoners did heavy work, and the ill disappeared. In October 1944, Anne, her sister Margot, and Mrs. Van Daan were transferred to Belsen, a concentration camp in Germany. Mrs. Frank was left at Auschwitz where she died. In March 1945, Margot died at Belsen. A few days later, Anne, who was not yet sixteen, died as well.

Of the eight people who hid in the secret annex, Otto Frank was the only survivor. When he returned to Amsterdam after the war, Miep and Elli, two of the friends who had aided the hiding families, gave him Anne's diary and writings. He originally published *The Diary of a Young Girl* as a memorial to his family.

About the AUTHOR

Anne Frank (1929–1945) was born in Frankfurt, Germany. To escape the Nazi persecution of the Jews, her family moved to Amsterdam, Holland, in 1933. There Anne attended school, made friends, and lived a normal life. In 1940, however, the Germans invaded Holland, changing the lives of Anne and many others. She had to leave her school and attend one especially for Jewish students. Soon roundups of Jews began. Anne's father prepared to go into hiding in some rooms in the building where his former business was housed. When Anne's sister, Margot, was called to report for deportation on July 5, 1942, the family went into hiding with the Van Daan family. Loyal friends in the building helped the two hiding families by bringing them food, news, and other necessities.

VOCABULARY FROM THE SELECTION

ardent	conditionally	frail	predominate	sabotage
barbarous	deprive	incessantly	privation	somber
beseech	dismal	indifferently	refrain	sufficiently
blithely	diversion	isolate	renowned	supercilious
boisterous	embody	oppress	repellent	superficial
capitulation	enhance	overawed	reserve	superfluous
compel	estrangement	patronage	retiring	

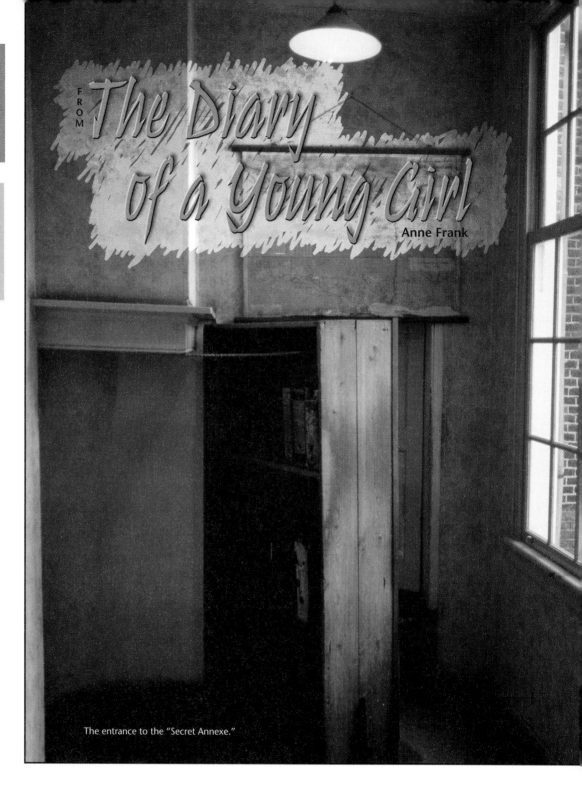

FROM

The Diary of a Young Girl

Anne Frank

The entrance to the "Secret Annexe."

Saturday, 20 June, 1942

I haven't written for a few days, because I wanted first of all to think about my diary. It's an odd idea for someone like me to keep a diary; not only because I have never done so before, but because it seems to me that neither I—nor for that matter anyone else— will be interested in the unbosomings[1] of a thirteen-year-old schoolgirl. Still, what does that matter? I want to write, but more than that, I want to bring out all kinds of things that lie buried deep in my heart.

> How did Anne feel about keeping a diary? What was her purpose for doing so?

There is a saying that "paper is more patient than man"; it came back to me on one of my slightly melancholy days, while I sat chin in hand, feeling too bored and limp even to make up my mind whether to go out or stay at home. Yes, there is no doubt that paper is patient and as I don't intend to show this cardboard-covered notebook, bearing the proud name of "diary," to anyone, unless I find a real friend, boy or girl, probably nobody cares. And now I come to the root of the matter, the reason for my starting a diary: it is that I have no such real friend.

Let me put it more clearly, since no one will believe that a girl of thirteen feels herself quite alone in the world, nor is it so. I have darling parents and a sister of sixteen. I know about thirty people whom one might call friends—I have strings of boy friends, anxious to catch a glimpse of me and who, failing that, peep at me through mirrors in class. I have relations, aunts and uncles, who are darlings too, a good home, no—I don't seem to lack anything. But it's the same with all my friends, just fun and joking, nothing more. I can never bring myself to talk of anything outside the common round.[2] We don't seem to be able to

> What type of friendships did Anne have? What type of friendship did she long to have?

get any closer, that is the root of the trouble. Perhaps I lack confidence, but anyway, there it is, a stubborn fact and I don't seem to be able to do anything about it.

Hence, this diary. In order to <u>enhance</u> in my mind's eye the picture of the friend for whom I have waited so long, I don't want to set down a series of bald facts in a diary like most people do, but I want this diary itself to be my friend, and I shall call my friend Kitty. No one will grasp what I'm talking about if I begin my letters to Kitty just out of the blue, so, albeit[3] unwillingly, I will start by sketching in brief the story of my life.

My father was thirty-six when he married my mother, who was then twenty-five. My sister Margot was born in 1926 in Frankfort-on-Main,[4] I followed on June 12, 1929, and, as we are Jewish, we emigrated to Holland in 1933, where my father was appointed Managing Director of Travies N.V. This firm is in close relationship with the firm of Kolen & Co. in the same building, of which my father is a partner.

The rest of our family, however, felt the full impact of Hitler's anti-Jewish laws, so life was filled with anxiety. In 1938 after the pogroms,[5] my two uncles (my mother's brothers) escaped to the U.S.A. My old grandmother came to us, she was then seventy-three. After May 1940 good times rapidly fled: first the war, then the <u>capitulation</u>, followed by the arrival of the Germans, which is when the sufferings of us Jews really began. Anti-Jewish decrees followed each other in quick succession. Jews must wear a yellow star,[6] Jews must hand in their bicycles, Jews are banned from

---

1. **unbosomings.** Innermost secrets
2. **common round.** Everyday subjects; small talk
3. **albeit.** Although
4. **Frankfort-on-Main.** City in Germany on the Main River
5. **pogroms.** Organized massacres
6. **yellow star.** Jews were forced to wear a six-pointed yellow star to distinguish them from others.

---

words for everyday use

en • hance (en hans´) vt., improve. *Mr. Kim was able to <u>enhance</u> his position at work by taking a course that improved his skills.*

ca • pit • u • la • tion (kə pich´yoo lā´shən) n., surrender. *The <u>capitulation</u> of a losing army is vital to negotiating a peaceful surrender.*

LITERARY NOTE

The Diary of a Young Girl was first published as *Het Achterhuis* in 1947. The first English translation was published in 1953. It is considered the most famous diary of the twentieth century. The most famous diary ever written in English was by Samuel Pepys, a civilian official of the British navy. Pepys made regular entries between 1660 and 1669. His diary describes many of the court intrigues and scandals of his day. He wrote his entries in a combined code and shorthand that was not solved until more than one hundred years after his death.

trams[7] and are forbidden to drive. Jews are only allowed to do their shopping between three and five o'clock and then only in shops which bear the placard "Jewish shop." Jews must be indoors by eight o'clock and cannot even sit in their own gardens after that hour. Jews are forbidden to visit theaters, cinemas, and other places of entertainment. Jews may not take part in public sports. Swimming baths, tennis courts, hockey fields, and other sports grounds are all prohibited to them. Jews may not visit Christians. Jews must go to Jewish schools, and many more restrictions of a similar kind.

So we could not do this and were forbidden to do that. But life went on in spite of it all. Jopie used to say to me, "You're scared to do anything, because it may be forbidden." Our freedom was strictly limited. Yet things were still bearable.

> What was Anne's attitude toward the anti-Jewish decrees?

Granny died in January 1942; no one will ever know how much she is present in my thoughts and how much I love her still.

In 1934 I went to school at the Montessori Kindergarten[8] and continued there. It was at the end of the school year, I was in form 6B, when I had to say good-by to Mrs. K. We both wept, it was very sad. In 1941 I went, with my sister Margot, to the Jewish Secondary School, she into the fourth form and I into the first.[9]

So far everything is all right with the four of us and here I come to the present day.

Saturday, 20 June, 1942

Dear Kitty,

I'll start straight away. It is so peaceful at the moment, Mummy and Daddy are out and Margot has gone to play ping-pong with some friends.

I've been playing ping-pong a lot myself lately. We ping-pongers are very partial to an ice cream, especially in summer, when one gets warm at the game, so we usually finish up with a visit to the nearest ice-cream shop, Delphi or Oasis, where Jews are allowed. We've given up scrounging for extra pocket money. Oasis is usually full and among our large circle of friends we always manage to find some kindhearted gentleman or boy friend, who presents us with more ice cream than we could devour in a week.

I expect you will be rather surprised at the fact that I should talk of boy friends at my age. Alas, one simply can't seem to avoid it at our school. As soon as a boy asks if he may bicycle home with me and we get into conversation, nine out of ten times I can be sure that he will fall head over heels in love immediately and simply won't allow me out of his sight. After a while it cools down of course, especially as I take little notice of <u>ardent</u> looks and pedal <u>blithely</u> on.

If it gets so far that they begin about "asking Father" I swerve slightly on my bicycle, my satchel falls, the young man is bound to get off and hand it to me, by which time I have introduced a new topic of conversation.

> How did Anne deal with boys who were getting too serious?

These are the most innocent types; you get some who blow kisses or try to get hold of your arm, but then they are definitely knocking at the wrong door. I get off my bicycle and refuse to go further in their company, or pretend to be

---

7. **trams.** Open railway cars
8. **Montessori Kindergarten.** Maria Montessori (1870–1952), an Italian educator, founded the Montessori method, based on the ideal of teaching children self-respect and independence at an early age.
9. **fourth form . . . the first.** Since Anne's sister is now about fifteen, fourth form is the same as ninth or tenth grade; Anne is twelve, so first form is the same as sixth or seventh grade.

---

words for everyday use

ar • dent (ärd´ nt) *adj.,* passionate. *He was an <u>ardent</u> supporter of equal rights for everyone and passionately defended his beliefs.*

blithe • ly (blīth´ lē) *adv.,* cheerfully, in a carefree way. *While picnicking in the woods, the happy couple was <u>blithely</u> unaware of the bear who watched from behind a tree.*

insulted and tell them in no uncertain terms to clear off.

There, the foundation of our friendship is laid, till tomorrow!

Yours, Anne

Wednesday, 24 June, 1942

Dear Kitty,

It is boiling hot, we are all positively melting, and in this heat I have to walk everywhere. Now I can fully appreciate how nice a tram is; but that is a forbidden luxury for Jews—shank's mare[10] is good enough for us. I had to visit the dentist in the Jan Luyken-straat in the lunch hour yesterday. It is a long way from our school in the Stadstimmertuinen; I nearly fell asleep in school that afternoon. Luckily, the dentist's assistant was very kind and gave me a drink—she's a good sort.

How had Anne come to view the convenience of a tram?

We are allowed on the ferry and that is about all. There is a little boat from the Josef Israelskade, the man there took us at once when we asked him. It is not the Dutch people's fault that we are having such a miserable time.

I do wish I didn't have to go to school, as my bicycle was stolen in the Easter holidays and Daddy has given Mummy's to a Christian family for safekeeping. But thank goodness, the holidays are nearly here, one more week and the agony is over. Something amusing happened yesterday, I was passing the bicycle sheds when someone called out to me. I looked around and there was the nice-looking boy I met on the previous evening, at my girl friend Eva's home. He came shyly towards me and introduced himself as Harry Goldberg. I was rather surprised and wondered what he wanted, but I didn't have to wait long. He asked if I would allow him to accompany me to school. "As you're going my way in any case, I will," I replied and so we went together. Harry is sixteen and can tell all kinds of amusing stories. He was waiting for me again this morning and I expect he will from now on.

Yours, Anne

Sunday morning, 5 July, 1942

Dear Kitty,

Our examination results were announced in the Jewish Theater last Friday. I couldn't have hoped for better. My report is not at all bad, I had one *vix satis*,[11] a five for algebra, two sixes, and the rest were all sevens or eights. They were certainly pleased at home, although over the question of marks my parents are quite different from most. They don't care a bit whether my reports are good or bad as long as I'm well and happy, and not too cheeky:[12] then the rest will come by itself. I am just the opposite. I don't want to be a bad pupil; I should really have stayed in the seventh form in the Montessori School, but was accepted for the Jewish Secondary. When all the Jewish children had to go to Jewish schools, the headmaster took Lies[13] and me underlined conditionally after a bit of persuasion. He relied on us to do our best and I don't want to let him down. My sister Margot has her report too, brilliant as usual. She would move up with *cum laude* if that existed at school, she is so brainy. Daddy has been at home a lot lately, as there is nothing for him to do at business; it must be rotten to feel so superfluous. Mr. Koophuis has taken over Travies

What motivated Anne to do well in school? What does Anne's motivation reveal about her character?

---

10. **shank's mare.** Walking
11. *vix satis.* With satisfactory force, or effort (Latin)
12. **cheeky.** Fresh; impertinent
13. **Lies.** Lies Goosens, Anne's best friend, was discussed in a previous passage of the diary that does not appear in this selection.

---

words for everyday use

con • di • tion • al • ly (kən dish′ən əl lē) *adv.*, based on certain conditions. *The striking workers conditionally agreed to return to work, provided that they received better pay and medical benefits.*

su • per • flu • ous (sə pʉr′flo͞o əs) *adj.*, unnecessary. *The guest felt completely superfluous at the party; nobody noticed or talked to her and she felt it didn't matter if she was there.*

1. Anne viewed the convenience of a tram as a luxury because of the intense heat that made walking difficult.
2. Anne was motivated by the expectations of her headmaster, whom she didn't want to let down. Her motivation shows the reader that Anne was concerned with meeting the expectations and desires of others.

CROSS-CURRICULAR ACTIVITIES

SOCIAL STUDIES. Have students explore other aspects of the Holocaust. What groups besides Jews were persecuted? Why? How was the founding of the state of Israel related to the Holocaust? Why was the creation of Israel significant to Jews throughout the world?

1. Anne's father presented the idea of the family going into hiding from the Nazis.
2. Anne's father told her not to worry and to enjoy her carefree life while she could.
3. Anne was told her father received a call-up notice from the German special police on Sunday. It conjured up images for her of concentration camps and lonely cells.

ADDITIONAL QUESTIONS AND ACTIVITIES

What major change has occurred in Anne's life since Sunday? What caused this change? What attitude does Anne have toward the change?
Answers
Anne and her family have gone into hiding with the Van Daan family following a call-up notice for Anne's sister Margot. Anne says that her world has been turned upside down but remains positive in her attitude because she is alive.

---

and Mr. Kraler the firm Kolen & Co. When we walked across our little square together a few days ago, Daddy began to talk of us going into hiding. I asked him why on earth he was beginning to talk of that already. "Yes, Anne," he said, "you know that we have been taking food, clothes, furniture to other people for more than a year now. We don't want our belongings to be seized by the Germans, but we certainly don't want to fall into their clutches ourselves. So we shall disappear of our own accord and not wait until they come and fetch us."

> *What idea did her father present?*

"But, Daddy, when would it be?" He spoke so seriously that I grew very anxious.

"Don't you worry about it, we shall arrange everything. Make the most of your carefree young life while you can." That was all. Oh, may the fulfillment of these somber words remain far distant yet!

> *What advice did her father give her?*

Yours, Anne

Wednesday, 8 July, 1942

Dear Kitty,

Years seem to have passed between Sunday and now. So much has happened, it is just as if the whole world had turned upside down. But I am still alive, Kitty, and that is the main thing, Daddy says.

Yes, I'm still alive, indeed, but don't ask where or how. You wouldn't understand a word, so I will begin by telling you what happened on Sunday afternoon.

At three o'clock (Harry had just gone, but was coming back later) someone rang the front doorbell. I was lying lazily reading a book on the veranda[14] in the sunshine, so I didn't hear it.

A bit later, Margot appeared at the kitchen door looking very excited. "The S.S.[15] have sent a call-up notice for Daddy," she whispered. "Mummy has gone to see Mr. Van Daan already." (Van Daan is a friend who works with Daddy in the business.) It was a great shock to me, a call-up; everyone knows what that means. I picture concentration camps[16] and lonely cells—should we allow him to be doomed to this? "Of course he won't go," declared Margot, while we waited together. "Mummy has gone to the Van Daans to discuss whether we should move into our hiding place tomorrow. The Van Daans are going with us, so we shall be seven in all." Silence. We couldn't talk any more, thinking about Daddy, who, little knowing what was going on, was visiting some old people in the Joodse Invalide;[17] waiting for Mummy, the heat and suspense, all made us very overawed and silent.

> *What shocking thing happened on Sunday? What frightening image did this conjure up?*

Suddenly the bell rang again. "That is Harry," I said. "Don't open the door." Margot held me back, but it was not necessary as we heard Mummy and Mr. Van Daan downstairs talking to Harry, then they came in and closed the door behind them. Each time the bell went, Margot or I had to creep softly down to see if it was Daddy, not opening the door to anyone else.

Margot and I were sent out of the room. Van Daan wanted to talk to Mummy alone. When we were alone together in our bedroom, Margot told me that the call-up was not for Daddy, but

---

14. **veranda.** Open porch
15. **S.S.** *Schutzstaffel* (German); German special police used by the Nazi Party during Hitler's regime
16. **concentration camps.** Prison camps where political prisoners or members of ethnic minorities are confined
17. **Joodse Invalide.** Hospital for Jews

---

words for everyday use

som • ber (säm′bər) *adj.*, depressing, grave. *The funeral was a somber affair; many people were sad and gravely expressed their sorrow.*

o • ver • awed (ō vər ôd′) *adj.*, overcome by awe or fearful respect. *We were overawed by the sight of the tornado; its fearsome power and speed made us run for cover.*

for her. I was more frightened than ever and began to cry. Margot is sixteen; would they really take girls of that age away alone? But thank goodness she won't go, Mummy said so herself; that must be what Daddy meant when he talked about us going into hiding.

Into hiding—where would we go, in a town or the country, in a house or a cottage, when, how, where . . . ?

These were questions I was not allowed to ask, but I couldn't get them out of my mind. Margot and I began to pack some of our most vital belongings into a school satchel. The first thing I put in was this diary, then hair curlers, handkerchiefs, schoolbooks, a comb, old letters; I put in the craziest things with the idea that we were going into hiding. But I'm not sorry, memories mean more to me than dresses.

What did Anne pack to take into hiding? What do the objects she packed reveal about her?

At five o'clock Daddy finally arrived, and we phoned Mr. Koophuis to ask if he could come around in the evening. Van Daan went and fetched Miep. Miep has been in the business with Daddy since 1933 and has become a close friend, likewise her brand-new husband, Henk. Miep came and took some shoes, dresses, coats, underwear, and stockings away in her bag, promising to return in the evening. Then silence fell on the house; not one of us felt like eating anything, it was still hot and everything was very strange. We let our large upstairs room to a certain Mr. Goudsmit, a divorced man in his thirties, who appeared to have nothing to do on this particular evening; we simply could not get rid of him without being rude; he hung about until ten o'clock. At eleven o'clock Miep and Henk Van Santen arrived. Once again, shoes, stockings, books, and underclothes disappeared into Miep's bag and Henk's deep pockets, and at eleven-thirty they too disappeared. I was dog-tired and although I knew that it would be my last night in my own bed, I fell asleep imme-

Who helped them to smuggle their belongings to the hiding place?

diately and didn't wake up until Mummy called me at five-thirty the next morning. Luckily it was not so hot as Sunday; warm rain fell steadily all day. We put on heaps of clothes as if we were going to the North Pole, the reason being to take clothes with us. No Jew in our situation would have dreamed of going out with a suitcase full of clothing. I had on two vests, three pairs of pants, a dress, on top of that a skirt, jacket, summer coat, two pairs of stockings, lace-up shoes, woolly cap, scarf, and still more, I was nearly stifled before we started, but no one inquired about that.

Margot filled her satchel with schoolbooks, fetched her bicycle, and rode off behind Miep into the unknown, as far as I was concerned. You see I still didn't know where our secret hiding place was to be. At seven-thirty the door closed behind us. Moortje, my little cat, was the only creature to whom I said farewell. She would have a good home with the neighbors. This was all written in a letter addressed to Mr. Goudsmit.

There was one pound of meat in the kitchen for the cat, breakfast things lying on the table, stripped beds, all giving the impression that we had left helter-skelter. But we didn't care about impressions, we only wanted to get away, only escape and arrive safely, nothing else. Continued tomorrow.

Yours, Anne

Thursday, 9 July, 1942

Dear Kitty,

So we walked in the pouring rain, Daddy, Mummy, and I, each with a school satchel and shopping bag filled to the brim with all kinds of things thrown together anyhow.

We got sympathetic looks from people on their way to work. You could see by their faces how sorry they were they couldn't offer us a lift; the gaudy yellow star spoke for itself.

Only when we were on the road did Mummy and

How did people driving by react?

1. Anne packed her diary, hair curlers, handkerchiefs, school books, a comb, and old letters in her satchel to take into hiding. The objects reveal that she placed great store on memories, some on appearance, and was not considering what she might really need in hiding.
2. Miep, Anne's father's business partner, and Miep's husband, Henk, helped the family smuggle their belongings to the hiding place.
3. People driving by reacted with sympathy for Anne's family because of the difficulties, threats, and fear associated with the yellow stars they were forced to wear.

ADDITIONAL QUESTIONS AND ACTIVITIES

- Prompt students to think about Anne's character. What qualities do they admire in her the most? the least? If students could give Anne one piece of advice about her experiences, what would it be?
- Ask students to consider what things are important to them. If they had to pack only a few belongings as Anne did, what would they choose? Students can discuss the reasons for their choices.

ANSWER TO GUIDED READING QUESTION

1. The hiding place was in Anne's father's office building. Only Mr. Kraler, Koophuis, Miep, and Elli Vossen, who worked for Anne's father, knew its location.

CROSS-CURRICULAR CONNECTIONS

HISTORY. Out of an estimated 8.3 million Jews living in Europe after 1939, about 6 million were killed during the Holocaust. It was said of the concentration camps that "Death seemed to guard all exits."

Daddy begin to tell me bits and pieces about the plan. For months as many of our goods and chattels[18] and necessities of life as possible had been sent away and they were <u>sufficiently</u> ready for us to have gone into hiding of our own accord on July 16. The plan had had to be speeded up ten days because of the call-up, so our quarters would not be so well organized, but we had to make the best of it. The hiding place itself would be in the building where Daddy has his office. It will be hard for outsiders to understand, but I shall explain that later on. Daddy didn't have many people working for him: Mr. Kraler, Koophuis, Miep, and Elli Vossen, a twenty-three-year-old typist who all knew of our arrival. Mr. Vossen, Elli's father, and two boys worked in the warehouse; they had not been told.

Where was the hiding place? Who knew about the hiding place?

I will describe the building: there is a large warehouse on the ground floor which is used as a store. The front door to the house is next to the warehouse door, and inside the front door is a second doorway which leads to a staircase (A). There is another door at the top of the stairs, with a frosted glass window in it, which has "Office" written in black letters across it. That is the large main office, very big, very light, and very full. Elli, Miep and Mr. Koophuis work there in the daytime. A small dark room containing the safe, a wardrobe, and a large cupboard leads to a small somewhat dark second office. Mr. Kraler and Mr. Van Daan used to sit here, now it is only Mr. Kraler. One can reach Kraler's office from the passage, but only via a glass door which can be opened from the inside, but not easily from the outside.

From Kraler's office a long passage goes past the coal store, up four steps and leads to the showroom of the whole building: the private office. Dark, dignified furniture, linoleum and carpets on the floor, radio, smart lamp, everything first-class. Next door there is a roomy kitchen with a hot-water faucet and a gas stove. Next door the W.C.[19] That is the first floor.

A wooden staircase leads from the downstairs passage to the next floor (B). There is a small landing at the top. There is a door at each end of the landing, the left one leading to a storeroom at the front of the house and to the attics. One of those really steep Dutch staircases runs from the side to the other door opening on to the street (C).

The right-hand door leads to our "Secret Annexe."[20] No one would ever guess that there would be so many rooms hidden behind that plain gray door. There's a little step in front of the door and then you are inside.

There is a steep staircase immediately opposite the entrance (E). On the left a tiny passage brings you into a room which was to become the Frank family's bed-sitting-room, next door a smaller room, study[21] and bedroom for the two young ladies of the family. On the right a little room without windows containing the washbasin and a small W.C. compartment, with another door leading to Margot's and my room. If you go up the next flight of stairs and open the door, you are simply amazed that there could be such a big light room in such an old house by the canal. There is a gas stove in this room (thanks to the fact that it was used as a laboratory) and a sink. This is now the kitchen for the Van Daan cou-

---

18. **chattels.** Property; belongings
19. **W.C.** Lavatory; literally "water closet"
20. **"Secret Annexe."** The secret annex in Anne's diary was really an *achterhuis*, meaning "house behind" in Dutch. The hiding place of the Franks was a separate upstairs apartment that overlooked a backyard. *Het Achterhuis* is the Dutch title of this book.
21. **study.** Room for reading or studying

---

words for everyday use

suf • fi • cient • ly (sə fish´ənt lē) *adv.*, adequately. *After participating in spring training, the baseball players were <u>sufficiently</u> ready to start the season.*

The Secret Annexe

- - - - - - Window
≣ Staircase
⬚ Lavatory
／ Door
▬ Bookcase

1st floor

Private office | Kitchen
Rear office
Small storeroom
Office of Miep, Elli, and Mr. Koophuis

2nd floor

Frank's bed-sitting room
Anne and Margot's study-bedroom
Landing
Storeroom
Storeroom
Storeroom

3rd floor

Van Daan's kitchen-living room
Peter's room
Flat roof
Attic

ple, besides being general living room, dining room, and scullery.[22]

A tiny little corridor room will become Peter Van Daan's apartment. Then, just as on the lower landing, there is a large attic. So there you are, I've introduced you to the whole of our beautiful "Secret Annexe."

Yours, Anne

Despite the cramped quarters, why might the annex have been beautiful to Anne?

Friday, 9 October, 1942

Dear Kitty,

I've only got <u>dismal</u> and depressing news for you today. Our many Jewish friends are being taken away by the dozen. These people are treated by the Gestapo[23] without a shred of decency, being loaded into cattle trucks and sent to Westerbork, the big Jewish camp[24] in Drente. Westerbork sounds terrible: only one washing

What dismal news did Anne have?

cubicle for a hundred people and not nearly enough lavatories. There is no separate accommodation. Men, women, and children all sleep together. One hears of frightful immorality because of this; and a lot of the women, and even girls, who stay there any length of time are expecting babies.

It is impossible to escape; most of the people in the camp are branded as inmates by their shaven heads and many also by their Jewish appearance.

If it is as bad as this in Holland whatever will it be like in the distant and <u>barbarous</u> regions they are sent to? We assume that most of them are murdered. The English radio speaks of their being gassed.[25]

---

22. **scullery.** Room for preparing meals
23. **Gestapo.** Secret police force of the Nazi state
24. **camp.** Concentration camp
25. **gassed.** Killed by poisonous gas

words for everyday use

dis • mal (diz'məl) *adj.*, depressing. *We didn't want to go outside on the <u>dismal</u>, rainy day.*
bar • ba • rous (bär'bə rəs) *adj.*, cruel; brutal. *The crowd's <u>barbarous</u> behavior resulted in riot police being sent to arrest them and stop their cruelty.*

1. Anne was outraged that innocent
   people were being executed by the
   Germans. She felt that she no
   longer was German, as Germans
   and Jews were now enemies.
2. Families were torn apart by the war.
3. Anne assessed her situation by
   deciding that she and her family
   were luckier than the millions in the
   concentration camps.

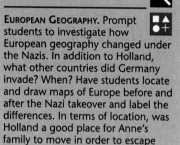

**CROSS-CURRICULAR
ACTIVITIES**

EUROPEAN GEOGRAPHY. Prompt
students to investigate how
European geography changed under
the Nazis. In addition to Holland,
what other countries did Germany
invade? When? Have students locate
and draw maps of Europe before and
after the Nazi takeover and label the
differences. In terms of location, was
Holland a good place for Anne's
family to move in order to escape
the Nazis? Why, or why not?

Perhaps that is the quickest way to die. I feel
terribly upset. I couldn't tear myself away while
Miep told these dreadful stories; and she herself
was equally wound up for that matter. Just
recently for instance, a poor old crippled Jewess
was sitting on her doorstep; she had been told to
wait there by the Gestapo, who had gone to fetch
a car to take her away. The poor old thing was
terrified by the guns that were shooting at English planes overhead, and by the glaring beams of
the searchlights. But Miep did not dare take her
in; no one would undergo such a risk. The Germans strike without the slightest mercy. Elli too is
very quiet: her boy friend has got to go to Germany. She is afraid that the airmen who fly over
our homes will drop their bombs, often weighing
a million kilos,[26] on Dirk's head. Jokes such as
"he's not likely to get a million" and "it only takes
one bomb" are in rather bad taste. Dirk is certainly not the only one who has to go: trainloads
of boys leave daily. If they stop at a small station
en route, sometimes some of them manage to get
out unnoticed and escape; perhaps a few manage
it. This, however, is not the end of my bad news.
Have you ever heard of hostages? That's the latest
thing in penalties for <u>sabotage</u>. Can you imagine
anything so dreadful?

Prominent citizens—innocent people—are
thrown into prison to await their fate. If the
saboteur can't be traced, the Gestapo simply put
about five hostages against the wall. Announcements of their deaths appear in the papers frequently. These outrages are described as "fatal
accidents." Nice people, the Germans! To think
that I was once one of them too! No, Hitler
took away our nationality
long ago. In fact, Germans
and Jews are the greatest
enemies in the world.

Yours, Anne

> What latest action
> outraged Anne? How
> did she feel about being
> German?

Wednesday, 13 January, 1943

Dear Kitty,

Everything has upset me again this morning,
so I wasn't able to finish a single thing properly.

It is terrible outside. Day and night more of
those poor miserable people are being dragged
off, with nothing but a rucksack[27] and a little
money. On the way they are <u>deprived</u> even of
these possessions. Families are torn apart, the
men, women, and children
all being separated. Children coming home from
school find that their parents have disappeared.
Women return from shopping to find their
homes shut up and their families gone.

> What effect did the war
> have on families?

The Dutch people are anxious too, their sons
are being sent to Germany. Everyone is afraid.

And every night hundreds of planes fly over
Holland and go to German towns, where the
earth is plowed up by their bombs, and every
hour hundreds and thousands of people are
killed in Russia and Africa. No one is able to
keep out of it, the whole globe is waging war and
although it is going better for the Allies,[28] the
end is not yet in sight.

And as for us, we are fortunate. Yes, we are luckier
than millions of people. It is quiet and safe here,
and we are, so to speak, living on capital. We are
even so selfish as to talk about "after the war,"
brighten up at the thought of having new clothes
and new shoes, whereas we really ought to save
every penny, to help other people, and save what
is left from the wreckage after the war.

> How did Anne assess
> her situation?

---

26. **a million kilos.** A little over two million pounds, a little over
eleven hundred tons
27. **rucksack.** Knapsack strapped over the shoulders
28. **the Allies.** In World War II, the primary countries allied
against Nazi Germany and Fascist Italy were Great Britain, the
Soviet Union, and the United States.

**words
for
everyday
use**

sab • o • tage (sab′ ə täzh) *n.*, destruction of machinery, bridges, and roads by enemy forces. *The enemy spy was
charged with <u>sabotage</u> for plotting to blow up the railroad bridge just before the train crossed.*
de • prive (dē priv′) *vt.*, take something away from. *After their parents took away the television, the children felt
<u>deprived</u> of entertainment and went to bed.*

The children here run about in just a thin blouse and clogs;[29] no coat, no hat, no stockings, and no one helps them. Their tummies are empty; they chew an old carrot to stay the pangs, go from their cold homes out into the cold street and, when they get to school, find themselves in an even colder classroom. Yes, it has even got so bad in Holland that countless children stop the passers-by and beg for a piece of bread. I could go on for hours about all the suffering the war has brought, but then I would only make myself more dejected. There is nothing we can do but wait as calmly as we can till the misery comes to an end. Jews and Christians wait, the whole earth waits; and there are many who wait for death.

Yours, Anne

Thursday, 6 January, 1944

Dear Kitty,

My longing to talk to someone became so intense that somehow or other I took it into my head to choose Peter.

Sometimes if I've been upstairs into Peter's room during the day, it always struck me as very snug, but because Peter is so <u>retiring</u> and would never turn anyone out who became a nuisance, I never dared stay long, because I was afraid he might think me a bore. I tried to think of an excuse to stay in his room and get him talking, without it being too noticeable, and my chance came yesterday. Peter has a mania for crossword puzzles at the moment and hardly does anything else. I helped him with them and we soon sat opposite each other at his little table, he on the chair and me on the divan.

It gave me a queer feeling each time I looked into his deep blue eyes, and he sat there with that mysterious laugh playing round his lips. I was able to read his inward thoughts. I could see on his face that look of helplessness and uncertainty as to how to behave, and, at the same time, a trace of his sense of manhood. I noticed his shy manner and it made me feel very gentle; I couldn't <u>refrain</u> from meeting those dark eyes again and again, and with my whole heart I almost <u>beseeched</u> him: oh, tell me, what is going on inside you, oh, can't you look beyond this ridiculous chatter?

But the evening passed and nothing happened, except that I told him about blushing[30]—naturally not what I have written, but just so that he would become more sure of himself as he grew older.

When I lay in bed and thought over the whole situation, I found it far from encouraging, and the idea that I should beg for Peter's <u>patronage</u> was simply <u>repellent</u>. One can do a lot to satisfy one's longings, which certainly sticks out in my case, for I have made up my mind to go and sit with Peter more often and to get him talking somehow or other.

Whatever you do, don't think I'm in love with Peter—not a bit of it! If the Van Daans had had a daughter instead of a son, I should have tried to make friends with her too.

I woke at about five to seven this morning and knew at once, quite positively, what I had dreamed. I sat on a chair and opposite me sat

---

29. **clogs.** Open wooden shoes worn in the Netherlands
30. **blushing.** In a previous passage of the diary that does not appear in this selection, Anne wrote about the way her adolescent emotions sometimes caused her to blush.

words for everyday use

re • tir • ing (ri tīr′ iŋ) *adj.,* private, withdrawn. *He was considered to be a shy, <u>retiring</u> type by his friends because he was often quiet and solitary.*

re • frain (ri frān′) *vi.,* hold back; curb an impulse. *The teacher asked the students to <u>refrain</u> from asking questions during the lecture, saying that she would answer them at the end.*

be • seech (bē sēch′) *vt.,* ask, implore. *After pleading for mercy, the lawyer <u>beseeched</u> the judge not to give her client the maximum sentence.*

pa • tron • age (pā′ trən ij) *n.,* goodwill; kindness. *In past centuries many poets and artists depended for their livelihood on the <u>patronage</u> of wealthy noblemen.*

re • pel • lent (ri pel′ ənt) *adj.,* distasteful; repulsive. *Though many considered her brother handsome, she found him <u>repellent</u> because of his disgusting eating habits.*

ANSWERS TO GUIDED READING QUESTIONS

1. Anne dreamed about a boy named Peter Wessel.
2. Anne was overwhelmed by a feeling of love, which she described as a mixture of confusion and longing.
3. Anne's longing was lessened by noticing that Peter was looking at her all the time in a way she couldn't explain.

ADDITIONAL QUESTIONS AND ACTIVITIES

One of the difficulties Anne must deal with is being confined for a long period of time. Prompt students to recall an experience during which they had to spend a long time in one place. What kinds of feelings did they experience? Would they respond differently now after reading Anne's diary? Why, or why not?

Peter . . . Wessel. We were looking together at a book of drawings by Mary Bos.

Whom did Anne dream about?

The dream was so vivid that I can still partly remember the drawings. But that was not all—the dream went on. Suddenly Peter's eyes met mine and I looked into those fine, velvet brown eyes for a long time. Then Peter said very softly, "If I had only known, I would have come to you long before!" I turned around brusquely[31] because the emotion was too much for me. And after that I felt a soft, and oh, such a cool kind cheek against mine and it felt so good, so good. . . .

I awoke at this point, while I could still feel his cheek against mine and felt his brown eyes looking deep into my heart, so deep, that there he read how much I had loved him and how much I still love him. Tears sprang into my eyes once more, and I was very sad that I had lost him again, but at the same time glad because it made me feel quite certain that Peter was still the chosen one.

It is strange that I should often see such vivid images in my dreams here. First I saw Grandma so clearly one night that I could even distinguish her thick, soft, wrinkled velvety skin. Then Granny[32] appeared as a guardian angel; then followed Lies, who seems to be a symbol to me of the sufferings of all my girl friends and all Jews. When I pray for her, I pray for all Jews and all those in need. And now Peter, my darling Peter—never before have I had such a clear picture of him in my mind. I don't need a photo of him, I can see him before my eyes, and oh, so well!

Yours, Anne

Saturday, 12 February, 1944

Dear Kitty,

The sun is shining, the sky is a deep blue, there is a lovely breeze and I'm longing—so longing—for everything. To talk, for freedom, for friends, to be alone. And I do so long . . . to cry! I feel as if I'm going to burst, and I know

that it would get better with crying; but I can't, I'm restless, I go from one room to the other, breathe through the crack of a closed window, feel my heart beating, as if it is saying, "Can't you satisfy my longings at last?"

I believe that it's spring within me, I feel that spring is awakening, I feel it in my whole body and soul. It is an effort to behave normally, I feel utterly confused, don't know what to read, what to write, what to do, I only know that I am longing . . . !

Yours, Anne

What feeling overwhelmed Anne?

Sunday, 13 February, 1944

Dear Kitty,

Since Saturday a lot has changed for me. It came about like this. I longed—and am still longing—but . . . now something has happened, which has made it a little, just a little, less.

What lessened Anne's longing?

To my great joy—I will be quite honest about it— already this morning I noticed that Peter kept looking at me all the time. Not in the ordinary way, I don't know how, I just can't explain.

I used to think that Peter was in love with Margot, but yesterday I suddenly had the feeling that it is not so. I made a special effort not to look at him too much, because whenever I did, he kept on looking too and then—yes, then—it gave me a lovely feeling inside, but which I mustn't feel too often.

I desperately want to be alone. Daddy has noticed that I'm not quite my usual self, but I really can't tell him everything. "Leave me in peace, leave me alone," that's what I'd like to keep crying out all the time. Who knows, the day may come when I'm left alone more than I would wish!

Yours, Anne

31. **brusquely.** Quickly; roughly
32. **Grandma . . Granny.** Grandma is Anne's father's mother, Granny is her mother's mother.

Sunday, 27 February, 1944

Dearest Kitty,

From early in the morning till late at night, I really do hardly anything else but think of Peter. I sleep with his image before my eyes, dream about him and he is still looking at me when I awake.

I have a strong feeling that Peter and I are really not so different as we would appear to be, and I will tell you why. We both lack a mother. His is too <u>superficial</u>, loves flirting and doesn't trouble much about what he thinks. Mine does bother about me, but lacks sensitiveness, real motherliness.

Peter and I both wrestle with our inner feelings, we are still uncertain and are really too sensitive to be roughly treated. If we are, then my reaction is to "get away from it all." But as that is impossible, I hide my feelings, throw my weight about the place, am noisy and <u>boisterous</u>, so that everyone wishes that I was out of the way.

In what ways were Anne and Peter alike?

He, on the contrary, shuts himself up, hardly talks at all, is quiet, daydreams and in this way carefully conceals his true self.

But how and when will we finally reach each other? I don't know quite how long my common sense will keep this longing under control.

Yours, Anne

Sunday, 19 March, 1944

Dear Kitty,

Yesterday was a great day for me. I had decided to talk things out with Peter. Just as we were going to sit down to supper I whispered to him, "Are you going to do shorthand[33] this evening, Peter?" "No," was his reply. "Then I'd just like to talk to you later!" He agreed. After the dishes were done, I stood by the window in his parents' room awhile for the look of things, but it wasn't long before I went to Peter. He was standing on the left side of the open window, I went and stood on the right side, and we talked. It was much easier to talk beside the open window in semidarkness than in bright light, and I believe Peter felt the same.

We told each other so much, so very very much, that I can't repeat it all, but it was lovely; the most wonderful evening I have ever had in the "Secret Annexe." I will just tell you briefly the various things we talked about. First we talked about the quarrels and how I regard them quite differently now, and then about the <u>estrangement</u> between us and our parents.

Why was the evening wonderful for Anne?

I told Peter about Mummy and Daddy, and Margot, and about myself.

At one moment he asked, "I suppose you always give each other a good night kiss, don't you?"

"*One*, dozens, why, don't you?"

"No, I have hardly ever kissed anyone."

"Not even on your birthday?"

"Yes, I have then."

We talked about how we neither of us confide in our parents, and how his parents would have loved to have his confidence, but that he didn't wish it. How I cry my heart out in bed, and he goes up into the loft[34] and swears. How Margot and I really only know each other well for a little while, but that, even so, we don't tell each other everything, because we are always together. Over every imaginable thing—oh, he was just as I thought!

---

33. **shorthand.** Method of writing symbols and shortened versions of words to make note-taking more efficient
34. **loft.** Attic room

FROM THE DIARY OF A YOUNG GIRL **377**

ADDITIONAL QUESTIONS AND ACTIVITIES

Prompt students to recall a time when they had a crush on someone, the way Anne did on Peter. Have them freewrite about what kinds of feelings they experienced and how they feel about the object of their "crush" now. How is Anne's description of her feelings for Peter similar to or different from their own?

ANSWERS TO GUIDED READING QUESTIONS

1. Anne and Peter did not like each other in the beginning. They changed because they began to understand how similar they were.
2. April 15, 1944, was an important day for Anne because it was when she received her first kiss from Peter.

Quotables

" ...then I did the simplest thing in the world. I leaned down...and kissed him. And the world cracked open."

—Agnes de Mille

Then we talked about 1942, how different we were then. We just don't recognize ourselves as the same people any more. How we simply couldn't bear each other in the beginning. He thought I was much too talkative and unruly, and I soon came to the conclusion that I'd no time for him. I couldn't understand why he didn't flirt with me, but now I'm glad. He also mentioned how much he isolated himself from us all. I said that there was not much difference between my noise and his silence. That I love peace and quiet too, and have nothing for myself alone, except my diary. How glad he is that my parents have children here, and that I'm glad he is here. That I understand his reserve now and his relationship with his parents, and how I would love to be able to help him.

"You always do help me," he said. "How?" I asked, very surprised. "By your cheerfulness." That was certainly the loveliest thing he said. It was wonderful, he must have grown to love me as a friend, and that is enough for the time being. I am so grateful and happy, I just can't find the words. I must apologize, Kitty, that my style is not up to standard today.

I have just written down what came into my head. I have the feeling now that Peter and I share a secret. If he looks at me with those eyes that laugh and wink, then it's just as if a little light goes on inside me. I hope it will remain like this and that we may have many, many more glorious times together!

Your grateful, happy Anne

Sunday morning, just before eleven o'clock, 16 April, 1944

Darlingest Kitty,

> How did Anne and Peter see each other in the beginning? How did they change?

Remember yesterday's date, for it is a very important day in my life. Surely it is a great day for every girl when she receives her first kiss? Well, then, it is just as important for me too! Bram's kiss on my right cheek doesn't count any more, likewise the one from Mr. Walker on my right hand.

> Why was April 15, 1944, an important day for Anne?

How did I suddenly come by this kiss? Well, I will tell you.

Yesterday evening at eight o'clock I was sitting with Peter on his divan, it wasn't long before his arm went round me. "Let's move up a bit," I said, "then I don't bump my head against the cupboard." He moved up, almost into the corner, I laid my arm under his and across his back, and he just about buried me, because his arm was hanging on my shoulder.

Now we've sat like this on other occasions, but never so close together as yesterday. He held me firmly against him, my left shoulder against his chest; already my heart began to beat faster, but we had not finished yet. He didn't rest until my head was on his shoulder and his against it. When I sat upright again after about five minutes, he soon took my head in his hands and laid it against him once more. Oh, it was so lovely, I couldn't talk much, the joy was too great. He stroked my cheek and arm a bit awkwardly, played with my curls and our heads lay touching most of the time. I can't tell you, Kitty, the feeling that ran through me all the while. I was too happy for words, and I believe he was as well.

We got up at half past eight. Peter put on his gym shoes, so that when he toured the house he wouldn't make a noise, and I stood beside him. How it came about so suddenly, I don't know, but before we went downstairs he kissed me, through my hair, half on my left cheek, half on

words for everyday use	**i • so • late** (ī' sə lāt) *vt.*, set apart from others. *If you choose to isolate yourself, a mountain cabin set deep in the woods is an excellent place for a retreat.* **re • serve** (ri zurv') *n.*, practice of keeping one's thoughts to oneself. *Because of the coach's quiet reserve, the players never knew what he was thinking.*

my ear; I tore downstairs without looking round, and am simply longing for today!

Yours, Anne

Thursday, 25 May, 1944

Dear Kitty,

There's something fresh every day. This morning our vegetable man was picked up for having two Jews in his house. It's a great blow to us, not only that those poor Jews are balancing on the edge of an abyss, but it's terrible for the man himself.

The world has turned topsy-turvy, respectable people are being sent off to concentration camps, prisons, and lonely cells, and the dregs that remain[35] govern young and old, rich and poor. One person walks into the trap through the black market,[36] a second through helping the Jews or other people who've had to go "underground"; anyone who isn't a member of the N.S.B.[37] doesn't know what may happen to him from one day to another.

This man is a great loss to us too. The girls can't and aren't allowed to haul along our share of potatoes, so the only thing to do is to eat less. I will tell you how we shall do that; it's certainly not going to make things any pleasanter. Mummy says we shall cut out breakfast altogether, have porridge[38] and bread for lunch, and for supper fried potatoes and possibly once or twice per week vegetables or lettuce, nothing more. We're going to be hungry, but anything is better than being discovered.

Yours, Anne

What type of people did Anne see suffering? What type of people did she see in power?

What effects did the loss of the vegetable man have on the hiding families? What was Anne's attitude about this turn of events?

Tuesday, 6 June, 1944

Dear Kitty,

"This is D-day,"[39] came the announcement over the English news and quite rightly, "this is *the* day." The invasion has begun!

The English gave the news at eight o'clock this morning: Calais, Boulogne, Le Havre, and Cherbourg, also the Pas de Calais[40] (as usual), were heavily bombarded. Moreover, as a safety measure for all occupied territories,[41] all people who live within a radius of thirty-five kilometers from the coast are warned to be prepared for bombardments. If possible, the English will drop pamphlets one hour beforehand.

According to German news, English parachute troops have landed on the French coast, English landing craft are in battle with the German Navy, says the B.B.C.[42]

We discussed it over the "Annexe" breakfast at nine o'clock: Is this just a trial landing like Dieppe[43] two years ago?

English broadcast in German, Dutch, French, and other languages at ten o'clock: "The invasion has begun!"—that means the "real" invasion. English broadcast in German at eleven o'clock, speech by the Supreme Commander, General Dwight Eisenhower.[44]

The English news at twelve o'clock in English: "This is D-day." General Eisenhower said to the French people: "Stiff fighting will come now, but after this the victory. The year 1944 is the year of complete victory; good luck."

English news in English at one o'clock (translated): 11,000 planes stand ready, and are flying to and fro non-stop, landing troops and attacking behind the lines; 4000 landing boats, plus small craft, are landing troops and matériel[45] between

---

35. **dregs that remain.** Poorest examples of humanity
36. **black market.** System or place for buying and selling goods illegally
37. **N.S.B.** Official political party of the Dutch Nazis
38. **porridge.** Oatmeal
39. **D-day.** Day on which a military attack is scheduled; specifically, June 6, 1944, the day Allied forces invaded Europe
40. **Calais, Boulogne, . . . Pas de Calais.** Towns along the northern coast of France
41. **occupied territories.** Regions controlled by an enemy state, in this case the Nazi government of Germany
42. **B.B.C.** British Broadcasting Corporation
43. **Dieppe.** City on the northern coast of France
44. **Supreme Commander, General Dwight Eisenhower.** (1890–1969) Highest-ranking officer of Allied forces; later, president of the United States from 1953 to 1961.
45. **matériel.** Military supplies

1. D-day brought the hope of victory in the war and the possibility that the family would be liberated from hiding.
2. Anne felt filled with confidence about the invasion because she had the feeling that friends were approaching.

CROSS-CURRICULAR CONNECTIONS

In Denmark, heroic national efforts were made to save the Jewish population in spite of the German occupation. Most Danish Jews were sent to neutral Sweden to live out the war.

Swedish businessman-diplomat Raoul Wallenberg used his position as a neutral Swedish citizen to help about one hundred thousand Hungarian Jews escape deportation to Nazi death camps. For his selfless work he was granted honorary United States citizenship—the only foreigner other than Winston Churchill to be so honored.

Cherbourg and Le Havre incessantly. English and American troops are already engaged in hard fighting. Speeches by Gerbrandy,[46] by the Prime Minister of Belgium, King Haakon[47] of Norway, De Gaulle[48] of France, the King of England, and last, but not least, Churchill.[49]

Great commotion in the "Secret Annexe"! Would the long-awaited liberation that has been talked of so much, but which still seems *too* wonderful, *too* much like a fairy tale, ever come true? Could we be granted victory this year, 1944? We don't know yet, but hope is revived within us; it gives us fresh courage, and makes us strong again. Since we must put up bravely with all the fears, privations, and sufferings, the great thing now is to remain calm and steadfast. Now more than ever we must clench our teeth and not cry out. France, Russia, Italy, and Germany, too, can all cry out and give vent to their misery, but we haven't the right to do that yet!

What hope did D-day bring?

Oh, Kitty, the best part of the invasion is that I have the feeling that friends are approaching. We have been oppressed by those terrible Germans for so long, they have had their knives so at our throats, that the thought of friends and delivery fills us with confidence!

How did Anne feel about the invasion?

Now it doesn't concern the Jews any more; no, it concerns Holland and all occupied Europe. Perhaps, Margot says, I may yet be able to go back to school in September or October.

Yours, Anne

P.S. I'll keep you up to date with all the latest news!

Tuesday, 1 August, 1944

Dear Kitty,

"Little bundle of contradictions." That's how I ended my last letter and that's how I'm going to begin this one. "A little bundle of contradictions," can you tell me exactly what it is? What does contradiction mean? Like so many words, it can mean two things, contradiction from without and contradiction from within.

The first is the ordinary "not giving in easily, always knowing best, getting in the last word," *enfin*,[50] all the unpleasant qualities for which I'm renowned. The second nobody knows about, that's my own secret.

I've already told you before that I have, as it were, a dual personality. One half embodies my exuberant cheerfulness, making fun of everything, my high-spiritedness, and above all, the way I take everything lightly. This includes not taking offence at a flirtation, a kiss, an embrace, a dirty joke. This side is usually lying in wait and pushes away the other, which is much better, deeper and purer. You must realize that no one knows Anne's better side and that's why most people find me so insufferable.

---

46. **Gerbrandy.** Pieter Sjoerds Gerbrandy (1885–1961) was the prime minister-in-exile of the Netherlands during World War II.
47. **King Haakon.** King Haakon VII (1872–1957) refused to abdicate his throne and encouraged resistance to German occupation.
48. **De Gaulle.** Charles de Gaulle (1890–1970); French soldier and statesman who led the Free French Forces after France fell to Germany and restored French government; president of France from 1958 to 1969
49. **Churchill.** Sir Winston Churchill (1874–1965); British statesman and prime minister from 1940 to 1945 and 1951 to 1955
50. *enfin.* Finally (French)

words for everyday use

in • ces • sant • ly (in ses′ ənt lē) *adv.,* endlessly. *June bugs buzz incessantly on summer nights, often distracting people with their endless noise.*
pri • va • tion (prī vā′ shən) *n.,* deprivation; lack of necessities of life. *Despite the privations of monastery life, most monks do not feel that they lack the necessities they need to prosper.*
op • press (ə pres′) *part.,* hold down by unjust power. *Mrs. Clemm felt oppressed by her creditors.*
re • nowned (ri nound′) *adj.,* famous. *Renowned for his ability to make objects disappears, the magician drew crowds wherever he went.*
em • bod • y (em bäd′ ē) *vt.,* make concrete; give form to; bring together. *She embodies the spirit of a true nurse; her kindness, consideration, and support are essential in someone caring for sick patients.*

Certainly I'm a giddy clown for one afternoon, but then everyone's had enough of me for another month. Really, it's just the same as a love film is for deep-thinking people, simply a <u>diversion</u>, amusing just for once, something which is soon forgotten, not bad, but certainly not good. I loathe having to tell you this, but why shouldn't I, if I know it's true anyway? My lighter superficial side will always be too quick for the deeper side of me and that's why it will always win. You can't imagine how often I've already tried to push this Anne away, to cripple her, to hide her, because after all, she's only half of what's called Anne: but it doesn't work and I know, too, why it doesn't work.

I'm awfully scared that everyone who knows me as I always am will discover that I have another side, a finer and better side. I'm afraid they'll laugh at me, think I'm ridiculous and sentimental, not take me seriously. I'm used to not being taken seriously but it's only the "lighthearted" Anne that's used to it and can bear it; the "deeper" Anne is too <u>frail</u> for it. Sometimes, if I really <u>compel</u> the good Anne to take the stage for a quarter of an hour, she simply shrivels up as soon as she has to speak, and lets Anne number one take over, and before I realize it, she has disappeared.

Therefore, the nice Anne is never present in company, has not appeared one single time so far, but almost always <u>predominates</u> when we're alone. I know exactly how I'd like to be, how I am too . . . inside. But, alas, I'm only like that for myself. And perhaps that's why, no, I'm sure it's the reason why I say I've got a happy nature

Which side of herself did Anne prefer? What fear made it difficult for her to change?

What were the two sides of Anne's character?

within and why other people think I've got a happy nature without. I am guided by the pure Anne within, but outside I'm nothing but a frolicsome little goat who's broken loose.

As I've already said, I never utter my real feelings about anything and that's how I've acquired the name of chaser-after-boys, flirt, know-all, reader of love stories. The cheerful Anne laughs about it, gives cheeky answers, shrugs her shoulders <u>indifferently</u>, behaves as if she doesn't care, but, oh dearie me, the quiet Anne's reactions are just the opposite. If I'm to be quite honest, then I must admit that it does hurt me, that I try terribly hard to change myself, but that I'm always fighting against a more powerful enemy.

A voice sobs within me: "There you are, that's what's become of you: you're uncharitable, you look <u>supercilious</u> and peevish, people dislike you and all because you won't listen to the advice given you by your own better half." Oh, I would like to listen, but it doesn't work; if I'm quiet and serious, everyone thinks it's a new comedy and then I have to get out of it by turning it into a joke, not to mention my own family, who are sure to think I'm ill, make me swallow pills for headaches and nerves, feel my neck and my head to see whether I'm running a temperature, ask if I'm constipated and criticize me for being in a bad mood. I can't keep that up: if I'm watched to that extent, I start by getting snappy, then unhappy, and finally I twist my heart round again, so that the bad is on the outside and the good is on the inside and keep on trying to find a way of becoming what I would so like to be, and what I could be, if . . . there weren't any other people living in the world.

Yours, Anne ∎

words for everyday use

di • ver • sion (də vʉr' zhən) *n.*, distraction. *Our afternoon at the beach was a pleasant <u>diversion</u> from all the work we had to do.*
frail (frāl) *adj.*, delicate; weak. *The prolonged illness left the once-robust Roberto <u>frail</u>.*
com • pel (kəm pel') *vt.*, force. *Larry had to <u>compel</u> himself to finish the tedious project.*
pre • dom • i • nate (prē däm' ə nāt') *vt.*, have authority over. *She let her positive thoughts and feelings <u>predominate</u> over her worries, which gave her a feeling of authority and control.*
in • dif • fer • ent • ly (in dif' ər ənt lē) *adv.*, without interest. *I thought Marnie would be excited at the concert, but she sat through it <u>indifferently</u>.*
su • per • cil • i • ous (soo pər sil' ē əs) *adj.*, full of pride or scorn. *Gary has always been proud, but lately his <u>supercilious</u> attitude is too much.*

---

1. Anne preferred the serious side of herself. The fear of being laughed at and not taken seriously, however, made it difficult for her to change.
2. The two sides of Anne's character were her exuberantly cheerful side and what she considered her deeper, more intellectual side.

SELECTION CHECK TEST 4.5.3 WITH ANSWERS

Checking Your Reading
1. Why did Anne keep a diary? **Anne wanted to write and record things buried deep within her heart.**
2. How old was Anne when she began her diary? **She was thirteen years old.**
3. With what other family did the Franks go into hiding? **They went into hiding with the Van Daans.**
4. Who, or what, is Kitty? **Kitty is the name Anne gives to her diary.**
5. According to Anne, what are the two sides of her personality? **She is cheerful and funny on one side and more serious and deep on the other side.**

Vocabulary in Context
Fill in each blank below with the most appropriate word from the following Words for Everyday Use. You may have to change the tense of the word.

ardent   capitulation   blithely
superfluous   enhance   somber

1. I wanted to **enhance** my writing skills, so I took a writing course in college.
2. Resistance was impossible: **capitulation** to the enemy forces was our only option.
3. Valerie was **ardent** about equal rights for women.
4. During our honeymoon, we **blithely** roamed the beach, hand in hand.
5. The jewelry was **superfluous**; it added nothing to the already stunning outfit.

Literary Tools
Fill in the blanks using the following terms.

diary   description   sensory details

1. A day-to-day record of a person's events and feelings is called a(n) **diary**.

SELECTION CHECK TEST 4.5.3 WITH ANSWERS (CONT.)

2. **Description** is used to portray a character, object, or a scene.
3. Words that describe how things look, feel, taste, smell, and sound are called **sensory details**.

RESPOND TO THE SELECTION

Based on the last lines of the selection, what would Anne "so like to be"? Why does she feel she cannot achieve it? Given her fate, what additional meaning can be taken from these lines?

ADDITIONAL QUESTIONS AND ACTIVITIES

Ask students the following questions:
1. What does Primo Levi say are the problems that young people face today?
2. In what way is the current generation skeptical?
3. Why is it important to speak on the things that happened during the Holocaust?

Answers
1. He says that today's young people encounter problems that have to do with unemployment, nuclear threat, technological and demographic changes, and the depletion of resources.
2. The current generation is skeptical because it has become distrustful of grand and universal truths and certainties (i.e., nothing in this world is for certain).
3. It is important to speak on the events that happened during the Holocaust because it happened. Because it happened, it can happen again—at any place and at any time.

Respond *to the* SELECTION

What feelings did you have toward Anne as you read this selection? Did they change as you read more of her diary? How did you feel about the ending of her diary and the events that followed?

RELATED READING

ABOUT THE RELATED READING

Primo Levi was born in Turin, Italy, in 1919 and trained as a chemist. He was arrested during World War II as a member of the anti-Fascist resistance and deported to the concentration camp in Auschwitz, Poland in 1944. Fortunately, Levi survived, and went on to write powerful memoirs, fiction, and poetry about his experience in the death camp and his subsequent travels through Eastern Europe. He died in April 1987. *The Drowned and the Saved,* his last book, was published the same year. In this book, Levi concentrated on the moral collapse that occurred in Auschwitz. He asks how people can allow such atrocities to recur again and again. Is human memory so weak that we cannot learn form history? The Related Reading is an excerpt from the conclusion of his book.

FROM The Drowned and the Saved

Primo Levi

The experiences that we survivors of the Nazi Lagers carry within us are extraneous to the new Western generation and become ever more extraneous as the years pass. For the young people of the 1950s and 1960s these were events connected with their fathers: they were spoken about in the family; memories of them still preserved the freshness of things seen. For the young people of the 1980s, they are matters associated with their grandfathers: distant, blurred, "historical." These young people are besieged by today's problems, different, urgent: the nuclear threat, unemployment, the depletion of resources, the demographic explosion, frenetically innovative technologies to which they must adjust. The world's configuration is profoundly changed; Europe is no longer the center of the planet. The colonial empires have yielded to the pressure of the peoples of Asia and Africa thirsting for independence, having been dissolved not without tragedies and struggles between the new nations. Germany, split in two for an indefinite future, has become "respectable," and in fact holds the destiny of Europe in its hands. The United States–Soviet Union diarchy, born out of World War II, persists; but the ideologies on which the governments of the two sole victors of the last conflict are based have lost much of their credibility and splendor. A skeptical generation stands at the threshold of adulthood, bereft not of ideals but of certainties, indeed distrustful of the grand revealed truth: disposed instead to accept the small truths, changeable from month to month on the convulsed wave of cultural fashions, whether guided or wild.

For us to speak with the young becomes ever more difficult. We see it as a duty and, at the same time, as a risk: the risk of appearing anachronistic, of not being listened to. We must be listened to: above and beyond our personal experiences, we have collectively witnessed a fundamental, unexpected event, fundamental precisely because unexpected, not foreseen by anyone. It took place in the teeth of all forecasts; it happened in Europe; incredibly, it happened that an entire civilized people, just issued from the fervid cultural flowering of Weimar, followed a buffoon whose figure today inspires laughter, and yet Adolf Hitler was obeyed and his praises were sung right up to the catastrophe. It happened, therefore it can happen again: this is the core of what we have to say.

It can happen, and it can happen everywhere. I do not intend to nor can I say that it will happen; as I pointed out earlier, it is not very probable that all the factors that unleashed the Nazi madness will again occur simultaneously but precursory signs loom before us. Violence, "useful" or "useless," is there before our eyes: it snakes either through sporadic and private episodes, or government lawlessness, both in what we call the first and the second worlds, that is to say, the parliamentary democracies and countries in the Communist bloc. In the Third World it is endemic or epidemic. It only awaits its new buffoon (there is no dearth of candidates) to organize it, legalize it, declare it necessary and mandatory, and so contaminate the world. Few countries can be considered immune to a future tide of violence generated by intolerance, lust for power, economic difficulties, religious or political fanaticism, and racialist attritions. It is therefore necessary to sharpen our senses, distrust the prophets, the enchanters, those who speak and write "beautiful words" unsupported by intelligent reasons.

It has obscenely been said that there is a need for conflict: that mankind cannot do without it. It has also been said that local conflicts, violence in the streets, factories, and stadiums, are an equivalent of generalized war and preserve us from it, as petit mal, the epileptic equivalent, preserves from grand mal. It has been observed that never before in Europe did forty years go by without a war: such a long European peace is supposedly an historical anomaly.

These are captious and suspect arguments. Satan is not necessary: there is no need for wars or violence, under any circumstances. There are no problems that cannot be solved around a table, provided there is good will and reciprocal trust—or even reciprocal fear, as the present interminable stalled situation seems to demonstrate, a situation in which the greatest powers confront each other with cordial or threatening faces but have no restraint when it comes to unleashing (or allowing the unleashing) of bloody wars among those "protected" by them, supplying sophisticated weapons, spies, mercenaries, and military advisers instead of arbiters of peace.

Nor is the theory of preventive violence acceptable: from violence only violence is born, following a pendular action that, as time goes by, rather than dying down, becomes more frenzied. In actuality, many signs lead us to think of a genealogy of today's violence that branches out precisely from the violence that was dominant in Hitler's Germany. Certainly it was not absent before, in the remote and recent past: nevertheless, even in the midst of the insensate slaughter of World War I there survived the traits of a reciprocal respect between the antagonists, a vestige of humanity toward prisoners and unarmed citizens, a tendential respect for treaties: a believer might say "a certain fear of God." The adversary was neither a demon nor a worm. After the Nazi *Gott mit uns*, everything changed. Goering's terrorist bombings were answered by the "carpet" bombings of the Allies. The destruction of a people and a civilization was proven to be possible and desirable both in itself and as an instrument of rule. Hitler learned the massive exploitation of slave labor in the school of Stalin, but in the Soviet Union it was brought back again, multiplied, at the end of the war. The exodus of minds from Germany and Italy, together with the fear of being surpassed by Nazi scientists, gave birth to nuclear bombs. Desperate, the Jewish survivors in flight from Europe after the great shipwreck have created in the bosom of the Arab world an island of Western civilization, a portentous palingenesis of Judaism, and the pretext for renewed hatred. After the defeat, the silent Nazi diaspora has taught the art of persecution and torture to the military and political men of a dozen countries, on the shores of the Mediterranean, the Atlantic, and the Pacific. Many new tyrants have kept in their drawer Adolf Hitler's *Mein Kampf*: with a few changes perhaps, and the substitution of a few names, it can still come in handy.

The Hitlerian example demonstrated to what an extent a war fought in the industrial era can be devastating even without having recourse to nuclear weapons. During the last twenty years the ill-fated Vietnamese enterprise, the Falkland conflict, the Iran-Iraq war, and the events in Cambodia and Afghanistan confirm it. Yet, it has also demonstrated (not in the rigorous sense of mathematicians, unfortunately) that, at least sometimes, at least in part, historical crimes are punished: the powerful of the Third Reich ended on the gallows or in suicide; the German people suffered a Biblical "massacre" of the first born that decimated a generation and a partition of their country that put an end to century-old German pride. It is not absurd to assume that, had Nazism not shown itself so very ruthless from the start, the alliance among its adversaries would not have been formed, or would have broken up before the end of the conflict, shattered. The world war willed by the Nazis and Japanese was a suicidal war: all wars should be feared as such. ∎

ADDITIONAL QUESTIONS AND ACTIVITIES

Ask students the following questions:
1. What are some factors that instigate violence?
2. What is Levi's response to the argument, "There is a need for conflict...mankind cannot do without it"?
3. What are some of the effects brought on by the Holocaust and WWI?

Answers
1. Intolerance, thirst for power, economic difficulties, and religious, political, and racial fanaticism generate violence.
2. He thinks this is an absurd statement because he believes that "there are no problems that cannot be solved around a table, provided there is good will and reciprocal trust—or even reciprocal fear."
3. Because of the Holocaust and WWI, the destruction of an entire people and civilization proved possible and desirable, nuclear bombs were invented, and the art of persecution and torture became more refined.

RECALL

1a. Anne's purpose for keeping a diary was to bring out all the things she secretly thought and felt. She named it "Kitty." The anti-Jewish laws she mentioned include Jews having to wear yellow stars, handing in their bicycles, not being allowed to take trams or drive, and other severe restrictions.

2a. Anne's father discussed the family going into hiding from the Nazis. The plans were moved up after her sister received a call-up notice from the S.S. The family clothes were secretly smuggled to the hiding place by Miep, who worked for Anne's father. The family also wore as many layers of clothing as possible to transport them to the hiding place. The hiding place was in the building where Anne's father had his office.

3a. Anne wanted to reach Peter on a deep personal level. She had an overpowering feeling of love for him. When they first met, Peter thought Anne was too talkative and she thought he was too quiet and reserved.

INTERPRET

1b. Anne was a highly intelligent, clever, funny and passionate person. The reader learns that Anne's family did not care if her school marks were good or bad. All they cared about was whether she was happy. However, Anne did not feel she could confide in them about her fears, dreams, and desires.

2b. Anne's attitude about going into hiding was fearful. She did not know what to think about giving up her life, except that it was better than going to a concentration camp. She was very grateful to be in the "Secret Annexe," where it was quiet and safe.

3b. The relationship between Anne and Peter developed over time, starting with a dislike that turned slowly into friendship and then into romance. Their close proximity and lack of other companionship played a major role in allowing them to get to know each other so well.

ANALYZE

4a. *Responses will vary.* The most likely experiences that students have shared with Anne are feelings of being misunderstood, being unable to confide in their parents, and experiencing first love.

Investigate, Inquire, and Imagine

Recall: GATHERING FACTS

1a. What was Anne's purpose for keeping a diary? What did she call her diary? What anti-Jewish laws did she mention?

2a. What plans did her father start to discuss? What moved up these plans? How did the Franks get their clothes to their hiding place? Where was their hiding place?

3a. What did Anne want from Peter? What overpowering feeling did she have? What did Anne and Peter think of each other when they first met?

Interpret: FINDING MEANING

1b. What type of person do you think Anne was? What does the reader learn about Anne's family from her diary?

2b. How did Anne feel about going into hiding? What was her attitude about being in the "Secret Annexe"?

3b. How did the relationship between Anne and Peter develop? What part did their close proximity play in their relationship?

Analyze: TAKING THINGS APART

4a. Anne lived in a dangerous, trying time, but her diary is not merely a historical chronicle; it is a personal one as well. In what ways do you feel she is like you? What experiences have you shared?

Synthesize: BRINGING THINGS TOGETHER

4b. How might the cramped quarters and limited contact with others affect relationships? How might they affect one's self-image?

Evaluate: MAKING JUDGMENTS

5a. What self-evaluation did Anne give herself in the last page of her diary? Based on what you can see of her in her diary, do you agree with Anne's evaluation of herself? Why, or why not?

Extend: CONNECTING IDEAS

5b. If every young person today were to read Anne Frank's diary, it would help to quell a fear that Primo Levi writes about in the Related Reading from *The Drowned and the Saved*. What is that fear, and why would reading the diary help?

Understanding Literature

DIARY. Review the definition for **diary** in the Handbook of Literary Terms. What do you learn about Anne through her diary? How might the view of Anne through her diary differ from a biography written about her from another person's point of view?

DESCRIPTION. Review the definition for **description** in Literary Tools in Prereading. Why do you think Anne wrote about the Secret Annexe with such specific details?

ANSWERS TO INVESTIGATE, INQUIRE, AND IMAGINE (CONT.)

SYNTHESIZE

4b. Cramped quarters and limited contact tend to put stress on people's relationships with others. Lack of opportunities to express oneself or interact with others might have negative effects on self-esteem.

EVALUATE

5a. Anne's self-evaluation was that she was really two people, one who was cheerful and lighthearted on the outside, and another who was deep and serious and only emerged through her writing when she was alone. Anne was extremely hard on herself in the self-evaluation she wrote in her diary. She was very insecure about her abilities, and what she saw as her dual personality was not so much a fault as it was a normal teenager's search for self-identity during a very difficult time.

(continued on page 385)

Writer's Journal

1. Write a **description** of a room in your home or apartment, as Anne does in her description of the Secret Annexe. Use specific details to describe the appearance of the room—whether it is cozy or cramped, spacious or empty, light or dark, etc.

2. What if you and your family were forced into hiding for an unknown amount of time like the Frank family? Imagine that you could pack only one suitcase and a school backpack with your belongings. What would you pack and why? Write your **packing list** along with your reasons for including each item.

3. Imagine that you are going to unveil a new memorial to Anne Frank. Write a brief **memorial dedication speech** to give on this occasion. The speech should tell something about Anne and why she is being honored.

Integrating the Language Arts

Collaborative Learning

PLAY. Anne Frank's diary has been adapted for stage, film, and television. Find a copy of the play *The Diary of Anne Frank* by Frances Goodrich and Albert Hackett. Perform a scene from it with some of your classmates. Afterwards, you may wish to compare how the diary and the adaptation affected you.

Media Literacy

SUMMARY OF MEDIA INTERVIEWS. Use the Internet or a newspaper or periodical index to locate interviews with Holocaust survivors. After reading several interviews, summarize the survivors' feelings about how their past experiences have shaped their current lives. It may be helpful to refer to the Language Arts Survey 5.26, "Using the Internet," and 5.30, "Evaluating Information and Media Sources."

Study and Research

HOLOCAUST RESEARCH. Explore other aspects of the Holocaust and share your findings with the class. Consider researching one or more of the following questions or another topic of interest: What groups besides Jews were persecuted? Why? How was the founding of the state of Israel related to the Holocaust? What happened to Jewish survivors of the Holocaust? What became of the Nazis? Who were the most infamous Nazi criminals to be captured and tried after the war? What were the results of the Nurenberg trial? What museums exist today in an effort to educate people about the Holocaust?

ANSWERS TO UNDERSTANDING LITERATURE

DIARY. The reader learns a tremendous amount about Anne through her diary. The reader learns about her fears, how she regards her family, her feelings about love, and most important, many qualities that she does not intend to reveal, including her intelligence and her cleverness. The reader also learns how she changes over a period of time. The view of Anne in her diary is much more personal and honest than a biography could be, because the diary is a firsthand account written by Anne, as opposed to another writer who does not know Anne the way she knows herself.

DESCRIPTION. The Secret Annexe was important to Anne and her family because it was their refuge. She also probably included the specific blueprints because it was such a secretive place, it would have been difficult for someone who hadn't seen it to understand the layout. Anne surely had no idea she'd be hiding for over two years, so at this point it was probably also somewhat of an adventure, albeit a frightening one.

ANSWERS TO INTEGRATING THE LANGUAGE ARTS

Collaborative Learning
To help students with this activity, refer students to the Language Arts Survey 4.1, "Verbal and Nonverbal Communication."

Media Literacy
Refer students to the Language Arts Survey 5.30, "Evaluating Information and Media Sources," for additional help with this activity.

ANSWERS TO INVESTIGATE, INQUIRE, AND IMAGINE (CONT.)

Additionally, if she were as shallow as she thought, her diary would not have stood the test of time.

EXTEND

5b. Primo Levi is concerned that the events of World War II are considered to be historical and distant by today's generation. Yet he feels that the events must be remembered because they could happen again. In reading Anne's diary, one realizes that Anne was a regular teenager with concerns about her inability to open up to her parents and dreams of first love. When you read of the humiliation and atrocities suffered by her family and people, the reader realizes that such atrocities could happen to any group of people. Levi feels that by having one's senses sharpened, one is in a better position to "distrust the prophets, the enchanters, those who speak and write 'beautiful words' unsupported by intelligent reasons."

GRAPHIC ORGANIZER

Students may include the following in their diagrams:

Harriet Tubman   **Moses**
Lived in 1800s   Lived in 1400s BC
          Both born as slaves

African American   Israelite man
woman living
in southern U.S.
Escaped on own first, then went back
      to deliver others from slavery

Had no good   Was adopted by
masters or   Pharaoh's
mistresses   daughter, didn't
                   live as a slave as a
                   youngster
Believed that God was using them to
          help slaves

Lived to see   Never got to set
Emancipation   foot on Promised
Proclamation   Land; God only
pronouncing   let him see it
all slaves free
      Both were successful in freeing
               their people

      Both died old—Moses at 120;

READER'S JOURNAL

Why is it important to have ideals? How do ideals relate to other concepts such as self-confidence? How would life be different if no one had any ideals?

BIOGRAPHY

 Literary
T O O L S

STYLE. Style is the manner in which something is said or written. Both the **diction**, or word choice, and the grammatical structure of "Harriet Tubman: The Moses of Her People" are simple and eloquent. Note how Hughes reveals his admiration for Tubman through his stylistic choices.

ALLUSION. An **allusion** is a rhetorical technique in which reference is made to a person, event, object, or work from history or literature. There is an allusion to Moses, a character from the Bible, in the title of this selection. Moses led the Israelites out of slavery in Egypt into the Promised Land. Think about this allusion as you read about Harriet Tubman's life.

Graphic **Organizer**

To understand the allusion between Moses and Harriet Tubman, create a Venn diagram to note some of their similarities and differences. (If you need more information on the life of Moses, consult a biblical concordance.)

Harriet Tubman   Moses

Lived in 1800s | Both born as slaves | Lived in 1400s BC

Reader's
Journal

To what lengths have you gone or would you go for your beliefs?

PREREADING

"HARRIET TUBMAN: THE MOSES OF HER PEOPLE"
by Langston Hughes

Reader's resource

AMERICAN HISTORY CONNECTION. During the mid-1800s, the Underground Railroad helped slaves escape into northern states and Canada. The Underground Railroad was not actually a railroad; it was so named because it helped slaves move quickly and secretly. Safe places where escaped slaves could hide were called stations, and people who helped slaves move to freedom were called conductors. Harriet Tubman, an escaped slave herself, was one of the most famous conductors on the Underground Railroad. She returned to the South nineteen times and helped hundreds of slaves to escape. Hughes featured Tubman in his book *Famous American Negroes*.

About the AUTHOR

Langston Hughes (1902–1967) was born in Joplin, Missouri, and grew up in Lawrence, Kentucky, and Cleveland, Ohio. He came from a family of abolitionists, people who fought for the end of slavery in the United States. Hughes started writing at an early age and published poetry and fiction in his high school magazine. After attending Columbia University for one year, he worked at a series of odd jobs while developing his skills as a writer. He then attended Lincoln University in Pennsylvania and graduated in 1929. By that time, he had published two books of poetry and had become known as a versatile and gifted poet. Hughes became concerned with political issues in the United States and other countries. For twenty years he worked as a columnist for an African-American weekly publication, *The Chicago Defender*. He also wrote the lyrics for a Broadway musical, *Street Scene*. Hughes eventually settled in Harlem, New York, and produced several volumes of poetry as well as a novel and an autobiography.

GOALS/OBJECTIVES

Studying this lesson will enable students to
- interpret and appreciate Harriet Tubman's experience of helping slaves to freedom on the Underground Railroad and fighting during the Civil War
- describe the literary accomplishments of Langston Hughes
- explain why Tubman became a conductor on the

Underground Railroad, and the historical significance of her work
- define *allusion* and *style* and explain how these relate to Hughes's writing
- research spirituals and explain what they meant to escaping slaves
- write a research report about other aspects of the Underground Railroad

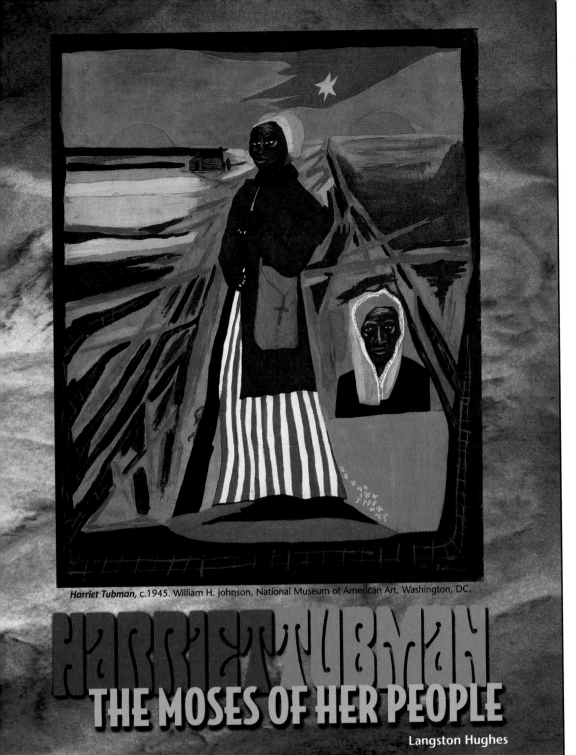

Harriet Tubman, c.1945. William H. Johnson. National Museum of American Art, Washington, DC.

HARRIET TUBMAN
THE MOSES OF HER PEOPLE

Langston Hughes

1. Harriet Tubman devoted herself to the cause of freedom, and the advancement of her people after the Civil War.

CROSS-CURRICULAR
CONNECTIONS

HISTORY. The Underground Railroad extended throughout fourteen Northern states from Maine to Nebraska. Its heaviest activities were concentrated in Pennsylvania, Ohio, Indiana, New York, and the New England states. During its forty years of existence, the total number of slaves who reached freedom by way of the Underground Railroad was between forty thousand and one hundred thousand.

"Then we saw the lightning, and that was the guns; and then we heard the thunder, and that was the big guns; and then we heard the rain falling, and that was the drops of blood falling; and when we came to get in the crops, it was dead men that we reaped." So the escaped slave, Harriet Tubman, described one of the battles of the War between the North and South in which she took part, for she was in the thick of the fighting. Before the War, like Frederick Douglass,[1] Harriet Tubman devoted her life to the cause of freedom, and after the War to the advancement of her people.

To what causes did Tubman devote herself?

Like Douglass she was born in Maryland a slave, one of eleven sons and daughters. No one kept a record of her birth, so the exact year is not known. But she lived so long and so much was written about her that most of the other facts of her life are accurately recorded. She was a homely child, morose, wilful, wild, and constantly in rebellion against slavery. Unlike Phillis Wheatley[2] or Douglass, Harriet had no teaching of any sort, except the whip. As a little girl, on the very first day that she was sent to work in the Big House,[3] her mistress whipped her four times. Once she ran away and hid in a pig sty for five days, eating the scraps thrown to the pigs. "There were good masters and mistresses, so I've heard tell," she once said, "but I didn't happen to come across any of them."

Harriet never liked to work as a servant in the house, so perhaps because of her rebellious nature, she was soon ordered to the fields. One day when she was in her early teens something happened that affected her whole life. It was evening and a young slave had, without permission, gone to a country store. The overseer[4] followed him to whip him. He ordered Harriet to help tie him up. As Harriet refused, the slave ran. The overseer picked up a heavy iron weight from the scales and threw it. But he did not hit the fellow. He struck Harriet's head, almost crushing her skull, and leaving a deep scar forever. Unconscious, the girl lingered between life and death for days. When at last she was able to work again, Harriet still suffered fits of unconsciousness. These lasted all her life. They would come upon her at any time, any place, and it would seem as if she had suddenly fallen asleep. Sometimes in the fields, sometimes leaning against a fence, sometimes in church, she would "go to sleep"[5] and no one could wake her until the seizure had passed. When she was awake, this did not affect her thinking. But her master thought the blow had made her half-witted. Harriet continued to let him believe this. Meanwhile, she prayed God to deliver her from bondage.

When she was about twenty-four years old, she married a jolly, carefree fellow named Tubman, who did not share her concern for leaving the slave country. A few years later, when her old master died, Harriet heard that she and two of her brothers were to be sold, so they decided to run away, together. It was dangerous to tell anyone. Harriet had no chance to let even her mother know directly. But on the evening that she was leaving, she went about the fields and the slaves quarters singing:

---

1. **Frederick Douglass.** (*circa* 1817–1895) African-American leader, writer, and diplomat
2. **Phillis Wheatley.** (1753?–1784) African-born American poet, who was brought to this country as a slave
3. **Big House.** Owner's house on a plantation
4. **overseer.** One who controlled and directed the slaves on the plantation
5. **"go to sleep."** Tubman was an epileptic; epilepsy, a disorder of the nervous system characterized by periods of unconsciousness, convulsions, or seizures, is often caused by brain damage resulting from a head injury.

words for everyday use

bon • dage (bän'dij) *n.*, slavery; involuntary servitude. *The <u>bondage</u> of slavery constrained the freedom of African Americans during the nineteenth century.*

*"When that old chariot comes
I'm gwine to leave you.
I'm bound for the Promised Land. . . ."*

And the way she sang that song let her friends and kinfolks[6] know that to Harriet the Promised Land right then meant the North, not heaven. That night she left the Brodas Plantation on the Big Buckwater River never to return. Before dawn her brothers became frightened and went back to the slave huts before their absence was discovered. But Harriet went on alone through the woods by night, hiding by day, having no map, unable to read or write, but trusting God, instinct, and the North star to guide her. By some miracle she eventually got to Philadelphia, found work there, and was never again a slave.

> What warning did Tubman give her family before leaving?

But Harriet could not be happy while all her family were slaves. She kept thinking about them. So, some months later, she went back to Maryland, hoping to persuade her husband to come North with her. He said he did not wish to go. She led others Northward, however, and, within two years of her own escape, she had secretly returned to the South three times to rescue two brothers, a sister and her children, and a dozen more slaves. The Fugitive Slave Law of 1850[7] now made it dangerous for runaways to stop anywhere in the United States, so Harriet led her followers to Canada where she spent a winter begging, cooking, and praying for them. Then she returned to Maryland to rescue nine more Negroes.

> How did Tubman escape fromm slavery?

> Why did Tubman return to the South?

During the first years of her own freedom, Harriet spent most of her time showing others how to follow in her footsteps. Her fame as a fearless leader of "freedom bands" spread rapidly. Shortly large rewards were offered by the slaveholders for her capture. But she was never captured, and she never lost any of her followers to the slave catchers. One reason for this was that once a slave made up his mind to go with her and started out, Harriet did not permit any turning back. Perhaps her experience with her two brothers when she first ran away accounted for this insistence. Her method of preventing frightened or weak travelers on the freedom road from returning to slavery, and perhaps being whipped into betraying the others, was simple. Harriet Tubman carried a pistol. When anyone said he could not, or would not go on, Harriet pulled her gun from the folds of her dress and said, "You *will* go on—or you'll die." The strength or the courage to continue was always forthcoming when her <u>faltering</u> companions looked into the muzzle of Harriet's gun. Through swamp and thicket, rain and cold, they went on toward the North. Thus everyone who started out with Harriet Tubman lived to thank her for freedom.

> What was one of the reasons for Tubman's success in leading others out of slavery?

Long before the War between the States came, so many slaves were escaping, and so many white people in the North were helping them, that the routes to freedom became known as the "Underground Railroad." Secret "stations" where escaping slaves might be hidden, warmed, and fed were established in homes, barns, and sometimes even churches along the way. The Quakers[8] were especially helpful and

> What name was given to the routes to freedom?

---

6. **kinfolks.** Family
7. **Fugitive Slave Law of 1850.** Law that made illegal the protection of escaping slaves
8. **Quakers.** Members of a Protestant sect who practice simplicity in their religious service and hold world peace as a primary goal

words for everyday use
fal • ter • ing (fôl´tər iŋ) *adj.,* hesitant; uncertain; wavering. *His <u>faltering</u> parents were hesitant about going to the concert with him; they doubted whether they would enjoy the music.*

1. Tubman sang a song to her family before leaving that revealed she was bound for the Promised Land, which to her meant the North.
2. Tubman escaped from slavery by walking through the woods by night and hiding by day, and trusting God, instinct, and the North Star to guide her.
3. Tubman returned to the South to persuade her husband and family to come North.
4. One of the reasons for Tubman's success in leading others out of slavery was that she did not permit any slaves to turn back after they had made up their minds to go with her.
5. The routes to freedom for slaves became known as the Underground Railroad.

active in this regard. And a strong Anti-Slavery Society supported such activities. Slave owners were losing thousands of dollars worth of slaves by escape every year. Harriet Tubman became known as a "conductor" on the Underground Railroad. She was not the only "conductor" but she was the most famous, and one of the most daring. Once she brought as many as twenty-five slaves in a single band to freedom.

Another time she had in her party of runaways a big strong slave worth $1500. His name was Josiah Bailey and the Maryland countryside was plastered with posters offering a reward for his capture. There were ads in the papers for his return. On the way through New York City a friend of freedom recognized Bailey from the description in the papers and said, "I'm glad to meet a man whose head is worth fifteen hundred dollars!" Josiah was so shocked at being recognized and so afraid that he would be captured that a mood of deep despair descended upon him and he would not speak the rest of the trip. When the train was carrying the runaways across the bridge at Buffalo into Canada, Bailey would not even look at the wonder of Niagara Falls.[9] But when they got on free soil and he was finally safe, he burst into song, and nobody could stop him from singing. He cried that at last, thanks to God, he was in Heaven! Harriet Tubman said, "Well, you old fool, you! You might at least have looked at Niagara Falls on the way to Heaven."

Harriet had a great sense of humor. She enjoyed telling the story on herself of how, not being able to read, she once sat down and went to sleep on a park bench right under a sign offering a big reward for her capture. When she began to make speeches to raise money for the cause of freedom, she often told jokes, sang, and sometimes even danced. She might have been a great actress, people said, because without makeup she could hollow out her cheeks and wrinkle her brow to seem like a very old woman. She would make her

> **What anecdote did Harriet enjoy retelling?**

body shrink and cause her legs to totter when she chose to so disguise herself. Once, making a trip to Maryland to rescue some relatives, she had to pass through a village where she was known. She bought two hens, tied them by their feet and hung them heads down around her neck, then went tottering along. Sure enough, a slave catcher came up the street who might, she thought, recognize her, tottering or not. So she unloosed the squalling chickens in the middle of the street and dived after them, purposely not catching them so she could run down the road in pursuit and out of the slave catcher's sight, while all the passersby laughed.

> **Why did she let the chickens loose?**

Sometimes, knowing that her band of fugitives was pursued by angry masters, she would get on a train headed South—because nobody would suspect that runaway slaves would be going South. Sometimes she would disguise the women in her party and herself as men. Babies would be given a sleeping medicine to keep them quiet and then wrapped up like bundles. Sometimes she would wade for hours up a stream to throw the hounds off scent. In the dark of night when there was no North star, she would feel the trunks of trees for the moss that grows on the northern side, and that would serve as a guide toward freedom. Often when all seemed hopeless—although she never told her followers she had such feelings—Harriet would pray. One of her favorite prayers was, "Lord, you've been with me through six troubles. Be with me in the seventh." Some people thought that Harriet Tubman led a charmed life because, within twelve years, she made nineteen dangerous trips into the South rescuing slaves. She herself said, "I never run my train off the track, and I never lost a passenger."

> **What was one of Tubman's favorite prayers?**

---

9. **Niagara Falls.** Giant waterfall (about 650 feet high) divided by an island; one side is in Niagara, New York, in the United States; the other side is in Niagara, Ontario, in Canada

Her father and mother were both over seventy years of age when she rescued them and brought her parents North to a home she had begun to buy in Auburn, New York. At first they stayed in St. Catharines, Canada, where escaped slaves were safe, since, in 1833, Queen Victoria[10] had declared all slavery illegal. But it was too cold for the old folks there. And Harriet's work was not on foreign soil. She herself seemed to have no fear of being captured. She came and went about the United States as she chose. And became so famous that, although she never sought the spotlight, it was hard for her not to be recognized wherever she was. Once at a great woman's suffrage meeting where her old head wound had caused her to go sound asleep in the audience, she was recognized, and awoke to find herself on the platform. Her speech for women's rights was roundly applauded. In those days neither Negroes nor women could vote. Harriet believed both should, so, like Frederick Douglass, she followed the woman's suffrage movement closely.

In appearance "a more ordinary specimen of humanity could hardly be found," but there was no one with a greater <u>capacity</u> for leadership than she had. Among the slaves, where she walked in secret, Harriet began to be known as Moses. And at the great public meetings of the North, as the Negro historian William Wells Brown wrote in 1854, "all who frequented anti-slavery conventions, lectures, picnics, and fairs, could not fail to have seen a black woman of medium size, upper front teeth gone, smiling <u>countenance</u>, attired in coarse but neat apparel, with an old-fashioned reticule or bag suspended by her side, who, on taking her seat, would at once drop off into a sound sleep. . . . No fugitive was ever captured who had Moses for a leader." She was very independent. Between rescue trips or speeches, she would work as a cook or a scrub-

woman. She might borrow, but she never begged money for herself. All contributions went toward the cause of freedom in one way or another, as did most of what she earned.

But when the War between the States began and she became a nurse for the Union Armies, and then a military scout and an invaluable intelligence agent behind the Rebel lines, she was promised some <u>compensation</u>. Technically she was not a registered nurse,[11] and being a woman, she could not be a soldier. Yet she carried a Union pass, traveled on government transports, did dangerous missions in Confederate territory, and gave advice to chiefs of staffs. But she never got paid for this, although she had been promised $1800 for certain assignments. To Harriet this made no difference until, after the War, she badly needed money to care for her aged parents. <u>Petitions</u> were sent to the War Department and to Congress to try to get the $1800 due her. But it was never granted.

> What roles did Tubman play in the War between the States?

Harriet Tubman's war activities were amazing. She served under General Stevens at Beaufort, South Carolina. She was sent to Florida to nurse those ill of dysentery, smallpox, and yellow fever.[12] She was with Colonel Robert Gould Shaw at Fort Wagner. She organized a group of nine Negro scouts and river pilots and, with Colonel Montgomery, led a Union raiding <u>contingent</u> of three gunboats and about 150 Negro troops up the Combahee River. As reported by

---

10. **Queen Victoria.** Alexandrina Victoria (1819–1901), queen of Great Britain and Ireland from 1837 to 1901
11. **registered nurse.** Nurse who has completed training and passed a state examination
12. **dysentery, smallpox, and yellow fever.** *Dysentery*—intestinal inflammation that can be caused by unsanitary conditions; *smallpox*—viral disease causing fever and skin eruptions; *yellow fever*—viral disease that causes high fever (carried by a mosquito)

words for everyday use

ca • pac • i • ty (kə pas′ i tē) *n.*, ability; qualifications. *The <u>capacity</u> for leadership of the president of the United States is respected throughout the world because of his abilities as a diplomat.*
coun • te • nance (koun′ tə nəns) *n.*, look on a person's face; face. *The marathon winner's smiling <u>countenance</u> revealed her perfect teeth and sparkling eyes.*
com • pen • sa • tion (käm pən sā′ shən) *n.*, payment for service. *After taking the job, he felt that the <u>compensation</u> he initially had agreed to was not adequate payment of his services.*
pe • ti • tion (pə tish′ ən) *n.*, formal document containing an earnest request. *The members of the English department signed a <u>petition</u> that showed support for their fired colleague and requested that he be given his job back.*
con • tin • gent (kən tin′ jənt) *n.*, group forming part of a larger group, such as troops. *The president ordered a <u>contingent</u> of tanks and soldiers to be sent to aid the situation.*

ANSWERS TO GUIDED READING QUESTIONS

1. Tubman organized and led a highly successful Union raiding contingent.
2. Tubman's reward was hearing the words "God bless you" from the people she led out of slavery. The witnesses to heroism were the midnight sky and the silent stars.
3. Tubman's statement about planting apples for others to eat meant that she had done the groundwork of fighting slavery, and that other generations would reap the benefits and hopefully continue to fight for equality.

SELECTION CHECK TEST 4.5.5 WITH ANSWERS

Checking Your Reading

1. Who is Harriet Tubman compared to in this selection? **She is compared to Moses.**
2. Where was Tubman born? **She was born in Maryland.**
3. What was the name of the escape route for slaves? **The name of the escape route was named the Underground Railroad.**
4. What did Tubman become known as along the escape route? **Tubman was known as a "conductor."**
5. What year did Tubman die? **Tubman died in 1913.**

Vocabulary in Context

Fill in each blank below with the most appropriate word from the following Words for Everyday Use. You may have to change the tense of the word.

faltering	countenance	petition
multitude	bondage	capacity

1. The **bondage** of slavery wounded the spirit of many African Americans.
2. You can tell when Josie is lying because of her **faltering** words.
3. Martin's joyful **countenance** revealed that the test had gone well.
4. Everybody signed a(n) **petition** to help gain our coach's job back.
5. A(n) **multitude** of people in the arena to support animal rights.

Literary Tools

Fill in the blanks using the following terms.

abolitionists	allusion	style

1. The manner in which something is said or written is called **style**.

---

the Boston *Commonwealth*,[13] for July 10, 1863, they "under the guidance of a black woman, dashed into the enemy's country, struck a bold and effective blow, destroying millions of dollars worth of commissary stores, cotton and lordly dwellings, and striking terror into the heart of rebeldom, brought off near 800 slaves and thousands of dollars worth of property." Concerning Harriet Tubman, it continued, "Many and many times she has penetrated the enemy's lines and discovered their situation and condition, and escaped without injury, but not without extreme hazard."

One of the songs Harriet sang during the War was:

> *Of all the whole creation in the East or in the West,*
> *The glorious Yankee nation is the greatest and the best.*
> *Come along! Come along! Don't be alarmed,*
> *Uncle Sam is rich enough to give you all a farm.*

But Harriet Tubman never had a farm of her own. Her generous nature caused her to give away almost all the money she ever got her hands on. There were always fugitives, or relatives, or causes, or friends in need. She was over forty years old when Abraham Lincoln signed the Emancipation Proclamation, making legal for all the freedom she had struggled to secure. She lived for almost fifty years after the War was over. Some people thought she was a hundred years old when she died in 1913. Certainly she was over ninety.

A number of books have been written about her. The first one, *Scenes in the Life of Harriet Tubman*, by Sarah H. Bradford, appeared in 1869, and the proceeds from its sale helped Harriet pay for her cottage. She wrote her friend, Frederick Douglass, who had hidden her and her runaway slaves more than once in his home in Rochester, for a letter about her book. In his reply he compared their two careers:

What remarkable feat did Tubman accomplish during the War?

"The difference between us is very marked. Most that I have done and suffered in the service of our cause has been in public, and I have received much encouragement at every step of the way. You, on the other hand, have labored in a private way. I have wrought in the day—you in the night. I have had the applause of the crowd and the satisfaction that comes of being approved by the multitude, while the most that you have done has been witnessed by a few trembling, scared and footsore bondsmen[14] and women, whom you have led out of the house of bondage, and whose heartfelt, *God bless you*, has been your only reward. The midnight sky and the silent stars have been the witnesses of your devotion to freedom and of your heroism."

What was Tubman's reward? Who witnessed her heroism?

When years later, in her old age, a reporter for *The New York Herald Tribune*[15] came to interview her one afternoon at her home in Auburn, he wrote that, as he was leaving, Harriet looked toward an orchard nearby and said, "Do you like apples?"

On being assured that the young man liked them, she asked, "Did you ever plant any apples?"

The writer confessed that he had not.

"No," said the old woman, "but somebody else planted them. I liked apples when I was young. And I said, 'Some day I'll plant apples myself for other young folks to eat.' And I guess I did."

Her apples were the apples of freedom. Harriet Tubman lived to see the harvest. Her home in Auburn, New York, is preserved as a memorial to her planting. ■

What did Tubman mean when she said she had planted apples for others to eat?

---

13. *Commonwealth.* Daily newspaper in Boston
14. **bondsmen.** Slaves
15. *The New York Herald Tribune.* Daily newspaper in New York City

---

words for everyday use

mul • ti • tude (mul´ tə tood) *n.*, masses; large number of people considered as a unit. *A multitude of protesters marched on Washington, where thousands of people raised their voices and spoke up collectively against injustice.*

392   *UNIT FIVE / NONFICTION*

SELECTION CHECK TEST 4.5.5 WITH ANSWERS (CONT.)

2. A(n) **allusion** is a technique in which a person, place, or work is referenced.
3. Langston Hughes's parents were **abolitionists** who fought against slavery.

Respond to the SELECTION

What surprised you about Tubman's life? If you were a slave trying to escape, would you want her to be your conductor? Why, or why not?

Investigate, Inquire, and Imagine

Recall: GATHERING FACTS

1a. Why did Tubman decide to run away? How did she let family and friends know what she was planning?

2a. What did Tubman do during her first few years of freedom? What tricks did she use to avoid being caught?

3a. How did Tubman describe one of the battles between the North and the South?

→ **Interpret:** FINDING MEANING

1b. What clues did Tubman's song hold? How did Tubman find her way to freedom?

2b. Why did Tubman first return to Maryland?

3b. What is surprising about Tubman's role in the battle? What compensation did she get for her wartime effort?

Analyze: TAKING THINGS APART

4a. Compare and contrast the deeds of Tubman and Frederick Douglass as noted in the text.

→ **Synthesize:** BRINGING THINGS TOGETHER

4b. Summarize the character traits that made Tubman such a successful conductor.

Evaluate: MAKING JUDGMENTS

5a. What motivated Tubman to take the risks that she took? How was she rewarded for her work?

→ **Extend:** CONNECTING IDEAS

5b. Why do you think Tubman followed the woman's suffrage movement? What did the two movements—freedom for the slaves and woman's suffrage—have in common?

Understanding Literature

STYLE. Review the definition for **style** in the Handbook of Literary Terms. Give some examples showing how the heroic nature of Harriet Tubman's character emerges from Hughes's simple and eloquent language.

ALLUSION. Review the definition for **allusion** and the Venn diagram you completed for Literary Tools in Prereading. Why is Tubman called the Moses of her people? What other reference is made to the Bible story?

"HARRIET TUBMAN: THE MOSES OF HER PEOPLE" **393**

RESPOND TO THE SELECTION

What qualities do you admire in Harriet Tubman? How did these qualities help her lead her people out of slavery? How do you think history would be different if she had not undertaken her work?

ANSWERS TO INVESTIGATE, INQUIRE, AND IMAGINE

RECALL
1a. Tubman decided to run away because she and two of her brothers were to be sold at an auction. She let her family and friends know what she was planning by singing a song whose lyrics had a double meaning.
2a. During her first few years of freedom, Tubman helped other slaves to escape. Tricks she used to avoid capture included disguising herself as an old woman or as a man, getting on trains headed South, and wading upstream to throw bloodhounds off her scent.
3a. Tubman described one of the battles between the North and South as violent, bloody, and full of dead soldiers.

INTERPRET
1b. Tubman's song held the clues that she was leaving and heading to the "promised Land" of the North. She found her way to freedom by traveling through the woods at night guided by the North Star.
2b. Tubman first returned to Maryland to persuade her husband to come with her.
3b. It is surprising that Tubman was able to penetrate enemy lines so many times and escape without injury. Tubman was promised that she would get eighteen hundred dollars in compensation, but it was never granted.

ANALYZE
4a. Tubman and Douglass were similar in that they both believed that African Americans and women should have the right to vote. Douglass noted that he had done most of his work in public, while Tubman had done most of hers in private.

SYNTHESIZE
4b. The traits that made Tubman a good conductor on the Underground Railroad were her strength, courage, and daring. She would not let slaves turn back, and

ANSWERS TO INVESTIGATE, INQUIRE, AND IMAGINE (CONT.)

her leadership paid off in freedom for many people. Her faith in God and her cleverness were also important qualities.

EVALUATE
5a. Tubman was motivated to take risks because of her desire for freedom for herself and others. The main reward she received for her work was the thanks of the people she helped.

EXTEND
5b. Harriet Tubman believed that both African Americans and women should have the right to vote. The two movements held the common belief that no one should be a second-class citizen. There should be one government *for* all the people *by* all the people.

Answers to Understanding Literature can be found on page 394.

ANSWERS TO UNDERSTANDING LITERATURE

STYLE. Hughes's discussion of how Tubman carried a pistol to scare frightened travelers away from returning to slavery, his account of Harriet chasing a chicken to keep from being noticed, and his examples of ways she would disguise herself and her party to prevent angry masters from following their trail are all examples of Hughes's direct and simple language describing Tubman's heroic nature.

ALLUSION. Tubman is considered the Moses of her people because she helped lead African Americans out of slavery and into the "Promised Land" of freedom. Tubman also alludes to the "Promised Land" in the song she sings when she is preparing to escape.

ANSWERS TO INTEGRATING THE LANGUAGE ARTS

Speaking and Listening
Suggest that students look in their local library for information about spiritual recording. Encourage students to bring recordings or other information on spirituals to class to share with other class members.

Study and Research
Encourage students to be creative with this project—especially with the visual aids they use. You may want to refer them to the Language Arts Survey 6.11, "Displaying Effective Visual Information."

Writer's Journal

1. Write an **allusion** that compares a friend, family member, teacher, or coach, to a character from history or literature.

2. Imagine that you are a former slave who has traveled north to freedom with Harriet Tubman. In the years since, you have been fortunate enough to get an education and a university degree. You recently read about Harriet Tubman in the newspapers, and you decide to write her a **thank-you letter** telling her what her personal sacrifice has meant to you and how it has changed your life.

3. What does courage mean to you? Choose a person you believe has courage. How does your subject display courage? Has the person "wrought in the day" like Douglass or in the night like Tubman? What motivates him or her to act as he or she does? Write a **biographical essay** that deals with this person's courage.

Integrating the Language Arts

Collaborative Learning

ROLE-PLAY. In his biography of Harriet Tubman, Hughes provides many examples of Tubman's interactions with other people. Divide into groups of two or three students and select different incidents from the story to act out—examples include Harriet trying to convince a frightened traveler not to return to slavery, Harriet rescuing her parents, Harriet chasing after the squalling chickens, etc. Try to capture the emotions of each character in your role play.

Speaking and Listening

SPIRITUALS. Spirituals are religious and emotional songs often based on biblical stories of deliverance. References to Moses, who led his people out of slavery in Egypt and to the Promised Land, are common in spirituals. Spirituals also allowed slaves to communicate their plans to flee with others. Tubman used a song for this purpose. Find other spirituals common during the period and explain the meaning they might have had to a slave thinking of escape. Try to find recordings of these spirituals to hear how they sound, and share your thoughts and the music with your class.

Study and Research

WRITTEN REPORT. Research other aspects of the Underground Railroad and how it contributed to ending slavery. What states did the Railroad travel through? What were some of the most famous "stations"? Who were some other "conductors" besides Harriet Tubman? You may want to include a map with your report. You can trace the general routes or "lines" of the Underground Railroad from South to North, including Canada, and indicate well-known stations and landmarks.

"Montgomery Boycott"
by Coretta Scott King

Reader's resource

HISTORY CONNECTION. The Montgomery Bus Boycott was an early action in the Civil Rights movement in the United States. A boycott is a planned refusal to buy, sell, or use something. Boycotts are meant to punish, persuade, or make some type of statement. In the 1950s, a movement of nonviolent protests began; the movement aimed at ending segregation, or forced separation of African Americans and white people, in public facilities such as lunch counters, bathrooms, and buses. Martin Luther King Jr. became the leader of this movement stressing nonviolent, Christian actions.

About the AUTHOR

Coretta Scott King (1927–) grew up in Alabama. She had to walk five miles a day to school and watch buses transporting white children pass by her. Early experiences such as these made King determined to gain acceptance and to be treated as an equal. King continued her education at Antioch College in Yellow Springs, Ohio, and then moved to Boston to study music. It was there that she met Martin Luther King Jr., whom she married in 1953.

King has fought for civil rights with courage and a fierce determination. Despite the bombing of her home in 1956 and the assassination of her husband in 1968, she has never hesitated to act on her beliefs. King continues to work with the Martin Luther King Jr. Center for Nonviolent Social Change.

Literary TOOLS

POINT OF VIEW. Point of view is the vantage point from which a story is told. This story is written from a *first-person point of view*, in which the narrator uses words such as *I* and *we*. Coretta Scott King is a participant or witness of the action. Think about how Mrs. King's point of view lends credibility and interest to the story.

AIM. A writer's **aim** is his or her purpose, or goal. As you read, consider what Coretta Scott King's aim may have been for writing "Montgomery Boycott."

Graphic Organizer

Make a chart listing the information Mrs. King provides about her husband. Then identify Mrs. King's aim in providing that information. One example has been done for you.

FACTS ABOUT MARTIN LUTHER KING JR.	AIM
He offered the Dexter church as a meeting place	To inform the reader of Martin's early involvement in the boycott.

Reader's Journal

What injustices do you feel are worth protesting?

ADDITIONAL RESOURCES

UNIT 5 RESOURCE BOOK
- Selection Worksheet 5.3
- Selection Check Test 4.5.7
- Selection Test 4.5.8

GRAPHIC ORGANIZER

Students should include the following information in their charts:
- **Fact:** Martin "hustled around town talking with other leaders" and arranged for transportation for people to get to work.
- **Aim:** To inform the reader of Martin's cooperation with other leaders
- **Fact:** Martin read in the paper that the NAACP was being accused of planting Mrs. Parks on the bus.
- **Aim:** To inform the reader of Martin's "awesome conscience"
- **Fact:** Martin drives around the city on the day of the boycott to gauge the success of the boycott.
- **Aim:** To inform the reader how moved Martin was by people's courage
- **Fact:** Martin accepts the presidency.
- **Aim:** To inform the reader of Martin's humility
- **Fact:** Martin delivers a speech "to rouse people to action and yet devoid of hate and resentment."
- **Aim:** To inform the reader of Martin's speaking skills and his commitment to nonviolent protest

READER'S JOURNAL

Why are protests important? How would life in the United States be different if no one ever protested?

GOALS/OBJECTIVES

Studying this lesson will enable students to
- understand the profound effect the Montgomery Boycott had on the advancement of the Civil Rights movement
- describe the accomplishments of Coretta Scott King
- define *aim* and *point of view* and recognize the use of

these techniques in the selection
- participate in a Civil Rights celebration
- write a comparison-contrast essay on Thoreau or Gandhi and Martin Luther King, Jr.
- conduct a media search about current Civil Rights activities

Rosa Parks at her trial on March 19, 1956.

Montgomery boycott

Coretta Scott King

Of all the facets of segregation in Montgomery,[1] the most _degrading_ were the rules of the Montgomery City Bus Lines. This Northern-owned corporation outdid the South itself. Although seventy percent of its passengers were black, it treated them like cattle—worse than that, for nobody insults a cow. The first seats on all buses were reserved for whites. Even if they were unoccupied and the rear seats crowded, Negroes would have to stand at the back in case some whites might get aboard; and if the front seats happened to be occupied and more white people boarded the bus, black people seated in the rear were forced to get up

> What did the bus segregation laws require?

and give them their seats. Furthermore—and I don't think Northerners ever realized this—Negroes had to pay their fares at the front of the bus, get off, and walk to the rear door to board again. Sometimes the bus would drive off without them after they had paid their fare. This would happen to elderly people or pregnant women, in bad weather or good, and was considered a great joke by the drivers. Frequently the white bus drivers abused their passengers, called

> What sometimes happened to pregnant or elderly African Americans?

them niggers, black cows, or black apes. Imagine what it was like, for example, for a black man to get on a bus with his son and be subjected to such treatment.

There had been one incident in March 1955 when fifteen-year-old Claudette Colvin refused to give up her seat to a white passenger. The high school girl was handcuffed and carted off to the police station. At that time Martin[2] served on a committee to protest to the city and bus-company officials. The committee was received politely—and nothing was done.

The fuel that finally made that slow-burning fire blaze up was an almost routine incident. On December 1, 1955, Mrs. Rosa Parks, a forty-two-year-old seamstress whom my husband _aptly_ described as "a charming person with a radiant personality," boarded a bus to go home after a long day working and shopping. The bus was crowded, and Mrs. Parks found a seat at the beginning of the Negro section. At the next stop more whites got on. The driver ordered Mrs. Parks to give her seat to a white man who boarded; this meant that she would have to stand all the way home. Rosa Parks was not in a revolutionary frame of mind. She had not

> What incident finally sparked a response?

planned to do what she did. Her cup had run over. As she said later, "I was just plain tired, and my feet hurt." So she sat there, refusing to get up. The driver called a policeman, who arrested her and took her to the courthouse. From there Mrs. Parks called E. D. Nixon, who came down and signed a bail bond[3] for her.

Mr. Nixon was a fiery Alabamian. He was a Pullman porter[4] who had been active in A. Philip Randolph's Brotherhood of Sleeping Car Porters and in civil-rights activities. Suddenly he also had had enough; suddenly, it seemed, almost every Negro in Montgomery had had enough. It was spontaneous combustion. Phones began ringing all over the Negro section of the city. The Women's Political Council suggested a one day boycott of

> What course of action was suggested?

---

1. **Montgomery.** Capital of Alabama, located on the Alabama River in the south central part of the state
2. **Martin.** Dr. Martin Luther King Jr. (1929–1968), leader of the American Civil Rights movement who was assassinated in 1968
3. **bail bond.** Formal pledge to pay the full amount of bail assigned by the court if the prisoner being released does not appear in court as scheduled
4. **Pullman porter.** Attendant in a railroad car that has seats that can be converted to berths for sleeping

---

words for everyday use

de • grad • ing (dē grād´iŋ) _adj._, depriving of dignity. _The use of whites-only water fountains was another _degrading_ aspect of segregation._

apt • ly (apt ´lē) _adv._, fittingly. _She was _aptly_ described in the yearbook as charming, popular, and smart, adjectives which fit her perfectly._

1. The bus segregation laws required that black people stand at the back of the bus and give up any seats in the back to whites.
2. Pregnant women or elderly people were often left behind by the bus after having paid their fares.
3. The incident that finally sparked a response involved Rosa Parks, a seamstress who boarded a bus and was ordered to give up her seat to a white man. She refused, and the police arrested her and took her to court.
4. A one-day boycott of buses to protest Rosa Parks's treatment was suggested.

1. Reverend Bennett believed it was
time to move and to act.

INTERNET RESOURCES

Will the Circle Be Unbroken? is a
radio documentary series
about the events of the Civil Rights
movement. It includes the
commentary of unsung heroes
throughout five southern states who
witnessed and participated in the
groundbreaking movement for
freedom and equality. Combined
with these oral histories, the
producers include music and rare
audiotape from the Civil Rights
years. Produced by the **Southern
Regional Council**, the thirteen-hour
series aired on National Public Radio
and can now be heard on the
Internet at
http://www.unbrokencircle.org/
home.htm. Encourage students to
log on to the site and listen to a
taped program.

ADDITIONAL QUESTIONS
AND ACTIVITIES

Interested students may want
to log on to http://www.unbro-
kencircle.org/scripts07.htm,
one of the pages of the *Will the
Circle Be Unbroken?* project
website. Here, they can read and
print out transcripts of the radio programs, including one that details the
Montgomery bus boycott.
Encourage students to form groups,
select a transcript, and then use that
transcript as the script for a play to
be enacted in front of the class. Each
student should take a role: one
would be the narrator, and each of
the others would play the different
people making comments about the
times.

Note: There are songs integrated
into each segment of the radio documentary. Students should be encouraged to find recordings of the songs
or sing the songs themselves as part
of their performance.

---

the buses as a protest. E. D. Nixon courageously
agreed to organize it.

The first we knew about it was when Mr. Nixon
called my husband early in the morning of Friday,
December 2. He had already talked to Ralph
Abernathy.[5] After describing the incident, Mr.
Nixon said, "We have taken this type of thing too
long. I feel the time has come to boycott the
buses. It's the only way to make the white folks see
that we will not take this sort of thing any longer."

Martin agreed with him and offered the Dexter Avenue Church as a meeting place. After
much telephoning, a meeting of black ministers
and civic leaders was arranged for that evening.
Martin said later that as he approached his
church Friday evening, he was nervously wondering how many leaders would really turn up.
To his delight, Martin found over forty people,
representing every segment of Negro life,
crowded into the large meeting room at Dexter.
There were doctors, lawyers, businessmen, fed-
eral-government employees, union leaders, and
a great many ministers. The latter were particularly welcome, not only because of their
influence, but because it meant that they were
beginning to accept Martin's view that "Religion deals with both heaven and earth. . . . Any
religion that professes to be concerned with the
souls of men and is not concerned with the
slums that doom them, the economic conditions
that strangle them, and the social conditions
that cripple them, is a dry-as-dust religion."
From that very first step, the Christian ministry
provided the leadership of our struggle, as
Christian ideals were its source.

The meeting opened with brief devotions.[6]
Then, because E. D. Nixon was away at work,
the Reverend L. Roy Bennett, president of the
Interdenominational[7] Ministerial Alliance, was
made chairman. After describing what had happened to Mrs. Parks, Reverend Bennett said,
"Now is the time to move. This is no time to
talk; it is time to act."

Martin told me after he
got home that the meeting
was almost wrecked because
questions or suggestions from the floor were cut
off. However, after a stormy session, one thing was
clear: however much they differed on details,
everyone was unanimously for a boycott. It was set
for Monday, December 5. Committees were organized; all the ministers present promised to urge
their congregations to take part. Several thousand
leaflets were printed on the church mimeograph
machine[8] describing the reasons for the boycott
and urging all Negroes not to ride buses "to work,
to town, to school, or anyplace on Monday,
December 5." Everyone was asked to come to a
mass meeting at the Holt Street Baptist Church
on Monday evening for further instructions. The
Reverend A. W. Wilson had offered his church
because it was larger than Dexter and more convenient, being in the center of the Negro district.

Saturday was a busy day for Martin and the other
members of the committee. They hustled around
town talking with other leaders, arranging with the
Negro-owned taxi companies for special bulk fares
and with the owners of private automobiles to get
the people to and from work. I could do little to
help because Yoki was only two weeks old, and my
physician, Dr. W. D. Pettus, who was very careful,
advised me to stay in for a month. However, I was
kept busy answering the telephone, which rang
continuously, and <u>coordinating</u> from that central
point the many messages and arrangements.

> *What did Reverend
> Bennett believe it was
> time to do?*

---

5. **Ralph Abernathy.** A leader of the Civil Rights movement
6. **devotions.** Prayers
7. **Interdenominational.** Cooperative effort among leaders of
different religious groups
8. **mimeograph machine.** Early form of copy machine that
used a roller with ink on it

**words
for
everyday
use**

co • or • di • nate (kō ôr´dǝ nāt´) *vt.,* harmonize in a common action or effort. *One of her functions as the director of
the program was to <u>coordinate</u> a reunion of its graduates.*

Our greatest concern was how we were going to reach the fifty thousand black people of Montgomery, no matter how hard we worked. The white press, in an outraged <u>exposé</u>, spread the word for us in a way that would have been impossible with only our resources.

As it happened, a white woman found one of our leaflets, which her Negro maid had left in the kitchen. The <u>irate</u> woman immediately telephoned the newspapers to let the white community know what the blacks were up to. We laughed a lot about this, and Martin later said that we owed them a great debt.

How was word spread about the boycott?

On Sunday morning, from their pulpits, almost every Negro minister in town urged people to honor the boycott.

Martin came home late Sunday night and began to read the morning paper. The long articles about the proposed boycott accused the NAACP[9] of planting Mrs. Parks on the bus—she had been a volunteer secretary for the Montgomery chapter—and likened the boycott to the tactics of the White Citizens' Councils.[10] This upset Martin. That awesome conscience of his began to gnaw at him, and he wondered if he were doing the right thing. Alone in his study, he struggled with the question of whether the boycott method was basically unchristian. Certainly it could be used for <u>unethical</u> ends. But, as he said, "We are using it to give birth to freedom . . . and to urge men to <u>comply</u> with the law of the land. Our concern was not to put the bus company out of business, but to put justice in business." He recalled Thoreau's words, "We can no longer lend our cooperation to an evil system," and he thought, "He who accepts evil without protesting against it is really coop-

erating with it." Later Martin wrote, "From this moment on I conceived of our movement as an act of massive noncooperation. From then on I rarely used the word *boycott*."

What problem did Reverend King have with the idea of a boycott? How did he come to terms with the idea?

<u>Serene</u> after his inner struggle, Martin joined me in our sitting room. We wanted to get to bed early, but Yoki began crying and the tele-

---

9. **NAACP.** National Association for the Advancement of Colored People
10. **White Citizens' Councils.** Groups started in Mississippi in 1954 that had the goal of defeating desegregation in the South

---

words for everyday use

ex • po • sé (eks´pō zā´) *n.*, public disclosure of a scandal or crime. *The newspaper ran an <u>exposé</u> revealing the truth about corruption in city hall.*

i • rate (ī rāt´) *adj.*, angry, wrathful. *It made him <u>irate</u> when his employer gave him misleading information, and he took his anger out on those around him.*

un • eth • i • cal (un eth´i kəl) *adj.*, not conforming to moral standards. *Plagiarism, or using the words and ideas of others without their permission, is <u>unethical</u> and can result in students being expelled from school.*

com • ply (kəm plī´) *vi.*, act in accordance with rule, command, or request. *The judge gave him thirty days to <u>comply</u> with the bicycle helmet law and warned him he would have to pay a fine if he refused.*

se • rene (sə rēn´) *adj.*, calm, peaceful. *Nature preserves are often considered to be <u>serene</u> places, allowing for quiet reflection.*

1. Leaflets were distributed to spread the word about the boycott. Word spread quickly when a white woman found a leaflet and called the papers in outrage.
2. Reverend King's problem with the boycott was whether or not it was unchristian. He came to terms with it by deciding that the boycott was in the name of justice against an evil system, and that to go along with the law without protesting it would have supported it.

CROSS-CURRICULAR CONNECTIONS

SOCIAL STUDIES. During the Montgomery bus boycott, the home of Martin Luther King, Jr., and his wife, Coretta Scott King, was bombed, but he persuaded his followers to remain nonviolent despite threats to their lives and property.

1. Reverend King found the courage of individuals willing to suffer for their freedom and dignity to be majestic.
2. Mrs. Parks's case was different because it was one of the first clearcut examples of a black person being convicted of disobeying the segregation laws.

CROSS-CURRICULAR ACTIVITIES

SOCIAL STUDIES. As a class, have students brainstorm a list of people who have sacrificed and suffered in exchange for freedom and dignity. Then have them pick one person from the list and conduct a research on that person. Ask students to find information on the sacrifice that person made and specific ways in which he or she suffered from the sacrifice(s) made. Did his or her sacrifice result in the achievement of freedom? Explain. Finally, have them present their information in an oral report to the class.

---

phone kept ringing. Between interruptions we sat together talking about the prospects for the success of the protest. We were both filled with doubt. Attempted boycotts had failed in Montgomery and other cities. Because of changing times and tempers, this one seemed to have a better chance, but it was still a slender hope. We finally decided that if the boycott was 60 percent effective we would be doing all right, and we would be satisfied to have made a good start.

A little after midnight we finally went to bed, but at five-thirty the next morning we were up and dressed again. The first bus was due at 6 o'clock at the bus stop just outside our house. We had coffee and toast in the kitchen; then I went into the living room to watch. Right on time, the bus came, headlights blazing through the December darkness, all lit up inside. I shouted, "Martin! Martin, come quickly!" He ran in and stood beside me, his face lit with excitement. There was not one person on that usually crowded bus!

We stood together waiting for the next bus. It was empty too, and this was the most heavily traveled line in the whole city. Bus after empty bus paused at the stop and moved on. We were so excited we could hardly speak <u>coherently</u>. Finally Martin said, "I'm going to take the car and see what's happening in other places in the city."

He picked up Ralph Abernathy, and they cruised together around the city. Martin told me about it when he got home. Everywhere it was the same. A few white people and maybe one or two blacks in otherwise empty buses. Martin and Ralph saw extraordinary sights—the sidewalks crowded with men and women trudging to work; the students of Alabama State College walking or thumbing rides; taxi cabs with people

clustered in them. Some of our people rode mules; others went in horse-drawn buggies. But most of them were walking, some making a round trip of as much as twelve miles. Martin later wrote, "As I watched them I knew that there is nothing more majestic than the determined courage of individuals willing to suffer and sacrifice for their freedom and dignity."

What did Reverend King find majestic?

Martin rushed off again at nine o'clock that morning to attend the trial of Mrs. Parks. She was convicted of disobeying the city's segregation ordinance and fined ten dollars and costs. Her young attorney, Fred D. Gray, filed an appeal. It was one of the first clearcut cases of a Negro being convicted of disobeying the segregation laws—usually the charge was disorderly conduct or some such thing.

What was different about Mrs. Parks's case?

The leaders of the movement called a meeting for three o'clock in the afternoon to organize the mass meeting to be held that night. Martin was a bit late, and as he entered the hall, people said to him, "Martin, we have elected you to be our president. Will you accept?"

It seemed that Rufus A. Lewis, a Montgomery businessman, had proposed Martin, and he had been unanimously elected. The people knew, and Martin knew, that the post was dangerous, for it meant being singled out to become the target of the white people's anger and vengeance. Martin said, "I don't mind. Somebody has to do it, and if you think I can, I will serve."

Then other officers were elected. Rev. L. Roy Bennett became vice-president; Rev. E. N. French, corresponding secretary; Mrs. Erna A. Dungee, financial secretary; and E. D. Nixon, treasurer. After that they discussed what to call

words for everyday use

co • her • ent • ly (kō hir´ənt lē) *adv.,* in a way capable of being understood. *The teacher tried to show his students how to write more <u>coherently</u> because their thoughts were always confused and disorganized when they put them down on paper.*

the organization. Someone suggested the Negro Citizens' Committee. Martin did not approve, because that sounded like an organization of the same spirit as the White Citizens' Council. Finally, Ralph Abernathy proposed calling the organization the Montgomery Improvement Association, the MIA, and this name was unanimously approved.

What organization was formed?

Fear was an invisible presence at the meeting, along with courage and hope. Proposals were voiced to make the MIA a sort of secret society, because if no names were mentioned it would be safer for the leaders. E. D. Nixon opposed that idea. "We're acting like little boys," he said. "Somebody's name will be known, and if we're afraid, we might just as well fold up right now. The white folks are eventually going to find out anyway. We'd better decide now if we are going to be fearless men or scared little boys."

That settled that question. It was also decided that the protest would continue until certain demands were met. Ralph Abernathy was made chairman of the committee to draw up the demands.

Martin came home at six o'clock. He said later that he was nervous about telling me he had accepted the presidency of the protest movement, but he need not have worried, because I sincerely meant what I said when I told him that night, "You know that whatever you do, you have my backing."

Reassured, Martin went to his study. He was to make the main speech at the mass meeting that night. It was now six-thirty, and—this was the way it was usually to be—he had only twenty minutes to prepare what he thought might be the most decisive speech of his life. He said afterward that thinking about the responsibility and the reporters and television cameras, he almost panicked. Five minutes wasted and only fifteen minutes left. At that moment he turned to prayer. He asked God "to restore my balance and be with me in a time when I need Your guidance more than ever."

How could he make his speech both militant enough to rouse people to action and yet devoid of hate and resentment? He was determined to do both.

What did Reverend King hope his speech would do?

Martin and Ralph went together to the meeting. When they got within four blocks of the Holt Street Baptist Church, there was an enormous traffic jam. Five thousand people stood outside the church listening to loudspeakers and singing hymns. Inside it was so crowded, Martin told me, the people had to lift Ralph and him above the crowd and pass them from hand to hand over their heads to the platform. The crowd and the singing inspired Martin, and God answered his prayer. Later Martin said, "That night I understood what the older preachers meant when they said, 'Open your mouth and God will speak for you.'"

First the people sang "Onward, Christian Soldiers" in a tremendous wave of five thousand voices. This was followed by a prayer and a reading of the Scriptures. Martin was introduced. People applauded; television lights beat upon him. Without any notes at all he began to speak. Once again he told the story of Mrs. Parks, and rehearsed some of the wrongs black people were suffering. Then he said, "But there comes a time when people get tired. We are here this evening to say to those who have mistreated us so long that we are tired, tired of being segregated and humiliated, tired of being kicked about by the brutal feet of oppression."

---

words for everyday use

de • void (di void´) adj., completely without. *Her blind date was devoid of charm, wit, or sophistication, and his utter lack of appeal made her wish the evening had never happened.*
op • pres • sion (ə presh´ən) n., something that holds down by unjust power. *For many decades, South Africa's policy of oppression against blacks was called apartheid.*

1. The organization that was formed was the Montgomery Improvement Association, or MIA.
2. Reverend King hoped his speech would rouse people to action without showing hate or resentment.

LITERARY NOTE

King was impressed by the teachings of Henry David Thoreau and Mohandas Gandhi on nonviolent resistance. He wrote, "I came to feel that this was the only morally and practically sound method open to oppressed people in their struggle for freedom."

1. The movement will be guided by the highest principles of law and order, people's consciences, and the principles of Christian faith, including nonviolence and love.
2. Reverend King wished to avoid becoming bitter and hating white people. According to Booker T. Washington, hate pulled one low.

SELECTION CHECK TEST 4.5.7 WITH ANSWERS

Checking Your Reading
1. Which Civil Rights activist wrote this selection? **Coretta Scott King wrote this selection.**
2. In what city do the events take place? **The events take place in Montgomery, Alabama.**
3. What do African-American leaders organize in the city after the bus incident? **They organize a boycott of the bus lines.**
4. What is the name of the woman who refuses to give up her seat? **The woman's name is Rosa Parks.**
5. What does Martin Luther King, Jr. ask his supporters to do? **He asks his supporters to protest in a nonviolent way.**

Vocabulary in Context
Fill in each blank with the most appropriate word from the following Words for Everyday Use. You may have to change the tense of the word.

| coordinate | unethical | irate |
| degrading | serene | aptly |

1. He was **aptly** introduced when the host described him as eloquent, passionate, and humble.
2. Treating women as objects rather than human beings is **degrading**.
3. We asked Victoria to **coordinate** the fundraiser.
4. I was **irate** over Pablo's apathetic attitude toward holidays.
5. Disclosing doctor-patient information is **unethical**.

Literary Tools
Fill in the blanks using the following terms.

| first-person | third-person |
| point of view | aim |

1. A writer's **aim** is his or her purpose or goal.
2. A selection that uses words such as *I* and *we* is written in the **first-person** point of view.
3. The vantage point from which a story is told is called **point of view**.

The audience cheered wildly, and Martin said, "We have no alternative but to protest. We have been amazingly patient . . . but we come here tonight to be saved from the patience that makes us patient with anything less than freedom and justice."

Taking up the challenging newspaper comparison with the White Citizens' Council and the Klan,[11] Martin said, "They are protesting for the perpetuation of injustice in the community; we're protesting for the birth of justice . . . their methods lead to violence and lawlessness. But in our protest there will be no cross burnings; no white person will be taken from his home by a hooded Negro mob and brutally murdered . . . we will be guided by the highest principles of law and order."

Having roused the audience for militant action, Martin now set limits upon it. His study of nonviolence and his love of Christ informed his words. He said, "No one must be intimidated to keep them from riding the buses. Our method must be persuasion, not <u>coercion</u>. We will only say to the people, 'Let your conscience be your guide.' . . . Our actions must be guided by the deepest principles of the Christian faith. . . . Once again we must hear

What will guide the movement?

the words of Jesus, 'Love your enemies. Bless them that curse you. Pray for them that despitefully use you.' If we fail to do this, our protest will end up as a meaningless drama on the stage of history, and its memory will be shrouded in the ugly garments of shame. . . . We must not become bitter and end up by hating our white brothers. As Booker T. Washington[12] said, 'Let no man pull you so low as to make you hate him.'" Finally, Martin said, "If you will protest courageously, and yet with dignity and Christian love, future historians will say, 'There lived a great people—a black people—who injected new meaning and dignity into the veins of civilization.' This is our challenge and our overwhelming responsibility."

What did Reverend King wish to avoid? What did Booker T. Washington warn against?

As Martin finished speaking, the audience rose cheering in <u>exaltation</u>. And in that speech my husband set the keynote and the tempo of the movement he was to lead from Montgomery onward. ∎

---

11. **the Klan.** Group begun as the Ku Klux Klan in Tennessee in 1866 for the purpose of militantly defeating any efforts of non-whites to attain equal rights with white Americans
12. **Booker T. Washington.** (1856–1915) Founder of the teacher's college for African Americans that later became Tuskegee Institute

words for everyday use

co • er • cion (kō ʉr´shən) *n.*, act of force through threats or violence. *The officer was accused of <u>coercion</u> because he threatened a suspect and forced him to confess to committing a crime.*

ex • al • ta • tion (eg´zôl tā´shən) *n.*, feeling of great joy and pride. *The crowd roared in <u>exaltation</u> when the home team came from behind to win the game and cap its undefeated season.*

Respond *to the* SELECTION

Which people introduced in this selection do you admire? What about them do you find admirable?

RESPOND TO THE SELECTION

Ask students to think of people they admire in their own lives. Which qualities do they admire? How are these qualities similar to or different from the qualities of the people they admire in the story?

Investigate, *Inquire,* and Imagine

Recall: GATHERING FACTS

1a. What part of segregation did Coretta Scott King find the most degrading? How were African-American passengers treated? What cruel joke did the bus drivers play?

2a. How was news spread about the boycott? What concerns did Reverend King have about the boycott? What term did he use instead?

3a. What organization was started? What were the two goals of Reverend King's speech?

Analyze: TAKING THINGS APART

4a. Why was Reverend King insistent that the protests be nonviolent?

Evaluate: MAKING JUDGMENTS

5a. In retrospect, was the Montgomery bus boycott a good decision for the organizers of the Civil Rights Movement? Why, or why not?

Interpret: FINDING MEANING

1b. What laws allowed the mistreatment of African-American bus passengers? How did people react to such laws?

2b. Why did Reverend King think it was a good sign that ministers were involved? How did he reconcile the idea of a boycott with his own beliefs?

3b. Why did the organization decide not to exist in secret? How did Reverend King achieve both the goals mentioned in his speech?

Synthesize: BRINGING THINGS TOGETHER

4b. Would Martin Luther King Jr. have considered the Montgomery boycott a success? Why, or why not?

Extend: CONNECTING IDEAS

5b. Have you ever done something (or if not, would you ever consider doing something) that caused you hardship in order to support a cause in which you believed? What did (or would) you do? How would you determine if your efforts were (would be) worthwhile?

Understanding *Literature*

POINT OF VIEW. Review the definition for **point of view** in the Handbook of Literary Terms. What private, internal thoughts of Reverend King's do we read in the selection that we might not have learned had another more distant biographer compiled this information?

AIM. Review the definition for **aim** in the Handbook of Literary Terms and the chart you made for Literary Tools on page 395. What was King's aim in writing this selection? What type of writing is this?

"MONTGOMERY BOYCOTT"   **403**

ANSWERS TO INVESTIGATE, INQUIRE, AND IMAGINE (CONT.)

SYNTHESIZE
4b. Because the black citizens of Montgomery succeeded in making the bus boycott a nonviolent protest against the segregation laws of the city, Martin Luther King, Jr. would probably have considered the boycott a success.

EVALUATE
5a. *Responses will vary.* The bus boycott turned out to be a good way to rally the masses to their cause.

By uniting, common individuals were able to show their support for the movement and to protest the injustices of segregation. And because so many African Americans were bus riders, their boycott did not go unnoticed by the white community.

EXTEND
5b. *Responses will vary.*

Answers to Understanding Literature can be found on page 404.

ANSWERS TO INVESTIGATE, INQUIRE, AND IMAGINE

RECALL
1a. King found the rules for riding the Montgomery City Bus Lines to be the most degrading part of segregation. African-American passengers were forced to stand in the back of the bus and give up any seats they had in back to whites. Bus drivers considered it a joke to drive away after African-American passengers had paid their fares in the front of the bus and were trying to board in back.

2a. The news about the boycott was spread through the newspapers after a white woman saw a leaflet her African-American maid had left on the table and called angrily to report it. Martin Luther King, Jr.'s concern about the boycott was that it was unchristian. The term he used instead of *boycott* was *massive noncooperation.*

3a. The organization that was started was the MIA, or Montgomery Improvement Association. The two goals of Reverend King's speech were to rouse people to take action and to remain free of hate or resentment.

INTERPRET
1b. The laws that allowed for the mistreatment of bus passengers were the segregation laws, specifically the city of Montgomery's segregation ordinance. There were several instances of people refusing to comply with the law. One such instance, that of Rosa Parks, led to the organization of a boycott of the bus lines.

2b. Reverend King thought it was a good sign that ministers were involved because it meant they were beginning to accept his view that religion dealt with the economic and social conditions of its followers. After much contemplation, King decided that the boycott was "massive noncooperation"— refusing to cooperate with laws that were wrong and unjust.

3b. Members decided that if they were afraid, there was no use in going on with the organization. They decided to be "fearless men." Reverend King achieved both of the goals mentioned in the speech by mobilizing people in Montgomery and throughout the country to protest in a nonviolent way.

ANALYZE
4a. Reverend King insisted that actions be guided by "the deepest principles of the Christian faith… If we fail to do this, our protest will end up as a meaningless drama on the stage of history, and its memory will be shrouded in the ugly garments of shame…"

TEACHER'S EDITION   **403**

POINT OF VIEW. Reverend King's internal struggle with the question of whether the boycott method was basically unchristian is probably best related by a witness personally close to King—as his wife certainly seemed to be. Also, the account about how King worried about his speech and finally left it in God's hands is a story only an insider would have known.

AIM. King's aim in writing "Montgomery Boycott" was to inform the reader of the beginnings of the Civil Rights movement and to show what a great man her husband was and how he was able to motivate people, even when he had doubts and insecurities. "Montgomery Boycott" is an example of expository/informational writing.

ANSWERS TO INTEGRATING THE LANGUAGE ARTS

Collaborative Learning
Students may want to check with their local chapter of the NAACP or other civil rights organization for information on the history of the movement. Students may also want to work together in groups to plan skits or films for the celebration. Remind students that all group members must participate and contribute ideas.

Study and Research
Have students read the "Comparison and Contrast Order" section of the Language Arts Survey 2.27, "Choosing a Method of Organization," to give them a better understanding of this activity.

Writer's Journal

1. Imagine that you are Coretta Scott King and that your spouse just came home to tell you he has accepted the presidency of the Montgomery Improvement Association and will become the foremost leader of the protest movement. Write a **diary entry** detailing some of your emotions regarding this announcement—perhaps pride in his abilities, excitement at the potential for change to occur, fear for his safety, etc.

2. Imagine that you are responsible for promoting the bus boycott. You need to get the proper information across to people and you need to convince them to join in the boycott. Prepare a **leaflet** for this purpose.

3. Pretend that you are a newspaper reporter for the *Montgomery Herald* in 1955 and that you are instructed to write an objective, unbiased **news report** of the bus boycott on December 5. You might wish to include interviews from individuals involved on both sides, giving their reactions/observations—i.e., a bus company executive, an African American supporting the boycott and walking six miles to work, etc.

Integrating the Language Arts

Collaborative Learning

CIVIL RIGHTS CELEBRATION. After further researching the Civil Rights movement in the United States, plan a civil rights celebration. Work together to plan skits that present several episodes of the Civil Rights movement or to create a film series about civil rights issues and leaders.

PANEL DISCUSSION. Hold a panel discussion with an emcee and five panelists, each representing a point of view toward the boycott. As a group identify roles and develop questions.

Study and Research

COMPARISON-CONTRAST ESSAY. Martin Luther King Jr. was impressed by the teachings of Henry David Thoreau and Mahatma Gandhi on nonviolent resistance. Research one of these men and write a report making comparisons and noting contrasts between the writings and teachings of Thoreau or Gandhi and King.

Media Literacy

MEDIA SEARCH. The Civil Rights movement has been ongoing since the time of Martin Luther King Jr. For example, Coretta Scott King works with the Martin Luther King Jr. Center for Nonviolent Social Change, and Jesse Jackson continually pursues social reform. Research current media—newspapers, radio, television, periodicals, the Internet, etc.—to find modern examples of civil rights activities. Then videotape a civil rights update to show to other classes.

PREREADING

"THE MAN WHO MISTOOK HIS WIFE FOR A HAT"
by Oliver Sacks

Reader's resource

SCIENCE CONNECTION. Neurology is the scientific study of the brain and the rest of the nervous system of the body. Neurologists like Dr. Sacks are experts in how the brain is structured, how it works, and how it sometimes goes wrong.

Agnosia is the loss of ability to recognize familiar objects, sounds, or smells. It is usually caused by brain damage. Although the senses of a person with agnosia work properly, his or her brain is unable to make a judgment about sensory information. Dr. P., the patient discussed in this selection, has visual agnosia, or the inability to recognize objects by sight. There is nothing wrong with his eyes, but his brain cannot make sense of what he sees. As a result, Dr. P. loses his ability to see objects as a whole. He is like a computer, which may be able to recognize patterns or abstract shapes, and can pick out certain details, but cannot make sense of a scene or even recognize a face. Dr. P. deals with his illness by making guesses about the world around him, sometimes with comical results, such as when he guesses that his wife's head must be his hat.

About the AUTHOR

Oliver Sacks was born in London and educated in London, Oxford, California, and New York. He is a professor of clinical neurology at the Albert Einstein College of Medicine and has written many books about working with neurological patients. Other than *The Man Who Mistook His Wife for a Hat,* the book from which this essay was taken, Sacks has written *Migraine* (1970), *Awakenings* (1974, revised edition 1987), *A Leg to Stand On* (1984), *Seeing Voices: A Journey into the World of the Deaf* (1989), and *An Anthropologist on Mars* (1995). *Awakenings* was made into a movie starring Robin Williams and Robert DeNiro.

Reader's Journal

What things do you find most amazing about the human brain?

Literary TOOLS

NARRATIVE WRITING AND CHRONOLOGICAL ORDER. Narrative writing is a type of nonfiction writing that aims to make a point by sharing a story about an event. Examples of narrative writing include a biography or a family history. **Chronological order** is the arrangement of details in order of their occurrence. It is the primary method of organization used in narrative writing. It is also common in nonfiction writing that describes processes, events, and cause-and-effect relationships. As you read this narrative, use the graphic organizer below to list the most important occurrences.

DIALOGUE. Dialogue is conversation involving two or more people or characters. In this selection, Oliver Sacks includes dialogue spoken by himself and his patient, Dr. P., as well as Dr. P.'s wife. Locate examples of dialogue in the selection.

Graphic Organizer

Make a chart like the one below. On the left side of the chart, list the important occurrences. On the right side, list what each occurrence reveals about Dr. P.'s illness. One example has been done for you.

OCCURRENCES IN THE CASE OF DR. P.	WHAT THEY REVEAL
Dr. P. fails to recognize some of his students until they speak, and he sees faces where there are none.	Something might be wrong with Dr. P.'s vision.

ADDITIONAL RESOURCES

UNIT 5 RESOURCE BOOK
- Selection Worksheet 5.4
- Selection Check Test 4.5.9
- Selection Test 4.5.10
- Language, Grammar, and Style Resource 3.44

GRAPHIC ORGANIZER

Responses will vary. Dr. P.'s ophthalmologist finds nothing wrong with his eyes—something is wrong with his brain. Dr. P. confuses his foot and his shoe—Dr. P. might be joking, crazy, or blind. Dr. P. fails to understand a picture of the Sahara Desert—Dr. P. does not see the whole, only details. Dr. P. mistakes his wife's head for his hat—Dr. P. often makes visual misjudgments, so often that his wife is used to it. Dr. P. sings the *Dichterliebe*—nothing is wrong with the musical parts of his brain. Dr. P. identifies Platonic solids—Dr. P. has no difficulty with abstract shapes. Dr. P. identifies playing cards—stylized designs are easy for Dr. P. to recognize. Dr. P. fails to understand scenes of movie—Dr. P. cannot recognize facial expressions or gender. Dr. P. fails to recognize photos of people he knows—unless someone has an obvious characteristic, Dr. P. cannot recognize him or her; he is blind to the outward appearance of people. Dr. P. describes, but cannot recognize, a rose and a glove—Dr. P. sees only lifeless abstractions, not familiar objects. Dr. P. describes a square in his town—Dr. P. cannot see or visualize things on the left side of his visual field. Dr. P. recalls novel *Anna Karenina*—visual descriptions lack meaning for him. Dr. P. stops eating when interrupted by a knock at the door and resumes when smelling coffee—Dr. P. uses music to perform everyday activities; also, he does recognize smells. Dr. Sacks views Dr. P.'s art—Dr. P.'s ability to paint has been affected by his disease.

GOALS/OBJECTIVES

Studying this lesson will enable students to
- empathize with the speaker who is suffering from agnosia
- describe the literary accomplishments of Oliver Sacks
- define *narrative writing, chronological order,* and *dialogue* and identify and explain examples of each

that they encounter in their reading
- demonstrate the ability to use the pronouns *who* and *whom* correctly
- conduct a research on the structure of the human brain

READER'S JOURNAL

Why is the brain an important organ? Do you think it is more or less important than the heart? Why?

1. Dr. P. failed to see, or recognize, faces. He sometimes saw faces where there were none.
2. Something is the matter with the visual parts of his brain. He must visit a neurologist.

VOCABULARY FROM THE SELECTION

abstract	genially
acuity	incisive
aghast	indomitable
amiably	ingenious
apprehend	linear
celluloid	omit
cognition	pathology
collusion	peremptory
comply	placidly
confabulate	renounce
construe	schematic
convoluted	stylized
deficit	symmetry
degenerative	tenacity
diffidently	torrid
elicit	trifle
farcical	verbatim
forbear	
frivolous	

THE MAN WHO MISTOOK HIS WIFE FOR A HAT

Oliver Sacks

Dr. P. was a musician of distinction, well-known for many years as a singer, and then, at the local School of Music, as a teacher. It was here, in relation to his students, that certain strange problems were first observed. Sometimes a student would present himself, and Dr. P. would not recognise him; or, specifically, would not recognise his face. The moment the student spoke, he would be recognised by his voice. Such incidents multiplied, causing embarrassment, perplexity, fear—and, sometimes, comedy. For not only did Dr. P. increasingly fail to see faces, but he saw faces when there were no faces to see: genially, Magoo-like,[1] when in the street, he might pat the heads of water-hydrants and parking meters, taking these to be the heads of children; he would amiably address carved knobs on the furniture, and be astounded when they did not reply. At first these odd mistakes were laughed off as jokes, not least by Dr. P. himself. Had he not always had a quirky sense of humour, and been given to Zen-like paradoxes[2] and jests? His musical powers were as dazzling as ever; he did not feel ill—he had never felt better; and the mistakes were so ludicrous—and so ingenious—that they could hardly be serious or betoken anything serious. The notion of there being "something the matter" did not emerge until some three years later, when diabetes developed. Well aware that diabetes could affect his eyes, Dr. P. consulted an ophthalmologist, who took a careful history, and examined his eyes closely. "There's nothing the matter with your eyes," the doctor concluded. "But there is trouble with the visual parts of your brain. You don't need my help, you must see a

What did Dr. P. fail to see, or recognize? What did he sometimes mistakenly see?

What is the matter with Dr. P.? What kind of doctor must he visit?

---

1. **Magoo-like.** Mr. Magoo is a cartoon character often shown making silly mistakes because of his poor eyesight.
2. **given to Zen-like paradoxes.** Zen is a type of Buddhism native to Japan which emphasizes the use of intuition. Students of Zen learn to look at things from a different point of view. A paradox is something contradictory. Dr. P tended to say and do things that were different or contrary to expectation.

---

words for everyday use

ge • nial • ly (jēn'yə lē) *adv.*, in a friendly way. *We had heard that Parisians were unfriendly, but the people we met in Paris behaved quite genially.*

ami • a • bly (ām'yə blē) *adv.*, in a friendly way. *"Hello there, Mike!" Bill said amiably.*

in • ge • nious (in jēn'yəs) *adj.*, original. *"What an ingenious idea!" I exclaimed to the inventor.*

The Readymade Bouquet, 1957. René Magritte.

neurologist." And so, as a result of this referral, Dr. P. came to me.

It was obvious within a few seconds of meeting him that there was no trace of dementia[3] in the ordinary sense. He was a man of great cultivation and charm, who talked well and fluently, with imagination and humour. I couldn't think why he had been referred to our clinic.

And yet there *was* something a bit odd. He faced me as he spoke, was oriented towards me, and yet there was something the matter—it was difficult to formulate. He faced me with his *ears*, I came to think, but not with his eyes. These, instead of looking, gazing, at me, "taking me in," in the normal way, made sudden strange fixations—on my nose, on my right ear, down to my chin, up to my right eye—as if noting (even studying) these individual features, but not seeing my whole face, its changing expressions,

---

3. **dementia.** Insanity

"me," as a whole. I am not sure that I fully realised this at the time—there was just a teasing strangeness, some failure in the normal interplay of gaze and expression. He saw me, he *scanned* me, and yet…

"What seems to be the matter?" I asked him at length.

"Nothing that I know of," he replied with a smile, "but people seem to think there's something wrong with my eyes."

"But *you* don't recognise any visual problems?"

"No, not directly, but I occasionally make mistakes."

I left the room briefly, to talk to his wife. When I came back Dr. P. was sitting <u>placidly</u> by the window, attentive, listening rather than looking out. "Traffic," he said, "street sounds, distant trains—they make a sort of symphony, do they not? You know Honegger's *Pacific 234*?"[4]

What a lovely man, I thought to myself. How can there be anything seriously the matter? Would he permit me to examine him?

"Yes, of course, Dr. Sacks."

I stilled my disquiet, his perhaps too, in the soothing routine of a neurological exam—muscle strength, co-ordination, reflexes, tone… It was while examining his reflexes—a <u>trifle</u> abnormal on the left side—that the first bizarre experience occurred. I had taken off his left shoe and scratched the sole of his foot with a key—a <u>frivolous</u>-seeming but essential test of a reflex—and then, excusing myself to screw my ophthalmoscope together, left him to put on the shoe himself. To my surprise, a minute later, he had not done this.

"Can I help?" I asked.

"Help what? Help whom?"

"Help you put on your shoe."

"Ach," he said, "I had forgotten the shoe," adding, *sotto voce*,[5] "The shoe? The shoe?" He seemed baffled.

"Your shoe," I repeated. "Perhaps you'd put it on."

He continued to look downwards, though not at the shoe, with an intense but misplaced concentration. Finally his gaze settled on his foot: "That is my shoe, yes?"

Did I mis-hear? Did he mis-see?

"My eyes," he explained, and put a hand to his foot. "*This* is my shoe, no?"

"No, it is not. That is your foot. *There* is your shoe."

"Ah! I thought that was my foot."

Was he joking? Was he mad? Was he blind? If this was one of his "strange mistakes," it was the strangest mistake I had ever come across.

I helped him on with his shoe (his foot), to avoid further complication. Dr. P. himself seemed untroubled, indifferent, maybe amused. I resumed my examination. His visual <u>acuity</u> was good: he had no difficulty seeing a pin on the floor, though sometimes he missed it if it was placed to his left.

He saw all right, but what did he see? I opened out a copy of the *National Geographic Magazine*, and asked him to describe some pictures in it.

His responses here were very curious. His eyes would dart from one thing to another, picking up tiny features, individual features, as they had done with my face. A striking brightness, a colour, a shape would arrest his attention and <u>elicit</u> comment—but in no case

What "strange mistake" does Dr. P. make when asked to put on his shoe?

---

4. **Honegger's *Pacific 234*.** Symphony, or piece of music, written by French composer Arthur Honegger (1892–1955)
5. *sotto voce.* Under his breath

<table>
<tr><td rowspan="5">**words for everyday use**</td><td>**plac • id • ly** (plaˈsəd lē) *adv.,* in a calm way. *Unlike most audiences, who erupted into cheers and wild applause, this audience sat <u>placidly</u> waiting for the band's first song.*</td></tr>
<tr><td>**tri • fle** (trīˈfəl) *adv.,* to a small degree; slightly. *I was a <u>trifle</u> annoyed when the pizza arrived late, but I didn't complain.*</td></tr>
<tr><td>**friv • o • lous** (friˈvə ləs) *adj.,* having little importance. *Enough with the <u>frivolous</u> details—let's get down to the important business of the day.*</td></tr>
<tr><td>**a • cu • i • ty** (a kyüˈə tē) *n.,* sharpness. *They called him the Razor because of his remarkable mental <u>acuity</u>.*</td></tr>
<tr><td>**e • lic • it** (ē liˈsət) *vt.,* call forth or bring out. *The offensive statements <u>elicited</u> boos from the audience.*</td></tr>
</table>

did he get the scene-as-a-whole. He failed to see the whole, seeing only details, which he spotted like blips on a radar screen. He never entered into relation with the picture as a whole—never faced, so to speak, *its* physiognomy.[6] He had no sense whatever of a landscape or scene.

I showed him the cover, an unbroken expanse of Sahara dunes.

"What do you see here?" I asked.

"I see a river," he said. "And a little guest-house with its terrace on the water. People are dining out on the terrace. I see coloured parasols here and there." He was looking, if it was "looking," right off the cover, into mid-air and <u>confabulating</u> non-existent features, as if the absence of features in the actual picture had driven him to imagine the river and the terrace and the coloured parasols.

I must have looked <u>aghast</u>, but he seemed to think he had done rather well. There was a hint of a smile on his face. He also appeared to have decided

What does Dr. P. say he "sees" in the National Geographic picture? Is this really what the picture looks like? What strange thing does he do next?

that the examination was over, and started to look round for his hat. He reached out his hand, and took hold of his wife's head, tried to lift it off, to put it on. He had apparently mistaken his wife for a hat! His wife looked as if she was used to such things.

I could make no sense of what had occurred, in terms of conventional neurology (or neuropsychology). In some ways he seemed perfectly preserved, and in others absolutely, incomprehensibly devastated. How could he, on the one hand, mistake his wife for a hat and, on the other, function, as apparently he still did, as a teacher at the Music School?

I had to think, to see him again—and to see him in his own familiar habitat, at home.

A few days later I called on Dr. P. and his wife at home, with the score of the *Dichterliebe* in my briefcase (I knew he liked Schumann),[7] and a variety of odd objects for the testing of perception. Mrs. P. showed me into a lofty apartment, which recalled fin-de-siècle Berlin.[8] A magnificent old Bösendorfer[9] stood in state in the centre of the room, and all round it were music-stands, instruments, scores… There were books, there were paintings, but the music was central. Dr. P. came in and, distracted, advanced with outstretched hand to the grandfather clock, but, hearing my voice, corrected himself, and shook hands with me. We exchanged greetings, and chatted a little of current concerts and performances. <u>Diffidently</u>, I asked him if he would sing.

"The *Dichterliebe!*" he exclaimed. "But I can no longer read music. You will play them, yes?"

I said I would try. On that wonderful old piano even my playing sounded right, and Dr. P. was an aged, but infinitely mellow Fischer-Dieskau,[10] combining a perfect ear and voice with the most <u>incisive</u> musical intelligence. It was clear that the Music School was not keeping him on out of charity.

What remarkable intelligence and ability does Dr. P. show?

---

6. **physiognomy.** Outward appearance
7. ***Dichterliebe…Schumann.*** Symphony written by German composer Robert Schumann (1810–1856)
8. **fin-de-siècle Berlin.** The décor of the apartment reminds him of Berlin, the capital of Germany, at the end of the 19th century.
9. **Bösendorfer.** Austrian-made grand piano
10. **Fischer-Dieskau.** Dietrich Fischer-Dieskau (1925–) a famed German singer with a low, baritone voice

1. Dr. P. claims to see a river, a guest-house, and people dining under colored parasols. His description does not match the picture whatsoever. Next, Dr. P. takes hold of his wife's head, thinking it is his hat.
2. Dr. P. shows remarkable musical intelligence. He has the ability to sing beautifully.

CROSS-CURRICULAR ACTIVITIES

MUSIC. You may wish to bring in a tape of Honegger's *Pacific 234* and have students listen to it. Do they hear a similarity between the sound of the music and the sound of traffic on a city street? They may also enjoy listening to Schumann's *Dichterliebe*, which Dr. P. so enjoyed singing.

CROSS-CURRICULAR
ACTIVITIES

GEOMETRY. Students can look up
the different Platonic solids
using an encyclopedia or
geometry book from the
library. What is a dodecahedron? an eikosihedron? What are the
names of the other solids?

Dr. P.'s temporal lobes were obviously intact:
he had a wonderful musical cortex.[11] What, I
wondered, was going on in his parietal and
occipital lobes,[12] especially in those areas where
visual processing occurred? I carry the Platonic
solids[13] in my neurological kit, and decided to
start with these.

"What is this?" I asked, drawing out the
first one.

"A cube, of course."

"Now this?" I asked, brandishing another.

He asked if he might examine it, which he
did swiftly and systematically: "A
dodecahedron, of course. And don't bother with
the others—I'll get the eikosihedron too."

<u>Abstract</u> shapes clearly presented no problems.
What about faces? I took out a pack of cards. All
of these he identified instantly, including the jacks,
queens, kings, and the joker. But these, after all,
are <u>stylized</u> designs, and it was impossible to tell
whether he saw faces or merely patterns. I
decided I would show him a
volume of cartoons which I
had in my briefcase. Here,
again, for the most part, he
did well. Churchill's cigar, Schnozzle's nose: as
soon as he had picked out a key feature he could
identify the face. But cartoons, again, are formal
and <u>schematic</u>. It remained to be seen how he
would do with real faces, realistically represented.

I turned on the television, keeping the sound
off, and found an early Bette Davis film. A love
scene was in progress. Dr. P. failed to identify
the actress—but this could have been because
she had never entered his world. What was
more striking was that he failed to identify the

*How does Dr. P. respond
to abstract shapes and
schematic drawings?*

expressions on her face or her partner's, though
in the course of a single <u>torrid</u> scene these
passed from sultry yearning through passion,
surprise, disgust and fury to a melting
reconciliation. Dr. P. could make nothing of
any of this. He was very unclear as to what was
going on, or who was who or even what sex
they were. His comments on the scene were
positively Martian.

It was just possible that some of his
difficulties were associated with the unreality of
a <u>celluloid</u>, Hollywood world; and it occurred
to me that he might be more successful in
identifying faces from his own life. On the walls
of the apartment there were photographs of his
family, his colleagues, his pupils, himself. I
gathered a pile of these together and, with
some misgivings, presented them to him. What
had been funny, or <u>farcical</u>, in relation to the
movie, was tragic in relation to real life. By and
large, he recognised nobody: neither his family,
nor his colleagues, nor his pupils, nor himself.
He recognised a portrait of Einstein, because
he picked up the characteristic hair and
moustache; and the same thing happened with
one or two other people. "Ach, Paul!" he said,
when shown a portrait of his brother. "That
square jaw, those big teeth, I would know Paul
anywhere!" But was it Paul he recognised, or
one or two of his features, on the basis of which
he could make a reasonable guess as to the
subject's identity? In the absence of obvious

---

11. **temporal lobes...musical cortex.** The musical areas of Dr.
P.'s brain were not damaged.
12. **parietal and occipital lobes.** The parietal lobes, located in
the central part of the brain, deal with bodily sensation; the occipital lobes, located in the back of the brain, contain the visual areas.
13. **Platonic solids.** Solid three-dimensional geometric shapes

---

**words
for
everyday
use**

ab • stract (ab′strakt) *adj.*, having only a simple form and not representing a picture or narrative content. *Thuy did not
like the <u>abstract</u> paintings, which just showed shapes and lines of color.*

styl • ized (stī′līzd) *adj.*, not realistic; conforming to a set pattern or design. *The company logo was a <u>stylized</u> sun: a yellow
circle with six lines that represented rays.*

sche • mat • ic (ski ma′ tik) *adj.*, following a set scheme or design. *The traveling speaker became bored quickly because her presentations were so <u>schematic</u>: the entire speech had to be said word-for-word.*

tor • rid (tôr′əd) *adj.*, hot; passionate. *Mom let me watch the rated R movie but covered my eyes when the <u>torrid</u> love scenes came on.*

cel • lu • loid (sel′yə loid) *adj.*, having to do with the movies or with celluloid, a tough plastic used for filmstrips. *The
actor's <u>celluloid</u> adventures were well known to all moviegoers.*

far • ci • cal (fär′ si kəl) *adj.*, resembling farce; laughably absurd. *The <u>farcical</u> behavior of the clowns made the children laugh.*

"markers," he was utterly lost. But it was not merely the cognition, the *gnosis*,[14] at fault; there was something radically wrong with the whole way he proceeded. For he approached these faces—even of those near and dear—as if they were abstract puzzles or tests. He did not relate to them, he did not behold. No face was familiar to him, seen as a "thou",[15] being just identified as a set of features, an "it." Thus there was formal, but no trace of personal, gnosis. And with this went his indifference, or blindness, to expression. A face, to us, is a person looking out—we see, as it were, the person through his *persona*, his face. But for Dr. P. there was no *persona* in this sense—no outward *persona*, and no person within.

> What is not familiar to Dr. P.? To what is Dr. P. blind?

I had stopped at a florist on my way to his apartment and bought myself an extravagant red rose for my buttonhole. Now I removed this and handed it to him. He took it like a botanist or morphologist[16] given a specimen, not like a person given a flower.

"About six inches in length," he commented. "A convoluted red form with a linear green attachment."

"Yes," I said encouragingly, "and what do you think it *is*, Dr. P. ?"

"Not easy to say." He seemed perplexed. "It lacks the simple symmetry of the Platonic solids, although it may have a higher symmetry of its own… I think this could be an inflorescence or flower."

"Could be?" I queried.

"Could be," he confirmed.

"Smell it," I suggested, and he again looked somewhat puzzled, as if I had asked him to smell a higher symmetry. But he complied courteously, and took it to his nose. Now, suddenly, he came to life.

"Beautiful!" he exclaimed. "An early rose. What a heavenly smell!" He started to hum "Die Rose, die Lillie…" Reality, it seemed, might be conveyed by smell, not by sight.

I tried one final test. It was still a cold day, in early spring, and I had thrown my coat and gloves on the sofa.

"What is this?" I asked, holding up a glove.

"May I examine it?" he asked, and, taking it from me, he proceeded to examine it as he had examined the geometrical shapes.

"A continuous surface," he announced at last, "infolded on itself. It appears to have"—he hesitated—"five outpouchings, if this is the word."

> How does Dr. P. describe the glove Dr. Sacks gives him? What does he think it is?

"Yes," I said cautiously. "You have given me a description. Now tell me what it is."

"A container of some sort?"

"Yes," I said, "and what would it contain?"

"It would contain its contents!" said Dr. P., with a laugh. "There are many possibilities. It could be a change-purse, for example, for coins of five sizes. It could…"

I interrupted the barmy[17] flow. "Does it not look familiar? Do you think it might contain, might fit, a part of your body?"

No light of recognition dawned on his face.

---

14. *gnosis.* Knowledge of truth
15. **"thou."** "You"
16. **botanist or morphologist.** Botanist—one who studies plants; morphologist—biologist who studies the form and structure of animals and plants
17. **barmy.** Full of froth; lacking substance

---

words for everyday use

cog • ni • tion (käg ni´shən) *n.*, knowing; having awareness and judgment. *Our brains provide us with cognition, while our bodies allow us to act on what we know.*

con • vo • lu • ted (kän´və lū´təd) *adj.*, having twists and coils; intricate or involved. *The professor's lecture was so convoluted that the students all became lost among its twists and turns.*

lin • e • ar (li´nē ər) *adj.*, in the form of a line. *The shortest distance between two points is a linear path.*

sym • me • try (si´mə trē) *n.*, quality of being equal on both sides of an imaginary center line. *The isosceles triangle has perfect symmetry; being exactly the same on either side.*

com • ply (kəm plī´) *vi.*, follow another's wishes or obey a rule. *The little boy was very obedient and complied when told to brush his teeth.*

1. Faces are not familiar to Dr. P., even the faces of loved ones. He is blind to facial expressions.
2. Dr. P. describes the glove as "a continuous surface infolded on itself," with "five outpouchings." He thinks it is a container that could hold coins.

BIBLIOGRAPHIC NOTE

Students may be interested in reading some of Oliver Sacks's other books about his work with patients. The books are listed in About the Author. They include: *Migraine* (1970), *Awakenings* (1974, revised edition 1987), *A Leg to Stand On* (1984), *Seeing Voices: A Journey into the World of the Deaf* (1989), and *An Anthropologist on Mars* (1995).

1. He has most difficulty with his left
   side.

No child would have the power to see and speak of "a continuous surface...infolded on itself," but any child, any infant, would immediately know a glove as a glove, see it as familiar, as going with a hand. Dr. P. didn't. He saw nothing as familiar. Visually, he was lost in a world of lifeless abstractions. Indeed he did not have a real visual world, as he did not have a real visual self. He could speak about things, but did not see them face-to-face. Hughlings Jackson, discussing patients with aphasia and left-hemisphere lesions,[18] says they have lost "abstract" and "propositional" thought[19]—and compares them with dogs (or, rather, he compares dogs to patients with aphasia). Dr. P., on the other hand, functioned precisely as a machine functions. It wasn't merely that he displayed the same indifference to the visual word as a computer but—even more strikingly—he construed the world as a computer construes it, by means of key features and schematic relationships. The scheme might be identified—in an "identiti-kit" way—without the reality being grasped at all.

The testing I had done so far told me nothing about Dr. P.'s inner world. Was it possible that his visual memory and imagination were still intact? I asked him to imagine entering one of our local squares from the north side, to walk through it, in imagination or in memory, and tell me the buildings he might pass as he walked. He listed the buildings on his right side, but none of those on his left. I then asked him to imagine entering the square from the south. Again he mentioned only those buildings that were on the right side, although these were the very buildings he had omitted before. Those he had "seen" internally before were not mentioned now; presumably, they were no longer "seen." It was evident that his difficulties with leftness, his visual field deficits, were as much internal as external, bisecting his visual memory and imagination.

What side of Dr. P.'s visual field does he seem to have the most difficulties with?

What, at a higher level, of his internal visualisation? Thinking of the almost hallucinatory intensity with which Tolstoy visualises and animates his characters, I questioned Dr. P. about *Anna Karenina*.[20] He could remember incidents without difficulty, had an undiminished grasp of the plot, completely omitted visual characteristics, visual narrative or scenes. He remembered the words of the characters, but not their faces; and though, when asked, he could quote, with his remarkable and almost verbatim memory, the original visual descriptions, these were, it became apparent, quite empty for him, and lacked sensorial, imaginal, or emotional reality. Thus there was an internal agnosia as well.

But this was only the case, it became clear, with certain sorts of visualisation. The visualisation of faces and scenes, of visual narrative and drama—this was profoundly impaired, almost absent. But the visualisation of *schemata*[21] was preserved, perhaps enhanced. Thus when I engaged him in a game of mental chess, he had no difficulty visualising the chessboard or the moves—indeed, no difficulty in beating me soundly.

---

18. **aphasia...lesions.** Aphasia—loss of ability to understand words and language; left-hemisphere lesions—lesions, or injuries, in the left side of the brain
19. **"abstract" and "propositional" thought.** These patients have lost the ability to think about ideas in the abstract or about things that might happen; they can only think about objects that are right in front of them or things that are happening right now. Like dogs, they live simply, and they live in the moment.
20. *Anna Karenina.* Famous novel by Russian author Leo Tolstoy
21. *schemata.* Schemes, set patterns

words for everyday use

con • strue (kən strü′) *vt.*, understand or explain the meaning of something using the circumstances or evidence. *Given the context clues in the sentence, which had to do with sea life, I was able to construe the meaning of the word conch.*

o • mit (ō mit′) *vt.*, leave out. *Gwen was hurt when I accidentally omitted her name from the guest list.*

de • fi • cit (de′fə sit) *n.*, lack of ability; disadvantage. *The basketball team overcame a 20-point deficit to win the game.*

ver • ba • tim (vər bā′təm) *adj.*, word for word. *I repeated the conversation verbatim.*

Luria said of Zazetsky[22] that he had entirely lost his capacity to play games but that his "vivid imagination" was unimpaired. Zazetsky and Dr. P. lived in worlds which were mirror images of each other. But the saddest difference between them was that Zazetsky, as Luria said, "fought to regain his lost faculties with the <u>indomitable</u> <u>tenacity</u> of the damned," whereas Dr. P. was not fighting, did not know what was lost, did not indeed know that anything was lost. But who was more tragic, or who was more damned—the man who knew it, or the man who did not?

When the examination was over, Mrs. P. called us to the table, where there was coffee and a delicious spread of little cakes. Hungrily, hummingly, Dr. P. started on the cakes. Swiftly, fluently, unthinkingly, melodiously, he pulled the plates towards him, and took this and that, in a great gurgling stream, an edible song of food, until, suddenly, there came an interruption: a loud, <u>peremptory</u> rat-tat-tat at the door. Startled, taken aback, arrested, by the interruption, Dr. P. stopped eating, and sat frozen, motionless, at the table, with an indifferent, blind, bewilderment on his face. He saw, but no longer saw, the table; no longer perceived it as a table laden with cakes. His wife poured him some coffee: the smell titillated his nose, and brought him back to reality. The melody of eating resumed.

What happens to Dr. P.'s enjoyment of lunch when there is a knock at the door? What snaps him back to reality?

How does he do anything, I wondered to myself? What happens when he's dressing, goes to the lavatory, has a bath? I followed his wife into the kitchen and asked her how, for instance, he managed to dress himself. "It's just like the eating," she explained. "I put his usual clothes out,

in all the usual places, and he dresses without difficulty, singing to himself. He does everything singing to himself. But if he is interrupted and loses the thread, he comes to a complete stop, doesn't know his clothes—or his own body. He sings all the time—eating songs, dressing songs, bathing songs, everything. He can't do anything unless he makes it a song."

While we were talking my attention was caught by the pictures on the walls.

"Yes," Mrs. P. said, "he was a gifted painter as well as a singer. The School exhibited his pictures every year."

I strolled past them curiously—they were in chronological order. All his earlier work was naturalistic and realistic, with vivid mood and atmosphere, but finely detailed and concrete. Then, years later, they became less vivid, less concrete, less realistic and naturalistic; but far more abstract, even geometrical and cubist.[23] Finally, in the last paintings, the canvasses became nonsense, or nonsense to me—mere chaotic lines and blotches of paint. I commented on this to Mrs. P.

What does Dr. Sacks think about Dr. P.'s final paintings? What does he think caused the change in Dr. P.'s artistic style?

"Ach, you doctors, you're such philistines!"[24] she exclaimed, "Can you not see *artistic development*—how he <u>renounced</u> the realism of his earlier years, and advanced into abstract, non-representational art?"

---

22. **Luria...Zazetsky.** The author is quoting Alexander Romanovich Luria (1902–1977), a Russian neuropsychologist, (psychologist who deals with neurology). Zazetsky was one of his patients.
23. **cubist.** In an abstract style, not meant to be realistic; such as some of the works of Spanish artist Pablo Picasso (1881–1973)
24. **philistines.** People who cannot understand artistic values; ignorant people

---

words for everyday use

in • dom • i • ta • ble (in dä′mə tə bəl) *adj.*, not defeatable. *Superman is* <u>indomitable</u> *except if kryptonite is used against him.*
te • na • ci • ty (tə na′sə tē) *n.*, courage; quality of not giving up. *At first the principal said no, but after seeing the* <u>tenacity</u> *of the students, he agreed to change the policy.*
per • emp • to • ry (pə remp′tə rē) *adj.*, urgent; commanding. *The general barked a* <u>peremptory</u> *order for troops to move forward.*
re • nounce (ri nouns′) *vt.*, give up or leave behind. *The vegetarian* <u>renounced</u> *eating meat.*

ANSWERS TO GUIDED READING QUESTIONS

1. When there is a knock at the door, Dr. P. becomes bewildered and frozen, forgetting what he is doing. The smell of the coffee reminds him that he is eating.
2. Dr. Sacks thinks that the final paintings are chaotic nonsense. He thinks Dr. P.'s disease caused the change.

CROSS-CURRICULAR ACTIVITIES

VISUAL ARTS. Show students slides or pictures of "realistic" works by painters such as Jan Vermeer, Adolphe-William Bouguereau, Rembrandt van Riijn, and Mary Cassatt. Then show them cubist, non-naturalistic works by Picasso, and finally abstract works such as those of Sam Francis and Jackson Pollock. Ask them what they like and don't like about each style of painting.

LITERARY NOTE

On the subject of brains and computers, Dr. Sacks writes in a postscript to this chapter: "Of course, the brain *is* a machine and a computer... But our mental processes, which constitute our being and life, are not just abstract and mechanical, but personal, as well—and, as such, involve not just classifying and categorizing, but continual judging and feeling also. If this is missing, we become computer-like, as Dr. P. was."

ANSWER TO GUIDED READING QUESTION

1. Dr. Sacks prescribes a life, that consists entirely of music.

SELECTION CHECK TEST 4.5.9 WITH ANSWERS

Checking Your Reading

1. What illness or sickness does Dr. P. have? **Dr. P has agnosia.**
2. What is this illness? **Agnosia is the loss of ability to recognize familiar objects, sounds, or smells.**
3. How does Dr. P. identify the glove Dr. Sacks gives him? **He identifies it as a container of some sort— possibly a change-purse.**
4. What kind of shapes presented no problem for Dr. P.? **Abstract shapes were not a problem for Dr. P.**
5. What does Dr. P. do in order to eat or dress himself? **He sings; he does everything singing to himself.**

Vocabulary in Context

Fill in each blank below with the most appropriate word from the Words for Everyday Use. You may have to change the tense of the word.

confabulated	placid	aghast
genially	diffidently	acuity

1. My kind grandpa behaves **genially** toward everybody, even strangers.
2. The **placid** lake was disturbed when the little kids jumped into it.
3. I couldn't remember what I did last night, so I **confabulated** a little bit.
4. Rinna was **aghast** when she heard that her dog ran away.
5. The little girl **diffidently** asked her babysitter for a piece of candy, knowing she probably would say no.

Literary Tools

Fill in the blank using the following terms.

chronological order	narrative writing
dialogue	irony

1. Nonfiction writing that is told in the form of a story is called **narrative writing**.
2. **Dialogue** occurs when two or more people converse with each other.
3. **Chronological order** is the arrangement of details in the order of their occurrence.

"No, that's not it," I said to myself (but <u>forbore</u> to say it to poor Mrs. P.). He had indeed moved from realism to non-representation to the abstract, but this was not the artist, but the <u>pathology</u>, advancing—advancing towards a profound visual agnosia, in which all powers of representation imagery, all sense of the concrete, all sense of reality, were being destroyed. This wall of paintings was a tragic pathological exhibit, which belonged to neurology, not art.

And yet, I wondered, was she not partly right? For there is often a struggle, and sometimes, even more interestingly, a <u>collusion</u> between the powers of pathology and creation. Perhaps, in his cubist period, there might have been both artistic and pathological development, colluding to engender an original form; for as he lost the concrete, so he might have gained in the abstract, developing a greater sensitivity to all the structural elements of line, boundary, contour— an almost Picasso-like power to see, and equally depict, those abstract organisations embedded in, and normally lost in, the concrete… Though in the final pictures, I feared, there was only chaos and agnosia.

We returned to the great music-room, with the Bösendorfer in the centre, and Dr. P. humming the last torte.

"Well, Dr. Sacks," he said to me. "You find me an interesting case, I perceive. Can you tell me what you find wrong, make recommendations?"

"I can't tell you what I find wrong," I replied, "but I'll say what I find right. You are a wonderful musician, and music is your life. What I would prescribe, in a case such as yours, is a life which consists entirely of music. Music has been the centre, now make it the whole, of your life."

What does Dr. Sacks prescribe for Dr. P.?

This was four years ago—I never saw him again, but I often wondered how he <u>apprehended</u> the world, given his strange loss of image, visuality, and the perfect preservation of a great musicality. I think that music, for him, had taken the place of image. He had no body-image, he had body-music: this is why he could move and act as fluently as he did, but came to a total confused stop if the "inner music" stopped. And equally with the outside, the world…

In *The World as Representation and Will* Schopenhauer[25] speaks of music as "pure will." How fascinated he would have been by Dr. P., a man who had wholly lost the world as representation, but wholly preserved it as music or will.

And this, mercifully, held to the end—for despite the gradual advance of his disease (a massive tumour or <u>degenerative</u> process in the visual parts of his brain) Dr. P. lived and taught music to the last days of his life. ∎

---

25. **Schopenhauer.** Arthur Schopenhauer (1788–1860), German philosopher

words for everyday use

for • bear (fôr bar') v., hold back from, abstain. *We ask that you <u>forbear</u> going out with your friends until your grades improve.*

pa • tho • lo • gy (pa thä' lə jē) n., abnormality caused by disease. *Compulsive lying is sometimes caused by a <u>pathology</u>: hence the term "pathological liar."*

col • lu • sion (kə lü' zhən) n., secret cooperation; conspiracy. *I became nervous because my friends were whispering so much, but then I found the reason for their <u>collusion</u> was a surprise party for me!*

ap • pre • hend (a' pri hend') v., grasp; understand. *Doug found it difficult to <u>apprehend</u> Carmen's point of view.*

de • gen • er • a • tive (di je' nə rə tiv) adj., something that degenerates, or destroys. *Alzheimer's is a <u>degenerative</u> disease that affects memory.*

Respond *to the* SELECTION

Which do you think is more tragic: someone who has lost the ability to perceive the world and knows it, or someone like Dr. P., who is unaware of what he or she is missing?

RESPOND TO THE SELECTION

Do you agree with the saying, "Ignorance is bliss"? Why, or why not? Do you think this saying applies to Dr. P.? Explain.

Investigate, Inquire, and Imagine

Recall: GATHERING FACTS

1a. Who is Dr. P.? Why does he need to see a neurologist? What unexpected mistakes does Dr. P. make on his first office visit?

2a. How does Dr. P. respond when shown solid geometrical shapes, playing cards, and cartoons? How does he respond when viewing a scene from a film and when shown photos? How does he respond when shown a rose and a glove?

3a. What does Dr. Sacks notice about Dr. P.'s paintings?

→ Interpret: FINDING MEANING

1b. Why do both Dr. Sacks and Dr. P. himself at first think nothing could be really wrong with Dr. P.? Why can't Dr. P. accurately describe the landscape in the *National Geographic* photo? Why do you think Dr. P. invents details in the photo?

2b. What do Dr. P.'s responses reveal about his ability to make sense of the visual world? What lack of ability does Dr. Sacks think is tragic, and why?

3b. What does Dr. Sacks think the paintings reveal? Why do you think Dr. P.'s wife disagrees with Dr. Sacks so strongly?

Analyze: TAKING THINGS APART

4a. List the tests Dr. Sacks performs on Dr. P. Which tests are easy for Dr. P., and why? Which tests are difficult or impossible for him to perform, and why?

→ Synthesize: BRINGING THINGS TOGETHER

4b. How is Dr. P. like a computer?

Evaluate: MAKING JUDGMENTS

5a. Evaluate the way Dr. P. has been able to function in life despite his disability. How well has he been able to adapt? Do you think Dr. Sacks's prescription is a good one for Dr. P.? Why, or why not?

→ Extend: CONNECTING IDEAS

5b. If you had agnosia, what things would you rely on to help you function in life and remain happy? Consider both physical and mental disabilities.

Understanding Literature

NARRATIVE WRITING AND CHRONOLOGICAL ORDER. Review the definitions for **narrative writing** and **chronological order** in the Handbook of Literary Terms. Why do you think it was important for Dr. Sacks to write his narrative in chronological order? What point do you think Oliver Sacks may have been making by writing about his patient Dr. P.? Was he making a point at all? Explain.

DIALOGUE. Review the definition for **dialogue** in Literary Tools in Prereading. In this selection, Oliver Sacks includes dialogue spoken by himself and his patient, Dr. P., as well as Dr. P.'s wife. What does the dialogue in the narrative reveal about Dr. P.? Why do you think the author chose to include dialogue rather than just summarize the conversations?

"THE MAN WHO MISTOOK HIS WIFE FOR A HAT" **415**

ANSWERS TO INVESTIGATE, INQUIRE, AND IMAGINE (CONT.)

EVALUATE
5a. *Responses will vary.* He is able to function in everyday life by singing his way through different tasks. He has adjusted well considering the seriousness of his disease. Students may say that Dr. Sacks's prescription fits Dr. P. very well. Dr. Sacks realizes that his "inner music" enables him to function. This is why he prescribes for Dr. P. "a life which consists entirely of music."

EXTEND
5b. *Responses will vary.*

Answers to Understanding Literature can be found on page 416.

RECALL
1a. Dr. P. is a gifted musician, singer, and music teacher. He needs to see a neurologist because he has lost the ability to recognize faces. Dr. P. confuses his foot with his shoe, describes a picture of the desert as showing a river and a guest-house and mistakes his wife's head for his hat.

2a. Dr. P. is able to identify these things. However, he is unable to understand what is happening in a film or recognize faces in photographs. He is able to pick out the features of a rose and a glove, but he does not have any idea what the objects are.

3a. He notices that the first paintings are realistic, but his paintings become more and more abstract.

INTERPRET
1b. Because Dr. P. speaks so fluently and demonstrates intelligence, Dr. Sacks thinks that nothing is wrong with his brain. Dr. P. thinks nothing is really wrong because his mistakes are so bizarre, and after all, he always has had a strange sense of humor. Dr. P. can't describe the scene accurately because he lacks the ability to process visual information. *Responses will vary.*

2b. Dr. P. can interpret abstract images but not complex images such as faces and facial expressions. He can see details, but not an image or object as a whole. Dr. Sacks thinks Dr. P.'s inability to recognize family and friends is tragic.

3b. Dr. Sacks thinks the paintings reveal the worsening of Dr. P.'s disease. *Responses will vary.*

ANALYZE
4a. Dr. Sacks performs many tests. Singing, identifying geometric shapes, playing cards, cartoon faces, and playing chess are easy for Dr. P. This is because he has no trouble with schematic, or abstract, forms and shapes. However, Dr. P. cannot describe a picture in *National Geographic,* make sense of a scene from a movie, or recognize photos of family and friends. This is because he cannot perceive a scene or an image as a whole: he can only pick out details.

SYNTHESIZE
4b. Dr. P. is like a computer in that he lacks common sense. Instead, he scans images for key features and set schemes or designs, just as a computer might.

TEACHER'S EDITION **415**

ANSWERS TO UNDERSTANDING LITERATURE

NARRATIVE WRITING AND CHRONOLOGICAL ORDER. It was important for the author to write in chronological order because as a doctor, he learned from each occurrence as it happened and acted accordingly. Therefore, the reader should learn from each occurrence as it really happened. Students may say that the author was making the point that when the brain is damaged, it can make up for the disability by becoming strong in other areas; in other words, humans are remarkably adaptable. He may also have been making the point that when dealing with patients, it is important to focus on what is *right* with the person, and not just what is wrong.

DIALOGUE. The dialogue reveals that Dr. P. has a German accent; he is light-hearted and yet thoughtful; he is also confident and upbeat. The author probably chose to include dialogue to give the reader a sense of his patient's personality.

ANSWERS TO INTEGRATING THE LANGUAGE ARTS

Language, Grammar, and Style
1. Who
2. who
3. whom
4. Who
5. whom

Collaborative Learning
Remind students not to use any hand gestures that might give away what the object is used for.

Writer's Journal

1. Close your eyes and imagine you are walking through a part of your house or through a familiar part of your city or town. Then, make a **list** of what you "see" on either side of you as you walk through this area. Note only things that you would *always* see, such as buildings or furniture, not transitory things such as people or cars.

2. Choose a familiar, ordinary object, and write a **description** of it as if you have never seen it before, using technical terms.

3. Imagine you are Dr. Sacks and you have just finished your first visit with Dr. P. Write **clinical notes** for the patient's file, describing your findings. You need not write in complete sentences, and you may use abbreviations as you would do in notes for class.

Integrating the Language Arts

Language, Grammar, and Style

DETERMINING WHO VS. WHOM. Review the Language Arts Survey 3.44, "Using *Who* and *Whom.*" Select the appropriate pronoun for each of the following sentences:

1. (Who/Whom) is Dr. Sacks's patient?
2. Dr. P., (who/whom) taught music for many years, no longer recognized his students.
3. The doctor (who/whom) Dr. Sacks quoted was Hughlings Jackson.
4. (Who/whom) wrote the novel *Anna Karenina*?
5. By (who/whom) were the paintings exhibited at the school?

Study and Research

RESEARCHING THE BRAIN. Research the structure of the human brain. You may consult resources in your library or on the Internet. Create a diagram of the brain, labeling its different lobes and areas, including the parietal and occipital lobes which are mentioned in the selection. Next, choose one of the five senses—sight, smell, taste, touch, or hearing. Research how the brain processes this type of sensory information. For example, what happens after you taste a sour pickle? How does the information about the pickle reach your brain, and what part of the brain receives the information? Prepare an oral report to be delivered to the class. Display your diagram of the brain during your presentation.

Collaborative Learning

IDENTIFYING OBJECTS. Divide the class into two teams and play a game that can help you understand the way Dr. P. "saw" objects. One student should think of and describe an everyday object as if the object were totally unfamiliar, just as Dr. P. described the rose and the glove given to him by Dr. Sacks. The teams must take turns guessing what the object is, based on the description of its features. The first team to give a correct answer wins one point.

"Ice and Light" from *Arctic Dreams*
by Barry Lopez

Reader's resource

Barry Lopez's **"Ice and Light"** is selected from his book of essays *Arctic Dreams: Imagination and Desire in a Northern Landscape* (1986), which won the National Book Award. In this work Lopez provides for our desire "not merely to know the sorts of things that are revealed in scientific papers but to know what is beautiful and edifying in a faraway place." According to Lopez, the natural world "retains an identity of its own, still deeper and more subtle than we can know. Our obligation toward it then becomes simple: to approach with an uncalculating mind, with an attitude of regard. . . . To intend from the beginning to preserve some of the mystery within it as a kind of wisdom to be experienced, not questioned. And to be alert for its openings, for that moment when something sacred reveals itself within the mundane, and you know the land knows you are there."

About the AUTHOR

Barry Lopez (1945–) has written *Of Wolves and Men* (1978), *Crow and Weasel* (1990), and the trilogy of story collections made up by *Desert Notes: Reflections in the Eye of a Raven* (1976), *River Notes: The Dance of Herons* (1979), and *Field Notes: The Grace Note of the Canyon Wren* (1994). He describes himself as "a writer who travels." His trips to Australia, Asia, Africa, and both the North and South Pole have provided a rich material for his books. Whether in the form of fiction or nonfiction, Lopez's work is intimately linked with natural history, a tradition he notes to be "as old as the history of coherent narrative" and speaking to "the fundamental issues of life." When not traveling, Lopez lives in the wilderness of Oregon.

Reader's Journal

What do you think about when looking at the night sky?

Literary TOOLS

NATURE WRITING. Nature writing is a genre of nonfiction concerned with the relationship between the human and the wild. It typically seeks to connect the reader with natural phenomena without recourse to personification or sentimentality, instead relying on the traditional tools of the literary essayist—style, form, and the allegiance to the significant and telling fact. Nature writing delights in both scientific precision and subjective description, seeking always to reveal the mysteries of nature without destroying them. As you read the selection, consider the ways in which nature writing is different from other forms of nonfiction you have read.

DESCRIPTION. Description is a type of writing that portrays a character, an object, or a scene. Descriptions make use of sensory details—words and phrases that describe how things look, sound, smell, taste, or feel. Effective descriptions contain precise nouns, verbs, adverbs, and adjectives. Descriptions often use imagery and figurative language. As you read, note the different kinds of descriptions Lopez uses.

Graphic Organizer

Make a cluster chart listing the visual descriptions Lopez uses in the first paragraph. One example has been done for you.

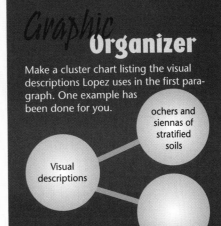

ochers and siennas of stratified soils

Visual descriptions

ADDITIONAL RESOURCES

UNIT 5 RESOURCE BOOK
- Selection Worksheet 5.5
- Selection Check Test 4.5.11
- Selection Test 4.5.12
- Language, Grammar, and Style Resource 3.87, 3.88
- Applied English Resource 6.5

GRAPHIC ORGANIZER

Students should list the following descriptions in their cluster charts:
- gray-greens of sparse plant life on bare soil
- greens, reds, yellows, and oranges of lichens
- whites of tundra swans and of sunlit ice in black water
- brilliant coloring of wildflowers and willow and bearberry
- iridescent colors of petroleum on a tundra puddle
- bright face of a king eider

READER'S JOURNAL

What is your favorite season? Explain.

GOALS/OBJECTIVES

Studying this lesson will enable students to
- enjoy and appreciate the natural world
- describe Barry Lopez's literary accomplishments and explain the significance of his writings
- define *nature writing* and *description* and recognize and explain examples of each in the selection
- demonstrate the ability to correctly use commas and semicolons
- conduct research on an aspect of nature
- write a letter of recommendation

INDIVIDUAL LEARNING STRATEGIES

MOTIVATION
Ask a science teacher to explain to your class how the northern lights are formed. What is the scientific and physiological explanation for this wondrous display of lights?

READING PROFICIENCY
This selection is filled with vivid imagery. Ask students to paint or draw a picture of a section they find especially vivid based on the descriptions Lopez uses.

ENGLISH LANGUAGE LEARNING
Some students may have trouble with the language and vocabulary. Have students get together with a partner to read through the vocabulary and footnotes and practice saying them aloud.

SPECIAL NEEDS
You may want to bring in several pictures of northern lights and sun dogs to give students a visual representation of what they are reading about.

ENRICHMENT
Ask students to observe some mysterious or wondrous aspect of nature. Then have them describe their encounter with that mysterious aspect including both the scientific explanation of it and the aesthetic and emotional effect it had on them.

VOCABULARY FROM THE SELECTION

abalone	pervasive
diaphanous	quiescent
evanescence	sienna
iridescent	subtend
ocher	tangible
penumbral	undulate

Ice and Light

from *Arctic Dreams*

Barry Lopez

At first it seems that, except for a brief few weeks in autumn, the Arctic is without color. Its land colors are the colors of deserts, the <u>ochers</u> and <u>siennas</u> of stratified soils, the gray-greens of sparse plant life on bare soil. On closer inspection, however, the monotonic rock of the polar desert is seen to harbor the myriad greens, reds, yellows, and oranges of lichens. The whites of tundra swans and of sunlit ice in black water are pure and elegant. Occasionally there is brilliant coloring—as with wildflowers in the summer, or a hillside of willow and bearberry in the fall; or a slick of vegetable oils shining with the <u>iridescent</u> colors of petroleum on a tundra puddle; or the bright face of a king eider.[1] But the bright colors are more often only points in a season, not brushstrokes; and they are absorbed in the paler casts of the landscape.

---

1. **king eider.** Large sea duck of the north

words for everyday use	**o • cher** (ō′ kər) *n.*, earthy, usually red or yellow and often impure iron ore used as a pigment. *The old barn had been painted with a mixture of <u>ocher</u>, lead, and mineral spirits.* **si • en • na** (sē e′ nə) *n.*, earthy substance containing oxides of iron and usually of manganese that is brownish-yellow when raw and orange-red or reddish-brown when burnt and is used as a pigment. *Because many of the children found the <u>sienna</u>-colored crayon to be ugly, they did not use it.* **ir • i • des • cent** (ir ə de′ sənt) *adj.*, having or exhibiting a play of colors producing rainbow effects. *Bob was fascinated by the <u>iridescent</u> soap bubbles floating on top of the bath water.*

Arresting color in the Arctic is found more often in the sky, with its vivid twilights and the aurora borealis. (The predominant colors of the aurora are a pale green and a soft rose. I turned over a weathered caribou antler once on the tundra and found these same two colors staining its white surface. Such correspondence, like that between a surfacing guillemot[2] and an Eskimo man rolling upright in his kayak, hold a landscape together.)

Where are the most vivid colors found in the Arctic?

Arctic skies retain the colors of dawn and dusk for hours in winter. On days when the southern sky is barely lit for a while around noon, layers of deep violet, of bruised purples and dense blues, may stretch across 80° of the horizon, above a familiar lavender and the thinnest line of yellow gold. The first sunrise/sunset of spring may glow "carmine and lake [red], fading off into crimsons, yellows, and saffrons," as a British naval surgeon wrote in his winter journal. In the spring and fall, when sunrises and sunsets are more widely separated, vivid reds, oranges, and yellows shine through washes of rose and salmon, of pale cyan, apricot and indigo, as they do in other latitudes. In summer, the skies have a nacreous[3] quality, like the inside of an abalone shell. The colors of summer skies are pastel; the temperature of the light, however, varies enough so that around midnight yellows in the landscape fade noticeably and blues deepen.

What are the Arctic skies like in the summer?

The striking phenomena in the arctic sky for a newcomer are the unsuspected variety of solar and lunar rings, halos, and coronas; the aurora borealis itself; and the mirages that occur at sea, including *fata morganas*. These events are especially apparent in the Far North for several reasons. The kinds of ice crystals that cause solar and lunar refraction are often present in the arctic sphere. The air itself is clear. Slight inversions in the lower atmosphere and sharp temperature differentials at the surface of the ocean in summer, which cause mirages, are common. And the arctic region lies directly underneath the part of the earth's atmosphere that makes the auroral display, or northern lights, visible.

When he was in winter quarters on the coast of Melville Island in 1819–20, William Parry[4] drew a picture of the sun's halos, arcs, and parahelia, or sun dogs, that is now famous. He captured in that single drawing many of the effects that are regularly seen in the Arctic either alone or in some combination. The sun, at the time, was about 22° above the southeastern horizon. It was surrounded by a halo that measured 44° across the horizon and by a second halo 92° across the horizon, part of which was cut off below by the line of the earth. (These are called, after their degree of radius, the 22° and 46° solar halos.) Both these halos were subtended by other arcs, while yet another arc cut across the sun and swept away east and west, parallel to the horizon (the parahelic arc). Where the parahelic arc crossed the 22° halo, two brilliant sun dogs appeared. And below the sun, just at the horizon gleamed a third sun dog (actually a subsun).

What is shown in William Parry's famous picture?

This picture can be readily explained by physicists in terms of ray mechanics, a precise

What explains the phenomena of light drawn by William Parry?

2. **guillemot.** Any of several narrow-billed birds of northern seas
3. **nacreous.** Having the quality of mother-of-pearl
4. **William Parry.** British explorer who searched for the Northwest Passage

words for everyday use	ab • a • lo • ne (a bə lō′ nē) *n.*, rock-clinging gastropod mollusk that has a flattened shell slightly spiral in form, lined with mother-of-pearl. *The handle of the steak knife was lined with pieces of abalone shell.* sub • tend (səb tend′) *vt.*, be opposite to and extend from one side to the other of. *The triangle's hypotenuse subtends a right angle.*

Quotables

"We can never have enough of nature. We must be refreshed by the sight of inexhaustible vigor, vast and titanic features, the sea-coast with its wrecks, the wilderness with its living and decaying trees, the thundercloud, and the rain which lasts three weeks and produces freshets. We need to witness our own limits transgressed, and some life pasturing freely where we never wander."

—Henry David Thoreau, from *Walden*

1. You need to train yourself to look at the right times and the right places.
2. Its delicacy is the transfixing aspect, rather than its dazzle.

CROSS-CURRICULAR CONNECTIONS

ASTRONOMY. Sun dogs, which are also referred to as "mock suns" or "false suns," are basically two brilliant images on either side of the sun. This optical illusion is formed only when there is high altitude, cold air with ice crystals in it, sunlight, and a good view. Sun dogs are caused by the reflection (of both vertical and horizontal light shafts) and refraction (bending) of light by the small ice crystals. However, unlike the sun, sun dogs are usually multicolored like a rainbow. The vertical light shafts refracting at an angle of 22 degrees from the sun produce this effect. This angle is resulted from the fact that the ice crystals are hexagonal (six-sided).

bending of sunlight through certain types of ice crystals aligned in a specific way. In fact, a physicist named Robert Greenler reproduced the elements of Parry's drawing almost perfectly in a computer illustration generated by the formulae involved—a tribute to the accuracy and completeness of Parry's work.

Francis M'Clintock, another British explorer, was presiding at a burial through the sea ice in Baffin Bay in 1857 when he took notice of a stark December moon. A "complete halo encircl[ed] the moon," wrote M'Clintock, "through which passed a horizontal band of pale light that encompassed the heavens; above the moon appeared the segments of two other halos, and there were also mock moons or paraselenae to the number of six. The misty atmosphere lent a very ghastly hue to this singular display, which lasted rather more than an hour."

The physics involved in the refraction and reflection of sunlight by ice crystals and water droplets, and its diffraction by air-borne particles, is dauntingly complex. The arcs and halos produced are sometimes very faint; they also occur in unexpected combinations. Seeing them, however, is largely a matter of training yourself to look. On a single spring day over Lancaster Sound I saw a soft, opaque white pillar or feather (the shape was like a passerine bird's tail feather) standing between the sun and the southeastern horizon (a sun pillar); and that evening, a few minutes after midnight, two long, rainbow-hued shields standing on the horizon on opposite sides of the sun, an unusual pair of sun dogs.

What do you need to train yourself to do in order to see the vivid lighting effects?

The aurora borealis, pale gossamer[5] curtains of light that seem to <u>undulate</u> across arctic skies, are transfixing in part because of their diffidence. "It is impossible to witness such a beautiful phenomenon without a sense of awe," wrote Robert Scott, the British Antarctic explorer, "and yet this sentiment is not inspired by its brilliancy but rather by its delicacy in light and colour, its transparency, and above all by its tremulous <u>evanescence</u> of form. There is no glittering splendour to dazzle the eye, as has been too often described; rather the appeal is to the imagination by the suggestion of something wholly spiritual…."

It is unusual in the literature of exploration to find a strictly consistent reaction, but virtually everyone who wrote down his thoughts about the aurora described, first, the inadequacy of his language and, second, a <u>pervasive</u> and stilling spiritual presence. Among Eskimos the descriptions are often of events that precede or follow life on earth, of the play of unborn children, or of torches held by the dead to help the living hunt in winter. In more southerly latitudes of the Northern Hemisphere, where the aurora is occasionally visible, its connotations are much different, largely because its predominant color when it becomes visible that far south is a deep red. The apparition suggested conflagration and holocaust to Europeans in the Middle Ages. Vikings thought it a reflection in the sky of Vulcan's forge. Miners in Alaska at the turn of the century, of a more scientific and prosaic bent,

What is the most impressive aspect of the aurora borealis?

---

5. **gossamer.** Something light, delicate, insubstantial, or tenuous or having the qualities of gossamer—a sheer fabric

words for everyday use

un • du • late (ən′ jə lāt) vi., form or move in waves. *The gentle breeze caused the flag to <u>undulate</u>.*
ev • a • nes • cence (e və ne′ sənts) n., process or fact of tending to vanish like vapor. *The owner of the baseball team was frustrated by the unpredictable <u>evanescence</u> of the fans' support.*
per • va • sive (pər vā′ siv) adj., quality or state of being diffused throughout every part of something. *The smell of perfume seemed <u>pervasive</u> in the doctor's waiting room.*

thought the aurora was a gaseous form of lightning or the glow from radium mines.

The first time I recognized the northern lights was on a flight from Seattle to Anchorage, when I saw them above the Wrangell Mountains. It was a clear night, and at first I thought it was only a long, moonlit orographic cloud, the kind one often sees isolated over a mountain. Then I saw it move. Completely absorbed, I watched the long banner of pale light, unfurling in lateral movements over the snow-white mountains until the plane turned away. The motions were like a t'ai chi[6] exercise: graceful, inward-turning, and protracted.

To what does Lopez compare his first sighting of the northern lights?

The bottom of an auroral display rarely comes as close as 100 miles above the earth. To the human eye, however, the thin wall of light sometimes appears actually to touch the earth because of a problem of depth perception with objects of unknown size in space. Accurate descriptions are further complicated by its overwhelming size, and its movement. The light wall is often hundreds of miles long and 150 miles or more high; as the intensity of auroral activity increases, the "curtain" of light begins to undulate in a horizontal direction, folding back on itself in huge S-curves and then unfurling again.

There are additional problems with perspective and scale. To someone underneath the display (the top of the wall is tipped toward the south), the aurora may appear like a convergence of rays toward an apex above. Seen edge-on (from directly beneath the bottom edge), the display may seem like luminous smoke rising from the earth. From a distance it may look like a weightless curtain of silk, hanging straight down and rippling in the night air.

The aurora occurs in a thin corridor called the auroral oval centered on the North Magnetic Pole. The display is created by electric discharge in the earth's ionosphere[7] and is apparent to us because some of the energy released is visible light. The most common tinting, of pale, whitish green and pinkish rose, is light emitted from oxygen atoms. During intense periods of auroral activity, nitrogen molecules release a crimson light, usually apparent only at the bottom edge of the auroral curtain.

What is the aurora borealis created by?

Imagine that your view is from the sun and that you are facing the earth. To your far left on the earth's surface are the penumbral shadows of dawn. Before you is the bright light of noon. To your far right the border between evening and night. Streaming outward from the sun is a gas of ionized, or charged, particles, mostly helium and hydrogen nuclei, called the solar wind. These particles pass around the earth as though it were a rock in a stream of water. In doing so they flatten the planet's magnetic field (the magnetosphere) on the near side (day) and elongate it on the far side (night). As it flows past the earth, the solar wind generates an electric current from left to right. The path of least resistance for the solar particles that carry this current is along force lines in the earth's magnetic field that curve down to the earth's surface in the polar regions (like the embrasure of an apple, where the stem is). Particles pouring into the polar regions from a positive terminal on the left create the aurora. As they flow up and out to a negative terminal on the right, they constitute a separate invisible phenomenon, the polar wind.

---

6. **t'ai chi.** Chinese system of physical discipline, related to the martial arts, that emphasizes slow, graceful movements
7. **ionosphere.** Part of the earth's atmosphere containing electrically charged particles

---

words for everyday use

pe • num • bral (pə nəm′ brəl) *adj.*, relating to a space of partial illumination (as in an eclipse) between the perfect shadow on all sides and the full light. *A penumbral shadow from the streetlight was cast over Eugenio's face.*

ANSWERS TO GUIDED READING QUESTIONS

1. Lopez compares the northern lights to a t'ai chi exercise.
2. It's created by an electric discharge in the earth's ionosphere; some of the energy is released as visible light.

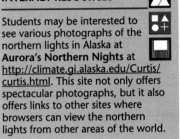

INTERNET RESOURCES

Students may be interested to see various photographs of the northern lights in Alaska at **Aurora's Northern Nights** at http://climate.gi.alaska.edu/Curtis/curtis.html. This site not only offers spectacular photographs, but it also offers links to other sites where browsers can view the northern lights from other areas of the world.

1. Varying intensities in the electric
   field produced by the solar wind
   make the lights appear to have
   folds.
2. Major magnetic storms on the sun
   cause the changes in color and
   motion.
3. The most remarkable effect is "to
   draw a viewer emotionally up and
   out of himself."

SELECTION CHECK TEST 4.5.11 WITH ANSWERS

Checking Your Reading
1. At first glance, what does the Arctic seem to be without? **It seems to be without color.**
2. Where are the most vivid colors found in the Artic? **They are found in the sky.**
3. To what does the speaker compare the movement of the northern lights? **He compares the motions to a t'ai chi exercise.**
4. How frequent do magnetic storms occur? **They occur in an eleven-year cycle.**
5. What do many people claim about the aurora? **They claim that it makes a muffled swish or crackling sound.**

Vocabulary in Context
Fill in each blank below with the most appropriate word from the following Words for Everyday Use. You may have to change the tense of the word.

quiescent   evanescence   sienna
diaphanous   iridescent   pervasive

1. The painter captured the **sienna**-colored mountains with a mixture of oranges, reds, and browns.
2. The kids were entranced by the **iridescent** colors formed when the sunlight hit the crystal.
3. The **quiescent** water was disturbed when the boat sped by.
4. A(n) **pervasive** smell of bread baking could be detected throughout the house.
5. The actor lamented the **evanescence** of fame, noting that he had been a star one month and all but forgotten the next.

As the stream of particles flows earthward down the funnel-shaped surface of the magnetosphere at the Pole, it excites electrons in oxygen atoms and nitrogen molecules which, as they settle back into a stable state, emit energy—X rays, infrared and ultraviolet light, radio waves, and visible light.

The still wall of light we perceive curved along an east-west arc is the calmest sort of auroral display. The more energetic the sun's streaming particles, the deeper they penetrate into the earth's ionosphere and the taller the wall of light becomes. Varying intensities in the electric field produced by the solar wind, and in the solar wind's own magnetic field, cause the wall to develop a series of fine corrugations and folds perpendicular to its east-west extension, to surge in several directions, and to break up into patches. The changes in the electric and magnetic fields that produce, respectively, the changes in color and motion are caused by magnetic storms on the sun. Major magnetic storms occur in an eleven-year cycle, in association with solar flares in the vicinity of sunspots and in solar features called coronal holes. Magnetic sub-storms, far more common, create the sequence of auroral events that arctic viewers think of as "typical" for an arctic winter evening. First, a sudden brightening resolves itself into a transparent auroral curtain. Its fine curruscations (rays) become more prominent. There are surges of movement east and west across the curtain, which starts to develop deep folds. The entire display may then move steadily north. Toward dawn it breaks up into isolated luminous patches, like clouds.

The power produced in this generator is astonishing—1 trillion watts with a current of 1 million amperes. The most violent solar storms affect magnetic compasses, wreak havoc with radio communications and certain navigational systems, and create induced electric currents in long conductors like the trans-Alaska pipeline.

Many people claim the aurora makes a sound, a muffled swish or "a whistling and crackling noise, like the waving of a large flag in a fresh gale of wind," as the explorer Samuel Hearne wrote. And some Eskimos say "the lights" will respond to a gentle whistling and come nearer. They easily evoke feelings of awe and tenderness; the most remarkable effect they seem to have, however, is to draw a viewer emotionally up and out of himself, because they throw the sky into a third dimension, on such a vast scale, in such a beautiful way, that they make the emotion of self-pity impossible.

I remember flying from Prudhoe Bay to Fairbanks one winter night. The sky was clear and the aurora borealis was very strong. With moonlight from the south the snow-covered landscape below was bright, its relief evident in ground shadows. Even the faint line separating the snow-covered tundra from the snow-covered ice was apparent. The auroral curtain stretched out to the west from my view, toward the village of Wainright and the Chukchi Sea. It was in its early, quiescent form of diaphanous rays, a long, pale ghost fire. I could see the edge of the Brooks Range and the plain of the North Slope below. I recalled days of camping in the mountains, of traveling on the tundra, and the times I'd camped on the arctic coast west of Prudhoe. I could see these places clearly, but it was the aurora, towering over the earth, that resolved what could have been only a map into a real landscape, making the memories seem immediate and tangible. ∎

> *What makes the northern lights appear to have "folds," like a curtain?*

> *What causes the changes in motion and color in the northern lights?*

> *What is the most remarkable effect of the lights?*

---

words for everyday use

qui • es • cent (kwī e′ sənts) *adj.*, inactive; peacefully at rest. *The volcano had been quiescent for centuries, but now it began to emit smoke and ash.*

di • aph • a • nous (dī a′ fə nəs) *adj.*, characterized by such fineness of texture as to permit seeing through. *For the photo shoot the model wore a diaphanous veil over her face.*

tan • gi • ble (tan′ jə bəl) *adj.*, definite; concrete; that can be seen or felt. *Because the government valued only programs with tangible benefits, it cut the funding for the arts.*

Respond *to the* SELECTION

What do Lopez's personal anecdotes add to the selection?

Investigate, Inquire, *and* Imagine

Recall: GATHERING FACTS

1a. What are the predominant colors of the aurora? Where else has Lopez found these colors?

2a. What aspects of the aurora borealis does Lopez describe?

3a. At the end of the essay, what effect does the aurora borealis have on the way Lopez perceives the landscape he sees from the airplane?

Interpret: FINDING MEANING

1b. What does Lopez mean when he says that similarities between the sky and other things in nature "hold a landscape together"?

2b. What is Lopez's attitude toward science?

3b. What does Lopez mean by a "real landscape"?

Analyze: TAKING THINGS APART

4a. Using specific examples from the text, identify and categorize the different kinds of descriptive material that Lopez uses to paint a picture of the aurora borealis and other such phenomena.

Synthesize: BRINGING THINGS TOGETHER

4b. What does the variety of descriptive materials that Lopez brings to the essay demonstrate?

Perspective: LOOKING AT OTHER VIEWS

5a. Evaluate the effect nature has on Lopez.

Empathy: SEEING FROM INSIDE

5b. Give examples of the ways in which nature is part of your life. How do you experience nature? What are your reactions to it?

Understanding Literature

NATURE WRITING. Review the definition for **nature writing** in the Handbook of Literary Terms. Why does Lopez choose this particular literary form in writing his essay? How does the form help make his point?

DESCRIPTION. Review the definition for **description** and the cluster chart you made for Literary Tools on page 417. Return to the Lopez essay and choose three different descriptive passages—either single sentences or whole paragraphs—that you find especially vivid and effective. In making your choices, consider such factors as the precise use of nouns, adjectives, adverbs, and adjectives as well as the effective use of figurative language or imagery. Explain why you chose these particular passages.

"ICE AND LIGHT" **423**

ANSWERS TO INVESTIGATE, INQUIRE, AND IMAGINE (CONT.)

SYNTHESIZE
4b. It demonstrates nature's and Lopez's ability to bring to the observer a unified vision of science and spirituality, of measurement and mystery.

EVALUATE
5a. *Responses will vary.* Lopez writes that the most remarkable effect of the aurora is "to draw the viewer emotionally up and out of himself" making "the emotion of self-pity impossible." Lopez seems

to suggest that being able to train ourselves to look beyond our own relatively puny concerns is a way of becoming part of the landscape, of finding meaning.

EXTEND
5b. *Responses will vary.*

Answers to Understanding Literature can be found on page 424.

RESPOND TO THE SELECTION

After reading this selection, do you have a better appreciation for nature and the mysteries surrounding it? Why, or why not?

ANSWERS TO INVESTIGATE, INQUIRE, AND IMAGINE

RECALL
1a. The predominant colors are "a pale green and a soft rose." Lopez has also found these colors on a caribou antler.

2a. He describes the scientific mechanisms of how the colors and movement are produced. He describes the emotional and spiritual effect of seeing them.

3a. The northern lights "resolved what could have been only a map into a real landscape, making the memories [of his camping experiences] seem immediate and tangible."

INTERPRET
1b. Lopez seems to suggest that finding similarities between otherwise unconnected things in nature is a way of seeing the world as a unified whole.

2b. For Lopez, science is not a way of distancing himself from the wonder of the natural world, but is a mode in which to experience it.

3b. For Lopez, the aurora seems to locate the landscape within the comprehensive vision of nature, within a world that is not confined by human limits. This is what makes it "real." "Real landscape" is landscape that is not just a grid, not just a visual trick of the altitude (he's flying in an airplane). Instead it is what exists beneath and within the sky.

ANALYZE
4a. *Responses will vary.* Lopez uses scientific information ("in terms of ray mechanics, a precise bending of sunlight through certain types of ice crystals aligned in a specific way"); Eskimo lore ("the descriptions are often of events that precede or follow life of earth," such as "the torches held by the dead to help the living hunt in winter"); metaphorical descriptions (the aurora looks like "a weightless curtain of silk, hanging straight down and rippling in the night air"); and anecdotes (the journals of explorers describe a "pervasive and stilling spiritual presence").

TEACHER'S EDITION **423**

ANSWERS TO UNDERSTANDING LITERATURE

NATURE WRITING. The form of nature writing is particularly effective because it allows Lopez to select details from his personal experience and from his scientific, historical, and cultural knowledge to underline what is mysterious and grand about the aurora borealis. The nature essay seeks to form a connection between the reader and nature, making the reader's experience "more immediate and tangible."

DESCRIPTION. *Responses will vary.*

ANSWERS TO INTEGRATING THE LANGUAGE ARTS

Language, Grammar, and Style
1. Its colors are the colors of deserts, the reds of stratified soils, the greens of plant life.
2. In summer, the skies have a nacreous quality, like the inside of an abalone shell.
3. The changes in the electric and magnetic fields that produce, respectively, the changes in color and motion are caused by magnetic storms on the sun.
4. The colors of summer skies are pastel; the temperature of the light, however, varies enough so that around midnight yellows fade noticeably.
5. The striking phenomena in the sky are the variety of solar and lunar rings, halos, and coronas; the aurora borealis itself; and the mirages that occur at sea, including fata morganas.

Study and Research
Refer students to the Language Arts Survey 5.19, "How to Locate Library Materials," and 5.26, "Using the Internet," for this activity.

Writer's Journal

1. Imagine you are a traveler visiting Alaska, where you have seen the northern lights for the first time. Write a **post card** to a friend describing what you've seen.
2. Imagine you are a member of one of the native peoples of Alaska. Write a **letter** to a pen pal in England explaining how the aurora borealis is important to you.
3. Imagine you are Barry Lopez and you have recently learned that the federal government has begun a program to drill for oil in a beautiful wilderness area of Alaska. Write a **letter of complaint** to the Secretary of Interior stating why you think the drilling is a bad idea.

Integrating the Language Arts

Language, Grammar, and Style

COMMAS AND SEMICOLONS. Read the Language Arts Survey 3.87, "Commas" and 3.88, "Semicolons." Then add the appropriate punctuation to the following sentences.

1. Its colors are the colors of deserts the reds of stratified soils the greens of plant life.
2. In summer the skies have a nacreous quality like the inside of an abalone shell.
3. The changes in the electric and magnetic fields that produce respectively the changes in color and motion are caused by magnetic storms on the sun.
4. The colors of summer skies are pastel the temperature of the light however varies enough so that around midnight yellows fade noticeably.
5. The striking phenomena in the sky are the variety of solar and lunar rings halos and coronas the aurora borealis itself and the mirages that occur at sea including fata morganas.

Study and Research

RESEARCHING NATURE. Think of an example of something in nature that has impressed, delighted, or troubled you (i.e., encountering a dangerous wild animal, finding a rare flower, watching a lunar eclipse). Using the resources of the library or the Internet, research your topic to find out more about it. One effective way to direct your research might be to brainstorm questions about the aspect of nature you are researching. Try to find answers to those questions. Then share your findings with the class.

Applied English

LETTER OF RECOMMENDATION. Write a letter recommending Barry Lopez for a job with an organization dedicated to protecting the environment. You may wish to review the Language Arts Survey 6.5, "Writing a Business Letter."

"The Last Bison"
by David Quammen

Reader's resource

HISTORY CONNECTION. Bison, or American buffalo, once roamed in great herds over North America from the Appalachians to the Rockies. In 1850, there were still almost twenty million bison left roaming free. White Americans slaughtered the animals indiscriminately in the late 1800s, almost wiping out the whole species. In "The Last Bison," Quammen traces the history of the bison and the measures taken to save the species from extinction.

About the AUTHOR

David Quammen (1948–) was born in Cincinnati, Ohio. He studied aquatic entomology, a branch of zoology that deals with insects that grow or live in or upon water, at Montana State University at Missoula. Quammen, who continues to live in Montana, claims to be a "follower of science" rather than a scientist, and he aims for unbiased, provable scientific claims. He has been a natural history columnist for *Outside* magazine. Quammen's books include *To Walk the Line* (1970), *Flight of the Iguana* (1988), *The Song of Dodo* (1996), *Natural Acts: A Sidelong View of Science and Nature* (1996), and *Wild Thoughts from Wild Places* (1998).

Literary TOOLS

ESSAY. An **essay** is a brief work of prose nonfiction. As you read this essay, decide what method of organization Quammen uses. Refer to the Language Arts Survey 2.27, "Choosing a Method of Organization."

AIM. A writer's **aim** is his or her purpose, or goal. Read more about aim in the Handbook of Literary Tools. As you read, determine the author's aim in writing "The Last Bison."

Graphic Organizer

Make a cluster chart listing facts about bison mentioned in the essay. One example has been done for you.

Facts about Bison

60 million existed during the 19th century

Reader's Journal

What impact do humans have on the natural environment?

ADDITIONAL RESOURCES

UNIT 5 RESOURCE BOOK
- Selection Worksheet 5.6
- Selection Check Test 4.5.13
- Selection Test 4.5.14
- Language, Grammar, and Style Resource 3.39
- Applied English Resource 6.9

GRAPHIC ORGANIZER

Students should include the following facts about the bison in their cluster charts:
- By 1889 there were only 541 bison left.
- Only parts of their carcasses were used.
- They were shot from trains for sport.
- Bison became harder to stalk as they became rare.
- Mountain bison survived in Yellowstone Park.
- Mountain bison were poached.
- Mountain bison were reduced to less than 25.
- Mountain bison were interbred.
- Mountain bison began to multiply naturally.
- Mountain bison now number 2,000.

READER'S JOURNAL

Students may begin by brainstorming a list of human impacts on nature, such as pollution, deforestation, and depletion of the ozone layer. What are the dangers of these impacts? If students could change one of them for the better, which one would it be? Why?

GOALS/OBJECTIVES

Studying this lesson will enable students to
- sympathize with the plight of the bison during the late nineteenth century
- describe the literary accomplishments of David Quammen
- define *essay* and *aim* and recognize and explain examples of each in the selection
- use colorful language in sentences
- conduct research on endangered species
- write a press release

MOTIVATION
Involve students in a debate about hunting. Is it ethical or unethical to hunt animals? What are some reasons people want to eliminate the killing of animals for sport? What are some reasons why hunting may be necessary? Finally, after the debate has ended, conduct a class survey on whether or not hunting should be banned in their state.

READING PROFICIENCY
Students may benefit from a discussion about developing a single idea in an essay or other piece of writing. Point out that the essay is carefully constructed, with each paragraph relating back to the central idea and establishing a tight focus.

ENGLISH LANGUAGE LEARNING
Give students the following additional vocabulary words:
excursion—short trip
idle—lazy; useless
remnant—small remaining quantity
reclusiveness—desire to remain alone
poached—hunted illegally
nostalgic—longing to go back to another place or time
doled—gave sparingly

SPECIAL NEEDS
To help students complete their graphic organizer activity, pair students with an advanced partner. Then encourage them to discuss the aim of David Quammen in writing this essay.

ENRICHMENT
Students may want to research the practice of hunting in the United States. How has hunting changed since the time of buffalo hunting? In what ways does hunting affect the environment? What animals are hunted most frequently? Why? Besides hunters, which groups are generally in favor of hunting? Interested students may give a presentation on hunting and how it is regarded today as opposed to the time of the buffalo hunts.

426 *UNIT FIVE / NONFICTION*

VOCABULARY FROM THE SELECTION

abundance	flagrant
accession	hindsight
carnage	prodigious
defunct	stalwart
distinction	superfluous
enterprising	

The Last Bison

David Quammen

It happened quickly. First there were 60 million, roaming the prairies and plains, blanketing whole valleys almost shoulder to shoulder for miles, the greatest abundance of any species of large mammal that modern humankind ever had the privilege to behold. And then, in 1889, there were (by one informed estimate) just 541 bison surviving throughout all the United States.

The slaughter had been conducted with prodigious efficiency and prodigious waste. Sometimes the meat was taken from a dead bison, sometimes only the hide, sometimes no more than the tongue, cut out and pickled in brine,[1] to be sent to New York in a barrel. Sometimes not even that: People shot them from train windows to relieve the boredom of crossing Nebraska by rail, and left them rotting untouched. In the 1870s, the wildest years of the carnage, certain booking agents for the railroads went so far as to advertise outings on that basis: "Ample time will be had for a grand BUFFALO HUNT. Buffaloes are so numerous along the road that they are shot from the cars nearly every day. On our last excursion our party killed twenty buffaloes in a hunt of six hours! Round trip

How were the buffalo killed in the 1870s?

1. **brine.** Water saturated with salt

words for everyday use

a • bun • dance (ə bun´dəns) n., great supply. An *abundance* of flowers covered the mountain, filling the scene with a great supply of colors and scents.
pro • di • gious (prə dij´əs) adj., amazing. The search for the missing boy was conducted with *prodigious* care, and he was located almost immediately.
car • nage (kär´nij) n., slaughter. As an endangered species, the bald eagle is protected from the kind of *carnage* that nearly resulted in the extinction of bison.

tickets from Leavenworth,[2] only $10!" In Montana and the Dakotas, last refuge of the big herds, the trade in hides peaked around 1882 and then suddenly, two years later, the professional hunters were coming back from a frustrating season having seen no buffalo.

What happened when the hunters went in search of buffalo in 1884?

None. They were gone or in hiding. Perhaps a final few desperate animals had retreated to high country, beyond the Absaroka Mountains, into Yellowstone Park.[3] At this point among the thrill-seekers, the railroad excursionists, those idle souls back in Wichita and St. Louis and Philadelphia who collected trophies and fancied themselves "sport hunters," there was a measure of interest in that supposed <u>distinction</u> which would attach to the man who killed the last American bison.

What interested "sport hunters"?

But no one did. Miracle of our good fortune: No one did.

Why not? Partly because of natural human sloth:[4] As bison grew more rare, the stalking of one became a matter of greater expense and inconvenience. Partly also because of collective good sense: Laws (belated and, at first, weak) were passed. And partly the last of the bison survived because they were not, for even an experienced and relentless hunter, so very easy to find. During that near brush with extinction at the end of the 1880s, when the species had fallen in this country to fewer than 600 individuals, and not many more in Canada, the high mountain meadows and steep woodlands of the Yellowstone plateau *did* shelter bison—probably more than 200 head, one-third of the entire national remnant.

These Yellowstone animals were not newcomers, however, not fugitives lately arrived in flight from the massacre below. They were a distinct subspecies now known as mountain bison. They had been there all along.

And they were a little different, the mountain bison, a little more cagey than their lowland relatives, perhaps more than a little better adapted to avoid terminal confrontation with man. Fossil evidence shows that they were slightly larger, on average, than plains bison (which is to say, larger than any animal on the continent), and yet from historical accounts we hear also that they were more agile and alert and wary. One observer in 1877 wrote: "These animals are by no means plentiful, and are moreover excessively shy, inhabiting the deepest, darkest defiles,[5] or the craggy, almost precipitous,[6] sides of mountains, inaccessible to any but the most practised mountaineers." Another writer, the park's superintendent in 1880, judged them "most keen of scent and difficult of approach of all mountain animals." The cloak of hair over their shoulders and hump was darker and finer than on plains buffalo, the alignment of horns was minutely different and, most important, the mountain bison were more hardy.

What was the most important difference about the mountain buffalo? What effect could this have on the declining buffalo population?

They had the evolved capability[7] to endure those bitter and long winters in the high Yellowstone valleys—above 7,500 feet with deep snow and temperatures often below minus

---

2. **Leavenworth.** City in northeastern Kansas on the Missouri River
3. **Yellowstone Park.** National park of about 3,500 square miles located mainly in northwestern Wyoming
4. **sloth.** Laziness
5. **defiles.** Deep stone valleys between cliffs or rock outcroppings
6. **precipitous.** Almost vertical; steep or sheer
7. **evolved capability.** Practical ability developed over many generations

---

words for everyday use

dis • tinc • tion (di stiŋk´shən) *n.*, special recognition. *He earned the <u>distinction</u> of being the only man to win the marathon three years in a row and was recognized with a special award for his achievement.*

40,000 buffalo hides stacked in Dodge City, Kansas, 1878.

ADDITIONAL QUESTIONS
AND ACTIVITIES

Prompt students to discuss Quammen's tone as a writer. How does he reveal his feelings about hunting? about bison? about nature?

Answers

Quammen reveals his feelings by being very direct. About hunting the last bison, he states, "Miracle of our good fortune: no one did." About bison, he says at the end of the essay, "These creatures were made for greatness," and calls them "America's most imposing and resolute and dignified beast." He reveals his powerful feeling for nature throughout the essay in his descriptions of the bison's place in nature: "They were made to scale the spine of a continent . . . and stand facing the driven snow."

25°—where a buffalo hunter, white or Indian, could too easily freeze to death in pursuit. They would face into a driving blizzard in open country and stand their ground—waiting, enduring, indomitable. They were living exempla of the word *stalwart*. They would plow snow aside with the muzzles of their massive heads to reach edible grass underneath. They would use the Firehole River and other natural geo-thermal features of Yellowstone as highways and oases during the worst of the winter. And in summer they climbed still higher, escaping the biting insects, grazing the sedges[8] and grasses of sub-alpine meadows, venturing even onto the alpine tundra above timberline. Hannibal[9] would have worshipped these creatures.

But despite their reclusiveness, despite their agility and power, despite the legislation that in 1872 had made Yellowstone our first national park, the mountain bison were still poached for their heads and their hides. Snowshoes[10] and Sharps rifles made this possible, if not easy, and trophy heads were now bringing high enough prices to justify the ordeal. It was illegal but the law allowed only token penalties, and the park budget allowed only token enforcement. In 1894, after an especially <u>flagrant</u> poaching case was reported in the journal *Forest and Stream*, spawning further coverage in newspapers around the country and a tardy <u>accession</u> of public concern, Congress finally

What did the government finally do? Why was this act almost too late?

---

8. **sedges.** Grasslike plants with triangular leaves that grow in wet ground
9. **Hannibal.** (*circa* 247–183 BC) North African general from the state of Carthage who crossed the Alps to invade Italy in 218 BC
10. **Snowshoes.** Flat, netted surfaces used for walking on snow

words for everyday use

stal • wart (stôl´wərt) *adj.,* strong; robust; unyielding. *Tonto was the trusted <u>stalwart</u> companion of the Lone Ranger.*
fla • grant (flā´grənt) *adj.,* outrageous. *The referee called the basketball player for a <u>flagrant</u> foul after she wrapped her arms around an opposing player about to score.*
ac • ces • sion (ak sesh´ən) *n.,* outburst. *An unusual <u>accession</u> of public concern followed the report that the town's drinking water was unsafe; the general outburst led to an emergency meeting.*

"THE LAST BISON" **429**

1. The surviving plains bison were preserved by ranchers. They were saddled and ridden, used in rodeos, crossbred with cattled, and killed for meat.
2. The Lamar Buffalo Ranch was superfluous because the wild bison that survived "saved themselves" and began to multiply again without human intervention.

SELECTION CHECK TEST 4.5.13 WITH ANSWERS

Checking Your Reading
1. How is the slaughter of the buffalo described? **It is described as efficient and wasteful.**
2. Who advertised buffalo hunts? **Railroad companies advertised buffalo hunts.**
3. What kind of buffalo lived on the Yellowstone plateau? **Mountain bison lived on the Yellowstone plateau.**
4. Of what word are the bison a living example? **They are a living example of the word** *stalwart*.
5. How long were the bison on the brink of extinction? **They were on the brink of extinction for two decades.**

Vocabulary in Context
Fill in each blank below with the most appropriate word from the following Words for Everyday Use. You may have to change the tense of the word.

prodigious   abundance   flagrant
accession   stalwart   distinction

1. There was a(n) **abundance** of food at the graduation party.
2. The new father handled the baby with **prodigious** care, as if the baby was breakable.
3. I chose Frank to be on my basketball team because he is **stalwart**; he is strong and never gives up.
4. The driver was pulled over for a(n) **flagrant** violation of traffic law; he had sped through a red light right in front of the police station.
5. Joelle had earned the **distinction** of being the first member of her family to attend college.

---

severe enough to protect the Yellowstone bison. Yet by then it was very nearly too late. Enforcement was still difficult in the Yellowstone backcountry, and by 1897 the entire park population had shrunk to less than twenty-five. These few animals were burdened with a double distinction. They were not only the last of the mountain bison. They were also the last wild bison, of any sort whatever, in all the United States.

Elsewhere the sole survivors were plains bison that had been preserved by **enterprising** ranchers for commercial stock-growing experiments. These private herds were dealt with like cattle: fed out on hay during hard weather, gathered periodically into corrals, the excess male calves castrated into steers. Saddled, some of them, for the amusement of their owners. Consigned to performing in rodeos. Cross-bred with domestic cattle. Doted on as nostalgic curios. And routinely slaughtered for their meat. When the century turned, there were still many buffalo in the United States, and the number increasing, but the only wild and free-living holdouts[11] were those two dozen in Yellowstone.

What happened to the survivors of the plains bison?

And then in 1902, with well-meaning folk convinced that the little group was doomed, stock-ranching practices came also to Yellowstone. Congress put up $15,000, twenty-one plains bison were purchased from private herds in Texas and Montana, and an official "Buffalo Ranch" was established in the gorgeous Lamar Valley of the park's northeast corner. Hay was doled out, there were corrals and roundups, castrations and cullings.[12] It became—judged on its own terms—a successful operation. Many

bison were raised at the Lamar Buffalo Ranch. Only **hindsight** could have shown us that it was an utterly **superfluous** enterprise.

Superfluous because, while this ranching proceeded in the Lamar, the two dozen wild bison went their own way, to the high woodlands and the tundra in summer, to the sheltered valleys and thermal areas in winter, and survived. Left alone, given nothing but peace, they saved themselves. Endured, as they always had done, and after two decades on the brink of extinction, began again to multiply naturally.

Why was the Lamar Buffalo Ranch "superfluous"?

The Buffalo Ranch is long since **defunct**. Its buildings now house a thriving institute for the study of Yellowstone's ecosystem. And today in Yellowstone Park, along the Lamar and the Firehole, amid the bunchgrass and sage[13] of the Hayden Valley, across the Mirror Plateau above Specimen Ridge and at the headwaters of the Bechler River, there live about two thousand bison.

Despite some past interbreeding with—adulteration by[14]—the old Lamar herd of coddled flatland outsiders, the Yellowstone animals represent our best and only remnant of wild bison, mountain bison, America's most imposing and resolute and dignified beast. These creatures were made for greatness. They were made to scale the spine of a continent, on tiny hooves below huge shoulders, and stand facing the driven snow. They were made to last. ∎

---

11. **holdouts.** Few remaining bison after the rest had been destroyed
12. **cullings.** Process of selecting, as for breeding
13. **bunchgrass and sage.** Tufts of grass and sagebrush, a composite plant with small flowers common in the dry, alkaline soil of western America
14. **adulteration by.** Impurification by; weakening by

---

words for everyday use

en • ter • pris • ing (ent ́ər prī ́zin) *adj.*, marked by an independent energetic spirit and by readiness to undertake an experiment. *He was considered an* enterprising *young businessman because he had ambitions of opening his own chain of restaurants.*

hind • sight (hīnd ́sīt ́) *n.*, ability to see, after an event, what should have been done. *"*Hindsight *is 20/20," his father told him after he failed the test and realized he should have studied harder for it.*

su • per • flu • ous (sə pʉr ́flo͞o əs) *adj.*, unnecessary. *Nora thought she was a* superfluous *member of the committee, since she never had anything to contribute.*

de • funct (dē funkt ́) *adj.*, no longer existing. *Drive-in movie theaters are largely* defunct; *only a few still exist.*

SELECTION CHECK TEST 4.5.13 WITH ANSWERS (CONT.)

Literary Tools
Fill in the blanks using the following terms.

aim   part-by-part   essay

1. A(n) **essay** is a brief work of prose nonfiction.
2. A writer's **aim** is his or her purpose, or goal.
3. Quammen organizes his information using **part-by-part** order.

Respond *to the* SELECTION

How did you feel when you heard about the way the bison were hunted during the nineteenth century?

Investigate, Inquire, and Imagine

Recall: GATHERING FACTS

1a. What was advertised as a buffalo hunt? What did bison hunters find around 1884?

2a. Where were there more than two hundred bison? How were these bison different? According to the author, what word did they exemplify?

3a. What measures were taken to preserve the bison?

→ Interpret: FINDING MEANING

1b. Why did people hunt the bison? What three things preserved the bison?

2b. Why were the bison in Yellowstone so hard to hunt?

3b. Why didn't preservation measures work? What was responsible for saving the bison?

Analyze: TAKING THINGS APART

4a. How did humans upset the balance of nature? Why were their efforts to amend this disruption ineffective?

→ Synthesize: BRINGING THINGS TOGETHER

4b. How might the message of this essay be applied to current practices regarding the environment?

Evaluate: MAKING JUDGMENTS

5a. Evaluate whether Quammen remains impartial about the bison. What attitude does he take toward them?

→ Extend: CONNECTING IDEAS

5b. Do you favor hunters' rights or environmentalists' concerns? Is there a way to arbitrate the disparate concerns of these two groups?

Understanding Literature

ESSAY. Review the definition for **essay** in the Handbook of Literary Terms. What method of organization does Quammen use in the essay? How is each paragraph related to the idea Quammen develops?

AIM. Review the definition for **aim** in Literary Tools and the cluster chart you made for that section. What is Quammen's aim in writing "The Last Bison"?

RESPOND TO THE SELECTION

Why do you think Quammen felt the need to write this essay? Do you agree or disagree with the perspective on hunting presented in this essay? How do you think a hunter would respond to this essay?

ANSWERS TO INVESTIGATE, INQUIRE, AND IMAGINE

RECALL

1a. Train rides were advertised as "Buffalo hunts" because bison could be shot from the passenger cars. In 1884, buffalo hunters found that most of their prey had disappeared.

2a. More than two hundred bison sought refuge in the high mountains meadows and steep woodlands of Yellowstone National Park. They were different because they were mountain bison, a stronger subspecies. They exemplified the word *stalwart*.

3a. Measures taken by Congress to preserve the bison included making Yellowstone the first national park and establishing penalties for hurting the bison that lived there. Additionally, crossbreeding was tried by ranchers and, in 1902, an official "Buffalo Ranch" was established in Yellowstone with plains bison purchased from private herds.

INTERPRET

1b. People hunted bison for sport, for food, for hides, and for relieving boredom. The three things that saved them from extinction were hunting expenses, passing of laws, difficulties in finding them.

2b. Mountain buffalo were so hard to hunt because they were better adapted to their habitat. They were able to endure long winters at high elevations, unlike hunters, and in the summers they climbed even higher.

3b. Preservation efforts did not work because the laws against hunting buffalo were weak and not regularly enforced. Ultimately, the bison saved themselves when they began to multiply in their natural habitat.

ANALYZE

4b. Humans upset the balance of nature by nearly wiping out an abundant species. Their efforts to make amends were ineffective because penalties were low, laws were not enforced, and hunting became a kind of trophy sport. The Buffalo Ranch was ineffective because no one realized that all the buffalo needed was to be left alone.

ANSWERS TO INVESTIGATE, INQUIRE, AND IMAGINE (CONT.)

SYNTHESIZE

4b. The message of the essay is that we must cultivate respect for all species and let them thrive in their natural habitats; people must care for the land and its animals, not wantonly destroy them or interfere with the balance of nature.

EVALUATE

5a. Quammen admires the bison, calling it "America's most imposing and resolute and dignified beast." He does not remain impartial when he states,

"These creatures were made for greatness. They were made to scale the spine of a continent, on tiny hooves below huge shoulders, and stand facing the driven snow. They were made to last."

EXTEND

5b. *Responses will vary.*

Answers to Understanding Literature can be found on page 432.

ANSWERS TO UNDERSTANDING LITERATURE

ESSAY. Quammen uses part-by-part order, beginning with the fact that in 1889 there were only 541 bison left in the United States. He then goes back in time to the 1870s to show what led up to this point. Each paragraph relates to the essay in that it provides more specific information about the main idea—that bison nearly became extinct.

AIM. Quammen's aim is to inform the reader that bison were nearly wiped out by hunting during the late nineteenth century, but in the end the bison saved themselves.

ANSWERS TO INTEGRATING THE LANGUAGE ARTS

Language, Grammar, and Style
1. White hunters <u>slaughtered</u> the bison.
2. Mountain bison survived <u>frigid</u> winters in Yellowstone.
3. The cold wind blew <u>furiously</u>.
4. Mountain bison <u>inhabited</u> inaccessible terrain.
5. The bison is America's most <u>imposing</u> beast.

Study and Research
Refer students to the Language Arts Survey 6.11, "Displaying Effective Visual Information" to help them make their presentation more effective.

Writer's Journal

1. Quammen says that the mountain bison "were living exempla of the word *stalwart*." Write a similar **definition** for another animal, such as a cat or a dog.
2. Write a **table of contents** for a book about endangered species.
3. Imagine you are a Native American warrior who has come across bison carcasses left to rot on the prairie. Write a **journal entry** about what you think of white hunters. Be sure to include your attitude toward the bison.

Integrating the Language Arts

Language, Grammar, and Style

USING COLORFUL LANGUAGE. Read the Language Arts Survey 3.39, "Adding Colorful Language to Sentences." Then rewrite the following sentences, replacing the underlined word with a colorful verb, adjective, or adverb.
1. White hunters <u>killed</u> the bison.
2. Mountain bison survived <u>cold</u> winters in Yellowstone.
3. The cold wind blew <u>hard</u>.
4. Mountain bison <u>lived</u> in inaccessible terrain.
5. The bison is America's most <u>impressive</u> beast.

Study and Research

ENDANGERED SPECIES. In this essay Quammen explores the history of an endangered species. Research another endangered species. Find out why it is endangered. Have humans killed too many? Is its habitat being destroyed? What conservation efforts are in effect to help preserve it? Are there any signs that these efforts are working? Present your findings to the class. You may want to use visual aids to make your presentation more effective. For example, you could draw a map showing where your species lives or make a chart tracing the population of the species over a specific time period.

Collaborative Learning

NATIVE AMERICAN BISON EXHIBIT. Imagine that your job is to design a museum exhibit explaining how the Plains Indians used the parts of the bison in their daily life and showing their attitude of reverence for the animal. Form small groups in order to plan your exhibit. Describe art, artifacts, songs, prayers, and interviews you want to use in your exhibit.

Applied English

PRESS RELEASE. Imagine it is 1872 and you are editor of a newspaper in Leavenworth, Kansas, where, as you learned in Quammen's essay, railroads advertised buffalo hunts. Read the Language Arts Survey 6.9, "Delivering a Press Release." Then write a press release protesting buffalo hunts on the train.

"YONDER SKY THAT HAS WEPT TEARS OF COMPASSION..."

by Chief Seattle

Reader's resource

HISTORY CONNECTION. Soon after the organization of the Washington Territory in 1853, Governor Stevens visited the town of Seattle. He addressed Chief Seattle's people about a proposed treaty—one that would relocate Seattle's people to a reservation. Chief Seattle responded to this address, and his response was recorded by Dr. Henry Smith, who had mastered the Duwamish language.

About the AUTHOR

Chief Seattle (1786–1866) was chief of the Suquamish and Duwamish tribes in the Northwest United States. Catholic missionaries converted him in the 1830s. In January 1855, Isaac Stevens, governor of the Washington Territory, proposed a treaty that would take control of the tribal lands and relocate tribal members to a reservation. Seeing little hope for the future, Seattle was one of the first to sign the Port Elliot Treaty. The city of Seattle was named for him despite his protests that his eternal rest would be disturbed every time his name was spoken.

Literary TOOLS

MOOD. Mood, or **atmosphere,** is the emotion created in the reader by part or all of a literary work. As you read the speech, think about the mood that Chief Seattle is conveying.

IMAGE AND IMAGERY. An **image** is language that creates a concrete representation of an object or an experience. The images in a literary work are referred to, collectively, as the work's **imagery.** Look for the nature imagery Seattle uses throughout his speech.

Graphic Organizer

To see the varying ways Chief Seattle uses imagery in his speech, read through the text jotting down examples of specific images that reference nature. Indicate a category—earth, water, or sky—for each image as shown in the example below. What does the imagery say about Chief Seattle?

IMAGE	CATEGORY
Today is fair. Tomorrow it may be overcast with clouds.	Sky

Reader's Journal

Imagine that somebody wanted to take over your house or your town and make you move to another place. How would you feel about this?

ADDITIONAL RESOURCES

UNIT 5 RESOURCE BOOK
• Selection Worksheet 5.7
• Selection Check Test 4.5.15
• Selection Test 4.5.16
• Language, Grammar, and Style Resource 3.32
• Speaking and Listening Resource 4.20

GRAPHIC ORGANIZER

Image	Category
My words are like the stars that never change.	Sky
His people are many. They are like the grass that covers the prairies	Earth
My people are few. They resemble the scattering trees of a storm-swept plain.	Earth
There was a time when our people covered the land as the waves of a wind-ruffled sea cover its shell-paved floor...	Water
Our people are ebbing away like a rapidly receding tide...	Water
The red man has ever fled the approach of the white man, as the morning mist flees before the morning sun.	Sky
The Indians' night promises to be dark. Not a single star of hope hovers above his horizon.	Sky
Chief Seattle's life is inextricably tied to all of nature.	

READER'S JOURNAL

Students may begin by brainstorming a list of things that would be different if someone took over their town. What could be improved? What might be made worse? What would best be left alone?

GOALS/OBJECTIVES

Studying this lesson will enable students to
• experience Chief Seattle's feelings about signing the Port Elliot Treaty
• describe the accomplishments of Chief Seattle during the nineteenth century
• explain the differences Chief Seattle sees between his people and white people

• define *mood* and *imagery* and recognize the use of these techniques in the selection
• identify nouns of direct address in sentences
• research Native American treaties
• tell a Native American myth

1. The white chief's people were numerous, like the grass that covers the prairies. Chief Seattle's people were few, like a scattering of trees on a storm-swept plain.
2. The white chief wanted to buy Chief Seattle's lands.

INDIVIDUAL LEARNING STRATEGIES

MOTIVATION
Invite a Native American student or adult who is knowledgeable in the area of historical treaties between the United States government and Native American tribes to speak about this topic. What was the aim or goal for most treaties? Did both parties stay loyal to the agreements made in the treaty?

READING PROFICIENCY
To help students better under the mood of this selection, students might benefit from hearing the selection read aloud. Also encourage students to read the Prereading page before they begin reading the selection on their own.

ENGLISH LANGUAGE LEARNING
Students may benefit from a discussion about imagery in speech writing. Encourage them to share any powerful or striking images from their cultures that would clearly illustrate something about their culture to other people. Also point out that the speech is translated from the Duwamish language.

SPECIAL NEEDS
Once students have answered the Guided Reading questions and the Recall questions from the Investigate, Inquire, and Imagine section, ask them to get together in small groups to discuss their answers.

ENRICHMENT
Students may want to research the growth of the city of Seattle since the time of Chief Seattle. What is the city like today? What are its main industries? Would Chief Seattle be satisfied with its development? Why, or why not? Students may want to look at maps or photographs to observe changes in Seattle's physical landscape.

YONDER SKY
THAT HAS WEPT TEARS OF COMPASSION...

Chief Seattle

Yonder sky that has wept tears of compassion upon my people for centuries untold, and which to us appears changeless and eternal, may change. Today is fair. Tomorrow it may be overcast with clouds. My words are like the stars that never change. Whatever Seattle says the great chief at Washington[1] can rely upon with as much certainty as he can upon the return of the sun or the seasons. The white chief says that big chief at Washington sends us greetings of friendship and goodwill. This is kind of him for we know he has little need of our friendship in return. His people are many. They are like the grass that covers vast prairies. My people are few. They resemble the scattering trees of a storm-swept plain. The great—and I presume—good white chief sends us word that he wishes to buy our lands but is willing to allow us enough to live comfortably. This indeed appears just, even generous, for the red man no longer has rights that he need respect, and the offer may be wise also, as we are no longer in need of an extensive country.

There was a time when our people covered the land as the waves of a wind-ruffled sea cover its shell-paved floor, but that time long since passed away with the greatness of tribes that are now but a mournful memory. I will not dwell on, nor mourn over, our untimely decay, nor <u>reproach</u> my paleface brothers with hastening it as we too may have been somewhat to blame.

Youth is impulsive. When our young men grow angry at some real or imaginary wrong, and <u>disfigure</u> their faces with black paint, it denotes that their hearts are black, and that they are often cruel and relentless, and our old men and old women are unable to restrain them. Thus it has ever been. Thus it was when the white man first began to push our forefathers westward. But let us hope that the hostilities between us may never return. We would have everything to lose and nothing to gain. Revenge by young men is considered gain, even at the cost of their own lives, but old men who stay at home in times of war, and mothers who have sons to lose, know better.

Our good father at Washington—for I presume he is now our father as well as yours, since King George has moved his boundaries further north—our great and good father, I say, sends us word that if we do as he desires he will protect us. His brave warriors will be to us a

> What were the white chief's people like? What were Chief Seattle's people like?

> What did the white chief wish to do?

---

1. **great chief at Washington.** President of the United States

words for everyday use
re • proach (ri prōch′) *vt.,* accuse, blame. *The minister <u>reproached</u> the boy for stealing from the collection plate.*
dis • fig • ure (dis fig′yər) *vt.,* hurt the appearance of. *Her appearance became frightening after she decided to <u>disfigure</u> herself with fake scars and white makeup.*

Scorched Earth, Clear-cut Logging on Native Sovereign Land, Shaman Coming to Fix, 1991.
Lawrence Paul Yuxweluptun, National Gallery of Canada, Ottawa.

bristling wall of strength, and his wonderful ships of war will fill our harbors so that our ancient enemies far to the northward—the Hydas and Tsimpsians—will cease to frighten our women, children, and old men. Then in reality will he be our father and we his children. But can that ever be? Your God is not our God! Your God loves your people and hates mine. He folds his strong protecting arms lovingly about the pale face and leads him by the hand as a father leads his infant son—but He has forsaken His red children—if they really are His. Our God, the Great Spirit, seems also to have forsaken us. Your God makes your people wax strong every day. Soon they will fill all the land. Our people are ebbing away like a rapidly

> How did Seattle feel about God and His relationship to Seattle's people?

art**note**

Scorched Earth, Clear-cut Logging on Native Sovereign Land, Shaman Coming to Fix, 1991. Lawrence Paul Yuxweluptun.

Lawrence Paul Yuxweluptun (1957–) of the Salish tribe of Canada uses his art to address the impact of environmental policies on Native peoples. His work encompasses painting, performance art, and virtual reality computer installations. In this painting he combines traditional Northwest Coast tribal imagery with European Surrealism. Faces of spirits can be found all around: in the sky, in trees and stumps, on the ground. What passages in Chief Seattle's letter also reflect this belief?

1. Seattle felt that God loved the white people but hated and had forsaken Seattle's people.

CROSS-CURRICULAR CONNECTIONS

HISTORY. In the fall of 1851, the crew of the schooner *Exact*, making their way to the Queen Charlotte Islands off the Canadian coast from Portland, Oregon, stopped at what is now known as Alki Point in West Seattle. The party that disembarked built the first primitive settlement, which was briefly called Duwamps after one of Chief Seattle's peoples.

ART NOTE

Scorched Earth, Clear-cut Logging on Native Sovereign Land, Shaman Coming to Fix, 1991. Lawrence Paul Yuxweluptun.

Responses will vary, but students might suggest the opening of the selection ("Yonder sky that has wept tears of compassion"), Chief Seattle's statement on page 436 that "Sad-voiced winds moan in the distance," and his closing on page 437, starting with his statement that "even the rocks . . . thrill with memories of stirring events . . ." His words that the white man's cities and villages "will throng with the returning hosts that once filled them and still love this beautiful land" especially relate to Yuxweluptun's painting.

ANSWERS TO GUIDED READING QUESTIONS

1. Seattle could not conceive of the two peoples being united under a single god because the white people did not protect Seattle's people or give them laws. Seattle said the two peoples had separate origins and destinies.
2. The land was important in Seattle's religion because the resting place of ancestors was considered sacred. The dead did not forget the land that gave them being, and often returned to visit, guide, console, and comfort the living.

LITERARY NOTE

Despite the Port Elliot Treaty, the city of Seattle's early growth was stunted by fear of hostile encounters with the local Native American population. During 1855–1858 there was a violent Native American uprising, which was a powerful deterrent to potential settlers. Significant growth came with the arrival of the railroads and the crucial decision that named Seattle—not Tacoma or Portland—the western terminus of the transcontinental rail system. The Klondike gold rush of 1897 also made Seattle the port of entry for prospectors heading to Alaska.

receding tide that will never return. The white man's God cannot love our people or He would protect them. They seem to be orphans who can look nowhere for help. How then can we be brothers? How can your God become our God and renew our prosperity and awaken in us dreams of returning greatness? If we have a common heavenly father He must be partial—for He came to His paleface children. We never saw Him. He gave you laws but had no word for his red children whose teeming multitudes once filled this vast continent as stars fill the firmament.[2] No; we are two distinct races with separate origins and separate destinies. There is little in common between us.

What did Seattle think about the possibility of his people and white people being related and united under a single god?

To us the ashes of our ancestors are sacred and their resting place is hallowed ground.[3] You wander far from the graves of your ancestors and seemingly without regret. Your religion was written upon tables of stone by the iron finger of your God[4] so that you could not forget. The Red Man could never comprehend nor remember it. Our religion is the traditions of our ancestors—the dreams of our old men, given them in the solemn hours of night by the Great Spirit; and the visions of our sachems,[5] and is written in the hearts of our people.

Your dead cease to love you and the land of their nativity[6] as soon as they pass the portals of[7] the tomb and wander way beyond the stars. They are soon forgotten and never return. Our dead never forget the beautiful world that gave them being. They still love its verdant

How did Seattle's dead ancestors feel about the land? Why was the land important in Seattle's religion?

valleys, its murmuring rivers, its magnificent mountains, sequestered vales and verdant-lined lakes and bays, and ever yearn in tender, fond affection over the lonely hearted living, and often return from the Happy Hunting Ground[8] to visit, guide, console and comfort them.

Day and night cannot dwell together. The red man has ever fled the approach of the white man, as the morning mist flees before the morning sun.

However, your proposition seems fair and I think that my people will accept it and will retire to the reservation you offer them. Then we will dwell in peace, for the words of the great white chief seem to be the words of nature speaking to my people out of dense darkness.

It matters little where we pass the remnant of our days. They will not be many. The Indians' night promises to be dark. Not a single star of hope hovers above his horizon. Sad-voiced winds moan in the distance. Grim fate seems to be on the red man's trail, and wherever he goes he will hear the approaching footsteps of his fell destroyer[9] and prepare stolidly to meet his doom, as does the wounded doe that hears the approaching footsteps of the hunter.

A few more moons. A few more winters—and not one of the descendants of the mighty hosts that once moved over this broad land or lived in happy homes, protected by the Great Spirit, will

---

2. **firmament.** Sky seen as an arch
3. **hallowed ground.** Sacred ground
4. **written . . . iron finger of your God.** Chief Seattle is referring to the stone tablets containing the Ten Commandments that, according to the Old Testament, were handed down from God to Moses.
5. **sachems.** Holy men
6. **nativity.** Birth
7. **portals of.** Opening to
8. **Happy Hunting Ground.** Heaven; place of afterlife
9. **fell destroyer.** Cruel murderer

words for everyday use

re • ced • ing (ri sēd´iŋ) *adj.*, moving back. *His receding hairline made everyone think he was going bald.*
ver • dant (vʉrd´´nt) *adj.*, green; covered in vegetation. *When we saw the verdant hills of Vermont, we understood why it was called the Green Mountain State.*
se • ques • tered (si kwes´tərd) *adj.*, secluded. *The sequestered valley was both beautiful and remote; its hidden lakes and secluded location made it a perfect spot for camping.*
rem • nant (rem´nənt) *n.*, small remaining part. *The discount store sold me a carpet remnant at a reasonable price.*
stol • id • ly (stäl´id lē) *adv.*, in a way that shows little emotion or excitability. *He thought stolidly about the high school prom, and did not participate in excited conversations about it.*

RESPOND TO THE SELECTION

If you had been in the original audience for his speech, do you think you would have agreed with him or do you think you would have had an opposing response?

remain to mourn over the graves of a people—once more powerful and hopeful than yours. But why should I mourn at the untimely fate of my people? Tribe follows tribe, and nation follows nation, like the waves of the sea. It is the order of nature, and regret is useless. Your time of decay may be distant, but it will surely come, for even the white man whose God walked and talked with him as friend with friend, cannot be <u>exempt</u> from the common destiny. We may be brothers after all. We will see.

What warning did Seattle give the white people?

We will ponder your proposition and when we decide we will let you know. But should we accept it, I here and now make this condition that we will not be denied the privilege without <u>molestation</u> of visiting at any time the tombs of our ancestors, friends, and children. Every part of this soil is sacred in the estimation of my people. Every hillside, every valley, every plain and grove, has been hallowed by some sad or happy event in days long vanished. Even the rocks, which seem to be dumb and dead as they swelter in the sun along the silent shore, thrill with memories of stirring events connected with the lives of my people, and the very dust upon which you now stand responds more lovingly to

What demand did Seattle make? Why was this request so important?

their footsteps than to yours, because it is rich with the blood of our ancestors and our bare feet are conscious of the sympathetic touch. Our departed braves, fond mothers, glad, happy-hearted maidens, and even our little children who lived here and rejoiced here for a brief season, will love these somber solitudes and at eventide[10] they greet shadowy returning spirits. And when the last red man shall have perished, and the memory of my tribe shall have become a myth among the white men, these shores will swarm with the invisible dead of my tribe, and when your children's children think themselves alone in the field, the store, the shop, upon the highway, or in the silence of the pathless woods, they will not be alone. In all the earth there is no place dedicated to solitude. At night when the streets of your cities and villages are silent and you think them deserted, they will throng with the returning hosts that once filled them and still love this beautiful land. The white man will never be alone.

Let him be just and deal kindly with my people, for the dead are not powerless. Dead, did I say? There is no death, only a change of worlds. ∎

How did Seattle view death?

_____

10. **eventide.** Evening

Respond *to the* SELECTION

To what idea in Chief Seattle's speech did you relate the most strongly?

Vocabulary in Context
Fill in each blank below with one of the words from the Words for Everyday Use. You may have to change the tense of the word.

verdant   receding   reproach   disfigure
remnant   sequestered

1. Ms. Teeslink **reproached** Billie for cheating on the math test.
2. Marcella's face became **disfigured** due to the car accident.
3. His **receding** hairline made the man look older than he really was.
4. The **verdant** golf course was lush and green.
5. We decided to go to a **sequestered** island so we could be alone.

Literary Tools
Fill in the blank using the terms below.

image   imagery   mood   aim

1. **Mood** is the emotion created in the reader by a literary work.
2. Language that creates a representation, or a "picture in words," of an object or experience is called a(n) **image**.
3. Nature **imagery** is used in Seattle's speech.

ANSWERS TO GUIDED READING QUESTIONS

1. Seattle warned the white people that they were mortal, and that their "time of decay" would surely come.
2. Seattle demanded to be able to visit the tombs of his peoples' ancestors, friends, and children at any time. This request was important because the soil was sacred to Seattle's people, and their connection to the land was powerful.
3. Seattle believed that there is no death, only a change of worlds.

SELECTION CHECK TEST 4.5.15 WITH ANSWERS

Checking Your Reading
1. Of which two Native American groups was Seattle chief? **Seattle was chief of the Duwamish and Suquamish peoples.**
2. What does the "white chief" want from Chief Seattle? **The white chief wants to buy the land where Chief Seattle's people have lived for generations, and says he will allow the people to keep enough land on which to "live comfortably."**
3. What has happened to Chief Seattle's people? **Chief Seattle says that the number of his people has been reduced and that their former greatness is now only "a mournful memory."**
4. Why have Seattle's people never been able to comprehend the white people's religion? **Chief Seattle's people cannot comprehend the white people's religion because it is so different from their own. They cannot understand why the whites wander away from the graves of their ancestors; they themselves hold the ashes of their ancestors sacred. They cannot understand why the whites needed to have the heavenly commandments written on tables of stone, because their own religion is written in their hearts. The white people's dead disappear and never return, whereas the Native American dead often return to visit, guide, console, and comfort their living relatives.**
5. Why will the white people never be alone after the Native Americans have all perished? **The white people will never be alone because at night, when their cities are silent and appear deserted, they will actually be filled with the ghosts of the Native Americans who were there before them.**

RECALL

1a. Life for Seattle's people will change as the weather does. However, Seattle's words will never change.

2a. The white chief wants to buy the land where Chief Seattle's people have lived for generations. He says that the number of his people has been reduced. The young considered revenge to be a gain, even at the cost of their own lives. Old men and mothers who have sons to lose know better.

3a. Both the white people's God and the Great Spirit seemed to have forsaken the speaker's people. Chief Seattle considers the resting place of his ancestors to be sacred. He believes that the dead of his people still love the natural world and return to visit, guide, console, and offer comfort to the living. The dead of the white people cease to love the living and the land of their birth.

INTERPRET

1b. Seattle compares his words to stars, the white people to the grass covering the prairies, and his own people to scattered trees. He makes these comparisons to make a point about the differences between the white man and his people and to emphasize the importance he and his people place on land.

2b. Seattle feels that the white chief's wish to buy Native American lands is just and generous. He does not mourn over the downfall of his people, conceding that they too may have been to blame for their fate.

3b. Ancestors are important because they are sacred. Chief Seattle's religion is made up of the traditions of ancestors, from the dreams of old men, and the visions of holy men.

ANALYZE

4a. Seattle expresses the religion of his people in terms of the traditions of ancestors. He expresses the white people's religion as written upon tables of stone by the iron finger of God, meaning the Ten Commandments.

SYNTHESIZE

4b. Seattle says it matters little where his people spend the rest of their days because their days are few. Seattle demands the right for his people to visit the tombs of their ancestors, friends, and children at any time without interference because this land is sacred.

PERSPECTIVE

5a. Chief Seattle is an intelligent and forceful leader. He understands how the world has changed for his tribe

Investigate, Inquire, and Imagine

Recall: GATHERING FACTS

1a. At the beginning of the speech, what is Chief Seattle referring to when he talks about the sky or weather changing? What things does Seattle say are "changeless and eternal"?

2a. What does the white chief want? What happened to the speaker's people? What do the young think of revenge? What do old men and mothers know about it?

3a. What did both the God of the white people and the Great Spirit do? How does Seattle feel about the resting place of his ancestors? How do the dead of his people differ from the dead of the white people?

Interpret: FINDING MEANING

1b. What comparisons does Chief Seattle make in the first paragraph? Why does he make these comparisons?

2b. How does Seattle feel about what the white chief wants? How does he feel about the downfall of his people?

3b. Why are ancestors so important? What comprises Chief Seattle's religion?

Analyze: TAKING THINGS APART

4a. As seen by Chief Seattle, compare and contrast his people's religion with the religion of the white people.

Synthesize: BRINGING THINGS TOGETHER

4b. Why does Seattle say it does not matter where his people spend the rest of their days? Why does Seattle ask for the condition of allowing his people to visit the land outside the reservation?

Perspective: LOOKING AT OTHER VIEWS

5a. Evaluate what characteristics of Chief Seattle are revealed by his speech.

Empathy: SEEING FROM INSIDE

5b. Compare and contrast the white people's relationship with the natural world to that of the Native Americans.

Understanding Literature

MOOD. Review the definition for **mood** in the Handbook of Literary Terms. What mood does Chief Seattle convey in his speech?

IMAGE AND IMAGERY. Review the definitions for **image** and **imagery** in Literary Tools and the chart you made for that section on page 433. What images does Chief Seattle use to compare white people to his people? What sky images does Seattle use? How does this imagery make Seattle's point more striking?

ANSWERS TO INVESTIGATE, INQUIRE, AND IMAGINE (CONT.)

even though he is saddened by it. In his speech he is diplomatic and poetic. Chief Seattle remains firm in his conviction that white people do not understand Native Americans.

EMPATHY

5b. The Native Americans have a very close association with the natural world as evidenced by the imagery in Seattle's speech. They only take what they need from the land. The land is sacred to them because

of all the events that have taken place there through time and because they believe the dead still visit and love the land. The white people tried to conquer the land—they chopped down many of the forests for wood to build, mined the earth, and built roads and railroads across the land.

Answers to Understanding Literature can be found on page 439.

Writer's Journal

1. Imagine you are Governor Stevens. Write a **telegram** of no more than six sentences to Washington summarizing Chief Seattle's speech.

2. Write a **monument inscription** for a statue of Seattle based on the details you've learned from his speech and the background information in this text.

3. Seattle believed that the dead were not powerless. Imagine that you are a white person who meets one of the invisible dead of Seattle's people. Would the ancestral ghost approve of the way your people are using the land and of your feelings for the natural environment? What do you think the ghost would say to you? Write a **dialogue** that incorporates this imaginary encounter.

Integrating the Language Arts

Language, Grammar, and Style

NOUNS OF DIRECT ADDRESS. Read the Language Arts Survey 3.32, "Avoiding Problems Caused by Understood Subjects and Nouns of Direct Address." Then identify the nouns of direct address in each of the following sentences.

1. Sam, are you going on the field trip to the Navajo reservation?
2. Can you see the silversmiths selling their jewelry, Anne?
3. Remember, everyone, that it costs a dollar to visit the hogan.
4. Michelle and Pam, are you buying a Navajo rug?
5. Remember, class, to meet at 2:00 for the tour of Monument Valley.

Study and Research

RESEARCHING TREATIES. The United States government signed treaties, like the Port Eliot Treaty, with many Native American groups. Many of these treaties were broken. Choose a Native American tribe and research the treaties made, whether they were broken, and if applicable, what is happening with those treaties today. When you have finished your research, make a presentation to the class.

Speaking and Listening

TELLING A NATIVE AMERICAN STORY. Read a Native American myth. Write the main events on an index card. Then practice telling the story to a small group of classmates. You may find it useful to read the Language Arts Survey 4.20, "Telling a Story."

ANSWERS TO INTEGRATING THE LANGUAGE ARTS

Language, Grammar, and Style
1. Sam
2. Anne
3. everyone
4. Michelle and Pam
5. class

Study and Research
Students may want to find copies of what Native American treaties looked like and use them as visual aids in their presentations. Also remind students that when working in groups, all group members must participate and contribute ideas.

ANSWERS TO UNDERSTANDING LITERATURE

MOOD. Chief Seattle seems saddened by, but accepting of, his people's fate. At the end of the speech, he impresses upon his listeners an atmosphere of respect for the sacredness of the land and the ancestors of his people.

IMAGE AND IMAGERY. The images that Seattle uses to compare white people to his people include "grass that covers vast prairies" for the white people and "scattered trees of a storm-swept plain" for his people.

Additionally, he mentions how the Native Americans fled from the white people the way the morning mist flies from the morning sun. The sky images he uses include a fair sky and an overcast sky with clouds, as well as stating "my words are like the stars that never change" and "not a single star of hope hovers above the horizon." The imagery makes Seattle's point more striking because it reinforces the importance of the natural world to his people.

VOCABULARY FROM THE SELECTION

anthropologist	meticulous
antiquity	obtuseness
barrage	reprehensible
dint	reticent
haphazardly	scrupulously
intersperse	

GRAPHIC ORGANIZER

Students should complete their chart as follows:

Tenor	Vehicle
ESA alphabet	hit parade
"	chorus line
past	the home shore gradually disappearing in the eyes of a sailor

also uses figures of speech in talking about letters as if they were alive

also
words in notebook/words of the Delphic Oracle
alphabet/artillery barrage

READER'S JOURNAL

How would your life change if you were paralyzed? How would you cope with your situation? How would you communicate?

MEMOIR

Literary TOOLS

MEMOIR. A **memoir** is a nonfiction narration that tells a story. A memoir can be autobiographical (about one's life) or biographical (about someone else's life). As you read "The Alphabet" and "Paris," decide what stories Bauby tells.

METAPHOR AND SIMILE. A **metaphor** is a figure of speech in which one thing is spoken or written about as if it were another. A **simile** is a comparison using _like_ or _as_. Both figures of speech invite the reader to make a comparison between two things. The two "things" involved are the writer's actual subject, the _tenor_ of the figure of speech, and another thing to which the subject is likened, the _vehicle_ of the figure of speech.

Graphic Organizer

As you read, make a chart like the one below listing the vehicle and tenor for the figures of speech you find in Bauby's memoir. One example has been done for you.

Tenor	Vehicle
paralysis	diving bell

Reader's Journal

When have you felt closed in or limited by your physical abilities?

"The Alphabet" and "Paris"
from The Diving Bell and the Butterfly
by Jean-Dominique Bauby

Reader's resource

"The Alphabet" and **"Paris"** are two chapters from Jean-Dominique Bauby's memoir _The Diving Bell and the Butterfly_, a book in which Bauby describes his experiences of living in virtually total paralysis. In "The Alphabet" Bauby describes the alphabet that helps him escape from the paralysis of his diving bell and free the butterflies of his imagination. In "Paris" he describes the city that is filled with memories for him on one occasion and the city that doesn't move him any more on another occasion.

About _the_ AUTHOR

In 1995 **Jean-Dominique Bauby** (1952–1997) had a successful career as the editor in chief of one of France's premier fashion magazines for women. A stroke to the brain stem left him in a coma. When he woke up, the only part of his body that still functioned was his left eye, with which he could communicate by blinking to select letters one by one as a special alphabet was slowly recited to him. In the same way, Bauby composed _The Diving Bell and the Butterfly_ (1997). He died two days after his book was published in France.

GOALS/OBJECTIVES

Studying this lesson will enable students to
- appreciate a memoir about a man's experiences with being paralyzed
- describe Bauby's literary accomplishments
- define _memoir, metaphor,_ and _simile_ and recognize the use of metaphor and simile in their reading
- identify action and linking verbs in sentences
- practice communicating using the ESA alphabet
- plan an itinerary for visiting Paris

THE ALPHABET

Jean-Dominique Bauby

I am fond of my alphabet letters. At night, when it is a little too dark and the only sign of life is the small red spot in the center of the television screen, vowels and consonants dance for me to a Charles Trenet[1] tune: "Dear Venice, sweet Venice, I'll always remember you…" Hand in hand, the letters cross the room, whirl around the bed, sweep past the window, wriggle across the wall, swoop to the door, and return to begin again.

E S A R I N T U L O M D P C F B
V H G J Q Z Y X K W

The jumbled appearance of my chorus line stems not from chance but from cunning calculation. More than an alphabet, it is a hit parade in which each letter is placed according to the frequency of its use in the French language. That is why E dances proudly out in front, while W labors to hold on to last place. B resents being pushed back next to V, and haughty J—which begins so many sentences in French—is amazed to find itself so near the rear of the pack. Rolypoly G is annoyed to have to trade places with H, while T and U, the tender components of *tu*,[2] rejoice that they have not been separated. All this reshuffling has a purpose: to make it easier for those who wish to communicate with me.

It is a simple enough system. You read off the alphabet (ESA version, not ABC) until, with a blink of my eye, I stop you at the letter to be noted. The maneuver is repeated for the letters that follow, so that fairly soon you have a whole word, and then fragments of more or less intelligible sentences. That, at least, is the theory. In reality, all does not go well for some visitors. Because of nervousness, impatience, or obtuseness, performances vary in the handling of the code (which is what we call this method of transcribing my thoughts). Crossword fans and Scrabble players have a head start. Girls manage better than boys. By dint of practice, some of them know the code by heart and no longer even turn to our special notebook—the one containing the order of the letters and in which all my words are set down like the Delphic oracle's.

Indeed, I wonder what conclusions anthropologists of the year 3000 will reach if they ever chance to leaf through these notebooks, where haphazardly scribbled remarks like "The physical therapist is pregnant," "Mainly on the legs," "Arthur Rimbaud,"[3] and "The French team

How does Bauby communicate with visitors?

---

1. **Charles Trenet.** Popular French singer
2. **tu.** French pronoun meaning *you* used when addressing friends and family members
3. **Arthur Rimbaud.** French Symbolist poet (1854-1891)

words for everyday use

ob • tuse • ness (äb tüs′ nəs) n., state of demonstrating slow intellect; dullness. *Jill's obtuseness in understanding the essay question made her lose ten points on the test.*

dint (dint) n., because; by dint of: because of. *By dint of hard work Mrs. Woodring rose to the head of the company.*

an • thro • pol • o • gist (an thrə pä′ lə jist) n., someone who studies human beings in relation to their characteristics and culture. *Margaret Mead was an anthropologist who studied puberty rites in Samoa.*

hap • haz • ard • ly (hap ha′ zərd lē) adv., done in a manner marked by lack of plan, order, or direction. *Dan's social studies teacher said he wrote his research paper haphazardly.*

---

1. Reticent people are more difficult for Bauby to communicate with. When asked how they are, they say only "Fine," which puts the ball back in Bauby's court.
2. Bauby sees the ultra-modern high rise where he used to work as editor in chief of a famous women's magazine.

CROSS-CURRICULAR
CONNECTION

MYTHOLOGY. Bauby compares the words that are contained in his notebooks to Delphic Oracles. Delphic Oracles are named after the village of Delphi, Greece. This is an important village because the famous Greek temple of Apollo resided here. People from all over the world would visit the temple of Apollo to consult the oracle (a person through whom a deity is believed to speak) that was there. The Delphic Oracles (collection of answers given by the oracle) are considered to be sacred because the oracles from Delphi were known to be the wisest and most respected of all oracles. The oracles were often ambiguous and could lead to disaster when misinterpreted.

played like pigs" are <u>interspersed</u> with unintelligible gibberish, misspelled words, lost letters, omitted syllables.

Nervous visitors come most quickly to grief. They reel off the alphabet tonelessly, at top speed, jotting down letters almost at random; and then, seeing the meaningless result, exclaim, "I'm an idiot!" But in the final analysis, their anxiety gives me a chance to rest, for they take charge of the whole conversation, providing both questions and answers, and I am spared the task of holding up my end. <u>Reticent</u> people are much more difficult. If I ask them, "How are you?" they answer, "Fine," immediately putting the ball back in my court. With some, the alphabet becomes an artillery <u>barrage</u>, and I need to have two or three questions ready in advance in order not to be swamped. <u>Meticulous</u> people never go wrong: they <u>scrupulously</u> note down each letter and never seek to unravel the mystery of a sentence before it is complete. Nor would they dream of completing a single word for you. Unwilling to chance the smallest error, they will never take it upon themselves to provide the "room" that follows "mush," the "ic" that follows "atom," or the "nable" without which neither "intermi" nor "abomi" can exist. Such scrupulousness makes for laborious progress, but at least you avoid the misunderstandings in which impulsive visitors bog down when they neglect to verify their intuitions. Yet I understood the poetry of such

What type of person does Bauby find it "more difficult" to communicate with? Why?

mind games one day when, attempting to ask for my glasses (*lunettes*), I was asked what I wanted to do with the moon (*lune*).

PARIS

I am fading away. Slowly but surely. Like the sailor who watches the home shore gradually disappear, I watch my past recede. My old life still burns within me, but more and more of it is reduced to the ashes of memory.

Yet since taking up residence in my diving bell,[4] I have made two brief trips to the world of Paris medicine to hear the verdict pronounced on me from the diagnostic heights. On the first occasion, my emotions got the better of me when my ambulance happened to pass the ultra modern high-rise where I once followed the <u>reprehensible</u> calling of editor in chief of a famous women's magazine. First I recognized the building next door—a sixties <u>antiquity</u>, now scheduled to be demolished, according to the billboard out front. Then I saw our own glass façade, airily reflecting clouds and airplanes. On the sidewalk were a few of those familiar-looking faces that one passes every day for ten

What building does Bauby see on his first trip to Paris?

---

4. **diving bell.** Diving apparatus consisting of a container open only at the bottom and supplied with compressed air by a hose

words for everyday use

in • ter • sperse (in tər spərs') *vt.*, placed at intervals in or among. *Fine art reproductions are <u>interspersed</u> throughout the selections of the textbook.*

ret • i • cent (re' tə sənt) *adj.*, inclined to be silent or uncommunicative in speech. *Because Jonah was <u>reticent</u> at his midterm conference, Mr. Washburn didn't know if he was going to try harder in electronics class.*

bar • rage (bə räzh') *n.*, vigorous or rapid outpouring or projection of many things at once. *The teacher could not ignore the <u>barrage</u> of protests from students after she assigned homework during vacation.*

me • tic • u • lous (mə ti' kyə ləs) *adj.*, marked by extreme or excessive care in the treatment of details; careful. *The lawyer maintained a <u>meticulous</u> personal appearance.*

scru • pu • lous • ly (skrü' pyə ləs lē) *adv.*, done in a painstakingly exact manner. *<u>Scrupulously</u>, the housekeeper swept up the broken glass.*

rep • re • hen • si • ble (re pri hen' sə bəl) *adj.*, worthy of or deserving disapproval or censure. *The judge was not looking forward to another day of hearing about the <u>reprehensible</u> acts of criminals.*

an • tiq • ui • ty (an ti' kwə tē) *n.*, something old, like relics, statues, or monuments. *The museum featured Greek and Roman <u>antiquities</u>.*

442 *UNIT FIVE / NONFICTION*

The Eiffel Tower, 1935. Raoul Dufy. Private Collection.

years without ever being able to put a name to them. When I thought I glimpsed someone I actually knew, walking behind a woman with her hair in a bun and a burly man in work clothes, I nearly unscrewed my head to see. Perhaps someone had caught sight of my ambulance from our sixth floor offices. I shed a few tears as we passed the corner café where I used to drop in for a bite. I can weep quite discreetly. People think my eye is watering.

The second time I went to Paris, four months later, I was unmoved by it. The streets were decked out in summer finery, but for me it was still winter, and what I saw through the ambulance windows was just a movie background. Filmmakers call the process a "rear screen projection," with the hero's car speeding along a road that unrolls behind him on a studio wall. Hitchcock films owe much of their poetry to the use of this process in its early, unperfected stages. My own crossing of Paris left me indifferent. Yet nothing was missing— housewives in flowered dresses and youths on roller skates, revving buses, messengers cursing on their scooters. The Place de l'Opéra, straight out of a Dufy[5] canvas. The treetops foaming like surf against glass building fronts, wisps of cloud in the sky. Nothing was missing, except me. I was elsewhere. ∎

How does Bauby's second visit to Paris differ from the first?

---

5. **Dufy.** Raoul Dufy, French painter (1877-1953), whose cityscapes are characterized by bright colors

FROM THE DIVING BELL AND THE BUTTERFLY **443**

ANSWER TO GUIDED READING QUESTION

1. He feels he is missing from the landscape, and Paris leaves him feeling "indifferent."

SELECTION CHECK TEST 4.5.17 WITH ANSWERS

Checking Your Reading
1. Of what is Bauby fond? **He is fond of his alphabet letters.**
2. How are the letters of his alphabet organized? **The letters of his "ESA" alphabet are organized according to the frequency of their use in the French language.**
3. How does Bauby communicate with visitors? **The visitor reads off Bauby's special alphabet and Bauby blinks with his left eye to indicate which letter he wants.**
4. Which types of people do well with Bauby's alphabet letters? **Crossword fans, Scrabble players, and girls manage to do well.**
5. What was missing during Bauby's second visit to Paris? **Nothing was missing, except Bauby.**

Vocabulary in Context
Fill in each blank below with the most appropriate word from the following Words for Everyday Use. You may have to change the tense of the word.

meticulous   obtuseness   reticent
scrupulously   anthropologist
haphazardly

1. The students **scrupulously** copied down all the vocabulary words, getting the spelling correct for each one.
2. The trainer was frustrated by Fifi's **obtuseness** in learning new tricks and finally concluded that Fifi was a rather dumb dog.
3. I chose to to be a(n) **anthropologist** because I'm interested in learning about different cultures throughout the world.
4. Because the project was put together **haphazardly**, our group had to do it over again.
5. Gwen is so **meticulous**; she remembers the slightest detail about everything.

Literary Tools
Fill in the blank using the following terms.

simile   autobiography   biography   memoir   metaphor

1. A(n) **memoir** can be autobiographical or biographical.
2. A(n) **biography** is about someone else's life.
3. "The Alphabet" is an example of a(n) **autobiography**.
4. A comparison that uses *like* or *as* is called a(n) **simile**.
5. A(n) **metaphor** is a type of figurative language in which one thing is written about as if it were another.

RESPOND TO THE SELECTION

After reading the selection, how have you become more sympathetic toward people who are limited in their physical abilities? How important is imagination and creativity for Bauby?

ANSWERS TO INVESTIGATE, INQUIRE, AND IMAGINE

RECALL

1a. The ESA alphabet is Bauby's lifeline to the outside world.

2a. There are nervous visitors, who reel off the alphabet tonelessly and jot down letters almost at random, resulting in miscommunication. Then there are reticent visitors, who put the burden of communication on Bauby. Finally, there are meticulous people, who write down each letter scrupulously and wait until the sentence is complete.

3a. Bauby describes "rear-screen projection" in which a scene is projected on a studio wall behind the actor.

INTERPRET

1b. Each letter of the ESA alphabet is placed according to the frequency of its use in the French language. This increases the likelihood that the letters Bauby's visitors want to use will appear quickly.

2b. Bauby prefers meticulous people with whom he never has any misunderstandings.

3b. Bauby no longer feels a part of Paris city life. It is as if the sights of Paris are being projected behind him.

ANALYZE

4a. Bauby works diligently and laboriously to communicate with his visitors. Even in his paralysis he wants to communicate with the people from his past life. This indicates that he has not given up on life.

SYNTHESIZE

4b. Bauby still has a full inner life. In "The Alphabet" he describes how his tool of communication dances for him like a "chorus line." In "Paris" he shows how the memories of his past still accompany him.

Respond to the SELECTION

Of the types of visitors Bauby describes, which would describe you if you went to visit him?

Investigate, Inquire, and Imagine

Recall: GATHERING FACTS

1a. In "The Alphabet," what is Bauby's lifeline to the outside world?

2a. How does Bauby categorize his visitors in terms of how they communicate with him?

3a. In "Paris," what cinematic technique does Bauby describe?

Interpret: FINDING MEANING

1b. How does the alphabet facilitate communication with Bauby's visitors?

2b. Which visitors does Bauby prefer?

3b. Why does Bauby compare his second trip to Paris to a "rear-screen projection"?

Analyze: TAKING THINGS APART

4a. Because of his paralysis, has Bauby given up on life? Explain your answer.

Synthesize: BRINGING THINGS TOGETHER

4b. What does Bauby have left to live for besides his visitors?

Evaluate: MAKING JUDGMENTS

5a. Why does Bauby cry during his first trip to Paris? What does this reveal about him?

Extend: CONNECTING IDEAS

5b. If you were Bauby and a friend questioned your reason for wanting to write a memoir of your experience, what would you tell your friend?

Understanding Literature

MEMOIR. Review the definition of **memoir** in Literary Tools in Prereading. What stories does Bauby tell? Is his memoir autobiographical or biographical?

METAPHOR AND SIMILE. Review the definitions of **metaphor** and **simile** in the Handbook of Literary Terms and the chart you made in Literary Tools on page 440. For what condition is the diving bell of the memoir's title a metaphor? Explain the comparison that Bauby makes between the ESA alphabet and a "hit parade." With what simile does Bauby describe his past? Which is your favorite figure of speech? Why?

ANSWERS TO INVESTIGATE, INQUIRE, AND IMAGINE (CONT.)

EVALUATE

5a. Bauby is contrasting his past life with his present life. This makes him cry because he misses what he no longer has. His crying reveals that he still has a full range of human emotion; he hasn't become apathetic toward life because of his paralysis.

EXTEND

5b. Students may say that Bauby would say he wanted to create a lasting testament to life. Others may say that Bauby would say he wanted people to understand what he was going through.

Writer's Journal

1. Imagine you are Bauby's nurse and you are preparing to welcome visitors for your patient for the first time after his stroke. Write **directions** explaining to visitors how to use the ESA alphabet.

2. Imagine you are Bauby and a reader has just written asking you to explain the title of your memoir. Write the reader a **letter** answering his or her question.

3. Bauby writes, "I once followed the reprehensible calling of editor in chief of a famous women's magazine." Imagine you are Bauby. Write a **journal entry** explaining why your view of your past profession has changed. Explain how your paralysis makes you look at things differently.

Integrating the Language Arts

Language, Grammar, and Style

ACTION VERBS AND LINKING VERBS. Read the Language Arts Survey 3.10, "Linking Verbs" and 3.60, "Action Verbs and State of Being Verbs." Then identify each verb in the sentences below as an action verb or a linking verb.

1. Bauby was paralyzed when he wrote *The Diving Bell and the Butterfly*.
2. In his mind, the letters of the ESA alphabet danced around his room.
3. Some of his visitors seemed nervous when they tried to communicate with him.
4. Bauby visited Paris twice after his paralysis.
5. He felt unmoved by the "City of Lights" during his second trip.

Speaking and Listening

USING THE ESA ALPHABET. With a classmate, play the roles of Bauby and one of his visitors. The visitor wants to update Bauby on events in his or her life. Bauby wants to "talk" about the memoir he wants to write. Communicate with each other using the ESA alphabet. When Bauby talks, he uses his left eye to indicate the letters he intends by blinking when that letter is reached in the alphabet. The visitor writes down each letter that Bauby selects and makes guesses at what Bauby is trying to express. When you have finished the "conversation," share with the class what you learned about Bauby's experiences in communication as a paralyzed man. What personality traits did he demonstrate in persisting in communicating in this manner? What personality traits did his visitors demonstrate in coming to see him?

Study and Research & Collaborative Learning

ITINERARY FOR PARIS VACATION. Before his paralysis, Jean-Dominique Bauby lived and worked in Paris, the capital of France. Imagine that you and a classmate have three days to spend in Paris. Read guidebooks of Paris to research the city. Then, with a classmate, plan a detailed itinerary of what you would see at what time. (Be sure to allow realistic time for travel between your different destinations.) Also note in which hotel you would stay and what restaurants you would visit. For an online list of Paris museums, monuments, restaurants, and hotels, access the website **Les Pages de Paris** at http://www.paris.org.

Language, Grammar, and Style
1. was (linking verb); wrote (action verb)
2. danced (action verb)
3. seemed (linking verb); tried (action verb)
4. visited (action verb)
5. felt (linking verb)

ANSWERS TO UNDERSTANDING LITERATURE

MEMOIR. In "The Alphabet" Bauby tells the story of visitors coming to see him. In "Paris" he tells the stories of his two trips to Paris. *The Diving Bell and the Butterfly* is autobiographical; it tells the story of Bauby's life after he became paralyzed.

METAPHOR AND SIMILE. The diving bell is a metaphor for Bauby's paralysis. The hit parade lists songs in order of their popularity in the same way that the alphabet organizes letters by their frequency of use. Bauby says his past is like the home shore gradually disappearing in the eyes of a sailor. *Responses will vary.*

THE UNITED NATIONS ESSAY CONTEST

The United Nations is an alliance that was established in 1945, right after World War II, by 51 countries who who were commited to working together to preserve peace. They hoped that by joining together, they could develop friendly relations among nations, cooperate in solving international problems, and promote respect for human rights. Today, nearly every nation in the world belongs to the UN: membership now totals 189 countries, from Afghanistan to Zimbabwe.

The United States is a powerful country, and it has an important role in the UN. In order to make sure the United States is doing all it can to help the UN, a special organization was formed, called the **United Nations Association of the United States of America (UNA-USA).** The UNA-USA is a nonprofit organization that is not connected to any political party. Its sole purpose is to make the United Nations stronger. The UNA-USA points out problems it sees in policies and offers alternative ways to resolve conflicts.

In helping the United Nations become a stronger force in achieving global change, the UNA-USA encourages people to participate in its cause. One way the UNA-USA gets the American people involved is through programs like Adopt-a-Minefield. This program allows Americans to contribute to the global effort of finding and eliminating hidden landmines in war-torn countries such as Iran and Iraq.

UNA-USA also works to educate citizens of the United States about the work that is being done to achieve global peace and the serious challenges the UN faces in achieving this goal. It strives to make Americans aware of their role as individuals to influence our country's policy of peace and democracy towards other nations. At the heart of these educational efforts is the annual **National High School Essay Contest** sponsored by UNA-USA and a number of philanthropic organizations.

Since 1986, this annual nationwide essay contest has given students the opportunity to think about America's role in world organization and global policies. The United Nations believe that establishing and maintaining peace must begin at the grassroots level—with individuals working in their communities. And because the UN considers high school students to be the future of America, they are passionate about educating students about the consequences of war and violence, oppression and racism. They believe that if they educate young people, they can prevent wars in the future.

The essay contest is one way to help educate young people and to get them thinking about global issues. Past essay topics have included "The United Nations and the Protection of Human Rights" (1998 topic); "Who Needs Whom: Why the U.S. Needs the UN" (1999 topic); "Culture of Peace" (2000); and "Global Health" (2001). Essays are required to be 1,500 words or fewer. The grand prize winner receives $1,000. Second and third prize winners are rewarded $750 and $500 respectively. For more details about the annual essay contest, log on to http://www.unausa.org/programs/nhsessay.htm. At this site, you can read past winning essays, such as those written by Jennie Lin and Ramya Murali, pictured above. Jennie Lin's "The United

Left to right: **Francois Coutu**, UNDP, **Ramya Murali**, 1999 Second Place winner, UNA of Greater Miami, **Jennie Lin**, 1999 First Place winner, UNA Houston Chapter, **Amb. Clay Constantinou**, Dean, Seton Hall University School of Diplomacy and International Relations, **William H. Luers**, Chairman and President, UNA-USA.

States and Its Responsibility" won the first prize in 1999, and Ramya Murali's essay, "Can One Thrive Without the Other?" won second prize that year. See below for an excerpt from Jennie Lin's essay.

Also at the site, you can learn about other programs and events sponsored by UNA-USA in which students can participate. UNA-USA's programs, including the National High School Essay Contest and the renowned Model United Nations program, are preparing new members of all ages for active participation in a world of global change and challenge.

excerpt from "The United States and its Responsibility"
by Jennie Lin, Grade 10, St. John's School, Houston, Texas

As the country that played a prominent role in the formation of the United Nations, the United States of America has been a leader in the UN community for the past five decades. The U.S. and the UN have shared and still share similar ideals of maintaining international peace, encouraging worldwide respect for equal rights and human rights, and achieving international cooperation in solving global problems. However, many critics have argued that the U.S. no longer needs the UN—that the U.S. should reduce its role in the only viable international organization whose foundation consists of so many American principles. Although these critics may have some valid concerns, the U.S. needs to remain a leader in the UN community for three main reasons: the UN affects Americans positively, UN successes and projects significantly outweigh the costs and failures, and U.S. leadership is important to global society.

GUIDED WRITING
Software

See the Guided Writing Software for an extended version of this lesson that includes printable graphic organizers, extensive student models and student-friendly checklists, and self-, peer, and teacher evaluation features.

"We see that words are tactile; we find rough words, smooth words, words with splintered edges, words to shout or whisper with, words that caress, words that strike."

—James J. Kilpatrick

EXAMINING THE MODEL. Chief Seattle's speech clearly stated the bereavement of his people at their great loss, and their acceptance of some responsibility for their own destiny. But it also sought to trigger compassion from the victors—white people—and to promote respect for Native American spirituality. His speech was meant to touch the hearts as well as the minds of his audience. He did this with a see-saw of words, contrasting Native American and white perspectives.

continued on page 449

448 UNIT FIVE

Guided Writing

COMPOSING AND DELIVERING A SPEECH

The very nature of being human is imbedded in speech, whether it is audible or expressed through sign language. We are human because we have ideas and perspectives we want to share. Words are our tools to make changes, remedy injustice, weigh alternative visions with one another, or improve the human condition.

Think of the ways you use your persuasive powers in daily conversations. You already know that words vary in intensity. You have a range of words to use in order to convey an idea, to soothe, to incite. And the intensity of your words is raised to a higher power when you *speak* them rather than write them merely to be read.

WRITING ASSIGNMENT. In this assignment, you will write and deliver a speech, aiming to persuade a larger audience to understand your perspective and consider your viewpoint about a subject that is important to you.

In 1853, Chief Seattle delivered a speech that still stands as a model of considered, deliberate consciousness-raising.

Professional Model

from Chief Seattle's speech, "Yonder sky that has wept tears of compassion...," page 434

The great—and I presume—good white chief sends us word that he wishes to buy our lands but is willing to allow us enough to live comfortably....

Then in reality will he be our father and we his children. But can that ever be? Your God is not our God! Your God loves your people and hates mine. He folds his strong protecting arms lovingly about the pale face and leads him by the hand as a father leads his infant son—but He has forsaken His red children—if they really are His. Our God, the Great Spirit, seems also to have forsaken us. Your God makes your people wax strong every day. Soon they will fill all the land. Our people are ebbing away like a rapidly receding tide that will never return. The white man's God cannot love our people or He would protect them. . . . How then can we be brothers? . . . . No; we are two distinct races with separate origins and separate destinies. There is little in common between us.

To us the ashes of our ancestors are sacred and their resting place is hallowed ground. You wander far from the graves of your ancestors and seemingly without regret. Your religion was written upon tables of stone by the iron finger of your God so that you could not forget. The Red Man could never comprehend nor remember it. Our religion is the traditions of our ancestors—the dreams of our old men, given them in the solemn hours of night by the Great Spirit; and the visions of our sachems, and is written in the hearts of our people. . . .

We will ponder your proposition and when we decide we will let you know. But should we accept it, I here and now make this condition that we will not be denied the privilege without molestation of visiting at any time the tombs of our ancestors, friends, and children.

Prewriting

FINDING YOUR VOICE. Chief Seattle's voice is true to his emotions and his heavy feelings of defeat. His figurative and vividly descriptive language reveal what we today would identify as a lyrically poetic voice. Your voice for your own speech must show similar concern. How you show that concern will depend on your own natural style. Write the first draft of your speech as you would say it to a friend.

Your speech must also demonstrate a reasonable approach to your subject. An audience can be convinced by emotion, but only for a short time. Depth of feeling must be accompanied by logic in a voice that convinces both the mind and emotions.

IDENTIFYING YOUR AUDIENCE. Your immediate audience will be your classmates and your teacher. You may decide there is a wider audience for your piece after you have polished what you want to say and after you have tested it in class.

WRITING WITH A PLAN. As you select a topic for your speech, keep two rules in mind. First, **choose something you care about.** Look around at how problems in our society affect you personally. For example, many Americans feel that the government is not setting aside enough funds for education. Is a lack of funding affecting the quality of your school? Or for example, some people feel that sports are overemphasized in American society, and that arts and music programs are

In the excerpt, you can also feel the back-and-forth nature of his speech as Chief Seattle moves from rich metaphors and images that draw a picture of his world, to straightforward declarations and proposals that draw conclusions. Chief Seattle moves back and forth between speaking as the poet of his people to speaking as their leader.

His speech aims to persuade his audience that the Red Man must be able to return to burial grounds, essentially the entire country he roamed before the White Man came. He does this by first arousing the feelings of his listeners, then making his demands.

"Write what you need to write, feed the hunger for meaning in your life."
—Donald M. Murray

FINDING YOUR VOICE. With a partner, have students discuss a topic with which they are concerned. Instruct them to conduct a discussion of the topic, expressing their own opinion and considering the opinions of others while using a reasonable, concerned, and informed tone of expression.

IDENTIFYING YOUR AUDIENCE. Ask students to read the Language Arts Survey 2.4, "Identifying Your Audience." Encourage them to think not only about their teacher and classmates as their audience, but also about people who might be capable of identifying with their viewpoint the subject they choose to write about.

WRITING WITH A PLAN. To help students conduct research on their subject, refer them to the Language Arts Survey 5.39, "Informal and Formal Note-taking." Students may also want to keep a research journal to help them organize their thoughts and questions they may have about the subject they choose. Refer students to the Language Arts Survey 5.37, "Keeping a Research Journal."

INDIVIDUAL LEARNING STRATEGIES

Motivation

As a class, have students brainstorm what tone and body language is most effective in persuading someone to do something you want him or her to do. Encourage students to use various tones. Then vote on which is most persuasive. Also have students display various types of body language. Again, vote on which stance or position of the body is most effective.

READING PROFICIENCY

Have students read the Language Arts Survey 1.12, "Seeking Knowledge as an Active Reader." Then have them practice these skills by reading the editorial sections of the newspaper to get a feel for persuasive writing.

ENGLISH LANGUAGE LEARNING

Students may be interested in composing and delivering a persuasive speech about a subject or problem that is related to their own culture or nation of origin. Explain to students that they may need to provide background information about the topic in their speech to help their classmates understand the nature of the problem.

SPECIAL NEEDS

You may want to simplify this assignment by asking students to do the writing part of the assignment only. Students may also need help completing their graphic organizer. You may want to pair them with a more proficient student to help them with this activity.

ENRICHMENT

Pair students with a partner and ask each of them to research and prepare a short rebuttal speech to their partner's persuasive speech. Have students participate in a debate in front of the class. Refer students to the Language Arts Survey 4.21, "Participating in a Debate," for this activity.

STUDENT MODEL— GRAPHIC ORGANIZER

See the Writing Resource book for a blackline master of the graphic organizer for this lesson.

Rehearsing Your Speech

As you prepare to write and deliver your speech, you may want to organize a rehearsal group. One of the most important factors in presenting a successful speech is practice, and the best type of practice is rehearsing a speech in front of a live audience.

Get together with other students in groups of three to five and plan to meet regularly outside of class. Use your rehearsal group to act as an audience, provide helpful feedback, and offer support to group members.

---

ignored. Is this problem affecting you? Your life might be affected by other societal problems, such as racism, sexism, pollution, insufficient public transportation, lack of medical care, or poverty. Think about how societal problems or societal demands affect you in school, on the job, or in your family.

Secondly, **know something about the subject you choose.** You will probably need to do some research. Remember to keep track of all your sources. This will show your audience that you know what you're talking about—you have an informed opinion. And your audience should be able to find and read for themselves any sources you used in your speech. As you research your topic, jot down important points on 4" x 6" index cards. Identify the source at the top right corner of the card. Use a separate card for each fact or quotation. Later, you can move the cards around as you construct your speech, deciding the best place for each point.

After you have done your research, bounce your ideas off someone else. Ask another student or a family member to play the role of a "heckler." They should listen to your points and argue against them. This will help you identify opposing viewpoints. Plan to get help from friends or family later when you are ready to rehearse the speech.

Now organize your ideas on paper. Yan Lin used the graphic organizer below to organize her speech on the need for more quietness in our lives.

Student Model—Graphic Organizer

SPEECH TOPIC:
Quietness

OUTLINE FOR THE BODY OF THE SPEECH

HISTORY:
a. quietness is poorly defined as "lack of noise"
b. one person's quietness is misunderstood by observers

MY IDEAS:
a. quietness is a means of finding our true selves
b. quietness helps us understand more about others

OBJECTIONS AND OVERCOMING THEM:
a. communication isn't possible without speech
b. overcoming the objection: the action of listening speaks louder than words

---

Drafting

Use the graphic organizer to help you write out the body of your speech. Your introduction and conclusion will evolve. Just as you grab the attention of your reader in a piece of writing, you must grab your listeners. You must also have a powerful punch in the conclusion of the speech. It is not unusual for the introduction and the conclusion to be the last parts you write.

Keep an eye out for effective anecdotes that would personalize the problem you will be addressing. A story could be part of an effective introduction.

Keep your focus on what you ultimately want your audience to do and choose supporting arguments that will lead the audience to that point in your conclusion.

Write freely and with emotion. Reach out for the kind of vivid language that fits your personality and writing style. Think in richer language than you would use in a late-night debate with a friend; writing allows you to experiment.

Student Model—Draft

> —Title?
>
> In today's life, there is nothing but noise, hurry and fear. ^We People are ~~still~~? ~~fighting~~ over trivia ^such as ~~bothering about~~ who was right about the result of last night's game. ➤ Need transition here ^We have invested in so ^When we are not involved in idle chatter, we play with machines. many high technologies not to ease our minds, but ^to ~~hasten~~ everyday li^ves ^And ^crowd more into our many times people are eager to take risks, not to learn more about life, but rather to intensify the action in the already existing chaos. "The practice of quietness is the only way to secure ourselves against breaking down from exhaustion." –Identify source.
>
> When the word "quietness" is defined, people usually refer to it as the "lack of noise." Indeed, that's the concrete definition for its physical aspect. ~~But~~

Self- and Peer Evaluation

Once you have finished your draft, look over your text. Let at least one peer read over your speech. Ask these questions to help focus the revision.

- Does the speech have a strong beginning, middle, and end?
- What method is used in the introduction to make the audience sit straighter in their chairs, or stop doodling on their papers and look up?
- Do ideas in the body of the speech flow from one to the other?
- Are transition words and phrases used to carry the listener from one idea to the next?
- Are your word choices on your major points strong enough to make the listener take note (or maybe even literally jot down a note!)?
- Do you think your conclusion will make them nod their heads in assent? Smile in responsive agreement?

> "It does not require many words to speak the truth."
>
> —Chief Joseph of the Nez Percé

Language, Grammar, and Style

Formal and Informal English
Lesson Overview
In this lesson, students will be asked to do the following:
- Identify Formal and Informal English, 452
- Revise Inconsistent Language Use, 453
- Use Formal and Informal English Effectively, 453

INTRODUCING THE SKILL. Explain to students that the language in which they speak is critical to expressing the credibility of their speech. When one accomplishes the skill of appropriating formal or informal English to a piece of writing or speech, effective and clear writing is the result.

PREVIEWING THE SKILL. For a direct definition of formal and informal English, refer students to the Language Arts Survey 3.2, "Formal and Informal English."

PRACTICING THE SKILL. Ask students to audiotape themselves delivering the speech they wrote. Does their speech accurately portray how they feel about the topic? Does their speech accurately address the intended audience? Have them correct any incorrect statements in their speech using the techniques learned from this lesson.

Language, Grammar, and Style

Formal and Informal English

IDENTIFYING FORMAL AND INFORMAL ENGLISH. The nature of a speech can be formal or informal, depending on the situation. An informal speech might be called for if you are telling a story among friends, giving a pep talk to your team at halftime, or presenting a toast at the dinner table. A formal speech might be called for when you are presenting an assigned speech to classmates, giving a presentation to a community group or organization, or speaking at an awards ceremony. When giving a formal speech, you might need to wear special attire such as a suit or dress.

If you are giving an informal speech, you would probably use **informal English**, the kind of English that is spoken in everyday conversation. Informal English is enlivened by colloquialisms and slang, and it allows grammatical constructions that would not be acceptable in formal English.

However, if you are giving a formal speech, you will need to use **formal English**, the kind of English used in school papers, some magazine articles and nonfiction books, and most literary works. It is the kind of English everyone can understand. Read the Language Arts Survey 3.2, "Formal and Informal English," for more information and some examples.

continued on page 453

~~in this speech we are more looking at its spiritual sense.~~ But there is a spiritual sense to it as well.

Gradually we have not only ignored the immediate need for silence, but we have also misunderstood its true spiritual meaning. If ~~you~~ we see a beautiful lady, nicely dressed, lying under a pine tree, alone, facing the sky and letting the sunshine bathe her, what would you think of her? ~~One~~ We would probably picture her as an artist or a poet enjoying nature in pleasant weather. Now let's change the setting. It's still the same person dressed more casually, only now she is resting by a library table in the corner with nothing in front of her and her eyes closed, while all her friends are having lunch and fun in the cafeteria. Now ~~one~~ we would probably describe her differently, as odd or weird. Possibly, she is only being quiet and trying to think. So what misleads our thoughts, confusing this silence, this tranquility, with being unusual, peculiar? It's the outer distraction, the distraction of the world, distractions beyond our physical selves, even our clothes are a big

disturbance). The writer, Steven
Taylor, says in the magazine New
Should italicize
Renaissance, "Modern humans have lost
touch with their inner 'true self.'
Silence and stillness are a means to
recovering happiness and contentment."

Revising and Proofreading

Check the transitions in your speech. *Now* works as a signpost, as do other words such as *so, and then*, or *therefore*. These are transitions we use in conversation, so they sound natural in a speech. Check your draft to see if you have covered all aspects of the topic. Have you finished your speech with a flourish?

Student Model—Revised

Quietness
by Yan Lin

In today's life, there lies nothing
but noise, hurry and fear. We endlessly
fight over trivia, such as who was right
about the result of last night's game.
When we are not involved in idle
chatter, we are playing with machines.
We have invested in so many high
technologies—not to ease our minds, but
to crowd more into our everyday lives.
And many times we are eager to take
risks, not to learn more about life,
but rather to intensify the action in
the already existing chaos. "The
practice of quietness is the only way
to secure ourselves against breaking
down from exhaustion," Minister John
Gunn suggests.
        When the word "quietness" is defined,
we usually refer to it as the "lack of
noise." That is a concrete definition
for its physical aspect. But there is a
spiritual sense to it as well.
        Gradually we have not only ignored
the immediate need for silence, but we
have also misunderstood its true
spiritual meaning. If you see a

Yan's speech is a formal presentation of her ideas. She must be sure to use formal English throughout. How would you label your speech? Have you used formal or informal English?

REVISING INCONSISTENT LANGUAGE USE. Yan's initial draft of her speech included a statement about the speech itself:

> When the word "quietness" is defined, people usually refer to it as the "lack of noise." Indeed, that's the concrete definition for its physical aspect. But in this speech we are more looking at its spiritual sense.

Yan changed the paragraph to retain the formal nature of her speech. She especially wanted to remove the informal and incorrect phrasing of "we are more looking." Rewrite the sentence to make it consistent with the rest of the speech.

USING FORMAL AND INFORMAL ENGLISH EFFECTIVELY. Rewrite one paragraph of your speech for a different audience. Go to extremes. If your speech is formal, rewrite it as an informal speech. Envision a complete change of setting and audience, and notice the changes in the flow of your speech and its tone. Now look at the entire manuscript for your speech. Find any inconsistencies in the formality of the wording.

GUIDED WRITING **453**

Revising and Proofreading

A handout of the proofreading checklist is available in the Teacher's Resource Kit, Writing Resource book 2.45.

Overcoming Speaking Anxiety

While some students thrive in the spotlight, many others report feeling terror at the thought of standing up to give a speech. As intimidating as it may seem, giving frequent speeches is one of the best ways to overcome this fear. It is also helpful to think of the worst possible things that can happen, and to address these fears. Here are specific fears students list concerning public speaking:

- going blank or forgetting my speech
- being laughed at or ridiculed
- visibly trembling or shaking
- fainting or passing out
- being disorganized or losing my place
- blushing
- making a fool of myself
- perspiring profusely
- boring my audience
- getting dry mouth

By naming your fears and recognizing that many other speakers have the same experience, you can gain confidence and give successful speeches. You may want to rehearse your speech privately and then join a rehearsal group (see "Rehearsing Your Speech," page 450). Speaking in public is an important life and career skill. Many people have overcome initial fears to be able to speak effectively—and without anxiety—in front of others.

beautiful young woman, nicely dressed, lying under a pine tree, alone, facing the sky and letting the sunshine bathe her, what would you think of her? You would probably picture her as an artist or a poet enjoying nature in pleasant weather. Now let's change the setting. It's still the same person, only now she is dressed more casually, resting by a library table in the corner with nothing in front of her and her eyes closed, while all her friends are having lunch and fun in the cafeteria. Now we would probably describe her differently, as odd or weird. Possibly, she is only being quiet and trying to think. So what misleads our thoughts, confusing this silence, this tranquility, with being unusual, peculiar? It's the outer distraction, the distraction of the world, distractions beyond our physical selves—even our clothes are a big disturbance. The writer, Steven Taylor, says in the magazine *New Renaissance*, "Modern humans have lost touch with their inner 'true self.' Silence and stillness are a means to recovering happiness and contentment."

Quietness is not just the state of being placid, but more the means to find our true selves. To really reach the true self, we have to overcome not only the outer distractions but the inner as well. Obviously, outer noises have completely obliterated silence from the modern world. Cars, trains, and all the cacophony of man-made noises have made us rush through life at a mad pace. Not only that, even in our houses media noises are trying to absorb all of our attention. Nowadays, it's become very rare to find a house where there isn't at least one TV set jabbering even though no one's really watching it. Consequently, what we have lost is conversation between residents themselves.

Now, what about inner noise? According to Taylor, it's the "endless stream of daydreams, memories, deliberations, worries, plans, etc., which we have no control over and which even continues (in the form of dreams) when we fall asleep." Every day we are either anticipating the future or remembering the past, but we never really live in the present. That means we never pay full attention to what we're presently doing. The only solution to such consequences is to be quiet. "We can remove ourselves from the extra stimuli," states Taylor, "by sitting in a quiet room and closing our eyes."

But in my opinion, inner noises are more distracting. If we can overcome the inner annoyances, the outer can be destroyed automatically. The inner self is what determines our progress toward quietness the most.

Other than with words, we can communicate in actions. And usually that's what will touch people the most. When we wait quietly for people to finish their sentences, we've shown our respect. When we listen silently to people's stories of depression, we've shown our care for them. When we suggest ideas to others, we've shown that we listened and we understood.

Once we've revived ourselves with silence, we are then capable of going to the spiritual zenith, revealed in the poem, "Quietness":

Some things are better left unsaid
Small talk is for the birds
For as many have said before
Actions speak louder than words
And that is why I understand
The quietness in you
For the feelings that you have inside
Are seen in all you do

(anonymous)

We can increase our intelligence and acumen with quietness. We can enlarge our social circles with quietness. We can, indeed, have happiness with quietness.

Giving a Speech
To practice delivering your speech, do this:

- Read your speech out loud to yourself. Pay attention to the phrasing. Remember that a comma or a semicolon dictates a pause. As you practice your speech, look at the positioning of your punctuation. Are you stopping where you intended? Does the punctuation indicate a pause or a complete stop? Have someone read your speech to you. Does it say what you want it to say?

- Put the main phrases from your speech on 4 x 6 note cards so that you have a reference point if you lose track of where you are. Memorizing, verbatim, is a good idea—but you do not want to be a robot when you speak. Be prepared *not* to recite the speech word for word. You want to appear natural. If you have your phrases on cards, you'll be able to comfortably maintain your momentum and not feel lost if you stumble—you can always find your place.

- Now practice your speech before a mirror. Where will hand gestures be appropriate? Where do you want to elongate a pause for emphasis? Which points do you want to emphasize with directed eye contact? Where is the point in your speech where you'll want to change your posture to visually emphasize a change in direction?

Giving a Speech

For additional practice giving a speech, refer to the Language Arts Survey 4.15, "Giving a Speech," and the related worksheets in the Speaking and Listening Resource book in the Teacher's Resource Kit.

Publishing and Presenting

Have students present their persuasive speeches in small groups or in front of the class. Hold a contest and have students vote to determine which speech is the most persuasive. You may want students to read the Language Arts Survey 4.6, "Adapting Listening Skills to Specific Tasks," before they listen to the speeches presented in class. Discuss which form of listening would be the most appropriate for a persuasive speech.

Reflecting

Consider videotaping speeches so students can review and reflect on their presentation.

Tips for More Effective Listening

Just as you can develop speaking skills, you can also develop listening skills. Follow these guidelines to become an active listener as others in your class deliver their speeches.

- Think of creative reasons to listen.
- Avoid jumping to conclusions or making assumptions; note questions to ask the speaker when he or she is finished.
- Communicate involvement to the speaker through eye contact, nonverbal feedback, and maintaining an attentive posture.
- Use listening time wisely to takes notes, review information mentally, restate ideas differently, and/or visualize the information presented.
- Accept and adapt to the speaker's delivery style.
- Avoid reacting emotionally to a message or speaker.
- Avoid classifying the speaker, context, or subject matter prematurely.
- Listen for major ideas; use the speaker's thesis, transitions, etc. as listening cues.
- Make a conscious effort to listen attentively to the message.
- Resist the temptation to demand entertainment.
- Practice active listening in your daily routine.

Publishing and Presenting

Your class will enjoy hearing each other's finalized speeches. If you have practiced your speech several times, it will go smoothly.

There are other forums in which you could present your speech. Forensics and debate teams in high schools provide platforms for developing your speaking skills. Your speech could immediately be used in informative speaking events which are part of forensics competition, as Yan's speech was. You could also publish your speech in the school newspaper or your local newspaper since you are illuminating an issue that you want others to care about.

Reflecting

What differences do you see between the language of a persuasive speech and the language of a research paper, or any work that is written only to inform? What differences are reflected because of the different purpose of each piece? Which has greater impact—reading a written speech or hearing one delivered orally?

UNIT 5 *review* — Nonfiction

Words for Everyday Use

Check your knowledge of the following vocabulary words from the selections in this unit. Write a short sentence using these words in context to make the meaning clear. To review the definition or usage of a word, refer back to the page number listed or the Glossary of Words for Everyday Use.

abalone, 419
abstract, 410
abundance, 427
accession, 429
acuity, 408
aghast, 409
amiably, 406
anthropologist, 441
antiquity, 442
apprehend, 414
aptly, 397
ardent, 368
barbarous, 373
barrage, 442
beseech, 375
blithely, 368
boisterous, 377
bondage, 388
capacity, 391
capitulation, 367
carnage, 427
celluloid, 410
coercion, 402
cognition, 411
coherently, 400
collusion, 414
compel, 381
compensation, 391
comply, 399, 411
conditionally, 369
confabulate, 409
construe, 412
contingent, 391

convoluted, 411
coordinate, 398
countenance, 391
deficit, 412
defunct, 430
degenerative, 414
degrading, 397
deprive, 374
devoid, 401
diaphanous, 422
diffidently, 409
dint, 441
disfigure, 434
dismal, 373
distinction, 428
diversion, 381
elicit, 408
embody, 380
enhance, 367
enterprising, 430
estrangement, 377
evanescence, 420
exaltation, 402
exempt, 437
exposé, 399
faltering, 389
farcical, 410
flagrant, 429
forbear, 414
frail, 381
frivolous, 408
genially, 406
haphazardly, 441

hindsight, 430
incessantly, 380
incisive, 409
indifferently, 381
indomitable, 413
ingenious, 406
interspersed, 442
irate, 399
iridescent, 418
isolate, 378
linear, 411
meticulous, 442
molestation, 437
multitude, 392
obtuseness, 441
ocher, 418
omit, 412
oppress, 380
oppression, 401
overawed, 370
pathology, 414
patronage, 375
penumbral, 421
peremptory, 413
pervasive, 420
petition, 391
placidly, 408
predominate, 381
privation, 380
prodigious, 427
quiescent, 422
receding, 436
refrain, 375

remnant, 436
renounce, 413
renowned, 380
repellent, 375
reprehensible, 442
reproach, 434
reserve, 378
reticent, 442
retiring, 375
sabotage, 374
schematic, 410
scrupulously, 442
sequestered, 436
serene, 399
sienna, 418
somber, 370
stalwart, 429
stolidly, 436
stylized, 410
subtend, 419
sufficiently, 372
supercilious, 381
superficial, 377
superfluous, 369, 430
symmetry, 411
tangible, 422
tenacity, 413
torrid, 410
trifle, 408
undulate, 420
unethical, 399
verbatim, 412
verdant, 436

Literary Tools

Define the following terms, giving concrete examples of how they are used in the selections in this unit. To review a term, refer to the page number indicated or the Handbook of Literary Terms.

aim, 395, 425
allusion, 386
chronological order, 405
description, 364, 417
dialogue, 405
diary, 364

essay, 425
image, 433
imagery, 433
memoir, 440
metaphor, 440
mood, 433

narrative writing, 405
nature writing, 417
point of view, 395
simile, 440
style, 386

ADDITIONAL RESOURCES

UNIT 5 RESOURCE BOOK
• Vocabulary Worksheet: Unit 5
• Study Guide: Unit 5 Test
• Unit 5 Test

VOCABULARY DEVELOPMENT

Give students the following exercise:
Using the Words for Everyday Use listed on page 457, write a test containing fifteen sentence-completion questions. Write three answer choices for each question. Vary the forms of the words as necessary. When you are done, exchange tests with a classmate.

EXAMPLE
1. The old man was _____, so I helped him up the steps.
a. elicit
b. frail
c. somber
(Answer: b)

Reflecting
on your reading

Genre Studies

1. **AUTOBIOGRAPHY AND SPEECH.** What experiences inspired *The Diary of a Young Girl* and "Yonder sky that has wept tears of compassion . . ."? How might a reader's perception of the events portrayed in a selection change if the events were presented from the perspective of an uninvolved observer? What might the reader lose by such a change in point of view?

2. **BIOGRAPHY.** Examine the biographies "Harriet Tubman: The Moses of Her People" and "The Montgomery Boycott." In what style are these works written? Describe the diction and grammatical structures used in each selection. Does the style suit the author's subject? How is the style of each piece related to the author's aim?

3. **ESSAY AND PERSONAL ESSAY.** Define *essay* and *personal essay* using examples from the excerpts of Barry Lopez's *Arctic Dreams* and Jean-Dominique Bauby's *The Diving Bell and the Butterfly*.

Thematic Studies

4. **OPPRESSION.** The biographies "Harriet Tubman: The Moses of Her People" and "Montgomery Boycott" tell the stories of people resisting oppression. Who were these people? Who led them? In what ways were they successful in their resistance of oppression?

5. **IDENTITY.** How did Anne Frank and Jean-Dominique Bauby define themselves? How were they transformed by their respective experiences of being confined in a hiding place and being confined by paralysis?

6. **PRESERVATION.** What do Barry Lopez and David Quammen want to preserve? What are their opinions of the Arctic and the bison? What descriptions or comments in their essays indicate that they feel this way?

---

for your READING LIST

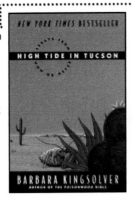

High Tide in Tucson by Barbara Kingsolver. From her hometown of Tucson, Arizona, this accomplished and popular novelist tries her hand at essays. In this collection, Kingsolver dives into topics she loves to puzzle over: motherhood, sports, exercise clubs, fashion, and writing itself, among others. If she has a question, she writes an essay to try to answer it. Here are twenty-five essays, all on completely different topics, yet her enjoyable and entertaining writing style is consistently quirky, feisty, and intelligent. Kingsolver is also the author of novels *The Bean Trees, Animal Dreams, Pigs in Heaven,* and of the short story collection, *Homeland and Other Stories.*

Independent Reading Activity

ESSAY TOPICS. There is more to write about in this world than any one person could ever think of. Each person's ideas are unique and reflect the way he or she sees the world. An **essay**, according to Webster's dictionary, is simply a short composition that deals with a subject from a personal point of view. Brainstorm a list of at least ten topics, themes, stories, and ideas you have that would make good essays. Think of possible titles, and write a short synopsis on each idea. Then choose one topic to research and write an essay about.

Selections for Additional Reading

The Man Who Mistook His Wife for a Hat, and Other Clinical Tales by Oliver Sacks. If you liked the essay by Oliver Sacks in this unit, you will enjoy reading his book, a collection of twenty essays, all on patients of his who have neurological disorders. Sacks does not see his patients as disabled; he sees them as having a different way of experiencing life, and often they are quite perceptive and gifted. In writing about them, Sacks wants his readers to see that as well.

Into Thin Air: A Personal Account of the Mount Everest Disaster by Jon Krakauer. This is a best-selling, first-hand account of the storm on Mount Everest that took the lives of six mountain climbers in May of 1996. Technology has changed mountain climbing tremendously, yet climbers still strive to experience nature in its most raw, extreme, and pure form. Check out the IMAX film of climbing Mount Everest that was made during the same time as this trip.

Autobiography of a Face by Lucy Grealy. When Lucy Grealy was a young girl growing up in New York, she found out she had jaw cancer and underwent a series of operations and chemotherapy which left her face permanently disfigured. She had to deal with things most people can't even imagine. Her scars have made her who she is today—a thoughtful, intelligent, sometimes lonely, funny, and charming person with true courage and a lot of spunk. This book is the story of her face, her life, and her spirit.

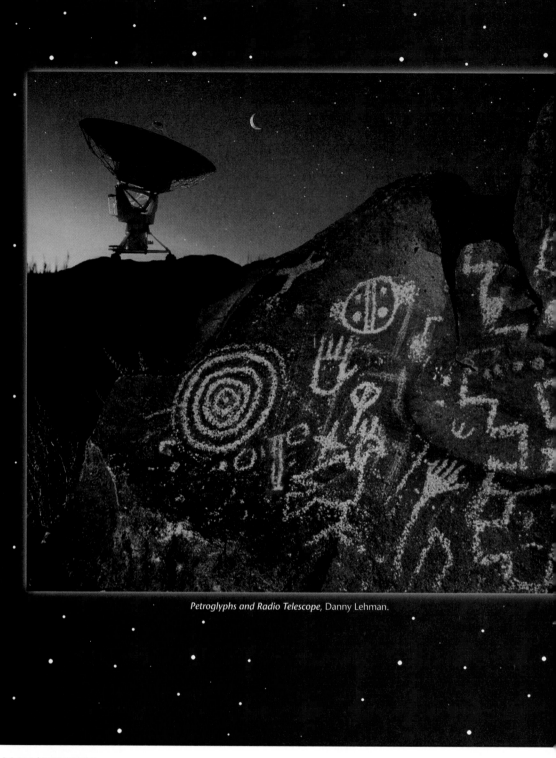

Petroglyphs and Radio Telescope, Danny Lehman.

GOALS/OBJECTIVES

Studying this unit will enable students to
- appreciate and experience several different kinds of informational and visual media
- understand the importance of informational and visual media in our society
- understand concepts such as *exposition, analysis,* and *aim,* and recognize them in informational and visual media
- define and explain elements of informational and visual media such as *electronic mail, fine art, webzines, periodical,* and *photojournalism*
- conduct a media campaign
- demonstrate the ability to use effective visual information

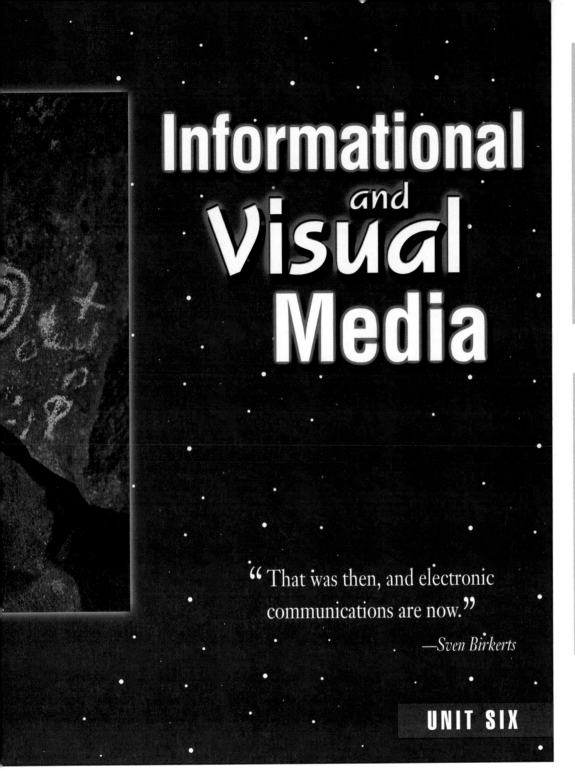

Informational *and* Visual Media

" That was then, and electronic communications are now. "

—*Sven Birkerts*

UNIT SIX

ELEMENTS of INFORMATIONAL AND VISUAL MEDIA

Informational Media

The term **media**, in most applications, is used as a plural of *medium*, which means a channel or system of communication, information, or entertainment. *Mass media* refers specifically to means of communication, such as **newspapers, magazines, radio,** or **television,** designed to reach the mass of the people. Today it includes electronic media used to distribute news, such as the Internet and computer news services.

Electronic media includes online magazines and journals, known as **webzines** or **e-zines, e-books, computer news services,** and many **web-based newspapers** that are available on the **Internet.** The **Web** is by far the most widely used part of the Internet. Consequently, people often use the terms *Net* and *Web* interchangeably. There is, however, a difference. Strictly speaking, the Internet is a system of computers, storage devices, and connections, along with the software that allows people to use these connections. The Web, in contrast, is the total collection of information available on that portion of the Internet that contains linked HTML documents. In addition to handling Web documents, the Internet also provides the physical basis for a number of other computer communications services, allowing people to send e-mail, access archives of files, and participate in discussion groups.

Multimedia is the presentation of information using the combination of text, sound, pictures, animation, and video. Common multimedia computer applications include **games, learning software, presentation software, reference materials,** and **web pages.**

Technical writing is a type of informational media that refers to scientific or process-oriented instructional writing of a technical or mechanical nature. Technical writing includes instruction manuals, such as computer software manuals, **how-to instructional guides,** and **procedural memos.**

Visual Media

In today's visually stimulating world, books and news media rely on **visual arts,** such as **fine art, illustrations, photographs, graphic aids,** and other visuals as well as the printed word to convey ideas. Visual arts offer insights into our world in a different way than print does. *Critical viewing* or careful examination of a painting or photograph can help you to comprehend its meaning and be able to compare and contrast the visual image with a literary work or other piece of writing. The Art Notes found throughout this book provide opportunities to critically view the fine art used to illustrate the literature selections.

ELEMENTS OF INFORMATIONAL MEDIA

NEWS ARTICLES. News articles are informational pieces of writing about a particular topic, issue, event, or series of events. News articles can be found in newspapers, magazines, journals, newsletters, and Internet sites such as news groups or information services. Broadcast reporters on television and radio verbally present forms of news articles.

EDITORIALS AND COMMENTARIES. An **editorial** is a newspaper or magazine article that gives the opinions of the editors or publishers. A **commentary** is a report of an event usually written by a participant or observer that expresses an opinion.

ESSAYS. An **essay** is a brief work of prose nonfiction that often appears in the media. An essay need not be a complete or exhaustive treatment of a subject but rather a tentative exploration of it. Examples of essays include "Beware the Unruly Sun" by Claudia Kalb (Unit 6) and "The Roots of Genius?" by Steven Levy (Unit 8).

INTERVIEWS. An **interview** is a meeting usually between a reporter and an individual that consists of a series of questions asked with the intention of getting to know personal details about the person being interviewed or to find out information about a news story or current event. Newspapers and magazines often contain **interviews** with famous celebrities, sports figures, and community leaders. The interview with Sven Birkerts in this unit is an example.

REVIEWS. A **review** or *critique* is a critical evaluation of a work, such as a book, play, movie, or musical performance or recording. See the book review "On Loan to the Lonely" by Barbara Gutierrez (Unit 9).

ELECTRONIC MAIL. **Electronic mail** or **e-mail** is the most widely used communication tool on the Internet. E-mail is used to send written messages between individuals or groups of individuals, often separated geographically by large distances. The proliferation of e-mail is changing the way people communicate as well as the structure of written correspondence.

WEB PAGES. A **web page** is an electronic "page" on the World Wide Web or Internet that may contain text, pictures, and sometimes animations related to a particular topic. A *website* is a collection of pages grouped together to organize the information offered by the person, company, or group that owns it. *URL* (Universal Resource Locator) refers to the

method of naming web pages or sites on the Internet. The URL or *Internet address* is a string of characters that identifies the type of document, the computer the document is on, the directories and subdirectories the document is in, and the name of the document.

INFORMATION SERVICES. **Information services** or *news services* are providers of electronic news, information, and e-mail services to customers connecting to the service with their computers over modems and telephone lines. Information services may also serve as gateways to other sources of information such as news groups, bulletin boards, chat groups, and the Internet.

ONLINE NEWSPAPERS. Most major newspapers are now available online and it is possible to read the morning news on your computer screen without a subscription. Online newspapers are updated continually and will have the most up-to-date news and weather reports available.

WEBZINES OR E-ZINES. **Webzines** or **e-zines** are basically periodicals such as magazines or journals that are available online. Some webzines

are available only online, while others are the electronic version of a print magazine that is distributed by traditional methods. An online magazine will usually contain all of the features of the print version, but may be more interactive and include more visual effects such as use

GENRE CHECK TEST 4.6.1 WITH ANSWERS

Checking Your Reading

SHORT ANSWER

1. Art is a two-part process; the first is creation by an artist. What is the second part? **The second part is interpretation by the viewer.**
2. What are graphic aids? **Graphic aids are charts, diagrams, drawings, etc. that present information visually.**
3. What does the *e* in *e-mail* stand for? **It stands for electronic.**
4. What is an editorial? **An editorial is an article that gives opinions.**
5. What does regular photography use that digital photography does not? **It uses film.**

Classifying Visual and Informational Media

MATCHING

Match each term with the best description. You may not use every term, and you may use some terms more than once.

a. newspapers
b. mass media
c. bulletin board system
d. Internet
e. technical writing
f. multimedia
g. visual arts
h. World Wide Web
i. periodicals
j. reviews

1. journals, newspapers, annual digests, magazines, newsletters; **i**
2. media designed to reach large numbers of people; **b**
3. computers and storage devices, connections between computers, software; **d**
4. fine art, illustrations, photographs; **g**
5. critical evaluations of books, plays, musical performances; **j**
6. central site where users read and post messages or play games together; **c**

of color and animation. Some webzines are available free of charge over the Internet, while others may require a subscription fee.

E-BOOKS. E-books or *electronic books* are books that are available on the Internet. Many publishers and book vendors are making many of their current and backlist titles available on the Internet in a downloadable format. *E-book* may also refer to the computer viewing device used to "read" the electronic texts, similar in size to a laptop computer.

ELEMENTS OF VISUAL MEDIA

GRAPHIC AIDS. Graphic aids are **drawings, illustrations, diagrams, charts, graphs, maps, spreadsheets,** and other visual materials that present information. Information presented in tables, charts, and graphs can help you see trends, discover facts, and uncover patterns. Learning to interpret graphics and images will help you to understand how things work, what things mean, and how things compare. See the Language Arts Survey 1.15, "Using Graphic Aids" for more information.

DOLLAR VALUE OF DONATED GOODS TO CANNED FOOD DRIVE

Grovers Corners
Bethel
Zion
Russell Springs
Jamestown
Springville

0   $200 $400 $600 $800

Sample Bar Graph

PHOTOGRAPHS. A photograph is a picture or likeness obtained by *photography*, the art or process of producing exact images on a sensitized surface (as a film) by the action of radiant energy and light. Photography was developed in the early nineteenth century; the word

photography comes from Greek words and means "drawing with light." Photographs serve as conveyers of news, historical documents, scientific evidence, works of art, and records of family life. The technology of photography continues to develop rapidly. Electronic technologies have not only changed the way most cameras work, but are changing the fundamental processing of photographs from the traditional developing of film to digital formats that can be stored on disk and downloaded to computers.

DIGITAL PHOTOGRAPHY. Digital photography is a method of making images without the use of conventional photographic film. Instead, a machine called a scanner records visual information and converts it into a code of ones and zeroes that a computer can read. Photographs in digital form can be manipulated by means of various computer programs. Digital photography has become widely used in advertising and graphic design and is quickly replacing conventional photographic technology in areas such as photojournalism.

PHOTOJOURNALISM. Photojournalism is documentary photography that tells a particular story in visual terms. Photojournalists usually work for daily and periodical newspapers, magazines, wire services, and other publications. Photojournalists cover cultural and news events in areas such as politics, war, business, sports, and the arts, striving to document news events as they happen.

VISUAL ARTS. The visual arts include objects that may be two-dimensional or three-dimensional, stationary or moving. Forms of art include painting, sculpture, drawing, printmaking, collage, photography, video, computer-assisted art, and other forms. Art is a two-part process consisting of the creation by the artist and the interpretation by the viewer. It conveys meaning in ways that draw differing interpretations for different viewers. Concepts and uses of art differ greatly throughout the world and throughout history, but every culture has created objects that have no practical function other than to be visually pleasing and to convey ideas or meaning to viewers.

SELECTION CHECK TEST 4.6.1 WITH ANSWERS (CONT.)

7. instructional manuals, how-to guides, procedural memos; **e**
8. all information available in the system of linked HTML documents; **h**
9. news articles, editorials, comic strips, weather, horoscopes; **a**
10. media that combines text, sound, pictures, animation, and video; **f**

ORDERING MEDIA COMPONENTS
Put the following components of electronic media in order, from SMALLEST to LARGEST. Put a (1) by the smallest and a (5) by the largest:

website **3**   web page **2**
Internet **5**   World Wide Web **4**
article **1**

"Under the Crack of Reality"

by Robert Hughes

Reader's resource

ART HISTORY CONNECTION. Although found even in early Greek art, *Realism,* the deliberate depiction of factual and realistic subjects, began in Europe in the mid–1800s, when artists no longer wanted their subjects idealized. They wanted to paint simple, ordinary, and commonplace scenes and people. At first their portrayals shocked audiences who were accustomed to a more romantic, idealized vision. People didn't initially know why artists wanted to paint real life, since so much of it seemed ugly and disturbing to them.

About the AUTHOR

Robert Hughes was born in Australia in 1938. He has lived in Europe and the United States since 1964, and has been an art critic for *Time* magazine since 1970. A prolific writer who has been publishing books about art since 1966, he counts *The Shock of the New* and *Nothing if Not Critical* among his recent books. Hughes now lives in New York City.

About the ARTIST

Edward Hopper (1882–1967) studied commercial art, and then studied painting under Robert Henri from 1900–1906. Influenced by European Realists, he went on to influence Pop art and New Realism of the 1960s and 1970s. His work is known for its large, geometric forms, strong vertical, horizontal, and diagonal lines, flat masses of color, and architectural elements. He often portrays his human subjects in a stark way that evokes in viewers a feeling of loneliness and isolation.

Literary TOOLS

COMPARISON-CONTRAST. Comparison and contrast order is a method of organization in which details about the similarities and differences between two subjects are presented in one of two ways. In the first method, the characteristics of one subject are presented, followed by the characteristics of a second subject. In the second method, both subjects are compared and contrasted with regard to one characteristic, then with regard to a second characteristic, and so on. In this essay, Hughes compares and contrasts Hopper's work to that of several other artists.

ANALYSIS. Analysis is a thinking strategy in which one divides a subject into parts and then examines the relationships among the parts and between individual parts and the whole. An analysis of a short story, for example, might consist of a division of the work into such parts as the exposition, the rising action, the climax, the resolution, and the dénouement, along with an examination of the role played by each of these parts in advancing the plot. An analysis of a line of poetry might consist of a careful examination of its rhythm, its figures of speech, its images, and its meaning or meanings. Hughes analyzes Hopper's art by discussing different aspects of it—subject, technique, and influences—and by discussing his art in historical and political context. Notice how Hughes talks as much about what Hopper's art is not as about what it is.

Reader's Journal

In your journal, describe in detail a realistic scene that you would like to paint.

ADDITIONAL RESOURCES

UNIT 6 RESOURCE BOOK
• Selection Worksheet 6.1
• Selection Check Test 4.6.3
• Selection Test 4.6.4

VOCABULARY FROM THE SELECTION

anarchist	portentous
demotic	prevalent
desolation	proscenium
diffident	ruminator
enigmatic	secession
epiphany	secular
ferment	tableau
ideology	vernacular
manifesto	vignette
nuance	
placid	

READER'S JOURNAL

You may want to suggest that students visualize a scene familiar to them—their home, a local grocery store, a park, or even the school or classroom.

GOALS/OBJECTIVES

Studying this lesson will enable students to
• appreciate and enjoy a brief analysis of art critiqued by Robert Hughes
• describe the influence Edward Hopper had on the Pop art and New Realism art

• define *comparison-contrast* and *analysis* and recognize examples of each in the selection
• compare and contrast two works of art
• write an art review

1. People thought he meant a political separation from French influence on art was needed. According to the author, he wanted simply to be more himself, to trust his own instincts.
2. Originality comes from hard work, and a lot of soul-searching.

INDIVIDUAL LEARNING STRATEGIES

MOTIVATION
Bring examples of art that are from the Realism period. Also bring examples of art that is considered Pop art to introduce students to the style of Edward Hopper's artwork.

READING PROFICIENCY
Have students summarize the main idea of each paragraph as they read the selection. You may also encourage them to read the selection aloud with a partner.

ENGLISH LANGUAGE LEARNING
The amount of Words for Everyday Use may be overwhelming for students. Ask them to pick ten words that interest them. Then have them create actions for each word as they play a game of charades.

SPECIAL NEEDS
To give students a preview of what the selection is about, have students read the Prereading page and the footnotes before they read the selection.

ENRICHMENT
Ask students to research an artist (sculptor, painter, graphic designer, architect, etc.) they feel has had a profound effect on art and on our culture. Have students include in their oral presentations examples of the artist's works, biographical information, and critical reviews given by art critics.

UNDER the CRACK of Reality

Robert Hughes

Edward Hopper died in 1967, nearly thirty years ago, but he remains one of those artists whose work—no matter how familiar and often reproduced it has become—comes up fresh whenever you see it. This <u>diffident</u> son of a Nyack, New York, dry-goods merchant had a long working life, almost all of it in America, and a sober style, some of which came from France and particularly from Manet and Daumier.[1] One of his few public utterances—in 1927, to the effect that "now or in the near future, American art should be weaned from its French mother"—used to be taken by cultural America-firsters[2] as a <u>manifesto</u> of <u>secession</u>, but it wasn't. He knew that real originality is made, not born; that it doesn't appear in spasms and tics but rather in a long digestive process, modified by anxiety. And he was a <u>ruminator</u>: <u>placid</u>, sometimes, on the surface, but an artist of incalculably deep feeling. Along with Jackson Pollock,[3] his polar opposite in every way, he was probably the most original American painter of the twentieth century.

> What did some people think Hopper meant by this quote?

> How does the author define originality?

1. **Manet and Daumier.** Édouard Manet (1832–1883), French Realist and Impressionist painter, and Honoré Daumier (1808–1879), French Realist illustrator
2. **America-firsters.** Reactionary group in the 1930s that preached American isolationism
3. **Jackson Pollock.** (1912–1956) American painter, leader of Abstract Expressionism who developed "drip" painting, his trademark

Nighthawks, 1942. Edward Hopper. Art Institute of Chicago.

INTERNET RESOURCES

For more information about Edward Hopper and his work, interested students may want to log on to **The Smithsonian's National Museum of American Art** website at http://nmaa-ryder.si.edu/collections/exhibits/hopper/. This website, done in a scrapbook-like style, provides biographical information on Hopper's life, his friends, and his artworks. Students can view some of his most popular work at this website.

words for everyday use

dif • fi • dent (dif' ə dənt) *adj.*, characterized by modest reserve; lacking confidence in oneself. *Her <u>diffident</u> manner made her seem shy.*

man • i • fes • to (man ə fe' stō) *n.*, public declaration of intentions, motives, or views. *He wrote his <u>manifesto</u> on school politics and read it on the playground.*

se • ces • sion (sə se' shən) *n.*, formal withdrawal from an organization. *The <u>secession</u> of states before the Civil War divided the country.*

ru • mi • na • tor (rü' mə nā dər) *n.*, one who ruminates—contemplates, ponders, mulls over, muses upon. *He was a <u>ruminator</u>, staring at the ocean for hours sometimes, just thinking.*

plac • id (pla' səd) *adj.*, serene, of a peaceful nature, meek, mild, calm. *He got no reaction from the man, who had a <u>placid</u> expression in his eyes.*

"UNDER THE CRACK OF REALITY" 467

Early Sunday Morning, 1930. Edward Hopper. Whitney Museum of American Art, New York.

Hopper's realism had nothing to do with the <u>prevalent</u> realisms of the 1930s and '40s in American painting. That is to say, it had no persuasive content; it was entirely free from <u>ideology</u>, left or right. He had studied painting with Robert Henri,[4] whose politics were romantically <u>anarchist</u>. But none of the political <u>ferment</u> of pre-World War I New York rubbed off on him, and none shows in his work. The only painting in this show that could be guessed to show an industrial worker is *Pennsylvania Coal Town*, 1947; and the bald man is posed like Millet's peasant with a hoe, raking grass outside his house in the sunlight, not hewing at the coal face in darkness. No hints of class conflict intrude on Hopper's vision of American society, which he painted one isolated person at a time.

How does the author describe Hopper's realism?

He kept his political views to himself. They were those of a conservative Wendell Willkie[5] Republican who, like his wife— the "Jo" whose presence pervades his paintings— loathed the New Deal and believed Roosevelt[6] was trying to become a dictator. Hopper rejected New Deal cultural programs; he didn't need work from the WPA[7] (his pictures were selling in the '30s for enough money to keep the Hoppers in frugal comfort and privacy, which was all he asked for), but he despised "improving" rhetoric in painting anyway. At the same time, he hated being classed with the equally rhetorical conservatives of "American Scene" painting, like Thomas Hart Benton.[8] "I never tried to do the American scene," Hopper said. "I think the American Scene painters caricatured America. I always wanted to do myself."

As a result, you won't find a stereotype anywhere in Hopper—though there are certainly

---

4. **Robert Henri.** (1865–1929) American Ashcan school painter
5. **Wendell Willkie.** Republican presidential candidate who ran unsuccessfully against Franklin Delano Roosevelt in 1940
6. **New Deal . . . Roosevelt.** Franklin D. Roosevelt, president of the U.S. from 1932 to 1945, to pull the nation out of the Depression through a series of work programs called the New Deal.
7. **WPA.** Works Progress Administration, part of Roosevelt's New Deal
8. **Thomas Hart Benton.** (1889–1975) One of America's foremost painters and muralists associated with the American Regionalists, because of his Midwestern landscapes and people, in the 1930s

---

words for everyday use

prev • a • lent (prev′ (ə)lent) *adj.*, widely accepted, favored. *Recycling is the <u>prevalent</u> approach to waste disposal in our neighborhood.*
i • de • ol • o • gy (ī dē ä′ lə jē) *n.*, ideas and concepts about human nature; the assertions, theories, and aims of an individual or group. *He joined the book group because its political <u>ideology</u> matched his own.*
an • ar • chist (an′ ər kəst) *n.*, one who rebels against any authority, established order, or ruling power. *He thought of himself as an <u>anarchist</u> and never voted.*
fer • ment (fər′ ment) *n.*, state of unrest. *The <u>ferment</u> over its contract divided the teacher's union.*

figures and nuances of human relationship that recur because they fascinated him, which is not at all the same thing.

Why are there no stereotypes in Hopper's paintings?

He saw an America no one else had got right; and now you can't see it without seeing him. His baking New York rooftops and rows of stumpy brownstones, his blue vistas of the sea at Wellfleet where yachts lean with plump sails into the light, his isolated people gazing from the windows of dull apartments or seedy motels, have become part of the very grain and texture of America's self-image. They capture what Hopper called "all the sweltering, tawdry life of the American small town, this sad desolation of our suburban landscape." Sometimes this transcends itself and leads to a sense of epiphany, as when the blond woman in the open blue robe appears

What was Hopper trying to capture?

in the dark doorway of *High Noon*, 1949, like some secular madonna drawn from sleep by a distant angelic voice.

Moreover, no American painter has influenced popular culture more deeply. A host of vernacular images, some famous (like the palace on the Texas plain in *Giant*, or Norman Bates' gaunt and brooding Victorian house in Hitchcock's *Psycho*), seem to grow from his work. Stage designers love him. Cameramen especially are drawn to what his friend, the critic Brian O'Doherty, called "that slanting, film-noir light." He loved movies and the stage, and was deeply influenced by them. He was capable of an enormous enthusiasm for players, not as stars but as workers in the mine of illusion. In that respect he was like a more demotic Watteau,[9]

tracing an American commedia dell'arte.[10] The stripper in *Girlie Show*, 1941, with her fine strong legs, haughty red trap of a mouth and ginger hair, fairly explodes into the spotlight, but there's an ironic memory of Botticelli[11] in the way she holds her veil.

Hopper's theatricality extends beyond his theater scenes. In a great Hopper there is always the moment of frozen time, literally a tableau, as though the curtain had just gone up but the narrative hasn't begun. It gives images of ordinary things their mystery and power, as in *Early*

What gives ordinary things their mystery and power?

Sunday Morning, 1930, with its long streaks of raking shadow cast by hydrant and barber's pole, its empty but never standardized windows. It's never portentous, as de Chirico's[12] cityscapes could be; you are in the real world but a stranger world than you imagined. The screwdriver slips under the lid of reality and lifts it a crack, no more. What's inside? Ask early Auden:[13]

> The glacier knocks in the cupboard,
> The desert sighs in the bed,
> And the crack in the tea-cup opens
> A lane to the land of the dead.

9. **Watteau.** Jean-Antoine Watteau (1684–1721), French artist whose work typified the graceful Rococo style
10. **commedia dell'arte.** Style of theater in Italy during the sixteenth to eighteenth centuries characterized by standardized situations and stock characters
11. **Botticelli.** (1445–1510) Sandro Botticelli, one of the greatest painters of the Florentine Renaissance
12. **de Chirico.** (1888–1978) Giorgio de Chirico, Italian painter; he founded Metaphysical painting.
13. **Auden.** (1907–1973) W. H. Auden, British and American poet; the selection is from the poem "One Evening."

---

words for everyday use

nu • ance (n(y)ü′ änts) *n.*, shade of difference; minute variation; subtle distinction. *It takes a long time to discover a person's unique nuances.*
des • o • la • tion (de sə lā′ shən) *n.*, condition of being deserted, abandoned, ruined, lifeless. *There was such desolation in the town after the tornado.*
e • piph • a • ny (ə pif′ ə nē) *n.*, sudden manifestation or perception of the essential nature or meaning of something. *As she watched it rain, she had an epiphany about the next decision in her life.*
sec • u • lar (sek′ yə lər) *adj.*, worldly or temporal, as opposed to spiritual; not sacred. *The camp songs were all of a secular nature.*
ver • nac • u • lar (vər nak′ yə lər) *adj.*, using a language or dialect native to a region or country; a mode of expression natural to or used by a group or class. *Her vernacular was charming.*
de • mot • ic (də mäd′ ik) *adj.*, of or relating to the people; popular and common, especially language. *Slang is part of each group's demotic expression.*
tab • leau (ta blō′) *n.*, artistic grouping; scene or arrangement. *She drew a tableau of the design for the living room.*
por • ten • tous (pōr ten′ təs) *adj.*, full of consequence or possibility. *The portentous message about his friend's whereabouts arrived late last night.*

ANSWERS TO GUIDED READING QUESTIONS

1. Hopper's paintings are free from stereotypes because he does not caricature America; he strives to be true to himself, which supports Hughes's point that Hopper is an original artist.
2. Hopper was trying to capture the feeling of desolation—of emptiness and isolation—in the American small town.
3. Ordinary things get their mystery and power from the feeling in them, and from the feeling that something is about to happen.

INTERNET RESOURCES

Hughes lists several of Hopper's paintings on this page. Students may be interested in logging on to **Artcyclopedia** at http://www.artcyclopedia.com/artists/hopper_edward.html. This website directly links students to various museums and art galleries where they can view Hopper's artwork online.

ANSWERS TO GUIDED READING QUESTIONS

1. The painting evokes the pleasure of seeing while being unnoticed. It creates this effect because of the perspective; the viewer is looking directly into the window.
2. Bold, strong diagonal lines are one of Hopper's trademarks. They are a structural brace but also add an element of a strange reality.

SELECTION CHECK TEST 4.6.3 WITH ANSWERS

Checking Your Reading
1. According to Hughes, what did Edward Hopper know about originality? **Hopper knew that originality was made, not born.**
2. With whom did Hopper study? **He studied with Robert Henri.**
3. What type of painter was Hopper? **He was a Realist painter.**
4. What won't the viewer see in any of Hopper's paintings? **The viewer won't see any stereotypes.**
5. What type of world does Hopper give us, according to Hughes? **Hopper gives us a world that is created, not recorded.**

Vocabulary in Context
Fill in each blank below with the most appropriate word from the following Words for Everyday Use. You may have to change the tense of the word.

placid   ruminator   diffident
nuance   secular   anarchist

1. Carla seems unfriendly, but she just has a **diffident** personality.
2. Henry likes to **ruminate** and be introspective.
3. The **placid** wind felt good on a spring day.
4. Nina could be considered a(n) **anarchist** because she rebels against authority.
5. I like to listen to **secular** music instead of sacred music.

Literary Tools
Fill in the blanks using the following terms.

comparison and contrast order
Realism   analysis

1. **Realism** is the deliberate depictions of factual and realistic subject.

Hopper excelled in painting, discreetly and from without, people who are outsiders to one another. You imagine him staring from the Second Avenue El[14] as it rattled past the lit brownstone windows, storing the enigmatic snapshots of home and business for later use. These are reconstructed scenes, emotion recollected in tranquility. In *Room in New York*, 1932, it is night; a man reads a paper at a round table, a woman turns away in her own absorption and boredom, touching the piano keyboard with one finger. They are out of synch, and their distance from each other is figured in the simple act of a woman with a shadowed face sounding a note (or perhaps only thinking about sounding it) to which there will be no response.

Room in New York, 1932. Edward Hopper. Sheldon Memorial Art Gallery, Lincoln, Nebraska.

No doubt Hopper saw something like this, yet not very like it. The space would not have been measured by his three exact and conscious patches of red: the armchair, the woman's dress, the lampshade. The figures would have been remote. In the picture they are large, and we are close to them, outside their window. You don't for a moment imagine Hopper on a scaffold outside the window or spying on the couple through a long lens. And yet the painting does evoke the pleasure, common to bird and people watchers, of seeing while being unnoticed; it does put your eye close to the window, several floors up; and this contributes a dreamlike tone to the image, as though you were levitating while the man and woman remained bound by gravity. This is not realism, but the scene is intensely real, a vignette framed in the dark proscenium of the window.

What does the painting evoke, and how does it create this effect?

Hopper gives us a created world, not one that is merely recorded. Everything in it is shaped by memory, sympathy, distance and formal imperatives. Nothing is there merely because it "was there." Mark Rothko[15] hated diagonals, but loved Hopper's. Richard Diebenkorn[16] loved diagonals and loved Hopper's too. As well anyone might: the diagonal, the slanting patch (especially of light) becomes a wonderfully expressive element in Hopper, acting both as a structural brace for the actual painted surface and as a sign of fugitive reality in imagined space. In *Morning Sun*, 1952, you are acutely aware that Jo, the long-limbed, middle-aged woman staring at nothing in particular from her bed, will move in a moment, that the patch of light will move too, that nothing will be the same again: but there it is, exactly the same. ■

How does the diagonal line function in Hopper's paintings?

---

14. **Second Avenue El.** The trains in Chicago are called the elevated, or El trains, because they travel above the street.
15. **Mark Rothko.** (1903–1970) Post World War II Abstract Expressionist painter
16. **Richard Diebenkorn.** (1922–1993) American painter

words for everyday use

en • ig • mat • ic (e nig mad' ik) *adj.*, inexplicable, obscure, puzzling. *She read the enigmatic message over and over.*

vi • gnette (vin yet') *n.*, short scene or incident, as from a movie. *The book opened with an intriguing vignette of the main character and her mother in a café.*

pro • sce • ni • um (prə sē' nē əm) *n.*, the front part, the foreground. *She placed flowers on the proscenium of the stage.*

SELECTION CHECK TEST 4.6.3 WITH ANSWERS (CONT.)

2. **Analysis** involves examining the relationship between individual parts.
3. Organizing information by its similarities and differences is called **comparison and contrast order**.

AS I WALKED OUT ONE EVENING

W. H. Auden

As I walked out one evening,
    Walking down Bristol Street,
The crowds upon the pavement
    Were fields of harvest wheat.

And down by the brimming river
    I heard a lover sing
Under an arch of the railway:
    "Love has no ending.

"I'll love you, dear, I'll love you
    Till China and Africa meet,
And the river jumps over the mountain
    And the salmon sing in the street.

"I'll love you till the ocean
    Is folded and hung up to dry,
And the seven stars go squawking
    Like geese about the sky.

"The years shall run like rabbits,
    For in my arms I hold
The Flower of the Ages,
    And the first love of the world."

But all the clocks in the city
    Began to whirr and chime:
"O let not Time deceive you,
    You cannot conquer Time.

"In the burrows of the Nightmare
    Where Justice naked is,
Time watches from the shadow
    And coughs when you would kiss.

"In headaches and in worry
    Vaguely life leaks away,
And Time will have his fancy
    To-morrow or to-day.

"UNDER THE CRACK OF REALITY" **471**

ADDITIONAL QUESTIONS AND ACTIVITIES

Ask students the following questions:
1. What metaphor does Auden use to describe the crowd as he walked down Bristol Street?
2. What are some images that represent the line "Love has no ending"?
3. Who or what is the lover's adversary?

Answers
1. He uses the metaphor of "fields of harvest wheat" to describe the crowd.
2. Some images that represent this line are: China and Africa meeting, the river jumping over the mountain, salmon singing in the street, the ocean drying out, and stars squawking like geese.
3. Time is the lover's adversary.

LITERARY TECHNIQUE

ALLUSION. An **allusion** is a rhetorical technique in which reference is made to a person, event, object, or work from history or literature. In this poem, Auden alludes to various Mother Goose nursery rhymes and stories such as *Jack in the Beanstalk* ("And the Giant is enchanting to Jack"), *Jack and Jill Went up the Hill* ("And Jill goes down on her back"), and *There Was a Crooked Man* ("You shall love Your crooked neighbour / With your crooked heart").

"Into many a green valley
    Drifts the appalling snow,
Time breaks the threaded dances
    And the diver's brilliant bow.

"O Plunge your hands in water,
    Plunge them in up to the wrist;
Stare, stare in the basin
    And wonder what you've missed.

"The glacier knocks in the cupboard,
    The desert sighs in the bed
And the crack in the tea-cup opens
    A lane to the land of the dead.

"Where the beggars raffle the banknotes
    And the Giant is enchanting to Jack,
And the Lily-white Boy is a Roarer,
    And Jill goes down on her back.

"O look, look in the mirror,
    O look in your distress;
Life remains a blessing
    Although you cannot bless.

'O stand, stand at the window
    As the tears scald and start;
You shall love your crooked neighbour
    With your crooked heart."

It was late, late in the evening
    The lovers they were gone;
The clocks had ceased their chiming,
    And the deep river ran on. ∎

ABOUT THE RELATED READING

Robert Hughes quotes lines from W. H. Auden's poem **"As I walked out one evening"** in his essay as he describes Edward Hopper's painting *Early Sunday Morning* (page 468). Just as Hopper often captured a moment of "frozen time" in his paintings, Auden's continuing subject in his poetry was the task of the present moment.

    Wystan Hugh (W. H.) Auden (1907–1973) was born in York, England, but came in 1939 to America and became a U.S. citizen in 1946. He taught poetry at a number of American colleges, and at Oxford University in England. The most active of the group of young English poets who brought new techniques and attitudes to English poetry in the late 1920s and early 1930s, Auden, it has been said, was the first poet writing in English who felt at home in the twentieth century. "One Evening" was written in November 1937 and has been published in several of Auden's poetry collections.

Respond *to the* SELECTION

Write a brief description of the effect looking at Edward Hopper's paintings has on you. How would you describe his work?

Investigate, Inquire, and Imagine

Recall: GATHERING FACTS

1a. In what way is Hopper a Realist?

2a. What movie sets were inspired by Hopper's paintings? How did Hopper feel about film?

3a. Hughes gives an extended interpretation of *Room in New York*. What elements does he see in the painting?

Interpret: FINDING MEANING

1b. How is Hopper's realism different from other forms of Realism?

2b. Why do you think his paintings influenced film scenes? Why do stage designers and cameramen love him?

3b. How does Hughes interpret the relationship between the man and woman in the painting?

Analyze: TAKING THINGS APART

4a. Hughes makes an important assertion in the first paragraph. What is the main point in this paragraph?

Synthesize: BRINGING THINGS TOGETHER

4b. What points does Hughes make to support his assertion?

Evaluate: MAKING JUDGMENTS

5a. Reread the last few paragraphs and note when and how Hughes goes from description to interpretation. Do you agree with his interpretation? Does it help you appreciate the painting? What can you add to his analysis?

Extend: CONNECTING IDEAS

5b. Hughes quotes from the W. H. Auden poem "As I walked out one evening" in his essay. Read the complete poem in the Related Reading following the selection. Why do you think Hughes quotes from this poem? How does the poem support his point about Hopper?

Understanding Literature

ANALYSIS. Review the definition for **analysis** in the Handbook of Literary Terms. Much of Hughes's analysis is based on what he sees as he looks at Hopper's work. He describes the work, and then takes description a step further when he discusses the meaning of the details. As you read through the essay again, what points seem factual to you? What points seem to be opinion, or interpretation? How does Hughes support his interpretations? Are his interpretations convincing?

COMPARISON-CONTRAST. Review the definition for **comparison-contrast** in Literary Tools in Prereading on page 465. Why does Hughes compare Hopper to other artists?

ANSWERS TO UNDERSTANDING LITERATURE (CONT.)

ANALYSIS. Point out that Hughes's assertions are educated, based on what he sees. He develops his analysis, taking it from one point to the next. For example, "In a great Hopper there is always the moment of frozen time, literally a tableau" is what he sees, and "as though the curtain had just gone up but the narrative hasn't begun" is his interpretation.

COMPARISON-CONTRAST. Hughes compares Hopper to other painters so that, in knowing what his work is not like, we will begin to see what it is like, and appreciate how unique and important his contribution is to art.

RESPOND TO THE SELECTION

What was the most interesting thing you learned about Edward Hopper? Do you think he was/is as significant as Hughes suggests in the development of realistic art and Pop art? Why, or why not?

ANSWERS TO INVESTIGATE, INQUIRE, AND IMAGINE

RECALL

1a. Hopper is a Realist in that he paints real scenes without romanticizing the subject.

2a. *Giant* and *Psycho* used sets reminiscent of Hopper. Hopper loved movies and the stage, and was influenced by them.

3a. Hughes's interpretation of *Room in New York* begins by describing what he sees—the room, the piano, the two people. Then he describes the colors, the furniture, the dress and lampshade.

INTERPRET

1b. Hopper's realism is different from other artists' in that he has no political or persuasive content.

2b. His paintings, while real, are so emotionally evocative. There is so much feeling in them. Stage designers can say a lot with one backdrop created by Hopper.

3b. Hughes interprets the woman turning away from the man. He portends that the man and woman are out of synch and distant from one another.

ANALYZE

4a. Hughes's assertion is that Hopper is one of the most original American painters of the 20th century.

SYNTHESIZE

4b. Hughes supports his assertion by describing Hopper's work as being influential and different from anyone else's work.

EVALUATE

5a. "It is night" is description. "They are out of synch" is analysis; it is Hughes educated impression, his opinion, his interpretation after looking at the painting for a long time.

EXTEND

5b. The images in Auden's poem are very unreal. Hughes's point is that although things seem real in Hopper, the world is stranger than it seems.

Collaborative Learning

Refer students to the Language Arts Survey 5.10, "Comparing and Contrasting." Students may also be interested in developing their scripts into a talk show where two people are chosen to represent Pollock and Hopper, and one person is chosen to be the talk show host. The rest of the class can participate by representing the audience who asks questions of the two artists.

Critical Thinking

For this activity, encourage students to read the Language Arts Survey 1.11, "'Reading' Art and Photographs."

Applied English

Encourage students to read samples of art reviews before they begin writing their own art review. This will give them a sense of style, tone, and art techniques they should address in their review. They can find art reviews in their city newspaper or online. One website that allows browsers to read art reviews by various art critics is **Art Connoisseur**, which is located at http://www.coe.missouri.edu/~jbenoit/art/. Students can view the art piece and read the art review for that particular artwork by renowned art critics.

Writer's Journal

1. Imagine you are either the man or the woman in the painting *Room in New York*. Write a **journal entry** describing the situation portrayed in the painting from your perspective.
2. Write a **description** of a painting by Hopper.
3. Write a **press release** announcing an exhibit of Hopper's paintings at a museum. Refer to the Language Arts Survey 6.9, "Delivering a Press Release."

Integrating the Language Arts

Collaborative Learning

COMPARING AND CONTRASTING ARTISTS. Hughes asserts that Jackson Pollock and Edward Hopper are two of the most original painters of the twentieth century. He also calls them "polar opposite[s] in every way." In your group, gather information about both artists, including historic time period, background information, and of course several reprints of their paintings. As a group, discuss the differences between the two great artists. Compare and contrast their work. Do they have anything in common whatsoever? Did they ever meet each other? Find out any information that you can. Write a script for a presentation that you can give your classmates. It can be in the form of a debate arguing Hughes's point, or a skit impersonating a meeting of these two great artists, or an informational lecture describing the work as if the class were seeing it in a museum.

Critical Thinking

ART ANALYSIS. In this essay, Hughes analyzes and interprets Hopper's painting, *Room in New York*. Choose another painting by Hopper and write a short analysis of it. You can use *Nighthawks* or *Early Sunday Morning*, reprinted in this selection, or you may want to go to the library and find a book with other reprints of Hopper's paintings. Spend some time looking carefully at the painting. To begin your analysis, describe each detail and element, the way that Hughes does. Then, to interpret the painting, try to determine what it might mean. What is implied (not directly stated) in the painting? What mood is created? What could be happening? What do the subjects seem to be thinking or feeling? Use the details of the painting to support your interpretive statements.

Applied English

ART REVIEW. Critics review and comment on all sorts of things—books, movies, art, music, food, etc. Hughes uses descriptive adjectives, precise language, and educated opinion to write his review of Edward Hopper's art. Pretend you are an art critic on an assignment with the local newspaper. Choose a piece of art in your school, a painting hanging on one of the walls, a piece of sculpture, or a piece of art done by a fellow student. Write a short newspaper review evaluating the work. You can include your interpretation of the piece, a short history of it, background information on the artist, and even a conversation with the artist if you can have one.

"Beware the Unruly Sun"
by Claudia Kalb

Reader's resource

This article first appeared in the June 21, 1999, issue of *Newsweek* magazine, a popular weekly news periodical. Although it contains medical terminology and technical information, the article is accessible and educational. Kalb wrote to be easily understood. The information presented in the article about the effects of the sun could save people's lives.

SCIENCE CONNECTION. The skin is the largest organ of the body. Its functions include protecting the inner organs from injury and invasion by bacteria, preventing the loss of fluids, and communicating with the brain on sensations having to do with temperature, touch, and pain. The skin consists of three layers. The top layer, the epidermis, is very thin. Below that, the dermis is thicker and contains hair follicles, sweat glands, blood vessels, and nerves. The deepest layer, the subcutis, forms a network of fat cells, conserves heat, and has a shock-absorbing effect that helps protect the body's organs from injury.

About the AUTHOR

Claudia Kalb writes for *Newsweek* magazine, primarily on topics of health. Kalb was named general editor for the magazine in June 1999. Kalb has been an associate editor, a correspondent and reporter in the Boston bureau, a researcher in New York, and a reporting intern in *Newsweek's* Chicago bureau. Prior to joining *Newsweek* in 1994, she worked as a researcher and reporter at the Freedom Forum Media Studies Center in New York. Kalb graduated *magna cum laude* from Amherst College before earning her master's degree in International Relations from Columbia University. While at Columbia, she was awarded a scholarship in the field of international media and communications.

Reader's Journal

What are some precautions you take now to protect your future health?

Literary TOOLS

PERIODICAL AND ARTICLE. A **periodical** is a newspaper, magazine, or newsletter that is published regularly (once a week, for example, as *Newsweek* is). An **article** is a brief work of nonfiction on a specific topic. Encyclopedia entries, newspaper reports, and nonfiction magazine pieces are examples of articles.

AIM. A writer's **aim** is his or her purpose, or goal. As you read "Beware the Unruly Sun," think about what the author's aim is.

Graphic Organizer

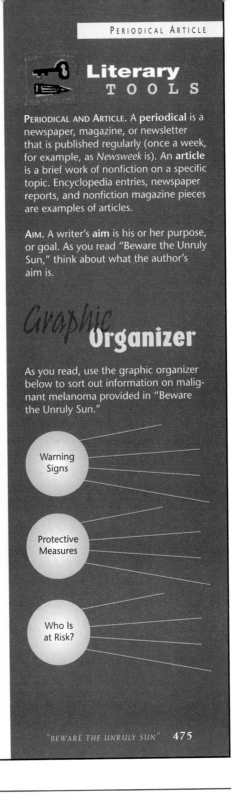

As you read, use the graphic organizer below to sort out information on malignant melanoma provided in "Beware the Unruly Sun."

Warning Signs

Protective Measures

Who Is at Risk?

"BEWARE THE UNRULY SUN" 475

ADDITIONAL RESOURCES

UNIT 6 RESOURCE BOOK
- Selection Worksheet 6.2
- Selection Check Test 4.6.5
- Selection Test 4.6.6
- Language, Grammar, and Style Resource 3.72

GRAPHIC ORGANIZER

Warning Signs: Moles that change color, grow, bleed, have abnormal shape, or are larger than 6mm
Protective Measures: Use sunscreen, wear a hat and protective clothing
Statistics of Occurrence: 44,000 people diagnosed in a year; 7300 could die; number of melanoma cases is twice as high today as twenty years ago; melanoma causes 6 out of 7 skin cancer deaths
Who Is at Risk: Everyone; fair skinned people are more apt; other risk factors are family history of melanoma, and sunburn

READER'S JOURNAL

What protective measures, if any, do you take when you go to the beach, or spend time in the sun? Why do you take these precautions? If you don't take protective measures, explain why.

GOALS/OBJECTIVES

Studying this lesson will enable students to
- appreciate the importance of being educated in health matters
- discuss the importance of taking protective measures against the sun
- define *periodical, article,* and *aim* and explain examples of each in the selection
- conduct research on the sun and its unique characteristics

1. She found a "funny-looking spot," probably a mole.
2. Malignant melanoma is rising faster than any other cancer.
3. If it is diagnosed early—before the melanoma has grown below the skin.

CROSS-CURRICULAR CONNECTIONS

WORLD HISTORY. In Egypt, the sun god was called *Re* or *Ra,* and in India, *Surya.* Native American Indians performed a Sun Dance in honor of the sun. Aztec religion called the sun gods *Huitzilopochtli* and *Tezcatlipoca* and built giant pyramids to honor them. Ancient cultures worshipped the sun because they recognized it as the source of light, warmth, and life, as well as a source of wisdom and natural harmony and unity with the cosmos.

VOCABULARY FROM THE SELECTION

burrow	malignant
derive	pigment
detection	plummet
immune	precursor
innocuous	prognosis
lesion	ravage

BEWARE
the unruly
Sun

Claudia Kalb

The summer sun. It warms the sand and the soul. But as Kathleen Black will remind you, those brilliant rays can also <u>ravage</u> the body. Just weeks before her 35th birthday last fall, Black was told that the funny-looking spot on her left shin—no bigger than a pencil eraser—was a deadly form of cancer called <u>malignant</u> melanoma. "Boy, those two words will echo in your brain," she says. "I saw my life flashing in front of me."

What did Ms. Black find on her shin?

In the United States, the incidence of melanoma is rising faster than almost any other cancer, striking Americans at twice the rate today as it did two decades ago. This year alone more than 44,000 people are expected to be diagnosed, and 7,300 could die. "The increase is absolutely astounding," says Dr. Martin Weinstock, chair of the American Cancer Society's (ACS) skin-cancer advisory group. "This is a major public-health problem."

What kind of cancer is rising faster than any other?

But there's good news, too. Melanoma offers its victims an unusual grace period: diagnosed early—before it's had time to <u>burrow</u> beneath the skin—it's almost totally curable. New tools, including computer imaging are helping dermatologists[1] detect melanoma. And new treatments, such as therapeutic vaccines, are

How is it curable?

now being tested to fight against it. Most important, you can easily learn the warning signs—and possibly save your own life.

Melanocytes, the body's <u>pigment</u> cells, generally do good, not harm. They give our skin its natural color and, when struck by the sun, churn out additional pigment (or melanin) to darken and protect us. Melanocytes also cluster together to form moles. Most are <u>innocuous</u>. But in some people, ultraviolet radiation[2] appears to help trigger melanocytes to multiply and turn cancerous, either in moles that already exist or in new skin <u>lesions</u>. More often than not, skin cancers turn out to be basal cell carcinoma or squamous cell carcinoma;[3] both are "nonmelanomas" and are usually not fatal. "It's the melanomas that kill," says Dr. John DiGiovanna, a dermatologist at Brown University School of Medicine. Accounting for

---

1. **dermatologists.** Doctors who specialize in skin
2. **ultraviolet radiation.** Energy waves produced by the sun, extending from the violet, or short-wavelength, end of the visible light range to the X-ray region
3. **basal cell carcinoma and squamous cell carcinoma.** Types of skin cancer

words for everyday use

rav • age (raʹ vij) *vt.,* lay waste to; destroy. *The fire <u>ravaged</u> the forest.*

ma • lig • nant (mə ligʹ nənt) *adj.,* severe, rapidly growing, potentially deadly. *Because the tumor was <u>malignant</u>, she began treatment immediately.*

bur • row (burʹ ō) *vi.,* dig; tunnel; delve beneath. *The tiny animal <u>burrowed</u> under the hay.*

pig • ment (pigʹ mənt) *n.,* coloring matter in cells and tissue. *The <u>pigment</u> of the mole changed from tan to brown almost overnight.*

in • noc • u • ous (in näʹ kyə wəs) *adj.,* harmless. *It was a rude but <u>innocuous</u> comment.*

le • sion (lēʹ zhən) *n.,* wound; flaw; abnormal change. *He noticed a red <u>lesion</u> on his arm and called the doctor.*

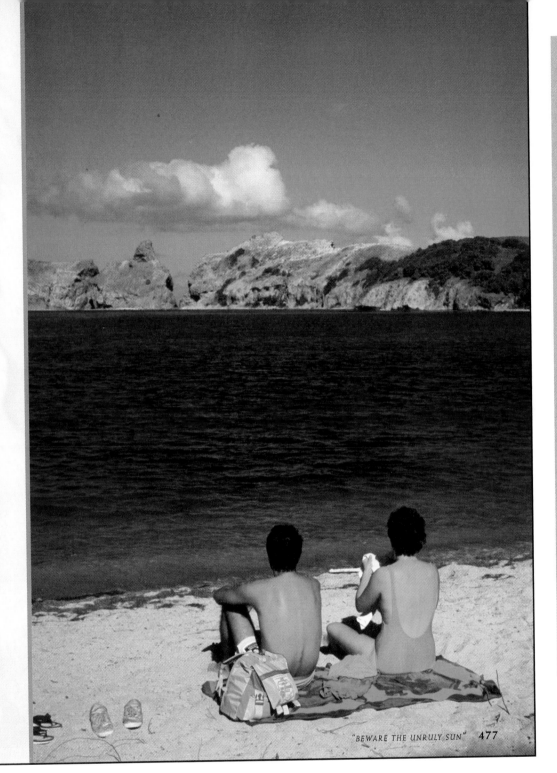

"BEWARE THE UNRULY SUN" 477

MOTIVATION
Ask students who are comfortable with this topic to share stories about people they know who have experienced illnesses due to the kind of lifestyle they live. Then as a class, brainstorm ways in which to stay healthy.

READING PROFICIENCY
Encourage students to skim over the scientific words they do not know—marking them down on their paper—during the first reading pass. During the second pass, have students go back to those words and try to figure them out based on the context. They may also look up the words in a dictionary.

ENGLISH LANGUAGE LEARNING
Encourage students to keep a journal of unfamiliar words as they read. If they are unable to grasp the meaning of the word from its context, define it for them.

SPECIAL NEEDS
Help put the selection in context for students. Also encourage them to focus on answering the Recall questions from the Investigate, Inquire, and Imagine section.

ENRICHMENT
Have students explore the work of a dermatologist. Suggest that they find information about dermatology on the Internet and/or interview a dermatologist from their community hospital. What is an average day like? What type of problems or illnesses are most common in the patients they see? How do lifestyle and environmental factors contribute to those skin problems? Have students present the answers to their questions in a written report.

just 4 percent of skin cancers, they cause six out of seven skin-cancer deaths.

Although no one is <u>immune</u> to melanoma, people with fair skin and light eyes and hair are at greater risk. Other factors include having a large number of moles, a family history of melanoma and bad sunburns as a child—especially in the first 15 years of life. The best weapon against the disease is early <u>detection</u>. But don't rely on your GP[4]: most have minimal training in skin cancer. Use the ABCD test to check yourself regularly (the Skin Cancer Foundation has visuals at www.skincancer.org): Is the mole asymmetrical? Is its border uneven or ragged? Is there more than one color present? Is the diameter greater than 6 millimeters? Also look for inflammation or bleeding. Check every inch of your body from your scalp down to the skin between your toes. Men are more likely to develop melanoma on their trunks (probably because they go shirtless in the sun), women on their legs.

If you see anything suspicious, call your doctor. The American Academy of Dermatology (www.aad.org or 888-462-DERM) can help you find a skin specialist in your area; the ACS

What are the risk factors for melanoma?

---
4. **GP.** General Practitioner, or doctor

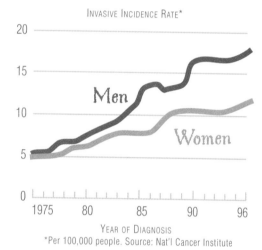

Melanoma: Rising Rates

It's the least common of the three major skin cancers, but it accounts for the most deaths.

INVASIVE INCIDENCE RATE*

Men

Women

1975 80 85 90 96

YEAR OF DIAGNOSIS

*Per 100,000 people. Source: Nat'l Cancer Institute

(www.cancer.org or 800-ACS-2345) offers information about what to expect during an exam. A key factor in <u>prognosis</u> is how deeply

words for everyday use

im • mune (i myün') *adj.*, protected; resistant to a disease. *Few people are <u>immune</u> to the common cold.*

de • tec • tion (di tek' shən) *n.*, discovery. *She visits the dentist regularly to ensure decay <u>detection</u>.*

prog • nos • is (präg nō' səs) *n.*, act or art of foretelling the course of a disease. *The doctor's <u>prognosis</u> was hopeful.*

the melanoma has invaded the skin. At less than three quarters of a millimeter,

What is a key factor in prognosis?

your chances are better than 95 percent. Beyond four millimeters, the odds <u>plummet</u> to less than 50 percent. Says AAD president Dr. Darrell Rigel: "That little difference is a big difference in survival."

If you do have a mole biopsied,[5] request that it be read by a specialist called a dermatopathologist. "In less trained hands, there have been problems," says Rigel. Seek a second opinion if you have any concerns. Dorothy Shaffer, 42, was told in 1990 that the mole on her calf was "nothing to worry about." But the lab made a mistake. Now a disease that might have been licked is threatening her life. "If I see 45," she says, "I'll be lucky."

You may be able to help ward off melanoma. Start by using sunscreen with an SPF[6] of at least 15. Dr. Mark Pittelkow of the Mayo Clinic recommends newer products containing zinc and avobenzone. Pay special attention to the kids, too.

What could potentially be the start of skin cancer?

Last week the ACS reported that 72 percent of 11- to 18-year-olds surveyed got sunburned last summer—a potential <u>precursor</u> to cancer. One third were wearing sunscreen at the time. The

FDA[7] ruled last month that sunscreens can no longer be labeled "sunblocks" because they're incapable of absolute protection. Use them liberally (about a shot glass full) and repeatedly. Ditch products more than three years old. And try to avoid direct sun between 10 A.M. and 4 P.M.

The future of melanoma may be better for all of us soon. New digital imaging can take a magnified snapshot or Melanomagram, helping doctors see deeper into a lesion and track it over time. Computers may soon be able to "read" moles and help make diagnoses. A genetic test is on the horizon, too. Drugs <u>derived</u> from the body's own chemicals are now being used to boost the immune system to attack advanced melanoma, and therapeutic vaccines are being tested. "From 15 years ago until now, we've taken quantum leaps"[8] says DiGiovanna.

Health officials, who are launching skin cancer-awareness campaigns this summer, hope increased vigilance and new research will one day kill off melanoma for good. It all starts with people like Kathleen Black—her cancer turned out to be early stage. "I really feel like I've dodged a bullet," she says. Now it's your turn. ■

5. **biopsied.** Examined body tissue, cells, and fluids
6. **SPF.** Sun Protection Factor
7. **FDA.** Food and Drug Administration
8. **quantum leaps.** Big steps; huge progress

words for everyday use

plum • met (plə' mət) *vi.*, fall or drop rapidly. *The value of the stock <u>plummeted</u>, and Mr. Robinson lost $10,000.*

pre • cur • sor (pri kur' sər) *n.*, person or thing that precedes and indicates the approach of another. *The nausea was usually the <u>precursor</u> of a headache.*

de • rived (di rīvd') *vi.*, taken, received, or made, especially from a specified source. *The expression is <u>derived</u> from Latin.*

Respond to the

SELECTION

How does reading the article influence how you will spend a day in the sun?

ANSWERS TO GUIDED READING QUESTIONS

1. A key factor in prognosis depends on how deeply the melanoma has grown below the skin.
2. A bad sunburn, especially in young people, could potentially be the start of skin cancer.

SELECTION CHECK TEST 4.6.5 WITH ANSWERS

Checking Your Reading
1. With what was Ms. Black diagnosed? **She was diagnosed with skin cancer.**
2. Where is melanoma rising fastest? **Melanoma is rising fastest in the United States.**
3. How is melanoma curable? **It is curable if the cancer is detected early.**
4. What type of person is at greatest risk? **People with fair skin and light eyes and hair are at greatest risk.**
5. What proof sunscreen should you use? **You should use sunscreen with at least SPF 15.**

Vocabulary in Context
Fill in each blank below with the most appropriate word from the following Words for Everyday Use. You may have to change the tense of the word.

innocuous	burrow	immune
ravage	prognosis	detection

1. I have a strong **immune** system because I hardly ever get sick.
2. During the scary scenes of the movie, I **burrow** my head in my pillow.
3. The chocolate chip cookies were **ravaged** by three starving toddlers.
4. The bull dog looks mean, but it is really **innocuous**.
5. The **prognosis** the doctor gave for recovery was encouraging.

Literary Tools
Fill in the blanks using the following terms.

periodical   article   aim

1. A writer's **aim** is his or her purpose.
2. *Newsweek* is an example of a(n) **periodical**.
3. A(n) **article** is a brief work of nonfiction on a specific topic.

RESPOND TO THE SELECTION

Ask students how they can enjoy being out in the sun and protect their skin at the same time.

RECALL

1a. A mole that is changing or growing on your skin is a warning sign of malignant melanoma.

2a. Check your skin frequently for signs of changing moles, use sunscreen, and stay out of the sun to protect yourself from melanoma.

3a. If the mole is less than 3 mm deep in the skin, it is 95% curable. If it grows beyond 4 mm deep, chances of survival are less than 50%.

INTERPRET

1b. If these signs appear, have it diagnosed immediately.

2b. You might not want to get a suntan or spend an extended amount of time out in the sun.

3b. The odds are significant because a very small amount of growth means the difference between life and death. Early detection and removal could easily and painlessly eliminate the cancer. Catching it when it is too late could mean prolonged illness, painful treatment, and death.

ANALYZE

4a. Prevention and early detection is crucial because you could die if symptoms go undiagnosed.

SYNTHESIZE

4b. A person needs to have respect for his or her own body, and to take precautions even when no sign of a problem exists.

EVALUATE

5a. The sun is the number one cause of melanoma because overexposure to it is harmful to skin cells.

EXTEND

5b. No, the sun is not at fault. We have become a culture of sun-bathers. We see tanned skin as a sign of beauty and health. We relish sun sports (swimming, surfing, beach-combing). We even have tanning salons. As a culture, we would need to change our definition of beauty, to stop promoting tanned skin as healthy, and to see protecting our skin as more beautiful and beneficial than tanning, burning, and possibly damaging it.

Investigate, Inquire, and Imagine

Recall: GATHERING FACTS

1a. List the warning signs of malignant melanoma.

2a. List the precautions that may protect you from melanoma.

3a. What are the survival odds depending on how deep the melanoma has invaded the skin?

Interpret: FINDING MEANING

1b. What should be done if these signs appear?

2b. How would these precautions change or determine certain behavior?

3b. What is significant about these odds, and what protection can be taken against them?

Analyze: TAKING THINGS APART

4a. In the case of malignant melanoma, why is prevention and early detection crucial?

Synthesize: BRINGING THINGS TOGETHER

4b. What attitude does a person need to have in order to carry out the suggestions for prevention?

Evaluate: MAKING JUDGMENTS

5a. Why is the sun the number one cause of melanoma?

Extend: CONNECTING IDEAS

5b. Is the sun to blame? As a culture, what is our attitude toward the sun and our bodies?

Understanding Literature

PERIODICAL AND ARTICLE. Review the definitions for **periodical** and **article** in Literary Tools in Prereading. Had you heard any of the information conveyed in "Beware the Unruly Sun" before you read the article? If so, from what sources?

AIM. Review the definition for **aim** in the Handbook of Literary Terms. What is the author's main purpose in writing "Beware the Unruly Sun"?

Writer's Journal

1. Imagine how you would feel if your doctor told you that you have malignant melanoma. Write a **journal entry** describing your first reaction.

2. Write a **poem** of praise to the sun.

3. Write a **letter** to a friend who is either a surfer or a tanning buff. Explain the hazards of getting too much sun and encourage him or her to be careful.

ANSWERS TO UNDERSTANDING LITERATURE

PERIODICAL AND ARTICLE. *Responses will vary.*

AIM. The author's main purpose in writing this article is to inform the reader. She includes a lot of medical information in her article, with the purpose of educating the reader.

Integrating the Language Arts

Language, Grammar, and Style

SUBORDINATING CONJUNCTIONS. Read the Language Arts Survey 3.72, "Subordinating Conjunctions." Then, for each sentence below, identify the subordinating conjunction and the subordinate clause.

1. People flock to the beach whenever the sun is out in summer.
2. Although no one is immune to melanoma, people with fair skin and light eyes and hair are at greater risk.
3. It's a good idea to avoid the sun unless you apply sunscreen.
4. If a mole becomes suspicious, consult a dermatopathologist.
5. Melanoma is completely curable when it is detected early.

Media Literacy

GRAPHIC AIDS. There is a lot of information in "Beware the Unruly Sun." Kalb uses statistics, data, measurements, time spans, and numbers to support the information. Sort out some of this data and, for one part of it, make a graphic aid—a chart, graph, drawing, diagram, or spreadsheet—that will help illustrate the article and educate the viewer.

Collaborative Learning & Study and Research

SUN REPORT. Without the sun, life on Earth would not exist. Working in small groups, prepare a report on an aspect of the sun, its benefits, its healing properties, and ways to protect your skin from overexposure. For example, you might research scientific data on the planet, or research how it makes plants grow. You might look up an ancient myth about a Sun god and report on the attitudes of ancient cultures toward the sun. To educate your classmates, gather a selection of sunscreen lotions and provide information on which is best.

Study and Research & Media Literacy

INTERNET RESEARCH. Log onto one of the websites cited in the article (www.aad.org or www.cancer.org) or look up more of Claudia Kalb's health articles on www.newsweek.com. Browse these sites until you find a related article or related information that interests you. Many of these informative articles are quite short. The emphasis of much cancer research is on prevention, and new information is constantly being presented on various ways to prevent illness. Prepare a brief report for your class on, for example, another common cancer that can be prevented by taking steps now.

ANSWERS TO INTEGRATING THE LANGUAGE ARTS

Language, Grammar, and Style
1. sub. conjunction: whenever; sub. clause: whenever the sun is out in summer
2. sub. conjunction: Although; sub. clause: Although no one is immune to melanoma
3. sub. conjunction: unless; sub. clause: unless you apply sunscreen
4. sub. conjunction: If; sub. clause: If a mole becomes suspicious
5. sub. conjunction: when; sub. clause: when it is detected early

Media Literacy
Refer students to the Language Arts Survey 1.15, "Using Graphic Aids," and 6.11, "Displaying Effective Visual Information," for helpful tips and guidelines in creating graphic aids.

Study and Research & Media Literacy
Topics could include smoking and lung cancer, breast cancer and the importance of breast exams, and healthy eating.

ADDITIONAL RESOURCES

UNIT 6 RESOURCE BOOK
- Selection Worksheet 6.3
- Selection Check Test 4.6.7
- Selection Test 4.6.8
- Language, Grammar, and Style Resource 3.17

VOCABULARY FROM THE SELECTION

anonymity
obligatory

GRAPHIC ORGANIZER

Other steps on writing a letter that students should include in their flow chart follow: Write promptly when you need to acknowledge a gift, a death, or a visit. Keep your writing stuff in one place. If you are intimidated by a large sheet of paper, use a small sheet or a note card with fine art on the front. Meditate on the person you want to write to. Use declarative sentences. Don't think about grammar and literary style. Tell where you went, whom you saw, what they said, and what you think. If you don't know where to begin, start with the present moment. Don't worry about form. When you come to the end of one episode, start a new paragraph. Don't tear up the page and start over if you write a bad line.

READER'S JOURNAL

Have students make a list of the five best letters they have received and choose one to describe. You might also ask students to identify problems they have with letter writing.

Literary TOOLS

AIM. A writer's **aim** is his or her purpose, or goal. People may write with the following aims: to inform (expository/informational writing); to entertain, enrich, enlighten, and/or use an artistic medium, such as fiction or poetry, to share a perspective (imaginative writing); to make a point by sharing a story about an event (narrative writing); to reflect (personal/expressive writing); to persuade readers or listeners to respond in some way, such as to agree with a position, change a view on an issue, reach an agreement, or perform an action (persuasive/argumentative writing). As you read, decide what Keillor's principal aim is in writing "How to Write a Letter."

EXPOSITION. Exposition is a type of writing that presents facts or opinions in an organized manner. Among the most common ways to organize exposition are the following: *analysis*; *classification*; *comparison-contrast*; and *process* or *how-to writing*. You may want to look up these methods of organization in the Handbook of Literary Terms.

Graphic Organizer

Keillor organizes much of his essay as process or how-to writing. As you read, make a flow chart like the one below, listing Keillor's tips for how to write a letter. One example has been done for you.

Get over the guilt of not writing →

"How to Write a Letter"
by Garrison Keillor

Reader's resource

"**How to Write a Letter**" is an essay that gives tips on how to write a personal letter. Garrison Keillor also comments on why it is important to keep the art of letter writing alive.

About the AUTHOR

Garrison Keillor (1942–) was born in Anoka, Minnesota, and studied at the University of Minnesota, where he began his radio career. In 1974, he started his weekly show "A Prairie Home Companion," broadcast on National Public Radio. With gentle, folksy humor each week he delivers news from Lake Wobegon, a fictional Midwestern town where "all the women are strong, all the men are good looking, and all the children are above average." The program won a Peabody Award and an Edward R. Murrow Award, while Keillor's recording of *Lake Wobegon Days* received a Grammy Award. In 1994 Keillor was inducted into the Radio Hall of Fame, and in 1999 he was awarded a National Humanities Medal. Of his radio work, Keillor has said, "The great blessing is to have work that is satisfying, and that's enough."

For many years Keillor has contributed to *The New Yorker* and other magazines. His books include *Happy to Be Here* (1982), *Lake Wobegon Days* (1985), *We Are Still Married: Stories and Letters* (1989), *The Book of Guys* (1993), *Wobegon Boy* (1997), and *Me: By Jimmy "Big Boy" Valente* (1999).

Reader's Journal

Do you like to receive personal letters? Why, or why not?

GOALS/OBJECTIVES

Studying this lesson will enable students to
- understand how to write a personal letter
- describe Garrison Keillor's accomplishments within informational media
- define *aim* and *exposition* and explain examples of each that they encounter in their reading
- demonstrate an ability to identify the function of sentences
- listen to an episode of Keillor's "A Prairie Home Companion"

How to write a letter

Garrison Keillor

We shy persons need to write a letter now and then, or else we'll dry up and blow away. It's true. And I speak as one who loves to reach for the phone, dial the number, and say, "Big Bopper here—what's shakin', babes?" The telephone is to shyness what Hawaii is to February, it's a way out of the woods, *and yet:* a letter is better.

How does Keillor describe himself?

Such a sweet gift—a piece of handmade writing in an envelope that is not a bill, sitting in our friend's path when she trudges home from a long day spent among wahoos and savages, a day our words will help repair. They don't need to be immortal, just sincere. She can read them twice and again tomorrow: *You're someone I care about, Corinne, and think of often and every time I do you make me smile.*

We need to write, otherwise nobody will know who we are. They will have only a vague impression of us as A Nice Person, because, frankly, we don't shine at conversation, we lack the confidence to thrust our faces forward and say, "Hi, I'm Heather Hooten: let me tell you about my week." Mostly we say "Uh-huh" and "Oh, really." People smile and look over our shoulder, looking for someone else to meet.

So a shy person sits down and writes a letter. To be known by another person—to meet and talk freely on the page—to be close despite distance. To escape from <u>anonymity</u> and be our own sweet selves and express the music of our souls.

Same thing that moves a giant rock star to sing his heart out in front of 123,000 people moves us to take ballpoint in hand and write a

words for everyday use

an • o • nym • i • ty (an' ə nim' ə tē) *n.*, quality or state of not being known. *Some writers use pen names to protect their <u>anonymity</u>.*

---

1. Keillor describes himself as a shy person.

INDIVIDUAL LEARNING STRATEGIES

MOTIVATION
Have students bring in letters they have received from family members or friends. Ask them to share what they like about receiving letters and if they like to write them.

READING PROFICIENCY
Pair students with an advanced reader and ask them to read the selection together, alternating each paragraph. Then have them work together on the Guided Reading questions.

ENGLISH LANGUAGE LEARNING
Students from different countries have mailing addresses that are styled differently from mailing addresses from the United States. Ask students to share how letters are written in their culture and the order of information that goes on an envelope.

SPECIAL NEEDS
Explain to students that this selection gives tips on and reasons for writing a letter. Ask them to find three tips or reasons Keillor gives for writing a letter.

ENRICHMENT
Have students get into groups. Using the tips and reasons given from this selection, ask students to develop a letter-writing promotional campaign in their school. Students' goal is to convince their school to participate in establishing pen pals through the Internet sites suggested on page 484 or with another school who is interested in having pen pals.

1. Keillor suggests trying a smaller page and writing boldly, or using a note card with a piece of fine art on the front.
2. One should start to write after meditating on the friend, when he or she becomes real in the writer's mind.

ADDITIONAL QUESTIONS AND ACTIVITIES

Establishing a pen pal is a great way to make friends and to practice the helpful tips that Keillor gives on letter writing. For those students who are interested in finding a pen pal, direct students to **World Pen Pals** at http://www.world-pen-pals.com/. This organization is one of the largest students-writing-students programs. Here, students can request a pen pal at a one time membership fee of $3.

few lines to our dear Aunt Eleanor. *We want to be known.* We want her to know that we have fallen in love, that we quit our job, that we're moving to New York, and we want to say a few things that might not get said in casual conversation: *Thank you for what you've meant to me, I am very happy right now.*

The first step in writing letters is to get over the guilt of *not* writing. You don't "owe" anybody a letter. Letters are a gift. The burning shame you feel when you see unanswered mail makes it harder to pick up a pen and makes for a cheerless letter when you finally do. *I feel bad about not writing, but I've been so busy,* etc. Skip this. Few letters are <u>obligatory</u>, and they are *Thanks for the wonderful gift and I am terribly sorry to hear about George's death* and *Yes, you're welcome to stay with us next month,* and not many more than that. Write those promptly if you want to keep your friends. Don't worry about the others, except love letters, of course. When your true love writes, *Dear Light of My Life, Joy of My Heart, O Lovely Pulsating Core of My Sensate[1] Life,* some response is called for.

Some of the best letters are tossed off in a burst of inspiration, so keep your writing stuff in one place where you can sit down for a few minutes and *(Dear Roy, I am in the middle of a book entitled* We Are Still Married *but thought I'd drop you a line. Hi to your sweetie, too)* dash off a note to a pal. Envelopes, stamps, address book, everything in a drawer so you can write fast when the pen is hot.

A blank white eight-by-eleven sheet can look as big as Montana if the pen's not so hot—try a smaller page and write boldly. Or use a note card with a piece of fine art on the front; if your letter ain't

What does Keillor suggest for the person intimidated by a white eight-by-eleven sheet of paper?

good, at least they get the Matisse.[2] Get a pen that makes a sensuous line, get a comfortable typewriter, a friendly word processor—whichever feels easy to the hand.

Sit for a few minutes with the blank sheet in front of you, and meditate on the person you will write to, let your friend come to mind until you can almost see her or him in the room with you. Remember the last time you saw each other and how your friend looked and what you said and what perhaps was unsaid between you, and when your friend becomes real to you, start to write.

At what moment should a person start to write?

Letters are a gift.

Write the salutation—*Dear You*—and take a deep breath and plunge In. A simple declarative sentence[3] will do, followed by another and another and another. Tell us what you're doing and tell it like you were talking to us. Don't think about grammar, don't think about lit'ry style; don't try to write dramatically, just give us your news. Where did you go, who did you see, what did they say, what do you think?

1. **Sensate.** Appealing to the senses
2. **Matisse.** (1869–1954) Henri Matisse, French painter
3. **declarative sentence.** Sentence that makes a direct statement and that is punctuated with a period

words for everyday use

oblig • a • to • ry (əb lig′ ə tôr′ ē) *adj.,* required. *Military service is* <u>obligatory</u> *in some European countries.*

If you don't know where to begin, start with the present moment: *I'm sitting at the kitchen table on a rainy Saturday morning. Everyone is gone and the house is quiet.* Let your simple description of the present moment lead to something else, let the letter drift gently along.

The toughest letter to crank out is one that is meant to impress, as we all know from writing job applications; if it's hard work to slip off a letter to a friend, maybe you're trying too hard to be terrific. A letter is only a report to someone who already likes you for reasons other than your brilliance. Take it easy.

Don't worry about form. It's not a term paper. When you come to the end of one episode, just start a new paragraph. You can go from a few lines about the sad state of pro football to the fight with your mother to your fond memories of Mexico to your cat's urinary-tract infection to a few thoughts on personal indebtedness and on to the kitchen sink and what's in it. The more you write, the easier it gets, and when you have a True True Friend to write to, a *compadre,*[4] a soul sibling, then it's like driving a car down a country road, you just get behind the keyboard and press on the gas.

> What is writing like when a person has a "True True Friend" to write to?

Don't tear up the page and start over when you write a bad line—try to write your way out of it. Make mistakes and plunge on. Let the letter cook along and let yourself be bold. Outrage, confusion, love—whatever is in your mind, let it find a way to the page.

Writing is a means of discovery, always, and when you come to the end and write *Yours ever* or *Hugs and kisses,* you'll know something you didn't when you wrote *Dear Pal.*

Probably your friend will put your letter away and it'll be read again a few years from now—and it will improve with age. And forty years from now, your friend's grandkids will dig it out of the attic and read it, a sweet and precious relic *of the ancient eighties* that gives them a sudden clear glimpse of you and her and

> What will your friend's grandkids feel when they read your letters in forty years?

the world we old-timers knew. You will then have created an object of art. Your simple lines about where you went, who you saw, what they said, will speak to those children and they will feel in their hearts the humanity of our times.

You can't pick up a phone and call the future and tell them about our times. You have to pick up a piece of paper. ∎

---

4. *compadre.* Spanish for close friend or pal

Respond *to the* SELECTION

If you were Keillor, what would you most want your readers to get out of your essay?

READER'S JOURNAL

After reading this selection, has Keillor persuaded you to write letters to friends and family members? Why, or why not?

---

1. Writing is like driving a car down a country road.
2. They will feel the "humanity of our times."

SELECTION CHECK TEST 4.6.7 WITH ANSWERS

Checking Your Reading
1. According to Keillor, why do shy people need to write? **Shy people need to write to make others know who they are.**
2. What is the first step in writing a letter? **The first step is to get over the guilt of not writing.**
3. What should you do before you begin to write? **You should sit and meditate on the person to whom you are writing.**
4. What type of information should you include in a letter? **You should include details that state what you are doing and what you think.**
5. What is the most difficult letter to write? **A letter that is meant to impress the reader is the most difficult to write.**

Vocabulary in Context
Write a contextual sentence for the following words:

1. anonymity
2. obligatory

Literary Tools
Fill in the blanks using the following terms.

imaginative   informational   narrative
aim   exposition   personal

1. A writer's **aim** is his or her purpose or goal.
2. **Imaginative** writing tries to entertain or enlighten the reader.
3. Making a point by sharing a story about an event is called **narrative** writing.
4. **Exposition** is a type of writing that presents facts or opinions in an organized manner.
5. **Personal** writing is usually reflective in nature.

RECALL

1a. A shy person needs to write a letter so he or she won't "dry up and blow away." A shy person gets "to meet and talk freely on the page," "to be close despite distance," "to escape from anonymity" and to express the music of his or her soul.

2a. The first step in writing letters is to get over the guilt of *not* writing.

3a. The "toughest letter to crank out" is one that is meant to impress.

INTERPRET

1b. In February, people like to escape the gloom and cold of winter in favor of tropical Hawaii. Talking on the telephone relieves the condition of shyness and, for the length of the call, allows the caller to be just as gregarious and outgoing as a non-shy person.

2b. Guilt prevents people from getting started on a letter because they become absorbed by the feeling of shame brought on by not writing and are unable to focus on what they want to share in the letter.

3b. The writer's attitude reveals that he or she feels inferior to the person addressed in the letter.

ANALYZE

4a. Keillor is referring to the experiences, hopes, and dreams of our generation that may be passed on to future generations if they read one of our letters.

SYNTHESIZE

4b. Keillor would probably be moved to read about the "humanity" of earlier times. As an author himself, Keillor might share a sense of camaraderie with those earlier authors.

EVALUATE

5a. Keillor sees work as a bad experience and coworkers as negative "wahoos and savages." Realistically, not every day at work can be bad. Keillor is purposely describing a bad day at work to demonstrate the effect a friendly letter can have on someone's life. He's saying that sometimes a personal letter can "repair" a bad day and, perhaps, put things in a better perspective.

EXTEND

5b. *Responses will vary.*

Investigate, Inquire, and Imagine

Recall: GATHERING FACTS

1a. What type of person needs to write a letter? Why? What does such a person gain by writing a letter?

2a. What is the first step in writing letters?

3a. What is the "toughest letter to crank out"?

Interpret: FINDING MEANING

1b. Keillor says, "The telephone is to shyness what Hawaii is to February. . . ." How would you explain this comparison?

2b. In what way does guilt prevent a person from getting started on a letter?

3b. If someone is trying to impress a friend in a letter, what does that say about the writer's attitude toward the friend?

Analyze: TAKING THINGS APART

4a. What does Keillor mean by the "humanity of our times"?

Synthesize: BRINGING THINGS TOGETHER

4b. How would Keillor likely respond to seeing letters in the Library of Congress by great authors such as George Washington and Abigail Adams?

Evaluate: MAKING JUDGMENTS

5a. Evaluate whether Keillor's view of work, described in paragraph 2, is realistic. What is his purpose in describing a workday in this manner?

Extend: CONNECTING IDEAS

5b. Watch the movie *84 Charing Cross Road* starring Anne Bancroft or read the book by the same title by Helene Hanff. Then write a short essay describing how letters enriched Helene's life.

Understanding Literature

AIM. Review the definition for **aim** in the Handbook of Literary Terms. What is Keillor's principal aim in writing "How to Write a Letter"?

EXPOSITION. Review the definition for **exposition** in the Handbook of Literary Terms and the flow chart you made in Literary Tools on page 482. What, for you, are the three most helpful tips that Keillor provides about how to write a letter? Are there any tips that you find useful for writing in general? What method of organization does Keillor use besides *process* or *how-to writing*? What is one example of this method of organization?

ANSWERS TO UNDERSTANDING LITERATURE

AIM. Keillor's principal aim in writing the essay is to change the reader's attitude toward letter writing and to persuade the reader to write letters. "How to Write a Letter" is an example of persuasive writing.

EXPOSITION. *Responses will vary.* Keillor also uses analysis when he discusses the obstacles to letter writing. For example, he analyzes the impediments of guilt when starting to write a letter.

Writer's Journal

1. Write the **script** for a filmstrip on how to write a letter.
2. Find a quote about letter writing. Then write a **journal entry** in which you speculate on Keillor's reaction to the quote.
3. Write a **letter** to Garrison Keillor describing how his essay improved your attitude toward letter writing. If you already liked to write letters, share some of your own perspectives about the importance of letter writing, and add any tips that Keillor might have overlooked.

Integrating the Language Arts

Language, Grammar, and Style

FUNCTIONS OF SENTENCES. Read the Language Arts Survey 3.17, "Functions of Sentences." Then identify each of the following sentences as declarative, interrogative, imperative, or exclamatory.

1. Give me a letter rather than a phone call any day.
2. The first step in writing letters is to get over the guilt of not writing.
3. Do you keep all your writing stuff in one place?
4. Don't worry about form.
5. What a lovely letter!

Media Literacy

GUIDE TO "A PRAIRIE HOME COMPANION." Listen to an episode of "A Prairie Home Companion" by accessing A Prairie Home Companion's Internet site at http://phc.mpr.org/. Then write a guide for that episode of "A Prairie Home Companion" for someone who has never heard the show. Summarize what each segment is about and identify the aim of each segment. Segments to include in your guide are advertisements, musical entertainment, "Guy Noir," and the "News from Lake Wobegon." Provide a brief biography of each of the musicians featured.

Collaborative Learning

PEN PAL INTRODUCTIONS. With several classmates, form a circle. Then take turns introducing someone to whom you write personal letters or e-mail messages. Describe your pen pal. Then identify his or her hobbies, tastes, opinions, and goals. Your pen pal might be a friend who has moved away, a cousin or grandparent, or someone from another country whom you have never met. If you have a picture of your pen pal, you might want to show it to the group.

ANSWERS TO INTEGRATING THE LANGUAGE ARTS

Language, Grammar, and Style
1. imperative
2. declarative
3. interrogative
4. imperative
5. exclamatory

Media Literacy
Students may be interested in e-mailing Keillor about their thoughts and reactions to "How to Write a Letter" and to the episode they choose to listen to. Students can e-mail Keillor directly at phc@mpr.org.

Collaborative Learning
Students interested in getting a pen pal may want to contact **PenPals** at http://www.penpals.com. If many students in your class do not write letters, you may want to postpone this activity until every student has a pen pal.

ADDITIONAL RESOURCES

UNIT 6 RESOURCE BOOK
- Selection Worksheet 6.4
- Selection Check Test 4.6.9
- Selection Test 4.6.10
- Language, Grammar, and Style Resource 3.61
- Speaking and Listening Resource 4.21

VOCABULARY FROM THE SELECTION

analogous	juxtapose
conglomerate	morbid
conjoining	obsolescence
conspicuous	omnipresence
corroboration	pliable
discourse	portend
eradicate	posit
exalt	relevance
imperative	stodgy
impinge	succumb
increment	surmount
inkling	vestigial
intrinsically	

GRAPHIC ORGANIZER

Students might include some of the following words in their cluster charts: vestigial, conjoining, eradicated, obsolescence, juxtapose, imperatives, lamentations.

READER'S JOURNAL

Students might discuss reading for pleasure versus reading for school.

Literary TOOLS

AIM. A writer's **aim** is his or her purpose, or goal. People may write with the following aims: to inform (expository/informational writing); to entertain, enrich, enlighten, and/or use an artistic medium, such as fiction or poetry, to share a perspective (imaginative writing); to make a point by sharing a story about an event (narrative writing); to reflect (personal/expressive writing); to persuade readers or listeners to respond in some way, such as to agree with a position, change a view on an issue, reach an agreement, or perform an action (persuasive/argumentative writing). As you read, determine Birkerts's primary aim in writing the essay.

DICTION. Diction, when applied to writing, refers to word choice. Much of a writer's style is determined by his or her diction, the types of words that he or she chooses. As you read, think of an adjective that describes Birkerts's diction.

Graphic Organizer

Make a cluster chart listing words that you think are characteristic of Birkerts's diction. One example has been done for you.

analogous

Diction

488 UNIT SIX

"Into the Electronic Millennium"
by Sven Birkerts

Reader's resource

Sven Birkerts's essay **"Into the Electronic Millennium"** first appeared, in slightly different form, in *The Boston Review* and was later included in a collection called *The Gutenberg Elegies: The Fate of Reading in an Electronic Age* (1994). In the introduction to that collection, Birkerts writes, "I speak as an unregenerate reader, one who still believes that language and not technology is the true evolutionary miracle. I have not yet given up on the idea that the experience of literature offers a kind of wisdom that cannot be discovered elsewhere. . . and that for a host of reasons the bound book is the ideal vehicle for the written word."

About the AUTHOR

Sven Birkerts (1951–) is a literary critic whose work has appeared in *The New York Times Book Review, The Atlantic, Harper's, The New Republic,* and many other literary journals and reviews. He is probably best known for his essay collection *The Gutenberg Elegies,* which the *Washington Post* called "a lament for literature and everything implicit in it." Since its publication, many other writers and critics have weighed in with their views on how the new technologies will affect the experience of reading and the functions of text. Though some have profoundly disagreed with Birkerts's claims, many have lauded him for his important cultural insights, which shine light on our collective sense of nostalgia, time, and place and which ask important questions about the future of the creative spirit. Other works by Birkerts include *Artificial Wilderness: Essays on 20th Century Literature* (1987), *American Energies: Essays in Fiction* (1992), *Tolstoy's Dictaphone: Technology and the Muse* (1996), and *Readings* (1999). Birkerts has taught literature at Emerson College and Mount Holyoke College.

Reader's Journal

What role does reading play in your life?

GOALS/OBJECTIVES

Studying this lesson will enable students to
- empathize with the author's concern for the printed word in a world of technological advances
- describe Sven Birkerts's criticism and attitude toward electronic media
- define *aim* and *diction* and recognize examples of each in the selection
- demonstrate the ability to identify transitive and intransitive verbs in sentences
- participate in a debate that argues for and against electronic technology

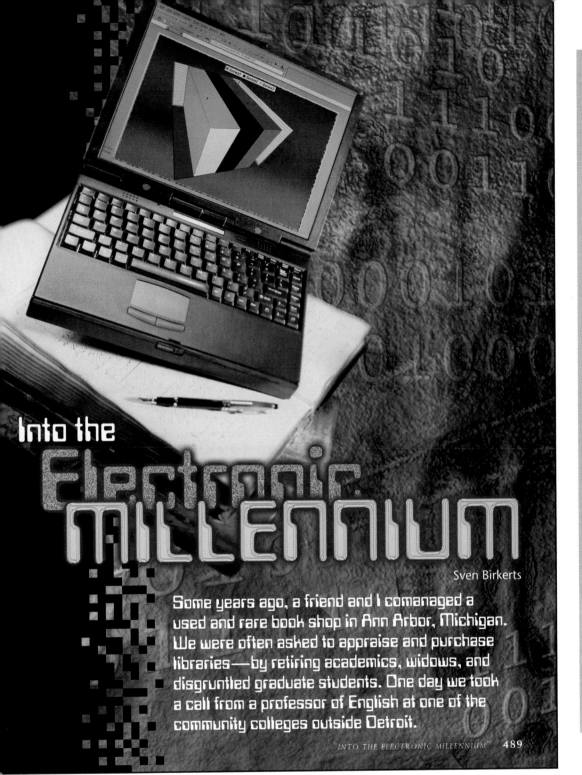

Into the
Electronic
MILLENNIUM

Sven Birkerts

Some years ago, a friend and I comanaged a used and rare book shop in Ann Arbor, Michigan. We were often asked to appraise and purchase libraries—by retiring academics, widows, and disgruntled graduate students. One day we took a call from a professor of English at one of the community colleges outside Detroit.

"INTO THE ELECTRONIC MILLENNIUM" 489

INDIVIDUAL LEARNING STRATEGIES

MOTIVATION
As a class, brainstorm the positive and negative effects of technology. Do students think that books and textbooks are going to be replaced with computers? Why, or why not?

READING PROFICIENCY
As students read this selection, ask them to mark the sections they have difficulty understanding. Then allow students to partner up with an advanced reader and work on answering the trouble spots.

ENGLISH LANGUAGE LEARNING
Have students pick five words of particular difficulty from the Words for Everyday Use. Then have them use those five words throughout the day in their everyday conversations. Finally, have students write down the contextual sentences they used that day.

SPECIAL NEEDS
Before students read the selection, have them thoroughly read the Prereading section. Explain to students that the selection is an essay trying to persuade readers about the importance of books and other printed texts, and how they are in danger of becoming obsolete due to technological advances.

ENRICHMENT
Ask students to conduct a school survey about what students think about the future of printed texts such as books, textbooks, and newspapers. Do they think printed texts are in as much danger as Birkerts believes they are? Have students summarize their survey by calculating the percentage of students who believe printed texts are in danger, those who do not believe in they are in danger, and those who are indifferent about this topic. Also ask them to chart their percentages using a pie graph.

1. The professor sold his books because he was getting out of the teaching business.

Quotables

"...the great national libraries and their buildings will go the way of the railroad stations and the movie palaces of an earlier era which were really vital institutions in their time...Somehow folks moved away from that when the technology changed."

—Robert Zich

When he answered the buzzer I did a double take—he looked to be only a year or two older than we were. "I'm selling everything," he said, leading the way through a large apartment. As he opened the door of his study I felt a nudge from my partner. The room was wall-to-wall books and as neat as a chapel.

The professor had a remarkable collection. It reflected not only the needs of his vocation—he taught nineteenth- and twentieth-century literature—but a book lover's sensibility as well. The shelves were strictly arranged, and the books themselves were in superb condition. When he left the room we set to work inspecting, counting, and estimating. This is always a delicate procedure, for the buyer is at once anxious to avoid insult to the seller and eager to get the goods for the best price. We adopted our usual strategy, working out a lower offer and a more generous fallback price. But there was no need to worry. The professor took our first offer without batting an eye.

As we boxed up the books, we chatted. My partner asked the man if he was moving. "No," he said, "but I am getting out." We both looked up. "Out of the teaching business, I mean. Out of books." He then said that he wanted to show us something. And indeed, as soon as the books were packed and loaded, he led us back through the apartment and down a

Why did the professor want to sell his books?

set of stairs. When we reached the basement, he flicked on the light. There, on a long table, displayed like an exhibit in the Space Museum,[1] was a computer. I didn't know what kind it was then, nor could I tell you now, fifteen years later. But the professor was keen to explain and demonstrate.

While he and my partner hunched over the terminal, I roamed to and fro, inspecting the shelves. It was purely a reflex gesture, for they held nothing but thick binders and paperbound manuals. "I'm changing my life," the ex-professor was saying. "This is definitely where it's all going to happen." He told us that he already had several good job offers. And the books? I asked. Why was he selling them all? He paused for a few beats. "The whole profession represents a lot of pain to me," he said. "I don't want to see any of these books again."

The scene has stuck with me. It is now a kind of marker in my mental life. That afternoon I got my first serious <u>inkling</u> that all was not well in the world of print and letters. All sorts of <u>corroborations</u> followed. Our professor was by no means an isolated case. Over a period of two years we met with several others like him. New men and new women who had glimpsed the future and had decided to get out while the getting was good. The selling off of books was sometimes done for financial reasons, but the need to burn bridges was usually there as well. It was as if heading to the future also required the destruction of tokens from the past.

A change is upon us—nothing could be clearer. The printed word is part of a <u>vestigial</u> order that we are moving away from—by choice and by societal compulsion. I'm not just talking about disaffected academics, either. This shift is happening

1. **Space Museum.** The Smithsonian's National Air and Space Museum in Washington, DC

words for everyday use

in • kling (in' kliŋ) *n.,* slight knowledge; vague notion. *Maria had an <u>inkling</u> that Justin would ask her to the dance.*

cor • rob • o • ra • tion (kə rä' bə rā' shən) *n.,* confirmation; something supported with evidence or authority. *The <u>corroboration</u> of the plaintiff's story by a key witness led to the conviction of the defendant.*

ves • tig • i • al (ve sti' jē əl) *adj.,* showing a trace, mark, or visible sign left by something vanished or lost. *From the <u>vestigial</u> ruins Daniel could imagine the temple as it looked in 45 BC.*

throughout our culture, away from the patterns and habits of the printed page and toward a new world distinguished by its reliance on electronic communications.

What is changing in our culture?

This is not, of course, the first such shift in our long history. In Greece, in the time of Socrates, several centuries after Homer, the dominant oral culture was overtaken by the writing technology. And in Europe another epochal transition was effected in the late fifteenth century after Gutenberg invented movable type. In both cases the long-term societal effects were overwhelming, as they will be for us in the years to come.

The evidence of the change is all around us, though possibly in the manner of the forest that we cannot see for the trees. The electronic media, while <u>conspicuous</u> in gadgetry, are very nearly invisible in their functioning. They have slipped deeply and irrevocably into our midst, creating sluices[2] and circulating through them. I'm not referring to any one product or function in isolation, such as television or fax machines or the networks that make them possible. I mean the interdependent totality that has arisen from the <u>conjoining</u> of parts—the disk drives hooked to modems, transmissions linked to technologies of reception, recording, duplication, and storage. Numbers and codes and frequencies. Buttons and signals. And this is no longer "the future," except for the poor or the self-consciously atavistic[3]—it is now. Next to the new technologies, the scheme of things represented by print and the snail-paced linearity of the reading act looks <u>stodgy</u> and dull. Many educators say that our students are less and less able to read, or analyze, or write with clarity and purpose. Who can blame the students? Every-

thing they meet with in the world around them gives the signal: That was then, and electronic communications are now.

Do I exaggerate? If all this is the case, why haven't we heard more about it? Why hasn't somebody stepped forward with a bow tie and a pointer stick to explain what is going on? Valid questions, but they also beg the question. They assume that we are all plugged into a total system—where else would that "somebody" appear if not on the screen at the communal hearth?

Media theorist Mark Crispin Miller has given one explanation for our situation in his discussions of television in *Boxed In: The Culture of TV.* The medium, he proposes, has long since diffused itself throughout the entire system. Through sheer <u>omnipresence</u> it has vanquished the possibility of comparative perspectives. We cannot see the role that television (or, for our purposes, all electronic communications) has assumed in our lives because there is no independent ledge where we might secure our footing. The medium has absorbed and <u>eradicated</u> the idea of a pretelevision past; in place of what used to be we get an ever-new and ever-renewable present. The only way we can hope to understand what is happening, or what has already happened, is by way of a severe and unnatural dissociation of sensibility.

Why can't we see the role television has assumed in our lives?

To get a sense of the enormity of the change, you must force yourself to imagine—deeply and in nontelevisual terms—what the world was like a hundred, even fifty, years ago. If the feat is too

---
2. **sluices.** Channels to drain or carry off surplus water
3. **atavistic.** Showing a recurrence of or reversion to a past style, manner, outlook, or approach

1. Our culture is drifting away from the "patterns and habits of the printed page" and toward electronic communications.
2. Because television has eradicated the sense of historical perspective, we are unable to see the role it plays in our lives.

CROSS-CURRICULAR CONNECTIONS

TECHNOLOGY. The printed book of the past is quickly turning into electronic cards that are fed into gadgets such as the hand-held electronic book created by Sony. Franklin Electronic Publishers has also created a miniature encyclopedia. With a punch of a few buttons, these electronic gadgets will do the rest. And when you are done reading or finding the information you are looking for, you can slip them back into your pocket.

words for everyday use

con • spic • u • ous (kən spi' kyü wəs) *adj.,* obvious to the eye or mind. *Jed's absence was <u>conspicuous</u> because it was his turn to give a speech.*
con • join • ing (kən join' iŋ) *n.,* joining together separate entities for a common purpose. *Romeo and Juliet hoped that the <u>conjoining</u> of their two families would occur after their marriage.*
stodg • y (stä' jē) *adj.,* moving in a slow plodding way. *The <u>stodgy</u> professor took his time in reaching the podium.*
om • ni • pres • ence (äm' ni pre' zən(t)s) *n.,* quality or state of being present in all places at all times. *The <u>omnipresence</u> of British soldiers on the streets of Belfast made Mrs. Conaghan feel that she was always being watched.*
e • rad • i • cate (i ra' də kāt) *vt.,* do away with as completely as if by pulling up by the roots. *Jim volunteers at an organization whose goal is to <u>eradicate</u> illiteracy.*

1. The natural world can now only be
seen dimly, can now only be
"perceived through a scrim." It has
become part of the past.
2. Large corporations are "waging
bitter takeover battles" to establish
global empires of media control.

difficult, spend some time with a novel from the period. Read between the lines and reconstruct. Move through the sequence of a character's day and then <u>juxtapose</u> the images and sensations you find with those in the life of the average urban or suburban dweller today.

Inevitably, one of the first realizations is that a communications net, a soft and <u>pliable</u> mesh woven from invisible threads, has fallen over everything. The so-called natural world, the place we used to live, which served us so long as the yardstick for all measurements, can now only be perceived through a scrim.[4] Nature

What has happened to the way we perceive the natural world?

was then; this is now. Trees and rocks have receded. And the great geographical Other, the faraway rest of the world, has been transformed by the pure possibility of access. The numbers of distance and time no longer mean what they used to. Every place, once unique, itself, is strangely shot through with radiations from every other place. "There" was then; "here" is now.

Think of it. Fifty to a hundred million people (maybe a conservative estimate) form their ideas about what is going on in America and in the world from the same basic package of edited images—to the extent that the image itself has lost much of its once-fearsome power. Daily news-

papers, with their long columns of print, struggle against declining sales. Fewer and fewer people under the age of fifty read them; computers will soon make packaged information a custom product. But if the printed sheet is heading for <u>obsolescence</u>, people are tuning in to the signals. The screen is where the information and entertainment wars will be fought. The communications <u>conglomerates</u> are waging bitter takeover battles in their

What are the big corporations now competing for?

zeal to establish global empires. As Jonathan Crary has written in "The Eclipse of the Spectacle," "Telecommunications is the new arterial network <u>analogous</u> in part to what railroads were for capitalism in the nineteenth century. And it is this electronic substitute for geography that corporate and national entities are now carving up." Maybe one reason why the news of the change is not part of the common currency is that such news can only sensibly be communicated through the more analytic sequences of print.

To underscore my point, I have been making it sound as if we were all abruptly walking out of one room and into another, leaving our books to the moths while we settle ourselves in front of our state-of-the-art terminals. The truth is that we are living through a period of overlap; one way of being is pushed athwart[5] another. Antonio Gramsci's often-cited sentence comes inevitably to mind: "The crisis consists precisely in the fact that the old is dying and the new cannot be born; in this interregnum,[6] a great variety

---

4. **scrim.** Theater drop that appears opaque when a scene in front is lighted and transparent when a scene in back is lighted
5. **athwart.** In opposition to
6. **interregnum.** Period of time between two reigns

words for everyday use

jux • ta • pose (juk' stə pōz) *vt.,* place side by side. *In her paintings, Clarisse <u>juxtaposes</u> unexpected combinations of colors and shapes.*
pli • a • ble (plī' ə bəl) *adj.,* supple enough to bend freely or repeatedly without breaking. *The toddler played with a <u>pliable</u> plastic toy.*
ob • so • les • cence (äb' sə le' sən(t)s) *n.,* process of becoming obsolete or the condition of being nearly obsolete, or no longer in use. *The thesis of the book is that American companies plan on <u>obsolescence</u> so that consumers will have to replace products periodically.*
con • glom • er • ate (kən gläm' rət) *n.,* widely diversified corporation. *The <u>conglomerate</u> had software, toy, and music entertainment divisions.*
a • nal • o • gous (ə na' lə gəs) *adj.,* showing a likeness that permits one to draw an analogy, or comparison. *A brain and a computer are <u>analogous</u> because both reason.*

of <u>morbid</u> symptoms appears." The old surely is dying, but I'm not so sure that the new is having any great difficulty being born. As for the morbid symptoms, these we have in abundance. The overlap in communications modes, and the ways of living that they are associated with, invites comparison with the transitional epoch in ancient Greek society, certainly in terms of the relative degree of disturbance. Historian Eric Havelock designated that period as one of "proto-literacy," of which his fellow scholar Oswyn Murray has written:

> To him [Havelock] the basic shift from oral to literate culture was a slow process; for centuries, despite the existence of writing, Greece remained essentially an oral culture. This culture was one which depended heavily on the encoding of information in poetic texts, to be learned by rote and to provide a cultural encyclopedia of conduct. It was not until the age of Plato[7] in the fourth century that the dominance of poetry in an oral culture was challenged in the final triumph of literacy.

That challenge came in the form of philosophy, among other things, and poetry has never recovered its cultural primacy. What oral poetry was for the Greeks, printed books in general are for us. But our historical moment, which we might call "proto-electronic," will not require a transition period of two centuries. The very essence of electronic transmissions is to <u>surmount</u> impedances[8] and to hasten transitions. Fifty years, I'm sure, will suffice. As for what the conversion will bring—and *mean*—to us, we might glean a few clues by looking to some of the "morbid symptoms" of the change. But to understand what these <u>portend</u>, we need to remark a few of the more obvious ways in which our various technologies condition our senses and sensibilities.

I won't tire my reader with an extended rehash of the differences between the print orientation and that of electronic systems. Media theorists from Marshall McLuhan to Walter Ong to Neil Postman have discoursed upon these at length. What's more, they are reasonably commonsensical. I therefore will abbreviate.

The order of print is linear, and is bound to logic by the <u>imperatives</u> of syntax. Syntax is the substructure of <u>discourse</u>, a mapping of the ways that the mind makes sense through language. Print communication requires the active engagement of the reader's attention, for reading is fundamentally an act of translation. Symbols are turned into their verbal referents and these are in turn interpreted. The print engagement is essentially private. While it does represent an act of communication, the contents pass from the privacy of the sender to the privacy of the receiver. Print also <u>posits</u> a time axis; the turning of pages, not to mention the vertical descent down the page, is a forward-moving succession, with earlier contents at every point serving as a ground for what follows. Moreover, the printed material is static—it is the reader, not the book, that moves forward. The physical arrangements of print are in accord with our traditional sense of history. Materials are layered; they lend themselves to rereading—and to sustained attention. The pace of reading is variable, with progress determined by the reader's focus and comprehension.

The electronic order is in most ways opposite. Information and contents do not simply move from one private space to another, but they travel along a network. Engagement is

---

7. **Plato.** Greek philosopher (*circa* 427–347 BC)
8. **impedances.** Hindrances; things that impede, or interfere with the progress of

---

words for everyday use

mor • **bid** (môr′ bəd) *adj.*, of, relating to, or characteristic of disease. *Because of her <u>morbid</u> condition, Mrs. Washburn sought a doctor's diagnosis.*
sur • **mount** (sər mount′) *vt.*, overcome; prevail over. *Suzie was in such a good mood she felt she could <u>surmount</u> any obstacle that came her way.*
por • **tend** (pôr tend′) *vt.*, give an omen or anticipatory sign of; indicate. *The black clouds <u>portend</u> a bad storm.*
im • **per • a • tive** (im per′ ə tiv) *n.*, something that is obligatory. *The <u>imperatives</u> of the scientific approach were neglected in the study.*
dis • **course** (dis′ kōrs) *n.*, verbal interchange of ideas; conversation. *Tim found the <u>discourse</u> of the guest speaker difficult to follow because he used a lot of compound-complex sentences and difficult vocabulary.*
pos • **it** (pä′ zət) *vt.*, suggest; propose as an explanation. *Galileo <u>posited</u> the observation that bodies do not fall with velocities proportional to their weights.*

Divide students into three groups. Each group will be assigned a media theorist to research: Group 1—Marshall McLuhan, Group 2—Walter Ong, and Group 3—Neil Postman. Have each group summarize the theory of their media theorist. Then have them compare his theory with the theory and viewpoints of Birkerts. Finally, have students present their information in an oral report.

1. Information that is presented to us in print requires the readers to actively engage with the work, whereas information that is presented to us through electronic communication subjects us to passive engagement.

SELECTION CHECK TEST 4.6.9 WITH ANSWERS

Checking Your Reading

1. Why did the ex-professor sell all his books? **He sold them because he was getting out of the teaching business.**
2. What shift is taking place in our society? **The shift from the written word to electronic communications is taking place.**
3. What evidences are there of this shift? **Electronic media, new and innovative gadgetry, and modems are evidence of this shift into electronic communications.**
4. Where will information and entertainment wars be fought? **These wars will be fought on the screen rather than the printed page.**
5. What is one way print order is different from electronic order? **Print order is linear while electronic order is circular.**

Vocabulary in Context

Fill in each blank below with the most appropriate word from the following Words for Everyday Use. You may have to change the tense of the word.

| stodgy | conjoining | vestigial |
| eradicate | inkling | conspicuous |

1. I had a(n) **inkling** that I'd get new skates for my birthday.
2. From the **vestigial** crumbs on Tasha's face, I could tell she sneaked a cookie.
3. It is **conspicuous** whenever Paul lies because he begins to stutter and turn red.
4. My ninety year-old grandmother walks in a **stodgy** way.
5. We spent one full day **eradicating** the weeds from the garden.

---

intrinsically public, taking place within a circuit of larger connectedness. The vast resources of the network are always there, potential, even if they do not <u>impinge</u> on the immediate communication. Electronic communication can be passive, as with television watching, or interactive, as with computers. Contents, unless they are printed out (at which point they become part of the static order of print) are felt to be evanescent.[9] They can be changed or deleted with the stroke of a key. With visual media (television, projected graphs, highlighted "bullets") impression and image take precedence over logic and concept, and detail and linear sequentiality are sacrificed. The pace is rapid, driven by jump-cut[10] <u>increments</u>, and the basic movement is laterally associative rather than vertically cumulative. The presentation structures the reception and, in time, the expectation about how information is organized.

Further, the visual and nonvisual technology in every way encourages in the user a heightened and ever-changing awareness of the present. It works against historical perception, which must depend on the inimical[11] notions of logic and sequential succession. If the print medium <u>exalts</u> the word, fixing it into permanence, the electronic counterpart reduces it to a signal, a means to an end.

> How does the way information is presented affect us?

Transitions like the one from print to electronic media do not take place without rippling or, more likely, *reweaving* the entire social and cultural web. The tendencies outlined above are already at work. We don't need to look far to find their effects. We can begin with the newspaper headlines and the millennial lamentations[12] sounded in the op-ed[13] pages: that our educational systems are in decline; that our students are less and less able to read and comprehend their required texts, and that their aptitude scores have leveled off well below those of previous generations. Tag-line communication, called "bite-speak" by some, is destroying the last remnants of political discourse; spin doctors and media consultants are our new shamans.[14] As communications empires fight for control of all information outlets, including publishers, the latter have <u>succumbed</u> to the tyranny of the bottom line; they are less and less willing to publish work, however worthy, that will not make a tidy profit. And, on every front, funding for the arts is being cut while the arts themselves appear to be suffering a deep crisis of <u>relevance</u>. And so on.

Every one of these developments is, of course, overdetermined, but there can be no doubt that they are connected, perhaps profoundly, to the transition that is underway. ∎

---

9. **evanescent.** Tending to vanish like vapor
10. **jump-cut.** Film term referring to the conclusion of a scene brought about by removing or accelerating the middle part
11. **inimical.** Hostile or unfriendly
12. **lamentations.** Acts or instances of expressing sorrow, mourning, or regret
13. **op-ed.** Page of special features usually opposite the editorial page of a newspaper
14. **shamans.** Priests who use magic for the purpose of curing the sick, divining the hidden, and controlling events

words for everyday use

in • trin • si • cal • ly (in trin' zi kə lē) adv., in a manner showing the essential nature or constitution of a thing. *Intrinsically, a diamond is worth more if it is not flawed.*
im • pinge (im pinj') vi., have an effect. *The rain impinged on my decision to take a walk.*
in • cre • ment (iŋ' krə ment) n., action or process of increasing in quantity or value. *Ted's wages increased in increments until he was finally making eight dollars an hour.*
ex • alt (ig zôlt') vt., elevate by praise or in estimation. *Joanna exalted her boyfriend and did not see him realistically.*
suc • cumb (sə kum') vi., yield to superior strength or force or overpowering appeal or desire. *Rob succumbed to his desire for chocolate and ate a Hershey bar.*
rel • e • vance (re' lə ven(t)s) n., pertinence; relation to the matter at hand. *The geometry teacher was used to students questioning the relevance of geometry to their everyday lives.*

SELECTION CHECK TEST 4.6.9 WITH ANSWERS (CONT.)

Literary Tools

Fill in the blanks using the following terms.

| aim | diction | persuasive | expository |

1. Writing that tries to change your viewpoint is called **persuasive** writing.
2. **Diction** refers to the words a writer chooses to use.
3. Informing is one type of **aim** a writer can have.

INSIGHTS
INSIGHTS INSIGHTS INSIGHTS INSIGHTS

from "The New Pandora's Box: An Interview with Sven Birkerts"
by Cliff Becker,
National Endowment for the Arts

Let's start with what may seem like an obvious question. Do you think the book is in trouble?
Often, I use the word *book* as the shorthand for a whole kind of cultural sensibility, and I think that particular sensibility which has been very much associated with the written word, the book, literature currently is being severely challenged by a whole new array of options—learning options and communications options.

Yet statistics from the book industry suggest that book-buying is on the rise. Is this perhaps a good sign for reading?
One would like to think that it's a good sign, but I find it hard to square with my own sense which is reaffirmed for me, every day in the world, that reading, by which I mean reading more than the newspaper or a book on gardening instruction, is in trouble. The book may triumph for a while in many different guises, but serious reading—the kind we associate with our cultural values—is under threat. It's not extinct, but there is a new set of pressures on it.

A large bookstore chain took out an ad in this weekend's *New York Times* boasting that it provides 150,000 channels in a 500 channel world. Do you see this as an example of printed culture coming into conflict with electronic culture?
Yes. I think advertising strategists are very cunning, and they're looking for the language of appeal. Channels now represent something very different than books. The ad is imaginative; a book is a channel in a way, but it's electronic channels and the accessed information one gets through such channels that are changing the entire dynamic right now in ways that threaten the kind of reading I'm talking about.

Would you differentiate between the current revolution of computers and electronic communication and previous technological revolutions?
I think there are two main features of this revolution that are key. First, more than the other revolutions and innovations, this one incorporates previous ones. It calls upon phone and screen technology, bringing together separate little revolutions that have already happened. The current technological revolution is a kind of synthetic event; some aspects of it obviously are exciting and attractive, and the opportunities it provides can make people dizzy.

Secondly, the rate of change has greatly accelerated, and we collectively are in a position where something which is rather enormous in its impact is being pushed at us over a short span of historical time. If you take the arrival of the automobile, which is now exactly one hundred years old, you'll see that we had a few long decades to gradually see the automobile encroaching before it overwhelmed us. What if the car had been invented in the 1890s, and then in 1905, there were already several hundred million automobiles? It's of that magnitude—this rate of change and adaptation.

In other words, it's happening so fast it's hard for us to keep up.
Well, yes, and there seems to be this tremendous kind of shoulder-shrugging. You can't fight city hall about this one because it's being introduced from the upper institutional level on down. At a corporate level, you have no choice—you must be online. It's also moving rapidly into the schools. While this is not necessarily tragic, neither is it a matter of choice. We have not had a chance to debate this new technology in the way television got debated in our culture for a good decade in its early years. Therefore, I see myself as an agent of

ADDITIONAL QUESTIONS AND ACTIVITIES

Ask students the following questions:
1. How does Birkerts explain the paradox of reading being threatened when book-buying is on the rise?
2. How is the current trend in technological advances different from past technological revolutions, according to Birkerts?

Answers
1. He explains this paradox by saying that serious reading—not the reading done in popular books, newspapers, or magazine, but "the kind we associate with our cultural values"—is being threatened.
2. The current trend is moving at a faster rate, forcing people to makes adaptations to their lives by incorporating computers and electronic communication into daily life. In the past, technological revolutions gradually affected society, but did not overwhelm us.

ADDITIONAL QUESTIONS
AND ACTIVITIES   π

Ask students to write a reaction
paper to Birkerts's view on
technology. Do they think that
our current technological
revolution has crossed a line so
that "a secondary system of
consequences" has been created? Or
do they think that the positive effects
of this revolution far outweigh the
consequences? Have them support
their opinions with specific concrete
examples.

discord trying to create a comparable debate, and overstating my position in order to make that happen. I sometimes take on a stronger polemical position than I might otherwise be inclined to, if I saw people looking at and debating these enormous changes, but I see so many people rushing in headlong that the alarmist in me wants to throw up a lot of flags quickly and say, "Wait a minute! Wait a minute!"

But can you see specific instances in which previous technological revolutions have had a positive influence on our culture?

That's an interesting question. I distinguish myself from neo-Luddite types in that I'm somewhat selective in my antipathies. Almost every particular technology reaps positive benefits up to a point where a line is crossed and a secondary system of consequences is created. For example, the telephone is a necessary and important invention. I wouldn't unplug my phone or get rid of it. When we got to the point, though, that items were piggybacked on top of it—the answering machine, the beeper, callwaiting, and conference calls, we began making the technology so flexible as to seep into our lives without recognizing its subversive effects. People now go around saying, "Gosh, I feel so distracted. I've got so much to do. I can't collect my thoughts." Much of this has to do with the invasion of an entire new layer of electronic agitations into their lives. They have ten times more stimuli with which to deal. Now there's fifteen e-mails and five messages on the machine, and telephone technology has overstepped its service function. It has begun to generate a secondary wave of effect.

Would you locate the emergence of this phenomena of secondary effect rather recently?

Yes. If I could wind history back, I'd wind it back to the rotary phone and stick with that, in terms of telephone technology. I'd wind the television back to three channels, and so on. We've opened the gates of proliferation, and we don't know how to begin to deal with it. This is the new Pandora's Box.

Earlier you mentioned that these new technologies were exciting. Can you conceive of a way in which they might offer positive new opportunities for the creation of art?

There are tremendous opportunities, and we are probably on the brink of the birth of whole new genres of art which will work through electronic systems. These genres will likely be multi-media in ways we can't imagine. Digitalization, the idea that the same string of digits can bring image, music, or text, is a huge revolution in and of itself. When artists begin to grasp the creative possibilities of works that are neither literary, visual, or musical, but exist using all three forms in a synthetic collage fashion, an enormous artistic boom will occur. This boom will endanger even further the old quiet pastime of reading mere words. I worry about this loss of reading mere words because the act of reading words on a page, the experience of language and literature serve reflective subjectivity in ways that nothing else really can.

• • •

Your book, *The Gutenberg Elegies*, ends with the command, "refuse it." Is this your command to yourself?

Yes. It is a command to myself, and it acknowledges the seduction which is part of the struggle I feel myself having. There's a very strong pressure from not only the outside, but also the inside, to get right in there and be with the times wherever they may go. Then I also feel the contrary force which is the force of needing to understand and sort things through. I feel the need to wait and the need of silence and subjective time to grasp the meaning of these enormous changes.

So you find yourself not so much refusing as resisting?

Yes. I resist it so that I can understand it; at some point after trying to understand it, I may conclude for myself that it's okay. For now, though, it's like being rushed into marriage. If I refuse it, it's not because I refuse the institution of marriage so much as that I'm not ready to get married. Though I am married, just to clarify that. ∎

Respond *to the* SELECTION

What do you think Birkerts would say about the immense expansion of the Internet that has largely occurred after this essay was published?

Investigate, Inquire, *and* Imagine

Recall: GATHERING FACTS

1a. Other than for financial gain, why did the people Birkerts met want to sell their books?

2a. Who was Gutenberg?

3a. On what was pre-literate Greek culture based?

Interpret: FINDING MEANING

1b. Why does Birkerts begin his essay with the anecdote of the English professor selling his books?

2b. The selection you have just read is taken from a book called *The Gutenberg Elegies.* Why do you think Birkerts gives the book this title?

3b. What is Birkerts's attitude toward the change that took place in Greece and the changes that are occurring in our society today?

Analyze: TAKING THINGS APART

4a. Analyze Birkerts's prognosis for literacy.

Synthesize: BRINGING THINGS TOGETHER

4b. What is Birkerts's attitude toward these changes?

Evaluate: MAKING JUDGMENTS

5a. Evaluate how realistically Birkerts portrays the electronic age in this essay.

Extend: CONNECTING IDEAS

5b. Read the Related Reading, "The New Pandora's Box: An Interview with Sven Birkerts." How does Birkerts's example of the automobile relate to changes in society today?

Understanding *Literature*

AIM. Review the definition for **aim** in the Handbook of Literary Terms. What is Birkerts's primary aim in writing this essay?

DICTION. Review the definition for **diction** in Literary Tools in Prereading and the cluster chart you made for that section. What adjectives best describe Birkerts's diction?

"INTO THE ELECTRONIC MILLENNIUM" **497**

RESPOND TO THE SELECTION

Before students respond to the question, you may want to make sure students understand Birkerts's attitude toward computers and the current technological revolution.

ANSWERS TO INVESTIGATE, INQUIRE, AND IMAGINE

RECALL

1a. Birkerts says the selling of books is often done to "burn bridges," to break people's connections to the past of print and connect them with the future of electronic media.

2a. Gutenberg invented movable type, which made literacy available to the masses.

3a. Pre-literate Greek culture was based on the oral tradition.

INTERPRET

1b. Birkerts says the scene is a "marker in my mental life," a scene which has for him become emblematic of the massive changes our society is undergoing as we enter the electronic age.

2b. Birkerts feels sorrow for what he sees as the death of books, for the passing of the great humanizing traditions of print culture that began with Gutenberg. "Elegies," or works that lament the dead, is appropriate in his title.

3b. Birkerts regrets the loss of Greek poetry, which "never recovered its cultural primacy." In the same way, Birkerts regrets the primacy of electronic media today since it is accompanied by "morbid symptoms" of which we need to be aware.

ANALYZE

4a. According to Birkerts, the complexity, distinctiveness, and subtlety of written language will diminish, eroding language. As our electronic links increase, our historical links will decrease, resulting in the disappearance of history.

SYNTHESIZE

4b. Birkerts fears and regrets these changes, believing that "language is the soul's ozone layer." He believes that if we diminish language, we diminish our individuality, or selfhood.

ANSWERS TO INVESTIGATE, INQUIRE, AND IMAGINE (CONT.)

EVALUATE

5a. Students who agree with Birkerts will say that he portrays the electronic age realistically. Others may feel that he is "making a mountain out of a molehill" and portraying an unrealistic view of the electronic age.

EXTEND

5b. Birkerts thinks that we are not being given enough time to assimilate the rapid changes in electronic

media. It would be preferable to him if people slowly got adjusted to electronic media in the same way that America was gradually introduced to the automobile. Birkerts believes we are being asked to change and adapt too rapidly to electronic media.

Answers to Understanding Literature can be found on page 498.

TEACHER'S EDITION **497**

AIM. Birkerts's primary aim is to inform the reader of changes threatening our cultural literacy and to persuade the reader to arm him- or herself against the dangers presented by the explosion of electronic media.

DICTION. Birkerts's diction is intellectual, formal, and complex.

**ANSWERS TO INTEGRATING
THE LANGUAGE ARTS**

Language, Grammar, and Style
1. sold (transitive)
2. impinges (intransitive)
3. are succumbing (intransitive)
4. relegated (transitive)
5. read (transitive)

Study and Research & Media Literacy
You may want to refer students to the Language Arts Survey 5.19, "How to Locate Library Materials," and 5.28, "Conducting an Internet Search," before they conduct their research.

Writer's Journal

1. Write an **anecdote** describing how your life is influenced by the electronic age.
2. Pretend you work in the field of computer technology. Write a **letter** to Birkerts defending why you think computer technology is beneficial to our culture.
3. Birkerts says, "What oral poetry was for the Greeks, printed books in general are for us." Write a **paragraph** explaining this analogy.

Integrating
the Language Arts

Language, Grammar, and Style

TRANSITIVE AND INTRANSITIVE VERBS. Read the Language Arts Survey 3.61, "Transitive and Intransitive Verbs." Then identify the verbs in the following sentences and tell whether they are transitive or intransitive.
1. The English professor sold all his books.
2. Electronic media impinge on our cultural literacy.
3. According to Birkerts, we are rapidly succumbing to technology.
4. In ancient Greece, literacy relegated oral poetry to a lesser role.
5. Fewer and fewer people under the age of fifty read newspapers.

Study and Research & Media Literacy

RESEARCHING OPINIONS ABOUT PRINT AND ELECTRONIC MEDIA. Using the resources of the library or Internet, research the works of other media theorists such as Marshall McLuhan, Walter Ong, and Neil Postman, who have all written about the differences between the cultures of print and electronics. Hold a class discussion about the viewpoints of these writers and Sven Birkerts.

Speaking and Listening & Collaborative Learning

DEBATE. Participate in a debate in which one group argues that the rise of electronic technology is beneficial to literacy, and the other group argues that it is harmful. Prepare both constructive and rebuttal speeches for your side. Before you begin, you might find it useful to review the Language Arts Survey 4.21, "Participating in a Debate."

NONFICTION

from The Victorian Internet
by Tom Standage

Reader's resource

This selection comes from a book by Tom Standage published in 1998. Entitled *The Victorian Internet: The Remarkable Story of the Telegraph and the Nineteenth Century's On-line Pioneers*, the book compares the nineteenth-century telegraph with the twentieth-century Internet and, in discovering how closely they are related, sheds a clearer understanding of the significance of both. The premise of the book is that sometimes examining the past can more clearly illumine the present as well as the future direction of an innovation.

TECHNOLOGY CONNECTION. The word *telegraph* is compiled of two Greek words: *tele* meaning "distant," and *graphein* meaning "to write." Coming into use in the late eighteenth century, the telegraph is now defined as any device or system that allows the transmission of information by coded signal over distance. The term most often refers to the electric telegraph, developed in the mid-nineteenth century. *Morse code* was invented by Samuel F. B. Morse in the 1830s. It uses a system of dashes and dots to represent letters and numbers. Morse code is still in use today for certain types of radiotelegraphy, including amateur radio.

About the AUTHOR

Tom Standage is a British journalist who writes about science and technology for many newspapers and magazines, including *The Guardian*, *The Independent*, and *Wired*. Now a science writer at *The Economist* in London, Standage lives in Greenwich, England. *The Victorian Internet* is his first book, published when he was twenty-nine years old.

Reader's Journal

For what purposes do you use the Internet?

Literary TOOLS

IRONY. Irony is a difference between appearance and reality, and one type of irony is when an event occurs that violates the expectations of a character, a reader, or an audience. In the case of "The Victorian Internet," two historic technological developments had some surprising results, both positive and negative.

COMPARISON-CONTRAST. Comparison-contrast presents similarities as it compares two things and presents differences as it contrasts them. A comparison-contrast essay is usually organized in one of two ways: either presenting all the characteristics of one subject and then of the other, or by comparing and contrasting both subjects with regard to one characteristic and then another. Standage is comparing and contrasting the telegraph with the Internet. Notice how in his essay, Standage compares both subjects on the point of one characteristic, then moves on to another.

Graphic Organizer

The book section compares and contrasts the Internet to the telegraph using many examples and much technical information. Make a Venn diagram like the one below to keep track of the parallels Standage makes. Refer to the Language Arts Survey 2.16, "Completing Venn Diagrams" for more information.

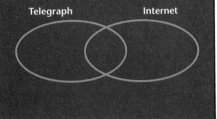

Telegraph   Internet

ADDITIONAL RESOURCES

UNIT 6 RESOURCE BOOK
- Selection Worksheet 6.5
- Selection Check Test 4.6.11
- Selection Test 4.6.12

VOCABULARY FROM THE SELECTION

encrypt
enmity
explicitly
facilitate
generic
gullibility
hype
impact
inaugurate

laud
obsolete
optimistic
panacea
protocol
purporting
quintessentially
skepticism
subsequently

GRAPHIC ORGANIZER

Some of the parallels Standage makes between the telegraph and the Internet are: both have two parts that exchange eight-digit numbers; the telegraph is the foundation for the Internet; both connect people easily no matter what the distance; both have special codes to increase or reduce the rate of transmission; both brought on a confused reaction from the public; both encounter scam artists who try to manipulate the transmission of information.

GOALS/OBJECTIVES

Studying this lesson will enable students to
- understand the relationship between the nineteenth century telegraph and the twentieth century Internet
- describe Tom Standage's literary accomplishments and explain the scientific and technological significance of his writings
- define *irony* and *comparison-contrast* and explain examples of each in the selection
- construct a technological time line

ANSWERS TO GUIDED READING QUESTIONS

1. The telegraph is the technological foundation for the phone, fax, and Internet.
2. People communicate across distances using interconnected networks.

INDIVIDUAL LEARNING STRATEGIES

MOTIVATION
Have students brainstorm past technological inventions that could be compared to present-day machines and gadgets. Then have them predict future technological inventions based on the machines we use today.

READING PROFICIENCY
Encourage students to write down the main idea of each paragraph as they read. You may want to give them an outline to fill in as they read the selection.

ENGLISH LANGUAGE LEARNING
Encourage students to preview the Words for Everyday Use and the footnotes before they read this selection.

SPECIAL NEEDS
Students may have a hard time understanding the parallels Standage makes between the Internet and the telegraph. Pair students with an advanced student to help them fill out the graphic organizer on page 499.

ENRICHMENT
Ask students to write a more complete About the Author for Tom Standage. Encourage them to look back at previous About the Author sections to get better acquainted with the writing style and the type of information that is included. They may need to do biographical research on the Internet or in the library.

The Victorian Internet

Tom Standage

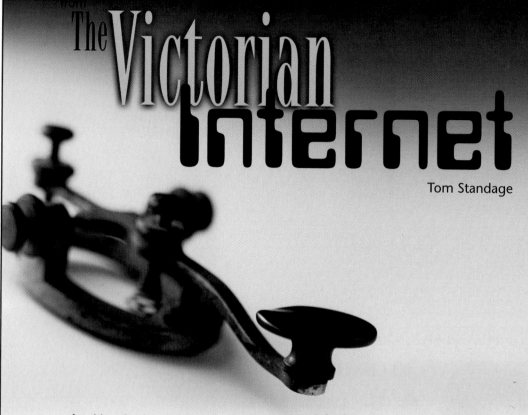

Although it has now faded from view, the telegraph lives on within the communications technologies that have <u>subsequently</u> built up on its foundations: the telephone, the fax machine, and, more recently, the Internet. And, ironically, it is the Internet—despite being regarded as a <u>quintessentially</u> modern means of communication—that has the most in common with its telegraphic ancestor.

What is the technological foundation for the phone, fax, and Internet?

Like the telegraph network, the Internet allows people to communicate across great distances using interconnected networks. (Indeed, the <u>generic</u> term *internet* simply means a group of interconnected networks.) Common rules and <u>protocols</u> enable any sort of computer to exchange messages with any other—just as messages could easily be passed from one kind of telegraph apparatus (a Morse printer, say) to another (a pneumatic tube). The journey of an e-mail mes

How do people communicate across distances?

words for everyday use	**sub • se • quent • ly** (sub' si kwent lē) *adv.*, following in order of time or place; succeeding. *College <u>subsequently</u> takes students into the work force.*
	quin • tes • sen • tial • ly (kwin tə sen(t)' shəl ē) *adv.*, most purely. *Writer Jack Kerouac expressed the essence of the Beat Generation <u>quintessentially</u> in* On the Road.
	ge • ner • ic (jə ner' ik) *adj.*, descriptive of all members of a group or category, not specific or individual, general. *She buys <u>generic</u> food brands because they are cheaper.*
	pro • to • col (prō' tə kol) *n.*, established, precise, and correct procedures. *Lawyers must follow <u>protocol</u> to defend their clients.*

sage, as it hops from mail server to mail server toward its destination, mirrors the passage of a telegram from one telegraph office to the next.

There are even echoes of the earliest, most primitive telegraphs—such as the optical system invented by Chappe[1]—in today's modems and network hardware. Every time two computers exchange an eight-digit binary number,[2] or byte, they are going through the same motions as an eight-panel shutter telegraph would have done two hundred years ago. Instead of using a codebook to relate each combination to a different word, today's computers use another agreed-upon protocol to transmit individual letters. This scheme, called ASCII (for American Standard Code for Information Interchange), says, for example, that a capital "A" should be represented by the pattern 01000001; but in essence the principles are unchanged since the late eighteenth century. Similarly, Chappe's system had special codes to increase or reduce the rate of transmission, or to request that garbled information be sent again—all of which are features of modems today. The protocols used by modems are decided on by the ITU, the organization founded in 1865 to regulate international telegraphy. The initials now stand for International Telecommunication Union, rather than International Telegraph Union.

More striking still are the parallels between the social impact of the telegraph and that of the Internet. Public reaction to the new technologies was, in both cases, a confused mixture of hype and skepticism. Just as many Victorians[3] believed the telegraph would eliminate misunderstanding between nations and usher in a new

In this example, how are the Internet and the telegraph alike?

era of world peace, an avalanche of media coverage has lauded the Internet as a powerful new medium that will transform and improve our lives.

What was the public reaction?

Some of these claims sound oddly familiar. In his 1997 book *What Will Be: How the New World of Information Will Change Our Lives*, Michael Dertouzos of the Laboratory for Computer Science at the Massachusetts Institute of Technology wrote of the prospect of "computer-aided peace" made possible by digital networks like the Internet. "A common bond reached through electronic proximity may help stave off future flareups of ethnic hatred and national breakups," he suggested. In a conference speech in November 1997, Nicholas Negroponte, head of the MIT Media Laboratory, explicitly declared that the Internet would break down national borders and lead to world peace. In the future, he claimed, children "are not going to know what nationalism is."

What may this common bond help prevent?

What does Negroponte claim children will not know in the future?

The similarities do not end there. Scam artists found crooked ways to make money by manipulating the transmission of stock prices and the results of horse races using the telegraph; their twentieth-century counterparts have used the Internet to set up fake "shop fronts" purporting

---

1. **optical system invented by Chappe.** Claude Chappe (1763–1805) was a French inventor who, with his brother Ignace, made a visual signal line, a visual telegraph, between two points on the war front during the French revolution. The device had two arms that formed positions representing the alphabet.

2. **binary number.** Number which has two as its base

3. **Victorians.** People who lived during the period of Queen Victoria's reign in England (1837–1901)

ANSWERS TO GUIDED READING QUESTIONS

1. The Internet and the telegraph are the same in that the two parts exchange 8-digit numbers.
2. Public reaction was mixed, both positive and negative—a combination of doubt and over-enthusiasm.
3. The common bond was theorized to prevent national strife and racism.
4. Nationalism is the sense of different nationalities, of belonging to one and not another, of being separate. This man's theory was that the Internet would connect everyone so strongly that it would break down national borders.

Quotables

"Modern Internet users are in many ways the heirs of the telegraphic tradition, which means that today we are in a unique position to understand the telegraph. And the telegraph, in turn, can give us a fascinating perspective on the challenges, opportunities, and pitfalls of the Internet."

—Tom Standage, preface to *The Victorian Internet*

CROSS-CURRICULAR CONNECTIONS

FIBER OPTICS. Patented in the 1920s, optical fibers are transparent rods of glass or plastic that are stretched long and are flexible. They can transmit light in the form of images to television or fax machines. Much research has been done on fiber optics since 1920 and it has improved telephone lines and cable television. Most personal computers are connected by phone lines. Fiber optic receiving equipment is currently too expensive to install fibers. In such a fast-moving field, that may all change very soon.

LITERARY NOTE

Standage calls the telegraph a "revolution in communications," and has termed it "the Victorian Internet" because of the Internet's relation to a system that is more than two hundred years old. He points out the telegraph's similarities to the current-day Internet, not only in design but in people's reaction to it. Telegraph lines spanned the whole world, and had a history of "scientific discovery, technological cunning, personal rivalry, and cutthroat competition," just like, Standage asserts, the Internet.

---

to be legitimate providers of financial services, before disappearing with the money handed over by would-be investors; hackers[4] have broken into improperly secured computers and made off with lists of credit card numbers.

People who were worried about inadequate security on the telegraph network, and now on the Internet, turned to the same solution: secret codes. Today software to compress files and <u>encrypt</u> messages before sending them across the Internet is as widely used as the commercial codes that flourished on the telegraph network. And just as the ITU placed restrictions on the use of telegraphic ciphers,[5] many governments today are trying to do the same with computer cryptography, by imposing limits on the complexity of the encryption available to Internet users. (The ITU, it should be noted, proved unable to enforce its rules restricting the types of code words that could be used in telegrams, and eventually abandoned them.)

What kind of software is used today and what does it prevent?

Why did the ITU abandon rules about code words?

On a simpler level, both the telegraph and the Internet have given rise to their own jargon and abbreviations. Rather than plugs, boomers, or bonus men, Internet users are variously known as surfers, netheads, or netizens. Personal signatures, used by both telegraphers and Internet users, are known in both cases as sigs.

Another parallel is the eternal <u>enmity</u> between new, inexperienced users and experienced old hands. Highly skilled telegraphers in city offices would lose their temper when forced to deal with hopelessly inept operators in remote villages; the same phenomenon was widespread on the Internet when the masses first surged on-line in the early 1990s, unaware of customs and traditions that had held sway on the Internet for years and capable of what, to experienced users, seemed unbelievable stupidity, <u>gullibility</u>, and impoliteness.

But while conflict and rivalry both seem to come with the on-line territory, so does romance. A general fascination with the romantic possibilities of the new technology has been a feature of both the nineteenth and twentieth centuries: On-line weddings have taken place over both the telegraph and the Internet. In 1996, Sue Helle and Lynn Bottoms were married on-line by a minister ten miles away in Seattle, echoing the story of Philip Reade and Clara Choate, who were married by telegraph 120 years earlier by a minister 650 miles away. Both technologies have also been directly blamed for causing romantic problems. In 1996, a New Jersey man filed for divorce when he discovered that his wife had been exchanging explicit e-mail with another man, a case that was widely reported as the first example of "Internet divorce."

After a period of initial skepticism, businesses became the most enthusiastic adopters of the telegraph in the nineteenth century and the Internet in the twentieth. Businesses have always been prepared to pay for premium services like private leased lines and value-added information—provided those services can provide a competitive advantage in the marketplace. Internet sites routinely offer stock prices and news headlines, both of which were available over a hundred years ago via stock tickers[6] and news wires.

What are businesses more readily prepared to do?

---

4. **hackers.** People who perform illegal activities and break-ins on computers
5. **cipher.** Message in code
6. **stock tickers.** Telegraphic receivers that print information, like stock prices, on paper

---

words for everyday use

en • crypt (en kript') *vt.*, encipher or encode. *The spy <u>encrypted</u> the message.*

en • mi • ty (en' mə tē) *n.*, ill will, hostility, antagonism. *Until she stomped out he hadn't realized he felt such <u>enmity</u> toward him.*

gul • li • bil • i • ty (gə lə bi' lə tē) *n.*, state of being easily deceived or cheated; naïveté. *Her <u>gullibility</u> made her believe him when he said the moon was bigger than the sun.*

And just as the telegraph led to a direct increase in the pace and stress of business life, today the complaint of information overload, blamed on the Internet, is commonplace.

The telegraph also made possible new business practices, <u>facilitating</u> the rise of large companies centrally controlled from a head office. Today, the Internet once again promises to redefine the way people work, through emerging trends like teleworking (working from a distant location, with a network connection to one's office) and virtual corporations (where there is no central office, just a distributed group of employees who communicate over a network).

How may the Internet redefine how people work?

The similarities between the telegraph and the Internet—both in their technical underpinnings and their social impact—are striking. But the story of the telegraph contains a deeper lesson. Because of its ability to link distant peoples, the telegraph was the first technology to be seized upon as a <u>panacea</u>. Given its potential to change the world, the telegraph was soon being hailed as a means of solving the world's problems. It failed to do so, of course—but we have been pinning the same hope on other new technologies ever since.

In the 1890s, advocates of electricity claimed it would eliminate the drudgery of manual work and create a world of abundance and peace. In the first decade of the twentieth century, aircraft inspired similar flights of fancy: Rapid intercontinental travel would, it was claimed, eliminate international differences and misunderstandings. (One commentator suggested that the age of aviation would be an "age of peace" because aircraft would make armies <u>obsolete</u>, since they would be vulnerable to attack from the air.) Similarly, television was expected to improve education, reduce social isolation, and enhance democracy. Nuclear power was supposed to usher in an age of plenty where electricity would be "too cheap to meter." The <u>optimistic</u> claims now being made about the Internet are merely the most recent examples in a tradition of technological utopianism[7] that goes back to the first transatlantic telegraph cables, 150 years ago.

Did any of these predictions come true? What point is the author making about Internet predictions?

That the telegraph was so widely seen as a panacea is perhaps understandable. The fact that we are still making the same mistake today is less so. The irony is that even though it failed to live up to the utopian claims made about it, the telegraph really did transform the world. It also redefined forever our attitudes toward new technologies. In both respects, we are still living in the new world it <u>inaugurated</u>. ∎

---

7. **utopianism.** Utopia is an imaginary place that has ideal laws and perfect social conditions. Utopianism refers to impossible schemes for social improvement.

words for everyday use

fa • cil • i • tate (fə si′ lə tāt) *vt.*, make easier. *Her research <u>facilitated</u> the discovery.*
pan • a • ce • a (pa nə sē′ ə) *n.*, universal remedy, cure-all. *Jokes are the <u>panacea</u> for sadness.*
ob • so • lete (äb sə lēt′) *adj.*, no longer active or in use. *Cash is almost becoming <u>obsolete</u> because of credit cards.*
op • ti • mis • tic (äp tə mis′ tik) *adj.*, anticipating the best. *She was <u>optimistic</u> about her college plans.*
in • au • gu • rate (i nä′ gyə rāt) *vt.*, begin, introduce, or mark a start of. *She <u>inaugurated</u> her business by having an open house.*

ABOUT THE RELATED READING

The New Way Things Work is the updated version of **David Macaulay's** book *The Way Things Work*, first published in 1988. Macaulay has created an accessible book for anyone who wants to understand how things work. He not only demonstrates how machines do what they do—from the simplest lever to the far-reaching capabilities of the Internet (see pages 504–505)—he also shows how the concept behind one invention is linked to the concept behind another. Macaulay is also the author and illustrator of a series of books about architecture and has written several children's books.

FROM THE VICTORIAN INTERNET 503

Literary Tools
Fill in the blanks with the following terms.

irony   comparison   contrast

1. **Irony** occurs when there is a difference between reality and appearance.
2. A(n) **contrast** is made when differences are identified between two things.
3. A(n) **comparison** is made when similarities are found in two things.

HOME COMPUTER 1
This user is sending an e-mail message to someone at Mammoth Corporation.

SERVICE PROVIDER
Home users subscribe to a service provider, which is a gateway to the Internet and e-mail services.

ROUTING COMPUTER

GOVERNMENT HOUSE WEB SITE

GROUND STATION

ROUTING COMPUTER

BACKBONE
A network of routing computers – the Internet backbone – links organizations and service providers. The routing computers decode addresses to connect users with each other and to sites throughout the Internet. The links are metal cables, fiber-optic cables, or radio links, possibly via satellites (see p.349).

UNDERSEA CABLE

SERVICE PROVIDER
The service provider is an organization with powerful computers that connect to the Internet and store users' web sites. A telephone line links each home computer via its modem to the service provider.

BRIGHT LIGHT WEB SITE

WEB SITE
Every web site has an Internet address, which takes the form http://www.mammoth.com/images. This is a web site at Mammoth Corporation showing images. http stands for HyperText Transport Protocol, which enables you to use the mouse to click on a word or image on the screen and instantly jump to another part of the web site or to a different web site. www is a code for the web site computer at mammoth.com, the code for the commercial organization Mammoth Corporation. Finally, the code word images takes the user to the part of the web site containing pictures to download or transfer from the web site.

BROWSER
To visit a web site, your computer must have a browser. This is a computer program that enables you to use all the facilities of the web site, such as jumping from one part of the site to another and downloading material.

HOME COMPUTER 2
This user first consults the search engine to find out about castles. The search engine provides the web site address of Grimm Castle, and the user jumps to the castle's web site.

TEACHEM SCHOOL WEB SITE

504

INTERNET AND E-MAIL

David Macaulay

All computer users, at home and at work, can link into the global computer communications network known as the Internet. Bits flash to and fro between the computers to provide people with a huge variety of services. People can send each other messages by electronic mail or e-mail; they can visit web sites on the World Wide Web to obtain information, entertainment, commercial services, and software of all kinds; and they can take part in discussion groups and chat via the computer. Organizations have computers that link directly to the Internet. Home computers link via a modem and phone line to a service provider.

COMMUNICATIONS SATELLITE

E-MAIL (ELECTRONIC MAIL)

Every person has an e-mail address which takes the form of his or her name, the symbol @ (at), and a domain name, such as jsmith@mammoth.com. The domain name contains the name of the person's service provider or organization followed by codes for the type of organization or provider and often its country, each separated by a dot. The domain name mammoth.com stands for Mammoth Corporation, which is a commercial organization (com). E-mail offers you more than a quick and easy way to send people written messages. It is possible to use e-mail to send computer data, such as word-processed documents and images.

SEARCH ENGINE

You can locate useful or interesting web sites by using a search engine. This is an organization with a web site containing a huge database of web site addresses. You key in a subject or a name that describes what you are seeking, and the search engine provides you with a list or selection of web site addresses that fit your inquiry. You then simply click on an address to jump to that web site.

GRIMM CASTLE WEB SITE

GROUND STATION

ROUTING COMPUTER

ROUTING COMPUTER

SERVICE PROVIDER

SEAVIEW HOTEL WEB SITE

HOPE CHURCH WEB SITE

MAMMOTH CORPORATION
This organization's powerful computers link up all its employees in an internal network and store its web site.

BUSINESS COMPUTER 1
The e-mail message arrives from home computer 1.

BUSINESS COMPUTER 2
This user is visiting the web site at Government House.

505

RECALL

1a. Positive effects of both: eliminate misunderstandings between nations and bring world peace.

2a. Both the Internet and telegraph are vulnerable to scam artists, thieves, hackers, and illegal operations.

3a. Businesses are competitive and want to earn money. They are always eager to try new technologies that promise a chance to do so.

INTERPRET

1b. Once people see the possibilities of new technology and other uses for it, it catches on quickly.

2b. Coded languages for both the Internet and the telegraph were developed to avoid these negative effects. Restrictions were placed on both, and laws were developed to prevent illegal operations.

3b. The area of business might indicate the future of people's personal lives as well. They are forerunners.

ANALYZE

4a. The telegraph and the Internet are most fundamentally alike in that they transmit signals from one port to another across great distances.

SYNTHESIZE

4b. There will be many different answers to this. One important point of comparing the two technologies is to show that while we have developed sophisticated technology, it never would have happened without ground-breaking discoveries. Things that we may take for granted today were brought to us by dedicated thinkers of the past. Inventors and inventions of the past are still as stunning as the inventions of today.

EVALUATE

5a. People say the Internet will change and improve our lives, that it will create a common bond that will eliminate racism. *Responses will vary.*

EXTEND

5b. An e-mail message hops from mail server to mail server toward its destination, similar to the way a telegraph message was passed from one telegraph apparatus to another.

RESPOND TO THE SELECTION

Based on this article, how important are past explorations in the making of future explorations? What is the relationship between the past and the future?

Respond to the SELECTION

Did you learn anything from this article? Explain.

Investigate, Inquire, and Imagine

Recall: GATHERING FACTS

1a. What positive effects did some believe both the Internet and telegraph would have?

2a. What were some of the negative effects that both the Internet and telegraph had?

3a. Why were businesses the first to embrace technological developments?

Interpret: FINDING MEANING

1b. How did the positive effects lead to the quick development of each form of communication?

2b. What ways to avoid these negative aspects were developed?

3b. What does this indicate about our society?

Analyze: TAKING THINGS APART

4a. Review the ways the telegraph and the Internet are most fundamentally alike.

Synthesize: BRINGING THINGS TOGETHER

4b. What might be the point of comparing the design of a cutting edge technological development to one that is now almost obsolete?

Evaluate: MAKING JUDGMENTS

5a. What are some of the positive predictions about the Internet, and why does the article suggest that they are overly optimistic?

Extend: CONNECTING IDEAS

5b. Review the diagram in the Related Reading "Internet and E-Mail" on page 504. How does the journey of an e-mail message mirror the passage of a telegram from one office to the next?

Understanding Literature

IRONY. Review the definition for **irony** in Literary Tools in Prereading. The author uses the word *irony* in the beginning of his essay. He says, "Ironically, it is the Internet—despite being regarded as a quintessentially modern means of communication—that has the most in common with its telegraphic ancestor." Why is that ironic? Standage uses the word again in his conclusion. What other examples of irony do you find in the essay?

COMPARISON-CONTRAST. Review the definition for **comparison-contrast** in the Handbook of Literary Terms. Often a valuable way to understand and see a subject is to compare it to a similar subject. Every time we make a decision we compare and contrast—what to eat for lunch, what to wear to school, what movie to watch. We weigh the pros and cons, and in so doing, we make connections. What decisions have you made that required you to compare and contrast?

ANSWERS TO UNDERSTANDING LITERATURE

IRONY. It is ironic because we always think we are light years ahead of the past centuries. It is ironic because two technologies that seem vastly different are based on the same foundation. There is irony in the fact that some people had such high hopes for the Internet, while some people used it to take advantage of others.

His concluding point is ironic because the Internet may be as significant a development as people predict, but just not in the ways they think.

COMPARISON-CONTRAST. *Responses will vary.*

Writer's Journal

1. Write a **journal entry** describing your own experience with the Internet—how you use it, how it has been helpful, and how it has been frustrating.

2. Write an **e-mail** to Bill Gates, founder of Microsoft, suggesting an Internet development idea of your own that you think would benefit the world.

3. Write a short **editorial essay** on how you think the Internet has changed the world, both in good and bad ways.

Integrating the Language Arts

Collaborative Learning

COMPARING FORMS OF COMMUNICATION. As a group, choose a topic related to *The Victorian Internet* and form a question for your group to discuss. Have an e-mail conversation with a classmate or a group of classmates about your question, or, if possible, schedule a chat room conversation with the whole group. After your online discussion, come back together as a group and have a follow-up conversation on the same topic. Then, discuss the differences between the online conversation and the face-to-face discussion you had. What problems did each form of communication pose? What benefits did each one offer? Was one type of discussion more successful and productive, and, if so, why? Weigh the similarities and differences of communicating on-line versus in person, and, using examples from the two kinds of discussions you had, report on your experience to the rest of the class.

Study and Research

RESEARCH PAPER. *The Victorian Internet* is a study of the evolution of long distance communication. Think of another important and related aspect of society and study and chart its evolution. Look at what has influenced its development and growth, and try to predict the next phase in the development of your subject. Jot down some of your ideas and connections, using a cluster map if you would like. Gather research on the pieces of your outline from different sources—encyclopedias, dictionaries, the Internet, or even from friends and family members. Ask them to help you make connections and to give you ideas. Once you have gathered your data, write a paper, organizing the information to show connections between the different phases of the evolution of the subject.

Media Literacy

TECHNOLOGY TIME LINE. Make a time line beginning with 1700 and going through the present day. Chart important technological advances on the time line, including information about its inventors. Gather as much information and data as you can. Search some of the topics listed in this unit on the Internet and find out what related topics your research links take you to. Once you have compiled all your information, begin to fill in the time line. This will enable you to make more connections and to see the evolution of other technological advances. Include things like developments in space exploration, electricity, automobiles, airplanes, telephones, fax machines, computers, etc.

ANSWERS TO INTEGRATING THE LANGUAGE ARTS

Collaborative Learning
To help students communicate effectively in their group conversations, refer students to the Language Arts Survey 4.4, "Listening in Conversations," and 4.7, "Communicating with Another Person."

Media Literacy
For more information on time lines, instruct students to read the Language Arts Survey 2.19, "Time Lines."

Language Arts *in Action*

The 21ST Century
A Literary Magazine
Written Entirely by Teens for Teens

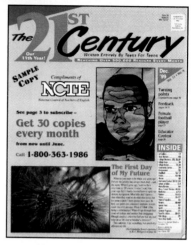

The 21st Century is a literary magazine published by The Young Authors Foundation that is written entirely by teens for teens. This magazine, which is celebrating its eleventh year of publication, is a creative alternative to traditional teen magazines that focus on fashion, romance, sports, and celebrities. *The 21st Century* provides young people with a chance to voice their views, and to know that their opinions, ideas, and creativity are of value and importance. The magazine has no staff writers, and depends completely on teen readers to submit work. More than 20,000 students have already been published. There is no charge to submit or to be published.

Most of the revenue to support the magazine is raised from grants and advertising, but there is also a subscription price for the printed magazine. The Young Authors Foundation is a nonprofit foundation and wants every school to have access to the magazine. If a school can't afford the standard subscription price a coupon is provided for a charity subscription. The 48-page monthly print magazine is shipped in class sets to 3,500 high schools and junior highs nationwide. Free sample copies are available to educators, librarians, and teenagers in the United States. *The 21st Century* also publishes a *Poetry Journal,* published in fall, winter, and spring, that includes at least 250 student poems per issue and is included with the subscription to the magazine.

Many community leaders, business executives, athletes, educators, artists, and authors receive *The 21st Century* and support the concept of a reader-supported publication for students to consider the ideas, talents, and concerns of their peers. Subscribers to the magazine have included President Bill Clinton and First Lady Hillary Rodham Clinton, poet Maya Angelou, Rev. Jesse Jackson, author Stephen King, tennis pro Andre Agassi, cellist Yo-Yo Ma, and newsanchor Dan Rather. *Jonathan Kozol,* author of *Amazing Grace,* said of the magazine, "*The 21st Century* is a solid, lively, and extremely candid publication. The writing is first-rate and fills an important need."

The 21st Century is now available online at www.TeenInk.com, in addition to the print version of the magazine. The slogan for the web magazine is "*Teen Ink, more than you think.*" The online version includes teen literature, along with interactive features, online resources, a color photo and art gallery, weekly opinion polls, and past issues of *The 21st Century*. Students can also search the site for their favorite book, movie, and music reviews. Another popular feature of the magazine is the section on college reviews written and submitted by teenagers across the country. The reviews include information about college academics, housing, food, sports, location, and atmosphere, all from the point of view of the student.

"Driving Lessons"
by Stephen Weber, Versailles, Kentucky

When the snow had fallen deep
In the dead-still silence of winter,
I would go crunching up the hill
Time and time again,
In stiff rubber boots,
Dragging myself behind me.
The air was bright and alive
And it tasted sweet in
The top of my mouth.
I admired the burning-blue sky
And squinted my eyes at
White-cotton clouds.
But when I pushed off and went sliding back down,
All of that shrank away
And left only me and
The sled.

Dear Editor,
    Your magazine is a wonderful way for teenagers to express themselves and their thoughts. Through writing and art they can help others understand what they are trying to convey.
    The community service section gives some teenagers a chance to share a good deed they have done. In the review sections, teenagers discover good movies, books, and even what type of college to look into. Your magazine is helping teenagers open up to one another.
    Miranda M.—Buffalo, New York

To submit your writing by mail, include your name, age, home address, telephone number and name of your school, along with your submission to *The 21st Century*, Box 30, Newton, MA 02461; or by e-mail to editor@TeenInk.com; or online at www.TeenInk.com. Contributors must be between the ages of thirteen and nineteen.

LESSON OVERVIEW

Conducting a Media Campaign

Language, Grammar, and Style
USING EFFECTIVE VISUAL INFORMATION

GUIDED WRITING
Software

See the Guided Writing Software for an extended version of this lesson that includes printable graphic organizers, extensive student models and student-friendly checklists, and self-, peer, and teacher evaluation features.

> "There is no material with which human beings work which has so much potential energy as words."
> —Ernest Elmo Calkins

Guided Writing

CONDUCTING A MEDIA CAMPAIGN

Sixteen-year-old twins Alyssa and James Meyer have a mission. After a trip to the animal shelter to pick out a dog, these two animal lovers decided to do something about the hundreds of sad faces they saw there locked inside cages. With the help of the Humane Society, they started a door-to-door campaign passing out flyers to convince pet owners to spay or neuter their animals and find good homes for the puppies and kittens they do breed.

All across America, teenagers like the Meyers are shaping their communities, using their powers of persuasion to change a bad situation or encourage people who are doing good work.

WRITING ASSIGNMENT. In this lesson you have the opportunity to make a difference in your world, to argue for a change or a new way of thinking. Using media such as public service announcements, posters, buttons, and flyers, you will work in groups to design and produce a media campaign for an issue that concerns you and your peers. When you are done with your campaign you will reflect on the process and the product you created.

Three students from Houston, Texas, decided to develop a campaign for recycling because students at their school were not using the recycling receptacles provided. People threw debris on the floors and school grounds that eventually ended up in the trashcan.

This was a personal issue for Jesse, Tom, and Jose because they had made visits to the local landfill with their social studies class and had seen the consequences of too much trash. They knew what an overflowing landfill could mean for the future of their community and that the consequences would affect their own lives.

The group collaborated to make several posters and each student wrote a separate campaign analysis. The student model on page 511 shows one of the posters and Jesse's campaign analysis.

Student Model

By Jesse Salas, Tom Poster, Jose Martinez

Your Garbage.
Your World.
Your Choice.
Recycle

Campaign Analysis
by Jesse Salas

Our cause was recycling. We wanted to get the people in our school to use the recycling boxes and barrels. More importantly, we wanted people to know why they should care. Many students at our school throw paper and cans on the floor. The janitor sweeps the mess up, puts it in the garbage cans, and it ends up in our landfill. We wanted to get the freshmen and sophomores especially to start recycling since they had the dirtiest halls. There were a few things I would do differently in our campaign, but basically I would say it was a success. Right now, all the hallways are cleaner than they were before our campaign and the recycling boxes are full.

For our campaign, we developed a slogan that put the responsibility on the individual person. A lot of kids don't think that their piece of paper or their empty soda can matters. It matters a lot. Americans dumped 150 million tons of garbage into landfills last year. This pollutes our soil, water, and air and everyone should care about that.

EXAMINING THE MODEL. Based on the sample poster, left, and Jesse's evaluation, what would you say is the main message of this campaign? Do you think the graphics and text on the poster help or hinder the message?

Do you agree with Jesse that scary statistics motivate people to change their behavior? What other techniques persuade viewers?

Avoiding False Arguments in Your Campaign

As you prepare your media campaign, find examples of successful campaigns that other people have prepared for print, broadcast, and electronic media. Which tactics do these campaigns use to get attention? Which present the truth in legitimate ways? Which use fact and which rely on opinion? Which present messages that depend on hype, false arguments, or propaganda?

To help you evaluate such presentations and prepare for your own, review the Language Arts Survey 5.2, "Distinguishing Fact from Opinion," and 5.3, "Avoiding False Arguments and Propaganda."

MOTIVATION
Ask students to think of an issue that causes concern in them. It can be a concern related to the environment, animals, cultural or societal values, etc. Then have them think about ways in which they could help solve the problems surrounding that issue.

READING PROFICIENCY
Refer students to the Language Arts Survey 5.30, "Evaluating Information and Media Sources." By knowing the guidelines by which media sources are critiqued, students will have a clearer idea of creating effective visuals for their media campaign.

ENGLISH LANGUAGE LEARNING
See strategies above for Reading Proficiency that will also benefit students who are English language learners. Also refer students to the Language Arts Survey 1.16, "Using Context Clues to Estimate Word Meaning," to help them find meaning to words that are unfamiliar to them as they read the lesson.

SPECIAL NEEDS
Some students may be physically limited in handing out flyers or putting up posters. You may want to simplify this activity by encouraging them to focus helping their group create posters, buttons, or flyers. Also make sure students understand the purpose of this lesson.

ENRICHMENT
Students may want to write a speech to complement their media campaign. Refer students to the Language Arts Survey 4.17, "Steps in Preparing an Extemporaneous Speech," and 4.18, "Guidelines for Giving a Speech," to help them write and present their speech effectively.

WRITING WITH A PLAN. Refer students to Language Arts Survey 4.13, "Collaborative Learning and Communication," to help them communicate effectively during the planning of this project. Also encourage students to review 2.9–2.23, "Gathering Ideas," to help them determine the issue they will argue.

FINDING YOUR VOICE. For more information on voice, refer students to the Language Arts Survey 3.3, "Register, Tone, and Voice."

IDENTIFYING YOUR AUDIENCE. Have students brainstorm characteristics of tone and voice they would use for the kind of audiences listed here in this section. How can students communicate their message to both adults and their peers at the same time?

FINDING YOUR VOICE. Your group will need to discuss and decide what its tone will be toward the topic it has chosen. The tone should fit your attitude and purpose. Graphics, photographs, and words will be different for a humorous approach than for a serious one.

IDENTIFYING YOUR AUDIENCE. Although you can choose to present your campaign to the general public, you have a ready-made audience in the students at your school. You can send a message to the teachers, parents, and other adults from the community who use your school building. Additionally, you will share reflections on your campaign with your classmates.

At first, we had a slogan that said, "Keep paper and cans out of our land." But after talking to other students we realized this slogan didn't really mean anything to them personally. So we switched to "Your garbage. Your world. Your choice. Recycle." We wanted people to change their behavior, so we came up with a contest to be judged by the vice principal: the class that had the cleanest hall for a week and used their recycling boxes the most would win a free noon concert with a local band.

We didn't want to use flyers for the campaign because that would create more trash. So we designed and hung posters all over the school and wrote announcements for the morning bulletin advertising our contest.

In our posters, we appealed to the viewers' sense of independence and imagination. We said, "Hey, this is your life. How do you want it to be?" We included some scary statistics in our posters like "Every American creates 4.3 pounds of trash *per day*."

The seniors won the contest and that was probably because they had been recycling all along. If I were to do this again, I would send people out to talk with the freshmen face to face. Jose wanted to make funny recycled hats and walk through the hallways telling people to recycle, but Tom and I thought that was dumb. I think now that may have worked by putting faces behind the posters.

Two other things might have helped our campaign. I think we should have put more posters near the recycling bins and maybe said more about what will happen to our land if we don't recycle. A landfill is a creepy place. I think we could have emphasized that more.

Prewriting

WRITING WITH A PLAN. To create a media campaign, you will need to decide on an issue and a message, write text, find the appropriate media to present your arguments, and distribute your information.

Determine what issue you will argue and gather information about your issue. Spend some time as a group discussing what issue you want to use for your campaign. You might want to draw on the information from the speeches you wrote in the previous lesson. Or you can start fresh, searching for background on a new topic of your choosing. Sources for information may include books, newspapers, television, magazines, the Internet, organizations, or public institutions.

Whatever you choose, be sure it is a topic that really matters to you, an issue or problem you have deep feelings about.

Make a campaign plan. A campaign or promotion plan is a clear statement of what you are going to do and how you are going to do it.

The Houston students used this graphic organizer to help them plan their campaign. Copy the categories and fill in your own plan.

Student Model—Graphic Organizer

Jesse, Tom, and Jose
Plan For Recycling Campaign

Goal: What do you want this campaign to do?
To convince people
- how much trash they are making
- why trash is a problem
- to use the paper recycling bins/barrels
- to stop throwing recyclables into the garbage cans
- to start thinking about recycling at home, too and to buy things that don't have so much packaging

Message: What is the message that will bring about your goal?
- recycle paper and cans
- reduce garbage, reduce landfills, reduce pollution
- reduce, reuse, recycle

Target Audience: Who do you want to hear this message?
- students and teachers
- other people who use our building

Strategies: How will you get your message out? Public service announcements, advertisements, articles, posters, skits, a web page?
- posters
- recycle buttons made out of recycled material
- an assembly/skit
- announcements in the morning bulletin
- a prize for the class that keeps its hall the cleanest: a noon concert in the gym

Resources: What equipment, materials, or people will you need for your campaign?
- poster board, paints, pens
- a band
- the vice principal if we put on an assembly or concert

Timetable: When will the campaign happen?
- January 5: get permission from vice principal for a recycling contest
- January 10: design and make posters; display them in strategic spots
- January 14: line up a band; write contest announcement for school bulletin
- January 20: announce winners of recycling contest
- January 31: band plays in gym for winning class

Language, Grammar, and Style

Using Effective Visual Information

IDENTIFYING EFFECTIVE VISUAL INFORMATION. Visual information can help your viewer understand and remember your message. Charts, photographs, and art are examples of the kinds of visuals that can enhance your text.

Visuals serve many purposes. They can:
- focus and hold audience attention
- make complex ideas easier to understand
- show comparison
- summarize main thoughts
- help the audience grasp facts quickly

continued on page 514

GUIDED WRITING **513**

Student Model—Graphic Organizer

See the Writing Resource book for a blackline master of the graphic organizer for this lesson.

Language, Grammar, and Style

Using Effective Visual Information
LESSON OVERVIEW
In this lesson, students will be asked to do the following:
- Identify Effective Visual Information, 513
- Fix Visual Information, 514
- Use Effective Visual Information, 515

INTRODUCING THE SKILL. Explain to students that people frequently learn things best and remember more when information is presented visually. Point out that the success of their media campaign will depend a lot on how effectively they use visual information.

PREVIEWING THE SKILL. Refer students to the Language Arts Survey 6.11, "Displaying Effective Visual Information." In their groups, ask them to analyze their visual aids based on the questions that are bulleted in the section.

PRACTICING THE SKILL. For more information on using visuals effectively, refer students to the Language Arts Survey 1.15, "Using Graphic Aids."

Look over the final draft of the students' poster and identify the purpose (or lack of purpose) of each element, including the text as well as the two graphics.

If you think about the purpose of your visuals, it will help you decide when and where to use them. In addition, here are some basic guidelines to help you create and display effective visuals:

- Keep the visuals simple. Avoid too many different fonts, many small pictures, or too many graphics.
- Make the visual big enough to be easily seen from the back of a classroom or down a long hallway.
- Use color with care. It can be distracting or make your graphics or text unreadable.
- Document all sources of graphic information just the way you would information from someone else's text. Give credit on any visual information that is not your own.

Rate the poster in the student model according to these guidelines. How effective do you think it is?

FIXING VISUAL INFORMATION. Examine the rough draft of a poster for recycling on page 515. What changes would you make to the text, graphics, and layout to make this poster clearer and more convincing?

continued on page 515

Self- and Peer Evaluation

After you have written the text for your media pieces, consider the questions below. If time allows, have other students complete a peer evaluation. Make any changes that will help your piece present a tight and effective message.

- What is the issue or cause this campaign addresses?
- Summarize the main message of the campaign.
- Who is the target audience and what does the campaign try to get them to do or think?
- Are there places where the text in the media elements could be clearer?
- Which visuals focus or clarify the message of the piece? Which detract from the message?
- Which visuals grab your attention? Where could visuals be stronger?
- Do the visuals and text fit together smoothly into an effective presentation? If not, how could they be better matched?
- Check to see that the analysis includes descriptions of how the campaign was developed along with its strengths and weaknesses. Where does the analysis need more examples or more explanation?

Drafting

With your issue and plan now clearly in mind, you are ready to begin writing and designing the components of your campaign. Concentrate on writing clear text that focuses on one aspect of an issue.

Create a Slogan

A slogan is your message condensed into an easy-to-remember phrase.

- Think about jingles or slogans you still remember from your childhood. What makes them memorable? rhyme? alliteration? strong verbs? specific images?
- Keep your slogan short. Get rid of extra words that take away from the meaning. Make it punchy.

Design Your Logo

This is a visual that represents you and your cause.

- Look through a magazine and find logos of famous brands. What do they try to tell you about the product?
- What visual best shows your message? Choose a picture or short text that makes your cause stand out.
- The logo can include an original cartoon character, a graphic, or even words, but keep it simple. Line drawings are easy to photocopy and clean graphics show up better than busy ones.
- Keep in mind what one top executive for a soft drink company has to say about a brand: "It's more than a name. It's show biz. It's theater. It's magic."

Produce Media for the Campaign

Create clean, short media pieces that convey your message at a glance—that's all the time you'll have to convince your viewers who are passing by in the halls or surfing the Internet.

You have many options for your media campaign. Consider videotaping a public service announcement or creating a short slide show that flashes on the wall in the cafeteria. Hang posters, make buttons and flyers, or design an ad for your school's website.

Evaluate Your Campaign

When your campaign is over, each student in your group will write a short analysis of what you did and how well it worked. Save your notes from your campaign so that you can refer to the steps you took to produce it.

Revising and Proofreading

Review your self- and peer evaluations. Revise your text and media elements after considering these comments and complete a final proofreading of your text and visuals. For more information, see the Language Arts Survey 2.45, "A Proofreading Checklist."

Publishing and Presenting

After days of planning and preparation, you are ready to start your campaign. Fill your school or web site with the words and images of your message and watch what happens.

Reflecting

It is customary and useful after a campaign to analyze what you did and how well it worked. This analysis helps you to know better how to improve future campaigns and also helps you understand human nature and the art of persuasion.

Each student should write his or her own reflection of the process. Below are suggestions for the kinds of information to include or consider in your evaluation:

- State the cause/issue you addressed.
- Tell who your target audience was.
- State the purpose of the campaign.
- To what emotions did you appeal?
- How did you develop your logo and your slogan?
- How successful was your campaign? Did you reach your target audience?
- What were the strengths and weaknesses of your campaign?
- What would you do differently?
- How was the campaign delivered

✿✿✿✿✿✿✿✿✿✿✿✿✿

We are depleting our natural resources, destroying animal habitat, ozone layers, and water quality. We've got acid rain and global warming.

Every day, Americans generate an average of 4.3 pounds of trash.

It's up to you. Will we use up our natural resources and pollute our land, air, and water?

Or will we reduce waste, reuse, and recycle?

Your garbage. Your world. Your choice.

Recycle.

✿✿✿✿✿✿✿✿✿✿✿✿✿

USING EFFECTIVE VISUAL INFORMATION. Look over your media for visuals that do not follow the guidelines on page 514. Does each visual serve a purpose? Are there any visuals that are hard to read or do not fit with the text? Is the font consistent? Are any of the visuals confusing or misleading? Adjust your media to achieve the best visual impact.

Revising and Proofreading

A proofreading checklist can be found in the Language Arts Survey 2.45. A handout of this checklist is available in the Teacher's Resource Kit, Writing Resource book.

Publishing and Presenting

To help students campaign their issue effectively, encourage them to review the Elements of Verbal and Nonverbal Communication in Language Arts Survey 4.1, "Verbal and Nonverbal Communication." Remind students that their audience will be paying attention to their words just as much as their posture, face expressions, and so on. Students should be aware of their nonverbal communication to make certain they send the right message to their audience.

Reflecting

Students should reflect on each of the bulleted items on page 515 in their journals. Then have them get into their groups and discuss their reactions to and reflections on their campaign.

UNIT 6 review
Informational & Visual Media

Words for Everyday Use

Check your knowledge of the following vocabulary words from the selections in this unit. Write a short sentence using these words in context to make the meaning clear. To review the definition or usage of a word, refer to the page number listed or the Glossary of Words for Everyday Use.

analogous, 492	exalt, 494	malignant, 476	prognosis, 478
anarchist, 468	explicitly, 501	manifesto, 467	proscenium, 470
anonymity, 483	facilitate, 503	morbid, 493	protocol, 500
burrow, 476	ferment, 468	nuance, 469	purport, 501
conglomerate, 492	generic, 500	obligatory, 484	quintessentially, 500
conjoining, 491	gullibility, 502	obsolescence, 492	ravage, 476
conspicuous, 491	hype, 501	obsolete, 503	relevance, 494
corroboration, 490	ideology, 468	omnipresence, 491	ruminator, 467
demotic, 469	immune, 478	optimistic, 503	secession, 467
derive, 479	imperative, 493	panacea, 503	secular, 469
desolation, 469	impinge, 494	pigment, 476	skepticism, 501
detection, 478	inaugurate, 503	placid, 467	stodgy, 491
diffident, 467	increment, 494	pliable, 492	subsequently, 500
discourse, 493	inkling, 490	plummet, 479	succumb, 494
encrypt, 502	innocuous, 476	portend, 493	surmount, 493
enigmatic, 470	intrinsically, 494	portentous, 469	tableau, 469
enmity, 502	juxtapose, 492	posit, 493	vernacular, 469
epiphany, 469	laud, 501	precursor, 479	vestigial, 490
eradicate, 491	lesion, 476	prevalent, 468	vignette, 470

Literary Tools

Define the following terms, giving concrete examples of how they are used in the selections in this unit. To review a term, refer to the page number indicated or the Handbook of Literary Terms.

aim, 475, 482, 488	comparison-contrast, 465, 499	irony, 499
analysis, 465	diction, 488	periodical, 475
article, 475	exposition, 482	

Reflecting on your reading

Genre Studies

1. **INFORMATIONAL AND VISUAL MEDIA.** Review the elements of informational and visual media on page 462–464. Find examples of ten of the items defined in your school. How are these terms used in your school? What purpose to they serve? Do you think information and visual media is the best way to convey a message? Why, or why not?

2. **MEDIA LITERACY.** Review the Language Arts Survey 5.28, "Conducting an Internet Search." Using the Internet, find a search engine and type in the keywords, "media literacy." Explore the sites that the search engine lists, looking at what each has to say about media literacy. Reflect on the following questions as you explore:

- Who is the intended audience of this site? What information does the site offer? What links does it list? What does the term "media literacy" mean to the site authors?
- Which of these sites are for high school students? How do you know?
- Based on your exploration of media literacy and the completion of this unit, how would you define media literacy? In what ways are you media literate? What aspects of informational and visual media would you like to know more about?

Thematic Studies

3. **ELECTRONIC MEDIA.** Based on Sven Birkerts's essay, "Into the Electronic Millennium," what is his perspective on technological advances and electronic media? How does his view differ from Tom Standage's perspective, which is conveyed in the excerpt from *The Victorian Internet*? Do you think the advantages of electronic media outweigh the disadvantages? Why, or why not?

4. **VISUAL MEDIA.** Often a graphic or visual representation of a topic is more effective than trying to write about it. In the first three selections of this unit, visuals such as photographs, charts, and the easily recognized essay format are deliberately used to convey specific information. Why do you think the author's chose to complement the written word with visuals? What are the advantages of using visual media?

for your READING LIST

American Heritage of Invention and Technology Magazine. The purpose of this quarterly magazine is to illustrate the importance of understanding the history of the process of change and innovation. The history of technological innovations offers valuable lessons about the nature of progress and the roots of problems facing this great nation. Read articles about how many of the inventions that we take for granted were developed, such as perfecting tin cans, making Teflon stick, the beginnings of the wire telephone, and more. Access the website at www.americanheritage.com/i&t.

Independent Reading Activity

BROWSE THE WEB. When a new technological advance catches on—the telephone, television, or computer, for example—we wonder what we did without it before it was invented. Today, the Internet provides information at the touch of a finger. It's a library in a box. Many books are published in their entirety on the web, and many encyclopedias are published online, such as britannica.com and artcyclopedia.com. Search for a few of your own invaluable resources. Type in the keyword of a topic you are studying and see what you find.

Selections for Additional Reading

http://owleyes.org/. Read a classic online. Log on to check out the list of authors whose books are published in their entirety on this website. You can read whole novels by Jack London, Ernest Hemingway, John Steinbeck, and Edith Wharton. Owleyes features a book a month, and offers biographical information, summaries, analyses, and term-paper help.

When We Were Kings, directed by Leon Gast. The 1996 Oscar-winning documentary on the historic "rumble in the jungle" boxing match between Muhammed Ali and George Foreman which took place in Zaire in 1974 shows the historic significance of this event.

poems.com. This site, http://www.poems.com/, is archived and organized by author, poem title, and date so you can easily look up any poem you want to find. It has links to the original publication, allowing you to browse other literary magazines on the web as well.

Themes in Literature
PART TWO

ART NOTE

Tahitian Pastoral Scene, 1893. Paul Gauguin.
Paul Gauguin (1848–1903) was a Post-Impressionist painter whose lush colors and two-dimensional forms helped form the basis of Modern art. He was born into a middle-class French family and became a successful stockbroker. In 1883, he gave up his secure existence to devote himself completely to painting. His style was inspired by the art of indigenous peoples, medieval stained glass, and Japanese prints. In 1891, Gauguin sailed for the South Pacific to escape European civilization and "everything that is artificial and conventional." Except for one visit to France from 1893 to 1895, he remained in the South Pacific islands for the rest of his life.

Tahitian Pastoral Scene, 1893. Paul Gauguin. The Hermitage, St. Petersburg, Russia.

GOALS/OBJECTIVES

Studying this unit will enable students to
- explore the theme of the examined life
- discuss different ways in which people learn about themselves
- define *repetition, paradox, dialogue, characterization, foreshadowing, central conflict, irony, internal monologue, antihero, motivation, symbol, aim, narration, description,* and *exposition* and explain examples of each that they encounter in their reading
- write a personal narrative
- demonstrate effective use of pronouns and antecedents

The Examined Life

" To live remains an art which everyone must learn, and which no one can teach. "

—*Havelock Ellis*

UNIT SEVEN

Introduce the unit by conducting a class discussion based on the quotations on page 522. Ask students the following questions:

- Which of these quotations, if any, have you read or heard before? Which are new to you?
- Which quotations can you identify with most? Which do you agree with most?
- Young people often ask the question, "What is the meaning of life?" How does Grandma Moses answer this question? Phillips Brooks? Kathleen Norris?

For students who are uncomfortable participating in the class discussion, suggest that they write their responses in their journals. These questions can also be used as essay prompts on the subject of examining one's life.

echoes

➤ Life is so largely controlled by chance that its conduct can be but a perpetual improvisation.

—W. Somerset Maugham

➤ One certainty we all accept is the condition of being uncertain and insecure.

—Doris Lessing

➤ Life is what we make it, always has been, always will be.

—Grandma Moses

➤ Life is easier than you'd think; all that is necessary is to accept the impossible, do without the indispensable, and bear the intolerable.

—Kathleen Norris

➤ What is life? It is the flash of a firefly in the night.

—Crowfoot, of the Blackfeet

➤ We learn from experience, that men never learn anything from experience.

—George Bernard Shaw

➤ Inside myself is a place where I live all alone and that's where you renew your springs that never dry up.

—Pearl S. Buck

➤ The ideal man bears the accidents of life with dignity and grace, making the best of circumstances.

—Aristotle

➤ Nothing in life is to be feared. It is only to be understood.

—Marie Curie

➤ A great part of life consists in contemplating what we cannot cure.

—Robert Louis Stevenson

➤ It is while you are patiently toiling at the little tasks of life that the meaning and shape of the great whole of life dawn on you.

—Phillips Brooks

"the waking"
by Theodore Roethke

Reader's resource

"**The Waking**" comments on the speaker's processes of learning as he or she goes through life. The poem was published in 1953 in Roethke's collection *The Waking: Poems, 1933–1953,* which won the Pulitzer Prize.

About the AUTHOR

Theodore Roethke (1908–1963), poet, was born in Saginaw, Michigan. His father and uncle owned greenhouses, which taught the young boy a reverence for nature. The greenhouse appears as a frequent subject in his poetry. Roethke once wrote that the greenhouse "is . . . my symbol for the whole of life, a womb, a heaven-on-earth."

Roethke attended the University of Michigan, where he was a reputed athlete. He dropped out of law school there and went to Harvard for graduate work. After graduation, he supported himself by teaching English at different universities. He was known for his public readings, which were enormously successful with students. Struggling to balance his vocation with his avocation, poetry, Roethke exhausted himself and suffered mental breakdowns. He was diagnosed with manic-depressive illness and spent time in mental institutions.

Roethke's first book, *Open House,* which appeared in 1941, was reviewed by the poet W. H. Auden, who said that Roethke had the ability to transform personal humiliation into something beautiful. The volume introduced the rich music, bitter wit, and dramatic themes that would characterize his work. The "greenhouse" lyrics of *The Lost Son and Other Poems* (1948) reveal the poet's empathy and search for oneness with all animate life: "I can hear, underground, that sucking and sobbing, / In my veins, in my bones I feel it." *Praise to the End* (1951) presented a sequence of dramatic pieces. Other collections of poetry included *The Waking* (1953), *Words for the Wind: The Collected Verse* (1958), and *The Far Field* (1964). The publication of *Collected Poems,* published posthumously in 1966, brought renewed interest in Roethke, who counted himself "among the happy poets."

POEM

Literary TOOLS

REPETITION. Repetition is the writer's conscious reuse of a sound, word, phrase, sentence, or other element. As you read, look for examples of repetition.

PARADOX. A **paradox** is a seemingly contradictory statement, idea, or event. Identify examples of paradox as you read this poem.

Graphic Organizer

Make a chart, listing paradoxes from the poem on the left. On the right explain why each statement is a paradox. One example has been done for you.

PARADOXICAL STATEMENTS	EXPLANATIONS
I wake to sleep	A person wakes in order to be active, not in order to go back to sleep.

Reader's Journal

How do you learn best, from example or from your own experience?

ADDITIONAL RESOURCES

UNIT 7 RESOURCE BOOK
- Selection Worksheet 7.1
- Selection Check Test 4.7.1
- Selection Test 4.7.2
- Language, Grammar, and Style Resource 3.34

GRAPHIC ORGANIZER

The following are other paradoxes students should list in their charts:
Paradoxical Statement
"We think by feeling."
"This shaking keeps me steady."
Explanation
Thinking and feeling are two different modes of experience. Shaking normally keeps a person unsteady.

READER'S JOURNAL

You might widen the topic to include educational learning theory. Point out that some students are visual learners while others are more aural. You might also discuss with students the theory of multiple intelligences.

GOALS/OBJECTIVES

Studying this lesson will enable students to
- appreciate a lyric poem
- describe Theodore Roethke's literary accomplishments
- define *repetition* and *paradox* and recognize the use of these techniques in the selection

- correct run-on sentences
- create a college class schedule
- orally interpret a relevant poem
- write a thesis statement

1. The speaker wakes up slowly, only
   to sleep again.

Melancholia: On the Beach, 1896. Edvard Munch. The Cleveland Art Museum.

the WAKING

Theodore Roethke

I wake to sleep, and take my waking slow.
I feel my fate in what I cannot fear.
I learn by going where I have to go.

How does the speaker wake up?

We think by feeling. What is there to know?
I hear my being dance from ear to ear.
I wake to sleep, and take my waking slow.

Of those so close beside me, which are you?
God bless the Ground! I shall walk softly there,
And learn by going where I have to go.

Light takes the Tree; but who can tell us how?
The lowly worm climbs up a winding stair;
I wake to sleep, and take my waking slow.

Great Nature has another thing to do
To you and me; so take the lively air,
And, lovely, learn by going where to go.

This shaking keeps me steady. I should know.
What falls away is always. And is near.
I wake to sleep, and take my waking slow.
I learn by going where I have to go. ∎

How does the speaker learn?

Respond *to the* SELECTION

Roethke says, "What falls away is always. And is near." Reread About the Author. What paradox in his own life might Roethke be referring to?

art n o t e

Melancholia: On the Beach, 1896. Edvard Munch.

The art of **Edvard Munch** (1863–1944) conveyed the anxiety of modern life. Munch became an important source for Expressionism, a style of art that uses color, shape, line, and texture to express emotion rather than create an accurate visual depiction. In Munch's time, *melancholia* was the word used for depression. How does this painting convey a sense of melancholy?

"THE WAKING" 525

---

1. The speaker says, "I learn by going where I have to go."

LITERARY TECHNIQUE

RHYME SCHEME AND ALLITERATION. A **rhyme scheme** is a pattern of end rhymes, or rhymes at the ends of lines of verse. The rhyme scheme of a poem is designated by letters, with matching letters signifying matching sounds. Ask students to determine the rhyme scheme of the poem.

Answers
The rhyme scheme of the poem is *aba aba abc abc abc abaa*. Students should also notice a pattern of rhyme between stanzas; for example, "fear" in stanza 1 rhymes with "ear" in stanza 2; "stair" in stanza 4 rhymes with "air" in stanza 5.

Alliteration is the repetition of initial consonant sounds. Ask students to identify the use of alliteration in line 2.

Answer
There is an alliteration of the *f* sound in *feel, fate,* and *fear.*

SELECTION CHECK TEST 4.7.1 WITH ANSWERS

Checking Your Reading
1. To what does the speaker wake? **The speaker wakes to sleep.**
2. How does the speaker learn? **The speaker learns by going where he or she has to go.**
3. To what animal does the speaker compare his journey? **The speaker compares it to the lowly worm that climbs up a winding stair.**
4. What keeps the speaker steady? **The shaking keeps the speaker steady.**

Literary Tools
1. Identify two lines that are repeated throughout the poem. **"I wake to sleep, and take my waking slow" and "I learn by going where I have to go" are repeated.**
2. Define *paradox.* **A paradox is a seemingly contradictory statement, idea, or event.**
3. Give an example of a paradox from "The Waking." *Responses will vary. but examples may include* **"I wake to sleep." "This shaking keeps me steady." "What falls away is always. And is near."**

RESPOND TO THE SELECTION

What things do you think the speaker has learned by examining his or her life?

ART NOTE

Melancholia: On the Beach, 1896. Edvard Munch.
Students may point out that Munch conveys a sense of melancholy with the expression and posture of the man and by using dark, somber colors.

RECALL

1a. The speaker feels that his or her fate resides "in what I cannot fear."

2a. The speaker feels his or her being dance "from ear to ear."

3a. The speaker emphasizes elements of nature by capitalizing them: "Ground," "Tree," and "Great Nature."

INTERPRET

1b. The line may mean that the speaker's fate is defined by his or her pursuit of the safer, less risky things in life.

2b. *Responses will vary.* Students may say that in line 1, the speaker says that people think by feeling. In line 2, the speaker illustrates this by saying that he or she "hears," or senses, his or her "being" or "self." In other words, knowing oneself or knowing the nature of life is not something we can know rationally, but rather feel intuitively.

3b. The lowly worm's climb "up a winding stair" symbolizes the speaker's journey. The speaker is insignificant like the worm and, also like the worm, has a difficult journey to make through life.

ANALYZE

4a. The speaker learns from his emotions ("We think by feeling") and nature ("Great Nature has another thing to do / To you and me"). The speaker also learns by doing; he learns by going where he has to go.

SYNTHESIZE

4b. The speaker is talking about learning how to live; he is developing an attitude toward life.

PERSPECTIVE

5a. The speaker is making a distinction between people who think by feeling and people who think by thinking. The speaker wants to know if the people in his or her life, those who are "so close beside me," experience life in the same manner.

EMPATHY

5b. Students might say that the speaker sees mystery in life as he or she does in the tree: "Light takes the Tree; but who can tell us how?" The speaker is open to what comes to him or her, especially gifts from nature, as he or she goes down the road of life.

Investigate, Inquire, and Imagine

Recall: GATHERING FACTS

1a. Where does the speaker feel that his or her fate resides?

2a. Where does the speaker feel his or her being dance?

3a. How does the speaker emphasize elements of nature?

Interpret: FINDING MEANING

1b. What does the line "I feel my fate in what I cannot fear" mean?

2b. In stanza 2, how is the meaning of line 2 connected to the meaning of line 1?

3b. What example in nature symbolizes the speaker's journey?

Analyze: TAKING THINGS APART

4a. Identify the speaker's modes of learning. Cite specific passages.

Synthesize: BRINGING THINGS TOGETHER

4b. What type of learning do you think the speaker is talking about?

Perspective: LOOKING AT OTHER VIEWS

5a. When the speaker asks ". . . which are you," what distinction is he or she making?

Empathy: SEEING FROM INSIDE

5b. If you were the speaker, how would you explain your philosophy of life?

Understanding Literature

REPETITION. Review the definition for **repetition** in the Handbook of Literary Terms. What two lines are repeated throughout the poem? How would you interpret these lines?

PARADOX. Review the definition for **paradox** and the chart you made for Literary Tools on page 523. What do the speaker's paradoxes add to the meaning of the poem?

Writer's Journal

1. Write a **journal entry** describing the twilight time between sleep and wakefulness. What thoughts go through your mind? How do your thoughts progress? What is the process of waking up like?

2. Add a four-line **stanza** to the poem, describing where the speaker went and what he or she experienced. Use the past tense: "I woke," "I felt," "I went," "I learned."

3. Imagine that you are the speaker's therapist. Write a **report** in which you describe the speaker's condition of thinking by feeling and the benefits that can be derived from having deep emotional responses that lead to thought.

ANSWERS TO UNDERSTANDING LITERATURE

REPETITION. The lines "I wake to sleep, and take my waking slow" and "I learn by going where I have to go" (with variations) are repeated throughout the poem. The purpose of the speaker's waking is to return to sleep, but while awake the speaker takes his or her waking "slow"; in other words, every moment of awake time is relished. The speaker does what he or she has to do and, in the process, learns. What the speaker has to do is determined by feelings and nature, the things from which the speaker learns the most.

(Continued on page 527)

Integrating the Language Arts

Language, Grammar, and Style

CORRECTING RUN-ONS. Read the Language Arts Survey 3.34, "Correcting Sentence Run-ons." Then revise the sentences below by changing punctuation and capitalization.

1. Theodore Roethke grew up loving greenhouses his father and uncle owned some.
2. Roethke was a good tennis player, he even gave tennis lessons.
3. He taught English at the university level his public readings were very popular with students.
4. The poet was diagnosed with manic-depressive illness he spent time in mental institutions.
5. W. H. Auden loved Roethke's first book of poetry he said Roethke had the ability to transform personal humiliation into something beautiful.

Applied English

CLASS SCHEDULE. Theodore Roethke taught during the last years of his life at the University of Washington. Imagine that you are an undergraduate student there. Access the University of Washington website at http://www.washington.edu. Create a class schedule for yourself based on the UW "course guide" for the following semester. Write down the names of the courses, the times they meet, and the names of the professors. Then write an essay describing your career goals, why you are taking each course, and what you think you will learn in each. Is the class a requirement that you need in order to graduate? Does the class apply toward your major or toward your minor?

Media Literacy & Study and Research

WRITING A THESIS STATEMENT. Like many writers, Theodore Roethke suffered from manic-depressive illness. Author Kay Redfield Jamison wrote *Touched with Fire: Manic-Depressive Illness and the Artistic Temperament*, a book about artistic geniuses suffering from this disease. Find a review of the book at the library or online. If you have access to the Internet, a good place to begin your research is with a large bookstore website. Then write a thesis statement that summarizes the book. (A thesis statement is the main idea that is supported in a work of nonfictional prose.)

Speaking and Listening

ORAL INTERPRETATION OF POETRY. Find a poem that relates to the theme "The Examined Life." Write an introduction to the poem that describes why it would fit well into this unit. Then practice reading your poem, deciding how you will use volume, pitch, stress, tone, gestures, facial expressions, and body language to present the poem effectively. Finally, present your poem to a small group of your classmates.

Language, Grammar, and Style
1. Theodore Roethke grew up loving greenhouses; his father and uncle owned some.
2. Roethke was a good tennis player; he even gave tennis lessons.
3. He taught English at the university level. His public readings were very popular with students.
4. The poet was diagnosed with manic-depressive illness; he spent time in mental institutions.
5. W. H. Auden loved Roethke's first book of poetry; he said Roethke had the ability to transform personal humiliation into something beautiful.

Applied English
Assign a score from 1 to 25 for each grading criterion below. (For more detailed evaluation, see the Assessment Resource for evaluation forms for writing, revising, and proofreading.)

ESSAY
- **CONTENT/UNITY.** The essay defines the student's career objectives, describes each course, and gives reasons for taking each course.
- **ORGANIZATION/COHERENCE.** The essay begins with the career objective, then moves on to a description of each course, and a reason for taking each course.
- **LANGUAGE/STYLE.** The essay is written in formal English.
- **CONVENTIONS.** The essay avoids errors in spelling, grammar, usage, and mechanics.

Media Literacy & Study and Research
Kay Redfield Jamison's thesis in *Touched with Fire: Manic-Depressive Illness and the Artistic Temperament* is that most great artists are manic depressives and doctors should promote a restrained, humanistic approach to treatment that does not cure the disorder at the expense of artistic inspiration.

ANSWERS TO UNDERSTANDING LITERATURE (CONT.)

PARADOX. With the phrase "I wake to sleep" the speaker is indicating the cycle of life, being asleep and being awake; "I take my waking slow" means that the speaker takes the time to find meaning in his or her life. The sentence "We think by feeling" underlines one mode of learning; for some people, deep emotional experiences resonate and lead to questioning thought about the nature of existence and how to lead one's life. The sentence "This shaking keeps me steady" means that the speaker's emotional responses are so deeply felt that they act as guideposts in his or her life.

ADDITIONAL RESOURCES

UNIT 7 RESOURCE BOOK
- Selection Worksheet 7.2
- Selection Check Test 4.7.3
- Selection Test 4.7.4

GRAPHIC ORGANIZER

Stuents may include the following in their charts:

Before
- Troubled by fear and anxiety
- Distracted while eating
- Only spoke to his servant, "Uncle" Bashir to give orders or ask a question.
- Angered, argumentative toward rival
- No balance, but mostly unhappy

After
- Filled with confident ability to succeed
- Attentive and ate with relish
- Smiled and spoke to him as a colleague or friend
- Full of forgiveness and tolerance
- No balance, fully happy

READER'S JOURNAL

Students may want to begin by freewriting a list of things that make them happy. They might include people, places, events, or things. Then they can choose a few things on the list and consider why those things make them happy.

 Literary TOOLS

DIALOGUE. Dialogue is conversation involving two or more characters. Pay attention to the way Mahfouz uses dialogue between the main character and several other characters to advance the plot.

CHARACTERIZATION. Characterization is the use of literary techniques to create a character. Writers use three major techniques to create characters: direct description, portrayal of characters' behavior, and representations of characters' internal states. As you read this story, note the techniques the author uses to develop the main character.

Graphic Organizer

Create a comparison/contrast chart like the one below to show how the main character's personality has changed since he woke up and discovered that he was happy.

BEFORE	AFTER
Usually woke up half asleep and strained	Woke up full of happiness

 Reader's Journal

What makes you happy and why?

"THE HAPPY MAN"
by Naguib Mahfouz

Reader's resource

"**The Happy Man**" explores the topic of happiness and asks whether it is possible to remain truly happy in this complicated world. Mahfouz tells the story of one man's experience dealing with an unexpected bout of "happiness" and how he attempts to deal with it and understand it.

About the AUTHOR

Naguib Mahfouz (1911–   ) was born in Egypt's large capital city, Cairo. He attended Cairo University and worked in the Egyptian Civil Service from 1934 until 1971. In all, Mahfouz has written over fifty novels and short story collections, thirty screenplays, and several plays for the stage. When Mahfouz won the Nobel Prize in 1988, his work had an audience of millions of readers, almost none of them in America. Since the prize, however, sixteen of Mahfouz's books—still only a fraction of his output—have been published in English translation. The "Cairo Trilogy," the early novels that established Mahfouz's reputation, won loyal readers here and sold more than 250,000 copies. Mahfouz today is considered one of the most important writers in the Arab world.

GOALS/OBJECTIVES

Studying this lesson will enable students to
- understand the effects of happiness on the main character
- describe Naguib Mahfouz's contributions to contemporary literature

- define *dialogue* and *characterization* and identify examples in the selection
- work as part of a group to create a children's book
- find stories in popular media

THE HAPPY MAN

Naguib Mahfouz

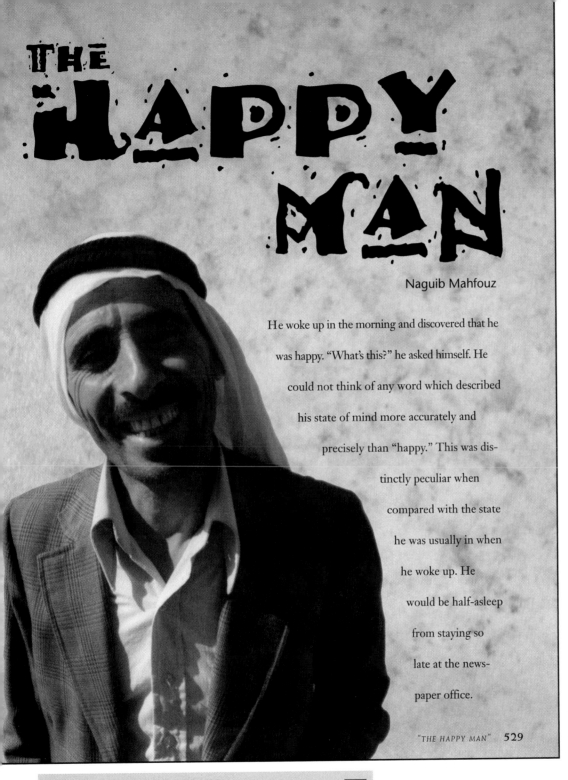

He woke up in the morning and discovered that he was happy. "What's this?" he asked himself. He could not think of any word which described his state of mind more accurately and precisely than "happy." This was distinctly peculiar when compared with the state he was usually in when he woke up. He would be half-asleep from staying so late at the newspaper office.

"THE HAPPY MAN" **529**

VOCABULARY FROM THE SELECTION

aspect	debilitating	renounce
assail	deranged	resound
colleague	enmity	savor
compel	imperishable	temperament
composure	impose	transcend
compunction	inconceivably	tyrannical
contemplation	plausible	zealous

Quotables

"We have no more right to consume happiness without producing it than to consume wealth without producing it."

—George Bernard Shaw,
Candida

ADDITIONAL QUESTIONS
AND ACTIVITIES

Share the quotation above with students. Ask them to discuss the idea presented by Shaw. Why should we be responsible for producing happiness? How can people produce happiness? Students might make a plan for one thing they could do to try to produce happiness.

He would face life with a sense of strain and <u>contemplation</u>. Then he would get up, whetting his determination to face up to all inconveniences and withstand all difficulties.

Today he felt happy, full of happiness, as a matter of fact. There was no arguing about it. The symptoms were quite clear, and their vigor and obviousness were such as to <u>impose</u> themselves on his senses and mind all at once. Yes, indeed; he was happy. If this was not happiness, then what was? He felt that his limbs were well proportioned and functioning perfectly. They were working in superb harmony with each other and with the world around him. Inside him, he felt a boundless power, an <u>imperishable</u> energy, an ability to achieve anything with confidence, precision, and obvious success. His heart was overflowing with love for people, animals, and things, and with an all-engulfing sense of optimism and joy. It was as if he were no longer troubled or bothered by fear, anxiety, sickness, death, argument, or the question of earning a living. Even more important than that, and something he could not analyze, it was a feeling which penetrated to every cell of his body and soul; it played a tune full of delight, pleasure, serenity, and peace, and hummed in its incredible melodies the whispering sound of the world, which is denied to the unhappy.

He felt drunk with ecstasy and <u>savored</u> it slowly with a feeling of surprise. He asked himself where it had come from and how; the past provided no explanation, and the future could not justify it. Where did it come from, then, and how?! How long would it last? Would it stay with him till breakfast? Would it give him enough

In what state is the man when he awakens? Why is this peculiar?

time to get to the newspaper office? Just a minute though, he thought . . . it won't last because it can't. If it did, man would be turned into an angel or something even higher. So he told himself that he should devote his attention to savoring it, living with it, and storing up its nectar before it became a mere memory with no way of proving it or even being sure that it had ever existed.

He ate his breakfast with a relish, and this time nothing distracted his attention while he was eating. He gave "Uncle" Bashir, who was waiting on him, such a beaming smile that the poor man felt rather alarmed and taken aback. Usually he would only look in his direction to give orders or ask questions, although, on most occasions, he treated him fairly well.

"Tell me, 'Uncle' Bashir," he asked the servant, "am I a happy man?"

The poor man was startled. He realized why his servant was confused; for the first time ever he was talking to him as a <u>colleague</u> or friend. He encouraged his servant to forget about his worries and asked him with unusual insistence to answer his question.

Why is "Uncle" Bashir startled and confused?

"Through God's grace and favor, you are happy," the servant replied.

"You mean, I should be happy. Anyone with my job, living in my house, and enjoying my health, should be happy. That's what you want to say. But do you think I'm really happy?"

The servant replied, "You work too hard, Sir"; after yet more insistence, "It's more than any man can stand. . . ."

He hesitated, but his master gestured to him to continue with what he had to say.

"You get angry a lot," he said, "and have fierce arguments with your neighbors. . . ."

words for everyday use

con • tem • pla • tion (kän´tǝm plā´shǝn) *n.*, thoughtful inspection. *The man's <u>contemplation</u> of his life included reflecting on his past achievements and considering his future goals.*

im • pose (im pōz´) *vt.*, force one's will on others. *She decided to <u>impose</u> herself on her friends by not telling them she was coming and staying long after they wanted her to leave.*

im • per • ish • a • ble (im per´ish ǝ bǝl) *adj.*, that will not die. *Many people used to believe that the Earth's resources were <u>imperishable</u>, but today we know it is important to conserve them to keep them from running out.*

sa • vor (sā´vǝr) *vt.*, enjoy with delight. *The delicious taste of the ice cream was something to <u>savor</u>; we enjoyed it even more with fudge sauce.*

col • league (käl´ēg´) *n.*, fellow worker. *He ran into a <u>colleague</u> in the hall, and they agreed to work together on the project.*

He interrupted him by laughing loudly. "What about you?" he asked. "Don't you have any worries?"

"Of course, no man can be free of worry."

"You mean that complete happiness is an impossible quest?"

"That applies to life in general. . . ."

How could he have dreamed up this incredible happiness? He or any other human being? It was a strange, unique happiness, as though it were a private secret he had been given. In the meeting hall of the newspaper building, he spotted his main rival in this world sitting down thumbing through a magazine. The man heard his footsteps but did not look up from the magazine. He had undoubtedly noticed him in some way and was therefore pretending to ignore him so as to keep his own peace of mind. At some circulation meetings,[1] they would argue so violently with each other that sparks began to fly and they would exchange bitter words. One stage more, and they would come to blows. A week ago, his rival had won in the union elections,[2] and he had lost. He had felt pierced by a sharp, poisoned arrow, and the world had darkened before his eyes. Now here he was approaching his rival's seat; the sight of him sitting there did not make him excited, nor did the memories of their dispute spoil his composure. He approached him with a pure and carefree heart, feeling drunk with his incredible happiness; his face showed an expression full of tolerance and forgiveness. It was as though he were approaching some other man

Does the servant think the main character is happy? What does the servant say to answer the man's question?

What had happened between the main character and his rival at work a week before? What is the first thing the main character says to him? How does he feel?

toward whom he had never had any feelings of enmity, or perhaps he might be renewing a friendship again. "Good morning!" he said without feeling any compunction.

The man looked up in amazement. He was silent for a few moments until he recovered, and then returned the greeting curtly. It was as though he did not believe his eyes and ears.

He sat down alongside the man. "Marvelous weather today. . . ." he said.

"Okay. . . ." the other replied guardedly.

"Weather to fill your heart with happiness."

His rival looked at him closely and cautiously. "I'm glad that you're so happy. . . ." he muttered.

"Inconceivably happy. . . ." he replied with a laugh.

"I hope," the man continued in a rather hesitant tone of voice, "that I shan't spoil your happiness at the meeting of the administrative council. . . ."

"Not at all. My views are well-known, but I don't mind if the members adopt your point of view. That won't spoil my happiness!"

"You've changed a great deal overnight," the man said with a smile.

"The fact is that I'm happy, inconceivably happy."

The man examined his face carefully. "I bet your dear son has changed his mind about staying in Canada?!" he asked.

"Never, never, my friend," he replied, laughing loudly. "He is still sticking to his decision. . . ."

What does the rival ask about the main character's son? Why does he ask?

---

1. **circulation meetings.** Meetings about newspaper circulation, or distribution
2. **union elections.** Vote for officers of unions; large daily newspapers often have, for example, a printer's union.

words for everyday use

en • mi • ty (en´mə tē) *n.*, hostility. *She felt a great deal of enmity toward the person who had stolen her bicycle.*
com • punc • tion (kəm puŋk´shən) *n.*, uneasiness brought on by sense of guilt. *Her compunction about leaving the office early was made worse by the fact that she was behind in her work.*
in • con • ceiv • a • bly (in kən sēv´ ə blē) *adv.*, unthinkably; unbelievably. *Science fiction writers are often inconceivably good at convincing their readers about future worlds that seem impossible now.*

ANSWERS TO GUIDED READING QUESTIONS

1. The servant does not think the man is happy. He answers the man's question by telling him why he is not happy—he works too hard and argues with his neighbors.
2. The rival had won in the union elections, and the main character had lost. The first thing the character says to his rival is "Good morning!" without feeling any hostility or guilt.
3. He asks if the man's son has decided to return from Canada. He poses the question because he knows that the main reason the man had been sad was because his son was so far away.

ADDITIONAL QUESTIONS AND ACTIVITIES

Do students agree that complete happiness is an "impossible quest," as the servant implies on page 531? If yes, what in the modern world prevents complete happiness? Do students know of people who seem to be extremely happy? If yes, what seems to be the source of their happiness? Do students feel there is a special formula for happiness? Invite students to discuss their responses with one another.

1. The rival had always thought that the main character was bad tempered.
2. The man's happiness is so over-whelming that he can't work at all.

ADDITIONAL QUESTIONS AND ACTIVITIES

One of the things the main character deals with in the story is his son moving to Canada. Have students think about a time when they moved, or a close friend or relative moved away. What kinds of feelings did they experience? Would they respond differently now? Why might the situation have been difficult for the main character?

CROSS-CURRICULAR ACTIVITIES

SOCIAL STUDIES. Have students learn about Egypt, Mahfouz's native country. What are positive and interesting aspects of the country? What problems does the country face? How is Egypt similar to or different from other Arab countries? Student may find newspapers, newsmagazines, and the Internet to be helpful sources for up-to-date information on Egypt and its place in the Arab world.

"But that was the principal reason for your being so sad. . . ."

"Quite true. I've often begged him to come back out of pity for me in my loneliness and to serve his country. But he told me that he's going to open an engineering office[3] with a Canadian partner; in fact, he's invited me to join him in it. Let him live where he'll be happy. I'm quite happy here—as you can see, inconceivably happy. . . ."

The man still looked a little doubtful. "Quite extraordinarily brave!" he said.

"I don't know what it is, but I'm happy in the full meaning of the word."

Yes indeed, this was full happiness; full, firm, weighty, and vital. As deep as absolute power, widespread as the wind, fierce as fire, bewitching as scent, <u>transcending</u> nature. It could not possibly last.

The other man warmed to his display of affection. "The truth is," he said, "that I always picture you as someone with a fierce and violent <u>temperament</u> which causes him a good deal of trouble and leads him to trouble other people."

> What had the rival thought of the main character until now?

"Really?"

"You don't know how to make a truce; you've no concept of intermediate solutions. You work with your nerves, with the marrow in your bones. You fight bitterly, as though any problem is a matter of life and death!"

"Yes, that's true."

He accepted the criticism without any difficulty and with an open heart. His wave expanded into a boundless ocean of happiness. He struggled to control an innocent, happy laugh, which the other man interpreted in a way far removed from its pure motives.

"So then," he asked, "you think it's necessary to be able to take a balanced view of events, do you?"

"Of course. I remember, by way of example, the argument we had the day before yesterday about racism. We both had the same views on the subject; it's something worth being <u>zealous</u> about, even to the point of anger. But what kind of anger? An intellectual anger, abstract to a certain extent; not the type which shatters your nerves, ruins your digestion, and gives you palpitations.[4] Not so?"

"That's obvious; I quite understand. . . ." He struggled to control a second laugh and succeeded. His heart refused to <u>renounce</u> one drop of its joy. Racism, Vietnam, Palestine, . . . no problem could <u>assail</u> that fortress of happiness which was encircling his heart. When he remembered a problem, his heart guffawed. He was happy. It was a tyrannical happiness, despising all misery and laughing at any hardship; it wanted to laugh, dance, sing, and distribute its spirit of laughter, dancing, and singing among the various problems of the world.

He could not bear to stay in his office at the newspaper; he felt no desire to work at all. He hated the very idea of thinking about his daily business and completely failed to bring his mind down from its stronghold in the kingdom of happiness. How could he possibly write about a trolley bus

> How does happiness affect the main character's work?

falling into the Nile when he was so intoxicated by this frightening happiness? Yes, it really was frightening. How could it be anything else,

---

3. **engineering office.** Company that contracts to plan building projects

4. **palpitations.** Rapid heartbeat

words for everyday use	**tran • scend** (tran send´) vt., go beyond the limits. *He was able to <u>transcend</u> the limits of his past by working hard and exceeding the goals he set.*
	tem • per • a • ment (tem´pər ə mənt) n., one's frame of mind. *The boss was known to have a difficult <u>temperament</u>, yelling at his employees and complaining about their laziness.*
	zeal • ous (zel´əs) adj., enthusiastic. *The <u>zealous</u> preacher enjoyed delivering passionate sermons that fired up his eager congregation.*
	re • nounce (ri nouns´) vt., give up. *Many people become vegetarians and <u>renounce</u> meat, choosing to eat a diet full of fruits, grains, and vegetables instead.*
	as • sail (ə sāl´) vt., attack with arguments or doubts. *Political candidates often <u>assail</u> each other, attacking the other's credibility and past record on important issues.*

when there was no reason for it at all, when it was so strong that it made him exhausted and paralyzed his will; apart from the fact that it had been with him for half a day without letting up in the slightest degree?!

He left the pages of paper blank and started walking backward and forward across the room, laughing and cracking his fingers. . . .

He felt slightly worried; it did not penetrate deep enough to spoil his happiness but paused on the surface of his mind like an abstract idea. It occurred to him that he might recall the tragedies of his life so that he could test their effect on his happiness. Perhaps they would be able to bring back some idea of balance or security, at least until his happiness began to flag a little. For example, he remembered his wife's death in all its various aspects and details. What had happened? The event appeared to him as a series of movements without any meaning or effect, as though it had happened to some other woman, the wife of another man, in some distant historical age. In fact, it had a contagious effect which prompted a smile and then even provoked laughter. He could not stop himself laughing, and there he was guffawing, ha . . . ha . . . ha!

The same thing happened when he remembered the first letter his son had sent him saying that he wanted to emigrate to Canada. The sound of his guffaws as he paraded the bloody tragedies of the world before him would have

> IT OCCURRED TO HIM THAT HE MIGHT RECALL THE TRAGEDIES OF HIS LIFE SO THAT HE COULD TEST THEIR EFFECT ON HIS HAPPINESS.

attracted the attention of the newspaper workers and passersby in the street, had it not been for the thickness of the walls. He could do nothing to dislodge his happiness. Memories of unhappy times hit him like waves being thrown onto a sandy beach under the golden rays of the sun.

What could the main character not stop doing? Why was this behavior odd?

He excused himself from attending the administrative council and left the newspaper office without writing a word. After lunch, he lay down on his bed as usual but could not sleep. In fact, sleep seemed an impossibility to him. Nothing gave him any indication that it was coming, even slowly. He was in a place alight and gleaming, resounding with sleeplessness and joy. He had to calm down and relax, to quiet his senses and limbs, but how could he do it? He gave up trying to sleep and got up. He began to hum as he was walking around his house. If this keeps up, he told himself, I won't be able to sleep, just as I can't work or feel sad. It was almost time for him to go to the club, but he did not feel like meeting any friends. What was the point of exchanging views on public affairs and private worries?! What would they think if they found him laughing at every major problem? What would they say? How would they picture things? How would they explain it? No, he did not need anyone, nor did he want to spend the evening talking. He should be by himself

words for everyday use

as • pect (as´pekt´) n., appearance or interpretation of an idea. *The lawyer knew that one aspect of the case might cause a problem, but she decided to play down its importance and appear unconcerned.*

re • sound (ri zound´) vi., extol loudly or widely. *As the curtain closed at the end of the play, the audience was resounding with their enjoyment of the production.*

"THE HAPPY MAN"   533

ANSWER TO GUIDED READING QUESTION

1. He could not stop guffawing, or laughing. It seems odd because he is remembering unhappy times, including his wife's death and his son's departure.

ADDITIONAL QUESTIONS AND ACTIVITIES

Have students discuss what makes them laugh. Encourage them to share jokes, anecdotes, or stories that they think are funny. What's funny about them? Does everyone laugh at the same things? Why, or why not? Prompt them to write about experiences during which they laughed a great deal, both with other people and by themselves.

Interested students may write an amusing story or song based on their experiences.

LITERARY TECHNIQUE

IRONY. **Irony** is the difference between appearance and reality. How does the main character begin to feel about his happiness? Why is this reaction ironic?
Answers
The main character begins to feel worried because he is so happy. This is ironic because feeling happy is a positive thing, not something one would normally worry about.

1. He does not want to meet them because he does not think they will understand his laughter. He decides to go for a long walk instead.
2. The doctor responds by laughing at the man's problem.
3. The doctor tells the main character to consult a gland specialist.

Quotables

"There is no duty we so much underrate as the duty of being happy."

—Robert Louis Stevenson,
An Apology for Idlers

ADDITIONAL QUESTIONS AND ACTIVITIES

Ask students to discuss the following questions:
Do most people place high value on being happy? What do people do to try to achieve happiness? What barriers stand in the way of happiness? In general, do you think you are a happy person? Why, or why not? What do you do, or what could you do, to be happy?

and go for a long walk to get rid of some of his excess vitality and think about his situation. What had happened to him? How was it that this incredible happiness had overwhelmed him? How long would he have to carry it on his shoulders? Would it keep depriving him of work, friends, sleep, and peace of mind?! Should he resign himself to it? Should he abandon himself to the flood to play with him as the whim took it? Or should he look for a way out for himself through thought, action, or advice?

> Why does the main character not want to meet his friends? What does he decide to do instead?

When he was called into the examination room in the clinic of his friend, the specialist in internal medicine, he felt a little alarmed. The doctor looked at him with a smile. "You don't look like someone who's complaining about being ill," he said.

"I haven't come to see you because I'm ill," he told the doctor in a hesitant tone of voice, "but because I'm happy!"

The doctor looked piercingly at him with a questioning air.

"Yes," he repeated to underline what he had said, "because I'm happy!"

There was a period of silence. On one side, there was anxiety, and on the other, questioning and amazement.

"It's an incredible feeling which can't be defined in any other way, but it's very serious. . . ."

The doctor laughed. "I wish your illness were contagious," he said, prodding him jokingly.

> How does the doctor react to the man's problem?

"Don't treat it as a joke. It's very serious, as I told you. I'll describe it to you. . . ."

He told him all about his happiness from the time he had woken up in the morning till he had felt <u>compelled</u> to visit him.

"Haven't you been taking drugs, alcohol, or tranquilizers?"

"Absolutely nothing like that."

"Have you had some success in an important sphere of your life: work . . . love . . . money?"

"Nothing like that either. I've twice as much to worry about as I have to make me feel glad. . . ."

"Perhaps if you were patient for a while. . . ."

"I've been patient all day. I'm afraid I'll be spending the night wandering around. . . ."

The doctor gave him a precise, careful, and comprehensive examination and then shrugged his shoulders in despair. "You're a picture of health," he said.

"And so?"

"I could advise you to take a sleeping pill, but it would be better if you consulted a nerve specialist. . . ."

The examination was repeated in the nerve specialist's clinic with the self-same precision, care, and comprehensiveness. "Your nerves are sound," the doctor told him. "They're in enviable condition!"

"Haven't you got a <u>plausible</u> explanation for my condition?" he asked hopefully.

"Consult a gland specialist!" the doctor replied, shaking his head.

> Where does the doctor tell the main character to go?

The examination was conducted for a third time in the gland specialist's clinic with the same precision, care, and comprehensiveness. "I congratulate you!" the doctor told him. "Your glands are in good condition."

He laughed. He apologized for laughing, laughing as he did so. Laughter was his way of expressing his alarm and despair.

He left the clinic with the feeling that he was alone, alone in the hands of his <u>tyrannical</u> hap-

words for everyday use	**com • pel** (kəm pel´) *vi.*, get or bring about by force. *The photographer wanted to <u>compel</u> his audience to respond by photographing groups of objects not ordinarily found with one another.*
	plau • si • ble (plô´zə bəl) *adj.*, seemingly true, acceptable. *The newspaper story was entirely <u>plausible</u>; it was the only account of the events that made sense.*
	ty • ran • ni • cal (tī ran´i kəl) *adj.*, oppressive, unjust. *The <u>tyrannical</u> ruler forced his subjects to live in poor conditions and work hard for little money.*

piness, with no helper, no guide, and no friend. Suddenly, he remembered the doctor's sign he sometimes saw from the window of his office in the newspaper building. It was true that he had no confidence in psychiatrists even though he had read about the significance of psychoanalysis.[5] Apart from that, he knew that their tentacles were very long and they kept their patients tied in a sort of long association. He laughed as he remembered the method of cure through free association and the problems which it eventually uncovers. He was laughing as his feet carried him toward the psychiatrist's clinic, and imagined the doctor listening

How does the main character feel as he leaves the clinic? Where does he decide to go?

to his incredible complaints about feeling happy, when he was used to hearing people complain about hysteria, schizophrenia,[6] anxiety, and so on.

"The truth is, Doctor, that I've come to see you because I'm happy!"

He looked at the doctor to see what effect his statement had had on him but noticed that he was keeping his <u>composure</u>. He felt ridiculous. "I'm inconceivably happy. . . ." he said in a tone of confidence.

He began to tell the doctor his story, but the latter stopped him with a gesture of his hand. "An overwhelming, incredible, <u>debilitating</u> happiness?" he asked quietly.

He stared at him in amazement and was on the point of saying something, but the doctor spoke first. "A happiness which has made you stop working," he asked, "abandon your friends, and detest going to sleep . . . ?"

"You're a miracle!" he shouted.

"Every time you get involved in some misfortune," the psychiatrist continued quietly, "you dissolve into laughter. . . ?"

"Sir . . . are you familiar with the invisible?"

"No!" he said with a smile, "nothing like that. But I get a similar case in my clinic at least once a week!"

"Is it an epidemic?" he asked.

Why does the psychiatrist understand the problem?

"I didn't say that, and I wouldn't claim that it's been possible to analyze one case into its primary elements as yet."

"But is it a disease?"

"All the cases are still under treatment."

"But are you satisfied without any doubt that they aren't natural cases. . . . ?"

"That's a necessary assumption for the job; there's only. . . ."

"Have you noticed any of them to be <u>deranged</u> in . . . ?" he asked anxiously, pointing to his head.

"Absolutely not," the doctor replied convincingly. "I assure you that they're all intelligent in every sense of the word. . . ."

The doctor thought for a moment. "We should have two sessions a week, I think?" he said.

"Very well. . . ." he replied in resignation.

"There's no sense in getting alarmed or feeling sad. . . ."

Alarmed, sad? He smiled, and his smile kept on getting broader. A laugh slipped out, and before long, he was dissolving into laughter. He was determined to control himself, but his resistance collapsed completely. He started guffawing loudly. . . . ∎

5. **psychoanalysis.** Psychiatric counseling technique originated by Austrian physician Sigmund Freud (1856–1939), based on the theory that the conscious mind rejects thoughts and emotions that remain in the unconscious mind, causing conflict in the individual. According to the theory, rejected feelings and thoughts can be brought to the conscious mind through psychoanalytic techniques such as free association and dream analysis.

6. **schizophrenia.** Major mental disorder of unknown cause typically characterized by distortions of reality

---

words for everyday use

com • po • sure (kəm pō´zhər) *n.,* calmness of mind or manner. *She tried to regain her <u>composure</u> after getting mad, but even a relaxing bath could not calm her down.*

de • bil • i • tat • ing (dē bil´ə tāt´iŋ) *adj.,* weakening. *The <u>debilitating</u> illness left him feeling tired and frail for months.*

de • ranged (dē rānjd´) *adj.,* insane. *The <u>deranged</u> fan began bothering the star athlete by following him around and shouting insults.*

1. The main character feels alone as he leaves the clinic, but still feels happy. He decides to go to a psychiatrist.
2. The psychiatrist understands the man's problem because he sees similar cases at least once a week.

SELECTION CHECK TEST 4.7.3 WITH ANSWERS

Checking Your Reading
1. Where does the main character work? **He works in a newspaper office.**
2. Who is "Uncle" Bashir? **He is the man's servant.**
3. Where did the main character's son go? **He went to Canada.**
4. Why does the main character go to the doctor? **He goes to the doctor because he is happy.**
5. Why isn't the psychiatrist surprised by the man's condition? **He sees such cases regularly.**

Vocabulary in Context
Fill in each blank below with the most appropriate word from the following Words for Everyday Use.

contemplation	colleague
compunction	plausible
deranged	zealous

1. After much **contemplation**, Luis made his decision.
2. Caleb doesn't really care about the environment, but Noreen is **zealous** about protecting it.
3. The explanation seemed **plausible**, but Jorge still wasn't convinced.
4. My **colleague** and I are up for the same promotion.
5. News reports indicated that the **deranged** killer was last seen by the marina.

Literary Tools
1. What is dialogue? **Dialogue is a conversation involving two or more characters.**
2. Name the three major techniques writers use to create character. **Writers use direct description, portrayal of characters' behavior, and representations of characters' internal states to create character.**

RESPOND TO THE SELECTION

Have you ever felt so happy that you began to worry about your happiness? How did you resolve your worries?

ANSWERS TO INVESTIGATE, INQUIRE, AND IMAGINE

RECALL

1a. The main character feels unexpectedly happy when he wakes up. He usually feels strained.

2a. The main character asks "Uncle" Bashir if the main character is a happy man. He says "Good morning!" to his rival without any feelings of hostility.

3a. The rival wonders if the main character's son has changed his mind about staying in Canada. The main character responds by saying that he has not. He recalls past tragedies to test their effects on his happiness.

INTERPRET

1b. The main character cannot think of a term to describe his new state of mind more accurately and precisely than "happy."

2b. "Uncle" Bashir responds that the main character works too hard and often gets angry. His rival describes him as someone with a fierce and violent temperament. From these descriptions, it seems that the main character is a difficult, troubled man.

3b. He keeps laughing because it is the only way he can express his alarm and despair. All the subjects he laughs at are tragic. He is unable to work because he is completely distracted by his happiness.

ANALYZE

4a. The main character's happiness is a cover for his intense sadness. He seeks treatment because he knows something is wrong. Reasons for his sadness include his wife's death and his son's departure. In short, he is laughing to keep from crying.

SYNTHESIZE

4b. The story seems to be saying that if you are happy all the time, you are thought to be insane. The author believes that there is a thin line between happiness and madness, in part because the modern world regards complete happiness as absurd.

EVALUATE

5a. He is diagnosed as needing

Respond to the SELECTION

How do you feel about the main character in this story? Do you feel that you understand what he is going through?

Investigate, Inquire, and Imagine

Recall: GATHERING FACTS

1a. What does the main character feel, unexpectedly, when he wakes up one morning? How does he usually feel?

2a. What does the main character ask his servant, "Uncle" Bashir? What does he say to his rival at the newspaper office?

3a. What does the rival say about the main character's son? How does the main character respond? Why does he decide to try to recall all of the tragedies in his life?

Analyze: TAKING THINGS APART

4a. Do you believe in the main character's happiness? Why does he seek treatment for his happiness? Give examples from the story that support your response.

Evaluate: MAKING JUDGMENTS

5a. How is the man finally diagnosed? Do you agree with this diagnosis? Why, or why not?

Interpret: FINDING MEANING

1b. How does the main character describe his new state of mind?

2b. What is "Uncle" Bashir's response to the main character's question? How does his rival at work react to him? Judging from these two instances, what kind of person is the main character normally?

3b. Why does the main character keep laughing? What do the subjects at which he laughs have in common? Why is he unable to work?

Synthesize: BRINGING THINGS TOGETHER

4b. What does this story seem to be saying about society and happiness? Do you think the author believes it is possible to be completely happy and also to function well in the modern world?

Extend: CONNECTING IDEAS

5b. What are some other ways that people cope with the despair and tragedy they are experiencing?

Understanding Literature

DIALOGUE. Review the definition for **dialogue** in the Handbook of Literary Terms. How does the dialogue in the story advance the plot?

CHARACTERIZATION. Review the definition for **characterization** in the Handbook of Literary Terms and the chart you made for Literary Tools in Prereading for this selection. How does the author let the reader know what the main character was like before the story began? What are the different ways in which we learn about this character?

ANSWERS TO INVESTIGATE, INQUIRE, AND IMAGINE (CONT.)

psychological treatment. It is a reasonable diagnosis, because he cannot stop himself from laughing. On the other hand, his laughter is helping him to cope with the despair and tragedy he's experienced.

EXTEND

5b. People may cry, withdraw, become depressed. They may immerse themselves in work or try to

drown out their sorrow with self-destructive behavior. They may take action to prevent another tragedy or to create a memorial for the subject of their loss.

Answers to Understanding Literature can be found on page 537.

Writer's Journal

1. Pretend that you are a friend of the main character in "The Happy Man." You hear that he is undergoing treatment for his unusual "condition" and you want to send a card to let him know that you are thinking of him. Write the words for the **greeting card** that you choose to send.

2. Write a short **poem** describing a time when you felt particularly happy or describing a person, place, or thing that brings you happiness.

3. Write a **character sketch** about the happiest person you know and what you think makes this person so happy.

Integrating the Language Arts

Applied English & Collaborative Learning

CHILDREN'S BOOK. Work with a group of other students to write, design, and illustrate a children's book that describes emotions—what an emotion is and what some common emotions are. Start by brainstorming a list of emotions such as sadness, happiness, embarrassment, anger, and so on. Then create a central character for your book, such as a child, a clown, an animal, or a stuffed bear. Next think of situations that would cause the character to feel the various emotions from your brainstorming list. Finally, create text and illustrations for each of these situations.

Media Literacy

MEDIA SEARCH. The main character in "The Happy Man" seemed to be using laughter to help him cope with the despair and tragedy he experienced in his life. A number of people dealing with tragedies such as the loss of a loved one to a rare disease or a senseless act of violence have turned their despair into positive action by starting or contributing to a foundation or working in another volunteer capacity for a related organization. Stories about such acts often appear in local newspapers, women's magazines, religious periodicals, and magazines like *Reader's Digest*. Find such a story to share with your class.

Collaborative Learning

WELLNESS FAIR. Plan a day of wellness and relaxation for your class, your school, or your community. As a class, discuss what you might feature at a wellness fair. Think about different displays or activities that might promote happiness or good spirits. You might consider displays on health and fitness, friends and relationships, volunteer work, and entertainment. You might also consider playing relaxing music, telling humorous stories, or providing refreshments. Hold a brainstorming session and think of ideas for this event. Decide if the event will be geared toward you and your classmates or if you would like it to be open to family, friends, and other members of your community. Then decide where it should take place and how long it should last.

Applied English & Collaborative Learning
Students might find it helpful to look at some children's books before writing their own. This may help them understand different styles in children's books and help them choose appropriate language for the age group they are targeting. They may want to share their books with younger students.

Media Literacy
Internet sites for some organizations describe the history of the organization or highlight people who have helped or benefited from the organization. This might be another source for students to check to find this type of story.

Collaborative Learning
Students may want to form groups to handle elements of their fair. Each group might do something different—music, food, games—but could also be responsible for a booth or display of its own choosing about wellness or happiness. After the fair is completed, have students give feedback about what they learned from putting on the fair, and whether it was different from what they expected.

ANSWERS TO UNDERSTANDING LITERATURE

DIALOGUE. The dialogue between the main character and "Uncle" Bashir presents the idea that no one can be fully happy. The dialogue between the main character and his rival shows that the main character has no balance and causes him to begin worrying about his happiness. The dialogues with the doctors continue to show the problem the man finds with his happiness.

CHARACTERIZATION. The author lets the reader know what the main character was like by supplying information through other characters such as "Uncle" Bashir and his rival at work. The reader learns about the main character through the perspectives of other characters, and through his own thoughts and observations about his condition.

GRAPHIC ORGANIZER

Cause: Overseer harassed neighboring peasants with large fines. **Effect:** Peasants decided to buy landowner's land when they heard she was selling.
Cause: Peasants began trespassing on his land. **Effect:** Pakhom politely asked them to stop at first but eventually began pressing charges which irritated the peasants. Pakhom began to feel crowded.
Cause: Visiting peasant told of new settlement. **Effect:** Pakhom sold everything and moved to new place, living ten times better than in the past.
Cause: Traveling merchant told of wonderful, cheap land in Bashkir country. **Effect:** Pakhom bought gifts and traveled for a week to check it out.
Cause: Bashkir elder told Pakhom that he could buy as much land as he could walk around in a day for a thousand rubles. **Effect:** Pakhom was greedy, walked too far, and killed himself trying to return by sunset.

READER'S JOURNAL

Suggest that students think about a specific time in their lives when greed played a role. Students may refer to personal greed or the greed of another person. Ask them to describe the event, the desired object, and the outcome. How does their own experience relate to the story?

Literary
T O O L S

FORESHADOWING. Foreshadowing is the act of hinting at events to occur later in the story. Watch for examples of foreshadowing as you read. Can you guess what might happen at the story's end?

CENTRAL CONFLICT. A **central conflict** is the primary struggle dealt with in the plot of a story or drama. As you read the story, note the various conflicts—both internal and external—that Pakhom experiences.

Organizer

Create a cause and effect chart like the one below to see how the various people with whom Pakhom came in contact fueled his selfish desires.

Cause	Effect
Sister-in-law boasted of life in town	Pakhom's wife became offended, inducing Pakhom to boast that if he had enough land even the Devil could not get him. This gave the Devil a challenge.
Overseer harassed neighboring peasants with large fines	
Peasants began trespassing on his land	
Visiting peasant told of new settlement	
Traveling merchant told of wonderful, cheap land in Bashkir country	
Bashkir elder told Pakhom that he could buy for 1000 rubles as much land as he could walk around in a day	

"Land Enough for a Man"
by Leo Tolstoy

Reader's
resource

"**Land Enough for a Man**" was written in 1885 and first appeared in the journal *Russian Wealth* in 1886. This story's theme reflects an attitude about greed, wealth, and worldly possessions that Tolstoy adopted late in life when he became a highly religious man and decided to sell his land, donate his money, and dress as a peasant. These actions were Tolstoy's attempt to find the true meaning of life and to move away from worldly symbols of power and prestige, such as money and land ownership.

About *the*
A U T H O R

Leo Tolstoy (1828–1910), a Russian writer and philosopher, is considered to be one of the world's greatest writers. He wrote close to one hundred volumes of novels, stories, plays, diaries, and essays. Two of his most famous novels are *War and Peace*, a novel set in Russia during the Napoleonic invasion of 1812, and *Anna Karenina,* a novel about the tragic life of a woman who, for love, defies the rules of the 19th-centure Russian society and is forced to pay the price. Born to a wealthy family, Tolstoy owned land and enjoyed his success as a writer for most of his adult life, until as an older man he became concerned with leading a simple, moral life, and gave away many of his worldly possessions.

Reader's
Journal

Where have you seen greed in the world around you? Where have you seen greed in your own life?

GOALS/OBJECTIVES

Studying this lesson will enable students to
- understand the impact of greed on the main character
- describe Leo Tolstoy's contributions to nineteenth-century Russian literature

- define *central conflict* and *foreshadowing* and interpret their uses in the story
- test new vocabulary words
- use various media to explore simple living trends and research Tolstoy's nineteenth-century Russia

The Pontine Marshes, 1850s. Alexander Ivanov. Courtesy of State Russian Museum, St. Petersburg, Russia.

Land Enough for a MAN

Leo Tolstoy

1

An older sister from town came to visit her younger sister in the country. The elder had married a merchant in town; the younger a peasant in the country. Drinking tea, the sisters chatted. The elder began to brag—to boast of her life in town; how spaciously and comfortably she lived, how well she dressed the children, how nicely she ate and drank, and how she went for drives, excursions, and to the theater.

The younger sister became offended and began <u>disparaging</u> the merchant's life and exalting her peasant life.

What do the sisters discuss?

"I wouldn't trade my life for yours," she said. "Our life is rough, I grant you, but we haven't a worry. You may live more neatly, and, perhaps, earn a lot at your trade, but you may lose it all. Remember the proverb: loss is gain's big brother. It often goes like that: one day you're rich and the day after, you're begging in the streets. But our peasant life is more stable: a meager life, but a long one. We won't be rich, but we'll always eat."

The older sister began to speak:

"Eat—like the pigs and calves! No elegance, no manners! No matter how hard your man works, you'll live and die in manure and so will your children."

"What of it," said the younger; "that's our way. Our life may be hard, but we bow to no one, are afraid of no one. While you in town are surrounded by temptations. It's all right now, but tomorrow it may turn ugly—suddenly you'll find your man tempted by cards, or wine, or some young charmer, and everything will turn to ashes. That's what often happens, doesn't it?"

What does the younger sister claim are the benefits of country life?

Pakhom, lying on top of the stove, listened to the women babbling.

"It's the absolute truth," he said. "We're so busy tilling mother earth from infancy, we don't get such nonsense in our heads. There's just one trouble—too little land! If I had all the land I wanted, I wouldn't fear the Devil himself!"

The women finished their tea, chatted some more about dresses, cleared the dishes, and went to bed. But the Devil sitting behind the stove had heard everything. He was delighted that the peasant wife had induced her husband to boast, and, particularly, to boast that if he had enough land even the Devil could not get him.

"All right," he thought, "we'll have a tussle, you and I; I'll give you plenty of land. And then I'll get you through your land."

2

Next to the peasants there lived a small landowner. She had three hundred and twenty-five acres of land. And she had always lived in peace with the peasants—never abusing them. Then she hired as <u>overseer</u> a retired soldier who began to harass the peasants with fines. No matter how careful Pakhom was, either his horses wandered into her oats, or his cattle got into her garden, or his calves strayed onto her meadow—and there was a fine for everything.

Pakhom would pay up and then curse and beat his family. Many were the difficulties Pakhom suffered all summer because of that overseer. Come winter, he was glad to stable the cattle—he begrudged them the <u>fodder</u>, but at least he was free from worry.

It was rumored that winter that the lady was selling her land, and that the innkeeper on the main road was arranging to buy it. The peasants heard this and groaned. "Well," they thought, "if the innkeeper gets the land, he'll pester us with worse fines than the lady. We can't get along without this land; we live too close."

A <u>delegation</u> of peasants representing the commune came to ask the lady not to sell the land to the innkeeper, but to give it to them. They promised to pay more. The lady agreed.

words for everyday use

dis • par • age (di spar′ ij) *vt.,* discredit; belittle. *The company attempted to <u>disparage</u> the employee's complaint, and to discredit and belittle him even further.*

o • ver • se • er (ō′ vər sē′ ər) *n.,* one who supervises the work of others. *The plant foreman was the <u>overseer</u> of the factory; he supervised all the workers on different shifts.*

fod • der (fäd′ ər) *n.,* coarse food for cattle, such as cornstalks, hay, and straw. *Cornstalks and hay make good <u>fodder</u> for the cattle; it keeps them well fed and nourished.*

del • e • ga • tion (del′ ə gā′ shən) *n.,* group of people authorized to speak and act for others. *A small <u>delegation</u> of citizens went to Washington to voice the opinions of their state on the issue.*

The peasants started making arrangements for the commune to buy the land; they held one meeting and another meeting—but the matter was still unsettled. The Evil One[1] divided them, and they were completely unable to agree. Then the peasants decided that each would buy individually as much as he could. To this, also, the lady agreed. Pakhom heard that his neighbor had bought fifty-five acres from the lady, and that she had loaned him half the money for a year. Pakhom became envious. "They're buying up all the land," he thought, "and I'll be left with nothing." He consulted his wife.

What did the peasants convince the landowner to do with her land?

"People are buying," he said, "so we must buy about twenty-five acres, too. Otherwise we can't exist—the overseer is crushing us with fines."

They figured out how they could buy. They had one hundred rubles[2] put aside, and they sold the colt and half the bee swarm, hired out their son as a worker, borrowed from their brother-in-law, and raised half the money.

Pakhom gathered up the money, chose his land—forty acres including a little woods—and went to bargain with the lady. He drove a bargain for his forty acres, and sealed it with his hand and a deposit. They went to town and signed the deed with half the money paid down and the rest due in two years.

So Pakhom had his own land. He borrowed seed, sowed the land he had bought: it produced well. In a year, he had settled his debts with both the lady and his brother-in-law. And so Pakhom became a landowner: he plowed and sowed his own land, mowed hay on his own land, cut timber from his own land, and pastured his herd on his own land. When Pakhom went out to plow the land which he now owned forever, or when he happened to glance over the sprouting fields and meadows, he could not rejoice enough. It seemed to him that the grass grew and the flowers flowered in a new way. When he had walked across this land before, it had been land like any land; now it had become completely exceptional.

How does land ownership make Pakhom feel?

3

So Pakhom lived and was pleased. Everything would have been fine, had the peasants not begun trespassing on his fields and meadows. He begged them politely to stop, but the trespassing continued. Either the cowherds let the cattle into the meadows, or the horses got into the wheat while grazing at night. Time after time, Pakhom chased them out and forgave without pressing charges; then he became tired of it and started to complain to the district court and he knew the peasants did not do these things deliberately, but only because they were crowded, yet he thought: "One still mustn't let them or they'll ravage everything. They must be taught."

What is troubling Pakhom?

To teach them, he sued once, and then again; one was fined, then another. Pakhom's neighbors began to hold a grudge against him; they started to trespass on purpose from time to time. One went to the grove at night and cut down a dozen linden trees for bast.[3] When Pakhom walked through the woods, he looked and saw a white glimmer. He approached— there lay the discarded peelings, and there stood the little stumps. If the villain had only cut the

---

1. **The Evil One.** Another name for the devil, or Satan
2. **rubles.** Russian currency
3. **bast.** Sturdy fiber used in making ropes and mats

---

words for everyday use

rav • age (rav' ij) *vt.*, destroy; pillage or rob. *Hurricanes and pirates had ravaged the coastal villages, but the coastal dwellers survived it all.*

ANSWERS TO GUIDED READING QUESTIONS

1. They convinced the land owner to sell the land to them instead of selling it to the innkeeper.
2. Landownership makes Pakhom feel very joyful and happy for a short time.
3. Pakhom is troubled by the peasants trespassing on his fields and meadows.

BIBLIOGRAPHIC NOTE

Interested students might choose to read other works by Tolstoy. The following is a selected bibliography of Leo Tolstoy's works.

Childhood, 1852
The Raid, 1853
Boyhood, 1854
Sevastopol Sketches, 1855–1856
Youth, 1857
Family Happiness, 1859
The Cossacks, 1863
War and Peace, 1863–1869
Anna Karenina, 1873–1877
A Confession, 1879–1882
What Men Live By, 1882
What I Believe, 1883
"The Death of Ivan Ilyich," 1886
The Kreutzer Sonata, 1889
Master and Man, 1895
What Is Art? 1898
Resurrection, 1899
Hadji Murad, 1904

1. Pakhom hears a rumor that people might be moving to new places. He decides to add the land of anyone who leaves to his own land.
2. He decides to leave and build himself a new, larger house in a new place. He makes the decision because he feels it is too crowded where he is.

LITERARY NOTE

Tolstoy is considered one of the great Russian writers. His first published work appeared in the Russian magazine *Contemporary* in 1852. It was based on his own memories and was titled *Childhood*.

ADDITIONAL QUESTIONS AND ACTIVITIES

Tolstoy's stories are written as though told by a narrator, so the reader sees reality through another person's perceptions. Discuss with students the advantages and disadvantages of using this technique. What is its impact on the story? How would the story be different if it were told by Pakhom in the first-person point of view?

---

edges of the bush, or left one standing, but he had razed them all, one after the other. Pakhom was enraged. He thought and thought: "It must be Semon," he thought. He went to search Semon's farm, found nothing, and quarreled with him. And Pakhom was even more certain Semon had done it. He filed a petition. Semon was called into court. The case dragged on and on; the peasant was <u>acquitted</u> for lack of evidence. Pakhom felt even more wronged and abused the elder and the judges.

"You're hand and hand with THIEVES"

"You're hand and hand with thieves," he said. "If you led honest lives, you wouldn't let thieves go free."

Pakhom quarreled with both the judges and his neighbors. The peasants started threatening to set fire to his place. Although Pakhom had more land than before, his neighbors were closing in on him.

Just then, there was a rumor that people were moving to new places. And Pakhom thought: "I have no reason to leave my land, but if some of us go, there'll be more space. I could take their land, add it

> *What rumor does Pakhom hear? What does he decide?*

to my place; life would be better. It's too crowded now."

Once when Pakhom was sitting at home, a peasant passing through dropped in. Pakhom put him up for the night, fed him, talked to him, and asked him where, pray, he came from. The peasant said he came from below, beyond the Volga, where he had been working. One thing led to another and the peasant gradually started telling how people were going there to settle. He told how his own people had gone there, joined the community, and divided off twenty-five acres a man.

"And the land is so good," he said, "that they sowed rye, and you couldn't see a horse in the stalks, it was so high; and so thick, that five handfuls make a sheaf.[4] One peasant," he said, "who hadn't a thing but his bare hands, came there and now has six horses, two cows."

Pakhom's heart took fire. He was thinking: "Why be poor and crowded here if one can live well there? We'll sell the house and land here; with this money, I'll build myself a house there and set up a whole establishment. There's only trouble in this crowded place. But I had better make the trip and look into it myself."

> *What does Pakhom decide to do? Why does he make this decision?*

That summer he got ready and went. He sailed down the Volga to Samara in a steamer, then walked four hundred versts[5] on foot. When he arrived, everything was just as described. The peasants were living amply on twenty-five acres per head, and they participated willingly in the activities of the community. And whoever had money could buy, in addition to his share, as much of the very best

---

4. **sheaf.** Cut stalks of grain bound up in a bundle
5. **versts.** Russian units of length equal to three thousand five hundred feet, or about two-thirds of a mile

---

words for everyday use

ac • quit (ə kwit´) *vt.*, clear a person of a charge or accusation. *The jury voted to <u>acquit</u> the robbery suspect because there was not enough evidence to show why she had been charged in the first place.*

land as he wanted at a ruble an acre; you could buy as much as you wanted!

After finding out everything, Pakhom returned home and began selling all he owned. He sold the land at profit, sold his own farm, sold his entire herd, resigned from the community, waited for spring, and set off with his family for a new place.

4

Pakhom arrived at the settlement with his family, and joined the community. He stood the elders drinks and put all the papers in order. They accepted Pakhom, divided off one hundred and twenty-five acres of land in various fields as his portion for his family of five—in addition to the use of the pasture. Pakhom built himself a farm and acquired a herd. His part of the common land alone was three times as large as before. And the land was fertile. He lived ten times better than in the past. You had <u>arable</u> land and fodder at will. And you could keep as many cattle as you wanted.

> What are the advantages of the new farmland?

At first, while he was busy building and settling himself, he was content; but after he became used to it, he felt crowded on this land, too. The first year, Pakhom sowed wheat on his share of the common land—it grew well. He wanted to sow wheat again, but there was not enough common land. And what there was, was not suitable. In that region, wheat is sown only on grassland or wasteland. They sow the land for a year or two, then leave it fallow until the grass grows back again. And there are many wanting that kind of land, and not enough of it for all. There were disputes over it, too; the richer peasants wanted to sow it themselves, while the poor people wanted to rent it to dealers to raise tax money. Pakhom wanted to sow more. The following year, he went to a dealer and rented land from him for a year. He sowed more—it grew well; but it was far from the village—you had to cart it about fifteen versts. He saw the peasant-dealers living in farmhouses and growing rich. "That's the thing," thought Pakhom; "if only I could buy land permanently for myself and build a farmhouse on my land. Everything would be at hand." And Pakhom began pondering over how he could buy freehold land.

So Pakhom lived for three years. He rented land and sowed wheat on it. The years were good ones, and the wheat grew well, and the surplus money accumulated. But Pakhom found it annoying to rent land from people every year and to have to move from place to place. Whenever there was a good piece of land, the peasants immediately rushed to divide up everything; if Pakhom did not hurry to buy, he had no land to sow. The third year, he and a dealer rented part of the common pasture from some peasants; he had already plowed when the peasants sued and the work was wasted. "If it had been my own land," he thought, "I'd bow to no one and there'd be no trouble."

And Pakhom began to inquire where land could be bought permanently. And he came across a peasant. The peasant had bought one thousand three hundred and fifty acres, then gone bankrupt, and was selling cheaply. Pakhom began talking terms with him. They haggled and haggled and agreed on fifteen hundred rubles, half of it payable later. They had just reached an agreement when a traveling merchant stopped at the farm for something to eat. They drank

> What does Pakhom wait to buy? Why?

ANSWERS TO GUIDED READING QUESTIONS

1. The advantages of Pakhom's land are that it is three times the size of what he had before, and it is fertile.
2. He waits to buy his own land so that he can save his money and build a farmhouse on the land he buys.

LITERARY NOTE

The Russian short-story tradition began in the 1830s. Nikolai Gogol is considered the father of the Russian short story. *Nevsky Prospect* (1835), *Diary of a Madman* (1835), and *The Overcoat* (1842) are considered his most enduring works.

Fyodor Dostoyevsky, a famous Russian novelist, is also respected as a short-story writer. His stories include "White Nights" (1848) and "The Dream of the Ridiculous Man" (1877).

---

words for everyday use

ar • a • ble (ar′ ə bəl) *adj.*, suitable for plowing. *Arable* soil is easy to plow and good for planting crops such as wheat and corn.

1. Pakhom gets advice about the importance of being nice to sellers when buying land.
2. The Bashkirs treat Pakhom as an honored guest.

CROSS-CURRICULAR CONNECTIONS

RUSSIAN LITERATURE. The first literary giant of Russia was the poet Alexander Pushkin. He absorbed the literary traditions of the West and used them to portray Russia's frequent inner turmoil as a nation. As the founder of modern Russian literature, Pushkin was known for such works as *Eugene Onegin*. He died in 1837.

---

and talked. The merchant said he was returning from the far-off Bashkir country. There, he said, he bought thirteen thousand five hundred acres of land from the Bashkirs. And all for one thousand rubles. Pakhom began asking questions. The merchant recounted.

"You just have to be nice to the old men," he said. "I distributed about a hundred rubles' worth of oriental robes and carpets and a case of tea, and gave wine to whoever wanted it. And I got the land for less than ten kopecks an acre." He showed Pakhom the deed. "The land," it read, "lies along a river, and the steppe is all grassland."

Pakhom began asking him how, where, and what.

"The land there—" said the merchant, "you couldn't walk around it in a year. The Bashkirs own it all. And the people are as silly as sheep. You can almost get it free."

"Well," Pakhom thought, "why should I buy thirteen hundred and fifty acres for my thousand rubles and saddle myself with a debt as well, when I can really get something for a thousand rubles."

5

Pakhom asked the way to the Bashkirs and as soon as he had escorted the merchant to the door, he began getting ready to go himself. He left the house in his wife's charge, made preparations, and set off with his hired hand. They went to town, bought a case of tea, gifts, wine— everything just as the merchant had said. They traveled and traveled, traversing five hundred versts. The seventh fortnight, they arrived at Bashkir camp. Everything was just as the merchant had said. They all lived in

> *What advice does Pakhom get about buying land from the Bashkirs?*

felt tents on the steppe near a stream. They themselves neither plowed nor ate bread, but their cattle and horses wandered over the steppes in herds. Twice a day they drove the mares to the colts tethered behind the huts; they milked the mares and made *kumiss*[6] out of it. The women beat the *kumiss* and made cheese, while all the men did was drink tea and *kumiss* and eat mutton and play reed pipes. They were all polite and jolly and they made merry all summer. A completely backward people, with no knowledge of Russian, but friendly.

As soon as the Bashkirs saw Pakhom, they came out of their tents and surrounded their guest. An interpreter was found; Pakhom told him he had come for land. The Bashkirs were delighted, seized Pakhom, conducted him to one of the best tents, placed him on a carpet, put feather pillows under him, sat down in a circle around him, and began serving him tea and *kumiss*. They slaughtered a sheep and fed him mutton. Pakhom fetched his gifts from the wagon and began distributing them among the Bashkirs. When Pakhom finished presenting his gifts to them, he divided up the tea. The Bashkirs were delighted. They jabbered and jabbered among themselves, then asked the interpreter to speak.

> *How do the Bashkirs treat Pakhom?*

"They ask me to tell you that they like you," said the interpreter, "and that it is our custom to give a guest every satisfaction, and to render gifts in kind. You have presented us with gifts; now tell us what we have that you like, so we can give a gift to you."

"What I like most of all," said Pakhom, "is your land. Our land is crowded, and, furthermore, all of it has been <u>tilled</u>, while your land is plentiful and good. I've never seen the like."

6. *kumiss.* Drink made of fermented mare's or camel's milk

The interpreter translated. The Bashkirs talked and talked among themselves. Pakhom did not understand what they were saying, but he saw that they were merry, were shouting something, and laughing. Then they became silent, turned to Pakhom, and the interpreter said, "They asked me to tell you that in return for your kindness they will be glad to give you as much land as you want. Just point it out and it will be yours."

They started to talk again and began to quarrel about something. Pakhom asked what the quarrel was about. And the interpreter said, "Some say the elder must be consulted about the land, that it can't be done without him. But others say it can be done."

6

The Bashkirs were still quarreling when, suddenly, out came a man in a fox fur cap. Everyone fell silent and stood up. And the interpreter said:

"That's the elder himself."

Pakhom immediately fetched the best robe and brought it to the elder along with five pounds of tea. The elder accepted and sat down in a seat of honor. And the Bashkirs immediately started telling him something. The elder listened and listened, requested silence with a nod, and said to Pakhom in Russian:

"Well," he said. "It can be done. Choose whatever you like. Land's plentiful."

"What does that mean: take what I want," thought Pakhom. "It has to be secured somehow. Or they'll say its yours, then take it away."

Does the elder offer opposition to Pakhom's request? What concern does Pakhom have about the arrangement?

"Thank you," he said, "for your kind words. You do have a lot of land, and I need only a little. But I'd like to know which is mine. It must be measured off somehow, and secured as mine. Our lives and deaths are in God's hands. What you, good people, are giving, your children may take back."

"You're right," said the elder; "it can be secured." Pakhom said:

"I heard there was a merchant here. You gave him a little piece of land too, and made a deed. I should have the same thing."

The elder understood.

"It can all be done," he said. "We have a scribe, and we'll go to the town to affix the seals."

"And what is the price?" said Pakhom.

"We've only one price: a thousand rubles a day."

Pakhom did not understand.

What is the price of the land? What questions does Pakhom have?

"What kind of measure is that—a day? How many acres does it have?"

"That," he said, "we don't know. But we sell by the day; as much as you can walk around in a day is yours, and the price is a thousand rubles a day."

Pakhom was astonished.

"But look," he said, "a day's walking is a lot of land."

The elder laughed.

"It's all yours!" he said. "There's just one condition: if you're not back where you started in a day, your money is lost."

"And how," Pakhom said, "will you mark where I go?"

"Well, we'll stand on the spot you choose, and stay there while you walk off a circle; and you'll take a spade with you, and, where convenient, dig holes

What does Pakhom have to do? What is the one condition?

to mark your path and pile the dirt up high; then we'll drive a plow from pit to pit. Make your circle wherever you want. What you walk around is all yours, as long as you're back where you started by sundown."

Pakhom was delighted. They decided to start off early. They chatted, drank more *kumiss*, ate mutton, drank tea again; night came on. They laid down a feather bed for Pakhom, and the Bashkirs dispersed, promising to assemble the next day at dawn to set out for the starting point before sunrise.

1. Pakhom plans how much land he will acquire in a day and what he will do with the land once he gets it.
2. Pakhom first sees the Bashkir elder, then the merchant who told him about the land, then the peasant who came from the South, and finally the Devil standing in front of Pakhom's own corpse.
3. Pakhom is pleased with the land.

BIOGRAPHICAL NOTE

Tolstoy joined the Russian army in 1852. In 1854, he was commissioned as an officer and served bravely in the Crimean War until 1856. His army experiences are described in many of his stories and novels.

Tolstoy was often in opposition to the Russian government and the church. Many of his works were censored, and his followers were persecuted. Tolstoy, however, was protected from harm by his worldwide fame and the love the Russian people had for him.

7

Pakhom lay on the feather bed, unable to sleep for thinking about the land. "I'll grab off a big piece of my own," he thought. "I can walk fifty versts in a day. The days are long now; there'll be quite a bit of land in fifty versts. What's poorest, I'll sell or let to the peasants, and I'll pick out the best to settle on myself. I'll get a plow and two oxen, and hire two laborers; I'll plow over a hundred acres and put cattle to graze on the rest."

> *What does Pakhom plan as he lies in bed?*

"Whatever you walk around will be YOURS"

All night Pakhom lay awake, drifting off to sleep only just before dawn. No sooner had he fallen asleep than he started to dream. He saw himself lying in that same hut and heard someone chuckling outside. And he wanted to see who was laughing, got up, went out of the hut, and there sat the Bashkir elder himself in front of the hut with both hands holding his sides, rocking back and forth, laughing at something.

Pakhom approached him and asked: "What are you laughing at?" Then he saw that it was not the Bashkir elder, but the merchant of the other day who had come to him and told him about the land. And he had barely asked the merchant, "Have you been here long?"—when it was no longer the merchant, but the peasant who had come on foot from the south long ago.

Then Pakhom saw that it was not the peasant, but the Devil himself, laughing, horns, hoofs, and all; and in front of him lay a barefoot man in shirt and trousers. And Pakhom looked closer to see what sort of man he was. He saw it was a corpse and that it was—he himself. Horrified, Pakhom woke up. "The things one dreams," he thought. He looked around; through the open door he saw the dawn; it was already turning white. "Must rouse the people," he thought; "time to go." Pakhom got up, woke his hired hand who was asleep in the wagon, ordered the horses harnessed, and went to wake the Bashkirs.

> *Whom does he see in his dream outside the hut?*

"It's time," he said, "to go to the steppe to measure off the land."

The Bashkirs got up, assembled everything, and the elder arrived. The Bashkirs began drinking *kumiss* again, and offered Pakhom tea, but he did not want to linger.

"If we're going, let's go," he said. "It's time."

8

The Bashkirs assembled, climbed on horseback and in wagons and set off. Meanwhile, Pakhom took a spade and set off with his laborer in his own wagon. They arrived at the steppe just as day was breaking. They went up a hillock (known as a *shikhan*[7] in Bashkir). The Bashkirs climbed out of their wagons, slid down from their horses, and gathered in a group. The elder went to Pakhom and pointed.

"There," he said; "everything the eye encompasses is ours. Take your pick."

Pakhom's eyes glowed. It was all grassland, level as the palm of the hand, black as a poppy seed, and wherever there was a hollow, there was grass growing chest-high.

> *What does Pakhom think of the land?*

The elder took off his fox cap and put it on the ground.

---

7. **shikhan.** Small hill

"That," he said, "will be the marker. Leave from here; return here. Whatever you walk around will be yours."

Pakhom draw out his money, placed it on the cap, unfastened his belt, took off his outer coat, girded his belt tightly over his stomach again, put a bag of bread inside his jacket, tied a flask of water to his belt, drew his bootlegs tight, took the spade from his laborer, and got set to go. He pondered and pondered over which direction to take—it was good everywhere. He was thinking: "It's all the same: I'll head toward the sunrise." He turned to face the sun and paced restlessly, waiting for it to appear over the horizon. He was thinking: "I must lose no time. And walking's easier while it's still cold." As soon as the sun's rays spurted over the horizon, Pakhom flung the spade over his shoulder and started off across the steppe.

He walked neither quickly nor slowly. He covered a verst; stopped, dug out a hole, and piled the turf up so it could be seen. He walked further. He loosened up and lengthened his stride. He covered still more ground; dug still another pit.

Pakhom glanced back. The *shikhan* was clearly visible to the sun, and the people stood there, and the hoops of the cart wheels glittered. Pakhom guessed that he had covered about five versts. It was getting warmer; he took off his jacket, flung it over his shoulder; and went on. He covered another five versts. It was warm. He glanced at the sun—already breakfast time.

"One lap finished," thought Pakhom. "But there are four in a day; it's too early to turn around yet. I'll just take my boots off." He sat down, took them off, stuck them in his belt, and went on. Walking became easier. He thought, "I'll just cover about five more versts, then start veering left. This is a very nice spot, too good to leave out. The farther away it is, the better it gets." He walked straight on. When he glanced around, the *shikhan* was barely visible, the people looked like black ants, and there was something faintly glistening on it.

What does Pakhom notice as he continues walking?

"Well," thought Pakhom, "I've taken enough on this side; I must turn. Besides, I've been sweating—I'm thirsty." He stopped, dug a bigger hole, stacked the turf, untied his flask, and drank. Then he veered sharply to the left. On and on he went; the grass grew taller and it became hot.

Pakhom began to feel tired; he glanced at the sun—it was already lunch time. He stopped; sat on the ground; ate bread and drank water, but did not lie down. "Lie down and you'll fall asleep," he thought. After a while, he walked on. Walking was easy at first. Eating had increased his strength. But it had gotten very hot and he was becoming sleepy. Still he pressed on, thinking—an hour of suffering for a lifetime of living.

When does Pakhom begin to feel tired? What does he do?

He walked a long way in this direction too, and when he was about to turn left, he came to a damp hollow, too nice to overlook. "Flax will grow well there," he thought. Again he went straight on. He took possession of the hollow, dug a hole beyond it, and turned the second corner. Pakhom glanced back at the *shikhan*; it was hazy from the heat, something seemed to be wavering in the air, and through the haze the people were barely visible on top of the *shikhan*—fifteen versts away. "Well," thought Pakhom, "I've taken long sides, I must take this one shorter." As he walked the third side, he increased his stride. He looked at the sun—it was already approaching tea-time, and he had only covered two versts on the third side. And it was still fifteen versts to the starting point. "No," he thought, "I'll have a lopsided place, but I must go straight back so I'll arrive in time, and not take anymore. There's lots of land already." Pakhom shoveled out a hole as quickly as he could and turned straight toward the *shikhan*.

Why does Pakhom continue beyond the place where he planned to turn?

"LAND ENOUGH FOR A MAN" 547

ANSWERS TO GUIDED READING QUESTIONS

1. Pakhom notices that he is quite far from the *shikhan*.
2. Pakhom begins to feel tired around lunch time. He stops, but does not go to sleep. He keeps walking.
3. Pakhom continues because he sees a hollow too good to overlook, where he thinks flax will grow.

ANSWERS TO GUIDED READING QUESTIONS

1. Pakhom regrets taking so much land. He begins to fear he won't make it.
2. Pakhom thinks he has failed. Then he realizes it is still light at the top of the *shikhan*.
3. Pakhom has exactly six feet of land in the end.

SELECTION CHECK TEST 4.7.5 WITH ANSWERS

Checking Your Reading

1. How much land does Pakhom get in the end? **He gets six feet.**
2. Where is the Devil sitting at the beginning of the story? **He is sitting behind Pakhom's stove.**
3. How much land does Pakhom buy? **He buys forty acres.**
4. Where does Pakhom go seeking more land? **He goes to the country of the Bashkirs.**
5. What does Pakhom realize about the sun near the story's end? **He realizes that it is still shining on top of the *shikhan*.**

Vocabulary in Context

Fill in each blank below with the most appropriate word from the following Words for Everyday Use.

disparage   delegation   arable
acquit   steppe   till

1. One part of the farmer's job is to **till** the soil.
2. The **delegation** was well received by the hosts, despite the touchy nature of their business.
3. Dry, arid land is generally not **arable**.
4. The attorney asked the jury to **acquit** her client instead of sending him back to jail.
5. Corbin's remarks **disparage** the hard work everyone else has done.

Literary Tools

1. What is foreshadowing? **Foreshadowing is the act of hinting at events to occur later in the story.**
2. What is a central conflict? **A central conflict is the primary struggle dealt with in the plot of a story or drama.**
3. What is the central conflict of "Land Enough for a Man"? **The central conflict is Pakhom's struggle with his own greed.**

As Pakhom walked straight toward the *shikhan*, he began having difficulties. He was perspiring, and his bare legs were cut and bruised and were beginning to fail him. He wanted to rest but could not—otherwise he would not arrive before sunset. The sun would not wait; it continued sinking, sinking. "Ah," he thought, "if only I haven't made a mistake and taken too much! What if I don't make it?" He glanced ahead at the *shikhan*, looked at the sun: the starting point was far away, and the sun was nearing the horizon.

> *What regret does Pakhom have? What does he fear?*

So Pakhom went on with difficulty; he kept increasing and increasing his stride. He walked, walked—and was still far away; he broke into a trot. He threw off his jacket, dropped his boots and flask; he threw off his cap, keeping only his spade to lean on. "Ah," he thought, "I've been too greedy, I've ruined the whole thing, I won't get there by sundown." And fear shortened his breath even more. Pakhom ran; his shirt and trousers clung to his body with sweat; his mouth was parched. His chest felt as though it had been inflated by the blacksmith's bellows; a hammer beat in his heart; and his legs no longer seemed to belong to his body—they were collapsing under him. Pakhom began to worry about dying of strain.

He was afraid of dying, but unable to stop. "I've run so far," he thought. "I'd be a fool to stop now." He ran and ran, and was very close when he heard a screeching—the Bashkirs shrieking at him—his heart became even more inflamed by their cries. Pakhom pressed forward with his remaining strength, but the sun was already reaching the horizon; and, slipping behind a cloud, it became large, red, and bloody. Now it was beginning to go down. Although the sun was close to setting, Pakhom was no longer far from the starting point either. He could

already see the people on the *shikhan* waving their arms at him, urging him on. He saw the fox cap on the ground and the money on it; and he saw the elder sitting on the ground, holding his sides with his hands. And Pakhom remembered his dream. "There is plenty of land," he thought, "if it please God to let me live on it. Oh, I've ruined myself," he thought. "I won't make it."

Pakhom glanced at the sun, but it had touched the earth and had already begun to slip behind the horizon which cut it into an arc. Pakhom overreached his remaining strength, driving his body forward so that his legs could barely move fast enough to keep him from falling. Just as Pakhom ran up to the base of the *shikhan*, it suddenly became dark. He glanced around—the sun had already set. Pakhom sighed. "My work has fallen through," he thought. He was about to stop when he heard the Bashkirs still shrieking. And he remembered that though it seemed below that the sun had set, it would still be shining on top of the *shikhan*. Pakhom took a deep breath and ran up the *shikhan*. It was still light there. As Pakhom reached the top, he saw the elder sitting in front of the cap, chuckling, holding his sides with his hands. Pakhom remembered his dream and groaned; his legs gave way, and he fell forward, his hands touching the cap.

> *What happens as Pakhom reaches the base of the shikhan? Why does he continue?*

"Aiee, good man!" cried the elder. "You have acquired plenty of land!"

Pakhom's laborer ran to lift him, but the blood was flowing from his mouth and he lay dead.

The Bashkirs clicked their tongues in commiseration.

The laborer took up the spade, dug Pakhom a grave just long enough to reach from his feet to his head—six feet in all—and buried him. ∎

> *How much land did Pakhom have in the end?*

Respond *to the*

SELECTION

If you could go back and talk to Pakhom before he attempts his last long walk, what advice would you give him?

Investigate, Inquire, and Imagine

Recall: GATHERING FACTS

1a. When the tale begins, what are the two sisters discussing? Where does each one live? About what does Pakhom boast?

2a. What does the small landowner agree to do with her land?

3a. Why do Pakhom's neighbors begin to dislike him? What do they do to challenge him? How does Pakhom learn of another opportunity to buy land?

Analyze: TAKING THINGS APART

4a. At the beginning of the story, all Pakhom wants is a chance to have his own land. When he finally gets some land, how do his attitude and his expectations change?

Evaluate: MAKING JUDGMENTS

5a. What is the meaning of the title? Could it have a double meaning? Explain why or why not.

→ Interpret: FINDING MEANING

1b. Who overhears Pakhom's boast? How does he respond to the boasting?

2b. Why at the end of the second part of the story has the land become "completely exceptional" to Pakhom? How does he feel?

3b. Why does Pakhom begin to feel crowded? What is his attitude toward the peasants? How does he feel as he thinks about buying more land somewhere else?

→ Synthesize: BRINGING THINGS TOGETHER

4b. How do the faces that Pakhom sees outside his hut in part seven of the story relate to different parts of the story and to the story as a whole?

→ Extend: CONNECTING IDEAS

5b. What consequences does a person's greed have for other people? What makes greed incompatible with caring for and about others?

Understanding *Literature*

FORESHADOWING. Review the definition for **foreshadowing** in the Handbook of Literary Terms. Where do you see examples of foreshadowing in this story? Do these examples prepare you for the story's ending?

CENTRAL CONFLICT. Review the definition for **central conflict** in Literary Tools in Prereading. On the surface, what is Pakhom's primary struggle? What does he claim over and over again to need? What is the story's true struggle, which takes place within Pakhom?

"LAND ENOUGH FOR A MAN" **549**

ANSWERS TO INVESTIGATE, INQUIRE, AND IMAGINE (CONT.)

EXTEND
5b. A greedy person is selfish, and a person's greed can influence him or her to acquire or possess something at all costs. The greedy person may not offer an honest trade or sale, may steal from others, and/or may use funds set aside for a legitimate purpose to acquire something else for him- or herself. A truly caring person would not be capable of dishonesty, theft, and misuse of funds because these actions hurt other people.

Answers to Understanding Literature can be found on page 550.

RESPOND TO THE SELECTION

Ask students to describe Pakhom's character. Does he deserve his fate? Why, or why not? Does his greed make him a good man, a bad man, or something in between?

ANSWERS TO INVESTIGATE, INQUIRE, AND IMAGINE

RECALL
1a. When the story begins, the sisters are discussing the differences in their lives. One sister lives in town, and the other on a farm. Pakhom boasts that there are no temptations to distract him, except wanting more land.
2a. The small landowner agrees to sell her land to the peasants.
3a. Pakhom's neighbors begin to dislike him because he sues them for trespassing on his land. They challenge him by cutting down a dozen of his linden trees. He learns of another opportunity to buy land from a traveling merchant returning from the Bashkir country.

INTERPRET
1b. The Devil overhears Pakhom's boast, and responds to it by catering to Pakhom's greed for more land. Ultimately, Pakhom's greed is what allows the Devil to get his soul.
2b. The land now seems exceptional because Pakhom owns it. He rejoices at knowing it is his forever.
3b. Pakhom begins to feel crowded because of his neighbors, who trespass on his land. He dislikes the peasants a great deal and considers them thieves. He likes the idea of buying land somewhere else because it is less crowded and he can live better.

ANALYZE
4a. After Pakhom finally gets some land, he becomes a person who is never satisfied. He always wants more land with fewer people around him, and he is never satisfied for very long with what he has.

SYNTHESIZE
4b. The faces are the guises in which the Devil has appeared in his attempt to collect Pakhom's soul.

EVALUATE
5a. Yes, the title may have a double meaning. Pakhom never seems to be satisfied with the amount of land he has. No amount of land is enough. At the end, it turns out that all he ultimately needs is six feet of land—enough for a grave.

TEACHER'S EDITION   **549**

Vocabulary
1. till
2. acquitted
3. disparage
4. overseer
5. arable
6. delegation

Writer's Journal

1. Imagine that you work for an advertising agency hired by the Bashkirs. Write an **advertisement** promoting their land to potential buyers. Include a description of the land and the terms of the selling agreement. You may want to include a warning about excessive greed.

2. Pakhom couldn't sleep most of the night before he was to walk the land. Imagine that he wrote in his journal about his good fortune, his thoughts about the amount of land he might acquire, what he might do with the land, his feelings towards the Bashkirs, etc. Write his **journal entry**.

3. The story of Pakhom teaches a lesson about one aspect of human nature. Create a short **lesson tale** or **parable** of your own. Like Tolstoy's tale, try to teach your lesson through the experience of a single character. Your character may be based on a real person, or he or she may be entirely fictional. Prior to writing your story, it may be helpful to make a diagram of what is going to happen in the story. Refer to the Language Arts Survey 2.20, "Story Maps."

Integrating the Language Arts

Vocabulary

SYNONYMS. Test your knowledge of the "Words for Everyday Use" from the story by filling in a vocabulary word for each of the underlined words for phrases in the sentences below.

1. It was difficult to <u>cultivate</u> the soil after such a dry winter and spring.

2. The court <u>cleared</u> the prisoner of the felony charges.

3. The candidate attempted to <u>discredit</u> her opponent's political experience.

4. Employees requesting vacation days or shift changes must see the plant <u>supervisor</u>.

5. The land on the mountainside was not <u>fit for plowing</u>; it was too rocky.

6. A student <u>group chosen to represent others</u> went to the school board meeting to object to the proposed budget cuts.

Media Literacy

SIMPLE LIVING. Though Leo Tolstoy was born to a wealthy family, as an older man he sold his land and most of his possessions and donated his money in order to lead a more simple, moral life. Possibly as a response to the rampant materialism of the last decades in the United States, the idea of simple living is becoming more attractive in modern days. Although most writers are not calling for the drastic changes that Tolstoy made in his later life, many are suggesting smaller living spaces, fewer possessions, and a change from high-powered, high-wage, stressful jobs to lower paying but more meaningful vocations. Check recent periodicals or Internet sites to find out what some of these advocates for simple living have to say. One site you may want to visit is *Simple Living: The Journal of Voluntary Simplicity* at http://www.simpleliving.com/. What are some of the suggested steps to take or changes to make if individuals or families want to live a simple life?

Study and Research

TOLSTOY'S RUSSIA. Research life in Russia during the time period that Tolstoy wrote "Land Enough for a Man" (1885). What was the class structure? How was life different for the people who worked the land and those who lived in the towns? What types of crops were grown? What kind of transportation was used? Who ruled Russia, and what was the political climate like? Did children go to school? Compile your findings in a written report.

ANSWERS TO UNDERSTANDING LITERATURE

FORESHADOWING. Foreshadowing occurs at the beginning of the story, when the Devil decides to punish Pakhom through his land. It also occurs in Pakhom's dream, when he sees his body at the Devil's feet. This latter example does prepare the reader for the end of the story.

CENTRAL CONFLICT. Pakhom's primary struggle is with his own greed and selfishness. He claims over and over to need more land, but the story's true struggle, as reflected within the character, is the individual's struggle to find value and satisfaction that does not come from material wealth.

"the thief"
by Junichiro Tanizaki

Reader's resource

The characters in "The Thief" are created by the use of two literary techniques of characterization: portrayal of characters' behavior and representations of characters' internal states. For the latter, Tanizaki uses internal monologue to reveal many of the narrator's private thoughts and emotions.

Central to the selection are the contradictory topics of trust and betrayal. The character of the narrator, an embodiment of both topics, tests the trust of his friends—and that of the reader as well.

About the AUTHOR

Junichiro Tanizaki (1886–1965) was born in Tokyo, Japan. His early and late works, particularly the novels *The Key* and *Diary of a Mad Old Man,* reveal his keen storytelling skills and his interest in the nature of beauty. The work of Tanizaki's middle period, generally considered to coincide with his move in 1923 to the more conservative area of Osaka, Japan, explores classical Japanese culture, including traditional Japanese ideals of beauty. The works from this period include *Some Prefer Nettles, A Portrait of Shunkin,* and *The Makioka Sisters.*

Reader's Journal

How would you react if a friend asked you to keep something secret that you knew was wrong?

Literary TOOLS

IRONY. **Irony** is a difference between appearance and reality. Types of irony include the following:

- *dramatic irony,* in which something is known by the reader or audience but unknown to the characters

- *verbal irony,* in which a statement is made that implies its opposite

- *irony of situation,* in which an event occurs that violates the expectations of the characters, the reader, or the audience.

Try to identify the type of irony used in this story.

INTERNAL MONOLOGUE. An **internal monologue** presents the private sensations, thoughts, and emotions of a character. The reader is allowed to step inside the character's mind and overhear what is going on in there. As you read, note how the narrator's internal monologues reveal different internal states of his mind.

Organizer

Make a cluster chart like the one below to document the narrator's thoughts.

I thought he flashed a suspicious look at me.

Narrator's internal monologues

ADDITIONAL RESOURCES

UNIT 7 RESOURCE BOOK
- Selection Worksheet 7.4
- Selection Check Test 4.7.7
- Selection Test 4.7.8

GRAPHIC ORGANIZER

Students may include the following items in their cluster charts:

- "If I were a prudent, clever thief— no I mustn't put it that way—if I were a thief with the least bit of conscience and consideration for other people, I'd try to keep my friendships untarnished, try to be open with my friends, treat them with a sincerity and warmth that I need never be ashamed of, while carrying out my thefts in secrecy."
- "Perhaps I'd be what people call 'a brazen thief,' but if you look at it from the thief's point of view, it's the most honest attitude to take."
- "But now, if only in my own mind, I was an outcast."
- "The more he trusted me, with his frank, open attitude, the more the gulf between us deepened."

READER'S JOURNAL

Students might imagine that a friend has betrayed their trust and write a letter to that person.

GOALS/OBJECTIVES

Studying this lesson will enable students to
- appreciate a story told by an unreliable narrator
- describe Junichiro Tanizaki's literary accomplishments
- define *internal monologue* and *irony* and identify these techniques as they encounter them in their reading

- write and perform a dramatic skit
- build vocabulary by learning the meanings of prefixes and suffixes

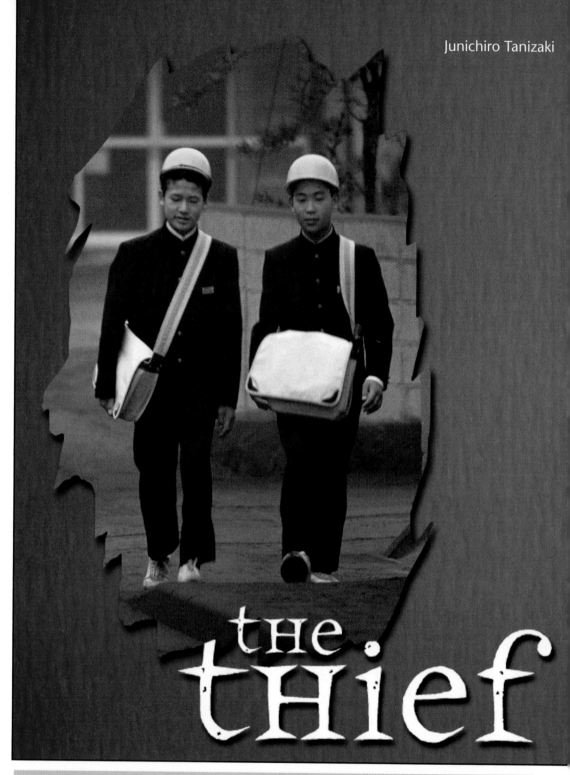

Junichiro Tanizaki

the thief

VOCABULARY FROM THE SELECTION

apt	emphatically	muster	proctor	taunting
brazen	enshroud	ominously	prudent	wry
confront	gullible	ostracize	reproachful	
debase	haughtily	persecute	roundabout	
elation	imploring	perverse	saunter	
elite	magnanimity	prestige	suppress	

It was years ago, at the school where I was preparing for Tokyo Imperial University. My dormitory roommates and I used to spend a lot of time at what we called "candle-light study" (there was very little studying to it), and one night, long after lights-out, the four of us were doing just that, huddled around a candle talking on and on.

I recall that we were having one of our confused, heated arguments about love—a problem of great concern to us in those days. Then, by a natural course of development, the conversation turned to the subject of crime: we found ourselves talking about such things as swindling, theft, and murder.

"Of all crimes, the one we're most likely to commit is murder." It was Higuchi, the son of a well-known professor, who declared this. "But I don't believe I'd ever steal—I just couldn't do it. I think I could be friends with any other kind of person, but a thief seems to belong to a different species." A shadow of distaste darkened his handsome features. Somehow that frown emphasized his good looks.

> *What does Higuchi say about thieves and stealing?*

"I hear there's been a rash of stealing in the dormitory lately." This time it was Hirata who spoke. "Isn't that so?" he asked, turning to Nakamura, our other roommate.

> *What has been happening in the dormitory lately?*

"Yes, and they say it's one of the students."

"How do they know?" I asked.

"Well, I haven't heard all the details—" Nakamura dropped his voice to a confidential whisper. "But it's happened so often it must be an inside job."

"Not only that," Higuchi put in, "one of the fellows in the north wing was just going into his room the other day when somebody pushed the door open from the inside, caught him with a hard slap in the face, and ran away down the hall. He chased after him, but by the time he got to the bottom of the stairs the other one was out of sight. Back in his room, he found his trunk and bookshelves in a mess, which proves it was the thief."

"Did he see his face?"

"No, it all happened too fast, but he says he looked like one of us, the way he was dressed. Apparently he ran down the hall with his coat pulled up over his head—the one thing sure is that his coat had a wisteria crest."[1]

"A wisteria crest?" said Hirata. "You can't prove anything by that." Maybe it was only my imagination, but I thought he flashed a suspicious look at me. At the same moment I felt that I instinctively made a <u>wry</u> face, since my own family crest is a wisteria design. It was only by chance that I wasn't wearing my crested coat that night.

"If he's one of us, it won't be easy to catch him. Nobody wants to believe there's a thief among us." I was trying to get over my embarrassment because of that moment of weakness.

> *What does the narrator say about catching a thief?*

"No, they'll get him in a couple of days," Higuchi said <u>emphatically</u>. His eyes were sparkling. "This is a secret, but they say he usually steals things in the dressing room of the bathhouse,[2] and for two or three days now the <u>proctors</u> have been keeping watch. They hide overhead and look down through a little hole."

---

1. **wisteria crest.** *Wisteria*—bluish-white or purplish flower native to the eastern United States and eastern Asia; *crest*—symbol or emblem of a family
2. **bathhouse.** Public bathing place. In Japan, bathhouses were common at the time this story was written.

---

words for everyday use	**wry** (rī) *adj.*, twisted or distorted. *Emma assumed a <u>wry</u> expression when she was asked her age.* **em • phat • i • cal • ly** (em fat' ik lē) *adv.*, in a forceful manner. *"That's my toy!" the child cried <u>emphatically</u>.* **proc • tor** (präk' tər) *n.*, school official who supervises students. *The <u>proctor</u> will be meeting with the parents of several students to discuss disciplinary problems.*

"Oh? Who told you that?" Nakamura asked.

"One of the proctors. But don't go around talking about it."

"If *you* know so much, the thief probably knows it too!" said Hirata, looking disgusted.

Here I must explain that Hirata and I were not on very good terms. In fact, by that time we barely tolerated each other. I say "we," but it was Hirata who had taken a strong dislike to me. According to a friend of mine, he once remarked scornfully that I wasn't what everyone seemed to think I was, that he'd had a chance to see through me. And again: "I'm sick of him. He'll never be a friend of mine. It's only out of pity that I have anything to do with him."

How do the narrator and Hirata get along? What has Hirata said about the narrator?

He only said such things behind my back; I never heard them from him directly, though it was obvious that he loathed me. But it wasn't in my nature to demand an explanation. "If there's something wrong with me he ought to say so," I told myself. "If he doesn't have the kindness to tell me what it is, or if he thinks I'm not worth bothering with, then I won't think of *him* as a friend either." I felt a little lonely when I thought of his contempt for me, but I didn't really worry about it.

Hirata had an admirable physique and was the very type of masculinity that our school prides itself on, while I was skinny and pale and high-strung. There was something basically incompatible about us: I had to resign myself to the fact that we lived in separate worlds. Furthermore, Hirata was a judo[3] expert of high rank and displayed his muscles as if to say: "Watch out, or I'll give you a thrashing!" Perhaps it seemed cowardly of me to take such a meek atti-

In what way are the narrator and Hirata different?

tude toward him, and no doubt I *was* afraid of his physical strength; but fortunately I was quite indifferent to matters of trivial pride or <u>prestige</u>. "I don't care how contemptuous the other fellow is; as long as I can go on believing in myself, I don't need to feel bitter toward him." That was how I made up my mind, and so I was able to match Hirata's arrogance with my own cool <u>magnanimity</u>. I even told one of the other boys: "I can't help it if Hirata doesn't understand me, but I appreciate his good points anyway." And I actually believed it. I never considered myself a coward. I was even rather conceited, thinking I must be a person of noble character to be able to praise Hirata from the bottom of my heart.

"A wisteria crest?" That night, when Hirata cast his sudden glance at me, the malicious look in his eyes set my nerves on edge. What could that look possibly mean? Did he know that my family crest was wisteria? Or did I take it that way simply because of my own private feelings? If Hirata suspected *me*, how was I to handle the situation? Perhaps I should laugh good-naturedly and say: "Then I'm under suspicion too, because I have the same crest." If the others laughed along with me, I'd be all right. But suppose one of them, say Hirata, only began looking grimmer and grimmer—what then? When I visualized that scene I couldn't very well speak out impulsively.

Why does the narrator suddenly feel he is under suspicion?

It sounds foolish to worry about such a thing, but during that brief silence all sorts of thoughts raced through my mind. "In this kind of situation what difference is there, really, between an innocent man and an actual criminal?" By then I

---

3. **judo.** Martial art that involves subtle methods of holding and overpowering an opponent

felt that I was experiencing a criminal's anxiety and isolation. Until a moment ago I had been one of their friends, one of the <u>elite</u> of our famous school. But now, if only in my own mind, I was an outcast. It was absurd, but I suffered from my inability to confide in them. I was uneasy about Hirata's slightest mood—Hirata who was supposed to be my equal.

What emotions is the narrator experiencing?

"A thief seems to belong to a different species." Higuchi had probably said this casually enough, but now his words echoed <u>ominously</u> in my mind.

"A thief belongs to a different species. . . ." A thief! What a detestable name to be called! I suppose what makes a thief different from other men is not so much his criminal act itself as his effort to hide it at all costs, the strain of trying to put it out of his mind, the dark fears that he can never confess. And now I was becoming <u>enshrouded</u> by that darkness. I was trying not to believe that I was under suspicion; I was worrying about fears that I could not admit to my closest friend. Of course it must have been because Higuchi trusted me that he told us what he'd heard from the proctor. "Don't go around talking about it," he had said, and I was glad. But why should I feel glad? I thought. After all, Higuchi has never suspected me. Somehow I began to wonder about his motive for telling us.

It also struck me that if even the most virtuous person has criminal tendencies, maybe I wasn't the only one who imagined the possibility of being a thief. Maybe the others were experiencing a little of the same discomfort, the same <u>elation</u>. If so, then Higuchi, who had been singled out by the proctor to share his secret, must have felt very proud. Among the four of us it was he who was most trusted, he who was thought least likely to belong to that "other species." And if he won that trust because he came from a wealthy family and was the son of a famous professor, then I could hardly avoid envying him. Just as his social status improved his moral character, so my own background—I was acutely conscious of being a scholarship student, the son of a poor farmer—<u>debased</u> mine. For me to feel a kind of awe in his presence had nothing to do with whether or not I was a thief. We *did* belong to different species. I felt that the more he trusted me, with his frank, open attitude, the more the gulf between us deepened. The more friendly we tried to be, joking with each other in apparent intimacy, gossiping and laughing together, the more the distance between us increased. There was nothing I could do about it.

What is the narrator's background? How is it different from the background of Higuchi?

For a long time afterward I worried about whether or not I ought to wear that coat of mine with the "wisteria crest." Perhaps if I wore it around nonchalantly no one would pay any attention. But suppose they looked at

What did the narrator worry about wearing?

"a thief belongs to a different species."

ANSWERS TO GUIDED READING QUESTIONS

1. The narrator is experiencing a criminal's anxiety and isolation.
2. The narrator comes from a poor, working-class family. Higuchi comes from a wealthy family and is the son of a famous professor.
3. The narrator worried about wearing his coat with the wisteria crest.

INTERNET RESOURCES

Students can learn more about crime prevention, including how to protect personal property and keep safe while traveling or remaining at home. A good place to start is the **National Crime Prevention Council On-Line Resource Center**, www.ncpc.org. Many law enforcement agencies have Internet sites as well that provide useful information. Students can choose one of the following ways to share the tips they learn:

- Create a booklet about protecting against theft
- Make posters about safeguarding home and property
- Write a series of public service announcements that give crime prevention tips

ANSWERS TO GUIDED READING QUESTIONS

1. The narrator says "spoiling a friendship" is a worse sin than stealing from a friend.
2. The narrator's thoughts make him more and more aware of the distance between him and his friends. He feels like a "full-fledged thief."
3. Nakamura tells the narrator that the proctors suspect him of being the thief.

LITERARY TECHNIQUE

DIALOGUE. Dialogue is conversation involving two or more people or characters. Dialogue is set apart by quotation marks and sometimes by tag lines, or expressions which indicate who is speaking and sometimes the manner in which the speaking is done. How does the content of the dialogue in this story differ from the narrator's internal monologue?

Answer
The dialogue does not reveal much about the narrator and his fears, which are revealed in his internal monologues. Some dialogue actually conflicts with the feelings and thoughts expressed in the narrator's internal monologue.

ADDITIONAL QUESTIONS AND ACTIVITIES

What do Nakamura's comments and reactions reveal about him and his beliefs about friendship? Provide evidence to support your answer.

Answer
Nakamura's comments and reactions reveal that he is a sympathetic and caring friend. The painful sigh and tears that precede his confession of the proctors' suspicions show that he is genuinely upset that his friend has been accused. He also tells the narrator that "I've never suspected you for a minute" and doesn't want the narrator to be angry with him.

me as much as to say: "Ah, he's wearing it!" Some would suspect me, or try to suppress their doubts of me, or feel sorry for me because I was under suspicion. If I became embarrassed and uneasy not only with Hirata and Higuchi but with all the students, and if I then felt obliged to put my coat away, that would seem even more sinister. What I dreaded was not the bare fact of being suspect, but all the unpleasant emotions that would be stirred up in others. If I were to cause doubt in other people's minds, I would create a barrier between myself and those who had always been my friends. Even theft itself was not as ugly as the suspicions that would be aroused by it. No one would want to think of me as a thief: as long as it hadn't been proved, they'd want to go on associating with me as freely as ever, forcing themselves to trust me. Otherwise, what would friendship mean? Thief or not, I might be guilty of a worse sin than stealing from a friend: the sin of spoiling a friendship. Sowing seeds of doubt about myself was criminal. It *was* worse than stealing. If I were a prudent, clever thief—no, I mustn't put it that way—if I were a thief with the least bit of conscience and consideration for other people, I'd try to keep my friendships untarnished, try to be open with my friends, treat them with a sincerity and warmth that I need never be ashamed of, while carrying out my thefts in secrecy. Perhaps I'd be what people call "a brazen thief," but if you look at it from the thief's point of view, it's the most honest attitude to take. "It's true that I steal, but it's equally true that I value my friends," such a man would say. "That is typical of a thief, that's why he belongs to a different species." Anyhow, when I started thinking that way, I couldn't help becoming more and more aware of the distance between me and my

> *What does the narrator say is a worse sin than stealing from a friend?*

friends. Before I knew it I felt like a full-fledged thief.

> *What effect do the narrator's thoughts have on him?*

One day I mustered up my courage and wore the crested coat out on the school grounds. I happened to meet Nakamura, and we began walking along together.

"By the way," I remarked, "I hear they haven't caught the thief yet."

"That's right," Nakamura answered, looking away.

"Why not? Couldn't they trap him at the bathhouse?"

"He didn't show up there again, but you still hear about lots of things being stolen in other places. They say the proctors called Higuchi in the other day and gave him the devil for letting their plan leak out."

"Higuchi?" I felt the color drain from my face.

"Yes. . . ." He sighed painfully, and a tear rolled down his cheek. "You've got to forgive me! I've kept it from you till now, but I think you ought to know the truth. You won't like this, but you're the one the proctors suspect. I hate to talk about it—I've never suspected you for a minute. I believe in you. And because I believe in you, I just had to tell you. I hope you won't hold it against me."

> *What information about the proctors does Nakamura share with the narrator?*

"Thanks for telling me. I'm grateful to you." I was almost in tears myself, but at the same time I thought: "It's come at last!" As much as I dreaded it, I'd been expecting this day to arrive.

"Let's drop the subject," said Nakamura, to comfort me. "I feel better now that I've told you."

"But we can't put it out of our minds just because we hate to talk about it. I appreciate your kindness, but I'm not the only one who's

words for everyday use	**sup • press** (sə pres´) *vt.*, keep from appearing or being known. *Although she tried to suppress her sneeze, it came out in a loud burst.* **pru • dent** (prōōd´ʼnt) *adj.*, cautious or discreet. *If you were prudent, you would save some of your money rather than spend it all.* **bra • zen** (brā´zən) *adj.*, showing no shame. *Older generations complain about the brazen behavior of today's youth.* **mus • ter** (mus´tər) *vt.*, gather together. *Can you muster the energy for a game of softball?*

556 UNIT SEVEN / THE EXAMINED LIFE

been humiliated—I've brought shame on you too, as my friend. The mere fact that I'm under suspicion makes me unworthy of friendship. Any way you look at it, my reputation is ruined. Isn't that so? I imagine you'll turn your back on me too."

"I swear I never will—and I don't think you've brought any shame on me." Nakamura seemed alarmed by my reproachful tone. "Neither does Higuchi. They say he did his best to defend you in front of the proctors. He told them he'd doubt himself before he doubted you."

"But they still suspect me, don't they? There's no use trying to spare my feelings. Tell me everything you know. I'd rather have it that way."

Then Nakamura hesitantly explained: "Well, it seems the proctors get all kinds of tips. Ever since Higuchi talked too much that night there haven't been any more thefts at the bathhouse, and that's why they suspect you."

"But I wasn't the only one who heard him!"— I didn't say this, but the thought occurred to me immediately. It made me feel even more lonely and wretched.

"But how did they know Higuchi told us? There were only the four of us that night, so if nobody else knew it, and if you and Higuchi trust me—"

"You'll have to draw your own conclusions," Nakamura said, with an imploring look. "You know who it is. He's misjudged you, but I don't want to criticize him."

What has Hirata shared with the proctors?

A sudden chill came over me. I felt as if Hirata's eyes were glaring into mine.

"Did you talk to him about me?"

"Yes. . . . But I hope you realize that it isn't easy, since I'm his friend as well as yours. In fact, Higuchi and I had a long argument with him last night, and he says he's leaving the dormitory. So I have to lose one friend on account of another."

I took Nakamura's hand and gripped it hard. "I'm grateful for friends like you and Higuchi," I said, tears streaming from my eyes. Nakamura cried too. For the first time in my life I felt that I was really experiencing the warmth of human compassion. This was what I had been searching for while I was tormented by my sense of helpless isolation. No matter how vicious a thief I might be, I could never steal anything from Nakamura.

After a while I said: "To tell you the truth, I'm not worth the trouble I'm causing you. I can't stand by in silence and see you two lose such a good friend because of someone like me. Even though he doesn't trust me, I still respect him. He's a far better man than I am. I recognize his value as well as anyone. So why don't I move out instead, if it's come to that? Please—let *me* go, and you three can keep on living together. Even if I'm alone I'll feel better about it."

"But there's no reason for you to leave," said Nakamura, his voice charged with emotion. "I recognize his good points too, but you're the one that's being persecuted. I won't side with him when it's so unfair. If *you* leave, *we* ought to leave too. You know how stubborn he is—once he's made up his mind to go he's not apt to change it. Why not let him do as he pleases? We might as well wait for him to come to his senses and apologize. That shouldn't take very long anyway."

"But he'll never come back to apologize. He'll go on hating me forever."

"THE THIEF" 557

ANSWER TO GUIDED READING QUESTION

1. Hirata has told the proctors that the narrator was present when Higuchi told of the proctors' plan and that he suspects the narrator of the thefts.

ADDITIONAL QUESTIONS AND ACTIVITIES

After Nakamura tells the narrator that Hirata has reported his suspicions to the proctors, Nakamura tells the narrator, "it isn't easy, since I'm his friend as well as yours… So I have to lose one friend on account of another." Have students write about or discuss this moral dilemma. Have they ever been in a similar situation with friends or family members? What was the source of the conflict? How did they resolve the conflict? Do they wish the situation had turned out differently?

LITERARY TECHNIQUE

POINT OF VIEW. Point of view is the vantage point from which a story is told. This story is told from a first-person limited point of view, meaning that the narrator can only reveal his thoughts and feelings and not those of any other character. How does this point of view affect the story? How does it affect your impression of the events, the narrator, and the other characters?
Answers
The first-person limited point of view restricts the reader to knowing just the narrator's opinions, thoughts, and feelings. The reader must trust the narrator because he is the only source of information.

1. The narrator decides not to leave because he would be disregarding his friends' kindness and making himself seem guilty.
2. The narrator finds money orders in Hirata's desk. He puts one of the money orders into his pocket and goes to bury it with the other things he stole. Hirata catches him.

LITERARY TECHNIQUE

MOOD. **Mood,** or **atmosphere,** is the emotion created in the reader by part or all of a literary work. A writer creates a mood with carefully chosen, concrete details. What mood is created by the following details: "It was evening and a light mist hung over the school grounds: we seemed to be on an island surrounded by endless gray seas"?

Answer
These details create an isolated mood, which reflects the narrator's loneliness. The image of an island underscores the narrator's belief that the students are ostracizing him.

ADDITIONAL QUESTIONS AND ACTIVITIES

Students in small groups can discuss the narrator's response to Hirata's punishment: "Somehow the pain was not wholly unpleasant. I felt suddenly relieved of the staggering burden I had been carrying." Why does he call it a "staggering burden"?

Answer
Students might surmise that the narrator wanted to be caught, that the "staggering burden" of concealing his identity in the face of growing suspicion had become too great. They might also suggest that the "staggering burden" is the guilt he feels for deceiving his friends.

Nakamura seemed to assume that I felt resentful toward Hirata. "Oh, I don't think so," he said quickly. "He'll stick to his word—that's both his strength and his weakness—but once he knows he's wrong he'll come and apologize, and make a clean breast of it. That's one of the likable things about him."

"It would be fine if he did . . . ," I said thoughtfully. "He may come back to you, but I don't believe he'll ever make friends with me again. . . . But you're right, he's really likable. I only wish he liked me too."

Nakamura put his hand on my shoulder as if to protect his poor friend, as we plodded listlessly along on the grass. It was evening and a light mist hung over the school grounds: we seemed to be on an island surrounded by endless gray seas. Now and then a few students walking the other way would glance at me and go on. They already know, I thought; they're ostracizing me. I felt an overwhelming loneliness.

That night Hirata seemed to have changed his mind; he showed no intention of moving. But he refused to speak to us—even to Higuchi and Nakamura. Yet for me to leave at this stage was impossible, I decided. Not only would I be disregarding the kindness of my friends, I would be making myself seem all the more guilty. I ought to wait a little longer.

Why does the narrator decide not to leave?

"Don't worry," my two friends were forever telling me. "As soon as they catch him the whole business will clear up." But even after another week had gone by, the criminal was still at large and the thefts were as frequent as ever. At last even Nakamura and Higuchi lost some money and a few books.

"Well, you two finally got it, didn't you? But I have a feeling the rest of us won't be touched." I remember Hirata's taunting look as he made this sarcastic remark.

After supper Nakamura and Higuchi usually went to the library, and Hirata and I were left to confront each other. I found this so uncomfortable that I began spending my evenings away from the dormitory too, either going to the library or taking long walks. One night around nine-thirty I came back from a walk and looked into our study. Oddly enough, Hirata wasn't there, nor did the others seem to be back yet. I went to look in our bedroom, but it was empty too. Then I went back to the study and over to Hirata's desk. Quietly I opened his drawer and ferreted out the registered letter that had come to him from his home a few days ago. Inside the letter were three ten-yen money orders, one of which I leisurely removed and put in my pocket. I pushed the drawer shut again and sauntered out into the hall. Then I went down to the yard, cut across the tennis court, and headed for the dark weedy hollow where I always buried the things I stole. But at that moment someone yelled: "Thief!" and flew at me from behind, knocking me down with a blow to my head. It was Hirata.

What does the narrator find in Hirata's desk? What does he do? Who catches him?

"Come on, let's have it! Let's see what you stuck in your pocket!"

"All right, all right, you don't have to shout like that," I answered calmly, smiling at him. "I admit I stole your money order. If you ask for it, I'll give it back to you, and if you tell me to come with you I'll go anywhere you say. So we understand each other, don't we? What more do you want?"

Hirata seemed to hesitate, but soon began furiously raining blows on my face. Somehow the pain was not wholly unpleasant. I felt suddenly relieved of the staggering burden I had been carrying.

---

words for everyday use	
os • tra • cize (äs´trə sīz´) *vt.*, banish or exclude. *Because of misconceptions about leprosy, lepers used to be <u>ostracized</u> from their communities.*
taunt • ing (tônt in) *adj.*, in a reproachful or sarcastic manner. *The <u>taunting</u> heckler drove the comedian from the stage.*
con • front (kən frunt´) *vt.*, meet face to face. *In tonight's match, the boxers will <u>confront</u> each other for the first time.*
saun • ter (sôn´tər) *vi.*, stroll. *The fashion models <u>sauntered</u> down the runway.*

"There's no use beating me up like this, when I fell right into your trap for you. I made that mistake because you were so sure of yourself—I thought: 'Why the devil can't I steal from *him*?' But now you've found me out, so that's all there is to it. Later on we'll laugh about it together."

I tried to shake Hirata's hand goodnaturedly, but he grabbed me by the collar and dragged me off toward our room. That was the only time Hirata seemed contemptible in my eyes.

"Hey, you fellows, I've caught the thief! You can't say I was taken in by him!" Hirata swaggered into our room and shoved me down in front of Naka-mura and Higuchi, who were back from the library. Hearing the commotion, the other boys in the dormi-tory came swarm-ing around our doorway.

> *How does the narrator feel when he is caught by Hirata?*

"i'm sorry, but stealing is one thing i can't control."

"Hirata's right!" I told my two friends, picking myself up from the floor. "I'm the thief." I tried to speak in my nor-mal tone, as casually as ever, but I realized that my face had gone pale.

"I suppose you hate me," I said to them. "Or else you're ashamed of me. . . . You're both hon-est, but you're certainly <u>gullible</u>. Haven't I been telling you the truth over and over again? I even said: 'I'm not the person you think I am. Hirata's the man to trust. He'll never be taken in.' But you didn't understand. I told you: 'Even if you become friendly with Hirata again, he'll never make friends with *me*.' I went as far as to say: 'I

know better than anyone what a fine fellow Hirata is!' Isn't that so? I've never lied to you, have I? You may ask why I didn't come out and tell you the whole truth. You probably think I was deceiving you after all. But try looking at it from my position. I'm sorry, but stealing is one thing I can't control. Still, I didn't like to deceive you, so I told you the truth in a <u>roundabout</u> way. I couldn't be any more hon-est than that—it's your fault for not taking my hints. Maybe you think I'm just being <u>perverse</u>, but I've never been more serious. You'll probably ask why I don't quit stealing, if I'm so anxious to be honest. But that's not a fair question. You see, I was born a thief. I tried to be as sincere as I could with you under the circum-stances. There was nothing else I could do. Even then my con-science bothered me—didn't I ask you to let *me* move out, instead of Hirata? I wasn't try-ing to fool you, I really wanted to do it for your sake. It's true that I stole from you, but it's also true that I'm your friend. I appeal to your friend-ship: I want you to understand that even a thief has feelings."

> *In what way does the narrator believe he has been truthful? Why does he believe he cannot stop stealing?*

Nakamura and Higuchi stood there in silence, blinking with astonishment.

"Well, I can see you think I've got a lot of nerve. You just don't understand me. I guess it can't be helped, since you're of a different species." I smiled to conceal my bitterness, and added: "But since I'm your friend, I'll warn you

words for everyday use	**gul • li • ble** (gul´ə bəl) *adj.*, easily cheated or tricked. *Con artists take advantage of <u>gullible</u> people.*
	round • a • bout (round´ə bout) *adj.*, not straightforward; indirect. *I wish you'd stop being <u>roundabout</u> and simply say what's on your mind.*
	per • verse (pər vʉrs´) *adj.*, deviating from what is considered right or good. *His sense of morality is so <u>perverse</u> that he no longer recognizes right from wrong.*

---

1. The narrator feels somewhat relieved when he is caught by Hirata.
2. The narrator believes he has been truthful because he has attested to Hirata's good judgment and gave his friends "hints." He believes he cannot stop stealing because he "was born a thief."

SELECTION CHECK TEST 4.7.7 WITH ANSWERS

Checking Your Reading
1. What do the narrator and his roommates do during the "candlelight study"? **They talk instead of studying.**
2. What family crest does the narrator wear on his coat? **He wears a wisteria crest.**
3. Where do most of the thefts occur? **They occur in the bathhouse.**
4. Whom does Hirata suspect is the thief? **Hirata suspects the narrator is the thief.**
5. What has the narrator stolen when he gets caught? **He has stolen a money order.**

Vocabulary in Context
Fill in each blank below with the most appropriate word from the following Words for Everyday Use.

taunting wry prestige
gullible brazen reproachful

1. Corey stammered an apology when met with Ursula's **reproachful** look.
2. There is no prize money, but the award carries significant **prestige**.
3. Try as he might, Clark found it difficult to ignore Regina's teasing and **taunting**.
4. Don't be **gullible** and fall for every old story in the book.
5. The **brazen** squirrel came and ate food right off my plate.

Literary Tools
1. In which type of irony is a statement made that implies its opposite? **In verbal irony a statement is made that implies its opposite.**
2. What is irony of situation? **Irony of situation is when an event occurs that violates the expectations of the characters, the reader, or the audience.**
3. Identify an example of irony of situation from this story. **The narrator being caught in the act of stealing violates the expectations of Higuchi, Nakamura, and the reader and is thus an example of irony of situation.**

SELECTION CHECK TEST 4.7.7 WITH ANSWERS (CONT.)

4. What is an internal monologue? **An internal monologue presents the private sensations, thoughts, and emotions of a character.**
5. What do the internal monologues reveal about the narrator in "The Thief"? **They reveal his growing** state of strain and fear while living under suspicion and that he does not think of himself as a thief.

1. The narrator believes Hirata to be a
   "better man" because he is able to
   see the truth in people. As an adult,
   the narrator pictures Hirata before
   he is about to commit a crime.
2. The narrator assures the reader that
   he has not written a single dishonest
   word.

RESPOND TO THE SELECTION

Pairs of students might role-play an
interview between a reporter and
one of the narrator's former
classmates. Students should ask and
answer questions about the
narrator's crimes and their effects on
his classmates.

---

that this isn't the last time a thing like this will happen. So be on your guard! You two made friends with a thief because of your gullibility. You're likely to run into trouble when you go out in the world. Maybe you get better grades in school, but Hirata is a better man. You can't fool Hirata!"

When I singled him out for praise, Hirata made a wry face and looked away. At that moment he seemed strangely ill at ease.

Many years have passed since then. I became a professional thief and have been often behind bars; yet I cannot forget those memories—especially my memories of Hirata. Whenever I am about to commit a crime I see his face before me. I see him swaggering about as <u>haughtily</u> as ever, sneering at me: "Just as I suspected!" Yes, he was a man of character with

> Why does the narrator believe Hirata to be a "better man"? As an adult, when does the narrator picture Hirata?

great promise. But the world is mysterious. My prediction that the naïve Higuchi would "run into trouble" was wrong: partly through his father's influence, he has had a brilliant career—traveling abroad, earning a doctoral degree, and today holding a high position in the Ministry of Railways. Meanwhile nobody knows what has become of Hirata. It's no wonder we think life is unpredictable.

I assure my reader that this account is true. I have not written a single dishonest word here. And, as I hoped Nakamura and Higuchi would, I hope you will believe that delicate moral scruples can exist in the heart of a thief like me.

> What does the narrator assure the reader? Do you believe him?

But perhaps you won't believe me either. Unless of course (if I may be pardoned for suggesting it) you happen to belong to my own species. ∎

words for everyday use

haugh • ti • ly (hôt´ə lē) *adv.*, in a proud or arrogant manner. *The rude man <u>haughtily</u> pushed his way to the front of the line.*

Respond *to the* SELECTION

Imagine that you are one of the narrator's friends—Nakamura, Higuchi, or Hirata. Discuss your thoughts about your friend, the thief. Express your feelings about the events related in the story.

ANSWERS TO UNDERSTANDING LITERATURE

IRONY. The event of the narrator being caught in the act of stealing violates the expectations of Higuchi, Nakamura, and the reader. This event is an example of situational irony.

INTERNAL MONOLOGUE. The narrator's internal monologue reveals his growing state of strain and fear while living under the suspicion of others. It also shows his surprise at the thought of being called a thief, which in light of the events is rather ironic, but perhaps more importantly reveals that he does not *think* of himself as a thief. A later internal monologue provides a glimpse of the narrator's belief system and his moral rationalizations: "If I were a prudent, clever

Investigate, Inquire, and Imagine

Recall: GATHERING FACTS

1a. What has been happening lately in the dormitory?

2a. What information does Higuchi provide about the thief at "candlelight study"?

3a. Who does Hirata suspect is the thief?

Interpret: FINDING MEANING

1b. What is the reason that a student is suspected of being the thief?

2b. What is the importance of the wisteria crest?

3b. What is probably the reason that Nakamura and Higuchi do not suspect the narrator?

Analyze: TAKING THINGS APART

4a. Analyze the internal conflicts the narrator experiences when he is under suspicion.

Synthesize: BRINGING THINGS TOGETHER

4b. What actions on the part of the narrator support his view that "moral scruples can exist in the heart of a thief like me"?

Perspective: LOOKING AT OTHER VIEWS

5a. Why do you think the narrator visualizes Hirata's face whenever he is about to commit a crime? What relationship between what we become and how others see us is suggested in the story?

Empathy: SEEING FROM INSIDE

5b. How important is trust in your relationship with family members? with friends? with teachers and coaches? with elected officials?

Understanding Literature

IRONY. Review the definition for **irony** in Literary Tools in Prereading. What event occurs at the end of the story that violates the expectations of Higuchi, Nakamura, and the reader? Of what type of irony is the event an example?

INTERNAL MONOLOGUE. Review the definition for **internal monologue** and the cluster chart you made for Literary Tools in Prereading. Consider one of the narrator's internal monologues:

> "A thief! What a detestable name to be called! I suppose what makes a thief different from other men is not so much his criminal act itself as his effort to hide it at all costs, the strain of trying to put it out of his mind, the dark fears that he can never confess. And now I was becoming enshrouded by that darkness. I was trying not to believe that I was under suspicion; I was worrying about fears that I could not admit to my closest friend."

What does the narrator reveal about his internal state through this monologue? Identify another internal monologue that reveals a different internal state of the narrator's mind.

ANSWERS TO UNDERSTANDING LITERATURE (CONT.)

thief—no, I mustn't put it that way—if I were a thief with the least bit of conscience and consideration for other people, I'd try to keep my friendships untarnished, try to be open with my friends, treat them with a sincerity and warmth that I need never be ashamed of, while carrying out my thefts in secrecy. Perhaps I'd be what people call 'a brazen thief,' but if you look at it from the thief's point of view, it's the most honest attitude to take."

ANSWERS TO INVESTIGATE, INQUIRE, AND IMAGINE

RECALL
1a. Lately "a rash of stealing" has taken place in the dormitory.
2a. Higuchi reveals that the proctors believe a student is suspected to be the thief. He also reveals the vital clue of the wisteria crest that is sewn on the thief's coat and the proctors' plan to hide above the bathhouse, watching for the thief.
3a. Hirata suspects the narrator is the thief.

INTERPRET
1b. A student is suspected to be the thief because "it's happened so often it must be an inside job."
2b. The wisteria crest was reportedly seen on the jacket of the thief. It is an important clue because it is specific and identifiable; the wisteria crest is also the crest of the narrator's family.
3b. Nakamura and Higuchi probably do not suspect the narrator because they are good friends—as Nakamura tells the narrator, "I believe in you."

ANALYZE
4a. The narrator is torn as to whether or not to wear the wisteria coat, and if he does wear it, how to act when others see it. He considers the possible emotional outcomes of wearing the coat.

SYNTHESIZE
4b. From the narrator's point of view, he has moral scruples because he told "the truth over and over again" when making comments such as "I'm not the person you think I am."

EVALUATE
5a. The narrator visualizes Hirata's face whenever he is about to commit a crime because the criminal action fulfills Hirata's view of him. This action suggests that one becomes the kind of person that others imagine one to be. On the other hand, the narrator wonders compellingly whether or not "even the most virtuous person has criminal tendencies." This would suggest that all humans have criminal tendencies and that it is due to the "unpredictable" nature of life whether or not those tendencies manifest themselves.

EXTEND
5b. *Responses will vary.*

ANSWERS TO INTEGRATING THE LANGUAGE ARTS

Vocabulary

magn-	great
en-	in or into
de-	down
con-	together
sup-	under
re-	back, return to previous state
im-	intensifier
-ty	quality of, condition
-ful	full of, characterized by

Speaking and Listening & Collaborative Learning

- Students should write scenes that present a conflict, a climax, and a resolution.
- Group members should collaborate on all aspects of creating the skit—brainstorming, writing, rehearsing, and presenting.

Writer's Journal

1. Imagine that you are Nakamura. People believe that your friend is a thief and your support of him is about to cost you your friendship with Hirata. Write a **letter to an advice columnist** requesting suggestions for handling this situation. Then write the **advice columnist's response**.

2. Write a page of **dialogue** based on a conversation among a group of friends who discuss a subject over the lunch table or at a sleepover. Include some internal monologue from the narrator (who may be yourself or an imagined person) who has thoughts about what his or her friends are saying but doesn't speak those thoughts out loud.

3. Imagine that you are an investigative reporter. Write a **profile** of the narrator in the story. Update the story imagining that he is currently a professional thief. Include in your profile childhood influences and experiences from the narrator's life.

Integrating the Language Arts

Vocabulary

PREFIXES AND SUFFIXES. Building vocabulary is easier if you know the building blocks of words. Many words are formed by adding prefixes or suffixes to a base word. Use a dictionary to look up the meaning of the prefixes and suffixes from the following list of vocabulary words found in this selection.

magnanimity	suppress
enshroud	reproachful
debase	imploring
confront	

Study and Research

JAPANESE EDUCATION. Research the Japanese public school system. How are classes organized? For how much of the year do students attend school? How much time are students generally expected to spend doing homework? Are boarding schools like the one described in this story common? How do Japanese schools differ from American schools? Share your findings in a written report.

Speaking and Listening & Collaborative Learning

DRAMATIC SKIT. Collaborate with three other students to write a dramatic scene that presents a meeting among the former friends—the narrator, Hirata, Nakamura, and Higuchi. (This scene will take place in the present time, many years after the school days in the dormitory.) In your scene, portray two of the characters as they are described at the end of the story—the narrator is a professional thief, and Higuchi holds a high position in the Ministry of Railways. Portray the other two characters—Hirata and Nakamura—according to what you think became of them. Write parts for each student in your group. Rehearse your skit and present it to the rest of the class.

"The Liar"
by Tobias Wolff

Reader's resource

"The Liar" is from Wolff's first collection of short stories, *In the Garden of the North American Martyrs* (1981). The subject of this story has a strong connection to Wolff's own life, since growing up he had only occasional contact with his real father, who was a habitual liar and was later imprisoned for fraud. Wolff's work often begins from his own experience, but by the time he is finished with a story, "the very act of writing has transformed the original experience into another experience, more 'real' to me than what I started with." He says, "The origins of my stories are always hard for me to pin down because the act of writing them inevitably tangles history and imagination in a way impossible for me to untangle later on. I tend to remember things in the past in narrative form, in story form, and I grew up around people who told stories all the time."

About the AUTHOR

Tobias Wolff (1945–   ) is known chiefly for his short story collections, *In the Garden of the North American Martyrs* (1981), *Back in the World* (1985), and *The Night in Question* (1996). He has also published a short novel, *The Barracks Thief* (1984), and two memoirs. Wolff won the Los Angeles Times Book Award for Biography for his first memoir *This Boy's Life* (1989), which recalled his parents' divorce and subsequent family dramas; it was also made into a movie. His second memoir, *In Pharaoh's Army: Memories of the Lost War* (1994), deals with his military service in Vietnam. Wolff won the prestigious PEN/Faulkner Award in 1985, the Saint Lawrence Award, and O. Henry Awards. Wolff teaches creative writing at Syracuse University.

Reader's Journal

Describe a time when you have been motivated to lie. If you lied, explain why. If you didn't, explain why you didn't.

Literary TOOLS

ANTIHERO. An **antihero** is a central character who lacks many of the qualities traditionally associated with heroes. An antihero may be lacking in beauty, courage, grace, intelligence, or moral scruples. Antiheroes are common figures in modern fiction and drama. As you read, consider whether or not you think the narrator of "The Liar" is an antihero.

MOTIVATION AND CHARACTERIZATION. A **motivation** is a force that moves a character to think, feel, or behave in a certain way. As you read, think of reasons why James may be telling lies. What is his motivation to do so? Keep in mind that we learn about James's motivations through **characterization**, the use of literary techniques to create a character. Writers use three major techniques to create characters: direct description, portrayal of characters' behavior, and representations of characters' internal states.

As you read, make a chart like the one below, noting the various ways in which we learn about James.

Direct description of James	Portrayal of James's behavior	James's internal state
	Writes letter saying his mother is dying	
	Says he doesn't know why he lies	

ADDITIONAL RESOURCES

UNIT 7 RESOURCE BOOK
• Selection Worksheet 7.5
• Selection Check Test 4.7.9
• Selection Test 4.7.10
• Language, Grammar, and Style Resource 3.33

GRAPHIC ORGANIZER

Direct description of James: Since the story is written in the first-person point of view, the narrator does not offer direct description of himself.
Portrayal of James's behavior: Writes fictitious letter claiming that his mother was dying; would hide to avoid getting hurt by playing rough; didn't cry at his father's funeral and showed signs of boredom during the eulogy; closed his eyes at school and refused to open them; tells morbid lies.
James's internal state: Says things were never easy between his mother and him; didn't like being thrown into the air as a child; thinks even things he does well get on his mother's nerves; thinks his mother is suspicious of him; thinks her distrust is what makes him forgetful.

READER'S JOURNAL

Students may also discuss the consequences of lying. They might consider whether there is ever a good reason to lie or if they consider all lies to be bad.

GOALS/OBJECTIVES

Studying this lesson will enable students to
• understand the motivations of the narrator
• describe Tobias Wolff's literary accomplishments
• define *antihero, motivation* and *characterization* and recognize examples of each that they encounter in their reading
• rewrite sentence fragments into complete sentences
• write a news story in two styles

ANSWERS TO GUIDED READING QUESTIONS

1. She finds a letter containing a lie.
2. They find the way she walks funny.

INDIVIDUAL LEARNING STRATEGIES

MOTIVATION
Students can write a list of "lies." These lies can be as realistic or as far-fetched as the student likes. For example, the student might write "my sister was adopted" or "my sister is an alien from the planet Zeboki." Students can save these lists in their writing portfolios as possible ideas for stories.

READING PROFICIENCY
Students should pay special attention to the Reader's Resource on the Prereading page. They should keep Wolff's ideas about writing and storytelling in mind as they read the story.

ENGLISH LANGUAGE LEARNING
Point out the following vocabulary words and expressions:
billboards—large signs for advertisements
notion—idea
persuade—convince
cradle—part of the phone where the receiver (ear and mouth piece) rest when not in use
choppy—rough
Yosemite—National Park in California
boom towns—towns that sprang up based on financial prosperity for a time
pun—play on words
staged—faked, acted
got his goat—angered or upset him
put him on the couch—psychoanalyze him, submit him to being examined by a psychiatrist
a lark—a game, fun

SPECIAL NEEDS
Students should pay special attention to the Guided Reading questions and the Recall questions in the Investigate, Inquire, and Imagine section. Remind students that James, the main character, is a liar. Some of the things he says are untrue.

ENRICHMENT
Interested students can read one of Wolff's memoirs, either *This Boy's Life* or *In Pharaoh's Army: Memories of the Lost War.* Students can give a brief report on the book they read.

the LIAR

Tobias Wolff

My mother read everything except books. Advertisements on buses, entire menus as we ate, billboards; if it had no cover it interested her. So when she found a letter in my drawer that was not addressed to her she read it. "What difference does it make if James has nothing to hide?"—that was her thought. She stuffed the letter in the drawer when she finished it and walked from room to room in the big empty house, talking to herself. She took the letter out and read it again to get the facts straight. Then, without putting on her coat or locking the door, she went down the steps and headed for the church at the end of the street. No matter how angry and confused she might be, she always went to four o'clock Mass and now it was four o'clock.

It was a fine day, blue and cold and still, but Mother walked as though into a strong wind, bent forward at the waist with her feet hurrying behind in short, busy steps. My brother and sisters and I considered this walk of hers funny and we smirked at one another when she crossed in front of us to stir the fire, or water a plant. We didn't let her catch us at it. It would have puzzled her to think that there might be anything amusing about her. Her one concession to the fact of humor was an insincere, startling laugh. Strangers often stared at her.

While mother waited for the priest, who was late, she prayed. She prayed in a familiar, orderly, firm way: first for her late husband, for my father's parents (just touching base; she had disliked them) and finally for her children in order of their ages, ending with me. Mother did not consider originality a virtue and until my name came up her prayers were exactly the same as on any other day.

> *What does the mother find in James's drawer?*

> *What do the children find funny about their mother?*

words for everyday use

smirk (smərk) *vi.,* smile in an affected or smug manner. *Phil* smirked *when he asked if he could help me with my report, insinuating I couldn't do it myself.*
con • ces • sion (kən se′ shən) *n.,* act of conceding or yielding. *Mr. Viterbo made no* concession *to caution when he drove.*

564

VOCABULARY FROM THE SELECTION

concession	grisly	loiter	pompous	shamble
consumptive	indifferent	magnanimous	psychoanalysis	smirk
discharge	indignant	mausoleum	reconciliation	underestimate
discreetly	irk	miser	relish	
eulogy	itinerary	morbidity	reproach	
furtive	leukemia	perverse	serenity	

Young Dane, c.1931. William H. Johnson. National Museum of American Art, Washington, DC.

But when she came to me she spoke up boldly. "I thought he wasn't going to do it any more. Murphy said he was cured. What am I supposed to do now?" There was <u>reproach</u> in her tone. Mother put great hope in her notion that I was cured. She regarded my cure as an answer to her prayers and by way of thanksgiving sent a lot of money to the Thomasite Indian Mission,[1] money she had been saving for a trip to Rome. She felt cheated and she let her feelings be known. When the priest came in Mother slid back on the seat and followed the Mass with concentration. After communion she began to worry again and went straight home without stopping to talk to Frances, the woman who always cornered Mother after Mass to tell about the awful things done to her by Communists, devil-worshippers, and Rosicrucians.[2] Frances watched her go with narrowed eyes.

Once in the house, Mother took the letter from my drawer and brought it into the kitchen. She held it over the stove with her fingernails, looking away so that she would not be drawn into it again, and set it on fire. When it began to burn her fingers she dropped it in the sink and watched it blacken and flutter and close upon itself like a fist. Then she washed it down the drain and called Dr. Murphy.

What does James's mother do with the letter?

---

1. **Thomasite Indian Mission.** Charity to which James's mother donates money
2. **Rosicrucians.** Followers of a movement that emphasizes psychic and spiritual enlightenment

words for everyday use

re • proach (ri prōch′) *n.*, expression of rebuke or disapproval. *According to his teachers, Sam's behavior in school was beyond <u>reproach</u>.*

565

ANSWER TO GUIDED READING QUESTION

1. She burns the letter.

INTERNET RESOURCE

Encourage students who are talented at writing fiction to enter their short stories in the Tobias Wolff Award for Fiction contest. You will find information about entering the contest at http://www.ac.wwu.edu/~bhreview/Contests/tobias-wolff.html.

ART NOTE

Young Dane, c.1931. William H. Johnson.
African-American artist William H. Johnson (1901–1970) began his career in the early days of the Harlem Renaissance and then spent many years in Europe. There, he was influenced by the paintings of Vincent van Gogh (see page 84) and Edvard Munch (see page 524), as exhibited in this expressionistic painting of a Danish boy. When he returned to New York in 1938, he began painting in a completely new style that he identified as "primitive" (see page 387), inspired by folk painting of the American South.

The letter was to my friend Ralphy in Arizona. He used to live across the street from us but he had moved. Most of the letter was about a tour we, the junior class, had taken of Alcatraz. That was all right. What got Mother was the last paragraph where I said that she had been coughing up blood and the doctors weren't sure what was wrong with her, but that we were hoping for the best.

This wasn't true. Mother took pride in her physical condition, considered herself a horse: "I'm a regular horse," she would reply when people asked about her health. For several years now I had been saying unpleasant things that weren't true and this habit of mine irked Mother greatly, enough to persuade her to send me to Dr. Murphy, in whose office I was sitting when she burned the letter. Dr. Murphy was our family physician and had no training in psychoanalysis but he took an interest in "things of the mind," as he put it. He had treated me for appendicitis and tonsilitis and Mother thought that he could put the truth into me as easily as he took things out of me, a hope Dr. Murphy did not share. He was basically interested in getting me to understand what I did, and lately he had been moving toward the conclusion that I understood what I did as well as I ever would.

What bothers James's mother about the letter?

What is Dr. Murphy's aim in treating James?

Dr. Murphy listened to Mother's account of the letter, and what she had done with it. He was curious about the wording I had used and became irritated when Mother told him she had burned it. "The point is," she said, "he was supposed to be cured and he's not."

"Margaret, I never said he was cured."

"You certainly did. Why else would I have sent over a thousand dollars to the Thomasite Mission?"

"I said that he was responsible. That means that James knows what he's doing, not that he's going to stop doing it."

"I'm sure you said he was cured."

"Never. To say that someone is cured you have to know what health is. With this kind of thing that's impossible. What do you mean by curing James, anyway?"

"You know."

"Tell me anyway."

"Getting him back to reality, what else?"

"Whose reality? Mine or yours?"

"Murphy, what are you talking about? James isn't crazy, he's a liar."

"Well, you have a point there."

"What am I going to do with him?"

"I don't think there's much you can do. Be patient."

"I've been patient."

"If I were you, Margaret, I wouldn't make too much of this. James doesn't steal, does he?"

What does Doctor Murphy think should be done about James's lying?

"Of course not."

"Or beat people up or talk back."

"No."

"Then you have a lot to be thankful for."

"I don't think I can take any more of it. That business about leukemia last summer. And now this."

"Eventually he'll outgrow it, I think."

"Murphy, he's sixteen years old. What if he doesn't outgrow it? What if he just gets better at it?"

---

words for everyday use

irk (ərk) vt., make weary, irritated, or bored. *Leslie irked her teacher when she asked to sharpen her pencil for the third time that hour.*

psy•cho•a•nal•y•sis (sī kō ə na′ lə səs) n., method of analyzing psychic phenomena and treating emotional disorders that involves treatment sessions during which the patient is encouraged to talk freely about personal experiences. *During psychoanalysis, the doctor encouraged Mr. Connell to talk about his childhood.*

leu•ke•mia (lü kē′ mē ə) n., acute or chronic disease characterized by an abnormal increase in the number of white blood cells in the tissues or blood. *Because of aggressive chemotherapy, the woman's leukemia went into remission.*

Finally Mother saw that she wasn't going to get any satisfaction from Dr. Murphy, who kept reminding her of her blessings. She said something cutting to him and he said something <u>pompous</u> back and she hung up. Dr. Murphy stared at the receiver. "Hello," he said, then replaced it on the cradle. He ran his hand over his head, a habit remaining from a time when he had hair. To show that he was a good sport he often joked about his baldness, but I had the feeling that he regretted it deeply. Looking at me across the desk, he must have wished that he hadn't taken me on. Treating a friend's child was like investing a friend's money.

According to the narrator, what is treating a friend's child like?

"I don't have to tell you who that was."

I nodded.

Dr. Murphy pushed his chair back and swiveled it around so he could look out the window behind him, which took up most of the wall. There were still a few sailboats out on the Bay, but they were all making for shore. A woolly gray fog had covered the bridge and was moving in fast. The water seemed calm from this far up, but when I looked closely I could see white flecks everywhere, so it must have been pretty choppy.

"I'm surprised at you," he said. "Leaving something like that lying around for her to find. If you really have to do these things you could at least be kind and do them <u>discreetly</u>. It's not easy for your mother, what with your father dead and all the others somewhere else."

FOR SEVERAL YEARS NOW I HAD BEEN SAYING UNPLEASANT THINGS THAT WEREN'T TRUE . . . .

"I know. I didn't mean for her to find it."

"Well." He tapped his pencil against his teeth. He was not convinced professionally, but personally he may have been. "I think you ought to go home now and straighten things out."

"I guess I'd better."

"Tell your mother I might stop by, either tonight or tomorrow. And James—don't <u>underestimate</u> her."

What does Dr. Murphy tell James to do?

While my father was alive we usually went to Yosemite for three or four days during the summer. My mother would drive and Father would point out places of interest, meadows where boom towns once stood, hanging trees, rivers that were said to flow upstream at certain times. Or he read to us; he had that grown-ups' idea that children love Dickens and Sir Walter Scott. The four of us sat in the back seat with our faces composed, attentive, while our hands and feet pushed, pinched, stomped, goosed, prodded, dug, and kicked.

What has happened to James's father?

One night a bear came into our camp just after dinner. Mother had made a tuna casserole and it must have smelled to him like something worth dying for. He came into the camp while we were sitting around the fire and stood swaying back and forth. My brother Michael saw him first and elbowed me, then my sisters saw him and screamed. Mother and Father had their

---

words for everyday use

pomp • ous (päm′ pəs) *adj.,* having or exhibiting self-importance. *With a <u>pompous</u> air, Claudia told the other students at her table that she was being inducted into National Honor Society.*

dis • creet • ly (di skrēt′ lē) *adv.,* done in an unobtrusive or unnoticeable manner. *The teacher took the student aside and told him <u>discreetly</u> he was missing five assignments.*

un • der • es • ti • mate (ən dər es′ tə māt) *vt.,* estimate as being less than the actual size or quantity. *The Bohens <u>underestimated</u> the time it would take to get from the hotel to the train station and consequently missed their train.*

"THE LIAR"   567

---

1. It's like investing a friend's money.
2. He tells James to "go home . . . and straighten things out."
3. James's father has died.

ADDITIONAL QUESTIONS AND ACTIVITIES

Students can prepare a guide about safety around animals. Students should first determine what animals people are likely to encounter in their area. Then they can do research to determine where the animal is likely to be encountered, when (what time of day), anything that is likely to attract the animal, and the best way to respond. Students should compile their findings into a brochure of safety tips.

ADDITIONAL QUESTIONS AND ACTIVITIES

Give students these additional examples of Swiftys and make sure they understand how the form works. Then have them try their hand at writing their own.

• "Stop!" Tom said haltingly.
• "I can see right through you," said Tom clearly.
• "Can you fix my watch?" Tom asked brokenly.

backs to him but Mother must have guessed what it was because she immediately said, "Don't scream like that. You might frighten him and there's no telling what he'll do. We'll just sing and he'll go away."

We sang "Row Row Row Your Boat" but the bear stayed. He circled us several times, rearing up now and then on his hind legs to stick his nose into the air. By the light of the fire I could see his doglike face and watch the muscles roll under his loose skin like rocks in a sack. We sang harder as he circled us, coming closer and closer. "All right," Mother said, "enough's enough." She stood abruptly. The bear stopped moving and watched her. "Beat it," Mother said. The bear sat down and looked from side to side. "Beat it," she said again, and leaned over and picked up a rock.

"Margaret, don't," my father said.

She threw the rock hard and hit the bear in the stomach. Even in the dim light I could see the dust rising from his fur. He grunted and stood to his full height. "See that?" Mother shouted: "He's filthy. Filthy!" One of my sisters giggled. Mother picked up another rock. "Please, Margaret," my father said. Just then the bear turned and <u>shambled</u> away. Mother pitched the rock after him. For the rest of the night he <u>loitered</u> around the camp until he found the tree where we had hung our food. He ate it all. The next day we drove back to the city. We could have bought more supplies in the valley, but Father wanted to go and would not give in to any argument. On the way home he tried to jolly everyone up by making jokes, but Michael and my sisters ignored him and looked stonily out the windows.

Things were never easy between my mother and me, but I didn't underestimate her. She

How does James's mother try to get rid of the bear?

underestimated me. When I was little she suspected me of delicacy, because I didn't like being thrown into the air, and because when I saw her and the others working themselves up for a roughhouse I found somewhere else to be. When they did drag me in I got hurt, a knee in the lip, a bent finger, a bloody nose, and this to Mother seemed to hold against me, as if I arranged my hurts to get out of playing.

Even things I did well got on her nerves. We all loved puns except Mother, who didn't get them, and next to my father I was the best in the family. My specialty was the Swifty[3]—" 'You can bring the prisoner down,' said Tom condescendingly." Father encouraged me to perform at dinner, which must have been a trial for outsiders. Mother wasn't sure what was going on, but she didn't like it.

What about James's behavior as a child gets on his mother's nerves?

She suspected me in other ways. I couldn't go to the movies without her examining my pockets to make sure I had enough money to pay for the ticket. When I went away to camp she tore my pack apart in front of all the boys who were waiting in the bus outside the house. I would rather have gone without my sleeping bag and a few changes of underwear, which I had forgotten, than be made such a fool of. Her distrust was the thing that made me forgetful.

And she thought I was cold-hearted because of what happened the day my father died and later at his funeral. I didn't cry at my father's funeral, and showed signs of boredom during the <u>eulogy</u>, fiddling around with the hymnals. Mother

What about James made his mother think he was cold-hearted?

---

3. **Swifty.** A type of pun that takes its name from a character named Tom Swift, the hero of a series of adventure stories. The play on words always involves an adverb.

words for everyday use

sham • ble (sham' bəl) *vi.,* walk awkwardly with dragging feet. *Mark <u>shambled</u> on his way to the principal's office.*
loi • ter (loi' tər) *vi.,* remain in an area for no obvious reason. *Before school, the students <u>loitered</u> in front of the convenience store.*
eu • lo • gy (yü' lə jē) *n.,* commendatory formal statement about the deceased person at a funeral. *In his <u>eulogy,</u> the pastor mentioned Mrs. Davies's years of charity work.*

put my hands into my lap and I left them there without moving them as though they were things I was holding for someone else. The effect was ironical and she resented it. We had a sort of <u>reconciliation</u> a few days later after I closed my eyes at school and refused to open them. When several teachers and then the principal failed to persuade me to look at them, or at some reward they claimed to be holding, I was handed over to the school nurse,

What did James refuse to do at school?

who tried to pry the lids open and scratched one of them badly. My eye swelled up and I went rigid. The principal panicked and called Mother, who fetched me home. I wouldn't talk to her, or open my eyes, or bend, and they had to lay me on the back seat and when we reached the house Mother had to lift me up the steps one at a time. Then she put me on the couch and played the piano to me all afternoon. Finally I opened my eyes. We hugged each other and I wept. Mother did not really believe my tears, but she was willing to accept them because I had staged them for her benefit.

My lying separated us, too, and the fact that my promises not to lie any

What is separating James and his mother?

more seemed to mean nothing to me. Often my lies came back to her in embarrassing ways, people stopping her in the street and saying how sorry they were to hear that such and such had happened. No one in the neighborhood enjoyed embarrassing Mother, and these situations stopped occurring once everybody got wise to me. There was no saving her from strangers, though. The summer after Father died I visited my uncle in Redding and when I got back I found to my surprise that Mother had come to

meet my bus. I tried to slip away from the gentleman who had sat next to me but I couldn't shake him. When he saw Mother embrace me he came up and presented her with a card and told her to get in touch with him if things got any worse. She gave him his card back and told him to mind his own business. Later, on the way home, she made me repeat what I had said to the man. She shook her head. "It's not fair to people," she said, "telling them things like that. It confuses them." It seemed to me that Mother had confused the man, not I, but I didn't say so. I agreed with her that I shouldn't say such things and promised not to do it again, a promise I broke three hours later in conversation with a woman in the park.

It wasn't only the lies that disturbed Mother; it was their <u>morbidity</u>. This was the real issue between us, as it had been between her and my father. Mother did volunteer work at Children's Hospital and St. Anthony's Dining Hall, collected things for the St. Vincent de Paul Society. She was a lighter of candles. My brother and sisters took after her in this way. My father was a curser of the dark. And he loved to curse the dark. He was never more alive than when he was <u>indignant</u> about something. For this reason the most important act of the day for him was the reading of the evening paper.

What was the most important thing the father did each day?

Ours was a terrible paper, <u>indifferent</u> to the city that bought it, indifferent to medical discoveries—except for new kinds of gases that made your hands fall off when you sneezed—and indifferent to politics and art. Its business was outrage, horror, gruesome coincidence. When my father sat down in the living room

words for everyday use

rec • on • cil • i • a • tion (re kən si lē ā′ shən) *n.*, act of restoring friendship or harmony. *The <u>reconciliation</u> between Mrs. Grabowski and her in-laws occurred when her first child was born.*

mor • bid • i • ty (mor biˈ də tē) *n.*, quality or state of being susceptible to gloomy or unwholesome feelings. *Seth's <u>morbidity</u> was evident in the gloomy stories and anecdotes he told.*

in • dig • nant (in digˈ nənt) *adj.*, filled or marked by anger at something unjust, unworthy, or mean. *The clerk's <u>indignant</u> remark indicated he was angered at being thought capable of stealing from the cash register.*

in • dif • fer • ent (in diˈ fərnt) *adj.*, marked by a lack of interest, enthusiasm, or concern. *At conferences, Martin's teacher told his parents that he did <u>indifferent</u> work in class.*

1. At school, James refused to open his eyes.
2. The "real issue" between James and his mother is the "morbidity" of his lies.
3. The most important thing the father did each day was read the newspaper.

ADDITIONAL QUESTIONS AND ACTIVITIES

Have students become familiar with their local newspaper by reading several issues. Students should write a critique of the paper that discusses its:
a) coverage (How much is devoted to world events vs. local events, news items vs. features, etc.),
b) tone and bias (Does it have a detached tone or an inviting local flair? Does it have a particular political bent?), and
c) accuracy (Does the paper print many retractions? Do the stories fit with what students have read and heard elsewhere? Are there many typographical errors or other mistakes that students can find?)

1. The newspaper makes him angry.
2. The parents didn't go out very often.

ADDITIONAL QUESTIONS
AND ACTIVITIES

Students can try this writing activity:

James's father is uncomfortable around people. This shows in the way he treats guests at his home. Imagine you are one of the guests. You have just come from a visit and don't want to go again. Write a letter to an advice columnist about your dilemma. Describe the visit and explain why you don't want to go again. Then write a response from the advice columnist.

---

with the paper Mother stayed in the kitchen and kept the children busy, all except me, because I was quiet and could be trusted to amuse myself. I amused myself by watching my father.

He sat with his knees spread, leaning forward, his eyes only inches from the print. As he read he nodded to himself. Sometimes he swore and threw the paper down and paced the room, then picked it up and began again. Over a period of time he developed the habit of reading aloud to me. He always started with the society section, which he called the parasite page. This column began to take on the character of a comic strip or a serial, with the same people showing up from one day to the next, blinking in chiffon, awkwardly holding their drinks for the sake of Peninsula orphans, grinning under sunglasses on the deck of a ski hut in the Sierras. The skiers really got his goat, probably because he couldn't understand them. The activity itself was inconceivable to him. When my sisters went to Lake Tahoe one winter weekend with some friends and came back excited about the beauty of the place, Father calmed them right down. "Snow," he said, "is overrated."

> What is James's father's reaction to the town's paper?

Then the news, or what passed in the paper for news: bodies unearthed in Scotland, former Nazis winning elections, rare animals slaughtered, <u>misers</u> expiring naked in freezing houses upon mattresses stuffed with thousands, millions; marrying priests, divorcing actresses, high-rolling oilmen building fantastic <u>mausoleums</u> in honor of a favorite horse, cannibalism. Through all this my father waded with a fixed and weary smile.

Mother encouraged him to take up causes, to join groups, but he would not. He was uncomfortable with people outside the family. He and my mother rarely went out, and rarely had people in, except on feast days[4] and national holidays. Their guests were always the same, Dr. Murphy and his wife and several others whom they had known since childhood. Most of these people never saw each other outside our house and they didn't have much fun together. Father <u>discharged</u> his obligations as host by teasing everyone about stupid things they had said or done in the past and forcing them to laugh at themselves.

> What were James's parents' social lives like?

Though Father did not drink, he insisted on mixing cocktails for the guests. He would not serve straight drinks like rum-and-Coke or even Scotch-on-the-rocks, only drinks of his own devising. He gave them lawyerly names like "The Advocate," "The Hanging Judge," "The Ambulance Chaser," "The Mouthpiece," and described their concoction in detail. He told long, complicated stories in a near-whisper, making everyone lean in his direction, and repeated important lines; he also repeated the important lines in the stories my mother told, and corrected her when she got something wrong. When the guests came to the ends of their own stories, he would point out the morals.

Dr. Murphy had several theories about Father, which he used to test on me in the course of our meetings. Dr. Murphy had by this time given up his glasses for contact lenses, and lost weight in the course of fasts which he undertook regularly. Even with his baldness he looked years younger than when he had come to the parties at our house. Certainly he did not look like my father's contemporary, which he was.

One of Dr. Murphy's theories was that Father had exhibited a classic trait of people who had

---

4. **feast days.** Religious celebrations commemorating particular Christian saints

---

words for everyday use	**mi • ser** (mī′ zər) *n.*, someone extremely stingy with money. *The most famous <u>miser</u> in English literature is Scrooge, who lived frugally and refused to donate to charities, even at Christmas.*
	mau • so • le • um (mo sə lē′ əm) *n.*, building for entombment of the dead above ground. *Amy visited the <u>mausoleum</u> to see where her grandfather was buried.*
	dis • charge (dis chärj′) *vt.*, throw off or deliver a duty or burden. *The bank officer <u>discharged</u> his duties before taking vacation.*

been gifted children by taking an undemanding position in an uninteresting firm. "He was afraid of finding his limits," Dr. Murphy told me: "As long as he kept stamping papers and making out wills, he could go on believing that he didn't *have* limits." Dr. Murphy's fascination with father made me uneasy, and I felt traitorous listening to him. While he lived, my father would never have submitted himself for analysis; it seemed a betrayal to put him on the couch now that he was dead.

What is one of Dr. Murphy's theories about James's father?

I did enjoy Dr. Murphy's recollections of Father as a child. He told me about something that happened when they were in the Boy Scouts. Their troop had been on a long hike and Father had fallen behind. Dr. Murphy and the others decided to ambush him as he came down the trail. They hid in the woods on each side and waited. But when Father walked into the trap none of them moved or made a sound and he strolled on without even knowing they were there. "He had the sweetest look on his face," Dr. Murphy said, "listening to the birds, smelling the flowers, just like Ferdinand the Bull."[5] He also told me that my father's drinks tasted like medicine.

W hile I rode my bicycle home from Dr. Murphy's office Mother fretted. She felt terribly alone but she didn't call anyone because she also felt like a failure. My

What is the effect of James's lying on his mother?

lying had that effect on her. She took it personally. At such times she did not think of my sisters, one happily married, the other doing brilliantly at Fordham.[6] She did not think of my brother Michael, who had given up college to work with runaway children in Los Angeles. She thought of me. She thought that she had made a mess of her family.

Actually she managed the family well. While my father was dying upstairs she pulled us together. She made lists of chores and gave each of us a fair allowance. Bedtimes were adjusted and she stuck by them. She set regular hours for homework. Each child was made responsible for the next eldest, and I was given a dog. She told us frequently, predictably, that she loved us. At dinner we were each expected to contribute something, and after dinner she played the piano and tried to teach us to sing in harmony, which I could not do. Mother, who was an admirer of the Trapp family,[7] considered this a character defect.

SHE THOUGHT OF ME. SHE THOUGHT SHE HAD MADE A MESS OF HER FAMILY.

Our life together was more orderly, healthy, while Father was dying than it had been before. He had set us rules to follow, not much different really than the ones Mother gave us after he got sick, but he had administered them in a fickle way. Though we were supposed to get an allowance we always had to ask him for it and then he would give us too much because he enjoyed seeming <u>magnanimous</u>.

5. **Ferdinand the Bull.** Cartoon character; a bull who prefers smelling pretty flowers to fighting matadors
6. **Fordham.** University in New York
7. **Trapp family.** World-famous family of singers depicted in the musical *The Sound of Music*

words for everyday use	**mag • nan • i • mous** (mag na′ nə məs) *adj.*, showing generosity. *The millionaire's <u>magnanimous</u> donation resulted in a new wing on the hospital.*

1. Dr. Murphy theorizes that James's father was "afraid of finding his limits."
2. James's lying makes his mother feel like a failure.

ADDITIONAL QUESTIONS AND ACTIVITIES

Ask students to create a list of their responsibilities. Then they should note which of them involve other people (for example, taking care of a younger sibling, being part of a team). Discuss the effects or consequences of not fulfilling their responsibilities.

ANSWERS TO GUIDED READING QUESTIONS

1. The family's life was more orderly and healthy while the father was dying.
2. His jokes are his way of holding himself together.
3. What they shared most was fear.
4. As his father dies, he becomes more tender and serene.

ADDITIONAL QUESTIONS AND ACTIVITIES

It took James a while to understand and feel connected to his father. Ask students to examine their own relationships with a parent or other adult who figures in their lives. Students should try to answer the question: What do we have in common?

Sometimes he punished us for no reason, because he was in a bad mood. He was apt to decide, as one of my sisters was going out to a dance, that she had better stay home and do something to improve herself. Or he would sweep us all up on a Wednesday night and take us ice-skating.

In what ways was James's life better while his father was dying?

He changed after he learned about the cancer, and became more calm as the disease spread. He relaxed his teasing way with us, and from time to time it was possible to have a conversation with him which was not about the last thing that had made him angry. He stopped reading the paper and spent time at the window.

He and I became close. He taught me to play poker and sometimes helped me with my homework. But it wasn't his illness that drew us together. The reserve between us had begun to break down after the incident with the bear, during the drive home. Michael and my sisters were furious with him for making us leave early and wouldn't talk to him or look at him. He joked: though it had been a <u>grisly</u> experience we should grin and bear it—and so on. His joking seemed <u>perverse</u> to the others, but not to me. I had seen how terrified he was when the bear came into the camp. He had held himself so still that he had begun to tremble. When Mother started pitching rocks I thought he was going to bolt, really. I understood—I had been frightened too. The others took it as a lark after they got used to having the bear around, but for Father and me it got worse through the night. I was glad to be out of there, grateful to Father for getting me out. I saw that his jokes were how he held himself together. So I reached out to him with a joke: " 'There's a bear outside,' said Tom

What was the purpose of the father's jokes?

intently." The others turned cold looks on me. They thought I was sucking up. But Father smiled.

When I thought of other boys being close to their fathers I thought of them hunting together, tossing a ball back and forth, making birdhouses in the basement, and having long talks about girls, war, careers. Maybe the reason it took us so long to get close was that I had this idea. It kept getting in the way of what we really had, which was a shared fear.

What did James share most with his father?

Toward the end Father slept most of the time and I watched him. From below, sometimes, faintly, I heard Mother playing the piano. Occasionally he nodded off in his chair while I was reading to him; his bathrobe would fall open then, and I would see the long new scar on his stomach, red as blood against his white skin. His ribs all showed and his legs were like cables.

I once read in a biography of a great man that he "died well." I assume the writer meant that he kept his pain to himself, did not set off false alarms, and did not too much inconvenience those who were to stay behind. My father died well. His irritability gave way to something else, something like <u>serenity</u>. In the last days he became tender. It was as though he had been rehearsing the scene, that the anger of his life had been a kind of stage fright. He managed his audience—us—with an old trouper's sense of when to clown and when to stand on his dignity. We were all moved, and admired his courage, as he intended we should. He died downstairs in a shaft of late afternoon sunlight on New Year's Day, while I was reading to him. I was alone in the

In what way does James's father "die well"?

words for everyday use

gris • ly (griz′ lē) *adj.*, inspiring disgust or distaste. *The <u>grisly</u> details of the murder were not released by the police.*
per • verse (pər vərs′) *adj.*, contrary; opposing what is right, reasonable, or accepted. *Showing his <u>perverse</u> sense of humor, Jed wore a military uniform to the pacifists' fancy dress ball.*
se • ren • i • ty (sə re′ nə tē) *n.*, quality or state of being tranquil. *The <u>serenity</u> of the garden made Sally fall asleep.*

house and didn't know what to do. His body did not frighten me but immediately and sharply I missed my father. It seemed wrong to leave him sitting up and I tried to carry him upstairs to the bedroom but it was too hard, alone. So I called up my friend Ralphy across the street. When he came over and saw what I wanted him for he started crying but I made him help me anyway. A couple of hours later Mother got home and when I told her that Father was dead she ran upstairs, calling his name. A few minutes later she came back down. "Thank God," she said, "at least he died in bed." This seemed important to her and I didn't tell her otherwise. But that night Ralphy's parents called. They were, they said, shocked at what I had done and so was Mother when she heard the story, shocked and furious. Why? Because I had not told her the truth? Or because she had learned the truth, and could not go on believing that Father had died in bed? I really don't know.

How does the mother react when she finds out that James did not tell her the truth about moving his father upstairs?

"Mother," I said, coming into the living room, "I'm sorry about the letter. I really am."

She was arranging wood in the fireplace and did not look at me or speak for a moment. Finally she finished and straightened up and brushed her hands. She stepped back and looked at the fire she had laid. "That's all right," she said. "Not bad for a <u>consumptive</u>."

"Mother, I'm sorry."

"Sorry? Sorry you wrote it or sorry I found it?"

"I wasn't going to mail it. It was a sort of joke."

"Ha ha." She took up the whisk broom and swept bits of bark into the fireplace, then closed the drapes and settled on the couch. "Sit down," she said. She crossed her legs. "Listen, do I give you advice all the time?"

"Yes."

"I do?"

I nodded.

"Well, that doesn't make any difference. I'm supposed to. I'm your mother. I'm going to give you some more advice, for your own good. You don't have to make all these things up, James. They'll happen anyway." She picked at the hem of her skirt. "Do you understand what I'm saying?"

What advice does the mother give to James?

"I think so."

"You're cheating yourself, that's what I'm trying to tell you. When you get to be my age you won't know anything at all about life. All you'll know is what you've made up."

I thought about that. It seemed logical.

She went on. "I think maybe you need to get out of yourself more. Think more about other people."

The doorbell rang.

"Go see who it is," Mother said. "We'll talk about this later."

It was Dr. Murphy. He and Mother made their apologies and she insisted that he stay for dinner. I went to the kitchen to fetch ice for their drinks, and when I returned they were talking about me. I sat on the sofa and listened. Dr. Murphy was telling Mother not to worry. "James is a good boy," he said. "I've been thinking about my oldest, Terry. He's not really dishonest, you know, but he's not really honest either. I can't seem to reach him. At least James isn't <u>furtive</u>."

"No," Mother said, "he's never been furtive."

Dr. Murphy clasped his hands between his knees and stared at them. "Well, that's Terry. Furtive."

"THE LIAR" 573

ANSWERS TO GUIDED READING QUESTIONS

1. James's mother is furious that he carried his father upstairs.
2. She tells him that he does not have to make things up—they will happen anyway.

ADDITIONAL QUESTIONS AND ACTIVITIES

One aspect of the Internet is that it allows people to communicate quickly and easily without having actual contact with one another. Some people suggest that users are likely to lie in this medium. For example, people may take on a persona very different from their real one. Hold a discussion about why people might do this and the effects such actions may have.

Before we sat down to dinner Mother said grace; Dr. Murphy bowed his head and closed his eyes and crossed himself at the end, though he had lost his faith in college. When he told me that, during one of our meetings, in just those words, I had the picture of a raincoat hanging by itself outside a dining hall. He drank a good deal of wine and persistently turned the conversation to the subject of his relationship with Terry. He admitted that he had come to dislike the boy. Then he mentioned several patients of his by name, some of them known to Mother and me, and said that he disliked them too. He used the word "dislike" with <u>relish</u>, like someone on a diet permitting himself a single potato chip. "I don't know what I've done wrong," he said abruptly, and with reference to no particular thing. "Then again maybe I haven't done anything wrong. I don't know what to think any more. Nobody does."

"I know what to think," Mother said.

"So does the solipsist.[8] How can you prove to a solipsist that he's not creating the rest of us?"

This was one of Dr. Murphy's favorite riddles, and almost any pretext was sufficient for him to trot it out. He was a child with a card trick.

"Send him to bed without dinner," Mother said. "Let him create that."

Dr. Murphy suddenly turned to me. "Why do you do it?" he asked. It was a pure question, it had no object beyond the satisfaction of his curiosity. Mother looked at me and there was the same curiosity in her face.

"I don't know," I said, and that was the truth.

Dr. Murphy nodded, not because he had anticipated my answer but because he accepted it. "Is it fun?"

When Dr. Murphy reveals his loss of faith, what mental picture forms in James's mind?

Does James enjoy his lying?

"No, it's not fun. I can't explain."

"Why is it all so sad?" Mother asked. "Why all the diseases?"

"Maybe," Dr. Murphy said, "sad things are more interesting."

"Not to me," Mother said.

"Not to me, either," I said. "It just comes out that way."

After dinner Dr. Murphy asked Mother to play the piano. He particularly wanted to sing "Come Home Abbie, the Light's on the Stair."

"That old thing," Mother said. She stood and folded her napkin deliberately and we followed her into the living room. Dr. Murphy stood behind her as she warmed up. Then they sang "Come Home Abbie, the Light's on the Stair," and I watched him stare down at Mother intently, as if he were trying to remember something. Her own eyes were closed. After that they sang "O Magnum Mysterium." They sang it in parts and I regretted that I had no voice, it sounded so good.

"Come on, James," Dr. Murphy said as Mother played the last chords. "These old tunes not good enough for you?"

"He just can't sing," Mother said.

When Dr. Murphy left, Mother lit the fire and made more coffee. She slouched down in the big chair, sticking her legs straight out and moving her feet back and forth. "That was fun," she said.

"Did you and Father ever do things like that?"

"A few times, when we were first going out. I don't think he really enjoyed it. He was like you."

---

8. **solipsist.** Person who believes the self can know nothing but its own modifications and is the only existent thing

---

words for everyday use

rel • ish (re′ lish) *n.,* enjoyment of or delight in something that satisfies one's tastes, inclinations, or desires. *Yvonne told the story of her trip with <u>relish</u>.*

I wondered if Mother and Father had had a good marriage. He admired her and liked to look at her; every night at dinner he had to move the candlesticks slightly to the right and left of center so he could see down the length of the table. And every evening when she set the table she put them in the center again. She didn't seem to miss him very much. But I wouldn't really have known if she did, and anyway I didn't miss him all that much myself, not the way I had. Most of the time I thought about other things.

Does James's mother miss her husband much?

"James?"

I waited.

"I've been thinking that you might like to go down and stay with Michael for a couple of weeks or so."

"What about school?"

"I'll talk to Father McSorley. He won't mind. Maybe this problem will take care of itself if you start thinking about other people."

What does James's mother suggest he do?

"I do."

"I mean helping them, like Michael does. You don't have to go if you don't want to."

"It's fine with me. Really. I'd like to see Michael."

"I'm not trying to get rid of you."

"I know."

Mother stretched, then tucked her feet under her. She sipped noisily at her coffee. "What did that word mean that Murphy used? You know the one?"

"Paranoid? That's where somebody thinks everyone is out to get him. Like that woman who always grabs you after Mass—Frances."

"Not paranoid. Everyone knows what that means. Sol-something."

"Oh. Solipsist. A solipsist is someone who thinks he creates everything around him."

Mother nodded and blew on her coffee, then put it down without drinking from it. "I'd rather be paranoid. Do you really think Frances is?"

"Of course. No question about it."

"I mean really *sick?*"

"That's what paranoid *is,* is being sick. What do you think, Mother?"

"What are you so angry about?"

"I'm not angry." I lowered my voice. "I'm not angry. But you don't believe those stories of hers, do you?"

"Well, no, not exactly. I don't think she knows what she's saying, she just wants someone to listen. She probably lives all by herself in some little room. So she's paranoid. Think of that. And I had no idea. James, we should pray for her. Will you remember to do that?"

I nodded. I thought of Mother singing "O Magnum Mysterium," saying grace, praying with easy confidence, and it came to me that her imagination was superior to mine. She could imagine things as coming together, not falling apart. She looked at me and I shrank; I knew exactly what she was going to say. "Son," she said, "do you know how much I love you?"

How is James's mother's imagination better than James's?

HE WAS A CHILD WITH A CARD TRICK.

The next afternoon I took the bus to Los Angeles. I looked forward to the trip, to the monotony of the road and the empty fields by the roadside. Mother walked with me down the long concourse. The station was crowded and oppressive. "Are you sure this is the right bus?" she asked at the loading platform.

1. According to James, she doesn't miss her husband very much.
2. She suggests he visit his brother for a couple of weeks.
3. She can imagine things as "coming together, not falling apart."

1. They both feel relieved.
2. The bus breaks down.
3. He tells her that he works with refugees from Tibet.

SELECTION CHECK TEST 4.7.9 WITH ANSWERS

Checking Your Reading

1. Which trait of the mother does James think is funny? **He thinks the way she walks is funny.**
2. What does James's mother do with the letter that contains the lie? **She burns it.**
3. What do James and his father share? **They share fear.**
4. What does James's mother do when the bear comes into their camp? **First she makes everyone sing, then she throws a rock at the bear.**
5. What does James tell the people on the bus he does? **He says he works with Tibetan refugees.**

Vocabulary in Context

Fill in each blank below with the most appropriate word from the following Words for Everyday Use.

| pompous | loiter | indifferent |
| miser | furtive | serenity |

1. After you go to the store, come right home. Do not **loiter**.
2. You can be frugal with your money without being a **miser**.
3. Mr. Nakamori knew something was up when he caught Jason sending me **furtive** signals.
4. The **serenity** of the lake was a welcome relief after the crowds of the city.
5. Tomas's casual presentation was greeted enthusiastically after the overblown speech by the **pompous** speaker.

Literary Tools

1. What is an antihero? **An antihero is a central character who lacks many of the qualities traditionally associated with heroes.**
2. What is a motivation? **A motivation is a force that moves a character to think, feel, or behave in a certain way.**
3. What is James's motivation to lie? *Responses may vary.* **James lies to put others at ease (as with the people on the bus and when he tells his mother that his father died in bed). He also lies to perhaps distance himself from difficult situations by making them up.**

"Yes."

"It looks so old."

"Mother—"

"All right." She pulled me against her and kissed me, then held me an extra second to show that her embrace was sincere, not just like everyone else's, never having realized that everyone else does the same thing. I boarded the bus and we waved at each other until it became embarrassing. Then Mother began checking through her handbag for something. When she had finished I stood and adjusted the luggage over my seat. I sat and we smiled at each other, waved when the driver gunned the engine, shrugged when he got up suddenly to count the passengers, waved again when he resumed his seat. As the bus pulled out my mother and I were looking at each other with plain relief.

> *What do both James and his mother feel as the bus pulls away?*

I had boarded the wrong bus. This one was bound for Los Angeles but not by the express route. We stopped in San Mateo, Palo Alto, San José, Castroville. When we left Castroville it began to rain, hard; my window would not close all the way, and a thick stream of water ran down the wall onto my seat. To keep dry I had to stay away from the wall and lean forward. The rain fell harder. The engine of the bus sounded as though it were coming apart.

In Salinas the man sleeping beside me jumped up but before I had a chance to change seats his place was taken by an enormous woman in a print dress, carrying a shopping bag. She took possession of her seat and spilled over onto half of mine, backing me up to the wall. "That's a storm," she said loudly, then turned and looked at me. "Hungry?" Without waiting for an answer she dipped into her bag and pulled out a piece of chicken and thrust it at me. "Hey, by

God," she hooted, "look at him go to town on that drumstick!" A few people turned and smiled. I smiled back around the bone and kept at it. I finished that piece and she handed me another, and then another. Then she started handing out chicken to the people in the seats near us.

Outside of San Luis Obispo the noise from the engine grew suddenly louder and just as suddenly there was no noise at all. The driver pulled off to the side of the road and got out, then got on again dripping wet. A few moments later he announced that the bus had broken down and they were sending another bus to pick us up. Someone asked how long that might take and the driver said he had no idea. "Keep your pants on!" shouted the woman next to me. "Anybody in a hurry to get to L.A. ought to have his head examined."

> *What happens to the bus?*

The wind was blowing hard around the bus, driving sheets of rain against the window on both sides. The bus swayed gently. Outside the light was brown and thick. The woman next to me pumped all the people around us for their itineraries and said whether or not she had ever been where they were from or where they were going. "How about you?" She slapped my knee. "Parents own a chicken ranch? I hope so!" She laughed. I told her I was from San Francisco. "San Francisco, that's where my husband was stationed." She asked me what I did there and I told her I worked with refugees from Tibet.

> *What lie does James tell the lady on the bus?*

"Is that right? What do you do with a bunch of Tibetans?"

"Seems like there's plenty of other places they could've gone," said a man in front of us.

words for everyday use

i • tin • er • ar • y (ī ti′ nə rer ē) n., route of a journey or the proposed outline of one. *Paris, where we would spend the most time on our trip, was the first destination on our itinerary.*

SELECTION CHECK TEST 4.7.9 WITH ANSWERS (CONT.)

4. Of which technique of characterization is this an example: "Her one concession to the fact of humor was an insincere, startling laugh." **It is an example of direct description.**

"Coming across the border like that. We don't go there."

"What do you do with a bunch of Tibetans?" the woman repeated.

"Try to find them jobs, locate housing, listen to their problems."

"You understand that kind of talk?"

"Yes."

"Speak it?"

"Pretty well. I was born and raised in Tibet. My parents were missionaries over there."

Everyone waited.

"They were killed when the Communists took over."

The big woman patted my arm.

"It's all right," I said.

"Why don't you say some of that Tibetan?"

"What would you like to hear?"

"Say 'The cow jumped over the moon.' " She watched me, smiling, and when I finished she looked at the others and shook her head. "That was pretty. Like music. Say some more."

"What?"

"Anything."

They bent toward me. The windows suddenly went blind with rain. The driver had fallen asleep and was snoring gently to the swaying of the bus. Outside the muddy light flickered to pale yellow, and far off there was thunder. The woman next to me leaned back and closed her eyes and then so did all the others as I sang to them in what was surely an ancient and holy tongue. ▪

What is the effect of James's "Tibetan" on the other passengers?

Respond *to the* SELECTION

Imagine that you are one of the passengers on the bus and that later you learn that James has lied to you about his involvement with Tibetans. How would that make you feel? Why?

"THE LIAR" 577

RESPOND TO THE SELECTION

Do you agree with the doctor's advice—that one shouldn't worry too much about James's lying? Why, or why not? Do you think his advice is good or bad?

RECALL

1a. He tells his friend Ralphy that his mother has been "coughing up blood" and that the doctors don't know what is wrong with her. Earlier, he said his mother had leukemia. Generally, his lies tend toward the tragic, sad, and morbid.

2a. She is furious.

3a. Wolff writes that "the woman next to me leaned back and closed her eyes and then so did all the others as I sang to them in what was surely an ancient and holy tongue."

INTERPRET

1b. By voicing potential griefs and losses as "lies," he makes them unavailable as truth, and thus attempts to shield himself from heartache. His lying makes his mother feel like a failure.

2b. James feels that it was important to his mother that he died in bed.

3b. By calling the Tibetan speech "ancient and holy," James (and by extension, the author) seems to be reminding us that lying can sometimes be positive. How can it matter whether or not James has told the truth when the lie has such a positive effect?

ANALYZE

4a. *Responses will vary.* No matter how she feels, she keeps to her schedule: she always attends four o'clock Mass. She tends to feel that life should proceed like a script.

SYNTHESIZE

4b. By telling lies, James attempts to introduce weakness and vulnerability into her life. For James, lying is perhaps an unconscious way of trying to get closer to his mother emotionally.

EVALUATE

5a. *Responses will vary.*

EXTEND

5b. Students may point out that at times it may be humane not to tell the truth when it may hurt someone else's feelings. Other stories or films that have the same theme include the short story "Like the Sun" by R. K. Narayan and the movie *Liar, Liar* starring Jim Carrey.

Investigate, *Inquire,* and Imagine

Recall: GATHERING FACTS

1a. What lies does James tell about his mother?

2a. What is the mother's reaction when she learns that James had carried his father upstairs after he died and that her husband had not actually died in bed?

3a. At the end of the story, what effect does James's pretending to speak Tibetan have on the other passengers on the bus?

Interpret: FINDING MEANING

1b. Why does James's lying upset his mother so much? Why is his lying such a betrayal for her?

2b. Why didn't James tell his mother the truth about this incident?

3b. What point do you think the author might be trying to make by his description of the way James speaks "Tibetan"?

Analyze: TAKING THINGS APART

4a. Wolff writes that James's mother prays "in a familiar, orderly way." Using specific examples from the story, identify other behaviors that demonstrate the mother's efforts to maintain an orderly life.

Synthesize: BRINGING THINGS TOGETHER

4b. How does James's lying work against his mother's need for an orderly life? Why do you think he wants to undo the orderliness of her life?

Evaluate: MAKING JUDGMENTS

5a. In your opinion, is James's lying justified? Support your answers with specific references from the text.

Extend: CONNECTING IDEAS

5b. Is it possible to be completely honest all the time? Is it sometimes better to tell a lie than to tell the truth? Why, or why not? What other stories or films do you know of that explore the theme of telling the truth?

Understanding *Literature*

ANTIHERO. Review the definition for **antihero** in the Handbook of Literary Terms. What other examples of antiheroes can you think of from stories, novels, films, or theater productions?

MOTIVATION AND CHARACTERIZATION. Review the definitions for **motivation** and **characterization** in the Handbook of Literary Terms and the chart you made for Literary Tools in Prereading. We learn about James's motivations not only through the standard techniques of characterization, but also through other characters' reactions. What we discover about the other characters may also give us clues about James. What do we learn about the motivations of James's parents?

ANSWERS TO UNDERSTANDING LITERATURE

ANTIHERO. *Responses will vary. Examples may include:* Billy Pilgrim from Vonnegut's *Slaughterhouse Five,* Gatsby from Fitzgerald's *The Great Gatsby,* the narrator of Poe's "The Tell-Tale Heart," Bart Simpson from *The Simpsons.*

MOTIVATION AND CHARACTERIZATION. From the incident with the bear, we learn that the father is motivated by fear.

Unlike James's mother, the father allows his fear to guide him toward a saner approach to the bear problem. Because she demands an orderly, tidy life, the mother does not allow fear to motivate her. Instead, she endangers the entire family by pitching rocks at the bear, while the father is honest enough to admit to himself that he has no business trying to intimidate a bear, no matter how "filthy" the bear might be.

Writer's Journal

1. Think of an incident in your life in which you have lost someone or something you loved. Write a **poem** in memoriam of this person or thing. Your poem may be lyric or narrative, rhymed or free verse.
2. Imagine you are James's father. Write James a brief **letter** describing the changes in your own personality you have experienced since finding out you were dying.
3. Read the Language Arts Survey 2.13, "Clustering." Then make two cluster charts: one about James's mother, the other about his father. Include as many details as you can about each character. Use the information in your charts to write a brief **character sketch** about each.

Integrating the Language Arts

Language, Grammar, and Style

SENTENCE FRAGMENTS. Read the Language Arts Survey 3.33, "Correcting Sentence Fragments." Rewrite the fragments as complete sentences, adding words as needed. If a sentence is not a fragment, write *OK* by its number.

1. To four o'clock Mass.
2. Said unpleasant things that weren't true.
3. Looking for help.
4. Discreetly was the way Dr. Murphy thought James should carry on.
5. One night came into their camp.

Speaking and Listening & Collaborative Learning

THE LYING GAME. Form a group of at least four people (groups consisting of an even number work best). On identical slips of paper, write "lie" on half of the slips and "truth" on the other half. Each player chooses a slip at random, being careful not to reveal to the others which word is written on his or her slip. Taking turns, each player then tells a brief story about a memorable family vacation. (Or choose some other topic to your liking.) Those who pick a "lie" must tell a false story; those who pick a "truth" must tell a true story. The object is to fool the other players into thinking that your lie is the truth (and vice versa). After everyone has told a story, each person tries to determine which of the stories were true, which false. Score one point for each correct determination.

Media Literacy

WRITING NEWSPAPER STORIES. Review the segment of "The Liar" in which James tells the reader about the bear invading his family's campground. Rewrite this story as if you were a top-notch reporter for a reputable newspaper (such as *The New York Times* or the *Washington Post*). Then, write the story as if you were writing for a sensational tabloid newspaper (such as *The National Enquirer* or *The Weekly World News*).

ANSWERS TO INTEGRATING THE LANGUAGE ARTS

Language, Grammar, and Style
Responses will vary.
1. James's mother went to four o'clock Mass.
2. James said unpleasant things that weren't true.
3. James's mother called Dr. Murphy, looking for help.
4. *OK*
5. One night a bear came into their camp.

Speaking and Listening & Collaborative Learning
After playing the game, students may wish to discuss the statement, "Truth is stranger than fiction." Did this statement hold true during their game? Were some of the funniest, strangest, or most outrageous stories the true ones?

Media Literacy
Suggest that students read several stories in each type of paper. This will help them get a grasp of the tone, diction, and style of each paper.

GRAPHIC ORGANIZER

The statement "We had to get accustomed to the idea of Father's being out on the river. We had to but we couldn't…" is paradoxical in that the family *must* do what is for them impossible to do. The fact that "Father did not come back. Nor did he go anywhere, really" is paradoxical because the idea of leaving is to go somewhere. The statement "It wasn't exactly accurate but it was a truthful sort of lie" is paradoxical in that a lie by its nature cannot be "truthful." The statement "Times changed, with… imperceptible rapidity" is paradoxical in that it calls rapidity "imperceptible." By its nature, rapidity is an observable quality. If it cannot be perceived, then it does not exist. The statement "My father always away and his absence always with me" portrays "absence" as "being." Absence is the state of not being present, so the statement is a paradox.

READER'S JOURNAL

Students might also write about how it might feel if somebody close to them decided to leave to escape responsibility. Students may speculate about the person's reasons for leaving and their feelings about leaving and discuss their own feelings toward the person and the situation.

SHORT STORY

Literary
T O O L S

SYMBOL. A **symbol** is a thing that stands for or represents both itself and something else. As you read, try to determine what you think the river might symbolize.

PARADOX. A **paradox** is a seemingly contradictory statement, idea, or event. All forms of irony involve paradox. An example of a paradox is the statement, "This sentence is a lie." If the sentence is true, then it is false; if it is false, then it is true. Consider the paradox presented by the first sentence of this story, given what the father does later in that same paragraph. Complete the graphic organizer below to explain the other paradoxes you find in the story.

Graphic
Organizer

Make a chart like the one below. In the left column write the paradoxical statements you find in the story. In the right column, explain why each statement is a paradox.

PARADOX	EXPLANATION
"We had to get accustomed to the idea of Father's being out on the river. We had to but we couldn't…"	

Reader's
Journal

Have you ever dreamed of escaping all your responsibilities? Where would you go?

PREREADING

'The Third Bank of the River'
by João Guimarães Rosa,
translated by William L. Grossman

Reader's
r e s o u r c e

"**The Third Bank of the River**" is a story about a boy whose father decides to take a most unusual journey. The father's reasons are unknown. He may be seeking a greater truth, such as the secret of eternity, or he may be insane, or even dead and traveling to the afterworld. The story is open to interpretation. As you read, come up with your own explanation of the father's river journey.

PHILOSOPHY CONNECTION. João Guimarães Rosa was fascinated by metaphysics, a branch of philosophy concerned with the nature of reality and existence. He wanted to explore a greater reality that lay beyond human perception. He also was fascinated by rivers, because he saw them as a symbol of eternity and infinite wisdom. He once said: "I would like to be a crocodile living in the river São Francisco. The crocodile comes to the world like a master in metaphysics, because for it each river is an ocean, a sea of wisdom, even if it reaches a hundred. I would like to be a crocodile because I love the great rivers, for they are deep as the human soul. On the surface they are lively and clear, but in the depths they are tranquil and dark like humanity's sufferings. I love another thing about our great rivers: their eternity. Yes, *river* is a magical word to conjugate eternity."

About the
A U T H O R

João Guimarães Rosa (1908–1967) was born in Cordisburgo, a small ranch town in Brazil. He loved languages and mastered seven of them: French, Latin, Greek, Russian, German, English, and Japanese. Guimarães Rosa also studied philosophy, religion, and the natural sciences. His knowledge of this array of subjects made his writings broad in vision, and revolutionary in scope.

As a young man, Guimarães Rosa was a medical doctor who practiced in rural, remote areas of Brazil, called the *sertao* or "backlands." It is said that he often accepted stories as payment. In fact, Guimarães Rosa wove into his work many stories from the oral tradition of the backlands. In 1946 he published his first book, entitled *Sagarana* (*saga* is Old Norse for "epic tale" and *rana* is native Brazilian for "in the manner of"). Then in 1956, he published both a 750-page series of novellas entitled *Corpo de Baile* (*Corps of Ballet*) and his greatest novel, *Grande Sertao: Veredas* (translated into English as *The Devil to Pay in the Backlands*). The novel is narrated by a man named Riobaldo, who has made a bargain with the Devil. This story is taken from the collection *The Third Bank of the River and Other Stories*, from which this story is taken, was published in 1962.

GOALS/OBJECTIVES

Studying this lesson will enable students to
• empathize with the sense of loss and confusion experienced by the speaker
• understand the literary accomplishments of João Guimarães Rosa
• define *symbol* and *paradox* and interpret examples of both in their reading

• demonstrate the ability to combine two sentences to make one
• use a library to conduct research
• discuss different interpretations of a story

The Third Bank of the River

João Guimarães Rosa,
translated by William L. Grossman

My father was a dutiful, orderly, straightforward man. And according to several reliable people of whom I inquired, he had had these qualities since adolescence or even childhood. By my own recollection, he was neither jollier nor more melancholy than the other men we knew. Maybe a little quieter. It was Mother, not Father, who ruled the house. She scolded us daily—my sister, my brother, and me. But it happened one day that Father ordered a boat.

He was very serious about it. It was to be made specially for him, of mimosa wood. It was to be sturdy enough to last twenty or thirty years and just large enough for one person. Mother carried on plenty about it. Was her husband going to become a fisherman all of a sudden? Or a hunter? Father said nothing. Our house was less than a mile from the river, which around there was deep, quiet, and so wide you couldn't see across it.

What does the father have made for himself?

I can never forget the day the rowboat was delivered. Father showed no joy or other emotion. He just put on his hat as he always did and said good-by to us. He took along no food or bundle of any sort. We expected mother to rant and rave, but she didn't. She looked very pale and bit her lip, but all she said was:

What are the mother's parting words to the father?

"If you go away, stay away. Don't ever come back!"

Father made no reply. He looked gently at me

Angel of Destiny, c.1900. Odilon Redon. Private collection.

art note

Angel of Destiny, c.1900. Odilon Redon.

Odilon Redon (1840–1916) was a Symbolist artist. He explained that his work was inspired by dreams, and that as in dreams, the meaning is not always clear. Redon said of his drawings that they "transport us to the ambiguous world of the indeterminate." As you read this story, decide whether Guimarães Rosa also transports us to such an ambiguous dreamlike world.

and motioned me to walk along with him. I feared mother's wrath, yet I eagerly obeyed. We headed toward the river together. I felt bold and exhilarated, so much so that I said: "Father, will you take me with you in your boat?"

What does the narrator ask his father?

He just looked at me, gave me his blessing, and by a gesture, told me to go back. I made as if to do so but, when his back was turned, I ducked behind some bushes to watch him. Father got into the boat and rowed away. Its

---

1. The father has a boat made for himself of mimosa wood.
2. The mother warns him that if he leaves, she doesn't want him back.
3. The narrator asks his father if he can go along in the boat.

INDIVIDUAL LEARNING STRATEGIES

MOTIVATION
Students can draw, paint, or create a three-dimensional representation of a place where they would like to go to escape or to seek peace. Students may choose to depict a real or imaginary place.

READING PROFICIENCY
Students may be confused by the title, "The Third Bank of the River." The role of the river is very important in this story. Have students focus on the Prereading page and the meaning of rivers to João Guimarães Rosa.

ENGLISH LANGUAGE LEARNING
Point out the following vocabulary words and expressions:
melancholy—gloomy
rant and rave—shout and carry on
wrath—anger
phenomenon—strange happening
vestments—robes for a priest
imperceptible—unnoticeable

SPECIAL NEEDS
Make sure students focus on the Guided Reading questions as they read and the Recall questions in the Investigate, Inquire, and Imagine section.

ENRICHMENT
Interested students can write an essay comparing and contrasting the relationships between the narrator of "The Third Bank of the River" and his father and that of James and his father in "The Liar."

VOCABULARY FROM THE SELECTION

annual	lull
capsize	obstinacy
composure	provisions
derelict	repent
impedimenta	rheumatism

CROSS-CURRICULAR ACTIVITIES

SOCIAL STUDIES. Students can work in small groups to research major rivers of the world, for example, the Nile, the Amazon, the Yangtze, and the Indus. Students should determine basic facts, such as length, volume, where the river starts and what body of water it empties into. They should also consider the effect of the river on civilizations that live near it. For example: What kinds of damage has flood caused? Why have cities been located where they have? What does the river provide? What special or symbolic meanings are associated with the river? Students can present their findings in oral presentations using visual aids.

shadow slid across the water like a crocodile, long and quiet.

Father did not come back. Nor did he go anywhere, really. He just rowed and floated across and around, out there in the river. Everyone was appalled. What had never happened, what could not possibly happen, was happening. Our relatives, neighbors, and friends came over to discuss the phenomenon.

What does the father do on the river?

Mother was ashamed. She said little and conducted herself with great composure. As a consequence, almost everyone thought (though no one said it) that Father had gone insane. A few, however, suggested that Father might be fulfilling a promise he had made to God or to a saint, or that he might have some horrible disease, maybe leprosy,[1] and that he left for the sake of the family, at the same time wishing to remain fairly near them.

Travelers along the river and people living near the bank on one side or the other reported that Father never put foot on land, by day or night. He just moved about on the river, solitary, aimless, like a <u>derelict</u>. Mother and our relatives agreed that the food which he had doubtless hidden in the boat would soon give out and that then he would either leave the river and travel off somewhere (which would be at least a little more respectable) or he would <u>repent</u> and come home.

How far from the truth they were! Father had a secret source of <u>provisions</u>: me. Every day I stole food and brought it to him. The first night after he left, we all lit fires on the shore and prayed and called to him. I was deeply distressed

What does the narrator do for his father?

and felt a need to do something more. The following day I went down to the river with a loaf of corn bread, a bunch of bananas, and some bricks of raw brown sugar. I waited impatiently a long, long hour. Then I saw the boat, far off, alone, gliding almost imperceptibly on the smoothness of the river. Father was sitting in the bottom of the boat. He saw me but he did not row toward me or make any gesture. I showed him the food and then I placed it in a hollow rock on the river bank; it was safe there from animals, rain, and dew. I did this day after day, on and on and on. Later I learned, to my surprise, that mother knew what I was doing and left food around where I could easily steal it. She had a lot of feelings she didn't show.

Mother sent for her brother to come and help on the farm and in business matters. She had the schoolteacher come and tutor us children at home because of the time we had lost. One day, at her request, the priest put on his vestments, went down to the shore, and tried to exorcise the devils that had got into my father. He shouted that Father had a duty to cease his unholy <u>obstinacy</u>. Another day she arranged to have two soldiers come and try to frighten him. All to no avail. My father went by in the distance, sometimes so far away he could barely be seen. He never replied to anyone and no one ever got close to him. When some newspapermen came in a launch to take his picture, Father headed his boat to the other side of the river and into the marshes, which he knew like the palm of his hand but in which other people quickly got lost. There in his private maze, which extended for miles, with heavy foliage

---

1. **leprosy.** Infectious disease caused by bacteria that can lead to skin sores and deformities

words for everyday use

der • e • lict (der' ə likt) *n.*, homeless social misfit; bum. *The man had become a <u>derelict</u> after many years of alcoholism had caused him to lose his job, family, and home.*

re • pent (ri pent') *vi.*, feel regret or change one's mind; turn away from sin. *Soon after he stole his friend's CD, Mike <u>repented</u> and put it back.*

pro • vi • sions (prə vi' zhəns) *pl. n.*, supplies, especially food. *Among our <u>provisions</u> for the camping trip were freeze-dried foods and marshmallows.*

ob • sti • na • cy (äb' stə nə sē) *n.*, stubbornness. *When Yuri refused to admit he was wrong, we all were annoyed by his <u>obstinacy</u>.*

582   *UNIT SEVEN / THE EXAMINED LIFE*

overhead and rushes on all sides, he was safe.

We had to get accustomed to the idea of Father's being out on the river. We had to but we couldn't, we never could. I think I was the only one who understood to some degree what our father wanted and what he did not want. The thing I could not understand at all was how he stood the hardship. Day and night, in sun and rain, in heat and in the terrible midyear cold spells, with his old hat on his head and very little other clothing, week after week, month after month, year after year, unheedful of the waste and emptiness in which his life was slipping by. He never set foot on earth or grass, on isle or mainland shore. No doubt he sometimes tied up the boat at a secret place, perhaps at the tip of some island, to get a little sleep. He never lit a fire or even struck a match and he had no flashlight. He took only a small part of the food that I left in the hollow rock—not enough, it seemed to me, for survival. What could his state of health have been? How about the continual drain on his energy, pulling and pushing the oars to control the boat? And how did he survive the <u>annual</u> floods, when the river rose and swept along with it all sorts of dangerous objects—branches of trees, dead bodies of animals—that might suddenly crash against his little boat?

He never talked to a living soul. And we never talked about him. We just thought. No, we could never put our father out of mind. If for a short time we seemed to, it was just a <u>lull</u> from which we would be sharply awakened by the realization of his frightening situation.

My sister got married, but mother didn't want a wedding party. It would have been a sad affair, for we thought of him every time we ate some especially tasty food. Just as we thought of him in our cozy beds on a cold, stormy night—out there, alone and unprotected, trying to bail out the boat with only his hands and a gourd. Now and then someone would say that I was getting to look more and more like my father. But I knew that by then his hair and beard must have been shaggy and his nails long. I pictured him thin and sickly, black with hair and sunburn, and almost naked despite the articles of clothing I occasionally left for him.

He didn't seem to care about us at all. But I felt affection and respect for him, and, whenever they praised me because I had done something good, I said: "My father taught me to act that way."

It wasn't exactly accurate but it was a truthful sort of lie. As I said, father didn't seem to care about us. But then why did he stay around there? Why didn't he go up the river or down the river, beyond the possibility of seeing us or being seen by us? He alone knew the answer.

My sister had a baby boy. She insisted on showing Father his grandson. One beautiful day we all went down to the river bank, my sister in her white wedding dress, and she lifted the baby high. Her husband held a parasol above them. We shouted to father and waited. He did not appear. My sister cried; we all cried in each other's arms.

My sister and her husband moved far away. My brother went to live in a city. Times changed, with their usual imperceptible rapidity. Mother finally moved too; she was old and went to live with her daughter. I remained behind, a leftover. I could never think of marrying. I just stayed there with the <u>impedimenta</u> of my life. Father, wandering alone and forlorn on the river, needed me. I knew he needed me, although he never even told me why he was

What does the narrator understand about his father's undertaking? What does he not understand?

1. He understood somewhat what his father wanted and did not want. He did not understand how his father could stand the hardship.

CROSS-CURRICULAR CONNECTIONS

SCIENCE. João Guimarães Rosa once said that he would like to be a crocodile. Students can research these animals to determine their habitats, eating habits, and mating habits. Students can also explore the threat crocodiles pose to humans and the threat humans pose to crocodiles. Students may also want to examine the difference between alligators and crocodiles.

words for everyday use	**an • nu • al** (an' yə wəl) *adj.,* occurring every year or once a year; yearly. *The Maple Street Theater will hold its tenth annual foreign film festival this month.* **lull** (ləl) *n.,* temporary pause in activity; temporary calm. *After lunch, the restaurant experienced a lull before the dinner rush.* **im • ped • i • men • ta** (im pe' də mən ta) *pl. n.,* implement, things that impede or prevent (plural of impediment). *"What are the major impedimenta standing in the way of this project?" the chairperson asked.*

1. The father explained his reasons to the man who built his boat. That man is now dead. Some people compare the father to Noah.

SELECTION CHECK TEST 4.7.11 WITH ANSWERS

Checking Your Reading

1. What kind of man was the narrator's father? **His father was dutiful, orderly, and straightforward.**
2. What specifications did the narrator's father give for his boat? **It was to be made of mimosa wood, just large enough for one man, and sturdy enough to last twenty or thirty years.**
3. What does the narrator's mother say when his father goes to his boat? **She tells him if he goes away, he should stay away and never come back.**
4. What major family events does the father miss? **He misses his daughter's wedding and the birth of his grandson.**
5. What does the narrator do when his father begins to row toward him at the end of the story? **He runs away.**

Vocabulary in Context

Fill in each blank below with the most appropriate word from the following Words for Everyday Use.

composure   repent   obstinacy
lull   capsize   annual

1. The rhythmic rocking will **lull** the child to sleep.
2. Don't rock the boat; it might **capsize**.
3. Yolanda's **obstinacy** makes it difficult to compromise.
4. Every year on the day after Thanksgiving, the school holds its **annual** Turkey Trot.
5. Always calm, Arial maintained her **composure** even when disaster struck.

Literary Tools

1. What is a symbol? **A symbol is a thing that stands for or represents both itself and something else.**
2. What thing is used as a symbol in this story? **The river is a symbol.**
3. Define *paradox*. **A paradox is a seemingly contradictory statement idea or event.**
4. Give an example of a paradox. *Responses will vary.*

doing it. When I put the question to people bluntly and insistently, all they told me was that they heard that father had explained it to the man who made the boat. But now this man was dead and nobody knew or remembered anything. There was just some foolish talk, when the rains were especially severe and persistent, that my father was wise like Noah[2] and had the boat built in anticipation of a new flood; I dimly remember people saying this. In any case, I would not condemn my father for what he was doing. My hair was beginning to turn gray.

> To whom did the father explain his reasons for going out on the river? To what person do some people compare the father?

I have only sad things to say. What bad had I done, what was my great guilt? My father always away and his absence always with me. And the river, always the river, perpetually renewing itself. The river, always. I was beginning to suffer from old age, in which life is just a sort of lingering. I had attacks of illness and of anxiety. I had a nagging <u>rheumatism</u>. And he? Why, why was he doing it? He must have been suffering terribly. He was so old. One day, in his falling strength, he might let the boat <u>capsize</u>; or he might let the current carry it downstream, on and on, until it plunged over the waterfall to the boiling turmoil below. It pressed upon my heart. He was out there and I was forever robbed of my peace. I am guilty of I know not what, and my pain is an open wound inside me. Perhaps I would know—if things were different. I began to guess what was wrong.

Out with it! Had I gone crazy? No, in our house that word was never spoken, never through all the years. No one called anybody crazy, for nobody is crazy. Or maybe everybody.

All I did was go there and wave a handkerchief So he would be more likely to see me. I was in complete command of myself. I waited. Finally he appeared in the distance, there, then over there, a vague shape sitting in the back of the boat. I called to him several times. And I said what I was so eager to say, to state formally and under oath. I said it as loud as I could:

"Father, you have been out there long enough. You are old. . . . Come back, you don't have to do it anymore. . . . Come back and I'll go instead. Right now, if you want. Any time. I'll get into the boat. I'll take your place."

And when I had said this my heart beat more firmly.

He heard me. He stood up. He maneuvered with his oars and headed the boat toward me. He had accepted my offer. And suddenly I trembled, down deep. For he had raised his arm and waved—the first time in so many, so many years. And I couldn't . . . In terror, my hair on end, I ran, I fled madly. For he seemed to come from another world. And I'm begging forgiveness, begging, begging.

I experienced the dreadful sense of cold that comes from deadly fear, and I became ill. Nobody ever saw or heard about him again. Am I a man, after such a failure? I am what never should have been. I am what must be silent. I know it is too late. I must stay in the deserts and unmarked plains of my life, and I fear I shall shorten it. But when death comes I want them to take me and put me in a little boat in this perpetual water between the long shores; and I, down the river, lost in the river, inside the river . . . the river . . . ■

2. **Noah.** Biblical figure who was told by God to build an ark in anticipation of a great flood

words for everyday use

rheu • ma • tism (rū′ mə ti zəm) *n.*, disease involving painful swelling of the muscles and joints; arthritis. *My grandfather's* <u>rheumatism</u> *caused him to walk with a limp.*
cap • size (kap′ sīz) *vi.*, become overturned. *The canoe* <u>capsized</u> *when Jeremy stood up in it.*

Respond *to the* SELECTION

Why do you think the son feels like a failure at the end of the story?

"HERACLITUS"

Jorge Luis Borges, translated by Norman Thomas di Giovanni

The day's second twilight.
Night that sinks into sleep.
Purification and oblivion.
The day's first twilight.
Morning that once was dawn.
Day that once was morning.
The crowded day that will become the weary
    evening.
The day's second twilight.
That other habit of time, night.
Purification and oblivion.
The day's first twilight...
The furtive dawn and in the dawn
the Greek's bewilderment.
What web is this

of *will be*, *is*, and *was*?
What river's this
through which the Ganges flows?
What river's this whose source is unimaginable?
What river's this
that bears along mythologies and swords?
No use in sleeping.
It runs through sleep, through deserts, through
    cellars.
The river bears me on and I am the river.
I was made of a changing substance, of mysteri-
    ous time.
Maybe the source is in me.
Maybe out of my shadow
the days arise, relentless and unreal. ■

ABOUT THE RELATED READING

Jorge Luis Borges (1899–1986) was an Argentinian poet, essayist, and short-story writer whose imaginative, fantastical, and mind-bending works are classics of twentieth-century world literature. Like fellow South American Guimarães Rosa, Borges was fascinated with metaphysical dilemmas, such as the nature of time, which he explores in this poem, **"Heraclitus."** The title, as well as the reference to "the Greek" in the poem, refer to Greek philosopher Heraclitus (*circa* 540–480 BC). Heraclitus famously compared the flow of time to the flow of a river, remarking: "You could not step twice into the same river; for other waters are ever flowing on to you." In "Heraclitus," Borges ponders this allegory of time as a river, a river "whose source is unimaginable" and which "runs through sleep, through deserts, through cellars."

RESPOND TO THE SELECTION

You may also ask students to discuss what would happen if the son had actually taken his father's place in the boat. When do sons typically take over for their fathers in real life? Is it always possible to relieve someone's else's burden?

LITERARY NOTE

Borges's poem was published in Spanish as "Heráclito" in his poetry collection *Elogio de la sombra* (*In Praise of Darkness*, 1969).

Japanese thinker Kamo no Chomei (AD 1153–1216) echoed Heraclitus's quote when he said, "The flow of the river is ceaseless and its water is never the same."

CROSS-CURRICULAR CONNECTIONS

MYTHOLOGY. In "Heraclitus," Borges draws upon the river as a mystical symbol for time-flow and eternity. In many cultures, rivers symbolize both eternity and constant change, and have appeared in mythology as routes connected to the afterlife. According to Greek mythology, the souls of the dead must cross the River Styx on their journey from the land of the living to the underworld, Hades.

For centuries, devout Hindus in India have held the Ganges River sacred. Many Hindus make pilgrimages to the holy city of Varanasi on the Ganges, and many bring their dead there to be cremated. The very poor, who cannot afford wood, often dump the bodies of loved ones directly into the river, where they believe the dead will pass on into the next life. This practice is less common now since people are aware of the environmental problems it causes.

RECALL

1a. The narrator says his father was a "dutiful, orderly, straightforward man."

2a. The father simply rows and floats around the river, never straying far from home and never coming in to shore. People think he is either insane, fulfilling a promise to God or to a saint, or that he has a horrible disease. While the father is on the river, the narrator's sister marries and has a son.

3a. The narrator offers to take his father's place in the boat, but when his father appears to accept, he runs away in terror.

INTERPRET

1b. Most students will say that the father's actions contradict the description of him as a "dutiful, orderly, straightforward man."

2b. The narrator provides food for his father because he feels "deeply distressed" and wants to do something more to help his father. The narrator's mother is upset and "ashamed" that her husband has left. The narrator's sister, too, is saddened that her father cannot be present for the events in her life, such as her marriage and the birth of his grandson.

3b. The narrator seems to feel guilty for allowing his father to remain on the river, especially now that he is so old. He runs from his father because he is terrified.

ANALYZE

4a. The narrator seems to feel a connection with his father, despite the fact that he does not know why his father decided to go out on the river. He says that his father needs him, and indeed his father depends on him for food. Students may say that the narrator's guilt is caused by a feeling that he should take over his father's duties and end his suffering.

SYNTHESIZE

4b. Clearly, the narrator is fearful and that is why he is finally unwilling to trade places with his father. It might be that the father actually is more dutiful than the son in the sense that he is unafraid to confront his own fate. It may be that the father is actually dead and had no choice, whereas the son, seeing him come "from another world" (literally the afterworld) is terrified, as all humans are, at the thought of confronting his own death.

Investigate, Inquire, and *Imagine*

Recall: GATHERING FACTS

1a. What kind of a man does the narrator say his father was?

2a. What does the narrator's father do out on the river? What reasons do people think might have caused the father to behave in this way? What events occur in the family while the father is out on the river?

3a. What offer does the narrator make his father? What does he do when his father accepts?

Interpret: FINDING MEANING

1b. Do the father's actions support the opening line of the story?

2b. Why do you think the narrator provides food for his father? How do the narrator's mother and sister feel about what the father has done? Explain.

3b. Why do you think the narrator makes such an offer? Why does he react as he does when his father actually accepts?

Analyze: TAKING THINGS APART

4a. Analyze the relationship between the narrator and his father. How does the narrator view his father's undertaking? What do you think causes the narrator's great guilt?

Synthesize: BRINGING THINGS TOGETHER

4b. Why do you think the father was willing to go out on the river, but the narrator was not, even when he had the chance? Explain, using evidence from the story.

Evaluate: MAKING JUDGMENTS

5a. Is the story realistic or fantastic? Which elements are fantastic? Are the townspeople and other relatives realistic characters? Explain.

Extend: CONNECTING IDEAS

5b. Compare the river in the story with the river described in the Related Reading, "Heraclitus" by Jorge Luis Borges. What kind of river does the poem refer to?

Understanding *Literature*

SYMBOL. Review the definition for **symbol** in the Handbook of Literary Terms. What do you think the river in this story might symbolize? Consider the appearance and size of the boat, made of wood and "just large enough for one person." What other wooden container could this boat symbolize? Consider the title of this story. Does a river actually have a third bank? What do you think the "third bank of the river" might symbolize? How is life similar to sitting in a boat on a river?

PARADOX. Review the definition for **paradox** in the Handbook of Literary Terms and the chart you made for Literary Tools. Explain how the father's journey is not actually a journey. How is the statement, "you can never step into the same river twice" a paradox?

ANSWERS TO INVESTIGATE, INQUIRE, AND IMAGINE (CONT.)

EVALUATE

5a. The story is mostly fantastic. The father's actions and his ability to survive for years on the river are not realistic. However, the townspeople and other relatives, and their reactions to the strange occurrence, are realistic.

EXTEND

5b. The river in the story is an actual river, whereas the river in the poem is the river of time, which goes on endlessly and drags everything along with it. However, students may say that in both selections, the river is intended to signify eternity in that it flows on forever and is too wide to be seen across.

> Answers to Understanding Literature can be found on page 587.

Writer's Journal

1. Imagine you are the father. Write a **stream-of-consciousness journal entry** describing what you see everyday and what thoughts go through your head.
2. If a third bank of the river existed, what would it be like? Would it be like heaven? Or would it be like a black hole in space? Write a **description** of the third bank.
3. Imagine you are the narrator's mother. Write a **conversation** between her and a friend in which she explains what she thinks of her husband's actions.

Integrating the Language Arts

Language, Grammar, and Style

COMBINING SENTENCES. Read the Language Arts Survey 3.36, "Combining and Expanding Sentences." Then combine each pair of sentences below to create a single sentence.

1. The narrator's father was a dutiful and orderly man. He was also straightforward.
2. The father was leaving. At the same time the narrator asked if he could go along.
3. The narrator stole food. Then he brought it to his father.
4. The narrator's mother knew what he was doing. She left food around where he could easily steal it.
5. The narrator asked himself questions. One question was "What bad had I done?"

Study and Research

RESEARCHING METAPHYSICS. Guimarães Rosa was very interested in the field of metaphysics. Research the study of metaphysics. Who first used the term *metaphysics*? Who were some of the most prominent philosophers of metaphysics and what were some of their main ideas? Are the ideas of metaphysics popular today? Share your findings with the class.

Critical Thinking & Collaborative Learning

HOLDING A CLASS DISCUSSION. Gather in groups of four or five students to discuss the mystery behind the story, "The Third Bank of the River." As a group, decide what you think motivates the father, supporting your theory with details from the story. Then, discuss the issue as a class. Consider the following possible explanations for his behavior.

- Father has gone insane. (What do other characters think? Who else might be insane, according to the narrator?)
- Father wishes to defy the laws of Time and thus avoid death. (How does avoiding death make him like Noah from the Bible?)
- Father is actually dead. (Why might people become angry with someone who has died? How can you explain the son's interactions with his father? How does this explanation account for why the son was not allowed to come along on the boat?)
- Father is searching for knowledge. (Consider the line: "[The boat's] shadow slid across the water like a crocodile, long and quiet" and compare it to the quote by Guimarães Rosa which was included in Prereading. What kind of knowledge is the father seeking, in your opinion?)

Language, Grammar, and Style
Responses will vary.
1. The narrator's father was a dutiful, straightforward, and orderly man.
2. As the father was leaving, the narrator asked if he could go along.
3. After the narrator stole food, he brought it to his father.
4. Because the narrator's mother knew what he was doing, she left food around where he could easily steal it.
5. The narrator asked himself questions such as "What bad had I done?"

ANSWERS TO UNDERSTANDING LITERATURE

SYMBOL. The river could symbolize the flow of time, never-ending yet always changing. The rowboat could symbolize a coffin. A river does not have a third bank. It simply flows on and then enters something larger. A river with a third bank is like eternity with an ending; it is unimaginable. Therefore, a "third bank" symbolizes eternity or the "unknowable." Life is similar to sitting in a boat on a river in that you are going in one direction, flowing with the current.

PARADOX. The father's "journey" is, paradoxically, a "non-journey" because he goes nowhere. The idea that you cannot step into the same river twice is a paradox because actually, the river itself is the same river, but the waters that make up the river are forever changing.

ADDITIONAL RESOURCES

UNIT 7 RESOURCE BOOK
- Selection Worksheet 7.7
- Selection Check Test 4.7.13
- Selection Test 4.7.14
- Language, Grammar, and Style Resource 3.90

GRAPHIC ORGANIZER

Description: Quindlen describes sitting in her favorite reading chair as a child.

Exposition: Quindlen analyzes the contribution of Gutenberg's printing press in order to point out how reading became available to the masses.

READER'S JOURNAL

You might put students in small groups to discuss the book or story that has had a positive effect on their life. Students who do not read outside of class might select a story or novel that they have read in class.

Literary TOOLS

AIM. A writer's **aim** is his or her purpose, or goal. People may write with the following aims: to inform (expository/informational writing); to entertain, enrich, enlighten, and/or use an artistic medium, such as fiction or poetry, to share a perspective (imaginative writing); to make a point by sharing a story about an event (narrative writing); to reflect (personal/expressive writing); to persuade readers or listeners to respond in some way, such as to agree with a position, change a view on an issue, reach an agreement, or perform an action (persuasive/argumentative writing).

NARRATION, DESCRIPTION, AND EXPOSITION. A writer may structure, or organize, a piece of writing in different ways in order to communicate more clearly. In her essay, Quindlen uses **narration**, **description**, and **exposition**. See the Handbook of Literary Terms for definitions of these terms.

Graphic Organizer

Fill in the chart below with an example of narration, description, and exposition in the essay. One example has been done for you.

Narration	Quindlen narrates her experiences of running away as a child.
Description	
Exposition	

from How Reading Changed My Life
by Anna Quindlen

Reader's resource

This essay is taken from *How Reading Changed My Life* (1998), an autobiography in which Anna Quindlen describes how her experiences with books and reading have enriched her life. She recounts how her passion for reading began in childhood and extends into her adulthood today, shaping her view of the world. "Reading has always been my home, my sustenance, my great invincible companion" says Quindlen. "Yet of all the many things in which we recognize some universal comfort . . . reading seems to be the one in which the comfort is most undersung, at least publicly, although it was really all I thought of, or felt, when I was eating up book after book, running away from home while sitting in [a] chair, traveling around the world and yet never leaving the room. I did not read from a sense of superiority, or advancement, or even learning. I read because I loved it more than any other activity on earth."

About the AUTHOR

Anna Quindlen (1953–) was born in Philadelphia, Pennsylvania. After graduating from Barnard College in 1974, she became a reporter. For *The New York Times* she wrote popular columns such as "About New York" and "Life in the 30's." Quindlen has also written three novels: *Object Lessons* (1991); *One True Thing* (1995) and *Black and Blue* (1998). *One True Thing* and *Black and Blue* were both made into motion pictures. In 1992 Quindlen won a Pulitzer Prize for her column "Public and Private." She has also written children's books.

Reader's Journal

What book or story has had a positive effect on your life?

GOALS/OBJECTIVES

Studying this lesson will enable students to
- appreciate an essay about reading
- describe Anna Quindlen's literary accomplishments
- define *aim, narration, description,* and *exposition* and recognize the use of these techniques in the selection

- identify possessive nouns and use apostrophes correctly
- write a composition about the Gutenberg printing press
- make a calendar with quotations about reading
- design a book jacket for *How Reading Changed My Life*

from
How READING
Changed My Life
Anna Quindlen

Woman Reading, 1922. Marc Chagall. Private collection.

The stories about my childhood, the ones that stuck, that got told and retold at dinner tables, to dates as I sat by red-faced, to my own children by my father later on, are stories of running away. Some are stories of events I can't remember, that I see and feel only in the retelling: the toddler who wandered down the street while her mother was occupied with yet another baby and was driven home by the police; the little girl who was seen by a neighbor ambling down the alley a block north of her family's home; the child who appeared on her grandparents' doorstep and wasn't quite sure whether anyone knew she'd come so far on her own.

> What episodes of Quindlen's childhood are still recounted today?

Other times I remember myself. I remember taking the elevated train to downtown Philadelphia because, like Everest, it was there, a spired urban Oz so other from the quiet flat streets of the suburbs where we lived. I remember riding my bicycle for miles to the neighborhood where my aunt and uncle lived, a narrow avenue of brick row houses with long boxcar backyards. I remember going to the airport with my parents when I was thirteen and reading the destinations board, seeing all the places I could go: San Juan, Cincinnati, Los Angeles, London. I remember loving motels; the cheap heavy silverware on airplanes; the smell of plastic, disinfectant, and mildew on the old Greyhound buses. I remember watching trains click by, a blur of grey and the diamond glitter of sunshine on glass, and wishing I was aboard.

The odd thing about all this is that I had a lovely childhood in a lovely place. This is the way I remember it; this is the way it was. The neighborhood where I grew up was the sort of place in which people dream of raising children—pretty, privileged but not rich, a small but satisfying spread of center-hall colonials, old roses, rhododendrons, and quiet roads. We

VOCABULARY FROM THE SELECTION

abate	covert	exclusivity	raucous
buttressed	disheartened	inveterate	sanction
compulsion	eloquent	invincible	solace
corollary	eponymous	plummeting	supplant
couch	ethos	pundit	sustenance

ANSWER TO GUIDED READING QUESTION

1. Episodes of Quindlen's running away as a child are still recounted today.

INDIVIDUAL LEARNING STRATEGIES

MOTIVATION
Students may enjoy creating posters that promote reading. Students can work as a group to brainstorm reasons for reading (to learn, to get information, for pleasure, to explore new worlds, etc.). Then they can use these reasons to create slogans for their posters.

READING PROFICIENCY
The information in the Reader's Resource on the Prereading page provides a good introduction to the author's main message. Students should focus on this section before they read the selection.

ENGLISH LANGUAGE LEARNING
Point out the following vocabulary words and expressions:
ambling—strolling
Oz—refers to a magical land told of by L. Frank Baum
interstate—highways or roads that go from state to state
guillotine—device used to behead people as a form of capital punishment
undersung—underrated, not given enough credit
domino effect—one thing leads to another

SPECIAL NEEDS
Make sure students pay special attention to the Guided Reading questions and the Recall questions from the Investigate, Inquire, and Imagine section.

ENRICHMENT
Interested students can write essays titled "How Reading Changed My Life." Students should focus on the kind of reading that is most important to them, whether it is reading for pleasure, or reading for learning, or reading for some other purpose.

walked to school, wandered wild in the summer, knew everyone and all their brothers and sisters, too. Some of the people I went to school with, who I sat next to in sixth and seventh grade, still live there, one or two in the houses that their parents once owned.

Not long ago, when I was in town on business, I determined to test my memories against the reality and drove to my old block, my old school, the homes of my closest friends, sure that I had inflated it all in my mind. But the houses were no smaller, the flowers no less bright. It was as fine as I had remembered—maybe more so, now when so much of the rest of the world has come to seem dingy and diminished.

Why did the author return to the setting of her childhood later in life?

Yet there was always in me, even when I was very small, the sense that I ought to be somewhere else. And wander I did, although, in my everyday life, I had nowhere to go and no imaginable reason on earth why I should want to leave. The buses took to the interstate without me; the trains sped by. So I wandered the world through books. I went to Victorian England in the pages of *Middlemarch* and *A Little Princess*, and to Saint Petersburg before the fall of the tsar with *Anna Karenina*. I went to Tara, and Manderley, and Thornfield Hall, all those great houses, with their high ceilings and high drama, as I read *Gone with the Wind*, *Rebecca*, and *Jane Eyre*.

How did Quindlen wander the world?

When I was in eighth grade I took a scholarship test for a convent school, and the essay question began with a quotation: "It is a far, far better thing that I do, than I have ever done; it is a far, far better rest that I go to, than I have ever known." Later, over a stiff and awkward lunch of tuna-fish salad, some of the other girls

at my table were perplexed by the source of the quotation and what it meant, and I was certain, at that moment, weeks before my parents got the letter from the nuns, that the scholarship was mine. How many times had I gone up the steps to the guillotine with Sydney Carton as he went to that far, far better rest at the end of *A Tale of Two Cities*?

Like so many of the other books I read, it never seemed to me like a book, but like a place I had lived in, had visited and would visit again, just as all the people in them, every blessed one—Anne of Green Gables, Heidi, Jay Gatsby, Elizabeth Bennet, Scarlett O'Hara, Dill and Scout, Miss Marple, and Hercule Poirot—were more real than the real people I knew. My home was in that pleasant place outside Philadelphia, but I really lived somewhere else. I lived within the covers of books and those books were more real to me than any other thing in my life. One poem committed to memory in grade school survives in my mind. It is by Emily Dickinson: "There is no Frigate like a Book / To take us Lands away / Nor any coursers like a Page / Of prancing Poetry."

Perhaps only a truly discontented child can become as seduced by books as I was. Perhaps restlessness is a necessary <u>corollary</u> of devoted literacy. There was a club chair in our house, a big one, with curled arms and a square ottoman;[1] it sat in one corner of the living room, catty-corner to the fireplace, with a barrel table next to it. In my mind I am always sprawled in it, reading with my skinny, scabby legs slung over one of its arms. "It's a beautiful day," my mother is saying; she said that always, often,

Where was the author's favorite place to read as a child?

---
1. **ottoman.** Cushioned footstool

words for everyday use

cor • ol • lar • y (kôr′ ə ler ē) *n.*, something that naturally follows; result. *One <u>corollary</u> of quitting smoking is improved physical health.*

autumn, spring, even when there was a fresh snowfall. "All your friends are outside." It was true; they always were. Sometimes I went out with them, coaxed into the street, out into the fields, down by the creek, by the lure of what I knew intuitively was normal childhood, by the promise of being what I knew instinctively was a normal child, one who lived, raucous, in the world.

I have clear memories of that sort of life, of lifting the rocks in the creek that trickled through Naylor's Run to search for crayfish, of laying pennies on the tracks of the trolley and running to fetch them, flattened, when the trolley had passed. But at base it was never any good. The best part of me was always at home, within some book that had been laid flat on the table to mark my place, its imaginary people waiting for me to return and bring them to life. That was where the real people were, the trees that moved in the wind, the still, dark waters. I won a bookmark in a spelling bee during that time with these words of Montaigne upon it in gold: "When I am reading a book, whether wise or silly, it seems to me to be alive and talking to me." I found that bookmark not long ago, at the bottom of a box, when my father was moving.

What quotation by Montaigne was printed on the bookmark that Quindlen won in a spelling bee when she was a child?

In the years since those days in that club chair I have learned that I was not alone in this, although at the time I surely was, the only child I knew, or my parents knew, or my friends knew, who preferred reading to playing kick-the-can or ice-skating or just sitting on the curb breaking sticks and scuffing up dirt with a sneaker in summer. In books I have traveled, not only to other worlds, but into my own. I learned who I was and who I wanted to be, what I might aspire to, and what I might dare to dream about my world and myself. More powerfully and persuasively than from the "shalt nots" of the Ten Commandments, I learned the difference between good and evil, right and wrong. One of my favorite childhood books, *A Wrinkle in Time*, described that evil, that wrong, existing in a different dimension from our own. But I felt that I, too, existed much of the time in a different dimension from everyone else I knew. There was waking, and there was sleeping. And then there were books, a kind of parallel universe in which anything might happen and frequently did, a universe in which I might be a newcomer but was never really a stranger. My real, true world. My perfect island.

Years later I would come to discover, as Robinson Crusoe did when he found Man Friday, that I was not alone in that world or on that island. I would discover (through reading, naturally) that while I was sprawled, legs akimbo,[2] in that chair with a book, Jamaica Kincaid was sitting in the glare of the Caribbean sun in Antigua reading in that same way that I did, as though she was starving and the book was bread. When she was grown-up, writing books herself, winning awards for her work, she talked in one of her memoirs of ignoring her little brother when she was supposed to be looking after him: "I liked reading a book much more than I liked looking after him (and even now I like reading a book more than I like looking after my own children . . .)."

While I was in that club chair with a book, Hazel Rochman and her husband were in South Africa, burying an old tin trunk heavy with hardcovers in the backyard, because the police might raid their house and search it for banned books. Rochman, who left Johannesburg for

---

2. **akimbo.** Set in a bent position

words for everyday use

rau • cous (rä′ kəs) *adj.*, boisterous. *The raucous pep rally energized the players for the game.*

1. The quotation reads: "When I am reading a book, whether wise or silly, it seems to me to be alive and talking to me."

ADDITIONAL QUESTIONS AND ACTIVITIES

Have students discuss the value of reading in relation to other activities. Students should present their own ideas for and against reading.

ANSWERS TO GUIDED READING QUESTIONS

1. Like Quindlen, Jamaica Kincaid and Oprah Winfrey preferred reading to any other childhood activity.
2. American culture suspects people who read for pleasure of being lazy and avoiding "real life."

INTERNET RESOURCES

To listen to an interview of Anna Quindlen discussing her novel *Black and Blue*, access **National Public Radio** at http://www.napr.org/programs/atc/980210.quindlen.html.

Chicago and became an editor for the American Library Association's *Booklist*, summed up the lessons learned from that night, about the power of reading, in a way I would have recognized even as a girl. "Reading makes immigrants of us all," she wrote years later. "It takes us away from home, but, most important, it finds homes for us everywhere."

While I was in that club chair with a book, Oprah Winfrey was dividing her childhood between her mother in Milwaukee and her father in Nashville, but finding her most consistent home between the covers of her books. Even decades later, when she had become the host of her <u>eponymous</u> talk show, one of the world's highest-paid entertainers, and the founder of an on-air book club that resulted in the sale of millions of copies of serious literary novels, Winfrey still felt the sting as she talked to a reporter from *Life* magazine: "I remember being in the back hallway when I was about nine—I'm going to try to say this without crying—and my mother threw the door open and grabbed a book out of my hand and said, 'You're nothing but a something-something bookworm. Get your butt outside! You think you're better than the other kids.' I was treated as though something was wrong with me because I wanted to read all the time!"

Reading has always been my home, my <u>sustenance</u>, my great <u>invincible</u> companion. "Book love," Trollope called it. "It will make your hours pleasant to you as long as you live." Yet of all the many things in which we recognize some universal comfort—God, sex, food, family, friends—reading seems to be the one in which the comfort is most undersung, at least publicly, although it was really all I thought of, or felt, when I was eating up book after book, running

> *What does the author have in common with Jamaica Kincaid and Oprah Winfrey?*

away from home while sitting in that chair, traveling around the world and yet never leaving the room. I did not read from a sense of superiority, or advancement, or even learning. I read because I loved it more than any other activity on earth.

By the time I became an adult, I realized that while my satisfaction in the sheer act of reading had not <u>abated</u> in the least, the world was often as hostile, or at least as blind, to that joy as had been my girlfriends banging on our screen door, begging me to put down the book—"that stupid book," they usually called it, no matter what book it happened to be. While we pay lip service to the virtues of reading, the truth is that there is still in our culture something that suspects those who read too much, whatever reading too much means, of being lazy, aimless dreamers, people who need to grow up and come outside to where real life is, who think themselves superior in their separateness.

> *According to Quindlen, what does American culture suspect of people who read for pleasure?*

There is something in the American character that is even secretly hostile to the act of aimless reading, a certain hale[3] and heartiness that is suspicious of reading as anything more than a tool for advancement. This is a country that likes confidence but despises hubris,[4] that associates the "nose in the book" with the same sense of <u>covert</u> superiority that Ms. Winfrey's mother did. America is also a nation that prizes sociability and community, that accepts a kind of psychological domino effect: alone leads to loner, loner to loser. Any sort of turning away from human contact is suspect, especially one that interferes with the go-out-and-getting <u>ethos</u> that seems to be at the heart of our

---

3. **hale.** Retaining exceptional health and vigor
4. **hubris.** Exaggerated pride or self-confidence

---

words for everyday use

e • pon • y • mous (i pä' nə məs) *adj.*, giving one's name to a people, institution, time period, nation, etc. *William Penn was the <u>eponymous</u> founder of Pennsylvania.*

sus • te • nance (səs' tə nən(t)s) *n.*, nourishment. *During his workouts, Jed depended on granola bars for <u>sustenance</u>.*

in • vin • ci • ble (in vin(t)' sə bəl) *adj.*, incapable of being conquered, overcome, or subdued. *The <u>invincible</u> team won all its games.*

a • bate (ə bāt') *vi.*, decrease in force or intensity. *When the rain <u>abated</u>, Julia walked to the subway station.*

co • vert (kō' vərt) *adj.*, not openly shown, engaged in, or avowed. *The book detailed the <u>covert</u> operations of the CIA in Central America.*

e • thos (ē' thäs) *n.*, distinguishing character, sentiment, moral nature, or guiding beliefs of a person, group, or institution. *In the <u>ethos</u> of ancient Greece, the individual was highly valued.*

national character. The image of American presidents that stick are those that portray them as men of action: Theodore Roosevelt on safari, John Kennedy throwing a football around with his brothers. There is only Lincoln as <u>solace</u> to the <u>inveterate</u> reader, a solitary figure sitting by the fire, saying, "My best friend is a person who will give me a book I have not read."

There also arose, as I was growing up, a kind of careerism in the United States that <u>sanctioned</u> reading only if there was some point to it. Students at the nation's best liberal arts colleges who majored in philosophy or English were constantly asked what they were "going to do with it," as though intellectual pursuits for their own sake had had their day, and lost it in the press of business. Reading for pleasure was replaced by reading for

What replaced reading for pleasure?

purpose, and a kind of dogged self-improvement: whereas an executive might learn far more from *Moby Dick* or *The Man in the Grey Flannel Suit*, the book he was expected to have read might by *The Seven Habits of Highly Successful People*. Reading for pleasure, spurred on by some interior <u>compulsion</u>, became as suspect as getting on the subway to ride aimlessly from place to place, or driving from nowhere to nowhere in a car. I like to do both those things, too, but not half so much as reading.

For many years I worked in the newspaper business, where every day the production of the product stands as a flimsy but <u>eloquent</u> testimony to the thirst for words, information, experience. But, for working journalists, reading in the latter half of the twentieth century was most often couched as a series of problems to be addressed in print: were children in public schools reading poorly? Were all Americans reading less? Was the printed word giving way to the spoken one? Had television and the movies <u>supplanted</u> books? The journalistic answer, most often, was yes, yes, yes, yes, <u>buttressed</u> by a variety of statistics that, as so often happens, were massaged to prove the point: reading had fallen upon hard times. And in circles devoted to literary criticism, among the professors of literature, the editors and authors of fiction, there was sometimes a kind of horrible <u>exclusivity</u> surrounding discussions of reading. There was good reading, and there was bad reading. There was the worthy and the trivial. This was always <u>couched</u> in terms of taste, but it tasted, smelled, and felt unmistakably like snobbery.

What kinds of questions did journalists ask about reading in the latter half of the twentieth century? Why did journalists explore these questions?

None of this was new, except, in its discovering, to me. Reading has always been used as a way to divide a country and a culture into the literati[5] and everyone else, the intellectually worthy and the hoi polloi.[6] But in the fifteenth century Gutenberg invented the printing press, and so began the process of turning the book from a work of art for the few into a source of information for the many. After that, it became more difficult for one small group of people to lay an exclusive claim to books, to

What view about reading suggested snobbery to Quindlen?

5. **literati.** Persons interested in literature or the arts
6. **hoi polloi.** General population; masses

words for everyday use

so • lace (sä′ ləs) *n.*, source of relief or consolation. *After losing, Kim took solace in the thought that she would win at the next meet.*

in • vet • er • ate (in ve′ t(ə) rət) *adj.*, firmly established by long persistence; habitual. *Sam was an inveterate liar.*

sanc • tion (saŋ(k)′ shən) *vt.*, give approval or consent to. *The School Board sanctioned a resting period for kindergartners.*

com • pul • sion (kəm pəl′ shən) *n.*, act of compelling, or urging forcefully. *Anne's doctor urged her to rethink her compulsion to get straight A's at the expense of her health.*

el • o • quent (e′ lə kwənt) *adj.*, marked by forceful and fluent expression. *Dr. Martin Luther King, Jr., was an eloquent preacher.*

sup • plant (sə plant′) *vt.*, take the place of and serve as a substitute. *The English teacher was frustrated in her efforts to supplant students' slang with standard, formal English.*

but • tressed (bə′ trəsd) *adj.*, strengthened. *Angelina's speech, buttressed with solid facts, was more convincing that Josh's.*

ex • clu • siv • i • ty (eks klü si′ və tē) *n.*, quality or state of being exclusive, or excluding. *Mrs. Carmichael scoffed at the exclusivity of the club that admitted new members by vote.*

couch (kauch) *part.*, phrased or expressed in a specified manner. *The memo was couched in strong language.*

SELECTION CHECK TEST 4.7.13 WITH ANSWERS (CONT.)

3. Give an example of how Quindlen uses narration in this selection. *Responses will vary.* **Quindlen narrates her experiences of running away as a child.**

4. Give an example of how Quindlen uses description in this selection. *Responses will vary.* **Quindlen describes sitting in her favorite reading chair as a child.**

5. Give an example of how Quindlen uses exposition in this selection. *Responses will vary.* **Quindlen analyzes the contribution of Gutenberg's printing press to point out how reading became available to the masses.**

ANSWERS TO GUIDED READING QUESTIONS

1. Reading for pleasure was replaced by reading for purpose.
2. "Were children in public schools reading poorly? Were all Americans reading less? Was the printed word giving way to the spoken one? Had television and the movies supplanted books?" Journalists asked these questions to prove that reading had "fallen upon hard times."
3. The view that there was good reading and bad reading suggested snobbery to Quindlen.

SELECTION CHECK TEST 4.7.13 WITH ANSWERS

Checking Your Reading

1. What stories are still told about the author? **Stories about her running away as a child are still told.**
2. Where did Quindlen like to read? **She liked to read in a club chair.**
3. Name two famous women Quindlen refers to who also love to read. **Quindlen refers to Jamaica Kincaid and Oprah Winfrey.**
4. What division does reading create in a country and culture? **It divides a country and culture into two groups: the literati and everyone else.**
5. What does Quindlen say she is at the end of the essay? **She says she is a bookworm.**

Vocabulary in Context
Fill in each blank below with the most appropriate word from the following Words for Everyday Use.

raucous	plummeting	invincible
covert	solace	eloquent

1. After her dog died, Nina took **solace** in volunteering at the animal shelter.
2. The floods could not drown the **invincible** spirit of the town.
3. The **covert** meeting took place in a secret location in the middle of the night.
4. We all breathed a sigh of relief when the **plummeting** plane leveled out and stopped falling.
5. The police came to break up the **raucous** party.

Literary Tools

1. In writing, what is an aim? **A writer's aim is his or her purpose, or goal.**
2. What is Quindlen's aim in this selection? **Quindlen's aim is to reflect on her experience and to share her opinion about the importance of reading.**

ANSWERS TO GUIDED READING QUESTIONS

1. Critics and scholars persisted in laying an exclusive claim to books.
2. Those who comprise the "real clan of the book" read to take the measure of themselves.

RESPOND TO THE SELECTION

Encourage students to rephrase Quindlen's arguments in their own words. For an additional activity, you might have students make a pro and con chart to answer the question "Should I spend my time reading?"

seize and hold reading as their own. But it was not impossible, and it continued to be done by critics and scholars. When I began to read their work, in college, I was <u>disheartened</u> to discover that many of them felt that the quality of poetry and prose, novels and history and biography, was <u>plummeting</u> into some intellectual bargain basement. But reading saved me from despair, as it always had, for the more I read the more I realized it had always been thus, and that apparently an essential part of studying literature, whether in 1840, 1930, or 1975, was to conclude that there had once been a golden age, and it was gone. "The movies consume so large a part of the leisure of the country that little time is left for other things," the trade magazine of the industry, *Publishers Weekly*, lamented in 1923. "The novel can't compete with cars, the movies, television, and liquor," the French writer Louis-Ferdinand Céline said in 1960.

There was certainly no talk of comfort and joy, of the lively subculture of those of us who forever fell asleep with a book open on our bedside tables, whether bought or borrowed. Of those of us who comprise the real clan of the book, who read not to judge the reading of others but to take the measure of ourselves. Of those of us who read because we love it more than anything, who feel about bookstores the way some people feel about jewelers. The silence about this was odd,

After Gutenberg invented the printing press, which group persisted in laying an exclusive claim to books?

For those who comprise the "real clan of the book," why do they read?

both because there are so many of us and because we are what the world of books is really about. We are the people who once waited for the newest installment of Dickens's latest novel and who kept battered copies of *Catcher in the Rye* in our back pockets and our backpacks. We are the ones who saw to it that *Pride and Prejudice* never went out of print.

But there was little public talk of us, except in memoirs like Ms. Kincaid's. Nothing had changed since I was a solitary child being given embossed[5] leather bookmarks by relatives for Christmas. It was still in the equivalent of the club chairs that we found one another: at the counters in bookstores with our arms full, at the front desks in libraries, at school, where teachers introduced us to one another—and, of course, in books, where book-lovers make up a lively subculture of characters. "Until I feared I would lose, it, I never loved to read. One does not love breathing," says Scout in *To Kill a Mockingbird*.

Reading is like so much else in our culture, in all cultures: the truth of it is found in its people and not in its <u>pundits</u> and its professionals. If I believed what I read about reading I would despair. But instead there are letters from readers to attend to, like the one from a girl who had been given one of my books by her mother and began her letter, "I guess I am what some people would call a bookworm."

"So am I," I wrote back. ■

---

5. **embossed.** Ornamented with raised work, such as gold lettering

words for everyday use	
dis • heart • ened (dis här' tənd) *adj.*, demoralized. *The debate team was <u>disheartened</u> when it learned Ridgevale High was its next opponent.*
plum • met • ing (plə' mət iŋ) *adj.*, dropping sharply and abruptly. *When the prices were <u>plummeting</u> after Christmas, Jerry bought a new stereo.*
pun • dit (pən' dət) *n.*, one who gives opinions in an authoritative manner; critic. *The <u>pundit</u> proclaimed that Internet stocks were overvalued.*

Respond *to the* SELECTION

What attitudes do readers for pleasure have to confront in our culture?

Recommended Reading by Anna Quindlen

10 Nonfiction Books That Help Us Understand the World

The Decline and Fall of the Roman Empire by Edward Gibbon
The Best and the Brightest by David Halberstam
Lenin's Tomb by David Remnick
Lincoln by David Herbert Donald
Silent Spring by Rachel Carson
In Cold Blood by Truman Capote
How We Die by Sherwin Nuland
The Unredeemed Captive by John Demos
The Second Sex by Simone de Beauvoir
The Power Broker by Robert A. Caro

10 Books That Will Help a Teenager Feel More Human

The Catcher in the Rye by J. D. Salinger
A Separate Peace by John Knowles
Lost in Place by Mark Salzman
What's Eating Gilbert Grape? by Peter Hedges
The World According to Garp by John Irving
Bloodbrothers by Richard Price
A Tree Grows in Brooklyn by Betty Smith
To Kill a Mockingbird by Harper Lee
The Heart is a Lonely Hunter by Carson McCullers
The Member of the Wedding by Carson McCullers

The 10 Books I Would Save in a Fire (If I Could Only Save 10)

Pride and Prejudice by Jane Austen
Bleak House by Charles Dickens
Anna Karenina by Leo Tolstoy
The Sound and the Fury by William Faulkner
The Golden Notebook by Doris Lessing
Middlemarch by George Eliot
Sons and Lovers by D. H. Lawrence
The Collected Poems of W. B. Yeats
The Collected Plays of William Shakespeare
The House of Mirth by Edith Wharton

10 Books I Just Love to Read, and Always Will

Main Street by Sinclair Lewis
My Ántonia by Willa Cather
The Lion, the Witch, and the Wardrobe by C. S. Lewis
Wuthering Heights by Emily Brontë
Jane Eyre by Charlotte Brontë
The Group by Mary McCarthy
The Blue Swallows by Howard Nemerov (poetry)
The Phantom Tollbooth by Norton Juster
A Christmas Carol by Charles Dickens
Scoop by Evelyn Waugh

FROM HOW READING CHANGED MY LIFE **595**

RECALL

1a. Quindlen's family members like to tell stories about when she ran away as a young child.

2a. Quindlen says, "I learned who I was and who I wanted to be, what I might aspire to, and what I might dare to dream about my world and myself . . . I learned the difference between good and evil, right and wrong."

3a. Reading divides a country and culture into the literati and everyone else, "the intellectually worthy and the hoi polloi." To Quindlen, there is an unmistakable snobbery in the definition of reading by the literati.

INTERPRET

1b. The author was adventurous and exploring as a child. Quindlen says, "There was always in me, even when I was very small, the sense that I ought to be somewhere else." The physical running away was paralleled by a mental running away, to new places, through reading.

2b. Reading continues to enrich Quindlen's life. She says, "Reading has always been my home, my sustenance, my great invincible companion." She probably gains new insights as she reads about other lives. Living a reflective life due to her reading probably makes Quindlen a better writer.

3b. Good reading is reading of which the "professors of literature, the editors and authors of fiction" approve. Bad reading is reading of which they disapprove.

ANALYZE

4a. Reading opens up new worlds to the reader. The result is that readers may feel they are not content with their own life and want to explore alternative lives, if only in their imagination.

SYNTHESIZE

4b. Quindlen probably read to her children when they were small. She probably took them to the library frequently and gave them books as gifts. It is likely that Quindlen had a lot of books around her house for her children to look at. Above all, she modeled reading by continuing to read good books in front of her children.

EVALUATE

5a. *Responses will vary. Possible responses are given.* She criticizes disapproval of reading that makes readers feel isolated, as she herself was in childhood. The author believes that reading for pleasure is just as

Investigate, Inquire, and Imagine

Recall: GATHERING FACTS

1a. What stories do Quindlen's family members like to recount about her early childhood?

2a. What has Quindlen learned about herself from reading?

3a. In what way does reading divide a country?

Interpret: FINDING MEANING

1b. What do these stories reveal about Quindlen's personality? How does Quindlen tie running away to reading?

2b. Now that Quindlen is an adult and knows who she is and has completed many of her aspirations, why does she continue to read?

3b. What is good reading and what is bad reading?

Analyze: TAKING THINGS APART

4a. Analyze the meaning behind the statement "Perhaps restlessness is a necessary corollary of devoted literacy."

Synthesize: BRINGING THINGS TOGETHER

4b. What do you think Quindlen does with her children to encourage a love of reading in them?

Evaluate: MAKING JUDGMENTS

5a. Evaluate whether in Quindlen's eyes the rewards of reading outweigh the censure of American popular opinion.

Extend: CONNECTING IDEAS

5b. Find a quote about reading not included in Quindlen's essay and explain whether it supports or refutes Quindlen's arguments about the value of reading.

Understanding *Literature*

AIM. Review the definition for **aim** in the Handbook of Literary Terms. What do you think is Quindlen's principal aim in writing "How Reading Changed My Life"? How does Quindlen accomplish this aim?

NARRATION, DESCRIPTION, AND EXPOSITION. Review the definitions for **narration**, **description**, and **exposition** in the Handbook of Literary Terms and the chart you made in Literary Tools on page 588. When Quindlen talks about her favorite reading chair as a child, is she using narration, description, or exposition? When she describes her episodes of running away as a child, which type of writing is she using? When she describes the effect of Gutenberg's printing press on society, which type of writing is she using?

ANSWERS TO INVESTIGATE, INQUIRE, AND IMAGINE (CONT.)

important as reading for purpose. She believes that reading is an end in itself: "I read because I loved it more than any other activity on earth." Unlike many Americans, Quindlen does not believe that reading for pleasure connotes laziness and an avoidance of "real life."

EXTEND

5b. *Responses will vary.*

> Answers to Understanding Literature can be found on page 597.

Writer's Journal

1. Write a **summer reading list** for students your age. Include five books you would recommend, and write a brief description of each book to make it sound interesting to your peers.
2. Write a **public service announcement** about the benefits of reading.
3. Complete the **letter** to Quindlen that begins "I guess I am what some people would call a bookworm." Explain why that is true, and discuss parts of *How Reading Changed My Life* with which you identify.

Integrating the Language Arts

Language, Grammar, and Style

POSSESSIVE NOUNS. Read the Language Arts Survey 3.90, "Apostrophes." Then, on your own paper, copy down the possessive nouns in the following sentences, adding apostrophes where they belong.

1. Anna Quindlens favorite chair was a club chair.
2. Her parents favorite stories are about the time she ran away.
3. On the bookmark she won at school was Montaignes quotation.
4. Oprah Winfrey, one of the worlds highest paid entertainers, also loved books as a child.
5. Would you have waited impatiently for the latest installment of Dickenss novel?

Media Literacy

RESEARCHING ON THE INTERNET. Look on the Internet for quotations about reading. Then make a year's calendar with a notable quote for each month. Be sure to identify the writer of each quote.

Collaborative Learning

BOOK JACKET. First, read the rest of *How Reading Changed My Life.* Then, working with a partner, design a book jacket. On the front cover draw an illustration that reflects the spirit of the book. On the inside cover summarize the book's content, using quotations from the book where appropriate. On the back cover write a biographical paragraph about Anna Quindlen.

Study and Research

RESEARCHING THE GUTENBERG PRESS. Write a composition about Gutenberg and the printing press he invented. Describe the main events of Gutenberg's life and answer the following questions: Where had printing existed in the world before it appeared in Europe? What European printers preceded Gutenberg? How did Gutenberg's press work? What was the masterpiece of Gutenberg's press? How did the invention of the printing press change European society?

ANSWERS TO INTEGRATING THE LANGUAGE ARTS

Language, Grammar, and Style
1. Quindlen's
2. parents'
3. Montaigne's
4. world's
5. Dickens's

Study and Research
Assign a score from 1 to 25 for each grading criterion below. (For more detailed evaluation, see the evaluation forms for writing, revising, and proofreading in the Assessment Resource book.)

Composition
- **CONTENT/UNITY.** The composition describes Gutenberg's life, his printing press, and the contributions of printing to European society.
- **ORGANIZATION/COHERENCE.** The main events of Gutenberg's life are presented chronologically in the composition.
- **LANGUAGE/STYLE.** The composition is written in formal English.
- **CONVENTIONS.** The composition avoids errors in spelling, grammar, usage, mechanics, and manuscript form.

ANSWERS TO UNDERSTANDING LITERATURE

AIM. Quindlen's principal aim is to reflect. *How Reading Changed My Life* is an example of personal/expressive writing. Quindlen accomplishes her aim by relating her personal experiences with reading and the personal experiences of Jamaica Kincaid and Oprah Winfrey. She refutes cultural criticisms of reading with insightful observations.

NARRATION, DESCRIPTION, AND EXPOSITION. When Quindlen talks about her favorite reading chair as a child, she is using description. When she describes her episodes of running away as a child, she is using narration. When she describes the effect of Gutenberg's printing press on society, she is using exposition.

GUIDED WRITING
Software

See the Guided Writing Software for an extended version of this lesson that includes printable graphic organizers, extensive student models and student-friendly checklists, and self-, peer, and teacher evaluation features.

"Wisdom is a life that knows it is living."
—Moravian prayer book

EXAMINING THE MODEL. There are many elements of skillful narration. One of the most important is the narrator's ability to create vivid images and use precise detail to relate the story. A narrator does more than simply list the *who, what, when* and *where* of an experience. Instead, a narrator makes very particular decisions to craft a series of detailed events into a complete story. If you look at the second and third paragraphs of Anna Quindlen's piece, you find excellent examples of selective and vivid detail:

I remember taking the elevated train to downtown Philadelphia because, like Everest, it was there, a spired urban Oz so other from the quiet flat streets of the suburbs...

I remember...where my aunt and uncle lived, a narrow avenue of brick row houses with long boxcar backyards

continued on page 599

Guided Writing

WRITING A PERSONAL NARRATIVE

You are a living story. All that you do, everywhere you go, all those you meet contribute to the growing story that is yours alone to tell.

As you spend time with others, think of yourself as a narrator with an audience hungry for details. Stories have always been an important part of the way humans communicate with each other. Stories can teach us experiences we might never know on our own and give us an opportunity to share our own unique experiences with others.

WRITING ASSIGNMENT. In this unit, you will be telling a personal narrative, a true story from your own life.

Professional Model

from *How Reading Changed my Life* by Anna Quindlen, page 589

The stories about my childhood, the ones that stuck, that got told and retold at dinner tables, to dates as I sat by red-faced, to my own children by my father later on, are the stories of running away. . . .

I remember taking the elevated train to downtown Philadelphia because, like Everest, it was there, a spired urban Oz so other from the quiet flat streets of the suburbs where we lived. I remember riding my bicycle for miles to the neighborhood where my aunt and uncle lived, a narrow avenue of brick row houses with long boxcar backyards... I remember loving motels; the cheap heavy silverware on airplanes; the smell of plastic, disinfectant, and mildew on the old Greyhound buses. I remember watching trains click by, a blur of grey and the diamond glitter of sunshine on glass, and wishing I was aboard.

The odd thing about all this is that I had a lovely childhood in a lovely place. This is the way I remember it, this is the way it was. The neighborhood where I grew up was the sort of place in which people dream of raising children—pretty, privileged but not rich, a small but satisfying spread of center-hall colonials, old roses, rhododendrons, and quiet roads. We walked to school, wandered wild in the summer, knew everyone and all their brothers and sisters, too. Some of the people I went to school with, who I sat next to in sixth and seventh grade, still live there, one or two in the houses that their parents once owned.

Prewriting

FINDING YOUR VOICE. The voice you choose for your narrative should fit the nature of your story. The professional model above is a good example. Quindlen's detail and choice of setting are matched by a voice that is as amazed and intrigued as the little girl in the story. Thus, your voice should match the general mood of the events of the tale.

IDENTIFYING YOUR AUDIENCE. The audience for your narrative may change as you develop your story. Sometimes you may write a story just for yourself. This can be a way of reliving difficult or exciting moments and using hindsight to reevaluate outcomes and consequences. Often you'll have others who will want to read your narrative. If you're writing about friends or family, it can be rewarding to have those involved be part of the drafting process. Personal narratives are also great ways for family histories to take shape.

WRITING WITH A PLAN. There are several prewriting activities that can make your search for a personal narrative topic fun and productive. One activity is to tap into the recorded history of your life that already exists. Talk to parents, siblings, and other relatives and have them refresh your memory about important events. Look through old photo albums, watch family videos, or look back at old calendars to see what you were doing, when, and with whom. Finally, make an "A time when_____" list by filling in the blank with whatever comes to mind: "A time when I was afraid. A time when I wasn't afraid but should have been. A time when I was forced to make a difficult choice. A time when I wanted to be accepted but wasn't."

After you have a range of topics, narrow the list by freewriting a few minutes on each one and testing the waters of your memory. This will help you to find a topic that is important to you and possibly to others, and will eliminate the topics that don't spark your immediate interest.

Joshua filled in the graphic organizer on page 600 to help him keep track of the details in his narrative.

I remember loving motels; the cheap heavy silverware on airplanes; the smell of plastic, disinfectant, and mildew on the old Greyhound buses. I remember watching trains click by, a blur of grey and the diamond glitter of sunshine on glass.

What is the purpose of all this vivid detail? If you look back at Quindlen's topic sentences, you can see that she is recalling stories and memories of her past that all have a common theme: running away. But she does not want the reader to mistake this as purposeless wanderlust. Instead, Quindlen is expressing how amazed and intrigued she was by the mystery of the world outside of her neighborhood. In order to make us feel this same amazement, she not only tells us, but *shows* us how she could be amazed and intrigued. Thus, she compares the urban grandeur of Philadelphia to Mt. Everest and Oz; she recalls the unique but peculiar smell and feel of motels, buses and planes; she sees on the side of a train not just the glare of the sun, but "diamond glitter." Such detail is more interesting to read and it lets the reader into the mind and, in this case, the childhood, of the narrator.

Prewriting

FINDING YOUR VOICE. Ask students to identify examples of natural but informed writing in this unit. Then ask them to emulate the voice and tone of those examples in their own writing.

IDENTIFYING YOUR AUDIENCE. In groups of four, ask students to brainstorm techniques or methods of generating interest among an audience that range from their own peers to elderly people.

WRITING WITH A PLAN. You may want to refer students to the Language Arts Survey 2.12, "Freewriting," to help them with this activity. Encourage students to write down all they can remember about the event they choose to write about (i.e. they way they felt, the people involved, the setting of the event, and the significance of the story they remember).

See the Writing Resource book for a
blackline master of the graphic organizer for this lesson.

Drafting

To help students write an effective
introduction that hooks the reader,
you may want to direct students to
Language Arts Survey 2.32,
"Drafting an Introduction."

Using the Graphic Organizer

The graphic organizer for this
personal narrative is a chart.
In order to keep your narrative
focused, make your chart
cover only five or ten minutes
and see if you can account for
the details and events that
emerge inside of those
minutes. Ask yourself what
you could hear, touch, smell,
taste, and see in this five- or
ten-minute event and put
these details, in order, in the
chart. This may sound difficult
at first, but often the most
important events in our life
occur in brief moments. Such
a short time frame can help
you realize how crowded with
meaningful detail such
moments can be. Early on, list
the circumstances that led up
to the event, and near the
end list the consequences or
outcomes of the event. These
will be used later for
introductory and concluding
paragraphs.

Student Model—Graphic Organizer

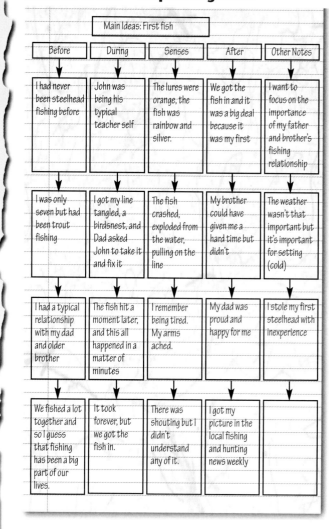

Main Ideas: First fish

Before	During	Senses	After	Other Notes
I had never been steelhead fishing before	John was being his typical teacher self	The lures were orange, the fish was rainbow and silver.	We got the fish in and it was a big deal because it was my first	I want to focus on the importance of my father and brother's fishing relationship
I was only seven but had been trout fishing	I got my line tangled, a birdsnest, and Dad asked John to take it and fix it	The fish crashed, exploded from the water, pulling on the line	My brother could have given me a hard time but didn't	The weather wasn't that important but it's important for setting (cold)
I had a typical relationship with my dad and older brother	The fish hit a moment later, and this all happened in a matter of minutes	I remember being tired. My arms ached.	My dad was proud and happy for me	I stole my first steelhead with inexperience
We fished a lot together and so I guess that fishing has been a big part of our lives.	It took forever, but we got the fish in.	There was shouting but I didn't understand any of it.	I got my picture in the local fishing and hunting news weekly	

Drafting

Drafting a narrative is like reconstructing a real experience with
words. As with all essays or stories, you need an inviting first
paragraph that provides background information and
introduces the story. Don't get into the plot of your narrative
until you reach the first body paragraph.

Before you move to the second paragraph, take a minute to
look back at the graphic organizer and remind yourself of where
your story really needs to start. If the event in your narrative
takes place on a particular day, will you begin the first body

paragraph at the beginning of that day, or will you need to give a little background information that wouldn't work in the introduction? If the event takes place in the afternoon or evening, can you start the story at those times? Asking these questions helps to eliminate the needless baggage that can make a narrative drag.

As the paragraphs unfold and as you reconstruct your story, keep this question in mind: Am I *telling* or am I *showing*?

You'll need to test the details. One effective way to do this is to read through your draft, highlighting in different colors images that use different senses: sight, hearing, smell, taste, and touch. Just the right details will show your reader the experience, not just tell about it.

Student Model—Draft

Give it a title

Even though I haven't lived too much of my life yet, it seems ~~like~~ *as though* most of the meaningful moments have happened when I ~~am~~ *was* fishing. ~~There have been early spring days on the mountain lakes, the river trips in scorching weather, and roller coaster rides on the ocean with my dad, brother and I all feeling pretty scared and pretty sick.~~ There has always

Probably off topic. Restrict the narrative to one event.

been something special that happens when the three of us go out fishing, and though it doesn't seem to matter if we catch fish or not, sometimes the fish itself is what makes it all special. This was the case when I was seven, and we were all fishing for winter steelhead in Washington.

If you fish with fanatics like my brother and my dad, the "morning" of a steelhead trip is really just the end of night. We would always get up before the day ever showed a sign of actually

Balancing Narration with Description

Sensory details are critical in helping your reader experience the event you are relating. At the same time, your assignment is not to write pure description but to use it to enhance your narrative.

Go back and reread Anna Quindlen's essay on page 589. Pay attention to the way she balances descriptive details with narrative techniques that chronicle her passion for reading.

INDIVIDUAL LEARNING STRATEGIES

MOTIVATION
Ask students to share their favorite selection from this unit. Then have them discuss the following questions with a partner: What made the selection interesting? What details and descriptions engaged you in the work? What did the author learn about himself or herself through the experience he or she wrote about? In what ways could you connect with the author and what he or she learned?

READING PROFICIENCY
Explain to students that personal narratives are often told in the first-person point of view. Ask them to read the definition of *point of view* in the Handbook of Literary Terms in order to prepare them for writing their narrative from this point of view.

ENGLISH LANGUAGE LEARNING
See strategies for Reading Proficiency above that will also benefit students who are English language learners. Also, allow students to discuss with the class the challenges of achieving literacy in their native language versus becoming literate in English.

SPECIAL NEEDS
Students with special needs may need assistance recalling details about past experiences that were meaningful to them. Encourage them to speak with family members or others who may be able to help them recall these events.

ENRICHMENT
Ask students to record their story on audiotape. Remind them that voice inflection and projection is critical since their audience will not be able to see their face. Refer them to Elements of Verbal Communication chart found in the Language Arts Survey 4.1, "Verbal and Nonverbal Communication." Then have them submit their tape to the school library, making their story available to others.

Use the checklist on page 602 for self- and peer evaluation. The checklist is intended to act as a student-friendly rubric to help students identify specific evidence of writing strengths and areas needing improvement. Make sure they provide concrete suggestions for improvement or specific evidence of why the writing works.

Self- and Peer Evaluation

Once you have finished your draft, read over your work. Let one or two of your peers do the same. Ask these questions about the essay:

- How many different senses are described in the draft?
- What is the climax of narrative?
- What is the source of tension, good or bad, in the story?
- Underline a sentence that shows more than tells.
- Which sentences use sensory details effectively?
- Is the story told in chronological order, or does it use a flashback?
- Is the order of events clear and logical?
- Find five sentences with pronouns and antecedents and check to see that they agree.
- What "things" in the narrative have distinctive shapes, sounds, or colors?

Revising and Proofreading

Check your draft against the questions above and make the necessary additions and deletions from your narrative. Keep in mind your goal of showing your audience the story, and of using sensory detail in your narrative.

happening and hit the river early enough to see the stars reflected in the water's darkness. These long mornings required *Perfect place for sensory detail.* more patience than I had at age seven, and I squirmed in my seat as the day started, trying to stay warm, while I listened to my brother become a steelhead fishing instructor.

Put this into dialog and bring it to life.
He explained that they hit hard, like I've never seen and that I should pay *"They hit hard, like you've never seen. Pay attention."* attention. I asked if they hit harder *"Harder than a trout?" I asked.* than a trout, but that just encouraged him to prove how smart he was.

He told me they hit—-like this, and *He scoffed knowingly. "Are you kidding? They hit like this," And he punched* he punched me in the shoulder really *me in the shoulder* hard. I complained to my dad. He just *"Ow! Dad!"* ignored us.

This does not move the story forward. Consider cutting.
~~My father usually sat in peace at the oars of our drift boat and pulled steadily upstream, keeping our pace downstream slow and even. Our fishing poles sat in holsters at the bow, pointing down river and the lines would travel into the water and end with a lure that would, like a little fish, wobble in the current. The idea, of course, was to attract the fish with the lure. My brother kept telling me it wouldn't happen.~~

This dialogue works beautifully! "You gotta put in a lot of fishing time to hook a steelhead."

Student Model—Revised

A First Fish
by Joshua Tanner

Even though I haven't lived too much of my life yet, it seems as though the most meaningful moments happen when I'm fishing. It doesn't seem to matter if we catch fish or not as there is just something special about fishing with my father and brother. Sometimes, however, the fish makes all the difference, and this was the case when I was seven, and we were out fishing for winter steelhead.

If you fish with fanatics like my brother and my dad, the "morning" of a steelhead trip is really just the end of night. We would always get up before the day ever showed a sign of actually happening and hit the river early enough to see the stars reflected in the water's darkness. These long mornings required a lot of clothing and even more patience. It was cold, and my brother always turned into some kind of Saturday morning steelhead guide with an attitude.

"They hit hard, like you've never seen. Pay attention."

"Harder than a trout?" I asked.

He scoffed, knowingly. "Are you kidding? They hit like this," and he punched me in the shoulder.

"Ow! Dad!"

My father ignored us and kept a steady pull on the oars.
My brother continued his lecture. I prepared for another punch.

"You gotta put in a lot of fishing time to hook a steelhead."

"How will I know when I've got one? Dad, can I check my bait?"

"Duh!" John scoffed again. " There is no bait, stupid, and I already told you how they hit." He raised his fist a second time to slug me.

"Knock it off!" My father's peace had been disturbed. "Josh, look at your reel. What d' ya got going there?"

I'd been too busy fending off the punch to realize I had released the spool on my reel and now had a "bird's nest," a tangle of line that unreeled

Language, Grammar, and Style

Getting Pronouns and Antecedents to Agree

IDENTIFYING AGREEMENT IN PRONOUNS AND ANTECEDENTS. A **pronoun** is a word that takes the place of a noun or stands in for an unknown noun. The noun that the pronoun replaces is called its **antecedent.** A pronoun must agree with or match its antecedent.

Look at the passage below from the professional model, an essay by Anna Quindlen.

> The odd thing about all this is that I had a lovely childhood in a lovely place. This is the way I remember <u>it</u>, this is the way it was.

In this passage, the pronoun *it* replaces the antecedent *childhood,* which was mentioned in the first sentence. The pronoun and antecedent agree in **number** and in **gender:** both are singular and gender-neutral. See the Language Arts Survey 3.45 for more information.

FIXING ERRORS IN PRONOUN–ANTECEDENT AGREEMENT. The following sentence, from Josh Tanner's rough draft, contains disagreement between pronouns and antecedents. Find the errors.

> The fish fought and fought. A few times they got close enough for us to see its black back and the

continued on page 604

Revising and Proofreading

A handout of the proofreading checklist is available in the Teacher's Resource Kit, Writing Resource book 2.45.

Language, Grammar, and Style

Getting Pronouns and Antecedents to Agree

LESSON OVERVIEW
In this lesson, students will be asked to do the following:
- Identify Agreement in Pronouns and Antecedents, 603
- Fix Errors in Pronoun–Antecedent Agreement, 604
- Use Pronouns that Agree with Their Antecedents, 604

INTRODUCING THE SKILL. Explain to students that using clear pronoun references in their writing will help their readers better understand the ideas or stories in their writing. If readers do not understand to whom or what a pronoun refers, they will be forced to stop reading to try to figure it out.

(continued on page 604)

ANSWERS TO EXERCISE

FIXING ERRORS IN PRONOUN–ANTECEDENT AGREEMENT: Josh's error is in the second sentence, where he uses the singular possessive pronoun its. This pronoun doesn't fit with the rest of the passage, in which Josh refers to the fish as plural and uses the plural pronoun they.

PREVIEWING THE SKILL. Refer students to the Language Arts Survey 3.45, "Getting Pronouns and Antecedents to Agree," 3.54, "Types of Pronouns," and 3.55, "Personal Pronouns." These sections of the Language Arts Survey form the basis of this lesson.

PRACTICING THE SKILL. Help students practice pronoun-antecedent agreement using Language, Grammar, and Style worksheets 3.45, 3.54, and 3.55 in the Teacher's Resource Kit. See also the Language, Grammar, and Style lesson for this unit in the Writing Resource book.

Publishing and Presenting

Encourage students to review the Language Arts Survey 2.6, "Choosing a Form," to help them explore different methods of publishing their work.

Reflecting

Ask students to read the Language Arts Survey 2.50, "Reflecting on Your Reading." Then have them write journal responses to the questions listed in the "Questions for Reflection" box.

---

pink lure hanging from its mouth, and then they would rocket off across the river and explode from the water again, trying to throw the hook.

Rewrite the sentence on your own paper, correcting the errors in pronoun-antecedent agreement. Then briefly explain your editing.

USING PRONOUNS THAT AGREE WITH THEIR ANTECEDENTS. Read over your narrative and make any needed corrections in pronoun-antecedent agreement.

Publishing and Presenting
The best part about writing stories is that it is always easy to find readers. Share your narrative with those who participated in the experience with you, or classmates who know the people in your story. Send a copy of your story to interested relatives, or keep a book of your narratives and start developing a family history from your perspective.

Reflecting
Your narrative is part of a vivid history of who you were at an important moment of your life. Keep adding to your collection. Keep a journal of those moments and those people who experienced life with you, and spend some quiet time reflecting on the stories that you want to pass along to others, of places you have been, and people you have known.

---

without tension. Every part of the nest I pulled on only made it tighten someplace else. My brother laughed.

"John, take your brother's pole."

"Huh?" We both couldn't believe it. I was being rescued.

We traded poles and John began working on my creation. I was feeling only slightly embarrassed when the fishing pole suddenly bent double and a huge steelhead shot out of the water thirty yards downstream. My instincts told me to stand-up, jab the pole into my gut and reel like mad. Immediately, John and Dad were yelling orders, telling me all sorts of things about keeping the rod tip up, and setting the drag—none of which made sense. The fish fought and fought. A few times it got close enough for us to see its black back and dangling pink lure, and then it would rocket off across the river and explode from the water again, trying to throw the hook.

In seven-year-old time, hours passed before the fish tired out enough to land. In reality it was probably twenty minutes. When the fish was finally captive, and dead, I looked around and noticed that my father had managed to get the boat to the bank, and that my brother had managed to untangle my bird's nest. We all stared at the fish. It was big, or so they said, with a beautiful rainbow painted down its side. It was the only fish we saw all day long.

The rest of that afternoon and evening was spent retelling the tale of how the fish jumped and fought and struggled, and how I persevered. I had caught my first steelhead and had been let into "the club." But the most amazing thing about the rest of that day was that my brother never said a thing about how the fish should have been his, about how I stole it from him with my inexperience, or how I hadn't really caught it at all. He probably punched me a few more times that day, but he kept his words to himself, and he let me have his fish.

UNIT 7 review
The Examined Life

Words for Everyday Use

Check your knowledge of the following vocabulary words from this unit. Write a short sentence using these words in context to make the meaning clear. To review the definition or usage of a word, refer to the page number listed or to the Glossary of Words for Everyday Use.

abate, 592
acquit, 542
annual, 583
apt, 557
arable, 543
aspect, 533
assail, 532
brazen, 556
buttressed, 593
capsize, 584
colleague, 530
compel, 534
composure, 535
compulsion, 593
compunction, 531
concession, 564
confront, 558
consumptive, 573
contemplation, 530
corollary, 590
couch, 593
covert, 592
debase, 555
debilitating, 535
delegation, 540
deranged, 535
derelict, 582
discharge, 570

discreetly, 567
disheartened, 594
disparage, 540
elation, 555
elite, 555
eloquent, 593
emphatically, 553
enmity, 531
enshroud, 555
eponymous, 592
ethos, 592
eulogy, 568
exclusivity, 593
fodder, 540
furtive, 573
grisly, 572
gullible, 559
haughtily, 500
impedimenta, 583
imperishable, 530
imploring, 557
impose, 530
inconceivably, 555
indifferent, 569
indignant, 569
inveterate, 593
invincible, 592
irk, 566

itinerary, 576
leukemia, 566
loiter, 568
lull, 583
magnanimity, 554
magnanimous, 571
mausoleum, 570
miser, 570
morbidity, 569
muster, 556
obstinacy, 582
ominously, 555
ostracize, 558
overseer, 540
persecute, 557
perverse, 559, 572
plausible, 534
plummeting, 594
pompous, 567
prestige, 554
proctor, 553
provisions, 582
prudent, 556
psychoanalysis, 566
pundit, 594
raucous, 591
ravage, 541
reconciliation, 569

relish, 574
renounce, 532
repent, 582
reproach, 565
reproachful, 557
resound, 533
rheumatism, 584
roundabout, 559
sanction, 593
saunter, 558
savor, 530
serenity, 572
shamble, 568
smirk, 564
solace, 593
steppe, 544
supplant, 593
suppress, 556
sustenance, 592
taunting, 558
temperament, 532
till, 544
transcend, 532
tyrannical, 534
underestimate, 567
wry, 553
zealous, 532

Literary Tools

Define the following terms, giving concrete examples of how they are used in this unit. To review a term, refer to the page number indicated or to the Handbook of Literary Terms.

aim, 588
antihero, 563
central conflict, 538
characterization, 528, 563
description, 588

dialogue, 528
exposition, 588
foreshadowing, 538
internal monologue, 551
irony, 551

motivation, 563
narration, 588
paradox, 523, 580
repetition, 523
symbol, 580

Reflecting on your reading

Genre Studies

1. **LYRIC POETRY.** Discuss the poems "The Waking" and "Heraclitus." How does the speaker of each poem regard the flow of time? What things, according to each speaker, are unknowable?

2. **SHORT STORY AND IRONY.** Writers of short stories often use irony to surprise the reader and create a story with impact. Discuss the use of **irony** in the short stories "The Happy Man," "Land Enough for a Man," and "The Thief." What happens in each of these stories that contradicted your expectations?

3. **PARADOX.** Consider the use of **paradox** in "The Waking" and "The Third Bank of the River." List examples of paradox from both works. What do the paradoxical ideas of each piece of writing convey about the nature of truth?

Thematic Studies

4. **HOW TO LEAD ONE'S LIFE.** What does each selection in this unit have to say about how a person should lead his or her life? Consider the message given by each story, and/or the lessons learned by the characters in the story. Give examples to support your answers.

5. **LIFE CHOICES AND PERSONAL PHILOSOPHIES.** Discuss the life choices made by the speaker of "The Waking," by the narrator of "The Thief," and by the father in "The Third Bank of the River." What is unusual about the choices each character makes? What personal philosophy underlies each character's choice? How are the characters' approaches to life similar or different?

6. **DISHONESTY.** Discuss the main characters of "The Happy Man," "The Thief," and "The Liar." In what way is each character dishonest, either with himself or with others? What causes each character to behave dishonestly? What does each character think about his own behavior? What do you think about each character's behavior? Can a person who is dishonest with himself or others actually be a good person, even a better one than most? Can such a person ever be truly happy?

for your...
READING LIST

An American Childhood by Annie Dillard. Annie Dillard was an inquisitive child and has always explored external events with her curious inner eye. This collection of untitled segments recalls her tomboyish childhood growing up in Pittsburg in the 1950s. She writes essays about her rock collection, her microscope, baseball mitt, and other important childhood artifacts. She begins one of her essays with the question, "What does it feel like to be alive?" It is a question she addresses fully in this book.

Independent Reading Activity

BOOK CLUB DISCUSSION. Form small groups and choose a book to read from these selections or another book with the theme of examining your life. It may be helpful to read Language Arts Survey 1.8, "Guidelines for Discussing Literature in a Book Club," before reading the book selected for your book club. When everyone has finished reading the book, take some time individually to prepare for your roles in the discussion. Write a response to your reading in a reading log. Note questions and comments in your log as you read to bring to the discussion group. You may find the following questions helpful to get the discussion started.

- What was the author's aim or purpose in writing the book? to inform? to entertain? to persuade?
- Who is the main character or protagonist in the book?
- What conflicts does the protagonist face? Are the conflicts internal or external? Why?
- Which character or characters in the book did you like or dislike? With which character did you identify the most?
- Is the story line or plot believable? Why or why not?
- Did the book end the way you anticipated? How did you expect it to end?
- Predict what might happen to the characters in the book if the story were continued.
- Did you like the book? Would you recommend it to your friends? Why or why not?
- What rating would you give the book on a scale of 1 to 10?

Selections for Additional Reading

The Meadow by James Galvin. Critics have called it a masterpiece, one of the best books on the American West. James Galvin has written about living on the rugged, wild landscape of Wyoming, combining storytelling, myth, history, and his own experience. Galvin is a poet, and *The Meadow* (1993), his first book of prose, is written in lyric poetic language. The short, intertwined chapters follow the lives of the people Galvin has grown to love, in the harsh and beautiful real world of Wyoming.

The Diary of a Young Girl by Anne Frank. In 1942, Anne Frank, a young Jewish girl, went into hiding in Amsterdam with her family to escape the Nazis during World War II. Her diary was discovered in the attic where the Franks hid for two years until the Nazis found them in 1944. She died in a concentration camp. There is honesty, intelligence, humor, and depth in this astonishing diary written by a girl just growing into and discovering herself, during one of the most horrific historic periods of the 20th century. Read an excerpt from Anne's diary in Unit 5.

Walden by Henry David Thoreau. "I went to the woods because I wanted to learn to live deliberately..." On July 4, 1845, Henry David Thoreau moved a few possessions from his home in Concord, Massachusetts, into a small cabin on Walden Pond to begin his experiment. In this book, he describes the most basic and fundamental aspects of daily life, and also articulates the profound insights he achieved simply by carrying them out. The account of the year he spent in solitude seeking to know the essence of life has become a classic.

UNIT REVIEW **607**

FOR YOUR READING LIST

Annie Dillard recalls her memories of childhood with vivid details in *An American Childhood*. She explores each stage of her childhood—from five years old to a teenager. Her exploration is so detailed that the *Chicago Tribune* described the book as all-consuming: "It consumes you as you consume it, so that, when you have put down this book, you're a different person, one who has virtually experienced another childhood."

Independent Reading Activity
Refer students to the freewriting exercise they did in the Unit 7 Guided Writing lesson under the "Writing with a Plan" section. Explain to them that the independent activity is similar to what they did in the freewriting activity. Students may want to use the technique used in the Student Model—Graphic Organizer section on page 600 to help them describe their surroundings and or to examine their life.

Wheatfield with Crows, 1890. Vincent van Gogh. National Museum of Van Gogh, Amsterdam.

GOALS/OBJECTIVES

Studying this unit will enable students to
- explore the concept of genius
- discuss different perspectives on genius
- give an example of an autobiography, a biography, and a personal essay
- define *characterization, simile, analysis, point of view,* *style, symbolism, description, satire, repetition, point of view, foreshadowing, colloquialism,* and *tone,* and identify and explain examples of each that they encounter in their reading
- write a narrative research paper that explores genius
- demonstrate the ability to use effective documentation

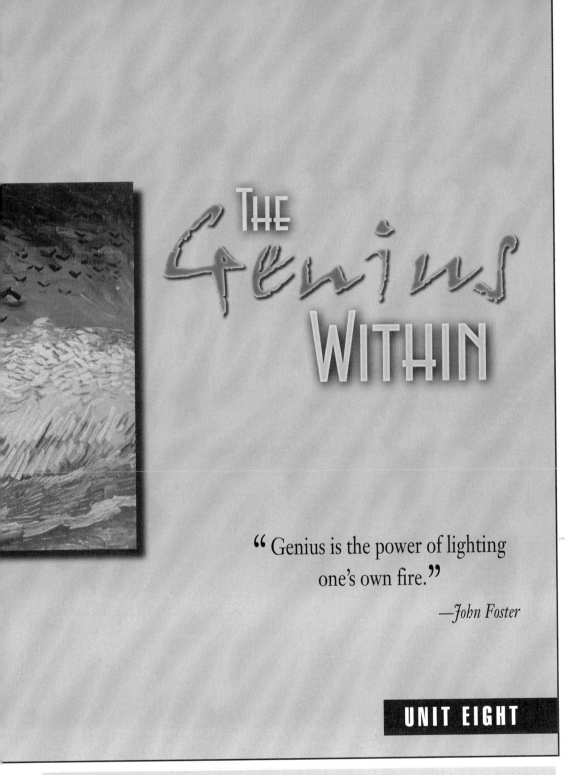

The Genius Within

"Genius is the power of lighting one's own fire."

—*John Foster*

UNIT EIGHT

(Continued on page 610)

echoes

➤ To believe your own thought, to believe that what is true for you in your private heart is true for all men—that is genius.

—Ralph Waldo Emerson

➤ It takes a lot of time to be a genius—you have to sit around so much doing nothing, really doing nothing.

—Gertrude Stein

➤ I have nothing to declare but my genius.

—Oscar Wilde at New York Customs

➤ Genius is one percent inspiration and ninety-nine percent perspiration.

—Thomas Edison

➤ Every production of genius must be the production of enthusiasm.

—Benjamin D'Israeli

➤ Everyone is a genius at least once a year. The real geniuses simply have their bright ideas closer together.

—G.C. Lichtenberg

➤ Genius without education is like silver in the mine.

—Benjamin Franklin

➤ There was never a genius without a tincture of madness.

—Aristotle

➤ There's a fine line between genius and insanity. I have erased this line.

—Oscar Levant

art note

Wheatfield with Crows, 1890, page 608. **Vincent van Gogh** (1853–1890) has become synonymous with the myth of the introspective genius. Van Gogh could not relate well with other people, but was consumed with a desire to express his deepest thoughts and feelings through art. Poverty, mental illness, and a lack of recognition wore him down, and he took his own life. *Wheatfield with Crows* is perhaps his last painting and is seen as symptomatic of the manic-depression (bipolar disorder) he suffered. He wrote of this painting, "I have formulated what I cannot express in words, namely how healthy and heartening I find the countryside," but at the same time: "I deliberately tried to express sadness and extreme loneliness."

"A Smart Cookie"
by Sandra Cisneros

Reader's
r e s o u r c e

MUSIC CONNECTION. An **allusion** is a figure of speech in which reference is made to a person, event, object, or work from history or literature. **"A Smart Cookie"** contains an allusion to *Madame Butterfly*, a well-known opera written in 1906 by the Italian composer Giacomo Puccini. The opera tells the story of Cho-Cho-San, a Japanese woman who becomes romantically involved with Pinkerton, an American naval lieutenant. The two have conflicting ideas about how committed their relationship is, and Pinkerton marries another woman while Cho-Cho-San waits for him in Japan. Esperanza's mother mentions this story as she talks about friends of hers who have not taken care of themselves as individuals or pursued their own dreams.

About *the* AUTHOR

Sandra Cisneros (1954–) is an American novelist, short-story writer, essayist, and poet whose works have brought the perspective of Chicana women into the mainstream of literary feminism. She is one of the first Hispanic-American women writers to achieve commercial success. Cisneros writes about conflicts directly related to her upbringing, including divided cultural loyalties, feelings of alienation, and degradation associated with poverty.

Cisneros was born in Chicago to a large Mexican-American family. Her six brothers tried to force her into a submissive feminine role that she rebelled against. After earning a B.A. from Loyola University, Cisneros attended the University of Iowa Writers' Workshop, where she earned an M.F.A.

The novel *The House on Mango Street* (1983), from which this selection is taken, is the author's first and most critically acclaimed work. Structured as a series of short, interconnected chapters, the work captures the hopes, desires, and disillusionments of a young female writer in an antagonistic environment. *Woman Hollering Creek and Other Stories* (1991) contains tales of beleaguered girls and women who nonetheless feel that they have power over their destinies. Cisneros's volumes of poetry include *Bad Boys* (1980), *The Rodrigo Poems* (1985), and *My Wicked Wicked Ways* (1987).

Literary
T O O L S

SIMILE. A **simile** is a comparison using *like* or *as*. Watch for the use of this literary technique as you read the novel excerpt.

CHARACTERIZATION. Characterization is the use of literary techniques to create a character. Writers use three major techniques to create characters: direct description, portrayal of characters' behavior, and representations of characters' internal states. See the Handbook of Literary Terms for information on how to identify each technique. As you read, decide which technique(s) Cisneros uses to characterize Esperanza's mother.

Graphic Organizer

Make a chart to list facts you learn about the mother and to tell which technique of characterization the author uses. One example has been done for you.

FACTS ABOUT THE MOTHER	TECHNIQUE
has lived in the city her whole life	direct description

Reader's
Journal

What makes you proud of who you are?

GRAPHIC ORGANIZER

Examples of direct description include: has lived in the city all her life, speaks two languages, can sing an opera, knows how to fix a TV, doesn't know which subway train to take to get downtown, used to draw, embroiders, would like to go to the ballet, would like to see a play, borrows opera records from the library.

Examples of portrayal of the character's behavior include: cooks oatmeal, tells her daughter to go to school, thinks Madame Butterfly was a fool, quit school because she was ashamed of her clothes.

READER'S JOURNAL

You might have students write the words *I'm somebody* at the top of a page in their journal. Then have them make a list of reasons they have for being proud of who they are. Students might read their journal entries to a classmate.

LITERARY TECHNIQUE

VIGNETTE. A **vignette** is a brief incident or scene. Explain to students that *The House on Mango Street* is a novel comprised of vignettes. "A Smart Cookie" is one of those vignettes. Ask students what point it makes.
Answer
This selection makes a point about the importance of education.

GOALS/OBJECTIVES

Studying this lesson will enable students to
• appreciate a vignette that makes use of allusion
• describe the literary accomplishments of Sandra Cisneros
• define *simile* and *characterization* and recognize the use of these techniques in the selection

• identify interrogative pronouns in sentences
• perform a dramatic skit
• research the opera *Madame Butterfly*
• write a college application essay

Agna Enters, 1900s. Abraham Walkowitz. National Museum of American Art, Washington, DC.

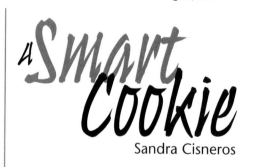

A Smart Cookie
Sandra Cisneros

I could've been somebody, you know? my mother says and sighs. She has lived in this city her whole life. She can speak two languages. She can sing an opera. She knows how to fix a T.V. But she doesn't know which subway train to take to get downtown. I hold her hand very tight while we wait for the right train to arrive.

What are some of the abilities of the narrator's mother?

She used to draw when she had time. Now she draws with a needle and thread, little knotted rosebuds, tulips made of silk thread. Someday she would like to go to the ballet. Someday she would like to see a play. She borrows opera records from the public library and sings with velvety lungs powerful as morning glories.[1]

Today while cooking oatmeal she is Madame Butterfly[2] until she sighs and points the wooden spoon at me. I could've been somebody, you know? Esperanza, you go to school. Study hard. That Madame Butterfly was a fool. She stirs the oatmeal. Look at my *comadres*.[3] She means Izaura whose husband left and Yolanda whose husband is dead. Got to take care all your own, she says shaking her head.

What is Esperanza told to do?

What has happened to Izaura and Yolanda?

Then out of nowhere:
Shame is a bad thing, you know. It keeps you down. You want to know why I quit school? Because I didn't have nice clothes. No clothes, but I had brains.

What has kept Esperanza's mother down?

Yup, she says disgusted, stirring again. I was a smart cookie then. ∎

1. **morning glories.** Trumpet-shaped flowers
2. **Madame Butterfly.** Main character in the famous opera of the same name
3. *comadres.* Spanish for fellow mothers

Respond *to the* SELECTION

Does Esperanza think her mother is still "a smart cookie"? Do you?

Investigate, Inquire, and Imagine

Recall: GATHERING FACTS

1a. Where has Esperanza's mother spent her life? What can she do? What does she have difficulty doing?

2a. What does Esperanza's mother say about her *comadres*, the women who are her friends?

3a. Why did Esperanza's mother quit school?

Interpret: FINDING MEANING

1b. How does Esperanza sound in the second paragraph as she describes her mother's abilities?

2b. Does Esperanza have respect for her mother? Explain.

3b. Why does Esperanza's mother say, "Got to take care all your own"?

Analyze: TAKING THINGS APART

4a. How does shame affect Esperanza's mother today?

Synthesize: BRINGING THINGS TOGETHER

4b. What can Esperanza do to take care of herself and not have regrets in her own life?

Evaluate: MAKING JUDGMENTS

5a. Evaluate the type of relationship Esperanza has with her mother.

Extend: CONNECTING IDEAS

5b. What difference does education make in a person's life? Does it make a person smarter? more worthy of respect? Does it give a person self-confidence and the means to reach his or her full potential? If so, how does it have this effect?

Understanding Literature

SIMILE. Review the definition for **simile** in the Handbook of Literary Terms. What simile does the daughter use to describe her mother's singing? What two things are compared in this simile? What makes this simile appropriate?

CHARACTERIZATION. Review the definition for **characterization** in Literary Tools on page 611 and the chart you made for Prereading. Which techniques of characterization does Cisneros use in depicting the mother? Give an example from the selection for each technique.

"A SMART COOKIE"   **613**

ANSWERS TO UNDERSTANDING LITERATURE

SIMILE. The narrator says that her mother "borrows opera records from the public library and sings with velvety lungs powerful as morning glories." This simile compares the power of the woman's voice to the bold color and shape of the flower and to the sound of the trumpet that the flower's shape suggests.

CHARACTERIZATION. Cisneros uses direct description and portrayal of the character's behavior in drawing the portrait of Esperanza's mother. The fact that she can speak two languages is an example of direct description. The advice she gives her daughter is an example of portrayal of the character's behavior.

ANSWERS TO INVESTIGATE, INQUIRE, AND IMAGINE

RECALL

1a. Esperanza's mother has spent her whole life in the city where she was born. She can speak two languages, sing an opera, and fix a TV, but she can't find her own way downtown on the subway.

2a. Esperanza's mother thinks her friends have wasted their lives by devoting themselves to the men they married.

3a. Esperanza's mother quit school because she was ashamed of her clothes.

INTERPRET

1b. Esperanza's tone is full of admiration and pride as she describes her mother's talents and interests.

2b. Esperanza's willingness to listen to her mother demonstrates she respects her.

3b. She means that all people, and especially all women, must learn to take care of themselves and not rely on anyone else to make their lives complete.

ANALYZE

4a. Today she may feel ashamed of her lack of education, and for this reason, she doesn't venture out to the ballet or the theater.

SYNTHESIZE

4b. Esperanza can learn from her mother's example that nothing, including acceptance by other people, is as important as being true to oneself.

PERSPECTIVE

5a. Esperanza and her mother are close. They listen to each other, know each other well, and are able to learn from each other.

EMPATHY

5b. There are cases of people who have become successful without formal education, but education is often looked at as the key to a good job and a successful life. *Responses will vary.*

Language, Grammar, and Style
1. Which
2. Whom
3. What
4. Who
5. What

Applied English
Assign a score from 1 to 25 for each grading criterion below. (For more detailed evaluation, see the evaluation forms for writing, revising, and proof-reading in the Assessment Resource book.)

COLLEGE APPLICATION ESSAY
- CONTENT/UNITY. The college application essay provides personal reasons for wanting to attend college.
- ORGANIZATION/COHERENCE. The college application essay is logically ordered, listing reasons from most to least important.
- LANGUAGE/STYLE. The college application essay is written in formal English.
- CONVENTIONS. The college application essay avoids errors in spelling, grammar, usage, mechanics, and manuscript form.

Writer's Journal

1. Imagine you are Esperanza's mother. Write a **wish list** that you have for yourself and one that you have for your daughter.

2. The narrator uses a simile to vividly describe the way her mother sings. Using a similar approach, write a **simile** to describe how a friend or family member does something.

3. Notice how much we learn about Esperanza's mother as she listens to records, stands at the stove, and stirs a pot of oatmeal. Our lives are full of short, everyday activities that may serve as backdrops for brief vignettes. Write your own **vignette** in the style of "A Smart Cookie."

Integrating the Language Arts

Language, Grammar, and Style

INTERROGATIVE PRONOUNS. Read the Language Arts Survey 3.57, "Interrogative Pronouns." Then identify each interrogative pronoun below.

1. Which opera is Esperanza's mother listening to?
2. Whom does Esperanza's mother want to continue her education?
3. What does Esperanza think of her mother?
4. Who lost their husbands?
5. What Esperanza's mother thinks is that she was a smart cookie when she was young.

Applied English

COLLEGE APPLICATION ESSAY. Imagine that you are Esperanza and that you are applying to several colleges. To be considered for acceptance, the colleges require you to submit an application that includes a short essay explaining your reasons for furthering your education. Write the essay based on your personal reasons for wanting to attend college.

Speaking and Listening & Collaborative Learning

DRAMATIC SKIT. Obtain a copy of *The House on Mango Street* from your school or local library. As a group, read the entire book out loud. Then vote on which chapters are your favorites. Organize into small groups and adapt each of the favorite chapters into skits. Rehearse your skits and perform them in order in your classroom. You may also want to invite other classes to see your performances. Elect one person to introduce the book.

Study and Research

Madame Butterfly. Obtain an audio recording or a video of the opera *Madame Butterfly* to listen to or view. Then make a list of several questions you have about the opera and its composer, Puccini. Research these questions and share your information with the class.

"Curiosità"

from *How to Think Like Leonardo da Vinci: Seven Steps to Genius Every Day*

by Michael J. Gelb

Reader's resource

How to Think Like Leonardo da Vinci, a book published in 1998, is an approach to learning and creativity that outlines ways to think better. Gelb begins with the theory that, as human beings, we use only a fraction of our potential brain power. He draws on Leonardo da Vinci's notebooks, inventions, and artwork to introduce the Seven da Vincian Principles—seven essential elements of genius that anyone can develop.

HISTORY CONNECTION. Leonardo da Vinci (1452–1519) was not only a great artist, architect, and scientist, but a great writer and thinker as well. Many of his ideas were ahead of his time. During the years 1490–1495 he thought it important to write down all the things that he was thinking, studying, and learning; his notebooks comprise the largest literary legacy any painter has offered. In them, four main topics took shape: painting, architecture, the elements of mechanics, and human anatomy. Da Vinci's notebooks were a unique accomplishment in art history, and an invaluable contribution to the world.

About *the* AUTHOR

Michael J. Gelb is also the author of *Lessons from the Art of Juggling* and *Thinking for a Change.* He lives outside Washington, DC, where he gives seminars on creative thinking at his High Performance Learning Center. IHe likes to juggle and to practice Aikido (a Japanese martial art).

Reader's Journal

Write a journal entry that describes how you like to think, how your mind works best, and how you come up with your own creative ideas.

Literary TOOLS

RENAISSANCE. The **Renaissance** was the period from the fourteenth to the early seventeenth century when Europe was making the transition from the medieval to the modern world. The word *renaissance* means "rebirth." The term refers to the rebirth of interest in ancient Greek and Latin writing that occurred during the period, a rebirth that is known as Humanism. This interest in classical knowledge inspired a reviewed interest in learning through direct observation and study of the natural world. Leonardo da Vinci pursued such studies in his passionate desire to discover these laws of nature. He was considered one of the greatest thinkers of the High Italian Renaissance.

ANALYSIS. Analysis is a thinking strategy in which one divides a subject into parts and then examines the relationships among the parts and between individual parts and the whole. In this selection, Gelb takes apart and examines Da Vinci's way of thinking in order to create a means for others to think better for themselves. By analyzing Da Vinci's work when he quotes from the notebooks, Gelb offers fresh insights on them. By analyzing Da Vinci's role in current thinking, he connects his ideas with the innovations of today.

ADDITIONAL RESOURCES

UNIT 8 RESOURCE BOOK
- Selection Worksheet 8.2
- Selection Check Test 4.8.3
- Selection Test 4.8.4

VOCABULARY FROM THE SELECTION

abate	insatiable
accessibly	phenomena
articulate	piety
assess	requisite
commission	rigor
confound	transmute
diverse	unfathomed
essence	
impulse	
inquisitiveness	

READER'S JOURNAL

Prompt students to think about *how* they think by asking them how they began, worked on, and completed specific projects they have done for the class. Tell them thinking is a process, and as they recognize their own process they can become more aware of how they think best.

GOALS/OBJECTIVES

Studying this lesson will enable students to
- appreciate the accomplishments and contributions of Leonardo da Vinci
- describe the Italian Renaissance period
- understand an analysis
- research Renaissance paintings
- use Leonardo da Vinci's method of assessment to review a work of art

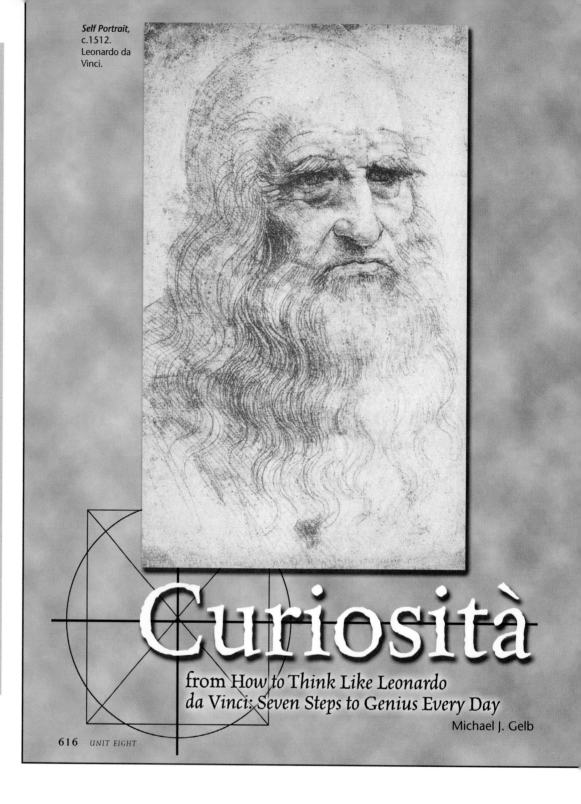

Self Portrait, c.1512. Leonardo da Vinci.

Curiosità

from *How to Think Like Leonardo da Vinci: Seven Steps to Genius Every Day*

Michael J. Gelb

A ll of us come into the world curious. Curiosità builds upon that natural <u>impulse</u>, the same impulse that led you to turn the last page—the desire to learn more. We've all got it; the challenge is using and developing it for our own benefit. In the first years of life our minds are engaged in an unquenchable thirst for knowledge. From birth—and some would argue, even before—the baby's every sense is attuned to exploring and learning.

What do babies do? Think of examples of this.

Like little scientists, babies experiment with everything in their environment. As soon as they can speak, children start <u>articulating</u> question after question: "Mommy, how does this work?" "Why was I born?" "Daddy, where do babies come from?"

As a child, Leonardo possessed this intense curiosity about the world around him. He was fascinated with nature, showed a remarkable gift for drawing, and loved mathematics. Vasari[1] records that the young Leonardo questioned his mathematics teacher with such originality that "he raised continuous doubts and difficulties for the master who taught him and often <u>confounded</u> him."

What kind of questions did Leonardo ask?

Great minds go on asking confounding questions with the same intensity throughout their lives. Leonardo's childlike sense of wonder and <u>insatiable</u> curiosity, his breadth and depth of interest, and his willingness to question accepted knowledge never <u>abated</u>. Curiosità fueled the wellspring of his genius throughout his adult life.

What were Leonardo's motives? In his book *The Creators: A History of Heroes of the Imagination*, Pulitzer Prize winner Daniel Boorstin tells us what they were not. "Unlike Dante,[2] he had no passion for a woman. Unlike Giotto,[3] Dante, or Brunelleschi,[4] he seemed to have had no civic loyalty. Nor devotion to church or Christ. He willingly accepted <u>commissions</u> from the Medici, the Sforzas, the Borgias,[5] or French kings—from the popes or their enemies. He lacked the sensual worldliness of a Boccaccio[6] or a Chaucer,[7] the recklessness of a Rabelais,[8] the <u>piety</u> of a Dante, or the religious passion of a Michelangelo."[9] Leonardo's loyalty, devotion, and passion were directed, instead, to the pure quest for truth and beauty. As Freud[10] suggested: "He <u>transmuted</u> his passion into <u>inquisitiveness</u>."

What is the purpose of the quote listing what Leonardo did not have?

---

1. **Vasari.** Giorgio Vasari (1511–1574), 16th century art historian
2. **Dante.** Dante Alighieri (1265–1321), Italian poet, author of *The Divine Comedy*
3. **Giotto.** Giotto di Bondone (1266–1337), Italian painter of frescoes
4. **Brunelleschi.** Filippo Brunelleschi (1377–1446), early Renaissance architect
5. **Medici, Sforzas, and Borgias.** All Italian rulers, leaders, and politicians during the 12th and 13th centuries
6. **Boccaccio.** Giovanni Boccaccio (1313–1375), Italian poet, author of *Decameron*, a collection of stories written in 1353
7. **Chaucer.** Geoffrey Chaucer (1343–1400), English author of *The Canterbury Tales*
8. **Rabelais.** François Rabelais (1494–1553), French poet
9. **Michelangelo.** Italian Renaissance painter, sculptor, architect and poet who lived rom 1475 to 1564
10. **Freud.** Dr. Sigmund Freud (1856-1939), father of psychoanalysis

---

words for everyday use

im • pulse (im' pəls) *n.*, sudden spontaneous inclination. *She could not resist the <u>impulse</u> to kiss the child.*
ar • tic • u • late (är tik' yoo lāt) *vt.*, give clear utterance to, speak. *By speaking out against the child's punishment, she <u>articulated</u> the thoughts of everyone.*
con • found (kən faund') *vt.*, baffle, stupify, perplex, confuse. *The child's silence in the classroom <u>confounded</u> the teacher.*
in • sa • tia • ble (in sā' shə bəl) *adj.*, incapable of being satisfied or appeased. *He had an <u>insatiable</u> appetite.*
abate (ə bāt') *vi.*, reduce; diminish; subside; lessen. *The storm finally <u>abated</u>, and they went outside.*
com • mis • sion (kə mish' ən) *n.*, fee paid to an agent or employee in exhange for a certain work. *The artist had accepted many <u>commissions</u> to paint portraits.*
pi • e • ty (pī' ə tē) *n.*, state of being pious, of having devoted loyalty to family, or religious zeal. *The man expressed his <u>piety</u> by attending church every day.*
trans • mute (tran(t)s myüt') *vt.*, change or alter in form, appearance, or nature. *The new laws would <u>transmute</u> society.*
in • quis • i • tive • ness (ən kwiz' ə tiv nes) *n.*, state of curiosity. *Mr. Farrell's <u>inquisitiveness</u> prompted the chairman to notice him.*

ANSWERS TO GUIDED READING QUESTIONS

1. Babies are naturally curious. They put things in their mouths, grab for things, and practice new skills.
2. Leonardo asked "original," or unique questions that stumped even his teachers. He didn't only learn what the teachers offered, but was actively engaged in his own learning.
3. The quote that lists what Leonardo did not have highlights the quality he did have—curiosity about everything. It was his curiosity that drove him to learn and excel in all different fields.

ADDITIONAL QUESTIONS AND ACTIVITIES

Students can work in small groups to research the people that Daniel Boorstin contrasts with Leonardo—Dante Alighieri, Filippo Brunelleschi, the Medici, the Sforzas, the Borgias, Giovanni Boccaccio, Geoffrey Chaucer, François Rabelais, and Michelangelo. Each group should learn more about the life and genius of their subject and present a short oral report of their findings.

1. His observations on nature trigger his curiosity.

Leonardo's inquisitiveness was not limited to his formal studies; it informed and enhanced his daily experience of the world around him. In a typical passage from the notebooks Da Vinci asks: "Do you not see how many and how varied are the actions which are performed by men alone? Do you not see how many different kinds of animals there are, and also of trees and plants and flowers? What variety of hilly and level places, of springs, rivers, cities, public and private buildings; of instruments fitted for man's use; of diverse costumes, ornaments and arts?"

Elsewhere he adds, "I roamed the countryside searching for answers to things I did not understand. Why shells existed on the tops of mountains along with the imprints of coral and plants and seaweed usually found in the sea. Why the thunder lasts a longer time than that which causes it, and why immediately on its creation the lightning becomes visible to the eye while thunder requires time to travel. How the various circles of water form around the spot which has been struck by a stone, and why a bird sustains itself in the air. These questions and other strange phenomena engage my thought throughout my life."

What triggers Leonardo's curiosity?

Leonardo's intense desire to understand the essence of things led him to develop an investigative style equally noteworthy for its depth of study as for its range of topics. Kenneth Clark,[11] who called him "undoubtedly the most curious man who ever lived," describes Da Vinci's uncompromising quest in accessibly contemporary terms:

"He wouldn't take Yes for an answer." In his anatomic investigations, for example, Leonardo dissected each part of the body from at least three different angles. As he wrote:

This depicting of mine of the human body will be as clear to you as if you had the natural man before you; and the reason is that if you wish thoroughly to know the parts of the man, anatomically, you, or your eye, require to see it from different aspects, considering it from below and from above and from its sides, turning it about and seeking the origin of each member. . . . Therefore by my drawings every part will be known to you, and by all means of demonstrations from three different points of view of each part.

But his curiosity didn't stop there: Da Vinci studied everything with the same rigor. If multiple perspectives yielded a deeper understanding of the body, for example, they would also help him evaluate his attempts to share that understanding. The result: layer upon layer of rigorous examination, all designed to refine not only his understanding but its expression, as he explains in his *Treatise on Painting*.

We know well that mistakes are more easily detected in the works of others than in one's own. . . . When you are painting you should take a flat mirror and often look at

---

11. **Kenneth Clark.** British art historian and leading authority on Italian Renaissance Art who lived rom 1903 to 1983

---

words for everyday use

di • verse (dī vərs') *adj.*, different in kind or species. *She had friends from everywhere, so there was a diverse crowd at her birthday party.*

phe • nom • e • na (fə nä' mə nə) *n., pl.* of phenomenon, observable facts or events. *He was always outside because he wanted to observe natural phenomena.*

es • sence (es' ən(t)s) *n.*, basic, underlying substance or form. *She wanted to get to know her aunt's true essence.*

ac • ces • si • bly (ak ses' ə blē) *adv.*, in a way that is easily understandable. *The complex information was accessibly presented in simple words and pictures.*

rig • or (rig' ər) *n.*, strictness; rigidity; severity. *She demanded that the chores be done with rigor.*

your work within it, and it will then be seen in reverse, and will appear to be by the hand of some other master, and you will be better able to judge of its faults than in any other way.

Why does Da Vinci suggest holding a painting up to a mirror?

Not content with just one strategy for <u>assessing</u> his work objectively, he adds: "It is also a very good plan every now and then to go away and have a little relaxation; for when you come back to the work your judgement will be surer, since to remain constantly at work will cause you to lose the power of judgement."

And finally, he suggests: "It is also advisable to go some distance away, because then the work appears smaller, and more of it is taken in at a glance, and a lack of harmony or proportion in the various parts and the colors of the objects is more readily seen."

His inexhaustible quest for truth also inspired him to look at reality from unusual and extreme perspectives. It took him under the water (he designed a snorkel, diving equipment, and a submarine) and into the sky (he designed a helicopter, a parachute, and his famous flying machine). He plunged into <u>unfathomed</u> depths and sought previously unimaginable heights in his passion to understand.

Leonardo's fascination with flight—his studies of the atmosphere, wind, and especially the movements of birds—offers a compelling metaphor for his life and work. A page of his notebooks depicts a bird in a cage

In what way is his study of flight a metaphor for his life and work?

with the caption "The thoughts turn towards hope." He observes poetically that a mother goldfinch, seeing her children caged, feeds them a bit of a poisonous plant, noting, "Better death than to be without freedom."

Giorgio Vasari informs us that in the course of his frequent strolls through the streets of Florence, Leonardo often encountered merchants selling caged birds. It was Da Vinci's custom to stop, pay the <u>requisite</u> price, and then open the door of the cage, releasing the prisoners to the endless blue sky. For Leonardo, the quest for knowledge opened the door to freedom. ∎

Parachute Experiments and Flying Machines, c.1519. Leonardo da Vinci.

---

words for everyday use

as • sess (ə ses') *vt.,* analyze critically and judge definitively the nature, significance, status, or merit of. *He <u>assessed</u> the damage with one look at the ruined building.*

un • fath • omed (un fath' əm) *adj.,* unsounded; undetermined; immense. *When she left home, she realized the <u>unfathomed</u> depth of her parents' love for her.*

req • ui • site (re' kwə zət) *adj.,* required by the nature of things. *She gave him the <u>requisite</u> tools for building the shed.*

"CURIOSITÀ" 619

Literary Tools

1. What does the term *Renaissance* mean? **It means rebirth.**
2. From what previous civilizations did the Renaissance draw its values, styles, and philosophies? **It drew upon the values, styles, and philosophies of the ancient Greek and Roman civilizations.**
3. How did Leonardo embody the Renaissance spirit?

Learning through direct observation and study of the natural world was important during the Renaissance. Leonardo passionately explored his world in this way.

4. What is analysis? **Analysis is a thinking strategy in which one divides a subject into parts and then examines the relationships among the parts and between individual parts and the whole.**

INSIGHTS

MAJOR ACCOMPLISHMENTS of Leonardo da Vinci

Michael J. Gelb

It would take an encyclopedia to begin to do justice to the full scope of Leonardo's accomplishments. We can get a glimpse of some of his most notable achievements through the categories of art, invention, military engineering, and science.

Leonardo *the artist* transformed the direction of art. He was the first Western artist to make landscape the prime subject of a painting. He pioneered the use of oil paints and the application of perspective, chiaroscuro, contrapposto, sfumato, and many other innovative and influential methods.

Leonardo's *Mona Lisa* and *The Last Supper* are recognized universally as two of the greatest paintings ever produced. They are certainly the most famous. Leonardo also created other wonderful paintings including *The Virgin of the Rocks, The Madonna and Child with St. Anne, The Adoration of the Magi, St. John the Baptist*, and his portrait of Ginevra de' Benci that hangs in the National Gallery in Washington, D.C.

Although Leonardo's paintings are few in number, his drawings are abundant and equally magnificent. Like the *Mona Lisa*, Leonardo's *Canon of Proportion* has become a universally familiar icon. His studies for *The Madonna and Child with St. Anne* and the heads of the apostles in *The Last Supper*, along with his drawings of flowers, anatomy, horses, flight, and flowing water, are unmatched.

Leonardo was also renowned as an architect and a sculptor. Most of his architectural work focused on general principles of design, although he did consult on a number of practical projects including cathedrals in Milan and Pavia, and the French king's château at Blois. While he is believed to have contributed to a number of sculptures, scholars agree that the only existing sculptures definitely touched by the maestro's hand are three bronzes on the north door of the Baptistery in Florence. The *Saint John the Baptist Preaching to a Levite and a Pharisee* was created in collaboration with the sculptor Rustici.

Leonardo *the inventor* made plans for a flying machine, a helicopter, a parachute, and many other marvels including the extendable ladder (still in use by fire departments today), the three-speed gear shift, a machine for cutting threads in screws, the bicycle, an adjustable monkey wrench, a snorkel, hydraulic jacks, the world's first revolving stage, locks for a canal system, a horizontal waterwheel, folding furniture, an olive press, a number of automated musical instruments, a water-powered alarm

620

clock, a therapeutic armchair, and a crane for clearing ditches.

More than any single invention, Leonardo deserves credit for pioneering the concept of automation. He designed myriad machines that could save labor and increase productivity. Although some were fanciful and impractical, others, like his automated looms, were portents of the Industrial Revolution.

As a *military engineer* Da Vinci made plans for weapons that would be deployed four hundred years later, including the armored tank, machine gun, mortar, guided missile, and submarine. As far as we know, however, nothing he designed was ever used to injure anyone during his lifetime. A man of peace, he referred to war as "*pazzia bestialissima*—beastly madness," and found bloodshed "infinitely atrocious." His instruments of war were designed "to preserve the chief gift of nature, which is liberty," he wrote. At times he shared them reluctantly, accompanying one design with a written glimpse of his ambivalence: "I do not wish to divulge or publish this because of the evil nature of men."

Mona Lisa, c.1503. Leonardo da Vinci. Louvre, Paris.

Mona Lisa, c.1503. Leonardo da Vinci. Louvre, Paris.

It is estimated that Leonardo da Vinci completed his famous portrait, *Mona Lisa*, in about 1503, and was so pleased with how it turned out that he carried it with him everywhere. Eventually he sold it to the French King Francois I, who ended up giving Leonardo a home and a place of honor and respect in the last years of the artist's life. The most captivating aspect of *Mona Lisa* is her mysterious, elusive, sad smile. In an essay called "On the Perfect Beauty of a Woman," sixteenth-century writer Firenuola tells us that the slight opening of the lips at the corners of the mouth was considered a sign of elegance in that period. To achieve it, Leonardo used his famous *sfumato* painting technique—a blending and dissolving of form, and interaction between light and shade, with mellow colors and blurred outlines that leave its interpretation up to the imagination of the viewer. In 1911, the painting was stolen from the Louvre Museum in Paris, France. It was found two years later in a hotel in Florence, Italy, and was reinstalled in the Louvre.

Leonardo *the scientist* is the subject of considerable scholarly debate. Some scholars suggest that if Leonardo had organized his scientific thoughts and published them, he would have had a massive influence on the development of science. Others argue that he was so far ahead of his time that his work would not have been appreciated even if it was formulated in comprehensible general theories. While Leonardo's science may best be appreciated for its intrinsic value as an expression of his quest for truth, most scholars agree that he can be credited with significant contributions to several disciplines:

Anatomy
- He pioneered the discipline of modern comparative anatomy.
- He was the first to draw parts of the body in cross section.
- He drew the most detailed and comprehensive representations of humans and horses.
- He conducted unprecedented scientific studies of the child in the womb.
- He was the first to make casts of the brain and the ventricles of the heart.

Botany
- He pioneered modern botanical science.
- He described geotropism (the gravitational attraction of the earth on some plants) and heliotropism (the attraction of plants toward the sun).
- He noted that the age of a tree corresponds to the number of rings in its cross section.
- He was the first to describe the system of leaf arrangement in plants.

Geology and Physics
- He made significant discoveries about the nature of fossilization, and he was the first to document the phenomenon of soil erosion. As he wrote, "Water gnaws at mountains and fills valleys."
- His physics studies anticipated the modern disciplines of hydrostatics, optics, and mechanics.

Leonardo's investigations led him to anticipate many great scientific discoveries including breakthroughs by Copernicus, Galileo, Newton, and Darwin.

40 years before Copernicus—Da Vinci noted, in large letters for emphasis, IL SOLE NO SI MUOVE," "The sun does not move." He added, "The earth is not in the center of the circle of the sun, nor in the center of the universe."

60 years before Galileo—He suggested that "a large magnifying lens" should be employed to study the surface of the moon and other heavenly bodies.

200 years before Newton—Anticipating the theory of gravitation, Leonardo wrote, "Every weight tends to fall towards the center by the shortest possible way." And elsewhere he added that because "every heavy substance presses downward, and cannot be upheld perpetually, the whole earth must become spherical."

400 years before Darwin—He placed man in the same broad category as monkeys and apes and wrote, "Man does not vary from the animals except in what is accidental."

More valuable than any of his specific scientific achievements, Leonardo's approach to knowledge set the stage for modern scientific thinking. ∎

622

Respond *to the* SELECTION

Write a journal entry describing an object—for example, half an apple, a tree, or a prize possession, from three different perspectives, or positions, for example, from above, below, close up, from a distance, from eye level, etc. If you would like, you can make three quick sketches of the object in your notebook as well.

Investigate, Inquire, and Imagine

Recall: GATHERING FACTS

1a. What, according to the selection, fueled Leonardo's genius throughout his life, and why?

2a. What types of things did Leonardo look at from three different sides?

3a. What ways does Leonardo suggest to evaluate one's own work?

Interpret: FINDING MEANING

1b. What do you think was the point of listing all the qualities Leonardo did not seem to have and that other great thinkers and artists did have?

2b. What are the advantages and benefits of seeing things from different sides?

3b. What importance does he place on evaluating his own work and why?

Analyze: TAKING THINGS APART

4a. Review Leonardo's major accomplishments. Why do you think he was able to excel in so many different fields?

Synthesize: BRINGING THINGS TOGETHER

4b. How would you categorize his major accomplishments? What does each of them have in common?

Evaluate: MAKING JUDGMENTS

5a. Evaluate why seeing was the most fundamental element of Leonardo's great work.

Extend: CONNECTING IDEAS

5b. What steps can one take to really see and think like Leonardo da Vinci?

Understanding Literature

RENAISSANCE. Review the definition of **Renaissance** in the Handbook of Literary Terms. A "Renaissance man" is a person who has wide interests and is expert in several areas. In what areas was Leonardo da Vinci an expert? According to Gelb, what fueled his interest in these areas? How did his mind work?

ANALYSIS. Review the definition of **analysis** in Literary Tools in Prereading. This selection is an analysis of the way Leonardo thinks, which means the author studied Leonardo, applied the insight he got from his study, and was able to come up with new ideas about it. How does Michael Gelb analyze Leonardo's work? How does he use the analysis to inspire others to think more creatively?

"CURIOSITÀ" **623**

ANSWERS TO INVESTIGATE, INQUIRE, AND IMAGINE

RECALL

1a. His deep curiosity fueled his life's work, his longing for knowledge, and his keen perception.

2a. He looked at things in nature from three perspectives, and especially the human body.

3a. He suggests that you make it seem as if it is someone else's; get some distance on it.; look at it backward in the mirror; take some time away from it.

INTERPRET

1b. Listing the qualities that he did not have showed that passion for learning does not have to be linked to a specific purpose. Leonardo was curious about everything, and merely for the sake of knowing, rather than for any other purpose or end.

2b. Leonardo himself said that to know an object you need to see it from different sides.

3b. Evaluating his own work was of utmost importance because he did not want to be blind to his own errors.

ANALYZE

4a. He was able to excel because of his curiosity for everything. It was as if he had an insatiable need to answer every question that came into his mind.

SYNTHESIZE

4b. His major accomplishments can be put into two categories: science and the arts. In both of these categories, creativity is the common thread.

EVALUATE

5a. Increased awareness due to direct observation of nature was a big part of the Renaissance period. Leonardo said that seeing made for more keen learning.

EXTEND

5b. Seeing can be practiced, like anything else; curiosity and questioning can be encouraged, and students can learn to honor their own curiosity by pursuing it creatively.

ANSWERS TO UNDERSTANDING LITERATURE

RENAISSANCE. Leonardo da Vinci was an expert in aviation, anatomy, painting, and writing. The desire to find the true essence of things fueled his interest in these areas. His mind was curious about everything, wanting to discover the true nature of things.

ANALYSIS. Gelb analyzes Leonardo's work by drawing on his notebooks, inventions, and artwork to support the theory that humans use only a fraction of their potential brainpower. In his analysis of Leonardo, he inspires others to think more creatively by setting Leonardo as a role model or example for us to follow.

Collaborative Learning
Direct students to read the Language
Arts Survey 5.9, "Analyzing and
Synthesizing," to help them with this
activity.

Media Literacy
Students may wish to discuss the
quotations before writing their essays.
They might do so in small groups.
Students may compile their essays in a
book titled *Thoughts on a Great
Thinker—Responses to Leonardo.*

Study and Research
Students might start by observing
several paintings from the Renaissance.
They should take notes on their
observations about the paintings,
including style, subject, and so on. Then
students can draw some conclusions
based on their own observations.
Students can then research the
Renaissance. They may make additional
conclusions or amend some of their
earlier thoughts based on the
information they gather.

Writer's Journal

1. Study the natural world. Sit outside, if you can, and watch. In your notebook, simply **record your observations** on an aspect of nature—a bird, an insect, or a plant.

2. In your notebook, write a **journal entry** about all the things in the world that you are curious about. Ask all the questions you have about those things.

3. Leonardo's notebooks were very important to him and contained invaluable information for future generations. He even wrote notes to future readers of his work in the notebooks. Write a **letter** to someone who will discover your notebook one or two hundred years from now. What would you want them to know about your life now?

Integrating the Language Arts

Collaborative Learning

ART REVIEW. As a group, review
Leonardo da Vinci's recommended
method of assessment, and then
choose a work of art for your group to assess and
analyze (maybe even *Mona Lisa*). The assessment
may take at least two days since one step is to go
away from the work for a short time. As you
proceed through each step—holding the work up
to a mirror, looking at it from a great distance, and
from more than one angle—jot down your own
notes. Discuss the painting together as a group,
and then come up with a complete analysis or
interpretation of the work of art.

Media Literacy

QUOTE ANALYSIS. One way that
Michael Gelb analyzes Leonardo
da Vinci's life and work is by
quoting from the notebooks he wrote. Go to
your library or log onto the Internet and look up
other quotes by Leonardo da Vinci. Find a quote
that intrigues you, even a very short one, and
write a brief analysis of it. How do you interpret
the quote? What associations does it have for
you? What did Leonardo mean by it? How does
the quote show his advanced thinking? Ask
yourself questions about the quote and, after
reflecting on it, respond to the quote in a short
essay about it.

Study and Research

RESEARCHING RENAISSANCE
PAINTING. Study the painting
style of the Renaissance period.
Look up some of the other painters listed in
the selection. What typifies the painting style
of that important era? What significant factors
influenced its style? What way of thinking
determined the style of painting? Do some
research in the library or on the Internet and
prepare a presentation on another
artist—perhaps Michelangelo, Raphael, or
Donatello—and include visual representations.

"Rules of the Game"
by Amy Tan

Reader's resource

"**Rules of the Game**" appears in Amy Tan's first novel, *The Joy Luck Club*. The novel weaves together the stories of four women who fled China in the 1940s and those of their American-born daughters. The setting for the novel is San Francisco's Chinatown, where the mothers form the Joy Luck Club, a group of friends who meet to play the Chinese game mah jong, invest in stocks, and share their stories about life in China.

About the AUTHOR

Amy Tan was born in Oakland, California, in 1952, just a few years after her mother and father immigrated from China. She studied English and linguistics at San Jose State University, earning her master's degree in 1974 and doing postgraduate studies at the University of California at Berkeley. She worked as a freelance technical writer and as a consultant to programs for children with disabilities.

In 1985, Amy Tan attended her first writers' workshop, and began writing fiction. Her first short story, "End Game," appeared in *FM Five,* a little magazine that is now defunct, and was later reprinted in *Seventeen* magazine. Then, in 1989, Tan published her first novel, *The Joy Luck Club.* To her surprise, the book was a huge success. It sold some spent forty weeks on the *New York Times* bestseller list, won several awards, and was made into a movie in 1993.

Tan went on to write the novels *The Kitchen God's Wife* (1991), *The Hundred Secret Senses* (1995), and *The Bonesetter's Daughter* (2001). She has also written two children's books, *The Moon Lady* (1992) and *The Chinese Siamese Cat* (1994). Her short stories and essays have appeared in many magazines. Tan lives in San Francisco and New York with her husband, Lou DeMattei, and their two Yorkshire terriers, Bubba Zoe and Lilliput.

Literary TOOLS

POINT OF VIEW. Point of view is the vantage point from which a story is told. In this story, Amy Tan uses the first-person point of view, in which the narrator uses pronouns such as *I* and *we.*

SYMBOL. A symbol is a thing that stands for or represents both itself and something else. In "Rules of the Game," the wind is a recurring symbol.

Graphic Organizer

As you read the story, make a chart like the one below, noting the reference to the wind and what you think the wind symbolizes, or represents.

REFERENCE TO WIND	WHAT THE WIND SYMBOLIZES
Waverly's mother says that a wise person does not go against the wind and that the strongest wind cannot be seen.	Her mother wants Waverly to show invisible strength like the wind.

Reader's Journal

What personal sacrifices would you be willing to make to be the best at something?

ADDITIONAL RESOURCES

UNIT 8 RESOURCE BOOK
- Selection Worksheet 8.3
- Selection Check Test 4.8.5
- Selection Test 4.8.6

VOCABULARY FROM THE SELECTION

adversary
ally
ancestral
benevolently
caption
concession
deftly
diminishing
elaborate
etiquette
flourish
fragrant
graciously
humility

impart
intricate
malodorous
prodigy
pungent
relent
replica
retort
solemnity
successive
tout
triumphant
vanity

GRAPHIC ORGANIZER

Reference to the Wind: While Waverly is playing at a chess tournament, she hears the wind say, "Blow from the South. The wind leaves no trail." **Symbol:** Wind symbolizes power and the ability to be cunning.
Reference to the Wind: The wind tells Waverly what moves to make: "Throw sand from the East to distract him...Blow, blow, blow." **Symbol:** Wind acts as a guide, teacher, and coach.

READER'S JOURNAL

What things are worth making sacrifices? Have you ever sacrificed something in order to achieve something, only to find out that you were unsuccessful in achieving your goal? How did that make you feel?

GOALS/OBJECTIVES

Studying this lesson will enable students to
- empathize with Waverly's struggles with her mother and her efforts to succeed at chess
- recognize the literary accomplishments of Amy Tan
- define *point of view* and *symbol* and identify these techniques in their reading
- experiment with point of view by using pronouns
- build vocabulary and dictionary skills

MOTIVATION
Have students discuss in small
groups the following questions:
What is your favorite hobby or
sport? What sacrifices do you
make in order to do these things?
What things do you do to increase
your abilities in a particular hobby or
sport?

READING PROFICIENCY
Assign each student a partner
(Try to include a proficient
reader in each pair). Then have
students read and summarize
what they've read in each section.
(Each section is marked by a large,
bold capital letter). Students should
share their summaries with one
another and note the differences and
similarities in their summaries.

ENGLISH LANGUAGE LEARNING
Allow students who were born
in the United States to parents
who are non-native English
speakers to share some of the
communication problems they
encounter with their parents. These
problems may be the result of a
language or cultural barrier.

SPECIAL NEEDS
Invite someone to visit your
class and show students how to play
chess. The visitor should
demonstrate the role of each chess
piece and what "check" and
"checkmate" means.

ENRICHMENT
What has been the most
meaningful advice you have
received from your parent(s) or
an adult friend? Identify that
advice and develop a short story
around it. Then share your story with
the rest of the class.

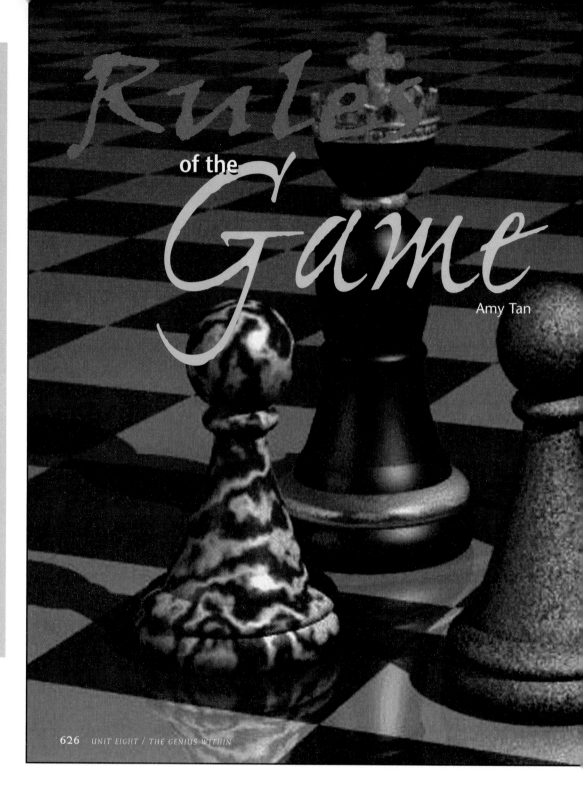

Rules of the Game

Amy Tan

I was six when my mother taught me the art of invisible strength. It was a strategy for winning arguments, respect from others, and eventually, though neither of us knew it at the time, chess games.

"Bite back your tongue," scolded my mother when I cried loudly, yanking her hand toward the store that sold bags of salted plums. At home, she said, "Wise guy, he not go against wind. In Chinese we say, Come from South, blow with wind—poom!—North will follow. Strongest wind cannot be seen."

INTERNET RESOURCES

Direct students to
http://www.fortunecity.com/
underworld/soundcard/1161/
History.htm. This web page is part of
Chesmayne, an online chess dictionary and encyclopedia web page.
Here, students will be able to read about the origin and history of chess.

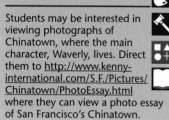
The next week I bit back my tongue as we entered the store with the forbidden candies. When my mother finished her shopping, she quietly plucked a small bag of plums from the rack and put it on the counter with the rest of the items.

What lessons does the narrator learn about wanting something?

⸻ ♜ ♞ ♝ ♛ ♚ ♝ ♞ ♜ ⸻

My mother <u>imparted</u> her daily truths so she could help my older brothers and me rise above our circumstances. We lived in San Francisco's Chinatown. Like most of the other Chinese children who played in the back alleys of restaurants and curio[1] shops, I didn't think we were poor. My bowl was always full, three five-course meals every day, beginning with a soup full of mysterious things I didn't want to know the names of.

We lived on Waverly Place, in a warm, clean, two-bedroom flat that sat above a small Chinese bakery specializing in steamed pastries and dim sum.[2] In the early morning, when the alley was still quiet, I could smell <u>fragrant</u> red beans as they were cooked down to a pastry sweetness. By daybreak, our flat was heavy with the odor of fried sesame balls and sweet curried chicken crescents. From my bed, I would listen as my father got ready for work, then locked the door behind him, one-two-three clicks.

At the end of our two-block alley was a small sandlot playground with swings and slides well-shined down the middle with use. The play area was bordered by wood-slat benches where old-country people sat crackling roasted watermelon seeds with their golden teeth and scattering the husks to an impatient gathering of gurgling pigeons. The best playground, however, was the dark alley itself. It was crammed with daily mysteries and adventures. My brothers and I would peer into the medicinal herb shop, watching old Li dole out onto a stiff sheet of white paper the right amount of insect shells, saffron-colored seeds, and <u>pungent</u> leaves for his ailing customers. It was said that he once cured a woman dying of an <u>ancestral</u> curse that had eluded the best of American doctors. Next to the pharmacy was a printer who specialized in gold-embossed wedding invitations and festive red banners.

Farther down the street was Ping Yuen Fish Market. The front window displayed a tank crowded with doomed fish and turtles struggling to gain footing on the slimy green-tiled sides. A hand-written sign informed tourists, "Within this store, is all for food, not for pet." Inside, the butchers with their bloodstained white smocks <u>deftly</u> gutted the fish while customers cried out their orders and shouted, "Give me your freshest," to which the butchers always protested, "All are freshest." On less crowded market days, we would inspect the crates of live frogs and crabs which we were warned not to poke, boxes of dried cuttlefish, and row upon row of iced prawns,[3] squid, and slippery fish. The sanddabs made me shiver each time; their eyes lay on one flattened side and reminded me of my mother's story of a careless girl who ran into a crowded street and was crushed by a cab. "Was smash flat," reported my mother.

At the corner of the alley was Hong Sing's, a four-table café with a recessed stairwell in front that led to a door marked "Tradesmen." My brothers and I believed the bad people emerged from this door at night. Tourists never went to Hong Sing's, since the menu was printed only in

---

1. **curio.** Something considered rare or unusual
2. **dim sum.** Traditional Chinese food consisting of a variety of items such as fried dumplings, chicken, or rice balls
3. **prawns.** Edible crustaceans resembling shrimp

---

words for everyday use

im • part (im part´) vt., give or communicate the knowledge of. *The teacher <u>imparted</u> his lessons to the class.*
fra • grant (fra´ grent) adj., marked by fragrance or pleasant odor. *The room was filled with the sweet smell of the <u>fragrant</u> flowers.*
pun • gent (pun´ jent) adj., sharp or pointed. *The aged cheese had a <u>pungent</u> odor.*
an • ces • tral (an ses´ trel) adj., relating to or inherited from an ancestor or family member. *She lived in her family's <u>ancestral</u> home.*
deft • ly (deft´ ly) adv., skillfully. *The skilled surgeon <u>deftly</u> performed the operation.*

Chinese. A Caucasian man with a big camera once posed me and my playmates in front of the restaurant. He had us move to the side of the picture window so the photo would capture the roasted duck

What does the man with the camera want the narrator and her friends to do?

with its head dangling from a juice-covered rope. After he took the picture, I told him he should go into Hong Sing's and eat dinner. When he smiled and asked me what they served, I shouted, "Guts and duck's feet and octopus gizzards!" Then I ran off with my friends, shrieking with laughter as we scampered across the alley and hid in the entryway grotto[4] of the China Gem Company, my heart pounding with hope that he would chase us.

My mother named me after the street that we lived on: Waverly Place Jong, my official name for important American docu-

How does the narrator get her name?

ments. But my family called me Meimei, "Little Sister." I was the youngest, the only daughter. Each morning before school, my mother would twist and yank on my thick black hair until she had formed two tightly wound pigtails. One day, as she struggled to weave a hard-toothed comb through my disobedient hair, I had a sly thought.

I asked her, "Ma, what is Chinese torture?" My mother shook her head. A bobby pin was wedged between her lips. She wetted her palms and smoothed the hair above my ear, then pushed the pin in so that it nicked sharply against my scalp.

"Who say this word?" she asked without a trace of knowing how wicked I was being. I shrugged my shoulders and said, "Some boy in my class said Chinese people do Chinese torture."

"Chinese people do many things," she said simply. "Chinese do business, do medicine, do painting. Not lazy like American people. We do torture. Best torture."

—————

My older brother Vincent was the one who actually got the chess set. We had gone to the annual Christmas party held at the First Chinese Baptist Church at the end of the alley. The missionary ladies had put together a Santa bag of gifts donated by members of another church. None of the gifts had names on them. There were separate sacks for boys and girls of different ages.

One of the Chinese parishioners had donned a Santa Claus costume and a stiff paper beard with cotton balls glued to it. I think the only children who thought he was the real thing were too young to know that Santa Claus was not Chinese. When my turn came up, the Santa man asked me how old I was. I thought it was a trick question; I was seven according to the American formula and eight by the Chinese calendar. I said I was born on March 17, 1951. That seemed to satisfy him. He then solemnly asked if I had been a very, very good girl this year and did I believe in Jesus Christ and obey my parents. I knew the only answer to that. I nodded back with equal solemnity.

Having watched the other children opening their gifts, I already knew that the big gifts were not necessarily the nicest ones. One girl my age got a large coloring book of biblical characters, while a less greedy girl who selected a smaller box received a glass vial of lavender toilet water. The sounds of the box were also important. A ten-year-old boy had chosen a box that jangled when he shook it. It was a tin globe of the world

---

4. **grotto.** Cave or artificial recess or structure built to resemble a cave

words for everyday use

so • lem • ni • ty (sə lem′ ne tē) *n.*, deep seriousness; formal or solemn observance. *The mourners were filled with solemnity at the funeral.*

1. He wanted to take a picture of them in front of the restaurant.
2. Her mother names her after the street that they live on.

ANSWERS TO GUIDED READING QUESTIONS

1. The mother did not want something that had been discarded by someone else. The boys were eager to play the game and didn't mind that it was used.
2. She offers him Life Savers as replacements for the missing pieces.

INTERNET RESOURCES

Did you know that there is poetry dedicated specifically to chess? Direct students to the **University of Pennsylvania Chess Club** website at http://chess.law.upenn.edu/chess_poetry.htm. Here students can read several poems devoted to chess.

with a slit for inserting money. He must have thought it was full of dimes and nickels, because when he saw that it had just ten pennies, his face fell with such undisguised disappointment that his mother slapped the side of his head and led him out of the church hall, apologizing to the crowd for her son who had such bad manners he couldn't appreciate such a fine gift.

As I peered into the sack, I quickly fingered the remaining presents, testing their weight, imagining what they contained. I chose a heavy, compact one that was wrapped in shiny silver foil and a red satin ribbon. It was a twelve-pack of Life Savers and I spent the rest of the party arranging and rearranging the candy tubes in the order of my favorites. My brother Winston chose wisely as well. His present turned out to be a box of <u>intricate</u> plastic parts; the instructions on the box proclaimed that when they were properly assembled he would have an authentic miniature <u>replica</u> of a World War II submarine.

Vincent got the chess set, which would have been a very decent present to get at a church Christmas party, except it was obviously used and, as we discovered later, it was missing a black pawn and a white knight. My mother graciously thanked the unknown benefactor, saying, "Too good. Cost too much." At which point, an old lady with fine white, wispy hair nodded toward our family and said with a whistling whisper, "Merry, merry Christmas."

When we got home, my mother told Vincent to throw the chess set away. "She not want it. We not want it," she said, tossing her head stiffly to the side with a tight, proud smile. My brothers had deaf ears. They were already lining up the chess pieces and reading from the dog-eared instruction book.

> How does the family regard the chess set?

I watched Vincent and Winston play during Christmas week. The chessboard seemed to hold <u>elaborate</u> secrets waiting to be untangled. The chessmen were more powerful than old Li's magic herbs that cured ancestral curses. And my brothers wore such serious faces that I was sure something was at stake that was greater than avoiding the tradesman's door to Hong Sing's.

"Let me! Let me!" I begged between games when one brother or the other would sit back with a deep sigh of relief and victory, the other annoyed, unable to let go of the outcome. Vincent at first refused to let me play, but when I offered my Life Savers as replacements for the buttons that filled in for the missing pieces, he <u>relented</u>. He chose the flavors: wild cherry for the black pawn and peppermint for the white knight. Winner could eat both.

> What does Waverly do to get her brothers to let her play chess?

As our mother sprinkled flour and rolled out small doughy circles for the steamed dumplings that would be our dinner that night, Vincent explained the rules, pointing to each piece. "You have sixteen pieces and so do I. One king and queen, two bishops, two knights, two castles, and eight pawns. The pawns can only move forward one step, except on the first move. Then they can move two. But they can only take men by moving crossways like this, except in the beginning, when you can move ahead and take another pawn."

"Why?" I asked as I moved my pawn. "Why can't they move more steps?"

"Because they're pawns," he said.

"But why do they go crossways to take other men? Why aren't there any women and children?"

---

words for everyday use

in • tri • cate (in' tri ket) *adj.*, complicated, having many complex parts. *It was an <u>intricate</u> puzzle with over 1000 tiny pieces.*
rep • li • ca (re' pli ka) *n.*, exact copy or reproduction. *The painting was a <u>replica</u> of the original.*
e • la • bor • ate (i la' be ret) *adj.*, marked by complexity, fullness of detail. *The man went to <u>elaborate</u> measures to plan every detail of his trip.*
re • lent (ri lent') *vi.*, give in or slacken. *Tired of Greg's pleading, Lora <u>relented</u> and told him the secret.*

"Why is the sky blue? Why must you always ask stupid questions?" asked Vincent. "This is a game. These are the rules. I didn't make them up. See. Here. In the book." He jabbed a page with a pawn in his hand. "Pawn. P-A-W-N. Pawn. Read it yourself."

My mother patted the flour off her hands. "Let me see book," she said quietly. She scanned the pages quickly, not reading the foreign English symbols, seeming to search deliberately for nothing in particular.

"This American rules," she concluded at last. "Every time people come out from foreign country, must know rules. You not know, judge say, Too bad, go back. They not telling you why so you can use their way go forward. They say, Don't know why, you find out yourself. But they knowing all the time. Better you take it, find out why yourself." She tossed her head back with a satisfied smile.

> How does Waverly's mother feel about American rules?

I found out about all the whys later. I read the rules and looked up all the big words in a dictionary. I borrowed books from the Chinatown library. I studied each chess piece, trying to absorb the power each contained.

I learned about opening moves and why it's important to control the center early on; the shortest distance between two points is straight down the middle. I learned about the middle game and why tactics between two adversaries are like clashing ideas; the one who plays better has the clearest plans for both attacking and getting out of traps. I learned why it is essential in the endgame to have foresight, a mathematical understanding of all the possible moves, and patience; all weaknesses and advantages become evident to a strong <u>adversary</u> and are obscured to a tiring opponent. I discovered that for the whole game one must gather invisible strengths and see the endgame before the game begins.

I also found out why I should never reveal "why" to others. A little knowledge withheld is a great advantage one should store for future use. That is the power of chess. It is a game of secrets in which one must show and never tell.

> What does Waverly say is the power of chess?

The chessboard seemed to hold elaborate secrets waiting to be untangled.

I loved the secrets I found within the sixty-four black and white squares. I carefully drew a handmade chessboard and pinned it to the wall next to my bed, where at night I would stare for hours at imaginary battles. Soon I no longer lost my games or Life Savers, but I lost my adversaries. Winston and Vincent decided they were more interested in roaming the streets after school in their Hopalong Cassidy[5] cowboy hats.

On a cold spring afternoon, while walking home from school, I detoured through the playground at the end of our alley. I saw a group of old men, two seated across a folding table playing a game of chess, others smoking pipes, eating peanuts, and watching. I ran home and grabbed Vincent's chess set, which was bound in a cardboard box with rubber bands. I also carefully selected two prized rolls of Life Savers. I came back to the park and approached a man who was observing the game.

---

5. **Hopalong Cassidy.** Fictional cowboy hero popularized by movies and television shows in the 1950s

words for everyday use

ad • ver • sar • y (ad' ve(r) ser ē) *n.*, one that contends with or opposes. *His enemy was a worthy <u>adversary</u>.*

1. She feels that Americans do not inform foreigners of the rules to help them get along in America. It is up to the foreigners to learn the rules on their own.
2. The power of chess is in withholding your knowledge and not revealing your strategy to others. "It is a game of secrets in which one must show and never tell."

INTERNET RESOURCES

Interested students may like to know about an interactive chess game that can be played on the Internet. Students can play chess with their friends online at http://www.hickenbotham.com/chess/index.html for free. They can even choose a chess board to play on or create their very own!

BIOGRAPHICAL NOTE

Interested students may want to read about more chess strategies and secrets in the following books written by grand masters. Both books cater to the needs of beginning and intermediate chess players. Detailed pictures and diagrams make it easy for the reader to understand and visualize the strategies explained.
- *The Game of Chess* by Siegbert Tarrasch (one of the original five grand masters)
- *Winning Chess Strategies: Proven Principles from One of the U.S.A.'s Top Chess Players (Winning Chess)* by Yasser Seirawa

Dragon Character, 1986. Wa Zuoren.
Collection of Robert A. Hefner III.

the names. The Double Attack from the East and West Shores. Throwing Stones on the Drowning Man. The Sudden Meeting of the Clan. The Surprise from the Sleeping Guard. The Humble Servant Who Kills the King. Sand in the Eyes of Advancing Forces. A Double Killing Without Blood.

There were also the fine points of chess <u>etiquette</u>. Keep captured men in neat rows, as well-tended prisoners. Never announce "Check" with <u>vanity</u>, lest someone with an unseen sword slit your throat. Never hurl pieces into the sandbox after you have lost a game, because then you must find them again, by yourself, after apologizing to all around you. By the end of the summer, Lau Po had taught me all he knew, and I had become a better chess player.

A small weekend crowd of Chinese people and tourists would gather as I played and defeated my opponents one by one. My mother would join the crowds during these outdoor exhibition games. She sat proudly on the bench, telling my admirers with proper Chinese <u>humility</u>, "Is luck."

A man who watched me play in the park suggested that my mother allow me to play in local chess tournaments. My mother smiled <u>graciously</u>, an answer that meant nothing. I desperately wanted to go, but I bit back my tongue. I knew she would not let me play

"Want to play?" I asked him. His face widened with surprise and he grinned as he looked at the box under my arm.

"Little sister, been a long time since I play with dolls," he said, smiling <u>benevolently</u>. I quickly put the box down next to him on the bench and displayed my <u>retort</u>.

Lau Po, as he allowed me to call him, turned out to be a much better player than my brothers. I lost many games and many Life Savers. But over the weeks, with each <u>diminishing</u> roll of candies, I added new secrets. Lau Po gave me

words for everyday use	**be • nev • o • lent • ly** (be nev′ lent lē) *adv.*, with kindness or goodwill. *She <u>benevolently</u> gave donations to the poor.* **re • tort** (ri tort′) *n.*, quick, witty, or cunning reply. *He gave a quick <u>retort</u> to the insult.* **di • min • ish • ing** (de mi′ nish ing) *adj.*, becoming smaller or less. *The poor investment gave <u>diminishing</u> returns.* **et • i • quette** (e′ ti ket) *n.*, proper social conduct or procedure. *She displayed good <u>etiquette</u> at the tea party.* **van • i • ty** (va′ ne tē) *n.*, inflated pride in oneself; conceit. *The boy accepted his trophy with a show of <u>vanity</u>.* **hu • mil • i • ty** (hu mi′ le tē) *n.*, state of being humble, not possessing pride. *With <u>humility</u>, she gave credit to her teacher.* **gra • cious • ly** (gra′ shes lē) *adv.*, with kindness and courtesy. *The gentleman <u>graciously</u> offered his seat to the elderly woman.*

among strangers. So as we walked home I said in a small voice that I didn't want to play in the local tournament. They would have American rules. If I lost, I would bring shame on my family.

> What does Waverly do to get her mother to let her play in the chess tournament?

"Is shame you fall down nobody push you," said my mother.

During my first tournament, my mother sat with me in the front row as I waited for my turn. I frequently bounced my legs to unstick them from the cold metal seat of the folding chair. When my name was called, I leapt up. My mother unwrapped something in her lap. It was her chang, a small tablet of red jade which held the sun's fire. "Is luck," she whispered, and tucked it into my dress pocket. I turned to my opponent, a fifteen-year-old boy from Oakland. He looked at me, wrinkling his nose.

> What does Waverly's mother give her for good luck?

As I began to play, the boy disappeared, the color ran out of the room, and I saw only my white pieces and his black ones waiting on the other side. A light wind began blowing past my ears. It whispered secrets only I could hear.

"Blow from the South," it murmured. "The wind leaves no trail." I saw a clear path, the traps to avoid. The crowd rustled. "Shhh! Shhh!" said the corners of the room. The wind blew stronger. "Throw sand from the East to distract him." The knight came forward ready for the sacrifice. The wind hissed, louder and louder. "Blow, blow, blow. He cannot see. He is blind now. Make him lean away from the wind so he is easier to knock down."

"Check," I said, as the wind roared with laughter. The wind died down to little puffs, my own breath.

My mother placed my first trophy next to a new plastic chess set that the neighborhood Tao[6] society had given to me. As she wiped each piece with a soft cloth, she said, "Next time win more, lose less."

"Ma, it's not how many pieces you lose," I said. "Sometimes you need to lose pieces to get ahead."

"Better to lose less, see if you really need."

At the next tournament, I won again, but it was my mother who wore the <u>triumphant</u> grin.

"Lost eight piece this time. Last time was eleven. What I tell you? Better off lose less!" I was annoyed, but I couldn't say anything.

I attended more tournaments, each one further away from home. I won all games, in all divisions. The Chinese bakery downstairs from our flat displayed my growing collection of trophies in its window, amidst the dust-covered cakes that were never picked up. The day after I won an important regional tournament, the window encased a fresh sheet cake with whipped-cream frosting and red script saying, "Congratulations, Waverly Jong, Chinatown Chess Champion." Soon after that, a flower shop, headstone engraver, and funeral parlor offered to sponsor me in national tournaments. That's when my mother decided that I no longer had to do the dishes. Winston and Vincent had to do my chores.

> How does Waverly's mother show that she values her daughter's skill as a chess player?

"Why does she get to play and we do all the work," complained Vincent.

"Is new American rules," said my mother. "Meimei play, squeeze all her brains out for win chess. You play, worth squeeze towel."

---

6. **Tao.** Chinese mystical philosophy founded in the 6th century BC

words for everyday use

tri • um • phant (trī em(p)′ fent) *adj.*, victorious, or relating to triumph. *The school held a celebration for the <u>triumphant</u> football team.*

ANSWERS TO GUIDED READING QUESTIONS

1. She tells her mother that she does not want to play in the tournament because they will have American rules and she doesn't want to bring shame on her family.
2. Her mother gives her her *chang*, a small red jade tablet that held the sun's fire.
3. She no longer makes her do the dishes and makes her brothers do her chores.

Quotables

"The highest art of the chess player lies in not allowing your opponent to show you what he can do."

—World champion Garry Kasparov

CROSS-CURRICULAR ACTIVITIES

CHESS HISTORY. The first person named grand master in chess was Czar (KI) Nicholas II in 1914.

Bobby Fischer is quoted on this page, saying that there will never be a woman grand master. He was wrong. In 1978, Nona Gapridashvilli of the USSR was the first woman to reach grand-master status. Today, there are over 600 chess players who have reached grand-master status. Out of the 600+ grand masters in the world, 108 of them are women.

By my ninth birthday, I was a national chess champion. I was still some 429 points away from grand master status, but I was <u>touted</u> as the Great American Hope, a child <u>prodigy</u> and a girl to boot. They ran a photo of me in *Life* magazine next to a quote in which Bobby Fisher said, "There will never be a woman grand master." "Your move, Bobby," said the <u>caption</u>.

The day they took the magazine picture I wore neatly plaited[7] braids clipped with plastic barrettes trimmed with rhinestones. I was playing in a large high school auditorium that echoed with phlegmy coughs and the squeaky wooden floors. Seated across from me was an American man, about the same age as Lau Po, maybe fifty. I remember that his sweaty brow seemed to weep at my every move. He wore a dark, <u>mal-odorous</u> suit. One of his pockets was stuffed with a great white kerchief on which he wiped his palm before sweeping his hand over the chosen chess piece with great <u>flourish</u>.

In my crisp pink-and-white dress with scratchy lace at the neck, one of two my mother had sewn for these special occasions, I would clasp my hands under my chin, the delicate points of my elbows poised lightly on the table in the manner my mother had shown me for posing for the press. I would swing my patent leather shoes back and forth like an impatient child riding on a school bus. Then I would pause, suck in my lips, twirl my chosen piece in midair as if undecided, and then firmly plant it in its new threatening place, with a triumphant smile thrown back at my opponent for good measure.

Dislocation, 1995. Kuange Jian.

art note

***Dislocation*, 1995. Kuange Jian.**
Contemporary artist **Kuange Jian** says that his painting represents the idea that young people "don't know which way they should go with their lives...as if they are 'dislocated' in society." What odd aspect of this painting suggests, or symbolizes, dislocation? In what way is the girl in Amy Tan's story becoming dislocated, or alienated, from her family and from her mother's traditional ideas?

---

7. **plaited.** Woven or braided

words for everyday use	
tout (taut') *vi.*, praised or publicized loudly. *Jill was <u>touted</u> for her scholastic abilities.*	

tout (taut') *vi.*, praised or publicized loudly. *Jill was <u>touted</u> for her scholastic abilities.*
prod • i • gy (prä' de jē) *n.*, highly talented child or youth. *His exceptional acting ability made him a child <u>prodigy</u>.*
cap • tion (kap' shen) *n.*, heading or comment accompanying a photograph. *The <u>caption</u> below the photograph explained what was happening.*
mal • o • dor • ous (mal ō' der es) *adj.*, having a bad odor. *The rotten fish made the room smell <u>malodorous</u>.*
flour • ish (fler' ish) *n.*, bold sweeping gesture. *The traffic guard waved his arms with a <u>flourish</u>.*

I no longer played in the alley of Waverly Place. I never visited the playground where the pigeons and old men gathered. I went to school, then directly home to learn new chess secrets, cleverly concealed advantages, more escape routes.

What is Waverly giving up to play chess?

But I found it difficult to concentrate at home. My mother had a habit of standing over me while I plotted out my games. I think she thought of herself as my protective <u>ally</u>. Her lips would be sealed tight, and after each move I made, a soft "Hmmmmph" would escape from her nose.

"Ma, I can't practice when you stand there like that," I said one day. She retreated to the kitchen and made loud noises with the pots and pans. When the crashing stopped, I could see out of the corner of my eye that she was standing in the doorway. "Hmmmph!" Only this one came out of her tight throat.

My parents made many <u>concessions</u> to allow me to practice. One time I complained that the bedroom I shared was so noisy that I couldn't think. Thereafter, my brothers slept in a bed in the living room facing the street. I said I couldn't finish my rice; my head didn't work right when my stomach was too full. I left the table with half-finished bowls and nobody complained. But there was one duty I couldn't avoid. I had to accompany my mother on Saturday market days when I had no tournament to play. My mother would proudly walk with me, visiting

What is the duty that Waverly has to perform for her mother?

many shops, buying very little. "This my daughter Wave-ly Jong," she said to whoever looked her way.

One day after we left a shop I said under my breath, "I wish you wouldn't do that, telling everybody I'm your daughter." My mother stopped walking. Crowds of people with heavy bags pushed past us on the sidewalk, bumping into first one shoulder, then another.

"Aiii-ya. So shame be with mother?" She grasped my hand even tighter as she glared at me.

I looked down. "It's not that, it's just so obvious. It's just so embarrassing."

"Embarrass you be my daughter?" Her voice was cracking with anger.

"That's not what I meant. That's not what I said."

"What you say?"

I knew it was a mistake to say anything more, but I heard my voice speaking, "Why do you have to use me to show off? If you want to show off, then why don't you learn to play chess?"

What does Waverly accuse her mother of doing?

My mother's eyes turned into dangerous black slits. She had no words for me, just sharp silence.

I felt the wind rushing around my hot ears. I jerked my hand out of my mother's tight grasp and spun around, knocking into an old woman. Her bag of groceries spilled to the ground.

"Aii-ya! Stupid girl!" my mother and the woman cried. Oranges and tin cans careened down the sidewalk. As my mother stooped to help the old woman pick up the escaping food, I took off.

I raced down the street, dashing between people, not looking back as my mother screamed

"Blow from the South," it murmured. "The wind leaves no trail."

ANSWERS TO GUIDED READING QUESTIONS

1. She never plays in the alley or the playground and spends all of her free time practicing her chess game.
2. She had to accompany her mother on Saturday market days when she had no tournament to play.
3. Waverly accuses her mother of using her to show off.

CROSS-CURRICULAR ACTIVITIES

To help students visualize the action that takes place between Waverly and her mother, show this scene from the film, *Joy Luck Club.* This scene in the movie is played out almost verbatim of what is written and described on this page.

words for everyday use

al • ly (a' lī) *n.,* one that is associated with another as a helper. *The doctor had become his <u>ally</u> in Ty's battle against cancer.*

con • ces • sion (ken se' shen) *n.,* something granted as a right or privilege. *Many <u>concessions</u> were made by both sides in order to reach an agreement.*

ANSWERS TO GUIDED READING QUESTIONS

1. She realizes she has no where to go and wasn't running from anything.
2. Her mother says the family should have no concern for her because she has no concern for them.
3. Her opponent is her mother. Her white pieces fell off the board as her mother's black pieces advanced. In her imagination Waverly rose up into the air, flew out the window, and continued to rise up into the night sky until everything below her disappeared and she was alone.

SELECTION CHECK TEST 4.8.5 WITH ANSWERS

Checking Your Reading
1. How does Waverly get her mother to buy the bag of plums? **She bites her tongue by not asking her for them.**
2. What other name is Waverly called? What does it mean? **She is called "Meimei," which means "little sister."**
3. From where did the chest set come? **The chess set came from a Christmas party held at a church.**
4. How did Waverly convince her brothers to let her play chess with them? **She convinces them with Life Savers.**
5. According to Waverly, where does the power of chess lie? **It lies in withholding a little knowledge and storing it for future use.**

Vocabulary in Context
Fill in each blank below with the most appropriate word from the Words for Everyday Use. You may have to change the tense of the word.

ally concession intricate
imparted adversary fragrant
elaborate

1. My tennis coach **imparted** the strategy of serve-and-volley to help me combat my opponent.
2. I could tell the melon was ripe because of its strong **fragrant** smell.
3. We used to be friends, but now we are **adversaries**.
4. The wedding reception was **elaborate**; there was a full-size orchestra, ice sculptures, and flowers from Guam.
5. Many people feel that driving is a **concession**, not something to be abused.

---

shrilly, "Meimei! Meimei!" I fled down an alley, past dark, curtained shops and merchants washing the grime off their windows. I sped into the sunlight, into a large street crowded with tourists examining trinkets and souvenirs. I ducked into another dark alley, down another street, up another alley. I ran until it hurt and I realized I had nowhere to go, that I was not running from anything. The alleys contained no escape routes.

My breath came out like angry smoke. It was cold. I sat down on an upturned plastic pail next to a stack of empty boxes, cupping my chin with my hands, thinking hard. I imagined my mother, first walking briskly down one street or another looking for me, then giving up and returning home to await my arrival. After two hours, I stood up on creaking legs and slowly walked home.

> *Why does Waverly decide to go home?*

The alley was quiet and I could see the yellow lights shining from our flat like two tiger's eyes in the night. I climbed the sixteen steps to the door, advancing quietly up each so as not to make any warning sounds. I turned the knob; the door was locked. I heard a chair moving, quick steps, the locks turning—click! click! click!—and then the door opened.

"About time you got home," said Vincent. "Boy, are you in trouble."

He slid back to the dinner table. On a platter were the remains of a large fish, its fleshy head still connected to bones swimming upstream in vain escape. Standing there waiting for my punishment, I heard my mother speak in a dry voice.

"We're not concerning this girl. This girl not have concerning for us."

> *How does Waverly's mother respond when Waverly returns home?*

Nobody looked at me. Bone chopsticks clinked against the insides of bowls being emptied into hungry mouths.

I walked into my room, closed the door, and lay down on my bed. The room was dark, the ceiling filled with shadows from the dinnertime lights of neighboring flats.

In my head, I saw a chessboard with sixty-four black and white squares. Opposite me was my opponent, two angry black slits. She wore a triumphant smile. "Strongest wind cannot be seen," she said.

Her black men advanced across the plane, slowly marching to each <u>successive</u> level as a single unit. My white pieces screamed as they scurried and fell off the board one by one. As her men drew closer to my edge, I felt myself growing light. I rose up into the air and flew out the window. Higher and higher, above the alley, over the tops of tiled roofs, where I was gathered up by the wind and pushed up toward the night sky until everything below me disappeared and I was alone.

> *Who is Waverly's opponent in her imaginary chess game? What happens during this game?*

I closed my eyes and pondered my next move. ∎

> **words for everyday use**
> suc • ces • sive (sək se′ siv) *adj.*, following in order. *He took the required classes in* <u>successive</u> *order.*

Respond *to the* SELECTION

What move do you think Waverly will make at the end of the story?

SELECTION CHECK TEST 4.8.5 WITH ANSWERS (CONT.)

Literary Tools
1. What is a symbol? **A symbol is a thing that represents both itself and something else.**
2. What is the recurring symbol in "Rules of the Game"? **The recurring symbol is the wind.**
3. From which point of view is the story told? **It is told from the first-person point of view.**

RESPOND TO THE SELECTION

Students should explain the strategy of the next move they think Waverly will make.

INSIGHTS

INSIGHTS INSIGHTS INSIGHTS

The Rules of Chess

Chess is played by two players beginning in the position shown below. The player with the light-colored pieces (usually referred to as white) moves first. Then each player takes a single turn. The players must move in turn. A move cannot be skipped.

When setting up the pieces, keep in mind two things. The light colored square goes on the player's right, and Queens go on their color next to the Kings on the center files.

You may not move a piece to a square already occupied by one of your own pieces. You may capture an opposing piece by replacing that piece with one of your own pieces, if the piece can legally move there.

THE KING

The King is the most important piece. When it is trapped so it cannot move without being captured, then the game is lost. The trap is called checkmate. The King can move one square in any direction. A King can never move into check or onto a square where it can be captured by an opponent's piece.

THE QUEEN

The Queen is the most powerful piece. She can move to any square in any direction if her path is not blocked. Her range and ability to attack many pieces at once are the source of her power.

THE ROOK

The Rook is a very powerful piece because it can move to any square along its file or row as long as its path is not blocked. Its range is the source of its power.

THE BISHOP

The Bishop is a powerful piece because it can move to any square along its diagonals as long as it is not blocked. Its range is the source of its power.

THE KNIGHT

The Knight is nearly as powerful as the Bishop not because of its range but because it is the only piece that can hop over other pieces. It does so in an L-shaped path. This ability makes it particularly powerful in the early stages of a game when the board is crowded with pieces.

THE PAWN

The Pawn is the least powerful piece because of its poor mobility. Ordinarily, it may move only one square forward. However, on its first move, it has the option of moving forward one or two squares. It may capture other pieces only by a diagonal move of one square. It may not capture forward. It may not move backward. The lowly Pawn usually does not last long, but if it is able to reach the eighth row or rank, then it can be promoted to any other piece except the King. A Pawn thus promoted is replaced by that piece. Therefore, it is possible to have more than one Queen or more than two Rooks, Bishops, or Knights on the board at one time.

THE OBJECTIVE IN CHESS

No one knows for certain where and when chess was invented, although a clue to its origins can be found in the word *checkmate*, a form of the Persian *shah-mat*, meaning, literally, "the king is dead." The objective in chess is to checkmate your opponent's King. When a King cannot avoid capture, then it is checkmated and the game is immediately over. If a King is threatened with capture but has a means to escape, then it is said to be in check. A King cannot move into check, and if in check must move out of check immediately. There are three ways to move out of check:

- By capturing the checking piece
- By blocking the line of attack by placing one's own piece between the checking piece and the King
- By moving the King out of check (away from its position)

If a King is not in check, and no other legal move is possible, then a stalemate, a draw or tie, occurs.

Over the years, various checkmate positions have acquired names given to them by players. The following illustration shows an example of a checkmate position known as the "Fool's Mate." Over the years, various checkmate positions have acquired names given to them by players. The following illustration shows an example of a checkmate position known as the "Fool's Mate." Only two moves into the game, the white player has foolishly left his or her King wide open. The black Queen slides down on a diagonal and traps the King to win the match.

ADDITIONAL INFORMATION

If you decide that you want to learn to play chess, you need, in addition, to learn the rules governing moves, known as *castling* and *capturing en passant*. You can find the Official Rules of Chess of the United States Chess Federation at the Federation's site on the World Wide Web. The address of the site is

http://www.uschess.org

A good introduction to the game is Snyder, Robert M. *Chess for Juniors: A Complete Guide for the Beginner*. New York: McKay, 1991. ∎

Investigate, Inquire, and Imagine

Recall: GATHERING FACTS

1a. What art does Waverly's mother teach her to use to get what she wants?

2a. How does Mrs. Jong react in public to the Christmas gift of a used chess game? What is her real opinion that she expresses privately when the family is at home?

3a. What does Waverly give up to become a champion chess player?

Interpret: FINDING MEANING

1b. How does Waverly use this art to get her mother to allow her to play in chess tournaments?

2b. Why does Mrs. Jong act as she does in public when that is not the way she really feels?

3b. Why do you think that Waverly becomes so obsessed with playing chess? Is it worth it for her to give up all of her free time to learn to play better? Explain why or why, not, using examples from the story.

Analyze: TAKING THINGS APART

4a. What problems do Waverly and her mother have when they try to communicate?

Synthesize: BRINGING THINGS TOGETHER

4b. Consider whether Mrs. Jong is a strong or weak communicator, citing examples from the story. How does her limited English affect her ability to communicate?

Evaluate: MAKING JUDGMENTS

5a. How effective are Mrs. Jong's rules in helping Waverly win at chess? Use evidence from the text to support your response.

Extend: CONNECTING IDEAS

5b. "Rules of the Game" and the related reading, "The Rules of Chess," outline various rules and game strategies. How do the actual game rules compare to Mrs. Jong's rules?

Understanding Literature

POINT OF VIEW. Review the definition for **point of view** in the Handbook of Literary Terms. Why do you think Amy Tan wrote "Rules of the Game" using the first-person point of view? What are the advantages and disadvantages of this approach? What types of point of view could reveal Mrs. Jong's inner thoughts? What point of view could a writer use to convey the inner thoughts of both Waverly and her mother?

SYMBOL. The wind serves as an important symbol in this story. Review the definition for **symbol** and the chart you completed as you read the story. Then answer the following questions:

- Waverly's mother says that a wise person does not go against the wind and that the "strongest wind cannot be seen." What does the symbol of the wind mean in terms of how Mrs. Jong expects her daughter to act?

RECALL

1a. Waverly's mother teaches her to bite back her tongue.

2a. She responds graciously saying that it is too good and costs too much money. In private, she says if the game was not good enough for the donor, it is not good enough for her family.

3a. She no longer played in the alley or stopped at the playground.

INTERPRET

1b. Waverly wants very much to play in the chess tournament, but she does not say so. Rather than beg her mother to let her participate, she suggests that she does not want to play because she might bring her family shame. Her mother lets her enter the tournament.

2b. Mrs. Jong is being polite and showing respect.

3b. *Responses will vary.*

ANALYZE

4a. Waverly and her mother have trouble being honest and direct in their communication because Waverly is taught to bite back her tongue.

SYNTHESIZE

4b. Mrs. Wong often does not communicate directly, which makes her a weak communicator. Her limited English does not seem to pose as much of a problem as her indirect means of communication and her metaphorical way of speaking.

EVALUATE

5a. Mrs. Jong's rules help Waverly. Waverly learns the sneak attack and learns that a seemingly less powerful piece can be very important.

EXTEND

5b. Mrs. Jong does not approach the rules from a traditional standpoint. In her mind, losing less pieces is important. She doesn't always believe that the most visible force is the most powerful force.

ANSWERS TO UNDERSTANDING LITERATURE

POINT OF VIEW. The first-person point of view allows the reader to associate closely with Waverly. The reader's perception of Mrs. Jong is colored by Waverly's opinion about or her relationship with her mother. An omniscient point of view could reveal Mrs. Jong's inner thoughts. A writer could use a changing point of view or an omniscient point of view to reveal the thoughts of both Waverly and Mrs. Jong.

SYMBOL. Mrs. Jong expects Waverly to be obedient and not challenge authority. The advice about the wind helps Waverly find an interesting move and distract her opponent. Waverly hears the wind whistling around her in her anger. Waverly's mother says "strongest wind cannot be seen." Waverly's mother could be the strongest wind or Waverly's anger could be seen as the strongest wind getting the best of her.

Language, Grammar, and Style
Responses will vary. Student responses should demonstrate an understanding of the omniscient point of view.
(Continued on page 641)

- During Waverly's first chess tournament, how does what her mother told her about the wind help her to defeat her opponent?
- How is the wind used as a symbol when Waverly accuses her mother of using her to show off?
- What does Waverly's mother say right before their imaginary chess game at the end of the story? Who represents the strongest wind at this point?

Writer's Journal

1. Write a **letter** to Waverly's mother advising her how you think she should treat her daughter.
2. Imagine you work at a store that sells board games. Write a **flyer** promoting the benefits of learning chess, aiming especially to attract young players to the game.
3. Write a **newspaper report** giving a play-by-play account of Waverly and her mother facing each other as if they are opponents in a chess game. In your account, state who appears to be the stronger player, and why.

Integrating the Language Arts

Language, Grammar, and Style

WORKING WITH PRONOUNS AND NOUNS. Part of the power of "Rules of the Game" comes from the fact that Amy Tan uses the first-person point of view. Try substituting the first-person pronouns in the story with third-person pronouns and nouns. Make your choices using the chart below:

I	she		we	they
me	her		us	them
my	her		our	their
mine	hers		ours	theirs

When you have finished, notice that the point of view is third person, but still limited to Waverly's view: her mother's inner thoughts are still not revealed. You may want to experiment with the **third-person unlimited**, or **omniscient point of view** by exploring the inner thoughts of the mother. Rewrite the first three paragraphs of the story using third-person omniscient point of view. Use words such as *Mrs. Jong, Waverly's mother, she, her,* and *hers* to describe what it is like for Mrs. Jong to scold Waverly for her tantrum when she wants the plums. What does she feel when Waverly acts up? Why does she decide not to allow Waverly to have the plum candies? How does Mrs. Jong feel when Waverly says nothing about them the following week, although she still clearly wants them? What satisfaction does Mrs. Jong experience seeing that Waverly at age six can learn the lesson her mother has taught her?

Applied English

TECHNICAL WRITING. "The Rules of Chess," on page 637, is an example of technical writing that describes how something is done. Try your hand at a piece of technical writing to explain some process—how to change a bicycle tire, how to make a quilt, or how to tune a guitar, for example. Make sure to include all the steps in chronological order. Use simple, straightforward sentence structure and vocabulary.

Media Literacy

NEWSPAPER RESEARCH. Newspapers contain stories that describe current events, but they also contain much more than that. What examples of games or descriptions of games can you find in newspapers? Go to the library or to a news-stand and search through some newspapers and find as many examples as you can. Clip or photocopy these to share in class.

Vocabulary

WORD ORIGINS. The word *checkmate* comes from the Persian *shah mat,* meaning "the king is dead." The study of the origins of words is called *etymology.* Many words have interesting origins. Use a dictionary or a book on etymologies to look up the origins of the following words.
On a piece of paper, write each word and its original meaning.

1. pungent
2. retort
3. vanity
4. touted
5. curio
6. fragrant
7. replica
8. grotto

Speaking and Listening & Collaborative Learning

ANALYZING COMMUNICATION. Working with another classmate, analyze the conversation between Waverly and Mrs. Jong shortly before Waverly runs away. Role-play the conversation between the two characters in the story. What miscommunication occurs between them? What does Mrs. Jong think that her daughter is saying? What is she actually saying? What steps could each person take to make sure that such miscommunication does not occur between them in the future?

Study and Research

RESEARCHING GAMES. Choose a game that interests you and research its origins. Possibilities include board games such as checkers or chess, or sports such as football, basketball, rugby, hockey, and lacrosse. Who invented the game? When and where was it invented? What were the original rules of the game? How has the game changed over the years? Present your findings in a small group in class.

Applied English
To help students with this writing activity, refer them to the Language Arts Survey 6.3, "Giving Directions," and 6.4, "Writing a Step-by-Step Procedure."

Vocabulary
pungent—prick or puncture
retort—twist back
vanity—emptiness, worthlessness
tout—peep, look out after
curio—care, diligence
fragrant—emit a sweet smell
replica—answer or reply
grotto—crypt

Speaking and Listening & Collaborative Learning
Refer students to the Language Arts Survey 4.7, "Communicating with Another Person." Have them use the guidelines listed in this section to analyze the communication between Waverly and her mother.

GRAPHIC ORGANIZER

Sight: The dull, murky sky stretched like a dark canopy, a vast infinity of grayness; Streets outside glistened with snow, the white sparkling flakes stuck and melted on the windowpanes and hung on the boughs of the trees like molten silver; Fire made giant shadows dance on the walls and ceiling; Chalk was a long, slender stick of vivid yellow; Christy looked about at the tense, excited faces that were at that moment frozen, immobile, eager, waiting for a miracle in their midst; Everything in the room swam till the faces around Christy were mere patches of white.

Hearing: The wind howled dismally; Christy looked up and became aware that everyone had stopped talking and was staring at him silently; Christy could hear the sound of the water tap dripping in the pantry, the loud ticking of the clock on the mantleshelf, and the soft hiss and crackle of the logs on the open hearth.

Touch: Big kitchen fire lit up the little room with a warm glow; Christy felt the sweat break out on his forehead; His hands were so tightly clenched that his fingernails bit into his flesh.

READER'S JOURNAL

Students should mention the result of the belief that the other person had in them. Students may also write a contrast piece about how they felt or how it affected them when somebody didn't have confidence in them.

AUTOBIOGRAPHY

AUTOBIOGRAPHY. An **autobiography** is the story of a person's life, written by that person. Decide what you learn about Christy Brown in his autobiography that you wouldn't learn from a biography about him.

DESCRIPTION. Description is a type of writing that portrays a character, an object, or a scene. Descriptions make use of *sensory details*—words and phrases that describe how things look, sound, smell, taste, or feel. Note how carefully and vividly Brown describes the scene when he writes the letter *A* for the first time.

Graphic Organizer

Christy Brown gives a very detailed description of the night he first wrote the letter *A*, thereby proving to his family that he was capable of intellectual activity. Make a sensory detail chart like the one below to show how the author appeals to your senses in providing vivid details describing the scene. One example has been done for you.

Sight:	
Hearing:	The wind howled dismally.
Touch:	
Taste:	
Smell:	

---

from ***My Left Foot***

by Christy Brown

Reader's resource

Christy Brown overcame many difficulties to become a writer and artist. The selection that follows describes Brown's birth and early childhood.

SCIENCE CONNECTION. Brown was born with cerebral palsy, paralysis caused by a brain disorder. **Cerebral palsy** is a disability that results from damage to the brain suffered before, during, or just after birth. People with cerebral palsy are mentally normal, but they have little control over their bodies. They typically cannot sit or hold their heads up without help. Their hands are clenched, they suffer uncontrollable bouts of clenched or slack jaw, and they move convulsively. When Christy Brown was born with this disorder, people advised his mother to send him to an institution. She firmly refused, and with the help of his family, Brown was able to overcome his physical problems and learn to read, write, and create art.

About *the* AUTHOR

Christy Brown (1932–1981) was born in Dublin, Ireland. One of twenty-two children, he was raised in the slums of the city. Because of his cerebral palsy, he was unable to walk, talk, eat, or drink unassisted. Over a fifteen-year period, using one toe to type, he wrote a novel. He was a poet and an artist as well and published seven books during his lifetime.

Reader's Journal

Describe a time when someone had confidence in your abilities.

GOALS/OBJECTIVES

Studying this lesson will enable students to
- empathize with Christy Brown's struggles to communicate
- recognize Brown's accomplishments as a writer
- define *autobiography* and *description* and recognize the use of these techniques in the selection
- learn about people who adapt or compensate for their disabilities
- research volunteerism and the disorder of cerebral palsy

from *My Left Foot* Christy Brown

I was born in the Rotunda Hospital on June 5th, 1932. There were nine children before me and twelve after me, so I myself belong to the middle group. Out of this total of twenty-two, seventeen lived, but four died in infancy, leaving thirteen still to hold the family fort.

Mine was a difficult birth, I am told. Both mother and son almost died. A whole army of relations queued up[1] outside the hospital until the small hours of the morning, waiting for news and praying furiously that it would be good.

After my birth, Mother was sent to recuperate for some weeks, and I was kept in the hospital while she was away. I remained there for some time, without name, for I wasn't baptized until my mother was well enough to bring me to church.

It was Mother who first saw that there was something wrong with me. I was about four months old at the time. She noticed that my head had a habit of falling backward whenever she tried to feed me. She attempted to correct this by placing her hand on the back of my neck to keep it steady. But when she took it away, back it would drop again. That was the first warning sign. Then she became aware of other defects as I got older. She saw that my hands were clenched nearly all of the time and were inclined to twine behind my back, my mouth couldn't grasp the teat of the bottle because even at that early age my jaws would either lock together tightly, so that it was impos-

> What was the first warning sign?

1. **queued up.** Joined a line of people

ANSWER TO GUIDED READING QUESTION

1. The first warning sign was that Brown could not support his own head.

INDIVIDUAL LEARNING STRATEGIES

MOTIVATION
Students can discuss stereotypes about people with physical or mental disabilities. They can list misconceptions about people with these disabilities. Students might also brainstorm ways to change these misconceptions.

READING PROFICIENCY
The information about cerebral palsy in the Reader's Resource should help students understand cerebral palsy and the misconceptions surrounding it. This background information may help students better understand Brown's situation.

ENGLISH LANGUAGE LEARNING
Point out the following vocabulary words to students before they read the selection:
inevitable—that cannot be avoided or evaded
contended—held to be fact; asserted
convulsed—moved violently and uncontrollably
molten—melted and made liquified by heat
profound—very deep; deeply or intensely felt

SPECIAL NEEDS
Students should focus on the Guided Reading questions and the Recall questions in the Investigate, Inquire, and Imagine section. Students might read a few paragraphs and then stop and give an oral summary of what they have read.

ENRICHMENT
Christy Brown was an artist and a poet. Students can research the written and visual works that Brown created. Students may wish to present Brown's work to the class. They can also do further research on Brown's life and present this information along with Brown's art.

VOCABULARY FROM THE SELECTION

bondage	inert
contention	involuntarily
conviction	momentous
immobile	taut
impertinence	volition

ANSWERS TO GUIDED
READING QUESTIONS

1. His mother also noticed that his hands were almost always clenched and twined behind his back, and his jaws locked tight or went completely slack. He was unable, at the age of six months, to sit up unsupported.
2. The doctor called him an interesting but hopeless case.
3. His mother set out to prove that her child was not an idiot. She was successful because she was motivated by love instead of duty.

Quotables

"Happy he
With such a mother! . . . trust in all things high

Comes easy to him, and tho' he trip and fall

He shall not blind his soul with clay."

—Alfred, Lord Tennyson

ADDITIONAL QUESTIONS AND ACTIVITIES

Brown's mother had a profound effect on the way his life turned out. He recognizes this in his autobiography. Students can make a Mother's Day card from Brown to his mother. The card should be personal and express Brown's recognition of how much his mother did for him. Alternately, students might choose to make a special card for their mothers or for someone else who has helped them immensely.

ADDITIONAL QUESTIONS AND ACTIVITIES

Have students view the film *My Left Foot* starring Daniel Day-Lewis and write a film review. In their film reviews, students should ask themselves:

• Does the film version remain true to the autobiography?
• Which are the best performances in the film? Which are the worst?
• What aspects of the autobiography are emphasized in the film?

---

sible for her to open them, or they would suddenly become limp and fall loose, dragging my whole mouth to one side.[2] At six months I could not sit up without having a mountain of pillows around me. At twelve months it was the same.

What other defects did Christy's mother notice?

Very worried by this, Mother told my father her fears, and they decided to seek medical advice without any further delay. I was a little over a year old when they began to take me to hospitals and clinics, convinced that there was something definitely wrong with me, something which they could not understand or name, but which was very real and disturbing.

Almost every doctor who saw and examined me labeled me a very interesting but also a hopeless case. Many told Mother very gently that I was mentally defective and would remain so. That was

What did the doctors say about Christy?

a hard blow to a young mother who had already reared five healthy children. The doctors were so very sure of themselves that Mother's faith in me seemed almost an <u>impertinence</u>. They assured her that nothing could be done for me. She refused to accept this truth, the inevitable truth—as it then seemed—that I was beyond cure, beyond saving, even beyond hope. She could not and would not believe that I was an imbecile, as the doctors told her. She had nothing in the world to go by, not a scrap of evidence to support her <u>conviction</u> that, though my body was crippled, my mind was not. In spite of all the doctors and specialists told her, she would not agree. I don't believe she knew why—she just knew, without feeling the smallest shade of doubt.

Finding that the doctors could not help in any way beyond telling her not to place her trust in

me, or, in other words, to forget I was a human creature, rather to regard me as just something to be fed and washed and then put away again, Mother decided there and then to take matters into her own hands. I was *her* child, and therefore part of the family. No matter how dull and incapable I might grow up to be, she was determined to treat me on the same plane as the others, and not as the "queer one" in the back room who was never spoken of when there were visitors present.

That was a <u>momentous</u> decision as far as my future life was concerned. It meant that I would always have my mother on my side to help me fight all the battles that were to come, and to inspire me with new strength when I was almost beaten. But it wasn't easy for her because now the relatives and friends had decided otherwise. They contended that I should be taken kindly, sympathetically, but not seriously. That would be a mistake. "For your own sake," they told her, "don't look to this boy as you would to the others; it would only break your heart in the end." Luckily for me, Mother and Father held out against the lot of them. But Mother wasn't content just to say that I was not an idiot: she set out to prove it, not because of any rigid sense of duty, but out of love. That is why she was so successful.

What did his mother set out to prove? Why was she successful?

At this time she had the five other children to look after besides the "difficult one," though as yet it was not by any means a full house. They were my brothers, Jim, Tony, and Paddy, and my two sisters, Lily and Mona, all of them very young, just a year or

---

2. **my jaws . . . whole mouth to one side.** These behaviors are typical of someone with severe cerebral palsy, a condition caused by lack of oxygen to the brain, which often occurs in a difficult childbirth.

words for everyday use
im • per • ti • nence (im pur'tʼn əns) *n.,* inappropriate, insolent action. *After his rude remarks, Leo was sent out of the room for his <u>impertinence</u>.*
con • vic • tion (kən vik'shən) *n.,* strong belief. *Edna said she thought we should go, but her spiritless voice lacked <u>conviction</u>.*
mo • men • tous (mō men'təs) *adj.,* very important. *The <u>momentous</u> decision was made only after long, sleepless hours of pacing and debating.*

so between each of them, so that they were almost exactly like steps of stairs.

Four years rolled by, and I was now five, and still as helpless as a newly born baby. While my father was out at bricklaying,[3] earning our bread and butter for us, Mother was slowly, patiently pulling down the wall, brick by brick, that seemed to thrust itself between me and the other children, slowly, patiently penetrating beyond the thick curtain that hung over my mind, separating it from theirs. It was hard, heart-breaking work, for often all she got from me in return was a vague smile and perhaps a faint gurgle. I could not speak or even mumble, nor could I sit up without support on my own, let alone take steps. But I wasn't <u>inert</u> or motionless. I seemed, indeed, to be convulsed with movement, wild, stiff, snakelike movement that never left me, except in sleep. My fingers twisted and twitched continually, my arms twined backwards and would often shoot out suddenly this way and that, and my head lolled and sagged sideways. I was a queer, crooked little fellow.

Mother tells me how one day she had been sitting with me for hours in an upstairs room, showing me pictures out of a great big story-book that I had got from Santa Claus last Christmas and telling me the names of different animals and flowers that were in them, trying without success to get me to repeat them. This had gone on for hours while she talked and laughed with me. Then at the end of it she leaned over me and said gently into my ear:

"Did you like it, Chris? Did you like the bears and the monkeys and all the lovely flowers?

> ## "It is his body that is shattered, not his mind."

Nod your head for yes, like a good boy."

But I could make no sign that I had understood her. Her face was bent over mine hopefully. Suddenly, <u>involuntarily</u>, my queer hand reached up and grasped one of the dark curls that fell in a thick cluster about her neck. Gently she loosened the clenched fingers, though some dark strands were still clutched between them.

Then she turned away from my curious stare and left the room, crying. The door closed behind her. It all seemed hopeless. It looked as though there was some justification for my relatives' <u>contention</u> that I was an idiot and beyond help.

They now spoke of an institution.

"Never!" said my mother almost fiercely, when this was suggested to her. "I know my boy is not an idiot. It is his body that is shattered, not his mind. I'm sure of that."

Sure? Yet inwardly, she prayed God would give her some proof of her faith. She knew it was one thing to believe but quite another thing to prove.

I was now five, and still I showed no real sign of intelligence. I showed no apparent interest in things except with my toes—more especially those of my left foot. Although my natural habits were clean, I could not aid myself, but in this respect my father took care of me. I used to lie on my back all the time in the kitchen or, on bright warm days, out in the garden, a little bundle of crooked muscles and twisted nerves,

> What was his mother's reply to suggestions that Christy be sent to an institution?

---

3. **bricklaying.** Building with layers of bricks and mortar

---

words for everyday use

in • ert (in ʉrt´) *adj.,* inactive. *The <u>inert</u> child came to life when I suggested that we might go to the beach.*
in • vol • un • tar • i • ly (in väl´ən ter´ə lē) *adv.,* unintentionally, uncontrollably. *When Jim hiccuped <u>involuntarily</u> throughout Clara's speech, she glared at him as though he did it on purpose.*
con • ten • tion (kən ten´shən) *n.,* argument. *Ira's <u>contention</u> that dogs are friendlier than cats angered Kim, who was a cat lover.*

ANSWER TO GUIDED READING QUESTION

1. His mother emphatically said, "Never!" and added that she knew her son was not an idiot. She said that his body was shattered, not his mind.

CROSS-CURRICULAR ACTIVITIES

PSYCHOLOGY. Students might comment upon Christy Brown's relationship with his mother. His mother shows a firm belief in her son's abilities despite the lack of any outward signs of intellect and the advice of doctors and relatives. In the twentieth century, the special relationship between a mother and her child has come into examination. One explanation of this relationship that has gained popular acceptance is attachment theory. This theory proposes that a "bonding" of mother and infant occurs soon after a child's birth, and this "bonding" is instrumental in the child's development. Students might research the psychological study of the relationships between mothers and their children. Some students might research John Bowlby's work on attachment theory. (Direct students to his *Attachment and Separation.*) Other students might research the imprinting theory of Konrad Lorenz. (Students might be particularly interested in the studies of ducklings that will follow any moving object, such as a balloon, upon hatching and will continue to follow this object even when shown their parents.) Students might also research the work of those who do not accept the attachment theory; while the theory gained popularity in the 1970s, many modern psychologists find fault with it. Students should report their findings to the class. When they have finished their presentations, generate a discussion on relationships between mothers and their children. Why do students think that mothers, like Christy Brown's, are willing to go to extreme lengths to support, protect, and help their children? Do they think that this was always the case, even in different time periods and cultures, or is it a twentieth-century phenomenon? Why might our society be fascinated with the love shared between a mother and her child?

ANSWER TO GUIDED READING QUESTION

1. Brown reached out and took the stick of chalk from his sister's hand with his left foot.

SELECTION CHECK TEST 4.8.7 WITH ANSWERS

Checking Your Reading

1. What was the first problem Brown's mother noticed when he was four months old? **She noticed that he was unable to hold his head up.**
2. What did the doctors say about Brown's case? **They said it was interesting but hopeless.**
3. What was Brown's mother determined to prove? **She was determined to prove that Brown was not an idiot.**
4. What surprising action did Brown perform with his left foot? **He took a piece of chalk out of his sister's hand.**
5. What does Brown call his road to a new world? **He calls the letter *A* that he scrawled with difficulty on the floor his road to a new world.**

Vocabulary in Context
Fill in each blank below with the most appropriate word from the following Words for Everyday Use.

conviction   momentous   inert
involuntarily   taut   volition

1. Grandpa pulled the sheets so **taut** you could bounce a quarter on them.
2. Flora could not be swayed from her **conviction**.
3. George was pretending to be asleep, but he **involuntarily** open his eyes with a start when I dropped the book.
4. Lacey called a family meeting to announce her **momentous** decision.
5. They didn't drag me away; I left of my own **volition**.

Literary Tools

1. What is an autobiography? **An autobiography is the story of a person's life, told by that person.**
2. What information can you get in an autobiography that you do not get in a biography? **You get a clearer sense of how the subject felt and what he or she thought during different situations.**
3. What are sensory details? **Sensory details are words that describe how things look, sound, smell, taste, and feel.**
4. Give two examples of sensory details from this selection. *Responses will vary.*

surrounded by a family that loved me and hoped for me and that made me part of their own warmth and humanity. I was lonely, imprisoned in a world of my own, unable to communicate with others, cut off, separated from them as though a glass wall stood between my existence and theirs, thrusting me beyond the sphere of their lives and activities. I longed to run about and play with the rest, but I was unable to break loose from my <u>bondage</u>.

Then, suddenly, it happened! In a moment everything was changed, my future life molded into a definite shape, my mother's faith in me rewarded and her secret fear changed into open triumph.

It happened so quickly, so simply after all the years of waiting and uncertainty, that I can see and feel the whole scene as if it had happened last week. It was the afternoon of a cold, gray December day. The streets outside glistened with snow, the white sparkling flakes stuck and melted on the windowpanes and hung on the boughs of the trees like molten silver. The wind howled dismally, whipping up little whirling columns of snow that rose and fell at every fresh gust. And over all, the dull, murky sky stretched like a dark canopy, a vast infinity of grayness.

Inside, all the family were gathered round the big kitchen fire that lit up the little room with a warm glow and made giant shadows dance on the walls and ceiling.

In a corner Mona and Paddy were sitting, huddled together, a few torn school primers[4] before them. They were writing down little sums onto an old chipped slate, using a bright piece of yellow chalk. I was close to them, propped up by a few pillows against the wall, watching.

It was the chalk that attracted me so much. It was a long, slender stick of vivid yellow. I had never seen anything like it before, and it showed up so well against the black surface of the slate that I was fascinated by it as much as if it had been a stick of gold.

Suddenly, I wanted desperately to do what my sister was doing. Then—without thinking or knowing exactly what I was doing, I reached out and took the stick of chalk out of my sister's hand—with my left foot.

I do not know why I used my left foot to do this. It is a puzzle to many people as well as to myself, for, although I had displayed a curious interest in my toes at an early age, I had never attempted before this to use either of my feet in any way. They could have been as useless to me as were my hands. That day, however, my left foot, apparently by its own <u>volition</u>, reached out and very impolitely took the chalk out of my sister's hand.

I held it tightly between my toes, and, acting on an impulse, made a wild sort of scribble with it on the slate. Next moment I stopped, a bit dazed, surprised, looking down at the stick of yellow chalk stuck between my toes, not knowing what to do with it next, hardly knowing how it got there. Then I looked up and became aware that everyone had stopped talking and was staring at me silently. Nobody stirred. Mona, her black curls framing her chubby little face, stared at me with great big eyes and open mouth. Across the open hearth,[5] his face lit by flames, sat my father, leaning forward, hands outspread on his knees, his shoulders tense. I felt the sweat break out on my forehead.

My mother came in from the pantry with a steaming pot in her hand. She stopped midway between the table and the fire, feeling the ten-

> *What surprising action did Christy make?*

---

4. **primers.** First books used to teach young children
5. **hearth.** Fireplace

words for everyday use	
bond • age (bän´dij) *n.*, constraint. *"Free at last!" shouted Marvin when he was released from <u>bondage</u>.*
vo • li • tion (vō lish´ən) *n.*, free will. *Though claiming to have been forced to join the club, Jerry really joined of his own <u>volition</u>.*

sion flowing through the room. She followed their stare and saw me in the corner. Her eyes looked from my face down to my foot, with the chalk gripped between my toes. She put down the pot.

Then she crossed over to me and knelt down beside me, as she had done so many times before.

"I'll show you what to do with it, Chris," she said, very slowly and in a queer, choked way, her face flushed as if with some inner excitement.

Taking another piece of chalk from Mona, she hesitated, then very deliberately drew, on the floor in front of me, *the single letter "A."*

"Copy that," she said, looking steadily at me. "Copy it, Christy."

What did Christy's mother tell him to do?

I couldn't.

I looked about me, looked around at the faces that were turned toward me, tense, excited faces that were at that moment frozen, <u>immobile</u>, eager, waiting for a miracle in their midst.

The stillness was profound. The room was full of flame and shadow that danced before my eyes and lulled my <u>taut</u> nerves into a sort of waking sleep. I could hear the sound of the water tap dripping in the pantry, the loud ticking of the clock on the mantelshelf, and the soft hiss and crackle of the logs on the open hearth.

I tried again. I put out my foot and made a wild jerking stab with the chalk which produced a very crooked line and nothing more. Mother held the slate steady for me.

"Try again, Chris," she whispered in my ear. "Again."

I did. I stiffened my body and put my left foot out again, for the third time. I drew one side of the letter. I drew half the other side. Then the stick of chalk broke and I was left with a stump. I wanted to fling it away and give up. Then I felt my mother's hand on my shoulder. I tried once more. Out went my foot. I shook, I sweated and strained every muscle. My hands were so tightly clenched that my fingernails bit into the flesh. I set my teeth so hard that I nearly pierced my lower lip. Everything in the room swam till the faces around me were mere patches of white. But—I drew it—*the letter "A."* There it was on the floor before me. Shaky, with awkward, wobbly sides and a very uneven center line. But it *was* the letter "A." I looked up. I saw my mother's face for a moment, tears on her cheeks. Then my father stooped and hoisted me on to his shoulder.

I had done it! It had started—the thing that was to give my mind its chance of expressing itself. True, I couldn't speak with my lips. But now I would speak through something more lasting than spoken words—written words.

That one letter, scrawled on the floor with a broken bit of yellow chalk gripped between my toes, was my road to a new world, my key to mental freedom. It was to provide a source of relaxation to the tense, taut thing that was I, which panted for expression behind a twisted mouth. ■

Why was this letter so significant?

ANSWERS TO GUIDED READING QUESTIONS

1. Brown's mother told him to copy the letter *A*.
2. The letter was significant because it was the key to his mental freedom.

RESPOND TO THE SELECTION

How would you describe Brown's mother? Would you consider her a heroic character? Why, or why not?

---

words for everyday use

im • mo • bile (im mō´bəl) *adj.,* not moving. *Louis remained <u>immobile</u> until the guard dog had passed, then he ran for his life.*
taut (tôt) *adj.,* tense. *Katie stretched and massaged her <u>taut</u> muscles until they relaxed.*

Respond *to the* **SELECTION**

What character traits did Christy show when he grabbed the chalk and proceeded to write the letter *A*?

ANSWERS TO INVESTIGATE, INQUIRE, AND IMAGINE

RECALL

1a. Brown says that he was born in Rotunda Hospital on June 5, 1932. His birth was difficult; both mother and child almost died. When he was four months old, his mother noticed he was unable to hold up his head. Doctors told her that his case was hopeless and that he should be institutionalized.

2a. Brown's mother decided to treat him as she would any other child. His other relatives thought he should be treated sympathetically, but not be taken seriously.

3a. Brown tells of a time his mother asked him if he liked a book she had shown him. She asked him to nod if he liked it. He was unable to do so, but involuntarily he reached out and grabbed a lock of her hair.

INTERPRET

1b. The doctors probably suggested this solution because they did not think that Brown would ever be able to communicate or take care of himself in any way.

2b. The decision of Brown's mother kept him from being institutionalized and also kept him from being dismissed as hopeless.

3b. Brown thought perhaps he was an idiot as others had said. It was a very frustrating and dispiriting event for him.

ANALYZE

4a. Brown's mother is indomitable, loving, tireless, and determined.

SYNTHESIZE

4b. Brown loves his mother and credits her selfless, loving, tireless efforts to get him to communicate with changing his life.

EVALUATE

5a. Brown's left foot was the part of his body over which he had control. It was the part of his body that opened the door to communication and a new future for him.

EXTEND

5b. Painstakingly, Christy Brown typed out *My Left Foot* using his left foot. Jean-Dominique Bauby wrote his memoir letter by letter using the ESA alphabet, having to stop his helper at each desired letter to form a word. Both men were so determined to tell their stories that they overcame enormous obstacles.

Investigate, Inquire, and Imagine

Recall: GATHERING FACTS

1a. What details does Christy Brown share about his own birth? What did his mother notice when he was about four months old? What did doctors tell her?

2a. How did Christy's mother decide to handle the situation? How did other relatives react?

3a. What incident does Christy share about his mother's efforts to make him respond? What was his response?

Interpret: FINDING MEANING

1b. Why do you think the doctors suggested this solution?

2b. Why was the decision made by Christy's mother so crucial?

3b. How did Christy feel about the incident that occurred when his mother was trying to get him to respond to the picture book?

Analyze: TAKING THINGS APART

4a. Identify the character traits of Christy's mother.

Synthesize: BRINGING THINGS TOGETHER

4b. How does Christy feel about his mother?

Evaluate: MAKING JUDGMENTS

5a. Of what importance is the title of Christy Brown's autobiography?

Extend: CONNECTING IDEAS

5b. What does the legacy of Christy Brown have in common with that of Jean-Dominique Bauby, the author of "The Alphabet" and Paris" (Unit 5)?

Understanding Literature

AUTOBIOGRAPHY. Review the definition for **autobiography** in the Handbook of Literary Terms. What information do you learn about Christy Brown that wouldn't be available in a biography?

DESCRIPTION. Review the definition for **description** in the Handbook of Literary Terms. Christy Brown gives a very detailed description of the night he first communicated by following his mother's instruction to write the letter *A*. What details does he use? Why is the description of this scene so detailed?

ANSWERS TO UNDERSTANDING LITERATURE

AUTOBIOGRAPHY. The autobiography shows how Brown was thinking when he relates events in his childhood, which a biographer would not have access to.

DESCRIPTION. Brown uses images such as the profound stillness of the room, the dancing flames and shadows, the sound of the water tap, and the ticking of the clock. These details create a vivid picture of the scene. The scene is probably described in such detail because it was such a momentous occasion.

Writer's Journal

1. Christy Brown's mother had a profound effect on the outcome of his life. He recognizes this in his autobiography. Make a special **Mother's Day card** from Christy to his mother that includes a short verse or statement of love and appreciation.

2. Write a **descriptive paragraph** about a momentous occasion in your life. Include sensory details that indicate how things looked, sounded, felt, tasted, and smelled at the time.

3. Imagine you are Christy Brown. Write a **paragraph** describing how you would like to be treated by others.

Integrating the Language Arts

Media Literacy & Speaking and Listening

ADAPTATION/COMPENSATION. Many people compensate for the inability to do something. For example, Christy Brown learned to write and type with his foot because he was unable to do so with his hands. There are many artists who paint with their feet or mouths because they are unable to do so with their hands. The outside world also can be adapted to the varied abilities and needs of others, as in the case of wheelchair basketball. Find other examples of compensation or adaptation by searching on the Internet. You may want to arrange interviews with people you know who have learned to compensate or adapt in some way. Share the results of your Internet search and/or interviews with your class.

Collaborative Learning

RESEARCHING VOLUNTEERISM. Together with a small group of classmates interview a representative of a local organization that serves a group of disabled people and find out what opportunities are available for volunteers. Prepare a handout to pass out to students interested in volunteering.

Study and Research

CEREBRAL PALSY. Research the disorder of cerebral palsy. What causes the disorder? How can it be treated? How common is it in the United States? In other countries? What is the life expectancy of a person with cerebral palsy? Are some individuals who suffer from the disorder still institutionalized? Are there other famous individuals who suffered from cerebral palsy?

ANSWERS TO INTEGRATING THE LANGUAGE ARTS

Media Literacy & Speaking and Listening
Students may also be interested to learn about the Americans with Disabilities Act. Students can learn about what adaptations are required in certain cases and people who have fought to remove barriers to people with disabilities.

Literary TOOLS

SOURCE. A **source** is a work from which an author takes his or her materials. As you read, determine what sources Fölsing uses.

BIOGRAPHY. A **biography** is the story of a person's life, told by someone other than that person. As you read, try to assess Einstein's character traits that were evident even in childhood.

Organizer

Make a chart listing facts about Einstein's life and what they reveal about his character.

Facts about Einstein's Life	What I Learned about Einstein's Character
Liked puzzles and building things	He enjoyed problem solving.

from Albert Einstein: A Biography
by Albrecht Fölsing

Reader's resource

This selection, which sheds light on Einstein's childhood development, is from the first chapter of a biography that Albrecht Fölsing wrote about Albert Einstein. The comprehensive biography, entitled *Albert Einstein: A Biography,* has seven sections, 39 chapters, and 860 pages.

SCIENCE CONNECTION. Albert Einstein (1879–1955), recognized as one of the greatest physicists of all time, grew up in Germany and graduated from the Federal Institute of Technology in Zürich, Switzerland. He earned his doctorate at the University of Zürich. After graduation, he became a professor of physics in Prague, Zürich, and Berlin. In 1921 he received the Nobel Prize in physics for his work on the photoelectric effect. However, he is most famous for his work on the theory of relativity. While Einstein was visiting the United States in 1933, the Nazis confiscated his home and property. For the rest of his life, he did his research at the Institute for Advanced Study at Princeton University, in New Jersey.

About the AUTHOR

Albrecht Fölsing (1940–) studied physics in Berlin, Philadelphia, and Hamburg. He became a science journalist and the head of the department of Science and Nature of a German public television show. In the foreword to the biography, Fölsing writes: "The most important aspect to me, always, was Einstein's physics. Physics was at the core of his identity, and only through physics can we get close to him as a seeker after truth, whose like we shall not see again." Fölsing has also written biographies about Galileo (1983), Wilhelm Conrad Röntgen (1995), and Heinrich Hertz (1997).

Reader's Journal

What story do you like that people tell about your childhood?

GOALS/OBJECTIVES

Studying this lesson will enable students to
- appreciate the development and background of an important historic figure
- make connections between Einstein's personal life and his contributions to the world
- understand that biography provides context for otherwise isolated events
- demonstrate the ability to combine and expand sentences
- write a credo

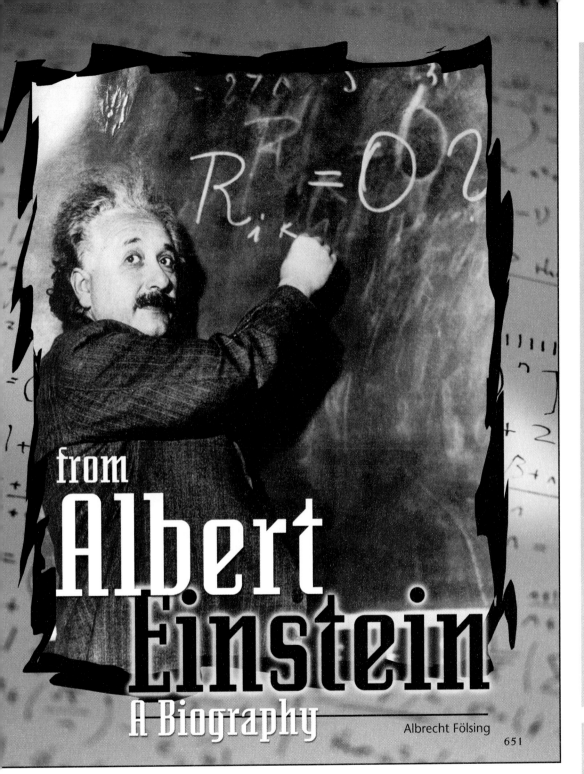

from
Albert Einstein
A Biography

Albrecht Fölsing

651

MOTIVATION
Encourage students to read a biography of another great scientist. If students are not particularly interested in science, they might choose a great mind in a field that does interest them. Students may read a full-length biography or they may find a shorter biographical article or biographical sketch. Students should give a summary of what they learned, including one interesting fact they did not know and anything they learned from the person's own words.

READING PROFICIENCY
You might begin by encouraging students to make a list of things they already know about Einstein. Students might make some guesses about what they think his childhood might have been like. They can check their predictions as they read.

ENGLISH LANGUAGE LEARNING
Point out the following vocabulary words:
formulation—way of forming something or putting it together
laborious—done with much effort
precede—go before
inhibit—slow or stop

SPECIAL NEEDS
Point out to students that although this is the story of Einstein's early life, it is not written in strict chronological order. Students should focus on the Guided Reading questions and the Recall questions in the Investigate, Inquire, and Imagine section.

ENRICHMENT
Encourage students to read more of Einstein's biography, speeches, and other writings. Students can then discuss why Einstein was so influential. As an alternate activity, students can present their ideas in a written report.

VOCABULARY FROM THE SELECTION

averse	perseverance
commend	plausible
conceptual	ramified
conspicuously	rigor
diminutive	roguish
facetiously	sarcasm
obstinacy	speculation
perpetuate	

1. Einstein's parents were concerned because Albert was born with such a big head.

2. Einstein credits his thinking powers to his own "curiosity, obsession and perseverance" and denies that it was inherited from any of his ancestors.

ADDITIONAL QUESTIONS AND ACTIVITIES

Students can try to trace their traits to various ancestors. Students might note physical traits, such as eye color, and personality or psychological traits, such as their sense of humor or musical ability. They can also list the ways their extended families have affected them in nongenetic ways. For example, a student might list an aunt who took him or her to a museum and helped develop an appreciation for art, or a cousin who explored pond life with him or her as a child.

He was born on March 14, 1879, in Ulm in southern Germany, on a cold but sunny Friday, half an hour before the church bells rang out midday. His parents and relatives, anxious to <u>perpetuate</u> the family name, were no doubt pleased that the first child was a boy. But as often happens with young couples who are facing parenthood for the first time, their joy was clouded by concern and even anxiety.

"When he was born"—his younger sister wrote many years later—"Mother was alarmed at the sight of his exceptionally large angular occiput[1] and at first thought he was a monster." The physician reassured the twenty-one-year-old mother, Pauline Einstein, that this peculiarity would soon disappear, and a few weeks later the size of the baby's skull was indeed quite normal, though a rather square occiput remained a lifelong characteristic.

Why were Albert Einstein's parents concerned when he was born?

The following morning the father, Hermann Einstein, put on his frock coat and went to the town hall to record the birth of his son. The boy was to be called Albert, only faintly echoing his grandfather's name, Abraham Einstein. Nothing, of course, suggested that the motto of Ulm, dating from its medieval prosperity, *Ulmenses sunt mathematici*—"The people of Ulm are mathematicians"—would be brilliantly confirmed by this Albert Einstein. In the column provided for religion, both parents and child were recorded as "Israelitic."[2]

• • •

In Einstein's case, perhaps more than with anybody else, one is tempted to engage in the popular game of asking what he might have inherited from whom. One obvious answer would be that with his mathematical gifts he took after his father and with his love of music he took after his mother. There have, of course, been attempts to find the first indications of Albert Einstein's exceptional talents somewhere in his family tree. But he himself refused to go along with such <u>speculations</u>:

√ It was curiosity, obsession, and sheer perseverance that brought me to my ideas.

First of all, I know virtually nothing about them, nor are there any people alive who could say a lot about them. If talents existed, then they could not emerge under their restricted living conditions. Besides, I know perfectly well that I myself have no special talents. It was curiosity, obsession, and sheer <u>perseverance</u> that brought me to my ideas. But as for any especially powerful thinking power ("cerebral muscles")—nothing like that is present, or only on a modest scale. Exploration of my ancestors therefore leads nowhere.

To what does Einstein credit his thinking powers, and what does he deny?

More significant, without any doubt, is the fact that both on his father's and on his mother's side, Albert Einstein was born into a large, widely <u>ramified</u> family, whose members were soon settled in many cities and several countries of Europe. We will meet some of these relatives later. They include an aunt in

---

1. **occiput.** Back part of the head
2. **Israelitic.** Jewish

words for everyday use

per • pet • u • ate (pər pe′ chə wāt) *vt.,* cause to last indefinitely; preserve. *Some say the Internet helps to perpetuate urban myths.*
spec • u • la • tion (spe kyə lā′ shən) *n.,* act or instance of guessing or surmising. *Marcia's theory about her friend's whereabouts was mere speculation.*
per • se • ver • ance (pər sə vir′ ən(t)s) *n.,* act of continuing, of pursuing to an end. *Julio's perseverance paid off when he won the race.*
ram • i • fied (ra′ mə fīd) *adj.,* branched; spread out; split up. *The ramified team reunited at soccer practice.*

Italy, who financed his studies; and his favorite uncle, Caesar Koch, a brother of his mother, whom the grain business had taken as far afield as St. Petersburg and Argentina, and who settled in Antwerp—where Albert, at age sixteen, sent him his first scientific essay.

These family connections were not only stimulating for young Einstein; they also helped him cope with many difficult phases in his life. And if in a city like Zurich there may have been no uncle, there would at least be a close friend of the family who looked after the young man. Much later, it was Professor Einstein, by then in America, who would try to help many of his relatives during the Nazis' persecution of the Jews.

After their marriage in 1876, Hermann Einstein and his young wife at first lived on Münsterplatz, the cathedral square, in the old part of Ulm. After two years, at the beginning of Pauline's first pregnancy, they moved into a bigger apartment. Early in 1879, with Pauline six months pregnant, they moved to the livelier Bahnhofstrasse 135B, to a comfortable apartment in a three-story building. We have already seen—thanks to his sister's notes—that Albert's birth was not without some alarm. From the same source, we learn that Grandmother Helene, on first seeing her grandson, exclaimed, "Much too fat! Much too fat!" Little Albert seems to have been a quiet baby, causing no trouble to those charged with looking after him.

Albert Einstein did not develop any particular feeling for his birthplace, because a year later the family moved to Munich. When, on his fiftieth birthday, the owner of the building presented him with a photograph, he responded, not without some <u>sarcasm</u>: "For a place to be born in, the house is pleasant enough, because on that occasion one makes no

great aesthetic demands yet; instead one first of all screams at one's dear ones, without bothering too much about reasons and circumstances."

Still, even though Einstein spent only the first year of his life in Ulm—growing up in Bavaria, and later in Italy and Switzerland—something Swabian[3] clung to him all his life. For one thing, there was the soft Swabian dialect, which the family never dropped after leaving Württemberg and which Einstein, if less markedly, kept to his old age. He himself became an object of its peculiar tendency toward <u>diminutives</u>: even as a grown man, he always remained, to his family and his second wife (his cousin Elsa), "der Albertl"—"Little Albert." Even during his final years in America, his English, which for him always remained a foreign language, seemed to have Swabian undertones.

In other respects, too, the Swabians would always have recognized him as one of their own: in his speculative brooding, in his often <u>roguish</u> and occasionally coarse humor, and in his pronounced, individualistic <u>obstinacy</u>. It was probably not just flattery when, as Ulm's most famous son, he was asked by the editor of the local paper for a comment, he readily came up with a compliment: "One's place of birth attaches to one's life as something just as unique

---

3. **Swabian.** Native of the German province of Swabia

SOCIAL STUDIES. Students can research how Einstein helped his relatives during the Nazi persecution of the Jews. Interested students can research other people or organizations who helped Jewish people during the Holocaust.

words for everyday use

sar • casm (sär' kə zəm) n., cutting remark in a tone of contempt; ironic or inverted language. *The stand-up comic's <u>sarcasm</u> was leveled against women.*
di • min • u • tive (də mi' nyə tiv) n., shortened name. *Frederick's <u>diminutive</u> is Fred.*
rog • uish (rōg' ish) adj., characteristic of a rogue, or scoundrel. *The <u>roguish</u> behavior of the trick-or-treaters came out when they threw eggs at people's houses.*
ob • sti • na • cy (ab' stə nə sē) n., stubbornness, persistence, or firmness. *Sophie's <u>obstinacy</u> resulted in her often getting her way.*

FROM ALBERT EINSTEIN: A BIOGRAPHY   653

1. His speech was slow to develop.
2. One explanation for his slowness was that he was thinking so carefully about what he was going to say, and wanted complete sentences to come out perfectly.
3. People thought Einstein was slow, even stupid, and maybe even had something wrong with him.

as one's origin from one's mother....I therefore think of Ulm with gratitude, because it combines artistic tradition with a simple and sound character."

This, then, was the environment in which Albert Einstein grew up—at first to the pure joy of his parents and relatives. The earliest characterization of his personality comes from his grandmother Jette Koch, who visited Munich in the summer of 1881 and said of her two-year-old grandson: "Little Albert is so sweet and so good that it pains me already not to be able to see him for such a long time." A week later, she wrote to Munich: "Little Albert is fondly remembered by us; he was so sweet and good, and we have to repeat his amusing ideas again and again." Unfortunately, the fond grandmother did not record any of those amusing ideas.

Little Albert's reaction to the birth of his sister Maria on November 18, 1881, was certainly amusing. No doubt the boy, then two years and eight months old, had been told of the arrival of a *Mädele*, a little girl, as a future playmate, because he promptly inquired where the *Rädele*, the wheels, of his new toy were. This may have been an early hint of his later delight in making up rhymes, or it may have been no more than a little boy's mishearing and being disappointed to find that the screaming bundle was not a plaything. Actually, the second explanation is more probable, since Einstein's speech development was strikingly slow, as he himself would later confirm: "It is true that my parents were worried because I began to speak relatively late, so much so they consulted a doctor. I can't say how old I was then, certainly not less than

What was slow to develop?

three." However, the delay seems to have been due to an early ambition to speak only in complete sentences. If someone asked him a question, he would first form the answer in his head, try it out in an undertone—deliberately, with obvious lip movements—and only after assuring himself that his formulation was

What was the explanation for his slowness?

Einstein grew up without the benefit of a therapist and developed his own distinctive character traits . . .

correct would he repeat the sentence aloud. This often gave the impression that he was saying everything twice, and the maidservant therefore called him "stupid." He gave up this habit only in his seventh year, or perhaps (according to some testimony) not until his ninth. One has the impression not only of particular thoroughness—the explanation his sister later gave for this peculiarity—but also of a boy's laborious and self-critical acquisition of language, in contrast to most children's natural, unproblematical learning.

What impression did people have of Einstein?

Albert's younger sister—nicknamed Maja—recorded in her warmhearted biographical notes that he was fondest of engrossing himself in all kinds of puzzles, making elaborate structures with building blocks and constructing houses of cards of breathtaking height. He was less interested in playing in the garden with young relatives who often came visiting, and he was totally <u>averse</u> to the fights

words for everyday use

averse (ə vərs´) *adj.*, having a dislike or distaste for something, and avoiding it. *Hans's neighbor was <u>averse</u> to gossip of any kind.*

of the boys in the street. These boys soon nicknamed him "the bore." If he could not avoid playing with other children, he deliberately sought the job of umpire, which, because of his instinctive sense of justice, was gladly assigned to him.

When Albert was five years old, a woman was engaged as a tutor to prepare him for the <u>rigors</u> of school life. She, however, found herself unequal to another trait in the boy's makeup—one that the family believed he had inherited from his grandfather Julius Koch.

What trait did Einstein exhibit? Where did his family think he got it?

Whenever something was not to Albert's liking, he was seized by a sudden temper, his face paled, his nose turned white, and the consequences were terrible. On one occasion, when he did not like a lesson, "he grabbed a chair and with it struck the woman tutor, who was so terrified that she ran away in fear and was never seen again." His little sister, too, had to suffer: "On another occasion he threw a large ninepin bowl at [her] head, and yet another time he used a child's pickaxe to strike a hole in [her] head." Fortunately, these tantrums receded during his seventh year and disappeared completely during his first years at school.

One might ask at this point how such a child—with <u>conspicuously</u> delayed speech development, averse to play and social behavior appropriate to his age, and moreover with an occasional total lack of self-control—would fare in the

How would teachers and psychologists today react to such a child?

tests and examinations that now precede enrollment in school. Such a child, in a fit of temper, might attack a teacher or a psychologist with a chair, just as occurred a century ago with young Albert Einstein and his tutor. In the accepted view of child psychologists, a child like this should be diagnosed long before starting school and given some form of therapy or other, when, as with little Albert, there are speech problems suggesting defective development. The psychoanalyst Erik H. Erikson, who has ventured to make this remote diagnosis on the strength of the records, believes that cases of this kind deserve or even demand careful attention. At the same time, he regards Albert Einstein's example as a warning against the present tendency to fit all children into the same mold; this could inhibit rather than promote the development of talent. In the event,

What does Einstein's example warn against?

Einstein grew up without the benefit of a therapist and developed his own distinctive character traits: his determination to apply his own yardstick, his intense brooding, and his profound way of wondering about things.

Einstein's receptiveness to "wonders" and "wondering" was of enormous importance to him throughout his life as a motivation for productive thought, especially in scientific matters. This was a trait which he felt he could not explain to himself, but he <u>commended</u> "wondering," and slowness, in a letter to a colleague, the Nobel Prize laureate James Franck:

> When I ask myself why it should have been me, rather than anyone else, who

---

words for everyday use

rig • or (ri′ gər) *n.,* strictness; demand. *The <u>rigors</u> of training stimulated Alexi.*
con • spic • u • ous • ly (kən spi′ kyə wəs lē) *adv.,* obviously; attracting attention; noticeably. *The assistant coach was <u>conspicuously</u> absent from practice.*
com • mend (kə mend′) *vt.,* praise; recommend as worthy. *The troop leader <u>commended</u> the boy scouts for their volunteer work.*

ANSWERS TO GUIDED READING QUESTIONS

1. He had a bad temper. His family thought he inherited it from his grandfather.
2. Teachers and psychologists today might think he needs therapy, even medication, and that there was something wrong with him.
3. It warns against trying to fit children into the same mold or making assumptions about them by using yardsticks to measure development.

Quotables

"The whole of science is nothing more than a refinement of everyday thinking."

—Albert Einstein

1. Einstein thinks he gained an ability to reflect and to think very deeply.
2. "Wonder" occurs when outer experience clashes with an inner idea.

SELECTION CHECK TEST 4.8.9 WITH ANSWERS

Checking Your Reading
1. Where was Albert Einstein born? **He was born in Ulm in southern Germany.**
2. What habit led the maidservants to call him stupid? **When speaking, he would say his answer to himself once with obvious lip movement. Then, he would say it out loud.**
3. What role did Einstein take when he played with other children? **He usually took the job of umpire.**
4. What did Einstein's father give him when he was sick? **His father gave him a compass.**
5. How old was Einstein when he propounded the Special Theory of Relativity? **He was twenty-six.**

Vocabulary in Context
Fill in each blank below with the most appropriate word from the following Words for Everyday Use. You may have to change the tense of the word.

speculation   perseverance
sarcasm   perpetuate
averse   commend

1. I was sure Alethea would give up, so I was surprised by her **perseverance**.
2. Ramon doesn't like team sports, but he is not **averse** to individual sports, like tennis.
3. Jim **commended** Amy for the extra effort she put in on the project.
4. Some jokes simply **perpetuate** stereotypes.
5. Before the award was announced, there was great **speculation** about who would receive it.

Literary Tools
1. What is a source? **A source is a work from which an author takes his or her materials.**
2. Name one source Fölsing used in writing this biography of Einstein. *Responses will vary.* **Fölsing used government records, notes written by Einstein's sister, and Einstein's own writings.**
3. What is a biography? **A biography is the story of a person's life told by another person.**
4. What element of this biography gives it the feel of an autobiography in some places? **The author quotes Einstein directly.**

discovered the relativity theory, I think that this was due to the following circumstance: An adult does not reflect on space-time problems. Anything that needs reflection on this matter he believes he did in his early childhood. I, on the other hand, developed so slowly that I only began to reflect about space and time when I was grown up. Naturally I then penetrated more deeply into these problems than an ordinary child would.

> *What does Einstein think he gained from his slow development?*

It is clear therefore that Einstein's notion of "wondering" is very different from the common meaning of that term—a noncommittal inability to understand. In his own view:

> It seems to occur whenever an experience comes into conflict with a conceptual world sufficiently fixated within us. If such a conflict is experienced strongly and intensively, then it reacts back in a decisive manner upon our mental world. In a certain sense, the development of that mental world is a continual flight from "wonder."—I experienced a wonder of just that kind as a child of four or five, when my father showed me a compass.

> *When does "wonder" occur?*

Thus in what Einstein facetiously called his "*Nekrolog*," his "Obituary"—published as *Autobiographisches*—he recalls an experience which he frequently related and which is recorded in several (basically agreeing) versions. He was sick in bed, when, no doubt to divert him, his father brought him a compass—not suspecting the lasting impression this instrument would make:

> The fact that the needle behaved in such a definite manner did not fit at all into the pattern of

occurrences which had established itself in my subconscious conceptual world (effects being connected with "contact"). I remember to this day—or think I remember—the deep and lasting impression this experience made on me. There had to be something behind the objects, something that was hidden.

Although the subject matter of Einstein's great accomplishment—the essay *Zur Elektrodynamik bewegter Körper (On the Electrodynamics of Moving Bodies)* of 1905, which contains the special theory of relativity—seems to be foreshadowed here, one should probably not read too much into this experience. A lot of children wonder about a rainbow, and some no doubt will have wondered about a compass needle, which seems to be moved by an invisible hand. A prism diffracting light or an apple dropping from a tree may evoke wonderment and clever questions. Altogether, as Sigmund Freud observed, the intelligence of adults pales against the brilliant intelligence of five-year-olds. Still, among all these children only one became an Isaac Newton and only one an Albert Einstein.

Einstein himself was unable to explain this powerful experience, because "a person has little insight into what goes on inside him. Seeing a compass for the first time may not produce a similar effect on a young dog, nor indeed on many a child. What then is it that determines a particular reaction from an individual? More or less plausible theories may be constructed about it, but one does not arrive at a deeper insight." We will have to content ourselves with the suggestion that a productive result probably depends both on the "wonder" and on the person "wondering." ∎

words for everyday use	**con • cep • tu • al** (kən sep' shə wəl) *adj.*, of or relating to concepts, an abstract idea, or intuitive thought. *Even at a young age, some children have a brilliant knack for <u>conceptual</u> thinking.*
	fa • ce • tious • ly (fə sē' shəs lē) *adv.*, in a joking or jesting manner, often inappropriately. *Mr. Cohen replied <u>facetiously</u> when Abdul asked for a job, and his feelings were hurt.*
	plau • si • ble (plô' zə bəl) *adj.*, believable; credible. *Martina gave her teacher a <u>plausible</u> excuse for being late.*

My Credo

Albert Einstein

Our situation on this earth seems strange. Every one of us appears here involuntarily and uninvited for a short stay, without knowing the whys and the wherefore. In our daily lives we only feel that man is here for the sake of others, for those whom we love and for many other beings whose fate is connected with our own. I am often worried at the thought that my life is based to such a large extent on the work of my fellow human beings and I am aware of my great indebtedness to them. I do not believe in freedom of the will. Schopenhauer's words: "Man can do what he wants, but he cannot will what he wills" accompany me in all situations throughout my life and reconcile me with the actions of others even if they are rather painful to me. This awareness of the lack of freedom of will preserves me from taking too seriously myself and my fellow men as acting and deciding individuals and from losing my temper. I never coveted affluence and luxury and even despise them a good deal. My passion for social justice has often brought me into conflict with people, as did my aversion to any obligation and dependence I do not regard as absolutely necessary. I always have a high regard for the individual and have an insuperable distaste for violence and clubmanship. All these motives made me into a passionate pacifist and anti-militarist. I am against any nationalism, even in the guise of mere patriotism. Privileges based on position and property have always seemed to me unjust and pernicious, as did any exaggerated personality cult. I am an adherent of the ideal of democracy, although I well know the weaknesses of the democratic form of government. Social equality and economic protection of the individual appeared to me always as the important communal aims of the state. Although I am a typical loner in daily life, my consciousness of belonging to the invisible community of those who strive for truth, beauty, and justice has preserved me from feeling isolated. The most beautiful and deepest experience a man can have is the sense of the mysterious. It is the underlying principle of religion as well as all serious endeavour in art and science. He who never had this experience seems to me, if not dead, then at least blind. To sense that behind anything that can be experienced there is a something that our mind cannot grasp and whose beauty and sublimity reaches us only indirectly and as a feeble reflection, this is religiousness. In this sense I am religious. To me it suffices to wonder at these secrets and to attempt humbly to grasp with my mind a mere image of the lofty structure of all that there is. ■

FROM ALBERT EINSTEIN: A BIOGRAPHY **659**

Quotables

"As long as there are sovereign nations possessing great power, war is inevitable."

"I do not believe that civilization will be wiped out in a war fought with the atomic bomb. Perhaps two thirds of the people of the earth might be killed, but enough men capable of thinking, and enough books, would be left to start again, and civilization could be restored."

"The unleashed power of the atom has changed everything save our modes of thinking, and we thus drift toward unparalleled catastrophes."

—Albert Einstein

ADDITIONAL QUESTIONS AND ACTIVITIES

Share the quotes above with students. Ask them if they agree with Einstein's ideas about war and atomic power. They might also discuss how they think Einstein would view the situation in the world today. Would his thoughts still hold up?

RESPOND TO THE SELECTION

In what ways is Einstein similar to and different from Leonardo da Vinci? What makes them both geniuses?

ANSWERS TO INVESTIGATE, INQUIRE, AND IMAGINE

RECALL

1a. He was slow. He began speaking late. He did not like to play with other children much. He had a bad temper.

2a. People today might think his behavior would require a therapist because it does not match the developmental and socialization standards people expect children to follow. There is more focus today on child development, which can be beneficial, but many children are wrongly diagnosed or not allowed to develop their unique skills and talents.

3a. His father showed him a compass.

INTERPRET

1b. One way people try to understand a person is to look at their childhood, what experiences might have shaped them or what traits they showed early on. In Einstein's case, a man who is considered a genius was, in contrast, considered to be slow or stupid as a child.

2b. If he had been forced to develop differently, then his mental growth might have been stunted. Einstein was able to develop in his own way and honor his own nature. He was able to "wonder" at will and examine the world around him. He wasn't forced to learn a certain way.

3b. The experience seems to have stopped Einstein. It was an idea he could not fathom, and so he pondered it deeply.

ANALYZE

4a. In the essay, Einstein's thinking process could be described as wondering, pondering, and reflecting. He talks about his perseverance. If he had a question, he pursued it deeply.

SYNTHESIZE

4b. This thinking process was key to all his scientific research and revelation. His idea of wondering went much deeper than most people's concept of wondering. It is unique in that he claims everyone has the same abilities, yet not everyone uses them.

EVALUATE

5a. There is a lot of emphasis in the essay on inherited traits, either from

Respond to the

SELECTION

What do you think was a formative childhood experience for Einstein?

Investigate, Inquire, and Imagine

Recall: GATHERING FACTS →

1a. What was Einstein like as a very young child?

2a. Why might people today think his behavior would require a therapist?

3a. What did Einstein's father show him when he was sick?

Interpret: FINDING MEANING

1b. Why does the author describe Einstein as a child?

2b. If experts had intervened to "retrain" Einstein when he was a child, what might have happened?

3b. Why did that experience have such a profound effect on Einstein?

Analyze: TAKING THINGS APART →

4a. Analyze Einstein's thinking process and his notion of "wondering."

Synthesize: BRINGING THINGS TOGETHER

4b. How did this way of thinking help him achieve so much in his life? What was his attitude toward his special gifts?

Evaluate: MAKING JUDGMENTS →

5a. What does the author stress when writing about Einstein's early formative years?

Extend: CONNECTING IDEAS

5b. Read the Related Reading "The Roots of Genius?". What scientific evidence exists that Einstein's brain was different from that of the average person?

Understanding Literature

SOURCE. Review the definition for **source** in the Handbook of Literary Terms. Upon what types of sources does Fölsing rely in writing the biography?

BIOGRAPHY. Review the definition for **biography** in Literary Tools in Prereading and the chart you made for that section. What type of a portrait of Einstein does Fölsing draw? When does the biography have the flavor of an autobiography? Do you agree or disagree that the biographical excerpt is a "serious yet highly readable and intimate account of a genius"?

immediate family or from his cultural heritage. The author also stresses that Einstein was considered slow or stupid as a child.

EXTEND

5b. Einstein had 73 percent more glial cells than the norm. His cortex was "more densely populated with neurons." He had a short sylvian fissure and his operculum was underdeveloped. His parietal

lobes, the parts of the brain that are believed to affect math, music, and visual images, were wider than average.

Answers to Understanding Literature can be found on page 661.

Writer's Journal

1. Write an autobiographical **paragraph** about an experience you had as a child that suggests who you would grow up to be.
2. Write Albert Fölsing a **letter** stating what you would like to know about Einstein's childhood that he does not describe in the biography.
3. Imagine you are a therapist who has just interviewed young Albert Einstein. Write a **report** stating how you assess his intelligence, maturity, and adjustment.

Integrating the Language Arts

Language, Grammar, and Style

COMBINING SENTENCES. Read the Language Arts Survey 3.36, "Combining and Expanding Sentences." Then combine each pair of sentences below to create a single sentence.

1. Einstein brooded speculatively and enjoyed coarse humor. He had a pronounced obstinacy.
2. His speech development was strikingly slow. He wanted to talk in complete sentences.
3. Rough boys nicknamed Einstein "the bore." Einstein avoided fighting with these children.
4. He was sick in bed. His father showed him a compass.
5. Einstein proved the veracity of the motto of Ulm. The motto states "The people of Ulm are mathematicians."

Study and Research

RESEARCHING MULTIPLE INTELLIGENCES THEORY. Albert Einstein demonstrates that people have different ways of learning. Recent explorations in brain research and human intelligence have provided a wealth of valuable information that is changing the perspectives of learning and teaching. The Multiple Intelligences Theory proposes a pluralized way of understanding the intellect. This theory states that there are eight basic intelligences: verbal-linguistic or "word smart," logical-mathematical or "logic smart," visual-spatial or "picture smart," body-kinesthetic or "body smart," musical-rhythmic or "music smart," interpersonal or "people smart," intrapersonal or "self-smart," and the naturalist or "nature smart." Research what each of these intelligences suggests about learning. Then write a paragraph describing the intelligence that fits you the best and give an example.

Speaking and Listening & Collaborative Learning

DISCUSSING "MY CREDO." Working with a partner, take turns reading out loud "My Credo" by Albert Einstein on page 659. As you listen, imagine Einstein delivering this speech to the German League of Human Rights, as he did in 1932. Afterwards, discuss the most significant points that Einstein raises. Finally, write your own credo, or statement of personal beliefs.

ANSWERS TO UNDERSTANDING LITERATURE

SOURCE. He refers to public records, such as the town hall's records of Einstein's birth, writings by Einstein himself, letters and biographical notes of family members, and psychological analysis by Erik Erikson.

BIOGRAPHY. Fölsing's portrait of Einstein shows genius and a desire to understand this great mind. The biography has a flavor of autobiography when Fölsing quotes Einstein directly. *Responses will vary.*

ANSWERS TO INTEGRATING THE LANGUAGE ARTS

Language, Grammar, and Style
1. Einstein brooded speculatively, enjoyed coarse humor, and had a pronounced obstinacy.
2. His speech development was strikingly slow because he wanted to talk in complete sentences.
3. Einstein avoided fighting with the rough boys who nicknamed him "the bore."
4. When we was sick in bed, his father showed him a compass.
5. Einstein proved the veracity of the motto of Ulm: "The people of Ulm are mathematicians."

ADDITIONAL RESOURCES

UNIT 8 RESOURCE BOOK
- Selection Worksheet 8.6
- Selection Check Test 4.8.11
- Selection Test 4.8.12
- Reading Resource 1.19
- Language, Grammar, and Style Resource 3.84

GRAPHIC ORGANIZER

Students should list the following examples of repetition in their cluster charts: No one knows, secrets, omnipresence, trained eyes, some officious person.

READER'S JOURNAL

Students should describe the situation that caused them to interact with a bureaucracy. They should also explain their feelings about the situation and how it was handled.

Literary TOOLS

STYLE. Style is the manner in which something is said or written. A writer's style depends upon many things, including his or her *diction*, selection of grammatical structures, and preference for *abstract* or *concrete* words. In this story look for characteristics of Barthelme's style.

SATIRE. Satire is humorous writing or speech intended to point out errors, falsehoods, foibles, or failings. It is written for the purpose of reforming human behavior or human institutions. As you read, notice the elements of the story that are satirical.

REPETITION. Repetition is a writer's conscious reuse of a sound, word, phrase, sentence, or other element. Look for examples of repetition in Barthelme's story.

Graphic Organizer

Make a cluster chart listing significant examples of repetition in the selection.

secrets

Repetition

Reader's Journal

Describe a time when you had to interact with a bureaucracy.

"Engineer-Private Paul Klee Misplaces an Aircraft Between Milbertshofen and Cambrai, March 1916"

by Donald Barthelme

Reader's resource

Barthelme once said that his favorite comedian was "the government." In this humorous story, an engineer-private "loses" an aircraft and decides on a course of action under the watchful eyes of the Secret Police.

ART CONNECTION. In "**Engineer-Private Paul Klee Misplaces an Aircraft Between Milbertshofen and Cambrai, March 1916**," the main character is the historical figure, Paul Klee (1879–1940), a Swiss expressionist painter, who actually did serve in the German Air Corps during World War I in an aircraft transport unit. Klee, like Barthelme, rejected tradition and experimented with abstract forms in his work.

About the AUTHOR

Donald Barthelme (1931–1989) is widely regarded as one of the most innovative and prolific fiction writers of the twentieth century. He wrote in what has come to be known as the Post–Modernist style—a style in which traditional forms and structures were rejected in favor of experimental ones. Barthelme used experimental structures and forms, along with humor and satire, to draw our attention to the absurdity of modern life. One of his stories, "Sentence," is in fact one very long sentence about the nature of sentences. Some of his other stories take the form of charts, lists, or groups of photographs with captions. Consequently, his work often seems fragmented and collage-like. Barthelme's quirky, humorous fiction was frequently published in the *New Yorker* magazine and came to be closely identified with that publication. His collections of short stories include *Come Back, Dr. Caligari* (1964), *Sadness* (1972), *Sixty Stories* (1981), and *Overnight to Many Distant Cities* (1983). He also wrote four novels.

GOALS/OBJECTIVES

Studying this lesson will enable students to
- enjoy a satirical short story
- recognize the literary accomplishments of Donald Barthelme
- define *style, satire,* and *repetition,* and recognize examples in their reading

- distinguish between simple, compound, and complex sentences
- build vocabulary using the prefix *omni*

Landschaftswagen No. 14, 1930. Paul Klee. Busch-Reisinger Museum, Harvard University, Cambridge, Massachusetts.

Engineer–Private
PAUL KLEE
Misplaces an Aircraft Between Milbertshofen and Cambrai, March 1916

Donald Barthelme

Paul Klee said:

"Now I have been transferred to the Air Corps. A kindly sergeant effected the transfer. He thought I would have a better future here, more chances for promotion. First I was assigned to aircraft repair, together with several other workers. We presented ourselves as not just painters but artist-painters. This caused some shaking of heads. We varnished wooden fuselages,[1] correcting old numbers and adding new ones with the help of templates. Then I was pulled off the painting detail and assigned to transport. I escort aircraft that are being sent to various bases in Germany and also

---

1. **fuselage.** Central body of an airplane, which holds the passengers, crew, and cargo

(I understand) in occupied territory. It is not a bad life. I spend my nights racketing across Bavaria[2] (or some such) and my days in switching yards. There is always bread and wurst[3] and beer in the station restaurants. When I reach a notable town I try to see the notable paintings there, if time allows. There are always unexpected delays, reroutings, backtrackings. Then the return to the base. I see Lily fairly often. We meet in hotel rooms and that is exciting. I have never yet lost an aircraft or failed to deliver one to its proper destination. The war seems <u>interminable</u>. Walden has sold six of my drawings."

What is Engineer-Private Paul Klee's job?

The Secret Police said:

"We have secrets. We have many secrets. We desire all secrets. We do not have your secrets and that is what we are after, your secrets. Our first secret is where we are. No one knows. Our second secret is how many of us there are. No one knows. <u>Omnipresence</u> is our goal.

What do the secret police have? What is their goal? What are their secrets?

art note

Landschaftswagen No. 14, 1930. Paul Klee, page 663.

In 1911, shortly before World War I, **Paul Klee** (1879–1940) joined The Blue Rider group (Der Blaue Reiter) which sought a new spiritual art through elemental forms and colors. They were in opposition to an intellectually rigid and increasingly mechanized world. Klee's work stood out from his colleagues' as being neither completely abstract nor expressionistic. Although he always stressed the importance of observation of nature, for Klee, the real world was just a springboard for his imagination, for example, this "landscape on wheels." What about Klee's work may have inspired Barthelme?

We do not even need real omnipresence. The theory of omnipresence is enough. With omnipresence, hand-in-hand as it were, goes <u>omniscience</u>. And with omniscience and omnipresence, hand-in-hand-in-hand as it were, goes <u>omnipotence</u>. We are a three-sided waltz. However our mood is melancholy. There is a secret sigh that we sigh, secretly. We yearn to be known, acknowledged, admired even. What is the good of omnipotence if nobody knows? However that is a secret, that sorrow. Now we are everywhere. One place we are is here watching Engineer-Private Klee, who is escorting three valuable aircraft, B.F.W. 3054/16-17-18, with spare parts, by rail from Milbertshofen[4] to Cambrai.[5] Do you wish to know what Engineer-Private Klee is doing at this very moment, in the baggage car? He is reading a book of Chinese short stories. He has removed his boots. His feet rest twenty-six centimeters from the baggage-car stove."

What do the Secret Police want? Why are they melancholy?

Paul Klee said:

"These Chinese short stories are slight and lovely. I have no way of knowing if the translation is adequate or otherwise. Lily will meet me in our rented room on Sunday, if I return in time. Our destination is Fighter Squadron Five. I have not had anything to eat since morning. The fine chunk of bacon given me along with my expense money when we left the base has been eaten. This morning a Red Cross lady with a squint gave me some very good coffee, however. Now we are entering Hohenbudberg."[6]

---

2. **Bavaria.** (bə ver′ ē ə) State in southwest Germany, the capital of which is Munich
3. **wurst.** Sausage (German)
4. **Milbertshofen.** (mil berts hof′ ən) Town in Bavaria
5. **Cambrai.** Town in northern France
6. **Hohenbudberg.** (hō ən bud′ berg) Small town in northwestern Germany

words for everyday use	
	in • ter • mi • na • ble (in tər′ mə nə bəl) *adj.,* having or seeming to have no end. *The sermon seemed <u>interminable</u> to the small child.*
	om • ni • pres • ence (äm ni pre′ zənts) *n.,* the quality or state of being everywhere at once. *The <u>omnipresence</u> of businessmen at the hotel told Mrs. Baker that there was a convention in town.*
	om • ni • science (äm ni′ shənts) *n.,* having universal or complete knowledge. *The <u>omniscience</u> of the contestant resulted in his winning a million dollars.*
	om • nip • o • tence (äm ni′ pə tənts) *n.,* quality or state of having unlimited power or influence. *No one questioned the <u>omnipotence</u> of the boxer when he got inside the ring.*

The Secret Police said:

"Engineer-Private Klee has taken himself into the station restaurant. He is enjoying a hearty lunch. We shall join him there."

Paul Klee said:

"Now I emerge from the station restaurant and walk along the line of cars to the flatcar on which my aircraft (I think of them as *my* aircraft) are carried. To my surprise and dismay, I notice that one of them is missing. There had been three, tied down on the flatcar and covered with canvas. Now I see with my trained painter's eye that instead of three canvas-covered shapes on the flatcar there are only two. Where the third aircraft had been there is only a puddle of canvas and loose rope. I look around quickly to see if anyone else has marked the disappearance of the third aircraft."

What does Paul Klee notice?

The Secret Police said:

"We had marked it. Our trained policemen's eyes had marked the fact that where three aircraft had been before, tied down on the flatcar and covered with canvas, now there were only two. Unfortunately we had been in the station restaurant, lunching, at the moment of removal, therefore we could not attest as to where it had gone or who had removed it. There is something we do not know. This is irritating in the extreme. We closely observe Engineer-Private Klee to determine what action he will take in the emergency. We observe that he is withdrawing from his tunic a notebook and pencil. We observe that he begins, very properly in our opinion, to note down in his notebook all the particulars of the affair."

What is "irritating in the extreme" to the Secret Police?

Paul Klee said:

"The shape of the collapsed canvas, under which the aircraft had rested, together with the loose ropes—the canvas forming hills and valleys, seductive folds, the ropes the very essence of looseness, lapsing—it is irresistible. I sketch for ten or fifteen minutes, wondering the while if I might not be in trouble, because of the missing aircraft. When I arrive at Fighter Squadron Five with less than the number of aircraft listed on the manifest,[7] might not some <u>officious</u> person become angry? Shout at me? I have finished sketching. Now I will ask various trainmen and station personnel if they have seen anyone carrying away the aircraft. If they answer in the negative, I will become extremely frustrated. I will begin to kick the flatcar."

What do the Secret Police believe Paul Klee is doing? What is he actually doing?

The Secret Police said:

"Frustrated, he begins to kick the flatcar."

Paul Klee said:

"I am looking up in the sky, to see if my aircraft is there. There are in the sky aircraft of several types, but none of the type I am searching for."

Where does Paul Klee search for the missing aircraft?

The Secret Police said:

"Engineer-Private Klee is searching the sky—an eminently sound procedure, in our opinion. We, the Secret Police, also sweep the Hohenbudberg sky, with our eyes. But find nothing. We are debating with ourselves as to whether we ought to enter the station restaurant and begin drafting our <u>preliminary</u> report for forwarding to higher headquarters. The knotty point, in terms of the preliminary report, is that we do not have the answer to the question

---

7. **manifest.** List of cargo or passengers

words
for
everyday
use

of • fi • cious (ə fi′ shəs) *adj.,* volunteering one's services where they are neither asked nor needed. *Officious people are considered meddlesome.*

pre • lim • i • nary (pri li′ mə ner ē) *adj.,* something that precedes or is introductory or preparatory. *Preliminary information suggested that a disgruntled employee was responsible for the shooting at the Veritech Corporation.*

"ENGINEER-PRIVATE PAUL KLEE MISPLACES AN AIRCRAFT BETWEEN MILBERTSHOFEN AND CAMBRAI, MARCH 1916" **665**

SELECTION CHECK TEST 4.8.11 WITH ANSWERS (CONT.)

Literary Tools
1. What is style? **Style is the manner in which something is said or written.**
2. Define *satire*. **Satire is humorous writing or speech intended to point out errors, falsehoods, or failings.**
3. What does this story satirize? **It satirizes bureaucracy.**
4. Give an example of repetition in this story. **No one knows, secrets, omnipresence, trained eyes, some officious person.**
5. What effect does the repetition have? **It helps create the satire of bureaucracy.**

ANSWERS TO GUIDED READING QUESTIONS

1. Paul Klee notices that one of the three aircraft he is transporting is missing from the truck.
2. The Secret Police are irritated because there is something they do not know—in this case, where the aircraft is.
3. The Secret Police believe that Paul Klee is writing down the details of the situation in his notebook. He is actually sketching the collapsed canvas that had covered the aircraft.
4. Paul Klee searches the air for the missing aircraft.

SELECTION CHECK TEST 4.8.11 WITH ANSWERS

Checking Your Reading
1. What was Paul Klee assigned to do when he was taken off paint detail? **He was assigned to transport.**
2. What are the sides to the three-sided waltz of the Secret Police? **The three sides are omnipresence, omnipotence, and omniscience.**
3. Where were Paul Klee and the Secret Police when the aircraft disappeared? **They were in the station restaurant.**
4. What is Paul Klee really doing when the Secret Police think he is noting the particulars of the affair? **He is sketching the canvas and ropes.**
5. What does Paul Klee do to cover up the missing aircraft? **He changes the number on the manifest and hides the canvas and ropes.**

Vocabulary in Context
Fill in each blank below with the most appropriate word from the following Words for Everyday Use.

interminable omnipotence
omniscience officious
preliminary ludicrous

1. I can't believe anyone accepted Horace's **ludicrous** explanation.
2. Because of several storms, our flight was subject to <u>**interminable**</u> delays.
3. Some people are real helpers, others are simply <u>**officious**</u>.
4. New findings are forcing us to reconsider our <u>**preliminary**</u> conclusions.
5. The king was surprised when a band of ruffians challenged his <u>**omnipotence**</u>.

1. The Secret Police consider omitting
   the fact that they do not know
   where the aircraft is. Somebody at
   the Central Bureau for Secrecy
   might notice the omission.
2. Paul Klee decides to apply reason.
   He decides to change the manifest
   to reflect conveyance of *two*
   aircrafts.
3. Paul Klee hides the extra canvas
   cover in an empty boxcar and walks
   through town to find a chocolate
   shop.
4. The Secret Police heartily support
   his solution and would like to
   "embrace him as a comrade and
   brother."
5. Paul Klee says, "The war is
   temporary. But drawings and
   chocolate go on forever."

'Where is the aircraft?' The damage potential to the theory of omniscience as well as potential to our careers, dictates that this point be omitted from the preliminary report. But if this point is omitted, might not some officious person at the Central Bureau for Secrecy note the omission? Become angry? Shout at us? Omissiveness is not rewarded at the Central Bureau. We decide to observe further the actions of Engineer-Private Klee, for the time being. "

> *What do the Secret Police consider omitting from their report? Why?*

Paul Klee said:

"I who have never lost an aircraft have lost an aircraft. The aircraft is signed out to me. The cost of the aircraft, if it is not found, will be deducted from my pay, meager enough already. Even if Walden sells a hundred, a thousand drawings, I will not have enough money to pay for this cursed aircraft. Can I, in the time the train remains in the Hohenbudberg yards, construct a new aircraft or even the simulacrum[8] of an aircraft, with no materials to work with or indeed any special knowledge of aircraft construction? The situation is <u>ludicrous</u>. I will therefore apply Reason. Reason dictates the solution. I will diddle the manifest. With my painter's skill which is after all not so different from a forger's, I will change the manifest to reflect conveyance of *two* aircraft, B.F.W. 3054/16 and 17, to Fighter Squadron Five. The extra canvas and ropes I will conceal in an empty boxcar—this one, which according to its stickers is headed for Essigny-le-Petit.[9] Now I will walk around town and see if I can find a chocolate shop. I crave chocolate."

> *What does Paul Klee decide to apply to the situation? What solution does he choose?*

The Secret Police said:

"Now we observe Engineer-Private Klee concealing the canvas and ropes which covered the former aircraft in an empty boxcar bound for Essigny-le-Petit. We have previously observed him diddling the manifest with his painter's skill which resembles not a little that of the forger. We applaud these actions of Engineer-Private Klee. The contradiction confronting us in the matter of the preliminary report is thus resolved in highly satisfactory fashion. We are proud of Engineer-Private Klee and of the resolute and manly fashion in which he has dealt with the crisis. We predict he will go far. We would like to embrace him as a comrade and brother but unfortunately we are not embraceable. We are secret, we exist in the shadows, the pleasure of the comradely/brotherly embrace is one of the pleasures we are denied, in our dismal service."

> *What does Paul Klee do after changing the manifest?*

> *What do the Secret Police think of Paul Klee's solution to the problem of the missing aircraft? What would they like to do to him?*

Paul Klee said:

"We arrive at Cambrai. The planes are unloaded, six men for each plane. The work goes quickly. No one questions my altered manifest. The weather is clearing. After lunch I will leave to begin the return journey. My release slip and travel orders are ready, but the lieutenant must come and sign them. I wait contentedly in the warm orderly room. The drawing I did of the collapsed canvas and ropes is really very good. I eat a piece of chocolate. I am sorry about the lost aircraft but not overmuch. The war is temporary. But drawings and chocolate go on forever."

> *What does Paul Klee say is temporary and what goes on forever?*

∎

---

8. **simulacrum.** Image of something; vague semblance
9. **Essigny-le-Petit.** (es sē nyē' lə pə tē') District of St. Quentin in northern France

---

words for everyday use	**lu • di • crous** (lü' də krəs) *adj.,* amusing or laughable through obvious absurdity, incongruity, exaggeration, or eccentricity. *The theater critic thought it was <u>ludicrous</u> the way the actors slid into position on a slanted stage.*

ANSWERS TO UNDERSTANDING LITERATURE

STYLE. Barthelme's style is unconventional, which is apparent in its reliance on dialogue alone and the lack of a narrator.

SATIRE. Barthelme has created a satire of self-important government officials who exist only to be officious or to create unnecessary bureaucracy. He would like to make the military a more humane or at least purposeful organization.

REPETITION. The repetition of words and phrases by the Secret Police and Paul Klee add to the humor and absurdity of the situation and are an element of the satire. They help create the sense of bureaucracy in the speech of the Secret Police.

Respond to the SELECTION

What do you think of Engineer-Private Paul Klee's solution to his problem?

Investigate, Inquire, and Imagine

Recall: GATHERING FACTS

1a. What is it that the Secret Police yearn for?

2a. What is it about the flat car, after the disappearance of the aircraft, which commands Paul Klee's attention? What does Paul Klee decide to apply in order to resolve the "ludicrous situation" in which he finds himself?

3a. What is the "resolute and manly fashion" in which Paul Klee has dealt with the crisis, according to the Secret Police?

→ Interpret: FINDING MEANING

1b. What is the irony of this desire?

2b. Why do you think this commands his attention? Why do you think this is the appropriate response in Paul Klee's judgment?

3b. Why are the Secret Police proud of Klee?

Analyze: TAKING THINGS APART

4a. Analyze the fashion in which both Klee and the Secret Police speak in this story.

→ Synthesize: BRINGING THINGS TOGETHER

4b. What is the importance of Klee's observations about war, drawings, and chocolates?

Evaluate: MAKING JUDGMENTS

5a. How effective are the Secret Police at being omniscient, omnipresent, and omnipotent?

→ Extend: CONNECTING IDEAS

5b. From the "Keystone Cops" of the 1930s to Barney Fife in the 1960s and the Secret Police in this story, bumbling police have been popular comic characters in American culture. Why do you think we like to laugh at portrayals of inept law enforcement officers?

Understanding Literature

STYLE. Review the definition of **style** in the Handbook of Literary Terms. Is Barthelme's style conventional or unconventional? What are examples of his style?

SATIRE. Review the definition of **satire** in Literary Tools on page 662. Whom or what do you believe Barthelme is satirizing? What do you think Barthelme would like to change about the target of his satire?

REPETITION. Review the definition for **repetition** in the Handbook of Literary Terms and the chart you made for Literary Tools on page 662. What purpose does repetition serve in this selection?

"ENGINEER-PRIVATE PAUL KLEE MISPLACES AN AIRCRAFT BETWEEN MILBERTSHOFEN AND CAMBRAI, MARCH 1916" **667**

Answers to Understanding Literature can be found on page 666.

Writer's Journal

1. Write a **job description** to be used by the office of military personnel to hire a new member of the Secret Police.

2. Imagine that you are a member of the Secret Police. Write the **report** to your supervisor that includes your observations of the events of Paul Klee's trip from Milbertshofen to Cambrai.

3. Imagine you are Paul Klee and you have just read the selection about yourself. Write a **letter** to Barthelme expressing your reactions to how he has characterized you.

Integrating the Language Arts

Language, Grammar, and Style

SIMPLE, COMPOUND, AND COMPLEX SENTENCES. Read the Language Arts Survey 3.84, "The Clauses of a Sentence: Simple, Compound, and Complex Sentences." Then identify the following sentences as simple, compound, complex, or compound-complex.

1. Paul Klee was an Engineer-Private in the German Air Corps.
2. After he finished his work, he liked to see the art museums, but there wasn't always time.
3. There had been three aircraft, but one was missing.
4. Paul diddled with the manifest, and he showed that only two aircraft were delivered.
5. After watching Paul Klee closely, the Secret Police approved of how he handled the situation.

Study and Research

RESEARCHING PAUL KLEE. Paul Klee has been called one of the most varied, complex, and brilliant artistic talents of the twentieth century. Research his life and work. With what artistic movement is he associated? Why? How did he feel about traditional forms and structures in art? What makes it easy to identify a Klee painting? Which is your favorite painting by Klee? Why? Present your findings to the class.

Vocabulary

THE PREFIX OMNI. Read the Language Arts Survey 1.19, "Learning Base Words, Prefixes, and Suffixes." The prefix *omni*, from Latin, means *all*. Using a dictionary, find the words that have the following definitions. Then write a contextualized sentence using each word.

1. having the authority or legal capacity to act in all matters
2. having virtually unlimited authority or influence
3. of all varieties, forms, or kinds
4. containing or including many items
5. unlimited in creative power

"Flowers for Algernon"

by Daniel Keyes

Reader's resource

"Flowers for Algernon" is considered a classic of science fiction. By the mid-1950s, the genre of science fiction was well established and typically concerned with subjects such as utopian (ideal) and dystopian (dehumanized) societies, lost worlds, and alien cultures. Through his character Charlie Gordon, who becomes intelligent because of a neurological operation, Keyes explores the theme of biological experimentation, another subject frequently examined in science fiction.

PSYCHOLOGY CONNECTION. The Rorschach Test was first introduced in 1921 by a Swiss psychiatrist named Hermann Rorschach. The test consists of a series of inkblots, which patients are asked to look at and to describe what they see in each design. These responses supposedly indicate to the person giving the test something about the patient's personality, intelligence, or emotional health. The test is based on the fact that humans often project their own ideas, interpretations, and feelings into obscure or ambiguous stimuli. Although the test has been popular over the years, it is considered by many to be an unreliable way of assessing people.

About *the* AUTHOR

Daniel Keyes (1927–) was born in New York City. Fascinated by the complexities of the human mind, Keyes earned a degree in psychology from Brooklyn College. Keyes has worked as a purser in the U.S. Maritime Service, a fiction editor for a New York publishing house, the co-owner of a photography company, a professor of English and director of creative writing at Ohio University, and a writer.

After receiving much praise for his short story "Flowers for Algernon," Keyes developed the story into a novel, published in 1966 under the same title. Later it was made into a movie, *Charlie*. Keyes's other works include the novels *The Touch* (1971) and *The Fifth Sally* (1981), and two works of nonfiction, *The Minds of Billy Milligan* (1981) and *Charlie, The True Story of a Serial Killer* (1986).

Literary TOOLS

POINT OF VIEW. Point of view is the vantage point from which a story is told. When stories are written from the *first-person point of view,* the narrator may be a participant or witness of the action. "Flowers for Algernon" is written in the first-person point of view from the vantage point of Charlie, the main character. As you read the story, consider the advantage of reading about Charlie's progress from his own point of view.

FORESHADOWING. Foreshadowing is the act of presenting materials that hint at events to occur later in a story. Look for examples of foreshadowing in "Flowers for Algernon."

Reader's Journal

What does the word *intelligence* mean to you? How important do you believe intelligence is? Are there different types of intelligence?

ADDITIONAL RESOURCES

UNIT 8 RESOURCE BOOK
- Selection Worksheet 8.7
- Selection Check Test 4.8.13
- Selection Test 4.8.14
- Language, Grammar, and Style Resource 3.80

VOCABULARY FROM THE SELECTION

applicability	regression
cower	sensibility
illiteracy	specialization
introspective	specter
justify	syndrome
neurosurgeon	tangible
obscure	vacuous
opportunist	verify
proportional	

READER'S JOURNAL

What are the different ways in which a person can be intelligent? When have you seen particular examples of these different intelligences? What sort of intelligence does the general public seem to value?

INDIVIDUAL LEARNING STRATEGIES

MOTIVATION
Ask students to discuss whether they would be willing to have an operation to make them smarter or more talented in a certain area. Would their answer change if they knew the effects were temporary? Students should explain their answers.

READING PROFICIENCY
Students should begin by reading the Reader's Resource, which presents the premise of the story. Have them watch for changes in Charlie's language and grammar as the selection continues.

GOALS/OBJECTIVES

Studying this lesson will enable students to
- empathize with Charlie Gordon and understand and appreciate his experience by reading his journal entries
- explore the life and work of Daniel Keyes
- define and understand the literary techniques of *point of view* and *foreshadowing*
- identify gerunds in sentences
- write and perform a dramatic skit
- research Gardner's theory of multiple intelligences

Flowers for Algernon

Daniel Keyes

PART 1

progris riport 1—martch 5 1965

Dr Strauss says I shud rite down what I think and evrey thing that happins to me from now on. I dont know why but he says its importint so they will see if they will use me. I hope they use me. Miss Kinnian says maybe they can make me smart. I want to be smart. My name is Charlie Gordon. I am 37 years old and 2 weeks ago was my birthday. I have nuthing more to rite now so I will close for today.

> *Why does Charlie start writing down his thoughts? What does he long to be?*

progris riport 2—martch 6

I had a test today. I think I failed it. and I think that maybe now they wont use me. What happind is a nice young man was in the room and he had some white cards with ink spilled all over them. He sed Charlie what do you see on this card. I was very skared even tho I had my rabits foot in my pockit because when I was a kid I always faled tests in school and I spilled ink to.

I told him I saw a inkblot. He said yes and it made me feel good. I thot that was all but when I got up to go he stopped me. He said now sit down Charlie we are not thru yet. Then I dont remember so good but he wantid me to say what was in the ink. I dint see nuthing in the ink but he said there was picturs there other pepul saw some picturs. I coudnt see any picturs. I reely tryed to see. I held the card close up and then far away. Then I said if I had my glases I coud see better I usally only ware my glases in the movies or TV but I said they are in the closit in the hall. I got them. Then I said let me see that card agen I bet Ill find it now.

I tryed hard but I still coudnt find the picturs I only saw the ink. I told him maybe I need new glases. He rote something down on a paper and I got skared of faling the test. I told him it was a very nice inkblot with littel points all around the eges. He looked very sad so that

> *What does Charlie fail to see in the inkblot? What does he see?*

wasnt it. I said please let me try agen. Ill get it in a few minits becaus Im not so fast somtimes. Im a slow reeder too in Miss Kinnians class for slow adults but Im trying very hard.

He gave me a chance with another card that had 2 kinds of ink spilled on it red and blue.

He was very nice and talked slow like Miss Kinnian does and he explained it to me that it was a *raw shok*.[1] He said pepul see things in the ink. I said show me where. He said think. I told him I think a inkblot but that wasnt rite eather. He said what does it remind you—pretend something. I closd my eyes for a long time to pretend. I told him I pretend a fowntan pen with ink leeking all over a table cloth. Then he got up and went out.

I dont think I passd the *raw shok* test.

progris riport 3—martch 7

Dr Strauss and Dr Nemur say it dont matter about the inkblots. I told them I dint spill the ink on the cards and I coudnt see anything in the ink. They said that maybe they will still use me. I said Miss Kinnian never gave me tests like that one only spelling and reading. They said Miss Kinnian told that I was her bestist pupil in the adult nite scool becaus I tryed the hardist and I reely wantid to lern. They said how come you went to the adult nite scool all by yourself Charlie. How did you find it. I said I askd pepul and sumbody told me where I shud go to lern to read and spell good. They said why did you want to. I told them becaus all my life I wantid to be smart and not dumb. But its very hard to be smart. They said you know it will probly be tempirery.[2] I said yes. Miss Kinnian told me. I dont care if it herts.

Later I had more crazy tests today. The nice lady who gave it me told me the name and I asked her how do you spellit so I can rite it in my progris riport. THEMATIC APPERCEPTION TEST.[3] I dont know the frist 2 words but I know what *test* means. You got to pass it or you get bad marks. This test lookd easy becaus I coud see the picturs. Only this time she dint want me to tell her

the picturs. That mixd me up. I said the man yesterday said I shoud tell him what I saw in the ink she said that dont make no difrence. She said make up storys about the pepul in the picturs.

I told her how can you tell storys about pepul you never met. I said why shud I make up lies. I never tell lies any more becaus I always get caut.

> *What is Charlie asked to do in the second test? Why can't he make up stories?*

She told me this test and the other one the raw shok was for getting personalty. I laffed so hard. I said how can you get that thing from inkblots and fotos. She got sore and put her picturs away. I dont care. It was sily. I gess I faled that test too.

Later some men in white coats took me to a difernt part of the hospitil and gave me a game to play. It was like a race with a white mouse. They called the mouse Algernon. Algernon was in a box with a lot of twists and turns like all kinds of walls and they gave me a pencil and a paper with lines and lots of boxes. On one side it said START

> *What is Algernon? What is Charlie asked to do with the pencil and paper?*

and on the other end it said FINISH. They said it was *amazed*[4] and that Algernon and me had the same *amazed* to do. I dint see how we could have the same *amazed* if Algernon had a box and I had a paper but I dint say nothing. Anyway there wasnt time because the race started.

One of the men had a watch he was trying to hide so I woudnt see it so I tryed not to look and that made me nervus.

Anyway that test made me feel worser than all the others because they did it over 10 times with diferent *amazeds* and Algernon won every time. I dint know that mice were so smart. Maybe thats because Algernon is a white

> *Why does the test with Algernon make Charlie feel bad?*

---

1. *raw shok*. Charlie means *Rorschach*.
2. *tempirery*. Charlie means *temporary*.
3. THEMATIC APPERCEPTION TEST. Personality test that involves asking the subject to make up a story after looking at a series of pictures
4. *amazed*. Charlie means *a maze*.

1. Charlie is asked to make up stories about people in pictures. He is unable to make up stories about people in pictures because he believes that making up stories about people he's never met is lying.
2. Algernon is a white mouse. Charlie is asked to do a maze with the pencil and paper.
3. The test with Algernon makes Charlie feel bad because the mouse is able to beat Charlie at the maze ten times.

CROSS-CURRICULAR CONNECTIONS

VIVISECTION. Vivisection, or animal testing, is a very old and well-known procedure. Scientists have been using vivisection since the beginning of scientific medicine. Mice, because of their small size and low cost, are ideal candidates for laboratory experiments. Using mice has contributed to the advancements in the areas of genetics, immunology, and virology. Mice have even helped in the research for finding a cure for AIDS. The benefits of animal testing prove to be astonishing, but many people feel that animal testing is wrong. And yet, human testing is considered even more unethical, making the alternatives to vivisection almost nil. However, the alternatives to animal testing have increased in the past decade due to scientific and technological advances.

1. Dr. Strauss believes that Charlie is a good candidate because he has good motivation.
2. Charlie's great achievement is having learned to read and write. The doctors compare this to other people learning Einstein's theory of relativity without help.

ADDITIONAL QUESTIONS AND ACTIVITIES

Why does Charlie bring a rabbit's foot, a lucky penny, and a horse shoe to the hospital with him? Why do these items provide comfort to him? Why do people adopt certain superstitions? Why might a scientist like Dr. Strauss be annoyed by superstitions?

Answers

Charlie brings the items for good luck. The items provide comfort to Charlie, who is entering a frightening situation of which he understands very little. Superstitions are generally based on fear, or a lack of understanding of a situation. They provide people with a superficial sense of comfort or control. Superstitions are seldom based upon laws of science. There is generally no logic or reason to them. Superstitions would seem strange or silly to a person who works in a career concerned with observation and experimentation.

ADDITIONAL QUESTIONS AND ACTIVITIES π

You may want to have students create a plot chart, like the one below, to help them organize the details of Charlie's transformation.

What is Charlie's personality like?
March 5–10
He feels inferior, lacks self-esteem, but is motivated. Tries hard to be smart.
March 14–June 4
Wants to be like everyone else; becomes more self-aware. Lonely; impatient to learn more.
June 5–July 28
Begins to notice signs of emotional instability and forgetfulness; touchy, irritable, suicidal.

What is Charlie's intelligence like?
March 5–10
IQ of 68

---

mouse. Maybe white mice are smarter than other mice.

progris riport 4—Mar 8

Their going to use me! Im so exited I can hardly write. Dr Nemur and Dr Strauss had a argament about it first. Dr Nemur was in the office when Dr Strauss brot me in. Dr Nemur was worryed about using me but Dr Strauss told him Miss Kinnian rekemmended me the best from all the pepul who she was teaching. I like Miss Kinnian becaus shes a very smart teacher. And she said Charlie your going to have a second chance. If you volenteer for this experament you mite get smart. They dont know if it will be perminint but theirs a chance. Thats why I said ok even when I was scared because she said it was an operashun. She said dont be scared Charlie you done so much with so little I think you deserv it most of all.

So I got scaird when Dr Nemur and Dr Strauss argud about it. Dr Strauss said I had something that was very good. He said I had a good *motor-vation*.[5] I never even knew I had that. I felt proud when he said that not every body with an eye-q[6] of 68 had that thing. I dont know what it is or where I got it but he said Algernon had it too. Algernons *motor-vation* is the cheese they put in his box. But it cant be that because I didnt eat any cheese this week.

Why does Dr. Strauss believe that Charlie is a good candidate for the experiment?

Then he told Dr Nemur something I dint understand so while they were talking I wrote down some of the words.

He said Dr Nemur I know Charlie is not what you had in mind as the first of your new brede of intelek**[7] (coudnt get the word) superman. But most pepul of his low ment** are host** and uncoop** and they are usualy dull apath** and hard to reach. He has a good natcher hes intristed and eager to please.

Dr Nemur said remember he will be the first human beeng ever to have his intelijence trippled by surgicle meens.

Dr Strauss said exakly. Look at how well hes lerned to read and write for his low mentel age its as grate an acheve** as you and I lerning einstines therey of **vity[8] without help. That shows the intenss motor-vation. Its comparat** a tremen** achev** I say we use Charlie.

What is Charlie's great achievement? To what do the doctors compare it?

I dint get all the words and they were talking to fast but it sounded like Dr Strauss was on my side and like the other one wasnt.

Then Dr Nemur nodded he said all right maybe your right. We will use Charlie. When he said that I got so exited I jumped up and shook his hand for being so good to me. I told him thank you doc you wont be sorry for giving me a second chance. And I mean it like I told him. After the operashun Im gonna try to be smart. Im gonna try awful hard.

progris riport 5—Mar 10

Im skared. Lots of people who work here and the nurses and the people who gave me the tests came to bring me candy and wish me luck. I hope I have luck. I got my rabits foot and my lucky penny and my horse shoe. Only a black cat crossed me when I was comming to the hospitil. Dr Strauss says dont be supersitis[9] Charlie this is sience. Anyway Im keeping my rabits foot with me.

I asked Dr Strauss if Ill beat Algernon in the race after the operashun and he said maybe. If the operashun works Ill show that mouse I can be as smart as he is. Maybe smarter. Then Ill be abel to read better and spell the words good and know lots of things and be like other people. I want to

---

5. *motor-vation.* Charlie means *motivation.*
6. **eye-q.** Charlie is trying to write *I.Q.*, short for "intelligence quotient," a number used to indicate relative intelligence as measured on a particular test.
7. **intelek**.** Charlie uses asterisks to complete words that he doesn't understand, in this case the word *intellectual.*
8. **einstines therey of **vity.** Charlie is trying to write *Einstein's Theory of Relativity*, meaning Albert Einstein's scientific theory about space and time.
9. **supersitis.** Charlie means *superstitious.*

ADDITIONAL QUESTIONS AND ACTIVITIES (CONT.)

March 14–June 4
He becomes so intelligent that it becomes difficult to communicate with people.
June 5–July 28
Deteriorates

How do others see and treat Charlie?
March 5–10
Miss Kinnian, Dr. Strauss think he's motivated, has a good nature, and is eager to please.

March 14–June 4
Coworkers make fun of him; later they avoid him and turn him out of the factory. Fanny sticks up for him but doesn't think what he has done is right. Dr. Nemur is

(Continued on page 673)

be smart like other people. If it works perminint they will make everybody smart all over the wurld.

They dint give me anything to eat this morning. I dont know what that eating has to do with getting smart. Im very hungry and Dr Nemur took away my box of candy. That Dr Nemur is a grouch. Dr Strauss says I can have it back after the operashun. You cant eat befor a operashun. . . .

Progress Report 6—Mar 15

The operashun dint hurt. He did it while I was sleeping. They took off the bandijis from my eyes and my head today so I can make a PROGRESS REPORT. Dr Nemur who looked at some of my other ones says I spell PROGRESS wrong and he told me how to spell it and REPORT too. I got to try and remember that.

I have a very bad memary for spelling. Dr Strauss says its ok to tell about all the things that happin to me but he says I shoud tell more about what I feel and what I think. When I told him I dont know how to think he said try. All the time when the bandijis were on my eyes I tryed to think. Nothing happened. I dont know what to think about. Maybe if I ask him he will tell me how I can think now that Im suppose to get smart. What do smart people think about. Fancy things I suppose. I wish I knew some fancy things already.

> About what does Charlie believe "smart people" think?

Progress Report 7—Mar 19

Nothing is happining. I had lots of tests and different kinds of races with Algernon. I hate that mouse. He always beats me. Dr Strauss said I got to play those games. And he said some time I got to take those tests over again. Those inkblots are stupid. And those pictures are stupid too. I like to draw a picture of a man and a woman but I wont make up lies about people.

I got a headache from trying to think so much. I thot Dr Strauss was my frend but he dont help me. He dont tell me what to think or when Ill get smart. Miss Kinnian dint come to see me. I think writing these progress reports are stupid too.

> Why does Charlie become discouraged after the operation?

Progress Report 8—Mar 23

Im going back to work at the factery. They said it was better I shud go back to work but I cant tell anyone what the operashun was for and I have to come to the hospitil for an hour evry night after work. They are gonna pay me mony every month for lerning to be smart.

Im glad Im going back to work because I miss my job and all my frends and all the fun we have there.

Dr Strauss says I shud keep writing things down but I dont have to do it every day just when I think of something or something speshul happins. He says dont get discoridged because it takes time and it happins slow. He says it took a long time with Algernon before he got 3 times smarter than he was before. Thats why Algernon beats me all the time because he had that operashun too. That makes me feel better. I could probly do that *amazed* faster than a reglar mouse. Maybe some day Ill beat Algernon. Boy that would be something. So far Algernon looks like he mite be smart perminent.

> What does Charlie learn about Algernon?

Mar 25

(I dont have to write PROGRESS REPORT on top any more just when I hand it in once a week for Dr Nemur to read. I just have to put the date on. That saves time)

We had a lot of fun at the factery today. Joe Carp said hey look where Charlie had his operashun what did they do Charlie put some brains in. I was going to tell him but I remembered Dr Strauss said no. Then Frank Reilly said

> Whom does Charlie consider to be his friends at work? What do these "friends" say to Charlie?

1. Charlie believes that smart people think about fancy things.
2. A noticeable change does not occur immediately after the operation, so Charlie becomes discouraged. He still cannot do the tests, and he still cannot beat the mouse at the maze.
3. Charlie learns that Algernon has had an operation to increase his intelligence.
4. Charlie considers his friends at work to be Joe Carp and Frank Reilly. These "friends" tease Charlie.

ADDITIONAL QUESTIONS AND ACTIVITIES (CONT.)

uncomfortable with the newly intelligent Charlie. Miss Kinnian is proud of him.
June 5–July 28
Dr. Strauss feels guilty. His coworkers now feel sorry for him. Miss Kinnian cries when she sees him.

What does Charlie think about other people?
March 5–10
Likes Miss Kinnian because she's smart. Perceptive enough to see that Dr. Strauss was more on his side than Dr. Nemur.
March 14–June 4
Thinks coworkers like him because they're always laughing at him. Later he learns that they are making fun of him and it makes him sick. Likes Miss Kinnian because she doesn't look down on him. Beginning to think she is beautiful. Surprised to learn that Dr. Strauss and Nemur aren't as knowledgeable as he thought.
June 5–July 28
Still loves Miss Kinnian, but is embarrassed to have her see him like he is. Doesn't want everyone to feel sorry for him. Wants to leave New York and go to a place where no one knows him.

What does Charlie think and feel about what is happening to him?
March 5–10
Very excited to be selected for the operation. Wants to be smart. Scared, though, of actual operation
March 14–June 4
Pleased that operation didn't hurt. At first disappointed that he isn't immediately smart. Later wants to help others with new-found knowledge.
June 5–July 28
Doesn't want deterioration to happen. Doesn't blame others, but "how it hurts."

1. Strauss gives him a device
resembling a television to turn on as
he sleeps.

LITERARY TECHNIQUE

EPONYM. An **eponym** is a person or character from whose name a word or title is derived, or a name that has become synonymous with some general characteristic or idea. Among Charlie's coworkers, *Charlie Gordon* becomes an eponym of a foolish action or an unintelligent person. For more information about eponyms, students should turn to the Handbook of Literary Terms in the back of their textbooks.

CROSS-CURRICULAR CONNECTIONS

NEUROLOGY. In this selection, Charlie experiences difficulty sleeping. Research on normal sleep led scientists to recognize and study sleep disorders, which afflict up to seventy million Americans. These disorders include insomnia, or difficulty in falling asleep, and sleep apnea, which causes breathing to stop for extended periods during sleep. These can cause behavior problems and accidents related to fatigue. Once sleep disorders became recognized, scientists began to find treatments for them. Almost everything known about the physiology of sleep has been learned by studying experimental animals. For example, scientists found that sleep phases are closely related to the activity of certain groups of nerve cells releasing brain chemicals that relay information from one neuron to another. Research on these specialized cell groups is helping scientists to devise specific drug treatments for sleep disorders.

what did you do Charlie forget your key and open your door the hard way. That made me laff. Their really my friends and they like me.

Sometimes somebody will say hey look at Joe or Frank or George he really pulled a Charlie Gordon. I dont know why they say that but they always laff. This morning Amos Borg who is the 4 man at Donnegans used my name when he shouted at Ernie the office boy. Ernie lost a packige. He said Ernie for godsake what are you trying to be a Charlie Gordon. I dont understand why he said that. I never lost any packiges.

Mar 28

Dr Strauss came to my room tonight to see why I dint come in like I was suppose to. I told him I dont like to race with Algernon any more.

He said I dont have to for a while but I shud come in. He had a present for me only it wasnt a present but just for lend. I thot it was a little television but it wasnt. He said I got to turn it on when I got to sleep. I said your kidding why shud I turn it on when Im going to sleep. Who ever herd of a thing like that.

What does Dr. Strauss give to Charlie?

But he said if I want to get smart I got to do what he says. I told him I dint think I was going to get smart and he put his hand on my sholder and said Charlie you dont know it yet but your getting smarter all the time. You wont notice for a while. I think he was just being nice to make me feel good because I dont look any smarter.

Oh yes I almost forgot. I asked him when I can go back to the class at Miss Kinnians school. He said I wont go their. He said that soon Miss Kinnian will come to the hospitil to start and teach me speshul. I was mad at her for not comming to see me when I got the operashun but I like her so maybe we will be frends again.

Mar 29

That crazy TV kept me up all night. How can I sleep with something yelling crazy things all night in my ears. And the nutty pictures. Wow. I dont know what it says when Im up so how am I going to know when Im sleeping.

Dr Strauss says its ok. He says my brains are lerning when I sleep and that will help me when Miss Kinnian starts my lessons in the hospitl (only I found out it isnt a hospitil its a labatory). I think its all crazy. If you can get smart when your sleeping why do people go to school. That thing I dont think will work. I use to watch the late show and the late late show on TV all the time and it never made me smart. Maybe you have to sleep while you watch it.

Progress Report 9—April 3

Dr Strauss showed me how to keep the TV turned low so now I can sleep. I don't hear a thing. And I still dont understand what it says. A few times I play it over in the morning to find out what I lerned when I was sleeping and I don't think so. Miss Kinnian says Maybe its another langwidge or something. But most times it sounds american. It talks so fast faster then even Miss Gold who was my teacher in 6 grade and I remember she talked so fast I coudnt understand her.

I told Dr Strauss what good is it to get smart in my sleep. I want to be smart when Im awake. He says its the same thing and I have two minds. Theres the *subsconscious* and the *conscious*[10] (thats how you spell it). And one dont tell the other one what its doing. They dont even talk to each other. Thats why I dream. And boy have I been having crazy dreams. Wow. Ever since that night TV. The late late late late late show.

I forgot to ask him if it was only me or if everybody had those two minds.

(I just looked up the word in the dictionary Dr Strauss gave me. The word is *subconscious. adj. Of the nature of mental operations yet not present in consciousness; as, subconscious conflict of desires.*) There's more but I still dont know what it means. This isnt a very good dictionary for dumb people like me.

Anyway the headache is from the party. My frends from the factery Joe Carp and Frank Reilly invited me to go with them to Muggsys Saloon for some drinks. I dont like to drink but they said we will have lots of fun. I had a good time.

Joe Carp said I should show the girls how I mop out the toilet in the factory and he got me a mop. I showed them and everyone laffed when I told that Mr Donnegan said I was the best janiter he ever

How is Charlie treated by Joe Carp and Frank Reilly? Does he realize how he is treated?

had because I like my job and do it good and never come late or miss a day except for my operashun.

I said Miss Kinnian always said Charlie be proud of your job because you do it good.

Everybody laffed and we had a good time and they gave me lots of drinks and Joe said Charlie is a card when hes potted. I dont know what that means but everybody likes me and we have fun. I cant wait to be smart like my best frends Joe Carp and Frank Reilly.

I dont remember how the party was over but I think I went out to buy a newspaper and coffe for Joe and Frank and when I came back there was no one their. I looked for them all over till late. Then I dont remember so good but I think I got sleepy or sick. A nice cop brot me back home. Thats what my landlady Mrs Flynn says.

But I got a headache and big lump on my head and black and blue all over. I think maybe I fell but Joe Carp says it was the cop they beat up drunks some times. I dont think so. Miss Kinnian says cops are to help people. Anyway I got a bad headache and Im sick and hurt all over. I dont think Ill drink anymore.

April 6

I beat Algernon! I dint even know I beat him until Burt the tester told me. Then the second time I lost because I got so exited I fell off the chair before I finished. But after that I beat him 8 more times. I must be getting smart to beat a smart mouse like Algernon. But I dont *feel* smarter.

I wanted to race Algernon some more but Burt said thats enough for one day. They let me hold him for a minit. Hes not so bad. Hes soft like a ball of cotton. He blinks and when he opens his eyes their black and pink on the eges.

I said can I feed him because I felt bad to beat him and I wanted to be nice and make frends. Burt said no Algernon is a very specshul mouse with an operashun like mine, and he was the first of all the animals to stay smart so long. He told me Algernon is so smart that every day he has to solve a test to get his food. Its a thing like a lock on a door that changes every time Algernon goes in to eat so he has to lern some-

---

10. **subsconscious** and the **conscious.** *Subconscious*—thoughts or feelings of which a person is not aware; *conscious*—thoughts or feelings of which a person is aware

1. Charlie is teased and made to look foolish by Joe Carp and Frank Reilly. Charlie continues to believe that when people laugh they are having fun with him, and he does not realize that they are laughing at him.

ADDITIONAL QUESTIONS AND ACTIVITIES

Ask students to have a discussion about the treatment of Charlie by his coworkers. Why is Charlie a target for the type of mistreatment he endures? Charlie says at one point, "I can't wait to be smart like my best friends Joe Carp and Frank Reilly." How do the students feel about this statement? How might they respond to it? If Joe and Frank and others who participate in the ridicule were able to read Charlie's journal and realize that he has his own thoughts and feelings, might they treat him differently? Why, or why not?
Answers
Students might respond by saying that Charlie is different from the others around him, and this makes him an easy target. Charlie is also overly trusting and eager for acceptance. The irony of the statement might anger students or make them sad. They might respond to Charlie's statement by telling him that Joe and Frank have a great deal to learn about being kind and decent and that they are not the best friends for him. Reading Charlie's journal might give people more insight into the fact that Charlie is a human being with thoughts and feelings like everyone else.

1. Charlie wants to befriend Algernon because he feels bad about beating him. Charlie doesn't think it is right to make Algernon pass a test to eat. These "friends" tease Charlie.
2. He is not satisfied with the ending and wants to read more.
3. Miss Kinnian tells Charlie that he shouldn't feel bad if he someday realizes that people aren't as nice as he thinks. Charlie responds by saying that his friends are good people who like him and who never did anything that wasn't nice.

LITERARY NOTE

British author Daniel Defoe published *Robinson Crusoe* in 1704, and the book immediately became successful. This adventure novel tells the story of a man who becomes shipwrecked on a desert island. With his own skills and some items salvaged from the ship, he is able to survive on the island. He builds a house, a boat, and is able to domesticate wild goats. Crusoe is eventually rescued by an English ship.

This story has been translated into many different languages. It has also served as the basis for other, similar tales, including the popular story *Swiss Family Robinson*.

---

thing new to get his food. That made me sad because if he coudnt lern he would be hungry.

I dont think its right to make you pass a test to eat. How would Dr Nemur like it to have to pass a test every time he wants to eat. I think Ill be frends with Algernon.

Why does Charlie want to befriend Algernon? What does Charlie think about the test Algernon must take to eat?

April 9

Tonight after work Miss Kinnian was at the laboratory. She looked like she was glad to see me but scared. I told her dont worry Miss Kinnian Im not smart yet and she laffed. She said I have confidence in you Charlie the way you struggled so hard to read and right better than all the others. At werst you will have it for a littel wile and your doing somthing for sience.

We are reading a very hard book. I never read such a hard book before. Its called *Robinson Crusoe*[11] about a man who gets merooned on a dessert Iland. Hes smart and figers out all kinds of things so he can have a house and food and hes a good swimmer. Only I feel sorry because hes all alone and has no frends. But I think their must be somebody else on the iland because theres a picture with his funny umbrella looking at footprints. I hope he gets a frend and not be lonly.

April 10

Miss Kinnian teaches me to spell better. She says look at a word and close your eyes and say it over and over until you remember. I have lots of truble with *through* that you say *threw* and *enough* and *tough* that you dont say *enew* and *tew*. You got to say *enuff* and *tuff*. Thats how I use to write it before I started to get smart. Im confused but Miss Kinnian says theres no reason in spelling.

Apr 14

Finished *Robinson Crusoe*. I want to find out more about what happens to him but Miss Kinnian says thats all there is. *Why*

How does Charlie feel after his first experience with a work of literature?

Apr 15

Miss Kinnian says Im lerning fast. She read some of the Progress Reports and she looked at me kind of funny. She says Im a fine person and Ill show them all. I asked her why. She said never mind but I shoudnt feel bad if I find out that everybody isnt nice like I think. She said for a person who god gave so little to you done more then a lot of people with brains they never even used. I said all my frends are smart people but there good. They like me and they never did anything that wasnt nice. Then she got something in her eye and she had to run out to the ladys room.

What does Miss Kinnian say to Charlie after she reads his progress reports? How does Charlie respond?

Apr 16

Today, I lerned the comma, this is a *comma* (,) a period, with a tail, Miss Kinnian, says its important, because, it makes writing, better, she said, somebody, coud lose, a lot of money, if a comma, isnt, in the, right place, I dont have, any money, and I dont see, how a comma, keeps you, from losing it,

But she says, everybody, uses commas, so Ill use, them too,

Apr 17

I used the comma wrong. Its punctuation. Miss Kinnian told me to look up long words in the dictionary to lern to spell them. I said whats the difference if you can read it anyway. She said its part of your education so now on Ill look up all the words Im not sure how to spell. It takes a long time to write that way but I think Im remembering. I only have to look up once and after that I get it right. Anyway thats how come I got the word *punctuation* right. (Its that way in the dictionary.) Miss Kinnian says a period is punctuation too, and there are lots of other

---

11. **Robinson Crusoe.** Daniel Defoe's adventure novel, first published in 1719, about a shipwrecked sailor and his struggle to survive on an island

marks to lern. I told her I thot all the periods had to have tails but she said no.

You got to mix them up. she showed? me" how. to mix! them(up,. and now; I can! mix up all kinds" of punctuation, in! my writing? There, are lots! of rules? to lern; but Im gettin'g them in my head.

One thing I? like about, Dear Miss Kinnian: (thats the way it goes in a business letter if I ever go into business) is she, always gives me' a reason" when—I ask. She's a gen'ius! I wish! I cou'd be smart" like, her;

(Punctuation, is; fun!)

Apr 18

What a dope I am! I didn't even understand what she was talking about. I read the grammar book last night and it explanes the whole thing. Then I saw it was the same way as Miss Kinnian was trying to tell me, but I didn't get it, I got up in the middle of the night, and the whole thing straightened out in my mind.

Miss Kinnian said that the TV working in my sleep helped out. She said I reached a plateau. Thats like the flat top of a hill.

After I figgered out how punctuation worked, I read over all my old Progress Reports from the beginning. Boy, did I have crazy spelling and punctuation! I told Miss Kinnian I ought to go over the pages and fix all the mistakes but she said, "No, Charlie, Dr. Nemur wants them just as they are. That's why he let you keep them after they were photostated,[12] to see your own progress. You're coming along fast, Charlie."

What does Charlie want to do with his old progress reports? Why is he not allowed to do this?

That made me feel good. After the lesson I went down and played with Algernon. We don't race any more.

April 20

I feel sick inside. Not sick like for a doctor, but inside my chest it feels empty like

To what does Charlie compare being emotionally hurt?

getting punched and a heartburn at the same time.

I wasn't going to write about it, but I guess I got to, because its important. Today was the first time I ever stayed home from work.

Last night Joe Carp and Frank Reilly invited me to a party. There were lots of girls and some men from the factory. I remembered how sick I got last time I drank too much, so I told Joe I didn't want anything to drink. He gave me a plain coke instead. It tasted funny, but I thought it was just a bad taste in my mouth.

We had a lot of fun for a while. Joe said I should dance with Ellen and she would teach me the steps. I fell a few times and I couldn't understand why because no one else was dancing besides Ellen and me. And all the time I was tripping because somebody's foot was always sticking out.

Then when I got up I saw the look on Joe's face and it gave me a funny feeling in my stomack. "He's a scream," one of the girls said. Everybody was laughing.

Frank said, "I ain't laughed so much since we sent him off for the newspaper that night at Muggsy's and ditched him."

"Look at him. His face is red."

"He's blushing. Charlie is blushing."

"Hey, Ellen, what'd you do to Charlie? I never saw him act like that before."

I didn't know what to do or where to turn. Everyone was looking at me and laughing and I felt naked. I wanted to hide myself. I ran out into the street and threw up. Then I walked home. It's a funny thing I never knew that Joe and Frank and the others liked to have me around all the time to make fun of me. Now I know what it means when they say "to pull a Charlie Gordon."

I'm ashamed.

Is there a negative side to becoming smarter? What does Charlie learn about Joe, Frank, and the others? How does he feel?

---

12. **photostated.** Photographically reproduced

1. He would like to go back and fix the punctuation on all his old progress reports. Miss Kinnian tells him that he should leave them as they are so that he can see his progress.
2. Charlie compares being emotionally hurt to being sick. He says, "Inside my chest it feels empty like getting punched and a heartburn at the same time."
3. Yes, as Charlie becomes smarter he realizes that Joe, Frank, and the others are making fun of him. He is ashamed.

ANSWER TO GUIDED READING QUESTION

1. Charlie does not think I.Q. tests are very useful because people giving him the test cannot explain what or where I.Q. is.

CROSS-CURRICULAR CONNECTIONS

PSYCHOLOGY. The definition of intelligence and the measurement thereof have long been subjects of considerable controversy. In 1904, Alfred Binet was commissioned by the French minister of education to develop a procedure to identify children in need of special instruction. In 1905 and again in 1911, Binet published the first intelligence tests. These tests measured abilities to perform a number of different tasks. Binet held that these tasks represented basic, innate abilities, not learned ones. Later, scores on the Binet tests were divided by children's chronological age to arrive at what is now known as the I.Q., or intelligence quotient.

The theory behind I.Q. tests, supported by mathematical analyses done by George Spearman, is that abilities on tests of different innate skills can be averaged to come up with a single score that represents a general quality called intelligence. However, that theory has come under attack in recent years based on reevaluation of the mathematical techniques used by Spearman. Today, many psychologists, such as Harvard's Howard Gardner, author of *Frames of Mind: The Theory of Multiple Intelligences,* argue that there is no single factor called intelligence that people possess in varying degrees. Such psychologists consider I.Q. tests extremely blunt instruments that do not properly reflect the diversity of human abilities. To these psychologists, there are many, many intelligences. For convenience, Gardner speaks of several large categories—linguistic intelligence, musical intelligence, logical-mathematical intelligence, spatial intelligence, bodily-kinesthetic intelligence, and the personal intelligences—although Gardner would be the first to say that these are rough categories and that no classification scheme can adequately represent the richness and diversity of human abilities.

Progress Report 10
April 21

Still didn't go into the factory. I told Mrs. Flynn my landlady to call and tell Mr. Donnegan I was sick. Mrs. Flynn looks at me very funny lately like she's scared of me.

I think it's a good thing about finding out how everybody laughs at me. I thought about it a lot. It's because I'm so dumb and I don't even know when I'm doing something dumb. People think it's funny when a dumb person can't do things the same way they can.

Anyway, now I know I'm getting smarter every day. I know punctuation and I can spell good. I like to look up all the hard words in the dictionary and I remember them. I'm reading a lot now, and Miss Kinnian says I read very fast. Sometimes I even understand what I'm reading about, and it stays in my mind. There are times when I can close my eyes and think of a page and it all comes back like a picture.

Besides history, geography, and arithmetic, Miss Kinnian said I should start to learn a few foreign languages. Dr. Strauss gave me some more tapes to play while I sleep. I still don't understand how that conscious and unconscious mind works, but Dr. Strauss say not to worry yet. He asked me to promise that when I start learning college subjects next week I wouldn't read any books on psychology—that is, until he gives me permission.

I feel a lot better today, but I guess I'm still a little angry that all the time people were laughing and making fun of me because I wasn't so smart. When I become intelligent like Dr. Strauss says, with three times my I.Q. of 68, then maybe I'll be like everyone else and people will like me and be friendly.

I'm not sure what an *I.Q.* is. Dr. Nemur said it was something that measured how intelligent you were—like a scale in the drugstore weighs pounds. But Dr. Strauss had a big argument with him and said an I.Q. didn't weigh intelligence at all. He said an I.Q. showed how much intelligence you could get, like the numbers on the outside of a measuring cup. You still had to fill the cup up with stuff.

Then when I asked Burt, who gives me my intelligence tests and works with Algernon, he said that both of them were wrong (only I had to promise not to tell them he said so). Burt says that the I.Q. measures a lot of different things including some of the things you learned already, and it really isn't any good at all.

So I still don't know what I.Q. is except that mine is going to be over 200 soon. I didn't want to say anything, but I don't see how if they don't know *what* it is, or *where* it is—I don't see how they know *how much* of it you've got.

Dr. Nemur says I have to take a *Rorshach Test* tomorrow. I wonder what *that* is.

> What does Charlie say about I.Q. tests as a means of measuring intelligence?

April 22

I found out what a *Rorshach* is. It's the test I took before the operation—the one with the inkblots on the pieces of cardboard. The man who gave me the test was the same one.

I was scared to death of those inkblots. I knew he was going to ask me to find the pictures and I knew I wouldn't be able to. I was thinking to myself, if only there was some way of knowing what kind of pictures were hidden there. Maybe there weren't any pictures at all. Maybe it was just a trick to see if I was dumb enough to look for something that wasn't there. Just thinking about that made me sore at him.

"All right, Charlie," he said, "you've seen these cards before, remember?"

"Of course I remember."

The way I said it, he knew I was angry, and he looked surprised. "Yes, of course. Now I want you to look at this one. What might this be? What do you see on this card? People see all sorts of things in these inkblots. Tell me what it might be for you—what it makes you think of."

I was shocked. That wasn't what I had expected him to say at all. "You mean there are no pictures hidden in those inkblots?"

He frowned and took off his glasses. "What?"

"Pictures. Hidden in the inkblots. Last time you told me that everyone could see them and you wanted me to find them too."

He explained to me that the last time he had used almost the exact same words he was using now. I didn't believe it, and I still have the suspicion that he misled me at the time just for the fun of it. Unless—I don't know any more—could I have been *that* feeble-minded?

We went through the cards slowly. One of them looked like a pair of bats tugging at something. Another one looked like two men fencing with swords. I imagined all sorts of things. I guess I got carried away. But I didn't trust him any more, and I kept turning them around and even looking on the back to see if there was anything there I was supposed to catch. While he was making his notes, I peeked out of the corner of my eye to read it. But it was all in code that looked like this:

WF + A DdF-Ad orig. WF-A SF + obj

The test still doesn't make sense to me. It seems to me that anyone could make up lies about things that they didn't really see. How could he know I wasn't making a fool of him by mentioning things that I didn't really imagine? Maybe I'll understand it when Dr. Strauss lets me read up on psychology.

What does Charlie see in the inkblots this time? Why does the test not make sense to him?

1. Charlie is finally able to see pictures in the inkblots. He sees the bats tugging at something and two men fencing with swords. The test does not make sense to Charlie because anyone could make up lies about things that they did not really see.

ADDITIONAL QUESTIONS AND ACTIVITIES

"Flowers for Algernon" was turned into a full-length motion picture in 1967. The movie, directed by Ralph Nelson, was called *Charly* and starred Cliff Robertson. You might want to show students this film and then ask them to compare the film with what they have just read. Is anything lost or gained by watching the film? How important to the story is being able to see the changes in Charlie's written English? Are different parts of the plot emphasized in the book and the movie? If so, why might this be the case? Ask students to answer these questions in writing by writing a movie review. Encourage students to read Language Arts Survey 5.32, "How to Evaluate a Film," before they watch the movie.

1. People at work such as Joe Carp and Frank Reilly avoid Charlie. Charlie thinks everyone is frightened of him.
2. Both doctors want to take credit for the experiment. Also, Dr. Nemur wants to publish the results of the experiment at the end of the month, and Dr. Strauss wants to wait until they are sure of the results. Dr. Strauss accuses Dr. Nemur of caring more about getting the distinction of being Chair of Psychology at Princeton than he cares about the entire experiment. Dr. Nemur accuses Dr. Strauss of being an opportunist riding on Nemur's coattails.
3. Charlie begins to notice that Miss Kinnian is attractive and younger than he thought. Also, he no longer feels that she is an "unreachable genius." He begins to see her as another human being.

ADDITIONAL QUESTIONS AND ACTIVITIES

Why might Charlie's coworkers be avoiding him? Ask students how they might feel if they were Charlie's coworkers. How does Charlie feel about the way in which he is being treated? What is slightly ironic about these feelings?

Answers
Students might say that Charlie's coworkers are frightened and confused by the dramatic changes in Charlie. They do not understand what has happened, so the situation seems strange and abnormal. Students might say that they, too, would find Charlie's transformation unsettling. They might also say that they would be curious about what has happened to him, and that they might ask him about his operation. Charlie feels lonely because suddenly everyone is avoiding him and nobody is laughing and joking with him. This is slightly ironic because, before his operation, people did laugh and joke with him, it was often because he was the object of ridicule.

April 25

I figured out a new way to line up the machines in the factory, and Mr. Donnegan says it will save him ten thousand dollars a year in labor and increased production. He gave me a $25 bonus.

I wanted to take Joe Carp and Frank Reilly out to lunch to celebrate, but Joe said he had to buy some things for his wife, and Frank said he was meeting his cousin for lunch. I guess it'll take a little time for them to get used to the changes in me. Everybody seems to be frightened of me. When I went over to Amos Borg and tapped him on the shoulder, he jumped up in the air.

How do people react to the changes in Charlie?

People don't talk to me much any more or kid around the way they used to. It makes the job kind of lonely.

April 27

I got up the nerve today to ask Miss Kinnian to have dinner with me tomorrow night to celebrate my bonus.

At first she wasn't sure it was right, but I asked Dr. Strauss and he said it was okay. Dr. Strauss and Dr. Nemur don't seem to be getting along so well. They're arguing all the time. This evening when I came in to ask Dr. Strauss about having dinner with Miss Kinnian, I heard them shouting. Dr. Nemur was saying that it was *his* experiment and *his* research, and Dr. Strauss was shouting back that he contributed just as much, because he found me through Miss Kinnian and he performed the operation. Dr. Strauss said that someday thousands of <u>neurosurgeons</u> might be using his technique all over the world.

Dr. Nemur wanted to publish the results of the experiment at the end of this month. Dr. Strauss wanted to wait a while longer to be sure. Dr.

Strauss said that Dr. Nemur was more interested in the Chair of Psychology at Princeton[13] than he was in the experiment. Dr. Nemur said that Dr. Strauss was nothing but an <u>opportunist</u> who was trying to ride to glory on *his* coattails.

About what do Dr. Strauss and Dr. Nemur argue?

When I left afterward, I found myself trembling. I don't know why for sure, but it was as if I'd seen both clearly for the first time. I remember hearing Burt say that Dr. Nemur had a shrew[14] of a wife, who was pushing him all the time to get things published so that he could become famous. Burt said that the dream of her life was to have a big shot husband.

Was Dr. Strauss really trying to ride on his coattails?

April 28

I don't understand why I never noticed how beautiful Miss Kinnian really is. She has brown eyes and feathery brown hair that comes to the top of her neck. She's only thirty-four! I think from the beginning I had the feeling that she was an unreachable genius—and very, very old. Now, every time I see her she grows younger and more lovely.

How do Charlie's views of Miss Kinnian change?

We had dinner and a long talk. When she said that I was coming along so fast that soon I'd be leaving her behind, I laughed.

"It's true, Charlie. You're already a better reader than I am. You can read a whole page at a glance, while I can take in only a few lines at a time. And you remember every single thing you read. I'm lucky if I can recall the main thoughts and the general meaning."

---

13. **Chair of Psychology at Princeton.** Head of the psychology department at Princeton University
14. **shrew.** Insulting term meaning "mean-spirited woman"

---

words for everyday use

neu • ro • sur • geon (nōō′rō sʉr′jən) *n.*, physician who operates on the brain and other parts of the nervous system. *Lena's fascination with the brain led her to become a <u>neurosurgeon</u>.*

op • por • tu • nist (äp′ər tōō′nist) *n.*, one who adapts his or her actions to circumstances to gain an advantage. *Gary is an <u>opportunist</u> who is trying to cash in on the daytrader market.*

"I don't feel intelligent. There are so many things I don't understand."

She took out a cigarette, and I lit it for her. "You've got to be a *little* patient. You're accomplishing in days and weeks what it takes normal people to do in half a lifetime. That's what makes it so amazing. You're like a giant sponge now, soaking things in. Facts, figures, general knowledge. And soon you'll begin to connect them, too. You'll see how the different branches of learning are related. There are many levels, Charlie, like steps on a giant ladder that take you up higher and higher to see more and more of the world around you.

"I can see only a little bit of that, Charlie, and I won't go much higher than I am now, but you'll keep climbing up and up, and see more and more, and each step will open new worlds that you never even knew existed." She frowned. "I hope . . . I just hope to God—"

"What?"

"Never mind, Charles. I just hope I wasn't wrong to advise you to go into this in the first place."

> What does Miss Kinnian hope?

I laughed. "How could that be? It worked, didn't it? Even Algernon is still smart."

We sat there silently for a while, and I knew what she was thinking about as she watched me toying with the chain of my rabbit's foot and my keys. I didn't want to think of that possibility any more than elderly people want to think of death. I *knew* that this was only the beginning. I knew what she meant about levels, because I'd seen some of them already. The thought of leaving her behind made me sad.

I'm in love with Miss Kinnian.

PART 2

Progress Report 11
April 30

I've quit my job with Donnegan's Plastic Box Company. Mr. Donnegan insisted that it would be better for all concerned if I left. What did I do to make them hate me so?

The first I knew of it was when Mr. Donnegan showed me the petition. Eight hundred and forty names, everyone connected with the factory, except Fanny Girden. Scanning the list quickly, I saw at once that hers was the only missing name. All the rest demanded that I be fired.

Joe Carp and Frank Reilly wouldn't talk to me about it. No one else would either, except Fanny. She was one of the few people I'd known who set her mind to something and believed it no matter what the rest of the world proved, said, or did—and Fanny did not believe that I should have been fired. She had been against the petition on principle and despite the pressure and threats she'd held out.

> Who is the only person who doesn't sign the petition to get Charlie fired? Why doesn't she sign it?

"Which don't mean to say," she remarked, "that I don't think there's something mighty strange about you, Charlie. Them changes. I don't know. You used to be a good, dependable, ordinary man—not too bright maybe, but honest. Who knows what you done to yourself to get so smart all of a sudden. Like everybody around here's been saying, Charlie, it's not right."

> What do others think of Charlie's new-found intelligence?

"But how can you say that, Fanny? What's wrong with a man becoming intelligent and wanting to acquire knowledge and understanding of the world around him?"

She stared down at her work, and I turned to leave. Without looking at me, she said: "It was evil when Eve listened to the snake and ate from the tree of knowledge. It was evil when she saw that she was naked. If not for that none of us would ever have to grow old and sick, and die."[15]

---

15. **"It was evil when Eve listened . . . old and sick, and die."** Biblical reference to Adam and Eve in the Garden of Eden, from Genesis

1. Miss Kinnian hopes it wasn't a mistake for her to have advised him to go into the experiment in the beginning.
2. Fanny Girden is the only one who doesn't sign the petition. She does not believe that it is right for him to be fired.
3. People are confused by the change in Charlie. They think his change is strange and "not right."

ADDITIONAL QUESTIONS AND ACTIVITIES

- Ask students to discuss why Charlie was fired from Donnegan's Plastic Box Company. Did the owner of the company make a fair decision? Why, or why not? Encourage students to discuss the role of Fanny Girden in this incident. Do they admire her? Why might she be the only one who did not go along with the crowd?
- What do they think of the comparison Fanny makes to Eve and the tree of knowledge? Is knowledge good or bad? Is there a point at which knowledge becomes dangerous? Are Charlie and the scientists wrong to interfere with nature?

LITERARY NOTE

Tell students that the quest for knowledge, power, beauty, fame, and fortune has long been a popular plot in literature. This plot comes originally from the story of Adam and Eve (Genesis 2:15–3:24). As Fanny describes on page 681, Eve tasted a fruit from the forbidden tree of knowledge in the garden of Eden. Because of this act, Adam and Eve lost their innocence and realized that they were naked. As punishment for tasting the forbidden fruit, they were cast out of Eden.

The Tragical History of Doctor Faustus is an influential play in English literature derived from the plot of the story of Adam and Eve. In this play, Doctor Faustus sells his soul to the devil in exchange for

LITERARY NOTE (CONT.)

knowledge and the ability to change the world. Although at first his intentions are good, he is gradually overcome by greed and the desire for power and attention. Faustus agonizes over his decision, and by the end of the play he realizes the mistake he has made. He feels his soul cannot be saved. The story of Doctor Faustus influenced other works of literature, particularly works in the science fiction genre.

1. No, Charlie does not know what people expect of him. He thinks that people laughed at him before for his ignorance and dullness, and they now despise him for his knowledge.

2. Charlie looks at his doctors, sees their faults and insecurities, and begins to understand that being a genius is not everything.

LITERARY TECHNIQUE

IRONY. Irony is a difference between appearance and reality. In *irony of situation*, an event occurs that violates the expectations of the characters, the reader, or the audience. Irony of situation can be found in "Flowers for Algernon." Before the operation, Charlie has trouble communicating with people both orally and on paper. After the operation, as he becomes more and more intelligent, Charlie finds himself again having trouble communicating. This time, it is because he is thinking, speaking, and writing at levels much higher than that of the general population.

Once again now I have the feeling of shame burning inside me. This intelligence has driven a wedge between me and all the people I once knew and loved. Before, they laughed at me and despised me for my ignorance and dullness; now, they hate me for my knowledge and understanding. What in God's name do they want of me?

> *Has his intelligence had the effect on others that Charlie had hoped it would have?*

They've driven me out of the factory. Now I'm more alone than ever before. . . .

May 15

Dr. Strauss is very angry at me for not having written any progress reports in two weeks. He's justified because the lab is now paying me a regular salary. I told him I was too busy thinking and reading. When I pointed out that writing was such a slow process that it made me impatient with my poor handwriting, he suggested that I learn to type. It's much easier to write now because I can type nearly seventy-five words a minute. Dr. Strauss continually reminds me of the need to speak and write simply so that people will be able to understand me.

I'll try to review all the things that happened to me during the last two weeks. Algernon and I were presented to the American Psychological Association sitting in convention with the World Psychological Association last Tuesday. We created quite a sensation. Dr. Nemur and Dr. Strauss were proud of us.

I suspect that Dr. Nemur, who is sixty—ten years older than Dr. Strauss—finds it necessary to see tangible results of his work. Undoubtedly, the result of pressure by Mrs. Nemur.

Contrary to my earlier impressions of him, I realize that Dr. Nemur is not at all a genius. He has a very good mind, but it struggles under the specter of self-doubt. He wants people to take him for a genius. Therefore, it is important for him to feel that his work is accepted by the world. I believe that Dr. Nemur was afraid of further delay because he worried that someone else might make a discovery along these lines and take the credit from him.

Dr. Strauss, on the other hand, might be called a genius, although I feel that his areas of knowledge are too limited. He was educated in the tradition of narrow specialization; the broader aspects of background were neglected far more than necessary—even for a neurosurgeon.

> *What does Charlie think of Dr. Nemur and Dr. Strauss now?*

I was shocked to learn that the only ancient languages he could read were Latin, Greek, and Hebrew and that he knows almost nothing of mathematics beyond the elementary levels of the calculus of variations.[16] When he admitted this to me, I found myself almost annoyed. It was as if he'd hidden this part of himself in order to deceive me, pretending—as do many people I've discovered—to be what he is not. No one I've ever known is what he appears to be on the surface.

Dr. Nemur appears to be uncomfortable around me. Sometimes when I try to talk to him, he just looks at me strangely and turns away. I was angry at first when Dr. Strauss told me I was giving Dr. Nemur an inferiority complex.[17] I thought he was mocking me, and I'm oversensitive at being made fun of.

---

16. **calculus of variations.** Branch of higher mathematics that involves finding a value representing the highest or lowest limit for a given expression
17. **inferiority complex.** Neurotic condition marked by feelings of inadequacy

---

words for everyday use

jus • ti • fy (jus´tə fī´) *vt.*, show to be right. *Ana said, "How do you justify spending so much money on clothing?"*

tan • gi • ble (tan´jə bəl) *adj.*, that can be seen or felt. *Money and bonus points are some of the tangible rewards of Sydney's job.*

spec • ter (spek´tər) *n.*, object of dread or fear. *A specter of unhappiness seemed to shroud the town after the funeral.*

spe • cial • i • za • tion (spesh´əl īz ā´shən) *n.*, concentration on only one part of a subject. *I want to be a doctor, but I do not yet know what area of specialization I will pursue.*

---

682 *UNIT EIGHT / THE GENIUS WITHIN*

How was I to know that a highly respected psychoex-perimentalist like Nemur

Why is Dr. Nemur uncomfortable around Charlie?

was unacquainted with Hindustani and Chinese? It's absurd when you consider the work that is being done in India and China today in the very field of his study.

I asked Dr. Strauss how Nemur could refute Rehajamati's attack on his method and results if Nemur couldn't even read them in the first place. That strange look on Dr. Strauss's face can mean only one of two things. Either he doesn't want to tell Nemur what they're saying in India, or else—and this worries me—Dr. Strauss doesn't know either. I must be careful to speak and write clearly and simply so that people won't laugh.

May 18

I am very disturbed. I saw Miss Kinnian last night for the first time in over a week. I tried to avoid all

In what way has Charlie's relationship with Miss Kinnian changed?

discussions of intellectual concepts and to keep the conversation on a simple, everyday level, but she just stared at me blankly and asked me what I meant about the mathematical variance equivalent in Dorbermann's *Fifth Concerto.*

When I tried to explain she stopped me and laughed. I guess I got angry, but I suspect I'm approaching her on the wrong level. No matter what I try to discuss with her, I am unable to communicate. I must review Vrostadt's equations on *Levels of Semantic Progression.*[18] I find that I don't communicate with people much any more. Thank God for books and music and things I can think about. I am alone in my apartment at Mrs. Flynn's boarding house most of the time and seldom speak to anyone.

May 20

I would not have noticed the new dishwasher, a boy of about sixteen, at the corner diner where I take my evening meals if not for the incident of the broken dishes.

They crashed to the floor, shattering and sending bits of white china under the tables. The boy stood there, dazed and frightened, holding the empty tray in his hand. The whistles and catcalls[19] from the customers (the cries of "Hey, there go the profits!" . . . *"Mazeltov!"* . . . and "Well, *he* didn't work here very long . . ." which invariably seem to follow the breaking of glass or dishware in a public restaurant) all seemed to confuse him.

When the owner came to see what the excitement was about, the boy <u>cowered</u> as if he expected to be struck and threw up his arms as if to ward off the blow.

"All right! All right, you dope," shouted the owner, "don't just stand there! Get the broom and sweep that mess up. A broom . . . a broom, you idiot! It's in the kitchen. Sweep up all the pieces."

The boy saw that he was not going to be punished. His frightened expression disappeared, and he smiled and hummed as he came back with the broom to sweep the floor. A few of the rowdier customers kept up the remarks, amusing themselves at his expense.

"Here, sonny, over here there's a nice piece behind you. . . ."

"C'mon, do it again. . . ."

"He's not so dumb. It's easier to break 'em than to wash 'em. . . ."

As his vacant eyes moved across the crowd of amused onlookers, he slowly mirrored their

---

18. *Levels of Semantic Progression.* Linguist's book about different levels of meaning in speech
19. **catcalls.** Shrill noises expressing disapproval

words for everyday use

cow • er (kou´ər) *vi.,* shrink and tremble; cringe. *Afraid of the thunder and lightning, the puppy <u>cowered</u> under the bed.*

"FLOWERS FOR ALGERNON" 683

ANSWERS TO GUIDED READING QUESTIONS

1. Charlie seems to give Dr. Nemur an inferiority complex.
2. The conversations between Charlie and Miss Kinnian have changed because Charlie speaks on such a highly intellectual level.

CROSS-CURRICULAR ACTIVITIES

ARTS AND HUMANITIES. Find a copy of Dorbermann's *Fifth Concerto* and play it for the class. You might also ask students to find it on their own in a library or music store. Interested students can research this composer and learn more about his work.

1. He finds it strange that people who would never take advantage of someone born without arms and legs readily take advantage of someone born with low intelligence. Charlie vaguely remembers that he used to be in the position the dishwasher is in now. Charlie is ashamed and angry for having caused a scene and for almost forgetting that he had recently been in the boy's position.
2. It disturbs Charlie to think that when others laughed and made fun of him, he joined in with them.
3. He compares himself and his desire for intelligence to the hunger of the child who cannot feed himself yet or decide what to eat.
4. Charlie decides to use his knowledge to study in the field of increasing human intelligence levels.

ADDITIONAL QUESTIONS AND ACTIVITIES

This is a great opportunity to talk about people who are mentally challenged and to try to perceive the world from their point of view. Ask students to study and research the media's depiction of people who are mentally challenged. For example, you may suggest they analyze one or two of the following movies: *To Kill a Mockingbird, Forrest Gump, Rain Man,* or the media's coverage of the Special Olympics. How do media portray mentally challenged people? How does their portrayal impact your attitudes toward them? What stereotypes do you have toward mentally challenged people? What stereotypes were broken as you learned more about them? Have students present their information to the rest of the class. Researching this topic should make students aware of the importance in understanding and empathizing with people who are different from them.

---

smiles and finally broke into an uncertain grin at the joke which he obviously did not understand.

I felt sick inside as I looked at his dull, <u>vacuous</u> smile, the wide, bright eyes of a child, uncertain but eager to please. They were laughing at him because he was mentally retarded.

And I had been laughing at him too.

Suddenly, I was furious at myself and all those who were smirking at him. I jumped up and shouted, "Shut up! Leave him alone! It's not his fault he can't understand! He can't help what he is! But for God's sake . . . he's still a human being!"

The room grew silent; I cursed myself for losing control and creating a scene. I tried not to look at the boy as I paid my check and walked out without touching my food. I felt ashamed for both of us.

How strange it is that people of honest feelings and <u>sensibility</u>, who would not take advantage of a man born without arms or legs or eyes—how such people think nothing of abusing a man born with low intelligence. It infuriated me to think that not too long ago, I, like this boy, had foolishly played the clown. And I had almost forgotten.

> What does Charlie find strange about how people treat the dishwasher? How does he feel about his own past behavior?

I'd hidden the picture of the old Charlie Gordon from myself because now that I was intelligent, it was something that had to be pushed out of my mind. But today in looking at that boy, for the first time I saw what I had been. *I was just like him!*

Only a short time ago, I learned that people laughed at me. Now I can see that unknowingly I joined with them in laughing at myself. That hurts most of all.

> What disturbs Charlie most about his past?

I have often reread my progress reports and seen the <u>illiteracy</u>, the childish naïveté—the mind of low intelligence peering from a dark room, through the keyhole, at the dazzling light outside. I see that even in my dullness I knew that I was inferior, and that other people had something I lacked—something denied me. In my mental blindness, I thought that it was somehow connected with the ability to read and write, and I was sure that if I could get those skills I would automatically have intelligence too.

Even a feeble-minded man wants to be like other men.

A child may not know how to feed itself or what to eat, yet it knows of hunger.

> To what does Charlie compare his desire for intelligence?

This, then, is what I was like. I never knew. Even with my gift of intellectual awareness, I never really knew.

This day was good for me. Seeing the past more clearly, I have decided to use my knowledge and skills to work in the field of increasing human intelligence levels. Who is better equipped for this work? Who else has lived in both worlds? These are my people. Let me use my gift to do something for them.

> How does Charlie decide to use his knowledge?

Tomorrow, I will discuss with Dr. Strauss the manner in which I can work in this area. I may be able to help him work out the problems of widespread use of the technique which was used on me. I have several good ideas of my own.

There is so much that might be done with this technique. If I could be made into a genius, what about thousands of others like myself? What fantastic levels might be achieved by using this technique on normal people? on *geniuses?*

---

words for everyday use

vac • u • ous (vak´yoo əs) *adj.,* devoid of interest or thought; empty. *By the <u>vacuous</u> look in her eyes, I could tell that my speech was boring.*

sen • si • bil • i • ty (sen´sə bil´ə tē) *n.,* capacity for being affected emotionally or intellectually. *A person of honest feeling and <u>sensibility</u> would never have left those people behind.*

il • lit • er • a • cy (il lit´ər ə sē) *n.,* state of being unable to read and write. *Jacob wants to be a teacher, so he decided to join an organization that helps to fight <u>illiteracy</u> in his city.*

684   UNIT EIGHT / THE GENIUS WITHIN

There are so many doors to open. I am impatient to begin.

Progress Report 12
May 23

It happened today. Algernon bit me. I visited the lab to see him, as I do occasionally, and when I took him out of his cage, he snapped at my hand. I put him back and watched him for a while. He was unusually disturbed and vicious.

May 24

Burt, who is in charge of the experimental animals, tells me that Algernon is changing. He is less cooperative; he refuses to run the maze anymore; general motivation has decreased. And he hasn't been eating. Everyone is upset about what this may mean.

May 25

They've been feeding Algernon, who now refuses to work the shifting-lock problem. Everyone identifies me with Algernon. In a way we're both the first of our kind. They're all pretending that Algernon's behavior is not necessarily significant for me. But it's hard to hide the fact that some of the other animals who were used in this experiment are showing strange behavior.

Dr. Strauss and Dr. Nemur have asked me not to come to the lab any more. I know what they're thinking, but I can't accept it. I am going ahead with my plans to carry their research forward. With all due respect to both of these fine scientists, I am well aware of their limitations. If there is an answer, I'll have to find it out for myself.

> **What do people pretend?**

> **What is becoming important to Charlie? Why might this be?**

Suddenly, time has become very important to me.

May 29

I have been given a lab of my own and permission to go ahead with the research. I'm onto something. Working day and night. I've had a cot moved into the lab. Most of my writing time is spent on the notes which I keep in a separate folder, but from time to time I feel it necessary to put down my moods and my thoughts out of sheer habit.

I find the *calculus of intelligence* to be a fascinating study. Here is the place for the application of all the knowledge I have acquired. In a sense it's the problem I've been concerned with all my life.

May 31

Dr. Strauss thinks I'm working too hard. Dr. Nemur says I'm trying to cram a lifetime of research and thought into a few weeks. I know I should rest, but I'm driven on by something inside that won't let me stop. I've got to find the reason for the sharp <u>regression</u> in Algernon. I've got to know *if* and *when* it will happen to me.

> **What does Charlie hope to learn in his research?**

June 4
Letter to Dr. Strauss (copy)

Dear Dr. Strauss:

Under separate cover I am sending you a copy of my report entitled "The Algernon-Gordon Effect: A Study of Structure and Function of Increased Intelligence," which I would like to have you read and have published.

As you see, my experiments are completed. I have included in my report all of my formulae, as well as mathematical analyses in the appendix. Of course, these should be <u>verified</u>.

---

words for everyday use

re • gres • sion (ri gresh´ən) *n.*, reversion to a simpler or earlier form. *The four-year-old child's desire to drink from a baby bottle represented a serious <u>regression</u>.*

ver • i • fy (ver´ə fī´) *vt.*, check the accuracy or correctness of. *I called the bus station to <u>verify</u> the time of my brother's arrival.*

---

1. People pretend that Algernon's behavior is not necessarily significant for Charlie.
2. Time has become important to Charlie. Because of what is happening to Algernon, he senses that he does not have much time to find an answer to problems related to Dr. Strauss and Dr. Nemur's research.
3. Charlie hopes to understand the regression in Algernon's behavior and when and if such a regression will occur in him.

CROSS-CURRICULAR CONNECTIONS

PSYCHOLOGY. For most of the twentieth century, psychologists accepted the idea that intelligence was largely inherited. Their acceptance of this idea was based on studies performed by the British psychologist Cyril Burt. Burt claimed to have studied hundreds of identical twins raised separately from one another and to have found high correlations in their scores on intelligence tests. Burt's studies led psychologists to believe that as much as 85 percent of intelligence was due to hereditary factors. Such a figure would, of course, have dramatic social and political implications. However, Burt's data proved to have been falsified. Today, most people accept that intelligence is a combination of both hereditary and environmental factors, a more sanguine view because it leaves open the possibility that intelligence can be improved through such means as adequate prenatal care, nutrition during the growth years, and instruction.

Because of its importance to both you and Dr. Nemur (and need I say to myself, too?) I have checked and rechecked my results a dozen times in the hope of finding an error. I am sorry to say the results must stand. Yet for the sake of science, I am grateful for the little bit that I here add to the knowledge of the human mind and the laws governing the artificial increase of human intelligence.

I recall your once saying to me that an experimental *failure* or the *disproving* of a theory was as important to the advancement of learning as a success would be. I know now that this is true. I am sorry, however, that my own contribution to the field must rest upon the ashes of the work of two men I regard so highly.

> Yours truly,
>
> encl.: rept.   Charles Gordon

June 5

I must not become emotional. The facts and the results of my experiments are clear, and the more sensational aspects of my own rapid climb cannot obscure the fact that the tripling of intelligence by the surgical technique developed by Drs. Strauss and Nemur must be viewed as having little or no practical applicability (at the present time) to the increase of human intelligence.

As I review the records and data on Algernon, I see that although he is still in his physical infancy, he has regressed mentally. Motor activity[20] is impaired; there is a general reduction of glandular activity; there is an accelerated loss of coordination.

There are also strong indications of progressive amnesia.

What has happened to Algernon?

As will be seen by my report, these and other physical and mental deterioration syndromes

can be predicted with statistically significant[21] results by the application of my formula.

The surgical stimulus to which we were both subjected has resulted in an intensification and acceleration of all mental processes. The unforeseen development, which I have taken the liberty of calling the Algernon-Gordon Effect, is the logical extension[22] of the entire intelligence speedup. The hypothesis here proven may be described simply in the following terms: Artificially increased intelligence deteriorates at a rate of time directly proportional to the quantity of the increase.

I feel that this, in itself, is an important discovery.

As long as I am able to write, I will continue to record my thoughts in these progress reports. It is one of my few pleasures. However, by all indications, my own mental deterioration will be very rapid.

I have already begun to notice signs of emotional instability[23] and forgetfulness, the first symptoms of the burn-out.

What does Charlie see as the first signs of his mental deterioration?

June 10

Deterioration progressing. I have become absentminded. Algernon died two days ago. Dissection shows my predictions were right.

His brain had decreased in weight, and there was a general smoothing out of cerebral convolutions as well as a deepening and broadening of brain fissures.[24]

---

20. **Motor activity.** Muscular movement
21. **statistically significant.** Observed departure from a hypothesis too large to be attributed to chance
22. **logical extension.** Reasonable continuation
23. **emotional instability.** Unsteady mental state
24. **cerebral convolutions . . . brain fissures.** Flattening of the bulges on the surface of the brain and deepening of the grooves that separate the brain's sections

---

words for everyday use

ob • scure (əb skyoor´) vt., conceal or hide. *The dense fog obscured our view of the fireworks.*

ap • pli • ca • bil • i • ty (ap´li kə bil´ə tē) n., appropriateness; usefulness. *When filling out the questionnaire, be sure of the applicability of each numbered item.*

syn • drome (sin´drōm) n., multiple symptoms characterizing a specific disease or condition. *The syndrome mentioned in the medical book sounds unpleasant.*

pro • por • tion • al (prō pôr´shə nəl) adj., having the same ratio. *Sales are proportional to the effectiveness of the sales force.*

I guess the same thing is or will soon be happening to me. Now that it's definite, I don't want it to happen.

I put Algernon's body in a cheese box and buried him in the backyard. I cried.

June 15

Dr. Strauss came to see me again. I wouldn't open the door, and I told him to go away. I want to be left to myself. I have become touchy and irritable. I feel the darkness closing in. It's hard to throw off thoughts of suicide. I keep telling myself how important this <u>introspective</u> journal will be.

It's a strange sensation to pick up a book that you've read and enjoyed just a few months ago and discover that you don't remember it. I remembered how great I thought John Milton was, but when I picked up *Paradise Lost* I couldn't understand it at all. I got so angry I threw the book across the room.

I've got to try to hold on to some of it. Some of the things I've learned. Oh, God, please don't take it all away.

> How does Charlie feel about losing his intelligence?

June 19

Sometimes, at night, I go out for a walk. Last night I couldn't remember where I lived. A policeman took me home. I have the strange feeling that this has all happened to me before—a long time ago. I keep telling myself I'm the only person in the world who can describe what's happening to me.

June 21

Why can't I remember? I've got to fight. I lie in bed for days, and I don't know who or where I am. Then it all comes back to me in a flash. Fugues[25] of amnesia. Symptoms of senility—

second childhood. I can watch them coming on. It's so cruelly logical. I learned so much and so fast. Now my mind is deteriorating rapidly. I won't let it happen. I'll fight it. I can't help thinking of the boy in the restaurant, the blank expression, the silly smile, the people laughing at him. No—please—not that again. . . .

June 22

I'm forgetting things that I learned recently. It seems to be following the classic pattern—the last things learned are the first things forgotten. Or is that the pattern? I'd better look it up again. . . .

I reread my paper on the Algernon-Gordon Effect, and I get the strange feeling that it was written by someone else. There are parts I don't even understand.

Motor activity impaired. I keep tripping over things, and it becomes increasingly difficult to type.

June 23

I've given up using the typewriter completely. My coordination is bad. I feel that I'm moving slower and slower. Had a terrible shock today. I picked up a copy of an article I used in my research, Krueger's "Uber psychische Ganzheit," to see if it would help me understand what I had done. First I thought there was something wrong with my eyes. Then I realized I could no longer read German. I tested myself in other languages. All gone.

June 30

A week since I dared to write again. It's slipping away like sand through my fingers. Most of the books I have are too hard for me now. I get angry with them because I know that I read and understood them just a few weeks ago.

---

25. **Fugues.** Dream states in which people act unconsciously

ANSWER TO GUIDED READING QUESTION

1. He wants to try desperately to hold on to his intelligence.

ADDITIONAL QUESTIONS AND ACTIVITIES

You may want to read passages of John Milton's *Paradise Lost* in class. Then have discussion about why Daniel Keyes chose to include this particular title in the selection. Ask them to discuss the plot of "Flowers for Algernon" and how it is similar to *Paradise Lost*.

---

words for everyday use

in • tro • spec • tive (in′trō spek′tiv) *adj.*, looking within oneself in an analytical way. *Jamie is an <u>introspective</u> person who likes to record her thoughts in a journal.*

1. Charlie hopes that from his reports someone will be able to learn about what is happening to him. This task has become more difficult because Charlie is having trouble remembering words and spellings.
2. Charlie remembers his father's drunkenness and his parents' arguments about money.
3. Mrs. Flynn tells Charlie that she does not like loafers.
4. Charlie brings flowers to Algernon's grave because Algernon was special to him.

ADDITIONAL QUESTIONS AND ACTIVITIES

Ask students the following questions: What emotions is Charlie experiencing as the results of the operation begin to reverse? Why, at this particular time in his life, might Charlie be remembering his parents? Ask students to write about particular experiences and feelings that remind them of childhood. Encourage students to freewrite about particularly clear childhood memories.

Answers

Students might say that Charlie is lonely, hurt, confused, and afraid. These might be emotions that he regularly experienced when he was a child, and that might be why childhood memories are surfacing at this particular time. He is also in need of love and care, and might like to have loving parental figures at this time. Give students adequate time during which to freewrite about their own childhood memories.

I keep telling myself I must keep writing these reports so that somebody will know what is happening to me. But it gets harder to form the words and remember spellings. I have to look up even simple words in the dictionary now, and it makes me impatient with myself.

Why does Charlie keep writing the reports? In what way has this task become more difficult?

Dr. Strauss comes around almost every day, but I told him I wouldn't see or speak to anybody. He feels guilty. They all do. But I don't blame anyone. I knew what might happen. But how it hurts.

July 7

I don't know where the week went. Todays Sunday I know because I can see through my window people going to church. I think I stayed in bed all week but I remember Mrs. Flynn bringing food to me a few times. I keep saying over and over Ive got to do something but then I forget and maybe its just easier not to do what I say Im going to do.

I think of my mother and father a lot these days. I found a picture of them with me taken at a beach. My father has a big ball under his arm and my mother is holding me by the hand. I dont remember them the way they are in the picture. All I remember is my father drunk most of the time and arguing with mom about money.

What does Charlie remember about his mother and father?

He never shaved much and he used to scratch my face when he hugged me. My mother said he died but Cousin Miltie said he heard his mom and dad say that my father ran away with another woman. When I asked my mother she slapped my face and said my father was dead. I dont think I ever found out which was true but I dont care much. (He said he was going to take me to see cows on a farm once but he never did. He never kept his promises. . . .)

July 10

My landlady Mrs Flynn is very worried about me. She says the way I lay around all day and dont do anything I remind her of her son before she threw him out of the house. She said she doesnt like loafers. If Im sick its one thing, but if Im a loafer thats another thing and she wont have it. I told her I think Im sick.

What does Mrs. Flynn say to Charlie?

I try to read a little bit every day, mostly stories, but sometimes I have to read the same thing over and over again because I dont know what it means. And its hard to write. I know I should look up all the words in the dictionary but its so hard and Im so tired all the time.

Then I got the idea that I would only use the easy words instead of the long hard ones. That saves time. I put flowers on Algernons grave about once a week. Mrs Flynn thinks Im crazy to put flowers on a mouses grave but I told her that Algernon was special.

Why does Charlie bring flowers to Algernon's grave?

July 14

Its Sunday again. I dont have anything to do to keep me busy now because my television set is broke and I dont have any money to get it fixed. (I think I lost this months check from the lab. I dont remember)

I get awful headaches and asperin doesnt help me much. Mrs Flynn knows Im really sick and she feels very sorry for me. Shes a wonderful woman whenever someone is sick.

July 22

Mrs Flynn called a strange doctor to see me. She was afraid I was going to die. I told the doctor I wasnt too sick and that I only forget sometimes. He asked me did I have any friends or relatives and I said no I dont have any. I told him I had a friend called Algernon once but he was a mouse and we used to run races together.

He looked at me kind of funny like he thought I was crazy.

He smiled when I told him I used to be a genius. He talked to me like I was a baby and he winked at Mrs Flynn. I got mad and chased him out because he was making fun of me the way they all used to.

> How does the "strange doctor" treat Charlie?

July 24

I have no more money and Mrs Flynn says I got to go to work somewhere and pay the rent because I havent paid for over two months. I dont know any work but the job I used to have at Donnegans Plastic Box Company. I dont want to go back there because they all knew me when I was smart and maybe they'll laugh at me. But I dont know what else to do to get money.

July 25

I was looking at some of my old progress reports and its very funny but I cant read what I wrote. I can make out some of the words but they dont make sense.

Miss Kinnian came to the door but I said go away I dont want to see you. She cried and I cried too but I wouldnt let her in because I didnt want her to laugh at me. I told her I didn't like her any more. I told her I didnt want to be smart any more. Thats not true. I still love her and I still want to be smart but I had to say that so shed go away. She gave Mrs. Flynn money to pay the rent. I dont want that. I got to get a job.

> What happens when Miss Kinnian visits Charlie?

Please . . . please let me not forget how to read and write. . . .

July 27

Mr. Donnegan was very nice when I came back and asked him for my old job of janitor. First he was very suspicious but I told him what

happened to me then he looked very sad and put his hand on my shoulder and said Charlie Gordon you got guts.

> Why does Mr. Donnegan say that Charlie has guts?

Everybody looked at me when I came downstairs and started working in the toilet sweeping it out like I used to. I told myself Charlie if they make fun of you dont get sore because you remember their not so smart as you once thot they were. And besides they were once your friends and if they laughed at you that doesnt mean anything because they liked you too.

One of the new men who came to work there after I went away made a nasty crack he said hey Charlie I hear your a very smart fella a real quiz kid. Say something intelligent. I felt bad but Joe Carp came over and grabbed him by the shirt and said leave him alone you lousy cracker or Ill break your neck. I didnt expect Joe to take my part so I guess hes really my friend.

Later Frank Reilly came over and said Charlie if anybody bothers you or trys to take advantage you call me or Joe and we will set em straight. I said thanks Frank and I got choked up so I had to turn around and go into the supply room so he wouldnt see me cry. Its good to have friends.

> How do Frank and Joe treat Charlie?

July 28

I did a dumb thing today I forgot I wasnt in Miss Kinnians class at the adult center any more like I use to be. I went in and sat down in my old seat in the back of the room and she looked at me funny and she said Charles. I dint remember she ever called me that before only Charlie so I said hello Miss Kinnian Im redy for my lesin today only I lost my reader that we was using. She startid to cry and run out of the room and everybody looked at me and I saw they wasnt the same pepul who use to be in my class.

Literary Tools
1. What is point of view? **Point of view is the vantage point from which a story is told.**
2. Whose point of view is used in this story? **The story is told from Charlie's point of view.**
3. What is foreshadowing? **Foreshadowing is the act of presenting materials that hint at events to occur later in a story.**
4. What event foreshadows Charlie's regression? **Algernon's regression foreshadows Charlie's regression.**

1. The doctor treats Charlie in a condescending manner, as if the experience had not been real and as though he thinks Charlie is crazy.
2. Charlie refuses to let Miss Kinnian in when she comes to see him. He does not want her to laugh at him. He shouts through the door that he does not like her and that he does not want to be smart anymore.
3. Mr. Donnegan feels that Charlie has guts because of all he has been through.
4. Frank and Joe stick up for Charlie when others make fun of him or are mean to him. They say they will take care of him.

SELECTION CHECK TEST 4.8.13 WITH ANSWERS

Checking Your Reading
1. How old is Charlie? **He is thirty-seven years old.**
2. What kind of report does Charlie write every day? **He writes a progress report.**
3. Who is Algernon? **Algernon is a laboratory mouse.**
4. Why does Charlie feel sorry for Robinson Crusoe? **He feels sorry for Robinson Crusoe because he is alone and doesn't have any friends.**
5. What happens to Algernon? **He regresses and dies.**

Vocabulary in Context
Fill in each blank below with the most appropriate word from the following Words for Everyday Use.

opportunist   justify   tangible   cower regression   introspective

1. We were pleased with Cori's progress but upset by her **regression** a few days later.
2. The winner receives honor as well as a **tangible** award, a trophy.
3. I realized Lucky was afraid of thunderstorms when I saw him **cower** under the table at the first thunderclap.
4. I don't have to **justify** my reasons to you.
5. Ted is very outgoing, but Liam is more **introspective**.

Then all of a suddin I remembered some things about the operashun and me getting smart and I said holy smoke I reely pulled a Charlie Gordon that time. I went away before she come back to the room.

Thats why Im going away from New York for good. I dont want to do nothing like that agen. I dont want Miss Kinnian to feel sorry for me. Evry body feels sorry at the factery and I dont want that eather so Im going someplace where nobody knows that Charlie Gordon was once a genius and now he cant even reed a book or rite good.

Im taking a cuple of books along and even if I cant reed them Ill practise hard and maybe I wont forget every thing I lerned. If I try reel hard maybe Ill be a littel bit smarter then I was before the operashun. I got my rabits foot and my luky penny and maybe they will help me.

If you ever reed this Miss Kinnian dont be sorry for me Im glad I got a second chanse to be smart becaus I lerned a lot of things I never even new were in this world and Im grateful that I saw it all for a littel bit. I dont know why Im dumb agen or what I did wrong maybe its becaus I dint try hard enuff. But if I try and practis very hard maybe Ill get a littl smarter and know what all the words are. I remember a little bit how nice I had a feeling with the blue book that has the torn cover when I red it. Thats why Im gonna keep trying to get smart so I can have that feeling agen. Its a good feeling to know things and be smart. I wish I had it rite now if I did I woud sit down and reed all the time. Anyway I bet Im the first dumb person in the world who ever found out somthing importent for sience. I remember I did something but I dont remember what. So I gess its like I did it for all the dumb pepul like me.

Goodby Miss Kinnian and Dr. Strauss and evreybody. And P.S. please tell Dr Nemur not to be such a grouch when pepul laff at him and he woud have more frends. Its easy to make frends if you let pepul laff at you. Im going to have lots of frends where I go.

What advice does Charlie give Dr. Nemur?

P.P.S. Please if you get a chanse put some flowers on Algernons grave in the bak yard. . . . ∎

Respond *to the* SELECTION

Would it have been better for Charlie never to have had intelligence than to have lost it in such a dramatic way? Why, or why not?

Investigate, Inquire, and Imagine

Recall: GATHERING FACTS

1a. What might happen to Charlie if he is selected for the experiment?

2a. With whom do the doctors identify Charlie?

3a. What "unforeseen development" does Charlie call the "Algernon-Gordon Effect"?

Interpret: FINDING MEANING

1b. Why does Charlie think he has failed all the tests?

2b. What actions on the part of Algernon show that he is regressing?

3b. What actions on the part of Charlie show that his intelligence is deteriorating?

Analyze: TAKING THINGS APART

4a. Irony is a difference between appearance and reality. In irony of situation, an event occurs that violates the expectations of the characters, the reader, or the audience. What is the irony of situation in "Flowers for Algernon"?

Synthesize: BRINGING THINGS TOGETHER

4b. Why does Charlie think that he's going to have lots of friends when he leaves New York? What sort of relationship between intelligence and happiness is described in the story?

Perspective: LOOKING AT OTHER VIEWS

5a. Imagine that you are Miss Kinnian in the selection. How did you feel on July 28 when you saw Charlie sitting in his old seat at the adult center class? What was particularly difficult about watching Charlie decline?

Empathy: SEEING FROM INSIDE

5b. What aspects of Charlie's deteriorating intelligence are the most painful for him? Why? What aspects of the regression does Charlie seem to welcome? Why?

Understanding Literature

POINT OF VIEW. Review the definition for **point of view** in the Handbook of Literary Terms. Consider the following passage from the selection:

> "Once again now I have the feeling of shame burning inside me. This intelligence has driven a wedge between me and all the people I once knew and loved. Before, they laughed at me and despised me for my ignorance and dullness; now, they hate me for my knowledge and understanding. What in God's name do they want of me?"

What private thoughts does Charlie reveal? With what emotional conflict is he struggling? Would a different point of view change the reader's conception of this conflict? Why, or why not?

FORESHADOWING. Review the definition for **foreshadowing** in the Handbook of Literary Terms. How does what happens to Algernon after the operation foreshadow what will happen to Charlie? What does the image of Algernon's grave foreshadow?

"FLOWERS FOR ALGERNON" 691

Answers to Understanding Literature can be found on page 690.

ANSWERS TO INVESTIGATE, INQUIRE, AND IMAGINE

RECALL

1a. His intelligence rate may increase (he'll get smarter), but it may not be permanent.

2a. The doctors identify Charlie with Algernon, the laboratory mouse.

3a. The "unforeseen development" of the "Algernon-Gordon Effect" is the deterioration of artificially increased intelligence "at a rate of time directly proportional to the quantity of the increase."

INTERPRET

1b. He thinks he has failed all the tests because he doesn't "see" pictures in an inkblot, he can't make up stories about pictures, and Algernon beats him at the maze.

2b. Algernon's regression shows in his increased irritability, disinterest in food, refusal to run the maze, and decreased motivation.

3b. Charlie's regression shows in his forgetfulness, inability to focus, declining motor skills, and declining spelling and language skills.

ANALYZE

4a. The irony of the situation is that before the operation, Charlie has trouble communicating with people both orally and on paper. After the operation, as he becomes more and more intelligent, Charlie finds himself again having trouble communicating. This time, it is because he is thinking, speaking, and writing at a level much higher than that of the general population.

SYNTHESIZE

4b. Charlie believes that "its easy to make frends if you let pepul laff at you." Charlie thinks that he will have many friends wherever he goes because people will be laughing at him. The story describes a world in which intelligence does not necessarily ensure happiness, nor does the lack of intelligence ensure it.

PERSPECTIVE

5a. Miss Kinnian probably feels upset and disappointed that this has happened to Charlie. She may feel guilty about her role in his situation.

EMPATHY

5b. For Charlie, his regressing intelligence is made painful by losing what he loved most about his intelligence—the ability to read and understand books and the ability to think and remember. Perhaps the most painful aspect for Charlie is that he remembers what it feels like to be "the boy in the restaurant, the blank expression, the silly smile, the people laughing at him. No— please—not that again..."

ANSWERS TO INTEGRATING THE LANGUAGE ARTS

Language, Grammar, and Style
1. gerund: experimenting, modifier: dangerous
2. gerund: writing, modifier: diary
3. gerund: thinking, modifier: subconscious and conscious
4. gerund: blushing, modifier: his
5. gerund: forgetting, modifier: progressive

Speaking and Listening & Collaborative Learning
Students might do a freewriting exercise from Charlie's point of view. Ideas gathered in this freewrite could be developed for the skit. After the dramatic presentations, students can discuss the difficulties Charlie would face in a new location and whether he made a wise move in leaving the city.

Writer's Journal

1. Imagine that you are Charlie. Write an **obituary** for Algernon to publish in the laboratory's newsletter, commenting on Algernon's contributions to science.
2. Pretend that you are Dr. Strauss. Charlie refuses to talk to you once his brain deterioration sets in, yet you want to convey to him your sincere apology for the turn of events. Write Dr. Strauss's **letter of apology**.
3. What was Charlie like before the operation? after? Write a **character analysis** of Charlie before and after the experiment.

Integrating the Language Arts

Language, Grammar, and Style

MODIFIERS FOR GERUNDS. Review the Language Arts Survey 3.80, "Verbals: Participles, Gerunds, and Infinitives." Then identify the gerunds and their modifiers in the following sentences.

1. Is human experimenting dangerous?
2. Charlie's diary writing reveals increased intelligence.
3. The doctor explained both subconscious and conscious thinking to Charlie.
4. Charlie was ashamed of his blushing.
5. Progressive forgetting bothered Charlie.

Speaking and Listening & Collaborative Learning

DRAMATIC SKIT. With three or four other students, write a brief play about one day in Charlie's life. Set the time one month from the end of the story and in the town to which you think Charlie has moved. Break the play, by scene, into the three major divisions of the day: morning, afternoon, and evening. Show Charlie as you imagine him in his new life, perhaps with new friends, perhaps looking for another job or a place to live. Write a part for each person in your group. After rehearsing your three-scene play, present it to the rest of the class.

Study and Research

RESEARCHING COUNTRIES. The word *Hindustani* means, literally, "dweller in northern India." It is also the word for a dialect of Western Hindi. This dialect is used as the language for trade in northern India. Charlie mentions the scientific work being done in India and China. Look up these countries and try to find information about their science and technology programs. You may also want to research the history, people, geography, and social customs of these countries.

"SHORT ASSIGNMENTS"
by Anne Lamott

Reader's resource

Anne Lamott's essay **"Short Assignments"** is taken from her book *Bird by Bird: Some Instructions on Writing and Life.* In *Bird by Bird*, Lamott wants to share "everything that has helped me along the way and what [writing] is like for me on a daily basis." In doing so she also gives us "the excuse to do things, go places and explore." "Short Assignments" teaches us how to focus on manageable objectives when we write.

About the AUTHOR

Anne Lamott (1954–) was raised in Northern California. She credits her father, also a writer, for teaching her how to "be bold and original and to let [herself] make mistakes." Her father's example and her own love of reading helped her realize, at a relatively early age, the sense of power and connection that good books can elicit. "I came to know," she writes in *Bird by Bird,* "what it was like to have someone speak for me, to close a book with a sense of both triumph and relief, one lonely isolated social animal finally making contact." And it was writing about her father's death that brought Lamott to her first published work, when she was twenty-six.

Lamott has published several novels, including *Hard Laughter* (1980), *Rosie* (1983), *Joe Jones* (1985), *All New People* (1989) and *Crooked Little Heart* (1997). In addition, she has written memoirs, *Operating Instructions* (1993) and *Traveling Mercies* (1999), and many articles and reviews for magazines. *Bird by Bird: Some Instructions on Writing and Life* (1994), is perhaps her best-known work to date.

Reader's Journal

What problems have you encountered when given a writing assignment?

Literary TOOLS

PERSONAL ESSAY. A **personal essay** is a short work of nonfictional prose on a single topic related to the life or interests of the writer. Personal essays are often, but not always, written in the first person. Also, review the definition for *essay* in the Handbook of Literary Terms. As you read the selection, note the use of personal material taken from the writer's experience.

COLLOQUIALISM AND **TONE. Colloquialism** is the use of informal language. **Tone** is the emotional attitude toward the reader or toward the subject implied by a literary work. As you read, look for examples of colloquialism in Lamott's writing and identify the tone she uses.

Organizer

Make a chart of colloquial expressions used in the essay and their equivalents in standard, formal English.

Colloquialisms	Formal English
Maybe I could find some boyfriend who is not a total and complete *fixer-upper.*	Maybe I could find some boyfriend who does not need much improvement.

ADDITIONAL RESOURCES

UNIT 8 RESOURCE BOOK
- Selection Worksheet 8.8
- Selection Check Test 4.8.15
- Selection Test 4.8.16
- Language, Grammar, and Style Resource 3.2

VOCABULARY FROM THE SELECTION

arresting
leering

GRAPHIC ORGANIZER

Students should include the following examples in their charts:
Colloquialism: get a grip
Formal: calm down and focus

Colloquialism: make a dent
Formal: make inroads in

Colloquialism: right up there with
Formal: is equal to

READER'S JOURNAL

You may have students brainstorm a list of problems together. Then if students have any suggestions for dealing with these problems, they can offer them to the class.

GOALS/OBJECTIVES

Studying this lesson will enable students to
- gain perspective on their own writing process
- understand how Lamott approaches writing
- define *personal essay,* and explain how the term relates to the selection
- define *colloquialism* and *tone* and recognize the use of these techniques in the selection
- rephrase informal English into formal English
- write a personal essay

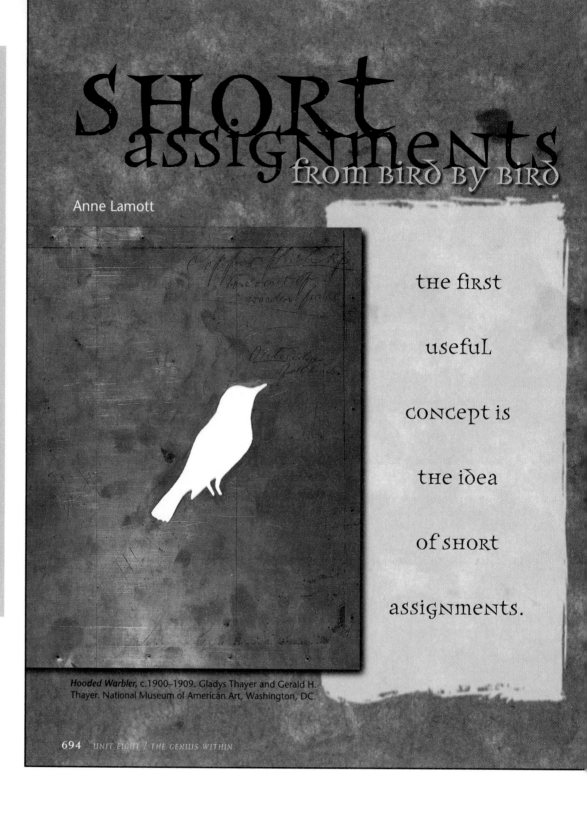

Hooded Warbler, c.1900–1909. Gladys Thayer and Gerald H. Thayer. National Museum of American Art, Washington, DC.

INDIVIDUAL LEARNING STRATEGIES

MOTIVATION
Lamott uses the image of a one-inch picture frame to create a small assignment for herself. Have students try this. If students have trouble getting to a small piece, have them start off thinking about a place they know well, for example, a city or their house. Then have them zoom in on a smaller part of this place (the corner of 12th and Broadway or their kitchen).

READING PROFICIENCY
Students should note the two main images in this selection that Lamott applies to writing. One is the image of a one-inch picture frame. The other is the image of taking things bird by bird.

ENGLISH LANGUAGE LEARNING
Lamott uses many colloquialisms in her writing. Students can work with other students when filling out their graphic organizers to understand the meaning of these expressions.

SPECIAL NEEDS
Students should pay special attention to the Guided Reading questions and the Recall questions in the Investigate, Inquire, and Imagine section.

ENRICHMENT
Interested students can read the rest of *Bird by Bird*. Ask students to identify the advice from Lamott that they feel is most helpful. Then ask students to try to follow the advice. Students can discuss their experiences doing so.

Often when you sit down to write, what you have in mind is an autobiographical novel about your childhood, or a play about the immigrant experience, or a history of—oh, say—say women. But this is like trying to scale a glacier. It's hard to get your footing, and your fingertips get all red and frozen and torn up. Then your mental illnesses arrive at the desk like your sickest, most secretive relatives. And they pull up chairs in a semicircle around the computer, and they try to be quiet but you know they are there with their weird coppery breath, leering at you behind your back.

> To what does the author compare the act of sitting down to write?

What I do at this point, as the panic mounts and the jungle drums begin beating and I realize that the well has run dry and that my future is behind me and I'm going to have to get a job only I'm completely unemployable, is to stop. First I try to breathe, because I'm either sitting there panting like a lapdog or I'm unintentionally making slow asthmatic death rattles. So I just sit there for a minute, breathing slowly, quietly. I let my mind wander. After a moment I may notice that I'm trying to decide whether or not I am too old for orthodontia[1] and whether right now would be a good time to make a few calls, and then I start to think about learning to use makeup and how maybe I could find some boyfriend who is not a total and complete fixer-upper and then my life would be totally great and I'd be happy all the time, and then I think about all the people I should have called back before I sat down to work, and how I should probably at least check in with my agent and tell him this great idea I have and see if *he* thinks it's a good idea, and see if *he* thinks I need orthodontia—if that is what he is actually

thinking whenever we have lunch together. Then I think about someone I'm really annoyed with, or some financial problem that is driving me crazy, and decide that I must resolve this before I get down to today's work. So I become a dog with a chew toy, worrying it for a while, wrestling it to the ground, flinging it over my shoulder, chasing it, licking it, chewing it, flinging it back over my shoulder. I stop just short of actually barking. But all of this only takes somewhere between one and two minutes, so I haven't actually wasted that much time. Still, it leaves me winded. I go back to trying to breathe, slowly and calmly, and I finally notice the one-inch picture frame that I put on my desk to remind me of short assignments.

> What helps Lamott to calm down enough to focus on writing?

It reminds me that all I have to do is to write down as much as I can see through a one-inch picture frame. This is all I have to bite off for the time being. All I am going to do right now, for example, is write that one paragraph that sets the story in my hometown, in the late fifties, when the trains were still running. I am going to paint a picture of it, in words, on my word processor. Or all I am going to do is to describe the main character the very first time we meet her, when she first walks out the front door and onto the porch. I am not even going to describe the expression on her face when she first notices the blind dog sitting behind the wheel of her car—just what I can see through the one-inch picture frame, just one paragraph describing this woman, in the town where I grew up, the first time we encounter her.

---

1. **orthodontia.** Branch of dentistry dealing with irregularities of the teeth and their correction (as by means of braces)

---

words for everyday use

leer • ing (lēr′ iŋ) *adj.,* casting a sidelong glance that is lascivious, knowing, or wanton. *Carol looked away from the stranger's leering expression.*

1. She compares writing to scaling a glacier: "It's hard to get your footing, and your fingertips get all red and frozen and torn up."
2. Breathing slowly and thinking about filling a one-inch picture frame with her story helps Lamott focus her thoughts.

INTERNET RESOURCE

Some students may be interested in reading more by Anne Lamott. In addition to her books, she has written a column called *Word by Word.* Students can access past articles at www.salon.com.

1. Doctorow says that writing is "like
driving a car at night. You can see
only as far as your headlights, but
you can make the whole trip that
way."
2. The story sometimes gives her
students hope, so that they do not
feel overwhelmed.
3. Writing can be desperate "because
it is about some of our deepest
needs" as human beings.
4. She suggests that readers should
display "Lighten up" on their wall as
a reminder not to take things too
seriously or too hard.

SELECTION CHECK TEST 4.8.15 WITH ANSWERS

Checking Your Reading
1. To what does Lamott compare sitting down to write something? **She compares it to trying to scale a glacier.**
2. What, according to Lamott, is the first useful concept? **The first useful concept is the idea of short assignments.**
3. What visual clue does Lamott have to help her remember not to be overwhelmed? **She has a one-inch picture frame.**
4. Why did her father say "bird by bird"? **He said it to help Lamott's brother who was overwhelmed by a project on birds.**
5. What advice from the movie *Stripes* does Lamott suggest we follow? **She suggests we "lighten up."**

Literary Tools
1. What is the subject of this personal essay? **This personal essay offers advice about writing based on the author's experience.**
2. Define *colloquialism*. **Colloquialism is the use of informal language.**
3. Give an example of a colloquialism. *Responses will vary.*
4. What is tone? **Tone is the emotional attitude toward the subject implied by a literary work.**
5. What tone does Lamott use in this essay? **Lamott uses a casual, conversational tone.**

E. L. Doctorow[2] once said that "writing a novel is like driving a car at night. You can see only as far as your headlights, but you can make the whole trip that way." You don't have to see where you're going, you don't have to see your destination or everything you will pass along the way. You just have to see two or three feet ahead of you. This is right up there with the best advice about writing, or life, I have ever heard.

> *What is the good advice she gets from E. L. Doctorow?*

So after I've completely exhausted myself thinking about the people I most resent in the world, and my more <u>arresting</u> financial problems, and, of course, the orthodontia, I remember to pick up the one-inch picture frame and to figure out a one-inch piece of my story to tell, one small scene, one memory, one exchange. I also remember a story that I know I've told elsewhere but that over and over helps me to get a grip: thirty years ago my older brother, who was ten years old at the time, was trying to get a report on birds written that he'd had three months to write, which was due the next day. We were out at our family cabin in Bolinas, and he was at the kitchen table close to tears, surrounded by binder paper and pencils and unopened books on birds, immobilized by the hugeness of the task ahead. Then my father sat down beside him, put his arm around my brother's shoulder, and said, "Bird by bird, buddy. Just take it bird by bird."

I tell this story again because it usually makes a dent in the tremendous sense of being overwhelmed that my students experience. Sometimes it actually gives them hope, and hope, as Chesterton[3] said, is the power of being cheerful in circumstances that we know to be desperate. Writing can be a pretty desperate endeavor,

> *What does the telling of the "bird by bird" story sometimes give Lamott's students?*

because it is about some of our deepest needs: our need to be visible, to be heard, our need to make sense of our lives, to wake up and grow and belong. It is no wonder if we sometimes tend to take ourselves perhaps a bit too seriously. So here is another story I tell often.

> *How is writing a "desperate endeavor"?*

In the Bill Murray[4] movie *Stripes*, in which he joins the army, there is a scene that takes place the first night of boot camp, where Murray's platoon is assembled in the barracks. They are supposed to be getting to know their sergeant, played by Warren Oates, and one another. So each man takes a few moments to say a few things about who he is and where he is from. Finally it is the turn of this incredibly intense, angry guy named Francis. "My name is Francis," he says. "No one calls me Francis—anyone here calls me Francis and I'll kill them. And another thing. I don't like to be touched. Anyone here ever tries to touch me, I'll kill them," at which point Warren Oates jumps in and says, "Hey—lighten up, Francis."

This is not a bad line to have taped to the wall of your office.

Say to yourself in the kindest possible way, Look, honey, all we're going to do for now is to write a description of the river at sunrise, or the young child swimming in the pool at the club, or the first time the man sees the woman he will marry. That is all we are going to do for now. We are just going to take this bird by bird. But we are going to finish this *one* short assignment. ∎

> *What does Lamott suggest that readers should do with the movie phrase she quotes?*

2. **E. L. Doctorow.** (1931–) American novelist
3. **Chesterton.** G. K. Chesterton (1874–1936) was a British writer and critic.
4. **Bill Murray.** American film and television comedian

words for everyday use	**ar • rest • ing** (ə rest' iŋ) *adj.*, catching the attention; striking; impressive. *For officer Nelson, seeing the dog at the wheel of the Chevrolet was an <u>arresting</u> experience.*

ANSWERS TO UNDERSTANDING LITERATURE

PERSONAL ESSAY. Lamott's use of the personal essay is an effective way to demonstrate to readers that she understands the difficulties they often face when first attempting to write. By relating her own frustrations, Lamott is able to earn the reader's trust and offer tools that they will be more likely to try because they have worked for her.

COLLOQUIALISM AND TONE. Lamott refers to a "fixer-upper" boyfriend, talks about how to "get a grip" on a writing assignment, how to "make a dent" in that assignment, and calls a writing tip "right up there" with the best advice about writing. This use of colloquial language contributes to the intimate, conversational tone of the essay.

Respond *to the* SELECTION

What are some examples of short assignments that Lamott would approve of if you were writing a short story?

Investigate, *Inquire,* and Imagine

Recall: GATHERING FACTS

1a. What does Lamott say writers often have in mind when they first sit down to write?

2a. What thoughts often distract Lamott while she writes?

3a. What movie phrase helps keep Lamott and her students from taking themselves too seriously?

Interpret: FINDING MEANING

1b. What does Lamott mean when she compares one's first attempts at writing to "trying to scale a glacier"?

2b. Characterize the kind of thoughts that go through Lamott's mind. Why do these thoughts keep her from writing?

3b. Think about the quote from the movie *Stripes.* What makes this quote an especially apt way for Lamott to make her point? What point might she be making that she doesn't state directly?

Analyze: TAKING THINGS APART

4a. Identify the potential obstacles writers face when starting a new writing project.

Synthesize: BRINGING THINGS TOGETHER

4b. What is the ultimate goal of Lamott's advice about "short assignments"? What does she want writers to be able to do?

Evaluate: MAKING JUDGMENTS

5a. Do you think Lamott's advice for writing is helpful? Why, or why not?

Extend: CONNECTING IDEAS

5b. How might Lamott's advice apply to other aspects of your own life? In what other circumstances might the "bird by bird" approach help you to reach your goals?

Understanding *Literature*

PERSONAL ESSAY. Review the definition for **personal essay** in Literary Tools in Prereading. What makes the personal essay an effective way for Lamott to express her ideas about how to write short assignments?

COLLOQUIALISM AND TONE. Review the definitions for **colloquialism** and **tone** in the Handbook of Literary Terms and the chart you made for Literary Tools on page 693. What colloquialisms does Lamott employ? How does her use of colloquial language contribute to the tone of the essay?

"SHORT ASSIGNMENTS" **697**

RESPOND TO THE SELECTION

What did you learn from reading this selection? How will Lamott's advice help you in your next writing assignment?

ANSWERS TO INVESTIGATE, INQUIRE, AND IMAGINE

RECALL

1a. Writers will often have in mind "an autobiographical novel about your childhood, or a play about the immigrant experience, or a history of… women."

2a. Her mind worries over getting her teeth fixed, making phone calls, learning how to use makeup, and finding an appropriate boyfriend.

3a. "Hey—lighten up, Francis."

INTERPRET

1b. Often writers' first attempts are plagued by taking on a subject that is too large, too grand, or too abstract. Writers often don't know how to give themselves a manageable assignment to get started.

2b. Lamott is distracted by thoughts about her everyday life. These mundane worries interrupt her writing because Lamott has been trying to take on too large or too indistinct a subject. The everyday thoughts shove their way into consciousness because they are concrete and immediate, as opposed to her writing topic.

3b. The Francis character wants to prohibit anyone from using his real name and from even touching him. This seems to suggest that when we take ourselves too seriously, as Francis does, we end up unable to express ourselves and gain recognition.

ANALYZE

4a. Writers may feel overwhelmed by the immensity of a chosen subject or lost in its abstractness. Because it is often difficult to address a large subject, writers may find themselves distracted by mundane concerns. Since writing often speaks to many of our deepest needs, a writer may take him- or herself too seriously. Too much intensity can deaden one's writing.

SYNTHESIZE

4b. At the most basic level, Lamott hopes her advice will help writers simply to begin, to get them past the big, white wall of the blank page. Yet even though she advises writers not

---

ANSWERS TO INVESTIGATE, INQUIRE, AND IMAGINE (CONT.)

to take themselves too seriously, she nevertheless offers a way to produce significant work by dividing it into manageable, smaller sections.

EVALUATE

5a. Students who find that Lamott's advice is helpful might mention that breaking up a writing assignment into manageable, smaller pieces is effective.

EMPATHY

5b. Students might find that other tasks that seem daunting, for example exploring and applying for college, or making another major decision, are easier if they break them into small parts. Students may also find that they are happier if they remember to "lighten up" and not take things too seriously.

Answers to Understanding Literature can be found on page 696.

Writer's Journal

1. Write a **letter** to Lamott, telling her which advice about writing in her essay you find helpful.
2. Write a **descriptive paragraph** about a friend. Describe your friend as he or she was at the very first moment the two of you met. Include only those details that you might see inside Lamott's "one-inch picture frame."
3. Write an **anecdote** about a writing tip that you find useful.

Integrating the Language Arts

Language, Grammar, and Style

USING FORMAL ENGLISH. Read the Language Arts Survey 3.2, "Formal and Informal English." Then replace the informal language in the following sentences with formal language.

1. Don't be put off by a new writing assignment.
2. You can't blow an assignment if you take the right approach.
3. Try to chill out in front of the computer.
4. When you're sick of a humungous topic, break it down into smaller assignments.
5. You can nail any assignment by taking it "bird by bird."

Applied English

WRITING A PERSONAL ESSAY. Write a personal essay that tells of a time when you learned to master a skill, such as piloting a sailboat, making a pizza, using a computer, or hitting a baseball. What was the experience like? What sorts of difficulties did you encounter? How did you solve your problems? What advice would you give someone who wants to learn this skill? What anecdotes can you include to reinforce the points you want to make?

Collaborative Learning

CALENDAR FOR WRITERS. With a classmate, look for helpful quotations about writing. Then make a calendar listing a quotation for each month. You may want to illustrate your calendar and highlight important literary dates.

Guided Writing

THE RESEARCH PAPER: WRITING A BIOGRAPHY/EXPLORING GENIUS

Go to your thesaurus and look up *genius*. If you have access to a computer, key the word *genius* in a word processing program and pull up the thesaurus. How many synonyms can you find for *genius*? Next, spend a few minutes brainstorming one or more names of real people who come to mind for each synonym. Discuss the words and names you generated with your classmates and teacher. What is your definition of *genius*?

Did you or some of your classmates suggest the noted scientist, Albert Einstein, as an example of genius? No other modern figure has so influenced our notion of science, mathematics, physics, and space. Einstein has become a cultural icon, too, featured in poetry, prose, movies, and posters. You may have heard people apologize for their own lack of genius by saying, "I'm no Einstein, but...."

While the world has known only one Albert Einstein, it has known many geniuses. Anyone who has extraordinary abilities or outstanding talent is a genius. Gifted musicians, athletes, scholars, leaders, scientists, mathematicians, and artists might all have levels of genius.

WRITING ASSIGNMENT. Your assignment is to research the life work of someone who you feel qualifies as a genius and write a paper that reports your findings. You will need to select sources, document them carefully, and prepare a final bibliography.

Student Model

> from "Albert Einstein: Nonconformist" by Cate Kyger
>
> Albert Einstein's fresh, nonconformist way of thinking allowed him to come up with astounding theories about the universe and to make significant contributions to international peace. How did this man who was born about one hundred and twenty-five years ago in Germany so radically change our understanding of the universe? What is his legacy to us?

> "Genius is the ability to put into effect what is in your mind."
> —F. Scott Fitzgerald

Writing Plan Checklist
- Select a fascinating subject
- Explore areas to develop (complete a graphic organizer)
- Narrow topic
- Locate sources (5–8 total, including at least one on-line)
- Take notes and document sources
- Write thesis statement
- Determine main points
- Organize information

EXAMINING THE MODEL. Cate starts her introduction by presenting her thesis statement: "Albert Einstein's fresh, nonconformist way of thinking allowed him to come up with astounding theories about the universe and to make significant contributions to international peace." She then poses two questions to

continued on page 700

GUIDED WRITING **699**

GUIDED WRITING
Software

See the Guided Writing Software for an extended version of this lesson that includes printable graphic organizers, extensive student models and student-friendly checklists, and self-, peer, and teacher evaluation features.

MOTIVATION
Ask students to define *genius* in their own words. Then have them explain how people that they have heard or read about influenced their definition.

READING PROFICIENCY
Encourage students to complete each step described in the lesson before they move on to the next step. Ask them to carefully review the Student Model section of this lesson to help them get a better sense of their goal for their assignment.

ENGLISH LANGUAGE LEARNING
See strategies for Reading Proficiency above that will also benefit students who are English language learners. Also review the students' drafts, pointing out problem areas that could be corrected with a dictionary or a grammar handbook.

SPECIAL NEEDS
Students with special needs may need assistance completing the graphic organizer in this lesson. Pair them with a more proficient student to help them complete it. You may also want the proficient student to help them in their research.

ENRICHMENT
Students may want to transform their biographies into an extemporaneous or persuasive essay—informing or persuading the audience about why they think the person they researched exemplifies genius.

Prewriting

IDENTIFYING YOUR AUDIENCE. To help students understand how audience affects the language they use, ask them to compare the words they use when telling a story to a friend with those they use when talking to a parent, teacher, or other authority figure. Explain that understanding what an audience expects or enjoys will help a writer please that audience.

FINDING YOUR VOICE. Remind students that a writer's voice is a unique and personal aspect of a written work. For more information on voice, refer students to the Language Arts Survey 3.3, "Register, Tone, and Voice."

---

capture the attention of her readers and to help them make the transition to the body of her research paper. Her voice shows her strong interest in Einstein in these initial paragraphs. Notice Cate's choice of words that shows her interest: "astounding theories," "his excitement for it blossomed," and "radically change our understanding."

Notice, too, that Cate provides citations for material she quotes in her paper.

FINDING YOUR VOICE. The research paper is the most formal piece of writing you will do, so you will need to use formal English. That means you should avoid using contractions, slang, and colloquialisms.

It is still important, however, to let your own voice come through in this paper. Perhaps you are astounded at the athletic genius of Babe Didrikson Zaharias or Jim Thorpe. Or you admire Ernest Hemingway, Frank Zappa, Mary Cassatt, or Laurence Olivier. Maybe you are amazed by the intellect of scientists such as Allen Turing, Robert Oppenheimer, or Marie Curie or amazed by the creative mind of Frank Lloyd Wright, Michelangelo, or Jules Verne. Let that admiration of your chosen subject show in your choice of words and sentence structure. Imagine that you are nominating your subject for the all-time genius award and convey your passion in your voice.

Prewriting (CONT.)

WRITING WITH A PLAN. To help students write their thesis statement, refer students to the Language Arts Survey 2.25, "Writing a Thesis Statement."

Einstein's passion for science began when he was a young child. When he was only four or five years old, he saw a magnetic compass. Fascinated by the arrow that always pointed to the north, he became convinced that there had to be "something behind things, something deeply hidden" (Physics).

At school, Einstein soon surpassed his classmates in many subjects, including math and science. Although he was very smart, he didn't enjoy school and even found it boring and intimidating. His uncle, an engineer, kept feeding his interest in science, however, and his excitement for it blossomed.

Prewriting

IDENTIFYING YOUR AUDIENCE. As your primary audience for your research paper, your teacher has a keen interest in the product you and your classmates produce. Keep your teacher in mind as you write, as well as your peers. What will interest your readers? Write to inform and enlighten this group.

WRITING WITH A PLAN. As always, finding a suitable topic is critical. Take some time to examine your list from above as well as to look further into the topic of genius. While the person you choose may still be living, you may find historical perspective lacking. Be aware, too, that true genius does not necessarily mean those who accumulate the most fame. Remember to use your curiosity regarding genius: Who interests you?

Once you have found a topic, you will need to find out what information is available. Gather information from the library and electronic sources and start reading. When you have some background information, you should be ready to narrow your topic by developing a focus for presenting information about this person. As you read about your narrowed topic, take notes and document the sources. You will need this information later. For more information on note taking and documenting sources, see the Language Arts Survey sections 5.36–5.44 in your textbook that deal with writing a research paper.

Next, write a thesis statement that states your topic and focus on that topic. Your thesis statement will serve as a guide to identify and develop the main points of support needed for your research paper. Thesis statements may change, of course, as you find more information that may not support your original intent.

After you have gathered information, organize it around the main points that support your thesis. Fill in a graphic organizer. Details for some parts of the outline, such as the introduction and conclusion, may best be filled in as you develop your draft for the paper.

Cate worked with the following graphic organizer as she took notes from her research materials and began to formulate her narrowed topic and thesis.

Student Model—Graphic Organizer

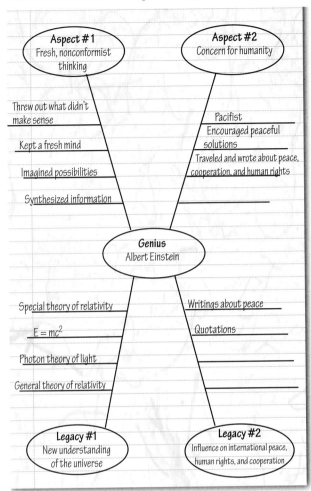

Aspect #1
Fresh, nonconformist thinking

Aspect #2
Concern for humanity

Threw out what didn't make sense

Kept a fresh mind

Imagined possibilities

Synthesized information

Pacifist

Encouraged peaceful solutions

Traveled and wrote about peace, cooperation, and human rights

Genius
Albert Einstein

Special theory of relativity

$E = mc^2$

Photon theory of light

General theory of relativity

Writings about peace

Quotations

Legacy #1
New understanding of the universe

Legacy #2
Influence on international peace, human rights, and cooperation

Drafting

It is easier to write a good introduction for your paper if you wait until the body of the paper is written; then you know what your paper says.

Begin with your thesis statement. What do you want to say about your subject? What aspects of genius are you trying to show to your reader? What is the person's legacy? What is the world still trying to understand about him/her? How does the genius continue to teach or impact us? Settle on the direction you think you want your paper to go. You can refine your thesis as the research reveals deeper understanding to you.

From the thesis statement write the main points that will show that your subject has achieved genius. Write about only one

Self- and Peer Evaluation

After you finish your first draft, complete a self-evaluation of your research paper. Try to read your draft as though you were uninformed on the subject. Identify background information or support that may be missing. Then obtain one or more peer evaluations.

As you evaluate your draft or that of a classmate, respond to the following questions:

- What aspects of genius does the paper cover?
- How does this subject relate to the reader?
- What additional information does the reader need for a more thorough understanding of this person as an example of genius?
- What would make the introduction more interesting or focused? What would make this introduction unlike others about the same general topic?
- How does the thesis reflect the writer's attitude about genius?
- What main point does each body paragraph develop?
- How does each body paragraph relate to the thesis?
- What questions does each body paragraph answer? What questions are left unanswered?
- What quotations enhance the paper? What additional quotations would add meaningful

continued on page 702

See the Writing Resource book for a blackline master of the graphic organizer for this lesson.

Self- and Peer Evaluation

Use the checklist on page 701 for self- and peer evaluation. The checklist is intended to act as a student-friendly rubric to help students identify specific evidence of writing strengths and areas needing improvement. Make sure they provide concrete suggestions for improvement or specific evidence of why the writing works.

Drafting

Refer students to the Language Arts Survey 2.25, "Writing a Thesis Statement," and 2.26, "Writing Main Ideas and Supporting Details," to help them with the drafting stage.

Revising and Proofreading

A handout of the proofreading checklist is available in the Teacher's Resource Kit, Writing Resource book 2.45.

support? Which quotations seem unnecessary?

- How logically do the main points support the thesis? What points might be missing? Which points might be extraneous to the thesis?
- How effective is the conclusion?

Revising and Proofreading

Review your self- and peer evaluations. Revise your writing after considering these comments. Proofread your revised draft for spelling, mechanical, and usage errors. Invite one or two friends to proofread, also.

For more information, see the Language Arts Survey 2.45, "A Proofreading Checklist."

point at a time. Be careful not to write a chronology of the person's life, since the assignment is not a simple biography. It is also an exploration of genius. As you write, insert the necessary parenthetical documentation for quotes or paraphrased information. Documenting sources as you proceed will ultimately save you time.

After you have developed and supported each main point, read through your draft to see if the points are coherent and work together. Then draft an introduction that develops interest in your subject. Include your thesis in the introduction. Finally, draft a conclusion that summarizes the essence of your paper.

Student Model (continued)

By 1902, Einstein had finished his public schooling and had graduated from the Polytechnic Institute in Switzerland. Surprisingly, he was unable to get an academic position so he worked as an examiner at the Swiss Patent Office in Bern. This job gave him much free time to ponder scientific questions. He didn't have a laboratory, nor were calculators or computers available back then. What he did have was knowledge of current scientific thought, a passion for scientific understanding, and imagination. His genius lay in his ability to keep a fresh mind, to throw out what didn't make sense, to rethink, to manipulate, and to creatively synthesize information until everything fit together. He worked out all of his ideas in his head and on scraps of paper! In 1905, by the time he was twenty-six years old, he had written several brilliant papers which transformed scientific thought (Levenson).

In his theory of relativity, Einstein explained that motion and time are relative to the observer. You can understand some of his brilliant thinking by examining his explanation of this theory. He said to imagine that you were traveling in a train at 50 miles per hour. Now imagine that you throw a ball out of the window at 10 miles per hour. To you, the ball is traveling at 10 miles per hour. To an observer standing beside the railroad, the ball is traveling at 60 miles per hour. The measurement is relative to the observer.

In a lighter vein, he explained relativity like this: "Put your hand on a hot stove for a minute, and it seems like an hour. Sit with a pretty girl for an hour, and it seems like a minute. That's relativity" (Magna).

Einstein's theory of relativity led to his famous equation: $E=mc^2$. The E stands for energy, the m stands for mass, and the c stands for the speed of light. This equation means that energy and mass are equivalent. This equation later led other scientists to develop nuclear power and the atomic bomb.

By 1916, Einstein published his general theory of relativity that explained relationships among space, time, motion, and gravity. These relationships helped Einstein explain to others the underlying order and simplicity that he saw in the universe. He received the Nobel Prize in 1921 for his photon theory of light.

Einstein's fresh way of thinking also influenced his commitment to international peace. After World War I, ninety-three German intellectuals signed a manifesto defending Germany's war conduct. Einstein, however, signed an antiwar counter-manifesto. He wanted a just peace and a supranational organization to prevent future wars. He said, "My pacifism is an instinctive feeling, a feeling that possesses me because the murder of men is disgusting. My attitude is not derived from any intellectual theory but is based on my deepest antipathy to every kind of cruelty and hatred" (Magna). Once again, Einstein was not afraid to think for himself, although there was pressure to go along with the majority.

By 1933, the Nazi government was starting to take over in Germany. While Einstein was on a visit to the United States and England, the Nazis broke into his home. Since Einstein was Jewish, the Nazis took his property and deprived him of his teaching positions and his citizenship in Germany. Einstein then became part of the staff at the Institute for Advanced Study in Princeton, New Jersey.

Language, Grammar, and Style

Effective Documentation
IDENTIFYING EFFECTIVE DOCUMENTATION. You need to credit authors and sources for the information that you use in your research. Citing your sources properly allows your readers to verify your research and protects you against plagiarism.

Directly quote when passages are precise, eloquent, or unique to a source. Put the exact words in quotation marks and reference the last name and the page where you found those words.

Direct Quotation
"This topic brings me to that worst outcrop of herd life, the military system, which I abhor" (Einstein 10).

At times, you may want to *paraphrase*, or tell in your own words, an author's idea. In paraphrasing, you must still credit the author by referencing the last name and page where you found the idea. If the author's name is unavailable, use a shortened form of the title.

Paraphrased statement
One week before his death in 1955, Einstein agreed that his name should go on a manifesto urging all nations to give up nuclear weapons. It was his last act for international peace (O'Connor).

continued on page 704

PREVIEWING THE SKILL. Refer students to the Language Arts Survey 5.43, "Paraphrasing, Summarizing, and Quoting." This is intended to reinforce the integrated Language, Grammar, and Style lesson in this unit.

PRACTICING THE SKILL. For additional practice, have students work through the exercise in the following section of the Language, Grammar, and Style Resource book located in the Teacher's Resource Kit: 5.43, "Paraphrasing, Summarizing, and Quoting."

If you use two or more articles or books with the same author, include the author, title of article or book, and page number in the parenthetical reference. Bracket any information you change or add to a quotation. You need not directly quote information that is common knowledge or that is found in several sources. Include all sources in your bibliography at the end of your paper in a works cited page.

FIXING INCORRECT DOCUMENTATION. Document sources correctly. Explain how you would fix the parenthetical documentation in each example below.

(Einstein, 10)
(p. 51 Tipler)
(Albert Einstein 23)

Avoid quotations that stand alone in your paper. Blend them into your writing.

Read the quotation from Einstein below. Then add your own words so that the quotations are not isolated from your writing.

"I know not with what weapons World War III will be fought, but World War IV will be fought with sticks and stones."

USING EFFECTIVE DOCUMENTATION. Read through your paper again. Have you handled quotations correctly? Check carefully for paraphrased ideas. Are there any places where you paraphrased material that you need to reference? Is your

continued on page 705

Although Einstein was a pacifist, he wrote a very controversial letter to President Franklin D. Roosevelt in 1939. In the letter he told the President that it was possible to build an atomic bomb and that Nazi Germany was planning to do so. He explained that he thought the United States should provide funds to help the research in this field. Einstein wrote this letter because he was concerned about the fate of humanity.

Einstein's letter influenced the United States to produce the first atomic bomb. Although Einstein wasn't ashamed of his letter, he worried about his decision to give the government so much information. Would they use it in a good or a bad way...? You can tell what Einstein was thinking when he said, "This topic brings me to that worst outcrop of herd life, the military system, which I abhor... This plague-spot of civilization ought to be abolished with all possible speed. Heroism on command, senseless violence, and all the loathsome nonsense that goes by the name of patriotism—how passionately I hate them!" (Einstein 10).

After the war with Germany ended, the United States was still fighting Japan. The U.S. government decided to drop two atomic bombs on Japan to end the war. After Einstein heard about this mass destruction on Japan, he was horrified. He worked tirelessly for peace and hoped that eventually the fear of an atomic bomb would prevent future wars: "Peace cannot be achieved through violence, it can only be attained through understanding" (Magna).

Einstein stayed at his position in Princeton for the rest of his life and obtained his United States citizenship in 1940. In 1952, he was offered the Presidency in Israel but declined, stating that he wasn't fit for such a prestigious position (The Nobel Foundation). One week before his death in 1955, Einstein agreed that his name should go on a manifesto urging all nations to give up nuclear weapons. It was his last act for international peace (O'Connor).

Albert Einstein's genius showed itself in his imaginative thinking about science and in his overwhelming concern for others' well-being. His legacy to us lies in his astonishing theories about the universe and in his commitment for international peace. His words, "Imagination is more important than knowledge. Knowledge is limited. Imagination encircles the world" (Magna), remind us to use our minds as our first resource, never to lose confidence in our dreams, and to believe in what we can accomplish.

Works Cited

A. Einstein: Image and Impact. Nov. 1996, revised Aug. 1998. American Institute of Physics. April 28, 2000. <http://www.aip.org/history/einstein/ early1.html>

Albert Einstein. The Nobel Foundation. April 28, 2000. <http://www.nobel.se/laureates/physics-1921-1-bio.html>

Albert Einstein – A Selection of Quotes. Mountain Man Graphics. Australia. April 28, 2000. <http://www.magna.com.au/~prfbrown/albert_e.html>

Einstein, Albert. *Ideas and Opinions*. New York: Bonanza Books. Originally published by Crown Publishers, 1954.

Levenson, Thomas. "Genius among Geniuses." Nova Online. April 28, 2000. <http://www.pbs.org/wgbh/nova/einstein/genius/index.html>

O'Connor, J. J. and Robertson, E. F. "Albert Einstein." School of Mathematics and Statistics, University of St. Andrews, Scotland. April 28, 2000. <http://www-history.mcs.st-andrews.ac.uk/history/Mathematicians/Einstein.html>

Tipler, Paul A. *Foundation of Modern Physics*. New York: Worth Publishers, Inc. 1969.

works cited page done correctly? See the chart "Formal Note-Taking" on page 1104. for additional information.

Publishing and Presenting

Your final product should be a paper that you are proud to present to your classmates. When you have done your best, share your work. You may wish to publish the papers as an anthology. Your high school library might wish to shelve a copy, or you might post your papers on your school's web site. Perhaps you and your classmates could create a bulletin board complete with portraits and papers.

Reflecting

Writing a good research paper is one of the more difficult tasks asked of students. What was the most difficult part of the project for you? What do you wish you would have done differently? What did you learn about your research and organizational skills? the subject matter? What future reading or research might you be compelled to do? How did your understanding of genius change or increase?

Publishing and Presenting

Encourage students to review the Language Arts Survey 2.6, "Choosing a Form," to help them explore different methods of publishing their work.

Reflecting

Encourage students to make a list of goals they plan to accomplish with this writing assignment. Have them put their papers away for a week. Then have them reread their biographical research paper and their list of goals. Ask them to write a paragraph reflecting on how their papers succeed in reaching those goals and how they might change them to better reach those goals.

ADDITIONAL RESOURCES

UNIT 8 RESOURCE BOOK
- Vocabulary Worksheet: Unit 8
- Study Guide: Unit 8 Test
- Unit 8 Test

VOCABULARY DEVELOPMENT

Give students the following exercise:
Using the Words for Everyday Use listed on page 706, make a fifteen question multiple choice test. Write the vocabulary word, and then write three choices, one of which should be a synonym of the vocabulary word. Be sure that the two incorrect choices are antonyms of the word, or choices that do not describe the word in any way. You may want to review the Language Arts Survey 5.50, "Synonym and Antonym Questions." When you are done, exchange tests with a partner.

EXAMPLE
Circle the letter of the word that most closely matches the meaning of the word in capital letters.
1. FLOURISH
   a. wilt
   b. die
   c. grow
(Answer: c)

REFLECTING ON YOUR READING

The prompts in Reflecting on Your Reading are suitable as topics for research papers. Refer to the Language Arts Survey 5.18–5.45, "Research Skills." (To evaluate research papers, see the evaluation forms for writing, revising, and proofreading in the Assessment Resource book.)
The prompts in Reflecting on Your Reading can also be adapted for use as topics or oral reports or debates. Refer student to the Speaking and Listening Resource in the Language Arts Survey. (To evaluate these projects, see the evaluation forms in the Assessment Resource book.)

UNIT 8 review
The Genius Within

Words for Everyday Use

Check your knowledge of the following vocabulary words from the selections in this unit. Write short sentences using these words in context to make the meaning clear. To review the definition or usage of a word, refer back to the page number listed or the Glossary of Words for Everyday Use.

abate, 617
accessibly, 618
adversary, 631
ally, 635
ancestral, 628
applicability, 686
arresting, 696
articulate, 617
assess, 619
averse, 654
benevolently, 632
bondage, 646
caption, 634
commend, 655
commission, 617
conceptual, 656
concession, 635
confound, 617
conspicuously, 655
contention, 645
conviction, 644
cower, 683
deftly, 628
diminishing, 632

diminutive, 653
diverse, 618
elaborate, 630
essence, 618
etiquette, 632
facetiously, 656
flourish, 634
fragrant, 628
graciously, 632
humility, 632
illiteracy, 684
immobile, 647
impart, 628
impertinence, 644
impulse, 617
inert, 645
inquisitiveness, 617
insatiable, 617
interminable, 664
intricate, 630
introspective, 687
involuntarily, 645
justify, 682
leering, 695

ludicrous, 666
malodorous, 634
momentous, 644
neurosurgeon, 680
obscure, 686
obstinacy, 653
officious, 665
omnipotence, 664
omnipresence, 664
omniscience, 664
opportunist, 680
perpetuate, 652
perseverance, 652
phenomena, 618
piety, 617
plausible, 656
preliminary, 665
prodigy, 634
proportional, 686
pungent, 628
ramified, 652
regression, 685
relent, 630
replica, 630

requisite, 619
retort, 632
rigor, 618, 655
roguish, 653
sarcasm, 653
sensibility, 684
solemnity, 629
specialization, 682
specter, 682
speculation, 652
successive, 636
syndrome, 686
tangible, 682
taut, 647
tout, 634
transmute, 617
triumphant, 633
unfathomed, 619
vacuous, 684
vanity, 632
verify, 685
volition, 646

Literary Tools

Define the following terms, giving concrete examples of how they are used in the selections in this unit. To review a term, refer to the page number indicated or to the Handbook of Literary Terms.

analysis, 615
autobiography, 642
biography, 650
characterization, 611
colloquialism, 693

description, 642
foreshadowing, 669
personal essay, 693
point of view, 625, 669

Renaissance, 615
repetition, 662
satire, 662
simile, 611

source, 650
style, 662
symbol, 625
tone, 693

Reflecting on your reading

Genre Studies

1. **BIOGRAPHY AND AUTOBIOGRAPHY.** The selection about Albert Einstein is a biography, while the selection from *My Left Foot* is an autobiography. From which point of view is each written? What insights do readers gain from the autobiography that they do not from the biography? Which selection do you think is more objective, and why?

2. **PERSONAL ESSAY.** "Short Assignments" by Anne Lamott can be considered a personal essay. Why? What personal information do you learn about the author in reading her essay?

3. **SHORT STORY.** "Flowers for Algernon" is told in the form of a journal. In what ways is this technique effective in portraying Charlie before and after the experiment? How does the author reveal that Charlie has become intelligent? How does the author reveal that Charlie has lost his intelligence? How would this story be different if it were told from a third-person point of view?

Thematic Studies

4. **FAMILY TIES.** How do the mothers of Esperanza in "Smart Cookie" and Christy Brown in the excerpt from *My Left Foot* influence their daughter and son? Why do Esperanza and Christy feel the way that they do about their mothers? How would their lives be different without their influence?

5. **TALENT.** What talent do Waverly Jong and Paul Klee have in common? How is their talent demonstrated in the short stories "Rules of the Game" and "Engineer-Private Paul Klee Misplaces an Aircraft Between Milbertshofen and Cambrai, March 1916"? Would the outcome of the stories be different if the characters did not have this talent?

for your READING LIST

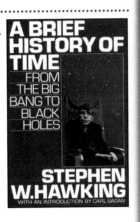

A Brief History of Time by Stephen J. Hawking. Stephen Hawking has been called the most brilliant physicist since Einstein. His purpose in this book is to inform his readers, in a clear, accessible way, about the progress being made in understanding the laws that govern the universe. Since it was published in 1988, it has been translated into thirty languages, and has sold five and a half million copies worldwide. In order to reach a still larger audience, Hawking made a documentary film to accompany the book.

Independent Reading Activity

READING COMPREHENSION. You are what you read. Or, as Sir Joshua Reynolds put it, "The more extensive your acquaintance is with the works of those who have excelled, the more extensive will be your powers of invention." Choose an excerpt from a book on a difficult concept, like time, science, or space. Choose a short passage and read it over several times. Look up the words you don't know in the dictionary. Paraphrase difficult sentences so that you understand them. Force your mind to understand the concept. Write a short essay that demonstrates your understanding of what you have read.

Selections for Additional Reading

Story of My Life by Helen Keller. When scarlet fever left her deaf and blind at age 19 months, Helen Keller was thrown into a dark, isolated world. Her teacher, Anne Sullivan, helped her find her way out of it. Keller's amazing accomplishments show that anything can be achieved, no matter what the odds.

Gandhi, an Autobiography: The Story of My Experiments with Truth by Mahatma Gandhi. One of the greatest spiritual leaders of the 20th century, Gandhi (1869–1948) was also a great thinker and a learned man. His autobiography documents his extraordinary life—his travels, his accomplishments, and his theories about the truth of life.

Smithsonian Visual Timeline of Inventions by Richard Platt. This book documents the history of invention and also explores why humans feel the impulse to invent. Clocks, airplanes, photography, safety pins, fiber optics, and telescopes—they are all in this illustrated book, plus much more.

UNIT REVIEW 707

The Farm, 1921–1922. Joan Miró. National Gallery of Art, Washington, DC.

GOALS/OBJECTIVES

Studying this unit will enable students to
- explore ideas related to the theme of diversity and community
- summarize the different ways fiction, nonfiction, poetry, and song lyrics express the theme of diversity and community
- define *dialogue, lyric poem, memoir, myth,* and *personal essay* and identify the characteristics of each as they encounter them in their reading
- define *theme, tone, characterization, irony, paradox,* and *stereotype* and identify and explain examples of each that they encounter in their reading
- write a cause and effect essay about increasing awareness of cultural diversity
- identify standard, formal English, correct errors in formal English, and use formal English in their writing when appropriate

Diversity and Community

" Civilization is the encouragement of differences. "

—*Mohandas Gandhi*

UNIT NINE

Ask students to work in groups to create a mural or bulletin board collage based on the ideas in the quotes. They may wish to research additional quotes having to do with diversity and community. Students should place the quote(s) and authors' names somewhere on their finished product. Encourage students to use various types of media visuals. For more artistic students, suggest that they create their own painting or drawing that reflects the ideas in the quotes.

echoes

➤ We must learn to live together as brothers or perish together as fools.
—Martin Luther King, Jr.

➤ There is nowhere you can go and only be with people who are like you. Give it up.
—Bernice Johnson Reagon

➤ If we cannot end now our differences, at least we can help make the world safe for diversity.
—John Fitzgerald Kennedy

➤ If we are to achieve a richer culture, rich in contrasting values, we must recognize the whole gamut of human potentialities, and so weave a less arbitrary social fabric, one in which each diverse human gift will find a fitting place.
—Margaret Mead

➤ It is never too late to give up your prejudices.
—Henry David Thoreau

➤ Always remember others may hate you but those who hate you don't win unless you hate them. And then you destroy yourself.
—Richard Nixon

➤ It is in part the very uniqueness of every individual that makes him, not only a member of a family, race, nation, or class, but a human being.
—Helen Merrell Lynd

➤ Every man is more than just himself; he also represents the unique, the very special and always significant and remarkable point at which the world's phenomena intersect, only once in this way and never again.
—Hermann Hesse

➤ There were never in the world two opinions alike, any more than two hairs or two grains. Their most universal quality is diversity.
—Michel Eyquem de Montaigne

➤ We must indeed all hang together, or most assuredly, we will all hang separately.
—Benjamin Franklin, remark on signing the Declaration of Independence, July 4, 1776

➤ Without a sense of caring, there can be no sense of community.
—Anthony J. D'Angelo

"Simple Song"
by Marge Piercy

Reader's resource

"Simple Song," like most of Marge Piercy's poetry, is a **free verse poem**, meaning that it does not follow regular rhyme, meter, or division into stanzas. The poem was included in Piercy's book *Circles on the Water,* which contains selected poems written between 1963 and 1982.

Piercy explains that poetry is a part of her everyday life. "I make up poems for our cats . . . I say poems to the peas and the day lilies. I make up poems for houses on the street in Cambridge-port." *Circles on the Water* reflects these "little grace notes of thanksgiving and praise and cursing during the day." It is a collection of love poems, feminist poems, poems about animals and vegetables, and poems about living on Cape Cod.

About the AUTHOR

Marge Piercy (1936–) was born in Detroit, Michigan, during the days of the Great Depression. While Piercy was growing up, she heard many stories from her mother and from her her grandmother, who was known as a great storyteller. This shaped her ability to create stories in her novels, which include *Woman on the Edge of Time, Going Down Fast,* and *Dance the Eagle to Sleep,* and *City of Darkness, City of Life.* Piercy is also well known for her poetry. She credits her mother with making her a poet by encouraging her to read and to develop her imagination. Her mother also encouraged her to observe sharply and remember what she observed, which are qualities common in successful writers and poets. Her collections of poetry include *Circles on the Water, Available Light* and *What Are Big Girls Made Of?*

Piercy and her husband, writer Ira Wood, currently live on Cape Cod, writing plays, novels, and running a small literary publishing company together. Piercy once said that she "can never imagine living without poetry." Her words prove true in that she has written fourteen poetry collections and has published hundreds of poems in magazines and newspapers since she began writing at age fifteen.

Literary TOOLS

SPEAKER AND FIRST-PERSON POINT OF VIEW. The **speaker** is the character who speaks in, or narrates, a poem—the voice assumed by the writer. The speaker and the writer of a poem are not necessarily the same person. **Point of view** is the vantage point from which a story is told. When a story is written from the **first-person point of view,** the narrator uses words such as *I* and *we.* In stories told from a *third-person point of view,* the narrator uses words such as *he, she, it,* and *they.* As you read "Simple Song," consider what point of view is used by the speaker in the poem.

THEME. A **theme** is a central idea in a literary work. As you read this poem, try to find the central ideas in the poem. What important ideas does the story convey? Use the graphic organizer below to help you find the central ideas

Graphic Organizer

Summarize the central idea from each stanza to help you find the theme(s) in the poem:

stanza 1 —

stanza 2 — [   ]

stanza 3 — [   ]

Reader's Journal

How would you respond to someone who is similar to you? to someone who is different from you?

ADDITIONAL RESOURCES

UNIT 9 RESOURCE BOOK
- Selection Worksheet 9.1
- Selection Check Test 4.9.1
- Selection Test 4.9.2
- Speaking and Listening Resource 4.14

GRAPHIC ORGANIZER

Students might identify the following ideas and themes in "Simple Song":
Stanza 1: When two people meet, they notice their similarities.
Stanza 2: When two people part, they notice their differences.
Stanza 3: People are unique and individual. Love is not strong enough to stop someone from wanting something new. People are always "open" to a new experience despite the love that binds them to the old.

READER'S JOURNAL

Encourage students to write a reflection about a friend with whom they no longer spend time.

INDIVIDUAL LEARNING STRATEGIES

MOTIVATION
Ask students to write about their network of friends in a journal entry. Which friend is most like them? Which friend is least like them? Did they face any obstacles in establishing a friendship?

READING PROFICIENCY
Explain to students that this poem can be separated into three sections. Have students tackle each stanza separately, summarizing the important ideas from each in their own words.

ENGLISH LANGUAGE LEARNING
Make sure students grasp the figurative meaning of "the open hand/the open eye/the door in the chest standing open." Explain that these expressions describe the speaker's idea that people are always open to new experiences and connections with others.

(Continued on page 712)

GOALS/OBJECTIVES

Studying this lesson will enable students to
- respond to a poem that describes the patterns of feelings people have for one another
- define *speaker* and summarize the speaker's ideas and discuss personal opinions on the different ways people relate to one another
- define *first-person point of view* and discuss how it

affects an interpretation of a poem
- define *theme* and identify the main themes in a poem
- work collaboratively to create a workplace diversity training program
- research the life and career of the poet and role-play a talk-show interview

1. We say that the other person is just like us, thinking and saying the same things.
2. We say that he or she is strange and that we can never agree or communicate with him or her.

INDIVIDUAL LEARNING STRATEGIES (CONT.)

SPECIAL NEEDS
Students will benefit from hearing or reading the poem aloud. Encourage the reader to pause after each stanza to allow time to grasp the meaning.

ENRICHMENT
Encourage students to write a response to "Simple Song" in the form of an original short poem. To prompt students' thinking, ask them to decide whether they agree or disagree with the ideas put forth by Piercy.

RESPOND TO THE SELECTION

Do you think love can be strong enough to keep people together despite their differences?

SELECTION CHECK TEST 4.9.1 WITH ANSWERS

Checking Your Reading
1. In your opinion, what does Piercy mean by "When we are going toward someone"? **Piercy possibly means when we fall in love.**
2. How do we perceive the person "we are going toward," according to Piercy? **We percieve the person as like us and easy to spend time with.**
3. How do we perceive the person we are leaving, according to Piercy? **We perceive the person as hard to talk to, hard to be around, and opposite of us.**
4. Are either of those perceptions correct, according to the last stanza? **According to the last stanza, neither of those perceptions is exactly correct.**
5. What do you think lines 14–18 mean? **Students may say that the lines mean that love is not as strong as our need for newness and excitement.**

Simple Song

Marge Piercy

When we are going toward someone we say
You are just like me
your thoughts are my brothers
word matches word
5   how easy to be together.

When we are leaving someone we say:
how strange you are
we cannot communicate
we can never agree
10 how hard, hard and weary to be together.

We are not different nor alike
But each strange in his leather body
sealed in skin and reaching out clumsy hands
and loving is an act
15 that cannot outlive
the open hand
the open eye
the door in the chest standing open. ∎

> *What do we say when we are moving toward someone?*

> *What do we say when we are leaving someone?*

Respond *to the* SELECTION

Do you have any friends with whom it is "easy to be together"? What makes them so easy to get along with? Do you have any friends who are very different from you? How do you get along with them?

Literary Tools
Match each literary term with the best description.

    a. speaker   b. first-person point of view   c. third-person point of view d. theme

1. a central idea in a literary work; **d**
2. the character who narrates a poem; **a**
3. uses words such as *he, she,* and *it*; **c**
4. uses words such as *I* and *we*; **b**

Investigate, Inquire, and Imagine

Recall: GATHERING FACTS

1a. When two people move toward each other, what are they thinking and feeling? What are they thinking and feeling as they end their relationship?

2a. In stanza 3, what words or phrases does the speaker use to describe each of us?

3a. What is love not able to outlive?

Interpret: FINDING MEANING

1b. What does it mean to say "your thoughts are my brothers"? Should this line be taken literally or figuratively? When is it easy for people to be together, and when is it difficult?

2b. What do these words or phrases suggest about people's ability to relate to one another?

3b. What does it mean to have an open hand and an open eye? What does the speaker mean by "the door in the chest standing open"? Should this be taken literally or figuratively?

Analyze: TAKING THINGS APART

4a. Identify the relationship between stanza 1 and stanza 2. What changes take place from stanza 1 to stanza 2? What does each stanza represent? What does the speaker mean when he or she says, in stanza 3, "We are not different nor alike"? What does the speaker say we are instead?

Synthesize: BRINGING THINGS TOGETHER

4b. In your own words, summarize stanzas 1 and 2. What is the speaker saying about what brings people together and what pushes them apart? How does stanza 3 serve as a response to stanzas 1 and 2?

Perspective: LOOKING AT OTHER VIEWS

5a. Do you agree or disagree with the speaker that "loving is an act / that cannot outlive / the open hand / the open eye / the door in the chest standing open" (lines 14–18)? Explain. Do you agree or disagree with the speaker that people are neither different nor alike? If you agree, what do you think we are instead? If you disagree, what makes us different? What makes us alike?

Empathy: SEEING FROM INSIDE

5b. What could you conclude about the speaker's experience with love based on lines 14–18? What advice is the speaker giving about relationships?

Understanding Literature

SPEAKER AND FIRST-PERSON POINT OF VIEW. Review the definitions for **speaker** and **first-person point of view** in the Handbook of Literary Terms. Who do you think is the speaker of this poem? Whom is the

---

ANSWERS TO INVESTIGATE, INQUIRE, AND IMAGINE (CONT.)

differences is what pushes them apart. In stanza 3, the speaker responds to stanzas 1 and 2 by saying that both approaches are mistakes, because in fact we are not entirely similar nor different from each other. Instead, we are all individuals.

PERSPECTIVE
5a. *Responses will vary.*

EMPATHY
5b. *Responses will vary.* Students may say that the speaker has seen love relationships end due to selfishness and closed-mindedness. The speaker advises people to be open to others and to appreciate the whole person.

ANSWERS TO INVESTIGATE, INQUIRE, AND IMAGINE

RECALL
1a. When two people move toward each other, their thoughts and words match and they are able to get along very easily. When two people are leaving each other, they call one another strange and say they cannot communicate or agree.
2a. The speaker says that we are "strange" in our leather bodies, "sealed in skin," and "reaching out clumsy hands."
3a. Love is not able to outlive "the open hand, the open eye, the door in the chest standing open."

INTERPRET
1b. The word *brothers* should not be taken literally, but figuratively. In speaking of thoughts that are "brothers," the speaker probably means thoughts that are closely related.
2b. The words or phrases "strange," "leather," "sealed in skin," and "clumsy hands" suggest that people are alienated from one another.
3b. Having an open hand means to be generous and giving, while having an open eye means to be aware and observant, open to learning new things and able to see the truth. "The door in the chest standing open" should be taken figuratively. It symbolizes a willingness or desire to have new experiences and feelings.

ANALYZE
4a. In stanza 1, two people are bound by similarities. But in stanza 2, they see no similarities between them—only differences. Stanza 1 represents what happens at the beginning of a relationship: people rejoice in the similarities. Stanza 2 shows what happens later: people are dismayed as they find they are actually not as alike as they thought. When the speaker says that we are neither different nor alike, the speaker means that we should not judge others by comparing them to ourselves, but see and accept them as they are. The speaker says that we are all "strange."

SYNTHESIZE
4b. In stanza 1, the speaker says that when we connect with someone, we feel that this person is very similar to us. In stanza 2, the speaker says that when we begin to grow apart from someone or are unable to connect with that person, we conclude that that person is a stranger. The speaker is saying that perceived similarities are what attract people to one another, and the disappointment of finding

ANSWERS TO UNDERSTANDING LITERATURE

SPEAKER AND FIRST-PERSON POINT OF VIEW. Students may say that the speaker of the poem is the author, Marge Piercy. The speaker is referring to people in general by using the word *we.* If she had used *I* instead of *we,* the audience may not be able to connect as strongly with the things she is saying because the word *I* is extremely exclusive, whereas *we* is inclusive. By using *we,* the author lets the reader know that her ideas are universal, that they apply to every human being.

THEME. *Responses will vary.* Students may say that the theme is the idea that similarities and differences should not be the driving forces in making or breaking relationships, but rather the need for communication with another human being is what should bring people together.

ANSWERS TO INTEGRATING THE LANGUAGE ARTS

Study and Research & Collaborative Learning
Before they begin their research, students should consult the Language Arts Survey 1.10, "Reading Newspapers, Journals, and Newsmagazines," and 5.26, "Using the Internet."

Media Literacy
If students have access to video equipment, you might want to have them work in small groups to make a recording of the interview. Students can delegate responsibilities. For example, all students can perform research and create a list of interview questions, but one student might be in charge of operating the camera and another student might direct the production.

---

speaker referring to when he or she uses the word *we?* How might the poem be different if the speaker had used *I* instead of *we?*

THEME. Review the definition for **theme** in Literary Tools on page 711 and the graphic organizer you made for that section. Identify one major theme that runs through this poem.

Writer's Journal

1. Write a **statement of belief** about one of the following: friendship, diversity, or interpersonal communication.
2. Create an **image** for an abstract noun such as *peace, justice, love, hate,* and so on.
3. Write a **poem** about how it feels to begin a new relationship with someone or how it feels to separate from a relationship.

Integrating the Language Arts

Study and Research & Collaborative Learning

CREATING A WORKPLACE DIVERSITY TRAINING PROGRAM. Form groups of five or six people, and imagine that your group is the human resources department for a major corporation. In order to react to the rapid cultural and sociological changes in our world, your company has asked your department to create a training program to educate employees about diversity and help them communicate with people different from them. In what ways can you help your company move toward ethnic diversity, political correctness, and cultural consciousness? Find the answers to these questions to help you create a training program. Begin by searching the Internet or finding books or magazine articles that discuss affirmative action and workplace diversity. Organize your information and then think of creative ways to teach the information to your employees. You could use role-play, quizzes, games, group discussion, presentations, a special speaker, or a combination of all of these strategies. When you have outlined a plan for your training program, try out one of your strategies on your class.

Media Literacy

CONDUCTING A TALK-SHOW INTERVIEW. With a partner, research the life and career of Marge Piercy. Be aware that she is both a poet and a novelist. You can find a wealth of information on Piercy by logging onto her home page at http://www.capecod.net/~tmpiercy/. One person will play the role of interviewer. He or she should create a list of questions to ask Piercy. The other person will play the role of Piercy, answering questions about her life and work, and how her experiences have proved useful in supplying ideas for her poems and novels. Refer to the Language Arts Survey 4.14, "Conducting an Interview."

"Prayer to the PACIFIC"

by Leslie Marmon Silko

Reader's resource

In **"Prayer to the Pacific,"** Silko celebrates nature and tells a myth that explains Native American migration to America. The poem was published in *Storyteller,* Silko's 1981 collection of poetry.

About the AUTHOR

Leslie Marmon Silko (1948–   ), poet, novelist, and short story writer, grew up on the Laguna Pueblo Reservation in New Mexico. She attended Bureau of Indian Affairs elementary schools, a Catholic high school, and the University of New Mexico. Silko, who left law school in order to work on her writing, published her first story in 1969. Among her honors is a prestigious MacArthur Foundation Fellowship. She has taught at several colleges, including the University of New Mexico.

Silko's writings reflect themes from her Native American heritage, including the relationship between humans and nature and the tensions of living within different cultures. Her first novel, *Ceremony* (1977), tells of the feelings of a World War II veteran of mixed parentage who seeks advice from a Native American sage. *Almanac of the Dead* (1991) is perhaps Silko's most talked about novel. One of the issues it discusses is the European conquest of Native Americans.

Literary TOOLS

SIMILE. A **simile** is a comparison using *like* or *as*. As you read, identify the simile in stanza 1.

MYTH. A **myth** is a story that explains objects or events in the natural world as resulting from the action of some supernatural force or entity, most often a god. As you read, pay attention to the myth contained in this poem.

Graphic Organizer

As you read, make a cluster chart listing what you learn about the sea turtles. One example has been done for you.

Reader's Journal

What story can you tell about the ocean?

ADDITIONAL RESOURCES

UNIT 9 RESOURCE BOOK
- Selection Worksheet 9.2
- Selection Check Test 4.9.3
- Selection Test 4.9.4
- Language, Grammar, and Style Resource 3.81, 3.82
- Speaking and Listening Resource 4.20

VOCABULARY FROM THE SELECTION

immemorial

GRAPHIC ORGANIZER

Students might list in their charts the following information about sea turtles:
- Thirty thousand years ago, Indians rode the sea turtles across the oceans.
- Turtles waded slowly out from the "gray sundown sea."
- Grandfather Turtle "rolled in the sand four times" before "swimming into the sea."

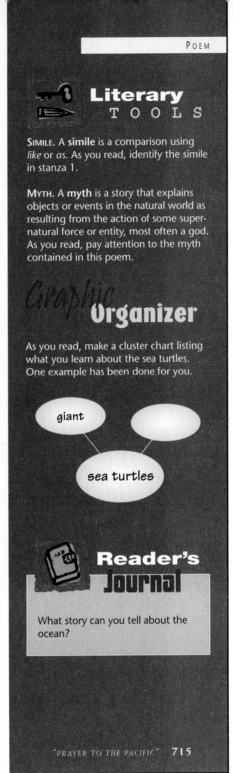

READER'S JOURNAL

You might also encourage students to think of some associations they have with the ocean. Ask them: What is the first thing that comes to mind when you hear the word *ocean*? What does the ocean represent to you? Have students freewrite about these associations in their journals.

GOALS/OBJECTIVES

Studying this lesson will enable students to
- interpret a poem in which the speaker shares personal associations with the ocean
- discuss how the speaker's cultural background influences her reactions to the ocean
- define *simile* and recognize an example they find in their reading
- define *myth* and explain how the term relates to the selection
- demonstrate an ability to recognize clauses and phrases in sentences
- conduct research on Native American myths and share one myth orally with classmates

1. She traveled to the ocean.
2. She carries back "four round stones"
   in her pocket.

INDIVIDUAL LEARNING STRATEGIES

MOTIVATION
Ask students to work with a partner to create a myth for the origin of rain. Make sure some aspect of the myth is grounded in reality, or what we today know about rain. Have students share their rain myths with the rest of the class.

READING PROFICIENCY
Before students read the poem, explain that they might view it as having three distinct sections. Encourage students to create a chart that separates and summarizes these three sections of the poem.

ENGLISH LANGUAGE LEARNING
Review with students the Prereading information on page 715, emphasizing that this poem draws on some important themes associated with Silko's Native American heritage.

SPECIAL NEEDS
Read "Prayer to the Pacific" aloud to students, pausing frequently to allow students time to grasp its meaning. Consider reading the poem one time, pausing at each period you encounter and asking volunteers to rephrase the ideas in their own words. Once you feel students understand the imagery and ideas, read the poem a second time without pauses.

ENRICHMENT
Have students locate and read another poem by Silko that shares the themes found in "Prayer to the Pacific." Students can write a brief comparison and contrast essay and share their ideas in small groups.

PRAYER TO THE PACIFIC

Leslie Marmon Silko

I traveled to the ocean
    distant
       from my southwest land of sandrock
       to the moving blue water
5   Big as the myth of origin.
  Pale
pale water in the yellow-white light of
      sun floating west
      to China
10   where ocean herself was born.
Clouds that blow across the sand are wet.

Squat in the wet sand and speak to the Ocean:
 I return to you turquoise the red coral you sent us,
     sister spirit of Earth.
15 Four round stones in my pocket I carry back the ocean
     to suck and to taste.

To where did the speaker travel?

What does the speaker carry back?

LITERARY TECHNIQUE

PERSONIFICATION. Personification is a figure of speech in which an idea, animal, or thing is described as if it were a person. Ask students how the ocean is personified in line 13.

Answer
The ocean "sends" turquoise and red coral, like gifts from one person to another.

Thirty thousand years ago
　　　　　Indians came riding across the ocean
　　　　　carried by giant sea turtles.

20　Waves were high that day
　　　　　great sea turtles waded　slowly out
　　　　　　　　　from the gray sundown sea.

Grandfather Turtle rolled in the sand　four times
　　　　　and disappeared
25　　　　　　　　　swimming into the sun.

And so　from that time
　　immemorial,
　　　　　as the old people say,
rain clouds drift from the west
30　　　　　gift from the ocean.

Green leaves in the wind
Wet earth on my feet
　　　　　swallowing raindrops
　　　　　　　　clear from China.　■

words for everyday use

im • me • mo • ri • al (i mə mōr′ ē əl) *adj.,* extending or existing since beyond the reach of memory, record, or tradition. *Christians believe that God has existed since time immemorial.*

Respond *to the* SELECTION

What gift of nature finds its source in the myth of the sea turtles?

LITERARY TECHNIQUE

CONCRETE POEM. A **concrete poem** is one printed or written in a shape that suggests its subject matter. Ask students what "Prayer to the Pacific" resembles.

Answer
Help students see that the shape of the poem resembles ocean waves.

SELECTION CHECK TEST 4.9.3 WITH ANSWERS

Checking Your Reading
1. Where does the speaker travel? **The speaker travels to the ocean.**
2. What does the speaker return to the earth? **She returns turquoise and red coral.**
3. What do the round stones symbolize for the speaker? **They symbolize the ocean.**
4. What do lines 6–10 describe? **They describe the sunset over the Pacific Ocean.**
5. According to lines 17–19, how did the Indians reach the Americas? **They were carried across the ocean on the backs of giant sea turtles.**

Literary Tools
1. What is a simile? **A simile is a comparison using *like* or *as.***
2. What is a myth? **A myth is a story that explains objects or events in the natural world as resulting from the action of some supernatural force or entity.**
3. Which myth does Silko mention in line 5? **She mentions the myth of origin.**

RESPOND TO THE SELECTION

What are some "gifts" that the ocean gives us? that nature gives us?

RECALL
1a. She lives in the "southwest land of sandrock."
2a. She takes "four round stones."

INTERPRET
1b. The speaker mentions where she is from because it is so different from the land of the ocean.
2b. The taste will remind her of the taste of the ocean. Once she has returned home the stones will help her remember the ocean.

ANALYZE
3a. The speaker understands the importance of myth in her culture. Her trip to the ocean recalls the myth of the sea turtles, which explains how her people came to America. She demonstrates feelings of love for Mother Earth, which is evident in her description of the ocean. She sees the earth as being interconnected when she swallows raindrops that come "clear from China."

SYNTHESIZE
3b. The speaker appreciates nature with intense physicality. For example, she intends "to suck and to taste" the stones she brings back from the ocean. She swallows raindrops and steps barefoot on the earth.

PERSPECTIVE
Responses will vary. Possible responses are given.
4a. The speaker's reaction to the ocean is understandable because she is affected by its beauty and by the connection to her people through the myth of the sea turtles.

EMPATHY
4b. Responses will vary.

Investigate, Inquire, and Imagine

Recall: GATHERING FACTS

1a. Where does the speaker live?

2a. What does the speaker take from the ocean?

Interpret: FINDING MEANING

1b. Why does the speaker mention where she is from?

2b. Why does the speaker intend "to suck and to taste" the stones?

Analyze: TAKING THINGS APART

3a. What evidence can you find that demonstrates the speaker's understanding and feelings toward her culture?

Synthesize: BRINGING THINGS TOGETHER

3b. How does the speaker appreciate nature, intellectually or physically? Give evidence to support your answer.

Perspective: LOOKING AT OTHER VIEWS

4a. Is the speaker's reaction to the ocean understandable?

Empathy: SEEING FROM INSIDE

4b. If you were the speaker, what would you remember about the ocean once you went back to the "southwest land of sandrock"?

Understanding Literature

SIMILE. Review the definition for **simile** in the Handbook of Literary Terms. To what is the largeness of the ocean compared in the first stanza? What is the purpose of this simile?

MYTH. Review the definition for **myth** in the Handbook of Literary Terms and the cluster chart you made for Literary Tools on page 715. What event in the history of Native Americans does the myth in stanza 3 attempt to explain? What modern explanation might science give to explain this migration?

ANSWERS TO UNDERSTANDING LITERATURE

SIMILE. The largeness of the ocean is compared to the bigness of the "myth of origin." The purpose of this simile is to introduce the myth that is told later in the poem.

MYTH. The myth explains how Native Americans came to America on the backs of "giant sea turtles." Science might suggest that Native Americans crossed on landlocked passages that were later submerged by the ocean.

Writer's Journal

1. Imagine you are the speaker and have returned home. Write a **journal entry** expressing what your trip to the ocean meant to you.

2. Write **interview questions** to ask the speaker about her beliefs.

3. Write a **myth** that explains the migration of Native Americans to America in a different way from that of the sea turtles.

Integrating the Language Arts

Language, Grammar, and Style

RECOGNIZING CLAUSES AND PHRASES. Read the Language Arts Survey 3.81, "Groups of Words that Function as One Part of Speech," and 3.82, "Phrases." Then identify the underlined parts of the folllowing sentences as clauses (C) or phrases (P).

1. <u>When the speaker left her "southwest land of sandrock,"</u> she went to the ocean.

2. She looked at the "pale water" <u>with discerning eyes</u>.

3. <u>To her way of thinking</u>, the ocean was as big as "the myth of origin."

4. The Indians <u>who came east to America</u> rode across the ocean on giant sea turtles.

5. <u>If you hold out your tongue</u>, you too can swallow raindrops "clear from China."

Speaking and Listening & Study and Research

STORYTELLING. Research several Native American myths. Then select one to tell a small group of classmates. Prepare an introduction that explains which Native American group developed the myth and what it explains about the natural world. Then decide what tone, facial expressions, and gestures to use in presenting your myth. Before you present your myth, you might find it useful to read the Language Arts Survey 4.20, "Telling a Story."

Media Literacy

TYING ORAL TRADITION TO FICTION. In the introduction to one of Leslie Marmon Silko's works, LaVonne Ruoff states, "Silko emphasizes the need to return to rituals and oral traditions of the past in order to rediscover the basis for one's cultural identity." Read about Silko's writings on the Internet and make a list of her writings for which this statement proves true. You can find information about Leslie Marmon Silko at the University of Minnesota's Internet site "Voices from the Gaps: Women Writers of Color" Internet site at http://voices.cla.umn.edu/authors/LeslieMarmonSilko.html.

ANSWERS TO INTEGRATING THE LANGUAGE ARTS

Language, Grammar, and Style
1. C
2. P
3. P
4. C
5. C

Speaking and Listening & Study and Research
To create a comfortable, informal storytelling environment, have groups arrange their chairs in a circle and allow students to retell their myths from their seats.

Media Literacy
To extend this activity, encourage students to choose another work by Silko to read. Have them formulate a thesis statement about tying oral tradition to fiction and express their ideas in a short essay.

GRAPHIC ORGANIZER

The information students include in their charts will vary. Below are a few examples:

Facts about Cabuliwallah	Technique
1. He wore loose, soiled clothing and a tall turban.	1. direct description
2. He greeted the narrator with a smile.	2. character's behavior
3. He joked about what was in his bag.	3. character's behavior
4. Rahmun struck a customer.	4. character's behavior
5. The idea suddenly came to him that his daughter has grown up, too.	5. internal state

READER'S JOURNAL

Students without an adult friend can write about a relationship with an adult relative. They may want to write their thoughts in the form of a letter to the adult.

Literary
TOOLS

THEME. A **theme** is a central idea in a literary work. A father's love for his child is one of the themes central to the story. What underlying theme is highlighted by the change in Mini, as seen by the Cabuliwallah, at the end of the story?

CHARACTERIZATION. Characterization is the use of literary techniques to create a character. Writers use three major techniques to create characters: direct description, portrayal of characters' behavior, and representations of characters' internal states. To learn how to recognize each of these techniques, read more about characterization in the Handbook of Literary Terms. As you read, determine which techniques Tagore employs to characterize the Cabuliwallah.

Graphic Organizer

Make a chart listing facts you learn about the Cabuliwallah and the technique of characterization that they demonstrate. One example has been done for you.

Facts about Cabuliwallah	Technique
Wore the loose, soiled clothing of his people and a tall turban; carried a bag on his back and boxes of grapes in his hand.	direct description

Reader's Journal

Describe a friendship you have had with an adult. What topics did you talk about?

"The Cabuliwallah"
by Rabindranath Tagore

Reader's resource

"The Cabuliwallah" is a short story about the friendship between a young girl and an itinerant peddler, told by the young girl's father. The story comes from Tagore's collection *Galpaguccha* ("A Bunch of Stories"), in which the author writes about "humble lives and their small miseries."

GEOGRAPHY CONNECTION. Cabuliwallahs are peddlers or fruit sellers from Kabul, Afghanistan. Kabul became the capital city of Afghanistan in 1773. Since then, it has been destroyed many times by civil wars and rebuilt again. Because of Kabul's location, fighting for the control of the Khyber Pass (a passage way through the mountains between Afghanistan and Pakistan) among the British, Persians, and Russians has also led to the cycle of destroying and rebuilding this city. Kabul continues to be the center of much turmoil and fighting centered around religious, political, and military ideals.

About the AUTHOR

Rabindranath Tagore (1861–1941), the son of the Great Sage Devendranath Tagore, was born in Calcutta, India. Tagore began to write early in his life, publishing in 1890 a collection of verse, *Manasi,* which marked the maturing of his genius. The next year, Tagore moved to Shilaidah and Saiyad-pur, where he wrote several collections of verse, stories, and two plays. He won the Nobel Prize for literature in 1913 for his collection *Gitanjali* ("Song Offering"). In his country, Tagore is widely known for his lyrics and songs on nature, love, and childhood. Also a gifted composer, he set hundreds of poems to music. Seeking to blend the best in Indian and Western traditions, Tagore founded the "world university," Santiniketan, one hundred miles outside of Calcutta. English translations of Tagore's work include *The Crescent Moon, One Hundred Poems of Kabir, The Gardener, Red Oleanders,* and *Fireflies.* His *Collected Poems and Plays* was published in 1936 and again in 1976.

GOALS/OBJECTIVES

Studying this lesson will enable students to
- appreciate a story about a peddler's relationship with a young girl
- describe Rabindranath Tagore's literary accomplishments and explain how his environment influenced his writing
- define *theme* and identify the main themes in a short story

- define *characterization* and recognize the characterization techniques used to create well-developed characters
- demonstrate an ability to distinguish between the active and the passive voice in writing
- present to the class an oral interpretation of a poem

"The Cabuliwallah"

Rabindranath Tagore

Mini, my five-year-old daughter, cannot live without chattering. I really believe that in all her life she has not wasted one minute in silence. Her mother is often vexed at this and would stop her prattle, but I do not. To see Mini quiet is unnatural and I cannot bear it for long. Because of this, our conversations are always lively.

What does Mini do all the time? How do her parents feel about this tendency?

One morning, for instance, when I was in the midst of the seventeenth chapter of my new novel, Mini stole into the room and putting her hand into mine, said: "Father! Ramdayal the door keeper calls a crow a krow! He doesn't know anything, does he?"

Before I could explain the language differences in this country, she was on the trace of another subject. "What do you think, Father? Shola says there is an elephant in the clouds, blowing water out of his trunk, and that is why it rains!"

The child had seated herself at my feet near the table and was playing softly, drumming on her knees. I was hard at work on my seventeenth chapter, where Pratap Singh, the hero, had just caught Kanchanlata, the heroine, in his arms and was about to escape with her by the third-story window of the castle, when all of a sudden Mini left her play and ran to the window, crying, "A Cabuliwallah! A Cabuliwallah!"[1] Sure enough, in the street below was a Cabuliwallah passing slowly along. He wore the loose, soiled clothing of his people and a tall turban; there was a bag on his back, and he carried boxes of grapes in his hand.

I cannot tell what my daughter's feelings were at the sight of this man, but she began to call him loudly. Ah, I thought, he will come in and my seventeenth chapter will never be finished! At this exact moment the Cabuliwallah turned and looked up at the child. When she saw this she was overcome by terror, fled to

Why is Mini frightened of the Cabuliwallah?

her mother's protection, and disappeared. She had a blind belief that inside the bag which the big man carried were two or three children like herself. Meanwhile, the peddler entered my doorway and greeted me with a smiling face.

So <u>precarious</u> was the position of my hero and my heroine that my first impulse was to stop and buy something, especially since Mini had called to the man. I made some small purchases, and a conversation began about Abdurrahman, the Russians, the English, and the Frontier Policy.[2]

---

1. **Cabuliwallah.** Peddler or fruit seller from Kabul (also spelled Cabul), the capital of Afghanistan
2. **Abdurrahman . . . the Frontier Policy.** Abdurrahman became ruler of Afghanistan in 1880, after regaining control of his country from the English and the Russians.

---

words for everyday use

pre • car • i • ous (prē ker´ē əs) *adj.,* insecure; unsure. *The <u>precarious</u> nature of their friendship can be seen in the uncertain gestures they make toward one another.*

VOCABULARY FROM THE SELECTION

composure	formidable	judicious
euphemism	impending	pervade
fettered	implore	precarious

INDIVIDUAL LEARNING STRATEGIES (CONT.)

ENRICHMENT
Ask students to research Calcutta. Students might choose to research one of the following topics: people, culture, climate, economy, or history. Students can present their information in written or oral reports.

---

1. Mini chatters, or talks, all the time. Mini's mother is confused by Mini's chatter, but her father enjoys it.
2. Mini believed the Cabuliwallah carried children like herself in his bag.

INDIVIDUAL LEARNING STRATEGIES

MOTIVATION
Have students work in small groups to discuss the experience of seeing an adult whom they have not seen since they were young children. Ask students to say how they feel when adults say "I haven't seen you since you were a baby!" or "My, how you've grown!" Ask students whether it is easy or difficult to communicate with adults they have not seen for years.

READING PROFICIENCY
To help students understand the context, explain that "The Cabuliwallah" is set in Calcutta, India's largest city. Have students locate India on a map. Then direct students to eastern India, the location of Calcutta. Point out that Calcutta is located near the Bay of Bengal and is one of India's major ports.

ENGLISH LANGUAGE LEARNING
Point out to students that this story deals with a man from one country living and working in a different country. While the Cabuliwallah can communicate with the people in Calcutta, he faces discrimination based on cultural and social class differences. Help students connect with the Cabuliwallah by encouraging them to share stories of their experiences in a new culture. They might draw from the stories of friends or relatives, as well.

SPECIAL NEEDS
Explain to students that the story covers a lengthy time period (nearly ten years). Point out that, at one point in the story, the time setting jumps to the future. Ask students to be on the lookout for this jump. You might have them make a two-column chart with the headings *Young Mini* and *Older Mini*. Students can record and separate the main story events from each time period.

BIOGRAPHICAL NOTE

Rabindranath Tagore is still considered Calcutta's most noteworthy citizen. Tagore expressed the complexity of life in Calcutta, a city strongly influenced by European cosmopolitanism, colonialism, and its own vibrant sense of identity.

Quotables

"At my dying hour, and over my long life,

A clock strikes somewhere at the city's edge."

—Rabindranath Tagore

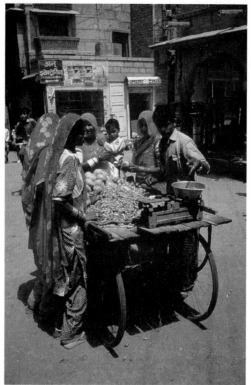

Fruit Sellers, Jaisalmer, India.

As he was about to leave, he asked: "And where is the little girl, sir?"

I, thinking that Mini must get rid of her false fear, had her brought out. She stood by my chair, watching the Cabuliwallah and his bag. He offered her nuts and raisins but she would not be tempted, and only clung closer to me, with all her doubts increased. This was their first meeting.

One morning, however, not many days later, as I was leaving the house I was startled to find Mini seated on a bench near the door, laughing and talking with the great Cabuliwallah at her feet. In all her life, it appeared, my small daughter had never found so patient a listener, except for her father. Already the corner of her little sari[3] was stuffed with almonds and raisins, gifts from her visitor. "Why did you give her those?" I said, and taking out an eight-anna piece,[4] handed it to him. The man accepted the money without delay and slipped it into his pocket.

> What does the narrator do when he sees his daughter with the Cabuliwallah's gifts? What does the Cabuliwallah do in return?

Alas, on my return an hour later, I found the unfortunate coin had made twice its own worth of trouble! The Cabuliwallah had given it to Mini, and her mother, seeing the bright, round object, had pounced on the child with: "Where did you get that eight-anna piece?"

"The Cabuliwallah gave it to me," said Mini cheerfully.

"The Cabuliwallah gave it to you!" cried her mother, much shocked. "Oh, Mini! How could you take it from him?"

Entering at this moment, I saved her from <u>impending</u> disaster and proceeded to make my own inquiries. I found that it was not the first or the second time the two had met. The Cabuliwallah had overcome the child's first terror by a <u>judicious</u> bribery of nuts and almonds, and the two were now great friends.

> How does the Cabuliwallah overcome Mini's fears?

They had many quaint jokes which afforded them great deal of amusement. Seated in front of him, and looking with all her tiny dignity on

---

3. **sari.** Full-length, robed dress, often of silk, worn by women in India
4. **eight-anna piece.** Coin once used in India

---

words for everyday use

im • pend • ing (im pend´ in) *adj.,* about to happen; imminent. *Having cleaned the house, she felt prepared for the <u>impending</u> visit from her relatives.*

ju • di • cious (joo dish´əs) *adj.,* reasoned, wise; calculated. *Always mindful of his health, he applied a <u>judicious</u> amount of butter to his toast.*

his gigantic frame, Mini would ripple her face with laughter and begin, "O Cabuliwallah! Cabuliwallah! what have you got in your bag?"

He would reply in the nasal accents of a mountaineer: "An elephant!" Not much cause for merriment, perhaps, but how they both enjoyed their joke! And for me, this child's talk with a grown-up man always had in it something strangely fascinating.

Then the Cabuliwallah, not to be caught behind, would take his turn with: "Well, little one, and when are you going to the father-in-law's house?"

Now most small Bengali maidens have heard long ago about the father-in-law's house, but we, being a little modern, had kept these things from our child, and at this question Mini must have been a trifle bewildered. But she would not show it, and with instant <u>composure</u> replied: "Are you going there?"

Among men of the Cabuliwallah's class, however, it is well known that the words "father-in-law's house" have a double meaning. It is a <u>euphemism</u> for jail, the place where we are well cared for at no expense. The sturdy peddler would take my daughter's question in this sense. "Ah," he would say, shaking his fist at an invisible policeman, "I will thrash my father-in-law!" Hearing this, and picturing the poor, uncomfortable relative, Mini would go into peals of laughter, joined by her <u>formidable</u> friend.

These were autumn mornings, the time of year when kings of old went forth to conquest; and I, never stirring from my little corner in Calcutta,[5] would let my mind wander over the whole world. At the very name of another country, my heart would go out to it, and at the sight

[marginal question] What is the double meaning of the words "father-in-law's house"?

of a foreigner in the streets, I would fall to weaving a network of dreams: the mountains, the glens, the forests of his distant homeland with a cottage in its setting, and the free and independent life of faraway wilds. Perhaps these scenes of travel pass in my imagination all the more vividly because I lead a vegetable existence[6] such that a call to travel would fall upon me like a thunderbolt. In the presence of this Cabuliwallah I was immediately transported to the foot of mountains, with narrow defiles[7] twisting in and out amongst their towering, arid peaks. I could see the string of camels bearing merchandise, and the company of turbaned merchants carrying queer old firearms and some of their spears down toward the plains. I could see—but at this point Mini's mother would intervene, <u>imploring</u> me to "beware of that man."

Unfortunately Mini's mother is a very timid lady. Whenever she hears a noise in the street or sees people coming toward the house, she always jumps to the conclusion that they are either thieves, drunkards, snakes, tigers, malaria, cockroaches, caterpillars, or an English sailor. Even after all these years of experience, she is not able to overcome her terror. Thus she was full of doubts about the Cabuliwallah and used to beg me to keep a watchful eye on him.

[marginal question] What are Mini's mother's feelings about the Cabuliwallah?

I tried to gently laugh her fear away, but then she would turn on me seriously and ask solemn questions.

Were children never kidnapped?

---

5. **Calcutta.** Seaport city in northeast India
6. **vegetable existence.** Dull life
7. **defiles.** Mountain passes

---

words for everyday use

com • po • sure (kəm pō´zhər) n., calmness. *Even when surrounded by jittery, inexperienced actors, the star maintained her well-practiced <u>composure</u>.*

eu • phe • mism (yōō´fə miz´em) n., word or phrase that is used in place of another, more offensive expression. *The dinner guest used the <u>euphemism</u> "interesting" to describe the suspicious-looking lumps floating in his soup bowl.*

for • mi • da • ble (fôr´mə də bəl) adj., imposing in size. *To the dismay of the prosecutor, the district attorney was building a <u>formidable</u> defense.*

im • plore (im plôr´) vt., beg. *After <u>imploring</u> me to drive carefully, my mother gave me the keys to the car.*

"THE CABULIWALLAH" **723**

1. "Father-in-law's house" could mean getting married. It was also a euphemism for jail.
2. Mini's mother was doubtful of the Cabuliwallah's intentions.

CROSS-CURRICULAR CONNECTIONS

SOCIAL STUDIES. In India, the major religion is Hinduism. Throughout Indian history, Hinduism has unified the many religions, races, languages, and cultures of India's diverse population. However, Hinduism has also created sharp divisions between people with its caste system. In the caste system, a person is born into a particular social class, from which he or she cannot separate. The class into which a person is born determines or restricts education, social associations, and occupations. In the story, the Cabuliwallah and the narrator belong to two different castes.

1. A neighbor owed Rahmun money for a shawl, but when Rahmun went to collect the money, the neighbor denied buying it. In the course of the argument, Rahmun struck the man and was charged for murderous assault.

CROSS-CURRICULAR ACTIVITIES

MATHEMATICS AND SCIENCES. Ask pairs of students to calculate the distance Rahmun traveled every January from Calcutta to his home in the mountains of Afghanistan. Students might use library or Internet resources to locate a map and a distance chart.

LITERARY TECHNIQUE

TRANSITION. A **transition** is a word, phrase, sentence, or paragraph used to connect ideas and to show relationships between them. Tagore uses transitions frequently in "The Cabuliwallah." Ask students to identify a few examples of transitions on pages 724–725.

Answer
Students might cite the phrases "once a year in the middle of January" and "one morning, a few days before he had made up his mind to go." They might also cite the sentences "time passed and he was forgotten" and "many years passed."

Was it, then, not true that there was slavery in Cabul?

Was it so very absurd that this big man should be able to carry off a tiny child?

I told her that, though not impossible, it was highly improbable. But this was not enough, and her dread persisted. As her suspicion was unfounded, however, it did not seem right to forbid the man to come to the house, and his familiarity went unchecked.

> *After the rains, there was a sense of cleanness in the air, and the rays of the sun looked like pure gold*

Once a year in the middle of January, Rahmun the Cabuliwallah was in the habit of returning to his country, and as the time approached he would be very busy going from house to house collecting his debts. This year, however, he always found time to come and see Mini. It would have seemed to an outsider that there was some conspiracy between them, for when he could not come in the morning, he would appear in the evening.

Even to me it was a little startling now and then, to suddenly surprise this tall, loose-garmented man of bags in the corner of a dark room; but when Mini would run in, smiling, with her "O Cabuliwallah! Cabuliwallah!" and the two friends so far apart in age would subside into their old laughter and their old jokes, I felt reassured.

One morning, a few days before he had made up his mind to go, I was correcting my proof sheets[8] in my study. It was chilly weather. Through the window the rays of the sun touched my feet, and the slight warmth was very welcome. It was almost eight o'clock, and the early pedestrians were returning home with their heads covered. All at once I heard an uproar in the street and, looking out, saw Rahmun bound and being led away between two policemen, followed by a crowd of curious boys. There were bloodstains on the clothes of the Cabuliwallah, and one of the policemen carried a knife. Hurrying out, I stopped them and inquired what it all meant. Partly from one, partly from another, I gathered that a certain neighbor had owed the peddler something for a Rampuri shawl but had falsely denied having bought it, and that in the course of the quarrel Rahmun had struck him. Now, in the heat of his excitement, the prisoner began calling his enemy all sorts of names. Suddenly, from a verandah of my house my little Mini appeared, with her usual exclamation: "O Cabuliwallah! Cabuliwallah!" Rahmun's face lighted up as he turned to her. He had no bag under his arm today, so she could not discuss the elephant with him. She at once therefore proceeded to the next question: "Are you going to the father-in-law's house?" Rahmun laughed and said: "Just where I am going, little one!" Then seeing that the reply did not amuse the child,

Why is Rahmun arrested?

---

8. **proof sheets.** Typeset copy of a manuscript on which an editor or author marks changes while comparing the proof to the original manuscript

he held up his <u>fettered</u> hands. "Ah," he said, "I would have thrashed that old father-in-law, but my hands are bound!"

How does the situation change the joke the Cabuliwallah and Mini had shared?

On a charge of murderous assault, Rahmun was sentenced to many years of imprisonment.

Time passed and he was forgotten. The accustomed work in the accustomed place was ours, and the thought of the once-free mountaineer spending his years in prison seldom occurred to us. Even my lighthearted Mini, I am ashamed to say, forgot her old friend. New companions filled her life. As she grew older she spent more of her time with girls, so much in fact that she came no more to her father's room. I was scarcely on speaking terms with her.

Many years passed. It was autumn once again and we had made arrangements for Mini's marriage; it was to take place during the Puja[9] holidays. With the goddess Durga returning to her seasonal home in Mount Kailas, the light of our home was also to depart, leaving our house in shadows.

The morning was bright. After the rains, there was a sense of cleanness in the air, and the rays of the sun looked like pure gold, so bright that they radiated even to the sordid brick walls of our Calcutta lanes. Since early dawn, the wedding pipes had been sounding, and at each beat my own heart throbbed. The wailing tune, Bhairavi, seemed to intensify my pain at the approaching separation. My Mini was to be married tonight.

From early morning, noise and bustle <u>pervaded</u> the house. In the courtyard the canopy had to be slung[10] on its bamboo poles; the tinkling chandeliers should be hung in each room and verandah; there was great hurry and excitement. I was sitting in my study, looking through the accounts, when someone entered, saluting respectfully, and stood before me. It was Rahmun the Cabuliwallah, and at first I did not recognize him. He had no bag, nor the long hair, nor the same vigor that he used to have. But he smiled, and I knew him again.

Who appears on the night of Mini's wedding? In what ways has he changed? How does the narrator recognize him?

"When did you come, Rahmun?" I asked him.

"Last evening," he said, "I was released from jail."

The words struck harsh upon my ears. I had never talked with anyone who had wounded his fellow man, and my heart shrank when I realized this, for I felt that the day would have been better omened if he had not turned up.

How does Mini's father feel about Rahmun's arrival?

"There are ceremonies going on," I said, "and I am busy. Could you perhaps come another day?"

At once he turned to go, but as he reached the door he hesitated and said: "May I not see the little one, sir, for a moment?" It was his belief that Mini was still the same. He had pictured her running to him as she used to do, calling, "O Cabuliwallah! Cabuliwallah!" He had imagined that they would laugh and talk together, just as in the past. In fact, in memory of those former days he had brought, carefully wrapped up in paper, a few almonds and raisins and grapes, somehow obtained from a countryman—his own little fund was gone.

I said again: "There is a ceremony in the house, and you will not be able to see anyone today."

---

9. **Puja.** Hindu holiday set aside for worshipping a god or goddess

10. **canopy . . . slung.** Cloth cover had to be suspended; a canopy over the bride and groom is typical in traditional wedding ceremonies.

---

words for everyday use	**fet • tered** (fet´ərd) *adj.,* handcuffed. *Before performing the illusion, the magician displayed his <u>fettered</u> hands to the audience.*
	per • vade (pər vād´) *vt.,* fill, spread through. *Smells of simmering tomatoes and garlic <u>pervaded</u> the kitchen.*

ANSWERS TO GUIDED READING QUESTIONS

1. The joke is changed because Rahmun is actually going to "father-in-law's house," or jail.
2. Rahmun, the Cabuliwallah, appears on the night of Mini's wedding. He no longer had his bag, long hair, or the vigor he once had.
3. Mini's father feels it is a bad omen that a man who wounded someone else has shown up on Mini's wedding day.

CROSS-CURRICULAR ACTIVITIES

SOCIAL STUDIES

- Ask students to skim the section of the story they have read thus far and take notes on the narrator's explanations of the social class differences between his family and the Cabuliwallah. Have students work in small groups to discuss the lines that separate social classes. Pose the following questions: Is money the main factor that separates social classes? What common bonds can bring people of separate social classes together?

- Have students research the caste system and discuss their thoughts about it. Ask students to analyze the similarities and differences between the caste system as it exists in India and the socioeconomic classes as they exist in the United States.

1. For years, Rahmun has carried with him a small piece of paper with the impression of his young daughter's hand on it. Mini's father realizes that he and the Cabuliwallah are similar in that they are both fathers.
2. Mini and Rahmun's joke has changed because Mini knows the double meaning of "father-in-law's house," or jail.
3. Mini's father gave Rahmun money that enabled Rahmun to return to his family. Because of this gift, Mini's father could not afford the electric lights and a military band. Mini's father hopes his generosity will bring Mini good fortune.

RESPOND TO THE SELECTION

What signs of discrimination against Rahmun are evident in the story?

SELECTION CHECK TEST 4.9.5 WITH ANSWERS

Checking Your Reading

1. How old is Mini when she meets the Cabuliwallah? **She is five years old.**
2. How does Mini react to the Cabuliwallah at first? **First, she calls him to the house. Then, she reacts with fear.**
3. How does their relationship change in the following weeks? **They become good friends, constantly talking and joking.**
4. What happens to the Cabuliwallah as he is trying to collect his debts? **He is arrested and taken to jail because he struck one of his customers who refused to pay for goods.**
5. How does Mini react to the Cabuliwallah when he returns on her wedding day? **She is shy and seems fearful, as she was during their first meeting.**

Vocabulary in Context

Fill in each blank below with the most appropriate word from the following Words for Everyday Use. You may need to change the tense of the word.

> precarious   impending   judicious
> composure   formidable   implore
> pervade

1. She faced the **formidable** task of cleaning the long-neglected attic.

The man's face fell. He looked wistfully at me for a moment, said "Good morning," and went out.

I felt a little sorry and would have called him back but saw that he was returning of his own accord. He came close up to me, holding out his offerings, and said: "I brought these few things, sir, for the little one. Will you give them to her?"

I took them and was going to pay him, but he caught my hand and said: "You are very kind, sir! Keep me in your recollection; do not offer me money! You have a little girl; I too have one like her in my own home. I thought of my own and brought fruits to your child, not to make a profit for myself."

Saying this, he put his hand inside his big loose robe and brought out a small dirty piece of paper. With great care he unfolded this and smoothed it out with both hands on my table. It bore the impression of a little hand, not a photograph, not a drawing. The impression of an ink-smeared hand laid flat on the paper. This touch of his own little daughter had been always on his heart, as he had come year after year to Calcutta to sell his wares in the streets.

> *What has Rahmun carried with him all these years? How does this change Mini's father's feelings?*

Tears came to my eyes. I forgot that he was a poor Cabuli fruitseller, while I was—but no, was I more than he? He was also a father.

That impression of the hand of his little Parbati in her distant mountain home reminded me of my own little Mini, and I immediately sent for her from the inner apartment. Many excuses were raised, but I would not listen. Clad in the red silk of her wedding day, with the sandal paste on her forehead, and adorned as a young bride, Mini came and stood bashfully before me.

Respond *to the* SELECTION

Was the Cabuliwallah's imprisonment just or unjust?

The Cabuliwallah was staggered at the sight of her. There was no hope of reviving their old friendship. At last he smiled and said: "Little one, are you going to your father-in-law's house?"

But Mini now understood the meaning of the word "father-in-law," and she could not reply to him as in the past. She flushed at the question and stood before him with her bride's face looking down.

> *What new meaning does Mini and Rahmun's old joke have?*

I remembered the day when the Cabuliwallah and my Mini first met, and I felt sad. When she had gone, Rahmun heaved a deep sigh and sat down on the floor. The idea had suddenly come to him that his daughter also must have grown up during this long time, and that he would have to make friends with her all over again. Surely he would not find her as he used to know her; besides, what might have happened to her in these eight years?

The marriage pipes sounded, and the mild autumn sun streamed around us. But Rahmun sat in the little Calcutta lane and saw before him the barren mountains of Afghanistan.

I took out a bank note and gave it to him, saying: "Go back to your own daughter, Rahmun, in your own country, and may the happiness of your meeting bring good fortune to my child!"

After giving this gift, I had to eliminate some of the festivities. I could not have the electric lights, nor the military band,[11] and the ladies of the house were saddened. But to me the wedding feast was brighter because of the thought that in a distant land a long-lost father met again with his only child. ■

> *What happens as a result of Mini's father giving money to Rahmun? What effect does Mini's father think it has on the festivities?*

---

11. **giving this gift, . . . military band.** Traditional weddings in India are very costly for the father of the bride.

SELECTION CHECK TEST 4.9.5 WITH ANSWERS (CONT.)

2. The tragic hero faced **impending** doom.
3. The jurors must make a **judicious** decision concerning the guilt of the defendant.
4. Even in the face of danger, the woman kept her **composure**.
5. The smell of garbage **pervaded** the neighborhood next to the landfill.

Literary Tools

1. What is the definition of *theme*? **A theme is a central idea in a literary work.**
2. What is characterization? **Characterization is the use of literary techniques to create a character.**
3. What are the three major techniques of characterization? **Direct description, portrayal of characters' behavior, and representation of**

Investigate, Inquire, and Imagine

Recall: GATHERING FACTS

1a. What can Mini, the narrator's five-year-old daughter, not live without doing?

2a. What is Mini's first reaction to the Cabuliwallah?

3a. What gift does Rahmun bring to Mini on her wedding day?

Interpret: FINDING MEANING

1b. What troubles the narrator when Mini is silent?

2b. What actions on the part of Mini and the Cabuliwallah show that they enjoy one another's friendship?

3b. What actions on the part of Mini show that she has grown up?

Analyze: TAKING THINGS APART

4a. Analyze the relationship between Rahmun and Mini. What things do they do with each other? How do they feel toward one another? Back up your answers with examples from the text.

Synthesize: BRINGING THINGS TOGETHER

4b. Based on the relationship between Rahmun and Mini you described in question 4a., predict what their relationship would have been like if Rahmun had never gone to jail. In what ways would Rahmun's life be different if they never separated? In what ways would Mini's life be different?

Evaluate: MAKING JUDGMENTS

5a. What is the reason Rahmun develops a special friendship with young Mini? Do you think this is a good reason? Why, or why not?

Extend: CONNECTING IDEAS

5b. Why do you think the narrator reacts the way he does when Rahmun shows him the impression of his daughter's hand on the piece of paper? How do you think the narrator's reaction would have been different if he, himself, were not a father of a daughter?

Understanding Literature

THEME. Review the definition for **theme** in the Handbook of Literary Terms. What underlying theme is highlighted by the change in Mini, as seen by Rahmun, at the end of the story?

CHARACTERIZATION. Review the definition for **characterization** in Literary Tools in Prereading and the chart you made for that section. What techniques does Tagore use to characterize Rahmun? Which of Rahmun's behaviors show that he dearly loves his only daughter?

Answers to Understanding Literature can be found on page 728.

Answers to Understanding Literature can be found on page 728.

ANSWERS TO INVESTIGATE, INQUIRE, AND IMAGINE

RECALL
1a. Mini cannot live without chattering.
2a. At first, Mini is frightened of the Cabuliwallah.
3a. Rahmun brings to Mini a gift of "a few almonds and raisins and grapes" on her wedding day.

INTERPRET
1b. Because Mini's silence seems "unnatural," he is troubled when she isn't chattering.
2b. They share laughter and jokes.
3b. Mini's shyness and embarrassed blush at understanding the "adult" meaning of the phrase "father-in-law's house" shows that she has grown up.

ANALYZE
4a. Rahmun and Mini's relationship with each other is positive. They share jokes, stories, and laugh a lot. Rahmun treats Mini like his own daughter by giving her gifts of fruits and nuts and by listening to her chattering. Mini is always excited to see Rahmun, calling out "O Cabuliwallah! O Cabuliwallah!" It is clear that she loves to spend time with him and he with her.

SYNTHESIZE
4b. If they never separated, Rahmun and Mini probably would have remained close friends. Rahmun would have been a second father to Mini, protecting her and giving her advice as she grew up through the years. They would still joke and laugh because they share the same humor. Rahmun's life would have been happier if they never separated. He would have played an integral part in her wedding. Mini would have had the opportunity to have two father figures in her life, protecting and loving her. Her life would have been filled with more love and laughter if they had never separated.

EVALUATE
5a. Rahmun develops a friendship with Mini because she reminds him of his own daughter. This is a good reason because the relationship allows him to fill the void and emptiness of having to be separated from daughter. The relationship is also good for Mini because it provides a companion who listens to her chattering.

ANSWERS TO INVESTIGATE, INQUIRE, AND IMAGINE (CONT.)

EXTEND
5b. He reacts this way because he can sympathize with Rahmun and Rahmun's pain of being away from his daughter for so long since the narrator is a father also. The narrator would not have been so understanding or sympathetic to Rahmun if he did not have a daughter himself. He probably would have dismissed Rahmun like he did the first time.

ANSWERS TO UNDERSTANDING LITERATURE

THEME. The change in Mini, as seen by Rahmun, at the end of the story highlights the theme of lost childhood and lost innocence. Mini blushes when she sees the Cabuliwallah again after all this time, showing an awareness of her womanhood.

CHARACTERIZATION. Tagore uses direct description and portrayal of the character's behavior to characterize Rahmun. Examples of his behavior that show his love for his daughter include how he unfolds the paper "with great care," how he places the paper "with both hands" on the narrator's table, and how he keeps the ink-smeared impression "always on his heart."

ANSWERS TO INTEGRATING THE LANGUAGE ARTS

Language, Grammar, and Style
1. The narrator created a hero and a heroine for his story.
2. The people of Calcutta called Rahmun the Cabuliwallah.
3. OK
4. The police took him to jail for hitting a customer.
5. The jailers released Rahmun on the day of Mini's wedding.

Applied English
Assign a score from 1 to 25 for each grading criterion below. (For more detailed evaluation, see the evaluation forms for writing, revising, and proofreading in the Assessment Resource book.)

THANK-YOU LETTER
- **CONTENT/UNITY.** The thank-you letter thanks an adult for help or a service rendered.
- **ORGANIZATION/COHERENCE.** The thank-you letter is well-organized.
- **LANGUAGE/STYLE.** The thank-you letter is written in formal English and uses clear and concise language.
- **CONVENTIONS.** The thank-you letter avoids errors in spelling, grammar, usage, mechanics, and manuscript form.

Speaking and Listening
You might ask students to write a one-page essay explaining their ideas about and interpretations of the poem. Once they read the poem to classmates, they can present their personal ideas. Encourage the class to ask the reader questions about his or her reading and interpretation.

Writer's Journal

1. Pretend you are Rahmun. Write a **letter** to your daughter in the mountains of Afghanistan, telling her how you feel about her, what you keep always in your possession, and why you have been separated.
2. Write a **wedding invitation** for Mimi's wedding. Include a special note to Rahmon explaining why he has been invited.
3. Imagine Rahmun returns to see the narrator after he has seen his daughter. Write a **dialogue** between the two men in which they discuss what their daughters were like when they were little and the relationship they have with them now that they are grown. Did Rahmun's daughter forgive him after his long absence? Did Mini forgive her father after he pared down her wedding celebration?

Integrating the Language Arts

Language, Grammar, and Style

USING THE ACTIVE VOICE. Read the Language Arts Survey 3.37, "Making Passive Sentences Active." Determine whether each of the following sentences is written in the passive or the active voice. Rewrite those that are in the passive voice, using the active voice instead. Write *OK* if a sentence needs no correction.

1. A hero and a heroine were created by the narrator for his story.
2. Ruhman was called the Cabuliwallah by the people of Calcutta.
3. Ruhman accepted the money for the almonds and raisins that the narrator handed him.
4. He was taken to jail by the police for hitting a customer.
5. Ruhman was released by his jailers on the day of Mini's wedding.

Applied English

LETTER OF THANKS. In this story, the narrator helps Rahmun by giving him money to go back home to see his daughter. Write a thank-you letter to an adult who has helped you in some way. It could be a coach, a teacher, a counselor, a tutor, a neighbor, or an employer. Express in your letter why that person's help or friendship has been meaningful to you. After you complete the letter, proof it for errors in spelling, grammar, usage, mechanics, and manuscript form. Then put the correct postage, address, and return address on the envelope and send your letter.

Speaking and Listening

ORAL INTERPRETATION. Select a poem by Tagore that you like. Read the Language Arts Survey 4.19, "Oral Interpretation." Then decide what verbal and nonverbal communication to use in an oral interpretation of the poem. Practice your interpretation. Then present your interpretation to the class or a small group of classmates.

"New Dog"

by Mark Doty

Reader's resource

"New Dog" was published in 1995 in Mark Doty's collection of poems *Atlantis*. It tells about his friend Wally's dying wish for a new dog and is recounted with a sense of immediacy. "Before Wally's diagnosis," says Doty, "lots of my work had been about memory and trying to gain some perspective on the past. Suddenly that was much less important and I felt pushed to pay attention to now, what I could celebrate or discern in the now."

About the AUTHOR

Mark Doty (1953–), poet and nonfiction writer, was born in Memphis, Tennessee, and grew up in Arizona, Florida, and California. He has written several books of poetry, including *Turtle, Swan* (1987); *Bethlehem in Broad Daylight* (1991); *My Alexandria* (1993), winner of the National Book Critics Circle Award, and a finalist for the National Book Award; *Atlantis* (1995), a *New York Times* and American Library Association Notable Book, recipient of the Ambassador Book Award, the Bingham Poetry Prize, and a Lambda Literary Award; and *The Sweet Machine* (1998), which has received critical acclaim. Doty has also written memoirs: *Heaven's Coast* (1996), *Firebird* (1999), and *Still Life with Oysters and Lemon* (2001). Of his writing, Doty says, "I've written a good deal, in recent years, along intensely personal lines. Those poems move through my own experiences of grief to connect with readers' experiences of the evanescence of what we love—or at least I hope they do! The work of the poet investigating personal experience is always to find such points of connection, to figure out how to open the private out to the reader." Doty currently teaches at the University of Houston.

POEM

Literary TOOLS

PARADOX. A **paradox** is a seemingly contradictory statement, idea, or event. As you read "New Dog," look for a paradox in the poem.

LYRIC POEM. A **lyric poem** is a highly musical verse that expresses the emotions of a speaker. As you read, try to identify the speaker's emotions.

Graphic Organizer

Make a cluster chart to list statements from the poem that point to the speaker's emotion. One example has been done for you.

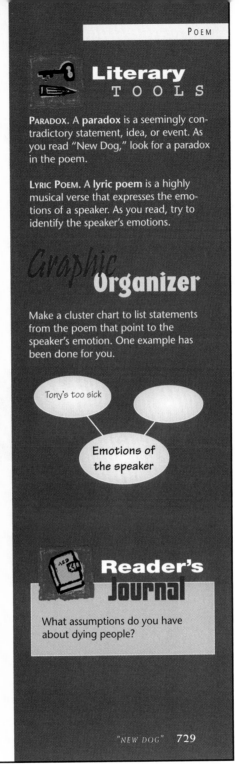

Tony's too sick

Emotions of the speaker

Reader's Journal

What assumptions do you have about dying people?

ADDITIONAL RESOURCES

UNIT 9 RESOURCE BOOK
• Selection Worksheet 9.4
• Selection Check Test 4.9.7
• Selection Test 4.9.8
• Language, Grammar, and Style Resource 3.39

VOCABULARY FROM THE SELECTION

concatenation
tentative

GRAPHIC ORGANIZER

Other statements that reveal the speaker's emotion include: "He's paralyzed now / from the waist down," "we don't know / how much longer / he'll be able to pet a dog," "Wally can no longer / feed himself," "I have never seen a touch so deliberate," "this gesture / toward the restless splendor, / the unruly, the golden, / the animal, the new."

READER'S JOURNAL

Encourage students to think about dogs or pets in general. Ask students to write about some of the positive aspects pets can add to human lives. For students without much experience with pets, ask them to recall portrayals about which they have heard, read, or watched onscreen.

GOALS/OBJECTIVES

Studying this lesson will enable students to
• appreciate a poem about the bond that is often forged between animals and humans
• summarize and discuss the speaker's perspectives on dying
• define *paradox* and identify this technique in poetry

• define *lyric poem* and explain how the term relates to the selection
• demonstrate an ability to make sentences more colorful by adding modifiers
• conduct research on the stages of dying

1. Wally wants to adopt a new dog. He also says he'd like "Some lizards, a talking bird, some fish. A little rat."

INDIVIDUAL LEARNING STRATEGIES

MOTIVATION
Have students work in small groups to share stories about the bond between dogs and humans. (You might broaden the discussion by allowing students to discuss all kinds of animals.) For example, students might suggest that companionship, loyalty, and humor are factors in the bonds humans form with animals.

READING PROFICIENCY
Point out to students that, while this poem exhibits the qualities of a lyric poem, "New Dog" also tells a story. Suggest that students make a chart with the headings *The Story* and *The Emotions*. Students can read the poem twice: once to summarize the action, or the story Doty tells, and again to identify and record the emotions he describes.

ENGLISH LANGUAGE LEARNING
Share with students these additional vocabulary words from the poem:
obligation—commitment; something one must do
bounding—leaping or jumping
boundless—having no limits
unmediated—not controlled or regulated
gilt—gold
flanks—body parts between ribs and hips
deliberate—purposeful
summoned—called forth
unruly—not disciplined; out of control

SPECIAL NEEDS
Explain that Doty uses italics in this poem for words that are traditionally placed in quotation marks. These lines are descriptions of what someone says.

ENRICHMENT
Have students research companion dogs (dogs that help people with physical or visual disabilities or medical conditions) and locate a story of how a dog helped its companion. Students might search magazine, newspaper, or Internet sources. Then, hold a class storytelling festival in which each student shares with the class the story they chose.

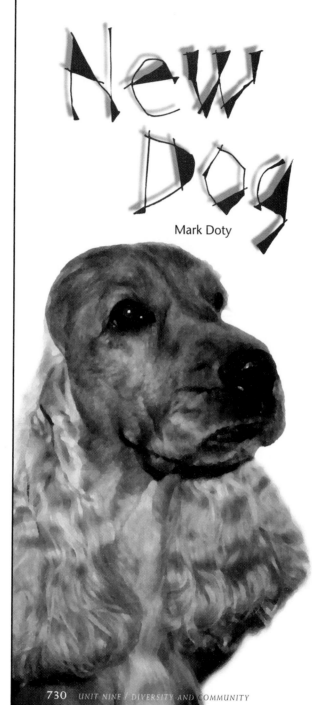

New Dog

Mark Doty

Jimi and Tony
can't keep Dino,
their cocker spaniel;
Tony's too sick,
the daily walks
more pressure
than pleasure,
one more obligation
that can't be met.

And though we already
have a dog, Wally
wants to adopt,
wants something small
and golden to sleep
next to him and
lick his face.
He's paralyzed now
from the waist down,

whatever's ruining him
moving upward, and
we don't know
how much longer
he'll be able to pet
a dog. How many men
want another attachment,
just as they're
leaving the world?

Wally sits up nights
and says, *I'd like
some lizards, a talking bird,
some fish. A little rat.*

So after I drive
to Jimi and Tony's
in the Village and they
meet me at the door and say,
*We can't go through with it,
we can't give up our dog,*
I drive to the shelter
—just to look—and there
is Beau: bounding and
practically boundless,

What does Wally want?

one brass <u>concatenation</u>
of tongue and tail,
unmediated energy,
too big, wild,

perfect. He not only
licks Wally's face
but bathes every
irreplaceable inch
of his head, and though
Wally can no longer
feed himself he can lift
his hand, and bring it
to rest on the rough gilt

How is Wally able to interact with the dog?

flanks when they are,
for a moment, still.
I have never seen a touch
so deliberate.
It isn't about grasping;
the hand itself seems
almost blurred now,
softened, though
<u>tentative</u> only

because so much will
must be summoned,
such attention brought
to the work—which is all
he is now, this gesture
toward the restless splendor,
the unruly, the golden,
the animal, the new. ■

words for everyday use

con • cat • e • na • tion (kän ka tə nā′ shən) *n.,* state of being linked together in a series or chain. *The <u>concatenation</u> of clues led the inspector to the murderer.*

ten • ta • tive (ten′ tə tiv) *adj.,* not fully worked out or developed. *Clarissa had <u>tentative</u> plans to play tennis in the afternoon.*

Respond *to the* SELECTION

What process has the speaker been witnessing?

ANSWER TO GUIDED READING QUESTION

1. The dog licks every inch of Wally's head. Wally musters up enough strength to rest his hand on Beau's body.

SELECTION CHECK TEST 4.9.7 WITH ANSWERS

Checking Your Reading
1. What is wrong with Wally? **He has a neurological illness that causes paralysis.**
2. Why does the narrator go to Jimi and Tony's home? **He goes to pick up the dog they can't keep.**
3. What happens when he arrives? **They say they cannot give up their dog.**
4. Where does the speaker go after he leaves Jimi and Tony's home? **He goes to an animal shelter "just to look."**
5. What does the speaker find there? **He finds Beau, the "perfect" dog for Wally.**

Literary Tools
1. What is a paradox? **A paradox is a seemingly contradictory statement, idea, or event.**
2. What is a lyric poem? **A lyric poem is a highly musical verse that expresses the emotions of a speaker.**
3. What emotions does the speaker express in this poem? **The speaker expresses confusion over Wally's want of a new attachment and wonder over Wally's ability to pet Beau.**

RESPOND TO THE SELECTION

You might ask students to write in their journals a brief paragraph explaining how they would feel if they were in the speaker's position.

RECALL

1a. They feel they can't keep their cocker spaniel because Tony is too sick.

2a. He "wants something small / and golden to sleep / next to him and / lick his face."

3a. He wonders, "How many men want another attachment, just as they're leaving the world?"

INTERPRET

1b. Although Jimi and Tony realize the difficulty of caring for a dog while Tony is so sick, they ultimately cannot give up the dog. Tony's attachment to life via his dog foreshadows the love Wally feels for his new dog, Beau.

2b. He is full of life and Wally wants to be reminded that, though dying, he is still alive.

3b. The speaker's efforts on behalf of Wally to find a new dog for him indicate that he approves of Wally's wanting a new dog and his attachment to life as he dies.

ANALYZE

4a. The compelling image of this poem is Wally reaching out to touch the new dog, a "gesture / toward the restless splendor, / the unruly, the golden, / the animal, the new."

SYNTHESIZE

4b. He is trying to understand how Wally, so close to death, can still cling to life.

EVALUATE

5a. The speaker takes an active role in taking care of Wally in his illness. He goes to the animal shelter to find a new dog for Wally to make him happy. As a caregiver, he helps make Wally's last days memorable and comfortable.

EXTEND

5b. The poems are different because in "The Legend" the Asian man is dead, while in "New Dog" Wally is still alive. Yet the underlying feeling of the speaker is the same, one of remorse about death. Both speakers feel grief at the senseless loss of life.

Investigate, Inquire, and Imagine

Recall: GATHERING FACTS

1a. What do Jimi and Tony feel they can't keep? Why?

2a. Why does Wally want a new dog?

3a. What does the speaker wonder?

Interpret: FINDING MEANING

1b. How does the situation of Jimi and Tony foreshadow what happens to Wally?

2b. Why can the speaker say that Beau is "perfect" for the dying Wally?

3b. Does the speaker approve or disapprove of Wally's wanting a new dog?

Analyze: TAKING THINGS APART

4a. About his poetic inspiration, Mark Doty says, " I wait to be haunted, as it were, by an image. What happens is something I see registers on a deeper level than most experience does. A seal in the harbor, or the wreck of a fishing boat. I'll feel this tug in my memory. Then I'll begin describing it to try to capture it. In the process of describing it I begin to understand what it is about the image that's compelling. It's not enough to describe it: the image is a vehicle for something I'm trying to understand." Identify the compelling image of Wally that informs this poem.

Synthesize: BRINGING THINGS TOGETHER

4b. What is Mark Doty trying to understand by writing this poem?

Evaluate: MAKING JUDGMENTS

5a. Evaluate the role the speaker plays in Wally's life.

Extend: CONNECTING IDEAS

5b. Compare and contrast the attitude toward death in Garrett Hongo's "The Legend" (page 74) and Mark Doty's "New Dog."

Understanding Literature

PARADOX. Review the definition for **paradox** in the Handbook of Literary Terms. What is the paradox in this poem?

LYRIC POEM. Review the definition for **lyric poem** in the Handbook of Literary Terms and the cluster chart you made for Literary Tools on page 729. What emotions of the speaker are implied in this lyric poem?

ANSWERS TO UNDERSTANDING LITERATURE

PARADOX. The paradox in this poem is that Wally wants something new and alive, a dog, when he is dying. It seems contradictory that someone so close to death would want something so full of life.

LYRIC POEM. The speaker feels remorse at his friend's terminal illness and wonder at his friend's ability to appreciate life as he faces death.

Writer's Journal

1. Imagine you are the speaker and Wally has died. Write a **eulogy** in which you remember your friend and his attitude toward life.
2. Imagine you are Wally. Write a **journal entry** in which you explain what your new dog, Beau, means to you.
3. Write a **paragraph** explaining whether or not Wally fits your image of a dying person.

Integrating the Language Arts

Language, Grammar, and Style

ADDING MODIFIERS. Read the Language Arts Survey 3.39, "Adding Colorful Language to Sentences." Then rewrite each of the following sentences, adding an appropriate adjective or adverb.

1. Tony is ill.
2. The speaker is a friend of Wally.
3. Beau is a dog.
4. Wally touches the dog.
5. Wally fights death.

Media Literacy

PETS AND THEIR IMPACT. Using the Internet, find other poems that explore the impact pets have on people. Enter "pets + poetry" or "animals + poetry" to find suitable sites. Then choose one poem that interests you and explain the impact of that pet on the speaker to the class. You might want to recite parts of the poem to prove your points.

HYPERTEXT. Mark Doty says, "I've always been a poet who wrote about urban life because I love the layers and surprises and the jangly complexities of cities." Locate the University of Texas's Internet site at http://ccwf.cc.utexas.edu/~jeffj/hypertext_version.html. For Doty's poem "Broadway" explain all the underlined references.

Study and Research

ON DEATH AND DYING. Research the stages of dying as described by Elisabeth Kübler-Ross. In a report, identify and describe each stage. Then determine which stage you think Wally is in in "New Dog" and explain your assessment in a written report.

ANSWERS TO INTEGRATING THE LANGUAGE ARTS

Language, Grammar, and Style
Possible responses are given.
1. Tony is deathly ill.
2. The speaker is a concerned friend of Wally.
3. Beau is a lively dog.
4. Wally touches the dog deliberately.
5. Wally fights death courageously.

Media Literacy
Encourage students to review the Language Arts Survey 5.26, "Using the Internet." This section offers more detailed instruction for performing successful Internet searches.

Study and Research
Assign a score from 1 to 25 for each grading criterion below. (For more detailed evaluation, see the evaluation forms for writing, revising, and proofreading in the Assessment Resource book.)

REPORT
- CONTENT/UNITY. The report identifies and describes each stage of dying as delineated by Elizabeth Kübler-Ross.
- ORGANIZATION/COHERENCE. The stages are described in order.
- LANGUAGE/STYLE. The report is written in formal language.
- CONVENTIONS. The report avoids errors in spelling, grammar, usage, mechanics, and manuscript form.

INDIVIDUAL LEARNING STRATEGIES

MOTIVATION
Engage students in an impromptu debate on this question: Is revenge for an injustice ever justified? After students read the poem, ask them if their opinions changed.

READING PROFICIENCY
Before students begin reading the selection, work with them to identify and pronounce the unfamiliar words in the poem, such as *Doña Luz, mercado, Juarez,* and *Villa.* Once students have finished reading, ask them to write a one-paragraph summary of the action in the poem.

ENGLISH LANGUAGE LEARNING
You might ask Spanish-speaking students to demonstrate the correct pronunciation of the Spanish words in "1910." Also, point out to students that a five-and-dime is a store that sells a variety of basic products at low prices. This term was used primarily to describe these stores during the early to mid-1900s.

SPECIAL NEEDS
Ask students to focus on the Guided Reading and Recall questions that accompany the selection. You might have students work with a partner to discuss the Interpret questions that follow the selection.

(Continued on page 735)

READER'S JOURNAL

You might ask students to think of stories they know about other people who were treated unfairly for similar reasons. They might recall stories about people they know or stories about which they have heard or read.

POEM

Literary
T O O L S

CHARACTERIZATION. Characterization is the use of literary techniques to create a character. Writers use three major techniques to create characters: direct description, portrayal of characters' behavior, and representations of characters' internal states. When using direct description, the writer, through a speaker, a narrator, or another character, simply comments on the character, telling readers about such matters as the character's appearance, habits, dress, background, personality, motivations, and so on. In portrayal of a character's behavior, the writer presents the actions and speech of the character, allowing the reader to draw his or her own conclusions from what the character says or does. When using representations of internal states, the writer reveals directly the character's private thoughts and emotions, often by means of what is known as the *internal monologue.* As you read this poem, consider what methods Pat Mora used to create the character of Doña Luz.

IRONY AND IRONY OF SITUATION. Irony is a difference between appearance and reality. **Irony of situation** is when an event occurs that violates the expectations of the characters, the reader, or the audience. As you read, consider what is ironic about the judgment Upton makes of Doña Luz.

Reader's
Journal

Have you ever been wrongly accused of something or been judged unfairly because of race, sex, or ethnic background? Explain.

"1910"

by Pat Mora

Reader's
r e s o u r c e

Pat Mora explains that the poem "1910" is "indeed based on a true story told to me by my aunt, Ygnacia Delgado. She was a wonderful storyteller, and I've written poems and essays about her."

HISTORY CONNECTION. The poem "1910" tells of a Mexican woman of privilege and dignity who had to flee her country, with her family, running "from Villa laughing at their terror." Pancho Villa was one of the leaders of the Mexican Revolution of 1910. The primary goal of the revolution was to oust dictator Porfirio Díaz, who had ruled Mexico for over thirty years, and to restore the system of democratic elections. Díaz fled the country in 1911.

Another important reason for the revolution was the extreme social inequality that had existed in Mexico ever since the arrival of the Spanish. The majority of the land in Mexico was owned either by the Catholic Church or by wealthy landowners. These landowners, or *hacendados,* treated the common people, many of them of Indian descent, like slaves. The peasants worked for them in exchange for food and a place to live, while the landowners gained all the profits. Rebels Emiliano Zapata and Pancho Villa led the common people in a full-scale war against the rich, crusading for a redistribution of wealth and land. This war caused many of the upper-class Mexicans to flee the country for the United States.

About *the*
A U T H O R

Pat Mora is an award-winning author of poetry, essays, and children's books. She is a native of El Paso, Texas, the border city to which her grandparents migrated during the Mexican Revolution.

Mora loves to write about her native Southwest, about women's identity, and about her travels. In her own words: "I write, in part, because Hispanic perspectives need to be a part of our literary heritage. . . . I want to be part of that process. I also write because I am fascinated by the pleasure and power of words."

"1910" is from the poetry collection Chants. Mora's other books of poetry include *Borders, Communion, Agua Santa: Holy Water,* and *Aunt Carmen's Book of Practical Saints.* She has recently put together a poetry collection for young adults, entitled *My Own True Name* (2000). Find more titles, and more about Pat Mora, at her website: http://www.patmora.com.

GOALS/OBJECTIVES

Studying this lesson will enable students to
• appreciate a poem in which a character fights back against racism
• summarize and explain the racism that the character in the poem experiences
• define *characterization* and identify the elements of characterization that the writer uses to create the poem's main character

• define *irony* and *irony of situation* and identify these techniques in poetry
• demonstrate an understanding of proper nouns and adjectives
• conduct research on the Mexican Revolution of 1810

The Gossip, 1900s. William Penhallow Henderson.
Courtesy, National Museum of American Art, Washington, DC.

Pat Mora

In Mexico they bowed
 their heads when she passed.
 Timid villagers stepped aside
  for the Judge's mother, Doña Luz,

who wore her black shawl, black
 gloves whenever she left her home—
  at the church, the *mercado*, and the *plaza*
   in the cool evenings when she strolled
    barely touching her son's wrist
     with her fingertips.

With whom did Doña
Luz walk in the
evenings?

"1910" 735

ANSWER TO GUIDED READING QUESTION

1. She walked with her son in the evenings.

LITERARY TECHNIQUE

REPETITION. Repetition is a writer's conscious reuse of a sound, word, phrase, sentence, or other element. Writers often use this technique to emphasize, or highlight, important ideas or themes. Point out to students that Mora repeats the phrase "who wore her black shawl, black gloves" several times throughout the poem. Ask students: Why might Mora want to highlight the fact that Doña Luz always wore her gloves and shawl? How does this fact about her play into the discrimination she faces near the end of the poem?

Answer
Help students see that, as Mr. Upton discriminates against Doña Luz, he forces her to take off the gloves that are so important to her.

INTERNET RESOURCES

Students interested in learning more about Pat Mora can visit her official Internet site at http://www.patmora.com.

INDIVIDUAL LEARNING STRATEGIES (CONT.)

ENRICHMENT
Ask students to work in small groups to create a TV news report of the events described in "1910." Ask students to present the news of Upton's Five-and-Dime burning, to report Doña Luz as a suspect, and to give some biographical background for Doña Luz. Encourage students to present their news stories to the class, using music and graphics, if possible.

1. Mr. Upton forced her to remove her gloves and shawl in order to shop in his store.

SELECTION CHECK TEST 4.9.9 WITH ANSWERS

Checking Your Reading
1. How would you describe Doña Luz's character? **She is a strong woman who is not easily affected by events that surround her.**
2. How does she react when she and her family must flee from Villa? **She laughs at her terror.**
3. What event causes her to show a sign of weakness? **Her lips quiver when Upton accuses her of being a thief.**
4. What do you think the black shawl and black gloves symbolize? **Students may say they symbolize the dignity of Doña Luz or that they symbolize her protection from the events that surround her.**
5. What happens to Upton's Five-and-Dime? **It burns down.**

Literary Tools
Match each literary term with the best description.

    a. characterization b. irony
        c. irony of situation

1. the difference between appearance and reality; **b**
2. the use of literary techniques to create a character; **a**
3. when an event occurs that violates the expectations of the characters, the reader, or the audience; **c**

RESPOND TO THE SELECTION

What else might Doña Luz have done to protect herself from Mr. Upton's racism?

---

who wore her black shawl, black
  gloves in the carriage that took her
    and her family to Juarez, border town, away
    from Villa[1] laughing at their terror when
    he rode through the village shouting,
      spitting dust.

who wore her black shawl, black
  gloves when she crossed the Rio Grande
    to El Paso, her back straight, chin high,
    never watching her feet,

who wore her black shawl, black
  gloves into Upton's Five-and-Dime,

who walked out, back straight, lips quivering,
  and slowly removed her shawl and gloves,
    placed them on the sidewalk with the other
    shawls and shopping bags
      "You Mexicans can't hide
      things from me," Upton would say.
      "Thieves. All thieves.
      Let me see those hands."

who wore her black shawl, black
  gloves the day she walked, chin high,
    never watching her feet, on the black

    beams and boards, still smoking,
      that had been Upton's Five-and-Dime. ■

What did Mr. Upton force Doña Luz to do?

---

1. **Villa.** Pancho Villa, hero of the Mexican Revolution of 1910

Respond *to the* SELECTION

Do you think Mr. Upton deserved what happened to him? Why, or why not?

Not Knowing, in Aztlán

Tino Villanueva

the way they look at you
      the schoolteachers
the way they look at you
      the City Hall clerks
the way they look at you
      the cops
      the airport marshals
the way they look at you

you don't know if it's something you did

or something you are   ■

ABOUT THE RELATED READING

Tino Villanueva was born in 1941 in San Marcos, Texas. As a child, he moved around with his parents who were migrant farm workers. He finished high school, was drafted into the army, and after his military service enrolled at Southwest Texas State University and began to write poetry. Villanueva's childhood and his Mexican-American heritage have inspired his writing. Aztlán was the mythological home of the Aztec people, a highly developed civilization that flourished in central Mexico before the arrival of the Spanish. In 1521, the Aztecs were defeated and their city destroyed by the Spanish conquistadores. However, Aztlán has remained a symbolic ideal for many Mexican people.

"1910"   737

RECALL

1a. Doña Luz was the elderly mother of a judge. She was regarded as a dignified lady and held in great respect.

2a. When Doña Luz goes into the Five-and-Dime, Mr. Upton searches her to make sure she hasn't stolen anything and says, "You Mexicans can't hide things from me. Thieves. All thieves."

3a. In the last five lines of the poem, Doña Luz walks over the burnt beams and boards of Upton's Five-and-Dime, which has been destroyed in a fire.

INTERPRET

1b. You can tell because people bowed their heads and stepped aside when Doña Luz passed.

2b. Upton is ignorant and prejudiced against Mexican people.

3b. Students may say that people were angry about what Mr. Upton had said to Doña Luz and burned down his store as revenge.

ANALYZE

4a. Doña Luz is a very dignified, poised woman, as evidenced by the way she walks with her back straight, chin high. She always wore black, which shows that she was a widow. She was very proud of her son, a well-respected judge. When she lived in Mexico, she was treated with respect and deference. When she moved to El Paso, she was treated like a criminal.

SYNTHESIZE

4b. This poem shows that some Americans were prejudiced against immigrants from Mexico. They did not judge the immigrants by their characters but by their foreign appearance. Without knowing anything about the immigrants as individuals, and without knowing about these people's lives in Mexico, they assumed that the newcomers were thieves, and treated them with utter contempt.

EVALUATE

5a. *Responses will vary.*

EXTEND

5b. *Responses will vary.* Like the speaker in "Not Knowing, in Aztlán," Doña Luz had done nothing wrong, but was the target of suspicion simply because of her ethnic background. She was judged for something she was—a Mexican immigrant—rather than for anything she had done. Students may say it is worse to be judged for something you are, because you cannot change what you are, but you can change what you do.

Investigate, Inquire, and Imagine

Recall: GATHERING FACTS

1a. Who was Doña Luz, and how was she regarded in her hometown in Mexico?

2a. What happens when Doña Luz goes into Upton's Five-and-Dime? What does Mr. Upton say to her?

3a. Where does Doña Luz walk in the last five lines of the poem?

Interpret: FINDING MEANING

1b. How can you tell how Doña Luz was regarded by those in her home town?

2b. What does the encounter with Mr. Upton reveal about him?

3b. What do you think happened to Mr. Upton's store?

Analyze: TAKING THINGS APART

4a. What details show you what kind of a person Doña Luz is? Compare how Doña Luz was treated in her native town to how she was treated when she arrived in El Paso.

Synthesize: BRINGING THINGS TOGETHER

4b. What does this poem show about the attitudes some Americans held toward immigrants from Mexico? How did they judge the newcomers?

Evaluate: MAKING JUDGMENTS

5a. Predict what Mr. Upton will do next. Do you think he will guess who is responsible for what happened to his store?

Extend: CONNECTING IDEAS

5b. How is the experience of Doña Luz similar to that of the speaker in "Not Knowing, in Aztlán"? Which do you think is worse—to be judged harshly for "something you did" or because of "something you are"? Explain.

Understanding Literature

CHARACTERIZATION. Review the definition for **characterization** in the Handbook of Literary Terms. What method or methods did the author of "1910" use to create the character of Doña Luz? Explain, giving examples. Do you get a complete picture of who this woman is, or just a glimpse?

IRONY AND IRONY OF SITUATION. Review the definitions for **irony** and **irony of situation** in Literary Tools on page 734. What is ironic about the judgment Upton makes of Doña Luz? How might this be considered an example of irony of situation?

ANSWERS TO UNDERSTANDING LITERATURE

CHARACTERIZATION. Students may say that the author of "1910" uses direct description and portrayal of a character's behavior. Doña Luz is depicted in a black shawl and gloves, and as walking with her son in a very dignified manner. The author does not reveal Doña Luz's internal states. Students may say that the poem does not give a complete picture of who the woman is, but rather, just a glimpse.

IRONY AND IRONY OF SITUATION. Students may say that Upton's judgment of Doña Luz is ironic, considering that she is actually a very important woman who would never be accused of such crimes in her home country. This can be considered an example of irony of situation, because Upton's harsh words violate the expectations of the reader. The reader would not expect a woman who is as dignified as Doña Luz to be treated so disrespectfully.

Writer's Journal

1. Imagine that Upton is being taken to court for discriminating against Mexican immigrants. Write the **opening statement** that might be delivered by the prosecuting attorney in this case.

2. Imagine that you are Doña Luz. Write a **letter of complaint** addressed to Mr. Upton, protesting the way you were treated when you visited his store. Use correct business letter format, inventing the addresses for Doña Luz and for the store.

3. Mr. Upton's policy of searching all Mexican customers is obviously unfair. Write a **store policy** for his Five-and-Dime that would instruct employees to treat all customers fairly. Include guidelines for how an employee should deal with an actual shoplifter.

Integrating the Language Arts

Language, Grammar, and Style

PROPER NOUNS AND ADJECTIVES. Read the Language Arts Survey 3.95, "Proper Nouns and Adjectives." You will notice that in the poem "1910" *Mexico* is a proper noun and *Mexican* is a proper adjective. *Judge* is another proper noun in the poem. It normally should not be capitalized unless it is used with a name, as in "Judge Luz." Write down the other proper nouns you find in "1910." Then form a proper noun and a proper adjective for each of the following common nouns.

EXAMPLE: Political party: Democrat (noun); Democratic (adjective)

1. state
2. country
3. scientist
4. literary movement
5. writer

Study and Research

MEXICAN HISTORY. Mexico has had not one revolutionary war, but two. Research the Mexican Revolution of 1810. How and where did the movement begin? Who were some of the heroes of the revolution? How did the war finally end? Write a report about your findings. Be sure to document your sources in a bibliography. For correct bibliographic format, see the Language Arts Survey 5.40, "Making Bibliographies and Bibliography Cards." As an alternative, you may wish to research the siege that took place from March to May 1867, which Mexicans commemorate as Cinco de Mayo, or you may choose to research the more recent uprising of Zapatista rebels based in Chiapas, a southern state of Mexico.

ANSWERS TO INTEGRATING THE LANGUAGE ARTS

Language, Grammar, and Style
Other proper nouns in "1910": Doña Luz, Juarez, Villa, Rio Grande, El Paso, Upton's Five-and-Dime, Mexicans. *Responses will vary. Sample responses are listed below.*

1. Texas, Texan
2. France, French
3. Darwin, Darwinian
4. romanticism, romantic
5. Shakespeare, Shakespearean

Study and Research
To meet the needs of individual students, you might have students work in small groups to complete this assignment. Each group member could research a different aspect of Mexican history, according to their strengths and interests. For example, students with strong logical-mathematical skills might report on statistics associated with the Mexican Revolution of 1810, while students with strong spatial skills might create a map that details pivotal towns and battles. Note that Mexicans celebrate their independence day on September 16. This is the day that the Revolution of 1810 began when revolutionary priest Father Hidalgo y Costilla issued a tract calling for racial equality and the redistribution of land. Cinco de Mayo commemorates the Mexicans' driving out of the French ruling monarchy in 1867.

GRAPHIC ORGANIZER

Students should include the following sensory details in their charts:
Sight: wrinkled shopping bag; neatly folded clothes; a Rembrandt glow on his face; a triangle of orange in the hollow of his cheeks; sunset / blazes the storefronts and lit windows of the street; Asian; very skinny; rumpled pants suit and a plaid mackinaw, dingy and too large; dumbfounded man; foot traffic / dappling the snow with fresh prints
Sound: flurry of footsteps; cries of pedestrians; babbling
Touch: warm laundry and crinkled paper, flannel-like

READER'S JOURNAL

Students might begin by describing a specific violent act in the news. Encourage them to recall how they felt when they heard the story.

VOCABULARY FROM THE SELECTION

array
mackinaw

POEM

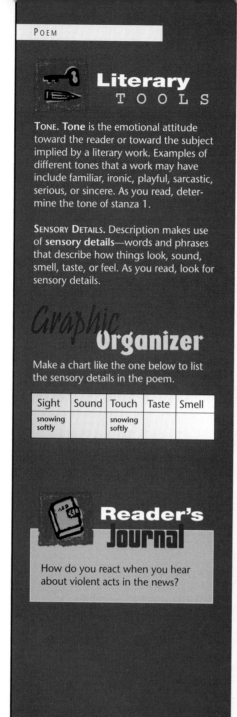

Literary TOOLS

TONE. Tone is the emotional attitude toward the reader or toward the subject implied by a literary work. Examples of different tones that a work may have include familiar, ironic, playful, sarcastic, serious, or sincere. As you read, determine the tone of stanza 1.

SENSORY DETAILS. Description makes use of **sensory details**—words and phrases that describe how things look, sound, smell, taste, or feel. As you read, look for sensory details.

Graphic Organizer

Make a chart like the one below to list the sensory details in the poem.

Sight	Sound	Touch	Taste	Smell
snowing softly		snowing softly		

Reader's Journal

How do you react when you hear about violent acts in the news?

740 *UNIT NINE*

PREREADING

"The Legend"
by Garrett Hongo

Reader's resource

"The Legend" was published in 1988 in Garrett Hongo's poetry collection *The River of Heaven*. Hongo was inspired to write the poem after seeing a TV news story about an Asian man killed in an act of street violence. The poet says "The Legend" is about "my own needs for mercy, for a fulfillment to a broad, urban, and contemporary story that baffled me."

CULTURE CONNECTION. In the poem, Hongo's reference to the "weaver girl" in the final stanza recalls an Asian myth in which she is the creator of the stars.

About the AUTHOR

Garrett Hongo (1951–), a Japanese American, was born in Hawaii and raised in Los Angeles. He received an MFA from the University of California at Irvine and currently teaches creative writing at the University of Oregon at Eugene. He is the author of two books of poetry: *Yellow Light* (1982) and *The River of Heaven* (1988), which was the Lamont Poetry Selection of The Academy of American Poets and a finalist for the Pulitzer Prize.

Hongo's most recent book is *Volcano: A Memoir of Hawaii* (1995), an evocation of his childhood in a Japanese-American household in Hawaii. Explaining his need to write *Volcano,* Hongo says, "The only way to cope was to write of my highly marginalized facts and events and create a land out of language." He found inspiration in a type of Japanese essay from the fourteenth century, on which he began modeling his prose. Hongo is also the editor of two major Asian-American anthologies: *Under Western Eyes: Personal Essays from Asian America* and *The Open Boat: Poems from Asian America*. Hongo's honors include fellowships from the Guggenheim Foundation, the National Endowment for the Arts, and the Rockefeller Foundation.

GOALS/OBJECTIVES

Studying this lesson will enable students to
• respond to a speaker's description of a tragedy and his or her personal feelings about it
• explain how a cultural myth relates to modern times
• define *tone* and describe the tone of a stanza of poetry

• define *sensory details* and recognize examples in their reading
• demonstrate an understanding of adverb clauses
• conduct research on the internment of Japanese Americans during World War II

The Legend

Garrett Hongo

In Chicago, it is snowing softly
and a man has just done his wash for the week.
He steps into the twilight of early evening,
carrying a wrinkled shopping bag
full of neatly folded clothes,
and, for a moment, enjoys
the feel of warm laundry and crinkled paper,
flannellike against his gloveless hands.
There's a Rembrandt[1] glow on his face,
a triangle of orange in the hollow of his cheek,
as a last flash of sunset
blazes the storefronts and lit windows of the street.

He is Asian, Thai or Vietnamese,
and very skinny, dressed as one of the poor
in rumpled suit pants and a plaid <u>mackinaw</u>,
dingy and too large.
He negotiates the slick of ice
on the sidewalk by his car,
opens the Fairlane's back door,
leans to place the laundry in,

> What did the man just do?

---

1. **Rembrandt.** (1606–1669) Dutch painter famous for his dramatic use of color and of light and shadow

mack • i • naw (ma′ kə nô) *n.,* short coat made of heavy fabric. *The heavy fabric of his* <u>mackinaw</u> *protected the man from the penetrating wind.*

"THE LEGEND"   741

1. He dies after being shot by a young man leaving a liquor store.

SELECTION CHECK TEST 4.9.11
WITH ANSWERS

Checking Your Reading

1. What is the setting of the poem? **The poem is set in Chicago outside of a laundromat during the winter.**
2. What has the man just finished? **He has just finished doing his wash for the week.**
3. What does the man look like? **He is a thin Asian man who is dressed in rumpled pants and a dingy coat.**
4. What happens to the man as he is placing his laundry in his car? **He is shot by a boy.**
5. How does the speaker feel about the wounded man? **The speaker is ashamed because he feels so distinctly separate from the wounded man.**

Literary Tools

1. What is tone? **Tone is the emotional attitude toward the reader or toward the subject implied by a literary work.**
2. What tone does the poem take toward the shooting? **Students may say the tone is one of disbelief, separation, or seriousness, to name a few.**
3. What are sensory details? **Sensory details are words and phrases that describe how things look, sound, smell, taste, or feel.**

and turns, for an instant,
toward the flurry of footsteps
and cries of pedestrians
as a boy—that's all he was—
backs from the corner package store
shooting a pistol, firing it,
once, at the dumbfounded man
who falls forward,
grabbing at his chest.

A few sounds escape from his mouth,
a babbling no one understands
as people surround him
bewildered at his speech.
The noises he makes are nothing to them.
The boy has gone, lost
in the light <u>array</u> of foot traffic
dappling the snow with fresh prints.
Tonight, I read about Descartes'[2]
grand courage to doubt everything
except his own miraculous existence
and I feel so distinct
from the wounded man lying on the concrete
I am ashamed.

Let the night sky cover him as he dies.
Let the weaver girl cross the bridge of heaven
and take up his cold hands.

In Memory of Jay Kashiwamura.

What happens to the man?

---

2. **Descartes.** René Descartes (1596–1650), French philosopher who said "I think, therefore I am"

words
for
everyday
use

ar • ray (ə rā′) *n.,* regular grouping or arrangement. *The <u>array</u> of soldiers in perfect alignment signaled drill practice was about to begin.*

ANSWERS TO UNDERSTANDING LITERATURE

TONE. The tone in the first stanza is peaceful and serene. "Snowing softly," "neatly folded," "warm," and "glow" are phrases and words that help create this tone.

SENSORY DETAILS. In About the Selection, students learn that Hongo based his poem on a real occurrence. The man's ethnicity, his being Asian, is probably factual, as is indicated at the end of the poem when Hongo pays tribute to the victim by saying "In memory of Jay Kashiwamura." It is likely that the other details, aside from perhaps the weather, are imagined by the poet.

Respond *to the* SELECTION

What emotion does the speaker probably feel about imagining the victim in the hands of the weaver girl after his death?

Investigate, *Inquire,* and Imagine

RECALL: GATHERING FACTS

1a. How is the man described?

2a. What is the man's ethnic origin?

3a. What do the suffering man's noises mean to the bystanders?

 Interpret: FINDING MEANING

1b. What does the description of the man reveal about his frame of mind?

2b. Why does the speaker mention the man's ethnic origin?

3b. What does the reaction of the bystanders reveal about them?

Analyze: TAKING THINGS APART

4a. Identify associations that come to mind from the title.

Synthesize: BRINGING THINGS TOGETHER

4b. Why do you think the poem is entitled "The Legend"?

Evaluate: MAKING JUDGMENTS

5a. Evaluate Hongo's attitude toward violence in contemporary society.

Extend: CONNECTING IDEAS

5b. Robert Frost liked to distinguish between grievances (complaints) and griefs (sorrows). He even suggested that grievances, which are propagandistic, should be restricted to prose, "leaving poetry free to go its way in tears." In what way does "The Legend" "go its way in tears"?

Understanding *Literature*

TONE. Review the definition for **tone** in the Handbook of Literary Terms. What is the tone of stanza 1? What phrases and words create this tone?

SENSORY DETAILS. Review the definition for **sensory details** in the Handbook of Literary Terms and the sensory details chart you made for Literary Tools on page 740. Which sensory details do you think are factual, and which do you think are imagined by the poet?

"THE LEGEND" **743**

ANSWERS TO INVESTIGATE, INQUIRE, AND IMAGINE (CONT.)

EXTEND
5b. Although Hongo's description of the murder is relatively objective, his reactions to it show deep emotion. He feels compelled to leave a verbal record of the crime, as well as his reactions to it. He shares his shame at feeling "so distinct / from the wounded man lying on the concrete." His empathy for the man's suffering is evident in his prayer that "the weaver girl cross the bridge of heaven / and take up his cold hands."

RESPOND TO THE SELECTION

As an alternate activity, you might encourage students to discuss or write in their journals about a time when a tragic story in the news affected them emotionally.

ANSWERS TO INVESTIGATE, INQUIRE, AND IMAGINE

RECALL
1a. He is "very skinny" and has a "Rembrandt glow on his face."
2a. He is Asian, Thai, or Vietnamese.
3a. "The noises he makes are nothing to them." They are "bewildered" at his speech.

INTERPRET
1b. The "Rembrandt glow on his face" indicates contentment with accomplishing his task (the laundry) and contentment with his life.
2b. He might be implying that the murder was a hate crime against a minority.
3b. *Responses will vary.* Students may say that the bystanders are apathetic and unmoved by the fate of the victim. Or, it may be that the bystanders simply do not understand the man's language and feel helpless to do or say anything to comfort him.

ANALYZE
4a. The title suggests ancient myths such as the knights of the Round Table, or a heroic contemporary person who has achieved greatness in sports, politics, entertainment, or some other arena.

SYNTHESIZE
4b. At first it seems that Hongo is playing with the reader by suggesting greatness in an ordinary man of unexceptional accomplishments. But by the conclusion of the poem it becomes clear that what happens to the man after his death is what makes him exceptional and legendary when the weaver girl takes up "his cold hands."

EVALUATE
5a. He is concerned that people have become insensitive to violence. His poem is a renunciation of this attitude. It shows the grief that a caring human being can express toward a victim he has never met. Because the victim did not anticipate any violence, the poet conveys an abhorrence of the randomness of the crime.

ANSWERS TO INTEGRATING THE LANGUAGE ARTS

Language, Grammar, and Style
1. adjective clause
2. adverb clause
3. adjective clause
4. adverb clause
5. noun clause

Speaking and Listening
Have each group of students first write a script of their scene, based on the information they learn in the poem. Encourage students to add as much dialogue as possible. Then students can work together to assign roles and practice their scenes before presenting to the class.

Study and Research
Ask students to review the Language Arts Survey 4.17, "Steps in Preparing an Extemporaneous Speech." Encourage students to add interest to their presentations by using visuals or multimedia technology.

Writer's Journal

1. Imagine you are one of the bystanders who has witnessed the man's murder. Write a **news article** about what you have observed.

2. Imagine you are the man doing his laundry. Write a **journal entry** describing how your day went and your plans for the evening.

3. Focus on a person or a scene that you can observe closely. Take notes on what you actually see and what you imagine about what you see. Then write a lyric **poem** about your experience.

Integrating the Language Arts

Language, Grammar, and Style

CLAUSES. Read about adjective, adverb, and noun clauses in the Language Arts Survey 3.83, "Clauses within a Sentence." Then identify the type of clause in each of the following sentences.

1. An Asian man <u>who has just done his wash for the week</u> steps into the twilight of early evening.
2. A triangle of orange lights his face <u>when the sunset blazes the storefronts.</u>
3. He negotiates the ice <u>which is slick.</u>
4. Another man shoots the Asian man <u>after exiting the corner package store.</u>
5. <u>Whoever shot the man</u> should be punished, don't you think?

Speaking and Listening

ROLE-PLAY. With several classmates, play the roles of the man who is murdered, the murderer, and the bystanders in "The Legend." Have another classmate play the role of a TV reporter who comes upon the scene after the murder, interviewing the bystanders about what they saw and their reactions to the crime.

Study and Research

INTERNMENT CAMPS. In his introduction to *Under Western Eyes: Personal Essays from Asian America,* Hongo writes about the necessity of telling individual stories. He writes about the internment of Japanese Americans during World War II: "There had been so much pain, losses so incredible, that to acknowledge them might have withered hope completely, and our elders wished to spare their children this kind of despair. *Kodomo no tame* is the phrase in Japanese—sacrifice for the sake of the children—which I grew to admire as a generational code that grew out of these very real and deep feelings of shame." Research the internment of Japanese Americans during World War II. Topics to include in your presentation include causes for internment, the condition of the camps, the impact of internment on Japanese Americans, and restitution. Then make an oral presentation of your findings. If you chose to do your research on the Internet, one site you will find useful is The Detroit News at http://detnews.com/menu/stories/13546.htm. To find more articles on the Internet, key in the words "Japanese Internment Camps."

"A White Woman of Color"

by Julia Álvarez

Reader's resource

"A White Woman of Color" is taken from the book *Half and Half: Writers on Growing Up Biracial and Bicultural* (1998). In this personal essay, Álvarez explores the meaning of race and identity.

HISTORY CONNECTION. The Dominican Republic forms the eastern two-thirds of the island Hispaniola. Haiti forms the remaining third. The island of Hispaniola is located in the Caribbean Sea between the islands of Jamaica and Puerto Rico. Tainos, a group of native people, originally occupied the Dominican Republic when Columbus set foot on the island in 1492. Spanish colonists, who soon took over, treated the natives brutally, reducing the Taino population from one million to 500. As a result, the Spanish soon brought African slaves to the island beginning in 1503 to ensure adequate labor for plantations. During the next century, the French occupied and colonized Haiti. Beginning in 1822, Haitians conquered the whole island, but forces led by Juan Pablo Duarte, the Dominican Independence hero, drove them out and established the Dominican Republic as an independent state in 1844.

About the AUTHOR

Julia Álvarez (1950–), poet, novelist, and nonfiction writer, was born in the Dominican Republic and emigrated to the United States with her family at the age of ten. Books provided a way for her to avoid feeling isolated, and by the time she was a teenager, Álvarez knew that she wanted to be a writer.

Álvarez uses her writing to discuss her experience as a person of two cultures, yet her audience is not targeted to one population. Although her novels have Latino characters, her treatment of them is not narrow; rather, Álvarez focuses on the intercultural idea of identity formation. A prolific writer, Álvarez has had essays, poems, and stories published in *The New Yorker, Allure,* and *Hispanic Magazine.* She has also written several novels, including *How the García Girls Lost Their Accents* (1991), *In the Time of the Butterflies* (1994), and *¡Yo!* (1997). Her first book of nonfiction, *Something to Declare* (1998), is about the atrocities of the dictator Trujillo in the Dominican Republic. Currently, Álvarez teaches English at Middlebury College.

Literary TOOLS

STYLE AND TONE. Style is the manner in which something is said or written. **Tone** is the emotional attitude toward the reader or toward the subject implied by a literary work. Examples of the different tones that a work may have include familiar, ironic, playful, sarcastic, serious, and sincere. As you read, identify the style and tone of the essay.

PERSONAL ESSAY. A **personal essay** is a short work of nonfictional prose on a single topic related to the life or interests of the writer. As you read, try to put the author's experiences and perceptions about race into categories.

Graphic Organizer

Make a cluster chart like the one below listing the author's experiences and perceptions that inform her concept of race. One example has been done for you.

lighter was better in her family

Experiences and Perceptions about Race

Reader's Journal

Have you ever witnessed or personally experienced racism or discrimination? Describe your experience. How did it make you feel?

VOCABULARY FROM THE SELECTION

acculturation	genocide
aesthetic	intrinsic
aquiline	lank
atrocity	malapropping
belligerence	paradigm
commodity	patronage
cosmopolitan	proliferate
diaphanous	protocol
elite	relegate
emulate	replenish
entrepreneur	sacrosanct
garish	solidarity

GRAPHIC ORGANIZER

Students' charts will vary. Examples are listed below.
- Manners and etiquette were clues to class distinction within her race
- Different types of education signaled class/race differences
- People had to deny their racial backgrounds to protect themselves from genocide during Trujillo's reign
- In America, all peoples of color were grouped together and judged the same way
- When ethnicity was "in," writer was more accepted, but she felt like a commodity

READER'S JOURNAL

You might have students expand their journal entries by asking them to write a "definition of me." Ask each student to think about his or her own cultural heritage and write about how that heritage defines him or her.

GOALS/OBJECTIVES

Studying this lesson will enable students to
- empathize with and understand a writer's perspective
- summarize the writer's ideas about discrimination and self-identity
- define *style* and *tone* and describe the style and tone of a personal essay
- demonstrate an understanding of the simple tenses

- define *personal essay* and explain how it relates to the selection
- work collaboratively to research the Civil Rights movement, the Women's movement, or the Anti-Vietnam War movement
- conduct research on a Latino writer and discuss his or her ideas about identity and racism

1. The youngest daughter is the pride and joy of the family because she most resembles a white person with silky hair and pale skin.
2. The mother eats with knives and forks, while the father thinks it is all right to eat with one's hands.

INDIVIDUAL LEARNING STRATEGIES

MOTIVATION
Ask students to think about a few of their characteristic personal traits, including aspects of their personality, their looks, and their attitudes. Have students consider how they established these traits. Do they think these traits were inherited? Did they "learn" them? Did they choose to be a certain way? Have students record their thoughts in their journals.

READING PROFICIENCY
Review carefully with students the information provided in the Reader's Resource and About the Author sections on page 745 in the text. Once students understand the selection's context, suggest that they read and summarize it one section at a time.

ENGLISH LANGUAGE LEARNING
Encourage students from other cultures to connect with this selection by asking them to think about their position between their native culture and their American culture. Have students describe, either in writing or orally, how their feelings are similar to or different from Álvarez's feelings.

SPECIAL NEEDS
Have students focus their attention on the Guided Reading and Recall questions that accompany this selection. Check students' work frequently to ensure that they are grasping the most important ideas in the selection.

ENRICHMENT
Students might be surprised to learn that while America is celebrated as a "melting pot," many immigrants of various cultures faced discrimination when they arrived here. Ask students to choose an ethnic group to research, aside from African Americans or Hispanics. Students might research Jewish, Polish, Italian, Irish, or Asian people, for example. Have each student report on any discrimination associated with the group he or she chooses.

A White Woman of Color

Julia Álvarez

Growing up in the Dominican Republic, I experienced racism within my own family—though I didn't think of it as racism. But there was definitely a hierarchy of beauty, which was the main currency in our daughters-only family. It was not until years later, from the vantage point of this country and this education, that I realized that this hierarchy of beauty was dictated by our coloring. We were a progression of whitening, as if my mother were slowly bleaching the color out of her children.

The oldest sister had the darkest coloring, with very curly hair and "coarse" features. She looked the most like Papi's side of the family and was considered the least pretty. I came next, with "good hair," and skin that back then was a deep olive, for I was a tomboy—another dark mark against me—who would not stay out of the sun. The sister right after me had my skin color, but she was a good girl who stayed indoors, so she was much paler, her hair a golden brown. But the pride and joy of the family was the baby. She was the one who made heads turn and strangers approach asking to feel her silken hair. She was white white, an adjective that was repeated in describing her color as if to deepen the shade of white. Her eyes were brown, but her hair was an unaccountable towheaded blond. Because of her coloring, my father was teased that there must have been a German milkman in our neighborhood. How could *she* be *his* daughter? It was

Who was the "pride and joy" of the Álvarez family? What made her so special?

clear that this youngest child resembled Mami's side of the family.

It was Mami's family who were *really* white. They were white in terms of race, and white also in terms of class. From them came the fine features, the pale skin, the lank hair. Her brothers and uncles went to schools abroad and had important businesses in the country. They also emulated the manners and habits of North Americans. Growing up, I remember arguments at the supper table on whether or not it was proper to tie one's napkin around one's neck, on how much of one's arm one could properly lay on the table, on whether spaghetti could be eaten with the help of a spoon. My mother, of course, insisted on all the protocol of knives and forks and on eating a little portion of everything served; my father, on the other hand, defended our eating whatever we wanted, with our hands if need be, so we could "have fun" with our food. My mother would snap back that we looked like *jibaritas*[1] who should be living out in the country. Of course, that was precisely where my father's family came from.

What differences did the mother and father have in regard to eating?

Not that Papi's family weren't smart and enterprising, all twenty-five brothers and sisters. (The size of the family in and of itself was considered very country by some members of Mami's family.) Many of Papi's brothers had

---

1. *jibaritas.* Term used by Dominicans for peasant females

---

words for everyday use

lank (laŋk) *adj.*, straight and limp. *After Tonya's shower, her lank hair hung down her back.*
em • u • late (em′ yə lāt) *vt.*, strive to equal or excel; imitate. *Can you emulate a British accent?*
pro • to • col (prō′ tə kəl) *n.*, code entailing strict adherence to correct etiquette. *Before meeting Queen Elizabeth, the actor was informed of the proper protocol for greeting Her Highness.*

View, 1962. Alex Katz. Private Collection.

ADDITIONAL QUESTIONS AND ACTIVITIES

Ask students the following questions:
1. How does the author describe the education of her father's siblings?
2. How did the members of her father's family look different from the members of her mother's family?

Answers
1. She explains that their education was "totally island." In other words, they got their education in the Dominican Republic, instead of at a prestigious school in America.
2. The members of her father's family had darker skin, less aquiline features, and coarse, curly hair. Some people in her father's family had an extra finger on one hand, too.

CROSS-CURRICULAR ACTIVITIES

ARTS AND HUMANITIES. Ask students to sketch a picture of the narrator. Encourage them to skim the parts of the story they have read thus far, jotting down details about the narrator's looks. Some students might even enjoy creating a "family portrait" of the narrator, her parents, and her sisters.

gone to the university and become professionals. But their education was totally island—no fancy degrees from Andover and Cornell and Yale, no summer camps or school songs in another language. Papi's family still lived in the interior versus the capital, in old-fashioned houses without air conditioning, decorated in ways my mother's family would have considered, well, tasteless. I remember antimacassars[2] on the backs of rocking chairs (which were the living-room set), <u>garish</u> paintings of flamboyant trees, ceramic planters with plastic flowers in bloom. They were *criollos*—creoles—rather than <u>cosmopolitans</u>, expansive, proud, colorful. (Some members had a sixth finger on their right—or was it their left hand?) Their features were less <u>aquiline</u> than Mother's family's, the skin darker, the hair coarse and curly. Their

---

2. **antimacassars.** Covers used to protect the back or arms of furniture

words for everyday use	gar • ish (gar' ish) *adj.,* excessively vivid. *Las Vegas is known for its <u>garish</u> neon lights.* cos • mo • pol • i • tan (käz mə pä' lə tən) *n.,* person having worldwide rather than limited or provincial scope or bearing. *<u>Cosmopolitans</u> from many European countries gathered at the gala to celebrate the opening of the new opera house.* aq • ui • line (a' kwə līn) *adj.,* curving like an eagle's beak. *The professor had an <u>aquiline</u> nose.*

money still had the smell of the earth on it and was kept in a wad in their back pockets, whereas my mother's family had money in the Chase Manhattan Bank, most of it with George Washington's picture on it, not Juan Pablo Duarte's.

It was clear to us growing up then that lighter was better, but there was no question of discriminating against someone because he or she was dark-skinned. Everyone's family, even an <u>elite</u> one like Mami's, had darker-skinned members. All Dominicans, as the saying goes, have a little black behind the ears. So, to separate oneself from those who were darker would have been to divide *una familia*, a <u>sacrosanct</u> entity in our culture. Neither was white blood necessarily a sign of moral or intellectual or political superiority. All one has to do is page through a Dominican history book and look at the number of dark-skinned presidents, dictators, generals, and <u>entrepreneurs</u> to see that power has not resided exclusively or even primarily among the whites on the island. The leadership of our country has been historically "colored."

But being black was something else. A black Dominican was referred to as a "dark Indian" (*indio oscuro*)—unless you wanted to come to blows with him, that is. The real blacks were the Haitians[3] who lived next door and who occupied the Dominican Republic for twenty years, from 1822 to 1844, a fact that can still so

As the saying goes, what do all Dominican have behind their ears? What does the saying mean?

inflame the Dominican populace you'd think it had happened last year. The denial of the Afro-Dominican part of our culture reached its climax during the dictatorship of Trujillo,[4] whose own maternal grandmother was Haitian. In 1937, to protect Dominican race purity, Trujillo ordered the overnight <u>genocide</u> of thousands (figures range from 4,000 to 20,000) of Haitians by his military, who committed this <u>atrocity</u> using only machetes[5] and knives in order to make this planned extermination look like a "spontaneous" border skirmish. He also had the Dominican Republic declared a white nation despite the evidence of the mulatto[6] senators who were forced to pass this ridiculous measure.

So, black was not so good, kinky hair was not so good, thick lips not so good. But even if you were *indio oscuro con pelo malo y una bemba de aquí a Baní*[7] you could still sit in the front of the bus and order at the lunch counter—or the equivalent thereof. There was no segregation of races in the halls of power. But in the <u>aesthetic</u> arena—the one to which we girls were <u>relegated</u> as females—lighter was better. Lank hair and pale skin and small, fine features were better. All I had to do was stay out of the sun and behave myself and I could pass as a pretty white girl.

---

3. **Haitians.** Natives or inhabitants of Haiti
4. **Trujillo.** Rafael Leónidad Trujillo Molino (1819–1961), dictator of the Dominican Republic from 1930 until his assassination in 1961.
5. **machetes.** Large heavy knives used as weapons or for cutting sugarcane and underbrush
6. **mulatto.** Person of mixed white and black ancestry
7. *indio oscuro con pelo malo y una bemba de aquí a Baní.* Spanish for "A dark Indian with bad hair and lips from here to Baní"

words for everyday use

elite (ā lēt′) *adj.*, best of a class. *The <u>elite</u> members of the movie industry arrived at the Academy Awards in limousines.*

sac • ro • sanct (sa′ krō saŋkt) *adj.*, sacred or holy. *The legislature approved three million dollars for the politically <u>sacrosanct</u> programs.*

en • tre • pre • neur (än trə prə nər′) *n.*, one who organizes, manages, and assumes the risks of a business or enterprise. *The <u>entrepreneur</u> started a software company that he still manages.*

geno • cide (je′ nə sīd) *n.*, deliberate and systematic destruction of a racial, political, or cultural group. *Hitler's attempt to exterminate all Jews is the most well known example of <u>genocide</u> in the world.*

atroc • i • ty (ə trä′ sə tē) *n.*, wicked or cruel act, object, or situation. *The book described the <u>atrocities</u> of trench warfare during World War I.*

aes • thet • ic (es the′ tik) *adj.*, of, relating to, or dealing with the beautiful. *The art students debated the <u>aesthetic</u> value of Expressionism over Impressionism.*

rel • e • gate (re′ lə gāt) *vi.*, assign to a place of insignificance or oblivion. *After swearing at the umpire, Brad was <u>relegated</u> to the bench for the rest of the game.*

Another aspect of my growing up also greatly influenced my thinking on race. Although I was raised in the heart of a large family, my day-to-day caretakers were the maids. Most of these women were dark-skinned, some of Haitian background. One of them, Misiá, had been spared the machetes of the 1937 massacre when she was taken in and hidden from the prowling *guardias*[8] by the family. We children spent most of the day with these women. They tended to us, nursed us when we were sick, cradled us when we fell down and scraped an elbow or knee (as a tomboy, there was a lot of this scraping for me), and most important, they told us stories of *los santos*[9] and *el barón del cementerio*,[10] of *el cuco*[11] and *las ciguapas*, beautiful dark-skinned creatures who escaped capture because their feet were turned backwards so they left behind a false set of footprints. These women spread the wings of our imaginations and connected us deeply to the land we came from. They were the ones with the stories that had power over us.

What was the most important thing the maids did for the Álvarez children?

We arrived in Nueva York in 1960, before the large waves of Caribbean immigrants created little Habanas, little Santo Domingos, and little San Juans in the boroughs of the city. Here we encountered a whole new kettle of wax—as my malapropping Mami might have said. People of color were treated as if they were inferior, prone to violence, uneducated, untrustworthy, lazy—all the "bad" adjectives we were learning in our new language. Our dark-skinned aunt, Tía Ana, who had lived in New York for several decades and so was the authority in these matters, recounted stories of discrimination on buses and subways. These Americans were so blind! One drop of black and you were black. Everyone

back home would have known that Tía Ana was not black: she had "good hair" and her skin color was a light *indio*. All week, she worked in a *factoria* in the Bronx, and when she came to visit us on Saturdays to sew our school clothes, she had to take three trains to our nice neighborhood where the darkest face on the street was usually her own.

We were lucky we were white Dominicans or we would have had a much harder time of it in this country. We would have encountered a lot more prejudice than we already did, for white as we were, we found that our Latino-ness, our accents, our habits and smells, added "color" to our complexion. Had we been darker, we certainly could not have bought our mock Tudor house in Jamaica Estates. In fact, the African American family who moved in across the street several years later needed police protection because of threats. Even so, at the local school, we endured the bullying of classmates. "Go back to where you came from!" they yelled at my sisters and me in the playground. When some of them started throwing stones, my mother made up her mind that we were not safe and began applying to boarding schools where privilege transformed prejudice into patronage.

Despite being white Dominicans, what added "color" to their complexion?

"So where are you from?" my classmates would ask.

"Jamaica Estates," I'd say, an edge of belligerence to my voice. It was obvious from my accent, if not my looks, that I was not *from* there in the way they meant being from somewhere.

---

8. *guardias.* Spanish for guards
9. *los santos.* Spanish for saints
10. *el barón del cementerio.* Spanish for the baron or nobleman of the cemetery
11. *el cuco.* Spanish for ghost

---

words for everyday use

mal • a • prop • ping (ma' lə prä piŋ) *adj.,* unintentionally misusing a word or phrase. *My malapropping sister consistently misuses clichés.*

pa • tron • age (pa' trə nij) *n.,* kindness done with an air of superiority. *Many homeless men and women want work rather than patronage.*

bel • lig • er • ence (bə lij' rənts) *n.,* aggressive or truculent attitude, atmosphere, or disposition. *The coach encouraged belligerence in his football players.*

1. They told stories that encouraged imagination and connected the children to their land.
2. Their accents, habits, and smells added "color" to their complexion.

LITERARY NOTE

The term *malaprop* appears in a Restoration-era play called *The Rivals* (1775) by Richard Brinsley Sheridan. His character, Mrs. Malaprop, was famous for her often humorous misuse of words. Sources trace the term back to the French *malapropos,* meaning "inappropriate."

1. The narrator's loss of her Catholic
faith, her gain of feminist ideals, her
new lifestyle, wardrobe, and "hippy
ways" all led to her separation from
her culture.

Quotables

"I've been pegged as a writer who
writes solely about women...And
yet, as Flaubert said, Madame
Bovary, c'est moi! We do become
our characters: male, female; old,
young; anglo, Latina. But it might
just be that the imaginative
challenge is greater when we have
to cross that autobiographical line
and become the opposite sex."

—Julia Álvarez

"I mean *originally*."

And then it would come out, the color, the accent, the cousins with six fingers, the smell of garlic.

By the time I went off to college, a great explosion of American culture was taking place on campuses across the country. The civil rights movement, the Vietnam War and subsequent peace movement, the women's movement, were transforming traditional definitions of American identity. Ethnicity was in: my classmates wore long braids like Native Americans and peasant blouses from Mexico and long, diaphanous skirts and dangly earrings from India. Suddenly, my foreignness was being celebrated. This reversal felt affirming but also disturbing. As huipils,[12] serapes,[13] and embroidered dresses proliferated about me, I had the feeling that my ethnicity had become a commodity. I resented it.

When I began looking for a job after college, I discovered that being a white Latina made me a nonthreatening minority in the eyes of these employers. My color was a question *only* of culture, and if I kept my cultural color to myself, I was "no problem." Each time I was hired for one of my countless "visiting appointments"—they were never permanent "invitations," mind you—the inevitable questionnaire would accompany my contract in which I was to check off my RACE: CAUCASIAN, BLACK, NATIVE AMERICAN, ASIAN, HISPANIC, OTHER. How could a Dominican divide herself in this way? Or was I really a Dominican anymore? And what was a Hispanic? A census

creation—there is no such culture—how could it define who I was at all? Given this set of options, the truest answer might have been to check off OTHER.

For that was the way I had begun to think of myself. Adrift from any Latino community in this country, my culture had become an internal homeland, periodically replenished by trips "back home." But as a professional woman on my own, I felt less and less at home on the island. My values, the loss of my Catholic faith, my lifestyle, my wardrobe, my hippy ways, and my feminist ideas separated me from my native culture. I did not subscribe to many of the mores[14] and constraints that seemed to be an intrinsic part of that culture. And since my culture had always been my "color," by rejecting these mores I had become not only Americanized but whiter.

What things separated the author from her native culture?

If I could have been a part of a Latino community in the United States, the struggle might have been, if not easier, less private and therefore less isolating. These issues of acculturation and ethnicity would have been struggles to share with others like me. But all my North American life I had lived in shifting academic communities—going to boarding schools, then college, and later teaching wherever I could get those yearly appointments—and these commu-

---

12. **huipils.** Mayan style of dresses or blouses with colorful embroidery
13. **serapes.** Colorful woolen shawls worn over the shoulders, usually by Mexican men
14. **mores.** Fixed morally binding customs of a particular group

words for everyday use

di • aph • a • nous (dī aʹ fə nəs) *adj.*, characterized by such fineness of texture as to permit seeing through. *Julie was aghast when she realized her swimsuit was diaphanous when wet.*

pro • lif • er • ate (prə liʹ fə rāt) *vi.*, grow by rapid production of new parts, cells, buds, or offspring. *Dandelions proliferate on my lawn each spring.*

com • mod • i • ty (kə mäʹ də tē) *n.*, economic good or product. *The general store sold salt, tea, flour, and other commodities.*

re • plen • ish (ri pleʹ nish) *vi.*, fill or build up again. *Mom replenished the glasses with lemonade.*

in • trin • sic (in trinʹ zik) *adj.*, belonging to the essential nature or constitution of a thing. *Our teacher says she would be happy if we were concerned about the intrinsic value of learning rather than learning just to take a test.*

ac • cul • tur • a • tion (ə kəl chə rāʹ shən) *n.*, cultural modification of an individual or group by adapting or borrowing traits from another culture. *The acculturation of new immigrants may take many years.*

nities reflected the dearth[15] of Latinos in the profession. Except for friends in Spanish departments, who tended to have come from their countries of origin to teach rather than being raised in this country as I was, I had very little daily contact with Latinos.

Where I looked for company was where I had always looked for company since coming to this country: in books. At first the texts that I read and taught were the ones prescribed to me, the canonical[16] works which formed the content of the bread-and-butter courses that as a "visiting instructor" I was hired to teach. These texts were mostly written by white male writers from Britain and the United States, with a few women thrown in and no Latinos. Thank goodness for the occasional creative writing workshop where I could bring in the multicultural authors I wanted. But since I had been formed in this very academy, I was clueless where to start. I began to educate myself by reading, and that is when I discovered that there were others out there like me, hybrids who came in a variety of colors and whose ethnicity and race were an evolving process, not a rigid paradigm or a list of boxes, one of which you checked off.

This discovery of my ethnicity on paper was like a rebirth. I had been going through a pretty bad

What did the author discover through reading books?

writer's block: the white page seemed impossible to fill with whatever it was I had in me to say. But listening to authors like Maxine Hong Kingston, Toni Morrison, Gwendolyn Brooks, Langston Hughes, Maya Angelou, June Jordan, and to Lorna Dee Cervantes, Piri Thomas, Rudolfo Anaya, Edward Rivera, Ernesto Galarza (that first wave of Latino writers), I began to hear the language "in color." I began to see that literature could reflect the otherness

I was feeling, that the choices in fiction and poetry did not have to be bleached out of their color or simplified into either/or. A story could allow for the competing claims of different parts of ourselves and where we came from.

Ironically, it was through my own stories and poems that I finally made contact with Latino communities in this country. As I published more, I was invited to read at community centers and bilingual programs. Latino students, who began attending colleges in larger numbers in the late seventies and eighties, sought me out as a writer and teacher "of color." After the publication of *How the García Girls Lost Their Accents*, I found that I had become a sort of spokesperson for Dominicans in this country, a role I had neither sought nor accepted. Of course, some Dominicans refused to grant me any status as a "real" Dominican because I was "white." With the color word there was also a suggestion of class. My family had not been among the waves of economic immigrants that left the island in the seventies, a generally darker-skinned, working-class group, who might have been the maids and workers in my mother's family house. We had come in 1960, political refugees, with no money but with "prospects": Papi had a friend who was the doctor at the Waldorf Astoria and who helped him get a job; Mami's family had money in the Chase Manhattan Bank they could lend us. We had changed class in America—from Mami's elite family to middle-class spics—but our background and education and most especially our pale skin had made mobility easier for us

What aspects of the Álvarez family made their race struggle easier than that of other Dominicans living in the United States?

15. **dearth.** Scarcity or inadequate supply
16. **canonical.** Relating to a group of literary works considered to be authentic or worthy of study

ANSWERS TO GUIDED READING QUESTIONS

1. She discovered that there were other people in the world struggling with the same issues of identity in terms of ethnicity and race.
2. Their pale skin, background, and education made their race struggle easier than other Dominicans' living in the United States.

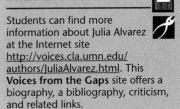

INTERNET RESOURCES

Students can find more information about Julia Alvarez at the Internet site http://voices.cla.umn.edu/authors/JuliaAlvarez.html. This **Voices from the Gaps** site offers a biography, a bibliography, criticism, and related links.

words for everyday use

par • a • digm (pärˊ ə dīm) *n.*, philosophical or theoretical framework consisting of theories and generalizations. *Shifts in paradigms are often painful because people are resistant to change.*

1. The very definition of *Latino* includes the mixture of European, indigenous, African, and other races. Latino is not exclusively one race; it is a mixture of several races.

RESPOND TO THE SELECTION

You might encourage students to discuss this question in small groups and then summarize the discussion in their journals.

SELECTION CHECK TEST 4.9.13 WITH ANSWERS

Checking Your Reading

1. What does the author experience within her own family? **She experiences racism.**
2. How does this experience manifest? **The racism manifests in the hierarchy of beauty—the lighter the skin and the straighter the hair, the more beautiful a girl was considered.**
3. Describe Álvarez's mother. **She was a white woman, both in terms of race and class. She was proper and considered part of the elite class.**
4. Describe Álvarez's father. **He was dark-skinned with coarse hair. He came from a country family of twenty-five children. His family was educated, but only in the Dominican Republic.**
5. What word has Álvarez learned to fear? Why? **She has learned to fear the word *exclusive* because it breeds racism and hatred.**

Vocabulary in Context

Fill in each blank below with the most appropriate word from the following Words for Everyday Use. You may need to change the tense of the word.

emulate protocol elite entrepreneur relegate replenish solidarity

1. The teacher explained the **protocol** for the standardized test.
2. The restaurant caters to an **elite** crowd.
3. My classmate can **emulate** many famous actors.
4. At the end of the school year, the art instructor must **replenish** her supplies.
5. The boy who was afraid of the baseball was **relegated** to the right field position.

---

here. We had not undergone the same kind of race struggles as other Dominicans; therefore, we could not be "real" Dominicans.

What I came to understand and accept and ultimately fight for with my writing is the reality that ethnicity and race are not fixed constructs or measurable quantities. What constitutes our ethnicity and our race—once there is literally no common ground beneath us to define it—evolves as we seek to define and redefine ourselves in new contexts. My Latino-ness is not something someone can take away from me or leave me out of with a definition. It is in my blood: it comes from that mixture of biology, culture, native language, and experience that makes me a different American from one whose family comes from Ireland or Poland or Italy. My Latino-ness is also a political choice. I am choosing to hold on to my ethnicity and native language even if I can "pass." I am choosing to color my Americanness with my Dominicanness even if it came in a light shade of skin color.

I hope that as Latinos, coming from so many different countries and continents, we can achieve <u>solidarity</u> in this country as the mix that we are. I hope we won't shoot ourselves in the foot in order to maintain some sort of false "purity" as the glue that holds us together. Such an enterprise is bound to fail. We need each other. We can't afford to reject the darker or lighter varieties, and to do so is to have absorbed a definition of ourselves as exclusively

one thing or the other. And haven't we learned to fear that word "exclusive"? This reductiveness is absurd when we are talking about a group whose very definition is that of a mestizo[17] race, a mixture of European, indigenous, African, and much more. Within this vast circle, shades will lighten and darken into overlapping categories. If we cut them off, we diminish our richness and we plant a seed of ethnic cleansing[18] that is the root of the bloodshed we have seen in Bosnia and the West Bank and Rwanda and even our own Los Angeles and Dominican Republic.

How is the word "exclusive" ironic when used to define Latinos?

As we Latinos redefine ourselves in America, making ourselves up and making ourselves over, we have to be careful, in taking up the promises of America, not to adopt its limiting racial paradigms. Many of us have shed customs and prejudices that oppressed our gender, race, or class on our native islands and in our native countries. We should not replace these with modes of thinking that are divisive and oppressive of our rich diversity. Maybe as a group that embraces many races and differences, we Latinos can provide a positive multicultural, multiracial model to a divided America. ∎

---

17. **mestizo.** Referring to a person of mixed blood
18. **ethnic cleansing.** Expulsion, imprisonment, or killing of ethnic minorities by a dominant majority group

---

words for everyday use

sol • i • dar • i • ty (sä lə dar′ ə tē) *n.*, unity based on community interests, objectives, and standards. *Solidarity among Polish workers was achieved under the leadership of Lech Walesa.*

Respond *to the* SELECTION

How do you think you as an individual can help provide a positive multicultural model for a divided America?

SELECTION CHECK TEST 4.9.13 WITH ANSWERS (CONT.)

Literary Tools
Match each literary term with the best description.
a. style   b. tone   c. personal essay

1. the emotional attitude toward the reader or toward the subject implied by a literary work; **b**
2. a short work of nonfictional prose on a single topic related to the life or interests of the writer; **c**
3. the manner in which something is said or written; **a**

Investigate, Inquire, and Imagine

Recall: GATHERING FACTS

1a. In what ways is the narrator's father "black"? In what ways is the narrator's mother "white"?

2a. Being a white Latina, how is the narrator a "colored" person?

3a. What did Maxine Hong Kingston, Toni Morrison, Gwendolyn Brooks, Langston Hughes, and other "colored" writers help the narrator realize?

Interpret: FINDING MEANING

1b. Why do you think being black or having qualities that are "black" is looked down upon?

2b. What does the narrator mean by "culture color"?

3b. How did the narrator's life change after reading these authors' works?

Analyze: TAKING THINGS APART

4a. Compare and contrast the racism experienced by the narrator in the Dominican Republic with the racism she experienced in the United States. How are they similar? How are they different?

Synthesize: BRINGING THINGS TOGETHER

4b. How would the author's life be different if she had never moved to the United States?

Perspective: LOOKING AT OTHER VIEWS

5a. Álvarez says that in her writing she ultimately fights for "the reality that ethnicity and race are not fixed constructs or measurable quantities." Do you think she successfully conveys this message in the selection? Explain.

Empathy: SEEING FROM INSIDE

5b. What examples of diversity do you find in our culture?

Understanding Literature

STYLE AND TONE. Review the definitions for **style** and **tone** in the Handbook of Literary Terms. What are the style and tone of this essay?

PERSONAL ESSAY. Review the definition for **personal essay** in Literary Tools in Prereading and the cluster chart you made for this section. Into what categories did you put the author's experiences and perceptions? What is an example for each category?

ANSWERS TO INVESTIGATE, INQUIRE, AND IMAGINE (CONT.)

SYNTHESIZE

5a. The struggle to define herself may not have been so great because her culture was accepted in the Dominican Republic. She also may not have become a writer since writing and reading were activities done to help her cope with the racism she endured in the United States.

EVALUATE

5a. *Responses will vary.*

EXTEND

5b. *Responses will vary.*

Answers to Understanding Literature can be found on page 754.

ANSWERS TO INVESTIGATE, INQUIRE, AND IMAGINE

RECALL

1a. The father is seen as "black" because of his dark skin color and coarse and curly hair. He also was brought up living in old-fashioned houses and living off the earth. The mother is seen as "white" because of her pale skin, fine features, and cosmopolitan habits and ways.

2a. The narrator is a colored person because her culture "colors" her.

3a. These writers made her realize there were others like her who were struggling to define themselves without the use of boxes and restrictions of racial paradigms. They also helped her to realize that literature could be used to express her feelings in a language that included her cultural color.

INTERPRET

1b. *Responses may vary.* Historically, being black or having qualities that are "black" have been equated with being barbaric or savage. The white Europeans came to "civilize" the darker race, equating whiteness with being educated and having a superior position over black people. So throughout history, blacks have been seen as less than or a lower class of people or race. Unfortunately, those stereotypes have lasted throughout the centuries.

2b. She means that her culture colors her by the accent, habits, and smells she has.

3b. It rectified her writer's block and allowed her to write whatever she wanted, bringing "color" to her stories and poems. This ultimately led her to connect with the Latino community in the United States.

ANALYZE

4a. The racism experienced by the narrator in these countries is similar because they both discriminated her by skin color and gave the message that pale skin is beautiful whereas dark skin is despised. The racism experienced by the narrator in these countries is different because in the United States, the racism was more overt. For example, kids yelled to the narrator, "Go back to where you came from!" Also in the United States, the racism stemmed from the "color" of her culture because it was threatening and different, whereas in the Dominican Republic, her culture was colorless since it was the norm.

ANSWERS TO UNDERSTANDING LITERATURE

STYLE AND TONE. The style of this essay could be described as high style, because Álvarez writes about complex and abstract ideas such as finding one's identity and the oppressive nature of racism. She also uses complex sentences and words in her writing. The tone of this essay is serious and introspective as she reflects back on how racism has influenced her life.

PERSONAL ESSAY. The narrator reveals that she thinks about racism, ethnicity, and culture and how those things have shaped her as an individual. The reader can conclude that she is a deeply introspective and passionate woman who has strong desire to define herself as a Latina woman and human being. The reader can also conclude that she has qualities of a leader because she is unwilling to conform to societal stereotypes and norms.

ANSWERS TO INTEGRATING THE LANGUAGE ARTS

Language, Grammar, and Style
1. *resembled*: past
2. *maintains*: present; *are*: present
3. *will provide*: future
4. *told*: past; *had*: past; *was*: past
5. *finds*: present; *connects*: present

Collaborative Learning & Study and Research
Consider assigning each group a different movement to research. Ask students to use their imaginations to come up with a creative way to present their information. For example, one group might present their information in the form of a television news report. Another group might share information by role-playing an interview with some key figures in the movement.

Study and Research
You might allow students to choose other Latino writers not mentioned in the selection. Encourage some students to choose Latino writers that have risen more recently, such as Sandra Cisneros, Gary Soto, or Jimmy Santiago Baca. Students can compare how ideas on Latino identity have changed over time.

Writer's Journal

1. Write a **letter** to Julia Álvarez explaining how you reacted to her essay.
2. Write an **anecdote** of what it was like to grow up with your ethnicity.
3. Write a **plan** for fighting racism that you can take as an individual or as a group.

Integrating the Language Arts

Language, Grammar, and Style

SIMPLE TENSES. Read the Language Arts Survey 3.62, "Properties of Verbs: Tense." Then, in the following sentences, identify the verbs and tell which tense they are in.
1. The youngest Álvarez daughter resembled her mother's side of the family.
2. In her essay, Álvarez maintains that ethnicity and race are not fixed constructs or measurable quantities.
3. With other Latinos, the author will provide a positive multicultural, multiracial model to a divided America.
4. The Dominican maids told Álvarez stories that had power over her when she was little.
5. The author finds that writing connects her with Latino communities.

Collaborative Learning & Study and Research

RESEARCHING A MOVEMENT. With several classmates, research one of the following movements mentioned in "A White Woman of Color": the Civil Rights Movement, the Women's Movement, or the Antiwar Movement (Vietnam). What led to the development of the movement? Who were the major figures in the movement? What changes occurred in American society because of the movement? How does the movement continue to affect us today? Refer to the Language Arts Survey 5.18–5.20, "Research Skills," to help you find the answers to these questions. Then present your findings in an oral presentation.

Study and Research

RESEARCHING LATINO WRITERS. Among the Latino writers who influenced Julia Álvarez are Lorna Dee Cervantes, Piri Thomas, Rudolfo Anaya, Edward Rivera, and Ernesto Galarza. Read a selection by one of these writers. Then, with several classmates, discuss what your author adds to the discussion of Latino identity in particular and racism in general in the United States.

"SOMETHING COULD HAPPEN TO YOU"

from *Almost a Woman*

by Esmeralda Santiago

Reader's resource

"Something Could Happen to You" is a warning that young Esmeralda Santiago frequently hears from her mother when she moves to Brooklyn, a borough of New York City, from Puerto Rico. The selection is taken from Santiago's memoir *Almost a Woman* (1998).

GEOGRAPHY CONNECTION. Puerto Rico is an island in the Caribbean (its name means "Rich Port") and a U.S. Commonwealth. The United States acquired Puerto Rico in 1898 as a result of the Spanish-American War. Puerto Rico is allowed a certain degree of self-government, but remains under the direct authority of the U.S. Congress. Since this has advantages and disadvantages for Puerto Ricans, the future status of Puerto Rico is currently being debated. As it stands now, when Puerto Ricans move to the United States, they have the same rights as any U.S. citizen.

About *the* AUTHOR

Esmeralda Santiago (1948–), originally from Macun, Puerto Rico, moved with her family to New York City when she was 13 years old. The oldest of eight children, she worked very hard in junior high school in Brooklyn, struggling to learn English. Her hard work paid off, and she was chosen to attend The High School of Performing Arts, a prestigious school in Manhattan. A graduate of Harvard University and Sarah Lawrence College, she lives in Westchester County, New York. Besides *Almost a Woman*, Santiago has written another memoir, *When I Was Puerto Rican* (1993), and a novel, *America's Dream* (1996).

Literary TOOLS

DIALOGUE. Dialogue is conversation involving two or more people or characters. As you read, notice how the dialogue between the author and the neighbor girl changes the author's self-identity.

MEMOIR. A memoir is a nonfiction narration that tells a story. A memoir can be autobiographical or biographical. As you read, pay attention to the formative experiences that Santiago recounts about her experiences as an immigrant.

Organizer

Make a cluster chart like the one below to list the formative experiences the author has shortly after coming to the United States. One example has been done for you.

```
   ( Learns to identify )        (            )
   ( herself as Hispanic )       (            )
              \            /
           ( Formative )
           ( Experiences )
```

Reader's Journal

Have you ever visited a place different from the one where you live? Write a journal entry about what it felt like to be a newcomer in a strange place.

ADDITIONAL RESOURCES

UNIT 9 RESOURCE BOOK
- Selection Worksheet 9.8
- Selection Check Test 4.9.15
- Selection Test 4.9.16
- Language, Grammar, and Style Resource 3.80
- Speaking and Listening Resource 4.21

GRAPHIC ORGANIZER

Students should list the following formative experiences in their cluster charts:
- realizes the darkness and the "aggressive two-dimensionality" of Brooklyn differs from Puerto Rico
- is unable to understand English on television
- wishes she could have an extra gym suit
- gets placed in a class for lower-ability students
- learns "The Star Spangled Banner" by heart

READER'S JOURNAL

Students should consider whether their initial feelings changed over time with familiarity.

VOCABULARY FROM THE SELECTION

demerit	pungent
ephemeral	sever
fastidious	subdue
gait	substantial
lanky	subtle
marred	vacate
mesmerized	

GOALS/OBJECTIVES

Studying this lesson will enable students to
- empathize with the speaker's experience of immigrating to the United States
- describe the obstacles faced by the author as a recent immigrant
- define *dialogue* and recognize how an author uses dialogue to illustrate important themes and ideas in writing
- define *memoir* and explain how the term relates to the selection
- demonstrate an ability to identify gerunds and participles in sentences
- participate in a debate about the Spanish language's place in the United States

1. The author and her family came from Puerto Rico.

Portrait of a Girl, 1900s. Jesús Guerrero Galván. Private collection.

"SOMETHING COULD HAPPEN TO YOU"
from *Almost a Woman*

Esmeralda Santiago

We came to Brooklyn in search of medical care for my youngest brother, Raymond, whose toes were nearly <u>severed</u> by a bicycle chain when he was four. In Puerto Rico, doctors wanted to amputate the often red and swollen foot, because it wouldn't heal. In New York, Mami hoped doctors could save it.

Where did the author and her family come from?

The day we arrived, a hot, humid afternoon had splintered into thunderstorms as the last rays of the sun dipped into the rest of the United States. I was thirteen and superstitious enough to believe thunder and lightning held significance beyond the meteorological. I stored the sights and sounds of that dreary night into memory as if their meaning would someday be revealed in a flash of insight to forever

words for everyday use

sev • er (se′ vər) vi., remove; cut. *Relations with her family were <u>severed</u> by Gong when she left China.*

transform my life. When the insight came, nothing changed, for it wasn't the weather in Brooklyn that was important, but the fact that I was there to notice it.

One hand tightly grasped by Mami, the other by six-year-old Edna, we squeezed and pushed our way through the crowd of travellers. Five-year-old Raymond clung to Mami's other hand, his unbalanced <u>gait</u> drawing sympathetic smiles from people who moved aside to let us walk ahead of them.

> *Why does Raymond walk with an "unbalanced gait"?*

At the end of the tunnel waited Tata, Mami's mother, in black lace and high heels, a pronged rhinestone pin on her left shoulder. When she hugged me, the pin pricked my cheek, pierced <u>subtle</u> flower-shaped indentations that I rubbed rhythmically as our taxi hurtled through drenched streets banked by high, angular buildings.

> *What is Tata's relation to the author?*

New York was darker than I expected, and, in spite of the cleansing rain, dirtier. Used to the sensual curves of rural Puerto Rico, my eyes had to adjust to the regular, aggressive two-dimensionality of Brooklyn. Raindrops pounded the hard streets, captured the dim silver glow of street lamps, bounced against sidewalks in glistening sparks, then disappeared, like tiny <u>ephemeral</u> jewels, into the darkness. Mami and Tata teased that I was disillusioned because the streets were not paved with gold. But I had no such vision of New York. I was disappointed by the darkness, and fixed my hopes on the promise of light deep within the sparkling raindrops.

Two days later, I leaned against the wall of our apartment building on McKibbin Street wondering where New York ended and the rest of the world began. It was hard to tell. There was no horizon in Brooklyn. Everywhere I looked my eyes met a vertical maze of gray and brown straight-edged buildings with sharp corners and deep shadows. Every few blocks there was a cement playground surrounded by chain link fence. And in between, weedy lots mounded with garbage and rusting cars.

> *What did the author see everywhere she looked in Brooklyn?*

A girl came out of the building next door, a jump rope in her hand. She appraised me shyly; I pretended to ignore her. She stepped on the rope, stretched the ends overhead as if to measure their length, then began to skip, slowly, grunting each time she came down on the sidewalk. Swish splat grunt swish, she turned her back to me, swish splat grunt swish, she faced me again and smiled. I smiled back and she hopped over.

"*¿Tú eres hispana?*" she asked, as she whirled the rope in lazy arcs.

"No, I'm Puerto Rican."

"Same thing. Puerto Rican, Hispanic. That's what we are here." She skipped a tight circle, stopped abruptly and shoved the rope in my direction. "Want a turn?"

"Sure." I hopped on one leg, then the other. "So, if you're Puerto Rican, they call you Hispanic?"

"Yeah. Anybody who speaks Spanish."

I jumped a circle, like she had done, but faster. "You mean, if you speak Spanish, you're Hispanic?"

"Well, yeah. No, I mean your parents have to be Puerto Rican or Cuban or something."

I whirled the rope to the right, then the left, like a boxer. "Okay, your parents are Cuban, let's say, and you're born here, but you don't speak Spanish. Are you Hispanic?"

---

words for everyday use

gait (gāt) *n.*, manner of walking or moving. *The tall man had a dignified* <u>gait</u>.

sub • tle (sə′ təl) *adj.*, difficult to perceive or understand. *The sound was so* <u>subtle</u> *that Julio couldn't be sure if his neighbors were home.*

ephem • er • al (i fem′ rəl) *adj.*, lasting briefly; temporary; fleeting. *The* <u>ephemeral</u> *beauty of the fireworks lasted for seconds only.*

1. Raymond walks with an unbalanced gait because he nearly severed his toes on a bicycle chain when he was four, and his foot never healed properly.
2. Tata is the author's maternal grandmother.
3. Everywhere she looked the author saw a "vertical maze of gray and brown straight-edged buildings with sharp corners and deep shadows."

LITERARY TECHNIQUE

SYMBOL. A **symbol** is a thing that stands for or represents both itself and something else. A *conventional symbol* is one with traditional, widely recognized associations, such as a dove symbolizing peace. A *personal* or *idiosyncratic symbol* is one that assumes its secondary meaning because of the special use to which it is put by a writer. Point out to students that Santiago uses personal symbols in the paragraph that begins, "New York was darker than I expected...." Ask students: What might the darkness of New York represent to the young Santiago? What might she mean by "the promise of light deep within the sparkling raindrops"?

Answers
Help students see that the darkness of New York might represent Santiago's feelings about her future in this strange country. Point out that "the promise of light deep within the sparkling raindrops" probably stands for the positive things that Santiago hoped she would find in her future.

She bit her lower lip. "I guess so," she finally said. "It has to do with being from a Spanish country. I mean, you or your parents, like, even if you don't speak Spanish, you're Hispanic, you know?" She looked at me uncertainly. I nodded and returned her rope.

But I didn't know. I'd always been Puerto Rican, and it hadn't occurred to me that in Brooklyn I'd be someone else.

Later, I asked. "Are we Hispanics, Mami?"

"Yes, because we speak Spanish."

"But a girl said you don't have to speak the language to be Hispanic."

She scrunched her eyes. "What girl? Where did you meet a girl?"

"Outside. She lives in the next building."

"Who said you could go out to the sidewalk? This isn't Puerto Rico. *Algo te puede suceder.*"

"Something could happen to you" was a variety of dangers outside the locked doors of our apartment. I could be mugged. I could be dragged into any of the dark, abandoned buildings on the way to or from school, and be raped and murdered. I could be accosted by gang members into whose turf I strayed. I could be seduced by men who preyed on unchaperoned girls too willing to talk to strangers. I listened to Mami's lecture with downcast eyes and the necessary, respectful expression of humility. But inside, I quaked. Two days in New York, and I'd already become someone else. It wasn't hard to imagine that greater dangers lay ahead.

Our apartment on McKibbin Street was more <u>substantial</u> than any of our houses in Puerto Rico. Its marble staircase, plaster walls, and tiled floors were bound to the earth, unlike the wood and zinc rooms on stilts where I'd grown up. Chubby angels with bare buttocks danced around plaster wreaths on the ceiling.

There was a bathtub in the kitchen with hot and cold running water, and a toilet inside a closet with a sink and a medicine chest.

An alley between our bedroom window and the wall of the next building was so narrow that I stretched over to touch the bricks and left my mark on the greasy soot that covered them. Above, a sliver of sky forced vague yellow light into the ground below, filled with empty detergent boxes, tattered clothes, unpaired shoes, bottles, broken glass.

Mami had to go look for work, so Edna, Raymond, and I went downstairs to stay with Tata in her apartment. When we knocked on her door, she was just waking up. I sat at the small table near the cooking counter to read the newspapers that Don Julio, Tata's boyfriend, brought the night before. Edna and Raymond stood in the middle of the room and stared at the small television on a low table. Tata switched it on, fiddled with the knobs and the antenna until the horizontal lines disappeared and black and white cartoon characters chased each other across a flat landscape. The kids sank to the floor cross-legged, their eyes on the screen. Against the wall, under the window, Tata's brother, Tío Chico, slept with his back to us. Every so often, a snore woke him, but he chewed his drool, mumbled, slept again.

Who is Tío Chico, and where does he sleep?

While Tata went to wash up in the hall bathroom, I tuned in to the television. A dot bounced over the words of a song being performed by a train dancing along tracks, with dogs, cats, cows, and horses dangling from its windows and caboose. I was hypnotized by the dot skipping over words that looked nothing like they sounded. "Shilbee cominrun demuntin wenshecoms, toot-toot" sang the locomotive, and the ball dipped and rose over "She'll be

words for everyday use
sub • stan • tial (səb stan(t)′ shəl) *adj.,* sturdy; firmly constructed. *The new <u>substantial</u> roof was made of slate.*

coming 'round the mountain when she comes," with no toots. The animals, dressed in cowboy hats, overalls, and bandannas, waved pick axes and shovels in the air. The toot-toot was replaced by a bow-wow or a miaow-ow, or a moo-moo. It was joyous and silly, and made Edna and Raymond laugh. But it was hard for me to enjoy it as I focused on the words whizzing by, on the dot jumping rhythmically from one syllable to the next, with barely enough time to connect the letters to the sounds, with the added distraction of an occasional neigh, bark, or the kids' giggles.

> Why was it hard for the author to enjoy the song on TV?

When Tata returned from the bathroom, she made coffee on the two-burner hot plate. Fragrant steam soon filled the small room, and, as she strained the grounds through a well-worn flannel filter, Tío Chico rose as if the aroma were an alarm louder and more insistent than the singing animals on the television screen, the clanking of pots against the hot plate and counter, the screech of the chair legs as I positioned myself so that I could watch both Tata and the cartoons.

"Well, look who we have here," Tío Chico said as he stretched until his long, bony fingers scraped the ceiling. He wore the same clothes as the day before, a faded pair of dark pants and a short-sleeve undershirt, both wrinkled and giving off a <u>pungent</u> sweaty smell. He stepped over Edna and Raymond, who barely moved to let him through. In two long-legged strides, he slipped out to the bathroom. As he shut the door, the walls closed in, as if his <u>lanky</u> body added dimension to the cramped room.

Tata hummed the cartoon music. Her big hands reached for a pan, poured milk, stirred briskly as it heated and frothed. I was <u>mesmerized</u> by her grace, by how she held her head, by the disheveled ash-color curls that framed her high cheekbones. She looked up with mischievous caramel eyes, and grinned without breaking her rhythm.

Tío Chico returned showered and shaved, wearing a clean shirt and pants as wrinkled as the ones he'd taken off. He dropped the dirty clothes in a corner near Tata's bed and made up his cot. Tata handed me a cup of sweetened *café con leche*, and, with a head gesture, indicated I should <u>vacate</u> the chair for Tío Chico.

"No, no, that's okay," he said, "I'll sit here." He perched on the edge of the cot, elbows on knees, his fingers wrapped around the mug Tata gave him. Steam rose from inside his hands in a transparent spiral.

I couldn't speak English, so the school counselor put me in a class for

> What class was the author put in, and why?

students who'd scored low on intelligence tests, who had behavior problems, who were marking time until their sixteenth birthday when they could drop out. The teacher, a pretty black woman only a few years older than her students, pointed to a seat in the middle of the room. I didn't dare look anyone in the eyes. Grunts and mutters followed me, and, while I had no idea what they meant, they didn't sound friendly.

The desk surface was elaborately carved. There were many names, some followed by an apostrophe and a year. Several carefully rendered obscenities meant nothing to me, but I appreciated the workmanship of the shadowed letters, the <u>fastidious</u> edges around the *f* and *k*. I guessed a girl had written the cursive message

"SOMETHING COULD HAPPEN TO YOU" 759

1. The author didn't have enough time to connect the letters to the sounds.
2. The author was placed in a "class for students who'd scored low on intelligence tests, who had behavior problems, who were marking time until their sixteenth birthday when they could drop out."

LITERARY TECHNIQUE

SENSORY DETAILS. Sensory details are words and phrases that describe how things look, sound, smell, taste, or feel. Point out to students that Santiago uses sensory details throughout this memoir. For example, the narrator describes "singing animals...the clanking of pots...[and] the screech of chair legs." Ask students to locate other examples of sensory details.

SELECTION CHECK TEST 4.9.15
WITH ANSWERS

Checking Your Reading

1. What was the weather like when
Santiago arrived in New York? **It
was hot, humid, and stormy.**
2. When Santiago first arrived, what
was her impression of New York?
**She thought New York was darker
and dirtier than she expected. She
was struck by the right angles and
the two-dimensional nature of
Brooklyn.**
3. What does the neighbor girl tell
Santiago? **She tells Santiago that**
Hispanic **and** *Puerto Rican* **are the
same thing.**
4. How does Santiago feel about this
revelation? **She feels as if she is
someone else, and knowing that
made her fear the dangers that
lay ahead.**
5. Why is Santiago placed in a class for
students with behavior problems?
**She is placed in the class because
she spoke no English.**

Vocabulary in Context
Fill in each blank below with the most
appropriate word from the following
Words for Everyday Use. You may need
to change the tense of the word.

sever subtle substantial mesmerized
vacate subdue marred

1. She dropped <u>subtle</u> hints about
what she wanted for her birthday.
2. When the fire alarm rang, we were
forced to <u>**vacate**</u> the building.
3. The child was <u>**mesmerized**</u> by the
light dancing off the crystal unicorn.
4. When he changed jobs, he <u>**severed**</u>
all ties with his former employer.
5. After feeling anxious for hours, she
was <u>**subdued**</u> by the good news.

Literary Tools

1. What is dialogue? **Dialogue is
conversation involving two or
more characters.**
2. What is a memoir? **A memoir is a
nonfiction narration that tells a
story.**
3. Is Santiago's memoir biographical or
autobiographical? **Her memoir is
autobiographical.**

---

whose *i*s were dotted with hearts and daisies.
Below it, several lines of timid, chicken-scratch
writing alternated with an aggressive line of
block letters.

I pressed my hands together under the desk
to <u>subdue</u> their shaking, studied the straight
lines and ragged curves chiseled into the
desktop by those who sat there before me. Eyes
on the <u>marred</u> surface, I focused on the
teacher's voice, on the unfamiliar waves of
sound that crested over my head. I wanted to
float up and out of that classroom, away from
the hostile air that filled every corner of it,
every crevice. But the more I tried to disappear,
the more present I felt, until, exhausted, I gave
in, floated with the words, certain that if I
didn't, I would drown in them.

On gym days, girls had to wear grass-green,
cotton, short-sleeve, bloomer-leg, one-
piece outfits that buttoned down the front to an
elastic waistband covered with a sash too short
to tie into anything but a bulky knot. Grass
green didn't look good on anyone, least of all
adolescent girls whose faces broke out in red
pimples. The gym suit had elastic around the
bottom to keep our panties from showing when
we fell or sat. On those of us with skinny legs,
the elastic wasn't snug enough, so the bloomers
hung limply to our knees, where they flapped
when we ran.

The uniform, being one piece, made it
impossible to go to the bathroom in the three
minutes between classes. Instead of wearing it
all day, we could bring it to school and change
before gym, but no one did, since boys
periodically raided the locker room to see our
underwear. Proper hygiene during "the curse"

was impossible, as we needed at least three
hands, so most girls brought notes from their
mothers. The problem was that if you didn't
wear the uniform on gym days, everyone knew
you were menstruating.

One girl bought two gym suits, chopped off
the bottom of one, seamed around the selvage,
and wore the top part under her blouse so that
no one could tell if she had her period or not. I
asked Mami to do that for me, but she said we
didn't have money to waste on such foolishness.

Friday mornings we had Assembly. The first
thing we did was to press our right hands to our
breasts and sing "The Star Spangled Banner."
We were encouraged to sing as loud as we
could, and within a couple of weeks, I learned
the entire song by heart.

Ojo sé. Can. Juice. ¿Y?
Bye de don surly lie.
Whassoprowow we hell
Add debt why lie lass gleam in.
Whosebrods tripe sand bye ¿Stars?
True de perro los ¡Ay!
Order am parts we wash,
Wha soga lang tree streem in.

> What song did the
> author learn by heart?

I had no idea what the song said or meant,
and no one bothered to teach me. It was one of
the things I was supposed to know, and, like the
daily recitation of "The Pledge of Allegiance,"
it had to be done with enthusiasm, or teachers
gave out <u>demerits</u>. The pledge was printed in
ornate letters on a poster under the flag in
every classroom. "The Star Spangled Banner,"
however, remained a mystery for years, its
nonsense words the only song I could sing in
English from beginning to end. ∎

**words
for
everyday
use**

sub • due (səb dü') *vt.,* bring under control; reduce the intensity or degree of. *The principal* <u>subdued</u> *the class.*
marred (märd) *adj.,* damaged or defaced. *Painters were restoring the* <u>marred</u> *wall.*
de • mer • it (di mer' ət) *n.,* mark entailing a loss of privilege. *The teacher gave Assad a* <u>demerit</u> *for being late.*

On Loan to the Lonely

Esmeralda Santiago remembers what life was like for a Puerto Rican girl trying to survive in a borrowed country.
by Barbara Gutierrez

I still remember the initial shock of sitting in my fifth-grade class in New York City and realizing that I could not understand a word the teacher was saying.

I was a newly arrived Cuban refugee, and learning English became a monumental and painful task. Esmeralda Santiago brings back those initial moments of life in the United States in her new memoir, *Almost a Woman*.

A sequel to Santiago's well-received *When I Was Puerto Rican*, the book details the story of a teenager's arrival in Brooklyn from her hometown of Macun and her slow and often painful assimilation into U.S. society. This is a universal tale familiar to thousands of immigrants to this country, but it is made special by Santiago's simplicity and honesty in the telling.

"Negi," as her family affectionately calls the young Santiago, is the oldest of eight children who arrive with their mother to seek medical care for one of the youngest. Negi leaves behind a father whom she loves but who is separated from her mother and has become emotionally distant from his daughter, as well. She also cherishes her warm memories of island life.

For Negi, 13 at the time, life in this borrowed homeland is full of incongruities and challenges.

Two days after her arrival, a young neighbor asks her if she is Hispanic.

"No, I am Puerto Rican," Negi retorts.

"Same thing. Puerto Rican. Hispanic. That's what we are here."

"Two days in New York, and I'd already become someone else. It wasn't hard to imagine that greater dangers lay ahead," Santiago writes.

Life becomes a constant balancing act as Negi tries to embrace an independent lifestyle without giving up the protective values of her upbringing. Each time she pushes the issue—wanting to date without a chaperone, for instance—her mother warns her: "Algo te puede suceder" or "Something can happen to you."

When her mother loses her factory job, and the only financial sustenance for the family, Negi accompanies her to the local welfare office to act as a translator. The scene is heart-wrenching as the daughter musters the little English she knows to help her family get assistance while retaining integrity and self-respect.

This encounter is a self-defining moment for Negi, who vows to learn enough English to never get "caught between languages."

Headstrong and intelligent, Negi manages not only to learn English but also to excel in school, and she gains acceptance to the prestigious High School of Performing Arts (eventually, she graduates from Harvard).

By far the most interesting part of the work is watching Negi develop her own moral compass in the face of her "mami," a single mother who bore several children out of wedlock but wanted her daughters to fare better and to leave the house in "a white gown en route to a cathedral."

Negi manages to fulfill most of the obligations imposed on her, acting as a role model for her many siblings, working full time and studying part time at a community college and still making the trip home to sleep safely under her mother's roof.

Santiago writes in a straightforward, honest tone without much flourish. Yet her language conveys intimate details of her emotional maturing that allows us to feel privy to a private woman. ∎

ABOUT THE RELATED READING

"On Loan to the Lonely" was written by **Barbara Gutierrez** and distributed by the Knight Ridder News Service. It appeared in the *St. Paul Pioneer Press* on October 4, 1998. In the article, Gutierrez reviews Esmeralda Santiago's *Almost a Woman*, a memoir about Santiago's experiences as an immigrant from Puerto Rico adjusting to life in New York City. According to Gutierrez, the most interesting part of the memoir is watching young Negi develop "her own moral compass" as she decides which of her mother's advice to follow.

ADDITIONAL QUESTIONS AND ACTIVITIES

Ask students the following questions:
1. What does Gutierrez have in common with Santiago?
2. What aspects of Santiago's writing style does Gutierrez repeatedly praise in this review?

Answers
1. At nearly the same age, both Gutierrez and Santiago emigrated from a Spanish-speaking homeland to the United States.
2. Gutierrez repeatedly praises the simplicity and honesty of Santiago's writing style.

CROSS-CURRICULAR ACTIVITIES

ARTS AND HUMANITIES. Ask students to choose a selection from this unit to review. Have students reread the piece they choose, and use "On Loan to the Lonely" by Barbara Gutierrez as a model. You might encourage students to read one or two simple literary reviews from other sources, as well. Once students have finished their reviews, have them work in groups with other students who reviewed the same selection to compare and contrast their ideas.

RESPOND TO THE SELECTION

How do you think the author feels about America? How is your attitude toward America similar to or different from the author's?

ANSWERS TO INVESTIGATE, INQUIRE, AND IMAGINE

RECALL

1a. The author and her family come to the United States to get medical help for Raymond. The doctors in Puerto Rico wanted to amputate his foot, but the family wants to save his foot if possible.

2a. The author's mother says "Algo te puede suceder," which means, "Something could happen to you."

3a. The author felt that she needed to float with the words or she would drown in them.

INTERPRET

1b. The United States offers state-of-the-art medical facilities, which are one of the benefits of a higher standard of living than that in Puerto Rico.

2b. The mother's attitude toward her new home is suspicious. She is afraid harm may come to her children.

3b. She was not given bilingual instruction and was being thrown into a "sink or swim" situation in which she would have to master English on her own.

ANALYZE

4a. The author is surprised to learn she is no longer considered Puerto Rican but belongs to a larger group called Hispanic. She forces the issue with her new friend to learn just how far this label extends. According to the young neighbor girl, Hispanic can mean Spanish-speaking, or just having parents who are. Eager to verify this newly-acquired information, the author seeks verification from her mother. But this categorization isn't as important to the mother as the author's safety, and she changes the topic when she learns the author has been playing outside.

SYNTHESIZE

4b. From the author's childhood experiences which she relates, it is unclear whether she is proud of her heritage. But the fact that the author has written a book about being Hispanic indicates she grew to be proud of her heritage and wants to share her experiences with others.

Respond to the SELECTION

If you were the author, what would you find the most upsetting about your first few months in Brooklyn?

Investigate, Inquire, and Imagine

Recall: GATHERING FACTS

1a. Why do the author and her family come to the United States?

2a. What does the author's mother caution her after learning she has gone outside to play?

3a. What reaction did the author have toward her teacher's words?

Interpret: FINDING MEANING

1b. What does the United States offer that Puerto Rico does not?

2b. What is the mother's attitude toward her new home? Why?

3b. What does this tell you about the kind of attention she was getting in school?

Analyze: TAKING THINGS APART

4a. Analyze what the author learns about being Hispanic.

Synthesize: BRINGING THINGS TOGETHER

4b. Is the author proud of being Hispanic? Explain.

Evaluate: MAKING JUDGMENTS

5a. What are the author's greatest obstacles as a recent immigrant?

Extend: CONNECTING IDEAS

5b. Read the Related Reading. In what capacity does Negi serve when her mother loses her factory job? Compare Santiago's experience with Julie Álvarez's in "A White Woman of Color."

Understanding Literature

DIALOGUE. Review the definition for **dialogue** in the Handbook of Literary Terms. What makes dialogue an effective way to show the author's newly acquired understanding of the term *Hispanic*? What do we learn about the author from this dialogue?

MEMOIR. Review the definition for **memoir** in Literary Tools in Prereading and the cluster chart you made for that section. How would you categorize the author's experiences that she recounts in this selection? Is her memoir autobiographical or biographical?

EVALUATE

5a. Students might say that learning English and learning how to feel safe are the author's greatest obstacles.

EXTEND

5b. Negi acts as a go-between between the Hispanic and white cultures, using her meager English to help the family get public assistance.

> Answers to Understanding Literature can be found on page 763.

Writer's Journal

1. Imagine you are 13-year-old Esmeralda. Write a **postcard** to a friend back in Puerto Rico telling him or her your perceptions of your new home and relating an interesting anecdote.

2. Imagine you are Esmeralda's mother. Write a **letter** to your husband back in Puerto Rico explaining how the children are adapting to life in the United States. Express the fears and hopes you have for your children.

3. About *Almost a Woman* Esmeralda Santiago has said, "When I began writing this book, I had no idea it would result in a dialogue about cultural identity." Write a **dialogue** between yourself and an imaginary teenager who is a young immigrant in your school. Discuss each of your cultural identities.

Integrating
the Language Arts

Language, Grammar, and Style

GERUNDS AND PARTICIPLES. Read the Language Arts Survey 3.80, "Verbals: Participles, Gerunds, and Infinitives." Then identify the gerunds and present participles in the following sentences.

1. Esmeralda likes jumping rope with the neighbor girl.
2. On TV she watches the bouncing ball move from one word to the next.
3. Touching the building next door is easy because it is so close.
4. She began singing "The Star Spangled Banner" at school.
5. The drinking mug is for *café con leche*.

Speaking and Listening & Study and Research

DEBATE. Hold a debate about whether bilingual education should be financed by your local school board or whether Spanish should be considered an official language in the United States. Write constructive and rebuttal speeches for your position. Before you begin, research your topic in the library or on the Internet and read the Language Arts Survey 4.21, "Participating in a Debate."

Study and Research

RESEARCHING IMMIGRATION. Research immigration to the United States today. Where do today's immigrants come from? How do they get here? Why did they leave their native country? Then research patterns of immigration one hundred years ago. Make a presentation to the class comparing immigration today with immigration one hundred years ago.

Language, Grammar, and Style
1. jumping (gerund)
2. bouncing (present participle)
3. touching (gerund)
4. singing (gerund)
5. drinking (present participle)

Speaking and Listening & Study and Research
You might encourage students to research bilingual education on the Internet, beginning with the **National Clearinghouse for Bilingual Education** Internet site at http://ncbe.gwu.edu. This site offers an online library, success stories, and links to other language and education links.

Study and Research
When students begin their research, direct them to the University of Minnesota's **Immigration History Research Center** Internet site at http://www1.umn.edu/ihrc/. This site provides students with research collections of information and a list of links to other sites about immigration.

ANSWERS TO UNDERSTANDING LITERATURE

DIALOGUE. By using dialogue between two young Hispanic girls, the author is able to introduce the idea of cultural identity in a simple, childish way. The author pushes the envelope to see just how far the Hispanic label reaches, showing herself to be an inquisitive, intelligent child.

MEMOIR. The selection reveals intimate details of a young Hispanic girl's adjustments to life in the United States which appeared dangerous to her the moment she learned she was no longer Puerto Rican but Hispanic. The selection is autobiographical.

ADDITIONAL RESOURCES

UNIT 9 RESOURCE BOOK
- Selection Worksheet 9.9
- Selection Check Test 4.9.17
- Selection Test 4.9.18
- Language, Grammar, and Style Resource 3.36

VOCABULARY FROM THE SELECTION

foreman
foxhole
impulse
kindling
stewed

GRAPHIC ORGANIZER

- **Assumption:** Boyd will eat stewed tomatoes. **Stereotype:** African-American boys are hungry and will eat anything.
- **Assumption:** Boyd's father does manual labor. **Stereotype:** African-American men do not have responsible positions.
- **Assumption:** Boyd's mother works outside the home. **Stereotype:** African-American wives cannot afford to stay home and raise their families.
- **Assumption:** Boyd's mother can sew. **Stereotype:** African-American mothers need to sew because they can't afford to buy clothes for their family.
- **Assumption:** Boyd has many siblings. **Stereotype:** African Americans always have large families.
- **Assumption:** Boyd and his family need clothes. **Stereotype:** African Americans are poor.

READER'S JOURNAL

You might want to initiate a class discussion about assumptions and stereotypes. Encourage students to share their opinions about the subject, and lead students to the idea that quick assumptions can be erroneous and often dangerous.

Literary TOOLS

CHARACTER. A **character** is a person who figures in the action of a literary work. A *static character* is one who does not change during the course of the action. A *dynamic character* is one who does change. As you read, decide whether Mrs. Wilson is a static character or a dynamic character.

STEREOTYPE. A **stereotype** is an uncritically accepted, fixed, or conventional idea, particularly an idea held about whole groups of people. As you read, think about the stereotypes Mrs. Wilson has about African Americans.

Graphic Organizer

Make a chart to list the assumptions made by Mrs. Wilson about Boyd and the stereotypes about African Americans that she has. One example has been done for you.

Assumptions	Stereotypes
Johnny made Boyd carry the wood	Whites order African Americans around

Reader's Journal

When have you made an assumption about another person only to discover later that you were wrong?

"After You, My Dear Alphonse"
by Shirley Jackson

Reader's resource

In **"After You, My Dear Alphonse"** Shirley Jackson shows that assuming things about another person can be a subtle, yet powerful form of prejudice. The saying "After you, my dear Alphonse" originated with a comic strip that first appeared in 1905. The expression is generally used when two people go back and forth, suggesting the other go first, as a way of being polite. It is sometimes used humorously. "After You, My Dear Alphonse" was published in Jackson's short story collection *The Lottery* in 1949.

About the AUTHOR

Shirley Jackson (1919–1965) is best known for her stories and novels of horror and the occult, rendered more terrifying because they are set against realistic, commonplace backgrounds. After graduating from Syracuse University, Jackson married literary critic Stanley Edgar Hyman. *Life Among the Savages* (1953) and *Raising Demons* (1957) are witty and humorous fictionalized memoirs about their life with their four children. Her most famous works include the short story collection *The Lottery* (1949) and the novel *The Haunting of Hill House* (1959). *The Haunting of Hill House* was made into a movie in 1966. A remake of the film, starring Liam Neeson, was released in 1999.

GOALS/OBJECTIVES

Studying this lesson will enable students to
- appreciate a short story about stereotypes
- describe Shirley Jackson's literary accomplishments
- define *character* and *stereotype* and recognize the use of these techniques in the selection
- identify compound, complex, and compound-complex sentences
- analyze comic strips from the past and compare them to modern comic strips
- write an agenda for a meeting

After You, My Dear Alphonse

Shirley Jackson

Mrs. Wilson was just taking the gingerbread out of the oven when she heard Johnny outside talking to someone.

What is Mrs. Wilson baking?

"Johnny," she called, "you're late. Come in and get your lunch."

"Just a minute, Mother," Johnny said. "After you, my dear Alphonse."

"After *you*, my dear Alphonse," another voice said.

"No, after *you*, my dear Alphonse," Johnny said.

Mrs. Wilson opened the door. "Johnny," she said. "You come in this minute and get your lunch. You can play after you've eaten."

Johnny came in after her, slowly. "Mother," he said, "I brought Boyd home for lunch with me."

"Boyd?" Mrs. Wilson thought for a moment. "I don't believe I've met Boyd. Bring him in, dear, since you've invited him. Lunch is ready."

Who is Johnny's friend?

"Boyd!" Johnny yelled. "Hey, Boyd, come on in!"

"I'm coming. Just got to unload this stuff."

"Well, hurry, or my mother'll be sore."[1]

"Johnny, that's not very polite to either your friend or your mother," Mrs. Wilson said. "Come sit down, Boyd."

As she turned to show Boyd where to sit, she saw he was a Negro boy, smaller than Johnny but about the same age. His arms were loaded with split <u>kindling</u> wood. "Where'll I put this stuff, Johnny?" he asked.

Mrs. Wilson turned to Johnny. "Johnny," she said, "what did you make Boyd do? What is that wood?"

"Dead Japanese," Johnny said mildly. "We stand them in the ground and run over them with tanks."

What game were the boys playing?

---

1. **sore.** Angry

---

words for everyday use

kin • dling (kind' liŋ) *adj.*, small pieces of wood or paper used to start a fire. *Janet used <u>kindling</u> sticks placed beneath the large logs to get the fire going.*

ANSWERS TO GUIDED READING QUESTIONS

1. She is baking gingerbread.
2. Johnny's friend is Boyd, an African-American boy.

INDIVIDUAL LEARNING STRATEGIES

MOTIVATION
Ask students to recall a time when a parent or guardian embarrassed them in front of one of their friends. Have students write about the incident in their journals. To spur their thinking, ask students: Do you feel your parent insulted your friend? Or were you just embarrassed by your parent's behavior? Did your friend notice? Did you tell your parent that you were embarrassed by the incident?

READING PROFICIENCY
Consider allowing students to work with a partner to read the story and complete the graphic organizer on page 764. Explain to students that by completing this graphic organizer, they will grasp the most important points of the story.

ENGLISH LANGUAGE LEARNING
Before students begin reading this selection, carefully review with them the information in the Reader's Resource on page 764. You might pair students with a partner who can help them uncover the prejudice behind Mrs. Wilson's subtle comments.

SPECIAL NEEDS
Ask students to focus their attention on the Guided Reading and Recall questions for the selection. Allow them ample time to complete the questions, and check their answers when they have finished. For incorrect answers, guide students in identifying the correct ones. For example, you might ask them additional questions that lead them to the correct answers.

ENRICHMENT
Ask students to learn more about Jackson by reading another of her stories. Have students choose a short story or a memoir and write a brief essay that summarizes the story and identifies its main themes. You might ask students to close the essay with their personal review of the story they read.

LITERARY TECHNIQUE

SETTING. The **setting** of a literary work is the time and place in which it occurs, together with all the details used to create a sense of a particular time and place. Ask students to fix the time period of the short story and to explain what details led them to that conclusion.

Answers
The word "Negro" dates the story to before the 1960s. The phrase "Dead Japanese" indicates a time around World War II, when the United States was at war with Japan. Consequently, the short story probably takes place in the 1940s or shortly thereafter.

1. The boys were playing war.
2. He offers the scrambled eggs to Boyd before he serves himself.
3. She assumes he will eat anything, including stewed tomatoes.
4. He's a foreman in a factory.
5. She plans to become a teacher.

LITERARY TECHNIQUE

CHARACTERIZATION. Characterization is the use of literary techniques to create a character. Writers use three major techniques to create characters: direct description, portrayal of characters' behavior, and representations of characters' internal states. Ask students to identify which techniques Jackson uses to draw the character of Mrs. Wilson and to identify an example for each.

Answer
Jackson uses portrayal of Mrs. Wilson's behavior, particularly through dialogue. On page 767, Jackson describes Mrs. Wilson taking away the gingerbread from Boyd. She also uses representation of Mrs. Wilson's internal state, as when she describes Mrs. Wilson as feeling "defeated."

ADDITIONAL QUESTIONS AND ACTIVITIES

Ask students the following questions:
1. What is Mrs. Wilson's attitude toward Boyd and his family?
2. Describe the relationship between Johnny and Boyd. What do the boys have in common?

Answers
1. Mrs. Wilson feels she is superior to Boyd and his family.
2. Johnny and Boyd treat each other as equals and seem to respect each other.

"How do you do, Mrs. Wilson?" Boyd said.

"How do you do, Boyd? You shouldn't let Johnny make you carry all that wood. Sit down now and eat lunch, both of you."

"Why shouldn't he carry the wood, Mother? It's his wood. We got it at his place."

"Johnny," Mrs. Wilson said, "go on and eat your lunch."

"Sure," Johnny said. He held out the dish of scrambled eggs to Boyd. "After you, my dear Alphonse."

> *What action indicates that Johnny is polite?*

"After *you*, my dear Alphonse," Boyd said.

"After *you*, my dear Alphonse," Johnny said. They began to giggle.

"Are you hungry, Boyd?" Mrs. Wilson asked.

"Yes, Mrs. Wilson."

"Well, don't you let Johnny stop you. He always fusses about eating, so you just see that you get a good lunch. There's plenty of food here for you to have all you want."

"Thank you, Mrs. Wilson."

"Come on, Alphonse," Johnny said. He pushed half the scrambled eggs onto Boyd's plate. Boyd watched while Mrs. Wilson put a dish of <u>stewed</u> tomatoes beside his plate.

"Boyd don't eat tomatoes, do you, Boyd?" Johnny said.

"*Doesn't* eat tomatoes, Johnny. And just because you don't like them, don't say that about Boyd. Boyd will eat *anything*."

> *What does Mrs. Wilson assume about Boyd?*

"Bet he won't," Johnny said, attacking his scrambled eggs.

"Boyd wants to grow up and be a big, strong man so he can work hard," Mrs. Wilson said. "I'll bet Boyd's father eats stewed tomatoes."

"My father eats anything he wants to," Boyd said.

"So does mine," Johnny said. "Sometimes he doesn't eat hardly anything. He's a little guy, though. Wouldn't hurt a flea."

"Mine's a little guy, too," Boyd said.

"I'll bet he's strong, though," Mrs. Wilson said. She hesitated. "Does he . . . work?"

"Sure," Johnny said. "Boyd's father works in a factory."

"There, you see?" Mrs. Wilson said. "And he certainly has to be strong to do that—all that lifting and carrying at a factory."

"Boyd's father doesn't have to," Johnny said. "He's a <u>foreman</u>."

> *What job does Boyd's father have?*

Mrs. Wilson felt defeated. "What does your mother do, Boyd?"

"My mother?" Boyd was surprised. "She takes care of us kids."

"Oh. She doesn't work, then?"

"Why should she?" Johnny said through a mouthful of eggs. "You don't work."

"You really don't want any stewed tomatoes, Boyd?"

"No, thank you, Mrs. Wilson," Boyd said.

"No, thank you, Mrs. Wilson, no, thank you, Mrs. Wilson, no, thank you, Mrs. Wilson," Johnny said. "Boyd's sister's going to work, though. She's going to be a teacher."

> *What does Boyd's sister plan to do?*

"That's a very fine attitude for her to have, Boyd." Mrs. Wilson restrained an <u>impulse</u> to pat Boyd on the head. "I imagine you're all very proud of her?"

"I guess so," Boyd said.

"What about all your other brothers and sisters? I guess all of you want to make just as much of yourselves as you can."

"There's only me and Jean," Boyd said. "I don't know yet what I want to be when I grow up."

---

words for everyday use

stewed (stüd) *adj.*, cooked with simmering heat. *Bill's uncle ate* <u>stewed</u> *prunes for breakfast that he simmered the night before.*

fore • man (fōr' mən) *n.*, person in charge of other workers or a section of a plant. *The* <u>foreman</u> *informed his workers of the production quota for the shift.*

im • pulse (im' pəls) *n.*, sudden spontaneous inclination to an unpremeditated action. *Jan's* <u>impulse</u> *was to throw a glass of water in her date's face after his rude remark.*

"We're going to be tank drivers, Boyd and me," Johnny said. "Zoom." Mrs. Wilson caught Boyd's glass of milk as Johnny's napkin ring, suddenly transformed into a tank, plowed heavily across the table.

"Look, Johnny," Boyd said. "Here's a <u>foxhole</u>. I'm shooting at you."

Mrs. Wilson, with the speed born of long experience, took the gingerbread off the shelf and placed it carefully between the tank and the foxhole.

"Now eat as much as you want to, Boyd," she said. "I want to see you get filled up."

"Boyd eats a lot, but not as much as I do," Johnny said. "I'm bigger than he is."

"You're not much bigger," Boyd said. "I can beat you running."

Mrs. Wilson took a deep breath. "Boyd," she said. Both boys turned to her. "Boyd, Johnny has some suits that are a little too small for him, and a winter coat. It's not new, of course, but there's lots of wear in it still. And I have a few dresses that your mother or sister could probably use. Your mother can make them over into lots of things for all of you, and I'd be very happy to give them to you. Suppose before you leave I make up a big bundle and then you and Johnny can take it over to your mother right away . . ." Her voice trailed off as she saw Boyd's puzzled expression.

"But I have plenty of clothes, thank you," he said. "And I don't think my mother knows how to sew very well, and anyway I guess we buy about everything we need. Thank you very much, though."

"We don't have time to carry that old stuff around, Mother," Johnny said. "We got to play tanks with the kids today."

Mrs. Wilson lifted the plate of gingerbread off the table as Boyd was

What does Mrs. Wilson do when Boyd rejects her offer of clothing?

about to take another piece. "There are many little boys like you, Boyd, who would be very grateful for the clothes someone was kind enough to give them."

What does Mrs. Wilson tell Boyd? Why?

"Boyd will take them if you want him to, Mother," Johnny said.

"I didn't mean to make you mad, Mrs. Wilson," Boyd said.

"Don't think I'm angry, Boyd. I'm just disappointed in you, that's all. Now let's not say anything more about it."

She began clearing the plates off the table, and Johnny took Boyd's hand and pulled him to the door. "Bye, Mother," Johnny said. Boyd stood for a minute, staring at Mrs. Wilson's back.

"After you, my dear Alphonse," Johnny said, holding the door open.

"Is your mother still mad?" Mrs. Wilson heard Boyd ask in a low voice.

"I don't know," Johnny said. "She's screwy sometimes."

"So's mine," Boyd said. He hesitated. "After *you*, my dear Alphonse." ∎

"AFTER YOU, MY DEAR ALPHONSE"   767

ANSWERS TO GUIDED READING QUESTIONS

1. She takes the gingerbread cookies off the table just as Boyd is about to take another.
2. She tells Boyd she's disappointed in him for not accepting the offer of used clothing.

SELECTION CHECK TEST 4.9.17 WITH ANSWERS

Checking Your Reading
1. What is the first assumption Mrs. Wilson makes about Boyd? **She assumes that Boyd was forced to carry the wood.**
2. What does Mrs. Wilson say to Boyd about lunch? **She says that there is plenty of food and that he can have all he wants.**
3. Does she mean what she says about lunch? How do you know? **She obviously does not mean it because she takes away the gingerbread as Boyd is reaching for another piece.**
4. What does Mrs. Wilson's response to Boyd's statement that his sister is going to be a teacher imply? **Her response implies that she believes his sister will not actually be able to teach. She is condescending to him by patting him on the head.**
5. Why do you think Mrs. Wilson is disappointed in Boyd? **Students may say that she is disappointed because he and his family have not lived up to the stereotype she has set in her mind.**

Vocabulary in Context
Fill in each blank below with the most appropriate word from the following Words for Everyday Use. You may need to change the tense of the word.

> kindling stewed foreman
> impulse foxhole

1. The <u>foxhole</u> saved the troopers' lives.
2. I tried to stave off the <u>impulse</u> to buy the expensive shoes.
3. They were unable to start the fire because they didn't have <u>kindling</u>.

SELECTION CHECK TEST 4.9.17 WITH ANSWERS (CONT.)

Literary Tools
Choose the letter of the term that best fits each definition.

a. dynamic character b. static character c. stereotype

c 1. an uncritically accepted, fixed, or conventional idea
a 2. a character who changes during the course of action
b 3. a character who does not change during the course of the action

RESPOND TO THE SELECTION

Extend the activity by asking students to explain how Johnny felt about the incident. Encourage students to look for hints in the selection as to Johnny's reaction to his mother's behavior.

ANSWERS TO INVESTIGATE, INQUIRE, AND IMAGINE

RECALL

1a. He invites his friend Boyd, an African-American boy.
2a. She offers Boyd used clothing for himself, his mother, and his sister, thinking Boyd's mother "can make them over."
3a. He rejects the offer, saying he has enough clothes and his family buys what they need.

INTERPRET

1b. She begins to make assumptions about Boyd that are not based on reality but on traditional stereotypes of African Americans.
2b. A racist attitude underlies Mrs. Wilson's seemingly generous gesture. She is assuming that all African Americans are poor and cannot afford to buy their own clothes.
3b. She is angry at him. She takes the gingerbread off the table before Boyd can take another piece. She says, "Don't think I'm angry" which indicates she is more concerned about what Boyd thinks of her than being honest with her emotions.

ANALYZE

4a. Johnny is not suspicious or angry when his mother suggests that he made Boyd carry the wood. He thinks it's perfectly logical that Boyd carried the wood because it was wood from Boyd's place. Boyd calmly and politely answers Mrs. Wilson's questions, even when a pattern of racism develops in her questioning. For example, when he refuses the used clothing she has offered, he is more concerned that he might have made Mrs. Wilson mad than concerned that Mrs. Wilson might think of him as inferior.

SYNTHESIZE

4b. Some students may point out that Boyd is polite and wants to treat his friend's mother with respect. Others may point out that, since Boyd himself is not prejudiced, he cannot recognize prejudice in Mrs. Wilson. Still others may suggest that Boyd realizes that Mrs. Wilson's intentions are generous even though they may be ignorant.

Respond *to the* SELECTION

If you were Johnny, what would you say to your mother about what happened at lunch? Would you be angry or happy with how she treated Boyd?

Investigate, *Inquire,* and Imagine

Recall: GATHERING FACTS

1a. Whom does Johnny invite home for lunch?

2a. What does Mrs. Wilson offer Boyd?

3a. How does Boyd respond to the offer of used clothing?

→ **Interpret: FINDING MEANING**

1b. How does Mrs. Wilson's behavior change once she sees the guest and why?

2b. What attitude underlies Mrs. Wilson's seemingly generous gestures?

3b. How does Mrs. Wilson feel when Boyd rejects the clothes? How can you tell?

Analyze: TAKING THINGS APART

4a. Are Johnny and Boyd aware of Mrs. Wilson's racist attitudes? Support your answer with evidence from the story.

→ **Synthesize: BRINGING THINGS TOGETHER**

4b. Why doesn't Boyd get angry with Mrs. Wilson?

Evaluate: MAKING JUDGMENTS

5a. Mrs. Wilson tells Boyd, "I'm just disappointed in you." Evaluate the cause of Mrs. Wilson's disappointment.

→ **Extend: CONNECTING IDEAS**

5b. What role did Mrs. Wilson want Boyd to play? What roles do you play in your life? How do you decide how to play these roles? Which roles are decided for you?

Understanding *Literature*

CHARACTER. Review the definition for **character** in the Handbook of Literary Terms. Is Mrs. Wilson a static or a dynamic character? Why? What character traits does she possess?

STEREOTYPE. Review the definition for **stereotype** in the Handbook of Literary Terms and the chart you made for Literary Tools on page 764. What stereotypes are presented in this short story? How does Boyd defy these stereotypes? What is his experience with stereotypes?

ANSWERS TO INVESTIGATE, INQUIRE, AND IMAGINE (CONT.)

EVALUATE

5a. Some students may point out that Mrs. Wilson is disappointed with Boyd because he does not fit her stereotype of what an African-American boy should be like. His father does not do manual labor, his mother stays at home, he is not poor and hungry, nor does he come from a large, uneducated family. Boyd breaks all of Mrs. Wilson's preconceived, prejudiced ideas. Such ideas are dangerous because they do not take the individual into account.

EXTEND

5b. Students might say the Mrs. Wilson wanted Boyd to play a role that fit her assumptions and expectations of African Americans, even though her assumptions were incorrect.

Writer's Journal

1. Imagine that you are Johnny. Write a **journal entry** describing your friend Boyd and explaining why you value his friendship.

2. Imagine that Boyd talks to his mother about Mrs. Wilson's offer of clothes and about the other questions she asked him. Write a **letter** that Boyd's mother mails to Mrs. Wilson.

3. Write a **dialogue** between Mr. and Mrs. Boyd in which Mrs. Boyd describes what transpired at lunch and Mr. Boyd poses questions and makes comments.

Integrating
the Language Arts

Language, Grammar, and Style

COMPOUND, COMPLEX, AND COMPOUND-COMPLEX SENTENCES. Read about compound, complex, and compound-complex sentences in the Language Arts Survey 3.36, "Combining and Expanding Sentences." Then identify each of the following sentences as a compound sentence, a complex sentence, or a compound-complex sentence.

1. Mrs. Wilson told Johnny to bring in his friend, since Johnny had invited him.
2. The boy didn't know yet what he wanted to be.
3. Boyd's father had given him the wood; therefore, he carried it.
4. After leaving the house, Boyd was relieved.
5. After they have eaten lunch, the boys will be soldiers, and they will play with tanks.

Applied English

AGENDA. Imagine that you belong to an organization called "Youth for Understanding," which has the aim of bringing together the different racial groups in your community. Write an agenda for the organization's first meeting. An agenda outlines things to be considered or done. What is your organization's goal? What groups do you want to bring together? What activities do you want to plan?

Media Literacy

CARTOONS. The title of this short story is an expression that comes from a comic strip from the early 1900s called *Alphonse and Gaston.* Find a copy of this comic strip and analyze the type of humor it presents. Compare its humor to the humor in a contemporary comic strip with which you are familiar. What things from *Alphonse and Gaston* are still funny today? How has American humor changed? How would you analyze the humor in the contemporary comic strip you chose to discuss?

Study and Research

"THE LOTTERY." Shirley Jackson's most famous short story is called "The Lottery." Read the story. You can find it on the Internet or at the library. Research the reaction the story engendered when it was first published. Then consult a biography of Jackson in your school library or on the Internet. Explain the reader's emotional reaction to "The Lottery" based on your understanding of the story. Why were people upset? What was Jackson's reason for writing the story?

ANSWERS TO INTEGRATING THE LANGUAGE ARTS (CONT.)

Study and Research
Have students organize their research and ideas in a two- or three-page essay. Encourage them to include in their essays their personal reactions to the story.

ANSWERS TO UNDERSTANDING LITERATURE

CHARACTER. Mrs. Wilson is a static character because she does not change. She does not learn from her conversation with Boyd that her attitudes are prejudicial; consequently, she does not reform them. Mrs. Wilson is formal, since she insists on correct speech from her son; she is strict, since she scolds Johnny for being late and for not being polite; she is racist, since she makes assumptions about Boyd based on the fact that he is African American.

STEREOTYPE. The stereotypes that are presented in this short story include: White people order African Americans around; African Americans are hungry and will eat anything; African-American men do not have responsible positions; African-American wives cannot afford to stay home and they need to sew in order to clothe their families; African Americans are poor. Boyd defies these stereotypes because he is well fed at home, his father is a foreman who does not do manual labor, his mother stays at home to raise the family, and his parents can afford to buy the things they need and do not have to rely on handouts. Boyd seems genuinely puzzled by Mrs. Wilson's behavior and is too innocent to know its true cause; he does not appear to have much experience with stereotypes of himself and other members of his race.

ANSWERS TO INTEGRATING THE LANGUAGE ARTS

Language, Grammar, and Style
1. compound sentence
2. compound sentence
3. compound-complex sentence
4. complex sentence
5. complex sentence

Applied English
Remind students that the agenda must be both informative and persuasive if they want to get people interested in the organization. Encourage students to use formal English, but to try to keep the tone light, positive, and courteous.

Media Literacy
Extend this activity by asking students to present their evaluations orally to the class. Students might enjoy making handouts of the comic strips they are comparing. Each oral presentation can conclude with a question-and-answer session about related topics not covered in the presentation.

ADDITIONAL RESOURCES

UNIT 9 RESOURCE BOOK
- Selection Worksheet 9.10
- Selection Check Test 4.9.19
- Selection Test 4.9.20
- Language, Grammar, and Style Resource 3.90
- Speaking and Listening Resource 4.14

GRAPHIC ORGANIZER

Students should include the following items in their charts: how my father stood his ground; how my people survived slavery; why the rivers overflow their banks; why the snow falls and covers the ground; why the hurricane sweeps through the land every now and then; why the angels woke me up this morning soon; why the blood still runs through my veins; how I rate to run another day

READER'S JOURNAL

What things about life are puzzling to you? What questions do you have about life that you would like answered?

INDIVIDUAL LEARNING STRATEGIES

MOTIVATION
Ask students to think about a song that has deeply affected them. Ask volunteers to share their stories about the song with the class.

READING PROFICIENCY
Have students read the song one stanza at a time. Point out that each stanza centers around a different theme. Ask students to jot down a few words that describe the theme of each stanza.

ENGLISH LANGUAGE LEARNING
Pair students with English-proficient partners and have them take turns reading the song aloud, with the proficient reader reading first.

(Continued on page 771)

SONG LYRICS

Literary TOOLS

REPETITION. Repetition is the writer's conscious reuse of a sound, word, phrase, sentence, or other element. What words and phrases are repeated in "I Remember; I Believe"?

THEME. A theme is a central idea in a literary work. Themes commonly address universal topics that people around the world share—things like love, death, family, and friendship. As you read, think about the theme or themes of the song. What part does repetition play in revealing the theme or themes? Use the Graphic Organizer below to help you connect the use of repetition to possible themes.

Graphic Organizer

Make a cluster chart to list what the speaker does not know.

"how my mother walked her trouble down"

Speaker Doesn't Know

Reader's Journal

What type of things do you remember? Do you think memories are important? Why, or why not?

770 *UNIT NINE*

PREREADING

"I REMEMBER; I BELIEVE"
by Bernice Johnson Reagon

Reader's resource

MUSIC CONNECTION. Dr. Bernice Reagon is not only a professor of history, she is also a singer and songwriter. In 1973, she founded Sweet Honey in the Rock, a Grammy Award-winning African-American female a cappella ensemble with deep musical roots in the sacred music of the black church—spirituals, hymns, gospel—as well as jazz and blues. Five African-American women join their powerful voices, along with hand percussion instruments, to create a blend of lyrics, movement, and narrative that weaves in the history of African Americans and women. Their songs, like "I Remember; I Believe," point the finger at justice, encourage activism, and sing the praises of love. The music speaks out against oppression and exploitation of every kind. The quintet, whose words are simultaneously interpreted in uniquely expressive American Sign Language, demands a just and human world for all.

About the AUTHOR

Bernice Johnson Reagon (1942–), born in Albany, Georgia, is a lover of two things: music and history. As a musician, Reagon sang with the original SNCC (Student Nonviolent Coordinating Committee) Freedom Singers. This experience gave her the desire and confidence to take control of her own music career; her most distinguishing act was founding the a cappella ensemble Sweet Honey in the Rock. As a historian, she teaches history at American University and is also the Curator Emeritus at the National Museum of American History in the Smithsonian Institution. Reagon fuses both her love for music and history in Sweet Honey in the Rock by writing songs that address the African-American experience and by weaving traditional music techniques such as African chant, field hollers, and the blues.

GOALS/OBJECTIVES

Studying this lesson will enable students to
- empathize with and understand a speaker's ideas
- explain how repetition is used in song lyrics to highlight important ideas
- define *repetition* and recognize examples in their reading
- define *theme* and identify the main themes in "I Remember; I Believe"
- demonstrate an ability to use apostrophes correctly
- conduct research on important moments in African-American history

I REMEMBER, I BELIEVE

Bernice Johnson Reagon

Autobiography: Water/Ancestors/Middle Passage/Family Ghosts, 1988. Howardena Pindell. Wadsworth Athenaeum, Hartford.

art note

Autobiography: Water/Ancestors/ Middle Passage/Family Ghosts, 1988. Howardena Pindell.

In this painted autobiography, **Howardena Pindell** (1943–) painted autobiography includes the central figure of herself immersed in water, her arms moving as if swimming. She is surrounded by pictures of relatives and ancestors, and by texts of racist laws of the past. The "middle passage" in the work's title refers to the route across the ocean taken by slave ships. A diagram of a slave ship is shown in the lower left. In the context of these elements, what do you think Pindell means by the metaphor of swimming?

I don't know how my mother
  walked her trouble down
I don't know how my father stood
  his ground
I don't know how my people survived slavery
I do remember, that's why I believe

What doesn't the speaker know about her mother?

I don't know why the rivers overflow their banks
I don't know why the snow falls and covers the ground
I don't know why the hurricane sweeps thru the land
  every now and then
Standing in a rainstorm, I believe

I don't know why the angels woke me up this morning
  soon
I don't know why the blood still runs through my veins
I don't know how I rate to run another day
I am here still running, I believe

My God calls to me in the
  morning dew
The power of the universe knows my name
Gave me a song to sing and sent me on my way
I raise my voice for justice, I believe

What does God do for the speaker?

RESPOND TO THE SELECTION

You might encourage students to respond to these questions in the form of song lyrics or a short poem.

ANSWERS TO INVESTIGATE, INQUIRE, AND IMAGINE

RECALL
1a. The speaker does not know how her people survived the injustice and oppression of slavery.
2a. The speaker does not know why she is able to live another day.
3a. The speaker says she raises her voice for justice and that she believes.

INTERPRET
1b. Students might suggest that, in light of what people today know about the horrors of slavery, it is difficult to understand how anyone survived it.
2b. Students might say that the speaker seems grateful for every day she is able to live.
3b. Students might assert that strong, determined people raise their voice for justice. People who remember past injustices will fight to prevent similar injustices from happening again.

ANALYZE
4a. Stanza 1: The speaker doesn't know how her parents endured the suffering and hardships they faced, or how her people survived slavery. Stanza 2: The speaker doesn't know why floods, storms, and hurricanes occur. Stanza 3: The speaker doesn't know why she has been chosen to have life.

SYNTHESIZE
4b. The speaker is able to believe because of experience—whether it be through primary experience such as living through natural disasters, or by bearing witness to experiences through the medium of memories.

EVALUATE
5a. *Responses will vary.* Most students should find the title appropriate for the song because it focuses on how remembering past struggles and triumphs leads people to believe in the strength of the human spirit. The title also suggests one major theme in the song—the importance of keeping the memory of the past alive.

Respond *to the* SELECTION

What do you believe you are called to do? Do you believe you are put on this Earth for a specific reason? Why, or why not?

Investigate, Inquire, *and* Imagine

Recall: GATHERING FACTS

1a. What does the speaker not know about her people?

2a. In stanza 3, what does the speaker say she does not know about herself?

3a. In stanza 4, what does the speaker say she is going to do?

Interpret: FINDING MEANING

1b. Why is this hard to perceive?

2b. Based on her thoughts in stanza 3, what do you think is her attitude toward life?

3b. What type of person raises his or her voice for justice?

Analyze: TAKING THINGS APART

4a. Describe the things that the speaker doesn't know.

Synthesize: BRINGING THINGS TOGETHER

4b. How is the speaker able to "believe" when she does not know why or how things are the way they are?

Evaluate: MAKING JUDGMENTS

5a. Do you think the title is appropriate for this song? Why, or why not?

Extend: CONNECTING IDEAS

5b. For decades after the Holocaust, many Holocaust survivors kept silent for various reasons—to forget or to hide their shame are just two of those reasons. Today, there is a whole genre in literature entitled Holocaust Literature that speaks against this silence. Why do you think oppressed peoples want to remember their past? their history? Why do you think they fight against silence?

Understanding *Literature*

REPETITION. Review the definition for **repetition** in the Handbook of Literary Terms. What does the repetition in this selection indicate about the speaker's focus? What is the speaker dwelling on?

THEME. Review the definition for **theme** in Literary Tools in Prereading and the cluster chart you made for that section. What possible themes from this song can you name? What is the speaker saying about memory and remembering the past? How does repetition work toward emphasizing the themes in the song?

ANSWERS TO INVESTIGATE, INQUIRE, AND IMAGINE (CONT.)

EXTEND
5b. *Responses will vary.* There are many reasons why oppressed peoples deliberately remember their past. Some remember to confront the group or country that oppressed them—forcing them to face their mistakes so that they will not repeat them. Openly recognizing past injustices also paves the way toward healing. Some remember in order to educate people about both the depravity of social injustices and racism. Others remember to validate their experience, and in so doing, validate their own humanity. They fight against silence because to be silent is to forget. To forget is to deny the pain and suffering the people went through, which ultimately leads to the denial of their humanity.

Writer's Journal

1. Write a **letter** to Dr. Reagon, describing the effect her song had on you.
2. Write a **memorial** to those people in history (people with which you most identify) who sacrificed and endured hardships fighting for the rights you now have.
3. Pretend you are a high school teacher. Write a **recommendation** to your choir director requesting that the song "I Remember; I Believe" be sung during next year's Black History Month at your school.

Integrating the Language Arts

Language, Grammar, and Style

APOSTROPHES. Read the Language Arts Survey 3.90, "Apostrophes." Then write out the correctly punctuated word for each of the following sentences.

1. Dr. Bernice (Reagons', Reagon's) interests are music and history.
2. Sweet Honey in the Rock? (Its', It's) an a cappella ensemble comprised of five African-American women.
3. They (cant', can't) sing without hand percussion instruments.
4. The group (doesn't, does'nt) use anything but traditional music techniques.
5. (That's, Thats') how Reagon fuses her love of music and history—by writing songs that address the African-American experience.

Speaking and Listening

CONDUCTING AN INTERVIEW. The song you just read spoke about the importance of remembering the past—even if the past is horrific and painful. We remember for many reasons—to educate, to heal, and to validate the sufferings a people went through. Validate someone's past sufferings by interviewing a person you feel has endured injustice. Refer to the Language Arts Survey 4.14, "Conducting an Interview," to help you in your interview process. If you do not know anyone personally who has been a victim of injustice, you might research the life of a well-known figure who fought against injustice, someone such as Mohandas Gandhi, Martin Luther King, Jr., or Malcolm X. Then give an oral report, sharing the experiences of the person you interviewed or researched with the rest of the class.

Study and Research

RESEARCHING A HISTORICAL BLACK MOVEMENT OR EVENT. In small groups, research a historical black movement or event. What incidents, ideas, and/or attitudes led to the development of the movement or event? Who were the most important figures in the movement? What was the movement or event about? How did it impact or change race relations among Americans? Is our society continuing to feel the effects from the movement or event? If yes, how so? If no, why not? Write a report based on the information you gathered and exchange your written report with a group who did their research on a different topic. In your groups, take time to discuss the movement or event and the impact it has had on our society.

ANSWERS TO UNDERSTANDING LITERATURE

REPETITION. The speaker repeats the phrases "I don't know" and "I believe." The repetition emphasizes her focus: she is able to believe in the possibility of that which, intellectually, she cannot understand or explain. She doesn't know how it is possible for people to endure and survive cruelty and injustice, or why nature itself can be so powerful, and even cruel. On the other hand, she is able to believe in the human capacity to survive, to fight, and to speak out for justice despite incredible oppression.

THEME. There are many different themes that can be taken from this song. One major theme is the importance of memory—remembering the past to help present and future generations believe in the possibility of justice and equality; to heal; and to validate our ancestors' struggles. The act of writing this song accomplishes the assignment the speaker received from God, that of raising her voice for justice. The importance of raising one's voice for justice is another possible theme. Another theme is that faith, or belief, triumphs over confusion and despair. Despite a person's struggle to understand how people are able to survive atrocities, it is still possible to believe in the value of surviving, fighting against oppression, and singing for justice.

ANSWERS TO INTEGRATING THE LANGUAGE ARTS

Language, Grammar, and Style
1. Reagon's
2. It's
3. can't
4. doesn't
5. That's

Speaking and Listening
Ask students to also review the Language Arts Survey 4.17, "Steps in Preparing an Extemporaneous Speech." If you ask students to include a recording of their interview or some other multimedia element in their presentations, you might have them read 4.22, "Preparing a Multimedia Presentation," as well.

ANSWERS TO INTEGRATING THE LANGUAGE ARTS (CONT.)

Study and Research
Refer students to the Language Arts Survey 5.19, "How to Locate Library Materials," and 5.26, "Using the Internet," to help them in their research. You may want to suggest that the students select topics from the following list:
- Jim Crow Laws
- Civil Rights movement
- Harlem Renaissance
- Black Arts movement
- Black Power movement
- MOVE and the 1985 police bombing in Philadelphia

GUIDED WRITING
Software

See the Guided Writing Software for an extended version of this lesson that includes printable graphic organizers, extensive student models and student-friendly checklists, and self-, peer, and teacher evaluation features.

INDIVIDUAL LEARNING STRATEGIES

MOTIVATION
Do students feel that their community is relatively culturally diverse? How are they personally affected by diversity? How has the appearance of more people from different backgrounds on television shows and movies, in advertising, and in magazines and newspapers helped to broaden the consciousness of white Americans?

READING PROFICIENCY
Encourage students who are working to become more efficient readers to read this Guided Writing lesson one section at a time. Emphasize that they should complete each step described in the lesson before they move on to the next section. Ask them to carefully

INFORMATIVE WRITING

"America has been in the best sense of the term a melting pot, every element adding its particular element of strength. The constant infusion of new blood has enriched our cultural life, speeded our material growth, and produced some of our ablest statesmen. . . . America has demonstrated for everyone with eyes to see that those things which unite peoples are greater than those which divide them, that war is not the inevitable fate of mankind."

—Arthur Schlesinger

EXAMINING THE MODEL. Tammy starts her essay with an introductory paragraph that contains the controlling, or central idea, of her paper. Her controlling idea is that each cultural group has made

continued on page 775

774 UNIT NINE

Guided Writing

WRITING A CAUSE AND EFFECT ESSAY

As you walk into the lunchroom, the aroma of pizza greets you. It smells especially appealing today, so you wait in line impatiently, hoping that there will still be some pizza left for you. Finally you bite in and taste the piping hot melted cheese and the spicy pepperoni. Your lunch, whether you are aware of it or not, is based on a recipe brought to this country many years ago by Italian immigrants.

Cultural diversity affects more than what you eat, however. You are probably aware that diverse cultural groups influence advertisements, computer games, music, art, and literature. Fifty years ago, almost everyone on television, movies, or in newspapers and magazines was white. Immigrants were pressured to blend in with the mainstream culture, to hide their ethnicity. Today, that is no longer the case. While intolerance of difference still exists, cultural diversity is more widely recognized and accepted. You are a part of the first generation of Americans raised to be fully aware of the value of cultural diversity. What are some effects that cultural diversity has had on your life?

WRITING ASSIGNMENT. For this lesson, you will analyze some effects of cultural diversity in American culture. Your writing will take the form of an informative essay.

An **essay** is a short nonfiction work that expresses a writer's thoughts about a single subject. The writer focuses the essay on a single, controlling idea. An essay is usually organized into an introduction, a body, and a conclusion. The aim of an informative essay is to inform, not to persuade.

In this excerpt, Tammy, a tenth grade student, examines some of the ways her Asian-American culture has affected America. As you read the first two paragraphs of her essay, look for the effects that she notes.

Student Model

from "From Familiarity to Acceptance" by Tammy Cha

The people who became the American Indians arrived via land bridges from Asia and, possibly, from Polynesia. Since that time, people have arrived from many

INDIVIDUAL LEARNING STRATEGIES (CONT.)

review the Student Model sections of the lesson to help them get a better sense of their goal in the assignment.

ENGLISH LANGUAGE LEARNING
Make sure that students thoroughly understand the concept of diversity. You might point out that their expe-

riences as newcomers to the country give them the opportunity to share a valuable perspective.

SPECIAL NEEDS
Students with special needs may need help thinking of a cause and effect relationship that is appropriate for this assignment.

You may need to help these students fill out their graphic organizer.

ENRICHMENT
To expand this assignment so that it includes more critical thinking, students may explore how America's cultural diversity is

(Continued on page 775)

lands and many cultures. Each group has brought its cultural traditions and its unique perspectives. The contributions of each group are important because they enrich the lives of all Americans.

About fifty years ago, my grandparents emigrated from Asia to this country. Like immigrants from many other countries, they were looking for economic opportunities. Since they strove to learn English and be like other Americans, they gradually became part of the American "melting pot." They also tried to retain some of their distinct cultural traditions because those traditions were part of their identity. In order to preserve this sense of identity, my grandmother told my father stories about her life in China. Those stories were consequently passed on to me.

Prewriting

FINDING YOUR VOICE. For this type of essay, you will need to use a respectful, honest, and informed voice. Your voice also needs to be logical because you are analyzing the causes and effects of a given event.

Look at the two examples below. Although each example contains a cause and an effect, one of the examples is logical and the other is not. Can you identify the logical example? Why is the other example illogical?

Teenagers are lazy because most of them do not have a part-time job.

When the economy is healthy, a lot of people are employed.

IDENTIFYING YOUR AUDIENCE. Your peers would be a good audience for this essay. They will want to hear your perspective and think about how it is similar to or different from their own. As you write, consider the information that will be important to your audience, keep their interest, and help them see the value in what you have to say.

WRITING WITH A PLAN. You may already know a specific effect of cultural awareness you can examine. John, for example, was aware of one effect of the local newspaper's interest in various cultures: each week the food section featured recipes from a different ethnic group. He thought that he would write about that effect in his essay.

Carmen was aware of one effect that happened as a result of the 1990 Native American Graves Protection and Repatriation Act: museums started to return cultural items to American Indian tribes. That effect, in turn, became a cause. Some of the returned artifacts are now presenting health problems to the tribes because of the treatments that had been used to preserve the artifacts. Carmen also planned to consider what new effects that could have on the tribes.

contributions that have enriched the lives of all Americans. In the first paragraph of the body of the essay, she explains that because her grandparents strove to learn English and be like other Americans, they gradually became part of the American "melting pot." She also notes that they wanted to retain some of their distinct cultural traditions because those traditions were part of their identity. Tammy uses the words *because, since, in order to,* and *consequently* to show the cause and effect relationship.

How can you tell a cause from an effect?

A **cause** makes something happen. The **effect** is what happens.

Turning the volume of a radio up makes the music louder. *Turning the volume up* is the cause. *The music getting louder* is the effect. Sometimes an effect becomes a cause. For example, the music getting louder might cause someone to say, "Turn it down!"

GUIDED WRITING 775

INDIVIDUAL LEARNING STRATEGIES (CONT.)

reflected in the media. For example, do they feel there are enough role models on television and in the movies for people of different cultures and for people of color? Do they feel that the roles on television programs or in movies provide realistic or stereotypical views of people of different cultures and ethnic backgrounds?

STUDENT MODEL—
GRAPHIC ORGANIZER

See the Writing Resource book for a
blackline master of the graphic
organizer for this lesson.

If you are still uncertain about which effect to write about, take some time to freewrite so that you generate several ideas.

Although some cause and effect essays start by examining an effect and analyzing the cause, you will be starting this essay with the cause (cultural awareness) and following with one or more effects.

Remember that events that simply follow one another are often not caused by the previous event. They might just happen to follow each other sequentially. The effects that you write about in this essay must not only follow each other, they *must* be a logical result of the cause. Those effects, in turn, can cause other effects and create a cause-and-effect chain.

Tammy filled in the graphic organizer below to help her analyze the cause and effect relationships.

Student Model—Graphic Organizer

Copy the graphic organizer onto your own paper. Fill in the organizer with the causes and the effects.

Words that show cause and effect relationships
after this
as a result
consequently
if
in order that
since
so
then
therefore
thus
while

"In reality, society and the individual are not antagonists. Culture provides the raw material of which individuals make their lives. If it is meager, the individual suffers. If it is rich, the individual has a chance to rise to the opportunity."
—*Ruth Benedict*

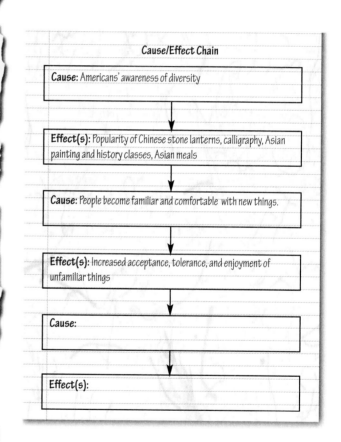

Cause/Effect Chain

Cause: Americans' awareness of diversity

Effect(s): Popularity of Chinese stone lanterns, calligraphy, Asian painting and history classes, Asian meals

Cause: People become familiar and comfortable with new things.

Effect(s): Increased acceptance, tolerance, and enjoyment of unfamiliar things

Cause:

Effect(s):

Drafting

Your essay should contain an introductory paragraph, several body paragraphs, and a concluding paragraph. The introduction should present the controlling idea, secure the reader's interest, and lead into the body of the paper. The last sentence of the introductory paragraph should contain a transitional "hook" that moves the reader to the first paragraph of the body.

Each paragraph in the body of the essay should contain one idea of support for your controlling idea. The body paragraphs can be organized in different ways. You could present your ideas in the order of their value. In other words, you could present your most important cause and effect in the first paragraph, your next most compelling cause and effect in the second paragraph and so on. You could also reverse the order and present your least compelling cause and effect first and proceed to the strongest cause and effect in the last paragraph.

The conclusion should repeat your controlling idea and summarize your main points of support. It should also leave your reader thinking about what you have said Use the information on your graphic organizer to guide you as you write the rough draft of your essay. Do not focus at this point on the details of spelling, grammar, usage, and mechanics. You will fix those problems when you revise and proofread your draft. At the drafting stage, simply concentrate on getting your ideas down on paper.

After finishing the introduction to her essay (shown on pages 774–775), Tammy continued her essay with a number of paragraphs detailing the influences of Asian-American culture on contemporary American life. Here is part of her draft.

Student Model—Draft

As a modern American teenager, ~~it is~~ *misplaced modifier*
watch slang ~~so cool~~ to see the contributions that Asian-Americans have made. Novelist Bette Bao Lord, cellist Yo-Yo Ma, football professional Eugene Chung, and film producer Janet Yang have made awesome contributions that ~~really rock~~.

It is clear to me that ~~folks~~ across America are ~~hip~~ to Asian culture. I know this because I see ~~folks~~ buying *Do you really want to mix informal with formal English?*

Self- and Peer Evaluation

After finishing your rough draft, you can do a self-evaluation of your work. If time allows, you may want to get one or two peer evaluations. See the Language Arts Survey 2.37–2.40 for more details about self- and peer evaluation. As you evaluate your draft, ask yourself these questions:

Introduction
- Can you clearly identify the controlling idea? If not, why not?
- How does the introduction secure the reader's interest?
- Does the introduction contain a transition to the body paragraphs?

Body
- How does each body paragraph support the controlling idea?
- What cause and effect words illustrate the relationships? What additional cause and effect words are needed to show the relationships?
- Are the cause and effect relationships logical? Is each effect truly a result of each cause?

Conclusion
- Does the conclusion repeat the controlling idea and summarize the main points of support?
- Does the conclusion leave the reader thinking about its ideas?

Entire Essay
- Does the essay use formal English?

GUIDED WRITING **777**

Drafting

Emphasize to students that the drafting phase of the writing process is an experimental phase. Point out that it is an opportunity for them to interweave their ideas, sample their organizational plan, and play with words. Remind them that they will refine all of these aspects of their essay later. You can refer students to the following Language Arts Survey sections, which deal with drafting: 2.31, "Drafting," 2.32, "Drafting an Introduction," 2.33, "Drafting Body Paragraphs," and 2.34, "Drafting a Conclusion."

Self- and Peer Evaluation

Have students use the checklist on page 777 for self- and peer evaluation. The checklist is intended to serve as a student-friendly rubric that should help students identify specific evidence of writing strengths and areas needing improvement. Make sure they provide concrete suggestions for improvement or specific evidence of why the writing works. A blackline master of the self- and peer evaluation checklist is available in the Writing Resource book.

Language, Grammar, and Style

Standard, Formal English

LESSON OVERVIEW
In this lesson, students will be asked to do the following:
- Identify Errors in Formal English, 778
- Fix Errors in Formal English, 779
- Use Formal English, 779

INTRODUCING THE SKILL. Explain to students that using formal English enables them to reach a wider audience than they would by using informal English. For example, magazines that younger people read may not be accessible or appealing to older adults because of their tone and unfamiliar references. Slang terms that may be familiar to their peer group might not be understood by older people or by people whose first language is not English. Informal English also tends to give their writing a lighter, more offhand tone, which could undermine the serious ideas they are attempting to present.

PREVIEWING THE SKILL. Refer students to the Language Arts Survey 3.2, "Formal and Informal English," if you have not already done so.

PRACTICING THE SKILL. For additional practice, have students work through the exercise in the following section of the Study and Research Resource located in the Teacher's Resource Kit: 3.2, "Formal and Informal English."

Revising and Proofreading

A handout of the proofreading checklist is available in the Teacher's Resource Kit, Writing Resource book 2.45. Students critiquing their classmates' work might be interested in using common proofreader's symbols, which are found in the Language Arts Survey 2.44, "Using Proofreader's Marks."

Language, Grammar, and Style

Standard, Formal English

IDENTIFYING FORMAL ENGLISH.
Formal English is the type of language that is appropriate for school essays, newspapers, and magazine articles, some literary works, oral or written reports, and test answers.

Informal English is appropriate when speaking with a friend or writing personal letters or notes. It is used in some e-mails, some newspapers and magazines, and some types of creative writing especially those including dialogue. Informal English is enriched by colloquialisms, dialect, and slang, which provide color and flavor. Informal English allows grammatical constructions that would not be acceptable in formal English. For more information, see the Language Arts Survey 3.2, "Formal and Informal English."

Look at each situation below. Explain if you should use formal or informal English in each situation.
1. You are interviewing for a job.
2. You are speaking with a good friend.
3. You are asking a teacher for more time to complete an assignment.
4. You are writing a personal letter to a friend.
5. You are asking for a refund at a store.

continued on page 779

and decorating their gardens with those cool Chinese stone lanterns. It's neat the way Chinese calligraphy is so popular. I notice that community colleges are offering classes in Asian painting and history. I know that many local restaurants are serving up [Change—American restaurants adapt traditional dishes] menus based on ∧traditional Asian dishes. These effects, in turn, cause people to become familiar and comfortable with something new. *Carry cause and effect further here.*

Part of who I am as an American is due to my heritage. Part of who I am as an American is due to the contributions of many other cultures. I think it's *change—make more formal* fantastic when we enrich each other's lives by sharing our cultural *More conclusive language here* traditions. Our cultural diversity in America benefits everyone.

Revising and Proofreading

As you consider your self-evaluation and peer reviews, think about the suggested changes. Which changes are needed to make your essay clearly understood by your readers? Which changes do you need to make to engage the reader and to help him or her gain additional understanding? Make revisions according to your decisions.

Next, proofread the copy for errors in spelling, grammar, usage, punctuation, capitalization, and paragraph form. Use formal English throughout your essay. See the Language Arts Survey 2.45 for a proofreading checklist.

Student Model—Revised

As a modern American teenager, I am aware of the contributions that Asian-Americans have made. Novelist Bette Bao Lord, cellist Yo-Yo Ma, football professional Eugene Chung, and film producer Janet Yang are just a few well-known Asians-Americans who have made significant contributions that enrich American life.

It is clear to me that people across America are aware of and interested in Asian culture. I know this because I see people buying and decorating their gardens with Chinese stone lanterns. I see the popularity of Chinese calligraphy. I notice that community colleges are offering classes in Asian painting and history. I know that many local restaurants are serving menus based on traditional Asian dishes. These effects, in turn, cause people to become familiar and comfortable with new things. The result of that effect is increased acceptance, tolerance, and enjoyment.

Part of who I am as an American is due to my heritage. Part of who I am as an American is due to the contributions of many other cultures. We enrich each other's lives by sharing our cultural traditions. As a result, our cultural diversity benefits everyone.

Publishing and Presenting

Write or print a final copy of your essay. You and your classmates may want to share your ideas and insights by reading them to each other in your classroom. You may also want to create a book of essays for others to read.

Reflecting

The experience of logically analyzing a chain of causes and effects helps you grow as a writer and a thinker. One of the values of an informative essay is that you and your readers have an opportunity to gain great insights. What have you learned about yourself through this writing experience? What insights have you gained from your classmates' essays? Were the effects you and your classmates noted logical results or were they simply events that sequentially followed one another? What new thoughts do you have about cultural diversity in America?

FIXING ERRORS IN FORMAL ENGLISH. Look at the following examples from Tammy's rough draft. Try to identify several errors in formal English. Explain how you could remedy these flaws.

As a modern American teenager, it is so cool to see the contributions that Asian-Americans have made.

Novelist Bette Bao Lord, cellist Yo-Yo Ma, football professional Eugene Chung, and film producer Janet Yang have made awesome contributions that really rock.

It is clear to me that people across America are hip to Asian culture. I know this because I see folks buying and decorating their gardens with those cool Chinese stone lanterns.

It's neat the way Chinese calligraphy is so popular.

USING FORMAL ENGLISH. Review your essay for instances of formal English and informal English. Look carefully, because colloquialisms, slang, and jargon are often difficult to spot because they occur so frequently in everyday language. Revise any instances of informal English that you find. Make sure that you use standard, formal English throughout your essay.

Publishing and Presenting

For more ideas, refer students to the Language Arts Survey 2.49, "Sharing Your Work with Others." If appropriate, students may wish to create visuals to display as they read their essays.

Reflecting

Encourage students to write a journal entry that considers the questions asked in Reflecting.

UNIT 9 *review*
Diversity and Community

Words for Everyday Use

Check your knowledge of the following vocabulary words from the selections in this unit. Write short sentences using these words in context to make the meaning clear. To review the definition or usage of a word, refer to the page number listed or the Glossary of Words for Everyday Use.

acculturation, 750	entrepreneur, 748	impulse, 766	proliferate, 750
aesthetic, 748	ephemeral, 757	intrinsic, 750	protocol, 746
aquiline, 747	euphemism, 723	judicious, 722	pungent, 759
array, 742	fastidious, 760	kindling, 765	relegate, 748
atrocity, 748	fettered, 725	lank, 746	replenish, 750
belligerence, 749	foreman, 766	lanky, 759	sacrosanct, 748
commodity, 750	formidable, 723	mackinaw, 741	sever, 756
composure, 723	foxhole, 767	malapropping, 749	solidarity, 752
concatenation, 731	gait, 757	marred, 760	stewed, 766
cosmopolitan, 747	garish, 747	mesmerize, 759	subdue, 760
demerit, 760	genocide, 748	paradigm, 751	substantial, 758
diaphanous, 750	immemorial, 717	patronage, 749	subtle, 757
elite, 748	impending, 722	pervade, 725	tentative, 731
emulate, 746	implore, 723	precarious, 721	vacate, 759

Literary Tools

Define the following terms, giving concrete examples of how they are used in the selections in this unit. To review a term, refer to the page number indicated or to the Handbook of Literary Terms.

character, 764	irony, 734	paradox, 729	speaker, 711
characterization, 720, 734	irony of situation, 734	personal essay, 745	stereotype, 764
dialogue, 755	lyric poem, 729	repetition, 770	style, 745
first-person point of view, 711	memoir, 755	sensory details, 740	theme, 711, 720, 770
	myth, 715	simile, 715	tone, 740, 745

VOCABULARY DEVELOPMENT

Give students the following exercise:
  Choose ten words from the Words for Everyday Use listed on page 780. For each word, write an antonym and a contextual sentence that uses the antonym.

EXAMPLE
mesmerized
antonym: disinterested
Not being a fan of auto racing, I was hardly mesmerized by the Indy 500; on the contrary I was completely <u>disinterested</u>.

Reflecting *on your reading*

Genre Studies

1. **LYRIC POEM.** A lyric poem is a highly musical verse that expresses the emotions of a speaker. Select a lyric poem from this unit that you like and describe what emotions the speaker is expressing. What examples of language use illustrate these emotions the best?

2. **NONFICTION.** Both "A White Woman of Color" and "Something Could Happen to You" explore the cultural identity of a Hispanic woman. How would you describe the approach each author takes toward expressing her experience? For example, is it narrative, reflective, or analytical? Which do you find the most effective? Why?

3. **SHORT STORY.** In "The Cabuliwallah," Tagore chose the first-person point of view. In "After You, My Dear Alphonse," Jackson chose the third-person point of view. What makes these points of view appropriate for the stories they relate?

REFLECTING ON YOUR READING

The prompts in Reflecting on Your Reading are suitable as topics for research papers. Refer to the Language Arts Survey 5.18–5.45, "Research Skills." (To evaluate research papers, see the evaluation forms for writing, revising, and proofreading in the Assessment Resource book.)
  The prompts in Reflecting on Your Reading can also be adapted for use as topics for oral reports or debates. Refer students to the Speaking and Listening Resource in the Language Arts Survey. (To evaluate these projects, see the evaluation forms in the Assessment Resource book.)

Thematic Studies

4. **THE IMMIGRANT EXPERIENCE.** In "The Cabuliwallah," "A White Woman of Color," and "Something Could Happen to You," the fruit peddler, Álvarez, and Santiago all confront life in a new land. What challenges do they face? What do they have to give up? Who adjusts the best? Why? Who has the most difficulty adjusting? Why? In what way are their lives more rich than those of people who have never moved to another country? What can we learn from their experiences?

5. **VIOLENCE.** How is violence central to "The Cabuliwallah" and "The Legend"? Was the violence justified? Do the authors take a position for or against violence? What do they say is the price of violence?

6. **DISCRIMINATION.** Who is discriminated against in "The Cabuliwallah" and "After You, My Dear Alphonse"? What is the basis for this discrimination—race, religion, nationality? Who does the discriminating? Are the perpetrators of the discrimination aware of their discrimination? How can you tell?

7. **FRIENDSHIP.** Which stanza of Marge Piercy's poem "Simple Song" reflects the status of the relationship between Mini and Rahmun at the beginning of "The Cabuliwallah"? Which stanza of Piercy's poem reflects the status of the relationship between Mini and Rahmun at the end of the story? What factors account for their separation and distance at the end of the story?

for your READING LIST

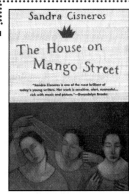

Sandra Cisneros

The House on Mango Street

"Sandra Cisneros is one of the most brilliant of today's young writers. Her work is sensitive, alert, nuanced... rich with music and picture."—Gwendolyn Brooks

The House on Mango Street by Sandra Cisneros. The short chapters in this book are narrated by Esperanza Cordero, who is growing up in a Latino neighborhood in Chicago. She is the oldest of four children and more than anything, she wants to live in a real house—but for now the house on Mango Street will have to do. Her father says it's temporary, but she knows how those things go. A "witch woman" reads her fortune and tells her she will have "a home in the heart." These stories are full of heart, laughter and sadness, tragedy and joy.

Independent Reading Activity

Immigrants in America. America is a country of immigrants. Most of us are originally from somewhere else. Where is your family from? Where are your neighbors from? Interview an older relative about your family's immigrant heritage. Or, if you prefer, talk to a member of your community. Find out when and why these people immigrated to the United States. Research their home country to determine what historical or current events may have prompted people to leave.

Selections for Additional Reading

The Education of Little Tree by Forrest Carter. After his parents die, in the 1930s, his Cherokee grandparents take this boy home to live with them and call him Little Tree. He learns more about life living with them in their small house in the woods than he ever would in school.

The Color of Water: A Black Man's Tribute to His White Mother by James McBride. This book is a son's loving tribute to his mother, Ruth McBride Jordan, a Polish immigrant who was raised as an Orthodox Jew in Virginia. When she moved to Harlem and married a black man, she battled both racism and poverty, yet managed to stay strong and raise a loving family.

Poet and novelist Sandra Cisneros was born in 1954 in Chicago. She is from a large Mexican-American family that includes her mother, father, and six brothers. Cisneros has worked as a teacher, a college recruiter, and an arts administrator. In addition to *The House on Mango Street,* originally published in 1985, Cisneros has published two volumes of poetry, *My Wicked Wicked Ways* and *Loose Woman,* and another collection of stories titled *Woman Hollering Creek.* She has also published a children's book, *Hairs/Pelitos,* which is based on one of the vignettes in *House on Mango Street.* Students who enjoy Cisneros's writing should be encouraged to read her other works. However, since some of her other work may not be age-appropriate, you may wish to select individual stories and poems to share with students.

Independent Reading Activity
Refer students to the Language Arts Survey 4.11, "Being Considerate of Other Cultures and Communication Styles," 4.12, "Overcoming Barriers to Effective Multicultural Communication," and 4.14, "Conducting an Interview." Students may be interested in writing short memoir pieces or short stories based on the experiences of one of their interview subjects.

A Successful Life, 1995. Cheri Samba. Private collection.

GOALS/OBJECTIVES

Studying this unit will enable students to
- experience several selections that explore the theme of cultural conflict
- discuss a speaker's experience of cultural conflict
- define terms such as *foreshadowing, narrator, symbol, tone, stereotype, irony, setting,* and *chronological order* and identify and explain examples of each that they encounter in their reading
- write an in-class answer to an essay question
- demonstrate the ability to use comparison and contrast order

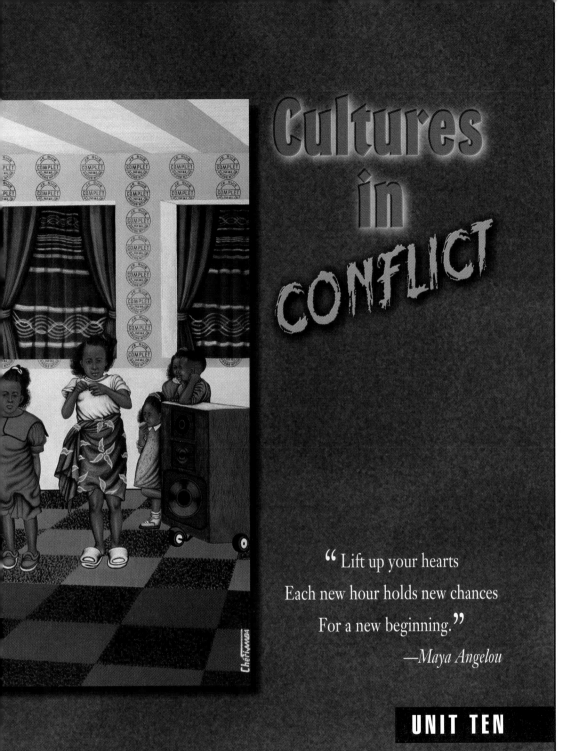

Cultures in CONFLICT

" Lift up your hearts
Each new hour holds new chances
For a new beginning. "

—*Maya Angelou*

UNIT TEN

Have students break into small groups, read the quotes aloud, and discuss them. Which quotes do they find most meaningful? Are there any they don't understand? What does Mohandas Gandhi mean when he says, "No culture can live, it if attempts to be exclusive"? To what extent do they agree with Eugene Ionesco?

ART NOTE

A Successful Life, 1995. Cheri Samba, page 782.
Cheri Samba (1956–) is a painter from Kinshasa, Congo, who portrays contemporary African life. His work is avidly collected by an international audience. Here, Samba portrays himself, his family, and their possessions against the backdrop of a traditional Congo village. He suggests the possibility of European/American culture and African culture coexisting. In the French text (the language of Congo), Samba explains his criteria for a successful life: being born, having children, and making a place for one's children.

echoes

➤ The conflict of forces and the struggle of opposing wills are of the essence of our universe and alone hold it together.

—*Havelock Ellis*

➤ As the traveler who has once been from home is wiser than he who has never left his own doorstep, so a knowledge of one other culture should sharpen our ability to scrutinize more steadily, to appreciate more lovingly our own.

—*Margaret Mead*

➤ A round man cannot be expected to fit in a square hole right away. He must have time to modify his shape.

—*Mark Twain*

➤ The art of life is a constant readjustment to our surroundings.

—*Kakuzo Okakaura*

➤ No culture can live, if it attempts to be exclusive.

—*Mahandas Gandhi*

➤ I have been a stranger in a strange land.

—*Bible, Exodus 2:22*

➤ I, a stranger and afraid
In a world I never made.

—*A. E. Housman, from "The laws of God, the laws of man"*

➤ The best
Thing we can do is to make wherever we're lost in
Look as much like home as we can.

—*Christopher Fry, from* The Lady's Not for Burning

➤ Ideologies separate us. Dreams and anguish bring us together.

—*Eugene Ionesco*

➤ If we have no peace, it is because we have forgotten that we belong to each other.

—*Mother Teresa*

"Dead Men's Path"
by Chinua Achebe

Reader's resource

"Dead Men's Path" is the story of a "progressive" African headmaster (principal) who takes on a new job in a village where the people are superstitious and cling to traditional tribal ways. The story addresses the cultural conflicts between "new" British ideas and "old" African customs. "Dead Men's Path" was published in Chinua Achebe's short story collection *Girls at War* (1972).

WORLD HISTORY CONNECTION. "Dead Men's Path" takes place in 1949 during the period when Great Britain ruled Nigeria. British intervention in Nigeria dates to the eighteenth century when the British displaced the Portuguese as leaders of the slave trade there. After the British parliament banned slavery in 1807, the British began making treaties with African tribal leaders to gain control of the territory. By 1906 Britain controlled all of Nigeria. The Colonial Office adopted the system of indirect rule, with traditional leaders continuing in power while owing allegiance to the colonial authority. Nigeria gained its independence from Great Britain in 1960. Chinua Achebe summarizes postcolonial consciousness in Nigeria: "It would be foolish to pretend that we have fully recovered from the traumatic effects of our first confrontation with Europe. . . ."

About *the* AUTHOR

Chinua Achebe (1930–) was born in Nigeria. The son of Christian missionaries, he was educated at the Church Missionary Society school where his father taught until, at 14, he was selected to attend the Government College at Umuahia, one of the best schools in West Africa. Educated in English at the University of Ibadan, Achebe taught for a short time before joining the staff of the Nigerian Broadcasting Corporation in Lagos. After cofounding a publishing company, he became a professor of English at the University of Nigeria.

Achebe has said that his duty as an African writer is "to help my society regain belief in itself and put away the complexes of the years of denigration and self-abasement" resulting from British colonialism. His novels include *Things Fall Apart* (1958), *No Longer at Ease* (1960), *Arrow of God* (1964), *A Man of the People* (1966), and *Anthills of the Savannah* (1988). His early novels show cultural clashes between traditional Igbo life and British missionaries and government. His later novels deal with corruption and other aspects of postcolonial African life. Achebe has also published collections of short stories, poetry, essays, and books for juvenile readers.

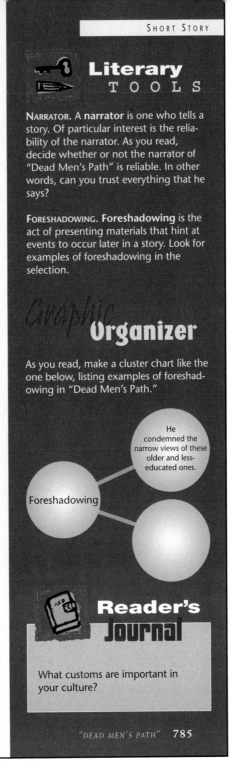

Literary TOOLS

NARRATOR. A **narrator** is one who tells a story. Of particular interest is the reliability of the narrator. As you read, decide whether or not the narrator of "Dead Men's Path" is reliable. In other words, can you trust everything that he says?

FORESHADOWING. Foreshadowing is the act of presenting materials that hint at events to occur later in a story. Look for examples of foreshadowing in the selection.

Graphic Organizer

As you read, make a cluster chart like the one below, listing examples of foreshadowing in "Dead Men's Path."

> Foreshadowing
>
> He condemned the narrow views of these older and less-educated ones.

Reader's Journal

What customs are important in your culture?

ADDITIONAL RESOURCES

UNIT 10 RESOURCE BOOK
- Selection Worksheet 10.1
- Selection Check Test 4.10.1
- Selection Test 4.10.2
- Language, Grammar, and Style Resource 3.41

VOCABULARY FROM THE SELECTION

eradicate	propitiate
denigration	superannuated
pivotal	

GRAPHIC ORGANIZER

Students should also note the following example in their cluster charts: The teacher says that "there was a big row some time ago when we attempted to close [the footpath]."

READER'S JOURNAL

You might encourage students to write about customs related to major life events such as birth, confirmation or bar mitzvah, marriage, and death. How are these events commemorated?

GOALS/OBJECTIVES

Studying this lesson will enable students to
- appreciate a short story from Nigeria
- describe Achebe's literary accomplishments and explain the historical significance of his writing
- define *narrator* and *foreshadowing* and recognize the use of these techniques in the selection
- change irregular verbs into the past tense
- research facts about Nigeria
- research postcolonial literature in Africa

1. Michael Obi is appointed to the position of headmaster of Ndume Central School.

INDIVIDUAL LEARNING STRATEGIES

MOTIVATION
Ask students how important the following personal qualities are to one's success in the working world: enthusiasm, flexibility, perceptiveness, energy, determination, decisiveness, tactfulness, caution, firmness, respect for others. Do these qualities always have a positive effect? Have them list other qualities that can help a person be effective on the job.

READING PROFICIENCY
Ask students to try to infer the meanings of the following vocabulary words from the context in the story:
colleague—coworker
downcast—in low spirits
skeptical—doubtful
row—noisy quarrel
zeal—enthusiasm

ENGLISH LANGUAGE LEARNING
Select sentences from the first page of the selection to illustrate different verb tenses for active verbs, including past, past perfect, and future.

SPECIAL NEEDS
To make sure students understand the historical context of the story, draw a simple flowchart on the board to summarize the sequence of events described in Reader's Resource.

ENRICHMENT
Have students investigate the part that missionaries have played in the history of Africa. What positive and negative effects have they had on the welfare of native Africans? In discussing these effects, students should cite specific individuals, countries, and impacts. Students may wish to present the results of their research in a written essay, pro and con chart, or a short debate.

Hidden Treasure, 1991. Emmanuel Ekong Ekefrey. Private Collection.

Chinua Achebe

Michael Obi's hopes were fulfilled much earlier than he had expected. He was appointed headmaster of Ndume Central School in January 1949. It had always been an unprogressive school, so the Mission authorities decided to send a young and energetic man to run it. Obi accepted this responsibility with enthusiasm. He had many wonderful ideas and this was an opportunity to put them into practice. He had had sound secondary school education which designated him a "<u>pivotal</u> teacher" in the official records and set him apart from the other headmasters in the mission field. He was outspoken in his condemnation of the narrow views of these older and often less-educated ones.

> To what position is Michael Obi appointed in January 1949?

"We shall make a good job of it, shan't we?" he asked his young wife when they first heard the joyful news of his promotion.

"We shall do our best," she replied. "We shall have such beautiful gardens and everything will be just *modern* and delightful…" In their two years of married life she had

words for everyday use

piv • o • tal (pi' və təl) *adj.*, on which something depends. *The <u>pivotal</u> new evidence helped to solve the crime.*

become completely infected by his passion for "modern methods" and his <u>denigration</u> of "these old and <u>superannuated</u> people in the teaching field who would be better employed as traders in the Onitsha[1] market." She began to see herself already as the admired wife of the young headmaster, the queen of the school.

How does Nancy Obi see herself when she learns of her husband's promotion?

The wives of the other teachers would envy her position. She would set the fashion in everything… Then, suddenly, it occurred to her that there might not be other wives. Wavering between hope and fear, she asked her husband, looking anxiously at him.

"All our colleagues are young and unmarried," he said with enthusiasm which for once she did not share. "Which is a good thing," he continued.

"Why?"

"Why? They will give all their time and energy to the school."

Nancy was downcast. For a few minutes she became skeptical about the new school; but was only for a few minutes. Her little personal misfortune could not blind her to her husband's happy prospects. She looked at him as he sat folded up in a chair. He was stoop-shouldered and looked frail. But he sometimes surprised people with sudden bursts of physical energy. In his present posture, however, all his bodily strength seemed to have retired behind his deep-set eyes, giving them an extraordinary power of penetration. He was twenty-six, but looked thirty or more. On the whole, he was not unhandsome.

"A penny for your thoughts, Mike," said Nancy after a while, imitating the woman's magazine she read.

"I was thinking what a grand opportunity we've got at last to show these people how a school should be run."

Ndume School was backward in every sense of the word. Mr. Obi put his whole life into the work, and his wife hers too. He had two aims. A high standard of teaching was insisted upon, and the school compound[2] was to be turned into a place of beauty. Nancy's dream-gardens came to life with the coming of the rains, and blossomed. Beautiful hibiscus and allamanda hedges in brilliant red and yellow marked out the carefully tended school compound from the rank neighborhood bushes.

What are Michael Obi's two foremost goals?

One evening as Obi was admiring his work he was scandalized to see an old woman from the village hobble right across the compound, through a marigold flower bed and the hedges. On going up there he found faint signs of an almost disused path from the village across the school compound to the bush on the other side.

What does Obi see one night as he is admiring his work?

"It amazes me," said Obi to one of his teachers who had been three years in the school, "that you people allowed the villagers to make use of this footpath. It is simply incredible." He shook his head.

"The path," said the teacher apologetically, "appears to be very important to them. Although it is hardly used, it connects the village shrine with their place of burial."

Why is the path across the school important to the villagers?

"And what has that got to do with the school?" asked the headmaster.

"Well, I don't know," replied the other with a shrug of the shoulders. "But I remember there

---

1. **Onitsha.** Commercial center in Nigeria
2. **compound.** Enclosed space within a building or group of buildings

1. She sees herself as the admired wife of the young headmaster, the "queen of the school."
2. He wants to insist upon a high standard of teaching and turn the school compound into a place of beauty.
3. He sees an old woman from the village hobble right across the school compound through a marigold flower bed and the hedges.
4. The path is important to the villagers because it connects the village shrine with their place of burial.

CROSS-CURRICULAR ACTIVITIES

WORLD CULTURES. Have students locate pictures of rural and urban areas in Nigeria today, and then share and discuss them in small groups.

1. He has sticks planted closely across the path at the two places where it entered and left the school premises. These are further strengthened with barbed wire.
2. The village priest of Ani comes to protest about the closed footpath. Obi tells him that the purpose of the school is to eradicate old beliefs, such as the idea that dead men require footpaths.
3. Two days after the priest's visit, a young woman in the villages dies in childbirth.
4. The villagers tear down the beautiful hedges, trample the flowers, and pull down one of the school buildings.
5. The white Supervisor reports that a "tribal-war" situation is developing between the school and the village, "arising in part from the misguided zeal of the new headmaster."

SELECTION CHECK TEST 4.10.1 WITH ANSWERS

Checking Your Reading
1. What kind of school had Ndume Central School been before Michael Obi arrived? **It had always been an unprogressive school.**
2. How did Obi feel toward the views of the older and less-educated residents? **He condemned them for their beliefs and was outspoken about his condemnation.**
3. Why is Obi happy that all the other teachers are "young and unmarried"? **He is happy because they will dedicate all of their time to teaching.**
4. What is the significance of the path to the villagers? **The villagers' dead relatives depart by the path, and the children being born come through the path to the village. The life of the village depends on the path.**
5. What results from Obi's unwillingness to compromise? **The villagers believe that a woman's death in childbirth is caused by the closing of the path, so they destroy the school compound.**

Vocabulary in Context
Fill in each blank below with the most appropriate word from the following Words for Everyday Use. You may have to change the tense of the word.

pivotal denigration superannuated
eradicate propitiate

---

was a big row some time ago when we attempted to close it."

"That was some time ago. But it will not be used now," said Obi as he walked away. "What will the Government Education Officer think of this when he comes to inspect the school next week? The villagers might, for all I know, decide to use the schoolroom for a pagan ritual during the inspection."

Heavy sticks were planted closely across the path at the two places where it entered and left the school premises. These were further strengthened with barbed wire.

> What does Obi have done to the compound?

Three days later the village priest of *Ani* called on the headmaster. He was an old man and walked with a slight stoop. He carried a stout walking stick which he usually tapped on the floor, by way of emphasis, each time he made a new point in his argument.

"I have heard," he said after the usual exchange of cordialities, "that our ancestral footpath has recently been closed…"

"Yes," replied Mr. Obi. "We cannot allow people to make a highway of our school compound."

"Look, here, my son," said the priest bringing down his walking stick, "this path was here before you were born and before your father was born. The whole life of this village depends on it. Our dead relatives depart by it and our ancestors visit us by it. But most important, it is the path of children coming in to be born…"

Mr. Obi listened with a satisfied smile on his face.

> Who comes to see the headmaster to protest closing the footpath? What does Obi tell him is the purpose of the school?

"The whole purpose of our school," he said finally, "is to <u>eradicate</u> just such beliefs as that. Dead men do not require footpaths. The whole

---

idea is just fantastic. Our duty is to teach your children to laugh at such ideas."

"What you say may be true," replied the priest, "but we follow the practices of our fathers. If you reopen the path we shall have nothing to quarrel about. What I always say is: let the hawk perch and let the eagle perch." He rose to go.

"I am sorry," said the young headmaster. "But the school compound cannot be a thoroughfare. It is against our regulations. I would suggest your constructing another path, skirting our premises. We can even get our boys to help in building it. I don't suppose the ancestors will find the little detour too burdensome."

"I have no more words to say," said the old priest, already outside.

Two days later a young woman in the village died in childbed. A diviner[3] was immediately consulted and he prescribed heavy sacrifices to <u>propitiate</u> ancestors insulted by the fence.

> What happens two days after the priest's visit?

Obi woke up the next morning among the ruins of his work. The beautiful hedges were torn up not just near the path but right round the school, the flowers trampled to death and one of the school buildings pulled down…That day, the white Supervisor came to inspect the school and wrote a nasty report on the state of the premises but more seriously about the "tribal-war situation developing between the school and the village, arising in part from the misguided zeal of the new headmaster." ■

> What do the villagers do to the school?

> What does the white Supervisor report?

---

3. **diviner.** Religious person to whom prophetic powers are attributed

---

words for everyday use	e • rad • i • cate (i ra′ də kāt) *vt.*, do away with. *Because she wants to <u>eradicate</u> illiteracy, Mrs. Koslowski volunteers to tutor adults who want to learn to read.*
	pro • pi • ti • ate (prō pi′ shē āt) *vt.*, win or regain the good will of. *After disobeying an order, the soldier <u>propitiated</u> her captain by giving him tickets to a concert.*

SELECTION CHECK TEST 4.10.1 WITH ANSWERS (CONT.)

1. The farmers sprayed their fields with herbicide to <u>eradicate</u> weeds.
2. His home run was a **pivotal** play in the game.
3. The **superannuated** man preferred his rotary phone to a new touch-tone model.

Literary Tools
1. Define *narrator*. **A narrator is one who tells a story.**

2. What is foreshadowing? **Foreshadowing is the act of presenting materials that hint at events to occur later in the story.**
3. Do you think the narrator of the story is reliable? Explain. **Students may say that the narrator seems to be reliable, however, somewhat biased toward the villagers. He subtly indicates his disdain for Michael Obi in both descriptions of Obi and of Obi's actions.**

Respond to the SELECTION

If you were Michael Obi, how might you have avoided the destruction of school property?

Investigate, Inquire, and Imagine

Recall: GATHERING FACTS

1a. What source prompts Nancy to say "A penny for your thoughts, Mike"? What idea does she have to beautify the school compound?

2a. What does the teacher who has been at the school three years remember?

3a. How does the priest explain the importance of the path to the village?

Interpret: FINDING MEANING

1b. Is Nancy more influenced by modern Western culture or by traditional African culture? Are her views different from her husband's? What character traits do the garden reveal about Nancy?

2b. Is Obi willing to learn from others? What adjectives describe him?

3b. Is Obi or the priest more tolerant of the other's beliefs?

Analyze: TAKING THINGS APART

4a. Analyze Obi's motivations in valuing the flowerbeds and hedges more than the villagers' beliefs.

Synthesize: BRINGING THINGS TOGETHER

4b. What does the path mean to the villagers?

Evaluate: MAKING JUDGMENTS

5a. Evaluate whether the Ani community was justified in destroying the flowerbeds, hedges, and school building.

Extend: CONNECTING IDEAS

5b. One way that the destruction of the school property might have been avoided is if the priest and Obi had compromised. Describe a conflict in your personal life, in government, in fiction, or in the movies. Tell what each side wanted and explain how the conflict was resolved.

Understanding Literature

NARRATOR. Review the definition for **narrator** in the Handbook of Literary Terms. Whose opinion is presented in the sentence "Ndume School was backward in every sense of the word"? How reliable is the narrator of "Dead Men's Path"? With whom do the narrator's sympathies lie?

FORESHADOWING. Review the definition for **foreshadowing** in the Handbook of Literary Terms and the cluster chart you made in Literary Tools on page 785. What events do the sentences you found foreshadow?

"DEAD MEN'S PATH" 789

ANSWERS TO INVESTIGATE, INQUIRE, AND IMAGINE (CONT.)

villagers, telling the village priest that the whole purpose of the school is to eradicate beliefs like the one the villagers hold about the path.

SYNTHESIZE
4b. The path symbolizes the body of rituals, beliefs, and feelings that bind the village people together.

EVALUATE
5a. Students may say the villagers were justifed because the tradition is so important to their

identity and Obi did not listen to the priest. Others may say the villagers had no right to destroy school property.

EXTEND
5b. *Responses will vary.*

Answers to Understanding Literature can be found on page 790.

RESPOND TO THE SELECTION

Encourage students to recognize Obi's lack of respect for the beliefs of the villagers in his community. Students might discuss in small groups how Obi and the priest might have reached a compromise.

ANSWERS TO INVESTIGATE, INQUIRE, AND IMAGINE

RECALL
1a. Nancy gets the idea from a woman's magazine. She wants to plant flower beds at the school.
2a. The teacher remembers there was a big row "some time ago" when the school attempted to close the path.
3a. The priest says, "The whole life of this village depends on [the path]. Our dead relatives depart by it and our ancestors visit us by it. But most important, it is the path of children coming in to be born."

INTERPRET
1b. Nancy's reading of the magazine shows that she is more influenced by modern Western culture than by traditional African culture. Her views are similar to her husband's; he favors progressive Western ideas in education. The carefully tended garden reveals that Nancy values beauty and order; she seems more interested in the look of the school than the teaching that goes on there.
2b. Obi does not seem very willing to learn from others. The teacher warns him of past conflict over the path. Then the priest relates the importance of the path to the village. Obi listens to neither of them. He decides that the flower beds and hedges will stay and does not concede that it might be prudent to allow the villagers access to the path. He is uncompromising, insensitive, close-minded, or overzealous.
3b. The priest is more tolerant. He admits to Obi, "What you say may be true" before stating the village's position on the footpath. He also hints that they should find a way to coexist: "Let the hawk perch and let the eagle perch." Obi is condescending as he listens with a "satisfied smile on his face."

ANALYZE
4a. Obi is motivated by "progressive" British educational ideals and a desire to beautify the school. He thinks he knows what is best for the

ANSWERS TO UNDERSTANDING LITERATURE

NARRATOR. Obi's opinion is presented in the sentence. Achebe narrates this story from the "modern" point of view. The story calls into question the true meaning of "progress." By presenting the story through Obi's consciousness, the reliability of the narrator is brought into question as his plans to modernize the school backfire. The reader must decide which attitudes presented in the story are really "backward."

FORESHADOWING. The sentence "[Obi] was outspoken in his condemnation of the narrow views of these older and often less-educated [headmasters]" foreshadows the conflict that Obi has with the priest. The sentence, "I remember there was a big row some time ago when we attempted to close [the path]," foreshadows the destruction of the school property.

ANSWERS TO INTEGRATING THE LANGUAGE ARTS

Language, Grammar, and Style
1. Michael Obi felt confident about his abilities to improve Ndume Central School.
2. His wife saw herself as the admired wife of the young headmaster.
3. Villagers sometimes ran through the flower beds of the compound.
4. The village priest brought a new perspective about the old village footpath.
5. Obi made a mistake by ignoring the desires of the villagers.

Study and Research & Collaborative Learning
Before students begin, ask them to list three to five questions they would like to find answers to in each topic area. Remind students to check to make sure their information sources are up to date. Encourage them to consult sources other than general encyclopedias.

Media Literacy
Ask students to select authors from different countries. Have students write a one-page summary of each author's work. Suggest that students obtain works by the authors they chose to research and take turns reading excerpts aloud.

Writer's Journal

1. Imagine you are a student reporter at Ndume Central School. Write a **newspaper article** describing the destruction of school property and explaining why it happened. You may want to include an interview with one of the villagers.
2. Write a **dialogue** in which Michael and Nancy discuss the destruction of school property and the superintendent's report.
3. Imagine you are Michael Obi. Write a **journal entry** after the Supervisor's report, explaining what you have learned about yourself and the village.

Integrating the Language Arts

Language, Grammar, and Style

IRREGULAR VERBS. Read the Language Arts Survey 3.41, "Using Irregular Verbs." Then rewrite the following sentences, putting the irregular verbs into the past tense.
1. Michael Obi feels confident about his abilities to improve Ndume Central School.
2. His wife sees herself as the admired wife of the young headmaster.
3. Villagers sometimes run through the flower beds of the compound.
4. The village priest brings a new perspective about the old village footpath.
5. Obi makes a mistake by ignoring the desires of the villagers.

Media Literacy

POSTCOLONIAL LITERATURE IN AFRICA. Using the Internet, research postcolonial literature in Africa. Select two authors and read about their lives and work. How do these authors show clashes between African and European cultures in their literature? What changes do they describe in African culture after the coming of Europeans? What recurring themes do they deal with in their literary works? You will find it useful to access Brown University's African Postcolonial Literature in English Internet site at http://landow.stg.brown.edu/post/misc/authors.html.

Study and Research & Collaborative Learning

RESEARCHING NIGERIA. With several students, research the population, religion, language, education, health, and employment in Nigeria. Have each student prepare a fact sheet about the topic he or she selects. Then write the facts on a piece of poster board. Present your findings to the class.

"One of Grandma Selma's Stories"

by Mary Lockwood

Reader's resource

"**One of Grandma Selma's Stories**" records an oral story told to the author. It is a short short, or extremely brief short story. Like many short shorts, this selection takes the form of an anecdote, or retelling of a single incident.

GEOGRAPHY CONNECTION. During winter months in the arctic region of Alaska, temperatures dip down to a blustery –56 degrees Fahrenheit; the average summer temperature is 40 degrees Fahrenheit. Total darkness prevails in this area from November 18 to January 24, while the sun never sets from May 10 to August 2.

About *the* AUTHOR

Mary Lockwood (1952–   ) was born in the arctic region of Alaska at a time when her people, the Inupiaq Malemuit, were facing the end of their traditional way of life. When Alaska became a state in 1959, the lives of Lockwood's family and community changed dramatically. New laws governing hunting and gathering hampered their ability to feed and clothe themselves, and they often went cold and hungry. As a young woman, Lockwood came to feel great anger about the decimation of her culture and resolved to write about that culture as a way of preserving it.

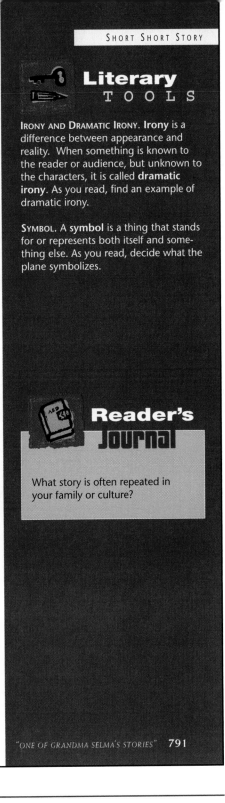

SHORT SHORT STORY

Literary TOOLS

IRONY AND DRAMATIC IRONY. Irony is a difference between appearance and reality. When something is known to the reader or audience, but unknown to the characters, it is called **dramatic irony.** As you read, find an example of dramatic irony.

SYMBOL. A **symbol** is a thing that stands for or represents both itself and something else. As you read, decide what the plane symbolizes.

Reader's Journal

What story is often repeated in your family or culture?

"ONE OF GRANDMA SELMA'S STORIES"   **791**

GOALS/OBJECTIVES

Studying this lesson will enable students to
- appreciate a recorded oral story about the clash of two cultures
- describe the role of storytelling in a Native American culture
- define *irony, dramatic irony,* and *symbol* and identify examples of each in the story
- define words using context clues
- identify and retell a story told by native peoples in far-northern North America

READER'S JOURNAL

What is your favorite story? Tell a classmate your story and explain why it is your favorite.

ANSWER TO GUIDED READING QUESTION

1. The dogs' ears prick up and their hair stands on end. The reader knows that the object making the sound is unusual because the people and animals who hear it are afraid or uneasy.

VOCABULARY FROM THE SELECTION

harpoon
pristine

reverberation
tundra

SELECTION CHECK TEST 4.10.3 WITH ANSWERS

Checking Your Reading
1. What kind of stove is Grandma Selma using? **She is using either a wood or coal burning stove.**
2. What kind of weapon does Bennijack have? **He has a harpoon.**
3. What do the stove and the weapon indicate about the lifestyle of the characters? **These indicate that the characters live a basic lifestyle without the use of guns or electricity.**

Literary Tools
1. What is irony? **Irony is the difference between appearance and reality.**
2. What is dramatic irony? **Dramatic irony is when the reader or audience knows something that is not known by the characters.**
3. What is a symbol? **A symbol is a thing that stands for or represents both itself and something else.**

One of Grandma Selma's STORIES

Mary Lockwood

O ne day, during the long, bright arctic summer, Grandma Selma was tending to her fire out on the beach at her summer camp. She heard a faint, strange sound that hummed constantly, and looked around. The dogs were awake and had their ears and fur standing up.

"That must be coming from my stove," she thought, and poked at the fire with a stick.

Still the sound continued; and even amplified.

She was beginning to be frightened, and the dogs paced nervously.

Further down the gravel beach, Bennijack halted his easy gait to listen. Something was different. Of all the familiar sounds, there was a new tone— and it didn't stop. He clutched his <u>harpoon</u> and fidgeted nervously. His sharp eyes scanned the <u>pristine</u> landscape of the arctic. Somewhere in the south, following the coastline, was a little speck in the sky. The <u>reverberations</u> grew as it became larger.

Soon it was apparent that this was the source of the intrusion into all that he knew. As the tremendous roar of the airplane engulfed him, he let out a cry and threw his harpoon up with all his might. The harpoon tangled in a propeller. Down the airplane pummeled, and with incredible explosions, crashed onto the <u>tundra</u>! ∎

How do the dogs react to the sound? How do you know that the object making the sound is unusual or unknown in this place?

words for everyday use

har • poon (här pōōn´) n., spear with a line attached for hunting large sea animals. *From his kayak, the fisherman flung the <u>harpoon</u> at the seal.*

pris • tine (pris´tēn´) adj., pure; unspoiled. *Jagged cuts from strip mining scar what was once a <u>pristine</u> hillside.*

re • ver • ber • a • tion (ri vur bə rā´shən) n., reechoed sound. *When the explorer called out a greeting into the cave; she was answered only by the <u>reverberation</u> of her own voice.*

tun • dra (tun´drə) n., treeless plains of the arctic region. *Because the <u>tundra</u> offers little protection from predators, many arctic creatures rely on their white coloring for camouflage on the open plains.*

Respond *to the* SELECTION

What emotion do you think prompted this story?

Investigate, Inquire, and Imagine

Recall: GATHERING FACTS

1a. Where does Grandma Selma live?

2a. From where does Grandma Selma think the noise is coming?

3a. What does Bennijack do when he hears the noise? What does he do when he sees the source of the noise?

 Interpret: FINDING MEANING

1b. What adjective best describes this location?

2b. What is her reaction when the noise grows louder? Why does she feel this way?

3b. Why does Bennijack attack the plane?

Analyze: TAKING THINGS APART

4a. What is the role of the hunter in the culture of the Inupiaq Malemuit?

 Synthesize: BRINGING THINGS TOGETHER

4b. How does Bennijack embody this role?

Evaluate: MAKING JUDGMENTS

5a. Evaluate whether Bennijack's attack on the plane is realistic. What purpose does this anecdote serve?

Extend: CONNECTING IDEAS

5b. What made the villagers in "Dead Men's Path" feel threatened? Is there any similarity in their response with Bennijack's?

Understanding *Literature*

IRONY AND DRAMATIC IRONY. Review the definitions for **irony** and **dramatic irony** in the Handbook of Literary Terms. What does the reader know about the source of the sound? How does Bennijack feel about the airplane? Why is it ironic that Bennijack throws his harpoon at the airplane?

SYMBOL. Review the definition for **symbol** in Literary Tools in Prereading. What might the plane symbolize?

ANSWERS TO INVESTIGATE, INQUIRE, AND IMAGINE (CONT.)

living and the dead, was replaced with flower beds. Like Bennijack, they fought against the encroachment of new ways that conflict with their traditional way of life.

ANSWERS TO UNDERSTANDING LITERATURE

IRONY AND DRAMATIC IRONY. The reader knows that the source of the sound is an airplane. Bennijack has never seen an airplane, so he is frightened by the plane and the noise it makes. There is dramatic irony in the fact that Bennijack thinks of the plane as a dangerous animal, while the reader knows that it is just a machine that flies.

SYMBOL. The plane might symbolize the intrusion of modern ways, including using machines for convenience, on the Inupiaq Malemuit way of life.

RESPOND TO THE SELECTION

Have students skim the story for words and phrases that hint at the author's emotions. They might also reflect on their own feelings at times when they were intruded upon unexpectedly or faced something totally unknown.

ANSWERS TO INVESTIGATE, INQUIRE, AND IMAGINE

RECALL

1a. Grandma Selma lives in the arctic.

2a. She thinks the noise is coming from her stove.

3a. Bennijack stops to listen as he clutches his harpoon, fidgets nervously, and then scans the landscape. When he sees the plane, he hurls his harpoon at it.

INTERPRET

1b. The location is isolated.

2b. When the noise grows louder, she becomes frightened because she doesn't know what the noise is.

3b. Bennijack attacks the plane because it is unfamiliar and seems menacing.

ANALYZE

4a. *Responses will vary.* The role of the hunter is to find and kill animals for food and other needs of the community and to protect the group from harm.

SYNTHESIZE

4b. In attacking the plane, Bennijack acts to protect his community. He shows courage in the face of a seeming danger and skill in hitting and bringing down the plane, as if it were a giant predator.

EVALUATE

5a. *Responses will vary.* Bennijack's attack on the plane is unrealistic. Even an expert hunter could not throw a harpoon so far. And even if the harpoon had tangled in the propeller, it might not have crashed the plane, since a plane with a dead motor can coast to a landing. The anecdote shows listeners that the Inupiaq Malemuit can conquer a powerful, unknown intruder. This anecdote would provide comfort to a people whose way of living is being threatened by outside influences.

EXTEND

5b. The villagers felt threatened when their traditional footpath, which represented a link between the

Writer's Journal

1. Pretend you are Bennijack. Write a **postcard** to a friend in a nearby village about the "intruder" in the sky.

2. Imagine you are a news reporter from Anchorage, Alaska. You have been flown into Grandma Selma's village to report the plane crash. Write a **newspaper article** that provides a rational Western reason for the crash.

3. Imagine you are Grandma Selma and that many years have elapsed since the plane crash. In that time period you have seen many changes in your culture. Write an **introduction** to your story about the airplane crash that explains its importance to your culture.

Integrating
the Language Arts

Vocabulary

USING CONTEXT CLUES. Read the Language Arts Survey 1.16, "Using Context Clues to Estimate Word Meaning." Then read each of the following sentences. Write the definition of each underlined word, using context clues to deduce its meaning.

1. Among the Eskimo, <u>infanticide</u> used to be a way of keeping the population down.

2. Most of the Greenland Eskimo have mixed with the white population, but elsewhere the Eskimo have tended to remain of pure <u>stock</u>.

3. Except for a small group of Caribou Eskimo living in central Canada, they are a <u>littoral</u>, or coastal, people who rove inland in the summer for freshwater fishing and game hunting.

4. Traditionally, the hunting life of the Eskimo has been <u>nomadic</u>, and they use dogsleds to move their possessions from place to place.

5. In earlier times the Eskimos wrote in <u>pictographs</u>, but these symbols were replaced with the Roman and Cyrillic alphabets in the eighteenth century.

Study and Research & Collaborative Learning

TRAVEL GUIDE. With several classmates, prepare a guide to Alaska that could be used by someone planning a trip there. Include information on geography and climate, the people who live there, key historic events such as immigration and statehood, native foods, sports, and places to visit and how to get there. Compile your travel guide and prepare a table of contents. If you wish to do your research online, access the state of Alaska home page at http://www.state.ak.us/.

Speaking and Listening

TELLING A STORY. Find a story important to the culture of the native peoples of Alaska, or other residents of the arctic in the world. Write the names of the characters and the main events on an index card. Then tell the story to a group of your classmates. Prepare an introduction that explains the values expressed in the story. You may find it useful to research the values of the native people of Alaska by visiting the Alaska Native Knowledge Network at http://www.ankn.uaf.ed/spiral.html. Before telling your story, you may find it useful to review the Language Arts Survey 4.20, "Telling a Story."

"The Gift of Cochise"
by Louis L'Amour

Reader's resource

In **"The Gift of Cochise,"** white settler Angie Lowe comes face to face with the Apache chief Cochise, who gives her a surprising gift.

HISTORY CONNECTION. "The Gift of Cochise" is set in the Arizona Territory, probably in the mid-1860s. In the nineteenth century, thousands of settlers of European descent moved into the western frontier, placing pressure on the Native-American populations there. One of the principal characters in the story is Cochise, the famous chief of southern Arizona's Chiricahua Apaches. Little is known about his early life. In 1861, a U.S. Army officer arrested Cochise and five other Native-American leaders in connection with a cattle raid. One of the five men was killed, but Cochise managed to escape, despite three bullet wounds that he had received. Over the next decade, during the time period of this story, Cochise led a fierce and largely successful offensive against the white settlers and soldiers in his territory, eluding capture by hiding in the Dragoon Mountains. Today, as in his own time, Cochise is revered as a great chief and warrior. In 1872, he voluntarily surrendered himself when the Chiricahua Apache Reservation was established.

> "When I was young I walked all over this country, east and west, and saw no other people than the Apaches. After many summers I walked again and found another race of people had come to take it. How is it? Why is it that the Apaches wait to die? . . . The Apaches were once a great nation; they are now but few."

—Cochise, 1866

About the AUTHOR

Louis L'Amour (1908–1988) was born in Jamestown, North Dakota. He traveled the world, working at an amazing variety of jobs that included being a lumberjack and an elephant handler. Always fascinated by stories of the western frontier, he became, along with Zane Grey, one of the two best-known writers of westerns. Altogether, L'Amour wrote eighty-six novels, over four hundred short stories, and many, many scripts for television and the movies. Among his most famous films is the award-winning *How the West Was Won*.

Literary TOOLS

STEREOTYPE. A **stereotype** is an uncritically accepted fixed or conventional idea, particularly an idea held about whole groups of people. As you read, find two examples of stereotype used to portray the characters in this selection.

GENRE. A **genre** is one of the types or categories into which literary works are divided. Literary works are sometimes classified into genres based on subject matter. Such a classification might describe detective stories, mysteries, romances, or westerns. "The Gift of Cochise" is a western. As such, it contains predictable elements that you can look for as you read the story.

Graphic Organizer

Create a cluster chart listing the elements that identify this story as a western. One example has been done for you.

Native American raids on white settlers

Elements of a Western

Reader's Journal

Think of a culture other than your own. In your journal, write about what you admire or respect about that culture and why.

ADDITIONAL RESOURCES

UNIT 10 RESOURCE BOOK
- Selection Worksheet 10.3
- Selection Check Test 4.10.5
- Selection Test 4.10.6
- Language, Grammar, and Style Resource 3.51
- Speaking and Listening Resource 4.18

VOCABULARY FROM THE SELECTION

acrid	inhibition
amiable	irresolute
antagonist	malevolent
contemptuously	plaintively
deference	resolutely
deflect	shiftless
disintegrate	sporadic
fatigue	

GRAPHIC ORGANIZER

Students should include the following elements in their cluster charts: western frontier setting, white settlers and Indians as characters, gunfight in a saloon, knife fights and shoot-outs between Indians and cowboys.

READER'S JOURNAL

Students might begin by brainstorming a list of the cultures that are represented in their school and community.

GOALS/OBJECTIVES

Studying this lesson will enable students to
- enjoy a short story set on the western frontier
- identify Louis L'Amour as a leading writer of westerns
- define *stereotype* and recognize examples of stereotypical characters in the selection
- define *genre* and identify features of the western genre
- identify common and proper nouns in sentences
- write a review of a western film
- give a speech

MOTIVATION

Have students give examples of western films, television shows, and books that are familiar to them. What do they recall about the characters, plots, and themes in these works? Ask them if they think these depictions of life in the Old West are generally accurate and to explain their answers.

READING PROFICIENCY

Have students keep a character chart as they read. For each character ask them to list words and phrases the author uses to describe the character, including his or her appearance, background, and thoughts. They should also note traits of the characters that are revealed through the character's own actions and speech.

ENGLISH LANGUAGE LEARNING

Have students read portions of the story out loud with a partner.

SPECIAL NEEDS

Encourage students to focus on the Guided Reading questions and the Recall questions in the Investigate, Inquire, and Imagine section.

ENRICHMENT

Invite students to write a western of their own. Alternatively, students might write a narrative song that retells the story of "The Gift of Cochise." For inspiration, they might listen to the American folk song "The Streets of Laredo." Encourage students to come up with a chorus in addition to verses for their song.

ADDITIONAL QUESTIONS AND ACTIVITIES

Ask students what words they would use to describe Cochise as he is portrayed in the portrait.

Answer
Students might say that the portrait shows someone who is calmly confident and dignified.

Chief Cochise.

The Gift of Cochise

Louis L'Amour

Tense, and white to the lips, Angie Lowe stood in the door of her cabin with a double-barreled shot gun in her hands. Beside the door was a Winchester '73,[1] and on the table inside the house were two Walker Colts.[2]

Facing the cabin were twelve Apaches on ragged calico ponies, and one of the Indians had lifted his hand palm outward. The Apache sitting on the white-splashed bay pony was Cochise.

Beside Angie were her seven-year-old son, Jimmy, and her five-year-old daughter, Jane.

Cochise sat on his pony in silence. His black, unreadable eyes studied the woman, the children, the cabin, and the small garden. He looked at the two ponies in the corral and the three cows. His eyes strayed to the small stack of hay cut from the meadow and to the few steers farther up the canyon.

Three times the warriors of Cochise had attacked this solitary cabin, and three times they had been turned back. In all, they had lost seven men, and three had been wounded. Four ponies had been killed. His braves reported that there was no man in the house, only a woman and two children, so Cochise had come to see for himself this woman who was so certain a shot with a rifle and who killed his fighting men.

These were some of the same fighting men who had outfought, out-

> **Why does Cochise go to this particular cabin?**

guessed, and outrun the finest American army on record, an army outnumbering the Apaches by a hundred to one. Yet a lone woman with two small children had fought them off, and the woman was scarcely more than a girl. And she was prepared to fight now. There was a glint of admiration in the old eyes that appraised her. The Apache was a fighting man, and he respected fighting blood.

"Where is your man?"

"He has gone to El Paso." Angie's voice was steady, but she was frightened as she had never been before. She recognized Cochise from descriptions, and she knew that if he decided to kill or capture her it would be done. Until now, the sporadic attacks she had fought off had been those of casual bands of warriors who raided her in passing.

> **Why does Cochise respect this woman?**

"He has been gone a long time. How long?"

Angie hesitated, but it was not in her to lie. "He has been gone four months."

Cochise considered that. No one but a fool would leave such a woman and such fine children. Only one thing could have prevented his return. "Your man is dead," he said.

> **Why does Angie hesitate? What does the fact that she answers the question reveal about her? What does Cochise's answer reveal about him? Is he a sentimental man?**

---

1. **Winchester '73.** Type of rifle that can repeat shots without reloading
2. **Walker Colts.** Types of revolvers or handguns

---

words for everyday use

spor • a • dic (spə rad´ik) adj., occasional. *The politician's speech was interrupted by* sporadic *outbursts from protesters.*

1. The return of the ponies reveals that Cochise is a reasonable man who keeps his word.

After the return of the ponies, what other signs reveal that Cochise has kept his promise that his people will not bother Angie?
Answer
She sees Apaches several times, but they leave her alone. She notices that Apaches have been to the spring, but they have not bothered her. They even leave meat occasionally on her doorstep.

Angie waited, her heart pounding with heavy, measured beats. She had guessed long ago that Ed had been killed, but the way Cochise spoke did not imply that Apaches had killed him, only that he must be dead or he would have returned.

"You fight well," Cochise said. "You have killed my young men."

"Your young men attacked me." She hesitated, then added, "They stole my horses."

"Your man is gone. Why do you not leave?"

Angie looked at him with surprise. "Leave? Why, this is my home. This land is mine. This spring is mine. I shall not leave."

"This was an Apache spring," Cochise reminded her reasonably.

"The Apache lives in the mountains," Angie replied. "He does not need this spring. I have two children, and I do need it."

"But when the Apache comes this way, where shall he drink? His throat is dry and you keep him from water."

The very fact that Cochise was willing to talk raised her hopes. There had been a time when the Apache made no war on the white man. "Cochise speaks with a forked tongue," she said. "There is water yonder." She gestured toward the hills, where Ed had told her there were springs. "But if the people of Cochise come in peace, they may drink at this spring."

The Apache leader smiled faintly. Such a woman would rear a nation of warriors. He nodded at Jimmy. "The small one—does he also shoot?"

"He does," Angie said proudly, "and well, too!" She pointed at an upthrust leaf of prickly pear. "Show them, Jimmy."

The prickly pear was an easy two hundred yards away, and the Winchester was long and heavy, but he lifted it eagerly and steadied it against the doorjamb as his father had taught him, held his sight an instant, then fired. The bud on top of the prickly pear <u>disintegrated</u>.

There were grunts of appreciation from the dark-faced warriors. Cochise chuckled.

"The little warrior shoots well. It is well you have no man. You might raise an army of little warriors to fight my people."

"I have no wish to fight your people," Angie said quietly. "Your people have your ways, and I have mine. I live in peace when I am left in peace. I did not think," she added with dignity, "that the great Cochise made war on women!"

The Apache looked at her, then turned his pony away. "My people will trouble you no longer," he said. "You are the mother of a strong son."

"What about my two ponies?" she called after him. "Your young men took them from me."

Cochise did not turn or look back, and the little cavalcade of riders followed him away. Angie stepped back into the cabin and closed the door. Then she sat down abruptly, her face white, the muscles in her legs trembling.

When morning came, she went cautiously to the spring for water. Her ponies were back in the corral. They had been returned during the night.

What does the return of the ponies reveal about Cochise?

Slowly, the days drew on. Angie broke a small piece of the meadow and planted it. Alone, she cut hay in the meadow and built another stack. She saw Indians several times, but they did not bother her. One morning, when she opened her door, a quarter of antelope lay on the step, but no Indian was in sight. Several times, during the weeks that followed, she saw moccasin tracks near the spring.

Once, going out at daybreak, she saw an Indian girl dipping water from the spring. Angie called to her, and the girl turned quickly, facing

words for everyday use

dis • in • te • grate (dis in′tə grāt′) *vi.,* break apart. *This thin plastic <u>disintegrates</u> in very hot water.*

her. Angie walked toward her, offering a bright red silk ribbon. Pleased at the gift, the Apache girl left.

And the following morning there was another quarter of antelope on her step—but she saw no Indian.

Ed Lowe had built the cabin in West Dog Canyon in the spring of 1871, but it was Angie who chose the spot, not Ed. In Santa Fe they would have told you that Ed Lowe was good-looking, <u>shiftless</u>, and agreeable. He was also, unfortunately, handy with a pistol.

Angie's father had come from County Mayo[3] to New York and from New York to the Mississippi, where he became a tough, brawling riverboatman. In New Orleans, he met a beautiful Cajun[4] girl and married her. Together, they started west for Santa Fe, and Angie was born en route. Both parents died of cholera[5] when Angie was fourteen. She lived with an Irish family for the following three years, then married Ed Lowe when she was seventeen.

Santa Fe was not good for Ed, and Angie kept after him until they started south. It was Apache country, but they kept on until they reached the old Spanish ruin in West Dog. Here there were grass, water, and shelter from the wind.

There was fuel, and there were pinyons and game.[6] And Angie, with an Irish eye for the land, saw that it would grow crops.

The house itself was built on the ruins of the old Spanish building, using the thick walls and the floor. The location had been admirably chosen for defense. The house was built in a corner of the cliff, under the sheltering overhang, so that approach was possible from only two directions both covered by an easy field of fire from the door and windows.

For seven months, Ed worked hard and steadily. He put in the first crop, built the house, and proved himself a handy man with tools. He repaired the old plow they had bought, cleaned out the spring, and paved and walled it with slabs of stone. If he was lonely for the carefree companions of Santa Fe, he gave no indication of it. Provisions were low, and when he finally started off to the south, Angie watched him go with an ache in her heart.

She did not know whether she loved Ed. The first flush of enthusiasm had passed, and Ed Lowe had proved something less than she had believed. But he had tried, she admitted. And it had not been easy for him. He was an <u>amiable</u> soul, given to whittling and idle talk, all of which he missed in the loneliness of the Apache country. And when he rode away, she had no idea whether she would ever see him again. She never did.

What did Ed Lowe miss? Why might Angie have wondered whether she would see him again?

Santa Fe was far and away to the north, but the growing village of El Paso was less than a hundred miles to the west, and it was there Ed Lowe rode for supplies and seed.

He had several drinks—his first in months—in one of the saloons. As the liquor warmed his stomach, Ed Lowe looked around agreeably. For a moment, his eyes clouded with worry as he thought of his wife and children back in Apache country, but it was not in Ed Lowe to worry for long. He had another drink and leaned on the bar, talking to the bartender. All Ed had ever asked of life was enough to eat, a horse to ride, an occasional drink, and companions to talk with. Not that he had anything

---

3. **County Mayo.** County in Ireland
4. **Cajun.** Descended from Acadian French immigrants; a native of Louisiana
5. **cholera.** Intestinal disease
6. **pinyons and game.** *Pinyons*—small pine trees with edible seeds; *game*—wild animals and birds that are hunted

1. Ed Lowe missed his friends and the bustle of Santa Fe. Angie probably wondered whether she would see him again because she believed he was discontent with their quiet life.

CROSS-CURRICULAR ACTIVITIES

MUSIC. Have students compile an anthology of folk songs about the Old West. Students who play instruments, such as guitar or piano, might like to find sheet music for these songs and hold a sing-along concert. Others might like to take turns playing recorded songs in small groups and sing along with the ones they especially like. As a third alternative, which might be especially effective with English language learners, teach students a cowboy folk song such as "I Ride an Old Paint," "The Old Chisholm Trail," "Red River Valley," "Get Along Little Dogie," or "Home on the Range."

1. The fact that Ed remembers Angie only after the fight indicates that he is impulsive and thoughtless.

LITERARY TECHNIQUE

CHARACTERIZATION. **Characterization** is the use of literary techniques to create a character. Writers use three major techniques to create characters: direct description, portrayal of characters' behavior, and representations of characters' internal states. Which techniques does the writer use to create the character of Ches Lane? of the Tolliver brothers? Provide evidence from the story to support your answer.
Answers
L'Amour uses direct description to create the character of Ches Lane: he is a "lean, powerful man with a shock of uncut black hair and a torn, weather-faded shirt." He describes one of the Tolliver brothers as a "broad-chested man" with "broken teeth." The writer also portrays the characters' behavior. Ches Lane, who reacts angrily to the Tollivers' accusation and explains his actions as self-defense, seems reasonable but proud and defiant. The Tollivers, who gang up on Ches and refuse to listen to his arguments, seem cruel and vengeful.

---

important to say. He just liked to talk.

Suddenly a chair grated on the floor, and Ed turned. A lean, powerful man with a shock of uncut black hair and a torn, weather-faded shirt stood at bay.[7] Facing him across the table were three hard-faced young men, obviously brothers.

Ches Lane did not notice Ed Lowe watching from the bar. He had eyes only for the men facing him. "You done that deliberate!" The statement was a challenge.

The broad-chested man on the left grinned through broken teeth. "That's right, Ches. I done it deliberate. You killed Dan Tolliver on the Brazos."[8]

"He made the quarrel." Comprehension came to Ches. He was boxed, and by three of the fighting, blood-hungry Tollivers.

"Don't make no difference," the broad-chested Tolliver said. "'Who sheds a Tolliver's blood, by a Tolliver's hand must die!'"

Ed Lowe moved suddenly from the bar. "Three to one is long odds," he said, his voice low and friendly. "If the gent in the corner is willin', I'll side him."

Two Tollivers turned toward him. Ed Lowe was smiling easily, his hand hovering near his gun. "You stay out of this!" one of the brothers said harshly.

"I'm in," Ed replied. "Why don't you boys light a shuck?"[9]

"No, by—!" The man's hand dropped for his gun, and the room thundered with sound.

Ed was smiling easily, unworried as always. His gun flashed up. He felt it leap in his hand,

The sound stopped, and the room was quiet, and there was the acrid smell of powder smoke.

saw the nearest Tolliver smashed back, and he shot him again as he dropped. He had only time to see Ches Lane with two guns out and another Tolliver down, when something struck him through the stomach and he stepped back against the bar, suddenly sick.

The sound stopped, and the room was quiet, and there was the <u>acrid</u> smell of powder smoke. Three Tollivers were down and dead, and Ed Lowe was dying. Ches Lane crossed to him.

"We got 'em," Ed said, "we sure did. But they got me."

Suddenly his face changed. "Oh Lord in heaven, what'll Angie do?" And then he crumpled over on the floor and lay still, the blood staining his shirt and mingling with the sawdust.

Stiff-faced, Ches looked up. "Who was Angie?" he asked.

"His wife," the bartender told him. "She's up northeast somewhere, in Apache country. He was tellin' me about her. Two kids, too."

Ches Lane stared down at the crumpled, used-up body of Ed Lowe. The man had saved his life.

One he could have beaten; two he might have beaten; three would have killed him. Ed Lowe,

> What does it say about Ed that he remembers Angie only after the fight?

---

7. **at bay.** With no way of escape
8. **Brazos.** River in Texas that flows into the Gulf of Mexico
9. **light a shuck.** A shuck is the material stripped away from an ear of corn. This material, when dried and bound together, can be used as a torch, leading the way of someone leaving through darkness.

---

words for everyday use

ac • rid (ak´rid) *adj.*, stinging. *The lab students wrinkled their noses as they smelled <u>acrid</u> chemicals.*

---

800   *UNIT TEN / CULTURES IN CONFLICT*

stepping in when he did, had saved the life of Ches Lane.

"He didn't say where?"

"No."

Ches Lane shoved his hat back on his head. "What's northeast of here?"

The bartender rested his hands on the bar. "Cochise," he said. . . .

For more than three months, whenever he could rustle the grub, Ches Lane quartered the country over and back. The trouble was, he had no lead to the location of Ed Lowe's homestead. An examination of Ed's horse revealed nothing. Lowe had bought seed and ammunition. The seed indicated a good water supply, and the ammunition implied trouble. But in the country there was always trouble.

A man had died to save his life, and Ches Lane had a deep sense of obligation. Somewhere that wife waited, if she was still alive, and it was up to him to find her and look out for her. He rode northeast, cutting for sign, but found none. Sandstorms had wiped out any hope of back-trailing Lowe. Actually, West Dog Canyon was more east than north, but this he had no way of knowing.

North he went, skirting the rugged San Andreas Mountains. Heat baked him hot; dry winds parched his skin. His hair grew dry and stiff and alkali-whitened. He rode north, and soon the Apaches knew of him. He fought them at a lonely water hole, and he fought them on the run. They killed his horse, and he switched his saddle to the spare and rode on. They cornered him in the rocks, and he killed two of them and escaped by night.

They trailed him through the White Sands, and he left two more for dead. He fought fiercely and bitterly and would not be turned from his quest. He turned east through the lava beds and still more east to the Pecos. He saw only two white men, and neither knew of a white woman.

The bearded man laughed harshly. "A woman alone? She wouldn't last a month! By now the Apaches got her, or she's dead. Don't be a fool! Leave this country before you die here."

Lean, wind-whipped, and savage, Ches Lane pushed on. The Mescaleros[10] cornered him in Rawhide Draw, and he fought them to a standstill. Grimly, the Apaches clung to his trail.

The sheer determination of the man fascinated them. Bred and born in a rugged and lonely land, the Apaches knew the difficulties of survival; they knew how a man could live, how he must live. Even as they tried to kill this man, they loved him, for he was one of their own.

Lane's jeans grew ragged. Two bullet holes were added to the old black hat. The slicker was torn; the saddle, so carefully kept until now, was scratched by gravel and brush. At night he cleaned his guns, and by day he scouted the trails. Three times he found lonely ranch houses burned to the ground, the buzzard- and coyote-stripped bones of their owners lying nearby.

Once he found a covered wagon, its canvas flopping in the wind, a man lying sprawled on the seat with a pistol near his hand. He was dead and his wife was dead, and their canteens rattled like empty skulls.

Leaner every day, Ches Lane pushed on. He camped one night in a canyon near some white oaks. He heard a hoof click on stone, and he backed away from his tiny fire, gun in hand.

The riders were white men, and there were two of them. Joe Tompkins and Wiley Lynn were headed west, and Ches Lane could have guessed why. They were men he had known before, and he told them what he was doing.

Lynn chuckled. He was a thin-faced man with lank yellow hair and dirty fingers. "Seems a mighty strange way to get a woman. There's some as comes easier."

> **What do others say about Ches Lane's chances of finding Angie?**

> **Why do the Apaches come to admire Ches?**

_____
10. **Mescaleros.** Apaches of Texas and New Mexico

"THE GIFT OF COCHISE" **801**

1. Angie's face shows marks of worry
   and struggle.
2. Angie can't leave her home because
   Apaches from other tribes would
   not willingly treat her peacefully or
   protect her as Cochise has.

What offer does Cochise make to
Angie? What reason does she give
for refusing his offer?
Answer
Cochise offers Angie the opportunity
to live with the Apaches and marry
an Apache man. She refuses because
she believes the Apaches and whites
are each suited to their own ways of
living.

"This ain't for fun," Ches replied shortly. "I got to find her."

Tompkins stared at him. "Ches, you're crazy! That gent declared himself in of his own wish and desire. Far's that goes, the gal's dead. No woman could last this long in Apache country."

At daylight, the two men headed west, and Ches Lane turned south. . . .

The lonely rider who fought so desperately and knew the desert so well soon became a subject of gossip among the Apaches. Over the fires of many a rancheria they discussed this strange rider who seemed to be going nowhere but always riding, like a lean wolf dog on a trail. He rode across the mesas and down the canyons; he studied signs at every water hole; he looked long from every ridge. It was obvious to the Indians that he searched for something—but what?

Cochise had come again to the cabin in West Dog Canyon. "Little warrior too small," he said, "too small for hunt. You join my people. Take Apache for man."

"No." Angie shook her head. "Apache ways are good for the Apache, and the white man's ways are good for white men—and women."

They rode away and said no more, but that night, as she had on many other nights after the children were asleep, Angie cried. She wept silently, her head pillowed on her arms. She was as pretty as ever, but her face was thin, showing the worry and struggle of the months gone by, the weeks and months without hope.

> What does Angie's face show?

The crops were small but good. Little Jimmy worked beside her. At night, Angie sat alone on the steps and watched the shadows gather down the long canyon, listening to the coyotes yap-ping from the rim of the Guadalupes,[11] hearing the horses blowing in the corral. She watched, still hopeful, but now she knew that Cochise was right: Ed would not return.

But even if she had been ready to give up this, the first home she had known, there could be no escape. Here she was protected by Cochise. Other Apaches from other tribes would not so willingly grant her peace.

> Why can't Angie leave her home?

At daylight she was up. The morning air was bright and balmy, but soon it would be hot again. Jimmy went to the spring for water, and when breakfast was over, the children played while Angie sat in the shade of a huge, old cottonwood and sewed. It was a Sunday, warm and lovely. From time to time, she lifted her eyes to look down the canyon, half smiling at her own foolishness.

The hard-packed earth of the yard was swept clean of dust; the pans hanging on the kitchen wall were neat and shining. The children's hair had been clipped, and there was a small bouquet on the kitchen table.

After a while, Angie put aside her sewing and changed her dress. She did her hair carefully, and then, looking in her mirror, she reflected with sudden pain that she *was* pretty and that she was only a girl.

Resolutely, she turned from the mirror and, taking up her Bible, went back to the seat under the cottonwood. The children left their playing and came to her, for this was a Sunday ritual, their only one. Opening the Bible, she read slowly,

"Though I walk through the valley of the shadow of death, I will fear no evil; for thou art with me; thy rod and thy staff, they comfort me.

---

11. **Guadalupes.** Mountain range in Texas and New Mexico

words for everyday use

res • o • lute • ly (rez ə lo͞ot′lē) *adv.*, firmly; determinedly. *The gymnast focused resolutely on her program in the moments before the contest.*

Thou preparest a table before me in the presence of mine enemies: thou . . ."

"Mommy." Jimmy tugged at her sleeve. "Look!"

Why might Angie have chosen this particular passage to read?

Ches Lane had reached a narrow canyon by midafternoon and decided to make camp. There was small possibility he would find another such spot, and he was dead tired, his muscles sodden with <u>fatigue</u>. The canyon was one of those unexpected gashes in the cap rock that gave no indication of its presence until you came right on it. After some searching, Ches found a route to the bottom and made camp under a wind-hollowed overhang. There was water, and there was a small patch of grass.

After his horse had a drink and a roll on the ground, it began cropping eagerly at the rich, green grass, and Ches built a smokeless fire of some ancient driftwood in the canyon bottom. It was his first hot meal in days, and when he had finished he put out his fire, rolled a smoke, and leaned back contentedly.

Before darkness settled, he climbed to the rim and looked over the country. The sun had gone down, and the shadows were growing long. After a half-hour of study, he decided there was no living thing within miles, except for the usual desert life. Returning to the bottom, he moved his horse to fresh grass, then rolled in his blanket. For the first time in a month, he slept without fear.

He woke up suddenly in the broad daylight. The horse was listening to something, his head up. Swiftly, Ches went to the horse and led it back under the overhang. Then he drew on his boots, rolled his blankets, and saddled the horse. Still he heard no sound.

Climbing the rim again, he studied the desert and found nothing. Returning to his horse, he mounted up and rode down the canyon toward the flatland beyond. Coming out of the canyon mouth, he rode right into the middle of a war party of more than twenty Apaches—invisible until suddenly they stood up behind rocks, their rifles leveled. And he didn't have a chance.

Swiftly, they bound his wrists to the saddle horn and tied his feet. Only then did he see the man who led the party. It was Cochise.

He was a lean, wiry Indian of past fifty, his black hair streaked with gray, his features strong and clean-cut. He stared at Lane, and there was nothing in his face to reveal what he might be thinking.

Several of the younger warriors pushed forward, talking excitedly and waving their arms. Ches Lane understood some of it, but he sat straight in the saddle, his head up, waiting. Then Cochise spoke and the party turned, and, leading his horse, they rode away.

The miles grew long and the sun was hot. He was offered no water and he asked for none. The Indians ignored him. Once a young brave rode near and struck him viciously. Lane made no sound, gave no indication of pain. When they finally stopped, it was beside a huge anthill swarming with big red desert ants.

Roughly, they quickly untied him and jerked him from his horse. He dug in his heels and shouted at them in Spanish: "The Apaches are women! They tie me to the ants because they are afraid to fight me!"

An Indian struck him, and Ches glared at the man. If he must die, he would show them how it should be done. Yet he knew the unpredictable nature of the Indian, of his great respect for courage.

"Give me a knife, and I'll kill any of your warriors!"

They stared at him, and one powerfully built Apache angrily ordered them to get on with it.

"THE GIFT OF COCHISE" 803

ANSWER TO GUIDED READING QUESTION

1. Angie's choice of Bible passage, from the Psalms, may show that she realizes she has been protected from her enemies during a difficult time and is grateful. She may also have chosen the passage because she is still uneasy about her situation and needs comfort.

LITERARY TECHNIQUE

SUSPENSE. Suspense is the feeling of expectation, anxiousness, or curiosity created by questions raised in the mind of a reader. What feeling is created at the end of the scene where Angie reads aloud from the Bible? What happens to this feeling when the scene shifts to Ches in the canyon?
Answers
The end of the scene, when Jimmy spots something in the distance, creates a feeling of expectation and anxiousness. Knowing that Ches is looking for Angie, the reader might assume that Jimmy has seen Ches. However, the passage that Angie read with references to death and evil also makes the reader anxious that something bad may happen. When the scene shifts to Ches in the canyon, this feeling of anxiousness increases because the reader realizes that Ches is not near Angie's cabin to offer help.

1. Ches believes he should be allowed
   to fight for his freedom or die
   fighting because he has both
   evaded and beaten the warriors
   until this point and has only been
   captured by accident.

CROSS-CURRICULAR
CONNECTIONS

HISTORY. Like many Native American
groups, the Apaches came to be
known by a name that was assigned
to them by whites or other tribes.
The name Apache derives from the
Zuni word *apachu,* which means
"enemy." The Apache call themselves N'de or Dineh, which means
"The People."

Cochise spoke, and the big
warrior replied angrily.

Ches Lane nodded
at the anthill. "Is this
the death for a fight-
ing man? I have
fought your strong
men and beaten them. I
have left no trail for them
to follow, and for months I
have lived among you, and
now only by accident have
you captured me. Give me a
knife," he added grimly,
"and I will fight *him!*" He indicated the big,
black-faced Apache.

The warrior's cruel mouth hardened, and he
struck Ches across the face.

The white man tasted blood and fury.
"Woman!" Ches said. "Coyote! You are afraid!"
Ches turned on Cochise, as the Indian stood
irresolute. "Free my hands and let me fight!" he
demanded. "If I win, let me go free."

Cochise said something to the big Indian.
Instantly, there was stillness. Then an Apache
sprang forward and, with a slash of his knife,
freed Lane's hands. Shaking loose the thongs,
Ches Lane chafed his wrists to bring back the
circulation. An Indian threw a knife at his feet. It
was his own bowie knife.

Ches took off his riding boots. In sock feet,
his knife gripped low in his hand, its cutting
edge up, he looked at the big warrior.

"I promise you nothing," Cochise said in
Spanish, "but an honorable death."

The big warrior came at him on cat feet.
Warily, Ches circled. He had not only to defeat
this Apache but to escape. He permitted himself
a side glance toward his horse. It stood alone.
No Indian held it.

The warrior's cruel mouth hardened, and he struck Ches across the face.

*Why does Ches believe
he should be allowed to
fight for his freedom?*

The Apache closed
swiftly, thrusting
wickedly with the
knife. Ches, who had
learned knife fight-
ing in the bayou
country of
Louisiana, turned his
hip sharply, and the
blade slid past him. He
struck swiftly, but the
Apache's forward movement deflected the blade,
and it failed to penetrate. However, as it swept
up between the Indian's body and arm, it cut a
deep gash in the warrior's left armpit.

The Indian sprang again, like a clawing cat,
streaming blood. Ches moved aside, but a back-
hand sweep nicked him, and he felt the sharp
bite of the blade. Turning, he paused on the
balls of his feet.

He had had no water in hours. His lips were
cracked. Yet he sweated now, and the salt of it
stung his eyes. He stared into the malevolent
black eyes of the Apache, then moved to meet
him. The Indian lunged, and Ches sidestepped
like a boxer and spun on the ball of his foot.

The sudden side step threw the Indian past
him, but Ches failed to drive the knife into the
Apache's kidney when his foot rolled on a stone.
The point left a thin red line across the Indian's
back. The Indian was quick. Before Ches could
recover his balance, he grasped the white man's
knife wrist. Desperately, Ches grabbed for the
Indian's knife hand and got the wrist, and they
stood there straining, chest to chest.

Seeing his chance, Ches suddenly let his knees
buckle, then brought up his knee and fell back,
throwing the Apache over his head to the sand.
Instantly, he whirled and was on his feet, standing over the Apache. The warrior had lost his

**words
for
everyday
use**
ir • res • o • lute (ir rəz´ə loͦot) *adj.,* undecided. *The store clerk became impatient with the* irresolute *customer.*
de • flect (dē flekt) *vt.,* turn to one side. *The press secretary calmly* deflected *the reporters' questions.*
ma • lev • o • lent (mə lev´ə lənt) *adj.,* wishing evil or harm to others. *The mysterious visitor assured the detective that
he had no* malevolent *intentions.*

knife, and he lay there, staring up, his eyes black with hatred.

Coolly, Ches stepped back, picked up the Indian's knife, and tossed it to him <u>contemptuously</u>. There was a grunt from the watching Indians, and then his <u>antagonist</u> rushed. But loss of blood had weakened the warrior, and Ches stepped in swiftly, struck the blade aside, then thrust the point of his blade hard against the Indian's belly.

Black eyes glared into his without yielding. A thrust, and the man would be disemboweled,[12] but Ches stepped back. "He is a strong man," Ches said in Spanish. "It is enough that I have won."

> What does Ches do when he has the advantage over the Apache warrior?

Deliberately, he walked to his horse and swung into the saddle. He looked around, and every rifle covered him.

So he had gained nothing. He had hoped that mercy might lead to mercy, that the Apache's respect for a fighting man would win his freedom. He had failed. Again they bound him to his horse, but they did not take his knife from him.

> What did Ches hope? What happens instead?

When they camped at last, he was given food and drink. He was bound again, and a blanket was thrown over him. At daylight they were again in the saddle. In Spanish he asked where they were taking him, but they gave no indication of hearing. When they stopped again, it was beside a pole corral, near a stone cabin.

When Jimmy spoke, Angie got quickly to her feet. She recognized Cochise with a start of relief, but she saw instantly that this was a war party. And then she saw the prisoner.

Their eyes met and she felt a distinct shock. He was a white man, a big, unshaven man who badly needed both a bath and a haircut, his clothes ragged and bloody. Cochise gestured at the prisoner.

"No take Apache man, you take white man. This man good for hunt, good for fight. He strong warrior. You take 'em."

> What does Cochise intend to do with Ches?

Flushed and startled, Angie stared at the prisoner and caught a faint glint of humor in his dark eyes.

"Is this here the fate worse than death I hear tell of?" he inquired gently.

"Who are you?" she asked, and was immediately conscious that it was an extremely silly question.

The Apaches had drawn back and were watching curiously. She could do nothing for the present but accept the situation. Obviously they intended to do her a kindness, and it would not do to offend them. If they had not brought this man to her, he might have been killed.

> Why does Angie "accept the situation"?

"Name's Ches Lane, ma'am," he said. "Will you untie me? I'd feel a lot safer."

"Of course." Still flustered, she went to him and untied his hands. One Indian said something, and the others chuckled; then, with a whoop, they swung their horses and galloped off down the canyon.

Their departure left her suddenly helpless, the shadowy globe of her loneliness shattered by this utterly strange man standing before her, this big, bearded man brought to her out of the desert.

---

12. **disemboweled.** Having had the inner organs of the abdomen removed

---

words for everyday use

con• temp • tu • ous • ly (kən temp′cho͞o əs lē) *adv.,* scornfully. *How can you speak so <u>contemptuously</u> of your friends?*

an• tag • on • ist (an tag′ə nist) *n.,* opponent. *I'd prefer not to confront such an intimidating <u>antagonist</u>.*

1. Ches chooses to wound rather than kill the Apache warrior.
2. Ches had hoped that by allowing the warrior to live, he would gain his own freedom. Instead, the Apaches bound him to his horse again.
3. Cochise intends for Ches to stay with Angie.
4. Angie accepts the situation because she doesn't want to offend the Apaches, who intended to do her a kindness, and she realizes they might have killed the white man if they had not brought her to him.

CROSS-CURRICULAR CONNECTIONS

WESTERNS. Most westerns were published as dime novels from the mid-nineteenth century to the early twentieth century. The most successful western dime novels were written during and after the Civil War. In the twentieth century, formula westerns gained enormous popularity in pulp fiction magazines such as *Wild West Weekly* (1927) and *Zane Grey's Western Magazine* (1947).

1. Ches may be thinking about
   staying with Angie.

Checking Your Reading
1. Who were surrounding Angie
   Lowe's house at the beginning of
   the story? **Twelve Apaches, one of
   whom was Cochise, were
   surrounding her house.**
2. Where does Angie tell Cochise her
   husband has gone? **She says that
   he has gone to El Paso.**
3. How long has her husband been
   gone? **He has been gone for four
   months.**
4. What happened to Ed in El Paso?
   He was killed in a gun fight.
5. What is the main gift Cochise gives
   Angie? **He gives her Ches Lane.**

Vocabulary in Context
Fill in each blank below with the most
appropriate word from the following
Words for Everyday Use. You may have
to change the tense of the word.

sporadic disintegrate shiftless amiable
acrid resolutely deflect

1. He was able to **deflect** the sword
   with his shield.
2. The **shiftless** man was unable to
   keep a job.
3. Her **amiable** nature allowed her to
   meet many unusual people.
4. Her ice sculpture **disintegrated** in
   the heat.
5. The student faced failure because of
   his **sporadic** school attendance.

Literary Tools
Match each literary term with the best
description.
   a. genres b. stereotypes c. westerns
        d. detective stories
1. uncritically accepted or
   conventional ideas, particularly
   when held about whole groups of
   people; **b**
2. the name for the categories into
   which literary works are divided; **a**
3. "The Gift of Cochise" is one of
   these; **c**

She smoothed her apron, suddenly pale as she
realized what his delivery to her implied. What
must he think of her? She turned away quickly.

"There's hot water," she said hastily, to prevent his speaking. "Dinner is almost ready."

She walked quickly into the house and
stopped before the stove, her mind a blank. She
looked around her as if she had suddenly waked
up in a strange place. She heard water being
poured into the basin by the door and heard
him take Ed's razor. She had never moved the
box. To have moved it would—

"Sight of work done here, ma'am."

She hesitated, then turned with determination
and stepped into the doorway. "Yes, Ed—"

"You're Angie Lowe."

Surprised, she turned toward him and recognized his own startled awareness of her. As he
shaved, he told her about Ed and what had happened that day in the saloon.

"He—Ed was like that. He never considered
consequences until it was too late."

"Lucky for me he didn't."

He was younger looking with his beard gone.
There was a certain quiet dignity in his face.
She went back inside and began putting plates
on the table. She was conscious that he had
moved to the door and was watching her.

"You don't have to stay," she said. "You owe me
nothing. Whatever Ed did, he did because he was
that kind of person. You aren't responsible."

He did not answer, and when she turned again
to the stove, she glanced swiftly at him. He was
looking across the valley.

There was a studied <u>deference</u> about him
when he moved to a place at the table. The children stared, wide-eyed and silent; it had been so
long since a man had sat at this table.

Angie could not remember when she had felt
like this. She was awkwardly conscious of her
hands, which never seemed to be in the right
place or doing the right things. She scarcely
tasted her food, nor did the children.

Ches Lane had no such <u>inhibitions</u>. For the
first time, he realized how hungry he was. After
the half-cooked meat of lonely, trailside fires,
this was tender and flavored. Hot biscuits,
desert honey . . . Suddenly he looked up, embarrassed at his appetite.

"You were really hungry," she said.

"Man can't fix much, out on the trail."

Later, after he'd got his bedroll from his saddle and unrolled it on the hay in the barn, he
walked back to the house and sat on the lowest
step. The sun was gone, and they watched the
cliffs stretch their red shadows across the valley.
A quail called <u>plaintively</u>, a mellow sound
of twilight.

"You needn't worry about Cochise," she said.
"He'll soon be crossing into Mexico."

"I wasn't thinking about Cochise."

That left her with noth-
ing to say, and she listened
again to the quail and
watched a lone bright star
in the sky.

> What is Ches thinking
> about at the end of the
> story?

"A man could get to like it here," he
said quietly.

---

words for everyday use	**def • er • ence** (def´ər əns) *n.*, courteous regard or respect. *The panel members showed* <u>deference</u> *to the Nobel Prize-winning scientist.* **in • hi • bi • tion** (in hi bish´ən) *n.*, restraint. *Speaking in front of such a large audience brought out the speaker's* <u>inhibitions</u>. **plain• tive • ly** (plān´tiv lē) *adv.*, sadly. *The wind, blowing* <u>plaintively</u> *through the abandoned lighthouse, sounded eerily human.*

Respond *to the* SELECTION

Predict whether Angie will accept Cochise's gift or send Ches Lane packing. Try to base your prediction on some evidence in the story.

Investigate, *Inquire,* and Imagine

Recall: GATHERING FACTS

1a. At the beginning of the story, what has happened three times in the recent past?

2a. Where does Ed Lowe go? What happens to him there?

3a. What does Ches Lane do after the gunfight?

Interpret: FINDING MEANING

1b. How does Cochise feel about Angie, and why?

2b. Ed Lowe leaves in order to get supplies and seed. What other possible motivation for his leaving is hinted at in the story? Why is it irresponsible for him to leave his wife and children alone?

3b. Why does Ches Lane seek out Angie?

Analyze: TAKING THINGS APART

4a. Analyze the relationship between Ches Lane and the Apaches.

Synthesize: BRINGING THINGS TOGETHER

4b. What is the "gift of Cochise"?

Evaluate: MAKING JUDGMENTS

5a. Evaluate Cochise's motives in giving the gift to Angie.

Extend: CONNECTING IDEAS

5b. Compare what is happening to Cochise and his people with what is happening to Grandma Selma and her people in "One of Grandma Selma's Stories."

Understanding *Literature*

STEREOTYPE. Review the definition for **stereotype** in the Handbook of Literary Terms. What aspects of characterizations of Angie, Ed, Ches, and Cochise are stereotypical? How does the characterization of Cochise rise above the traditional western stereotypes of Native Americans in general?

GENRE. Review the definition for **genre** in Literary Tools in Prereading and the cluster chart you made for that section. What elements of "The Gift of Cochise" make it typical of the genre known as the western? What elements of the story are not typical of westerns? What values do westerns typically promote and celebrate? How might these values be related to frontier life?

"THE GIFT OF COCHISE" **807**

ANSWERS TO INVESTIGATE, INQUIRE, AND IMAGINE

RECALL

1a. Three times in the recent past Apache warriors have attacked the Lowe cabin and been turned back.

2a. Ed Lowe goes to El Paso. He is killed in a fight in a saloon there.

3a. After the gunfight, Ches Lane goes in search of Angie Lowe.

INTERPRET

1b. Cochise admires Angie because she has fended off the Apache warriors, killing seven men and wounding three, even though she is scarcely more than a girl and lives alone with two small children.

2b. The story hints that Ed, who enjoys talking to people, might have left because he was bored living on an isolated farm. It is irresponsible for him to leave his wife and children alone because they live in Apache country, where the Apache are known to attack white settlers.

3b. Ches Lane seeks out Angie because he feels indebted to her husband Ed for saving his life. He wants to return the favor by protecting Angie.

ANALYZE

4a. *Responses will vary.* As the Apaches trail and fight Ches on his wanderings, they come to admire his determination, his fierce fighting, and his ability to survive in a rugged and lonely land. Still, seeing him as an enemy in their territory, they capture him and mistreat him. Even after Ches succeeds in killing the biggest Apache warrior, Cochise does not grant him his freedom.

SYNTHESIZE

4b. Ches Lane is the "gift of Cochise." Cochise wanted Angie to take an Apache man for a husband. When she refused, he found her a worthy white "warrior" to care for her and protect her and her children.

EVALUATE

5a. *Responses will vary.* Cochise seems selfless in thinking of Angie's needs.

ANSWERS TO INVESTIGATE, INQUIRE, AND IMAGINE (CONT.)

He is motivated by what is right and proper in his own culture, in which a woman isn't left to fend for herself, and by his respect for Angie's self-sufficiency. Cochise may also want to maintain friendly relations with Angie, because she allows Apache who come in peace to drink at her spring.

EXTEND

5b. In both stories, the ways of native people are being threatened by the encroachment of whites.

Bennijack and the Apaches try to fight off the encroachment, but they will not succeed because the whites are too numerous.

Answers to Understanding Literature can be found on page 808.

TEACHER'S EDITION **807**

ANSWERS TO UNDERSTANDING LITERATURE

STEREOTYPE. The characterization of Angie as a tough and self-sufficient frontier woman, though "scarcely more than a girl," is stereotypical of some westerns. Ed's bravado in the saloon seems stereotypical, as does Ches's characterization as a brave, solitary, proud man. The characterization of Cochise rises above the usual western stereotype of Native Americans as war-loving and violent toward whites by depicting him as a thoughtful, reasonable, and respectful man.

GENRE. "The Gift of Cochise" has typical western elements such as a gunfight in a saloon, a cowboy fighting Indians on the trail, and Native American raids on white settlers. Unlike most westerns, the story also depicts communication and understanding between white settlers and Native Americans. Westerns typically promote values such as physical courage, determination, and self-sufficiency. These qualities were needed because frontier life was physically demanding and life-and-death conflicts could occur at any moment.

ANSWERS TO INTEGRATING THE LANGUAGE ARTS

Language, Grammar, and Style
1. *Common Nouns:* north, village, miles, west; *Proper Nouns:* Santa Fe, El Paso
2. *Common Nouns:* chief. *Proper Nouns:* Cochise, Apaches.
3. *Common Nouns:* homestead; *Proper Nouns:* Angie Lowe, Ed
4. *Common Nouns:* antelope, cabin; *Proper Nouns:* Apaches, West Dog Canyon
5. *Common Nouns:* surprise; *Proper Nouns:* Ches Lane

Collaborative Learning & Speaking and Listening
Suggest that students jot down a few notes as they watch the film. They can keep these notes organized by deciding ahead of time what aspects of the film they want to evaluate. Have them create a note-taking form on a single sheet of paper that is divided into six or eight sections, each with a topic heading such as Characters, Plot, Setting, Theme, Acting, Script, and Photography.

Speaking and Listening & Study and Research
Assign a score from 10 to 25 points for each grading criterion below. (See the evaluation forms for writing, revising, and proofreading in the Assessment Resource book.)

Writer's Journal

1. Pretend you are Angie. Write a **thank-you note** to Cochise for all that he has done for you.
2. Imagine you work for the El Paso sheriff's department. Write a **report** about the murders that took place at the local saloon.
3. Write a **dialogue** between Angie and Ches as they get to know each other. Try to show what they have in common and what potential conflicts they might have.

Integrating the Language Arts

Language, Grammar, and Style

COMMON AND PROPER NOUNS. Read the Language Arts Survey 3.51, "Common Nouns and Proper Nouns." Then make two lists of the nouns in the sentences below, one headed *Common Nouns* and the other *Proper Nouns*.

1. Santa Fe was far and away to the north, but the growing village of El Paso was less than a hundred miles to the west.
2. Cochise was the chief of the Apaches.
3. Angie Lowe never saw Ed at the homestead again.
4. Twice the Apaches brought antelope to the cabin in West Dog Canyon.
5. But the biggest surprise of all was Ches Lane.

Collaborative Learning Media Literacy

FILM REVIEW. Watch *How the West Was Won* or another western film written by Louis L'Amour. Then, with a partner, videotape a review of the film in the manner of two TV movie reviewers. One reviewer gives reasons for seeing the film, and the other reviewer gives reasons not to see it.

Speaking and Listening & Study and Research

GIVING A SPEECH. Imagine you are Angie. The year is 1866. Cochise is meeting in a council with General Gordon Granger of the United States Army. The purpose of the meeting is to find a resolution between the Apaches and the white settlers. Write a speech you might deliver at the council meeting in which you present your view of Cochise and his people. You may want to find more information on General Gordon Granger and his army in order to know your audience better. Include in your speech a possible resolution you feel would be fair and beneficial to both parties. You might find it helpful to review the Language Arts Survey 4.18, "Guidelines for Giving a Speech" before delivering your speech to the rest of class.

ANSWERS TO INTEGRATING THE LANGUAGE ARTS (CONT.)

SPEECH
- **CONTENT/UNITY.** The speech presents a position and two or three strong arguments to support it.
- **ORGANIZATION/COHERENCE.** The speech begins with a topic sentence that presents the writer's position. It then presents two or three arguments in a logical order.
- **LANGUAGE/STYLE.** The speech uses vivid and precise nouns, verbs, and modifiers.
- **CONVENTIONS.** The speech avoids errors in spelling, grammar, usage, mechanics, and manuscript form.

"CHEE'S DAUGHTER"

by Juanita Platero and Siyowin Miller

Reader's resource

"Chee's Daughter" is the story of a traditional Navajo farmer, Chee, whose ways come into conflict with modern society and materialistic values. When Chee's wife dies, his daughter is taken by his in-laws to live with them, according to a Navajo custom which maintains that a girl child belongs with her mother's relatives. Chee struggles to maintain his belief in the promise of the land as he plans how to get his daughter back. "Chee's Daughter" was first published in 1948.

CULTURE CONNECTION. Traditional Navajo culture is matrilineal; a family traces its ancestry back through the mother's line, and children belong to the mother's clan. Several generations of a family might live together. Women have an important position in Navajo society; the oldest woman in the family enjoys a place at the center of family life. The largest Native American tribe in the United States, the Navajo have adopted peaceful arts—from the Mexicans metalworking, from the Pueblo Indians weaving. The Navajo reside on reservations in northeastern Arizona, northwestern New Mexico, and southeastern Utah.

About the AUTHORS

Juanita Platero, a Navajo writer, lived at one time on a reservation in New Mexico, the setting for "Chee's Daughter." She began working in collaboration with California writer Siyowin Miller in 1929. Most of the stories the two wrote together show the conflict in values between the old Navajo ways and the new ways of industrial society. Platero and Miller also wrote a novel, *The Winds Erase Your Footprints*.

Literary TOOLS

IRONY AND IRONY OF SITUATION. **Irony** is a difference between appearance and reality. **Irony of situation** occurs when an event violates the expectations of the characters, the reader, or the audience. As you read, find two examples of irony of situation in the story.

SETTING AND TONE. The **setting** of a literary work is the time and place in which it occurs, together with all the details used to create a sense of a particular time and place. **Tone** is the emotional attitude toward the reader or toward the subject implied by a literary work. As you read, decide what tone the authors use when describing the property of Chee and Old Man Fat.

Graphic Organizer

Make a chart describing Chee's and Old Man Fat's property. One example has been done for you.

CHEE'S PROPERTY	OLD MAN FAT'S PROPERTY
levels of jagged rock and levels of rich red earth	mushroom growth along the highway

Reader's Journal

Have you ever lost something you valued? What were you willing to do to get it back?

ADDITIONAL RESOURCES

UNIT 10 RESOURCE BOOK
• Selection Worksheet 10.4
• Selection Check Test 4.10.7
• Selection Test 4.10.8
• Language, Grammar, and Style Resource 3.39

GRAPHIC ORGANIZER

Students might note the following descriptions in their charts:
Chee's Property
"Here was the old feeling of wholeness and of oneness with the sun and earth and growing things"; "indistinct furrows of the fields beside the stream, where each year the corn and beans and squash drank thirstily of the overflow from summer rains"; his mother's hogan was "secure in a recess of overhanging rock"; the dome-shaped hogan was made of "red rock and red adobe like the ground on which it nestled"; a corral for sheep and goats; a "horse corral made of heavy cedar branches sternly interlocked"
Old Man Fat's Property
"drab, treeless land"; trading store with gas pumps in front; hogan of logs with "pseudo-Navajo designs on the roof"; "smoke-smudged windows"; and a "garish blue door"; "gaudy Navajo rugs" hung out to attract tourists

READER'S JOURNAL

You might have students make a sequence chart to show how they got something precious back that they had lost. Students who have not lost anything precious can write about what they fear losing. Encourage students to consider things such as friendship and self-respect, not just objects.

GOALS/OBJECTIVES

Studying this lesson will enable students to
• empathize with and understand a narrator's perspective
• discuss how the story reflects cultural traditions and lifestyles among the Navajo
• define *irony* and recognize examples of *irony of situation* in the selection
• define *setting* and *tone* and explain the importance of the two contrasting settings in the story and the writer's tone in describing them
• make sentences more colorful by adding modifiers
• write travel materials about the southwestern United States
• research Navajo heritage

MOTIVATION

Have students compare and contrast two different family settings in which they spend time. Some students, for example, may live part time in two different households because of divorce. Other students may have spent extended periods visiting at a relative's house or living with a friend's family. Have students compare and contrast the two settings. How do the settings compare physically? How do the settings reflect the activities and values of those who live there?

READING PROFICIENCY

Have pairs of students read the definitions of the vocabulary words out loud, as well as the context sentences. Ask them to then take turns composing their own oral sentences using the words.

ENGLISH LANGUAGE LEARNING

Provide students with these additional definitions:

curio—something considered unusual or bizarre
acrid—sharp and harsh
haste—careless hurry

SPECIAL NEEDS

Help students focus on the Guided Reading questions from the selection.

ENRICHMENT

Have students stage a tribal council meeting or a hearing before a government judge in which Chee brings his case. To be decided is whether Chee's daughter will be returned to him. Students should play the roles of Chee, his parents and sister, his in-laws, his daughter, and any other characters they think appropriate. Three council members or a presiding judge should be elected.

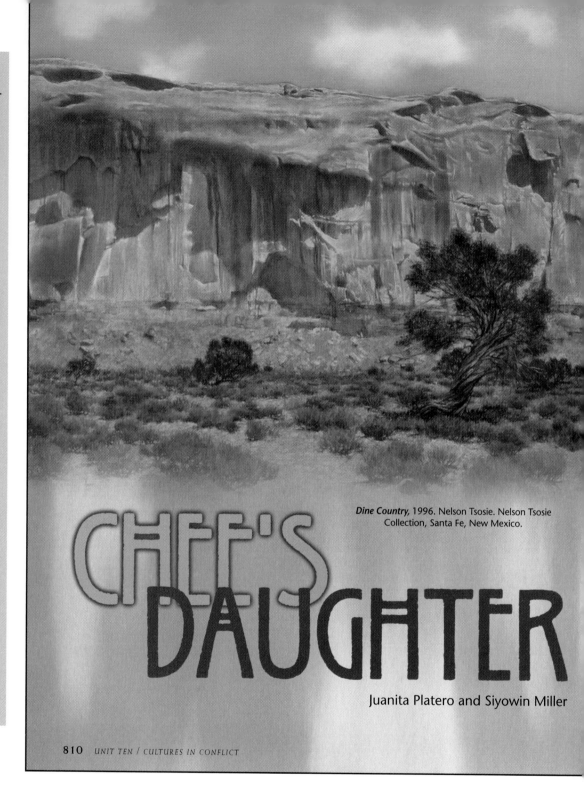

Dine Country, 1996. Nelson Tsosie. Nelson Tsosie Collection, Santa Fe, New Mexico.

CHEE'S DAUGHTER

Juanita Platero and Siyowin Miller

810 UNIT TEN / CULTURES IN CONFLICT

The hat told the story, the big, black, drooping Stetson. It was not at the proper angle, the proper <u>rakish</u> angle for so young a Navajo. There was no song, and that was not in keeping either. There should have been at least a humming, a faint, all-to-himself "he he he heya," for it was a good horse he was riding, a slender-legged, high-stepping buckskin that would race the wind with light knee-urging. This was a day for singing, a warm winter day, when the touch of the sun upon the back belied the snow high on distant mountains.

What is the first indication that something is wrong?

Wind warmed by the sun touched his high-boned cheeks like flicker[1] feathers, and still he rode on silently, deeper into Little Canyon, until the red rock walls rose straight upward from the stream bed and only a narrow piece of blue sky hung above. Abruptly the sky widened where the canyon walls were pushed back to make a wide place, as though in ancient times an angry stream had tried to go all ways at once.

This was home—this wide place in the canyon—levels of jagged rock and levels of rich red earth. This was home to Chee, the rider of the buckskin, as it had been to many generations before him.

Where is the man's home?

He stopped his horse at the stream and sat looking across the narrow ribbon of water to the bare-branched peach trees. He was seeing them each springtime with their age-<u>gnarled</u> limbs transfigured beneath veils of blossom pink; he was seeing them in autumn laden with their yellow fruit, small and sweet. Then his eyes searched out the indistinct furrows of the fields beside the stream, where each year the corn and beans and squash drank thirstily of the overflow from summer rains. Chee was trying to outweigh today's bitter betrayal of hope by gathering to himself these reminders of the <u>integrity</u> of the land. Land did not cheat! His mind lingered deliberately on all the days spent here in the sun caring for the young plants, his songs to the earth and to the life springing from it— "…In the middle of the wide field…Yellow Corn Boy…He has started both ways…" then the harvest and repayment in full measure. Here was the old feeling of wholeness and of oneness with the sun and earth and growing things.

What crops does Chee grow?

How does Chee feel about the land?

Chee urged the buckskin toward the family compound where, secure in a recess of overhanging rock, was his mother's dome-shaped hogan,[2] red rock and red adobe like the ground on which it nestled. Not far from the hogan was the half-circle of brush like a dark shadow against the canyon wall-corral for sheep and goats. Farther from the hogan, in full circle, stood the horse corral made of heavy cedar branches sternly interlocked. Chee's long thin lips curved into a smile as he passed his daughter's tiny hogan squatted like a round Pueblo oven beside the corral. He remembered the summer day when together they sat back on their heels and plastered wet adobe all about the circling wall of rock and the woven dome of piñon[3] twigs. How his family laughed when the Little One herded the bewildered chickens into her tiny hogan as the first snow fell.

---

1. **flicker.** Woodpecker
2. **hogan.** Traditional cone-shaped Navajo house made of logs or strips of wood and covered with mud
3. **piñon.** Small pine tree native to the Southwest

ANSWERS TO GUIDED READING QUESTIONS

1. The man's hat is not at the proper "rakish angle" for so young a Navajo and he is not singing to himself, as Navajo often do.
2. The man's home is in Little Canyon where "levels of jagged rock and levels of rich red earth" are visible.
3. Chee grows peaches, corn, beans, and squash.
4. He feels a wholeness and oneness with "the sun and earth and growing things."

VOCABULARY FROM THE SELECTION

banter	integrity
belligerently	meager
bluster	pseudo
deference	rakish
flaunt	shorn
forage	smoldering
froth	surmise
garish	thriftlessness
gnarled	truant
indolence	zealously

words for everyday use

rak • ish (rā′ kish) *adj.*, dashingly or carelessly unconventional; jaunty. *Karim's <u>rakish</u> clothes made him stand out at the dance.*

gnarled (närld) *adj.*, full of knots or gnarls. *Grandpa's <u>gnarled</u> hands are the result of rheumatoid arthritis.*

in • teg • ri • ty (in te′ grə tē) *n.*, completeness; soundness; incorruptibility. *City council members were impressed by the <u>integrity</u> of the mayor's plan to draw new businesses to the downtown area.*

1. Chee's wife died of tuberculosis, "the coughing sickness." His daughter was taken by his in-laws, in keeping with the custom that girl children who lose their mother go to live with her mother's people.

Then the smile faded from Chee's lips and his eyes darkened as he tied his horse to a corral post and turned to the strangely empty compound. "Someone has told them," he thought, "and they are inside weeping." He passed his mother's deserted loom on the south side of the hogan and pulled the rude wooden door toward him, bowing his head, hunching his shoulders to get inside.

His mother sat sideways by the center fire, her feet drawn up under her full skirts. Her hands were busy kneading dough in the chipped white basin. With her head down, her voice was muffled when she said, "The meal will soon be ready, Son."

Chee passed his father sitting against the wall, hat over his eyes as though asleep. He passed his older sister, who sat turning mutton ribs on a crude wire grill over the coals, noticed tears dropping on her hands. "She cared more for my wife than I realized," he thought.

Then because something must be said sometime, he tossed the black Stetson upon a bulging sack of wool and said, "You have heard, then." He could not shut from his mind how confidently he had set the handsome new hat on his head that very morning, slanting the wide brim over one eye: he was going to see his wife, and today he would ask the doctors about bringing her home; last week she had looked so much better.

His sister nodded but did not speak. His mother sniffled and passed her velveteen sleeve beneath her nose. Chee sat down, leaning against the wall. "I suppose I was a fool for hoping all the time. I should have expected this. Few of our people get well from the coughing sickness.[4] But she seemed to be getting better."

His mother was crying aloud now and blowing her nose noisily on her skirt. His father sat up, speaking gently to her.

Chee shifted his position and started a cigarette. His mind turned back to the Little One. At least she was too small to understand what had happened, the Little One who had been born three years before in the sanitarium[5]

where his wife was being treated for the coughing sickness, the Little One he had brought home to his mother's hogan to be nursed by his sister, whose baby was a few months older. As she grew fat-cheeked and sturdy-legged, she followed him about like a shadow; somehow her baby mind had grasped that of all those at the hogan who cared for her and played with her, he—Chee—belonged most to her. She sat cross-legged at his elbow when he worked silver at the forge; she rode before him in the saddle when he drove the horses to water; often she lay wakeful on her sheep pelts until he stretched out for the night in the darkened hogan and she could snuggle warm against him.

Chee blew smoke slowly, and some of the sadness left his dark eyes as he said, "It is not as bad as it might be. It is not as though we are left with nothing."

Chee's sister arose, sobs catching in her throat, and rushed past him out the doorway. Chee sat upright, a terrible fear possessing him. For a moment his mouth could make no sound. Then: "The Little One! Mother, where is she?"

His mother turned her stricken face to him. "Your wife's people came after her this morning. They heard yesterday of their daughter's death through the trader at Red Sands."

What happened to Chee's wife? What happened to his daughter?

Chee started to protest, but his mother shook her head slowly. "I didn't expect they would want the Little One either. But there is nothing you can do. She is a girl child and belongs to her mother's people; it is custom."

Frowning, Chee got to his feet, grinding his cigarette into the dirt floor. "Custom! When did my wife's parents begin thinking about custom? Why, the hogan where they live doesn't even face the east!"[6] He started toward the door.

---

4. **coughing sickness.** Tuberculosis, a disease affecting the lungs
5. **sanitarium.** Institution where tuberculosis patients go to recover their health
6. **"Why, the hogan . . . face the east."** According to Navajo custom, the door of a hogan faces the east.

"Perhaps I can overtake them. Perhaps they don't realize how much we want her here with us. I'll ask them to give my daughter back to me. Surely, they won't refuse."

His mother stopped him gently with her outstretched hand. "You couldn't overtake them now. They were in the trader's car. Eat and rest, and think more about this."

"Have you forgotten how things have always been between you and your wife's people?" his father said.

That night, Chee's thoughts were troubled—half-forgotten incidents became disturbingly vivid—but early the next morning he saddled the buckskin and set out for the settlement of Red Sands. Even though his father-in-law, Old Man Fat, might laugh, Chee knew that he must talk to him. There were some things to which Old Man Fat might listen.

Chee rode the first part of the fifteen miles to Red Sands expectantly. The sight of sandstone buttes[7] near Cottonwood Spring reddening in the morning sun brought a song almost to his lips. He twirled his reins in salute to the small boy herding sheep toward many-colored Butterfly Mountain, watched with pleasure the feathers of smoke rising against treedarkened western mesas[8] from the hogans sheltered there. But as he approached the familiar settlement sprawled in mushroom growth along the highway, he began to feel as though a scene from a bad dream was becoming real.

Several cars were parked around the trading store, which was built like two log hogans side by side, with red gas pumps in front and a sign across the tar-paper roofs: Red Sands Trading Post—Groceries Gasoline Cold Drinks Sandwiches Indian Curios. Back of the trading post an unpainted frame house and outbuildings

Where is Chee going?

squatted on the drab, treeless land. Chee and the Little One's mother had lived there when they stayed with his wife's people. That was according to custom—living with one's wife's people—but Chee had never been convinced that it was custom alone which prompted Old Man Fat and his wife to insist that their daughter bring her husband to live at the trading post.

Beside the post was a large hogan of logs, with brightly painted pseudo-Navajo designs on the roof—a hogan with smoke-smudged windows and a garish blue door which faced north to the highway. Old Man Fat had offered Chee a hogan like this one. The trader would build it if he and his wife would live there and Chee would work at his forge, making silver jewelry where tourists could watch him. But Chee had asked instead for a piece of land for a cornfield and help in building a hogan far back from the highway and a corral for the sheep he had brought to this marriage.

A cold wind blowing down from the mountains began to whistle about Chee's ears. It flapped the gaudy Navajo rugs which were hung in one long bright line to attract tourists. It swayed the sign *Navajo Weaver at Work* beside the loom where Old Man Fat's wife sat hunched in her striped blanket, patting the colored thread of a design into place with a wooden comb. Tourists stood watching the weaver. More tourists stood in a knot before the hogan where the sign said: *See Inside a Real Navajo Home 25¢.*

Then the knot seemed to unravel as a few people returned to their cars; some had cameras; and there against the blue door Chee saw

7. **buttes.** Isolated hills or mountains with steep or precipitous sides
8. **mesas.** Isolated relatively flat-topped natural elevations usually more extensive than buttes and less extensive than plateaus

words for everyday use

pseu • do (sü′ dō) *adj.*, being apparently rather than actually as stated; false; deceptive. *Gina's pseudo-intellectual attitude in class perplexed her friends, who knew her as less than serious.*

gar • ish (gar′ ish) *adj.*, offensively or distressingly bright; flashy. *Everyone commented that Mrs. Ross's garish dress was not appropriate for a funeral.*

"CHEE'S DAUGHTER" 813

1. He is going to the settlement of Red Sands to see his father-in-law, Old Man Fat.

INTERNET RESOURCES

Encourage students to browse the **Four Corners Post Card** at http://www.ausbcomp.com/redman/index.htm. This website offers viewers information about the history of Navajos—their religion, language, and even the history of weaving. Students can also read the Navajo creation story at this website.

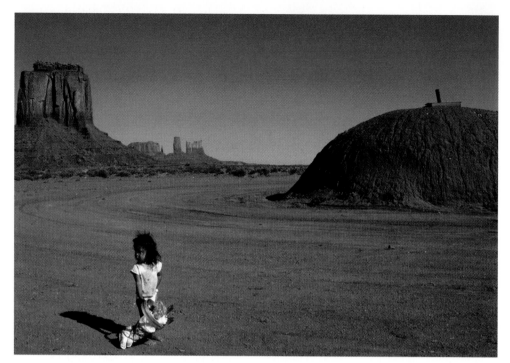

the Little One standing uncertainly. The wind was plucking at her new purple blouse and wide green skirt; it freed <u>truant</u> strands of soft dark hair from the <u>meager</u> queue[9] into which it had been tied with white yarn.

"Isn't she cunning!" one of the women tourists was saying as she turned away.

Chee's lips tightened as he began to look around for Old Man Fat. Finally he saw him passing among the tourists collecting coins.

Then the Little One saw Chee. The uncertainty left her face, and she darted through the crowd as her father swung down from his horse. Chee lifted her in his arms, hugging her tight. While he listened to her breathless chatter, he watched Old Man Fat bearing down on them, scowling.

As his father-in-law walked heavily across the graveled lot, Chee was reminded of a statement his mother sometimes made: "When you see a fat Navajo, you see one who hasn't worked for what he has."

Old Man Fat was fattest in the middle. There was <u>indolence</u> in his walk even though he seemed to hurry, indolence in his cheeks so plump they made his eyes squint, eyes now <u>smoldering</u> with anger.

Some of the tourists were getting into their cars and driving away. The old man said <u>belligerently</u> to Chee, "Why do you come here? To spoil our business? To drive people away?"

---

9. **queue.** Braid

words for everyday use	tru • ant (trü′ ənt) *adj.*, characteristic of someone who shirks duty. *The <u>truant</u> sentinel was found asleep at his post.* mea • ger (mē′ gər) *adj.*, deficient in quality or quantity. *The family subsisted on a <u>meager</u> diet of rice and vegetables.* in • do • lence (in′ də lənts) *n.*, inclination to laziness. *Mr. Kidman's <u>indolence</u> kept him from getting promoted.* smol • der • ing (smōl′ dər iŋ) *adj.*, showing suppressed anger, hate, or jealousy. *<u>Smoldering</u> with jealousy, Leslie's eyes stared at Kevin and Amy.* bel • lig • er • ent • ly (bə lij′ rənt lē) *adv.*, done in a manner inclined to or exhibiting assertiveness, hostility, or combativeness. *Three-year-old Matthew pushed Sally <u>belligerently</u> when she took his pail and shovel.*

"I came to talk with you," Chee answered, trying to keep his voice steady as he faced the old man.

"We have nothing to talk about," Old Man Fat <u>blustered</u> and did not offer to touch Chee's extended hand.

"It's about the Little One." Chee settled his daughter more comfortably against his hip as he weighed carefully all the words he had planned to say. "We are going to miss her very much. It wouldn't be so bad if we knew that *part* of each year she could be with us. That might help you too. You and your wife are no longer young people and you have no young ones here to depend upon." Chee chose his next words remembering the <u>thriftlessness</u> of his wife's parents, and their greed. "Perhaps we could share the care of this little one. Things are good with us. So much snow this year will make lots of grass for the sheep. We have good land for corn and melons."

Chee's words did not have the expected effect. Old Man Fat was enraged. "Farmers, all of you! Long-haired farmers! Do you think everyone must bend his back over the shorthandled hoe in order to have food to eat?" His tone changed as he began to brag a little. "We not only have all the things from cans at the trader's, but when the Pueblos come past here on their way to town, we buy their salty jerked[10] mutton, young corn for roasting, dried sweet peaches."

Chee's dark eyes surveyed the land along the highway as the old man continued to brag about being "progressive." *He* no longer was tied to the land. He and his wife made money easily and could *buy* all the things they wanted. Chee realized too late that he had stumbled into the old argument between himself and his wife's parents. They had never

What does Old Man Fat brag about?

understood his feeling about the land—that a man took care of his land and it in turn took care of him. Old Man Fat and his wife scoffed at him, called him a Pueblo farmer, all during that summer when he planted and weeded and harvested. Yet they ate the green corn in their mutton stews, and the chili paste from the fresh ripe chilis, and the tortillas from the cornmeal his wife ground. None of this working and sweating in the sun for Old Man Fat, who talked proudly of his easy way of living—collecting money from the trader who rented this strip of land beside the highway, collecting money from the tourists.

What does Chee believe about the land?

How does Old Man Fat earn his money?

Yet Chee had once won that argument. His wife had shared his belief in the integrity of the earth, that jobs and people might fail one, but the earth never would. After that first year she had turned from her own people and gone with Chee to Little Canyon.

Old Man Fat was reaching for the Little One. "Don't be coming here with plans for my daughter's daughter," he warned. "If you try to make trouble, I'll take the case to the government man in town."

The impulse was strong in Chee to turn and ride off while he still had the Little One in his arms. But he knew his time of victory would be short. His own family would uphold the old custom of children, especially girl children, belonging to the mother's people. He would have to give his daughter up if the case were brought before the headman of Little Canyon, and certainly he would have no better chance before a strange white man in town.

He handed the bewildered Little One to her grandfather who stood watching every move-

10. **jerked.** Preserved by being cut into strips and dried in the sun

"CHEE'S DAUGHTER" 815

ANSWERS TO GUIDED READING QUESTIONS

1. Old Man Fat brags about being "progressive" and no longer tied to the land. He and his wife make money easily and can buy the food that they need.
2. Chee believes that if a man took care of his land, it in turn took care of him.
3. Old Man Fat earns his money renting his strip of land beside the highway and collecting money from tourists.

ADDITIONAL QUESTIONS AND ACTIVITIES

Ask students why Chee doesn't rely on outside forces to get his daughter back.
Answer
If Chee went to the tribal council, the members would side with his wife's parents in keeping with Navajo custom. If he went to the "government man," he would have no better chance because that person would be a total stranger and might rule against him because of his poverty and lack of fluent English.

LITERARY TECHNIQUE

CONFLICT. A **conflict** is a struggle between two forces in a literary work. Ask students which two characters are in conflict. Is the conflict between them a new one or an old one? Explain.
Answers
Chee and Old Man Fat are in conflict over who should look after Chee's daughter. This disagreement revives a deep and long-standing "argument" between Chee and his wife's parents about whether the old Navajo way of life based on farming or a more modern way of life away from the land is better. Chee's wife shared his belief in that "jobs and people might fail one, but the earth never would."

1. Chee questions the land because he thinks it can't give him back his daughter.

LITERARY TECHNIQUE

INTERNAL CONFLICT. An **internal conflict** is a struggle that takes place within a character. Have students identify the internal conflict within Chee.
Answer
The internal conflict is between Chee's faith in the land, which has served him well in the past, and his doubt that the land can help him with his current problem. He thinks he may need another kind of wisdom than the land can offer.

ment suspiciously. Chee asked, "If I brought you a few things for the Little One, would that be making trouble? Some velvet for a blouse, or some of the jerky she likes so well…this summer's melon?"

Old Man Fat backed away from him. "Well," he hesitated, as some of the anger disappeared from his face and beads of greed shone in his eyes. "Well," he repeated. Then as the Little One began to squirm in his arms and cry, he said, "No! No! Stay away from here, you and all your family."

The sense of his failure deepened as Chee rode back to Little Canyon. But it was not until he sat with his family that evening in the hogan, while the familiar bustle of meal preparing went on about him, that he began to doubt the wisdom of the things he'd always believed. He smelled the coffee boiling and the oily fragrance of chili powder dusted into the bubbling pot of stew; he watched his mother turning round crusty fried bread in the small black skillet. All around him was plenty—a half of mutton hanging near the door, bright strings of chili drying, corn hanging by the braided husks, cloth bags of dried peaches. Yet in his heart was nothing.

He heard the familiar sounds of the sheep outside the hogan, the splash of water as his father filled the long drinking trough from the water barrel. When his father came in, Chee could not bring himself to tell a second time of the day's happenings. He watched his wiry, soft-spoken father while his mother told the story, saw his father's queue of graying hair quiver as he nodded his head with sympathetic exclamations.

Chee's doubting, acrid thoughts kept forming: Was it wisdom his father had passed on to him, or was his inheritance only the stubbornness of a long-haired Navajo resisting change? Take

care of the land and it will take care of you. True, the land had always given him food, but now food was not enough. Perhaps if he had gone to school, he would have learned a different kind of wisdom, something to help him now. A schoolboy might even be able to speak convincingly to this government man whom Old Man Fat threatened to call, instead of sitting here like a clod of earth itself—Pueblo farmer indeed. What had the land to give that would restore his daughter?

Why does Chee question the land?

In the days that followed, Chee herded sheep. He got up in the half-light, drank the hot coffee his mother had ready, then started the flock moving. It was necessary to drive the sheep a long way from the hogan to find good winter forage. Sometimes Chee met friends or relatives who were on their way to town or to the road camp where they hoped to get work; then there was friendly banter and an exchange of news. But most of the days seemed endless; he could not walk far enough or fast enough from his memories of the Little One or from his bitter thoughts. Sometimes it seemed his daughter trudged beside him, so real he could almost hear her footsteps—the muffled pad-pad of little feet in deerhide. In the glare of a snowbank he would see her vivid face, brown eyes sparkling. Mingling with the tinkle of sheep bells he heard her laughter.

When, weary of following the small sharp hoof marks that crossed and recrossed in the snow, he sat down in the shelter of a rock, it was only to be reminded that in his thoughts he had forsaken his brotherhood with the earth and sun and growing things. If he remembered times when he had flung himself against the earth to rest, to lie there in the sun until he could no longer feel where he left off and the earth

words for everyday use	for • age (fōr′ ij) *n.*, food for animals that graze. *The farmer depended on alfalfa for forage.* ban • ter (ban′ tər) *n.*, good-natured and usually witty and animated joking. *From their teacher's banter before class, students could tell he was in a good mood.*

began, it was to remember also that now he sat like an alien against the same earth; the belonging together was gone. The earth was one thing and he was another.

It was during the days when he herded sheep that Chee decided he must leave Little Canyon. Perhaps he would take a job silversmithing for one of the traders in town. Perhaps, even though he spoke little English, he could get a job at the road camp with his cousins; he would ask them about it.

Springtime transformed the mesas. The peach trees in the canyon were shedding fragrance and pink blossoms on the gentled wind. The sheep no longer foraged for the yellow seeds of chamiso[11] but ranged near the hogan with the long-legged new lambs, eating tender young grass.

Chee was near the hogan on the day his cousins rode up with the message for which he waited. He had been watching with mixed emotions while his father and his sister's husband cleared the fields beside the stream.

"The boss at the camp says he needs an extra hand, but he wants to know if you'll be willing to go with the camp when they move it to the other side of the town?" The tall cousin shifted his weight in the saddle.

The other cousin took up the explanation. "The work near here will last only until the new cutoff beyond Red Sands is finished. After that, the work will be too far away for you to get back here often."

That was what Chee had wanted—to get away from Little Canyon—yet he found himself not so interested in the job beyond town as in this new cutoff which was almost finished. He pulled a blade of grass, split it

What interests Chee more than talk of a job?

thoughtfully down the center, as he asked questions of his cousins. Finally he said: "I need to think more about this. If I decide on this job, I'll ride over."

Before his cousins were out of sight down the canyon, Chee was walking toward the fields, a bold plan shaping in his mind. As the plan began to flourish, wild and hardy as young tumbleweed, Chee added his own voice softly to the song his father was singing: "…In the middle of the wide field…Yellow Corn Boy…I wish to put in."

Chee walked slowly around the field, the rich red earth yielding to his footsteps. His plan depended upon this land and upon the things he remembered most about his wife's people.

Through planting time Chee worked <u>zealously</u> and tirelessly. He spoke little of the large new field he was planting, because he felt so strongly that just now this was something between himself and the land. The first days he was ever stooping, piercing the ground with the pointed stick, placing the corn kernels there, walking around the field and through it, singing, "…His track leads into the ground… Yellow Corn Boy…his track leads into the ground." After that, each day Chee walked through his field watching for the tips of green to break through; first a few spikes in the center and then more and more, until the corn in all parts of the field was above ground. Surely, Chee thought, if he sang the proper songs, if he cared for this land faithfully, it would not forsake him now, even though through the lonely days of winter he had betrayed the goodness of the earth in his thoughts.

What does Chee believe about the land?

---

11. **chamiso.** Shrub that forms dense thickets

---

words for everyday use

zeal • ous • ly (zē′ ləs lē) *adv.*, fervently; ardently. *Students worked <u>zealously</u> on the math problems because the exercise was a contest.*

ANSWERS TO GUIDED READING QUESTIONS

1. The new cutoff that was almost finished interests Chee more than talk of a job.
2. Chee believes that if he sings the proper songs and cares for the land faithfully, it will not forsake him now.

ADDITIONAL QUESTIONS AND ACTIVITIES

Chee's cousins both work in road construction. Why might these young men have chosen this type of work rather than farming? Is it realistic to expect most Navajo to live as Chee does? Why, or why not? Ask students to write a paragraph in which they answer these questions.

1. His whole family waits with him because he told them of his plan for the crops.

Through the summer Chee worked long days, the sun hot upon his back, pulling weeds from around young corn plants; he planted squash and pumpkin; he terraced a small piece of land near his mother's hogan and planted carrots and onions and the moisture-loving chili. He was increasingly restless. Finally he told his family what he hoped the harvest from this land would bring him. Then the whole family waited with him, watching the corn: the slender graceful plants that waved green arms and bent to embrace each other as young winds wandered through the field, the maturing plants <u>flaunting</u> their pollen-laden tassels in the sun, the tall and sturdy parent corn with new-formed ears and a <u>froth</u> of purple, red, and yellow corn beards against the dusty emerald of broad leaves.

Who waits with Chee? Why?

Summer was almost over when Chee slung the bulging packs across two pack ponies. His mother helped him tie the heavy rolled pack behind the saddle of the buckskin. Chee knotted the new yellow kerchief about his neck a little tighter, gave the broad black hat brim an extra tug, but these were only gestures of assurance and he knew it. The land had not failed him. That part was done. But this he was riding into? Who could tell?

When Chee arrived at Red Sands, it was as he had expected to find it—no cars on the highway. His cousins had told him that even the Pueblo farmers were using the new cutoff to town. The barren gravel around the Red Sands Trading Post was deserted. A sign banged against the dismantled gas pumps: *Closed until further notice.*

Old Man Fat came from the crude summer shelter built beside the log hogan from a few branches of scrub cedar and the sides of wooden crates. He seemed almost friendly when he saw Chee.

"Get down, my son," he said, eyeing the bulging packs. There was no bluster in his voice today, and his face sagged, looking somewhat saddened, perhaps because his cheeks were no longer quite full enough to push his eyes upward at the corners. "You are going on a journey?"

Chee shook his head. "Our fields gave us so much this year, I thought to sell or trade this to the trader. I didn't know he was no longer here."

Old Man Fat sighed, his voice dropping to an injured tone. "He says he and his wife are going to rest this winter; then after that he'll build a place up on the new highway."

Chee moved as though to be traveling on, then jerked his head toward the pack ponies. "Anything you need?"

"I'll ask my wife," Old Man Fat said as he led the way to the shelter. "Maybe she has a little money. Things have not been too good with us since the trader closed. Only a few tourists come this way." He shrugged his shoulders. "And with the trader gone—no credit."

Chee was not deceived by his father-in-law's unexpected confidences. He recognized them as a hopeful bid for sympathy and, if possible, something for nothing. Chee made no answer. He was thinking that so far he had been right about his wife's parents: their thriftlessness had left them with no resources to last until Old Man Fat found another easy way of making a living.

Old Man Fat's wife was in the shelter working at her loom. She turned rather wearily when her husband asked with noticeable <u>deference</u> if she would give him money to buy supplies. Chee <u>surmised</u> that the only income here was from his mother-in-law's weaving.

---

words for everyday use

flaunt (flänt') *vt.*, display to public notice. *<u>Flaunting</u> the school colors, the mascot paraded around the field during halftime.*

froth (fräth) *n.*, something light and airy like bubbles on a liquid. *A <u>froth</u> of milk left a mustache on Joy's lip.*

def • er • ence (de' fə rəns) *n.*, respect and esteem due another. *Because of the <u>deference</u> Chris showed her classmates, she was elected to Student Council.*

sur • mise (sər mīz') *vi.*, imagine or infer on slight grounds. *From the number of students absent, the teacher <u>surmised</u> the flu was going around again.*

She peered around the corner of the shelter at the laden ponies, and then she looked at Chee. "What do you have there, my son?"

Chee smiled to himself as he turned to pull the pack from one of the ponies, dragged it to the shelter where he untied the ropes. Pumpkins and hard-shelled squash tumbled out, and the ears of corn—pale yellow husks fitting firmly over plump ripe kernels, blue corn, red corn, yellow corn, many-colored corn, ears and ears of it—tumbled into every corner of the shelter.

"Yooooh," Old Man Fat's wife exclaimed as she took some of the ears in her hands. Then she glanced up at her son-in-law. "But we have no money for all this. We have sold almost everything we own—even the brass bed that stood in the hogan."

Old Man Fat's brass bed. Chee concealed his amusement as he started back for another pack. That must have been a hard parting. Then he stopped, for, coming from the cool darkness of the hogan was the Little One, rubbing her eyes as though she had been asleep. She stood for a moment in the doorway, and Chee saw that she was dirty, barefoot, her hair uncombed, her little blouse <u>shorn</u> of all its silver buttons. Then she ran toward Chee, her arms outstretched. Heedless of Old Man Fat and his wife, her father caught her in his arms, her hair falling in a dark cloud across his face, the sweetness of her laughter warm against his shoulder.

It was the haste within him to get this slow waiting game played through to the finish that made Chee speak unwisely. It was the desire to swing her before him in the saddle and ride fast to Little Canyon that prompted his words. "The money doesn't matter. You still have something…"

What state does Chee find his daughter in?

Chee knew immediately that he had overspoken. The old woman looked from him to the corn spread before her. Unfriendliness began to harden in his father-in-law's face. All the old arguments between himself and his wife's people came pushing and crowding in between them now.

Old Man Fat began kicking the ears of corn back onto the canvas as he eyed Chee angrily. "And you rode all the way over here thinking that for a little food we would give up our daughter's daughter?"

Chee did not wait for the old man to reach for the Little One. He walked dazedly to the shelter, rubbing his cheek against her soft dark hair, and put her gently into her grandmother's lap. Then he turned back to the horses. He had failed. By his own haste he had failed. He swung into the saddle, his hand touching the roll behind it. Should he ride on into town?

Then he dismounted, scarcely glancing at Old Man Fat, who stood uncertainly at the corner of the shelter, listening to his wife. "Give me a hand with this other pack of corn, Grandfather," Chee said, carefully keeping the small bit of hope from his voice.

Puzzled, but willing, Old Man Fat helped carry the other pack to the shelter, opening it to find more corn as well as carrots and round, pale yellow onions. Chee went back for the roll behind the buckskin's saddle and carried it to the entrance of the shelter, where he cut the ropes and gave the canvas a nudge with his toe. Tins of coffee rolled out, small plump cloth bags; jerked meat from several butcherings spilled from a flour sack; and bright red chilis splashed like flames against the dust.

"I will leave all this anyhow," Chee told them. "I would not want my daughter nor even you old people to go hungry."

"CHEE'S DAUGHTER" 819

ANSWER TO GUIDED READING QUESTION

1. Chee finds his daughter dirty, barefoot, her hair uncombed, and her little blouse shorn of all its silver buttons.

ANSWER TO GUIDED READING QUESTION

1. Old Man Fat and his wife decide that Chee can have his daughter back because they cannot spare the food to feed her.

SELECTION CHECK TEST 4.10.7 WITH ANSWERS

Checking Your Reading

1. Where does Chee live? **He lives in Little Canyon in the American Southwest. His home is a hogan.**
2. What does he do for a living? **Chee farms for a living. He also forges silver.**
3. What happens to Chee's wife? **She dies of tuberculosis.**
4. What happens to Chee's daughter as a result of this event? Why? **Chee's daughter is taken to live with his late wife's parents. It is Navajo tradition that a child be with her mother's parents after the mother's death.**
5. How are Chee and his family different from his wife's family? **Chee and his family are farmers and hard workers. They closely observe Navajo tradition in their daily lives. His wife's family are traders and strive to make easy money without working hard. They do not observe Navajo tradition in their daily lives.**

Vocabulary in Context
Fill in each blank below with the most appropriate word from the following Words for Everyday Use.

integrity garish meager indolence
bluster thriftlessness flaunt

1. The **meager** portions were not enough to sustain the health of the child.
2. The bejeweled woman **flaunted** her wealth.
3. The boy's **indolence** infuriated both his parents and his teachers.
4. Her **garish** outfit brought disapproving glances from her peers.
5. When voting for a politician, you should choose the one with the most **integrity**.

Literary Tools

1. What is irony of situation? **Irony of situation is when an event occurs that violates the expectation of the characters, the reader, or the audience.**

Old Man Fat picked up a shiny tin of coffee, then put it down. With trembling hands he began to untie one of the cloth bags—dried sweet peaches.

The Little One had wriggled from her grandmother's lap, unheeded, and was on her knees, digging her hands into the jerked meat.

"There is almost enough food here to last all winter." Old Man Fat's wife sought the eyes of her husband.

Chee said, "I meant it to be enough. But that was when I thought you might send the Little One back with me." He looked down at his daughter noisily sucking jerky. Her mouth, both fists, were full of it. "I am sorry that you feel you cannot bear to part with her."

Old Man Fat's wife brushed a straggly wisp of gray hair from her forehead as she turned to look at the Little One. Old Man Fat was looking too. And it was not a thing to see. For in that moment the Little One ceased to be their daughter's daughter and became just another mouth to feed.

"And why not?" the old woman asked wearily.

What do Old Man Fat and his wife decide? Why?

Chee was settled in the saddle, the barefooted Little One before him. He urged the buckskin faster, and his daughter clutched his shirtfront. The purpling mesas flung back the echo: "…My corn embrace each other. In the middle of the wide field…Yellow Corn Boy embrace each other." ∎

Respond *to the* SELECTION

If you were Chee, what would you state you have learned from your experience of getting your daughter back?

ABOUT THE RELATED READING ➤

The speaker of **"Freeway 280"** is caught between two cultures, that of Mexican Americans and that of mainstream white Americans. In her quest for self-identity, the speaker visits her old neighborhood and is overwhelmed by nostalgia for how things used to be. **Lorna Dee Cervantes,** is a Mexican-American poet who published her first collection of poems, *Emplumada,* in 1981. She has also established her own small press and poetry magazine, *Mango.* Concerned for her cultural heritage, Cervantes also has a keen awareness of the struggles faced by women—especially Hispanic women—in contemporary American society.

SELECTION CHECK TEST 4.10.7 WITH ANSWERS (CONT.)

2. What is the setting of "Chee's Daughter"? **"Chee's Daughter" is set in the American Southwest in modern times.**
3. What is tone? **Tone is the emotional attitude implied by the literary work toward the reader or toward the subject.**

RESPOND TO THE SELECTION

Students may say that Chee learned that determination and thoughtful planning are rewarded.

Freeway 280

Lorna Dee Cervantes

Las casitas[1] near the gray cannery,
nestled amid wild abrazos[2] of climbing roses
and man-high red geraniums
are gone now. The freeway conceals it
all beneath a raised scar.

But under the fake windsounds of the open lanes,
in the abandoned lots below, new grasses sprout,
wild mustard remembers, old gardens
come back stronger than they were,
trees have been left standing in their yards.
Albaricoqueros, cerezos, nogales . . .[3]
Viejitas[4] come here with paper bags to gather greens.
Espinaca, verdolagas, yerbabuena . . .[5]

I scramble over the wire fence
that would have kept me out.
Once, I wanted out, wanted the rigid lanes
to take me to a place without sun,
without the smell of tomatoes burning
on swing shift[6] in the greasy summer air.

Maybe it's here
en los campos extraños de esta ciudad[7]
where I'll find it, that part of me
mown under
like a corpse
or a loose seed.

■

---

1. **Las casitas.** Little houses (Spanish)
2. **abrazos.** Embraces
3. **Albaricoqueros, cerezos, nogales.** Apricot, cherry, and walnut trees
4. **Viejitas.** Old women
5. **Espinaca, verdolagas, yerbabuena.** Spinach, purslane (an edible weed), and mint
6. **swing shift.** Work shift between the day and night shifts, for example, 4 PM to midnight
7. **en los campos extraños de esta ciudad.** In the strange fields of this city

"CHEE'S DAUGHTER" **821**

RECALL

1a. Chee and his family live off the land in the traditional Navajo way. Old Man Fat and his wife live at the trading post near a highway, rent their land to a trader, collect money from tourists, and buy all their food.

2a. Chee is mourning the death of his wife and the loss of his daughter whom his in-laws have taken, according to Navajo custom.

3a. The new cutoff means Old Man Fat and his wife will no longer have enough income from tourists, who will no longer be passing their way.

INTERPRET

1b. *Responses will vary.* Old Man Fat cheapens his Navajo heritage and treats it as a salable commodity, even using his granddaughter as a tourist attraction. Chee follows the farming and herding ways of his ancestors; he deeply respects and embraces his Navajo heritage.

2b. At first Chee believes in the integrity of the land, but he begins to doubt his beliefs because it seems that the land has nothing to give that could restore his daughter. However, once he has the Little One with him again, Chee sings the traditional Navajo corn song, showing that his belief in the promise of the land remains strong.

3b. Old Man Fat is characterized by greed and indolence. When Chee offers him a winter's food supply, he decides he would rather give up his granddaughter than stretch the bounty to feed three mouths instead of two.

ANALYZE

4a. Chee lives in a hogan that faces east in a canyon. He sings to his plants to make them grow, especially the corn song. He herds sheep, like generations of Navajo before him.

SYNTHESIZE

4b. The Navajo revere the land, seeing spiritual qualities in natural things. Chee believes that "a man took care of his land and it in turn took care of him." At the end of the story, Chee wins back his daughter as a direct result of his faith in the land.

EVALUATE

5a. *Responses will vary.* Chee is being manipulative. Giving his produce in exchange for his daughter is part of a well-thought-out plan he developed when he heard about the new cutoff. Knowing that Old

---

Investigate, Inquire, and Imagine

Recall: GATHERING FACTS

1a. How do Chee and his family live? How do Old Man Fat and his wife live?

2a. What two events is Chee mourning?

3a. What does the new cutoff mean to Chee?

Interpret: FINDING MEANING

1b. What do the differences in the two men's ways of life tell you about their attitudes toward their Navajo heritage?

2b. What transformation occurs in Chee's feelings about the land?

3b. Does Old Man Fat act true to character at the end of the story?

Analyze: TAKING THINGS APART

4a. Analyze in what manner Chee lives according to Navajo tradition.

Synthesize: BRINGING THINGS TOGETHER

4b. What is the traditional Navajo attitude toward the land? How does the story's conclusion reinforce this attitude?

Evaluate: MAKING JUDGMENTS

5a. Is Chee being generous or manipulative when he gives his produce to Old Man Fat and his wife?

Extend: CONNECTING IDEAS

5b. Read the Related Reading, "Freeway 280." What has the speaker lost? How is her loss comparable to Old Man Fat's loss?

Understanding Literature

IRONY AND IRONY OF SITUATION. Review the definitions for **irony** and **irony of situation** in the Handbook of Literary Terms. What examples of irony of situation did you find in the story?

SETTING AND TONE. Review the definitions for **setting** and **tone** in the Handbook of Literary Terms. In the descriptions of Chee's and Old Man Fat's property, what tone do the authors use? What specific words establish that tone? Through whose point of view does the reader see Old Man Fat's property? How do descriptions of the setting help to establish the conflict between Chee and Old Man Fat?

ANSWERS TO INVESTIGATE, INQUIRE, AND IMAGINE (CONT.)

Man Fat is greedy and lazy, he expects him to be more interested in obtaining the food he offers than in keeping the Little One.

EXTEND

5b. The speaker of the poem has lost the houses in the neighborhood where she lived to the construction of a freeway. She has also lost her emotional connection to the place, which she had once wanted to escape. Old Man Fat has also lost touch with his roots, but he does not feel the loss of them, only the loss of his money, food, and possessions.

Writer's Journal

1. Imagine you are Chee's daughter at age fifteen. Write a **journal entry** in which you describe what it was like to live with your mother's parents when you were three. What did you like about your new life? What did you miss from your old life? How did you feel about having your life uprooted?

2. Imagine you are Chee in winter when he loses his faith in the land. Describe a **daydream** in which your life is as you want it to be. What are you doing? Who is present? What happens?

3. In this story, we are given descriptions of two contrasting settings: the trading post and Chee's home in Little Canyon. Write two **paragraphs** describing two contrasting settings that create different emotions in you, such as calmness and excitement. Use specific details that will help your readers visualize the two settings. Try to communicate your feelings about the two different places.

Integrating the Language Arts

Language, Grammar, and Style

ADDING MODIFIERS. Read the Language Arts Survey 3.39, "Adding Colorful Language to Sentences." Then rewrite each of the following sentences, adding an appropriate adjective or adverb. Some sentences may require more than one modifier.

1. Chee's hat was not at the proper angle for so young a Navajo.
2. The sky widened where the canyon walls were pushed back to make a wide place.
3. Back of the trading post a frame house and outbuildings squatted on the land.
4. Chee lifted the Little One in his arms, hugging her.
5. Through planting time Chee worked to actualize his plan.

Applied English & Study and Research

TRAVEL WRITING. Imagine that you work for a company that makes travel books. A new project is to create a travel book about the United States. Your job is to write a description of an area in the Southwest where the Navajo live, either northeastern Arizona or northwestern New Mexico. Describe what the terrain is like and what plants and animals your readers will see when they go there. You may want to do some additional research on the Southwest before you begin writing.

Study and Research & Collaborative Learning

RESEARCHING NAVAJO CULTURE. Select a topic such as Navajo customs, way of life, arts, or beliefs for each member of your group. Research your topic and depict what you have learned on a poster board. Report on what you have learned to your group, using your poster board as an organizational tool for your presentation. Then give a group presentation to the class.

ANSWERS TO INTEGRATING THE LANGUAGE ARTS (CONT.)

- **ORGANIZATION/COHERENCE.** The information is arranged in a clear and sensible order. Paragraphs have clear topic sentences.
- **LANGUAGE/STYLE.** The writer uses vivid and precise nouns, verbs, and modifiers.
- **CONVENTIONS.** The writing avoids errors in spelling, grammar, usage, mechanics, and manuscript form.

Study and Research & Collaborative Learning
Encourage students to use online resources as well as printed materials in their research. You may wish to have them review the Language Arts Survey 5.30, "Evaluating Information and Media Sources," before they begin. The following websites may be especially useful:
Navajo Nation Home Page at http://www.navajo.org
Navajo Nation at http://crystal.nec.cc.nm.us/~vino/NN

ANSWERS TO UNDERSTANDING LITERATURE

IRONY AND IRONY OF SITUATION. Irony of situation occurs when Old Man Fat and his wife take the Little One to live with them after their daughter dies, in keeping with the Navajo custom. This is ironic because Chee does not expect them to think about custom, based on the fact that they have rejected the traditional Navajo way of life. Irony of situation also occurs when Chee works to get his daughter back. This is ironic because the reader might expect Chee, who embraces traditional Navajo ways, to accept the loss of his daughter.

SETTING AND TONE. The authors use a respectful tone when describing Chee's property with words such as *wholeness, oneness, secure, nestled,* and *interlocked.* They use a critical tone when describing Old Man Fat's property with words such as *garish, pseudo, drab, treeless,* and *smoke-smudged.* The reader sees Old Man Fat's property through Chee's disapproving eyes. Descriptions of Chee's property emphasize his spiritual relationship to the land and the old Navajo life of farming. Descriptions of Old Man Fat's property emphasize his acceptance of questionable materialistic values. These two ways of life come into conflict as the two characters argue about where and with whom the Little One should live.

ANSWERS TO INTEGRATING THE LANGUAGE ARTS

Language, Grammar, and Style
Responses will vary.
1. Chee's hat was not at the proper <u>rakish</u> angle for so young a Navajo.
2. <u>Abruptly</u> the sky widened where the canyon walls were pushed back to make a wide place.
3. Back of the trading post an unpainted frame house and outbuildings squatted on the <u>drab, treeless</u> land.
4. Chee lifted the Little One in his arms, hugging her <u>tightly</u>.
5. Through planting time Chee worked <u>zealously</u> and <u>tirelessly</u> to actualize his plan.

Applied English & Study and Research
Assign a score from 1 to 25 for each grading criterion below. (For more detailed evaluation, see the evaluation forms for writing, revising, and proofreading in the Assessment Resource book.)

- **CONTENT/UNITY.** The travel writing describes the terrain, plants, and animals of northeastern Arizona or northwestern New Mexico.

Literary TOOLS

AIM. A writer's **aim** is his or her purpose, or goal. People may write with the following aims: to inform (expository/informational writing); to entertain, enrich, enlighten, and/or use an artistic medium, such as fiction or poetry, to share a perspective (imaginative writing); to make a point by sharing a story about an event (narrative writing); to reflect (personal/expressive writing); to persuade readers or listeners to respond in some way, such as to agree with a position, change a view on an issue, reach an agreement, or perform an action (persuasive/argumentative writing). As you read, try to assess the author's aim(s) in writing this personal essay.

STYLE. Style is the manner in which something is said or written. A writer's style depends upon many things, including diction, or the words the writer chooses, and the way her or she structures sentences. Look for evidence in this selection that would help you determine the writer's style.

Graphic Organizer

Make a cluster chart listing examples that you believe to be representative of the author's diction.

psychocultural suicide

Diction

824 UNIT TEN

"The Road from Ballygunge"
by Bharati Mukherjee

Reader's resource

In **"The Road from Ballygunge,"** Mukherjee explores the meaning of cultural identity in India and the United States. The essay is taken from the book *Half and Half: Writers on Growing Up Biracial and Bicultural* (1998).

HISTORY CONNECTION. The British Raj ruled India from 1858 to 1947. After World War II, England lost its imperial power in the world when many of its former colonies became independent. As Prime Minister, Clement Attlee announced his intention to grant independence to India. In March 1946, negotiations for the transfer of power began between the Cabinet Mission of England and Indian leaders. On the stroke of midnight on August 14, 1947, India became independent. Pandit Jawaharial Nehru became the first prime minister, and Dr. Rajendra Prasad became the first president of the country. On January 26, 1950, India became democratic and is the largest democracy in the world today.

About the AUTHOR

Bharati Mukherjee (1940–) grew up in a wealthy traditional Indian family in Calcutta. She learned English at a private girls' school run by Irish nuns. It wasn't until she attended the University of Iowa Writers' Workshop that she began to write professionally. Since her graduation, she has written several novels and collections of short stories, including *The Middleman and Other Stories* (1988), which won the National Book Critics' Circle Award for best fiction. Mukherjee has lived as a colonial in India, then as a post-colonial Indian in Canada, and finally as an immigrant and eventual citizen in the United States. She now tries to fuse her several lives together by writing "new immigrant" literature. Mukherjee is currently a professor of English at the University of California at Berkeley.

Reader's Journal

What difficulties have you experienced when moving?

ADDITIONAL RESOURCES

UNIT 10 RESOURCE BOOK
- Selection Worksheet 10.5
- Selection Check Test 4.10.9
- Selection Test 4.10.10
- Language, Grammar, and Style Resource 3.62
- Speaking and Listening Resource 4.21
- Study and Research 5.30

VOCABULARY FROM THE SELECTION

benevolently	nostalgia
biculturalism	parochial
colonial	patriarchy
deplore	perimeter
despotic	periphery
euphoria	resilient
expatriate	sovereign
integrity	vigorous

GRAPHIC ORGANIZER

Students might include some of the following words and phrases in their cluster charts: psychic integrity, peripheries, benevolently despotic, colonial context, backlot-constructed "America," and gritty aggravations of every day

READER'S JOURNAL

Students who have never moved might speculate about what it would be like if they were uprooted from their home.

GOALS/OBJECTIVES

Studying this lesson will enable students to
- appreciate how a bicultural upbringing could affect one's outlook as an immigrant
- identify Bharati Mukherjee as a writer of "new immigrant" literature
- define *aim* and *style* and recognize the use of these techniques in the selection
- identify perfect tense verbs in sentences
- research an aspect of Indian culture or recent Indian history

The Road from Ballygunge

Bharati Mukherjee

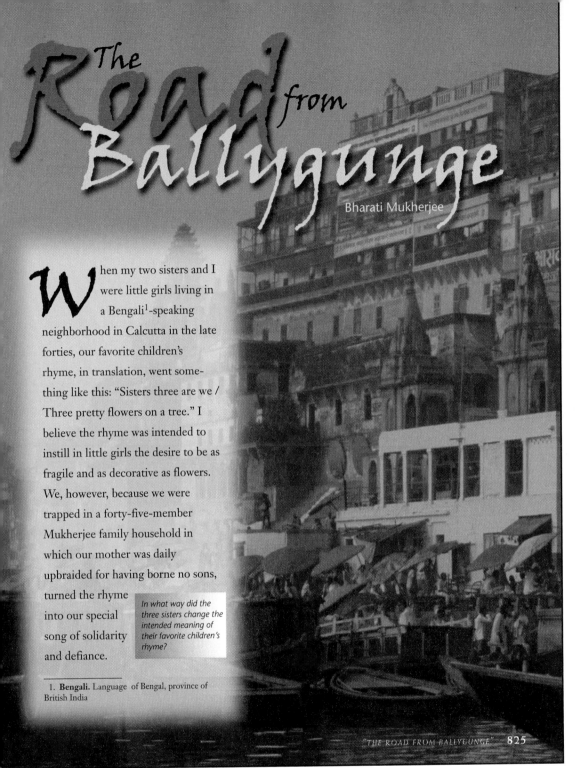

When my two sisters and I were little girls living in a Bengali[1]-speaking neighborhood in Calcutta in the late forties, our favorite children's rhyme, in translation, went something like this: "Sisters three are we / Three pretty flowers on a tree." I believe the rhyme was intended to instill in little girls the desire to be as fragile and as decorative as flowers. We, however, because we were trapped in a forty-five-member Mukherjee family household in which our mother was daily upbraided for having borne no sons, turned the rhyme into our special song of solidarity and defiance.

> In what way did the three sisters change the intended meaning of their favorite children's rhyme?

---

1. **Bengali.** Language of Bengal, province of British India

"THE ROAD FROM BALLYGUNGE" 825

ANSWER TO GUIDED READING QUESTION

1. They changed the intended meaning, "to instill in little girls the desire to be as fragile and decorative as flowers," into a song of "solidarity and defiance."

INDIVIDUAL LEARNING STRATEGIES

MOTIVATION
Encourage students to read additional essays from the anthology *Half and Half: Writers on Growing Up Biracial and Bicultural.* In small groups, have students compare the experiences and points of view in the essays they have read. Encourage biracial and bicultural students to comment on similarities and differences between their own lives and those of the writers in the collection.

READING PROFICIENCY
While reading the selection, have students make a chart comparing the attitudes of the narrator and her sister Mira toward taking up residence in the United States.

ENGLISH LANGUAGE LEARNING
Invite students who are immigrants to the United States to describe their feelings about their new country. Students might also describe the experiences and attitudes of friends or family members who are immigrants.

SPECIAL NEEDS
Before students read, put the selection into historical context for them. Tell students that the narrator and main character in the story comes from a well-to-do family living in an attractive neighborhood in Calcutta, a large city in India, and eventually settles in the United States.

ENRICHMENT
The national debate over illegal immigration has also raised questions about U.S. policy on legal immigration. Ask students to find and read several articles about recent national or state legislation that has affected, or could affect, legal immigrants. Have them summarize what is at stake and present arguments made by those who want to increase and those who want to decrease legal immigration.

1. The Raj arrested boys for reciting
banned nationalist poems and
raided clubhouses for homemade
bombs.

ADDITIONAL QUESTIONS
AND ACTIVITIES

Mukherjee uses an advanced vocabulary that students may find challenging. Give students a list of additional vocabulary words and definitions that includes the following:
homogeneously—uniformly
intuit—sense or grasp without using
reasoning
pharmaceutical—relating to medical
drugs
mentality—way of thinking
eccentric—strange
enunciate—pronounce words very
clearly
patronize—look down on

Pose questions in which you use the
vocabulary word, and ask students
to answer using the word, as in this
example:
You: Do you think wearing a
saucepan as a hat is *eccentric?*
Student: Yes, I think wearing a
saucepan as a hat is *eccentric.*

Before the fifteenth of August, when India
became a <u>sovereign</u> nation, our block of Rash
Behari Avenue constituted our entire world.
Rash Behari Avenue is a wide, boulevarded
artery in the comfortably middle-class neighborhood of Ballygunge, which includes the
Dhakuria Lakes for boating and grassy stretches
for strolling. Our block of one-, two-, and
three-story stucco houses, many with storefronts, was self-sufficient. In addition to "variety" shops where we could buy everything from
candies to smelling salts,[2] our block accommo-
dated a homeopath's[3] and a doctor's storefront
clinics, a photographer's studio, and a tea shop.
The freshwater fish we ate twice a day came
from nearby Gariahat Market, famous in the
city for selling the freshest fish and vegetables.
Our male cousins played <u>vigorous</u> boys' games
in the muddy furrows of wartime trenches in
the small park three houses down, while our girl
cousins took singing or sitar[4]-playing lessons at
home. As the sun went down every evening, my
cymbals-clanking sisters and I followed our widowed paternal grandmother as she, a stern
champion of Hindu tradition, lit the cotton
wicks of a multiheaded, cobra-shaped brass oil
lamp and with the holy glow of lamplight
chased ghosts out of every room.

Our block of Ballygunge was so homogeneously Hindu and Bengali-speaking that as a
very small child I never saw any foreigner other
than an Afghan[5] peddler who came by once a
winter with baskets of dried fruits and nuts. All
the same, the Raj[6] assaulted the innocent self-
centeredness of my <u>parochial</u> childhood with its
sloganeering: "British is Best"; "Britannica
Rules." In that colonial context, I intuited that
<u>biculturalism</u> was a fixed contest between two
cultures of opposing values:
ours and *theirs.* Even in
Ballygunge, the Raj cast a
bullying shadow. *They*
arrested our neighborhood boys for reciting
banned nationalist poems; in the trench-scarred
park where members of a youth club worked
out, *they* raided the clubhouse for homemade
bombs. *We* avenged ourselves through films and
novels in which the villain was a ruddy-faced,
pith-helmeted, women-molesting, sadistic
English planter of indigo or jute.[7] Sometimes
the contest touched me directly. In the kindergarten school run by Bengali-speaking
Protestant missionaries that I, the middle sister,
briefly attended, I saw Jack and Jill tumbling
down the hill in an illustrated book of British
nursery rhymes, and though Mira, my older sister, and I were always dressed in pretty, just-
sewn frocks my mother kept turning out on her
brand-new Singer sewing machine, I couldn't
help envying just a little bit Jill's perky pinafore
outfit made of cloth not available in fabric stalls
in Ballygunge.

That envy for Jill's pinafore, I now realize, was
exactly the emotion that the colonizer aims for.
<u>Colonial</u> insistence on race-based biculturalism
reinforces ghetto identity and ghetto mentality.
Any erasure of the ghetto's boundaries becomes

*In what ways did the
Raj "cast a bullying
shadow"?*

---

2. **smelling salts.** Scented aromatic salts used to restore someone who has fainted
3. **homeopath.** One who administers minute doses of a remedy
that would in a healthy person produce symptoms similar to those
of the disease
4. **sitar.** Long-necked Indian lute with varying number of strings
5. **Afghan.** Native or resident of Afghanistan, a country located
northwest of Pakistan
6. **Raj.** British rule in India from 1858 to 1947
7. **indigo or jute.** Common East Indian plants

**words
for
everyday
use**

sov • er • eign (sā′ və rən) *adj.,* enjoying autonomy; independent. *In 1963, Kenya became a <u>sovereign</u> country.*
vig • or • ous (vi′ g(ə) rəs) *adj.,* full of physical or mental strength or active force. *Our social studies teacher encourages <u>vigorous</u> debates in class.*
pa • ro • chi • al (pə rō′ kē əl) *adj.,* limited in range or scope. *My grandfather's <u>parochial</u> background did not prepare him well for the rigors of college.*
bi • cul • tur • al • ism (bī kəlch′ rəl izm) *n.,* two distinct cultures existing in one nation. *<u>Biculturalism</u> is prevalent in Canada with the existence of both French and Anglo cultures.*
co • lo • nial (kə lō′ nē əl) *adj.,* characteristic of one power having control over a dependent area or people. *England's <u>colonial</u> power was so extensive that it was said the sun never sat on the British Empire.*

an erasure of personal identity, any border-crossing amounts to betrayal.

Before Independence, like most children on our block, Mira and I had never ventured into the necklace of ghettos beyond. We knew, of course, that Bengalis with Westernized attitudes and close connections to the colonial government lived in neighborhoods with English names, such as Sunny Park, Rainy Park, and Mandeville Gardens; Europeans corralled themselves in Chowringhee, a "White Town" of garden-ringed bungalows, spacious apartment buildings, swept-clean roads, and colonial monuments; Muslims clustered in beef-eating neighborhoods of twisted alleys full of *burqua*[8]-wearing women and henna[9]-bearded men; and Anglo-Indians, a small Eurasian community of Empire loyalists who claimed Britain (which they were not ever likely to make their pilgrimage to) as their "homeland," hovered in the shabby peripheries of Chowringhee, self-segregating themselves from us Hindus and Muslims.

How would you describe the relationship among the various ethnic groups before India gained independence?

If Mira and I had not come of age in the post-Independence Calcutta of the fifties when the euphoria of nation building threw reactionary women like my paternal grandmother temporarily off balance, we would have been married off as teenagers, as had been our mother, to carefully selected Bengali Brahmin bridegrooms. Our maternal grandmother had been seven years old on her wedding day, and her younger sister only five on hers. At seven, Mother's mother had been scorned as an aged bride by the community, the victim of the progressive views of a father eccentric enough to encourage literacy for women.

We sisters were born at a lucky moment in the city's history. Independence opened up business opportunities for Indian men of energy and vision like our father, who in the fifties came to be known in the Calcutta Chamber of Commerce as the Bengal Tiger. The pharmaceutical company that Father, a biochemist by training, had founded in the mid-forties, prospered, requiring the relocation of the manufacturing plant to a large site outside the city limits. Workaholic Father's need to be on site at all hours eased our nuclear family's breakout from the crowded household in Ballygunge. For Mother, the move meant quarrel-free permission to enroll us in a girls-only school where the cultivation of intelligence would be as important a goal as the refinement of femininity and manners. The school she picked was Loreto House, an exclusive English-language establishment run by Irish nuns who promised Mother, the muzzled feminist, "Our girls can compete with the best anywhere in the world."

What makes the author say that she and her sisters were born at a lucky time?

My years in Loreto House School and Loreto House College exposed me to a postcolonial variant of Raj-style biculturalism that required continual and complex readjustments to ensure survival with psychic integrity. During the schoolday, except during French class, we spoke only English; learned only European history because no India-friendly but not Britain-unfriendly textbook of Indian history satisfactory to the Loreto House nuns had yet been published; performed Gilbert and Sullivan in music class; acted in plays by Shakespeare, Oscar Wilde, J. M. Barrie in perfectly mimicked

---

8. *burqua*. Head-to-toe garment with only a mesh opening to see through worn by Muslim women
9. **henna**. Reddish-brown dye used to color hair

---

words for everyday use

pe • riph • ery (pə riˈ f(ə) rē) *n.*, outward bounds of something as distinguished from its internal regions or center. *On the periphery of the Twin Cities is a freeway designed to skirt downtown.*

eu • pho • ria (yu fōrˈ ē ə) *n.*, feeling of well-being or elation. *The euphoria of the crowd was evident when Pele scored another goal.*

1. The ethnic groups segregated themselves by staying within their own areas of the city.
2. They were born during the Independence era of India. Independence opened up business opportunities for men and encouraged women to be educated.

LITERARY TECHNIQUE

CHARACTERIZATION. Characterization is the use of literary techniques to create a character. To characterize her parents, Mukherjee primarily uses the technique of direct description. How does she describe her mother and father?
Answers
She describes her father as "eccentric enough to encourage literacy for women," a biochemist by training and head of a pharmaceutical company, and a workaholic. She describes her mother as a "muzzled feminist" who wants her girls to go to a school where their intelligence will be cultivated.

upper-class British accents; memorized Christian scriptures, including the Acts of the Apostles; played unfeminine sports like volleyball and basketball; and sang songs like "Home on the Range" at school socials. At home, we spoke a mixture of Bengali and English, and on weekend visits to Ballygunge relatives, a carefully enunciated, formally phrased Bengali; we tried to keep up with Bengali-language plays, songs, movies, and celebrity gossip; we scouted the city for stores selling the trendiest saris.[10] Biculturalism ballooned into triculturalism every Thursday afternoon when we took in the matinee at the Metro Cinema in Chowringhee. The Metro Cinema showed only MGM musicals, costumed extravaganzas usually starring Doris Day, and made us daydream of a backlot-constructed "America" where the big-boned heroine with the frank face and toothy smile pursued love and happiness without having to step over homeless families and maimed beggar children sleeping on sidewalks. Loreto House was my accidental laboratory for experimenting with how and what new cultural elements to incorporate into my Ballygunge-self and how and what to reject so I could survive adolescence in transitional times.

What language(s) were spoken during school? at home? on weekend visits to Ballygunge relatives?

Father, who liked to think of himself as a benevolently despotic head of the family, was touched by the promise and excitement of those improvisational times. He took what he later described as the biggest gamble of his life: he sent each of us three sisters to American campuses to study whatever subjects we wanted for two years while he searched for bridegrooms for us.

Mira and my younger sister, Ranu, arrived as "for-

What was the largest gamble ever made by the author's father?

eign students" at what was then known as Idlewild Airport in the fall of 1960. Ranu, who had just turned sixteen, was met by a friendly alumna of Vassar College and driven to Poughkeepsie to start her sophomore year. Vassar dorms were filled with what I imagine were American equivalents of Loreto House women and Ranu expected to fit in with them, but their cultural tolerances turned out to be totally alien. When Ranu learned that she had to fulfill the school requirement that entering students be photographed in the nude, she rushed back in tears to India.

Mira changed planes at Idlewild Airport for Detroit, gritted her teeth when she saw how different a neighborhood downtown Detroit was from Ballygunge, made friends with other international students, got her graduate degree in child psychology and preschool education, and just as Dad announced that he had found the perfect East Bengali groom for her, she surprised him by marrying a Bombay-born, Marathi-speaking Indian graduate student getting his business administration degree at Wayne State University.

I arrived in the United States exactly a year after Mira had. On my way to the University of Iowa in Iowa City, where I was to study for a master of fine arts degree for two years, I stopped off in Detroit to visit with Mira. In that one year away from Mukherjee-style benevolent patriarchy, Mira had evolved into a confident, independent-thinking woman who had stepped out of the secured perimeters of our Calcutta compound into a bold, unchaperoned new world. The

What major changes did Mira undergo while living in America?

---

10. **saris.** Garments consisting of two sets of cloth—one is used for a skirt and the other a head or shoulder covering—worn by Indian women

words for everyday use

be • nev • o • lent • ly (bə nev′ lənt lē) *adv.*, marked by or disposed to doing good. *Mrs. Cadbury contributed benevolently to charities.*
des • pot • ic (des pä′ tik) *adj.*, characteristic of a ruler or person with absolute authority and power. *My despotic sister thinks she can tell me what to do.*
pa • tri • ar • chy (pā′ trē är kē) *n.*, social organization marked by the supremacy of the father or males. *During the 1970s women's libbers struggled against the existing patriarchy.*
pe • rim • e • ter (pə ri′ mə tər) *n.*, line or strip bounding or protecting an area. *A vegetable garden formed the perimeter of the backyard.*

night I arrived in Detroit, she gathered her friends in her tiny apartment off Woodward Avenue for a "Welcome, Bharati!" potluck dinner. The kitchen alcove was crowded with Hong Kong Chinese, Algerians, Moroccans, Tunisians, Chaldean Christians, Indians from states in India that we Bengalis had traditionally patronized, two white American women, and one African American man. Except for the three native-born Americans, all the guests—like Mira, like me—were "foreign students" on student visas, though the few who were nearing the end of their medical school or engineering school degree programs were hoping to stay on as immigrants.

I stayed two weeks with Mira, then continued my journey to Iowa City. Before my two years of study at the Writers' Workshop were over, like Doris Day in my favorite MGM matinees, I found love and happiness with a fellow student,

which led to a lunchtime marriage in a lawyer's office above a coffee shop. Because the man I so impulsively married happened to be an American citizen of Canadian parents, I was forced to choose between life with my husband on an alien continent and life back in India, my homeland. I chose husband over homeland. I don't think I had any idea when I first made that choice that I was acknowledging my willingness to transform myself from expatriate to immigrant, from aloof spectator to responsible participant, and in that process to transform the America I'd adopted into a homeland I would be proud to claim.

What was the author forced to choose between due to her marriage to an American?

It is assumed in many parts of the world that to become an "American" demands jumping into the mythical melting pot—a kind of cultural electric chair—and committing psychocultural

---

words for everyday use

ex • pa • tri • ate (ek spā′ trē ət) *n.*, person living in a foreign land. *Jamal became an* _expatriate_ *after moving from his native land, Algeria, to France.*

---

1. Mira feels that the United States treats its immigrants unfairly and as if they aren't valuable. She feels that immigrants are manipulated and discarded in America.
2. The narrator considers the stubborn resistance to America shown by some immigrants a "sad waste."

SELECTION CHECK TEST 4.10.9 WITH ANSWERS

Checking Your Reading
1. How many sisters does Bharati Mukherjee have? **She has two sisters.**
2. How does the author describe her neighborhood of Ballygunge? **She describes it as a middle-class neighborhood that was self-sufficient. It is homogeneously Hindu and Bengali-speaking.**
3. How does the author view biculturalism as a child? **She sees biculturalism as a contest between us and them.**
4. Where do the author and her sisters attend school? What kind of a school is it? **They attend school at Loreto House. It is an all-girls, English-speaking school.**
5. Where does the author attend college in the United States? **She attends the University of Iowa in Iowa City.**

Vocabulary in Context
Fill in each blank below with the most appropriate word from the following Words for Everyday Use from "The Road from Ballygunge." You may have to change the tense of the word.

> vigorous deplore euphoria
> perimeter expatriate nostalgia
> resilient

1. Most plants are **resilient**; they can weather storms and pruning.
2. The woman planted marigolds around the **perimeter** of the garden.
3. He was overcome by a feeling of **euphoria** when he heard that he had passed the difficult exam.
4. T. S. Elliot was considered an **expatriate** because he was born in the United States but spent most of his life in Europe.
5. When I think of my childhood home, I am overcome with **nostalgia**.

---

suicide. Resistance to change, to a McWorld of blue jeans and hamburgers, the deliberate barricading of oneself within ones original culture, is seen as heroic. In those circles, expatriation is a sign of <u>integrity</u>. Using the Old Culture as a shield against the New is a temptation I understand, but which I <u>deplore</u>.

Mira, who has lived in Detroit since 1960 and who now practices there as a child psychologist, and her Indian-born husband belong in the circle of expatriates. In the late nineties as the United States embroils itself in shrill debates over the rights of legal immigrants, Mira rages to me over the phone: "I feel used. I feel manipulated and discarded. This is such an unfair way to treat a person who was *invited* to stay and work here because of her talent… For over thirty years, I've invested my creativity and skills in the improvement of America's preschool system. I've obeyed all the rules, I've paid my taxes, I love my work, I love my students, I love the friends I've made. But I want to go home to India when I'm ready to retire. I still feel I have an Indian heritage. I feel some kind of an irrational attachment to India that I don't to America."

How does Mira feel the United States treats its immigrants?

I wonder if Mira's "irrational attachment" comes from having lived the past thirty-seven years in a bicultural city like Detroit, where the only cultures that matter are African American and European American, and where to be an Indo-American is to feel irrelevant.

In bicultural, bilingual countries like Canada, Belgium, or Sri Lanka, the debate about "nationhood" automatically generates bitterness, and sometimes blood. In theory, bilingualism should be an advantage, a gift; yet bilingual nations face the greatest challenge to stability. Slovakia has already made a "Slovak Only in Public Spaces" decision. In officially bilingual Canada, the war between the Anglophones and the Francophones[11] continues to be fought in a climate of catastrophic national breakup.

I recognize Mira's pain as real. I understand her survivor's need of <u>nostalgia</u> for a homeland she doesn't have to live in and experience the gritty aggravations of every day. But in multicultural states like California, where I make my home, her expatriate stance of stubborn resistance to America seems a sad waste. A tragedy for all Americans, not just herself. In cities like San Francisco, where immigrants from Central America and South America jostle elbows with refugees from Cambodia and Vietnam, I've eavesdropped on thickly accented, enthusiastic conversation about "drive-through diagnostics" and "bun management" between people wearing fast-food-company logos on their shirt pockets. I want to think that in our multicultural United States, immigrants like them will play the stabilizing role that pride and history deny the major players.

What does the narrator consider a "sad waste"?

The point is not to adopt the mainstream American's easy ironies nor the expatriate's self-protective contempt for the "vulgarity" of immigration. The point is to stay <u>resilient</u> and compassionate in the face of change. ■

---

11. **Anglophones and the Francophones.** Persons belonging to an English-speaking country and a French-speaking country

---

words for everyday use

in • teg • ri • ty (in te′ grə tē) *n.*, firm adherence to a code of moral or artistic values. *Monica demonstrated her <u>integrity</u> when she refused to cheat on the exam.*
de • plore (di plôr′) *vi.*, feel grief for; consider unfortunate. *I <u>deplore</u> the fact that people waste food when there are starving people in this world.*
nos • tal • gia (nä stal′ jə) *n.*, homesickness. *Tyrone experienced <u>nostalgia</u> during his month stay at the summer camp.*
re • sil • ient (ri zil′ yənt) *adj.*, ability to recover from or adjust easily to misfortune or change. *Monica proved to be <u>resilient</u> when she adjusted easily to her new job in another state.*

SELECTION CHECK TEST 4.10.9 WITH ANSWERS (CONT.)

Literary Tools
1. What is a writer's aim? **A writer's aim is his or her purpose or goal in writing.**
2. What are some possible aims a writer might have? **A writer might aim to inform, to persuade, to** entertain, to reflect, or to make a point, for example.
3. What is style? **Style is the manner in which something is said or written.**

Respond *to the* SELECTION

Why do you think the author deplores "using the Old Culture as a shield against the New"?

Investigate, *Inquire,* and Imagine

Recall: GATHERING FACTS

1a. What girls-only school did Mukherjee's mother pick for her daughters to attend?

2a. What would have happened if the author and her sister had not come of age during the post-Independent era?

3a. What did the author and her sisters do every Thursday afternoon?

Interpret: FINDING MEANING

1b. What type of education did the author receive at this school?

2b. What does this suggest about the influence Western culture has had on India?

3b. Why does the narrator say that biculturalism turned into triculturalism every Thursday afternoon?

Analyze: TAKING THINGS APART

4a. Identify the frustrations Mira has with the United States.

Synthesize: BRINGING THINGS TOGETHER

4b. What advice do you think Mira would give girls at the Loreto House who planned to immigrate to the United States?

Evaluate: MAKING JUDGMENTS

5a. Evaluate why the author thinks it is important for an expatriate "to stay resilient and compassionate in the face of change."

Extend: CONNECTING IDEAS

5b. What made it easier for Mukherjee to immigrate to the United States than for Esmeralda Santiago (Unit 9)?

Understanding *Literature*

AIM. Review the definition for **aim** in the Handbook of Literary Terms. What are the author's aim(s) in writing this personal essay?

STYLE. Review the definition for **style** in Literary Tools in Prereading and the cluster chart you made for that section. What words and phrases are representative of the author's diction? How would you describe Mukherjee's style?

"THE ROAD FROM BALLYGUNGE" 831

ANSWERS TO INVESTIGATE, INQUIRE, AND IMAGINE (CONT.)

"psychocultural suicide" and therefore they barricade themselves within their original culture. Such rigid thinking keeps expatriates from feeling like they belong in their new culture and keeps them from playing a role in transforming and stabilizing that culture.

EXTEND
5b. Esmeralda Santiago came to the United States as a child and didn't have the cognitive skills to assess

the benefits and problems of life in the United States. In addition, unlike Bharati Mukherjee, she did not speak English, which prevented her from understanding instruction and interactions with non-Hispanics.

Answers to Understanding Literature can be found on page 832.

RESPOND TO THE SELECTION

Think back to a time you were in a new place. How did you feel? How was your experience similar to or different from the experiences described of Mira and the narrator?

ANSWERS TO INVESTIGATE, INQUIRE, AND IMAGINE

RECALL
1a. The girls attended Loreto House School and College, an exclusive English-language school run by Irish nuns who claim their girls "can compete with the best anywhere in the world."
2a. The author and her sisters would have been married off as teenagers to carefully selected Bengali Brahmin men.
3a. Every Thursday afternoon the author and her sisters went to the matinee at the cinema to see an MGM musical.

INTERPRET
1b. At the school, she received a Western-style education with a heavy British influence, speaking only English and learning European history and literature.
2b. It suggests that Western culture was influential in post-colonial India and helped promote and encourage education and independence for women.
3b. The narrator's life is bicultural in that she is steeped in British culture at school and Bengali culture at home. Her life becomes tricultural on Thursday afternoons because the American movies she sees then expose her to American culture.

ANALYZE
4a. Mira, who settles in Detroit as a legal immigrant but (the narrator implies) never becomes a U.S. citizen, doesn't feel accepted in the country in which she has invested so much of herself.

SYNTHESIZE
4b. *Responses will vary.* Mira may advise girls who plan to immigrate to the United States to consider the strength of their attachment to India when they are faced with the choice of becoming U.S. citizens and adopting the United States as their homeland.

EVALUATE
5a. The author notes that many immigrants think that becoming an "American" means committing

AIM. Mukherjee's aims are to inform the reader of her experiences and perceptions with immigration and to persuade other expatriates to stay "resilient and compassionate in the face of change."

STYLE. Words and phrases such as "peripheries," "benevolently despotic," and "psychocultural suicide" are representative of Mukherjee's elevated diction. This elevated diction combined with moderately complex sentence structure and the use of both concrete and abstract words give the selection a semiformal style.

ANSWERS TO INTEGRATING THE LANGUAGE ARTS

Language, Grammar, and Style
1. has been living (present perfect)
2. will have written (future perfect)
3. had been (past perfect)
4. had left (past perfect)
5. has said (present perfect)

Collaborative Learning & Study and Research
In presenting their findings, students should look for ways to engage the senses of their audience. For example, they might have audience members sample Indian foods, listen to excerpts of traditional music, or try on traditional Indian clothing.

Speaking and Listening & Collaborative Learning
Encourage students to gather quotations from persons who have firsthand experience or knowledge of arranged marriages to use in supporting their arguments.

Media Literacy
Students might want to create a time line or maps to accompany their oral presentation.

Writer's Journal

1. Imagine you are the author at the time she visits her sister in the United States. Write a **postcard** to your other sister in India describing how Mira has adapted to life in the United States and who her friends are.
2. Imagine you are the author living in the United States. Write a **journal entry** in which you describe the nostalgia you have for your childhood in India.
3. Imagine you work for the student paper at the University of California at Berkeley. You have been assigned to interview Mukherjee about "The Road from Ballygunge." Write five **interview questions** you'd like to ask Mukherjee about the selection you just read, and indicate why you would like to ask each of those questions.

Integrating the Language Arts

Language, Grammar, and Style

PERFECT TENSES. Read about perfect tenses in the Language Arts Survey 3.62, "Properties of Verbs: Tense." Then identify each perfect tense verb in the following sentences and tell which tense it is in.

1. Mukherjee has been living in the United States for many years.
2. With her next collection of short stories, she will have written six books.
3. Her father had been progressive to send his daughters to school in the United States.
4. Ranu had left the United States shortly after her arrival.
5. Of her writing, the author has said, "Mine is not minimalism, which strips away, but compression, which reflects many layers of meaning."

Collaborative Learning & Study and Research

RESEARCHING INDIAN CULTURE. With a partner, research an aspect of Indian culture such as traditional music, the Hindu religion, food, or holidays. Then present your findings to the class.

Speaking and Listening & Collaborative Learning

PARTICIPATING IN A DEBATE. Traditionally, in India, fathers find husbands for their daughters, as Mukherjee's grandfather did for her mother and aunt. Hold a debate about the benefits of arranged marriages.

Prepare constructive and rebuttal speeches to defend your position. You may find it useful to review the Language Arts Survey 4.21, "Participating in a Debate."

Media Literacy

HISTORY OF INDIA. What led to the British Raj? What led to India's independence? What is the present political, economic, and social situation of India? Use the Internet to help you find the answers to these questions. Read the Language Arts Survey 5.30, "Evaluating Information and Media Sources" to help you find quality web sites such as www.historyofindia.com/ britrule.html and www.itihaas.com. Present your findings in an oral presentation.

from **Desert Exile: The Uprooting of a Japanese-American Family**

by Yoshiko Uchida

Reader's **resource**

Yoshiko Uchida describes the early days of life in the relocation center at Tanforan racetrack in this excerpt from her autobiography, *Desert Exile: The Uprooting of a Japanese-American Family.*

HISTORY CONNECTION. During World War II, more than 100,000 Japanese Americans were sent to relocation centers in remote areas where they were forced to live in hastily made, shoddily constructed barracks. This massive group relocation and incarceration happened as a result of Executive Order 9066, signed by President Franklin D. Roosevelt, which ordered all Japanese Americans to be interned for security reasons. Claims that such a roundup was a wartime necessity are belied by the fact that the United State was also at war with Germany and Italy, yet descendants of persons from those nations were not imprisoned. The United States government has since admitted its mistake and offered reparations to families who were dislocated.

About *the* AUTHOR

Yoshiko Uchida (1921–1992) was a senior at the University of California at Berkeley when the United States entered World War II and the federal government ordered people of Japanese descent to be incarcerated. She was sent with her family to a detention center at the Tanforan racetrack in California. Five months later, they were moved to a guarded camp in Utah called Topaz. At Topaz, Uchida taught in an elementary school until she was released in 1943 to accept a fellowship for graduate study at Smith College. She earned a master's degree in education, but decided not to teach because it took too much time away from her writing. She wrote many children's books, most of which deal with Japanese folklore and other Japanese themes. In her later writings, she focused more on the experience of Japanese Americans in the United States. Both *Journey to Topaz: A Story of the Japanese-American Evacuation* and *Desert Exile: The Uprooting of a Japanese-American Family* focus on the Japanese-American experience in the detention camps of World War II.

Literary TOOLS

AUTOBIOGRAPHY. An **autobiography** is the story of a person's life, written by that person. As you read, consider Uchida's purpose in writing about her experiences in a relocation center.

CHRONOLOGICAL ORDER. Chronological order is the arrangement of details in order of their occurrence. It is the primary method of organization used in narrative writing. As you read, pay attention to the order in which events occur.

Graphic Organizer

Place the events listed below on a time line in chronological order:

- ate for the first time in the smaller mess hall
- ate fried chicken and ice cream
- unpacked bundle of belongings
- sewed curtains
- read telegram from father

moved into
horse stall
apartment

left
Tanforan

Reader's Journal

Describe communal living you have experienced outside your family. What are the positive and negative aspects of such an arrangement?

ADDITIONAL RESOURCES

UNIT 10 RESOURCE BOOK
- Selection Worksheet 10.6
- Selection Check Test 4.10.11
- Selection Test 4.10.12
- Language, Grammar, and Style Resource 3.35
- Speaking and Listening Resource 4.20

GRAPHIC ORGANIZER

Students should place events in the following order on their time lines:
- unpacked bundle of belongings
- ate for the first time in the smaller mess hall
- read telegram from father
- sewed curtains
- ate fried chicken and ice cream

READER'S JOURNAL

Some students will have had experiences living in summer camps. Other students can write about what they would and would not like if they attended one.

GOALS/OBJECTIVES

Studying this lesson will enable students to
- empathize with the speaker's feelings as her life undergoes an upheaval
- describe Yoshiko Uchida's literary accomplishments
- explain the historical events surrounding the internment of Japanese Americans during World War II

- define *autobiography* and identify and analyze elements of an autobiography
- define *chronological order* and recognize its use in their reading
- reduce wordiness in sentences
- write a survey

American Diary: October 16, 1942, 1997. Roger Shimomura. Private Collection.

From

Desert
EXILE

The Uprooting of a Japanese-American Family

Yoshiko Uchida

artnote

 An American Diary, 1997. Roger Shimomura. **Roger Shimomura** (1939–) is an American artist and teacher who was interned with his family at Camp Minidoka in Idaho. His series of paintings, *An American Diary,* is based on the diary his grandmother kept during their internment.

As the bus pulled up to the grandstand, I could see hundreds of Japanese Americans jammed along the fence that lined the track. These people had arrived a few days earlier and were now watching for the arrival of friends or had come to while away the empty hours that had suddenly been thrust upon them.

As soon as we got off the bus, we were directed to an area beneath the grandstand where we registered and filled out a series of forms. Our baggage was inspected for contraband,[1] a <u>cursory</u> medical check made, and our living quarters assigned. We were to be housed in Barrack 16, Apartment 40. Fortunately, some friends who had arrived earlier found us and offered to help us locate our quarters.

It had rained the day before, and the hundreds of people who had trampled on the track had turned it into a miserable mass of slippery mud. We made our way on it carefully, helping my mother, who was dressed just as she would have been to go to church. She wore a hat, gloves, her good coat, and her Sunday shoes, because she would not have thought of <u>venturing</u> outside our house dressed in any other way.

> How was the narrator's mother dressed? Why was she dressed this way?

Everywhere there were black tar-papered barracks[2] that had been hastily erected to house the eight thousand Japanese Americans of the area who had been uprooted from their homes. Barrack 16, however, was not among them, and we couldn't find it until we had traveled half the length of the track and gone beyond it to the northern rim of the racetrack compound.

Finally one of our friends called out, "There it is, beyond that row of eucalyptus trees." Barrack 16 was not a barrack at all, but a long stable raised a few feet off the ground with a broad ramp the horses had used to reach their stalls. Each stall was now numbered, and ours was number 40. That the stalls should have been called "apartments" was a <u>euphemism</u> so <u>ludicrous</u> it was comical.

> What made the word "apartment" ludicrous in this context?

When we reached stall number 40, we pushed open the narrow door and looked uneasily into the vacant darkness. The stall was about ten by twenty feet and empty except for three folded army cots lying on the floor. Dust, dirt, and wood shavings covered the linoleum that had been laid over manure-covered boards, the smell of horses hung in the air, and the whitened corpses of many insects still clung to the hastily whitewashed walls.

High on either side of the entrance were two small windows, which were our only source of daylight. The stall was divided into two sections by Dutch doors[3] worn down by teeth marks, and each stall in the stable was separated from the <u>adjoining</u> one only by rough partitions that stopped a foot short of the sloping roof. The space, while perhaps a good source of <u>ventilation</u> for the horses, deprived us of all but visual privacy, and we couldn't even be sure of that because of the crevices and knotholes in the dividing walls.

> Why did the narrator and her family lack privacy?

Because our friends had already spent a day as residents of Tanforan, they had become <u>adept</u> at

---

1. **contraband.** Smuggled goods
2. **barracks.** Large, plain, often temporary housing
3. **Dutch doors.** Doors split across the middle so the top and bottom halves can be opened separately

---

words for everyday use

cur • so • ry (kʉr´sə rē) *adj.*, superficial; done rapidly with little attention to detail. *Having made only a <u>cursory</u> review of her notes, the student was not prepared for the exam.*
ven • ture (ven´chər) *vi.*, go at some risk. *Few people <u>ventured</u> outdoors during the brutal cold snap.*
eu • phe • mism (yōō´fə miz´əm) *n.*, word or phrase substituted for a more offensive word or phrase. *Some theatergoers used the <u>euphemism</u> "interesting" to describe the unusual, disturbing play.*
lu • di • crous (lōō´di krəs) *adj.*, absurd, ridiculous. *The prosecuting attorney called the defendant's unlikely alibi <u>ludicrous</u>.*
ad • join • ing (ə join´iŋ) *adj.*, next to each other. *The <u>adjoining</u> hotel rooms are connected by doors inside the rooms.*
ven • ti • la • tion (vent ´l ā´shən) *n.*, circulation of fresh air. *Perhaps you should open the windows to increase the <u>ventilation</u> in the room.*
a • dept (ə dept´) *adj.*, expert; highly skilled. *After twenty years in the entertainment business, the talent scout was <u>adept</u> at spotting potential stars.*

ANSWERS TO GUIDED READING QUESTIONS

1. The narrator's mother was dressed as if she were going to church. By continuing to act as she would under normal circumstances, the narrator's mother is attempting to maintain her dignity.
2. The word *apartment* is ludicrous because the room was really a horse stall.
3. The narrator and her family lacked privacy because the partitions between the stalls did not reach all the way to the roof and had crevices and knotholes.

LITERARY TECHNIQUE

EUPHEMISM. A **euphemism** is an indirect word or phrase used in place of a direct statement that might be considered offensive. An example in the story is the camp authority's use of the term "apartment" to describe the only slightly improved horse stall where the Uchidas must live. Have students think of other euphemisms that might be used to describe aspects of the camp.

1. The Uchidas, and Mrs. Uchida in particular because of her neuralgia, faced the real danger of exposure to the cold night air as they slept.

scrounging for necessities. One found a broom and swept the floor for us. Two of the boys went to the barracks where mattresses were being issued, stuffed the ticking with straw themselves, and came back with three for our cots.

Nothing in the camp was ready. Everything was only half-finished. I wondered how much the nation's security would have been threatened had the army permitted us to remain in our homes a few more days until the camps were adequately prepared for occupancy by families.

By the time we had cleaned out the stall and set up the cots, it was time for supper. Somehow, in all the confusion, we had not had lunch, so I was eager to get to the main mess hall,[4] which was located beneath the grandstand.

The sun was going down as we started along the muddy track, and a cold, piercing wind swept in from the bay. When we arrived, there were six long, weaving lines of people waiting to get into the mess hall. We took our place at the end of one of them, each of us clutching a plate and silverware borrowed from friends who had already received their baggage.

Shivering in the cold, we pressed close together trying to shield Mama from the wind. As we stood in what seemed a bread line for the destitute, I felt degraded, humiliated, and overwhelmed with a longing for home. And I saw the unutterable sadness on my mother's face.

This was only the first of many lines we were to endure, and we soon discovered that waiting in line was as inevitable a part of Tanforan as the north wind that swept in from the bay, stirring up all the dust and litter of the camp.

Once we got inside the gloomy, cavernous mess hall, I saw hundreds of people eating at wooden picnic tables, while those who had

already eaten were shuffling aimlessly over the wet cement floor. When I reached the serving table and held out my plate, a cook reached into a dishpan full of canned sausages and dropped two onto my plate with his fingers. Another man gave me a boiled potato and a piece of butterless bread.

With five thousand people to be fed, there were few unoccupied tables, so we separated from our friends and shared a table with an elderly man and a young family with two crying babies. No one at the table spoke to us, and even Mama could seem to find no friendly word to offer as she normally would have done. We tried to eat, but the food wouldn't go down.

"Let's get out of here," my sister suggested.

We decided it would be better to go back to our barrack than to linger in the depressing confusion of the mess hall. It had grown dark by now, and since Tanforan had no lights for nighttime occupancy, we had to pick our way carefully down the slippery track.

Once back in our stall, we found it no less depressing, for there was only a single electric light bulb dangling from the ceiling, and a one-inch crevice at the top of the north wall admitted a steady draft of the cold night air. We sat huddled on our cots, bundled in our coats, too cold and miserable even to talk. My sister and I worried about Mama, for she wasn't strong and had recently been troubled with neuralgia,[5] which could easily be aggravated by the cold. She in turn was worrying about us, and of course we all worried and wondered about Papa.

What real danger was faced by the Uchidas in their new living quarters?

---

4. **mess hall.** Room or building where a group, such as soldiers, eats
5. **neuralgia.** Pain along the path of a nerve

---

words for everyday use

des • ti • tute (des´tə tōōt´) n., those living in poverty. *The city has opened ten new shelters for the destitute.*

de • grad • ed (dē grād´id) adj., disgraced; humiliated. *Have you ever felt degraded by unkind remarks?*

in • ev • i • ta • ble (in ev´i tə bəl) adj., certain to occur. *Mistakes are inevitable when workers are tired and overworked.*

Suddenly we heard the sound of a truck stopping outside.

"Hey, Uchida! Apartment 40!" a boy shouted.

I rushed to the door and found the baggage boys trying to heave our enormous "camp bundle" over the railing that fronted our stall.

"What ya got in here anyway?" they shouted good-naturedly as they struggled with the <u>unwieldy</u> bundle. "It's the biggest thing we got on our truck!"

I grinned, embarrassed, but I could hardly wait to get out our belongings. My sister and I fumbled to undo all the knots we had tied into the rope around our bundle that morning and eagerly pulled out the familiar objects from home.

We unpacked our blankets, pillows, sheets, tea kettle, and, most welcome of all, our electric hot plate.[6] I ran to the nearest washroom to fill the kettle with water, while Mama and Kay made up the army cots with our bedding. Once we hooked up the hot plate and put the kettle on to boil, we felt better. We sat close to its warmth, holding our hands toward it as though it were our fireplace at home.

Before long some friends came by to see us, bringing with them the only gift they had—a box of dried prunes. Even the day before, we wouldn't have given the prunes a second glance, but now they were as welcome as the boxes of Maskey's chocolates my father used to bring home from San Francisco.

> *What made the prunes taste so good?*

Mama managed to make some tea for our friends, and we sat around our steaming kettle, munching gratefully on our prunes. We spent most of the evening talking about food and the lack of it, a concern that grew <u>obsessive</u> over the next few weeks, when we were constantly hungry.

Our stable consisted of twenty-five stalls facing north, which were back to back with an equal number facing south, so we were surrounded on three sides. Living in our stable were an assortment of people—mostly small family units—that included an artist, my father's barber and his wife, a dentist and his wife, an elderly retired couple, a group of Kibei bachelors (Japanese born in the United States but educated in Japan), an insurance salesman and his wife, and a widow with two daughters. To say that we all became intimately acquainted would be an understatement. It was, in fact, <u>communal</u> living, with semiprivate cubicles provided only for sleeping.

Our neighbors on one side spent much of their time playing cards, and at all hours of the day we could hear the sound of cards being shuffled and money changing hands. Our other neighbors had a teenage son who spent most of the day with his friends, coming home to his stall at night only after his parents were asleep. Family life began to show signs of strain almost immediately, not only in the next stall but throughout the entire camp.

> *Why would family life become strained under these circumstances?*

One Sunday our neighbor's son fell asleep in the rear of his stall with the door bolted from inside. When his parents came home from church, no amount of shouting or banging on the door could awaken the boy.

"Our stupid son has locked us out," they explained, coming to us for help.

I climbed up on my cot and considered pouring water on him over the partition, for I knew he slept just on the other side of it. Instead I dangled a broom over the partition and poked

---

6. **hot plate.** Small, portable cooking device

words for everyday use	**un • wield • y** (un wēl′dē) *adj.*, hard to manage because of shape or weight. *The father helped his four-year-old daughter swing the <u>unwieldy</u> baseball bat.* **ob • ses • sive** (əb ses′iv) *adj.*, persistent to an abnormal degree. *School officials have questioned the football coach's <u>obsessive</u> rivalry with neighboring schools.* **com • mu • nal** (käm′yŏŏ nəl) *adj.*, of or shared by all; in the community. *Although the apartment building has a <u>communal</u> kitchen and living room, each tenant has a separate bedroom.*

and prodded with it, shouting, "Wake up! Wake up!" until the boy finally bestirred himself and let his parents in. We became good friends with our neighbors after that.

About one hundred feet from our stable were two latrines and two washrooms for our section of camp, one each for men and women. The latrines were crude wooden structures containing eight toilets, separated by partitions but having no doors. The washrooms were divided into two sections. In the front section was a long tin trough spaced with spigots of hot and cold water, where we washed our faces and brushed our teeth. To the rear were eight showers, also separated by partitions but lacking doors or curtains. The showers were difficult to adjust, and we either got scalded by torrents of hot water or shocked by an icy blast of cold. Most of the Issei[7] were unaccustomed to showers, having known the luxury of soaking in deep, pine-scented tubs during their years in Japan, and found the showers virtually impossible to use.

Our card-playing neighbor scoured the camp for a container that might serve as a tub and eventually found a large wooden barrel. She rolled it to the showers, filled it with warm water, and then climbed in for a pleasant and leisurely soak. The greatest compliment she could offer anyone was the use of her private tub.

The lack of privacy in the latrines and showers was an embarrassing hardship especially for the older women, and many would take newspapers to hold over their faces or squares of cloth to tack up for their own private curtain. The army, obviously ill-equipped to build living quarters for women and children, had made no attempt to introduce even the most common of life's civilities into these camps for us.

---

7. **Issei.** Japanese who immigrated to the United States after 1907. They were not granted citizenship until 1952.

During the first few weeks of camp life, everything was <u>erratic</u> and in short supply. Hot water appeared only <u>sporadically</u>, and the minute it was available, everyone ran for the showers or the laundry. We had to be clever and quick just to keep clean, and my sister and I often walked a mile to the other end of the camp, where hot water was in better supply, in order to boost our morale with a hot shower.

Even toilet paper was at a premium, for new rolls would disappear as soon as they were placed in the latrines. The shock of the evacuation compounded by the short supply of every necessity brought out the <u>baser</u> instincts of the internees,[8] and there was little <u>inclination</u> for anyone to feel responsible for anyone else. In the early days, at least, it was everyone for himself or herself.

What effect did the internment have on interpersonal relationships?

One morning I saw some women emptying bed pans into the troughs where we washed our faces. The sight was enough to turn my stomach, and my mother quickly made several large signs in Japanese cautioning people against such unsanitary practices. We posted them in <u>conspicuous</u> spots in the washroom and hoped for the best.

Across from the latrines was a double barrack, one containing laundry tubs and the other equipped with clotheslines and ironing boards. Because there were so many families with young children, the laundry tubs were in constant use. The hot water was often gone by 9:00 A.M., and many women got up at 3:00 and 4:00 in the morning to do their wash, all of which, including sheets, had to be done entirely by hand.

We found it difficult to get to the laundry before 9:00 A.M. and by then every tub was taken and there were long lines of people with bags of dirty laundry waiting behind each one. When we finally got to a tub, there was no more hot water. Then we would leave my mother to hold the tub while my sister and I rushed to the washroom, where there was a better supply, and carried back bucketfuls of hot water, as everyone else learned to do. By the time we had finally hung our laundry on lines outside our stall, we were too exhausted to do much else for the rest of the day.

For four days after our arrival, we continued to go to the main mess hall for all our meals. My sister and I usually missed breakfast because we were assigned to the early shift, and we simply couldn't get there by 7:00 A.M. Dinner was at 4:45 P.M., which was a terrible hour, but not a major problem, as we were always hungry. Meals were uniformly bad and skimpy, with an abundance of starches such as beans and bread. I wrote to my non-Japanese friends in Berkeley shamelessly asking them to send us food, and they obliged with large cartons of cookies, nuts, dried fruit, and jams.

How did the narrator get extra food?

We looked forward with much anticipation to the opening of a half dozen smaller mess halls located throughout the camp. But when ours finally opened, we discovered that the preparation of smaller quantities had absolutely no effect on the quality of the food. We went eagerly to our new mess hall only to be confronted at our first meal with chili con carne, corn, and butterless bread. To <u>assuage</u> our disappointment, a friend and I went to the main

---

8. **internees.** Prisoners, especially during wartime

words for everyday use

er • rat • ic (er rat´ik) *adj.,* having no fixed purpose. *My friend's <u>erratic</u> schedule prevents him from making plans with friends.*
spo • rad • i • cal • ly (spə rad´ik lē) *adv.,* occasionally; in scattered instances. *Because of a broken antenna, the television receives clear signals <u>sporadically</u>.*
bas • er (bāsr) *adj.,* meaner or less decent. *The goal of civilization is to rid people of their <u>baser</u> instincts.*
in • cli • na • tion (in klə nā´shən) *n.,* tendency. *My <u>inclination</u> is to give others the benefit of the doubt.*
con • spic • u • ous (kən spik´yōō əs) *adj.,* easy to see. *Their bright yellow jackets make the security guards <u>conspicuous</u> in the crowded stadium.*
as • suage (ə swāj´) *vt.,* calm; pacify. *Take a few deep breaths to <u>assuage</u> your nervousness.*

1. The internment camp brought out the "baser instincts" of the internees. People had little inclination to feel responsible for anyone else, at least at first.
2. The narrator got extra food by writing to non-Japanese friends and asking them to send some.

ADDITIONAL QUESTIONS AND ACTIVITIES

Students might imagine that they are the narrator's non-Japanese friend. How would they feel about the narrator's situation? Have students write a letter to the narrator that might have been sent along with a package of tasty foods.

1. The narrator was amazed to find fresh vegetables in the main mess hall.
2. The wonderful gift was the unexpected news that the narrator's father would be joining the family in the camp.

SELECTION CHECK TEST 4.10.11 WITH ANSWERS

Checking Your Reading
1. What does Uchida see when the bus pulls up to the grandstand? **She sees hundreds of Japanese Americans along the fence of the track, looking for friends and relatives or simply whiling away time.**
2. What is the "apartment" assigned to the author and her family like? **It is a horse stall with a Dutch door and two small windows. There are three cots on the floor. The walls do not reach the ceiling. The "apartment" is surrounded by others like it.**
3. What are three main problems the author and other residents encounter at Tanforan? **There is a severe lack of hot water, there is not enough food, and there are long lines for everything.**
4. Whom does the author ask for food? **She asks her non-Japanese friends in Berkeley to send food.**
5. Where was the author's father? **He was in jail in Montana and had been released on parole. He would accompany them soon.**

Vocabulary in Context
Fill in each blank below with the most appropriate word from the following Words for Everyday Use. You may have to change the tense of certain verbs.

venture euphemism ludicrous inevitable obsessive sporadically adept

1. "Passed away" is a(n) **euphemism** for "died."
2. The young bird **ventured** out of the nest to learn to fly.
3. The ballerina proved she was a(n) **adept** dancer in that amazing performance.
4. The college student called home too **sporadically** according to his mother.
5. Many thought that Christopher Columbus's belief that Earth was round was **ludicrous**.

Literary Tools

---

mess hall, which was still in operation, to see if it had anything better. Much to our amazement and delight, we found small lettuce salads, the first fresh vegetables we had seen in many days. We ate raven-ously and exercised enormous self-control not to go back for second and third helpings.

What amazed the narrator?

The food improved gradually, and by the time we left Tanforan five months later, we had fried chicken and ice cream for Sunday dinner. By July tubs of soapy water were installed at the mess hall exits so we could wash our plates and utensils on the way out. Being slow eaters, however, we usually found the dishwater tepid and dirty by the time we reached the tubs, and we often rewashed our dishes in the washroom.

Most internees got into the habit of rushing for everything. They ran to the mess halls to be first in line; they dashed inside for the best tables and then rushed through their meals to get to the washtubs before the suds ran out. The three of us, however, seemed to be at the end of every line that formed and somehow never managed to be first for anything.

One of the first things we all did at Tanforan was to make our living quarters as comfortable as possible. A pile of scrap lumber in one corner of camp melted away like snow on a hot day as residents salvaged whatever they could to make shelves and crude pieces of furniture to supplement the army cots. They also made ingenious containers for carrying their dishes to the mess halls, with handles and lids that grew more and more elaborate in a sort of unspoken competition.

Because of my father's absence, our friends helped us in camp, just as they had in Berkeley, and we relied on them to put up shelves and build a crude table and two benches for us. We put our new camp furniture in the front half of our stall, which was our "living room," and put our three cots in the dark, windowless rear section, which we promptly dubbed "the dungeon." We ordered some print fabric by mail and sewed curtains by hand to hang at our windows and to cover our shelves. Each new addition to our stall made it seem a little more like home.

One afternoon about a week after we had arrived at Tanforan, a messenger from the administration building appeared with a telegram for us. It was from my father, telling us he had been released on parole from Montana and would be able to join us soon in camp. Papa was coming home. The wonderful news had come like an unexpected gift, but even as we hugged each other in joy, we didn't quite dare believe it until we actually saw him. ■

What was the unexpected gift?

---

words for everyday use

rav • e • nous • ly (rav′ə nəs lē) *adv.*, in a wildly hungry manner. *After being stranded for three days without food, the rescued hikers ate* ravenously.

sal • vage (sal′vij) *vt.*, save; rescue. *Luckily, we were able to* salvage *a photo album from the fire.*

Respond *to the* SELECTION

What do you think the author missed the most when she lived in Tanforan?

SELECTION CHECK TEST 4.10.11 WITH ANSWERS (CONT.)

1. What is an autobiography? **An autobiography is the story of a person's life, written by that person.**
2. What is chronological order? **Chronological order is the arrangement of details in order of their occurrence.**
3. Why might an author choose chronological order for an autobiography? **Chronological order presents a linear picture of the events of his or her life.**

RESPOND TO THE SELECTION

As an alternative activity, ask students to put themselves in Uchida's place. Which aspect of living at the relocation camp would have been hardest for them to adjust to?

Investigate, Inquire, and Imagine

Recall: GATHERING FACTS

1a. Where were the narrator and her family sent? Where did they finally find their housing?

2a. How did they feel when they first went to the mess hall? What lifted their spirits?

3a. What were some of the problems of communal living?

Interpret: FINDING MEANING

1b. What made their new situation bearable?

2b. Why was the situation at the mess hall so depressing? Why did receiving their household goods have such a cheering effect?

3b. What did people do to deal with the problems of communal living? How were relationships between people affected by the lifestyle in the camp?

Analyze: TAKING THINGS APART

4a. Identify and classify the improvements made in the internees' living conditions.

Synthesize: BRINGING THINGS TOGETHER

4b. What do these improvements suggest? How would you summarize the character of the Uchida family and the other Japanese-American families who tried to create a better environment in which to live?

Evaluate: MAKING JUDGMENTS

5a. Evaluate the tone of the following statement made by Uchida: "I wondered how much the nation's security would have been threatened had the army permitted us to remain in our homes a few more days until the camps were adequately prepared for occupancy by families." What attitude toward the forced relocation does this sentence imply?

Extend: CONNECTING IDEAS

5b. Do you think the forcing of Japanese-Americans into detention centers is similar to the forcing of Jews into concentration camps? Explain. What similarities and differences do you see?

Understanding Literature

AUTOBIOGRAPHY. Review the definition for **autobiography** in the Handbook of Literary Terms. What do you learn about Yoshiko Uchida from this selection? What do you learn about life in an internment camp? What do you think was her purpose in writing this account?

CHRONOLOGICAL ORDER. Review the definition for **chronological order** in Literary Tools in Prereading and the time line you made for that section. What transitions are used to sequence the story? Why do you think Uchida used **chronological order** to tell her story? What parts of the autobiography are not written in chronological order?

FROM DESERT EXILE: THE UPROOTING OF A JAPANESE-AMERICAN FAMILY **841**

ANSWERS TO INVESTIGATE, INQUIRE, AND IMAGINE (CONT.)

was angry at the U.S. government about the relocation.

EXTEND

6a. *Responses will vary.* Among the similarities are that both groups were forced to abandon their homes, to evacuate quickly, with little time to gather their belongings, and to live communally away from the rest of the population. Both groups were singled out because of their ethnic identity. Differences include the fact that Jews were forced to do hard labor at the concentration camps and many died of starvation or were killed there, whereas Japanese Americans were not forced to work or physically harmed.

Answers to Understanding Literature can be found on page 842.

RECALL

1a. The narrator and her family were sent to an internment camp at Tanforan Racetrack in California. They finally found their housing in a stall of a horse stable.

2a. When they first went to the mess hall, they felt "degraded, humiliated, and overwhelmed with a longing for home." Their spirits are lifted when they receive their bundle of belongings from home and are able to hook up their hot plate and put the kettle on to boil.

3a. Problems of communal living included lack of privacy in their living quarters, bathrooms, and showers; a short supply of hot water and toilet paper, inadequate washing facilities; and poor food quality.

INTERPRET

1b. The presence of friends made their new situation bearable.

2b. The situation at the mess hall was depressing because the internees had to stand in long lines, the room was gloomy and cavernous, and food was poor in quality and skimpy in quantity. Receiving their household goods made their living space seem more homelike and comfortable.

3b. One woman found a wooden barrel to serve as a bathing tub. People learned where the larger supplies for hot water were, and some tacked up cloth to make the latrine stalls more private. Waiting in line and rushing for things became a part of life. Because of the short supply of everything, many people often forget about others and fended for themselves. At the same time, friends of Uchida's family helped them.

ANALYZE

4a. Improvements can be classified as those the internees made themselves, such as making furniture, shelves, and curtains, and those the camp officials made, such as setting up smaller mess halls and serving better quality food.

SYNTHESIZE

4b. The improvements suggest that the Uchida family and other Japanese Americans tried to make the best of a bad situation. Their character could be summarized as resourceful.

EVALUATE

5a. Uchida's tone is sarcastic or critical. This sentence implies that Uchida

ANSWERS TO UNDERSTANDING LITERATURE

AUTOBIOGRAPHY. The reader learns about Uchida's adaptability and patience. She adjusts to her new situation and does not grow bitter in her unpleasant surroundings. She is also innovative in the face of adversity. About life in an internment camp, the reader learns about the uncomfortable living quarters, lack of privacy, competition for resources, and unpleasant food that gradually improves. Uchida's likely purpose in writing this account is to tell people about the injustice that was done to Japanese Americans and to inform people about the conditions they experienced at the internment camps and their effects.

CHRONOLOGICAL ORDER. Transitional phrases include "As soon as we got off the bus," "During the first few weeks," and "Four days after our arrival." Uchida may have used chronological order to help readers better understand the process of events that took place at the detention camp. Parts of the autobiography not written in chronological order include the descriptions of general conditions that remained the same throughout their time in the camps, such as the lack of privacy in the latrines and showers.

ANSWERS TO INTEGRATING THE LANGUAGE ARTS

Language, Grammar, and Style
1. The officials inspected for and confiscated contraband.
2. Eight thousand Japanese Americans of the area had been uprooted from their homes.
3. Barrack 16 was a horse stall.
4. The stall was divided into two sections by Dutch doors.
5. Uchida's neighbor's stall was bolted from inside.

Speaking and Listening
Some students might enjoy creating a traditional Japanese costume to wear as they tell their folk tale.

Collaborative Learning
Have students brainstorm a list of possible topics for questions before they begin writing. Multiple-choice questions should be used to ensure that students can quantify the results of their survey. After writing the questions, have students review and edit the questions to make sure that the questions are clear and answer choices are unambiguous and do not overlap.

Writer's Journal

1. Imagine you are Uchida. Write a **letter** to your father describing your living quarters and conditions in the camp.
2. Pretend you are Uchida's mother. Write a **journal entry** describing what you find to be the greatest indignities in living in the camp.
3. Imagine you are a Japanese American living in Tanforan. Write an **appeal** to the President to abolish Executive Order 9066. Explain why the order is unfair and why Japanese Americans do not present a threat to U.S. security.

Integrating the Language Arts

Language, Grammar, and Style

REDUCING WORDINESS. Good writers use only as many words as needed to convey their thoughts clearly. They correct for wordiness when editing their writing. Read the Language Arts Survey 3.35, "Correcting Wordy Sentences." Then reduce the wordiness in the following sentences.

1. The officials inspected for contraband and confiscated any smuggled goods.
2. Eight thousand Japanese Americans of the area had been uprooted and made to leave their homes.
3. Barrack 16 was a horse stall where horses had been stabled.
4. The stall was divided into two sections by Dutch doors that were split across the middle so the top and bottom halves could be opened separately.
5. The locked door of Uchida's neighbor's stall was bolted from inside.

Speaking and Listening

TELLING A JAPANESE FOLK TALE. Yoshiko Uchida wrote a number of stories for children based on Japanese folk tales. Read her version of one of the folk tales or another version in a volume of Japanese folk tales. Then tell your selected story to a small group of classmates. You may want to review the Language Arts Survey 4.20, "Telling a Story."

Collaborative Learning

WRITING A SURVEY. Imagine that the military were interested in how interned Japanese Americans found life in the camps. As a class write a survey that the military might have administered. Then interview classmates pretending to be interned Japanese Americans and total the results of the survey. What recommendations would you make for administering changes in the camp?

Media Literacy

CLASS DISCUSSION. Watch the film *Snow Falling on Cedars.* Which character is the go-between of the white and Japanese-American community? What tie connects him to the Japanese-Americans? What character traits does he exhibit when he helps the Japanese-American family? What feelings does he have to push aside in order to help them? Discuss these and other questions after viewing the film.

ANSWERS TO INTEGRATING THE LANGUAGE ARTS (CONT.)

Media Literacy
You might have students contrast the tone of the film with the tone of Uchida's autobiography. Students should note that the selection has a documentary quality.

from *When Heaven and Earth Changed Places*
by Le Ly Hayslip

Reader's resource

When Heaven and Earth Changed Places is an autobiographical account of Hayslip's experiences during the Vietnam War. This selection examines her relationship with her father as well as the difficulties of surviving the ravages of war. Hayslip continued her autobiography in a book called *Child of War, Woman of Peace*, which explores her adaptation to life in the United States.

HISTORY CONNECTION. Throughout its history, Vietnam has struggled under the threat of conquest and war. In 111 BC, Vietnam was conquered by the Chinese, who controlled the country for more than twelve hundred years. A period of civil war and other invasions then followed. French efforts to colonize the country began in the late nineteenth century. Colonization ended in 1954 when the Vietminh, an organization of nationalist and communist parties that aimed at securing independence for Vietnam, defeated the French and seized political power for their leader, Ho Chi Minh, who became president of North Vietnam. At that time the country was divided into North Vietnam and the Republic of South Vietnam. American forces joined with Republican forces in Vietnam to fight against the communist Viet Cong, who were backed by the North Vietnamese government.

About the AUTHOR

Le Ly Hayslip (1949–   ) was born the youngest of six children in a traditional farming village in Vietnam. She was twelve years old when Americans landed in her village, beginning the nightmare of the Vietnam War for her. She survived terrible abuse, imprisonment, and torture. Her father was not as fortunate. After separation from his family, cruel treatment by soldiers on both sides of the war, and distress over the loss of his village, he died by his own hand. In 1970, Hayslip married an American serviceman and moved to the United States. She now lives in Los Angeles, where she has started a relief and world peace organization called the East Meets West Foundation.

Literary TOOLS

AIM. A writer's **aim** is his or her purpose, or goal. As you read, try to determine the author's aim in writing this selection.

ANECDOTE. An **anecdote** is a usually short narrative of an interesting, amusing, or biographical incident. In this selection, Hayslip includes several anecdotes that she heard from her father. As you read, try to determine why he tells her these stories.

Organizer

Make a chart listing the anecdotes Hayslip's father tells and why he tells them. One example has been done for you.

SUMMARY OF ANECDOTE	WHY HE TOLD IT
Female ancestor was a warrior	So that she will revere her ancestors

Reader's Journal

What is important to your parents?

ADDITIONAL RESOURCES

UNIT 10 RESOURCE BOOK
- Selection Worksheet 10.7
- Selection Check Test 4.10.13
- Selection Test 4.10.14
- Language, Grammar, and Style Resource 3.83

GRAPHIC ORGANIZER

Students may include the following additional examples in their charts:
Summary of Anecdote
Parents were forced to help build a runway for the French
Father admired his wife's industriousness
Father saved belongings from enemy soldiers and avoided capture
Why He Told It
So that she will appreciate freedom
So that she will honor her mother
So that she will appreciate that survival takes both determination and luck

READER'S JOURNAL

As an alternate activity, ask students what ideals and values their parents hold. How do they know they hold these ideals and values?

GOALS/OBJECTIVES

Studying this lesson will enable students to
- appreciate an autobiographical selection that highlights personal and family strength in wartime
- describe how Le Ly Hayslip's life was influenced by the Vietnam War
- define *aim* and determine the author's aim in the selection
- define *anecdote* and recognize examples of anecdotes in the selection
- identify adjective clauses in sentences
- use interviews to learn about the experiences of Vietnamese immigrants both in their home country and in the United States

MOTIVATION

Ask students to reread the second paragraph of the selection, in which Hayslip describes her father. They should note that the description covers his appearance, his behavior, and his internal qualities. Ask students to come up with a similar, one-paragraph description of someone they know very well.

READING PROFICIENCY

The many anecdotes the father tells and the lively dialogue between father and daughter, as well as the author's use of everyday language and generally simple sentences, make this selection engaging and highly accessible. Encourage students to read the selection aloud in pairs or small groups.

ENGLISH LANGUAGE LEARNING

Select sentences from the selection to illustrate independent and subordinate clauses.

SPECIAL NEEDS

Explain that the narrator in this selection recounts inspiring stories about family members and ancestors told to her by her father. Make sure students understand the terms *ancestor* and *descendant*.

ENRICHMENT

Some students might like to do research on Hayslip's East Meets West Foundation. Have them find out the foundation's mission and its main activities. The website for the foundation is http://www.eastmeetswest.org.

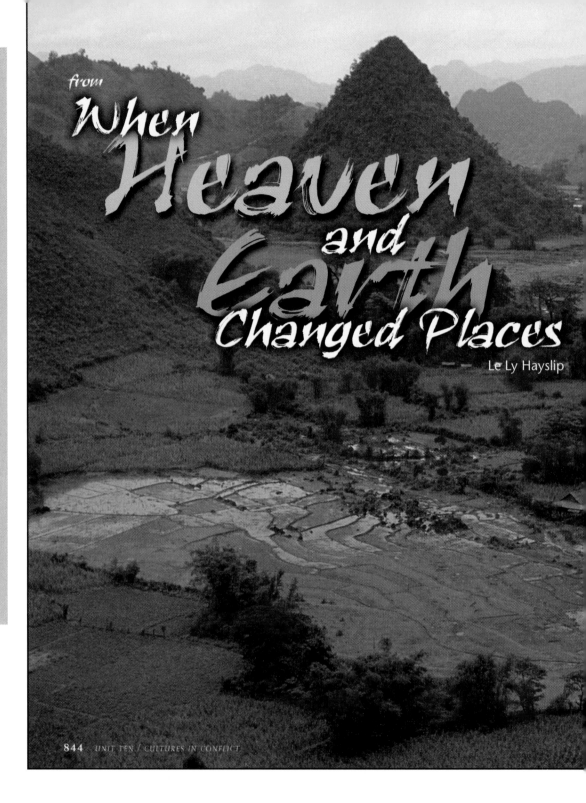

from
When
Heaven
and
Earth
Changed Places

Le Ly Hayslip

844   UNIT TEN / CULTURES IN CONFLICT

1. The narrator admired her father's
noble and handsome appearance,
his easygoing personality, his
diligence, honesty, and empathy.

A fter my brother Bon went North, I began to pay more attention to my father.

He was built solidly—big-boned—for a Vietnamese man, which meant he probably had well-fed, noble ancestors. People said he had the body of a natural-born warrior. He was a year younger and an inch shorter than my mother, but just as good-looking. His face was round, like a Khmer or Thai,[1] and his complexion was brown as soy from working all his life in the sun. He was very easygoing about everything and seldom in a hurry. Seldom, too, did he say no to a request—from his children or his neighbors. Although he took everything in stride, he was a hard and <u>diligent</u> worker. Even on holidays, he was always mending things or tending to our house and animals. He would not wait to be asked for help if he saw someone in trouble. Similarly, he always said what he thought, although he knew, like most honest men, when to keep silent. Because of his honesty, his <u>empathy</u>, and his openness to people, he understood life deeply. Perhaps that is why he was so easy-going. Only a half-trained mechanic thinks everything needs fixing.

> What characteristics did the narrator admire in her father?

He loved to smoke cigars and grew a little tobacco in our yard. My mother always wanted him to sell it, but there was hardly ever enough to take to market. I think for her it was the principle of the thing: smoking cigars was like burning money. Naturally, she had a song for such gentle vices—her own habit of chewing betel nuts[2] included:

---

1. **Khmer or Thai.** *Khmer*—native of Cambodia; *Thai*—native of Thailand
2. **betel nuts.** Red palm seeds, the fruit of the betel palm; commonly chewed in Southeast Asia

**VOCABULARY FROM
THE SELECTION**

avenge	empathy
defect	entitle
diligent	prospect

**words
for
everyday
use**

dil • i • gent (dil´ə jənt) *adj.,* hard-working; industrious. *The <u>diligent</u> student was rewarded with good grades.*
em • pa • thy (em´pə thē) *n.,* ability to share in another's emotions. *The counselor demonstrated her <u>empathy</u> by listening to the students' problems.*

1. The father's treatment of his daughter was unusual because he shared knowledge with her that is customarily shared only with a son.
2. The narrator was amazed by her ancestor's bravery. She was even more amazed that her father took pride in her ancestor's accomplishments and that he believed that his daughter was worth of her example.
3. The narrator didn't ever cry after a nap again because she wants to follow in the footsteps of the Phung Thi women and be strong.

CROSS-CURRICULAR ACTIVITIES

HISTORY. Ask students to investigate other women in history who have served as soldiers on the battlefield, or in other unusual roles, in times of war. Ask them to create a poster depicting and describing one or more of the most notable examples they find.

Get rid of your tobacco,
And you will get a water buffalo.
Give away your betel,
And you will get more paddy land.

Despite her own good advice, she never abstained from chewing betel, nor my father from smoking cigars. They were rare luxuries that life and the war allowed them.

My father also liked rice wine, which we made, and enjoyed an occasional beer, which he purchased when there was nothing else we needed. After he'd had a few sips, he would tell jokes and happy stories and the village kids would flock around. Because I was his youngest daughter, I was <u>entitled</u> to listen from his knee—the place of honor. . . .

Once, when I was the only child at home, my mother went to Da Nang[3] to visit Uncle Nhu, and my father had to take care of me. I woke up from my nap in the empty house and cried for my mother. My father came in from the yard and reassured me, but I was still cranky and continued crying. Finally, he gave me a rice cookie to shut me up. Needless to say, this was a tactic my mother never used.

The next afternoon I woke up, and although I was not feeling cranky, I thought a rice cookie might be nice. I cried a fake cry, and my father came running in.

"What's this?" he asked, making a worried face. "Little Bay Ly[4] doesn't want a cookie?"

I was confused again.

"Look under your pillow," he said with a smile.

I twisted around and saw that, while I was sleeping, he had placed a rice cookie under my pillow. We both laughed, and he picked me up like a sack of rice and carried me outside while I gobbled the cookie.

In the yard, he plunked me down under a tree and told me some stories. After that, he got some scraps of wood and showed me how to make things: a doorstop for my mother and a toy duck for me. This was unheard of—a father doing these things with a child that was not a son! Where my mother would instruct me on cooking and cleaning and tell stories about brides, my father showed me the mystery of hammers and explained the customs of our people.

> What was unusual about the way in which the narrator's father treated her?

His knowledge of the Vietnamese went back to the Chinese Wars in ancient times. I learned how one of my distant ancestors, a woman named Phung Thi Chinh, led Vietnamese fighters against the Han. In one battle, even though she was pregnant and surrounded by Chinese, she delivered the baby, tied it to her back, and cut her way to safety wielding a sword in each hand. I was amazed at this warrior's bravery and impressed that I was her descendant. Even more, I was amazed and impressed by my father's pride in her accomplishments (she was, after all, a humble female) and his belief that I was worthy of her example. *"Con phai theo got chan co ta"* ("follow in her footsteps"), he said. Only later would I learn what he truly meant.

> What amazed the narrator about her ancestor Phung Thi Chinh?

Never again did I cry after my nap. Phung Thi women were too strong for that. Besides, I was my father's daughter, and we had many things to do together.

> Why didn't the narrator ever cry after a nap again?

---

3. **Da Nang.** Seaport in central Vietnam
4. **Little Bay Ly.** Narrator's childhood nickname

words for everyday use

en • ti • tle (en tīt´l) vt., give a right to. *With this pass, I was <u>entitled</u> to enter the movie theater without paying.*

On the eve of my mother's return, my father cooked a feast of roast duck. When we sat down to eat it, I felt guilty and my feelings showed on my face. He asked why I acted so sad.

"You've killed one of mother's ducks," I said. "One of the fat kind she sells at the market. She says the money buys gold, which she saves for her daughters' weddings. Without gold for a dowry[5]—*con o gia*—I will be an old maid!"

My father looked suitably concerned, then brightened and said, "Well, Bay Ly, if you can't get married, you will just have to live at home forever with me!"

I clapped my hands at the happy <u>prospect</u>.

My father cut into the rich, juicy bird and said, "Even so, we won't tell your mother about the duck, okay?"

I giggled and swore myself to secrecy.

The next day, I took some water out to him in the fields. My mother was due home any time, and I used every opportunity to step outside and watch for her. My father stopped working, drank gratefully, then took my hand and led me to the top of a nearby hill. It had a good view of the village and the land beyond it, almost to the ocean. I thought he was going to show me my mother coming back, but he had something else in mind.

He said, "Bay Ly, you see all this here? This is the Vietnam we have been talking about. You understand that a country is more than a lot of dirt, rivers, and forests, don't you?"

I said, "Yes, I understand." After all, we had learned in school that one's country is as sacred as a father's grave.

"Good. You know, some of these lands are battlefields where your brothers and cousins are fighting. They may never come back. Even your sisters have all left home in search of a better life. You are the only one left in my house. If the enemy comes back, you must be both a daughter and a son. I told you how the Chinese used to rule our land. People in this village had to risk their lives diving in the ocean just to find pearls for the Chinese emperor's gown. They had to risk tigers and snakes in the jungle just to find herbs for his table. Their payment for this hardship was a bowl of rice and another day of life. That is why Le Loi, Gia Long, the Trung Sisters, and Phung Thi Chinh fought so hard to expel the Chinese. When the French came, it was the same old story. Your mother and I were taken to Da Nang to build a runway for their airplanes. We labored from sunup to sundown and well after dark. If we stopped to rest or have a smoke, a Moroccan would come up and whip our behinds. Our reward was a bowl of rice and another day of life. Freedom is never a gift, Bay Ly. It must be won and won again. Do you understand?"

What did the narrator's father teach her about freedom?

I said that I did.

"Good." He moved his finger from the patchwork of brown dikes, silver water, and rippling stalks to our house at the edge of the village. "This land here belongs to me. Do you know how I got it?"

I thought a moment, trying to remember my mother's stories, then said honestly, "I can't remember."

He squeezed me lovingly. "I got it from your mother."

"What? That can't be true!" I said. Everyone in the family knew my mother was poor and my father's family was wealthy. Her parents were dead, and she had to work like a slave for her

---

5. **dowry.** Property transferred from a woman's family to her husband upon their marriage

words for everyday use

pros • pect (prä´spekt´) *n.*, anticipated outcome. *The <u>prospect</u> of failure gave the young musician stage fright.*

1. He taught her that freedom must be won and won again by constantly defending oneself against those who want to take away that freedom.

ADDITIONAL QUESTIONS AND ACTIVITIES

Students can discuss the instruction they received as a child from male and female relatives. In their experience, did boys and girls, or brothers and sisters, learn the same things? What explanations do students have for these differences in instruction?

1. Bay Ly's father said that her mother managed land and her household so well that his parents gave them the biggest share of the family land. In this way, the narrator's father says, the land came from her mother.

mother-in-law to prove herself worthy. Such women don't have land to give away!

"It's true." My father's smile widened. "When I was a young man, my parents needed someone to look after their lands. They had to be very careful about whom they chose as wives for their three sons. In the village, your mother had a reputation as the hardest worker of all. She raised herself and her brothers without parents. At the same time, I noticed a beautiful woman working in the fields. When my mother said she was going to talk to the matchmaker about this hard-working village girl she'd heard about, my heart sank. I was too attracted to this mysterious tall woman I had seen in the rice paddies. You can imagine my surprise when I found out the girl my mother heard about and the woman I admired were the same.

"Well, we were married and my mother tested your mother severely. She not only had to cook and clean and know everything about children, but she had to be able to manage several farms and know when and how to take the extra produce to the market. Of course, she was testing her other daughters-in-law as well. When my parents died, they divided their several farms among their sons, but you know what? They gave your mother and me the biggest share because they knew we would take care of it best. That's why I say the land came from her, because it did."

In what way did the land come from the narrator's mother?

I suddenly missed my mother very much and looked down the road to the south, hoping to see her. My father noticed my sad expression.

"Hey." He poked me in the ribs. "Are you getting hungry for lunch?"

> *I suddenly missed my mother very much and looked down the road to the south, hoping to see her.*

"No. I want to learn how to take care of the farm. What happens if the soldiers come back? What did you and Mother do when the soldiers came?"

My father squatted on the dusty hilltop and wiped the sweat from his forehead. "The first thing I did was to tell myself that it was my duty to survive—to take care of my family and my farm. That is a tricky job in wartime. It's as hard as being a soldier. The Moroccans were very savage. One day the rumor passed that they were coming to destroy the village. You may remember the night I sent you and your brothers and sisters away with your mother to Da Nang."

"You didn't go with us!" My voice still held the horror of the night I thought I had lost my father.

"Right! I stayed near the village—right on this hill—to keep an eye on the enemy and on our house. If they really wanted to destroy the village, I would save some of our things so that we could start over. Sure enough, that was their plan.

"The real problem was to keep things safe and avoid being captured. Their patrols were everywhere. Sometimes I went so deep in the forest that I worried about getting lost, but all I had to do was follow the smoke from the burning huts and I could find my way back.

"Once, I was trapped between two patrols that had camped on both sides of a river. I had to wait in the water for two days before one of them moved on. When I got out, my skin was shriveled like an old melon's. I was so cold I could hardly move. From the waist down, my body was black with leeches. But it was worth all the pain. When your mother came back, we still had some furniture and tools to cultivate

848   *UNIT TEN / CULTURES IN CONFLICT*

the earth. Many people lost everything. Yes, we were very lucky."

My father put his arms around me. "My brother Huong—your uncle Huong—had three sons and four daughters. Of his four daughters, only one is still alive. Of his three sons, two went north to Hanoi and one went south to Saigon. Huong's house is very empty. My other brother, your uncle Luc, had only two sons. One went north to Hanoi, the other was killed in the fields. His daughter is deaf and dumb. No wonder he has taken to drink, eh? Who does he have to sing in his house and tend his shrine[6] when he is gone? My sister Lien had three daughters and four sons. Three of the four sons went to Hanoi and the fourth went to Saigon to find his fortune. The girls all tend their in-laws and mourn slain husbands. Who will care for Lien when she is too feeble to care for herself? Finally, my baby sister Nhien lost her husband to French bombers. Of her two sons, one went to Hanoi and the other joined the Republic, then <u>defected</u>, then was murdered in his house.

Nobody knows which side killed him. It doesn't really matter."

My father drew me out to arm's length and looked me squarely in the eye. "Now, Bay Ly, do you understand what your job is?"

I squared my shoulders and put on a soldier's face. "My job is to <u>avenge</u> my family. To protect my family by killing the enemy. I must become a woman warrior like Phung Thi Chinh!"

My father laughed and pulled me close. "No, little peach blossom. Your job is to stay alive—to keep an eye on things and keep the village safe. To find a husband and have babies and tell the story of what you've seen to your children and anyone else who'll listen. Most of all, it is to live in peace and tend the shrine of our ancestors. Do these things well, Bay Ly, and you will be worth more than any soldier who ever took up a sword." ∎

> *Which did the narrator's father admire more, the arts of war or the arts of peace and survival? How do you know?*

---

6. **shrine.** Altar; place of worship

Respond *to the* SELECTION

How has the author lived up to her father's advice?

RESPOND TO THE SELECTION

As an alternative activity, ask students if they agree the statement made by Bay Ly's father: "Freedom is never a gift. It must be won and won again."

ANSWER TO GUIDED READING QUESTION

1. Her father admires the arts of peace and survival more than the arts of war. When his daughter tells him she will become a warrior and avenge her family, he tells her that if she keeps peace and looks after her family, she will "be worth more than any soldier who ever took up a sword."

SELECTION CHECK TEST 4.10.13 WITH ANSWERS

Checking Your Reading
1. How does Hayslip describe her father? **She describes him as solidly built, with a dark complexion and a round face. She says that he was easygoing because he understood life so deeply.**
2. Why does the author's father have to take care of her? **He has to take care of her because her mother went to Da Nang to visit a relative.**
3. What advice does the author's father give her after he tells her the story of Phung Thi Chinh? **He tells Hayslip to "Follow in her footsteps."**
4. Where does Hayslip's father say he got his land? **He says it came from his wife.**
5. What does Hayslip's father tell her that her job is? **He says her job is to stay alive and make sure the village is safe. He also says her job is to tell her story to anyone who will listen.**

Vocabulary in Context
Fill in each blank below with the most appropriate word from the following Words for Everyday Use. You may have to change the tense of the words.

diligent empathy entitle prospect defect avenge

1. Because she was an outstanding citizen, she was <u>entitled</u> to our respect.
2. I was excited by the **prospect** of visiting Australia.
3. The warrior promised to **avenge** the suffering of his comrade.
4. The **diligent** worker received a handsome raise.
5. My **empathy** for the woman in the movie manifested itself in tears.

SELECTION CHECK TEST 4.10.13 WITH ANSWERS (CONT.)

Literary Tools
1. What is a writer's aim? **A writer's aim is his or her purpose or goal for writing.**
2. What is an anecdote? **An anecdote is a short narrative of an interesting, amusing, or biographical incident.**
3. Give one example of an anecdote from the selection. **The story of spending two days in the river is an example of a biographical anecdote.**

RECALL
1a. The author's brother went north.
2a. Her father was easygoing because he "understood life deeply." A "half-trained mechanic" thinks that everything needs fixing.
3a. Her father taught her to make things out of wood and told her about the history and customs of her people. He taught her that freedom "is never a gift" but must be "won and won again."

INTERPRET
1b. She began to pay more attention to her father because her brother, who had previously received his attention, or hers, was gone.
2b. *Responses will vary.* The author's mother relished the small pleasure of chewing betel nuts, and her father enjoyed smoking cigars. They demonstrated wisdom about what is really important in life by being loving and attentive to their children and being hard-working. The narrator's father strives to pass on his pride in the family ancestors and their country and his knowledge that freedom is precious.
3b. Phung Thi Chinh, one of the author's ancestors, was a great woman warrior who fought against the Chinese while pregnant, delivered her baby during a battle, and defeated her enemies. Bay Ly is amazed by her ancestor's bravery and by the fact that her father takes pride in a woman's accomplishments and wants her to follow in Phung Thi Chinh's footsteps.

ANALYZE
4a. Bay Ly says her job is to avenge her family, many of whom have died in the war, to protect them by killing the enemy, or becoming a woman warrior. According to her father, her job is to stay alive, to keep an eye on things and keep the village safe, to find a husband and have children, to tell them and others what she has seen, and to live in peace and tend the shrine of their ancestors.

SYNTHESIZE
4b. The major difference between the two job descriptions is that Bay Ly's is focused on fighting and war whereas her father's is focused on life and peace.

EVALUATE
5a. *Responses will vary.* Bay Ly's father is a good father. He is attentive to her needs when she wakes up crying

Investigate, Inquire, and Imagine

Recall: GATHERING FACTS

1a. Where did the author's brother go?

2a. Why, according to the author, was her father easygoing? What does a "half-trained mechanic" think?

3a. What did the author's father teach her even though she was not a son? What did her father teach her about freedom?

Interpret: FINDING MEANING

1b. Why did the author start to pay more attention to her father?

2b. What small pleasures did the author's mother and father relish? In what ways did they demonstrate wisdom about what is really important in life?

3b. What did Phung Thi Chinh do? How did Bay Ly feel about this woman?

Analyze: TAKING THINGS APART

4a. Compare and contrast what Bay Ly believes to be her job with what her father desires for her.

Synthesize: BRINGING THINGS TOGETHER

4b. What is the major difference between these two job descriptions?

Evaluate: MAKING JUDGMENTS

5a. Evaluate whether the author's father is a good father. If not, why not? If so, why does he qualify?

Extend: CONNECTING IDEAS

5b. What does the author's father have in common with Angie Lowe in "The Gift of Cochise"?

Understanding Literature

AIM. Review the definition for **aim** in the Handbook of Literary Tools. What did the author tell you in this autobiographical story? What purpose does this work achieve? Is this selection principally an example of expository, imaginative, narrative, personal, or persuasive writing?

ANECDOTE. Review the definition for **anecdote** in Literary Tools in Prereading and the chart you made for that section. What anecdotes does Hayslip's father tell her? Why does he tell her these anecdotes?

ANSWERS TO INVESTIGATE, INQUIRE, AND IMAGINE (CONT.)

from her nap. He jokes with her, listens to her, and tells her stories. He believes his daughter can do something great in her life, as her ancestor Phung Thi Chinh did. He teaches her about the customs of her people and how to build things. He gives her advice about how to live her life at the end of the selection.

EXTEND
5b. Hayslip's father had to defend his home against the enemy just as Angie Lowe had to defend her homestead against the Apaches. Both Hayslip's father and Lowe show resourcefulness, determination, and good survival skills.

Answers to Understanding Literature can be found on page 851.

Writer's Journal

1. Pretend you are the adult Bay Ly. Write a **thank you note** to your father for sharing the stories he told you at the top of the hill when you were a little girl. Describe how those stories shaped you into the person you are today.

2. Bay Ly's mother wrote a song about why she should stop chewing betel nuts and why her husband should stop smoking tobacco. Write **song lyrics** that explain why you or someone you know should stop a particular habit.

3. Write an **anecdote** about how you learned a life lesson from a parent, grandparent, or friend.

Integrating the Language Arts

Language, Grammar, and Style

ADJECTIVE CLAUSES. Read about adjective clauses in the Language Arts Survey 3.83, "Clauses within a Sentence." Then identify the adjective clauses in the following sentences.

1. The rice cookie that Bay Ly's father gave her made her stop crying.
2. She admired the ancestor whose childbirth did not interrupt her fighting.
3. The shrine which her father wanted her to tend was dedicated to her ancestors.
4. Her father admired the pretty woman who worked in the fields.
5. Her father gave her advice that would help her.

Study and Research

THE CULTURE OF ANCESTORS. Hayslip's father wanted her to tend the shrine of their ancestors. Research how the Vietnamese honor their ancestors. What practices do they partake in to honor their ancestors? Are there holidays reserved for honoring ancestors? Is honoring ancestors part of their religion? How does the Vietnamese attitude toward ancestors compare with that of other Asian cultures such as those of China and Japan?

Speaking and Listening

INTERVIEWING. To find out more about life in Vietnam, interview Vietnamese immigrants in your community. What was their life like in Vietnam? Why did they leave their country? What was their trip to the United States like? Why did they choose to come to this country? How have they adapted to life in the United States? Which aspects of American culture at first seemed strange to them? What elements of Vietnamese culture remain a part of their life? Have they been back to visit Vietnam? If so, do they perceive Vietnam differently now that they have lived in another country? Ask the Vietnamese immigrants these and other questions. Then present your findings to the class.

ANSWERS TO UNDERSTANDING LITERATURE

AIM. Hayslip tells about her childhood, her relationship with her father, and the family stories that he passed on to her. The author's purpose is to inform, to pass on the wisdom and experiences contained in the stories to others, as her father had urged her to do. This selection is an example of narrative writing.

ANECDOTE. Hayslip's father tells her anecdotes about a female warrior ancestor, how he and his wife were forced to help build a runway for the French, how he met and married his wife, and how he kept some things safe and avoided being captured when the enemy came to destroy their village. He tells his daughter these anecdotes so that she will revere her ancestors, value hard work and freedom, honor her mother, and know that staying alive is important.

ANSWERS TO INTEGRATING THE LANGUAGE ARTS

Language, Grammar, and Style
1. that Bay Ly's father gave her
2. whose childbirth did not interrupt her fighting
3. which her father wanted her to tend
4. who worked in the fields
5. that would help her

Study and Research
Ask students to prepare a one- or two-page report on their findings.

Speaking and Listening
Students who cannot interview Vietnamese immigrants directly can locate interviews in magazines and newspapers as well as in online sources.

GUIDED WRITING
Software

See the Guided Writing Software for an extended version of this lesson that includes printable graphic organizers, extensive student models and student-friendly checklists, and self-, peer, and teacher evaluation features.

"Words are the legs of the mind; they bear it about, carry it from point to point, bed it down at night, and keep it off the ground and out of the marsh and mists."

—*Richard Eder*

Refer to the Language Arts Survey 5.53, "Taking Essay Tests" for additional information.

EXAMINING THE MODEL. Angela's "Obi and Achebe" model is an example of a question based on a specific selection. Her model follows the two-step rule. The author states a thesis in the first two sentences that constitute the first paragraph. Her essay begins with a generalization of

continued on page 853

Guided Writing

RESPONDING TO ESSAY TEST QUESTIONS

It has been said that there is a simple two-step secret to getting high grades on essay exams:
1) State a thesis.
2) Prove it.

While this is clearly meant to be a little humorous, it is true. It really *is* that simple (provided you've studied the right things). Sometimes people forget that essay tests are about demonstrating that you understand a subject enough to write about it.

Since this is a condensation of the basic formula for all essay writing, you already know the steps involved in this process—prewriting, drafting, evaluating, and revising.

WRITING ASSIGNMENT. Your assignment is to prepare an in-class answer to an essay question about cultures in conflict. Unless your teacher supplies an essay question based on one of the selections in this unit, answer the following question. It is similar to one you might be asked to answer in a standardized test.
Question: Analyze a cultural conflict that you and another person have had as a result of your different cultural views.

Angela Jackson was asked the following question for her essay: Compare and contrast the vision of "culture" of Obi and his wife to that of the priest and the villagers, as Achebe describes their respective perspectives in "Dead Men's Path." In this story, what are the differences in their values?

Student Model

Essay Response by Angela Jackson

Culturally, Obi and the priest in Achebe's story "Dead Men's Path" are different in almost every way. Two ways in particular, the way they view birth and death and the way they view other cultures, cause the problems when they come in contact with each other.

The priest and the villagers apparently view death as a kind of earthly transition, one that does not stop the person who "died" from visiting the village along a path that leads through Obi's garden. New babies also come down this path on their way to being born in the village. To Obi, however, this belief is silly. He feels that dead men and unborn babies have no use for a path, and states this belief directly to the priest. Then he even goes further and says he hopes to teach the children of the village to laugh at those ideas.

This inability to accept a different culture is the second main characteristic that separates Obi from the priest. While the priest thinks that Obi's culture and his own can exist side by side, Obi cannot allow that path to continue through his garden. When, as he leaves, the priest says something about hawks and eagles both having a place to perch, he seems confident he has settled the issue. However, Obi presses the matter and states flatly that he cannot allow the path to continue. He does offer to help build an alternate path, but by saying this he only highlights his inability to accept and understand other cultures. The priest then realizes the futility of further discussion and walks out without saying anything else.

The two sides in Achebe's story have many cultural differences, not the least of which is the very important issue of what birth and death mean. However, one of the cultures—the priest's—provides room for coexistence with other cultures, as long as they do not interfere. The other —Obi's—has no such value, and this causes the conflict. It is the one difference in value that, if eradicated, might have made the others insignificant.

Prewriting

You are already familiar with the idea of prewriting, so you know that a great deal of normal prewriting—gathering information—should be done well before you sit down to the essay exam. You have done this part by reading your assignments, listening in class, and engaging in discussions.

However, in the few minutes you will take before you actually start writing your essay answer, it is very important to run through a shortened version of the entire prewriting process. This will help you formulate your answer and structure your essay.

IDENTIFYING YOUR AUDIENCE. Your audience is the test evaluator—whoever will be reading your essay and looking for certain points presented in a clear, coherent manner. Sometimes you know the evaluator—your teacher, for example—so you can use phrases and concepts you've shared as a class or in discussions. On the other hand, on some tests like the SAT, you'll never meet the evaluator. In this case, assume that the evaluator knows the subject and will understand the phrases usually used to discuss it.

the two men, and then lists two supports of this generalization. The rest of her essay follows the structure suggested in these two sentences.

In the body of the essay, she fleshes out these two supports with specific examples that compare and contrast the two characters and their cultural views. She paraphrases remembered examples of dialogue and uses particular actions by each man.

Finally, Angela concludes with a fuller version of the same generalization with which she began. In the last sentence, she offers a kind of "what if…" that further expands the thesis and provides a nice exit to the essay.

FINDING YOUR VOICE. Essay exams are intended to provoke thoughtful, but plain, answers. While some essays you write depend heavily on style for making a point, essay exam answers do not; instead essay answers should emphasize the fact or analysis to be communicated. The best way to do that is in an honest, committed, but objective voice—much like a newspaper reporter's voice. Remember that you need to take a stance toward your subject, but you also need to support that stance objectively.

INDIVIDUAL LEARNING STRATEGIES

MOTIVATION
Ask students how they feel about taking essay tests. Many students will respond negatively. Ensure them that this lesson will help them to be successful in taking essay tests and to make essay test-taking less scary.

READING PROFICIENCY
Encourage student to read this Guided Writing lesson one section at a time. Emphasize that they should complete each step described in the lesson before they move on to the next section.

ENGLISH LANGUAGE LEARNING
The strategies for Reading Proficiency listed above will also benefit English language learners.

SPECIAL NEEDS
Students may have an especially hard time understanding the concept of a thesis statement. Pair them with an enrichment student to help them understand what a thesis statement is and to help them write their thesis statement.

ENRICHMENT
Encourage students to take their essay test answer a step further by brainstorming ways in which to prevent cultural conflicts from happening. What could be done to minimize cultural conflict? Have them develop one type of "cultural conflict prevention." Then have them present their ideas in an oral report. (Note: Research may be required for this activity.)

Prewriting

IDENTIFYING YOUR AUDIENCE. Because students will be writing for test evaluators or teachers, remind students that they will need to use formal English when writing their essay answers. Correct spelling and grammar usage is just as important as the essay itself. You may want to refer students to the Language Arts Survey 3.2, "Formal and Informal English."

FINDING YOUR VOICE. Refer students to the Language Arts Survey 2.5, "Finding Your Voice," and 3.3, "Register, Tone, and Voice."

WRITING WITH A PLAN. Refer students the to the Language Arts Survey 2.9–2.23, "Gathering Ideas," for more ideas on gathering, brainstorming, and organizing ideas.

Drafting

Refer students to the Language Arts Survey 2.25, "Writing a Thesis Statement," and 2.26, "Writing Main Ideas and Supporting Details," to help them with the drafting stage.

Self-Evaluation

Use the checklist on page 856 for self-evaluation. The checklist is intended to act as a student-friendly rubric to help students identify specific evidence of writing strengths and areas needing improvement. Make sure they look objectively at their work and develop concrete suggestions for improvement or specific evidence of why the writing works.

Key Words in Essay Prompts

analyze; identify: break into parts and describe the parts and their relationships

compare: look for qualities or characteristics that resemble each other and emphasize similarities among them, but in some cases also mention differences

contrast: stress the dissimilarities of things, qualities, events, or problems

define; describe; explain: classify and tell the features of; clarify with supporting details and examples

evaluate; assess; justify; argue; prove: tell and evaluate reasons for believing a statement

interpret: tell the meaning and significance of; infer meaning based on facts

summarize: retell very briefly, stating only the main points; condense an event, concept, or debate to its most important points and relate them in an objective manner

synthesize: bring parts together into an understanding of the larger whole

Although both situations suggest an audience with extensive knowledge of your subject, you cannot rely on that knowledge to fill in what you leave out of your answer. Keep in mind that the purpose of an exam is to demonstrate your knowledge and/or analysis of a subject.

WRITING WITH A PLAN. Confident and successful test-takers follow the same routine every time they sit down to an essay exam. By following a rhythm and plan during the exam, you can turn a possibly stressful experience into a familiar, stress-free experience.

1) Preview the Entire Test

First, read all of the questions and directions on the exam to get an overview of what is expected of you. Determine which essay prompts are worth more points and which will require extra time to properly respond. Then budget your time accordingly, and stick to your plan.

2) Analyze the Questions

The essay prompts provide clues about what is expected of you. Read them carefully and decide exactly what is being asked by paying special attention to the meanings of the *key words*.

In the example above, Angela was prompted to "compare and contrast" the priest and Obi. This is a clear direction that she needs to analyze how the two are alike and different. However, a good thesis statement goes beyond just stating the differences. It argues the reasons those differences are significant.

Look again at the general question for your writing assignment: "Analyze a cultural conflict that you and another person have had as a result of your different cultural views." This, too, provides clear direction that you should analyze the differences in your culture and someone else's. Consider how your thesis statement can go beyond just stating the conflict to explaining the reasons those differences are or are not significant.

3) Brainstorm/Collect/Recollect

Once you've figured out what the question is asking, and well before you start writing, you will need to gather your thoughts about it. As a first step, use clustering, listing, or other idea-generation techniques you have learned. For instance, you might try writing concepts you'll be examining in a circle, and then spidering out from there. In the model, the concepts might be "culture," "Obi," and "the priest"—how are they connected? What do you remember from the story?

In the case of your essay prompt, you have been asked to write about a cultural conflict that you and another person have had as a result of your different cultural views. Therefore, the concepts might be "culture," "my views," "_____'s views."

Resist the temptation to skip straight from the brainstorm to writing the answer. Taking the time to organize your thoughts now will mean the difference between an average answer and that really great answer.

For a compare/contrast essay like the model, make a graphic organizer like a simple chart. In an exam, you don't have time to make an elaborate chart. After she brainstormed, Angela quickly sketched out this graphic organizer:

Student Model—Graphic Organizer

Subject	Obi's view	The Priest's view	Similar/different?
Death	The end/departure	Transition/stay here in different form	Different
Other cultures	No tolerance — only one way	Others should just be left alone	Very different — main difference
The other guy	Sadly superstitious and wrong, needs correction	Different, but entitled to his own view	Very different

Organizing ideas in this way is very simple, but when Angela was done making this chart, she had already accomplished two things. First, she had found her thesis statement. Second, the structure her answer should take became apparent—she would use an introduction, two main paragraphs that dealt with two cultural aspects and how the two men differed in regard to them, and then a conclusion.

Drafting

Writing an exam differs a bit from usual essay writing in that you should start with your thesis statement right up front—don't prepare for it and put it at the end of your introductory paragraph. On many exam answers, your thesis statement will be your entire introductory paragraph.

Another difference is that you will have little or no chance to revise. Your first draft should be nearly complete—that's why it is so important to follow your prewriting routine before you start writing. Do plan a couple of minutes to look over your paper at the end of the examination period, however, to make sure you can attend to glaring errors.

Write freely and quickly. Follow the structure created by your brainstorming and graphic organizing, but don't hesitate to add additional ideas as they occur to you.

Self-Evaluation

There are a couple of ways to handle self-evaluation in an exam setting. Some people like to read through each essay answer immediately after they are done writing it, while the facts are still fresh in their mind. Others wait until they are done with all the answers, and then read through them all at once. The second

Language, Grammar, and Style

Comparison and Contrast Order

IDENTIFYING COMPARISON AND CONTRAST ORDER. Comparison and contrast essays like the model are useful for organizing and presenting information and analysis that deals with two distinct subjects. There are two basic ways to organize a comparison/contrast essay:

1) Block Organization (by subject)

In this model, you start by describing one of the two subjects completely, and then describing the second subject using the same characteristics, mentioning some similarities and differences. Then, in the third part of the essay, you bring the two subjects together and briefly summarize the differences and similarities.

EXAMPLE

"Florida is hot, southern and lush. Alaska is cold and northern, but also covered in green growth. Thus, we can see that while the two states differ in temperature and location, they both share an abundance of vegetation."

2) Point-by-point organization (by characteristic)

In this model, you first describe how the two subjects relate to a single characteristic, then how the same two subjects relate to a second characteristic, and so on.

EXAMPLE

"Meteorologically, Florida is hot while Alaska is cold. Geographically, Florida lies far south, but Alaska is in the

continued on page 856

Student Model— Graphic Organizer

See the Writing Resource book for a blackline master of the graphic organizer for this lesson.

Language, Grammar, and Style

Comparison and Contrast Order
LESSON OVERVIEW
In this lesson, students will be asked to do the following:
- Identify Comparison and Contrast Order, 855
- Fix Ineffective Use of Comparison and Contrast Order, 855
- Use Comparison and Contrast Order, 856

INTRODUCING THE SKILL. Explain to students that the comparison and contrast order is one of the most popular ways to analyze literary works and to organize essays. Since most essays require students to compare and contrast two ideas or works, mastering the comparison and contrast order will ensure success in taking essay tests.

PREVIEWING THE SKILL. You may want to refer students to the Grade 10 Resource Book. Direct them to the Critical Writing section of the selection tests. Have them examine previously completed essays that required them to use comparison and contrast order to organize their essays.

PRACTICING THE SKILL. Ask students to exchange papers with a partner. Then have them identify the thesis, the supporting details, and the two ideas or opposing thoughts they are comparing and contrasting.

north. As far as vegetation goes, however, they are much the same; both are covered with lush greenery. Thus, we can see that while the two states differ in temperature and location, they share an abundance of vegetation."

When noting similarities, you'll use words like "both" and "likewise." When outlining differences, you'll use words like "although," "while," and "but." These types of words will help build smooth transitions between ideas and subjects.

FIXING INEFFECTIVE USE OF COMPARISON AND CONTRAST ORDER. Look again at the Student Model on pages 852–853. Has the student used block or point-by-point organization? Does the organizational method she chose fit with her subject matter? Explain. Rewrite the Student Model using a different organizational scheme. Which version is more effective?

USING COMPARISON AND CONTRAST ORDER EFFECTIVELY. Look over the comparison-contrast paper you have written for this assignment. Make sure the form of organization you used is clear, whether it is point-by-point or block. Determine if you have gone beyond just stating the differences, to explaining the reasons those differences are significant.

method has two distinct advantages. First, you'll bring a more objective eye to the essay after even a brief break from it. Second, at the end of the test you will know which essays were really successful and which could use a little work. In either case, be sure to budget time for evaluation and revision back at the first step of your prewriting exercises.

No matter which method you use, ask yourself these questions as you look over your work:

Have I...

- answered the question? Is that answer *in my thesis statement*?
- provided detailed facts to support my answer?
- covered all that I brainstormed and organized?
- summarized and restated the answer?

Revising and Proofreading

You obviously won't have a great deal of time to revise, so spend it wisely. Remember that the purpose of the exam is to determine your level of knowledge, so first look for higher order concerns like content and organization.

When you are satisfied with these issues, move on to lower order concerns like grammar and mechanics. Use proofreading marks to make your changes. A marked-up but correct essay is preferable to a clean essay that has grammatical mistakes.

Publishing and Presenting

Too often after we turn in an essay exam, we just forget about it and move on. Maybe we talk to our friends about how we think we have done, or what we missed, but rarely do we really look at what we've written. This is unfortunate because exam writing is often a real glimpse into our own thought processes. With little time and more questions waiting, exams sometimes bring out our most natural writing.

Next time you take an essay exam, take a close look at your answer afterwards. You might be surprised at the thoughts you generated under a little pressure.

Reflecting

Think of a time you felt uneasy in an essay exam situation. Why were you uncomfortable? Did you prepare yourself by reading the material and participating in class? What sort of analysis of the questions did you do? How long did you spend on prewriting?

Go through the steps you took on your last essay exam, and consider whether or not that was the best way to do it. What might you change for next time?

UNIT 10 review
Cultures in Conflict

Words for Everyday Use

Check your knowledge of the following vocabulary words from the selections in this unit. Write a short sentence using these words in context to make the meaning clear. To review the definition or usage of a word, refer back to the page number listed or the Glossary of Words for Everyday Use.

acrid, 800
adept, 835
adjoining, 839
amiable, 799
antagonist, 805
assuage, 839
avenge, 849
banter, 816
baser, 839
belligerently, 814
benevolently, 828
biculturalism, 826
bluster, 815
colonial, 826
communal, 837
conspicuous, 839
contemptuously, 805
cursory, 835
defect, 849
deference, 806, 818
deflect, 804
degraded, 836
denigration, 787
deplore, 830
despotic, 828
destitute, 836
diligent, 845
disintegrate, 798
empathy, 845

entitle, 846
eradicate, 788
erratic, 839
euphemism, 835
euphoria, 827
expatriate, 829
fatigue, 803
flaunt, 818
forage, 816
froth, 818
garish, 813
gnarled, 811
harpoon, 792
inclination, 839
indolence, 814
inevitable, 836
inhibition, 806
integrity, 811, 830
irresolute, 804
ludicrous, 835
malevolent, 804
meager, 814
nostalgia, 830
obsessive, 837
parochial, 826
patriarchy, 828
perimeter, 828
periphery, 827
pivotal, 786

plaintively, 806
pristine, 792
propitiate, 788
prospect, 847
pseudo, 813
rakish, 811
ravenously, 840
resilient, 830
resolutely, 802
reverberation, 792
salvage, 840
shiftless, 799
shorn, 819
smoldering, 814
sovereign, 826
sporadic, 797
sporadically, 839
superannuated, 787
surmise, 818
thriftlessness, 815
truant, 814
tundra, 792
unwieldy, 837
ventilation, 835
venture, 835
vigorous, 826
zealously, 817

Literary Tools

Define the following terms, giving concrete examples of how they are used in the selections in this unit. To review a term, refer to the page number indicated or to the Handbook of Literary Terms.

aim, 824, 843
anecdote, 843
autobiography, 833
chronological order, 833
dramatic irony, 791

foreshadowing, 785
genre, 795
irony, 791, 809
irony of situation, 809
narrator, 785

setting, 809
stereotype, 795
style, 824
symbol, 791
tone, 809

REFLECTING ON YOUR READING

The prompts in Reflecting on Your Reading are suitable as topics for research papers. Refer to the Language Arts Survey 5.18–5.45, "Research Skills." (To evaluate research papers, see the evaluation forms for writing, revising, and proofreading in the Assessment Resource book.)

The prompts in Reflecting on Your Reading can also be adapted for use as topics or oral reports or debates. Refer student to the Speaking and Listening Resource in the Language Arts Survey. (To evaluate these projects, see the evaluation forms in the Assessment Resource.)

Reflecting on your reading

Genre Studies

1. **SHORT STORY.** Do Angie in "The Gift of Cochise" and Chee in "Chee's Daughter" experience internal or external conflict? How do they attempt to resolve their conflict? What difficulties do they have in dealing with a culture different from their own? How are the characters' conflicts eventually resolved? How does their understanding of the other culture help them to resolve their conflict?

2. **NONFICTION.** What are the aims for Mukherjee, Uchida, and Hayslip in writing their nonfiction selections? How does the use of anecdotes reinforce their aims?

3. **POETRY.** How does "Freeway 280" tie in to the theme of this unit—cultures in conflict? According to the speaker of the poem, which cultures are in conflict? Which culture is winning the contest for the speaker's soul? What is the speaker looking for at the end of the poem?

Thematic Studies

4. **STEREOTYPES.** What role does stereotyping play in "Dead Men's Path" and "Chee's Daughter"? What do the people doing the stereotyping assume? What is the danger of stereotyping for Michael Obi in the former story and the tourists in the latter?

5. **FATHERLY LOVE.** In which selections do fathers demonstrate love for their childhood? How do they show their love for their children? What character traits do the fathers exhibit that make them good role models for their children?

6. **CULTURES IN CONFLICT.** For Mira in "The Road from Ballygunge," which cultures are in conflict? How does she feel treated by her adopted country? Why does she want to retire to her homeland?

7. **COMMUNAL LIVING.** Based on the observations of Yoshiko Uchida, does communal living bring out the best or the worst in people? Does Uchida show herself to be adaptable to communal living? How can you tell?

for your READING LIST

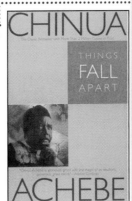

CHINUA
THINGS
FALL
APART
ACHEBE

Things Fall Apart by Chinua Achebe. A simple story of a strong man whose life is dominated by fear and anger. Uniquely and richly African, it reveals at the same time Achebe's keen awareness of the human qualities common to men of all times and places. This is Achebe's masterpiece and is often compared to the great Greek tragedies. More than two million copies of *Things Fall Apart* have been sold in the United States since it was first published here in 1959, and worldwide over eight million copies are in print in fifty different languages. Cited in the London *Sunday Times* as one of the "1,000 Makers of the Twentieth Century" for defining "a modern African literature that was truly African" and thereby making "a major contribution to world literature," Chinua Achebe has published novels, short stories, essays, poetry, and children's books.

Independent Reading Activity

CULTURAL EXPRESSIONS. Every aspect of our society is an expression of one culture or another, or a combination of many. Different cultures express themselves in different ways, often many in the same neighborhood. What different cultural expressions are there in your city or neighborhood? Do you listen to music from other countries? Do you like ethnic food? What art exhibits have you seen? Explore a cultural expression in your neighborhood or city, and find out as much as you can from it, either by reading about it or by talking to people. Prepare a report on the event or location you chose, and present it to your class.

Selections for Additional Reading

Grass Dancer by Susan Power. Grass Dancing is a Native American tradition, and the characters of this novel assemble at the powwow to watch and to compete against each other. Susan Power, of the Sioux tribe, interweaves stories about the young and old, dreams and life, men and women, revenge and love. Some of the characters have a dark, rich history that would try to doom them, but it is the same history that ultimately gives them triumphant life.

Desert Exile: The Uprooting of a Japanese-American Family by Yoshiko Uchida.
If you found the excerpt in this unit on page 833 interesting, you may want to read Uchida's memoir about the more than one hundred thousand Japanese Americans who were taken from their homes and sent to detention centers during World War II. Uchida and her family were among them, and *Desert Exile* is her autobiographical story of that time.

Cry, the Beloved Country by Alan Paton. This is the story of a Zulu pastor, Stephen Kumalo, and his son, Absalom, in turbulent South Africa in the 1940s. It is a story of racial inequality and the injustice of apartheid.

FOR YOUR READING LIST

Things Fall Apart discusses the impacts of colonialism on a traditional Nigerian village. It explores the consequences that take place when white men force their ways on to a tribe that is deeply rooted in tribal customs and old ways. Students will appreciate the accessible writing style Achebe uses to describe what life was like for the Ibo tribe before and after colonialism.

Independent Reading Activity
To help them with this activity, have students do some prereading on how to communicate effectively with people from a different culture. Refer them to the Language Arts Survey 4.11, "Being Considerate of Other Cultures and Communication Styles," and 4.12, "Overcoming Barriers to Effective Multicultural Communication." You may also want to encourage students who are non-native English speakers to share some suggestions on how to communicate effectively with someone from their culture.

ART NOTE

The Neoclassical artist Jacques-Louis David (1748–1825) painted *The Death of Socrates* as a lesson in sacrifice for moral principles. The Athenian government accused Socrates of corrupting the young through his teachings and gave him the choice of renouncing his beliefs or drinking deadly hemlock. David shows him calmly discoursing on the immortality of the soul with his grief-stricken disciples as he reaches for the cup of poison.

TEACHING THE MULTIPLE INTELLIGENCES

Continued on page 861

The Death of Socrates, 1787. Jacques-Louis David. Metropolitan Museum of Art, New York.

GOALS/OBJECTIVES

Studying this unit will enable students to
- appreciate and interpret a Greek tragedy
- identify Sophocles as a great Greek tragedian
- name and describe elements of plot, and trace their development in a drama
- describe the role of the chorus in classical Greek drama
- study the Golden Age of Greece
- connect theater today with the contributions of ancient playwrights
- write a review of a performance
- identify and use parallel structure in writing as well as fix errors in parallelism

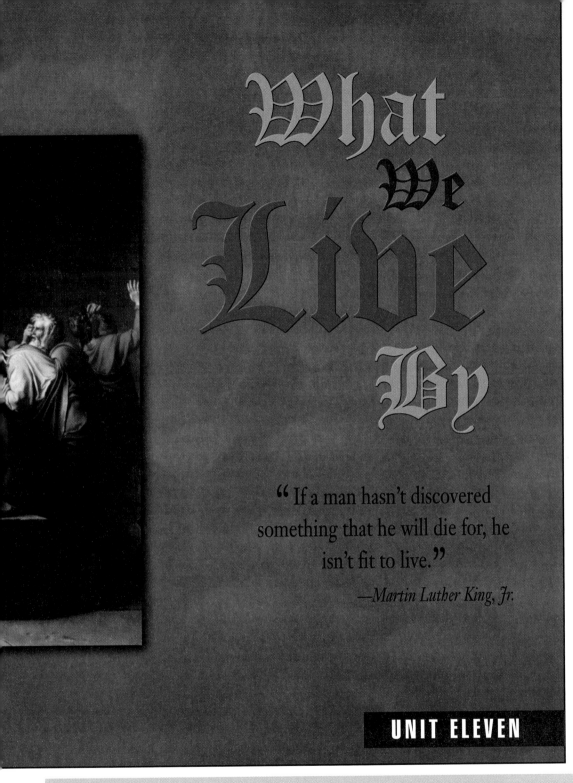

What We Live By

" If a man hasn't discovered something that he will die for, he isn't fit to live. "

—*Martin Luther King, Jr.*

UNIT ELEVEN

echoes

▶ Pride is hateful before God and man.

—The Bible, Apocrypha, Ecclesiasticus 10:7

▶ The tyrant is a child of Pride
Who drinks from his great sickening cup
Recklessness and vanity,
Until from his high crest headlong
He plummets to the dust of hope.

—Sophocles, Oedipus Rex

▶ He who rules by moral force is like the pole star, which remains in its place while all the lesser stars do homage to it.

—Confucius

▶ The gods
Visit the sins of the fathers upon the children.

—Euripedes, Phrixus, fragment 830

▶ We are going to have to decide what kind of people we are—whether we obey the law only when we approve of it or whether we obey it no matter how distasteful we may find it.

—Harry S. Ashmore, on integration of Little Rock High School, Arkansas Gazette, Sept. 4, 1957

▶ Extreme law is often extreme injustice.

—Terence (Publius Terentius Afer, c.190–159 BC.)

▶ The being who patiently endures injustice, and silently bears insults, will soon become unjust, or unable to discern right from wrong.

—Mary Wollstonecraft, in Vindication of the Rights of Woman

▶ It is better to die on your feet than to live on your knees.

—Delores Ibarruri

▶ The one thing that doesn't abide by majority rule is a person's conscience.

—Harper Lee

▶ Life is made up of constant calls to action, and we seldom have time for more than hastily contrived answers.

—Judge Learned Hand

862 *UNIT ELEVEN / WHAT WE LIVE BY*

ANTIGONE

by Sophocles,
translated by Dudley Fitts and Robert Fitzgerald

Reader's resource

Antigone (an tig' ə nē) is the middle play in a trilogy of classical Greek tragedies called the Theban Plays. The trilogy, written by Sophocles (sä' fə clēz'), also includes *Oedipus the King* and *Oedipus at Colonus*. At the end of the first play, *Oedipus the King*, Oedipus (ed' ə pəs), fictional king of the city of Thebes, is forced into exile. At that time, according to the story, he left Thebes under the rule of his two sons, Polyneices (päl i nē' sēz) and Eteocles (ē tē' ə klēz). Both, however, wanted to be the sole ruler. Polyneices attacked Thebes, and the two brothers killed each other in the ensuing battle. Creon, brother-in-law to Oedipus, was installed as king, and his first act as leader was to punish Polyneices posthumously for attacking the kingdom by refusing to have him buried. As *Antigone* begins, Polyneices's sister Antigone declares that she will bury him. According to ancient Greek tradition, not being buried is a horrifying dishonor, and Antigone feels obliged to bury her brother no matter what the consequences. The play centers on the conflict between Creon and Antigone. Neither is able to yield to the other, and tragic consequences result.

About the AUTHOR

Sophocles (*circa* 496–406 BC) wrote more than 125 plays, and, although only seven of them have survived, he remains to this day one of the most important playwrights in literature. Sophocles's first tragedy was performed in 468 BC at the festival of Dionysos, and was awarded first prize over a play written by the older and more known Aeschylus. From that time on Sophocles held a high place in Athenian drama. This great tragedian is known to have been a talented athlete and musician, and an active member of the community of Athens, Greece. He was born into a wealthy family, was well educated, was a personal friend of prominent statesmen, and was popular for his grace and charm. Sophocles lived to be ninety years old—witnessing almost the entire fifth century, which was a glorious time in the history of Athens—and remained an active leader of the great city for his whole life. All his surviving plays were written after he was fifty years old, and *Oedipus at Colonus* was written when he was ninety. One of his last known acts was to lead a chorus in public mourning for the death of his rival, Euripides. Sophocles died that same year.

Literary TOOLS

TRAGEDY AND TRAGIC HERO. A **tragedy** is a drama that tells the story of the fall of a person of high status. It celebrates the courage and dignity of a *tragic hero* in the face of inevitable doom. A **tragic hero** is a character who possesses noble qualities but who also has a *tragic flaw* that brings about his or her fall in a tragedy. As you read, determine who might be the tragic hero, or heroes, of *Antigone*.

PLOT, EXPOSITION, INCITING INCIDENT, AND RISING ACTION. A **plot** is a series of events related to a central *conflict*, or struggle. A typical plot involves the introduction of a conflict, its development, and its eventual resolution. The **exposition**, or **introduction**, in a plot sets the tone or mood, introduces the characters and the setting, and provides necessary background information. The **inciting incident** is the event that introduces the central conflict. The **rising action**, or **complication**, develops the conflict to a high point of intensity. Look for these elements of plot as you read through the first three scenes of *Antigone*.

CHORUS AND ODE. In classical Greek drama, a **chorus** was a group of people who spoke directly to the audience to convey the author's viewpoint or to introduce story details. The chorus traditionally made its entrance singing a song called the *parodos*, the first of a number of **odes**, or lofty, serious lyric poems, it would sing throughout the play. These choral odes had alternating stanzas called the *strophe*, the *antistrophe*, and the *epode*. The chorus moved up one side of the stage while singing the strophe, down the other during the antistrophe, and stood in place during the epode. As you read, examine the odes delivered by the Chorus and consider the role of the Chorus, and its leader, the Choragos.

HISTORICAL/ CULTURAL NOTE

The Birth of Drama in the West
One of the greatest contributions that ancient Greece made to Western culture was the invention of drama. In the West, as in other parts of the world, drama grew out of ritual religious performances. In early Greece, festivals honoring Dionysos, the god of the vine and revelry, included performances by choruses, or troupes of dancers who would chant and sing. According to legend, in the early sixth century BC, a chorus leader named **Thespis** separated himself from the chorus and gave himself individual lines. This innovation made possible dramatic interaction between the chorus and the lone actor, and thus drama was born. To this day, actors are sometimes called **thespians**. The first great Athenian playwright, **Aeschylus** (525–456 BC), introduced a second actor into his scenes. Sophocles changed drama the most when he introduced a third actor, reduced the importance of the chorus, and added scene paintings as props on stage.

Greek Theaters, Scenery, and Costumes
The audience of a Greek play sat in an amphitheater, open to the sky, with tiered, stone seats arranged in a semicircle around the **orchestra**, a circular stage where the chorus performed. Behind the orchestra was a wooden building called the *skene*, from which we get our modern word *scene*. The *skene* was used as a changing area for the actors and as a place to store props. It also served as part of the set, representing a temple, a shrine, a cave, or a home.

   Greek theaters seated as many as 15,000 people, so elaborate measures had to be taken to make sure that everyone in the audience could see and hear the action. The actors wore expensive costumes and large masks fitted with small brass megaphones for projecting their voices. They also wore padding, headpieces, and platform shoes to increase their size. Because of the masks, actors did not depend on facial expressions as they do today but rather communicated feelings by means of exaggerated gestures, body movements, and tones of voice.

Dramatists of the Golden Age
Greek drama reached its peak in the Golden Age of Greece, 477–431 BC.

HISTORICAL/CULTURAL NOTE (CONT.)

During this time, four great playwrights emerged: **Aeschylus** (es' kə ləs), **Sophocles**, **Euripides** (480–406 BC), and **Aristophanes** (448–385 BC). Aristophanes was a master of the **comedy**—his works were wild and hilarious satires of Greek customs, politics, and even the gods. The other three playwrights were masters of the **tragedy**, a play that explores the heights of noble beliefs and heroic action on the one hand, and the depths of despair over human existence on the other. Of the three tragedians, many consider Sophocles to be the "purest" artist, the one whose plays are truest to actual human experience.

READER'S JOURNAL

Ask students to recall a time when they defied a parent or authority figure. Did they do so because they strongly believed they were right, or did they do so knowing they were in the wrong? How can a person tell when they are making the correct judgment? As an alternative, students may write about someone they know who believes he or she is always right.

INDIVIDUAL LEARNING STRATEGIES

MOTIVATION
Ask students to discuss what their definition of *tragedy* is. What makes something tragic, instead of merely sad?

READING PROFICIENCY
Although the language used in this play is relatively straightforward, students may have trouble with the allusions to places and people of ancient Greece. Go over with them the Words for Everyday Use and the footnotes, then encourage them to read through each scene with a partner, answering the Guided Reading questions as they go and summing up the main point of each scene.

ENGLISH LANGUAGE LEARNING
In addition to going over the Words for Everyday Use and footnotes, you may wish to review with students the archaic language and the additional vocabulary below.
sentry—soldier standing guard
carrion birds—birds like vultures, who eat dead and decaying flesh
fiery—hot with anger
helms—helmets
sated—satisfied
auspicious—favorable
impassively—emotionlessly
doddering—trembling from weakness or age
demoralizing—corrupting of the morals
prow—front part of a boat
expansively—with readiness to talk
folly—foolishness

SPECIAL NEEDS
Students will find it helpful to hear the selection read out loud. Either read out loud to students, have them alternate reading aloud, or have them listen to a dramatic reading on audiotape. Make sure

ANTIGONE

Sophocles, translated by Dudley Fitts and Robert Fitzgerald

Antigone, 1900s. Marie Spartali Stillman. Simon Carter Gallery, Woodbridge, UK.

Reader's Journal

When have you done something you strongly believed was right, although it went against someone else's belief, a rule, or even a law? What were the consequences of your actions?

art note

Antigone, 1900s. Marie Spartali Stillman.

Marie Spartali Stillman (1844–1927), the daughter of a Greek family living in London, studied under Pre-Raphaelite painters Dante Gabriel Rossetti and Ford Madox Brown. Her subjects include historical and literary figure groups such as that in *Antigone*, above. As you read the play, identify the figures in the painting and describe the action it portrays.

INDIVIDUAL LEARNING STRATEGIES (CONT.)

students focus on the Guided Reading questions and the Recall questions in the Investigate, Inquire, and Imagine section.

ENRICHMENT
Ask students to compile a bibliography of works for each of the great Golden Age dramatists,

Sophocles, Aeschylus, Euripedes, and Aristophanes. They should use proper bibliographic form. Then, they should select a play by one of the dramatists and write a synopsis of the play.

CAST OF CHARACTERS

ANTIGONE (an tig′ ə nē), daughter of Oedipus, former King of Thebes

ISMENE (is mē′ nē), another daughter of Oedipus

EURYDICE (yo͞o rid′ ə sē), wife of Creon

CREON (krē′ än), King of Thebes, uncle of Antigone and Ismene

HAIMON (hī′ mən), Creon's son, engaged to Antigone

TEIRESIAS (tī rē′ sē əs), a blind prophet

A SENTRY

A MESSENGER

CHORUS

CHORAGOS (kō rā′ gəs), leader of the chorus

A BOY, who leads Teiresias

GUARDS

SERVANTS

Scene. Before the palace of CREON, *King of Thebes. A central double door, and two lateral doors. A platform extends the length of the facade, and from this platform three steps lead down into the "orchestra," or chorus-ground.* **Time.** *Dawn of the day after the repulse of the Argive[1] army from the assault on Thebes.*

Prologue

[ANTIGONE and ISMENE *enter from the central door of the Palace.*]

ANTIGONE. Ismene, dear sister,
You would think that we had already suffered enough
For the curse on Oedipus:
I cannot imagine any grief
5   That you and I have not gone through. And now—
Have they told you of the new <u>decree</u> of our King Creon?

ISMENE. I have heard nothing: I know
That two sisters lost two brothers, a double death
In a single hour; and I know that the Argive army
10   Fled in the night; but beyond this, nothing.

ANTIGONE. I thought so. And that is why I wanted you
To come out here with me. There is something we must do.

ISMENE. Why do you speak so strangely?

---

1. **Argive.** From Argos, a capital city in ancient Greece

words for everyday use

de • cree (di krē′) *n.,* order set forth by one in authority. *The judge issued a new <u>decree</u>.*

For the Prologue through scene 2:

anarchist	lithe
comprehensive	meddle
compulsive	reverence
conscience	sententiously
decree	statecraft
endure	vengeance
insolence	waver

LITERARY NOTE

The Curse on Oedipus
In line 3 of the Prologue, Antigone refers to the "curse on Oedipus." Oedipus was Antigone's father, and a great tragic hero. His story is told in ***Oedipus the King,*** the first play in Sophocles's Theban trilogy, although it was in fact written some years after *Antigone.* Greek audiences were very familiar with the legend of Oedipus, because it had been an important part of the Greek oral tradition for centuries. The famous oral poet Homer told the story of Oedipus in his epic poems *The Iliad* and *The Odyssey,* which date back to the seventh or eighth centuries BC.

The story of Oedipus goes thus: The city of Thebes was founded by Cadmus, who angered the god Apollo. In retaliation, Apollo placed a curse upon the city. According to Apollo's oracle at Delphi, the son of King Laius and Queen Jocasta would kill his father and marry his mother. When Oedipus was born, his parents sent a servant to abandon the baby in the woods. However, the servant took pity on him and delivered the boy to King Polybus of Corinth. When Oedipus was a young man, he learned of the prophecy, and he fled Corinth in horror, determined never to fulfill it. However, while on the road to Thebes, he got into an argument and killed a stranger— who was in fact his father, King Laius. Thinking no more about the incident, he proceeded to Thebes, where he ended up marrying his mother, Jocasta, taking his father's place as King of Thebes. Together they had four children, Antigone, Ismene, Eteocles, and Polyneices. Oedipus's incest, although unintentional, caused the gods to bring a terrible plague onto the city of Thebes. In investigating the reason behind this curse, Oedipus discovered the horrible truth about his life. He plucked out his own eyes to punish himself for having been blind to the truth, while his

Continued

LITERARY NOTE (CONT.)

wife/mother Jocasta killed herself. Oedipus, who is truly noble at heart, does finally die peacefully in Colonus under the protection of King Theseus, a story that is told in the final chapter of Sophocles's trilogy, *Oedipus at Colonus.*

The story of Oedipus is one of an individual struggling against his own fate and against the will of the gods. Ultimately, Oedipus finds there is no escape. He accepts that he is at the mercy of the gods. From the very beginning of *Antigone,* there are hints that Oedipus's curse is still alive and will continue to destroy the lives of his children. Ask students to watch for references to fate and to the anger of the gods as they read *Antigone.* Which events in the play seem to be the result of the "curse on Oedipus"?

HISTORICAL/CULTURAL NOTE

Types of Greek Theater

The Greeks created the major types, or genres, of theater—tragedy, comedy, and farce. Plays were an integral part of many festivals, and on a given festival day, an ancient Greek audience would see three tragedies and a satyr play by a single playwright, followed by a comedy by a different playwright. Hence, tragedies were usually written in a cycle of three.

Inform students that the best definition we have of Greek **tragedy** was written by the philosopher and critic **Aristotle** in a work called the *Poetics*. (The definition of *tragedy* included in the Handbook of Literary Terms is based on Aristotle's definition.) Greek tragedy depicts the downfall of a character of high status who is neither completely good nor completely evil. The hero's fall is brought about by some flaw in his or her character, known as a **tragic flaw.** Aristotle's term for the tragic flaw, *hamartia,* has also been translated as "an error in judgment." One of the most commonly presented tragic flaws is that of *hubris,* or excessive pride. Aristotle believed that witnessing the downfall of a basically good but flawed individual, not unlike ourselves, would evoke the emotions of pity and fear in the audience (pity for the suffering the hero experiences and fear for ourselves—that we could be in the hero's situation). Aristotle stated that the emotions of pity and fear bring about "the **catharsis** of such emotions," meaning that in watching a tragedy the viewer experiences a sort of emotional cleansing or release.

Classical Greek **comedies** often contained humorous satires of public figures or of types of people, and this humorous side of the classical comedy prefigured our current use of the word *comedy* to refer to any funny enactment. **Satyr plays** were wild, humorous romps dealing with

---

ANTIGONE. Listen, Ismene:

15 Creon buried our brother Eteocles
With military honors, gave him a soldier's funeral,
And it was right that he should; but Polyneices,
Who fought as bravely and died as miserably,—
They say that Creon has sworn

20 No one shall bury him, no one mourn for him,
But his body must lie in the fields, a sweet treasure
For carrion birds to find as they search for food.
That is what they say, and our good Creon is coming here
To announce it publicly; and the penalty—
Stoning to death in the public square!

25   There it is,
And now you can prove what you are:
A true sister, or a traitor to your family.

ISMENE. Antigone, you are mad! What could I possibly do?

ANTIGONE. You must decide whether you will help me or not.

30 ISMENE. I do not understand you. Help you in what?

ANTIGONE. Ismene, I am going to bury him. Will you come?

ISMENE. Bury him! You have just said the new law forbids it.

ANTIGONE. He is my brother. And he is your brother, too.

ISMENE. But think of the danger! Think what Creon will do!

35 ANTIGONE. Creon is not strong enough to stand in my way.

ISMENE. Ah sister!
Oedipus died, everyone hating him
For what his own search brought to light, his eyes
Ripped out by his own hand; and Iocaste[2] died,

40 His mother and wife at once; she twisted the cords
That strangled her life; and our two brothers died,
Each killed by the other's sword. And we are left:
But oh, Antigone,
Think how much more terrible than these

45 Our own death would be if we should go against Creon
And do what he has forbidden! We are only women;
We cannot fight with men, Antigone!
The law is strong, we must give in to the law
In this thing, and in worse. I beg the Dead

50 To forgive me, but I am helpless: I must yield

What is Antigone going to do?

What will Creon do if Antigone carries out her plan?

---

2. **Iocaste** (yō kä′ stä). Iocaste, the mother of Antigone and Ismene, hanged herself when she learned that her husband, Oedipus, was actually her son.

HISTORICAL/CULTURAL NOTE (CONT.)

ludicrous situations and characters. The name of this type of play comes from the characters, who were dressed as satyrs, creatures half human and half goat. Satyr plays were the first examples of the modern theatrical form known as **farce,** in which ludicrous, improbable, funny situations are the norm.

HISTORICAL NOTE

The rich men of Athens, or **choregoi,** were appointed to finance particular plays. Since these men were also politicians, their political views were often reflected in the play. Attendance to the plays was mandatory for the citizens of Athens, and public money was allocated to people who couldn't afford admission.

To those in authority. And I think it is dangerous business
To be always <u>meddling</u>.

ANTIGONE. If that is what you think,
I should not want you, even if you asked to come.
You have made your choice and you can be what you want to be.
55 But I will bury him; and if I must die,
I say that this crime is holy: I shall lie down
With him in death, and I shall be as dear
To him as he to me.
It is the dead,
Not the living, who make the longest demands:
We die for ever. . . .
60 You may do as you like,
Since apparently the laws of the gods mean nothing to you.

ISMENE. They mean a great deal to me; but I have no strength
To break laws that were made for the public good.

ANTIGONE. That must be your excuse, I suppose. But as for me,
I will bury the brother I love.

Why does Ismene refuse to help Antigone?

65 **ISMENE.** Antigone,
I am so afraid for you!

ANTIGONE. You need not be:
You have yourself to consider, after all.

ISMENE. But no one must hear of this, you must tell no one!
I will keep it a secret, I promise!

ANTIGONE. Oh tell it! Tell everyone!
70 Think how they'll hate you when it all comes out
If they learn that you knew about it all the time!

ISMENE. So fiery! You should be cold with fear.

ANTIGONE. Perhaps. But I am doing only what I must.

ISMENE. But can you do it? I say that you cannot.

75 **ANTIGONE.** Very well: when my strength gives out, I shall do
no more.

ISMENE. Impossible things should not be tried at all.

ANTIGONE. Go away, Ismene:

**words
for
everyday
use**
med • dle (med əl) *vi.,* interfere in something that is not one's business. *Don't try to set Patrick up on a blind date—he resents people who <u>meddle</u> in his personal life.*

ANSWER TO GUIDED READING QUESTION

1. Ismene says she is afraid to break laws that were made for the public good. She feels she is not strong enough to defy Creon.

HISTORICAL/CULTURAL NOTE

Inform or remind students of the following information about some of the Greek gods referred to in *Antigone.*
Aphrodite was the goddess of love and beauty. She was the mother of **Eros**, or **Cupid**, the god of love.
Apollo was the god of music, poetry, wisdom, light, and truth. Often, especially in later myths, he was called Phoebus Apollo. *Phoebus* means "shining," and in these later myths, Apollo was often called the god of the sun.
Ares was the cruel god of war, who delighted in slaughter. His companions included Discord, Strife, Terror, and Panic. He was associated with the vulture and the dog.
Pallas Athene, or **Athena**, was the goddess of wisdom, justice, war, civilization, and peace. She sprang from the head of her father, Zeus.
Dionysus, or **Dionysos**, was the god of revelry and of the vine. He was often pictured as a handsome youth with grape leaves and vines in his hair and pan pipes in his hands. His worshippers, the fierce female maenads, honored him with ecstatic, frenzied, and often brutal rituals.
Hades, or **Pluto**, was the dreaded god of the underworld. He owned a helmet that made its wearer invisible. His wife was **Persephone**. **Hecate** is a goddess of the underworld and a companion of Persephone.
Zeus was the leader of the Olympian gods. When "God" is referred to in *Antigone,* Zeus is meant. Zeus was god of the sky and of thunder. He carried a thunderbolt, wore a breastplate called the *aegis,* and was associated with the oak tree and the eagle. His palace was on Mount Olympus.

CROSS-CURRICULAR ACTIVITIES

SOCIAL STUDIES. The central conflict of *Antigone* involves Creon's violation of Greek burial tradition. In ancient Greece it was considered very important that a person's body be buried properly—that ensured that the deceased would be allowed to enter the underworld. Ask students to discuss the funeral customs and beliefs about death held by different cultures. They may conduct research on the subject and share their findings with the class. What kind of funeral ceremonies are held around the world? Are there cultures in which bodies are not buried, but are left in the open or treated in some other way? What types of monuments have been built? For example, students may learn about the Mausoleum at Halicarnassus, one of the seven wonders of the ancient world.

1. Ismene thinks Antigone is foolish.
   She is frightened by her actions,
   but she admires her noble loyalty to
   her family.
2. Polyneices and his army are
   described as brash, overly confident
   men who brag and swagger.

LITERARY TECHNIQUE

DESCRIPTION AND MOOD.
Description is a type of writing
that portrays a character, an object,
or a scene. Descriptions make use of
sensory details—words and phrases
that describe how things look,
sound, smell, taste, or feel. Effective
descriptions contain precise nouns,
verbs, adverbs, and adjectives.
Mood, or *atmosphere*, is the emotion
created in the reader by part or all of
a literary work. The writer can evoke
in the reader an emotional
response—such as fear, discomfort,
longing, or anticipation—by working
carefully with descriptive language
and sensory details. Students should
note and name some of the precise
nouns, verbs, and adjectives used in
the description of the battle between
Polyneices and Eteocles. You may
also have them create a sensory
detail chart listing the sensory details
in the Parodos. Refer them to the
Language Arts Survey 2.18, "Sensory
Detail Charts," for guidance. Finally,
ask students to describe the mood
that is created by the description.
Answers
Some of the precise nouns, verbs,
and adjectives include: *marching,
striking, eddy, blaze, roused, windy,
yawning, famished, pinefire, garland,
bray, swagger, blasted, clanging, fury.*
The sensory details include descriptions of sight, sound, and touch. All
of these details, students might suggest, contribute to a mood of high
tension, awe, and dread.

LITERARY TECHNIQUE

METAPHOR AND SIMILE. A
metaphor is a figure of speech
in which one thing is written or spoken about as if it were another. This
figure of speech invites the reader to
make a comparison between the two
things. A **simile** is a comparison that
uses *like* or *as*. Ask students to identify some of the metaphors used in

---

I shall be hating you soon, and the dead will too,
For your words are hateful. Leave me my foolish plan:
80 I am not afraid of the danger; if it means death,
It will not be the worst of deaths—death without honor.

ISMENE. Go then, if you feel that you must.
You are unwise,
But a loyal friend indeed to those who love you.

[*Exit into the Palace.* ANTIGONE *goes off, left. Enter the* CHORUS.]

Parodos

CHORUS.   [STROPHE 1]
Now the long blade of the sun, lying
Level east to west, touches with glory
Thebes of the Seven Gates.[3] Open, unlidded
Eye of golden day! O marching light
5 Across the eddy and rush of Dirce's stream.[4]
Striking the white shields of the enemy
Thrown headlong backward from the blaze of morning!

CHORAGOS. Polyneices their commander
Roused them with windy phrases,
10 He the wild eagle screaming
Insults above our land,
His wings their shields of snow,
His crest their marshalled helms.

CHORUS.   [ANTISTROPHE 1]
Against our seven gates in a yawning ring
15 The famished spears came onward in the night;
But before his jaws were sated with our blood,
Or pinefire took the garland of our towers,
He was thrown back; and as he turned, great Thebes—
No tender victim for his noisy power—
20 Rose like a dragon behind him, shouting war.

CHORAGOS. For God hates utterly
The bray of bragging tongues;
And when he beheld their smiling,
Their swagger of golden helms,
25 The frown of his thunder blasted
Their first man from our walls.

CHORUS.   [STROPHE 2]

---

3. **Seven Gates.** Seven entrances through the wall that
surrounded and protected Thebes
4. **Dirce's stream.** Small river into which Dirce, an early
queen of Thebes, was thrown after she was murdered

> *How does Ismene feel
> about Antigone?*

> *Paraphrase this
> description of Polyneices
> and his army.*

LITERARY TECHNIQUE (CONT.)

the Parodos. How does each metaphor contribute to
the mood of the description?
Answers
Responses will vary. Students may note any of the following metaphors: "the long blade of the sun";
"unlidded / Eye of golden day"; "[Polyneices] the
wild eagle screaming insults above the land...His

wings their shields...His crest their [helmets]"; and
"jaws," used as a metaphor for Polyneices's warlike
troops. They may note the following simile:
"Thebes...Rose like a dragon behind him, shouting
war." These figures of speech contribute to the mood
of danger and excitement.

We heard his shout of triumph high in the air
Turn to a scream; far out in a flaming arc
He fell with his windy torch, and the earth struck him.
30 And others storming in fury no less than his
Found shock of death in the dusty joy of battle.

CHORAGOS. Seven captains at seven gates
Yielded their clanging arms to the god
That bends the battle-line and breaks it.
35 These two only, brothers in blood,
Face to face in matchless rage,
Mirroring each the other's death,
Clashed in long combat.

CHORUS.   [ANTISTROPHE 2]
But now in the beautiful morning of victory
40 Let Thebes of the many chariots sing for joy!
With hearts for dancing we'll take leave of war:
Our temples shall be sweet with hymns of praise,
And the long night shall echo with our chorus.

SCENE 1

CHORAGOS. But now at last our new King is coming:
Creon of Thebes, Menoikeus'[5] son.
In this auspicious dawn of his reign
What are the new complexities
5 That shifting Fate has woven for him?
What is his counsel? Why has he summoned
The old men to hear him?

[*Enter* CREON *from the Palace, center. He addresses the* CHORUS *from the top step.*]

CREON. Gentlemen: I have the honor to inform you that our
Ship of State, which recent storms have threatened to destroy,
10 has come safely to harbor at last, guided by the merciful
wisdom of Heaven. I have summoned you here this morning
because I know that I can depend upon you: your devotion to
King Laïos[6] was absolute; you never hesitated in your duty to
our late ruler Oedipus; and when Oedipus died, your loyalty
15 was transferred to his children. Unfortunately, as you know,
his two sons, the princes Eteocles and Polyneices, have killed
each other in battle; and I, as the next in blood, have
succeeded to the full power of the throne.
I am aware, of course, that no Ruler can expect complete loyalty
20 from his subjects until he has been tested in office.

---

5. **Menoikeus** (me noi' kē əs). Father of Creon and Iocaste
6. **King Laïos** (lā' əs). Father of Oedipus

ANSWERS TO GUIDED READING QUESTIONS

ANSWERS TO GUIDED READING QUESTIONS

1. Creon does not expect complete loyalty from his subjects, since he is so new to the office. However, he expects his subjects to do what is "best for the State," and to value the "public welfare" above any "private friendship."
2. Eteocles will be honored with a traditional burial and full military honors.
3. Creon's command is that Polyneices must have no burial. Creon will reward those who are loyal to his command by showing them respect in their lifetime and reverence when they are dead.

ADDITIONAL QUESTIONS AND ACTIVITIES

Ask students what they think Creon is implying when he says he will show respect and reverence to those people who obey his command. Do his words contain an unspoken threat? Is Creon prepared to earn respect as a leader, or is he simply going to demand it? Explain.
Answer
Responses will vary. Students may say that there is an implied threat in Creon's words. He is implying that he is able to punish any disobedient person both in life and in death. Although Creon says that he is prepared to earn loyalty, he is demanding that the people respect him and his laws.

LITERARY TECHNIQUE

DIALOGUE. Dialogue is conversation involving two or more people or characters. Plays are made up of dialogue and stage directions. In the conversation between the Choragos and Creon (lines 49–56), what is revealed about the Choragos's attitude toward Creon's edict?
Answer
The Choragos does not support or condemn the edict outright. He simply says that if that is Creon's will, the elders will follow it because they recognize that Creon has the right to enforce it.

---

25   Nevertheless, I say to you at the very outset that I have nothing but contempt for the kind of Governor who is afraid, for whatever reason, to follow the course that he knows is best for the State; and as for the man who sets private friendship above the public welfare—I have no use for him, either. I call God to witness that if I saw my country headed for ruin, I should not be afraid to speak out plainly; and I need hardly remind you that I would never have any dealings with an enemy of the people. No one values friendship more highly

30   than I; but we must remember that friends made at the risk of wrecking our Ship are not real friends at all.

   These are my principles, at any rate, and that is why I have made the following decision concerning the sons of Oedipus: Eteocles, who died as a man should die, fighting for his

35   country, is to be buried with full military honors, with all the ceremony that is usual when the greatest heroes die; but his brother Polyneices, who broke his exile to come back with fire and sword against his native city and the shrines of his fathers' gods, whose one idea was to spill the blood of his blood and

40   sell his own people into slavery—Polyneices, I say, is to have no burial: no man is to touch him or say the least prayer for him; he shall lie on the plain, unburied; and the birds and the scavenging dogs can do with him whatever they like.

   This is my command, and you can see the wisdom behind it. As

45   long as I am King, no traitor is going to be honored with the loyal man. But whoever shows by word and deed that he is on the side of the State—he shall have my respect while he is living, and my <u>reverence</u> when he is dead.

   CHORAGOS. If that is your will, Creon son of Menoikeus,

50   You have the right to enforce it: we are yours.

   CREON. That is my will. Take care that you do your part.

   CHORAGOS. We are old men: let the younger ones carry it out.

   CREON. I do not mean that: the sentries have been appointed.

   CHORAGOS. Then what is it that you would have us do?

55   **CREON.** You will give no support to whoever breaks this law.

   CHORAGOS. Only a crazy man is in love with death!

What does Creon expect from his subjects? What does he say should be ranked above private friendship?

How will Eteocles be honored?

What does Creon command with regard to Polyneices? How will he reward loyalty to his command?

---

words for everyday use	**rev • er • ence** (rev' rəns) *n.*, profound respect, love, and awe. *The great leader was treated with <u>reverence</u> by the people of her country.*

CROSS-CURRICULAR ACTIVITIES

SOCIAL STUDIES. Creon's speech at the beginning of scene 1 is essentially political, similar to the State of the Union Address given by the President of the United States each year. Ask students to compare Creon's speech with a State of the Union address. Transcripts of the State of the Union addresses delivered in recent years are available on the Internet. Students could print a copy of the most recent speech or find another political speech. Have students pair up to compare the speech, in terms of information, purpose, and tone, with Creon's. For additional information on purpose and tone, see the Language Arts Survey 2.3, "Identifying Your Purpose," and 4.1, "Verbal and Nonverbal Communication."

CREON. And death it is; yet money talks, and the wisest
Have sometimes been known to count a few coins too many.

[*Enter* SENTRY *from left.*]

SENTRY. I'll not say that I'm out of breath from running, King,
60   because every time I stopped to think about what I have to tell
      you, I felt like going back. And all the time a voice kept
      saying, "You fool, don't you know you're walking straight into
      trouble?"; and then another voice: "Yes, but if you let
      somebody else get the news to Creon first, it will be even
65   worse than that for you!" But good sense won out, at least I
      hope it was good sense, and here I am with a story that makes
      no sense at all; but I'll tell it anyhow, because, as they say,
      what's going to happen's going to happen, and—

CREON. Come to the point. What have you to say?

70 SENTRY. I did not do it. I did not see who did it. You must not
      punish me for what someone else has done.

CREON. A <u>comprehensive</u> defense! More effective, perhaps,
If I knew its purpose. Come: what is it?

SENTRY. A dreadful thing . . . I don't know how to put it—

CREON. Out with it!

75 SENTRY.   Well, then;
The dead man—
                    Polyneices—

[*Pause. The* SENTRY *is overcome, fumbles for words.* CREON *waits
impassively.*]
                              out there—
                                        someone,—

New dust on the slimy flesh!

[*Pause. No sign from* CREON.]

Someone has given it burial that way, and
Gone . . .

[*Long pause.* CREON *finally speaks with deadly control.*]

CREON. And the man who dared do this?

What has happened to
Polyneices's body?

---

words
for
everyday
use

com • pre • hen • sive (käm′ prə hen′ siv) *adj.,* covering a matter completely, inclusive. *The caterer had a
<u>comprehensive</u> list of bakeries in the area.*

1. Polyneices's body has been covered
   with dirt.

LITERARY TECHNIQUE

DIALOGUE AND COMIC RELIEF.
Dialogue is conversation
involving two or more characters.
Plays are made up of dialogue and
stage directions. Ask students what
impression they get of the sentry, the
soldier who was guarding
Polyneices's body, from reading the
dialogue in lines 59–77. Writers
sometimes insert into a serious work
of fiction or drama a humorous
scene that is said to provide **comic
relief**, because it relieves the seriousness or emotional intensity felt by the
audience. Paradoxically, a scene introduced for comic relief can sometimes, because of the contrast it provides, increase the perceived intensity or seriousness of the action
around it. Do students think that the
character of the sentry provides
comic relief? Why, or why not? Does
Creon's dialogue with the sentry provide a contrast to the other dialogue
in scene 1?
Answers
Responses will vary. Students will
probably say that the sentry is
extremely nervous and frightened of
talking to Creon. His fear makes him
frantic and he rambles nonsensically.
Students may say that the character
of the sentry provides comic relief
because he is almost ridiculously
scatterbrained and he irritates Creon.
A contrast is provided between the
solemn speeches of the Chorus and
Creon and the wordy, confused lines
of the sentry.

ADDITIONAL QUESTIONS AND ACTIVITIES

Ask students to form pairs to enact the scene
between Creon and the sentry—from the sentry's
entrance until line 104—as a skit. They should use
exaggerated gestures and body language in order to
convey the emotions felt by each character. Be sure
the students note the stage directions when

preparing to enact the skit. If you wish to have
them continue the skit through the end of the
scene, you may read line 105 (spoken by the
Choragos). When they have rehearsed their
performances, each pair should perform the skit for
the class.

1. The sentry is afraid of Creon and dreads his mission. He is honest in a way that is comical.
2. Creon thinks that the gods would never do such a thing for Polyneices because Polyneices was a bad person who tried to loot the gods' temples, burn their images, and take over Thebes.

ADDITIONAL QUESTIONS AND ACTIVITIES

Ask students the following question: Why does Creon become so enraged at the Choragos's suggestion (lines 105–110)? Is the Choragos's suggestion reasonable, given the beliefs of the ancient Greeks? Why does Creon dismiss it so quickly?
Answers
Creon is angry because the Choragos is suggesting another way of seeing the situation. The problem in the play hinges on the fact that Creon cannot see any other way but his own. *Responses will vary.* Students will probably say that the suggestion is reasonable, considering that the Greeks believed their gods to be active in human affairs. Creon probably dismisses the suggestion so quickly because he is stubborn and proud and does not like being contradicted.

Ask students to discuss the logic Creon uses in his rebuttal to the Choragos's suggestion. Is Creon's rebuttal a logically valid argument, or is it a fallacy? In other words, is the assumption on which he bases his argument a reasonable one? Does he back up his argument with any evidence? Does Creon have any logical reason to conclude that "anarchists" have bribed someone to bury Polyneices? Explain. What does Creon's style of arguing reveal about his character?
Answers
Responses will vary, but students should note that Creon bases his argument on the assumption that he knows what the gods think. He assumes that they share his values and point of view, while in reality he has no way of knowing whether or not this is true, nor does he have any concrete evidence that the gods support him. Therefore, his argument is not valid; it is a fallacy. Creon has no logical reason to

---

80 **SENTRY.**   I swear I
Do not know! You must believe me!
                                Listen:
The ground was dry, not a sign of digging, no,
Not a wheeltrack in the dust, no trace of anyone.
It was when they relieved us this morning and one of them,
The corporal, pointed to it.
85   There it was,
The strangest—
                        Look:
The body, just mounded over with light dust: you see?
Not buried really, but as if they'd covered it
Just enough for the ghost's peace. And no sign
90 Of dogs or any wild animal that had been there.
And then what a scene there was! Every man of us
Accusing the other: we all proved the other man did it,
We all had proof that we could not have done it.
We were ready to take hot iron in our hands,
95 Walk through fire, swear by all the gods,
It was not I!
I do not know who it was, but it was not I!

[CREON'S *rage has been mounting steadily, but the* SENTRY *is too intent upon his story to notice it.*]

And then, when this came to nothing, someone said
A thing that silenced us and made us stare
100 Down at the ground: you had to be told the news,
And one of us had to do it! We threw the dice,
And the bad luck fell to me. So here I am,
No happier to be here than you are to have me:
Nobody likes the man who brings bad news.

> What is the sentry's attitude toward Creon?

105 **CHORAGOS.** I have been wondering, King: can it be that the gods
    have done this?

CREON. [*Furiously*] Stop!
Must you doddering wrecks
Go out of your heads entirely! "The gods!"
110 Intolerable!
The gods favor this corpse? Why? How had he served them?
Tried to loot their temples, burn their images,
Yes, and the whole State, and its laws with it!
Is it your senile opinion that the gods love to honor bad men?

> Why does Creon think the gods could not be responsible for burying Polyneices?

ADDITIONAL QUESTIONS AND ACTIVITIES (CONT.)

believe that anarchists were behind the crime. He has no evidence of this; he is only speculating and theorizing. Creon's style of arguing reveals that he is not a reasonable person; he refuses to weigh different points of view. He angers quickly and is quick to punish.

A pious thought!—

115   No, from the very beginning
There have been those who have whispered together,
Stiff-necked <u>anarchists</u>, putting their heads together,
Scheming against me in alleys. These are the men,
And they have bribed my own guard to do this thing.

120 Money!   [*Sententiously*]
There's nothing in the world so demoralizing as money.
Down go your cities,
Homes gone, men gone, honest hearts corrupted,
Crookedness of all kinds, and all for money!
[*To* SENTRY]

                           But you—!

125 I swear by God and by the throne of God,
The man who has done this thing shall pay for it!
Find that man, bring him here to me, or your death
Will be the least of your problems: I'll string you up
Alive, and there will be certain ways to make you

130 Discover your employer before you die;
And the process may teach you a lesson you seem to have missed:
The dearest profit is sometimes all too dear:
That depends on the source. Do you understand me?
A fortune won is often misfortune.

    SENTRY. King, may I speak?

135 CREON.   Your very voice distresses me.

    SENTRY. Are you sure that it is my voice, and not your <u>conscience</u>?

    CREON. By God, he wants to analyze me now!

    SENTRY. It is not what I say, but what has been done, that hurts you.

    CREON. You talk too much.

    SENTRY.   Maybe; but I've done nothing.

140 CREON. Sold your soul for some silver: that's all you've done.

    SENTRY. How dreadful it is when the right judge judges wrong!

    CREON. Your figures of speech
May entertain you now; but unless you bring me the man,

ANTIGONE / *SCENE 1*   **873**

---

1. Humans cannot secure themselves against death.
2. The city is strong, and "stands," when laws are kept. It can be assumed by the equation that the city is weakened, and "falls," when laws are broken.

Quotables

"What a piece of work is a man, how noble in reason, how infinite in faculties; in form and moving how express and admirable, in action how like an angel, in apprehension, how like a god: the beauty of the world, the paragon of animals!"

—Spoken by Hamlet in Shakespeare's *Hamlet, Prince of Denmark*

ADDITIONAL QUESTIONS AND ACTIVITIES

Ask students to compare the above quote from *Hamlet* to Ode I. How are the sentiments expressed in each passage similar? In what sense are humans *not* like the gods, as pointed out in the ode?
Answers
Both passages express the sentiment that humans are wonderful creatures, the greatest creatures on the earth. However, as pointed out in Ode I, humans are mortal.

LITERARY TECHNIQUE

THEME. A **theme** is a central idea in a literary work. What theme or central idea regarding human beings does the Chorus communicate in Ode I? What laws do you think the Chorus refers to in the second antistrophe? Whose point of view do you think the Chorus is supporting in this last stanza, Creon's or Antigone's?
Answers
The theme dealt with in the ode is that humans are mighty and great, but yet, they are mortal and are subject to the laws of good and evil. Humans are capable of conquering the sea, the land, and the beasts; of using words and creating great cities

---

You will get little profit from them in the end.

[*Exit* CREON *into the Palace.*]

145   **SENTRY.** "Bring me the man"—!
I'd like nothing better than bring him the man!
But bring him or not, you have seen the last of me here.
At any rate, I am safe!

[*Exit* SENTRY.]

Ode I

CHORUS.   [STROPHE 1]
Numberless are the world's wonders, but none
More wonderful than man; the stormgray sea
Yields to his prows, the huge crests bear him high;
Earth, holy and inexhaustible, is graven
5   With shining furrows where his plows have gone
Year after year, the timeless labor of stallions.

                                  [ANTISTROPHE 1]
The lightboned birds and beasts that cling to cover,
The <u>lithe</u> fish lighting their reaches of dim water,
All are taken, tamed in the net of his mind;
10   The lion on the hill, the wild horse windy-maned,
Resign to him; and his blunt yoke has broken
The sultry shoulders of the mountain bull.

                                [STROPHE 2]
Words also, and thought as rapid as air,
He fashions to his good use; <u>statecraft</u> is his,
15   And his the skill that deflects the arrows of snow,
The spears of winter rain: from every wind
He has made himself secure—from all but one:
In the late wind of death he cannot stand.

                              [ANTISTROPHE 2]
O clear intelligence, force beyond all measure!
20   O fate of man, working both good and evil!
When the laws are kept, how proudly his city stands!
When the laws are broken, what of his city then?
Never may the anarchic man find rest at my hearth,
Never be it said that my thoughts are his thoughts.

> *What force can humans not predict or withstand?*

> *What happens when laws are kept? What happens when they are broken?*

---

words for everyday use	**lithe** (līth′) *adj.,* mild, gentle, or agile. *Her <u>lithe</u> voice floated through the air.* **state • craft** (stāt kraft′) *n.,* art of conducting state affairs. *The governor was skilled in the art of <u>statecraft</u>.*

LITERARY TECHNIQUE (CONT.)

that protect them from the elements—but they cannot conquer death. *Responses will vary.* Students might say that the Chorus is speaking of the laws of government, the laws people make in order to prevent their societies from falling apart. They may point out that the Chorus is supporting Creon here in saying that laws are important and that anarchy leads to the crumbling of cities. Other students might suggest that the laws the Chorus refers to are moral laws, ones that deal with good and evil, and which are laid down by the gods. If so, the Chorus is echoing Antigone's point of view and may be suggesting that humans, however powerful they may be, must obey the laws of the gods.

SCENE 2

[*Re-enter* SENTRY *leading* ANTIGONE.]

CHORAGOS. What does this mean? Surely this captive woman
Is the Princess, Antigone. Why should she be taken?

SENTRY. Here is the one who did it! We caught her
In the very act of burying him.—Where is Creon?

CHORAGOS. Just coming from the house.
[*Enter* CREON, *center.*]

5   **CREON.**   What has happened?
Why have you come back so soon?

SENTRY. [*Expansively*]   O King,
A man should never be too sure of anything:
I would have sworn
That you'd not see me here again: your anger
10   Frightened me so, and the things you threatened me with;
But how could I tell then
That I'd be able to solve the case so soon?
No dice-throwing this time: I was only too glad to come!

Here is this woman. She is the guilty one:
15   We found her trying to bury him.
Take her, then; question her; judge her as you will.
I am through with the whole thing now, and glad of it.

CREON. But this is Antigone! Why have you brought her here?

SENTRY. She was burying him, I tell you!

CREON. [*Severely*]   Is this the truth?

20   **SENTRY.** I saw her with my own eyes. Can I say more?

CREON. The details: come, tell me quickly!

SENTRY.   It was like this:
After those terrible threats of yours, King,
We went back and brushed the dust away from the body.
The flesh was soft by now, and stinking,
25   So we sat on a hill to windward and kept guard.
No napping this time! We kept each other awake.
But nothing happened until the white round sun
Whirled in the center of the round sky over us:
Then, suddenly,
30   A storm of dust roared up from the earth, and the sky

> What information does the sentry bring to Creon?

1. The sentry informs Creon that Antigone has been caught trying to bury Polyneices.

ADDITIONAL QUESTIONS AND ACTIVITIES

How do the Choragos and Creon react when they see that the sentry has brought in Antigone? Why do you think they react this way?
Answers
The Choragos and Creon are both stunned and confused to see Antigone brought in. They apparently never suspected the Princess to have committed the crime. *Responses will vary.* Perhaps the two men are shocked that a woman would dare defy Creon, particularly a woman of Creon's own court. Perhaps they assume that women are not brave enough to commit such acts of defiance.

1. Antigone was not afraid and denied nothing when captured.
2. The sentry was relieved, because he knew he was now safe from punishment. However, he was troubled because he regarded Antigone as a friend and knew her arrest could lead to her death.
3. Antigone says the gods of the underworld would never make a law such as the one Creon made; they would never make a law that called for dishonoring someone after death.

LITERARY TECHNIQUE

SIMILE. A **simile** is a comparison using *like* or *as*. What simile does the sentry use in lines 35–41 when describing Antigone's actions? What does his choice of imagery suggest about his attitude toward Antigone?
Answers
The sentry compares Antigone to a mother bird who returns to her nest to find her babies stolen, all her love's work lost. His choice of imagery suggests that the sentry sympathizes with Antigone. He understands her sorrow—he finds it as natural as that of a mother bird who has lost her young.

CROSS-CURRICULAR ACTIVITIES

SOCIAL STUDIES. Ask students to research the Greek beliefs about the underworld, or Hades. Did Greeks believe in both a place of punishment and a place of reward—an equivalent to the Judeo-Christian heaven and hell? What were some famous punishments delivered in Hades? What myths were associated with the underworld?

To answer these questions, students might visit the library and find a book or encyclopedia of Greek mythology. Some obvious choices are Edith Hamilton's *Mythology,* Robert Graves's work *The Greek Myths,* or *Book of Greek Myths* by Ingri and Edgar Parin d'Aulaire. Or, students may consult one of many Internet resources about Greek mythology to learn about the Greek conception of the underworld. One

---

Went out, the plain vanished with all its trees
In the stinging dark. We closed our eyes and <u>endured</u> it.
The whirlwind lasted a long time, but it passed;
And then we looked, and there was Antigone!
35 I have seen
A mother bird come back to a stripped nest, heard
Her crying bitterly a broken note or two
For the young ones stolen. Just so, when this girl
Found the bare corpse, and all her love's work wasted,
40 She wept, and cried on heaven to damn the hands
That had done this thing.
            And then she brought more dust
And sprinkled wine three times for her brother's ghost.
We ran and took her at once. She was not afraid.
Not even when we charged her with what she had done.
She denied nothing.
45   And this was a comfort to me,
And some uneasiness: for it is a good thing
To escape from death, but it is no great pleasure
To bring death to a friend.
            Yet I always say
There is nothing so comfortable as your own safe skin!

50 CREON. [*Slowly, dangerously*] And you, Antigone,
You with your head hanging,—do you confess this thing?

ANTIGONE. I do. I deny nothing.

CREON. [*To* SENTRY]   You may go.

[*Exit* SENTRY.]

[*To* ANTIGONE] Tell me, tell me briefly:
Had you heard my proclamation touching this matter?

55 ANTIGONE. It was public. Could I help hearing it?

CREON. And yet you dared defy the law.

ANTIGONE.   I dared.
It was not God's proclamation. That final Justice
That rules the world below makes no such laws.

Your edict, King, was strong,

> **How did Antigone react when captured?**

> **Why did her reaction both comfort the sentry and make him uneasy?**

> **What law would not be made in the "world below"?**

words for everyday use

en • dure (ən dyər′) *vt.,* bear up under great hardship; remain firm; tolerate. *Laura* <u>endured</u> *her boss's irrational behavior for as long as she could, and then she quit.*

CROSS-CURRICULAR ACTIVITIES (CONT.)

good site is the **Greek Mythology Link** at http://hsa.brown.edu/~maicar/Underworld.html. Students should present their findings in a visual way. They could draw a map of the underworld with explanatory captions, draw pictures of various sights there, or they could create a travel brochure explaining and illustrating all of the sights that a traveler might see on a trip through Hades.

Teaching Note: Students may read myths associated with Hades, such as the myth of Persephone and Demeter. Students may include some of the following elements of Hades in their projects: Persephone, the Rivers Styx, Acheron, and Phlegethon, the spring of Lethe, Tartarus, Kronos, the avenging Erinyes, the Elysian fields, Prometheus, and Sisyphus.

60 But all your strength is weakness itself against
The immortal unrecorded laws of God.
They are not merely now: they were, and shall be,
Operative forever, beyond man utterly.

I knew I must die, even without your decree:
65 I am only mortal. And if I must die
Now, before it is my time to die,
Surely this is no hardship: can anyone
Living, as I live, with evil all about me,
Think Death less than a friend? This death of mine
70 Is of no importance; but if I had left my brother
Lying in death unburied, I should have suffered.
Now I do not.
            You smile at me. Ah Creon,
Think me a fool, if you like; but it may well be
That a fool convicts me of folly.

75 **CHORAGOS.** Like father, like daughter: both headstrong, deaf to
    reason!
She has never learned to yield.

According to the Choragos, how is Antigone like her father?

CREON.   She has much to learn.
The inflexible heart breaks first, the toughest iron
Cracks first, and the wildest horses bend their necks
At the pull of the smallest curb.
                           Pride? In a slave?
80 This girl is guilty of a double <u>insolence</u>,
Breaking the given laws and boasting of it.
Who is the man here,
She or I, if this crime goes unpunished?
Sister's child, or more than sister's child,
85 Or closer yet in blood—she and her sister
Win bitter death for this!

[*To* SERVANTS]   Go, some of you,
Arrest Ismene. I accuse her equally.
Bring her: you will find her sniffling in the house there.
Her mind's a traitor: crimes kept in the dark
90 Cry for light, and the guardian brain shudders;
But how much worse than this
Is brazen boasting of barefaced anarchy!

Of what does Creon accuse Antigone?

words for everyday use

in • so • lence (in′ sə ləns) *n.*, haughtiness, impudence, disrespect. *The student's <u>insolence</u> led to a visit to the principal.*

ANSWERS TO GUIDED READING QUESTIONS

1. According to the Choragos, Antigone is like her father, Oedipus, in that she is headstrong and refuses to listen to reason.
2. Creon accuses Antigone of a "double insolence," breaking the law and then boasting about it.

LITERARY NOTE

When Creon calls Antigone "Sister's child, or more than sister's child / Or closer yet in blood...," he is referring to the incest committed by Oedipus, which caused Antigone to be born both child and grandchild of Jocasta, Creon's sister.

ADDITIONAL QUESTIONS AND ACTIVITIES

How does Antigone regard the possibility of her own death? According to Creon, who has committed the worse crime, Antigone or Ismene? Explain.
Answers
Antigone boldly faces her own death and welcomes it. She says that she knew she must die anyway, being mortal, and that she would rather die before her time than live "with evil all about [her]" and with her brother lying unburied. For this reason she views death as "a friend." He says he blames them both equally, but then he admits that he finds Antigone's "brazen boasting of barefaced anarchy" much worse than Ismene's secret thoughts of treason.

LITERARY TECHNIQUE

TRAGIC FLAW. Remind students that a **tragic flaw** is a personal weakness that brings about the fall of a character in a tragedy. Antigone's father, Oedipus, possessed the tragic flaw of stubbornness and pride. In the tragedy *Oedipus the King*, Oedipus brings about his own tragic

---

LITERARY TECHNIQUE (CONT.)

fall by insisting on seeking out the person who is responsible for killing King Laios, despite warnings that he would be better off not knowing. When he asks for the help of Teiresias, the blind prophet, Teiresias, knowing that Oedipus himself is responsible, says, "Alas, how terrible is wisdom when it brings no profit to the man that's wise." He refuses to tell Oedipus what he knows, but Oedipus, stubborn and headstrong, insists on knowing. When Teiresias tells him, Oedipus, in his foolish pride, seeks to prove the prophet wrong, thereby leading him to the horrible truth and his own tragic fall. The Choragos compares Antigone to her father in that they both possess this flaw of stubbornness.

1. Antigone and Creon disagree as to whether Polyneices, a traitor, deserves to be honored in death as much as does Eteocles, who defended his country. Creon believes that Eteocles deserves the honors but Polyneices does not, while Antigone believes that "there are honors due all the dead."

ADDITIONAL QUESTIONS AND ACTIVITIES

Point out to students Antigone's line "Which of us can say what the gods hold wicked?" What is she pointing out about Creon's argument? Of what is she accusing him here?
Answers
Antigone is pointing out that Creon's argument is a fallacy, because he cannot know what the gods think. She is accusing him of arrogance. He must be terribly arrogant to believe he can speak for the gods.

ANTIGONE. Creon, what more do you want than my death?

CREON.   Nothing.
That gives me everything.

ANTIGONE.   Then I beg you: kill me.
95 This talking is a great weariness: your words
Are distasteful to me, and I am sure that mine
Seem so to you. And yet they should not seem so:
I should have praise and honor for what I have done.
All these men here would praise me
100 With their lips not frozen shut with fear of you.

[*Bitterly*]

Ah the good fortune of kings,
Licensed to say and do whatever they please!

CREON. You are alone here in that opinion.

ANTIGONE. No, they are with me. But they keep their tongues
in leash.

105 **CREON.** Maybe. But you are guilty, and they are not.

ANTIGONE. There is no guilt in reverence for the dead.

CREON. But Eteocles—was he not your brother too?

ANTIGONE. My brother too.

CREON.   And you insult his memory?

ANTIGONE. [*Softly*] The dead man would not say that I insult it.

110 **CREON.** He would: for you honor a traitor as much as him.

ANTIGONE. His own brother, traitor or not, and equal in blood.

CREON. He made war on his country. Eteocles defended it.

ANTIGONE. Nevertheless, there are honors due all the dead.

CREON. But not the same for the wicked as for the just.

115 **ANTIGONE.** Ah Creon, Creon,
Which of us can say what the gods hold wicked?

CREON. An enemy is an enemy, even dead.

ANTIGONE. It is my nature to join in love, not hate.

On what point do Antigone and Creon disagree?

CROSS-CURRICULAR ACTIVITIES

ARTS AND HUMANITIES. Have students view a film version of *Antigone* and compare and contrast the film with Sophocles's version. Some films available for rental include the 1962 production starring Irene Pappas and directed by George Tzavellas and the 1984 BBC version directed by Don Taylor and starring Juliet Stevenson. Ask students to comment on the way a film production, with its use of special effects and camera techniques, might differ from a stage production. Students should also discuss how the director interpreted Sophocles's work. Were there elements of the play that were left out, or interpreted in a surprising way?

Antigone and Ismene.

CLASSICAL GREEK ART. Locate and
share with students images of
classical Greek art such as black
and red figure ware pottery,
statues, busts, and reliefs of
gods, goddesses, and important people. Emphasize that the
orderliness and precision of Greek art
and architecture are the basis of
what is known as the **classic style**.
Students might enjoy discussing the
art and talking about how the techniques and skills used in the art, and
the mood individual pieces create. If
possible, arrange a trip to the local
art museum, get transparencies or
art books from your school's art history teacher, or find a site on the
Internet that displays examples of
classical Greek art. Two possibilities
include a page managed by the
Detroit Institute of Arts, at
http://www.dia.org/collections/
ancient/greece/greece.html and
"19th-Century Photography of
Ancient Greece," maintained by the
Getty Research Institute, which is
at http://www.getty.edu/gri/greece/.

INTERNET RESOURCES

The illustration on this page
shows Antigone and Ismene
wearing hairstyles and dress
popular in ancient Greece.
Students may be interested in
researching the clothing, hairstyles,
and jewelry of ancient Greek times.
A wealth of information is available
on the Internet. One excellent site is
the **Tulane University Theater
Pages**, which contain information
about costume, hairstyles, and
jewelry from different time periods—
illustrated with art and sculpture of
the day. Take a look at the following
address and click on the link for the
costumes of Greece: http://ps.
theatre.tulane.edu/Period.Styles/
Costumes/text/Cost.Per_Styles.html.
Another site is the **Timeline of
Costume History** at http://www.
costumes.org/pages/timelinepages/ti
meline.htm. Other links can be
found at http://www.costumes.org/
pages/histlink.htm. Students might
visit these sites and then imagine
they are costume designers for a
production of Antigone. They could
then describe, or draw and label,
costume and hairstyle designs for
each of the major characters. if
students do not have access to the
Internet, they may find many print
resources at the local library.

ART NOTE

Ask students to examine the illustration of Antigone
and Ismene and interpret what the picture shows
about the sisters' states of mind. How would students
describe Ismene's facial expression and body
language? How would they describe Antigone's?

Does Antigone look determined and brave to them,
or does she look stubborn and arrogant? With which
sister do they most identify? Which would be a better
friend?

1. Ismene chooses to take part of the blame for what Antigone has done.
2. Antigone rejects Ismene's offer. She says that if Ismene shares the blame, Antigone's own death will lose some of its meaning.

LITERARY TECHNIQUE

FOIL. A **foil** is a character whose attributes, or characteristics, contrast with and therefore throw into relief the attributes of another character. Point out to students that Ismene serves as a foil to Antigone; her weakness emphasizes Antigone's strength.

SELECTION CHECK TEST 4.11.1 WITH ANSWERS

Checking Your Reading

1. What does Antigone tell Ismene she intends to do? **She tells Ismene that she intends to bury their brother, Polyneices.**
2. What does Ismene think of Antigone's plans? **Ismene is afraid for Antigone because she knows that Antigone will be sentenced to death if caught.**
3. For what reason has Creon forbidden this act? **Creon has forbidden anyone to bury Polyneices because Polyneices was a traitor who attacked and tried to take over Thebes.**
4. Whom does Creon suspect of breaking his law? **Creon suspects that "anarchists" who are scheming against him, have bribed his sentry into breaking the law.**
5. Who discovers what Antigone has done? What will happen to Antigone? **The sentry who is assigned to guard Polyneices's body discovers Antigone in the act of sprinkling dirt on the corpse. Creon says that Antigone must be sentenced to die.**

Vocabulary in Context
Fill in each blank below with the most appropriate word from the following Words for Everyday Use from the first half of *Antigone*. You may have to change the tense of the word.

sententiously   meddle   lithe
insolence   anarchist   comprehensive
conscience   endure

CREON. [*Finally losing patience*] Go join them, then; if you must
    have your love,
120 Find it in hell!

CHORAGOS. But see, Ismene comes:

[*Enter* ISMENE, *guarded.*]

Those tears are sisterly, the cloud
That shadows her eyes rains down gentle sorrow.

CREON. You too, Ismene,
125 Snake in my ordered house, sucking my blood
Stealthily—and all the time I never knew
That these two sisters were aiming at my throne!
                         Ismene,
Do you confess your share in this crime, or deny it?
Answer me.

130 ISMENE. Yes, if she will let me say so. I am guilty.

ANTIGONE. [*Coldly*] No, Ismene. You have no right to say so.
You would not help me, and I will not have you help me.

ISMENE. But now I know what you meant; and I am here
To join you, to take my share of punishment.

What choice does Ismene make?

135 ANTIGONE. The dead man and the gods who rule the dead
Know whose act this was. Words are not friends.

ISMENE. Do you refuse me, Antigone? I want to die with you:
I too have a duty that I must discharge to the dead.

ANTIGONE. You shall not lessen my death by sharing it.

How does Antigone respond?

140 ISMENE. What do I care for life when you are dead?

ANTIGONE. Ask Creon. You're always hanging on his opinions.

ISMENE. You are laughing at me. Why, Antigone?

ANTIGONE. It's a joyless laughter, Ismene.

ISMENE.   But can I do nothing?

ANTIGONE. Yes. Save yourself. I shall not envy you.
145 There are those who will praise you; I shall have honor, too.

ISMENE. But we are equally guilty!

SELECTION CHECK TEST 4.11.1 WITH ANSWERS (CONT.)

1. Glenda's **conscience** bothered her so much after she lied to her sister that she finally confessed the truth.
2. Stephan considered himself an **anarchist**—he believed all government and laws should be abolished.
3. Our chemistry teacher announced that the final test will be **comprehensive**—it will cover all of the concepts we learned over the entire year.
4. After I snapped back at my soccer coach, I immediately regretted my **insolence**.
5. Lorna wished her co-workers would stop asking about her personal life—why did they have to **meddle** in what was none of their business?

Continued on page 881

ANTIGONE.   No more, Ismene.
You are alive, but I belong to Death.

CREON. [*To the* CHORUS] Gentlemen, I beg you to observe these
   girls:
One has just now lost her mind: the other,
150 It seems, has never had a mind at all.

ISMENE. Grief teaches the steadiest minds to <u>waver</u>, King.

CREON. Yours certainly did, when you assumed guilt with the
   guilty!

ISMENE. But how could I go on living without her?

CREON.   You are.
She is already dead.

ISMENE.   But your own son's bride!

155 **CREON.** There are places enough for him to push his plow.
I want no wicked women for my sons!

ISMENE. O dearest Haimon, how your father wrongs you!

CREON. I've had enough of your childish talk of marriage!

CHORAGOS. Do you really intend to steal this girl from your son?

CREON. No; Death will do that for me.

160 **CHORAGOS.**   Then she must die?

CREON. [*Ironically*] You dazzle me.
                          —But enough of this talk!
[*To* GUARDS] You, there, take them away and guard them well:
For they are but women, and even brave men run
When they see Death coming.

[*Exit* ISMENE, ANTIGONE, *and* GUARDS.]

Ode II

CHORUS.   [STROPHE 1]
Fortunate is the man who has never tasted God's <u>vengeance</u>!
Where once the anger of heaven has struck, that house is shaken
Forever: damnation rises behind each child

> How has Ismene's mind wavered from the beginning of the play?

---

words for everyday use

wa • ver (wā′ vər) *vi.*, move back and forth; hesitate; be undecided. *The server stood there patiently as I <u>wavered</u> between choosing lasagna or a chicken sandwich.*

ven • geance (ven′ jəns) *n.*, act of taking revenge, inflicting punishment. *The war dragged on for centuries, as each side continued to take <u>vengeance</u> for every act of violence.*

ANTIGONE / SCENE 2   **881**

ANSWER TO GUIDED
READING QUESTION

1. Ismene has wavered between wanting to help Antigone and being too afraid to defy Creon. She has now decided to stand up to Creon and share the blame for what Antigone has done.

LITERARY TECHNIQUE

VERBAL IRONY. Verbal irony occurs when a statement is made that implies its opposite. How is Creon's statement in line 161 an example of verbal irony?
Answer
Creon's statement is an example of verbal irony because when he says that the Choragos's intelligence dazzles him, he actually means to say that the Choragos is being extremely slow and stupid.

ADDITIONAL QUESTIONS AND ACTIVITIES

Ask students to evaluate Antigone's behavior at this point in the play. How would they describe her attitude toward both Creon and Ismene? Is her attitude justifiable? Could she modify her behavior to get better responses? Do they find her an admirable character, or a foolish and headstrong one? Why?
Answers
Responses will vary. Some students will say that Antigone is behaving rudely and disrespectfully to a king and uncle, while others will see her attitude as defiant, challenging, and bold. Students may describe Antigone's attitude toward her sister as sarcastic, bitter, and vindictive. Students may debate whether Antigone's behavior and attitude are justifiable. Some may suggest that if Antigone had behaved more diplomatically or humbly, she may have gotten a better response from Creon, but others may disagree.

SELECTION CHECK TEST 4.11.1 WITH ANSWERS (CONT.)

Literary Tools
Fill in the blanks using the following terms. You may not use every term, and you may use some terms more than once.

tragedy   exposition   chorus   choragos   parodos
   tragic hero   strophe   ode   complication   plot

1. A(n) **plot** is a series of events related to a central conflict, or struggle.

2. A(n) **ode** is a serious lyric poem sung by the chorus in a Greek tragedy.
3. A stanza in a choral ode is called a **strophe**.
4. The chorus traditionally made its entrance singing an ode called the **parodos**.
5. A(n) **tragedy** tells the story of the fall of a person of high status.

TEACHER'S EDITION   **881**

ANSWER TO GUIDED READING QUESTION

1. The Chorus compares Antigone to a flower which is now going to "close up," or die, over a "handful of dust."

ADDITIONAL QUESTIONS AND ACTIVITIES

Ask students the following questions about Ode II:
What looms upon Oedipus's children? What do all of Oedipus's children have in common? Whose mortal arrogance, or pride, does the Chorus suggest will be punished by Zeus? Read lines 26–27. How do you interpret these lines? What does a person's folly, or foolishness, contribute to his or her fate?
Answers
"[G]athering sorrow from time long past" is looming upon Oedipus's children. Oedipus has passed down a legacy of sorrow and tragedy onto his children. All of Oedipus's children take on the "rage of the enemy god"—in other words, they are filled with the pride and combativeness of Ares, the god of war, and this pride leads them to tragedy. The Chorus suggests that all arrogance is punished by Zeus. Students might say that the pride of both Antigone and of Creon as well are bound to be punished. People's own foolish pride leads to a woeful fate.

ANSWERS TO UNDERSTANDING LITERATURE

TRAGEDY AND TRAGIC HERO. Students will probably say that they can tell this is a tragedy because Antigone, a person of high status, faces a tragic fate for having broken a decree. Students may say that Antigone is the tragic hero and that her flaw is being overly bold and prideful. Creon can also be considered a tragic hero whose flaw is his arrogance toward the gods.

PLOT, EXPOSITION, INCITING INCIDENT, AND RISING ACTION. The central conflict of *Antigone* is the conflict between Creon and Antigone over whether Polyneices deserves a proper burial. The exposition occurs in the Prologue, as the reader learns of the recent events in Thebes. The inciting incident occurs when Antigone announces her plan to defy

---

Like a wave cresting out of the black northeast,
5 When the long darkness undersea roars up
And bursts drumming death upon the windwhipped sand.

[ANTISTROPHE 1]

I have seen this gathering sorrow from time long past
Loom upon Oedipus' children: generation from generation
Takes the <u>compulsive</u> rage of the enemy god.
10 So lately this last flower of Oedipus' line
Drank the sunlight! but now a passionate word
And a handful of dust have closed up all its beauty.

[STROPHE 2]

> To what does the Chorus compare Antigone?

What mortal arrogance
Transcends the wrath of Zeus?[7]
15 Sleep cannot lull him, nor the effortless long months
Of the timeless gods: but he is young forever,
And his house is the shining day of high Olympos.[8]
    All that is and shall be,
    And all the past, is his.
20 No pride on earth is free of the curse of heaven.

[ANTISTROPHE 2]

The straying dreams of men
    May bring them ghosts of joy:
But as they drowse, the waking embers burn them;
Or they walk with fixed eyes, as blind men walk.
25 But the ancient wisdom speaks for our own time:
    Fate works most for woe
    With Folly's fairest show.
Man's little pleasure is the spring of sorrow.

---

7. **Zeus.** Son of Saturn, chief of the Greek gods, ruler of gods and mortals
8. **Olympos.** Mountain in Greece; the home of the gods

words for everyday use

com • pul • sive (kəm' pəl siv) *adj.*, as if driven by a force. <u>Compulsive</u> gambling is as serious an addiction as alcoholism; it can be impossible to stop the habit without professional help.

Respond *to the*

Consider how you might persuade a person of Creon's mindset to show mercy and to see another point of view. What arguments would you use to appeal to Creon and help him to see the good in Antigone's action?

ANSWERS TO UNDERSTANDING LITERATURE (CONT.)

Creon's edict. The rising action includes Creon's discovery that his law has been broken, his further discovery that the lawbreaker was Antigone, and his argument with her, in which he declares she must die.

CHORUS AND ODE. The Chorus represents the opinion of the people of Thebes, providing commentary on the action of the play in Ode I and Ode II and background information in the Parodos. The Chorus treats Creon with respect, praising his words, yet also tries to persuade him to change his mind about his decree. The Chorus often seems fickle or changeable. They are watching the events very intently, pointing out how complex the conflict is. There is no right or wrong necessarily, although the combination of events leads to disaster.

Investigate, Inquire, and Imagine

Recall: GATHERING FACTS

1a. What reasons does Creon give for why Polyneices is to have no burial? What law is Antigone obeying in wanting to bury Polyneices? What law is she breaking?

2a. What are the differences in opinion between Ismene and Antigone?

3a. What does Antigone say in scene 1 about the possibility of her own death? In scene 3, what does she say would make her suffer more than dying would?

Interpret: FINDING MEANING

1b. How do the people of Thebes seem to regard Creon's decree? How do they view him? Do they side with Antigone or with Creon? Give evidence to support your answer.

2b. What do these differences reveal about Antigone's character? Why does Antigone refuse to let Ismene share the blame for the act of burying Polyneices?

3b. Why was Antigone willing to risk her life to bury Polyneices?

Analyze: TAKING THINGS APART

4a. Analyze the discussion between Creon and Antigone in scene 3. What arguments does Creon present for why Polyneices should be desecrated? How does Antigone respond to each of his points? Of what does each accuse the other?

Synthesize: BRINGING THINGS TOGETHER

4b. What are the attitudes of Antigone, Creon, Ismene, and the Chorus toward the laws of the gods? toward those of kings?

Evaluate: MAKING JUDGMENTS

5a. Evaluate Creon as a leader and a judge. What words and actions reveal his values, priorities, and moral character?

Extend: CONNECTING IDEAS

5b. Is it justifiable to disobey an unfair law or to protest when "the right judge judges wrong"? Name some figures from history who have committed civil disobedience in protest of unfair laws.

Understanding *Literature*

TRAGEDY AND TRAGIC HERO. Review the definition for **tragedy** and **tragic hero** on page 863. What elements introduced so far hint that *Antigone* is a tragedy? Identify the tragic hero or heroes of the play and what his or her tragic flaw might be. Predict what will happen to this person or these people.

PLOT, EXPOSITION, INCITING INCIDENT, AND RISING ACTION. Review the definitions for **plot, exposition, inciting incident,** and **rising action** in the Handbook of Literary Terms. Name the central conflict of *Antigone*. Then identify and describe the exposition, inciting incident, and rising action of the play.

CHORUS AND ODE. Review the definitions for **chorus** and **ode** on page 863. What role does the Chorus play in *Antigone?* Why is the Chorus important? Consider the information the Chorus gives in the Parodos, the message it delivers in Ode I and Ode II, and how it interacts with Creon. What is the position of the Chorus in relation to the conflict between Creon and Antigone? Explain.

RECALL

1a. Creon says that Polyneices must have no burial because he was a traitor to Thebes. In wanting to bury Polyneices, Antigone is following the laws of the gods but breaking the law of the government.

2a. Antigone is determined to stand up to Creon in order to bury Polyneices. Ismene shares Antigone's belief that Polyneices should have a proper burial, but is afraid to defy Creon.

3a. Antigone says that if she must die, she is glad that her death will be honorable. In scene 3, she says that she would suffer more if she had left her brother unburied than she will suffer by facing her own death.

INTERPRET

1b. *Responses will vary.* The people of Thebes seem to think that Creon's decree is harsh. They seem to fear him and to feel sorry for Antigone.

2b. In comparison with Ismene, Antigone is strong, bold, and honorable. She is not afraid to risk her life for her beliefs. Because Ismene did not help her bury Polyneices, Antigone thinks she does not deserve to share the honor of a righteous death.

3b. Antigone was willing to risk her life because of her love for her brother and her faith that what she is doing corresponds to the will of the gods. Students may say that Antigone's willingness to die is also in part due to her own stubbornness in refusing to yield to Creon.

ANALYZE

4a. Creon says that Polyneices should be desecrated because he was a traitor, and that honoring Polyneices would insult Eteocles. Antigone responds that there are honors due all the dead. Creon accuses Antigone of pride and insolence, while Antigone accuses him of daring to hold his laws above those of God.

SYNTHESIZE

4b. Antigone views the laws of the gods as "immortal" and "beyond man utterly"—to her, they are stronger than the laws of humankind. Creon believes that his own laws are supreme, and that they must be obeyed over private friendship and private beliefs. Ismene says that the laws of the gods mean a lot to her, but that she is not strong enough to "break laws that were made for the public good." The Chorus believes that laws must be followed, or cities will fall.

ANSWERS TO INVESTIGATE, INQUIRE, AND IMAGINE (CONT.)

EVALUATE

5a. As a leader, Creon expects absolute obedience to his laws, believing that only he knows what is best for the State. As a judge, Creon is harsh and hasty. His quick anger clouds his judgment. He expects his subjects to value "the public welfare" above private friendships, as he does. When Creon says "An enemy is an enemy, even dead," he reveals his inflexibility and his reluctance to forgive.

EXTEND

5b. *Responses will vary.* Students may say that it is not only justifiable, but vital that people be allowed to protest a law or a judgment they view as unfair. Leaders such as Mahatma Gandhi, Rosa Parks, Martin Luther King, Jr., and Nelson Mandela committed civil disobedience in order to protest unfair laws.

ART NOTE

In the late nineteenth century, at the apex of the British empire, artists became interested in the ancient empires of Greece and Rome. Although his style was still very Romantic, the English painter Frederic Leighton (1830–1896) tried to depict classical themes realistically. He and other artists of the period benefited from their studies of recent archeological discoveries, which gave their paintings a sense of historical accuracy.

READER'S JOURNAL

Students may say that they would risk death to defend a friend or family member. However, they will probably say that if they were Antigone, they would feel very frightened and would doubt they were doing the right thing.

VOCABULARY FROM THE SELECTION

For scene 3 through the end of the play:

aphorism	lamentation
astray	malicious
blasphemy	piety
clement	prevail
consenting	profane
deference	subordinate
dirge	transgress
implacable	trifle
instinct	vile

PLAY

Literary TOOLS

IMAGE AND IMAGERY. An **image** is language that creates a concrete representation of an object or experience. An image is also the vivid mental picture created in the reader's mind by that language. The images in a literary work are referred to, collectively, as the work's *imagery.* As you read the last half of *Antigone,* notice the imagery used in the Chorus's odes.

PLOT, CLIMAX, CRISIS, FALLING ACTION, AND CATASTROPHE. A **plot** is a series of events related to a central *conflict,* or struggle. A typical plot involves the introduction of a conflict, its development, and its eventual resolution. The **climax** is the high point of interest or suspense in the plot. The **crisis,** or **turning point,** often the same event as the climax, is the point in the plot where something decisive happens to determine the future course of events and the eventual working out of the conflict. The **falling action** is all of the events that follow the climax. The **catastrophe,** in tragedy, is the event that marks the ultimate tragic fall of the central character. Often this event is the character's death. As you read the rest of this play, look for each of these elements.

 Reader's Journal

Do you have beliefs for which you would be willing to die? Write an entry in your journal describing how you might feel if you were Antigone at this point in the play.

Brave Antigone, 1882. Frederic Leighton.

SCENE 3

CHORAGOS. But here is Haimon, King, the last of all
   your sons.
Is it grief for Antigone that brings him here,
And bitterness at being robbed of his bride?

[*Enter* HAIMON.]

CREON. We shall soon see, and no need of diviners.[1]
                                             —Son,

---

1. **diviners.** Those who can tell the future

LITERARY TECHNIQUE

CHARACTERIZATION. Characterization is the use of literary techniques to create a character. After they read scene 3, ask students to discuss what is revealed about the character of Creon through his speech to his son Haimon. How would they describe him as a father, and as a leader? What does he want, and what does he fear?

Answers
Creon is an authoritarian father, who expects absolute obedience from his son. He does not take into account Haimon's feelings and desires. He is also an authoritarian ruler—a tyrant and a dictator. He wants absolute obedience and respect, and fears being seen weak before the people.

5   You have heard my final judgment on that girl:
     Have you come here hating me, or have you come
     With <u>deference</u> and with love, whatever I do?

     HAIMON. I am your son, father. You are my guide.
     You make things clear for me, and I obey you.

10   No marriage means more to me than your continuing wisdom.

How does Creon want his son Haimon to think of him?

     CREON. Good. That is the way to behave: <u>subordinate</u>
     Everything else, my son, to your father's will.
     This is what a man prays for, that he may get
     Sons attentive and dutiful in his house,

15   Each one hating his father's enemies,
     Honoring his father's friends. But if his sons
     Fail him, if they turn out unprofitably,
     What has he fathered but trouble for himself
     And amusement for the <u>malicious</u>?

                                   So you are right

20   Not to lose your head over this woman.
     Your pleasure with her would soon grow cold, Haimon,
     And then you'd have a hellcat in bed and elsewhere.
     Let her find her husband in Hell!
     Of all the people in this city, only she

25   Has had contempt for my law and broken it.
     Do you want me to show myself weak before the people?
     Or to break my sworn word? No, and I will not.
     The woman dies.
     I suppose she'll plead "family ties." Well, let her.

What does Creon fear will happen if he does not go through with Antigone's punishment?

30   If I permit my own family to rebel,
     How shall I earn the world's obedience?
     Show me the man who keeps his house in hand,
     He's fit for public authority.

                         I'll have no dealings
     With lawbreakers, critics of the government:

35   Whoever is chosen to govern should be obeyed—
     Must be obeyed, in all things, great and small,
     Just and unjust! Oh Haimon,
     The man who knows how to obey, and that man only,
     Knows how to give commands when the time comes.

Why are these lines ironic? What laws has Creon refused to obey?

40   You can depend on him, no matter how fast
     The spears come: he's a good soldier, he'll stick it out.

words for everyday use

def • er • ence (def' ər əns) *n.*, attitude of yielding to another. *I treated my beloved grandmother with <u>deference</u>, allowing her to choose what she wanted to do for our visits together.*

sub • ord • i • nate (sə' bord ən āt) *vt.*, place in a lower class, order, or rank. *Josh got poor grades because he <u>subordinated</u> his studies to his social life.*

ma • lic • ious (mə lish' əs) *n.*, those who act with malice, or evil intention. *The <u>malicious</u> shall never win out over the virtuous.*

ANTIGONE / SCENE 3   **885**

ANSWERS TO GUIDED READING QUESTIONS

1. Creon wants Haimon to think of him as an absolute ruler. He expects him to obey him unquestioningly.
2. Creon fears that the people will view him as weak if he does not go through with Antigone's punishment.
3. The irony is that while Creon demands total obedience from his subjects, while he himself has refused to obey a law of the gods, of whom he is a subject.

Quotables

" 'Reverence for parents' stands written among the three laws of most revered righteousness."

—Aeschylus (525–456 BC)

ADDITIONAL QUESTIONS AND ACTIVITIES

Ask students to read lines 47–48 and discuss what they reveal about Creon's attitudes toward women. Point out to them that earlier in the play, Ismene says to Antigone, "We are only women, / We cannot fight with men, Antigone!" What do these lines suggest about the role of women in ancient Greece? Does Antigone's act appear even more daring in this context?

CROSS-CURRICULAR ACTIVITIES

SOCIAL STUDIES. Ask students to form small groups to research the position of women in ancient Greek society. Many books are available on the subject of women in classical times. Refer to the teacher's note on page 287 of your teacher's edition for a list of titles. Students should present their findings in an oral report. They should distinguish between the position of the average woman and that of women such as Antigone who were members of the nobility.

CROSS-CURRICULAR ACTIVITIES (CONT.)

Teaching Note: Students should learn that women in ancient Greece were completely dependent on males. They had no legal rights and could not inherit property, so they were financially dependent first on their fathers and then on their husbands. They were likely to marry very young—at thirteen or fourteen years of age—and their husbands were usually at least twice their age.

1. Creon's temper terrifies people. The people think Antigone has acted in an honorable, noble, and admirable way, and that her sentence is completely unfair.
2. Haimon says that such a man has an empty soul.

ADDITIONAL QUESTIONS AND ACTIVITIES

Ask students to evaluate Haimon's attitude toward his father based on their dialogue in scene 3.
Answer
Responses will vary. Haimon really loves and respects his father. He is concerned for him, and wants to persuade him not to be so hard-headed and stubborn. He tries to do so with grace and tact.

Quotables

"Reason is immortal, all else mortal."
—Pythagoras
(c.582–500 BC)

"Reason in man is rather like God in the world."
—Saint Thomas Aquinas
(c.1225–1274)

CROSS-CURRICULAR ACTIVITIES

LOGIC. Students may be interested in researching the origins of logic. Logic deals with the rules that govern whether statements and arguments are true, false, or nonsensical. A logical fallacy is a logical mistake. A fallacy occurs with an invalid inference, one unwarranted by the facts at hand. Ask students to research the Greek philosopher Aristotle's contributions to the science of logic. They should define the term *syllogism* and give examples of simple syllogisms. Students should also learn the difference between deductive and inductive reasoning, and provide an example of each.

Ask students to determine whether the following argument presented by Creon is valid or invalid, and why. Is

---

Anarchy, anarchy! Show me a greater evil!
This is why cities tumble and the great houses rain down,
This is what scatters armies!
45 No, no: good lives are made so by discipline.

We keep the laws then, and the lawmakers,
And no woman shall seduce us. If we must lose,
Let's lose to a man, at least! Is a woman stronger than we?

CHORAGOS. Unless time has rusted my wits,
50 What you say, King, is said with point and dignity.

HAIMON. [*Boyishly earnest*] Father:
Reason is God's crowning gift to man, and you are right
To warn me against losing mine. I cannot say—
I hope that I shall never want to say!—that you
55 Have reasoned badly. Yet there are other men
Who can reason, too; and their opinions might be helpful.
You are not in a position to know everything
That people say or do, or what they feel:
Your temper terrifies them—everyone
60 Will tell you only what you like to hear.
But I, at any rate, can listen; and I have heard them
Muttering and whispering in the dark about this girl.
They say no woman has ever, so unreasonably,
Died so shameful a death for a generous act:
65 "She covered her brother's body. Is this indecent?
She kept him from dogs and vultures. Is this a crime?
Death?—She should have all the honor that we can give her!"

This is the way they talk out there in the city.

You must believe me:
70 Nothing is closer to me than your happiness.
What could be closer? Must not any son
Value his father's fortune as his father does his?
I beg you, do not be unchangeable:
Do not believe that you alone can be right.
75 The man who thinks that,
The man who maintains that only he has the power
To reason correctly, the gift to speak, the soul—
A man like that, when you know him, turns out empty.

It is not reason never to yield to reason!

80 In flood time you can see how some trees bend,
And because they bend, even their twigs are safe,
While stubborn trees are torn up, roots and all.

What about Creon terrifies people? What is the people's opinion of Antigone's sentence?

What does Haimon say is true of a man who thinks he alone can be right?

CROSS-CURRICULAR ACTIVITIES (CONT.)

reasoning employed in the arguments?
Years and experience make a person wise. I am older and more experienced than Haimon. Therefore, I am wiser and will always be right when arguing with him.
Answers
Students will say that the argument is a fallacy because the antecedent, that years and experience make a person wise, does not imply that a person

without years and experience is not wise. The argument uses inductive reasoning, whereby one starts with a generalization and uses it to make a statement about the particular. Students may identify other fallacies in Creon's reasoning, such as his conclusion that since Haimon loves Antigone and has her interests at heart, he cannot have Creon's own interests at heart as well.

And the same thing happens in sailing:
Make your sheet fast, never slacken—and over you go,
85 Head over heels and under: and there's your voyage.
Forget you are angry! Let yourself be moved!
I know I am young; but please let me say this:
The ideal condition
Would be, I admit, that men should be right by <u>instinct</u>;
90 But since we are all too likely to go <u>astray</u>
The reasonable thing is to learn from those who can teach.

CHORAGOS. You will do well to listen to him, King,
If what he says is sensible. And you, Haimon,
Must listen to your father.—Both speak well.

What advice does the Choragos give?

95 CREON. You consider it right for a man of my years and experience
To go to school to a boy?

HAIMON.   It is not right
If I am wrong. But if I am young, and right,
What does my age matter?

CREON. You think it right to stand up for an anarchist?

100 HAIMON. Not at all. I pay no respect to criminals.

CREON. Then she is not a criminal?

HAIMON. The City would deny it, to a man.

CREON. And the City proposes to teach me how to rule?

HAIMON. Ah. Who is it that's talking like a boy now?

105 CREON. My voice is the one voice giving orders in this City!

HAIMON. It is no City if it takes orders from one voice.

CREON. The State is the King!

HAIMON.   Yes, if the State is a desert.

[*Pause*]

CREON. This boy, it seems, has sold out to a woman.

HAIMON. If you are a woman: my concern is only for you.

110 CREON. So? Your "concern"! In a public brawl with your father!

---

words for everyday use

in • stinct (inz' tinkt) *n.*, impulse, natural tendency, response arising from below the conscious level. *Monarch butterflies travel by <u>instinct</u> to warmer climates.*

a • stray (ə strā') *adv.*, out of the right way, off the path. *The marked trail kept the hikers from going <u>astray</u>.*

CROSS-CURRICULAR ACTIVITIES

POLITICS. Students may be interested in researching current governments run by an absolute leader, or dictator. They should examine what basic rights the people retain under a dictatorship. For example, is free speech and freedom of the press allowed, or are these suppressed? Have any human rights abuses been reported? Are there rebel groups protesting the government, or do the people generally seem in favor of the regime? What positive developments came from the dictatorship? Why might people sometimes support a dictator as opposed to a republic based on representation?

ANSWER TO GUIDED READING QUESTION

1. The Choragos advises both father and son to listen to each other.

LITERARY TECHNIQUE

ANALOGY. An **analogy** is a comparison of two things that are alike in some respects. What two analogies does Haimon use to explain why people who are inflexible often meet with disaster? Compare his lines with those of Creon in scene 2, lines 76–79. What is ironic about the similarity between these lines?
Answer
Haimon uses analogies of trees in a flood and a ship sailing at sea. The flexible tree survives the force of the water, while an inflexible one breaks. A ship with slackened sails is able to take in wind, while a ship with tight sails is blown over. These examples illustrate how a flexible person is able to weather opposition in life, while an inflexible one is destroyed. Creon echoes these lines in scene 2 when he uses the analogies of an inflexible heart, tough iron, and wild horses to illustrate why Antigone in her inflexibility is headed for disaster. It is ironic that Creon clearly understands this principle, but is unable to apply it to his own actions.

HISTORICAL NOTE

Students may note that in this argument between Haimon and Creon, Haimon seems to be arguing for a democratic form of government, while his father advocates a dictatorship. The Athenian audience of the play would have applauded Haimon. They despised tyrants like Creon, having been ruled by tyrants up until 508 BC, when the leader **Cleisthenes** (6th century BC) introduced democracy into Athens. A council of 500 people was elected each year to make laws and to run the state. All male citizens had the right to vote on laws put forth by the council. Direct rule by the people or by their elected representatives flowered in Athens under Pericles. The Greeks are credited with introducing democracy to the Western world. In fact, the word *democracy* comes from the Greek words *demos*, meaning "people," and *kratein*, meaning "to rule or govern."

1. Creon supports his own rights, while Haimon supports the rights of God. Creon believes that Haimon is a fool for agreeing with a woman, Antigone.
2. Haimon implies that if Antigone dies, he will take his own life.

ADDITIONAL QUESTIONS
AND ACTIVITIES

Ask students to describe how Haimon's attitude toward his father has changed from the beginning of the scene.
Answer
Students should note that while before, Haimon was polite and deferential toward his father, he now openly shows his disgust. He says that his father is "perverse" and that he is raving.

CROSS-CURRICULAR
ACTIVITIES

PSYCHOLOGY. Ask students to take on the role of a family therapist or psychiatrist. How might they help Haimon and Creon to work through their disagreement? Students might brainstorm ideas, and then put together a role-play in groups of three, with the "therapist" making suggestions for the feuding father and son.

HAIMON. How about you, in a public brawl with justice?

CREON. With justice, when all that I do is within my rights?

HAIMON. You have no right to trample on God's right.

CREON. [*Completely out of control*] Fool, adolescent fool! Taken in by a woman!

115 HAIMON. You'll never see me taken in by anything <u>vile</u>.

CREON. Every word you say is for her!

HAIMON. [*Quietly, darkly*]   And for you.
And for me. And for the gods under the earth.

CREON. You'll never marry her while she lives.

HAIMON. Then she must die.—But her death will cause another.

120 CREON. Another?
Have you lost your senses? Is this an open threat?

HAIMON. There is no threat in speaking to emptiness.

CREON. I swear you'll regret this superior tone of yours!
You are the empty one!

HAIMON.   If you were not my father,
125 I'd say you were perverse.

CREON. You girlstruck fool, don't play at words with me!

HAIMON. I am sorry. You prefer silence.

CREON.   Now, by God—!
I swear, by all the gods in heaven above us,
You'll watch it, I swear you shall!

[*To the* SERVANTS]   Bring her out!
130 Bring the woman out! Let her die before his eyes!
Here, this instant, with her bridegroom beside her!

HAIMON. Not here, no; she will not die here, King.
And you will never see my face again.
Go on raving as long as you've a friend to endure you.

[*Exit* HAIMON.]

CHORAGOS. Gone, gone.

> *Whose rights does Creon support? Whose rights does Haimon honor? Why does Creon think his son is a fool?*

> *What does Haimon imply?*

words for everyday use   vile (vīl′) *adj.*, foul; mean; base; cheap; contemptible. *The two-week old soup was <u>vile</u>.*

ADDITIONAL QUESTIONS AND ACTIVITIES

Ask students to form pairs to enact the scene between Creon and Haimon as a skit. Recalling that Greek actors could not rely solely on facial expressions, students should concentrate on developing exaggerated gestures and body language in order to convey the emotions felt by each character. How might they convey persuasion, lecturing, rage, and disgust? Be sure the students note the stage directions when preparing to enact the skit. When they have rehearsed their performances, each pair should perform the skit for the class.

Creon, a young man in a rage is dangerous!

CREON. Let him do, or dream to do, more than a man can.
He shall not save these girls from death.

CHORAGOS. These girls?
You have sentenced them both?

CREON. No, you are right.
140 I will not kill the one whose hands are clean.

How does Creon revise his plan?

CHORAGOS. But Antigone?

CREON. [*Somberly*] I will carry her far away
Out there in the wilderness, and lock her
Living in a vault of stone. She shall have food,
145 As the custom is, to absolve the State of her death.
And there let her pray to the gods of hell:
They are her only gods:
Perhaps they will show her an escape from death,
Or she may learn,
                though late,
150 That <u>piety</u> shown the dead is piety in vain.

[*Exit* CREON.]

Ode III

CHORUS.   [STROPHE]
Love, unconquerable
Waster of rich men, keeper
Of warm lights and all-night vigil
In the soft face of a girl:
5 Sea-wanderer, forest-visitor!
Even the pure Immortals cannot escape you,
And mortal man, in his one day's dusk,
Trembles before your glory.

What force, or natural law, does the Chorus speak of in this ode?

                    [ANTISTROPHE]

Surely you swerve upon ruin
10 The just man's <u>consenting</u> heart,
As here you have made bright anger
Strike between father and son—
And none has conquered but Love!
A girl's glance working the will of heaven:

---

words for everyday use

pi • e • ty (pī′ əd ē) *n.*, devoted loyalty or duty to family or religion. *The saints are known for their exceptional <u>piety</u>.*

con • sent • ing (kən sent′ iŋ) *adj.*, agreeing; approving. *The <u>consenting</u> students took the experimental exam, while those who decided to opt out were allowed to study quietly.*

ANTIGONE / SCENE 3   **889**

ANSWERS TO GUIDED READING QUESTIONS

1. Creon decides that he will not sentence Ismene to death along with Antigone.
2. The Chorus speaks of love.

ADDITIONAL QUESTIONS AND ACTIVITIES

Why does Creon decide to spare Ismene's life? What do you think of this sudden reversal, considering how Creon has been characterized thus far in the play? What does he decide to do with Antigone? Why does he not execute her outright?
Answers
Creon decides to spare Ismene at the prompting of the Choragos. He realizes that he cannot kill Ismene, since she did not participate in the crime. Students may find Creon's reversal surprising, since thus far in the play Creon has been unwilling to budge from his decisions. Creon decides to lock Antigone in a stone vault in the wilderness. She will have food. *Responses will vary.* Students may say that he does not execute her outright because he wants to "absolve the State of her death," meaning that he does not want to be directly responsible for her death and thus possibly incur the outrage of the Theban people. He probably hopes that she will kill herself or die eventually in the vault.

CROSS-CURRICULAR ACTIVITIES

FINE ARTS. Ask students to create a work of art reflecting their impression of Ode III. They may, for example, paint Aphrodite laughing down as father and son fight over the fate of Antigone. Or, their work might be more abstract. Students can display their work in the classroom. Students who play a musical instrument might want to select a piece of music that they feel would fit the theme and mood of the ode, and play this piece for the class. If they compose music, they may be able to compose a short tune that reflects the mood of the ode. If they wish, students might explain to the class why they feel their art or music reflects the mood or theme of the ode.

ANSWER TO GUIDED READING QUESTION

1. The double negatives make it somewhat ambivalent. The Chorus says that Antigone has never been "unpraised," or dishonored.

LITERARY TECHNIQUE

Mood. Mood, or *atmosphere*, is the emotion created in the reader by part or all of a literary work. Ask students to describe the mood that is created in scene 4. What specific details convey this mood?

ADDITIONAL QUESTIONS AND ACTIVITIES

Antigone accuses the Chorus of laughing at her. Does the Chorus really mean to laugh at Antigone? Why might Antigone think this? Ask students to discuss the Chorus's attitude toward Antigone in scene 4.

Pleasure to her alone who mocks us,
Merciless Aphrodite.[2]

SCENE 4

CHORAGOS. [*As* ANTIGONE *enters guarded*] But I can no longer
  stand in awe of this,
Nor, seeing what I see, keep back my tears,
Here is Antigone, passing to that chamber,
Where all find sleep at last.

ANTIGONE.   [STROPHE 1]
5   Look upon me, friends, and pity me
Turning back at the night's edge to say
Good-by to the sun that shines for me no longer;
Now sleepy Death
Summons me down to Acheron,[3] that cold shore:
10   There is no bridesong there, nor any music.

CHORUS. Yet not unpraised, not without a kind of honor,
You walk at last into the underworld;
Untouched by sickness, broken by no sword.
What woman has ever found your way to death?

> What does the Chorus say has never yet happened to Antigone in her short life?

ANTIGONE.   [ANTISTROPHE 1]
15   How often I have heard the story of Niobe,[4]
Tantalos' wretched daughter, how the stone
Clung fast about her, ivy-close: and they say
The rain falls endlessly
And sifting soft snow; her tears are never done.
20   I feel the loneliness of her death in mine.

CHORUS. But she was born of heaven, and you
Are woman, woman-born. If her death is yours,
A mortal woman's, is this not for you
Glory in our world and in the world beyond?

ANTIGONE.   [STROPHE 2]
25   You laugh at me. Ah, friends, friends,
Can you not wait until I am dead? O Thebes,
O men many-charioted, in love with Fortune,
Dear springs of Dirce, sacred Theban grove,
Be witnesses for me, denied all pity,
30   Unjustly judged! and think a word of love
For her whose path turns

---

2. **Aphrodite** (af rə dī′ tē). Goddess of beauty and love
3. **Acheron** (ak′ ə ron). River in the underworld over which the dead are ferried
4. **Niobe** (nī′ ō bē). Mother whose children were slain by Latona and Apollo because of her arrogance. Zeus turned her to stone, but she continued to mourn for her children, and a stream formed from her tears.

890   *UNIT ELEVEN / WHAT WE LIVE BY*

CROSS-CURRICULAR ACTIVITIES

MYTHOLOGY. In this scene, Antigone refers to the myth of Niobe. Ask students to locate the entire myth in a book of Greek mythology. They might then write a paragraph comparing Niobe to Antigone. You may ask them to find other myths that involve humans being punished by the gods. What behavior or attitude do the gods most often punish?

Under dark earth, where there are no more tears.

CHORUS. You have passed beyond human daring and come at last
Into a place of stone where Justice sits.

35   I cannot tell
What shape of your father's guilt appears in this.

ANTIGONE.   [ANTISTROPHE 2]
You have touched it at last: that bridal bed
Unspeakable, horror of son and mother mingling:
Their crime, infection of all our family!

40   O Oedipus, father and brother!
Your marriage strikes from the grave to murder mine.
I have been a stranger here in my own land:
All my life
The <u>blasphemy</u> of my birth has followed me.

45   CHORUS. Reverence is a virtue, but strength
Lives in established law: that must prevail.
You have made your choice,
Your death is the doing of your conscious hand.

ANTIGONE.   [EPODE]
Then let me go, since all your words are bitter,

50   And the very light of the sun is cold to me.
Lead me to my vigil, where I must have
Neither love nor <u>lamentation</u>; no song, but silence.

[CREON *interrupts impatiently*.]

CREON. If <u>dirges</u> and planned lamentations could put off death,
Men would be singing forever.

[*To the* SERVANTS]   Take her, go!

55   You know your orders: take her to the vault
And leave her alone there. And if she lives or dies,
That's her affair, not ours: our hands are clean.

ANTIGONE. O tomb, vaulted bride-bed in eternal rock,
Soon I shall be with my own again

60   Where Persephone[5] welcomes the thin ghosts underground:
And I shall see my father again, and you, mother,

---

5. **Persephone** (pər sef′ ə nē). Queen of the underworld and wife of Pluto, king of the underworld

words for everyday use

blas • phe • my (blas′ fə mē) *n.*, irreverence toward God. *Cursing like that is <u>blasphemy</u>!*

lam • en • ta • tion (lam ən tā′ shən) *n.*, vocal expression of sorrow. *Her <u>lamentation</u> was heartbreaking.*

dirge (dərj′) *n.*, song, hymn, or piece of writing expressing deep and solemn grief. *Mozart wrote the <u>dirge</u> that was performed at his own funeral.*

> *Whose guilt does the Chorus mention as possibly having caused Antigone's cruel end?*

> *Now whom does the Chorus blame for Antigone's fate?*

1. The Chorus suggests that Oedipus's guilt may have led to his own daughter's cruel end.
2. Now they tell Antigone that this was all her own conscious doing, that she is solely responsible for her actions.

ADDITIONAL QUESTIONS AND ACTIVITIES

Ask students to discuss what they think led to Antigone's fate. Was it the curse of Oedipus, or her own actions? Could it have been both? Why, or why not? What might Antigone have done to avoid this fate?

CROSS-CURRICULAR ACTIVITIES

MUSIC. Ask students to research the type of instruments and music used at a Greek funeral. If possible, they may locate recordings of traditional Greek music and play it for the class.

LITERARY NOTE

Antigone compares her tomb to a bridal bed—"O tomb, vaulted bride-bed in eternal rock"—suggesting that she will be married to Death. The idea that a girl who died unmarried was a bride of Death was a common, if morbid, idea. In Shakespeare's *Romeo and Juliet* (act 4, scene 5) Juliet's father says, upon believing Juliet dead: "Death is my son-in-law, Death is my heir, / My daughter he hath wedded."

1. Antigone repeats that she has
refused to disobey the laws of
heaven, which in her mind are
higher than Creon's.

And dearest Polyneices—
                             dearest indeed
To me, since it was my hand
That washed him clean and poured the ritual wine:
65   And my reward is death before my time!

And yet, as men's hearts know, I have done no wrong,
I have not sinned before God. Or if I have,
I shall know the truth in death. But if the guilt
Lies upon Creon who judged me, then, I pray,
May his punishment equal my own.

70   **CHORAGOS.**   O passionate heart,
Unyielding, tormented still by the same winds!

CREON. Her guards shall have good cause to regret their delaying.

ANTIGONE. Ah! That voice is like the voice of death!

CREON. I can give you no reason to think you are mistaken.

75   **ANTIGONE.** Thebes, and you my fathers' gods,
And rulers of Thebes, you see me now, the last
Unhappy daughter of a line of kings,
Your kings, led away to death. You will remember
What things I suffer, and at what men's hands,
80   Because I would not <u>transgress</u> the laws of heaven.

[*To the* GUARDS, *simply*]

Come: let us wait no longer.

[*Exit* ANTIGONE, *left, guarded.*]

Ode IV

CHORUS.   [STROPHE 1]
All Danaë's beauty[6] was locked away
In a brazen cell where the sunlight could not come;
A small room, still as any grave, enclosed her.
Yet she was a princess too.
5   And Zeus in a rain of gold poured love upon her.

> *These are Antigone's
> last lines. What does
> she again assert?*

---

6. **Danaë's beauty** (dan ā′ ē). Danaë was locked in a tower to escape a prophecy that
her son would kill her father. Zeus, drawn by her beauty, visited her in the form of a
shower of gold, and fathered her son Perseus. Years later, Perseus killed the man he did
not know was his grandfather. The story echoes that of Oedipus.

**words
for
everyday
use**   trans • gress (trans gres′) *vt.*, go beyond limits set; break, violate. *Do not <u>transgress</u> the rules or you will be disqualified
from the race.*

O child, child,
No power in wealth or war
Or tough sea-blackened ships
Can <u>prevail</u> against untiring Destiny!

[ANTISTROPHE 1]

10   And Dryas' son[7] also, that furious king,
Bore the god's prisoning anger for his pride:
Sealed up by Dionysos in deaf stone,
His madness died among echoes.
So at the last he learned what dreadful power
15   His tongue had mocked:
For he had <u>profaned</u> the revels,
And fired the wrath of the nine
<u>Implacable</u> Sisters[8] that love the sound of the flute.

[STROPHE 2]

And old men tell a half-remembered tale
20   Of horror done where a dark ledge splits the sea
And a double surf beats on the gray shores:
How a king's new woman, sick
With hatred for the queen he had imprisoned,
Ripped out his two sons' eyes with her bloody hands
25   While grinning Ares[9] watched the shuttle plunge
Four times: four blind wounds crying for revenge,

[ANTISTROPHE 2]

Crying, tears and blood mingled. —Piteously born,
Those sons whose mother was of heavenly birth!
Her father was the god of the North Wind
30   And she was cradled by gales,
She raced with young colts on the glittering hills
And walked untrammeled in the open light:
But in her marriage deathless Fate found means
To build a tomb like yours for all her joy.

According to the Chorus, who or what was ultimately responsible for what happened to Danaë, to Dryas's son, and to Phineas's wife?

---

7. **Dryas' son.** Dryas' son Lycorgos, was locked up and driven mad by the gods for objecting to the worship of Dionysos, the god of wine
8. **nine Implacable Sisters.** Also called the Muses, these nine goddesses were daughters of Zeus and Mnemosyne (Memory). They inspired invention and art and were unforgiving to those who offended them.
9. **king's . . . Ares.** According to the myth, King Phineas imprisoned his wife, the Queen, and allowed his jealous new wife to blind the sons of the Queen while Ares, the god of war, looked on with glee.

words for everyday use

pre • vail (prē vāl′) *vi.*, grow strong, gain victory, triumph. *Justice <u>prevailed</u>.*

pro • fane (prō fān′) *vt.*, violate, abuse, or make impure. *A black scar <u>profaned</u> the burned forest.*

im • pla • ca • ble (im pla′ kə bəl) *adj.*, unable to be appeased; relentless. *I apologized many times, but Ramona was <u>implacable</u>—she said she could never forgive me.*

ANSWER TO GUIDED READING QUESTION

1. The Chorus blames Fate, or Destiny.

LITERARY TECHNIQUE

MOOD. Mood, or *atmosphere*, is the emotion created in the reader by part or all of a literary work. The writer can evoke in the reader an emotional response—such as fear, discomfort, longing, or anticipation—by working carefully with descriptive language and sensory details. Ask students what mood is conveyed in Ode IV, and then cite some of the descriptive and sensory details that contribute to the mood.

CROSS-CURRICULAR ACTIVITIES

MYTHOLOGY. Students might read the myths of Danaë, Dryas's son, and King Phineas in a book of mythology.

CROSS-CURRICULAR ACTIVITIES

DANCE. The Chorus did not only sing or chant the lines of the odes, but they also danced. Ask interested students to choreograph a simple, ritual dance to go along with the ode and to perform it for the class while chanting the lines of the ode. They may select music to accompany their performance. Remind them that the Chorus traditionally went up one side of the stage during the strophe and returned during the antistrophe.

1. Creon's line is ironic because he has not listened to anyone in the entire play. There are many things about himself that he is not aware of—his pride and vanity and stubbornness.

2. Teiresias believes that the gods are rejecting the Thebans' offerings because they are angry that Creon has left "the corpse of Oedipus' son" to lie without proper burial. He blames Creon for the calamity.

LITERARY NOTE

The blind seer Teiresias was a familiar figure in the Greek oral tradition. He appeared in Homer's *Odyssey* and in Sophocles's later play, *Oedipus Rex*. Ask students to note the paradox of a blind person who actually "sees" more than other humans can see.

HISTORICAL NOTE

Consulting a prophet or oracle in order to get advice from the gods was very common in ancient Greece. Greeks and people from other lands traveled to Delphi, located on Mount Parnassos, to receive advice or answers from the god Apollo.

LITERARY TECHNIQUE

MOOD AND IMAGERY. Mood, or *atmosphere,* is the emotion created in the reader by part or all of a literary work. The writer can evoke in the reader an emotional response—such as fear, discomfort, longing, or anticipation—by working carefully with descriptive language and sensory details. **Imagery** is the images in a literary work. Ask students what mood is conveyed in Teiresias's speech to Creon, and then cite some of the descriptive and sensory details that contribute to the mood. What imagery does Teiresias use in his speech to Creon?
Answers
Responses will vary.

SCENE 5

[*Enter blind* TEIRESIAS, *led by a boy. The opening speeches of* TEIRESIAS *should be in singsong contrast to the realistic lines of* CREON.]

TEIRESIAS. This is the way the blind man comes, Princes, Princes, Lock-step, two heads lit by the eyes of one.

CREON. What new thing have you to tell us, old Teiresias?

TEIRESIAS. I have much to tell you: listen to the prophet, Creon.

5   **CREON.** I am not aware that I have ever failed to listen.

TEIRESIAS. Then you have done wisely, King, and ruled well.

CREON. I admit my debt to you. But what have you to say?

TEIRESIAS. This, Creon: you stand once more on the edge of fate.

CREON. What do you mean? Your words are a kind of dread.

10   **TEIRESIAS.** Listen, Creon:
I was sitting in my chair of augury,[10] at the place
Where the birds gather about me. They were all a-chatter,
As is their habit, when suddenly I heard
A strange note in their jangling, a scream, a
15   Whirring fury; I knew that they were fighting,
Tearing each other, dying
In a whirlwind of wings clashing. And I was afraid.
I began the rites of burnt-offering at the altar,
But Hephaistos[11] failed me: instead of bright flame,
20   There was only the sputtering slime of the fat thigh-flesh
Melting: the entrails dissolved in gray smoke,
The bare bone burst from the welter. And no blaze!
This was a sign from heaven. My boy described it,
Seeing for me as I see for others.
25   I tell you, Creon, you yourself have brought
This new calamity upon us. Our hearths and altars
Are stained with the corruption of dogs and carrion birds
That glut themselves on the corpse of Oedipus' son.
The gods are deaf when we pray to them, their fire
30   Recoils from our offering, their birds of omen
Have no cry of comfort, for they are gorged
With the thick blood of the dead.
                        O my son,

---

10. **chair of augury.** Seat where he practices augury, the art of telling fortunes from omens
11. **Hephaistos** (hi fes' təs). God of fire

> *Why is Creon's line ironic?*

> *According to Teiresias, why do the gods reject the Thebans' offerings? Who has caused this calamity?*

LITERARY TECHNIQUE

ALLITERATION. Alliteration is the repetition of initial consonant sounds. How does alliteration help to emphasize some of the imagery of Teiresias's speech?
Answer
Students may note the lines "whirlwind of wings"; "sputtering slime"; "fat thigh-flesh"; "bare bone burst." The alliteration emphasizes some of the more disturbing and gruesome imagery, intensifying their horror.

These are no <u>trifles</u>! Think: all men make mistakes,
But a good man yields when he knows his course is wrong.
35 And repairs the evil. The only crime is pride.

Give in to the dead man, then: do not fight with a corpse—
What glory is it to kill a man who is dead?
Think, I beg you:
It is for your own good that I speak as I do.
40 You should be able to yield for your own good.

CREON. It seems that prophets have made me their especial
    province.
All my life long
I have been a kind of butt for the dull arrows
Of doddering fortunetellers!
               No, Teiresias:
45 If your birds—if the great eagles of God himself
Should carry him stinking bit by bit to heaven,
I would not yield. I am not afraid of pollution:
No man can defile the gods.
             Do what you will,
Go into business, make money, speculate
50 In India gold or that synthetic gold from Sardis,[12]
Get rich otherwise than by my consent to bury him.
Teiresias, it is a sorry thing when a wise man
Sells his wisdom, lets out his words for hire!

TEIRESIAS. Ah Creon! Is there no man left in the world—

55 CREON. To do what?—Come, let's have the <u>aphorism</u>!

TEIRESIAS. No man who knows that wisdom outweighs any wealth?

CREON. As surely as bribes are baser than any baseness.

60 TEIRESIAS. You are sick, Creon! You are deathly sick!

CREON. As you say: it is not my place to challenge a prophet.

TEIRESIAS. Yet you have said my prophecy is for sale.

CREON. The generation of prophets has always loved gold.

---

12. **Sardis.** Where the first coins made from an alloy of gold and silver were produced

> Of what does Creon accuse Teiresias?

words for everyday use

tri • fle (trī′ fəl) n., something inconsequential, of little value. *Don't get bothered by trifles.*

a • phor • ism (a fə rizəm) n., short, insightful saying. *She took to heart the aphorism "You are what you eat."*

1. He accuses Teiresias of having been bribed into delivering this ominous prophecy.

ADDITIONAL QUESTIONS AND ACTIVITIES

How is Creon's accusation of Teiresias similar to his accusation of his own son earlier in the play?
Answer
In scene 3, line 108, Creon says Haimon has "sold out" for love of a woman. Here, he accuses Teiresias of selling out for money. Creon insults the intelligence of both men, and refuses to see that they are trying to help him.

CROSS-CURRICULAR ACTIVITIES

GEOGRAPHY. Ask students to locate Sardis on a map of the ancient Greek world. Such maps are often included in world atlases. In what kingdom was Sardis located during ancient Greek times? In what country is the site located today?
Answer
Sardis was an ancient city in western Asia Minor, the capital city of the ancient kingdom of Lydia. Today, it is located east of Izmir, Turkey.

ADDITIONAL QUESTIONS AND ACTIVITIES

Teiresias repeats some Greek aphorisms when talking to Creon. Ask students to discuss some aphorisms popular today.

LITERARY TECHNIQUE

MOTIF. A **motif** is any element that recurs in one or more works of literature or art. In literature, disturbances in nature commonly signify disorder in the political state, and foreshadow disaster. Recall that in Shakespeare's *Julius Cæsar* in Unit 4, Cæsar's death was foreshadowed by strange and unnatural occurrences—such as a man all in flames but not burning, a lion at the Capitol, and the dead rising from their graves. Note the disturbances in nature that Teiresias recounts (the birds tearing each other apart, the fire that refused to light) and ask students what these disturbances mean.
Answer
The disturbances point to Creon's violation of divine law.

LITERARY NOTE

In line 64, Teiresias points out that he was responsible for Creon becoming king. Here, he is referring to his role in the legend of Oedipus, as told by Sophocles in *Oedipus the King.* Teiresias set into motion all the events that led to Creon's becoming king. He was the one who revealed to Oedipus that he himself had killed his father, King Laius. Oedipus did not believe Teiresias; in fact, like Creon, he accused the blind seer of having been paid to give false prophecies. But, Oedipus finally learned that Teiresias was right, and once he did, he blinded himself and went into exile from Thebes, leaving his throne to Eteocles and Polyneices. When those two killed each other, Creon became king.

HISTORICAL/CULTURAL NOTE

In Greek religion, the Furies or Erinyes (i rin' ē ēz) were goddesses of vengeance, born from the blood of Uranus. Their names were Megaera (meaning envious), Tisiphone (blood avenger), and Alecto (unceasing pursuit). They were most often represented as three ugly old women with the heads of dogs, bat's wings, and snakes for hair. The three Furies punished wrongs people committed against relatives, regardless of the motive. When called upon to act, they tormented their victim to death.

TEIRESIAS. The generation of kings has always loved brass.

CREON. You forget yourself! You are speaking to your King.

TEIRESIAS. I know it. You are a king because of me.

65   **CREON.** You have a certain skill; but you have sold out.

TEIRESIAS. King, you will drive me to words that—

CREON. Say them, say them!
Only remember: I will not pay you for them.

TEIRESIAS. No, you will find them too costly.

CREON.   No doubt. Speak:
70   Whatever you say, you will not change my will.

TEIRESIAS. Then take this, and take it to heart!
The time is not far off when you shall pay back
Corpse for corpse, flesh of your own flesh.
You have thrust the child of this world into living night,
75   You have kept from the gods below the child that is theirs:
The one in a grave before her death, the other,
Dead, denied the grave. This is your crime:
And the Furies[13] and the dark gods of Hell
Are swift with terrible punishment for you.

Do you want to buy me now, Creon?
80   Not many days,
And your house will be full of men and women weeping,
And curses will be hurled at you from far
Cities grieving for sons unburied, left to rot
Before the walls of Thebes.

85   These are my arrows, Creon: they are all for you.

But come, child: lead me home.   [*To* BOY]
Let him waste his fine anger upon younger men.
Maybe he will learn at last
To control a wiser tongue in a better head.

[*Exit* TEIRESIAS.]

90   **CHORAGOS.** The old man has gone, King, but his words
Remain to plague us. I am old, too,
But I cannot remember that he was ever false.

CREON. That is true. . . . It troubles me.
Oh it is hard to give in! but it is worse

What is Teiresias's prophecy?

What does Creon admit is worse than the shame of giving in?

---

13. **Furies.** Goddesses of vengeance who punished those who sinned against their own families by making them insane

95   To risk everything for stubborn pride.

CHORAGOS. Creon: take my advice.

CREON.   What shall I do?

CHORAGOS. Go quickly: free Antigone from her vault
And build a tomb for the body of Polyneices.

CREON. You would have me do this?

CHORAGOS.   Creon, yes!
100   And it must be done at once: God moves
Swiftly to cancel the folly of stubborn men.

CREON. It is hard to deny the heart! But I
Will do it: I will not fight with destiny.

CHORAGOS. You must go yourself, you cannot leave it to others.

CREON. I will go.
105   —Bring axes, servants:
Come with me to the tomb. I buried her, I
Will set her free.
                    Oh quickly!
My mind misgives—
The laws of the gods are mighty, and a man must serve them
110   To the last day of his life!

[*Exit* CREON.]

Pæan

CHORAGOS.   [STROPHE 1]
God of many names

CHORUS.   O Iacchos
                              son
of Kadmeian Semele
                    O born of the Thunder![14]
Guardian of the West
                    Regent
of Eleusis' plain[15]
                    O Prince of maenad[16] Thebes
and the Dragon Field[17] by rippling Ismenos:

> **What laws are mighty? How has Creon changed?**

---

14. **Iacchos** (ē yä′ kəs) . . . **Kadmeian Semele** (sem′ ə lē) . . . **Thunder.** Iacchos is another name for Dionysos. His mother was Kadmeian Semele, daughter of Kadmos, the founder of Thebes; his father was Zeus, who controlled thunder
15. **Eleusis' plain.** Site of worship for Dionysos and Demeter
16. **maenad.** Female follower of Dionysos, god of wine
17. **Dragon Field.** Field near the River Ismenos

1. The laws of the gods are mighty. This is a reversal of Creon's earlier attitude.

LITERARY TECHNIQUE

CRISIS, CLIMAX, AND DRAMATIC IRONY. As students may note in their plot pyramids for *Antigone*, the moment in which Creon's "mind misgives" and he admits that "the laws of the gods are mighty" is the **crisis**, or turning point, of the play. It may also be identified as the **climax**, or high point of interest and suspense in the play, since Creon now calls for axes to free Antigone, and the audience wonders what he will find there. Point out to students, however, that Greek audiences would not be feeling suspense at this point in the play. They were already familiar with the events portrayed in *Antigone*, and their emotions were created by the **dramatic irony** present in the play at this point. Dramatic irony is created when the reader or audience knows something that the characters do not. The Greek audience knew quite well that Creon would find something terrible when he went to free Antigone from her vault, and they felt pity and fear for Creon. Then, according to Aristotle, they experienced a catharsis, or cleansing, of such emotions.

CROSS-CURRICULAR ACTIVITIES

GEOGRAPHY AND HISTORY. In the Pæan, the Choragos mentions many sites in ancient Greece and refers to the history of Thebes. Have students research the history and geography of ancient Greece by completing one or more of the following activities individually or in groups:
- Create a map of ancient Greece including the following places: Athens, Colonus, Corinth, Crete, Delphi, Doris, Macedonia, Peloponnesus, Sparta, Thebes, and Thrace.
- Compare and contrast the cultures of Sparta and Athens.
- Make a time line of events in Greek history including but not

---

CROSS-CURRICULAR ACTIVITIES (CONT.)

limited to the following: the first Olympic games, the birth and death of Sophocles, the birth and death of Pericles, the beginning and end of the Persian Wars, the beginning and end of the Peloponnesian War, the Battle of Salamis, and the Battle of Thermopylae.

- Present in comic book or picture book form the events of the Battle of Salamis, including the events leading up to the battle.
- Read or view a performance of a play by Sophocles other than *Antigone*. Write a review of the work or the performance.

CHORAGOS.   [ANTISTROPHE 1]
God of many names

CHORUS.   the flame of torches
flares on our hills
                         the nymphs of Iacchos
dance at the spring of Castalia:[17]
from the vine-close mountain
                                   come ah come in ivy:
10   *Evohe evohe!*[19] sings through the streets of Thebes

CHORAGOS.   [STROPHE 2]
God of many names

CHORUS.   Iacchos of Thebes
heavenly Child
                    of Semele bride of the Thunderer!
The shadow of plague is upon us:
                                   come
with <u>clement</u> feet
                         oh come from Parnasos[20]
down the long slopes
15   across the lamenting water

CHORAGOS.   [ANTISTROPHE 2]
Io[21] Fire! Chorister of the throbbing stars!
O purest among the voices of the night!
Thou son of God, blaze for us!

CHORUS. Come with choric rapture of circling Maenads
Who cry *Io Iacche!*
20   *God of many names!*

Exodos

[*Enter* MESSENGER, *left.*]

MESSENGER. Men of the line of Kadmos, you who live
Near Amphion's citadel:[22]

---

18. **Castalia** (kas tä′ lē ə). Site sacred to Apollo where his followers would worship
19. *Evohe evohe* (ē vō e)*!* Exclamation of triumph used during festivals of Dionysos
20. **Parnasos** (pär na′ səs). Mountain in central Greece sacred to Dionysos and Apollo
21. **Io** (ē ō′). Greek for "Behold" or "Hail"
22. **Amphion's citadel** (am fī′ ən). Fortress built by King Amphion of Thebes who used his lyre to magically move the stones into place

words for everyday use

clem • ent (klem ənt) *adj.,* kind, gentle, or favorable. *They love the <u>clement</u> weather of the South.*

I cannot say
Of any condition of human life "This is fixed,
This is clearly good, or bad." Fate raises up,
5   And Fate casts down the happy and unhappy alike:
No man can foretell his Fate.
                                    Take the case of Creon:
Creon was happy once, as I count happiness:
Victorious in battle, sole governor of the land,
Fortunate father of children nobly born.
10   And now it has all gone from him! Who can say
That a man is still alive when his life's joy fails?
He is a walking dead man. Grant him rich,
Let him live like a king in his great house:
If his pleasure is gone, I would not give
15   So much as the shadow of smoke for all he owns.

CHORAGOS. Your words hint at sorrow: what is your news for us?

MESSENGER. They are dead. The living are guilty of their death.

CHORAGOS. Who is guilty? Who is dead? Speak!

MESSENGER.   Haimon.   Who is dead, and how
Haimon is dead; and the hand that killed him   did he die?
Is his own hand.

20   CHORAGOS.   His father's? or his own?

MESSENGER. His own, driven mad by the murder his father had
        done.

CHORAGOS. Teiresias, Teiresias, how clearly you saw it all!

MESSENGER. This is my news: you must draw what conclusions
        you can from it.

CHORAGOS. But look: Eurydice, our Queen:
25   Has she overheard us?

[Enter EURYDICE from the Palace, center.]

EURYDICE. I have heard something, friends:
As I was unlocking the gate of Pallas'²³ shrine,
For I needed her help today, I heard a voice,
Telling of some new sorrow. And I fainted,
30   There at the temple with all my maidens about me.
But speak again: whatever it is, I can bear it:
Grief and I are no strangers.

─────────────
23. **Pallas.** Pallas Athene, goddess of wisdom

ANTIGONE / *EXODOS*   **899**

4. What does Teiresias report is happening at the
   hearths and altars where sacrifices are burned?
   Why is this happening? **The offerings will not
   catch flame. Teiresias believes the gods are
   refusing the sacrifices because they are angry
   that Creon has not given Polyneices proper
   burial.**

5. What happens to Antigone, Eurydice, and Haimon
   by the end of the play? Why? **All three kill
   themselves in grief.**

LITERARY TECHNIQUE

CLIMAX. The **climax** is the high point
of interest or suspense in the play.
Students may find it odd that the
climactic moment of the play—the
point when Creon opens the vault to
find Antigone dead and Haimon
strikes at him with his sword—is not
shown on stage but rather, is
recounted by a messenger. Inform
them that, as noted in the Literary
Note on this page, it was a
convention of Greek theater to keep
all violence offstage. It might also
have been difficult for actors to
remove the "bodies" from the stage
without it seeming odd to the
audience, since Greek theaters did
not have curtains that could be
drawn between scenes.

LITERARY NOTE

Conventions of Greek Drama
Every type of literature has its
conventions, or characteristics that
most works of that type share. The
use of masks, costumes, scenery,
music, and choral dancing are some
of the conventions of Greek drama.
Also, although plots often deal with
cataclysmic events, violent actions,
according to Greek convention, took
place offstage and were reported to
the actors and the audience rather
than witnessed. Typically, a Greek
drama alternated between scenes
with actors and scenes in which the
chorus danced and sang
commentaries on the action of the
drama. As students read in
Prereading, an *ode* sung by the
chorus was itself divided into
alternating parts, the **strophe** and
the **antistrophe.** (During the
strophe, the chorus sang and turned
from stage right to stage left. During
the antistrophe, the chorus sang in
answer to the previous strophe and
returned from stage left to stage
right.) On the next page, the Chorus

MESSENGER.   Dearest Lady,
I will tell you plainly all that I have seen.
I shall not try to comfort you: what is the use,
35 Since comfort could lie only in what is not true?
The truth is always best.
                              I went with Creon
To the outer plain where Polyneices was lying,
No friend to pity him, his body shredded by dogs.
We made our prayers in that place to Hecate[24]
40 And Pluto,[25] that they would be merciful. And we bathed
The corpse with holy water, and we brought
Fresh-broken branches to burn what was left of it,
And upon the urn we heaped up a towering barrow
Of the earth of his own land.
                              When we were done, we ran
45 To the vault where Antigone lay on her couch of stone.
One of the servants had gone ahead,
And while he was yet far off he heard a voice
Grieving within the chamber, and he came back
And told Creon. And as the King went closer,
50 The air was full of wailing, the words lost,
And he begged us to make all haste. "Am I a prophet?"
He said, weeping, "And must I walk this road,
The saddest of all that I have gone before?
My son's voice calls me on. Oh quickly, quickly!
55 Look through the crevice there, and tell me
If it is Haimon, or some deception of the gods!"

We obeyed; and in the cavern's farthest corner
We saw her lying:
She had made a noose of her fine linen veil
60 And hanged herself. Haimon lay beside her,
His arms about her waist, lamenting her,
His love lost underground, crying out
That his father had stolen her away from him.

When Creon saw him the tears rushed to his eyes
65 And he called to him: "What have you done, child? Speak to me.
What are you thinking that makes your eyes so strange?
O my son, my son, I come to you on my knees!"
But Haimon spat in his face. He said not a word,
Staring—
                              And suddenly drew his sword
70 And lunged. Creon shrank back, the blade missed; and the boy,

---

24. **Hecate** (hek′ ə tē). Goddess of the underworld
25. **Pluto.** King of the underworld

LITERARY NOTE (CONT.)

sings its first ode, called the Parodos.
Another convention of Greek drama was its
observance of the **three unities of action, space,** and
time. According to Greek poetic theory, a play should
represent a unified action (that is, events all related to
the working out of a central conflict or struggle). This
action should occur in a single place and at a single
time, usually in the course of one day. In the words of
Aristotle, a well-made play is a unified "imitation of
an action" and has a definite "beginning, middle, and
end."

Desperate against himself, drove it half its length
Into his own side, and fell. And as he died
He gathered Antigone close in his arms again,
Choking, his blood bright red on her white cheek.
75   And now he lies dead with the dead, and she is his
At last, his bride in the houses of the dead.

[*Exit* EURYDICE *into the Palace.*]

CHORAGOS. She has left us without a word. What can this mean?

MESSENGER. It troubles me, too; yet she knows what is best,
Her grief is too great for public lamentation,
80   And doubtless she has gone to her chamber to weep
For her dead son, leading her maidens in his dirge.

What has happened at Antigone's stone vault?

CHORAGOS. It may be so: but I fear this deep silence.

[*Pause*]

What does the Choragos fear?

MESSENGER. I will see what she is doing. I will go in.

[*Exit* MESSENGER *into the Palace.*]

[*Enter* CREON *with attendants, bearing* HAIMON'S *body.*]

CHORAGOS. But here is the King himself: oh look at him,
85   Bearing his own damnation in his arms.

CREON. Nothing you say can touch me any more.
My own blind heart has brought me
From darkness to final darkness. Here you see
The father murdering, the murdered son—
90   And all my civic wisdom!

What has brought Creon darkness?

Haimon my son, so young, so young to die,
I was the fool, not you; and you died for me.

CHORAGOS. That is the truth; but you were late in learning it.

CREON. The truth is hard to bear. Surely a god
95   Has crushed me beneath the hugest weight of heaven,
And driven me headlong a barbaric way
To trample out the thing I held most dear.

The pains that men will take to come to pain!

[*Enter* MESSENGER *from the Palace.*]

MESSENGER. The burden you carry in your hands is heavy,
100   But it is not all: you will find more in your house.

CREON. What burden worse than this shall I find there?

---

1. Antigone has hung herself and Haimon has killed himself with a sword.
2. The Choragos fears the deep silence.
3. Creon admits that his own blindness has brought him this darkness.

Quotables

"Truth is mighty and will prevail."
—Thomas Brooks

"The truth shall make you free."
—the Bible, John 7:32

SELECTION CHECK TEST 4.11.3 WITH ANSWERS (CONT.)

Quote Identification
Tell which character in *Antigone* said each of the following quotes, and explain what is meant by the quote. If relevant, include the name of the person being spoken to.

1. "There is no happiness where there is no wisdom. / No wisdom but in submission to the gods." **This quote is spoken by the Choragos as a moral at the end of the play.**
2. "It is not reason never to yield to reason!" **Haimon says this to his father as he attempts to persuade Creon to rethink his harsh sentencing of Antigone.**
3. "My mind misgives— / The laws of the gods are mighty, and a man must serve them / To the last day of his life!" **This quote is spoken by Creon after he realizes that Teiresias is right and that he must submit to the gods or suffer their wrath. He has decided to build a tomb for Polyneices and set Antigone free.**
4. "Not many days, / And your house will be full of men and women weeping, / And curses will be hurled at you from far / Cities grieving for sons unburied, left to rot / Before the walls of Thebes." **Teiresias says this as a warning to Creon that if he does not give in to the will of the gods, there will be terrible suffering in Thebes and in his own home.**
5. "O tomb, vaulted bride-bed in eternal rock, / Soon I shall be with my own again / Where Persephone welcomes the thin ghosts underground." **Antigone says this as she is being led to the stone vault in the wilderness, as ordered by Creon. Students might recall that Persephone is the Queen of the Underworld.**

Vocabulary in Context
Fill in each blank below with the most appropriate word from the following Words for Everyday Use. You may have to change the tense of the word.

clement   deference   implacable   lamentation
malicious   piety   prevail   transgress   vile

1. We celebrated after our soccer team **prevailed** over the highest-ranking team in the finals.
2. As was expected in Chinese society, Boun showed **deference** to her parents by bowing to their opinion on certain matters.
3. The baby spat out the **vile** medicine.
4. Sherice was furious when she learned that her so-called best friend was spreading **malicious** rumors about her.
5. Burt was a natural-born rebel who would **transgress** any rule you set forth.

ANSWER TO GUIDED READING QUESTION

1. Eurydice has killed herself in grief.

ART NOTE

Ask students whether they think the illustration shows an ancient Greek theater. How can they tell?
Answer
This illustration shows a modern stage set and production, not a Greek theater. They should be able to tell this because the Greek theaters did not have curtains. They were outdoor amphitheaters. Also, all the actors in Greek plays wore masks.

ADDITIONAL QUESTIONS AND ACTIVITIES

Read lines 109–110. How do these lines contradict what Creon says in line 86, and to what Eurydice says in lines 31–32?
Answer
Both Creon and Eurydice claim to be able to bear the truth, but then they cannot. Point out what Ismene said in scene 2, line 287, that "grief teaches the steadiest mind to waver."

LITERARY NOTE

Aeschylus's *Prometheus Bound* serves as a fine example of Greek tragedy. In this drama, the Titan Prometheus helps human beings by bringing them fire and by teaching them useful arts such as writing and building. In his pride, Prometheus ignores the warnings of Zeus, who does not want human beings to have such power, and as a result, Zeus condemns Prometheus to be chained to a rock and tortured. Some common themes that appear not only in *Prometheus Bound* but throughout Greek tragedy are justice and injustice, the relationship between power and knowledge, and the struggle to exert one's will while caught in the web of fate. Usually, Greek tragedy pits the hero against one or more gods, and the hero's downfall in such a case is inevitable, a matter of fate in which the hero's character, or personality, becomes his or her destiny.

Last scene of *Antigone:* Creon crying over the body of his son, Haimon.

MESSENGER. The Queen is dead.

CREON. O port of death, deaf world,
Is there no pity for me? And you, Angel of evil,
105   I was dead, and your words are death again.
Is it true, boy! Can it be true!
Is my wife dead? Has death bred death?

MESSENGER. You can see for yourself.

[*The doors are opened, and the body of* EURYDICE *is disclosed within.*]

CREON. Oh pity!
110   All true, all true, and more than I can bear!
O my wife, my son!

MESSENGER. She stood before the altar, and her heart
Welcomed the knife her own hand guided,
And a great cry burst from her lips for Megareus[26] dead,

What has happened to Eurydice?

26. **Megareus** (mə ga′ rē əs). Oldest son of Creon and Eurydice, who was killed in the civil war by Argive forces invading Thebes

902   *UNIT ELEVEN / WHAT WE LIVE BY*

Quotables

"A man's character is his fate."
—Heraclitus
(c.540–c.480 BC)

902   TEACHER'S EDITION

115 And for Haimon dead, her sons; and her last breath
Was a curse for their father, the murderer of her sons.
And she fell, and the dark flowed in through her closing eyes.

CREON. O God, I am sick with fear.
Are there no swords here? Has no one a blow for me?

120 MESSENGER. Her curse is upon you for the deaths of both.

CREON. It is right that it should be. I alone am guilty.
I know it, and I say it. Lead me in,
Quickly, friends.
I have neither life nor substance. Lead me in.

125 CHORAGOS. You are right, if there can be right in so much wrong.
The briefest way is best in a world of sorrow.

CREON. Let it come,
Let death come quickly, and be kind to me.
I would not ever see the sun again.

130 CHORAGOS. All that will come when it will; but we, meanwhile,
Have much to do. Leave the future to itself.

CREON. All my heart was in that prayer!

CHORAGOS. Then do not pray any more: the sky is deaf.

CREON. Lead me away. I have been rash and foolish.
135 I have killed my son and my wife.
I look for comfort; my comfort lies here dead.
Whatever my hands have touched has come to nothing.
Fate has brought all my pride to a thought of dust.

[*As* CREON *is being led into the house, the* CHORAGOS *advances and speaks directly to the audience.*]

CHORAGOS. There is no happiness where there is no wisdom.
140 No wisdom but in submission to the gods.
Big words are always punished,
And proud men in old age learn to be wise.

> What is the final message of the Choragos?

Respond *to the* SELECTION

Is Creon malicious or evil, or just misguided? What character flaw brought about his own ruin and that of his family?

RESPOND TO THE SELECTION

Some students may say that Creon is not evil or malicious, but misguided. He probably did not mean to cause such pain. His excessive pride brought about his own ruin and that of his family.

Quotables

"The most pathetic figure of the Greek theater, the unfortunate Oedipus, Sophocles takes to be a noble man called to error and alienation in spite of his wisdom, yet called too, in the end, through monstrous suffering, to radiate a magic power rich in a blessing which works even after he passes on. 'The noble man does not sin' is what the poet means. Though every natural law, the whole civilized world, fall to the ground through his actions, these very actions attract a higher, magical circle of influences which grounds a new world upon the rubble of the old. This is what the poet—inasmuch as he is a religious thinker—means."
—Friedrich Nietzsche, "Sophoclean Tragedy"

"Count no mortal happy till he has passed the final limit of his life secure from pain."
—Spoken by the Chorus at the end of Sophocles's *Oedipus the King*

ADDITIONAL QUESTIONS AND ACTIVITIES

Share with students the Quotables on this page. Then ask them the following questions:
- Do you view Creon as "a noble man called to error and alienation in spite of his wisdom"? Do you believe that after Creon's tragedy, a new world can be built up on the "rubble of the old"? Can any good come from Creon's tragedy?
- How do you interpret the words of the Chorus at the end of *Oedipus the King*?

Answers
Responses will vary. Creon is a noble and wise man who errs. He has learned a valuable lesson, and some good may come of his tragedy. He will serve as an example to future leaders that they must honor the laws of the gods. The Chorus is saying, count no person happy until he or she is dead. In other words, tragedy can strike at any time during a person's life.

RECALL

1a. Haimon is Creon's son and Antigone's fiancé. He begs his father to change his mind and forgive Antigone. He accuses his father of being too stubborn to see reason. His father accuses him of being weakened by love for a woman.

2a. Creon decides to lock Antigone away in a stone vault in the wilderness. The Chorus sings about love in Ode III.

3a. Creon changes his mind, tragically, when it is too late. Antigone, Haimon, and Eurydice all kill themselves.

INTERPRET

1b. Haimon respects his father, but clearly sees his father's error and attempts to point it out to him. Creon expects absolute obedience from both his son and his people. By refusing to give in, he hopes to make the point that those who betray Thebes will receive no mercy. *Responses will vary.*

2b. Creon hopes to use Polyneices and Antigone as examples to show that anyone who defies him will be punished. He hopes to earn the respect and fear of his subjects. The Chorus suggests that the gods are more powerful than his law.

3b. Creon finally changes his mind after Teiresias predicts that a terrible tragedy will befall him if he does not reverse his decision. While at first he refuses to believe Teiresias, he is deeply troubled by the old man's prophecy. The Choragos points out to him that Teiresias never lies. Finally Creon realizes that however humiliating it is to back down, it is worse to risk everything for stubborn pride. The events at the end of the play utterly destroy Creon. In his words, "Fate has brought all my pride to a thought of dust."

ANALYZE

4a. *Responses will vary.* The tragic events at the end of *Antigone* were partly dictated by Fate, and partly brought on by the actions of the characters. Antigone seems unsure whether her death was her own choice or whether it was an inescapable fate decreed by the gods because of her father's sins. In scene 4, lines 37–44, Antigone blames the curse of Oedipus as having caused her tragic end. However, the Chorus points out that she also made her own choice,

---

Investigate, Inquire, and Imagine

Recall: GATHERING FACTS

1a. Who is Haimon, and what is his relationship to Antigone? What does Haimon beg of his father? Of what does he accuse his father, and of what weakness does his father accuse him?

2a. What does Creon decide to do with Antigone? Of what does the Chorus sing in Ode III, after Creon has made his decision?

3a. When does Creon finally change his mind? What happens to Antigone? to Haimon? to Eurydice?

Interpret: FINDING MEANING

1b. How does Haimon treat his father? What does Creon expect of his son and of his people? What point is Creon trying to make by refusing to give in? With which man do you agree, and why?

2b. What does Creon hope he will accomplish by carrying out this decision? What does the Chorus suggest is more powerful than Creon's law?

3b. What finally persuades Creon to reverse his decision? How do the events at the end of the play affect Creon? What does he realize about himself?

Analyze: TAKING THINGS APART

4a. Analyze the role that fate played in *Antigone*. Which events do the characters blame on "fate"? Which events do you think the characters brought upon themselves? Which did they have no control over—in other words, which could have been caused by fate?

Synthesize: BRINGING THINGS TOGETHER

4b. Whom, if anyone, do you blame for the tragic events of *Antigone*? Did anyone in the play intend to cause such harm? What tragic flaws did the characters possess that led to their tragic fall?

Perspective: MAKING JUDGMENTS

5a. Describe the points of view of Antigone and Creon. How do the characters view each other? In what ways does pride affect the perspectives of each character?

Empathy: CONNECTING IDEAS

5b. If you were Antigone, what might you have done differently to avert the tragedy at the end of the play? if you were Creon? Which one of them has fallen most completely at the end of the play, and why?

Understanding Literature

IMAGE AND IMAGERY. Review the definition for **image** in the Handbook of Literary Terms. What imagery from nature does Haimon use in scene 3 when trying to persuade his father to see reason? What natural imagery is used in the Chorus's odes? What is the effect of this natural imagery on the meaning of the play?

PLOT, CLIMAX, CRISIS, FALLING ACTION, AND CATASTROPHE. Review the definition for **plot** in the Handbook of Literary Terms. What do you think caused the crisis, or turning point, in the play? Was Creon motivated by concern for Antigone or for his own fate when he changed his mind at this point? Were you able to predict what would occur in the play's catastrophe? What message, or lesson, was conveyed by the catastrophe? Complete a plot pyramid like the following showing where each plot element occurs in the play. Include the plot elements from the first half of *Antigone* as well.

ANSWERS TO INVESTIGATE, INQUIRE, AND IMAGINE (CONT.)

and asserts that her death was her own doing. In Ode IV, the Chorus conveys the moral that no one "can prevail against untiring destiny," suggesting that no one, including Antigone, can avoid his or her fate once it has been decreed by the gods.

SYNTHESIZE

4b. *Responses will vary.* Students will probably blame both Antigone, for her stubborn refusal to bend to the law or to apologize for her actions, and Creon, for his refusal to pardon Antigone or yield to reason. Neither Antigone nor Creon intended to cause such harm, but both possessed the tragic flaw of excessive pride which made them incapable of averting the tragedy.

(Continued on page 905)

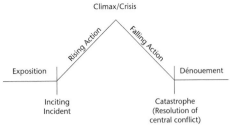

Climax/Crisis

Rising Action

Falling Action

Exposition

Dénouement

Inciting
Incident

Catastrophe
(Resolution of
central conflict)

Writer's Journal

1. Write a **speech** to be delivered by the Chorus, describing what might happen to Creon next.
2. Write a **monologue** Creon might deliver at the end of the play, revealing his remorse and repentance for his role in the tragedy.
3. Write a **letter** Antigone might have written before her death to both of her deceased brothers, Eteocles and Polyneices, in which she explains and justifies her thinking and her actions.

Integrating the Language Arts

Collaborative Learning & Speaking and Listening

DRAMATIC READINGS FROM *ANTIGONE*. *Antigone* is a play of high drama, and exquisite, direct dialogue which gets very quickly to the core of the conflict. It was intended to be acted on stage, so it is important to hear the words aloud. As a group, read the play, or parts of it, out loud. Have the readers stand—even simple drama has a powerful effect. Have a group of three or more read the parts of the Chorus. Then, as a whole group, read the Chorus's lines together. What is the dramatic effect of hearing a group of people recite the same lines together? How is it different from hearing just one person speaking, or reading it to yourself? Jot down your responses in your notebook, and then share your ideas in a group discussion.

Study and Research

RESEARCHING THE GOLDEN AGE OF ATHENS. The period from 477 BC – 431 BC is known as the Golden Age of Greece. During this time, art, politics, learning, and athleticism flourished. Research an aspect of fifth-century Athens and prepare an oral report. Collect material from a variety of sources. You might do an Internet search on Sophocles to find out about related topics, or check *Encyclopedia Britannica Online* at www.britannica.com. Visit the library to look at picture books on Greece, or see if there are any videos about ancient Greece. One topic you might research is fifth-century Greek drama. Find out what the stage used in the drama typically looked like, where the audience stood, and what the important elements of the performance were. Include visual representations in presenting your research to the rest of the class. Draw a picture or build a model of the stage. Describe what it must have been like to have attended such an event.

PERSPECTIVE

5a. Antigone is steadfastly determined to follow what she sees as the law of the gods and her duty as a loving sister to ensure that Polyneices receives a proper burial. She thinks Creon is foolish and stubborn. Creon believes that if he gives in to Antigone he will be seen as weak. He believes it is his duty to punish her in order to maintain the respect of his subjects. He sees Antigone as a spoiled, foolish woman with too much pride. Both characters are too proud to see the other's point of view.

EMPATHY

5b. *Responses will vary.* Students may say that Antigone should have been more diplomatic. Perhaps she could have appealed to Creon's mercy. Creon could have listened to his son and to the Choragos. If Haimon had reached Antigone before she killed herself, or if she hadn't killed herself, everything might have been righted. If Haimon hadn't killed himself, Eurydice might still be alive. Creon is the only character to witness all the events of the play. He suffers the most because he sees the full extent of the damage and realizes that he is responsible for all of it. Antigone, on the other hand, has the satisfaction of believing that she died for a noble cause. Point out to the students that this element completes the fullness of the Greek tragedy: the character most blind to his or her own tragic flaw is, in the end, the one who sees the full horror of the flaw as it has materialized. The tragedy reached its peak only because Creon witnessed its completion.

ANSWERS TO UNDERSTANDING LITERATURE

IMAGE AND IMAGERY. Haimon tells his father that some trees bend during flood time, and are saved from being broken by the strength of the waters, while "stubborn trees are torn up, roots and all." Imagery of the sea and of sunlight pervade the Chorus's odes. *Responses will vary.* The imagery reminds us that a natural order exists beyond the order imposed by humans.

PLOT, CLIMAX, CRISIS, FALLING ACTION, AND CATASTROPHE. The crisis was caused by Teiresias's warnings to Creon. These warnings made Creon finally see that he was in the wrong. *Responses will*

ANSWERS TO UNDERSTANDING LITERATURE (CONT.)

vary. Creon may have been more worried about his own fate, since he seemed to care little for what suffering Antigone would have to endure. The catastrophe teaches that humans must bow to the wisdom of the gods. Students should include the following events in their graphic organizer: **Crisis and Climax** (the same event in the play): Creon realizes he is risking everything for stubborn pride and announces that he will release Antigone from her vault. **Falling Action:** Eurydice learns that Antigone and Haimon have both killed themselves, and she kills herself in grief. **Catastrophe:** Creon realizes that he has caused the deaths of his entire family, and wishes he himself would die. **Dénouement:** Creon is led into the house and the Chorus sums up the moral of the play: "There is...no wisdom but in submission to the gods."

Guided Writing

GUIDED WRITING
Software

See the Guided Writing Software for an extended version of this lesson that includes printable graphic organizers, extensive student models and student-friendly checklists, and self-, peer, and teacher evaluation features.

> "Nature fits all her children with something to do.
>
> He who would write and can't write, can surely review."
>
> —James Russell Lowell, dramatist

EXAMINING THE MODEL. The opening paragraph of a review is always the most important, so look at Rohan Preston's introduction. What do you know about the play based on the introduction? You know that *The Darker Face of the Earth* deals with the complicated topic of slavery with some clarity. Preston is relieved to find something positive to report, signalling that on the whole the review will be favorable.

Notice the absence of specific details in the introduction. Instead of expanding on the specifics, the paragraph merely introduces them: the title, the playwright, the location, the general subject matter of slavery in America. With his

continued on page 907

906 *UNIT ELEVEN*

REVIEWING A DRAMATIC PERFORMANCE

Reviewers can reinforce what we already know about entertainment, anger us with strong opinions contrary to our own, or challenge us to think in a new way. A successful reviewer has two important skills. First, the reviewer has the ability to form opinions based on solid reasoning. Second, the reviewer persuades the reader to accept or at least consider his or her informed opinion. In this lesson you will work on both of these skills.

WRITING ASSIGNMENT. Your assignment in this lesson is to write a review of a performance. The performance can be either of a theater production or a film.

Professional Model

> from a drama review of *The Darker Face of the Earth* written by Rohan Preston/ *Minneapolis Star Tribune*
>
> Slavery in America is such a messy, unresolved issue— mucking up feelings of guilt and shame— that it is unfair to ask a single play to provide a totally clean and focused treatment on the subject. Still, it's a relief that Rita Dove's drama, *The Darker Face of the Earth*, which opened at the Guthrie Theater on Wednesday, finds some clarity after a dense, rambling start.
>
> The play, which uses the Oedipus story as a template, arcs a difficult course. . . . It's set on the Jennings plantation in South Carolina in 1820 and 1840. A black boy born to Amalia Jennings LaFarge, the plantation's white mistress, is quickly sold into slavery. Twenty years later she buys him back from a seafaring captain. Neither is aware that he, now the worldly and literate Augustus Newcastle, is her son.
>
> In this world, the noble Greeks have been replaced by Americans scratching for bits of human sanity, with captives finding freedom in juju and madness and murder while their overlords escape by turning to drink, astronomy and fairy tales.

Darker Face takes place in Douglas Stein's set, which suggests poplar trees. Marlies Yearby's choreography is smart in the field-work scenes and seems cluttered elsewhere. Cooper Moore's dulcet harmonies make slavery sound sweet.

The most impressive work comes from the acting company, with Lester Purry endowing Augustus with the ferocity of a revolutionary. . . . His performance is the show's center of gravity. Karen Landry's Amalia is dauntless and forceful without losing her femininity. . . . And Laurie Carlos' Scylla, a conjure woman, exhibits all the normalcy of a happily mad woman.

The shortcomings have to do with the amount of undeveloped characters—from the conjurer to mad Hector, the snake-catcher of the swamps to a free-flowing chorus. . . .

These elements delay and sometimes eject you from the roiling pathos of *Darker Face*, which takes you to a place of cleansing, if not tears.

Prewriting

FINDING YOUR VOICE. The way a review "sounds" to the reading audience is as important as the content of the review. Look again at the professional model above. What do you hear? Preston calls slavery "such a messy, unresolved issue," and thus avoids antagonizing his audience while at the same time noting the complexity of slavery. His word choice tells the audience that he respects them. Remember that your audience wants to know what you think. Tell them confidently and honestly.

IDENTIFYING YOUR AUDIENCE. Performance reviews are great opportunities for you to get published in your school or local newspaper or school website. When you identify your audience, the focus of the review should be more apparent to you. If you are writing a review for a drama class assignment, your focus will be more technically oriented than if you are writing a review for the school newspaper.

WRITING WITH A PLAN. When writing a review, get your first impressions on paper as soon after the performance as you can. These first impressions will serve to record your viewing experience and refresh your memory as you draft your review. As you record your notes, cover as many different elements as you can. Think about the lighting, the sound, where you sat in the theater, the scene transitions, costumes, music, or, for that matter, the lack of music. Naturally, you can't cover all of these topics, but you'll never know how important they are until you stop to think and take notes on them.

opinion and the basic information taken care of, Preston moves on to the body of the review.

Preston provides background information in the second paragraph, telling us character names, the central conflict, setting, and only a little plot. The reviewer's job is not to re-tell the story but to give the reader only the information necessary to help support the opinion stated in the first paragraph.

Preston chooses to discuss the set, choreography, the music, and the acting company. Most of Preston's commentary and strongest claims are saved for the performances. Vivid language describes the "ferocity" of the male lead and the "dauntless and forceful" nature of the female lead. In this way, Preston has saved the best or most important for last, a common technique used by almost all writers.

Taking Notes

Once your notes are complete, find an emphasis. Ask yourself, "What do I remember most vividly?" Was it the stage? the costumes? the bad seat you were given? the brilliant script? the way the performers played to this particular audience? These are only a few of dozens of questions you should ask as you form your first draft.

Next, go through and cross off all but a few of the most impressive or disappointing components. You will now have an idea of the tone of the review you will write. After

continued on page 908

selecting the elements of focus, you will have a rough outline of the content of the review.

Staying Focused

Remember the goal of your first paragraph. Stay focused on the general and not the specific. State your opinion clearly, keeping in mind the voice you want to maintain throughout the review. Grab your audience's attention.

In the paragraphs that follow the introduction, organize the important evidence from your notes into a persuasive whole. Start by presenting a brief summary of the story. Introduce characters, conflicts, and setting but don't go too far. All you need is a framework for the evidence supporting your opinion. Once the summary is complete, address the basic components of the performance. Be economical when you select the topics of your body paragraphs and write about what you know. Start with the least important element and finish with the most important.

Close your review with a brief reiteration of your opinion.

A simple graphic organizer can help to clarify how you feel about the various components of the performance. Sophomore David Klein chose to address the following elements in his review of a performance of Arthur Miller's *Death of a Salesman*.

Student Model—Graphic Organizer

Name of Performance/Director
Death of a Salesman (film, 1984)/directed by Volker Schlandorff

Overall Rating
Superb; even though the play is fifty years old, it still has power and anguish

Important plot elements
Willy is at the end of his rope, losing his grasp on reality. His sons /wife, (and Willy himself) have a difficult time accepting the family's past. Minor characters, Ben, Charlie and Bernard, all have a connection to Loman's past.

How the set enhances the production
The set was more movie-like and so camera work and editing took care of most of the parts where Willy was dreaming or having flashbacks. Still, the set is important to convey the way Willy feels trapped and boxed in.

Strongest component of this production
Performances by Dustin Hoffman as Willy and John Malkovich as Biff were the highlight. Hoffman's Willy carries the world on his shoulders/ beaten down. Malkovich makes certain that this play is about Biff as well as Willy.

Any weak element to the play
None. I had a difficult time understanding the role of Willy's dead brother, Ben, but I don't think that is a weakness worth mentioning.

Where you viewed the play and its impact on your opinion of the performance in general
In class, on a VCR, over a two-day period. Teacher stopped the tape too many times to discuss the film, interrupted the flow of the script and action.

Possible Thesis Statements
Willy and Biff Loman combine to show the power and pain that broken dreams can have.
Death of a Salesman still captivates audiences with its urgency and anguish over one man's fall from hope.
Arthur Miller's *Death of a Salesman* is still one of the great American dramas and certainly the best American tragedy.

Drafting

The drafting process is the next phase in writing your review. A draft is an unfinished, unpolished version, a working model of what you want to produce. Use your notes, your graphic organizer, and your remembered experience of seeing the play or film to help as you write.

Student Model—Draft

Review by David Klein

Title? You need an interesting grabber in the first ¶.

Even after fifty years, Arthur Miller's

"I am not a dime a dozen, I am Willie Loman!" It has been 50 years since an

classic tale of an ordinary American

actor has shouted those lines.

life and *Death of a Salesman* still

captivates audiences with its pain and

truth. In the 1984 production (now on

video), Dustin Hoffman, as Willy, and

John Malkovich, as Biff, both turn in

Maybe put all the actors together and then

excellent performances. This production

mention the director.

was directed by Volker Schlondorff and

also stars Stephen Lang as Happy, Kate

Reid as Linda, and Charles Durning as

Good—you include the key bits of info in the 1st ¶.

Charley, Willy's only friend. *the title, director & actors.*

Death of a Salesman takes place in

two different time frames. The ~~regular~~ *present*

time of the play covers about two

evenings. The other time frame is

Willy's fantasy world. In this frame

Willy flashes back to various parts of

his past to <u>relive visits</u> from <u>his</u>

<u>brother</u>, <u>he talks with his neighbor</u>,

and <u>shares moments of joy and pain</u> with

his sons....

Self- and Peer Evaluation

After you finish your first draft, complete a self-evaluation of your writing. If time allows, you may want to get one or two peer evaluations. See the Language Arts Survey 2.37 for more details about self- and peer evaluation.

- How does the introduction grab the attention of the reader?
- Where in the introduction does the reviewer make a clear statement of opinion?
- Where are examples of the reviewer's honest and engaged voice?
- What specific elements of the production does the reviewer cover?
- What specific details does the reviewer use to back up his or her opinion?
- Does the review follow a logical order, from the least important detail to the most important?
- What examples of strong and vivid language has the reviewer used?
- What specific background information about the performance does the reviewer include to give the audience some hints at the plot and conflict?
- What other elements from the performance might the reviewer cover as he or she considers revising?

Drafting

Encourage students to use their completed graphic organizer to help them make sure they have organized the main points of their review carefully. Remind students to include a synopsis of the play, but not to reveal the outcome of the film or play when providing a synopsis. One way to consider their synopsis is to see it as a motivation tool to get their audience to see or not see the film or play.

Self- and Peer Evaluation

Have students review the Language Arts Survey 2.37, "Self- and Peer Evaluation." Then have students use the checklist on page 909 for self- and peer evaluation. The checklist is intended to act as a student-friendly rubric that should help students identify specific evidence of writing strengths and areas needing improvement. Make sure they provide concrete suggestions for improvement or specific evidence of why the writing works.

Language, Grammar, and Style

Sentence Parallelism
IDENTIFYING PARALLELISM. A sentence has **parallelism** when it uses the same grammatical forms to express ideas of equal, or parallel, importance. A parallel sentence structure follows a consistent pattern. Look at a sample from the professional model to see what is meant by "consistent pattern."

> Reviewers can reinforce what we already know about entertainment, anger us with strong opinions, or challenge us to think in new ways.

If we take the detail away from this sentence and look only at the parts that keep it parallel, it would look like this:

> Reviewers can reinforce, (can) anger, or (can) challenge.

Each part of the list matches the others aligned by the helping verb *can*.

FIXING ERRORS IN PARALLELISM. Look at the sentence below from David's rough draft. Identify what makes it non-parallel and write a revised version, making sure the listed items match in case and number.

> In this frame, Willy flashes back to various parts of his past to relive visits from his brother, he talks with his neighbor, and shares moments of joy and pain with his sons.

continued on page 911

910   UNIT ELEVEN

Revising and Proofreading

Remember that in the Drafting section of this lesson you focused on voice, detail and organization. Use your self- and peer evaluations to make revision decisions. As you look back at your rough draft, be prepared to make major changes when necessary. See the Language Arts Survey 2.45 for a proofreading checklist.

Student Model—Revised

> *Death of a Salesman* by Arthur Miller
> Directed by Volker Shlondorff
> A Review by David Klein
>
> "I am not a dime a dozen! I am Willy Loman!" It has been fifty years since the first actor playing Willy shouted those painful lines. Even after fifty years, *Death of a Salesman*, Arthur Miller's classic tale of an ordinary American life, still captivates audiences with its pain and truth. In the 1984 production (now on video), Dustin Hoffman as Willy, and John Malkovich as Biff, both turn in excellent performances. This production was directed by Volker Schlondorff and also stars Stephen Lang as Happy, Kate Reid as Linda, and Charles Durning as Charley, Willy's only friend.
> *Death of a Salesman* takes place in two different time frames. The present time of the play covers about two evenings. The other time frame is a series of flashbacks from Willy's perspective. In this frame, Willy relives conversations with his neighbor, moments of joy and pain with his family, and secrets from his own dark past. In the present time frame, Willy is an old, slow man on the verge of losing everything. As the play goes back to his past, some of the reasons for Willy's present pain and mental stress are revealed to the audience.
> The set of *Salesman* must be able to show both time frames of the play. In this production, shot on film but with a play-like atmosphere, the camera does most of the work of convincing the audience that they are suddenly

seventeen years in the past. The differences between the stage production and this film are a little too obvious when the camera goes in for close-ups. After all, when you watch a play, you can't see what a camera close-up shows. So in that regard the film is not as challenging as the play, and it's maybe a little inauthentic.

The strength of this production comes from Hoffman's role as Willy and Malkovich's role as Biff. Willy is a small man with big aspirations. Hoffman plays this part very well. As the Willy in the flashback, Hoffman is youthful and energetic. But the Willy of the real time almost seems to crumble under the weight created by the world and his past.

Malkovich is excellent as Biff. In the flashbacks Biff is seventeen and on the verge of greatness. In present time, Biff is thirty-four and, like his father, slowed by broken dreams. Malkovich plays the Biffs like a pro. He's believable in both roles.

These actors tell Miller's simple but painful story. The director lets the play unfold with a mix of dignity but urgency. Between the directing, the set, and especially the acting, we are reminded of why this play was so great when it opened fifty years ago and why it will still be great fifty years from now.

Publishing and Presenting

Once you have finished your review, consider sharing it with your class, especially if it is a current or controversial performance. If the entire class has written a review of the same work, use the reviews as platforms for a debate on the merits of the actors, directors, etc. This same idea could be used to debate the relevancy of the subject matter of the play itself. *Death of Salesman* is a perfect example for a debate topic. The play explores themes of success and failure, appearances, adulthood, virtue and honesty.

Rewrite the sentence so that the elements are parallel.

USING PARALLEL STRUCTURE. Imagine if there were no such thing as parallel structure and you couldn't create lists or draw comparisons. Writing and speaking would be tedious and fragmented. Imagine trying to explain your morning: *For breakfast I ate eggs. I also had toast. For a drink I had orange juice.* Naturally, we would combine these sentences into one: *For breakfast I had eggs, toast, and orange juice.* Parallel structure allows a writer to fit more information into a smaller package. Go through your revised draft to check to see that your sentences contain parallel structures.

For more information, see the Language Arts Survey 3.38, "Achieving Parallelism."

Reflecting

As a reviewer you step into the role of critic and teacher. Consider the seriousness of this job. You are writing to a group, and are responsible for accuracy and sincerity. If you have ever made a decision based on a review, you know what it is like to rely on someone else's opinion. What does it mean to you to be heard? How do you want to sound?

Publishing and Presenting

Students may want to print all their reviews together, with a section for films and a section for plays, and distribute the collection to their friends and teachers. You might also talk to the librarian of your school and see about including the film and play reviews collection in the library.

Reflecting

Encourage students to analyze several reviews of plays and films written by professionals to see how they are judged by professional reviewers. Then have them compare those reviews with the reviews their class wrote.

UNIT 11 review
What We Live By

Words for Everyday Use

Check your knowledge of the following vocabulary words from the selections in this unit. Write a short sentence using each of these words in context to make the meaning clear. To review the definition or usage of a word, refer to the page number listed or to the Glossary of Words for Everyday Use.

anarchist, 873	consenting, 889	lamentation, 891	sententiously, 873
aphorism, 895	decree, 865	lithe, 874	statecraft, 874
astray, 887	deference, 885	malicious, 885	subordinate, 885
blasphemy, 891	dirge, 891	meddle, 867	transgress, 892
clement, 898	endure, 876	piety, 889	trifle, 895
comprehensive, 871	implacable, 893	prevail, 893	vengeance, 881
compulsive, 882	insolence, 877	profane, 893	vile, 888
conscience, 873	instinct, 887	reverence, 870	waver, 881

Literary Tools

Define each of the following terms, giving concrete examples of how they are used in the selections in this unit. To review a term, refer to the page number indicated or to the Handbook of Literary Terms.

catastrophe, 884	falling action, 884	plot, 863, 884
chorus, 863	image, 884	rising action, 863
climax, 884	imagery, 884	tragedy, 863
crisis, 884	inciting incident, 863	tragic flaw, 884
exposition, 863	ode, 863	tragic hero, 863

Reflecting *on your reading*

Genre Studies

1. TRAGEDY. What is a tragedy? What makes *Antigone* a tragic play? Who is the tragic hero and what is this hero's tragic flaw? Is there more than one tragic hero? Explain.

2. CHORUS. Greek tragedies were the first plays to employ the role of a chorus. Explain what a chorus is, and analyze the role of the Chorus and the Choragos in *Antigone.* Why is the Chorus necessary? What purpose does it serve? Be sure you describe the Chorus's point of view in regard to the main conflict of the play. Give examples from the text to support your analysis.

Thematic Studies

3. LAW. One theme dealt with in *Antigone* is the importance of following laws in order to maintain a healthy state or kingdom. What are the attitudes of Antigone, Creon, Ismene, and

the Chorus toward laws? Consider both the laws of the gods and those of kings. Which laws do you think the author of the play believed were supreme? Cite evidence from the play to support your answer.

4. **FATE.** Analyze the theme of fate in *Antigone*. Which events do the characters blame on "fate"? Which events do you think the characters brought upon themselves? Which did they have no control over—in other words, which could have been caused by fate? Whom do you blame for the tragic events of *Antigone*? Support your answer with examples from the play.

5. **PRIDE COMES BEFORE A FALL.** You may have heard the saying, "Pride goeth before destruction, and a haughty spirit before a fall" (The Bible, Proverbs 16:18). Would Sophocles have agreed with this axiom? Examine how this saying relates to the theme of *Antigone*. What happens in the play as a result of excessive pride or haughtiness? Support your answer with evidence from the play.

for your READING LIST

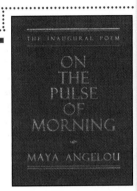

On the Pulse of Morning by Maya Angelou. Maya Angelou's poem *On the Pulse of Morning* was read by the poet at the Inauguration of President William Jefferson Clinton on January 20, 1993. In this poem, which has been published in booklet form, she asks us to "Lift up your eyes / Upon this day breaking for you. / Give birth again / to the dream." Angelou has written five volumes of autobiography, beginning with *I Know Why the Caged Bird Sings.* She has also published five collections of poetry: *And Still Rise, Just Give Me a Cool Drink of Water 'fore I Diiie, Oh Pray My Wings Are Gonna Fit Me Well, Shaker, Why Don't You Sing?,* and *I Shall Not be Moved.*

Independent Reading Activity

FINDING STORIES IN THE NEWS. It is said that truth is stranger than fiction. News stories are factual and are meant to inform, but they often contain high drama. We can also learn about human behavior from them, and often there is a good story behind the news articles. Spend a few days reading the daily news. Clip articles from it that you find intriguing and interesting. Perhaps you want to find an uplifting news story, or a human interest story, or a story where you feel an injustice is being righted. Find a story you like and write a short story or a play based on it. Try to figure out why this event happened. What led up to it? What motivated the people involved? What did they go through? How did they change?

Selections for Additional Reading

Opened Ground by Seamus Heaney. This collection includes the essential poems from Seamus Heaney's twelve previous volumes of poetry, as well as new sequences drawn from *The Cure at Troy* (Heaney's version of Sophocles' *Philocetes*) and *Sweeney Astray* (an adaptation of the medieval Irish poem *Buile Suibhne),* and a number of previously uncollected poems.

The Alchemist: A Fable about Following Your Dream by Paulo Coehlo. Brazilian novelist Paulo Coehlo's character Santiago has many adventures, including meeting an alchemist who becomes his greatest teacher.

Blood Wedding: A Tragedy in Three Acts and Seven Scenes by Federico García Lorca. This passionate story written in 1933 by Spanish playwright Lorca (1898–1936) is about two young people ruined by their love for each other. Not fate, not class differences, nor family ties can keep them apart, although the consequences are disastrous.

UNIT REVIEW 913

FOR YOUR READING LIST

On the Pulse of Morning is one of Angelou's most recent collections of poems. It quickly became a national bestseller and was hailed by some critics as her best collection so far. It includes the famous and captivating poem that was written specifically for President William Jefferson Clinton's inauguration. That poem was also entitled "On the Pulse of Morning."

Independent Reading Activity
Before students begin this activity, ask them to read the Language Arts Survey 1.10, "Reading Newspapers, Journals, and Newsmagazines" and 5.31, "How to Read a Newspaper or Newsmagazine." After they have spent a few days reading news articles, have students answer the questions in the form of an essay. Students may want to complement their essay with a collage of their clippings.

REFLECTING ON YOUR READING

The prompts in Reflecting on Your Reading are suitable topics for research papers. Refer to the Language Arts Survey 5.18–5.45, "Research Skills." (To evaluate research papers, see the evaluation forms for writing, revising, and proofreading in the Assessment Resource book.)

The prompts in Reflecting on Your Reading can also be adapted for use as topics for oral reports or debates. Refer students to the Speaking and Listening Resource in the Language Arts Survey. (To evaluate these projects, see the evaluation forms in the Assessment Resource book.)

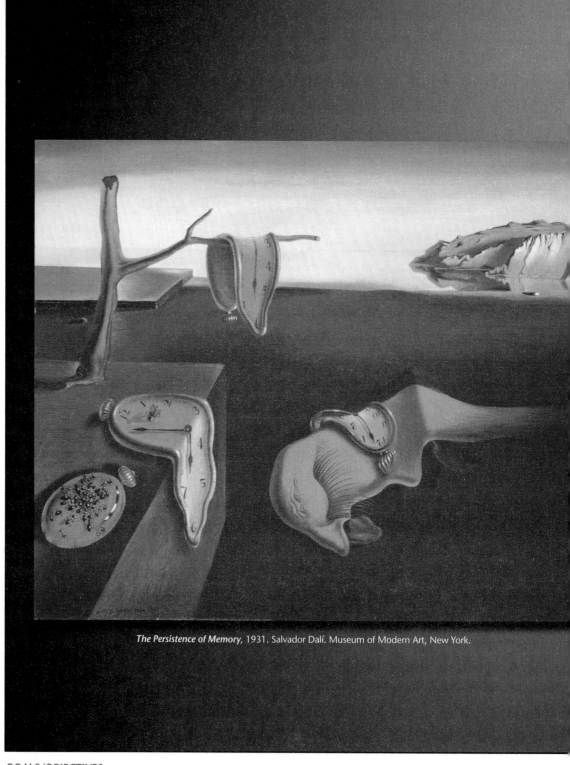

The Persistence of Memory, 1931. Salvador Dalí. Museum of Modern Art, New York.

GOALS/OBJECTIVES

Studying this unit will enable students to
• appreciate and enjoy various types of fiction such as mysteries, urban legends, science fiction, and Magical Realism
• discuss the mysteries and supernatural forces surrounding our world
• define literary terms such as *setting, mood, conflict,* *foreshadowing,* and *suspense* and identify and explain examples of each that they encounter in their reading
• write a science fiction story
• identify run-on sentences and comma splices and demonstrate the ability to use sentences effectively

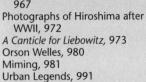

"Now comes the mystery."

—*Henry Ward Beecher*

UNIT TWELVE

Read the quotes aloud. Ask students
to discuss which quotations and
speakers they recognize. Of the
quotes on page 916, what attitudes
or expectations do the speakers
seem to have about the mysterious?
About the future? What do the
words "dark" or "darkness" seem to
symbolize for the speakers?

echoes

➤ There is a fifth dimension beyond that which is known to man. It is a dimension as vast as space, and as timeless as infinity. It is the middle ground between light and shadow—between science and superstition. And it lies between the pit of a man's fears and the summit of his knowledge. This is the dimension of the imagination.

—Rod Serling

➤ I am taking a fearful leap in the dark.

—Thomas Hobbes

➤ There is nothing to be learned from history anymore. We're in science fiction now.

—Allen Ginsberg

➤ Act boldly and unseen forces will come to your aid.

—Dorothea Brande

➤ The universe is a big place, perhaps the biggest.

—Kilgore Trout (Kurt Vonnegut)

➤ The mystical is not how the world is, but that it is.

—Ludwig Wittgenstein

➤ One does not discover new lands without consenting to lose sight of the shore for a very long time.

—André Gide

➤ Everything has its wonders, even darkness and silence, and I learn, whatever state I may be in, therein to be content.

—Helen Keller

➤ When it gets dark enough you can see the stars.

—Lee Salk

➤ Those who dwell among the beauties and mysteries of the Earth are never alone or weary of life.

—Rachel Carson

"House Taken Over"

by Julio Cortázar, translated by Paul Blackburn

Reader's resource

"House Taken Over" was originally published in a book of short stories titled *Bestiario,* which means "bestiary." A bestiary is a type of medieval literature which relates religious or moralistic stories, usually about animals that behave like humans.

The story takes place in Buenos Aires, the capital of Argentina, sometime after 1939. Cortázar was a student of Surrealism, and many of his stories seem to occur somewhere between the realistic world that we already know and a marvelous realm of fantasy. Cortázar has written that one of his aims in writing is to bring to the reader "instances of dislocation in which the ordinary ceases to be tranquilizing."

About the AUTHOR

Julio Cortázar (1914–1984) was born in Brussels, Belgium, to Argentine parents who returned to Argentina after World War I. After receiving a degree in literature in Buenos Aires, he taught in secondary schools and worked as a literary translator. In 1951 Cortázar moved to France, where he lived until his death, becoming a citizen in 1981. He published poems and plays in the thirties and forties but achieved his first major success with a book of short stories, *Bestiario,* published in 1951. Other short story collections include *Final del juego* (1956; translated into English as *End of the Game*) and *Las armas secretas* (1958; translated as *Secret Weapons*). His open-ended novel *Rayuela* (*Hopscotch*), published in 1963, is considered his masterpiece; the reader is invited to read the chapters of the novel in whatever order he or she chooses. The author recommends several ways to rearrange the novel, demonstrating in this way that stories need not be linear and chronological.

Literary TOOLS

SETTING. The **setting** of a literary work is the time and place in which it occurs, together with all the details used to create a sense of a particular time and place. As you read, decide what impact the house has on the characters.

MOOD. Mood, or **atmosphere,** is the emotion created in the reader by part or all of a literary work. As you read, determine the mood of the story.

Organizer

Make a cluster chart listing facts that contribute to the mood of the story. One example has been done for you.

- Mood
- Irene turned down suitors for no particular reason.

Reader's Journal

What is your favorite room in your house?

ADDITIONAL RESOURCES

UNIT 12 RESOURCE BOOK
- Selection Worksheet 12.1
- Selection Check Test 4.12.1
- Selection Test 4.12.2
- Language, Grammar, and Style Resource 3.10
- Speaking and Listening Resource 4.21

GRAPHIC ORGANIZER

Students may include the following facts in their cluster charts:
- The characters are content with just keeping the house clean.
- Irene knits too many things and then unravels them.
- The narrator can find "nothing worthwhile" to read.
- The narrator watches Irene knitting for hours.
- The characters remain calm and content when something takes over the back half of the house.
- The narrator says they "can live without thinking."
- Irene talks in her sleep and the narrator flails in his sleep.
- The characters abandon their house when they hear noises in the front half.

READER'S JOURNAL

As an alternate activity, ask students what it means to "kill time." What kinds of activities fall into the category of killing time? What is the alternative to killing time?

VOCABULARY FROM THE SELECTION

brusquely	indispensable
commune	nocturnal
dexterity	recessed
flail	skein
folio	vestibule
hurl	

GOALS/OBJECTIVES

Studying this lesson will enable students to
- appreciate a short story with surreal elements
- summarize Julio Cortázar's literary accomplishments
- define *setting* and *mood* and recognize and explain examples of each that they encounter in their reading
- demonstrate the ability to identify linking verbs in sentences
- research surrealism as an artistic and literary movement

1. The great-grandparents, a grandfather, and the parents of the narrator and his sister Irene previously lived in the house.
2. They didn't get married because they had enough to do just keeping the big house clean.
3. They will allow distant cousins to inherit the house and have it torn down, or they will have it torn down themselves.
4. Irene spends most of her days knitting.

INDIVIDUAL LEARNING STRATEGIES

MOTIVATION
Invite students to write or tell brief stories using the same basic story elements that Cortázar uses in "House Taken Over"—a middle-aged brother and sister, an old family house, and strange sounds heard in some part of the house.

READING PROFICIENCY
Have students make a list of words and phrases the author uses to describe Irene as they read. Once they have this list, have them use it to come up with a list of traits for the character. Then have them discuss whether Irene is a realistic character or a symbolic character.

ENGLISH LANGUAGE LEARNING
Provide students with these additional vocabulary words and their definitions:
topple—overthrow
ajar—slightly open
sinister—suggesting trouble or evil

SPECIAL NEEDS
Help students use the details on page 920 to create a drawing of the layout of the house, where all of the action takes place. The diagram should show the front and back sections, the corridor connecting them, the oak door leading to the rear part, and the front vestibule and gated door. Have students refer to their drawings as they read about what happens in different parts of the house.

HOUSE
Taken Over

Julio Cortázar, translated by Paul Blackburn

We liked the house because, apart from its being old and spacious (in a day when old houses go down for a profitable auction of their construction materials), it kept the memories of great-grandparents, our paternal grandfather, our parents and the whole of childhood.

Who lived in the house before the narrator and his sister Irene?

Irene and I got used to staying in the house by ourselves, which was crazy; eight people could have lived in that place and not have gotten in each other's way. We rose at seven in the morning and got the cleaning done, and about eleven I left Irene to finish off whatever rooms and went to the kitchen. We lunched at noon precisely; then there was nothing left to do but a few dirty plates. It was pleasant to take lunch and commune with the great hollow, silent house, and it was enough for us just to keep it clean. We ended up thinking, at times, that that was what had kept us from marrying. Irene turned down two suitors for no particular reason, and María Esther went and died on me before we could manage to get engaged. We were easing into our forties with the unvoiced concept that the quiet, simple marriage of sister and brother was the indispensable

What was it that kept both the narrator and his sister from getting married?

end to a line established in this house by our grandparents. We would die here someday, obscure and distant cousins would inherit the place, have it torn down, sell the bricks and get rich on the building plot; or more justly and better yet, we would topple it ourselves before it was too late.

What plans do the narrator and his sister have for the house?

Irene never bothered anyone. Once the morning housework was finished, she spent the rest of the day on the sofa in her bedroom, knitting. I couldn't tell you why she knitted so much; I think women knit when they discover that it's a fat excuse to do nothing at all. But Irene was not like that, she always knitted necessities, sweaters for winter, socks for me, handy morning robes and bedjackets for herself. Sometimes she would do a jacket, then unravel it the next moment because there was something that didn't please her; it was pleasant to see a pile of tangled wool in her knitting basket fighting a losing battle for a few hours to retain its shape. Saturdays I went downtown to buy wool; Irene had faith in my good taste, was pleased with the colors and never a skein had to be returned. I took advantage of these trips to make the rounds of the bookstores, uselessly asking if they had anything new in French literature.

How does Irene spend most of her days?

> **words for everyday use**
>
> com • mune (kə myün′) *vi.,* be in intimate relation or rapport. *Many Romantic poets* commune *with nature.*
> in • dis • pens • able (in di spen′ sə bəl) *adj.,* absolutely necessary. *A microscope is* indispensable *for biology class.*
> skein (skān) *n.,* loosely coiled length of wound yarn. *Grandma had to buy another* skein *of blue wool to finish my sweater.*

INDIVIDUAL LEARNING STRATEGIES (CONT.)

ENRICHMENT
Have students write an epilogue to the story that tells what eventually became of the narrator and his sister. For example, did they find a new house? Did they continue to live together? Are they still living the same kind of life? What are their feelings about losing the house? Have students imagine where the characters are ten or twenty years after the story ends.

The Rule of Light, 1944. René Magritte. Private collection.

CROSS-CURRICULAR CONNECTIONS

HISTORY. Between 1916 and 1930, Argentina was governed by moderate, democratically elected leaders. A military takeover in 1930 sparked a decade of unrest and repression. By 1946, popular leader Juan Perón had gained undisputed power. Although Perón introduced some economic reforms, such as wage increases for industrial workers, his regime was marked by corruption and strong-arm tactics that limited or revoked people's constitutional liberties.

Nothing worthwhile had arrived in Argentina since 1939.

But it's the house I want to talk about, the house and Irene; I'm not very important. I wonder what Irene would have done without her knitting. One can reread a book, but once a pullover is finished you can't do it over again, it's some kind of disgrace. One day I found that the drawer at the bottom of the chiffonier,[1] replete with mothballs, was filled with shawls, white, green, lilac. Stacked amid a great smell of camphor[2]—it was like a shop; I didn't have the nerve to ask her what she planned to do with them. We didn't have to earn our living, there was plenty coming in from the farms each month, even piling up. But Irene was only interested in the knitting and showed a wonderful <u>dexterity</u>,

How do they earn their living?

1. **chiffonier.** High narrow chest of drawers
2. **camphor.** Aromatic liniment used to ward off moths

words for everyday use

dex • ter • i • ty (dek ster′ ə tē) *n.*, skill and ease in using the hands. *The toddler demonstrated <u>dexterity</u> when playing with his tool set.*

1. They live in the front wing of the house. They only go to the rear part of the house beyond the oak door to do the cleaning.
2. The narrator hears the indistinct sounds of a chair knocked over or muffled conversation from the other part of the house.
3. In response to the sound, he quickly throws himself against the door and shuts it. He then locks and bolts the door.

CROSS-CURRICULAR ACTIVITIES

ENVIRONMENTAL SCIENCE. Have students locate Buenos Aires on a map and use reference works or Internet sources to find out whether it is a "clean" or smoggy city.

LITERARY TECHNIQUE

ALLEGORY. An **allegory** is a work in which each element symbolizes, or represents, something else. In a political allegory, the action, setting, and characters represent political events, places, and persons. Students may be familiar with George Orwell's *Animal Farm,* a political allegory about totalitarianism.

A number of clues suggest that "House Taken Over" can be read as a political allegory. First, the words "taken over" and "topple" that the author uses in reference to the house both have political overtones. Second, the setting is Argentina, a country that has experienced periods of military and civilian dictatorship. Third, the extreme behavior of the characters makes them seem more symbolic than realistic. Irene and the narrator could represent middle- or upper-class people living comfortably under a totalitarian government who ignore the gradual erosion of their rights and freedoms.

and for me the hours slipped away watching her, her hands like silver sea-urchins, needles flashing, and one or two knitting baskets on the floor, the balls of yarn jumping about. It was lovely.

How not to remember the layout of that house. The dining room, a living room with tapestries, the library, and three large bedrooms in the section most <u>recessed</u>, the one that faced toward Rodríguez Peña.[3] Only a corridor with its massive oak door separated that part from the front wing, where there was a bath, the kitchen, our bedrooms, and the hall. One entered the house through a <u>vestibule</u> with enameled tiles, and a wrought-iron grated door opened onto the living room. You had to come in through the vestibule and open the gate to go into the living room; the doors to our bedrooms were on either side of this, and opposite it was the corridor leading to the back section; going down the passage, one swung open the oak door beyond which was the other part of the house; or just before the door, one could turn to the left and go down a narrower passageway which led to the kitchen and the bath. When the door was open, you became aware of the size of the house; when it was closed, you had the impression of an apartment, like the ones they build today, with barely enough room to move around in.

> *What part of the house do they live in?*

Irene and I always lived in this part of the house and hardly ever went beyond the oak door except to do the cleaning. Incredible how much dust collected on the furniture. It may be Buenos Aires[4] is a clean city, but she owes it to her population and nothing else. There's too much dust in the air, the slightest breeze and it's back on the marble console tops and in the diamond patterns of the tooled-leather desk set. It's a lot of work to get it off with a feather duster; the motes rise and hang in the air, and settle again a minute later on the pianos and the furniture.

I'll always have a clear memory of it because it happened so simply and without fuss. Irene was knitting in her bedroom, it was eight at night, and I suddenly decided to put the water up for *mate*.[5] I went down the corridor as far as the oak door, which was ajar, then turned into the hall toward the kitchen, when I heard something in the library or the dining room. The sound came through muted and indistinct, a chair being knocked over onto the carpet or the muffled buzzing of a conversation. At the same time or a second later, I heard it at the end of the passage which led from those two rooms toward the door. I <u>hurled</u> myself against the door before it was too late and shut it, leaned on it with the weight of my body; luckily, the key was on our side; moreover, I ran the great bolt into place, just to be safe.

> *What does the narrator hear in the other part of the house?*

> *What does he do in response to the sound?*

I went down to the kitchen, heated the kettle, and when I got back with the tray of *mate*, I told Irene:

"I had to shut the door to the passage. They've taken over the back part."

She let her knitting fall and looked at me with her tired, serious eyes.

"You're sure?"

I nodded.

---

3. **Rodríguez Peña.** Street named after a South American historical figure
4. **Buenos Aires.** Capital city of Argentina
5. *mate.* Strong tea made from the dried leaves of a South American evergreen tree

"In that case," she said, picking up her needles again, "we'll have to live on this side."

I sipped at the *mate* very carefully, but she took her time starting her work again. I remember it was a gray vest she was knitting. I liked that vest.

The first few days were painful, since we'd both left so many things in the part that had been taken over. My collection of French literature, for example, was still in the library. Irene had left several <u>folios</u> of stationery and a pair of slippers that she used a lot in the winter. I missed my briar pipe,[6] and Irene, I think, regretted the loss of an ancient bottle of Hesperidin.[7] It happened repeatedly (but only in the first few days) that we would close some drawer or cabinet and look at one another sadly.

Why is it difficult to be restricted to one part of the house?

"It's not here."

One thing more among the many lost on the other side of the house.

But there were advantages, too. The cleaning was so much simplified that, even when we got up late, nine thirty for instance, by eleven we were sitting around with our arms folded. Irene got into the habit of coming to the kitchen with me to help get lunch. We thought about it and decided on this: while I prepared the lunch, Irene would cook up dishes that could be eaten cold in the evening. We were happy with the arrangement because it was always such a bother to have to leave our bedrooms in the

What is good about being restricted to one part of the house?

evening and start to cook. Now we made do with the table in Irene's room and platters of cold supper.

Since it left her more time for knitting, Irene was content. I was a little lost without my books, but so as not to inflict myself on my sister, I set about reordering papa's stamp collection; that killed some time. We amused ourselves sufficiently, each with his own thing, almost always getting together in Irene's bedroom, which was the more comfortable. Every once in a while, Irene might say:

"Look at this pattern I just figured out, doesn't it look like clover?"

After a bit it was I, pushing a small square of paper in front of her so that she could see the excellence of some stamp or another from Eupen-et-Malmédy.[8] We were fine, and little by little we stopped thinking. You can live without thinking.

What do they gradually stop doing as they live in their part of the house?

Whenever Irene talked in her sleep, I woke up immediately and stayed awake. I never could get used to this voice from a statue or a parrot, a voice that came out of the dreams, not from a throat. Irene said that in my sleep I <u>flailed</u> about enormously and shook the blankets off. We had the living room between us, but at night you could hear everything in the house. We heard each other

---

6. **briar pipe.** Pipe made of briarroot; used for smoking tobacco
7. **Hesperidin.** Sugar compound found in unripe citrus fruits, often used for medicinal purposes
8. **Eupen-et-Malmédy.** Region of France

words for everyday use

fo • lio (fō′ lē ō) *n.*, case or folder for loose papers. *Bertrand kept his loose poems in a <u>folio</u>.*
flail (flāl′) *vi.*, swing around or beat about wildly. *The drowning sailor <u>flailed</u> his arms frantically.*

ANSWERS TO GUIDED READING QUESTIONS

1. It is difficult to be restricted to one part of the house because the narrator and Irene left many things in the part that was taken over and now they regret the loss of those items.
2. It is good to be restricted to one part of the house because the cleaning is simplified, and they don't have to leave their bedrooms for meals.
3. They gradually stop thinking.

LITERARY TECHNIQUE

DRAMATIC IRONY AND VERBAL IRONY. Dramatic irony exists when the reader or audience knows something that a character does not know. Ask students what is ironic about the narrator's comment, "We were fine, and little by little we stopped thinking." Are the characters really fine? Why is this statement also humorous? **Verbal irony** exists when a statement is made that implies its opposite. Is this an example of verbal irony on the part of the author?
Answers
The dramatic irony comes from the fact that the narrator may think he and his sister are fine, but the reader knows they are not fine. They behave very oddly, such as responding calmly to the noises and yielding to whatever has taken over the house. Their solitary lifestyle and Irene's constant knitting are also strange. If these characters were real people, we would probably call them mentally unbalanced. The inability of the characters to see the absurdity of their situation is humorous. The statement also shows verbal irony on the part of the author because he is implying the opposite of what he has written.

ADDITIONAL QUESTIONS AND ACTIVITIES

Ask students to reflect on the narrator's statement "You can live without thinking." Have them give examples of how this might apply to a real person living today. How would someone who lives without thinking behave? How would he or she spend their time? What would he or she talk about?

1. They talk loudly in the part that adjoins the part taken over, that is, in the kitchen and bathroom.
2. The balls of yarn connected to her knitting are left behind the closed front door, so she drops her knitting.
3. The narrator tosses the key down the sewer.

LITERARY TECHNIQUE

IRONY AND IRONY OF SITUATION. **Irony** is the difference between appearance and reality. In **irony of situation,** an event occurs that violates the expectations of the characters, the reader, or the audience. Ask students to find examples of situational irony in Cortázar's story. Have them focus on specific events as well as the overall plot of the story.
Answers
Situational irony exists in the fact that the brother and sister are extremely wealthy but live like servants, cleaning the huge house and living in smaller quarters. Also ironic is the fact that the characters appear busy but really accomplish nothing. Another ironic feature is that the narrator expects that he and his sister might "topple," or destroy, the house someday, but it ends up toppling them.

RESPOND TO THE SELECTION

As an alternate activity, ask students what events or effects in the story are similar to those in dreams.

---

breathing, coughing, could even feel each other reaching for the light switch when, as happened frequently, neither of us could fall asleep.

Aside from our <u>nocturnal</u> rumblings, everything was quiet in the house. During the day there were the household sounds, the metallic click of knitting needles, the rustle of stamp-album pages turning. The oak door was massive, I think I said that. In the kitchen or the bath, which adjoined the part that was taken over, we managed to talk loudly, or Irene sang lullabies. In a kitchen there's always too much noise, the plates and glasses, for there to be interruptions from other sounds. We seldom allowed ourselves silence there, but when we went back to our rooms or to the living room, then the house grew quiet, half-lit, we ended by stepping around more slowly so as not to disturb one another. I think it was because of this that I woke irremediably and at once when Irene began to talk in her sleep.)

In what part of the house do they not remain silent?

Except for the consequences, it's nearly a matter of repeating the same scene over again. I was thirsty that night, and before we went to sleep, I told Irene that I was going to the kitchen for a glass of water. From the door of the bedroom (she was knitting) I heard the noise in the kitchen; if not the kitchen, then the bath, the passage off at that angle dulled the sound. Irene noticed how <u>brusquely</u> I had paused, and came up beside me without a word. We stood listening to the noises, growing more and more sure that they were on our side of the oak door, if not the kitchen then the bath, or in the hall itself at the turn, almost next to us.

We didn't wait to look at one another. I took Irene's arm and forced her to run with me to the wrought-iron door, not waiting to look back. You could hear the noises, still muffled but louder, just behind us. I slammed the grating and we stopped in the vestibule. Now there was nothing to be heard.

"They've taken over our section," Irene said. The knitting had reeled off from her hands and the yarn ran back toward the door and disappeared under it. When she saw that the balls of yarn were on the other side, she dropped the knitting without looking at it.

What happens to Irene's knitting?

"Did you have time to bring anything?" I asked hopelessly.

"No, nothing."

We had what we had on. I remembered fifteen thousand pesos[9] in the wardrobe in my bedroom. Too late now.

I still had my wrist watch on and saw that it was 11 P.M. I took Irene around the waist (I think she was crying) and that was how we went into the street. Before we left, I felt terrible; I locked the front door up tight and tossed the key down the sewer. It wouldn't do to have some poor devil decide to go in and rob the house, at that hour and with the house taken over. ∎

What does the narrator do after he locks the front door?

---

9. **pesos.** Currency in Argentina

---

words for everyday use

noc • tur • nal (näk tər′ nəl) *adj.,* of, relating to, or occurring in the night. *The raccoon made a <u>nocturnal</u> journey to our trash can at midnight.*

brusque • ly (brusk′ lē) *adv.,* done in a markedly short or abrupt manner. *The waitress <u>brusquely</u> took our order without giving me time to say how I wanted my steak cooked.*

Respond to the SELECTION

What or who do you think took over the house?

SELECTION CHECK TEST 4.12.1 WITH ANSWERS

Checking Your Reading

1. Who lives with the narrator in the huge, old house, and what do the two of them intend to do with the house eventually? **The narrator's sister Irene lives with him. The two of them intend to die in the house and let the house be inherited by distant cousins who will knock it down; or, they may knock down the house themselves.**

2. What do the two inhabitants of the house do all day? What does the narrator say they eventually live without doing? **Irene knits constantly, making things that no one needs. The narrator goes down to buy wool and watches her knit; rearranges his father's stamp collection; and does little else. The two eventually live without thinking.**

3. How do the two earn their money? **They do not need to work because they earn money from the farms owned by their family.**

(Continued on page 923)

Casa Pablo Neruda

Tal vez ésta es la casa en que viví
cuando yo no existí ni había tierra,
cuando todo era luna o piedra o sombra,
cuando la luz inmóvil no nacía.
Tal vez entonces esta piedra era
mi casa, mis ventanas o mis ojos.
Me recuerda esta rosa de granito,
algo que me habitaba o que habité,
cueva o cabeza cósmica de sueños,
copa o castillo o nave o nacimiento.
Toco el tenaz esfuerzo de la roca,
su baluarte golpeado en la salmuera,
y sé que aquí quedaron grietas mías,
arrugadas sustancias que subieron
desde profundidades hasta mi alma,
y piedra fui, piedra seré, por eso
toco esta piedra, y para mí no ha muerto:
es lo que fui, lo que seré, reposo
de un combate tan largo como el tiempo.

House Pablo Neruda

Perhaps this is the house I lived in
when neither I nor earth existed,
when all was moon or stone or darkness,
when still light was unborn.
Perhaps then this stone was
my house, my windows or my eyes.
This rose of granite reminds me
of something that dwelled in me or I in it,
a cave, or cosmic head of dreams,
cup or castle, ship or birth.
I touch the stubborn spirit of rock,
its rampart pounds in the brine,
and my flaws remain here,
wrinkled essence that rose
from the depths to my soul,
and stone I was, stone I will be. Because of this
I touch this stone, and for me it hasn't died:
it's what I was, what I will be, resting
from a struggle long as time. ∎

ABOUT THE RELATED READING

Pablo Neruda is the pen name of Neftalí Ricardo Reyes Basoalto (1904–1973), a Chilean poet who won the Nobel Prize for literature in 1971. His most widely read poetry collection, *Veinte poemas de amor y una canción desesperada* (*Twenty Love Poems and a Song of Despair*), was published in 1924. His *Canto general* (*General Song*, 1950) is one of the greatest epic poems written about the American continent. In addition to being a preeminent poet, Neruda served as a diplomat representing Chile in Argentina, Spain, and Mexico. After losing favor with the rightist government of his homeland, he went into exile in Italy, a period in his life depicted in the movie *The Postman* (1995). Neruda's poem "House" was published posthumously in the poetry collection *Neruda at Isla Negra* (1998). The poem appears here in the original Spanish and in its English translation.

"HOUSE TAKEN OVER" 923

SELECTION CHECK TEST 4.12.1 WITH ANSWERS (CONT.)

4. Why does the narrator have to close off the back part of the house? **The narrator and his sister hear noises and voices coming from the back part of the house and conclude that "they"—perhaps some mysterious people or ghosts—have taken over that part.**
5. What finally happens to the house at the end of the story? What do the narrator and Irene do? **The house gets completely taken over. The narrator and Irene are forced to flee the house. They throw the key down the sewer so that no one can get inside it again.**

Vocabulary in Context
Fill in each blank below with the most appropriate word from the following Words for Everyday Use. You may have to change the tense of the word.

dexterity indispensable nocturnal
flail commune hurl brusquely

1. Kayla's dad hung up the phone so **brusquely** that I had no chance to leave a message for Kayla.
2. People feel a special bond with dogs; they feel they can **commune** with them as with no other animal.
3. The protesters were arrested when they **hurled** rocks at the police.
4. A typical kindergartener does not yet have the **dexterity** needed to write in cursive.
5. Cats are **nocturnal** creatures; that is why you often see them napping during the day.

SELECTION CHECK TEST 4.12.1 WITH ANSWERS (CONT.)

Literary Tools
1. What is the setting of a literary work? **The setting is the time and place in which the work occurs, together with all the details used to create a sense of that particular time and place.**
2. What is mood? **Mood is the emotion created in the reader by part or all of a literary work.**
3. What is another word for the mood of a literary work? **Another word for mood is *atmosphere*.**

ANSWERS TO INVESTIGATE, INQUIRE, AND IMAGINE

RECALL

1a. He quickly shuts the door to the part of the house where the sounds are coming from.

2a. He describes the sounds as muted and indistinct, like "a chair being knocked over onto the carpet or the muffled buzzing of a conversation."

3a. She is knitting.

INTERPRET

1a. He may react this way because he feels unprepared or unable to face what has happened or wants to ignore it. He may be afraid that some harm will come to him and his sister.

2b. The knocked-over chair suggests a disruption to the orderliness and comfortable routine of the house. The buzzing conversation contrasts with the lack of words or significant conversation between the narrator and his sister. By ignoring these sounds and doing nothing about them, the narrator shows that simply carrying on with the household routine is what is most important to him.

3b. Irene's excessive knitting of things no one will use, which occupies all of her time, shows that her life does not have a useful purpose.

ANALYZE

4a. Evidence of being satisfied with their lives includes the fact that Irene is content with only knitting, and the narrator is content to spend hours watching her. The narrator also says, "We amused ourselves sufficiently, each with his own thing."

SYNTHESIZE

4b. The house is being taken over because its owners are absorbed in their own mindless activities. They do not investigate the sounds they hear or challenge the outside force that has entered the house. The author may be warning us to stay alert to what is happening around us and to take action when outside forces deprive us of something important. More broadly, he may be urging us to live an active, engaged, and meaningful life, rather than remaining passive, isolated, and unthinking.

EVALUATE

5a. Some students may say the ancestors would not approve of the narrator's life in the house because he is not doing anything productive and, by not marrying, has chosen not to continue the family line.

924 TEACHER'S EDITION

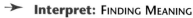

Investigate, Inquire, and Imagine

Recall: GATHERING FACTS ➝ **Interpret: FINDING MEANING**

1a. What does the narrator do after he hears the first sounds in the house?

1b. Why do you think he reacts this way? What is he afraid of?

2a. Exactly how does Cortázar describe the sounds that the narrator hears?

2b. Why do you think Cortázar uses these particular details to describe the sounds? What meaning is he trying to get at here?

3a. What is Irene doing throughout most of the story?

3b. What is the significance of her knitting an entire bureau full of clothes, which is obviously far more than she and her brother can use?

Analyze: TAKING THINGS APART ➝ **Synthesize: BRINGING THINGS TOGETHER**

4a. What evidence do you see in the story that the brother and sister are satisfied with the way things are in their lives? Cite evidence from the story to support your answer.

4b. Why is the house being taken over? What warning is the author giving us about our own lives?

Evaluate: MAKING JUDGMENTS ➝ **Extend: CONNECTING IDEAS**

5a. Do you think the narrator's ancestors would approve of the life he is leading in this house? Explain your answer.

5b. Read the poem "House" by Pablo Neruda. In what ways is the house in the poem like the house in "House Taken Over"? Use details from both the story and poem to support your answer.

Understanding Literature

SETTING. Review the definition for **setting** in the Handbook of Literary Tools. How does the setting reflect the meaning of "House Taken Over"?

MOOD. Review the definition for **mood** in Literary Tools in Prereading and the cluster chart you made for that section. What is the mood of the story?

ANSWERS TO INVESTIGATE, INQUIRE, AND IMAGINE (CONT.)

Others may say the ancestors would approve of his quiet, comfortable, and disengaged life because it is like the lives they themselves led earlier.

EXTEND

5b. In both works, the house can be seen as a symbolic stand-in for the narrator himself. In Neruda's poem, a stone is "the house I lived in / when neither I nor earth existed" whose stones were "my windows or my eyes." This stone, this house, contains the narrator's "wrinkled essence," including his soul and his flaws. In Cortázar's story, the house seems to be symbolic of how the narrator is pitted against himself, of the struggle between the narrator's desire for comfort and complacency and the part of himself that refuses to allow for such a blindly comfortable, unexamined life.

> Answers to Understanding Literature can be found on page 925.

Writer's Journal

1. Imagine that you are the narrator and you have just received a letter from a friend asking how you are and what you are up to. Write a **letter** answering your friend's questions.
2. Imagine you are Irene. Write the **journal entry** that you might have written following the first sign of the house being taken over.
3. Write a **description** of a location, paying attention to describing the mood you want to convey.

Integrating the Language Arts

Language, Grammar, and Style

LINKING VERBS. Read the Language Arts Survey 3.10, "Linking Verbs." Identify the linking verb in each of the following sentences.

1. At the beginning of the story, the narrator and his sister are ready to move into the house.
2. They appear complacent about life.
3. They remain isolated in one wing of the house when the other section of the house is taken over.
4. At first they seem unaffected by the new occupants.
5. Do they leave the house because they grow afraid of the occupants?

Study and Research & Media Literacy

RESEARCHING SURREALISM. Julio Cortázar was heavily influenced by Surrealism, an artistic movement that took place between WWI and WWII. Surrealist artists were interested in the products of the unconscious mind, such as fantasy and dreams, and often used such elements in their art. Using the resources of the library or the Internet, put together a short report on Surrealism. Who began the movement? What were the basic ideas of the movement, and where did they come from? How is it possible to recognize a surreal literary or artistic work? Who were some of the movement's most famous artists and writers? What aspects of "House Taken Over" are surreal? Present your findings to the class.

Collaborative Learning & Speaking and Listening

HOLDING A DEBATE. Conduct a debate in which one group argues for the reality of ghosts, and the other argues that ghosts are mere figments of the imagination. If you are arguing for the reality of ghosts, research witness accounts of ghost sightings. If you are arguing that ghosts do not exist, research expert opinions about why people think they see ghosts. Whichever side you are on, prepare both constructive and rebuttal speeches. In preparation for the debate, you might find it useful to review the Language Arts Survey 4.21, "Participating in a Debate."

ANSWERS TO UNDERSTANDING LITERATURE

SETTING. We are given many details about the house, where all of the action happens. It is too large for the two persons who live in it. The fact that so little is mentioned about the country and time period, or any details about life outside the house, underscores the empty contentment and social and emotional isolation of the characters. In the end, the house literally takes over the house by throwing the brother and sister out onto the streets.

MOOD. The mood of the story is complacent and ironic. The many signs of complacency in the characters' lives seem to indicate that something is wrong with them. The house "decides" to take matters into its own hands, both to avoid its own destruction and to force the brother and sister out onto the street, where presumably they will be challenged in new ways. The irony of the mood is evident when the narrator expresses his peculiar delight in Irene's constant knitting.

ANSWERS TO INTEGRATING THE LANGUAGE ARTS

Language, Grammar, and Style
1. are
2. appear
3. remain
4. seem
5. grow

Study and Research & Media Literacy
Students might tackle this project in pairs or small groups. Pairs might have one student research artists (and photographers) and one research writers. Groups might assign a different artist or writer to each member.

Collaborative Learning & Speaking and Listening
Before assigning this project, ask students whether they would consider Cortázar's work a ghost story, and why.

ADDITIONAL RESOURCES

UNIT 12 RESOURCE BOOK
- Selection Worksheet 12.2
- Selection Check Test 4.12.3
- Selection Test 4.12.4
- Language, Grammar, and Style Resource 3.27

VOCABULARY FROM THE SELECTION

affliction	impertinence
cataclysm	infamy
catechism	ingenuous
celestial	iridescent
consolation	magnanimous
decrepit	penitent
decrepitude	proliferate
deign	providential
exasperated	prudence
frivolity	robust
grandeur	supernatural
haughty	terrestrial
hermetic	

GRAPHIC ORGANIZER

Students should include these examples in their cluster charts:
- Girl is changed into a spider by a lightning bolt.
- Angel performs consolation miracles.

READER'S JOURNAL

Students might describe the criteria they would use in deciding whether or not to aid the stranger. Students might consider facial expressions, speech, clothing, and the feeling they get from the stranger.

Literary TOOLS

POINT OF VIEW. Point of view is the vantage point from which a story is told. As you read, think about how the story would be different if it were told from the angel's point of view.

OXYMORON. An **oxymoron** is a statement that contradicts itself. While reading, look for an example of an oxymoron.

MAGICAL REALISM. Magical Realism is a kind of fiction that is for the most part realistic but that contains elements of fantasy. It originated in the works of Latin American writers who wished to communicate non-European world views. Magical Realism reflects the fact that many Latin Americans accept what Europeans would consider "fantastical occurrences" as a part of everyday reality.

Graphic Organizer

Create a cluster chart listing the examples of Magical Realism in the story. One example has been done for you.

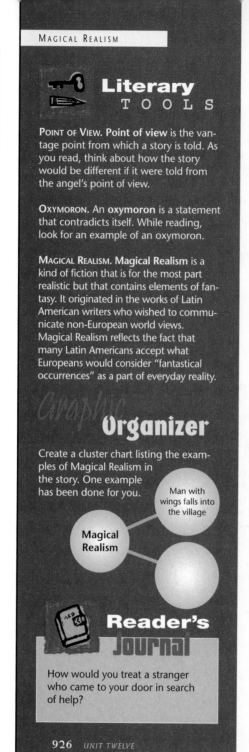

Reader's Journal

How would you treat a stranger who came to your door in search of help?

"a very old man with enormous wings"
by Gabriel García Márquez

Reader's resource

The short story "A Very Old Man with Enormous Wings," like many of García Márquez's stories, takes place in a rural Latin American village. The setting is important because the people in this fictional village are isolated from outside influences and seek understanding of their world through folklore and supernatural events. For them, the supernatural and the incredible do not need to be explained because they are considered perfectly common.

CULTURE CONNECTION. In many religions such as Judaism, Christianity, and Islam, it is believed that there are supernatural beings called angels who take on a human form, possess swanlike wings, and provide peace and protection to those who believe in them.

About the AUTHOR

Gabriel García Márquez (1928–) was born in Aracataca, Colombia, a town that made its living from banana production. One of sixteen children born to the town telegrapher, he put himself through high school on a scholarship, quit law school out of boredom after a year, and became a newspaper reporter. "I have been told by the family that I started telling about things, stories and so on, almost ever since I was born," said the author. "I guess that's what got me into journalism and fiction writing, and the two went together all my life." For most of his life, García Márquez has lived in self-imposed exile in Barcelona, Paris, Rome, New York, and Mexico City.

In *Leaf Storm* (1955), his first book, García Márquez introduced the fictional town of Macondo, a symbol of all underdeveloped Latin countries and the setting for many of his later works. His epic masterpiece, *One Hundred Years of Solitude* (1967), took twenty years to complete and has sold more copies around the world than any other work by a contemporary Spanish-speaking author. Other notable works by García Márquez include *Love in the Time of Cholera* (1985), *The General in His Labyrinth* (1989), and *Strange Pilgrims* (1992). In 1982 García Márquez was awarded the Nobel Prize in literature "for his novels and short stories in which the fantastic and the realistic are combined in a richly composed world of imagination, reflecting a continent's life and conflicts."

GOALS/OBJECTIVES

Studying this lesson will enable students to
- enjoy and interpret a short story by a South American author
- describe the literary accomplishments of Gabriel García Márquez
- define *point of view* and discuss the point of view used in the selection
- define *oxymoron* and identify an example in their reading
- define *Magical Realism* and cite elements of Magical Realism in the story
- identify subjects and verbs in sentences
- conduct research on angels

The Winged Man, 1800s. Odilon Redon.
Musée des Beaux-Arts, Bordeaux, France.

a very old man with ENORMOUS WINGS

Gabriel García Márquez

On the third day of rain they had killed so many crabs inside the house that Pelayo had to cross his drenched courtyard and throw them into the sea, because the newborn child had a temperature all night and they thought it was due to the stench. The world

INDIVIDUAL LEARNING STRATEGIES

MOTIVATION
Ask students to make a list of words or images they associate with the word *angel*.

READING PROFICIENCY
Students might benefit from listening to a recording of the story or having the story read aloud to them. When students read on their own, encourage them to read the entire story in one sitting.

ENGLISH LANGUAGE LEARNING
Have students pronounce each vocabulary word aloud after you pronounce it first. Then ask students a question using the word. Students should answer using a complete sentence that also contains the vocabulary word. Example: What is something that is *iridescent?* The wings of certain butterflies are *iridescent.*

SPECIAL NEEDS
Tell students that the story describes how people in a small seaside village react to the sudden arrival of an extraordinary and puzzling visitor. As they read, have them make a list of how the villagers react to the mysterious visitor. Ask them to think about whether these reactions are unusual or typical of human beings based on their own experience.

ENRICHMENT
Have students gather additional information about the life of Gabriel García Márquez and then create a print or media interview with the author. If they decide to prepare a television interview, they might want to watch a few author interviews on the program "Booknotes" on the C-SPAN network to get ideas for questions and format.

LITERARY TECHNIQUE (CONT.)

Answers
The mood is one of unpleasant strangeness and uneasiness. This mood is established by the image of crabs crawling around inside a wet house, a highly unusual event, and the details of the heavy rain, the child's fever, and the terrible smell. This mood creates an expectation that some disturbing and supernatural event may unfold in the story.

LITERARY TECHNIQUE

MOOD. Mood, or *atmosphere*, is the emotion created in the reader by part or all of a literary work. Descriptive language and sensory details both contribute to the mood of a work. Ask students what mood is established in the first paragraph of the story. What details and images help to create this mood? How does the mood established create a certain expectation in the reader?

had been sad since Tuesday. Sea and sky were a single ash-gray thing and the sands of the beach, which on March nights glimmered like powdered light, had become a stew of mud and rotten shellfish. The light was so weak at noon that when Pelayo was coming back to the house after throwing away the crabs, it was hard for him to see what it was that was moving and groaning in the rear of the courtyard. He had to go very close to see that it was an old man, a very old man, lying face down in the mud, who, in spite of his tremendous efforts, couldn't get up, impeded by his enormous wings.

Frightened by that nightmare, Pelayo ran to get Elisenda, his wife, who was putting compresses on the sick child, and he took her to the rear of the courtyard. They both looked at the fallen body with mute stupor. He was dressed like a ragpicker. There were only a few faded hairs left on his bald skull and very few teeth in his mouth, and his pitiful condition of a drenched great-grandfather had taken away any sense of <u>grandeur</u> he might have had. His huge buzzard wings, dirty and half-plucked, were forever entangled in the mud. They looked at him so long and so closely that Pelayo and Elisenda very soon overcame their surprise and in the end found him familiar. Then they dared speak to him, and he answered in an incomprehensible dialect with a strong sailor's voice. That was how they skipped over the inconvenience of the wings and quite intelligently concluded that he was a lonely castaway from some foreign ship wrecked by the storm. And yet, they called in a neighbor woman who knew everything about life and death to see him, and all she needed was one look to show them their mistake.

"He's an angel," she told them. "He must have been coming for the child, but the poor fellow is so old that the rain knocked him down."

On the following day everyone knew that a flesh-and-blood angel was held captive in Pelayo's house. Against the judgment of the wise neighbor woman, for whom angels in those times were the fugitive survivors of a <u>celestial</u> conspiracy, they did not have the heart to club him to death. Pelayo watched over him all afternoon from the kitchen, armed with his bailiff's club, and before going to bed he dragged him out of the mud and locked him up with the hens in the wire chicken coop. In the middle of the night, when the rain stopped, Pelayo and Elisenda were still killing crabs. A short time afterward the child woke up without a fever and with a desire to eat. Then they felt <u>magnanimous</u> and decided to put the angel on a raft with fresh water and provisions for three days and leave him to his fate on the high seas. But when they went out into the courtyard with the first light of dawn, they found the whole neighborhood in front of the chicken coop having fun with the angel, without the slightest reverence, tossing him things to eat through the openings in the wire as if he weren't a <u>supernatural</u> creature but a circus animal.

Father Gonzaga arrived before seven o'clock, alarmed at the strange news. By that time onlookers less frivolous than those at dawn had already arrived and they were making all kinds of conjectures concerning the captive's future. The simplest among them thought that he should be named mayor of the world. Others of sterner mind felt that he should be promoted to the rank of five-star general in order to win all wars. Some visionaries hoped that he could be put to stud in order to implant on earth a race

words for everyday use	**gran • deur** (gran′ jer) *n.*, quality or state of being magnificent. *Ansel Adams captures the <u>grandeur</u> of the Rocky Mountains in his photographs.* **ce • les • tial** (sə les′ chəl) *adj.*, of or relating to heaven. *For the Wise Men, the star in the east was a <u>celestial</u> sign indicating Jesus' birth.* **mag • nan • i • mous** (mag na′ nə məs) *adj.*, showing or suggesting nobility of feeling and generosity of mind. *The <u>magnanimous</u> gesture of the businessman, who gave a hundred dollars to a homeless man, was noticed by a reporter.* **su • per • nat • u • ral** (sü pər na′ chə rəl) *adj.*, of or relating to a god, spirit, or devil. *Primitive people interpret lunar eclipses as <u>supernatural</u> events.*

of winged wise men who could take charge of the universe. But Father Gonzaga, before becoming a priest, had been a <u>robust</u> woodcutter. Standing by the wire, he reviewed his <u>catechism</u> in an instant and asked them to open the door so that he could take a close look at that pitiful man who looked more like a huge <u>decrepit</u> hen among the fascinated chickens. He was lying in a corner drying his open wings in the sunlight among the fruit peels and breakfast leftovers that the early risers had thrown him. Alien to the <u>impertinences</u> of the world, he only lifted his antiquarian eyes and murmured something in his dialect when Father Gonzaga went into the chicken coop and said good morning to him in Latin. The parish priest had his first suspicion of an imposter when he saw that he did not understand the language of God or know how to greet His ministers. Then he noticed that seen close up he was much too human: he had an unbearable smell of the outdoors, the back side of his wings was strewn with parasites and his main feathers had been mistreated by <u>terrestrial</u> winds, and nothing about him measured up to the proud dignity of angels. Then he came out of the chicken coop and in a brief

What do the villagers throw at the angel?

What human aspects does the angel demonstrate?

the curious came from far away.

sermon warned the curious against the risks of being <u>ingenuous</u>. He reminded them that the devil had the bad habit of making use of carnival tricks in order to confuse the unwary. He argued that if wings were not the essential element in determining the difference between a hawk and an airplane, they were even less so in the recognition of angels. Nevertheless, he promised to write a letter to his bishop so that the latter would write to his primate so that the latter would write to the Supreme Pontiff[1] in order to get the final verdict from the highest courts.

His <u>prudence</u> fell on sterile hearts. The news of the captive angel spread with such rapidity that after a few hours the courtyard had the bustle of a marketplace and they had to call in troops with fixed bayonets to disperse the mob that was about to knock the house down. Elisenda, her spine all twisted from sweeping up so much marketplace trash, then got the idea of fencing in the yard and charging five cents admission to see the angel.

The curious came from far away. A traveling carnival arrived with a flying acrobat who buzzed over the crowd several times, but no one paid any attention to him because his wings were not those of an angel but, rather, those of a sidereal bat. The most unfortunate invalids on earth came in search of health: a poor woman

---

1. **Supreme Pontiff.** Pope in Rome

words for everyday use

ro • bust (rō bəst′) *adj.*, having or exhibiting strength or vigorous health. *The <u>robust</u> hiker walked for fifty miles.*
cat • e • chism (ka′ tə ki zəm) *n.*, summary of Christian doctrine often in the form of questions and answers. *Before being confirmed, Angie had to learn her <u>catechism</u> and recite portions of it by heart.*
de • crep • it (di krə′ pət) *adj.*, wasted and weakened by or as if by the infirmities of old age. *The <u>decrepit</u> man had a hump on his back, and he walked with a cane.*
im • per • ti • nence (im pər′ tən ənts) *n.*, quality or state of being unrestrained within due or proper bounds; insolence. *Ramón had the <u>impertinence</u> to ask his teacher if he could borrow fifty dollars until pay day.*
ter • res • tri • al (tə res′ trē əl) *adj.*, of or relating to the earth or its inhabitants. *After examining <u>terrestrial</u> wonders, the scientist turned his eyes to the sky.*
in • gen • u • ous (in jen′ yə wəs) *adj.*, artless; innocent; naive. *In Paris, the <u>ingenous</u> tourist asked what the Eiffel Tower was.*
pru • dence (prü′ dənts) *n.*, ability to govern and discipline oneself by the use of reason. *Mr. Chin's <u>prudence</u> was evident when he studied the company before investing in it.*

---

1. The villagers throw the angel scraps of food.
2. The angel smells bad and has parasites on its wings.

who since childhood had been counting her heartbeats and had run out of numbers; a Portuguese man who couldn't sleep because the noise of the stars disturbed him; a sleepwalker who got up at night to undo the things he had done while awake; and many others with less serious ailments. In the midst of that shipwreck disorder that made the earth tremble, Pelayo and Elisenda were happy with fatigue, for in less than a week they had crammed their rooms with money and the line of pilgrims waiting their turn to enter still reached beyond the horizon.

The angel was the only one who took no part in his own act. He spent his time trying to get comfortable in his borrowed nest, befuddled by the hellish heat of the oil lamps and sacramental candles that had been placed along the wire. At first they tried to make him eat some mothballs, which, according to the wisdom of the wise neighbor woman, were the food prescribed for angels. But he turned them down, just as he turned down the papal lunches[2] that the <u>peni-tents</u> brought him, and they never found out whether it was because he was an angel or because he was an old man that in the end he ate nothing but eggplant mush. His only super-natural virtue seemed to be patience. Especially during the first days, when the hens pecked at him, searching for the stellar parasites that <u>pro-liferated</u> in his wings, and the cripples pulled out feathers to touch their defective parts with, and even the most merciful threw stones at him, trying to get him to rise so they could see him standing. The only time they succeeded in arousing him was when they burned his side with an iron for branding steers, for he had

been motionless for so many hours that they thought he was dead. He awoke with a start, ranting in his <u>hermetic</u> language and with tears in his eyes, and he flapped his wings a couple of times, which brought on a whirlwind of chicken dung and lunar dust and a gale of panic that did not seem to be of this world. Although many thought that his reaction had been one not of rage but of pain, from then on they were careful not to annoy him, because the majority under-stood that his passivity was not that of a hero taking his ease but that of a <u>cataclysm</u> in repose.

Father Gonzaga held back the crowd's <u>frivo-lity</u> with formulas of maidservant inspiration while awaiting the arrival of a final judgment on the nature of the captive. But the mail from Rome showed no sense of urgency. They spent their time finding out if the prisoner had a navel, if his dialect had any connection with Aramaic,[3] how many times he could fit on the head of a pin, or whether he wasn't just a Norwegian with wings. Those meager letters might have come and gone until the end of time if a <u>providential</u> event had not put an end to the priest's tribulations.

It so happened that during those days, among so many other carnival attractions, there arrived in town the traveling show of the woman who had been changed into a spider for having dis-obeyed her parents. The admission to see her was not only less than the admission to see the angel, but people were permitted to ask her all

> *How does the angel react when it is branded?*

---

2. **papal lunches.** Expensive meals
3. **Aramaic.** Ancient Jewish language

words for everyday use

pen • i • tent (pe′ nə tənt) *n.*, person who repents of sin. *The <u>penitent</u> went to confession regularly.*
pro • lif • er • ate (prə li′ fə rāt) *vi.*, grow by rapid production of new parts, cells, buds, or offspring. *Weeds <u>profiler-ated</u> in Mrs. Jensen's garden unless she pulled them out every week.*
her • met • ic (hər me′ tik) *adj.*, difficult or impossible to comprehend. *Jon could not do the <u>hermetic</u> calculus problem.*
cat • a • clysm (ka′ tə kli zəm) *n.*, momentous and violent event marked by overwhelming upheaval and demolition. *In the <u>cataclysm</u> twenty homes and a road were destroyed.*
fri • vol • i • ty (fri vä′ lə tē) *n.*, inappropriate silliness, triviality. *The teacher ended the class's <u>frivolity</u> because students needed to concentrate on reviewing what would be on the test.*
prov • i • den • tial (prä və dent′ shəl) *adj.*, occurring by or as if by an intervention of Providence, or heaven. *The prisoner's <u>providential</u> escape was made possible when a rowboat washed onto the island.*

manner of questions about her absurd state and to examine her up and down so that no one would ever doubt the truth of her horror. She was a frightful tarantula the size of a ram and with the head of a sad maiden. What was most heartrending, however, was not her outlandish shape but the sincere affliction with which she recounted the details of her misfortune. While still practically a child she had sneaked out of her parents' house to go to a dance, and while she was coming back through the woods after having danced all night without permission, a fearful thunderclap rent the sky in two and through the crack came the lightning bolt of brimstone that changed her into a spider. Her only nourishment came from the meatballs that charitable souls chose to toss into her mouth. A spectacle like that, full of so much human truth and with such a fearful lesson, was bound to defeat without even trying that of a haughty angel who scarcely deigned to look at mortals. Besides, the few miracles attributed to the angel showed a certain mental disorder, like the blind man who didn't recover his sight but grew three new teeth, or the paralytic who didn't get to walk but almost won the lottery, and the leper whose sores sprouted sunflowers. Those consolation miracles, which were more like mocking fun, had already ruined the angel's reputation when

the woman who had been changed into a spider finally crushed him completely. That was how Father Gonzaga was cured forever of his insomnia and Pelayo's courtyard went back to being as empty as during the time it had rained for three days and crabs walked through the bedrooms.

The owners of the house had no reason to lament. With the money they saved they built a two-story mansion with balconies and gardens and high netting so that crabs wouldn't get in during the winter, and with iron bars on the windows so that angels wouldn't get in. Pelayo also set up a rabbit warren close to town and gave up his job as bailiff[4] for good, and Elisenda bought some satin pumps with high heels and many dresses of iridescent silk, the kind worn on Sunday by the most desirable women in those times. The chicken coop was the only thing that didn't receive any attention. If they washed it down with creolin[5] and burned tears of myrrh[6] inside it every so often, it was not in homage to the angel but to drive away the dungheap stench that still hung everywhere like a ghost and was turning the new house into an old one. At first, when the child learned to walk, they were careful that he not get too close to the

the angel was the only one who took no part in his own act.

----

4. **bailiff.** Government official
5. **creolin.** Disinfectant
6. **myrrh.** Fragrant, bitter-tasting powder used in making incense and perfumes

words for everyday use

af • flic • tion (ə flik′ shən) n., state of being in persistent pain or distress. *My great-aunt's affliction made her unable to walk.*

haugh • ty (hô′ tē) adj., blatantly and disdainfully proud. *The haughty cheerleader refused to talk to students who were not popular.*

deign (dān′) vi., condescend reluctantly, with a strong sense of one's own superiority. *The opera star deigned to take the roses that a fan offered her.*

con • so • la • tion (kän(t) sə lā′ shən) adj., something that consoles, or alleviates pain or suffering. *Contestants on the game show won a consolation prize if they didn't win any money.*

ir • i • des • cent (ir′ ə de′ sənt) adj., having a lustrous rainbowlike play of color. *The iridescent prism cast its colors on the wall.*

1. They build a mansion, Pelayo quits his job, and Elisenda buys expensive clothes and shoes.

What do Pelayo and Elisenda do with their newly acquired wealth?

CROSS-CURRICULAR ACTIVITIES

ART. Ask students to create one or more illustrations for the story in a form of their own choosing. Some possibilities are illustrations of key events in the story or circus-type posters promoting the "spectacles" of the spider woman and the winged man. Encourage them to choose colors and materials that will help convey the "magical" qualities of the story.

chicken coop. But then they began to lose their fears and got used to the smell, and before the child got his second teeth he'd gone inside the chicken coop to play, where the wires were falling apart. The angel was no less standoffish with him than with other mortals, but he tolerated the most ingenious <u>infamies</u> with the patience of a dog who had no illusions. They both came down with chicken pox at the same time. The doctor who took care of the child couldn't resist the temptation to listen to the angel's heart, and he found so much whistling in the heart and so many sounds in his kidneys that it seemed impossible for him to be alive. What surprised him most, however, was the logic of his wings. They seemed so natural on that completely human organism that he couldn't understand why other men didn't have them too.

When the child began school it had been some time since the sun and rain had caused the collapse of the chicken coop. The angel went dragging himself about here and there like a stray dying man. They would drive him out of the bedroom with a broom and a moment later find him in the kitchen. He seemed to be in so many places at the same time that they grew to think that he'd been duplicated, that he was reproducing himself all through the house, and the <u>exasperated</u> and unhinged Elisenda shouted that it was awful living in that hell full of angels. He could scarcely eat and his antiquarian eyes had also become so foggy that he went about bumping into posts. All he had left were the bare cannulae[7] of his last feathers. Pelayo threw a blanket over him and extended him the charity of letting him sleep in the shed, and only then did they notice that he had a temperature at night, and was delirious with the tongue twisters of an old Norwegian. That was one of the few times they became alarmed, for they thought he

was going to die and not even the wise neighbor woman had been able to tell them what to do with dead angels.

And yet he not only survived his worst winter, but seemed improved with the first sunny days. He remained motionless for several days in the farthest corner of the courtyard, where no one would see him, and at the beginning of December some large, stiff feathers began to grow on his wings, the feathers of a scarecrow, which looked more like another misfortune of <u>decrepitude</u>. But he must have known the reason for those changes, for he was quite careful that no one should notice them, that no one should hear the sea chanteys[8] that he sometimes sang under the stars.

What does the angel sing?

One morning Elisenda was cutting some bunches of onions for lunch when a wind that seemed to come from the high seas blew into the kitchen. Then she went to the window and caught the angel in his first attempts at flight. They were so clumsy that his fingernails opened a furrow in the vegetable patch and he was on the point of knocking the shed down with the ungainly flapping that slipped on the light and couldn't get a grip on the air. But he did manage to gain altitude. Elisenda let out a sigh of relief, for herself and for him, when she saw him pass over the last houses, holding himself up in some way with the risky flapping of a senile vulture. She kept watching him even when she was through cutting the onions and she kept on watching until it was no longer possible for her to see him, because then he was no longer an annoyance in her life but an imaginary dot on the horizon of the sea. ∎

---

7. **cannulae.** Tubular, hollow understructure of a feather
8. **sea chanteys.** Songs sung by sailors in rhythm with their work

---

words for everyday use

in • fa • my (in′ fə mē) *n.*, something grossly criminal, shocking, or brutal. *The infamy of the conclusion of* Braveheart *leaves the moviegoer wondering how people could be so cruel as to torture another human being.*

ex • as • per • at • ed (ig zas′ pə rāt əd) *adj.*, excited to anger, annoyance, or irritation. *The exasperated judge pounded his gavel.*

de • crep • i • tude (di kre′ pə tüd) *n.*, quality or state of being wasted and weakened. *The decrepitude of the nursing home resident led to him being confined to a wheelchair.*

EAST Song

Álvaro Mutis

At any turn

an invisible angel waits;

a vague fog, a faded vision

will tell you words of the past.

Like water in a ditch, time

carves in you a gentle labor

of days and weeks,

of years without name or souvenir.

At any turn

the one you never were, the one that died

of you so much being what you are,

will continue waiting, uselessly, for you.

Not even a hint,

not even the slightest shadow

tells you what that encounter

could have been. There, however,

there was the key

to your brief happiness on earth. ■

ABOUT THE RELATED READING

Like his countryman Gabriel García Márquez, **Álvaro Mutis,** born in 1923, focuses on the occurrence of the supernatural in ordinary circumstances. His poems suggest that the unexplainable and the fantastic play an integral role in understanding reality, perhaps as much as the laws of nature and our senses do. In the poem "**East Song,**" the line between fantasy and reality is not clear. The poem navigates the reader through a dreamlike world where the possibilities of what might be lurking just out of reach of the present, where "At any turn / an invisible angel waits." In addition to poetry, Mutis has written short stories and novels.

"A VERY OLD MAN WITH ENORMOUS WINGS" 933

ADDITIONAL QUESTIONS AND ACTIVITIES

Students may be familiar with Robert Frost's poem "The Road Not Taken." Ask them to reread that poem and comment on whether that poem and "East Song" have a similar theme. You may wish to have students compare the tone of the two poems as well.

SELECTION CHECK TEST 4.12.3 WITH ANSWERS

Checking Your Reading
1. What strange person does Pelayo find in his courtyard? **Pelayo finds an old man with wings lying face down in the courtyard.**
2. What is Father Gonzaga's opinion of the man? What evidence does he have for feeling this way? **The priest believes that the man is not a true angel, since he does not understand Latin or know how to greet a priest, and in addition, he smells and has parasites.**
3. How do the people in the village react to the winged man? What do they want from him? **The villagers mob the winged man. They want him to help cure their ailments.**
4. What new attraction comes to town? **A woman who had been changed into a spider comes.**
5. What finally happens to the winged man? **He flies away to sea.**

Vocabulary in Context
Fill in each blank below with the most appropriate word from the following Words for Everyday Use. You may have to change the tense of the word.

infamy   penitent   haughty
ingenuous   iridescent   celestial
proliferate   magnanimous

1. The oil splotches on the pavement were **iridescent** in the sunlight.
2. Years later, Raul felt **penitent** and apologized to his younger sister for having picked on her when they were kids.
3. The **ingenuous** child was shocked to learn that her grandmother was her father's "mommy."
4. In the summertime, weeds **proliferate** in our backyard.
5. The **haughty** actor carried himself with an air of superiority, and waved away his fans with a sneer of disgust.

SELECTION CHECK TEST 4.12.3 WITH ANSWERS (CONT.)

Literary Tools
1. From which point of view is "A Very Old Man with Enormous Wings" told? **This story is told from the third-person point of view.**
2. Give an example of an oxymoron. **Students may give examples such as "freezer burn," "act naturally," "sweet sorrow," and "genuine imitation."**
3. What is Magical Realism? **Magical Realism is a kind of fiction that is for the most part realistic but that contains elements of fantasy.**

RESPOND TO THE SELECTION

As an alternate activity, ask students what the angel might have been saying to those around him each time he spoke in his foreign tongue.

ANSWERS TO INVESTIGATE, INQUIRE, AND IMAGINE

RECALL

1a. Pelayo finds an old man lying face down in the mud who cannot get up because he is impeded by his huge wings.

2a. People from the neighborhood as well as Father Gonzaga, the village priest, come to see the angel.

3a. The onlookers lose interest when a traveling show of a woman who was turned into a spider comes to town.

INTERPRET

1b. Pelayo and Elisenda think the old man is a castaway from a foreign ship because he speaks a language they don't understand and has a strong "sailor's voice."

2b. The priest doubts the good intentions of the old man because he does not understand when the priest speaks to him in Latin and does not know how to greet a priest. The old man also does not have the "proud dignity of angels."

3b. The lesson she teaches is that children should obey their parents or they may end up being turned into a spider as she was.

ANALYZE

4a. When Pelayo and Elisenda's child recovers, the parents think it might be due to the intervention of the angel and they think of helping him escape on a raft. Then greed overcomes them and they decide to make money off the angel by charging the curious to see him. At the end of the story, once the angel no longer brings them income, Pelayo and Elisenda barely put up with him; he has become an "annoyance" that they are only too glad to be rid of when he flies away.

SYNTHESIZE

4b. Several times the author mentions the decrepit state of the angel. He is probably too weak and ill to try to leave.

EVALUATE

5a. The angel, in a sick and weakened state, has lost his full power. He cannot even fly until the end of the

---

Respond to the SELECTION

If you were the angel, how would you assess your stay with Pelayo and Elisenda?

Investigate, Inquire, and Imagine

Recall: GATHERING FACTS

1a. What does Pelayo find in his courtyard?

2a. Who comes to see the angel?

3a. What happens to make the onlookers lose interest in the angel?

Interpret: FINDING MEANING

1b. Why do Pelayo and Elisenda think the angel is a "lonely castaway from some foreign ship wrecked by the storm"?

2b. Why does the priest doubt the good intentions of the angel?

3b. What lesson does the spider woman teach children?

Analyze: TAKING THINGS APART

4a. Analyze Pelayo and Elisenda's motivations for treating the angel as they do.

Synthesize: BRINGING THINGS TOGETHER

4b. Why does the angel stay with Pelayo and Elisenda if he is not treated well?

Evaluate: MAKING JUDGMENTS

5a. Evaluate the potency of the angel's powers.

Extend: CONNECTING IDEAS

5b. Read the Related Reading, "East Song." What does the "invisible angel" represent in an individual's life? How is the angel of the poem different from the one in the short story?

Understanding Literature

POINT OF VIEW. Review the definition for **point of view** in Literary Tools in Prereading. How would the story be different if it were told from the angel's point of view? What things might we learn about the angel?

OXYMORON. Review the definition for **oxymoron** in the Handbook of Literary Terms. What does Elisenda say when the angel comes to live in the house? What makes this an oxymoron?

MAGICAL REALISM. Review the definition for **Magical Realism** in Literary Tools and the cluster chart you made for that section. What elements of Magical Realism does García Márquez incorporate in his story?

934   UNIT TWELVE / OTHER WORLDS

ANSWERS TO INVESTIGATE, INQUIRE, AND IMAGINE (CONT.)

story. When he tries to perform miracles on the believers who come for him to help, they go awry.

EXTEND

5b. The "invisible angel" is referred to as "the one you never were, the one that died of you so much being what you are." It seems to represent a path

in life not taken or some part of the self that the individual never embraced. The angel in Mutis's poem is spiritual rather physical, unlike García Márquez's angel. It also seems to be a more powerful and positive force, unlike the physical angel, who is a very weak old man.

---

934   TEACHER'S EDITION

Writer's Journal

1. Imagine you work in the traveling circus. Write an **advertisement** for the local village newspaper advertising the attraction of the spider-woman so that people will want to pay to see her.

2. Imagine you are the angel. Write a **journal entry** about your incarceration in the chicken coop. What do you think of Pelayo, Elisenda, and the villagers? What do you think they think of you?

3. Imagine you are the village priest. Write a **letter** to the Pope asking for direction on what to do about the angel. What are your concerns?

Integrating the Language Arts

Language, Grammar, and Style

THERE SENTENCES. Read the Language Arts Survey 3.27, "Working with *There* Sentences." Then identify the subject and verb for each of the following sentences.

1. After Pelayo returned from the beach, there was a man with enormous wings in his courtyard.
2. Has there ever been a more surprising sight than an angel in a chicken coop?
3. There was a circus that came to town.
4. Many curiosity seekers came, and there were now more people interested in the spider woman.
5. There was an incidence of chicken pox.

Study and Research & Collaborative Learning

RESEARCHING ANGELS. With several classmates, research how angels are portrayed in religion, literature, and the media. What human characteristics do they possess? What spiritual characteristics do they possess? How do people who claim to have seen angels describe them? Report on your findings to the class.

Media Literacy & Study and Research

MAGICAL REALISM READING LIST. Create a reading list for students interested in reading other stories and novels with Magical Realism. If you wish to do your research online, you might begin by accessing the Gabriel José García Márquez web page at http://www.TheModernWord.com.

ANSWERS TO UNDERSTANDING LITERATURE

POINT OF VIEW. If the story were told from the angel's point of view, we would learn about the angel's thoughts and motivations instead of Pelayo and Elisenda's and the villagers'. We might find out where the angel has been, how he finds his new surroundings, and what his tasks on Earth are.

OXYMORON. Elisenda says that the house is a "hell full of angels." This is an oxymoron because hell is usually considered the place where Satan and his worshippers, not angels, live.

MAGICAL REALISM. The angel, with his consolation miracles and ability to fly, and the spider woman's supernatural transformation are examples of Magical Realism.

ANSWERS TO INTEGRATING THE LANGUAGE ARTS

Language, Grammar, and Style
1. *subject:* man; *verb:* was
2. *subject:* sight; *verb:* has been
3. *subject:* circus; *verb:* came
4. *subject:* people; *verb:* were interested
5. *subject:* incidence; *verb:* was

Study and Research & Collaborative Learning
Before students begin, ask them to brainstorm ideas for their research. Have them consider what they already know about angels in religion, literature, and the media and jot this information down in the form of a list or concept web. They can then use their list or web to guide their research. Alternatively, they could brainstorm a list of questions about angels and possible sources of information.

Media Literacy & Study and Research
Remind students to use the correct form for bibliography entries when they gather information for their list. For examples, direct them to the Language Arts Survey 5.40, "Making Bibliographies and Bibliography Cards." You may wish to ask students to annotate each entry with a one- or two-sentence summary of the work.

GRAPHIC ORGANIZER

Students should include the following in their plot charts:
Exposition—Watson introduces Sherlock Holmes and the case; Helen Stoner describes her stepfather's unusual background and violent temper and her sister's mysterious death.
Inciting Incident—Helen, sleeping in her sister's room, has heard the same low whistle that preceded her sister's death; she feels in danger and has come to Holmes for help.
Rising Action—Dr. Roylott warns Holmes not to meddle. Holmes and Watson go to the Roylott house, discover the fake bell-pull and small ventilator in the sister's room, then hide out alone in the room at night.
Climax—They hear a low whistle, then a hiss. Holmes lashes out furiously at the bell-pull.
Falling Action—They discover Dr. Roylott in the room next door, killed by a speckled snake he kept in his safe.
Resolution—Holmes and Watson tell Helen that the doctor caused her sister's death.
Dénouement—Holmes sums up solution of the case.

READER'S JOURNAL

As an alternate activity, ask students to describe someone they know well who, in their opinion, has an interesting mind. What mental or intellectual qualities make the person interesting?

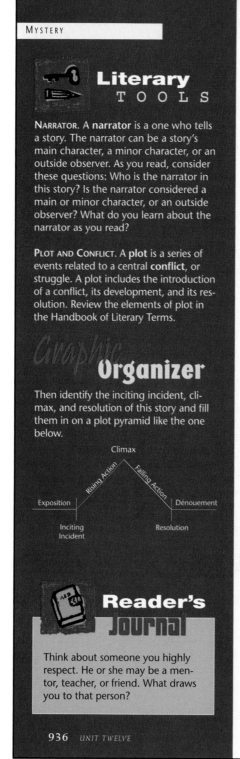

MYSTERY

Literary TOOLS

NARRATOR. A **narrator** is a one who tells a story. The narrator can be a story's main character, a minor character, or an outside observer. As you read, consider these questions: Who is the narrator in this story? Is the narrator considered a main or minor character, or an outside observer? What do you learn about the narrator as you read?

PLOT AND CONFLICT. A **plot** is a series of events related to a central **conflict,** or struggle. A plot includes the introduction of a conflict, its development, and its resolution. Review the elements of plot in the Handbook of Literary Terms.

Graphic Organizer

Then identify the inciting incident, climax, and resolution of this story and fill them in on a plot pyramid like the one below.

```
                    Climax
                     /\
         Rising     /  \   Falling
         Action    /    \   Action
                   /      \
   Exposition ____/        \____ Dénouement
        |                         |
     Inciting              Resolution
     Incident
```

Reader's Journal

Think about someone you highly respect. He or she may be a mentor, teacher, or friend. What draws you to that person?

"The Adventure of the Speckled Band"
by Sir Arthur Conan Doyle

Reader's resource

"The Adventure of the Speckled Band" is included in the genre of detective fiction which is also known as mystery story, whodunit, thriller, crime novel, and police procedural. Credit for the invention of the modern detective story is given to Edgar Allan Poe, who published "The Murders in the Rue Morgue" in 1841. In that story, Poe introduced his intellectual detective, C. Auguste Dupin. Sherlock Holmes is Dupin's most famous successor.

HISTORY CONNECTION. During the late 1880s in Britain, popular journalism and fiction boomed, due primarily to the rapid spread of literacy among the population. The increased number of readers prompted publishers to start new magazines, newspapers, and journals and to hire known and unknown writers to write articles, anecdotes, adventure tales, and mysteries. Sir Arthur Conan Doyle was one of those unknown writers, and the *Strand* was a new monthly magazine. The collection now known as *The Adventures of Sherlock Holmes* contains the first twelve stories, including "The Adventure of the Speckled Band," that Conan Doyle published serially in the *Strand.* "The Adventure of the Speckled Band" appeared in the February 1892 issue.

About the AUTHOR

Sir Arthur Conan Doyle (1859–1930) was born in Edinburgh, Scotland. After graduating from the University of Edinburgh, Doyle practiced medicine in Southsea, Portsmouth. In 1886, Doyle wrote his first detective story, a novel titled *A Study in Scarlet,* in which he introduced the characters Sherlock Holmes and Dr. Watson. However, the novel received very little attention at the time it was published. After returning from Vienna and Paris in 1891, Doyle began seeing patients again. To the good fortune of the reading world, Doyle's medical services were rarely required. He spent the days in his office writing what would become the first stories in the collection now known as *The Adventures of Sherlock Holmes.* The detective stories became wildly popular in England and the United States. At one point in his career, Doyle attempted to "retire" Sherlock Holmes, but public outcry for Holmes's return was so enormous that Doyle could only oblige; the Holmes stories continued to appear until 1927.

GOALS/OBJECTIVES

Studying this lesson will enable students to
- appreciate a work of detective fiction
- describe Sir Arthur Conan Doyle's contributions to the genre of detective fiction
- define *narrator* and identify and analyze the

narrative voice of literature they read
- define *plot* and *conflict* and identify the central conflict in the selection
- use quotation marks correctly in sentences
- investigate a long-standing Sherlock Holmes fan club

The Adventure of the Speckled Band

Sir Arthur Conan Doyle

On glancing over my notes of the seventy-odd cases in which I have during the last eight years studied the methods of my friend Sherlock Holmes, I find many tragic, some comic, a large number merely strange, but none commonplace: for, working as he did rather for the love of his art than for the acquirement of wealth, he refused to associate himself with any investigation which did not tend

Why does Holmes work?

towards the unusual, and even the fantastic. Of all these varied cases, however, I cannot recall any which presented more singular features than that which was associated with the well-known Surrey family of the Roylotts of Stoke Moran. The events in question occurred in the early days of my association with Holmes, when we were sharing rooms as bachelors in Baker Street. It is possible that I might have placed them upon record before, but a promise of secrecy was made at the time, from which I have only been freed during the last month by the untimely death of the lady to whom the pledge was given. It is perhaps as well that the facts should now come to light, for I have reasons to know that there are widespread rumors as to the death of Dr. Grimesby Roylott which tend to make the matter even more terrible than the truth.

It was early in April in the year '83[1] that I woke one morning to find Sherlock Holmes standing, fully dressed, by the side of my bed. He was a late riser, as a rule, and as the clock on the mantelpiece showed me that it was only a quarter-past seven, I blinked up at him in some surprise, and perhaps just a little resentment, for I was myself regular in my habits.

"Very sorry to knock you up,[2] Watson," said he, "but it's the common lot this morning. Mrs. Hudson has been knocked up, she retorted upon me, and I on you."

"What is it, then—a fire?"

"No; a client. It seems that a young lady has arrived in a considerable state of excitement, who insists upon seeing me. She is waiting now in the sitting-room. Now, when young ladies wander about the metropolis at this hour of the morning, and knock sleepy people up out of their beds, I presume that it is something very pressing which they have to communicate. Should it prove to be an interesting case, you would, I am sure, wish to follow it from the outset. I thought, at any rate, that I should call you and give you the chance."

---

1. '83. 1883
2. knock you up. British for "call on you" or "knock on your door"

ANSWER TO GUIDED
READING QUESTION

1. Watson admires the "rapid deduction" based on logic that Holmes uses to solve cases.

LITERARY NOTE

Conan Doyle chronicled the first meeting between Watson and Holmes in *A Study in Scarlet,* the first story in the Sherlock Holmes series.

VOCABULARY FROM
THE SELECTION

allied	livid
allusion	loathing
aperture	manifold
apparition	massive
averse	minutely
averted	parapet
blanch	pending
blandly	pittance
compliance	prolong
confide	protrude
confound	provision
coroner	recoil
deduce	reverie
deduction	scaffolding
dispel	scruple
dissolute	sear
endeavor	somber
erroneous	successive
haggard	suggestive
herald	tangible
impassable	ventilator
impending	vigil
imperturbably	whitewashed
imprudence	wretched
invaluable	

A reconstruction of Sherlock Holmes's study at the Sherlock Holmes Pub in London.

"My dear fellow, I would not miss it for anything."

I had no keener pleasure than in following Holmes in his professional investigations, and in admiring the rapid <u>deductions</u>, as swift as intuitions, and yet always founded on a logical basis, with which he unravelled the problems which were submitted to him. I rapidly threw on my clothes and was ready in a few minutes to accompany my friend down to the sitting-room. A lady dressed in black and heavily veiled, who had been sitting in the window, rose as we entered.

What does Watson admire about Holmes?

"Good-morning, madam," said Holmes cheerily. "My name is Sherlock Holmes. This is my intimate friend and associate, Dr. Watson, before whom you can speak as freely as before myself. Ha! I am glad to see that Mrs. Hudson has had the good sense to light the fire. Pray draw up to it, and I shall order you a cup of hot coffee, for I observe that you are shivering."

"It is not cold which makes me shiver," said the woman in a low voice, changing her seat as requested.

"What, then?"

words for everyday use

de • duc • tion (dē duk´shən) *n.,* reasoning from the general to the specific; conclusion reached by such reasoning. *After they gather clues, the investigators use* <u>deduction</u> *to develop theories about a crime.*

"It is fear, Mr. Holmes. It is terror." She raised her veil as she spoke, and we could see that she was indeed in a pitiable state of agitation, her face all drawn and gray, with restless, frightened eyes, like those of some hunted animal. Her features and figure were those of a woman of thirty, but her hair was shot with premature gray, and her expression was weary and <u>haggard</u>. Sherlock Holmes ran her over with one of his quick, all-comprehensive glances.

"You must not fear," said he soothingly, bending forward and patting her forearm. "We shall soon set matters right, I have no doubt. You have come in by train this morning, I see."

"You know me, then?"

"No, but I observe the second half of a return ticket in the palm of your left glove. You must have started early, and yet you had a good drive in a dog-cart[3] along heavy roads, before you reached the station."

The lady gave a violent start and stared in bewilderment at my companion.

"There is no mystery, my dear madam," said he, smiling. "The left arm of your jacket is spattered with mud in no less than seven places. The marks are perfectly fresh. There is no vehicle save a dog-cart which throws up mud in that way, and then only when you sit on the left-hand side of the driver."

"Whatever your reasons may be, you are perfectly correct," said she. "I started from home before six, reached Leatherhead at twenty past, and came in by the first train to Waterloo. Sir, I can stand this strain no longer; I shall go mad if it continues. I have no one to turn to—none, save only one, who cares for me, and he, poor fellow, can be of little aid. I have heard of you, Mr. Holmes; I have heard of you from Mrs. Farintosh, whom you helped in the hour of her sore need. It was from her that I had your

address. Oh, sir, do you not think that you could help me, too, and at least throw a little light through the dense darkness which surrounds me? At present it is out of my power to reward you for your services, but in a month or six weeks I shall be married, with the control of my own income, and then at least you shall not find me ungrateful."

Holmes turned to his desk and, unlocking it, drew out a small case-book, which he consulted.

"Farintosh," said he. "Ah yes, I recall the case; it was concerned with an opal tiara.[4] I think it was before your time, Watson. I can only say, madam, that I shall be happy to devote the same care to your case as I did to that of your friend. As to reward, my profession is its own reward; but you are at liberty to defray whatever expenses I may be put to, at the time which suits you best. And now I beg that you will lay before us everything that may help us in forming an opinion upon the matter."

"Alas!" replied our visitor, "the very horror of my situation lies in the fact that my fears are so vague, and my suspicions depend so entirely upon small points, which might seem trivial to another, that even he to whom of all others I have a right to look for help and advice looks upon all that I tell him about it as the fancies of a nervous woman. He does not say so, but I can read it from his soothing answers and <u>averted</u> eyes. But I have heard, Mr. Holmes, that you can see deeply into the <u>manifold</u> wickedness of the human heart. You may advise me how to walk around the dangers which encompass me."

Why do the young woman's fears and suspicions seem silly to other people to whom she turns for advice?

---

3. **dog-cart.** Two-wheeled open cart
4. **opal tiara.** Small crown covered with opals, which are milky, luminous, semiprecious stones

---

words for everyday use	**hag • gard** (hag´ərd) *adj.,* having a wild, worn look. *Your <u>haggard</u> appearance betrays your lack of sleep.*
	a • vert • ed (ə vʉrt´id) *adj.,* turned away. *The mourners' <u>averted</u> faces showed their respect for the grief-stricken family.*
	man • i • fold (man´ə fōld´) *adj.,* having many and various forms. *The salesperson demonstrated the vacuum cleaner's <u>manifold</u> functions.*

"THE ADVENTURE OF THE SPECKLED BAND" 939

1. Miss Stoner's stepfather isolated himself in his house and became violent. As a result of his uncontrollable anger, he got involved in a series of brawls and was arrested twice.

LITERARY TECHNIQUE

DETECTIVE STORY. Tell students that another name for a **detective story**, or mystery that involves the solving of a murder, is "whodunit." Usually there are a number of suspects who might have "done it," and the detective must evaluate their motives as well as the evidence. One common question that the detective in a murder mystery asks is "Who would stand to benefit from the person's death?" This question often leads to an investigation of wills, legal documents that spell out who will inherit the deceased person's wealth. Ask students who would benefit from Julia Stoner's death, and how.
Answer
Julia's stepfather would benefit. He inherited a large sum of money from his wife when she died. According to her will, an "annual sum" out of that money will go to each daughter if they marry. If they died before marrying, the stepfather can keep all the family wealth for himself.

"I am all attention, madam."

"My name is Helen Stoner, and I am living with my stepfather, who is the last survivor of one of the oldest Saxon families in England, the Roylotts of Stoke Moran, on the western border of Surrey."

Holmes nodded his head. "The name is familiar to me," said he.

"The family was at one time among the richest in England, and the estates extended over the borders into Berkshire in the north, and Hampshire in the west. In the last century, however, four <u>successive</u> heirs were of a <u>dissolute</u> and wasteful disposition, and the family ruin was eventually completed by a gambler in the days of the Regency.[5] Nothing was left save a few acres of ground, and the two-hundred-year-old house, which is itself crushed under a heavy mortgage. The last squire[6] dragged out his existence there, living the horrible life of an aristocratic pauper; but his only son, my stepfather, seeing that he must adapt himself to the new conditions, obtained an advance from a relative, which enabled him to take a medical degree and went out to Calcutta,[7] where, by his professional skill and his force of character, he established a large practice. In a fit of anger, however, caused by some robberies which had been perpetrated in the house, he beat his native butler to death and narrowly escaped a capital sentence.[8] As it was, he suffered a long term of imprisonment and afterwards returned to England a morose and disappointed man.

"When Dr. Roylott was in India he married my mother, Mrs. Stoner, the young widow of Major-General Stoner, of the Bengal Artillery. My sister Julia and I were twins, and we were only two years old at the time of my mother's remarriage. She had a considerable sum of money—not less than £1000[9] a year—and this she bequeathed to Dr. Roylott entirely while we resided with him, with a <u>provision</u> that a certain annual sum should be allowed to each of us in the event of our marriage. Shortly after our return to England my mother died—she was killed eight years ago in a railway accident near Crewe. Dr. Roylott then abandoned his attempts to establish himself in practice in London and took us to live with him in the old ancestral house at Stoke Moran. The money which my mother had left was enough for all our wants, and there seemed to be no obstacle to our happiness.

"But a terrible change came over our stepfather about this time. Instead of making friends and exchanging visits with our neighbors, who had at first been overjoyed to see a Roylott of Stoke Moran back in the old family seat, he shut himself up in his house and seldom came out save to indulge in ferocious quarrels with whoever might cross his path. Violence of temper approaching to mania has been hereditary in the men of the family, and in my stepfather's case it had, I believe, been intensified by his long residence in the tropics. A series of disgraceful brawls took place, two of which ended in the police-court until at last he became the terror of the village, and the folks would fly at his approach, for he is a man of immense strength, and absolutely uncontrollable in his anger.

What change occurred in Miss Stoner's stepfather? What happens as a result of this change?

"Last week he hurled the local blacksmith over a <u>parapet</u> into a stream, and it was only by paying over all the money which I could gather

---

5. **the Regency.** Period of English history from 1811 to 1820
6. **squire.** Landowner
7. **Calcutta.** Seaport city in northeast India
8. **capital sentence.** Death sentence
9. **£1000.** One thousand pounds sterling. The pound is the main unit of English currency.

words for everyday use

suc • ces • sive (sək ses´iv) *adj.*, following one after another in sequence. *The title of the <u>successive</u> films were indicated by Roman numerals.*

dis • so • lute (dis´ə lōōt´) *adj.*, immoral. *Although he was once <u>dissolute</u>, the young man reformed himself and abandoned his former lifestyle.*

pro • vi • sion (prō vizh´ən) *n.*, condition; agreement. *Does the apartment lease have a special <u>provision</u> regarding pets?*

par • a • pet (par´ə pet´) *n.*, low wall or railing. *Over the years, ivy had grown up the <u>parapet</u> and covered it entirely.*

together that I was able to avert another public exposure. He had no friends at all save the wandering gypsies, and he would give these vagabonds leave to encamp upon the few acres of bramble-covered land which represent the family estate, and would accept in return the hospitality of their tents, wandering away with them sometimes for weeks on end. He has a passion also for Indian animals, which are sent over to him by a correspondent, and he has at this moment a cheetah and a baboon, which wander freely over his grounds and are feared by the villagers almost as much as their master.

Who are Dr. Roylott's friends?

"You can imagine from what I say that my poor sister Julia and I had no great pleasure in our lives. No servant would stay with us, and for a long time we did all the work of the house. She was but thirty at the time of her death, and yet her hair had already begun to whiten, even as mine has."

"Your sister is dead, then?"

"She died just two years ago, and it is of her death that I wish to speak to you. You can understand that, living the life which I have described, we were little likely to see anyone of our own age and position. We had, however, an aunt, my mother's maiden sister, Miss Honoria Westphail, who lives near Harrow,[10] and we were occasionally allowed to pay short visits at this lady's house. Julia went there at Christmas two years ago, and met there a half-pay major of marines,[11] to whom she became engaged. My stepfather learned of the engagement when my sister returned and offered no objection to the marriage; but within a fortnight of the day which had been fixed for the wedding, the terrible event occurred which has deprived me of my only companion."

Sherlock Holmes had been leaning back in his chair with his eyes closed and his head sunk in a cushion, but he half opened his lids now and glanced across at his visitor.

"Pray[12] be precise as to details," said he.

"It is easy for me to be so, for every event of that dreadful time is <u>seared</u> into my memory. The manor-house is, as I have already said, very old, and only one wing is now inhabited. The bedrooms in this wing are on the ground floor, the sitting-rooms being in the central block of the buildings. Of these bedrooms the first is Dr. Roylott's, the second my sister's, and the third my own. There is no communication between them, but they all open out into the same corridor. Do I make myself plain?"

Why does Holmes want her to be precise about the details of her story?

"Perfectly so."

"The windows of the three rooms open out upon the lawn. That fatal night Dr. Roylott had gone to his room early, though we knew that he had not retired to rest, for my sister was troubled by the smell of the strong Indian cigars which it was his custom to smoke. She left her room, therefore, and came into mine, where she sat for some time, chatting about her approaching wedding. At eleven o'clock she rose to leave me, but she paused at the door and looked back.

"'Tell me, Helen,' said she, 'have you ever heard anyone whistle in the dead of the night?'"

"'Never,'" said I.

"'I suppose that you could not possibly whistle, yourself, in your sleep?'

"'Certainly not. But why?'"

What does Julia ask Helen?

---

10. **Harrow.** Section of London
11. **half-pay major of marines.** Marine major who earns half the salary of a full-pay major
12. **Pray.** Please

words for everyday use

sear (sir') *vt.*, brand as by burning. *That brilliant painting is <u>seared</u> in my mind.*

"THE ADVENTURE OF THE SPECKLED BAND" **941**

ANSWERS TO GUIDED READING QUESTIONS

1. After the scream, she hears a low whistle, like the one her sister had described, and a few moments later a clanging sound.
2. Helen's sister's last words were "It was the band! The speckled band!"

LITERARY TECHNIQUE

DESCRIPTION. A **description**, one type of writing, portrays a character, an object, or a scene. A description uses sensory details and vivid nouns and verbs to convey an image. What sensory details and vivid language create the scene of Julia's death?
Answers
Sensory details such as "her face blanched with terror" and "her whole figure swaying to and fro like that of a drunkard" and vivid language such as "stabbed with her finger" and "a fresh convulsion seized her and choked her words" help create the scene of Julia's death.

"'Because during the last few nights I have always, about three in the morning, heard a low, clear whistle. I am a light sleeper, and it has awakened me. I cannot tell where it came from—perhaps from the next room, perhaps from the lawn. I thought that I would just ask you whether you had heard it.'

"'No, I have not. It must be those <u>wretched</u> gypsies in the plantation.'

"'Very likely. And yet if it were on the lawn, I wonder that you did not hear it also.'

"'Ah, but I sleep more heavily than you.'

"'Well, it is of no great consequence, at any rate.' She smiled back at me, closed my door, and a few moments later I heard her key turn in the lock."

"Indeed," said Holmes. "Was it your custom always to lock yourselves in at night?"

"Always."

"And why?"

"I think that I mentioned to you that the doctor kept a cheetah and a baboon. We had no feeling of security unless our doors were locked."

"Quite so. Pray proceed with your statement."

"I could not sleep that night. A vague feeling of <u>impending</u> misfortune impressed me. My sister and I, you will recollect, were twins, and you know how subtle are the links which bind two souls which are so closely <u>allied</u>. It was a wild night. The wind was howling outside, and the rain was beating and splashing against the windows. Suddenly, amid all the hubbub of the game, there burst forth the wild scream of a terrified woman. I knew that it was my sister's voice. I sprang from my bed, wrapped a shawl round me, and rushed into the corridor. As I opened my door I seemed to hear a low whistle, such as my sister described, and

What does Miss Stoner hear after the scream?

a few moments later a clanging sound, as if a mass of metal had fallen. As I ran down the passage, my sister's door was unlocked, and revolved slowly upon its hinges. I stared at it horror-stricken, not knowing what was about to issue from it. By the light of the corridor-lamp I saw my sister appear at the opening, her face <u>blanched</u> with terror, her hands groping for help, her whole figure swaying to and fro like that of a drunkard. I ran to her and threw my arms round her, but at that moment her knees seemed to give way and she fell to the ground. She writhed as one who is in terrible pain, and her limbs were dreadfully convulsed. At first I thought that she had not recognized me, but as I bent over her she suddenly shrieked out in a voice which I shall never forget, 'Oh, my God! Helen! It was the band! The speckled band!' There was something else which she would fain[13] have said, and she stabbed with her finger into the air in the direction of the doctor's room, but a fresh convulsion seized her and choked her words. I rushed out, calling loudly for my stepfather, and I met him hastening from his room in his dressing-gown. When he reached my sister's side she was unconscious, and though he poured brandy down her throat and sent for medical aid from the village, all efforts were in vain, for she slowly sank and died without having recovered her consciousness. Such was the dreadful end of my beloved sister."

What were Helen's sister's last words?

"One moment," said Holmes; "are you sure about this whistle and metallic sound? Could you swear to it?"

"That was what the county <u>coroner</u> asked me at the inquiry. It is my strong impression that I heard it, and yet, among the crash of the gale

---

13. **fain.** Have wished to

words for everyday use
wretch • ed (rech' id) *adj.*, contemptible; despicable. *That <u>wretched</u> bus driver shut the door in my face.*
im • pend • ing (im pend iŋ) *adj.*, about to happen. *The <u>impending</u> lottery drawing filled the audience with excited anticipation.*
al • lied (ə līd´) *adj.*, related; united by kinship. *The two families are <u>allied</u> by marriage.*
blanch (blanch) *vi.*, turn pale. *Ron <u>blanched</u> with nervousness at the thought of making a speech.*
cor • o • ner (kôr´ə nər) *n.*, public officer whose duties include determining the causes of deaths. *Has the <u>coroner</u> determined how the victims died?*

and the creaking of an old house, I may possibly have been deceived."

"Was your sister dressed?"

"No, she was in her night-dress. In her right hand was found the charred stump of a match, and in her left a match-box."

What conclusion does Holmes draw? on what basis?

"Showing that she had struck a light and looked about her when the alarm took place. That is important. And what conclusions did the coroner come to?"

"He investigated the case with great care, for Dr. Roylott's conduct had long been notorious in the county, but he was unable to find any satisfactory cause of death. My evidence showed that the door had been fastened upon the inner side and the windows were blocked by old-fashioned shutters with broad iron bars, which were secured every night. The walls were carefully sounded, and were shown to be quite solid all round, and the flooring was also thoroughly examined, with the same result. The chimney is wide, but is barred up by four large staples. It is certain, therefore, that my sister was quite alone when she met her end. Besides, there were no marks of any violence upon her."

"How about poison?"

"The doctors examined her for it, but without success."

"What do you think that this unfortunate lady died of, then?"

"It is my belief that she died of pure fear and nervous shock, though what it was that frightened her, I cannot imagine."

"Were there gypsies in the plantation at the time?"

"Yes, there are nearly always some there."

"Ah, and what did you gather from this <u>allusion</u> to a band—a speckled band?"

"Sometimes I have thought that it was merely the wild talk of delirium, sometimes that it may have referred to some band of people, perhaps to these very gypsies in the plantation. I do not know whether the spotted handkerchiefs which so many of them wear over their heads might have suggested the strange adjective which she used."

Holmes shook his head like a man who is far from being satisfied.

"These are very deep waters," said he; "pray go on with your narrative."

"Two years have passed since then, and my life has been until lately lonelier than ever. A month ago, however, a dear friend, whom I have known for many years, has done me the honour to ask my hand in marriage. His name is Armitage—Percy Armitage—the second son of Mr. Armitage, of Case Water, near Reading. My stepfather has offered no opposition to the match, and we are to be married in the course of the spring. Two days ago some repairs were started in the west wing of the building, and my bedroom wall has been pierced, so that I have had to move into the chamber in which my sister died, and to sleep in the very bed in which she slept. Imagine, then, my thrill of terror when last night, as I lay awake, thinking over her terrible fate, I suddenly heard in the silence of the night the low whistle which had been the <u>herald</u> of her own death. I sprang up and lit the lamp, but nothing was to be seen in the room. I was too shaken to go to bed again, however, so I dressed, and as soon as it was daylight I slipped down, got a dog-cart at the Crown Inn, which is opposite, and drove to Leatherhead, from whence I have

Where is Miss Stoner sleeping? What is significant about the noise she hears? In what way is her situation similar to that of her sister just before her death?

ANSWERS TO GUIDED READING QUESTIONS

1. Holmes concludes that Julia had struck a match and looked around the room when she heard the sound. He makes the conclusion based on the fact that she was holding a burnt match and a match box in her hands when she died.
2. Miss Stoner is sleeping in the room her sister used to have. She hears the same noise her sister heard just before she died. Like her sister just before her death, Miss Stoner is engaged to be married.

words for everyday use

al • lu • sion (ə lü´zhən) *n.,* casual or indirect reference. *Critics have long debated the meaning of some <u>allusions</u> in the poet's writing.*

her • ald (her´əld) *n.,* messenger or harbinger. *Warmer and sunnier days are a <u>herald</u> of spring.*

ANSWERS TO GUIDED READING QUESTIONS

1. Holmes doesn't want the stepfather to know about his examining the room because he suspects that the stepfather is involved in the strange events Miss Stoner has described.

2. At this point, Holmes might have the theory that the doctor enlisted the gypsies to break into Julia's room and cause her death.

CROSS-CURRICULAR CONNECTIONS

HISTORY. According to his creator, the character of Sherlock Holmes was partly inspired by Dr. Joseph Bell, who taught at the University of Edinburgh when Conan Doyle was a medical student. Like Holmes, Dr. Bell possessed uncanny deductive powers. Dr. Bell, however, applied his skills to diagnosing illnesses rather than to solving crimes.

come on this morning with the one object of seeing you and asking your advice."

"You have done wisely," said my friend. "But have you told me all?"

"Yes, all."

"Miss Roylott, you have not. You are screening your stepfather."

"Why, what do you mean?"

For answer Holmes pushed back the frill of black lace which fringed the hand that lay upon our visitor's knee. Five little <u>livid</u> spots, the marks of four fingers and a thumb, were printed upon the white wrist.

"You have been cruelly used," said Holmes.

The lady colored deeply and covered over her injured wrist. "He is a hard man," she said, "and perhaps he hardly knows his own strength."

There was a long silence, during which Holmes leaned his chin upon his hands and stared into the crackling fire.

"This is a very deep business," he said at last. "There are a thousand details which I should desire to know before I decide upon our course of action. Yet we have not a moment to lose. If we were to come to Stoke Moran today, would it be possible for us to see over these rooms without the knowledge of your stepfather?"

> Why do you think Holmes doesn't want the stepfather to know about his examining the rooms?

"As it happens, he spoke of coming into town today upon some most important business. It is probable that he will be away all day, and that there would be nothing to disturb you. We have a housekeeper now, but she is old and foolish, and I could easily get her out of the way."

"Excellent. You are not <u>averse</u> to this trip, Watson?"

"By no means."

"Then we shall both come. What are you going to do yourself?"

"I have one or two things which I would wish to do now that I am in town. But I shall return by the twelve o'clock train, so as to be there in time for your coming."

"And you may expect us early in the afternoon. I have myself some small business matters to attend to. Will you not wait and breakfast?"

"No, I must go. My heart is lightened already since I have <u>confided</u> my trouble to you. I shall look forward to seeing you again this afternoon." She dropped her thick black veil over her face and glided from the room.

"And what do you think of it all, Watson?" asked Sherlock Holmes, leaning back in his chair.

"It seems to me to be a most dark and sinister business."

"Dark enough and sinister enough."

"Yet if the lady is correct in saying that the flooring and walls are sound, and that the door, window, and chimney are <u>impassable</u>, then her sister must have been undoubtedly alone when she met her mysterious end."

"What becomes, then, of these nocturnal whistles, and what of the very peculiar words of the dying woman?"

"I cannot think."

"When you combine the ideas of whistles at night, the presence of a band of gypsies who are on intimate terms with this old doctor, the fact that we have every reason to believe that the doctor has an interest in preventing his stepdaughter's marriage, the dying allusion to a band, and, finally, the fact that Miss Helen Stoner heard a metallic clang, which might have been caused by one of those metal bars that secured the shutters falling back into its place, I think that there is good ground to think

> What theory might Holmes have at this point about the cause of the sister's death?

words for everyday use	**liv • id** (liv´id) *adj.*, black and blue; colored like a bruise. *A vitamin deficiency can cause <u>livid</u> marks to appear as a result of even the slightest bump.* **a • verse** (ə vurs´) *adj.*, reluctant or opposed. *Are you <u>averse</u> to trying unusual cuisines?* **con • fide** (kən fīd´) *vi.*, trust, especially by sharing secrets. *The twin sisters <u>confided</u> in each other.* **im • pass • a • ble** (im pas´ə bəl) *adj.*, that cannot be passed or traveled through. *On the day of the move, mountains of boxes made the hallway nearly <u>impassable</u>.*

that the mystery may be cleared along those lines."

"But what, then, did the gypsies do?"

"I cannot imagine."

"I see many objections to any such theory."

"And so do I. It is precisely for that reason that we are going to Stoke Moran this day. I want to see whether the objections are fatal, or if they may be explained away. But what in the name of the devil!"

The ejaculation had been drawn from my companion by the fact that our door had been suddenly dashed open, and that a huge man had framed himself in the <u>aperture</u>. His costume was a peculiar mixture of the professional and of the agricultural, having a black top-hat, a long frock-coat, and a pair of high gaiters, with a hunting-crop[14] swinging in his hand. So tall was he that his hat actually brushed the cross bar of the doorway, and his breadth seemed to span it across from side to side. A large face, seared with a thousand wrinkles, burned yellow with the sun, and marked with every evil passion, was turned from one to the other of us, while his deep-set, bile-shot[15] eyes, and his high, thin, fleshless nose, gave him somewhat the resemblance to a fierce old bird of prey.

"Which of you is Holmes?" asked this <u>apparition</u>.

"My name, sir; but you have the advantage of me," said my companion quietly.

"I am Dr. Grimesby Roylott, of Stoke Moran."

"Indeed, Doctor," said Holmes <u>blandly</u>. "Pray take a seat."

"I will do nothing of the kind. My stepdaughter has been here. I have traced her. What has she been saying to you?"

"It is a little cold for the time of the year," said Holmes.

"What has she been saying to you?" screamed the old man furiously.

"But I have heard that the crocuses promise well," continued my companion <u>imperturbably</u>.

"Ha! You put me off, do you?" said our new visitor, taking a step forward and shaking his hunting-crop. "I know you, you scoundrel! I have heard of you before. You are Holmes, the meddler."

My friend smiled.

"Holmes, the busybody!"

His smile broadened.

"Holmes, the Scotland Yard Jack-in-office!"[16]

Holmes chuckled heartily. "Your conversation is most entertaining," said he. "When you go out, close the door, for there is a decided draught."

"I will go when I have said my say. Don't you dare to meddle with my affairs. I know that Miss Stoner has been here. I traced her! I am a dangerous man to fall foul of![17] See here." He stepped swiftly forward, seized the poker, and bent it into a curve with his huge brown hands.

"See that you keep yourself out of my grip," he snarled, and hurling the twisted poker into the fireplace, he strode out of the room.

Why does Dr. Roylott bend the steel poker?

"He seems a very amiable person," said Holmes, laughing. "I am not quite

---

14. **long frock-coat . . . hunting-crop.** *Long frock-coat*—men's dress coat with a full skirt reaching to the knees in front and back; *gaiters*—high overshoes with cloth uppers; *hunting-crop*—short whip used for horseback riding, especially for a fox hunt on horseback

15. **bile-shot.** Bile is a yellow or brown fluid produced by the liver. In ancient medicine, too much yellow bile was said to produce a choleric, or angry, spirit. The whites of the man's eyes have a yellowish cast that reflects his anger.

16. **Scotland Yard Jack-in-office.** *Scotland Yard*—detective department of the London police; *Jack-in-office*—insulting term for an "employee." In nineteenth-century England, men who worked as employees were looked down upon by the wealthy.

17. **fall foul of.** Dr. Roylott means "become enemy of."

---

words for everyday use

ap • er • ture (ap′ər chər) *n.*, opening. *The detective spied on the suspects through a well-disguised <u>aperture</u> in the wall.*

ap • pa • ri • tion (ap′ə rish′ən) *n.*, anything eerie that appears suddenly and unexpectedly. *When she developed her film, the paranormal researcher discovered that she had captured the image of the <u>apparition</u>.*

bland • ly (bland′ lē) *adv.*, smoothly. *The hostess <u>blandly</u> introduced her guests to one another.*

im • per • turb • a • bly (im′pər tʉr′bə blē) *adv.*, without being excited or disturbed. *Although he was nervous, the contestant spoke <u>imperturbably</u>.*

ANSWER TO GUIDED READING QUESTION

1. Dr. Roylott bends the steel poker to demonstrate his strength and intimidate Holmes.

ADDITIONAL QUESTIONS AND ACTIVITIES

How does Holmes treat Dr. Grimesby Roylott when he comes to his office? Why might he have chosen to treat the doctor this way?
Answers
Holmes acts uninterested in what the doctor has to say and quickly invites him to leave. He seems to be trying to provoke the doctor by being rude, to test the truth of Miss Stoner's report that her stepfather has a violent temper.

so bulky, but if he had remained I might have shown him that my grip was not much more feeble than his own." As he spoke he picked up the steel poker and, with a sudden effort, straightened it out again.

"Fancy his having the insolence to <u>confound</u> me with the official detective force! This incident gives zest to our investigation, however, and I only trust that our little friend will not suffer from her <u>imprudence</u> in allowing this brute to trace her. And now, Watson, we shall order breakfast, and afterwards I shall walk down to Doctors' Commons, where I hope to get some data which may help us in this matter."

It was nearly one o'clock when Sherlock Holmes returned from his excursion. He held in his hand a sheet of blue paper, scrawled over with notes and figures.

"I have seen the will of the deceased wife," said he. "To determine its exact meaning I have been obliged to work out the present prices of the investments with which it is concerned. The total income, which at the time of the wife's death was little short of £1100, is now, through the fall in agricultural prices, not more than £750. Each daughter can claim an income of £250, in case of marriage. It is evident, therefore, that if both girls had married, this beauty would have had a mere <u>pittance</u>, while even one of them would cripple him to a very serious extent. My morning's work has not been wasted, since it has proved that he has the very strongest motives for standing in the way of anything of the sort. And now, Watson, this is too serious for dawdling, especially as the old man is aware that we are interesting ourselves in his affairs; so if you are ready, we shall call a cab and drive to

> *What motivation does Dr. Roylott have for committing murder?*

Waterloo.[18] I should be very much obliged if you would slip your revolver into your pocket. An Eley's No. 2[19] is an excellent argument with gentlemen who can twist steel pokers into knots. That and a toothbrush are, I think, all that we need."

At Waterloo we were fortunate in catching a train for Leatherhead, where we hired a trap at the station inn and drove for four or five miles through the lovely Surrey lanes. It was a perfect day, with a bright sun and a few fleecy clouds in the heavens. The trees and wayside hedges were just throwing out their first green shoots, and the air was full of the pleasant smell of the moist earth. To me at least there was a strange contrast between the sweet promise of the spring and this sinister quest upon which we were engaged. My companion sat in the front of the trap, his arms folded, his hat pulled down over his eyes, and his chin sunk upon his breast, buried in the deepest thought. Suddenly, however, he started, tapped me on the shoulder, and pointed over the meadows.

"Look there!" said he.

A heavily timbered park stretched up in a gentle slope, thickening into a grove at the highest point. From amid the branches there jutted out the gray gables and high roof-tree of a very old mansion.

"Stoke Moran?" said he.

"Yes, sir, that be the house of Dr. Grimesby Roylott," remarked the driver.

"There is some building going on there," said Holmes; "that is where we are going."

"There's the village," said the driver, pointing to a cluster of roofs some distance to the left; "but if you want to get to the house, you'll find it shorter to get over this stile,[20] and so by the

---

18. **Waterloo.** One of the largest train stations in London
19. **Eley's No. 2.** Type of gun
20. **stile.** Step or set of steps used for climbing over a fence or wall

---

words for everyday use	**con • found** (kən found´) *vt.*, mix up indiscriminately. *How could anyone possibly <u>confound</u> Impressionism with Cubism?* **im • pru • dence** (im prü´dəns) *n.*, lack of judgment; thoughtlessness. *Although we disapprove of your <u>imprudence</u>, we think you've learned from your mistake.* **pit • tance** (pit´ns) *n.*, small amount. *After taxes, my paycheck is reduced to a <u>pittance</u>.*

foot-path over the fields. There it is, where the lady is walking."

"And the lady, I fancy, is Miss Stoner," observed Holmes, shading his eyes. "Yes, I think we had better do as you suggest."

We got off, paid our fare, and the trap rattled back on its way to Leatherhead.

"I thought it as well," said Holmes as we climbed the stile, "that this fellow should think we had come here as architects, or on some definite business. It may stop his gossip. Good-afternoon, Miss Stoner. You see that we have been as good as our word."

Our client of the morning had hurried forward to meet us with a face which spoke her joy. "I have been waiting so eagerly for you," she cried, shaking hands with us warmly. "All has turned out splendidly. Dr. Roylott has gone to town, and it is unlikely that he will be back before evening."

"We have had the pleasure of making the doctor's acquaintance," said Holmes, and in a few words he sketched out what had occurred. Miss Stoner turned white to the lips as she listened.

"Good heavens!" she cried, "he has followed me, then."

"So it appears."

"He is so cunning that I never know when I am safe from him. What will he say when he returns?"

"He must guard himself, for he may find that there is someone more cunning than himself upon his track. You must lock yourself up from him tonight. If he is violent, we shall take you away to your aunt's at Harrow. Now, we must make the best use of our time, so kindly take us at once to the rooms which we are to examine."

The building was of gray, lichen-blotched[21] stone, with a high central portion and two curving wings, like the claws of a crab, thrown out on each side. In one of these wings the windows were broken and blocked with wooden boards, while the roof was partly caved in, a picture of ruin. The central portion was in little better repair, but the right-hand block was comparatively modern, and the blinds in the windows, with the blue smoke curling up from the chimneys, showed that this was where the family resided. Some scaffolding had been erected against the end wall, and the stone-work had been broken into, but there were no signs of any workmen at the moment of our visit. Holmes walked slowly up and down the ill-trimmed lawn and examined with deep attention the outsides of the windows.

"This, I take it, belongs to the room in which you used to sleep, the center one to your sister's, and the one next to the main building to Dr. Roylott's chamber?"

"Exactly so. But I am now sleeping in the middle one."

"Pending the alterations, as I understand. By the way, there does not seem to be any very pressing need for repairs at that end wall."

"There were none. I believe that it was an excuse to move me from my room."

"Ah! that is suggestive. Now, on the other side of this narrow wing runs the corridor from which these three rooms open. There are windows in it, of course?"

| *What does Holmes mean when he says, "that is suggestive"?* |

"Yes, but very small ones. Too narrow for anyone to pass through."

"As you both locked your doors at night, your rooms were unapproachable from that side. Now, would you have the kindness to go into your room and bar your shutters?"

---

21. **lichen-blotched.** Covered with small, spongelike green plants that belong to the plant group *Lichenes*

---

1. He means that using the excuse of the repairs to move Miss Stoner into her sister's bedroom is an important and revealing detail that may help him figure out who caused the sister's death.

Miss Stoner did so, and Holmes, after a careful examination through the open window, <u>endeavored</u> in every way to force the shutter open, but without success. There was no slit through which a knife could be passed to raise the bar. Then with his lens[22] he tested the hinges, but they were of solid iron, built firmly into the <u>massive</u> masonry. "Hum!" said he, scratching his chin in some perplexity, "my theory certainly presents some difficulties. No one could pass these shutters if they were bolted. Well, we shall see if the inside throws any light upon the matter."

A small side door led into the <u>whitewashed</u> corridor from which the three bedrooms opened. Holmes refused to examine the third chamber, so we passed at once to the second, that in which Miss Stoner was now sleeping, and in which her sister had met with her fate. It was a homely little room, with a low ceiling and a gaping fireplace, after the fashion of old country houses. A brown chest of drawers stood in one corner, a narrow white-counterpaned[23] bed in another, and a dressing table on the left-hand side of the window. These articles, with two small wickerwork chairs, made up all the furniture in the room save for a square of Wilton carpet in the centre. The boards round and the paneling of the walls were of brown, worm-eaten oak, so old and discolored that it may have dated from the original building of the house. Holmes drew one of the chairs into a corner and sat silent, while his eyes traveled round and round and up and down, taking in every detail of the apartment.

"Where does that bell communicate with?" he asked at last, pointing to a thick bell-rope[24] which hung down beside the bed, the tassel actually lying upon the pillow.

"It goes to the housekeeper's room."

"It looks newer than the other things?"

"Yes, it was only put there a couple of years ago."

"Your sister asked for it, I suppose?"

"No, I never heard of her using it. We used always to get what we wanted for ourselves."

"Indeed, it seemed unnecessary to put so nice a bell-pull there. You will excuse me for a few minutes while I satisfy myself as to this floor." He threw himself down upon his face with his lens in his hand and crawled swiftly backward and forward, examining <u>minutely</u> the cracks between the boards. Then he did the same with the woodwork with which the chamber was paneled. Finally he walked over to the bed and spent some time in staring at it and in running his eye up and down the wall. Finally he took the bell-rope in his hand and gave it a brisk tug.

"Why, it's a dummy," said he.

"Won't it ring?"

"No, it is not even attached to a wire. This is very interesting. You can see now that it is fastened to a hook just above where the little opening for the <u>ventilator</u> is."

"How very absurd! I never noticed that before."

"Very strange!" muttered Holmes, pulling at the rope. "There are one or two very singular points about this room. For example, what a fool a builder must be to open a ventilator into another room, when, with the same trouble, he might have communicated with the outside air!"

"That is also quite modern," said the lady.

---

22. **lens.** Holmes's famous magnifying glass
23. **white-counterpaned.** Covered with a white embroidered quilt
24. **bell-rope.** Tasseled rope attached to a bell in another room, usually in servant quarters or the kitchen of a large house and used for calling servants

---

words for everyday use

en • deav • or (en dev´ər) *vi.,* make an earnest attempt. *The honest employee <u>endeavored</u> to return the wallet to its rightful owner.*

mas • sive (mas´iv) *adj.,* big and solid. *A <u>massive</u> monument stands at the entrance to the cemetery.*

white • washed (hwīt´ wôshd´) *adj.,* painted with a white mixture of lime, water, and other elements. *The <u>whitewashed</u> fence had begun to chip and peel, revealing the brown wood.*

mi • nute • ly (mī nūt´lē) *adv.,* closely; in a manner attentive to tiny details. *The appraiser studied the antique <u>minutely</u> for any signs of damage.*

ven • ti • la • tor (vent´'l āt´ər) *n.,* opening through which air can pass. *This smoky room could use a <u>ventilator</u>.*

1. Holmes observes the bell-rope that
doesn't ring and the ventilator that
doesn't ventilate, both relatively
new additions to the room.

"Done about the same time as the bell-rope?" remarked Holmes.

"Yes, there were several little changes carried out about that time."

"They seem to have been of a most interesting character—dummy bell-ropes, and ventilators which do not ventilate. With your permission? Miss Stoner, we shall now carry our researches into the inner apartment."

What unusual details does Holmes observe in the room?

Dr. Grimesby Roylott's chamber was larger than that of his stepdaughter, but was as plainly furnished. A camp-bed, a small wooden shelf full of books, mostly of a technical character, an armchair beside the bed, a plain wooden chair against the wall, a round table, and a large iron safe were the principal things which met the eye. Holmes walked slowly round and examined each and all of them with the keenest interest.

"What's in here?" he asked, tapping the safe.

"My stepfather's business papers."

"Oh! you have seen inside, then?"

"Only once, some years ago. I remember that it was full of papers."

"There isn't a cat in it, for example?"

"No. What a strange idea!"

"Well, look at this!" He took up a small saucer of milk which stood on the top of it.

"No; we don't keep a cat. But there is a cheetah and a baboon."

"Ah, yes, of course! Well, a cheetah is just a big cat, and yet a saucer of milk does not go very far in satisfying its wants, I daresay. There is one point which I should wish to determine." He squatted down in front of the wooden chair and examined the seat of it with the greatest attention.

"Thank you. That is quite settled," said he, rising and putting his lens in his pocket. "Hello! Here is something interesting!"

1. Holmes finds odd the fact that the dog lash is tied so as to make a loop. Holmes might infer that the lash was tied in this way so it could be used on something other than a dog.
2. *Responses will vary.* Students should use details presented thus far to make their deductions.

ADDITIONAL QUESTIONS AND ACTIVITIES

What comments from Holmes hint that he has solved the mystery? What do his comments tell the reader about the mystery?
Answers
After examining the seat of the chair, Holmes says, "That is quite settled." After looking at the dog lash, he exclaims, "Ah, me! it's a wicked world, and when a clever man turns to crime, it is the worst of all. I think that I have seen enough now." His comments indicate that the chair and the lash are keys to the mystery.

The object which had caught his eye was a small dog lash[25] on one corner of the bed. The lash, however, was curled upon itself and tied so as to make a loop of whipcord.

"What do you make of that, Watson?"

"It's a common enough lash. But I don't know why it should be tied."

"That is not quite so common, is it? Ah, me! it's a wicked world, and when a clever man turns his brains to crime, it is the worst of all. I think that I have seen enough now, Miss Stoner, and with your permission we shall walk out upon the lawn."

> What does Holmes find odd about the dog lash? What might he infer from this clue?

I had never seen my friend's face so grim or his brow so dark as it was when we turned from the scene of this investigation. We had walked several times up and down the lawn, neither Miss Stoner nor myself liking to break in upon his thoughts before he roused himself from his <u>reverie</u>.

"It is very essential, Miss Stoner," said he, "that you should absolutely follow my advice in every respect."

"I shall most certainly do so."

"The matter is too serious for any hesitation. Your life may depend upon your <u>compliance</u>."

"I assure you that I am in your hands."

"In the first place, both my friend and I must spend the night in your room."

Both Miss Stoner and I gazed at him in astonishment.

"Yes, it must be so. Let me explain. I believe that that is the village inn over there?"

"Yes, that is the Crown."

"Very good. Your windows would be visible from there?"

"Certainly."

"You must confine yourself to your room, on pretence of a headache, when your stepfather comes back. Then when you hear him retire for the night, you must open the shutters of your window, undo the hasp,[26] put your lamp there as a signal to us, and then withdraw quietly with everything which you are likely to want into the room which you used to occupy. I have no doubt that, in spite of the repairs, you could manage there for one night."

"Oh, yes, easily."

"The rest you will leave in our hands."

"But what will you do?"

"We shall spend the night in your room, and we shall investigate the cause of this noise which has disturbed you."

"I believe, Mr. Holmes, that you have already made up your mind," said Miss Stoner, laying her hand upon my companion's sleeve.

"Perhaps I have."

"Then, for pity's sake, tell me what was the cause of my sister's death."

> Holmes seems at this point to have solved the mystery. Based on the details presented so far in the story, what do you think the solution to the mystery is?

"I should prefer to have clearer proofs before I speak."

"You can at least tell me whether my own thought is correct, and if she died from some sudden fright."

"No, I do not think so. I think that there was probably some more <u>tangible</u> cause. And now, Miss Stoner, we must leave you, for if Dr. Roylott returned and saw us, our journey would be in vain. Good-bye, and be brave, for if you will do what I have told you, you may rest assured that we shall soon drive away the dangers that threaten you."

Sherlock Holmes and I had no difficulty in engaging a bedroom and sitting room at the

---

25. **lash.** Leash
26. **hasp.** Latch (in this case, window latch)

words for everyday use

rev • er • ie (rev′ər ē) *n.*, daydream. *The student's <u>reverie</u> was interrupted by her teacher abruptly saying her name.*
com • pli • ance (kəm plī′əns) *n.*, giving in to a request. *Can we expect your <u>compliance</u> in following these new rules?*
tan • gi • ble (tan′jə bəl) *adj.*, definite; concrete. *These fresh tracks are <u>tangible</u> evidence that a wolf has been in the area.*

Crown Inn. They were on the upper floor, and from our window we could command a view of the avenue gate,[27] and of the inhabited wing of Stoke Moran Manor House. At dusk we saw Dr. Grimesby Roylott drive past, his huge form looming up beside the little figure of the lad who drove him. The boy had some slight difficulty in undoing the heavy iron gates, and we heard the hoarse roar of the doctor's voice and saw the fury with which he shook his clinched fists at him. The trap drove on, and a few minutes later we saw a sudden light spring up among the trees as the lamp was lit in one of the sitting rooms.

"Do you know, Watson," said Holmes as we sat together in the gathering darkness, "I have really some <u>scruples</u> as to taking you tonight. There is a distinct element of danger."

"Can I be of assistance?"

"Your presence might be <u>invaluable</u>."

"Then I shall certainly come."

"It is very kind of you."

"You speak of danger. You have evidently seen more in these rooms than was visible to me."

"No, but I fancy that I may have <u>deduced</u> a little more. I imagine that you saw all that I did."

"I saw nothing remarkable save the bell-rope, and what purpose that could answer I confess is more than I can imagine."

"You saw the ventilator, too?"

"Yes, but I do not think that it is such a very unusual thing to have a small opening between two rooms. It was so small that a rat could hardly pass through."

What might be small enough to pass through the ventilator?

"I knew that we should find a ventilator before ever we came to Stoke Moran."

"My dear Holmes!"

"Oh, yes, I did. You remember in her statement she said that her sister could smell Dr. Roylott's cigar. Now, of course that suggested at once that there must be a communication between the two rooms. It could only be a small one, or it would have been remarked upon at the coroner's inquiry. I deduced a ventilator."

"But what harm can there be in that?"

What detail led Holmes to infer the existence of the ventilator?

"Well, there is at least a curious coincidence of dates. A ventilator is made, a cord is hung, and a lady who sleeps in the bed dies. Does not that strike you?"

"I cannot as yet see any connection."

"Did you observe anything very peculiar about that bed?"

"No."

"It was clamped to the floor. Did you ever see a bed fastened like that before?"

"I cannot say that I have."

"The lady could not move her bed. It must always be in the same relative position to the ventilator and to the rope— or so we may call it, since it was clearly never meant for a bell-pull."

What had Holmes noticed about the bed? What explanation does he give Watson?

"Holmes," I cried, "I seem to see dimly what you are hinting at. We are only just in time to prevent some subtle and horrible crime."

"Subtle enough and horrible enough. When a doctor does go wrong he is the first of criminals. He has nerve and he has knowledge. Palmer and Pritchard[28] were among the heads of their profession. This man strikes even deeper, but I think, Watson, that we shall be able to

---

27. **avenue gate.** Gate between the manor's property and the public road
28. **Palmer and Pritchard.** Two English doctors accused of vicious crimes

---

words for everyday use

scru • ple (skrü´pəl) *n.*, doubt in deciding what is proper or ethical. *Her <u>scruples</u> led her to seek the advice of a minister.*

in • val • u • a • ble (in val´ yü ə bəl) *adj.*, priceless. *Although this ring isn't worth much money, I consider it <u>invaluable</u> because it belonged to my great-grandmother.*

de • duce (dē düs´) *vt.*, infer by logical reasoning. *The logician challenged his students to <u>deduce</u> the answer.*

1. A rat, or an animal smaller than it, might be small enough to pass through the ventilator.
2. The detail of Miss Stoner's sister being able to smell the doctor's cigar smoke led Holmes to infer the existence of a ventilator.
3. Holmes noticed that the bed was fastened to the floor. He explains that the bed was always in the same position relative to the ventilator and to the rope, or bell-pull.

1. Holmes has brought a cane, a box
of matches, and the stump of a
candle. *Responses will vary.* Students
might suggest that Holmes has
brought the candle and matches
for light and the cane for protection
or to help him walk.

LITERARY TECHNIQUE

SUSPENSE. **Suspense** is a feeling
of expectation, anxiousness, or
curiosity created by questions raised
in the mind of a reader or viewer.
What feeling is being created in this
scene? What questions is the reader
asking?
Answers
This scene creates a feeling of anxiousness about what Holmes and
Watson will find in Miss Stoner's
room, and whether they are in danger. The reader might be asking
questions such as: Will the doctor's
wild animals harm Holmes and
Watson? Do the animals have something to do with Julia's murder?
What will happen in the dark room?
Will Dr. Watson have to use his
pistol?

ADDITIONAL QUESTIONS
AND ACTIVITIES

Some students might like to
work in pairs to create a sound-
effects tape for a radio presentation of "The Adventure of the
Speckled Band." First, have them
make a photocopy of the story and
note in the margins what sounds
would be appropriate at different
points. Next they should jot down
ideas for how they will create these
sounds. If students have access to
recording equipment, have them
make a sample tape on which they
record short sections of dialogue or
narrative along with the appropriate
sound effects.

strike deeper still. But we shall have horrors
enough before the night is over; for goodness'
sake let us have a quiet pipe and turn our minds
for a few hours to something more cheerful."

About nine o'clock the light among the
trees was extinguished, and all was dark
in the direction of the Manor House.
Two hours passed slowly away, and then, suddenly, just at the stroke of eleven, a single bright
light shone out right in front of us.

"That is our signal," said Holmes, springing
to his feet; "it comes from the middle window."

As we passed out, he exchanged a few words
with the landlord, explaining that we were
going on a late visit to an acquaintance and that
it was possible that we might spend the night
there. A moment later we were out on the dark
road, a chill wind blowing in our faces and one
yellow light twinkling in front of us through
the gloom to guide us on our <u>somber</u> errand.

There was little difficulty in entering the
grounds, for unrepaired breaches gaped in the
old park wall. Making our way among the trees,
we reached the lawn, crossed it, and were about
to enter through the window when out from a
clump of laurel bushes there darted what
seemed to be a hideous and distorted child, who
threw itself upon the grass with writhing limbs
and then ran swiftly across the lawn into the
darkness.

"My God!" I whispered; "did you see it?"

Holmes was for the moment as startled as I.
His hand closed like a vise upon my wrist in his
agitation. Then he broke into a low laugh and
put his lips to my ear.

"It is a nice household," he murmured. "That
is the baboon."

I had forgotten the strange pets which the
doctor affected. There was a cheetah, too; per-

haps we might find it upon our shoulders at any
moment. I confess that I felt easier in my mind
when, after following Holmes's example and
slipping off my shoes, I found myself inside the
bedroom. My companion noiselessly closed the
shutters, moved the lamp onto the table, and
cast his eyes round the room. All was as we had
seen it in the daytime. Then creeping up to me
and making a trumpet of his hand, he whispered
into my ear again so gently that it was all that I
could do to distinguish the words:

"The least sound would be fatal to our plans."

I nodded to show that I had heard.

"We must sit without light. He would see it
through the ventilator."

I nodded again.

"Do not go asleep; your very life may depend
upon it. Have your pistol ready in case we
should need it. I will sit on the side of the bed,
and you in that chair."

I took out my revolver and laid it on the corner of the table.

Holmes had brought up a long thin cane, and
this he placed upon the bed beside him. By it he
laid the box of matches and the stump of a candle. Then he turned down the lamp, and we
were left in darkness.

> What items has Holmes
> brought in preparation
> for their vigil? Why do
> you think he brought
> these things?

How shall I ever forget
that dreadful <u>vigil</u>? I could
not hear a sound, not even
the drawing of a breath,
and yet I knew that my companion sat open
eyed, within a few feet of me, in the same state
of nervous tension in which I was myself. The
shutters cut off the least ray of light, and we
waited in absolute darkness. From outside came
the occasional cry of a night bird, and once at
our very window a long drawn catlike whine,
which told us that the cheetah was indeed at liberty. Far away we could hear the deep tones of

---

**words
for
everyday
use**

som • ber (säm´bər) *adj.,* dark and gloomy. *The <u>somber</u> movie opens with a shot of an abandoned castle at night.*
vig • il (vij´əl) *n.,* purposeful staying awake during the usual hours of sleep. *We should take turns keeping <u>vigil</u> while
we camp.*

the parish clock, which boomed out every quarter of an hour. How long they seemed, those quarters! Twelve struck, and one and two and three, and still we sat waiting silently for whatever might befall.

Suddenly there was the momentary gleam of a light up in the direction of the ventilator, which vanished immediately, but was succeeded by a strong smell of burning oil and heated metal. Someone in the next room had lit a dark-lantern. I heard a gentle sound of movement, and then all was silent once more, though the smell grew stronger. For half an hour I sat with straining ears. Then suddenly another sound became audible—a very gentle, soothing sound, like that of a small jet of steam escaping continually from a kettle. The instant that we heard it, Holmes sprang from the bed, struck a match, and lashed furiously with his cane at the bell-pull.

> **What sound do Holmes and Watson hear? What is Holmes's reaction? What second sound do they hear?**

"You see it, Watson?" he yelled. "You see it?"

But I saw nothing. At the moment when Holmes struck the light I heard a low, clear whistle, but the sudden glare flashing into my weary eyes made it impossible for me to tell what it was at which my friend lashed so savagely. I could, however, see that his face was deadly pale and filled with horror and <u>loathing</u>.

He had ceased to strike and was gazing up at the ventilator when suddenly there broke from the silence of the night the most horrible cry to which I have ever listened. It swelled up louder and louder, a hoarse yell of pain and fear and anger all mingled in the one dreadful shriek. They say that away down in the village, and even in the distant parsonage,[29] that cry raised the sleepers from their beds. It struck cold to our hearts, and I stood gazing at Holmes, and he at me, until the last echoes of it had died away into the silence from which it rose.

"What can it mean?" I gasped.

"It means that it is all over," Holmes answered. "And perhaps, after all, it is for the best. Take your pistol, and we will enter Dr. Roylott's room."

> **What do you think has happened?**

With a grave face he lit the lamp and led the way down the corridor. Twice he struck at the chamber door without any reply from within. Then he turned the handle and entered, I at his heels, with the cocked pistol in my hand.

It was a singular sight which met our eyes. On the table stood a dark-lantern with the shutter half open, throwing a brilliant beam of light upon the iron safe, the door of which was ajar. Beside this table, on the wooden chair, sat Dr. Grimesby Roylott, clad in a long gray dressing-gown, his bare ankles <u>protruding</u> beneath, and his feet thrust into red heelless Turkish slippers.[30] Across his lap lay the short stock with the long lash which we had noticed during the day. His chin was cocked upward and his eyes were fixed in a dreadful, rigid stare at the corner of the ceiling. Round his brow he had a peculiar yellow band, with brownish speckles, which seemed to be bound tightly round his head. As we entered he made neither sound nor motion.

"The band! the speckled band!" whispered Holmes.

I took a step forward. In an instant his strange headgear began to move, and there reared itself from among his hair the squat diamond-shaped head and puffed neck of a loathsome serpent.

---

29. **parsonage.** Home of a parson, or minister
30. **Turkish slippers.** House slippers of the kind made or worn in Turkey

---

words for everyday use	
	loath • ing (lōth′ iŋ) *n.*, intense hatred; disgust. *The animal trainer coaxed students to overcome their <u>loathing</u> of snakes.*
	pro • trude (prō trüd′) *vt.*, thrust out. *The child's mittened hands, <u>protruding</u> stiffly from her coat, looked like paws.*

ANSWERS TO GUIDED READING QUESTIONS

1. It is dangerous to draw conclusions upon insufficient data because such conclusions are often wrong.
2. His observation that no one could enter the room from the outside caused Holmes to reject his first theory about the murder.

SELECTION CHECK TEST 4.12.5 WITH ANSWERS

Checking Your Reading

1. Whose death does Miss Stoner wish Sherlock Holmes to investigate, and where did this person die? **She wishes him to investigate the death of her sister, Julia, who died in her bedroom at the family's estate, Stoke Moran.**
2. What noise did the victim hear in the dead of night? What were her last words before she died? What noises did Miss Stoner hear on the night the victim died? **The victim, Julia, heard a whistle in the dead of night. Her last words were, "It was the band! The speckled band!" Miss Stoner heard the whistle and a metallic clanging sound.**
3. Who stands to benefit from the deaths of Miss Stoner and her sister? Explain. **Miss Stoner's stepfather, Dr. Roylott, stands to benefit from the deaths of his two stepdaughters, because if they die they will not collect their inheritance, leaving more money for him.**
4. What three strange details does Sherlock Holmes notice when inspecting Miss Stoner's bedroom? **He notices a ventilator that leads to the next room rather than outside; a bell-pull that is not connected to any bell; and he notices that the bed is bolted to the floor.**
5. What was the speckled band? Who was guilty of the murder, and how did he accomplish it? **The speckled band was actually a deadly snake from India. Dr. Roylott was guilty of the murder. He sent the snake through the ventilator, from whence it crept down the false bell-rope and bit Julia.**

Vocabulary in Context

Fill in each blank below with the most appropriate word from the following Words for Everyday Use. You may have to change the tense of the word.

"It is a swamp adder!" cried Holmes; "the deadliest snake in India. He has died within ten seconds of being bitten. Violence does, in truth, <u>recoil</u> upon the violent, and the schemer falls into the pit which he digs for another. Let us thrust this creature back into its den, and we can then remove Miss Stoner to some place of shelter and let the county police know what has happened."

As he spoke he drew the dog-whip swiftly from the dead man's lap, and throwing the noose round the reptile's neck he drew it from its horrid perch and, carrying it at arm's length, threw it into the iron safe, which he closed upon it.

Such are the true facts of the death of Dr. Grimesby Roylott, of Stoke Moran. It is not necessary that I should <u>prolong</u> a narrative which has already run to too great a length by telling how we broke the sad news to the terrified girl, how we conveyed her by the morning train to the care of her good aunt at Harrow, of how the slow process of official inquiry came to the conclusion that the doctor met his fate while indiscreetly playing with a dangerous pet. The little which I had yet to learn of the case was told me by Sherlock Holmes as we traveled back next day.

"I had," said he, "come to an entirely <u>erroneous</u> conclusion which shows, my dear Watson how dangerous it always is to reason from insufficient data. The presence of the gypsies, and the use of the word 'band,' which was used by the poor girl, no doubt to explain the appearance which she had caught a hurried glimpse of by the light of her match, were sufficient to put me upon an entirely wrong scent. I can only claim the merit that I instantly reconsidered my position when, however, it became clear to me that whatever

Why is it dangerous to draw conclusions upon insufficient data?

danger threatened an occupant of the room could not come either from the window or the door. My attention was speedily drawn, as I have already remarked to you, to this ventilator, and to the bell-rope which hung down to the bed. The discovery that this was a dummy, and that the bed was clamped to the floor, instantly gave rise to the suspicion that the rope was there as a bridge for something passing through the hole and coming to the bed. The idea of a snake instantly occurred to me, and when I coupled it with my knowledge that the doctor was furnished with a supply of creatures from India, I felt that I was probably on the right track. The idea of using a form of poison which could not possibly be discovered by any chemical test was just such a one as would occur to a clever and ruthless man who had had an Eastern training. The rapidity with which such a poison would take effect would also, from his point of view, be an advantage. It would be a sharp-eyed coroner, indeed, who could distinguish the two little dark punctures which would show where the poison fangs had done their work. Then I thought of the whistle. Of course he must recall the snake before the morning light revealed it to the victim. He had trained it, probably by the use of the milk which we saw, to return to him when summoned. He would put it through this ventilator at the hour that he thought best, with the certainty that it would crawl down the rope and land on the bed. It might or might not bite the occupant; perhaps she might escape every night for a week, but sooner or later she must fall a victim.

"I had come to these conclusions before ever I had entered his room. An inspection of his chair showed me that he had been in the habit of

What observation caused Holmes to reject his first theory about the murder?

---

words for everyday use

re • coil (ri koil´) *vi.*, spring back. *Deathly afraid of spiders, the man <u>recoiled</u> when he saw the tarantula.*
pro • long (prō lôŋ´) *vt.*, lengthen or extend in time. *The school year will be <u>prolonged</u> because of several snow days.*
er • ro • ne • ous (ər rō´nē əs) *adj.*, mistaken, wrong. *Some people in the fourteenth century held the <u>erroneous</u> belief that the world was flat.*

954 UNIT TWELVE / OTHER WORLDS

SELECTION CHECK TEST 4.12.5 WITH ANSWERS (CONT.)

averse   dissolute   sear   deduction   manifold
aperture   tangible   impending

1. The **aperture** in the wall of the fort enabled soldiers to shoot at the enemy while being shielded from counterattack.
2. The detective believed the suspect was guilty, but was unable to prove it without having found **tangible** evidence, such as a dropped item or fingerprints, at the scene of the crime.
3. Stan was **averse** to hard work, and would avoid it whenever possible.
4. Benjamin Franklin's legacy to American society was **manifold**: he passed down witticisms and philosophy, discoveries, inventions, and theories.
5. The details of the accident were **seared** in the driver's memory—it was impossible for her to forget.

standing on it, which of course would be necessary in order that he should reach the ventilator. The sight of the safe, the saucer of milk, and the loop of whipcord were enough to finally <u>dispel</u> any doubts which may have remained. The metallic clang heard by Miss Stoner was obviously caused by her stepfather hastily closing the door of his safe upon its terrible occupant. Having once made up my mind, you know the steps which I took in order to put the matter to the proof. I heard the creature hiss as

What clues did Holmes use to confirm his theory?

I have no doubt that you did also, and I instantly lit the light and attacked it."

"With the result of driving it through the ventilator."

"And also with the result of causing it to turn upon its master at the other side. Some of the blows of my cane came home and roused its snakish temper, so that it flew upon the first person it saw. In this way I am no doubt indirectly responsible for Dr. Grimesby Roylott's death, and I cannot say that it is likely to weigh very heavily upon my conscience." ■

words for everyday use

 dis • pel (di spel´) *vt.*, cause to vanish or disappear. *Learning more about sharks helped me <u>dispel</u> my misconceptions.*

Respond *to the* **SELECTION**

From Miss Stoner's narrative, what guesses did you make about the cause of her death? What do you think of Holmes's reasoning? Do you detect any flaws in explanation?

ANSWER TO GUIDED READING QUESTION

1. Holmes used the following clues: the chair, the sight of the safe, the saucer of milk, the loop of whipcord, and the metallic clang that Miss Stoner heard.

SELECTION CHECK TEST 4.12.5 WITH ANSWERS (CONT.)

Literary Tools
Fill in the blanks using the following terms. You may not use every term, and you may use some terms more than once.

resolution   plot   conflict   narrator
   climax   inciting incident

1. A **plot** is a series of events related to a central conflict, or struggle.
2. The **narrator** of this story is Dr. Watson, Sherlock Holmes's sidekick.
3. The **climax** of a story is the high point of interest or suspense in the plot.

RESPOND TO THE SELECTION

Some students might take issue with the assumption that the snake would inevitably bite a sleeping human.

RECALL

1a. On the night of Julia's death, she hears a low whistle and then a clanging sound.

2a. The bell-rope is a dummy; it does not ring.

3a. The "speckled band" is a swamp adder, "the deadliest snake in India."

INTERPRET

1b. The three events that prompt Miss Stoner's urgent visit to Holmes are her engagement, her move into her sister's room, and the sound of a low whistle in the night. These are the same circumstances that preceded her sister's death.

2b. The facts that suggest a horrible crime to Holmes are a bed that is clamped to the floor, the dummy bell-pull, and a ventilator going to a room next door instead of to the outside. Holmes infers that these three elements "must always be in the same relative position" in preparation for a horrible crime.

3b. The "erroneous conclusion" is the idea that the band of gypsies camping on the estate had something to do with Julia's death. This conclusion was based on the presence of the gypsies, with whom the doctor was on close terms, and on Julia's reference to a "band" in her dying words.

ANALYZE

4a. Dr. Grimesby Roylott is a violent man with a short temper. He is motivated by greed to murder one stepdaughter and to attempt the murder of the other. If either of his stepdaughters marries, according to his wife's will they will each inherit a large part of the family fortune. By murdering them, he will prevent their marriages and thus ensure his control of his wife's fortune.

SYNTHESIZE

4b. Dr. Roylott was an intelligent man who earned a medical degree in India. He is clever in devising an intricate plan for a murder that makes use of his specialized knowledge. The situation is the "worst of all" because as an intelligent man, he is capable of concealing the murder so cleverly that he nearly gets away with it.

EVALUATE

5a. *Responses will vary.*

EXTEND

5b. *Responses will vary.*

Investigate, *Inquire* and Imagine

Recall: GATHERING FACTS ➔

1a. What two sounds does Miss Stoner hear on the night of Julia's death?

2a. What is unusual about the bell-rope?

3a. What is "the speckled band"?

Interpret: FINDING MEANING

1b. What three events cause Miss Stoner to fear for her life and prompt her urgent visit to Holmes?

2b. What facts about the furnishings in Miss Stoner's bedroom suggest a horrible crime to Holmes?

3b. What "erroneous conclusion" reminds Holmes of the dangers of reasoning from "insufficient data"?

Analyze: TAKING THINGS APART ➔

4a. What kind of man is Dr. Grimesby Roylott? What motivates him to commit such horrible crimes?

Synthesize: BRINGING THINGS TOGETHER

4b. Holmes says, "Ah me! it's a wicked world, and when a clever man turns his brains to crime, it is the worst of all." In what ways does this quote apply to Dr. Roylott?

Perspective: LOOKING AT OTHER VIEWS ➔

5a. Pretend Holmes went to trial for the murder of Dr. Roylott. Imagine you are the judge. Would you find him guilty or innocent of the murder? Why, or why not?

Empathy: SEEING FROM INSIDE

5b. Imagine you are Holmes. Would you feel guilty for being indirectly responsible for Dr. Roylott's death? Why, or why not?

Understanding *Literature*

NARRATOR. Review the definition of **narrator** in Literary Tools in Prereading on page 936. A narrator is one who tells a story. Who is the narrator of this story? What is that narrator's relationship to the main character? What special circumstances give this narrator access to the details related in the story?

PLOT AND CONFLICT. Review the definition of **plot** and **conflict** in the Handbook of Literary Terms. A plot is a series of events related to a central conflict, or struggle. In this story, what is the struggle that the main character undertakes? What techniques does the main character use to resolve the conflict?

ANSWERS TO UNDERSTANDING LITERATURE

NARRATOR. The narrator is Dr. Watson. He is assistant and friend to Sherlock Holmes. This narrator has worked with Holmes over the last eight years on more than seventy cases, including the case of the speckled band. He has access to the details related in the story because he was sharing rooms with Holmes at the time and was involved in the case.

PLOT AND CONFLICT. The struggle that Sherlock Holmes undertakes is the struggle to reveal the murderer of his

client's sister. Holmes uses questioning, observation, forming and testing hypotheses, research, and reasoning (deduction) to resolve the conflict. For example, Holmes observes the details of Julia's room from the outside as well as from the inside. He also observes Dr. Roylott's room. He connects the details he has heard from Miss Stoner, including the fact that Dr. Roylott acquired animals from India. Holmes then uses these direct observations to make his deductions and solve the mystery of Julia's death.

Writer's Journal

1. Create three possible **headlines** used for a newspaper article that might be written about the night's events that took place at the Stoke Moran Manor House.
2. Imagine you are a coroner. Write a **death report** describing the cause of Dr. Roylott's death.
3. Pretend you are Helen Stoner. Write a **thank-you letter** to both Holmes and Watson for destroying your fears and saving your life.

Integrating the Language Arts

Language, Grammar, and Style

USING QUOTATION MARKS. Use quotation marks in your writing to enclose the exact words spoken by a person or character. Read the Language Arts Survey 3.92, "Quotation Marks," for more information. Then copy the sentences below, adding quotation marks where needed.

1. I'm very sorry to wake you, said Holmes, but we need to get started with the investigation.
2. Watson said, I am willing to help you in any way you need.
3. My name is Helen Stoner, said the woman with fear on her face.
4. My dear fellow, Watson said in earnest, I would not miss it for the world.
5. It is a swamp adder! cried Holmes; the most poisonous snake in India!

Study and Research

FAN CLUB. More than a century after first appearing in print, the character of Sherlock Holmes is enthusiastically kept alive by devoted readers and fan clubs. One of the most well-known clubs in the United States is the Baker Street Irregulars in New York. You can learn about this and other American Sherlockian societies at the San Francisco Sherlockian Societies Home Page (http://www.lafterhall.com/sherlock.html). You may also visit the website of The Sherlock Holmes Society of London at http://www. sherlock-holmes.org.uk. As a class, research the Baker Street Irregulars and the Sherlock Holmes Society of London and find the names and addresses of other clubs devoted to Sherlock Holmes. Form small groups, assigning one club to each group, and write a letter to the club's president. In your letter, explain your group's interest in the club and request information regarding the club's history, activities, and membership. Refer to Language Arts Survey 5.26, "Using the Internet" to help you in your research.

Collaborative Learning

DETECTIVE STORY. Working with a partner, write a detective story involving a detective and his "sidekick." Remember that a detective story is a form of narrative fiction that focuses on crimes and their solutions. Before you begin to write, brainstorm crimes you may want to explore and ways in which the crimes could be solved. Then make a list of characters you want to create. Finally, put it all together by establishing a setting that is appropriate with the tone of your story.

ANSWERS TO INTEGRATING THE LANGUAGE ARTS

Language, Grammar, and Style

1. "I'm very sorry to wake you," said Holmes, "but we need to get started with the investigation."
2. Watson said, "I am willing to help you in any way you need."
3. "My name is Helen Stoner," said the woman with fear on her face.
4. "My dear fellow," Watson said in earnest, "I would not miss it for the world."
5. "It is a swamp adder!" cried Holmes; "the most poisonous snake in India!"

Study and Research & Collaborative Learning

Assign a score from 1 to 25 for each grading criterion below. (For more detailed evaluation, see the evaluation forms for writing, revising, and proofreading in the Assessment Resource book.)

1. FAN CLUB—BUSINESS LETTER
   CONTENT/UNITY. The body of the letter gives a reason for writing and requests information about the club's history, activities, and membership. The address of the fan club is correct.
   ORGANIZATION/COHERENCE. The main points in the body of the letter are presented clearly and concisely.
   LANGUAGE/STYLE. The letter uses formal language and an appropriate salutation and closing.
   CONVENTIONS. The letter is typed in a standard business letter form and avoids errors in spelling, grammar, usage, and mechanics.

2. DETECTIVE STORY
   CONTENT/UNITY. The story features a detective and his or her sidekick, a crime that they solve, and a distinctive setting.
   ORGANIZATION/COHERENCE. The story has a clear plot, including an exposition, rising action, climax, and denouement, and the characters behave consistently throughout the story.
   LANGUAGE/STYLE. The language of the story contributes to the story's tone.
   CONVENTIONS. The story avoids errors in spelling, grammar, usage, mechanics, and manuscript form.

ADDITIONAL RESOURCES

UNIT 12 RESOURCE BOOK
- Selection Worksheet 12.4
- Selection Check Test 4.12.7
- Selection Test 4.12.8

GRAPHIC ORGANIZER

Students may include the following details in their charts:

Sight: "tomb-like building," "skeletal pattern" of a leaf, streets like "dry river beds," uneven sidewalk, "fierce white cone of light," "a little black jail with bars," one house with "all of its electric lights brightly lit"

Hearing: "whisperings and murmurs," "faint push of his soft shoes through autumn leaves," "cold, quiet whistle between his teeth," "cloverleaf intersection which stood silent," "thunderous surge of cars," "metallic voice called to him," "...its radio throat faintly humming," "a faint whirring click"

Touch/Feeling: "good crystal frost in the air . . . cut the nose and made the lungs blaze," "there was nothing soft there [in the police car]"

Taste: No details given

Smell: "rusty smell" of fallen leaves, "...a faint incense puttering from their exhausts," police car "smelled of riveted steel . . . of harsh antiseptic"

READER'S JOURNAL

As an alternate activity, ask students if they think television will be more important or less important in people's lives fifty years from now. Have them explain the reasons for their prediction.

VOCABULARY FROM THE SELECTION

alibi	revue
illumination	riveted
jockey	

Literary TOOLS

MOOD. **Mood,** or **atmosphere**, is the emotion created in the reader by part or all of a literary work. Think about what emotions you feel as you read this story.

SETTING. The **setting** of a literary work is the time and place in which it occurs, together with all the details used to create a sense of a particular time and place. Note the details Bradbury uses to create this unusual setting.

Graphic Organizer

Make a sensory details chart like the one below. As you read the story, record the various details that give you a better sense of the particular time and place of the setting and the mood evoked.

Sight	"...it was not unequal to walking through a graveyard where only the faintest glimmers of firefly light appeared in flickers behind the windows."
Hearing	
Touch/ Feeling	
Taste	
Smell	

"The Pedestrian"
by Ray Bradbury

Reader's resource

Science fiction is highly imaginative fiction containing fantastic elements based upon scientific principles, discoveries, or laws. Often, science fiction deals with the future, the distant past, or with worlds other than our own. The genre allows writers to suspend or alter certain elements of reality in order to create fascinating and sometimes instructive alternatives. **"The Pedestrian"** is set in the year AD 2053. As you read the selection, consider the ways in which the world Bradbury created is similar to the world you know.

About the AUTHOR

Ray Bradbury (1920–   ) was born in Waukegan, Illinois. Best known for his science fiction and fantasy stories, he has published scores of books, including novels, children's books, and collections of short stories, poetry, and plays. Bradbury's science fiction stories offer social criticism and warnings against the dangers of losing control of technology. For his work in science fiction and fantasy, he has won the World Fantasy Award for lifetime achievement and the Grand Master Award from the Science Fiction Writers of America.

Reader's Journal

What do you think an automated world might be like?

GOALS/OBJECTIVES

Studying this lesson will enable students to
- empathize with a character's feelings about his world
- describe Ray Bradbury's literary accomplishments and the social themes of his writings
- explain the elements of science fiction and identify and interpret these in a literary work

- define *mood* and *setting* and recognize their function in the selection
- write a police report, a prediction, and a poem
- plan a celebration of reading, research recent scientific discoveries on the Internet, and experience a TV-free week and write an essay about their efforts

Night Shadows, 1921. Edward Hopper. Whitney Museum of American Art, New York.

The PEDESTRIAN

Ray Bradbury

To enter out into that silence that was the city at eight o'clock of a misty evening in November, to put your feet upon that buckling concrete walk, to step over grassy seams and make your way, hands in pockets, through the silences, that was what Mr. Leonard Mead most dearly loved to do. He would stand upon the corner of an intersection and peer down long moonlit avenues of sidewalk in four directions, deciding which way to go, but it really made no difference; he was alone in this world of AD 2053, or as good as alone, and with a final decision made, a path selected, he would stride off, sending patterns of frosty air before him like the smoke of a cigar.

Sometimes he would walk for hours and miles and return only at midnight to his house. And on his way he would see the cottages and homes with their dark windows, and it was not unequal to walking through a graveyard where only the

> Who else is in Leonard's world? What might the phrase "as good as alone" indicate?

"THE PEDESTRIAN" 959

1. Leonard compares walking through
   the dark city to walking through a
   graveyard.
2. He imagines himself to be in the
   center of a wintry, windless
   American desert plain.
3. He has never met another person
   walking in his ten years of walking
   by night or day.
4. Leonard is stunned and entranced
   by the light the police car shines on
   him.

INTERNET RESOURCES

Students can learn more about
Ray Bradbury's life, works, and
awards at the **Brookings Books Ray
Bradbury Page**, http://www.brook-
ingsbook.

ADDITIONAL QUESTIONS
AND ACTIVITIES

What does Leonard seem to enjoy
about his walks?
Answer
He seems to enjoy the physical sensations, the quietness, and contact
with nature.

---

faintest glimmers of firefly light appeared in
flickers behind the win-
dows. Sudden gray phan-
toms seemed to manifest
upon inner room walls
where a curtain was still undrawn against the
night, or there were whisperings and murmurs
where a window in a tomb-like building was still
open.

To what does Leonard compare walking through the dark city?

Mr. Leonard Mead would pause, cock his
head, listen, look, and march on, his feet making
no noise on the lumpy walk. For long ago he
had wisely changed to sneakers when strolling
at night, because the dogs in intermittent squads
would parallel his journey with barkings if he
wore hard heels, and lights might click on and
faces appear and an entire street be startled by
the passing of a lone figure, himself, in the early
November evening.

On this particular evening he began his journey in a westerly direction, toward the hidden
sea. There was a good crystal frost in the air; it
cut the nose and made the lungs blaze like a
Christmas tree inside; you could feel the cold
light going on and off, all the branches filled
with invisible snow. He listened to the faint
push of his soft shoes through autumn leaves
with satisfaction, and whistled a cold quiet whistle between his teeth, occasionally picking up a
leaf as he passed, examining its skeletal pattern
in the infrequent lamplights as he went on,
smelling its rusty smell.

"Hello, in there," he whispered to every house
on every side as he moved. "What's up tonight
on Channel 4, Channel 7, Channel 9? Where
are the cowboys rushing, and do I see the
United States Cavalry over the next hill to the
rescue?"

The street was silent and long and empty, with
only his shadow moving like the shadow of a
hawk in midcountry. If he closed his eyes and
stood very still, frozen, he could imagine himself
upon the center of a plain, a
wintry, windless American
desert with no house in a
thousand miles, and only dry river beds, the
streets, for company.

Where does Leonard imagine himself to be?

"What is it now?" he asked the houses, noticing his wrist watch. "Eight-thirty P.M.? Time for
a dozen assorted murders? A quiz? A <u>revue</u>? A
comedian falling off the stage?"

Was that a murmur of laughter from within a
moonwhite house? He hesitated, but went on
when nothing more happened. He stumbled
over a particularly uneven section of sidewalk.
The cement was vanishing under flowers and
grass. In ten years of walk-
ing by night or day, for
thousands of miles, he had
never met another person
walking, not once in all that time.

What has Leonard noticed that is strange about his walks?

He came to a cloverleaf intersection which
stood silent where two main highways crossed
the town. During the day it was a thunderous
surge of cars, the gas stations open, a great
insect rustling and a ceaseless <u>jockeying</u> for
position as the scarab-beetles,[1] a faint incense
puttering from their exhausts, skimmed homeward to the far directions. But now these highways, too, were like streams in a dry season, all
stone and bed and moon radiance.

He turned back on a side street, circling
around toward his home. He was within a block
of his destination when the lone car turned a
corner quite suddenly and flashed a fierce white
cone of light upon him. He
stood entranced, not unlike

How does Leonard react to seeing the police car?

---

1. **scarab-beetles.** Any of a family of large, brightly colored
beetles

**words
for
everyday
use**

re • vue (ri vyü´) *n.*, musical show parodying topical matters. *In the highly amusing political <u>revue</u> now playing at an
off-Broadway theater, the politicians look like wolves who prey on sheeplike voters.*
jock • ey (jäk´ē) *vi.*, maneuver, as for position or advantage. *As the marathon began, thousands of runners began
<u>jockeying</u> for the best position.*

a night moth, stunned by the <u>illumination</u>, and then drawn toward it.

A metallic voice called to him:

"Stand still. Stay where you are! Don't move!"

He halted.

"Put up your hands!"

"But—" he said.

"Your hands up! Or we'll shoot!"

The police, of course, but what a rare, incredible thing; in a city of three million, there was only *one* police car left, wasn't that correct? Ever since a year ago, 2052, the election year, the force had been cut down from three cars to one. Crime was ebbing; there was no need now for the police, save for this one lone car wandering and wandering the empty streets.

"Your name?" said the police car in a metallic whisper. He couldn't see the men in it for the bright light in his eyes.

"Leonard Mead," he said.

"Speak up!"

"Leonard Mead!"

"Business or profession?"

"I guess you'd call me a writer."

"No profession," said the police car, as if talking to itself. The light held him fixed, like a museum specimen, needle thrust through chest.

"You might say that," said Mr. Mead. He hadn't written in years. Magazines and books didn't sell any more. Everything went on in the tomblike houses at night now, he thought, continuing his fancy. The tombs, ill-lit by television light, where the people sat like the dead, the gray or multicolored lights touching their faces, but never really touching *them*.

"Stand still. Stay where you are! Don't move!"

"No profession," said the phonograph voice, hissing. "What are you doing out?"

"Walking," said Leonard Mead.

"Walking!"

"Just walking," he said simply, but his face felt cold.

"Walking, just walking, walking?"

"Yes sir."

"Walking where? For what?"

"Walking for air. Walking to see."

"Your address!"

"Eleven South Saint James Street."

"And there is air *in* your house, you have an *air conditioner*, Mr. Mead?"

"Yes."

"And you have a viewing screen in your house to see with?"

"No."

"No?" There was a crackling quiet that in itself was an accusation.

"Are you married, Mr. Mead?"

"No."

"Not married," said the police voice behind the fiery beam. The moon was high and clear among the stars and the houses were gray and silent.

"Nobody wanted me," said Leonard Mead with a smile.

"Don't speak unless you're spoken to!"

Leonard Mead waited in the cold night.

"Just *walking*, Mr. Mead?"

"Yes."

"But you haven't explained for what purpose."

"I explained; for air, and to see, and just to walk."

"Have you done this often?"

Why does Leonard walk?

words for everyday use

il • lu • mi • na • tion (i lü′mə nā′shən) *n.*, lighting up. *The powerful lights of the helicopter cast a bright <u>illumination</u> on the smugglers in the boat below.*

1. He walks for air, to see, and just to walk.

CROSS-CURRICULAR CONNECTIONS

TECHNOLOGY. Bradbury wrote this story before the advent of personal computers or cable television. For example, in describing the sounds of the police car, he refers to "punch-slotted" cards. Punch cards, perforated with tiny slots that encode information, were used for entering data into early computers.

Bradbury (on page 960) also refers to just three television channel numbers as well as the types of programs that were common in the 1960s. Today many households have access to dozens of television channels transmitted by cable or satellite and thousands of programs of every type.

1. He notices that no one is in the car.
2. Unlike the other houses in the city, Leonard's house is brightly lit.

SELECTION CHECK TEST 4.12.7 WITH ANSWERS

Checking Your Reading

1. What does Leonard Mead like to do at night? **He likes to go for walks.**
2. What do the other people in his city do at night? **They stay inside and watch television.**
3. What does Leonard say to explain to the police car why he is out walking at night? Why doesn't the car believe him? **Leonard says that he goes out for air and to see things. The police car doesn't believe him because it thinks he should have enough air from his air conditioner and should be able to see anything he wants on his "viewing screen," or television.**
4. What does Leonard notice about the police car when he approaches it? **He notices there is nobody inside the police car.**
5. Where does the police car take Leonard? **It takes him to the "Psychiatric Center for Research on Regressive Tendencies."**

Vocabulary in Context
Fill in each blank below with the most appropriate word from the following Words for Everyday Use. You may have to change the tense of the word.

illumination   jockey   alibi
riveted   revue

1. The huge neon sign cast a red **illumination** into the windows across the street.
2. The reporters **jockeyed** for the best vantage point from which to photograph the celebrity.
3. When my parents asked who had left the mess in the kitchen, I pointed out that I had an **alibi**: I had been at the softball tournament all day.

Literary Tools
1. What is *mood*? **Mood, or atmosphere, is the emotion created in the reader by part or all of a literary work.**
2. How does a writer create mood? **A writer can create mood through descriptive language and sensory details.**

"Every night for years."

The police car sat in the center of the street with its radio throat faintly humming.

"Well, Mr. Mead," it said.

"Is that all?" he asked politely.

"Yes," said the voice. "Here." There was a sigh, a pop. The back door of the police car sprang wide. "Get in."

"Wait a minute, I haven't done anything!"

"Get in."

"I protest!"

"Mr. Mead."

He walked like a man suddenly drunk. As he passed the front window of the car he looked in. As he had expected there was no one in the front seat, no one in the car at all.

> *What does he notice as he approaches the car?*

"Get in."

He put his hand to the door and peered into the back seat, which was a little cell, a little black jail with bars. It smelled of <u>riveted</u> steel. It smelled of harsh antiseptic; it smelled too clean and hard and metallic. There was nothing soft there.

"Now if you had a wife to give you an <u>alibi</u>," said the iron voice. "But—"

"Where are you taking me?"

The car hesitated, or rather gave a faint whirring click, as if information, somewhere, was dropping card by punch-slotted card[2] under electric eyes. "To the Psychiatric Center for Research on Regressive Tendencies."[3]

He got in. The door shut with a soft thud. The police car rolled through the night avenues, flashing its dim lights ahead.

They passed one house on one street a moment later, one house in an entire city of houses that were dark, but this one particular house had all of its electric lights brightly lit, every window a loud yellow illumination, square and warm in the cool darkness.

"That's *my* house," said Leonard Mead.

No one answered him.

The car moved down the empty river-bed streets and off away, leaving the empty streets with empty sidewalks, and no sound and no motion all the rest of the chill November night. ∎

> *What is different about Leonard's house?*

---

2. **puncch-slotted card.** Cards with tiny perforations were used for entering data in early computers.
3. **Regressive Tendencies.** Moving back to earlier behavior patterns or habits

words for everyday use

riv • et • ed (rivʹit əd) *adj.*, fastened with metal pins called rivets. *Bridges are commonly made of <u>riveted</u> steel beams.*
al • i • bi (alʹə bīʹ) *n.*, excuse; proof of activities. *When I accused Dwight of robbing the candy machine, he offered as his <u>alibi</u> the evidence that he had been on vacation with his family at the time of the crime.*

Respond *to the* SELECTION

What do you find most disturbing about the world in which Mr. Mead lives?

SELECTION CHECK TEST 4.12.7 WITH ANSWERS (CONT.)

3. What is setting? What is the setting of "The Pedestrian"? **The setting of a literary work is the time and place in which it occurs, together with all the details used to create a sense of a particular time and place. The setting of "The Pedestrian" is outside in a city at night, in the year AD 2053.**

RESPOND TO THE SELECTION

As an alternate activity, take a class poll to find out how many hours per day students spend watching television on average and how many hours they spend walking or doing some other type of physical activity.

Investigate, Inquire, and Imagine

Recall: GATHERING FACTS

1a. What does Leonard Mead like to do at night? What does he learn to do to be less noticeable?

2a. What is Leonard Mead's profession? What two reasons does Leonard give for walking?

3a. What does the police car do after questioning Leonard? Where does it take him?

Interpret: FINDING MEANING

1b. Why does Leonard want to avoid drawing attention to himself? Why are the streets deserted?

2b. Why does the police car say he has no profession? Why does the police car find Leonard's reasons unbelievable? What might have helped him?

3b. How is Leonard's house different from those around it? Why is Leonard seen as possessing "regressive tendencies"?

Analyze: TAKING THINGS APART

4a. Why is crime ebbing in this large city?

Synthesize: BRINGING THINGS TOGETHER

4b. What are the people in this city lacking? What does Leonard have that they do not?

Evaluate: MAKING JUDGMENTS

5a. What comment might Bradbury be making about society? How valid is this comment? Explain.

Extend: CONNECTING IDEAS

5b. Now that we have entered the twenty-first century, do you think Bradbury is accurate with some of his predictions and warnings? In what ways are his predictions true? In what ways have his predictions not yet come to pass?

Understanding Literature

MOOD. Review the definition for **mood** in the Handbook of Literary Terms. The writer can evoke in the reader an emotional response—such as fear, discomfort, longing, or anticipation—by writing carefully with descriptive language and sensory details. To what does the author compare the city in the second paragraph? What kind of mood does this create?

SETTING. Review the definition for **setting** and the sensory details chart you made for Literary Tools in Prereading. Writers create setting by various means. In fiction, setting is most often revealed by means of description of such elements as landscape, scenery, building, furniture, clothing, the weather, and the season. Where and when is this story set? What is strange about this place?

Answers to Understanding Literature can be found on page 964.

ANSWERS TO UNDERSTANDING LITERATURE

MOOD. The author compares the city to a graveyard filled with tombs inhabited by phantoms. This description creates a somber mood because it suggests that the city and its people are essentially dead to the world around them.

SETTING. The story is set in a city of three million people in an unidentified land much like the United States in the year 2053. The setting is strange because the streets are empty and the houses are dark.

ANSWERS TO INTEGRATING THE LANGUAGE ARTS

Collaborative Learning
As part of planning their reading promotion event, have students think of a way to measure the results of the promotion, such as number of children read to or books sold at a used book sale. Point out that developing a tool for measuring results will help them assess the success of their efforts.

Media Literacy & Speaking and Listening
Students might investigate how new technology is changing medicine, transportation, work, sports, and how people spend their leisure time, as well as other areas.

Applied English
Encourage students to read their essays aloud with other students.

Writer's Journal

1. Write a **police report** to describe the interaction between Mr. Leonard Mead and the automated police car. Include a description of Mr. Mead's "unusual" behavior, the answers he gave to the questions asked, and the reasons for transporting him to the Psychiatric Center for Research on Regressive Tendencies.

2. Write a **prediction** of what you think life will be like in 2053. Will things have changed very much? What role will technological and scientific advances play in the near future? Explain why you think your predictions will come true.

3. Imagine a day, a week, or longer during which you avoided any contact with electronic media—no TV, no videos, no e-mail, no phone conversations, no web-browsing, etc. Do you think the experience would be an ordeal? an inconvenience? a freeing experience? Write a **poem** describing your imagined mood at the end of the time period.

Integrating the Language Arts

Collaborative Learning

CELEBRATION OF READING. Leonard Mead states that he is a writer, but he has not written in years because nobody reads anymore. Promote reading in your school and community by organizing a celebration of books and of reading. With your classmates, you might create a display of your favorite books and vivid posters that promote reading, host a reading at which each student can read a favorite piece or writing, arrange to read to a small group of younger students, volunteer with an organization that promotes or teaches literacy, or create a publication of book reviews and essays about the importance of reading.

Media Literacy & Speaking and Listening

MEDIA SEARCH. Use the Internet or the library to find electronic or print articles to read about recent scientific discoveries or emerging technologies. Imagine ways that these developments could affect life as we know it if they were to become widespread. Share some of your most interesting findings with the class.

Applied English

ESSAY WRITING. Participate in a TV-free week where you substitute other activities such as reading, being with friends, or physical activities in place of television watching. During the week, take notes on the activities you enjoyed instead of TV and note any negative reactions you may have experienced (such as being unable to join in on a conversation about an episode of a favorite TV show or missing a big televised sporting event). At the end of the week, write an essay on the pros and cons of life without television.

"By the Waters of Babylon"
by Stephen Vincent Benét

Reader's resource

"By the Waters of Babylon" is a science-fiction story that is a noteworthy example of what has become a stock science-fiction tale, a vision of the future after some great holocaust.

WORLD HISTORY CONNECTION. The title of this story, "By the Waters of Babylon," refers to an ancient city in Mesopotamia. The city was a bustling, vibrant place; the capital of a mighty empire; and for many years, the most famous city in the world. Babylon reached its peak during the seventh century BC, but declined thereafter. Much of what we know about this once great city comes from excavations of the ruins of the city that began during Benét's lifetime.

About the AUTHOR

Stephen Vincent Benét (1898–1943) was born in Bethlehem, Pennsylvania. Because his father was a soldier, the family moved frequently from one army base to the next. Those early travels and an interest in history greatly affected Benét's writing. He began writing at age fifteen and two years later published his first book of poetry. He continued to write poetry while a student at Yale. Later Benét received a Guggenheim Fellowship and went to Paris, where he finished a narrative poem about the Civil War, *John Brown's Body* (1928), for which he won a Pulitzer Prize. Later in his career, Benét turned to writing stories and novels. His story "Sobbin Women" (1926) was made into the musical *Seven Brides for Seven Brothers,* and his short story "The Devil and Daniel Webster" (1937) was made into an opera and a movie. In 1944, Benét was awarded a second Pulitzer Prize posthumously for his epic poem on the westward migration, *Western Star.*

Literary TOOLS

SIMILE. A **simile** is a comparison using *like* or *as.* Note the author's use of this descriptive technique as you read the story.

APHORISM. An **aphorism** is a short saying or pointed statement. Aphorisms are often clever ways of passing on advice. What aphorism does the father pass on to his son (the narrator) near the end of the story?

DIALECT. A **dialect** is a version of a language spoken by the people of a particular place, time, or social group. The narrator uses his own dialect to describe many places and objects he finds unfamiliar that we consider ordinary and know by our own modern-day terminology.

Organizer

As you read, make a chart of the objects and places the narrator describes, and see if you can determine what it is he is depicting.

NARRATOR'S DESCRIPTION	OUR TERMINOLOGY
god-roads	highway

Reader's Journal

Have you ever come to an important discovery or realization? If so, describe the experience.

ADDITIONAL RESOURCES

UNIT 12 RESOURCE BOOK
- Selection Worksheet 12.5
- Selection Check Test 4.12.9
- Selection Test 4.12.10

GRAPHIC ORGANIZER

Students may include some or all of the following objects and places in their charts: god-roads—highways; Ou-dis-sun—Hudson River; Place of the Gods—New York City; Great Burning—nuclear war; Bitter Water—Atlantic Ocean; high towers of the gods—skyscrapers; stones carved with magical numbers or words—remains of statues or signs; enchanted boxes and jars of food—canned, boxed, frozen food; mighty temple that goes down into great caves and tunnels—New York City's Grand Central Station, leading to the city subway system; coverings on the floor—rugs; washing place with no water—sink; a thing that says "Hot" but is not hot to touch—hot-water faucet; cooking place with no wood—stove/oven; "strong magic in things…but magic was gone"—electricity, gas, running water; bronze door without a handle in a hallway—door of an elevator; chariots—cars; UBTREAS—perhaps the word "subtreasury"; a man or god named ASHING—George Washington (his name on a plaque must have been partially destroyed)

READER'S JOURNAL

As an alternate activity, ask students to write about why human beings throughout history have been driven by a desire to know more.

VOCABULARY FROM THE SELECTION

chamber	perplexed
enchantment	summon

GOALS/OBJECTIVES

Studying this lesson will enable students to
- appreciate a science fiction story about a future world
- describe Stephen Vincent Benét's literary accomplishments
- describe the elements of science fiction and identify and interpret these in a literary work

- define *simile, aphorism* and *dialect* and recognize examples of these literary techniques in the selection
- write a simile, a descriptive paragraph, and a speech
- review a science fiction movie or TV show, study the history of Babylon, and collaborate with other students to create a list of aphorisms

MOTIVATION

Ask students to try describing what their town, city, or neighborhood might look like after a devastating event like the one that has taken place in Benét's story. What might they see and recognize in the ruins? What would be changed or missing? What signs of life would there be? Ask students to imagine this situation and then write a descriptive paragraph.

READING PROFICIENCY

Students may have trouble identifying the places and objects indirectly described in the story. Ask them to list each puzzling object or place the narrator mentions in their charts and to identify as many as they can. To fill in the holes in their chart, ask them to review the clues they were able to figure out and see if these can help them figure out others. Alternatively, go through the items in the chart with students one by one and offer additional hints or ways of thinking about the narrator's descriptions.

ENGLISH LANGUAGE LEARNING

The story is told in simple and flowing language. Invite students to read passages from the story aloud to reinforce their reading skills.

SPECIAL NEEDS

Read the first paragraph or two aloud to students. Before you begin, ask students to listen for at least one word or phrase that suggests the time and place of the story and write it down when they hear it. Then have students give their examples. Point out that although the story appears to be set in the long-ago past, they will find out otherwise as they read further.

ENRICHMENT

The narrator says that "perhaps, in the old days, they ate knowledge too fast." Ask students if they think people in American society today "eat knowledge too fast." If they agree, have them give examples and write a short essay in which they reflect on the social, economic, and personal effects of the rapid increase in knowledge.

Interrupted Journey, c.1971. Samuel Bak. Pucker Gallery, Boston.

By the Waters of Babylon

Stephen Vincent Benét

The north and the west and the south are good hunting ground, but it is forbidden to go east. It is forbidden to go to any of the Dead Places except to search for metal, and then he who touches the metal must be a priest or the son of a priest. Afterwards, both the man and the metal must be purified. These are the rules and the laws; they are well made. It is forbidden to cross the great river and look upon the place that was the Place of the Gods—this is most strictly forbidden. We do not even say its name though we know its name. It is there that spirits live, and demons—it is there that there are the ashes of the Great Burning. These things are forbidden—they have been forbidden since the beginning of time.

What is most strictly forbidden?

My father is a priest; I am the son of a priest. I have been in the Dead Places near us, with my father—at first, I was afraid. When my father went into the house to search for the metal, I stood by the door and my heart felt small and weak. It was a dead man's house, a spirit house. It did not have the smell of man, though there were old bones in a corner. But it is not fitting that a priest's son should show fear. I looked at the bones in the shadow and kept my voice still.

Then my father came out with the metal—a good, strong piece. He looked at me with both eyes but I had not run away. He gave me the metal to hold—I took it and did not die. So he knew that I was truly his son and would be a priest in my time. That was when I was very young—nevertheless, my brothers would not have done it, though they are good hunters. After that,

How does the narrator's father know the narrator will be a priest?

they gave me the good piece of meat and the warm corner by the fire. My father watched over me—he was glad that I should be a priest. But when I boasted or wept without a reason, he punished me more strictly than my brothers. That was right.

After a time, I myself was allowed to go into the dead houses and search for metal. So I learned the ways of those houses—and if I saw

art note

Interrupted Journey, c.1971.
Samuel Bak.
Samuel Bak (1933–) is a Holocaust survivor whose father and grandparents were among the 100,000 Jews murdered by Nazis in the infamous Vilna Ghetto. It was in Vilna that Bak began to draw, and the Holocaust has always haunted his work. His paintings evoke a post-apocalyptic world where human achievements have become petrified and broken.

LITERARY NOTE

The title of Benét's story comes from Psalm 137 in the Bible, which opens with the line: "By the waters of Babylon, there we sat down and wept, when we remembered Zion." Benét plays off several themes in the psalm, including the destruction of the mighty, living in a strange land, being estranged from one's past, and the importance of remembering and keeping faith with one's past beliefs.

Quotables

"What experience and history teach is this—that people and governments never have learned anything from history, or acted on principles deduced from it."

—Georg Wilhelm Hegel

1. The narrator wishes to know more; his lack of knowledge burns in him.
2. The narrator sees a river and beyond it "a great Dead Place" where the gods are walking about.

CROSS-CURRICULAR ACTIVITIES

SOCIAL STUDIES. The narrator of this story embarks on a vision quest, or journey of initiation. This type of journey is a traditional feature of many Native American cultures as well as the aboriginal culture of Australia. Have students do research to find out about the purpose and characteristics of the vision quest in one of these cultures.

bones, I was no longer afraid. The bones are light and old—sometimes they will fall into dust if you touch them. But that is a great sin.

I was taught the chants and the spells—I was taught how to stop the running of blood from a wound and many secrets. A priest must know many secrets—that was what my father said. If the hunters think we do all things by chants and spells, they may believe so—it does not hurt them. I was taught how to read in the old books and how to make the old writings—that was hard and took a long time. My knowledge made me happy—it was like a fire in my heart. Most of all, I liked to hear of the Old Days and the stories of the gods. I asked myself many questions that I could not answer, but it was good to ask them. At night, I would lie awake and listen to the wind—it seemed to me that it was the voice of the gods as they flew through the air.

We are not ignorant like the Forest People—our women spin wool on the wheel, our priests wear a white robe. We do not eat grubs from the tree; we have not forgotten the old writings, although they are hard to understand. Nevertheless, my knowledge and my lack of knowledge burned in me—I wished to know more.

How does the narrator feel about his knowledge?

When I was a man at last, I came to my father and said, "It is time for me to go on my journey. Give me your leave."

He looked at me for a long time, stroking his beard; then he said at last, "Yes. It is time." That night, in the house of the priesthood, I asked for and received purification.[1] My body hurt, but my spirit was a cool stone. It was my father himself who questioned me about my dreams.

He bade[2] me look into the smoke of the fire and see—I saw and told what I saw. It was what I have always seen—a river, and, beyond it, a great Dead Place and in it the gods walking. I have always thought about that.

What does the narrator see in his dream?

His eyes were stern when I told him—he was no longer my father but a priest. He said, "This is a strong dream."

"It is mine," I said, while the smoke waved and my head felt light. They were singing the Star song in the outer <u>chamber</u> and it was like the buzzing of bees in my head.

He asked me how the gods were dressed and I told him how they were dressed. We know how they were dressed from the book, but I saw them as if they were before me. When I had finished, he threw the sticks three times and studied them as they fell.

"This is a very strong dream," he said. "It may eat you up."

"I am not afraid," I said and looked at him with both eyes. My voice sounded thin in my ears but that was because of the smoke.

He touched me on the breast and the forehead. He gave me the bow and the three arrows.

"Take them," he said. "It is forbidden to travel east. It is forbidden to cross the river. It is forbidden to go to the Place of the Gods. All these things are forbidden."

"All these things are forbidden," I said, but it was my voice that spoke and not my spirit. He looked at me again.

"My son," he said. "Once I had young dreams. If your dreams do not eat you up, you may be a great priest. If they eat you, you are still my son. Now go on your journey."

I went fasting,[3] as is the law. My body hurt but not my heart. When the dawn came, I was

---

1. **purification.** Method of freeing from guilt or sins
2. **bade.** Asked
3. **fasting.** Not eating food or eating only limited amounts of food for a period of time

words for everyday use

cham • ber (chām′bər) *n.*, reception room in an official residence. *When the ambassador went to see the king of Lunonia, he was kept waiting in the outer <u>chamber</u> for an hour before being allowed into the royal court.*

out of sight of the village. I prayed and purified myself, waiting for a sign. The sign was an eagle. It flew east.

Sometimes signs are sent by bad spirits. I waited again on the flat rock, fasting, taking no food. I was very still—I could feel the sky above me and the earth beneath. I waited till the sun was beginning to sink. Then three deer passed in the valley, going east—they did not wind me or see me. There was a white fawn with them—a very great sign.

I followed them, at a distance, waiting for what would happen. My heart was troubled about going east, yet I knew that I must go. My head hummed with my fasting—I did not even see the panther spring upon the white fawn. But, before I knew it, the bow was in my hand. I shouted and the panther lifted his head from the fawn. It is not easy to kill a panther with one arrow, but the arrow went through his eye and into his brain. He died as he tried to spring—he rolled over, tearing at the ground. Then I knew I was meant to go east—I knew that was my journey. When the night came, I made my fire and roasted meat.

What sign convinces the narrator that he is meant to go east?

It is eight suns' journey to the east and a man passes by many Dead Places. The Forest People are afraid of them, but I am not. Once I made my fire on the edge of a Dead Place at night and, next morning, in the dead house, I found a good knife, little rusted. That was small to what came afterward but it made my heart feel big. Always when I looked for game, it was in front of my arrow, and twice I passed hunting parties of the Forest People without their knowing. So I knew my magic was strong and my journey clean, in spite of the law.

Toward the setting of the eighth sun, I came to the banks of the great river. It was half-a-day's journey after I had left the god-road—we do not use the god-roads now for they are falling apart into great blocks of stone, and the forest is safer going. A long way off, I

had seen the water through trees, but the trees were thick. At last, I came out upon an open place at the top of a cliff. There was the great river below, like a giant in the sun. It is very long, very wide. It could eat all the streams we know and still be thirsty. Its name is Ou-dis-sun, the Sacred, the Long. No man of my tribe had seen it, not even my father, the priest. It was magic and I prayed.

What does the narrator see that no man of his tribe has seen before?

Then I raised my eyes and looked south. It was there, the Place of the Gods.

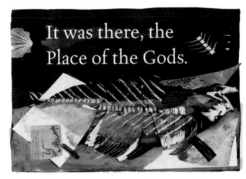

It was there, the Place of the Gods.

How can I tell what it was like—you do not know. It was there, in the red light, and they were too big to be houses. It was there with the red light upon it, mighty and ruined. I knew that in another moment the gods would see me. I covered my eyes with my hands and crept back into the forest.

Surely, that was enough to do, and live. Surely it was enough to spend the night upon the cliff. The Forest People themselves do not come near. Yet, all through the night, I knew that I should have to cross the river and walk in the places of the gods, although the gods ate me up. My magic did not help me at all, and yet there was a fire in my bowels, a fire in my mind. When the sun rose, I thought, "My journey has been clean. Now I will go home from my journey." But, even as I thought so, I knew I could not. If I went to the Place of the Gods, I would surely die, but, if I did not go, I could never be

1. He killed a panther that was following a white fawn in an eastward direction.
2. The narrator sees the sacred river that is known as Ou-dis-sun.

ANSWERS TO GUIDED READING QUESTIONS

1. He is afraid to continue his journey because he is certain he will die if he goes to the Place of the Gods. He continues because he knows he will never be at peace again if he does not.
2. The narrator describes the broken bridges across the river that were damaged in the time of the Great Burning.
3. The gods teach the narrator to cross the river by paddling with the pole on one side of the raft.

CROSS-CURRICULAR ACTIVITIES

Music. Students might enjoy setting the narrator's song to music. Have them experiment with different melodies or chants until they find one that fits the mood and tone of the words of John's song. You may wish to have students review the definitions of *mood* and *tone* before they begin. Invite volunteers to sing their songs before the class.

LITERARY TECHNIQUE

Style. Style is the manner in which something is said or written. A writer's style depends on things such as word choice, grammatical structures, and a preference for abstract or concrete words. Ask students to identify the recurring features that define Benét's style in "By the Waters of Babylon."
Answers
One successful feature of Benét's style in the story is the use of descriptive imagery, words, and sentence structures that are consistent with the narrator's experience. For example, the narrator speaks of a tower that is not broken as being like a "great tree in a forest" and refers to the Atlantic Ocean as "the Bitter Water." Benét also uses simple language and sentence structures that fit the speech of someone who lives in a primitive society. In keeping with his identity as a future priest, or wise man of his culture, the narrator sometimes uses abstract words, such as "spirit," as well as concrete terms.

at peace with my spirit again. It is better to lose one's life than one's spirit, if one is a priest and the son of a priest.

 Why is the narrator afraid to continue his journey? Why does he continue?

Nevertheless, as I made the raft, the tears ran out of my eyes. The Forest People could have killed me without fight, if they had come upon me then, but they did not come. When the raft was made, I said the sayings for the dead and painted myself for death. My heart was cold as a frog and my knees like water, but the burning in my mind would not let me have peace. As I pushed the raft from the shore, I began my death song—I had the right. It was a fine song.

"I am John, son of John," I sang. "My people are the Hill People. They are the men.
I go into the Dead Places but I am not slain.
I take the metal from the Dead Places but I am not blasted.
I travel upon the god-roads and am not afraid. E-yah! I have killed the panther, I have killed the fawn!
E-yah! I have come to the great river. No man has come there before.
It is forbidden to go east, but I have gone, forbidden to go on the great river, but I am there.
Open your hearts, you spirits, and hear my song.
Now I go to the Place of the Gods, I shall not return.
My body is painted for death and my limbs weak, but my heart is big as I go to the Place of the Gods!"

All the same, when I came to the Place of the Gods, I was afraid, afraid. The current of the great river is very strong—it gripped my raft with its hands. That was magic, for the river itself is wide and calm. I could feel evil spirits about me, in the bright morning; I could feel their breath on my neck as I was swept down the stream. Never have I been so much alone—I

tried to think of my knowledge, but it was a squirrel's heap of winter nuts. There was no strength in my knowledge any more and I felt small and naked as a new-hatched bird—alone upon the great river, the servant of the gods.

Yet, after a while, my eyes were opened and I saw. I saw both banks of the river—I saw that once there had been god-roads across it, though now they were broken and fallen like broken vines. Very great they were, and wonderful and broken—broken in the time of the Great Burning when the fire fell out of the sky. And always the current took me nearer to the Place of the Gods, and the huge ruins rose before my eyes.

 What does the narrator describe?

I do not know the customs of rivers—we are the People of the Hills. I tried to guide my raft with the pole but it spun around. I thought the river meant to take me past the Place of the Gods and out into the Bitter Water of the legends. I grew angry then—my heart felt strong. I said aloud, "I am a priest and the son of a priest!" The gods heard me—they showed me how to paddle with the pole on one side of the raft. The current changed itself—I drew near to the Place of the Gods.

Who teaches the narrator how to cross the river?

When I was very near, my raft struck and turned over. I can swim in our lakes—I swam to the shore. There was a great spike of rusted metal sticking out into the river—I hauled myself up upon it and sat there, panting. I had saved my bow and two arrows and the knife I found in the Dead Place but that was all. My raft went whirling downstream toward the Bitter Water. I looked after it, and thought if it had trod me under, at least I would be safely dead. Nevertheless, when I had dried my bowstring[4] and restrung it, I walked forward to the Place of the Gods.

---

4. **bowstring.** String that can be pulled taut and then released to shoot an arrow from a bow

It felt like ground underfoot; it did not burn me. It is not true what some of the tales say, that the ground there burns forever, for I have been there. Here and there were the marks and stains of the Great Burning, on the ruins, that is true. But they were old marks and old stains. It is not true either, what some of our priests say, that it is, an island covered with fogs and <u>enchantments</u>. It is not. It is a great Dead Place—greater than any Dead Place we know. Everywhere in it there are god-roads, though most are cracked and broken. Everywhere there are the ruins of the high towers of the gods.

In what way is the Place of the Gods different from the stories about it?

How shall I tell what I saw? I went carefully, my strung bow in my hand, my skin ready for danger. There should have been the wailings of spirits and the shrieks of demons, but there were not. It was very silent and sunny where I had landed—the wind and the rain and the birds that drop seeds had done their work—the grass grew in the cracks of the broken stone. It is a fair island—no wonder the gods built there. If I had come there, a god, I also would have built.

How shall I tell what I saw? The towers are not all broken—here and there one still stands, like a great tree in a forest, and the birds nest high. But the towers themselves look blind, for the gods are gone. I saw a fish-hawk, catching fish in the river. I saw a little dance of white butterflies over a great heap of broken stones and columns. I went there and looked about me—there was a carved stone with cut-letters, broken in half. I can read letters but I could not understand these. They said UBTREAS. There was also the shattered image of a man or a god. It had been made of white stone and he wore his hair tied back like a woman's. His name was ASHING, as I read on the cracked half of a stone. I thought it wise to pray to ASHING, though I do not know that god.

How shall I tell what I saw? There was no smell of man left, on stone or metal. Nor were there many trees in that wilderness of stone. There are many pigeons, nesting and dropping in the towers—the gods must have loved them, or, perhaps, they used them for sacrifices. There are wild cats that roam the god-roads, green-eyed, unafraid of man. At night they wail like demons, but they are not demons. The wild dogs are more danger-ous, for they hunt in a pack, but them I did not meet till later. Everywhere there are the carved stones, carved with magical numbers or words.

What possible explanations does the narrator have for the large number of pigeons he finds?

I went North—I did not try to hide myself. When a god or demon saw me, then I would die, but meanwhile I was no longer afraid. My hunger for knowledge burned in me—there was so much that I could not understand. After awhile, I knew that my belly was hungry. I could have hunted for my meat, but I did not hunt. It is known that the gods did not hunt as we do—they got their food from enchanted boxes and jars. Sometimes these are still found in the Dead Places—once, when I was a child and foolish, I opened such a jar and tasted it and found the food sweet. But my father found out and punished me for it strictly, for often that food is death. Now, though, I had long, gone past what was forbidden, and I entered the likeliest towers, looking for the food of the gods.

I found it at last in the ruins of a great temple in the mid-city. A mighty temple it must have been, for the roof was painted like the sky at night with its stars—that much I could see, though the colors were faint and dim. It went down into great caves and tunnels—perhaps

words for everyday use

en • chant • ment (en chant´mant) *n.*, magic spell or charm. *Housman wrote a poem about an evil queen who was defeated by a warrior when her magic <u>enchantments</u> against him failed.*

1. The ground of the Place of the Gods does not burn forever.
2. He thinks the gods must have loved the pigeons or used them for sacrifices.

they kept their slaves there. But when I started to climb down, I heard the squeaking of rats, so I did not go—rats are unclean, and there must have been many tribes of them, from the squeaking. But near there, I found food, in the heart of a ruin, behind a door that still opened. I ate only the fruits from the jars—they had a very sweet taste. There was drink, too, in bottles of glass—the drink of the gods was strong and made my head swim. After I had eaten and drunk, I slept on the top of a stone, my bow at my side.

What stops the narrator from further exploration?

When I woke, the sun was low. Looking down from where I lay, I saw a dog sitting on his haunches. His tongue was hanging out of his mouth; he looked as if he were laughing. He was a big dog, with a gray-brown coat, as big as a wolf. I sprang up and shouted at him but he did not move—he just sat there as if he were laughing. I did not like that. When I reached for a stone to throw, he moved swiftly out of the way of the stone. He was not afraid of me; he looked at me as if I were meat. No doubt I could have killed him with an arrow, but I did not know if there were others. Moreover, night was falling.

I looked about me—not far away there was a great, broken god-road, leading North. The towers were high enough, but not so high, and while many of the dead-houses were wrecked, there were some that stood. I went toward this god-road, keeping to the heights of the ruins, while the dog followed. When I had reached the god-road, I saw that there were others behind him. If I had slept later, they would have come upon me asleep and torn out my throat. As it was, they were sure enough of me; they did not hurry. When I went into the dead-house, they kept watch at the entrance—doubtless they thought they would have a fine hunt. But a dog cannot open a door, and I knew, from the books, that the gods did not like to live on the ground but on high.

I had just found a door I could open when the dogs decided to rush. Ha! They were surprised when I shut the door in their faces—it was a good door, of strong metal. I could hear their foolish baying beyond it, but I did not stop to answer them. I was in darkness—I found stairs and climbed. There were many stairs, turning around till my head was dizzy. At the top was another door—I found the knob and opened it. I was in a long, small chamber—on one side of it was a bronze door that could not be opened, for it had no handle. Perhaps there was a magic word to open it, but I did not have the word. I turned to the door in the opposite side of the wall. The lock of it was broken and I opened it and went in.

Why can't the narrator open the bronze door? What do you think the bronze door is?

Within, there was a place of great riches. The god who lived there must have been a powerful god. The first room was a small ante-room—I waited there for some time, telling the spirits of the place that I came in peace and not as a robber. When it seemed to me that they had had time to hear me, I went on. Ah, what riches! Few, even, of the windows had been broken—it was all as it had been. The great windows that looked over the city had not been broken at all though they were dusty and streaked with many years. There were coverings on the floors, the colors not greatly faded, and the chairs were soft and deep. There were pictures upon the walls, very strange, very wonderful—I remember one of a bunch of flowers in a jar—if you came close to it, you could see nothing but bits of color, but if you stood away from it, the flowers might have been picked yesterday. It made my heart feel strange to look at this picture—and to look at the figure of a bird, in some hard clay, on a table and to see it so like our birds. Everywhere there were books and writings, many in tongues that I could not read. The god who lived there must have been a wise god and full of knowledge. I felt I had a right there, as I sought knowledge also.

Nevertheless, it was strange. There was a washing-place but no water—perhaps the gods washed in air. There was a cooking-place but no wood, and though there was a machine to cook food, there was no place to put fire in it. Nor were there candles or lamps—there were things that looked like lamps but they had neither oil nor wick. All these things were magic, but I touched them and lived—the magic had gone out of them. Let me tell one thing to show. In the washing-place, a thing said "Hot" but it was not hot to the touch—another thing said "Cold" but it was not cold. This must have been a strong magic but the magic was gone. I do not understand—they had ways—I wish that I knew.

What are the things the narrator finds in the god's house?

It was close and dry and dusty in their house of the gods. I have said the magic was gone, but that is not true—it had gone from the magic things, but it had not gone from the place. I felt the spirits about me, weighing upon me. Nor had I ever slept in a Dead Place before—and yet, tonight, I must sleep there. When I thought of it, my tongue felt dry in my throat, in spite of my wish for knowledge. Almost I would have gone down again and faced the dogs, but I did not.

In what way is the magic of the place still there?

I had not gone through all the rooms when the darkness fell. When it fell, I went back to the big room looking over the city and made fire. There was a place to make fire and a box with wood in it, though I do not think they cooked there. I wrapped myself in a floor-covering and slept in front of the fire—I was very tired.

Now I tell what is very strong magic. I woke in the midst of the night. When I woke, the fire had gone out and I was cold. It seemed to me that all around me there were whisperings and voices. I closed my eyes to shut them out. Some will say that I slept again, but I do not think that I slept. I could feel the spirits drawing my spirit out of my body as a fish is drawn on a line.

Why should I lie about it? I am a priest and the son of a priest. If there are spirits, as they say, in the small Dead Places near us, what spirits must there not be in that great Place of the Gods? And would not they wish to speak? After such long years? I know that I felt myself drawn as a fish is drawn on a line. I had stepped out of my body—I could see my body asleep in front of the cold fire, but it was not I. I was drawn to look out upon the city of the gods.

It should have been dark, for it was night, but it was not dark. Everywhere there were lights—lines of light—circles and blurs of light—ten thousand torches would not have been the same. The sky itself was alight—you could barely see

Everywhere there were lights—lines of light—circles and blurs of light . . .

the stars for the glow in the sky. I thought to myself "This is strong magic," and trembled. There was a roaring in my ears like the rushing of rivers. Then my eyes grew used to the light and my ears to the sound. I knew that I was seeing the city as it had been when the gods were alive.

That was a sight indeed—yes, that was a sight: I could not have seen it in the body—my body would have died. Everywhere went the gods, on foot and in chariots—there were gods beyond number and counting and their chariots blocked the streets. They had turned night to day for their pleasure—they did not sleep with the sun. The noise of their coming and going was the noise of many waters. It was magic what they could do—it was magic what they did.

What does the narrator find magical about his vision?

ANSWERS TO GUIDED READING QUESTIONS

1. In the god's house, the narrator finds unbroken windows, unfaded rugs, soft chairs, pictures on the walls, books, a washing-place, a cooking-place, and things that looked like lamps.
2. Although the magic is gone from the "magic things," the magic of the place is still there.
3. In his vision the gods went everywhere on foot and in chariots, and there were huge numbers of them. They had lit up the night sky as through it were day, and their coming and going creates a huge noise.

BIBLIOGRAPHIC NOTE

For another look at a future world after a fiery nuclear holocaust, students might like to read *A Canticle for Liebowitz* by Walter M. Miller, Jr. (Bantam, 1997). This grim but funny science fiction classic, originally published in 1959, covers a period of about 600 years as monks at a Utah abbey go about rebuilding civilization.

ANSWERS TO GUIDED READING QUESTIONS

1. The narrator says the gods had "wisdom beyond wisdom," but not everything they did was done well.
2. The Place of the Gods was destroyed during a war between the gods. Fire fell from the sky along with a poisonous mist.

CROSS-CURRICULAR ACTIVITIES

MATH AND GEOGRAPHY. The narrator says the Place of the Gods (New York City) is "eight suns' journey" to the east of where he lives. He also describes himself as one of the People of the Hills. Have students estimate how many miles per day a fit person might walk on foot over open ground. Using this estimate, the details given in the story, and a map of the eastern seaboard states, have them make guesses about where the narrator's people lived.

Answers

Some possibilities are the Appalachian Mountains of Pennsylvania, such as the Poconos or Blue Mountains.

I looked out of another window—the great vines of their bridges were mended and the god-roads went East and West. Restless, restless, were the gods and always in motion! They burrowed tunnels under rivers—they flew in the air. With unbelievable tools they did giant works—no part of the earth was safe from them, for, if they wished for a thing, they summoned it from the other side of the world. And always, as they labored and rested, as they feasted and made love, there was a drum in their ears—the pulse of the giant city, beating and beating like a man's heart.

Were they happy? What is happiness to the gods? They were great, they were mighty, they were wonderful and terrible. As I looked upon them and their magic, I felt like a child—but a little more, it seemed to me, and they would pull down the moon from the sky. I saw them with wisdom beyond wisdom and knowledge beyond knowledge. And yet not all they did was well done—even I could see that—and yet their wisdom could not but grow until all was peace.

How does the narrator sum up the nature of the gods?

Then I saw their fate come upon them and that was terrible past speech. It came upon them as they walked the streets of their city. I have been in the fights with the Forest People—I have seen men die. But this was not like that. When gods war with gods, they use weapons we do not know. It was fire falling out of the sky and a mist that poisoned. It was the time of the Great Burning and the Destruction. They ran about like ants in the streets of their city—poor gods, poor gods! Then the towers began to fall. A few escaped—yes, a few. The legends tell it. But, even after the city became a

How was the Place of the Gods destroyed?

Dead Place, for many years the poison was still in the ground. I saw it happen, I saw the last of them die. It was darkness over the broken city and I wept.

All this, I saw. I saw it as I have told it, though not in the body. When I woke in the morning, I was hungry, but I did not think first of my hunger for my heart was perplexed and confused. I knew the reason for the Dead Places but I did not see why it had happened. It seemed to me it should not have happened, with all the magic they had. I went through the house looking for an answer. There was so much in the house I could not understand—and yet I am a priest and the son of a priest. It was like being on one side of the great river, at night, with no light to show the way.

Then I saw the dead god. He was sitting in his chair, by the window, in a room I had not entered before and, for the first moment, I thought that he was alive. Then I saw the skin on the back of his hand—it was like dry leather. The room was shut, hot and dry—no doubt that had kept him as he was. At first I was afraid to approach him—then the fear left me. He was sitting looking out over the city—he was dressed in the clothes of the gods. His age was neither young nor old—I could not tell his age. But there was wisdom in his face and great sadness. You could see that he would have not run away. He had sat at his window, watching his city die—then he himself had died. But it is better to lose one's life than one's spirit—and you could see from the face that his spirit had not been lost. I knew that, if I touched him, he would fall into dust—and yet, there was something unconquered in the face.

That is all of my story, for then I knew he was a man—I knew then that they had been men, neither gods nor demons. It is a great knowl-

---

words for everyday use

sum • mon (sum´ən) *vt.,* order to come or appear. *The king summoned the ambassador to come from his embassy and to appear before him instantly.*

per • plexed (pər pleksd´) *adj.,* uncertain or hesitant. *The traveler stood perplexed for a long time at the fork in the road, studying a sign that indicated she could reach her destination by following either path.*

edge, hard to tell and believe. They were men—they went a dark road, but they were men. I had no fear after that—I had no fear going home, though twice I fought off the dogs, and once I was hunted for two days by the Forest People. When I saw my father again, I prayed and was purified. He touched my lips and my breast; he said, "You went away a boy. You come back a man and a priest." I said, "Father, they were men! I have been in the Place of the Gods and seen it! Now slay me, if it is the law—but still I know they were men."

What does the narrator realize about the gods?

He looked at me out of both eyes. He said, "The law is not always the same shape—you have done what you have done. I could not have done it my time, but you come after me. Tell!"

I told and he listened. After that, I wished to tell all the people but he showed me otherwise. He said, "Truth is a hard deer

What advice does the narrator's father give him? How does the narrator respond to this advice?

to hunt. If you eat too much truth at once, you may die of the truth. It was not idle that our fathers forbade the Dead Places." He was right—it is better the truth should come little by little. I have learned that, being a priest. Perhaps, in the old days, they ate knowledge too fast.

Nevertheless, we make a beginning. It is not for the metal alone we go to the Dead Places now—there are the books and the writings. They are hard to learn. And the magic tools are broken—but we can look at them and wonder. At least, we make a beginning. And, when I am chief priest we shall go beyond the great river. We shall go to the Place of the Gods—the place newyork—not one man but a company. We shall look for the images of the gods and find the god ASHING and the others—the gods Lincoln and Biltmore and Moses. But they were men who built the city, not gods or demons. They were men. I remember the dead man's face. They were men who were here before us. We must build again. ■

Respond *to the* SELECTION

What can you learn by studying the past?

SELECTION CHECK TEST 4.12.9 WITH ANSWERS (CONT.)

enchantment that had frozen all movement.
4. The coach **summoned** the quarterback to his office after practice.

Literary Tools
1. What is an aphorism? **An aphorism is a short saying or pointed statement.**
2. Give one example of an aphorism. *Responses will vary.* **Students should be able to think of at least**

one example, such as "You can lead a horse to water, but you can't make him drink."
3. What is dialect? **A dialect is a version of a language spoken by the people of a particular time, place, or social group.**
4. What is a simile? **A simile is a comparison using** *like* **or** *as.*
5. Give one example of a simile. *Responses will vary.*

---

1. The narrator realizes that the gods were not gods, but human beings.
2. The father advises his son not to reveal everything he knows at once. The narrator feels his father is right and decides to "make a beginning" in rebuilding civilization.

RESPOND TO THE SELECTION

Students might say that they can learn from situations in the past that are similar to present-day situations. They may also learn about leaders and other persons they admire.

SELECTION CHECK TEST 4.12.9 WITH ANSWERS

Checking Your Reading
1. To what forbidden place does the narrator travel? **The narrator travels to the Place of the Gods.**
2. What signs assure the narrator that his journey is meant to be? **He sees an eagle flying east and three deer going east with a white fawn, and he kills a panther with one arrow before it can kill the fawn.**
3. What does the narrator do before crossing the river? **He says the sayings of the dead, he paints himself for death, and he sings a death song.**
4. What does the narrator see while he sleeps in the dead house? **He sees the city as it had been and how it was destroyed.**
5. What does the narrator realize about the gods? **He realizes that they were just people like himself.**

Vocabulary in Context
Fill in each blank below with the most appropriate word from the following Words for Everyday Use. You may have to change the tense of the word.

chamber   summon   perplexed
enchantment

1. Julian was **perplexed** when I put his king in check; he had no idea what move to make.
2. During our class field trip to the governor's mansion, we were kindly ushered into the governor's **chamber** while we waited to shake hands with him.
3. Everything in the garden was peaceful and still, as if under some

RECALL

1a. It is forbidden to travel east. Metal can be taken from the Dead Places. Only a priest or the son of a priest is allowed to do this.

2a. The narrator sees an eagle flying east and three deer going east with a white fawn; he is able to kill a panther that attacks the white fawn. When he sees the Place of the Gods, at first he covers his eyes with his hands and creeps back into the forest. Then he prepares to go there by making a raft, reciting the sayings for the dead, and painting himself for death. As he pushes off, he sings a death song.

3a. He finds a corpse sitting before a window.

INTERPRET

1b. He goes to the forbidden place because he has always thought about it. When he sets out, he believes it is a place where gods live, and he expects to be killed merely for looking upon it.

2b. He is frightened to continue his journey because he is certain he will die if he goes to the Place of the Gods. He continues because his spirit, or desire to know, drives him on.

3b. The narrator realizes the gods were actually humans. The narrator decides that he and his people must rebuild their lost civilization.

ANALYZE

4a. The narrator is fascinated with the Place of the Gods because, as a priest, he seeks knowledge, and he senses that the place contains great wisdom that has been lost.

SYNTHESIZE

4b. The title refers to the ancient city of Babylon, which was once mighty and vibrant, but now exists only in ruins. The author's choice of title suggests a parallel between Babylon and New York City, another grand and busy city that for Benét seems to represent a high point of modern civilization.

EVALUATE

5a. The rules may have originally been imposed because the areas were still contaminated with radiation and anyone who traveled there could become sick or die from radiation sickness. Later, though, the people were probably forbidden to travel to the Place of the Gods out of an unfounded fear of the unknown.

EXTEND

5b. The narrator says that he could see in the dead man's face that he had

---

Recall: GATHERING FACTS

1a. In which direction is it forbidden to travel? What can be taken from the Dead Places? Who is allowed to do this?

2a. What signs does the narrator receive that make him believe that his journey was meant to be? What does he do after seeing the Place of the Gods from across the river? How does he prepare to go there?

3a. What startling thing does the narrator find in the dead house in the morning after his vision?

Interpret: FINDING MEANING

1b. Why does the narrator go to the forbidden place? What are his ideas about this place when he sets out?

2b. Why is the narrator frightened to continue his journey? Why does he do so anyway?

3b. What realization does the narrator come to about the gods? What decision does the narrator come to because of this realization?

Analyze: TAKING THINGS APART

4a. What causes the narrator's fascination with the Place of the Gods?

Synthesize: BRINGING THINGS TOGETHER

4b. How is the title related to the story? In what way is the historical background related to the story?

Evaluate: MAKING JUDGMENTS

5a. Why do you think the Hill People forbade their tribe members from journeying to the east, crossing the river, and going to the Place of the Gods?

Extend: CONNECTING IDEAS

5b. The narrator believed that he would die when he set foot in the Place of the Gods, but he felt compelled to go there anyway. Otherwise he would never be at peace with his spirit. How would you compare the narrator's feelings with the imagined feelings of the dead man whom the narrator found looking out the window of the house?

Understanding *Literature*

SIMILE. Review the definition for **simile** in the Handbook of Literary Terms. What simile does the narrator use to describe his feelings about crossing the river into the Place of the Gods? Why might the narrator use images from nature with which to compare himself? How do these similes describe his physical condition? his mental state?

APHORISM. Review the definition for **aphorism** in the Handbook of Literary Terms. The narrator's father tells him, "Truth is a hard deer to hunt." What does he mean by this? What might make it difficult for people to accept the truths the narrator wishes to share?

DIALECT. Review the definition of **dialect** and the chart you made for Literary Tools in Prereading. How does the author's use of dialect give the story a more realistic flavor?

ANSWERS TO INVESTIGATE, INQUIRE, AND IMAGINE (CONT.)

not lost his spirit even though he had died watching his city die. The dead man could have run away, but may have felt that it was better to watch his city die and die himself than to run away with a broken spirit. Earlier, when the narrator decides to risk his life and enter the Place of the

Gods, he says, "It is better to lose one's life than one's spirit." These remarks suggest that the narrator and the dead man share the same feelings.

Answers to Understanding Literature can be found on page 977.

Writer's Journal

1. Write a **simile** to help describe some modern technological innovation to a person who has no understanding of modern technology.
2. Write a **descriptive paragraph** depicting how your house, local park, school, or town center might look if it were abandoned for fifty or a hundred years.
3. At the end of the story the narrator says, "We must build again." Write a **speech** the narrator might give to his people to rally their support and excite them about building again. As a prewriting suggestion, make a list of reasons for building again. Think of ways life might be improved for the narrator's people. Imagine the world of the "gods" as the narrator saw it. In your speech show why this world is so wonderful. Think of the structural things which need to be rebuilt, but consider the societal changes that will occur as well.

Integrating the Language Arts

Media Literacy & Speaking and Listening

SCIENCE FICTION ON SCREEN. Watch a science fiction movie or television show and review it for your class. Give a brief plot summary and explain why the movie or show is classified as science fiction. What do you think is the purpose of the movie or show? How well is this purpose carried out? What special effects are used to create this fictional world? If you and a classmate watch the same movie, compare your reactions.

Study and Research

A STUDY OF BABYLON. Find out more about the ancient city of Babylon and the excavation efforts of the twentieth century. Why was Babylon chosen as the capital of Mesopotamia? What made it the most famous city in the world during its peak? What brought about the city's decline? When and how were the excavation efforts begun? Prepare a written report on your findings.

Collaborative Learning

APHORISMS. One of the literary terms for this selection is *aphorism*—a short saying or pointed statement. Examples of aphorisms include "A penny saved is a penny earned" and "Don't look a gift horse in the mouth." Gather into groups with four to six students each. See how many aphorisms each group can come up with in a fifteen minute time period. Have one group member be the secretary and record them all. At the end of the time period, compare notes with the other groups. Were there several common aphorisms that all or most groups had on their lists?

ANSWERS TO INTEGRATING THE LANGUAGE ARTS (CONT.)

CONVENTIONS. The report avoids errors in spelling, grammar, usage, mechanics, and manuscript form.

Collaborative Learning
Students might also like to locate books of aphorisms on different topics at the library. Have them share sayings that especially appeal to them.

ANSWERS TO UNDERSTANDING LITERATURE

SIMILE. The narrator says his heart is "cold as a frog" and his knees "like water." He also says that his knowledge is "a squirrel's heap of winter nuts" and that he feels "small and naked as a new-hatched bird." These similes suggest that he is weak with fear and feels defenseless and that his knowledge is inadequate for what he is about to face.

APHORISM. The father means that not everyone is ready to accept the truth. The traditions and superstitions that the people cling to would make it difficult for them to accept the truths the narrator has discovered.

DIALECT. The narrator's choice of words show that he does not know the names of places and objects that are familiar to contemporary readers. His dialect—which uses simple language, repetition, and terms such as "the Forest People" and "the Great Burning"—realistically conveys the simple hunting society he lives in and that society's limited worldview.

ANSWERS TO INTEGRATING THE LANGUAGE ARTS

Media Literacy & Speaking and Listening
Ask students to read at least two movie or television reviews in the media before they watch and review the movie or show they have selected. Remind them that a review is more than a plot summary; at the same time, they should be careful not to give away important events in the plot. Encourage students to prepare a note-taking form before they watch and record their notes under headings such as "Plot," "Characters," "Setting," "Special Effects," and "Purpose."

Study and Research
Assign a score from 1 to 25 for each grading criterion below. (For more detailed evaluation, see the evaluation forms for writing, revising, and proofreading in the Assessment Resource book.
WRITTEN REPORT
CONTENT/UNITY. The written report gives information about the ancient city of Babylon that has been revealed through excavations.
ORGANIZATION/COHERENCE. The report follows a logical sequence of topics and uses logical transitions between topics.
LANGUAGE/STYLE. The report uses vivid and precise nouns, verbs, and modifiers.

VOCABULARY FROM THE SELECTION

nondescript   outset
ominous   phosphorescent

READER'S JOURNAL

Ask students why a hitchhiker might be a good character to include in a ghost story. What feelings or thoughts do they associate with hitchhikers?

Literary TOOLS

NARRATOR AND SOUND EFFECTS. A **narrator** is one who tells a story. In a play, the narrator is the character or person who introduces the work. Not all plays have narrators, but narrators are quite common in radio plays. **Sound effects** are sounds used in the production of a play to make the action seem realistic or to signal the presence of something. As you read, consider what the narrator and the use of sound effects add to this radio play.

FORESHADOWING AND SUSPENSE. **Foreshadowing** is the act of presenting materials that hint at events to occur later in a story. **Suspense** is a feeling of expectation, anxiousness, or curiosity created by questions raised in the mind of a reader, viewer, or listener. A writer evokes these questions through emotion-producing concrete details. By raising questions, the writer keeps the audience engaged in the action, wondering how the questions will be answered. As you read *The Hitchhiker,* look for foreshadowing and suspense. Do these elements keep you engaged in the action of the radio play?

Reader's JOURNAL

Do you enjoy ghost stories and thrillers? Why do you think such stories are so popular?

THE HITCHHIKER

by Lucille Fletcher

Reader's resource

The Hitchhiker is a **radio play**. As such, it depends entirely on sound, for there is no visual component to the audience's experience. Bear this in mind as you read the play. Everything that you read is meant to be heard. In place of the written program that one might receive when going to the theater, the script contains a narrator, who introduces the play. In place of visual presentations of people, objects, and scenes, the script calls for sound effects and descriptions given by the characters. As you read the play, notice how the scenes are carefully painted by the characters, so that a listener can recreate each scene in his or her mind's eye. Many people find that listening to a radio play can be an even more powerful experience than seeing a movie or a television program, because a radio play allows the audience to imagine the action. Often what we imagine is more intense than anything that we might actually see.

About the AUTHOR

Lucille Fletcher (1912–) wrote radio dramas during the so-called "Golden Age of Radio" in the 1930s and 1940s. She has also written short stories, novels, and screenplays for movies and for television. Her most famous works are *Sorry, Wrong Number* and *The Hitchhiker.* The former work has appeared in stage, television, and movie versions.

GOALS/OBJECTIVES

Studying this lesson will enable students to
- enjoy reading a radio play
- identify radio plays as an important form of art and entertainment in the 1930s and 1940s
- define *narrator* and *sound effects* and explain their role in a radio play

- define *foreshadowing* and *suspense* and recognize examples of these literary techniques in the selection
- identify parts of speech for words or phrases in sentences
- stage a radio play
- research urban legends

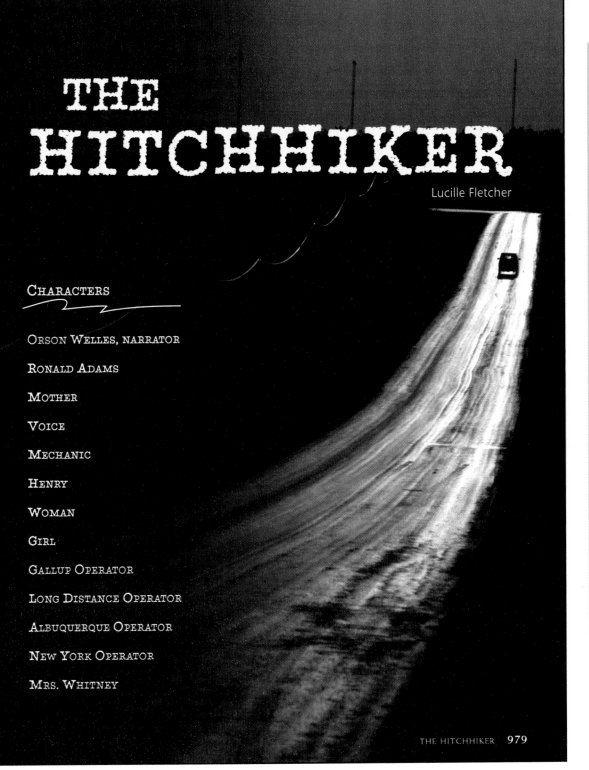

THE HITCHHIKER

Lucille Fletcher

CHARACTERS

ORSON WELLES, NARRATOR

RONALD ADAMS

MOTHER

VOICE

MECHANIC

HENRY

WOMAN

GIRL

GALLUP OPERATOR

LONG DISTANCE OPERATOR

ALBUQUERQUE OPERATOR

NEW YORK OPERATOR

MRS. WHITNEY

THE HITCHHIKER 979

BIOGRAPHICAL NOTE

Orson Welles (1915–1985) was an American writer, actor, director, and producer. He is best known for his groundbreaking film *Citizen Kane* (1941); his 1938 radio version of H. G. Wells's *War of the Worlds,* which caused widespread panic because many listeners believed this fictional account of an alien attack on New Jersey was a real news report; and his acting in films such as *Jane Eyre* (1944), *A Man for All Seasons* (1966), and *Catch-22* (1970).

WELLES. (*narrating*)   Good evening, this is Orson Welles. . . .

MUSIC.   *In.*

WELLES.   Personally I've never met anybody who didn't like a good ghost story, but I know a lot of people who think there are a lot of people who don't like a good ghost story. For the benefit of these, at least, I go on record at the <u>outset</u> of this evening's entertainment with the sober assurance that, although blood may be curdled on the program, none will be spilt. There's no shooting, knifing, throttling, axing, or poisoning here. No clanking chains, no cobwebs, no bony and/or hairy hands appearing from secret panels or, better yet, bedroom curtains. If it's any part of that dear old <u>phosphorescent</u> foolishness that people who don't like ghost stories don't like, then again, I promise you we haven't got it. What we do have is a thriller. If it's half as good as we think it is, you can call it a shocker, and we present it proudly and without apologies. After all, a story doesn't have to appeal to the heart—it can also appeal to the spine. Sometimes you want your heart to be warmed—sometimes you want your spine to tingle. The tingling, it's to be hoped, will be quite audible as you listen tonight to *The Hitchhiker*—That's the name of our story, *The Hitchhiker*—

> How will this ghost story differ from others?

SOUND.   *Automobile wheels humming over concrete road.*

MUSIC.   *Something weird and shuddery.*

ADAMS. (*narrating*)   I am in an auto camp[1] on Route Sixty-Six just west of Gallup, New Mexico. If I tell it, perhaps it will help me. It will keep me from going mad. But I must tell this quickly. I am not mad now. I feel perfectly well, except that I am running a slight temperature. My name is Ronald Adams. I am thirty-six years of age, unmarried, tall, dark, with a black mustache. I drive a 1940 Ford V-8, license number 6V-7989. I was born in Brooklyn.[2] All this I know. I know that I am, at this moment, perfectly sane. That it is not I who has gone mad—but something else—something utterly beyond my control. But I must speak quickly . . . very quickly. At any moment the link with life may break. This may be the last thing I ever tell on earth . . . the last night I ever see the stars. . . .

> How does the writer communicate the setting and build suspense and mystery at the beginning of the play?

MUSIC.   *In.*

ADAMS. (*narrating*)   Six days ago I left Brooklyn to drive to California. . . .

MOTHER.   Goodbye, son. Good luck to you, my boy. . . .

ADAMS.   Goodbye, mother. Here—give me a kiss, and then I'll go. . . .

MOTHER.   I'll come out with you to the car.

ADAMS.   No. It's raining. Stay here at the door. Hey—what is this? Tears? I thought you promised me you wouldn't cry.

MOTHER.   I know dear. I'm sorry. But I—do hate to see you go.

ADAMS.   I'll be back. I'll only be on the coast three months.

MOTHER.   Oh—it isn't that. It's just—the trip. Ronald—I really wish you weren't driving.

ADAMS.   Oh—mother. There you go again. People do it every day.

---

1. **auto camp.** Highway rest area
2. **Brooklyn.** One of the five boroughs of New York City; located south of the island of Manhattan

---

words for everyday use	**out • set** (outʹsetʹ) *n.,* beginning; start. *Though he tried his best, Randall knew from the <u>outset</u> that he would never persuade the queen of the prom to join his rock band.*
	phos • pho • res • cent (fäsʹfə resʹsənt) *adj.,* luminescent, giving off light. *Warm sea waters often glow at night when <u>phosphorescent</u> plankton are agitated.*

MOTHER. I know. But you'll be careful, won't you. Promise me you'll be extra careful. Don't fall asleep—or drive fast—or pick up any strangers on the road. . . .

What does Adams's mother fear?

ADAMS. Lord, no. You'd think I was still seventeen to hear you talk—

MOTHER. And wire me as soon as you get to Hollywood, won't you, son?

ADAMS. Of course I will. Now don't you worry. There isn't anything going to happen. It's just eight days of perfectly simple driving on smooth, decent, civilized roads, with a hotdog or a hamburger stand every ten miles. . . . *(Fade)*

SOUND. *Auto hum.*

MUSIC. *In.*

ADAMS. *(narrating)* I was in excellent spirits. The drive ahead of me, even the loneliness, seemed like a lark. But I reckoned without *him.*

MUSIC. *Changes to something weird and empty.*

ADAMS. *(narrating)* Crossing Brooklyn Bridge that morning in the rain, I saw a man leaning against the cables. He seemed to be waiting for a lift. There were spots of fresh rain on his shoulders. He was carrying a cheap overnight bag in one hand. He was thin, <u>nondescript</u>, with a cap pulled down over his eyes. He stepped off the walk right in front of me and, if I hadn't swerved hard, I'd have hit him.

SOUND. *Terrific skidding.*

MUSIC. *In.*

How do the sound effects help to communicate the action?

ADAMS. *(narrating)* I would have forgotten him completely, except that just an hour later, while crossing the Pulaski Skyway over the Jersey flats,[3] I saw him again. At least, he looked like the same person. He was standing now, with

one thumb pointing west. I couldn't figure out how he'd got there, but I thought probably one of those fast trucks had picked him up, beaten me to the Skyway, and let him off. I didn't stop for him. Then—late that night, I saw him again.

MUSIC. *Changing.*

ADAMS. *(narrating)* It was on the New Pennsylvania Turnpike between Harrisburg and Pittsburgh. It's two hundred and sixty-five miles long, with a very high speed limit. I was just slowing down for one of the tunnels—when I saw him—standing under an arc light by the side of the road. I could see him quite distinctly. The bag, the cap, even the spots of fresh rain spattered over his shoulders. He hailed me this time. . . .

VOICE. *(very spooky and faint)* Hall-ooo. . . . *(It echoes as though coming through the tunnel.)* Hall-ooo. . . !

ADAMS. *(narrating)* I stepped on the gas like a shot. That's lonely country

What is unusual about the hitchhiker's voice?

through the Alleghenies, and I had no intention of stopping. Besides, the coincidence, or whatever it was, gave me the willies. I stopped at the next gas station.

SOUND. *Auto tires screeching to stop . . . horn honk.*

MECHANIC. Yes, sir.

ADAMS. Fill her up.

MECHANIC. Certainly, sir. Check your oil, sir?

ADAMS. No, thanks.

SOUND. *Gas being put into car.*

MECHANIC. Nice night, isn't it?

---

3. **Pulaski Skyway . . . Jersey flats.** Name of an overpass that crosses a marshy area in northeastern New Jersey

<table>
<tr><td>**words
for
everyday
use**</td><td>**non • de • script** (nän´di skript´) *adj.,* lacking in recognizable characteristics or qualities. *When I saw the <u>nondescript</u> car following ours for the third time that day, I began to think I was in a spy story.*</td></tr>
</table>

THE HITCHHIKER **981**

ANSWERS TO GUIDED READING QUESTIONS

1. Adams's mother fears that her son will have an accident while driving.
2. The sound effects here indicate the violence with which Adams swerved on the bridge; in general, they help to convey actions that cannot easily or naturally be conveyed through dialogue.
3. The hitchhiker's voice sounds very spooky and faint; it echoes as if coming through a tunnel.

CROSS-CURRICULAR ACTIVITIES

GEOGRAPHY. Students can obtain a road atlas and trace the probable route that Adams took on his cross-country trip from Brooklyn, New York, to Gallup, New Mexico.

ADDITIONAL QUESTIONS AND ACTIVITIES

Have groups of students perform the first four pages of the play using mime only. Instead of speaking or using sound effects, they should convey the action, the characters' conversations, and Adams's thoughts and feelings nonverbally, using movement, gesture, facial expression, and posture. Have them begin with Adams's first lines and end with the train incident. Students may wish to designate one student to serve as director.

ANSWERS TO GUIDED READING QUESTIONS

1. Adams is asking about the rain because the hitchhiker he just saw had fresh rain on his shoulders, like the one he saw earlier in New Jersey, even though it has been dry in the area for quite some time.
2. The mechanic's comments suggest that people do not hitchhike on the lonely stretch of highway Adams is traveling.

Quotables

"A good scare is worth more to a man than good advice."

—Ed Howe

ADDITIONAL QUESTIONS AND ACTIVITIES

Have students skim the play for details that indicate that the story is not contemporary. Ask them to estimate the time period of the story based on the details they find.
Answers
Details that indicate the time period include the following: Orson Welles (d. 1985) serving as narrator; Adams's car, a 1940 Ford V-8; the cost of gasoline (a fill-up for $1.49); a highway driving speed of 45 miles per hour; the term "auto camp" instead of "rest stop"; the use of "Route 66" as a cross-country route; the long procedure for making a long-distance pay-telephone call; the use of a name ("Beechwood") in the telephone number. The time period is probably the 1940s.

ADAMS. Yes. It—hasn't been raining here recently, has it?

MECHANIC. Not a drop of rain all week.

Why is Adams asking about the rain?

ADAMS. I suppose that hasn't done your business any harm.

MECHANIC. Oh—people drive through here all kinds of weather. Mostly business, you know. There aren't many pleasure cars out on the Turnpike this season of the year.

ADAMS. I suppose not. (*casually*) What about hitchhikers?

MECHANIC. (*laughing*) Hitchhikers here?

ADAMS. What's the matter? Don't you ever see any?

MECHANIC. Not much. If we did, it'd be a sight for sore eyes.

ADAMS. Why?

MECHANIC. A guy'd be a fool who started out to hitch rides on this road. Look at it. It's two hundred and sixty-five miles long, there's practically no speed limit, and it's a straightaway. Now what car is going to stop to pick up a guy under those conditions? Would you stop?

ADAMS. No. (*He answers slowly, with puzzled emphasis.*) Then you've never seen anybody?

MECHANIC. Nope. Mebbe they get the lift before the Turnpike starts—I mean, you know—just before the toll house—but then it'd be a mighty long ride. Most cars wouldn't want to pick up a guy for that long a ride. And you know—this is pretty lonesome country here—mountains, and woods. . . . You ain't seen anybody like that, have you?

How do the mechanic's comments add to the mystery?

ADAMS. No. (*quickly*) Oh no, not at all. It was—just a—technical question.

MECHANIC. I see. Well—that'll be just a dollar forty-nine—with the tax. . . . (*Fade*)

SOUND. *Auto hum up.*

MUSIC. *Changing.*

ADAMS. (*narrating*) The thing gradually passed from my mind, as sheer coincidence. I had a good night's sleep in Pittsburgh. I did not think about the man all next day—until just outside of Zanesville, Ohio, I saw him again.

MUSIC. *Dark, ominous note.*

ADAMS. (*narrating*) It was a bright sun-shiny afternoon. The peaceful Ohio fields, brown with the autumn stubble, lay dreaming in the golden light. I was driving slowly, drinking it in, when the road suddenly ended in a detour. In front of the barrier, he was standing.

MUSIC. *In.*

ADAMS. (*narrating*) Let me explain about his appearance before I go on. I repeat. There was nothing sinister about him. He was as drab as a mud fence. Nor was his attitude menacing. He merely stood there, waiting, almost drooping a little, the cheap overnight bag in his hand. He looked as though he had been waiting there for hours. Then he looked up. He hailed me. He started to walk forward.

VOICE. (*far off*) Hall-ooo . . . Hall-ooo. . . .

ADAMS. (*narrating*) I had stopped the car, of course, for the detour. And for a few moments, I couldn't seem to find the new road. I knew he must be thinking that I had stopped for him.

VOICE. (*sounding closer now*) Hall-ooo . . . Hallll . . . ooo. . . .

words for everyday use om • i • nous (äm´ə nəs) *adj.*, threatening, sinister. *The captain of the field hockey team thought the buzzards circling overhead at the start of the game were* ominous.

SOUND. *Gears jamming . . . sound of motor turning over hard . . . nervous accelerator.*

VOICE. (*closer*)   Hall . . . oooo. . . .

ADAMS. (*with panic in his voice*)   No. Not just now. Sorry. . . .

VOICE. (*closer*)   Going to California?

SOUND. *Starter starting . . . gears jamming.*

ADAMS. (*as though sweating blood*)   No. Not today. The other way. Going to New York. Sorry . . . sorry. . . .

SOUND. *Car starts with squeal of wheels on dirt . . . into auto hum.*

MUSIC. *In.*

ADAMS. (*narrating*)   After I got the car back onto the road again, I felt like a fool. Yet the thought of picking him up, of having him sit beside me was somehow unbearable. Yet, at the same time, I felt, more than ever, unspeakably alone.

SOUND. *Auto hum up.*

ADAMS. (*narrating*)   Hour after hour went by. The fields, the towns ticked off, one by one. The lights changed. I knew now that I was going to see him again. And though I dreaded the sight, I caught myself searching the side of the road, waiting for him to appear.

SOUND. *Auto hum up . . . car screeches to a halt . . . impatient honk two or three times . . . door being unbolted.*

SLEEPY MAN'S VOICE.   Yep? What is it? What do you want?

ADAMS. (*breathless*)   You sell sandwiches and pop here, don't you?

VOICE. (*cranky*)   Yep. We do. In the daytime. But we're closed up now for the night.

ADAMS.   I know. But—I was wondering if you could possibly let me have a cup of coffee—black coffee.

VOICE.   Not at this time of night, mister. My wife's the cook and she's in bed. Mebbe further down the road—at the Honeysuckle Rest. . . .

SOUND. *Door squeaking on hinges as though being closed.*

ADAMS.   No—no. Don't shut the door. (*shakily*) Listen—just a minute ago, there was a man standing here—right beside this stand—a suspicious looking man. . . .

WOMAN'S VOICE. (*from distance*)   Henry? Who is it, Henry?

HENRY.   It's nobuddy, mother. Just a feller thinks he wants a cup of coffee. Go back into bed.

ADAMS.   I don't mean to disturb you. But you see, I was driving along—when I just happened to look—and there he was. . . .

HENRY.   What was he doing?

ADAMS.   Nothing. He ran off—when I stopped the car.

HENRY.   Then what of it? That's nothing to wake a man in the middle of his sleep about. (*sternly*) Young man, I've got a good mind to turn you over to the local sheriff.

> *Why does Henry react in this way? What is peculiar about the way in which Adams is behaving?*

ADAMS.   But—I—

HENRY.   You've been taking a nip,[4] that's what you've been doing. And you haven't got anything better to do than to wake decent folk out of their hard-earned sleep. Get going. Go on.

ADAMS.   But—he looked as though he were going to rob you.

HENRY.   I ain't got nothin' in this stand to lose. Now—on your way before I call out Sheriff Oakes. (*Fade*)

SOUND. *Auto hum up.*

---

4. **taking a nip.** Having a drink of something alcoholic

1. Henry cannot understand the cause of Adams's alarm and thus is suspicious of him. Adams is clearly disturbed and not acting politely or rationally.

ADAMS. (*narrating*)   I got into the car again, and drove on slowly. I was beginning to hate the car. If I could have found a place to stop . . . to rest a little. But I was in the Ozark Mountains of Missouri now. The few resort places there were closed. Only an occasional log cabin, seemingly deserted, broke the monotony of the wild wooded landscape. I had seen him at that roadside stand; I knew I would see him again— perhaps at the next turn of the road. I knew that when I saw him next, I would run him down. . . .

SOUND.   *Auto hum up.*

ADAMS.   But I did not see him again until late next afternoon. . . .

SOUND.   *Warning system at train crossing.*

ADAMS. (*narrating*)   I had stopped the car at a sleepy little junction just across the border into Oklahoma—to let a train pass by—when he appeared, across the tracks, leaning against a telephone pole.

SOUND.   *Distant sound of train chugging . . . bell ringing steadily.*

ADAMS. (*narrating, very tensely*)   It was a perfectly airless, dry day. The red clay of Oklahoma was baking under the southwestern sun. Yet there were spots of fresh rain on his shoulders. I couldn't stand that. Without thinking, blindly, I started the car across the tracks.

SOUND.   *Train chugging closer.*

ADAMS. (*narrating*)   He didn't even look up at me. He was staring at the ground. I stepped on the gas hard, veering the wheel sharply toward him. I could hear the train in the distance now, but I didn't care. Then something went wrong with the car. It stalled right on the tracks.

SOUND.   *Train chugging closer. Above this, sound of car stalling.*

ADAMS. (*narrating*)   The train was coming closer. I could hear its bell ringing, and the cry of its whistle. Still he stood there. And now—I knew that he was beckoning—beckoning me to my death.

SOUND.   *Train chugging close. Whistle blows wildly. Then train rushes up and by with pistons going.*

ADAMS. (*narrating*)   Well—I frustrated him that time. The starter had worked at last. I managed to back up. But when the train passed, he was gone. I was all alone in the hot dry afternoon.

SOUND.   *Train retreating. Crickets begin to sing in background.*

MUSIC.   *In.*

ADAMS. (*narrating*)   After that, I knew I had to do something. I didn't know who this man was or what he wanted of me. I only knew that from now on, I must not let myself be alone on the road for one single moment.

SOUND.   *Auto hum up. Slow down. Stop. Door opening.*

ADAMS.   Hello, there. Like a ride?

GIRL.   Well, what do you think? How far you going?

ADAMS.   Amarillo . . . I'll take you all the way to Amarillo.

GIRL.   Amarillo, Texas?

ADAMS.   I'll drive you there.

GIRL.   Gee!

SOUND. *Door closes—car starts.*

MUSIC.   *In.*

GIRL.   Mind if I take off my shoes? My dogs[5] are killing me.

ADAMS.   Go right ahead.

GIRL.   Gee, what a break this is. A swell car, a decent guy, and driving all the way to Amarillo. All I been getting so far is trucks.

ADAMS.   Hitchhike much?

GIRL.   Sure. Only it's tough sometimes, in these great open spaces, to get the breaks.

---

5. **dogs.** Feet (slang)

ADDITIONAL QUESTIONS AND ACTIVITIES

What word does Adams use to describe the man he keeps seeing? What does he say he is trying to do about the man?
Answers
He describes him as a sort of phantom. He is trying to get rid of him ("run him down") or prove that he is real.

ADAMS. I should think it would be. Though I'll bet if you get a good pick-up in a fast car, you can get to places faster than—say, another person, in another car?

GIRL. I don't get you.

ADAMS. Well, take me, for instance. Suppose I'm driving across the country, say, at a nice steady clip of about forty-five miles an hour. Couldn't a girl like you, just standing beside the road, waiting for lifts, beat me to town after town—provided she got picked up every time in a car doing from sixty-five to seventy miles an hour?

GIRL. I dunno. Maybe and maybe not. What difference does it make?

ADAMS. Oh—no difference. It's just a—crazy idea I had sitting here in the car.

GIRL. (*laughing*) Imagine spending your time in a swell car thinking of things like that!

ADAMS. What would you do instead?

GIRL. (*admiringly*) What would I do? If I was a good-looking fellow like yourself? Why—I'd just enjoy myself—every minute of the time. I'd sit back, and relax, and if I saw a good-looking girl along the side of the road . . . (*sharply*) Hey! Look out!

ADAMS. (*breathlessly*) Did you see him too?

GIRL. See who?

ADAMS. That man. Standing beside the barbed wire fence.

GIRL. I didn't see—anybody. There wasn't nothing but a bunch of steers—and the barbed wire fence. What did you think you was doing? Trying to run into the barbed wire fence?

ADAMS. There was a man there, I tell you . . . a thin gray man, with an overnight bag in his hand. And I was trying to—run him down.

GIRL. Run him down? You mean—kill him?

ADAMS. He's a sort of—phantom. I'm trying to get rid of him—or else prove that he's real.

THE HITCHHIKER 985

1. The girl runs away from Adams because he asks her strange questions, is apparently seeing things that do not exist, and runs the car off the road in an attempt to "get rid of" the thin gray man he has been seeing. She thinks he needs sleep, is out of control, and that it would be unsafe to travel with him.

But (*desperately*) you say you didn't see him back there? You're sure?

GIRL. (*queerly*) I didn't see a soul. And as far as that's concerned, mister . . .

ADAMS. Watch for him the next time, then. Keep watching. Keep your eyes peeled on the road. He'll turn up again—maybe any minute now. (*excitedly*) There. Look there—

SOUND. *Auto sharply veering and skidding. Girl screams.*

SOUND. *Crash of car going into barbed wire fence. Frightened lowing of steer.*

GIRL. How does this door work? I—I'm gettin' outta here.

ADAMS. Did you see him that time?

GIRL (*sharply*) No. I didn't see him that time. And personally, mister, I don't expect never to see him. All I want to do is to go on living—and I don't see how I will very long driving with you—

ADAMS. I'm sorry. I—I don't know what came over me. (*frightened*) Please—don't go. . . .

GIRL. So if you'll excuse me, mister—

ADAMS. You can't go. Listen, how would you like to go to California? I'll drive you to California.

GIRL. Seeing pink elephants all the way? No thanks.

ADAMS. (*desperately*) I could get you a job there. You wouldn't have to be a waitress. I have friends there—my name is Ronald Adams—You can check up.

SOUND. *Door opens.*

GIRL. Uhn-hunh. Thanks just the same.

ADAMS. Listen. Please. For just one minute. Maybe you think I am half cracked. But this man. You see, I've been seeing this man all the way across the country. He's been following me. And if you could only help me—stay with me—until I reach the coast—

GIRL. You know what I think you need, big boy? Not a girl friend. Just a good dose of sleep. . . . There, I got it now.

SOUND. *Door opens . . . slams.*

ADAMS. No. You can't go.

GIRL. (*screams*) Leave your hands offa me, do you hear! Leave your—

ADAMS. Come back here, please, come back.

SOUND. *Struggle . . . slap . . . footsteps running away on gravel . . . lowing of steer.*

> Why does the girl run away?

ADAMS. (*narrating*) She ran from me, as though I were a monster. A few minutes later, I saw a passing truck pick her up. I knew then that I was utterly alone.

SOUND. *Lowing of steer up.*

ADAMS. (*narrating*) I was in the heart of the great Texas prairies. There wasn't a car on the road after the truck went by. I tried to figure out what to do, how to get hold of myself. If I could find a place to rest. Or even, if I could sleep right here in the car for a few hours, along the side of the road . . . I was getting my winter overcoat out of the back seat to use as a blanket, (Hall-ooo), when I saw him coming toward me (Hall-ooo), emerging from the herd of moving steer . . .

VOICE. Hall-ooo . . . Hall-oooo . . .

SOUND. *Auto starting violently . . . up to steady hum.*

MUSIC. *In.*

ADAMS. (*narrating*) I didn't wait for him to come any closer. Perhaps I should have spoken to him then, fought it out then and there. For now he began to be everywhere. Whenever I stopped, even for a moment—for gas, for oil, for a drink of pop, a cup of coffee, a sandwich—he was there.

MUSIC. *Faster.*

ADAMS. (*narrating*) I saw him standing outside the auto camp in Amarillo that night, when I dared to slow down. He was sitting near the drinking fountain in a little camping spot just inside the border of New Mexico.

MUSIC. *Faster.*

ADAMS. (*narrating*) He was waiting for me outside the Navajo Reservation,[6] where I stopped to check my tires. I saw him in Albuquerque where I bought twelve gallons of gas . . . I was afraid now, afraid to stop. I began to drive faster and faster. I was in lunar landscape now—the great arid mesa country of New Mexico. I drove through it with the indifference of a fly crawling over the face of the moon.

MUSIC. *Faster.*

ADAMS. (*narrating*) But now he didn't even wait for me to stop. Unless I drove at eighty-five miles an hour over those endless roads—he waited for me at every other mile. I would see his figure, shadowless, flitting before me, still in its same attitude, over the cold and lifeless ground, flitting over dried-up rivers, over broken stones cast up by old glacial upheavals, flitting in the pure and cloudless air. . . .

What does this passage confirm or deny about Adams's previous theory that the hitchhiker was getting fast rides and so staying ahead of him?

MUSIC. *Strikes sinister note of finality.*

ADAMS. (*narrating*) I was beside myself when I finally reached Gallup, New Mexico, this morning. There is an auto camp here—cold, almost deserted at this time of year. I went inside, and asked if there was a telephone. I had the feeling that if only I could speak to someone familiar, someone I loved, I could pull myself together.

SOUND. *Nickel put in slot.*

OPERATOR. Number, please?

Why does Adams make the telephone call?

ADAMS. Long distance.

SOUND. *Return of nickel: buzz.*

LONG DISTANCE. This is long distance.

ADAMS. I'd like to put in a call to my home in Brooklyn, New York. My name is Ronald

Adams. The number there is Beechwood 2-0828.

LONG DISTANCE. Thank you. What is your number?

ADAMS. 312.

ALBUQUERQUE OPR. Albuquerque.

LONG DISTANCE. New York for Gallup. (*Pause*)

NEW YORK OPR. New York.

LONG DISTANCE. Gallup, New Mexico, calling Beechwood 2-0828. (*Fade*)

ADAMS. I had read somewhere that love could banish demons. It was the middle of the morning. I knew Mother would be home. I pictured her, tall, white-haired, in her crisp house dress, going about her tasks. It would be enough, I thought, merely to hear the even calmness of her voice. . . .

LONG DISTANCE. Will you please deposit three dollars and eighty-five cents for the first three minutes? When you have deposited a dollar and a half, will you please wait until I have collected the money?

SOUND. *Clunk of six coins.*

LONG DISTANCE. All right, deposit another dollar and a half.

SOUND. *Clunk of six coins.*

LONG DISTANCE. Will you please deposit the remaining twelve cents?

SOUND. *Clunk of four coins.*

LONG DISTANCE. Ready with Brooklyn—go ahead, please.

ADAMS. Hello.

MRS. WHITNEY. Mrs. Adams's residence.

ADAMS. Hello. Hello—Mother?

---

6. **Navajo Reservation.** Land reserved for the Navajo tribe by the United States government during the period of westward expansion, similar to other reservations for Native American tribes

THE HITCHHIKER **987**

1. Adams receives the information
that he himself was killed in an
automobile accident six days ago
on the Brooklyn Bridge.

SELECTION CHECK TEST 4.12.11
WITH ANSWERS

Checking Your Reading
1. On what bridge did Adams swerve
to avoid hitting a hitchhiker? **He
swerved on the Brooklyn Bridge.**
2. Who keeps appearing to Adams as
he is traveling? **A male hitchhiker
keeps appearing to Adams.**
3. What happens just before the
female hitchhiker leaves Adams?
**Adams drives off the road and
through a fence.**
4. To whom does Adams wish to
speak when he calls home? **He
wishes to speak to his mother.**
5. What does Adams learn about
himself when he calls home? **He
learns that he died in an accident
on the Brooklyn Bridge.**

Vocabulary in Context
Fill in each blank below with the most
appropriate word from the following
Words for Everyday Use. You may have
to change the tense of the word.

phosphorescent   nondescript
ominous   outset

1. The **phosphorescent** mushrooms
glowed in the pitch-black cave.
2. At the **outset** of their journey, the
Donner party was optimistic, but
once they had traveled many miles,
they began to despair.
3. The house was **nondescript**; it
looked like most of the other
houses in the suburban
neighborhood.
4. Rain had been predicted and the
sky indeed looked **ominous**, so we
decided to postpone the picnic.

Literary Tools
Fill in the blanks using the following
terms. You may not use every term, and
you may use some terms more than
once.

sound effects   foreshadowing
narrator   suspense

1. Playwrights sometimes call for
s**ound effects** to make the action in
a play seem more realistic.
2. A feeling of anxiousness or curiosity
in the mind of the reader, viewer,
or listener is called **suspense**.

MRS. WHITNEY. (*very flat and rather proper . . .
dumb, too, in a flighty sort of way*) This is Mrs.
Adams's residence. Who is it you wished to speak
to, please?

ADAMS. Why—who's this?

MRS. WHITNEY. This is Mrs. Whitney.

ADAMS. Whitney? I don't know
any Mrs. Whitney. Is this Beechwood 2-0828?

MRS. WHITNEY. Yes.

ADAMS. Where's my mother? Where's Mrs.
Adams?

MRS. WHITNEY. Mrs. Adams is not at home.
She is still in the hospital.

ADAMS. The hospital!

MRS. WHITNEY. Yes. Who is this calling
please? Is it a member of the family?

ADAMS. What's she in the hospital for?

MRS. WHITNEY. She's been prostrated[7] for
five days. Nervous breakdown. But who is this
calling?

ADAMS. Nervous breakdown? But—my
mother was never nervous . . .

MRS. WHITNEY. It's all taken place since the
death of her oldest son, Ronald.

Respond *to the* SELECTION

Did you guess the ending before you finished reading? Discuss with other students in your class
what you thought would happen.

ADAMS. The death of her oldest son, Ronald . . . ?
Hey—what is this? What number is this?

MRS. WHITNEY. This is Beechwood 2-0828.
It's all been very sudden. He was killed just six
days ago in an automobile accident on the
Brooklyn Bridge.

OPERATOR. (*breaking in*)
Your three minutes are up,
sir. (*Silence*)

> *What inexplicable
information does Adams
receive from Mrs.
Whitney?*

OPERATOR. Your three
minutes are up, sir. (*pause*) Your three minutes
are up, sir. (*fade*) Sir, your three minutes are up.
Your three minutes are up, sir.

ADAMS. (*narrating in a strange voice*) And so, I am
sitting here in this deserted auto camp in Gallup,
New Mexico. I am trying to think. I am trying
to get hold of myself. Otherwise, I shall go
mad . . . Outside it is night—the vast, soulless
night of New Mexico. A million stars are in the
sky. Ahead of me stretch a thousand miles of
empty mesa, mountains, prairies—desert.
Somewhere among them, he is waiting for me.
Somewhere I shall know who he is, and who . . .
I . . . am. . . .

MUSIC. Up.   ∎

---

7. **prostrated.** The character means *prostrate*, lying flat.

SELECTION CHECK TEST 4.12.11 WITH ANSWERS (CONT.)

3. The **narrator** of a play introduces the work and piques
interest in it.
4. **Foreshadowing** is the act of presenting materials that
hint at events to occur later.
5. The writer keeps the audience interested in a story by
raising questions that produce **suspense**.

RESPOND TO THE SELECTION

Ask students if they agree with the
statement by Orson Welles in his
introduction that the story is a
"thriller." Did they find the story
spine-tingling? Why or why not?

from
THE VANISHING HITCHHIKER

Roadside Ghosts: "The Vanishing Hitchhiker"

Jan Harold Brunvand

A prime example of the adaptability of older legends is "The Vanishing Hitchhiker"—*the* classic automobile legend. This returning-ghost tale was known by the turn of the century both in the United States and abroad. It acquired the newer automobile motif by the period of the Great Depression, and thereafter spawned a number of subtypes with greatly varied and oddly interlocking details, some of which themselves stemmed from earlier folk legends. Merely sampling some of the many "Vanishing Hitchhiker" variants that have been collected over a period of some forty years can help us trace the legend's incredible development. Surely most readers already know a local "true" account (or maybe two or three) similar to Example A, as told by a teenager in Toronto, Canada in 1973:

Example A

Well, this happened to one of my girlfriend's best friends and her father. They were driving along a country road on their way home from the cottage when they saw a young girl hitchhiking. They stopped and picked her up and she got in the back seat. She told the girl and her father that she just lived in the house about five miles up the road. She didn't say anything after that but just turned to watch out the window. When the father saw the house, he drove up to it and turned around to tell the girl they had arrived—but she wasn't there! Both he and his daughter were really mystified and decided to knock on the door and tell the people what had happened. They told them that they had once had a daughter who answered the description of the girl they supposedly had picked up, but she had disappeared some years ago and had last been seen hitchhiking on this very road. Today would have been her birthday.

This version has the basic elements—not necessarily "original" ones—well known in oral tradition and occasionally reported in newspapers since the early 1930s. The stable story units have been labeled in brackets in the following text from South Carolina collected by workers of the South Carolina Writers' Project (Work Projects Administration) sometime between 1935 and 1941:

According to the author of this essay, what is "The Vanishing Hitchhiker"?
Answers
It is an old legend about a roadside ghost with many subtypes. The legend is based on a returning-ghost tale known by the turn of the century and is passed on in the oral tradition.

LITERARY NOTE

Many urban legends began as "lesson tales," stories meant to frighten people, especially young people, from doing certain things. For example, the story of a ghostly hitchhiker might have spread because it contains a useful lesson against picking up strange hitchhikers while driving alone. Another well-known urban legend involves spiders nesting in a girl's heavily hair-sprayed "bee hive" hairdo; this legend may have been spread by parents who believed the 1960s fad hairstyle to be unhealthy and unattractive and who wished to discourage their children from wearing it. Other well-known urban legends involve tragedies occurring while a teenage couple sits alone in a car—another activity parents often wish to discourage.

Example B

A traveling man [driver] who lived in Spartanburg [authentication] was on his way home one night [setting] when he saw a woman walking along the side of the road [hitchhiker]. He stopped his car and asked the woman if he could take her where she was going. She stated that she was on her way to visit her brother who lived about three miles further on the same road [her address]. He asked her to get in the car and sit by him, but she said she would sit in the back of the car [her choice of seat]. Conversation took place for a while as they rode along, but soon the woman grew quiet. The man drove on until he reached the home of the woman's brother, whom he knew [more authentica-tion]; then stopped his car to let the woman alight. When he looked behind him, there was no one in the car [disap-pearance]. He thought that rather strange [curiosity or concern], so went into the house and informed the brother that a lady had gotten into his car to ride to see him, but when he arrived at the house the lady had disappeared. The brother was not alarmed at all and stated that the lady was his sister who had died two years before [identification]. He said that this traveling man was the seventh to pick up his sister on the road to visit him, but that she had never reached his house yet.

Variations on the basic story are endless, and trying to sort them out into any kind of possible chronological development is hampered by the fact that the date when a version happened to be collected and published bears little relationship to its possible age in tradition, and by the prin-ciple that legends become highly localized and rationalized with many circumstantial details whenever they are adopted into a particular context. For instance, the plot has several differ-ent twists and turns in this 1935 version (para-phrased by the collector) from Berkeley, California:

Example C

This story was heard in a Durant Avenue boarding house, told several times as a true story. It happened to a friend of the narrator. This friend was driving up Hearst Avenue one rainy night. As he came to North Gate (Hearst and Euclid avenues) he saw a girl, a student with books under her arm, waiting for the streetcar. Since these had stopped running, he offered her a ride. She lived up on Euclid. They drove out along Euclid quite a way with some conversation. As they were crossing an intersection, another car came down the steep hill and they would have crashed if the girl had not pulled on the emergency brake [a unique detail in the story]. The fellow was flabbergasted and sat looking at the other car, which pulled around him and went on. When he remem-bered his companion and looked over, she was gone. Since it was near her home, he assumed she had simply gotten out to walk the rest of the way; but she had left a book on the seat. The next day he went to return the book. He found her father, an English professor, at home. He said that the girl was his daughter, that she had been killed in an auto accident at the same corner one or two years ago that very day. But since the fellow had the book, the father took it into the library, to look on the shelves for it—he found the place where it should have been vacant.

A strictly urban setting for the story allows for more precise and thorough double-checking of factual details. In 1941 Rosalie Hankey of the University of California, who was gathering materials for a lengthy study of "The Vanishing Hitchhiker," tried to verify specific accident reports from Berkeley. In one version the automobile crash in which the girl was killed was supposed to have happened in 1935 or 1936 at the corner of College and Bancroft. But in checking the Berkeley city records from 1934 to 1937, Hankey found that only a single accident involving personal injury, non-fatal, had occurred at that corner during the five-year period. . . .

"The Vanishing Hitchhiker" is unusual among urban legends in deriving from earlier supernatural folk legends with foreign antecedents. Many ghosts, in fact, are said to be on endless quests—such as The Flying Dutchman's—for peace and contentment back home. Folklorist Louis C. Jones established this link to traditional ghostlore by citing a number of New York state versions—some of them associated with European immigrant storytellers—reliably dated to the late nineteenth century and involving travelers on horseback. Here is one of his examples:

Example H
(Collected by Catherine S. Martin, 1943, from her mother Grace C. Martin, who lived as a girl in and near Delmar, a small town, eight miles southwest of Albany, New York. The story was current in the 1890s.)

Mother has told of tales that she has heard of a ghost rider who used to jump on young men's horses as they went past a certain woods near Delmar on their way to parties. The rider, a woman, always disappeared when they arrived at their destination. She was believed to have been a jealous one, but did little harm except riding behind the young man.

. . . Three other versions, from Illinois (2) and Georgia (1) dated by storytellers as having been known in 1876, 1912, and 1920 place the hitchhiker in a horse-drawn vehicle; Professor Jones has also called attention to a Chinese story collected from immigrants in California in which the ghost of a beautiful young girl *walks* with a young man along the road to her parents' home, whereupon she disappears. In an interesting counterpart to the American legend, the Chinese girl walks *behind* the man (just as the hitchhiker almost invariably sits in the car's backseat or rumble seat), so that he must turn around in order to notice her disappearance. Also, the Chinese father's reaction is a clear parallel of the scene in later accounts: "Yes, that is the precise place where she was killed. It was her spirit which led you here." ■

ABOUT THE RELATED READING
The Related Reading from *The Vanishing Hitchhiker* analyzes a classic urban legend involving a ghostly hitchhiker much like the one in the play you just read. The author presents several versions of the urban legend and traces the story back to early supernatural folk legends. **Jan Harold Brunvand** is a professor emeritus of folklore at the University of Utah and the foremost expert on urban legends, having written numerous books on the subject. Brunvand defines urban legends as "realistic stories concerning recent events (or alleged events) with an ironic or supernatural twist. They are an integral part of white Anglo-American culture and are told and believed by some of the most sophisticated 'folk' of modern society—young people, urbanites, and the well educated. The storytellers assume that the true facts of each case lie just one or two informants back down the line with a reliable witness, or in a news media report." How can you tell if a story is actually an urban legend? The easiest way to test it, Brunvand says, is to simply ask yourself, "Is it too good to be true?" If it *is* too good, it probably isn't true. There are about 500 of these stories currently being told, says Brunvand, a sign that "the storytelling urge is alive and well." His latest book is *The Truth Never Stands in the Way of a Good Story* (2000).

RECALL

1a. Adams tells his mother he will be careful driving on his long trip—that he will not fall asleep, drive fast, or pick up any strangers on the road. As Adams is crossing the Brooklyn Bridge in the rain, he sees a man who appears to be hitchhiking at the side of the road. When the man steps off the walk in front of him, Adams swerves hard to avoid hitting him.

2a. Adams picks up a young woman while driving. He tells her he sees a thin gray man with an overnight bag in his hand by the roadside and that he is trying to "run him down." Adams crashes into a fence at the side of the road where he thinks he sees the man standing.

3a. Adams telephones his mother. He wants to call her because he thinks that talking to someone familiar, whom he loves, will help him pull himself together. He learns from Mrs. Whitney that he died six days ago in a car accident on the Brooklyn Bridge.

INTERPRET

1b. She is worried that he might have an accident on the road. Her fears prove to be justified. Adams thinks he avoided hitting the man on the bridge and kept on driving.

2b. The young woman Adams picks up runs away because she is frightened. She has reason to fear Adams because he is acting irrationally, claiming to see a man that she doesn't see, and is driving unsafely.

3b. *Responses will vary.* Adams was killed in a crash on the bridge.

ANALYZE

4a. The figure beside the road is frightening because he repeatedly appears ahead of Adams, he is spattered with fresh rain even when there is no rain falling, he hails Adams in a strange voice, and he disappears as inexplicably as he appears.

SYNTHESIZE

4b. Adams wonders who the hitchhiker is and who he himself is. *Responses will vary.*

EVALUATE

5a. *Responses will vary.*

EXTEND

5b. *Responses will vary.* The idea for the play could have come from urban legends about a mysterious hitchhiker. Brunvand says that the legend goes back to the turn of the century and he gives two examples of the legend from the 1930s, so it

Investigate, Inquire, and Imagine

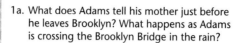

Recall: GATHERING FACTS → **Interpret: FINDING MEANING**

1a. What does Adams tell his mother just before he leaves Brooklyn? What happens as Adams is crossing the Brooklyn Bridge in the rain?

2a. Whom does Adams pick up while driving? What does he tell this person? What crazy act does Adams perform?

3a. Whom does Adams telephone near the end of the play? What reason does he give for making this call? What does he learn from Mrs. Whitney?

1b. What is Adams's mother worried about at the beginning of the play? Given the later events of the play, were her fears justified? What does Adams think happened on the bridge?

2b. Why does the person whom Adams picks up run away? Does this person have reason to fear Adams? Why, or why not?

3b. What do you think happened to Adams when he swerved on the Brooklyn Bridge?

Analyze: TAKING THINGS APART → **Synthesize: BRINGING THINGS TOGETHER**

4a. What makes the figure beside the road so frightening?

4b. What question does Adams raise at the end of the play? How would you answer the question?

Evaluate: MAKING JUDGMENTS → **Extend: CONNECTING IDEAS**

5a. Do you agree with the narrator that this is a spine-tingling tale? Why, or why not?

5b. Compare the play *The Hitchhiker* with the urban legends from *The Vanishing Hitchhiker*. Do you think the idea for the play could have come from urban legends about mysterious hitchhikers? Why, or why not? What similarities and differences are there between the legends and the radio play?

Understanding Literature

NARRATOR AND SOUND EFFECTS. Reread the definitions for **narrator** and **sound effects** on page 978. Who is the narrator of this play? What information does the narrator provide about the play to come? What does the narrator say to capture the attention of the audience and keep them tuned in? What are some of the sound effects used in this play? Why are such effects especially important in a radio play?

FORESHADOWING AND SUSPENSE. Reread the definitions for **foreshadowing** and **suspense** on page 978. How does the conversation between Adams and his mother at the beginning of the play foreshadow later events? What aspects of the hitchhiker raise questions in the minds of Adams and the audience for this play? What question does Adams repeat about the hitchhiker at the end of the play? What question does he have about himself at the end of the play? What do you think the answers to these questions might be? What other questions do you have that were never answered in the play?

ANSWERS TO INVESTIGATE, INQUIRE, AND IMAGINE (CONT.)

could have influenced the author of a radio play who was writing in the 1930s and 1940s. People probably find stories about vanishing travelers to be especially spooky because many people have had the experience of driving alone along a dark highway and can easily imagine strange things happening. The legend may be especially scary because it does carry a ring of truth—it *is* dangerous to pick up hitchhikers. As in the legend, the play involves a driver and a hitchhiker who

vanishes. In the play, however, the hitchhiker reappears over and over again. Also, the hitchhiker is a man instead of a young woman, as in Brunvand's examples. Perhaps the biggest difference is that in the play it is the driver, not the hitchhiker, who turns out to have died earlier.

Answers to Understanding Literature can be found on page 993.

Writer's Journal

1. Imagine you wanted to tell this story around a campfire. Create a **prose retelling** of the play, being sure to include all of the chilling details.

2. Imagine that the hitchhiker appeared again at the end of the play and delivered his lines in the form of a poem. Write the **poem** he would recite to Adams, explaining to his listener what has happened to him and where he must now go.

3. Think of a ghost story you know—perhaps one that you heard when you were a child. Now rewrite it in the form of a short **radio play**, using *The Hitchhiker* as a model.

Integrating the Language Arts

Language, Grammar, and Style

PARTS OF SPEECH. Review the Language Arts Survey 3.7, "Parts of Speech Overview." Then identify the part of speech for each underlined word or phrase in the sentences below.

1. Orson Welles, a <u>famous actor, writer, and director</u>, read the <u>part</u> of the narrator <u>in</u> *The Hitchhiker*.

2. In this radio play, <u>Ronald Adams,</u> the main character, experiences a nightmarish <u>drive</u> <u>from</u> Brooklyn to New Mexico.

3. <u>Radio</u> plays <u>were</u> <u>very</u> popular in the years before television was invented.

4. <u>Say,</u> have <u>you</u> ever heard of Lucille Fletcher's <u>other</u> well-known work, *Sorry, Wrong Number*?

5. <u>It</u> was made into a movie, <u>but</u> I haven't seen it yet. Would you like <u>to rent</u> it?

Collaborative Learning & Speaking and Listening

STAGING A RADIO PLAY. Work with other students to stage all or part of *The Hitchhiker*. Choose a director, actors, and sound effects people. Prepare scripts. Rehearse the play. Then present it to other students. You may wish to tape-record your presentation, listen to the recording, and then do a critique of your performance. If your class is large, you should divide into teams and have each team produce its own recording. If you wish, you may rewrite the roles slightly so that the lead is a woman (Veronica Adams, for example).

Study and Research & Media Literacy

RESEARCHING URBAN LEGENDS. With a partner, visit the library and check out one of Jan Brunvald's books about urban legends. Prepare an oral report about one of the legends he discusses in his book. As an alternative, find your legend on the Urban Legends Reference Pages on the Internet at http://www.snopes.com, a site run by Barbara and David P. Mikkelson. You may wish to create visuals to go along with your presentation. Encourage other students to share any stories they may have heard that are similar to the legend you chose to research.

NARRATOR AND SOUND EFFECTS. The narrator of the play is Orson Welles. The narrator tells the audience that the play is a ghost story without the violence and other stereotypical features of ghost stories, such as cobwebs and bony hands. To capture the attention of the audience, he says that the story is a thriller and a shocker that will tingle the spine.

Sound effects include automobile sounds that signal what Adams's car is doing and weird music that reinforces the spooky mood of the story. These effects are especially important in a radio play because listeners must rely entirely on their ears to understand the action and picture the scenes in the story. Music is important for establishing mood because a play generally consists of dialogue and does not contain descriptive passages that could set the mood through language and sensory details.

FORESHADOWING AND SUSPENSE. In the conversation, the mother worries that some harm will come to her son on his driving trip, perhaps because of driving fast or picking up a hitchhiker. This conversation foreshadows the son's fatal car accident, as well as his speeding and encounter with a hitchhiker.

Two aspects of the hitchhiker raise questions in the mind of Adams and the audience. First, his shoulders are sprinkled with rain no matter where he appears, even when it has not been raining. Second, he always seems to be one step ahead of Adams on his cross-country trip and is following the same route. Since both of these aspects defy common sense and probability, they raise the question of whether the hitchhiker may be a figment of Adams's imagination or a supernatural character. At the end of the play, Adams wonders who the hitchhiker is and who he himself is. The hitchhiker may be Death, and Adams may be a ghost. *Responses will vary.*

ANSWERS TO INTEGRATING THE LANGUAGE ARTS

Language, Grammar, and Style
1. appositive, noun, preposition
2. noun, noun, preposition
3. adjective, verb, adverb
4. interjection, pronoun, adjective
5. pronoun, conjunction, verbal (infinitive)

ANSWERS TO INTEGRATING THE LANGUAGE ARTS (CONT.)

Collaborative Learning & Speaking and Listening
Students will need to convey the feelings and attitudes of the characters strictly through voice. In addition, have them think about how the pace of the dialogue might change in different scenes. Remind them that brief silences or pauses can be used effectively in a radio play—to indicate transitions, to vary the pace of the dialogue, and to help convey a character's reaction.

Study and Research & Media Literacy
In their oral reports, students should briefly retell the legend. They may also discuss the origin of the legend if known, typical features of the legend, and any variations that exist.

LESSON OVERVIEW

Writing a Short Story/Science Fiction

GUIDED WRITING
Software

See the Guided Writing Software for an extended version of this lesson that includes printable graphic organizers, extensive student models and student-friendly checklists, and self-, peer, and teacher evaluation features.

INDIVIDUAL LEARNING STRATEGIES

MOTIVATION
To pique students' interest, you might read several short science fiction stories in class, or play a short clip from a science fiction movie. Ask them to discuss science fiction books and movies they enjoy. What elements made these books or movies particularly unique or exciting? What larger social issues or issues of human nature did their plots explore?

"What good are all the objects in the universe if there is no subject?"
—Ursula K. LeGuin

EXAMINING THE MODEL. In Ray Bradbury's "The Pedestrian," Leonard Mead finds himself in the strange situation of having to explain to an empty police car why he's out walking at night while everyone else in his town is glued to their "viewing screens."

Bradbury examines one significant factor in the world of "The Pedestrian" in the year 2053: almost everybody spends every evening watching his or her "viewing screen." From there, Bradbury
continued on page 995

Guided Writing

WRITING A SHORT STORY/ SCIENCE FICTION

Science fiction gives you writing power in a wild way—you can bend time, mince space, and mutate bodies at will. When we write or read sci-fi, all rules are off—or are they? What makes a science fiction story really good, anyway? Is it the oddity of the surrounding phenomena or the magnitude of the intergalactic explosions? While those things certainly help us through the story and boost our interest, in the end they alone can't carry the story. Science fiction is, like all fiction, about solid, believable characters—how they think and what they do in their weird worlds that tell us about the life we live here and now. Science fiction takes relatively normal people and throws them forward into unseen worlds and watches what happens.

WRITING ASSIGNMENT. For this assignment, you will explore worlds of your own making and write them into a science fiction story. As you write, have fun with the wild and weird. Indulge your creative greatness. At the same time, keep in mind that the deeper value of sci-fi is in its ability to help us understand our world.

Professional Model

from "The Pedestrian" by Ray Bradbury, page 958

A metallic voice called to him:
"Stand still. Stay where you are! Don't move!"
He halted.
"Put up your hands!"
"But—" he said.
"Your hands up! Or we'll shoot!"
The police, of course, but what a rare, incredible thing; in a city of three million, there was only *one* police car left, wasn't that correct? Ever since a year ago, 2052, the election year, the force had been cut down from three cars to one. Crime was ebbing; there was no need now for the police, save for this one lone car wandering and wandering the empty streets. . . .

INDIVIDUAL LEARNING STRATEGIES (CONT.)

READING PROFICIENCY
Encourage students to read both the Professional Model and the Student Model—Revised aloud to get a sense of how the dialogue and descriptive language sounds. Ask them to summarize what they are asked to do in the Prewriting section, to make sure they understand the assignment.

ENGLISH LANGUAGE LEARNING
See strategies for Reading Proficiency above that

will also benefit students who are English language learners. Make sure that students thoroughly understand the concept of science fiction. Some of the terms related to technology and space or time travel may be unfamiliar to students whose first language is not English. You may wish to list some common science fiction terms on the board and discuss them along with concepts associated with science fiction.

continued on page 995

[The police car doesn't accept Mead's explanation that he was walking just to walk.]

"Well, Mr. Mead," [the police car] said.

"Is that all?" he asked politely.

"Yes," said the voice. "Here." There was a sigh, a pop. The back door of the police car sprang wide. "Get in."

"Wait a minute, I haven't done anything!"

"Get in."

"I protest!"

"Mr. Mead."

He walked like a man suddenly drunk. As he passed the front window of the car he looked in. As he had expected, there was no one in the front seat, no one in the car at all.

"Get in."

He put his hand to the door and peered into the back seat, which was a little cell, a little black jail with bars. It smelled of riveted steel. It smelled of harsh antiseptic; it smelled too clean and hard and metallic. There was nothing soft there.

"Now if you had a wife to give you an alibi," said the iron voice. "But—"

"Where are you taking me?"

The car hesitated, or rather gave a faint whirring click, as if information, somewhere, was dropping card by punch-slotted card under electric eyes. "To the Psychiatric Center for Research on Regressive Tendencies."

He got in. The door shut with a soft thud. The police car rolled through the night avenues, flashing its dim lights ahead.

Prewriting

WRITING WITH A PLAN. Creating a science fiction world is no small task. To create a believable new world, there are many details to consider. The details may be big (what is the atmosphere of your world?) or small (what color are the butterflies?), but they are all important because if they don't fit together, your readers will notice. Humans are fairly attuned to their worlds, and when introduced to another one, they quickly notice incongruities.

In Bradbury's world, everything fits into place—the police are rarely needed since most people spend their time glued to television, so when Mead is out walking, the police car has no idea how to deal with him. Bradbury mentions an election in a specific year, 2052, that helped create this situation. His world is believable and real, even though it is many years in the future.

Another good way to plan before writing is to outline a plot before you start. You will remember from unit three that a basic plot has seven essential elements: exposition, inciting incident,

extrapolates the other differences this would make. For instance, there would be less need for police, since crime would drop, since all the criminals would be home, watching their viewing screens also. However, Bradbury sees at least one dark side of the new world: people who don't watch their viewing screens, like writers, are seen as "regressive." What does "regressive" mean? Is Bradbury's world really that fantastic? Does it resemble our current world in any way? Clearly, Bradbury created a strange but believable future to comment on his concerns about actual, contemporary life.

Notice also that Mead is a relatively normal person. This helps Bradbury show the abnormality of the situation in which Mead finds himself. We readers can identify with Mead because of his normalcy, and therefore understand the abnormality, the near-horror, of Mead's situation.

SPECIAL NEEDS
Encourage students to create a cluster chart in order to brainstorm "crazy" ideas about what the future might be like. You may wish to simplify the assignment by asking them to create and describe the setting of their story, without worrying about the plot.

ENRICHMENT
Direct students to the Language Arts Survey 4.20, "Telling a Story," and ask them to present their short stories to their classmates. Classmates can tell what they like and didn't like about the story, and which parts they would like to see developed into a longer story. Based on the feedback from classmates, students could expand their short stories into novellas or even novels. You might also encourage them to submit their work to a science fiction magazine for publication.

Prewriting

WRITING WITH A PLAN. Most science fiction writing has some basis in reality. Students who have difficulty coming up with ideas for a story might benefit from creating a list of current problems facing humans, recent advances in science (such as cloning and the decoding of the human genome), and ingenious inventions they would like to see created. With a little imagination, these lists can provide useful ideas for science fiction plots. You might have students brainstorm for such ideas in small groups. Similarly, they might try asking "what if" questions to spark their imagination, as explained in the Language Arts Survey 2.15, "Imagining: Asking *What If* Questions."

continued on page 996

FINDING YOUR VOICE. Ask students to consider the following questions: What will be the aura of the world you would like to introduce? Will there be a threatening undertone? Will there be a solemn or a carefree attitude? Will you want to make the reader comfortable, with a false sense of peace that might be destroyed later? Or will you want the reader to laugh and find your story humorous? The mood and the voice of students' stories depends upon the message their stories are written to convey. For more information on voice, refer students to the Language Arts Survey 2.5, "Finding Your Voice," and 3.3, "Register, Tone, and Voice." Ask them to identify the mood or tone conveyed in the Professional Model and Student Model—Revised. How are these created through language?

IDENTIFYING YOUR AUDIENCE. Students will find a chart, "Thinking about Your Audience," in the Language Arts Survey 2.4, "Identifying Your Audience." What emotions will they try to engage—awe and surprise, fear of the unknown, or discomfort and uneasiness? They should also consider whether they are writing a story that will simply entertain an audience, keep them occupied for a time, or one that will instruct or provide ideas to contemplate.

Student Model— Graphic Organizer

See the Writing Resource book for a blackline master of the graphic organizer for this lesson.

FINDING YOUR VOICE. Voice is the quality of a work that tells you that one person in particular wrote it. Your attitude toward your topic will be reflected in the voice you project through sentence structure and word choice. Your voice will also play a big part in the tone of your story. Will your story be scary or humorous, or both? sarcastic or sincere? what kinds of sentence structure create a scary feeling? What kinds of words? Also, remember that well-developed characters have distinctive, realistic voices themselves.

IDENTIFYING YOUR AUDIENCE. Your audience will be your fellow class members, but also the larger world of your high school community. You'll want to address a topic that interests them, and in a way that they will understand.

---

rising action, climax, resolution, falling action, and dénouement. Nicholas sketched out this plot outline for his story. After he had a bare-bones version down on paper, he went back and added other layers, other lines of details.

Student Model—Graphic Organizer

Exposition: Kyle's on the moon
-on vacation
–is exploring
——he's a lieutenant

Inciting Incident: He finds a wormhole
-it's a white light, a tunnel
–exciting discovery
——he decides to risk entering the wormhole

Rising Action: Kyle goes through a wormhole
-he comes out on an astral plane
–meets another being on the same bodiless plane
——discovers that he's bodiless

Climax: Kah tries to make Kyle a slave
-communicates telepathically
–Kah has made the wormhole
——Kah is very loud and obnoxious

Resolution: Kyle tricks Kah into taking a solid form
-pricks his pride ("you're afraid . . .")
–discovers that Kah isn't so menacing
——trusts new friend to find a way home

Falling Action: Kyle gets away while Kah screams curses

Dénouement: Returns safely home

Nicholas continued in this manner for a couple more levels, each time adding more details to his plot and his world. He solved problems such as, "How can Kah be loud on a bodiless plane?" and "Why is Kyle on the moon anyway?" In this way, he made sure that each plot point flowed reasonably and smoothly into the next.

By using a plot outline as a graphic organizer and a brainstorming tool, you can help create believable, well-rounded worlds and characters.

Drafting

Now comes the fun part. As you explore your new world and bring it to life, enjoy it! If you've prepared by brainstorming about your new world and writing a plot outline, you should have no problem writing a full draft in one or two sittings. Don't worry too much about fine details right now—your prewriting should have created enough depth to get you started. Just get something down on paper that you can work with later. Don't delete or cross out anything. Even if you decide to go in a very different direction, keep the original; often you'll return to your first thoughts later.

Student Model—Draft

from "The Wormhole" by Nicholas McLean

Kyle Brent stepped out of the wormhole, which disappeared behind him. He almost didn't notice it because *Darkness and a feeling of weightlessness* the new environment was so strange. He *surrounded him.* was surrounded by darkness and flooded

Try to use an active verb here—not passive
over by a feeling of weightlessness, it was disorienting at first, but he soon grew used to it because he had been weightless before, during his zero-G training at the Astronautical Naval Academy. Somehow, though, this felt *He couldn't quite determine how...euphoric...* different. Explain how it felt

He decided *ing* he should try to take some readings with his MDC, he tried to reach into his pocket. To his great surprise, *with which* he found he had no arm to reach ~~with~~ ~~and~~, in fact no body whatsoever. It was an incredibly freeing sensation. He felt as if he could do anything--that he had somehow been freed from all

Planning the Details

To avoid confusing your readers, it is more important than ever to plan well ahead, to envision your world before you try to commit it to paper.

- pick a definite time and place in which your story will happen
- avoid overly-simple descriptions like "the future"
- brainstorm about what that time and place looks like using sensory details
- circle the details that most intrigue you
- for the details you circled, freewrite a paragraph describing and explaining each one in depth
- include at least brief histories that explain the events in your story—why are these things the way they are?

Finally, write a paragraph that describes your world, incorporating the results of your brainstorm. Whether or not this paragraph will make it into your story is up to you, but you should keep it close by for your own reference; it is the first and, so far, only record that your new, unseen world exists!

Drafting

Encourage students to use their completed graphic organizer to help them make sure they have laid out the essential elements of their plot. They may also wish to summarize the story out loud to a friend before beginning to write it down so that they can resolve any contradictions.

Planning the Details

As they attempt to flesh out the details of their story, students may find it useful to employ the techniques discussed in the Language Arts Survey 2.14, "Questioning: Using the 5 *W*s and an *H*." A sensory detail chart, as explained in the Language Arts Survey 2.18, may also prove useful in developing details for the setting. Finally, students might wish to consult a thesaurus to refine and improve their word choice. Encourage them to read the Language Arts Survey 5.22, "Using a Thesaurus."

Following the Rules of Your Own Universe

C. S. Lewis (author of the science fiction trilogy *Perelandra, Out of the Silent Planet,* and *That Hideous Strength*), once said that in creating a world of fantasy and science fiction, a writer could make any rules he or she desired, but then would have to abide by them or lose all credibility.

You started this lesson by examining the ways Ray Bradbury had made his world in "The Pedestrian" authentic. Now do the same thing for Nicholas's student model. How does he explain the world of the wormhole? How does he use Kyle's encounter with the alien Rahn Metah to provide an explanation of what has happened? Does Kah's presence and Kyle's and Metah's sudden escape from Kah seem believable, according to what Nicholas explains about their situation? Why, or why not?

Finally, look at the rules you have constructed for your own universe. What are those rules? What are the implications of those rules? Is there any place where you have broken the rules or suddenly changed them in a way that defies the logic needed to make your story believable?

Explain his background so you can provide
responsibility. He was on Luna to relax.
                                    motivation of character
He had just been out exploring and
1. Mother haed been President
enjoying the lunar landscape when his
(model kid) 2. Responsible for sister 3. as officer on the ship
MDC had detected the initial signs of
                                    That was the purpose of
the wormhole's presence. the trip—

The thought of the wormhole suddenly

caused him to wonder where he was. Was

he alone? Without doing anything but

thinking about it, Kyle Brent suddenly
Yes, your language is descriptive
found himself next to—or the closest

thing to being next to in this non-

physical universe—a life form.

Revising and Proofreading

If possible, wait a day before you revise your story. Review your self- and peer evaluations. Revise your writing according to decisions you make about these comments. Science fiction writing offers the opportunity and responsibility to use vivid descriptions. Go back through your story and look for places where you might add more descriptive words, especially adjectives and adverbs. In the paragraphs where you describe your new world, try adding an adjective to every noun, just to see how it sounds. You'll want to take many of them out later, but play around with them to determine which adjectives help provide context and meaning.

Student Model—Revised

                The Wormhole
              by Nicholas McLean

    Lieutenant Kyle Brent studied the
readings on his hand-held Mobile
Display Console (more commonly called
the MDC) and sighed joyfully. What a
discovery! He'd found a wormhole—an
actual stable wormhole—on the moon! It
was a scientific discovery of immense
proportions. He couldn't pass it up

just because he was technically on vacation.

A perfect circle with a diameter of two meters, the wormhole hung in mid-"air" before him. It consisted solely of brilliant white light, giving no indication of being anything spectacular, but Kyle knew differently. He knew he shouldn't—that it was against the rules—but he wanted more than anything to enter that gateway through existence now and explore what lay beyond.

There was no telling where it would lead. It could let out in another time, another dimension, another point in space, or most likely a combination of all three. But he couldn't help it. He deserved an adventure and didn't really have anything to lose. He'd deal with the consequences of it if and when he got back. The danger was great, but he'd played it safe and done as he'd been told his entire life. It was time to take a risk.

He stepped through the wormhole.

Kyle Brent stepped out of the wormhole, which disappeared behind him. He almost didn't notice it because the new environment was so strange. Darkness and a feeling of weightlessness flooded over him. It was disorienting at first, but he soon grew used to it because he had been weightless before, during his zero-G training at the Astronautical Naval Academy. Somehow, though, this felt different. He couldn't quite determine how, but it was like nothing he had ever experienced in his life—almost euphoric.

Deciding he should try to take some readings with his MDC, he tried to reach into his pocket. To his great surprise, he found he had no arm with which to reach and, in fact, no body whatsoever. It was an incredibly freeing sensation. He felt as if he could do anything—that he had somehow been freed from all responsibility. All

Self- and Peer Evaluation

After you finish your rough draft, complete a self-evaluation of your writing. If time allows, you may want to get one or two peer evaluations. See the Language Arts Survey 2.37 for more details about self- and peer evaluation. As you evaluate your science fiction story, or that of a classmate, answer the following questions:

- What changes in the present world has the writer created in his or her new world?
- Where, if anywhere, do elements of the new world fail to fit together?
- Where in the story is the action believable?
- Where in the story do characters seem believable?
- Where do the motivations for characters seem reasonable?
- Where are the setting, characters and actions vividly described?
- Where can adjectives be added to the description of the setting?
- Identify each of the essential elements of plot in the story.
- Where, if anywhere, do run-on sentences or comma splices occur?

Self- and Peer Evaluation

Have students use the checklist on page 999 for self- and peer evaluation. The checklist is intended to serve as a student-friendly rubric that should help students identify specific evidence of writing strengths and areas needing improvement. Make sure they provide concrete suggestions for improvement or specific evidence of why the writing works. A blackline master of the self- and peer evaluation checklist is available in the Writing Resource book.

Run-on Sentences and Comma Splices

LESSON OVERVIEW

In this lesson, students will be asked to do the following:

- Identify Run-ons and Comma Splices, 1000
- Fix Run-ons and Comma Splices, 1001
- Use Sentences Effectively, 1001

INTRODUCING THE SKILL. Explain to students that effective sentence structure demonstrates clear thinking, and that the ability to write well-constructed sentences is one of the most essential skills in writing.

continued on page 1001

Language, Grammar, and Style

Run-ons and Comma Splices

IDENTIFYING RUN-ONS AND COMMA SPLICES. While there is nothing wrong with long sentences, they must be grammatically correct. Sentences that have multiple independent clauses joined without appropriate conjunctions or punctuation are called *run-ons*, and are grammatically incorrect.

If you make a long sentence by joining two smaller sentences, you need more than just a comma to make the combination work. This kind of run-on is called a *comma splice*.

EXAMPLE

> "It was an incredibly freeing sensation, he felt as if he could do anything."

Revise a run-on by adding appropriate conjunctions or punctuation. The above run-on could be fixed a few different ways:

REVISED

Divide it into two independent clauses separated by a period:

> "It was an incredibly freeing sensation. He felt as if he could do anything."

Divide it into two independent clauses separated by a semicolon:

> "It was an incredibly freeing sensation; he felt as if he could do anything.

continued on page 1001

---

his life he had been responsible. When his mother had been President in the early 2110s, he had felt the need to be responsible for maintaining the public's positive view of his family. When his parents had died, he'd felt responsible for caring for his sister, despite the fact that they were the same age. Then, too, for the past three years as security officer aboard the USS Odyssey, he had been responsible for protecting the ship and crew from harm. He was ready for a break from responsibility. That had been why he had come to Luna, to relax. He had just been out exploring and enjoying the lunar landscape when his MDC had detected the initial signs of the wormhole's presence.

The thought of the wormhole suddenly caused him to wonder where he was. Was he alone? Without doing anything but thinking about it, Kyle Brent suddenly found himself next to—or the closest thing to being next to in this nonphysical universe—a life form.

"Ummm...Hi," he said in a way best described as telepathically. "I'm Kyle Brent."

"I am Rahn Metah," replied the being.

"Do you know where we are?" Kyle asked, hoping for an encouraging answer.

"I'm not sure. I just reached out to touch this weird circle I'd found and fell through. Next thing I knew, I was here." He paused a moment in doubt, then continued, "Could we be on an astral plane?"

"Yes!" exclaimed Kyle. "So we're slightly out of phase with our respective dimensions! Why didn't I see it before? I was so caught up in my own feelings of euphoria that I didn't realize the obvious!"

"So we know where we are," Metah interjected. "Now what do we do?"

Before Kyle could respond, a telepathic voice rang out in his (and Metah's) mind.

"I AM KAH! I AM RESPONSIBLE FOR YOUR BEING HERE! YOU WILL NOW BEGIN YOUR ETERNAL DUTIES AS MY PERSONAL SLAVES!" the "voice" roared, making the apparent slaves-to-be cringe inwardly.

Before Kyle could react beyond that, Metah "whispered" into his mind. "Stall him," was the message. "I think I know how to get us out of here, but I need time. I'm going to try to will myself into physical form and use my cybernetic implants to create a new wormhole and get us out of here."

The entire message came in a split second, and it came more as a thought than a paragraph. He had just met Metah, but he decided he'd rather risk trusting Metah than become Kah's eternal slave. And, of course, he'd rather return to his life of responsibility than stay here.

"Show yourself!" Kyle ordered Kah, hoping to buy the time Metah needed.

"I WILL NOT!"

"Are you afraid if we see you that we won't be scared enough to become your slaves?"

"I FEAR NOTHING! MOST CERTAINLY NOT THE LIKES OF YOU!"

"Then prove it. Show yourself and prove your fearlessness to us."

"I ACCEPT YOUR CHALLENGE, DESPITE ITS FOOLISH NATURE!"

Kah revealed himself, appearing as a physical entity. No more than five feet in height, he had slimy, dark gray skin and a menacing appearance, but nothing overly threatening. He seemed to be more angry than actually dangerous or frightening. Kyle continued in his goading strategy.

"How are we to know that this is your true appearance and not a ruse developed to frighten us into submission?"

"YOU DO NOT! ENOUGH OF YOUR FOOLISH GAMES! YOUR ATTEMPTS TO STALL FOR TIME ARE USELESS! YOU WILL BOW DOWN TO ME!"

Kyle was out of ideas. He didn't know

Make one clause subordinate to the other:

"Because of an incredibly freeing sensation, he felt as if he could do anything."

Insert a conjunction:

"It was an incredibly freeing sensation, and he felt as if he could do anything."

FIXING RUN-ONS AND COMMA SPLICES. Fixing errors in sentence structure not only cleans up the writing but also improves its flow. Nicholas found the following errors in his sentences.

It was disorienting at first, he soon grew used to it because he had been weightless before, during his zero-G training at the Astronautical Naval Academy.

He decided he should try to take some readings with his MDC, he tried to reach into his pocket.

Rewrite each of the sentences above in three different ways. Decide which way sounds best to you.

USING SENTENCES EFFECTIVELY. Read through your story and look for run-ons and comma splices. If you find any, fix them according to the directions in this lesson.

For more information, see the Language Arts Survey 3.34, "Correcting Sentence Run-ons."

Language, Grammar, and Style (CONT.)

PREVIEWING THE SKILL. Have students read the Language Arts Survey 3.34, "Correcting Sentence Run-ons." The Language, Grammar, and Style Resource book 3.34 also provides additional review exercises.

PRACTICING THE SKILL. For additional practice, have students work through the exercise in the following section of the Study and Research Resource book located in the Teacher's Resource Kit: 3.34, "Correcting Sentence Run-ons."

Publishing and Presenting

For more ideas, refer students to the Language Arts Survey 2.49, "Sharing Your Work with Others." Also refer students to the Language Arts Survey 4.19, "Oral Interpretation," if they are planning to record their story as a radio program.

Reflecting

Encourage students to write a journal entry that considers the questions asked in Reflecting. Lead a class discussion on the cultural significance of science fiction. Is science fiction merely an entertaining form of literary expression, or can it have social and political value as well?

Publishing and Presenting

To share your work, your class might wish to gather your stories together in an anthology and present them to the school or other classes.

Science fiction has also been frequently adapted to radio and screenplay formats. Consider doing this with your story. You could write an introduction as if it were for an old radio show and read your story into a tape recorder, complete with occasional pauses for commercials and sound effects. You might play your recording to your class, or even over the public address system on a special day. You might also adapt your creation to video format, creating costumes and scenery to make your unseen world come alive.

what to do. His brave front and his military training broke down. He had never been trained to deal with an evil entity! So great was his terror that his mind accidentally shook him back into physical form, and he began to tremble. He broke out in a cold sweat. His knees began to buckle. He would have collapsed had there been any gravity or ground beneath him.

He was relieved beyond human comprehension when Metah suddenly appeared along with a wormhole. Kyle wasted no time; he floated for the wormhole.

Less than five seconds after Metah appeared with the wormhole, the two wayward explorers departed, leaving a furious Kah behind to scream his enraged curses at them. They did not hear the curses, however, for they had returned safely home.

Reflecting

Science fiction short stories can be powerful works of art. Think back on some of your favorite sci-fi movies or books. Which one was the best? Freewrite a paragraph describing its main character. Can you imagine that character in another situation, like on a pirate ship or in the Civil War? What universal qualities do good sci-fi characters have?

Words for Everyday Use

Check your knowledge of the following vocabulary words from this unit. Write a short sentence using these words in context to make the meaning clear. To review the definition or usage of a word, refer to the page number listed or to the Glossary of Words for Everyday Use.

affliction, 931	flail, 921	penitent, 930
alibi, 962	folio, 921	perplexed, 974
allied, 942	frivolity, 930	phosphorescent, 980
allusion, 943	grandeur, 928	pittance, 946
aperture, 945	haggard, 939	proliferate, 930
apparition, 945	haughty, 931	prolong, 954
averse, 944	herald, 943	protrude, 953
averted, 939	hermetic, 930	providential, 930
blanch, 942	hurl, 920	provision, 940
blandly, 945	illumination, 961	prudence, 929
brusquely, 922	impassable, 944	recessed, 920
cataclysm, 930	impending, 942	recoil, 954
catechism, 929	impertinence, 929	reverie, 950
celestial, 928	imperturbably, 945	revue, 960
chamber, 968	imprudence, 946	riveted, 962
commune, 918	indispensable, 918	robust, 929
compliance, 950	infamy, 932	scaffolding, 947
confide, 944	ingenuous, 929	scruple, 951
confound, 946	invaluable, 951	sear, 941
consolation, 931	iridescent, 931	skein, 918
coroner, 942	jockey, 960	somber, 952
decrepit, 929	livid, 944	successive, 940
decrepitude, 932	loathing, 953	suggestive, 947
deduce, 951	magnanimous, 928	summon, 974
deduction, 938	manifold, 939	supernatural, 928
deign, 931	massive, 948	tangible, 950
dexterity, 919	minutely, 948	terrestrial, 929
dispel, 955	nocturnal, 922	ventilator, 948
dissolute, 940	nondescript, 981	vestibule, 920
enchantment, 971	ominous, 982	vigil, 952
endeavor, 948	outset, 980	whitewashed, 948
erroneous, 954	parapet, 940	wretched, 942
exasperated, 932	pending, 947	

Literary Tools

Define the following terms, giving concrete examples of how they are used in this unit. To review a term, refer to the page number indicated or to the Handbook of Literary Terms.

aphorism, 965	mood, 917, 958	setting, 917, 958
conflict, 936	narrator, 936, 978	simile, 965
dialect, 965	oxymoron, 926	sound effects, 978
foreshadowing, 978	plot, 936	suspense, 978
Magical Realism, 926	point of view, 926	

Reflecting on your reading

Genre Studies

1. **SURREALISM AND MAGICAL REALISM.** Discuss the surreal qualities and supernatural elements in the stories "House Taken Over" and "A Very Old Man with Enormous Wings." Which elements in the stories are realistic, and which are not? Define **Magical Realism**. What characteristics of Magical Realism are present in "A Very Old Man..."? Do you think "House Taken Over" can be considered a Magical Realist story? Why, or why not?

2. **MYSTERY AND DETECTIVE FICTION.** What are some other names for the genre of **detective fiction**? Name some elements you associate with detective fiction. Which of these are present in "The Adventure of the Speckled Band"? Which elements in "The Adventure of the Speckled Band" make it exciting and suspenseful to read? Why do you think the genre of detective fiction has been so popular over the years?

3. **SCIENCE FICTION.** Define **science fiction** and discuss the elements of science fiction that can be found in the stories "The Pedestrian" and "By the Waters of Babylon."

4. **URBAN LEGENDS AND POPULAR CULTURE.** Compare the Related Reading from *The Vanishing Hitchhiker* to the radio play *The Hitchhiker*. How does the mysterious hitchhiker figure into the urban legends retold in the Related Reading, and how does he appear in the radio play? Do you think it is possible that the author of the play, Lucille Fletcher, drew inspiration from urban legends about hitchhikers? Why do you think the idea of an eerie hitchhiker appears in so many legends and in stories in our popular culture? What is it about that type of story that appeals to people today?

5. **ROLE OF THE NARRATOR IN FICTION.** Compare the roles of the narrators in the detective story "The Adventure of the Speckled Band," "By the Waters of Babylon," and *The Hitchhiker*. What is the purpose of each narrator? Which narrators are omniscient, or all-knowing, and which are not? Which narrator best reflects the point of view of the reader, and why?

Thematic Studies

6. **INVASION OF THE SUPERNATURAL.** Compare the relationship of the real to the supernatural in "House Taken Over," "A Very Old Man with Enormous Wings," "East Song," and *The Hitchhiker.* How do the characters in each story regard the supernatural elements? Are they perplexed or frightened, or do they take these happenings at face value? Is the reader supposed to take these unreal elements at face value or is there some hidden meaning or trick the reader must figure out?

7. **VISIONS OF THE FUTURE.** Compare the vision of the future depicted in "The Pedestrian" with that depicted in "By the Waters of Babylon." What does each author forsee might happen in the future? Which aspects of each story reflect events that have actually happened in the real world? What evils in human nature or in today's society could actually lead to such a nightmarish future as that depicted in each story?

8. **Logic and Reasoning as a Means to Solving Life's Mysteries.** Compare the mysteries in "The Adventure of the Speckled Band," "House Taken Over," and "A Very Old Man with Enormous Wings." What happens to dispel the mystery in the first story? How would Sherlock Holmes deal with the mysteries in the other two stories? Can logic and deductive reasoning solve those mysteries? How does the narrator of "By the Waters of Babylon" solve the mystery of who inhabited the Place of the Gods?

for your READING LIST

The Illustrated Man by Ray Bradbury. This book of intertwined stories of suspense, science fiction, and the supernatural was published in 1951 and is just as gripping, as sometimes frightening, today as it was fifty years ago. The stories are linked together by an anonymous narrator who meets a man tattooed from head to toe. As the narrator looks, the tattoos become alive and tell these stories. "The Veldt" is about children who go too far with a virtual reality room. "Kaleidoscope" tells about astronauts stranded in space. The book and has become a classic, perhaps because of how closely the stories ring true. The human experience is the same no matter what year it is or what planet we are on.

Independent Reading Activity

Predicting the Future. Science fiction often explores what the future will be like. Important science fiction writers such as Ray Bradbury and George Orwell, writing in the twentieth century, made predictions about the future. Now that we are in the twenty-first century, how many of their predictions have already come true? Has anything happened in the new millennium that no one could possibly have predicted, say, fifty years ago? Go to the library and locate novels or short stories by science fiction authors. Make a list of their predictions. Note which ones have come true, and which are totally outrageous and have not come true. Finally, list some of the things you see in our world now that no one predicted. Write a short report on your findings.

Selections for Additional Reading

Cosmicomics by Italo Calvino. Calvino takes complex scientific concepts and transforms them into magical fiction in these highly imaginative short stories. They are hilarious, intelligent, and unfathomable. He plays games with time and space, as his character, old Qfwfq, narrates a strange, wonderful history of the cosmos. His cosmic comedies open the mind to wonder. They are like nothing you will have read before.

Instead of Three Wishes by Megan Whalen Turner. The seven short stories in this collection each take the natural, "real" world to a place of supernatural phenomena. Leprechauns, nightmares, and ghosts turn the ordinary world upside down. The surprising endings make for highly entertaining reading.

1984 by George Orwell. Read the futuristic classic that shocked audiences when it came out in 1949 and made them fear the future. This is the story of Winston Smith who lives in a world of controlled information and thought. When he joins a secret brotherhood he becomes a hunted enemy of Big Brother. The year 1984 has come and gone, and we've crossed into the new millennium. The book is still a classic, and still thought-provoking.

FOR YOUR READING LIST

Although *The Illustrated Man* was published in 1951, the stories stand the test of time not only because of Bradbury's wonderful use of language and mastery of the short story, but also because of his ability to comment on the universal human condition. In short, the book is a classic. The book contains eighteen stories, all told by the tattoos on the illustrated man. The man claims that his tattoos were created by a woman from the future, and that they have the power to tell about the future—even to predict the end of the world.

Students may be interested in viewing the movie *The Illustrated Man* (1969), which was directed by Jack Smight and stars Rod Steiger. The film depicts three of the short stories from Bradbury's collection, "The Long Rain," "The Veldt," and "The Last Night Of The World."

Independent Reading Activity
In addition, students may wish to make a list of their own predictions about the future. They may select one prediction and plan a way to present it to the rest of the class, using drawings, models, or other forms of media in their presentations. Refer them to the Language Arts Survey 6.11, "Displaying Effective Visual Information," as they prepare these visuals.

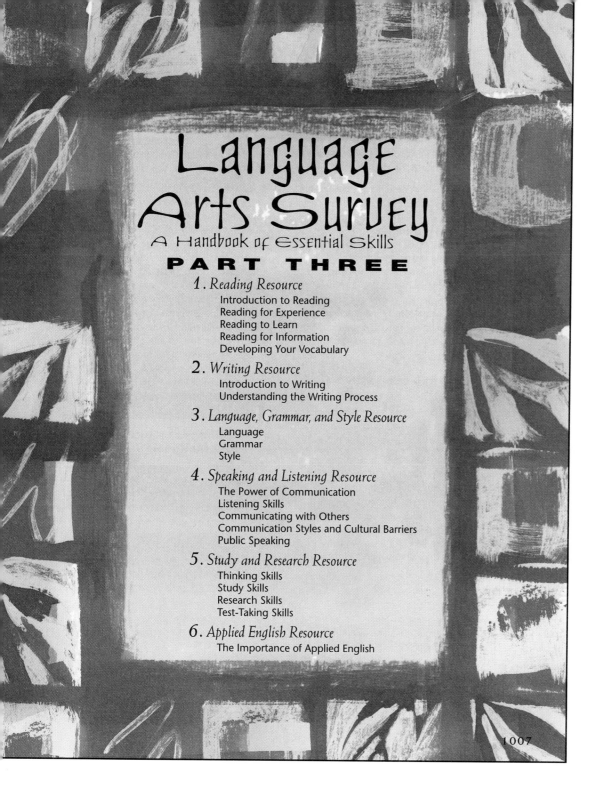

Language Arts Survey

A Handbook of Essential Skills

PART THREE

1. *Reading Resource*
Introduction to Reading
Reading for Experience
Reading to Learn
Reading for Information
Developing Your Vocabulary

2. *Writing Resource*
Introduction to Writing
Understanding the Writing Process

3. *Language, Grammar, and Style Resource*
Language
Grammar
Style

4. *Speaking and Listening Resource*
The Power of Communication
Listening Skills
Communicating with Others
Communication Styles and Cultural Barriers
Public Speaking

5. *Study and Research Resource*
Thinking Skills
Study Skills
Research Skills
Test-Taking Skills

6. *Applied English Resource*
The Importance of Applied English

1007

RESPOND TO THE SELECTION

The Respond to the Selection questions and critical thinking prompts following each selection provide students with the opportunity to be active readers by asking questions that get the students involved in the literature, like the questions mentioned in section 1.4, "Educating Your Imagination as an Active Reader." See pages 382 and 393 in Unit 5 for examples.

READING Resource

INTRODUCTION TO READING

1.1 Purposes of Reading

You as a reader read for different purposes. You might **read for experience**—for insights into ideas, other people, and the world around you. You can also **read to learn**. This is the kind of reading done most often in school. When you read to learn, you may read textbooks, newspapers and newsmagazines, and visual "texts" such as art and photographs. The purpose of this type of reading is to gain knowledge. Third, you can **read for information**. When you read in this way, you are looking for specific data in such things as reference materials, tables, databases, and diagrams.

1.2 Reading Independently

Learning to know and value your own response to what you read is one of the rewards of becoming an independent reader. Scanning, skimming, and reading slowly and carefully are three different ways of reading.

SCANNING. When you **scan**, you look through written material quickly to locate particular information. Scanning is useful when you want to find an entry in an index or a definition in a textbook chapter. To scan, simply run your eye down the page, looking for a key word. When you find the key word, slow down and read carefully.

SKIMMING. When you **skim**, you glance through material quickly to get a general idea of what it is about. Skimming is an excellent way to get a quick overview of material. It is useful for previewing a chapter in a textbook, for surveying material to see if it contains information that will be useful to you, and for reviewing material for a test or essay. When skimming, look at titles, headings, and words that appear in boldface or colored type. Also read topic sentences of paragraphs, first and

last paragraphs of sections, and any summaries or conclusions. In addition, glance at illustrations, photographs, charts, maps, or other graphics.

SLOW AND CAREFUL READING. When you **read slowly and carefully**, you look at each sentence, taking the time to absorb its meaning before going on. Slow and careful reading is appropriate when reading for pleasure or when studying a textbook chapter for the first time. If you encounter words that you do not understand, try to figure them out from context or look them up in a dictionary. You may want to write such words in a notebook. The act of writing a word will help you to remember it later. When reading for school, take notes using a rough outline form. Writing the material will help you to remember it. For more information, see the Language Arts Survey 5.17, "Taking Notes, Outlining, and Summarizing Information."

READING FOR EXPERIENCE

1.3 Reading Literature: Educating Your Imagination

The most important reason to read literature is to educate your imagination. Reading literature will train you to think and feel in new ways. In the process of reading literary works and thinking about your own and others' responses to them, you will exercise your imagination and grow in ways that might otherwise have been impossible.

1.4 Educating Your Imagination as an Active Reader

Reading literature actively means thinking about what you are reading as you are reading it. Here are some important strategies for reading actively.

ASK QUESTIONS AS YOU READ.

• How does what I am reading make me feel?

• What is the setting of this work? How do things look, sound, taste, feel, or smell?

- Do I identify with any of the characters? What would I do if I were in their place?
- Does what I am reading involve a conflict? If so, what is it? How might it be resolved?
- What main images, ideas, symbols, or themes appear in the work?
- What can be learned from the experiences of these characters?

MAKE PREDICTIONS AS YOU READ. While reading, think often about what will come next. Think about how situations might turn out and what characters might do.

SUMMARIZE PARTS AS YOU READ. Especially when reading longer works, it is a good idea to stop, perhaps at the end of each chapter or section, to summarize on paper what you have read so far. Doing so will help you remember complicated literary works.

1.5 Keeping a Reader's Journal

Keeping a reader's journal will help you get the most out of your experience with literature. A reader's journal can first act as a log in which you record the title and author of the work you are reading. You may want to briefly summarize the work. You can write a journal response to questions such as those in the Reader's Journal and Respond to the Selection features of this textbook. Or you might write your own questions and respond to them.

What story is often repeated in your family or culture? My family often repeats the story of my going down a hill in my little red wagon at the age of four. The speed resulted in the wagon going into the street. Scared for my safety, my father spanked me and told me not to go down the hill again. I did not speak to my father for a week because I was so angry at him. I thought it was enough punishment to have a scraped knee from my fall when the wagon tipped over after going over the curb. My family likes to tell this story because it shows the love of adventure and willfulness that became my trademark characteristics when I got older.

1.6 Reading Silently versus Reading Out Loud

At times you will find it best to read silently and at other times to read out loud. When reading independently, you will probably make the most progress by reading silently. However, you may find it most helpful to read difficult passages out loud, even if softly. Hearing the words spoken can help make sense of complex passages. Another good time to read out loud is with poetry. By speaking the lines, you will be able to hear the rhythm and rhyme. Plays are also intended to be performed, and as with poetry, they are best appreciated when they are read out loud. This can be particularly helpful when different people take on the roles of different characters.

1.7 Reading with a Book Club or Literature Circle

No two people are exactly alike. Because of this, the experience that you have when reading a particular story, poem, or play will be different from the experience of each of your classmates. That's what makes discussing literature with other students interesting.

In a classroom literature circle, students get together in a small group to exchange insights, interpretations, and questions about literature they have read independently. Students in a literature circle may gather to discuss a selection and work together to understand it. Or they might read different literary works and meet to compare themes, writing styles of different authors, or different selections by the same author. Personal insights recorded in a reading log or journal can be shared when the literature circle meets.

1.8 Guidelines for Discussing Literature in a Book Club

At first, your literature group might need help from your teacher to get started, but soon your group should be able to conduct its own sessions if you follow these guidelines.

BEFORE THE SESSION
- Finish reading the assignment on time.
- Write down ideas in your reader's journal to help yourself get ready for the discussion.

READING RESOURCE **1009**

READING RESOURCE

READER'S JOURNAL. The Reader's Journal questions in the Prereading section of each selection provide students with response questions and writing prompts that they can use to get started writing in their own reading journals. See pages 528 and 538 in Unit 7 for examples.

BOOK CLUB. You might have your students read the books suggested in the For Your Reading List section at the end of each unit and have students conduct a book club in small groups. See pages 607 and 781.

- Mark places in the reading that you don't understand or want to discuss with your group. Also mark passages that you like, disagree with, or find especially worth remembering.
- Make sure you bring the literature to school instead of leaving it home on discussion day.

DURING THE SESSION
- Share your ideas and offer suggestions.
- Speak clearly, loudly, and slowly enough.
- Make eye contact with others.
- Answer questions other people ask.
- Ask questions to help other members clarify or expand on their points.
- Help keep the group on track and focused.
- Encourage others to talk.
- Disagree when you find it necessary without hurting others' feelings.
- Summarize and repeat your ideas when necessary.
- Give reasons for your opinions.
- Listen politely and ask follow-up questions.
- Try to understand and carry out other members' suggestions.

AFTER THE SESSION
- Evaluate your contribution to the group.
- Evaluate the overall success of your group.
- List ways to improve the next time.

READING TO LEARN

When you are reading to learn, you have two main goals: to expand your knowledge on a particular topic and to remember the information later. When you read to learn, you will often work with textbooks, nonfiction library books, newspapers, or journals, newsmagazines, and related art and photographs.

1.9 Reading Textbooks and Nonfiction Books

Textbooks provide a broad overview of a course of study. Textbooks should provide as much material as possible in an objective, factual way. Other nonfiction books provide information about actual people, places, things, events, and ideas. Types of nonfiction books include histories, biographies, autobiographies, and memoirs.

THE PARTS OF A BOOK. When previewing an entire book, you might want to glance at all of its parts. Every book will have some or all of the following parts:

THE PARTS OF A BOOK

Title page	Gives the title, author, and publisher
Copyright page	Gives information regarding the publication of the book and the copyrights protecting it from being copied or sold illegally
Table of contents	Lists the units, chapters, and/or subjects of the book and the page numbers where they are found
Preface, introduction, or foreword	Introduces the book
Text	Contains main part of the book
Afterword or epilogue	Gives conclusion or tells what happened later
Appendix	Gives additional information about subjects covered in the book, often in chart or table form
Glossary	Lists key words used in the book and their definitions
Bibliography	Lists sources used in writing the book or sources for further study
Index	Lists in alphabetical order the subjects mentioned in the book and pages where these subjects are treated

1.10 Reading Newspapers, Journals, and Newsmagazines

Newspapers, journals, and newsmagazines contain an enormous amount of information. Few people have time to read everything that appears in a newspaper each day. Nonetheless, staying aware of the news is important.

To get an overview of a newspaper, journal, or newsmagazine, skim the headlines and leads (the first sentence in a news story that explains the who, what, where, why, and how of the story). Read any news summaries included in the publication. Then read in depth any stories that seem particularly important or interesting. Also take advantage of the features and entertainment sections, which often reflect contemporary culture or the particular flavor of a community.

When reading news stories and editorials, make sure to distinguish between facts and opinions. **Facts** are statements that can be proved by observation or by consulting a reliable and objective source. **Opinions** are predictions or statements of value or belief. When you encounter opinions in the news, try to determine whether they are sound. Sound opinions are supported by facts. For more information, see the Language Arts Survey 5.2, "Distinguishing Fact from Opinion."

1.11 "Reading" Art and Photographs

In today's visually stimulating world, books and news media rely on art, photographs, and other visuals as well as the printed word to convey ideas. Being able to understand and interpret graphic images is important in today's society. Visual arts offer insights into our world in a different way than print does.

Careful examination of a painting can lead you to discover meaning in it and to compare and contrast the painting's meaning with that of a literary work or other piece of writing. The same thing happens with photographs. Learning to interpret other graphics or images—drawings, diagrams, charts, and maps—will help you to understand more easily how things work, what things mean, and how things compare.

1.12 Seeking Knowledge as an Active Reader

Reading to learn requires you to develop and use key skills to acquire knowledge. Reading actively means thinking about what you are reading as you read it. Slow and careful reading—and sometimes rereading—is necessary when reading to understand new and complex material. There are five key skills required for active reading:

- asking questions
- using your prior knowledge to make inferences and predictions about what you are reading
- recognizing what you do not know
- being able to synthesize information or create summaries, and
- knowing when to adapt your reading approach.

ASK QUESTIONS. Questioning allows you to realize what you understand about what you are reading. Before you read, think about your prior knowledge about the subject. When confronted with new information, your mind is doing many things at once. It is trying to figure out what it already knows about the topic and how this information connects to the information already in your brain. During reading, your mind is trying to answer these questions: What is the essential information presented here? How is this new information organized? After reading, you need to examine how your knowledge has grown, and identify the questions you still have about the material.

BEFORE READING

What is this going to be about?
What do I already know about the topic?
What's my purpose for reading this?

DURING READING

What does the author want me to know?
What is the significance of what I am reading?
What do I need to remember from this material?

AFTER READING

What have I learned?
What else do I want to know about this topic?

USE YOUR PRIOR KNOWLEDGE TO MAKE INFERENCES AND PREDICTIONS. While you are reading, you need to use what you already know about the topic to make inferences about what the author is saying. As you read, think about what might come next and try to make predictions about the next section of material.

KNOW WHAT YOU DO NOT KNOW. Recognizing when you do not understand something is as important as knowing that you do understand it. Try to form questions about the material you do not understand. Reread the text. Explain the topic to another student. Teaching someone else forces you to work to understand the material in deeper ways.

SUMMARIZE OR SYNTHESIZE TEXT. Summarizing what you are reading not only helps you identify and understand the main and subordinate points in the text, it is essential for storing and retrieving the information from long-term memory. Write a summary for each major section of the text you read. Create meaningful labels for a list of things or actions.

ADAPT YOUR READING APPROACH. If you become aware that you are not comprehending the material, you need to try another approach. Expert readers alter their reading strategies to compensate for any problems they have. You may need to experiment with different tactics like speeding up, slowing down, rereading, standing up and reading, reading the same material from another book, reading with a dictionary in your lap, or generalizing or visualizing what you are reading.

1.13 Strategies for Reading to Learn: SQ3R

A five-step reading strategy called SQ3R can help you reduce your study time and increase your ability to understand the essential information. The main steps of SQ3R are **S**URVEY, **Q**UESTION, **R**EAD, **R**ECALL, and **R**EVIEW.

SURVEY
- Preview the organization of material.
- Glance at visuals and assess how they contribute to the meaning of the text.
- Skim headings and introductory paragraphs.

- Notice words in italics, boldface, and other terms that stand out.
- Ask yourself: What is the scope of the reading task? What should I learn from this material?

QUESTION
- Turn chapter titles and headings into questions.
- Ask yourself what the text is offering and what the author is saying.
- Ask yourself what you should know about the material and what you already know about it.
- Question graphics and visual materials. Try to translate the information they offer into your own words.
- Use words like *who, what, when, where, why,* and *how* to retrieve information.

READ
- Read and interact with the text.
- Underline or copy in your journal the main points.
- Make note of unusual or interesting ideas.
- Jot down words you need to define.
- Write your reactions to what you read.

RECALL
- Condense the major points of the text by writing recall cues.
- Summarize the material you have read. Reread any sections you don't clearly remember.
- Use graphic organizers to visualize or map out the material.
- Reread the text aloud if you need help recalling.

REVIEW
- After you have finished the chapter or book, go back and reread main headings and compare them to your notes.
- Review your notes, summaries, and definitions. Answer any questions you wrote.
- Ask yourself: What do I now understand? What is still confusing?

READING FOR INFORMATION

1.14 Reading Internet Materials, Reference Works, Graphic Aids, and Other Visuals

When you are reading for information, you are looking for information that answers a specific, immediate question; that helps you learn how to do something; or that will help you make a decision or draw a conclusion about something. One of the most important tasks for you to learn in school is how to access, process, and think about the vast amount of information available to you on the Internet and in online and print reference works, graphic aids, and other visuals.

Skills critical to reading for information include:
- determining your specific purpose for reading or viewing
- determining the creator's or author's purpose
- knowing how to interpret symbols and numeric data, and
- using an appropriate approach for the reading or viewing task.

DETERMINE YOUR SPECIFIC PURPOSE FOR READING OR VIEWING. Know why you are reading and what information you seek. State your purpose for reading as clearly as you can. Are you searching the Internet for a review of the movie you're unsure whether to see? Are you learning to operate a computer program? Are you researching data to determine if city regulations allow pet ferrets?

DETERMINE THE CREATOR'S OR AUTHOR'S PURPOSE. It is important to interpret the creator's or author's viewpoint. Ask yourself what the writer or illustrator wants the reader to think, believe, or do after reading this piece. Ask yourself if the author has bias on the topic that is affecting his or her views. If you are on the Internet, check for the following: Who is sponsoring the site? What hyperlinks are embedded in the site? Can you contact the website? When was the content on the site developed, and how might that affect the information it provides?

DETERMINE HOW THE AUTHOR USES SYMBOLS AND NUMERIC DATA. Work to understand how the creator or author uses symbols, icons, and abbreviated headings on tables. Use any icons as shortcuts for navigating through the text and also for identifying the important from unimportant material.

USE THE SEARCH APPROACH. Although your reading and viewing strategies should vary and relate

directly to your purpose, you may find the SEARCH method helpful when you are reading for information. SEARCH stands for Scan, Examine, Act, Review, Connect, and Hunt.

SCAN
- Look over the text and determine how the material is structured.
- Look for a table of contents, a glossary, an index, and other helpful sections.
- For an Internet site, look for a site map.

EXAMINE
- Do directions appear in a sequence of steps? Are there diagrams? Do directions reveal exactly what to do, or do you need to experiment a little?
- Is there a pattern in headings or icons?
- Are there any references to other sources of information?
- If you are on the Internet, does the site provide any links?

ACT
- Explore the procedures you are reading and learn by doing.
- If you are seeking data, take notes about the information. Is it exactly what you were looking for, or do you need to keep looking?

REVIEW
- Revisit the steps of a procedure to make sure you have them clear in your head.
- Compare similar resources and read any additional references or links provided.

CONNECT
- Connect the information to what you previously knew about the topic. How did you build on what you knew?
- Connect text with visual aids. How do the visual aids supplement the text? What additional information do they provide?

HUNT
- Look up the meanings of any new words you found.
- Use the help feature on a computer program to find answers to your questions.
- Make a visual diagram of a procedure if it will help you remember it.

READING INTERNET MATERIALS, REFERENCE WORKS, GRAPHIC AIDS, AND OTHER VISUALS. Students are asked to use these resources in the Media Literacy activity on page 404.

1.15 Using Graphic Aids

Graphic aids are pictures, maps, illustrations, charts, graphs, diagrams, spreadsheets, and other visual materials that present information. Many people, including scientists, sociologists, economists, business analysts, and school administrators, use graphic aids to present data in understandable ways. Information presented in tables, charts, and graphs can help you find information, see trends, discover facts, and uncover patterns. Here are some common types of structures for presenting data.

PIE CHARTS. A pie chart is a circle that stands for a whole group or set. The circle is divided into parts to show the divisions of the whole. When you look at a pie chart, you can see the relationships of the parts to one another and to the whole.

BAR GRAPHS. A bar graph compares amounts of something by representing the amounts as bars of different lengths. In the bar graph below, each bar represents the value in dollars of canned goods donated by several communities to a food drive. To read the graph, simply draw in your imagination a line from the edge of the bar to the bottom of the graph. Then read the number. For example, the bar graph below shows that the community of Russell Springs donated $600 worth of goods during the food drive.

MAPS. A map is a representation, usually on a surface such as paper or a sheet of plastic, of a geographic area, showing various significant features of that area.

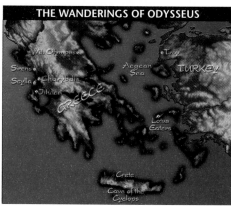

SAMPLE MAP

ARLINGTON HIGH SCHOOL POETRY SURVEY

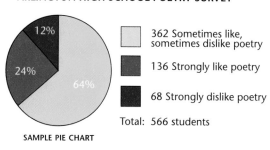

12%
24%
64%

362 Sometimes like, sometimes dislike poetry

136 Strongly like poetry

68 Strongly dislike poetry

Total: 566 students

SAMPLE PIE CHART

DOLLAR VALUE OF DONATED GOODS TO CANNED FOOD DRIVE

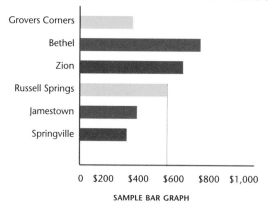

Grovers Corners
Bethel
Zion
Russell Springs
Jamestown
Springville

0   $200 $400 $600 $800 $1,000

SAMPLE BAR GRAPH

Here are guidelines for working with graphics:

BEFORE READING

- Determine the subject of the graphic by reading the title, headings, and other textual clues.
- Determine how the data are organized, classified, or divided by reading the labels along rows or columns.
- Ask yourself: Why am I reading this document? What do I need to find? Where in this graphic is that information located?

DURING READING

- Survey the data and look for trends by comparing columns and rows, noting changes among information fields, looking for patterns, or navigating map sections.
- Use legends, keys, and other helpful sections in the graphic.
- Ask yourself: How do the data I need compare to other data on the graphic? What do those comparisons mean to me? What in this graphic can I skim or skip?

AFTER READING

- Check footnotes or references for additional information about the data and its sources.
- Ask yourself: Did this graphic answer my questions? If so, what are the answers? If not, where do I go to find the answers?

DEVELOPING YOUR VOCABULARY

1.16 Using Context Clues to Estimate Word Meaning

If you come across an unfamiliar word in your reading and you can't access a dictionary, you can often figure out the meaning of a word by using context clues.

One type of context clue is **restatement**. The author may tell you the meaning of the word you do not know by using different words to express the same idea in another sentence.

EXAMPLES

The dog snarled at Donald malevolently.
The dog's vicious behavior warned Donald to stay away.

The restatement provides a context clue that malevolently means "maliciously, with intent to do harm."

Another type of context clue is **apposition**. An apposition is renaming something in different words. Look for a word or phrase that has been placed in the sentence to clarify the word you do not know.

EXAMPLE

Evan's conclusion was based on a fallacy, a false idea about how Maggie felt toward him.

Examples given in a sentence can also be used as context clues.

EXAMPLE

The words *dad*, *radar*, *noon*, and *tenet* are all palindromes; so is the phrase "A man, a plan, a canal, Panama!"

1.17 Using a Dictionary

Dictionary entries provide much more information about words than just their spelling and definitions.

The **pronunciation** is given immediately after the entry word. You can find a complete key to pronunciation symbols in the dictionary's table of contents. In some dictionaries, a simplified key is provided at the bottom of each page.

An abbreviation of the **part of speech** usually follows the pronunciation. This label tells the ways in which a word can be used (see the Language Arts Survey 3.7, "Parts of Speech Overview"). If a word can be used in more than one way, definitions are grouped by part of speech.

An **etymology** is the history of a word. In the first entry, the word *pole* can be traced back through Middle English (ME) and Old English (OE) to the Latin (L) word *palus*, which means "stake." In the second entry, the word *pole* can be traced back through Middle English to the Latin word *polus*, which comes from the Greek word *polos*, meaning "axis of the sphere."

Each **definition** in the entry gives a different meaning of the word. When a word has more than one meaning, the different definitions are numbered. The first definition in an entry is the most common meaning of the word.

Sometimes the entry will include a list of **synonyms**. The entry may also include an **illustration of usage**, which is an example of how the word is used.

USING A DICTIONARY. Students are asked to use their dictionary skills in the Language, Grammar, and Style activity on page 562 and the Vocabulary activity on page 641.

USING CONTEXT CLUES TO ESTIMATE WORD MEANING. Students are asked to estimate the meaning of unfamiliar words using context clues in the Vocabulary activity on page 794.

1.18 Using Glossaries and Footnotes

A **glossary** is an alphabetized list of words and their definitions. Glossaries usually appear at the end of an article, chapter, or book. **Footnotes** appear at the foot, or bottom, of a page. Sometimes they cite a source of information. Other times they define annotated words in order of appearance.

1.19 Learning Base Words, Prefixes, and Suffixes

Many words are formed by adding prefixes or suffixes to base words. (See the Language Arts Survey 3.101, "Using Spelling Rules I.") If you are unfamiliar with a word that is formed with a prefix or a suffix, check to see if you recognize the meaning of the base word and the meaning of its prefix or the suffix.

PREFIX	MEANING	EXAMPLE	MEANING
anti–	"against"	antibacterial	against bacteria
dis–	"not, opposite"	disagreeable	not agreeable
hyper–	"over, excessively"	hyperactive	excessively active
im–, un–	"not"	unusual	not usual
post–	"after"	postseason	after the season
re–	"again"	reprint	print again

SUFFIX	MEANING	EXAMPLE	MEANING
–er, –or	"one who"	narrator	one who narrates
–ful	"full of"	graceful	full of grace
–ish	"like"	childish	like a child
–ity, –ty	"state of, quality"	captivity	state of being captive
–less	"without"	fearless	without fear
–ment	"act of, state of"	achievement	act of achieving

1.20 Learning Synonyms, Antonyms, and Homonyms

A **synonym** is a word that has the same or nearly the same meaning as another word.

EXAMPLES   discover, find, locate, pinpoint

An **antonym** is a word that means the opposite of another word.

EXAMPLES   discover, conceal   give, take   success, defeat

A **homonym** is a word that has the same pronunciation as another word but with a different meaning, origin, and, usually, spelling.

EXAMPLES   bight, bite, byte

1016   *LANGUAGE ARTS SURVEY*

1.21 Exploring Word Origins and Word Families

The English language gains new words from many different sources. One source is the names of people and places. Another source of words in the English language is **acronyms**. Acronyms are words formed from the first letter or letters of the major parts of terms.

EXAMPLES

sonar, from sound navigation ranging; NATO, from North Atlantic Treaty Organization; NASA, from National Aeronautic and Space Administration

Some words in the English language are **borrowed** from other languages.

EXAMPLES **deluxe** (French), **Gesundheit** (German), **kayak** (Eskimo)

Many words are formed by **shortening** longer words.

EXAMPLES

ad, from advertisement; auto, from automobile; lab, from laboratory; phone, from telephone; stereo, from stereophonic

Brand names are often taken into the English language. People begin to use these words as common nouns, even though most of them are still brand names.

EXAMPLES Scotch tape, Xerox, Rollerblade

HAMBURGER

Originally known as "Hamburg steak," the hamburger takes its name from the city of Hamburg, Germany.

SPOONERISM

A slip of the tongue whereby the beginning sounds of words are switched; named after the Rev. William A. Spooner, who was noted for such slips. For example, after officiating at a wedding, he told the groom, "It is kisstomary to cuss the bride."

1.22 Jargon and Gobbledygook

Jargon is the specialized vocabulary used by members of a profession. It tends to be difficult for people outside the profession to understand. A plumber may speak of a "hubless fitting" or a "street elbow" (kinds of pipe). A computer programmer may talk of "ram cache" (part of computer memory) or a "shell" (a type of operating software for computers).

Jargon is useful to writers who want to describe authentically situations in which jargon would naturally be used. A novel about fighter pilots would probably be full of aviation jargon. A science fiction film might include futuristic jargon about warps in space and energy shields.

Gobbledygook is unclear, wordy jargon used by bureaucrats, government officials, and others. For example, the failure of a program might be called an "incomplete success." A bureaucrat might say, "We are engaged in conducting a study with a view to ascertaining which employees might be assigned to the mobility pool and how we might create revenue enhancement," when he means, "We are planning to cut jobs and increase taxes." Avoid the use of gobbledygook. Effective communication involves using precise language instead of muddy, vague vocabulary.

1.23 Clichés and Euphemisms

A **cliché** is an expression that has been used so often it has been colorless and uninteresting. The use of clichés instantly makes writing dull.

EXAMPLES quick as a wink, pretty as a picture

A **euphemism** is an inoffensive term that substitutes for one considered offensive.

EXAMPLES aerial mishap (for "plane crash") building engineer (for "janitor")

1.24 Connotation and Denotation

A **connotation** of a word is all the associations it has in addition to its literal meaning. For example, the words *cheap* and *economical* both denote "inexpensive," but *cheap* connotes shoddy and inferior while *economical* connotes a good value for the money. A **denotation** of a word is its dictionary definition. Writers and speakers should be aware of the connotations as well as the denotations of the words they use. Contrast these denotations and connotations:

EXAMPLES

curious: nosy, snoopy, prying, inquisitive, inquiring

THE SEVEN STAGES IN THE WRITING PROCESS are developed thoroughly in each of the Guided Writing lessons that appear at the end of each unit. See pages 756–763 at the end of Unit 8 for an example.

WRITING *Resource*

INTRODUCTION TO WRITING

2.1 The Writing Process

We live in an information age in which success in most fields requires well-developed writing skills. The most important action that you can take to shape a successful future for yourself is to learn how to write clearly and effectively. Almost anyone can learn to write well by learning the writing process. The writing process is simply the steps that a person takes to compose a piece of writing.

SEVEN STAGES IN THE PROCESS OF WRITING

PREWRITING · DRAFTING · SELF- AND PEER EVALUATION · REVISING · PROOFREADING · PUBLISHING AND PRESENTING · REFLECTING

STAGE	TASKS
1. Prewriting	Plan your writing: choose a topic, audience, purpose, and form; gather ideas; arrange them logically.
2. Drafting	Get your ideas down on paper.
3. Self- and Peer Evaluation	Evaluate, or judge, the writing piece and suggest ways to improve it. Judging your own writing is called **self-evaluation**. Judging a classmate's writing is called **peer evaluation**.
4. Revising	Work to improve the content, organization, and expression of your ideas.
5. Proofreading	Check your writing for errors in spelling, grammar, capitalization, and punctuation. Correct these errors, make a final copy of your paper, and proofread it again.
6. Publishing and Presenting	Share your work with an audience.
7. Reflecting	Think through the writing process to determine what you learned as a writer, what you accomplished, and what you would like to strengthen the next time you write.

While writing moves through these seven stages, it is also is a continuing cycle. You might need to go back to a previous stage before going on to the next step. Returning to a previous stage will strengthen your final work. Note also that the Reflecting stage can be done between any of the other stages. The more you reflect on your writing, the better your writing will become.

UNDERSTANDING THE WRITING PROCESS

2.2 Prewriting

In the **prewriting** stage of the writing process, you make a writing plan. You decide on a purpose, audience, form, and topic. You also begin to discover your voice and gather and organize ideas.

THE PARTS OF A WRITING PLAN

Purpose	A **purpose**, or **aim**, is the goal that you want your writing to accomplish.
Audience	An **audience** is the person or group of people intended to read what you write.
Voice	**Voice** is the quality of a work that tells you that one person wrote it.
Form	A **form** is a kind of writing. For example, you might write a paragraph, an essay, a short story, a poem, or a news article.
Topic	A **topic** is simply something to write about. For example, you might write about a sports hero or about a cultural event in your community.

2.3 IDENTIFYING YOUR PURPOSE. A **purpose**, or **aim,** is the goal that you want your writing to accomplish. For example, you might write to inform, to entertain, to tell a story, to reflect, or to persuade. Your writing might have more than one purpose. For example, a piece of writing might inform about an important event while persuading the audience to respond in a specific way.

MODES AND PURPOSES OF WRITING

MODE	PURPOSE	EXAMPLE
expository/informative writing	to inform	news article, research report
imaginative writing	to entertain, enrich, and enlighten by using a form such as fiction or poetry to share a perspective	poem, short story
narrative writing	to make a point by sharing a story about an event	biography, family history
personal/expressive writing	to reflect	diary entry, personal letter
persuasive/argumentative writing	to persuade readers or listeners to respond in some way, such as to agree with a position, change a view on an issue, reach an agreement, or perform an action	editorial, petition

2.4 IDENTIFYING YOUR AUDIENCE. An **audience** is the person or group of people intended to read what you write. For example, you might write for yourself, for a friend, for a relative, or for your classmates. The best writing usually is intended for a specific audience. Choosing a specific

PREWRITING. The Parts of a Writing Plan: Purpose, Audience, Voice, Form, and Topic, are discussed in depth in each of the Guided Writing lessons that appear at the end of each unit. For examples see pages 63–64 and 150.

IDENTIFYING YOUR PURPOSE. Students are asked to identify authors' aims in the Literary Tools section on pages 395 and 425.

IDENTIFYING YOUR AUDIENCE. The Guided Writing lessons at the end of each unit contain instruction about identifying your audience as part of the prewriting process. For examples, see pages 232 and 512.

audience beforehand will help you make important decisions about your work. For example, for an audience of young children, you would use simple words and ideas. For an audience of fellow members of a technology club, you would use jargon and other specialized words that they already know. For more information, see the the Language Arts Survey 3.3, "Register, Tone, and Voice."

THINKING ABOUT YOUR AUDIENCE

- What people would be most interested in my topic?
- How much does the audience that I am considering already know about the topic?
- How much background information do I need to provide?
- What words, phrases, or concepts in my writing will my audience not understand? For which ones will I have to provide clear explanations?
- What can I do at the beginning of my writing to capture my audience's interest?

2.5 FINDING YOUR VOICE. Voice is the quality of a work that tells you that one person in particular wrote it. Voice makes a person's writing unique. Beginning with the prewriting stage and continuing through the rest of the writing process, a writer discovers his or her own unique voice. For more information, see the section about voice in the Language Arts Survey 3.3, "Register, Tone, and Voice."

2.6 CHOOSING A FORM. Another important decision that a writer needs to make is what form his or her writing will take. A form is a kind of writing. For example, you might write a paragraph, an essay, a short story, a poem, or a newspaper article. The following chart lists some forms of writing that you might want to consider.

FORMS OF WRITING

Adventure	Directions	Letter	Rap
Advertisement	Dream report	Magazine article	Recipe
Advice column	Editorial	Memorandum	Recommendation
Agenda	Epitaph	Menu	Research report
Apology	Essay	Minutes	Résumé
Appeal	Eulogy	Movie review	Schedule
Autobiography	Experiment	Mystery	Science fiction
Biography	Fable	Myth	Short story
Book review	Family history	Narrative	Slide show
Brochure	Fantasy	Newspaper article	Slogan
Calendar	Greeting card	Obituary	Song lyric
Caption	Headline	Parable	Speech
Cartoon	History	Paraphrase	Sports story
Character sketch	Human interest story	Petition	Statement of belief
Children's story	Instructions	Play	Summary
Comedy	Interview questions	Police/Accident report	Tall tale
Consumer report	Invitation	Poem	Thank-you note
Debate	Itinerary	Poster	Tour guide
Detective story	Joke	Proposal	Want ad
Dialogue	Journal entry	Radio or TV spot	Wish list

FINDING YOUR VOICE. Sections on finding your voice are found in each of the Guided Writing lessons at the end of each unit. See pages 63 and 150 for examples.

CHOOSING A FORM. Students are asked to use various forms of writing in the Writer's Journal found after each selection. For example, students are asked to write a newspaper article on page 790 and a police report on page 808.

2.7 CHOOSING A TOPIC. A topic is simply something to write about. For example, you might write about a sports hero or about a cultural event in your community. Here are some ideas that may help you find interesting writing topics:

WAYS TO FIND A WRITING TOPIC	
Check your journal	Search through your journal for ideas that you jotted down in the past. Many professional writers get their ideas from their journals.
Think about your experiences	Think about people, places, or events that affected you strongly. Recall experiences that taught you important lessons or that you felt strongly about.
Look at reference works	Reference works include printed or computerized dictionaries, atlases, almanacs, and encyclopedias.
Browse in a library	Libraries are treasure houses of information and ideas. Simply looking around in the stacks of a library can suggest good ideas for writing.
Use the mass media	Newspapers, magazines, radio, television, and films can suggest good topics for writing. For example, a glance at listings for public television programs might suggest topics related to the arts, to history, or to nature.
Talk to people	Friends, relatives, teachers, and other people you know can be valuable sources for writing.
Do some freewriting	Simply put your pen or pencil down on a piece of paper and write about whatever pops into your mind. Write for two to five minutes without pausing to worry about whether your writing is perfect. Then look back over what you have written to see if you can find any good topics there.
Ask "What if" questions	Ask questions beginning with "What if" to come up with topics for creative writing. For example, you might ask, "What if a kid with a ham radio set received a message from space? Would people believe her?"
Make a cluster chart	Write some general subject such as music or sports in the middle of a piece of paper. Circle this subject. Then, around it, write other ideas that come into your mind as you think about the subject. Circle these and draw lines to connect the outer circles to the inner one.

2.8 FOCUSING A TOPIC. Sometimes a topic is too broad to be treated in a short piece of writing. When you have a topic that is too broad, you must **focus**, or limit, the topic.

WAYS TO FOCUS A WRITING TOPIC	
Break the topic into parts	For example, the topic "newspapers" could be broken down into reporting, copyediting, advertising, circulation, and so on.
Ask questions about the topic	Begin your questions with the words *who, what, where, when, why,* and *how.* Then ask what stands out about your topic or what interests you most.
Make a cluster chart or do some freewriting	For information on these techniques, see the Language Arts Survey 2.7, "Choosing a Topic."

WRITING RESOURCE

CHOOSING A TOPIC. Students can learn more about freewriting by reading the Language Arts Survey 2.12, "Freewriting." Students can read more about making a cluster chart in the Language Arts Survey 2.13, "Clustering."

Brainstorming. Students are asked to brainstorm for objects to put into a time capsule in the Unit 1 Guided Writing lesson on page 65.

Learning from Professional Models. The Guided Writing lessons at the end of each unit contain professional or student writing models as the basis for writing instruction. See an example on page 598.

Once you have made your writing plan by identifying your purpose, form, audience, and topic, the next step in the prewriting stage is to **gather ideas**. There are many ways to gather ideas for writing. This section will introduce you to some of the most useful ones.

2.9 Brainstorming. When you **brainstorm,** you think of as many ideas as you can, as quickly as you can, without stopping to evaluate or criticize the ideas. In brainstorming, anything goes. Sometimes even silly-sounding ideas can lead to productive ones. When you brainstorm in a group, often one person's idea will help another person to build on that concept. It is a good way to come up with creative, new ideas and innovative solutions to problems. Remember that no idea should be rejected in the brainstorming stage. Welcome all ideas with an encouraging response such as, "Great! Any other ideas?" Be sure to get contributions from everyone in your group and to record all ideas so they can be considered and judged later.

2.10 Learning from Professional Models. Professional models are works by published authors. They can be an excellent way to gather your own ideas. For example, one student was impressed by the way Sven Birkerts wrote about electronic technology in his essay "Into the Electronic Millennium" in Unit 6. He analyzed this informative essay and used it as a model when he wrote his own piece on the Internet for a computer class. For more examples, see the way Professional Models are used in the Guided Writing lessons at the end of each unit in this textbook.

2.11 Keeping a Journal. A **journal** is a record of your ideas, dreams, wishes, and experiences. Composition books, spiral notebooks, looseleaf binders, and bound books with blank pages all make excellent journal books. Some people even keep electronic journals on computers.

TYPES OF JOURNALS	
A Diary, or Day-to-day Record of Your Life	August 3, 2003. Today I started keeping a journal. My brother Sean saw me writing and asked me what I was doing. When I told him, he said, "Don't go writing about me in that thing!" I guess he thinks he has all kinds of fascinating secrets! In a family as large as ours, though, it is pretty difficult to have any privacy. . . .
A Reader Response Journal	When I think about what Angie will do at the end of "The Gift of Cochise," I think about how independent and strong she is in the face of danger. This makes me think she does not need Ches Lane in her life. But what about the tears Angie sheds in private? This seems to indicate that she is really afraid even though she never lets it show. I think Ches Lane is going to make himself indispensable to Angie, that he'll grow on her, she will become used to his company, and will welcome a man's help in running the farm.
A Commonplace Book, or Book of Quotations	"Many a thing is despised that is worth more than is supposed." —Chrétien de Troyes, <u>Arthurian Romances</u> "Who knows why people do what they do?" —Barbara Kingsolver, <u>Animal Dreams</u>
A Writer's Lab, or Collection of Ideas for Writing	What if some new supercomputer fell in love with one of its programmers? That could be a very funny or a very sad story. How would it begin? Let's see. One day Randall Meeks, a programmer for the Department of Defense, goes in to work and sits down at a terminal connected to ERICA, a new top-secret computer whose name means Efficient Risk-Instruction Computational Automaton. He logs onto the computer. A message appears, reading, "Good morning. You are looking quite handsome today." He thinks that one of the other programmers is playing a joke on him—but he's wrong.

CONTINUED

A Learning Log, or Record of What You Have Learned	Science: I read today in my science textbook that at the top of Mt. Everest, the highest point on the planet, there are rocks that were formed when sediment fell to the bottom of an ocean. How could the bottom of an ocean get pushed up to the top of the highest mountain? I'll have to ask in class tomorrow about that. Wow, Earth really is a turbulent thing, constantly changing. I wonder what it will look like millions of years into the future?
A Record of Questions	What causes the sky to glow at sunset? Chandra seems unhappy lately. How could I cheer her up? How does a person get a job as a zookeeper? Do you have to study animal behavior or biology or something like that in college? I think it would be fun to work with animals and to help save endangered species.
A Daily Organizer	Things to do tomorrow: • Go to library for book on Gandhi for social studies report • Go to football practice after school • Call Pete about concert tickets • Turn in overdue math homework

2.12 FREEWRITING. Freewriting is simply taking a pencil and paper and writing whatever comes into your mind. Try to write for several minutes without stopping and without worrying about spelling, grammar, usage, or mechanics. If you get stuck, just repeat the last few words until something new pops into your mind.

I really don't get this freewriting stuff. Just write? About what? Hum. I don't think of myself as a writer. I mean, sure, I can write and all, but . . . OK, I'm stuck . . . OK, I'm stuck. Funny, I was just thinking, what if some character in a short story kept saying that this was just a story that he was stuck in and the other characters thought he was crazy, and maybe he manages to figure out a way to pop in and out of the story that he was in, or maybe he can get into different stories at different times. Weird idea, I know it's like that idea that "maybe this is all just a dream." Dreams are interesting. There's that nursery rhyme, "Life is but a dream." What's that called. Oh, Row, Row, Row Your Boat. We used to sing that on the bus in elementary school.

To gather ideas about a specific topic, you might want to try **focused freewriting**. In a focused freewrite, you still write nonstop for a few minutes, but you stick with one topic and write whatever comes to mind as you think about that topic.

2.13 CLUSTERING. Another good way to tap what you already know is to make a **cluster chart**. To make a cluster chart, draw a circle in the center of your paper. In it write a topic you want to explore. Draw more circles branching out from your center circle, and fill them with subtopics related to your main topic. See the sample cluster chart on the following page.

CLUSTERING. Students often practice clustering in the Prereading stage under the graphic organizer on the first page of the selection. For examples, see pages 715 and 729.

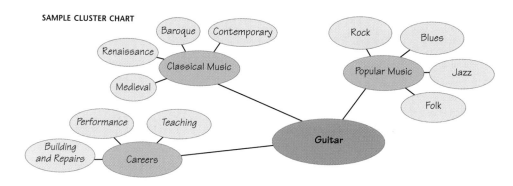

SAMPLE CLUSTER CHART

2.14 QUESTIONING: USING THE 5 Ws AND AN H. Using the 5 Ws and an *H* means asking the **reporting questions** *who, what, where, when, why,* and *how* about your topic. This questioning strategy is especially useful for gathering information about an event or for planning a story.

USING QUESTIONING (TOPIC: THE HARLEM RENAISSANCE)	
Who	African-American writers and artists
What	Period of outstanding literary and artistic vigor and creativity
Where	The vast black ghetto of Harlem, New York
When	1920s
Why	To promote literary and artistic works by African Americans
How	The Harlem Renaissance altered the character of black literature and art, moving from conventional imitations of white novelists, poets, and artists to sophisticated explorations of black life and culture that revealed and stimulated a new confidence and racial pride.

Sample paragraph using this information:

African-American writers and artists partook in a period of outstanding literary and artistic vigor and creativity during the Harlem Renaissance in the 1920s. Centered in the vast black ghetto of Harlem, New York, the movement was to promoted literary and artistic works by African Americans. The Harlem Renaissance altered the character of black literature and art, moving from conventional imitations of white novelists, poets, and artists to sophisticated explorations of black life and culture that revealed and stimulated a new confidence and racial pride.

2.15 IMAGINING: ASKING *WHAT IF* QUESTIONS. If you are doing imaginative or creative writing, ask questions that begin with the words *what if*. "What if" questions can spark your imagination and lead you down unexpected and interesting paths. It can also help you see another side of things and strengthen your own when writing a persuasive piece.

EXAMPLES	What if I could run school for a week? What changes would I make?
	What if I could go back in time to speak with a historical figure?
	What if the greenhouse effect melted the polar icecaps and raised the levels of the oceans around the world? How would people respond?
	What if the city council rejects the proposal for a teen center? How will this affect me and the kids I know?

2.16 COMPLETING VENN DIAGRAMS. If you are writing a comparison and contrast essay, one of the best ways to gather ideas is by completing a Venn diagram. A Venn diagram shows two slightly overlapping circles. The outer part of each circle shows what aspects of two things are different from each other. The inner, or shared, part of each circle shows what aspects the two things share.

"CHEE'S DAUGHTER"
BY JUANITA PLATERO AND
SIYOWIN MILLER

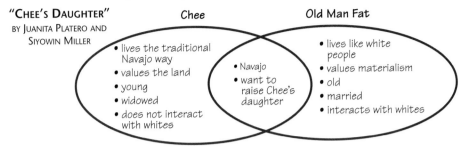

2.17 ANALYZING. To **analyze** is to break something down into its parts and then think about how the parts are related. Analyzing is a way to sort out information about a topic. An **analysis chart** can help you to list the parts and to describe each one.

ANALYSIS OF "FREEWAY 280" BY LORNA DEE CERVANTES		
PART	**DESCRIPTION**	**RELATION OF PART TO WHOLE**
Stanza 1	Description of how the speaker's neighborhood used to look.	Explains how the freeway changed the neighborhood forever.
Stanza 2	Description of the land beneath the freeway.	Explains how the land remembers the past.
Stanza 3	Description of the speaker's return to her old neighborhood.	Explains how the speaker has changed. Once she wanted to escape her old neighborhood; now nostalgia brings her back there.
Stanza 4	Description of the speaker's search.	Explains how the speaker is seeking her cultural identity by returning to her roots.

2.18 SENSORY DETAIL CHARTS. Most people have the use of five major **senses**: sight, sound, touch, taste, and smell. The larger the number of these senses you use to observe something, the more you will notice about it. A **sensory detail chart** can help you to collect information about something so that you can describe it thoroughly. To make a sensory detail chart, begin by writing your subject at the top of the page. Make a box with a column for each of the five senses. In the column under each heading, list details about the subject that you learn from that sense.

SENSORY DETAILS OF A MARATHON				
SIGHT	**SOUND**	**TOUCH**	**TASTE**	**SMELL**
hundreds of runners of all ages	starting gun	hot, sore feet from standing so long	hot dogs and lemonade from vendor carts	hot asphalt
news reporters and onlookers	crowds clapping	stinging face from sun and wind		perspiration
running clothes	running shoes slapping on asphalt			

SENSORY DETAIL CHARTS. In the graphic organizer activity on page 958, students are asked to complete a sensory detail chart.

TIME LINES. Students are asked to make a time line in the graphic organizer on page 833.

PRO AND CON CHARTS. Students are asked to make a pro and con chart in the Study and Research activity on page 287.

2.19 TIME LINES. A **time line** can be useful when you are planning to write a story or a historical account. It gives you an overview of the sequence of events during a particular time period. To make a time line, draw a line on a piece of paper and divide it into equal parts. Label each part with a date or a time. Then add key events at the right places along the time line.

Landmark Events in the History of the Civil Rights Movement (1950–1975)

1950	1955	1960	1965	1970	1975
	1954 *Brown* v. *Board of Education*: U.S. Supreme Court bans racial segregation in public schools	**1960** Sit-in at Greensboro, NC, lunch counter	**1965** March for voting rights from Selma to Montgomery, AL; Voting Rights Act passed; Malcolm X assassinated; race riots in Watts section of Los Angeles	**1971** Supreme Court rules that busing of students may be ordered to achieve desegregation	

2.20 STORY MAPS. A **story map** is a chart that shows the various parts of a fable, myth, tall tale, legend, short story, or other fictional work. Most story maps include the following elements:

ELEMENTS OF A STORY MAP

ELEMENT	DESCRIPTION
Setting	The time and place in which the story occurs
Mood	The emotion created in the reader by the story
Conflict	A struggle between two forces in the story
Plot	The series of events taking place in the story
Characters	The people (or sometimes animals) who play roles in the story
Theme	The main idea of the story

2.21 PRO AND CON CHARTS. A **pro and con chart** shows arguments for and against taking a particular position on some issue. To create a pro and con chart, begin by writing a statement, called a **proposition**, at the top of a piece of paper. Under the proposition, make two columns, one labeled *Pro* and the other, *Con*. In the pro column, list arguments in favor of the proposition. In the con column, list arguments against the proposition.

PRO AND CON CHART

Proposition: All students should take an hour of physical education each day.

Pro	Con
—would keep students in good physical condition	—would take time away from academic studies
—improved health would also improve students' ability to think clearly and work hard	—the same ends might be achieved in less time per day

2.22 INTERVIEWING. In an **interview**, you meet with someone and ask him or her questions. Interviewing experts is an excellent way to gain information about a particular topic. For example, if you are interested in writing about the making of pottery, you might interview an art teacher, a professional potter, or the owner of a ceramics shop. When planning an interview, list the questions you would like to ask, including some about the person's background as well as about your topic. Other questions might occur to you as the interview proceeds. See the Language Arts Survey 4.14, "Conducting an Interview."

2.23 RESEARCHING FOR IDEAS. No matter what your subject, you can probably find information about it by doing research in reference works. **Reference works** include encyclopedias, dictionaries, almanacs, atlases, indexes, Internet sites, and more. For additional information about reference materials and how to find them, see the Language Arts Survey 5.20, "Using Reference Works," and 5.37, "Keeping a Research Journal."

ORGANIZING IDEAS

2.24 WRITING PARAGRAPHS. After you have gathered ideas for a piece of writing, the next step is to organize these ideas in a useful and reader-friendly way. The most basic organization of ideas occurs in forming paragraphs. A good paragraph is a carefully organized unit of writing. It develops a sequence in narrative writing or develops a particular topic in informational or persuasive writing.

PARAGRAPHS WITH TOPIC SENTENCES. Many paragraphs include a topic sentence that presents a main idea. The topic sentence can be placed at the beginning, middle or end of the paragraph. Topic sentences usually appear early on in the paragraph and are commonly followed by one or more supporting sentences. Often these supporting sentences begin with transitions that relate them to the other sentences or to the topic sentence. This type of paragraph may end with a clincher sentence, which sums up what has been said in the paragraph.

EXAMPLE

TOPIC SENTENCE	*Antigone* by Sophocles tells the story of the end of the life of the daughter born of the incestuous union of Oedipus and his mother, Jocasta.
SUPPORTING SENTENCES	The play concerns that part of the Oedipus story that occurs after Eteocles and Polyneices have killed each other over the succession to the throne of Thebes. Antigone's uncle Creon succeeds to the throne and decrees that anyone who buries the dishonored Polyneices will face capital punishment. Antigone, however, obeys her instincts of love and loyalty and defies the orders of her uncle, willing to face the consequences of her act of humanity. Believing that civic duty outweighs family ties, Creon refuses to commute Antigone's death sentence.
CLINCHER SENTENCE	Antigone's bravery in the face of impending death makes her one of the most memorable classical heroines.

PARAGRAPHS WITHOUT TOPIC SENTENCES. Most paragraphs do not have topic sentences. In a narrative piece of writing, many paragraphs state a series of events, and no sentence in the paragraph sums up the events. In good narrative writing, the sequence of events appears in chronological order. Descriptive writing may contain paragraphs organized spatially—in the order in which the speaker or narrator sees, hears, feels, smells, and tastes things in a given situation.

EXAMPLE

I asked her, "Ma, what is Chinese torture?" My mother shook her head. A bobby pin was wedged between her lips. She wetted her palms and smoothed the hair above my ear, then pushed the pin in so that it nicked sharply against my scalp.

Amy Tan, from "Rules of the Game"

ORGANIZING IDEAS: WRITING WITH A PLAN. For instruction on different types of writing organization, see the Writing with a Plan section of the Guided Writing lessons at the end of each unit. For examples, turn to pages 232 and 700.

PARAGRAPHS WITH TOPIC SENTENCES. Students are asked to focus on writing paragraphs with topic sentences in the Unit 1 Guided Writing Language, Grammar, and Style lesson on pages 67–69.

WRITING RESOURCE

PARAGRAPH UNITY. The ideas in a paragraph should be tightly linked, or "together." They should be ordered and linked in a logical and easily understandable way. You can organize a paragraph in the order of time (chronologically), in the order of importance, or in order to achieve a specific purpose, such as describing or comparing and contrasting. To link the ideas in a paragraph, use connective words and phrases. In informational or persuasive paragraphs, *for example, as a result, finally, therefore,* and *in fact* are common connectives. In narrative and descriptive paragraphs, words like *first, then, suddenly, above, beyond, in the distance,* and *there* are common connectives. In comparison-contrast paragraphs, common phrases include *similarly, on the other hand,* and *in contrast.* In cause and effect paragraphs, linkers include *one cause, another effect, as a result, consequently, finally,* and *therefore.*

2.25 WRITING A THESIS STATEMENT. One way to start organizing your writing, especially if you are writing an informative or persuasive essay, is to identify the main idea of what you want to say. Present this idea in the form of a sentence or two called a thesis statement. A **thesis statement** is simply a sentence that presents the main idea or the position you will take in your essay.

THESIS FOR A PERSUASIVE ESSAY

The development at Rice Creek Farm should be stopped because it will destroy one of the best natural areas near the city.

THESIS FOR AN INFORMATIVE ESSAY

Wilma Rudolph was an athlete who succeeded in the elite sport of tennis before the world was willing to recognize her.

2.26 WRITING MAIN IDEAS AND SUPPORTING DETAILS. Once you have a thesis statement, the next step is to select several main ideas to support your thesis statement. Begin by writing your thesis at the top of a piece of paper. Then list the main points that you will use to support your thesis. For each main idea, list several supporting details—statements, facts, examples, quotes, and illustrations that explain or demonstrate your idea.

THESIS: The development at Rice Creek Farm should be stopped because people will be unable to enjoy the area, a considerable amount of wildlife will be harmed, and an important water resource will be lost.

- People will be unable to enjoy the area.
  - Hundreds of people of all ages now bike, run, and swim in the area in the summer and ski in the winter. Last year's recreation survey was completed by 653 people. Eighty-five percent said that they visited Rice Creek Farm at least twice a month.
  - The development of an industrial park would ban people from using the area. It will become a factory site instead of a wooded recreation area. "The industrial park site would be strictly off limits to the public for their own protection," developer Orrin Q. Smedley said in the *Rice Creek Times.*

- A considerable amount of wildlife will be harmed.
  - The wooded area will be completely eliminated, destroying habitat.

CONTINUED

— The species that will be lost will include deer, fox, racoons, skunks, and wild birds, according to the parks board supervisor.

• An important water resource will be lost.
   — The water resource has many uses, including recreational and agricultural.
   — The quality of our city water supply depends on the preservation of this habitat.

2.27 CHOOSING A METHOD OF ORGANIZATION. Writing can be organized in different ways.

METHOD	DESCRIPTION
Chronological Order	Give events in the order in which they happen or should be done; connect events by using transition words such as *first, second, next, then,* and *finally.* Chronological organization would be a good method for relating a narrative, giving a recipe, writing a how-to article on building a bird-feeder, or to describe a process, such as what happens when a volcano erupts.
Spatial Order	Describe parts in order of their location in space, for example, from back to front, left to right, or top to bottom; connect your descriptions with transition words or phrases such as *next to, beside, above, below, beyond,* and *around.* Spatial order would be a useful form for an article describing a kitchen renovation, or a descriptive passage in a science fiction story set in a space station.
Order of Importance	List details from least important to most important or from most important to least important; connect your details with transition phrases such as *more important, less important, most important,* and *least important.* A speech telling voters why they should elect you class president could be organized from the least important reason and build to the most important reason.
Comparison and Contrast Order	Details of two subjects are presented in one of two ways. In the first method, the characteristics of one subject are presented, followed by the characteristics of the second subject. This method would be useful to organize an essay that compares and contrasts two fast-food chains. You could use this method to say why one is superior to another. "BurgerWorld has the most restaurants. They broil their hamburgers, and offer a line of low-fat meals. Ma's Burgers has far fewer restaurants, fries their hamburgers, and offers no low-fat choices." In the second method, both subjects are compared and contrasted with regard to one quality, then with regard to a second quality, and so on. An essay organized according to this method could compare the platforms of two political parties, issue by issue: the environment, the economy, and so on. Ideas are connected by transitional words and phrases that indicate similarities or differences, such as *likewise, similarly, in contrast, a different kind,* and *another difference.*
Cause and Effect Order	One or more causes are presented followed by one or more effects, or one or more effects are presented followed by one or more causes. A public health announcement warning about the dangers of playing with fire would be usefully organized by cause-and-effect. An essay discussing the outbreak of World War I and the events that led up to it could be organized by effect and causes. Transitional words and phrases that indicate cause and effect include *one cause, another effect, as a result, consequently,* and *therefore.*

CONTINUED

CHOOSING A METHOD OF ORGANIZATION. Students are asked to reflect on the effects of using chronological order in narrative writing in the Literary Tools section on page 833. Students are also asked to use the cause and effect order in the Unit 9 Guided Writing lesson on page 774.

OUTLINING. Students are encouraged to outline their essay before they begin the drafting process in the Unit 1 and Unit 3 Guided Writing lesson. See pages 64 and 233 for examples.

Part by Part Order	Ideas are presented according to no *overall* organizational pattern. However, each idea is connected logically to the one that precedes it and/or to the one that follows it. A letter to a friend might be organized part by part. One paragraph might discuss a party the writer just attended and the next could focus on the writer's feelings about a person he or she met there. After chronological order, this is the most common method for organizing ideas in writing. Transitional words or phrases include anything that indicates the relationship or connection between the ideas.

2.28 OUTLINING. An **outline** is an excellent framework for highlighting main ideas and supporting details. Rough and formal outlines are the two main types of outlines writers commonly use.

2.29 ROUGH OUTLINES. To create a **rough outline**, simply list your main ideas in some logical order. Under each main idea, list the supporting details set off by dashes.

What Is Drama?

Definition of Drama
—Tells a story
—Uses actors to play characters
—Uses a stage, properties, lights, costumes, makeup, and special effects

Types of Drama
—Tragedy
  —Definition: A play in which the main character meets a negative fate
  —Examples: <u>Antigone</u>, <u>Romeo and Juliet</u>, <u>Death of a Salesman</u>
—Comedy
  —Definition: A play in which the main character meets a positive fate
  —Examples: <u>A Midsummer Night's Dream</u>, <u>Cyrano de Bergerac</u>, <u>The Odd Couple</u>

2.30 FORMAL OUTLINES. A **formal outline** has headings and subheadings identified by numbers and letters. One type of formal outline is the **topic outline**. Such an outline has entries that are words or phrases rather than complete sentences.

What Is a Myth?

I. Definition of myth
    A. Ancient story involving gods
       1. Multiple gods in mythology
       2. Gods given human characteristics
    B. Often about origins
       1. Reflect prescientific worldview
       2. Gods and humans actively participate
    C. Often about heroes
II. Creation myths
    A. The Greek myth of the origins of the universe
    B. The Greek myth of the origins of human beings
III. Origin myths
    A. Arachne and the origins of spiders
    B. Phaëthon and the origins of deserts
IV. Hero myths
    A. Theseus and the Minotaur
    B. Herakles and the twelve labors

2.31 Drafting

After you have gathered your information and organized it, the next step in writing is to produce a draft. A **draft** is simply an early attempt at writing a paper. When working on a draft, keep in mind that you do not have to get everything just right the first time through. The beauty of a draft is that you can rework it many times until you are satisfied with the final product.

Different writers approach drafting in different ways. Some prefer to work slowly and carefully, perfecting each part as they go. Producing such a **careful draft** can be rewarding because you get to see a finished, polished piece emerging part by part. However, many writers find that perfecting each part as they come to it bogs down the process. These writers prefer to write a discovery draft, getting all their ideas down on paper in rough form and then going back over the paper to work it into shape. When writing a **discovery draft**, you do not focus on spelling, grammar, usage, and mechanics. You can take care of those matters during revision.

2.32 DRAFTING AN INTRODUCTION. The purpose of an introduction is to capture your reader's attention and establish what you want to say. An effective introduction can start with a quotation, a question, an anecdote, an intriguing fact, or a description that hooks the reader to keep reading.

An effective introduction can open with:

A QUOTE	"That's one small step for man, one giant leap for mankind." With these words, Neil Armstrong signaled his success as the first human to set foot on the moon...
A QUESTION	What would it be like if all the birds in the world suddenly stopped their singing?
AN ANECDOTE	When my brother was nineteen, he volunteered in a homeless shelter making sure people had a safe place to spend the night. He told me once that he would never forget the time he met...
A FACT	More than a million new web pages appear each day on the Internet...
A DESCRIPTION	Along the murky bottom of the ocean floor, at the deepest part of the ocean, lies the giant squid, a creature so elusive that few people have ever seen it. For hundreds of years, no one knew it really existed—although tales of sea monsters had long hinted of it.

2.33 DRAFTING BODY PARAGRAPHS. When writing the body of an essay, refer to your outline. Each heading in your outline will become the main idea of one of your paragraphs. To move smoothly from one idea to another, use transitional words or phrases. As you draft, include evidence from documented sources to support the ideas that you present. This evidence can be paraphrased, summarized, or quoted directly. For information on documenting sources, see the Language Arts Survey 5.36, "Documenting Sources," and 5.43, "Paraphrasing, Summarizing, and Quoting."

2.34 DRAFTING A CONCLUSION. In the conclusion, bring together the main ideas you included in the body of your essay and create a sense of closure to the issue you raised in your thesis. There is no single right way to conclude a piece of writing. Possibilities include:

- making a generalization
- restating the thesis and major supporting ideas in different words
- summarizing the points made in the rest of the essay
- drawing a lesson or moral
- calling on the reader to adopt a view or take an action
- expanding on your thesis or main idea by connecting it to the reader's own interests
- linking your thesis to a larger issue or concern

2.35 USING TRANSITIONS EFFECTIVELY. Transitions are words and phrases that help you move smoothly from one idea to the next in your writing. The transition words themselves depend on the method of organization you are using in your paper. For lists of these words and when to use them, see the Language Arts Survey 2.27, "Choosing a Method of Organization."

WRITING RESOURCE

DRAFTING. The Guided Writing lessons at the end of each unit allow students the opportunity to go through the drafting process of writing. For examples, see pages 233 and 514.

DRAFTING AN INTRODUCTION. Students are asked to draft an introduction in the Unit 3 Guided Writing lesson on page 233.

2.36 WRITING NARRATIVE, DIALOGUE, DESCRIPTION, AND EXPOSITION. Some writing purposes do not require a thesis or a formal outline. They rely on other types of writing to present their ideas effectively. These types include narration, dialogue, description, and exposition.

TYPE OF WRITING	DESCRIPTION AND ORGANIZATION
Narrative	As with the narrative mode, this method tells a story or presents events using time, or **chronological order**, as a way of organization.
Dialogue	Writing using this method presents words as they were actually spoken by people. Quotation marks are usually used to set off direct speech.
Description	Writing with this method portrays a character, an object, or a scene. Descriptions make use of sensory details—words and phrases that describe how things look, sound, smell, taste, or feel. Descriptive writing frequently uses **spatial order** as a method of organization.
Exposition	Writing using this method presents facts or opinions in an organized manner. There are many ways to organize exposition. Among the most common are the following: **Analysis** breaks something into its parts and shows how the parts are related. **Cause and effect order** identifies and analyzes the causes and effects of something. **Classification** involves placing subjects into categories, or classes, according to their properties or characteristics. These groups are then presented, one-by-one, in some reasonable order. **Comparison and contrast order** is a method of organization in which details about the similarities and differences between two subjects are presented in one of two ways. In the first method, characteristics of one subject are presented, followed by the characteristics of a second subject. In the second method, both subjects are compared and contrasted with regard to one characteristic, then with regard to a second characteristic, and so on. **Definition** explains a concept or idea and examines its qualities. **Problem/Solution** writing analyzes a problem and proposes possible solutions. It can be objective or persuasive. **Process/How-to** writing presents the steps in a process or gives the reader directions on how to do something.

2.37 Self- and Peer Evaluation

When you evaluate something, you examine it carefully to find its strengths and weaknesses. Evaluating your own writing is called **self-evaluation**. A **peer evaluation** is an evaluation of a piece of writing done by a classmate, or peer.

2.38 HOW TO EVALUATE A PIECE OF WRITING. After producing a rough draft of a piece of writing, the next step is to evaluate that draft to find out what you or the writer you are evaluating should improve.

A good evaluation practice is to read through the piece of writing three times:

- **First, check for content.** If you are evaluating your own writing, make sure that you have said all that you want to say, that you have not left out important details, and that you have not included unimportant or unrelated details. If you are evaluating a peer's writing, make sure the content is clear, that nothing is missing to prevent the work from carrying the reader forward, and that the writer has not included any unrelated details.

- **Second, check for organization.** Make sure that the ideas in the writing are presented in a reasonable order.
- **Third, check the style and language** of the piece. Make sure that the language is appropriately formal or informal, that the tone is appropriate to the message and the audience the piece addresses, and that the writer has defined any key or unfamiliar terms.

As you check the writing piece, make notes about what the writer needs to revise, or change. See the Language Arts Survey 2.42, "A Revision Checklist," for further information on what to look for as you evaluate your or a peer's writing.

2.39 How to Deliver Helpful Criticism

- **Be focused.** Concentrate on content, organization, and style. Do not concentrate at this point on proofreading matters such as spelling and punctuation; they can be fixed later.
- **Be positive.** Let the writer know what he or she has done right. Show how the paper could be improved by making the changes that you are suggesting.
- **Be specific.** Give the writer concrete ideas for improving his or her work. For example, if you think that two ideas seem unconnected, suggest a way in which they might be connected clearly.
- **Be tactful.** Consider the other person's feelings, and use a pleasant tone of voice. Do not criticize the writer. Instead, focus on the writing.

2.40 How to Benefit from Helpful Criticism

- **Tell your evaluator specific concerns.** For example, if you are wondering whether something you have written is clear, ask the evaluator if he or she understands that part of what you have written.
- **Ask questions to clarify comments** that your evaluator makes.
- **Accept your evaluator's comments graciously.** Remember that criticisms can be helpful. They can help you to identify weaknesses and produce a better piece through revision. If, on the other hand, you think that a given suggestion will not truly improve your writing, you do not have to follow it. There are many ways to strengthen writing. By reflecting on reviewer comments and your own self-evaluation, you will be ready to go on to the next step: revision.

2.41 Revising

After identifying weaknesses in a draft through self-evaluation and peer evaluation, the next step is to **revise** the draft. Here are four basic ways to improve meaning and content:

Adding or Expanding. Sometimes writing can be improved by adding details, examples, or transitions to connect ideas. Often a single added adjective, for example, can make a piece of writing clearer or more vivid.

UNREVISED	Wind whistled through the park.
REVISED	A **bone-chilling** wind whistled through the park.

At other times, you will find you will need to add details to back up your main idea.

UNREVISED	Everyone uses the park so its destruction would be a major loss to the community.
REVISED	Of the 653 people who responded to the survey, 85 percent said they would consider the destruction of the park a major loss to the community.

Revising. Instruction on revising and proofreading is given in each of the Guided Writing lessons at the end of the units. For examples, see pages 234 and 515.

CUTTING OR CONDENSING. Often writing can be improved by cutting unnecessary or unrelated material.

UNREVISED	Watson was firmly determined to find the structure of the DNA molecule.
REVISED	Watson was determined to find the structure of the DNA molecule.

REPLACING. Sometimes weak writing can be made stronger through more concrete, more vivid, or more precise details.

UNREVISED	Several things had been bothering Bill.
REVISED	Several personal problems had been bothering Bill.
UNREVISED	Chandra lived in a house down the street.
REVISED	Chandra lived in a Garrison colonial down Mulberry Street.

MOVING. Often you can improve the organization of your writing by moving part of it so that related ideas appear near one another.

UNREVISED	Mince the garlic in very fine pieces. Then heat a tablespoon of olive oil in a small skillet. Stir it with a wooden spoon and saute just until it starts to brown. Then remove it. Oh—before you put it in the skillet, heat some oil. Use about a tablespoon. Olive oil is best. Use medium-low heat.
REVISED	Mince the garlic in very fine pieces. Heat a tablespoon of olive oil in a small skillet at a medium-low temperature. When the oil is hot, add the garlic. Stir it with a wooden spoon and saute it just until it starts to brown. Then remove the garlic.

When you mark a piece of writing for revision, use the standard proofreading symbols. The symbols for adding, cutting, replacing, and moving are the first four symbols in the Language Arts Survey 2.44, "Using Proofreader's Marks."

2.42 A REVISION CHECKLIST. The following chart lists some questions to ask yourself whenever you are revising your writing. If you cannot answer *yes* to any of these questions, then you need to revise your work. Continue revising until you can answer *yes*.

REVISION CHECKLIST	
Content	• Does the writing achieve its purpose?
	• Are the main ideas clearly stated and supported by details?
Organization	• Are the ideas arranged in a sensible order?
	• Are the ideas connected to one another within paragraphs and between paragraphs?
Style	• Is the language appropriate to the audience and purpose?
	• Is the mood appropriate to the purpose of the writing?

2.43 Proofreading

When you proofread your writing, you read it through to look for errors and mark corrections. When you mark corrections to your writing, use the standard proofreading symbols. With just a little practice you'll find them very easy and convenient.

2.44 USING PROOFREADER'S MARKS. Consult the chart below for standard proofreading marks.

PROOFREADER'S SYMBOLS

Symbol and Example	Meaning of Symbol
The very first time	Delete (cut) this material.
cat cradle	Insert (add) something that is missing.
George	Replace this letter or word.
All the horses king's	Move this word to where the arrow points.
french toast	Capitalize this letter.
the vice-President	Lowercase this letter.
housse	Take out this letter and close up space.
book keeper	Close up space.
gerbil	Change the order of these letters.
end. "Watch out," she yelled.	Begin a new paragraph.
Love conquers all	Put a period here.
Welcome friends.	Put a comma here.
Getthe stopwatch	Put a space here.
Dear Madam	Put a colon here.
She walked he rode.	Put a semicolon here.
name brand products	Put a hyphen here.
cats meow	Put an apostrophe here.
cat's cradle (stet)	Let it stand. (Leave as it is.)

2.45 A PROOFREADING CHECKLIST. After you have revised your draft, make a clean copy of it and proofread it for errors in spelling, grammar, and punctuation. Use the following proofreading checklist.

PROOFREADING CHECKLIST

Spelling	• Are all words, including names, spelled correctly?
Grammar	• Does each verb agree with its subject?
	• Are verb tenses consistent and correct?
	• Are irregular verbs formed correctly?
	• Are there any sentence fragments or run-ons?
	• Have double negatives been avoided?
	• Have frequently confused words, such as *affect* and *effect*, been used correctly?
Punctuation	• Does every sentence end with an end mark?
	• Are commas used correctly?
	• Do all proper nouns and proper adjectives begin with capital letters?

WRITING RESOURCE

USING PROOFREADER'S MARKS.
Encourage students to use proofreader's marks when they do peer evaluations. A blackline master of the Proofreader's Symbols is provided in the Writing Resource book 2.44 in the Teacher's Resource Kit.

PROPER MANUSCRIPT FORM. Encourage students to read the Language Arts Survey 2.46, "Proper Manuscript Form," after they are done revising and proofreading their written assignments.

PUBLISHING AND PRESENTING. Ideas for publishing and presenting student writing are suggested in each of the Guided Writing lessons at the end of the units. For examples, see pages 69 and 155.

MAINTAINING A WRITING PORTFOLIO. You might find additional suggestions for helping students maintain a writing portfolio in *Portfolio Keeping: A Guide for Students* by Nedra Reynolds.

2.46 PROPER MANUSCRIPT FORM. After proofreading your draft, you will want to prepare your final manuscript. Follow the guidelines given by your teacher or, if your teacher tells you to do so, the guidelines given here. After preparing a final manuscript according to these guidelines, proofread it one last time for errors.

GUIDELINES FOR PREPARING A MANUSCRIPT

- Keyboard your manuscript using a typewriter or word processor, or write it out neatly using blue or black ink.
- Double-space your paper. Leave one blank line between every line of text.
- Use one side of the paper.
- Leave one-inch margins on all sides of the text.
- Indent the first line of each paragraph.
- In the upper right-hand corner of the first page, put your name, class, and date. On every page after the first, include the page number in this heading, as follows:
  Keanna Pérez
  English 7
  October 3, 2001
  p. 2
- Make a cover sheet listing the title of the work, your name, the date, and the class.

2.47 Publishing and Presenting Your Work

In the **publishing and presenting stage**, you share your work with an audience.

2.48 MAINTAINING A WRITING PORTFOLIO. A **writing portfolio** is a collection of your writing. Usually, a portfolio is a file folder with your name on it and your writing in it. Your teacher may ask you to keep a complete portfolio, one that includes all the pieces that you write. Another possibility is that your teacher will ask you to keep a selected portfolio, one that contains only your very best pieces of writing.

When you put a piece of writing in your portfolio, make sure that your name and the date are on it. Attach any notes or earlier versions of the writing that you have.

From time to time, you and your teacher will evaluate, or examine, your portfolio. You will meet in a student-teacher conference and talk about your pieces of writing. Your teacher will help you to find strengths and weaknesses in your writing. He or she also will help you to make plans for improving your writing in the future.

Keeping a writing portfolio can be exciting. In very little time, you can build a collection of your work. Looking over this work, you can take pride in your accomplishments. You can also reflect on how you are growing as a writer.

2.49 SHARING YOUR WORK WITH OTHERS. Some writing is done just for one's self. Journal writing usually falls into that category. Most writing, however, is meant to be shared with others. There are many ways in which to share your work. Here are several ways in which you can publish your writing or present it to others:

- Find a local publication that will accept your work. (A school literary magazine, a school newspaper, or a community newspaper are possibilities.)

- Submit the work to a regional or national publication. Check a reference work such as *Writer's Market* to find information on types of manuscripts accepted, manuscript form, and methods and amounts of payment.
- Enter the work in a contest. Your teacher may be able to tell you about writing contests for students. You can also find out about such contests by looking for announcements in writers' magazines and literary magazines.
- Read your work aloud to classmates, friends, or family members.
- Obtain permission to read your work aloud over the school's public address system.
- Work with other students to prepare a publication—a brochure, online literary magazine, anthology, or newspaper.
- Prepare a poster or bulletin board, perhaps in collaboration with other students, to display your writing.
- Make your own book by typing or word processing the pages and binding them together. Or copy your work into a blank book.
- Hold a reading or performance of student writing as a class or schoolwide project.
- Share your writing with other students in a small writers' group that meets periodically to discuss one or two students' recent work. (Members of the group should receive the work to be discussed beforehand so they can read it and make notes on it.)
- If the work is dramatic in nature, work with other students to present a performance of it, either as straight drama or as readers' theater. If the work is poetry, fiction, or nonfiction, work with others to present it as an oral interpretation.

2.50 Reflecting on Your Writing

In the **reflecting** stage, you think through the writing process to determine what you learned as a writer, what you accomplished, and what skills you would like to strengthen the next time you write. Reflection can be done in a journal, on a self-evaluation form for writing, in small group discussion, or simply in your own thoughts. Here are some questions to ask as you reflect on the writing process and yourself as a writer.

QUESTIONS FOR REFLECTION

- What have I learned in writing about this topic?
- What have I learned in writing for this purpose?
- What have I learned by using this form?
- How do I perceive my audience? What would I like my audience to gain from my writing?
- What kind of voice does my writing have?
- How have I developed as a writer while writing this piece?
- What strengths have I discovered in my work?
- What aspects of my writing do I want to strengthen? What can I do to strengthen them?

REFLECTING ON YOUR WRITING. Students are asked to reflect on their writing at various stages of the writing process in the Guided Writing lessons at the end of each unit. For examples, turn to pages 604 and 705.

LANGUAGE, GRAMMAR, AND STYLE *Resource*

LANGUAGE

3.1 Appropriate Uses of English

Language is a powerful tool for conveying meaning. It is also a complex tool that must be used appropriately if genuine communication is to occur. In deciding how to communicate most effectively, a speaker must make choices concerning use of formal or informal English; what tone to use, the effects of irony, sarcasm, and rudeness; and how dialect affects the communicated message.

3.2 Formal and Informal English

Depending on the situation, you might use either formal English or informal English when you speak or write. Formal English is appropriate for school essays, newspaper and magazine articles, some literary works, oral or written reports, and test answers. Informal English is appropriate when speaking with a friend or writing personal letters or notes; it can also be used in some literary works.

How do you decide whether to use formal or informal English? You will naturally tend to use informal English, so all you need to remember are the situations just described in which formal English may be expected instead. Your audience and purpose help determine whether to use formal or informal English. For example, you would use formal English to discuss a grade with a teacher or to ask for a refund from a store manager. You would use informal English talking with your friends. You might use somewhat formal English in getting to know a new friend, and then relax and use more informal English as the friendship developed.

How do you tell the difference between formal and informal English? Informal English allows grammatical constructions that would not be acceptable in formal English. Many of these constructions are described in the Grammar Handbook on page 1055, where they are labeled "nonstandard." Informal English also uses *colloquialisms* and *slang*.

A **colloquialism** is a word or phrase used in everyday conversation.

COLLOQUIAL ENGLISH
You guys must be **sick of** doing the same thing day after day.
He was **totally turned off** by the movie.

FORMAL ENGLISH
All of you must be **weary** of doing the same thing day after day.
He was completely **displeased** by the movie.

Slang is a form of speech made up of invented words or old words that are given a new meaning.

SLANG
You better **chill out** for a while—you're too angry to talk to him now.

FORMAL ENGLISH
You had better **relax** for a while—you're too angry to talk to him now.

3.3 Register, Tone, and Voice

To understand the concept of register, imagine that all the different kinds of usage in a language—both formal and informal—form one large set. A **register** is a subset of language usage specific to a particular relationship between people. In talking to a friend, for example, you speak in a register that is casual, warm, and open. In speaking to a young child, you speak in a register that is nonthreatening and simple to understand. In speaking to an official such as a police officer or a government clerk, you speak in a register that is polite but forthright—the same register that person should use with you. The words you choose, the grammar you employ to say those words, and your tone of voice will change depending on the register in which you are speaking.

Another way to understand register is to examine its meaning as a musical term. In music, register means the range of notes a singer or instrument is capable of producing. Your speaking and writing, however, are not limited to one range of usage. You can call on any part of a broad scale of usage, ranging from a grunt to a complex and formal declaration of your thought.

One hallmark of people who know how to use the power of language is their ability to choose and use the appropriate register for whatever situation they are in. They do not offend strangers by being too familiar or puzzle their friends by being too formal.

Tone is a writer's or speaker's attitude toward a subject. The tone of a message should reflect the speaker's attitude toward the subject and his or her audience. The speaker shapes the tone of a message by carefully choosing words and phrases. *Diction*, or choice of words, determines much of a speaker's tone. For instance, when writing a letter of complaint, do you want to say, "Your new product is so disgusting that I'll never buy anything you make ever again" or "I am concerned with the danger your new product poses to young children"? The tone you convey will depend greatly upon word choice.

The following examples give two different descriptions of the same scene. In one the scene is described in a tone of fear, and in the other it is described in a tone of awe. If you were telling a story about someone who was afraid of the ocean, you might use the more negative description. If you were writing about someone who enjoyed the ocean, you would probably use the more positive description.

TONE OF FEAR

Menacing black waves rolled in relentlessly, crashing down upon the rocks and threatening to sweep everything in their path out to sea. Mountainous and savage, the waves pounded the shore with a fury that sent a chill of dread through my soul.

TONE OF AWE

Powerful breakers rolled in majestically, splashing against the rocks and sending fountains of spray high into the air. I stood in awe of this force so mighty that nothing could stop it.

Voice is the quality of a work that tells you that one person in particular wrote it—not several, and not just anyone. Voice is one feature that makes a spoken or written work unique. The voice of a work can be difficult to define; it may have to do with the way a writer or speaker views people, events, objects, ideas, the passage of time, even life itself. If this treatment of the subject is consistent throughout, despite variations in tone, register, point of view, and topic, then the writer or speaker has established a voice, a sense of individuality, in the work.

In your own communication, whether in speaking or writing, you should strive to develop your own voice, not to imitate the voices of others. What that voice is, and how it compares to others, are matters no one can decide for you. "To thine own self be true," says Polonius in Shakespeare's *Hamlet*, "and thou canst not then be false to any man." Be true to your own voice, and your experience will speak directly to the experience of others.

3.4 Irony, Sarcasm, and Rudeness

It is easy to mistake the term *rude* to mean anything that is crude, distasteful, or not pleasing to someone. The word *rude* has been adapted and expanded into a general slang term. The standard definition of *rude* means bad-mannered, impolite, or inconsiderate. If someone says something a listener doesn't like, that person is not rude in the original meaning of the word. However, a person who interrupts someone else's conversation, curses, or forgets to say "please," "thank you," or "excuse me" is being selfish and inconsiderate—all characteristics of rude behavior within the original meaning of the word.

REGISTER, TONE, AND VOICE. Refer students to the Language Arts Survey 3.3, "Register, Tone, and Voice" when they are reading the Finding Your Voice section of each Guided Writing lesson. See pages 512 and 700 for examples.

Frequently students confuse sarcasm or irony with rudeness. **Verbal irony** is present when someone says or writes the opposite of what he or she means in order to create humor or to make a point. It can be funny or serious. For example, if someone pushes to the front of a line, and someone else says, "What polite behavior," the speaker is expressing verbal irony. **Sarcasm** is a specialized kind of irony; the difference is the speaker's intentions. Sarcastic people say the opposite of what they mean in order to criticize, hurt, or humiliate someone. Sarcasm differs from other forms of irony because it is usually unkind.

Tobias Wolff uses verbal irony in "The Liar" when James lies to the people on the bus:

EXAMPLE

"What do you do with a bunch of Tibetans?" the woman repeated.
"Try to find them jobs, locate housing, listen to their problems."
"You understand that kind of talk?"
"Yes."
"Speak it?"
"Pretty well. I was born and raised in Tibet. My parents were missionaries over there."

3.5 Dialects of English

A **dialect** is a version of a language spoken by people of a particular place, time, or group. Dialects are characterized by differences in pronunciation, word choice, grammar, and accent. They are usually based on social differences (upper class, middle class, and lower class) or on regional differences. In the United States, the major regional dialects are northern, southern, midland, and western.

All dialects are equally capable of expressing thought, which is what language is for. Therefore, no dialect is better than any other dialect. The dialect used by the most powerful social class is usually considered the **standard**, and other dialects are considered **nonstandard**. But standard does not mean "correct" or "better than others." Knowledge of the standard dialect is useful because it is widely understood, and because in many situations, speaking or writing in the standard dialect will ensure that people focus on what you say rather than how you say it. They will understand your meaning, without being distracted by your use of an unfamiliar dialect.

Knowing nonstandard dialect is also useful to writers. Consider the way Amy Tan uses dialect to make her writing more authentic.

EXAMPLE

"This American rules," she concluded at last. "Every time people come out from foreign country, must know rules. You not know, judge say, Too bad, go back. They not telling you why so you can use their way go forward. They say, Don't know why, you find out yourself. But they knowing all the time. Better you take it, find out why yourself."   from "Rules of the Game"

Differences in dialect show up especially in the terms speakers use to refer to certain objects in various areas of the country. For example, the generic term for a carbonated beverage is "soda" in Florida and Washington, DC, "pop" in Ohio and Minnesota, "coke" in Georgia and Tennessee, and "tonic" in Boston. Similarly, the grassy strip separating the lanes of an interstate highway is called a "mall" in upstate New York, a "median" in Ohio, a "medial strip" in Pennsylvania, a "meridian" in the upper Midwest, and "neutral ground" in Louisiana.

GRAMMAR

In English the basic unit of meaning is the sentence. In this integrated approach to grammar you will examine sentences to determine what they mean. This should help you to be a better reader and more skillful writer. This approach may be new to you, so here are a series of charts and references to help you as you begin. Do not memorize these charts. The more you use them, the less you will need them. With time, you will develop a feeling for the way language works so you will not need them at all.

3.6 Identifying the Parts of Speech

Each word in a sentence has one of four basic functions: it **names**, **modifies**, **expresses action or state of being**, or **links**.

A fifth "extra" function is to interrupt for effect; words that **interrupt** will be discussed at the end of this section.

English also has words that can work as more than one part of speech. Words that can take on different parts of speech are called **hybrids**. These words will be explained at the end of this section.

Below is an overview of the parts of speech. For a more detailed description of what each part of speech does, see the "Parts of Speech Summary" on page 1071.

3.7 Grammar Reference Chart—Parts of Speech Overview

GRAMMAR REFERENCE CHART—PARTS OF SPEECH OVERVIEW. Students are asked to review the Parts of Speech in the Language, Grammar, and Style activities on pages 44 and 53.

PARTS OF SPEECH	EXAMPLE(S)
NAMERS (nouns and pronouns) are subjects and objects.	
NOUN. A **noun** names a person, place, thing, or idea.	Adam, journalist, mountain, India, rose, motorcycle, honesty, feeling
PRONOUN. A **pronoun** is used in place of a noun to name a person, place, thing, or idea.	**I** bought the bricks and used **them** to build a wall. Take Schuyler to the ice cream shop and buy **him** (used in place of Schuyler) a cone.
EXPRESSERS (verbs) name an action or state of being plus the conditions around it.	
VERB. A **verb** expresses action or state of being.	bake, glance, give, build, compose, think, look, feel, am
MODIFIERS (adjectives and adverbs) make other parts of speech more specific.	
ADJECTIVE. An **adjective** modifies, or changes the meaning of, a noun or pronoun.	**gray** skies, **deep** water, **eerie** laughter
ADVERB. An **adverb** modifies, or changes the meaning of, a verb, an adjective, or another adverb.	Leanne gripped the wheel **nervously**. Elliot thought the exam was **extremely** easy. Giovanni peered over the edge of the cliff **very** cautiously.
LINKERS (prepositions and conjunctions) join all the constructions of the English language.	
PREPOSITION. A **preposition** is used to show how a noun or a pronoun is related to other words in the sentence. Common prepositions are *in, after, among, at, behind, beside, off, through, until, upon,* and *with.*	Pablo enjoyed the concert **at** the Wang Center. Theresa squeezed **through** the opening **of** the cave and crawled **into** the narrow passage.
CONJUNCTION. A **conjunction** joins words or groups of words. Common conjunctions are *and, but, for, nor, or, so,* and *yet.*	Wilhelm plays the guitar, **but** Leonard plays drums. Wilhelm **and** Leonard play loudly.
INTERRUPTERS (interjections and other constructions) interrupt a sentence for emphasis.	
INTERJECTION. An **interjection** is a word used to express emotion. Common interjections are *oh, ah, well, say,* and *wow.*	**Hey!** What are you doing in there? **Oh well,** I didn't expect to win the election anyway.
APPOSITIVE. An **appositive** is an interrupter that renames a noun.	My friend **Yang Yardley** did a beautiful project on birds. Mrs. Cokely, **my favorite teacher**, will retire.
NOUN OF DIRECT ADDRESS. **A noun of direct address** says the name of the person or group spoken to and is never the subject of the sentence.	Wait until dark, **Audrey**. **Class**, listen to the instructions. (*Class* is a noun of direct address; the subject of the sentence is *you*; the pronoun *you* is understood.)

CONTINUED

LANGUAGE, GRAMMAR, AND STYLE RESOURCE **1041**

PARTS OF SPEECH	EXAMPLE(S)

HYBRIDS (such as possessive nouns, pronouns, verbals) can act as more than one part of speech.

POSSESSIVE NOUNS AND PRONOUNS. Possessive nouns and **pronouns** are nouns and pronouns that function as adjectives.	Angela read **Scott's** essay. (*Scott's* is a possessive noun modifying *essay*.) Angela read **his** essay. (*His* is a possessive pronoun modifying *essay*.)
VERBALS. Verbals are verb forms such as participles, gerunds, and infinitives that can function as adjectives, nouns, and adverbs.	I love the **swimming** pool. (*Swimming* is a verbal called a participle and acts as an adjective.) **Swimming** is my favorite sport. (*Swimming* is a verbal called a gerund and acts as a noun.) I like **to swim**. (*To swim* is a verbal called an infinitive.)

To understand how a sentence works, here are other groups of words that you should know about.

3.8 Grammar Reference Chart—Helping Verbs

A **helping verb** helps a main verb to express action or state of being.

HELPING VERBS		
be (am, are, is, was, were, being, and been)	have (has, had)	shall
	may	should
can	might	will
could	must	would
do (does, did)		

3.9 Grammar Reference Chart—The Verb *To Be*

Most languages use the verb *to be* more than any other verb because its forms have more uses than any other verb form. It can be the main verb of a sentence, used to express existence. It also can be a helping verb used with action verbs. Here are some forms of *to be:*

THE VERB *TO BE*	
Present: am, is, are **Past:** was, were, has been, had been **Future:** will be, shall be, will have been	**Other Expressions and Forms that use *Be*:** being, can be, could be, could have been, may be, may have been, might be, might have been, must be, must have been, would be, would have been

3.10 Grammar Reference Chart—Linking Verbs

A **linking verb** connects a noun with another noun, a pronoun, or pronoun adjective that describes or defines it. Note that some linking verbs can also be action verbs. For example, *I grow tired* uses *grow* as a linking verb. *I grow flowers* uses *grow* as an action verb. Notice how <u>I am a junior</u> and <u>A junior am I</u> mean exactly the same thing. This is because *am* is a linking, not an action verb. Sentences with action verbs cannot be reversed in the same way: *I made a bookshelf* and *A bookshelf*

GRAMMAR REFERENCE CHART—LINKING VERBS. Students are asked to identify the linking verb in each sentence in the Language, Grammar, and Style activity on page 925.

made me do not mean the same thing. Here is a list of common linking verbs. *Be* is the most common of all.

LINKING VERBS		
appear	grow	smell
be (am, is, are, was, were, been)	look	sound
become	remain	stay
feel	seem	taste

3.11 Grammar Reference Chart—Prepositions

These are the most commonly used prepositions. Remember, though, that any word on this list may not always be used as a preposition. If it is a preposition, it will always have an object.

PREPOSITIONS				
aboard	at	concerning	off	until
about	before	down	on	up
above	behind	during	over	upon
across	below	except	past	with
after	beside	for	since	within
against	besides	from	through	without
along	between	in	throughout	
amid	beyond	into	to	
among	but	like	under	
around	by	of	underneath	

3.12 What Is Grammar?

The **grammar** of a language refers to two different language areas. First, grammar is the collection of rules and standards that careful speakers use as they write and speak. Second, a **grammar** is any one of several possible descriptions of a language.

Classical grammar has troubled English students because it was originally designed to fit Latin, an inflected language. In Latin every word has an ending or inflection that defines its sentence function, so word order doesn't matter. About the middle of this century, different English grammars began to appear. The most successful of the new grammars were based upon rules of English word order, but frequently the terms used were too confusing to be widely used.

Consequently, the grammar presented here uses elements of both. It demands that students label words and language groups according to what language is doing (which we know by word order). Many terms are familiar because they come from classical grammar, but their meaning may change to fit the grammar of a syntactic language, English.

3.13 English Is a Syntactic Language

Scholars who study language have classified European languages into two major categories: **inflected languages** and **syntactic languages.** The words of **inflected** languages change their forms to tell speakers how the word is used. Word order isn't all that important to meaning. Some inflected languages are Latin and German. English is a **syntactic language**. Word order **(syntax)** determines meaning for **syntactic languages.**

3.14 The Importance of Syntax, or Word Order

EXAMPLE   The junior class plans the prom each spring.

In English sentences words are arranged in specific patterns. In the most frequently used sentence, the sentence tells who *(The junior class)*, and then it tells what that *who* does *(plans the prom each spring)*. When word order changes, the sentence changes meaning; if the pattern rules are ignored, the sentence may become awkward, or even meaningless.

EXAMPLES

Class the the prom plans each spring junior.
Plans the junior spring the prom class each.
Class the plans each the prom junior spring.

A change in syntax results in a change in meaning; different sentence positions of the same word results in different meanings.

EXAMPLES

Junior prom <u>plans</u> are finished by March.
<u>Plans</u> for our house were completed last fall.
Our family <u>plans</u> a vacation every summer.

In the first two sentences, *plans* names something. In the first sentence it is used to mean arrangements; in the second, it means blueprints. In the third sentence, *plans* is an action. In all sentences the word form is the same, but different positions signal different meanings.

3.15 Inflections in English

English does have some **inflections**, or changes in form, but word order is most important! English verbs, adjectives, and pronouns are inflected. Sometimes we add a suffix (add *-ed* to *work*, *-er* or *-est* to *hard*), other times interior letters or the entire forms change: *drive* becomes *drove*, *my* becomes *mine*, *was* becomes *were*.

EXAMPLES

INFLECTED VERBS

Today I *carry* my lunch. Yesterday I *carried* it, too. (The *y* is replaced by *i*, and the suffix *-ed* is added.)

Today I *have* lots of homework; yesterday I *had* very little. (The entire verb form changes.)

<u>Inflected adjectives</u>

My sister is *wise;* my mother is *wiser,* but my grandmother is the *wisest* woman in the family. (The suffixes *-er* and *-est* are added to indicate higher degrees of quality.)

Kevin's day was *good;* Tua's was *better,* but mine turned out *best.* (The form changes altogether.)

<u>Inflected Pronouns</u>

Most pronouns change forms: *me, mine; they, them.* A specialized group of pronouns, the reflexive and intensive pronouns, add the suffix *-self* to the singular possessive pronoun forms *my, him, her, it,* and *your;* and add *-selves* to the plural forms *them, your,* and *our.*

3.16 The Sentence: The Basic Building Block of the English Language

Since first grade you have been encouraged to write and speak in sentences because they are the basic units of meaning. English sentences are organized to tell us whom or what a speaker is talking about and information about that whom or what. Classical grammar defines a sentence as "a group of words that expresses a complete thought."

3.17 Functions of Sentences

English speakers use four kinds of sentences to express four different kinds of complete thoughts:

- A **declarative sentence** informs us. First, it tells whom or what a speaker is writing or speaking about, and second, it gives information about that whom or what.

- An **interrogative sentence** asks a question.

- An **imperative sentence** gives orders or makes requests.

- An **exclamatory sentence** expresses strong feeling.

EXAMPLES

Declarative	I am ready to eat dinner.
Interrogative	Is dinner ready?
Imperative	Give me my food.
Exclamatory	I'm starving to death!

3.18 Subjects and Verbs: The Basic Building Blocks in a Sentence

Good readers and writers analyze meaning by examining the structure of sentences. Finding the parts of a sentence is a basic tool for people who use language well.

3.19 Finding the Complete Subject and Complete Predicate in a Sentence

All simple English sentences can be divided into two parts, the subject and the predicate. In the most common English sentence, the first part of the sentence tells us what it is talking about. This is the **complete subject**. Then it gives us information about the subject; this second part of the sentence is called the **complete predicate**. In the following examples, the complete subject is underlined once and the complete predicate is underlined twice.

EXAMPLES

One of my brothers fixed his own car.
Sharyl and Ken will be presenting Friday's history lesson.
Lala might have been given a wrong classroom number.

NOTE: Every word in every sentence is a part of the complete subject or the complete predicate.

3.20 Finding the Simple Subject and Simple Predicate in a Sentence

Most people need more specific information than that given by the complete subject and the complete predicate. The basic units of meaning are found in the **simple subject** and the **simple predicate** (more frequently called the **verb**). The **simple subject** is the **complete subject** without any of its modifiers. The **verb** is the **complete predicate** without any complements or modifiers.

The **simple subject** is the complete subject without any modifiers or linkers—the extra words.

EXAMPLES

Little **kids** like pet kittens and puppies.
Telly's **mother** wants a new car.

The **simple predicate** or **verb** is the complete predicate without any complements, linkers, or modifiers.

EXAMPLES

Little kids **like** pet kittens and puppies.
Telly's mother **wants** a new car.

NOTE: Verbs may have more than one word—they may have as many as four! Each of the examples is one verb.

EXAMPLES

play (one word)
is playing (two words)
has been playing (3 words)
may have been playing (4 words)

3.21 How to Find the Simple Subject and Verb

The following four-step method will help you to find the simple subject and verb.

EXAMPLE

My older sister might not get a motorcycle for high school graduation.

1. Ask, "What is the action of this sentence?" The action is *get*.

2. Using the Language Arts Survey 3.8, "Helping Verbs," check some of the words around the action word. For the sample sentence, you might want to check *might* and *not*. *Might* is on the list; *not* isn't. Only *might* is a helping verb. The verb of the sentence is *might get*.

3. After finding the verb, ask who (what) did the action? Who *might get*? *My older sister*.

4. Finally, what words aren't necessary for simplest meaning? *Older sister* makes sense, so omit *my*; *older* can be left out, too. *Sister* is the simple subject of the sentence.

3.22 Sentence Completers for Action Verbs: Direct and Indirect Objects

A sentence must have a subject and a verb, but sometimes sentences have other parts that complete the meaning. The completers for action verbs are **direct objects** and **indirect objects**.

First, it is important to realize that not all sentences have objects. Here are some examples of sentences without objects. In each of these sentences there is no receiver of the action. The verb expresses the total concept.

EXAMPLES

Birds fly south.

HOW TO FIND THE SIMPLE SUBJECT AND VERB. Students are asked to identify the simple subject and verb in sentences in the Language, Grammar, and Style activities on pages 87 and 91.

SENTENCE COMPLETERS FOR ACTION VERBS: DIRECT AND INDIRECT OBJECTS. Students are asked to identify the direct and indirect object in sentences in the Language, Grammar, and Style activities on pages 100 and 105.

LANGUAGE, GRAMMAR, AND STYLE RESOURCE

Work fast.
I have been walking.

DIRECT OBJECTS. A **direct object** receives the action in the sentence. The following sentences do have receivers of the action, or direct objects. In each case, once the verb is found, the direct object answers the question *what?* about the verb.

Birds ate grain. (Birds ate what? *grain*)
Work the problems fast. (Work what? *problems*)
I walked the dog. (Walked what? *dog*)

The last step was to get rid of any modifiers. That tells you what the direct object itself is. Also note that a direct object is *never* in a prepositional phrase.

INDIRECT OBJECTS. Sometimes the direct object is received by someone or something. This receiver is called the **indirect object**. A sentence without a direct object cannot have an indirect object.

EXAMPLE   Mike gave me a red pencil.

What is the *action* (the verb)? *gave*
Who gave? (the subject) *Mike*
What did he give? (the direct object) *pencil*

To find the indirect object, check to see if the direct object had a receiver. Who got the direct object? In this sentence we ask, "Who got the pencil?" The answer is *me*.

Who received the pencil? (the indirect object) *me*

3.23 Sentence Completers for Linking Verbs: Predicate Nouns, Pronouns, and Adjectives

Unlike action verbs, **linking verbs** do not describe an *action*. They simply join a subject to another word that describes or identifies it. Since no action is being performed, there are no objects or direct objects. Instead, the first noun, or naming word, is assumed to be the subject while the renaming or describing word is called its **complement**.

Because a linking verb has no object or direct object, the order of the sentence can sometimes be reversed without affecting the meaning. For example, *I am a student* and *A student am I* mean

the same thing. *Am* is merely linking the two nouns, no matter what the order. On the other hand, *I made dinner* and *Dinner made me* mean very different things. Because *made* is an action verb, the sentence cannot be reversed. There are three types of sentence completers for linking verbs: predicate nouns, predicate pronouns, and predicate adjectives.

PREDICATE NOUN	Tala is my best <u>friend</u>.
PREDICATE PRONOUN	We are the <u>ones</u>!
PREDICATE ADJECTIVE	Tierre felt <u>ill</u>.

3.24 Predicate Nouns and Pronouns as Sentence Completers

Sentences with predicate nouns and pronouns do not use action verbs: they use forms of the verb *to be*. (Forms of *to be* are listed in 3.9, "Grammar Reference Chart—The Verb *To Be*.") To find a **predicate noun** or **predicate pronoun**, ask the same questions asked to find a **direct object**.

EXAMPLE   Mary will have been my friend for six years.

To find the predicate noun, ask, "Mary will have been what?" The answer is *friend*.

EXAMPLE   The most dangerous criminal was he.

To find the predicate pronoun, ask, "The most dangerous criminal was who?" The answer is *he*.

NOTE: Direct and indirect objects include *me, her, him,* and so on. Predicate pronouns include *I, she, he,* and so forth, the same forms as subjects.

3.25 Predicate Adjectives as Sentence Completers

A **predicate adjective** modifies, or describes, the subject of a sentence. Sentences with predicate adjectives may use a variety of linking verbs. Consult 3.10, the "Grammar Reference Chart— Linking Verbs," for a list of linking verbs. Most of these are used just with predicate adjectives, not with predicate nouns or pronouns.

EXAMPLE   Della feels blue today.

To find the predicate adjective, ask, "Della feels what?" The answer is *blue*. *Blue* describes Della.

SUBJECTS AND VERBS: PROBLEM CONSTRUCTIONS

English speakers often rearrange or use different kinds of sentences. Some of these constructions can be challenging!

3.26 Working with Inverted Sentences

A sentence is **inverted** when all or part of the complete predicate comes before the subject. When you ask a question, you automatically invert your sentence. Usually, part of the verb is in front of the subject.

EXAMPLES

DECLARATIVE SENTENCE	Sitka did study the math problem.
INTERROGATIVE SENTENCE	Did Sitka study the math problem?

In both sentences, the verb is *did study*. Part of the verb comes before the subject.

Other sentences may be inverted so that a modifier comes before the subject.

EXAMPLE Sitka studied the math problem today.
Today Sitka studied the math problem.
Today modifies *studied* in both sentences.

Be sure to find all the words in the verb of an inverted sentence.

3.27 Working with *There* Sentences

The word *there* often appears as the first word or as one of the first few words in a sentence. *There* will never be a basic part of the sentence; it is a modifier. To make finding the subject and verb easier, cross out *there* before determining the basic parts of the sentence.

EXAMPLE
There will be two standardized tests given this week.

Remove *there*:
will be two standardized tests given this week

Rearrange words:
two standardized tests will be given this week

Now the subject and verb are easy to find. The subject is *tests*; the verb is *will be given*.

3.28 Working with Compound Subjects, Verbs, and Sentences

If a sentence has more than one subject, together they are called a **compound subject**.

EXAMPLE
Frank and Jesus work at a carwash.

If a sentence has more than one verb, the verbs together are called a **compound verb**.

EXAMPLE
Helen cooked dinner, washed dishes, and swept the floor.

Notice that each verb has its own direct object. Sentences can have both a compound subject and a compound verb.

EXAMPLE
Mikka and Juan cut the grass and washed the car.
Subjects: Mikka, Juan; Verbs: cut, washed.

A **compound sentence** refers to two sentences that are either 1) connected by a semicolon *or* 2) connected with a coordinating conjunction and a comma. Each part of the compound sentence has its own subject and verb.

EXAMPLES
Sally wanted a car, but her family wouldn't buy one.
Sally wanted a car; her family wouldn't buy one.

In both sentences, the subjects are *Sally* and *family*; the verbs are *wanted* and *would buy*. (*Not* is not part of the verb; it only modifies the verb.)

For more information, see the Language Arts Survey 3.36, "Combining and Expanding Sentences."

3.29 Working with Negatives and Contractions

NEGATIVES. **Negatives** such as *not* and *never* frequently affect verbs. They are adverbs, because they add to the meaning of the verb. The verb tells what an action is, and the negative says that the writer or speaker means the opposite of that.

EXAMPLES
I play basketball.
Negative: I do not play basketball.

Make sure to use only one negative in each sentence. Check your writing to be sure that you

WORKING WITH *THERE* SENTENCES. Students are asked to work with *There* sentences in the Language, Grammar, and Style activity on page 935.

WORKING WITH NEGATIVES AND CONTRACTIONS. Students are asked to work with negative contractions in the Language, Grammar, and Style activity on page 439.

IDENTIFYING PREPOSITIONAL PHRASES.
Students are asked to work with
prepositional phrases in the
Language, Grammar, and Style
activity on page 223.

have not used a negative word such as *not,*
nobody, none, nothing, hardly, barely, can't,
doesn't, won't, isn't, or *aren't* with another
negative word.

DOUBLE NEGATIVE (NONSTANDARD)

I hardly never eat my lunch at school.

Didn't Joyce never go to Chicago?

It doesn't make no difference!

Why wasn't Jerry hurt no worse when the car was
destroyed?

CORRECTED SENTENCES (STANDARD)

I hardly ever eat my lunch at school.

Didn't Joyce ever go to Chicago?

It doesn't make any difference!

Why wasn't Jerry hurt any worse when the car was
destroyed?

CONTRACTIONS. Contractions combine two words
by shortening and joining them with an
apostrophe.

EXAMPLES

isn't, aren't, don't, can't

When you are trying to determine subjects and
verbs in a sentence, contractions need to be
written out into the two words that they
represent. After the contraction is written out,
each word should be considered separately. Each
of the contractions above contains a negative.
Remember that a negative is never part of a verb
but is an adverb.

CONTRACTION	WORDS CONTRACTED	PARTS OF SPEECH
isn't	is not	is (verb or helping verb), not (negative; adverb)
aren't	are not	are (verb), not (negative; adverb)
don't	don not	do (verb), not (negative; adverb)
can't	can not	can (helping verb), not (negative; adverb)

**AVOIDING PROBLEMS CAUSED BY
UNDERSTOOD SUBJECTS AND NOUNS OF
DIRECT ADDRESS.** Students are asked to
identify nouns of direct address in
sentences in the Language, Grammar,
and Style activity on page 439.

3.30 Identifying Prepositional Phrases

The simple subject and verb is *never* in a
prepositional phrase. If you think a word might
be a preposition, check the chart of common
prepositions in the Language Arts Survey 3.11,
Grammar Reference Chart, "Prepositions." If the
word is there, find its object.

The prepositional phrases have been underlined
in the example below:

EXAMPLE

One <u>of my brothers</u> is planning a medical career
<u>after college.</u>

NOTE: The simple subject, verb, and complements
are *never* in prepositional phrases, so
before determining the subject and verb of a sentence, if you cross out the prepositional phrases,
you will have fewer words to consider.

3.31 Using Indefinite Pronouns

You seldom have problems with personal pronouns
in sentences because they are easy to recognize.
When you encounter an indefinite pronoun (used
to replace a person or a group of people not
specifically identified), you might make errors in
subject and verb agreement. Subjects and objects
are particularly tricky when they are followed by a
prepositional phrase, as shown below.

EXAMPLES

<u>Some</u> of the students wrote excellent short stories.
<u>Ten</u> from the senior class were chosen for a
legislative workshop.
Mr. James gave <u>several</u> of my friends top grades on
their papers.

You might want to cross out prepositional
phrases in a sentence before you determine
subjects and verbs.

3.32 Avoiding Problems Caused by Understood Subjects and Nouns of Direct Address

Understood subjects are sometimes used in
sentences that make requests or give commands.
The subject is *you,* but it is not written out,
because both the speaker/writer and
listener/reader understand who is meant.

EXAMPLES

Open your books. Give me your attention.
Run outside; the school is burning down!

In each of these the speaker does not have to say the *you* because it is understood.

If you are not sure that the subject is understood, try using *you* in front of the verb.

Nouns of direct address are never a part of the basic sentence. They name the person talked to, and they are always set off from the rest of the sentence using commas. They can appear at any place in a sentence.

EXAMPLES

<u>Hank</u>, when did you plan to finish your project?
Have you seen the new science lab, <u>Carrie</u>?
I need to know, <u>class</u>, if you had any problems with today's homework.

By paying attention to the comma clues—that is, the way the noun of direct address is set off from the rest of the sentence—you will realize that these nouns are not actually a part of the basic sentence.

WRITER'S WORKSHOP: BUILDING EFFECTIVE SENTENCES

3.33 Correcting Sentence Fragments

A sentence contains a subject and a verb and should express a complete thought. A **sentence fragment** is a phrase or clause that does not express a complete thought but has been punctuated as though it did.

SENTENCE FRAGMENT

So he could explore the clear waters of the lake.

COMPLETE SENTENCE

Teddy bought a new mask and snorkel so he could explore the clear waters of the lake.

SENTENCE FRAGMENT

Looking for the lost little girl.

COMPLETE SENTENCE

The searchers combed the woods looking for the lost little girl.

3.34 Correcting Sentence Run-ons

A **sentence run-on** is made up of two or more sentences that have been run together as if they were one complete thought. You can fix a run-on by dividing it into two separate sentences. Mark the end of each idea with a period, question mark, or exclamation point. Capitalize the first word of each new sentence.

RUN-ON

Jason tried to jump across the swollen stream he slipped in the mud on the other side.

TWO SENTENCES

Jason tried to jump across the swollen stream. He slipped in the mud on the other side.

RUN-ON

Mr. Strauss refused to reconsider his decision, he had made up his mind and didn't want to be bothered with the facts.

TWO SENTENCES

Mr. Strauss refused to reconsider his decision. He had made up his mind and didn't want to be bothered with the facts.

You can also correct a sentence run-on with a semicolon.

RUN-ON

I went to bed early I got up late.

CORRECTED WITH SEMI-COLONS

I went to bed early; I got up late.

A **sentence string** is a sentence run-on formed of several sentences strung together with conjunctions. Edit sentence strings by breaking them into separate sentences and subordinate clauses.

STRINGY

When I decided to audition for the part, I had no idea how to do it so I asked my friend Eileen who has some acting talent what to do and she said to practice in front of a mirror, but I tried that and it didn't help, so I had Eileen come over instead and when I read my lines to her that really helped.

CORRECTING SENTENCE RUN-ONS.
Students are asked to correct sentence run-ons in the Language, Grammar, and Style activity on page 527.

CORRECTING SENTENCE FRAGMENTS.
Students are asked to correct sentence fragments in the Language, Grammar, and Style activities on pages 22 and 579.

LANGUAGE, GRAMMAR, AND STYLE RESOURCE

CORRECTING WORDY SENTENCES. In the Language, Grammar, and Style activity on page 842, students are asked to reduce wordiness in sentences.

COMBINING AND EXPANDING SENTENCES. Students are asked to combine sentences in the Language, Grammar, and Style activities on pages 587 and 661.

REVISED

When I decided to audition for the part, I had no idea how to do it. I asked my friend Eileen, who has some acting talent, what to do. She said to practice in front of a mirror, but I tried that and it didn't help. I had Eileen come over instead. When I read my lines to her, that really helped.

3.35 Correcting Wordy Sentences

As you write, avoid **wordy sentences**. Use only the words necessary to make your meaning clear to a reader. Edit your sentences so that they are not wordy and complicated. Replace complicated or general words with simple and specific words.

WORDY

Make sure that you are very careful not to forget to lock the door to the house when you leave the house.

CLEAR AND DIRECT

Don't forget to lock the door as you leave.

3.36 Combining and Expanding Sentences

There are many ways to combine and expand sentences to achieve smooth writing and sentence variety.

COMBINING SENTENCES. If you use several short sentences in a paragraph, your writing might sound choppy, and your reader might have trouble understanding how ideas are connected.

Combining sentences is a good way to bring two sentences together that deal with the same main idea. If you combine short sentences, your writing will sound smooth and clear, and your reader will see how ideas are connected to one another.

One way of combining sentences is to take a word or phrase from one sentence and insert it into another sentence. You might need to change the form of the word.

BORING, SHORT SENTENCES

The cowboys walked into the saloon. Their walk was more like a swagger. They were boisterous.

COMBINED SENTENCE

The boisterous cowboys swaggered into the saloon.

Another way of combining sentences is to merge two related sentences into one sentence

that states both ideas. Your two sentences can be combined with a comma and a **conjunction** such as *and, or, for, nor, but, so,* or *yet.*

BORING, SHORT SENTENCES

The storm was fierce. The captain brought the ship to safety.

COMBINED SENTENCE

The storm was fierce, but the captain brought the ship to safety.

EXPANDING SENTENCES. You can expand sentences and achieve sentence variety by knowing how to use different types of clauses and sentences. These include independent clauses, compound sentences, complex sentences, and compound-complex sentences.

An **independent clause** expresses a complete thought and can stand by itself as a sentence.

INDEPENDENT CLAUSES

The geese flew away.
The geese flew away at the sound of the plane.

A **compound sentence** is formed by two or more independent clauses joined by a conjunction and a comma; or by a semicolon followed by a transition word such as *however* or *therefore* and a comma.

COMPOUND SENTENCES

The geese flew away at the sound of the plane, and all was quiet.
The geese flew away at the sound of the plane; however, the crows remained.

You can also expand a sentence that has only one independent clause by adding a subordinate clause. You will then have a **complex sentence**—one formed of an independent clause and at least one subordinate clause. In the following examples, the subordinate clauses are underlined.

COMPLEX SENTENCES

<u>After the geese flew away</u>, the crows remained.
The geese flew away, <u>scared by the noise</u>.

If you combine a compound sentence and a complex sentence, you will have a **compound-complex sentence**. This kind of sentence must have two or more independent clauses and at least one subordinate clause. In the following examples, the subordinate clauses are underlined.

COMPOUND-COMPLEX SENTENCES

Although they were accustomed to loud noises, the geese flew away at the sound of the plane; however, the crows remained.

The geese flew away at the sound of the plane; however, the crows remained, greedily eating the corn in the fields.

3.37 Making Passive Sentences Active

A verb is **active** when the subject of the verb performs the action. It is **passive** when the subject of the verb receives the action.

ACTIVE   Caroline delivered a powerful speech.
PASSIVE A powerful speech was delivered by Caroline.

Poor writing uses too many passive verbs. Use active verbs unless you have a good reason for using the passive voice. In the examples that follow, note how the active verbs make the writing more natural and interesting.

WITH PASSIVE VERBS

The school was flooded with requests from students for a longer vacation. It was not decided by the school board until later to give them a hearing. The meeting was begun by the student council. The vote was unanimous to extend spring break an extra week. It was considered an unprecedented move favoring all students suffering spring fever.

WITH ACTIVE VERBS

Students flooded the school with requests for a longer vacation. The school board did not decide until later to give them a hearing. The student council began the meeting. Everyone voted to extend spring break an extra week. The unprecedented move favored all students suffering spring fever.

Note that the writer could still combine, expand, and add variety to these sentences. Making such sentences active instead of passive, however, is a good start toward livelier writing.

3.38 Achieving Parallelism

A sentence has **parallelism** when it uses the same grammatical forms to express ideas of equal, or parallel, importance. When you edit your sentences during revision, check to be sure that your parallelism is not faulty.

FAULTY

The teacher told me to think better and having more focus.

PARALLEL

The teacher told me to think better and to have more focus.

FAULTY

Being too late for the bus and to get something to eat, I decided to walk to the mall.

PARALLEL

Being too late for the bus and wanting to get something to eat, I decided to walk to the mall.

FAULTY

I really like playing chess, walking my dog, and vacations in Florida.

PARALLEL

I really like playing chess, walking my dog, and taking vacations in Florida.

3.39 Adding Colorful Language to Sentences

When you write, use words that tell your reader exactly what you mean. Precise and lively language makes your writing more interesting to your reader.

DULL

The people made noise.

COLORFUL

The mob made an uproar.

Specific verbs also help to create a clear picture in a reader's mind. Use verbs that tell the reader exactly what you mean.

DULL

He took the pitcher and drank the cool water.

COLORFUL

He grabbed the pitcher and gulped the cool water.

A modifier is a word that modifies—that is, changes or explains—the meaning of another word. Adjectives and adverbs are modifiers. Colorful modifiers can turn dull reading into dynamic reading.

DULL

The cold wind blew hard.

MAKING PASSIVE SENTENCES ACTIVE. In the Language, Grammar, and Style activity on page 727 students change passive sentences to active ones.

ADDING COLORFUL LANGUAGE TO SENTENCES. Students are asked to work with vivid words in sentences in the Language, Grammar, and Style activities on pages 432 and 823.

ACHIEVING PARALLELISM. Students are asked to achieve parallelism in sentences in the Language, Grammar, and Style activity on page 170.

EDITING FOR GRAMMAR AND USAGE ERRORS

3.40 Getting Subject and Verb to Agree

A word that describes or stands for *one* person, place, thing, or idea is **singular**. A word that describes or stands for *more than one* person, place, thing, or idea is **plural**.

SINGULAR NOUNS	prize, child, instrument
PLURAL NOUNS	prizes, children, instruments

In a sentence, a verb must be singular if its subject is singular and plural if its subject is plural. **A verb must agree in number with its subject.**

SINGULAR AGREEMENT	<u>Charles</u> <u>needs</u> forty more dollars.
PLURAL AGREEMENT	<u>They</u> <u>need</u> forty more dollars.
SINGULAR AGREEMENT	<u>She</u> <u>exercises</u> every day.
PLURAL AGREEMENT	The <u>girls</u> <u>exercise</u> every day.

The pronouns *I* and *you*, although singular, almost always take the same verb forms as for the plural pronouns *we* and *they*. The only exceptions are the forms *I am* and *I was*.

EXAMPLES
I <u>believe</u> the car industry will continue to rebound.
You <u>sense</u> my uneasiness.

AGREEMENT WITH COMPOUND SUBJECTS. A **compound subject** is formed of two or more nouns or pronouns that are joined by a conjunction and have the same verb. A compound subject joined by the conjunction *and* usually takes a plural verb.

EXAMPLE   <u>Salt</u> and <u>acid rain</u> <u>are</u> hard on a car's body.

A compound subject in which the subjects are joined by the conjunction *and* takes a singular verb if the compound subject really names only one person or thing.

EXAMPLE   His <u>work and love</u> <u>is</u> writing.

A compound subject formed of two singular subjects joined by the conjunctions *or* or *nor* takes a singular verb.

EXAMPLES
Neither <u>Streep</u> nor <u>Foster</u> <u>is</u> usually guilty of underpreparing.
Either <u>poetry</u> or <u>drama</u> <u>is</u> appropriate for public performance.

A compound subject formed of a singular subject and a plural subject joined by the conjunctions *or* or *nor* takes a verb that agrees in number with the subject nearer the verb.

EXAMPLES
Either <u>Kim</u> or the backup <u>vocalists</u> <u>are</u> responsible for the recording.
Either the backup <u>vocalists</u> or <u>Kim</u> <u>is</u> responsible for the recording.

AGREEMENT WITH INDEFINITE PRONOUNS. These indefinite pronouns are singular and take a singular verb: *anybody, anyone, anything, each, either, everybody, everyone, everything, neither, nobody, no one, nothing, one, somebody, someone,* and *something.*

EXAMPLES
<u>Nobody wants</u> to take the exam on Friday.
<u>Everybody enjoys</u> some kind of music.

These indefinite pronouns are plural and take a plural verb: *both, few, many,* and *several.*

EXAMPLES
<u>Both</u> of these choices <u>are</u> unacceptable.
<u>Several</u> new students <u>are</u> on the honor roll.

The following indefinite pronouns can be singular or plural: *all, any, most, none,* and *some.*

EXAMPLES
<u>All</u> of the cookies <u>were saved</u>. (*All* is plural.)
<u>All</u> of the pie <u>was eaten</u>. (*All* is singular.)

AGREEMENT IN INVERTED SENTENCES. When you invert sentences for emphasis, make sure you maintain agreement in number between subject and verb.

EXAMPLES
For those ghastly performances <u>he takes</u> full credit.
The last straw <u>she took</u>.

AGREEMENT WITH DOESN'T AND DON'T. The contraction *doesn't* (from *does not*) is third-person singular and should be used only with a third-person singular subject (*he, she,* or *it,* for example). The contraction *don't* (from *do not*) should be used with all other subjects.

EXAMPLES

She doesn't want material things.
They don't understand the procedure.
I don't find the subject boring.

OTHER PROBLEMS IN SUBJECT-VERB AGREEMENT. When a sentence begins with *here, there, when,* or *where,* often the subject follows the verb. In editing your writing, use extra care to check that the subject and verb of such sentences agree in number. Remember that the contractions *here's, there's, when's,* and *where's* contain a singular verb (is) and should only be used with a singular subject.

EXAMPLES

Here's the team.
There is one more exam being given.
When's the test?
When are the band members joining us?
Where's the rub?

Also check to be sure a verb in a sentence with a predicate nominative agrees in number with the subject and not with the predicate nominative.

EXAMPLES

Essays are the hardest part of school.
The hardest part of school is essays.

A collective noun takes a singular verb when the noun refers to the group as a unit, and it takes a plural verb when it refers to the members of the group as individuals.

| AS SINGULAR | The team runs laps every day. |
| AS PLURAL | The team joke among themselves behind the coach's back. |

While editing your work, check for nouns that are plural in form but singular in meaning. They should take singular verbs.

EXAMPLES   cryogenics, slacks, measles

The title of a creative work such as a book or song takes a singular verb, as does a group of words used as a unit.

EXAMPLES

The book *Aphorisms* has been on the bestseller list for two weeks.

Sidney and Austen is the smallest firm in Chicago.

An expression stating an amount is singular and takes a singular verb when the amount is considered as one unit. It is plural and takes a plural verb when the amount is considered as something with many parts.

AS SINGULAR

Three eggs is a high-cholesterol breakfast.

AS PLURAL

Three eggs were found splattered across the windshield.

A fraction or a percentage is singular when it refers to a singular word and plural when it refers to a plural word.

AS SINGULAR

One-fourth of the text was footnotes.

AS PLURAL

One-fourth of all the pages were footnotes.

AS SINGULAR

Over 60 percent of the nation is hopeful about the economy.

AS PLURAL

Over 60 percent of all citizens are hopeful about the economy.

Expressions of measurement, such as area, length, volume, and weight, are usually singular.

EXAMPLE

Two quarts is a lot of milk to drink in one sitting.

3.41 Using Irregular Verbs

To write about something that happened in the past, use past tense verbs (tense means *time* in grammar). For regular verbs, add *-ed* or *-d* to the present form of the verb. For more information, see the Language Arts Survey 3.62, "Properties of Verbs: Tense."

EXAMPLES

The bandit guarded the hideout.
guard (base form) + ed

Carmen gazed at the distant mountains.
gaze (base form) + d

USING IRREGULAR VERBS. In the Language, Grammar, and Style activity on page 790, students are asked to work with irregular verbs in sentences.

Irregular verbs often have different past tense forms and are formed using a different spelling. The following chart lists some of the most common irregular verbs.

IRREGULAR VERBS	
begin/began	grow/grew
bring/brought	have/had
burst/burst	hurt/hurt
choose/chose	know/knew
come/came	lay/laid
cut/cut	make/made
do/did	ride/rode
draw/drew	run/ran
drink/drank	see/saw
eat/ate	sing/sang
fall/fell	take/took
feel/felt	teach/taught
fly/flew	wear/wore
give/gave	write/wrote
go/went	

When using irregular verbs in the perfect tense (with *has* or *have*), make sure you do not use the past form instead of the past participle.

NONSTANDARD
I have knew him since I was in middle school.

STANDARD
I have known him since I was in middle school.

Another error to avoid is using the past participle form without a helping verb, or mistaking the past participle for the past.

| NONSTANDARD | I flown this plane dozens of times. |
| STANDARD | I have flown this plane dozens of times. |

| NONSTANDARD | I done all I could do to convince him. |
| STANDARD | I did all I could do to convince him. |

Finally, do not add *-d* or *-ed* to the past form of an irregular verb.

| NONSTANDARD | I ated an apple. |
| STANDARD | I ate an apple. |

3.42 Avoiding Split Infinitives

In the English language, the infinitive is often in the form of two words, *to* and the base word.

EXAMPLES   to catch, to succeed, to entertain

USING *WHO* AND *WHOM*. In the Language, Grammar, and Style activity on page 416, students are asked to determine whether to use *Who* or *Whom* in sentences.

Under traditional rules of grammar, the infinitive should not be "split." In other words, adverbs or other sentence components should not come between *to* and the base word.

| NONSTANDARD | Irving begged me to immediately show him the photos. |
| STANDARD | Irving begged me to show him the photos immediately. |

3.43 Using *I* and *Me*

Before you use the words *I* and *me* in a sentence, remember that *I* is always the subject of a verb and *me* is always the object of a verb or of a preposition.

EXAMPLES
I went sailing in Florida.
Amber and I went sailing in Florida.

I is the subject in both of these sentences.

Lester helped me set up for the party.
Lester helped Brianna and me set up for the party.

In both sentences, *me* is the object of the verb *helped*.

If you are not sure which pronoun to use with a compound subject, drop the other part of the subject and use your pronoun separately with the verb.

EXAMPLE
Sam and (I, me) went sledding at the golf course.

After dropping out Sam:
I went sledding at the golf course. OR Me went sledding at the golf course.

Correct: Sam and I went sledding at the golf course.

EXAMPLE
Please apologize for Carol and (I, me).

After dropping out Carol:
Please apologize for me. OR Please apologize for I.

Correct: Please apologize for Carol and me.

3.44 Using *Who* and *Whom*

The pronoun *who* has two different forms. *Who* is used as a subject of a sentence. *Whom* is used as the direct object of a verb or of a preposition.

SUBJECT

<u>Who</u> knows the answer?

Where is the boy <u>who</u> looks after the sheep?

DIRECT OBJECT

<u>Whom</u> did the police arrest?

The plumber <u>whom</u> we called charged a huge fee.

OBJECT OF PREPOSITION

By <u>whom</u> is this painting?

From <u>whom</u> is that gift?

3.45 Getting Pronouns and Antecedents to Agree

Make sure pronouns in your writing agree with their antecedents (the words they refer back to) in number and gender.

Number refers to singular and plural. If the antecedent is singular, the pronoun must also be singular; if the antecedent is plural, the pronoun must also be plural.

INCORRECT NUMBER

One of the boys <u>need</u> tennis shoes.

CORRECT NUMBER

One of the boys <u>needs</u> tennis shoes.

Gender is the form a word takes to show whether it is masculine, feminine, or neutral (neither masculine nor feminine). The pronoun must match its antecedent in terms of gender.

3.46 Avoiding Dangling and Misplaced Modifiers

A **dangling modifier** seems to modify a word it is not intended to modify. If this error occurs when the modifier is too far away from the word it is supposed to modify, it is called a **misplaced modifier**. Edit a dangling or misplaced modifier by rewording the sentence or moving the modifier closer to the phrase it modifies.

DANGLING

Valerie drove to the airport while <u>taking a nap.</u>

WORDS ADDED

Valerie drove to the airport while <u>I was taking a nap.</u>

MISPLACED

Alex walked his dog <u>wearing shorts</u>.

REWORDED

Alex, <u>wearing shorts</u>, walked his dog.

3.47 Recognizing Other Problems with Modifiers

Them is a personal pronoun. *Those* is a demonstrative pronoun, which means it points out a particular person, place, or thing.

NONSTANDARD	Them cars have four-wheel drive.
STANDARD	Those cars have four-wheel drive.

The words *bad* and *badly* often confuse writers. Use *bad* as an adjective, and *badly* as an adverb. The adjective *bad* should follow a linking verb such as *feel, see, smell, sound,* or *taste.*

NONSTANDARD

Reports of the forest fire sounded badly.

STANDARD

Reports of the forest fire sounded bad.

NONSTANDARD

Ricky behaved bad for the babysitter.

STANDARD

Ricky behaved badly for the babysitter.

The words *good* and *well* also tend to confuse writers. *Good* is an adjective used to modify a person, place, thing, or idea, not an action verb. *Well* is an adverb meaning "successfully" or "skillfully" and an adjective meaning "healthy" or "of a satisfactory condition."

NONSTANDARD

Allen swims good.

STANDARD

Allen swims well.

Allen is a good swimmer.

Allen is well now that he is over his cold.

Each modifier has a **positive, comparative,** and **superlative** form of comparison. Most one-syllable modifiers and some two-syllable modifiers form comparative and superlative degrees by adding *-er* and *-est.* Other two-syllable modifiers, and all modifiers of more than two syllables, use *more* and *most* to form these degrees.

	POSITIVE	COMPARATIVE	SUPERLATIVE
ADJECTIVES	hungry	hungrier	hungriest
	daring	more daring	most daring
ADVERBS	late	later	latest
	fully	more fully	most fully

RECOGNIZING OTHER PROBLEMS WITH MODIFIERS. Students are asked to correct and avoid errors in modifier usage in sentences in the Language, Grammar, and Style activity on page 334.

GETTING PRONOUNS AND ANTECEDENTS TO AGREE. In the Language, Grammar, and Style activity on page 145, students are asked to get pronouns and antecedents to agree in sentences.

LANGUAGE, GRAMMAR, AND STYLE RESOURCE

To show a decrease in the quality of any modifier, form the comparative and superlative degrees by using *less* and *least*.

EXAMPLES   dense, less dense, least dense
skeptically, less skeptically, least skeptically

Some modifiers form comparative and superlative degrees irregularly. Check the dictionary if you are unsure about the comparison of a modifier.

EXAMPLES   good, better, best
well, better, best
bad, worse, worst

Use the comparative degree when comparing two things. Use the superlative degree when comparing more than two things.

COMPARATIVE
Santha was the **more easily** intimidated of the two sisters.
SUPERLATIVE
The skin is the **largest** organ of the human body.

3.48 Correcting Common Usage Problems

Watch for these words and learn their correct usage as you edit your own writing.

accept, except. To *accept* is to "welcome something" or to "receive something willingly." To *except* is to "exclude or leave something out." *Except* is also used as a preposition meaning "but."

The Tigers accept our challenge to a rematch.
She excepted Roland from the guest list.
I will eat any vegetable except collard greens.

advice, advise. *Advice* is a noun meaning "guidance or recommendation regarding a decision." To *advise* is to "recommend or inform."

I took your advice about the movie.
I would advise you to avoid that movie.

affect, effect. *Affect* is a verb meaning "have an effect on." *Effect* is a noun meaning "the result of an action."

The short story <u>affected</u> me strangely.
The short story had a strange <u>effect</u> on me.

altogether, all together. *Altogether* is an adverb meaning "thoroughly." Something *done all together* is done as a group or mass.

She was altogether frustrated waiting all day.
We were all together awaiting news of the surgery.

among, between. Use the word *between* when talking about two people or things at a time. Use the word *among* when talking about a group of three or more.

Oscar and Lucas had five dollars between them.
There was disagreement among the team members.

can, may. Use the word *can* to mean "able to do something." Use the word *may* to ask or give permission.

Can you swim across Gull Pond?
May I go swimming? Yes, you may go.

fewer, less. *Fewer* refers to the number of units of something. *Less* refers to bulk quantity.

I have fewer than eight items.
I have less energy when it is very humid.

in, into. The preposition *in* indicates location. The preposition *into* indicates direction from the outside to the inside.

The meeting is being held in the gym.
The students are going into the gym now.

its, it's   The word *its* is a possessive pronoun. The word *it's* is a contraction of *it is*.

The turtle dug its nest.
The sun will be up by the time it's over.

lay, lie. *Lay* means to "put" or to "place" and always takes a direct object. *Lie* means to "rest" or to "be in a lying position." *Lie* never takes a direct object. (Note that the past tense of *lie* is *lay*.)

Lay the map on the table.
Gretchen laid the map on the table.
Lie down and keep quiet.
Oliver lay down and kept quiet.

like, as. *Like* is a preposition meaning "similar to." *Like* usually introduces a phrase. *As* should be used as a conjunction. *As* usually introduces a clause that has a subject and a verb.

NONSTANDARD
The sun came out earlier, just like I had hoped.
STANDARD
The sun came out earlier, just as I had hoped.

Rodney has been acting as a spoiled brat.
Rodney has been acting like a spoiled brat.

their, they're, there. These three *homonyms* (words that sound alike but that have different spellings and meanings) sometimes confuse writers. The word *their* is a possessive pronoun. The word *they're* is the contracted form of *they are*. The word *there* refers to a place.

Marsupials carry their young in a pouch.
They're complaining about the noise.
The lamp should go over there.

to, too, two. *To* is a preposition that can mean "in the direction of." *Too* is an adverb that means both "extremely, overly" and "also." *Two* is the spelling for the number 2.

Take the basket to Granny's house.
Ivan has too many fish in his tank.
Sharon is invited, too.
I have two wishes left.

your, you're. *Your* is a possessive pronoun. *You're* is the contracted form of *you are*.

Your mittens are in the dryer.
You're the winner!

PARTS OF SPEECH SUMMARY

As you have seen, the meanings of words depend on their positions in a sentence. As their positions change, both meaning and function change. You have looked at function to determine parts of the sentence.

You can now go one step further. By looking at the relationship of a word to the rest of the words in a sentence, you can determine the parts of speech for individual words. Once again, you will be examining what a word does; then you will label its part of speech.

Remember two important facts: 1) words have four primary functions—they **name**, **express**, **modify**, and **link**. They can also **interrupt**. 2) Groups of words can function as one individual part of speech.

3.49 Namers—Nouns and Pronouns

Namers are **nouns** and **pronouns**, parts of speech that name people, places, ideas, and things or refer to them; you can tell what they are by what they do. Nouns and pronouns are subjects and objects: direct objects, indirect objects, objects of prepositions, and objects of infinitives. Namers:

NAME PEOPLE	Dylan, principal, father, choreographer
NAME PLACES	home, Central Park, Joe's Tacos
NAME IDEAS	love, multiplication, tonality, smell
NAME THINGS	basketball, dance, orbit, trading card

3.50 Specific Kinds of Nouns

There are many kinds of nouns. They include common and proper nouns, concrete and abstract nouns, and collective nouns.

3.51 COMMON NOUNS AND PROPER NOUNS. **Common nouns** are the names given to general objects. **Proper nouns** are names of specific people or things. They are always capitalized.

COMMON NOUNS
girl, monument, government agency

PROPER NOUNS
Michelle, Washington Monument, United States Supreme Court

Some proper nouns may have more than one word. *Michelle Adams, Central High School,* and the *United States Department of the Interior* are all names of one person or one place or organization. These multiword names are still considered to be one noun because they name only one person or thing.

3.52 CONCRETE NOUNS AND ABSTRACT NOUNS. A **concrete noun** names anything you can physically taste, touch, smell, see, or hear. An **abstract noun** names something that cannot be physically sensed.

CONCRETE NOUNS	automobile, textbook, lunchbox
ABSTRACT NOUNS	sadness, suffering, mood

3.53 COLLECTIVE NOUNS. **Collective nouns** name groups—family, committee, class. Collectives are interesting nouns because, in their singular forms, they can be either singular or plural, depending upon how the group acts. When the group acts together as one unit to do something, the group is considered singular.

COMMON NOUNS AND PROPER NOUNS. Students are asked to identify common and proper nouns in sentences in the Language, Grammar, and Style activity on page 808.

CONCRETE AND ABSTRACT NOUNS. Students are asked to work with concrete and abstract nouns in sentences in the Language, Grammar, and Style activity on page 105.

Because the committee acted as one unit (by everyone doing the same one thing at the same time), the noun is singular and takes a singular verb form. The possessive pronoun *its* also reflects that the noun is collective.

When the group acts as individuals instead of as one unit, the group is considered plural.

EXAMPLE   The <u>committee</u> <u>were</u> giving their reports.

Because individual members gave their reports at different times and functioned as individuals, the group is considered plural. Note how the verb *were giving* and the possessive pronoun *their* reflect this.

3.54 Types of Pronouns

Pronouns replace names (nouns) with reference words. Because we use these references in so many situations, there are four different kinds of pronouns and three hybrids. The four kinds of pronouns are **personal pronouns, indefinite pronouns, interrogative pronouns,** and **reflexive pronouns**.

The three kinds of hybrids are **possessive pronouns, relative pronouns,** and **intensifying pronouns. Possessive pronouns** are hybrids because they take pronoun forms but act as modifiers; **relative pronouns** are hybrids because they are pronoun forms that act as linkers; and **intensifying pronouns** are hybrids because they use the same forms as reflexive pronouns but act as interrupters. The three hybrids are discussed in the hybrids section (see Language Arts Survey 3.78, "Hybrids").

3.55 PERSONAL PRONOUNS. A **personal pronoun** is a substitute for the name of a person or thing. The personal pronouns are *I, me, we, us, he, she, it, him, her, you, they,* and *them.* Personal pronouns refer to three groups of speakers: first, second, and third person.

FIRST PERSON:	the speaker or speakers talks about themselves: *I, me, we, us*
SECOND PERSON:	the speaker talks about the person talked to: *you*
THIRD PERSON:	the speaker talks about someone or something else: *he, she, it, they*

All personal pronouns require clear **antecedents**, or nouns that come before the pronoun. That means that the person or thing that the pronoun refers to must be obvious.

EXAMPLE   Have you seen <u>Mary</u>? Yes, I saw <u>her</u> yesterday.
(<u>Mary</u> is the antecedent of <u>her</u>.)

3.56 INDEFINITE PRONOUNS. Indefinite pronouns are pronouns used when we may not be sure whom we are talking about. They include *somebody, anybody, few,* and *many.* They also include numbers. Frequently they are used when the reference word is in a prepositional phrase. Below are some indefinite pronouns.

INDEFINITE PRONOUNS		
all	few	nothing
another	many	one
any	neither	other
anyone	no one	some
both	nobody	someone
each	none	something
either		

EXAMPLES

A <u>few</u> in our English class are reviewing a new textbook.
We asked for <u>some</u> of the details about the news story.
<u>Nobody</u> knows where the homecoming decorations were stored.
<u>Three</u> of the swimmers qualified for the state meet.

3.57 INTERROGATIVE PRONOUNS. Interrogative pronouns are the question-askers of the pronoun family. *Who, whom, whose, which,* and *what* are the interrogative pronouns.

EXAMPLES

<u>Which</u> of these buses do I take to reach my school?
<u>Whom</u> do I ask for directions?
<u>What</u> do I do now?

Be careful when identifying interrogative pronouns. The same words are used as relative pronouns (discussed in 3.79), but relative pronouns do not ask a question.

TYPES OF PRONOUNS. Students are asked to work with various types of pronouns in the Language, Grammar, and Style activities on pages 115 and 133.

PERSONAL PRONOUNS. In the Language, Grammar, and Style activities on pages 115 and 640, students are asked to work with personal pronouns.

3.58 REFLEXIVE PRONOUNS. Reflexive pronouns refer back to a noun previously used and can be recognized because *-self* and *-selves* have been added to other pronoun forms. Some reflexive pronouns include *myself, herself, yourself, themselves,* and *ourselves.*

EXAMPLES
I talk to <u>myself</u>.
Mike and James helped <u>themselves</u> to more food.

Reflexive pronouns are often parts of the basic sentence or objects of prepositions. (Note that **intensifying pronouns**, discussed in 3.78, "Hybrids," use the same forms, but they are interrupters and are neither a part of a basic sentence nor an object of a preposition.)

3.59 Expressers—Verbs

Verbs are the **expressers** of the English language, and they carry more information than any other single part of speech because they have three major properties: *tense, mood,* and *voice.* They reveal the time something happened or will happen, whether the action is finished or continuing, whether the subject is the actor or receiver of the action, and the manner in which the action occurred. English verbs can be from one to four words long.

EXAMPLES
    runs
    has run
    has been running
    may have been running

NOTE: The same verb may fit into several of the classes below, depending on its uses in different sentences.

3.60 ACTION VERBS AND STATE OF BEING VERBS. The verb of any sentence is either an **action verb** or a **state of being verb**, depending on the message the verb expresses in the sentence. **Action verbs** are all of the words that refer to actions and to things you can do.

EXAMPLES   have, get, drive, run, sleep

State of being verbs indicate that something exists. These are all the forms of the verb *to be* that are listed on your Grammar Reference Chart in the Language Arts Survey 3.9, "The Verb *To Be.*"

3.61 TRANSITIVE AND INTRANSITIVE VERBS. Transitive verbs are action verbs that have completers. If a verb has a direct object, it is a transitive verb.

EXAMPLE   Jamie writes short stories.

   (*Short stories* is a direct object, so the verb *writes* is transitive.)

  Intransitive verbs are action verbs that do not take objects.

EXAMPLE   The sun shines every day in Mexico.

The action *shines* is complete in itself; no extra material is necessary. This makes *shines* an intransitive verb.

3.62 Properties of Verbs: Tense

Verbs carry a concept of time, called **tense**. The simple tenses express simple past, present, and future. The perfect tenses give information about actions that take place over time.

SIMPLE TENSES. **Present tense** shows that something is happening now. **Past tense** verbs talk about something that happened before now, and **future tense** verbs talk about something that will happen in the future:

SIMPLE TENSES FOR THE VERB *TO STUDY*	
PRESENT	
I / You / We / They	study. / do study.
He/She/It	studies. / does study.
PAST	
I / You / He/She/It / We / They	studied. / did study.

CONTINUED

PROPERTIES OF VERBS: TENSES. Students are asked to work with simple and perfect tenses in the Language, Grammar, and Style activities on pages 754 and 832.

ACTION VERBS AND STATE OF BEING VERBS. On page 445 in the Language, Grammar, and Style activity students are asked to identify action and state of being verbs in each sentence.

FUTURE

I
You
He/She/It } will study.
We
They

PERFECT TENSES. The **perfect tenses** express past, present, and future, but they add information about actions that continued over a period of time and were completed in the past or will be completed in the present or future. All perfect tenses use some form of the helping verb *to have* with a past participle.

SIMPLE TENSES FOR THE VERB *TO SLEEP*

PRESENT PERFECT

I
You
We } have slept.
They

He/She/It   has slept.

PAST PERFECT

I
You
He/She/It } had slept.
We
They

FUTURE PERFECT

I
You
He/She/It } will have slept.
We
They

PROGRESSIVE VERB FORMS. Each of the simple and perfect tenses has a **progressive** form that shows continuing action. The progressive form is made by using a tense of the helping verb *be* with the present participle (*–ing* form).

PROGRESSIVE TENSES FOR THE VERB *TO WORK*

PRESENT PROGRESSIVE

I   am working.

He/She/It }   is working.

You
We } are working.
They

PAST PROGRESSIVE

I
He/She/It } was working.

You
We } were working.
They

FUTURE PROGRESSIVE

I
You
He/She/It } will be working.
We
They

PRESENT PERFECT PROGRESSIVE

I
You
We } have been working.
They

He/She/It }   has been working.

CONTINUED

PAST PERFECT PROGRESSIVE

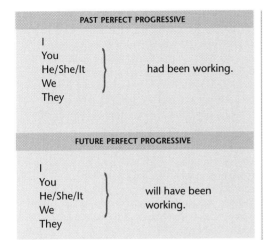

I
You
He/She/It   } had been working.
We
They

FUTURE PERFECT PROGRESSIVE

I
You
He/She/It   } will have been
We   working.
They

3.63 Properties of Verbs: Voice

The **voice** of a verb refers to the relationship between the subject and the action. A verb is in the **active voice** if the subject did the acting. It is in the **passive voice** if someone or something else did the acting and the subject is the receiver of the action.

ACTIVE   Mary gave her sister Ronda a new skirt.
PASSIVE   Ronda was given a new skirt for her birthday.

If the sentence is in the active voice, the subject of the sentence, Mary, did the acting—she gave a skirt to Rhonda. The first sentence is in the active voice. In the second sentence, Ronda did nothing at all. Someone else, not named, did the acting. The second sentence is in the passive voice.

Writing in the active voice strengthens writing; writing in the passive voice usually weakens it. The passive voice can be very effective in many cases, but it should be used seldomly and carefully. For more information, see the Language Arts Survey 3.37, "Making Passive Sentences Active."

3.64 Properties of Verbs: Mood

The **mood** of a verb is the manner in which the verb relates the action. English uses three moods: the **indicative**, the **imperative**, and the **subjunctive**.

The **indicative mood** (notice how close this word is to *indicate*) is used most frequently. This is the mood used to make a statement or ask a

question. Most declarative and interrogative sentences fall into this mood.

Imperative sentences are in the **imperative mood**. These make requests or give commands.

IMPERATIVE
Please, hand me the salt.
Run before the flood gets you!

The **subjunctive mood** has few uses in English, and is used much less frequently than it is used in other languages. It is used to express a wish, a possible condition, or a condition contrary to a fact.

SUBJUNCTIVE
If I were you, I would dress more warmly in this weather.
If I had a million dollars, I would buy an airplane and fly around the world.
It is necessary that you be on time.
If they were here, they would win the prize.

Notice the verb form in the first sentence. The only verb that has a unique form in the subjunctive is the verb *to be*. *Were* is used with all pronouns, not just the singular.

3.65 Modifiers—Adjectives and Adverbs

Adjectives and **adverbs**, two kinds of **modifiers**, add meaning to nouns, adjectives, verbs, and adverbs. To determine whether the word is an adjective or adverb, use the following procedure:

1. Look at the word that is modified.
2. Ask yourself, "Is this modified word a noun or a pronoun?"

If the answer is *yes*, the modifier is an adjective. **Adjectives** modify only nouns and pronouns. If the answer is *no*, the modifier is an **adverb**. **Adverbs** modify verbs, adjectives, and other adverbs.

3.66 ADJECTIVES. Adjectives modify nouns or pronouns by making them more specific.

GENERAL REFERENCE	puppy
A LITTLE MORE SPECIFIC	the puppy

LANGUAGE, GRAMMAR, AND STYLE RESOURCE

MODIFIERS—ADJECTIVES AND ADVERBS. In the Language, Grammar, and Style activity on page 119, students are asked to identify adjectives and adverbs.

MORE SPECIFIC YET	the little puppy
EVEN MORE SPECIFIC	the little, black-spotted puppy
WITH A PREPOSITIONAL PHRASE	the little, black-spotted puppy with the shaggy coat

As each step adds more modifiers (more information), it becomes more possible for the listener or reader to visualize the actual dog.

3.67 ADVERBS. Adverbs are the generalists of the modifier family. They modify anything that is not a namer (noun or pronoun)—verbs, adjectives, and other adverbs. Many times they will specify *where* or *when;* nouns and pronouns specify *who* or *what.*

ADVERBS MODIFY VERBS

Katie came home <u>quickly</u>.

Quickly tells how Katie came home.

ADVERBS MODIFY ADJECTIVES

She wore a <u>really</u> new dress.

New modifies *dress; really* modifies the modifier, *new.* Since *new* is an **adjective**, not a **noun** or **pronoun**, *really* has to be an **adverb**.

ADVERBS MODIFY OTHER ADVERBS

Katie scurried home <u>really fast</u>.

Fast modifies the verb *scurried; really* modifies *fast.* In this sentence, one adverb modifies another.

3.68 Linkers / Joiners

Conjunctions and **prepositions** are the joiners of the English language. These words join everything from individual words to complete sentences to create compound sentences. Because there are many kinds of links that need to be made, there are many kinds of linkers: prepositions, coordinating conjunctions, correlative conjunctions, and subordinating conjunctions.

3.69 PREPOSITIONS. Prepositions are easy to identify because they have objects. If the word does not have an object, then it is another part of speech. See the Language Arts Survey 3.11 for a list of prepositions. If you find one of these words in a sentence, find its object. If it has an object, then the preposition and its object(s)—it may have more than one—form a prepositional phrase.

EXAMPLE   I went [to the store] [for a loaf] [of sandwich bread].

In this sentence, three words are on the preposition list: *to, for,* and *of.* Does *to* have an object? Ask, "*to* what?" The answer is *the store. To* has an object, so it is a preposition. *To the store* is a prepositional phrase. After you apply the same test to *for* and *of,* you will find that they are both prepositions and that the sample sentence has three prepositional phrases. These are *to the store, for a loaf,* and *of sandwich bread.*

3.70 COORDINATING CONJUNCTIONS. Coordinating conjunctions join words and groups of words of equal importance. The most common coordinating conjunctions are *and, or, nor, for, but, yet,* and *so.* The word is not important; what is important is that both words or word groups are equally important.

EXAMPLE

Her morning schedule included math <u>and</u> history <u>and</u> music <u>and</u> home room.

Note that joining a series of words using coordinating conjunctions between them is perfectly acceptable grammar. Most writers use commas, however, and save multiple conjunctions for sentences with special emphasis. (Note: All but the last *and* could be replaced by commas.)

When a coordinating conjunction plus a comma joins two or more complete thoughts that could be separate sentences, the resulting structure is called a **compound sentence**.

COMPOUND SENTENCE

I wanted to go to a movie, <u>but</u> nothing sounded very good.

Here a comma plus *but* join two short, complete, independent thoughts. Each of the two parts could be a sentence of its own. Since their ideas are closely related, they can be joined using proper punctuation.

3.71 CORRELATIVE CONJUNCTIONS. Correlative conjunctions travel in pairs that belong together. Some of these pairs are *both...and, neither...nor, either...or,* and *not only...but also.*

EXAMPLES

<u>Both</u> art <u>and</u> graphic design are electives in our school.

<u>Neither</u> Latin <u>nor</u> Greek languages are studied by

most high school students.
She wanted to study <u>either</u> architecture <u>or</u> industrial design.
He spoke <u>not only</u> German, <u>but also</u> spoke French and Spanish.

3.72 SUBORDINATING CONJUNCTIONS. Subordinating conjunctions join two phrases or clauses that are not of equal importance. Subordinating conjunctions are used to establish that one idea in a sentence is more important than the other. Subordinating conjunctions include *after, before, if, than, since, unless, when,* and *while;* there are many more. All of the following examples contain subordinating conjunctions.

SUBORDINATING CONJUNCTIONS
We will go on a picnic on Saturday <u>unless</u> it rains.
<u>Whenever</u> the pollen count is high, I start to sneeze and get itchy eyes.
I want to visit my grandmother in Detroit <u>if</u> I can save enough money.
<u>When</u> the deadline arrives, students need to get their projects handed in.

Even though both clauses have subjects and verbs, the parts of the sentence of the most important clause (called the **main clause**) will be the subject and verb of the sentence. The parts of the sentence found in the less important clause (called the **subordinate clause**) can be ignored. These are NOT the main subject and verb of the sentence; they are only the subject and verb of a **dependent clause**.

3.73 Interrupters

Sometimes you will want to interrupt the flow of your sentences and thoughts by adding a word or phrase for emphasis. Most **interrupters** are set off from the rest of the sentences by commas because they are not basic building blocks of meaning. **Interrupters** include **interjections, parenthetical expressions, nouns of direct address,** and **appositives.** Another interrupter, **intensifying pronouns,** is discussed in the Language Arts Survey 3.78, "Hybrids."

Interrupters (with the exception of one-word appositives) are set off from other parts of the sentence using commas. It is important to note that no interrupter is ever a basic part of a sentence.

3.74 INTERJECTIONS. Interjections are parts of speech that express strong feeling or enhance meaning.

EXAMPLES
<u>Yes</u>, I finished my homework.
<u>Good grief</u>, you did what again?
<u>Wow</u>, Sam got a new car for his birthday.

Note that omitting the interjection does not affect the basic meaning of the sentence. Each interjection is set off from the rest of the sentence by commas.

3.75 PARENTHETICAL EXPRESSIONS. Parenthetical expressions are those comments (set off by commas) that explain, comment, or qualify the ideas contained in the sentence. Common parenthetical expressions include *by the way, however, on the other hand, incidentally.*

EXAMPLES
I went right home after school; <u>however</u>, my sister went shopping for school supplies.
Mary misplaced her coat. <u>By the way</u>, have you seen a red raincoat in your closet?

3.76 NOUNS OF DIRECT ADDRESS. A noun of direct address says the name of the person or group spoken to. A noun of direct address is *never* the subject of the sentence. This becomes especially tricky when the subject is understood.

EXAMPLE   <u>Class</u>, listen to the instructions.

Class is a noun of direct address; the understood subject is *you.*

3.77 APPOSITIVES. Appositives rename a noun. Like all interrupters, appositives are enclosed or set off from the rest of the sentence by commas. In some cases, word names do not require commas.

EXAMPLES
My friend <u>Yang</u> did a beautiful project on birds. (No punctuation is required.)

Mrs. Cokley, <u>my favorite teacher</u>, will retire this year. (Commas are needed.)

SUBORDINATING CONJUNCTIONS.
Students are asked to identify the subordinating conjunction in sentences in the Language, Grammar, and Style activity on page 481.

LANGUAGE, GRAMMAR, AND STYLE RESOURCE

3.78 Hybrids

Hybrids are words usually thought of as one part of speech that occasionally function as another. Each word form should be labeled according to what it does in the sentence. Some common hybrids include **possessive nouns** and **possessive pronouns, relative pronouns, intensifying pronouns,** and a group of verb forms called **verbals**.

3.79 POSSESSIVE NOUNS AND PRONOUNS. Possessive nouns and **possessive pronouns** are namer forms that work as modifiers. To form a possessive noun, an apostrophe plus an *s* is added to a singular; an apostrophe is added to a plural. Notice how the possessive noun uses a noun form, but with the suffix it becomes a modifier.

EXAMPLE   Linda proofread <u>Marty's</u> assignment.

Marty's modifies *assignment.* Consequently this construction is a hybrid: it looks like a noun, but it functions as an adjective. When listing parts of the sentence, label a possessive noun as an adjective.

Possessive pronouns act much the same way. Many possessive forms are the same as other pronouns, but a few pronoun forms are uniquely possessive. Some of the unique forms include *mine, your, yours, hers, its, our, their,* and *theirs.* Two other possessive forms, *her* and *him,* are not always possessive.

EXAMPLE   I ate <u>my</u> pizza.

My modifies *pizza. My* looks like a pronoun, but here it works as a modifier by telling whom the pizza belongs to. Because we label parts of speech according to what they are doing in the sentence, this word should be considered a modifier—in this case, an adjective.

Relative pronouns are pronoun forms that function like **subordinating conjunctions.** The commonly used relative pronouns are *who, whom, whose, which,* and *that.* These words can connect a subordinate clause to the main clause of the sentence. But they also will function as a subject, object, or predicate pronoun—these are exactly the same functions as naming parts of speech.

EXAMPLE
I want to meet the person <u>who painted that picture</u>.

Who is the **relative pronoun** that connects the subordinate clause (underlined) with the main clause. Also notice that *who* is the subject of the clause; the verb is *painted.*

EXAMPLE
I want to meet the cousin <u>whom you described</u>.

Whom, the **relative pronoun,** is the connection between the two clauses; it also is the direct object of the verb *described.*

EXAMPLE
Kate was the one <u>with whom I designed my art sculpture</u>.

In this sentence, *whom* is the object of the preposition *with;* it also connects the two clauses.

3.80 VERBALS: PARTICIPLES, GERUNDS, AND INFINITIVES. Verbals are verb forms that act as namers or modifiers. There are three different forms of verbals. These include participles (that act as modifiers), gerunds (that act like nouns), and infinitives (that can act like nouns, adjectives and adverbs).

To determine if a verb is used as a verbal, you must be aware of what the word is actually doing in the sentence. Like other verbs, verbals can take objects, modifiers or both. When a verbal has modifiers and/or objects, the group of words is called a participial phrase, a gerund phrase, or an infinitive phrase. Like all phrases, verbal phrases function as one part of speech.

Participles are action adjectives. They have two forms: the present participle and the past participle. Both are used the same way.

The **present participle** uses the *–ing* form.

EXAMPLES   Jana jumped off the <u>diving</u> board.
My uncle has a <u>hearing</u> aid.
I love to listen to that <u>marching</u> band.

The **past participle** uses the *–ed* form.

EXAMPLES   A <u>raided</u> cookie jar is not a pretty sight.
The <u>forgotten</u> language will never be recovered.
A <u>watched</u> pot never boils.

Note that you can find the object of a participle by using the same questioning strategy you use to find the verb of a sentence. The participle and its object form a construction called a **participial phrase**. It acts as one part of speech, an adjective.

VERBALS: PARTICIPLES GERUNDS, AND INFINITIVES. Students are asked to identify participles and gerunds in sentences in the Language, Grammar, and Style activities on pages 692 and 763.

The student taking notes got an *A* last semester.

Taking is a participle. If you ask, "*taking* what?", the answer is *notes*. The object of *taking*, the **participle**, is *notes*. Since *taking notes* modifies *student*, the entire construction (called a participial phrase) is working as an adjective.

Gerunds are verb forms used as namers. When you use any action as a name (running, jumping, writing, singing, playing), you use a gerund.

EXAMPLES

Running was her favorite activity.
(The gerund is the subject of the sentence.)

He liked high jumping.
(The gerund is the direct object.)

She wanted a tutor for writing.
(The gerund is the object of a preposition.)

Like participles, gerunds can take objects. You can find the object of a gerund just as you find the object of a verb.

EXAMPLE

Buying a prom dress took all of Katy's money.

Buying is a **gerund**. If you ask, "Buying what?", the answer is *a prom dress*. After you eliminate the modifiers, you will see that the object of the gerund *buying* is *dress*.

Gerunds can also take modifiers; since the gerund acts as a noun, the modifiers are adjectives.

EXAMPLE Dan began ice skating.

In this case, *ice* modifies *skating*.

EXAMPLE Senna began complaining to her mother.

Note that the prepositional phrase *to her mother* modifies *complaining*. This makes the modifier a prepositional phrase.

In both of the sentences above, the entire **gerund phrase** (the gerund + objects and/or modifiers) acts as one noun. In both these sentences, the phrases are direct objects.

Infinitives are verbals that use the form *to* + the verb. Each of the examples below illustrates a different use of infinitives. Infinitives can be used as nouns or as modifiers (adjectives and adverbs).

EXAMPLES

Her desire to win dominated her entire life. (Adjective)

The entire family gathered to celebrate my grandmother's birthday. (Adverb)

To attend college is my ultimate goal. (Noun)

When I turned sixteen, my parents allowed me to drive my car to school. (Adverb)

Like other verbals, infinitives can take modifiers and objects. In the second and third sample sentences, the infinitives have objects. *To celebrate* has an object, *my grandmother's birthday;* the object of *to attend* is *college.* The fourth, *to drive,* has an object, *my car,* and a modifier, *to school.*

Infinitives can get tricky because speakers and writers may leave out *to* when it follows some commonly used verbs. Sometimes the *to* is omitted in infinitives that follow *dare, do, feel, hear, help, let, make, need, see, watch.* These constructions, called **bare infinitives**, are usually direct objects that name an action. The *to* is understood.

EXAMPLES

I heard her (to) play the piano.
Help me (to) carry this table.

Be careful. The *to* is not always left out after these verbs, and no dependable rule seems to exist. Native speakers with good ears will have a sense of this, but others may find it difficult. Fortunately, it is never wrong to include the *to* with an infinitive, although it may sound a little awkward.

3.81 Groups of Words That Function as One Part of Speech

Sometimes groups of words function as one part of speech. These groups fall into two categories: **phrases** and **clauses. Clauses** have both subjects and verbs; **phrases** do not.

EXAMPLES

I need to get another spiral notebook. (Phrase)

She will be elected to the Student Council. (Phrase)

I will watch television when I finish my homework. (Clause)

GROUPS OF WORDS THAT FUNCTION AS ONE PART OF SPEECH. Students are asked to recognize clauses in sentences in the Language, Grammar, and Style activity on page 719.

PHRASES. Students are asked to recognize phrases in sentences in the Language, Grammar, and Style activity on page 719.

Do you know <u>who will be our next class president</u>? (Clause)

Most clauses and phrases are named after the functions that they perform.

3.82 PHRASES. **Phrases** are groups of words that do not contain a subject and verb and that function as one part of speech. The following kinds of phrases are used in the English language:

Adjective phrases are prepositional phrases that modify nouns or pronouns.

> EXAMPLE   Slim wanted a job <u>with good hours</u>.

Adverb phrases are prepositional phrases that modify anything except nouns and pronouns.

> EXAMPLE   I spoke <u>to the two-headed alien</u>.

Participial phrases are verbal phrases that function as adjectives.

> EXAMPLE   <u>Their recently remodeled</u> house is the jewel of the neighborhood.

Gerund phrases are verbal phrases that function as nouns.

> EXAMPLE   <u>Getting good grades</u> is important to many students.

Infinitive phrases are verbal phrases that function as nouns, adjectives, or adverbs.

> EXAMPLES   <u>To see angels</u> is to believe in them. (Noun)
> The ride <u>to go on</u> is the Ferris wheel. (Adjective)
> We are ready <u>to go home</u>. (Adverb)

3.83 CLAUSES WITHIN A SENTENCE. The **clauses** within a sentence are groups of words that 1) contain a subject and verb and that 2) function as one part of speech. The following kinds of clauses are used in the English language:

Adjective clauses are subordinate clauses that function as adjectives; they modify nouns and pronouns.

> EXAMPLE
> I admired the girl <u>who won the speech contest</u>.

Adverb clauses are subordinate clauses that function as adverbs, modifiying anything except nouns and pronouns.

> EXAMPLE
> My mother got upset <u>when she learned where I was going</u>.

Noun clauses function as subjects and objects.

> EXAMPLE
> <u>Whoever gets straight *A*'s in math</u> gets a four-year scholarship from the school's foundation.

3.84 THE CLAUSES OF A SENTENCE: SIMPLE, COMPOUND, AND COMPLEX SENTENCES. The **independent clauses**, or **main clauses**, of a sentence are the parts that contain a subject and verb. Without coordinating and/or subordinating words, they could stand alone. A sentence with only one independent clause is called a **simple sentence**.

> SIMPLE SENTENCE
> Mabel made a broccoli pizza.

A sentence with two or more independent, or main, clauses—two ideas of equal importance—is called a **compound sentence.** The independent clauses are usually connected with a comma and a **coordinating conjunction** such as *and, but, for, nor, or,* or *yet.*

> COMPOUND SENTENCE
> Mabel made a broccoli pizza, <u>but</u> I didn't eat it!

A sentence with one independent clause and one or more **dependent,** or **subordinate, clauses** (less important clauses) is called a **complex sentence.** The dependent clauses are usually connected to the independent clause with a **subordinating conjunction** such as *after, because, if,* or *when,* or a **relative pronoun** such as *this* or *that.* The dependent clause may either begin or end a complex sentence, but when it begins the sentence, a comma must follow it. If a sentence contains both kinds of clauses, it is called a **compound-complex sentence.**

> COMPLEX SENTENCE
> After I returned home, I ate a cheese pizza.
> I ate a cheese pizza after I returned home.

If a sentence contains both kinds of clauses, it is called a **compound-complex sentence.**

> COMPOUND-COMPLEX SENTENCE
> I ate a cheese pizza after I returned home, and Mabel was insulted because I didn't eat the one she cooked.

For more information, see the Language Arts Survey 3.36, "Combining and Expanding Sentences."

CLAUSES WITHIN A SENTENCE. Students are asked to work with adverb clauses in the Language, Grammar, and Style activity on page 744 and adjective clauses on page 851.

3.85 Editing for Punctuation Errors

To avoid punctuation errors, you should know how to use end marks, commas, semicolons, colons, apostrophes, underlining, italics, quotation marks, dashes, and hyphens.

3.86 END MARKS. End marks tell the reader where a sentence ends. An end mark also shows the purpose of the sentence. The three end marks are the period, the question mark, and the exclamation point.

A **declarative sentence** ends with a period.

DECLARATIVE

> For many years the Empire State Building was the tallest skyscraper in the world.

An **interrogative sentence** ends with a question mark.

INTERROGATIVE

> When did World War I begin?
> How do you spell your name?

An **exclamatory sentence** ends with an exclamation point.

EXCLAMATORY

> The view from the top is breathtaking!
> Help! Marvin is choking!

3.87 COMMAS. A **comma** separates words or groups of words within a sentence. Commas tell the reader to pause at certain spots in the sentence. These pauses help keep the reader from running together certain words and phrases when these phrases should be kept apart for clarity. Following is a list of the most common ways commas should be used.

RULES	EXAMPLES
Use commas to separate **items in a series**. Three or more words make a series.	The primary particles in an atom are protons, neutrons, and electrons. Choices include carrots, green beans, and asparagus.
Use commas when you **combine sentences using** *and, but, or, nor, yet, so,* or *for.* Place the comma before these words.	Casey was confident that he could hit a home run. He struck out. Casey was confident that he could hit a home run, but he struck out. Joanna will sing in the talent show. Margaret will accompany her. Joanna will sing in the talent show, and Margaret will accompany her.
Use a comma to **set off words or phrases that interrupt sentences**. Use two commas if the word or phrase falls in the middle of the sentence. Use one comma if the word or phrase comes at the beginning or at the end of a sentence.	Emily's twin brothers, Eric and Derrick, look exactly alike. Hercules, a hero of classical mythology, was said to be the strongest man on earth. After the first quarter, the Knicks dominated the game. How did you solve that problem, Jared?

CONTINUED

COMMAS. Students are asked to work with commas in the Language, Grammar, and Style activities on pages 287 and 424.

RULES	EXAMPLES
Use commas to **separate the parts of a date**. Do not use a comma between the month and the day.	The Germans surrendered on May 8, 1945. My appointment is on Wednesday, January 7.
Use commas to **separate items in addresses**. Do not put a comma between the state and the ZIP code.	Francisco was born in Caracas, Venezuela. They live at 210 Newfield Road, DeWitt, New York 13214.

3.88 SEMICOLONS. You have seen how two related sentences can be combined into one using a conjunction such as *and, but, so,* and *or*. Another way to join two related sentences into one is to use a semicolon. The **semicolon** can be used in place of the comma and the conjunction.

EXAMPLES

A fin was spotted moving through the water, so the bathers scrambled onto the beach.
A fin was spotted moving through the water; the bathers scrambled onto the beach.

Danielle is an exchange student from Paris, and everyone is enjoying getting to know her.
Danielle is an exchange student from Paris; everyone is enjoying getting to know her.

3.89 COLONS. Use a **colon** to introduce a list of items.

EXAMPLES

Don't forget the following items for the hike: water bottle, food, first-aid kit, extra sweater, and rain gear.
Make sure you have all your paperwork in order: passport, visa, and tickets.

You should also use a colon between numbers that tell hours and minutes.

1:07 P.M.   6:00 A.M.   9:54 P.M.

A colon is often used after the greeting in a business letter.

Dear Sirs: Dear Ms. Flanagan:

3.90 APOSTROPHES. An **apostrophe** is used to form the possessive of nouns. To form the possessive of a singular noun, you should add an apostrophe and an *s* to the end of the word.

EXAMPLES

The sun's diameter is about 864,000 miles.
(sun + 's = sun's)

Isaac's room is plastered with posters of the Pacers.
(Isaac + 's = Isaac's)

The possessive of a plural noun is formed two different ways. If the plural noun does not end in *s*, you add an apostrophe and an *s* to the end of the word. If the plural noun ends with an *s*, add only an apostrophe.

EXAMPLES

The women's volleyball team is undefeated.
(women + 's = women's)

The Vikings' star quarterback is on the injured list.
(Vikings + ' = Vikings')

There are some words that end in *s* and are singular, such as *species* or *Jesus*, that have an irregular possessive form. Form the possessive of these words by adding only an apostrophe.

EXAMPLES

Moses' staff
Euripedes' tragedies

3.91 UNDERLINING AND ITALICS. Italics are a type of slanted printing used to make a word or phrase stand out. In handwritten documents, or in forms of printing in which italics are not available, underlining is used. You should underline or italicize the titles of books, magazines, works of art, movies, and plays.

BOOKS	*The Joy Luck Club, Almost a Woman* or The Joy Luck Club, Almost a Woman
MAGAZINES	*Reader's Digest, Sports Illustrated* or Reader's Digest, Sports Illustrated

WORKS OF ART	*Mona Lisa*, *The Thinker* or <u>Mona Lisa</u>, <u>The Thinker</u>
MOVIES	*Gone with the Wind*, *Casablanca* or <u>Gone with the Wind</u>, <u>Casablanca</u>
PLAYS	*Antigone*, *Julius Caesar*, or <u>Antigone</u>, <u>Julius Caesar</u>

3.92 QUOTATION MARKS. When you use a person's exact words in your writing, you are using a **direct quotation**. Enclose the words of a direct quotation in quotation marks.

EXAMPLES

"It looks as if thunderclouds are gathering," Sylvia remarked.
Pietro said, "It's good to be back home."

A direct quotation should always begin with a capital letter. Separate a direct quotation from the rest of the sentence with a comma, question mark, or exclamation point. Do not separate the direct quotation from the rest of the sentence with a period. All punctuation marks that belong to the direct quotation itself should be placed inside the quotation marks.

EXAMPLES

"Your golf game has really improved," Avram remarked.
Victor lamented, "I wish Uncle Don were here."
"Did I turn off the iron?" wondered Mrs. Cameron.
Joy asked, "Have you seen my red blouse?"

Use quotation marks to enclose the titles of short works such as short stories, poems, songs, articles, and parts of books.

SHORT STORIES
"The Open Window," "The Necklace"

POEMS
"Dream Variations," "The Legend"

SONGS
"I Remember; I Believe," "You'll Be in My Heart"

ARTICLES, ESSAYS
"Beware the Unruly Sun," "The Road from Ballygunge"

PARTS OF BOOKS
"Curiosità "

3.93 HYPHENS AND DASHES. A **hyphen** is used to make a compound word.

EXAMPLES

four-year-old boy, great-grandmother, run-of-the-mill, seventh-grade student, three-time winner

A **dash** is used to show a sudden break or change in thought.

EXAMPLE

Juan surprised his teacher—and himself—by getting an *A* on the science test.

3.94 Editing for Capitalization Errors

To avoid capitalization errors, you should know how to capitalize proper nouns and adjectives; geographical names, directions and historical names; and titles of art and history books.

3.95 PROPER NOUNS AND ADJECTIVES. Using capital letters is called **capitalization**. Always capitalize proper nouns and adjectives. A proper noun names a specific person, place, or thing. A **proper adjective** is an adjective formed from a proper noun.

PROPER NOUNS
Lebanon, Queen Elizabeth, Democrat
PROPER ADJECTIVES
Lebanese, Elizabethan, Democratic

Capitalize the names of people and pets.

PEOPLE AND PETS
Charles A. Lindbergh, Marie Curie, Smoky

There are many different kinds of proper nouns. The chart below should help you to recognize some of them.

PROPER NOUNS

TITLES USED WITH NAMES
Dr. Stetson, Ms. Dixon, Mr. Meletiadis
MONTHS, DAYS, HOLIDAYS
January, Wednesday, Labor Day
RELIGIONS
Hinduism, Catholicism, Buddhism

CONTINUED

QUOTATION MARKS. In the Language, Grammar, and Style activities on page 975, students are asked to use quotation marks.

EDITING FOR CAPITALIZATION ERRORS. Students are asked to edit capitalization errors in sentences in the Language, Grammar, and Style activity on page 189.

PROPER NOUNS AND ADJECTIVES. Students are asked to change common nouns to proper nouns and adjectives in the Language, Grammar, and Style activity on page 739.

PROPER NOUNS

SACRED BEINGS AND WRITINGS
the Great Spirit, the Bible, the Koran

CITIES, STATES, COUNTRIES
Seattle, Louisiana, Peru

NATIONALITIES
Danish, Brazilian, Greek

STREETS, BRIDGES
Highland Street, Tappan Zee Bridge

BUILDINGS, MONUMENTS
World Trade Center, Washington Monument

CLUBS, ORGANIZATIONS, BUSINESSES
Kiwanis Club, National Audubon Society, Sears Roebuck

3.96 *I* AND FIRST WORDS. Capitalize the first word of every sentence.

EXAMPLES

Did you see that meteor?
The river rose over its banks.

Capitalize the word *I* whenever it appears.

EXAMPLES

Janice and I will buy the present.
Whenever I see horses, I think of Uncle Sherman.

3.97 FAMILY RELATIONSHIPS AND TITLES OF PERSONS. A word for a family relation such as *Mom, Dad,* or *Grandpa* should be capitalized if it is used as the name or part of the name of a particular person. Do not capitalize a word for a family relation if a modifier such as *the, a, my,* or *your* comes before it.

CAPITALIZED

When they were children, Dad, Aunt Polly, and Uncle Richard went down the Grand Canyon on mules.

NOT CAPITALIZED

My grandma has a cousin who lives in Germany.

Capitalize the official title of a person when it is followed by the person's name or when it is used instead of a name in direct address.

President James Polk, Queen Mary, Sir Winston Churchill, Pope Paul
"I am honored to meet you, Ambassador."

Do not capitalize references to occupations.

the electrician, the doctor, the sergeant, the judge, the chef, the editor

3.98 GEOGRAPHICAL NAMES, DIRECTIONS, AND HISTORICAL NAMES. Capitalize the names of specific places, including terms such as *lake, mountain, river,* or *valley* if they are used as part of a name.

BODIES OF WATER	Colorado River, Black Sea
CITIES AND TOWNS	Kansas City, Fayetteville
COUNTIES	Cayuga County, Kosciusko County
COUNTRIES	Switzerland, Indonesia
ISLANDS	Ellis Island, Isle of Wight
MOUNTAINS	Pike's Peak, Mount Rainier
STATES	Montana, South Carolina
STREETS, HIGHWAYS	Erie Boulevard, Route 71

Do not capitalize general names for places.

EXAMPLES

The still lake beautifully reflected the white-capped mountain.
Follow this road for two more miles and you will reach a small town.

Capitalize geographical directions if they are part of a specific name or a commonly recognized region. Do not capitalize words such as east(ern), west(ern), north(ern), and south(ern) if they are used only to indicate direction.

CAPITALIZED

<u>Western</u> Samoa, <u>East</u> Africa, <u>South</u> Bend, <u>Northern</u> Ireland

NOT CAPITALIZED

<u>west</u> of Denver, <u>eastern</u> face of the mountain, <u>south</u> side of the city, <u>northern</u> regions

Capitalize historical events, special events, and recognized periods of time.

HISTORICAL EVENTS

Continental Congress, Boxer Rebellion

HISTORICAL PERIODS

Paleozoic Era, Industrial Age

SPECIAL EVENTS

Empire State Games, Rose Bowl

3.99 TITLES OF ARTWORKS AND LITERARY WORKS. Apply title capitalization to titles of artworks and literary works. In title capitalization, capitalize the first word, the last word, and all other words except articles (*a, an,* and *the*) and prepositions.

EXAMPLES

DaVinci's *Mona Lisa*, van Gogh's *Cornfield with Crows*, Rembrandt's *The Night Watch*, Shakespeare's *The Tragedy of Romeo and Juliet*, Tolstoy's *War and Peace*, Bradbury's "The Pedestrian"

3.100 Editing for Spelling Errors

You can improve your spelling by following the rules given here, and by memorizing the list of commonly misspelled words.

3.101 USING SPELLING RULES I. Always check your writing for spelling errors, and try to recognize the words that give you more trouble than others. Adding prefixes and suffixes often causes spelling errors. A prefix is a letter or a group of letters added to the beginning of a word to change its meaning. When adding a prefix, do not change the spelling of the word itself.

dis + similar = dissimilar
un + necessary = unnecessary

A **suffix** is a letter or group of letters added to the end of a word to change its meaning. The spelling of most words is not changed when the suffix *–ness* or *–ly* is added.

even + ness = evenness
usual + ly = usually

If you are adding a suffix to a word that ends with *y*, and that *y* follows a vowel, you should usually leave the *y* in place. (**Vowels** are the letters *a, e, i, o,* and *u.*)

employ + ment = employment
stay + ing = staying
destroy + ed = destroyed

If you are adding a suffix to a word that ends with *y*, and that *y* follows a consonant, you should usually change the *y* to *i.* (**Consonants** are all letters that are not vowels.)

silly + est = silliest
sticky + ness = stickiness
cry + ed = cried
cheery + ly = cheerily

If you are adding a suffix that begins with a vowel to a word that ends with a silent *e*, you should usually drop the *e*.

shave + ing = shaving
value + able = valuable
rose + y = rosy
take + ing = taking

If you are adding a suffix that begins with a consonant to a word that ends with a silent *e*, you should usually leave the *e* in place.

tire + less = tireless
sincere + ly = sincerely
fate + ful = fateful
place + ment = placement

3.102 USING SPELLING RULES II. When a word is spelled with the letters *i* and *e* and has the long *e* sound, it is spelled *ie* except after the letter *c*.

thief, relieve, yield, pierce
ceiling, conceive, receipt, deceive

The only word in the English language that ends in *–sede* is *supersede*. Only the following three words end in *–ceed*: *exceed, proceed,* and *succeed*. Every other word that ends with the "seed" sound is spelled *–cede*.

precede, recede, concede, accede

Most noun plurals are formed by simply adding *–s* to the end of the word.

stairs, ducklings, kites, rockets

The plurals of nouns that end in *o, s, x, z, ch,* or *sh* should be formed by adding *–es*.

tomatoes, classes, taxes, topazes, beaches, flashes

An exception to the rule above is that musical terms (and certain other words that end in *o*) are usually pluralized by adding *–s*.

pianos, solos, concertos, sopranos, banjos, radios

Form the plurals of nouns that end in *y* following a vowel by adding *–s*.

EXAMPLES   toy + s = toys
donkey + s = donkeys
Thursday + s = Thursdays
ray + s = rays

Form the plurals of nouns that end in *y* following a consonant by changing the *y* to an *i* and adding –es.

EXAMPLES
pony + s = ponies
spy + s = spies
country + s = countries
story + s = stories

3.103 COMMON SPELLING ERRORS. Some English words are often misspelled. The following box contains a list of 150 commonly misspelled words. If you master this list, you will avoid many errors in your spelling.

COMMONLY MISSPELLED ENGLISH WORDS

absence	biscuit	enormous	liquefy	parallel	siege
abundant	breathe	enthusiastically	magnificent	pastime	significance
academically	business	environment	manageable	peasant	souvenir
accessible	calendar	exhaust	maneuver	permanent	sponsor
accidentally	camouflage	existence	meadow	persistent	succeed
accommodate	catastrophe	fascinating	mediocre	phenomenon	surprise
accurate	cellar	finally	miniature	physician	symbol
acknowledgment	cemetery	forfeit	mischievous	pneumonia	synonymous
acquaintance	changeable	fulfill	misspell	prestige	temperature
adequately	clothes	guidance	mortgage	privilege	tomorrow
adolescent	colossal	guerrilla	mysterious	procedure	transparent
advantageous	column	hindrance	naive	prophesy	twelfth
advisable	committee	hypocrite	necessity	prove	undoubtedly
ancient	conceivable	independent	nickel	receipt	unmistakable
annihilate	conscientious	influential	niece	referred	unnecessary
anonymous	conscious	ingenious	noticeable	rehearsal	vacuum
answer	consistency	institution	nucleus	relieve	vehicle
apparent	deceitful	interference	nuisance	resistance	vengeance
article	descendant	irrelevant	nutritious	resources	villain
attendance	desirable	irresistible	obedience	responsibility	vinegar
bankruptcy	disastrous	judgment	occasionally	rhythm	weird
beautiful	discipline	league	occurrence	schedule	whistle
beggar	efficiency	leisure	orchestra	seize	withhold
beginning	eighth	license	outrageous	separate	yacht
behavior	embarrass	lightning	pageant	sergeant	yield

SPEAKING AND LISTENING Resource

THE POWER OF COMMUNICATION

Humans are by nature social creatures. **Communication** is a form of behavior that fulfills the basic human need to connect and interact with other individuals in society. Because democratic government requires the free exchange of ideas, communication is also fundamental to the political way of life in the United States.

4.1 Verbal and Nonverbal Communication

Human beings use both verbal and nonverbal communication to convey meaning and exchange ideas. When a person expresses meaning through words, he or she is using **verbal communication**. When a person expresses meaning without using words, for example by standing up straight or shaking his or her head, he or she is using **nonverbal communication**. When we speak to another person, we usually think that the meaning of what we say comes chiefly from the words we use. However, as much as 60 percent of the meaning of a message may be communicated nonverbally.

ELEMENTS OF VERBAL COMMUNICATION		
ELEMENT	**DESCRIPTION**	**GUIDELINES FOR SPEAKERS**
Volume	loudness or softness	Vary your volume, but make sure that you can be heard.
Melody, Pitch	highness or lowness	Vary your pitch. Avoid speaking in a monotone (at a single pitch).
Pace	speed	Vary the speed of your delivery to suit what you are saying. Excitement, for example, can be communicated by a fast pace, and seriousness can be communicated by slowing down and saying something forcefully.
Tone	emotional quality	Suit your tone to your message, and vary it appropriately as you speak. For example, you might use a light tone for a happy message and a heavier one for a sad message.
Enunciation	clearness with which words are spoken	When speaking before a group, pronounce your words more precisely than you would in ordinary conversation.

INTERNET RESOURCES

Access **Teaching Online's** *Confidence in Public Speaking* oral language lesson for middle or high school at http://www.teachingonline.org/publicspeaking.html.

VERBAL AND NONVERBAL COMMUNICATION. Students are asked to use verbal and nonverbal skills in the Speaking and Listening and Collaborative Learning activities on pages 127 and 385.

ELEMENTS OF NONVERBAL COMMUNICATION

ELEMENT	DESCRIPTION	GUIDELINES FOR SPEAKERS
Eye contact	Looking audience members in the eye	Make eye contact regularly with people in your audience. Try to include all audience members.
Facial expression	Using your face to show your emotions	Use expressions to emphasize your message—raised eyebrows for a question, pursed lips for concentration, eyebrows lowered for anger, and so on.
Gesture	Meaningful motions of the arms and hands	Use gestures to emphasize points. Be careful, however, not to overuse gestures. Too many can be distracting.
Posture	Position of the body	Keep your spine straight and head high, but avoid appearing stiff. Stand with your arms and legs slightly open, except when adopting other postures to express particular emotions.
Proximity	Distance from audience	Keep the right amount of distance between yourself and the audience. You should be a comfortable distance away, but not so far away that the audience cannot hear you.

LISTENING SKILLS

Learning to listen well is essential not only for success in personal life, but also for success in school and, later, on the job. It is estimated that high school and college students spend over half their waking time listening to others, yet most people are rather poor listeners.

4.2 Active versus Passive Listening

Effective listening requires skill and concentration. The mind of a good listener is focused on what a speaker is trying to communicate. In other words, an effective listerner is an active listener. Ineffective listeners view listening as a passive activity, something that simply "happens" without any effort on their part. Passive listening is nothing more than hearing sounds. This type of listening can cause misunderstanding and miscommunication.

Different situations require different listening skills. The following suggestions can help you become a better listener in particular situations.

4.3 Listening to a Lecture or Demonstration

• Think of creative reasons to listen. It can be difficult to pay attention to a lecture or demonstration if you do not think the information being presented is important to you. Try to think of reasons why the information is important by asking yourself: How can I use this information?

• As you listen, show the speaker that you are involved. Remember that in a lecture or demonstration, as in a conversation, the speaker depends on you for positive feedback or response. Try to maintain an attentive posture by sitting up straight, making eye contact, and nodding when you understand.

• Listen for major ideas. Try to identify the speaker's main points and the facts or materials that are offered to support them. Check your understanding of what the speaker is saying by putting it into your own words, in your head, as you listen.

- Take notes as you listen. Note the major ideas and related details. Do not try to write down what the speaker says word for word. Use phrases, symbols, and abbreviations such as w/ for *with, Amer.* for *American,* and & or + for *and.* (For more information, see the Language Arts Survey 5.17, "Taking Notes, Outlining, and Summarizing Information.")

- When you do not understand something that the speaker is saying, make a note. Save questions and comments for an appropriate time, usually when the speaker pauses or when he or she invites questions. Then raise your hand before asking your question or making your comment.

- Do not let yourself become distracted. Avoid such things as daydreaming, focusing on the speaker's delivery, or listening to background noise. Giving in to distractions can prevent you from understanding the speaker's message.

4.4 Listening in Conversations

- Do not monopolize the conversation. Give the other person plenty of opportunities to speak.

- When the other person is speaking, pay attention to what he or she is saying. Show through eye contact, body language, and facial expressions that you are interested and attentive.

- Avoid mentally debating the other person while he or she is speaking. This may distract you from truly hearing what the person has to say. Try to withhold judgment until the other person has finished.

- Ask the other person questions. Asking questions is a good way to start a conversation, to keep the conversation going, and to show the other person that you are really listening. The best questions are usually ones that directly relate to what the speaker has been saying.

- When you speak, respond to what the other person has been saying. Relate what you say to what he or she has said.

- Take time to think about what the other speaker has said before responding. Do not be afraid of a lull in the conversation while you think about what has been said and about your response.

- If you find yourself becoming overly emotional during a conversation, stop, take a deep breath, and bring your emotions under control before continuing. If controlling your emotions seems too difficult, consider continuing the conversation at a later time.

4.5 Listening to the Media

- Avoid being a "couch potato." Television, movies, and radio programs can be powerful manipulators. As you watch or listen, think critically about what you are seeing or hearing by evaluating these messages.

- When watching or listening to news programs or commercial advertisements, make sure to distinguish facts from opinions. *Facts* are statements that can be proved by checking a reference work or making observations. *Opinions* are statements of value or statements of policy that express personal beliefs. A statement of value expresses positive or negative attitudes toward a person, object, or idea. For example, "Albert Einstein was a great humanitarian" is a statement of value because it expresses a positive attitude toward Einstein. A statement of policy says what should or should not be done. "Congress should spend more money on education" is a statement of policy because it suggests what Congress should do. When you hear an opinion, ask yourself whether it is supported by the facts. For more information, see the Language Arts Survey 5.2, "Distinguishing Fact from Opinion."

- When watching or listening to an entertainment program, think about the quality of the program. Consider the quality of the acting, directing, and writing. Also consider the production qualities of the program—the lighting, sound effects, staging, camera work, costuming, properties, and music.

- Think about what message or messages are being delivered by the program and whether you agree or disagree with them. Do not assume that just because a program is entertaining, it does not communicate a message.

LISTENING IN CONVERSATIONS. Students are encouraged to follow the guidelines for listening in conversations in the Speaking and Listening & Collaborative Learning activity on page 87 and the Media Literacy activity on page 842.

1076 *TEACHER'S EDITION*

- Set standards about what you will watch or listen to. Learn to turn off a program or to switch to another program when something does not meet your standards.

- Limit the time that you spend watching or listening to the broadcast media. Remember that there is much more that you might be doing with your life such as reading, learning a new hobby or skill, writing in your journal, exercising, interacting with other people, creating works of art, or simply thinking.

4.6 Adapting Listening Skills to Specific Tasks

Just as different situations require different types of listening, different tasks or goals may also require different listening strategies and skills.

LISTENING FOR COMPREHENSION means listening for information or ideas communicated by other people. For example, you are listening for comprehension when you try to understand directions to a friend's house or your teacher's explanation of how to conduct a classroom debate. When listening for comprehension, your goal is to reach understanding, so it is important to recognize and remember the key information or ideas presented. Concentrate on getting the main points or major ideas of a message rather than all the supporting details. This can prevent you from becoming overwhelmed by the amount of information presented.

You might also use a technique called clarifying and confirming to help you better remember and understand information. The technique involves paraphrasing or repeating back to the speaker in your own words the key information presented to make sure that you have understood correctly. If the situation prevents you from using the technique—for instance, if there is no opportunity for you to respond directly to the speaker—it can still be helpful to rephrase the information in your own words in your head to help you remember and understand it.

LISTENING CRITICALLY means listening to a message in order to comprehend and evaluate it. When listening for comprehension, you usually assume that the information presented is true. Critical listening, on the other hand, includes comprehending and judging the arguments and appeals in a message in order to decide whether to accept or reject them. Critical listening is most useful when you encounter a persuasive message such as a sales pitch, advertisement, campaign speech, or news editorial. When evaluating a persuasive message, you might consider the following: Is the speaker trustworthy and qualified to speak about this subject? Does the speaker present logical arguments supported by solid facts? Does the speaker use unproven assumptions to make a case? Does the speaker use questionable motivational appeals, such as appeals to fear or to prejudice? These questions can help you decide whether or not to be convinced by a persuasive message.

LISTENING TO LEARN VOCABULARY involves a very different kind of listening because the focus is on learning new words and how to use them properly. For instance, if you were to hear a presentation on hip-hop music, the speaker might introduce some of the many slang terms used in this musical style and explain what they mean. Or you might have a conversation with someone who has a more advanced vocabulary and use this as an opportunity to learn new words. The key to listening in order to learn vocabulary is to pay attention to how words are used in context. Sometimes it is possible to figure out what an unfamiliar word means based simply on how the word is used in a sentence. Once you learn a new word, try to use it several times so it becomes more familiar and you become comfortable using it. Also be sure to look up the word in a dictionary to find out whether it has other meanings or connotations of which you are not aware.

LISTENING FOR APPRECIATION means listening purely for enjoyment or entertainment. You might listen appreciatively to a singer, a comedian, a storyteller, an acting company, or a humorous speaker. Appreciation is a very individual matter and there are no rules about how to appreciate something. However, as with all forms of listening, listening for appreciation requires attention and concentration.

COMMUNICATING WITH OTHERS

4.7 Communicating with Another Person

The ordinary human interactions that take place in daily life involve a great deal of interpersonal communication, or communication between two individuals. The following guidelines will help you to communicate more effectively in such daily interactions.

- **Make eye contact** and maintain a relaxed posture.

- **Provide feedback as you listen**. Smile or nod to show understanding and/or agreement. Ask questions or make comments when the speaker pauses for feedback. Try not to interrupt or to finish the speaker's sentences for him or her.

- **Reflect back or rephrase what the speaker has said** to make sure that you understand him or her. For example, suppose that the speaker says, "Crazy Horse never allowed anyone to make a likeness of him or take his photograph." You could reflect back, "So, nobody ever made a likeness of Crazy Horse or took his photograph? That's interesting. Why do you think he felt that way?"

- **Control your emotions**. If you become angry while listening to the speaker, take a deep breath and count to ten. Make sure you haven't misunderstood by rephrasing the statement that angered you. If you can contain your anger, express your objections calmly. If you cannot contain your anger, end your conversation and say that you would like to continue it at another time.

- **Distinguish between facts and opinions**. Facts are statements that can be proven true, whereas opinions are expressions of personal belief that may or may not be true. When presenting factual information in a conversation, it is helpful to explain what the basis for the fact is. When presenting opinions, try to indicate this by introducing these ideas with phrases like "I believe that . . ." or "In my opinion . . ." If you are unsure whether another person is stating a fact or opinion, ask what his or her statement is based on.

4.8 Communicating in a Small Group

Much human activity takes place in small groups. A small group is defined as a group of three to fifteen people, interacting in a face-to-face situation, who have an awareness of a group identity. Everyone is involved in a small group at one point or another in their lives, whether it be a high school clique, an after-school organization, an athletic team, or a family. Although many of the principles of interpersonal communication hold true in small group situations, there are additional factors to consider because of the number of people involved. The following guidelines will help you become a better communicator and participant in small group situations.

- **Respect group norms and culture**. Most groups have norms or rules that govern appropriate behavior for group members. Groups also have their own culture or way of life that may include certain beliefs, rituals, or behaviors. When participating in a small group, be sure to pay attention to and respect the norms and culture of the group.

- **Understand group roles**. Individual members are likely to fulfill particular roles in a group based on what they do best. Constructive roles help the group to achieve its goals. These include the **leader** (directs the work of the group), **secretary** (keeps minutes of group meetings), **gatekeeper** (keeps communication open by encouraging and discouraging participation), and **harmonizer** (helps to resolve conflict or reduce tension between group members). Destructive roles may prevent the group from achieving its goals. These include the **joker** (distracts the group by engaging in horseplay), **dominator** (tries to control the group for his or her own interests), **blocker** (puts down the ideas of others or refuses to cooperate), and **deserter** (withdraws from the group and does not participate). Successful group participants attempt to fulfill positive and constructive roles within the group and encourage others to do so.

COMMUNICATING IN A SMALL GROUP. Examples of Integrating the Language Arts activities that require communication in small groups can be found on pages 189 and 308.

COMMUNICATING WITH ANOTHER PERSON. Students are required to communicate with another person in the Speaking and Listening activity on page 445.

SPEAKING AND LISTENING RESOURCE

- **Take turns participating**. Good group members make contributions to the discussion, but also allow others to participate. If an overly talkative person seems to dominate the discussion, be willing to take on the role of gatekeeper and gently suggest that others be allowed to contribute. For instance, you might say, "I've been interested in what you have to say, Ed. What do other people think about this issue?"

- **Help to foster a positive group climate**. Group climate refers to the degree of warmth or coldness that group members feel toward each other. You have probably been in a group with a cold climate before, where members constantly bicker and argue and never seem to accomplish anything. Positive or warm group climates are characterized by trust, cooperation, and concern for others. Negative or cold group climates are characterized by suspicion, competition, and selfishness. As a good group member, you can help to create a positive and warm climate by being supportive of others ideas, empathizing with others, treating others as equals, and remaining flexible and open to new ideas and information.

- **Establish group goals**. Some groups have a difficult time accomplishing anything because it is not clear what the goals of the group are. Without goals, a group is like a ship that sets sail with no clear destination. Chances are the ship and the group will drift aimlessly until they run aground. You can help your group stay focused by encouraging its members to establish clear goals at the beginning, and referring to these goals whenever the group seems to run aground or lose its way.

4.9 Communicating in a Large Group

Large groups are those that contain more than fifteen people. Generally the larger the size of the group, the less opportunity there is for each individual to participate. However, there are still principles that can help you become a better communicator in large group situations.

- **Share group roles**. In larger groups, it may be difficult to decide who takes what role as many

members may have the skills needed for any one role. Sharing roles and responsibilities can allow everyone to contribute to the group.

- **Focus on key relationships**. It may not be possible to get to know everyone in a large group setting. Identify those key individuals in the group that you will most need to interact with in carrying out your assignments or duties, and focus on getting to know them.

- **Emphasize group identity, norms, and goals**. As groups become larger in size, they are likely to become less cohesive. Cohesiveness refers to the level of commitment and attraction members feel to each other and the group. Groups that experience low cohesion are usually not productive or successful. Try to increase cohesion by reinforcing the identity, norms, and goals of the group at every opportunity.

- **Stand up when speaking**. Make sure that everyone in the room can see and hear you. If there is a microphone available, use it. Speak in a normal tone four to six inches from the microphone.

- **Avoid the pressure to conform**. In larger groups, individuals are less comfortable speaking out if they disagree with an idea or decision. This can produce "groupthink," where members give in to the pressure to conform and do not critically evaluate information and/or decisions. If you disagree with an expressed idea or decision, do not hesitate to speak out and share your reservations.

- **Foster responsibility**. In large groups, it is relatively easy for individual members to shirk their duties and avoid responsibility. If something goes wrong, there are usually many people to blame so no one feels individually responsible for the outcomes of the group. Take responsibility yourself, and encourage others in the group to carry out their assigned duties.

4.10 Asking and Answering Questions

There are many situations in which you will find it useful to ask questions of a speaker, or in which you will be asked questions about a presentation. Often a formal speech or presentation will be

COMMUNICATING IN A LARGE GROUP. Students are asked to hold a class discussion in the Critical Thinking & Collaborative Learning activity on page 587.

followed by a question-and-answer period. Keep the following guidelines in mind when asking or answering questions.

ASKING QUESTIONS

- **Wait to be recognized.** In most cases, it is appropriate to raise your hand if you have a question and to wait for the speaker or moderator to call on you.

- **Make questions clear and direct.** The longer your question, the less chance a speaker will understand it. Make your questions short and to the point.

- **Do not debate or argue.** If you disagree with a speaker, the question-and-answer period is not the time to hash out an argument. Ask to speak with the speaker privately after the presentation is over, or agree on a later time and place to meet.

- **Do not take others' time.** Be courteous to other audience members and allow them time to ask questions. If you have a follow-up question, ask the speaker if you may proceed with your follow-up.

- **Do not give a speech.** Sometimes audience members are more interested in expressing their own opinion than in asking the speaker a question. Do not give in to the temptation to present a speech of your own.

ANSWERING QUESTIONS

- **Come prepared** for a question-and-answer period. Although you can never predict the exact questions that people will ask you, you can anticipate many questions that are likely to be asked. Rehearse aloud your answers to the most difficult questions.

- **Be patient.** It may take some time for audience members to formulate questions in response to your speech. Give the audience a moment to do so. Don't run back to your seat the minute your speech is over, or if there is an awkward pause after you invite questions.

- **Be direct and succinct.** Be sure to answer the question directly as it has been asked, and to provide a short but clear answer.

- **Rephrase difficult or ambiguous questions.** If you are not sure what an audience member's question is, repeat the question back to them to clarify. You may also want to repeat the question if not everyone in the audience could hear it.

- **Be courteous.** Sometimes audience members will ask a question you have already answered in your speech. Be tactful in such situations. Briefly repeat the information from your speech in case the audience member did not hear or understand you the first time.

- **Handle difficult audience members gracefully.** Sometimes audience members hog the stage or try to pick a verbal fight with a speaker. In such situations, keep your cool and gently suggest that the audience member talk to you privately after the presentation so you can discuss the issue with him or her more fully.

COMMUNICATION STYLES AND CULTURAL BARRIERS

4.11 Being Considerate of Other Cultures and Communication Styles

Communication styles and behaviors vary greatly between people of different cultures—even those who live and were raised in the same country. There are many possible verbal and nonverbal sources of miscommunication between cultural groups. In some cultures, emotionally intense discussions and insults are expected forms of behavior. In other cultures, such behavior is considered rude. In traditional Asian cultures, a slap on the back is considered insulting and it is not customary to shake hands with people of the opposite sex. In other cultures, a slap on the back expresses friendliness and it is customary to shake hands with anyone you meet for the first time. When listening to someone speak, Native Americans consider a bowed head a sign of respect. In other cultures, lack of eye contact may be seen as a sign of shyness, weakness, or disrespect. In Latino cultures, two speakers in conversation may stand very close and even touch each other. In other cultures, standing close is considered an intrusion on personal space and

SPEAKING AND LISTENING RESOURCE

thought to be rude, and touching is generally acceptable only with close friends or relatives.

These are only a few of the many communication differences that exist among people of different cultures. When interacting with a person from another culture, it is important to remember that such differences may exist and to respect the other individual's cultural practices and behaviors.

4.12 Overcoming Barriers to Effective Multicultural Communication

The following guidelines and suggestions will help you to overcome some common barriers and stumbling blocks to communicating with people of different cultural backgrounds.

- **Treat people as individuals**. Do not assume that everyone is "the same" as you are, or even that people with similar cultural backgrounds are the same. Avoid relying on preconceptions and stereotypes when interacting with someone from another culture. Regardless of what cultural practices, physical characteristics, or behaviors they might share, human beings are individuals and should always be treated as such.

- **Be sensitive to sources of miscommunication**. Remember that both verbal and nonverbal behaviors send messages to others, and that both can lead to miscommunication and misunderstanding. If you think you have done or said something that has offended someone from another culture, ask if this is the case. It may be uncomfortable to do so at first, but you are more likely to overcome your error and become friends if you show respect and sensitivity to the other person.

- **Seek common ground**. One reason people from different cultures may have difficulty communicating is because they focus on differences rather than similarities. A simple way to overcome this problem is to find some common interest, belief, or activity that you share with the other person and that can help to bridge differences.

- **Accept others as they are**. Avoid the temptation to evaluate or judge the behavior, beliefs, feelings, or experiences of others. Instead, learn to accept differences as valid, even if you personally disagree with what someone

else thinks or feels. It is also helpful to remember that the other person is probably doing the best he or she can with whatever resources are available at the time.

- **Avoid provoking language**. Racial, ethnic, or gender slurs have no place in an enlightened society and should never be used. Profanity or swearing is unacceptable, even among close friends, and should be avoided. You-statements ("You are not listening to me," "You should not do that," "You don't know what you're talking about") can feel like an attack, even when they are well intentioned. People often react to you-statements by becoming defensive or hostile. Try to use I-statements instead ("I feel like you aren't listening to me," "I don't think you should do that," "I'm not sure I agree with you").

4.13 Collaborative Learning and Communication

Collaboration is the act of working with one or more other people to achieve a goal. Many common learning situations involve collaboration:

- participating in a small-group discussion
- doing a small-group project
- tutoring another student or being tutored
- doing peer evaluation

GUIDELINES FOR DISCUSSION

- **Listen actively during the discussion**. Maintain eye contact with the speakers. Make notes on what they say. Mentally translate what they say into your own words. Think critically about whether you agree or disagree with each speaker, and why.

- **Be polite**. Wait for your turn to speak. Do not interrupt others. If your discussion has a group leader, ask to be recognized before speaking by raising your hand.

- **Participate in the discussion**. At appropriate times, make your own comments or ask questions of other speakers.

- **Stick to the discussion topic**. Do not introduce unrelated or irrelevant ideas.

- **For a formal discussion, assign roles**. Choose a group leader to guide the discussion and a secretary to record the minutes (the main ideas and proposals made by group members). Also draw up an agenda before the discussion, listing items to be discussed.

GUIDELINES FOR PROJECTS

- **Choose a group leader** to conduct the meetings of your project group.

- **Set a goal** for the group, some specific outcome or set of outcomes that you want to bring about.

- **Make a list of tasks** that need to be performed.

- **Make a schedule** for completing the tasks, including dates and times for completion of each task.

- **Make an assignment sheet**. Assign certain tasks to particular group members. Be fair in distributing the work to be done.

- **Set times for future meetings**. You might want to schedule meetings to evaluate your progress toward your goal as well as meetings to actually carry out specific tasks.

- **Meet to evaluate your overall success** when the project is completed. Also look at the individual contributions of each group member.

GUIDELINES FOR TUTORING

- **Find out what the other student needs to learn.** Help him or her clarify assignments and areas of strength and weakness.

- **Break down your teaching into steps** that can be followed easily. Then help the other student to follow through on each step.

- **Review basic concepts, terms, and processes.** Encourage the other student to explain these to you in his or her own words.

- **Give the other student practice activities or exercises**, and help him or her to complete them.

- **Be patient.** Give the other student time to respond, to make mistakes, and to ask questions.

- **Be encouraging and supportive.** Remember that your job is to help someone else to learn, not to display your own knowledge.

GUIDELINES FOR BEING TUTORED

- **Bring with you all the materials that you need**, such as your textbook, study guides, notes, worksheets, pencils, and paper.

- **Explain as clearly as you can what you need help with**. Prepare questions beforehand.

- **Ask questions about anything that you do not understand.** Remember that no question is silly if it is sincere.

- **Be patient.** Learning takes time.

- **Do not give up if you do not understand immediately.** Practice makes perfect.

- **Be polite** and thank your tutor for his or her help.

GUIDELINES FOR PEER EVALUATION. For more information on peer evaluation, see the Language Arts Survey 2.37, "Self- and Peer Evaluation," 2.39, "How to Deliver Helpful Criticism," and 2.40, "How to Benefit from Helpful Criticism."

4.14 Conducting an Interview

In an interview, you meet with someone and ask him or her questions. Interviewing experts is an excellent way to gain information about a particular topic. For example, if you are interested in writing about the art of making pottery, you might interview an art teacher, a professional potter, or the owner of a ceramics shop.

When planning an interview, you should do some background research on your subject and think carefully about questions you would like to ask. Write out a list of questions, including some about the person's background as well as about your topic. Other questions might occur to you as the interview proceeds, but it is best to be prepared. For guidelines on being a good listener, read the Language Arts Survey 4.2, "Active versus Passive Listening," and 4.4, "Listening in Conversations." Here are some more tips for interviewing:

- **Set up a time for the interview in advance**. Don't just try to work questions into a regular conversation. Set aside time to meet in a quiet place where both you and the person you are interviewing can focus on the interview.

- **Explain the purpose of the interview**. Be sure the person you are interviewing knows what you want to find out and why you need to know it. This will help him or her to answer your questions in a way that is more useful and helpful to you.

CONDUCTING AN INTERVIEW. For practice, see the interviewing activities in Integrating the Language Arts activities on pages 9 and 22.

CONDUCTING AN INTERVIEW. Additional interviewing activities are found in Integrating the Language Arts activities on pages 115 and 649.

- **Ask mostly open-ended questions**. These are questions that allow the person you are interviewing to express a personal point of view. They cannot be answered with a simple "yes" or "no" nor a brief statement of fact. The following are all examples of open-ended questions: "Why did you become a professional potter?" "What is the most challenging thing about owning your own ceramics shop?" "What advice would you give to a beginning potter?" One of the most valuable questions to ask at the end of the interview is, "What would you like to add that I haven't asked about?" This can provide some of the most interesting or vital information of all.

- **If possible, tape-record the interview**. Then you can review the interview at your leisure. Be sure to ask the person you are interviewing whether or not you can tape-record the session. If the person refuses, accept his or her decision.

- **Take notes during the interview**, whether or not you are also tape-recording it. Write down the main points and some key words to help you remember details. Record the person's most important statements word for word.

- **Clarify spelling and get permission for quotes**. Be sure to get the correct spelling of the person's name and to ask permission to quote his or her statements.

- **End the interview on time**. Do not extend the interview beyond the time limits of your appointment. The person you are interviewing has been courteous enough to give you his or her time. Return this courtesy by ending the interview on time, thanking the person for his or her help, and leaving.

- **Write up the results of the interview as soon as possible after you conduct it**. Over time, what seemed like a very clear note may become unclear or confusing. If you are unclear of something important that the person said, contact him or her and ask for clarification.

PUBLIC SPEAKING

4.15 Giving a Speech

The fear of speaking in public, although quite common and quite strong in some people, can be overcome by preparing a speech thoroughly and practicing positive thinking and relaxation. Learning how to give a speech is a valuable skill, one that you most likely will find much opportunity to use in the future.

The nature of a speech, whether formal or informal, is usually determined by the situation or context in which it is presented. **Formal speeches** usually call for a greater degree of preparation, might require special attire such as a suit or dress, and are often presented to larger groups who attend specifically to hear the presentation. A formal speech situation might exist when presenting an assigned speech to classmates, giving a presentation to a community group or organization, or presenting a speech at an awards ceremony. **Informal speech** situations are more casual and might include telling a story among friends, giving a pep talk to your team at halftime, or presenting a toast at the dinner table.

4.16 Types of Speeches

The following are the three main types of speeches:

- **Impromptu speech**. This is a speech given without any advance preparation. For example, if you were surprised by a gift or an award, you might be called upon to give a brief speech that was not written or rehearsed.

- **Memorized speech**. This is a speech that has been written out and memorized word for word. Your teacher may ask you to prepare a memorized speech on a topic you are studying at school.

- **Extemporaneous speech**. This is a speech in which the speaker refers to notes occasionally. Most professional speakers prefer to deliver extemporaneous speeches because they combine the liveliness of an impromptu speech with the careful preparation of a memorized or manuscript speech. While the speaker does not plan what he or she will say word for word, the speaker does create an overall plan for the speech, records important points on cards, and rehearses until she or he is comfortable with the material. You might give an extemporaneous speech at a city council meeting about funding for your school.

4.17 Steps in Preparing an Extemporaneous Speech

1. **Choose a topic for your speech**. Consider the audience, occasion, and your own strengths and weaknesses as a speaker when choosing a topic.

2. **Do prewriting to identify what you know or think about the topic**. As you write, think about different ways to approach the topic.

3. **Do research on the topic**. Use a variety of source materials, including newspapers, magazines, books, interviews, Internet sources, and personal experience.

4. **Determine your specific purpose in speaking about your topic**. What are you trying to accomplish in speaking to your audience? Are you trying to demonstrate something to them? Compare and contrast two things or ideas? Strengthen their commitment to something? Spur them to take action?

5. **Organize your material into three to five main points**. Use a clear, logical, and interesting organizational strategy that is suited to your specific purpose, the audience, and the occasion. Be sure each point flows logically and smoothly from the one that comes before it. Include transitions between main points, and between the introduction, body, and conclusion of the speech.

6. **Create visual aids**. Some material is too difficult to present orally and is best presented visually. Visual aids should be neat, attractive, visible from a distance, and relevant to your speech. For more information, see the Language Arts Survey 6.11, "Displaying Effective Visual Information."

7. **Prepare note cards**. Notecards should be no larger than 4 x 6 inches and should contain as much information as you need to present your speech, but not so much that you are tempted to read from the cards. Write clearly and legibly so you can read your notes at a distance.

8. **Rehearse with your note cards**. Never attempt to speak at length on a subject without practicing what you will say. If possible, practice a few times in front of a live audience. Otherwise, use a mirror or recording device. Rehearse until you feel comfortable with the material and can present the speech with minimal use of notecards. Be sure to rehearse with visual aids if you are using them.

9. **Deliver your speech**.

4.18 Guidelines for Giving a Speech

A speech should always include a beginning, a middle, and an end. The beginning, or introduction, of your speech should spark the audience's interest, present your central idea, and briefly preview your main points. The middle, or body, of your speech should expand upon each of your main points in order to support the central idea. The end, or conclusion, of your speech should be memorable and should give your audience a sense of completion.

TIPS FOR SUCCESSFUL PUBLIC SPEAKING

- **Be sincere and enthusiastic**. Feel what you are speaking about. Apathy is infectious and will quickly spread to your audience.

- **Maintain good but relaxed posture**. Don't slouch or lean. It's fine to move around a bit; it releases normal nervous tension. Keep your hands free to gesture naturally instead of holding on to note cards, props, or the podium so much that you will "tie up" your hands.

- **Speak slowly**. Oral communication is more difficult than written language and visual images for audiences to process and understand. Practice pausing. Don't be afraid of silence. Focus on communicating with the audience. By looking for feedback from the audience, you will be able to pace yourself appropriately.

- **Maintain genuine eye contact**. Treat the audience as individuals, not as a mass of people. Look at individual faces.

- **Speak in a genuine, relaxed, conversational tone**. Don't act or stiffen up. Just be yourself.

- **Communicate**. Focus on conveying your message, not "getting through" the speech. Focus on communicating with the audience, not speaking at or to it.

- **Use strategic pauses**. Pause briefly before proceeding to the next major point, before

STEPS IN PREPARING AN EXTEMPORANEOUS SPEECH. For practice working on and presenting speeches, see the Integrating the Language Arts activities on pages 230, 308, and 808.

direct quotations, and to allow important or more complex bits of information to sink in.

- **Remain confident and composed.** Remember that listeners are generally "for you" while you are speaking, and signs of nervousness are usually undetectable. To overcome initial nervousness, take two or three deep breaths as you are stepping up to speak.

4.19 Oral Interpretation

Oral interpretation is the process of presenting a dramatic reading of a literary work or group of works. The presentation should be sufficiently dramatic to convey to the audience a sense of the particular qualities of the work. Here are the steps you need to follow to prepare and present an oral interpretation:

1. **Choose a cutting.** The cutting may be a single piece; a selection from a single piece; or several short, related pieces on a single topic or theme.

2. **Write the introduction and any necessary transitions.** The introduction should mention the name of each piece, the author, and, if appropriate, the translator. It should also present the overall topic or theme of the interpretation. Transitions should introduce and connect the parts of the interpretation.

3. **Rehearse, using appropriate variations in volume, pitch, pace, stress, tone, gestures, facial expressions, and body language.** If your cutting contains different voices (a narrator's voice and characters' voices, for example), distinguish them. Try to make your verbal and nonverbal expression mirror what the piece is saying. However, avoid movement—that's for drama. Practice in front of an audience or mirror or use a video camera or tape recorder.

4. **Present your oral interpretation.** Before actually presenting your interpretation, relax and adopt a confident attitude. If you begin to feel stage fright, try to concentrate on the work you are presenting and the audience, not on yourself.

INTERPRETING POETRY. Here are some additional considerations as you prepare to interpret a poem. The way you prepare your interpretation of a

poem will depend on whether the poem you have chosen is a lyric poem, a narrative poem, or a dramatic poem.

- A **lyric poem** has a single speaker who reports his or her own emotions.
- A **narrative poem** tells a story. Usually a narrative poem has lines belonging to narrator, or person who is telling the story. The narrator may or may not take part in the action.
- A **dramatic poem** contains characters who speak. A dramatic poem may be a lyric, in which characters simply report emotions, or a narrative, which tells a story. A dramatic monologue presents a single speaker at a moment of crisis or self-revelation and may be either lyric or narrative.

Before attempting to dramatize any poem, read through the poem carefully several times. Make sure that you understand it well. To check your understanding, try to paraphrase the poem, or restate its ideas, line by line, in your own words.

ANALYZING THE SPEAKER OF A LYRIC POEM. When dramatizing a lyric or dramatic poem, think about the speaker of the poem. Ask yourself:

- Who is the speaker?
- How old is the speaker?
- Is the speaker male or female?
- What is the situation in which the speaker finds himself or herself?
- What does the speaker think about his or her situation?
- What values, opinions, beliefs, wishes, or needs does the speaker have?
- Is the speaker fully aware of the implications of what he or she is saying, or does the reader know more than the speaker?

Try to form a clear image of the speaker in your mind. Think about how such a person might sound, feeling and thinking as he or she does.

ANALYZING THE NARRATOR AND CHARACTERS OF A NARRATIVE OR DRAMATIC POEM. When analyzing a narrative or dramatic poem, ask about the narrator and the characters the same questions that you would ask about the speaker of a lyric poem. How are the narrator and the characters related to one another? In what ways are they different? Is there anything that the narrator understands that one or more of the characters do not?

List the narrator and each of the characters in the poem. After each, list his or her characteristics. Then try to form a clear image of each in your mind. Again, think about how each might sound, feeling and thinking as he or she does. If the poem is narrative, think of how each character reacts to the events in the story that the poem tells.

USING VERBAL AND NONVERBAL COMMUNICATION TO INTERPRET THE POEM. After analyzing the speaker (in a lyric poem) or the narrator and characters (in a narrative or dramatic poem), make a copy of the poem and mark it to show

- the different voices you will use when reading
- the emotions that you will express
- places to increase or decrease your pace
- places to raise or lower your volume
- gestures and facial expressions to use to communicate emotions

MEMORIZING A POEM. To memorize a poem, work line by line. Look at one line. Look away and repeat it. Then check to see that you got it right. Once you get that line right, add a second line. Look away and repeat both lines. Then check them. Continue in this manner until the entire poem is memorized. You may wish to have someone else look at a copy of the poem while you recite it out loud. This second person can prompt you when you forget a line. Memorize the poem thoroughly before you begin working on the qualities of your reading. If you have not thoroughly memorized the lines, you will not be able to concentrate on how you sound.

4.20 Telling a Story

A **story** or **narrative** is a series of events linked together in some meaningful fashion. We use narratives constantly in our daily lives: to make a journal entry, to tell a joke, to report a news story, to recount an historical event, to record a laboratory experiment, and so on. When creating a narrative, consider all of the following elements:

- **Decide on your purpose.** Every story has a point or purpose. It may be simply to entertain or to share a personal experience, but it may have a moral or lesson. Your purpose in telling a story will shape many other parts of the narrative, so it is important to know your purpose before you construct your narrative.

- **Select a focus.** The focus for your narrative will depend largely on your purpose in telling it. For example, if you were telling the story of Abraham Lincoln's life, and your purpose was to show how someone could rise from humble roots to a position of greatness, you would probably choose a broad focus for the story. You might begin with Lincoln's birth in a Kentucky log cabin and end with his eventual rise to the position of president of the United States and his many accomplishments in office. If your purpose was to show that perseverance is an important virtue, you might choose a narrower focus. Your story could ignore Lincoln's early life and instead focus on his long political career and his many defeats on the way to the presidency.

- **Choose your point of view.** The storyteller or narrator determines the point of view from which the story will be told. You can choose to speak in the first person, either as a direct participant in the events or as an observer (real or imagined) who witnessed the events first hand. You can also use the third-person voice to achieve greater objectivity. Once again, your purpose in telling the story may affect your decision about what point of view you choose.

- **Determine sequence of events.** The sequence of events refers to the order in which they are presented. Although it might seem obvious that stories should "begin at the beginning," this is not always the best approach. Some narratives begin with the turning point of the story to create a sense of drama and capture the listener's interest. Others begin at the end of the story and present the events leading up to this point in hindsight. Wherever you choose to begin the story, your narrative should present events in a logical fashion and establish a clear sense of direction for your listeners.

- **Determine duration of events.** Duration refers to how long something lasts. Everyone has experienced an event that seemed to last for hours, when in reality it only took minutes to

SPEAKING AND LISTENING RESOURCE

TELLING A STORY. Storytelling activities are found in the Integrating the Language Arts activities on pages 9, 31, and 439.

occur. A good storyteller can likewise manipulate the duration of events in order to affect the way listeners experience them.

- **Select details carefully**. Make them consistent with your focus and make sure they are necessary to your purpose. A well-constructed story should flow smoothly, and should not get bogged down by irrelevant or unnecessary detail. Details can also establish the tone and style of the story and affect how listeners react to the events being described.

- **Choose characters**. All stories include characters, who need to be developed so that they become real for listeners. Try to provide your listeners with vivid, concrete descriptions of the mental and physical qualities of important characters in the story. Remember that listeners need to understand and relate to the characters in order to appreciate their behavior.

- **Create dialogue**. Although it is possible to tell a story in which the characters do not speak directly, conversation and dialogue help to add life to a story. As with detail, dialogue should be used carefully. It is important that dialogue sound authentic, relate to the main action of the story, and advance the narrative. When telling a story, you might choose to enact the characters by creating an individual voice for each one.

4.21 Participating in a Debate

A **debate** is a contest in which two people or groups of people defend opposite sides of a proposition in an attempt to convince a judge or audience to agree with their views. **Propositions** are statements of fact, value, or policy that usually begin with the word *resolved*. The following are examples of typical propositions for debate:

RESOLVED	That lie detector tests are inaccurate. (proposition of fact)
RESOLVED	That imagination is more important than knowledge. (proposition of value
RESOLVED	That Congress should prohibit the sale of handguns to private citizens. (proposition of policy)

The two sides in a debate are usually called the affirmative and the negative. The **affirmative**

takes the "pro" side of the debate and argues in favor of the proposition, while the **negative** takes the "con" side and argues against the proposition. Using a single proposition to focus the debate ensures that the two sides argue or clash over a common topic. This allows the participants in the debate to develop their logic and ability to argue their positions persuasively.

Sometimes you may find that you are defending a side of a proposition that you do not personally agree with. For example, you may be asked to defend gun control in class even though you believe that the Second Amendment to the Constitution prohibits regulations on the sale of guns. Although some people may find this distasteful, there is good reason to play the "devil's advocate." First, defending a position you do not believe in will allow you to better understand the position of those who disagree with you. Although you may not change your stance, you may come to appreciate why others see the issue differently. Second, in a society based on the free and open exchange of ideas, debate is a fundamental method for arriving at just and reasonable decisions. Every idea deserves consideration, even if it is ultimately rejected.

Typically, both sides in a debate are allowed an equal amount of time to prepare for the debate and to state their case for or against the proposition. To ensure fairness, the affirmative and negative teams take turns presenting speeches. There are two basic types of speeches: **constructive speeches** in which each side states its case for or against the proposition, and **rebuttal speeches** in which each side refutes or attacks its opponent's arguments, while defending its own case. Sometimes debaters are allowed to cross-examine or ask questions of their opponents during the debate. A typical debate might be organized as follows:

AFFIRMATIVE CONSTRUCTIVE	7 minutes
Cross-Examination by Negative	2 minutes
Negative Constructive	7 minutes
Cross-Examination by Affirmative	2 minutes
Affirmative Rebuttal	3 minutes
Negative Rebuttal	5 minutes
Affirmative Rebuttal	2 minutes

PARTICIPATING IN A DEBATE. For practice debating, see Integrating the Language Arts activities on pages 344 and 498.

In addition, each side might be granted 4 or 5 minutes of preparation time during the debate to prepare its upcoming speeches. Preparation time may only be used between speeches.

Once the debate is finished, the audience or judge is asked to consider the arguments that have been made and to vote for which side made the more persuasive case. Ideally, judges or audience members will try to be objective and make their decision based not on their personal views of the issue, but rather based on the arguments made by the debaters in the contest.

SUGGESTIONS FOR PARTICIPATING IN A DEBATE

- **Be prepared.** In a debate, it will never be possible to anticipate all the arguments your opponent might make. However, by conducting careful and through research on both sides of the issue, you should be able to prepare for the most likely arguments you will encounter. You can prepare briefs or notes on particular issues in advance of the debate to save yourself preparation time during the debate.

- **Be organized.** Because a debate involves several speeches that concern the same basic arguments or issues, it is important that you remain organized during the debate. When attacking or refuting an opponent's argument, or when advancing or defending your own argument, be sure to follow a logical organizational pattern to avoid confusing the audience or the other team.

- **Take notes** by turning a long sheet of paper sideways. Draw one column for each speaker, taking notes on each speech going down one column, and recording notes about a particular argument or issue across the page as it is discussed in each successive speech.

- **Be audience-centered.** In the argument with your opponent it is easy to forget the goal of the debate: to persuade your audience that your case is correct.

- **Prepare in advance** for the most likely arguments your opponents will raise. Use time sparingly to organize your materials and think of responses to unanticipated arguments. Save time for the end of the debate, during rebuttal speeches, when it will be more valuable.

4.22 Preparing a Multimedia Presentation

Whether you use a simple overhead projector and transparencies or a PowerPoint presentation that involves graphics, video, and sound, multimedia technology can add an important visual element to a presentation. Consider the following guidelines to create a multimedia presentation:

- **Ensure that audio-visual elements enhance understanding.** The multimedia elements should add to the verbal elements, not distract from them. Be sure the content of the presentation is understandable, and that the amount of information—both verbal and visual—will not overwhelm audience members.

- **Make sure the presentation is clearly audible and visible.** Video clips or graphics may appear blurry on a projection screen, or may not be visible to audience members in the back or on the sides of the room. Audio clips may sound muffled or may echo in a larger room or a room with different acoustics. When creating a multimedia presentation, be sure the presentation can be easily heard from all parts of the room.

- **Become familiar with the equipment.** Well before the presentation, be sure you know how to operate the equipment you will need, that you know how to troubleshoot if the equipment malfunctions, and that the equipment you will use during the presentation is the same as that which you practiced with.

- **Be sure the room can accommodate your needs.** Once you know where you will make your presentation, be sure the necessary electrical outlets and extension cords are available, that lights can be dimmed or turned off as needed, that the room can accommodate the equipment you will use, and so forth.

- **Rehearse with the equipment.** Make sure that you can operate the equipment while speaking at the same time. Be sure that the multimedia elements are coordinated with other parts of your presentation. If you will need to turn the lights off in the room, make sure you can operate the equipment in the dark and can still see your note cards.

PREPARING A MULTIMEDIA PRESENTATION. Students are asked to create a multimedia presentation in the Integrating the Language Arts activity on page 308.

STUDY AND RESEARCH
Resource

THINKING SKILLS

Everyone thinks, but not everyone realizes that thinking—like hitting a baseball or playing the piano—is a skill that you can improve by learning and practicing. This section gives you some tips that can greatly improve your ability to make decisions, to solve problems, and to learn and think critically.

5.1 Making Decisions and Solving Problems

MAKING DECISIONS. When you have a decision to make, the best approach is to weigh the alternatives available to you. You can do this by making a **criteria analysis chart**. To make such a chart, list the results that you want to achieve down the left side of the chart. List your choices across the top of the chart. Then assign points from 1 to 5 to each choice, with 1 being the lowest and 5 being the highest. Add up the points for each choice to see which one is best.

CRITERIA ANALYSIS CHART		
Purchase of Portable Radio	**Brand A**	**Brand B**
1. Low cost	2	3
2. Good warranty	2	1
3. Attractive design	3	1
4. Many features	2	3
Total	**9**	**8**

When making a decision, you often must weigh several factors. You can compare your options by making a **pro and con** chart on paper. First make a list of all your options. For each option list the reasons for choosing it (the pros) and the reasons for not choosing it (the cons). Then compare the lists.

PROS AND CONS		
Painting Yearbook Illustration or Drawing It in Pencil		
	Painting	**Drawing in Pencil**
Pros	colorful	easier less expensive
Cons	more expensive more difficult	not colorful

SOLVING PROBLEMS. There are many ways to solve problems. To solve a complex problem, you will probably need to use more than one strategy. Here are two approaches you can try:

• **Trial and error**. Sometimes when you have to solve a problem, you just make a guess and see if it works. In a **trial-and-error approach**, you try one possible solution and if it doesn't work you try another. If you don't know how to solve a particular math problem, you could guess the answer, plug it back into the problem, and then revise your answer as necessary.

Brainstorm a list of possible solutions.

↓

Try one.

↓

Did it work?

↙ Yes → Done   ↘ No →

• **Divide and conquer**. Another strategy for problem solving is to divide the problem into parts and then solve each part one at a time in a logical sequence. Here is an example:

PROBLEM
A friend is coming to stay at your house for a few days and you need to prepare a room for him.

SOLUTION
Break down the job into small, manageable goals:

STRATEGY
(1) Move desk and computer from small downstairs room.
(2) Remove storage boxes from closet and put in basement.
(3) Clean the room.
(4) Put cot in room and make bed.

5.2 Distinguishing Fact from Opinion

What is the difference between the following statements?

The language with the greatest number of speakers, over nine hundred million, is Mandarin Chinese.

Mandarin Chinese is the greatest language in the world.

The first statement expresses a **fact**. You can prove this fact by looking in a reference book. The second statement expresses an **opinion**. This statement can be supported but not proved.

A fact is a statement that, at least in principle, could be proved by direct observation. Every statement of fact is either true or false. The following statement is an example of a fact:

Edgar Allan Poe wrote "The Pit and the Pendulum." (This statement can be proved by getting a published copy of the story to see who the author is.)

An opinion is a statement that expresses not a fact about the world, but rather an attitude or desire. Three common types of opinions are value statements, policy statements, and certain types of predictions.

A **value statement** expresses an attitude toward something. Such statements often include judgment words such as the following:

attractive	honest	ugly
awesome	junk	unattractive
beautiful	kind	valuable
cheap	mean	wonderful
dishonest	nice	worthless
excellent	petty	worthwhile
good	treasure	

Ancient Greece produced some <u>beautiful</u> and <u>inspiring</u> myths.
Those violent "action films" are just <u>awful</u>.

A **policy statement** tells not what is, but what someone believes should be. Such statements usually include words such as *should, should not, ought to, ought not to, must,* or *must not.* Examples of policy statements include the following:

The president <u>should be</u> reelected.
You <u>must not</u> play your radio during study hall.

Closely related to policy statements are **requests** and **commands**:

Reelect the president.
Do not play your radio during study hall.

A **prediction** makes a statement about the future. Because the future is unpredictable, most predictions can be considered opinions:

People will live longer in the future.
Tomorrow will be partly cloudy.

EVALUATING FACTS AND OPINIONS. When evaluating a fact, ask yourself whether it can be proved

STUDY AND RESEARCH RESOURCE

INTERNET RESOURCES

You can now access **Merriam-Webster Online** at http://www.m-w.com/. Webster's online site is an excellent reference for information about the English language, including basic word definitions, pronunciation, etymology, spelling, and usage. It also includes a Word of the Day feature and transcripts of their *Word for the Wise* radio program.

The **American Library Association** home page can be accessed at http://www.ala.org/. This site also hosts the online version of *American Libraries: The Magazine of the American Library Association,* and the digital counterpart of the American Library Association's *Booklist* magazine. For more than ninety years, *Booklist* has provided reviews of the latest books and (more recently) electronic media.

School Library Journal Online, the web companion to *School Library Journal,* one of the top print resources for librarians who work with children and young adults, is available at http://www.slj.com/.

DISTINGUISHING FACT FROM OPINION. Encourage students to distinguish fact from opinion in About the Author sections. Students might make a column listing facts and another column listing opinions. Then ask students to assess the section as being objective or subjective in its approach. Students will find that there are more facts than opinions in the About the Author sections.

through direct observation or by checking a reliable source such as a reference work or an unbiased expert. An opinion is as good as the facts that support it. The opinion that Mandarin Chinese is the greatest language in the world is supported by such facts as the number of speakers that it has. However, others might argue that English is the greater language because it is spoken more widely around the globe. Of course, no list of facts would conclusively prove or disprove the opinion.

When you write and speak, express opinions sparingly. Usually, you can make a stronger case by substituting related facts for opinions. For example, instead of saying, "This was a wonderful day," you could say something like, "Today the sun was shining, it was 74 degrees outside, and I got an *A* on my math test. That's what made it a great day." When you express an opinion, especially in writing, include facts to back up or support that opinion.

When reading or listening, be critical about the statements that you encounter. Ask yourself, "Is this a fact or an opinion?" If it is a statement of fact, consider whether it can be proved or seems likely. If it is an opinion, consider whether it is supported by facts.

5.3 Avoiding False Arguments and Propaganda

Another very important thinking skill is learning to use good logic. Life is a process of trying to learn what is true and then to live according to what you believe to be true. Not only do you need good facts, but you also need to know how to put those facts together to come up with the right conclusions. Learning how to think clearly will enable you to avoid errors in logic and to arrive at true conclusions. It will also help you to recognize the faulty thinking of others (especially advertisers) who might be trying to persuade you of something. The intentional use of false arguments to persuade others is called **propaganda**. Here are some of the many faulty arguments of which you should be aware.

GLITTERING GENERALITIES AND "SPIN." Glittering **generalities** are statements given to make

something sound more appealing. Such statements can be hard to prove, as they appeal to the emotions.

EXAMPLE

These trading cards are the best ever in this limited-time collection!

ANALYSIS

Nothing in this statement tells the listener why the trading cards are the best ever. Adding "limited-time collection" to the statement vaguely implies that the trading cards will be available for only a short while, and that the listener should buy them quickly before they are unavailable.

Spin is a technique used to slant public perception of the news. Public relations firms and advertisers use this technique to create a favorable perception of a product or organization. Unlike more obvious forms of advertising, spin is hard to recognize because it can be invisible. It is important to know how to recognize such manipulative and misleading statements.

EXAMPLE

The accident was a minor incident because only twenty-five people were injured.

ANALYSIS

The fact is that twenty-five people were injured. This does not make it a minor incident; someone is merely interpreting the accident as minor.

STEREOTYPES. An overgeneralization about a group of people is known as a **stereotype**. Stereotypes are one of the most dangerous of all overgeneralizations. Remember that the differences among people within a single race or ethnic background are greater than the average differences between races or ethnic groups as a whole. Stereotyping is always based on lack of knowledge or experience. It is the basis of prejudice and is unacceptable in a civilized society.

UNSOUND OPINIONS. A fact is a statement that can be proved. An opinion is a statement that cannot be proved. An opinion is someone's personal idea of what is right and may or may not be true. A sound opinion is one that can be supported by facts. An **unsound opinion** is one that cannot be supported by facts. Always be sure that you make

AVOIDING FALSE ARGUMENTS AND PROPAGANDA. Students are asked to avoid false arguments and propaganda in the Unit 6 Guided Writing lesson on page 511.

a clear distinction between facts and opinions and that you can back up your opinions with facts.

FACT

Miss Rivers won this year's award for excellence in teaching.

OPINION

Miss Rivers is the best teacher at Jordan High School.

ANALYSIS

The statement that "Miss Rivers is the best teacher at Jordan High School" is someone's personal feeling about her. However, it is probably a sound opinion because it is backed up by the fact that she received the award for excellence in teaching.

CIRCULAR REASONING. Circular reasoning is the error of trying to support an opinion by restating it in different words. You can avoid circular reasoning by always backing up your opinions with facts.

EXAMPLE

That adventure book was exciting because it was full of action.

ANALYSIS

The "reason" the speaker gives for saying that the book was exciting is really just another way of saying it was exciting. He or she should mention some specific examples to show what makes the story exciting.

LOADED WORDS. In trying to argue for or against something, people will often use **loaded words**, or words that stir up strong feelings, whether positive or negative. Be careful not to let your feelings interfere with your understanding of the facts.

EXAMPLE

Representative Philbert is a lazy, good-for-nothing imbecile.

ANALYSIS

This statement, an emotional attack on the representative uses loaded words that will stir up feelings against him. It is not a reasonable evaluation of his policies or actions in office.

BANDWAGON APPEAL. Bandwagon appeal plays to your desire to be part of the crowd—to be like everyone else and to do what everyone else is doing. Beware of advertisements or arguments that try to get you to think or act like everyone else. Just because "everybody" believes or does something does not make it good or right for you.

EXAMPLE

Those who want to be cool wear Star jeans.

ANALYSIS

This statement suggests that you aren't really part of the "in" crowd unless you wear this brand of jeans. It does not prove, or even say, anything about the quality of the clothing.

5.4 Classifying

One of the many higher-level thinking skills you can develop is the ability to classify. To **classify** is to put into classes or categories. Items in the same category should share one or more characteristics. For example, whales are classified by their method of eating as baleen or toothed whales. The key step in classifying is choosing categories that fit your purpose. Make sure you clearly define your categories.

5.5 Generalizing

To **generalize** is to make a broad statement based on one or more particular observations. For example, suppose that you observe that several cats like to stare through windows. You might generalize, based on this discovery, that "cats like to stare through windows." Such generalizations are also called **inferences**. People have learned most of what they know about the world by making generalizations based on their experiences.

Generalizing is therefore an extremely important thinking tool. Unfortunately, it is not a perfect one. Generalizations can be proved false by only one exception. Since generalizations can be proved false by a new experience, avoid making generalizations based on too little evidence. Keep an open mind and be willing to revise your ideas about the world.

5.6 Making Inferences, Predictions, and Hypotheses

From careful observation, it is possible to make generalizations, or **inferences**, about the world around us. From there it is possible to **predict** what will happen and to form hypotheses. A **hypothesis** is an educated guess about a cause or an effect. A prediction based on a theory is a hypothesis. A possible explanation for an observed event is also a hypothesis. A hypothesis always needs to be tested against experience. You can test hypotheses the following ways:

- Conduct actual experiments to see if your prediction will occur.
- Examine many relevant examples.
- Conduct a "thought experiment" by asking "What if" questions. (See 2.15, "Imagining: Asking 'What If' Questions.")

Notice that a hypothesis can be disproved by only one exception. However, a hypothesis cannot be proved merely by gathering examples. Theories and hypotheses can change if a discovery shows them to be inadequate.

5.7 Deductive versus Inductive Reasoning

Deduction and induction are two types of logical reasoning. **Deductive reasoning** starts with a generalization to make a statement or statements about something specific. **Inductive reasoning** examines specific facts or instances to make a generalization.

DEDUCTIVE

All whales live in the sea. **(general)**
The beluga whale must live in the sea. **(specific)**

All students have signed the school policy statement. **(general)**
Tom is a student at the school. Therefore, he has signed the policy statement. **(specific)**

INDUCTIVE

The blue whale, beluga, and orca live in the sea. **(specific)**
Therefore, all whales live in the sea. **(general)**

More than 100 students have signed the school policy statement. **(specific)**

Therefore, all students have signed the policy statement. **(general)**

Note that with inductive reasoning, only one specific example is needed to prove the generalization false. See the Language Arts Survey 5.5, "Generalizing."

5.8 Estimating and Quantifying

To support an argument, you need to provide facts, and often facts are strengthened by numbers or quantities. If you claim, for instance, that too many people are without health insurance, you should **quantify** your claim by stating how many. The numbers you need may be available in reference works. If not, you might be able to **estimate**, or find the approximate quantity. Sometimes you will have only enough knowledge to estimate a range within which the actual number actually falls. If you need to estimate, always make clear that you are doing so.

QUANTIFYING

The science fair had 314 registered participants.

ESTIMATING

The science fair was attended by about 300 students and their parents.

5.9 Analyzing and Synthesizing

When you **analyze** something, you break it down into parts and then think about how the parts are related to each other and to the whole. For example, you might analyze a painting by describing its composition, shapes, lines, colors, and subject. You might analyze a short story by describing its conflict, plot, characters, setting, and theme. You might analyze a movie by describing its acting, directing, writing, settings, and costumes.

When you **synthesize** something, you bring everything that you were considering together into a whole.

5.10 Comparing and Contrasting

Comparing and contrasting are closely related processes. When you **compare** one thing to another, you describe similarities between the two things. When you **contrast** two things, you describe their differences.

To compare and contrast, begin by listing the features of each subject. Then go down both lists and check whether each feature is shared or not. You can also show similarities and differences in a Venn diagram. For more information, see the Language Arts Survey 2.16, "Completing Venn Diagrams," and 2.27, "Choosing a Method of Organization: Comparison and Contrast Order."

5.11 Evaluating

When you evaluate, you make a judgment about something. You may be asked to compare two things to determine which is more valuable or effective. Evaluate questions use such words as *evaluate, judge, justify, critique, determine whether, decide the effectiveness of,* and *appraise.*

> Determine whether Hawthorne believably portrays Beatrice in "Rappaccini's Daughter," using evidence from the text to support your response.

5.12 Extending

When you **extend** your knowledge, you connect one experience to another. In the study of literature, you extend your knowledge by making connections between two pieces of literature, between the literary work and your own experience, or between a literary work and a cultural or current event. Extend questions use such words as *extend your knowledge, connect, relate,* and *apply.*

> In popular culture and throughout history, people have been accused of being poisonous, like Dr. Rappaccini. Name examples of such people and the ways they have influenced the world around them. Then name people who have countered them.

5.13 Perspective, Empathy, and Self-Understanding

When you are asked to use perspective, empathy, and self-understanding to answer a question, you are exercising an important ability to connect the experience of one person or group to your own. Such thinking allows you to see multiple perspectives, generate alternative viewpoints, and understand another person's feelings and

worldview. These questions also allow you to understand your own perspective.

> Why do you think Susan B. Anthony was willing to be arrested for her convictions? How would you react if you lost your rights as a citizen? Would you be willing to risk arrest to fight for your rights, as Susan B. Anthony did? Why, or why not?

STUDY SKILLS

5.14 Developing Good Study Habits

Success in a future career depends largely on success in school. No matter what your experience in school so far, you can improve your performance enormously by developing good study habits. Doing so will make learning easier and more enjoyable.

Find a place to work. Homework is best done in a special study area. Follow these guidelines for picking an appropriate place to study:

- Choose a quiet location, away from distractions such as conversation, television, or loud music.

- Choose a place that is well lit and comfortable. Adequate lighting will help you to avoid eyestrain and headaches.

- Choose a study area that is available at regular times. Set aside a specific time each day for study.

- Have all the tools that you will need, such as paper, pencils, textbooks, handouts, and reference works, ready and at hand.

Make a study plan. Many of your assignments will be due on the following day. Others will be long-term projects. At the end of each school day, make a habit of looking over your assignment notebook. Decide what tasks you need to complete for the following day. Break down longer assignments into specific steps that need to be completed by specific times. Record all of these assignments on a calendar or study plan.

5.15 Keeping an Assignment Notebook

Keeping track of assignments in your head can be dangerous because of the possibility of forgetting important details. Instead, write down all your assignments in an assignment notebook. For each assignment, record:

- the name of the subject
- details of the assignment, including what, precisely, you need to do
- the date of the assignment
- the date when the assignment is due

5.16 Understanding the Assignment

Understanding an assignment depends on your ability to follow directions.

FOLLOWING SPOKEN DIRECTIONS. Often teachers give assignments orally. When listening to spoken assignments,

- Listen carefully. Write down the directions as you hear them.
- Notice what steps are involved in the assignment. Also notice the order of these steps.
- Listen for the key word in each step. A key word is one that tells you what to do. Examples are *read, write, organize,* and *memorize.*
- If you do not understand the directions, ask your teacher to explain them.

FOLLOWING WRITTEN DIRECTIONS. Directions for tests usually are written down. Assignment directions also sometimes appear in written form on the board, overhead transparencies, or handouts. When reading written directions,

- Read all the directions completely before you begin the assignment.
- Ask questions to clarify any points not covered in the directions.
- Divide the assignment into steps. Put these steps in a logical order.
- Decide what materials you will need, and assemble them before you begin.
- Reread each step before you actually do it.

5.17 Taking Notes, Outlining, and Summarizing Information

When **taking notes** in class or while conducting your own research, you may find it helpful to use a

rough outline, or modified outline, form. Write main ideas, capitalizing the first letter of the first word and all proper nouns and proper adjectives. Beneath the main ideas, write related subordinate ideas, preceded by dashes.

Major Cultures in N. Amer., 1492
  —Eastern woodland (incl. Iroquois & Algonquians)
  —Southeastern (incl. Cherokee & Chicasaw)
  —Plains (incl. Dakota, Pawnee, & Kiowa)
  —Southwestern (incl. Navajo, Hopi, & Apache)
  —Great Basin (incl. Ute & Paiute)
  —Plateau (incl. Nez Perce & Yakima)
  —Northwestern (incl. Chinook & Yurok)
  —California (incl. Shasta, Pomo, & Chumash)

Origins
  —Came to Amer. by land bridge across Bering Strait
  — ~ 35,000 bc
  —May have followed herds, mammoths, musk oxen, etc.

To review the material, you might find it helpful to read over your notes and outline, and then to **summarize** what you have learned. Writing a summary of the material is more powerful than thinking through your summary or even saying it out loud. The act of writing reinforces your memory of what you have learned.

RESEARCH SKILLS

Learning is a lifelong process, one that extends far beyond school. Both in school and on your own, it is important to remember that your learning and growth are up to you. One good way to become an independent lifelong learner is to master research skills. Research is the process of gathering ideas and information. One of the best resources for research is the library.

5.18 How Library Materials Are Organized

Each book in a library is assigned a unique number, called a **call number**. The call number is printed on the **spine** (edge) of each book. The numbers serve to classify books as well as to help the library keep track of them.

Libraries commonly use one of two systems for classifying books. Most school and public libraries use the **Dewey Decimal System.** Most college libraries use the **Library of Congress Classification System** (known as the LC system).

5.19 How to Locate Library Materials

If you know the call number of a book or the subject classification number you want, you can usually go to the bookshelves, or stacks, to obtain the book. Use the signs at the ends of the rows to locate the section you need. Then find the

THE LIBRARY OF CONGRESS SYSTEM

Call Letters	Subjects
A	Reference and General Works
B–BJ	Philosophy, Psychology
BK–BX	Religion
C–DF	History
G	Geography, Autobiography, Recreation
H	Social Sciences
J	Political Science
K	Law
L	Education
M	Music
N	Fine Arts
P	Language, Literature
Q	Science, Mathematics
R	Medicine
S	Agriculture
T	Technology
U	Military Science
V	Naval Science
Z	Bibliography, Library Science

THE DEWEY DECIMAL SYSTEM

Call Numbers	Subjects
000–099	Reference and General Works
100–199	Philosophy, Psychology
200–299	Religion
300–399	Social Studies
400–499	Language
500–599	Science, Mathematics
600–699	Technology
700–799	Arts
800–899	Literature
900–999	History, Geography, Biography[1]

1. Biographies (920s) are arranged alphabetically by the name of the person whose life is treated in each biography.

INTERNET RESOURCES

Let your fingers do the walking and visit the **Internet Public Library** at http://www.ipl.org/. The Internet Public Library is the first public library of the Internet. This site provides library services to the Internet community by finding, evaluating, selecting, organizing, describing, and creating quality information resources; teaches what librarians have to contribute in a digital environment; and promotes the importance of libraries.

THE DEWEY DECIMAL SYSTEM. Have students locate a book for each subject and write down its title and call number.

particular shelf that contains call numbers close to yours.

Library collections include many other types of publications besides books, such as magazines, newspapers, audio and video recordings, and government documents. Ask a librarian to tell you where to find the materials you need.

To find the call numbers of books that will help you with your research, use the library's catalog. The catalog lists all the books in the library (or a group of libraries if it is part of a larger system).

COMPUTERIZED CATALOGS. Many libraries today use computerized catalogs. Systems differ from library to library, but most involve using a computer terminal to search through the library's collection. You can usually search by author, title, subject, or key word. If your library has a computerized catalog, you will need to learn how to use your library's particular system. A librarian can help you to master the system. Here is a sample book entry screen from a computerized catalog.

Author	Wallace, David Rains, 1945-
Title	The Quetzal and the Macaw: The story of Costa Rica's National Parks
Publication info.	Sierra Club Books, 1992
No. of pages/size	xvi, 222p. : maps : 24 cm.
ISBN	ISBN 0-87156-585-4
Subjects	National Parks and reserves—Costa Rica—History
	Costa Rica. Servicio de Parques Nacionales—History
	Nature conservation—Costa Rica—History
Dewey call number	333.78

COMPUTERIZED CATALOG SEARCHES

Search By	Example	Hints
Author	gould, stephen j	Type last name first. Type as much of the name as you know.
Title	mismeasure of man	Omit articles such as *a, an,* or *the* at the beginning of titles.
Subject	intelligence tests; ability-testing	Use the list of subjects provided by the library.
Key words	darwin; intelligence; craniology	Use related topics if you can't find anything in your subject.

CARD CATALOGS. Like a computerized catalog, a card catalog contains basic information about each book in the library. In a card catalog the information is typed on paper cards, which are arranged alphabetically in drawers. For each book there is a title card, one author card for each author, and at least one subject card. All of these cards show the book's title, author, and call number, so you can search for a book by title, author, or subject. The following illustration shows a typical title card.

A TITLE CARD

333.78　The Quetzal and the Macaw : the story of
　　　　Costa Rica's national parks.
　　　　Wallace, David Rains, 1945–
　　　　The Quetzal and the Macaw : the story of
　　　　Costa Rica's national parks.—San
　　　　Francisco: Sierra Club Books, 1992
　　　　xvi, 222 p. : maps : 24 cm.
　　　　1. National parks and reserves—Costa Rica—
　　　　History. 2. Costa Rica. Servicio de
　　　　Parques nacionales—History. 3. Nature
　　　　conservation—Costa Rica—History. I. Title.
　　　　ISBN 0-394-57456-7

When you find the entries for the books you want, write down the call number of each book and then go to the shelves. If you cannot find a particular book you need in the catalog, ask the librarian if your library can request books from another library through an interlibrary loan.

INTERLIBRARY LOANS. Many libraries are part of larger library networks. In these libraries, the computerized catalog covers the collections of several libraries. If you want a book from a different library, you will need to request the book at the library's request desk or by using its computer. Ask your librarian to help you if you have questions. He or she will be able to tell you when the book will be shipped to your library.

5.20 Using Reference Works

Most libraries have an assortment of reference works in which knowledge is collected and organized so that you can find it easily. Usually, reference works cannot be checked out of the library.

5.21 TYPES OF DICTIONARIES. You will find many types of dictionaries in the library reference section. The most common is a dictionary of the English language. Examples include the *American Heritage Dictionary*, *Webster's New World Dictionary*, and the multi-volume *Oxford English Dictionary*. Other word dictionaries focus on slang, abbreviations and acronyms, English/foreign language translation, and spelling. Biographical, historical, scientific, and world language dictionaries are also some of the works you will find in the reference section.

For more information on using a dictionary to look up specific words in English, see the Language Arts Survey 1.17, "Using a Dictionary."

5.22 USING A THESAURUS. A thesaurus is a reference book that groups synonyms, or words with similar meanings. Suppose that you are writing an essay and have a word that means almost but not quite what you want, or perhaps you find yourself using the same word over and over. A thesaurus can give you fresh and precise words to use. For example, if you look up the word *sing* in a thesaurus, you might find the following synonyms listed:

> **sing** (v.)　carol, chant, croon, hum,
> vocalize, warble, yodel

5.23 USING ALMANACS, YEARBOOKS, AND ATLASES. **Almanacs** and **yearbooks** are published each year. An almanac provides statistics and lists, often related to recent events. In an almanac you can find facts about current events, countries of the world, famous people, sports, entertainment, and many other subjects. An overview of the events of the year can be found in a yearbook.

Some of the more widely used almanacs and yearbooks are *The Guinness Book of World Records;* the *Information Please, Almanac, Atlas, and Yearbook;* the *World Almanac and Book of Facts;* and the *World Book Yearbook of Events.*

An **atlas** is a collection of maps and other geographical information. Some atlases show natural features such as mountains and rivers; others show political features such as countries and cities. If you need to locate a particular feature on a map in an atlas, refer to the gazetteer, an index that lists every item shown on the map.

TITLE CARDS. Have students make a title card for a book they are interested in.

USING AN ALMANAC. You might want to prepare a list of questions that students could find answers for by using an almanac. Have students work with a partner to find answers for the worksheet.

USING REFERENCE WORKS. For activities using various reference works, see the Study and Research activity on page 507 and the Applied English and Study and Research activity on page 823.

USING THE INTERNET. Internet research activities are found in the Integrating the Language Arts activities on pages 22, 61, and 498.

5.24 USING BIOGRAPHICAL REFERENCES, ENCYCLOPEDIAS, AND PERIODICALS. A **biographical reference** contains information on the lives of famous people. Examples include *Who's Who*, the *Dictionary of American Biography*, and *Contemporary Authors*.

Encyclopedias provide a survey of knowledge. General encyclopedias, such as *World Book*, contain information on many different subjects. Specialized encyclopedias, such as the *LaRousse Encyclopedia of Mythology*, contain information on one particular area of knowledge.

The topics in an encyclopedia are treated in articles, which are usually arranged in alphabetical order. If you look up a topic and do not find it, check the index (usually in the last volume). The index will tell you where in the encyclopedia your topic is covered.

A **periodical** is a publication that comes out regularly, usually once a week, once a month, or four times a year. Magazines and newspapers are periodicals. Because they are published frequently and quickly, periodicals are an excellent source for the latest news and information, but they may not be as accurate as some other sources.

5.25 USING INDEXES, APPENDICES, AND GLOSSARIES. An **index** lists in alphabetical order the subjects mentioned in a book or collection of periodicals and pages where these subjects are treated. Indexes help you locate possible sources of information about your topic. An index can be at the back of a book of nonfiction, or it can be a published book itself.

An example of a published index is *The Reader's Guide to Periodic Literature*, a comprehen-sive index to popular magazine and journal articles. Some periodicals, such as the *New York Times* and *National Geographic*, publish their own indexes, listing articles in past issues. Most indexes are published in sequential volumes that are issued yearly or monthly. Indexes are available as bound books, on microfilm, and online on the Internet.

An **appendix** provides additional material, often in chart or table form, at the end of a book or other writing.

A **glossary** lists key words in a book and their definitions.

5.26 Using the Internet

The **Internet** is a vast collection of computer networks that can provide you with a great wealth of information from libraries, government agencies, high schools and universities, non-profit and educational organizations, museums, user groups, and individuals around the world. The Internet provides a valuable way to do research--if you know how to use it. Here are some guidelines.

5.27 BROWSING VERSUS SEARCHING ON THE INTERNET. Browsing means sifting through Internet sites by means of an Internet browser, or software that connects you to the Internet. **Searching** means conducting focused research by using an Internet search engine. By both browsing and searching, you can gain access to the information you want. Browsing allows you to navigate through different sites, either before or after you have conducted a search. Searching allows you to narrow and expand your research in a focused way to find the particular information you need.

Internet Search Engines

www.alltheweb.com
This enormous engine tracks more than 200 million URLs, (Universal Resource Locators, or Internet addresses).

www.altavista.digital.com
This engine claims to index 30 million Web pages.

www.infoseek.com
This search engine also contains a large database and an associated directory, Infoseek Guide.

www.yahoo.com
This popular search service is maintained by online editors who sift through Internet sites and keep only the valuable ones.

5.28 CONDUCTING AN INTERNET SEARCH

• Access a reliable search engine.

• Browse the search engine's links or do a keyword search.

• Use Boolean search strategies (see the Language Arts Survey 5.29) or other specialized search tools to narrow and expand your search as needed.

• Browse the results of your search.

CONDUCTING AN INTERNET SEARCH. Students are encouraged to use the search tips in conducting research in Integrating the Language Arts activities on pages 649 and 773.

- Repeat this process using different search engines until you find what you want.

To keep track of your Internet research, see the Language Arts Survey 5.41, "Documenting and Mapping Internet Research."

5.29 USING BOOLEAN SEARCH STRATEGIES. Boolean logic refers to the logical relationship among search terms. It is named for the mathematician George Boole. To conduct a focused search on the Internet, you should know Boolean operators such as AND, OR, NOT, and NEAR. These operators allow you to limit or expand your research. There are several guides to using Boolean search strategies on the Internet. They can be found by searching with the keyword "Boolean."

Boolean Operators	
" "	Quote marks help limit your search to just the phrase in quotes. "Hitchhiker's Guide to the Galaxy" will find references to that specific book title. Without the quotes, a search engine might list numerous other sites, including those related to hitch-hikers, guide, and galaxy.
AND	This operator lets you join two ideas. "Greece" AND "travel" would provide you with travel information to Greece. The two words by themselves would give you listings too general to be helpful.
OR	This operator gives you sites that carry information about one or the other of two groups. "Rottweilers OR Huskies" will give you sites that include either one of these dog breeds. "Rottweilers AND Huskies" will list only sites that include both dog breeds.
NOT	This command lets you eliminate certain sites. "American food NOT pizza" will find sites on American food but exclude sites related to pizza.

5.30 Evaluating Information and Media Sources

To conduct your research efficiently, you need to evaluate your sources and set priorities among them. Ideally, a source will be:

- **Unbiased.** When an author has a personal stake in what people think about a subject, he or she may withhold or distort information. Investigate the author's background to see if she or he is liable to be biased. Using loaded language and overlooking obvious counterarguments are signs of author bias.

- **Authoritative.** An authoritative source is reliable and trustworthy. An author's reputation, especially among others who conduct research in the same field, is a sign of authority. Likewise, periodicals and publishers acquire reputations for responsible or poor editing and research.

- **Timely.** Information about many subjects changes rapidly. An astronomy text published last year may already be out of date. In other fields—for instance, algebra—older texts may be perfectly adequate. Consult with your teacher and your librarian to decide how current your sources must be.

- **Available.** Borrowing through interlibrary loan, tracing a book that is missing, or recalling a book that has been checked out to another person takes time. Make sure to allow enough time for these materials.

- **Appropriate for your level.** Find sources that present useful information that you can understand. Materials written for "young people" may be too simple to be helpful. Books written for experts may presume knowledge that you do not have. Struggling with a difficult text is often worth the effort, but if you do so, monitor your time and stay on schedule.

5.31 HOW TO READ A NEWSPAPER OR NEWSMAGAZINE. Newspapers and news magazines contain an enormous amount of information. Few people who are not professional politicians or news personnel have the time to read all or most of what appears in a newspaper each day. Nonetheless, reading the news is important. Only by doing that can you take

EVALUATING INFORMATION AND MEDIA SOURCES. For practice evaluating media sources, see the Media Literacy activity on page 385.

advantage of democratic freedoms and make informed voting decisions.

An excellent way to approach reading a newspaper is as follows: Skim the headlines and leads for world, national, state, and local news stories. Read any news summaries included in your paper. Then read in depth any stories that seem particularly important or interesting. You may also wish to read the feature or entertainment sections of the newspaper, according to your own interests.

When reading news stories and editorials, make sure to distinguish between facts and opinions. Facts are statements that can be proved by observation or by consulting a reliable and objective source. Opinions are predictions or statements of value or policy. When you encounter opinions in a newspaper, try to determine whether these opinions are sound. Sound opinions are ones supported by facts. For more information on distinguishing between facts and opinions, see the Language Arts Survey 5.2, "Distinguishing Fact from Opinion."

5.32 How to Evaluate a Film. We watch movies for a multitude of reasons, but perhaps the most common is that a movie allows us to escape our own realities for a couple of hours. It lets us visit new places, see and try exciting new things, and experience life in someone else's shoes. A great film gives us insight into the lives of others and so expands our understanding and our sympathies. Some films, however, are created solely for the purpose of making money through exploiting sensational elements or gimmicks. Although you cannot control the types of movies Hollywood decides to make, you can control the types of movies you choose to watch. The following guidelines will enable you to become a more discriminating consumer of films.

- **Plan ahead**. Decide in advance which films you would like to see. Don't settle for just any movie that happens to be playing at your local theater or on television.

- **Listen, watch, and read what the critics have to say.** Take what the critics have to say into consideration to help you decide which movies to see. Once you have seen the movie, decide for

yourself whether you agree or disagree with a particular critic. Consider what elements of the movie you liked or disliked, and what could have been altered to make it better. If, after a while, you find one particular critic with whom you tend to agree on a regular basis, use his or her opinion to help you choose which movies to see.

- **Be a critic yourself**. Be critical of dialogue and story lines. Many films recycle conventional story lines and dialogue. Many contain sensational scenes that provoke audiences but forfeit quality in story line, dialogue, and content. When you see a film, ask yourself questions such as the following:

  - Does each scene move the story forward?

  - Do the characters' actions fit their motives? Is their dialogue believable?

  - Are the themes raised in the film fully developed?

  - What effects do lighting, camera angle, and musical background produce?

- **Be aware of previews and coming attractions**. These are designed with the help of the production company's marketing and sales departments to motivate you to see their film. Previews can make a film seem more humorous, exciting, and powerful than it really is by showing only the best dialogue and action.

- **Try something new!** Try viewing a film that is much different from the type and genre that you usually see. Keep an open mind; you might just surprise yourself and enjoy it.

- **Never substitute**. Never see a film adaptation of a literary work as a substitute for reading the work itself. While seeing such an adaptation can be a good introduction to a literary work, do not rely on it to capture all the richness of the original.

5.33 How to Evaluate Radio and Television. Television and radio are other communication media. You may not be able to respond directly to the broadcaster, but you can still control the broadcast message. Follow the guidelines below to effectively control television output:

- **Plan your television and radio time.** Rather

How to Evaluate a Film. For practice in evaluating films, see the Integrating the Language Arts activities on pages 44 and 977.

than accepting whatever program happens to be on, look at broadcast listings and choose programs that are of interest to you.

- **Be a critic.** Question what you see and hear. What criticisms do you have about a program: its quality, its message, its originality, the depth and reliability of its coverage?

- **Remember that advertisers pay for most broadcast programs.** They also control the content of the programs they sponsor and pay for your attention because they want to sell you something. Listen to and watch these advertisements and programs critically. Read the Language Arts Survey 5.2, "Distinguishing Fact from Opinion," for tips on evaluating information critically.

5.34 HOW TO EVALUATE ADVERTISEMENTS. Advertising messages are everywhere in the media. To sharpen your skills in evaluating them, see the Language Arts Survey 5.2, "Distinguishing Fact from Opinion," and 5.3, "Avoiding False Arguments and Propaganda."

5.35 HOW TO UNDERSTAND INTERNET SITES. Most published print materials have been checked carefully before publication. But anyone can publish something on the Internet—without having to verify facts or guarantee quality. When you use the Internet for research, be careful to evaluate your sources. Here are some guidelines.

Consider the resource's domain name.
Documents that end with .edu and .gov are generally reliable, since they come from educational and governmental organizations. Commercial sites end in .com. They can be reliable, too, but watch for biases that favor the company's product. Sites ending in .org or .net can be trusted if they are from a reliable organization, but watch for special interest group sites that slant or "spin" information to their advantage.

KEY TO INTERNET DOMAINS

.com	commercial entitity
.edu	educational institution
.firm	business entity
.gov	government agency or department

.info	organizations that provide information
.mil	military organization
.net	network resource
.org	other type of organization, usually nonprofit
.store	online stores

Consider the author.
- Is the author's name listed?
- What are this person's credentials?
- What makes him or her qualified to provide this information?
- Does the author provide a way for you to contact him or her?

Evaluate the quality of information.
- How accurate is the information? Does it appear to be reliable and without errors?
- Are there links to other reliable sources? Do the links really work?
- How current is the information? Is the date provided for when the site was authored or revised? Is this the latest information on this topic?
- How clearly does the author provide information?
- How well does the author cover the topic, based on what you know from other sources?
- How does the author support the information—with charts, graphs, a bibliography?

Look for objectivity.
- Is the information given without bias?
- Is the author objective, or does he or she try to influence the way you think?

5.36 Documenting Sources

As you use your research in your writing, you must document your sources of information. Remember to:
- Credit the sources of all ideas and facts that you use.
- Credit original ideas or facts that are expressed in text, tables, charts, and other graphic information.
- Credit all artistic property, including works of literature, song lyrics, and ideas.

HOW TO UNDERSTAND INTERNET SITES. An activity that requires students to understand Internet sites is found in the Media Literacy activity on page 487.

DOCUMENTING SOURCES. Direct instruction on effectively documenting sources can be found in the Language, Grammar, and Style section of the Guided Writing lesson at the end of Unit 8, pages 703–705.

STUDY AND RESEARCH RESOURCE

5.37 KEEPING A RESEARCH JOURNAL. Just as a writing journal can help you track your thoughts, experiences, and responses to literature, a research journal can help you track your research. A research journal is a notebook, electronic file, or other means to track the information you find as you conduct research. A research journal can include: a list of questions you want to research. (Such questions can be an excellent source of writing topics.)

EXAMPLES

> How did the Vietnam Veterans Memorial come to be? Why is it one of the most visited memorials in America?
>
> Where can I find more artwork by Faith Ringgold?
>
> Why was Transcendentalism such an important literary movement in America but not in Europe?

5.38 USING YOUR RESEARCH JOURNAL FOR DOCUMENTATION. As you conduct your research, rely on your research journal as a place to take notes on the sources you find and your evaluation of them. Keeping a research journal can be an invaluable way to track your research and to take notes.

5.39 INFORMAL AND FORMAL NOTE-TAKING. Informal note-taking is for when you want information for your own use only, and when you will not need to quote or document your sources. You would take informal notes when preparing materials to use in studying, for instance, as you watch a film or listen to a lecture.

Informal note-taking is much like outlining (see 2.29, "Rough Outlines"). Use important ideas as headings, and write relevant details below. You will not be able to copy every word, nor is there any need to. Write phrases instead of sentences.

QUOTATION	"Jerzy Kosinski came to the United States in 1957, and in 1958 he was awarded a Ford Foundation fellowship."
NOTES	Jerzy Kosinski —came to US 1957 —Ford Foundation fellowship 1958

You will also want to record information about the event or performance, including the date, time, place, speaker, and title, as applicable. After you are done taking notes, read them over to ensure that they are legible and meaningful. If you have used idiosyncratic shorthand or abbreviations that you may not later recall, write out your notes more fully.

Formal note-taking is for when you may need to quote or document your sources. When you are keeping formal notes for a project—for instance, for a debate or a research paper—you should use 4" x 6" index cards.

PREPARING NOTE CARDS

1. Identify the source at the top right corner of the card. (Use the source numbers from your bibliography cards.)

2. Identify the subject or topic of the note on the top line of the card. (This will make it easier to organize the cards later.)

3. Use a separate card for each fact or quotation.

4. Write the pertinent source page number or numbers after the note.

SAMPLE NOTE CARD

Topic — Similes — Source number (from bibliography cards) ⑧

"My best friend is like the sister I never had; she is always there for me through the good times and the bad, always making me feel that I am not alone." — Note

Quotation marks

p. 26 — Page reference

FORMAL NOTE-TAKING

TYPE OF NOTE	WHEN TO USE	WHAT TO WATCH FOR
Quotation	When the exact wording of a primary source is important to your topic	Copy spelling, capitalization, punctuation, and numbers exactly as in the source.
	When you are providing a definition	Place quotation marks around all direct quotations.
Paraphrase	When the wording of a secondary source is particularly memorable or insightful	Record, when appropriate, explanatory background information about the speaker or the context of a quotation.
	Most of the time	Focus on your main purpose, and note only points related to your topic.
		Place quotation marks around any quoted words or phrases.
Summary	When the point you are making does not require the detail of a paraphrase	Reread the source after writing your summary to be sure that you have not altered the meaning.

5.40 MAKING BIBLIOGRAPHIES AND BIBLIOGRAPHY CARDS. If you are writing a research paper, your teacher will ask you to include a bibliography to tell where you got your information. A **bibliography** is a list of sources that you used for your writing. A **source** is a book, a magazine, a film, or any other written or audio-visual material that you use to get information. As you work on your paper, you should be writing down on note cards the information for each source that you use. The chart below shows the correct form for different types of bibliography entries.

FORMS FOR BIBLIOGRAPHY ENTRIES

A. A book
Douglass, Frederick. Escape from Slavery: The Boyhood of Frederick Douglass in His Own Words. New York: Alfred A. Knopf, 1994.

B. A magazine article
Reston, James, Jr. "Orion: Where Stars Are Born." National Geographic. December 1995: 90-101.

C. An encyclopedia entry
"Lewis and Clark Expedition." Encyclopedia Americana. Jackson, Donald. 1995 ed.

D. An interview
Campbell, Silas. Personal interview. 6 February 1997.

E. A film
The Big Heat. Dir. Fritz Lang. With Glenn Ford and Gloria Grahame. Writ. Sidney Boehm. Based on the novel of the same title by William P. McGiven. 90 min. Columbia, 1953.

F. The Internet
Durham, Dacia. The Charles A. and Anne Morrow Lindbergh Foundation. 24 Oct. 1995, updated 18 June 1999. <http://www.mtn.org/lindfdtn/>.

STUDY AND RESEARCH RESOURCE **1103**

MAKING BIBLIOGRAPHIES AND BIBLIOGRAPHY CARDS. Students are asked to make bibliography cards in the Media Literacy activity on page 87 and the Study and Research

For each source used, prepare a bibliography card using an index card. Include all of the information in the following chart when preparing your cards.

INFORMATION TO INCLUDE ON A BIBLIOGRAPHY CARD	
Author(s)	Write the complete name(s) of all author(s), editor(s), and translator(s).
Title	Write the complete title. If the piece is contained in a larger work, include the title of the larger work. (For example, write the name of the encyclopedia as well as the name of the article you used.)
Publisher	Write exactly as it appears on the title page.
Place and date of publication	Copy this information from the title page or copyright page of a book. For a magazine, write the date of the issue that you used.
Location and call number	Note where you found the book. If it is in a library collection, write the call number.
Card number	Give a number to each bibliography card that you prepare. Write that number in the top right corner of the card and circle it. When you take notes from the source, include this number on each note card so that you will be able to identify the source of the note later on.

SAMPLE BIBLIOGRAPHY CARD

Van Lawick-Goodall, Jane.
    In the Shadow of Man

       Boston: Houghton, 1971.

    Peabody Institute Library

599.8

5.41 DOCUMENTING AND MAPPING INTERNET RESEARCH. Your research journal is an excellent tool for tracking how you find information. It can be especially invaluable for documenting and mapping Internet research. As you browse and search on the Internet, it can be easy to jump from one Internet site to the next and to lose track of how you got from place to place. Especially as you conduct research, it is important to map your path. Here is one way to do so.

- Write a brief statement of the topic of your research.

- Write key words or phrases that will help you search for this information.

- Note the search engines that you will use.

- As you conduct a search, note how many "hits" or Internet sites the search engine has accessed. Determine whether you need to narrow or expand your search. Write down new key words accordingly, and the results of each new search.

- When you find promising sites, write them down.

- Access each promising site. Evaluate its information using the guidelines in 5.35, "How to Understand Internet Sites."

- Once you find information to include in your work, document it carefully. For more information on how to document Internet sites, see the Language Arts Survey 5.40, "Making Bibliographies and Bibliography Cards."

5.42 AVOIDING PLAGIARISM. Plagiarism is taking someone else's words or thoughts and pretending that they are your own. Plagiarism is a very serious problem and has been the downfall of many students and even famous people. Whenever you use someone else's writing to help you with a paper or a speech, you must be careful either to put the ideas in your own words or to use quotation marks. In either case, you must give credit to the person whose ideas you are using. Giving such credit to others is called documenting your sources.

5.43 PARAPHRASING, SUMMARIZING, AND QUOTING. As you do research, your notes will include paraphrases, summaries, and quotations.

5.44 PARENTHETICAL DOCUMENTATION. Parenthetical documentation is currently the most widely used form of documentation. To use this method to document the source of a quotation or an idea, you place a brief note identifying the source in parentheses immediately after the borrowed material. This type of note is called a **parenthetical citation**, and the act of placing such a note is called **citing a source**.

The first part of a parenthetical citation refers the reader to a source in your List of Works Cited or Works Consulted. For the reader's ease in finding the source in your bibliography, you must cite the work according to how it is listed in the bibliography.

PARAPHRASING, SUMMARIZING, AND QUOTING. You will find activities that require students to paraphrase and summarize their research in the Study and Research activities on pages 105 and 197.

SAMPLE PARENTHETICAL CITATIONS

A. For works listed by title, use an abbreviated title.

Sample bibliographic entry
"History." *Encyclopedia Britannica: Macropædia*. 1992 ed.

Sample citation
Historians go through three stages in textual criticism ("History" 615).

B. For works listed by author or editor, use the author's or editor's last name.

Sample bibliographic entry
Brown, Dee. *Bury My Heart at Wounded Knee: An Indian History of the American West*. New York: Holt, 1970.

Sample citation
"Big Eyes Schurz agreed to the arrest" (Brown 364).

C. When the listed name or title is stated in the text, cite only the page number.
Brown avers that Big Eyes Schurz agreed to it (364).

D. For works of multiple volumes, use a colon after the volume number.

Sample bibliographic entry
Pepys, Samuel. *The Diary of Samuel Pepys*. Ed. Robert Latham and William Matthews. 10 vols. Berkeley: University of California Press, 1972.

Sample citation
On the last day of 1665, Pepys took the occasion of the new year to reflect, but not to celebrate (6: 341–2).

E. For works quoted in secondary sources, use the abbreviation "qtd. in."

Sample citation
According to R. Bentley, "reason and the facts outweigh a hundred manuscripts" (qtd. in "History" 615).

F. For classic works that are available in various editions, give the page number from the edition you are using, followed by a semicolon; then identify the section of the work to help people with other editions find the reference.

STUDY AND RESEARCH RESOURCE

5.45 FOOTNOTES AND ENDNOTES. Parenthetical documentation, described in 5.44, is the most common of many accepted systems. Footnoting and endnoting are two other accepted methods.

FOOTNOTES. Instead of putting citations in parentheses within the text, you can place them at the bottom or foot of the page; hence the term **footnote**. In this system, a number or symbol is placed in the text where the parenthetical citation would otherwise be, and a matching number or symbol at the bottom of the page identifies the citation. This textbook, for example, uses numbered footnotes in its literature selections to define obscure words and to provide background information.

ENDNOTES. Many books use endnotes instead of footnotes. Endnotes are like footnotes in that a number or symbol is placed within the text, but the matching citations are compiled at the end of the book, chapter, or article rather than at the foot of the page.

Footnote and endnote entries begin with the author's (or editor's) name in its usual order (first name, then last) and include publication information and a page reference.

SAMPLE FOOTNOTE OR ENDNOTE CITATIONS	
A BOOK WITH ONE AUTHOR	[1]Jean Paul-Sartre, *Being and Nothingness* (New York: The Citadel Press, 1966) 149-151.
A BOOK WITH ONE EDITOR AND NO SINGLE AUTHOR	[2]Shannon Ravenel, ed., *New Stories from the South: The Year's Best, 1992* (Chapel Hill, NC: Algonquin Books, 1992) 305.
A MAGAZINE ARTICLE	[3]Andrew Gore, "Road Test: The Apple Powerbook," *MacUser* December 1996: 72.

TEST-TAKING SKILLS

5.46 Preparing for Tests

Tests are a common part of school life. These guidelines will help you to prepare for and take a test.

PREPARING FOR A TEST

- **Know exactly what you will be tested on.** If you have questions, ask your teacher.
- **Make a study plan** to allow yourself time to go over the material. Avoid last-minute cramming.
- **Review the subject matter.** Use your notes, your SQ3R strategy, and any study questions given by your teacher.
- **Make lists** of important names, dates, definitions, or events. Ask a friend or family member to quiz you on them.
- **Try to predict questions** that may be on the test. Make sure you can answer them.
- **Get plenty of sleep** the night before the test.

Eat a nutritious breakfast on the morning of the test.

TAKING A TEST

- **Survey the test** to see how long it is and what types of questions are included.
- **Read all directions and questions** carefully. Make sure that you know exactly what to do.
- **Plan your time.** Answer easy questions first. Allow extra time for complicated questions. If a question seems too difficult, skip it and go back to it later. Work quickly, but do not rush.
- **Save time for review.** Once you have finished, look back over the test. Double-check your answers, but do not change answers too often. Your first ideas are often the correct ones.

5.47 Taking Objective Tests

Objective tests require simple right-or-wrong answers. This chart describes the kinds of questions you may see on objective tests.

QUESTIONS FOUND ON OBJECTIVE TESTS

DESCRIPTION	GUIDELINES
True/False. You are given a statement and asked to tell whether the statement is true or false.	• If any part of a statement is false, then the statement is false. • Words like *all, always, never,* and *everyone* often appear in false statements. • Words like *some, usually, often,* and *most* often appear in true statements. • If you do not know the answer, guess. You have a 50/50 chance of being right.
Matching. You are asked to match items in one column with items in another column.	• Check the directions. See if each item is used only once. Also check to see if some are not used at all. • Read all items before starting. • Match those you know first. • Cross out items as you match them.
Multiple Choice. You are asked to choose the best answer from a group of answers given.	• Read *all* choices first. • Rule out incorrect answers. • Choose the answer that is most complete or accurate. • Pay particular attention to choices such as *none of the above* or *all of the above.*
Short Answer. You are asked to answer the question with a word, a phrase, or a sentence.	• Read the directions to find out if you are required to answer in complete sentences. • Use correct spelling, grammar, punctuation, and capitalization. • If you cannot think of the answer, move on. Something in another question might remind you of the answer.

TRUE/FALSE QUESTIONS. Point out that the word *not* completely changes the meaning of a sentence. To evaluate a sentence that contains a negative, students should see if its opposite makes sense or is plausible. If it does, the original must be false. Also point out that excessive wordiness might point to a statement's being false. Only one part of the statement needs to be false to make the entire statement false.

INTERNET RESOURCES

An excellent online resource for note-taking and test-taking tips (excerpts from *The Confident Student* by Carol Kanar) can be accessed at http://www. mscc.cc.ar.us/ studentserv/notetaki.htm. This site also contains many other links for note-taking and test preparation tips.

5.48 Strategies for Taking Standardized Tests

Standardized tests are given to many students in a school district, a state, or a country. You may already have taken a standardized test, such as the Iowa Test of Basic Skills, and you certainly will take more during your school career. Some standardized tests, such as the Scholastic Aptitude Test, or SAT, are used to help determine entrance to colleges and universities. Others must be passed to enter certain vocations or professions. A standardized test measures overall ability, or achievement over a period of time. Learning how to take standardized tests well can help you to achieve your academic and career goals.

When selecting an answer on a standardized test, remember these points:

• If you do not know the answer, try to rule out some choices and then guess from those remaining.

• If a question seems too difficult, skip it and go back to it later. Be aware, however, that most

STUDY AND RESEARCH RESOURCE

tests allow you to go back to questions only within a section.

- Always follow the instructions of the test monitor.

5.49 ANALOGY QUESTIONS. Analogy questions ask you to find the relationship between a given pair of words and then to recognize a similar relationship between another pair of words. In an analogy question, the symbols : and :: mean "is to" and "as," respectively. The example below would be "Mare is to horse as . . ." when read aloud. To answer an analogy question, examine all of the answers. If more than one answer seems correct, choose the best one.

To answer an analogy question, think of a sentence that relates the two words. For example, you might think of the sentence "A *mare* is a female *horse*." Then look for another pair of words that would make sense in that sentence: "A *doe* is a female *deer*."

EXAMPLE

MARE : HORSE ::
(A) lamb : sheep
(B) man : woman
(C) boy : girl
(D) bee : wasp
(E) doe : deer

The answer is E.

5.50 SYNONYM AND ANTONYM QUESTIONS. Synonym and **antonym** questions give you a word and ask you to select the word that has the same meaning (for a synonym) or the opposite meaning (for an antonym). You must select the best answer, even if none is exactly correct. For this type of question, you should try all the choices to see which one works best. Always know whether you are looking for a synonym or an antonym, because you will usually find both among the answers.

EXAMPLE

Write the letter of the word that is most nearly the opposite in meaning to the word in capital letters.
1. AMIABLE
   (A) capable
   (B) friendly
   (C) hostile
   (D) lovely

The answer is C.

5.51 SENTENCE COMPLETION QUESTIONS. Sentence-completion questions present you with a sentence that has two words missing. You must select the pair of words that best completes the sentence.

EXAMPLE

The expansion of Cedar Hospital was largely_____by the citizens of Minor county, even though it was a major_____for the taxpayers.
   (A)   needed...contribution
   (B)   cheered...burden
   (C)   criticized...expense
   (D)   welcomed...dilemma

The answer is B.

5.52 READING COMPREHENSION QUESTIONS. Reading comprehension questions give you a short piece of writing and then ask you several questions about it. The questions may ask you to figure out something based on information in the passage. Use the following strategies when answering reading comprehension questions:

STEPS IN ANSWERING READING COMPREHENSION QUESTIONS

1. Read all the questions quickly.
2. Read the passage with the questions in mind.
3. Reread the first question carefully.
4. Scan the passage, looking for key words related to the question. When you find a key word, slow down and read carefully.
5. Answer the first question.
6. Repeat this process to answer the rest of the questions.

SYNONYM AND ANTONYM QUESTIONS. Students are asked to select synonyms for various words in the Vocabulary activity on page 550.

5.53 Taking Essay Tests

An **essay** is a short piece of writing that expresses the writer's thoughts about a particular subject. To answer an essay question, follow these guidelines.

- **Analyze each question.** Once you understand clearly what you have to do, you will be able to organize and write more effective essays in the time available.

  First, read the *entire* question carefully. Look for key words in the question that tell you what is expected. Underline these words or write them on your own note paper. Then make sure to answer *all* parts of the question.

- **Organize your answer.** Determining how you will spend the time available is an important part of planning an essay. Allow time for planning, writing, and reviewing. Before you begin writing, make a rough outline of the main points you will make. Include main points and key details. Later, if you find yourself running out of time, try at least to state your remaining main points and to add a conclusion.

- **Write a clear introduction.** This will help to keep you on track as you write each paragraph. Your introduction should state the thesis, or main idea, of your essay and should briefly answer the question. In the rest of the essay, you can elaborate on your answer, providing evidence to support it.

- **Review your answer.** Before you turn in your completed essay, take time to review and polish it.

UNDERSTANDING AN ESSAY QUESTION

TYPE OF ESSAY QUESTION	TASKS OF ESSAY
analyze	break into parts and describe the parts and their relationships
compare; compare and contrast	identify and describe similarities and differences
describe; explain	tell the steps in a process; identify causes and effects
define; describe; identify	classify and tell the features of
interpret	tell the meaning and significance of
summarize	retell very briefly, stating only the main points
argue; prove; show	tell and evaluate reasons for believing a statement

QUESTIONS FOR REVIEWING AN ANSWER TO AN ESSAY QUESTION

- Does the essay answer all parts of the question?
- Does the introduction state clearly the main idea of the essay?
- Does the body of the essay provide evidence to support the main idea?
- Does the essay cover all the points in my rough outline?
- Are there any points that could be made more strongly or clearly?
- Is every word in the essay easily readable?
- Is the essay free of errors in grammar, usage, and mechanics?

APPLIED ENGLISH
Resource

THE IMPORTANCE OF APPLIED ENGLISH

Applied English is English in the world of work, or practical English. When you apply English skills to real-world situations, you are using your reading, writing, speaking, and listening abilities for practical reasons.

6.1 Filling Out Forms

Entering a new school, going to a new doctor, registering computer software, applying for a job—these are but a few of the thousands of activities that involve filling out forms. The following guidelines will help you to complete a form in a way that will make a good impression.

GUIDELINES FOR COMPLETING FORMS:

- Get an extra copy or make a photocopy of the form so that you can complete a practice form.

- Read through the directions and the form itself before completing it.

- Gather the information you will need to complete the form. This information may include former addresses, dates of events, or a social security number.

- Complete the form neatly. Avoid smudges or cross-outs. Use the writing method requested on the form. Most forms request that you either type or use black or blue ink.

- Do not leave any lines blank. Use N.A. for "not applicable" if a request for information does not apply to you. For example, if you have always lived at the same address, you would write N.A. in the blank following "Previous Addresses."

- Proofread your information for errors in punctuation, spelling, or grammar. Make sure all information is correct.

- Submit the form to the appropriate person or address. Use an envelope or folder to keep the form neat and clean.

- Keep a copy of the form for your own records.

6.2 Following Directions

Every day people all over the world face the challenge of doing something they have never done before. Despite their inexperience, many people are able to succeed because they are able to follow directions. At the same time, someone must be able to give them clear, precise directions. Consider these guidelines before you begin following or giving directions.

GUIDELINES FOR FOLLOWING DIRECTIONS

- If the directions are being given in written form, read them carefully before beginning the procedure. If they are being given in spoken form, take notes as you listen. Ask for clarification if something is confusing.

- If written directions include any vocabulary or technical words you do not understand, look them up in a dictionary, or see if the materials include footnotes, a glossary, or an appendix. If an instructor uses words you do not understand, ask him or her to rephrase.

- Take your time and make sure you have performed each step carefully and accurately before proceeding to the next step.

- If you get stuck following directions, retrace your steps or reread the step you are on. If they are available, consult diagrams, maps, or illustrations. You might find it helpful to ask someone else to read the directions and see if he or she arrives at the same conclusion as you do. If the directions include a "help hotline" or other contact information, you may want to use it.

6.3 Giving Directions

GUIDELINES FOR GIVING DIRECTIONS

- Think through the directions completely, from start to finish, before you begin.

- Give each step in the order in which it should be taken.

- Include all necessary steps. Do not assume that your reader or listener already knows any part of the directions unless you are absolutely sure that this is the case.

- Do not include any unnecessary steps.

- Use simple language that can be understood easily.

- Use transition words such as *first, second, third, next, then,* and *finally* to connect your ideas.

- When possible, use a parallel or similar sentence structure for each part of the directions.

- When giving directions orally, ask the listener to repeat the directions to you when you have finished. This way you can check to make sure that your directions have been understood.

- If the directions that you are giving are complicated, put them into writing. Number each direction to help you and your reader to keep the steps separate and clear. You may also wish to include a map, diagram, or other illustration to accompany the written directions. For more information, see the Language Arts Survey 6.11, "Displaying Effective Visual Information."

6.4 Writing a Step-by-Step Procedure

A **step-by-step procedure** is a how-to or process piece that uses directions to teach someone something new. Written procedures include textual information and sometimes graphics. Spoken procedures can be given as oral demonstrations. They can include textual and graphic information and other props.

Examples of step-by-step procedures include an oral demonstration of how to saddle a horse; instructions on how to treat a sprained ankle; a video showing how to do the perfect lay-up in

basketball; and an interactive Internet site allowing the user to design and send a bouquet of flowers.

To write a step-by-step procedure, review the Language Arts Survey 6.3, "Giving Directions" and 6.11, "Displaying Effective Visual Information."

GUIDELINES FOR WRITING A STEP-BY-STEP PROCEDURE

- If you are showing how to make something, create several different samples to show each step of the procedure. For example, if you are showing how to make a wooden basket, you might want to display the raw materials, the started basket, the basket halfway finished, and then the finished product. You might also want to have a sample showing a variation—a different type of weaving, for example, that the finished product may not have.

- Be prepared. The best way to prevent problems is to anticipate and plan for them. Rehearse an oral demonstration several times. If you are preparing the procedure in written form, go through your directions as if you knew nothing about the process. Anticipate what it would be like to learn this procedure for the first time. See if you can follow your own directions, or have a friend work through the procedure and offer suggestions for improvement.

- Acknowledge mistakes. If you are sharing a procedure "live" as an oral demonstration and you can't talk around or correct a mistake, tell your audience what has gone wrong, and why. If you handle the situation in a calm, direct way, the audience may also learn from your mistake.

- Know your topic well. The better you know it, the better you will be able to teach others.

6.5 Writing a Business Letter

A **business letter** is usually addressed to someone you do not know personally. Therefore, a formal tone is appropriate for such a letter.

Following appropriate form is especially important when writing business letters. If you follow the correct form and avoid errors in spelling, grammar, usage, and mechanics, your letter will sound professional and make a good impression.

WRITING A STEP-BY-STEP PROCEDURE. Students are asked to give directions using a step-by-step procedure in the Applied English activity on page 641.

WRITING A BUSINESS LETTER. Students are asked to write business letters in the Applied English activities on pages 217, 424, and 957.

Above the salutation, a business letter should contain the name and title of the person to whom you are writing and the name and address of that person's company or organization (see the model on the following page).

One common form for a business letter is the block form. In the block form, each part of the letter begins at the left margin. The parts are separated by line spaces.

Begin the salutation with the word *Dear*, followed by the courtesy or professional title used in the inside address, such as *Ms., Mr.,* or *Dr.,* and a colon. If you are not writing to a specific person, you may use a general salutation such as *Dear Sir or Madam.*

In the body of your letter, use a polite, formal tone and standard English. Make your points clearly, in as few words as possible.

End with a standard closing such as *Sincerely, Yours truly,* or *Respectfully yours.* Capitalize only the first word of the closing. Type your full name below the closing, leaving three or four blank lines for your signature. Sign your name below the closing in blue or black ink (never in red or green). Proofread your letter before you send it. Poor spelling, grammar, or punctuation can ruin an otherwise well-written business letter.

GUIDELINES FOR WRITING A BUSINESS LETTER

- Outline your main points before you begin.

- Word process your letter, if at all possible. Type or print it on clean 8 1/2" x 11" white or off-white paper. Use only one side of the paper.

- Use the block form or another standard business letter form.

- Single space, leaving a blank line between each part, including paragraphs.

- Use a standard salutation and a standard closing.

- Stick to the subject. State your main idea clearly at the beginning of the letter. Keep the letter brief and informative.

- Check your spelling, grammar, usage, and punctuation carefully.

STUDENT MODEL

Jorge loves snorkeling and wants to get a summer job working part time in a dive shop. This is a copy of the letter that he sent to the owner of the shop.

498 Blue Key Rd.
Charleston, SC 02716

October 3, 2001

Mr. Davy Jones, Owner
Deep Sea Divers, Inc.
73 Ocean St.
Charleston, SC 02716

Dear Mr. Jones:

Please consider me for a position as a part-time clerk in your store for the coming summer. I understand that in the summer your business increases considerably and that you might need a conscientious, hard-working clerk. I can offer you considerable knowledge of snorkeling and diving equipment and experience working in a retail shop.

I will be available for work three days per week between June 1 and August 12. I am enclosing a résumé and references. Please contact me if you wish to set up an interview.

Sincerely,

Jorge Alvarez

Jorge Alvarez

6.6 Writing a Memo

In businesses, schools, and other organizations, employees, students, and others often communicate by means of **memoranda**, or **memos**. For example, the director of a school drama club might write a memo to the editor of the student newspaper announcing tryouts for a new play.

Some memos will be more informal than others. If you know the person to whom you are writing well or if the memo has only a social function such as announcing a party, the tone can be fairly informal. Most memos, however, have a fairly formal tone.

A memo begins with a header. Often this header contains the word *memorandum* (the singular form of memoranda) and the following words and abbreviations:

TO:
FR: (from)
DT: (date)
RE: (regarding)
cc: (copy)

STUDENT MODEL

Jack Hart, the president of the drama club at Wheaton High School, wishes to have the upcoming tryouts for his club's production of *Oklahoma!* announced in the school newspaper. He decides to write a memo to the editor of the paper, Lisa Lowry.

MEMORANDUM

TO: Lisa Lowry
FR: Jack Hart
RE: Tryouts for the spring production of *Oklahoma!*
DT: February 12, 2001
cc: Ms. Wise

Please include the following announcement in the upcoming issue of the *Wheaton Crier*: Tryouts for the Wheaton Drama Club's spring production of *Oklahoma!* will be held on Friday, February 26, at 6:00 P.M. in the Wheaton High School Auditorium. Students interested in performing in this musical should come to the auditorium at that time prepared to deliver a monologue less than two minutes long and to sing one song from the musical. Copies of the music and lyrics can be obtained from the sponsor of the Wheaton Drama Club, Ms. Wise. For additional information, please contact Ms. Wise or any member of the Drama Club.

Thank you.

6.7 Writing a Proposal

A **proposal** outlines a project that a person wants to complete. It presents a summary of an idea, the reasons why the idea is important, and an outline of how the project would be carried out. Because the proposal audience is people who can help carry out the proposal, a proposal is both informative and persuasive.

EXAMPLES
- You want funding for an art project that would benefit your community
- Your student council proposes a clothing drive for disaster relief
- You and a group of your friends want to help organize a summer program for teens your age

Proposal: To host a community arts day at the park behind Jordan High School that would allow high school artists to try new art forms and to exhibit their work.

Rationale: The art students at Jordan High School have shown there is a lot of talent here worth sharing. An Arts Day would let everyone interested get involved, and build school and community pride. Art students could lead others through simple art projects, and people could learn new things. At the end, the art could be displayed in an art fair at the community park. Artwork and refreshments could be sold, with all proceeds going to the Jordan High School Art Scholarship.

Schedule/Preparation Outline

Present proposal to School Pride Committee	April 1
Meet with art students to organize event	April 6–15
Contact area businesses for donations	April 6–15
Advertise event and sell tickets	April 16–25
Have practice day to make sure art activities work	April 20
Hold community Arts Day	April 26

BUDGET
Expenses

Posters, mailings, tickets	$30
Art supplies	$200
Refreshments	$75

Note: Expenses will be fewer if we ask area businesses to help sponsor event

Total estimated expenses	$305

Income

Ticket sales (estimated 150 tickets sold @ $3 each)	$450
Refreshment sales	$100
Earnings from art sold at exhibit	$200
Total estimated income	$750
Net proceeds	$445

Note: All proceeds will be donated to the Jordan High School Art Scholarship Fund

GUIDELINES FOR WRITING A PROPOSAL
- Keep the tone positive, courteous, and respectful.
- State your purpose and rationale briefly and clearly.
- Give your audience all necessary information. A proposal with specific details makes it clear what you want approved, and why your audience—often a committee or someone in authority—should approve it.
- Use standard, formal English.
- Format your proposal with headings, lists, and schedules to make your proposed project easy to understand and approve.

6.8 Writing a Résumé

A **résumé** is a summary of a job applicant's career objectives, previous employment experience, and education. Its purpose is to help the applicant obtain the job he or she seeks. A résumé should be accompanied by a cover letter to the employer (see an example in the Language Arts Survey 6.5, "Writing a Business Letter"). Many helpful books and articles are available in libraries and bookstores on writing a résumé. Here are some guidelines.

GUIDELINES FOR WRITING A RÉSUMÉ

- Keep your information brief—to one page if possible. The goal of the resume is to give a potential employer a quick snapshot of your skills and abilities.

- Include all vital contact information—name, address, phone number, and e-mail address, if applicable—at the top of the page.

- Use headings to summarize information regarding job or career objective, education, work experience, skills, extracurricular activities, awards (if applicable), and references. Note that work experience should be listed starting with your most recent job and working backward.

- Key or type your résumé on white or cream-colored paper. Proofread it carefully for any errors; all facts must be accurate as well. Make it as neat as possible.

- You may list references, or simply state that they are available on request.

Pat Mizos
5555 Elm Street
Anytown, NY 20111
(212) 555-5555

Objective:
To gain employment working in a summer camp program for children

Education:
Orchard High School, 2001 graduate

Major area of study: College preparatory, with concentration in science and physical education classes

Grade point average: 3.5 (B+)

Work experience:
Summer 1999   Summer youth counselor, Anytown Parks and Recreation Department

Summer 1998   Dishwasher, the Lobster Shack Anytown, NY

Skills:
Intermediate-level Spanish (three years in high school)
Beginning-level American Sign Language (one semester at Anytown Vocational School)
Certified in CPR

Extracurricular activities:
Swim team, tennis team, youth hotline crisis volunteer

References:
Available on request

DELIVERING A PRESS RELEASE. Students can practice writing a press release in the Applied English activity on page 432.

WRITING A PUBLIC SERVICE ANNOUNCEMENT. Students are asked to write a public service announcement in the Unit 6 Guided Writing lesson on page 510.

6.9 Delivering a Press Release

A **press release** is an informative piece intended for publication in local news media. A press release is usually written to promote an upcoming event or to inform the community of a recent event that promotes, or strengthens, an individual or organization.

EXAMPLES
- a brief notice from the choir director telling the community of the upcoming spring concert
- an informative piece by the district public information officer announcing that your school's art instructor has been named the state Teacher of the Year

GUIDELINES FOR WRITING A PRESS RELEASE
- Know your purpose. What do you want your audience to know from reading your piece?
- Use the 5 *Ws* and an *H—who, what, where, when, why,* and *how*—questioning strategy to convey the important information at the beginning of your story. (For more information, see the Language Arts Survey 2.14, "Questioning: Using the 5 *Ws* and an *H.*")
- Keep the press release brief. Local media are more likely to publish or broadcast your piece if it is short and to the point.
- Include contact information such as your name, phone number, and times you can be reached. Make this information available to the media representative or, if applicable, to the reading public.
- Type your press release using conventional manuscript form. Make sure the text is double-spaced and that you leave margins of at least an inch on all sides of the page.
- At the beginning of the press release, key the day's date and the date the information is to be released. (You can type "For immediate release" or designate the date you would like the press release to be printed in the newspaper.)
- At the end of the press release, key the word "END."

- Check a previous newspaper for deadline information or call the newspaper office to make sure you get your material there on time. Address the press release to the editor.

6.10 Writing a Public Service Announcement

A **public service announcement**, or PSA, is a brief, informative article intended to be helpful to the community. PSAs are written by nonprofit organizations and concerned citizens for print in local newspapers, for broadcast by television and radio stations, and for publication on the Internet.

EXAMPLES
- an article by the American Cancer Society outlining early warning signs of cancer
- an announcement promoting Safety Week
- an informative piece telling coastal residents what to do during a hurricane

GUIDELINES FOR WRITING A PUBLIC SERVICE ANNOUNCEMENT
- Know your purpose. What do you want your audience to know from reading or hearing your piece?
- State your information as objectively as possible.
- As with most informative writing, use the 5 *Ws* and an *H—who, what, where, when, why,* and *how*—questioning strategy to get your important information at the beginning of your story.
- Keep your announcement brief. Local media are more likely to publish or broadcast your piece if it is short and to the point.
- Include contact information in case the media representative has any questions. You might also include contact information in the PSA itself.
- Key or type your PSA in conventional manuscript form. Make sure the text is double-spaced and that you leave margins of at least an inch on all sides of the page.
- At the end of the PSA, key "END" to designate the end of the announcement.
- Be aware of print and broadcast deadlines and make sure your material is sent on time.

6.11 Displaying Effective Visual Information

People frequently learn things best and remember more when information is presented visually. Whenever possible, use charts, tables, pictures, slides, photographs, models, and art to express key points.

PURPOSES OF VISUALS

- focus and hold audience attention
- help the audience grasp facts quickly
- clarify something complicated
- show comparisons
- emphasize key points
- summarize main thoughts
- serve as an outline or guide in a presentation

The quality of your visuals will affect your presentation. Depending on their use, visuals can detract from a presentation or enhance it. Before you use a visual, ask yourself:

- Is it attention-grabbing?
- Is it simple and neat?
- Does it serve a real purpose?
- Can I use it easily?
- Does it fit smoothly into the presentation?

The success of your presentation will depend on how you display visual information. Here are some guidelines.

GUIDELINES FOR DISPLAYING VISUAL INFORMATION

- Keep visual information simple. Do not clutter visual display with multiple lettering or font styles, too many small images, or too much textual or graphic information.
- Design your visual display in a way that the
- Clearly label your visual display. Make it easy for the viewer to know what you are showing. Include a title or caption, labels for different parts, and simple, main points when needed.
- Make the visual visible. Type or graphics that are too small can make the best visual presentation useless. If the display is on a computer screen, make sure you can read it. If the display is for a speech or exhibit, stand back and see if you can see it from the back of the room or wherever your audience members will be. (A general rule is that one-inch letters can be read at 32 feet, two-inch letters at 64 feet, and three-inch letters at 128 feet.)

- Use bullets or numbering to organize your text. For simple presentations, use either one or the other; don't use both.
- Use color carefully. Color can add visual interest, but it can also be distracting or make a graphic or text area illegible.
- Document all sources of graphic information. The ideas in visual information are someone's intellectual property, just like the ideas in text material. Make sure you give proper credit for all work not your own.

For more information on types of visual presentations, see the Language Arts Survey 1.15, "Using Graphic Aids."

6.12 Working on a Team

Working on a team, or doing collaborative learning, is an essential Applied English skill that depends on a strong ability to communicate. This ability can be strengthened with practice.

Individual members of a team or small group are likely to fulfill particular roles or positions based on what they know or do best. Sometimes a group decides before it starts a project who should take on what role. For instance, a group might choose someone to lead it or to act as secretary. At other times, roles emerge as a group progresses. Often, one person fulfills many roles in a group.

Constructive group roles help the group achieve its goals and objectives. These include:

- **leader:** directs the work of the group by assigning tasks or roles to other group members
- **implementer:** carries out or implements group tasks
- **information seeker:** asks for facts, information, or opinions
- **information giver:** offers facts, information, or opinions
- **coordinator:** pulls ideas together, identifies relationships between ideas

DISPLAYING EFFECTIVE VISUAL INFORMATION. Students are asked to create a visual display of the brain in the Study and Research activity on page 416. The Language, Grammar, and Style lesson in the Unit 6 Guided Writing activity also gives students tips on creating effective visual information. See pages 513–515.

WORKING ON A TEAM. Collaborative Learning activities follow many of the selections in the Integrating the Language Arts section of the Post-Reading. Also refer to the Speaking and Listening Resource 4.7–4.13 for more information on group communication and collaborative learning.

- **summarizer:** summarizes group discussions, calls attention to tasks that need to be fulfilled
- **evaluator:** analyzes data, reasoning, conclusions, or decisions of the group
- **energizer:** motivates the group, stimulates greater productivity and discussion
- **administrator:** keeps meetings on track, makes members aware of time and other constraints
- **secretary:** keeps minutes or a record of what occurs at group meetings
- **encourager:** provides understanding, positive reinforcement, and group solidarity
- **harmonizer:** helps to resolve conflict or misunderstandings between group members; encourages compromise
- **gatekeeper:** keeps communication open by encouraging and discouraging participation
- **tension reliever:** uses humor in a productive way to reduce tension and relax group members

Destructive group roles are counterproductive and prevent the group from achieving its goals or objectives.

- **blocker:** puts down others or their ideas; refuses to cooperate
- **aggressor:** picks fights with other members; is too negative and critical
- **recognition seeker:** uses group to boast about personal accomplishments
- **self-confessor:** unloads personal problems on group members, or otherwise uses the group to gain sympathy
- **joker:** uninvolved in group work; creates distractions, and engages in "horseplay"

- **dominator:** tries to control group and monopolize its time to advance his or her own interests
- **distractor:** goes off on tangents; offers irrelevant information or ideas
- **deserter:** withdraws from the group; does not participate in group discussions or decision making

TASKS FOR BEING A PRODUCTIVE TEAM MEMBER

AS A PARTICIPANT
- share personal experience
- contribute relevant ideas
- support statements with evidence
- respond to others with respect
- try to understand others' views
- show willingness to change views when appropriate
- show willingness to clarify and defend views
- allow others to speak
- maintain focus on discussion

AS A LEADER
- help the group keep on track
- help ensure that everyone gets a chance to speak
- help the group achieve its goals

AS A RECORD KEEPER
- keep accurate records of the discussion
- make sure all group members have records useful to the project

For more information, see the Language Arts Survey 4.7–4.9, "Communicating with Others," and 4.13, "Collaborative Learning and Communication."

ABRIDGMENT. An **abridgment** is a shortened version of a work. When doing an abridgment, an editor attempts to preserve the most significant elements of the original. See also *abstract* and *paraphrase.*

ABSTRACT. 1. *n.* An **abstract,** *précis,* or *summary* is a brief account of the main ideas or arguments presented in a work. A well-made abstract presents those ideas or arguments in the same order as in the original. Writing an abstract is an excellent way to commit to memory the major ideas of a nonfiction work, such as an essay or a chapter in a textbook. See *paraphrase.* 2. *adj.* An **abstract** word or phrase is one that refers to something that cannot be directly perceived by the senses. *Freedom, love, integrity, honesty,* and *loyalty* are examples of abstract terms. The opposite of *abstract* in this sense is *concrete.* See *concrete.*

ACCENT. See *stress.*

ACRONYM. An **acronym** is a word created from the first, or initial, letters of a series of words. Examples of acronyms include *scuba,* from the words *self-contained underwater breathing apparatus,* and *radar,* from *radio detecting and ranging.*

ACROSTIC. An **acrostic** is a poem organized so that the first or last letters of each line form a word, a phrase, or a regular sequence of letters of the alphabet.

ACT. An **act** is a major division of a drama. The first dramas were not divided into acts, but rather into scenes in which the actors performed and scenes in which the chorus spoke. The dramas of ancient Rome were generally divided into five acts. In modern times, plays are most often divided into three acts, and short plays called "one-acts" are common. There are five acts in Shakespeare's play *The Tragedy of Julius Cæsar* (Unit 4).

ACTION. The **action** is the sequence of events that actually occur in a literary work, as opposed to those that occur off-scene or that precede or follow the events in the work itself. A common literary technique, inherited from the classical *epic,* is to begin a work *in medias res,* in the middle of the action, and to fill in the background details later through flashbacks. See *flashback.*

ACTOR. An **actor** is one who performs the role of a character in a play. The term is now used both for male and female performers.

ADAGE. See *proverb.*

ADAPTATION. An **adaptation** is a rewriting of a literary work in another form. In modern times, adaptations for film are often made of successful novels, musicals, and plays. Anne Frank's *The Diary of a Young Girl* (Unit 5) has been successfully adapted for the stage and screen.

AFTERWORD. An **afterword** is a statement made at the end of a work, often an analysis, a summary, or a celebration of the preceding work. See *epilogue.*

AIM. A writer's **aim** is his or her purpose, or goal. People may write with the following aims:
- to inform (expository/informative writing)
- to entertain, enrich, enlighten, and/or use an artistic medium, such as fiction or poetry, to share a perspective (imaginative writing)
- to share a story, about an event, often to make a point (narrative writing)
- to reflect (personal/expressive writing)
- to persuade readers or listeners to respond in some way, such as to agree with a position, change a view on an issue, reach an agreement, or perform an action (persuasive/argumentative writing)

Here are examples of writing that reflect these five aims:

expository/informative
  news article, research report
imaginative
  poem, short story
narrative
  biography, family history
personal/expressive
  diary entry, personal letter
persuasive/argumentative
  editorial, petition

ALLEGORY. An **allegory** is a work in which each element symbolizes, or represents, something else. One interpretation of João Guimarães

Rosa's "Third Bank of the River" (Unit 7) is that it is an allegory about death. In one sense, all literature can be viewed as allegorical in that individual characters, objects, places, and actions can be seen as types representing others of their kind. See *concrete universal* and *extended metaphor*.

ALLITERATION. **Alliteration** is the repetition of initial consonant sounds. Some writers also use the term to describe repeated initial vowel sounds. The following lines from Langston Hughes's "Dream Variations" (Unit 2) contain an example of alliteration:

> To fling my arms wide
> In the face of the sun

ALLUSION. An **allusion** is a rhetorical technique in which reference is made to a person, event, object, or work from history or literature. For example, Denise Levertov's "A Tree Telling of Orpheus" (Unit 2) makes allusions to the Greek myth of Orpheus. Robert Hughes's article "Under the Crack of Reality" (Unit 6) makes an allusion to W. H. Auden's poem "One Evening."

AMBIGUITY. An **ambiguity** is a statement that has a double meaning or a meaning that cannot be clearly resolved. In English, the word *cleave* is oddly ambiguous, for it can mean either "to cling together" or "to cut apart." Many literary figures of speech, including *metaphors, similes, personifications,* and *symbols,* are examples of intentional ambiguity, speaking of one thing when another is intended.

ANACHRONISM. An **anachronism** is a reference to something that did not exist at the time being described. Thus, a reference to a computer in a story taking place during the Civil War would be an anachronism because computers had not been invented during the nineteenth century.

ANAGRAM. An **anagram** is a word or a phrase created by rearranging the letters of another word or phrase. The title of Samuel Butler's novel *Erewhon* is an anagram for *nowhere.* See *palindrome*.

ANALOGY. An **analogy** is a comparison of two things that are alike in some respects. Often an analogy explains or describes something unfamiliar by comparing it to something more familiar. A *simile* is an expressed analogy; a *metaphor* is an implied analogy. In "How to Write a Letter" (Unit 6), Garrison Keillor makes an analogy between a giant rock star who sings "his heart out in front of 123,000 people" and a person who writes a letter. See *simile* and *metaphor*.

ANALYSIS. 1. **Analysis** is a thinking strategy in which one divides a subject into parts and then examines the relationships among the parts and between individual parts and the whole. An analysis of a short story, for example, might consist of a division of the work into such parts as the *exposition,* the *rising action,* the *climax,* the *resolution,* and the *dénouement,* along with an examination of the role played by each of these parts in advancing the plot. An analysis of a line of poetry might consist of a careful examination of its rhythm, its figures of speech, its images, and its meaning or meanings. 2. **Analysis** is also a way to organize exposition, a type of nonfiction writing.

ANAPEST. An **anapest** is a poetic foot containing two weakly stressed syllables followed by one strongly stressed syllable, as in the words *unimpressed* and *correlate.* A line of poetry made up of anapests is said to be *anapestic.*

ANECDOTE. An **anecdote** is a usually short narrative of an interesting, amusing, or biographical incident. Although anecdotes are often the basis for short stories, an anecdote differs from a short story in that it lacks a complicated plot and relates a single episode. Anecdotes are sometimes used in nonfiction writing as examples to help support an idea or opinion. In her memoir "Something Could Happen to You" (Unit 9), Esmeralda Santiago tells several anecdotes about being a new immigrant in the United States to illustrate the problems people living in two cultures face.

ANTAGONIST. See *character*.

ANTIHERO. An **antihero** is a central character who lacks many of the qualities traditionally associated with heroes. An antihero may be lacking in beauty, courage, grace, intelligence, or moral scruples. Antiheroes are common figures in modern fiction and drama. In Tobias Wolff's "The Liar" (Unit 7), James, the narrator of the story, is an antihero because he lies. See *hero*.

APHORISM. An **aphorism** is a short saying or pointed statement. Examples of aphorisms by Benjamin Franklin include "The early bird catches the worm" and "Time is money." An aphorism that gains currency and is passed from generation to generation is called a *proverb* or *adage*. See *proverb*.

APOSTROPHE. An **apostrophe** is a rhetorical device by which a speaker turns from the audience as a whole to address a single person or thing.

APPOSITION. An **apposition** is a grammatical form in which a thing is renamed in a different word, phrase, or clause.

ARCHAIC LANGUAGE. **Archaic language** consists of old or obsolete words or phrases such as *smote* for *hit*.

ARCHETYPE. An **archetype** is an inherited, often unconscious, ancestral memory or motif that recurs throughout history and literature. The notion of the archetype derives from the psychology of Carl Jung, who described archetypes as symbols from humanity's "collective unconscious." The term is often used, more generally, to refer to any element that recurs throughout the literature of the world. Thus the story of the journey, in which someone sets out on a path, experiences adventures, and emerges wiser, may be considered archetypal, for it is found in all cultures and in all times. See *motif*.

ARGUMENT. 1. An **argument** is a summary, in prose, of the plot or meaning of a poem or drama. 2. In nonfiction writing, an **argument** is the case for accepting or rejecting a proposition or course of action.

ARGUMENTATION. **Argumentation** is a type of writing that presents reasons or arguments for accepting a position or for adopting a course of action.

ARGUMENTATIVE WRITING. See *aim*.

ARTICLE. An **article** is a brief work of nonfiction on a specific topic. The term *article* is typically used for encyclopedia entries and short nonfiction works that appear in newspapers and popular magazines. The term is sometimes used as a synonym of *essay*, though the latter term often connotes a more serious, important, or lasting work. "Under the Crack of Reality" and "Beware the Unruly Sun" (Unit 6) are examples of magazine articles. See *essay*.

ASIDE. An **aside** is a statement made by a character in a play, intended to be heard by the audience but not by other characters on the stage.

In Shakespeare's *The Tragedy of Julius Cæsar*, Cæsar makes an aside to the audience in act 2, scene 2, lines 1–3.

ASSONANCE. **Assonance** is the repetition of vowel sounds in stressed syllables that end with different consonant sounds. An example is the repetition of the short *i* sound in the following line from Gwendolyn Brooks's "The Bean Eaters" (Unit 2):

Remembering, with twinklings and twinges

ATMOSPHERE. See *mood*.

AUTOBIOGRAPHY. An **autobiography** is the story of a person's life, written by that person. Some editors and critics distinguish between autobiographies, which focus on personal experiences, and *memoirs*, which focus on public events, though the terms are often used interchangeably. The excerpt from *My Left Foot* by Christy Brown in Unit 8 is an example of an autobiography, as is the excerpt from *Desert Exile: The Uprooting of a Japanese-American Family* by Yoshiko Uchida in Unit 10.

BACKGROUND INFORMATION. See *flashback*, *plot*, and *setting*.

BALLAD. A **ballad** is a simple narrative poem in four-line stanzas, usually meant to be sung and usually rhyming *abcb*. *Folk ballads*, composed orally and passed by word of mouth from generation to generation, have enjoyed enormous popularity from the Middle Ages to the present. Examples of popular American ballads include "The Ballad of Casey Jones" and "Bonny Barbara Allan." *Literary ballads*, written in imitation of folk ballads, have also been very popular. The folk ballad stanza usually alternates between lines of four and three feet. Common techniques used in ballads include repeated lines, or *refrains*, and *incremental repetition*, the repetition of lines with slight, often cumulative, changes throughout the poem. See *refrain*.

BIBLIOGRAPHY. A **bibliography** is a list of works on a given subject or of works consulted by an author. See *List of Works Cited*.

BIOGRAPHY. A **biography** is the story of a person's life, told by someone other than that person. The excerpt from *Albert Einstein: A Biography* by Albrecht Fölsing in Unit 8 is an example of a biography.

BLANK VERSE. Blank verse is unrhymed poetry written in iambic pentameter. An *iambic pentameter* line consists of five *feet*, each containing two syllables, the first weakly stressed and the second strongly stressed.

BLEND. A blend, or *portmanteau,* is a word created by joining together two previously existing words, such as *smoke* and *fog* for *smog.*

CACOPHONY. Cacophony is harsh or unpleasant sound. Writers sometimes intentionally use cacophony for effect.

CÆSURA. A cæsura is a major pause in a line of poetry.

CARICATURE. In literature, a **caricature** is a piece of writing that exaggerates certain qualities of a character in order to satirize or ridicule that character or type. See *satire.*

CATALOG. A catalog is a list of people or things.

CATASTROPHE. The **catastrophe** is a conclusion of a work, particularly of a tragedy, marked by the fall of the central character. In the catastrophe, the central conflict of the work is ended, or resolved. The catastrophe of Sophocles's *Antigone* (Unit 11) occurs when Creon learns of the deaths of his wife and son and recognizes that his life is ruined. See *plot.*

CATHARSIS. The ancient Greek philosopher Aristotle described tragedy as bringing about a **catharsis**, or purging, of the emotions of fear and pity. Some critics take Aristotle's words to mean that viewing a tragedy causes the audience to feel emotions of fear and pity, which are then released at the end of the play, leaving the viewer calmer, wiser, and perhaps more thoughtful. The idea that catharsis calms an audience has been contradicted by recent psychological studies that suggest that people tend to imitate enacted feelings and behaviors that they witness. Much of the current debate over violence on television and in movies centers on this question of whether viewing such violence has a cathartic (calming) or an arousing effect on the viewer.

CENSORSHIP. Censorship is the act of examining works to see if they meet predetermined standards of political, social, or moral acceptability. Official censorship is aimed at works that will undermine authority or morals and has often in the past resulted in the suppression of works considered dangerous or licentious. Famous American novels that have been targets of censorship include *Adventures of Huckleberry Finn* by Mark Twain and *The Catcher in the Rye* by J. D. Salinger.

CENTRAL CONFLICT. A **central conflict** is the primary struggle dealt with in the plot of a story or drama. The central conflict in Sophocles's *Antigone* (Unit 11) is Creon's dispute with Antigone over the burial of her brother Polyneices. See *conflict* and *plot.*

CHARACTER. A **character** is a person (or sometimes an animal) who figures in the action of a literary work. A *protagonist,* or *main character,* is the central figure in a literary work. An *antagonist* is a character who is pitted against a protagonist. *Major characters* are those who play significant roles in a work. *Minor characters* are those who play lesser roles. A *one-dimensional character, flat character,* or *caricature* is one who exhibits a single dominant quality, or *character trait.* In the Aztec myth "Popocatépetl and Ixtacihuatl" (Unit 1), the two young lovers are one-dimensional characters. A *three-dimensional, full,* or *rounded character* is one who exhibits the complexity of traits associated with actual human beings, like James in Tobias Wolff's "The Liar" (Unit 7). A *static character* is one who does not change during the course of the action. A *dynamic character* is one who does change. A *stock character* is one found again and again in different literary works. An example of a stock character is the mad scientist of nineteenth- and twentieth-century science fiction.

CHARACTERIZATION. Characterization is the use of literary techniques to create a character. Writers use three major techniques to create characters: direct description, portrayal of characters' behavior, and representations of characters' internal states. When using direct description, the writer, through a speaker, a narrator, or another character, simply comments on the character, telling the reader about such matters as the character's appearance, habits, dress, background, personality, motivations, and so on. In portrayal of a character's behavior, the writer presents the actions and speech of the character, allowing the reader to draw his or her own conclusions from what the character says or does. When using representations of internal states, the writer reveals directly the character's private thoughts and emotions, often by means of what is known as the *internal monologue*. See *character* and *internal monologue*.

CHORUS. A **chorus** is a person or group of people who speaks directly to the audience to convey the author's viewpoint or to introduce story details. In classical Greek drama, the chorus traditionally made its entrance singing a song called the *parodos*, the first of a number of *odes*, or lofty, serious lyric poems it would sing throughout the play. These choral odes had alternating stanzas called the *strophe*, the *antistrophe*, and the *epode*. The chorus moved up one side of the stage while singing the strophe, down the other during the antistrophe, and stood in place during the epode. In *Antigone* (Unit 11), the leader of the chorus is called the Choragos.

CHRONOLOGICAL ORDER. **Chronological order** is the arrangement of details in order of their occurrence. It is the primary method of organization used in narrative writing. It is also common in nonfiction writing that describes processes, events, and cause and effect relationships.

CLASSIC. A **classic** is a work of literature that is widely held to be one of the greatest creations within a given literary tradition. The question of what works are to be considered classic is a much-debated one. Shakespeare's *The Tragedy of Julius Cæsar* (Unit 4) and Sophocles's *Antigone* (Unit 11) are traditionally considered drama classics.

CLASSIFICATION ORDER. **Classification order** is a method of organization in which subjects are divided into groups, or classes. These groups are then presented, one-by-one, in some reasonable order. Classification order is commonly used in exposition, or expository writing. See *exposition*, #1.

CLICHÉ. A **cliché** is an overused or unoriginal expression such as *quiet as a mouse* or *couch potato*. Most clichés originate as vivid, colorful expressions but soon lose their interest because of overuse. Careful writers and speakers avoid clichés, which are dull and signify lack of originality.

CLIMAX. The **climax** is the point of highest interest and suspense in a literary work. The term also is sometimes used to describe the *turning point* of the action in a story or play, the point at which the rising action ends and the falling action begins. The climax in Sophocles's *Antigone* (Unit 11) occurs when Creon decides he must free Antigone, only to learn that he is too late. See *crisis* and *plot*.

CLOSED COUPLET. See *couplet*.

COHERENCE. **Coherence** is the logical arrangement and progression of ideas in a speech or piece of writing. Writers achieve coherence by presenting their ideas in a logical sequence and by using transitions to show how their ideas are connected to one another. See *transition*.

COINED WORDS. **Coined words** are those that are intentionally created, often from the raw materials provided by already existing words and word parts. Examples of recently coined words include *spacewalk* and *e-mail*.

COLLOQUIALISM. **Colloquialism** is the use of informal language. Much modern poetry is characterized by its use of colloquialism. Garrison Keillor uses colloquialisms in "How to Write a Letter" (Unit 6) when he says, "Big Bopper here—what's shakin', babes?"

COMEDY. Originally a literary work with a happy ending, a **comedy** is any lighthearted or humorous work, especially one prepared for the stage or the screen. Comedy is often contrasted with *tragedy*, in which the hero meets an unhappy fate. (It is perhaps only a slight exaggeration to say that comedies end with wedding bells and tragedies with funeral bells.) Comedies typically present less-than-exalted characters who display human limitations, faults, and misunderstandings. The typical progression of the action in a comedy is from initial order to a humorous misunderstanding or confusion and back to order again. Stock elements of comedy include mistaken identities, word play, satire, and exaggerated characters and events. See *tragedy*.

COMIC RELIEF. Writers sometimes insert into a serious work of fiction or drama a humorous scene that is said to provide **comic relief**, because it relieves the seriousness or emotional intensity felt by the audience. Paradoxically, a scene introduced for comic relief can sometimes, because of the contrast it provides, increase the perceived intensity or seriousness of the action around it.

COMPARISON AND CONTRAST ORDER. See *exposition*, #1.

COMPLICATION. The **complication** is the part of a plot in which the conflict is developed or built to its high point of intensity. See *plot*.

CONCRETE. A **concrete** word or phrase is one that names or describes something that can be directly perceived by one or more of the five senses. *Buffalo, geranium, storm,* and *heron* are examples of concrete terms. See *abstract.*

CONCRETE POEM. A **concrete poem,** or *shape poem,* is one printed or written in a shape that suggests its subject matter.

CONCRETE UNIVERSAL. A **concrete universal** is a particular object, person, action, or event that provides an instance or example of a general type.

CONFESSIONAL POETRY. Confessional poetry is verse that describes, sometimes with painful explicitness, the private or personal affairs of the writer.

CONFLICT. A **conflict** is a struggle between two forces in a literary work. A *plot* involves the introduction, development, and eventual resolution of a conflict. One side of the *central conflict* in a story or drama is usually taken by the *main character.* That character may struggle against another character, against the forces of nature, against society or social norms, against fate, or against some element within himself or herself. In "The Moment Before the Gun Went Off" (Unit 3), the main character experiences man-against-himself conflict. A struggle that takes place between a character and some outside force is called an *external conflict.* A struggle that takes place within a character is called an *internal conflict.* In Tillie Olsen's short story "I Stand Here Ironing" (Unit 3), the narrator has an internal conflict about whether or not she has been a good mother to her daughter.

CONNOTATION. A **connotation** is an emotional association or implication attached to an expression. For example, the word *inexpensive* has positive emotional associations, whereas the word *cheap* has negative ones, even though the two words both *denote,* or refer to, low cost. Good writers choose their words carefully in order to express appropriate connotations. See *denotation.*

CONSONANCE. Consonance is a kind of slant rhyme in which the ending consonant sounds of two words match, but the preceding vowel sound does not, as in the words *wind* and *sound.* The following lines from Garrett Hongo's poem "The Legend" (Unit 9) provide an example:

as a last flash of sunset / blazes the storefronts and lit windows of the street.

CONVENTION. A **convention** is an unrealistic element in a literary work that is accepted by readers or viewers because the element is traditional. One of the conventions of fiction, for example, is that it uses the past tense to describe current or present action. Rhyme schemes and organization into stanzas are among the many commonly employed conventions of poetry.

CONVENTIONAL SYMBOL. See *symbol.*

COUPLET. A couplet is two lines of verse that usually rhyme. These lines from Shakespeare's *The Tragedy of Julius Cæsar* (Unit 4) provide an example:

So call the field to rest, and let's away,
To part the glories of this happy day

A *closed couplet* is a pair of rhyming lines that present a complete statement. A pair of rhyming iambic pentameter lines is also known as a *heroic couplet.*

CRISIS. In the plot of a story or a drama, the **crisis** is that point in the development of the conflict at which a decisive event occurs that causes the main character's situation to become better or worse. The crisis in Sophocles's *Antigone* (Unit 11) occurs when Creon decides to free Antigone, only to learn that he is too late. See *plot.*

CRITIC. A literary **critic** is a person who evaluates or interprets a work of literature. See *criticism.*

CRITICAL ESSAY. A **critical essay** is a type of informative or persuasive writing that presents an argument in support of a particular interpretation or evaluation of a work of literature. A well-constructed critical essay presents a clear *thesis,* or main idea, supported by ample evidence from the work or works being considered. See *thesis.*

CRITICISM. Criticism is the act of evaluating or interpreting a work of art or the act of developing general guidelines or principles for such evaluation or interpretation. Over the centuries, many schools, or philosophies, of criticism have been developed. However, most readers and teachers are eclectic critics, drawing consciously or unconsciously upon various schools of critical thought.

DACTYL. A **dactyl** is a poetic foot made up of a strongly stressed syllable followed by two weakly stressed syllables, as in the word *feverish*. A line of poetry made up of dactyls is said to be *dactylic*.

DEAD METAPHOR. A **dead metaphor** is one that is so familiar that its original metaphorical meaning is rarely thought of when the expression is used. An example is the word *nightfall*, which describes the coming of darkness as a falling object.

DEFINITION. A **definition** is an explanation of the meaning of a word or phrase. A dictionary definition typically consists of two parts: the *genus*, or class to which the thing belongs, and the *differentia*, or differences between the thing and other things of its class.

DENOTATION. The **denotation** is the basic meaning or reference of an expression, excluding its emotional associations, or *connotations*. For example, the words *dirt* and *soil* share a single common denotation. However, *dirt* has negative connotations of uncleanliness, whereas *soil* does not. See *connotation*.

DÉNOUEMENT. See *plot*.

DESCRIPTION. **Description** is a type of writing that portrays a character, an object, or a scene. Descriptions make use of *sensory details*—words and phrases that describe how things look, sound, smell, taste, or feel. Effective descriptions contain precise nouns, verbs, adverbs, and adjectives. When Garrett Hongo describes the Asian man's suit pants as "rumpled" in "The Legend" (Unit 9), he is appealing to the sense of sight. Descriptions often use *imagery* and *figurative language*.

DIALECT. A **dialect** is a version of a language spoken by the people of a particular place, time, or social group. Writers often use dialect, as in Amy Tan's "Rules of the Game" (Unit 8), to give their works a realistic flavor. A *regional dialect* is one spoken in a particular place. A *social dialect* is one spoken by members of a particular social group or class. The *vernacular* is the speech of the common people.

DIALOGUE. 1. **Dialogue** is conversation involving two or more people or characters. Plays are made up of dialogue and stage directions. Fictional works are made up of dialogue, narra-

tion, and description. 2. **Dialogue** is also used to describe a type of literary composition in which characters debate or discuss an idea.

DIARY. A **diary** is a day-to-day record of a person's activities, experiences, thoughts, and feelings. Anne Frank's *The Diary of a Young Girl* (Unit 5) is written in the form of a diary. See *journal*.

DICTION. **Diction**, when applied to writing, refers to word choice. Much of a writer's style is determined by his or her diction, the types of words that he or she chooses. Diction can be formal or informal, simple or complex, contemporary or archaic, ordinary or unusual, foreign or native, standard or dialectical, coarse or refined, euphemistic or blunt. See *style*.

DIMETER. See *meter*.

DOMINANT IMPRESSION. See *effect*.

DRAMA. A **drama** is a story told through characters played by actors. The script of a drama typically consists of characters' names, dialogue spoken by the characters, and stage directions. Because it is meant to be performed before an audience, drama can be distinguished from other literary works by the central role played in it by the *spectacle*—the sensory presentation to the audience, which includes such elements as lighting, costumes, makeup, properties, set pieces, music, sound effects, and the movements and expressions of actors. Another important distinguishing feature of drama is that it is collaborative. The interpretation of the work depends not only upon the author and his or her audience, but also upon the director, the actors, and others involved in mounting a production. Two major types of drama are *comedy* and *tragedy*. Both Shakespeare's *The Tragedy of Julius Cæsar* (Unit 4) and Sophocles's *Antigone* (Unit 11) are tragedies. See *comedy, dialogue, spectacle, stage directions,* and *tragedy*.

DRAMATIC CONVENTION. A **dramatic convention** is an unreal element in a drama that is accepted as realistic by the audience because it is traditional. Such conventions include the impersonation of characters by actors, the use of a curtain to open or close an act or a scene, the revelation of a character's thoughts through *asides* and *soliloquies*, and the removal of the so-called *fourth wall* at the front of the stage that allows the audience to see action taking place in an imagined interior. See *convention* and *suspension of disbelief*.

DRAMATIC IRONY. See *irony*.

DRAMATIC MONOLOGUE. A **dramatic monologue** is a poem that presents the speech of a single character in a dramatic situation. The speech is one side of an imagined conversation. See *soliloquy*.

DRAMATIC POEM. A **dramatic poem** is a verse that relies heavily on dramatic elements such as monologue (speech by a single character) or *dialogue* (conversation involving two or more characters). Often dramatic poems are narratives as well. In other words, they often tell stories. Types of dramatic poetry include the *dramatic monologue* and the *soliloquy*. See *poetry, lyric poem,* and *narrative poem*.

DRAMATIS PERSONAE. **Dramatis personae** are the characters in a literary work. The term is most often used for the characters in a drama. See page 246 for a list of the dramatis personae in Shakespeare's *Julius Cæsar* and page 865 for a list of the dramatis personae in Sophocles's *Antigone*.

DREAM RECORD. A **dream record** is a diary or journal in which a writer records his or her dreams. See *diary* and *journal*.

DYNAMIC CHARACTER. See *character*.

DYSTOPIA. A **dystopia** is an imaginary, horrible world, the opposite of a *utopia*. Dystopias are common in science fiction. A famous example of a dystopia is the society described in Ray Bradbury's *Fahrenheit 451*. See *utopia*.

EDITORIAL. An **editorial** is a short, persuasive piece that appears in a newspaper, magazine, or other periodical.

EFFECT. The **effect** of a literary work is the general impression or emotional impact that it achieves. Some writers and critics, notably Edgar Allan Poe, have insisted that a successful short story or poem is one in which each detail contributes to the overall effect, or *dominant impression*, produced by the piece.

ELABORATION. **Elaboration**, or **amplification**, is a writing technique in which a subject is introduced and then expanded upon by means of repetition with slight changes, the addition of details, or similar devices.

ELEGY. An **elegy** is a poem that laments the dead. It is frequently long and formal in tone, but other poems can mourn death or loss as well.

ELIZABETHAN SONNET. See *sonnet*.

EMPHASIS. **Emphasis** is importance placed on an element in a literary work. Writers achieve emphasis by various means, including *repetition, elaboration,* stress, restatement in other words, and placement in a strategic position at the beginning or end of a line or a sentence.

END RHYME. **End rhyme** is rhyme that occurs at the ends of lines of verse. See *rhyme*.

ENGLISH SONNET. See *sonnet*.

EPIC. An **epic** is a long story, often told in verse, involving heroes and gods. Grand in length and scope, an epic provides a portrait of an entire culture, of the legends, beliefs, values, laws, arts, and ways of life of a people. Famous epic poems include Homer's *Iliad* and *Odyssey*, Virgil's *Aeneid*, Dante's *The Divine Comedy*, the anonymous Old English *Beowulf*, and Milton's *Paradise Lost*. The *Kalevala* (Unit 2) is a Finnish epic.

EPIC HERO. See *hero*.

EPIGRAM. An **epigram** is a short, often witty, saying. An example of an epigram is Benjamin Franklin's "Three may keep a secret, if two of them are dead."

EPIGRAPH. An **epigraph** is a quotation or motto used at the beginning of the whole or part of a literary work to help establish the work's theme.

EPILOGUE. An **epilogue** is a concluding section or statement, often one that comments on or draws conclusions from the work as a whole.

EPIPHANY. When applied to literature, the term **epiphany** refers to a moment of sudden insight in which the essence, or nature, of a person, thing, or situation is revealed. The use of the term in this sense was introduced by the Irish author James Joyce.

EPISODE. An **episode** is a complete action within a literary work.

EPISTLE. An **epistle** is a letter, especially one that is highly formal. Letters in verse are sometimes called epistles.

EPITAPH. An **epitaph** is an inscription or verse written to be used on a tomb or written in commemoration of someone who has died. The epitaph on the grave of Benjamin Franklin, written by Franklin himself, reads as follows:

The body of
Benjamin Franklin, printer,
(Like the cover of an old book,
Its contents worn out,
And stript of its lettering and gilding)
Lies here, food for worms!
Yet the work itself shall not be lost,
For it will, as he believed, appear once more
In a new
And more beautiful edition,
Corrected and amended
By its Author!

EPITHET. An **epithet** is a characteristic word or phrase used alongside the name of a person, place, or thing. "Spring, the season of new beginnings," is an example. Sometimes an epithet is so familiar that it can be used in place of a name.

EPONYM. An **eponym** is a person or character from whose name a word or title is derived, or a name that has become synonymous with some general characteristic or idea. Narcissus is the eponym of the word *narcissism*, which means extreme preoccupation with one's own appearance and importance. In Keyes's "Flowers for Algernon" (Unit 8), *Charlie Gordon* is an eponym of an unintelligent person or a foolish action.

ESSAY. An **essay** is a brief work of prose nonfiction. The original meaning of essay was "a trial or attempt," and the word retains some of this original force. An essay need not be a complete or exhaustive treatment of a subject but rather a tentative exploration of it. A good essay develops a single idea and is characterized by *coherence* and *unity*. Bharati Mukherjee's "The Road from Ballygunge" (Unit 10) is an example of a personal essay, or an essay related to the life or interests of the writer. See *coherence* and *unity*.

EUPHEMISM. A **euphemism** is an indirect word or phrase used in place of a direct statement that might be considered too harsh or offensive. The phrase *pass away*, used instead of *die*, and the phrase *waste management*, used in place of *garbage collection*, are euphemisms. In *Desert Exile: The Uprooting of a Japanese-American Family* (Unit 10), Yoshiko Uchida considers "apartment" a euphemism since her family's

living quarters in the internment camp are no more than a horse stall.

EUPHONY. **Euphony** is pleasing sound. Writers achieve euphony by various means, including repetitions of vowel and consonant sounds, *rhyme*, and *parallelism*. See *cacophony*.

EXPOSITION. 1. **Exposition** is a type of writing that presents facts or opinions in an organized manner. Among the most common ways to organize exposition are the following: analysis classification, comparison contrast, and process or how-to writing. See Types of Nonfiction Writing, page 427, for more information. 2. In a plot, the **exposition** is that part of a narrative that provides background information, often about the characters, setting, or conflict. See *plot*.

EXPOSITORY WRITING. See *aim*.

EXPRESSIVE WRITING. See *aim*.

EXTENDED METAPHOR. An **extended metaphor** is a point-by-point presentation of one thing as though it were another. The description is meant as an implied comparison, inviting the reader to associate the thing being described with something that is quite different from it.

EXTERNAL CONFLICT. See *conflict*.

EYE RHYME. See *sight rhyme*.

FABLE. A **fable** is a brief story, often with animal characters, told to express a moral. Famous fables include those of Æsop and Jean de La Fontaine.

FAIRY TALE. A **fairy tale** is a story that deals with mischievous spirits and other supernatural occurrences, often in medieval settings. The name is generally applied to stories of the kinds collected by Charles Perrault in France and the Brothers Grimm in Germany or told by Hans Christian Andersen in Denmark. "Cinderella" and "The Little Mermaid" are famous examples.

FALLING ACTION. See *plot*.

FANTASY. A **fantasy** is a literary work that contains highly unrealistic elements. Fantasy is often contrasted with *science fiction*, in which the unreal elements are given a scientific or pseudoscientific basis. Gabriel García Márquez's "A Very Old Man with Enormous Wings" (Unit 12) contains elements of fantasy. See *Magical Realism* and *science fiction*.

FARCE. A **farce** is a type of comedy that depends heavily on so-called low humor and on improbable, exaggerated, extreme situations or characters.

FICTION. Fiction is prose writing about imagined events or characters. The primary forms of fiction are the *novel* and the *short story*. See *novel* and *short story*.

FIGURATIVE LANGUAGE. Figurative language is writing or speech meant to be understood imaginatively instead of literally. Many writers, especially poets, use figurative language to help readers to see things in new ways. Figurative language includes such literary techniques as *apostrophe, hyperbole, irony, metaphor, metonymy, oxymoron, paradox, personification, simile, synecdoche,* and *understatement.*

FIGURES OF SPEECH. Figures of speech, or **tropes,** are expressions that have more than a literal meaning. Hyperbole, metaphor, personification, simile, and understatement are all figures of speech. See *hyperbole, metaphor, personification, simile,* and *understatement.*

FIRST-PERSON POINT OF VIEW. See *point of view.*

FLASHBACK. A **flashback** is a section of a literary work that presents an event or series of events that occurred earlier than the current time in the work. Writers use flashbacks for many purposes, but most notably to provide *background information,* or exposition. In popular melodramatic works, including modern romance fiction and detective stories, flashbacks are often used to end suspense by revealing key elements of the plot such as a character's true identity or the actual perpetrator of a crime. One common technique is to begin a work with a final event and then to tell the rest of the story as a flashback that explains how that event came about. Another common technique is to begin a story *in medias res* (in the middle of the action) and then to use a flashback to fill in the events that occurred before the opening of the story.

FLASH FICTION. See *short short.*

FLAT CHARACTER. See *character.*

FOIL. A **foil** is a character whose attributes, or characteristics, contrast with, and therefore throw into relief, the attributes of another character. In Shakespeare's *Julius Cæsar* (Unit 4),

Mark Antony may be seen as a foil for Brutus in that the former is a persuasive and charismatic speaker whereas the latter is straightforward and less showy.

FOLK BALLAD. See *ballad.*

FOLK SONG. A **folk song** is a traditional or composed song typically made up of stanzas, a refrain, and a simple melody. A form of folk literature, folk songs are expressions of commonly shared ideas or feelings and may be narrative or lyric in style. Traditional folk songs are anonymous songs that have been transmitted orally. Examples include the ballad "Bonny Barbara Allan," the sea chantey "Blow the Man Down," the children's song "Row, Row, Row Your Boat," the railroad song "Casey Jones," and the cowboy song "The Streets of Laredo." Contemporary composers of songs in the folk tradition include Bob Dylan, Joan Baez, Pete Seeger, and Joni Mitchell. See *ballad.*

FOLK TALE. A **folk tale** is a brief story passed by word of mouth from generation to generation. Writers often make use of materials from folk tales. Famous collections of folk tales include the German *Märchen,* or fairy tales, collected by the Brothers Grimm; Yeats's collection of Irish stories, *Mythologies;* and Zora Neale Hurston's collection of African-American folk tales and other folklore materials, *Of Mules and Men.* "Popocatépetl and Ixtacihuatl" in Unit 1 can be considered a folk tale. See *fairy tale, folklore,* and *oral tradition.*

FOLKLORE. Folklore is a body of orally transmitted beliefs, customs, rituals, traditions, songs, verses, or stories. *Folk tales, fables, fairy tales, tall tales, nursery rhymes, proverbs, legends, myths, parables, riddles,* charms, spells, and *ballads* are all common kinds of folklore, though each of these can be found, as well, in literary forms made in imitation of works from the oral tradition. See *folk tale, fable, fairy tale, tall tale, nursery rhyme, proverb, myth, parable, riddle,* and *ballad.*

FOOT. In a poem, a **foot** is a unit of rhythm consisting of strongly and weakly stressed syllables. See *meter* and *scansion.* Also see the specific types of feet: *anapest, dactyl, iamb, spondee,* and *trochee.*

FORESHADOWING. Foreshadowing is the act of presenting materials that hint at events to occur later in a story. The narrator of "Dead Men's Path" (Unit 10) foreshadows Michael Obi's failure in his role as headmaster when he states, "He condemned the narrow views of these older and less-educated ones."

FOREWORD. See *preface.*

FRAME TALE. A **frame tale** is a story that itself provides a vehicle for the telling of other stories.

FREE VERSE. **Free verse**, or *vers libre,* is poetry that avoids use of regular rhyme, meter, or division into stanzas. Much of the poetry written in the twentieth century is in free verse. Free verse is also referred to as *open verse.* The poems "New Dog" by Mark Doty and "The Legend" by Garrett Hongo (Unit 9) use free verse.

FULL CHARACTER. See *character.*

GENRE. A **genre** (zhän' rə) is one of the types or categories into which literary works are divided. Some terms used to name literary genres include *autobiography, biography, comedy, drama, epic, essay, lyric, narrative, novel,* pastoral, *poetry, short story,* and *tragedy.* Literary works are sometimes classified into genres based on subject matter. Such a classification might describe *detective stories, mysteries, adventure stories, romances, westerns,* and *science fiction* as different genres of fiction.

HAIKU. A **haiku** is a traditional Japanese three-line poem containing five syllables in the first line, seven in the second, and five again in the third. A haiku presents a picture, or image, in order to arouse in the reader a specific emotional and/or spiritual state.

HALF RHYME. See *slant rhyme.*

HEPTAMETER. See *meter.*

HEPTASTICH. A **heptastich** is a stanza with seven lines. See *stanza.*

HERO. A **hero** is a character whose actions are inspiring and courageous. An epic hero represents the ideals of the culture that creates it. In early literature, a hero is often part divine and has remarkable abilities, such as magical power, superhuman strength, or great courage. A tragic hero is a character of high status who possesses noble qualities but who also has a tragic flaw, or personal weakness. Creon in Sophocles's *Antigone* (Unit 11) can be considered a tragic

hero. In much contemporary literature, the term hero often refers to any main character. Madame Loisel is the hero of Guy de Maupassant's "The Necklace" (Unit 3).

HEROIC COUPLET. See *couplet.*

HEROIC EPIC. A **heroic epic** is an epic that has a main purpose of telling the life story of a great hero. See *epic.*

HEXAMETER. See *meter.*

HIGH STYLE. See *style.*

HOW-TO WRITING. See *exposition,* #1.

HYMN. A **hymn** is a song or verse of praise, often religious.

HYPERBOLE. A **hyperbole** (hī pʉr' bə lē) is an exaggeration made for rhetorical effect.

IAMB. An **iamb** is a poetic foot containing one weakly stressed syllable followed by one strongly stressed syllable, as in the words *afraid* and *release.* A line of poetry made up of iambs is said to be *iambic.*

IAMBIC. See *iamb.*

IMAGE. An **image** is language that creates a concrete representation of an object or an experience. An image is also the vivid mental picture created in the reader's mind by that language. The images in a literary work are referred to, collectively, as the work's *imagery.*

IMAGERY. See *image.*

IMAGINATIVE WRITING. See *aim.*

IN MEDIAS RES. See *action* and *flashback.*

INCITING INCIDENT. See *plot.*

INCREMENTAL REPETITION. See *ballad.*

INFORMATIVE WRITING. See *aim.*

INTERNAL CONFLICT. See *conflict.*

INTERNAL MONOLOGUE. An **internal monologue** presents the private sensations, thoughts, and emotions of a character. The reader is allowed to overhear what is going on in the character's mind. Which characters' internal states can be revealed in a work of fiction depends on the *point of view* from which the work is told. See *point of view.*

INTRODUCTION. See *preface.*

INVERSION. An **inversion** is a poetic technique in which the normal order of words in an utterance is altered. Robert Frost's famous line "Whose woods these are, I think I know" is an inversion of the usual order of expression: "I think I know whose these woods are."

IRONY. **Irony** is a difference between appearance and reality. Types of irony include the following: *dramatic irony*, in which something is known by the reader or audience but unknown to the characters; *verbal irony*, in which a statement is made that implies its opposite; and *irony of situation*, in which an event occurs that violates the expectations of the characters, the reader, or the audience. Verbal irony occurs in act 3 of Julius Cæsar (Unit 4) when Antony repeatedly was the word "honorable" while describing dishonorable acts. Irony of situation occurs in "Like the Sun" (Unit 3) when Sekhar experiences his "first test" at his morning meal.

IRONY OF SITUATION. See *irony*.

JOURNAL. A **journal**, like a *diary*, is a day-to-day record of a person's activities, experiences, thoughts, and feelings. In contrast to diary, the word *journal* connotes an outward rather than an inward focus. However, the two terms are often used interchangeably. See *diary*.

LEGEND. A **legend** is a story coming down from the past, often based on real events or characters from older times. Unlike myths, legends are popularly regarded as historical; however, they may contain elements that are fantastic or unverifiable. "Popocatépetl and Ixtacihuatl" in Unit 1 is an example of a Central American legend.

LIMITED POINT OF VIEW. See *narrator* and *point of view*.

LIST OF WORKS CITED. A **List of Works Cited** is a type of bibliography that lists works used or referred to by an author. A standard feature of a research paper, the List of Works Cited appears at the end of the paper and is arranged in alphabetical order. See *bibliography*.

LOW STYLE. See *style*.

LYRIC POEM. A **lyric poem** is a highly musical verse that expresses the emotions of a speaker. Lyric poems are often contrasted with narrative poems, which have storytelling as their main pur-pose. In Unit 2, Gwendolyn Brooks's "The Bean Eaters" and Langston Hughes's "Dream Variations" are examples of lyric poetry. See *poetry*.

MAGICAL REALISM. **Magical Realism** is a kind of fiction that is for the most part realistic but that contains elements of fantasy. It originated in the works of Latin American writers who wished to communicate non-European worldviews. Magical Realism reflects the fact that Latin American culture often accepts what Europeans would consider "fantastic occurrences" as a part of everyday reality. "A Very Old Man with Enormous Wings" by Gabriel García Márquez (Unit 12) is an example of Magical Realism.

MAIN CHARACTER. See *character*.

MAJOR CHARACTER. See *character*.

MEMOIR. A **memoir** is a nonfiction narration that tells a story. A memoir can be autobiographical (about one's life) or biographical (about someone else's life). Memoirs are based on a person's experiences and reactions to historical events. Esmeralda Santiago's "Something Could Happen to You" (Unit 9) is taken from her memoir *Almost a Woman*. See *autobiography* and *biography*.

METAPHOR. A **metaphor** is a figure of speech in which one thing is spoken or written about as if it were another. This figure of speech invites the reader to make a comparison between the two things. The two "things" involved are the writer's actual subject, the *tenor* of the metaphor, and another thing to which the subject is likened, the *vehicle* of the metaphor. In Unit 2 Gabriela Mistral uses this metaphor in her poem "Afternoon": "slow oil, not wine, / my veins." The tenor of the metaphor is "my veins," and the vehicle of the metaphor is "slow oil."

Personification and *similes* are types of metaphor. See *dead metaphor, mixed metaphor, personification,* and *simile*.

METER. The **meter** of a poem is its rhythmical pattern. English verse is generally described as being made up of rhythmical units called feet, as follows:

TYPE OF FOOT	STRESS PATTERN	EXAMPLE
iamb, or iambic	⌣ /	insist

foot		
trochee, or trochaic foot	/ ˘	freedom
anapest, or anapestic foot	˘ ˘ /	unimpressed
dactyl, or dactylic foot	/ ˘ ˘	feverish
spondee, or spondaic foot	/ /	baseball

Some scholars also use the term *pyrrhee*, or *pyrrhic* foot, to describe a foot with two weak stresses. Using this term, the word *unbelievable* might be described as consisting of two feet, an anapest followed by a pyrrhic:

˘ ˘ / | ˘ ˘
un be liev | a ble

Terms used to describe the number of feet in a line include the following:

monometer for a one-foot line
dimeter for a two-foot line
trimeter for a three-foot line
tetrameter for a four-foot line
pentameter for a five-foot line
hexameter, or Alexandrine, for a six-foot line
heptameter for a seven-foot line
octameter for an eight-foot line

A seven-foot line of iambic feet is called a *fourteener*.

A complete description of the meter of a line includes both the term for the type of foot that predominates in the line and the term for the number of feet in the line. The most common English meters are iambic tetrameter and iambic pentameter. The following are examples of each:

IAMBIC TETRAMETER:
˘ / ˘ / ˘ / ˘ /
O slow | ly, slow | ly rose | she up

IAMBIC PENTAMETER:
˘ / ˘ / ˘ / ˘ /
The cur | few tolls | the knell | of part |
˘ /
ing day,

METONYMY. **Metonymy** is the naming of an object associated with a thing in place of the name of the thing itself. Speaking of the *White House* when one means *the administrative* or *executive branch of the United States government* is an example of metonymy.

MIDDLE STYLE. See *style*.

MINOR CHARACTER. See *character*.

MIXED METAPHOR. A **mixed metaphor** is an expression or passage that garbles together two or more metaphors. An example of mixed metaphor would be the sentence "The chariot of the sun screamed across the sky," in which the sun is described, inconsistently, as both a chariot and as something that screams. See *metaphor*.

MODE. A **mode** is a form of writing. One common classification system, based on purpose or aim, divides types of writing into five modes: expository/informative, imaginative, narrative, personal/expressive, and persuasive/argumentative. See *aim*.

MONOMETER. See *meter*.

MOOD. **Mood,** or *atmosphere,* is the emotion created in the reader by part or all of a literary work. The writer can evoke in the reader an emotional response—such as fear, discomfort, longing, or anticipation—by working carefully with descriptive language and sensory details. Ray Bradbury evokes a somber mood in "The Pedestrian" (Unit 12).

MORAL. A **moral** is a practical or moral lesson, usually relating to the principles of right and wrong, to be drawn from a story or other work of literature. The moral of "The Necklace" (Unit 3) is to live your life honestly and to communicate openly.

MOTIF. A **motif** is any element that recurs in one or more works of literature or art. Examples of common folk tale motifs found in oral traditions throughout the world include grateful animals or the thankful dead, three wishes, the trial or quest, and the magical metamorphosis, or transformation of one thing into another. "Cinderella," "The Ugly Duckling," and the Arthurian "Sword in the Stone" are examples of the transformation motif, in which persons or creatures of humble station are revealed to be exceptional. Much can be revealed about a literary work by studying the motifs within it. In *The Tragedy of Julius Cæsar* (Unit 4), the motif of disorder in nature is significant because it reflects the moral disorder in Rome.

MOTIVATION. A **motivation** is a force that moves a character to think, feel, or behave in a certain way. Chee, in "Chee's Daughter" (Unit 10), is motivated by love to get his daughter back from his in-laws.

MUSE. In ancient Greek and Roman myth, the **Muses**—the nine daughters of Zeus and Mnemosyne, or Memory—were believed to provide the inspiration for the arts and sciences. Calliope was the Muse of epic poetry; Clio, the Muse of history; Erato, the Muse of lyrical poetry; Euterpe, the Muse of music; Melpomene, the Muse of tragedy; Polyhymnia, the Muse of sacred choral poetry; Terpsichore, the Muse of choral dance and song; Thalia, the Muse of comedy; and Urania, the Muse of astronomy. The idea of the Muse has often been used by later writers to explain the vagaries and mysteries of literary inspiration. The connection of the Muses with entertainments and the arts survives in our English words *amusing* and *amusement*.

MYTH. A **myth** is a story that explains objects or events in the natural world as resulting from the action of some supernatural force or entity, most often a god. Every early culture around the globe has produced its own myths. "The Five Ages of Man" and "Orpheus" in Unit 1 are Greek myths. *The Popol Vuh*, also in Unit 1, is an example of a Central American myth.

NARRATION. **Narration** is a type of writing that tells a story, or describes events, most often using time, or *chronological order*, as a way of organization. See *chronological order*.

NARRATIVE POEM. A **narrative poem** is a verse that tells a story. Denise Levertov's "A Tree Telling of Orpheus" (Unit 2) is an example of a narrative poem. See *poetry*.

NARRATIVE WRITING. See *aim*.

NARRATOR. A **narrator** is one who tells a story. In a drama, the narrator may be a character who introduces, concludes, or comments upon the action of the play. However, dramas typically do not have narrators. Works of fiction, on the other hand, always do, unless they consist entirely of dialogue without tag lines, in which case they cease to be fictions and become closet dramas, drama meant to be read but not performed. The narrator in a work of fiction may be a central or minor character or simply someone who witnessed or heard about the events being related. Writers achieve a wide variety of ends by varying the characteristics of

the narrator chosen for a particular work. Of primary importance is the choice of the narrator's *point of view*. Will the narrator be omniscient, knowing all things, including the internal workings of the minds of the characters in the story, or will the narrator be limited in his or her knowledge? Will the narrator participate in the action of the story or stand outside that action and comment on it? Will the narrator be reliable or unreliable? That is, will the reader be able to trust the narrator's statements? These are all questions that a writer must answer when developing a narrator. In Tobias Wolff's "The Liar" (Unit 7), the narrator is James, the boy who does the lying. See *point of view* and *speaker*.

NATURE WRITING. **Nature writing** is a genre of nonfiction concerned with the relationship between the human and the wild. It typically seeks to connect the reader with natural phenomena without recourse to personification or sentimentality, instead relying on the traditional tools of the literary essayist—style, form, and the allegiance to the significant and telling fact. Nature writing delights in both scientific precision and subjective description, seeking always to reveal the mysteries of nature without destroying them.

NEAR RHYME. See *slant rhyme*.

NONFICTION. **Nonfiction** is writing about real events. *Essays, autobiographies, biographies*, and *news articles* are all types of nonfiction. Unit 5 is comprised of nonfiction selections. See *prose*.

NONSENSE VERSE. A **nonsense verse** is a kind of light verse that contains elements that are silly, absurd, or meaningless as in this example from "The Owl and the Pussycat" by Edward Lear:

> And there in a wood a Piggy-wig stood,
> With a ring at the end of his nose,
>   His nose
>   His nose,
> With a ring at the end of his nose.

NOVEL. A **novel** is a long work of prose fiction. Often novels have involved plots; many characters, both major and minor; and numerous settings. "A Smart Cookie" and "Rules of the Game," both in Unit 8, are excerpts from Sandra Cisneros's and Amy Tan's novels *The House on Mango Street* and *The Joy Luck Club*.

NOVELLA. A **novella** is a short novel.

NURSERY RHYME. A **nursery rhyme** is a children's verse.

OBJECTIVE CORRELATIVE. An **objective correlative** is a group of images that together create a particular emotion in the reader. The term was coined by T. S. Eliot. See *image*.

OCCASIONAL VERSE. An **occasional verse** is one written to celebrate or commemorate some particular event. For example, for President Clinton's first inauguration in 1993, Maya Angelou read a poem she wrote for the occasion, "On the Pulse of Morning."

OCTAMETER. See *meter*.

OCTAVE. An **octave** is an eight-line stanza. A Petrarchan sonnet begins with an octave. See *meter* and *sonnet*.

OFF RHYME. See *slant rhyme*.

OMNISCIENT POINT OF VIEW. See *narrator* and *point of view*.

ONE-ACT. See *act*.

ONE-DIMENSIONAL CHARACTER. See *character*.

ONOMATOPOEIA. **Onomatopoeia** is the use of words or phrases that sound like the things to which they refer. Examples of onomatopoeia include words such as *buzz, click,* and *pop.* Poets and other writers often make use of onomatopoeia.

ORAL TRADITION. An **oral tradition** is a work, an idea, or a custom that is passed by word of mouth from generation to generation. Materials transmitted orally may be simplified in the retelling. They also may be sensationalized because of the tendency of retellers to add to or elaborate upon the materials that come down to them. Often, works in an oral tradition contain miraculous or magical elements. Common works found in the oral traditions of peoples around the world include *folk tales, fables, fairy tales, tall tales, nursery rhymes, proverbs, legends, myths, parables, riddles,* charms, spells, and *ballads.* "Magic Words" in Unit 1 belongs to the Inuit oral tradition. "Sundiata Keita, the Legend and the King," also in that unit, belongs to the oral tradition of Mali. See *folklore.*

OXYMORON. An **oxymoron** is a statement that contradicts itself. Words like *bittersweet, tragicomedy,* and *pianoforte* (literally, "soft-loud") are oxymorons that develop a complex meaning from two seemingly contradictory elements.

PALINDROME. A **palindrome** is a word, a phrase, or a sentence that reads the same backward as forward. Examples include the word *radar* and the phrase *A man, a plan, a canal—Panama.*

PARABLE. A **parable** is a very brief story told to teach a moral lesson. The most famous parables are those told by Jesus in the Bible.

PARADOX. A **paradox** is a seemingly contradictory statement, idea, or event. All forms of *irony* involve paradox. An *oxymoron* is a paradoxical statement. Some paradoxes present unresolvable contradictory ideas. An example of such a paradox is the statement, "This sentence is a lie." If the sentence is true, then it is false; if it is false, then it is true. See *irony* and *oxymoron.*

PARALLELISM. **Parallelism** is a rhetorical technique in which a writer emphasizes the equal value or weight of two or more ideas by expressing them in the same grammatical form. Gwendolyn Brooks uses parallelism in the following lines from "The Bean Eaters" in Unit 2:

> Two who are Mostly Good.
> Two who have lived their day.

PARAPHRASE. A **paraphrase** is a rewriting of a passage in different words. A paraphrase is often distinguished from an *abstract* or summary as follows: a summary is shorter than the original, whereas a paraphrase may be as long as or longer than the original. See *abstract.*

PARODY. A **parody** is a literary work that imitates another work for humorous, often satirical, purposes.

PENTAMETER. See *meter.*

PERIODICAL. A **periodical** is a newspaper, magazine, journal, newsletter, or other publication that is produced on a regular basis. *Poetry* magazine has been a leading force in shaping the course of modern American poetry.

PERSONA. A **persona** consists of the qualities of a person or character that are shown through speech or actions.

PERSONAL ESSAY. A **personal essay** is a short work of nonfictional prose on a single topic related to the life or interests of the writer. Personal essays are characterized by an intimate and informal style and tone. They are often, but not always, written in the first person. See *essay.*

PERSONAL SYMBOL. See *symbol.*

PERSONAL WRITING. See *aim.*

PERSONIFICATION. **Personification** is a figure of speech in which an idea, animal, or thing is described as if it were a person. In Denise Levertov's "A Tree Telling of Orpheus" in Unit 2, a tree that can talk and move is personified.

PERSUASIVE WRITING. See *aim.*

PLAGIARISM. **Plagiarism** is the act of using material gathered from another person or work without crediting the source of the material.

PLOT. A **plot** is a series of events related to a central *conflict,* or struggle. A typical plot involves the introduction of a conflict, its development, and its eventual resolution. Terms used to describe elements of plot include the following:

- The **exposition,** or *introduction,* sets the tone or mood, introduces the characters and the setting, and provides necessary background information.
- The **inciting incident** is the event that introduces the central conflict.
- The **rising action,** or **complication,** develops the conflict to a high point of intensity.
- The **climax** is the high point of interest or suspense in the plot.
- The **crisis,** or *turning point,* often the same event as the climax, is the point in the plot where something decisive happens to determine the future course of events and the eventual working out of the conflict.
- The **falling action** is all the events that follow the climax.
- The **resolution** is the point at which the central conflict is ended, or resolved.
- The **dénouement** is any material that follows the resolution and that ties up loose ends.
- The **catastrophe,** in tragedy, is the event that marks the ultimate tragic fall of the central character. Often this event is the character's death.

Plots rarely contain all these elements in precisely this order. Elements of exposition may be introduced at any time in the course of a work. A work may begin with a catastrophe and then use flashback to explain it. The exposition or dénouement or even the resolution may be missing. The inciting incident may occur before the beginning of the action actually described in the work. These are but a few of the many possible variations that plots can exhibit. See *conflict.*

POETIC LICENSE. **Poetic license** is the right, claimed by writers, to change elements of reality to suit the purposes of particular works that they create. Such things do not happen in reality, but they are accepted by readers willing to suspend disbelief in order to have imaginary experiences. For example, Levertov uses poetic license when she gives speech and movement to the tree in "A Tree Telling of Orpheus" (Unit 2). See *suspension of disbelief.*

POETRY. **Poetry** is imaginative language carefully chosen and arranged to communicate experiences, thoughts, or emotions. It differs from prose in that it compresses meaning into fewer words, and often uses *meter, rhyme,* and techniques such as *metaphor* and *simile.* Poetry is usually arranged in lines and stanzas as opposed to sentences and paragraphs, and it can be more free in the ordering of words and the use of punctuation. Types of poetry include *narrative, dramatic,* and *lyric.* See *meter, rhyme, narrative poem, dramatic poem,* and *lyric poem.*

POINT OF VIEW. **Point of view** is the vantage point from which a story is told. Stories are typically written from a *first-person point of view,* in which the narrator uses words such as *I* and *we;* from a *second-person point of view,* in which the narrator uses *you;* or from a *third-person point of view,* in which the narrator uses words such as *he, she, it,* and *they.* In stories written from a first-person point of view, the narrator may be a participant or witness of the action. In stories told from a third-person point of view, the narrator generally stands outside the action. In some stories, the narrator's point of view is *limited.* In such stories, the narrator can reveal his or her private, internal thoughts or those of a single character. In other stories, the narrator's point of view is *omniscient.* In such stories the narrator can reveal the private, internal thoughts of any character.

PORTMANTEAU. See *blend.*

PRÉCIS. See *abstract.*

PREFACE. A **preface** is a statement made at the beginning of a literary work, often by way of introduction. The terms *foreword, preface,* and *introduction* are often used interchangeably.

PROCESS WRITING. See *exposition, #1.*

PROLOGUE. A **prologue** is an introduction to a literary work, often one that sets the scene and introduces the conflict or the main characters. Sophocles's *Antigone* (Unit 11) begins with a prologue between Antigone and her sister Ismene.

PROSCENIUM STAGE. See *stage*.

PROSE. **Prose** is the broad term used to describe all writing that is not drama or poetry, including fiction and nonfiction. Types of prose writing include novels, short stories, essays, and news stories. Most biographies, autobiographies, and letters are written in prose. See *fiction*.

PROSE POEM. A **prose poem** is a work of prose, usually a short work, that makes such extensive use of poetic language, such as figures of speech and words that echo their sense, that the line between prose and poetry becomes blurred. "Holidays" by Jamaica Kincaid (Unit 2) is an example of a prose poem.

PROTAGONIST. See *character*.

PROVERB. A **proverb**, or **adage**, is a traditional saying, such as "You can lead a horse to water, but you can't make it drink" or the title of Shakespeare's play *All's Well That Ends Well*.

PSEUDONYM. A **pseudonym** is a name assumed by a writer. For example, Mark Twain was the pseudonym of Samuel Clemens.

PSYCHOLOGICAL FICTION. **Psychological fiction** is fiction that emphasizes the interior, subjective experiences of its characters, and especially such fiction when it deals with emotional or mental disturbance or anguish.

PUN. A **pun** is a play on words, one that wittily exploits a double meaning. Act 1, scene 1 of Shakespeare's *Julius Cæsar* (Unit 4) contains several puns. One example is the line, "yet if you be out, sir, I can mend you." "If you be out" means both "if your shoes are worn out" and "if you are put out, or angry."

PURPOSE. See *aim*.

PYRRHIC. See *meter*.

QUATRAIN. A **quatrain** is a stanza containing four lines.

QUINTAIN. A **quintain**, or **quintet**, is a stanza containing five lines.

QUINTET. See *quintain*.

RAP. **Rap** is improvised, rhymed verse that is chanted or sung, often to a musical accompaniment.

REALISM. **Realism** is the attempt to render in art an accurate portrayal of reality.

REDUNDANCY. **Redundancy** is needless repetition. The phrase *firmly determined* is redundant because the word *determined* already implies firmness.

REFRAIN. A **refrain** is a line or group of lines repeated in a poem or song. Many *ballads* contain refrains.

REGIONAL DIALECT. See *dialect*.

REGIONAL FICTION. **Regional fiction** is writing in which particular settings play an important role. The details used to create a particular regional setting are called *local color*. Many American novels and short stories deal with particular regions of the country (New York City, the western frontier, small towns in the South or Midwest, and so on).

RENAISSANCE. The **Renaissance** was the period from the fourteenth to the early seventeenth century when Europe was making the transition from the medieval to the modern world. The word *renaissance* means "rebirth." The term refers to the rebirth of interest in ancient Greek and Latin writing that occurred during the period, a rebirth that is known as Humanism.

REPETITION. **Repetition** is the writer's conscious reuse of a sound, word, phrase, sentence, or other element.

RESOLUTION. See *plot*.

REVERSAL. A **reversal** is a dramatic change in the direction of events in a drama or narrative, especially a change in the fortunes of the protagonist. See *plot*.

REVIEW. A **review** is a written evaluation of a work of art, a performance, or a literary work, especially one that appears in a periodical or on a broadcast news program. Common subjects of reviews include books, films, art exhibitions, restaurants, and performances of all kinds, from rock concerts to ballets.

RHETORIC. **Rhetoric** is the art of speaking or writing effectively. It involves the study of ways in which speech and writing affect or influence audiences. Rhetoric has also been defined as the art of persuasion.

RHETORICAL QUESTION. A **rhetorical question** is one asked for effect but not meant to be answered because the answer is clear from context.

RHETORICAL TECHNIQUE. A **rhetorical technique** is an extraordinary but literal use of language to achieve a particular effect on an audience. Common rhetorical techniques include *apostrophe, catalog, parallelism, repetition*, and the *rhetorical question*.

RHYME. **Rhyme** is the repetition of sounds at the ends of words. Types of rhyme include *end rhyme* (the use of rhyming words at the ends of lines), *internal rhyme* (the use of rhyming words within lines), *exact rhyme* (in which the rhyming words end with the same sound or sounds), and *slant rhyme* (in which the rhyming sounds are similar but not identical). An example of exact rhyme is the word pair *moon/June*. Examples of slant rhyme are the word pairs *rave/rove* and *rot/rock*. See *poetry, slant rhyme* and *rhyme scheme*.

RHYME SCHEME. A **rhyme scheme** is a pattern of end rhymes, or rhymes at the ends of lines of verse. The rhyme scheme of a poem is designated by letters, with matching letters signifying matching sounds. For example, the rhyme scheme for Emily Dickinson's poem "Success is counted sweetest. . ." (Unit 2) is *abcb* for all three stanzas.

RHYTHM. **Rhythm** is the pattern of beats or stresses in a line of verse or prose. See *meter*.

RIDDLE. A **riddle** is a word game in which something is described in an unusual way and the reader or listener must figure out what that something is. Riddles are common in folklore and myth throughout the world.

RISING ACTION. See *plot*.

ROMANCE. **Romance** is a term used to refer to four types of literature: 1. medieval stories about the adventures and loves of knights; 2. novels and other fictions involving exotic locales and extraordinary or mysterious events and characters; 3. nonrealistic fictions in general; and 4. in popular, modern usage, love stories of all kinds. Today, the term is quite widely used to refer to love stories, especially popular, sentimental stories.

ROUNDED CHARACTER. See *character*.

RUN-ON LINE. A **run-on line** is a line of verse in which the sense or the grammatical structure does not end with the end of the line but rather is continued on one or more subsequent lines. The following lines from Emily Dickinson's "Success is counted sweetest. . ." (Unit 2) form a single sentence:

> Not one of all the purple Host
> Who took the Flag today
> Can tell the definition
> So clear of Victory
>
> As he defeated—dying—
> On whose forbidden ear
> The distant strains of triumph
> Burst agonized and clear!

The act of continuing a statement beyond the end of a line is called *enjambment*.

SATIRE. **Satire** is humorous writing or speech intended to point out errors, falsehoods, foibles, or failings. It is written for the purpose of reforming human behavior or human institutions.

SCANSION. **Scansion** is the art of analyzing poetry to determine its meter. See *meter*.

SCENE. A **scene** is a short section of a literary work that presents action that occurs in a single place or at a single time. Long divisions of dramas are often divided into scenes.

SCIENCE FICTION. **Science fiction** is highly imaginative fiction containing fantastic elements based on scientific principles, discoveries, or laws. It is similar to fantasy in that it deals with imaginary worlds but differs from fantasy in having a scientific basis. Often science fiction deals with the future, the distant past, or with worlds other than our own, such as other planets, parallel universes, and worlds under the ground or the sea. The genre allows writers to suspend or alter certain elements of reality in order to create fascinating and sometimes instructive alternatives. Important writers of science fiction include H. G. Wells, Jules Verne, Ray Bradbury, Arthur C. Clarke, Isaac Asimov, Ursula K. Le Guin, Robert Heinlein, and Kurt Vonnegut, Jr. In Unit 12, Bradbury's "The Pedestrian," Stephen Vincent Benét's "By the Waters of Babylon," and Lucille Fletcher's "The Hitchhiker" are all examples of science fiction. See *fantasy*.

SENSORY DETAIL. See *description*.

SENTIMENTALITY. **Sentimentality** is an excessive expression of emotion. Much popular literature of the nineteenth and twentieth centuries is characterized by sentimentality.

SEPTET. A **septet** is a stanza with seven lines.

SESTET. A **sestet** is a stanza with six lines, such as the second part of a Petrarchan sonnet. See *meter* and *sonnet*.

SET. A **set** is a collection of objects on a stage arranged in such a way as to create a scene.

SETTING. The **setting** of a literary work is the time and place in which it occurs, together with all the details used to create a sense of a particular time and place. Writers create setting by various means. In drama, the setting is often revealed by the stage set and the costumes, though it may be revealed through what the characters say about their environs. In fiction, setting is most often revealed by means of description of such elements as landscape, scenery, buildings, furniture, clothing, the weather, and the season. It can also be revealed by how characters talk and behave. In its widest sense, setting includes the general social, political, moral, and psychological conditions in which characters find themselves. A Navajo homestead and a trading post for tourists in the Southwest provide the setting for "Chee's Daughter" (Unit 10). See *set*.

SHAKESPEAREAN SONNET. See *sonnet*.

SHAPE POEM. See *concrete poem*.

SHORT SHORT. A **short short**, or *flash fiction,* is an extremely brief short story. This recently recognized genre of the short story is currently enjoying considerable popularity among readers of literary magazines and short story collections published in the United States. Short shorts sometimes take the form of anecdotes, or retellings of single incidents. Alternatively, they may attempt to develop an entire plot within the compass of a few paragraphs. Many short shorts are highly poetic and may be considered prose poems. See *anecdote* and *prose poem*.

SHORT STORY. A **short story** is a form of short prose fiction that relates a narrative. Short stories are typically crafted carefully to develop a plot, a conflict, characters, a setting, a mood, and a theme, all within relatively few pages. This form of literature gained popularity in the nineteenth century. See *conflict, character, mood, plot, setting,* and *theme*.

SIGHT RHYME. A **sight rhyme**, or **eye rhyme**, is a pair of words, generally at the ends of lines of verse, that are spelled similarly but pronounced differently. The words *lost* and *ghost* and *give* and *thrive* are examples. The end rhyme between *do* and *go* in Theodore Roethke's "The Waking" (Unit 7) provides an example:

> Great Nature has another thing to **do**
> To you and me; so take the lively air
> And lovely, learn by going where to **go.**

SIMILE. A **simile** is a comparison using *like* or *as*. Archibald MacLeish uses several similes in his poem "Ars Poetica" (Unit 2). For example, he says "A poem should be wordless / As the flight of birds." A simile is a type of *metaphor,* and like any other metaphor, can be divided into two parts, the *tenor* (or subject being described), and the *vehicle* (or object being used in the description). In MacLeish's simile, the tenor is "A poem" and the vehicle is "the flight of birds." They can be compared because they share some quality, in this case, wordlessness. See *metaphor*.

SLANG. **Slang** is extremely colloquial speech not suitable for formal occasions and usually associated with a particular group of people. An example of slang current among young people in the United States in the 1920s is "the bee's knees," for something uniquely attractive or wonderful. Among young people in the northeastern United States, the word *wicked* is now sometimes used as a slang term meaning "extremely," as in "That song is wicked good." Writers sometimes use slang in an attempt to render characters and setting vividly.

SLANT RHYME. A **slant rhyme,** *half rhyme, near rhyme,* or *off rhyme* is the substitution of assonance or consonance for true rhyme. The pairs *world/boiled* and *bear/bore* are examples. See *assonance, consonance,* and *rhyme*.

SOCIAL DIALECT. See *dialect*.

SOLILOQUY. A **soliloquy** is a speech delivered by a lone character that reveals the speaker's thoughts and feelings. Antony's speech over the dead body of Cæsar in act 3, scene 1 of Shakespeare's *Julius Cæsar* (Unit 4) is an example of a soliloquy.

SONNET. A **sonnet** is a fourteen-line poem, usually in iambic pentameter, that follows one of a number of different rhyme schemes. The *English, Elizabethan,* or *Shakespearean* sonnet is divided into four parts: three *quatrains* and a final *couplet.* The rhyme scheme of such a sonnet is *abab cdcd efef gg.* The *Italian* or *Petrarchan sonnet* is divided into two parts: an *octave* and a *sestet.* The rhyme scheme of the octave is *abbaabba.* The rhyme scheme of the sestet can be *cdecde, cdcdcd,* or *cdedce.* Rainer Maria Rilke's sonnet "The Gazelle" (Unit 2) is comprised of two quatrains and two tercets that rhyme *abab cdcd efe gfg.*

SOURCE. A **source** is a work from which an author takes his or her materials. In writing *Albert Einstein: A Biography,* Albrecht Fölsing used sources such as Einstein's own letters, diaries, and unpublished manuscripts to create an accurate, penetrating portrait of the scientific genius (Unit 8).

SPEAKER. The **speaker** is the character who speaks in, or narrates, a poem—the voice assumed by the writer. The speaker and the writer of a poem are not necessarily the same person.

SPECTACLE. In drama, the **spectacle** is all the elements that are presented to the senses of the audience, including the lights, setting, costumes, makeup, music, sound effects, and movements of the actors.

SPIRITUAL. A **spiritual** is a folk song of deep religious and emotional character. Spirituals were developed among African Americans in the southern United States during slavery. The words are most often related to biblical passages and frequently reflect patient, profound melancholy, even though the songs seldom refer to slavery itself. Spirituals influenced blues, jazz, and gospel songs.

SPONDEE. A **spondee** is a poetic foot containing two strongly stressed syllables, as in the words *compound* and *roughhouse.* Such a foot is said to be *spondaic.*

STAGE. A **stage** is any arena on which the action of a drama is performed. In the Middle Ages, stages often consisted of the beds of wagons, which were wheeled from place to place for performances. From the use of such wagons in inn yards, the *thrust stage* developed. This was a platform that extended out into the audience and that was closed at the back. In front of the platform in the first English theaters, such as Shakespeare's Globe Theatre, was an open area, the pit, where common people stood. Around the pit were balconies in imitation of the balconies of inns. The modern *proscenium stage* typically is closed on three sides and open at the front, as though the *fourth wall* had been removed. Sometimes contemporary plays are performed as *theater in the round,* with the audience seated on all sides of the playing area.

STAGE DIRECTIONS. **Stage directions** are notes included in a play, in addition to the dialogue, for the purpose of describing how something should be performed on stage. Stage directions describe setting, lighting, music, sound effects, entrances and exits, properties, and the movements of characters. They are usually printed in italics and enclosed in brackets or parentheses.

STANZA. A **stanza** is a group of lines in a poem. The following are some types of stanza:

two-line stanza	*couplet*
three-line stanza	*triplet* or *tercet*
four-line stanza	*quatrain*
five-line stanza	*quintain* or *quintet*
six-line stanza	*sestet*
seven-line stanza	*heptastich* or *septet*
eight-line stanza	*octave*

STATIC CHARACTER. See *character.*

STEREOTYPE. A **stereotype** is an uncritically accepted, fixed or conventional idea, particularly such an idea held about whole groups of people. A *stereotypical,* or *stock,* character is one who does not deviate from conventional expectations of such a character. Examples of stereotypical characters include the merciless villain, the mad scientist, and the hard-boiled private eye. See *character.*

STOCK CHARACTER. See *character* and *stereotype.*

STORY. A **story,** or **narrative,** is writing or speech that relates a series of events. When these events are causally connected and related to a conflict, they make up a *plot.* See *plot.*

STREAM-OF-CONSCIOUSNESS WRITING. **Stream-of-consciousness writing** is literary work that attempts to render the flow of feelings, thoughts, and impressions within the minds of characters. Modern masters of stream-of-consciousness writing include Virginia Woolf, James Joyce, and William Faulkner.

STRESS. **Stress,** or **accent**, is the level of emphasis given to a syllable. In English metrics, the art of *rhythm* in written and spoken expression, syllables are generally described as being strongly or weakly stressed, in other words, accented or unaccented. A strongly stressed or accented syllable receives a strong emphasis. A weakly stressed or unaccented syllable receives a weak one. In the following lines from Dickinson's "Success is counted sweetest. . ." (Unit 2), the strongly stressed or accented syllables are marked with a slash mark (/).

    /   /   /
Success is counted sweetest
     /   /   /
By those who ne'er succeed.

STYLE. **Style** is the manner in which something is said or written. Traditionally, critics and scholars have referred to three levels of style: high style, for formal occasions or lofty subjects; middle style, for ordinary occasions or subjects; and low style, for extremely informal occasions or subjects. A writer's style depends upon many things, including his or her *diction* (the words that the writer chooses), selection of grammatical structures (simple versus complex sentences, for example), and preference for *abstract* or *concrete* words. Any recurring feature that distinguishes one writer's work from another can be said to be part of that writer's style. See *abstract* and *fiction*.

SUBPLOT. A **subplot** is a subordinate story told in addition to the major story in a work of fiction. Often a subplot mirrors or provides a *foil* for the primary plot. See *plot* and *story*.

SUMMARY. See *abstract*.

SURREALISM. **Surrealism** is a movement in literature and art characterized by the juxtaposition of seemingly unrelated images. The movement began in 1924 as a reaction against "rational" middle-class values, which Surrealists felt had led to the devastation of World War I. Influenced by Sigmund Freud's exploration of the subconscious mind, Surrealists sought to give expression to the world of dream and fantasy and connect it to the everyday, rational world. An example of Surrealist literature is Julio Cortázar's "House Taken Over" (Unit 12).

SUSPENSE. **Suspense** is a feeling of expectation, anxiousness, or curiosity created by questions raised in the mind of a reader or viewer.

SUSPENSION OF DISBELIEF. **Suspension of disbelief** is the act by which the reader willingly sets aside his or her skepticism in order to participate imaginatively in the work being read. Readers may not believe that trees can talk and walk, but they are willing to suspend that disbelief when reading poems such as Levertov's "A Tree Telling of Orpheus" (Unit 2). The willingness to suspend disbelief, to participate imaginatively in a story being read, is the most important attribute, beyond literacy, that a person can bring to the act of reading literature.

SYMBOL. A **symbol** is a thing that stands for or represents both itself and something else. Writers use two types of symbols—conventional, and personal or idiosyncratic. A *conventional symbol* is one with traditional, widely recognized associations. Such symbols include doves for peace; laurel wreaths for heroism or poetic excellence; the color green for jealousy; winter, evening, or night for old age; wind for change or inspiration; the moon for fickleness or inconstancy; roads or paths for the journey through life; woods or darkness for moral or spiritual confusion. A *personal* or *idiosyncratic symbol* is one that assumes its secondary meaning because of the special use to which it is put by a writer. In "One of Grandma Selma's Stories" (Unit 10), the plane symbolizes the intrusion of Western civilization into traditional Inuit ways of life.

SYNAESTHESIA. **Synaesthesia** is a figure of speech that combines in a single expression images related to two or more different senses.

SYNECDOCHE. A **synecdoche** (sin ek' də kē´) is a figure of speech in which the name of part of something is used in place of the name of the whole or vice versa. In the command "All hands on deck!" *hands* is a synecdoche in which a part (hands) is used to refer to a whole (people, sailors). Addressing a representative of the country of France as *France* would be a synecdoche in which a whole (France) is used to refer to a part (one French person).

SYNTAX. **Syntax** is the pattern or arrangement of words in a statement. Poets often vary the syntax of ordinary speech or experiment with unusual syntactic arrangements. See *inversion*.

TAG LINE. A **tag line** is an expression in a work of fiction that indicates who is speaking and sometimes indicates the manner of speaking. Examples include the familiar *she said* as well as more elaborate expressions such as *Raoul retorted angrily.*

TALL TALE. A **tall tale** is a story, often lighthearted or humorous, that contains highly exaggerated, unrealistic elements. Stories about Paul Bunyan are tall tales.

TENOR. See *metaphor.*

TERCET. See *triplet.*

TETRAMETER. See *meter.*

THEATER (playing area). See *stage.*

THEATER IN THE ROUND. See *stage.*

THEME. A **theme** is a central idea in a literary work. The theme of Tillie Olsen's short story "I Stand Here Ironing" (Unit 3) is that failure is self-perpetuating, often being passed down to the next generation. In R. K. Narayan's short story "Like the Sun," also in Unit 3, the theme centers on the consequences of telling the truth.

THESIS. A **thesis** is a main idea that is supported in a work of nonfictional prose. The thesis of Bharati Mukherjee's "The Road from Ballygunge" (Unit 10) is that living in a second culture requires resilience and compassion.

THIRD-PERSON POINT OF VIEW. See *point of view.*

THREE-DIMENSIONAL CHARACTER. See *character.*

THRUST STAGE. See *stage.*

TONE. **Tone** is the emotional attitude toward the reader or toward the subject implied by a literary work. Examples of the different tones that a work may have include familiar, ironic, playful, sarcastic, serious, and sincere. In describing the traditional Navajo way of life, the authors of "Chee's Daughter" (Unit 10) use a reverent and respectful tone.

TRAGEDY. A **tragedy** is a drama (or by extension any work of literature) that tells the story of the fall of a person of high status. It celebrates the courage and dignity of a tragic hero in the face of inevitable doom. Sometimes that hero's doom is made inevitable by a *tragic flaw,* a personal weakness that brings about the fall of a character in his or her fall. In the twentieth century, writers have extended the definition of tragedy to cover works that deal with the fall of any sympathetic character, despite his or her status. Both Shakespeare's *Julius Cæsar* (Unit 4) and Sophocles's *Antigone* (Unit 11) are tragedies.

TRAGIC FLAW. See *tragedy.*

TRAGIC HERO. See *hero* and *tragedy.*

TRANSITION. A **transition** is a word, phrase, sentence, or paragraph used to connect ideas and to show relationships between them. *However, therefore, in addition,* and *in contrast* are common transitions. Repeated nouns, synonyms, and pronouns can also serve as transitions.

TRANSLATION. **Translation** is the art of rendering speech or writing into another language.

TRIMETER. See *meter.*

TRIPLET. A **triplet**, or *tercet,* is a stanza of three lines.

TROCHEE. A **trochee** is a poetic foot consisting of a strongly stressed syllable followed by a weakly stressed syllable, as in the word *winter.* A line of poetry made up of trochees is said to be *trochaic.*

TROPE. See *figures of speech.*

TURNING POINT. See *plot.*

UNDERSTATEMENT. An **understatement** is an ironic expression in which something of importance is emphasized by being spoken of as though it were not important, as in "He's sort of dead, I think."

UNITY. A work has **unity** when its various parts all contribute to creating an integrated whole. An essay with unity, for example, is one in which all the parts help to support the thesis statement, or main idea. See *essay.*

UNRELIABLE NARRATOR. An **unreliable narrator** is one whom the reader cannot trust. See *narrator.*

UTOPIA. A **utopia** is an imaginary, idealized world. The term comes from the title of Sir Thomas More's *Utopia,* which described what More believed to be an ideal society. More took the word from the Greek roots meaning "no-place." See *dystopia.*

VEHICLE. See *metaphor.*

VERBAL IRONY. See *irony.*

VERNACULAR. See *dialect.*

VERS LIBRE. See *free verse.*

VOICE. **Voice** is the way a writer uses language to reflect his or her unique personality and attitude toward topic, form, and audience. A writer expresses voice through tone, word choice, and sentence structure.

GLOSSARY
Of Words For Everyday Use

PRONUNCIATION KEY

VOWEL SOUNDS

a	hat	i	sit	o͞o (or ü)	blue, stew	ə	extra
ā	play	ī	my	oi (or ȯi)	boy		under
ä	star	ô	go	ou (or aů)	wow		civil
e	then	ô (or ȯ)	paw, born	u	up		honor
ē	me	o͝o (or ů)	book, put	ʉ	burn		bogus

CONSONANT SOUNDS

b	but	j	jump	p	pop	th	the
ch	watch	k	brick	r	rod	v	valley
d	do	l	lip	s	see	w	work
f	fudge	m	money	sh	she	y	yell
g	go	n	on	t	sit	z	pleasure
h	hot	ŋ	song, sink	th	with		

ab • a • lo • ne (a bə lō′ nē) *n.*, rock-clinging gastropod mollusk that has a flattened shell slightly spiral in form, lined with mother-of-pearl.

abate (ə bāt′) *vi.*, reduce; diminish; subside; lessen.

ab • stract (ab′ strakt) *adj.*, having only a simple form and not representing a picture or narrative content.

a • bun • dance (ə bun′ dəns) *n.*, great supply.

ac • ces • si • bly (ak ses′ ə blē) *adv.*, easily understandable.

ac • ces • sion (ak sesh′ ən) *n.*, outburst.

ac • cul • tur • a • tion (ə kəl chə rā′ shən) *n.*, cultural modification of an individual or group by adapting or borrowing traits from another culture.

ac • quit (ə kwit′) *vt.*, clear a person of a charge or accusation.

ac • rid (ak′rid) *adj.*, stinging.

a • cu • ity (ə kyü′ ə tē) *n.*, sharpness.

ad • a • mant (ad′ ə mənt) *adj.*, unshakeable; not giving in.

a • dept (ə dept′) *adj.*, expert; highly skilled.

ad • join • ing (ə join′ iŋ) *adj.*, next to each other.

ad • ver • sar • y (ad′ ve(r) ser ē) *n.*, one that contends with or opposes.

aes • thet • ic (es the′ tik) *adj.*, of, relating to, or dealing with the beautiful.

af • flic • tion (ə flik′ shən) *n.*, state of being in persistent pain or distress.

a • ghast (ə gast′) *adj.*, horrified; shocked.

al • i • bi (al′ ə bī) *n.*, excuse; proof of activities.

al • lied (ə līd′) *adj.*, related; united by kinship.

al • lu • sion (ə lü′ zhən) *n.*, casual or indirect reference.

al • ly (a′ lī) *n.*, one that is associated with another as a helper.

am • i • a • ble (ā′ mē ə bəl) *adj.*, friendly.

ami • a • bly (ām′ yə blē) *adv.*, in a friendly way.

a • miss (ə mis′) *adv.*, wrongly; improperly.

a • nal • o • gous (ə na′ lə gəs) *adj.*, showing a likeness that permits one to draw an analogy, or comparison

an • ar • chist (an′ ər kəst) *n.*, one who rebels against any authority, established order, or ruling power.

an • ces • tral (an ses′ trel) *adj.*, relating to or inherited from an ancestor or family member.

an • guish (aŋ′ gwish) *n.*, great suffering from worry or pain.

an • nu • al (an′ yə wəl) *adj.*, occurring every year or once a year; yearly.

a • nom • a • lous (ə näm′ ə ləs) *adj.*, inconsistent or contradicting.

an • o • nym • i • ty (an ə nim′ ə tē) *n.*, quality or state of not being known or having no special or distinguishing qualities.

an• tag • on • ist (an tag′ ə nist) *n.*, opponent.

an • thro • pol • o • gist (an thrə pä′ lə jist) *n.*, someone who studies human beings in relation to their characteristics and culture.

an • tiq • ui • ty (an ti′ kwə tē) *n.*, something old, like relics, statues, or monuments.

ap • er • ture (ap′ ər chər) *n.*, opening.

a • phor • ism (a′ fə rizəm) *n.*, short, insightful saying.

ap • par • el (ə per′əl) *n.*, clothing.

ap • pa • ri • tion (ap ə rish′ ən) *n.*, anything that appears suddenly, or in an extraordinary way; ghost.

ap • pli • ca • bil • i • ty (ap li kə bil′ ə tē) *n.*, appropriateness; usefulness.

ap • pre • hend (a pri hend') v., grasp; understand.

ap • pre • hen • sive (ap rē hen' siv) adj., fearful; nervous.

apt (apt) adj., likely or inclined.

apt • ly (apt´ lē) adv., fittingly.

aq • ui • line (a' kwə līn) adj., curving like an eagle's beak.

ar • a • ble (ar' ə bəl) adj., suitable for plowing.

ar • dent (ärd´ 'nt) adj., passionate.

ar • ray (ə rā') n., regular grouping or arrangement.

ar • rest • ing (ə rest' iŋ) adj., catching the attention; striking; impressive.

ar • tic • u • late (är tik´yōō lit) adj., able to express oneself easily and clearly.

ar • tic • u • late (är tik´yōō lāt) vt., give clear utterance to, speak.

as • pect (as´ pekt) n., appearance or interpretation of an idea.

as • sail (ə sāl´) vt., attack with arguments or doubts.

as • sess (ə ses') vt., analyze critically and judge definitively the nature, significance, status, or merit of.

as • suage (ə swāj´) vt., calm; pacify.

a • stray (ə strā') adv., out of the right way, off the path.

a • sun • der (ə sun' dər) adv., into pieces or parts.

a • troc • i • ty (ə träs´ ə tē) n., cruel or evil act, object, or situation.

aug • ment (ôg men´t) vt., increase; add to.

a • venge (ə venj´) vt., get revenge for.
revenge for an injury or wrong.

a • verse (ə vʉrs´) adj., reluctant or opposed; having a dislike or distaste for something, and avoiding it.

a • ver • sion (ə vʉr´ zhən) n., loathing or revulsion.

a • vert • ed (ə vʉrt´ id) adj., turned away.

ban • ter (ban' tər) n., good-natured and usually witty and animated joking.

bar • ba • rous (bär' bə rəs) adj., cruel; brutal.

bar • rage (bə räzh') n., vigorous or rapid outpouring or projection of many things at once.

bas • er (bāsr) adj., meaner or less decent.

be • hest (bē hest') n., command.

bel • lig • er • ence (bə lij' rənts) n., aggressive or truculent attitude, atmosphere, or disposition.

bel • lig • er • ent • ly (bə lij' rənt lē) adv., done in a manner inclined to or exhibiting assertiveness, hostility, or combativeness.

be • nev • o • lent (bə nev' ə lənt) adj., kindly or charitable.

be • nev • o • lent • ly (bə nev' lənt lē) adv., marked by or disposed to doing good; with kindness or goodwill.

be • queath (bē kwēth´) vt., hand down; pass on.

be • seech (bē sēch') vt., ask, implore.

be • siege (bē sēj') vt., close in on and attack.

bi • cul • tur • al • ism (bī kəlch' rəl izm) n., two distinct cultures existing in one nation.

blanch (blanch) vi., turn pale.

bland • ly (bland´ lē) adv., smoothly.

blas • phe • my (blas' fə mē) n., irreverence toward God.

blithe • ly (blīth´ lē) adv., cheerfully, in a carefree way.

blus • ter (bləs' tər) vi., utter with noisy self-assertiveness.

bois • ter • ous (bois' tər əs) adj., lively and exuberant; stormy or turbulent.

bon • dage (bän' dij) n., slavery; involuntary servitude; constraint.

bran • dish (bran' dish) vt., wave; exhibit.

bra • va • do (brə vä´ dō) n., false courage.

bra • zen (brā´zən) adj., showing no shame.

brine (brīn) n., salt water.

brusque • ly (brusk' lē) adv., done in a markedly short or abrupt manner.

bur • row (bʉr' ō) vi., dig; tunnel; delve beneath.

but • tressed (bə' trəsd) adj., strengthened.

cal • lous • ly (ka' ləs lē) adv., insensitively, uncaringly.

ca • pac • i • ty (kə pas' i tē) n., ability; qualifications.

ca • pit • u • la • tion (kə pich yōō lā´ shən) n., surrender

cap • size (kap' sīz) vi., become overturned.

cap • tion (kap' shen) n., heading or comment accompanying a photograph.

car • cass (kär´ kəs) n., body of a slain animal.

car • nage (kär´ nij) n., slaughter.

cat • a • clysm (ka' tə kli zəm) n., momentous and violent event marked by overwhelming upheaval and demolition.

cat • e • chism (ka' tə ki zəm) n., summary of Christian doctrine often in the form of questions and answers.

ce • les • tial (sə les' chəl) adj., of or relating to heaven.

cel • lu • loid (sel' yə loid) adj., having to do with the movies or with celluloid, a tough plastic used for filmstrips.

cha • grin (shə grin´) n., feeling of severe embarrassment and annoyance.

cham • ber (chām´ bər) n., reception room in an official residence.

chas • tise • ment (chas tīz' mənt) n., scolding; condemnation.

cher • ish (cher´ ish) vt., hold dear.

churl (chʉrl) n., surly, mean person.

clem • ent (klem' ənt) adj., kind, gentle, or favorable.

co • erce (kō ʉrs') vt., force by intimidation to do something.

co • er • cion (kō ʉr´ shən) n., act of force through threats or violence.

cog • i • ta • tion (käj ə tā´shən) n., thought.

cog • ni • tion (käg ni' shən) n., knowing; having awareness and judgment.

co • her • ent (kō hir´ ənt) adj., logically connected; making sense.

co • her • ent • ly (kō hir´ ənt lē) adv., in a way capable of being understood.

col • league (käl ēg´) n., fellow worker.

col • lu • sion (kə lü' zhən) n., secret cooperation; conspiracy.

co • lo • nial (kə lō' nē əl) adj., characteristic of one power having control over a dependent area or people.

com • mend (kə mend') vt., praise; recommend as worthy.

com • mis • sion (kə mish' ən) n., fee paid to an agent or employee in exhange for a certain work.

com • mod • i • ty (kə mä' də tē) n., economic good or product.

com • mon • wealth (käm´ ən welth´) n., republic.

com • mu • nal (käm´ yōō nəl) adj., of or shared by all; in the community.

com • mune (kə myün') vi., be in intimate relation or rapport.

com • mu • ni • ca • tive (kə myü' ni kā tiv, kə myü' ni kə tiv) adj., talkative; giving information readily.

com • pel (kəm pel') vi., get or bring about by force; vt., force.

com • pen • sa • tion (käm pən sā' shən) n., payment for service.

com • pli • ance (kəm plī´ əns) n., giving in to a request.

com • ply (kəm plī´) vi., follow another's wishes or obey a rule; act in accordance with a rule, command, or request.

com • po • sure (kəm pō´ zhər) n., calmness of mind or manner.

com • pre • hen • sive (käm prə hen´ siv) adj., covering a matter completely, inclusive.

com • pul • sion (kəm pəl´ shən) n., act of compelling, or urging forcefully.

com • pul • sive (kəm´ pəl siv) adj., as if driven by a force.

com • punc • tion (kəm puŋk´ shən) n., uneasiness brought on by sense of guilt.

con • cat • e • na • tion (kän ka tə nā´ shən) n., state of being linked together in a series or chain.

con • cave (kän kāv´) adj., curved inward.

con • cep • tu • al (kən sep´ shə wəl) adj., of or relating to concepts, an abstract idea, or intuitive thought.

con • ces • sion (kən se´ shən) n., act of conceding or yielding; something granted as a right or privilege.

con • demn (kən dem´) vt., pronounce judgment against; sentence.

con • di • tion • al • ly (kən dish´ ən əl lē) adv., based on certain conditions.

con • fab • u • late (kən fa´ byə lāt) vt., fill in gaps in memory by fabricating, or inventing, information.

con • fide (kən fīd´) vi., trust, especially by sharing secrets.

con • fla • gra • tion (kän flə grā´ shən) n., large, destructive fire.

con • found (kən found´) vt., mix up indiscriminately; baffle, stupify, perplex, or confuse.

con • front (kən frunt´) vt., meet face to face.

con • glom • er • ate (kən gläm´ rət) n., widely diversified corporation.

con • join • ing (kən join´ iŋ) n., joining together separate entities for a common purpose.

con • joint • ly (kən joint´ lē) adv., in a united or combined manner.

con • science (kän´ chəns) n., sense of right or wrong within an individual.

con • sci • en • tious (kän´ she enshəs) adj., scrupulous; governed by what one knows is right.

con • sent • ing (kən sent´ iŋ) adj., agreeing; approving.

con • sign (kən sīn´) vt., hand over or deliver.

con • so • la • tion (kän(t) sə lā´ shən) adj., something that consoles, or alleviates pain or suffering.

con • spic • u • ous (kən spi´ kyu wəs) adj., obvious to the eye or mind; easy to see.

con • spic • u • ous • ly (kən spi´ kyə wəs lē) adv., obviously; attracting attention; noticeably.

con • stan • cy (kän´ stən sē) n., faithfulness; resolve; unchangeableness.

con • sti • tute (kän´stə tōōt) vt., form the components or elements of.

con • strue (kən strü´) vt., understand or explain the meaning of something using the circumstances or evidence; analyze; interpret.

con • sump • tive (kən səmp´ tiv) n., person affected with consumption, or tuberculosis.

con • tem • pla • tion (kän təm plā´ shən) n., thoughtful inspection.

con• temp • tu • ous • ly (kən temp´chōō əs lē) adv., scornfully.

con • ten • tion (kən ten´ shən) n., argument.

con • tin • gent (kən tin´ jənt) n., group forming part of a larger group, such as troops.

con • vey (kən vā´) vt., make known.

con • vic • tion (kən vik´ shən) n., strong belief.

con • vo • lu • ted (kän və lü´ təd) adj., having twists and coils; intricate or involved.

co • or • di • nate (kō ôr´ də nāt) vt., harmonize in a common action or effort.

cor • ol • lar • y (kōr´ ə ler ē) n., something that naturally follows; result.

cor • o • ner (kôr´ ə nər) n., public officer whose duties include determining the causes of deaths.

cor • por • al (kôr´ pə rəl) adj., having to do with the body.

cor • rob • o • ra • tion (kə rä´ bə rā´ shən) n., confirmation; something supported with evidence or authority.

cor • rode (kə rōd´) vt., eat away; weaken or destroy gradually.

cos • mo • pol • i • tan (käz mə pä´ lə tən) n., person having worldwide rather than limited or provincial scope or bearing.

couch (kauch) vt., phrase or express in a specified manner.

coun • te • nance (koun´ tə nəns) n., look on a person's face; face.

co • vert (kō´ vərt) adj., not openly shown, engaged in, or avowed.

cow • er (kou´ ər) vi., shrink and tremble; cringe.

cull (kul´) vt., to select from a group.

cur (kʉr) n., dog; mongrel.

cur • so • ry (kʉr´ sə rē) adj., superficial; done rapidly with little attention to detail.

de • base (dē bās´) vt., make lower in value or quality.

de • bauch (dē bôch´) n., extreme indulgence of one's appetites.

de • bil • i • tat • ing (dē bil´ə tāt iŋ) adj., weakening.

de • cree (di krē´) n., an order set forth by one in authority; vt., order officially..

de • crep • it (di krə´ pət) adj., wasted and weakened by or as if by the infirmities of old age.

de • crep • i • tude (di kre´ pə tüd) n., quality or state of being wasted and weakened.

de • duce (dē düs´) vt., infer by logical reasoning.

de • duc • tion (dē duk´ shən) n., reasoning from the general to the specific; conclusion reached by such reasoning.

de • fect (dē fekt´) vi., leave one's country because one disapproves of its political policies.

def • er • ence (de´ fə rənts) n., respect and esteem due another.

de • fi • cit (de´ fə sit) n., lack of ability; disadvantage.

de • flect (dē flekt´) vt., turn to one side.

deft • ly (deft´ ly) adv., skillfully.

de • funct (dē fuŋkt´) adj., no longer existing.

de • gen • er • ate (dē jen´ ər it) adj., having sunk below a former condition.

de • gen • er • a • tive (di je´ nə rə tiv) adj., something that degenerates, or destroys.

de • grad • ed (dē grād´ id) adj., disgraced; humiliated.

de • grad • ing (dē grād´ iŋ) adj., depriving of dignity.

deign (dān´) vi., condescend reluctantly, with a strong sense of one's own superiority.

del • e • ga • tion (del ə gā´ shən) n., group of people authorized to speak and act for others.

de • lib • er • ate (di lib´ər āt) vt., think about or consider carefully.

de • lir • i • ous (di lir´ ē əs) adj., hallucinating; restless and confused.

de • lu • sion (di lōō´ zhən) n., false belief or opinion.

de • mer • it (di mer´ ət) n., mark entailing a loss of privilege.

de • mot • ic (də mäd´ ik) adj., of or relating to the people; popular and common, especially language.

den • i • gra • tion (de ni grä´ shən) n., belittling.

de • nun • ci • a • tion (dē nun sē ā´ shən) n., criticism; speaking against.

de • plore (di plōr´) vi., feel grief for; consider unfortunate.

de • prive (dē priv´) vt., take something away from.

de • ranged (dē rānjd´) adj., insane.

der • e • lict (der´ ə likt) n., homeless social misfit; bum.

de • rive (di rīv´) vi., take, receive, or make, especially from a specified source.

des • o • la • tion (de sə lā´ shən) n., condition of being deserted, abandoned, ruined, lifeless.

des • pot • ic (des pä´ tik) adj., characteristic of a ruler or person with absolute authority and power.

des • ti • tute (des´ tə tōōt) n., those living in poverty.

de • tain (di tān´) vt., hold or keep as if in custody.

de • tec • tion (di tek´ shən) n., discovery.

de • void (di void´) adj., completely without.

dex • ter • i • ty (dek ster´ ə tē) n., skill and ease in using the hands.

di • aph • a • nous (dī a´ fə nəs) adj., characterized by such fineness of texture as to permit seeing through.

dif • fi • dent (dif´ ə dənt) adj., characterized by modest reserve; lacking confidence in oneself.

dif • fi • dent • ly (di´ fə dənt lē) adv., in a hesitant, shy way.

di • late (dī lāt) vi., become larger or wider.

dil • i • gent (dil´ ə jənt) adj., hard-working; industrious.

di • min • ish • ing (de mi´ nish ing) adj., becoming smaller or less.

di • min • u • tive (də mi´ nyə tiv) n., shortened name.

dint (dint) n., because; by dint of: because of.

dirge (dərj´) n., song, hymn, or piece of writing expressing deep and solemn grief.

dis • charge (dis chärj´) vt., throw off or deliver a duty or burden.

dis • con • so • late (dis kän´ sə lit) adj., unhappy; not to be comforted.

dis • course (dis´ kōrs) n., verbal interchange of ideas; conversation; vi., speak.

dis • creet • ly (di skrēt´ lē) adv., done in an unobtrusive or unnoticeable manner.

dis • fig • ure (dis fig´ yər) vt., hurt the appearance of.

dis • heart • ened (dis här´ tənd) adj., demoralized.

dis • in • te • grate (dis in´ tə grāt´) vi., break apart.

dis • mal (diz´ məl) adj., depressing.

dis • par • age (dis spar´ ij) vt., discredit; belittle.

dis • pel (di spel´) vt., cause to vanish or disappear.

dis • perse (dis pʉrs´) vi., break up and scatter about.

dis • so • lute (dis´ ə lōōt) adj., immoral.

dis • tinc • tion (di stiŋk´ shən) n., special recognition.

di • verse (dī vʉrs´) adj., different in kind or species.

di • ver • sion (də vʉr´ zhən) n., distraction.

di • vest • ment (dī vest´ mənt) n., deprivation of property, authority, or title.

di • vin • er (də vīn´ ər) n., one who tries to foretell the future.

do • cil • i • ty (dō sil´ ə tē) n., state of being easily managed.

do • mes • tic (də məs´ tik) adj., of or relating to the household or the family.

dredge (drej) vt., dig up (in search of something).

du • ly (dōō´ lē) adv., as required, sufficiently.

eaves (ēvz) n., the lower border of a roof that overhangs the wall.

ed • dy (ed´ ē) v., move with a circular motion against the main current.

ed • i • fice (ed´ i fis) n., structure.

e • la • bor • ate (i la´ be ret) adj., marked by complexity, fullness of detail.

e • lat • ed (ē lāt´ ed) part., filled with joy.

e • la • tion (ē lā´ shən) n., feeling of joy or pride.

e • lic • it (ē li´ sət) vt., call forth or bring out.

elite (ā lēt´) n., regarded as the finest; adj., best of a class.

el • o • quent (e´ lə kwənt) adj., marked by forceful and fluent expression.

e • mit (ē mit´) vt., discharge; send out; give off.

em • pa • thy (em´ pə thē) n., ability to share in another's emotions.

em • phat • i • cal • ly (em fat´ ik lē) adv., in a forceful manner.

em • bod • y (em bäd´ ē) vt., make concrete; give form to; bring together.

em • u • late (em´ yə lāt) vt., strive to equal or excel; imitate.

en • chant • ed (en chant´ əd) adj., invested with magical powers.

en • chant • ment (en chant´ mənt) n., magic spell or charm.

en • crypt (en kript´) vt., encipher or encode.

en • deav • or (en dev´ ər) vi., make an earnest attempt.

en • dure (ən dyər´) vt., bear up under great hardship; remain firm; tolerate; live through.

en • gen • der (en jen´ dər) vt., give birth to; produce.

en • gulf (en gulf´) vt., overwhelm; swallow up.

en • hance (en hans´) vt., improve.

en • ig • mat • ic (e nig mad´ ik) adj., inexplicable, obscure, puzzling.

en • mi • ty (en´ mə tē) n., ill will; hostility; antagonism.

en • shroud (en shroud´) vi., cover; hide.

en • sign (en sīn´) n., flag; banner.

en • ter • pris • ing (ent´ər prī´ ziŋ) adj., marked by an energetic spirit and by readiness to undertake an experiment.

en • ti • tle (en tīt´ 'l) vt., give a right to.

en • trails (en´ trālz) n. pl., inner organs, viscera.

en • treat (en trēt´) vt., implore; strongly request.

en • tre • pre • neur (än trə prə nər´) n., one who organizes, manages, and assumes the risks of a business or enterprise.

en • voy (än´ voi) n., agent who transacts diplomatic business.

e • phem • er • al (i fem´ rəl) adj., lasting briefly; temporary; fleeting.

e • piph • a • ny (ə pif´ ə nē) n., sudden manifestation or perception of the essential nature or meaning of something.

e • pon • y • mous (i pä´ nə məs) adj., giving one's name to a people, institution, time period, nation, etc.

e • quiv • o • cal (ē kwiv´ ə kəl) adj., uncertain; undecided.

e • rad • i • cate (i ra´ də kāt) vt., do away with as completely as if by pulling up by the roots.

er • rat • ic (er rat´ ik) adj., having no fixed purpose.

er • ro • ne • ous (ər rō´ nē əs) adj., mistaken, wrong.

es • sence (es´ ən(t)s) n., basic, underlying substance or form.

es • trange • ment (e strānj´ mənt) n., alienation of affection.

e • thos (ē´ thäs) n., distinguishing character, sentiment, moral nature, or guiding beliefs of a person, group, or institution.

e • ti • quette (e´ ti ket) n., proper social conduct or procedure.

eu • lo • gy (yü´ lə jē) n., commendatory formal statement about the deceased person at a funeral.

eu • phe • mism (yōō´ fa miz em) n., word or phrase that is used in place of another, more offensive expression.

eu • pho • ria (yu fōr´ ē ə) n., feeling of well-being or elation.

ev • a • nes • cence (e və ne´ sənts) n., process or fact of tending to vanish like vapor.

ex • alt (ig zōlt´) vt., elevate by praise or in estimation.

ex • al • ta • tion (eg zōl tā´ shən) n., feeling of great joy and pride.

ex• as • per • at • ed (ig zas´ pə rāt əd) adj., excited to anger, annoyance, or irritation.

ex • clu • siv • i • ty (eks klü si´ və tē) *n.*, quality or state of being exclusive, or excluding.

ex • empt (eg zempt´) *adj.*, excused, released.

ex • pa • tri • ate (ek spā´ trē ət) *n.*, person living in a foreign land.

ex • pe • di • ent (ek spē´dē ənt) *n.*, resource suited to the occasion.

ex • plic • it • ly (ik spli´ sət lē) *adv.*, clearly expressed, directly stated.

ex • po • sé (eks pō zā´) *n.*, public disclosure of a scandal or crime.

ex • pound (eks pound´) *vt.*, explain in detail point by point.

fa • ce • tious • ly (fə sē´ shəs lē) *adv.*, in a joking or jesting manner, often inappropriately.

fa • cil • i • tate (fə si´ lə tāt) *vt.*, make easier.

fal • ter • ing (fôl´ tər iŋ) *adj.*, hesitant; uncertain; wavering.

fal • ter • ing • ly (fôl´ tər iŋ lē) *adv.*, uncertainly, unsteadily.

far • ci • cal (fär´ si kəl) *adj.*, resembling farce; laughably absurd.

fas • tid • i • ous (fa sti´ dē əs) *adj.*, meticulous; showing attention to detail.

fa • tigue (fə tēg´) *n.*, weariness from labor or exertion.

fawn (fôn) *vi.*, show excessive friendliness; flatter.

fea • ture (fē´ chər) *n.*, distinct part or quality.

fell (fel) *vt.*, knock or cut down.

fer • ment (fur´ ment) *n.*, state of unrest.

fet • tered (fet´ ərd) *adj.*, handcuffed.

fi • nesse (fə nes´) *n.*, ability to handle difficult situations diplomatically.

fla • grant (flā´ grənt) *adj.*, outrageous.

flail (flāl) *vi.*, swing around or beat about wildly.

flaunt (flänt) *vt.*, display to public notice.

flour • ish (fler´ ish) *n.*, bold sweeping gesture.

fod • der (fäd´ ər) *n.*, coarse food for cattle, such as cornstalks, hay, and straw.

fo • li • o (fō´ lē ō) *n.*, case or folder for loose papers.

for • age (fôr´ ij) *n.*, food for animals that graze.

for • ay (fôr´ ā) *n.*, raid; attack.

for • bear (fôr bar´) *v.*, hold back from, abstain.

fore • man (fōr´ mən) *n.*, person in charge of other workers or a section of a plant.

for • mi • da • ble (fôr´mə də bəl) *adj.*, imposing in size.

fox • hole (fäks´ hōl) *n.*, pit dug for protection from enemy fire.

fra • grant (fra´ grent) *adj.*, marked by fragrance or pleasant odor.

frail (frāl) *adj.*, delicate; weak.

fri • vol • i • ty (fri vä´ lə tē) *n.*, inappropriate silliness, triviality.

friv • o • lous (fri´ və ləs) *adj.*, having little importance.

froth (fräth) *n.*, something light and airy like bubbles on a liquid.

fur • tive (fər´ tiv) *adj.*, done by stealth or in secret; shifty.

gait (gāt) *n.*, manner of walking or moving.

gar • ish (gar´ ish) *adj.*, offensively or distressingly bright; flashy; excessively vivid.

gar • land (gär´lənd) *n.*, wreath or chain of flowers or leaves.

ge • ner • ic (jə ner´ ik) *adj.*, descriptive of all members of a group or category, not specific or individual, general.

ge • nial • ly (jēn´ yə lē) *adv.*, in a friendly way.

ge • no • cide (je´ nə sīd) *n.*, deliberate and systematic destruction of a racial, political, or cultural group.

ghast • ly (gast´ lē) *adj.*, horrible; frightful.

glib (glib) *adj.*, able to speak in a smooth, easy manner.

gnarled (närld) *adj.*, full of knots or gnarls.

goad • ed (gōd´ əd) *part.*, prodded into action.

gra • cious • ly (gra´ shes lē) *adv.*, with kindness and courtesy.

gran • deur (gran´ jer) *n.*, quality or state of being magnificent.

griev • ous (grēv´ əs) *adj.*, very serious; grave.

gris • ly (griz´ lē) *adj.*, inspiring disgust or distaste.

gul • li • bil • i • ty (gə lə bi´ lə tē) *n.*, state of being easily deceived or cheated; naïveté.

gul • li • ble (gul´ ə bəl) *adj.*, easily cheated or tricked.

hag • gard (hag´ ərd) *adj.*, having a wild, worn look.

hap • haz • ard • ly (hap ha´ zərd lē) *adv.*, done in a manner marked by lack of plan, order, or direction.

har • poon (här po͞on´) *n.*, spear with a line attached for hunting large sea animals.

haugh • ti • ly (hôt´ə lē) *adv.*, in a proud or arrogant manner.

haugh • ty (hô´ tē) *adj.*, blatantly and disdainfully proud.

her • ald (her´ əld) *n.*, messenger or harbinger.

her • met • ic (hər me´ tik) *adj.*, difficult or impossible to comprehend.

hind • sight (hīnd´ sīt´) *n.*, ability to see, after an event, what should have been done.

hom • age (häm´ ij) *n.*, acts done to show honor and respect.

hor • rid (hōr´ id) *adj.*, terrible; horrible.

hu • mil • i • ty (hu mi´ le tē) *n.*, state of being humble, not possessing pride.

hurl (hərl) *vt.*, send or thrust with great vigor.

hype (hīp) *n.*, *slang*, promotion or attention from, for example, the media.

i • de • ol • o • gy (ī dē ä´ lə jē) *n.*, ideas and concepts about human nature; the assertions, theories, and aims of an individual or group.

il • lit • er • a • cy (il lit´ ər ə sē) *n.*, state of being unable to read and write.

il • lu • mi • na • tion (i lü´ mə nā´shən) *n.*, lighting up.

im • me • mo • ri • al (i mə mōr´ ē əl) *adj.*, extending or existing since beyond the reach of memory, record, or tradition.

im • mi • nent (im´ə nənt) *adj.*, impending; threatening; about to occur.

im • mo • bile (im mō´ bəl) *adj.*, not moving.

im • mod • er • ate (im mäd´ ər it) *adj.*, excessive, unrestrained.

im • mune (i myün´) *adj.*, protected; resistant to a disease.

im • pact (im´ pakt) *n.*, the force of impression of one thing on another.

im • part (im part´) *vt.*, give or communicate the knowledge of.

im • pass • a • ble (im pas´ ə bəl) *adj.*, that cannot be passed or traveled through.

im • ped • i • men • ta (im pe´ də mənt) *pl. n.*, impediments, things that impede or prevent (plural of impediment).

im • pend • ing (im pend´ iŋ) *adj.*, about to happen; imminent.

im • pen • e • tra • ble (im pen´i trə bəl) *adj.*, incapable of being passed through.

im • per • a • tive (im per´ ə tiv) *n.*, something that is obligatory.

im • per • cep • ti • ble (im pər sep´ tə bəl) *adj.*, subtle; so as not to be easily perceived.

im • per • ish • a • ble (im per´ ish ə bəl) *adj.*, that will not die.

im • per • ti • nence (im pər´ tən ənts) *n.*, quality or state of being unrestrained within due or proper bounds; insolence.

im • per • turb • a • bly (im pər tur´ bə blē) *adv.*, without being excited or disturbed.

im • pinge (im pinj´) *vi.*, have an effect.

im • pla • ca • ble (im pla´ kə bəl) *adj.*, unable to be appeased; relentless.

im • plore (im plôr´) *vt.*, beg.

im • plor • ing (im plôr´ iŋ) *adj.*, in an earnest or beseeching manner.

im • pose (im pōz´) *vt.*, force one's will on others.

im • pru • dence (im prü´ dəns) *n.,* lack of judgment; thoughtlessness.

im • pulse (im´ pəls) *n.,* sudden spontaneous inclination to an unpremeditated action; act of driving onward.

in • au • gu • rate (i nä´ gyə rāt) *vt.,* begin, introduce, or mark a start of.

in • ces • sant • ly (in ses´ ənt lē) *adv.,* constantly, endlessly.

in • ci • sive (in sī´ səv) *adj.,* sharp.

in • cli • na • tion (in klə nā´ shən) *n.,* tendency.

in • con • ceiv • a • bly (in kən sēv´ ə blē) *adv.,* unthinkably; unbelievably.

in • cre • ment (iŋ´ krə ment) *n.,* action or process of increasing in quantity or value.

in • cum • bent (in kum´ bənt) *n.,* lying or pressing with its weight on something else.

in • del • i • ble (in del´ ə bəl) *adj.,* permanent; incapable of being erased or removed.

in • dif • fer • ence (in dif´ ər əns) *n.,* lack of concern.

in • dif • fer • ent (in di´ fərnt) *adj.,* marked by a lack of interest, enthusiasm, or concern.

in • dif • fer • ent • ly (in dif´ ər ənt lē) *adv.,* without interest.

in • dig • nant (in dig´ nənt) *adj.,* filled or marked by anger at something unjust, unworthy, or mean.

in • dis • pens • able (in di spen´ sə bəl) *adj.,* absolutely necessary.

in • do • lence (in´ də lənts) *n.,* inclination to laziness.

in • dom • i • ta • ble (in dä´mə tə bəl) *adj.,* not defeatable.

in • ert (in ʉrt´) *adj.,* inactive.

in • es • ti • ma • ble (in es´ tə mə bəl) *adj.,* too valuable to be measured; invaluable.

in • ev • i • ta • ble (in ev´ i tə bəl) *adj.,* certain to occur.

in • fa • my (in´ fə mē) *n.,* something grossly criminal, shocking, or brutal.

in • fir • mi • ty (in fʉr´ mə tē) *n.,* sickness; weakness.

in • fuse (in fyo͞oz´) *vt.,* inspire; fill.

in • gen • ious (in jēn´ yəs) *adj.,* original.

in • gen • u • ous (in jen´ yə wəs) *adj.,* artless; innocent; naive.

in • gra • ti • at • ing (in grā´ shē āt iŋ) *adj.,* seeking another's favor by conscious effort.

in • hi • bi • tion (in hi bish´ ən) *n.,* restraint.

in • kling (iŋ´ kliŋ) *n.,* slight knowledge; vague notion.

in • noc • u • ous (in nä´ kyə wəs) *adj.,* harmless.

in • quis • i • tive • ness (ən kwiz´ ət iv nes) *n.,* state of curiosity.

in • sa • tia • ble (in sā´ shə bəl) *adj.,* incapable of being satisfied or appeased.

in • scru • ta • bil • i • ty (in skro͞ot´ ə bil´ ə tē) *n.,* complete obscurity.

in • so • lence (in´ sə lənts) *n.,* haughtiness; impudence; disrespectfulness.

in • so • lent (in´ sə lənt) *adj.,* boldly disrespectful.

in • sti • ga • tion (in stə gā´shən) *n.,* incitement; something that urges one to act.

in • stinct (inz´ tiŋkt) *n.,* impulse, natural tendency, response arising from below the conscious level.

in • sur • rec • tion (in sə rek´ shən) *n.,* rebellion.

in • teg • ri • ty (in te´ grə tē) *n.,* firm adherence to a code of moral or artistic values; completeness; soundness; incorruptibility.

in • tem • per • ate (in tem´pər it) *adj.,* lacking restraint.

in • ter (in tʉr´) *vt.,* bury.

in • ter • im (in´ tər im) *n.,* in-between time.

in • ter • mi • na • ble (in tər´ mə nə bəl) *adj.,* having or seeming to have no end.

in • ter • pose (in tər pōz´) *vt.,* place or come between.

in • ter • sperse (in tər spərs´) *vt.,* place at intervals in or among.

in • tri • cate (in´ tri ket) *adj.,* complicated, having many complex parts.

in • trin • sic (in trin´ zik) *adj.,* belonging to the essential nature or constitution of a thing.

in • trin • si • cal • ly (in trin´ zi kə lē) *adv.,* in a manner showing the essential nature or constitution of a thing.

in • tro • spec • tive (in trō spek´ tiv) *adj.,* looking within oneself in an analytical way.

in • val • u • a • ble (in val´ yü ə bəl) *adj.,* priceless.

in • vet • er • ate (in ve´ t(ə) rət) *adj.,* firmly established by long persistence; habitual.

in • vin • ci • ble (in vin(t)´ sə bəl) *adj.,* incapable of being conquered, overcome, or subdued.

in • voke (in vōk´) *vt.,* call on for blessing, help, inspiration, or support.

in • vol • un • tar • i • ly (in väl ən ter´ ə lē) *adv.,* unintentionally, uncontrollably.

i • rate (ī rāt´) *adj.,* angry, wrathful.

ir • i • des • cent (ir ə de´ sənt) *adj.,* having a lustrous rainbowlike play of color.

irk (ərk) *vt.,* make weary, irritated, or bored.

ir • res • o • lute (ir rəz´ ə lo͞ot) *adj.,* undecided.

i • so • late (ī´ sə lāt) *vt.,* set apart from others.

i • so • lat • ed (ī´ sə lāt əd) *adj.,* separate; remote.

i • tin • er • ar • y (ī ti´ nə rer ē) *n.,* route of a journey or the proposed outline of one.

jeop • ard • ize (jep´ ər dīz) *vt.,* risk; endanger.

jock • ey (jäk´ ē) *vi.,* maneuver, as for position or advantage.

ju • di • cious (jo͞o dish´ əs) *adj.,* reasoned, wise; calculated.

jus • ti • fy (jus´ tə fī) *vt.,* show to be right.

jux • ta • pose (juk´ stə pōz) *vt.,* place side by side.

kin • dling (kind´ liŋ) *adj.,* small pieces of wood or paper used to start a fire.

knoll (nōl) *n.,* mound.

lac • er • a • tion (las´ər ā´shən) *n.,* wound; distress.

la • ment (lə ment´) *vi.,* express sorrow or grieve; regret strongly.

lam • en • ta • tion (lam ən tā´ shən) *n.,* vocal expression of sorrow.

lank (laŋk) *adj.,* straight and limp.

lank • y (laŋk´ ē) *adj.,* tall; spare; loose-jointed.

lat • ter (lat´ ər) *adj.,* last mentioned.

laud (lôd) *vt.,* sing the praises of.

leer • ing (lēr´ iŋ) *adj.,* casting a sidelong glance that is lascivious, knowing, or wanton.

le • sion (lē´ zhən) *n.,* wound; flaw; abnormal change.

leu • ke • mia (lü kē´ mē ə) *n.,* acute or chronic disease characterized by an abnormal increase in the number of white blood cells in the tissues or blood.

lime (līm) *n.,* calcium oxide, a white substance used in making mortar and cement.

lin • e • ar (li´ nē ər) *adj.,* in the form of a line.

lithe (līth) *adj.,* mild, gentle, or agile.

liv • id (liv´id) *adj.,* black and blue; colored like a bruise.

loath • ing (lōth´ iŋ) *n.,* intense hatred; disgust.

loi • ter (loi´ tər) *vi.,* remain in an area for no obvious reason.

lu • di • crous (lü´ də krəs) *adj.,* amusing or laughable through obvious absurdity, incongruity, exaggeration, or eccentricity.

lull (ləl) *n.,* temporary pause in activity; temporary calm.

mack • i • naw (ma´ kə nô) *n.,* short coat made of heavy fabric.

mag • na • nim • i • ty (mag nə nim′ə tē) *n.,* quality of being generous or noble.

mag • nan • i • mous (mag na′ nə məs) *adj.,* showing or suggesting nobility of feeling and generosity of mind.

mal • a • prop • ping (ma′ lə prä piŋ) *adj.,* unintentionally misusing a word or phrase.

ma • lev • o • lent (mə lev′ə lənt) *adj.,* wishing evil or harm to others.

mal • ice (mal′ is) *n.,* desire to do harm.

ma • lic • ious (mə lish′ əs) *n.,* those who act with malice, or evil intention.

ma • lig • nant (mə lig′ nənt) *adj.,* severe, rapidly growing, potentially deadly.

mal • o • dor • ous (mal ō′ der es) *adj.,* having a bad odor.

man • i • fes • to (man ə fe′ stō) *n.,* public declaration of intentions, motives, or views.

man • i • fold (man′ ə fōld) *adj.,* having many and various forms.

marred (märd) *adj.,* damaged or defaced.

mas • sive (mas′ iv) *adj.,* big and solid.

mau • so • le • um (mo sə lē′ əm) *n.,* building for entombment of the dead above ground.

mea • ger (mē′ gər) *adj.,* deficient in quality or quantity.

med • dle (med′ əl) *vi.,* interfere in something that is not one's business.

mes • mer • ize (mez′ mə rīz) *vt.,* hypnotize; fascinate.

me • tic • u • lous (mə ti′ kyə ləs) *adj.,* marked by extreme or excessive care in the treatment of details; careful.

mi • grate (mī′grāt) *vi.,* move from one place to another.

mi • nute • ly (mī nüt′ lē) *adv.,* closely; in a manner attentive to tiny details; to a very small degree.

mis • con • strue (mis′ kən strōō′) *vt.,* misinterpret; misunderstand.

mi • ser (mī′ zər) *n.,* someone extremely stingy with money.

mo • les • ta • tion (mō les tā′ shən) *n.,* interference with intent to trouble or harm.

mo • men • tous (mō men′ təs) *adj.,* very important.

mor • bid (môr′ bəd) *adj.,* of, relating to, or characteristic of disease.

mor • bid • i • ty (mor bi′ də tē) *n.,* quality or state of being susceptible to gloomy or unwholesome feelings.

mul • ti • tude (mul′ tə tōod) *n.,* masses; large number of people considered as a unit.

mus • ter (mus′ tər) *vt.,* gather together.

neu • ro • sur • geon (nōō′rō sur jən) *n.,* physician who operates on the brain and other parts of the nervous system.

noc • tur • nal (näk tər′ nəl) *adj.,* of, relating to, or occurring in the night; active at night.

non • de • script (nän di skript′) *adj.,* lacking in recognizable characteristics or qualities.

nos • tal • gia (nä stal′ jə) *n.,* homesickness.

nu • ance (n(y)ü′ änts) *n.,* shade of difference; minute variation; subtle distinction.

ob • lig • a • to • ry (əb lig′ə tôr ē) *adj.,* required.

ob • scure (əb skyōōr′) *vt.,* conceal or hide.

ob • ses • sive (əb ses′ iv) *adj.,* persistent to an abnormal degree.

ob • so • les • cence (äb′ sə le′ sən(t)s) *n.,* process of becoming obsolete or the condition of being nearly obsolete, or no longer in use.

ob • solete (äb sə lēt′) *adj.,* no longer active or in use.

ob • sti • na • cy (ab′ stə nə sē) *n.,* stubborness, persistence, or firmness.

ob • tuse • ness (äb tüs′ nəs) *n.,* state of demonstrating slow intellect; dullness.

o • cher (ō′ kər) *n.,* earthy, usually red or yellow and often impure iron ore used as a pigment.

o • di • ous (ō′ dē əs) *adj.,* disgusting; offensive.

of • fi • cious (ə fi′ shəs) *adj.,* volunteering one's services where they are neither asked nor needed.

om • i • nous (äm′ ə nəs) *adj.,* threatening, sinister.

om • i • nous • ly (äm′ə nəs lē) *adv.,* in a threatening or sinister manner.

o • mit (ō mit′) *vt.,* leave out.

om • nip • o • tence (äm ni′ pə tənts) *n.,* quality or state of having unlimited power or influence.

om • ni • pres • ence (äm′ ni pre′ zən(t)s) *n.,* quality or state of being present in all places at all times.

om • ni • science (äm ni′ shənts) *n.,* having universal or complete knowledge.

op • por • tu • nist (äp ər tōō′ nist) *n.,* one who adapts his or her actions to circumstances to gain an advantage.

op • press (ə pres′) *part.,* hold down by unjust power.

op • pres • sion (ə presh′ən) *n.,* something that holds down by unjust power.

op • ti • mistic (äp tə mis′ tik) *adj.,* anticipating the best.

os • tra • cize (äs′ trə sīz) *vt.,* banish or exclude.

o • ver • awed (ō vər ôd′) *adj.,* overcome by awe or fearful respect.

o • ver • se • er (ō′ vər sē′ ər) *n.,* one who supervises the work of others.

out • set (out′ set) *n.,* beginning; start.

over • seas (ō vər sēz′) *adj.,* situated, originating in, or relating to lands beyond the sea.

pal • pa • ble (pal′ pə bəl) *adj.,* easily perceived; obvious; clear, capable of being handled, touched, or felt.

pan • a • ce • a (pa nə sē′ ə) *n.,* universal remedy, cure-all.

par • a • digm (par′ ə dīm) *n.,* philosophical or theoretical framework consisting of theories and generalizations.

par • a • pet (par′ ə pet) *n.,* low wall or railing.

pa • ro • chi • al (pə rō′ kē əl) *adj.,* limited in range or scope.

par • ti • cle (pärt′ i kəl) *n.,* tiny bit.

pa • tho • lo • gy (pa thä′ lə jē) *n.,* abnormality caused by disease.

pa • tri • ar • chy (pā′ trē är kē) *n.,* social organization marked by the supremacy of the father or males.

pa • tron • age (pā′ trən ij) *n.,* goodwill; kindness done with an air of superiority.

pend • ing (pen′ diŋ) *adj.,* while awaiting; until.

pen • i • tent (pe′ nə tənt) *n.,* person who repents of sin.

pe • num • bral (pə nəm′ brəl) *adj.,* relating to a space of partial illumination (as in an eclipse) between the perfect shadow on all sides and the full light.

per • emp • to • ry (pə remp′ tə rē) *adj.,* urgent; commanding.

pe • rim • e • ter (pə ri′ mə tər) *n.,* line or strip bounding or protecting an area.

pe • riph • ery (pə ri′ f(ə) rē) *n.,* outward bounds of something as distinguished from its internal regions or center.

per • pet • u • ate (pər pe′ chə wāt) *vt.,* cause to last indefinitely; preserve.

per • plexed (pər pleksd′) *adj.,* uncertain or hesitant.

per • se • cute (pʉr′ si kyōōt) *vt.,* cruelly oppress.

per • se • ver • ance (pər sə vir′ ən(t)s) *n.,* act of continuing, of pursuing to an end.

per • vade (pər vād′) *vt.,* fill, spread through.

per • va • sive (pər vā′ siv) *adj.,* quality or state of being diffused throughout every part of something.

per • verse (pər vərs´) *adj.*, contrary; opposing what is right, reasonable, or accepted; deviating from what is considered right or good.

per • verse • ness (pər vurs´ nəs) *n.*, deviation from what is considered right or good.

pe • ti • tion (pə tish´ ən) *n.*, formal document containing an earnest request.

phe • nom • e • na (fə nä´ mə nə) *n.*, *pl. of phenomenon,* observable facts or events.

phos • pho • res • cent (fäs fə re´ sənt) *adj.*, luminescent, giving off light.

pi • e • ty (pī´ ə tē) *n.*, state of being pious, of having devoted loyalty to family, or religious zeal.

pig • ment (pig´ mənt) *n.*, coloring matter in cells and tissue.

pit • tance (pit´ ´ns) *n.*, small amount.

piv • o • tal (pi´ və təl) *adj.*, on which something depends.

plac • id (pla´ səd) *adj.*, serene, of a peaceful nature, meek, mild, calm.

plac • id • ly (pla´ səd lē) *adv.*, in a calm way.

plain • tive (plān´ tiv) *adj.*, mournful; sad.

plain• tive • ly (plān´ tiv lē) *adv.*, sadly.

plau • si • ble (plô´ zə bəl) *adj.*, believable; credible.

pli • a • ble (plī´ ə bəl) *adj.*, supple enough to bend freely or repeatedly without breaking.

plum • met (plə´ mət) *vi.*, fall or drop rapidly.

plum • met • ing (plə´ mət iŋ) *adj.*, dropping sharply and abruptly.

pomp • ous (päm´ pəs) *adj.*, having or exhibiting self-importance.

por • tend (pôr tend´) *vt.*, give an omen or anticipatory sign of; indicate.

por • tent (pôr´ tent) *n.*, sign; omen.

por • ten • tous (pôr ten´ təs) *adj.*, full of consequence or possibility; ominous; foreboding; predictive.

pos • it (pä´ zət) *vt.*, suggest; propose as an explanation.

pre • car • i • ous (prē ker´ ē əs) *adj.*, insecure; unsure.

pre • cur • sor (pri kur´ sər) *n.*, person or thing that precedes and indicates the approach of another.

pre • dom • i • nate (prē däm´ ə nāt) *vt.*, have authority over.

preen (prēn) *vi.*, dress or groom oneself in a fussy, vain way.

pre • lim • i • nary (pri li´ mə ner ē) *adj.*, something that precedes or is introductory or preparatory.

prem • is • es (prem´is əs) *n.*, house and its land.

pres • sage (prē säj´) *vi.*, foretell; warn.

pres • tige (pres tēzh´) *n.*, reputation; power to impress.

pre • vail (prē vāl´) *vi.*, grow strong, gain victory, triumph.

prev • a • lent (prev´ (ə)lent) *adj.*, widely accepted, favored.

pris • tine (pris tēn´) *adj.*, pure, unspoiled.

pri • va • tion (prī vā´ shən) *n.*, deprivation; lack of necessities of life.

proc • tor (präk´ tər) *n.*, school official who supervises students.

pro • cure (prō kyo͝or´) *vt.*, get or obtain.

pro • di • gious (prə dij´ əs) *adj.*, amazing.

pro • di • gy (präd´ ə jē) *n.*, exceptional person or thing; highly talented child or youth.

pro • fane (prō fān´) *vt.*, violate, abuse, or make impure.

prof • fer (präf´ ər) *vi.*, offer.

prog • nos • is (präg nō´ səs) *n.*, act or art of foretelling the course of a disease.

pro • lif • er • ate (prə li´ fə rāt) *vi.*, grow by rapid production of new parts, cells, buds, or offspring.

pro • long (prō lôŋ´) *vt.*, lengthen or extend in time.

prom • i • nence (prom´ ə nəns) *n.*, conspicuousness.

pro • pi • ti • ate (prō pi´ shē āt) *vt.*, win or regain the good will of.

pro • por • tion • al (prō pôr´ shə nəl) *adj.*, having the same ratio.

pro • sce • ni • um (prə sē´ nē əm) *n.*, the front part, the foreground.

pros • pect (prä´ spekt) *n.*, anticipated outcome.

pro • to • col (prō´ tə kol) *n.*, established, precise, and correct procedures; code entailing strict adherence to correct etiquette.

pro • tract (prō trakt´) *vt.*, prolong.

pro • trude (prō trüd´) *vt.*, thrust out.

prov • i • den • tial (prä və dent´ shəl) *adj.*, occurring by or as if by an intervention of Providence, or heaven.

pro • vi • sion (prō vizh´ ən) *n.*, condition; agreement.

pro • vi • sions (prə vi´ zhəns) *pl. n.*, supplies, especially food.

pru • dence (prü´ dənts) *n.*, ability to govern and discipline oneself by the use of reason.

pru • dent (prüd´ ´nt) *adj.*, cautious or discreet.

pseu • do (sü´ dō) *adj.*, being apparently rather than actually as stated; false; deceptive.

psy • cho • a • nal • y • sis (sī kō ə na´ lə səs) *n.*, method of analyzing psychic phenomena and treating emotional disorders that involves treatment sessions during which the patient is encouraged to talk freely about personal experiences.

pu • is • sant (pyü´ i sənt) *adj.*, strong; powerful.

pun • dit (pən´ dət) *n.*, one who gives opinions in an authoritative manner; critic.

pun • gent (pən´ jənt) *adj.*, causing a sharp sensation; prickly; acrid; sharp or pointed.

pur • port (pər pōrt´) *vt.*, claim or imply something that might not be true.

qui • es • cent (kwī e´ sənt) *adj.*, inactive; peacefully at rest.

quin • tes • sen • tial • ly (kwin´ tə sen(t)´ shəl ē) *adv.*, most purely.

rak • ish (rā´ kish) *adj.*, dashingly or carelessly unconventional; jaunty.

ram • i • fied (ra´ mə fīd) *adj.*, branched; spread out; split up.

rau • cous (rä´ kəs) *adj.*, boisterous.

ra • vage (rav´ ij) *vt.*, lay waste to; destroy; ruin; pillage or rob.

rav • aged (rav´ ijd) *adj.*, ruined; devastated.

rav • e • nous • ly (rav´ ə nəs lē) *adv.*, in a wildly hungry manner.

ra • vine (rə vēn´) *n.*, long, deep hollow in the earth's surface.

re • ced • ing (ri sēd´ iŋ) *adj.*, moving back.

re • cessed (rē´ sesd) *adj.*, hidden or set apart.

re • coil (ri koil´) *vi.*, spring back.

rec • on • cil • i • a • tion (re kən si lē ā´ shən) *n.*, act of restoring friendship or harmony.

re • dress (ri dres´) *vt.*, right a wrong; rectify.

re • frain (ri frān´) *vi.*, hold back; curb an impulse.

ref • uge (ref´ yo͞oj) *n.*, place of shelter and safety.

re • fute (ri fyoot´) *vt.*, prove to be wrong.

re • gime (rə zhēm´) *n.*, government; administration in power.

re • gres • sion (ri gresh´ ən) *n.*, reversion to a simpler or earlier form.

re • ju • ve • nate (ri jü´ və nāt) *vt.*, make feel young again.

rel • e • gate (re´ lə gāt) *vi.*, assign to a place of insignificance or oblivion.

re • lent (ri lent´) *vi.*, give in or slacken.

rel • e • vance (re´ lə ven(t)s) *n.*, pertinence; relation to the matter at hand.

rel • ish (re´ lish) *n.*, enjoyment of or delight in something that satisfies one's tastes, inclinations, or desires.

rem • nant (rem´ nənt) *n.*, small remaining part.

re • morse (ri môrs´) n., deep sense of guilt.

ren • der (ren´dər) vt., cause to be or become.

re • nounce (ri nouns´) vt., give up or leave behind.

re • nowned (ri nound´) adj., famous.

re • pel • lent (ri pel´ ənt) adj., distasteful; repulsive.

re • pent (ri pent´) vi., feel regret or change one's mind; turn away from sin.

re • plen • ish (ri ple´ nish) vi., fill or build up again.

re • pli • ca (re´ pli kə) n., exact copy or reproduction.

rep • li • ca • tion (rep lə kā´ shən) n., repetition, echo.

re • pose (ri pōz´) vt., lie, rest, or be supported on.

rep • re • hen • si • ble (re pri hen´ sə bəl) adj., worthy of or deserving disapproval or censure.

re • proach (ri prōch´) n., expression of rebuke or disapproval; vt., accuse; blame.

re • proach • ful (ri prōch´ fəl) adj., expressing blame.

req • ui • site (re´ kwə zət) adj., required by the nature of things.

re • serve (ri zurv´) n., practice of keeping one's thoughts to oneself.

res • i • due (rez´ ə dōō) n., leftover or remainder.

re • sil • ient (ri zil´ yənt) adj., ability to recover from or adjust easily to misfortune or change.

res • in • ous (rez´ ən əs) adj., having resin—a clear, yellowish-brown substance that comes from trees or plants.

re • solve (ri zälv´) n., intention.

re • sound (ri zound´) vi., extol loudly or widely.

res • o • lute • ly (rez ə lōōt´ lē) adv., firmly; determinedly.

res • o • lu • tion (rez´ ə lōō shən) n., determination.

ret • i • cent (re´ tə sənt) adj., inclined to be silent or uncommunicative in speech.

re • tir • ing (ri tīr´ iŋ) adj., private, withdrawn.

re • tort (ri tort´) n., quick, witty, or cunning reply.

re • ver • ber • a • tion (ri vur bər ā´ shən) n., echoed sound.

rev • er • ence (rev´ rəns) n., profound respect, love, and awe.

rev • er • ent • ly (rev´ ər ənt lē) adv., in a manner suggesting deep respect, love, or awe.

rev • er • ie (rev´ ər ē) n., daydream.

rev • o • lu • tion • ar • y (rev´ ə lōō shən er ē) n., one who seeks to overthrow a government.

re • vue (ri vyü´) n., musical show parodying topical matters.

rheu • ma • tism (rü´ mə ti zəm) n., disease involving painful swelling of the muscles and joints; arthritis.

ri • gid • i • ty (ri jid´ə tē) n., state of being inflexible.

rig • or (rig´ ər) n., strictness; rigidity; severity.

rig • or • ous (rig´ ər əs) adj., extremely harsh or severe.

riv • er • y (riv´ ər ē) adj., riverlike.

riv • et • ed (riv´ it əd) adj., fastened with metal pins called rivets.

ro • bust (rō bəst´) adj., having or exhibiting strength or vigorous health.

rogu • ish (rōg´ ish) adj., characteristic of a rogue, or scoundrel.

round • a • bout (round´ ə bout) adj., not straightforward; indirect.

ru • mi • na • tor (rü´ mə nā dər) n., one who ruminates—contemplates, ponders, mulls over, muses upon.

sab • o • tage (sab´ ə täzh) n., destruction of machinery, bridges, and roads by enemy forces.

sac • ro • sanct (sa´ krō saŋkt) adj., sacred or holy.

sal • vage (sal´vij) vt., save; rescue.

sanc • tion (saŋ(k)´ shən) vt., give approval or consent to.

sar • casm (sär´ ka zəm) n., cutting remark in a tone of contempt; ironic or inverted language.

saun • ter (sôn´ tər) vi., stroll.

sa • vor (sā´ vər) vt., enjoy with delight.

scaf • fold • ing (skaf´ əld iŋ) n., temporary framework for supporting workers while repairing a building.

sche • mat • ic (ski ma´ tik) adj., following a set scheme or design.

scru • ple (skrü´ pəl) n., doubt in deciding what is proper or ethical.

scru • pu • lous • ly (skrü´ pyə ləs lē) adv., done in a painstakingly exact manner.

scru • ti • nize (skroo ti ´n īz´) vt., look at carefully.

sear (sir) vt., brand as by burning.

se • ces • sion (sə se´ shən) n., formal withdrawal from an organization.

sec • u • lar (sek´ yə lər) adj., worldly or temporal, as opposed to spiritual; not sacred.

self- • pos • sessed (self´ pə zesd´) adj., confident, composed.

sen • si • bil • i • ty (sen sə bil´ ə tē) n., capacity for being affected emotionally or intellectually.

sen • ten • tious • ly (sen ten´ shəs lē) adv., in an overly moralizing way.

se • pia (sē´ pē ə) adj., brownish gray to dark olive brown color.

se • ques • tered (si kwes´ tərd) adj., secluded.

se • rene (sə rēn´) adj., calm, peaceful.

se • ren • i • ty (sə re´ nə tē) n., quality or state of being tranquil.

ser • vile (sur´ vəl or sur vīl´) adj., slavelike, submissive.

sev • er (se´ vər) vt., remove; cut.

sham • ble (sham´ bəl) vi., walk awkwardly with dragging feet.

shift • less (shift´ lis) adj., lazy.

shod • dy (shäd´ ē) adj., poorly made; cheap, inferior.

shorn (shorn) vi., past tense of shear, cut or clipped.

si • en • na (sē e´ nə) n., earthy substance containing oxides of iron and usually of manganese that is brownish-yellow when raw and orange-red or reddish-brown when burnt and is used as a pigment.

sin • ew (sin´ yü) n., muscle.

skein (skān) n., loosely coiled length of wound yarn.

skep • ti • cism (skep´ tə si zəm) n., attitude of doubt or suspended judgment.

smirk (smərk) vi., smile in an affected or smug manner.

smol • der • ing (smōl´ dər iŋ) adj., showing suppressed anger, hate, or jealousy.

so • lace (sä´ ləs) n., source of relief or consolation.

so • lem • ni • ty (sə lem´ ne tē) n., deep seriousness; formal or solemn observance.

so • lic • it (sə lis´ it) vt., ask earnestly or pleadingly.

sol • i • dar • i • ty (sä lə dar´ ə tē) n., unity based on community interests, objectives, and standards.

som • ber (säm´ bər) adj., dark and gloomy; depressing; grave.

sooth • say • er (sooth´ sā ər) n., person who professes to foretell the future.

sov • er • eign (sä´ və rən) adj., enjoying autonomy; independent.

spe • cial • i • za • tion (spesh əl īz ā´shən) n., concentration on only one part of a subject.

spec • ter (spek´ tər) n., object of dread or fear.

spec • u • la • tion (spe kyə lā´ shən) n., act or instance of guessing or surmising.

spon • ta • ne • ous • ly (spän tā´ nē əs lē) adv., in a natural way, without outside influence.

spor • a • dic (spə rad´ ik) adj., occasional.

spo • rad • i • cal • ly (spə rad´ ik lē) *adv.,* occasionally; in scattered instances.

stal • wart (stôl´ wərt) *adj.,* strong; robust; unyielding.

state • craft (stāt kraft´) *n.,* art of conducting state affairs.

steppe (step) *n.,* any of the great plains of southeast Europe and Asia having few trees.

stewed (stüd) *adj.,* cooked with simmering heat.

stodg • y (stä´ jē) *adj.,* moving in a slow plodding way.

stol • id • ly (stäl´ id lē) *adv.,* in a way that shows little emotion or excitability.

stu • pe • fied (stoo´ pə fīd) *adj.,* stunned; bewildered.

styl • ized (stīl´ īzd) *adj.,* not realistic; conforming to a set pattern or design.

sub • due (səb dü´) *vt.,* bring under control; reduce the intensity or degree of.

sub • ord • i • nate (sə´ bord ən āt) *vt.,* place in a lower class, order, or rank.

sub • se • quent • ly (sub´ si kwent lē) *adv.,* following in order of time or place; succeeding.

sub •´ side (səb sīd´) *vi.,* become less intense.

sub • stan • tial (səb stan(t)´ shəl) *adj.,* sturdy; firmly constructed.

sub • tend (səb tend´) *vt.,* be opposite to and extend from one side to the other of.

sub • tle (sə´ təl) *adj.,* difficult to perceive or understand.

suc • ces • sive (sək ses´ iv) *adj.,* following one after another in sequence.

suc • cinct • ly (suk siŋkt´ lē) *adv.,* in a concise manner.

suc • cumb (sə kum´) *vi.,* yield to superior strength or force or over-powering appeal or desire; give way to.

suf • fice (sə fīs´) *vi.,* be enough; be sufficient.

suf • fi • cient • ly (sə fish´ ənt lē) *adv.,* adequately.

sug • ges • tive (səg jes´ tiv) *adj.,* revealing; telling.

sum • mon (sum´ ən) *vt.,* order to come or appear.

su • per • an • nu • at • ed (sü pər an´ yə wāt əd) *adj.,* old-fashioned; outdated.

su • per • cil • i • ous (soo pər sil´ ē əs) *adj.,* full of pride or scorn.

su • per • fi • cial (soo pər fish´ əl) *adj.,* shallow.

su • per • flu • ous (sə pʉr´ floo əs) *adj.,* unnecessary.

su • per • nat • u • ral (sü pər na´ chə rəl) *adj.,* of or relating to a god, spirit, or devil.

sup • plant (sə plant´) *vt.,* take the place of and serve as a substitute.

sup • ple • ness (sup´ əl nes) *n.,* flexibility.

sup • press (sə pres´) *vt.,* keep from appearing or being known.

sur • ly (sʉr´ lē) *adj.,* bad-tempered; rude; hostile.

sur • mise (sər mīz´) *vi.,* imagine or infer on slight grounds.

sur • mount (sər mount´) *vt.,* overcome; prevail over.

sus • te • nance (səs´ tə nən(t)s) *n.,* nourishment.

sym • me • try (si´ mə trē) *n.,* quality of being equal on both sides of an imaginary center line.

syn • drome (sin´ drōm) *n.,* multiple symptoms characterizing a specific disease or condition.

tab • leau (ta blō´) *n.,* artistic grouping; scene or arrangement.

tan • gi • ble (tan´ jə bəl) *adj.,* definite; concrete; capable of being perceived by the senses, especially by the sense of touch.

taunt • ing (tônt´ iŋ) *adj.,* in a reproachful or sarcastic manner.

taut (tôt) *adj.,* tense.

tem • per (tem´ pər) *vt.,* reduce in intensity; moderate.

tem • per • a • ment (tem´ pər ə mənt) *n.,* one's frame of mind.

tem • pest (tem´ pist) *n.,* storm.

te • na • ci • ty (tə na´ sə tē) *n.,* courage; quality of not giving up.

ten • an • cy (ten´ ən sē) *n.,* occupation of something by right.

ten • ta • tive (ten´ tə tiv) *adj.,* not fully worked out or developed.

ten • ta • tive • ly (ten´ tə tiv lē) *adv.,* hesitantly, timidly; uncertainly.

ter • res • tri • al (tə res´ trē əl) *adj.,* of or relating to the earth or its inhabitants.

thrift • less • ness (thrift´ ləs nəs) *n.,* carelessness, wastefulness, or incompetence in handling money or resources.

throng (thrôŋ) *n.,* crowd, gang; group.

till (til) *vt.,* plow and fertilize land for the raising of crops; cultivate.

tor • rid (tôr´ əd) *adj.,* hot; passionate.

tout (taut) *vi.,* praised or publicized loudly.

tran • quil (tran´ kwil) *adj.,* calm; serene.

tran • scend (tran send´) *vt.,* go beyond the limits.

trans • gress (trans gres´) *vt.,* go beyond limits set; break, violate.

trans • mute (tran(t)s myüt´) *vt.,* change or alter in form, appearance, or nature.

tre • bly (treb´ lē) *adv.,* extremely; three times as.

trend (trend) *n.,* line of development; current tendency.

tri • fle (trī´ fəl) *adv.,* to a small degree; slightly; *n.,* something inconsequential; of little value.

tri • um • phant (trī em(p)´ fent) *adj.,* victorious, or relating to triumph.

triv • i • al • i • ty (triv ē al´ i tē) *n.,* something insignificant.

tru • ant (trü´ ənt) *adj.,* characteristic of someone who shirks duty.

tun • dra (tun´ drə) *n.,* treeless plains of the arctic region.

ty • ran • ni • cal (tī ran´ i kəl) *adj.,* oppressive, unjust.

u • nan • i • mous (yoo nan´ ə məs) *adj.,* in complete agreement.

un • con • ge • ni • al (un kən jēn´ yəl) *adj.,* incompatible.

un • der • es • ti • mate (ən dər es´ tə māt) *vt.,* estimate as being less than the actual size or quantity.

un • der • ling (un´ dər liŋ) *n.,* person of low status; servant.

un • du • late (ən´ jə lāt) *vi.,* form or move in waves.

un • eth • i • cal (un eth´ i kəl) *adj.,* not conforming to moral standards.

un • fath • omed (un fath´ əm) *adj.,* unsounded; undetermined; immense.

un • gov • ern • a • ble (un guv´ ərn ə bəl) *adj.,* unable to be controlled.

un • wield • y (un wēl´ dē) *adj.,* hard to manage because of shape or weight.

u • sur • er (yoo´ zhər ər) *n.,* person who lends at an extremely high interest rate.

ut • ter • ance (ut´ ər əns) *n.,* speech.

va • cate (vā´ cāt) *vt.,* deprive of an occupant; make free.

vac • u • ous (vak´ yoo əs) *adj.,* devoid of interest or thought; empty.

val • iant (val´ yənt) *adj.,* full of courage; brave.

val • id (val´ id) *adj.,* sound; just.

val • or (val´ ər) *n.,* courage or bravery.

van • i • ty (va´ ne tē) *n.,* inflated pride in oneself; conceit.

van • quish (vaŋ´ kwish) *vt.,* conquer.

van • quished (vaŋ´ kwishd) *adj.,* beaten or conquered in battle.

ven • er • ate (ven´ ər āt) *vt.,* worship.

ven • geance (ven´ jəns) *n.,* act of taking revenge; inflicting punishment.

ven • ti • la • tion (vent ʼl ā´ shən) *n.,* circulation of fresh air.

ven • ti • la • tor (vent´ 'l āt´ ər) *n.*, opening through which air can pass.

ven • ture (ven´ chər) *vi.*, do at some risk.

ver • ba • tim (vər bā´ təm) *adj.*, word for word.

ver • dant (vʊrd´ 'nt) *adj.*, green; covered in vegetation.

ver • i • fy (ver´ ə fī) *vt.*, check the accuracy or correctness of.

ver • nac • u • lar (vər nak' yə lər) *adj.*, using a language or dialect native to a region or country; a mode of expression natural to or used by a group or class.

ves • ti • bule (ves´ tə byül) *n.*, foyer or hall entrance.

ves • tig • i • al (ve sti' jē əl) *adj.*, showing a trace, mark, or visible sign left by something vanished or lost.

vig • il (vij´ əl) *n.*, purposeful staying awake during the usual hours of sleep.

vi • gnette (vin yet') *n.*, short scene or incident, as from a movie.

vig • or • ous (vi' g(ə) rəs) *adj.*, full of physical or mental strength or active force.

vile (vīl) *adj.*, foul; mean; base; cheap; contemptible.

vi • rid • i • an (və ri' dē ən) *adj.*, chrome green.

vis • age (viz' ij) *n.*, face; appearance.

vo • li • tion (vō lish´ ən) *n.*, free will.

wa • ver (wā' vər) *vi.*, move back and forth; hesitate; be undecided.

white • washed (hwīt' wôshd') *adj.*, painted with a white mixture of lime, water, and other elements.

wrench (rench) *vt.*, pull or strain at something with violent twisting or straining.

wretch • ed (rech´ id) *adj.*, miserable; deeply unhappy; contemptible; despicable.

wry (rī) *adj.*, twisted or distorted.

yoke (yōk) *n.*, anything that harnesses or reduces to servitude, like the wooden yoke used around the necks of cattle.

zeal • ous (zel´ əs) *adj.*, enthusiastic.

zeal • ous • ly (ze' ləs lē) *adv.*, fervently; ardently.

INDEX
Of Titles and Authors

INDEX Of Skills

READING

abstract, 101, 104
accent, 1139
act, 240
active reading, 1008–1009, 1011–1012
aim, 362, 395, 403, 425, 431, 475, 480, 482, 486, 488, 497, 588, 596, 824, 831, 843, 850, 1119
allegory, 1119–1120
alliteration, 77, 1120
allusion, 120, 126, 386, 393, 1120
analogy, 1120
analysis, 465, 473, 615, 623, 1120
anapest, 76, 1120, 1130
anecdote, 843, 850
antagonist, 162
antihero, 563, 578, 1120
aphorism, 965, 976, 1120–1121
apostrophe, 1121
apposition, 1015
arena stage, 240
argumentative writing, 363
art, 1011
article, 475, 480
aside, 240, 1121
assonance, 77, 1121
atmosphere, 164, 433, 917, 958, 1131
autobiography, 362, 642, 648, 833, 841
ballad, 1121
bar graphs, 1014
biography, 362, 650, 660
blank verse, 242, 1121–1122
blocking, 241
book club, 1009–1010
caricature, 162
catastrophe, 326, 343, 884, 904, 1122, 1134
catharsis, 1122
central conflict, 242, 266, 538, 549, 1122
character, 162, 198, 206, 242, 265, 764, 768, 1122
characterization, 162, 183, 208, 216, 528, 536, 563, 578, 611, 613, 720, 727, 734, 738, 1122
charts, 464

chorus, 863, 883, 1123
chronological order, 16, 21, 405, 415, 833, 841, 1123
cliché, 1123
climax, 163, 232, 288, 308, 884, 904, 1123, 1134
colloquialism, 693, 697, 1123
comedy, 240, 1123
commentary, 462
comparison-contrast, 465, 473, 499, 506
complication, 163, 268, 286, 863, 1134
computer games, 462
computer news service, 462
concrete, 101, 104
concrete poem, 1124
confessional poetry, 1124, 1140
conflict, 163, 171, 181, 183, 188, 936, 956, 1124
connotation, 1017, 1124
consonance, 77, 1124
constitutions, 362
context clue, 1015
contracts, 362
convention, 1124
couplet, 76, 1124
creative nonfiction, 362
crisis, 163, 288, 308, 884, 904, 1124, 1134
criticism, 1124
dactyl, 76, 1124–1125, 1131
dead metaphor, 1125
deeds, 362
denotation, 1017, 1125
dénouement, 163, 232, 1134
description, 363, 364, 384, 417, 423, 588, 596, 642, 648, 1125
diagrams, 464
dialect, 965, 976, 1125
dialogue, 54, 61, 74, 240, 363, 405, 415, 528, 536, 755, 762, 1125
diary, 362, 364, 384
diction, 488, 497, 1125
dictionary, 1015
digital photography, 464
dimeter, 1131
drama, 240–241, 1125

dramatic convention, 1125
dramatic irony, 45, 52, 183, 551, 791, 793
dramatic monologue, 74, 1126
dramatic poem, 74, 1126
dramatic reading, 359
dramatis personae, 1126
drawings, 464
dynamic character, 162, 764
dystopia, 1126
e-books, 462, 464
editorials, 462
effect, 1126
elaboration, 1126
electronic mail, 463
electronic media, 462
elegiac lyric, 76
elegy, 1126
e-mail, 463
emphasis, 1126
end rhyme, 77, 111, 1126
epics, 5
epigram, 1126
epigraph, 1126
epiphany, 1126
epistle, 1126
epitaph, 1126–1127
epithet, 1127
eponym, 1127
essay, 362, 425, 431, 462–463, 1127
etymology, 1015
euphemism, 1127
euphony, 1127
exposition, 163, 232, 363, 482, 486, 588, 596, 863, 1127, 1134
expository writing, 363
expressive writing, 363
extended metaphor, 1127
external conflict, 163, 171
e-zines, 462, 463–464
fable, 4, 1127
fairy tale, 4, 1127
falling action, 163, 232, 309, 324, 884, 904, 1134
fantasy, 1127–1128
farce, 1128
fiction, 160–162, 1128
figurative language, 1128

INDEX OF SKILLS

INDEX
Of Internet Sites

At the time of publication, the following were valid, working Internet sites. Due to the changing nature of the Internet, some of these sites may no longer be accessible via the listed address. If an address does not work, try conducting a keyword search by the name of the site, author, or topic. If you find a non-working site, please notify us at educate@emcp.com so that we can update this index.

INDEX OF INTERNET SITES **1163**

INDEX
Of Fine Art

ACKNOWLEDGMENTS

ART ACKNOWLEDGMENTS
Cover *The Persistence of Memory*, 1931. Salvador Dali. © 2000 Estate of Salvador Dali/Artists Rights Society (ARS), New York/DEMART PRO ARTE, Paris; *The Farm*, 1921-1922. Joan Miro. © 2000 Artists Rights Society (ARS), New York/ADAGP, Paris/ National Gallery of Art, Washington, DC.; *Tahitian Pastoral Scene*, 1893. Paul Gauguin. Planet Art; *The Human Condition*, 1934. René Magritte. © 2000 Charly Herscovici, Brussels / Artists Rights Society (ARS), New York.; **2** National Gallery of Art, Washington, DC. Gift of Edgar William and Bernice Chrysler Garbisch.; **5** © Luca I. Tettoni/CORBIS; **7** © Kevin Fleming/CORBIS; **10** © Hulton-Deutsch Collection/CORBIS; **12** SuperStock; **18** © Hans Georg Roth/CORBIS; **24** © AFP/CORBIS; **33** Wellesley College Library; **46** Wellesley College Library; **55** © Nik Wheeler/CORBIS; **72** Corcoran Gallery of Art, Washington, DC. Museum Purchase, Gallery Fund.; **75** © The State Russian Museum/CORBIS; **78** AP/Paula Alye Scully/Wide World Photos; **79** © Tony Arruza/CORBIS; **83** Library of Congress; **84** Van Gogh Museum, Amsterdam. Vincent Van Gogh Foundation; **88** Library of Congress; **89** Art Resource, NY; **92** Library of Congress; **93** © Francis G. Mayer/CORBIS; **96** © Oscar White/CORBIS; **97** © Brett Weston Archive/CORBIS; **101** Library of Congress. Photo by George Platt Lynes, 1935.; **102** © Francis G. Mayer/CORBIS; **106** © Bettmann/CORBIS; **107** © Kevin Schafer/CORBIS; **108** © Bettmann/CORBIS; **111** Amherst College Archives and Special Collections. Used by permission of the Trustees of Amherst College; **117** © Burstein Collection/CORBIS; **120** AP/Wide World Photos; **121** © Kimbell Art Museum/ CORBIS; **128** Archive Photos; **131** Art Resource, NY; **135** Photo: The Central Art Archives; **143** Ann Marsden; **158** © Richard Estes; **161** © 2000 Charly Herscovici, Brussels / Artists Rights Society (ARS), New York; **165** © 2000 Artists Rights Society (ARS), New York / ADAGP, Paris; **171** Library of Congress; **172** Corcoran Gallery of Art, Museum Purchase; **182** Archive Photos; **184** SuperStock; **190** Archive Photos; **193** © Contemporary African Art Collection/ CORBIS; **198** © Chris Hellier/CORBIS; **199** Museum of Fine

Arts, Boston. Zoe Oliver Sherman; **208** © Roger Ressmeyer/CORBIS; **209** © The Estate of Alice Neel. Museum of Art, Rhode Island School of Design. Gift of Richard and Hartley Neel. Photograph by Del Bogart.; **218** Reuters/Stringer/ Archive Photos; **219** © Arvind Garg/CORBIS; **224** AP; **227** National Gallery of Art, Washington, D.C.; **243** Bridgeman Art Library; **245** Wellesley College Library, Special Collections; **264** © Robbie Jack/CORBIS; **345** Steve Estensen; **346** Steve Estensen; **361** © Graham Dean/CORBIS; **365** Archive Photos; **367** © Wolfgang Kaehler/CORBIS; **386** Library of Congress; **387** National Museum of American Art, Washington, DC/Art Resource, NY; **395** Library of Congress; **396** © Bettmann/ CORBIS; **399** © Bettmann/CORBIS; **405** Archive Photos; **407** © 2000 Charly Herscovici, Brussels / Artists Rights Society (ARS), New York. / Bridgeman Art Library; **417** © Galen Rowell/CORBIS; **418** © Tim Thompson/CORBIS; **425** © Michael Llewellyn; **426** © Yogi, Inc./CORBIS; **429** © CORBIS; **433** © Museum of Flight/CORBIS; **435** © Lawrence Paul Yuxweluptun. Photo: National Gallery of Canada, Ottawa; **438** © Bass Museum of Art/CORBIS; **440** Jean-Loup Sieff; **443** © 2000 Artists Rights Society (ARS), New York / ADAGP, Paris / © Edimédia/CORBIS; **447** Camera One; **460** © Danny Lehman/ CORBIS; **465** Hughes: Mario Ruiz/Time/ TimePix; **465** Hopper: © Oscar White/ CORBIS; **466** Art Institute of Chicago; **468** Photograph © 2000: Whitney Museum of American Art, New York. Purchase with funds from Gertrude Vanderbilt Whitney; **470** Oil on canvas 29" x 36" Sheldon Memorial Art Gallery. UNL-F.M. Hall Collection; **475** Newsweek; **482** © Philip Gould/CORBIS; **483** © Julie Delton; **488** © Richard Howard; **489** PhotoDisc; **499** Walker and Company; **500** PhotoDisc; **520** Planet Art; **523** AP/World Wide Photos; **524** © 2000 Artists Rights Society (ARS), New York / BONO Oslo/The Cleveland Art Museum; **528** Rueters/Fredric Neema/Archive Photos; **529** © David Turnley/CORBIS; **538** Library of Congress; **539** © The State Russian Museum/CORBIS; **551** Hiroshi Mamamoto; **552** © Roger Ressmeyer/ CORBIS; **563** AP/World Wide Press; **565** National Museum of American Art,

Washington, DC./Art Resource, NY; **581** Bridgeman Art Library; **588** UPI/CORBIS-Bettmann; **589** © Araldo de Luca/CORBIS; **608** Planet Art; **612** National Museum of American Art, Washington, DC./Art Resource; **615** © Ed Pierce; **616** © Bettmann/CORBIS; **619** © Baldwin H. Ward & Kathryn C. Ward/CORBIS; **621** PictureQuest; **625** Photo by Robert Foothorap © 1995; **642** Secker & Warburg Ltd.; **643** The Random House Group; **651** © Bettmann/CORBIS; **659** © Bettmann/CORBIS; **662** © Nancy Crampton; **664** © 2000 Artists Rights Society (ARS), New York/VG Bild-Kunst, Bonn. © Burstein Collection/CORBIS; **674** © Richard T. Nowitz/CORBIS; **679** © Richard T. Nowitz/CORBIS; **693** © Mallory Geitheim; **694** National Museum of American Art, Washington, DC./Art Resource, NY; **708** © 2000 Artists Rights Society (ARS), New York/ADAGP, Paris/National Gallery of Art, Washington, DC.; **711** © Debi Milligan; **715** Arb; **716** © Jack Fields/CORBIS; **720** © E. O. Hoppe/ CORBIS; **722** Corel; **729** © Jill Krementz; **734** Arte Público Press; **735** Art Resource, NY; **740** © Ellen Foscue Johnson; **745** © Daniel Cima; **747** © Geoffrey Clements/CORBIS; **755** © Frank Cantor; **756** Christie's Images/ SuperStock; **767** PhotoDisc; **771** © Howardena Pindell. Wadsworth Athenaeum, Hartford. The Ella Gallup Sumner and Mary Catlin Sumner Collection Fund.; **782** © Contemporary African Art Collection/CORBIS; **785** Steve Miller/New York Times Co./ Archive Photos; **786** © Contemporary African Art Collection/CORBIS; **791** Mary Lockwood; **792** Corel; **795** UPI/CORBIS-Bettmann; **797** © Bettmann/CORBIS; **810** © AINACO/ CORBIS; **814** © The Purcell Team/CORBIS; **824** Jerry Bauer; **833** Bancroft Library, UC Berkeley, Berkeley, CA.; **834** © Roger Shimomura. Photo courtesy of the artist.; **844** © Owen Franken/CORBIS; **860** © Francis G. Mayer/CORBIS; **863** © Gianni Dagli Orti/CORBIS; **864** © Bridgeman Art Library; **879** © Bettmann/CORBIS; **884** © Wood River Gallery/ PictureQuest; **902** © Bettmann/CORBIS; **914** © 2000 Estate of Salvador Dalí/Artists Rights Society (ARS), New York/DEMART PRO ARTE, Paris; **917** © Bettmann/CORBIS; **919** © Archivo Iconografico, S.A./CORBIS; **926**

Sophie Baker; **927** Bridgeman Art Library; **936** © E. O. Hoppe/CORBIS; **938** Bridgeman Art Library; **949** Rodney Busch; **958** Library of Congress; **965** Archive Photos; **966** © Samuel Bak. © Burstein Collection/CORBIS; **979** © Robert Holmes/CORBIS; **985** © D. Boone/CORBIS; **969, 973** © Julie Delton

LITERARY ACKNOWLEDGMENTS
Americas Magazine. "Lather and Nothing Else" by Hernando Téllez. Reprinted from *Americas*, a bimonthly magazine published by the General Secretariat of the Organization of American States in English and Spanish. **Arte Público Press.** "1910" by Pat Mora is reprinted with permission from the publisher of *Chants* (Houston, Texas: Arte Público Press—University of Houston, 1985). **Bancroft Library.** From *Desert Exile: The Uprooting of a Japanese-American Family*, by Yoshiko Uchida. Copyright © by Yoshiko Uchida. University of Washington Press. Courtesy of The Bancroft Library, University of California, Berkeley. **Marvin Bell.** "The Mystery of Emily Dickinson" from *A Marvin Bell Reader*. Copyright © 1994 by Marvin Bell. Reprinted by permission. **Susan Bergholz Literary Services.** "A Smart Cookie" by Sandra Cisneros from *The House on Mango Street*. Copyright © 1989 by Sandra Cisneros. Published by Vintage Books, a division of Random House, Inc. and in hardcover by Alfred A. Knopf in 1994. Reprinted by permission of Susan Bergholz Literary Services, New York. All rights reserved. "A White Woman of Color", copyright © 1998 by Julia Álvarez. Published in *Half and Half: Writers on Growing up Biracial and Bicultural*, ed. Claudine Chiawei O'Hearn, Pantheon Books, July 1998. Reprinted by permission of Susan Bergholz Literary Services, New York. All rights reserved. **Bibliotheca Islamica.** "The Happy Man" from *God's World* by Naguib Mahfouz, translated by Akef Abadir and Roger Allen. Copyright © 1973, 1988 by Akef Abadir and Roger Allen. Published by Bibliotheca Islamica, Box 14474, Minneapolis, MN 55414. **Sophie Cabot Black.** "East Song" by Álvaro Mutis, trans. Sophie Cabot Black and Maria Negroni. Copyright © 1993 by Sophie Cabot Black and Maria Negroni. **Brandt & Brandt Literary Agents, Inc.** "By the Waters of Babylon" by Stephen Vincent Benét. From *The Selected Works of Stephen Vincent Benét*. Copyright © 1937 by Stephen Vincent Benét. Copyright renewed © 1965 by

Thomas C. Benét, Stephanie B. Mahin, and Rachel Benét Lewis. Reprinted by permission of Brandt & Brandt Literary Agents, Inc. **Gwendolyn Brooks.** "The Bean Eaters" from *Blacks* by Gwendolyn Brooks, © 1991, Third World Press. Reprinted by permission of CSA II Enterprises on behalf of Gwendolyn Brooks. **Carcanet Press Limited.** "The Five Ages of Man" and "Orpheus" from *The Greek Myths* by Robert Graves. Copyright © 1960 by Robert Graves. Reprinted by permission of Robert Graves and Carcanet Press Ltd. **Don Congdon Associates.** "The Pedestrian" by Ray Bradbury. Reprinted by permission of Don Congdon Associates, Inc. Copyright © 1951 by the Fortnightly Publishing Co., renewed 1979 by Ray Bradbury. **Joan Daves Agency.** "Afternoon" by Gabriela Mistral. Reprinted by arrangement with Doris Dana, c/o Joan Daves Agency/Writers House as agent for the proprietor. **Faber and Faber, Inc.** "Into the Electronic Millennium" from *The Gutenberg Elegies* by Sven Birkerts. Copyright © 1994 by Sven Birkerts. Reprinted by permission of Faber and Faber, Inc., an affiliate of Farrar, Straus & Giroux, LLC. **Farrar, Straus & Giroux, LLC.** "After You, My Dear Alphonse" from *The Lottery* by Shirley Jackson. Copyright © 1948, 1949 by Shirley Jackson. Copyright renewed 1976, 1977 by Laurence Hyman, Barry Hyman, Mrs. Sarah Webster and Mrs. Joanne Schnurer. Reprinted by permission of Farrar, Straus & Giroux, LLC. "Holidays" from *At the Bottom of the River* by Jamaica Kincaid. Copyright © 1979, 1983 by Jamaica Kincaid. Reprinted by permission of Farrar, Straus & Giroux, LLC. "In late-afternoon light the tops of the bread-fruit leaves" from "A Santa Cruz Quartet" from *The Bounty* by Derek Walcott. Copyright © 1997 by Derek Walcott. "The Moment Before the Gun Went Off" from *Jump and Other Stories* by Nadine Gordimer. Copyright © 1991 by Nadine Gorimer. Reprinted by permission of Farrar, Straus & Giroux, LLC. **Fundación Pablo Neruda.** "Casa" (vol. *Las piedras de Chile*) by Pablo Neruda. Spanish version. Copyright © 1960. Reprinted by permission of Agencia Literaria Carmen Balcells S.A., Barcelona on behalf of the Fundación Pablo Neruda, Santiago, Chile. **Harcourt, Inc.** *Antigone* from *Sophocles, The Oedipus Cycle: An English Version* by Dudley Fitts and Robert Fitzgerald, copyright 1939 by Harcourt, Inc. and renewed 1967 by

Dudley Fitts and Robert Fitzgerald, reprinted by permission of the publisher. CAUTION: All rights, including professional, amateur, motion picture, recitation, lecturing, performance, public reading, radio broadcasting, and television are strictly reserved. Inquiries on all rights should be addressed to Harcourt, Inc., Permissions Department, Orlando, FL 32887-6777. "The Enchanted Garden" from *Difficult Loves* by Italo Calvino, copyright 1949 by Giulio Einaudi editore, Torino, copyright © 1958 by Giulio Einaudi editore, s.p.a., Torino, English translation copyright © 1984 by Harcourt Inc. Reprinted by permission of Harcourt, Inc. "Magic Words" from *Magic Words,* copyright © 1968, 1967 by Edward Field, reprinted by permission of Harcourt, Inc. "The Necklace" by Guy de Maupassant from *Adventures in Reading*, Laureate Edition, Grade 9, by Evan Lodge, Marjorie Braymer, Mary R. Bowman, and Herbert Potell, copyright © 1963 by Harcourt, Inc. and renewed 1991 by Deborah Jean Lodge, Alice Lodge, Jeanne M. Shutes, Jessica Sand, Lydia Winderman, Florence F. Potell and Mary Rives Bowman. Reprinted by permission of Harcourt, Inc. **HarperCollins Publishers.** "The Liar" from *In the Garden of the North American Martyrs* by Tobias Wolff. Copyright © 1981 by Tobias Wolff. Reprinted by permission of HarperCollins Publishers, Inc. "New Dog" from "Atlantis" from *Atlantis Poems* by Mark Doty. Copyright © 1995 by Mark Doty. Reprinted by permission of HarperCollins Publishers, Inc. All pages from "A Very Old Man with Enormous Wings" from *Leaf Storm and Other Stories* by Gabriel García Márquez. Copyright © 1971 by Gabriel García Márquez. Reprinted by permission of HarperCollins Publishers, Inc. **Harvard University Press.** "Success is counted sweetest..." by Emily Dickinson. Reprinted by permission of the publishers and the Trustees of Amherst College from *The Poems of Emily Dickinson,* Ralph W. Franklin, ed., Cambridge, Mass.: The Belknap Press of Harvard University Press. Copyright © 1998 by the President and Fellows of Harvard College. Copyright © 1951, 1955, 1979 by the President and Fellows of Harvard College. **Henry Holt and Company.** "The Montgomery Boycott" from *My Life with Martin Luther King, Jr.*, revised edition by Coretta Scott King. Copyright, © 1993 by Coretta Scott King. Reprinted by permission of Henry Holt and Company, LLC. "Sundiata

Keita, the Legend and the King" from *The Royal Kingdoms of Ghana, Mali and Songhay: Life in Medieval Africa* by Patricia and Fredrick McKissack. Copyright © 1994 by Patricia and Fredrick McKissack. Reprinted by permission of Henry Holt and Company, LLC. **Houghton Mifflin Company.** "Ars Poetica" from *Collected Poems 1917–1982* by Archibald MacLeish. Copyright © 1985 by the Estate of Archibald MacLeish. Reprinted by permission of Houghton Mifflin Co. All rights reserved. "Internet and E-Mail" from *The New Way Things Work* by David Macaulay. Compilation copyright © 1988, 1998 Dorling Kindersley, Ltd., London. Text copyright © 1988, 1998 David Macaulay, Neil Ardley. Illustrations copyright © 1988, 1998 David Macaulay. Reprinted by permission of Houghton Mifflin Co. All rights reserved. **Immigration & Refugee Services of America.** "Chee's Daughter" by Juanita Platero and Siyowin Miller from *Common Ground*, Volume 8, Winter 1948. Copyright © 1948 by the American Council for Nationalities Service. Reprinted by permission of Immigration & Refugee Services of America. **Daniel Keyes.** "Flowers for Algernon", © 1959, 1987, by Daniel Keyes. **Alfred A. Knopf.** "The Alphabet" and "Paris" from *The Diving Bell and the Butterfly* by Jean-Dominique Bauby, trans., Jeremy Leggatt. Copyright © 1997 by Editions Robert Laffont, S. A., Paris. Reprinted by permission of Alfred A. Knopf, a division of Random House, Inc. "Dream Variations" from *Selected Poems* by Langston Hughes. Copyright © 1926 by Alfred A. Knopf, Inc. and renewed 1954 by Langston Hughes. Reprinted by permission of the publisher. "The Legend" from *The River of Heaven* by Garrett Hongo, copyright © 1988 by Garret Hongo, reprinted by permission of Alfred A. Knopf, a division of Random House, Inc. "Simple Song" from *Circles on the Water* by Marge Piercy. Copyright © 1982 by Marge Piercy. Reprinted by permission of Alfred A. Knopf, a division of Random House, Inc. "The Thief" from *Seven Japanese Tales* by Junichiro Tanizaki, trans., Howard Hibbett. Copyright © 1963 by Alfred A. Knopf, Inc. Reprinted by permission of Alfred A. Knopf, a division of Random House, Inc. **Latin American Literary Review.** "Freeway 280" by Lorna Dee Cervantes. Reprinted by permission of the publisher, *Latin American Literary Review*, Vol. 15, No. 10, 1977. Pittsburgh, PA. **Ellen Levine Literary**

Agency. "How to Write a Letter" from *We Are Still Married* by Garrison Keillor, published by Viking Penguin Inc. Reprinted by permission of International Paper Company. Copyright © 1987 by International Paper Company. Originally titled "How to Write a Personal Letter." Used by permission of the Ellen Levine Literary Agency. **Mary Lockwood.** "One of Grandma Selma's Stories" by Mary Lockwood, as published in *Raven Tells Stories*, by Greenfield Review Press, 1991. Reprinted by permission of the author. **Ruth MacKenzie.** Lyrics to "In the Blue Woodland" from the compact disc *Kalevala: Dream of the Salmon Maiden*. Copyright by Ruth MacKenzie. Reprinted by permission. **William Morris Agency.** "The Hitchhiker" by Lucille Fletcher. Copyright © 1947 by Lucille Fletcher. Reprinted by permission of the William Morris Agency, Inc. on behalf of the author. **Bharati Mukherjee.** "The Road from Ballygunge" by Bharati Mukherjee. Copyright © 1999 by Bharati Mukherjee. Reprinted with permission of author. **National Endowment for the Arts.** "The New Pandora's Box: An Interview with Sven Birkerts" by Cliff Becker, National Endowment for the Arts. Reprinted by permission of Cliff Becker. **New Directions Publishing Corp.** "The Dance" by William Carlos Williams from *Collection Poems, Volume II: 1939–1962.* Copyright © 1944 by William Carlos Williams. Reprinted by permission of New Directions Publishing Corp. "A Tree Telling of Orpheus" from *Denise Levertov: Poems 1968–1972.* Copyright © 1968 by Denise Levertov Goodman. Reprinted by permission of New Directions Publishing Corp. **Newsweek, Inc.** From "Beware the Unruly Sun" by Claudia Kalb, *Newsweek,* June 21, 1999, pp. 81–82. Reprinted by permission of Newsweek, Inc. "The Roots of Genius?" by Steven Levy, *Newsweek,* June 23, 1999. Reprinted by permission. **W. W. Norton & Company.** From *The Vanishing Hitchhiker: American Urban Legends and Their Meanings* by Jan Harold Brunvand. Copyright © 1981 by Jan Harold Brunvand. Used by permission of W. W. Norton & Company, Inc. **Thien-bao Thuc Phi.** "Where Is Our Blues?" Copyright © 2001 by Thien-bao Thuc Phi. Used by permission of the author. **Harold Ober Associates.** "Harriet Tubman: The Moses of Her People" from *Famous American Negroes* by Langston Hughes. Copyright © 1954 by Langston Hughes. Copyright

renewed 1982 by George Houston Bass. Reprinted by permission of Harold Ober Associates, Inc. **Oxford University Press.** "The Drowned Maid" © Keith Bosley 1989. Reprinted from *The Kalevala* translated by Keith Bosley (World's Classics 1989) by permission of Oxford University Press. **Penguin Putnam, Inc.** From *Albert Einstein: A Biography* by Albrecht Fölsing, translation by Ewald Osers. Translation copyright © 1997 by Ewald Osers. Used by permission of Viking Penguin, a division of Penguin Putnam, Inc. "Heraclitus" from *In Praise of Darkness* by Jorge Luis Borges, translated by Norman Thomas di Giovanni, copyright © 1969, 1970, 1971, 1972, 1973, 1974 by Emece Editores, S.A., and Norman Thomas di Giovanni. Used by permission of Dutton, a division of Penguin Putnam Inc. "Like the Sun" from *Under the Banyan Tree* by R. K. Narayan. Copyright © 1985 by R. K. Narayan. Used by permission of Viking Penguin, a division of Penguin Putnam, Inc. "My Credo" by Albert Einstein, speech given in Berlin in 1932 to the German League of Human Rights. Reprinted in *Einstein* by Michael White and John Gribbon, 1994. Used by permission of Penguin Putnam, Inc. "Rules of the Game" from *The Joy Luck Club* by Amy Tan. Copyright 1989 by Amy Tan. Used by permission of Putnam Berkley, a division of Penguin Putnam Inc. "The Two Swords" from *King Arthur & His Knights of the Round Table*, copyright by Robert Lancelyn Green, 1953. First published by Penguin Books Ltd. Reprinted by permission. **Perseus Books, LLC.** From *Almost a Woman* by Esmeralda Santiago. Copyright © 1997 by Canto-Media, Inc. Reprinted by permission of Perseus Book Publishers, a division of Perseus Books, LLC. **David Quammen.** "The Last Bison" by David Quammen. Originally appeared in *Outside Magazine.* Reprinted by permission of David Quammen. All rights reserved. Copyright © 1982 by David Quammen. **Random House, Inc.** "As I walked out one evening" from *W. H. Auden Selected Poems,* by W. H. Auden. Copyright © 1940 & renewed 1968 by W. H. Auden. Reprinted by permission of Random House, Inc. "Curiosità" and "Major Accomplishments" from *How to Think Like Leonardo da Vinci in Seven Steps* by Michael J. Gelb. Copyright © 1998 by Michael J. Gelb. Used by permission of Dell Publishing, a division of Random House, Inc. "Dead Men's Path" from *Girls at War and Other Stories* by Chinua Achebe, copyright © 1972, 1973 by

Chinua Achebe. Used by permission of Doubleday, a division of Random House, Inc. From *The Diary of a Young Girl: The Definitive Edition* by Anne Frank. Otto H. Frank & Mirjam Pressler, Editors, translated by Susan Massotty. Translation copyright © 1995 by Doubleday, a division of Bantam Doubleday Dell Publishing Group, Inc. Used by permission of Doubleday, a division of Random House, Inc. From "Einstein" by Denis Brian from *Booknotes: Life Stories* by Brian Lamb, edit. Copyright © 1999 by National Cable Satellite Corporation. Reprinted by permission of Times Books, a division of Random House, Inc. "The Gazelle" from *The Selected Poetry of Rainer Maria Rilke* by Rainer Maria Rilke, edited and translated by Stephen Mitchell. Copyright © 1982 by Stephen Mitchell. Reprinted by permission of Random House, Inc. "The Gift of Cochise" by Louis L'Amour. First appeared in *Collier's*, July 5, 1952. Copyright © 1952 by the Cromwell-Collier Publishing Company, from *War Party* by Louis L'Amour. Used by permission of Bantam Books, a division of Random House, Inc. "House Taken Over" from *End of the Game and Other Stories* by Julio Cortázar, translation by Paul Blackburn. Copyright © 1967 by Random House, Inc. Reprinted by permission of Pantheon Books, a division of Random House, Inc. From *How Reading Changed My Life* by Anna Quindlen. Copyright © 1998 by Anna Quindlen. Reprinted by permission of Ballantine Books, a division of Random House, Inc. "I Stand Here Ironing" from *Tell Me a Riddle* by Tillie Olsen. Copyright © 1956, 1957, 1960, 1961 by Tillie Olsen. Used by permission of Delacorte Press/Seymour Lawrence, an imprint of Bantam Doubleday Dell Publishing Group, a division of Random House, Inc. "Short Assignments" by Anne Lamott from *Bird by Bird* by Anne Lamott. Copyright © 1994 by Anne Lamott. Reprinted by permission of Pantheon Books, a division of Random House, Inc. "The Waking" from *The Collected Poems of Theodore Roethke*. Copyright © 1953 by Theodore Roethke. Reprinted by permission of Doubleday, a division of

Random House, Inc. From *When Heaven and Earth Changed Places* by Le Ly Hayslip. Copyright © 1989 by Le Ly Hayslip and Charles Jay Wurts. Used by permission of Doubleday, a division of Random House, Inc. **Random House UK.** "The Letter *A*" from *My Left Foot* by Christy Brown, published by Martin Secker & Warburg Ltd. Copyright © 1954 by Christy Brown. Reprinted by permission of Random House UK. **The Estate of João Guimarães Rosa.** "The Third Bank of the River" from *Modern Brazilian Short Stories*, translated by William L. Grossman. Copyright © 1967 by The Regents of the University of California. **Seaver Books.** "Prayer to the Pacific" from *Storyteller* by Leslie Marmon Silko. Copyright © 1981 by Leslie Marmon Silko. Published by Seaver Books, New York, NY. **Simon & Schuster.** "The Cabuliwallah" by Rabindranath Tagore from *A Tagore Reader*, edited by Amiya Chakravarty. Copyright © 1961 by Macmillan Publishing Company. Reprinted with the permission of Scribner, a division of Simon & Schuster. "Conclusion" from *The Drowned and the Saved* by Primo Levi, reprinted with permission of Simon & Schuster. Translated by Raymond Rosenthal, English translation copyright © 1988 by Simon & Schuster, Inc. "The Man Who Mistook His Wife for a Hat" from *The Man Who Mistook His Wife for a Hat and Other Clinical Tales* by Oliver Sacks. Reprinted with the permission of Simon & Schuster. Copyright © 1970, 1981, 1983, 1984, 1985 by Oliver Sacks. "Poetry" by Marianne Moore. Reprinted with the permission of Simon & Schuster from *The Collected Poems* by Marianne Moore. Copyright © 1935 by Marianne Moore. Copyright renewed © 1963 by Marianne Moore and T. S. Eliot. **Songtalk Publishing Company.** "I Remember; I Believe" by Bernice Johnson Reagon. Copyright © Songtalk Publishing Co. (BMI). Used by permission of the publisher. **Sterling Lord Literistic.** "Ice and Light", pages 228–236 from *Arctic Dreams: Imagination and Desire in a Northern Landscape* by Barry Lopez. Reprinted by permission of Sterling Lord Literistic, Inc. Copyright © 1986 by Barry

Holstun Lopez. **Time, Inc.** Adapted from "Under the Crack of Reality" by Robert Hughes from *Time*, July 17, 1995. Reprinted by permission of Time, Inc. **Tribune News Service.** "On Loan to the Lonely" by Barbara Gutierrez. Reprinted with permission of Knight Ridder/Tribune Information Services. **University of Oklahoma Press.** From *Popol Vuh: The Sacred Book of the Ancient Quiche Maya*. English version by Delia Goetz and Sylvanus G. Morley from the translation of Adrián Recinos. Copyright © 1950 by the University of Oklahoma Press. "Yonder sky that has wept tears of compassion..." from *Indian Oratory: Famous Speeches by Noted Indian Chieftains*, compiled by W. C. Vanderwerth. Copyright © 1971 by the University of Oklahoma Press. Used by permission. **Tino Villanueva.** "Not Knowing, in Aztlán" by Tino Villanueva. Originally appeared in *Tejidos*, University of Texas-Austin (Vol. I, No. 2, March 1974). Copyright © 1974 by Tino Villanueva. Used by permission of the author. **Walker Publishing Company, Inc.** From *The Victorian Internet* by Tom Standage, pp. 205–211. Copyright © 1998 by Tom Standage. Reprinted by permission of Walker Publishing Company, Inc. **White Pine Press.** "House" from *Neruda at Isla Negra*, by Pablo Neruda. Translated by Maria Jacketti, Dennis Maloney and Clark Zlotchew. Copyright © 1998 by White Pine Press. Reprinted by permission of the publisher. **Wylie Agency, Inc.** "Engineer-Private Paul Klee Misplaces an Aircraft between Milbertshofen and Cambrai" from *Sadness* by Donald Barthelme. Copyright © 1979 Donald Barthelme. Reprinted by permission of the Wylie Agency.

We have made every effort to trace the ownership of all copyrighted material and to secure permission from copyright holders. In the event of any question arising as to the use of any material, we will be pleased to make the necessary corrections in future printings. Thanks are due to the aforementioned authors, publishers, and agents for permission to use the materials indicated.

CURRICULUM